A 11 HAS

Language Typology and Language Universals

HSK 20.2

Handbücher zur Sprach- und Kommunikationswissenschaft

Handbooks of Linguistics
and Communication Science

Manuels de linguistique et
des sciences de communication

Mitbegründet von
Gerold Ungeheuer

Herausgegeben von / Edited by / Edités par
Armin Burkhardt
Hugo Steger
Herbert Ernst Wiegand

Band 20.2

Walter de Gruyter · Berlin · New York
2001

Language Typology and Language Universals
Sprachtypologie und sprachliche Universalien
La typologie des langues et les universaux linguistiques

An International Handbook /
Ein internationales Handbuch / Manuel international

Edited by / Herausgegeben von / Edité par
Martin Haspelmath · Ekkehard König
Wulf Oesterreicher · Wolfgang Raible

Volume 2 / 2. Halbband / Tome 2

Walter de Gruyter · Berlin · New York
2001

∞ Gedruckt auf säurefreiem Papier, das die
US-ANSI-Norm über Haltbarkeit erfüllt.

Library of Congress Cataloging-in-Publication Data

Language typology and language universals : an international handbook /
edited by Martin Haspelmath ... [et al.] = Sprachtypologie und sprachli-
che Universalien : ein internationales Handbuch / herausgegeben von
Martin Haspelmath ... [et al.].
   v. cm. − (Handbooks of linguistics and communication science =
   Handbücher zur Sprach- und Kommunikationswissenschaft ;
   Bd. 20)
English, French, and German.
Includes bibliographical references and indexes.
ISBN 3-11-011423-2 (v. 1 : alk. paper) − ISBN 3-11-017154-6 (v. 2 :
alk. paper)
   I. Typology (Linguistics) − Handbooks, manuals, etc. 2. Universals
(Linguistics) − Handbooks, manuals, etc. I. Title: Sprachtypologie
und sprachliche Universalien. II. Haspelmath, Martin, 1963 − III.
Handbücher zur Sprach- und Kommunikationswissenschaft ; Bd. 20.

P204 .L3 2001
410′.1−dc21
                                                    2001047665

Die Deutsche Bibliothek − *CIP-Einheitsaufnahme*

Language typology and language universals : an international handbook
= Sprachtypologie und sprachliche Universalien / ed. by Martin Haspel-
math .... − Berlin ; New York : de Gruyter
   (Handbücher zur Sprach- und Kommunikationswissenschaft ; Bd. 20)
Vol. 2. − (2001)
   ISBN 3-11-017154-6

© Copyright 2001 by Walter de Gruyter GmbH & Co. KG, D-10785 Berlin
Dieses Werk einschließlich aller seiner Teile ist urheberrechtlich geschützt. Jede Verwertung außerhalb der
engen Grenzen des Urheberrechtsgesetzes ist ohne Zustimmung des Verlages unzulässig und strafbar. Das
gilt insbesondere für Vervielfältigungen, Übersetzungen, Mikroverfilmungen und die Einspeicherung und
Verarbeitung in elektronischen Systemen.
Printed in Germany
Satz: Arthur Collignon GmbH, Berlin
Druck: WB-Druck, Rieden/Allgäu
Buchbinderische Verarbeitung: Lüderitz & Bauer-GmbH, Berlin
Einbandgestaltung und Schutzumschlag: Rudolf Hübler, Berlin

Contents/Inhalt/Contenu

Volume 2/2. Halbband/Tome 2

X. Syntactic Typology
Syntaktische Typologie
Typologie syntaxique

64.	Beatrice Primus, Word order typology	855
65.	Gilbert Lazard, Le marquage différentiel de l'objet	873
66.	Leonid I. Kulikov, Causatives	886
67.	Konstantin I. Kazenin, The passive voice	899
68.	Konstantin I. Kazenin, Verbal reflexives and the middle voice	916
69.	Vladimir P. Nedjalkov, Resultative constructions	928
70.	Ray Freeze, Existential constructions	941
71.	Leon Stassen, Predicative possession	954
72.	Maria Koptjevskaja-Tamm, Adnominal possession	960
73.	Ekkehard König, Internal and external possessors	970
74.	Kaoru Horie, Complement clauses	979
75.	Leon Stassen, Comparative constructions	993
76.	Vera I. Podlesskaya, Conditional constructions	998
77.	Peter Siemund, Interrogative constructions	1010
78.	Viktor S. Xrakovskij, Hortative constructions	1028
79.	Laura A. Michaelis, Exclamative constructions	1038
80.	Knud Lambrecht, Dislocation	1050
81.	Hans Bernhard Drubig, Wolfram Schaffar, Focus constructions	1079
82.	Leon Stassen, Noun phrase coordination	1105
83.	Bertil Tikkanen, Converbs	1112
84.	Andrej A. Kibrik, Reference maintenance in discourse	1123

XI. Lexical typology
Lexikalische Typologie
La typologie lexicale

85.	Peter Koch, Lexical typology from a cognitive and linguistic point of view	1142
86.	Cecil H. Brown, Lexical typology from an anthropological point of view	1178
87.	Cliff Goddard, Universal units in the lexicon	1190
88.	Niklas Jonsson, Kin terms in grammar	1203
89.	Brenda Laca, Derivation	1214
90.	Robert MacLaury, Color terms	1227
91.	Ewald Lang, Spatial dimension terms	1251

92.	David Gil, Quantifiers	1275
93.	Åke Viberg, Verbs of perception	1294

XII. Phonology-based typology
Typologie auf phonologischer Basis
Typologie du domaine phonologique

94.	David Restle, Theo Vennemann, Silbenstruktur	1310
95.	Thomas Krefeld, Phonologische Prozesse	1336
96.	Aditi Lahiri, Metrical patterns	1347
97.	Larry M. Hyman, Tone systems	1367
98.	D. Robert Ladd, Intonation	1380

XIII. Salient typological parameters
Typologisch besonders markante Parameter
Paramètres typologiques particulièrement saillants

99.	Peter Auer, Silben- und akzentzählende Sprachen	1391
100.	Walter Bisang, Finite vs. non-finite languages	1400
101.	Aleksandr E. Kibrik, Subject-oriented vs. subjectless languages	1413
102.	Johannes Helmbrecht, Head-marking vs. dependent-marking languages	1424
103.	Mark C. Baker, Configurationality and polysynthesis	1433
104.	Katalin É. Kiss, Discourse configurationality	1442

XIV. Typological characterization of language families and linguistic areas
Typologische Charakterisierung von Sprachfamilien und Sprachbünden
La caractéristique typologique de familles et d'aires linguistiques

105.	Östen Dahl, Principles of areal typology	1456
106.	Hans Goebl, Arealtypologie und Dialektologie	1471
107.	Martin Haspelmath, The European linguistic area: Standard Average European	1492
108.	Jack Feuillet, Aire linguistique balkanique	1510
109.	Karen H. Ebert, Südasien als Sprachbund	1529
110.	Christel Stolz, Thomas Stolz, Mesoamerica as a linguistic area	1539

XV. Diachronic aspects of language types and linguistic universals
Diachronische Aspekte von Sprachtypologie und Universalienforschung
Aspects diachroniques de la recherche typologique et universaliste

111.	Wulf Oesterreicher, Historizität – Sprachvariation, Sprachverschiedenheit, Sprachwandel	1554
112.	Andreas Blank, Pathways of lexicalization	1596

113.	Claude Hagège, Les processus de grammaticalisation	1609
114.	John Ole Askedal, Conceptions of typological change	1624
115.	Sarah Grey Thomason, Contact-induced typological change	1640
116.	Peter Mühlhäusler, Typology and universals of Pidginization	1648
117.	Pieter Muysken, Creolization	1656
118.	Hans-Jürgen Sasse, Typological changes in language obsolescence .	1668
119.	Helmut Lüdtke, 'Tote' Sprachen	1678
120.	Dieter Wanner, From Latin to the Romance languages	1691
121.	Jan Terje Faarlund, From Ancient Germanic to modern Germanic languages	1706
122.	Lars Johanson, Vom Alttürkischen zu den modernen Türksprachen	1719
123.	Antonio Loprieno, From Ancient Egyptian to Coptic	1742
124.	Stefan Weninger, Vom Altäthiopischen zu den neuäthiopischen Sprachen	1762
125.	Wolfgang Schulze, Die kaukasischen Sprachen	1774

Indexes / Register / Indexes

Index of names / Namenregister / Index des noms	1797
Index of languages / Sprachenregister / Index des langues	1823
Index of subjects / Sachregister / Index des matières	1837

Volume 1/1. Halbband/Tome 1

Preface	V
Vorwort	VII
Préface	IX
Common abbreviations/Häufige Abkürzungen/Abréviations fréquentes	XIX

I.	Foundations: Theoretical foundations of language universals and language typology Grundlagen: Die sprachtheoretische Fundierung von Universalienforschung und Sprachtypologie Fondements: les bases théoriques de la typologie linguistique et de la recherche universaliste	
	1. Wolfgang Raible, Language universals and language typology	1
	2. Bernard Comrie, Different views of language typology	25
II.	Foundations: Points of contact between language universals/language typology and other disciplines Grundlagen: Berührungspunkte von Universalien- forschung und Sprachtypologie mit anderen Disziplinen Fondements: les points de contact entre la recherche universaliste, la typologie linguistique et d'autres disciplines	
	3. Doris Tophinke, Handlungstheorie, Kommunikationstheorie, Lebenswelt	40

4.	Kai Buchholz, Sprachphilosophie	62
5.	François Rastier, Sciences cognitives et Intelligence Artificielle	75
6.	Heiner Böhmer, Künstliche Sprachen und Universalsprachen	85
7.	Derek Bickerton, Biological foundations of language	95
8.	Wolfgang Raible, Linguistics and Genetics: Systematic parallels	103
9.	Jürgen Dittmann, Sprachpathologie	123
10.	Franz Dotter, Gebärdensprachforschung	141
11.	Wolfgang Schnotz, Textproduktions- und Textverstehensforschung	154
12.	Harald Haarmann, Sprachtypologie und Schriftgeschichte	163

III. History and prehistory of universals research
Geschichte und Vorgeschichte der Universalienforschung
Histoire et préhistoire de la recherche universaliste

13.	Pierre Swiggers, Alfons Wouters, Philosophie du langage et linguistique dans l'Antiquité classique	181
14.	Jakob Hans Josef Schneider, Sprachtheorien im Mittelalter	192
15	Werner Hüllen, Reflections on language in the Renaissance	210
16.	Lia Formigari, Theories of language in the European Enlightenment	222
17.	N. N., Schulen des Strukturalismus	entfällt

IV. History and approaches of language typology
Geschichte und Richtungen der Sprachtypologie
Histoire et écoles de la typologie linguistique

18.	Werner Hüllen, Characterization and evaluation of languages in the Renaissance and in the Early Modern Period	234
19.	Georg Bossong, Die Anfänge typologischen Denkens im europäischen Rationalismus	249
20.	Martin Haase, Sprachtypologie bei Edward Sapir	264
21.	Heidi Aschenberg, Typologie als Charakterologie	266
22.	Esa Itkonen, The relation of non-Western approaches to linguistic typology	275

V. Current approaches to language typology and universals research
Gegenwärtige Ansätze von Sprachtypologie und Universalienforschung
Les tendences actuelles dans le domaine de la typologie linguistique et de la recherche universaliste

23.	Martin Haase, Sprachtypologie und Universalienforschung bei Joseph H. Greenberg	280
24.	Hubert Haider, Parametrisierung in der Generativen Grammatik	283
25.	Daniel Jacob, Die Hegersche Noematik	293
26.	Yakov G. Testelets, Russian works on linguistic typology in the 1960-1990s	306

27.	Hansjakob Seiler, The Cologne UNITYP project	323
28.	Christiane Pilot-Raichoor, Gilbert Lazard, le RIVALC et la revue *Actances*	344

VI. Explanatory principles, principles of organization, and methods in typology and language universals
Erklärungsprinzipien, Ordnungsprinzipien und Methoden für universalistische und typologische Fragestellungen
Les principes d'explication, les principes structurants et les méthodes appliquées aux questions d'ordre universaliste et typologique

29.	John A. Hawkins, The role of processing principles in explaining language universals	360
30.	Claus D. Pusch, Ikonizität	369
31.	Wolfgang Ullrich Wurzel, Ökonomie	384
32.	Ralph Ludwig, Markiertheit	400
33.	Revere D. Perkins, Sampling procedures and statistical methods	419

VII. Communication-theoretic prerequisites and language-independent *tertia comparationis* as bases of typological coding
Kommunikationstheoretische 'Vorgaben' und außersprachliche *tertia comparationis* als Grundlage sprachtypenbezogener Kodierung
Fondements du codage typologique: les données communicatives et les *tertia comparationis*

34.	Heidi Aschenberg, Sprechsituationen und Kontext	435
35.	Doris Tophinke, Sprachliches Handeln, Kommunikantenrollen, Beziehungsaspekte	444
36.	Raymund Wilhelm, Diskurstraditionen	467
37.	Waldfried Premper, Universals of the linguistic representation of situations ('participation')	477
38.	Hans-Jürgen Sasse, Scales between nouniness and verbiness	495
39.	Anne Reboul, Foundations of reference and predication	509
40.	Jan Rijkhoff, Dimensions of adnominal modification	522
41.	José Luis Iturrioz Leza, Dimensionen der verbalen Modifikation	533
42.	Robert I. Binnick, Temporality and aspectuality	557
43.	Peter Mühlhäusler, Universals and typology of space	568
44.	Wolfgang Klein, Deiktische Orientierung	575
45.	Wolfgang Raible, Linking clauses	590
46.	Jorunn Hetland, Valéria Molnár, Informationsstruktur und Reliefgebung	617
47.	Elisabeth Stark, Textkohäsion und Textkohärenz	634

VIII. Morphological techniques
Morphologische Techniken
Les techniques morphologiques

48.	Georg Bossong, Ausdrucksmöglichkeiten für grammatische Relationen	657
49.	Vladimir A. Plungian, Agglutination and flection	669
50.	Johanna Rubba, Introflection	678
51.	Laurie Bauer, Compounding	695
52.	Gregory Stump, Affix position	708
53.	José Luis Iturrioz Leza, Inkorporation	714

IX. Typology of morphological and morphosyntactic categories
Typologie morphologischer und morphosyntaktischer Kategorien
La typologie des catégories morphologiques et morphosyntaxiques

54.*	Jan Anward, Parts of speech	726
55.	Martin Haase, Lokalkasus und Adpositionen	736
56.	Peter Mühlhäusler, Personal pronouns	741
57.	Ekkehard König, Intensifiers and reflexive pronouns	747
58.	Martin Haase, Local deixis	760
59.	Jouko Lindstedt, Tense and aspect	768
60.	Dietmar Zaefferer, Modale Kategorien	784
61.	Greville G. Corbett, Number	816
62.	Nikolaus P. Himmelmann, Articles	831
63.	Bernd Kortmann, Adverbial conjunctions	842

* We apologize for the misprint in the volume 1 of Jan Anward's name.

X. Syntactic Typology
Syntaktische Typologie
Typologie syntaxique

64. Word order typology

1. Historical overview
2. Heads
3. Major constituents of the clause
4. References

1. Historical overview

The work of Greenberg (1963) is generally viewed as marking the beginning of word order typology as a discipline of modern linguistics. But observations about cross-language word order patterns and their variation had been published much earlier. Interest in word order typology arose mainly within historical linguistics from the comparison of the classical languages with modern descendants. Some of the major claims of modern word order typology had been formulated centuries ago (cf. Lehmann 1995: 1150f.), for instance, the claim that word order is fixed when case endings are lost or that the determining element regularly either precedes or follows the determined element (cf. notably Weil 1844 and Behaghel 1932). Schmidt (1926) deserves special mention as he compiled a world atlas of languages showing the position of the possessive and genitive relative to the head noun and the position of the pronominal subject relative to the verb. Greenberg (1963) proposed 45 linguistic universals based on a sample of 30 languages and supplemented with basic information about 112 more languages. He introduced the basic theoretical concepts of modern approaches to typology and universals, such as the distinction between strict and statistical universal, the concept of a universal correlation and that of an implicational universal (→ Art. 23).

Since Greenberg's (1963) influential paper, word order typology has become a major topic in the field of linguistic typology. The major empirical and methodological developments were the improvement of the sampling methodology (cf. Bell 1978, Dryer 1989) and an increase in the sample to some 350 languages in Hawkins (1983), and to over 600 languages in Tomlin (1986) and Dryer (1992). The range of word order phenomena covered by typological studies has expanded considerably and an increasing number of correlations with other properties of grammar have been shown to exist (cf. § 3.). On the theoretical level, many linguists were engaged in explaining Greenberg's findings (cf. § 2.2.). A number of studies pointed to the role of word order typology for other fields of linguistics such as language change and genetic classification (cf. Givón 1971, Lehmann 1972, 1973, Vennemann 1975, 1984, Hawkins 1983, Nichols 1992) as well as areal linguistics (Dryer 1992, 1998, Nichols 1992). The Word Order Group of the EUROTYP Program on the typology of European languages also deserves special mention for its empirical and theoretical contributions (cf. the papers in Siewierska 1998 discussed further below).

2. Heads

2.1. Basic facts

Greenberg's major contribution was the insight that the basic order of the major constituents of the clause (subject, object, and verb) correlates with the basic order of minor elements relative to each other, such as noun and genitive, noun and adjective, adposition and noun. It was only later that a principle underlying these correlations was formulated in terms of the distinction 'head' vs. 'dependents', cf. (1):

(1)   Consistent Head Serialization (CHS): For all phrasal categories X, the head of X either precedes or follows all dependents.

The CHS leads to a typological distinction in terms of ideally consistent head-final vs. head-initial word order, and as a consequence, to a distinction between head-initial and head-final languages. Table 64.1 summarizes the basic facts and shows languages that can be associated with the two patterns:

Table 64.1:

Consistent head-initial order:	Consistent head-final order:
verb − object (VO)	object − verb (OV)
inflected auxiliary − main verb (AuxV)	main verb − inflected auxiliary (VAux)
preposition − noun (Pr)	noun − postposition (Po)
noun − genitive/possessor (NG)	genitive/possessor − noun (GN)
adjective − object of comparison	object of comparison − adjective
article − noun	noun − article
noun − adjective (NA)	adjective − noun (AN)
noun − numeral (NNum)	numeral − noun (NumN)
noun − demonstrative (NDem)	demonstrative − noun (DemN)
noun − relative clause (NRel)	relative clause − noun (RelN)
complementizer − clause (CompS)	clause − complementizer (SComp)
verb − adverb (VAdv)	adverb − verb (AdvV)
adjective − adverb (AAdv)	adverb − adjective (AdvA)
Languages approaching this ideal: Berber, Biblical Hebrew, Chinook, Irish, Maori, Maasai, Welsh, Zapotec	Languages approaching this ideal: Basque, Burmese, Burushaski, Hindi, Japanese, Kannada, Laz, Turkish
Less consistent languages: English (AN, GN/NG, AdvA) Rumanian (AN/NA, NumN, DemN, AdvA)	Less consistent languages: Finnish (SVO, AuxV, NRel/RelN) Guarani (SVO, NRel, NA, NumN/NNum)

Greenberg (1963) noticed that some orders are dominant, i.e. they co-occur with both head-initial and head-final patterns, and thus depart from the cross-categorial harmony shown in Table 64.1. Greenberg (1963) and subsequent studies (Hawkins 1983, chap. 3; Dryer 1988, 1992) have established that adjectives, demonstratives, numerals and sentence-modifying adverbs (e.g. negation particles, time adverbs) depart quite often from the cross-categorial harmony shown in Table 64.1 (cf. § 2.2. and § 2.3.2. below). Such elements will be called bad patterners. Some patterners, such as the suffixes, are bad only for a particular language type. The subject is a bad patterner in VO languages since it often precedes V yielding SVO (cf. § 3.3. below). Finally, relative and complement clauses and complementizers are bad patterners in head-final languages, but good patterners in head-initial languages (cf. § 2.2. further below).

As shown by Greenberg (1963), morphological affixes also enter the word order correlations in Table 64.1 (→ Art. 52) and behave like heads (cf. Williams 1981 for an analysis of affixes as heads). Prefixes are found almost exclusively in head-initial languages. Inconsistencies come from suffixes, which are found in both head-final and head-initial languages. This reflects an overall preference for suffixation over prefixation (cf. for explanations Hawkins & Cutler 1988, Hall 1988, Bybee et al. 1990). More recent studies have shown that the different types of affixes pattern differently (cf. Dahl 1993: 918 for affixed negation, Siewierska & Bakker 1996: 147f. and Dryer 1995: 1058 for verb agreement affixes). A plausible explanation is the historical origin of the affixes. Thus, for instance, the weak preference for affixed negators to be prefixed rather than suffixed to the verb is assumed by Dahl (1993: 918) to be due to their emergence from negative particles, which also show the same preference to precede the verb.

Hawkins (1983) formulates stronger descriptive generalizations, most of which have no counterexamples in his sample of ca. 350 languages (but cf. Dryer 1991 for a small number of exceptions). A recurrent schema of such implicational universals is the following:

(2) $P \rightarrow (P' \rightarrow Q)$, logically equivalent to $(P \& P') \rightarrow Q$
P − good patterner, P' worse patterner than P and Q

Examples: Pr → (NA → NG); VSO → (NA → NG); Po → (AN → GN); SOV → (AN → GN)

The (in)stability relations between P′ and Q established by these statements follow from the logic of the implicational relation. A statement like P → (P′ → Q) can only be falsified if P and P′ are true and Q false. Note that, given that P is true, P′ may be false and Q true, but if Q is false P′ must also be false. Thus, for example, if the adjective (P′) alone departs from the adposition serialization, the general statement still holds. But if the genitive (Q) departs from the adpositional serialization, the adjective has to depart as well.

2.2. Explanations

Greenberg's main contribution is of empirical and methodological nature. Nevertheless, he offers some tentative proposals for more general notions and principles underlying the different universals he formulated as unrelated empirical generalizations. One of the crucial notions for the typological facts under discussion is, according to Greenberg, the concept of harmony between various word order rules. In his opinion, this concept is connected to analogy and to the psychological concept of generalization. He illustrates this with the connection between genitive order and Pr/Po and suggests that the word order correlations are due to the analogy between possessive and spatial relationships and to the fact that prepositions often evolve from nouns. In German for example the preposition *wegen* as in *wegen der Verbesserung* 'because of the improvement' evolved from the noun *Weg* as in *Weg der Verbesserung* 'way of improvement'. According to Greenberg, an initial correlation between PrN and NG can be generalized via the subjective and objective genitive to verbal phrases, i.e. to VO. A later proponent of this type of diachronic explanation is Givón (1971). This line of explanation has been repeatedly criticized, mainly on the grounds that it is highly questionable that the diachronic evolution of the various elements involved in the correlations illustrated in Table 64.1 is uniform within and across languages.

Bartsch and Vennemann (1972: 131 f., Vennemann 1974) have contributed towards a better understanding of the basic facts by stating that there is a synchronic syntactic Principle of Natural Serialization, such that all operators tend either to precede or follow their operand. Within the framework of categorial grammar proposed by Bartsch and Vennemann, syntactic structures are determined by semantic structures, and accordingly, the notions of operator and operand are defined on the basis of semantic functor-argument representations. In more general terms, a specifying element is identified as the operator and the specified element as the operand. The problem with the notions of operator (or specifier, modifier) and operand (or specified, modified) is that they cannot be identified by a set of coherent criteria on the basis of functor-argument structures (cf. Keenan 1979). Thus, on purely semantic grounds, one can treat either NP or V as the operator (cf. Montague 1974). Under the assumption that the object NP is the operator, it maps a transitive verb onto an intransitive verb (cf. Bartsch & Vennemann 1972: 136). Under the standard view, it is an argument or operand of a verbal functor. The interchangeability of operator and operand also holds for other constructions (cf. Jacobs 1994: 17 f. for adverb and verb).

Later, Vennemann (1977, Vennemann & Harlow 1977) turned to the syntactic head concept for the clarification of the specifier-specified relation, which substitutes the operator-operand relation of earlier work. The specifier is identified with the non-head element, the specified element with the head. The principle under discussion states that all specifiers tend either to precede or follow the element they specify (cf. CHS in (1) above). The syntactic head notion has the advantage that it is more readily identifiable. Vennemann (1977) and other linguists (cf. Jackendoff 1977, Gazdar et al. 1985, Zwicky 1985, Corbett et al. 1993, Pollard & Sag 1994) have contributed towards the clarification of the head concept within modern syntactic theories and have worked out viable criteria for its identification. Cf. some of the criteria in (3):

(3) (a) the head determines the category of the phrase (i.e. head and phrasal node share the major categorial features)
  (b) the head is the determining category in terms of case government or other valency-related phenomena in which one element determines the presence, syntactic or semantic function of another element
  (c) the head expresses the syntactic function of the phrase by inflection (i.e. head and phrasal node share the functional inflectional features)

By these criteria taken in conjunction one can establish the heads in Table 64.1 (cf. for a discussion of equivocal cases § 2.3.3. below). Vennemann (1977) and Vennemann & Harlow (1977) also claim that inflected auxiliary verbs, articles, and complementizers are heads. This has become a common assumption in recent approaches to syntax.

Alternative explanations based on completely different distinctions have also been put forward. Maxwell (1984) tries to capture the correlations shown in Table 64.1 on the basis of the concept of a semantic link and the principle that an element which serves as a semantic link between two other elements is likely to occur in linear order between them. Linking elements are, according to Maxwell, case affixes, adpositions, complementizers and auxiliary verbs. These elements constitute a subclass of heads. Therefore, it is not surprising that his principle covers some of the data captured by the CHS, such as V-preposition-NP and NP-postposition-V. But, as Maxwell himself admits, his proposal cannot capture all the data that are correctly predicted by the CHS. Thus, for instance, his principle fails to explain the strongly preferred position of auxiliaries in V-initial languages (Aux-V-NP) as well as other characteristics of V-initial languages. And since Maxwell's proposal also fails where the CHS fails (e. g. the bad patterns mentioned above), it is obviously empirically inferior to the CHS.

Another approach that has serious empirical disadvantages is Gil's (1986) prosodic theory. The preliminary assumption is that languages fall into two rhythmic patterns, iambic (i. e. weak-strong) vs. trochaic (i. e. strong-weak). The ordering correlations that are supposed to follow from this typological prosodic distinction are based on the empirically false assumption that heads occur, in general, in stronger prosodic constituents than do their dependents (1986: 174). On the basis of this assumption, iambic languages would tend to be head-final while trochaic languages would show the opposite tendency towards head-initial serialization. Contrary to Gil's claim, a number of linguists (cf. Deszö 1982, Harlig & Bardovi-Harlig 1988) have established that the object is in stronger prosodic position than the verb, in general, and this yields the exactly opposite correlations: OV languages are assumed to be trochaic and VO languages iambic (cf. German *weil Peter [VP das BUCH kaufte]* vs. English *because Peter [VP bought the BOOK]*). As shown by Jacobs (1992), this supposed correlation between accent placement and head position is accidental and an epiphenomon of universal accentuation rules.

We conclude that the head-based CHS is empirically superior to the approaches referred to above. Various proposals have been put forward as an ultimate rationale for the observed cross-categorial consistency associated with the CHS. The proposals in (i)−(iii) below deserve special mention, as they have gained wider acceptance or have been incorporated into more recent proposals:

(i) a consistent direction of modification to the left or to the right, as suggested by the approaches of Behaghel (1932), Lehmann (1972, 1973) and Vennemann (1974, 1977);
(ii) a consistent left-branching vs. right-branching in terms of phrase structure (Dryer 1988, 1992);
(iii) a consistent direction of case assignment or semantic-role assignment to the left or to the right.

The common trait of these proposals is that they are based on syntactic structural notions. Despite their merits, they are not free of shortcomings. The weakness of the proposal (i) is that it cannot cope with the bad patterners. The consistent branching hypothesis mentioned in (ii) fares better as it makes the same predictions as the CHS for head-dependent pairs in which the dependent is a branching, expandable constituent. It also seems to explain why non-branching dependents such as demonstratives and numerals are bad patterners. A nonbranching constituent that does not pattern along the CHS does not yield a structure with a deeply embedded mixed branching. Dryer (1992: 128) assumes that his principle reflects the nature of the human parser but the exact nature of the processing advantage remains unclear. As shown by Frazier & Rayner (1988), mixed branching per se does not give rise to substantial processing complexity.

The claim of a unidirectional case or semantic-role assignment mentioned in (iii) originated in the work of Travis (1984) and Kayne (1984) and has become a major typological parameter within generative grammar (cf. Haider 1986, Fanselow 1987). This parameter captures only a subset of the data that fall under the CHS and makes no predictions for a dependent element whose case or semantic role is not assigned by its head (e.g. adverbial, noun modifier). The advantage of treating such dependents separately will be discussed in connection with (10) later in this section.

Some of the approaches in (i)−(iii) implicitly or explicitly suggest that there is a psycholinguistic, i.e. parsing, advantage in the cross-categorical harmony at issue, but the exact nature of this advantage remains unclear. Proposals (i) and (iii) rely heavily on the notion of unidirectionality, but the fact that there are two types of languages instead of one does not seem to be straightforwardly explicable by unidirectionality alone.

A recent proposal for the latter problem is offered withing generative grammar by postulating a uniform universal basic order (cf. Kayne 1994). Other patterns of word order are derived by movement transformations from the universal basic order. Unfortunately, as expected by the facts in Table 64.1, evidence for a head-final, i.e. right-branching, universal base (cf. Haider 1993) competes with evidence for a head-initial, i.e. left-branching, universal base (cf. Zwart 1997).

A more attractive explanation for the CHS is offered by Hawkins (1990, 1994, 1998, → Art. 29). According to Hawkins, the principle underlying the CHS is a performance principle of parsing efficiency. The basic ideas of Hawkins' approach are the following. The parsing of a phrasal node (= constituent recognition domain) X begins mandatorily as soon as one has identified the first immediate constituent (IC) of X (beginning from the left), proceeds with the further ICs of X and ends as soon as one has identified the last IC of X. ICs are identified by mother-node-constructing categories, which are heads in the unmarked case. Hawkins' principle captures the intuitively appealing idea that the human parser prefers to resolve the recognition of a syntactic phrase by parsing as few words as possible. More specifically, the human parser prefers orderings that present all ICs of a node in as rapid a succession as possible, thereby maximizing left-to-right IC-to-word ratios. (4) presents the formulation of Hawkins (1990: 233):

(4) Early Immediate Constituents (EIC)
The human parser prefers linear orders that maximize the left-to-right IC-to-word ratios of the phrasal nodes that it constructs.

Hawkins further assumes that the EIC principle explains the most frequent orders within phrases with free word order as well as the only grammatical order within phrases with rigid order. Let us look at the various orderings of the German example 'went along the river':

(5) (a) [$_{VP}$ [$_V$ *ging*] [$_{PP}$ *entlang des Flusses*]]
        1/1   2/2   100%
    (b) [$_{VP}$ [$_V$ *ging*] [$_{PP}$ *den Fluß entlang*]]
        1/1   2/2 2/3 2/4   79%
    (c) [$_{VP}$ [$_{PP}$ *entlang des Flusses*] [$_V$ *ging*]]
        1/1   1/2 1/3   2/4 58%
    (d) [$_{VP}$ [$_{PP}$ *den Fluß entlang*] [$_V$ *ging*]]
        1/1   2/2 100%

In order to recognize (or produce) the ICs of the VP in (5a) one has to parse (or produce) 2 words. The verb is the first IC on the left that constructs the mother node V. It gets the IC-to-word ratio 1/1 (= 100%). The second IC is a PP which is immediately identified by the preposition. It gets the IC-to-word ratio 2/2 (= 100%). The average IC-to-word ratio of the whole VP is 100%. Note that Hawkins' principle is formulated for structural recognition domains. The parser does not have to parse all the words of the VP (e.g. *des Flusses* in (5a)) in order to recognize its structure. The structural recognition job is done as soon as one has recognized the ICs of the structure. The structure in (5a) has several properties which makes it optimal in terms of EIC: the heads of the ICs are peripheral, on the same side of the ICs and close to each other, and additionally, the longer IC follows the shorter IC. The structures in (5b−c) are less optimal because the heads are on different sides of the ICs. The difference in the IC-to-word ratios in (5b) and (5c) is of typological relevance. The co-occurrence of verb-initial order in VP and postpositions in (5b) has a better EIC ratio than the mirror image of verb-final order in VP and prepositions in (5c). There are correspondingly more languages of type (5b) than of type (5c). The structure in (5d) is again optimal: adjacent final heads lead to a rapid recognition of the VP structure. The two-word window in (5d) is explained by the fact that the PP is constructed only as soon as its head is encountered. (5d) also shows that in consistent head-final structures it is more advantageous to place longer ICs before shorter ICs.

In sum, the EIC principle correctly predicts a tendency to place heads peripherally and as close as possible to each other (cf. for similar ideas Frazier 1979, Rijkhoff 1992, 1998). It also predicts the preference for consistent branching direction, i.e. that the heads should be on the same side of each phrasal category. It shares the advantage of the branching direction proposal in explaining the fact that light, non-branching constituents that are not aligned along the CHS (e.g. numerals, demonstratives) are more readily tolerated than heavier, branching categories (dependent noun or adpositional phrases). Additionally, EIC predicts that short ICs tend to precede longer ICs in head-initial languages (cf. Behaghel's (1932) Law of Increasing Constituents). In consistent head-final languages longer ICs are preferred before shorter ICs (cf. Hawkins 1994, chap. 4 for corroborating data from Japanese, Turkish, Hungarian and Korean). Hawkins' approach copes with the major unsolved problems of alternative proposals. It clarifies the nature of the psycholinguistic advantage that comes from heads that are positioned peripherally on the same side of the phrase by demonstrating that this pattern leads to more rapid language processing. Furthermore, it also shows that head-final languages are equally well apt to contribute to more rapid language processing, and thus explains why the languages currently existing in the world are roughly equally divided between the head-initial and the head-final types.

A comparison of Hawkins' proposal with alternative proposals may help to assess the merits of the different approaches. According to Vennemann's proposal, the languages of the world fall into one of two ideal types: consistently head-final languages, i.e. prespecifying languages in Vennemann's terminology, and consistently head-initial, i.e. postspecifying languages. As repeatedly shown in the literature, the strong consistency claim is false as an empirical generalization. This can be demonstrated by the simple fact that in Greenberg's extended sample of 142 languages, 50 languages have 25% inconsistency and 24 languages have 50% inconsistency with respect to the pairs V-O, N-A, N-G and Pr/Po (cf. Hawkins 1983: 40). But the fact is that Vennemann did not formulate his principle as a descriptive generalization, but rather as an explanatory principle defining a more abstract notion of an ideal language type (cf. for an explicit discussion Vennemann 1983). As pointed out by Vennemann, strong versions of universal preferences are necessary not only to uncover the ultimate rationale for the explanandum, but also for an appropriate formulation of the goal of diachronic processes. The same holds true for Dryer's branching direction principle, which is explicitly meant to explain ideal configurations (cf. 1992: 89).

Despite repeated criticism of Vennemann on this issue (cf. Comrie 1981: 93 f., Hawkins 1983, chap. 2), more recent studies on word order show that explanatory principles do not coincide with descriptive generalizations. Note that Hawkins himself explains the descriptive universal implications put forward in 1983 (cf. (2) for some examples) by EIC, a very general performance principle. This principle incorporates not only Vennemann's principle, Dryer's consistent branching hypothesis and the assumption of a consistent unidirectional case or semantic-role assignment of generative grammar, but also Behaghel's Law of Increasing Constituents. The appeal of EIC as an explanatory principle is precisely the fact that it is of greater generality and thus stronger than the alternative proposals.

The different kinds of explanations can also be evaluated with respect to the bad patterners mentioned above. In order to explain the inconsistent patterns, Lehmann (1973) and Vennemann (1975, 1984) resort to diachronic change from one consistent serialization pattern to the other. Thus, for instance, the notorious inconsistency of Modern German is assumed by Vennemann to be due to the fact that German is moving from a consistent head-final to a consistent head-initial pattern. Another example is the inconsistent position of V and Aux in Modern Finnish (cf. Table 64.1) that is due to a relatively recent development from SOV, which is still found in some Finnic languages (e.g. Udmurt). There is no doubt that diachrony is an important factor of explanation (cf. also Givón 1971, Hawkins 1983, chap. 5–7). Nevertheless, the diachronic hypothesis alone cannot explain the class of bad patterners. Recall that the same categories seem to be bad patterners across languages. This calls for a principled way of dealing with the bad patterners.

Hawkins' EIC and Dryer's consistent branching hypothesis cope with the fact that numeral-noun and demonstrative-noun pairs are more inconsistently placed than noun-genitive and noun-adposition pairs. Numeral and demonstratives are light, usually non-branching dependents that do not lead to very bad IC-to-word ratios or to deeply embedded mixed branching, if they are not placed along the CHS. These arguments are less convincing as an explanation for the instability of adjectives, which, contrary to the assumption of Hawkins and Dryer, are readily modified, conjoined or stacked (e.g. *a very fresh and cool beer, an expensive light lager beer*). Furthermore, EIC and the unidirectional branching hypothesis cannot explain the good patterning of manner adverbs (e.g. *walks slowly*), since fully recursive or very complex phrases headed by an adverb are less common than complex adjectival phrases. These principles also fail to capture the fact that complementizers, relative and complement clauses are good patterners in head-initial languages but bad ones in head-final languages.

Hawkins (1988, 1990) resorts to a parsing principle connected to minimal attachment in order to explain the asymmetry in the location of complementizers and embedded clauses. Cf. (6):

(6) Minimal Attachment Principle (Hawkins 1990: 252)
The human parser prefers linear orderings that invite correct minimal attachments of words and ICs to nodes on-line.

A gross violation of this principle is found in the English example *John knew the answer to the difficult problem was correct*, since the number of wrongly attached words and ICs that must be reassigned to other nodes is rather high. Consider languages with prenominal relative clauses, such as Japanese:

(7) Japanese (Hawkins 1990: 253)
Zoo-ga   kirin-o
elephant-SUBJ giraffe-OBJ
taoshi-ta   shika-o nade-ta
knocked down deer-OBJ patted
'The elephant patted the deer that knocked down the giraffe'

Such structures invite regular misanalysis of the highlighted portion as a main clause with the meaning 'the elephant knocked down the giraffe'. Postposing the relative clause will serve the Minimal Attachment Principle, but violate EIC. It is clear that head-final languages, OV languages in particular, cannot satisfy both principles simultaneously, whereas head-initial languages can obey both. This explains why head-initial languages almost invariably employ NRel order while head-final languages use NRel in addition to RelN. (6) can also be satisfied if a head-final language uses sentence-initial complementizers. By the same reasoning, the two principles correctly predict that head-initial languages will have almost only CompS order whereas head-final languages will have both CompS and SComp.

Another factor that intervenes with EIC (or the CHS) is captured by the Principle of Syntactic Expression of Semantic Dependencies, as stated in Primus (1996, 1998):

(8) Syntactic Expression of Semantic Dependencies (SESD)
If a non-head constituent Y depends semantically on a non-head constituent X, then X tends to precede and/or c-command Y.

X c-commands Y if and only if X and Y do not dominate each other, and the first branching node that dominates X dominates Y.

An explanation of principle (8) in terms of language processing is offered by Hawkins (1998). (8) is meant to explain the position of dependents relative to each other. A classical case of semantic dependency is that between an antecedent and its reflexive pronoun. (8) explains the fact that antecedents tend to precede and/or c-command their reflexive anaphors (cf. Reinhart 1983). Another type of semantic dependency is established by scopal operators (e.g. quantifiers) or modifiers and their semantic domain. Quantified NPs and modifiers also tend to precede and/or c-command the elements within their scope (cf. Pafel 1993). The scope of a modifier depends on the function of the modifier. Thus, for example, time modifiers (e.g. *works all day*) may have larger scope than modal modifiers (*works diligently*), and this explains, in conjunction with (8), the empirical observation that time modifiers tend to precede and c-command the whole clause, whereas modals are preferably placed closer to the predicate (cf. Tomlin 1986).

Let us now discuss and illustrate the claims of the SESD and the CHS (or EIC) for the relative order of the demonstrative, numeral, adjective and head noun. In Hawkins' (1983) and Rijkhoff's (1992, 1998) world samples, the basic order pattern shown in (9) is statistically most dominant within integral NPs, i.e. NPs which are not constructed appositively (cf. § 2.3.2. below):

(9) Dem Num A N

Rijkhoff's principles of Head Proximity and Domain Integrity as well as the EIC principle explain the adjacent position of the adjectival and nominal heads and the fact that the nominal modifiers are not placed discontinuously. But these principles fail to explain the relative order of the modifiers in (9). This order is best explained by a Principle of Scope as formulated by Rijkhoff and, in more general terms, by the SESD. Demonstratives have intrinsic scope over the rest of the NP, numerals scope over the AN-subphrase, and adjectives over their head noun (cf. Croft 1990: 117f., 174f. for a discussion of such intrinsic semantic relationships). Thus, for example, *these three cold beers*, cannot have a meaning in which the numeral or the adjective is outside the scope of the demonstrative. Although Rijkhoff (1992, 1998) does not explicitly use the structural notion of c-command, his universal semantic NP-structure implicitly follows the principle (8) in terms of c-command. But is is c-command in conjunction with precedence that predicts why the relative order of modifiers exhibited in (9) is universally preferred.

(8) is relevant for the typological word order characteristics of modifiers, since the SESD competes with the CHS (or EIC) in determining their order. This explains why modifiers are, in general, less consistently ordered along the CHS than complements. The interaction between the SESD and the CHS seems to be guided by the degree of valency-bonding between head and dependent, as captured in (10):

(10)   Interaction Hypothesis: The more determined the dependent-head relationship is in terms of the presence, subcategorization, syntactic or semantic function of the dependent (cf. the head criterion (3b)), the greater the impact of the CHS (or EIC).

(10) avoids the dichotomy between complements and modifiers of traditional valency grammars, since valency has proved to be a multi-factor concept (cf. Jacobs 1994). (3b) and (10) mention only some of the major factors involved in the valency-based relationship between head and dependent. On the far end of the scale of valency-free dependents are verb and adjective modifying adverbs, negators, adjectives and other noun modifiers except for genitives. Despite suggestions to the contrary (cf. Dryer 1992: 106f.), the pairs consisting of auxiliary − main verb, adjective − standard of comparison, genitive − noun are rather head-complement pairs, and as predicted by (10), these pairs show a strong tendency to follow the CHS (or EIC). The valency-bonding may have different manifestations though. Thus, for example, auxiliary verbs require the presence of a main verb as do certain verbs that require the presence of an object. Neither main verbs in Aux-V pairs nor standards of comparison in adjective phrases can be adjoined recursively. As to genitives, their semantic function as possessor, agent or patient is established by the head noun. Furthermore, a genitive with the same semantic function cannot be adjoined recursively. Even the traditional class of modifiers does not seem to be uniform. Adverbs of time or cause or those modifying the truth value of the sentence have the least valency-bonding to the verb and can be combined with virtually any verb lexeme. Among the adverbs, manner adverbs are most likely to exhibit selectional restrictions (cf. *sleeps soundly* vs. **walks soundly*). This might explain why manner adverbs tend to pattern along the CHS (cf. Dryer 1992: 93).

The discussion in this section draws attention to the fact that the inconsistencies relative to the CHS (or EIC) may reflect the interaction of these principles with other competing principles. The competition model of word order has gained a wide acceptance among linguists of various research traditions. This section presented two plausible competing principles regarding Minimal Attachment and the Syntactic Expression of Semantic Dependencies that seem to overrule the CHS under certain conditions. These principles make good predictions about the class of bad patterners for the CHS, but the preceding discussion is not intended to claim that these are the only competitors (cf. Siewierska 1988 for a survey of word order rules and principles).

2.3.   Problems

2.3.1. Variable word order

A serious problem for the typological distinction under discussion is word order variation. One possible solution is to register all word order variants as relevant. This does not seem unproblematic in view of the fact that the variants are, in general, not evenly distributed; some are used more often and show less grammatical or stylistic restrictions than others. Thus, it has become common practice to consider one word order variant as basic. Rumanian, for instance, has both AN and NA order. Since AN is restricted to a single adjective which often exhibits meaning idiosyncrasies, the NA order is considered basic. But the fact that typological word order surveys very rarely mention the other option hinders a better understanding of the subtler and surprisingly consistent structure of the Rumanian noun phrase (cf. the discussion in the following section). No matter how well chosen the basic order is, by the neglect of the other variants one may miss generalizations or typologically interesting traits of the language under investigation.

2.3.2. Cross-language categorization

A well-known methodological and theoretical problem for typology is the cross-language comparability of linguistic categories. This includes apparently well-established terms such as adjective, noun or subject, whose universality has been contested in a number of studies. A popular way to avoid, rather than solve the problem is to employ semantic factors in identifying the syntactic categories at issue (cf. Greenberg 1963: 59, Hawkins 1983: 9, Croft 1990: 11 f.).

Let us illustrate the problem with negators, which seem to qualify for a uniform categorization across languages if one takes their uniform semantic function into consideration. But negators fall into disparate syntactic categories across languages (cf. Payne 1985, Dahl 1979, 1993). Consequently, their typologically relevant ordering properties are disparate too (cf. Dahl 1979, 1993). Negation words that are like verbs behave like superordinate heads to the verb, i.e. they pattern, in general, before the verb in VO languages and after the verb in OV languages. Negation words that are affixes tend to be ordered like affixes (cf. § 2.1. above). Negators that are free particles or adverbs tend to c-command and/or precede their scope (cf. Jacobs 1991: 572) as predicted by the SESD in (8) above. In addition to this preference, negative particles also have a tendency to be placed in immediately preverbal position (cf. Dahl 1979: 91 f., Jacobs 1991: 573, Dahl 1993: 916, Dryer 1998: 313).

Another critical issue is the analysis of adjectives. The adjectives pose at least three different kinds of problems pertaining to their syntactic categorization, to their status as modifier or head of the noun phrase, and to the structure of the noun phrase. As to categorization, it is a well-known fact that in some languages words with adjectival meanings pattern more like nouns (e.g. Latin, Rumanian, Modern Greek) and in others more like verbs (e.g. Guarani and other Tupi-Guarani languages). Nevertheless, this distinction is neglected in the actual word order classification of these different types of languages. Thus, for instance, both Rumanian and Guarani are classified as NA-languages (Greenberg 1963, Hawkins 1983). The NA order in Guarani is inconsistent with the noun-postposition order and the other head-final traits of the language (cf. Table 64.1). In order to assess NA order appropriately it is crucial to take into account that Guarani does not have a distinct class of adjectives. When used adnominally, adjectival notions are expressed by uninflected stative verbs, such as *poti* 'to be clean' in *ao poti* 'clean clothes' (Gregores & Suárez 1967: 148). In conclusion, instead of NA, Guarani uses NV, and this pattern matches the basic NP-V order in intransitive clauses. This kind of explanation seems to be available for other languages as well. As mentioned by Dryer (1988: 198), in the V-final languages in which adjectives are verbs they tend to follow the noun.

As to the functional status of adjectives and other noun modifiers, let us illustrate the point with Rumanian and Basque. When looked at superficially, prenominal demonstratives and adjectives in Rumanian are inconsistent with the basic head-initial pattern of the language. The prenominal elements are inflected exactly like the head-noun, if it occurs in NP-initial position, and are in complementary distribution with each other. In fact, nominal inflection appears on the first element in the NP irrespective of its category, as shown in (11):

(11) Rumanian
copil-ul-lui frumos
child-DEF-OBL beautiful
'the beautiful child'
acest-ui copil frumos
this-OBL child beautiful
'this beautiful child'
mic-ul-ui copil
small-DEF-OBL child
'the small child'
**frumosului copilului*
'the beautiful child'
**acestui frumosului copil*
'this beautiful child'
**micului frumosului copil*
'the small beautiful child'

The illustrated noun phrases are in the genitive-dative case (OBL), and some of them show the suffixed definite article (DEF). Note that the definite article is also attached to the semantically appropriate first element in the NP irrespective of its category.

The data in (11) suggest that inflected prenominal elements are heads by the inflectional criterion (3c) above (cf. for a similar proposal Mallinson 1986: 203, Radford 1993: 90). They are also mother-node-constructing categories for the NP in the sense of Hawkins' EIC. Under this interpretation, $\text{Dem}_{\text{infl}}\text{N}$, $\text{A}_{\text{infl}}\text{N}$ and $\text{N}_{\text{infl}}\text{A}$ turn out to be consistent with the dominant head-initial pattern of the language.

As to the adjectives and demonstratives in Basque, they are a mirror image of the situation in Rumanian. The case affix is attached to the last element of the noun phrase, no matter whether it is a demonstrative, adjective or noun. This is illustrated in (12). The order AN, as in (12b), is restricted to a few adjectival lexemes.

(12)   Basque (Saltarelli 1988: 75–77)
  (a) *ohe zabal-ak*
      bed wide-PL.ABS
      'wide beds'
  (b) *amerikar hiri-a*
      American city-ABS
      'American city'
  (c) *hiri amerikarr-a*
      city American-ABS
      'American city'
  (d) *liburu berri hari-ek*
      book new that-PL.ABS
      'those new books'

As with Rumanian, the apparently aberrant word orders turn out to be consistent with the overall word order pattern of the language, if one analyses the last inflected element of the NP as its head (cf. Householder 1988 for more head-final languages with NP-final inflectional marking).

The problems involving the head status of noun modifiers have been acknowledged in the literature (cf. Radford 1993 for adjectives, and Dryer 1992: 119 for numerals). The preceding discussion is intended not so much to claim that demonstratives and adjectives are heads in all languages, but rather to suggest that they are heads in some languages. While they may constitute a fairly well-defined category from a semantic point of view, the grammatical properties of noun modifiers seem to vary from language to language, so that they do not constitute a homogeneous category with respect to the CHS.

The situation illustrated in Rumanian and Basque has theoretical implications for the syntactic notion of head. One can either extend the notion of head to cover the inflected demonstratives and adjectives in Rumanian and Basque, or one has to give up the idea that heads are the relevant concepts in the typological distinction at issue (cf. Hawkins 1993 for the latter option and in favour of his processing concept of mother-node-constructing category).

Let us follow the first option and discuss a distinction that seems of greater relevance for word order typology. The distinction at issue is that between functional and lexical heads. As a first approximation, functional heads can be identified as heads without a lexical semantic content such as articles, complementizers, auxiliary verbs and adpositions serving a purely syntactic function as with adpositional objects (e. g. *depends on X, complains about X*). Lexical heads such as verbs, nouns and adjectives have a rich semantic content. More important than this semantic distinction are the syntactic characteristics of functional heads (cf. Haider 1993: 25 f.):

(13) (a) Functional heads take lexical phrases as their complement, i. e. functional phrases are more complex phrases with embedded lexical phrases.
      (b) Functional head positions can be filled by different (even lexical) categories under restricted conditions
      (c) The functional head (instead of or additionally to the further embedded lexical head) expresses the syntactic function of the phrase by inflection if it belongs to an inflecting cateogry (cf. also (3c) above).

The NP-initial position in Rumanian and the NP-final position in Basque qualify as functional head positions by the criteria in (13). Property (13b) characterizes functional heads as purely structural notions, since a syntactic head position of this kind can be filled with different categories under restricted conditions. Such a condition is the presence of functional inflection, i. e. inflectional features that identify the syntactic function of the whole phrase (cf. (13c)).

The distinction between functional and lexical heads also helps to uncover a regular pattern in the typological inconsistencies of

German. Functional heads such as articles and complementizers must occupy a left-peripheral position. Note that adpositions that serve a purely syntactic function (e. g. *denkt an dich* 'thinks of you') are always prepositions in German. Some lexical heads such as uninflected verbs (*ohne dem Kind das Buch zu geben* 'without giving the child the book') and adjectives in the adjective phrase (*der [vermutlich des Mordes **verdächtige**] Mann* 'the man that is presumably suspected to be the murderer') occur only on the right periphery of the phrase.

Another problem pertaining to adjectives and other noun modifiers is the fact that in some languages what seems to be a regular noun phrase is a string of loosely, i. e. appositively connected elements. Each of these elements can represent the noun phrase and, therefore, can appear as a major constituent of the sentence (e. g. Kalkatungu, Mangarayi, Ngiyambaa, Nunggubuyu and other Australian languages, Yimas and possibly other Papuan languages of New Guinea, but also some of the European languages such as Latin or Polish, cf. Rijkhoff 1992, 1998). In such languages, the elements semantically modifying a noun can be freely moved within the sentence.

These observations hint at the possibilities of improving the typological characterization of languages by a more thorough analysis of the category and function of the elements involved in the Greenbergian correlations. The discussion focused on noun modifiers because these show cross-language categorization problems which are not matched to the same extent by verbs, adpositions and nouns.

2.3.3. Linguistic areas and genera

The relatively recent discovery of broader areal and genetic patterns in the distribution of the different word order types confronts typologists with a new challenging aspect. Neither the rather consistent patterns, nor the bad patterners mentioned in the preceding sections seem to be randomly distributed over the areas and genera of the world (cf. Dryer 1992, 1998, Nichols 1992, Bakker 1998). Australia and New Guinea, for example, show a prevalence for GN that leads to inconsistencies in the VO languages of this area. In Africa, NAdj and NDem is prevalent, and this explains why the ratio of consistent languages with VO and N-Modifier (NMod) is higher in this area than in the rest of the world.

Dryer (1998) offers a more detailed discussion of the areal and genetic patterns of NMod/ModN in the VO languages of Europe. He proposes the following scale with Celtic, as the most consistent head-initial representative, to Baltic and Finnic as the least consistent representatives (VO and ModN, GN in particular):

(14) Celtic < Albanian, Romance < Greek, Slavic < Germanic < Baltic, Finnic

Dryer (1998: 303 f.) explains the position of the Celtic languages in (14) by their geographical and chronological distance from an Eurasian stock of languages with a consistent OV-ModN pattern. Additionally, an Afroasiatic substratum with head-initial traits may have influenced the development of the modern Celtic languages (cf. Dryer 1998: 317, Fn. 16): By contrast, the Finnic and Baltic languages are geographically and chronologically closer to the Eurasian OV-type. Despite its preliminary and tentative character, this line of explanation offers a fascinating view on the possibilities offered by interdisciplinary studies on language typology, language contact and historical-comparative linguistics.

The discussion in the preceding sections has shown that the patterns that are inconsistent with the Greenbergian word order correlations may have various sources. Such patterns may be due to the effect of competing principles (cf. § 2.2.), to a misanalysis of the categories involved in the correlations (§ 2.3.2.) or to language contact and a subsequent diachronic change (this section).

3. Major constituents of the clause

3.1. Variable vs. rigid order

One of the topics in typological research is the distinction between languages with rigid word order and languages with free word order and its possible explanation. It is only more recently that word order variation has been studied more systematically within typological research (cf. Steele 1978, Nichols 1992, Bakker 1998, Siewierska 1998 and the studies within generative grammar mentioned below).

Within the framework of generative grammar, the distinction between variable and rigid order at the clausal level was introduced as a typological configurationality parameter by Hale (1983) and Chomsky (1981) (→ Art. 103). Languages with rather rigid word order at clausal level such as English and French are assumed to have a configurational sentence structure with a structural asymmetry between subject and object. For non-configurational languages such as Warlpiri, Hale proposes flat structures that do not form intermediate phrases such as VP. An alternative proposal is Jelinek (1984). She claims that non-configurational languages lack nominal verbal arguments. Instead, pronominal clitics or agreement affixes attached to the verb serve as verbal arguments. This account is meant to explain not only free word order in non-configurational languages but also some of their further properties such as free deletion of argument NPs and absence of expletives (i.e. elements such as German *es kamen drei Männer*, Engl. *there came three men*). The correlation between rich agreement inflection, absence of expletives and free deletion of pronominal arguments is also part of the typological pro-drop parameter in generative grammar (cf. Jaeggli & Safir 1989). The configurationality issue has been abandoned in more recent generative research in favor of the pro-drop parameter, Baker's (1995) polysynthesis parameter and the option of freely scrambling the major constituents of the clause.

The studies mentioned above do not pursue the Greenbergian methodology as they are not based on larger language samples. Nevertheless, Jelinek's work in particular points to a correlation between rich agreement marking and word order freedom which has also been demonstrated to exist within the Greenbergian research tradition by Steele (1978), and more recently on a larger sample, by Siewierska (1998). The last mentioned authors have considered variation in the permissible permutations of nominal S, O and finite V relative to each other in main, affirmative, declarative clauses.

Siewierska's study (1998: 507 f.) establishes a direct correlation between absence of morphological marking (case marking and agreement with S or S and O) and rigid word order as stated in (15):

(15) If morphological marking of the distinction between S and O is absent, then with more than chance frequency the relative order of S, O and V is restricted or rigid (logically equivalent to the statement that if a language has flexible order of S, O, and V, then with more than chance frequency it distinguishes S and O by morphological marking).

(15) generalizes Steele's (1978) and Jelinek's (1984) observations about the role of agreement for word order flexibility. Siewierska's findings corroborate the closer correlation between agreement marking and word order flexibility as opposed to case marking. Thus, 81% of the languages without agreement and 69% of the languages without case marking are restricted or rigid order languages. Correspondingly, among the languages with flexible and highly flexible word order, 84% have agreement and 63% case marking.

The common explanation for these correlations is as follows: Grammatical functions may be signalled morphologically or by word order. A language without morphological marking of S and O has to distinguish S and O by word order. This explanation is based on the one-form-one-meaning principle and is intuitively appealing, but it is founded on the false assumption that morphological marking and word order are functionally equivalent (cf. Primus 1996 for arguments against this assumption). The fact that these coding devices do not serve the same function explains why rigid word order may co-occur with morphological marking.

An alternative explanation for the correlations in (15) is Jelinek's proposal discussed above, which is restricted to agreement marking. Another proposal was developed for case-marking languages (cf. Primus 1996, 1998). This proposal allows case-marking languages to have rigid order under certain conditions and also predicts which order of verbal arguments will occur in the absence of morphological marking. It is grounded on the common assumption that word order is a multifactor phenomenon. There are several competing linearization factors and each factor determines a particular word order. A word order ⟨X, Y⟩ obeying a linearization factor F is reversed to ⟨Y, X⟩ only if there is another linearization factor F′ that motivates ⟨Y, X⟩. There are at least two relevant grammatical factors determining the basic order of verbal arguments: thematic roles and formal relations established by the case or adpositional marking of a verbal argument.

As to semantic or thematic roles, this approach can be viewed as a further development of Dowty's (1991) analysis. Under this view, thematic roles are treated as cluster concepts of prototype theory involving more basic concepts such as control, causation, sentience, etc. The Thematic Hierarchy (16) captures the thematic linearization factor:

(16) The Thematic Hierarchy
Proto-Agent $<\theta$ Proto-Recipient $<\theta$ Proto-Patient
controller   recipient   controlled
causer   addressee   caused
experiencer   benefactive   stimulus
possessor   possessed

(16) also specifies the more basic roles falling under the proto-role above them. The list is not exhaustive, but it suffices to illustrate the main assumptions of this approach. The hierarchy relation "<" is specified with respect to the type of relational concept involved in the hierarchy: $<\theta$ alignes thematic roles, $<m$ in (17) below alignes syntactic relations that are expressed morphologically or adpositionally.

The second linearization factor is the hierarchy of formal relational concepts in (17):

(17) The 'Case' Hierarchy
(a) nominative/absolutive argument $<m$ accusative/ergative argument $<m$ dative or other oblique case argument $<m$ ...
(b) inflectional case argument $<m$ adpositional argument

Within cross-linguistic research it has become common practice to use the concept of case not only for inflectional forms but also for adpositions or other particles attached to syntactic arguments. Therefore, 'case' is used in this broader sense in the name of the hierarchy. (17b) does not establish a second hierarchy; it only clarifies the formal asymmetry between inflectional case marking and adpositional marking, if a language uses both marking devices. The 'Case' Hierarchy (17) holds for many languages, but it is not universally valid. The most common variation of (17) comes from the fact that a language may lack one of the categories involved or may collapse categories into one hierarchy position. The word order rule in (18) below is universally applicable, even if each language has its own formal hierarchy.

The word order universal that captures these two grammatical factors can be formulated as follows (cf. Primus (1996) for its explanation in terms of the SESD in (8) above):

(18) For any pair of verbal co-arguments X, Y: if X $<\theta$ Y or X $<m$ Y, then X tends to c-command and/or precede Y.

The difference between more rigid order and more flexible order of verbal arguments can be explained in this kind of approach by the interaction between the Thematic Hierarchy and the 'Case' Hierarchy. If they are in conflict with each other, i.e. X $<\theta$ Y and Y $<m$ X, the resulting order is rather free. The impression of freedom comes from the fact that no matter which order is chosen, the choice is motivated by one ordering factor, either $<\theta$ or $<m$. When they operate in conjunction, i.e. X $<\theta$ Y and X $<m$ Y, a departure from the order predicted by the two factors has no grammatical motivation. Since grammatical linearization factors are stronger than pragmatic ones in languages which are not discourse-configurational in the sense discussed below, a grammatically rigid order has less chance of being reversed for pragmatic reasons. The word order rule (18) also predicts more rigid order along the Thematic Hierarchy, if there is no distinction between X and Y in terms of the 'Case' Hierarchy (X = m Y).

By this reasoning, no languages are predicted to have a rigid order in canonical transitive clauses in which a patient that is causally affected or controlled by the agent precedes a controlling or causing agent. In nominative languages, this kind of agent is coded canonically by the nominative and cannot be outranked by the patient on the Thematic or 'Case' Hierarchy. In ergative languages, this kind of agent is canonically coded by the ergative and is outranked only on the 'Case' Hierarchy by the patient that is canonically coded by the absolutive. In the canonical transitive clauses of nominative and ergative languages, the coding constellation is such that it does not motivate a rigid patient-agent order. (18) also predicts that in virtue of their canonical coding, the relative order of agent and patient is more often reversed in ergative languages than in nominative languages. These predictions are borne out by the facts. Among the languages with basic patient-agent order (i.e. O before S order, cf. Derbyshire & Pullum 1981), the order is never rigid, and ergative languages are statistically more dominant than average (cf. Primus 1995: 1088 f.).

Rigid word order in the absence of a formal 'case' asymmetry can be illustrated with recipient-patient order in English and Swedish:

(19)   She gave John a book. *She gave a book John.
(20)   Swedish: Hon gav Johan en bok. *Hon gav en bok Johan.

As shown in Primus (1998) for European languages, a Proto-Recipient (R) rigidly precedes a Proto-Patient (P) in those constructions that lack a formal distinction for these roles. By contrast, the order of R and P is free if and only if P <m R, as is the case when R and P are canonically marked by cases and/or adpositions:

(21)   She gave a book to John. She gave to John the book I bought yesterday.

This approach also captures the fact that morphological marking may co-occur with rigid word order if a pair of verbal arguments are aligned as X <θ Y and X <m Y. The different ditransitive constructions in Icelandic in (22)–(23) will serve as an illustration:

(22)   Icelandic (Ottósson 1991: 78)
        Jón gaf Maríu (DAT) bókina (ACC).
        'John gave Mary the book.'

(23)   (a) þeir leyndu Ólaf (ACC) sannleikanum (DAT).
            'They concealed Olaf the truth.'
        (b) Jón bað Ólaf (ACC) bónar (GEN)
            'John asked Olaf a favour.'
        (c) Jón skilaði Maríu (DAT) bókinni (DAT).
            'John returned the book to Mary.'
        (d) María óskaði Ólafi (DAT) alls góðs (GEN).
            'Mary wished Olaf all the best.'

The two objects in (22) can be inverted under certain conditions, whereas the relative order of the two objects in (23) is rigid. The explanation of this difference is straightforward within the approach defended here. The case-marking of R and P in (22) is canonical: R is in the dative, P in the accusative. This leads to the constellation X <θ Y and Y <m X, and as a consequence, to free word order. As in all languages in the European sample with this type of marking for P and R, the order of R and P is rather free with a slight preference for the thematically determined RP order, as illustrated in (22). Other verbs belonging to this class in Icelandic are *segja* 'tell', *senda* 'send', *synja* 'show', a. o. The verbs in (23) show the constellation X <θ Y and X <m Y or X =m Y, and as a consequence, rigid word order.

The approach presented above not only captures the fact that rigid order may be conditioned by the absence of case distinctions, but also that the order is invariantly in accordance with the Thematic Hierarchy (16). It also captures the fact that morphological marking may cooccur with rigid word order under certain conditions. But this approach deals only with languages with case and adpositional marking. The role of agreement marking in determining word order variation is possibly of a different nature. Recall that according to Jelinek's proposal, languages with rich agreement marking are non-configurational. Non-configurational languages have not only a free word order of verbal arguments in all types of constructions, but also further properties which are absent in languages such as English, Icelandic and German: free deletion of nominal arguments and absence of expletives. This suggests that flexible word order may have different sources in different types of languages.

Yet another source of word order flexibility of S, O, and V is discourse configurationality (→ Art. 104). Linguists from different research traditions (cf. Mithun 1987, Payne 1992, Kiss 1995, 1998) have drawn attention to the fact that there are languages in which the relative order of verbal arguments is solely determined by their discourse function. More specifically, there are languages in which the topic and/or focused constituent is restricted to a particular structural position. Languages with a rather rigid topic position are, for example, Rumanian, Catalan, and Modern Greek. There are also languages with a fairly rigid topic and focus position: Amele, Basque, Georgian, Laz, Hungarian, and Turkish (cf. Primus 1993, Kiss 1995 for references). In these discourse-configurational languages, there are no palpable grammatical restrictions for the relative order of verbal arguments, but the interplay between discourse-based and grammatically based serialization has not been studied systematically enough to allow a firm conclusion.

The discussion in this section suggests that word order flexibility at the clausal level may be conditioned by various factors. There are a number of recent studies that point to the factors that seem relevant for the issue: agreement or case marking of grammatical functions, syntactic configurationality, and discourse configurationality.

3.2. Wh-words

As Greenberg (1963) observed, the position of wh-word correlates with the head-serialization type of the language, cf. (24):

(24)   Universal 12: If a language has dominated order VSO in declarative sentences, it always puts interrogative words or phrases first in interrogative word questions; if it has dominant order SOV in declarative sentences, there is never such an invariant rule.

Subsequent studies found exceptions to this universal (cf. Dryer 1991: 466), but the correlation between V-initial languages and sentence-initial wh-words is still valid as a strong preference.

The sentence-initial wh-words are treated within generative grammar as being in complementizer position or in a position immediately preceding the complementizer (cf. Haegeman 1991, chap. 7, for a survey of different approaches). Since V-initial languages strongly favour CompS, this analysis is a plausible explanation for the sentence-initial placement of wh-words in this type of languages. V-final languages have either sentence-initial wh-words or wh-words that are placed in immediately preverbal position. Kim (1988) mentions the following SOV languages with preverbal wh-words: Turkish, Sherpa, Telugu, Tamil, Laccadive Malayalam, Gujarati, Hindi-Urdu and other Indo-Aryan languages, Korean, Japanese, Basque. In Hungarian and Georgian, the position of wh-words is also immediately preverbal, but the position of the verb itself is variable (SOV/SVO).

It seems then that wh-words are preferably located in a position that immediately precedes a sentential head, i.e. Comp or V. This would explain their strongly preferred sentence-initial position in V-initial languages, which are also consistently Comp-initial. As mentioned above in connection with Minimal Attachment phenomena (cf. (6)), many V-final languages have Comp-initial sentence structures. This would explain why both sentence-initial wh-words and preverbal wh-words are found within this class of languages.

As to the adjacency of wh-words to sentential heads, Kiss (1995: 20f.) offers a survey of various structural explanations within generative grammar which are based on the association of wh-words with focus (cf. also Horvath 1986, Kim 1988), and indeed, in some focus-configurational languages, the wh-words appear in the structural focus position. Under this assumption, focused constituents are expected to show the same ordering asymmetries as wh-words. They are expected to occur, in general, in sentence-initial position in V-initial languages. V-final languages are predicted to have either sentence-initial or preverbal focus positions. But this does not seem to be the case, and an explanation for their different behaviour is the fact that wh-words and focused constituents differ considerably in their word-order relevant properties. Wh-words are light, non-branching elements, they usually do not carry the main sentence stress and show limited word order variation within and across languages. Their main function is to mark the wh-interrogative sentence type. By contrast, focused constituents are not sentence type markers. They have a variable extension from one word to the whole clause, must carry the main stress of the clause and show more word order variation even in focus-configurational languages. Their position seems to depend heavily on the extension of the focus, and as a consequence, on their syntactic weight (cf. Primus 1993). In the light of these observations, the association of wh-words with focus is not a straightforward matter and considerably more empirical work is needed in order to assess the common word order properties of wh-words and focused constituents.

An alternative plausible explanation for the adjacency of wh-words to sentential heads is based on the syntactic and semantic function of wh-words to express the interrogative sentence type. As the cross-linguistic survey of Sadock & Zwicky (1985) shows, the characteristic forms that mark grammaticalized sentence types are associated with sentential heads: verb inflection (especially for imperatives), verb or auxiliary position, verb affixes, and particles which preferably occur sentence initially or close to the verb or the auxiliary.

3.3. Subjects

As shown by Dryer (1991), SVO languages have by far more word order properties in common with V-initial languages than with V-final languages. Therefore, the subject seems to be a bad patterner relative to the CHS in SVO languages. An explanation that has been repeatedly invoked in the literature is the prominent discourse function of the subject as the most topical constituent. In conformity with this line of explanation, SVO order should be related to the discourse-configurational languages. The fact that in such languages the subject, i. e. Proto-Agent, typically precedes the verb and the other arguments of the verb is an epiphenomenon of the canonical topic selection and the canonical sentence-initial location of topics (cf. Primus 1993, Kiss 1995). In the light of this explanation discourse-configurational languages prefer SVO order over VSO due to the canonical topic-predication structure. This explanation seems to be plausible in view of the fact that many discourse-configurational SVO languages have VSO order in sentences without a topic (cf. Sasse 1987, Primus 1993). Space limitation prohibits the discussion of the pro-drop parameter, which has also been associated with the presence of VS as a variant to SV in SVO languages such as Italian (cf. Jaeggli & Safir 1989).

This line of reasoning is a plausible explanation for the distinction between SV and VS in discourse-configurational languages, but not in languages such as English and French, which have a grammatically determined SVO order and no pro-drop option. A more recent grammatical explanation is proposed by Ouhalla (1991). Following Pollock (1989), Ouhalla assumes that elements such as subject agreement (SAgr) and Tense (T) are syntactic heads, each with its own phrasal category (AgrP and TP), and that the location of SAgr and T relative to each other is a major typological parameter which, among other things, determines the surface order of subject and verb. The two relevant structures are shown in a simplified version in (25):

(25) (a) [$_{AgrP}$ subject ... [$_{TP}$ ... [$_T$ verb] [$_{VP}$ ...]]]
 (b) [$_{TP}$ ... [$_T$ verb] [$_{AgrP}$ subject ... [$_{VP}$ ...]]]

Within the framework of recent generative grammar, the subject is obligatorily moved from a base-generated VP-internal position to a node immediately dominated by AgrP in order to receive nominative case, and the verb is obligatorily moved to the T-head position. This explains why the different relative orders of SAgr and T yield different surface positions of S and V, as shown in (25). Crucial for an adequate assessment of Ouhalla's proposal is the fact that the actual affixation procedure for T and SAgr is a separate transformation that does not necessarily lead to a relative affix order that directly mirrors the relative order of T and SAgr in the configurations (25). But it would be a welcome finding if this would be the case.

Siewierska (1994) tested Ouhalla's parameter on the relative order of SAgr and T in 218 languages which have both markers on the same side of the verb stem. SV comprises SOV and SVO, and VS includes VSO and VOS. The correlation Agr[T] ↔ SV is valid in Siewierska's sample as a statistical generalization: it holds for 108 out of 136 Agr[T] languages (= 79%) and 152 SV languages (= 71%). The correlation is even stronger when T or Agr or both are free forms (e. g. clitics). Note that the relative position of free forms is more revealing for Ouhalla's proposal which analyses Agr and T as syntactically free nodes. The correspondence T[Agr] ↔ VS is less clear in the sample: it holds only for 31 out of 54 T[Agr] languages (= 57%) and 57 VS languages (= 54%). This correspondence is much clearer with free forms: it holds for 12 out of 13 T[Agr] languages (= 92%) and 15 VS languages (= 80%).

The asymmetry in the correlations involving affixed forms seems to show the effect of the frequency asymmetry of the elements involved. Agr[T] is much more frequent than T[Agr] universally (cf. Bybee 1985: 35) and in Siewierska's sample (75% vs. 25%), and SV is strongly preferred over VS universally (cf. Tomlin 1986) and in Siewierska's sample (73% vs. 27%). The correlation Agr[T] ↔ SV involves preferred members, and this enhances the probability of their co-occurrence. The correlation T[Agr] ↔ VS involves dispreferred members, and this lowers the probability of their co-occurrence. Taking these frequency asymmetries and the situation with free forms into account, the statistical results are by far more promising for Ouhalla's proposal than Siewierska is willing to admit. Nevertheless, it is premature to claim that these results are explicable only by Ouhalla's proposal. As mentioned by Siewierska, diachronic explanations in the vein of Givón (1971) are also appealing.

As with other word order phenomena discussed in this article, recent proposals for the SV/VS distinction span the range of explanations from discourse-based considerations to syntactic structural factors. This polarity may have an empirical basis in the phenomenon itself or may be a theoretical artefact due to the polarization of the two most prominent research traditions in the field of language typology and universals: generative grammar, which strongly favours formal structural explanations, and functional typology, which concentrates on explanations in terms of the communicative (discourse-pragmatic) functions of language.

4. References

Baker, Mark C. 1995. *The polysynthesis parameter.* Oxford: Oxford University Press.

Bakker, Dik. 1998. "Flexibility and consistency in word order patterns in the languages of Europe". In: Siewierska (ed.), 383−419.

Bartsch, Renate & Vennemann, Theo. 1972. *Semantic structures.* Frankfurt a. M.: Athenäum.

Behaghel, Otto. 1932. *Deutsche Syntax. Eine geschichtliche Darstellung.* Vol. IV. Heidelberg: Winter.

Bell, Alan. 1978. "Language samples". In: Greenberg et al. (eds.) Vol. I, 123−156.

Bybee, Joan & Pagliuca, William & Perkins, Revere. 1990. "On the asymmetries in the affixation of grammatical material". In: Croft, William & Denning, Keith & Kemmer, Suzanne (eds.). *Studies in typology and diachrony.* Amsterdam: Benjamins, 1−42.

Bybee, Joan. 1985. *Morphology.* Amsterdam: Benjamins.

Chomsky, Noam. 1981. *Lectures on government and binding.* Dordrecht: Foris.

Comrie, Bernard. 1981. *Language universals and linguistic typology.* Chicago: University of Chicago Press.

Corbett, Greville & Fraser, Norman & McGlashan, Scott (eds.) 1993. *Heads in grammatical theory.* Cambridge: Cambridge University Press.

Croft, William. 1990. *Typology and universals.* Cambridge: Cambridge University Press.

Dahl, Östen. 1979. "Typology of sentence negation". *Linguistcs* 17: 79−106.

−. 1993. "Negation". In: Jacobs et al. (eds.), 914−923.

Derbyshire, Desmond C. & Pullum, Geoffrey. 1981. "Object initial languages". *International journal of American linguistics* 47: 192−214.

Deszö, László. 1982. *Studies in syntactic typology and contrastive grammar.* The Hague: Mouton.

Dowty, David R. 1991. "Thematic proto-roles and argument selection". *Language* 67: 547−619.

Dryer, Matthew. 1988. "Object-verb order and adjective-noun order: dispelling a myth". *Lingua* 74: 77−109.

−. 1989. "Large linguistic areas and language sampling". *Studies in Language* 13: 257−92.

−. 1991. "SVO languages and the VO:OV typology". *Journal of Linguistics* 27: 443−482.

−. 1992. "The Greenbergian word order correlations". *Language* 68: 81−138.

−. 1995. "Word order typology". In: Jacobs et al. (eds.). Vol. II, 1050−1065.

−. 1998. "Word order in the languages of Europe". In: Siewierska (ed.), 283−319.

Fanselow, Gisbert. 1987. "Über Wortstellungstypologie anläßlich eines Buches von J. Hawkins". *Zeitschrift für Sprachwissenschaft* 6: 114−133.

Frazier, Lyn. 1979. *On comprehending sentences: Syntactic parsing strategies.* IUCL. Bloomington.

Frazier, Lyn & Rayner, Keith. 1988. "Parametrizing the language processing system: Left- vs. right-branching within and across languages". In: Hawkins (ed.), 247−279.

Gazdar, Gerald & Klein, Ewan & Pullum, Geoffrey. 1985. *Generalized Phrase Structure Grammar.* Cambridge: Harvard University Press.

Gil, David. 1986. "A prosodic typology of language". *Folia Linguistica* 20: 165−231.

Givón, Talmy. 1971. "Historical syntax and synchronic morphology: an archeologist's field trip". *Proceedings from the 7th regional meeting of the Chicago Linguistic Society,* 394−415.

Greenberg, Joseph H. 1963. "Some universals of grammar with particular reference to the order of meaningful elements". In: Greenberg, Joseph H. (ed.). *Universals of language.* Cambridge/Mass: MIT Press, 58−90.

Greenberg, Joseph H. & Ferguson, Charles A. & Moravcsik, Edith A. (eds.) 1978. *Universals of human language.* 4 vols. Stanford: Stanford University Press.

Gregores, Emilio & Suárez, Jorge A. 1967. *A description of Colloquial Guaraní.* The Hague: Mouton.

Haegeman, Liliane. 1991. *Introduction to government and binding theory.* London: Blackwell.

Haider, Hubert. 1986. "Who is afraid of typology?" *Folia Linguistica* 20: 109−145.

−. 1993. *Deutsche Syntax − Generativ.* Tübingen: Narr.

Hale, Kenneth. 1983. "Warlbiri and the grammar of non-configurational languages". *Natural language and linguistic theory* 1: 5−47.

Hall, Christopher. 1988. "Integrating diachronic and processing principles in explaining the suffixing preference". In: Hawkins (ed.), 321−349.

Hammond, Michael & Moravcsik, Edith A. & Wirth, Jessica R. (eds.) 1988. *Studies in syntactic typology.* Amsterdam: Benjamins.

Harlig, Jeffrey & Bardovi-Harlig, Kathleen. 1988. "Accentuation typology, word order and theme-rheme structure". In: Hammond et al. (eds.), 125−146.

Hawkins, John A. 1983. *Word order universals.* New York: Academic Press.

−. 1988. "On explaining some right-left asymmetries in syntactic and morphological universals". In: Hammond et al. (eds.), 321−358.

—. (ed.) 1988. *Explaining language universals*. Oxford: Blackwell.

—. 1990. "A parsing theory of word order universals". *Linguistic Inquiry* 21: 223–261.

—. 1993. "On heads, parsing, and word order universals. In: Corbett et al. (eds.), 231–265.

—. 1994. *A performance theory of order and constituency*. Cambridge: Cambridge University Press.

—. 1998. "Some issues in a performance theory of word order". In: Siewierska (ed.), 729–781.

Hawkins, John A. & Cutler, Anne. 1988. "Psycholinguistic factors in morphological asymmetry". In: Hawkins (ed.), 280–320.

Horvath, Julia. 1986. *Focus in the theory of grammar and the syntax of Hungarian*. Dordrecht: Foris.

Householder, Fred. 1988. "The group genitive and type 24 languages". In: Duncan-Rose, Caroline & Vennemann, Theo (eds.). *A Festschrift for Robert P. Stockwell*. London: Routledge, 381–388.

Jackendoff, Ray. 1977. *X-bar-syntax: a study of phrase structure*. Cambridge/Mass: MIT Press.

Jacobs, Joachim. 1991. "Negation". In: von Stechow, Arnim & Wunderlich, Dieter (eds.). *Semantik. Ein internationales Handbuch der zeitgenössischen Forschung*. Berlin: de Gruyter, 560–596.

—. 1992. "Neutral stress and the position of heads". In: Jacobs, Joachim (ed.). *Informationsstruktur und Grammatik* (Linguistische Berichte, special issue 4), 220–244.

—. 1994. *Kontra Valenz*. Trier: Wissenschaftlicher Verlag.

Jacobs, Joachim & von Stechow, Arnim & Sternefeld, Wolfgang & Vennemann, Theo (eds.) 1993/1995. *Syntax. Ein internationales Handbuch zeitgenössischer Forschung*. Vol. I (1993), vol. II (1995). Berlin: de Gruyter.

Jaeggli, Osvaldo & Safir, Ken (eds.) 1989. *The null subject parameter*. Dordrecht: Kluwer Academic Publishers.

Jelinek, Eloise. 1984. "Empty categories, case and configurationality". *Natural language and linguistic theory* 2: 39–76.

Kayne, Richard. 1984. *Connectedness and binary branching*. Dordrecht.

—. 1994. *The antisymmetry of syntax*. Cambridge/Mass.: MIT Press.

Keenan, Edward. 1979. "On surface form and logical form". *Studies in the Linguistic Sciences* 8. Dept. of Linguistics, University of Illinois.

Kim, Alan Hyun-Oak. 1988. "Preverbal focusing and type XXIII languages". In: Hammond et al. (eds.), 147–172.

Kiss, Katalin E. 1995. "Introduction". In: Kiss, Katalin E. (ed.). *Discourse configurational languages*. Oxford: Oxford University Press, 3–27.

—. 1998. "Discourse configurationality in the languages of Europe". In: Siewierska (ed.), 681–727.

Lehmann, Winfred. 1972. "Contemporary linguistics and Indo-European studies". *Publications of the Modern Language Association* 87: 967–993.

—. 1973. "A structural principle of language and its implications". *Language* 49: 42–66.

—. 1995. "Objectives of a theory of syntactic change". In: Jacobs et al. (eds.), 1116–1126.

Mallinson, Graham. 1986. *Rumanian*. London: Croom Helm.

Maxwell, Daniel. 1984. "A typologically based principle of linearization". *Language* 60: 251–285.

Mithun, Marianne. 1987. "Is basic order universal?" In: Tomlin, Russel (ed.). *Coherence and foregrounding in discourse*. Amsterdam: Benjamins, 281–328.

Montague, Richard. 1974. "The proper treatment of quantification in ordinary English". In: Thomason, Richmond (ed.). *Formal philosophy*. New Haven: Yale University Press, 247–270.

Nichols, Johanna. 1992. *Linguistic diversity in space and time*. Chicago: University of Chicago Press.

Ottósson, Kjartan G. 1991. "Icelandic double objects as small clauses". In: *Working papers in Scandinavian syntax* 48: 77–97.

Ouhalla, Jamal. 1991. *Functional categories and parametric variation*. London: Routledge.

Pafel, Jürgen. 1993. "Scope and word order". In: Jacobs et al. (eds.). Vol. I, 867–880.

Payne, Doris L. (ed.) 1992. *Pragmatics of word order flexibility*. Amsterdam: Benjamins.

Payne, John R. 1985. "Negation". In: Shopen (ed.). Vol. I, 197–242.

Pollard, Carl & Sag, Ivan A. 1994. *Head-driven phrase structure grammar*. Chicago: University of Chicago Press.

Pollock, J.-Y. 1989. "Verb movement, UG and the structure of IP". *Linguistic Inquiry* 20: 365–424.

Primus, Beatrice. 1993. "Word order and information structure: A performance-based account of topic positions and focus positions". In: Jacobs et al. (eds.). Vol. I, 880–896.

—. 1995. "Relational typology". In: Jacobs et al. (eds.). Vol. II, 1076–1109.

—. 1996. "Dependenz und Serialisierung: das Deutsche im Sprachvergleich". In: Lang, Ewald & Zifonun, Gisela (eds.). Deutsch – typologisch. Berlin: de Gruyter, 57–91.

—. 1998. "The relative order of recipient and patient in the languages of Europe". In: Siewierska (ed.), 421–473.

Radford, Andrew. 1993. "Head-hunting: on the trail of the nominal yanus". In: Corbett et al. (eds.), 73–113.

Reinhart, Tanya. 1983. *Anaphora and semantic interpretation*. London: Croom Helm.

Rijkhoff, Jan. 1992. *The noun phrase. A typological study of its form and structure.* Phd thesis. University of Amsterdam.

—. 1998. "The noun phrase in the languages of Europe". In: Siewierska (ed.), 321–382.

Sadock, Jerold M. & Zwicky, Arnold M. 1985. "Speech act distinctions in syntax". In: Shopen (ed.). Vol. I, 155–196.

Saltarelli, Mario. 1988. *Basque.* London: Croom Helm.

Sasse, Hans-Jürgen. 1987. "The thetic/categorical distinction revisited". *Linguistics* 25: 511–580.

Schmidt, Wilhelm. 1926. *Die Sprachfamilien und Sprachenkreise der Erde.* Heidelberg: Winter.

Shopen, Timothy (ed.) 1985. *Language typology and syntactic description.* 3 vols. Cambridge: Cambridge University Press.

Siewierska, Anna. 1988. *Word order rules.* London: Croom Helm.

—. 1994. "Affix and main clause constituent order". In: Haftka, Brigitta (ed.). *Was determiniert Wortstellungsvariation?* Berlin: Akademie Verlag, 63–76.

—. 1998. "Variation in major constituent order: a global and a European perspective". In: Siewierska (ed.), 475–551.

—. (ed.) 1998. *Constituent order in the languages of Europe.* Berlin: de Gruyter.

Siewierska, Anna & Bakker, Dik. 1996. "The distribution of subject and object agreement and word order type". *Studies in Language* 20: 115–161.

Steele, Susan. 1978. "Word order variation: A typological study". In: Greenberg et al. (eds.). Vol. IV, 585–624.

Tomlin, Russel. 1986. *Basic word order. Functional principles.* London: Croom Helm.

Travis, Lisa. 1984. *Parameters and effects on word order variation.* Phd thesis. Cambridge/Mass.

Vennemann, Theo. 1974. "Theoretical word order studies: results and problems". *Papiere zur Linguistik* 7: 5–25.

—. 1975. "An explanation of drift". In: Li, Charles N. (ed.). *Word order and word order change.* Austin, 269–306.

—. 1977. "Konstituenz und Dependenz in einigen neueren Grammatiktheorien". *Sprachwissenschaft* 2: 259–301.

—. 1983. "Causality in language change. Theories of linguistic preferences as a basis for linguistic explanations". *Folia Linguistica Historica* 6: 5–26.

—. 1984. "Typology, universals, and change in language". In: Fisiak, Jan (ed.). *Historical syntax.* Berlin: Mouton, 593–612.

Vennemann, Theo & Harlow, Ray. 1977. "Categorial grammar and consistent basic VX serialization". *Theoretical Linguistics* 4: 227–254.

Weil, Henri. 1844. *De l'ordre des mots dans les langues anciennes comparées aux langues modernes.* Paris: Univ. Diss.

Williams, Edwin. 1981. "On the notions 'lexically related' and 'head of a word'". *Linguistic Inquiry* 12: 245–274.

Zwart, Jan-Wouter. 1997. "The germanic SOV languages and the universal base hypothesis". In: Haegeman, Liliane (ed.). *New comparative syntax.* London: Longman, 246–267.

Zwicky, Arnold. 1985. "Heads". *Journal of Linguistics* 21: 1–29.

Beatrice Primus, Universität zu Köln
(Germany)

65. Le marquage différentiel de l'objet

1. Introduction
2. Formes de la variation
3. Corrélats de la variation
4. Variations connexes
5. Facteurs associés
6. Abréviations
7. Références

1. Introduction

On appelle « marquage différentiel de l'objet » (expression introduite par Bossong 1985) le fait que, dans une langue donnée l'objet (dit souvent « objet direct ») est susceptible d'apparaître soit sans marque morphologique soit affecté d'une marque. Les deux constructions peuvent en général apparaître avec le même verbe: la variation n'est donc pas liée à la valence du verbe.

Cette définition suppose une définition préalable de l'objet. Nous posons par hypothèse que la construction des phrases « d'action », c'est-à-dire exprimant une action exercée par un agent sur un patient qui en est affecté, constitue, dans la plupart des langues, la « construction biactancielle majeure », qui sert de modèle à toutes sortes de phrases exprimant autre chose que des actions. Nous définissons l'objet comme l'actant représentant le patient et tout actant traité de même dans cette construction.

Le marquage différentiel de l'objet est attesté dans de nombreuses langues (cf., notamment, Thomson 1912; Moravcsik 1978; Bossong 1985; Nocentini 1992; Bossong 1998). L'objet marqué par un cas accusatif ou par une particule pré- ou postposée s'oppose à un objet au cas zéro ou sans adposition. Voici trois exemples:

(1) Espagnol
  (a) *ha matado tres perros*
    a tué   trois chiens
    'Il a tué trois chiens.'
  (b) *ha matado a   mi perro*
    a tué   PREP mon chien
    'Il a tué mon chien.'

(2) Mongol (Beffa & Hamayon 1975: 134, 209)
  (a) *ter xün   delgüürees nom*
    ce homme du.magasin livre
    avav
    acheter:PAS
    'Cet homme a acheté des livres au magasin.'
  (b) *ene nom-yg tand ögsön*
    ce livre-ACC à.vous avoir.donné
    '(Je) vous ai donné ce livre.'

(3) Aymara (Porterie-Gutierrez 1980: 8−9)
  (a) *ajca   manq'aski*
    viande a.mangé
    'Il a mangé de la viande.'
  (b) *k'usilu-ca qamaqʰi-ru ñac'antatajna*
    singe-TH renard-SFX attacha
    'Le singe attacha le renard.'

Dans ce qui suit, nous examinerons successivement les formes de la variation (§ 2.), ses corrélats sémantiques et pragmatiques (§ 3.), des variations connexes concernant l'objet (§ 4.) et quelques autres facteurs associés à ces mêmes variations, qui conduisent à intégrer l'ensemble de ces variations dans une théorie de la transitivité (§ 5.).

2. Formes de la variation

On considérera dans cette section la nature des marques morphologiques affectant l'objet (§ 2.1.), les fonctions syntaxiques qu'elles sont susceptibles de remplir en synchronie (§ 2.2.), leurs origines possibles (§ 2.3.), la position de l'objet marqué et de l'objet non marqué dans la proposition (§ 2.4.).

2.1. Nature des marques

Les marques affectant l'objet sont, selon les langues, de différentes sortes (la famille des langues iraniennes offre un bel échantillon de marques diverses, cf. Bossong 1985). La marque peut être:

a) Un affixe de déclinaison (agglutiné ou amalgamé). C'est le cas en mongol (ex. (2)), dans toutes les langues turques, dans les langues dravidiennes, dans une partie des langues et dialectes iraniens (ossète, ishkâshimi, wakhi, dialectes du nord-ouest), en arménien oriental, en oudi (caucasique du nord-est), dans une partie des langues ouraliennes (mordve, zyriène, lapon méridional, dialectes vogouls, samoyède yourak), en albanais, en amharique, en guarani, en aymara.

b) Une préposition, ainsi dans des langues romanes (*a* dans les langues ibériques et dans divers dialectes, *pe* en roumain), dans des dialectes arabes (maltais, irakien), en hébreu, en araméen, en arménien classique, en chinois mandarin, dans des dialectes iraniens de l'est.

c) Une postposition, comme en persan et dans divers dialectes iraniens, en hindi (avec cas oblique) et dans d'autres langues indo-aryennes. Il va de soi qu'il n'y a pas de distinction tranchée entre les postpositions et les suffixes de cas des langues agglutinantes comme le turc, le guarani ou l'aymara (ex. (3)).

d) Un morphème sans valeur casuelle propre. C'est le cas en dogon, où le morphème ŋ, qui est analysé comme ayant proprement une valeur constrastive, sert à caractériser l'objet dans certaines conditions (Plungian 1993: 230; 1995: 12−13), ex.:

(4) *sana kanda ŋ boe*
  NPR NPR   a.appelé
  'Sana a appelé Kanda.'

2.2. Fonctions des marques

Dans une partie des langues concernées (environ la moitié, selon les échantillons recensés par Bossong (1985: 116), la marque de l'objet n'a pas d'autre fonction casuelle (ou n'en a qu'accessoirement) et peut donc s'analyser comme un accusatif: c'est le cas dans les langues turques (à l'exception du tchouvache), en mongol, dans les langues dravidiennes (toutes ces langues ont un cas accusatif), en persan contemporain (postposition *râ*), en hébreu (préposition *'et*), en albanais (cas accusatif), en chinois (préposition *ba*). Dans les autres langues, elle fonctionne aussi comme génitif ou comme datif, allatif, etc., ou assume plusieurs de ces valeurs casuelles.

En ossète et en mordve, il s'agit d'un génitif-accusatif au sein d'une déclinaison d'une dizaine de cas: c'est une marque abstraite de dépendance adverbale ou adnominale. Dans la plupart des autres langues, la marque en question fonctionne couramment comme datif. En tchouvache, c'est un suffixe casuel d'accusatif-datif. En espagnol et dans d'autres dialectes romans, la préposition *a* fonctionne comme datif et allatif (et locatif). Dans les dialectes arabes et en araméen la préposition *l-* est marque de datif. De même, en hindi/ourdou, la postposition *ko*. Semblablement, les suffixes *ru* en aymara et *pe* en guarani s'emploient en valeur de datif et d'allatif (et, en guarani, de locatif). En arménien oriental, le cas dit datif fonctionne aussi comme génitif et marque l'objet défini.

Les autres cas sont plus rares. En roumain, la préposition *pe* signifie «sur». Dans des dialectes iraniens du nord-ouest, il s'agit d'un cas oblique général, opposé seulement au cas direct; ce cas oblique fonctionne aussi comme ergatif. Dans des dialectes iraniens du groupe shughni (Pamir), la préposition *az*, qui marque l'objet, s'emploie aussi en valeur ablative.

2.3. Origines des marques

Le bref tableau précédent indique clairement une affinité entre le datif et le marquage de l'objet. Partout où la marque objectale fonctionne aussi comme datif et où la diachronie est accessible, l'emploi datif est antérieur à l'emploi accusatif. La même évolution est connue aussi dans des cas où la marque en question n'est plus qu'un accusatif. Ainsi, si, en persan contemporain, la postposition *râ* ne s'emploie plus guère que pour marquer l'objet, elle fonctionnait comme datif en persan classique.

On peut expliquer cette affinité entre marque d'objet et datif par le fait que le complément au datif est généralement le plus proche du verbe après l'objet. D'autre part, on sait que ce complément est souvent un humain et, comme on verra (§ 3.2.), l'humanitude est un des facteurs favorisant le marquage.

Cependant la marque objectale peut avoir des origines diverses, même si, comme il est probable, son évolution sémantique et fonctionnelle passe généralement (mais pas toujours) par un emploi datif. Le *râ* du persan remonte à un morphème signifiant «pour, à cause de». La postposition *ko* du hindi signifie originellement «pour, en considération de, en ce qui concerne». La préposition *pe* du roumain dérive du latin *per* «à travers, par». La préposition *az* du shughni est originellement ablative: on peut présumer que son fonctionnement comme marque objectale dérive d'emplois où elle indique le thème du propos, «du côté de, en ce qui concerne». La préposition *ma* d'un autre dialecte iranien (parâči) provient probablement d'un morphème signifiant «quant à, pour le compte de». La valeur ancienne de *z-* en arménien classique était sans doute «par rapport à» (Meillet 1936: 94). En lapon méridional, la désinence d'accusatif pluriel dérive d'un ancien partitif, apparemment devenu sans fonction et récupéré pour marquer l'objet défini (Comrie 1977: 11–12).

La marque objectale peut aussi provenir d'une particule de discours. On saisit l'évolution en cours en dogon. La particule postposée *ŋ* sert principalement à indiquer la valeur rhématique d'un élément de la phrase, ex. (5) (Plungian 1993: 229; 1995: 13), mais peut aussi marquer un nom propre ou un pronom objet (cf. ci-dessus, § 2.1.).

(5) (a) *gamma ge ay awe*
    chat DEF souris a.saisi
    'Le chat a attrapé une souris.'
  (b) *gamma ge ay (no) ŋ awe*
                    ce
    'C'est cette souris que le chat a attrapée.'

C'est aussi une valeur rhématique originelle qu'on a cru reconnaître dans des emplois de *'et* en hébreu biblique.

Une troisième origine est attestée par le cas du chinois mandarin, où la préposition *ba* provient d'un ancien verbe employé en série avec le verbe principal et signifiant «prendre» (cf. Lord 1982).

On peut conclure de ce qui précède que, lorsque, à un certain moment de l'évolution d'une langue, le besoin se fait sentir de marquer l'objet dans certaines conditions, l'activité langagière «capte», pour remplir cet emploi, soit un morphème casuel soit une particule de discours soit encore un verbe sériel, dont la valeur se prête à ce glissement de fonction.

2.4. Position de l'objet

Outre la présence ou l'absence de la marque, une autre caractéristique importante sépare, au moins dans une partie des langues en question, objet marqué et objet non marqué: c'est leur place dans la proposition ou, le plus souvent, leur plus ou moins grande aptitude à se déplacer au sein de la proposition. Le cas le plus évident est celui du chinois, où l'objet non marqué suit immédiatement le verbe, tandis que l'objet marqué par la préposition *ba* le précède nécessairement.

D'autre part, en turc, en persan, en indo-aryen, et dans les langues dravidiennes, toutes langues à verbe final, l'objet non marqué se place immédiatement devant le verbe et peut difficilement se déplacer. L'objet marqué au contraire peut se trouver séparé du verbe par d'autres termes, voire figurer en tête (dans ce cas il est généralement thématique), ou même, dans un style un peu relâché, se trouver rejeté après le verbe. Autrement dit, l'objet non marqué, en quelque manière, fait corps avec le verbe, alors que l'objet marqué jouit d'une relative autonomie. Nous décrivons cette situation en disant que l'objet marqué constitue une terme majeur, disons un «pôle», de la proposition, au même titre que le sujet (et que le verbe); l'objet non marqué au contraire est «dépolarisé»; il est simplement adjoint au verbe et fait partie du «pôle» verbal (la notion de polarisation a été introduite par Hincha 1961, à propos de l'objet persan). La phrase à objet marqué comporte donc trois pôles: elle est «tripolaire», tandis que la phrase à objet non marqué est «bipolaire» (cf. Lazard 1982; 1984: 1994a: 231−232; Pilot-Raichoor 1994: 380−385). La différence peut être schématisée par les formules suivantes, où X et Y représentent respectivement le sujet et l'objet, V le verbe (l'ordre des sigles est arbitraire):

(6) *objet marqué:*   X − Y − V
     objet non marqué: X − YV

Le lexique tire d'ailleurs parti de cette situation, car il existe dans toutes ces langues un grand nombre de locutions verbales constituées d'un verbe plus ou moins vidé de son contenu sémantique et accompagné d'un objet non marqué. Ces locutions se comportent souvent comme des verbes simples et même peuvent à leur tour régir un objet, marqué ou non. Comparer, en persan (7a) et (7b):

(7) (a) *tabrik   goftand*
         bénédiction dirent
         'Ils prononcèrent des bénédictions.'
     (b) *pedar-râ   tabrik goftand*
         père-POSTP
         'Ils félicitèrent (bénirent) le père.'

La lexicalisation de séquences formées d'un objet non marqué et d'un verbe est peut-être propre aux langues du même type que le persan ou le turc, mais la distinction entre phrase tripolaire et phrase bipolaire est probablement généralisable à des langues d'autre type qui connaissent le marquage différentiel de l'objet. Ainsi, en mordve, langue où l'ordre des mots est très souple et se prête ainsi à exprimer les nuances de la visée communicative, l'objet non marqué tend à se placer après le verbe, tandis que l'objet marqué «jouit d'une autonomie plus grande» (Perrot 1993: 194).

Tout cela indique que le marquage différentiel de l'objet n'est pas seulement une particularité morphologique, mais qu'il met en cause l'organisation même de la proposition.

3. Corrélats de la variation

Nous rappellerons d'abord les règles données par les grammaires (§ 3.1.), puis nous examinerons plus en détail les différents facteurs en cause dans quelques langues où la question a fait l'objet d'études détaillées (§ 3.2.), pour dégager une conclusion (§ 3.3.) et esquisser une typologie (§ 3.4.).

3.1. La doctrine traditionnelle

Les grammaires des langues où l'objet peut être marqué ou non indiquent généralement, de manière sommaire, soit que la marque apparaît quand l'objet désigne un être humain ou un animé, soit qu'elle affecte l'objet défini. Les catégories en cause sont donc l'humanitude ou l'animation et la définitude, ou, dans la terminologie de Bossong, l'«inhérence» et la «référence».

La marque est généralement donnée comme caractérisant l'objet défini en turc, en mongol, dans les langues ouraliennes, en persan, en albanais, en arménien classique, en arabe maltais et en arabe oriental, en araméen, en hébreu. L'emploi de *ba* en chinois a donné lieu à d'abondantes discussions, mais les auteurs sont d'accord sur le fait que l'objet ainsi marqué est défini. Dans le cas d'autres langues, les grammaires donnent généralement pour règle que l'objet est marqué quand il désigne une personne ou un être animé: c'est le cas du hindi et des langues indo-aryennes, des langues dravidiennes, de l'arménien oriental, de l'ossète, de l'espagnol (avec des nuances), du guarani, de l'aymara. Dans quelques langues (dogon, malgache), l'emploi de la marque est limité aux noms propres et aux pronoms, qui sont par nature humains (en général) et définis.

Qu'elles réfèrent à la définitude ou à l'humanitude, ces règles sont certainement trop simples. Il est presque toujours très facile de trouver des contre-exemples, qui embarrassent les grammairiens et donnent lieu à des commentaires confus. La raison en est que le marquage de l'objet est conditionné par une pluralité de facteurs, qui peuvent jouer ensemble, mais avec des différences de langue à langue. Il faut donc considérer en détail et langue par langue le fonctionnement du marquage différentiel de l'objet.

3.2. Les facteurs en cause

Dans l'examen des facteurs en cause je prendrai ici pour point de départ une étude faite sur le persan (Lazard 1982) et ferai des rapprochements avec quelques études sur d'autres langues, pour indiquer les similitudes et les différences.

a) Définitude. Cette notion doit être entendue comme comportant des degrés, depuis le pleinement défini, c'est-à-dire entièrement identifiable pour le locuteur et l'allocutaire, jusqu'au non-référentiel en passant par l'indéfini spécifique, l'indéfini membre d'un ensemble défini, etc. En persan, tout objet défini, soit par un déterminant soit par le contexte (le persan n'a pas d'article défini), est affecté de la postposition *râ*; il en va de même de l'objet indéfini spécifique; l'objet non référentiel est normalement sans marque. On a donc par exemple:

(8) (a) *ketâb xândam*
    livre j'ai.lu
    'J'ai lu un/des livre(s).'
  (b) *ketâb-i-râ xândam ke xeyli*
    livre-INDEF-POSTP j'ai.lu que très
    jâleb bud
    intéressant était
    'J'ai lu un livre qui était très intéressant.'
  (c) *ân ketâb-râ xândam*
    ce
    'J'ai lu ce livre.'

La définitude est en persan le facteur majeur: c'est dans la zone de l'objet indéfini et, le plus souvent, non référentiel, que jouent, secondairement, d'autres facteurs. Il en va de même en turc (Nilsson 1985). En arabe d'Irak, l'objet défini est facultativement marqué, l'objet indéfini ne l'est jamais. En tamoul, un objet, humain ou non, défini ou précédé de *oru* « un » et spécifique est ordinairement affecté du suffixe d'accusatif (Murugaiyan 1993: 180). En badaga, autre langue dravidienne, un objet défini est marqué s'il est humain ou si, humain ou non, il est déterminé par un déictique (Pilot-Raichoor 1994: 366).

b) Humanitude (ou animation). Cette catégorie aussi doit être entendue comme scalaire: elle va de l'humain (dont le plus haut degré est formé du locuteur et de l'allocutaire) aux noms de substances massives et aux noms abstraits, avec, dans l'intervalle, ceux qui désignent les animés (supérieurs et inférieurs) et les inanimés discrets. La différence est, dans tous les cas, entre les entités traitées comme des personnes et celles qui ne le sont pas. En persan, un objet générique peut être marqué s'il est humain ou humanisé en quelque mesure: comparer (9a) et (9b).

(9) (a) *xarguš dust dâram*
    lapin ami j'ai
    'J'aime le lapin (cuisiné).'
  (b) *xarguš-râ dust dâram*
    lapin-POSTP
    'J'aime les lapins (ce sont des animaux sympathiques).'

Dans des parlers romans (gascon et autres dialectes occitans, catalan, sarde, dialectes d'Italie méridionale, ladin des Grisons), les objets (noms ou pronoms) les plus fréquemment marqués sont ceux qui désignent des personnes (Rohlfs 1971: 325−326). En badaga, les objets humains (ou divins), définis ou non, sont toujours marqués; d'autre part, toutes choses égales d'ailleurs, un animé sera plus facilement marqué qu'un inanimé (Pilot-Raichoor 1994: 364; 367).

Les deux catégories de définitude et d'humanitude ont des affinités: leurs échelles coïncident dans leur partie supérieure, celle où se situent les pronoms personnels et les noms propres de personnes. Il n'est donc pas étonnant qu'il y ait des langues où seules ces deux classes d'unités reçoivent la marque objectale: c'est le cas du dogon, du malgache. On peut y joindre aussi les langues comme le pashto, où les pronoms objets de 1re et 2ème personne sont au cas oblique, tandis que les noms objets restent au cas direct, et enfin les langues où les pronoms, mais non les noms, sont pourvus d'une forme accusative, comme l'anglais (ce n'est pas par hasard que les pronoms masculins et feminins ont un cas régime, mais non le pronom neutre). Rappelons aussi que, en finnois, les noms en fonction d'objet peuvent se trouver au nominatif (si la phrase ne comporte pas d'autre nominatif), mais que, en revanche, les pronoms objets ont toujours une forme différente du nominatif. En roman même, c'est aux pronoms objets que s'est d'abord appliquée la marque (Rohlfs (1971: 331).

c) Prégnance du verbe et rapport sémantique entre verbe et objet. Toutes choses égales d'ailleurs, la postposition persane *râ* a plus de chances d'être omise avec des verbes de contenu sémantique ténu (« avoir, faire, etc. ») qu'avec des verbes d'un sémantisme plus prégnant. D'autre part, il semble que la marque soit plus facilement omise lorsqu'il y a une affinité entre le verbe et l'objet, en d'autres termes lorsque, avec un objet donné, un certain verbe est « attendu ». C'est le cas d'expressions telles que « fermer porte », « ouvrir porte », « manger pain », « donner leçon », « faire travail », etc. De telles expressions désignent des actions courantes, coutumières, fortement institutionnalisées. Elles sont, on le conçoit, facilement lexicalisées.

En espagnol, l'« efficience » du verbe a été invoquée pour rendre compte du marquage de l'objet: un même verbe, pris dans un sens figuré affaibli, s'accommode d'un objet non marqué, même humain, alors que, lorsqu'il est au sens propre, la marque est obligatoire (Pottier 1968: 85, 90). On a pu dresser un tableau de probabilité d'apparition de la marque, fondé sur la combinaison des propriétés de l'objet (animation, singularisation) et de celles du verbe (efficience) (*ibid.*: 87 sqq.). On constate des faits analogues en turc (Nilsson 1985: 45; Taylan & Zimmer 1994) et dans les langues dravidiennes. En tamoul, l'expression « voir fille » sera sans marque d'accusatif si elle réfère à des visites faites en vue d'un mariage, selon l'usage traditionnel (Passerieu Bordeneuve 1991: 156). C'est de même que l'on a « tuer poulet » sans accusatif si c'est pour le manger (action courante), mais avec accusatif si c'est un poulet écrasé sur la route par accident (Murugaiyan 1993: 173–174). En chinois, les grammairiens disent que la construction de l'objet avec la préposition *ba* n'est possible que si le patient est en quelque manière affecté par le procès désigné par le verbe (cf. Lazard 1994b: 172).

d) Consistance matérielle de l'objet et du verbe. Il semble que, en persan, le fait que le syntagme objet et/ou le verbe ou le groupe verbal soient relativement longs favorise l'apparition de la marque; mais, il est vrai, ce facteur se laisse difficilement isoler, car il va généralement de pair avec une certaine consistance sémantique. Il est possible que des faits analogues se laissent apercevoir dans des langues dravidiennes.

e) Thématicité de l'objet. Un objet thématique, même générique et non référentiel, est toujours marqué en persan par la postposition *râ*, alors que l'objet non marqué fait, au contraire, partie du membre rhématique de la phrase; comparer (10a) et (10b) (qui sont intonés, accentués et rythmés différemment). L'objet thématique tend à figurer en tête de phrase et à se trouver ainsi séparé du verbe par d'autres termes.

(10) (a) *ketâb mixânand*
    livre ils.lisent
    'On lit un/des livre(s).'
(b) *ketâb-râ mixânand*
    livre-POSTP ils.lisent
    'Les livres, on les lit.'

La thématicité est un des facteurs les plus importants et les plus fréquents du marquage de l'objet. Elle est clairement attestée dans les langues romanes: l'objet thématisé en tête de phrase ou rejeté en queue et coréférent d'un pronom est très fréquemment marqué (type *à ton père je l'ai vu* et *tu me le donnes, à ton petit frère*, en français populaire du midi) (Rohlfs 1971: 327). En catalan, où l'objet marqué est plus rare qu'en espagnol, « l'emploi de la préposition est ancien et légitime quand il s'agit d'un objet mis en relief par anticipation ou répétition (reprise) du régime » (*ibid.*: 322). En tamoul, un objet thématique, même non humain et non référentiel, peut être marqué (Murugaiyan 1993: 179). Il en va de même en badaga (Pilot-Raichoor 1994: 386). En samoyède yourak, il semble que l'objet ne soit à l'accusatif que s'il est thématique (Comrie 1977: 11). En chinois, l'objet marqué par le préposition *ba* est toujours thématique (Frei 1956–57).

f) Rhématicité de l'objet. Il semble que, en persan, la marque puisse aussi caractériser un objet pourvu d'une valeur rhématique contrastive (Lazard 1982: 190–191). C'est, apparemment, ce même emploi qu'il faut reconnaître dans cet exemple badaga (Pilot-Raichoor 1994: 386):

(11) *iddu, nooda beeku nara*
    étant voir il.faut humain
    looka-va, sattu, nooda beeku
    monde-ACC mor voir il.faut
    soga looka-va
    divin monde-ACC
    'Vivant, c'est le monde humain qu'il faut voir; mort, c'est le paradis qu'il faut voir.'

En arabe d'Irak, en cas d'objet pronominal, on emploie, en plus d'un clitique, un pronom introduit par une préposition pour souligner sa valeur rhématique contrastive, ex. (Erwin 1963: 332):

(12) (a) *laazim ašuuf-a*
 il.faut que.je.voie-lui
 'Il faut que je le voie.'
 (b) *laazim ašuuf-a 'il-a*
 PRÉP-lui
 'C'est lui qu'il faut que je voie (litt. il faut que je le voie à lui).'

3.3. Conclusion: conditions de la polarisation de l'objet

Ainsi, le marquage de l'objet est conditionné par des facteurs sémantiques (définitude, humanitude, rapport avec le sémantisme du verbe) et pragmatiques (thématicité et, parfois, rhématicité contrastive de l'objet).

Considérons d'abord le conditionnement sémantique. Dans certains cas, on aperçoit une règle simple. C'est ainsi que, en persan, tout objet défini est marqué; en badaga, tout objet humain, défini ou non, est marqué. Mais ces règles ne couvrent pas l'ensemble des faits. Il reste une zone de flottement, où jouent diversement d'autres facteurs et où le locuteur a la liberté d'exprimer des nuances subtiles. Il en va ainsi probablement dans toutes les langues concernées. Cependant, à considérer l'ensemble des faits dans un ensemble de langues, on constate une régularité constante: le marquage différentiel de l'objet étant corrélatif d'une différence qui consiste en ce qu'il se situe plus ou moins haut sur l'échelle de définitude et/ou plus ou moins haut sur celle d'humanitude et/ou en ce qu'il forme avec le verbe un procès plus ou moins institutionnalisé, l'objet marqué est toujours celui qui a le référent le plus défini et/ou le plus humain et/ou le moins associé au sémantisme verbal dans un procès institutionnalisé, et l'objet non marqué est toujours celui qui a les caractéristiques opposées.

Les catégories d'humanitude et de définitude peuvent être unies dans une super-catégorie d'« individuation » (cf. Lazard 1984). Il est clair que plus une entité est humaine ou proche de l'humain et plus elle est définie, plus elle est individualisée, plus elle a de poids et d'autonomie sémantiques. Un objet dont le référent est haut en humanitude et en définitude tend donc, en vertu de ce poids sémantique, à entrer en contraste avec le verbe. Un objet dont, au contraire, le référent se situe plus bas sur ces échelles se prête à s'associer et à se subordonner au verbe: son sémantisme tend à se fondre avec celui du verbe dans une représentation unique. Dans le cas des expressions exprimant des procès institutionalisés, l'association habituelle de l'objet (même défini et parfois humain) avec le verbe a le même effet. Dans le cas d'un objet hautement individué, l'individuation et le poids sémantique qui en résulte ont pour corrélat, sur le plan de la syntaxe, la « polarisation » de l'objet (§ 2.4.); au contraire, l'objet faiblement individué n'est pas polarisé et il fait corps avec le verbe.

Les facteurs pragmatiques ont des effets semblables. Prototypiquement, l'objet fait partie, avec le verbe, du membre rhématique de la phrase; les phrases où l'objet est thématique, sans être rares, sont donc fonctionnellement marquées. L'objet thématique entre en contraste avec le verbe, qui est rhématique par vocation. Il en est d'ailleurs souvent disjoint dans la chaîne, puisqu'il tend à figurer en tête de phrase, ou, en cas de « rappel », en fin de phrase. En outre, il est ordinairement défini, comme le sont le plus souvent les termes thématisés, quels qu'ils soient. Il est donc naturel qu'il soit polarisé.

Quant au cas, plus rare et encore mal attesté, de l'objet rhématique contrastif, il se sépare par là même du verbe, qui n'est pas contrastif (cf. ex. (11)), et il est donc aussi polarisé.

Il faut compléter ces conclusions par une considération fonctionnelle. Dans beaucoup de langues, le sujet grammatical est obligatoirement défini; dans les autres, il l'est le plus souvent. Il tend aussi, au moins dans les phrases d'action, à être humain ou animé. Il est donc caractérisé prototypiquement par un haut degré de définitude et d'humanitude. Il est aussi prototypiquement thématique. Dans la phrase à deux actants, quand l'objet est indéfini et/ou inanimé, il n'y a pas de confusion possible. Mais s'il est haut situé sur les échelles de définitude et d'humanitude et/ou s'il est thématique, il se trouve posséder les mêmes caractéristiques que le sujet et la phrase peut être ambiguë, si le marquage grammatical et/ou l'ordre des mots ne suffisent pas à indiquer clairement les fonctions. On a déduit de ces circonstances l'idée raisonnable que le marquage différentiel de l'objet, qui apparaît justement quand l'objet possède des propriétés subjectales, est fondé sur la nécessité de distinguer les fonctions de sujet et d'objet (Tomson 1928; Velten 1932; Comrie 1977: 9; Bossong 1991: 162–163; la question est théorisée par Bossong 1998).

3.4. Typologie

Si, dans toutes les langues concernées, le marquage différentiel de l'objet est conditionné par tout ou partie du même ensemble de paramètres recensés ci-dessus (§ 3.2. et 3.3.), elles diffèrent quant à l'importance respective de chacun de ces paramètres et quant à l'extension du marquage de l'objet. Ces différences donnent la possibilité d'esquisser une typologie.

En persan, le marquage a une assez grande extension, puisqu'il s'étend depuis le haut de l'échelle de définitude jusqu'à l'indéfini spécifique et a lieu aussi dans le cas de l'objet thématique (ou rhématique?), même générique. Il semble fonctionner de même en turc. En hébreu, il est un peu plus restreint, puisqu'il ne s'applique qu'aux objets définis. En badaga, le facteur dominant est plutôt l'humanitude: tout objet humain est marqué, ainsi que tout objet, humain ou non, affecté d'un déictique; dans les autres cas, il y a flottement; mais l'objet thématique (ou rhématique constrastif) est marqué. Le marquage semble moins étendu, quoique encore assez fréquent, en espagnol et dans les dialectes romans occidentaux: les objets humains sont généralement marqués; dans les autres cas, il y a une large marge de flottement. Il est plus restreint en arabe irakien: l'objet défini est marqué facultativement, l'objet indéfini ne l'est pas; le pronom objet est marqué s'il est rhématique. Dans certaines langues, le marquage est limité aux objets qui se situent en haut des échelles d'individuation. En dogon, il ne concerne que les pronoms et les noms propres. Restent enfin les langues où seuls les pronoms (désignant des personnes) sont marqués, comme le pashto et l'anglais.

4. Variations connexes

Le marquage différentiel proprement dit, tel qu'il a été décrit ci-dessus, doit être situé par rapport à d'autres variations conditionnées par des catégories de l'objet. Dans cette section, nous passerons une revue sommaire des suivantes: l'accord objectal « différentiel » (§ 4.1.), l'alternance de l'objet avec un complément partitif ou oblique (§ 4.2.), l'incorporation et la coalescence (§ 4.3.), la construction antipassive (§ 4.4.), et nous esquisserons une première conclusion (§ 4.5.).

4.1. L'accord objectal

Dans diverses langues accusatives, la forme verbale comporte, outre l'accord avec le sujet, une marque d'accord avec l'objet. Dans certaines d'entre elles, cet accord est variable, c'est-à-dire a lieu ou non selon le cas. Le facteur déterminant est la définitude de l'objet: l'accord n'a lieu qu'avec un objet défini. C'est le cas en swahili et d'autres langues bantoues, en amharique, en palau, en mordve. Le hongrois et d'autres langues finno-ougriennes ont une conjugaison « objective », qui peut être analysée comme comportant une marque d'objet (de 3ème personne en hongrois) et ne s'emploie qu'avec objet défini. On peut aussi ranger ici le « redoublement de l'objet » dans les langues balkaniques, albanais, grec, bulgare, macédonien, roumain, c'est-à-dire l'emploi d'un clitique « redoublant » un objet nominal: ce phénomène a lieu avec un objet thématique et même, en macédonien, avec tout objet défini (cf. Bossong 1998; Lazard 1998a: 49–51).

Dans les langues où existe l'« accord objectal différentiel », l'objet, en cas d'accord, peut se déplacer plus ou moins librement dans la phrase; en l'absence d'accord, l'objet reste généralement au voisinage du verbe (Lazard 1996). On saisit la parenté de cet accord objectal variable et du marquage différentiel de l'objet: même conditionnement par la définitude (et/ou la thématicité) et même polarisation de l'objet défini. Il y a d'ailleurs des langues où les deux procédés se combinent: ainsi en amharique, en mordve, en roumain. L'accord n'y a lieu qu'avec un objet marqué (mais non inversement, cf. § 5.1.).

4.2. L'objet partitif

En finnois, l'objet est, non à l'accusatif, mais au partitif lorsqu'il est pluriel indéfini ou lorsque, au singulier indéfini, il a un référent « massif », ex.:

(13) *luen hyvi-ä kirjo-ja*
je.lis bon-PART livre-PL.PART
'Je lis de bons livres.'

(14) *juon maitoa*
je.bois lait.PART
'Je bois du lait.'

Des emplois analogues existent en russe, en polonais et dans les langues baltiques, où l'on emploie le génitif au sens d'un partitif. En turc on emploie l'ablatif. Dans des langues dépourvues de déclinaison, on utilise une préposition locative ou ablative, par exemple en arabe d'Alger, où « manger dans orange » signifie « manger de l'orange ».

La variation est ici encore conditionnée par les catégories de définitude et d'humanitude, mais autrement que le marquage différentiel au sens strict. L'objet se situe vers le bas de l'échelle de définitude, puisqu'il désigne une portion indéfinie d'un ensemble (indéfini ou défini). D'autre part, il réfère à du massif et le massif est le plus bas degré de l'humanitude/animation, à l'opposé de l'humain, au-dessous même de l'inanimé discret. Alors que le marquage évoqué ci-dessus est déclenché par le fait que l'objet est fortement individué, c'est ici au contraire le faible degré d'individuation qui conditionne l'emploi du partitif. Les deux types de marquage peuvent d'ailleurs coexister dans la même langue et indiquer différents degrés d'individuation, p. ex. en turc (Nilsson 1985: 45):

(15) (a) *peynir yedik*
fromage nous.avons.mangé
'Nous avons mangé du fromage.'
(b) *peynir-den yedik*
fromage-ABL
'Nous avons mangé du fromage (en question).'
(c) *peynir-i yedik*
fromage-ACC
'Nous avons mangé le fromage.'

Les mêmes relations se retrouvent dans des langues de structure toute différente, p. ex. en tongien: (16a) est la construction à coalescence (cf. § 4.3.), (16b) la construction oblique, (16c) la construction de base (ergative) (Hopper & Thompson 1980: 257−258, 263).

(16) (a) *na'e kai ika 'a Sione*
ASP manger poisson ABS NPR
'John a mangé du poisson (a fait consommation de poisson).'
(b) *na'e kai 'a e tamasi'i 'i*
ABS ART enfant PREP
he ika
ART poisson
'L'enfant a mangé du poisson (en question).'
(c) *na'e kai e Sione 'a e ika*
ERG ABS ART
'John a mangé le poisson.'

4.3. L'objet coalescent

Une autre variation consiste en l'incorporation de l'objet au sein de la forme verbale, procédé attesté notamment dans diverses langues amérindiennes, nahuatl, iroquois, etc, mais aussi en tchouktche. L'objet incorporé s'oppose à l'objet actanciel, ainsi en nahuatl, qui distingue jusqu'à trois constructions, ex. (Launey 1979: 40, 166):

(17) (a) *ni-naca-cua*
je-viande-mange
'Je mange de la viande.'
(b) *Ø-qui-cua nacatl in pilli*
il-la-mange viande ART enfant
'L'enfant mange de la viande.'
(c) *Ø-qui-cua in nacatl in pilli*
ART
'L'enfant mange la viande.'

Dans (17c) l'objet, défini, est « actancialisé » (polarisé) au moyen de l'« article » *in*. Dans (17b), indéfini, il est simplement apposé au verbe. Dans (17a), le tour à incorporation tend à exprimer un concept unifié et réfère à une activité particulière, institutionalisée (« faire gras »): l'objet est non référentiel. Il en va de même en général dans les langues incorporantes.

Certaines langues, sans aller jusqu'à l'incorporation proprement dite, ont des constructions dans lesquelles l'objet est en quelque manière coalescent avec le verbe. Dans des langues océaniennes, l'objet non référentiel suit immédiatement le verbe et ne peut en être séparé (cf. § 4.2., ex. (16a)); en outre, dans certaines langues, le lexème verbal prend alors une forme particulière; l'objet référentiel au contraire est libre. La séquence verbe + objet coalescent peut se lexicaliser et fonctionner comme un verbe simple. On oppose ainsi, par exemple, « conduire voiture », au sens de « être conducteur de voiture », à « conduire la/une voiture ».

Signalons en outre que certaines de ces langues connaissent un autre type de coalescence, concernant les pronoms et les noms propres en fonction d'objet; mais il s'agit d'un phénomène tout différent, plutôt assimilable à une sorte de conjugaison objectale (cf. Lazard 1984: 276; 1994a: 198−199).

4.4. La diathèse antipassive

Dans les langues ergatives, la diathèse antipassive va souvent de pair avec un objet plus ou moins faiblement individué. Le passage de la construction de base ergative (l'actif) à l'antipassif consiste généralement en ce que le verbe prend une forme spécifique, l'agent passe de l'ergatif à l'absolutif et l'objet soit disparaît soit passe de l'absolutif à un cas oblique. Lorsque l'objet subsiste, il est souvent non référentiel. En bezhta (Caucase), il est générique: on peut dire à l'antipassif «il tue des moutons», mais non «il tue le mouton». Il se comporte plus ou moins de même dans des langues australiennes. En esquimau, il est rhématique et ordinairement indéfini: (18b) à l'antipassif s'oppose à (18a) à l'actif (construction ergative) (Mennecier 1995: 335).

(18) (a) *qimmi-p niqi-q niiva-a-Ø*
 chien-ERG viande-ABS mange-il-la
 'Le chien mange la viande.'
 (b) *qimmi-q niqi-mi niivu-q*
 chien-ABS viande-INSTR mange-il
 'Le chien mange de la viande.'

Dans d'autres langues ergatives, la construction antipassive comporte un objet à l'absolutif (cas zéro) placé obligatoirement au voisinage du verbe, p. ex. en basque (Rebuschi 1986: 182−183); cet objet est toujours rhématique:

(19) (a) *Peio-k liburu asko*
 NPR-ERG livre beaucoup:ABS
 irakurria-k ditu (constr.ergative)
 lu-PL il.les.a
 'Peio a lu beaucoup de livres.'
 (b) *Peio liburu asko irakurria*
 NPR-ABS lu:SG
 da (constr.antipassive)
 il.est
 'Peio a lu beaucoup de livres (est un grand lecteur).'

Cette construction se trouve aussi dans des langues maya.

Ainsi, dans les constructions antipassives, l'objet est soit à un cas oblique soit au cas zéro et étroitement lié au verbe; dans les deux cas il est situé plus ou moins bas sur le gradient d'individuation et il tend à être rhématique. Ces deux types d'objets sont évidemment comparables, respectivement, à l'objet oblique des constructions «indirectes» (§ 4.2.) et à l'objet dépolarisé des langues où joue le marquage différentiel proprement dit (§ 2.4., § 3.3.).

4.5. Conclusion: l'échelle objectale

Récapitulons. Les types d'objets qui peuvent entrer en opposition entre eux sont les suivants:

a) objet affecté d'une marque objectale spécifique (polarisé) (§ 2., § 3.), éventuellement avec accord verbal (§ 4.1.),
b) objet affecté d'une marque de partitif ou de cas oblique (§ 4.2.), y compris l'objet oblique de l'antipassif (§ 4.4.),
c) objet non marqué (dépolarisé) (§ 2., § 3.), y compris l'objet à cas zéro de l'antipassif (§ 4.4.),
d) objet coalescent ou incorporé (§ 4.3.).

Il est évident que les deux derniers ont d'étroites affinités. L'objet coalescent est non référentiel; l'objet dépolarisé peut l'être. L'objet dépolarisé, dans les langues du type persan, est étroitement lié au verbe, et les séquences objet dépolarisé + verbe sont souvent lexicalisées et se comportent comme les expressions avec objet incorporé. L'objet dépolarisé est ou tend à être quasi-coalescent.

Les deux premiers types d'objets portent l'un et l'autre une marque, mais ils sont différents. L'objet marqué$_1$ se situe dans la partie supérieure du gradient d'individuation; pragmatiquement, il tend à être mis en relief comme thématique (ou parfois rhématique); syntaxiquement, il constitue un pôle de la proposition; morphologiquement, il porte une marque qui est soit propre à la fonction objectale soit une marque d'accusatif-datif. L'objet marqué$_2$ est plutôt bas en individuation; syntaxiquement, il est marginalisé comme un terme oblique; morphologiquement, il porte une marque (partitif, génitif, instrumental, préposition locative ou autre) qui n'est pas propre à la fonction objectale, mais remplit d'autres fonctions. Il entre dans une construction «indirecte» qui le rapproche des termes locatifs ou instrumentaux.

Si l'on prend en considération la «distance grammaticale» du verbe à ces différents types d'objets (cf. Lazard 1994a: 90 ss.; 1995), le plus proche est évidemment l'objet coalescent (voire incorporé), puis vient l'objet non marqué, puis l'objet marqué$_1$, enfin l'objet oblique (marqué$_2$):

(20) ⎯⎯⎯⎯⎯⎯⎯⎯⎯⎯⎯⎯⎯⎯→
 objet: coalescent non marqué marqué$_1$ oblique

5. Facteurs associés

Jusqu'ici il n'a été question que de l'objet. Mais il se trouve que certaines des constructions qui sont conditionnées par les catégories de l'objet peuvent l'être aussi par d'autres facteurs, que nous évoquerons sommairement: aspect (§ 5.1.), négation (§ 5.2.), caractéristiques du procès et de l'agent (§ 5.3.), ce qui conduit à intégrer les variations de la construction de l'objet dans une théorie plus générale (§ 5.4.).

5.1. L'aspect

En finnois, la construction de l'objet au partitif sert non seulement dans les conditions indiquées ci-dessus (§ 4.2., cf. aussi § 5.2.), mais aussi, même dans le cas d'un objet défini, pour exprimer l'aspect progressif, ex.:

(21) *äiti pesee paitaa*
mère lave chemise:PART
'Le mère est en train de laver la chemise (litt. lave de la chemise).'

En mordve, l'emploi de la conjugaison « subjective » (§ 4.1.) avec un objet marqué, donc défini, exprime l'aspect imperfectif. En arabe d'Alger et d'autres dialectes arabes et berbères d'Afrique du Nord, le marquage prépositionnel de l'objet (§ 4.2.) donne au verbe (à l'inaccompli) un sens progressif. En bezhta, la construction antipassive (§ 4.4.) exprime une action habituelle, courante. Dans diverses langues australiennes ergatives, elle se prête particulièrement à indiquer l'habitude, le procès en cours, l'activité continue ou encore l'action tentée. Si l'on réunit sous l'étiquette d'incomplétif ces diverses nuances aspectuelles, qui ont en commun de s'opposer à l'action unique, effective et complète, il est clair que la construction indirecte de l'objet est fréquemment associée à l'aspect incomplétif. Il est évident qu'il y a une étroite affinité entre l'idée d'objet partiel et celle de procès incomplet: c'est pourquoi ces deux idées peuvent se trouver exprimées par les mêmes procédés.

5.2. La négation

La construction de l'objet au partitif (§ 4.2.) est obligatoire en finnois avec un verbe négatif. De même en russe et dans les langues baltiques, l'objet, même défini, peut se trouver au génitif dans les phrases négatives; en polonais, c'est une règle générale. L'effet de la négation se manifeste aussi en français avec un objet indéfini: on dit *je vois une maison*, mais *je ne vois pas de maison*, où l'objet est prépositionnel et sans article. En basque, langue ergative, on trouve, en phrase négative, l'objet indéfini au partitif.

5.3. Caractéristiques de l'action et de l'agent

Dans diverses langues ergatives, l'antipassif, avec construction indirecte de l'objet, est aussi en rapport avec certaines caractéristiques de l'action et de l'agent. En tchouktche, par opposition à l'actif (la construction ergative), il s'emploie volontiers quand l'agent n'est pas un être conscient agissant volontairement; les relations sont les mêmes en esquimau (cf. Lazard 1994a: 188). De même encore, dans des langues australiennes ergatives (yidiny, Dixon 1977: 276; kuku-yalanji, Dixon 1994: 151; etc.), si l'action n'est pas exercée volontairement par un agent bien individué, l'antipassif est préféré à la construction active.

5.4. Conclusion: degrés de transitivité

Nous avons vu (§ 4.5.) que l'objet marqué$_1$ est susceptible d'entrer dans une double opposition: d'une part avec l'objet oblique, d'autre part avec l'objet non marqué ou coalescent. Le corrélat sémantique de cette double opposition est que l'objet marqué$_1$ est plus fortement individué que l'objet oblique, qui est partiel, indéfini, non référentiel ou générique, et que l'objet non marqué, qui tend à être non humain, indéfini, non référentiel ou à se fondre avec le verbe dans l'expression d'un procès institutionnalisé, et, à plus forte raison, que l'objet coalescent, qui est non référentiel. Tout cela suggère de considérer l'objet marqué$_1$ (et/ou commandant l'accord verbal) comme l'objet prototypique et les autres, à savoir d'un côté l'objet oblique et de l'autre l'objet coalescent ou tendant à la coalescence, comme des formes objectales dégradées. Dans les langues qui ignorent le marquage différentiel, la position d'objet prototypique est occupée par l'objet non marqué, qui peut avoir le même poids sémantique et syntaxique que l'objet marqué des langues à marquage différentiel. Il s'oppose comme lui d'un côté à l'objet oblique, de l'autre à l'objet coalescent ou tendant à la coalescence (qu'on trouve, p. ex., en français dans des locutions comme *prendre feu*, *porter plainte*, etc.). Il en va à peu près de même dans les langues où le marquage est limité au degré supérieur d'individuation (pronoms, noms propres). L'objet prototypique, marqué ou non, se trouve toujours dans la zone médiane du continuum (20).

Nous avons constaté d'autre part que les constructions où entrent l'objet oblique (constructions indirectes) servent souvent à exprimer aussi un aspect incomplétif, une action incomplète en quelque manière, une action involontaire ou dont la cause n'est pas un agent typique, voire une action niée, c'est-à-dire nulle. D'autre part les constructions à incorporation, à coalescence ou tendant à la coalescence expriment normalement des procès habituels, institutionnalisés. Les constructions à objet prototypique, par opposition, sont propres à exprimer des actions complètes, émanant d'un agent doué de volonté et portant sur un patient bien individué, qu'elles affectent réellement. Nous pouvons considérer que les constructions à objet prototypique se caractérisent, par rapport aux autres constructions, comme exprimant des actions prototypiques.

Il semble indiqué de rendre compte de cette situation en termes de transitivité. La situation étant complexe, on la représentera d'autant mieux qu'on concevra la transitivité, non pas comme une question de oui ou non, mais comme une grandeur susceptible de degrés, comme l'ont proposé plusieurs auteurs (Hopper & Thompson 1980; Hagège 1982: 49−51; Givón 1990: 565−566; cf. Lazard 1998b). Il est naturel de poser les constructions à objet prototypique, exprimant des actions prototypiques, comme les plus transitives. Ce choix est en bon accord avec la notion traditionnelle et avec l'intuition. Les constructions à objet « dégradé » seront considérées comme de transitivité moindre, mais non nulle, puisqu'elles comportent encore un objet. Les constructions intransitives sont celles qui ne comportent pas d'objet, c'est-à-dire les constructions uniactancielles.

Si l'on parcourt le continuum (20) en partant de la gauche, on voit que la transitivité est d'abord presque nulle, avec l'objet incorporé, car les verbes incorporant leur objet se comportent à peu près comme des verbes uniactanciels. Elle croît ensuite, faible d'abord avec l'objet coalescent ou tendant à la coalescence, puis plus forte avec l'objet non marqué non coalescent, puis elle passe par un maximum dans la zone médiane, où se situe l'objet prototypique, puis elle redevient faible avec l'objet oblique, qui est traité comme un terme périphérique (cf. Lazard 1994a: 251−253).

Tel est, je crois, le cadre général des variations évoquées ci-dessus sommairement. Naturellement, le fonctionnement des langues est indéfiniment varié et tous les faits évoqués ne se trouvent pas dans toutes les langues: certaines n'ont pas de marquage différentiel de l'objet, d'autres peut-être ignorent toute tendance à la coalescence, etc. Mais il n'est pas déraisonnable de penser que toutes les variations peuvent *grosso modo* être situées dans le tableau ci-dessus. Reste à faire l'analyse détaillée des faits pertinents dans le plus grand nombre possible de langues. Ce sont ces analyses qui permettront d'affiner et de corriger le tableau.

6. Abréviations spéciales

INDEF	indéfini
INSTR	instumental
NPR	nom propre
PART	partitif
PAS	passé
POSTP	postposition
PREP	préposition
SFX	suffixe
TH	thème

7. Références

Beffa, Marie-Lise & Hamayon, Roberte. 1975. *Éléments de grammaire mongole.* Saint-Sulpice de Favières: Dunod.

Bossong, Georg. 1985. *Empirische Universalienforschung. Differentielle Objektmarkierung in den neuiranischen Sprachen.* Tübingen: Narr.

Bossong, Georg. 1991. « Differential object marking in Romance and beyond ». In: Wanner, Dieter & Kibbee, Douglas A. (eds.). *New analyses in Romance linguistics.* (Current issues in linguistic theory, 69.) Amsterdam: Benjamins, 143−170.

Bossong, Georg. 1998. In: Feuillet, Jack (éd.) *Actance et valence dans les langues de l'Europe.* (Empirical Approaches to Language Typology, EUROTYP 20−2.) Berlin/New York: Mouton de Gruyter, 193−258.

Comrie, Bernard. 1977. « Subjects and direct objects in Uralic languages: a functional explanation on case marking systems ». *Études finno-ougriennes* 12: 5−17.

Dixon, R. M. W. 1977. *A grammar of Yidiñ.* Cambridge: Cambridge University Press.

Dixon, R. M. W. 1994. *Ergativity.* Cambridge: Cambridge University Press.

Erwin, W. M. 1963. *A short reference grammar of Iraqi Arabic.* Washington: Georgetown University Press.

Frei, Henri. 1956−57. « The ergative construction in Chinese: theory of Pekinese BA$_3$ ». *Genko Kenkyu* 31: 22−50; 32: 83−115.

Givón, Talmy. 1990. *Syntax, volume II.* Amsterdam/Philadelphia: Benjamins.

Hagège, Claude. 1982. *La structure des langues.* (Que sais-je?) Paris: PUF.

Hincha, Georg. 1961. « Beiträge zu einer Morphemlehre des Neupersischen ». *Der Islam* 37: 136−201.

Hopper, Paul J. & Thompson, Sandra A. 1980. « Transitivity in grammar and discourse ». *Language* 56: 253−299.

Launey, Michel. 1979. *Introduction à la langue et à la littérature aztèques.* Paris: Harmattan.

Lazard, Gilbert. 1982. « Le morphème *râ* en persan et les relations actancielles ». *Bulletin de la Société de linguistique de Paris* 77.1: 177–208.

Lazard, Gilbert. 1984. « Actance variations and categories of the object ». In: Plank, Frans (ed.). *Objects. Towards a theory of grammatical relations.* London: Academic Press, 269–292.

Lazard, Gilbert. 1994a. *L'actance.* Paris: Presses Universitaires de France. (English translation: *Actancy.* Berlin/New York: Mouton de Gruyter 1998).

Lazard, Gilbert. 1994b. « Le *râ* persan et le *ba* chinois ». *Cahiers de linguistique Asie orientale* 23 (*Mélanges offerts à Alexis Rygaloff*): 169–176.

Lazard, Gilbert. 1995. « La notion de distance actancielle ». In: Bouscarel, Janine & Franckel, Jean-Jacques & Robert, Stephane (édd.). *Langues et langage. Problèmes et raisonnement en linguistique, Mélanges offerts à Antoine Culioli.* (Linguistique nouvelle.) Paris: Presses Universitaires de France, 135–146.

Lazard, Gilbert. 1996. « Fonction de l'accord verbe-actant », *Faits de langue* 8: 151–160.

Lazard, Gilbert. 1998a. « Définition des actants dans les langues européennes ». In: Feuillet, Jack (éd.). *Actance et valence dans les langues de l'Europe.* (Empirical Approaches to Language Typology, EUROTYP 20–2.) Berlin/New York: Mouton de Gruyter, 11–146.

Lazard, Gilbert. 1998b « De la transitivité restreinte à la transitivité généralisée ». In: Rousseau, André (éd.). *La transitivité.* Lille: Presses du Septentrion, 55–84.

Lord, Carol. 1982. « The development of object markers in serial verb languages ». In: Hopper, Paul J. & Thompson, Sandra A. (eds.). *Studies in transitivity.* (Syntax and Semantics, 15.) New York: Academic Press, 277–299.

Meillet, Antoine. 1936. *Esquisse d'une grammaire comparée de l'arménien classique*, Vienne: Impr. des Pp. mekhitharistes.

Mennecier, Philippe. 1995. *Le tunumiisut, dialecte inuit du Groenland oriental.* Paris: Klincksieck.

Moravcsik, Edith A. 1978. « On the case marking of objects ». In: Greenberg, Joseph H. & Ferguson, Charles A. & Moravcsik, Edith A. (eds.): *Universals of human language.* Palo Alto: Stanford University Press, IV, 249–289.

Murugaiyan, Appasamy. 1993. « Marquage différentiel de l'objet et variation actancielle en tamoul ». *Actances* 7: 161–183.

Nilsson, Birgit. 1985. *Case marking semantics in Turkish.* Stockholm: Department of Linguistics.

Nocentini, Alberto. 1992. « Oggetto marcato vs. oggetto non-marcato: stato ed evoluzione di una categoria nell'area euro-asiatica ». In: *L'Europa linguistica: contatti, contrasti, affinità di lingue.* (Società di linguistica italiana. SLI 30) 227–246.

Passerieu Bordeneuve, Jean-Claude. 1991. « L'objet marqué en tamoul. Autonomie énonciative et dépendance prédicative ». *LINX* (Université Paris Nanterre) 24: 147–160.

Perrot, Jean. 1993. « L'objet en mordve erza ». *Actances* 7: 183–193.

Pilot-Raichoor, Christiane. 1994. « L'objet en badaga ». *Bulletin de la Société de linguistique de Paris* 89.1: 359–397.

Plungian, Vladimir A. 1993. « Relations actancielles en dogon ». *Actances* 7: 227–238.

Plungian, Vladimir A. 1995. *Dogon.* München, Newcastle: Lincom Europa.

Porterie-Gutierrez, Liliane. 1980. « Les relations actancielles en aymara ». *Amerindia* 5: 7–29.

Pottier, Bernard. 1968. « L'emploi de la préposition *a* devant l'objet en espagnol ». *Bulletin de la Société de linguistique de Paris* 63.1: 83–95.

Rebuschi, Georges. 1986. « Diathèse et (non-)configurationnalité: l'exemple du basque ». *Actances* 2: 175–207.

Rohlfs, Gerhard. 1971. « Autour de l'accusatif prépositionnel dans les langues romanes ». *Revue de linguistique romane* 35: 312–334.

Taylan, Eser E. & Zimmer, Karl. 1994. « Case marking in Turkish: indefinite object construction ». *Berkeley Linguistics Society* 20: 547–552.

Thomson, Alexander. 1912. « Beiträge zur Kasuslehre IV. Ueber die Neubildung des Akkusativs ». *Indogermanische Forschungen* 30: 65–79.

Tomson, A. I. 1928: « Ob upotreblenii časticy *ra* v vinitel'nom padeže v persidskom jazyke ». *Doklady Akademii nauk SSSR* 11: 227–232.

Velten, H. V. 1932. « The accusative case and its substitutes in various types of languages ». *Language* 8: 255–270.

Gilbert Lazard,
École Pratique des Hautes Études,
Paris, France

66. Causatives

1. Definitions
2. Formal types of causatives
3. Causative and related categories
4. Syntax of causative constructions
5. The semantics of causative verbs
6. Diachronic sources of causative affixes
7. Special abbreviations
8. References

1. Definitions

Causatives can be defined as verbs which refer to a **causative situation**, that is, to a causal relation between two events, one of which (P_2) is believed by the speaker to be caused by another (P_1); cf. e.g. Nedjalkov & Sil'nickij 1969a, 1973; Kastovsky 1973. In other words, a causative is a verb or verbal construction meaning 'cause to V_o', 'make V_o', where V_o stands for the embedded base verb. (For other possible definitions of causatives, see § 3.1.). Examples of **causative constructions** (hereafter, CC) are (1–3):

(1) *John opened the door*

(2) *Peter made John go*

(3) Turkish (Comrie 1976: 263)
Ali Hasan-ı öl-dür-dü
Ali:NOM Hasan-ACC die-CAUS-PAST
'Ali killed Hasan.'

Opened, made go, and *öl-dür-dü* in (1–3) are causative verbs, because they refer to causal relations between causing events ('John did sth.', 'Peter did sth.', 'Ali did sth.') and caused events ('the door opened', 'John went', 'Hasan died') and thus all mean 'CAUSE to V_o' ('cause to open', 'cause to go', 'cause to die').

In some languages causative markers apply to both verbs and nominals (nouns, adjectives), forming verbs with the meaning 'make Q', where Q is a quality or the like (*transformatif* in Mel'čuk 1994: 323–324). This is, for instance, the case in Lakota, Nahuatl (cf. Tuggy 1987: 607–614) and many Austronesian languages. So, for example, in Karo Batak we find *galang* 'big' – *pe-galang* 'expand' and similarly in Acehnese *duek* 'sit' – *peu-duek* 'to place', *raja* 'king' – *peu-raja* 'make king; treat as a king', *dit* 'few' – *peu-dit* 'make few' (Durie 1985: 78–81); see also § 5.1.4.

The term **factitive** used to be employed in nearly the same sense as *causative*, particularly often to refer to causatives meaning 'make Q' ('make red', 'make angry', etc.). Nowadays it occurs rarely, except perhaps in the French and Semiticist traditions (cf., for instance, a detailed discussion of the causative/factitive distinction in Kouwenberg 1997: 237 ff.), although some grammars still use it to denote denominal causatives (see above). For a special sense of the term *factitive* adopted within the tradition of the Leningrad/St.Petersburg Typological School, see § 5.1.2.

2. Formal types of causatives

Formal types of causatives can be distinguished according to how the meaning 'cause' is expressed (for a survey, see Nedjalkov & Sil'nickij 1969b: 20–28 [= 1973: 1–10], Baron 1974: 302–310, Song 1996: 20–72).

2.1. Morphological causatives

In **morphological** causatives the causative morpheme is an affix which applies to the base (non-causative) verb, as in Turkish (cf. (3)), Sanskrit (cf. *pat-* 'fly' – *pāt-áya-ti* 'makes fly'), Arabic (cf. *fariha* 'be glad' – *farraha* 'make glad'); for a survey of morphological processes for marking causatives, see e.g. Dixon 2000: 33f.

2.2. Syntactic causatives

In **syntactic** causatives (other terms: *periphrastic,* or *analytic, causatives*) the causative morpheme is a free form, typically a verb meaning 'cause', 'make', 'let', 'give', etc.; cf. English *make go, let know,* German *gehen lassen,* French *faire aller, laisser aller.* Syntactic causatives are distinguished by many authors from constructions which refer to causative situations but do not represent cohesive units, thus being biclausal sentences. (The latter type of construction is sometimes also regarded as a syntactic causative, but this terminological use is less common; cf., for instance, Song's (1996: 35–67) *AND* type and *PURP(ose)* type as opposed to *COMPACT* type as well as the discussion in Moore & Polinsky 1998: 235 ff.). For instance, English *make* + INF, German *lassen* + INF, French *faire* + INF constructions are syntactic causatives, while English *cause to* + INF, German *zwingen zu* + INF, Russian *zastavljat'* + INF are not. There are a number of syntactic and morphological criteria and features for distinguishing syntactic causatives (monoclausal CCs) from non-fused biclausal CCs; cf. Nedjalkov & Nikitina 1965, Nedjalkov 1971: 25—28 [= 1976: 35—39], Comrie 1976: 296—303, De Wolf 1985, Dixon 2000: 34—37 (where biclausal CCs are called 'periphrastic causatives' as opposed to 'same predicate' causatives) and the extensive literature on the clause union features (e. g. Fauconnier 1983, Zubizarreta 1985, Davies & Rosen 1988). Thus, verbs like German *lassen* or French *faire* in syntactic causatives lack many typical features of independent (non-auxiliary) verbs; in particular, they cannot have their own arguments, and they typically do not passivize (cf. (4 d)), etc.:

(4) (a) *Man zwang den Studenten abzureisen.*
'One forced the student to leave.'
(b) *Der Student wurde gezwungen abzureisen.*
'The student was forced to leave.'
(c) *Man ließ den Studenten abreisen.*
'One made/let the student leave.'
(d) **Der Student wurde abreisen gelassen.*
'The student was made leave.'

The distinction between syntactic causatives and non-fused CCs is by no means clear-cut; on the contrary, here we are obviously confronted with a continuum of degrees of fusion, rather than with a 'monoclausal/biclausal CCs' dichotomy.

2.3. Lexical causatives

Lexical causatives are verbs meaning 'CAUSE V₀' but lacking any regular and productive causative marker. They typically are in a suppletive relation with their non-causative counterparts, cf. *kill* — *die*. Historically, lexical causatives may go back to morphological causatives with a marker which was regular and productive in the older language, cf. Old English *cwellan* (> English *kill*) — *cwelan* 'die', English *fell* — *fall*, *lay* — *lie*, Russian *suš-i-t'* 'make dry' — *sox-nu-t'* 'become dry' (the suffix *-i-* in the Russian example is likely to go back to the same Indo-European source as the Sanskrit causative marker in *pāt-áya-ti* quoted in § 2.1., namely to IE *-eie/o-*). Lexical (lexicalized) causatives can even synchronically co-exist with the morphological causatives in which they originate, cf. Imbabura Quechua *wañu-* 'die' — *wañu-chi-* 'cause to die' (morphological causative) — *wanchi-* 'kill' (lexical causative) (Muysken 1981: 450). In some cases it is difficult to draw a clear-cut distinction between morphological and lexical causatives; see e. g. Shibatani (2000: 525—528) on Japanese causatives.

There is a rich literature dealing with the problem of why lexical causatives like *kill* cannot be semantically derived from their non-lexicalized paraphrases. The discussion on why *kill* does not mean *cause to die*, triggered by McCawley (1968), arose chiefly in the framework of generative semantics; for a survey, see e. g. Shibatani (1976). The most comprehensive treatment of the issue and detailed argumentation against McCawley's approach can be found in Wierzbicka (1975); cf. also Horn (1984: 27—29). In particular, unlike lexical causatives, analytical CCs of the type *cause to die* lack such features as unity of place (*John caused Peter to die in Africa* does not imply that John was in Africa, while *John killed Peter in Africa* does), implication of physical contact, etc.

2.4. Labile verbs

A special subtype of lexical causatives are those which are formally indistinguishable from their non-causative counterparts, cf. English verbs like *open* and *move* which can be used both intransitively and transitively (as in (1)). There is, however, neither any consensus on whether such verbs should be treated as one lexical unit with two different syntactic uses or as two separate lexical units (cf. e. g. Kastovsky 1973), nor is there any generally accepted term for such verbs/pairs. Some typologists have borrowed the term **labile** from Caucasian linguistics to denote verbs which can be employed in different syntactic constructions (e. g. both as causatives and corresponding non-causatives) with no formal change in the verb. Other terms occurring in the literature are, for instance, *causative-decausative* (Dolinina 1989: 26 f.), *voice-neutral* (Theckhoff 1980), *optionally transitive* (Miller 1993: 179 f.), *ambitransitive* (Dixon 1994: 18, 54, 217 f. et passim; 2000: 38 f.). In the English tradition of the last few decades the intransitive member of pairs like *The door opened* — *John opened the door* is often termed **ergative** (cf. Keyser & Roeper 1984); see Dixon (1994: 18—21) for a criticism of this terminological use and Kulikov 1999 a for a general survey.

2.5. Causative vs. anticausative (decausative)

The label **anticausative** is used to refer to the non-causative member of the opposition in the case where the directions of the semantic ('V₀' → 'CAUSE V₀') and formal derivation do not match, i.e. in those instances where the non-causative is morphologically more complex than the causative, cf. Russian *lomat'* 'break' — *lomat'-sja* 'break, get broken'. This term (introduced in Nedjalkov & Sil'nickij 1969b: 20) is not as widely accepted as *causative*; other terms used in (nearly) the same sense are *decausative, inchoative, (pure) intransitive, middle, pseudo-passive, eventive, fientive,* etc. In Indo-European studies of the last ten years written in German the term 'fientive' has become the standard term used to refer to intransitive verbs expressing spontaneous event; this is due to the influential monograph Gotō 1987 (cf. p. 25 ff. et passim). For a survey and analysis of anticausatives, see Haspelmath (1987), Kulikov (1998b), Padučeva (2001) and (→ Art. 52); see also Abraham (1997) for a discussion of the causative/anticausative opposition and labile patterns in Germanic languages.

2.6. Formal types of causative oppositions in the languages of the world and productivity of the causative derivation

According to whether the causative or non-causative member of the opposition is typically marked formally, languages can be divided into two classes, i.e. a fundamentally intransitive class in which formally marked causatives are preferred and a fundamentally transitive class in which formally marked anticausatives are preferred; see Haspelmath 1993 for a survey. Descriptive and typological studies have revealed that the (morphological) causative belongs to the most frequently occurring derivational verbal categories (cf. Nichols 1992: 154 f.). In many languages morphological causatives can be derived from all (non-derived) verbs, whereas in other languages there are restrictions on the derivational possibilities. Specifically, in some languages causatives can be derived only from intransitives (early Vedic, Arabic, Indonesian, Mayan, Klamath) and in others they can be derived from intransitive and transitive but not ditransitive verbs (Abkhaz, Basque). However, we probably will not find languages where causatives can be derived from transitives but not intransitives; in fact, this is a universal formulated by Nedjalkov (1966); cf. also Nedjalkov & Sil'nickij (1969b: 25–26 [= 1973: 7–8]) and Song (1996: 170–174). The modern Indo-European languages of Europe, most of which either have syntactic causatives (Germanic, Romance languages) and lack productive morphological causatives or have morphological anticausatives instead (Slavic), thus represent quite a rare language type.

3. Causative and related categories

3.1. Causatives *sensu latiore*, *sensu stricto* and "(just) transitives": a terminological note

The definition given in § 1. encompasses all verbs and constructions which refer to causal situations, regardless of their formal features and position within the verbal system of a given language, i.e. causatives in a wider sense (*causatives sensu latiore*). This terminological use is quite common, for instance, in general typological and semantic studies, but in grammatical descriptions of individual languages the term *causative* is more often employed in a narrower sense. By *causatives sensu stricto* one typically means only those verbs which (i) stand in regular opposition both formally and semantically to the corresponding non-causatives within the verbal system of a given language, (ii) are formally more complex than their non-causative counterparts, and (iii) represent a more or less productive formation. Thus, only morphological (cf. Turkish *öl-dür-* 'kill') and syntactic (cf. *make go*) causatives qualify as *causatives sensu stricto*, while lexical causatives (*kill, open*), as well as verbs which are morphologically simpler than the corresponding non-causatives (anticausatives, cf. Russian *lomat'* — *lomat'-sja*) and non-fused CCs (*cause to go*) do not. Furthermore, in many languages where causatives can double up (see § 5.2.), first (simple) causatives are typically less regular and productive than second causatives and/or can be built only or mostly on intransitive verbs (see § 2.6.). Correspondingly, in a variety of descriptive studies on verbal systems of individual languages only second (double) causatives are regarded as causatives properly speaking, while first causatives are termed *(just) transitives* and treated separately from *causatives (proper)* (although not always consistently; see the diagram below). Since this terminological convention appears to be quite inconsistent and confusing, the author does not see any good reasons to abandon the use of the term *causative* in those cases where the meaning of the verb in question can be rendered as 'CAUSE V_o'; cf. Nedjalkov & Sil'nickij 1969b: 34 [= 1973: 16], fn. 17. For a general discussion of the distinction between causativity and transitivity, see e.g. Zide 1972, Desclés & Guentchéva 1998, Shibatani 2000: 525−528, 548−563.

The relation between the wider and narrow concepts of causatives can be schematized as in Table 66.1:

Table 66.1

causatives sensu latiore	lexical	suppletive (*kill*)	("non-causative") transitives
		labile (*open*)	
		non-productive morphological (*fell*)	
	morphological	less productive	**causatives sensu stricto**
		more productive	
	syntactic (*make go*)		
	biclausal CCs (*cause to go*)		

3.2. Causative and voice

In a number of grammatical descriptions (in particular, in many Altaic and Uralic grammars) the causative is considered as one of the voices (*causative voice, kauzativnyj/ponuditel'nyj zalog*); see, in particular, Shibatani (2000: 547−548). Given a more rigorous definition of voice, however (see especially Mel'čuk 1993), there are several reasons for treating the causative separately. Unlike prototypical voices, such as the passive, the causative changes the lexical meaning of the base verb (see § 1.). The causative can also be combined with several voices within one form as, for example, in the case of passives derived from causatives, causatives derived from reflexives, etc.; see, for instance, Muysken 1981: 457 ff. on the interaction between the causative and other derivational processes in Quechua. Moreover, the causative can double up (see § 5.2.2.); cf. Mel'čuk (1993: 11; 1994: 324−326). See also Babby 1983 where the causative in Turkish is regarded as a grammatical voice, in contrast with the (anti)causative in Russian.

4. Syntax of causative constructions

Leaving aside biclausal CCs and assuming that a causative structure results from a fusion of a matrix and an embedded predicate (cf. Comrie 1976: 262; for a different view, see Song 1996: 166 ff.), the causativization scenario can be represented as follows. The predication referring to the caused event P_2 is embedded into the matrix predication (C_o CAUSE [X], whereby C_o is the causer and [X] is some unspecified event) as its second argument. (Cf., e.g., (2) which results from *Peter* CAUSED [*John went*], i.e. P_2 = [*John went*]). This process of embedding one clause into another to produce a single, derived clause has an important syntactic repercussion. With respect to the structure of the caused event, causativization entails the introduction of a new subject, i.e. the *causer* of the matrix predication, into the underlying structure of the clause. This in turn forces an alteration in the status of the subject of the original clause. Semantically, its role is changed to that of a *causee* (the one who is caused to do/undergo something); syntactically, it is ousted as subject of the derived clause and relegated to some other syntactic function within the clause. The syntactic properties and, above all, the case marking of the causee depend on the syntactic and semantic structure of the embedded clause (for a survey of case marking in CCs, see Dixon 2000: 45−59) and are one of the most widely discussed topics in contemporary syntactic studies. Nearly all syntactic theories have raised this issue, as some kind of "testing ground" for their theoretical apparatus, and even an enumeration of different approaches to the syntax of CCs would be impossible within this article. I will only focus on the two most influential approaches, which will be referred to, for convenience, as the *grammatical relations approach* and the *semantic roles approach*.

4.1. The grammatical relations approach

4.1.1. "Paradigm case": syntactic demotion

The grammatical relations approach was most explicitly elaborated by Comrie (1976) (cf. also Comrie 1985: 335 ff.). The basic principle (labelled by Comrie "paradigm case") determining the syntactic changes accompanying causativization can be formulated as follows: the causee, ousted from the subject position by the causer, is demoted down the grammatical relations hierarchy (other terms: *case hierarchy*, *noun phrase accessibility hierarchy*) (Subject > Direct object > Indirect object > Oblique object) to the highest (= leftmost) free position. This means that if the embedded verb is intransitive, transitive, or ditransitive (i. e. is constructed with both DO and IO), the causee appears as DO, IO, or Oblique object, respectively. Paradigm cases are provided by Romance languages (French (cf. (5)), Italian) or Turkish (cf. (6−8) from another Turkic language, Tuvan):

(5) French (Comrie 1976: 262−263)
 (a) *Je ferai courir* **Henriette** (DO)
  'I shall make Henriette run.'
 (b) *Je ferai manger les gâteaux **à Jean*** (IO)
  'I shall make Jean eat the cakes.'
 (c) *Je ferai écrire une lettre au directeur **par Jean*** (Oblique Object)
  'I'll get Jean to write a letter to the director.'

Cf. also the Tuvan examples (6−8), where all the three grammatical relations in question (DO, IO, Oblique object) are encoded by case suffixes only (Kulikov 1998a: 260):

(6) (a) *ool doŋ-gan*
  boy freeze-PAST
  'The boy froze.'
 (b) *ašak* **ool-du** *doŋ-ur-gan*
  old.man boy-ACC freeze-CAUS-PAST
  'The old man made the boy freeze.'

(7) (a) *ašak ool-du ette-en*
  old.man boy-ACC hit-PAST
  'The old man hit the boy.'

 (b) *Bajïr **ašak-ka** ool-du ette-t-ken*
  Bajïr old.man-DAT boy-ACC hit-CAUS-PAST
  'Bajïr made the old man hit the boy.'

(8) (a) *Bajïr ool-ga bižek-ti ber-gen*
  Bajïr boy-DAT knife-ACC give-PAST
  'Bajïr gave the knife to the boy.'
 (b) *ašak **Bajïr-dan** ool-ga bižek-ti ber-gis-ken*
  old.man Bajïr-ABL boy-DAT knife-ACC give-CAUS-PAST
  'The old man made Bajïr give the knife to the boy.'

However, probably no language conforms exactly to what Comrie calls the "paradigm case" (cf. Song 1996: 160, Dixon 2000: 54−56), and even in languages which, at first glance, meet Comrie's generalization perfectly, like French, we are often faced with an alternative case marking, cf. (5 b) as opposed to (5 d) below. Exceptions to the "paradigm case" fall into two main classes, *extended demotion* and *syntactic doubling*.

4.1.2. Extended demotion

In some languages, the causee can "skip" one or more free positions in the hierarchy and hence be demoted more than necessary according to the "paradigm case". The most frequent type of extended demotion results in the marking of the causee in the same manner as the agent in passive constructions, as if causativization applied to the passivized embedded clause. This alternative "passive marking" competes in some languages with that conforming to the "paradigm case"; for instance, in French both (5 b) and (5 d) are acceptable:

(5) (d) *Je ferai manger les gâteaux **par Jean***

For a possible way of accounting for "passive marking" see e. g. Saksena 1980 b.

Rarer are other types of marking of the causee and still rarer are languages like Gilyak (Nivkh), where the special case ending *-ax* is used solely to express the embedded subject of CCs (cf. Nedjalkov, Otaina & Xolodovič 1969: 195 [= 1995: 77]).

4.1.3. Syntactic doubling

The causee can be demoted to a position which is already occupied − for instance, it can appear as another NP in the accusative alongside the embedded DO (cf. Aissen 1979: 156−201). However, some sophisticated syntactic tests and criteria may reveal differences between NPs which show the same case marking, for instance, between the embedded DO and "new DO". In particular, in many languages only one of these may become a subject in passive constructions (e. g. only the causee), control possessive reflexives, as in (9), etc.:

(9) Korean (Kozinsky & Polinsky 1993: 197)
ku salam-i$_i$ apeci-lul$_j$ acessi-lul$_k$
the man-NOM father-ACC uncle-ACC
caki(-uy)$_{i/j/*k}$ pang-eyse ttayli-key
self(-GEN) room-LOC hit-PURP
hay-ess-ta
do-PAST-DEC
'This man$_i$ made **the father**$_j$ hit the uncle$_k$ in his$_{i/j/*k}$ room.'

Thus, only one of the two identically marked NPs bears a DO relation and there is no true syntactic doubling. For a comprehensive treatment of this issue, see Kozinsky & Polinsky (1993), Polinsky (1994). Moreover, syntactic criteria reveal that the causee may behave differently from any other (prototypical) object and retain a number of subject properties − even in cases where there is no coding conflict in terms of case marking (cf. Falk 1991).

4.2. The semantic roles approach

The semantic roles approach, most explicitly elaborated by Cole (1983) (cf. also Saksena 1980a, Böhm 1981, Alsina 1992, Alsina & Joshi 1991, Kemmer & Verhagen 1994), is an alternative to Comrie's "paradigm case". The grammatical relation of the causee in a CC is said to be primarily determined by its semantic role ("theta role"), specifically by its position in the Agency Hierarchy (Agent > Experiencer > Patient), rather than by the syntactic structure of the embedded clause, as in (10):

(10) Quechua (Cole 1983: 118−119; cf. also Muysken 1981: 451−453)
(a) *nuqa **Fan-wan** rumi-ta*
    I   Juan-INS rock-ACC
    apa-či-ni
    carry-CAUS-1SG
    'I had Juan carry the rock.'
(b) *nuqa **Fan-ta** rumi-ta*
    I   Juan-ACC rock-ACC
    apa-či-ni
    carry-CAUS-1SG
    'I made Juan carry the rock.'
(c) *nuqa **runa-man** rik^{h}u-či-ni*
    I   man-DAT see-CAUS-1SG
    'I showed it to the man.'

Case marking on the causee is said to correspond to its semantic role (more Agent-like causee in (10 a), more Patient-like causee in (10 b), Experiencer in (10 c)). The cases where the marking on the causee is better accounted for by the "paradigm case", rather than in terms of semantic roles, are treated as resulting from the grammaticalization of the semantically based principle. For instance, subjects of intransitive verbs are said to be prototypical patients, therefore the embedded subject (causee) may tend to be marked as DO in all cases where the embedded clause is intransitive, regardless of whether it is a patient or not.

4.3. Other approaches

The majority of other approaches can be characterized according to whether the grammatical relation or semantic role is regarded as the salient parameter or whether these two explanatory strategies are combined to a lesser or greater degree (for a survey, see Kulikov 1994). For instance, Foley & Van Valin (1984) introduced within the framework of Role and Reference Grammar a hierarchy of accessibility of semantic roles to the Actor/Undergoer layer, which thus serves as an interface between semantic roles and grammatical relations; by combining elements of the two aforementioned approaches, this theory provides an explanation for some exceptions to Comrie's "paradigm case". A similar approach ('a proto-role account' of argument selection) is presented in Ackerman (1994). For yet another approach to the problem see Song 1996: 174 ff. (but also see Moore & Polinsky 1998: 245−247 for some criticism).

5. The semantics of causative verbs

5.1. Semantic types of causatives

The main semantic types of causatives occurring in the languages of the world are most comprehensively discussed by Nedjalkov & Sil'nickij (1969b: 28−35 [= 1973: 10−17]), Shibatani (1975: 40−72), Dixon (2000: 61−74) (mainly from a typological perspective) and Talmy (1976) (mainly from a logical perspective, illustrated by English examples only). The linguistically relevant types of causative meaning (i. e. those which can be distinguished by means of distinct morphemes within some languages) are the following.

5.1.1. Direct vs. indirect causatives

According to whether the causer physically manipulates the causee in bringing about the caused event or not, one may distinguish between direct and indirect causatives; other pairs of terms employed to refer to these types of causatives are *manipulative* vs. *directive* causation (cf. Shibatani 1976: 31−38), *contact* vs. *distant* and *immediate* vs. *mediated* causation. The following examples from Zyrjan (Finno-Ugric) illustrate this difference:

(11)   Zyrjan (Lytkin 1957: 105)
        puk- 'sit' − *puk-t-* 'lay' − *puk-öd-* 'cause to sit.'

To put it differently, direct and indirect causatives can be distinguished as *causer-controlled* and *causee-controlled*; for this and other related features, see, e. g., Wierzbicka 1988: Ch. 3; Li 1991; Dixon 2000: 67−70; Shibatani 2000: 549−563.

A special subtype of indirect causation is the *curative* meaning ('ask someone to bring about P₂') attested e. g. in Finnish (cf. Pennanen 1986) and some other Finno-Ugric languages, as in (12):

(12)   Mansi (Rombandeeva 1973: 156 ff.)
        ūnt(u)- 'sit down' − *ūnt-t(u)-* 'seat' − *ūnt-t-u-*pt(a)- 'ask to sit down.'

Very few languages distinguish between other, even more subtle types of indirect causation, as, for instance, Naukan Eskimo, which has several curative suffixes (*-hjka-*, *-sihjka-* 'ask to do sth.', *-hjqur(a)-* 'order to do sth.', *-hjqusar(a)-* 'persuade to do sth.'; see Menovščikov & Xrakovskij 1970).

5.1.2. Permissive

Permissive causatives express the situation where the causer permits the causee to bring about the caused event (P₂), without actually causing the causee to do so. In logical terms, the permissive of V₀ can be defined as 'non-causing [somebody] not to bring about V₀' (e. g. *allow to sleep* ≈ 'not cause not to be awake'), i. e. NOT(CAUSE(NOT(V₀))). The non-permissive causative (causative proper) can be termed **coercive**. Yet another term for coercive, introduced within the tradition of the Leningrad/St.Petersburg Typological School, is **factitive** (cf. Nedjalkov & Sil'nickij 1969b: 28 [= 1973: 10]), but this terminological use is not widely accepted. A causative morpheme can express both permissive and coercive (factitive) meanings (as in Georgian, Quechua, Turkish, etc.), and verbs of permission (like English *let*) can easily develop into normal (non-permissive) causative auxiliaries (as was the case with German *lassen* or Dutch *laten*). Languages with special markers for permissive are very rare (cf. Kulikov & Nedjalkov 1992: 142).

5.1.3. Assistive

Assistive (cooperative) meaning ('help to bring about P₂', 'assist at bringing about P₂') does not incorporate the meaning 'CAUSE' and, strictly speaking, should be treated separately from causatives *sensu stricto*, but it is often rendered by the same marker as ordinary causatives (as in Georgian). In some languages this meaning is expressed by special morphemes (Quechua, Guarani, Cashibo (Peru) and some other Amerindian languages).

5.1.4. Declarative

Yet another meaning often expressed by the causative marker is **declarative**: 'speak about sb. as if s/he were bringing about P₂' (instead of 'cause sb. to bring about P₂'), 'consider Q' (e. g. 'consider bad' instead of the proper causative 'make bad'), attested, for instance, in Arabic, Lakota. As is the case with the assistive, the declarative does not incorporate the meaning 'CAUSE' and thus does not belong to causatives *sensu stricto*, but their close relationship is obvious ('speak about sb. as if s/he were bringing about P₂' ≈ 'cause P₂ to come about in someone's mind'). The declarative usage is common for both causatives and non-causative transitives in literary texts, where "a poet or storyteller is regarded as actually bringing about the events of which he speaks" (Ingalls 1991: 202). Ingalls presents evidence for this from Sanskrit and Latin; cf., e. g., the following Latin example (ibid.: 203):

(13)   Latin
        Turgidus Alpinus jugulat dum Memnona, dumque defingit Rheni luteum caput ... (Horace)
        'While the turgid [poet] Alpinus cuts the throat of [King] Memnon; while he disfigures the muddy headwaters of the Rhine ...'

Declaratives and some other meanings close to them, such as 'treat as P', 'provide with

P', 'use P on sth.', are typical of denominal causatives (see § 1.); cf. Acehnese ***peu***-raja 'make king' (causative proper), 'treat as a king' (declarative); *nan* 'name' − ***peu***-nan 'to name', *taloe* 'rope' − ***peu***-taloe 'tie up'.

5.1.5. Deliberate vs. accidental causation and other semantic oppositions

The opposition between **deliberate** (intentional) vs. **accidental** causation (attested, e. g., in Kashmiri, Bella Coola, Squamish; for a semantic discussion of this distinction, see Paducheva 1997), as well as the semantically related opposition between the non-agentive (inanimate) and agentive causer (e. g. in Swahili and Karo Batak), is much more rarely morphologically relevant than those discussed under § 5.1.1.−3. See also Wierzbicka (1988: Ch. 3) for other semantic contrasts within the systems of causatives.

5.2. Second causative, double causative and iconicity in the form-meaning relation

5.2.1. First vs. second causatives

In the case where two or more causatives differing in meaning can be derived from the same verbal root, they can be termed **first causative**, **second causative**, etc. respectively (for a general survey, see Kulikov 1993). First and second causatives are ordered in terms of their formal (morphological) complexity and degree of fusion, according to the following hierarchy:

lexical causative < morphological causative (with one or more causative affixes) < syntactic causative (monoclausal CC) < biclausal causative sentence

The main semantic types of opposition between first and second causatives are listed under § 5.1. Assuming that contact (direct) and coercive (factitive) causation is more elementary than distant (indirect) and permissive, semantic and formal (morphological) complexity can be said to correlate iconically with each other, as well as with the productivity and regularity of the causative verb formation (see e. g. Wachowicz 1976: 77−90, Kulikov 1999b, Shibatani 2000: 549−571). In particular, indirect causatives are typically more complex from the morphological point of view, whereby the corresponding marker often incorporates that of the direct ("first") causative as, for instance, in Hindi (cf. causative suffixes -*ā*- and -*vā*-; see Saksena 1982a; 1983 for discussion), Mansi (cf. (12)), etc. Furthermore, the morphologically simpler first causatives are often less regular from the semantic point of view. In particular, they can show some idiomatic semantic changes, denoting pragmatically more common unmarked (conventional) situations than second causatives do (e. g. 'play with [a child]' or 'amuse [a child]', instead of 'make [a child] play'; cf. Kulikov 1999b: 53−55, Shibatani 2000: 561−562). Such oppositions can be interpreted in terms of the division of pragmatic labor; cf. Horn 1984: 27−29. Likewise, English periphrastic *make*-causatives are syntactically and semantically simpler than *have*-causatives, which, in turn, are simpler than biclausal causative sentences with *cause*; cf. Baron 1974: 333−334, Givón 1975; Shibatani 1976, Terasawa 1985. On the subtle semantic differences between *make*- and *have*-causatives (and similar oppositions in other languages), which do not amount to the direct/indirect distinction, see Wierzbicka (1988: Ch. 3); see also Verhagen & Kemmer (1997) for an interpretation of the distinction between Dutch *doen*- and *laten*-causatives (= direct vs. indirect causation) in cognitive terms. For a general interpretation of the complexity of causatives in terms of iconicity (i. e. greater linguistic distance between cause and effect signals greater conceptual distance between cause and result and between causer and cause), see Comrie (1985: 332−334), Haiman (1985: 108−111), Kulikov (1999b), Dixon (2000: 74−78); cf. also Song (1992) for some counter-evidence.

5.2.2. Double causatives

Double causatives are derived from the first ("simple") causative by adding a second causative morpheme, thus representing a special subtype of the second causative with a complex causative marker incorporating the first causative marker. Such formations are especially common in agglutinative languages where affixes easily combine with each other and iterate. Double causatives (as well as rarer triple etc. causatives) typically express a double (triple, etc.) causative chain, as in (14):

(14)   Chuvash (Kornilov et al. 1969: 247 f.)
       xïr- 'shave' − *xïr-tar*- 'ask to shave'
       − *xïr-tar-tar*- 'cause to ask to shave.'

Less trivial, but no less iconic, are the cases where iteration of the causative marker expresses intensivity, iterativity, plurality of some participants of the causative situation or semantically more complex causative meanings discussed under § 5.1. such as the distant causation (cf. Kulikov 1993: 128−134; 1999b: 52−53).

5.3. Polysemy of causative markers

Alongside causative meanings proper, causative markers have other functions in some languages; for a survey of this polysemy, see Nedjalkov (1966), Nedjalkov & Sil'nickij (1969b: 35−43 [= 1973: 17−25]), Kulikov & Nedjalkov (1992: 143−145).

5.3.1. Valence-increasing derivations

Most such secondary functions belong together with causatives to the sphere of **valence-increasing** (transitivizing) **derivations**. These include the assistive and the declarative (both are often treated as subtypes of the causative meaning, see § 5.1.3.−4.) as well as the applicative. The applicative is attested, e. g., in Chukchee, some Australian languages, such as Pitta-Pitta, Kalkatungu and Yidiny (see Austin 1997), and in Uto-Aztecan languages, cf. Nahuatl *ni-mēwa* 'I arise' − *ni-k-mēwi-liya* 'I raise him', *ni-ȼahȼi* 'I shout' − *ni-k-ȼahȼi-liya* 'I shout to him' (see Tuggy 1987). The applicative includes different subtypes, in particular, the benefactive ('do' − 'do for someone', attested e. g. in Indonesian) and the comitative ('come' − 'come with someone', attested e. g. in Chukchee and many Amazonian (Arawak) languages, such as Tariana; see Wise 1990, Aikhenvald 1998: 56−58), sometimes treated as separate valence-increasing categories. For the causative/applicative polysemy, see, in particular, Austin (1997), Dixon & Aikhenvald (1997: 77 ff.), Shibatani (2000: 563−571).

5.3.2. Causative/passive polysemy

In Korean, some Altaic languages of Siberia (Tuvan, Yakut, Mongolian, Manchu and other Tungusic languages), some West African languages (Songhai, Dogon), Bella Coola (Amerindian) and some other languages of the world, verbs with causative markers can also function as **passives**, as in (15):

(15) Manchu (I. Nedjalkov 1991: 5)
 (a) *Bata i-mbe va-ha*
   enemy he-ACC kill-PAST
   'The enemy killed him.'
 (b) *I bata-be va-bu-ha*
   he enemy-ACC kill-CAUS/PASS-PAST
   'He made (somebody) kill the enemy.'
 (c) *I (bata-de) va-bu-ha*
   he (enemy-DAT) kill-CAUS/PASS-PAST
   'He is/was killed (by the enemy).'

The passive usage is likely to have developed, most often and quite naturally, from the permissive (e. g. 'I let someone catch my hand' → 'I was grabbed by the hand', etc.) and/or from the reflexive-causative meanings ('I let someone photograph myself' → 'I was photographed'). For a general discussion, see Nedjalkov (1964), Andersen (1991: 75−82) (on cognitive sources of the causative/passive polysemy), I. Nedyalkov (1991), Plungian (1993), Washio (1993), Knott (1995).

5.3.3. Reciprocal

Yet another meaning of the valence-changing type which can be expressed by causative markers is the **reciprocal**. This rare type of polysemy occurs, for instance, in some Austronesian (e. g. Nakanai, Tanga; cf. Li 1991: 347−349) and Maipuran Arawakan languages (e. g. Piro, cf. Wise 1990).

5.3.4. Intensive, iterative, distributive

Some other functions, such as the **intensive** (as in (16)), the **iterative** or the **distributive** appear less motivated, since, unlike causatives, they do not imply any valence change:

(16) Arabic (Premper 1987: 89−90)
 (a) *'alima* 'learn' − *'allama* 'teach' (causative);
 (b) *daraba* 'hit' − *darraba* 'hit strongly' (intensive).

This type of polysemy can probably be accounted for within the approach to transitivity as a complex set of features all concerned with the effectiveness with which an action takes place (Hopper & Thompson 1980). Causativization is a transitivity-increasing derivation and therefore may be secondarily associated with aspectual meanings (or *aktionsarten*) corresponding to a greater degree of effectiveness. Causing someone to do something implies channelling extra force from outside into the situation, the meaning 'more forcefully', 'more effectively' being thus the common semantic denominator shared by the causativity, on the one hand, and intensivity, iterativity etc., on the other; for more evidence and discussion, see Li (1991: 349−351), Golovko (1993), Maslova (1993), Kulikov (1999c).

6. Diachronic sources of causative affixes

In some languages causative markers can be traced back to certain free forms or affixes with other functions. In particular, causative affixes can go back to syntactic causatives built with separate verbs meaning 'make', 'let', 'give', etc.; see under § 2.2. Other typical sources of causative morphemes are directional or benefactive affixes; cf. Song 1990: 169−193 [≈ 1996: 80−106]. For instance, in Lamang (Chadic) the causative suffix -ŋà may be related to the benefactive preposition -ŋgà; in Kxoe (Central Khoisan) the causative suffix -kà is identical to the directional preposition -kà. Finally, causative markers can develop from the verbal affixes with non-causative meanings listed under § 5.3.3. (intensive, iterative); cf. Li 1991.

Acknowledgements

I am much indebted to W. Abraham, W. F. H. Adelaar, P. K. Andersen, T. Bynon, M. Haspelmath, K. Kiryu, E. König, F. H. H. Kortlandt, A. M. Lubotsky, V. P. Nedjalkov, N. Nicholas, I. A. Nikolaeva, V. A. Plungian, N. M. Rodina, Th. C. Schadeberg, M. Shibatani, J. J. Song, T. Tsunoda, H. Vater, V. Velupillai and T. Zehnder for critical remarks and valuable comments on earlier drafts of this paper.

7. Special abbreviations

CC	causative construction
DEC	declarative
INS	instrumental
PURP	purpose

8. References

Abraham, Werner. 1997. "Kausativierung und Dekausativierung: zu Fragen der verbparadigmatischen Markierung in der Germania". In: Birkmann, Th. et al. (eds.). *Vergleichende germanische Philologie und Skandinavistik. Festschrift für Otmar Werner.* Tübingen: Niemeyer, 13−28.

Abraham, Werner & Kulikov, Leonid (eds.). 1999. *Tense-aspect, transitivity and causativity. Essays in honour of Vladimir Nedjalkov.* (Studies in Language Companion Series, 50). Amsterdam: Benjamins.

Ackerman, Farrell. 1994. "Entailments of predicates and the encoding of causees". *Linguistic Inquiry* 25.3: 535−547.

Aikhenvald, Alexandra Y. 1998. "Transitivity increasing operations in Tariana". In: Kulikov & Vater (eds.), 47−59.

Aissen, Judith L. 1979. *The syntax of causative constructions.* New York: Garland.

Alsina, Alex. 1992. "On the argument structure of causatives". *Linguistic Inquiry* 23.4: 517−555.

Alsina, Alex & Joshi, Smita. 1991 [1993]. "Parameters in causative constructions". In: Dobrin, Lise M. et al. (eds.). *Papers from the 27th regional meeting of the Chicago Linguistic Society.* Pt. 1: The General Session. Chicago: Chicago Linguistic Society, 1−15.

Andersen, Paul Kent. 1991. *A new look at the passive.* (Duisburger Arbeiten zur Sprach- und Kulturwissenschaft, 11). Frankfurt am Main etc.: Peter Lang.

Austin, Peter. 1997. "Causatives and applicatives in Australian Aboriginal languages". In: Matsumura, Kazuto & Hayasi, Toru (eds.). *The dative and related phenomena.* Tokyo: Hitsuji Shobo, 165−225.

Babby, Leonard H. 1983. "The relation between causative and voice: Russian vs. Turkish". *Wiener Slawistischer Almanach* 11 [Fs. I. Mel'čuk]: 61−88.

Baron, Naomi S. 1974. "The structure of English causatives". *Lingua* 33: 299−342.

Bennett, David C.; Bynon, Theodora & Hewitt, B. George (eds.). 1995. *Subject, voice and ergativity: Selected essays.* London: School of Oriental and African Studies, University of London.

Böhm, Roger. 1981. "On causing without a subject". *Lingua* 53.1: 3−31.

Cole, Peter. 1983. "The grammatical role of the causee in universal grammar". *International Journal of American Linguistics* 49.2: 115−133.

Comrie, Bernard. 1976. "The syntax of causative constructions: Cross-language similarities and divergencies". In: Shibatani (ed.), 261−312.

−. 1985. "Causative verb formation and other verb-deriving morphology". In: Shopen, Timothy (ed.). *Language typology and syntactic description.* Vol. III. *Grammatical categories and the lexicon.* Cambridge: Cambridge University Press, 309−348.

Comrie, Bernard & Polinsky, Maria (eds.). 1993. *Causatives and transitivity.* (Studies in Language Companion Series, 23). Amsterdam: Benjamins.

Davies, William & Rosen, Carol. 1988. "Unions as multi-predicate clauses". *Language* 64.1: 52−88.

Desclés, Jean-Pierre & Guentchéva, Zlatka. 1998. "Causalité, causativité, transitivité". In: Kulikov & Vater (eds.), 7−27.

De Wolf, Charles M. 1985. "Case marking, causatives, and constituency: A non-transformational approach". *General Linguistics* 25.4: 236−272.

Dixon, Robert M. W. 1994. *Ergativity.* (Cambridge Studies in Linguistics, 69). Cambridge: Cambridge University Press.

—. 2000. "A typology of causatives: form, syntax and meaning". In: Dixon & Aikhenvald (eds.), 30–83.

Dixon, Robert M. W. & Aikhenvald, Alexandra Y. 1997. "A typology of argument-determined constructions". In: Bybee, Joan et al. (eds.). *Essays on language function and language type: Dedicated to T. Givón*. Amsterdam: Benjamins, 71–113.

Dixon, Robert M. W. & Aikhenvald, Alexandra Y. (eds.). 2000. *Changing valency: case studies in transitivity*. Cambridge: Cambridge University Press.

Dolinina, Inga B. 1989. *Sintaksičeski-značimye kategorii anglijskogo glagola*. Leningrad: Nauka.

Durie, Mark. 1985. *A grammar of Acehnese*. (Verhandelingen van het Koninklijk Instituut voor Taal-, Land- en Volkenkunde, 112). Dordrecht: Foris.

Eilfort, William H. et al. (eds.). *Causatives and agentivity. Papers from the Parasession on causatives and agentivity at the 21st regional meeting of the Chicago Linguistic Society*. Chicago: Chicago Linguistic Society.

Falk, Yehuda N. 1991. "Causativization". *Journal of Linguistics* 27.1: 55–79.

Fauconnier, Gilles. 1983. "Generalized union". In: Tasmowski, Liliane & Willems, Dominique (eds.). *Problems in syntax*. (Studies in language, 2). New York: Plenum Press; Ghent: Communication and Cognition, 195–229.

Foley, William A. & Van Valin, Robert D., Jr. 1984. *Functional syntax and universal grammar*. (Cambridge Studies in Linguistics, 38). Cambridge etc.: Cambridge University Press.

Givón, Talmy. 1975. "Cause and control: On the semantics of interpersonal manipulation". In: Kimball, John P. (ed.). *Syntax and semantics*, vol. 4. New York etc.: Academic Press, 59–89.

Golovko, Evgeniy V. 1993. "On non-causative effects of causativity in Aleut". In: Comrie & Polinsky (eds.), 385–390.

Gotō, Toshifumi. 1987. *Die "I. Präsensklasse" im Vedischen: Untersuchung der vollstufigen thematischen Wurzelpräsentia*. (Österreichische Akademie der Wissenschaften. Philos.-Hist. Klasse. Sitzungsberichte, 489). Wien: Verlag der Österreichischen Akademie der Wissenschaften.

Haiman, John. 1985. *Natural syntax: Iconicity and erosion*. (Cambridge Studies in Linguistics, 44). Cambridge etc.: Cambridge University Press.

Haspelmath, Martin. 1987. *Transitivity alternations of the anticausative type*. (Institut für Sprachwissenschaft, Arbeitspapier, 5 (Neue Folge)). Köln.

—. 1993. "More on the typology of inchoative/causative verb alternation". In: Comrie & Polinsky (eds.), 87–120.

Hopper, Paul J. & Thompson, Sandra A. 1980. "Transitivity in grammar and discourse". *Language* 56.2: 251–299.

Horn, Laurence R. 1984. "Toward a new taxonomy for pragmatic inference: Q-based and R-based implicature". In: Schiffrin, Deborah (ed.). *Meaning, form, and use in context: Linguistic applications*. Washington: Georgetown University Press, 11–42.

Ingalls, Daniel H. H. 1991. "A note on Pāṇini 3.1.26, *Vārttika* 8." In: Deshpande, Madhav M. & Bhate, S. (eds.). *Pāṇinian studies. Professor S. D. Joshi felicitation volume*. (Michigan papers on South and Southeast Asia, 37). Ann Arbor: Center for South and Southeast Asian studies, The University of Michigan, 201–208.

Kastovsky, Dieter. 1973. "Causatives". *Foundations of Language* 10: 255–315.

Kemmer, Suzanne & Verhagen, Arie. 1994. "The grammar of causatives and the conceptual structure of events". *Cognitive Linguistics* 5.2: 115–156.

Keyser, Samuel Jay & Roeper, Thomas. 1984. "On the middle and ergative constructions in English". *Linguistic Inquiry* 15.3: 381–416.

Knott, Judith. 1995. "The causative-passive correlation". In: Bennett et al. (eds.), 53–59.

Kornilov, G. E.; Xolodovič, A. A. & Xrakovskij, V. S. 1969. "Kauzativy i antikauzativy v čuvašskom jazyke". In: Xolodovič (ed.), 238–259.

Kouwenberg, Norbertus J. C. 1997. *Gemination in the Akkadian verb*. (Studia Semitica Neerlandica, 32). Assen: Van Gorcum.

Kozinsky, Isaac & Polinsky, Maria. 1993. "Causee and patient in the causative of transitive: Coding conflict or doubling of grammatical relations?" In: Comrie & Polinsky (eds.), 177–240.

Kulikov, Leonid I. 1993. "The "second causative": A typological sketch". In: Comrie & Polinsky (eds.), 121–154.

—. 1994. "Tipologija kauzativnyx konstrukcij v sovremennyx sintaksičeskix teorijax". In: Belikov, Vladimir I. et al. (eds.). *Znak: Sbornik statej po lingvistike, semiotike i poėtike pamjati A. N. Žurinskogo*. Moskva: Russkij učebnyj centr MS, 48–60.

—. 1998a. "Causative constructons in Tuvinian: towards a typology of transitivity". In: Johanson, Lars et al. (eds.). *The Mainz Meeting. Proceedings of the Seventh International Conference on Turkish Linguistics*. (Turcologica, 32). Wiesbaden: Harrassowitz, 258–264.

—. 1998b. "Passive, anticausative and classification of verbs: the case of Vedic". In: Kulikov & Vater (eds.), 139–153.

—. 1999a. "May he prosper in offspring and wealth (A few jubilee remarks on the typology of labile verbs and Sanskrit *púṣyati* 'prospers; makes prosper')". In: Rakhilina, Ekaterina V. & Testelets, Yakov G. (eds.). *Tipologija i teorija jazyka: Ot opisanija k ob'jasneniju. K 60-letiju A. E. Kibrika*. [Typology and linguistic theory: From description to explanation. For the 60th birthday of Aleksandr

E. Kibrik]. Moskva: "Jazyki russkoj kul'tury", 224–244.

—. 1999b. "Remarks on double causatives in Tuvan and other Turkic languages". *Journal de la Société Finno-Ugrienne* 88: 49–58.

—. 1999c. "Split causativity: remarks on correlations between transitivity, aspect, and tense". In: Abraham & Kulikov (eds.), 21–42.

Kulikov, Leonid I. & Nedjalkov, Vladimir P. 1992. "Questionnaire zur Kausativierung". *Zeitschrift für Phonetik, Sprachwissenschaft und Kommunikationsforschung* 45.2: 137–149.

Kulikov, Leonid & Vater, Heinz (eds.). 1998. *Typology of verbal categories: Papers presented to Vladimir Nedjalkov on the occasion of his 70th birthday.* (Linguistische Arbeiten, 382). Tübingen: Niemeyer.

Li, Fengxiang. 1991. "An examination of causative morphology from a cross-linguistic and diachronic perspective". In: Dobrin, Lise M. et al. (eds.). *Papers from the 27th regional meeting of the Chicago Linguistic Society.* Pt. 1: The General Session. Chicago: Chicago Linguistic Society, 344–359.

Lytkin, Vasilij I. 1957. "Ponuditel'nyj zalog v permskix jazykax". *Učenye zapiski Udmurtskogo NII IÈLJa* 18: 93–113.

Maslova, Elena S. 1993. "The causative in Yukaghir". In: Comrie & Polinsky (eds.), 271–285.

McCawley, James D. 1968. "Lexical insertion in a transformational grammar without deep structure". In: Darden, Bill J. et al. (eds.). *Papers from the 4th regional meeting of the Chicago Linguistic Society.* Chicago: Chicago Linguistic Society, 71–80.

Mel'čuk, Igor A. 1993. "The inflectional category of voice: towards a more rigorous definition". In: Comrie & Polinsky (eds.), 1–46.

—. 1994. *Cours de morphologie générale (théorique et descriptive).* Vol. II/2: Significations morphologiques. Montréal: Les Presses de l'Université de Montréal.

Menovščikov, Georgij A. & Xrakovskij, Viktor S. 1970. "Kauzativnye glagoly i kauzativnye konstrukcii v èskimosskom jazyke". *Voprosy jazykoznanija* 4: 102–110.

Miller, J. Gary. 1993. *Complex verb formation.* Amsterdam: Benjamins.

Moore, John & Polinsky, Mary. 1998. Review of: Song 1996. *Linguistic Typology* 2.2: 231–251.

Muysken, Pieter. 1981. "Quechua causatives and logical form: a case study of markedness". In: Belletti, Adriana et al. (eds.). *Theory of markedness in generative grammar: proceedings of the 1979 GLOW conference.* Pisa: Scuola Normale Superiore di Pisa, 445–473.

Nedjalkov, Vladimir P. 1964. O svjazi kauzativnosti i passivnosti. *Učenye zapiski Baškirskogo universiteta* 21. Serija filologičeskix nauk 9 (13): 301–310.

—. 1966. Ob areal'nyx universalijax (na materiale kauzativnyx glagolov). In: *Konferencija po problemam izučenija universal'nyx i areal'nyx svojstv jazykov. Tezisy dokladov.* Moskva, 55–58.

—. 1971. *Kauzativnye konstrukcii v nemeckom jazyke: Analitičeskij kauzativ.* Leningrad: Nauka. (German translation: *Kausativkonstruktionen.* (Studien zur Deutschen Grammatik, 4). Tübingen: Narr, 1976).

Nedjalkov, Vladimir P. & Nikitina, Tamara N. 1965. "O priznakax analitičnosti i služebnosti (na materiale kauzativnyx konstrukcij)". In: Žirmunskij, V. M. & Sunik, O. P. (eds.). *Analitičeskie konstrukcii v jazykax različnyx tipov.* Moskva – Leningrad: Nauka, 170–193.

Nedjalkov, Vladimir P.; Otaina, Galina A. & Xolodovič, Aleksandr A. 1969. "Morfologičeskij i leksičeskij kauzativy v nivxskom jazyke". In: Xolodovič (ed.), 179–199. (English translation: "Morphological and lexical causatives in Nivkh". In: Bennett et al. (eds.), 60–81).

Nedjalkov, Vladimir P. & Sil'nickij, Georgij G. 1969a. "Tipologija kauzativnyx konstrukcij". In: Xolodovič (ed.), 5–19. (German translation: "Typologie der kausativen Konstruktionen". *Folia Linguistica* 6.3/4 (1973): 273–290).

—. 1969b. "Tipologija morfologičeskogo i leksičeskogo kauzativov". In: Xolodovič (ed.), 20–50. (English translation: "The typology of morphological and lexical causatives". In: Kiefer, Ferenc (ed.). 1973. *Trends in Soviet theoretical linguistics.* Dordrecht etc.: Reidel, 1–32).

Nedyalkov, Igor V. 1991. Recessive-accessive polysemy of verbal affixes. *Languages of the world* 1: 4–31.

Nichols, Johanna. 1992. *Linguistic diversity in space and time.* Chicago – London: The University of Chicago Press.

Paducheva [Padučeva], Elena V. 1997. "Verb categorization and the format of a lexicographic definition (semantic types of causative relations)". In: Wanner, Leo (ed.). *Recent trends in meaning-text theory.* (Studies in Language Companion Series, 39). Amsterdam: Benjamins.

—. 2001. "Russkij dekauzativ i ego formal'nye modeli". *Naučno-texničeskaja informacija* (Ser. 2): 1, 23–34.

Pennanen, Esko V. 1986. "On the so-called curative verbs in Finnish". *Finnisch-ugrische Forschungen* 47.2–3: 163–182.

Plungian, Vladimir A. 1993. "Three causatives in Dogon and the overlapping of causative and passive markers". In: Comrie & Polinsky (eds.), 391–396.

Polinsky, Maria. 1994. "Double objects in causatives: Towards a study of coding conflict". *Studies in Language* 19.1: 129–221.

Premper, Waldfried. 1987. *KAUSATIVIERUNG im Arabischen (Ein Beitrag zur sprächlichen Dimen-*

sion der PARTIZIPATION). (Arbeiten des Kölner Universalien-Projekts [AKUP], 66). Köln: Institut für Sprachwissenschaft.

Rombandeeva, Evdokija I. 1973. *Mansijskij (vogul'skij) jazyk*. Moskva: Nauka.

Saksena, Anuradha. 1980a. "The affected agent". *Language* 56.4: 812–826. (= Ch. 4–5 in Saksena 1982b).

–. 1980b. "The source of causative contrast". *Lingua* 51: 125–136. (= Ch. 3 in Saksena 1982b).

–. 1982a. "Contact in causation". *Language* 58.4: 820–831. (= Ch. 6 in Saksena 1982b).

–. 1982b. *Topics in the analysis of causatives: with an account of Hindi paradigms*. (University of California Publications in Linguistics, 98). Berkeley: University of California Press.

–. 1983. "A semantic model of causative paradigms". *Lingua* 59.1: 77–94. (= Ch. 7 in Saksena 1982b).

Shibatani, Masayoshi. 1975. *A linguistic study of causative constructions*. Bloomington, Indiana.

–. 1976. "The grammar of causative constructions: A conspectus". In: Shibatani (ed.), 1–40.

–. 2000. "Issues in transitivity and voice: Japanese perspective". *Bull. Faculty of Letters, University of Kobe* 27: 523–586.

Shibatani, Masayoshi (ed.). 1976. *The grammar of causative constructions*. (Syntax and semantics, 6). New York etc.: Academic Press.

Song, Jae Jung. 1990. "On the rise of causative affixes: a universal-typological perspective". *Lingua* 82: 151–200. (≈ Ch. 3 in Song 1996).

–. 1992. "A note on the iconicity in causatives". *Folia Linguistica* 26.3–4: 333–338.

–. 1996. *Causatives and causation: A universal typological perspective*. London etc.: Longman.

Talmy, Leonard. 1976. "Semantic causative types". In: Shibatani (ed.), 43–116.

Tchekhoff, Claude. 1980. The organization of a voice-neutral verb: An example in Avar. *International Review of Slavic Linguistics* 5: 219–230.

Terasawa, Jun. 1985. "The historical development of the causative use of the verb *make* with an infinitive". *Studia Neophilologica* 57: 133–143.

Tuggy, David. 1987. "Náhuatl causative/applicative in cognitive grammar". In: Rudzka-Ostyn, Brygida (ed.). *Topics in cognitive linguistics*. (Current Issues in Linguistic Theory, 50). Amsterdam: Benjamins, 587–618.

Verhagen, Arie & Kemmer, Suzanne. 1997. "Interaction and causation: Causative constructions in modern standard Dutch". *Journal of Pragmatics* 27: 61–82.

Wachowicz, Krystyna. 1976. "Some universal properties of morphological causatives". *Working Papers on Language Universals* (Stanford) 20: 59–106.

Washio, Ryuchi. 1993. "When causatives mean passive: A cross-linguistic perspective". *Journal of East Asian Linguistics* 2: 45–90.

Wierzbicka, Anna. 1975. "Why 'kill' does not mean 'cause to die': The semantics of action sentences". *Foundations of Language* 13: 491–528. (= Ch. 5 in: Wierzbicka, Anna. 1980. *Lingua mentalis*. Sydney: Academic Press).

–. 1988. *The semantics of grammar*. (Studies in Language Companion Series, 18). Amsterdam: Benjamins.

Wise, Mary Ruth. 1990. "Valence-changing affixes in Maipuran Arawakan languages". In: Payne, Doris L. (ed.). *Amazonian linguistics: Studies in lowland South American languages*. Austin: University of Texas Press, 89–116.

Xolodovič, Aleksandr A. (ed.). *Tipologija kauzativnyx konstrukcij. Morfologičeskij kauzativ*. Leningrad: Nauka.

Zide, Arlene R. K. 1972. "Transitive and causative in Gorum". *Journal of Linguistics* 8: 201–215.

Zubizarreta, Maria Luisa. 1985. "The relation between morphophonology and morphosyntax: The case of Romance causatives". *Linguistic Inquiry* 16.2: 247–289.

Leonid I. Kulikov, Leiden (The Netherlands)

67. The passive voice

1. Introduction
2. Morphology of the passive voice
3. Syntax of the passive construction
4. Functions of the passive voice
5. Derived vs. basic status of the passive voice
6. Cross-linguistic distribution of the passive voice
7. The passive in relation to some other grammatical phenomena
8. Special abbreviations
9. References

1. Introduction

The passive voice is one of the most important types of voice alternations attested across languages. The majority of languages with voice alternations also have the passive voice. The definition of the passive voice which we will adopt in the present article largely follows Haspelmath (1990: 27). A construction is called passive if:

(i) the verbal form used in that construction is morphologically derived in some way from the form used in the unmarked (active) voice construction; and
(ii) the actor is either unexpressed or expressed by a non-obligatory oblique phrase with the derived verbal form; and
(iii) the subject, if any, is not the actor;
(iv) the construction is somehow restricted vis-à-vis the unmarked (active) voice construction in its distribution; and
(v) the propositional semantics of the construction is identical to that of the unmarked (active) voice; specifically, the number of participants and their roles do not change.

(Here and below, we prefer to use the term "actor" rather than "agent"; the former comprises not only agents of action verbs, but also experiences and subjects of mental states denoted by transitive verbs; see Foley & Van Valin 1985 for a similar use of this term.)

It is easy to see that the constructions traditionally recognized as passive satisfy this definition; consider the English passive as an example:

(1) (a) the active voice
The mother washed the child.
(b) the passive voice
The child was washed (by the mother).

In (1b) the analytic verbal form *was washed* is derived from the form used in the active voice (1a). The agent of (1b) is expressed by the oblique prepositional phrase and can be omitted, whereas the subject of (1b) is a patient NP. Finally, the construction illustrated in (1b) is less frequent than its active correlate in (1a).

At the same time, it is easy to notice that the above definition subsumes under the label of the passive voice certain constructions which are traditionally not considered as passives. Specifically, it allows subjectless passives as well as passive constructions which prohibit the expression of the actor. Besides, it does not specify the morphological nature of passive marking, stipulating only that passive verbal forms must be derived from their active counterparts. Considered against the background of "Standard Average European" (→ Art. 107), this could seem an unnecessary extension of the domain of the passive voice. However, a typological survey of passive constructions warrants marking the criteria for passive more loose: As the reader of the present article will see, the construction traditionally labeled "the passive voice" constitutes a part of the large and complex continuum of de-transitivizing grammatical devices, which differ from one another in form and in meaning. Searching for a typological account of the de-transitivizing grammatical devices, we find it appropriate to make the passive domain wider than it appears from the Standard Average European perspective. The above definition of the passive voice aims exactly at capturing the cross-linguistic diversity of passives. At the same time, the proposed definition allows to draw a distinction between the passive voice and the middle voice — another large domain of the de-transitivizing continuum (see § 4.2.1.; see also Art. 68).

One further consequence of the definition proposed above is that morphological and syntactic properties are equally essential for the passive voice. In this respect the passive voice differs from tense, aspect, modality and other verbal categories which generally do not affect the syntactic characteristics of the verb. On the other hand, our definition implies that transitivity alternations similar to the passive voice in their syntactic effect, but lacking morphological marking on the verb do not count as passives. This disagrees with Dryer's (1982) view that the universal and essential part of the passive is its syntactic properties only; it is remarkable, however, that most if not all of the putative passives lacking passive morphology in fact cannot be identified as passives not only on morphological grounds, but on syntactic grounds as well (see the list of such sonstructions with summaries of their relevant properties in Haspelmath 1990: 27 ff.).

The article is organized as follows: In § 2 the morphological diversity of the passive voice is considered; § 3 deals with the syntactic typology of passives. In § 4, syntactic and semantic functions of the passive voice are considered, and differences between the passive voice and other de-transitive constructions are identified. In § 5, the question of the derived status of the passive voice is discussed. The cross-linguistic distribution of the passive voice is considered in § 6. Finally, § 7 deals with typologically valid categories close to the passive voice and highlights differences between them.

2. Morphology of the passive voice

2.1. Synthetic passive

In the synthetic expression of the passive, several subtypes can be distinguished, depending upon the kind of morphological markers.

2.1.1. Additional morpheme

An additional morpheme is by far the most widespread type of synthetic expression of the passive voice. Within it, in turn, two subtypes exist: the one where the passive morpheme is attached directly to the verbal stem, i.e. more "internally" than aspect, tense and agreement markers (Haspelmath's "additional stem affix"), and the one where the passive morpheme is less close to the root than those markers (Haspelmath's "extra-inflectional affix"). As noted by Haspelmath, the former type is much more frequent than the latter. A passive form with an additional stem affix is illustrated for Classical Greek, and a passive form with an extra-inflectional affix is illustrated for Modern Icelandic:

(2) Classical Greek
(a) ho kúrios é-lu-se
ART lord.NOM PRET-release-AOR.3sg
tòn doũlo-n
ART.ACC slave-ACC
'The lord released the slave.'

(b) ho doũlos
ART slave.NOM
e-lú-thē:-Ø hupò
PRET-release-PASS.AOR-3sg by
toũ kurí-ou
ART.GEN lord-GEN
'The slave was released by the lord.'

(3) Modern Icelandic
(a) ég kall-a
I call-1sg
'I call.'
(b) ég kall-a-st
I call-1sg-PASS
'I am called.'

Additional stem affixes also mark passives in e.g. Turkish, Vedic, Modern Greek, Inuit (Fortescue 1984), Jacaltec (Mayan; Craig 1977), Navajo (Athabaskan; A. A. Kibrik 1996), Nepali (Indo-Aryan; Bandhu 1973), Fula (Bantu; Koval' & Njalibuli 1997), and Yaqui (Uto-Aztecan; Langacker 1976). Passives with an extra-inflectional affix are reported by Haspelmath (1990), apart from Modern Icelandic and its relative Danish, also for 'O'odham (Aztec-Tanoan) and Shuswap (Salish). Another instance of this type of passive is the Russian construction with the marker -sj(a) following verbal inflection; its passive function, however, is restricted to a very limited class of verbs. Haspelmath (1990: 30) observes that passives of this type usually are derived from reflexive pronouns cliticized to the verbal form.

In Bybee (1985), the cross-linguistic tendency towards the "internal" position of passive markers receives a functional explanation, based on the assumption that the more intimately a category interacts with the lexical meaning of a verb, the more probable it is for markers of that category to occur in contact position with the verbal stem. Clearly, the passive as well as other voice alternations (valence-changing categories, in Bybee's terms) is semantically "fused" with the verb much more closely than, for instance, tense or modality: The former change the semantic interpretation of core verbal dependents, whereas the latter only change characteristics semantically external to the action, such as its temporal reference or truth value.

As far as the position of the passive affix with respect to the stem is concerned, languages seem to allow all the logically possible alternatives. Passive suffixes are attested e.g. in Turkic languages and in Finno-Ugric languages. Passive prefixes occur e.g. in Sre (Mon-Khmer; Keenan 1985: 252) and in Navajo. A passive infix is illustrated by *-h-* in some Mayan languages (Haspelmath 1990: 31), and a passive circumfix is illustrated by the Georgian complex *i-stem-eb* (see Harris 1981: 191).

2.1.2. Differential agreement inflections

A smaller number of languages, instead of employing a special passive morpheme, mark the passive voice by means of a passive inflectional paradigm. A salient example is Latin and Classical Greek, where the active and the passive voices differ in subject agreement markers (in Classical Greek this is the case for a limited number of tenses, excluding the Aorist and the Futurum, where the passive is expressed by an additional stem suffix).

Overall, however, this way of passive marking is not very common cross-linguistically. Interestingly, while present in the "classical" European languages, it is not attested in modern languages of Europe (except in Modern Greek).

2.1.3. Sound replacement

This way of passive marking is well-known in Semitic languages, cf. Biblical Hebrew:

(4)   *hevî* 'he brought' – *huvâ* 'he was brought'

Haspelmath (1990) cites the Sinhala passive as an example of the same type.

2.1.4. Other types of synthetic passives

Another possible type of synthetic passive involves the alternation of a stem affix: instead of mere addition of a passive affix to a non-passive stem, a passive affix can replace some affix of that stem. However, as Haspelmath (1990: 31) notes, in such cases the direction of derivation can never be determined, and for none of the alleged passives of this type is it clear that they indeed are passives.

Reduplication as a means to mark a synthetic passive is attested only for participles, e.g. in Hausa (Kraft & Kirk-Greene 1973: 178).

2.2. Analytic passives

Analytic or periphrastic passives consist of an auxiliary plus a non-finite verbal form, usually a participle. Analytic passives vary with respect to the types of auxiliaries they employ.

2.2.1. Intransitive auxiliaries

Among intransitive auxiliaries, the most frequent in passives are 'be' (e.g. in Basque, English, Russian), 'become' (German, Persian), and verbs of motion (Italian, Hindi). Consider a Basque active sentence (5a), with the auxiliary 'have', and its passive counterpart with the auxiliary 'be' in (5b) (Moreno Cabrera 1998: 172):

(5) (a) *Jon-ek   telesail-a   ikusi du*
       John-ERG TV.series-ART seen has
       'John has watched the TV series.'
    (b) *Telesail-a   Jon-ek   ikusi-a   da*
       TV.series-ART John-ERG seen-ART is
       'The TV series has been watched by John.'

2.2.2. Transitive auxiliaries

The following transitive auxiliaries are most often used in analytic passives: 'get, receive' (e.g. in Welsh, Tzeltal, Vietnamese), 'suffer' (another passive auxiliary in Vietnamese), 'touch' (Thai). For instance:

(6)   Thai
       Mary thùuk (John) kóot
       Mary touch (John) embrace
       'Mary was embraced (by John).'

A more exotic auxiliary, which is nevertheless attested in analytical passives, is a verb with the meaning 'eat'. An example is (7) from Sinhala (Shibatani 1998: 131):

(7)   Sinhala
       Chitra Ranjit-gen guTi ka-nawa.
       Chitra Ranjit-ABL hit   eat-IND
       'Chitra is hit by Ranjit.'

2.3. Distribution of synthetic and analytic passives

2.3.1. Cross-linguistic distribution

In general, synthetic passives seem to be more widespread than analytic passives across languages. Dryer (1982: 55) claims that analytic passives are rare outside Indo-European. Non-Indo-European languages with analytic passives are mainly concentrated in South East Asia. Siewierska (1984: 149–159) cites passives of this kind for Thai, Vietnamese, Mandarin Chinese and Burmese. Interestingly, in all these languages passives use transitive auxiliaries (cf. § 2.2.2). Although the SEA-passives falsify Dryer's claim, the general statistical predominance of synthetic passives is evident.

At the same time, Haspelmath (1990: 38–39) notes that in a number of languages (Korean, Tamil and some others), morphemes marking synthetic passives are diachronically derived from (mainly intransitive) auxiliaries. Thus it appears that the present distribution of synthetic and analytic passives can differ considerably from the one observed at earlier historical stages.

2.3.2. Language-internal distribution

In some languages, both an analytic and a synthetic passive are attested. Consider Russian:

(8) Russian
 (a) analytic passive
    dom byl postroen rabočimi
    house was built   workers.INSTR
    'The house was built by the workers.'
 (b) synthetic passive
    dom stroil-sja rabočimi
    house built-PASS workers.INSTR
    'The house was built by the workers.'

The language-internal distribution of the two types of passives with respect to tense, aspect, syntactic constructions etc. has not yet received much attention. However, the difference in *lexical* distribution of the two types of constructions is obvious. The analytic passive usually is highly productive — with some restrictions, it can apply to the majority of verbs that in principle allow the passive. Synthetic passives, by contrast, are often restricted to a rather limited group of verbs. The reason for this probably is that synthetic passive markers are usually polysemous. Thus, Russian -*sja*, marking passive with some verbs, marks anticausative, reflexive, reciprocal, potential and some other categories of the middle domain with others (cf. Art. 68, § 4).

3. Syntax of the passive construction

3.1. Typology of passives with respect to promoted entities

As stated in § 1, the subject of the passive construction is usually the patient. There are, however, some languages where non-patients can also be promoted to the subject position as a result of passivization. Thus, Japanese (Shibatani 1985) and Classical Greek (Feldman 1978) allow passives with promotion of a dative indirect object. Promotion of dative arguments also is possible in English, where it is discussed in much details by Larson (1988). This type of passives is usually called *indirect*:

(9) Japanese
 (a) direct passive
    hon-wa marii-ni atae-rare-ta
    book-TOP Mary-DAT give-PASS-PAST
    'The book was given to Mary.'
 (b) indirect passive
    marii-wa hon-o   atae-rare-ta
    Mary-TOP book-ACC give-PASS-PAST
    'Mary was given a book.'

Promotion to subject position is still less restricted in Malagasy (Keenan 1976), where not only any non-actor argument, but also most adjuncts (beneficiary, locative, instrument, etc.) can be promoted. Passive morphemes vary with respect to the semantic role of the promoted phrase (i.e. there are "direct", "dative", "locative" etc. passives):

(10) Malagasy
 (a) active
    manasa ny lamba amin'ity savony
    washed the clothes with-the soap
    Rasoa
    Rasoa
    'Rasoa washed the clothes with the soap.'
 (b) "patient" passive
    nosasan-dRasoa   amin'ny
    washed.PASS-by.Rasoa with.the
    savony ny lamba
    soap   the clothes
    'The clothes were washed with the soap by Rasoa.'
 (c) "instrumental" passive
    anasan-dRasoa   ny lamba
    washed.with.PASS-by.Rasoa the clothes
    ny savony
    the soap
    lit. 'The soap was washed the clothes with by Rasoa'.

Languages with conditions on promoted phrases that are so loose in passives are very rare. In all probability, they all belong to the Austronesian family. Moreover, in most of them, the treatment of the corresponding promotional constructions as passives is questionable. Thus, in Malagasy the putative passive verbal forms are not derived morphologically from their active counterparts (Keenan 1976: 255–259). The passive nature of similar promotional constructions in Philippine languages has been the subject of an extensive debate since the 1970s, because the promoted phrase possesses only a limited number of properties normally associated with subjects (see Schachter 1976, de Wolf 1988, Kroeger 1993).

As shown in Keenan (1985: 277), if a language allows promotion of constituents other than direct objects in a passive construction, it also allows promotion of direct objects, either with the same or with a different morphological formation of the passive construction. In other words, the existence of an indirect passive implies the existence of a direct passive, but not the other way round. Moreover, the comparison between English, Classical Greek and Japanese on the one hand and Malagasy on the other hand shows that the promotion of phrases in the passive construction obeys the following implicational hierarchy:

(11)   Accessibility to Promotion in Passivization
       DIRECT OBJECT > INDIRECT OBJECT > ADJUNCT

A phenomenon possibly different from both the direct and the indirect passive is observed in passives derived from raising (or "Exceptional Case Marking") constructions, cf. (12)−(13) for English:

(12)   *They believe him to be a liar.*

(13)   *He is believed to be a liar.*

Under the analysis proposed in Chomsky (1981), the pronoun *him* in (12) does not raise into the position of the matrix direct object. Instead, it occupies the subject position within the infinitive clause, where it is "exceptionally case marked" by the matrix verb. If this is true, the passive in (13) promotes an element of an embedded clause. This possibility is precluded even in Malagasy, a language with generally very loose restrictions on promoted phrases. Therefore, typological observations support the alternative raising analysis, in which the NP *him* in (12) is treated as the matrix direct object. Such constructions can hardly serve as counterevidence against the clause-boundness of the passive promotion.

3.2. The actor in the passive voice

When an intransitive verb is derived from a transitive verb in the passive construction, the patient remains the only core argument of the derived verb. The actor may either be omitted or expressed by an oblique NP. The English passive allows both options:

(14)   *John was kissed (by Mary).*

As noted by Keenan (1985: 249), the passive never requires the expression of the actor. There are languages where an actor NP in the passive construction is impossible, and there are languages where it is optional.

3.2.1. Passives which prohibit expression the actor

The languages where the passive construction does not allow an actor NP phrase include Latvian (Keenan 1985: 249), Ute (Givón 1988), Fula (Koval' & Njalibuli 1998), Nahuatl (Sullivan 1988), Ulcha (Manchu-Tungus; Nichols 1979), and Classical Arabic, among others. It is important to note that although passives of this kind do not allow the expression of the actor, they nevertheless imply its existence. The action expressed in such passives cannot be spontaneous: The construction shows unambiguously that the action was carried out by some actor, which only remains unspecified in the construction.

3.2.2. Actor expressed as an oblique NP

If the actor is expressed in a passive construction, it is most commonly marked as an oblique NP. Usually languages avoid employing a special marker associated only with the demoted actor; instead, the actor is marked by an adposition or a case morpheme otherwise introducing some other oblique elements. Below the most widely attested types of polysemy of the actor markers are listed.

(i) Instrumental
Instrumental marking of the actor can be found in Basque, Russian and Bantu languages. Consider (15) from Basque:

(15)   Basque (Keenan 1985: 248−249)
       (a) active
       gizon-a-k   txakurr-a   maluskatu
       man-the-ERG dog-the(ABS) beat
       zuan
       AUX(3sg.Sub:3sg.Ob)
       'The man beats the dog.'
       (b) passive
       gizon-a-k   txakurr-a
       man-the-INSTR dog-the(ABS)
       maluskatu-a zan
       beat-PASS   AUX(3sg.Sub)
       'The dog was beaten by the man.'

(ii) Locative
Locative case marking is common for Standard Average European languages, where locative prepositions are used with actor

phrases; this is the case in English (preposition *by*), French (*de*) and German (*von*). The same option can perhaps be identified in Japanese, where the actor is followed by the postposition *-ni*, which also marks indirect objects and certain types of locatives.

(iii) Genitive
Genitive case-marking of the actor is less common cross-linguistically. It is attested in Malagasy (Keenan 1976, 1985: 259), where the actor is cliticized on the verb in the same way as the possessor is cliticized onto a noun phrase (cf. (10)). Keenan suggests that the use of the genitive marking of the actor correlates with nominal sources of verbal morphology.

(iv) Special marker of actor
This option seems to be the most infrequent one: Normally, the marking of the actor coincides with the marking of one of the obliques. This tendency, however, is apparently violated in Bahasa Indonesia, where the preposition *oleh* is restricted to Agent phrases in the passive.

3.2.3. Incorporation of actor

Incorporation of the actor instead of its demotion to the status of an oblique NP is observed in very few languages, probably because incorporation normally corresponds to a prominent syntactic status of the element undergoing it. Keenan (1985: 264) mentions actor incorporation as a productive phenomenon in Quechua and Toba Batak (Malayo-Polynesian) passives; but see a somewhat different interpretation of the relevant constructions in Toba Batak in Manning & Sag 1998.

4. Functions of the passive voice

4.1. Syntactic functions of passive; the impersonal passive

According to the definition of the passive proposed in § 1, the formation of a passive construction includes two distinct syntactic processes: *pro*motion of a non-subject NP into the subject position and *de*motion of the initial subject (actor). The question arises whether the core function of the passive may be universally reduced to any one of these two processes. This problem may be approached either from a syntactic or from a semantic perspective. Put in a syntactic perspective, it can be resolved if it is shown that either promotion or demotion alone is sufficient for passivization. The only function which will appear to be obligatory for all instances of the passive would be treated as the only core function of the passive.

All the instances of passives considered so far do not allow us to recognize either promotion of a non-subject or demotion of the subject as the core syntactic function of the passive voice. Indeed, in all of them both processes take place obligatorily. However, this is not always the case with passives: In some languages, passives may be derived from intransitive verbs having only one argument. This is the case e. g. in Dutch (see Kirsner 1976), Fula (see Koval' & Njalibuli 1997), Athabaskan languages (A. A. Kibrik 1996: 266 ff.), German, Irish (Noonan 1994), Lithuanian, Norwegian (Åfarli 1992), northern dialects of Russian (Timberlake 1976), some Manchu-Tungus languages (Nichols 1979), Polish, Finnish (Comrie 1977), Turkish (Biktimir 1986), Ute (Givón 1988), Welsh (Awbery 1976), plus a number of other languages (for some valuable observations on the cross-linguistic distribution and the functions of the impersonal passive, see Frajzyngier 1982, Shibatani 1998). Consider (16) from Dutch:

(16)   Dutch
Er   wordt   (door de jongens)
there becomes by   the young.men
gefloten
whistled
'The young men whistle.'
(lit. 'There gets whistled by the young men.')

Here the intransitive verb displays the same analytical passive formation as transitives do in Dutch. The subject, as expected in passives, may be either deleted or expressed by an oblique phrase. However, at least on the surface, no promotion of a non-subject is observed here: Since the verb has only one argument, there is in fact nothing to promote into the subject position.

The existence of this type of passives led Comrie (1977) to the conclusion that subject demotion is the only core syntactic function of the passive voice. Promotion of a non-subject, according to their view, is not the essential syntactic function of the passive voice and accompanies subject demotion only in the formation of passives from transitive verbs. Moreover, it was argued that even there promotion of a non-subject is not obligatory: in a number of languages demotion of transitive subjects is not accompanied by promotion of a non-subject either. This is the case e.g. in Norwegian, Welsh, Ute and Kannada. Consider (17) from Welsh (cited from Perlmutter & Postal 1983b: 139):

(17) *lladdwyd dyn (gan ddraig)*
 was-killed man by dragon
 'A man was killed (by a dragon).'

In this passive construction the patient is not the subject: First, the verb does not agree with the patient in person and number, as it does with subjects in Welsh. Secondly, when the patient is a pronoun, it can cliticize to one of the mood markers in the way direct objects do, but subjects never do in Welsh. It can be shown that in constructions of this kind the patient does not possess the syntactic properties associated with subjects, e.g. the ability to control zero anaphora (Foley & Van Valin 1985: 319–325).

Passives without promotion of a non-subject are usually termed *impersonal passives*. It should be noted, however, that not all scholars agree that the existence of the impersonal passive implies that the core function of passive is always subject demotion. Specifically, this view was rejected in Relational Grammar (Perlmutter & Postal 1983a), where the nonexistence of *spontaneous demotion* is a basic grammatical "law". Perlmutter & Postal have suggested an alternative analysis of impersonal passives, which rescues that law. According to their analysis, promotion (in their terms, advancement) to subject position in fact takes place in impersonal passives, but that is promotion of a dummy, which may be invisible, as in Welsh, or visible, as in Dutch (*er*).

In fact, the positions of the proponents of both the "promotional" and of the "demotinal" analysis of the passive voice may need serious amendments in the light of evidence adduced by Keenan (1976). Keenan argues that in some languages, the NP promoted in a passive construction acquires not the complete set of the subject properties, but only some of them. Specifically, he shows this to be the case in Maasai (but see the arguments of Perlmutter & Postal (1983b: 159–165) against this interpretation of the passive voice in that language). More recently, the "non-complete" subjecthood of the patient was reported for the passive voice in Chepang (Thompson 1990) and in Bella Coola (Forrest 1994). Given this, we have something like "semi-promotional" passives apart from standard and impersonal passives, and the opposition between passives with and without promotion of a (non-dummy) NP becomes scalar rather than binary.

A further problem is related to the status of impersonal passives with respect to "standard" promotional passives. Although in most languages impersonal and promotional passives coincide in their morphological manifestation on the verb, in some languages the impersonal passive is a category morphologically distinct from the promotional passive. Unlike Dutch (see (16)), where the two passives coincide in form, in Irish the promotional passive is expressed with an analytical verbal form, whereas the impersonal passive is expressed by means of a synthetic verbal form:

(18) Irish (Noonan 1994: 280)
 (a) active
 bhí Liam ag bualadh Sheáin
 be-PAST Bill at hit-NOMIN John-GEN
 'Bill was hitting John.'
 (b) promotional passive
 bhí Seán á bhualadh
 be-PAST John to+his hit-NOMIN
 (agLiam)
 (at Bill)
 'John was being hit (by Bill).'
 (c) impersonal passive
 bualadh Seán (le Liam)
 hit-PAST-IMPERS John with Bill
 'John was hit (by Bill).'

For all these reasons, the conclusion seems plausible that the existence of the impersonal passive can hardly be as decisive for the argument about functions of the passive voice as it was assumed earlier. The relation between the impersonal and the standard promotional passive appears to be more complex than it seemed at the beginning.

A typologically valid observation concerning impersonal passives is that they most often do not express the actor, cf. Siewierska (1984: 100). However, the above Dutch and Welsh examples show that this is not obligatorily the case. Besides, the following restrictions on the distribution of personal and impersonal passives hold true: (1) no language has impersonal passives of transitives without having (impersonal) passives of intransitives; (2) no language has (impersonal) passives of intransitives without having some type of passive of transitives; see Ackema & Neeleman 1998 for an explanation of these restrictions in the spirit of Optimality Theory.

4.2. Semantic function(s) of the passive voice

Since the "demotional" or "promotional" nature of the passive voice cannot be detected merely by syntactic evidence, a semantic rather than a purely syntactic study of the problem is called for.

The first serious attempts to approach the problem from a semantic perspective were undertaken by Langacker & Munro (1975) and Shibatani (1985). An important premise of these studies was the hypothesis of iconicity in morphology: If some categories regularly receive the same formal manifestation, then their meanings should also be related. On this assumption, the passive voice was studied in its relation with those categories with which it often has identical marking.

Before discussing the semantic interpretation of passive arrived at by this line of research, we need to consider the question of polysemy of passive morphology in more detail.

4.2.1. Polysemy of passive markers: Middle voice and adversative passive

The concept of the middle voice is discussed in Art. 68. The middle voice is a label for a big cluster of meanings, which include among others reflexive, reciprocal, anticausative (or spontaneous), and potential. It is very common across languages that some or even all the categories of this set receive the same morphological marking. A semantic characteristic that all these categories apparently have in common and that distinguishes the middle voice from "direct" transitives is the lack of an actor distinct from the patient — either the actor does not exist at all (anticausative), or it coincides with the patient (reflexive, reciprocal), or it is perceived as a potential, not actual participant. (For some other semantic characteristics of the middle voice see Art. 68, § 5.).

The semantic distinction between the passive voice and the categories of "the middle domain" is straightforward: The passive always implies the existence of two distinct participants — the actor and the patient, even if the actor is not expressed or cannot be expressed. By contrast, the middle voice never has this implication. This difference can be illustrated by a comparison between the passive voice and the anticausative (for details on the anticausative and its synchronic and diachronic relation with the passive voice, see Art. 68, § 4.12.). Cf. the two forms derived from one and the same verb in Russian:

(19) Russian
(a) passive
dom byl razrušen (neprijatelem)
building was destroyed enemy.INSTR
'The building was destroyed by the enemy.'
(b) anticausative
dom razrušil-sja
building destroyed-ANTICAUS
'The building was destroyed (spontaneously).'

In (19b), it is not clear whether the house was ruined as a result of somebody's efforts or spontaneously (in the latter case the predicate has only one argument not just in syntax, but also in semantics). By contrast, (19a) means that the house was ruined by some actor, not spontaneously.

Given this important distinction between the passive and the middle voice, it is not at all surprising that the two voices have distinct morphological manifestations in many languages. This is the case in Classical Greek, Imbabura Quechua, West Greenlandic Eskimo, Georgian, Fula, and many others. Nevertheless, in a large number of languages the two voices have identical morphological marking. Passive morphology is employed in marking (some meanings from) the middle domain in Spanish, Diyari (Australia), Latin, Udmurt, Modern Greek, Tigre (Afroasiatic), and some other languages. As often noted (Barber 1975, Klaiman 1988: 36, Haspelmath 1987: 35, 1990: 35), the passive function is usually a late development for middle morphology. The passive voice develops out of the anticausative function of the middle, i.e. out of the instance of the middle where the subject is merely an affected entity, as it is in the passive voice.

In a small number of languages, passive morphology (both on the verb and in marking of the agent) is used in a special **adversative** construction, where the subject is an entity affected by the situation, possibly not being its participant. A salient example of a language with an adversative passive is Japanese (Shibatani 1998: 125):

(20) *Taroo-wa kyuuni Hanako-ni*
Taro-TOP suddenly Hanako-DAT
hasira-re-ta.
run-PASS-PAST
'Taro was adversely affected by Hanako's running suddenly.'

4.2.2. Towards the core function(s) of the passive voice

The frequent formal identity of the passive voice with the middle voice and the adversatives leads one to the hypothesis that the semantics of the passive voice has some important points of proximity with these two categories. Shibatani (1985), in particular, suggested on the basis of this polysemy that actor de-focusing is the only essential function of the passive voice. According to Shibatani, in all the key meanings of the middle voice (reflexive, reciprocal, anticausative), the actor is suppressed – in fact, these constructions lack an actor distinct from the patient (cf. Art. 68). The adversative construction can also be treated as an actor de-focusing device: As soon as an affected entity promoted into the subject position is foregrounded, the actor is de-focused. Since actor de-focusing takes place in categories often formally identical with the passive voice, one can suggest that actor de-focusing is the essential function of the passive voice as well.

Although the analysis suggested by Shibatani accounted quite well for the polysemy of the passive markers, the restriction of functions of the passive to only de-focusing of the actor was not fully confirmed by discourse studies. This is particularly clear from the results obtained by Givón (1981, 1983 (ed.), 1984), who has studied the discourse status of the actor and the patient both in the direct voice and in the passive voice of various languages. The central quantitative parameters measured by Givón for every participant of the situation in a given construction are **referential distance** and **topic persistence**. Referential distance is the gap (counted in clauses) between the present and the previous references to the participant in the discourse. Topic persistence is the number of clauses to the right – i.e. in subsequent discourse – in which the participant continues an uninterrupted presence as a semantic argument of the clause.

Givón argues that pragmatic prominence of a participant expressed in some construction correlates with low referential distance and high topic persistence calculated for that participant. It turns out that in the passive voice, the actor is systematically characterized by high referential distance and low topic persistence; by contrast, the patient of the passive voice normally demonstrates small referential distance and high topic persistence. The statistical studies in Givón (ed.) 1983 as well as many subsequent publications within the Givonian paradigm show that this tendency is observed for passive constructions in very many languages.

Clearly, this result shows that the passive voice can equally be used for pragmatic demotion of the actor and for pragmatic promotion of the patient. Any attempt to choose one of these two functions as the "core", motivated though it is by considerations of polysemy of passive morphology, is not justified by the statistical study of discourse.

Similarly, Foley & Van Valin (1985) also acknowledge two independent functions of the passive voice – backgrounding of the actor and foregrounding of a non-actor. They claim that any passive construction has either one of these functions or both, supporting this claim mainly by syntactic evidence: In some languages passivization leads to the transmission of subject properties to a non-actor (marking a non-actor the syntactic "pivot" of the clause, in Foley & Van Valin's terms), but in some other languages it does not have this effect.

Furthermore, claiming that actor demotion *and* patient promotion (interchangeably) constitute the core function(s) of the passive would also be undesirable for several reasons. First, voice is a verbal category, so it would not be natural for it to have demotion or promotion of an argument, rather than marking of some characteristic of the event in general, as the core meaning.

Secondly, identification of any kind of (de-)focusing as the basic meaning of the passive is not supported by diachronic considerations. As shown by Haspelmath (1990: 60–61), passive morphology never arises diachronically from markers of topicalization or focusing, as would be expected if one of the foregrounding/backgrounding operations were the basic function of the passive voice.

Finally, the passive voice demonstrates regular structural asymmetries with the foregrounding/backgrounding syntactic rules *par excellence*, i.e. topicalization and focus fronting (including focus of questions, called WH-movement). These asymmetries were studied in much detail within the generative paradigm (in generative terms, they correspond to asymmetries between A- and A'-movement; cf. the summary in Corver & van Riemsdijk 1994). The most important among them are:

(1) only NPs can be moved to the subject position of a passive clause; by contrast,

topicalization, focus fronting etc. applies freely to any kind of constituents, including adverbs, prepositional phrases, etc.;
(2) the passive can be applied only to elements of a matrix clause (see § 3.1); by contrast, matrix topicalization and its congeners can be applied to elements of a subordinate clause (cf. *Whom did Bill say John saw?*).

Putting together all these considerations coming from various linguistic approaches, one should suggest that the invariant meaning of the passive voice is related to parameters of the event rather than of its participants. The first candidate here was stativization, listed by Givón (1981) among basic meanings of the passive voice. Passives have the stativization effect e. g. in Chichewa (Bantu) and in Choctaw (see Foley & Van Valin 1985: 322). However, data obtained from some languages show that this meaning is not inherent in the passive voice: The passive can well denote processes on a par with states (this is the case, for instance, in Navajo, cf. A. A. Kibrik 1996: 269).

Another attempt to discern an event parameter which constitutes the meaning of the passive voice was made in Haspelmath (1990), where it was argued that the actual invariant characteristic of the passive voice is inactivization of the situation. This conclusion is mainly based on historical facts: Inactiveness of the situation is a common feature of the elements which grammaticize into passive markers. Interestingly, Haspelmath substantiates this claim not only for passive morphemes derived from markers of the middle "domain", but also for passive auxiliaries: They normally develop from verbs with inactive meanings (cf. § 2.2).

If inactivization is indeed the basic function of the passive voice, then the two other functions — actor de-focusing and patient focusing — fall out for free. Indeed, if a situation is inactive, it cannot have an actor, at least a foregrounded one — hence the passive voice serves for backgrounding of the actor. Given this, the patient remains the only core NP which can be foregrounded — hence the passive voice can be used to focus the patient.

5. Derived vs. basic status of the passive voice

The definition of the passive proposed in § 1 requires that any passive verbal form be morphologically derived from an active form. A natural suggestion would be that the morphologically derived status of the passive voice should be reflected by its syntactic status as well. If that is the case, a passive sentence can be treated as derived from the corresponding active sentence.

In actual fact, however, things do not appear to be that simple. In this connection, it is worth mentioning that traditional conceptions of the passive voice, predominant before the structuralist concept of derivation became common in linguistic theory, said nothing on its derived status. Consider e. g. the definition suggested by Kruisinga (1925: 167−168; cit. Shibatani 1998: 117): "Voice is the name of a verbal form according as it primarily expresses the action or state with regard to its subject, which may be represented as acting (*active voice*), undergoing (*passive voice*), or affected by its own action (*reflexive* [middle] *voice*)." It turns out that the research of the last decades has to some extent revived this "pre-derivational" view of the passive. In § 5.1 syntactic aspects of the problem are discussed. In § 5.2, a semantic view on the voice category which does not presuppose its derived status is outlined.

5.1. Derived vs. non-derived syntactic nature of the passive voice

The global view of the passive voice as a syntactically derived category was accepted in the earliest work on generative grammar. Thus, Chomsky (1965) considered the passive as one of the transformations, replacing the active verbal form by its passive counterpart and changing positions of the arguments. However, in the course of the later development of generative grammar, the transformational account of the passive voice was rejected. Put most briefly, the motivation for this move was as follows.

Lees (1960) noticed that in English nominalized clauses, a syntactic alternation, similar to the passive in several respects, is possible:

(21) (a) *the enemy's destruction of the city*
(b) *the city's destruction by the enemy*

In (21b), the patient precedes the noun in the same way as it precedes the verb in English passives; besides, the agent is introduced by the preposition *by*, also typical of the actor in the passive construction. For that reason, (21b) was treated as a passive nominalization.

A few years later, Chomsky (1970) argued that English nominalizations are not derived from finite clauses by means of any transformation, that is, structures containing nominalizations are base-generated, with nominalized forms inserted directly from the lexicon. Given this, (21b) could not be treated as a nominalization of the corresponding passive sentence. Nevertheless, the theory had to capture the parallelism between phrases like (21b) and passive clauses; for that reason, a treatment of the passive was required under which (21b) would also be counted as an instance of the passive. In order to achieve this, it was suggested to treat (21b) as the passive correlate of (21c):

(21) (c) *the destruction of the city by the enemy*

(21c) was considered as base generated, and the role of the passive transformation was preposing of the NP *city* to the head noun. The same transformation was adopted for sentential passives: It was assumed that passive verbal forms are inserted directly from the lexicon, active subject phrases are base generated as dependents of the preposition *by*, and the passive merely preposes the NP base generated as a direct object. That means that the passive sentence in (22b) is generated by the passive transformation from the base generated structure in 22a):

(22) (a) *The city was destroyed by the enemy.*
(b) [s [vp *was destroyed* [*the city*] [*by the enemy*]]

In this way, a unified account of passive sentences and nominalizations was achieved. At the same time some independent evidence was adduced in favor of passive verbal forms being base generated in English (Freidin 1975; cf. Wasow 1977). The proponents of the outlined account of the passive voice also noted that, defined in this way, the passive transformation is general enough in its form, as its description is not overloaded with construction-specific morphological material (a summary of arguments in favor of this account of the passive transformation is given in van Riemsdijk & Williams 1986, Ch. 3).

A very important consequence of this account is that the actor NP takes an oblique position at all stages of derivation of the passive construction. This predicts, in particular, that the actor NP cannot have any properties associated with subjects. However, some typological evidence has cast some doubt on this treatment of the actor in passives.

Perlmutter (1983) showed that in Russian passives, reflexive pronouns can be coreferent not only with subjects, but also with oblique actors, as in (23):

(23) *Èta kniga byla kuplena Borisom*
this book was bought Boris.INSTR
dlja sebja.
for himself
'The book was bought by Boris$_i$ for him$_i$ (lit. for himself).'

If the agent was oblique at all stages of derivation, the coreference in (23) could not be accounted for, as usual obliques never bind reflexives in Russian. By contrast, if the agent occupies the subject position at some stage of derivation, (23) is accounted for as soon as it is assumed that coreference relations can be established at that level. According to Perlmutter, this gives evidence against any account of passives under which the agent is base-generated as an oblique.

Further typological studies have revealed that passives in different languages may differ with respect to the possibility for actors to be antecedents of reflexive pronouns. As shown in Dalrymple 1993, Manning 1996, the possibility for the oblique actor to be coreferent with reflexive pronouns in passive constructions is attested in a large number of languages, e. g. Inuit, Sanskrit, Turkish, Lithuanian. An appropriate generalization could be that if the actor in a passive construction can bind a reflexive pronoun, then the subject can bind it as well. An apparent counterexample, however, is Marathi (Darlymple 1993: 11−13), where one of the reflexive pronouns can be bound by the actor, but not by the subject in passive constructions. Anyway, it is clear that the predictions of the strict non-derivational account of the passive voice are not completely borne out, seen from a typological perspective.

5.2. Voice as a semantic category

Quite a different view of the opposition between derived and basic voices is found in modern functional studies, especially in Klaiman (1988) and Croft (1994). These authors explicitly reject the "syntactic" view of voice as a category merely changing the relation between semantic roles and syntactic arguments of a predicate. Instead, they treat voice as a manifestation of the semantic and/or pragmatic status of the subject (its control over the action, its affectedness by the action, its topicality, etc.) in the verb form.

Morphological marking of the status of the subject does not always allow one to determine the direction of derivation. Thus, as shown by Klaiman 1988, Tamil makes use of the so called "strong" and "weak" verbal stems; the "weak" stem is used when the subject is affected by the actor; the "strong" stem is used otherwise. Tamil morphology does not allow us to treat either of these two stems as derived from the other. However, despite the lack of a derivational relation, the two forms correspond to two voices in Klaiman's understanding.

Klaiman (1988: 46 ff.) explicitly rejects the view that in voice systems (with the term "voice" understood in the way outlined immediately above) only one voice is non-derived, others being derived from it. The similarity between the passive and the middle voices consists, according to Klaiman, in the fact that in both voices the subject is an affected entity. The main distinction between the two voices, apart from the obligatory existence of the actor in the passive (see § 4.2), is that the passive voice is morphologically derived, whereas the middle may be non-derived. Croft (1994: 110 ff.) states that conceptually the middle and the passive voices are quite close due to the affectedness of the subject, which also explains the frequently observed diachronic relation between the two voices. When voice is understood as a category which manifests the semantic status of the subject rather than a mere "switch" of the syntactic coding of arguments, the opposition between derived and non-derived voices becomes marginal for the grammatical system.

6. Cross-linguistic distribution of the passive voice

In general, the passive voice is cross-linguistically one of the common categories. However, quite a few languages lacking the passive voice have been described. They include many languages of Australia, Nakh-Daghestanian languages (see A. E. Kibrik 1979, 1997), languages of Papua New Guinea (see Li & Lang 1979 for Enga), and many Chadic languages (Keenan 1985: 247) as well as Tongan, Samoan, and Hungarian (Siewerska 1984). The question arises as to what properties of a language imply the lack of the passive voice.

The list of the language families above could create the impression that the lack of the passive voice correlates with ergativity (Hungarian looks as the only exception, being a nominative language). However, this impression is false since the passive voice is attested in a number of ergative languages, e.g. in many Mayan languages (England 1988), in Eskimo (Woodbury 1977), and in Basque (cf. (15) above). On the other hand, some languages lacking the passive are nominative, like the Chadic languages. This calls for some other account for the cross-linguistic distribution of passives, which would not relate it directly to ergativity (for further discussion of the relation between the passive voice and ergativity see § 7.2).

Such an account as suggested within a large-scale typological survey of clause-patterning undertaken in Kibrik (1997) (cf. Art. 101). The central assumption of Kibrik's model is that the notion of subject (as well as that of direct object and other syntactic relations) is not universal. Kibrik shows that it is not possible to distinguish the syntactically most "prominent" NP in all languages of the world, i.e. the NP with roughly those properties which are associated with subjects in Standard Average European: In a number of languages these properties are split between two NPs, in some others they are not restricted to any syntactic position at all. The prediction of this model is that the passive voice, as well as any other voice alternation changing the syntactic relations like subject and object, can be attested only in languages where these syntactic relations exist.

According to A. E. Kibrik 1997, this prediction is borne out in a large sample of languages. For example, the passive is never attested in the so-called topic-prominent languages (Li & Thompson 1976; Kibrik's term for this language type is "flow-oriented"), which lack the subject and object opposition. Also, in many ergative languages which lack the passive voice (e.g. Daghestanian) there are no grounds for identifying the category of subject: coding of arguments in those languages is uniquely determined by their semantic roles, rather than by syntactic relations such as subject, object, etc.

7. The passive in relation to some other grammatical phenomena

7.1. Passive and inverse

Since the pragmatic demotion of the agent as well as the promotion of the patient are the essential functions of the passive voice, the question arises whether the same or a similar function can be expressed by any other grammatical means. It turns out that in a number of languages a construction exists which resembles the passive in an important respect but contrasts with it in another respect:

(1) like the passive voice, this construction is used when the pragmatic status of the patient outranks that of the agent; BUT:
(2) unlike the passive voice, this construction does not make the verb intransitive.

Consider the system of case marking in Algonquian languages, e. g. Plains Cree (Dahlstrom 1976). If both arguments of a transitive verb are 3rd person, then the more topical one is case-marked as "proximate", and the less topical one as "obviative". Thus in (24a) the agent bears the proximate case marker, and the patient the obviative case marker; in (24b) this is the other way round:

(24) (a) *aya.hciniw-ah nisto e.h-nipaha.t*
Blackfoot-OBV three kill.DIR-3.OBV
awa na.pe.sis
this boy.PROX
'The boy [PROX] killed three Blackfoot (men) [OBV].'

(b) *osa.m e.-sa.khikot ohta.wiy-ah*
much love.INV.OBV-3 his.father-OBV
wa o.skini.kiw
this young.man.PROX
'(For) his father [OBV] loved his young man [PROX].'

Verb agreement in both sentences also signals the relative topicality of the arguments: (24a) has the "direct" agreement marker, and (24b) has the "inverse" agreement marker, used when the patient is more topical than the agent. However, it is crucial that the agreement markers both in (24a) and (24b) are compatible only with transitive verbs. By contrast, in the passive construction of Plains Cree the verb is marked as derived *in*transitive:

(25) *awa na.pe.sis e.kwaaw*
this boy.PROX and this
o.skini.kiw mawi.hka.ta.wak
young.man.PROX mourn.PASS-3p.PROX
'This boy [PROX] and this young man [PROX] are being mourned.'

Thus, in the construction illustrated by (25), unlike the passive construction, pragmatic demotion of the agent and promotion of the patient does not lead to de-transitivization of the verb.

Transitive constructions marking the pragmatic priority of the patient are reported for Athabaskan (Thompson 1989), Tupí-Guaraní (Payne 1994), Squamish (Jacobs 1994), Nepali (Givón 1994), and Tibeto-Burman (DeLancey 1981), among other languages. From the formal point of view, the construction in question may be triggered either by a verbal morpheme (e. g. in Tupí-Guaraní), or by a combination of a verbal morpheme with special case-marking of arguments (e. g. in Algonquian).

Givón (1994) calls the constructions in question in the above-mentioned languages **inverse** constructions. Givón claims that in these constructions the patient outranks the agent not as strongly as it does in passive constructions. Givón's general view of the relation between the inverse, the passive voice and other constructions is summarized in the following table (where ">" means pragmatic priority, and ">>" means high degree of this priority):

Table 67.1: (Givón 1994: 8)

Relative topicality of the actor (Givón's agent) and the patient in the four main voices:

Voice	Relative topicality
active/direct	AGT > PAT
inverse	AGT < PAT
passive	AGT << PAT
antipassive	AGT >> PAT

In Givón's view, a construction with any kind of formal properties should be qualified as inverse as long as it satisfies the functional definition of this category. As a consequence, the domain of the inverse is in fact not restricted to the constructions characterized above: Givón also recognizes a "promotional inverse", where the patient becomes the subject and which, at least formally, is closer to the passive, and a "word-order inverse", where the priority of the patient over the agent is expressed only by means of linear precedence of the patient. However, we concentrate only on those instances of the Givonian inverse which, being manifested as a morphological category, are at the same time most clearly distinguishable from the passive voice.

Apart from inverse constructions which mark discourse priority of the patient over the actor, there are inverse constructions obligatorily used when the patient outranks the actor on some semantic hierarchy, most often on the hierarchy of persons, which usually is 1>2>3. Thus, in Tupí-Guaraní (Payne 1994) a special form of the verb must be used when the patient is higher than the actor on this hierarchy. Givón (1994: 23) calls this type of inverse semantic (as opposed to pragmatic). It is plausible to suggest that the semantic inverse diachronically develops from the pragmatic inverse: Since a 1st or 2nd person participant often has higher pragmatic priority than a 3rd person participant, the pragmatic inverse should be frequent in sentences with 1st or 2nd person patient, to the effect that the use of the inverse in them can grammaticalize as obligatory. Studies of complex polypersonal agreement systems in a number of languages have shown that they may be interpreted in the most natural and elegant way if some morphemes are treated as semantic inverse markers rather than as inflections (cf. A. E. Kibrik 1997a for Aljutor, Bynon 1998 for Dumi).

The inverse, at least as long as it is understood as a strictly morphological category and does not subsume, for instance, mere word order change of the agent and the patient, is cross-linguistically much less common than the passive voice. This might be explained by the "Principle of Maximization of Contrast" proposed by Shibatani (1998: 120), which states that languages should maximize contrasts of grammatical meanings as much as possible. Obviously, the position of the inverse between the direct and the passive voices (cf. Table 1) makes it less than optimal from the point of view of this principle.

7.2. Passives, ergativity and antipassives

The ergative construction is in a number of respects very similar to the passive construction. Indeed, in an ergative case-marking system, the patient of a transitive verb bears the same case as the subject of an intransitive verb. In a passive construction (at least in the case of the promotional passive) the patient's case is also identical with that of an intransitive subject, whereas the actor, if expressed at all, is marked differently. This led the pioneers of ergativity studies to claim that the ergative construction is equivalent with the passive construction, i. e. that ergative languages are in fact languages where the passive has become the basic construction of the clause (see Schuchardt 1896).

However, in-depth studies of ergativity, mainly undertaken in the 1970s and 1980s, have completely undermined this analysis. There are at least three reasons to reject it.

First, the passive was defined in §1 as a construction derived from an active counterpart. For the ergative construction, of course, this is not true since it is unmarked, not derived from any other construction (at least synchronically).

Secondly, in the ergative construction the patient does not always possess the key syntactic priorities of the subject (control of coordinate deletion, priority in relativization, prominent (leftmost) linear position, etc.). This is the case only in a minority of languages with ergative morphology, called syntactically ergative languages (see Dixon 1994: 143−181). In most of the ergative languages, however, syntactic priorities associated with the subject in nominative languages are either assigned to the actor (as in some languages of Papua New Guinea − Li & Lang 1979), or distributed in some way between core arguments (Dixon 1994: 175−177, A. E. Kibrik 1997, Kazenin 1994). By contrast, in the passive construction the actor, if expressed, never retains any syntactic priorities associated with the subject, as they are always transmitted to the patient. A contrast between the ergative construction in Lak (Caucasus, Nakh-Daghestanian family) and a passive construction in Russian in the context of coordination illustrates this point. In Lak, the actor of the ergative construction is the most probable antecedent for a gap in the subsequent clause; in Russian, the actor of the passive construction can never be the antecedent, since that is a property of the subject only:

(26) Lak
rasul-lul qaĩa buwša-r
Rasul-ERG house build.PAST-3sg
lawgša-r
leave.PAST-3sg
'Rasul has built the house and (Rasul) left.'

(27) Russian
**Dom byl postroen Ivanom i*
house was built Ivan.INSTR and
ušel.
left

((27) can only mean that, after Ivan built the house, the house left, which makes the sentence ridiculous.)

Thirdly, as already mentioned in §6, a number of ergative languages possess a passive construction derived from the ergative construction; naturally, this would not be expected if the ergative construction itself was an instance of the passive voice.

Despite the non-identity between the passive voice and the ergative construction, they often are historically related: a passive construction can become an ergative construction in the course of its diachronic development. Dixon (1994: 187–192) shows that this is one of the ways of accusative-to-ergative historical shift. It has taken place e.g. in Indian and Iranian languages (see Anderson 1977, Masica 1991: 339–346) as well as in many Polynesian languages (see Hohepa 1969). For this shift to take place, the passive construction has to become the unmarked, standard construction of the sentence, thus leading to the elimination of the active construction or at least to a restriction of its distribution. As soon as the construction becomes unmarked, it cannot count as an instance of the passive voice anymore; due to the formal similarity between the (promotional) passive and the ergative construction, the marked passive construction becomes an unmarked ergative.

One more phenomenon has to be mentioned in relation to the problem of the passive and ergativity. In many ergative languages the so-called antipassive transitivity alternation is observed, which puts the actor in the nominative case and the patient in an oblique case; the verb in the antipassive construction bears special morphological marking:

(28) Dyirbal
 (a) ergative construction
  yabu nguma-nggu bura-n
  mother.ABS father-ERG see-NONFUT
  'Father saw mother.'
 (b) antipassive construction
  nguma bural-nga-nʸu
  father.ABS see-ANTIPASS-NONFUT
  yabu-gu
  mother-DAT
  'Father saw mother.'

The term "antipassive" was suggested by Silverstein (1976) because this process was treated as the "inverted" equivalent of the passive in ergative languages: it promotes the actor into the subject position, in the same way as the passive promotes the patient into that position. However, it turned out in subsequent research that the antipassive exists in many languages without syntactic ergativity, where the patient is not the subject, and for that reason a change of the actor's case from ergative to nominative cannot be treated as syntactic "promotion". The antipassive in Samoan, a language where subject properties in the ergative construction are predominantly concentrated on the actor, is illustrative (see Chung 1980); data on antipassives in other languages without syntactic ergativity are discussed in Cooreman (1994). In that study, it is also argued that the core function of the antipassive, at least in languages where the patient is not the subject in the ergative construction, serves the purpose of patient de-focusing. Under this interpretation, the antipassive remains an "inverted" equivalent of the passive, but this relates to pragmatic functions of these voice alternations rather than to their syntactic nature.

At the same time, identifying the core function of the antipassive as patient de-focusing admittedly makes the high frequency of antipassives in ergative languages and their low frequency in other types of languages enigmatic. The strong preference for antipassives in ergative languages materializes in the following universal proposed by Nichols (1992: 158): if a language has an antipassive but has no passive, then that language is ergative. This important typological observation probably should be explained together with the relative infrequency of the passive voice in ergative languages (see § 6).

8. Special abbreviations

ANTICAUS	anticausative
ANTIPASS	antipassive
IMPERS	impersonal
IND	indicative
INSTR	instrumental
INV	inverse
NOMIN	nominalization
OBV	obviative
PROX	proximate
SEA	South East Asia

9. References

Ackema, Peter & Neeleman, Ad. 1998. "Conflict resolution in passive formation." *Lingua* 104: 13–29.

Åfarli, T. 1992. *The Syntax of Norwegian Passive Constructions.* Amsterdam: Benjamins.

Anderson, Stephen R. 1977. "On mechanisms by which languages become ergative." In: Li, Charles (ed.) *Mechanisms of syntactic change.* Austin: University of Texas Press, 1−23.

Awbery, G. M. 1976. *The Syntax of Welsh.* Cambridge: Cambridge University Press.

Bandhu, C. 1973. "Clause patterns in Nepali." In: Hale, A. & Watters, D. (eds.). *Clause, Sentence and Discourse Patterns in Selected Languages of Nepali.* Summer Institute of Linguistics, 1−80.

Barber, E. 1975. "Voice beyond the Passive." *Berkeley Linguistics Society* 1: 16−24.

Biktimir, T. 1986. "Impersonal passives and the -ArAk construction in Turkish." In: Slobin, Dan I. & Zimmer, K. (eds.). *Studies in Turkish Linguistics.* Amsterdam: Benjamins, 53−75.

Bybee, Joan L. 1985. *Morphology: A study of the relation between meaning and form.* Amsterdam: Benjamins.

Bynon, Theodora. 1998. "Inverse direction and second person in Dumi." In: Kulikov, Leonid & Vater, Heinz (eds.) *Typology of verbal categories* (Linguistische Arbeiten, 382). Tübingen: Max Niemeyer, 85−94.

Chomsky, Noam. 1965. *Aspects of the theory of syntax.* Cambridge/MA: MIT Press.

Chomsky, Noam. 1970. "Remarks on nominalization." In: Jacobs, R. & Rosenbaum, P. S. (eds.) *Readings in English Transformational Grammar.* Waltham/MA.

Chomsky, Noam. 1981. *Lectures on government and binding.* (Studies in Generative Grammar, 9.) Dordrecht: Foris.

Chung, S. 1980. "Transitivity and surface filters." In: Hollyman, Jim & Pawley, Andrew (eds.) *Studies in Pacific languages and cultures.* Auckland, 311−332.

Comrie, Bernard. 1977. "In defense of spontaneous demotion: the impersonal passive." In: Cole, Peter & Sadock, J. M. (eds.) *Grammatical relations* (Syntax and Semantics, 8.) New York: Academic Press, 47−58.

Cooreman, Ann. 1994. "A functional typology of antipassives." In: Fox, Barbara & Hopper, Paul (eds.) *Voice: form and function* (Typological Studies in Language, 27). Amsterdam: Benjamins, 49−88.

Corver, Norbert & van Riemsdijk, Henk. 1994. "Introduction." In: Corver, Norbert & van Riemsdijk, Henk (eds.) *Studies on scrambling.* Dordrecht: Foris.

Craig, Colette G. *The structure of Jacaltec.* Austin: University of Texas Press.

Croft, William. 1994. "Voice: beyond control and affectedness." In: Fox, Barbara & Hopper, Paul (eds.) *Voice: form and function* (Typological Studies in Language, 27). Amsterdam: Benjamins, 89−118.

Dahlstrom, Amy. 1976. *Plains Cree Morphosyntax.* Ph.D. dissertation. University of California at Berkeley.

Dalrymple, Mary. 1993. *The Syntax of Anaphoric Binding.* Stanford: CSLI Publications.

DeLancey, Scott. 1981. "The category of direction in Tibeto-Burman." *Linguistics of the Tibeto-Burman Area* 6.1: 83−101.

Dixon, R. M. W. 1994. *Ergativity.* (Cambridge Studies in Linguistics, 69.) Cambridge: Cambridge University Press.

Dryer, Matthew. 1982. "In defence of universal passive." *Linguistic Analysis* 10(1): 53−60.

England, Nora. 1988. "Mam voice." In: Shibatani, Masayoshi (ed.) *Passive and voice.* (Typological Studies in language, 16.) Amsterdam: Benjamins, 525−546.

Feldman, H. 1978. "Passivizing on Datives in Greek." *Linguistic Inquiry* 9: 499−502.

Foley, William A. & Van Valin, Robert D. 1985. "Information packaging in the clause." In: Shopen, Timothy (ed.) *Language typology and syntactic description.* Vol. 1. Cambridge: Cambridge University Press, 282−364.

Forrest, Linda. 1994. "The de-transitive clauses in Bella Coola: Passive vs. Inverse." In: Givón, Talmy (ed.). *Voice and inversion.* (Typological Studies in Language, 28.) Amsterdam: Benjamins, 147−168.

Fortescue, Michael. 1984. *West Greenlandic.* (Croom Helm Decriptive Grammars.) London: Croom Helm.

Frajzyngier, Z. 1982. "Indefinite Agent, passive and impersonal passive: A functional study." *Lingua* 58: 267−290.

Freidin, Robert. 1975. "The analysis of passives." *Language* 51: 384−405.

Givón, T. 1981. "Typology and functional domains." *Studies in Language* 5.1: 163−193.

Givón, T. (ed.) 1983. *Topic continuity in discourse: A quantitative cross-linguistic study.* (Typological Studies in Language, 3.) Amsterdam: Benjamins.

Givón, T. 1984. *Syntax: A functional-typological introduction.* Vol. 1. Amsterdam.

Givón, T. 1988. "Tale of two passives in Ute." In: Shibatani, Masayoshi (ed.) *Passive and voice.* (Typological Studies in language, 16.) Amsterdam: Benjamins, 417−440.

Givón, T. 1994. "The pragmatics of de-transitive voice: Functional and typological aspects of inversion." In: Givón, T. (ed.) *Voice and inversion.* (Typological Studies in Language, 28.) Amsterdam: Benjamins, 3−44.

Harris, Alice. 1981. *Georgian syntax: A study in Relational Grammar.* Cambridge: Cambridge University Press.

Haspelmath, Martin. 1987. *Transitivity Alternations of the Anticausative Type.* (Institut für Sprachwissenschaft der Universität zu Köln, Arbeitspapiere, N. F. 3.) Köln: Universität zu Köln.

Haspelmath, Martin. 1990. "The grammaticization of passive morphology." *Studies in Language* 14: 25–72.

Hohepa, P. W. 1969. "The accusative-to-ergative drift in Polynesian languages." *Journal of Polynesian Society* 78: 297–329.

Jacobs, Peter. 1994. "The inverse in Squamish." In: Givón, T. (ed.). *Voice and inversion.* (Typological Studies in Language, 28.) Amsterdam Benjamins, 121–146.

Kazenin, Konstantin. 1994. "Split syntactic ergativity: toward an implicational hierarchy." *Sprachtypologie und Universalienforschung* 47: 78–98.

Keenan, Edward. 1976. "Remarkable subjects in Malagasy." In: Li, Charles (ed.) *Subject and topic.* New York: Academic Press, 247–301.

Keenan, Edward. 1985. "Passive in the world's languages." In: Shopen, Tymothy (ed.) *Language typology and syntactic description.* Vol. 1. Cambridge: Cambridge University Press, 243–281.

Kibrik, Aleksandr E. 1979. "Canonical ergativity and Daghestan languages." In: Plank, Frans (ed.) *Ergativity.* London: Academic Press, 61–77.

Kibrik, Aleksandr E. 1997. "Beyond subject and object: toward a comprehensive clause relational typology." *Linguistic Typology* 1.3: 279–346.

Kibrik, Aleksandr E. 1997a. "Ierarxii, roli, markirovannost' i "anomal'naja" upakovka grammatičeskoj informacii" [Hierarchies, roles, markedness, and "abnormal" packaging of grammatical information.] *Voprosy Jazykoznanija* no. 4: 27–57.

Kibrik, Andrej A. 1996. "Transitivity decrease in Navajo and Athabaskan: actor-affecting propositional derivations." In: Jelinek, Eloise & Midgette, Sally & Rice, Keren & Saxon, Leslie (eds.) *Athabaskan language studies: Essays in honor of Robert W. Young.* Albuquerque, 259–303.

Kirsner, Robert S. 1976. "On the subjectless "pseudopassive" in standard Dutch and the semantics of background agents." In: Li, Charles (ed.) *Subject and Topic.* New York: Academic Press, 387–415.

Klaiman, M. H. 1988. "Affectedness and control: A typology of voice systems." In: Shibatani, Masayoshi (ed.) *Passive and voice.* (Typological Studies in language, 16.) Amsterdam: Benjamins, 25–83.

Koval', Antonina I. & Njalibuli, D. 1997. *Glagol fula v tipologičeskom osveščenii [The Fula verb in typological perspective.]* Moskva: Nauka.

Kraft, Charles H. & Kirk-Greene, A. H. M. 1973. *Hausa.* London.

Kroeger, P. 1993. *Phrase Structure and Grammatical relations in Tagalog.* Stanford: CSLI Publications.

Kruisinga, E. 1925. *A Handbook of Present-day English.* Part 3. Utrecht.

Langacker, Ronald & Munro, Pamela. 1975. "Passives and their meaning." *Language* 51: 789–830.

Langacker, Ronald W. 1976. *Non-distinct arguments in Uto-Aztecan.* Berkeley.

Larson, Richard K. 1988. "On the double object constructions." *Linguistic Inquiry* 19: 589–632.

Lees, Robert B. 1960. *The grammar of English nominalizations.* The Hague: Mouton.

Li, Charles N. & Lang, R. 1979. "The syntactic irrelevance of an ergative case in Enga and other Papuan languages." In: Plank, Frans (ed.) *Ergativity.* London: Academic Press, 207–324.

Li, Charles & Thompson, Sandra. 1976. "Subject and topic: A new typology of languages." In: Li, Charles (ed.) *Subject and topic.* New York: Academic Press, 457–489.

Manning, Christopher. 1996. *Ergativity: argument structure and grammatical relations.* Stanford: CSLI Publications.

Manning, Christopher & Sag, Ivan. 1998. "Argument structure, valence, and binding." *Nordic Journal of Linguistics* 21: 107–144.

Masica, C. P. 1991. *The Indo-Aryan languages.* Cambridge: Cambridge University Press.

Moreno Cabrera, Juan C. 1998. "Allocutivity and voice in the Basque verb." In: Kulikov, Leonid & Vater, Heinz (eds.) *Typology of verbal categories* (Linguistische Arbeiten, 382). Tübingen: Max Niemeyer, 169–178.

Nichols, Johanna. 1979. "Syntax and pragmatics in Manchu-Tungus language." In: *The elements: a parasession on linguistic units and levels, including papers from the conference on Non-Slavic languages of the USSR.* Chicago, 420–428.

Nichols, Johanna. 1992. *Language diversity in space and time.* Chicago: Chicago University Press.

Noonan, Michael. 1994. "A tale of two passives in Irish." In: Fox, Barbara & Hopper, Paul (eds.) *Voice: form and function* (Typological Studies in Language, 27). Amsterdam: Benjamins, 279–312.

Payne, Doris. 1994. "The Tupí-Guaraní inverse." In: Fox, Barbara & Hopper, Paul (eds.). *Voice: form and function* (Typological Studies in Language, 27). Amsterdam: Benjamins, 313–344.

Perlmutter, David. 1983. "The inadequacy of some monostratal theories of passive." In: Perlmutter, David & Rosen, Carol (eds.) *Studies in Relational Grammar* 2. Chicago: University of Chicago Press, 3–37.

Perlmutter, David & Postal, Paul. 1983a. "Toward a universal characterization of passivization." In: Perlmutter, David (ed.) *Studies in Relational grammar* 1. Chicago: University of Chicago Press, 3–29.

Perlmutter, David & Postal, Paul. 1983b. "Impersonal passives and some relational laws." In: Perlmutter, David & Rosen, Carol. *Studies in Relational Grammar* 2. Chicago: University of Chicago Press, 126–170.

van Riemsdijk, Henk & Williams, Edwin. 1986. *Introduction to the theory of grammar.* (Current

Studies in Linguistics, 12.) Cambridge/MA: MIT Press.

Schachter, Paul. 1976. "The subject in Philippine languages: topic, actor, actor-topic, or none of these." In: Li, Charles (ed.). *Subject and topic.* New York: Academic Press, 491–518.

Schuchardt, Hugo. 1896. *Über den passiven Charakter des Transitivs in den kaukasischen Sprachen.* (Sitzungsberichte der philosophisch-historischen Classe der Akademie der Wissenschaften zu Wien, 133. 1–191). Wien: Akademie der Wissenschaften.

Shibatani, Masayoshi. 1985. "Passives and related constructions." *Language* 61: 821–848.

Shibatani, Masayoshi. 1998. "Voice parameters." In: Kulikov, Leonid & Vater, Heinz (eds.). *Typology of verbal categories* (Linguistische Arbeiten, 382). Tübingen: Narr, 117–138.

Siewierska, Anna. 1984. *The passive: A comparative linguistic analysis.* London: Croom Helm.

Silverstein, Michael. 1976. "Hierarchy of features and ergativity." In: Dixon, Robert M. W. (ed.) *Grammatical categories in Australian languages.* Canberra, 112–171. [Reprinted in: Muysken, Pieter & van Riemsdijk, Henk (eds.) 1986. *Features and projections.* Dordrecht: Foris, 163–232.]

Sullivan, T. 1988. *Compendium of Nahuatl Grammar.* Salt Lake City: University of Utah Press.

Thompson, Chad. 1989. *Voice and obviation in Athabaskan and other languages.* Ph. D. Dissertation, University of Oregon.

Thompson, Chad. 1990. "On the treatment of topical objects in Chepang: passive or inverse?" *Studies in Language* 14: 405–427.

Timberlake, Alan 1976. "Subject properties in the North Russian passive." In: Li, Charles (ed.). *Subject and topic.* New York: Academic Press, 545–570.

Wasow, Thomas. 1977. "Transformations and the lexicon." In: Culicover, Peter & Akmajian, Adrian & Wasow, Thomas (eds.) *Formal syntax.* New York: Academic Press.

Wolf, Charles de. 1988. "Voice in Austronesian languages of Philippine type: passive, ergative or neither." In: Shibatani, Masayoshi (ed.) *Passive and voice.* (Typological Studies in Language, 16.) Amsterdam: Benjamins, 143–193.

Woodbury, Anthony. 1977. "Greenlandic Eskimo, Ergativity and Relational Grammar." In: Cole, Peter & Sadock, J. M. (eds.) *Grammatical relations* (Syntax and Semantics, 8.) New York: Academic Press, 307–336.

Konstantin I. Kazenin,
Moscow (Russian Federation)

68. Verbal reflexives and the middle voice

1. Verbal reflexives vs. reflexive pronouns
2. Morphological types of verbal reflexives
3. Syntactic types of verbal reflexives
4. Polysemy of verbal reflexive markers
5. Accounts of the polysemy; the middle voice
6. Valence-increasing vs. valence-decreasing languages
7. Special abbreviations
8. References

1. Verbal reflexives vs. reflexive pronouns

It is a universal tendency that languages avoid using two or more coreferent full NPs within one clause. Whatever account this is given in a particular theory of grammar, instead of sentences like *John saw John* languages normally make use of sentences where the full NP *John* occurs only once. The coreferentiality of the NPs can be marked in two different ways:

(a) one of the coreferential NPs is replaced by a reflexive pronoun; this is the case in English:

(1) *John$_i$ saw **himself**$_i$*

(b) one of the coreferential NPs is deleted, and the verb receives special marking which signals coreferentiality of the two participants; this is the case in (2) from Russian:

(2) Russian
  (a) *Mat' odela syn-a*
    mother dressed son-ACC
    'Mother dressed the son.'
  (b) *Mat' odela-s'*
    mother dressed-REFL
    'Mother dressed herself.'

The (a) case is discussed in Art. 57 and 84. The present article concentrates on the (b) case, which is termed **verbal reflexive**.

So far verbal reflexives have received much less attention than anaphoric reflexives. Especially few attempts have been made to discover relations between the two types of reflexives in languages where both are present. The consistently separate treatment of the two types of reflexives, however, is misleading because a historical relation between them is obvious in a large number of cases (see § 2.).

An important property of verbal reflexive markers is that they are normally polysemous: a marker with which reflexives are derived from some verbs can often be used in the derivation of some other categories from other verbs. What most of these categories have in common is that they decrease the number of core arguments of the verb, i. e. they are **recessive** (cf. § 3. for details). The nature of the verbal reflexive should be studied in connection with reflexive pronouns, on the one hand, and with the wide range of other recessive categories, on the other.

2. Morphological types of verbal reflexives

2.1. Derived and non-derived reflexives

The morphological typology of verbal reflexives involves the following major distinction:

(i) reflexives derived from their non-reflexive counterparts vs.
(ii) reflexives not derived from their non-reflexive counterparts.

Derived reflexives are by far more numerous than non-derived ones. Within derived reflexives, we find the following division:

(a) verbal reflexives historically related to reflexive pronouns;
(b) verbal reflexives with other diachronic sources.

Russian and Spanish derived verbal reflexives are examples of the first class — the Russian reflexive suffix -*s'l-sja* (cf. 3) and the Spanish reflexive clitic *se* (cf. (22) below) are historically derived from anaphors; cf. (3a) with the verbal reflexive and (3b) with the reflexive pronoun historically related to it:

(3) Russian
 (a) *Ivan moet-sja*
  Ivan washes-REFL
  'Ivan washes himself.'
 (b) *Ivan moet sebja*
  Ivan washes self
  'Ivan washes himself.'

The suffix *-ri* in Imbabura Quechua is an example of the second class, as it cannot be treated as derived from a reflexive pronoun, at least not from a pronoun attested in modern Imbabura Quechua (Cole 1982: 92):

(4) *mana ali runa-ka*
  not good man-TOPIC
  wañu-chi-ri-rka
  die-CAUS-REFL-PAST.3
  'The bad man killed himself.'

Non-derived reflexives are in an equipollent opposition with their non-reflexive counterparts. Usually reflexives of this type differ from the corresponding transitives in inflectional paradigms. Consider the "active" inflection of a transitive verb and the so-called "middle" inflection of its reflexive counterpart in Classical Greek:

(5) Classical Greek
 (a) *loú-ō*
  wash-1sg.ACTIVE
  'I wash something (tr.).'
 (b) *loú-omai*
  wash-1sg.MIDDLE
  'I wash myself.'

An interesting subtype of non-derived reflexives is observed in languages where transitive verbs cross-reference both the agent and the patient, and some stems (usually called labile) allow both transitive and intransitive uses. Transitivity alternations of this kind usually show different semantic effects depending upon the meaning of the verbal stem. Reflexivity is one of the possible effects of such transitivity alternations e. g. in West Greenlandic Eskimo, where some stems followed by an intransitive inflection (i. e. cross-referencing the only core NP of an intransitive verb) denote a reflexive event if the same stem with transitive inflection (cross-referencing both the agent and the patient) corresponds to a normal two-place event:

(6) West Greenlandic Eskimo (Fortescue 1984: 157)
 (a) *tuqqur-paa*
  hide-3sg/3sg.INDIC
  'He$_i$ hid it$_j$.'
 (b) *tuqqur-puq*
  hide-3sg.INDIC
  'He$_i$ hid himself$_i$.'

On the whole, however, equipollent oppositions between reflexive and transitive uses are much less common cross-linguistically than derivation of reflexives. In terms of markedness theory (Greenberg 1966), this means that coreference of arguments is the marked option against their non-coreference — this is viewed as the reason for reflexives to be morphologically more complex than their non-reflexive counterparts.

Treating a derivational relation of reflexives with their non-reflexive counterparts as the standard case is further confirmed by the fact that there are derivational means that serve for reflexive marking only, i. e. are not polysemous (e. g. the suffix -cə in Abkhaz — see Speas 1986: 64). By contrast, equipollent oppositions like those in (5)–(6) always have reflexive only as one of a rather wide range of meanings (see Bakker 1993 for Classical Greek, Fortescue 1984: 157 for Eskimo).

2.2. The morphological asymmetry between verbal and anaphoric reflexives

An important difference between verbal and anaphoric reflexives is that the former express the reflexive relation by a morpheme within the verb, whereas the latter express this relation by means of a separate word (reflexive pronoun). Therefore the verbal reflexivity always is a morphologically "lighter" device than anaphoric reflexivity (see Kemmer 1993: 25–28, Faltz 1977/85: 53 ff.). This fact plays a crucial role in the explanation of some essential properties of verbal reflexives (cf. §§ 3.–4.).

3. Syntactic types of verbal reflexives

3.1. Direct and indirect reflexives

The syntactic classification of reflexives reflects the syntactic positions of the participant deleted under coreference and of the antecedent. The type of reflexive in which the Agent is coreferential with the Patient is called **direct**. The reflexive which marks coreferentiality of the Agent with a participant other than the Patient (Benificiary, Recipient) is called **indirect**. The direct reflexive is a detransitivizing device, because it conflates the Agent and the Patient into a single core NP.

In general, the expression of indirect reflexivity has been studied in much less detail than the expression of direct reflexivity (thus, Kemmer 1993: 75 names only two grammars in which it is explicitly stated that some particular reflexive marker is used for direct, but is not used for indirect reflexive). For verbal reflexives the core meaning is direct, whereas the indirect meaning is relatively seldom expressed in verbal form. There are languages where the verbal reflexive only can be direct. Russian is an example: reflexive use of the verbal marker -*sja* is possible when the agent and the patient coincide, but is excluded when the agent coincides with some other participant, whereas the patient is expressed by a full NP — in this case a reflexive pronoun must be used (cf. (8a) vs. (8b)):

(7) *Ivan odel-sja   v pal'to*
    Ivan dressed-REFL in coat
    'Ivan (Agent) dressed himself (Patient) in the coat.'

(8) (a) *Ivan kupil   sebe   pal'to*
        Ivan bought to.himself coat
        'Ivan bought a coat for himself.'
    (b) **Ivan kupil-sja   pal'to*
        Ivan bought-REFL coat.ACC
        'Ivan bought a coat for himself.'

In contrast to this, there is no language where verbal reflexive can denote indirect but not direct reflexive. The implicational universal, therefore, is that if a language allows verbal marking of indirect reflexives, it allows verbal marking of direct reflexives as well. An explanation of this implication will be proposed in § 5.

Normally indirect reflexives employ the same morphological device that is used in direct reflexives. Thus, the suffix -*ri* in Imbabura Quechua, marking direct reflexive in (4) above, can also mark indirect reflexive:

(9) Imbabura Quechua (Cole 1982: 92)
    marya-ka   kwintu-ta
    Mary-TOPIC story-ACC
    yupa-ri-rka
    recount-REFL-PAST.3
    'Mary told herself a story.'

The example in (10) from Classical Greek illustrates an interesting subtype of indirect verbal reflexive, where the agent acts upon some part of his/her own body (thus the coreference between the agent and the possessor of the patient is entailed):

(10) *loúo-mai   t-às*
     wash-1sg.MIDDLE.PRES ART-ACC.PL
     kheĩr-as
     hand-ACC.PL
     'I wash my hands.'

In this case verbal marking of the indirect reflexives is more common than elsewhere (thus, the Classical Greek indirect reflexive is restricted to the body action verbs). This is probably for reasons of economy: Note, first, that, as mentioned above, verbal reflexives are typically "lighter" morphologically than reflexives pronouns. Second, coreference of the agent with the possessor of the patient is highly expected exactly in body action verbs (see Kemmer 1993: 53–67). Therefore, it is natural that language chooses the "lighter" way to mark this coreferentiality in the context where it occurs especially often.

In some languages verbal reflexives which normally occur in direct function can occasionally be used in indirect function. This is the case in Biblical Hebrew, where one of derivational verbal forms (*hitpaʾel*), frequently marking direct reflexives and reciprocals, has indirect meaning at least in the following example:

(11)   wə-**hit**-ḥalləq-û   ʾot-ah
       and-REFL-divide.IMP-3PL   ACC-3fm
       lə-šiʿah   ḥəlaq-îm
       into-seven   part-PL
       '... and divide it [the land] for yourself into seven parts.' (Joshua 18:5)

3.2. The position of the antecedent

Another syntactic parameter by which verbal reflexives vary is **the syntactic position of the antecedent**. In nominative languages, the agent is uniformly retained and the patient is deleted in verbal reflexive construction, cf. (7) vs. the ungrammatical (12) in Russian:

(12)   *Ivan-a odel-**sja**
       Ivan-ACC dressed-REFL
       'Ivan dressed himself.'

In ergative languages, verbal reflexives show some variability in this respect. Most often, the ergative NP (i.e. the Agent) is deleted in verbal reflexives, cf. Dyirbal (Dixon 1972: 90):

(13)   (a) bala yugu   bangul yarangu
           that stick.NOM that.ERG man.ERG
           buyban
           hides
           'The man hides the stick.'
       (b) bayi yara   buyba-**yiringu**
           that man.NOM hide-REFL
           'That man hides himself.'

Since ergative case marking in Dyirbal is available with all and only transitive verbs, reflexive here is a detransitivizing device, as it is expected to be. However, in some other ergative languages the ergative NP is retained and the patient absolutive NP is deleted. Obviously, in such kind of verbal reflexives the verb remains transitive:

(14)   Kabardian (Kazenin, in press)
       a:-bə   z(ə) -e   -tx'as'-∅
       he-ERG   REFL -3.SG.ERG -wash-PRES
       'He is washing himself.'

One could notice that ergative languages retaining the ergative NP in verbal reflexives follows the general rule observed for reflexive *pronouns*, according to which pronouns are always inserted in the patient position, and the coreferent agent is expressed with a full NP. It would be tempting to hypothesize that all the verbal reflexives retaining ergative NPs are historically derived from constructions with reflexive pronouns. However, the study necessary for evaluation of this hypothesis has not yet been undertaken.

In languages without case marking, it is sometimes difficult to distinguish what is the syntactic position of the antecedent and what is the position of the deleted NP. In a number of cases some indirect evidence can show the right solution. Thus, in Mohawk, a language without case marking, the argument of the direct reflexive can be incorporated into the verb (Baker 1996: 200):

(15)   w-atat-aʾshar-othiyo-s
       NsA-REFL-knife-sharpen-HAB
       'The knife sharpens itself.'

Since only patients (theme-objects, in Baker's terms) can undergo noun incorporation in Mohawk, Baker concludes that the patient is preserved, but the agent is deleted in Mohawk verbal reflexives.

3.3. The scope of verbal reflexives

In the previous section, it was argued that verbal reflexives can occur in a rather wide set of syntactic configurations, contrary to the usual assumption that they only can mark coreferentiality between the agent and the patient. However, an important restriction on verbal reflexives is their **clause-boundness**. In this respect verbal reflexives differ from reflexive pronouns, which in some languages can have antecedents outside their clause ("long-distance anaphora," in generative terms — see Koster & Reuland (eds.) 1991). This asymmetry is illustrated by the following Russian examples:

(16)   (a) Ivan nazval-**sja**/ nazval **sebja**
           Ivan called-REFL/ called himself
           predstavitel-em   prezident-a
           representative-INSTR president-GEN
           'Ivan claimed to be (lit. called himself) a representative of the president.'

(b) *Gubernator razrešil Ivan-u*
governor allowed Ivan-DAT
nazvat'-sja predstavitel-em
call-REFL representative-INSTR
prezident-a
president-GEN
'The governor$_i$ allowed Ivan$_j$ to call himself$_{*i/j}$ a representative of the president.'

(c) *Gubernator razrešil Ivan-u*
governor allowed Ivan-DAT
nazvat' **sebja** *predstavitel-em*
call self representative-INSTR
prezident-a
president-GEN
'The governor$_i$ allowed Ivan$_j$ to call himself$_{i/j}$ a representative of the president.'

The interpretation of (16b) shows that the verbal reflexive requires an antecedent in its own clause (to the effect that the non-expressed subject of the infinitive obligatorily becomes the antecedent of the embedded verbal reflexive).

The only case when verbal reflexives can be not clause-bound is their logophoric use. The term 'logophoric', originally introduced in Hagège 1974, refers to contexts of reportative verbs where the speaker is coreferential with the protagonist of the reported situation. A number of languages employ particular morphosyntactic devices for this kind of contexts, cf.:

(17) Modern Icelandic (Andrews 1982, cit. Kemmer 1993: 91)
Haraldur segi-st hafa skrifað
Harald say-REFL to.have written
itgerð-ina
thesis-the.ACC
'Harald says that he has written the thesis.'

This use of verbal reflexives, however, also appears to be somewhat marginal: logophoric pronouns are considerably more frequent across languages than logophoric verbal markers (for the functional specificity of this type of reflexive uses see Faltz 1977/1985, Sells 1987). Note also that (17) is not quite parallel to (16b) in its ungrammatical interpretation, because in (17) it is the matrix, but not the embedded verb that takes the reflexive form in the case of extra-clausal ('long distance') coreferentiality. Besides, under certain interpretation (17) could be treated as the result of raising of the embedded subject into the matrix clause, in which case, of course, (17) will not violate the clause-boundness requirement for verbal reflexives.

4. Polysemy of verbal reflexive markers

Polysemous verbal reflexive markers are more frequent than verbal markers denoting only reflexives. Languages demonstrate important similarities with respect to additional functions available to verbal reflexive markers. Most of the types of polysemy listed below are very frequent, and the rest are frequent enough for them not to be called exotic. An important characteristic of all these instances of polysemy is that various meanings are lexically distributed: a normally polysemous marker can have only one (at most, two) meaning in combination with any given verb. This often made linguists suggest that this polysemy is the realization of some invariant grammatical function, which is related to detransitivization. Following Lyons (1968: 373), this invariant function was called **'the middle voice'** (this meaning of the term "middle" should be properly distinguished from the notion of "middle constructions", corresponding e.g. to English sentences like *Bureaucrats bribe easily* — see e.g. Fagan 1988). The detailed study of function and form of the various detransitivizing devices brought in important refinements of the initial simple analysis. This will be discussed in the next section. Before that, I will introduce the most important types of the polysemy. Most of these types are discussed in greater detail in Haspelmath (1987) and Geniušienė (1987).

4.1. Reflexive and passive

This type of polysemy is rather common cross-linguistically (see Haspelmath 1990, Keenan 1985: 253—255). The Diyari (Australia) suffix *-tadi-* demonstrates it in the following examples (Austin 1981: 152ff.):

(18) (a) *ŋani muduwa-ṯadi-yi*
1sgs scratch-REFL-PRES
'I scratch myself."

(b) *ŋawu maṇa*
3sg.NF.S door-ABS
ŋandawalka-ṯadi-ṇa wara-yi
close-PASS-PART AUX-PRES
waṯara-ṇi
wind-LOC
'The door was closed by the wind.'

The historical relation between reflexive and passive has been studied in detail in a large number of languages (see Haspelmath 1990: 42−46 and references there). It has been shown that the development always goes unidirectionally from reflexive to passive (via anticausative − cf. § 4.2.), but never the other way round. Semantically, this transition is viewed as loss of the agentivity meaning typical of reflexives. As soon as the subject becomes a mere undergoer, the resultant meaning is passive (or anticausative) instead of reflexive.

When verbal reflexive marking is distinct from passive markers, two possibilities exist:

(i) passive and reflexive are expressed with distinct verbal affixes:

(19) Fula (Koval' & Njalibuli 1997: 115−144)
  (a) *o yeggiti-**ke***
   he forgot-REFL
   'He forgot himself.' (reflexive)
  (b) *rendere ndee ess-**aama***
   water-melon into.parts divide-PASS
   'The water-melon was devided into parts.' (passive)

(ii) reflexivity is expressed by an affix, but the passive voice is expressed by an auxiliary:

(20) Georgian (Harris 1981)
  (a) *rezo i-mal-**eb**-a*
   Rezo PREF-hide-PASS-3sgSubj
   'Rezo hides himself.' (reflexive)
  (b) *rezo damxrčvali-**a** vanos mier*
   Rezo drowned-AUX Vano by
   'Reso is (or: has been) drowned by Vano.'

The opposite situation, where reflexivity would be expressed by an auxiliary and passive voice by an affix, is not attested across languages. This shows that verbal reflexive marking cannot be 'heavier' than the marking of passive. An account of this will be suggested in § 5.

Another important tendency, also to be discussed in section 5, is that in case passive and reflexive have distinct verbal marking the latter, but not the former, marker is usually polysemous.

4.2. Reflexives and anticausatives

The difference between anticausativity (or spontaneous) and passive voice is that the latter always implies existence of an agent (even when the agent is not expressed), whereas the former does not. The reflexive/anticausative polysemy may be observed in the following uses of the Russian suffix -*sj(a)*:

(21) (a) *mat' odela-**s'***
   mother dressed-SUFF
   'Mother dressed herself.' (reflexive)
  (b) *dver' otkryla-**s'***
   door opened-SUFF
   'The door opened.' (anticausative)

In Haspelmath (1987: 30), the generalization was proposed that if a verbal morpheme has both the reflexive and the passive use, then it will also have the anticausative use. This is so because anticausative is semantically intermediate between passive and reflexive: on the one hand, in anticausative, as in passive constructions (but unlike reflexives) the subject is not agentive; on the other hand, the anticausative like the reflexive (but unlike the passive) has only one core argument. Therefore the historical development from reflexive to passive, mentioned in § 4.1., always goes via the anticausative.

The reflexive and anticausative have a common marker distinct from passive markers e. g. in Imbabura Quechua (Cole 1981: 91), West Greenlandic Eskimo (Fortescue 1984: 157), Fula (Koval', Njalibuli 1997: 120−126). The reflexive/anticausative/passive polysemy exists in Latin, Udmurt, Modern Greek, 'O'odham (Aztec-Tanoan) and Tigre (Afroasiatic), among other languages (see Haspelmath 1990: 36).

4.3. Reflexives and reciprocals

This type of polysemy is illustrated by the following Spanish examples:

(22) Spanish (Givón 1979: 194)
  (a) ***Se** curaron los brujos*
   REFL cured.3pl the sorcerers
   'The sorcerers cured themselves.' (reflexive)
  (b) *Juan y Maria **se** vieron en la calle*
   Juan and Mary REFL saw.3pl in the street
   'Juan and Mary saw each other in the street.' (reciprocal)

A less standard case of the relation between reflexives and reciprocals is found in Kabardian (Kazenin, in press). In that language with a polypersonal agreement system, the NP omitted in reciprocals and reflexives is cross-referenced on the verb by the marker -*za*- (with the allomorphs -*zary*- and -*zy*- distributed between various agreement positions). As illustrated by (14) above, the patient NP in Kabardian verbal reflexives is omitted, and the marker appears in the patient agreement slot. In reciprocals, by contrast, the agent NP is omitted, and the marker appears in the agent agreement slot:

(23) Kabardian (Kazenin, in press)
      a:xa-r   ∅
      the-ABS(Object) 3.PL.ABS
      -zar -*o* -*cəx* -∅
      -REC-DYN-know-PRES
      'They know each other.'

Thus in Kabardian reflexives and reciprocals, although related morphologically, appear to be in an asymmetric relation in syntax.

A detailed analysis of reciprocals in their relation to other categories in languages of different types is suggested in Nedjalkov (ed.) (in press). Specifically, that collective monograph studies the relation of reciprocals to other recessive categories, on the one hand, and to the categories of the collective/sociative domain, on the other.

4.4. Reflexives and potentials

This type of polysemy is less common. An example from Russian can be provided:

(24) *Detj-am*   *ne spit-sja*
      children-DAT NEG sleep.3SG-REFL
      'The children cannot go to sleep.'

The potential meaning of reflexive markers is also reported for Spanish, Danish, Kanuri (Nilo-Saharan) and some other languages. According to Haspelmath (1987: 31, 35), the potential meaning is an intermediate stage between the passive and anticausative. If this view is correct, the relation between reflexive and potential is indirect.

4.5. Reflexives and indefinite object deletion

The indefinite object deletion is a transitivity alternation which is traditionally acknowledged as very restricted lexically (sometimes it is called "deobjective", "absolutive" or 'antipassive"; the latter term, however, is associated with one more type of transitivity alternation, characterized in § 4.6.). The reflexive markers can have this function almost exclusively with verbs of manipulative activity. The deleted Patient is understood as generic. This function is attested e. g. for the Udmurt reflexive morpheme -*śk*- (Haspelmath 1990: 34): *vur-yny* 'sew something' (transitive) vs. *vuri-śk-yny* 'sew, be engaged in sewing' (intransitive).

4.6. Reflexives and antipassives

Antipassive is a transitivity alternation which demotes the patient (changes its syntactic status from the direct object for an oblique) and retains the agent as a core argument. Initially this term was proposed by Silverstein (1976) in reference to this type of transitivity alternations only found in ergative languages, where it puts the agent in nominative (instead of ergative) and the patient in one of the oblique cases. The term "antipassive" was justified by the concept of ergativity viewing the nominative patient as the subject: under this view, questioned seriously in subsequent discussions (Anderson 1976, A. E. Kibrik 1997), antipassive promotes the agent into the subject position, indeed being the reverse image of the passive.

Productive patient-demoting transitivity alternations indeed are attested predominantly in languages with ergative morphology. In some of them this transitivity alternation is signalled by the same verbal marker as the one used in reflexives. The Diyari suffix -*tadi*-, the reflexive and passive uses of which were illustrated in (18), can also mark the antipassive (Austin 1981: 152−153):

(25) (a) *ŋatu ŋana   wiḻa   kaḻka-yi*
         1sgA 3sgfo woman-ABS wait-PRES
         'I wait for the woman.'
     (b) *ŋani kaḻka-tadi-yi   ŋaŋkaṉu*
         1sgs wait-ANTIPASS-PRES   3sgfLOC
         wiḻa-ṉi
         woman-LOC
         'I wait for the woman.'

4.7. Reflexive markers in deponent verbs

The above list, however, does not exhaust the possibilities of use of reflexive verbal markers in non-reflexive meaning. The widely known phenomenon of the so-called **deponent verbs** is attested in Hungarian, Classical Greek, Latin, Turkish, Fula, Russian and some other languages. These verbs have the form of verbal reflexives, but, at least synchronically, do not correlate with any non-reflexive verb. E. g., the following reflexive forms are basic means to express the corresponding non-reflexive situations: Latin *vereo-r* 'fear', Russain *bojat-sja* 'fear', Fula *'oppin-o* 'squat', *hiim-o* 'think, reflect'.

Deponent verbs have often been treated as a marginal, non-essential use of verbal reflexive markers. This treatment was to a large extent induced by the strongly "syntactic" approach to reflexives and other verbal categories of this kind, which treated change of valence-type as the "core", and all the other uses as the "periphery". However, there are some regularities in the use of deponents which cast serious doubt on treating them in this way. Indeed, deponents regularly occur in one and the same semantic groups of verbs in non-related languages — most frequently they are encountered among speech verbs, verbs of translational motion, verbs of body care, and verbs of cognition. More recent functional study of the middle voice, sketched in the next section, has shown that viewing deponents as the "periphery" of "syntactic" uses of verbal reflexives was to a large extant erroneous.

5. Accounts of the polysemy; the middle voice

We have seen that the possibilities for polysemy of verbal reflexives are impressive indeed. As already mentioned, verbal forms with some set of the meanings listed above are often called **middle voice** forms. This term, coming from the grammar of Classical Greek, has frequently been used without any explication of what makes the various meanings listed above related. The most popular informal definition of the middle voice was given by Lyons (1968: 373), who characterized the middle voice as indicating that "the 'action' or 'state' affects the subject of the verb or his interests".

The array of functions available for the middle voice is often called **the middle domain**. Regular marking of these functions with identical formal devices makes one search for a shared meaning. Crucially, it is almost impossible to discern any syntactic core of all the functions from the middle domain. Specifically, valence-decrease, which takes place in reflexives, reciprocals, passives, anticausatives and indefinite object deletion, is not obligatory in potential constructions, not unproblematic with logophoric middles (its existence there depends upon whether the protagonist of the reported event is treated as the subject of the embedded verb or the "raised" object of the logophorically marked matrix verb — see § 3.3.) and surely does not take place with deponents. This shows that in order to give an account for really all the functions from the middle domain, a semantic rather than structural explanation is called for.

The first serious attempts to discern a functional core of the middle domain were undertaken in Givón (1981) and Shibatani (1985). These authors were in the first turn concerned with the regular morphological coincidence between passives, on the one hand, and reflexives, reciprocals, anticausatives, potentials etc. on the other. Shibatani (1985) argued that all these constructions defocus the agent. His arguments for the passive as an agent de-focusing device are outlined in Art. 67. Agent de-focusing is obvious for anticausative and potential constructions and is shown to take place also in reciprocal and reflexive ones. According to Givón (1981), the passive has a wider range of pragmatic functions, including, apart from the agent de-focusing, also topicalization of the patient, stativization of the whole event, etc. Givón argued that all the other grammatical constructions from the middle domain share with the passive at least one of its functions.

These accounts have made it impossible to further overlook the regular morphological coincidence between the categories under investigation. Also, they prove beyond any doubt that this coincidence has deep semantic sources. However, the proposed accounts failed to explain why many languages which have identical morphological devices for reflexive, reciprocal, anticausative etc. constructions have a distinct device only for marking the passive (see § 4.1.–4.2.). This is totally unpredictable if the function viewed as shared by reflexive, reciprocal and anticausative constructions is at the same time a core function of passive. Besides, the accounts of Givón and Shibatani treat all the categories of the domain under investigation as derivational — at least semantically, if not morphologically. Indeed, de-focusing of the Agent, topicalization of the Patient etc. presuppose some alternative grammatical construction where these operations do not take place. This approach, however, is unable to explain the existence of deponent verbs, which do not manifest any derivational recessive category but nevertheless have reflexive markers.

A serious attempt to resist the pressure of the derivational approach was made in Klaiman (1988) (see also Klaiman 1992). Klaiman noted that the active and the middle differ primarily in conceptual status of the subject: in the active it is not affected, but in the middle it is affected. This conclusion was shown to be correct both for the derived and deponent middles.

Another analysis which to a large extent resolves these problems was undertaken in Kemmer (1993), a cognitively-based study of the middle domain, giving a systematic account of form and function relations within it. For Kemmer, the passive is neither the starting point nor the focus of the investigation. She attempts to discern semantic correspondence in the uses of the middle morphology, irrespective of whether this or that use of a middle marker corresponds to a derivational category or not. This allows Kemmer to treat deponent verbs together with the transitivity alternations listed above. She classifies verbs on the basis of their semantics rather than of their derivational history. She observes that the following verbs regularly occur with markers referring to one or several categories of the middle domain:

(1) verbs of grooming and body care: Latin *orno-r* 'adorn oneself', *perluo-r* 'bathe', Turkish *yik-an* 'wash', *giy-in* 'dress', Russian *odevat'-sja* 'dress', *myt'-sja* 'wash';
(2) verbs of change in body posture: Djola *lak-* 'sit down', Bahasa Indonesian *ber-lutut* 'kneel down', Russian *sadit'-sja* 'sit down';
(3) verbs of non-translational motion: Fula *tam-o* 'clench one's fist', Russian *vertet'-sja* 'turn around';
(4) verbs of translational motion: Fula *ma'y'y-o* 'climb, mount', Bahasa Indonesian *ber-djalan* 'walk, stroll'.

Already among the verbs listed above, some are derived and some are deponent. For instance, the Russian verbs *myt'-sja* 'wash oneself' and *odevat'-sja* 'dress oneself' are derived reflexives from the corresponding transitives *myt'* 'wash somebody' and *odevat'* 'dress somebody'; in the same way *vertet'-sja* 'turn' is an anticausative derived from *vertet'* 'turn something/somebody'; but the verb *sadit'-sja* 'sit down' is a deponent, since the corresponding transitive **sadit'* is not attested. However, what only is crucial for Kemmer is the semantic similarity between these verbs. Attempting to account for the unitary coding of these types of verbs across languages, Kemmer notes: "Actions that are carried out by human entities on or through their bodies tend to be conceived of as unary or atomic actions, rather than complex actions distinguished into their component parts of acting and acted on entities" (p. 58). The reason for this is that action expressed by such verbs is directed upon the agent's body or some part of it. Naturally, this is not the case for verbs with a high degree of semantic transitivity according to Hopper & Thompson (1980), such as 'kill', 'build' etc., where the agent and the patient are clearly distinct. Therefore, Kemmer concludes that common semantic feature of the above listed groups of verbs is **the low distinguishability of participants**.

Naturally, not all reflexives have this property: e. g. the reflexive derived from the verb 'see' still denotes an action with quite distinct (albeit coreferential) agent and patient, as in a sentence meaning 'John saw himself in the mirror'. Therefore, Kemmer goes on to study the relation between marking of verbs with low distinguishability of participants and marking of other kinds of reflexive and reciprocal situations. Her main observation is that languages here can choose between the following two strategies: (1) **the one-form strategy**, under which the marker occuring in verbs with low distinguishability of participants is also used throughout all reflexives (and reciprocals); (2) **the two-form strategy**, where the marker used in reflexives (and reciprocals) is distinct from the marker used in verbs with low distinguishability of participants. The one-form strategy is attested e. g. in German, French, Guugu Yimidhirr (Pama-Nyungan family, Australia), Changana and Pangwa (Niger-Kongo). Languages characterized by the two-form strategy include, among others, the Scandinavian languages, Russian, Turkish, Bahasa Indonesia, Latin, Classical Greek, Hungarian, Sanskrit, and Georgian.

It is the two-form strategy that is crucial for definition and theoretical motivation of the notion 'middle voice'. Kemmer notes that if a language chooses the two-form strategy, one of the two markers is morphologically "lighter" than the other one. E. g. Djola (Niger-Kongo) employs the suffixes *ərə* (the "heavy" one) and *-ə* (the "light" one) in this area of meanings. Studying distribution of these markers, Kemmer suggests that functions of "light" markers correspond to the core of the middle domain. The most important observation about the two-form languages is that the "light" markers are employed in verbs with low distinguishability of participants, whereas the "heavy" marker is employed in other kinds of reflexives. Interestingly, Kemmer means by "heavy markers" both the morphemes used on verb and anaphoric pronouns. Thus, in Russian verbs with high distinguishability of the agent and the patient employ the "heavy" marker – the reflexive pronoun rather than the "light" marker -*sja*:

(26) Russian
*Ivan uvidel sebja/*uvidel-sja v*
Ivan saw himself saw-REFL in
zerkale
the.mirror.
'Ivan saw himself in the mirror.'

Studying expression of reciprocals, Kemmer discerns the class of verbs which denote "naturally reciprocal events", i.e. events which are necessarily or frequently semantically reciprocal ('meet', 'fight', 'converse', 'kiss'). She observes that such verbs are again typically marked by the "light" markers in two-form languages, whereas with other types of events the reciprocal normally is expressed with a "heavy" marker. This leads Kemmer to identify a more general semantic property corresponding to middle, which she calls **low distinguishability of events**.

The "lightness" of markers is explained by economy reasons, since they are used in verbs where coincidence of the agent and the patient in one entity is expected (often because the agent and the patient are not properly distinguished). Heavy markers, by contrast, are used with those verbs with which this option is infrequent.

Kemmer's semantic rather than derivational account of the middle voice allows her to see important similarities between marking of various categories, which hardly would ever have received attention in the derivational approach. Thus, she notes that indirect verbal reflexives have "light" marking when distinguishability of the agent and the beneficiary/recipient is low (verbs like 'acquire for oneself'), and "heavy" markers otherwise. The distribution is virtually the same as in direct verbal reflexives.

In this way, Kemmer accounts for the middle voice irrespective of whether certain instances of it mark grammatical derivation or not. The middle domain corresponds to some semantic properties of the event, which may be or not be induced by some derivational process. Middles differ from transitive verbs in that the latter have at least two entirely distinct participants, which are conceived separately even in the case where they are coreferential; their coreferentiality is marked by reflexive rather than by middle morphology (of course, in a one-form system, where middle and reflexive are collapsed in one form, this distinction is not morphologically manifested). At the same time, middles differ from bare intransitive verbs, since in the latter distinguishability of the agent and patient is missing, whereas in middles it exists, although it is low note that, the verbs marked by the middle voice in some languages are expressed by bare intransitives in some other languages – cf. the Russian middle *ložit'-sja* and its English intransitive equivalent *lie down*, the Russian middle *celovat'-sja* and its English equivalent *kiss* in sentences like *John and Mary kissed*).

Although Kemmer does not discuss the passive at great length, it seems that her account of the middle voice is able to explain why reflexives, but not the passive tend to be polysemous in languages where the two categories are morphologically distinct (see § 4.1.). Indeed, reflexives can have much in common with some other types of verbs from Kemmer's middle domain (reciprocals, many deponents), but passive is not characterized by low distinguishability of participants (or events), thus it is less semantically related to the middle domain.

However, Kemmer's analysis also fails to account for a number of important cross-linguistic tendencies. She does not suggest any insightful explanation of why the same "light" markers which are used in naturally reflexive and reciprocal events are also used with high regularity in anticausatives (we have seen in § 4.2. that this is the case). It seems doubtful that the same semantic properties which Kemmer discovers in "lightly marked" reflexives and reciprocals are at work in the anticausative part of the middle domain as well: anticausatives have only one core NP, hence distinction between an agent and a patient is out of the question, as in mere intransitives. Besides, those instances of morphological coincidence between the passive and Kemmer's middle voice which exist (see section § 4.1.) remain almost unaccounted for, since in passive both the agent and the patient may be present and not at all be clearly distinguishable.

An account of the middle taking into closer consideration its anticausative function as well as its relation to the passive is represented in Arce-Arenales, Axelrod & Fox (1994). There, much in the spirit of Klaiman (1988) (see Art. 67), it is suggested that a distinction should be drawn between the passive voice and a syntactically active voice in which the subject "also exhibits the conceptual status 'affected entity'" (p. 2). The latter is called *the middle diathesis*. This analysis readily explains why the anticausative is regularly marked by the same devices as reflexives and reciprocals are: the subject of an anticausative is an affected entity in the same way as the subject of a reflexive or a reciprocal is. However, it seems to predict a wider scope of the middle markers than they really have: middle marking can be expected at any verb where the subject is an affected entity, including mere one-place intransitives. This, of course, is not the case. Kemmer's distinction between middle and intransitive, allowing her to explain, among a number of other things, why middle marking takes place only with a rather limited number of underived intransitives, is lost in the account of Arce-Arenales et al.

To conclude, a functional account of middle has now been developed, attempting to explain as many of the various uses of middle morphology as possible. There seems to be no account proposed so far that would cover the whole middle domain. It is now undeniable that the derivational account, treating valence-decrease as the core function and all the rest uses as marginal, fails to predict very important and higly regular cross-linguistic correlations.

6. Valence-increasing vs. valence-decreasing languages

Although the relations between verbal and anaphoric reflexive in languages where both exist reveal much about the nature of middle voice, coexistence of the two types of reflexive marking in a language is not at all universal. In general, the following combinations of possibilities can be expected:

(i) + verbal reflexive + anaphoric reflexive
(ii) − verbal reflexive + anaphoric reflexive
(iii) + verbal reflexive − anaphoric reflexives

The possibility in (iii) is very rare. It shows up in some polysynthetic languages, e. g. in Mohawk (Baker 1996: 51), where at least direct reflexives can only have verbal marking.

The distribution of the remaining languages between options (i) and (ii) correlates with a general typological opposition which is usually labelled as opposition between **valence-increasing** and **valence-decreasing** languages. Recent typological studies have revealed that a large number of languages show clear preference either for valence-increasing or for valence-decreasing morphological devices. According to Haspelmath (1993: 100−103), languages where causative and detransitivization derivational processes are equally productive constitute a minority against languages where one of these derivational processes surpasses the other one in productivity. Haspelmath shows that most of the languages preferring valence decreasing verbal morphology are concentrated in the European area, whereas languages preferring valence increasing verbal derivation prevail outside Europe.

Since verbal reflexives are an instance of valence-decreasing morphology, verbal reflexives are expected only in languages which prefer valence decrease. This expectation is strengthened by the fact that, as shown in § 4, verbal reflexives most often employ markers which at the same time have other valence-decreasing functions. Although no special studies of this problem have been done, this expectation is borne out at least in so far that verbal reflexives exist in most European languages. On the other hand, languages showing strong preference for valence increase lack verbal reflexives, always marking coreferentiality of arguments by means of anaphoric reflexives. This is the case e. g. in the Nakh-Daghestanian family (A. A. Kibrik 1996).

7. Special abbreviations

ANTIPASS	antipassive
HAB	habitual
INDIC	indicative
INSTR	instrumental
PREF	prefix
REC	reciprocal
SUFF	suffix

8. References

Austin, Peter. 1981. *A grammar of Diyari*. (Cambridge Studies in Linguistics, 32) Cambridge: Cambridge University Press.

Anderson, Stephen R. "On the notion of subject in ergative languages." In: Li, Charles (ed.). *Subject and Topic*. New York: Academic Press.

Andrews, Avery. 1982. "The representation of case in Modern Icelandic." In: Bresnan, Joan (ed.). *The mental representation of grammatical relations*. Cambridge/MA: MIT Press.

Arce-Arenales, Manuel & Axelrod, Melissa & Fox, Barbara. 1994. "Active voice and middle diathesis: a cross-linguistic study." In: Fox, Barbara & Hopper, Paul (eds.). *Voice: form and function.* (Typological Studies in Language, 27) Amsterdam/Philadelphia: Benjamins, 1–22.

Baker, Mark. 1996. *The Polysynthesis Parameter.* (Oxford Studies in Comparative Syntax.) New York/Oxford: Oxford University Press.

Bakker, Egbert. 1993. "Voice, aspect and actionsart: middle and passive in Ancient Greek." In: Fox, Barbara & Hopper, Paul (eds.). *Voice: form and function.* (Typological Studies in Language, 27) Amsterdam/Philadelphia: Benjamins, 23–48.

Cole, Peter. 1982. *Imbabura Quechua.* (LINGUA descriptive series.) Amsterdam: North Holland.

Dixon, Robert M. W. 1972. *The Dyirbal language of North Queensland.* Cambridge: Cambridge University Press.

Faltz, Leonard. 1977/1985. *Reflexivization: A study in universal syntax.* Doctoral dissertation, University of California, Berkeley. [Reprinted in 1985 by Garland Publishing, New York.]

Fortescue, Michael D. 1984. *West Greenlandic.* London: Croom Helm.

Geniušienė, Emma. 1987. *The typology of reflexives.* Berlin: Mouton de Gruyter.

Givón, Talmy. 1981. "Typology and functional domain." *Studies in Language* 5: 163–193.

Greenberg, Joseph. 1966. *Language universals, with special reference to feature hierarchies.* (Janua Linguarum series minor, 59.) The Hague: Mouton.

Hagège, Claude. 1974. "Les pronoms logophoriques." In: *Bulletin de la Societe de Linguistique de Paris* 69. 287–310.

Haspelmath, Martin. 1987. *Transitivity alternations of the anticausative type.* (Institut für Sprachwissenschaft der Universität zu Köln, Arbeitspapiere, N. F. 5). Cologne: University of Cologne.

Haspelmath, Martin. 1990. "The grammaticization of passive morphology." *Studies in Language* 14.1: 25–72.

Haspelmath, Martin. 1993. "More on the typology of inchoative/causative verb alternations." In: Comrie, Bernard & Polinsky, Maria (eds.). *Causatives and transitivity.* (Studies in Language Companion Series, 23.) Amsterdam/Philadelphia: Benjamins, 87–120.

Hopper, Paul & Thompson, Sandra. 1980. "Transitivity in grammar and discourse." *Language* 56: 251–299.

Kazenin, Konstantin. In press. "Reciprocal, reflexive, sociative, comitative, and relativization in Kabardian." In: Nedjalkov, Vladimir (ed.). *A typology of reciprocal constructions.*

Keenan, Edward L. 1985. "Passive in the world's languages." In: Shopen, Timothy (ed.). *Language typology and syntactic description.* Vol. 1. Cambridge: Cambridge University Press, 243–281.

Kemmer, Suzanne. 1993. *The middle voice.* (Typological studies in language, 23.) Amsterdam/Philadelphia: Benjamins.

Kibrik, Aleksandr E. 1997. "Beyond subject and object: toward a comprehensive relational typology." *Linguistic Typology* 1.3: 279–346.

Kibrik, Andrej A. 1996. "Transitivity in lexicon and grammar". In: Kibrik, Alexandr E. (ed.). *Godoberi.* (LINCOM Studies in Caucasian Linguistics 02.) München/Newcastle: LINCOM Europa, 107–146.

Klaiman, M. H. 1988. "Affectedness and control: a typology of voice systems." In: Shibatani, Masayoshi (ed.). *Passive and voice.* (Typological Studies in Language, 16.) Amsterdam/Philadelphia: Benjamins, 25–83.

Koster, Jan & Reuland, Eric. (eds.). 1991. *Long-distance anaphora.* Cambridge, Mass.: MIT Press.

Koval', Antonina & Njalibuli, Burejma. 1997. *Glagol fula v tipologiceskom osvescenii.* (The Fula verb in typological perspective.) Moskva.

Lyons, John. 1968. *Introduction to theoretical linguistics.* Cambridge: Cambridge University Press.

Nedjalkov, Vladimir P. (ed.). In press. *A typology of reciprocal constructions.*

Sells, Peter. 1987. "Aspects of logophoricity." *Linguistic Inquiry* 18.3: 445–79.

Shibatani, Masayoshi. 1985. "Passives and related constructions." *Language* 61: 821–848.

Silverstein, Michael. 1976. "Hierarchy of features and ergativity". In: Dixon, Robert M. W. (ed.). *Grammatical categories in Australian languages.* Canberra: Australian National University, 112–171.

Speas, Arie. 1986. *Abkhaz Studies.* Leiden.

*Konstantin I. Kazenin, Moscow
(Russian Federation)*

69. Resultative constructions

1. Introduction
2. Distinctions between the resultative and contiguous categories
3. The resultative form
4. Agent-oriented resultative
5. Resultative proper and statives
6. Principal resultative meanings
7. Restrictions on resultative formation
8. Polysemy of resultative markers
9. The agentive complement (AC) with Patient-oriented resultatives
10. Special abbreviations
11. References

1. Introduction

1.1. Resultative

The prototypical **resultative** (or **resultative proper**) is defined as a verb form or a more or less regular derivative from terminative verbs that expresses a state implying a previous event (action or process) it has resulted from (see Nedjalkov & Jaxontov 1988: 3–8). Thus (1c), (2b) and (3c) are logical consequences of (1a–b), (2a) and (3a) respectively:

(1) (a) *He **has opened** the window*
 (b) *Suddenly the window **was opened***
 (c) *The window **was** still **opened**;*

(2) (a) *He **has** (*still) **gone***
 (b) *He **is** still **gone**.*

1.2. Stative

The resultative (see (3c)) differs from **derived statives** (see (3b)) in that the latter express a state of an entity without implying a previous event. Therefore, in Georgian the stative *a-b-i-a* 'is fastened/tied' (the marker is the suffix *-i-* in the present and the prefix *e-* in the past and future, and a copula which has the reduced form *-a* in the 3rd. p. < *aris* 'is') under (3b) and not RES *da-b-m-ul-i-a* 'is fastened/tied' (the marker is the suffix *-ul-* of the passive participle and the reduced copula) under (3c) may be used in a sentence meaning 'Only one apple is growing (lit. 'is fastened') on this branch'. (In (3a) and (3c) *da-* is a perfectivizing preverb and *-am-/-m-* is a thematic suffix).

(3)   Georgian (M. Mačavariani, p. c.)
 (a) *mama-m   ʒaɣl-i   da-a-b-al*
     father-ERG dog-NOM PREV-CAUS-tie-3.SG
     a -b -am-s
     CAUS-tie-TH-3.SG
     'Father has tied/is tying the dog'

 (b) *ʒaɣl-i   a-b-i-a   /e-b-a*
     dog-NOM CAUS-tie-STAT-3.SG STAT-tie-3.SG
     'The dog is/was on a leash'
 (c) *ʒaɣl-i   da-b-m-ul-i-a*
     dog-NOM PREV-tie-TH-PAST.PTCP-NOM-3.SG
     'The dog is leashed/tied'.

Both categories express states and they share a number of important properties, many claims about the resultative being valid for the stative. Moreover, it is not always easy to distinguish between the two meanings (cf. the conflicting opinions about the Active Perfect in Ancient Greek as stative and resultative in Perel'muter (1988: 280) and Haspelmath (1992: 207) respectively). Since they are very close to each other, in languages that possess both categories they are often interchangeable. Below, the term **resultative** is used in the broad sense (unless it is otherwise specified) to cover both categories.

1.3. Subject- and object-oriented resultative

Two main syntactic types of resultatives are distinguished: (1) **object-oriented resultative**, whose subject corresponds to the direct object (patient) of the base verb (see (1), (3), (4)); they involve **intransitivization**, which makes them syntactically similar to passives; (2) **subject-oriented resultative**, retaining the underlying subject. The latter type is subdivided into two subtypes: (a) an intransitive subtype (see (2), (5)) and (b) a transitive one (see (6)), according to the valency of the base verb. In the latter subtype, the previous action affects the agent rather than the object (see § 4.). This subtype may be termed **possessive** because it is most commonly derived from transitives whose object is a body part or a thing in immediate contact with the agent, which results in a possessive (in a broad sense) relation between agent and patient, as in (6). Alternative terms for object-oriented, intransitive subject-oriented and transitive subject-oriented (possessive) resultatives are **P-oriented**, **S-oriented** and **A-oriented** resultatives respectively (cf. Comrie 1981: 68–70), abbreviated as **P-resultative**, **S-resultative** and **A-resultative**.

A-resultatives are not as common as the other two syntactic types. Thus, they are not attested in Standard Russian, but in a number of northern dialects possessive relations can be expressed (by forms identical with the S- and P-resultative). The following examples are from the Torzhok dialect of Russian (to the best of my knowledge, it is the only Slavic dialect where all the three syntactic types have the same marker, viz. the converbal suffix (*-ši*/*-vši*)):

(4) Russian (Trubinskij 1988: 389–90)
  (a) *On pomyl pol*
    'He (has) washed the floor'
  (b) *Pol pomy-**vši***
    'The floor is washed'.

(5) (a) *On upal*
    'He has fallen'
  (b) *On upa-**vši***
    'He is fallen'.

(6) (a) *On nadel šapku*
    'He has put on a cap'
  (b) *On byl nade-**vši** šapku*
    'He had a cap on'.

There are also a number of less common syntactic types of resultatives, e.g. the one in which the subject corresponds to the underlying indirect object. In this type a direct object is retained, like in the A-resultative, and semantically it is also similar to the latter, due to a kind of possessive relation between subject and object, cf. (6b) and (7b):

(7) Japanese (M. Shibatani, p.c.)
  (a) *Boku-wa **fune-ni** nimotu-o nose-ta*
    I-TOP   ship-DAT cargo-ACC load-PAST
    'I have loaded cargoes on the ship'
  (b) ***Fune-wa** nimotu-o nose-te i-ru*
    ship-TOP cargo-ACC load-CONV be-PRES
    'The ship is loaded with cargoes'
    (also 'The ship is loading cargoes [onto itself]').

1.4. Ambiguous types of resultatives

There are resultatives that allow two interpretations, as derived 1) from a transitive or an intransitive verb, on the one hand, and 2) from an actional or a statal verb, on the other. In each case both base verbs have the same form.

(1) **P-** or **S-resultative**? A resultative may be related to two verbs, one intransitive denoting a process (transition from one state into another), and the other transitive denoting causation of the latter process. In such cases the semantic boundary between S-resultatives and P-resultatives vanishes. For instance, (1c) is relatable not only to (1a) but also to *The window (has) opened*. S/P ambiguity of resultatives is also attested in Armenian, Norwegian, German, Georgian, etc.

(2) **Resultative or quasi-resultative?** The latter term refers to cases when the base verb is inherently stative (see (12)). A great many languages have verbs of dual terminative/durative aspectual value denoting (depending on the context) either an action or a state that may result from this action. The relevant derived form is resultative if related to the actional meaning and it is quasi-resultative if related to the statal meaning of the same base verb. It is reasonable to consider these ambiguous forms resultatives proper.

(2.1) **Quasi-resultative** or **S-/A-resultative**? This type is abundant in Nivkh; cf. *polm-* 'to be/become blind', *řik-* 'to take into/hold in one's arms', etc. Needless to say, their resultative form expresses a resultant state exclusively. (*-d'* is a sentence-final marker; in (8c) a form of the progressive consisting of a converb and the copula is used):

(8) Nivkh (G. Otaina, p.c.)
  (a) *If nana por-d'*
    'He has just lain down'
  (b) *If t'ək por-d'*
    'He lay for a long time'
  (c) *If por-r hum-d'*
    'He is lying'
  (d) *If por-ɣəta-d'*
    'He was/is lying'.

Compare a standard resultative opposition:

(9) (a) *If mu-d'* 'He died'
  (b) *If mu-ɣəta-d'* 'He is dead'.

(2.2) **Quasi-** or **P-resultative**? Here we find mostly verbs of two lexical groups. One group compreses **emotive verbs**, cf.:

(10) (a) *This surprised me*
   (b) *This surprises me*
   (c) *I **am surprised** at this.*

(10c) is related to (10a) as a P-resultative proper and to (10b) as a **quasi-resultative**, in this case as a **converse** (which involves synonymy), i.e. two valencies are retained but the position of the arguments is reversed.

The second group comprises verbs implying **physical contact** of two entities; the relation between (11c) and (11a) as well as (11b) is analogous to that holding between the examples under (10):

(11) (a) *Water is slowly filling the tub*
   (b) *Water fills the tub to the brim*
   (c) *The tub **is filled** with water.*

The interpretation of (11c) becomes even more complicated if we take into account that it is relatable to two more basic constructions:

(d) *He filled the tub with water*
(e) *The tub filled with water.*

If natural states are described, where no previous action or process can be implied, a derived construction can be interpreted as a quasi-resultative only; cf.:

(12) (a) *Hills surround the town*
 (b) *The town **is surrounded** by hills.*

The relations considered under (2.2) are also encountered in German, Armenian, Hindi, Chukchi, etc.

1.5. Terms used for the resultative

The phenomenon referred to here as **resultative** is considered in the literature under a variety of names, depending on its relation to other categories in a particular language: (1) **stative**; (2) **resultative**; **resultative Aktionsart**, including (2a) **resultative stative** (as a special variety of resultative and stative, a combination of (1) and (2)) and, as an abbreviation, **resultative**; (3) **perfect**; (3a) **statal perfect** (a combination of (1) and (3)); (4) **passive**, including **statal passive** or the **passive of state** (a combination of (1) and (4)); **Zustands-passiv**; (5) **continuous (durative) aspect**; **durative accomplishment**.

As we see, these terms show that the resultative is mostly associated with three categories: **perfect**, **passive**, and **progressive**.

The literature on the resultative and its relation to other categories in individual languages is quite extensive (to name but a few studies: Öberg 1907; Engelhardt 1969; Brinker 1971; Helbig 1980: 197–212; Milan 1985; Lemos 1987; Schubert 1982; Payne 1990: 429–53), and theoretical issues have also been given a good deal of attention in generative grammar (cf. Wasow 1977: 327–60; Anderson 1977: 361–377; Dubinsky & Simango 1996: 749–81; see also References in these papers).

To my knowledge, the first to use the term "resultative" in the sense close to that defined above was E. Sapir who described the suffix *-q'ai* in Southern Paiute as follows: "This suffix indicates a durative state or activity which is the result of the action predicated by the verb stem; e. g. *to HOLD* as a resultative of *to GRASP*. Resultative verbs are very common in Paiute" (Sapir 1930: 150).

2. Distinctions between the resultative and contiguous categories

2.1. Perfect and resultative

The **perfect** is defined here as a form that expresses an action (process, or state) in the past which has continuing relevance for the present. The distinctive features of the perfect are the following:

(1) the after-effects of a perfect action are non-specific, and they are not necessarily attributed to any particular participant of the situation, whereas the meaning of the resultative always directly depends on the lexical meaning of the base verb, being a component of the latter meaning;
(2) the perfect form, unlike the resultative which is lexically restricted, can be derived from any verb irrespective of its lexical meaning, valency and aspect, including verbs meaning 'to work', 'to love', etc.;
(3) the perfect does not involve any valency change, while the resultative from most transitive verbs is intransitive (excepting the rare A-resultative; see § 4.) as the state resulting from a previous event is attributed to one participant; thus preferential intransitivity is characteristic of resultatives (in these cases there is formal and semantic affinity with predicative adjectives);
(4) adverbials of duration (e. g. *for two hours, all day long*), if they combine with perfects at all, occur mostly with those of durative verbs and denote duration of the event, while with RES (including the perfect of a resultative) they express duration of the state. Adverbials meaning 'still' freely collocate with resultatives of temporary states (see (1c) and (2b)), but not as a rule with those of permanent or irreversible states (see (2) in § 6.1.)) and with perfects. Compare Armenian, where the two categories differ formally:

(13) Armenian (Kozinceva 1988: 455)
 (a) *Na (*der) ənk-el   e*
  he (still) fall-PERF is
  'He has (*still) fallen'
 (b) *Na der ənk-aç   e*
  he still fall-RES.PART is
  'He is still fallen/lying'.

(5) There are also differences in combinability with locative adverbials.

2.2. Passive and resultative

The term **passive** is applied to verb forms indicating that the surface subject does not encode the agent or that the latter is not expressed in the surface structure. The passive involves a valency change, but no change in the lexical meaning. This term thus covers actional but not statal passives (in traditional terms). The resultative itself is voice-neutral, but P-resultatives involve a valency change since the patient surfaces as subject and the agent expression is deleted. This results in an overlapping of the properties of resultative and passive.

2.3. Progressive and resultative

The term **progressive** is used here in a broad sense to denote a temporary ongoing action or state at the moment of utterance or some other relevant moment. The meanings of progressive and RES share the feature of **homogeneous duration**, the former lacking, needless to say, prior reference (see § 8.3.).

3. The resultative form

3.1. Non-combined and combined forms

A resultative can (a) be expressed by a special form not used in any other function, or (b) share its form with some other category or categories. The former case is referred to here as **non-combined** (non-polysemous) and the latter as **combined** (polysemous) **resultative**. The resultative and non-resultative meanings of a combined marker may be distributed among different verbs (cf. Chinese (46) and (47)) or within one and the same verb (cf. English (1), (44a)).

In Japanese, the marker of P-resultative *-te a-ru* (which involves intransitivisation) is non-combined (see (23), (43), (48b)), while the S-/A-resultative marker *-te i-ru* is used in four meanings: (i) resultative, (ii) progressive, (iii) perfect, and (iv) secondary A-resultative (see (24), (50), (25), (49)).

3.2. Morphological types of resultative forms

Cross-linguistically, resultative forms can be periphrastic or bound (simple). Here is a list of the most common morphological types of these forms (a language may have more than one form).

(1) Periphrastic resultative forms, with verbs meaning 'to be', 'to have', etc. commonly used as auxiliaries:
(a) "(perfective) converb + auxiliary", as in Japanese (23), Archi (31), Uzbek, Abkhaz, Mongolian, Nivkh, dialectal Russian (4b), (5b), (6b), etc.;

(b) "(perfective) participle + auxiliary", as in English (1c), Armenian (13b), Mongolian, Hindi (39), German (34) and (43a), Russian (45), Georgian (3c), Lithuanian (41), (43), etc.;
(c) root reduplication + copula:

(14) Ewe (K. Agbodjo, p.c.)
(a) *tu* 'to close'
(b) *le tutu* 'is closed'.

(2) Bound resultative forms:
(a) marked with an affix, as in Nivkh (8d), (33) and (35), Chukchi (15b), Selkup (20—22), Chinese (30b), also in Eskimo, Uzbek, Tongan, etc.;

(15) Chukchi
(a) *vakʔo-* 'to sit down' →
(b) *vakʔo-tva-* 'to sit, be seated';

(b) containing two affixes, mostly those of the passive and past tense (including perfect), as in Evenki (29c), (36), also in Arabic, etc.; as a rule, this is a polysemous form;
(c) with root reduplication (without a copula), cf.:

(16) Efik (Welmers 1973: 336)
(a) *nă-* 'to lie down' →
(b) *ná-nà-* 'to be lying down';

(d) reduplication of the initial consonant, as in Ancient Greek (active and middle Perfect):

(17) A. Greek (Perel'muter 1988: 277, 280)
(a) *lagkhánō* 'to get (possession of)'
(b) *lé-logkhe* 'he possesses (sth)';

(18) (a) *peíthō* 'to convince'
(b) *pé-poitha* 'I believe';

(e) agreement alternation, cf.:

(19) Ket (Kreinovič 1968: 42, 248—52)
(a) *kassat* **d-a-v-oɣon**
shoe.sole I-PRES-it-attach
'I am mending a shoe sole'
(b) *kassat* **a-v-oɣon**
shoe.sole PRES-it-attach
'The shoe sole is mended'.

3.3. Marking of syntactic types

Two cases are distinguished here.

(1) **Identical marking** for all the syntactic types: this seems to be the most common case across languages, attested in Chinese, Nivkh, Chukchi, Hausa, Hindi, Southern Paiute, Ancient Greek, Abkhaz, some Russian dialects (see (4), (5), (6)); cf. the use of

the suffix -*mpə*- (after vowels) /-*pə*- (after consonants) in Selkup:

(20) Selkup (A. Kuznecova, p. c.)
      P-resultative
      (a) *tu-qo* 'to close' (tr)
      (b) *tu-**mpə**-qo* 'to be closed';

(21) S-resultative
      (a) *cu-qo* 'to melt' (intr)
      (b) *cu-**mpə**-qo* 'to be melted';

(22) A-resultative
      (a) *orqəl-qo* 'to grasp'
      (b) *orqəl-**pə**-qo* 'to hold'.

Identical marking has a functional explanation: it is due to the fact that in all the three cases the derived subject is identical with that underlying constituent which is the most affected by the previous action. In the case of S-resultatives it is the only constituent, and in P- and A-resultatives it is the most affected one (see Comrie 1981: 66−71).

(2) **Special marking** for P-resultatives; thus in Japanese the P-resultative differs from both S- and A-resultatives in the choice of the auxiliary (*a-ru* and *-i-ru* respectively in combination with a converb in *-te/-de*). Sometimes, the P-resultative marker is supplemented by the passive suffix (see (43); cf. also Armenian: case (i) in § 8.1.1.):

(23) Japanese: P-resultative
      (a) *kake-ru* 'to hang' (tr)
      (b) *kake-**te ar**-u* 'to be hanging';

(24) S-resultative
      (a) *sin-u* 'to die'
      (b) *sin-**de i**-ru* 'to be dead';

(25) A-resultative
      (a) *ki-ru* 'to put on (clothes)'
      (b) *ki-**te i**-ru* i. 'to be wearing'
                          ii. 'to be putting on'
                          (Jacobsen 1982: 378).

Lithuanian also belongs here: the P-resultative is rendered by the passive form (like in English), while the S- and A-resultatives formally coincide with the perfect active form (see (40)). In Aleut, P-resultatives are marked with the suffix *-ĝi-*, and *S*- and A-resultatives with the suffix *-x̂ta-* (see Golovko 1988: 185).

3.4. Resultative in relation to other categories

The most common cases here seem to be the following. (1) A resultative form is part of the system of tense forms; a likely case is Archi where it is called the perfect. (2) It is one of the voice forms; this may be the case in German. (3) It is one of the members of a special category, neither tense nor voice; this seems to be the case in pre-literary Ancient Greek where the perfect (resultative form) was in opposition to the non-perfect (dynamic form). (4) It is one of the functions of a polysemous form entering into either the voice, the aspect, or the tense system as in Russian, Chinese, and Selkup. (5) It occurs at a juncture of two categories; a possible example may be Evenki, where the resultative meaning is rendered by passive perfect forms (i. e. forms with a perfective participle) only.

4. Agent-oriented resultative

This syntactic type merits special attention since it is transitive and may play an important role in the evolution of the resultative into the perfect. It is a less common type than the S-resultative, while the latter is less common than the P-resultative. The direction of implication is **A-resultative** → **S-resultative** → **P-resultative** (the only exception found so far is Dogon which displays the latter two types and no A-resultative; see § 8.4.).

(1) **Lexical restrictions**. As pointed out in § 1.3., A-resultatives are typically derived from transitives which describe situations changing (mostly or exclusively) the state of the agent rather than that of the patient (cf. (6), (39c), (40c)). In this respect they are close to S-resultatives. This peculiarity is determined by the lexical meaning and/or semantic type of the object of the base verbs. Eight lexical groups can be distinguished: (1) verbs meaning 'to take', 'to lose', 'to receive'; (2) verbs meaning 'to put on (clothes)'; (3) verbs denoting motion of body parts, like 'to lower one's head'; (4) verbs denoting actions upon body parts, cf. 'to break one's leg'; (5) verbs of affinity, contact or attachment, like 'to surround', 'to follow (sb)'; (6) verbs meaning 'to eat', 'to drink'; (7) verbs of mental acquisition like 'to see', 'to learn', 'to study (sth)'; (8) verbal collocations like 'to make a mistake', 'to perform a deed', 'to win a victory', etc. (a) The first six groups share the feature of (organic) physical contact between agent and patient; (b) in group (7) the contact is "mental", and (c) in the last group the verb and direct object function as a single semantic unit and the object does not encode any semantic role.

Verbs of the first two types are not numerous in the Indo-European languages but they are quite numerous in some (East) Asian languages, therefore the A-resultative is rather common here. Thus in Nivkh type (1) comprises verbs like *ev-* 'to take', *ilk-* 'to put (sth) behind the belt', *ilm-* 'to take into one's mouth', *yaz-* 'to grasp with one's teeth', *lez-* 'to take under one's arm', *yin-* 'to put on one's shoulders', *řik-* 'to take into one's arms', *řo-* 'to take into one's hands', etc. The lists of transitives from which A-resultatives can be formed are astonishingly similar across languages. This applies to languages such as Japanese, Korean, Chinese, Hindi, Hausa, Nivkh, Akkadian.

(2) **Expansion of the lexical base**. Sometimes resultatives may denote putting a thing into a place that belongs to the agent (rather than is on him) or is accessible to him, i.e. situations like "There is a picture in *his* room", "He has a pen in *his* pocket", "He has a book on *his* desk". These cases involve a deviation from the standard A-resultative meaning, due to the expansion of the range of base verbs.

(26) Evenki (I. Nedjalkov, p. c.)
Omōlgi evikēn-me tadū
boy   toy-ACC   there
d'ajū-ča-ča-n
hide-STAT-PAST-3.SG
'The boy kept a toy hidden there.'

The role of the subject referent as possessor diminishes here and its role as agent becomes more prominent. Therefore it is highly probable that the resultative could develop into transitive (plu)perfect via A-resultatives, a type that is transitive and involves no valency change.

(3) **Secondary A-resultative**. This type presents another possible way of a resultative developing into a perfect. The principal case is the one considered in (1) above, where the result of a prior action affects the agent in the first place, due to the lexical meaning of the verb and/or the semantic type of object. In the secondary A-resultative the state expressed by the P-resultative or, even, S-resultative happens to be important for the person who is in some way involved in the resultant state. This person can be loosely called **possessor**. The possessor may or may not be the agent of the prior action and surfaces either as subject or some other constituent. Accordingly, the subject and non-subject subtypes of the secondary A-resultative that differ syntactically are distinguished: they are types "A has B" and "B is in A's possession".

(3.1) The **subject type** of secondary A-resultative is exemplified by (27d), where the agent is not known:

(27) Slovak (Isačenko 1960: 373)
(a) *X uvari-l   polievku*
    X cook-PAST soup
    'X has cooked soup'
(b) *Polievka je uvare-n-á*
    soup   is cook-PASS-F
    'The soup is ready'
(c) *Otec má polievku*
    father has soup
    'Father has (some) soup'
(d) *Otec **má** polievku **uvarenú***
    'Father has the soup cooked'.

This variety of A-resultatives has developed into the perfect in the Romance and Germanic languages.

(3.2) The **non-subject type**, where the possessor surfaces as an oblique object (*u menja* lit. 'on/at me'):

(28) Russian
(a) *U menja vzja-ty   bilet-y*
    at me   take-PAST.PTCP tickets-NOM
    'I've got tickets.'

An oblique object here has a tendency to develop into the surface subject. This type of resultatives has developed into the ergative perfect in the Indo-Iranian languages (see, e. g., Pirejko 1979: 481−88). This course of development seems to characterize the northern Russian dialects.

5. Resultative proper and statives

In this section, the term **resultative** is used in its narrow sense (cf. § 1.2.) and is opposed to the term **stative**. Four types of relations between the two categories are possible.

(1) **There are both resultatives and statives, each with a special marker**. In this case the resultative tends to have "heavier" marking than the stative. Besides, statives tend to comprise a closed set. Thus in Georgian and Uzbek their number does not exceed 70. In Evenki (about 200 statives), the stative marker is *-ča-/-če-/-čo* (see (29b)), the resultative being marked by a combination of two suffixes, passive *-v-/-p-* and perfective participle marker *-čā-/-če-/-čō-* which forms perfects with the copula *bi-* 'to be' omitted in the 3rd p. (for Georgian see (3)):

(29)   Evenki (I. Nedjalkov, p. c.)
   (a) *uj-* 'to tether'
   (b) *uju-ča-* 'is tethered'
   (c) *uj-v-čā-* 'is tethered'.

(2) **There is only a stative marker**. This is the case in Chinese and in Chukchi. As the stative form does not indicate if there has been any prior action or not, it can be used to express resultant states as well (see § 1.3. and (15b)).

(30)   Chinese (S. Jaxontov, p. c.)
   (a) *Tāmen bǎ méi zai zhuāng chē*
       they BA coal on load cart
       shang le
       top PERF
       'They loaded the coal on the cart'
   (b) *chē shang zhuāng-zhe méi*
       cart top load-STAT coal
       'The cart is loaded with coal.'

(3) **There is only a resultative marker**. This may be the case in Archi where the resultative marker is the suffix *-li* of a terminative converb and the auxiliary *-i*:

(31)   Archi (Al. Kibrik, p. c.)
       NoIš zabollir-ši ebt'ni-li b-i
       horse fence-ALL tie-CONV CL-be
       'The horse is tied to the fence.'

(4) **A marker is resultative with some verbs and stative with other verbs**. This is the case in Russian, German, English and Arabic, where the stative meaning is characteristic of quasi-resultatives (cf. *was opened* in (1b) and *is surrounded* in (12b)).

6. Principal resultative meanings

The following semantic distinctions are relevant, in the first place, for languages with a developed system of resultatives (as a kind of grammatical category). These distinctions can also serve as a semantic background for resultatives in those languages where they are attested only for some semantic subclasses of verbs.

Resultative meanings can be of two types, specific and general.

A **specific-resultative** meaning implies that the observable state of an entity allows us to deduce the particular action or process that has brought it about. For instance, if something is "cooked" or "tied" we can deduce that someone has cooked or tied it first.

In the case of **general-resultative** meaning the speaker describes the state of an entity through an action which he has witnessed or deduced. Thus, we can assert that a person is killed only if we know that someone has killed him, while the body may bear no signs of inflicted death. This meaning is characteristic of resultatives derived from verbs of "non-physical" actions and those which result in destruction or disappearance of the patient. It is a feature of resultatives proper, while statives cannot have it. Thus,

(32)   *Das Geld ist gestohlen.*

means "The money is not where is should be, and I know (or at least suppose) that someone has stolen it".

6.1. Specific-resultative meanings

Three subtypes can be distinguished.

(1) Resultatives denoting **observable states**. They are attested in all the languages, and they are often the prevalent type (cf. (1c), (3b), (6b), etc.). In Nivkh, nearly all the resultatives seem to be of this type. It is interesting to note that the resultative form of some verbs of destruction denotes a kind of "intermediate" state resulting from an action which has not been brought to an end (if it were, the resultant state would be unobservable); cf.:

(33)   Nivkh (P-resultative)
       Arak ra -ɣəta-d'
       vodka drink -RES-FIN
       'The vodka is not quite finished.'

(2) Resultatives of **temporary state. Reversible** resultatives. They denote states that can be discontinued. The range of these resultatives limits the range of those that express observable states. They can be termed **reversible**, as opposed to those of irreversible states. They are typical of Chinese and Mongolian where resultatives are not formed from verbs with the meanings 'to fry', 'to tear', 'to wipe (up)', 'to break', 'to build', etc.

(3) Resultatives expressing **position in space** of one thing relative to another **in physical contact** with it. This feature implies the above two and limits the number of potentially possible resultatives. They are bivalent and derive from trivalent verbs. They are particularly numerous, if not the most numerous, in Chinese. They can be sometimes replaced by verbs of being (somewhere); e. g., (30b) is interchangeable with the sentence meaning 'Their reeds are in the boat'. Bivalent locative statives are typical of Georgian, Evenki, etc. (see (3b), (29), (31)).

6.2. General-resultative meanings

States expressed by "specific" resultatives can be defined without reference to the previous action (cf. '(is) leashed' = '(is) on a leash', '(is) nailed' = '(is) held by nails', '(is) broken' = '(is) in pieces', etc.). States expressed by "general" resultatives, by contrast, do not lend themselves to such paraphrasing; cf. (30b) and (34):

(34) *Die Thesen sind gebilligt.*
'The theses are approved of'.

(For a detailed survey of general-resultative meanings on the basis of German data see Litvinov & Nedjalkov 1988: 58—92.)

6.3. Implicational hierarchy

If a language has resultatives of unobservable states (see § 6.2.) it also has resultatives of observable states (see § 6.1.). Within the latter type, the implicational hierarchy corresponds to the order of consideration: 1) observable states → 2) reversible states → 3) position in space.

7. Restrictions on resultative formation

Formation of resultatives is subject to a number of restrictions.

(1) **Lexical restrictions**: rigid and non-rigid. These two main types of restrictions are imposed by the two basic types of resultative meanings, specific and general. In some languages with **specific-resultative** meanings, it seems possible to give a (nearly) complete list of resultatives.

In languages with **general-resultative** meanings a necessary condition is terminativity, though not all terminatives produce resultatives. For instance, Norwegian and Armenian seem to have weaker restrictions on resultative formation than German. Thus in German the P-resultative form *ist getötet* 'is killed' is hardly ever used and requires a very special context, while its Norwegian and Armenian counterparts *er drept* (← *drepe*) and *spanv-ač e* (← *span-el*) respectively are quite common. On the whole, in languages with lax restrictions on the range of lexical meanings it is rather hard to demarcate the boundaries of possible restrictions.

(2) **Violation of restrictions** imposed by terminativity. Pragmatic factors may determine formation of resultatives from non-terminative verbs. Thus, such events as "to cry" and "to work" do not necessarily produce resultant states "tear-stained (in tears)" and "tired", but such resultatives occur in quite a number of languages: in Nivkh, Evenki, Abkhaz, Georgian, etc.; cf.:

(35) Nivkh
to- 'to cry' → *to-ɣəta-* 'tear-stained' (cf. (8d), (33));

(36) Evenki
soŋo- 'to cry' → *soŋo-p-čō* 'tear-stained' (cf. 29c)).

(3) **Syntactic restrictions**. Some languages lack one or another of the syntactic types of resultatives. Thus in Standard Russian there is no A-resultative, and in Dogon there seems to be no P-resultative.

(4) **Tense-aspect restrictions**. The probability of tense forms of the resultative is described by the implication: future → past → present tense. Thus in Archi instead of 'he will sit' a form meaning 'he will sit down' is used. In Abkhaz and Akkadian the tense-aspect paradigm of statives is markedly less developed than that of dynamic predicates. The past tense of a resultative may change its meaning in comparison with the present in some languages (Archi, Dogon, Russian; see (45) and § 8.4.).

(5) **Negation restrictions**. As negation points to the absence of the state named and, therefore, to the absence of a prior action, an indication of the latter action can be the only possible or, at least, preferable way of expressing a resultant state. For instance, in Chinese instead of the form meaning '(is) not closed', *méi guān* '(they) did not close' is used. Resultatives in Nivkh, Mongolian and Yukaghir do not take negation, either.

8. Polysemy of resultative markers

8.1. Resultative and perfect

8.1.1. Patterns across languages

Four types of linguistic situation are possible: (a) a language may have neither a perfect nor a resultative; (b) a language may have a perfect and no special resultative form; (c) a language may have a resultative form only (e. g. Nivkh, Evenki, Chinese, Ket, Asiatic Eskimo, etc.); (d) a language may have both resultative and perfect (Hindi, Armenian, Lithuanian, Chukchi, etc.).

In the latter case, which alone is of interest here, three variants are possible: (i) each category has distinct marking (Armenian (13),

(37), Chukchi); (ii) the resultative may share the same marking with the perfect in all the syntactic types (see Hindi (40)) or (iii). The S- and A-resultative share their marking with active perfect, and P-resultative with passive perfect (see Lithuanian (40b−c) and (40a) respectively); (iv) it may share its marking with perfect only in some of the syntactic types (see Japanese (48b) and (49ii).

Case (i): In Armenian, the perfect and resultative are formed with participles in *-el* and *-ač* respectively plus auxiliary *em* (as a rule, the P-resultative also contains the passive marker *-v-*):

(37)   Armenian (N. Kozinceva, p. c.)
   (a) *gr-el e* 'has written'
       gr-[v]-ač e 'is written'
   (b) *nst-el e* 'has sat down'
       nst-ač e 'is sitting'.

The resultative can in principle have all the (seven) tense-aspect forms. In the following example the perfect marker is the perfect participle *jeγ-el* of the copula, but person is marked on the auxiliary of the resultative:

(38)   Armenian (N. Kozinceva, p. c.)
       Na nst-ač e jeγ-el
       'He has been sitting (but not any longer).'

Case (ii): In Hindi, the perfect and resultative are both expressed by a perfective participle (in (39a) *-ā* is F.SG) of the lexical verb + copula *honā*, provided that the optional perfective participle *huā* is absent; the three syntactic types look as follows:

(39)   Hindi
   (a) *likhā hai*   i. 'has written'
                    ii. 'is written'
   (b) *baiṭhā hai* i. 'has sat down'
                    ii. 'is sitting'
   (c) *pahnā hai*   i. 'has put on'
                    ii. 'is wearing'.

In (39a) and (39c) the perfect and resultative differ syntactically: in (39a) the P-resultative is intransitive while the perfect is transitive; in (39c) both are transitive but the perfect has an ergative construction, and the A-resultative a nominative one. In (39b) both are intransitive and the interpretation may be determined by context; in this case the more common reading is ii. 'is sitting', and the perfect reading i. 'has sat down' may be indicated by an adverb meaning 'just', and the like.

Case (iii): In Lithuanian, passive perfect and P-resultative are expressed by a passive perfective participle (marked by the suffix *-t-*) and copula (usually omitted in the present tense), while the active perfect and S-/A-resultative are rendered by an active perfective participle with a copula; cf.:

(40)   Lithuanian (E. Geniušienė, p. c.)
   (a) *[yra] parašy-t-a*
       i. 'has been written'
       ii. 'is written'
   (b) *[yra] atsisėd-ęs* i. 'has sat down'
                           ii. 'is sitting'
   (c) *[yra] apsivilk-ęs* i. 'has put on'
                           ii. 'is wearing'.

Naturally enough, these resultatives cannot be used in the perfect form.

8.1.2. Genetic relationship

The possibility that verb forms expressing (1) resultant states (often termed statal perfect) could develop into forms expressing (2) actions that have continuing relevance for the subsequent period of time (actional perfect) and, further on, into (3) aorists or preterites, has been repeatedly pointed out in the literature. Evolution of resultative into perfect is determined by the loss (to a certain degree and in various combinations) of the features discussed in § 2.1., viz. lexical restrictions, valency change, the meaning of state as an aspectual characteristic of a verb form. Four main types of relations between resultative and perfect are attested.

(1) **Resultative with no properties of the perfect**. This is the state of things in Nivkh and it seems to be characteristic of the pre-literary Ancient Greek Active Perfect.

(2) **Perfect with no properties of the resultative**. This is the case in English and Uzbek, where the perfect has no features considered under § 2.1. But this is not to say that a perfect (or some other verbs form) cannot occur in a typically resultative context.

(3) **Resultative with properties of the perfect.** This is observed in a number of Russian dialects in which the prevalent form of resultative is the converb in *-šil-vši* (see (4), (5), (6)). This form is in the process of acquiring perfect features: this is evident in the extended lexical base, viz. non-terminative verbs, such as 'to be', 'to be ill', 'to walk', 'to know', 'to love', etc.

(4) **Perfect with properties of the resultative**. This type, the most controversial of the four, can be illustrated by Lithuanian data, where verbs are used in the perfect without restrictions and generally render meanings typical

of English perfects, but unlike the latter they are also used in the resultative meaning and take adverbials of duration; cf.:

(41) Lithuanian (E. Geniušienė, p. c.)
Jis [yra] mir-ęs
i. 'He has died' (perfect if, for instance, we add *kątik* 'just')
ii. 'He is dead' (S-resultative, if we add *jau metai* 'already for a year').

8.2. Resultative and passive

(1) The greatest formal and semantic proximity between resultatives and perfects is observed in intransitive verbs (cf. (41)), while resultatives (excepting A-resultatives, which are not numerous; see § 4.) and perfects from transitive verbs differ syntactically (see 3) in § 2.1.; cf. (39a)). In the case of resultatives and passives, the reverse is true. Both forms from intransitives here are unlikely to have any points of similarity, either formally or semantically.

As regards resultatives and passives of transitive verbs, they often have the same expression, the passive form being used to express the resultative meaning (in grammars, the latter case is usually called **statal passive** and is opposed to **actional passive**). Moreover, not infrequently, if they are not combined and differ formally, resultatives and passives "compete" with one another in the sense that they can be interchangeable in certain contexts, the differences in the overall meaning being insignificant or very subtle. This is particularly common in cases where the passive occurs in the perfect, as this form usually implies the present tense of a resultative, cf.:

(42) P-resultative
 (a) *Das Glas ist halb geleert.*
 (b) *Das Glas ist geleert worden.*

The likeliest interpretation for (42a) is that the speaker has done it himself, whereas in (42b) someone other than the speaker has done it.

(2) **Relationship between resultatives and passives across languages**. Three types of linguistic situation are possible: (a) a language may possess the passive and no resultative; (b) a language may possess the resultative and no passive (here belong Nivkh, Asiatic Eskimo, Chukchi, Archi, Ket, etc.); (c) a language may have both categories.

In the latter case (i) each category may have distinct marking or (ii) the P-resultative may share its marking with passive.

Case (i): The two forms may be entirely different, as in Mongolian, or they may partly coincide, in which case the common part is a form of the base verb and the auxiliaries are different, as in Hindi, Spanish, Norwegian, German (cf. (44b)), etc. Armenian (see (37a)) is more complicated in this respect, as a P-resultative form may contain a passive marker as well (to emphasize the valency shift). Similar instances are registered in the specialist literature on Japanese, and they are accepted by some native speakers; cf.:

(43) Japanese (M. Shibatani, p. c.)
Denwa-mo sumi-ni
telephone corner-DAT
kakus-are-te at-ta
hide-PASS-CONV be-PAST
'The telephone was hidden in the corner'.

Case (ii): This is encountered in Russian, Arabic, English, French, Lithuanian, Evenki, etc. Compare the following English example taken from Jespersen (1924: 274), where the same form is used both as resultative and passive, and its German equivalent, where they are formally distinct:

(44) (a) *When I came in at five, the door **was shut**, but I do not know when it **was shut**.*
 (b) *Als ich um fünf kam, **war** die Tür **geschlossen**, aber ich weiß nicht, wann sie **geschlossen wurde**.*

The probability of resultative interpretation of passive forms diminishes from the present to past to future tense. Besides, in Russian the forms in question may differ in combinability with actional adverbials: the past and future tense forms collocate with them, as in (45a), while the present tense form (with the copula omitted) is not quite acceptable, which points to its preferable resultative interpretation:

(45) Russian
 (a) *Dver' byla/budet bystro zakryta*
 'The door was/will be quickly shut'
 (b) *?Dver' bystro zakryta*
 'The door is quickly shut'.

(For a detailed analysis of actualisation of resultative and passive meanings of combined forms in Russian and other Slavic languages see Knjazev (1989: 82—217)).

(3) It seems likely that the resultative is historically an older category not only in the opposition "resultative:perfect", but also in the

opposition "resultative:passive". Evidence in support of this claim is to be found in some works on the history of German.

8.3. Resultative and progressive

Verbal forms with the resultative and progressive meanings of the same marker are encountered in many languages: Chinese, Japanese, Uzbek, Balkar, Mongolian, Iroquoian (Chafe 1980: 43–9), etc. A resultative marker homonymous with an expression of progressive may be used alongside another which may be a more important means of expression. Thus, in Chinese the resultative marker *zhe* (see (46b)) may also mark the progressive meaning, its principal marker being the auxiliary *zài*, cf. (47a) and (47b). It should be noted that the suffix *zhe* acquired the progressive meaning quite recently.

(46)   Chinese (S. Jaxontov, p. c.)
    (a) *guà* 'to hang' (tr)
    (b) *guà-zhe* 'to hang' (intr);

(47) (a) *Ta chī-zhe fàn* 'He is dining'
    (b) *Ta zài chī fàn* 'He is dining'.

Actualisation of the progressive meaning may be dependent on non-terminativity of the base verb (cf. (47a) and (48), (24) and (50)), and in the case of a terminative transitive verb it may be determined by retained transitivity and/or context; cf. (49) which, unlike (48b) which is a P-resultative, allows three readings: i) progressive, ii) perfect, iii) secondary A-resultative (see also (23), (25)). If we take into account the fourth meaning of the marker *-te i-ru* mentioned above (see the S-resultative in (24)), we obtain a very special case of polysemy.

(48)   Japanese
    (a) *Kare wa denki o tuke-ta*
        'He switched on the lights'
    (b) *Denki ga tuke-te ar-u*
        'The lights are switched on';

(49)   Japanese (Jacobsen 1982: 376)
    Kare wa denki o tuke-te i-ru (tr)
    i. 'He is turning the lights on'
    ii. 'He has turned the lights on'
    iii. 'He keeps the lights turned on.'

(50)   Japanese
    (a) *nom-u* 'to smoke'
    (b) *non-de i-ru* 'to be smoking'.

8.4. Other cases of polysemy

There are also some less common cases of polysemy involving other meanings which seem to be less intimately related to the resultative meaning, and similar patterns of polysemy recur in unrelated languages. Most likely, the related meanings are derivatives of the resultative meaning. (The latter meaning itself may in its turn have descended from forms with a perfective meaning.) The cases given below are of interest for the theory of unidirectionality, but at the same time they raise difficulties for explanation within the framework of this theory.

Resultative forms can express the following meanings in the languages named.

Dogon (S- and A-resultatives only): 1) inferential (visible trace of the prior event) and 2) experiential, if used in the past tense (Plungian 1988: 481–93).

Yukaghir: 1) passive, 2) inferential, 3) previous action (with a post-position), 4) advance of a transitive subject to focus position (in this case a verb acquires the simple past tense meaning) (Maslova 1992: 77–106).

Aleut (P-resultative is non-polysemous): 1) secondary A-resultative, 2) experiential meaning (in which case the suffix is repeated), 3) the meaning of two-directional motion ('to go somewhere and return') (Golovko 1988: 191–6).

Nanai: the meaning of two-directional motion.

Nivkh: periphrastic resultative forms (converb + copula) express the progressive; bound forms (converb without a copula) are used to express 1) the meaning of previous action with continuing relevance for the subsequent period of time (the syntactic structure in this case is retained); 2) intensity (Nedjalkov & Otaina 1988: 147–9).

Evenki and Selkup: in these languages the resultative suffix is materially identical (hopefully, not accidentally) with that of the past tense; both markers may co-occur in the same (past tense of a resultative) verb form, which makes this a case of homonymy mentioned here with reservations. Compare Evenki *d'ajū-ča-ča-n* 'kept hidden' in (26) and Selkup *orqəl-pə-mpa-tə* 'held' (cf. *orqəl-pə-* 'to hold' in (22b); E. Helimski, p. c.). This case of homonymy is probably a diachronic continuation of the polysemy of the resultative and perfect (see § 8.1.).

9. The agentive complement (AC) with Patient-oriented resultatives

(1) **The AC across languages**. The AC is a constituent of a derived structure which encodes (or can encode) the subject referent of

the corresponding active construction, whatever its semantic role (see (51)). In the majority of our sample languages outside the Indo-European family, an AC cannot be used with P-resultatives. This is true for a number of languages which have (1) the resultative and no passive: Eskimo, Chukchi, Ket, Nivkh; (2) both passive and non-combined resultative: Mongolian, Japanese, and Aleut in which an AC does not occur with the passive, either; (3) a resultative combined with passive: Arabic, Uzbek and (Indo-European) Latvian (in the latter two languages an AC does not usually occur in passives, either). In Nivkh, for instance, on hearing a sentence meaning 'The cups are washed up' you cannot ask "by whom?". This is also the case in Archi. In Georgian, an AC cannot be used with statives but it can occur with resultatives. Characteristically, most of the languages mentioned in which the P-resultative does not allow an AC lack emotive and contact quasi-resultatives (see § 1.4.). For languages with both passives and resultatives, an implication can be suggested: if an AC is excluded with passives it is also excluded with resultatives. The reverse is not necessarily true.

Since an AC practically does not occur with special-resultative meanings, the following concerns general-resultative meanings.
(2) Semantic types of AC with P-resultatives. Two types of AC can be distinguished by the feature "the AC referent does not participate in the (resultant) state".
(2.1) An AC lacking this feature can be termed **dynamic**. It can be a) **canonical** and b) **non-canonical**.
(a) A canonical AC refers to an active agent, usually human:

(51) (a) *Ich kann Ihnen ein Buch darüber geben, es ist **von einem Arzt** verfasst.*
(b) *Dieses Buch hat **ein Arzt** verfasst.*

The most common examples are those in which an AC acquires a kind of **qualitative force**, as it describes the subject referent: the **meaning** of (51a) **is to show who is the author of the** book and if the AC is deleted the sentence will make little sense, because if it were not written it would not have existed.
(b) A non-canonical AC refers to an active force, e. g., animals, machines, an explosion, flood, vermin, etc. The referent can usually be inferred from an observable state; e. g.:

(52)   *Das Ufer war **vom Vieh** zerstampft.*

(2.2) The referent of a **static** (quasi-agentive) AC does participate in the (resultant) state. Two semantic sub-types can be distinguished: a) emotive-causal AC, as in (53), and b) contact-locative AC, as in (54), which are related mostly to the types of bivalent quasi-resultatives (emotive and contact; see 2.2) in § 1.6.4.):

(53)   *Ich war **von Ihrem Schicksal** erschüttert.*
(54)   *Die Stadt war **vom Feind** besetzt.*

The four semantic variants of AC are listed here in the order of diminishing agentive force and, accordingly, increasing probability of their occurrence with P-resultatives (or quasi-resultatives) (for details, see also Litvinov & Nedjalkov 1988: 148–185).

10. Abbreviations

AC	agentive complement
ALL	allative
A-resultative	agent-oriented resultative
CL	noun class
FIN	marker of finite verb
P-resultative	patient-oriented resultative
PREV	preverb
RES	resultative
S-resultative	subject-oriented resultative
STAT	stative
TH	thematic suffix

11. References

Anderson, Stephen R. 1977. "Comments on the paper by Wasow". In: P. W. Culicover et al. (eds.) *Formal Syntax*. New York, etc.: Academic Press Inc. 361–377.

Brinker, Klaus. 1971. *Das Passiv im heutigen Deutsch. Form und Funktion* (= Heutiges Deutsch. Reihe 1,2). München: Hueber, Düsseldorf: Schwann.

Chafe, Wallace L. 1980. "Consequential verbs in the Northern Iroquoian languages and elsewhere". In: K. Klar et al. (eds.). *American Indian and Indoeuropean Studies*. The Hague: Mouton, 43–9.

Comrie, Bernard. 1981. "Aspect and voice: some reflexions on perfect and passive". In: Ph. Tedeschi, A. Zaenen (eds.). *Tense and aspect.* (Syntax and Semantics, 14). New York: Academic Press, 65–78.

Dubinsky, Stanley & Simango, Silvester Ron. 1996. "Passive and stative in Chichewa: evidence for modular distinctions in grammar". *Language* 72, 749–81.

Engelhardt, Hiltraud. 1969. *Realisiertes und Nichtrealisiertes im System des deutschen Verbs. Das syn-*

taktische Verhalten des zweiten Partizips (= Göppinger Arbeiten zur Germanistik 5). Göppingen: Kümmerle.

Golovko, Jevgenij V. 1988. "Resultative and Passive in Aleut". In: Nedjalkov (1988), 185−98.

Haspelmath, Martin. 1992. "From Resultative to Perfect in Ancient Greek". *Función* 11−12: 187−224.

Helbig, Gerhard. 1980. "Zustandspassiv, *sein*-Passiv oder Stativ?" *Kopenhagener Beiträge zur germanistischen Linguistik.* Sonderband 1: *Festschrift für Gunnar Bech zum 60. Geburtstag.* København: Akademisk Forlag, 197−212.

Isačenko, Alexandr V. 1960. *Grammatičeskij stroj russkogo jazyka v sopostavlenii s slovackim. Morfologija II* [The grammatical structure of Russian in comparison with Slovak. Morphology II]. Bratislava: Vydavateľstvo Slovenskej Akadémie Vied.

Iturrioz Leza, José Luis (ed.). 1992. *Nuevos estudios sobre construcciones resultativas [= Función, 11−2].*

Jacobsen, Wesley M. 1982. "Vendler's Verb Classes and the Aspectual Character of Japanese *te-iru*". *Berkeley Linguistic Society* 8: 373−84.

Jaxontov, Sergej Je. 1988. "Resultative in Chinese". In: Nedjalkov (1988), 113−33.

Jespersen, Otto. 1924. *The Philosophy of Grammar.* New York: Allen & Unwin.

Knjazev, Jurij P. 1989. *Akcional'nost' i statal'nost'. Ix sootnošenie v russkix konstrukcijax s pričastijami na -n, -t.* [Action and State: their interrealtion in Russian constructions with *-n, -t* participles]. München: Verlag Otto Sagner.

Kozinceva, Natalia A. 1988. "Resultative, Passive and Perfect in Armenian" In: Nedjalkov (1988), 449−68.

Kreinovič, Jeruhim A. 1968. *Glagol ketskogo jazyka* [The verb in Ket]. Leningrad: Nauka.

Lemos, Cláudia T. G. de. 1987. *Ser and estar in Brazilian Portuguese. With Particular Reference to Child Language Acquisition.* Tübingen: Gunter Narr Verlag.

Litvinov, Viktor & Nedjalkov, Vladimir. 1988. *Resultativkonstruktionen im Deutschen* (= Studien zur deutschen Grammatik 34). Tübingen: Gunter Narr Verlag.

Maslova, Elena, S. 1992. "Resultative and Combined Meanings in Kolyma Yukaghir". *Función* 11−12: 77−106.

Milan, Carlo. 1985. *Das Passiv im Deutschen und Italienischen. Die Partizipialkonstruktionen mit werdenlsein und esserelvenire.* Heidelberg: Carl Winter Universitätsverlag.

Nedjalkov, Vladimir P. (ed.). 1988. *Typology of Resultative Constructions.* (Typological Studies in Languages, 12) Amsterdam/Philadelphia: John Benjamins.

Nedjalkov, Vladimir P. & Jaxontov, Sergej Je. "The Typology of Resultative Constructions". In: Nedjalkov (1988), 3−62.

Nedjalkov, Vladimir P. & Otaina, Galina A. 1988. "Resultative and continuative in Nivkh". In: Nedjalkov (1988), 135−51.

Öberg, A. B. 1907. *Über die hochdeutsche Passivumschreibung mit sein und werden. Historische Darstellung.* Lund: Berlingska Boktryckeriet.

Payne, Thomas E. 1990. "Transitivity and Ergativity in Panare". In: D. L. Payne (ed.). *Amazonian Linguistics: Studies in Lowland South American Languages.* Austin: Univ. of Texas Press, 429−53.

Perel'muter, Ilja A. 1988. "Stative, Resultative, Passive and Perfect in Ancient Greek (Homeric Greek)". In: Nedjalkov (1988), 277−87.

Pirejko, L. A. 1979. "On the Genesis of the Ergative Construction in Indo-Iranian". In: F. Plank (ed.). *Ergativity. Towards A Theory Of Grammatical Relations.* London, etc.: Academic Press, 481−88.

Plungian, Vladimir A. 1988. "Resultative and Apparent Evidential in Dogon". In: Nedjalkov (1988), 481−93.

Sapir, Edward. 1930. *Southern Paiute. A Shoshonean language.* Proceedings of the American Academy of Arts and Sciences 65, No. 1.

Schubert, Klaus. 1982. *Aktiv und Passiv im Deutschen und Schwedischen.* Diss. Kiel: Christian-Albrechts-Universität.

Trubinskij, Valentin I. 1988. "Resultative, Passive and Perfect in Russian Dialects". In: Nedjalkov (1988), 389−409.

Wasow, Thomas. 1977. "Transformations and the Lexicon". In: P. W. Culicover et al. (eds.). *Formal Syntax.* New York, etc.: Academic Press Inc., 327−60.

Welmers, William E. 1973. *African Language Structures.* Berkeley: University of California Press.

Vladimir P. Nedjalkov, Sankt Petersburg (Russia)

70. Existential constructions

1. Overview
2. Conventional analyses
3. Extended view of the existential
4. The locative proform
5. The existential and the predicate locative
6. A theoretical proposal
7. The *'have'* existential
8. 'My helicopter is'
9. Summary
10. Special abbreviations
11. References

1. Overview

The **existential** construction is a sentence in which some entity (the theme argument) is associated with some location (the location argument). The theme must be indefinite. The existential in most languages has a 'be' copula. In some languages, there is a proform in the existential. An example from English is given in (1).

(1) There is a pterodactyl in her barn.

In (1), 'a pterodactyl' is the indefinite theme, and 'her barn' is the location.

I will show in § 6.3. that the overall form of the English existential is actually anomalous, but I begin with example (1) since it has been the focus of the initial and still widely accepted analysis of the existential.

The world's languages present considerable variety of form in the construction that functions as the existential. This article will attempt to cover much of that variety. Though the form may differ, existentials all have the same semantics: they encode the relation of the two arguments and the indefinite feature noted above. Here we give a structural analysis of existentials, leaving aside pragmatic or functional explanations (for the latter type of analysis, see, e. g., Heine 1997).

In many languages, the subject of the existential is a locative phrase or is marked with some oblique case; in the examples in (2), the leftmost phrase is the subject of the existential.

(2) (a) Japanese:
kono kyooshitsu-ni denki
this classroom-DAT electric
dokei-ga arimasu
clock-NOM is
'There is an electric clock in this classroom.'

(b) Hindi:
kamree-mẽẽ aadmii hai
room.OBL-in man is.3SG
'There is a man in the room.'

(c) Russian:
na stole byla kniga
on table.LOC was book
'There was a book on the table.'

That the locative phrase is actually the subject in these languages will be demonstrated in detail in this chapter. It is the role of the locative phrase in the wider class of locative expressions in the world's languages that will establish that it is the subject of the existential construction.

In addition, some existentials contain a characteristic proform (in bold below):

(3) (a) French:
*il **y** a des chocolats sur*
3SG there have some chocolates on
la table
the table
'There are some chocolates on the table.'

(b) Italian:
***ci** sono uomini nella casa*
there are men in.the house
'There are (some) men in the house.'

(c) Palauan (Western Austronesian):
*ŋ-ŋar **er** ŋii a bilis er a*
3SG-be P 3SG NP dog P NP
sers-ek
garden-1SG
'There is a dog in my garden.'

Below I give a cross-linguistic perspective on the existential, which will show that it is universally locative. In doing so, it will be necessary to examine its relation to other locative constructions. This will yield a unified analysis of locatives which establishes the **locative paradigm**. Placing the existential within the locative paradigm will reveal the essential character of the function and syntax of the existential, for language in general as well as for individual languages.

2. Conventional analyses

This section discusses the analysis of existentials in terms of English, but applies generally (see the parallel analyses of various languages in Reuland & ter Meulen (1987), for example). In the last thirty years, several analyses of existential sentences have appeared. They may be divided roughly into two groups. In the first, an existential has an expletive (e.g. *there*) in subject position (see, inter alia, Chomsky 1981, pp. 85ff., Milsark 1974). The focus of these treatments is often an account of *there* and its correlation with the (indefinite) theme argument. In the second group, the existential and the predicate locative sentence are treated as derivationally related, thus claiming a syntactic relationship between (1) and (4) (e.g., Fillmore 1968, Kuno 1971, Lyons 1967; see also Hoekstra & Mulder (1990) for a movement analysis of the existential ("locative preposing") which contrasts Dutch and English).

(4)   The pterodactyl is in her barn.

In the first type of analysis, also informally known as *there*-insertion, the **theme** argument is assumed to be the underlying subject of the sentence. The theme moves into verb phrase, in some versions, or begins the derivation as specifier of VP in others. In either case, the subject position is empty, has no thematic role, and is filled with expletive *there* during the derivation. The expletive and the theme are often considered to be coindexed, which allows *there* to receive Case and thereby take on some of the properties of the subject: it may trigger agreement, raise, invert, and so on:

(5) (a) *There **is** a pterodactyl in her barn.*
    (b) *There **are** pterodactyls in her barn.*
    (c) ***There seem** to be pterodactyls in her barn.*
    (d) ***Is there** a pterodactyl in her barn?*

A focus of this type of analysis is the indefiniteness of the theme (see the articles in Reuland & ter Meulen 1987, including the editors' introduction). In Milsark (1974), the relation of *there* and the theme is discussed in terms of **quantification**: *there (be)* represents an existential quantifier binding a variable, which is the indefinite theme. In Safir (1982) the existential analysis reflects a generalized **definiteness effect** in which *there* is an expletive subject and the relevant properties of the sentence arise essentially from the theme. In Stowell (1978), the *there*-sentence (1) is basic and the corresponding predicate locative ((4) above) is derived from it by movement of the theme to subject; here too, *there* is expletive. In Moro (1997), as for Safir, the properties of the existential sentence arise from the theme; though Moro sees the expletive as a raised predicate rather than a subject, it is correlated to the theme, and the locative phrase is optional and an adjunct.

Analyses in this group argue that *there* has no semantic content and does not contribute to interpretation; it is licensed by (i.e. appears in the sentence by virtue of its relation to) the theme, and its number-agreement properties are also linked to the theme. It is explicitly unrelated to the locative argument. Conventionally, *there* deletes at LF or becomes an LF-affix adjoining to the theme (see, inter alia, Chomsky 1989; there are many variants on the LF-adjunction analysis; see also the various sources cited).

In the second type of analysis, the focus is on the **location** argument, rather than the relation of *there* and the theme. This type of analysis has been the minority view. In what follows, I will show that, cross-linguistically, the syntax of the existential *must* be interpreted as centering on locativity. The existential indisputably manifests indefiniteness, but as a semantic feature. That is, the syntax of these expressions does not link *there* with the indefinite theme, but rather with the location. Furthermore, I will suggest an explanation for the fact that indefinite themes are associated in the existential with a particular locative structure. Finally, we will see that an expletive subject like *there* is essentially irrelevant to the analysis of existentials.

3. Extended view of the existential

In many, perhaps most languages, the existential and the **possessive** sentence share a startling structural resemblance. Consider Russian:

(6)   Russian:
    a. *na stole   byla kniga*   existential
       on table.LOC COP book
       'There was a book on the table.'
    b. *u menja   byla sestra*   possessive
       at 1SG.GEN   COP sister
       'I had a sister.'

The existential and the possessive sentence contain the same constituents: a locative argument, a theme argument, and a copula; and the constituents appear in the same order. This suggests the working hypothesis that the location is in subject position in both the existential and the possessive. This hypothesis will receive further support as we continue our analysis.

It has long been recognized that a possessor is treated as a location in human language. Consider, for example, the fact that the possessor in many languages is marked with a preposition or given an oblique case form; more detail on its locativity is found in Freeze (1992).

The essential difference between the possessive and the existential is that the location argument in the possessive is typically [+human] while in the existential it is not. The [±human] feature of the locative argument is central to the analysis of locativity; it has at least equal weight with the [±definite] feature of the theme. Its importance can further be seen in the fact that it determines the choice of preposition, or the presence vs. absence of an overt preposition, marking the subject. For example, Russian *u* marks a [+human] possessive subject, as seen in (6b), while the [−human] locative subject takes some other preposition. Note that if a [+human] location is not interpreted as a possessor, the sentence need not be possessive (e. g., *'There's a flea on Mary.'*), though it will still be existential.

The contrasting value of this feature is responsible for the differences in function. Except for the [±human] feature, *the possessive and the existential are the same structure* in these languages (examples (8) through (11) display four more languages that are like Russian in this way). In § 6. I will show that they are abstractly the same structure in all languages. In the face of the structural identity of the existential and the possessive, we would predict other morphological commonalities. This is borne out in the fact that, in many languages, the existential and the possessive have the same copula form, even though other copulas may exist in the language. A sampling appears in the list below; this list is of course not exhaustive:

(7)   Sampling of locative copulas

Chichewa (Bantu)	*li*	similarly for other Bantu
Chinese	*you*	
Finnish	*on*	
French	*avoir*	
Hebrew	*yeʃ*	
Hindi	*hoona*	
Japanese	*ar-/i-*	
K'ekchi?	*wan*	similarly for other Mayan
Lezgian	*awa*	
Modern Greek	*exei*	
Navajo	*hóló̜*	
Palauan	*ŋar*	
Portuguese	*ter*	
Quechua	*tiya*	
Russian	*est'*	
Scots Gaelic	*bi*	
Tongan	∅	similarly for other Polynesian
Shanghainese	*yu*	
Tagalog	*may*	
Trukese	*mei*	
Turkish	*var*	
Vietnamese	*co*	
Yosondua Mixtec (Oto-Mangue)	*yo*	

Following are examples from several other disparate languages, illustrating the identity of the existential and the possessive.

(8)   Hindi (=2b)
a. *kamree-mẽẽ aadmii hai*
   room.OBL-in man   COP.3SG
   'There is a man in the room.'
b. *larkee-kee paas kuttaa hai*
   boy.OBL-GEN by   dog   COP.3SG
   'The boy has a dog.'

(9)   Tagalog
a. *may gera sa ewropa*
   COP war in Europe
   'There is a war in Europe.'
b. *may relos ang naanai*
   COP watch Art mom
   'Mom has a watch.'

(10)   Finnish
a. *pöydä-llä   on kyna*
   table-ADESSIVE COP pencil
   'There is a pencil on the table.'
b. *Liisa-lla   on mies*
   Lisa-ADESSIVE COP man
   'Lisa has a husband.'

(11)   Scots Gaelic
a. *tha min   anns a' phoit*
   COP oatmeal in   the pot
   'There is oatmeal in the pot.'
b. *tha peann aig Mairi*
   COP pen   at Mary
   'Mary has a pen.'

The examples in (6) and (8) through (11) illustrate the most widespread cross-linguistic pattern. They show that not only is the possessive sentence an existential, but in all, the semantic relationship of the location and the theme arguments is the same (for further arguments and supporting linguistic evidence, see Freeze 1992). In § 7., I will provide an explanation of possessive sentences containing a lexical 'have' copula, such as that found in English.

This section has shown that existentials and possessives are the same, except for the semantic features of the subject. So far, then, we have established one part of the evidence that the locative in a sentence like Russian (6) is the subject. Another strong support for this is found in § 8., where I describe *the possessed-theme existential*.

4. The locative proform

In the introduction to this article I mentioned that the existential in some languages has a "characteristic proform". Hereafter I will refer to it as the **locative proform**, and the structure in which it occurs the **proform existential**. The proform actually occurs in a distinct minority of languages: it is represented in Romance, a few Germanic, in Arabic and in a few Austronesian languages; it is not found in other Indo-European languages nor in a dozen other unrelated language families represented in this study. No such proform has been reconstructed for Indo-European. In Romance, these proforms are decaying to some extent. I do not include English *there* among locative proforms, for reasons which will become clear in § 6.

Languages with a proform existential include the three illustrated in (3) above: French, Italian, and Palauan. The proform also occurs in Palestinian Arabic and Tongan. These are exemplified in (12) (the proform is in boldface, glossed "P"):

(12) (a) Palestinian Arabic:
 kaan **fii** *ʔulad ʕa(la) l*
 COP.PRET.SG P boys on the
 maktab
 desk
 'There were boys on the desk.'
 (b) Tongan:
 ʔoku **ʔi ai** *ʔae kurii ʔi he*
 TNS P3SG ABS.Art dog P Art
 poopao
 canoe
 'There's a dog in the canoe.'

I will return to the question of English *there* after I establish the properties of the proform cross-linguistically. Two questions that arise with respect to the proform are: (1) is it locative? and (2) what position does it occupy?

4.1. Is it locative?

First, all such proforms are lexically locative. In Romance we find French *y* 'there', allied with Catalan *hi*, Italian *ci*, and Spanish *-y* (this form in Spanish is not synchronically analyzable). Proforms in Palauan, Arabic, and Tongan, exemplified above, are explicitly locative, since they either consist of a prepositional phrase with a third person singular complement, or a form historically derived from such a phrase: Palauan *er ŋii* 'P+3SG', Palestinian Arabic *fii* 'in it', and Tongan *ʔi ai* 'P+3SG'. Germanic expletive pronouns found in the existential are not locative (e. g., German *es*, Icelandic *βað*; Swedish *det*, all meaning 'it'); see § 6.2. on English *there* and Dutch *er*.

Second, this lexically locative proform occurs only in locative expressions, assuming that my presentation of the existential and the possessive as locative is correct. Note that the identity of the existential and the possessive, and the occurrence of the same locative copula in both, requires that the underlying structure be locative (or non-locative) for both. The association of the existential, the possessive, and the predicate locative in the next section considerably strengthens the locative analysis. On the other hand, the presence of the proform is optional from the point of view of universal grammar, and is not relevant to the syntax (though when it *is* present, it may affect the syntax; this will be shown in § 7.).

4.2. Where is it?

The locative proform is not found in SOV languages, and in other languages it obeys strict positional constraints. Where it occurs at all, it is always adjacent to inflectional elements (auxiliary or copula) and always precedes the locative phrase. Its position with respect to inflection suggests that it is a manifestation of the **second position** effect ("V2") (see Freeze and Georgopoulos 2000), and that it in some sense agrees with the locative subject of the existential.

Typically, the proform is not in subject position. It occurs in SVO languages that have empty or dummy subjects (e. g., French (see (3a) above)), and in other languages that have locative subjects in the existential/possessive. Table 70.1 will illustrate this for a representative sample of languages (p = the proform; e = empty subject; L = location; T = theme; D = dummy; subject position is aligned vertically):

70. Existential constructions

Table 70.1: Position of the existential proform:

Basic order	Language	Existential order			
			subject		
SVO	Finnish		L	COP T	
	Russian		L	COP T	
	Catalan		e	**p** COP T	
	French		D	**p** COP T	
VOS	Palauan	COP **p** T	L		
	Chamorro	COP T	L		
VSO	Pal. Arabic	COP **p** T	L		
	Tagalog	COP T	L		
SOV	Hindi		L	T COP	
	Japanese		L	T COP	

Furthermore, the proform does not have subject properties (see (5)): it does not raise, trigger agreement, and so on. Note that English *there* is excluded from this discussion, since it does act like a subject.

The lexical specification of the proform, its distribution, and the constraints on its linear position, all must be stated with reference to a locative phrase or a locative feature. The simplest and most obvious explanation is that the proform is locative. This follows naturally from the hypothesis on which the existential is locative.

5. The existential and the predicate locative

The discovery that the existential and the possessive are identical in many languages was based on cross-linguistic evidence that they share the same argument structure, copula, and constituent order. Another construction with at least the same argument structure is the **predicate locative**. Like its sister constructions, it contains a theme and a location. Example (4) is repeated here:

(4)   *The pterodactyl is in her barn.*

It has long been noticed that the theme of the existential is indefinite while that of the predicate locative is typically definite. In addition, as discussed above, the predicate locative and the existential have traditionally been associated by movement analyses ('*there*-insertion', etc.), which account for the different position of the theme in the two structures (subject in predicate locative, nonsubject in the existential). While I associate them differently, I do recognize the fact that they alternate according to the definiteness of the theme. I illustrate with the predicate locative in Russian, Hindi, and Tagalog, and repeat the existential and possessive for each language, for comparison.

(13)   Russian:
   kniga byla na stole predicate locative
   book COP on table.LOC
   'The book was on the table.'
   b. *na stole byla kniga* existential
   on table.LOC COP book
   'There was a book on the table.'
   c. *u menja byla sestra* possessive
   at 1SG.GEN COP sister
   'I had a sister.'

(14)   Hindi:
   a. *mãĩ hindustaan-mẽẽ thaa* predicate
   I India-in COP.PAST locative
   'I was in India.'
   b. *kamree-mẽẽ aadmii hai* existential
   room.OBL-in man COP.PRES
   'There is a man in the room.'
   c. *laṛkee-kee paas kuttaa*
   boy.OBL-GEN by dog
   hai possessive
   COP.PRES
   'The boy has a dog.'

(15)   Tagalog:
   a. *na sa baabaʔi ang*
   COP at woman NP
   sanggol predicate locative
   baby
   'The baby is with the woman.'
   b. *may gera sa ewropa* existential
   COP war in Europe
   'There is a war in Europe.'

c. *may relos ang naanai* possessive
   COP watch Art mom
   'Mom has a watch.'

Since the possessive is prototypically an existential with a [+human] location, the possessive should also alternate with the predicate locative. By definition, the predicate locative positions the location (usually [-human]) in the predicate. However, the alternation of the possessive with the predicate locative is more subtle, since the predicate locative typically, from a cross-linguistic viewpoint, has a [+definite] subject. (I. e., in many languages a sentence like *A boy is in the room* is ungrammatical and the content of this sentence must be expressed with an existential.) At this point I would remind the reader that the [±human] feature belongs to the locative argument, while the [±definite] feature belongs to the theme argument. The following schemata should clarify things; assume the subject is the leftmost argument:

(16) (a) predicate locative:
       THE THEME IS IN THE LOCATION.
       [+definite]   [±human]
       ?[-definite]
     (b) existential:
       IN THE LOCATION IS A THEME.
       [-human]   [-definite]
     (c) possesive:
       THE LOCATION be/has THE/A THEME.
       [+human]   [±definite]

A number of generalizations emerge from these schemata. Obviously, given the same set of underlying constituents, the choice of **subject** typically depends on distribution of certain feature-value pairs: [+definite] theme for the predicate locative, [-human] location for the existential, and [+human] location for the possessive. In this sense, as an existential, the possessive does alternate with the predicate locative. However, the two features do not strictly covary according to their ±value: if the theme is [+definite] and the possessor-location is [+human], either structure could be chosen, according to these schemata. What determines the choice appears to be a reflex of the universal linguistic tendency to foreground or subjectivize a [+human] argument, part of a more general **animacy hierarchy** that governs much linguistic phenomena. This tendency elects the possessive over the predicate locative. These facts can be illustrated in some way in practically any language; I will give only the following example:

(17)
A: "Where's my book?" [+definite] theme
B: "It's on the shelf." predicate locative, [-human] location
   or
   "I have it." possessive, [+human] location
*"The shelf has it (on it)." Or
*"It's with me." (≠ *I have it*)

Though all possession is location, not all location is possession. *Mary has a flea on her* gives Mary as the location of the flea, but not as its possessor. In *I have a knife on me*, 'on me' designates location but not necessarily possession; such expressions can also be used for alienable but not inalienable possession (see § 8.).

Interestingly, though the predicate locative alternates with the existential and the possessive, it never contains a locative proform. This is further evidence that the proform is a property of the existential, and that it is locative: the existential/possessive has a locative subject, the predicate locative does not.

To conclude this section, I propose that the three structures examined so far constitute the **locative paradigm**. They are variations on a single underlying array of elements.

I now turn to the analysis that unites these three structures, and other structures as well.

6. A theoretical proposal

This section presents a syntactic analysis of the locative paradigm. This analysis makes use of the predicate-internal subject theory as articulated for various languages by Belletti & Rizzi (1988); Fukui & Speas (1986); Georgopoulos (1991); Kuroda (1986); Koopman & Sportiche (1988); and others. The phrase structure follows the theory of Chomsky (1986). In adopting a classical Government & Binding theory framework, I do not exclude the possibility that my proposals can be presented in some other syntactic framework; note also that the tree diagrams in this section omit some nonessential detail.

6.1. The analysis

The schemata in Chomsky (1986) provide for the following minimal structure for a syntactic phrase, where X may be noun (N), verb (V), adjective (A), preposition (P), determiner (D), inflection (I), or complementizer (C). The practice is to name the various positions as follows:

(18) Phrase structure schemata (Chomsky 1986):

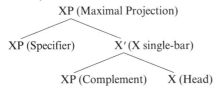

The phrase marked 'Specifier' is the conventional position of the subject.

Each of the members of the locative paradigm is derived from the single underlying structure in (19), which is composed according to (18). The subject position in this structure is empty (*e*) and is not assigned a thematic role; the predicate phrase is overtly or abstractly repositional (PP). The theme argument is the specifier of the predicate phrase and the location is the complement. I is [+locative].

(19)

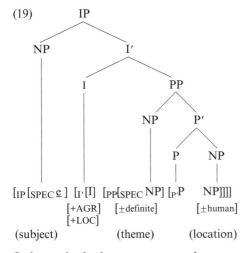

Order varies by language, as usual.

Order in the locative paradigm appears to be more rigid than other word-order-dependent syntactic phenomena. That is, even a language that appears to have more or less free word order is likely to have invariant order throughout the locatives (e. g., Szabolcsi 1981).

For our purposes, the copula arises in I and consists of morphological and syntactic features which, in the locative paradigm, includes a locative feature. I assume that the copula is given phonological form at PF, following Anderson (1982). The actual form of the copula in particular languages is subject to its usual unpredictable irregularity.

This universal underlying structure accounts for the locative paradigm as follows; refer also to the schemata in (16) for further guidance as to feature values. The reader should keep in mind that the derivations in this section apply within the (universal) grammar, not in a particular language; particular languages will instantiate various possible surface structures.

If the theme is [−definite], the locative phrase moves to the empty specifier of IP (subject position), yielding the common form of the existential; if the location in the existential is [+human], then the existential receives the possessive interpretation. If the theme is [+definite], either a predicate locative or a possessive could be derived. Typically, a [+definite] theme occurring with a [−human] location becomes subject, yielding a predicate locative. The possessive ranks the [+human] feature above a [+definite] feature, allowing for possessive structures in addition to predicate locatives. (It is possible that the entire locative paradigm is a group of rankings for subject position, an idea I won't pursue here.)

The following trees illustrate the essentials of these movements; I will first take the data from Russian (SVO):

(20) (a) Existential:

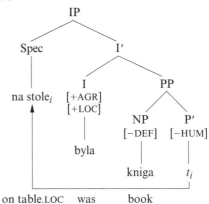

on table.LOC was book

'There was a book on the table.'

(b) Possessive:

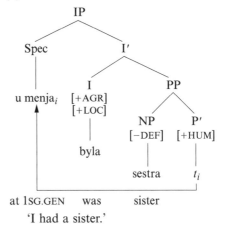

at 1SG.GEN was sister

'I had a sister.'

(c) Predicate locative:

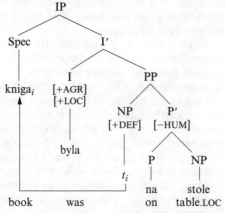

'The book was on the table.'

The same derivations are illustrated in the following three trees, this time for Hindi (Hindi is SOV); this language should make it clear that the analysis is not affected by constituent order.

(21) (a) Existential:

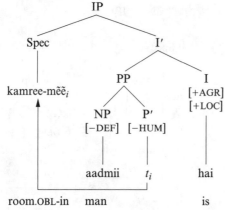

'There is a man in the room.'

(b) Possessive:

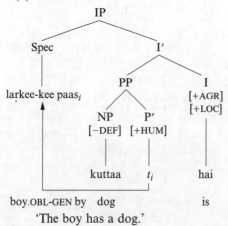

'The boy has a dog.'

(c) Predicate locative:

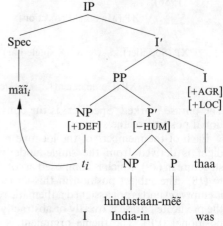

'I was in India.'

The trees for a language like Tagalog (VOS) would look essentially the same, except for the fact that the subject would be located at the right of the sentence, and the copula would be leftmost. In Tagalog, the surface form of the copula varies according to the locativity of the subject. As (15) shows, the form is *na* for a non-locative subject, and *may* for a locative subject (existential or possessive). These are both lexicalizations of the locative copula. In addition, the subject of the possessive has no overt preposition.

6.2. The proform

I now turn to the derivation of the proform existential. In essence, the proform is a lexicalization of the [+locative] feature of the copula. It is not an argument or linked to any argument. It is important to distinguish the various lexical forms of copulas, which are notoriously idiosyncratic, from the lexical form of one of its features, in this case [+locative]. The latter is always a locative proform or an unmarked third person pronoun ('it'), accompanied by a preposition (cf. § 4.1.).

Derivation of the proform existential is illustrated with French and Tongan. French has a dummy subject, a proform, and an unmoved locative phrase. This last fact may seem contradictory, since I have claimed that the existential has a locative *subject*. However, the French facts actually follow from the general analysis of the locative paradigm, as will be made clear; here I will just point out that French represents a variation on the prototypical derivation, in that it has a 'have' copula; such copulas do not have a morphologically locative subject.

(22) French proform existential:

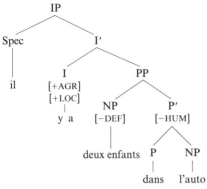

it there COP two children in the.car
'There are two children in the car.'

Since the subject of the French existential is empty, it is filled by expletive *il* '3SG'. The occurrence of *il* has no relation to the locative paradigm.

Tongan, a V-initial language, has *both* the locative proform and a locative subject in the existential; the locative copula is ø.

(23) a. Tongan proform existential:

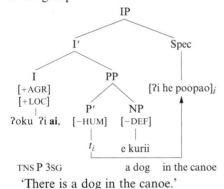

TNS P 3SG   a dog   in the canoe
'There is a dog in the canoe.'

The Tongan possessive has the same form, including the proform:

b. ʔoku ʔi **ai** ʔae faanau ʔa Sione
   TNS P 3SG   ABS.Art   GEN John

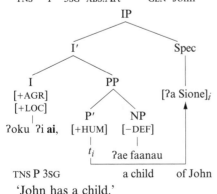

TNS P 3SG   a child   of John
'John has a child.'

The lexicalization of the [+locative] feature is unpredictable: the copula has the feature, whether or not it yields a proform. The proform has no other source in the sentence. Thus, a locative copula like Tagalog *may* is equivalent in morphosyntactic features to French *y#a* and Tongan *ʔi ai* though the Tagalog form does not show a proform.

6.3. Germanic

I give details of the Germanic case here to show the extremes of variation within the paradigm. Most Germanic existentials do not have a locative proform, but like French these languages have a non-locative expletive pronoun in subject position. This is the same expletive pronoun found in impersonal expressions throughout the rest of the language (see Freeze 1992):

(24) (a) Swedish:
       det fanns   inget postkontor i
       it find.PASS no   postoffice in
       den byn
       that town
       'There was no postoffice in that town.'
    (b) German:
       es gibt/ist ein Buch auf dem Tisch
       it gives/is a   book on the table
       'There is a book on the table.'
    (c) Icelandic:
       það eru mys í baðkerinu
       it   are mice in the-bathtub
       'There are mice in the bathtub.'

In addition, it appears that all Germanic languages have 'have' copulas in the possessive (see § 7.) and the verb agrees with the theme, as we would predict. Thus the Germanic locative paradigm seems comparatively unlocative structurally.

A few Germanic languages, e. g., English (*there*), Danish, and Dutch (*er*) have lexically locative existential proforms and they are, exceptionally, in subject position. But these few Germanic cases are not on a par with existential proforms cross-linguistically, as can be seen in the general survey contained in this chapter. Obviously these Germanic proforms are related to a feature of the locative paradigm. I assume that they have the same underlying structure as in other languages, but the subject pronoun must be linked to the locative argument by a process of predication (Williams 1980). *There* must be distinguished from the deictic *there*, which is referential and for which *here* may be substituted.

6.4. Summary of the Locative Paradigm

In our investigation of existential constructions, we have accounted for the close relations among the existential, the possessive sentence, and the predicate locative. This account amounts to a description of the **locative paradigm**, which effortlessly relates these three structures across human language. Besides the "default" existential, we find a rare alternative structure, the proform existential, and the extremely rare type exemplified by English.

A detail not yet explained is the nature of the possessive form of the existential with a 'have' copula.

7. The 'have' existential

Bach (1967), on comparing locative predications and their lexical copula forms cross-linguistically, asked why a language (e. g., English) should have different copulas in 'be' predications and 'have' predications when so many languages (e. g., Japanese) do not. Bach went so far as to term the 'have' form "pathological". Following Bach's ideas, I have distinguished the two lexical forms by referring to a **'be' copula**, on one hand, and a **'have' copula**, on the other. As a matter of fact, the existence of a separate 'have' possessive copula seems to present a problem for maintaining the general analytic integrity of the possessive sentence with the rest of the locative paradigm, which contains a 'be' copula. In this section I dispose of the problem.

Languages with a 'have' possessive are few: they include a minority of Indo-European languages: Germanic, Romance, and Persian. Add to these a precious few other languages in which the 'have' form is borrowed, or is a late development − often from a verb meaning 'hold, grasp'. Compare Spanish to Russian:

(25) (a) Spanish:
  Juan tiene caballo
  John has horse
  'John has a horse.'
 (b) Russian:
  u menja byla sestra
  at 1SG.GEN is sister
  'I had a sister.'

Here Spanish appears to have no locative 'be' copula, and no lexical preposition marks the subject, which bears nominative case. In these properties Spanish represents the general pattern of 'have' copula languages, including English. The theme is often treated as the object of 'have' in that it may bear morphological accusative case, and/or trigger object agreement. 'Have' agrees with the subject in some of these languages.

The universal locative structure in (19) also underlies the 'have' languages. Movement of the location argument to subject position may in some languages leave the preposition in the predicate phrase. The preposition then raises to I and may optionally incorporate into I. If incorporation does not take place, the theme may be appear to be the object of P. It is not, of course, because I_P is not transitive. Alternatively, P does incorporate into I, yielding what is written out morphologically as 'have', and the theme then appears to be or is reanalyzed as the object of 'have'. 'Have' is not transitive either, so both outcomes are basically intransitive. In all cases the subject is still *semantically* the location.

Note, in the Portuguese examples below, that [I_P + theme] cannot be extracted as a constituent. Portuguese has two possible possessive forms: (26a), with *está* + P, and a 'bare' location subject, or (26b), where *está* + P become *ter*, 'have':

(26) Portuguese:
 a. *o menino está com fome*
  the child is with hunger
  'The child is hungry.'
 b. *o menino tem fome*
  the child has hunger
  'The child is hungry.'

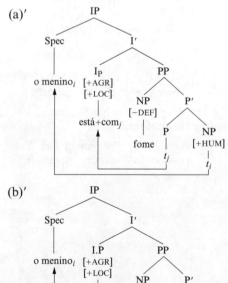

But P+theme is not a constituent:

    c. *Com que está o menino
       with what is the child
       (With what is the child?
       = What does the child have?)

The Portuguese example (26a) is a normal alternative of (26b) with *ter* 'have' (considered to be idiomatic). Thus the preposition in the (a) variant marks the location underlyingly but appears to mark the theme on the surface, as a result of reanalysis. In the (b) variant, as in English, 'be'+P is reanalyzed as a single lexical item and lexicalized as 'have'. 'Have' is always a derived form.

The difference between a language like Portuguese and a language like English is that in English the incorporation process is obligatory.

Something more should be said about the French variant (cf. (22)), which does have a locative in the predicate but also a 'have' copula in the existential. This copula probably was historically generalized to the existential, perhaps replacing 'be'. Such historical substitutions in Romance are well attested. In Spanish and Portuguese, *haber* 'have' was replaced by *tener* (Sp.) /*ter* (Port.) 'hold, grasp' in the possessive; this form in Portuguese then generalized to the existential. Portuguese still has the 'have' copula in the existential and possessive (optionally); but 'be' in the predicate locative (like French). In fact, Romance locatives show a great deal of historical structural change; little of the detail can be included here.

This solves the central mysteries of the 'have' predication: the subject does not appear to be a location, since it has no locative marking; there appears to be no locative copula, since the copula combines with P to spell out 'have'. Though this analysis does not amount to a claim that the 'have' possessive is an existential, the elements of this analysis are the same as those for the **locative paradigm** as a whole.

I will close this section by observing that the copula forms involved in the locative paradigm, 'be' and 'have', are the auxiliary forms familiar in Romance, Germanic, and also found outside of Indo-European. The analysis of their use as auxiliaries builds on the analysis given here (see, for example, Kayne 1993).

8. 'My helicopter is'

Linguists have noticed another relatively prevalent locative structure, the **possessed-theme** possessive. It at first seems exotic but upon examination it turns out to be familiar; it also turns out to be unambiguously an *existential*. Here is an example from Mayan (see Freeze 1992; this construction is also attested, inter alia, in Hindi, Turkish, Hungarian (all SOV), and Palauan (VOS)):

(27) K'ekchiʔ (Mayan):
    wan   iʃ-soʔsol-tʃ'itʃ'   li
    COP.LOC 3SG.GEN-dragonfly-metal the
    iʃq
    woman
    The woman has a helicopter.
    (Lit. 'The woman's helicopter is.')

In this structure the copula is locative, the possessor is a marked genitive (in a way characteristic of the particular language), and the (possessed) theme is subject. From the literal translation the reader can see that this sentence may actually be an existential − but an existential with apparently a single grammatical relation, the subject. In some languages having this construction, it is an alternate to the existential/possessive structure described above. In others, like K'ekchiʔ, it is the only available possessive construction. In any case, it contains all the essential elements of the locative paradigm.

Interestingly, in languages in which such morphology is overt, the theme argument even in this construction is indefinite. This fact demonstrates that the sentence is a true existential, and only the possessor can be semantically [±definite]:

(27)' ... [[the woman's] helicopter] is.
      [+def possessor] [−def theme]

Previously I have analyzed this structure as having a nominal predicate phrase (DP) rather than a PP predicate, since there is no preposition marking the location. I adopt the same analysis here (though one could be constructed using the locative structure in (19), assuming a null P). The possessor (location) is assigned to the specifier of N, whose N' is the theme. This possessed NP moves through specifier of D to specifier of I (underlying level and surface level of derivation shown; K'ekchiʔ is VOS):

(28) K'ekchi? (Maya)

(a)
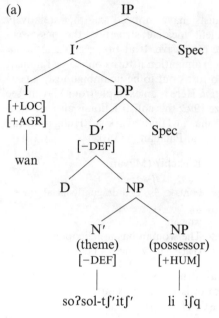
COP dragonfly-metal the woman

(b)
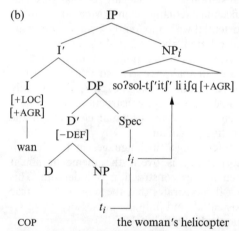
COP   the woman's helicopter

'The woman's helicopter is.'

The possessor is not necessarily definite, but this feature-value is not functional since the possessor and theme never dissociate; that is, there can be no 'have' in this construction.

Hindi is one language that has both the possessed theme-subject existential and the locative-subject existential; the former expresses inalienable possession and the latter alienable possession:

(29) Hindi:
  a. *meree doo bhaii hãi*
     my.PL two brother COP.3PL
     'I have two brothers.'
     (Lit. My two brothers are.)
  b. *laṛkee-kee paas kuttaa hai*
     boy.OBL-GEN by dog COP.3SG
     'The boy has a dog.'

Thus, in Hindi, inalienable possession has a theme subject, while alienable possession has a locative subject. This is typical of the phenomenon, though languages commonly allow arbitrary exceptions to alienable and inalienable class membership (see Freeze 1991 for more detail and discussion).

True to our analysis of the proform above, and consonant with the unity of the locative paradigm in general, it is reassuring to find that the possessed-theme structure may contain the locative proform: the Palauan (VOS) version is an example:

(30) Palauan:
  a. *ŋ-ŋar er ŋii a berruk*
     3SG-be P it NP raft.1SG
     'I have a raft.' (Lit. 'My raft is.')
  b. *ŋ-ŋar er ŋii a berrul a Sie me a Toki*
     3SG-be P it NP raft.3SG NP and
     NP
     'Sie and Toki have a raft.'
     (Lit. 'Sie and Toki's raft is.')

The possibility of the proform in this construction is further evidence that it is part of the locative paradigm, and more particularly, that it is an *existential*. Only existentials have the proform. Interestingly, the proform possessed-theme existential variant allows a critical distinction in word order. I have found that SOV languages (e. g., Japanese) have no proform existentials, and SVO languages (e. g., English) have no possessed-theme existentials. V-initial order may have both. It is necessary to recognize the V-initial type (such as Palauan) in order to bring out this evidence that the existential and the possessive are the same. As usual, the proform is in second position, preceding the subject.

The evidence of the possibility of the proform, taken together with the evidence that the theme must be indefinite in this structure, is conclusive: it is an existential.

9. Summary

A study of the existential turns out to implicate a surprising array of structures which were not previously considered related. The predicate locative and the existential have long been suspected of participating in some sort of regular pattern, but the possessive sentence with 'have' seemed unlocative and therefore unrelated. The locative paradigm, in unifying these structures, establishes a much wider linguistic relevance for the analysis of the existential. Extension of the analysis to possessed-theme-subject existentials, consideration of the role of the locative analysis in the alienable/inalienable distinction, discovery of the distinctions in word order made by the existential variants, the account of the distribution of the locative proform, and the possibility that the analysis of the existential may advance the analysis of auxiliaries, all of these contributions highlight the centrality of locative constructions in human language.

10. Special abbreviations

P   locative pro-form/preposition
TNS   tense

11. References

Anderson, Stephen. 1982. 'Where's morphology?' *Linguistic Inquiry* 13: 571−612.

Bach, Emmon. 1967. '*Have* and *be* in English syntax'. *Language* 43: 462−85.

Belletti, Adriana and Luigi Rizzi. 1988. 'Psych-verbs and theta theory'. *Natural Language and Linguistic Theory* 6. 291−352.

Bender, Ernest. 1968. *Hindi grammar and reader.* Philadelphia: University of Pennsylvania Press.

Bresnan, Joan & Kanerva, Jonni M. 1989: 'Locative inversion in Chicheŵa. A case study of factorization in grammar'. *Linguistic Inquiry* 20: 1−50.

Chomsky, Noam. 1981. *Lectures on government and binding.* Dordrecht: Foris.

− 1986. *Barriers.* Cambridge: MIT Press.

− 1995. 'Some notes on economy of derivation and representation', chapter 2 of *The minimalist program.* Cambridge: MIT Press.

Fillmore, Charles. 1968. 'The case for case' In: Bach, Emmon & Harms, Robert (eds.) *Universals in Linguistic Theory.* New York: Holt, 1−88.

Freeze, Ray. 1991. 'Existential in Austronesian.' Presented at the Sixth International Conference on Austronesian, Honolulu.

− 1992. 'Existentials and other locatives'. *Language* 68.3, 555−595.

Freeze, Ray and Georgopoulos, Carol (2000). 'Locus Operandi'. In: Carnie, Andrew & Guilfoyle, Eithne (eds.). *The syntax of verb-initial languages*, Oxford: Oxford University Press.

Fukui, Naoki and Speas, Margaret. 1986. 'Specifiers and projection'. In: Fukui, Naoki et al., (eds.). *Papers in theoretical linguistics*, MITWPL 8, Cambridge: MIT.

Georgopoulos, Carol. 1991. 'On psych predicates'. In: Georgopoulos, Carol & Ishihara, Roberta (eds.). *Interdisciplinary approaches to language: Essays in honor of S.-Y. Kuroda*: 217−238. Dordrecht, Kluwer Academic Publishers.

Haspelmath, Martin. 1993. *A Grammar of Lezgian.* Berlin: Mouton de Gruyter.

Heine, Bernd. 1997. *Possession: Cognitive sources, forces, and grammaticalization.* Cambridge: Cambridge University Press.

Hoekstra, Teun and Mulder, René. 1990. 'Unergatives as copular verbs; locational and existential predication'. *The Linguistic Review* 7: 1−79.

Kayne, Richard. 1993. 'Toward a modular theory of auxiliary selection'. *Studia Linguistica* 47:1: 3−31.

Koopman, Hilda and Sportiche, Dominique. 1988. 'The position of subjects', *Lingua* 85.2/3 211−258. Special issue: The syntax of verb-initial languages.

Kuno, Susumo. 1971. 'The position of locatives in existential sentences'. *Linguistic Inquiry* 2.333−378.

Kuroda, S.-Y. 1986. 'Whether we agree or not'. *Lingvisticae Investigationes* 12.1−47.

Lyons, John. 1967. 'A note on possessive, existential, and locative sentences'. *Foundations of Language* 3. 390−396.

Milsark, Gary. 1974. *Existential sentences in English*. Massachusetts Institute of Technology dissertation.

Moro, Andrea (1997). *The raising of predicates.* Cambridge, UK: Cambridge University Press.

Reuland, Eric and ter Meulen, Alice. 1987. *The representation of (in)definiteness.* Cambridge: MIT Press.

Safir, Ken. 1982. *Syntactic chains.* Cambridge University Press.

Stowell, Timothy. 1978. 'What was there before 'there' was there?' In: Farkas, Donka et al., (eds.)., *Papers from the fourteenth regional Meeting of the Chicago Linguistic Society.* University of Chicago.

Szabolcsi, Anna. 1981. 'The possessive Construction in Hungarian: A Configurational category in a non-configurational language'. *Acta Linguistica Academiae Scientiarum Hungaricae* 31: 261−289.

Williams, Edwin. 1980. 'Predication'. *Linguistic Inquiry.* 11. 203−238.

Ray Freeze, Salt Lake City
(USA)

71. Predicative possession

1. Definition of the domain
2. Major types of predicative possession
3. Transitivization
4. Adjectivalization
5. Correlations of the Possessive Typology
6. References

1. Definition of the domain

The typology of predicative possession has been addressed in recent literature by several authors, notably Locker (1954), Clark (1978), Seiler (1983), Lizotte (1983), Heine (1997) and Stassen (in preparation). Although these authors differ somewhat in their approaches and in the range of phenomena which they discuss, a consensus opinion is that the domain of possession must be subdivided into three semantically cognate, but nonetheless separate subdomains. It can be argued that these three subdomains are in fact the results of differences in settings on two more general cognitive/semantic parameters, viz. Time Stability (Givón 1984) and Control (Hopper & Thompson 1980). Thus, we can distinguish between

(i) **inalienable possession**, in which the relation between the possessor and the possessed object is [+ Time Stable] and [− Control]. Languages vary as to which possessive relationships they choose to encode as inalienable, but the core of this subdomain seems to belong to kinship relations, and part-whole relations, such as between a body and its parts. Other relations often encountered in inalienable possessive constructions are social relations ("friend", "leader", "name"), implements of material culture ("bow", "pet", "canoe", "clothing"), or agents c.q. objects of actions (see Seiler 1983).

(ii) **alienable possession**, in which the relation between possessor and possessed object must be characterized as [+ Time Stable] and [+ Control]. Roughly speaking, this is the domain of "ownership" in a narrow juridical or ethical sense; it comprises those cases in which the possessive relation can be disrupted, transferred or given up by acts of stealing, borrowing, selling or buying.

(iii) **temporary possession**, in which the relation between possessor and possessed object can be characterized as [− Time Stable] and [+ Control]. This domain comprises relations that may be circumscribed by phrases such as "to have on one's person", "to have at one's disposal" or "to carry with oneself". An English example which strongly invites this temporary possessive reading would be something like *Look out! He's got a knife!*

Although there are languages like English, which use, or can use, the same type of formal encoding for all three subdomains, quite a few languages match the semantic distinctions in the domain by different formal encoding strategies. This fact has led several (though not all) authors on the topic to single out one of the subdomains as their focus of attention. In this article, the exposition will be restricted to typological aspects of the encoding of alienable possession.

Apart from semantic considerations, there are also formal parameters which contribute to a further delineation of the domain of possession. First, there is the distinction between **predicative possession**, as illustrated in (1a), and **adnominal possession** (→ Art. 72), as illustrated in (1b):

(1)   English
    (a) *John has a motorcycle.*
    (b) *John's motorcycle (got stolen).*

This article will deal with predicative possession only. Secondly, within predicative alienable possession, it often matters whether the noun phrase that indicates the possessed item (the PD) is **indefinite** or not. English is a language in which this parameter gives rise to two radically different encoding options:

(2)   English
    (a) *John has a motorcycle.*
    (b) *This motorcycle is John's.*

In what follows, attention will be paid only to those constructions in which the PD has an indefinite reading. This decision is in keeping with the practice to which most authors on the subject have adhered, albeit sometimes tacitly.

2. Major types of predicative possession

Authors on the typology of predicative (alienable) possession do not agree fully on the number and the nature of possessive encoding types. However, there are at least four strategies that are recognized by everybody, as they are relatively frequent and clearly identifiable.

Among these four strategies, one stands apart, in that it encodes the possessive relationship between possessor and PD in the form of a **transitive construction**. In this **HAVE-Possessive**, the possessor NP and the PD function as the subject and direct object of a 'have'-verb which, in many cases, can be shown to derive from some verb indicating physical control or handling, such as 'take', 'grasp', 'hold', or 'carry'. The construction has a concentration in some western branches of modern Indo-European, such as Germanic, Romance, West and South Slavonic, Modern Greek, and Albanian, as well as in some, though not many, eastern Indo-European languages (Modern Persian). Heine (1997) reports a number of Have-cases for African language families, notably Khoisan. Apart from this, however, Have-possessives are only incidental occurrences in linguistic families. Although most linguistic groupings in the world allow a Have-strategy for at least some of their members, it can be demonstrated that nowhere else in genetic or areal language groupings it is the primary, or even a prominent, encoding option for predicative alienable possession. An example of the Have-Possessive is:

(3) Albanian (Indo-European)
     Une   kam   një   laps.
     1SG.NOM have.1SG.PRES INDEF   pencil
     'I have a pencil.' (Kacori 1979: 30)

Opposed to the Have-Possessive, the other three major types employ a strategy which is syntactically intransitive: the possessive construction has the basic form of an **existential sentence**. Thus, all three types feature a one-place predicate with a locational or existential meaning: its usual translation can be something like 'to be', 'to be there', 'to be present', or 'to exist'. The difference between them lies in the encoding of the possessor NP and the possessed NP.

In the **Locational Possessive**, the possessed NP functions as the grammatical subject of the "exist"-predicate. The possessor NP (PR) is constructed in some oblique case form, which has as its basic meaning the specification of a locational relation. Depending on the particular type of locational relation selected, it is possible to subcategorize this type into Locative Possessive (with the PR being marked by some item meaning 'at', 'on' or 'in') and Dative Possessive (with a marker 'to' or 'for' on the PR). The Locational Possessive is the prominent option in Eurasia and Northern Africa, as well as in Polynesia and the northern part of South America. A randomly chosen example is:

(4) Written Mongolian (Poppe 1954: 147)
     Na   -dur morin bui
     1SG -LOC horse be.3SG.PRES
     'I have a horse.'

With the Locational Possessive, the **Topic Possessive** shares the characteristic that the possessed NP is constructed as the grammatical subject of the existential predicate. The distinguishing feature of the Topic Possessive lies in the encoding of the possessor NP, which is constructed as the **discourse topic** of the sentence. As such, the possessor NP indicates the setting', or background' of the sentence, that is, the discourse frame which restricts the truth value of the sentence that follows it. Its function can thus be circumscribed by English phrases such as *given X, as for X, with regard to X, speaking about X, as far as X is concerned,* and the like. Topic-possessives show a concentration in South-East Asia, but the type is also found in West and North-East Africa, in Austronesian and Papuan languages, as well as in many Amerind language groups. An example is:

(5) Tondano (Austronesian, Philippine)
     (Sneddon 1975: 175)
     Si   tuama si   wewean wale   rua
     AN.SG man   TOP   exist   house two
     'The man has two houses.'

With the two other intransitive possessive types, the **Conjunctional Possessive** shares the feature of containing an existential predicate. In other respects, however, the Conjunctional Possessive contrasts with both the Locational Possessive and the Topic Possessive. For a start, the Conjunctional Possessive constructs the possessor NP as the grammatical subject. An even more conspicuous feature is the encoding of the possessed NP. In the Conjunctional Possessive this NP is accompanied by, and usually in construction with, a marker which can be analyzed neither as a locational item nor as an indicator of topics. Closer inspection reveals that this marker in all cases originates from an item which is, or at least has been, employed as a means to indicate **simultaneity between clauses**. Thus, we find markers which have their origin in a sentential adverb meaning 'also' or 'too', or in a subordinating conjunction 'when/while', or in a coordinating particle 'and'. A prominent option within the Conjunctional Possessive is the use of the comitative marker ('with') on the possessed NP, which is why the type is often referred to as the WITH-Possessive in the literature. It can be argued, however, that languages which employ this comitative marker on possessed NP's also use this marker as a means to coordinate noun phrases (see Stassen 1999), so that this WITH-strategy can be seen as a special case of a more general conjunctional format. Concentrations of the conjunctional Possessive are found in Sub-Saharan Africa and in eastern Austronesian and Papuan languages. Examples include:

(6) Daga (Papuan, South-East) (Murane 1974: 303)
Orup da agoe den
man one slave with/too
'A man had a slave.'

(7) Sango (Niger-Kordofanian, Ubangian) (Samarin 1967: 95)
Lo eke na bongo
3SG be and/with garment
'S/he has a garment.'

In addition to these four basic types, most authors on the subject distinguish a fifth strategy, which may be called the Genitive Possessive. The **Genitive Possessive** shares features with both the Locational Possessive and the Topic Possessive, in that the possessed NP is constructed as the grammatical subject of an existential predicate. The defining feature of the Genitive Possessive is the encoding of the possessor NP, which is constructed as an adnominal modifier to the possessed NP. Depending on the strategy which the language has for the encoding of such adnominal NP's, the Genitive Possessive may involve dependent marking on the possessor NP (as in Avar), head marking on the possessed NP by means of a pronominal affix (as in Tzutujil), both head marking and dependent marking (as in Turkish), or no marking at all (as in Lahu):

(8) Avar (Dagestanian) (Kalinina 1993: 97)
Dir mašina b -ugo
1SG.GEN car III-be.PRES
'I have a car.'

(9) Tzutujil (Mayan) (Dayley 1981: 200)
K'o jun ruu-keej n -ata?
exist a his -horse my-father
'My father has a horse.'

(10) Turkish (Altaic, Turkic) (Lewis 1967: 251)
Mehmed' -in para -sı var
M. -GEN money-his exist
'Mehmed has money.'

(11) Lahu (Sino-Tibetan, Burman) (Matisoff 1973: 385)
Yô-hi câ-tu mâ cò
3PL food NEG exist
'They have no food.'

There are, however, indications that these cases of 'genitival' possession are in fact grammaticalizations from the Locative Possessive or the Topic Possessive, so that they do not have to be considered as a separate encoding type (Stassen, in preparation).

3. Transitivization

A number of languages exhibit constructions which cannot be classified straightforwardly in terms of any of the basic types. Closer inspection reveals that these cases can be rated as the results of several grammaticalization processes. The first of these processes might be called **Transitivization** or **HAVE-Drift**, as it consists in a process of drifting towards a HAVE-Possessive from one of the other three basic types. Cases of HAVE-Drift from an erstwhile Conjunctional Possessive commonly involve the cliticization or incorporation of the conjunctional marker into the existential predicate; the newly formed predicate then acts as a transitive verb. An example is:

(12) Luganda (Niger-Kordofanian, North-East Bantu) (Ashton et al. 1954: 234)
O -li -na ekitabo
2SG -be -with book
'You have a book.'

HAVE-Drift from Topic Possessives commonly involves the reanalysis of the existential "be"- item as a transitive verb, and the reanalysis of the possessor NP and possessed NP as the subject and direct object of that verb. The process is helped along by the fact that, in the typical case, this "be"-item occupied the canonical position of transitive verbs in the original possessive construction. An example of this form of HAVE-Drift is given in (13). That the process is gradual and involves various intermediate stages can be seen from the Luiseño sentences in (14): here the reanalysis of the erstwhile topic into subject seems to be under way, but the construction is not fully transitive yet.

(13) Khasi (Austro-Asiatic, Mon-Khmer) (Rabel 1961: 139)
Nga don ka jaañsaw
1SG have/exist ART red cloth
'I have a red cloth.'

(14) Luiseño (Uto-Aztecan, Numic) (Steele 1977: 114, 122)
(a) *Noo -p no-toonav qala*
1SG-TOP my-basket be.INAN.PRES
'I have a basket.'
(b) *Noo-n no-toonav qala*
1SG-SUBJ my-basket be.INAN.PRES
'I have a basket.'

Instances of HAVE-Drift from Locational Possessives are not very frequent. Comrie (1989: 219–225) reports a case from Maltese, with an intermediate stage in which the possessor NP is topicalized. A similar process must have taken place in the Celtic languages Breton (see Press 1986: 139) and Cornish:

(15) Cornish (Indo-European, Celtic) (Lewis & Pedersen 1974: 211)
(a) *Ancow a -s byth*
death to -2SG be.3SG.FUT
'You will have death: you will die'
(b) *Why a -s byth ancow*
2SG.NOM to -2SG be.3SG.FUT death
(c) *An tekter a -s betheugh*
ART beauty to -2SG be.2SG.DEP
why
2SG.NOM
'The beauty which you will have.'

It is tempting to view the phenomenon of HAVE-Drift as being motivated by iconicity (Haiman 1980). After all, the relation between possessor and possessed is fairly high in Transitivity (Hopper & Thompson 1980). In particular, possession implies a high degree of Control of the possessor over the possessed item. Hence, languages may evolve to a situation in which this semantic transitivity is matched by formal transitivity; and the only major possessive type which is formally transitive is the HAVE-Possessive.

4. Adjectivalization

In some linguistic areas, we find possessive constructions in which the PD is constructed as the predicate (or part of the predicate) and treated in the same way as predicative adjectives are treated. Thus, depending on whether predicative adjectives are 'nouny' or 'verby' (Wetzer 1996, Stassen 1997), the possessed noun phrase shows up as (part of the) complement of the copula, or as (the lexical core of) a predicative verb. Examples include:

(16) Tiwi (Australian, Tiwi) (Osborne 1974: 60)
ŋawa mantani təraka
our friend wallaby
'Our friend has a wallaby.'

(17) Kanuri (Nilo-Saharan, Saharan) (Cyffer 1974: 122)
Kâm kúrà -tə̀ kúŋŋə́nà-
man big -the money
-nzə́-wà (gə̀nyí)
-his-ADJ/with (NEG.COP)
'The big man has (no) money.'

(18) Guajajara (Tupi) (Bendor-Samuel 1972: 162)
I -mukaw
3SG -gun
'He has a gun.'

(19) Yukaghir (Jochelson 1905: 405)
Met āče -n
1SG.NOM reindeer -with
-je
-1SG.PRES.INDEF.INTRANS
'I have (a) reindeer.'

Cases like these are probably best viewed as the results of a grammaticalization process by which the possessed noun phrase (together with its marker, if it has one) is gradually reanalyzed as the predicate of the construction. Depending on whether the possessed noun phrase carries a marker or not, the source of such products of **adjectivalization** can be traced back to a Conjunctional Possessive or a Topic Possessive. The process of adjectivalization may well be fostered by the fact that in the relevant languages the existential verb is either zero or identical to the copula.

5. Correlations of the Possessive Typology

Several bodies of facts seem to suggest that the typology of predicative possession is at least partially "modelled" on the encoding of a specific type of temporal sequence. Stassen (in preparation) argues that **simultaneous temporal sequences with non-identical subjects and identical predicates** form the structural template of three of the four basic possessive types. This author assumes that the universal semantic structure for these types is something like

(20) *Exist (PR) & Exist (PD)*

which is a special case of a general temporal sequence of the form

(21) $F(a) \& F(b)$

The claim is that the formal options which a language possesses for the encoding of sequences like (21) delimit the range of strategies that a language can employ in the encoding of predicative possession.

Preliminary evidence for this Modelling Analysis stems from the fact that at least one major type, viz. the Conjunctional Possessive, shows clear lexical and/or morphological relations to coordinative structures. Apart from that, there are a few languages in which the predicative possessive construction has the overt form of a simultaneous sequence such as (20). Thus, in Ixtlan Zapotec possessives can have the form of a (simultaneous) coordination of two existential sentences:

(22)   Ixtlan Zapotec (Oto-Manguean, Zapotecan) (De Angulo & Freeland 1935: 123)
Doa tu jrudi   , doa tu beku
exist one gentleman , exist one dog
to   kye
small his
'A certain gentleman had a little dog.'
(Lit.: 'There was a gentleman, there was his little dog')

In Daflā, the possessive construction shows the form of a simultaneous sequence of two existential sentences, in which one of the sentences has been deranked (i.e., reduced to a non-finite clause). As example (23b) illustrates, this strategy is used in Daflā for simultaneous sequences in general.

(23)   Daflā (Sino-Tibetan, Tibeto-Burman) (Grierson 1909: 603)
  (a) predicative possession:
Lok nyi ak da-t   -la, ka
one man one be-PRET.TCP -at, sons
anyiga da-tleya
two   be-3DU.PRET
'A man had two sons.'
(Lit.: 'While there was a man, there were two sons.')
  (b) simultaneous sequence: (Grierson 1909: 603)
Ha guda hä dema durre u
that country in great famine, become
-t   -la, mug ai   da -pa
-PAST.PCP -at, his stomach eat -get
-ma
-NEG
'When a great famine came to pass in that country, he could not get food.'

As a more general point, it appears that possessive types can be shown to be restricted to languages in which a certain encoding strategy for simultaneous sequences is available. Stassen adduces evidence for the following three implicational universals:

(i) If a language has a Locational Possessive, that language will have deranking of simultaneous sequences. That is, such a language has the possibility to encode the predicate in one of the clauses in the sequence as a non-finite, subordinate form.

An example which corroborates this universal is:

(24)   Latvian (Indo-European, Baltic) (Budina Lazdina 1966: 22)
  (a) possessive:
Tev -am ir   mja
father -DAT be.3SG.PRES house.NOM
'Father has a house.'
  (b) simultaneous sequence: (Endzelin 1922: 793)
Man   sienu   ved-dam   -ai
1SG.DAT hay.ACC enter-PCP.PRES -DAT
uznaca   lietus
come down.3SG.PRET rain.NOM
'As I was bringing in the hay, it started raining.'

(ii) If a language has a Topic Possessive, that language will have backgrounding of simultaneous sequences. That is, such a language has the possibility to encode one of the clauses in the sequence as the "scene-setting" background for the interpretation of the other clause. Formally, this usually implies preposing of the background clause, and topicalization marking of that clause, either by intonation alone, or by some overt topic marking device.

A case in which this correlation is directly visible is

(25)   Mandarin (Sino-Tibetan, Sinitic)
  (a) possessive: (Li & Thompson 1981: 513)
Tā yǒu sān -ge   háizi
he exist three -CLASS child
'He has three children.'
  (b) simultaneous sequence: (Li & Thompson 1981: 642)
Wǒ sǐ -le, nǐ zuì hǎo zài
I   die-PERF, you most good again
jià
marry
'When/if I die, you'd better marry again.'

(iii) If a language has a Conjunctional Possessive, that language will have predominant (and sometimes even exclusive) balancing of simultaneous sequences. That is, such a language prefers the encoding of its temporal sequences in the form of a *coordination*.

A language which provides a direct match between its encoding options for predicative possession and simultaneous sequencing is Bari.

(26) Bari (Nilo-Saharan, Nilotic) (Spagnolo 1933: 102)
   (a) possessive:
     Matat kata ko   kisuk jore
     chief exist and/with cattle much
     'The chief has much cattle.'
   (b) simultaneous sequence: (Spagnolo 1933: 212)
     Wani ko   Gore atu i
     W.   and/with G.   they PERF
     gwaja na kore
     go   to dance
     'Wani and Gore have gone dancing/ Wani has gone dancing with Gore.'

While the universals (ii) and (iii) are exceptionless in Stassen's 260 language sample, universal (i) meets with a few counter-examples. To be specific, Russian, Modern Arabic and Hebrew, and the Celtic languages have locational possessives but no synchronic possibilities of deranking under non-identical subjects. As it can be shown that, for all these languages, this 'absolute' deranking strategy was an encoding option in earlier stages of their history, one may hypothesize that, in these languages at least, the possessive construction is more conservative than its model.

A major problem for the Modelling Analysis of predicative possession is the status of the HAVE-Possessive. While the three other major possessive types have their counterpart in one of the options in the encoding of simultaneous sequencing, no such matching is available for HAVE-possessives. Now, the HAVE-Possessive constitutes a diachronically heterogeneous type, in that 'have'-verbs derive from different sources. These verbs stem from either 1) the grammaticalization or reanalysis of original Locational, Topic, or Comitative Possessives (see above), or 2) a (more or less) "bleached" form of a verb meaning 'to seize/hold/grasp/carry'. For at least a number of languages it can be documented that this transitive 'have'-verb has superseded a former non-transitive possessive construction (Latin > Romance, Classical Greek > Modern Greek). Thus, we can observe a general tendency among languages to change their possessive constructions into a HAVE-Possessive. The forces behind this tendency are probably manifold. On the one hand, a general iconic motivation to match a semantically transitive construction type with a formally transitive encoding may be at work here. Furthermore, the drift towards a HAVE-Possessive may be fostered by the need to eliminate possible ambiguities. For example, in languages with an unmarked Topic Possessive possible ambiguities between "I have a dog" and "I am a dog" arise when the existential 'be'-verb and the copula are (or come to be) identical. In languages with a Locative Possessive the same type of ambiguity threatens when the language loses its case system (and the copula and existential 'be'-verb are identical). It may be that, in order to eliminate ambiguities of this kind, the language resorts to an item c. q. construction type which was available anyway for the expression of temporary possession ('hold', 'carry'). In other words, in such languages the semantic range of the temporary possessive construction may have been expanded to include alienable possession as well.

6. References

Ashton, E. O. et al. 1954. *Luganda grammar*. London: Longmans, Green & Co.

Bendor-Samuel, D. 1972. *Hierarchical structures in Guajajara*. Norman, Okl.: Summer Institute of Linguistics.

Budina Lazdina, T. 1966. *Teach yourself Latvian*. London: The English Universities Press.

Clark, Eve V. 1978. "Locationals: existential. Locative and possessive constructions". In: Greenberg, Joseph C. Ferguson & Moravcsik, E. (eds.). *Universals of Human Language*. Volume 4. *Syntax*. Stanford: Stanford University Press, 86–126.

Comrie, Bernard. 1989. *Language universals and linguistic typology*. Oxford: Basil Blackwell.

Cyffer, N. 1974. *Syntax des Kanuri*. Hamburg: Helmut Buske.

Dayley, J. P. 1981. *Tzutujil grammar*. UC Berkeley/ Ph. D. Diss.

De Angulo, J. & Freeland, J. S. 1935. "The Zapotecan linguistic group". *International Journal of American Linguistics* 8: 1–38.

Endzelin, J. 1922. *Lettische Grammatik*. Riga: Gulbis.

Givón, T. 1984. *Syntax: a functional-typological introduction*. Volume 1. Amsterdam: Benjamins.

Grierson, G. A. (ed.). 1909. *Linguistic survey of India*. Part III. Tibeto-Burman family. Part I. *General introduction. Specimens of the Tibetan dialects, the Himalayan dialects and the North Assam group.* Calcutta: Government Printing Office.

Haiman, John. 1980. "The iconicity of grammar". *Language* 56: 515–540.

Heine, Bernd. 1997. *Possession: cognitive sources, forces and grammaticalization*. Cambridge: Cambridge University Press.

Hopper, Paul J. & Thompson, Sandra. 1980. "Transitivity in grammar and discourse". *Language* 56: 251–99.

Jochelson, W. 1905. "Essay on the grammar of the Yukaghir language". *American Anthropologist* 7,2: 369–424.

Kacori, T. 1979. *A handbook of Albanian*. Sofia: Sofia University "Kliment Ohridski", Faculty of Slavonic Studies.

Kalinina, Elena. 1993. "Sentences with non-verbal predicates in the Sogratl dialect of Avar". In: Kibrik, Aleksandr E. (ed.). The noun phrase in the Andalal dialect of Avar as spoken at Sogratl. Strasbourg: EUROTYP Working Papers 90–104.

Kibrik, A. E. (ed.). 1993. "The noun phrase in the Andalal dialect of Avar as spoken at Sogratl". *EUROTYP Working Papers*, Theme 7: *Noun Phrase Structure*, Working Paper No. 18. Konstanz: University of Konstanz.

Lewis, L. 1967. *Turkish grammar*. Oxford: Clarendon Press.

Lewis, H. & Pedersen, H. 1974. *A concise comparative Celtic grammar*. Göttingen: Vandenhoeck & Ruprecht.

Li, Charles N. & Thompson, Sandra A. 1981. *Mandarin Chinese: a functional reference grammar*. Berkeley etc.: University of California Press.

Lizotte, R. J. 1983. *Universals concerning existence, possession and location sentences*. Brown University/Ph. D. Diss.

Locker, E. 1954. "Être et avoir. Leurs expressions dans les languages". *Anthropos* 49: 481–510.

Matisoff, James A. 1973. *The grammar of Lahu*. Berkeley/Los Angeles: University of California Press.

Murane, E. 1974. *Daga grammar*. Norman, Okl.: Summer Institute of Linguistics.

Osborne, C. R. 1974. *The Tiwi language*. Canberra: Australian Institute of Aboriginal Studies.

Poppe, Nicholas. 1954. *Grammar of Written Mongolian*. Wiesbaden: Harrassowitz.

Press, Ian. 1986. *A grammar of modern Breton*. Berlin etc.: Mouton de Gruyter.

Rabel, L. 1961. *Khasi, a language of Assam*. Baton Rouge: Louisiana State University Press.

Samarin, William J. 1967. *A grammar of Sango*. The Hague: Mouton.

Seiler, Hansjakob. 1983. *Possession as an operational dimension of language*. Tübingen: Narr.

Sneddon, J. N. 1975. *Tondano phonology and grammar*. Canberra: The Australian National University.

Spagnolo, F. L. M. 1933. *Bari grammar*. Verona: Nigrizia.

Stassen, Leon. 1997. *Intransitive predication*. Oxford: Clarendon Press.

Stassen, Leon. 1999. "Some universal characteristics of noun phrase conjunction". In: Plank, Frans (ed.). *Noun phrase structure in the languages of Europe* (EUROTYP, Vol. 9). Berlin: Mouton De Gruyter.

Stassen, Leon. *Possession in language*. In Preparation.

Steele, Susan. 1977. "On being possessed'. *Berkeley Linguistics Society* 3: 114–31.

Wetzer, H. 1996. *Nouniness and verbiness: a typological study of adjectival predication*. Berlin: Mouton de Gruyter.

Leon Stassen, Nijmegen
(The Netherlands)

72. Adnominal possession

1. Adnominal possession and possessive noun phrases: prototypical cases
2. Structural types of possessive noun phrases
3. Functions of possessors within PNPs and possessor-article incompatibility
4. Splits in the possession area
5. Grammaticalization patterns
6. Connections with other grammatical phenomena
7. Special abbreviations
8. References

1. Adnominal possession and possessive noun phrases: prototypical cases

The phrases *Peter's hat*, *my son* and *the boy's leg* are all possessive noun phrases (henceforth PNPs) and exemplify adnominal possession whereby one entity, the possessee, referred to by the head of the noun phrase, is represented as possessed in one or another way by another entity, the possessor, referred to by the attribute. Moreover, all our examples present prototypical cases of PNPs in that the possessor is an individuated human being, the possessee is a specific concrete object and their relation includes legal ownership, as in *Peter's hat*, kinship relations (*my son*) or body-part relations (*the boy's leg*); the two latter are often opposed to the former as inalienable vs. alienable possession (cf. § 4.). Such examples, however, constitute only a minor part of what counts as possessive noun phrases, both in English and cross-linguistically. Thus, *Peter's train / thoughts / teacher* or *a dog's kennel* have the same structure as possessive noun phrases par excellence even though they hardly refer to possession strictu senso: the train is Peter's probably because he takes it regularly, abstract concepts like thoughts as well as other human beings are not included among people's belongings, and dogs will not count as possessors in the legal sense. In short, linguistic possession is generally difficult to grasp and at least a partial answer to what counts as possession should be sought in the bio-cultural sphere (Seiler 1983: 4−7). However, many people would agree that the core of this category is made up of cases where there is an exclusive asymmetric long-term relation between two entities − for each possessee there is only one possessor, who has the right to make use of the possessee − and the possessor is an individuated human being (cf. Taylor 1989: 202−203).

2. Structural types of possessive noun phrases

The expression of adnominal possession across languages has attracted considerable attention among typologists − Ultan (1978), Seiler (1983), Croft (1990: 28−39), Manzelli (1990), Plank (1995), Heine (1997) and Koptjevskaja-Tamm (2001) all present structural classifications of PNPs. This section lists the major types of such constructions.

A number of languages make use of **juxtapositional** PNPs, which lack any overt marker to specify the relation between the possessee and the possessor. In languages with nominal case the possessee and the possessor may receive the same case: this pattern is well attested among the Australian languages, where it is normally restricted to PNPs which refer to inalienable possession (1c). The same pattern, termed "**case attraction**" or "**case assimilation**", is also known from ancient Indo-European languages

(1) (a) Kobon (Trans-New Guinea, Davies 1981: 57)
 Dumnab ram
 Dumnab house
 'Dumnab's house'
 (b) Warrgamay (Pama-Nyungan, Dixon 1980: 293)
 ŋaja ŋulmburu bingany ŋunda-lma
 I:NOM woman:ABS foot:ABS look.at:FUT
 'I'll look at the woman's foot.'

Most PNPs, however, involve one or several **construction markers, CMs** − overt elements which show explicitly that the possessor and the possessee are related in a specific way (thus; *'s* is the CM in *Peter's house*). It may be convenient to classify such PNPs according to the degree of morpho-syntactic bondedness of their CM into **synthetic** ones, where CMs appear as bound elements, and **analytic** ones, in which the CM is not morphologically bound. This classification is of course a rude oversimplification of the facts: first, as in the case with other grammatical phenomena, there is normally a whole scale between clearly bound and clearly free markers (cf. Seiler 1983: 72 on a scale of techniques employed in possession); second, an analytic PNP may, in addition, involve bound CMs as well.

Within synthetic PNPs, CMs may attach to the possessee (the head of a PNP), to the possessor (one of its dependents), or to both. Following Nichols (1986), we will speak of **head-marking, dependent-marking** and **double-marking**.

Dependent-marking is a frequent technique within PNPs. When inflectional, such construction markers are often termed **genitive case** markers: in other words, the genitive case is identified across languages as the case of the possessor in PNPs (cf. (2)). There is, however, no terminological consensus on the label used for the case of the possessor in languages where the same case can be used for other functions as well, and different local traditions solve this problem in different ways. In descriptions of Modern Greek, for example, the term "genitive" traditionally applies to the case used both for marking possessors in PNP and goals/recipients in clauses, whereas a comparable multifunctional case in Gooniyandi is labelled "dative" in McGregor (1990: 179−180). Many languages have a special series of possessive pronouns, not directly comparable with lexical possessors. Possessive pronouns often agree with the head in number-gender-case; in such cases we may talk about dependent-marking **relatedness-indicators**, or **indexers**, i. e. construction markers which are chosen in accordance with some properties of the nominals involved — crucially, not only or not so much of the nominal to which they are morphologically bound (Plank 1995: 38). Interestingly, there are languages in which such agreement concerns even lexical possessors, as in (3) from Romani where possessors in the genitive case agree with the possessee in number, gender and case (this phenomenon is termed *Suffixaufnahme* after Nikolaus Finck, cf. Plank 1995). Thus, although dependent-markers in PNPs tend to be **relation identifiers**, i. e. simply mark the relation in a PNP as such, there are indexers among them too.

(2) Imbabura Quechua (Cole 1982: 115)
 José-paj wasi
 José-GEN house
 'José's house'

(3) Romani
 (a) *[e*
  the:OBL.M.SG
  manuś-es-qoro] *kher*
  man-OBL.SG.M-GEN:M.SG.NOM house_M
  'the man's house'
 (b) *[e*
  the:OBL.M.SG
  manuś-es-qiri *buzni*
  man-OBL.SG.M-GEN:M.SG.NOM goat_F
  'the man's goat'
 (c) *[e* *manuś-es-qere]*
  the:OBL.M.SG man-OBL.SG.M.GEN:PL
  ćhave
  children
  'The man's children'

Turning now to **head-marking**, in some languages nouns used as possessees appear in a special form, **a construct state**, contrasted to those used in other position, **an absolute state**. The terminological distinction between "states" originally comes from studies of Semitic and other Afro-Asiatic languages. In Luo, for example, the absolute and the construct states of the word 'pot' are *àgulu* vs. *àgund*. Nominals may also take special possessive morphemes which mark them as possessees (cf. (4a)), or **ezafe**-markers (known primarily from Iranian languages) which appear whenever a noun combines with attributes (and are thus not only restricted to PNPs). More frequently, possessees attach possessive suffixes or prefixes which vary according to the person-gender-number of the possessor (4b). Such indexing possessive affixes may often suffice as the only indication of a non-lexical possessor. Thus, in standard Finnish 'your (plural) house' will be either *teidän talo-nne* = '2PL.GEN house-2PL.POSS', especially when there is an additional emphasis on the possessor, or simply *talonne*. The possibility of deleting the dependent *teidän* altogether creates an extra dimension which is not accounted for by the straightforward distinction between head- and dependent-marking. The various head-marking phenomena may combine, so that possessive affixes appear on the nominal form which per se differs from the form used in other contexts, outside adnominal possession. Thus, head-marking, in contrast to dependent-marking, tends to involve indexers.

(4) (a) Western Tarahumara (Uto-Aztecan; Burgess 1984: 61)
  kantelário upí-la
  Candelario wife-POSS
  'Candelario's wife'
 (b) Mam (Mayan; England 1983: 142)
  t-kamb' meeb'a
  3SG-prize orphan
  'the orphan's prize'

Finally, the various head-marking and dependent-marking techniques can combine in **double-marked PNPs**, e. g.

(5) Imbabura Quechua (Equadorian Quechua; Cole 1982: 115)
 José-pa wayi-n
 José-GEN horse-3
 'José's horse'

Similarly to dependent-marking, head-marking and double-marking within synthetic PNPs, construction markers in analytic PNPs can be syntactically associated with the possessor, the possessee or both. A CM may also be a link which is not associated with either the possessee or the possessor. However, classifying analytic PNPs according to these criteria often turns out to be a much more complicated enterprise than it appears to be at first. This is because decisions about their constituent structure require a great deal of morphosyntactic information that is not always obvious and/or easily available.

The simplest examples of analytic PNPs involve pre- and postpositions and particles which pertain to the possessor. Sometimes the choice of a CM is sensitive to the properties of the possessee, i.e. the CM has an indexing function in addition to its relation-identifying functions. This is common, for example, among the Bantu languages in which the so called associative particle (normally -a) takes different class prefixes in accordance with the possessee's nominal class (cf. (6)). The Bantu PNP shares certain properties with PNPs in Standard Albanian, in which adnominal possessors in the genitive/dative case are obligatorily accompanied by the so called syntagmatic article − a misleading term since these elements have nothing to do with referential contrasts. These proclitic items appear as the first element in a possessor noun phrase and agree with the possessee in number, gender, case and definiteness (cf. (7)). PNPs involving possessive/relational classifiers which might probably also count as syntactically associated with the possessor will be treated separately in § 4.

(6) Swahili (Niger-Congo: Bantu; Plank 1995: 45)
  (a) *wa-toto w[a]-a Ali*
     CL.PL-child CL.PL-of Ali
     'Ali's child/children'
  (b) *ki-tanda ch-a Ali*
     CL.SG-bed CL.SG-of Ali
     'Ali's bed'

(7) Albanian
  (a) *shtëpi-a e një*
     house_F-DEF.NOM ATTR:F.SG.NOM a
     fshatar-i
     peasant-INDEF.GEN/DAT.SG
     'some/a peasant's house'
  (b) *libr-i i*
     book_M-DEF.SG.NOM ATTR:M.SG.NOM
     nxënës-it
     pupil-DEF.GEN/DAT.SG
     'the pupil's book'
  (c) *nëpërmjet libr-it*
     with book_M-DEF.SG.GEN/DAT
     të nxënës-it
     ATTR:M.SG.GEN/DAT pupil-DEF.GEN/DAT.SG
     '(with) the book of the pupil'

A completely different type of analytic PNPs involve "**linking pronouns**", i.e. possessive pronouns adjacent to the possessee and, thus, normally analyzed as being syntactically associated (building a co-constituent) with it. Linking pronouns may gradually give rise to full-fledged possessive affixes, whereby syntactic association with the head turns into head-marking. However, in many cases linking pronouns occur in-between the possessee and the possessor, which thus motivates their association with both (or with neither) with the result that superficially comparable and even genetically related structures in different languages suggest different constituency relations. An interesting case is presented by various Germanic varieties which use some local variant of the colloquial German construction *dem Vater sein Buch* 'the:DAT father his book'. While in some varieties the linking pronoun is unambiguously associated with the possessee, in others it behaves rather like a linker. In Modern Norwegian, extraction of interrogative words suggests syntactic association of linking (reflexive) pronouns to the possessee: thus, interrogative pronominal possessors, when extracted out of the PNP and fronted, are never accompanied by the linking pronoun, which has to be left behind together with the possessee (cf. (8a−c)). However, this is the only argument for such an analysis: other tests suggest that PNPs with the linking pronoun either are going through or have gone through the process of reanalysis, by which the reflexive pronoun becomes prosodically and syntactically attached to the possessor. Thus, Norwegian allows for predicative and elliptic (headless) uses of the combination "Possessor + reflexive pronoun", as in (8c).

(8) Norwegian
  (a) *Hvem er det si-n bil?*
     who is it REFL.POSS-M.SG car?
  (b) *Hvem sin bil er det?*
     who REFL.POSS.M.SG car is it?
  (c) **Hvem sin er det bil?*
     who REFL.POSS.M.SG is it car?
     'Whose car is it?'
  (d) *Per si-n bil er bedre*
     Per REFL.POSS-M.SG car is better
     enn Lisa si-n.
     than Lisa REFL.POSS-M.SG
     'Per's car is better than Lisa's.'

Constructions with linking pronouns are attested all over the world; among other things, they constitute a dominant PNP type among creole languages.

The structurally different PNP types are not evenly distributed among the languages of the world and lend themselves to a number of areal generalizations: thus, the European languages prefer dependent-marking PNPs, the second choice being double-marked and prepositional PNPs (Koptjevskaja-Tamm 2001a), while in North America head-marked and, to a lesser degree, doublemarked PNPs predominate (Nichols 1986, 1992).

3. Functions of possessors within PNPs and possessor-article incompatibility

As mentioned in § 1., PNPs across languages are employed for reference to a variety of relations, a large portion of which hardly have anything to do with possession in the strict sense. Part-whole relations ('the roof of the house'), location ('London's banks' or 'desert animals'), time ('yesterday's magazine' or 'a spring flower'), authorship ('Mozart's symphonies'), quality ('a man of power') — these are a subset of relations which are covered by PNPs in language after language. It has been repeatedly argued that any attempt to describe the semantics of PNPs is a hopeless enterprise; many studies suggest that the basic function of adnominal possession is simple reference to a relation between entities, which is lexically determined, involves world-knowledge and/or contextual properties. Thus, in Lithuanian, the genitive construction *stalo koja* 'a/the leg of a/the table' (table:GEN.SG leg/foot:NOM.SG) expresses part-whole relations due to the semantics of the word *koja*, while in the construction *aukso žiedas* 'a/the golden ring' (gold:GEN.SG ring:NOM.SG), the genitive dependent, mainly due to the semantics of the word *auksas*, names the material which makes up the referent of the head. This is particularly true of **relational nouns** (such as *leg, brother, middle*), which normally require an additional argument with which it conjures up one specific relation.

Even optimal candidates for prototypical PNPs, such as *Peter's hat*, may have a number of interpretations as well: 'a hat which Peter is wearing at the moment (but which does not necessarily belong to him)', 'a hat he has designed', 'a hat he dreams of and therefore constantly talks about', etc. This is typical of **non-relational nouns**, the referents of which may enter into different, multiple relations with other entities. However, some of these interpretations, though possible, are fairly unlikely, whereas others occur frequently and represent so to speak unmarked options. Also, the range of relations which can be expressed by adnominal possessors is subject to considerable cross-linguistic variation, which makes it meaningful to describe semantics of adnominal possession in a particular language and across languages in more precise terms than 'a relation between two entities' (a suggestion for a semantic map of genitival meanings in several languages is made in Nikiforidou 1991).

The core of linguistic possession is made up of cases where there is an exclusive asymmetric long-term relation between two entities, one of which is an individuated human being (Taylor 1989: 202–203). This basic asymmetry between prototypical possessors and possessees is often efficiently employed in discourse for identifying the referent of a nominal via its relation to the referent of the possessor. Thus, it is easy to identify the referents of the NPs *Peter's children / head / house* if we know which 'Peter' is meant. In other words, prototypical adnominal possessors are extremely suitable as **anchors** (in the sense of Hawkins 1991) or as **reference point entities** (Langacker 1995) for the identification of the referents of the head. Even other relations, which are normally expressed by PNPs across languages and which are not possessive in the strict sense, may be classified as anchoring relations, e. g. 'yesterday's newspaper' (temporal), 'the skyscraper's roof' (part-whole), 'Stockholm's banks' (local).

However, PNPs across languages may also cover non-anchoring relations, i. e. relations which do not serve to identify the referent of the head, but rather to characterize it. Thus, adnominal 'material' and 'purpose' relations are expressed in many languages in exactly the same way as possession, cf. *kavos puodelis* 'a coffee cup' (lit. coffee's cup') and *brolio puodelis* 'a/the brother's cup' in Lithuanian, even though 'golden rings' and 'coffee cups' are not necessarily more definite than 'rings' and 'cups'. The ability to serve as a reference point has, of course, to do with referential properties of adnominal possessors: 'gold' and 'coffee' are not definite and not even referential. Of significant typological interest here is the extent to which PNPs across languages are restricted to those involving definite / referential / specific attributes, as well as the relations that can actually be covered by PNPs.

In their functions as reference point entities, possessors are, of course, reminiscent of definite articles — and herein lies the functional explanation for the incompatibility of possessors and articles in PNPs which is known from a number of languages. Thus, in English, possessed nominals cannot take articles, as in *a/*the my house or my *a/*the house. Interestingly, such PNPs are normally interpreted as definite. Thus, *Peter's friend* refers to 'the friend of Peter's': the presence of the genitive induces definiteness of the possessee and of the whole PNP. When the possessee is indefinite, a more complex PNP has to be chosen – *a friend of Peter's* or *one of Peter's friends*. English has thus grammaticalized the similarity in the anchoring functions of genitives and articles and chosen an economical solution for the frequently occurring pattern whereby nominals are identified via their possessors (Haspelmath 1999, Koptjevskaja-Tamm 2001b).

Although this phenomenon is attested in quite a few languages – e. g. Swedish, Scottish Gaelic, Romani, Hebrew, Vai, to mention but a few examples, – most languages with articles allow articles to co-occur with possessors, like in Italian *un/il mio libro* 'one of my books/my book'. The two types of possessors – i.e., those which can co-occur with articles and those which cannot – are sometimes called **adjectival-genitives** vs. **determiner-genitives** (Lyons 1986). Interestingly, one and the same language can have both types of genitives, like the English *'s*-genitives and *of*-genitives, where the determiner-genitive is normally restricted to anchoring usages (the specifying *'s*-genitive); the situation is further complicated by the existence of a non-determiner *'s*-genitive, as in *a women's magazine*. A similar split between PNPs involving definite vs. indefinite possessees is attested even in languages where possessors co-occur with articles, as in Rumanian (cf. (9)). Here, indefinite possessees require the presence of a special agreeing attributive particle in addition to the possessor in the genitive case.

(9) Rumanian
 (a) *portret-ul   rege-lui*
  portrait-ART king-ART.GEN
  'the king's portrait'
 (b) **un portret rege-lui*
  a   portrait ling-ART.GEN
  'a portrait of the king'
 (c) *un portret a-l   rege-lui*
  a   portrait ATTR-M.SG king-ART.GEN
  'a portrait of the king'

4. Splits in the possession area

Co-occurrence of several different possessive constructions in one and the same language is a fairly frequent phenomena, and in addition to split possession caused by definiteness vs. indefiniteness of the possessee and the whole PNP, there are other recurring types of split possession systems in the world's languages. The alternating possessive constructions are thus opposed to each other according to various parameters. An important group of factors which may influence a choice among these different constructions have to do with the nature of the possessee and/or with its precise relation to the possessor.

A frequent type of possession splits is traditionally regarded as the opposition between alienable and inalienable possession, or the alienability split (10):

(10) Maltese (Semitic)
 a. Inalienable possession
  bin is-sultān id   ir-raġel
  son DEF-king hand DEF-man
  'the king's son' 'the man's hand'
 b. Alienable possession
  is-siġġu ta' Pietru
  DEF-chair of Peter
  'Peter's chair'

The traditional labels give the impression that the distinction is one between two kinds of possession, and there have been numerous attempts to characterize this opposition as a primarily semantic one, reflecting some basic difference between typically inalienable concepts and others, e. g. in their relationality (inalienable nominals have an additional argument as compared to others) or in the way their referents are conceived of (as being inherently cognitively or physically connected to other entities). However, all these semantic characterizations turn out to be too general from a cross-linguistic prospective. Typically, inalienables form a closed set, membership in which can be represented as an implicational hierarchy: "If an item on the hierarchy is inalienable, then all the items to the left are inalienable" (Nichols (1988: 572, cf. also Chappell & McGregor (eds.) 1996):

KIN TERMS AND/OR BODY PARTS	> PART-WHOLE AND/OR SPATIAL RELATIONS	> CULTURALLY BASIC POSSESSED ITEMS (CLOTHING, TOOLS, DOMESTIC ANIMALS)

Structurally, inalienable constructions tend to involve inflection of the possessee-nominal (head-marking) or to involve mere juxtaposition of the possessee and the possessor-nominals; whereas alienable constructions are often analytic or involve inflectional marking of the possessor-nominal (dependent-marking). In addition, inalienable nouns are in some languages obligatorily marked for being possessed. Thus, in Yucatec Maya inalienable body part terms simply never occur outside PNPs, whereas most kinship terms for such usages have to be absolutivized by attaching the suffix *-tsil*. Conversely, in some languages certain nominals can never be possessed unless they take special additional morphemes, as in Chemehuevi, where names for animals and plants have to be first compounded with *puŋku* 'pet' vs. *i-gapi-* 'plant' when used as possessees (Press 1980: 60—61).

(11) Yucatec Maya (Lehmann 1996: 50, 54)
 a. *in   chi'*
    1SG.POSS mouth
    'my mouth'
 b. **le   (chi'(-tsil)-o'*
    DEF mouth(-ABSOL)-DIST
    'the mouth'
 c. *in   tàatah*
    1SG.POSS father
    'my father'
 d. *le   tatah-tsil-o'*
    DEF father-ABSOL-DIST
    'the father'

The recurrent co-variation of form and meaning has received various explanations. Thus Haiman proposes a functional explanation based on **iconic motivation**, whereby "the greater the formal distance between X and Y, the greater the conceptual distance between the notions they represent" (Haiman 1985: 106). Nichols (1988, 1992) suggests that there is a high correlation between the presence of an alienability distinction in a language and the availability of head-marked possession and that head-marking patterns characteristic of inalienable nouns result from innovative fusion or conservative retention of the head-marked pattern with nouns of the closed set. Diachronic processes akin to those proposed by Nichols are developed further within **the grammaticalization** framework. Koptjevskaja-Tamm (1996) and Heine (1997) show in detail how the various properties frequently found in the alienability split can be explained by tracing the grammaticalization processes which give rise to such splits. Thus, there is sufficient evidence that alienability splits often involve an opposition between the **archaic**, inalienable construction and the **innovative**, alienable construction.

Alienability splits of the kind discussed above find semantic parallels in other constructions, not necessarily involving adnominal possession, e. g. constructions with external (→ Art. 73) and implicit possessors, like German *Die Mutter wäscht dem Kind die Haare* and Swedish *Jag skadade foten* 'I hurt my foot' (lit. 'the foot'). It is also difficult to define what exactly could count as an alienability split. Thus, certain kinship terms in Bulgarian, when modified by possessive clitics, cannot take suffixed definite articles, as opposed to all other possessed nominals, e. g. *majka(*-ta) mi* 'mother(*-DEF.SG.F) my' vs. *kola-ta mi* 'car-DEF.SG.F my' — and similar special behaviour of articles with kinship terms is attested in a number of languages. There is here a formal difference between possessed kinship terms, which correspond to shorter and less elaborated expressions, and other possessed nominals, similarly to other cases of alienability splits. However, the exact morpho-syntactic manifestation of this opposition is different from cases of alienability splits par excellence. All this creates problems for possible correlations between alienabiliy splits and other linguistic features as those in Nichols (1988, 192: 116—123).

In a number of languages an alienability split is further elaborated by a system of **possessive**, or **relational classifiers**, i. e. by special elements which specify "the real-world relation that obtains between the referents" of the possessor and possessee nominals (Lichtenberk 1983: 148), e. g. whether an object is used for eating raw or cooked, as a plant, as a prey etc. (cf. (12)). This specification is normally required only for alienable nominals: the relation between inalienables and their possessors follows from the semantics of the former.

(12) Iaai (Austronesian, Oceanic: the Loyalty Islands; Lichtenberk 1983: 159)
 (a) *lawu-yi yixi*
     CLASS-yi fish
     'my fish, that I am keeping'
 (b) *xala-yi yixi*
     CLASS-my fish
     'my cooked-fish food'
 (c) *xocaa-yi yixi*
     CLASS-my fish
     'my raw-fish food'
 (d) *xolo-yo yixi*
     CLASS-my fish
     'my fish, that I caught'

Such constructions occur primarily in Oceania, in particular among the Micronesian languages where relational classifier systems reach extreme elaboration and involve more than 20 members; they are also attested in a few indigenous American languages, e. g. in Cahuilla (Uto-Aztec, Seiler 1983: 36–37).

The relation between a possessor and a possessee within a noun phrase may also be specified temporally, by tense markers which occur in a few languages:

(13) Hixkaryana (Carib; Derbyshire 1979: 98)
    a. *ro-kanawa-ri*
       my-canoe-PRES.POSS
       'my canoe'
    b. *ro kanawa-tho*
       my-canoe-PAST.POSS
       'my former canoe'

The other major groups of splits in PNPs occur along the **animacy/referentiality scale**. To take a simple example, pronominal possessors in French precede possessees and agree with them; they do not co-occur with articles, e. g. *mon livre* vs. *ma table*. Other possessors attach the preposition *de* and follow the possessee, which freely combines with articles, as *un/le livre de Pierre*. A much more complicated case is presented by restrictions of the formation of agreeing possessive adjectives in Slavic. Although the exact conditions differ across the languages, they more or less obey the animacy and definiteness hierarchies: the higher the possessor's referent is on these hierarchies the more likely the possessive adjective can be formed. In other cases the possessor will be coded by a genitive case marker. The best case is provided by proper names inherently referring to definite humans, cf. in Russian *Pet-in-a golova* 'Peter-POSS.ADJ-F.SG.NOM head' vs. *golova kukl-y* '(a/the) head of a/the doll-GEN' (Corbett 1995).

A number of languages have a special PNP type reserved for proper names as possessors. This is the case in Rumanian, for example, where many personal names and names of months (i. e. proper names which cannot be marked for definiteness) express their functions through preposed particles which are identical to 3d person masculine pronouns in the genitive/dative (cf. (14) with (9)):

(14) Rumanian
    a. *coroan-a*   *lui*
       crown-DEF.F.SG his/PR.ART.GEN/DAT
       Vladimir
       Vladimir
       'Vladimir's crown'
    b. *casa*   *lui*   *Mary*
       house-DEF.F.SG his/PR.ART.GEN/DAT Mary
       'Mary's house'

5. Grammaticalization patterns

Linguistic possession is a fairly abstract cognitive domain and expressions for it are therefore normally derived from more concrete domains. Recurrent "overlappings" between PNPs and other constructions combined with what we actually know about the history of many particular languages suggest various **grammaticalization sources** for PNPs, or source event schemas used for expression of adnominal possession (Heine 1997: chapters 2, 3). The most important among these include the following five:

(i) Source Schema – constructions involving reference to the **source** of an object or the **starting point** of movement, as in French *la maison de Pierre* or German *das Haus von meinem Vater*.

(ii) Goal Schema – constructions involving reference to the **goal** of movement or a **recipient**. Thus, the use of the same case form for possessors in PNPs (referring to alienable possession) and for recipients with verbs of giving is well attested in the Australian languages, as in Dyirbal (ex. (15)).

(15) Dyirbal (Pama-Nyungan)
    (a) Recipient (Dixon 1980: 322)
       bala barri baŋgun yibi-ŋgu
       it:ABS axe:ABS she:ERG woman-ERG
       wuga-n baŋul yara-ŋu
       give-PRES he:GEN/DAT man-GEN/DAT
       'The woman is giving the axe to the man.'
    (b) Possessor (Dixon 1969: 36)
       badibadi-ŋu yabi
       Badibadi-GEN/DAT mother:ABS
       'Badibadi's mother'

In a similar vein, the analytic PNP *hatt-en till mann-en* 'hat-DEF.COMM to man-DEF.COMM ('the man's hat') in Standard Norwegian involves the preposition *till* 'to' which is otherwise used for reference to the goal of motion and recipients.

(iii) Location Schema – constructions involving reference to the **location** on/in an object or in its immediate vicinity. Thus, the PNP *hestur-in hjá Jógvan-i* (horse-DEF.SG.M. NOM at John-DAT.SG) 'John's horse' in Faroese involves the locative preposition *hjá* 'at' (Lockwood 1955: 104–105). Locative constructions serve as a very frequent grammaticalization source for PNPs.

(iv) Topic Schema — the possessor is introduced as a thematic element followed by the possessee, "as for X, (X's) Y". This schema underlies constructions with linking pronouns exemplified in (8).

(v) Anaphoric pronouns referring to the possessee ("X, Y's one") have e. g. given rise to the ezafe-suffixes in the Iranian and in a number of other languages (Aristar 1991: 1–33).

6. Connections with other grammatical phenomena

There is a huge literature on connections between adnominal possession and other grammatical phenomena, discussed within various theoretical frameworks. One prominent research domain here has been word order, which will not be discussed in the present article (→ Art. 64).

Another fruitful direction of research concerns possible connections between CMs employed in adnominal possession and in other constructions. Two examples will be considered here: connections between PNPs and clauses or verb-subject/verb-object combinations, and connections between PNPs and other instances of adnominal modification.

Nichols (1986: 75) proposes the following generalization on availability of head-marking in various types of constructions:

"If a language has major, salient, head-marking morphology anywhere, it will have it at the clause level".

For the purposes of the present discussion, this generalization can be reworded as follows:

"If a language uses head-marking in PNPs, it will use head-marking (i. e., verbal agreement) to relate arguments to verbs".

The question of whether markers themselves show proneness to be used cross-categorially has also received considerable attention. Thus, on the basis of North American Indian languages, Seiler (1983) described certain types of affinities between nominal possessive affixes and person markers of arguments (subject and/or object) on verbs, partly dependent on alienability splits, for which he suggested a semantic-conceptual explanation. According to him, every possessive structure involves both established possession, which has to be established by explicit means and calls for an active acquiring possessor, and inherent possession, whereby the possessor is not active, but rather experiencing when something happens to the possessee. The active possessor shares similarities with agents of dynamic verbs, while the inactive possessor is akin to patients and experiencers. This, in turn, explains why possessive affixes may be similar or even identical both to subject- and object markers on verbs. On the basis of a large-scale world-wide language sample, Siewierska (1998) confirms that possessive affixes in the majority of relevant languages show considerable affinities with verbal person marking. However, it is much more complicated to establish cross-linguistic preferences or statistical universals with respect to the identity of verbal arguments with which the possessor exhibits formal affinities, or to correlate such affinities with alienability splits.

Turning now to adnominal modification in general, there seems to be considerable cross-linguistic variation as to whether markers of adnominal possession are "exclusive" for PNPs. Thus, while the European languages in general tend to differentiate between PNPs and other cases of adnominal modification, the languages of South-Eastern Asia (Matisoff 1972) tend to use the same marker for various kinds of adnominal modification, illustrated by example (15) in which six different types of adnominal attributes (possessors, adjectives, demonstratives, numerals, locative modifiers and relative clauses) are related to their head by means of the same construction marker:

(15) Hokkien (Sino-Tibetan: Chinese; David Gil p. c.)
(a) $a^{44(>44)}$-$beŋ^{24}$ $e^{24>22}$ $p^heŋ^{24>22}$-ko^{53}
Ah Beng   CM   apple
'Ah Beng's apple'
(b) $aŋ^{24}$ $e^{24>22}$ $p^heŋ^{24>22}$-ko^{53}
red   CM   apple
'the/a red apple'
(c) cit^4 $e^{24>22}$ $p^heŋ^{24>22}$-ko^{53}
this   CM   apple
'this apple'
(d) $si^{21>53}$ $e^{24>22}$ $p^heŋ^{24>22}$-ko^{53}
four   CM   apple
'four apples'
(e) $touʔ^{21>53}$ $tieŋ^{53}$ $e^{24>22}$
table   top   CM
$p^heŋ^{24>22}$-ko^{53}
apple
'the/an apple on the table'

(f) $a^{44(>44)}$-$beŋ^{24}$ bue^{53} $e^{24>22}$
Ah Beng buy CM
$p^heŋ^{24>22}$-ko^{53}
apple
'the/an apple Ah Beng bought'

Another potentially fruitful research area would be possible connections between morphosyntactic and semantic properties of adnominal and sentential possession.

7. Special abbreviations

PNP possessive NP
CM construction marker

8. References

Aristar, Anthony Rodrigues. 1991. "On diachronic sources and synchronic pattern: An ivestigation into the origin of linguistic universals." *Language* 67.1: 1–33.

Burgess, Don. 1984. "Western Tarahumara." In: Langacker, Ronald (ed.). *Studies in Uto-Aztecan Grammar. Southern Uto-Aztecan Grammatical Sketches.* (Summer Institute of Linguistics Publications in Linguistics, 56, IV.) Dallas: Summer Institute of Linguistics, 1–149.

Chapell, Hillary & McGregor, William (eds.) 1996. *The grammar of inalienability. A typological perspective on body part terms and the part-whole relation.* (Empirical approaches to languages typology, 14.) Berlin: Mouton.

Cole, Peter. 1982. *Imbabura Quechua.* (Lingua Descriptive Studies.) Amsterdam: North Holland Publishing Company.

Corbett, Greville. 1995. "Slavonic's closest approach to Suffixaufnahme: The possessive adjective." In: Plank, Frans (ed.). *Double Case. Agreement by Suffixaufnahme.* New York/Oxford: Oxford University Press, 265–282.

Croft, William. 1990. *Typology and unversals.* Cambridge: Cambridge University Press.

Davies, J. 1981. *Kobon.* (Lingua Descriptive Studies, 3.) Amsterdam: North-Holland Publishing Company.

Derbyshire, Desmond C. 1979. *Hixkaryana.* (Lingua Descriptive Studies, 1.) Amsterdam: North-Holland Publishing Company.

Dixon, Robert M. W. 1969. "Relative clauses and possessive phrases in two Australian languages." *Language* 45: 35–44.

Dixon, Robert M. W. 1980. *The Languages of Australia.* (Cambridge Language Surveys.) Cambridge: Cambridge University Press.

England, Nora C. 1983. *A Grammar of Mam, a Mayan Language.* Austin: University of Texas Press.

Haiman, John. 1985. *Natural Syntax.* Cambridge: Cambridge University Press.

Halspelmath, Martin. 1999 "Explaining article-possessor incompatibility: economic motivation in noun phrase syntax." *Language* 75, 2: 227–243.

Hawkins, John. 1991. "On (in)definite articles: implicatures and (un)grammaticality prediction." *Journal of Linguistics* 27: 405–442.

Heine, Bernd. 1997. *Possession. Cognitive sources, forces, and grammaticalization.* Cambridge: Cambridge University Press.

Herslund, Michael. 1980. *Problèmes de syntaxe de l'ancien français. Compléments datifs et génitifs.* (Etudes Romanes de l'Université de Copenhague. Revue Romane numéro spécial 21.). Copenhague: Akademisk Forlag.

Koptjevskaja-Tamm, Maria. 1996. "Possessive NPs in Maltese: Alienability, Iconicity and Grammaticalization". In: Borg & Plank, Frans (eds.). The Maltese NP Meets Typology. *Rivista di Linguistica* 8.1: 245–274.

Koptjevskaja-Tamm, Maria. 2001a. "Genitives and possessive NPs in the languages of Europe". In: Plank, Frans (ed.).

Koptjevskaja-Tamm, Maria. 2001b. "'A woman of sin', 'a man of duty' and 'a hell of a mess': non-determiner genitives in Swedish". In: Plank, Frans (ed.).

Langacker, Ronald W. 1995. "Possession and Possessive Constructions". In: Taylor, John R. & MacLaury, Robert E. (eds.). *Language and the cognitive construal of the world.* Berlin and New York: Mouton, 51–79.

Lehmann, Christian. 1996 *Possession in Yucatec.* München/Newcastle: LINCOM.

Lichtenberk, Frantisek. 1983. "Relational classifiers." *Lingua* 60: 147–176.

Lockwood, W. B. 1955. *An Introduction to Modern Faroese.* Copenhague: Ejnar Munksgaard.

Lyons, Christopher. 1986. The syntax of English genitive constructions. *Journal of Linguistics* 22: 123–143.

Manzelli, Gianguido. 1990. "Possessive adnominal modifiers". In: Bechert, Johannes & Bernini, Giuliano & Buridant, Claude (eds.). *Towards a Typology of European Languages.* (Empirical Approaches to Language Typology, 8.) Berlin/New York: Mouton, 63–111.

Matisoff, James A. 1972. "Lahu nominalization, relativization and genitivization." In: Kimball, J. P. (ed.). *Syntax and Semantics,* 1. New York: Seminar Press Inc., 237–258.

McGregor, William. 1990. *A Functional Grammar of Gooniyandi.* Amsterdam/Philadelphia: John Benjamins Publishing Company.

Nichols, Johanna. 1986. "Head-marking and dependent-marking grammar". *Language* 62.1: 56–119.

Nichols, Johanna. 1988. "On alienable and inalienable possession." In: Shipley, W. (ed.). *In Honor of Mary Haas: From the Haas Festival Conference on Native American Linguistics.* Berlin: Mouton, 557–609.

Nichols, Johanna. 1992. *Linguistic Diversity in Space and Time.* Chicago and London: The University of Chicago Press.

Nikiforidou, Kiki. 1991. "The meanings of the genitive: A case study in semantic structure and semantic change." *Cognitive Linguistics* 2.2.: 149–205.

Plank, Frans. 1995. "(Re-)Introducing Suffixaufnahme." In: Plank, Frans (ed.). *Double Case. Agreement by Suffixaufnahme.* New York/Oxford: Oxford University Press, 3–110.

Plank, Frans. (ed.). 1995. *Double Case. Agreement by Suffixaufnahme.* New York/Oxford: Oxford University Press.

Plank, Frans. (ed.). ?2002 *The Noun Phrase in the Languages of Europe.* Berlin: Mouton.

Press, Margareth. 1980. *Chemehuevi. A grammar and lexicon.* (University of California Publications in Linguistics, 40). Berkeley: University of California Press.

Seiler, Hansjakob. 1983. *Possession as an Operational Dimension of Language.* Tübingen: Gunter Narr Verlag.

Siewierska, Anna. 1998. "On nominal and verbal person marking". *Linguistic Typology* 2.1: 1–56.

Taylor, John R. 1989. *Linguistic categorization: Prototypes in Linguistic Theory.* Oxford: Clarendon Press.

Ultan, Russel. 1978. "Towards a typology of substantival possession." In: Greenberg, Joseph et al. (eds.). *Universals of Human Language* 4: *Syntax.* Stanford: Standford University Press, 11–50.

Maria Koptjevskaja-Tamm, Stockholm (Sweden)

73. Internal and external possessors

1. Basic distinctions
2. Typical properties of external possessors
3. Typological variability
4. Areal Patterns
5. Theoretical issues
6. References

1. Basic distinctions

The following English sentences and their translations into German illustrate a general and pervasive contrast between the two languages:

(1) a. *Fred is washing his hands.*
    b. *My hands are shaking.*
    c. *I told him to his face.*

(2) German
   a. *Fritz wäsch-t   sich   die*
      Fred wash-3SG.PRES REFL.DAT the
      Hände.
      hands
   b. *Mir   zittern   die Hände.*
      me:DAT shake.3PL the hands
   c. *Ich habe es ihm   in-s   Gesicht*
      I   have it he.DAT into-DEF face
      gesagt.
      said

In English, **possessor** (Fred or the speaker) and **possessum** (the relevant body part) are encoded within the same phrase. As in most other cases where possessive relations are expressed by grammatical rather than lexical means, the possessor is encoded as a possessive pronoun or genitive phrase modifying a noun. In other words, **adnominal possessors** (→ Art. 72) or **internal possessors** are used in English to express both alienable (*John's house*) and inalienable possession (*John's face*). In German, by contrast, the possessor of the relevant body part is expressed by a separate clause-level constituent in the dative case that is not part of the same phrase as the possessum. Moreover, since German *waschen* and *zittern* are examples of a transitive and an intransitive verb, respectively, just as their English counterparts in (1), this extra argument in the dative is not licensed by the valence (argument structure) of the verb. Note furthermore that there is a syntactic and semantic dependency between the constituent encoding the body part and that encoding the possessor: The occurrence of the dative-marked NP depends on the selection of a suitable subject, object or PP. Among the terms that have been used for structures like (2) in German and other languages, the term **external possessors**, introduced by Vergnaud & Zubizarreta (1992), seems preferable to the older term 'possessor raising', primarily used for related structures in Non-European languages, since it is not committed to a specific view on their derivation. The particular use of the dative ('sympathetic dative' or 'possessive dative') found in structures like (2) can be distinguished from other uses of the so-called 'free dative' by several criteria: Unlike the ethical dative (cf. (3a)), the possessive dative characterizes phrases that manifest all the properties of genuine clause-level constituents, such as occurrence in the forefield in German (cf. (2b)) and unlike the *dativus in/commodi* (cf. (3b)) the possessive dative does not combine with noun phrases containing adnominal possessors, unless they are coreferent with the dative phrase (cf. Wegener, 1985; Podlesskaya & Rakhilina, 1999: 506):

(3) German
    a. *Fass mir ja nicht den*
       touch me:DAT PRTCL NEG the:ACC
       Hund an!
       dog:ACC PREF
       'Don't you touch the dog!'
    b. *Maria wusch ihr-em Sohn*
       Mary washed her-DAT son:DAT
       Papas altes Hemd.
       daddy's old shirt
       'Mary washed daddy's old shirt for her son.'
    c. **Maria wusch ihr-em Sohn*
       Mary washed her-DAT son:DAT
       Papas Füße.
       daddy's feet
       'Mary washed daddy's feet on/for her son.'

Since the encoding of external possessors by a dative phrase is a specific European phenomenon, a general, cross-linguistically applicable characterization of the relevant constructions must be given along the following lines (cf. Payne & Barshi, 1999: 3):

(3) Definition
    External possessor constructions are constructions in which a semantic possessor-possessum relation is expressed (i) by coding the possessor as a core grammatical relation of the verb and (ii) in a constituent separate from that which contains the possessum. (iii) Despite being coded as a core argument, the possessor phrase is not licensed by the argument frame of the verb root itself.

The definition given above comprises three conditions, which – taken together – restrict the class of phenomena to be analyzed as external possessors quite severely. Condition (ii) is the most basic and seems to be generally agreed on. Condition (i) excludes all cases where the possessor is not coded as a subject, direct object or indirect object, but as a locative phrase, as in the following example from Swedish:

(4) Swedish
    Någon bröt armen på honom.
    Someone broke the:arm on him.
    'Someone broke his arm'

Finally, condition (iii) excludes all cases from the class of external possessors where a subject is the understood possessor of a body part expressed by an object or oblique phrase. In König & Haspelmath (1997: 573 ff.) the term 'implicit-possessor constructions' is used for such structures:

(5) Spanish
    Carmen levantó la mano.
    Carmen raised the hand
    'Carmen raised her hand.'

(6) Russian
    Ja prikusil jazyk.
    I:NOM bit tongue:AKK
    'I bit my tongue.'

Similarly problematic in view of condition (iii) are cases like the following in English and other languages, called 'possessor splitting' by Podlesskaya & Rakhilina (1999):

(7) a. *Ben punched Jim on the nose.*
    b. *She grabbed him by the arm.*
    c. *He kissed her on the cheek.*

In cases such as these the possessor phrase IS licensed by the argument structure of the verb. What is lacking, however, is the relationship of syntactic and semantic dependency between possessor phrase and possessum phrase typical of external possessor constructions. In (7) the prepositional phrase containing the possessum is omissible in each case and provides a further (metonymic) specification of the precise endpoint of the action expressed by the verb. Existing studies of external possessor constructions differ in that they include all three or only a subset of the conditions given in the definition (3) and, as a consequence, in that they include none, some or all of the phenomena illustrated by (4)–(7).

2. Typical properties of external possessors

As already mentioned, external possessors are typically 'extra-thematic' arguments (cf. Shibatani, 1994) and thus not licensed by the argument structure of a verb. Moreover, they depend syntactically on the occurrence of a possessum phrase. Semantically, the possessum evokes the possessor and has no separate existence apart from it. In other words, the possessa have a relational meaning and can thus be assumed to have an argument structure of their own. This argument could be assumed to be saturated by the possessor phrase. In European languages which have such constructions, external possessors are invariably expressed by a dative phrase or an 'indirect object', whereas there are several options for encoding the possessum.

Languages with external possessor constructions typically do not employ such patterns to the complete exclusion of the corresponding internal possessor constructions. More often than not there is the possibility of choosing between these two constructions, depending on the meaning one wants to express. External possessor constructions typically imply that the possessor is strongly affected by the action or event denoted by the rest of the sentence (cf. Havers, 1911; Bally, 1926; König & Haspelmath, 1997; Wierzbicka, 1988). The following examples from German illustrate the typical semantic contrast between external possessor constructions and their counterparts with internal posessors:

(8) German
    a. *Ich habe meine Haare verbrannt.*
       I:NOM have my hair burnt
       'I (have) burnt my hair.'
    b. *Ich habe mir die Haare*
       I:NOM have me:DAT the hair
      verbrannt.
      burnt
      'I have burnt/singed my hair.'

(9) a. *Karl ist auf meinen Mantel*
      Charles is on my coat
      getreten.
      stepped
      'Charles stepped on my coat.'
    b. *Karl ist mir auf den Mantel*
      Charles is me:DAT on the coat
      getreten.
      stepped
      'Charles stepped on my coat.'

Sentence (9b) is only possible in a situation where the person identified as Karl is wearing the coat and (8b) suggests that the speaker got too close to a candle and singed his/her hair. A sentence like (8a), by contrast, would typically be used when referring to a wig or strand of hair that had been cut off before the event of burning took place and (9a) suggests that the coat in question is lying somewhere on the floor. Analogous subtle contrasts have been reported from many other languages. Roldán (1972: 27), for instance, observes that the first example of the following minimal pair could be used to describe the patient's reaction during eye surgery, whereas the second example would be used to describe a person's emotional involvement:

(10) a. *Sus ojos se llenaron de lágrimas.*
      his eyes REFL filled of tears
    b. *Los ojos se le llenaron de*
      the eyes REFL him:DAT filled of
      lágrimas.
      tears
      'His eyes filled with tears.'

The common denominator of the preceding three b-examples is that the possessor is (construed as being) affected by an event which affects some part of him/her, whereas in the a-examples the body part or garment is seen as a separate, autonomous entity.

The choice between external possessor constructions and internal possessor constructions is not available, however, whenever the possessum — typically an expression for a body part — is not used in its literal sense but forms an idiomatic expression together with the predicate. In other words, the internal possessor constructions do not have the range of transferred, idiomatic interpretations that the analogous external possessor constructions have:

(11) a. *Die Polizei sitzt mir*
      the police is.sitting me:DAT
      im Nacken.
      in.DEF.DAT neck
      'The police is breathing down my neck.'
    b. ?*Die Polizei sitzt in meinem Nacken.*
      'The police is sitting on my neck.'

(12) a. *Karl hat sich dar-über den*
      Charles has REFL there-over the
      Kopf zerbrochen.
      head broken
      'Charles has racked his brains over it.'

b. *Karl hat darüber seinen Kopf zerbrochen.*
'Charles has broken his head over it.'

3. Typological variability

3.1. Grammatical relation of the external possessor

(i) Languages without external possessor constructions

As is shown by the English examples listed above, external possessor constructions may be subjected to very tight restrictions in a language or they may be lacking altogether. In English the regular pattern of adnominal possession is employed indiscriminately for both alienable and inalienable possession and the only possible, if somewhat dubious, examples of external possessor constructions are sentences like (7), i. e. sentences in which the possessum is encoded separately as a prepositional phrase. Among the languages without clear instances of external possessor constructions we also find Finnish, Persian, Armenian, Kurdish, Turkish, Hindi and other Indic languages, as well as Amharic, Lezgian, Tsez, Yucatec Maya, Celtic, to name only a few examples. The following sentences from Finnish and Hindi provide some illustration (cf. Haspelmath, 1999: 118):

(13) Finnish (Ursula Lehmus, p.c.)
Lapse-n tukka leika-ttiin
child-GEN hair cut-PASS.PAST
'The child's hair was cut.'

(14) Hindi
Vah apne baal dho rah-ii hai.
s/he self's hair wash PROG-FEM.SG is
'She is washing her (own) hair.'

It is not quite clear whether this lack of external possessor constructions correlates significantly with other properties of the relevant languages, even though certain tendencies are visible: Languages without external possessors also tend to lack implicit possessors as well as a well-developed system of case distinctions. In Indo-European languages, at least, external possessors disappeared with the loss of case distinctions (cf. Havers, 1911). Instead of simply noting the absence of external possessor constructions in a language, one can analyze this absence as a strategy of unfolding, or stressing, interparticipant relations, i.e. those relations that exist between participants irrespective of the predicate. The availability of external possessor constructions, by contrast, can be seen as indicating that a given language follows the principle of unfolding participant relations, i. e. of expressing the involvement of each participant in the situation as far as possible, irrespective of coexisting relations to other participants in the situation (cf. Lehmann et al. 2000).

(ii) External possessors as indirect objects.

A second parameter of typological variation in the domain under discussion concerns the encoding of the external possessor in those languages which have such constructions. In most European languages the external possessor is expressed by a dative-marked argument (cf. König & Haspelmath, 1997; Haspelmath, 1999). In fact, this type of encoding external possessors is so pervasive in Europe and so rare outside this continent that M. Haspelmath regards it as a crucial property of a European Sprachbund (→ Art. 107):

(15) Italian
Mi lav-o le mani.
me:DAT wash-1SG.PRES the hands
'I wash my hands.'

(16) Hungarian
A kutya beleharapott a
the dog into.bit the
szomszéd-nak a lábá-ba.
neighbor-DAT the leg:3SG-LOC
'The dog bit the neighbour in the leg.'

(17) Russian (Podlesskaya & Raklilina, 1999: 508)
Babuška pomy-la
grandmother:NOM wash-PAST
vnuku ruki.
grandson:DAT hands:ACC
'Grandmother washed her grandson's hands.'

(iii) External possessors as locative adjuncts

Another fairly frequent type of coding external possessors, found at the periphery of Europe, is the use of a locative case or locative adposition, either the superessive (Scandinavian, Godoberi) or adessive (Estonian, Irish and partly Russian):

(18) Estonian
Ta-l jooks-eb nina-st
he-ADESS run-3SG.PRES nose-EL
ver-d.
blood-PART
'He is bleeding from the nose'

(19) Irish
Bhí an lámh ar crith aige.
was the hand on shaking at.3SG.M
'His hand was shaking.'

(iii) Relational inheritance (possessor raising)

A frequent type of external possessor constructions outside of Europe is often analyzed as the result of promoting (raising) the possessor to the grammatical relation occupied by the possessum. These are the so-called 'double subject' or 'double object' constructions:

(20) Korean
    a. *Mary-ka ku namwu-lul*
       Mary-NOM that tree-ACC
       kaci-lul cal-ass-ta.
       branch-ACC cut-PAST-DECL
       'Mary cut the branches of the tree.'
    b. *Na pay aphu-ta.*
       I stomach ache-DECL
       'My stomach aches.'

(21) Mandarin
    Tā tóu téng.
    he head painful
    'He has a headache.'

In languages with specific topic markers, such as Japanese, the possessor typically occurs as the topic of a main clause, but has the same inflectional affix and the same grammatical function as the possessum in subordinate clauses:

(22) Japanese (Shigehiro Kokutani, p.c.)
    a. *Watashi-wa atama-ga itai.*
       1SG-TOP head-NOM be.hurting
       'I have a headache'
    b. *Watashi-ga atama-ga*
       1SG-NOM head-NOM
       itai-tte doushite wakat-ta-no.
       be.hurting-COMP how guess-PERF-Q
       'How did you guess that I had a headache?'

Even though two 'subjects' or 'objects' are found in such structures, various tests show that typically only one of these constituents exhibits the normal subject or object properties, the other one having the status of a 'chômeur'.

(iv) Possessor raising and possessum demotion

The 'promotion' or raising of the possessor phrase to the grammatical function of subject or object can be accompanied by other syntactic processes, such as possessor demotion, the incorporation of the possessor into the verb or applicative marking on the verb (cf. Haspelmath, 1999: 119ff.). If the possessum in double subject constructions and double object constructions does not exhibit the normal properties of subjects or objects, these cases can also be analyzed as exhibiting both possessor promotion and possessum demotion. The latter effect is even more clearly visible in cases where the possessum exhibits oblique case-marking or no special case marking combined with reduced behavioral properties. In the following example from Yoruba, the possessor has the status of direct object, whereas the possessum is introduced by a locative preposition:

(23) Yoruba (Rowlands 1969: 22)
    ó jí mi l' ówó gbé.
    he steal me in money take
    'He stole my money.'

Sentences of type (7) (e.g. *He kissed her on the lips.*), the only possible instance of external possessor constructions in English, could also be analyzed along those lines.

(v) Possessor raising with possessum incorporation

A more radical form of demotion is the incorporation of the possessum into the verb. The following example is from Guaraní, a polysynthetic language spoken in Paraguay:

(24) Guaraní (Velázquez-Castillo, 1999: 97)
    a. *A-johei-ta pe-mitārova.*
       1ACT-wash-FUT that-child face
       'I'll wash that child's face.'
    b. *A-hova-hei-ta pe-mitā.*
       1ACT-face-wash-FUT that child
       'I'll face-wash that child.'

Example (24a) is an instance of an internal possessor construction, (24b) is the corresponding version with an incorporated possessum. Possessum-incorporation as a concomitant feature of external possessors seems to be a fairly frequent phenomenon in the indigenous languages of the Americas (cf. Baker, 1999; Levy, 1999). It has also been reported for Chukchi and Aceh. In English the closest we get to this phenomenon is the verb *brainwash* (*They brainwashed the prisoners.*). There are, however, also some phenomena in European languages with dative possessors that are related to possessum incorporation. As pointed out above, only external possessors permit a non-literal, metaphorical interpretation in these languages. The following German example is a case in point:

(25) German
Claudia hat vielen Männern
Claudia has many:DAT men:DAT
den Kopf verdreht.
the:AKK head:AKK turned
'Claudia has turned the head of many men.'

In cases like these, the verb and the direct object form a semantic unit (an idiom). Moreover, we find the article in the singular with a distributive interpretation and the object noun does not permit attributive modification.

(vi) Possessor raising with applicative marking on the verb

In some languages the promotion of the possessor and demotion of the possessum is accompanied by an applicative affix, i. e. by a marker that indicates that the direct object does not have the semantic role of a patient. In the second of the following examples from Tzotzil the applicative suffix *-be* indicates that the possessor rather than the possessum functions as direct (primary) object:

(26) Tzotzil
  a. *i- Ø- s- yaintas h- k'ob*
     COMPL-3ABS-3ERG-injure 1POSS-hand
     'He has injured my hand.'
  b. *l- i- s- yaintas- be h- k'ob*
     COMPL-1ABS-3ERG-injure- APPL 1POSS-hand
     'He has injured my hand.'

In Tzotzil, verbs manifest both subject- and object agreement. In (26a) the verb agrees with the possessum, as is indicated by the 3rd person absolutive affix. This shows that the possessum functions as direct (primary) object. In (26b), by contrast, the object marker (1st person absolutive) shows that the verb agrees with the possessor, which therefore must be analyzed as direct object. The following example from an Australian language is even clearer, since there is no possessive marking on the noun expressing the possessum:

(27) Kalkatungu (Australian)
Kalpin-tu lha-nytyama-mi-kin
man-ERG hit-APPL-FUT-INTERROG
nyini thuku?
you:ABS dog:ABS
'Will the man hit your dog?'

As is shown by the preceding examples, external possessors may assume a wide variety of grammatical relations in the clause (indirect object, direct object, intransitive subject, etc.) but there does not seem to be any clear pattern, expressible by an implicational hierarchy, governing the variation observable across languages (cf. Payne & Barshi, 1999: 9).

3.2. Grammatical relations of the possessum

While the grammatical relation of an external possessor phrase seems to be more or less constant across different types of clauses within a specific language, there typically is some variation in the syntactic status of the possessum phrase, depending on the type of predicate it combines with. The following examples from German show that the possessor is invariably expressed by a dative-marked indirect object, in contrast to the possessum phrase which may have the status of a direct object, a subject or an oblique phrase:

(28) a. *Der Arzt hat mir den Magen*
       the doctor has me:DAT the stomach
       geröngt.
       x-rayed
       'The doctor has x-rayed my stomach.'
    b. *Mir flattern die Nerven.*
       me:DAT are.shaking the nerves
       'My nerves are shaking.'
    c. *Er spuckte mir in-s Gesicht.*
       he spat me:DAT into-the face
       'He spat into my face.'

The preceding examples show that the encoding of the possessum depends on the valence (argument structure) of the relevant verb: Only with intransitive verbs may a possessum phrase show up as a subject. Additional patterns and constraints within languages and across languages seem to be a consequence of the specific meaning (the affectedness of the possessor by something happening to the possessum) typically associated with such constructions: Possessa rarely assume the relation of transitive subject, unaccusative subjects, i. e. intransitive subjects with a patient-like semantic role, are much more frequent than unergative subjects and indirect objects possessa have never been reported as being accessible to external possessors. The hierarchy formulated by Haspelmath (1999: 113) for the accessibility of possessa to external possessors in European languages seems to be at least partially valid also for a wider variety of languages:

(29) **The Syntactic Relations Hierarchy**
direct object > unaccusative subject > unergative subject > transitive subjects

3.3. Semantic properties

(i) Properties of possessors

External possessors are most typically animate, human and perhaps even speech-act participants. By and large, the patterns of variation observable across languages relative to the meaning of external possessors can be formulated in terms of the well-known animacy hierarchy: If an external possessor construction is possible for a type of possessor low on the hierarchy it is also possible for any possessor higher on the scale (cf. Havers, 1911; Seiler, 1983: 76; Haspelmath, 1999: 113):

(30) **The Animacy Hierarchy**
$1^{st}/2^{nd}$ pers. > 3rd pers. > proper name > other animate nouns > inanimate nouns

Languages differ with regard to the precise cut-off point in the admissibility of external possessor constructions, but the preference for the higher positions of the hierarchy seems to a universal phenomenon. One of the few languages that permit inanimate external possessors is Korean:

(31) Korean
Mary-ka ku namwu-lul
Mary-NOM that tree-ACC
kaci-lul cal-ass-ta.
branch-ACC cut-PAST-DECL
'Mary cut the branches of the tree.'

For many languages the cut-off point in the admissibility of external possessor constructions are higher animals or even human beings, as long as they are still alive:

(32) German
a. *Karl ist dem Hund auf die*
Charles is the:DAT dog:DAT on the
Pfote getreten.
paw stepped
'Charles stepped on the dogs paw.'
b. ?*Karl ist der Pflanze auf das*
Charles is the plant on the
Blatt getreten.
leaf stepped
'Charles has stepped on the leaf of the plant.'

The restriction of external possessor constructions to pronouns can be illustrated with examples from French, where sentences like (33 b) are of dubious acceptability or stylistic quality, unless they are used idiomatically. The corresponding sentence with an internal possessor (*la jambe de Jacques*) would of course be perfectly acceptable:

(33) French
a. *On lui a cassé la*
somebody him:DAT has broken the
jambe.
leg
'Somebody broke his leg.'
b. ?*On a cassé la jambe à Jacques.*
'Somebody broke Jacques's leg.'

(ii) Types of predicates

Given that the various semantic conditions governing external possessor constructions in various languages can be regarded as specific manifestations of a general affectedness condition, it is to be expected that these constructions should be best with event predicates rather than stative ones, in particular with those expressing an effect. Such a preference has been observed for European languages (König & Haspelmath, 1997) and many other cases, but does not hold for all languages. In Sinitic languages, in Japanese and Korean, as well as in some Amerindian languages it is stative intransitive predicates which provide the starting point for external possessor constructions. And even in European languages stative predicates are possible as long as the relevant state strongly affects the possessor. The following Italian example presents a situation of visual perception as a case of sexual harassment:

(34) Italian
Le ho visto le gambe.
her:DAT I:have seen the legs
'I saw her legs.'

(iii) Possessive relations

Adnominal possessors (→ Art. 72) may express a wide variety of possessive relations, from legal possession to very abstract relations of association. Most typically the relationship between external possessors and the relevant possessa is one of inalienable possession, body parts being the most frequently discussed case in the literature. So the simplest version of the hierarchy constraining accessible possessa in external possessor constructions can be formulated as inalienable < alienable. A more fine-grained version of this hierarchy is formulated by Payne & Barshi (1999: 14) as follows:

(35) **The Inalienability Hierarchy**
body-part > part-whole > other inalienable > alienable + proximate > alienable + distal

The fact that many analyses of external possessors in various languages have the term 'body parts' in the title clearly indicates that body parts are the most typical possessa in such constructions. Apart from permitting such cases, languages may differ in subtle ways. In German, for example, garments and all other entities surrounding the body ('tent', 'house', 'country') are permissible possessa in the relevant constructions, while kinship terms are somewhat marginal:

(36) German
   a. *Es regnete ihm in-s Zelt.*
      it rained him:DAT into-DEF tent
      'It was raining into his tent (with him inside).'
   b. ?*Sie haben mir den*
      they have me:DAT the:AKK
      Vater beleidigt.
      father:AKK insulted
      'They insulted my father.'
   c. *Sie haben ihm das Haus*
      they have him:DAT the house
      angezündet.
      burnt
      'They set fire to his house.'

In other languages kinship terms seem to be privileged (cf. Chappell, 1999).

4. Areal patterns

It is only since very recently that possessor raising in non-European languages and external possessor constructions in European languages have come to be seen as two manifestations of basically the same phenomenon. This reassessment of the facts has shown that external possessor constructions are found in all parts of the globe (cf. Payne & Barshi, 1999: 5f.). There are, however, clear areal patterns with regard to the distribution of those formal properties that have been shown to vary across languages. The encoding of the external possessor by a case-marked noun phrase in the dative is a characteristic feature of a European linguistic area, just like the opposition between definite and indefinite article or perfects with 'have' (→ Art. 107). Such dative external possessors are found in the core area of European languages, regardless of whether they are Indo-European languages or not, and they are lacking at the periphery of Europe as well as in the Indo-European languages outside of Europe (cf. Haspelmath, 1999). Relational inheritance ('usurpation'), by contrast, is a frequent phenomenon in East-Asian languages and possessum incorporation seems to be frequent in the indigenous languages of the Americas. Neither of these phenomena is found in Europe.

5. Theoretical issues

The ubiquity of external possessor constructions suggests that they must be some linguistically natural phenomenon, serving some important communicative need. Moreover, there is clearly some pragmatic or cognitive motivation behind the various formal properties discussed above. External possessor constructions express that a (typically) human experiencer or patient is affected by an event affecting a part of his body. Since the part identified by the possessum has no independent existence apart from the whole and since the whole (i. e. the possessor) is more salient than the part, it should not come as a surprise that this greater salience of the possessor is reflected in syntactic form.

No convincing and generally accepted solution, however, has so far been offered for the problems raised by the existence of external possessors for syntactic theory. In particular, external possessor constructions challenge the notion that clause-level syntax depends directly on the argument structure or valence of individual verbs, a notion that is part of many syntactic theories. Various syntactic, semantic and pragmatic explanations have been offered for the apparent mismatch between the argument structure of the verb and the extra ('unlicensed') argument found in external possessor constructions, none of which provides a convincing solution for all problems (cf. Barshi & Payne, 1999: 15 ff.). One proposal assumes that the argument structure of the verb is adjusted by some lexical operation (incorporation, addition of an applicative affix) and that the 'extra' argument is licensed as a result of this adjustment (Baker, 1999). A related proposal for European languages is the idea that the extra argument (the possessor) saturates an empty argument position introduced by the relational nouns expressing the possessum (cf. Wunderlich, 1996; Polinsky & Comrie, 1999).

A purely pragmatic explanation is the idea that an extra argument is licensed ('extra-thematic licensing') to the extent that the referent is relevant for and fits in with the scene depicted by the relevant clause (cf. Shibatani, 1994).

6. References

Baker, Mark. 1999."External Possession in Mohawk: Body parts, incorporation, and argument structure." In: Payne, Doris L. & Barshi, Immanuel (eds.), *External Possession*. Amsterdam: Benjamins, 294–323.

Bally, Charles. 1926. "L'expression des idées de sphère personnelle et de solidarité dans les langues indo-européennes." In: Fankhauser, F. & Jud, F. (eds.) *Festschrift Louis Gauchat*. Aarau: Sauerländer, 68–78.

Chappell, Hilary & McGregor, William (eds.) 1995. *The Grammar of Inalienability: A Typological Perspective on Body Part Terms and the Part-Whole Relation*. Berlin: Mouton de Gruyter.

Chappell, Hilary. 1999. "The double unaccusative construction in Sinitic languages". In: Payne, Doris L. & Barshi, Immanuel (eds.), *External Possession*. Amsterdam: Benjamins, 195–228.

Haspelmath, Martin. 1999. "External possession in a European areal perspective". In: Payne, Doris L. & Barshi, Immanuel (eds.), *External Possession*. Amsterdam: Benjamins, 109–135.

Havers, Wilhelm. 1911. *Untersuchungen zur Kasussyntax der indoeuropäischen Sprachen*. Straßburg: Trübner.

König, Ekkehard & Haspelmath, Martin. 1997. "Les constructions à possesseur externe dans les langues de l'Europe". In: Feuillet, Jack (ed.) *Actance et Valence dans les langues de l'Europe*. Berlin: Mouton, 525–606.

Krohn, Dieter. 1980. *Dativ und Pertinenzrelation*. Göteborg: Acta Universitatis Gothenburgensis.

Langacker, Ronald, W. 1999. "Double subject constructions.", In: Sung-Yun Bak (ed.). *Linguistics in the Morning Calm* 4. 83–104. Seoul: Hanshin.

Lehmann, Christian et al. 2000. "Unfolding of situation perspectives as a typological characteristic of languages." *Sprachtypologie und Universalienforschung* 53.71–79.

Levy, Paulette 1999. "'Where' rather than 'what': Incorporation of parts in Totonac." In: Payne, Doris L. & Barshi, Immanuel (eds.), *External Possession*. Amsterdam: Benjamins,

Payne, Doris L. & Barshi, Immanuel, (eds.) 1999. *The Grammar of External Possession*. Amsterdam: Benjamins.

Podlesskaya, Vera I. & Rakhilina, Ekaterina V. 1999. "External possession, reflexivization and body parts in Russian". In: Payne, Doris L. & Barshi, Immanuel (eds.), *External Possession*. Amsterdam: Benjamins, 505–521.

Polinsky, Maria & Comrie, Bernard. 1999. "Possessor raising in a language that does not have any." In: Payne, Doris L. & Barshi, Immanuel (eds.), *External Possession*. Amsterdam: Benjamins, 523–542.

Roldán, Mercedes. 1972. "Concerning Spanish datives and possessives." *Languages Sciences* 21: 27–32.

Rowlands, E. C. 1969. *Yoruba*. Sevenoaks: Hodder and Stoughton.

Seiler, Hansjakob. 1983. *Possession as an operational dimension of language*. (Language Universals Series, 2.) Tübingen: Gunter Narr.

Shibatani, Masayoshi. 1994. "An integrational approach to possessor raising, ethical datives and adversative passives", *Berkeley Linguistic Society* 20: 461–486.

Uehara, Keiko. 1999. "External possession constructions in Japanese: A psycholinguistic perspective." In: Payne, Doris L. & Barshi, Immanuel (eds.), *External Possession*. Amsterdam: Benjamins, 45–74.

Velázquez-Castillo, Maura. 1999. "Body part EP constructions: A cognitive/functional analysis." In: Payne, Doris L. & Barshi, Immanuel (eds.), *External Possession*. Amsterdam: Benjamins, 77–107.

Vergnaud, Jean-Roger & Zubizarreta, Maria-Louise. 1992. "The definite determiner and the inalienable constructions in French and English". *Linguistic Inquiry* 23: 595–652.

Wegener, Heide. 1985. *Der Dativ im heutigen Deutsch*. Tübingen: Narr.

Wierzbicka, Anna. 1988. *The Semantics of Grammar*. Amsterdam: Benjamins.

Wunderlich, Dieter. 1996. "Dem Freund die Hand auf die Schulter legen." In: Harras, Gisela & Bierwisch, Manfred (eds.), *Wenn die Semantik arbeitet*. Tübingen: Niemeyer.

Ekkehard König, Freie Universität Berlin (Germany)

74. Complement clauses

1. Introduction
2. Complement clauses in view of finiteness and clause combining
3. The semantics of complementation
4. Diachronic aspects of complementation
5. Distributional and other constraints on complement clauses: cross-linguistic variation
6. Complement clauses and relative clauses: cross-linguistic distributional patterning
7. Conclusion
8. Special abbreviations
9. References

1. Introduction

This section provides a survey of major typological findings on **complement clauses** (or **complements**), which are defined as clauses functioning syntactically as either a subject or an object:

(1) ***That David came in time*** *was surprising.*

(2) *Ann avoided **meeting her ex-girlfriend at the party.***

Some complement clauses include a **complementizer**, i.e. "a word, particle, clitic, or affix whose function it is to identify the entity as a complement" (Noonan 1985: 44), like *that* in (1).

The syntactic phenomenon represented by complement clauses is referred to as **complementation**, i.e. "the syntactic situation which arises when a notional sentence or predication is an argument of a predicate. [...] a predication can be viewed as an argument of a predicate if it functions as the subject or object of that predicate" (Noonan 1985: 43).

Not all languages possess constructions uniquely identifiable as complement clauses. Dixon (1995) proposes a typology of clause linking which comprises **co-ordinate and non-embedded subordinate constructions**, **complement clause constructions**, and **relative-clause constructions**. Languages may not have a construction uniquely identified as a complement clause "which has the internal structure of a clause but fills an object, subject, or post-object slot in a main clause" (1995: 181); however, these languages can use other constructions to express a meaning similar to the complement clause. Dixon refers to this phenomenon as a **complementation strategy**. For instance, Dyirbal employs a relative clause construction as a complement strategy:

(3) Dyirbal (Dixon 1995: 208)
ŋaja ŋamba-n **ŋinu-na**
I-NOM hear-PAST you-ACC
milga-ŋu
chastise (TR)-REL+ABS
'I heard you(r) being chastised.' (Lit. 'I heard you, who were ...')

Similarly, Mandarin Chinese employs a juxtaposed construction as a complementation strategy:

(4) Mandarin Chinese (Li & Thompson 1981: 164)
wǒ méi xiǎngdào **nǐ zhù zài**
I NEG realize you live in
Niǔyuè.
New York
'I didn't realize you lived in New York.'

The following sections will present the findings of major typological research on complement clauses, as well as of studies based on complement clauses in particular languages which have cross-linguistic implications.

2. Complement clauses in view of finiteness and clause combining

The first parameters of variation to be considered concern two syntactico-semantic aspects of complementation: finiteness and clause combining.

2.1. Finiteness

Complement clauses are distinguishable from main clauses in terms of the degree of **finiteness**, and show varying degrees of affinity to noun phrases (→ Art. 100). Givón (1990: 853) defines the finiteness of a clause as 'the degree of its similarity to the **prototype transitive clause**" (emphasis original – KH), which includes such syntactic features as **tense-aspect-modality** and **case-marking of the subject and object**. Complement clauses show varying degrees of **nouniness** as they lose syntactic features coding finiteness.

Noonan (1985: 29–65) provides a cross-linguistic typology of **complement types** on the basis of morphosyntactic features encoding finiteness, e.g. the part of speech of the predicate (i.e. verb, noun, or adjective), range of inflectional categories marked in the complement, syntactic relation of subject to predicate, etc. Noonan's typology consists of **indicative**, **subjunctive**, **paratactic**, **infinitive**, **participle**, and **nominalized** (shown by bold face in the examples below).

Indicative complement clauses most closely resemble declarative main clauses:

(5) (a) *It rained yesterday.* (declarative main clause)
 (b) *I heard **that it rained yesterday**.* (indicative complement clause)

Subjunctive is the term "given to special verb forms or markers that obligatorily occur in certain types of subordinate clauses" (Bybee, Perkins & Pagliuca 1994: 213), e.g. complement clauses and relative clauses which encode **irrealis** (see § 3.1., Art. 60):

(6) Spanish (Bybee, Perkins & Pagliuca 1994: 213)
 *Dice que **vengan** ahora.*
 say.3SG that come.SUBJ.3PL now
 'He says for them to come now.'

Paratactic complements are illustrated by the following Lango example, where a series of fully inflected verbs are linked without any marker of subordination (→ Art. 82):

(7) Lango (Noonan 1985: 55)
 *Dákó òkòbbì icó **òkwɔ̀rɔ̀***
 woman told.3SG.DAT man sifted.3SG
 kál
 millet
 'The woman said it to the man, he sifted millet.'
 (The woman told the man to sift millet (and he did))

According to Noonan (1985: 56−60), infinitive complements show cross-linguistic variation in terms of the range of inflectional categories allowed, e.g. tense, aspect, voice, object agreement, except that they cannot allow subject-verb agreement (see Mufwene & Dijkhoff 1989 for the argument against the existence of an infinitive in Atlantic pidgins and creoles; → Art. 100). The following example illustrates an infinitive complement in Russian, which generally shows opposition both in aspect and voice:

(8) Russian (Koptjevskaja-Tamm 1993: 33)
 *Ja ne ljublju gromk-o **čita-t'***
 I not like loud-ADV read-INF
 stix-i
 poem-ACC.PL
 'I do not like to read poems loudly.'

Participles, the use of which "in complementation is usually limited" (Noonan 1985: 62), are illustrated by the following Classical Greek perception verb complement:

(9) Classical Greek (Noonan 1985: 63)
 Eîde autòn
 saw (3SG) him (ACC)
 paúonta
 stop (PART, PRES, MASC, SG, ACC)
 'He saw him stopping.'

Nominalization is one of the most frequent means employed by languages to encode complementation (cf. Ross 1973, Horie 1997, Noonan 1997, Horie 2000a, b.

O'Dowd (1992) takes note of the crosslinguistic preference for employing nominalization to encode subordination, including complement clauses, and argues that the tendency is motivated by the **syntactic metaphor** EVENTS ARE OBJECTS.

Koptjevskaja-Tamm (1993) is one of the most comprehensive typological studies of one particular type of nominalized constructions, i.e. **action nominal constructions** (or ANCs) which include **action nominals** as their head. The latter are defined as "nouns derived from verbs (verbal nouns) with the general meaning of an action or process, 'capable of declining or taking prepositions or postpositions in the same way as non-derived nouns, and showing 'reasonable' productivity.'" (1993: 5).

Koptjevskaja-Tamm presents a cross-linguistic typology of ANCs arranged on a cline of finiteness. That is, the cross-linguistically attested ANC types range from the type most closely resembling finite clauses to the type most closely resembling non-derived noun phrases, with the other types plotted in between. The most finite ANC type, type 1 'Sentential,' is illustrated by the following Archi example, which retains both the dependent-marking and the head-marking strategies used in finite clauses:

(10) Archi (Koptjevskaja-Tamm 1993: 92)
 wez sini [un
 I.DAT know you.CL1.NOM
 wirx̄ₒinkul]
 work.AN.CL1.NOM
 'I know that you work.'

The most nominal ANC type, her type 4 'Nominal,' is illustrated by the following Finnish example, where both subject and object are put in the genitive case:

(11) Finnish (Koptjevskaja-Tamm 1993: 169)
[Vanhempien taloudellisen
parents.GEN economic
tuen antaminen] *on*
support.GEN give.AN is
riippuvaista tuloista
dependent incomes.PARTV
'Parents' giving of economic support is dependent on their incomes.'

Furthermore, Koptjevskaja-Tamm expands on Stassen's two strategies of clause chaining, **balanced constructions** vs. **deranked constructions**, and the typology of languages based on the strategies, **balancing languages** vs. **deranking languages** (Stassen 1985: 75–76). Balanced constructions are "chaining constructions in which predicates remain of the same rank" (1985: 76) and the languages which choose this encoding option are referred to as balancing languages. English has a balanced construction as follows:

(12) *John **jumped** out of his chair and **grabbed** a gun.*

Deranked constructions are those in which "only one of the predicates in the chain retains its finite verb form, whereas the other predicate is represented as a subordinate, usually non-finite, verbal construct" (1985: 77); languages which use this encoding option are called deranking languages. Tamil has a deranked construction, whereby one of the two predicates in the chain is deranked to a gerund as in *erudiittu* below:

(13) Tamil (Stassen 1985: 77)
*Avaru kavide **erudiittu***
he.NOM poetry.ACC write.PERF.GER
*naaval **moripeyarttaaru***
novel.ACC translate.PAST.IND.3SG
'He wrote poetry and then translated a novel.'

Based on this typology, Koptjevskaja-Tamm proposed the following classification of languages:

(i) **Complement-balancing languages** are those which "have both balanced and deranked noun clauses" (Koptjevskaja-Tamm 1993: 24). In these languages, "ANCs compete with finite clauses (and, perhaps, with some other types of noun clauses) for meanings and functions" (1993: 45);

(ii) **Strictly complement-balancing languages** are those "which only have balanced noun clauses" (1993: 26) like Chinese;

(iii) **Complement-deranking languages** are those which "obligatorily derank the predicates in their noun clauses" (1993: 26). In these languages, "(t)he resulting system of verbal nouns is especially intricate" (1993: 46).

2.2. Clause combining

Various languages are known to use the morpho-syntactic mechanism of **clause combining** to encode a variety of semantic relationships that hold between clauses. Complement clauses, which function as arguments of matrix clause predicates, tend to show a high degree of **clause integration** into matrix clauses compared to other subordinate clauses such as adverbial clauses. Typological research undertaken to describe cross-linguistically observed clause-combining phenomena includes the following (see also § 3.2.).

Foley & Van Valin (1984: 77–80) proposed a three-layer clause structure model consisting of **nucleus**, **core** and **periphery**, as shown in Fig. 74.1:

```
[(NP)...(NP)[NP(NP) [Predicate]]]
                     ───────── NUCLEUS
            ─────────────────  CORE
 ────────────────────────────  PERIPHERY
────────────────────────────
            CLAUSE
```

Fig. 74.1: The layered structure of the clause (Foley & Van Valin: 78)

Each layer is distinguishable from the other in terms of the set of **operators** on each layer, i.e. aspect and directionals (nuclear operators), modality (core operator), status, tense, evidentials, and illocutionary force (peripheral operators).

Foley & Van Valin also introduce the notions of **juncture** and **nexus**, the former referring to the constructions built up by tokens of the same layer, i.e. nuclear juncture, core juncture, peripheral juncture. Nexus refers to the syntactic linkage of two clauses. Foley's & Van Valin's notion of nexus is radically different from the traditional two-way distinction between **coordination** and **subordination** in that it introduces the third category **cosubordination**. In this framework, the three nexus types are characterized as follows: coordination [−embedded, −dependent], subordination [+embedded, +dependent], and cosubordination [−embedded, +dependent].

Core subordination, which may or may not involve the embedding of an entire clause, is most commonly employed to encode complement clauses cross-linguistically:

(14) *Mary regretted **having turned down the job**.* (core subordination: reduced clause embedding)

(15) *I suspect **that John will not attend the party**.* (core subordination: full clause embedding)

Less frequently, complement clauses may be realized by coordination, as shown below:

(16) Lango (Noonan 1985: 44)
Àtín òpòyò òcègò dɔ́gólá
child remembered.3SG closed.3SG door
'The child remembered to close the door.' (peripheral coordination: parataxis)

Lehmann (1988) proposed a cross-linguistic typology of clause linkage based on the following six parameters. Each of these parameters constitutes a continuum arranged between the two poles, i. e. maximal elaboration and maximal compression, as shown in Fig. 74.2:

elaboration ⟵⟶ **compression**
 (1) Downgrading of subordinate clause
weak parataxis ⟵⟶ strong embedding
 (2) Syntactic level
high ⟵⟶ low
sentence word
 (3) Desentantialization
weak ⟵⟶ strong
clause noun
 (4) Grammaticalization of main predicate
weak ⟵⟶ strong
lexical verb grammatical affix
 (5) Interlacing
weak ⟵⟶ strong
clauses disjunct clauses overlapping
 (6) Explicitness of linking
maximal ⟵⟶ minimal
syndesis asyndesis

Fig. 74.2. Parallelism of clause linkage continua (Lehmann 1988: 217)

The six parameters show a high degree of correlation and/or dependency relationship among them, e. g. the high integration of the subordinate into the main clause correlates positively with its desentantialization (ibid: 214).

Complement clauses are formed by various morpho-syntactic means cross-linguistically, but there are some features of clause linkage parameters which are characteristic of complement clauses, e. g. **embedding**, **desentantialization**, and **grammaticalization of the main verb**, as illustrated by the following sentences:

(17) Clause embedding in Latin complementation (Bolkestein 1989: 24)
laete fero quod Romani
gladly bear.1SG that Romans.NOM
vicerunt
have won.3PL
'I am happy that the Romans have won.'

(18) Desentantialization in English gerundive complement (Lehmann 1988: 197)
 (a) *She objected to [**his constantly reading** magazines].*
 (b) *She objected to [**his constant** reading of magazines].*

(19) Grammaticalization of a main verb as a causative verb in Italian (Lehmann 1988: 201)
*Ho **fatto** prendere a mio*
have.1SG made [take.INF to my
figlio un'altra professione.
son an other profession]
'I had my son choose another profession.'

3. The semantics of complementation

Next we will discuss some purely semantic distinctions. § 3.1. presents work on the logico-semantic distinctions encoded in complement clauses, in particular the distinction between realis and irrealis. § 3.2. introduces work on semantic distinctions between event and proposition, and their analogues. § 3.3. presents research on form-meaning interaction in complementation.

3.1. Realis/irrealis and related semantic distinctions in complementation

Primarily under the influence of transformational generative grammar, logico-semantic properties encoded in complementation such as **factivity**, **assertivity**, and **implicativity**, were productively studied during the 1970s with English as the primary language of investigation (cf. Kiparsky & Kiparsky 1970, Hooper 1975, Karttunen 1971). For instance, the following English examples illustrate the distinction between factive and non-factive complement clauses (Kiparksy & Kiparsky 1970: 147):

(20) (a) *I regret **that it is raining**.* (factive)
  (b) *I suppose **that it is raining*** (non-factive)

Sentence (20a) conveys the speaker's presupposition that the proposition ('it is raining') expressed in the complement is true, whereas sentence (20b) does not convey such a presupposition. The notion of factivity has also been investigated in various languages other than English, e.g. Japanese (Kuno 1973a), Korean (Kim 1984), Kinyarwanda (Givón & Kimenyi 1974).

Bolinger (1968: 124) notes that a similar semantic distinction, i.e. **reification** and **potentiality**, is encoded in English by the gerund complement and by the *to*-infinitive complement:

(21) (a) ***Waiting** was a mistake.* (reification)
  (b) ***To wait** would have been a mistake.* (potentiality)

Building on these earlier works, Frajzyngier & Jasperson (1991: 135) propose a semantic distinction, encoded in the English complement system, between **domain of reality (de re)** and **domain of speech (de dicto)**, the latter referring to "a semantic domain in which reference is made to the elements of speech rather than to the elements of reality." According to Frajzyngier and Jaspersen, Bolinger's "reification" and "potentiality" both belong in the domain of reality, whereas the notion of the *de dicto* domain is necessary to account for the differing syntactic-semantic behavior of *that*-clause complements in comparison to gerunds and *to*-infinitive complements. This difference is apparent in co-occurrence restrictions between verbs of thinking and saying (i.e. *de dicto* predicates) and co-occurring complements, as shown below (1991: 140, emphasis added):

(22) (a) *Phil **thought** that Broncos **prevailed**.*
  (b) **Phil **thought** the Broncos **prevailing**.*

The verb *think* requires a *that*-clause, the *de dicto* complement, and excludes the use of the gerund, which is a *de re* complement.

Frajzyngier (1991) takes note of the cross-linguistically recurrent use of the demonstrative as a complementizer, as in the following:

(23) Mupun (Frajzyngier 1991: 229)
   n-pan **nə** man wur
   1SG-think COMP know 3M
   'I think that I know him.'

Frajzyngier proposes that the function of the demonstrative as a complementizer is to indicate that the following complement clause belongs to the domain of *de dicto* (→ § 4.).

The semantic distinctions mentioned so far in this subsection center around the distinction between **realis** and **irrealis** (→ Art. 60). Dixon (1995: 183) makes the following remark on the cross-linguistic ubiquity of this distinction: "I suggest the following universal: for languages which have complement-clause constructions there are at least two possibilities: a 'potential (irrealis)' type, typically referring to something that has not happened but which people want or intend should happen [...]; and an 'actual (realis)' type, typically referring to some existing or certain event or state." This distinction is often invoked in the discussion of subjunctive mood widely observed in Romance languages.

Palmer (1986: 126–171) presents a cross-linguistic survey of major mood and modal meanings expressed in complement clauses in various languages, e.g. subjunctive mood, **epistemic modality**, **deontic modality**, and includes discussion of other topics related to complementation, e.g. non-finite clauses, deixis and indirect speech, and performatives (→ Art. 60).

Bybee, Perkins and Pagliuca (1994: 212–225) discuss the development of subjunctive mood. Specifically, they suggest that subjunctives were first used in "harmonic" contexts wherein their modal meanings are compatible with the meaning of the main verb. Subjunctives later became generalized and could be used in non-harmonic contexts until they became "an obligatory concomitant of subordination of a certain type" (1994: 214).

Givón (1994) argues that the subjunctive mood tends to encode two irrealis modality meanings cross-linguistically, i.e. lower certainty within the epistemic modality domain, and weaker manipulation within the deontic modality domain, as shown in the following Spanish complements (1994: 305, 281, emphasis in the original):

(24) (a) *Es mejor que lo **dejemos***
   be better COMP it leave.1PL.SUBJ
   para más tarde
   for more late
   'It **would** be better if we **left** it for later.' (weaker conviction)
  (b) *le aconsejaron que no*
   him advise COMP NEG
   ***dijera** nada*
   say.PAST.SUBJ.3SG nothing
   'They advised him that **he should not say** anything.' (weaker manipulation)

3.2. Event vs. proposition and related semantic distinctions in complementation

Another important semantic distinction encoded in complementation is that between **event** and **proposition**. Bolinger (1974) notes that English bare-infinitive and *to*-infinitive respectively encode **percept** and **concept** (cf. also Duffley 1992):

(25) (a) *I saw Mary jump.* (percept)
 (b) *I saw Mary to be uncooperative.* (concept)

A similar semantic contrast between **direct perception** and **indirect deduction**, respectively encoded by the bare-infinitive complement and the *that*-clause complement in English, is discussed by Kirsner & Thompson (1976: 206−207):

(26) (a) *We can see Bill solve the problem.* (direct perception)
 (b) *We can see that Bill solved the problem.* (indirect deduction)

Bickerton (1981: 100) reports the existence of a similar semantic distinction in Guyanese Creole, as shown below:

(27) (a) *mi hia drom a nak*
  I hear drum ASP beat
  'I heard drums beating.'
 (b) *mi hia se drom a nak*
  I hear THAT drum ASP beat
  'I heard that drums were beating.'

Lyons (1989: 172) also notes that a similar semantic distinction between **second-order entities** (i.e. "a hypostatized relation, event, process or state of affairs" (1989: 170)) and **propositions** (or **third-order entities**) is encoded respectively by the gerundive complements and the *that*-clause in English, as shown below:

(28) (a) *I heard John singing in his bath.* (second-order entity)
 (b) *I know that John is singing in his bath.* (proposition)

English is particularly rich in terms of complement clause constructions which can co-occur with the same predicate, particularly perception/cognition verbs and directive verbs, with subtly differing semantic implications. Extensive treatments of this phenomenon are found in Borkin (1973, 1984), Riddle (1974), Wierzbicka (1988), and Dixon (1991). Consider the following examples from Borkin (1973: 46):

(29) (a) *I find that this chair is uncomfortable.*
 (b) *I find this chair to be uncomfortable.*
 (c) *I find this chair uncomfortable.*

Borkin argues that the degree of clause integration, which progressively increases from (a) to (c), correlates with the degree of directness of the experience encoded in the complement.

Horie (1991, 1993) are among the first cross-linguistic studies, inspired by the above-mentioned primarily English-based studies, of the semantic distinction between **event** (directly perceived events) and **proposition** (indirectly perceived events) as encoded in perception and cognition verb complements. Horie argues that languages employ different strategies for encoding this distinction, frequently the use of non-finite and finite complement clauses for encoding event and proposition respectively, as shown below (Horie 1991: 235):

(30) (French)
 (a) *J'ai vu Jean traverser la rue.*
  I've seen Jean cross.INF the street
  'I saw Jean cross the street.' (event)
 (b) *Je pense que Jean a*
  I think COMP have
  traversé la rue.
  crossed
  'I think that Jean crossed the street.' (proposition)

Other strategies often employed include the use of different complementizers to distinguish event or propositional interpretation, as in Japanese (cf. also Kuno 1973a, Josephs 1976), or the use of a complementizer for only one semantic interpretation (i.e. proposition), as in Khmer:

(31) Japanese (Horie 1991: 237)
 (a) *John-wa Mary-ga toori-o*
  John-TOP Mary-NOM street-ACC
  wataru-no-o mi-ta.
  cross-COMP-ACC see-PAST
  'John saw Mary cross the street.' (event)
 (b) *John-wa Mary-ga toori-o*
  TOP NOM street-ACC
  watat-ta-koto-o sit-ta.
  cross-PAST-COMP-ACC know-PAST
  'John learned that Mary had crossed the street.' (proposition)

(32) Khmer (Horie 1991: 237)
 (a) No complementizer (event)
  knom khəən tidaa səmlap trəy
  I see Tidaa kill fish
  'I saw Tidaa kill the fish.'

(b) Complementizer *thaa* (proposition; cf. also section 4)
bophaa ciə **thaa** *tidaa səmlap*
Bophaa believe say Tidaa kill
trəy
fish
'Bophaa believes that Tidaa killed the fish.'

Dik & Hengeveld (1991) employ the framework of Functional Grammar to represent the different perceptual meanings exhibited by perception verb complements cross-linguistically. The Functional Grammar model adopted in their paper consists of a four-layered hierarchical structure of utterances consisting of **term**, **predication**, proposition, and clause. Each of these layers can be modified by a different set of operators (e.g. aspect, negation, mood, evidentials). Dik and Hengeveld use this model to account for the syntactic and semantic differences between **immediate perception constructions** and **mental perception constructions** as illustrated below:

(33) (a) *We saw the girl (*not) cry.* (immediate perception construction)
 (b) *We saw that the girl was (not) crying.* (mental perception construction)

Dik & Hengeveld attribute the syntactic and semantic differences between the two constructions to the representational differences triggered by the presence or absence of the operators (in this case, negation) available at different layers. Dik's & Hengeveld's cross-linguistic generalization of the difference between the two constructions is summarized as follows: "The distinction [...] is reflected in the different forms that these constructions may take in many languages. The differences in form may concern (i) the complement type, in particular the complement predicate; (ii) the complementizer" (ibid: 242).

3.3. Form-meaning interaction in complementation

Typologists have also investigated close correlations of form and meaning in complement clause constructions, which were noted in passing in § 3.2.

Givón (1980) is one of the first and most thorough cross-linguistic studies of form-meaning correlation in complementation (cf. also Givón 1990, Ch. 13, Horie 2000c). Specifically, Givón argues that an **iconic relationship** holds between the semantics of complement-taking verbs and the syntactic structure of their complements. He proposes the following semantic notion of **binding**: "The stronger the influence exerted over the agent of the complement clause by the agent of the main-clause verb, by whatever means, the higher is the main-verb on the binding scale" (1980: 335; → Art. 30).

Furthermore, Givón argues that there is a correlation between the position occupied by the complement-taking verb on the **binding hierarchy**, and the following morpho-syntactic phenomena exhibited in complement clauses: (i) case-marking options allowed for the complement subject, (ii) tense-aspect-modality possibilities expressible in the complement clause, and (iii) the degree of lexical fusion of main and complement verbs.

On a continuum of strongest to weakest degrees of binding, the hierarchy ranges from **manipulative verbs** (e.g. English *make*) to **modality verbs** (e.g. *manage*) to **cognition-utterance verbs** (e.g. *think*, *say*). The following English examples illustrate the correlation between the degree of semantic binding of the matrix verb and the syntactic form taken by its complement:

(34) (a) *I made {**John go**/*John to go/*that John would go}.*
 (b) *I caused {**John to go**/*John go/*that John would go}.*
 (c) *I advised {**John to go**/**that John go**/*John go}.*

Among the three matrix verbs in question, the verb highest on the binding hierarchy, i.e. *make*, takes the most reduced bare-infinitive sentential complement, whereas the verb lowest on the hierarchy, i.e. *advise*, is allowed to take the least reduced subjunctive *that*-clause complement. The syntactic behavior of the verb *cause* signals its intermediate position on the binding hierarchy between the two other verbs.

There is considerable variation in terms of the degree of intricacy of the binding hierarchy realized in each individual language. However, there is a constant correlation between the semantics of the complement-taking verb and the syntactic form of its co-occurring complement.

A similar correlation between form and meaning of complementation was noted by Foley & Van Valin (1984: 270), who argued for an Interclausal Relational Hierarchy, as shown in Fig. 74.3 (with labels added; cf. also § 2.2.):

Syntactic bondedness hierarchy	Interclausal semantic relations hierarchy
	strongest
Nuclear cosubordination	Causative
Nuclear coordination	Modality
Core cosubordination	Psych-action
Core subordination	Jussive
Core coordination	Direct perception complement
Peripheral cosubordination	Indirect discourse complement
Peripheral subordination	Temporal adverbial clause
Peripheral coordination	Conditionals
	Simultaneous action
	Sequential action: overlapping
	Sequential action: non-overlapping
	Action-action: unspecified
	weakest

Fig. 74.3. Interclausal Relational Hierarchy [IRH]

Regarding this hierarchy, Foley & Van Valin note that "the strongest semantic relations will be expressed in the most tightly linked syntactic configurations found in the language, the weaker relations in the less tightly linked constructions" (1984: 271).

Ransom (1986) proposes that matrix predicates and complementizers are lexically specified for specific modality meanings, i.e. information modalities (Truth, Future truth, Occurrence, Action) and evaluative modalities (Predetermined, Determined, Undetermined, Indeterminate), as illustrated below (1986: 209, 210):

(35) *regret*: NPa__[Predet Truth:S]
       that: [Predetermined/Determined/Undetermined; Truth]

Ransom suggests that co-occurrence of a particular complement-taking predicate and the co-occurring complementizer, e.g. the co-occurrence of the predicate *regret* and the complementizer *that*, is thus semantically predictable.

4. Diachronic aspects of complementation

Complement clauses do not suddenly emerge out of a vacuum, but are developed gradually on the basis of existing linguistic resources. Excluding some languages which employ simple juxtaposition to encode complementation, (e.g. Mandarin Chinese in (4)), complement clauses constitute complex syntactic construction in many languages of the world.

There are two historical aspects of complement clauses which can be studied from a diachronic perspective, the emergence of complementizers, and the concomitant creation of complement clauses as **complex constructions**.

Complementizers in many languages of the world are known to have derived from other grammatical words such as demonstrative pronouns, conjunctions, adpositions or case-markers, or from lexical words such as nouns and verbs. These developments can be regarded as instances of **grammaticalization**, "that subset of linguistic changes through which a lexical item in certain uses becomes a grammatical item, or through which a grammatical item becomes more grammatical" (Hopper & Traugott 1993: 2; → Art. 113).

The development of complementizers from demonstrative pronouns is documented in many languages (cf. 3.1.). The German complementizer *dass* in (36) is known to have historically derived from the Old High German neuter demonstrative pronoun *das*:

(36)   *das glaube ich wohl,* **dass** *du*
        that believe I truly that you
        dies gern möchtest
        this want
        'I really believe it, that you like this.'
        (Harris & Campbell 1995: 287)

The development of complementizers from case markers is discussed by Haspelmath (1989: 290), as shown in his following Old High German example:

(37)   *joh wer thih bitit thanne ouh*
        and who thee asks now also
        hiar zi drinkanne (Otfrid II, 14, 24)
        here to drink
        'And he who is asking you now here to drink (i.e. for a drink)'

The infinitive *zi* in verbal complement clause in (37) derives from the allative preposition *zi*, meaning 'to.'

Development of complementizers from lexical nouns is documented in languages like Japanese and Korean (see Horie 1991, 1995, 1997, Ransom 1985), as shown below:

(38) Japanese (Horie 1991: 240)
 John-wa Mary-ga toori-o
   TOP   NOM street-ACC
 *watat-ta **koto**-o omoidasi-ta.*
 cross-PAST COMP-ACC remember-PAST
 'John remembered that Mary had crossed the street.'

(39) Korean (Kim 1984: 61)
 John-un Mary-eykey cip-ey
   TOP   DAT   home-to
 *ka-l **kes**-ul*
 go-FUT.ADN COMP-ACC
 myenglyengha-yess-ta.
 order-PAST-DECL
 'John ordered Mary to go home.'

As pointed out by Horie (1991: 240) and Ransom (1985: 365−366), complementizers *koto* and *kes* developed from lexical nouns with similar phonological shapes, respectively meaning "abstract event" and "concrete thing."

Development of complementizers from verbs, particularly 'say' verbs, is amply attested in West African languages in particular, as well as in South East and South Asian languages, by Lord (1993). Consider the following Ewe sentence, in which the 'say' verb *bé* is used as a complementizer marking a desiderative complement clause:

(40) Ewe (Lord 1993: 186)
 *me-dí **bé** máfle awua ɖewó*
 I-want (say) i.SUBJ.buy dress some
 'I want to buy some dresses.'

Saxena (1995) argues for a cross-linguistically observed unidirectional grammaticalization process whereby a word meaning 'say' (as well as a word meaning 'thus') expands its grammatical functions from direct quote marker/complementizer ("Stage I") to reason/purpose marker ("Stage II") to conditional marker ("Stage III") to comparative marker ("Stage IV"). According to Saxena, this development of grammatical functions constitutes an **implicational hierarchy** whereby if a language has a 'say' verb encoding a certain function (e. g. conditional marking function), then that verb should encode other functions lower on the hierarchy (e. g. complementizer marking function), but the opposite may not hold. The following sentence illustrates the most advanced stage of grammaticalization whereby the 'say' verb in Newari functions as a comparative marker:

(41) Newari (Saxena (1995: 359)
 (a) *sita **dha**-k-a-a ram tɔr-i*
  Sita say-CAUSE-PART-NF Ram tall-PD
  'Ram is taller **than** Sita.'

As is predictable from the implicational hierarchy, *dha* functions also as a complementizer:

(Saxena 1995: 358)
 (b) *ram-ɔ̃ saroj cəlak*
  Ram-ERG Saroj intelligent
  ***dha**-ka-a-a dhal-ɔ*
  say-CAUSE-PART-NF say-PD
  'Ram said **that** Saroj is intelligent.'

Development of complementizers usually involves significant structural changes such as **reanalysis** of constituent structure (cf. Harris & Campbell 1995: 286−293, Frajzyngier 1996). Consider the following Tok Pisin sentences (Romaine 1988: 142, glosses added − KH):

(42) (a) *Elizabeth i tok **olsem**, 'Yumi*
    PM   spoke thus   we
  mas kisim ol samting pastaim.'
  must get them thing first
  'Elizabeth spoke thus, "We must get things first".'
 (b) *Na yupela i no save **olsem***
  and you (PL.) PM NEG know COMP
  ***em i** matmat?*
  it PM cemetery
  'And you (pl.) did not know that it was a cemetery?'

As noted by Romaine (1988: 142), *olsem* in (42a) functions as an adverb preceding a direct quote in the matrix clause. *Olsem* in (42b), in contrast, is reanalyzed as a complementizer preceding an embedded clause, thereby creating a complement clause construction [s' COMP S].

A newly created complement clause construction can be in competition with a less productive conservative complement construction during the transitional period. Horie (1995: 193) notes that, in Modern Japanese, the innovative complement construction with overt nominalizer *no* replaced the old complement construction formed by the bare adnominal predicate form in regular complementation environments such as (43a):

(43) (a) *Taroo-wa [Mariko-ga Amerika-ni*
Taro-TOP   Mariko-NOM America-to
it-ta]   no/*ɸ-o sit-ta.
go-PAST COMP ACC know-PAST
'Taro learned that Mariko had gone to America.'

However, the conservative bare adnominal predicate complement construction still survives in some syntactic environments, particularly idioms, as shown below (ibid: 194, see also Horie 1997, 1999):

(b) *[Mitome-zaru]-ɸ/*no -o*
admit-NEG   COMP   ACC
e-nai.
obtain-NEG
'(I) do not obtain not admitting (it),' i.e. '(I) cannot but admit (it).'

5. Distributional and other constraints on complement clauses: cross-linguistic variation

A complement clause, particularly a finite complement clause, tends cross-linguistically to be a relatively long constituent of a sentence. Various languages therefore show a tendency to place a complement clause at the sentence-final or sentence-initial position. The choice is crucially related to whether the basic word order of the language is VO or OV.

VO languages tend to place a finite complement clause in the sentence-final position, a phenomenon called **extraposition**, as shown in (44):

(44)   *I found it unbearable **that he would make such an announcement.***

As observed by Noonan (1985: 83), extraposition in languages like English is obligatory "in sentence-medial position of complements whose heads are verbs." Consider the following English examples (from Noonan 1985: 82−83, cf. also Kuno 1973b):

(45) (a) **Is **that Floyd left town** significant?*
    (b) *Is it significant **that Floyd left town**?*

Grosu & Thompson (1977: 134) note that the same restriction exists in many typologically diverse languages (e.g. Spanish, Modern Hebrew, Afrikaans, Malagasy, Tagalog), but that there are languages such as Japanese, Korean, Nama, Wappo, and Mojave, where the restriction doesn't hold, as shown below:

(46)   Mojave (Grosu & Thompson 1977: 134)
John-č   Mary-č   iva:-m
John-SUBJ Mary-SUBJ arrive-DIFFSUBJ
su:paw-m
know-TENSE
'John knows that Mary came.'

OV languages such as Japanese tend to place a complement clause at the sentence-initial position, though Japanese is more tolerant than English of a complement clause being placed in sentence-medial position:

(47) (a) *[S′ **Tyuutoo-de   sensoo-ga***
         Middle East-in war-NOM
         boppatusi-ta   to]
         break out-PAST COMP
         [NP Taroo-ga] [VP it-ta].
              Taro-NOM   say-PAST
'That the war had broken out in the Middle East, Taro said.'
    (b) *[NP Taroo-ga] [S′ **tyuutoo-de sensoo-ga boppatusi-ta to]** [VP it-ta].*
'Taro said that the war had broken out in the Middle East.'

Cross-linguistic tendencies illustrated above obviously call for an explanation. One of the most thorough explanatory attempts is found in Hawkins (1994). Hawkins argues that these cross-linguistic preferences in arranging a heavy constituent such as a complement clause are motivated by the human need to process constituents of the sentence as rapidly as possible, and are accomplished by placing the heavy constituent at the sentence-final position (in the case of VO languages) or at the sentence-initial position (in the case of OV languages). For instance, the order in (47a) in Japanese is preferred over that in (47b) because the former provides a more rapid identification of immediate constituents of the sentence than the latter. Specifically, in (47a), the three immediate constituents of the sentence (i.e. S′, NP, VP) are parsed on the basis of three words characterizing their structural identity, i.e. complementizer *to*, NP *Taroo-ga*, and VP *it-ta*. In (47b), by contrast, three additional words in the complement clause, i.e. *tyuutoo-de, sensoo-ga, boppatu-sita*, need to be processed sequentially to arrive at the complementizer *to* signalling S′. Therefore, the latter ordering, being more costly processing-wise, is less preferred (→ Art. 29).

Omission of a complementizer, which is cross-linguistically rather infrequent (e.g.

(French) *Je pense *(que) Jean a traversé la rue*), can also be governed by processing-related factors. The English complementizer *that*, for instance, is omissible in direct object position, but not in subject position (cf. Bolinger 1972, Haiman 1990):

(48) (a) **(That) Will mastered 500 Chinese characters in a month is known to everyone.*
(b) *I know (that) Will mastered 500 Chinese characters in a month.*

In subject position in (48a), omission of the complementizer is costly processing-wise because it would significantly delay the correct identification of S′ on-line until the main verb *surprised* is processed. In contrast, omission of the complementizer in direct object position in (48b) is not as costly since the main verb *know* has already been processed; the complement verb *mastered* can then signal the presence of a complement clause.

Furthermore, Ross (1986) proposed syntactic constraints on extraction of elements out of certain types of complement clauses, exhibited in the unacceptability of the following English sentences (from Ross 1986: 148, 75, modified):

(49) (a) **The teacher who **that the principal would fire ( )** was expected by the reporters is [...].*
(b) **The hat which I believed **the claim that Otto was wearing ( )** is red.*

In (49a), the NP *the teacher* was extracted from within the finite complement clause, which is in subject position, whereas in (49b), an NP *the hat* was extracted from within a complement clause with the nominal head *the claim*. Ross proposed that no extraction of elements is possible from within a sentential subject, as in (49a), or a sentence dominated by a noun phrase with a lexical head, as in (49b). These constraints are referred to as the **Sentential Subject Constraint** and the **Complex NP Constraint**. It is obvious that these "syntactic" constraints have a processing basis, though Ross does not elaborate on this point. That is, extraction of elements from these complex clause constructions will lead to processing difficulties and are dispreferred.

From a typological point of view, it is important to note that there are languages such as Japanese, which do not strictly observe the constraints:

(50) Japanese (Ross 1986: 149, 83, modified and glosses added)
(a) *Kore-wa **Mary-ga kabutte ita***
this-TOP Mary-NOM wear.GER existed
***koto-ga** akirakana boosi-da.*
COMP-NOM obvious hat-COP
'*This is the hat which that Mary was wearing is obvious.'
(b) *(?) **Kare-ga kabutte ita to iu***
he-NOM wear.GER existed COMP
***syutyoo-o** watakusi-ga sinzita*
claim-ACC I-NOM believed
boosi [...]
hat
'*the hat which I believed the claim that he was wearing'

Cross-linguistic differences in the applicability of syntactic operations such as **Raising** have been examined by typologists. Hawkins (1986: 75−85) argued that the applicability of raising in German complement constructions is more severely restricted than in English, as shown below:

(51) (a) *I believe **John** [( ) to be ill].*
(b) **Ich glaube **Johann** [( ) krank zu sein].* (ibid: 77, modified)

Comrie & Matthews (1990) inquired into the cross-linguistically variable acceptability of so-called **Tough Movement**, a syntactic operation also known as object-to-subject raising in the English-based transformational generative grammatical tradition, as shown below:

(52) **John** *is easy [to please ( )].*

Comrie and Matthews argue that, while it may be possible to give a functional definition of tough movement cross-linguistically, "the formal devices used to express this function are radically different from language to language, correlating with other syntactic typological distinctions among the languages in question" (1990: 55). For example, the analogous syntactic operation in Indonesian is not applicable straightforwardly because of the general constraint that only subjects can be extracted:

(53) Indonesian (1990: 56)
Buku ini mudah di-baca
book this easy PASS-read
/*mem-baca
ACC-read
'This book is easy to read.'

In (53), passivization is necessary to ensure that the extracted noun phrase *buku* be a subject.

That this constraint on extraction generally holds in other syntactic constructions in Indonesian is shown by the following relative clause examples (1990: 56):

(54) (a) *buku yang di-baca (oleh pelajar)*
book that PASS-read by student
'the book that is read (by the student)'

(b) **buku yang pelajar mem-baca*
book that student ACC-read
'the book that the student read'

6. Complement clauses and relative clauses: cross-linguistic distributional patterning

Complement clauses can have either a verbal or nominal head, as shown below:

(55) (a) *The president learned **that the plane crashed**.*
(b) *the news **that the plane crashed***

Few studies exist of the cross-linguistic patterning of complement clauses in relation to relative clauses save Comrie & Horie (1995) and Comrie (1996).

Comrie & Horie (1995) note that languages differ in terms of whether complement clauses with a nominal head are treated similarly to complement clauses with a verbal head, or similarly to relative clauses. Languages like English encode both types of complement clauses in a similar manner, as shown above in (55), in contrast with relative clauses, which are differently encoded:

(56) *the news **which surprised the world***

In contrast, languages like Japanese show the opposite patterning, in that complement clauses with a nominal head and relative clauses are encoded alike, whereas complement clauses with a verbal head can show a different pattern (Comrie & Horie 1995: 68, 71, cf. also Comrie 1996):

(57) (a) *[gakusei ga hon o kat-ta]*
student NOM book ACC buy-PAST
zizitu
fact
'the fact [that the student bought the book]'
(complement clause with a nominal head)

(b) *[gakusei ga kat-ta] hon*
student NOM buy-PAST book
'the book [that the student bought]'
(relative clause)

(c) *[Gakusei ga hon o kat-ta*
student NOM book ACC buy-PAST
to/tte] boku ga it-ta.
that I NOM say-PAST
'I said [that the student bought the book].'
(complement clauses with a verbal head)

As shown in (57a) and (57b), both the complement clause with a nominal head and the relative clause are directly attached to head nouns without any over linker. In contrast, the complement clause with a verbal head ends in an overt complementizer *to* or *tte* as in (57c).

Khmer shows an interesting distribution of complements with their nominal heads, unlike the patterning found either in English or Japanese, as shown below (Comrie & Horie 1995: 71–72):

(58) (a) *kamnit [dael tidaa baan səmlap*
idea REL Tidaa PAST kill
bopphaa]
Bopphaa
'the idea that Tidaa killed Bopphaa'
(complement clause with a nominal head)

(b) *damnəŋ [thaa qəwpuk baan slap]*
news COMP father PAST die
'the news that father had died'
(complement clause with a nominal head)

(c) *siəwphiu [dael koun-səs baan tiñ]*
book REL student PAST buy
'the book that the student bought'
(relative clause)

(d) *neəʔ-kruu dəŋ [thaa koun-səs*
teacher know COMP student
baan tiñ siəwphiu].
PAST buy book
'The teacher knew that the students bought the book.' (complement clause with a verbal head)

Complement clauses with nominal heads in Khmer are distributed between those which exhibit similar marking to relative clauses, as in (58a), and those which are marked similarly to complement clauses with verbal heads, as in (58b), with the distribution determined apparently by such factors as the semantics of the head noun of the complement clause.

Comrie (1996) notes that the distributional pattern illustrated in (57a) and (57b) in Japanese, i.e. "**noun-modifying constructions**" unifying both relative clauses and complement clauses with nominal heads, is an areal phenomenon widely observed in languages of Asia, e.g. Japanese, Korean, Ainu, Chinese, Thai, and the Dravidian languages.

7. Conclusion

This article presented a survey of major research topics and approaches found in the typological studies of complement clauses. Dixon (1995: 183) offers the following general impression on this topic: "(C)omplement-clause constructions are common among the languages of Europe, Oceania and Africa but rare in those of Australia and South America." Though few systematic studies have been done so far (except detailed studies on some specific areas, e.g. Joseph 1983 on the Balkan languages), cross-linguistic distribution of complement clauses is an intriguing area of inquiry.

Another potentially fruitful venue for research on complement clauses comes from the diachronic and cross-linguistic perspectives on form-meaning interaction examined by Bybee, Perkins & Pagliuca (1994). It seems very plausible that typological features of a language, particularly the morphological typology of the language (e.g. inflectional, agglutinating, isolating, etc.) can offer new insights into the type of complement clause(s), the lexical resources of complementizer(s), and the degree of grammaticalization of complementizers in the language. It is hoped that further systematic typological attempts will provide us with a better understanding of the cross-linguistic distribution of complement clauses.

8. Special abbreviations

ADN	adnominal form
AN	action nominal
ANCS	action nominal constructions
CL	class
COP	copula
DIFFSUB	different subject
FG	functional grammar
GER	gerundive form
NF	nonfinal
PART	participle
PARTV	partitive
PD	past disjunct
PM	predicative marker
SUBJ	subjunctive

9. References

Bickerton, Derek. 1981. *Roots of language*. Ann Arbor: Karoma.

Bolinger, Dwight. 1968. "Entailment and the meaning of structures". *Glossa* 2.2: 119−127.

−. 1972. *That's that*. The Hague: Mouton.

−. 1974. "Concept and percept: two infinitive constructions and their vicissitudes". In: *World papers in phonetics: festschrift for Dr. Onishi's kizyu*. Tokyo: The Phonetic Society of Japan, 65−91.

Bolkestein, Machtelt A. 1989. "Parameters in the expression of embedded predications in Latin". In: Calboli, Gualtiero (ed.). *Subordination and other topics in Latin*. Amsterdam: Benjamins 3−35.

Borkin, Ann. 1973. "To be and not to be". *Chicago Linguistic Society* 9: 44−56.

−. 1984. *Problems in form and function*. Norwood/NJ: Ablex.

Bybee, Joan & Perkins, Revere & Pagliuca, William. 1994. *The evolution of grammar*. Chicago: The University of Chicago Press.

Comrie, Bernard. 1996. "The unity of noun-modifying clauses in Asian languages". *Pan-Asiatic linguistics*. Salaya, Thailand, 1077−1088.

− & Horie, Kaoru. 1995. "Complement clauses versus relative clauses: some Khmer evidence. In: Abraham, Werner & Givón, Talmy & Thompson, Sandra A. (eds.). *Discourse grammar and typology*. (Studies in Language Companion Series, 27.) Amsterdam: Benjamins, 65−75.

− & Matthews, Steve. 1990. "Prolegomena to a typology of tough movement". In: Croft, William & Denning, Keith & Kemmer, Suzanne. (eds.). *Studies in typology and diachrony*. (Typological Studies in Language, 20.) Amsterdam: Benjamins, 43−58.

Dik, Simon C. & Hengeveld, Kees. 1991. "The hierarchical structure of the clause and the typology of perception-verb complements". *Linguistics* 29: 231−259.

Dixon, Robert W. 1991. *A new approach to English grammar, on semantic principles*. Oxford: Oxford University Press.

−. 1995. "Complement clauses and complement strategies." In: Palmer, F. R. (ed.). *Meaning and grammar*. Cambridge: Cambridge University Press, 174−220.

Duffley, Patrick J. 1992. *The English infinitive*. London: Longman.

Foley, Williams A. & Van Valin Jr., Robert. 1984. *Functional syntax and universal grammar*. Cambridge: Cambridge University Press.

Frajzyngier, Zygmunt. 1991. "The *de dicto* domain in language". In: Traugott, Elizabeth Closs & Heine, Bernd. (eds.). *Approaches to grammaticalization*, Vol. 1. (Typological Studies in Language, 19.) Amsterdam: Benjamins, 219−251.

—. 1996. *Grammaticalization of the complex sentences. A case study in Chadic.* (Studies in Language Campanion Series, 32.) Amsterdam: Benjamins.

— & Jasperson, Robert. 1991. "*That*-clauses and other complements". *Lingua* 83: 133—153.

Givón, Talmy. 1980. "The binding hierarchy and the typology of complements". *Studies in Language* 4.3: 333—377.

—. 1990. *Syntax.* Vol. II. Amsterdam: Benjamins.

—. 1994. "Irrealis and the subjunctive". *Studies in Language* 18.2: 265—337.

— & Kimenyi, Alexandre. 1974. "Truth, belief and doubt in Kinyarwanda". *Studies in African Linguistics, Supplement* 5: 95—113.

Grosu, Alexander & Thompson, Sandra A. 1977. "Constraints on the distribution of NP clauses". *Language* 53.1: 104—151.

Haiman, John. 1990. "Schizophrenic complementizers." In: Croft, William & Denning, Keith & Kemmer, Suzanne. (eds.). *Studies in typology and diachrony.* (Typological Studies in Language, 20.) Amsterdam: Benjamins, 79—94.

Harris, Alice C. & Campbell, Lyle. 1995. *Historical syntax in cross-linguistic perspective.* Cambridge: Cambridge University Press.

Haspelmath, Martin. 1989. "From purposive to infinitive — A universal path of grammaticalization". *Folia Linguistica Historica* 10.1—2: 287—310.

Hawkins, John A. 1986. *A comparative typology of English and German.* London: Croom Helm.

—. 1994. *A performance theory of order and constituency.* Cambridge: Cambridge University Press.

Hooper, Joan B. 1975. "On assertive predicates". In: Kimball, John (ed.). *Syntax and semantics* 4. New York: Academic Press, 91—124.

Hopper, Paul J. & Traugott, Elizabeth Closs. 1993. *Grammaticalization.* Cambridge: Cambridge University Press.

Horie, Kaoru. 1991. "Cognitive motivations for event nominalizations". *Chicago Linguistic Society* 27, Part 1: 233—245.

—. 1993. A cross-linguistic study of perception and cognition verb complements: a cognitive perspective. Unpublished doctoral dissertation, University of Southern California, Los Angeles.

—. 1995. "What the choice of overt nominalizer *no* did to Modern Japanese syntax and semantics". In: Andersen, Henning (ed.). *Historical Linguistics 93.* Amsterdam: Benjamins, 191—203.

—. 1997. "Three types of nominalization in Modern Japanese: *no, koto*, and zero". *Linguistics* 35.5: 879—894.

—. 1999. "From core to periphery: a study on the directionality os syntactic change in Modern Japanese". In: Fox, Barbara A. & Jurafsky, Dan & Michaelis, Laura A. (eds.). Cognition and function in language. Stanford: CSLI, 1—4.

—. 2000a. "Complementation in Japanese and Korean". In: Horie, Kaoru (ed.). *Complementation. Cognitive and functional perspectives.* Amsterdam: Benjamins, 11—31.

—. 2000b. "Core-oblique distinction and nominalizer choice in Japanese and Korean". *Studies in Language* 24.1: 77—102.

—. 2000c. (ed.) *Complementation. Cognitive and functional perspectives.* Amsterdam: Benjamins.

Joseph, Brian D. 1983. *The synchrony and diachrony of the Balkan infinitive.* Cambridge: Cambridge University Press.

Josephs, Lewis S. 1976. "Complementation". In: Shibatani, Masayoshi (ed.). *Syntax and semantics* 5. New York: Academic Press, 307—370.

Karttunen, Lauri. 1971. "Implicative verbs". *Language* 47: 340—358.

Kim, Nam-Kil 1984. *The grammar of Korean complementation.* Honolulu.

Kiparsky, Paul & C. Kiparsky. 1970. "Fact." In: Bierwisch, Manfred & Heidolph, Karl Erich (eds.). *Progress in linguistics.* The Hague: Mouton, 143—173.

Kirsner, Robert S. & Thompson, Sandra A. 1976. "The role of pragmatic inference in semantics: a study of sensory verb complements in English". *Glossa* 10.2: 200—240.

Koptjevskaja-Tamm, Maria. 1993. *Nominalizations.* London: Routledge.

Kuno, Susumu. 1973a. *The structure of the Japanese language.* Cambridge, Mass.: MIT Press.

—. 1973b. "Constraints on internal clauses and sentential subjects". *Linguistic Inquiry* 4.3: 363—385.

Lehmann, Christian. 1988. "Towards a typology of clause linkage". In: Haiman, John & Thompson, Sandra A. (eds.). *Clause combining in grammar and discourse.* (Typological Studies in Language, 18.) Amsterdam: Benjamins, 181—225.

Li, Charles & Thompson, Sandra A. 1981. *Mandarin Chinese. A functional reference grammar.* Berkeley and Los Angeles: University of California Press.

Lord, Carol. 1993. *Historical change in serial verb constructions.* (Typological Studies in Language, 26.) Amsterdam: Benjamins.

Lyons, John. 1989. "Semantic ascent: a neglected aspect of syntactic typology". In: Arnold, Doug & Atkinson, Martin & Durand, Jacques & Grover, Claire & Sadler, Louisa. (eds.). *Essays on grammatical theory and universal grammar.* Oxford: Oxford University Press, 153—186.

Mufwene, Salikoko S. & Dijkhoff, Marta B. 1989. "On the so-called 'infinitive' in Atlantic creoles". *Lingua* 77: 297—330.

Noonan, Michel. 1985. "Complementation". In: Shopen, Timothy. (ed.). *Language typology and syntactic description*, Vol. 2. *Complex constructions*. Cambridge: Cambridge University Press, 42–140.

–. 1997. "Versatile nominalizations". In: Bybee, Joan & Haiman, John & Thompson, Sandra A. (eds.). *Essays on language function and language type*. Amsterdam: Benjamins, 373–394.

O'Dowd, Elizabeth. 1992. "The syntactic metaphor of subordination". *Lingua* 86: 47–80.

Palmer, F. R. 1986. *Mood and modality*. Cambridge: Cambridge University Press.

Ransom, Evelyn N. 1985. "The grammaticalization of complementizers". *Berkeley Linguistics Society* 14: 364–374.

–. 1986. *Complementation: its meaning and form*. (Typological Studies in Language, 10.) Amsterdam: Benjamins.

Riddle, Elizabeth. 1974. "Some pragmatic conditions on complementizer choice." *Chicago Linguistic Society* 11: 467–474.

Romaine, Suzanne. 1988. *Pidgin and creole languages*. London: Longman.

Ross, John Robert. 1973. "Nouniness". In: Fujimura, Osamu. (ed.). *Three dimensions of linguistic theory*. Tokyo: TEC 137–258.

–. 1986. *Infinite syntax!* Norwood/NJ: Ablex.

Saxena, Anju. 1995. "Unidirectional grammaticalization: diachronic and cross-linguistic evidence". *Sprachtypologie und Universalienforschung* 48.4: 350–372.

Stassen, Leon. 1985. *Comparison and universal grammar*. Oxford: Blackwell.

Wierzbicka, Anna. 1988. "The semantics of English complementation in a cross-linguistic perspective". In: Wierzbicka, Anna. *The semantics of grammar*. (Studies in Language Companion Series, 18.) Amsterdam: Benjamins, 23–168.

Kaoru Horie, Tohoku University (Japan)

75. Comparative constructions

1. Definition of the domain
2. The Comparison of inequality: parameters
3. Predicate marking in comparative constructions
4. Explanation of the typology of comparative constructions
5. Comparison of equality
6. Special abbreviations
7. References

1. Definition of the domain

In semantic or cognitive terms, comparison can be defined as a mental act by which two objects are assigned a position on a predicative scale. Should this position be the same for both objects, then we have a case of the **comparison of equality**. If the positions on the scale are different, then we speak of the **comparison of inequality**. In both cases, however, the notion essentially involves three things: a predicative scale, which, in language, is usually encoded as a gradable predicate, and two objects. Although these objects can, in principle, be complex, the practice of typological linguistic research has been to restrict them to primary objects, which are typically encoded in the form of noun phrases. Thus, a comparative construction typically contains a predicate and two noun phrases, one of which is the object of comparison (the comparee NP), while the other functions as the yard-stick' of the comparison (the standard NP). In short, prototypical instances of comparative constructions in the languages of the world are sentences that are equivalent to the English sentences in (1), in which the noun phrase following the items *as* and *than* is the standard NP:

(1) English (Indo-European, Germanic)
 (a) *John is as tall as Lucy*
 (b) *John is taller than Lucy*

2. The comparison of inequality: parameters

Post-war literature on the typology of the comparison of inequality includes Ultan (1972), Andersen (1983) and Stassen (1984, 1985). This latter author presents a typology of comparative constructions which is based on a sample of 110 languages. A basic parameter in this typology is the encoding of the standard NP. First, one can make a distinction between instances of **fixed-case comparatives** and **derived-case comparatives**. In the former type, the standard NP is always in the same case, regardless of the case of the comparee NP. In the latter type, the standard NP derives its case assignment from the case of the comparee NP. Classical Latin is an example of a language in which both types were allowed. The sentences in (2) illustrate a construction type in which the standard NP is dependent on the comparee NP for its case marking. In contrast, sentence (3) shows a construction type in which the standard NP is invariably in the ablative case. As a result, sentence (3) is ambiguous between the readings of (2a) and (2b).

(2) Latin (Indo-European, Italic)
 (a) *Brutum ego   non minus*
     B.-ACC 1SG.NOM not less
     amo   quam Caesar
     love.1SG.PRES than C.-NOM
     'I love Brutus no less than Caesar (loves Brutus)'
 (b) *Brutum ego   non minus*
     B.-ACC 1SG.NOM not less
     amo   quam Caesarem
     love.1SG.PRES than C.-ACC
     'I love Brutus no less than (I love) Caesar'

(3) Latin (Indo-European, Italic)
     Brutum ego   non minus
     B.-ACC 1SG.NOM not less
     amo   Caesare
     love.1SG.PRES C.-ABL

Both types of comparative constructions can be subcategorized further, on the basis of additional parameters. Within the fixed-case comparatives, a first distinction is that between **direct-object comparatives** and **adverbial comparatives**. Direct-object comparatives (or, as Stassen (1985) calls them, Exceed-Comparatives) have as their characteristic that the standard NP is constructed as the direct object of a transitive verb with the meaning "to exceed" or "to surpass". Thus, the construction typically includes two predicates, one of which is the comparative predicate, and another which is the "exceed"-verb. The comparee NP is the subject of the "exceed"-verb. Concentrations of the Exceed-Comparative are found in Sub-Saharan Africa, in China and South-East Asia, and in Eastern Austronesia. An example is:

(4) Duala (Niger-Kordofanian, North-West Bantu)
     Nin ndabo e kolo buka nine
     this house it big exceed that
     'This house is bigger than that'

Adverbial comparatives, on the other hand, are characterized by the fact that the standard NP is invariably constructed in a case form which has a locational/adverbial function. Depending on the exact nature of this function, adverbial comparatives can be divided into three further subtypes. **Separative comparatives** mark the standard NP as the source of a movement, with a marker meaning "from", or "out of". **Allative comparatives** construct the standard NP as the goal of a movement ("to, towards", "over, beyond") or as a benefactive ("for"). Finally, **locative comparatives** encode the standard NP as a location, in which an object is at rest ("in", "on", "at", "upon"). Concentrations of (the various subtypes of) the Adverbial Comparative are found in Africa above the Sahara, in Eurasia (including the Middle East and India, but with the exception of the modern languages of Continental Europe), Eskimo, some Western North-American languages, Mayan, Quechuan, Carib, Polynesia, and some (but not many) Australian and Papuan languages. Illustrations of the various subtypes of adverbial comparatives are:

(5) Mundari (Austro-Asiatic, Munda)
     Sadom-ete hati   mananga-i
     horse-from elephant big   -3SG.PRES
     'The elephant is bigger than the horse'

(6) Breton (Indo-European, Celtic)
     Jazo bras-ox wid-on
     he big -AFF for-me
     'He is bigger than me'

(7) Tamazight
     Enta ihengrin   foull i
     he tall.3SG.MASC upon me
     'He is taller than me'

Within the derived-case comparatives, in which the case marking of the standard NP is derived from – or "parasitic on" – the case marking of the comparee NP, two subtypes can be distinguished. First, there is the **conjoined comparative**. Here the comparative construction consists of two structurally independent clauses, one of which contains the comparee NP, while the other contains the standard NP. Furthermore, the two clauses show a structural parallellism, in that the grammatical function of the comparee NP in one of the clauses is duplicated by the grammatical function of the standard NP in the other clause. If, for example, the comparee functions as the grammatical subject in its clause, the standard NP will also have subject status in its clause.

Since the construction has two clauses, it follows that the construction will also have two independent predicates. In other words, the comparative predicate is expressed twice. There are two ways in which this double expression may be effectuated. The language may employ antonymous predicates in the two clauses ("good-bad", "strong-weak"). Alternatively, the two predicates may show a positive-negative polarity ("good-not good", "strong-not strong"). In geographical terms, the conjoined comparative seems to be concentrated in the Southern Pacific, including Australian, Papuan, and Eastern Austronesian languages, but it is also common in large parts of the Americas, and there are also some cases in Eastern Africa. Examples include:

(8) Kobon (Papuan)
     U kub u   pro
     this big that small
     'This is bigger than that'

(9) Menomini (Algonquian)
     Tata'hkes-ew nenah teh kan
     strong -3SG   I   and not
     'He is stronger than me'

A second subtype of derived-case comparison is defined negatively, in that the standard NP has derived case, but the construction does not have the form of a coordination of clauses. Instead, the construction features a specific comparative particle which accompanies the standard NP. With a few, mostly West-Indonesian exceptions, this **particle comparative** appears to be restricted to Europe. The English *than*-comparative is a case in point. Another example is Hungarian:

(10) Hungarian (Uralic)
     Istvan magasa-bb mint Peter
     I.-NOM tall -AFF than P.-NOM
     'Istvan is taller than Peter'

In summary, the typology of comparison of inequality developed in Stassen (1984, 1985) can be presented in the following table:

(11)
FIXED CASE	direct object	EXCEED
	adverbial	SEPARATIVE
		ALLATIVE
		LOCATIVE
DERIVED CASE	conjoined	CONJOINED
	non-conjoined	PARTICLE

3. Predicate marking in comparative constructions

Apart from, or in addition to, case assignment of the standard NP, a further possible parameter in the typology of comparative constructions might be considered to be the presence or absence of comparative marking on the predicate. In the vast majority of languages, such overt marking is absent; predicative adjectives in comparatives retain their unmarked, 'positive' form. Some languages, however, mark a predicative adjective in a comparative construction by means of a special affix (e. g., *-er* in English, German and Dutch, *-ior* in Latin, *-bb* in Hungarian, *-ago* in Basque) or a special adverb (*more* in English, *plus* in French). Especially in the case of comparative affixes the etymological origin is largely unknown. As for the areal distribution of this predicate marking in comparatives, it can be observed that it is an almost exclusively European phenomenon, and that it is particularly frequent in languages that have a particle comparative construction. For a tentative explanation of this latter correlation see Stassen (1985, ch. 15).

4. Explanation of the typology of comparative constructions

Stassen (1985) advances the claim that the typology of comparative constructions is derived from (and hence predicted by) the typology of **temporal sequencing**. That is, the type(s) of comparative construction which a language may employ is argued to be limited by the options which the language has in the encoding of (simultaneous or consecutive) sequences of events. A first indication in favour of this hypothesis is that at least one of the attested comparative types, viz., the conjoined comparative, has the overt form of a temporal sequence (in this case, a simultaneous coordination). Moreover, for most of the other comparative types a correlation with a possible encoding of some temporal sequence can be established as well. Stassen (1985) produces detailed evidence for the correctness of the following set of universals:

(12) The universals of comparative type choice:
  (a) If a language has an adverbial comparative, then that language allows deranking (i. e. non-finite subordination) of one of the clauses in a tem-

poral sequence, even when the two clauses in that sequence have different subjects.
(b) If a language has an Exceed-Comparative, then that language allows deranking of one of the clauses in a temporal sequence only if the two clauses have identical subjects.
(c) If a language has a conjoined comparative, then that language does not allow deranking of clauses in temporal sequences at all.

The parallelism between these various options in temporal sequence encoding and corresponding comparative types is illustrated by examples from Naga, Dagomba and Kayapo:

(13) Naga (Tibeto-Burman, Tibeto-Burman)
(a) *A de   kepu ki themma lu   a*
    I words speak on man   that me
    vu -we
    strike-INDIC
    'As I spoke these words, that man struck me'
(b) *Themma hau lu ki vi -we*
    man   this than on good-INDIC
    'This man is better than that man'

(14) Dagomba (Niger-Kordofanian, Gur)
(a) *Nana   san -la   o -suli n -dum*
    scorpion take-HAB his-tail PREF-sting
    nira
    people
    'The scorpion stings people with its tail'
(b) *O-make dpeoo n   -gare   -ma*
    he-has strength PREF-exceed -me
    'He is stronger than me'

(15) Kayapo (Ge)
(a) *Ga -ja   nium-no*
    2SG -stand 3SG -lie down
    'You are standing, and/while he is lying down'
(b) *Gan ga-prik ba   i-pri*
    2SG 2SG-big 1SG 1SG-small
    'You are bigger than me'

Given that the universals in (12) meet with very few, and "incidental", counterexamples, Stassen (1985) concludes that the typology of comparative constructions is "modelled" on the typology of temporal sequencing, so that, in effect, comparative constructions appear to be a special case of the encoding of temporal sequences.

A residual problem for this 'modelling' analysis of comparative types is presented by the particle comparatives. Like conjoined comparatives, particle comparatives form a case of derived-case comparison, but unlike conjoined comparatives their surface structure form is not that of a coordination. Nonetheless, there are indications that even particle comparatives are coordinate in origin. In a number of cases, the particle used in particle comparatives has a clear source in a coordinating conjunction or adverb (e. g. *karo* "than/but" in Javanese, *dan* "than/then" in Dutch, *baino* "than/but" in Basque, *asa* "than/then" in Toba Batak, *noria* "than/after that" in Goajiro, *ngem* "than/but" in Ilocano, *na* "than/nor" in Scottish Gaelic, *nor* "than/nor" in Scottish English, *ē* "than/or" in Classical Greek). Furthermore, particle comparatives in at least some languages share a number of syntactic properties with coordinations. For example, the Dutch comparative allows Gapping, a rule which is commonly thought to be restricted to coordinate structures.

(16) Dutch (Indo-European, Germanic)
(a) *Ik verzamel boeken en mijn*
    I collect   books and my
    broer   verzamelt platen
    brother collects   records
    'I collect books and my brother collects records'
(b) *Ik verzamel boeken en mijn*
    I collect   books and my
    broer   Ø platen
    brother   records

(17) Dutch (Indo-European, Germanic)
(a) *Ik koop meer boeken dan mijn*
    I buy more books than my
    broer   platen koopt
    brother records buys
    'I buy more books than my brother buys records'
(b) *Ik koop meer boeken dan mijn*
    I buy more books than my
    broer   platen Ø
    brother records

One might argue, then, that particle comparatives must be seen as grammaticalizations from an underlying sequential construction. In this way, the particle comparative does not have to present a counterexample to the modelling analysis of comparative constructions, although it certainly forms a recalcitrant case.

5. Comparison of equality

In contrast to the comparison of inequality, other types of comparison have as yet not been the subject of extensive typological investigation. A number of exploratory observations on the encoding of equative sentences and superlatives can be found in Ultan (1972). Haspelmath & Buchholz (1998) consider a domain of constructions which center around the concepts of equality and similarity. Among others, this domain includes equative sentences such as (18a), similative sentences such as (18b), and sentences which contain role phrases, such as (18c):

(18) English: (Indo-European, Germanic)
(a) *Robert is as tall as Maria*
(b) *Fatmir sings like a nightingale*
(c) *He works as an engineer*

Since Haspelmath & Buchholz (1998) limit themselves largely to the languages of Europe, no globally applicable typological conclusions can be drawn from their observations. However, the authors succeed in identifying a number of typically "European" characteristics of the constructions in (18), which provide strong evidence for the existence of a European Sprachbund, called "Standard Average European (SAE)". Thus, in the core of this Sprachbund (which comprises West Germanic, Romance, Baltic, Slavic and Greek), equative and similative constructions are encoded in ways that are not attested in non-SAE languages of Europe, nor, presumably, anywhere else in the world. Important features of SAE encoding of the domain of equality and similarity are the following:

(i) equative sentences in SAE tend to show a double marking. Both the standard NP and the predicate in the construction are marked by an analytic item. Examples of this are *as ... as* in English, *aussi ... que* in French, or *tam ... quam* in Latin. In the typical case, the two markers are related, in that the marker on the predicate is the demonstrative form, and the marker on the standard NP the relative/interrogative form, of the same lexical stem. This construction type is largely absent from the languages outside the European Sprachbund, where single marking on either the predicate or the standard NP appears to be the rule.

(ii) similative constructions in SAE tend to mark standard NP's only, and for this they tend to use the same marker as is employed for the standard NP in the equative construction. Although French (*comme* vs. *que*) and English (*as* vs. *like*) are notable exceptions to this tendency, the overwhelming majority of SAE languages confirm to it, as can be illustrated by cases like Swedish *som*, German *wie*, and Serbocroat *kao*.

(iii) in role phrases in SAE the same marker tends to be used that is employed for the marking of the standard NP in equative and/or similative constructions. Examples of this state of affairs include Czech *jako*, and again Swedish *som*. In this feature, SAE languages differ sharply from non-SAE languages, in which usually quite different strategies for the encoding of role phrases are used, such as special "essive" case markings.

In conclusion, there is reason to assume that, in the languages of Standard Average European, the domain of equality and similarity has been formally generalized to a degree which is seldom, if ever, encountered outside this Sprachbund.

6. Special abbreviations

AFF	affix
INDIC	indicative
HAB	habital
PREF	prefix

7. References

Andersen, Paul Kent. 1983. *Word order typology and comparative constructions*. Amsterdam: Benjamins.

Haspelmath, Martin & Buchholz, Oda. 1998. "Equative and similative constructions in the languages of Europe". In: van der Auwera, Johan (ed.). *Adverbial constructions in the languages of Europe*. Berlin: Mouton de Gruyter, 277–334.

Stassen, Leon. 1984. "The comparative compared". *Journal of Semantics* 3: 143–182.

Stassen, Leon. 1985. *Comparison and Universal Grammar*. Oxford: Blackwell.

Ultan, Russell. 1972. "Some features of basic comparative constructions". In: *Working papers on Language Universals* (Stanford) 9: 117–162.

Leon Stassen, Nijmegen
(The Netherlands)

76. Conditional constructions

1. Introduction
2. Conditionals in logic and linguistics
3. Conditional markers
4. Tense, aspect, mood, modality and polarity in conditionals
5. "Conditionals are topics"
6. Conditionals, concessive conditionals and concessives
7. Special abbreviations
8. References

1. Introduction

Conditionals are a subclass of sentences that contain adverbial clauses of circumstance. The inventory of circumstantial relations that may be expressed by complex sentences with adverbial clauses traditionally includes conditional relations, in addition to causal, temporal, concessive, concessive conditional, comparative, purposive and resultative ones.

A prototypical conditional sentence, like (1)

(1) *If the weather is fine we shall go for a walk.*

consists of two clauses, one of which (*if the weather is fine*), usually called **protasis**, **antecedent** or, simply, ***if*-clause**, expresses a proposition whose fulfillment or non-fulfillment is relevant to the degree of reality assigned to the proposition expressed by another clause (*we shall go for a walk*), usually called **apodosis** or **consequent** (Trask 1993: 55).

There are not many systematic crosslinguistic studies of conditionals. Among the few are Traugott et al. 1986, Athanasiadou & Dirven 1997, Xrakovskij 1998.

Our overview of the structure of conditionals across languages will be organized as follows: In § 2., we shall briefly discuss how the conditional relation in natural languages differs from material implication as defined in logic. § 3. examines formal types of conditionals. In § 4., we will look at grammatical marking of protasis and apodosis. In § 5., discourse functions of conditionals are discussed. Finally, in § 6., we show how conditionals are related to concessive conditionals and concessives.

2. Conditionals in logic and linguistics

2.1. Truth values and irrealis expressions

Conditionals, together with coordinate conjunctions (*and*, *or*), negation and quantifiers, have been thoroughly studied both by linguists and logicians as an example of how the notions developed in the propositional calculus can be reflected in natural language and vice versa. The relationship of the protasis to the apodosis in conditional sentences is often analyzed as corresponding to the logical notion of (material) implication. But, as numerous scholars have pointed out (for references see, inter alia, Comrie 1986, Haiman 1994, van der Auwera 1997 and the bibliography there), conditionals in natural languages ("ordinary" conditionals) differ from the logical implication in many important respects. First and foremost, the truth-functional definition of implication given in the propositional calculus dictates that a compound statement $A \rightarrow B$ is true unless A is true and B is false, while components of ordinary conditionals often cannot be evaluated in terms of truth values. For example, they may refer not only to past and present situations in the real world but also to processes, states or events that are not directly perceived, but are rather remembered as previously experienced or imagined and therefore "judged not to accord with current objective reality" (Chafe 1995: 349). These include the so-called irrealis expressions, like questions, imperatives or suggestions:

(2) *If the weather is fine shall we go for a walk?*
    go for a walk!
    let us go for a walk!

Although the apodoses in (2) cannot be evaluated in terms of truth values, they form totally acceptable ordinary conditionals.

2.2. Truth values and the epistemic scale

Ordinary conditionals appeal not to the neat binary "true"/"false" division, but rather to the epistemic scale that represents speaker's subjective assessment of the reality of a given situation, with "true" and "false" being the two endpoints of the scale (cf., Akatsuka 1985, van der Auwera 1983, Givón 1995: 111–174). Prototypical, "hypothetical", conditionals, like (1), are based on situations separated from both endpoints of the scale, in that their reality is presented as unknown (other terms used for this type of conditionals are "open" or "real" conditionals, cf. Trask 1993, Palmer 1986). The so-called "counterfactual" conditionals are based on situations that are viewed as "contrary-to-fact", i.e. close to the "false" endpoint of the scale (another term often used for this type is "unreal" conditionals, cf. Palmer 1986). In the counterfactual conditional (3) below, the situation "I am you" is presented as false:

(3) *If I were you I would go there.*

Languages use both grammatical and lexical devices to express how the speaker estimates the degree of possibility of a given situation. In English, for example, the conditional conjunction *if* may introduce clauses with different degrees of possibility depending on the tense-aspect-mood verbal forms in the combined clauses. The following sentences are arranged in Givón (1995: 136) from higher to lower possibility (or, "degree of certainty"):

(4) *What **will** you **do** if I **tell** you that ...*
*What **would** you **do** if I **told** you that ...*
*What **would** you **do** if I **were to tell** you that ...*
*What **would** you **have done** if I **had told** you that ...*

In addition, in each of the above cases, the degree of certainty can be lowered by using modal verbs in the appropriate tense-aspect-mood form in the apodosis, cf. (Givón 1995: 135):

(5) *If she comes, we **will/may** consider it.*
*If she ever came, we **would/might** consider it.*
*If she had come, we **would have/might have** considered it.*

The degree of the speaker's certainty is determined by a set of pragmatic factors. One of them, as pointed out by Akatsuka (1985: 630−638), is the novelty of the information covered by a conditional: the speaker is usually more certain about the newly learned or actualized information. For example, the information obtained in the ongoing discourse is, cross-linguistically, usually marked as "almost" real. This can be illustrated by the Russian conditional conjunction *raz* (Iordanskaja 1988) or Japanese *nara* (Akatsuka 1985), which represent information that has just entered the speaker's consciousness at the time of the speech event. Conditionals "*raz Q, P*" in Russian or "*Q nara, P*" in Japanese are close in meaning to English *if*-clauses in sentences, like *If you are so smart, (then, I wonder) why are you not rich*, and can be interpreted in the following way: 'Usually, if *Q*, then *P*. I have just observed/learned (or, You have just told me) that *Q*. That is why, I believe that *P*':

(6) Russian
Ja   xote-l   pogovori-t' no
I.NOM want-PAST.SG.M talk-INF   but
raz   ty   zanjat-a
if/since you.NOM be.busy-F.SG
zajd-u   popozže
drop.in-1.SG.FUT later
'I wanted to talk, but if/since [as far as I can see, at the moment] you are busy, I will drop in later.'

The high certainty of the represented information usually associated with these conditionals explains why in descriptive grammars they fall between conditionals and causatives (cf. Švedova 1970: 719).

2.3. Evaluative modality and polarity

In ordinary conditionals the expression of conditionality is intimately bound up with the expression of other categories such as mood (modality) or polarity (e.g. Engl. negative conditional marker *unless* 'if not'). Modal meanings which are built into the meaning of ordinary conditionals often include not only epistemic attitudes (probability/certainty) but also evaluative/deontic attitudes. i.e. desirability, obligation, permission etc. For instance, the Korean temporal marker *-taka* may be used also as a conditional marker and, in this case, it implies the speaker's evaluation of the situation given in the apodosis as undesirable (Akatsuka & Sohn 1994, Akatsuka 1997). This is the reason why (7b) with a desirable situation in the apodosis is ungrammatical:

(7) Korean (Akatsuka 1997: 324−325)
 (a) *cam-man   ca-taka-(nun)*
     sleep-only sleep-COND-(TOP)
     nakceyha-keyss-ta
     flunk-FUT-DEC
     'If you just sleep, you will flunk (the exam).'
 (b) **cam-man   ca-taka-(nun)*
     sleep-only sleep-COND-(TOP)
     naaci-keyss-ta
     feel.better-FUT-DEC
     'If you just sleep, you will feel better.'

When the meaning of polarity is combined with the meaning of ordinary conditionals, it may influence its epistemic component. Thus, Wierzbicka (1997: 38—43) has shown that negative conditionals often represent lower possibility of a given situation than their positive counterparts. For instance, the following Polish negative conditional (8a) has exclusively counterfactual reading, while its positive counterpart (8b) can be both counterfactual and hypothetical:

(8) Polish (based on Wierzbicka 1997: 40)
  (a) *Gdyby nie posz-li w tę stronę*
   if.SBJV NEG go-PAST to that direction
   to by się nie zgubi-li
   then SBJV REFL NEG lose-PAST
   'If they hadn't gone in that direction, they wouldn't have got lost'
  (b) *Gdyby posz-li w tę stronę to*
   if.SBJV go-PAST to that direction then
   by się zgubi-li
   SBJV REFL lose-PAST
   'If they had gone in that direction, they would have got lost', or 'If they went in that direction, they would get lost'

2.4. Habitual conditionals

Ordinary conditionals may assign varying degrees of generality to the implicational relationship, i.e. the relationship between the introduced states of affairs may be unique (specific) as well as habitual (generic). Thus, in Russian, using subjectless infinitives instead of finite verbal forms in the protasis makes the relationship more general:

(9) Russian
  Esli derža-t' cvet-y   v
  if   keep-INF flower-PL.ACC in
  tepl-e   oni   bystro
  heat-LOC they.NOM quickly
  vjan-ut
  wither.away-PRES.3.PL
  'If [one] keep[s] flowers in the heat, they quickly wither away', lit. 'If to keep flowers ...'

Habitual conditionals display a number of similarities with other habitual and generic expressions, including temporal clauses and restrictive relative clauses on generic heads: *If flowers are kept in the heat, they quickly wither away* → *When flowers are kept in the heat, they quickly wither away* → *Flowers that are kept in the heat, quickly wither away* (among recent investigations on this topic see Ziv 1997, Langacker 1997). Clear evidence for the functional proximity between habitual conditionals and temporal expressions is provided by the fact that some markers are ambiguous between habitual conditional and temporal meanings (e.g. German *wenn*).

2.5. Causal relation between the protasis and the apodosis

Ordinary conditionals usually presuppose that the processes, states or events denoted by protasis and apodosis are somehow related in the speaker's world. Normally, this relationship can be interpreted as causal. Thus, sentence (1) receives a correct interpretation because of the general experience that fine weather can naturally be connected with going for a walk. This presupposed correlation between the protasis and the apodosis in ordinary conditionals does not carry over to material implication. Logically indisputable conditionals with a true protasis and a true apodosis tend to appear linguistically unacceptable if a causal relation cannot be established between the propositions, like in (10), taken from (Comrie 1986: 80):

(10) *If Paris is the capital of France, two is an even number.*

Furthermore, natural languages tend to impose a causal relation between the protasis and the apodosis whenever it is possible. This can be illustrated by the so-called "Dracula conditionals" such as (11), taken from (Akatsuka 1991: 25):

(11) *If Confucius was born in Texas, I'm Dracula.*

Both the protasis and the apodosis are false here, hence the truth of the conditional as a whole as predicted by the truth table. But the actual interpretation of Dracula conditionals in discourse normally imposes a correlation between the degree of absurdity in the protasis and the degree of absurdity in the apodosis, i.e. what is imposed is that the claim that Confucius was born in Texas is as absurd as the claim that the speaker is Dracula (see Akatsuka 1986, 1991 and the bibliography there).

2.6. "Speech act" conditionals and related phenomena

Ordinary conditionals, unlike material implications, may relate not only states of affairs but also the attitudes of interlocutors. The so-called "speech act", or "illocutionary", conditionals provide reasons, excuses or explanations for the speaker making a given assertion (cf., Iordanskaya 1988, Sweetser 1990):

(12) *I am not going, in case you haven't heard.*

The hearer's attitude can also be involved, as it happens in the so-called "observational" conditionals (Martin 1975: 557), like (13):

(13) Japanese
  Sono kado o   magar-eba mise
  this corner DO turn-COND shop
  ga   ar-u
  SUBJ be.located-PRES
  'If [you] turn round the corner, there will be a shop'

In (13), the conditional relationship is established not between "turning round the corner" and "the location of the shop", but rather between "turning round the corner" and the possibility for a hearer (or anyone in his position) to find ("observe") the shop.

3. Conditional markers

3.1. Main structural types of conditionals

Cross-linguistically, the most common conditional pattern exhibits the two following characteristics: First, the protasis precedes the apodosis, which is known as Greenberg's (1966: 84) Universal 14: "In conditional statements, the conditional clause precedes the conclusion as the normal order in all languages" (see § 5. for further discussion). Second, the overt marking of conditionality is built into the protasis. Conditionals that meet neither of the two requirements seem to have not been reported so far, i.e. an initial, marked consequent would be highly unusual. On the other hand, neither of the two requirements is absolute. First, under special circumstances (see § 5. for further discussion) the protasis may follow the apodosis:

(14) Polish
  Nie zgubi-li-by   sie   gdyby nie
  NEG lose-PAST-SBJV REFL if.SBJV NEG
  posz-li w   te   strone
  go-PAST to that   direction
  'They wouldn't have got lost if they hadn't gone in that direction'.

Second, conditionals can be overtly marked not only on the protasis, like in (15a), but also on the apodosis, like in (15b), or both in the protasis and in the apodosis (15c) (see § 3.3. for further discussion):

(15) (a) *IF you go, I will go too.*
  (b) *Maybe you will go, THEN I will go too.*
  (c) *IF you go, THEN I will go too.*

It is also possible that a relation between two combined clauses (phrases) obtains a conditional interpretation without any overt indication of conditionality. For example, a non-finite verbal form (e.g. the so-called "contextual converb", as defined in Nedjalkov V. 1995: 106) may have a wide variety of circumstantial interpretations including a conditional one. In many cases the irrealis expressions in the apodosis lead to the conditional interpretation of the contextual form in the protasis. The irrealis expressions may include questions, imperatives or subjunctives, as in (16) below, which is an example from Evenki (a Northern Tungusic language spoken in Siberia):

(16) Evenki (Nedjalkov I. 1995: 456)
  Asatkan-me ajav-mi   asila-mča-v.
  girl-ACC   love-CONV marry-SBJV-1.SG
  'If I loved this girl I would marry her.'
  Lit. 'Loving this girl, I would marry her.'

As will be shown below, in §§ 3.2.–3.4., conditionality can be signaled by means of segmental devices (affixes or function words) or (less frequently) by means of special word order patterns.

3.2. Overt marking of the protasis

3.2.1. Affixes as conditional markers

Conditional markers may be suffixed to the stem or prefixed to it. In languages that use non-finite verb forms as a clause combining strategy, the conditional marker is usually a verbal suffix, as in many Daghestanian languages, including Hinalugh, cf. (17). In languages with person-number agreement of the verb in the protasis, the conditional marker may be a prefix on the verb, as in Basque, Caddo (cf. (27) in § 4.), or in Bantu languages, like Dabida, cf. (18):

(17) Hinalugh (Kibrik et al. 1972: 209)
  q'ula gæʃ-q'aʁi zu ʃalkʰur-du-mæ
  rain   pour-COND   I   get.wet-1.SG-DEC
  'If it rains [which is very probable], I'll get wet.'

(18) Dabida (Rjabova 1998: 84–85)
  βi-ka-kumba   iβanu
  3.PL.SUBJ-COND-shoot arrow
  ji-'dima   ku-vika
  CL.SG.SUBJ-can   INF-fly
  'If they shoot an arrow, will it reach [the destination]?'

3.2.2. Function words as conditional markers

Function words (free morphemes) marking conditional protases are usually qualified as conjunctions and are typical of languages that tend to use finite verb forms as a clause combining strategy, like many Indo-European (e. g. English *if*, German *wenn*, Bulgarian *ako*, Persian *agar*, Modern Greek *ean*, *an*). Sometimes, though, the degree of "finiteness" of the forms to which free conditional morphemes are attached may be restricted. For example, the conditional conjunction *to* in Japanese is attached to a finite form but this form is obligatorily non-past (although this grammatical non-past tense form may refer to the situations that actually took place in the past), so the "finiteness" of this form is limited by the restrictions in tense marking.

In closely related languages, an expression that originally was the same conditional marker may appear as a bound morpheme in one language and as a free morpheme in another. An example is found in the Tibeto-Burman language Newari (Genetti 1994: 150–151), where conditional markers in two dialects have the same etymology (Classical Newari locative *sa*), but represent independent developments: *sa* in Dolakha suffixes to the stem while *sā* in Kathmandu is attached to the finite inflected verb.

Moreover, in some languages the same conditional marker can be used both as a free and a bound morpheme. In this case, the choice "free vs. bound" may iconically reflect the degree of clause integration (cf. "the binding scale" in Givón 1991: 95–97). In the Papuan language Amele, as described in Roberts 1988, the conditional marker *fi* is used as a conjunction when the appropriate verbal form is marked for a switch reference category Different Subject (lower integration), but is attached to the verbal form as an affix when the form is marked for Same Subject (higher integration):

(19) Amele (Roberts 1988: 84–85)
  (a) *Uqa ho-co-b fi ija*
     3.SG come-DS.3.SG COND 1.SG
     mad-ig-en
     say-1.SG-FUT
     'If he comes I will speak.'
  (b) *Ija hu-f-ig   mad-ig-en*
     1.SG come-COND.SS-1.SG say.1.SG-FUT
     'If I come I will speak."

3.3. Overt marking of the apodosis

Instead of (or together with) overt marking of the protasis, languages may also mark the apodosis, see (15b–c) above. Conditional markers that appear in the apodosis provide resumptive clause linking. Being responsible for reference-tracking, they often contain pronominal anaphoric elements, or at least, their pronominal origin remains diachronically transparent. Thus, as shown in Podlesskaya (1997), Russian has developed the following conditional resumptives.

1) Three negative conditional resumptives with a general meaning 'if not so': *inače* (which is originally a pronominal adverb meaning 'differently', cf. *Ja predstavljal sebe ego inače* 'I imagined him differently.'); *a to* (which consists of the adversative conjunction *a* plus the conditional resumptive *to* 'then'); and *a ne to* (which consists of the adversative conjunction *a* plus the negative particle *ne* plus the conditional resumptive *to*):

(20)   Russian
    Ja včera vsta-l
    I.NOM yesterday get.up.PERF-PAST-SG.M
    rano inače / a to / a ne to ja   by
    early otherwise   I.NOM SBJV
    ne uspe-l   na poezd
    NEG be.in.time.PERF.PAST.SG.M for train
    'I got up early yesterday, otherwise I would not have caught the train.'

2) Two positive conditional resumptives with a general meaning 'if so, [then ...].' which are the close equivalents to the English *then*, namely – *to* 'then' (which is originally the singular neuter demonstrative pronoun) and *togda* 'then' (which is originally a pronominal temporal adverb).

Of the two Russian positive conditional resumptives, *to* appears in the apodosis only when there is a conditional marker also in the protasis, while *togda* can appear in the apodosis alone without any support from the protasis. When there is a conditional marker in the protasis, both *to* and *togda* are optional. This is summarized in Table 76.1 below:

Table 76.1: Russian

protasis	apodosis
esli 'if'	*to* 'then'
esli 'if'	ø
esli 'if'	*togda* 'then'
ø	*togda* 'then'
(*ø	*to* 'then')

When the apodosis is marked explicitly, the protasis is often (though not always) "self-sufficient" in that it may contain no device signaling that its content will be somehow utilized in the further discourse. The protasis may even end in a period intonation, not a comma (cf. Chafe 1988). Thus, (21a) and (21b) below differ in that (21b) lacks the conditional conjunction in the protasis, and it is the conditional resumptive *togda* 'then' in the apodosis that defines the type of clause linkage. Sentences, like (21b) exhibit lower degree of clause integration and hence are less grammaticalized forms of conditionals in that the combination of clauses is restricted mainly by lexical and not by grammatical patterns:

(21) Russian
 (a) *Esli oni   ne   pried-ut*
   if they.NOM NEG come-PRES.3.PL
   ni   v subbotu, ni v
   neither on Saturday nor on
   voskresen'je, togda / to / ø ja
   Sunday   then   I.NOM
   bud-u   vynužden-a poex-at'
   be-PRES.1.SG forced-F.SG go-INF
   k nim   sam-a
   to their [place] myself-F.SG
   'If they come neither on Saturday nor on Sunday, I will have to go to their place myself.'
 (b) *Možet byt' oni   ne*
   maybe   they.NOM NEG
   pried-ut   ni   v subbotu
   come-PRES.3.PL neither on Saturday
   ni   v voskresen'je.
   nor on Sunday
   *Togda / *to / ø ja   bud-u*
   then   I.NOM be-PRES.1.SG
   vynužden-a poex-at' k nim
   forced-F.SG go-INF   to their [place]
   sam-a
   myself-F.SG
   'Maybe they come neither on Saturday nor on Sunday. Then (in that case) I will have to go to their place myself.'

With respect to most reliable tests for distinguishing between subordination and coordination, conditionals marked on the apodosis, cross-linguistically, show more symptoms of coordination than conditionals marked on the protasis. For instance, with respect to positional criteria, conditionals marked on the apodosis block transposition of clauses and inserting one clause into the other, while conditionals marked on the protasis allow these operations. Thus, in the Russian conditional (22), which is marked on the protasis, the conditional clause can be inserted into the consequent:

(22) Russian
 (a) *Esli Maš-a   zabole-et*
   if   Maša-F.SG.NOM fall.ill-PRES.3.SG
   Petj-a   ne   pried-et.
   Petja-M.SG.NOM NEG come-PRES.3.SG
 (b) *Petj-a   [esli Maš-a*
   Petja-M.SG.NOM if   Maša-F.SG.NOM
   zabole-et]   ne   pried-et
   fall.ill-PRES.3.SG NEG come-PRES.3.SG
   'Petja [if Maša falls ill] won't come.'

However, if the resumptive *to* 'then' appears in the consequent clause, as in (23), any clause order variations are forbidden:

(23) Russian
 (a) *Esli Maš-a   zabole-et*
   if   Maša-F.SG.NOM fall.ill-PRES.3.SG
   to   Petj-a   ne
   then Petja-M.SG.NOM NEG
   pried-et.
   come-PRES.3.SG
   'If Maša falls ill, then Petja won't come'.
 (b) **Petj-a   [esli Maš-a*
   Petja-M.SG.NOM if   Maša-F.SG.NOM
   zabole-et]   to   ne
   fall.ill-PRES.3.SG then NEG
   pried-et
   come-PRES.3.SG
   *'Petja [if Maša falls ill] then won't come.'

3.4. Word order patterns as conditional markers

Instead of (or together with) segmental markers, languages sometimes use special word order patterns to mark conditionality. Well-known examples are some Germanic languages with the so-called "verb-first conditionals":

(24) German (König & van der Auwera 1988: 116)
 (a) *Wäre ich in Paris, ich würde zum Louvre gehen.*
 (b) *Wäre ich in Paris, würde ich zum Louvre gehen.*

The conditionals with non-canonical verb-initial word order in the protasis are used in the absence of a conditional marker, while in the presence of a conditional marker, the protasis, like any other adverbial clause, exhibits verb-final word order:

(25) German
Wenn ich in Paris wäre, würde ich zum Louvre gehen.

When the word order in the protasis is verb-first, the word order in the apodosis may be either verb-second, as in the isolated simple sentence, cf. (24a), or verb-first, as in the main clause marked for having a preceding subordinate, cf. (24b). As was shown in König & van der Auwera (1988: 116–117), verb-first and verb-second apodoses are synonymous in German, while in Dutch they differ in epistemic modality: the verb-first apodosis exhibits a higher degree of the speaker's certainty in the denoted situation and therefore cannot receive a counterfactual reading. As a result, of the two German counterfactuals (24a) and (24b), only (24a) with the verb-second apodosis has a correct Dutch equivalent (26a), while (26b) with the verb-first apodosis is ungrammatical:

(26) Dutch (based on König & van der Auwera 1988: 116)
 (a) *Was ik in Parijs ik zou   naar*
  was I in Paris I would to
  het Louvre gaan.
  the Louver go
  'If I were in Paris, I would go to the Louvre.'
 (b) **Was ik in Parijs zou   ik naar*
  was I in Paris would I to
  het Louvre gaan.
  the Louvre go
  'If I were in Paris, I would go to the Louvre.'

It is important that in the Germanic languages the verb-first word order pattern is used not only in conditionals but also in yes-no questions. This is a cogent argument for the functional proximity of conditionals and yes-no questions: both relate to the epistemic attitude. Both in yes-no questions and in conditionals the speaker is not certain about the reality of the denoted state of affairs, but in yes-no questions this uncertainty is presented as a basis for seeking new information, while in conditionals, this uncertainty is presented as a basis for establishing a relationship between the degree of reality assigned to two different states of affairs (see § 5. for further discussion).

4. Tense, aspect, mood, modality and polarity in conditionals

As was pointed out in § 2., to get the adequate picture of a conditional in a given language at least the following pieces of information are necessary: the temporal status of combined clauses (do the introduced states of affairs refer to the past, present or future?); the epistemic status (how does the speaker assess the reality of the introduced states of affairs?), the evaluative status (the speaker's attitude towards of the introduced states of affairs in terms of (un)desirability, (dis)approval, etc.), the polarity status (is the reality of the state of affairs introduced in the apodosis based on fulfillment or on non-fulfillment of the state of affairs introduced in the protasis?) and the frequentativity status (is the relationship between the introduced states of affairs unique/specific or habitual/generic?).

Usually, this information is not exclusively covered by conditional markers but is rather distributed between the three relevant groups of devices: conditional markers proper, grammatical markers on the protasis or (and) on the apodosis (e.g. tense, aspect, mood and polarity markers), and "supporting" lexical devices (e.g. adverbial sentence modifiers, quantifiers, particles etc.). Parts of this information may be differently grouped together, depending on the grammaticalization strategy of a given language.

For example, Caddo (Macro-Siouan: Oklahoma, Texas), as reported in Chafe (1995), has prefixes for particular (unique) conditions, generic (habitual) conditions and for negative conditions, so that frequentativity and polarity status in Caddo is covered by conditional markers while the epistemic status is covered by a separate morpheme, namely by the irrealis marker:

(27) Caddo (Chafe 1995: 356–357)
 (a) *hi-t'a-yi-bahw*
  PARTICULAR.COND-1.AG-IRR-see
  'If I see it …'
 (b) *nas-t'a-yi-bahw*
  GENERIC.COND-1.AG-IRR-see
  'If, whenever I see it …'
 (c) *nadús-t'a-yi-bahw*
  NEG.COND-1.AG-IRR-see
  'If I don't see it …'

In many languages the epistemic status of conditionals can be expressed lexically, cf. the Chamorro (Austronesian) particle *mohon* 'as if, supposedly' that is attached to the protasis to switch it from hypothetical to counterfactual, i.e. to lower its degree of possibility (Chung & Timberlake 1985: 252). Likewise, Japanese uses the particle *moshi* 'supposedly' in the protasis to restrict the meaning of some implicational constructions to purely conditional, while in the absence of the particle, these constructions may have both conditional and temporal interpretations. In addition, Japanese has a lexical device to restrict the meaning of conditional constructions to purely counterfactual, namely, an adversative conjunction (e.g. *noni* 'but') positioned after the apodosis: in other words, to make a counterfactual conditional out of a conditional construction "If X then Y", in Japanese, you have to say *If X then Y but* (see for details Hasada 1997, Podlesskaya 1995: 85−107).

Some combinations of tense, aspect and mood markers in the protasis and/or in the apodosis may take over the function of indicating the conditional relationship itself, so that the two adjacent clauses receive the conditional meaning without a conditional marker proper. In the Australian languages Margany and Gunya (Breen 1981) the potential mood in the second of the two combined clauses introduces an undesirable consequence that might take place if the hearer does not follow the imperative protasis, and is, thus, responsible for the epistemic status, for the evaluative status, the polarity status, and for establishing the conditional relationship between propositions:

(28) Margany (Breen 1981: 340)
balga ṉuwa ḓambal baḓa:n^{y}d^{y}u
hit there snake bite.POT
inaṉa
2.SG.ACC
'Kill that snake [or if you don't do it] it'll bite you.'

Note that the same strategy of coding conditional meaning (the imperative in the protasis, the potential in the apodosis) is used for warnings in spoken English (and many other languages): *Don't go any closer − it might be dangerous!*, i.e. 'if you go any closer, it might be dangerous'.

Though verbal mood is cross-linguistically the most common device for representing the epistemic status of conditionals, some combinations of tense and aspect can be also used for this purpose. A well-known example is found in Indo-European languages, e.g. Germanic and Iranian, where past tenses (sometimes in combination with the perfect aspect) are used to mark conditionals of low certainty, i.e. hypothetical and counterfactual (for details, see, for example Givón 1995: 111−174, Xrakovskij 1994, Dahl 1997 and the bibliography given there).

For tense, aspect, mood and polarity marking in conditionals, a language can either use a subset of markers attested in simple (single) clauses, or may develop special markers that are used exclusively in combinations of clauses being, then, themselves signals of clause integration. Languages with sophisticated systems of conditionals often use both types of marking. An impressive example is the Archi language (Daghestan), briefly discussed below following (Kibrik et al. 1977).

The first device exploited in the Archi conditionals is the conditional converb marked with the suffix *-(e)nč'iš* which can be derived from the three different groups of verbal forms.

(a) When the conditional converb in *-(e)nč'iš* is derived from the perfective stem, it can be used either for habitual conditionals with the indicative apodosis ("Whenever you go, I go too"), or for unique conditionals with both protasis and apodosis being hypothetical and referring to the future ("If you go tomorrow, I will go too / I wish I could go too / take me with you"). The apodosis is either the future indicative in this case, or the imperative, or the approbative − a mood that expresses the speaker's positive evaluation of one situation in comparison with another. The approbative in Archi is one of the verbal moods used only in clause combinations (see (32) below), unlike the indicative and the imperative, which are used also in single clauses:

(29) Archi (Kibrik et al. 1977: 2.279)
zamāna   e=b=ī- enč'iš
time.NOM.SG can.PFV(=CL=)-COND
x̄Iele-ši   zaba
guest-ADV come.IMP
'If you have time, come [and] be [my] guest.'

(b) The conditional converb in *-(e)nč'iš* can be derived from the possibilitive which is an epistemic mood denoting that the speaker admits the possibility of the situation in question. The possibilitive in the conditional in its turn requires the perfective stem of the auxiliary. The tense-aspect-mood combination "perfective/possibilitive" is allowed only in clause combinations (e. g. conditionals), while the possibilitive in single clauses requires the so-called potential stem of the auxiliary. Conditional converbs derived from the possibilitive introduce hypothetical situations in the past or in the present:

(30) Archi (Kibrik et al. 1977: 2.281)
un,   ručka   b-ešde-li
you.ERG pen.NOM.SG CL-buy.PFV-CONV
bo-xo-nč'iš   b-ez
CL-AUX.PFV.PBL-COND CL-I.DAT
b-ak̄u-s   b-a
CL-see-INF CL-make.IMP
'If you have bought a pen (which is very probable), show it to me.'

(c) The conditional converb in *-(e)nč'iš* can be derived from indicative forms to express a counterfactual condition if the verb in the apodosis belongs to the fixed set of forms that introduce hypothetical situations. This set includes, for instance, the so-called past inceptive form, which is used when the speaker believes that the situation in question has most probably started by the moment of speech. The counterfactual conditional below exhibits a conditional converb in *-(e)nč'iš*, which is derived from the analytical presence indicative form in the protasis and the analytical past inceptive in the apodosis:

(31) Archi (Kibrik et al. 1977: 2.286)
hinc to-r   ši-a-r-ši
now she.NOM-CL write-do-DUR-CONV
d-i-nč'iš   učitel-li   zā-rši
CL-be-COND teacher-ERG I.OBL-ALL
bo-qi-ši   edi
tell.PERF-INC-CONV be.PAST
'If she had been writing now, the teacher would have told me [about it by now].'

Alongside conditional converbs Archi exploits two finite forms in the conditional protasis, namely the conjunctive and the optative. Both forms are allowed also in single clauses. The conjunctive combines the epistemic and the evaluative meaning: "I wish it is so, but I doubt that it is possible". The optative is a polite imperative, i. e. a category of "weak manipulation" (Givón 1995: 111–174): "we both think that it is good, why don't you do it?". The conjunctive as a clause combining device introduces the counterfactual protasis, expressing an unrealizable wish:

(32) Archi (Kibrik et al. 1977: 2.215)
w-ez   w-ak̄u-īu w-i-kini   zon
CL-I.DAT CL-see-ADJ CL-be-CONJ I.NOM
to-w-mu-x̌u   bāIbu-qi-di
(s)he-CL-OBL-COM talk.PFV-INC-APPR
'If I only knew [him] (lit. 'if for me there were the state of seeing'), I would have talked to him.'

The optative in the conditional protasis is always combined with negation while the optative in the single clause can be only positive. Thus, the negative optative in conditional sentences is a combination of mood and polarity that signals clause combining:

(33) Archi (Kibrik et al. 1977: 3.139)
noc'   sa-s   eīi-t'u-īan
bird.NOM catch-INF can.CL-NEG-OPT
immaq'₀i
leave.IMP
'If you can't catch the bird, leave [well alone, although it would be good if you could catch it].'

5. "Conditionals are topics"

The famous thesis that the conditional protasis functions as topic, in that it sets a framework within which the following sentence is valid, was first articulated by Haiman (1978), see also his later publications, e. g. Haiman (1994). Haiman based this claim on three important facts.

The first is Greenberg's (1966) universal 14 mentioned in § 3.1. – the conditional protasis almost invariably precedes the apodosis in the unmarked, or only permissible case, as the topic precedes the comment. The fact that clause order in conditionals iconically reflects the pragmatic sequence of the related events was noticed already in Greenberg (1966: 103): "The order of elements in language parallels that in physical experience or the order of knowledge. In the instance of conditionals, although the truth relations involved are timeless, logicians have always symbolized them in the order *implying, implied* exactly as in spoken language. If *modus ponens* is used in proof then we have a pragmatic example which follows the order of reasoning. No one thinks to write a proof backwards."

The second is the widespread morphological and syntactic identity of the conditional and topic marker in a large number of unrelated languages: Haiman (1994: 687) lists examples from Hua (*-mo*), Turkish (*-sA*) and Vietnamese (*thi*).

The third is the fact that conditionals and polar interrogative sentences often use the same or very similar marking devices. This was already illustrated by verb-first conditionals and yes-no questions in Germanic languages (§ 3.4.). Also well known is the fact that conditional conjunctions often serve as complementizers in indirect yes-no questions (*I was wondering IF you'd like to come to the cinema with me this evening?*). In some languages polar interrogative markers can give rise to conditional markers, e.g. Russian conditional marker *esli* 'if' is originally a grammaticalized combination of a copula *est'* with a polar interrogative marker *li* (on interrogatives and topic markers as the main sources from which conditional markers derive see Traugott 1985).

Three more facts should be added to this list of general considerations. First, conditional protases are easily cross-referenced by anaphoric pronouns that are the core arguments in the apodosis. In (34) the anaphoric pronoun *éto* being the subject of the consequent clause refers to the conditional protasis (the status of conditionals with respect to pronominalization and null-anaphora in cross-references to clauses is discussed in Iatridou & Embick 1997):

(34)   Russian
       [*Esli on   prid-ët   odin*]$_i$
       if   he.NOM come-3.SG alone
       éto$_i$ nikogo   ne   udiv-it.
       this.NOM nobody.ACC NEG surprise-3.SG
       '[If he comes alone]$_i$, this$_i$ will not surprise anybody.'

Second, the non-canonical word order — with the protasis following the apodosis — is often implied (or at least, favored) by the overt focus markers in the protasis, e.g. by restricting particles, like *only*: *I will go there **only** if you go with me*. Focus markers in these cases signal that the protasis loses its prototypical topical status.

Third, in the vast majority of languages, conditionals, unlike causatives, temporals or locatives, have no corresponding wh-questions. In some languages (e.g. Russian) the question can be put literally like "under which conditions?", but questions like this often sound somewhat artificial, like "teacher's questions", and even these questions cannot be answered with canonical conditionals. On the contrary, questions about possible consequences are easily formed following the "what if ..." model and are often reduced to the plain protasis: *And what will happen if he doesn't come? > And what if he doesn't come? > And if he doesn't come?* So again conditional protases appear to be topical in that they set the scene for the further discourse development.

Symptoms of a functional proximity between conditionals and interrogative sentences — and, hence, between conditionals and topics! — can be found also in so-called "concessive conditionals", or "even if" conditionals, like

(35)   *Even if it rains, we'll go for a walk.*

Like concessives proper, e.g.

(36)   *Although it rained, we went for a walk.*

concessive conditionals signify that the expected implication is not carried through ('raining' implies 'not going for a walk'). But concessive conditionals differ from concessives proper in the epistemic status of the protasis: the concessive protasis presents the denoted situation as "real" (in (36) the speaker knows that it rained), while the concessive conditional protasis presents the denoted situation as belonging to a set of possibilities, that are claimed to be irrelevant for the fulfillment of the apodosis. Thus, in (35), 'raining' is included into the set of conditions that, contrary to expectations, will not influence the speaker's intention to go for a walk, and, moreover, among these conditions 'raining' is presented as the most valuable possibility that could have influenced the speaker's intention.

As was shown very extensively in Haspelmath & König 1998, there are three types of concessive conditionals: scalar (cf. (35) and (37a)), alternative (37b), and universal (37c):

(37)   Haspelmath & König (1998: 563)
       (a) *Even if we do not get any financial support, we will go ahead with our project.*
       (b) *Whether we get any financial support or not, we will go ahead with our project.*
       (c) *No matter how much (/However much) financial support we get, we will go ahead with our project.*

Overt markers in concessive conditionals often have the same morphological and lexical sources as conditionals and/or concessives. One of the common marking devices in scalar concessive conditionals is the combination of a conditional marker with a restrictive particle, e. g. English *even if*. Devices similar to, or even identical with concessives proper are also not unusual: an example is found in Japanese where the verb form in *-temo* (a converb in *-te* plus the restrictive particle *mo* 'even/also') may have concessive, counterfactual concessive conditional and hypothetical concessive conditional interpretations. According to Fujii Yamaguchi (1990: 353—354), the choice between possible interpretations depends on the form of the apodosis: on its tense-aspect-mood marking, the presence of some pragmatic particle, like exclamative *yo*, or even the right intonation. Thus, the concessive interpretation in (38a) is due to the past tense of the verb, the counterfactual concessive conditional interpretation in (38b) is due to the particle *yo*, and the hypothetical concessive conditional interpretation in (38c) is due to the hypothetical mood of the verb:

(38) Japanese (Fujii Yamaguchi 1990: 354)
(a) *Syuzyutu o si-temo*
operation DO do-CONC/CONCCOND
naora-na-katta
recover-NEG-PAST
'Although he had an operation, he did not recover.'
(b) *Syuzyutu o si-temo*
operation DO do-CONC/CONCCOND
naora-na-katta yo
recover-NEG-PAST EXCL
'Even if he had had an operation, he would not have recovered!'
(c) *Syuzyutu o si-temo*
operation DO do-CONC/CONCCOND
(doose) naora-nai daroo
(anyway) recover-NEG HYP
'Even if he has an operation, he still will not recover.'

The most striking fact is that in many unrelated languages alternative concessive conditionals are based on the same patterns as interrogative sentences and universal concessive conditionals are based on the same patterns as sentences with universal quantifiers. As was pointed out in Haspelmath & König 1998 (see also König & van der Auwera 1988: 106—123, Thompson & Longacre 1985: 198—199, Longacre 1985: 244—245), these patterns in the protasis are usually either a disjunction 'P or not P' (sometimes introduced by a conditional marker), like in (39), or a free-choice expression based on a wh-question word (sometimes accompanied by a restrictive particle), like in (40):

(39) German (König & van der Auwera 1988: 118)
(Ganz gleich) ob wir ihm
(no matter) whether we him
helfen oder nicht, er schafft es
help or not he makes it
nie.
never
'Whether we help him or not, he will never make it.'

(40) Dutch (König & van der Auwera 1988: 118)
Hoeveel hij ook verdient, hij is
how.much he also earns he is
nooit tevreden.
never content
'However much he earns, he is never content.'

Here, again, the reason why concessive conditionals and questions share the same morpho-syntax is that both establish a framework within which the following portion of the discourse can develop — just like topics do.

7. Special abbreviations

AG	agent
ALL	allative
APPR	approbative
CL	noun class marker
COM	comitative
CONC	concessive
CONCCOND	concessive conditional
CONJ	conjunctive
CONV	converb
DEC	declarative
DO	direct object
DS	different subject
EXCL	exclamative
HYP	hypothetical
INC	inceptive
IRR	irrealis
OPT	optative
PAST	past
PBL	possibilitive
POT	potentialis
SBJV	subjunctive
SS	same subject

8. References

Akatsuka, Noriko. 1985. "Conditionals and the epistemic scale". *Language* 61.3: 625—639.

Akatsuka, Noriko. 1986. "Conditionals are discourse-bound". In: Traugott, Elizabeth Closs & ter

Meulen, Alice & Reilly, Judy Snitzer & Ferguson, Charles A. (eds.). *On conditionals.* Cambridge: Cambridge University Press, 333–351.

Akatsuka, Noriko. 1991. "Dracula conditionals and discourse". In: Georgopoulos, Carol & Ishihara, Roberta (eds.). *Interdisciplinary approaches to language.* (Essays in honor of S.-Y. Kuroda). Kluwer Academic Press: Dordrecht – Boston – London, 25–37.

Akatsuka, Noriko. 1997. "Negative conditionality, subjectification, and conditional reasoning". In: Athanasiadou & Dirven (eds.). 1997, 232–354.

Akatsuka, Noriko & Sohn, Sung-ock. 1994. "Negative conditionality: The case of Japanese *-tewa* and Korean *-taka*". In: Akatsuka, Noriko (ed.). *Japanese/Korean Linguistics, 4.* CSLI/Stanford, 203–220.

Athanasiadou, Angeliki & Dirven, René (eds.). 1997. *On conditionals again.* Amsterdam/Philadelphia: John Benjamins.

Breen, J. G. 1981. "Margany and Gunya". In: Dixon, R. M. W. & Blake, Barry J. (eds.). *Handbook of Australian languages.* Vol. 2. Canberra: The Australian National University Press, 274–393.

Chafe, Wallace. 1988. "Linking intonation units in spoken English". In: Haiman, John & Thompson, Sandra A. (eds.). *Clause combining in grammar and discourse.* (Typological studies in language, 18.). Amsterdam: John Benjamins, 1–27.

Chafe, Wallace. 1995. "The realis-irrealis distinction in Caddo, the Northern Iroquoian languages, and English". In: Bybee, Joan & Fleischman, Susanne (eds.). *Modality in grammar and discourse.* John Benjamins: Amsterdam/Philadelphia, 349–365.

Chung, Sandra & Timberlake, Alan. 1985. "Tense, aspect, and mood". In: Shopen, Timothy (ed.). *Language typology and syntactic description* (Volume III. Grammatical categories and the lexicon). Cambridge: Cambridge University Press, 250–255.

Comrie, Bernard. 1986. "Conditionals: a typology". In: Traugott, Elizabeth Closs & ter Meulen, Alice & Reilly, Judy Snitzer & Ferguson, Charles A. (eds.). *On conditionals.* Cambridge: Cambridge University Press, 77–99.

Dahl, Östen. 1997. "The relation between past time reference and counterfactuality: a new look". In: Athanasiadou & Dirven (eds.). 1997, 97–114.

Fujii Yamaguchi, Seiko. 1990. "Counterfactual concessive conditionals in Japanese". In: Hoji, Hajime (ed.). *Japanese/Korean Linguistics.* Stanford: The Stanford Linguistics Association, 353–367.

Genetti, Carol. 1994. *A descriptive and historical account of the Dolakha Newari dialect.* (Monumenta Serindica, 24). Tokyo: Institute for the Study of Languages and Cultures of Asia and Africa.

Givón, T. 1991. "Isomorphism in the grammatical code: cognitive and biological considerations". *Studies in Language* 15.1: 85–114.

Givón, T. 1995. *Functionalism and Grammar.* Amsterdam, Philadelphia: John Benjamins.

Greenberg, Joseph. 1966. "Some universals of grammar, with particular reference to the order of meaningful elements." In: Greenberg, J. (ed.). *Universals of Language*, 2nd edn. Cambridge (Mass.): MIT Press.

Haiman, John. 1978. "Conditionals are topics". *Language* 54.3: 564–589.

Haiman, John. 1994. "Conditionals, grammatical". In: *The encyclopedia of language and linguistics*: Oxford. New York: Pergamon Press, 685–688.

Hasada, Rie. 1997. "Conditionals and counterfactuals in Japanese". *Language Sciences* 19.3: 277–288.

Haspelmath, Martin & König, Ekkehard. 1998. "Concessive conditionals in the languages of Europe". In: van der Auwera, Johan (ed.). *Adverbial constructions in the languages of Europe.* Berlin, New York: Mouton de Gruyter, 563–640.

Iatridou, Sabine & Embick, David. 1997. "Apropos *pro*". *Language* 73.1: 58–78.

Iordanskaja, Lidija N. 1988. "Semantics of the Russian conjunction RAZ compared with some other conjunctions". *Russian Linguistics* 12.3: 239–267.

Kibrik, Alexandr E. & Kodzasov, Sandro V. & Olovjannikova, Irina P. & Samedov, Džalil. 1977. *Opyt strukturnogo opisanija arčinskogo jazyka* [Attempt of a structural description of Archi]. Moscow: Moscow State University.

Kibrik, Alexandr E. & Kodzasov, Sandro V. & Olovjannikova, Irina P. 1972. *Fragmenty grammatiki xinalugskogo jazyka* [Fragments of the grammar of Hinalugh]. Moscow: Moscow State University.

König, Ekkehard & van der Auwera, Johan. 1988. "Clause integration in German and Dutch conditionals, concessive conditionals and concessives". In: Haiman, John & Thompson, Sandra A. (eds.). *Clause combining in grammar and discourse.* (Typological studies in language, vol. 18). Amsterdam: John Benjamins, 101–133.

Langacker, Ronald W. 1997. "Generics and habituals". In: Athanasiadou & Dirven (eds.). 1997, 191–222.

Longacre, Robert E. 1985. "Sentences as combinations of clauses". In: Shopen, Timothy (ed.). *Language typology and syntactic description* (Volume II. Complex constructions). Cambridge: Cambridge University Press, 235–286.

Martin, Samuel. 1975. *A Reference Grammar of Japanese.* New Haven/London: Yale University Press.

Nedjalkov, Igor' V. 1995. "Converbs in Evenki" In: König, Ekkehard & Haspelmath, Martin (eds.). *Converbs in cross-linguistic perspective: Structure and meaning of adverbial verb forms (adverbial participles, gerunds)*. Berlin, New York: Mouton de Gruyter, 441–464.

Nedjalkov, Vladimir P. 1995. "Some typological parameters of converbs" In: König, Ekkehard & Haspelmath, Martin (eds.). *Converbs in cross-linguistic perspective: Structure and meaning of adverbial verb forms (adverbial participles, gerunds)*. Berlin, New York: Mouton de Gruyter, 97–136.

Palmer, Frank R. 1986. *Mood and modality*. Cambridge: Cambridge University Press.

Podlesskaya, Vera I. 1995. "K tipologii implikativnyx konstrukcij" [On a typology of implicative constructions]. *Voprosy jazykoznanija* 6: 77–84.

Podlesskaya, Vera I. 1997. "Syntax and semantics of resumption: some evidence from Russian conditional conjuncts". *Russian Linguistics* 21: 125–155.

Rjabova, Irina S. 1998 *Jazyk dabida* [The Dabida language]. Moscow: Ponovskij i partnery.

Roberts, John R. 1988. "Switch-reference in Papuan languages: a syntactic or extrasyntactic device?" *Australian Journal of Linguistics* 8.1: 75–117.

Švedova, Natal'ja J. (ed.) 1970. *Grammatika sovremennogo russkogo literaturnogo jazyka* [A grammar of the modern Russian literary language]. Moscow: Nauka.

Sweetser, Eve. 1990. *From etymology to pragmatics: Metaphorical and cultural aspects of semantic structure*. Cambridge: Cambridge University Press.

Thompson, Sandra A. & Longacre, Robert E. "Adverbial clauses". In: Shopen, Timothy (ed.). *Language typology and syntactic description* (Volume II. Complex constructions). Cambridge: Cambridge University Press, 171–234.

Traugott, Elizabeth C. & ter Meulen, Alice & Reilly, Judy Snitzer & Ferguson, Charles A. (eds.) 1986. *On conditionals*. Cambridge: Cambridge University Press.

Traugott, Elizabeth C. 1986. "Conditional markers." In: Traugott, Elizabeth Closs & ter Meulen, Alice & Reilly, Judy Snitzer & Ferguson, Charles A. *On conditionals*. Cambridge: Cambridge University Press. 289–307.

Trask, Robert L. 1993. *A dictionary of grammatical terms in linguistics*. Routledge: London–New York.

van der Auwera, Johan. 1983. "Conditionals and antecedent possibilities". *Journal of Pragmatics* 7: 297–309.

van der Auwera, Johan. 1997. "Conditional perfection". In: Athanasiadou & Dirven (eds.). 1997, 169–190.

Xrakovskij, Victor S. 1994. "Uslovnyje konstrukcii: vzaimodejstvije kondicional'nyx i temporal'nyx znachenij" [Conditional constructions: the interaction of conditional and temporal meanings]. *Voprosy jazykoznanija* 6: 129–139.

Xrakovskij, Victor S. (ed.). 1998. *Tipologija uslovnyx konstrukcij*. [Typology of conditional constructions]. St. Petersburg: Nauka.

Wierzbicka, Anna. 1997. "Conditionals and counterfactuals: conceptual primitives and linguistic universals". In: Athanasiadou & Dirven (eds.). 1997, 15–59.

Ziv, Yael. 1997. "Conditionals and restrictives on generics". In: Athanasiadou & Dirven (eds.). 1997, 223–239.

Vera Podlesskaya, Moscow (Russia)

77. Interrogative constructions

1. Introduction
2. Clause types and associated speech acts
3. Types of interrogative constructions
4. Polar interrogatives
5. Constituent interrogatives
6. Non-canonical uses of interrogative constructions
7. Special abbreviations
8. References

1. Introduction

To acquire information is very important to the human species. Apparently, most if not all languages have developed some particular means dedicated to eliciting information, henceforth called interrogative constructions or simply interrogatives. In addition, there is always the option to eschew interrogatives and use non-canonical means for obtaining information.

Depending on the kind of information sought, we can differentiate essentially three types of interrogatives across the world's languages. They may be used (i) to ask whether a proposition or its negation is true, (ii) to inquire which values (if any) instantiate the variables of an open proposition and (iii) to query which element of a set of alternatives makes an open sentence true:

(1) (a) *Does a platypus lay eggs?*
    (b) *What is a platypus?*
    (c) *Is a platypus a mammal or a bird?*

We will refer to these three types as 'polar interrogatives', 'constituent interrogatives' and 'alternative interrogatives' respectively, but it should be noted that there is a multiplicity of labels to be found in the literature. Polar interrogatives have also been called 'closed' or 'yes-no' interrogatives/questions and the set of labels used for constituent interrogatives includes items such as 'open', 'special', 'partial', 'question-word', '*wh*' and 'information' interrogatives.

Although the existence of interrogative constructions seems a universal property of natural languages, languages differ substantially in the strategies they employ for coding interrogatives. There are seven basic strategies of deriving interrogatives, some of them being restricted to particular types of interrogatives: (i) intonation, (ii) interrogative particles, (iii) interrogative tags, (iv) disjunctive constructions (v) the order of constituents, (vi) verbal inflection and (vii) interrogative words. Some of these strategies can occur in combination, others may be mutually exclusive.

Interrogative systems are related to many other subsystems of grammar (relative pronouns, indefinite pronouns, conditionals, etc.) and interrogative marking may be derived from or expand into these areas.

2. Clause types and associated speech acts

There are three basic clause types to be found in the languages of the world and interrogatives are one of them. Besides interrogative clauses, we find declarative and imperative clauses and with each of these clause types a prototypical speech act is associated. The speech act normally associated with declaratives is that of making a statement, with interrogatives that of asking a question and with imperatives it is the issuing of a command (directives), as the following English examples illustrate:

(2) (a) *She is a good student.* (declarative, statement)
    (b) *Is she a good student?* (interrogative, question)
    (c) *Be a good student!* (imperative, directive)

As is well-known, this conventionalised relationship between syntactic structure or clause type and conversational use is by no means isomorphic and in actual use declaratives and interrogatives (not so much imperatives, though) may be associated with various other speech acts (cf. Huddleston 1994 for a good summary). For instance, we frequently find declaratives used as questions and interrogatives in the function of directives:

(3) (a) *He has come today?* (declarative, question)
    (b) *Could you pass the salt?* (interrogative, directive)

In addition to the three clause types discussed so far, we find that some languages (English, German, etc.) have yet another clause type − exclamative clauses (→ Art. 79) − which, however, is not universal. The speech act prototypically associated with exclamative clauses is that of an evaluation:

(4)   *How good a student she is!*

3. Types of interrogative constructions

Common to all types of interrogatives is that the speaker uses them to elicit information from the addressee. Depending on the kind of information requested, we can distinguish between polar interrogatives, constituent interrogatives and alternative interrogatives.

The expected answer in the case of polar interrogatives is either 'yes' or 'no'. The speaker asks the addressee about the truth value of the proposition expressed by the relevant interrogative clause. Polar interrogatives may have either positive or negative polarity. In the unbiased case, the speaker has no expectations with respect to the answer, as in the following example:

(5)   *Is 761 a prime number?*

In many cases, however, the speaker's expectations are biased in favour of either a positive or a negative answer. As a rule, positive polar interrogatives carry negative conduciveness whereas positive conduciveness is associated with negative polar interrogatives:

(6) (a) *Have I ever let you down?*
    (b) *Can't you stay a little longer?*

With constituent interrogatives we find an interrogative word (*who, what, when*, etc.) in the position of the unknown information, which also specifies the kind of information queried. The speaker expects the addressee to supply adequate information for these variables. Constituent interrogatives can be used to query persons, things, times, locations, circumstances, etc. There are interrogatives with one or with multiple interrogative words:

(7) (a) *Who opened the door?*
    (b) *Who did what to whom?*

According to Hamblin (1973), a constituent interrogative such as *Who came?* denotes the set of propositions constituted by the possible answers to it (*John came*, *Maria came*, etc.). Karttunen (1977) refines Hamblin's proposal by restricting the propositions in the set to those that are true answers to the question. This approach easily accommodates constituent interrogatives with multiple interrogative words.

The third type of interrogatives to be briefly discussed are alternative interrogatives. With these the speaker offers the addressee a list of possible answers from which he is supposed to choose the correct one:

(8)   *Would you like tea or coffee?*

Alternative interrogatives are frequently subsumed under polar interrogatives and then come to be analysed as two (or more) coordinated polar interrogatives which have been reduced due to ellipsis. Although an analysis of alternative interrogatives in terms of polar interrogatives seems possible, it disregards the fact that they cannot be answered simply by 'yes' or 'no', but have to be answered by one of the conjuncts given. Interestingly enough, alternative interrogatives can be used as polar interrogatives once their typical intonation pattern (rise on first and subsequent conjuncts, fall on last conjunct) is replaced by normal question intonation (final rise). Since the differences and similarities between polar and alternative interrogatives are relatively unimportant from a typological perspective, no distinction will be drawn between these two types of interrogatives in the following discussion.

The three types of interrogatives introduced in this section can be found as both main clauses and subclauses, i. e. they can be either non-embedded or embedded. This article concentrates primarily on interrogatives as main clauses because much of what can be said about non-embedded interrogatives also holds for embedded structures. It should be borne in mind, however, that there are differences and that, for the marking of embedded interrogatives, languages may select a different subset from the set of strategies available. English embedded interrogatives, for instance, do not show the intonation typical of main clause interrogatives, nor do they undergo a change in word order (cf. (9)). Embedded polar interrogatives, in contrast to their non-embedded counterparts, must be introduced by the conjunctions *if* or *whether*.

(9) (a) *She wondered if she could trust him.*
    (b) *She wondered who she could trust.*

4. Polar interrogatives

The strategies for marking polar interrogatives in the languages of the world vary within clearly fixed bounds and comprise the use of special intonation patterns, interrogative particles, the addition of tags, disjunctive structures, a change in the order of constituents and particular verbal inflection. According to the empirical study conducted by Ultan (1978), intonation is by far the most widespread strategy and can be found in nearly all languages of his sample. As a matter of fact, most languages and maybe all seem able to mark polar interrogatives solely by intonation (see Geluykens 1988 for a more pessimistic view on the role of intonation). It is slightly less common to mark polar interrogatives with interrogative particles and tags, although these strategies are still very frequent in comparison to the three remaining ones. To indicate polar interrogatives by a disjunctive construction (x or not x) or a different order of constituents is relatively rare, and particularly the latter strategy is usually associated with European languages. Special verbal inflection is only reported from polysynthetic languages, such as Eskimo, where it does indeed make sense to talk of an interrogative mood. It is usually possible to use intonation in combination with one of the other strategies.

4.1. Intonation

The intonation contour most widely employed for polar interrogatives, and in fact, interrogatives in general, is a rising one (ca. 95% of the world's languages according to Ultan's 1978 sample) with the rise usually being placed towards the end of the contour. Greenberg (1966: 80) points out that intonational marking of interrogatives is typically found in clause-final position and accordingly includes this general property of languages into his set of language universals (#8). What is also frequently pointed out is that the rising intonation typically used for interrogatives reflects an iconic principle according to which rising intonation, due to its openness in terms of pitch or frequency, is tantamount to uncertainty with regard to the truth-conditions of the situation described and non-termination of the current turn, whereas the falling intonation usually used in declaratives signals conviction and termination.

(10) Italian
 (a) *Suo marito è ancora \malato.* (statement)
 (b) *Suo marito è ancora /malato?* (question)
 'Her husband is still ill./?'

Given that the marking of polar interrogatives with a rising intonation is such a pervasive tendency in the languages of the world, it should not come entirely unexpected to also find some variation within this parameter itself. In his sample, Ultan (1978) finds at least four strategies of placing the rise towards the end of the contour (cf. Table 77.1).

Table 77.1: Higher pitch towards end of contour

higher ultima	Vietnamese
higher penult	Chontal
higher pitch on last stressed vowel	Bashkir
rising toward last stressed vowel	Hebrew

And although the final rise certainly represents the dominant strategy cross-linguistically, there are also languages that mark polar interrogatives with a higher pitch towards the beginning of the contour (cf. Table 77.2). In fact, what seems relevant typologically is whether a language places the higher pitch on the left edge or on the right edge of the contour. The actual realisation of either setting can, in all likelihood, be predicted from the phonological rules relevant for a particular language.

Table 77.2: Higher pitch towards beginning of contour

higher initial syllable	Western Desert
higher stressed vowels	Finnish

Apart from these relatively clear intonational patterns, Ultan (1978: 220) also lists some more complex examples, notably the ones of Aramaic and Hausa, which employ a "higher ultima followed by a falling extra-high ultima falling to mid", and the interrogative pattern of Guaraní, which has "higher stressed vowels at any point within the contour".

Even more interesting, however, are those languages which do not use rising intonation for interrogatives and falling intonation for declaratives, but seem to be doing it exactly the other way round. In Chitimacha, apparently, interrogative intonation has a falling contour whereas declarative intonation has a rising contour. And with Fanti (Kwa) and Grebo (Niger-Congo), we have two additional languages which deviate in a similar manner.

4.2. Interrogative particles

Interrogative particles are expressions like French *est-ce que*, Polish *czy*, Finnish *kö*, Mandarin *ma*, Slavic *li*, Turkish *mi* (cf. Bazin 1984), Bengali *ki*, etc. and are, after intonation, the most widely employed device for marking polar interrogatives. They can also be found with constituent interrogatives, but are clearly preferred with polar interrogatives. Ultan (1978: 226 f.) argues that for some languages it would be more reasonable to talk of interrogative affixes or clitics because there these expressions are added to words, usually predicates. Interrogative particles, like interrogative intonation, can be analysed as operators which take a declarative as input and turn it into an interrogative.

(11) Japanese (Hinds 1984: 158)
 (a) *yamada-san wa ginkoo de*
  yamada-Mr. TOP bank at
  hataraite-imasu.
  working
  'Mr. Yamada works at the bank.'
 (b) *yamada-san wa ginkoo de*
  yamada-Mr. TOP bank at
  hataraite-imasu ka?
  working IP
  'Does Mr. Yamada work at the bank?'

Languages may have more than one interrogative particle. In Korean, for instance, which has grammaticalised several levels of formality (honorification), we find that different particles are used at different levels, namely *pnikka* (formal), *eyo* (polite), *e* (intimate), *nunya* (plain). The position indicated by 'X' in (12) below can be taken up by one of these expressions.

(12) Korean (Chang 1996: 84)
 Kui-nun cal cwumwusi-X
 he-TOP well sleep-IP
 'Does he sleep well?'

The position of interrogative particles varies from language to language although it tends to be relatively fixed for any particular language. Dominant positions for interrogative particles to occur in are the beginning or end of a clause with the clause-final position being slightly preferred (as e. g. in the Japanese example above). An example of a language that places interrogative particles at the beginning of a clause would be Yiddish (cf. (13)).

(13) Yiddish (Sadock & Zwicky 1985: 181)
 Ci hot Mojše gekojft a hunt?
 IP has Moses bought a dog
 'Did Moses buy a dog?'

Additional languages with clause-initial interrogative particles include Welsh (an), Indonesian (apa) and Hebrew (ha'im). It is customary to include into the group of languages with clause-initial particles also those in which the interrogative particle follows the first constituent of the clause (i. e. where the particle is enclitic to it). One such language is Russian (cf. (14)). Here the formation of a polar interrogative involves the preposing of the constituent that is the focus of the question to clause-initial position plus the insertion of the particle li immediately behind it.

(14) Russian (Comrie 1984: 20)
 Čital li ty ètu knigu?
 read IP you this book
 'Have you read this book?'

If some other constituent is the focus of the question, it can be placed into clause-initial position in a similar manner, again followed by li:

(15) Russian (Comrie 1984: 20)
 (a) Ty li čital ètu knigu?
 (b) Ètu li knigu ty čital?

The situation in Latin is quite comparable to the one found in Russian (cf. Sadock & Zwicky 1985: 182):

(16) Est-ne puer bonus?
 'Is the boy good?

(17) Puer-ne bonus est?
 'Is it the boy who is good?'

(18) Bonus-ne puer est?
 'Is it good that the boy is?'

Similar facts are also reported from Ute (and also Finnish), where the interrogative particle -aa is always enclitic to the first constituent:

(19) Ute (Givón 1984: 219 f.)
 (a) mamá-ci-aa 'u wúuka-pugá?
 woman-SUBJ-IP that.SUBJ work-REM
 'Did the woman work?'
 (b) kúaw-aa páĝa-kway-kya?
 yesterday-IP leave-go-ANT
 'Did (she) leave yesterday?'

The position that an interrogative particle occupies in a certain language also allows it to make some predictions with respect to the word order type of that languages. As observed by Greenberg (1966: 81) as well as Ultan (1978: 227 f.), initial particles tend to correlate with verb initial languages whereas final particles are most common with verb final languages. However, this generalisation is not without exceptions and what makes it even more complicated to formulate clear correlations is that various languages have more than one interrogative particle, which are usually restricted to either clause-initial or clause-final position. There seem to be no preferences for the position of interrogative particles in SVO languages. Thai and Yoruba, for instance, have final particles whereas the particle in Lithuanian is initial, but all belong to the basic type SVO.

Finally, a brief remark on the relation between interrogative particles and other domains of grammar seems in order. Traugott (1985: 291) points out that interrogative particles are one of the major sources of conditional markers. This is clearly visible in Russian, where the marker of the conditional protasis (esli) has been derived from the copula (est') and the interrogative particle (li). Similar observations can be made in Hua (a Papuan language), as the following example demonstrates:

(20) Hua (Haiman 1978: 570–571)
 E -si -ve baigu -e
 come 3SG.FUT IP will stay 1SG
 'If he comes, I will stay.'

The close relationship between conditionals and polar interrogatives is also observable in languages that grammaticalised their conditional marker from a different domain or where the etymology of this marker is unknown. In German it is possible to mark the protasis by the constituent order typical of polar interrogatives while dispensing with the actual conditional marker (cf. (21)). Viewed against this background, the inversion of subject and verb found in certain English conditionals finds a simple explanation.

(21)   German (Sadock & Zwicky 1985: 183)
       Ist das Buch rot, so muß es mir gehören.
       'If the book is red, it must belong to me.'

4.3. Interrogative tags

Another strategy for marking polar interrogatives are the so-called interrogative tags, as exemplified in (22) below.

(22)   (a) *He has gone to Tokyo, hasn't he?*
       (b) *She did not do that, did she?*

In many languages, these tags are clearly related to interrogative particles both in meaning and in distribution. Bengali *ki*, for instance, is used as interrogative particle and as part of the interrogative tag.

(23)   Bengali (Saha 1984: 131−132)
       (a) *beral pakhita dhorechilo, noy ki?*
           cat   bird.SG   caught   not-is IP
           'The cat caught the bird, didn't it?'
       (b) *ki beral pakhita dhorechilo?*
           IP cat   bird.SG   caught
           'Did the cat catch the bird?'

When tags are added to a sentence to mark it as a question, it usually receives the intonation pattern typical of polar interrogatives in that language. Still, there is a great number of differences between these two devices which shall be discussed in the following paragraphs.

In contrast to interrogative particles, for which the clause-initial position is no less likely than the clause-final position, interrogative tags are in the great majority of cases appended to a (declarative) clause. Out of the 32 languages in Ultan's (1978) sample, for which tags are clearly attested, there is only one example of a language with an unambiguous initial tag − Hebrew *halo* − and even here we find another tag which is bound to clause-final position. Another difference from interrogative particles is that tags are formally not particles, but occur as either (content) words (24), phrases (25) or clauses (26). There are negative tags as well as positive tags, with the negative tags frequently either including or being formally alike to the negative marker of that language (cf. French *n'est-ce pas* and Khasi *ʔeem*). Positive tags usually involve a copula or existential predicate (Rotuman *ne* (= predicative particle), Thai *chây mǎy* 'is it'), interjections (English *eh*) and words related to the predicate 'true' (Russian *pravda* 'true').

(24)   Russian
       Ty ego slyšal, pravda?
       'You heard him, didn't you?'

(25)   German
       Er ist sehr reich, nicht wahr?
       'He is very rich, isn't he?'

(26)   *John would not do that, would he?*

The most important difference, however, is that polar interrogatives based on tags are always biased with respect to the answer expected (cf. Hudson 1975: 22 ff.). As a rule of thumb, negative tags presuppose a positive answer, whereas positive tags bias expectations towards a negative answer (cf. (22)). Considered on a more detailed level, however, the situation observed in single languages like English and also cross-linguistically is much more complicated. Ultan (1978) observes that the answer induced by a tag question depends to a greater extent on the polarity of the declarative sentence used for forming the question and less so on the polarity of the tag (cf. Table 77.3). Although a majority of languages in his sample awaits a positive answer to a question formed by combining a positive declarative with a negative tag (reversed polarity tag), the next most frequent constellation is a positive declarative and a positive tag (constant polarity tag) inducing again a positive response, and only then do we find negative declarative, positive tag and negative answer. Languages that allow all three parameters being set to a negative value seem very rare.

Table 77.3: Tags and polarity

declarative	tag	response	number of languages
P	N	P	10 (+5?)
P	P	P	5 (+1?)
N	P	N	2 (+1?)
N	N	N	1

4.4. Disjunction

In some languages it can be observed that the disjunctive structures normally used for alternative interrogatives have become a possible device for posing polar interrogatives. Apparently, this has happened in Mandarin Chinese where the disjunction of an affirmative clause and its negative counterpart, the so-called A-not-A construction, has been grammaticalised and is now a common way of forming such interrogatives (cf. (27)). The disjunction is usually not overtly expressed, i. e. the disjunctive morpheme *háishi* is missing in most of the cases.

(27)　Mandarin (Li & Thompson 1984: 53)
　　　tā zài jiā bu zài jiā?
　　　3SG at home NEG at home
　　　'Is s/he at home?'

The complete formula exemplified in (27) is, however, rarely encountered in ordinary conversation and normally one of the reduced versions given in (28) is used. In other words, identical material may be omitted.

(28)　(a)　*ta zài bu zài jiā?*
　　　(b)　*tā zài jiā bu zài?*

Although the A-not-A construction is a perfectly adequate instrument for asking questions that are not biased with respect to their answer, i. e. that do not carry positive or negative conduciveness, the very same structure also finds application in the formation of interrogative tags, which, as illustrated in the previous section, do express expectations towards either a positive or a negative answer.

(29)　Mandarin (Li & Thompson 1984: 54)
　　　zhāng-sān xǐhuan hē jiǔ, duì
　　　Zhang-san like drink wine right
　　　bu duì?
　　　NEG right
　　　'Zhang-san likes to drink wine, right?'

(30)　Mandarin
　　　nǐ míngtiān lái kàn wǒ, hǎo
　　　you tomorrow come see me good
　　　bu hǎo?
　　　NEG good
　　　'You come to see me tomorrow, O. K.?'

(31)　Mandarin
　　　nǐ fùqin hěn lǎo, shì bu shì?
　　　you father very old be NEG be
　　　'Your father is very old, right?'

Given that essentially the same construction is used to mark polar interrogatives that are either biased or unbiased with respect to the answer expected, how is it possible to arrive at the contextually relevant interpretation of the A-not-A construction? In many cases, of course, the context will provide the necessary clues, but there are also clues within the relevant clauses themselves. First, the set of A-not-A structures used as tags is extremely limited and highly lexicalised. Apart from the examples cited in (29)–(31), there is only *kě bu kěyǐ* 'possible' and *xíng bu xíng* 'okay' that occur with significant frequency. Even more important is the fact that A-not-A tags are always added to complete propositions/clauses, whereas in the case of unbiased polar interrogatives, the A-not-A structure picks up part of the proposition, usually the predicator.

(32)　Mandarin
　　　nǐ huì bu huì dǎ-zì?
　　　you know.how NEG know-how hit-word
　　　'Can you type?'

Another interesting question concerns the differences in meaning and use between A-not-A interrogatives in Mandarin and those involving the interrogative particle *ma*. Evidently, in many contexts the two strategies can be interchanged:

(33)　Mandarin (Li & Thompson 1984: 57)
　　　nǐ hē bu hē píjiǔ?
　　　you drink NEG drink beer
　　　'Will you drink beer?'

(34)　Mandarin
　　　nǐ hē píjiǔ ma?
　　　you drink beer IP
　　　'Will you drink beer?'

In other contexts, however, only one of the two strategies can be employed to yield a fully acceptable interrogative clause. In the following example, the A-not-A construction would not be appropriate because the context does not allow the speaker to be neutral about the proposition in question (cf. § 6.):

(35)　Mandarin
　　　?? *nǐ shēngbìng bu shēngbìng?*
　　　you sick NEG sick
　　　'Are you sick?'

4.5. Order of constituents

One of the strategies of marking polar interrogatives that languages across the world are not particularly likely to manifest is a change in the order of their basic constituents (inversion). Speaking from a typological perspective, the constituent most likely to be affected by inversion is the finite verb. The verb may even be the only constituent for which this kind of reordering is possible. Provided a language allows inversion in order to mark polar interrogatives, what usually happens is that the finite verb is put into clause-initial position (cf. (36)).

(36) (a) *John is a policeman.*
     (b) *Is John a policeman?*

Thus, inversion of the verb-fronting type can only occur in languages whose basic word order type is either SVO or SOV; it is ruled out for VSO-languages. In addition, inversion with polar interrogatives is only found in those languages that also use inversion as a means for marking constituent interrogatives (cf. Greenberg 1966: 83, universal #11).

In English, inversion is restricted to auxiliaries and modals and *do*-support is necessary to convert clauses lacking such operators into polar interrogatives:

(37) (a) *John phoned me yesterday.*
     (b) *Did John phone you yesterday?*

There are only seven examples of inverting languages to be found in Ultan's (1978) sample, and six out of these seven languages come from Europe (English, Finnish, French, Hungarian, Rumanian, Russian). They belong to just two genetic groups, either Indo-European or Finno-Ugric. The only non-European language in this sample to demonstrate inversion is Malay, a SVO-language belonging to the Indonesian branch of the Austronesian family.

In some languages, the combination of two or more of the strategies for marking polar interrogatives is not possible. French, for instance, prohibits the simultaneous use of inversion and interrogative particle (cf. (38)).

(38) (a) *Allez-vous a Paris?*
     (b) *Est-ce que vous-allez a Paris?*
     (c) **Est-ce qu'allez vous a Paris?*
         'Are you going to Paris?'

Russian, on the other hand, can invert to VSO while marking the interrogative with the particle *li*. Note, however, that word order in Russian is relatively free and that the constituent on which the question focus is placed always comes in initial position.

4.6. Verbal inflection

Although, cross-linguistically speaking, relatively rare in terms of frequency, the strategy employed by West Greenlandic (Kalaallisut) and Eskimo languages (Inuit) in general for the formation of polar interrogatives seems rather interesting and totally different from the four strategies we have discussed so far. What we find here is special verbal morphology exclusively dedicated to interrogative formation so that it makes sense to assume an interrogative mood for this group of languages.

(39) West Greenlandic (Sadock 1984: 190)
     (a) *nerivutit*
         'you ate'
     (b) *nerivit*
         'Did you eat?'

Judged against the background that Eskimo languages are highly inflecting and polysynthetic, such a feature certainly cannot come entirely unexpected. Another language for which a verbal strategy of interrogative formation is attested is Blackfoot.

What is also interesting about such languages are the distributional gaps observable with interrogative morphology. According to Sadock (1984: 198), West Greenlandic shows independent interrogative morphology only in combination with subjects of the second and third person. It is not possible to find a morphological distinction between declarative and interrogative for clauses with first person subjects.

(40) West Greenlandic
     (a) *takuvoq*
         'He sees.'
     (b) *takua?*
         'Does he see?'

(41) West Greenlandic
     (a) *takuvutit*
         'You see.'
     (b) *takuit?*
         'Do you see?'

(42) West Greenlandic
     takuvunga
     'I see.' / 'Do I see?'

Such an imbalance in the system is probably not entirely unmotivated and may be explained on the basis of the function interrogative clauses have under normal circumstances. Their main function clearly is to elicit information from the addressee, i.e. to access the addressee's knowledge base. Since most knowledge relevant to the speaker about himself is contained in the speaker's knowledge base, the speaker will usually try to acquire information that does not pertain to himself. This explains why first person interrogatives are not really needed and can mostly be dispensed with.

5. Constituent interrogatives

Constituent interrogatives differ from polar interrogatives both in form and meaning. They cannot be answered simply by supplying a truth-value. In posing a constituent interrogative, speakers expect information that allows them to complete the interpretation of a proposition. This may be information central to the situation described by that proposition, viz. concerning the participants and objects involved in it, or more circumstantial information relating to the relevant locational or temporal setting, or to issues like the manner of execution and the purpose. Natural languages have specific devices dedicated to the function of eliciting such substantial information — interrogative words — which can be analysed as placeholders or variables in a proposition to be filled or assigned a value by the answer (cf. (43)).

(43) *Who killed the sheriff? — Bill killed the sheriff.*

Since there does not seem to exist a language without constituent interrogatives, it is safe to conclude that all languages have interrogative words, although languages differ heavily in the number of interrogative words they posess and in the semantic distinctions they draw.

Having said this, we have already identified the main formal feature of constituent interrogatives across languages: interrogative words. However, nearly all of the strategies used for marking clauses as polar interrogatives, as discussed in the previous section, can also be found with constituent interrogatives, although they play a less important role in this domain and are often optional. Before discussing interrogative words in some detail, let us therefore briefly consider these by now familiar strategies in the context of constituent interrogatives.

As far as intonation is concerned, it appears that this strategy is much less important for the characterisation of constituent interrogatives than polar interrogatives, if it is not even entirely insignificant. Out of 36 languages in Ultan's (1978) study for which intonation as a means for marking polar interrogatives is attested (mostly rising intonation or higher pitch), only 12 (or 33.3%) use the same or a similar intonational pattern also for marking constituent interrogatives. The overall impression that the data give is that most languages either do not mark constituent interrogatives by intonation at all (33.3%) or do so only optionally (33.3%). Languages that do not distinguish between declaratives and constituent interrogatives intonationally include Fula, Japanese and Tagalog; representatives of languages allowing optional marking of constituent interrogatives are Amharic, English and Turkish.

Saying that intonation plays only a minor role in the marking of constituent interrogatives, however, should not be taken to mean that there is no interesting variation to be found concerning this parameter across the world's languages. By way of exemplification, note that the intonation nucleus in Russian constituent interrogatives, in contrast to comparable English structures, usually falls on the interrogative word (cf. Comrie 1984: 24).

(44) Russian
      KTO ljubit Tanju?
      who loves Tanya
      'Who loves Tanya?'

The parsimonious use of intonation in constituent interrogatives may suggest that natural languages have a tendency to use grammatical marking in the most economical way possible (at least in this subdomain of grammar). After all, constituent interrogatives are clearly characterised as interrogatives through the presence of an interrogative word. However, the co-occurrence of interrogative particles with interrogative words in approximately half of the world's languages makes clear that interrogative marking may be employed redundantly.

(45) Japanese (Kuno 1978: 93)
  (a) *Taroo wa kita ka?*
      Taroo TOP came IP
      'Did Taroo come?'
  (b) *Taroo wa sono okane o dare ni ka?*
      Taroo TOP the money OBJ who to IP
      yatta
      gave
      'Who did Taroo give the money to?'

In contrast, the use of tags in constituent interrogatives is not attested and may even be ruled out entirely. This restriction may find an explanation in the fact that tags are mainly used to ask for confirmation and that this is incompatible with the meaning of constituent interrogatives.

As a matter of fact, the compatibility of the various strategies of interrogative formation with the two (three) types of interrogatives and also the combinatorial restrictions of these strategies between themselves has been an issue of much debate in the relevant literature (cf. Baker 1970, Wąsik 1982, Cheng 1997). What is clear is that not all combinations are possible; what is much less clear is what the relevant constraints are. For instance, it seems relatively uncontroversial that the use of more than one morphological strategy for the marking of polar interrogatives is ruled out. Li & Thompson (1984: 55) point out that the A-not-A construction of Mandarin, the interrogative tag of that language as well as the interrogative particle are mutually exclusive. In addition, these strategies are not compatible with constituent interrogatives. This latter observation from Mandarin, however, cannot be generalised because the interrogative particle of Japanese does occur in constituent interrogatives (cf. (45)). What can probably be said with reasonable certainty is that if a language uses a particle to mark constituent interrogatives, then this language will also allow the use of this particle in polar interrogatives.

How widespread inversion (i.e. the reordering of the major constituents of a clause) is in the formation of constituent interrogatives heavily depends on which constituents we put into focus. As the subsequent section will show, placing interrogative words in clause-initial position is very common, and from this perspective, inversion is nothing unusual. However, if we restrict the scope of the term 'inversion' to the recordering of subject and verb, as can be observed in languages like English and German, the number of languages that makes use of this strategy drops heavily and is in all likelihood restricted to selected representatives of Indo-European (mainly Germanic). As the following example demonstrates, in English this kind of inversion occurs only if a constituent other than the subject is questioned.

(46) (a) *Who saw him?*
    (b) *Who did he see?*
    (c) *When did he see him?*

Last but not least, it appears worth mentioning that the interrogative mood found in Eskimo is used in the formation of both polar interrogatives and constituent interrogatives:

(47) West Greenlandic (Sadock 1984: 199)
    (a) *neri-va-ø?*
        eat-INT-3SG
        'Did he eat?'
    (b) *su-mik   neri-va-ø*
        what-INST eat-INT-3SG
        'What did he eat?'

5.1. The position of interrogative words

According to the position of interrogative words, languages fall into three types: (i) those that put interrogative words obligatorily in clause-initial position, (ii) those in which interrogative words occupy the same position as the constituent questioned, and (iii) those languages that allow either of these two positions. The position of interrogative words has aroused much interest in generative studies (cf. Cheng 1997), where these three types of languages are referred to as (i) fronting languages, (ii) *in-situ* languages, and (iii) optional fronting languages. The following data exemplify these three types:

(48) Finnish (Sulkala and Karjalainen 1992: 12)
    (a) *Maija ottaa omenaa.*
        Maija take.3SG apple.PAR
        'Maija is taking an apple.'
    (b) *Mitä   Maija ottaa?*
        what.PAR Maija take.3SG
        'What is Maija taking?'

(49) Mandarin (Cheng 1997: 5)
    (a) *Hufei mǎi-le yī-běn-shū*
        Hufai buy-ASP one-CL-BOOK
        'Hufai bought a book.'
    (b) *Hufei mǎi-le shénme?*
        Hufei buy-ASP what
        'What did Hufai buy?'

(50) Swahili (Haiman 1985: 245)
    (a) *A-li-fika   lini?*
        3SG-PAST-arrive when
        'When did s/he arrive?'
    (b) *kwa nini chakula ki-me-chelewa?*
        why   food   3SG-PERF-late
        'Why is the food late?'

Additional fronting languages include English, German, Hebrew, Supyire, Yoruba, Zapotec. Further examples of *in-situ* languages are Indonesian, Japanese, Lezgian and Mandarin whereas Egyptian Arabic, Kannada,

Korean or Palauan belong to the group of optional fronting languages. Ultan (1978: 229) notes that 73.4% of the languages in his sample either place interrogative words in clause-initial position obligatorily or show a strong tendency to do so (i.e. fronting languages and optionally fronting languages taken together) whereas 25% of the languages investigated locate interrogative words in the position of the constituents for which they substitute (i.e. *in-situ* languages). The remaining 1.6% are filled by fairly exceptional languages like Khasi, where interrogative words are apparently found in clause-final position, and languages like Gujarati, which reserve special positions in the clause for them (preceding the verb phrase in this case). Interestingly enough, Gujarati behaves exactly like Hungarian in this respect.

To decide whether a language is strictly *in situ* or allows optional fronting of interrogative words is often not easy because what superficially looks like straightforward fronting may, on closer inspection, prove to be an entirely different construction type. Consider the case of Scottish Gaelic in (51). In this language interrogative words may stay *in situ*, but they can also occur in clause-initial position. However, fronting is only possible in relative constructions.

(51) Scottish Gaelic (Macaulay 1992: 173)
 (a) *Cheannaich Iain dè?*
  bought Iain what
 (b) *Dè a cheannaich Iain?*
  what REL bought Iain
  'What did Iain buy?'

Similar problems in the classification of optional fronting languages are reported by Cheng (1997: 43 ff.). In the three languages she discusses (Egyptian Arabic, Bahasa Indonesia, Palauan), fronted interrogative words are clearly related to relative clauses as well as clefts.

The position of the interrogative word in a given language correlates, to a certain extent at least, with the basic word order type of that language. In the sample compiled by Greenberg (1966: 82) we find the following distribution:

Table 77.4

position of interrogative word	VSO	SVO	SOV
initial	6	10	0
in situ	0	3	11

The preceding table shows that VSO-languages locate interrogative words in clause-initial position, but that they are usually found *in situ* in SOV-languages. No such correlation can be established for languages with the basic word order type SVO. In this set we find both *in-situ* languages and those with initial interrogative words. As long as the focus is on VSO-languages, apparently, the expectations that these correlations raise for additional languages are borne out well by the data. In the majority of cases, languages of this word order type seem to have initial interrogative words. In contrast, it is not difficult to find counterexamples to the generalisation that SOV-languages leave interrogative words *in situ*. Latin would be a case in point and the universal that Greenberg bases on these correlations is therefore formulated rather cautiously: "If a language has dominant order VSO in declarative sentences, it always puts interrogative words or phrases first in interrogative word questions; if it has dominant order SOV in declarative sentences, there is never such an invariant rule."

The position of interrogative words has also been proposed to correlate with the position of interrogative particles in polar interrogatives. Baker (1970: 207), based on Greenberg's (1966) data, hypothesises that only languages which locate interrogative particles, provided they have such particles, in clause-initial position permit interrogative words in positions other than those of the constituents they substitute for. According to Baker, the position of such particles predicts whether a language is *in situ* or not. Cheng (1997: 13 ff.) takes up Baker's idea, but cites Hopi, Bahasa Indonesia and Hindi as possible counterexamples to his generalisation. According to her own proposal, all *in-situ* languages possess special particles to mark constituent interrogatives, although this marking may be covert, and all languages with such particles are *in situ*.

5.2. Key properties of interrogative words

Although there is probably no language that lacks interrogative words, languages can vary greatly in the number of interrogative words they possess as well as in the kinds of distinctions they draw in that area. Nevertheless, one typically finds two basic kinds of interrogative words. On the one hand, there are those that substitute for the core arguments of a predication (English *who*, *what*), and which inquire about the central participants of the situations denoted by the relevant clauses. On the other hand, we also find interrogative words that seek circumstantial information of the situation in question and which, syntactically speaking, one would have to analyse as adjuncts (cf. (52a) vs. (52b)).

(52) (a) *Who invited him? / Who did he invite?*
(b) *When / where did he arrive?*

A number of parameters cut across the group of interrogative words in argument positions. One of the distinctions that virtually all languages make, and which seems almost universal, is the one between interrogative words used to inquire about human referents and those used for non-human referents, i. e. between *who* and *what* as shown in the example below:

(53)   *Who / what did he see?*

The relevant distinction in Russian is between *kto* and *što*, in Mandarin it is between *shéi* and *shénme*, in Georgian *vin* vs. *ra*, *kuka* and *mikä* in Finnish and *kina* vs. *suna* in West Greenlandic. The few languages that do not have this distinction, such as Ute, usually have distinct interrogative words for animate and non-animate referents instead:

(54)   Ute (Givón 1984: 226)
(a) *'áa   wųųka-x̂a?*
    IW.SG.ANIMATE   work.ANT
    'Who worked?' / 'Which one worked?'
(b) *'aĝé-rų   qorų́c'ąy-kya?*
    IW.INANIMATE break.ANT
    'Which thing broke?'

There are only three exceptions to this generalisation found in Ultan's (1978) sample, namely Khasi, Sango and Lithuanian, with Lithuanian probably being the only clear case of a language where interrogative words do not differ according to the human/non-human (animate/non-animate) parameter. In both Khasi and Sango we find interrogative words which clearly have a preferred interpretation. Another language which, like Lithuanian, does not distinguish *who* and *what* is the closely related Latvian:

(55)   Latvian
       Kas tas ir?
       'Who/what is that?'

Another parameter of variation according to which interrogative words can vary is gender and number marking. Unfortunately, we have very little systematic knowledge on this parameter and it is not possible to give general statements or to draw cast-iron statistical conclusions. Within the boundaries of Europe we find, at the one extreme, languages like English, which have neither number nor gender marking, and at the other extreme languages like Icelandic, which neatly differentiate between masculine, feminine and neuter as well as singular and plural in this domain. Evidently, this parameter correlates with the amount of inflection generally found in a language. The following table shows the interrogative words of Icelandic in the nominative case.

Table 77.5: Interrogative words in Icelandic

Icelandic	*masculine*	*feminine*	*neuter*
singular	hver	hver	hvað
plural	hverjir	hverjar	hver

The interrogatives in (56) exemplify some of these contrasts (cf. Kress 1982: 108):

(56)   Icelandic
(a) *Hverjir eru þessir menn?*
    'Who are these men?'
(b) *Hverjar eru þessar konur?*
    'Who are these women?'
(c) *Hver eru þessi börn?*
    'Who are these children?'

For a language like Finnish, which does not have grammatical gender, but distinguishes between human and non-human interrogative words, the distribution in the nominative looks as follows:

Table 77.6: Interrogative words in Finnish

Finnish	*human*	*non-human*
singular	kuka	ketkä
plural	mikä	mitkä

Two additional examples of languages that draw a distinction between singular and plural in this domain are West Greenlandic and Ute, with West Greenlandic exhibiting a singular/plural distinction with both human and non-human interrogative words. An English interrogative like *Who is here?* corresponds to two different interrogatives in West Greenlandic:

(57) West Greenlandic (Sadock 1984: 200 f.)
(a) *Kina maaniit-pa-Ø?*
    IW.SG be.here-INT-3SG
    'What single person is here?'
(b) *Ki-kkut maaniit-pa-t?*
    IW-PL be.here-INT-3PL
    'Which people are here?'

The relevant interrogative words in West Greenlandic for querying non-human referents are *suna* (SG) and *suut* (PL). Ute, by comparison, has the relevant contrast only for animate interrogative words. Here, the interrogative pronoun '*áa* is specified for animate and singular, '*áa-mu* for animate and plural, but '*agá-ru* is used for both singular and plural inanimates.

A very similar distribution is found in Swedish, which differentiates between singular (*vem*) and plural (*vilka*) in the case of human nouns (cf. (58)), but has *vad* to substitute both singular and plural non-human nouns.

(58) Swedish
(a) *Vem öppnade dörren?*
    'Who opened the door?'
(b) *Vilka öppnade fabriksportarna?*
    'Who (PL) openend the factory gates?'

It is important to bear in mind, however, that the interrogative words in many languages can be used both as nominals and as adjectives. In view of the fact that the adjectives in certain languages show agreement with their nominal head, it is little surprising that the interrogative words in these languages also show agreement. One example of such a language would be Icelandic. Many other languages, however, have different, though clearly related forms for the two uses and then only the adjectival forms show agreement marking (cf. German *welch-*, Swedish *vilk-* and Latin *qui*).

(59) German
(a) *Welcher Mann ist gekommen?*
    'Which (M.SG) man came?'
(b) *Welche Frau ist gekommen?*
    'Which (F.SG) woman came?'
(c) *Welches Kind ist gekommen?*
    'Which (NT.SG) child came?'
(d) *Welche Kinder sind gekommen?*
    'Which (PL) children came?'

Apart from distinguishing between interrogative words in the singular or plural, some languages also have special forms reserved for binary oppositions (remnants of a dual). An example would be Finnish *kumpi*, which literally means 'which one of the two', and forms with a comparable meaning are also found in Latin (*uter, utra, utrum*).

Another interesting contrast is found in Ute (cf. Givón 1984: 226 ff.), which, apparently, differentiates between referential and non-referential interrogative words, with the latter being used for type identification, and the former for token identification. Consider the following contrast between referential '*áa* and non-referential '*ípu̧*:

(60) Ute
(a) '*áa sivą̧ątu-ci paxâ-qa?*
    IW.SUBJ goat-OBJ kill-ANT
    'Who killed the goat?'
(b) '*ípu̧ wi'í-kya?*
    IW.SUBJ fall-ANT
    'What kind of a thing fell?'

The interrogative pronouns of Ute for subject and object position can be summarised as follows:

Table 77.7: Interrogative words in Ute

UTE	SUBJECT		OBJECT	
	REF	NON-REF	REF	NON-REF
ANIMATE SG	'áa	'íni	'áay	'iní
ANIMATE PL	'áa-mu̧	'iní-u	'áa-mu̧	'iní-u
INANIMATE	'aĝá-ru̧	'ípu̧	'aĝá-ru̧	'ípu̧

In languages with case systems that are more elaborate than the parsimonious systems of say English and Chinese, what one typically finds is that case marking also extends into the domain of interrogative words. Out of the 16 cases of Finnish, no fewer than 13 case forms can be differentiated in this domain, ranging from nominative (*kuka*) to abessive (*kenettä*). Another language with a fairly elaborate case system is West Greenlandic. The following table (77.8) shows the full paradigms of *kina* ('who') and *suna* ('what') found in this language (cf. Sadock 1984: 200).

As far as interrogative words in non-argument positions are concerned, languages around the globe appear to distinguish between at least four different types, seeking information about (i) the location of a situation, (ii) its temporal setting, (iii) the manner

Table 77.8: Interrogative words in West Greenlandic

WG	HUMAN		NON-HUMAN	
	SINGULAR	PLURAL	SINGULAR	PLURAL
ABS	kina	kikkut	suna	suut
ERG	kia(p)	kikkut	suup	suut
INST	kimik	kikunnik	sumik	suunnik
ABL	kimit	kikunnit	sumit	suunnit
ALL	kimut	kikunnut	sumut	suunnut
LOC		kikunni	sumi	sunni
PERL			sukkut	

of carrying it through and (iv) the reason for it. The four English sentences below exemplify these options:

(61) (a) *Where did he surprise her?*
   (b) *When did he surprise her?*
   (c) *How did he surprise her?*
   (d) *Why did he surprise her?*

In addition, languages frequently have interrogative words or case-inflected word forms that allow more precise inquiries concerning one or more of these four domains. As for location, for instance, Early Modern English draws a clear distinction between source and goal (cf. (62)). A similar distinction is found in German, Lezgian, Georgian and Finnish, with *woher/wohin*, *hinaj/hiniz*, *saidan/sait* and *mistä/mihin* being used to inquire about source and goal respectively. Swedish only codes the goal with a separate word (*vart*).

(62) (a) *O whither shall we fly from this reproach?*
   [Shakespeare, *Henry* VI, 1. 1. 97]
   (b) *Now; whence come you?* [Shakespeare, *The Merry Wives of Windsor*, 4. 5. 95]

Equally noteworthy is the way in which certain languages distinguish between several temporal interrogative words. West Greenlandic, apparently, uses *qanga* to inquire about states-of-affairs that happened before the moment of utterance and *qaqugu* for those that lie in the future (cf. Sadock 1984: 201). In Kannada, there is, apart from the interrogative word corresponding to English *when* (*ya:vattu*, *ya:va:ga*), a separate form dedicated to days (*endu* 'what day').

The semantic distinctions that languages typically draw in the domain of interrogative words are summarised in Table 77.9:

Table 77.9: Semantic distinctions

concept	gloss	concept	gloss
person	WHO	time	WHEN
object	WHAT	manner	HOW
location	WHERE	reason	WHY

In a small-scale and not very representative study, Heine et. al (1991: 55−59) try to establish correlations between the concept expressed by an interrogative word and its phonological and morphological properties. According to their findings, the interrogative words for person, object and location are the ones that exhibit the least phonological and morphological complexity. In the majority of languages in their sample these concepts are expressed by monomorphemic and monosyllabic forms. Interrogative words for time and manner are usually more complex. The prototypical case seems to be a monomorphemic, but polysyllabic word. Most complex in terms of morphological structure, however, are interrogative words coding reason or cause (and also purpose), which usually consist of more than one morpheme. In this respect, English *why* is clearly the exception rather than the rule.

5.3. Multiple occurrences of interrogative words

Particularly interesting parameters of cross-linguistic variation can be observed with those clauses that contain not just one interrogative word, but multiple occurrences of them. Hence, the subject of the subsequent discussion will be sentences like the following:

(63) *Who did what to whom?*

One parameter along which languages differ is the position of such multiple occurrences of interrogative words in a clause. As was discussed in § 5.1., languages also show variation in the position of interrogative words when just one of these words is present in a clause. What we mainly find is languages that obligatorily front interrogative words to clause-initial position (fronting languages) and languages in which interrogative words remain in the position of the constituents they substitute for (*in-situ* languages). A very similar pattern of variation can be observed when multiple occurrences of interrogative words are present in a clause. On the one hand, there are languages like English, which only front one interrogative word while leaving additional occurrences *in situ*. This is exemplified by the following pair of sentences:

(64) (a) *John gave the book to Mary.*
    (b) *Who gave what to whom?*

Additional languages following the English pattern include German, Dutch, Swedish, Italian, Spanish, etc. In languages such as these it is usually still possible to locate any of the interrogative words in clause-initial position while rearranging the remaining ones according to syntactic rules specific to the language in question (cf. (65)). Nevertheless, the non-fronted interrogative words will occur in exactly the same positions in which the substituted constituents would occur.

(65) (a) *What did who give to whom?*
    (b) *To whom did who give what?*

On the other hand, we find languages in which multiple occurrences of interrogative words all occur clause-initially, although often in a well-defined order. Such multiple fronting languages are most likely a proper subset of fronting languages because there is probably no language that is *in situ* for just one interrogative word, but which becomes fronting if there are more than one of these words contained in a clause. Within the group of European languages, it is the Slavic languages that most clearly demonstrate multiple fronting of interrogative words, as the examples below illustrate (cf. Cheng 1997: 64 ff.; for a recent treatment within optimality theory cf. Ackema & Neeleman 1998):

(66) Bulgarian
    Koj kogo e vidjal?
    who whom saw.3SG
    'Who saw whom?'

(67) Polish
    Co komu Monika dała?
    what to whom Monica gave
    'What did Monica give to whom?'

(68) Russian
    Kto kogo ljubit?
    who whom loves
    'Who loves whom?'

In these languages, there is a very strong requirement to front all interrogative words. Failing to do so either results in ungrammaticality, or the relevant sentence has to be interpreted in a different way, usually as an echo question:

(69) (a) **Koj e vidjal kogo?* (Bulgarian)
    (b) **Co Monika komu dała?* (Polish)
    (c) **Kto ljubit kogo?* (Russian)

Another language that obligatorily fronts multiple occurrences of interrogative words is Georgian:

(70) Georgian (Harris 1984: 71),
    (a) vin ras qidulobs?
        who what he.buy.it
        'Who is buying what?'
    (b) *vin qidulobs ras?
        who he.buy.it what

Interestingly enough, there also appear to be languages that clearly allow multiple fronting of interrogative words, while, at the same time, it does not seem obligatory for them to front all interrogative words. One of the languages for which optional multiple fronting has been reported is Finnish (cf. (71), (72)). Nevertheless, it is not entirely clear whether there is a difference in meaning or in distribution between the two sentences.

(71) Finnish (Sulkala and Karjalainen 1992: 16)
    Kuka nauroi kenelle?
    who laugh.IMPF (3SG) who-ALL
    'Who was laughing at whom?'

(72) Finnish
    Kuka kenelle nauroi?
    who who-ALL laugh.IMPF(3SG)
    'Who was laughing at whom?'

Another parameter of variation can be found in the group of multiple fronting languages itself. This parameter concerns the relative order of the adjacent interrogative words which, on the one hand, may be governed by strict rules and, on the other hand, be relatively unconstrained. One of the rules confining the order of multiple interrogative words in Bulgarian is that the one in the nominative has to come first, followed by an interrogative word in either the accusative or dative (cf. Cheng 1997: 77 ff.). Accusative interrogative words, in turn, occur before those in the dative (NOM > ACC > DAT).

(73) Bulgarian
    (a) *Koj kogo vizda*
        who whom sees
        'Who sees whom?'
    (b) **Kogo koj vizda*
        whom who sees

An additional rule in Bulgarian, apparently, regulates the relative order of arguments and adjuncts, with arguments always occurring before adjuncts:

(74) Bulgarian
(a) *Koj kude e otisul*
who where went.3SG
'Who went where?'
(b) **Kude koj e otisul*
where who went.3SG

In Czech and Polish, in contrast, the relative order of interrogative words is said to be relatively unconstrained (cf. (75), (76)). It should be borne in mind, however, that with respect to the parameter under discussion, the judgements of native speakers do not always coincide and that detailed studies dealing with this parameter from a typological point of view do not exist.

(75) Czech
Kdo kdy koho pozval, nevím
who when whom invited I don't know
'Who invited whom when, I don't know.'

(76) Czech
Kdy kdo koho pozval, nevím
when who whom invited I don't know

5.4. Additional uses of interrogative words

There are quite a few domains of grammar in which interrogative words can also be observed to play a role. In the following we will briefly consider their importance for relative clauses and indefinites.

In most European languages interrogative words are also used as relative pronouns. This kind of polysemy is not particularly frequent across the languages of the world, but in view of the fact that relative clause formation on the basis of relative pronouns is mainly restricted to European languages, this is certainly little surprising (cf. Comrie 1981: 142). Languages that do not draw a formal distinction between interrogative words and relative pronouns include English, Spanish, Italian, etc. (cf. (77)), although there is often no perfect overlap. English is relatively unrestricted in that it can use nearly all interrogative words as relativisers. German, in contrast, only allows for the adjectival interrogative words (*welch-* 'which') to be used in this way.

(77) (a) *Who did you meet?*
(b) *I met the man who you saw.*

In many languages there is a close relationship between interrogative words and indefinite pronouns (cf. Haspelmath 1997: 170 ff.):

(78) German
a. *Wer kommt da?*
'Who is coming?'
b. *Da kommt wer.*
'Someone is coming.'

As can be seen in Table 77.10, languages may either use interrogative words as a source for the development of indefinites or simply use the same form for either function.

Table 77.10: Interrogative words and indefinite pronouns

language	who	indefinite
Bulgarian	kój	njákoj
Hungarian	ki	valaki
Polish	kto	ktoś
Japanese	dare	dare
Korean	nwukwu	nwukwu
Mandarin	shéi	shéi

According to Haspelmath (1997), a pervasive strategy of deriving indefinites from interrogative words is reduplication. Examples include Vietnamese *ai ai* 'anybody', 'whoever' (*ai* 'who'), Latin *ubi-ubi* 'anywhere', 'wherever' (*ubi* 'where') and Khasi *kumnu-kumnu* 'somehow' (*kumnu* 'how'). Although this strategy is fairly common and freely distributed all over the world, it is not entirely clear why reduplication should be so suitable for the derivation of indefinites.

Depending on the limitations defined by a particular language as well as on the context in which such indefinites are used, they can receive mainly two interpretations, either as existential or universal quantifier (→ Art. 92). For instance, the preferred interpretation of Mandarin *shénme* under the scope of negation is as the existential quantifier (cf. (79)). This very sentence could also be read as a question (meaning *What did Guojing not buy?*).

(79) Mandarin (Cheng 1997: 97)
Guojing méi-yǒu mǎi shénme.
Guojing not-have buy what
'Guojing did not buy anything.'

In combination with the adverb *dou*, in contrast, *shénme* must receive a universal interpretation:

(80) Mandarin (Cheng 1997: 98)
Botong shénme dōu chī.
Botong what all eat
'Botong eats everything.'

The close connection between interrogative words and indefinites is also clearly visible in English indirect questions of the type *You're looking for something?*, which are often understood in the same way as constituent interrogatives (*What are you looking for?*). Note that replacing the interrogative word by an indefinite yields the presupposition of a question.

6. Non-canonical uses of interrogative constructions

Just as non-interrogative clauses can be used to elicit information, it is equally possible to employ interrogatives for purposes other than asking questions (i. e. as indirect speech acts). The use of interrogatives as directives was demonstrated in the beginning of this article (cf. (3b)), but apart from such well-known and widely used exploitations, we also find more specific applications. Attention shall be drawn in this final section to echo questions and rhetorical questions.

Echo questions are used as responses to either statements or questions. Uttered in response to a statement they typically express surprise about it and are used to seek confirmation. In English, this type of echo question is not coded by a usual interrogative clause. Instead, normal declarative word order is used (cf. (81)), which means that interrogative words stay *in situ*.

(81) (a) A: *I'll be 100 next year.* − B: *You'll be 100 next year?*
 (b) A: *I've seen a ghost.* − B: *You've seen what?*

In Russian, by contrast, no syntactic peculiarities are associated with such echo questions. Where they differ from normal interrogatives is in the intonation pattern used (cf. Comrie 1984: 38). More interesting from a typological point of view is Japanese, because here we find a particle (*tte*) exclusively dedicated to marking echo questions (cf. (82)). The particle *tte* is a truncated form of *tte ii-mashita ka*, with *tte* being the quotative particle, *ii-mashita* a verb meaning 'said' and *ka* the interrogative particle.

(82) Japanese (Hinds 1984: 165)
 dare deshita tte?
 who was PART
 'Who did you say it was?'

When echo questions are used in response to a preceding question, they are usually used to make sure that the question was understood correctly and/or to gain time to work out the relevant answer. With this type of echo question no syntactic modifications are observable in English (apart from adjusting the deictic expressions):

(83) A: *How much would you like to give?*
 − B: *How much would I like to give?*

As far as English is concerned, this is true of echo questions given in reply to both polar interrogatives and constituent interrogatives. By comparison, echo questions given in response to polar interrogatives in Russian, German and French obligatorily take a particle. In other words, in these languages this type of echo questions behaves like an embedded question.

(84) German
 A: *Hast du dieses Buch gelesen?*
  have you this book read
 B: *Ob ich dieses Buch gelesen habe? Ja.*
  PART I this book read have yes
 'A: Have you read this book? − B: Have I read this book? Yes.'

Rhetorical questions are interrogatives uttered in a context in which the answer to them is given. Therefore, they are frequently referred to as "questions that expect no answer". As (85) shows, negative rhetorical questions imply a positive answer whereas those with positive polarity expect a negative answer.

(85) (a) *Isn't the weather terrible?*
 (b) *Who cares, anyway?*

Arguably, rhetorical questions can be found in all languages and they also appear to be functioning in a comparable manner. However, very little typological work has been carried out in this area so that we have to confine ourselves to a few brief remarks.

One interesting observation is reported from Mandarin, where, as discussed in § 4.4., we find two strategies for coding polar interrogatives (the A-not-A construction and the particle *ma*). As Li & Thompson (1984: 57 ff.) point out, it is only polar interrogatives based on the particle *ma* that can be used rhetorically. In the following example, the A-not-A construction would be inadequate (cf. § 4.4.):

(86) Mandarin
he! nǐ yǐwéi wǒ érnǚquíngchǎng ma
ha you think I sentimental IP
'Ha! Do you suppose I'm sentimental?'

The reason for this division of labour, Li & Thompson argue, must be sought in the fact that A-not-A interrogatives are restricted to contexts in which the speaker makes no assumptions about the truth-value of the proposition in question (cf. § 4.4.). Given that the key property of rhetorical questions is that the speaker knows the answer, this condition cannot be fulfilled.

The main function that is usually attributed to rhetorical questions is to make an indirect statement (as demonstrated in (85)). However, they can also be used with a thematicising function in order to establish or reintroduce a discourse theme (cf. *And what happens to the girl? She gets pregnant.*). Drawing on a substantial corpus of oral narratives from Tamil, Herring (1991) argues that the frequent use of rhetorical questions in that language, particularly as a thematicising device, has resulted in the interrogative words involved being grammaticalised into conjunctions:

(87) Tamil (Herring 1991: 273)
Avan ēn inkē illai nnā avan
he why here NEG CONJ he
ūrukku pōnān
town.DAT go.3.SG.M
'Why he isn't here, he went to his village.'

(88) Tamil
Avan inkē illai ēnnā avan ūrukku
he here NEG CONJ he town.DAT
pōnān
go.3.SG.M
'He's not here because he went to his village.'

In example (88) above the interrogative word *ēn* ('why') has merged with the conditional conjunction *nnā* into an autonomous conjunction. Even more striking is that there are also contexts where interrogative elements occur as conjunctions on their own. Evidently, interrogative constructions across the world still leave ample room for new discoveries.

7. Special abbreviations

ALL	allative
ANT	anterior
CL	classifier
CONJ	conjunction
INST	instrumental
INT	interrogative
IP	interrogative particle
IW	interrogative word
LIG	ligature
NT	neuter
PAR	partitive
PART	particle
PAST	past tense
PERL	perlative
REF	referential
REM	remote

8. References

Ackema, Peter & Neeleman, Ad. 1998. "Optimal questions". *Natural Language & Linguistic Theory* 16: 3, 443–490.

Baker, Carl Lee. 1970. "Notes on the description of English questions". *Foundations of Language* 6, 197–219.

Bazin, Louis. 1984. "La particule interrogative -*mi* en Turc". In: Valentin, Paul (ed.) *L'interrogation. Actes du colloque tenu les 19 et 20 décembre 1983 par le Department de Linguistique de l'Université de Paris-Sorbonne*, 89–94.

Chang, Suk-Jin. 1996. *Korean.* Amsterdam: Benjamins.

Cheng, Lisa Lai-Shen. 1997. *On the typology of wh-questions.* New York: Garland.

Chisholm, William S. & Milic, Louis T. & Greppin, John A. C. (eds.). 1984. *Interrogativity: A colloquium on the grammar, typology and pragmatics of questions in seven diverse languages.* Amsterdam: Benjamins.

Comrie, Bernard. 1981. *Language universals and linguistic typology.* Oxford: Blackwell.

Comrie, Bernard. 1984. "Russian". In: Chisholm, William S. et al. (eds.), 7–46.

Givón, Talmy. 1984. "Ute". In: Chisholm, William S. et al. (eds.), 215–243.

Geluykens, R. 1988. "On the myth of rising intonation in polar questions". *Journal of Pragmatics* 12, 467–485.

Greenberg, Joseph H. 1966. "Some universals of grammar with particular reference to the order of meaningful elements". In: Greenberg, Joseph H. (ed.) *Universals of language.* Cambridge, Mass: MIT Press, 73–113.

Haiman, John. 1978. "Conditionals are topics". *Language* 54, 564–589.

Haiman, John. 1985. *Natural syntax.* Cambridge: Cambridge University Press.

Hamblin, C. L. 1973. "Questions in Montague English". *Foundations of Language* 10, 41–53.

Harris, Alice C. 1984. "Georgian". In: Chisholm, William S. et al. (eds.), 63–112.

Haspelmath, Martin. 1997. *Indefinite pronouns*. Oxford: Clarendon Press.

Heine, Bernd & Claudi, Ulrike & Hünnemeyer, Friederike. 1991. *Grammaticalization. A conceptual framework*. Chicago: Chicago University Press.

Herring, Susan C. 1991. "The grammaticalization of rhetorical questions in Tamil". In: Traugott, Elizabeth C. & Heine, Bernd (eds.). *Approaches to grammaticalization*, I, 253–284.

Hinds, John. 1984. "Japanese". In: Chisholm, William S. et al. (eds.), 145–188.

Huddleston, Rodney D. 1994. "Sentence types and clause subordination". In: Asher, R. E. (ed.) *The Encyclopedia of Language and Linguistics*. Oxford: Pergamon Press, vol. 7, 3845–3857.

Hudson, Richard A. 1975. "The meaning of questions". *Language* 51, 1–31.

Karttunen, Lauri. 1977. "Syntax and semantics of questions". *Linguistics and Philosophy* 1, 3–44.

König, Ekkehard & Siemund, Peter. To appear "Speech act distinctions in grammar". In: Shopen, Timothy (ed.). *Language typology and syntactic description*. Cambridge: Cambridge University Press.

Kress, Bruno. 1982. *Isländische Grammatik*. Leipzig: Verlag Enzyklopädie.

Kuno, Susumu. 1978. "Japanese: A characteristic OV language". In: Lehmann, Winfried P. (ed.). *Syntactic typology. Studies in the phenomenology of language*. Sussey: The Harvester Press, 57–138.

Li, Charles N. & Thompson, Sandra A. 1984. "Mandarin". In: Chisholm, William S. et al. (eds.), 47–61.

Macaulay, Donald. 1992. *The Celtic Languages*. Cambridge: Cambridge University Press.

Sadock, Jerrold M. 1984. "West Greenlandic". In: Chisholm, William S. et al. (eds.), 189–214.

Sadock, Jerrold M. & Zwicky, Arnold M. 1985. "Speech act distinctions in syntax". In: Shopen, Timothy (ed.). *Language typology and syntactic Description*. Cambridge: Cambridge University Press, Vol. I, 155–196.

Saha, P. K. 1984. "Bengali". In: Chisholm, William S. et al. (eds.), 113–143.

Sneddon, James Neil. 1996. *Indonesian*. London: Routledge.

Sulkala, Helena & Karjalainen, Merja. 1992. *Finnish*. London: Routledge.

Traugott, Elizabeth C. 1985. "Conditional markers". In: Haiman, John (ed.). *Iconicity in syntax*. Amsterdam: Benjamins, 289–307.

Ultan, Russell. 1978. "Some general characteristics of interrogative systems". In: Greenberg, Joseph H. (ed.). *Universal of human language*. Stanford, CA: Stanford University Press, Vol. IV, 211–248.

Wąsik, Zdzisław. 1982. "Zur strukturellen Typologie der Fragen (anhand ausgewählter Sprachen der Gegenwart)". *Zeitschrift für Phonetik, Sprachwissenschaft und Kommunikationsforschung* 35: 4, 466–475.

Peter Siemund, Berlin
(Germany)

78. Hortative constructions

1. Hortative constructions: definition and calculus
2. Classification of hortative constructions
3. Interpretations of hortative constructions
4. Semantics of verbs used in hortative constructions
5. The imperative paradigm
6. Description of the imperative paradigm
7. Actual imperative paradigms as contrasted with the ideal imperative paradigm
8. References

1. Hortative constructions: definition and calculus

Hortative constructions represent a substantial proportion of speech patterns generated by man and are instrumental in regulating joint activities in society. They are designed to stimulate a specific reaction, including a speech reaction. Despite the transparency of their meaning (*Bring me some water!*, *Silence!*, *Fire!*, etc.), the semantic structure of hortative constructions comprises three elements belonging to three different planes: Prescription (consisting of Prescriptor, Recipient of Prescription, and Performer of Prescribed Action); Communication (consisting of Speaker [= Prescriptor], Listener [= Recipient of Prescription], and Outside Person not included into the act of communication, or a third person); and Imposed State of Affairs whose minimum constituents are Action P and its Agent [= Performer of Prescribed Action]. The above semantic model is both necessary and sufficient to formulate a definition of hortative constructions.

Hortative constructions are constructions conveying the idea of direct speech causation that can be interpreted as: '*The speaker [= prescriptor], wishing action P (which is either being or not being performed at the moment of speech) to take place, informs the listener [= recipient of prescription] as to who should be the agent of action P [= performer of prescribed action], thus attempting to cause action P by the very fact of this information*'. According to this definition, the aim of any hortative construction consists in either changing or preserving the existing reality. Cf.: *Turn the TV off!* and *"Don't move, please!", said the doctor seeing that the patients were about to sit up.*

Despite the similarity of this definition to others found with various authors, it contradicts them at the stage of language-material analysis. The discrepancy results from conflicting notions as to which of the participants of a speech situation can be the agent of the prescribed action P [= performer of prescribed action]. The most widespread view is that only the listener [= recipient of prescription] can perform this role. Maintaining thereby that the listener [= recipient of prescription] and the agent [= performer of prescribed action] of an hortative construction must be co-referent, this approach excludes from the class of hortative constructions all sentences where the agent [= performer of prescribed action] is represented by: a) a third person, e.g. *Let John come in*, b) the speaker him/herself, e.g. *Let me turn the TV on*, or c) both the speaker and the listener, e.g. *Let us go*. These constructions can be classified as hortative only within conceptions which admit that not only the listener, but also the speaker, the listener + the speaker, or a third person can perform the function of their agent [= performer of prescribed action].

We believe that the general solution to this problem is that *any of the established participants of an act of communication or any theoretically admissible combination of such participants can appear in the function of the agent [= performer of prescribed action]*. In other words, we suggest a calculus comprising 17 models of hortative constructions. Theoretically each of these models could use a corresponding specific imperative verb form but in reality they are only attested for the first seven models of the calculus. Theoretically possible representations of the agent [= performer of prescribed action] are shown in the calculus in Table 78.1.

Speaking of this calculus in general, we must note that only the first seven models have empirically attested corresponding special imperative verb forms, with the second and third models being prototypical, accounting for over 80 percent of all hortative constructions found in texts. At the same time, this calculus covers all the theoretically possible ways to denote the agent [= performer of prescribed action].

Table 78.1: A calculus of hortative construction models

No	Performer of prescribed action
1	the speaker ~ the 1st person singular
2	the listener ~ the 2nd person singular
3	the listeners ~ the 2nd person plural (dual, trial)
4	an outside person ~ the 3rd person singular
5	outside persons ~ the 3rd person plural (dual, trial)
6	the speaker + the listener
7	the speaker + the listeners
8	the speaker + an outside person
9	the speaker + outside persons
10	the listener + an outside person
11	the listener + outside persons
12	the listeners + an outside person
13	the listeners + outside persons
14	the speaker + the listener + an outside person
15	the speaker + the listeners + an outside person
16	the speaker + the listener + outside persons
17	the speaker + the listeners + outside persons

2. Classification of hortative constructions

In principle, all hortative constructions can be classified into two groups. The first group comprises sentences with specific grammatical marking, e.g. *Paint well!*, *Let John go to London!*, *Silence!*, or *Ivanov, to the Director, right now!*, whose only (or primary) function is to convey commands. It is these sentences that are normally identified as hortative. In speech-act theory they are described as direct directive speech acts. The second group includes sentences of the type *Tomorrow you are going to Moscow*, or *You can go and apo-*

logise right now. These sentences lack the specific grammatical features of the first group, and conveying commands is not their only or primary function. In speech-act theory they are described as indirect directive speech acts. The nucleus of the first group is made up of sentences whose predicates are expressed by specialised imperative verb forms — either synthetic, like Russian *Risuj!* 'Paint! (2nd person sg.)' or Russian *Jedem!* 'Let us go!', or analytic, like *Let him go* or *Let us keep silence.*

3. Interpretations of hortative constructions

In hortative constructions with the listener as the agent [= performer of prescribed action] prescription is generally interpreted as command, demand, direction, instruction, request, supplication, errand, suggestion, advice, desire, permission, etc. Since verbs of speech causation are traditionally classified into factitive and permissive verbs, interpretations of directive constructions can also be divided into factitive and permissive interpretations. The former reflect situations where the hortative construction is uttered on the speaker's [= prescriptor's] own initiative; the latter reflect situations where the utterance of a hortative construction is solicited by the listener [= performer of prescribed action], who asks the speaker for a prescription. The most socially significant factitive interpretations are: command, demand, request, and suggestion; permission has permissive interpretation *per se*; and advice can be interpreted as either permissive or factitive.

Some authors insist that variations of the imperative meaning depend on intonation. If one agrees with this point of view, then one should regard supplication, command, advice, etc. as grammatical meanings with specialised intonations as their markers. However, the existence of a variety of hortative intonations has not been experimentally proven yet. Thus, in Russian, each of the seven established intonation patterns correlates as a rule with more than one interpretation of the hortative sentence. Taking the viewpoint above, we should infer that Russian has no special hortative intonation distinctive from the narrative and interrogative intonations, or special intonations for command, demand, direction, instruction, request, supplication, errand, suggestion, advice, desire, permission, etc., since the seven intonations can be also found with narrative and interrogative sentences.

Interpretation of hortative sentences with 2nd person imperative verbs is mainly based on an analysis of the speech situation taking into account the social status of the participants in a given situation. In a variety of cases, differently interpreted hortative sentences have special formal features setting them apart from other similar constructions.

Commands normally travel from "top to bottom", i.e. from the "boss" to the "subordinate", with both clearly differentiated in the speech situation. At the same time, commands can be given both in an institutional or in a personal environment. When issuing a command, the "boss" [= prescriptor], empowered to supervise the execution of the imposed action, presumes that the "subordinate" [= recipient of prescription] is obliged to comply. Nevertheless, hortative sentences expressing commands may contain special markers to strongly favour this particular interpretation, cf. Russian hortative particles like *a nu*, *nu-ka*, and *a nu-ka* (that can be translated as *now*, *now then*, *come on*, etc.). Due to the vertical pattern of subordination the reasons for, or motives of, a command are normally not explained, and the command itself is not subject to discussion. Another specific feature of commands is that they are often given in situations where there is a lack of time. And finally, the boss is in a position to punish the subordinate who fails to comply.

Demands are very close to commands except that they can travel both ways: not only "down", but also from "bottom to top", or they can occur in situations where there is no official subordination between the speaker and the listener. The specific feature of a demand is that it presupposes necessity to observe the existing social norms, rules or conventions — which, in reality, can be broken. The speaker [= prescriptor] presumes that the listener [= performer of the prescribed action] ought to comply with the prescription.

Requests are normally directed either horizontally (when there is no subordination at all) or from "bottom to top"; in principle, requests can also go from "top to bottom", but then a certain amount of hypocrisy is involved, as a request by the boss is invariably understood as a command. The speaker [= prescriptor] presumes that the listener

[= performer of the prescribed action] can (although he is not obliged to) comply with the prescription. To formally stress their unobliging character request sentences can use special politeness markers like *please, could you please*, etc. Requests can be validated by the explanation of their reasons or motives. Cf.: *Please! Speak! Teach me! I want to learn!*.

Advice normally comes from persons regarding themselves as authorities and/or well-wishers. Subordination between advice-givers and advice-receivers is not necessary; in fact, it is even irrelevant. When offering advice the speaker [= prescriptor] presumes that the listener [= performer of the prescribed action] can comply with the prescribed action which represents the option the speaker himself would choose, if he/she were in the listener's place. Cf.: *Futures trading is not for you. Quit that, or you'll go bust.* Advice can provoke negative reactions from the listener, as people in principle tend to oppose uninvited counsel limiting their choice. Cf.: *"You'd better take the box down for a while", somebody advised. "Take it down yourself", snapped the boy.*

Hortative sentences with permissive interpretation have their own distinctive features. Normally, they are immediately preceded by some extra-speech stimuli or an interrogative sentence (uttered by someone intending to be the performer of the prescribed action in the hortative act to follow) with a request for permission or advice. Requests for permission normally travel from "bottom to top". A distinctive formal feature of interrogative sentences requesting for permission is that they generally include permission verbs of speech causation of the type *allow, permit*, or permission modals like *may*. Cf.: *The girl asked in a polite voice: "Auntie, may I glue a paper-box?" "Glue, my dear, whatever you like"*. Another feature of permission hortatives is their brevity, there being no need for lengthy explanation as the speaker already knows all the participants and circumstances of the action to follow from both the request and the situation. Permission can also be expressed by a single imperative verb, or represented by a permission formula of the type *do, okay, of course, you are welcome*, etc. Normally, permissive hortative sentences do not use pronominal subjects found in factitive hortative sentences. Permission hortatives expressing advice differ from factitive hortatives only in that they are preceded by the listener's solicitation of advice. Cf.: *The boy glanced at him, and the man, having caught his eye, advised: "Tell the officer how you committed the robbery".*

Hortative sentences with 3rd person imperatives admit semantic interpretations similar to those of hortative sentences with 2nd person imperatives. The same is true for hortative sentences with 1st person imperative verb forms both in the dual and the plural except that they can express neither permission nor advice in situations where the speaker [= prescriptor] cannot be simultaneously the performer of the prescribed action. All other interpretations seem to be possible although these sentences appear to express invitation characteristic only of their type. Cf.: *Your room is ready. Let's go.* It should be noted that 1st person singular hortatives seem to level out all other semantic interpretations and convey only a general idea of autoprescription. Cf.: *Let me go and bring John! How could I forget about him?*

4. Semantics of verbs used in hortative constructions

Most languages appear to impose no fundamental formal restrictions on the structure of imperative verb forms. Normally, imperative markers can be found even with verbs which, due to their semantic features, are never used in hortative constructions; cf. the Russian verb *očutit'sja* 'find oneself somewhere': **Očutis' v Krymu!* **'Find yourself in the Crimea!'*. Actually, verbs appearing in hortative constructions have only one semantic restriction — they must designate controllable actions, i.e. actions which, in a given situation, can be performed in a controlled manner by any person based on his/her own or somebody else's experience. Accordingly, hortative constructions practically never use stative verbs, including permanent action or relation verbs like *own, belong, consist of*, modal verbs like *want* or *can*, verbs of passive perception like *see* or *hear*, verbs of measure like *weigh*, verbs denoting location in space like *find oneself*, etc., i.e. verbs that normally designate uncontrollable states of affairs.

At the same time, it must be noted that there is no impenetrable wall between controllable and uncontrollable actions. Certain actions which at first sight appear to be uncontrollable may turn out to be partially or temporarily controllable after more detailed analysis — thus allowing the relevant verbs to form hortative constructions. A typical example of transforming a normally uncontrollable action into a temporarily controllable one (with concomittant change of certain standard parameters) is the situation where the doctor asks his patient to breathe in, i.e. to breathe deeper than under normal circumstances when the process of breathing is totally uncontrollable. Some uncontrollable actions admit controllable imitation. Take, for instance, a theatre rehearsal where actors can be asked by the director to controllably perform normally uncontrollable actions which, during the show, should again appear natural and uncontrollable. Cf. *John, you should fall with more energy in the second act!*. Imitated action markers are adverbials like *intentionally* or *deliberately*. Their presence in hortative constructions allows the use of non-agentive "deficient behaviour" verbs like *blab out, confuse, lose*, etc.: *You lose their tickets deliberately, and then they won't be able to leave*. It should be noted also that some uncontrollable states can result from a string of preceding controllable actions. For instance, such states as *fall ill, get well, catch cold, have a nap, get thinner, grow taller*, etc. are uncontrollable and non-premeditated, although actions they can result from are often well-known. And a sentence like *Take a nap for half an hour!* conveys rather a wish than a prescription because its addressee cannot go to sleep or stay awake solely at his/her will. But at the same time one can deliberately undertake a number of controllable actions normally conducive to and preceding going to sleep like *wash, take off one's shoes, get into bed*, etc.

5. The imperative paradigm

A study of the existing imperative verb descriptions in various types of languages shows that their authors rarely agree on the composition of imperative paradigms distinguished in the same language. This fact is especially noteworthy as the descriptions of other paradigms (in the indicative, optative, conjunctive, and other moods) normally coincide. One of the reasons for this irregularity is that the inventory of hortative verb forms comprises not only verbs with hortation as their only or central meaning, but also verbs with optional hortative semantics. The latter produce polysemous (or homonymous) sentences whose ambiguity can be largely neutralized through intonation. There is no generally accepted view regarding the expediency of including or not including such semantically ambiguous forms into the imperative paradigm. Another reason for this irregular situation is the wary attitude linguists show toward analytical forms which are sometimes excluded from corresponding paradigms (in our case, the imperative paradigm) for want of clear identification criteria. For instance, Russian imperative sequences like *Davaj [budem] molčat'* 'let us keep silence', or *Pust' [on] molčit* 'let him keep silence' are sometimes excluded from the imperative paradigm based on purely formal criteria, one being the analytic character of these forms. A similar situation is true for English sequences like *Let's go*.

To simulate a universal imperative paradigm, we used two components: *constant* components inherent in all the forms of the paradigm, and *variable* components inherent in each individual form of the paradigm and contrasting it with all other forms. The constant semantic components of the imperative paradigm include: (1) the lexical meaning of the prescribed action; (2) the grammatical meaning of the 1st person singular, i.e. the meaning of the speaker [= prescriptor]; (3) the grammatical meaning of hortation interpreted as 'causation of the speaker's [= prescriptor] will'. The variable semantic components are: (1) the grammatical meanings of the person and number of the agent of the prescribed action [= performer of the prescribed action]; (2) the grammatical meaning of the number of the listener [= recipient of prescription]. Due to certain restricting factors, the above-mentioned ideal calculus is reduced to the maximum possible "actual" paradigm comprising seven person/number forms divided into the three groups shown in Table 78.2.

Members of each of these groups have similar referent/role structure. Group I forms signal that the agent of the action [= performer of prescribed action] is either a single (form 1) or a plural (form 2) listener. Group II forms signal that the agent of the action is the speaker (form 3), the speaker and a single listener (form 4), or the speaker and plural listeners (form 5). Group III forms signal that the agent of the action is either a single outside person not included into the act of communication (form 6), or plural outside persons not included into the act of communication (form 7).

78. Hortative constructions

Table 78.2: A maximum actual imperative paradigm

Group	No	Person and number	Example (Russian)
I	1	2nd person sg.	*spoj* 'sing'
	2	2nd person pl.	*spojte* 'sing'
II	3	1st person sg.	*spoju* 'let me sing'
	4	1st person du.	*spojom* 'let us sing'
	5	1st person pl.	*spojomte* 'let us sing'
III	6	3rd person sg.	*pust' [on/ona] spojot* 'let [him/her] sing'
	7	3rd person pl.	*pust' [oni] spojut* 'let [them] sing'

(Group I forms correspond to models 2 and 3 of the calculus; Group II forms, to models 1, 6, and 7; and Group III forms, to models 4 and 5 of the calculus).

By describing the paradigm of Table 78.2 as "actually" possible we wish to stress that its composition only provides a clue to what types of imperative forms can be found in various languages, while leaving aside the issue of imperative forms actually represented in any of the specific languages. To be included into the imperative paradigm, verb forms should, in our view, conform to only two formal requirements: (a) they must be regularly built on lexemes whose semantics admit the formation of imperative verb forms, and (b) they must be recognizable within the sentence as units with hortative meaning. There can be no restriction regarding the type of formal imperative markers which can be represented by affixes, adverbal particles, stress, word-order, actual actant environment, etc. and appear in hortative constructions both independently or in various combinations.

As far as we know, our rather "liberal" notional and formal imperative verb criteria differ from similar but more "rigid" ones implicitly applied by other researchers (cf. Wierzbicka 1972). The most rigorous semantic restriction originates in the narrow interpretation of hortative meaning. It insists that the only person/persons to follow prescription is/are its immediate addressee/addressees — the listener/listeners. Therefore the imperative paradigm can comprise no other components than 2nd person forms. At the same time, some grammatical descriptions suggest expanded imperative pardigms including 3rd person and 1st person forms as well. We believe, though, that their authors are led by formal rather than semantic considerations proceeding from the notion that any imperative paradigm must contain only formally homogeneous elements, with the latter's morphology distinctively differing from that of the members of other paradigms.

It is for this reason that all Turkologists without exception include into the imperative paradigm not only 2nd person forms like Tatar *bar* 'go (sg.)' and *bar-ygyz* 'go (pl.)', but also 3rd person forms like *bar-syn* 'let [him] go (sg.)' and *bar-syn-nar* 'let [them] go (pl.)', which are formally homogeneous with 2nd person forms and have no homonyms in other paradigms. Thus, for Turkologists, 3rd person imperatives represent an objective reality, whereas Slavists, in particular scholars of Russian, are divided on the issue. For instance, many outstanding scholars support the "semantic" point of view which excludes the 3rd person from the imperative paradigm and maintain that sequences like *Pust' on pridjot* 'Let him come' or *Pust' on sdelajet* 'Let him do', etc. cannot be recognized as imperative. However, they seem to be motivated by formal rather than semantic criteria. We presume that, if the Slavic languages had synthetic (instead of analytic) 3rd person imperatives formally homogeneous with 2nd person imperatives, the issue of their exclusion from the paradigm would hardly arise.

It deserves mentioning in this connection that the overwhelming majority of scholars of Russian include 1st person dual and plural imperatives like *Idjom* 'Let us go' (dual) and *Idjomte* 'let us go' (plural) into the imperative paradigm. A brief analysis can reveal that this classification is based not on formal, but on purely semantic criteria. Both forms are not analytic but synthetic, and both convey hortative meaning. In addition, forms like *idjomte* have no homonyms in other verb paradigms, while forms like *idjom*, from which *idjomte*-type verbs are derived, have 1st person plural present tense homonyms in the indicative. On the one hand, the inclusion of this form into the imperative paradigm defies the formal homogeneity requirement, on the other hand, however, it is perfectly justified from the semantic viewpoint – which in this case prevails. Turkologists, by contrast, have to grapple with the problem of *including* in their imperative paradigm the Turkic 1st person plural imperative of the type *bar-yjk* 'let us go' which, though synthetic, is optative in form and therefore formally not homogeneous with 2nd and 3rd person imperatives. That is why, proceeding from purely formal criteria, many well-known Turkologists exclude this form from the imperative paradigm despite the fact that (a) only this form can express this particular hortative meaning, (b) this form is regularly derived from lexemes that admit the formation of hortative verb forms, and (c) this form is generally recognized to convey hortative meaning. At the same time, other authors who base their analysis on both semantic and formal criteria, while excluding it from the imperative paradigm, describe it as a form designed to "fill in" the "defective" imperative paradigm. And lastly, authors who follow functional/semantic criteria and regard the above formal requirements as irrelevant naturally include the form in question into the imperative paradigm.

To summarize, we would like to stress that the imperative paradigms distinguished by different authors in various languages often inadequately reflect the actual situation, which is the result of unwarranted semantic and formal restrictions imposed on imperative forms. Casting aside those rigid restrictions and constructing imperative paradigms in accordance with the universal functional/semantic criteria suggested above – the latter based on very liberal formal requirements – one could construct a description to accommodate all imperative forms actually existing in languages.

Although the person and number categories are necessary and sufficient for the formation of an imperative paradigm, one should not forget that verbs in various languages may possess categories which, while not forming the imperative paradigm, may be instrumental in determining the number of forms it comprises, because oppositions built on their meanings are formally marked in the imperative paradigm (as well as in other verb paradigms of a given language). As a result, each of the seven forms of the actually possible imperative paradigm can be represented in specific languages by a number of variants whose composition is determined by the set of grammatical categories relevant for the imperative meaning. These categories are those of gender, class, aspect, "tense", and voice. For example, Arabic distinguishes masculine and feminine forms: *'uktub* (2nd person sg. masc.) 'write', and *'uktubī* (2nd person sg. femin.) 'write'. The Abkhaz language has different masculine and feminine class forms: *uca* (2nd person sg., addressed to a man) 'go', and *bca* 'go' (2nd person sg., addressed to a woman). The Russian language has imperfective forms (*poj* 'sing', 2nd person sg.) and perfective forms (*spoj* 'sing' 2nd person sg.). In Evenki there is an immediate-future imperative (*eme-kel* 'come') and a distant-future imperative (*eme-devi* 'come-later'). Actions prescribed by the former may begin at any point of the time axis after the moment of hortation, while actions denoted by the latter are to begin only after a certain lapse of time. A number of languages, e. g. Latin, distinguish active and passive imperative forms, cf.: *lauda* (2nd person sg., active) 'praise' and *laudāre* 'be praised by somebody'. It should also be noted that in some languages the category of number is represented by a larger inventory of forms than those used in the imperative paradigm model above, which adds to the number of forms in actual imperative paradigms. Cf. Nganasan 2nd person forms: *tu-"* 'come', *tuj-ŋuri* 'come you two', and *tuj-ŋuru"* 'come you many'.

Imperative form variability can also stem from semantic and pragmatic interpretations, which: (1) reflect etiquette-determined relations between the speaker and the listener; (2) specify the hortative meaning; (3) rank actions according to the level of emphasis. Examples illustrating these variants are given below.

(1) Various levels of the speaker's politeness to the listener are reflected, for instance, by 2nd person imperatives in Korean. Thus the verb *xa-da* 'do' has five 2nd person imperative forms: *xa-si-o* (grade I = politeness), *xa-o* (grade II – courtesy), *xa-ge* (grade III – intimacy), *xa-jɔ-ra* (grade VI – neutrality), and *xe* (grade V – familiarity).

(2) Special permissive imperative forms can be found in Nivkh (Amur dialect): forms in *-gira* (sg.), and forms in – *girla* (pl.). Cf.: *Viny-ğa vi-gira* 'If-you-want-to-go, go', and *Ev-d' hağa ev-girla* 'If-you-want-to take, take'.

(3) Neutral/emphatic imperative opposition with the auxiliary *do* is found in English, cf.: *Come in*, and *Do come in*. Unlike standard forms, emphatic imperatives normally prescribe expected action. In the speaker's view, such an action is going to happen anyway, with or without his/her (as a rule repeated) prescription. Therefore, emphatic imperatives have a stronger categorical connotation.

6. Description of the imperative paradigm

6.1. Second person forms

Second-person forms are normally represented by either the root (cf. Kazakh *kel-ø* 'come') or the stem of one of the verb forms, cf. Hebrew *saper-ø* 'tell' derived from the Imperfect. The widespread absence of formal markers with 2nd person singular imperatives (or one of the 2nd person singular imperatives, if there are more than one) may be explained by the pragmatic importance of the imperative, for the expression of which most (though not all) languages reserve the most concise form. At the same time, 2nd person forms may have specialised markers added to the stem (root). This is true, for instance, for Chukchi-Kamchatkan languages, cf.: Kerek *q-akkuj-ej* 'eat', and Chukchi *qy-čejvy-gi* 'go'. The imperative marker in these subjective forms is the prefix *q(y)-*.

In Armenian, 2nd person imperatives are formed by adding: (a) the suffix *-ir* to the infinitive stem in *-el*: *gr-el* 'to write' → *gr-ir* 'write!'; (b) the suffix *-a* to the infinitive stem in *-al*: *kard-al* 'to read' → *karda* 'read!'; and (c) the suffix *-u* to the aorist form with the causative suffix − *c-*: *ačecnel* 'to grow sth.' → *ače-cr-u* 'grow sth.!'

The most common way to build 2nd person plural imperatives is by adding a specialised plural marker to the 2nd person singular form, cf. Kazakh *kel* 'come' → *kel-inder* 'come (pl.)'. At the same time, the plural marker can be added to a stem different from the one with which the singular imperative marker is used − as in Armenian, where the singular imperative marker is normally added to the infinitive stem, and the plural imperative marker, to the Aorist stem, cf.: *gr-ir* 'write (sg.)' and *grec-ek* 'write (pl.)'. This means that in a general description one cannot reduce the process of 2nd person plural imperatives formation to simple formal derivation from 2nd person singular imperatives.

It should be noted that opposition by number is not basically compulsory for 2nd person imperatives. Thus an unmarked 2nd person imperative, which could be described as a general number form, is found in English: *Open* [sg.] *the door!* / *Open* [pl.] *the door!*, and in Mongolian: *buu* 'Come down (both sg. and pl.)'.

In some cases 2nd person imperatives partially or completely coincide with other mood forms, thus revealing the existence of polysemous (homonymous) forms. Compare for instance French where 2nd person singular imperatives in most cases either completely coincide with the present indicative (cf. *dis* and *tu dis*) or the subjunctive (cf. *sois* and *tu sois*), or have identical pronunciation, with the only difference in spelling being the absence of an *-s* ending (cf. *parle* and *tu parles*, or *aie* and *que tu aies*). On the other hand, French 2nd person plural imperatives completely coincide with the present indicative (cf. *parlez* and *vous parlez*) or the subjunctive (cf. *soyez heureux* and *que vous soyez heureux*). Specific forms for 2nd person singular and plural imperatives are found only with two French verbs: *sache* and *sachez*, and *veuille−veuillez*. In this connection it is important to note that both the present indicative and the subjunctive belong to forms whose meaning includes the component of 'action incomplete at the moment of speech', which is also characteristic of the semantics of the imperative. This explains why these forms are often used to convey hortative meaning.

To make the picture complete, we should also mention 2nd person dual number imperatives attested in some languages, including certain Slavic languages like Slovenian (*govorita* 'speak-you-two'), Upper Sorbian where these forms are additionally contrasted by gender (cf.: *spevaj-taj* 'sing-you-two masc.' and *spevaj-tej* 'sing-you-two femin.'), as well as Chukchi-Koryak, Samoyed, Semitic, and other languages.

6.2. First person forms

First person singular imperatives are fairly variegated in their morphology and can be represented by: (1) imperatives *per se*, which are morphologically homogeneous with other imperative forms including the basic 2nd person forms (cf. Kerek *m-akkui-k* 'let-me-eat', and Klamath *sdig-eek* 'let-me-smell'); (2) indirect mood forms like the optative, cf. Kazakh *kel-ejin* 'let-me-come' (optative), Armen. *gna-m* 'let me go' (future optative); (3) the indicative with present/future perspective, cf. Russian *Pojdu-ka ja* 'Let me go'; (4) analytical forms containing: (a) auxiliary causative verbs or particles historically derived from them, cf. English *Let me go*; (b) auxiliary verbs with the meaning '*give*' or particles historically derived from them, cf. Russian *Daj(te) projdu* 'let me pass', and (c) hortative particles, cf. Indonesian *biar/mari aku bersandar* 'Let me lean on something' with *bersandar* meaning '(You pl./sg.) lean!'.

First person singular imperatives are not found in descriptions of many languages. One of the possible reasons for this may be the fact that, as mentioned above, 1st person singular imperatives are often morphologically heterogeneous with other specific imperative forms, and are thus not included in the paradigm. Another reason may be that, although theoretically auto-prescription is quite possible (hence its inclusion in the calculus suggested above), in practice situations of auto-prescription are comparatively rare, with the result that a language (like, for instance, Aleut) may actually have no 1st person imperative forms. At the same time in languages, where this form is attested, it is profusely used in texts; e.g. in Kerek it accounts for about 30 percent of the total number of imperatives used.

Many languages have both 1st person dual and 1st person plural imperative forms (both are often described as plural) e.g. in Yakut: *bar-yax* 'let us go (you sg. and me)', and *bar-yağ-yng* 'let us go (you pl. and me)'. The former, the "excluding" imperative, is used to signal that the agent of the action is the speaker together with a single listener, and the second, the "including" imperative, shows that the agent of the action is the speaker together with plural listeners. Other languages have only one form that does not distinguish between the two above meanings, cf. Hungarian *men-j-ünk* 'Let us go from here'.

Some languages may have both an imperative form that does not distinguish the number of listeners taking part in the action, and forms that do. Thus in Hebrew forms of the type *nelex* 'Let's go' are indifferent to the number of listeners, while in combination with the 2nd person singular or plural imperative of the verb *ba* 'come' they take the number of the listeners into account, cf.: *bo nelex* 'Let's go (you masc. and me)', *bo'i nelex* 'Let's go (you femin. and me)', and *bo'u nelex* 'Let's go (you pl. and me)'. While on the subject of number neutralisation, we should mention some languages that always, when the speaker is the agent of the action (regardless of whether the listeners participate in the action or not) use one form, which may be classified as 1st person general number; cf. Mongolian *jav-ja* 'Let me/you-and-me/us-many go'. As to the composition of 1st person dual, plural, and general number forms, these can be: (1) purely imperative, i.e. morphologically homogeneous with the basic 2nd person forms (cf. Eskimo *tagi-l'-tun* 'Let us come you (sg.) and me', *tagi-l'-ta* 'Let us come you (pl.) and me'); (2) indirect mood forms like the optative, conjunctive, etc. (Armenian *gna-nk'* 'Let us go', future optative); (3) indicative forms with present/future perspective or their derivates (Russian *idjom* 'Let us go' (dual) and *idjomte* 'Let us go' (plural), French *parlons*); (4) analytical forms comprising: (a) auxiliary causative verbs or particles historically derived from them (English *Let us* (dual/plural) *go*); (b) "auxiliary" motion verbs with the meaning 'come', 'arrive', 'go' (Haitan Creole *an(u) mǎže* 'Let us (dual/plural) eat'); (c) auxiliary verbs with the meaning 'give' or particles historically derived from them (Ewe *na miyi* 'let us (you and me) go', 'Let us pl. go'); (d) auxiliary modal verbs (German *wollen wir arbeiten*); (e) hortative particles denoting the agent of the action (Indonesian *mari bersandar* 'Let us (dual or pl.) lean to sth.' with *bersandar* meaning '(You pl./sg.) lean!'.

6.3. Third-person forms

The opposition of 3rd person singular and plural imperatives is neutralized rather rarely: Mongolian *jav-ag* 'Let him/them go', or Lak *čiča-ča* 'Let him/them write'. It is interesting to note that sometimes, as in many Turkic languages, 3rd person singular forms are used instead of 3rd person plural forms (if the latter are represented in the paradigm), cf. Tofalar *al-syn* 'Let him/them take', and *al-syn-nar* meaning 'Let them take'. Some languages, in addition to 3rd person singular and plural imperatives, possess 3rd person dual forms, e.g. Nganasan *tuj-ŋe* 'Let him come', *tuj- ŋegej* 'Let them two come', and *tuj-ŋe″* 'Let them many come'.

From the morphological standpoint, 3rd person forms can be: (1) imperatives *per se*, i.e. imperatives morphologically homogeneous with the basic 2nd person forms (cf. Yakut *bar-dyn* 'let him go', *bar-dyn-lar* 'Let them go'); (2) indirect mood forms (cf. Aleut *xaka-a-xt(a)* 'Let him/them come near' — the optative (cf. French *qu'il parle* — *qu'ils parlent* — the subjunctive); (3) indicative forms with a present/future perspective (cf.

Hebrew *ye- saper* 'Let him tell', *te-saper* 'Let her tell', *ye-sapr-u* 'Let them tell'); (4) analytical forms containing: (a) auxiliary causative verbs or particles historically derived from them (cf. English *Let him/her take, Let them take*, Russian *Pust'/puskaj čitaet/čitajut* 'Let him/them read'); (b) hortative particles (cf. Indonesian *biar bersandar* 'Let him/her/them lean on sth.'); (c) markers historically derived from the conjunction of purpose 'so that' (cf. Ewe *ne yi* 'Let (= so that) he went', *ne woayi* 'Let (= so that) they went').

7. Actual imperative paradigms as contrasted with the ideal imperative paradigm

In contrasting imperative paradigms in specific languages with the ideal paradigm we wish to highlight the following features.

Morphological homogeneity is not characteristic of imperative paradigms in general. Although formally homogeneous imperative paradigms do occur (e. g. in Chukchi-Kamchatkan languages, Yukagir, and Hungarian), they should be treated rather as an exception; and the rule is that imperative paradigms normally comprise morphologically heterogeneous forms with homonyms in other verb paradigms. However, it should be pointed out that the range of these "formally" non-imperative forms is rather limited (indirect mood forms; indicative forms with present and future perspective; and analytic sequences including causative verbs, verbs of motion and "giving", modal verbs, and hortative particles historically derived from the above verbs or from a conjunction of purpose). They can be included in imperative paradigms, for all of them, like formal imperatives, denote actions that, although realizable, have not been realized at the moment of speech.

Imperatives can be classified into basic and peripheral forms. Basic forms are 2nd person imperatives which are a compulsory element of any imperative paradigm. Typically they do not allow number neutralization or general-number forms, although sometimes it is possible, cf. English *Go*. Being the markers of the most natural situation of prescription, these forms exceed all other imperatives by their frequency in texts. Basic imperatives practically have no analytical forms or homonyms in other verb paradigms. Their fundamental difference from peripheral forms is that peripherals may be absent from a specific imperative paradigm. This is most often the case with 1st person singular imperatives which are absent, for example, in Aleut, Ukrainian, and Byelorussian; the absence of 3rd person forms is attested less frequently (e. g. in Japanese). Thus specific paradigms may have fewer forms than the ideal paradigm. Another difference is the prevailing heterogeneity of peripheral imperatives which are also often represented by multivariant forms. The reason for the morphological heterogeneity of peripheral imperatives seems to be their occurrence in appellatives, i. e. forms whose function is to establish and maintain contacts between people and which, as is generally known, tend to quickly "wear out" and be replaced by new forms. This pre-determines the existing irregularity in the historical development of different imperative forms and explains why in synchrony imperative paradigms often display a wide morphological diversity of components.

In closing we would like to give a sample of two imperative paradigms: a formally homogeneous perfective imperative paradigm of the Kerek verb *akkuik* 'eat', and a formally heterogeneous perfective imperative paradigm of the Russian verb *spet'* 'sing'.

Table 78.3: Kerek and Russian imperative paradigms

Person	Number	Kerek: *akkuik* 'eat'	Russian: *spet'* 'sing'
2nd	singular	q-akkuj-Ø-ej	spoj (-ka)
2nd	dual	q-akkuj-Ø-tek	—
2nd	plural	q-akkuj-la-Ø-tek	spojte (-ka)
1st	singular	m-akkui-Ø-k	spoju (-ka)
1st	dual	mn-akkuj-Ø-mek	spojom (-ka), davaj (-ka) spojom
1st	plural	mn-akkuj-la-Ø-(mek)	spojomte (-ka), davajte (-ka) spojom
3rd	singular	n-akkuj-Ø-n	pust' (-ka) [on/ona] spojot
3rd	dual	n-akkuj-Ø-x'aj	—
3rd	plural	n-akkuj-la-Ø-j	pust' (-ka) [oni] spojut

8. References

Birjulin, Leonid. 1994. *Semantika i pragmatika russkogo imperativa* [Semantics and pragmatics of the Russian imperative] (Slavica Helsingiensia, 13.) Helsinki: University of Helsinki.

Bolinger, Dwight. 1974. "Do-Imperatives", *Journal of English Linguistics* 8: 1–5.

Davies, Eirlys. 1986. *The English imperative*. London: Croom Helm.

Hamblin, Charles L. 1987. *Imperatives*. New York: Blackwell.

Hare, Richard M. 1949. "Imperative sentence". *Mind*, 58: 21–39.

Šteling, Donat A. 1982. "O grammatičeskom statuse povelitel'nogo naklonenija" [On the grammatical status of the imperative mood]. *Izv. AN SSSR. Serija literatury i jazyka*, 41.3.

Wierzbicka, Anna. 1972. *Semantic primitives*. Frankfurt am Main: Athenäum.

Xrakovskij, Viktor S. (ed.) 1992. *Tipologija imperativnyx konstrukcij* [Typology of imperative constructions] St. Petersburg: Nauka.

Xrakovskij, Viktor S., Volodin, Aleksandr P. 1986. *Semantika i tipologija imperativa. Russkij imperativ.* [Semantics and typology of the imperative. The Russian imperative] Leningrad: Nauka.

Viktor S. Xrakovskij, Sankt Petersburg (Russia)

79. Exclamative constructions

1. Introduction
2. The conceptual basis of the exclamative category
3. The exclamative sentence type
4. The cross-linguistic expression of exclamative meaning
5. Conclusion
6. References

1. Introduction

Exclamative constructions form a variegated class, both within and across languages. This article presents a typological survey of the coding of exclamations. This survey will proceed in the following fashion. First, we will explore the conceptual basis of the category *exclamation*, and in particular the category of **degree exclamations** (section 2). Second, we will examine the formal, semantic and pragmatic constraints which jointly define the exclamative sentence type – a type whose characterization is based, as in Grimshaw (1979), on the degree class (section 3). Third, we will look at cross-linguistic manifestations of this type, with particular attention to those recurrent formal properties which reflect components of the exclamative sentence type and which suggest general tendencies in the grammaticalization of exclamative constructions (section 4). In a concluding section (section 5), we will consider the question of whether, on the basis of the data considered, one can establish the existence of a form-function fit in the area of exclamations.

2. The conceptual basis of the exclamative category

Any attempt to identify a sentence type in a given language, or to compare instances of a given sentence type across languages, relies on an understanding of the function pole of the form-function pairing. Such an understanding has been particularly elusive in the case of exclamations, since the terms *exclamation* and *exclamative* have often been taken to refer to emphatic or expressive utterances in general, as in the following definition from a study on exclamative intonation: "L'exclamation est généralement définie comme la manifestation linguistique d'un état émotionnel de l'énonciateur […]" (Morel 1995: 63). Further, the label *exclamation* has often been applied to related expressive phenomena, like interjections and news-reporting declaratives. For example, Makkai (1985) purports to examine the diachronic sources of exclamations, but focuses largely on interjections. Speech-act theory (Austin 1962, Searle 1979, Geis 1995) has not helped to refine our understanding of the exclamative type, since expressive speech acts, with the exception of formalized locutions like apologies, are not readily analyzed with regard to preparatory, essential and sincerity conditions.

It is perhaps because researchers lack a solid conceptual foundation for the exclamative type that this type has not figured prominently in typological syntactic research (exceptions being Elliott 1974 and Sadock &

79. Exclamative constructions

Zwicky 1985). Therefore, as a prelude to our typological exploration of exclamative constructions, we will now examine semantic and pragmatic criteria which define exclamations and distinguish them from interjections and declaratives.

2.1. The coding of surprise

Exclamations, like *The nerve of some people!* or the French *Comme il fait beau!* ('How lovely it is!'), are grammatical forms which express the speaker's affective response to a situation: exclamations convey surprise. Surprise may be accompanied by positive or negative affect. In the model assumed here, surprise is not merely a response (startled or otherwise) to a situation which the speaker had failed to predict. For example, I might not have predicted a hallway encounter with a colleague, but I would not necessarily find that encounter surprising (even if my colleague had startled me). Instead, surprise entails a **judgement** by the speaker that a given situation is **noncanonical**. A noncanonical situation is one whose absence a speaker would have predicted, based on a prior assumption or set of assumptions, e.g., a stereotype, a set of behavioral norms, or a model of the physical world (Michaelis 1994b).

In conveying surprise, exclamations resemble a subset of **interjections** (Ehlich 1986, Makkai 1985). Interjections resemble exclamations in that they express the speaker's appraisal of a situation. While some interjections (like *Yay!* or *Damn!*) express the speaker's **evaluation** (positive or negative) of the situation, some, like *Hey!* or *Oh my God!*, have a function like that of exclamatives — expressing what Fillmore & Kay & O'Connor (1988) call a **noncanonicity judgement**.

2.2. The expression of speaker viewpoint

The individual whose surprise is expressed by an interjection or exclamation is — by default — the speaker. A judgement expressible as an exclamation, like that expressible as an interjection, can, however, be attributed to someone other than the speaker, as in (1) and the presumably veridical quote in (2):

(1) *She couldn't believe how few people came to help her.*

(2) *He's like, 'Hey! You're not supposed to be here!'*

Sentence (1) is vague as to whether the speaker shares the judgement attributed to the subject-referent (that the paucity of helpers was surprising). Sentences like (3–4), however, appear to invite the hearer to share the speaker's judgement:

(3) *You won't believe who spoke up.*

(4) *Du würdest nicht glauben, wer sich zu Wort gemeldet hat.*
     'You wouldn't believe who spoke up.'

Exclamatives like (3–4), in which the hearer is the judge, have a marked status: such exclamations generally require a futurate or subjunctive main verb. This modal marking imparts a hypothetical flavor; sentences like (3–4) presuppose that the hearer is not currently in a position to make the relevant judgement. The modal marking appears to be crucial: utterances like (5) are anomalous, whether or not they are construed as exclamations:

(5) *??You don't believe who spoke up.*

The irrealis flavor of (3–4) suggests that the speaker is by default the source of the noncanonicity judgement, as does the interpretation of (6), in which the source of the relevant viewpoint is not overtly expressed:

(6) *It's incredible how little you can spend there.*

In (6) the relevant judgement (concerning the unusually low prices) is attributed to the speaker (at least), and perhaps also to people in general. The expression of speaker viewpoint appears intrinsic to the exclamative speech act, and utterances like (1), despite having formal hallmarks of exclamatives (e.g., a *wh*-complement following an epistemic predicator), are not clear examples of exclamations, just as (2), despite containing a form otherwise identifiable as an interjection, is not a prototypical example of an interjection. One can presume instead that examples like (1–2) involve **perspectival shift** (Fillmore 1982). Just as the demonstrative adjective *this* is not clearly proximal when the viewpoint of someone other than the speaker is invoked (as in, say, a narrative), so an exclamative form like (1) does not clearly perform an exclamative function when the viewpoint expressed is not the speaker's.

2.3. Propositional content

We have observed that exclamations and interjections share two semantico-pragmatic properties: the function of expressing a noncanonicity judgement and the indexical function of expressing speaker perspective. The major semantic feature which distinguishes exclamations from interjections is also the major semantic property that exclamations share with declaratives: **recoverable propositional content**. Both exclamations and declaratives linguistically encode a proposition which the speaker assumes to be true.

Interjections lack this property. For example, the interjection *Hey!* does not express a proposition. While one might analyze this interjection as conventionally expressing a meaning that can be represented by a proposition of the form 'I am surprised at some aspect of the present situation', such a proposition is not encoded, elliptically or otherwise, by the linguistic form in question. By contrast, the exclamation in (7):

(7) *It's so hot!*

denotes the proposition 'It's hot to a particular degree'. The claim that exclamations lexically encode a proposition requires some justification in light of examples like (8):

(8) *In The Mask, Carrey plays Stanley Ipkiss, a bank clerk whose timidity is quickly demonstrated in a series of opening sketches. Poor Ipkiss!* **The indignities that the world heaps on him!** − Michael Covino, The East Bay *Express* 8/15/94 (= Michaelis & Lambrecht 1996a (32 d))

Although the exclamation in (8) consists of a NP alone, the interpretation of this NP is identical to that of a clausal exclamation like *The world heaps so many indignities on him*. Grimshaw (1979) refers to exclamations like that in (8) as **hidden exclamatives**. The proposition conveyed by the hidden exclamative in (8) ('There is some number of inidignities') is distinct from propositions we might use to represent the speech-act force of the utterance, which in (8) is presumably the expression of surprise at the high number, etc. of indignities suffered by Ipkiss.

Thus, exclamatives and declaratives, unlike, say, questions and imperatives, express propositions. What properties distinguish exclamations from declaratives? Sadock & Zwicky (1985: 162) describe the difference between the two sentence types as follows:

Exclamations are intended to be expressive whereas declaratives are intended to be informative. Both represent a proposition as being true, but in an exclamation, the speaker emphasizes his strong emotional reaction to what he takes to be a fact, whereas in a declarative, the speaker emphasizes his intellectual appraisal that the proposition is true.

Sadock & Zwicky frame the distinction between the two sentence types as one of emphasis: the declarative emphasizes the truth of the proposition, while the exclamation emphasizes the speaker's emotional reaction to the proposition (*qua* situation). The different emphases of the two speech-act types can be described in terms of the well known semantico-pragmatic property of **presupposition**. Exclamations, unlike declaratives, presuppose that the proposition expressed is mutually known by speaker and hearer.

The presupposed proposition is one which involves a **scalar degree**. The degree itself is not mutually presupposed; the speaker purports to know it, but assumes that the hearer does not, since the speaker's purpose in exclaiming is to inform the hearer that the degree in question is extreme. Thus, the propositions which are presupposed in exclamative utterances can be represented as open propositions like 'It is hot to x degree'. The presupposed status of this open proposition is reflected in use conditions. A speaker could use (7) when the general ambient temperature is mutually known to be warm. A speaker would not be inclined to use (7) to report on the weather if neither the speaker nor the hearer know whether it is cold, hot or temperate outside.

On the view that exclamations presuppose the propositions which they express, news-reporting utterances (like *They dismissed the Paula Jones case!*) do not qualify as exclamations. Although this sentence does convey the affective stance associated with exclamations (surprise), it does not instantiate any exclamative construction. It also fails to qualify as an exclamation with respect to the scalarity criterion. However, scalarity, while a necessary condition for exclamative status, is not a sufficient one. Scalarity must be coupled with presupposition. Thus, (9) is not an exclamation on the view taken here:

(9) *It's very* HOT!

Although (9) contains a degree adverb, *very*, this degree adverb differs from anaphoric degree adverbs like *so*. As Zwicky (1995) observes, the syntactic behavior of degree adverbs of the *very*-class is systematically distinct from that of degree adverbs in the *so*-class. As shown in (10), degree adverbs of the *so*-

class have cataphoric reference in, e.g., the inverted resultative construction (10a), while degree adverbs of the *very*-class do not (10b):

(10) (a) *I almost* FAINTED, *the sun was so hot.*
    (b) **I almost* FAINTED, *the sun was very hot.*

With respect to exclamations in particular, the degree adverb *very* does not collocate with interjections (like *God!*) and matrix predicators (like *I can't believe*) which express the speaker's affective stance. This is shown in (11), where anomalous exclamations containing *very* are contrasted with well formed exclamations containing *so*.

(11) (a) ??GOD, *it's very* HOT!
    (a') GOD, *it's so* HOT!
    (b) ??*I can't* BELIEVE *it's very* HOT!
    (b') *I can't* BELIEVE *it's so* HOT!

The distinct behavior of two classes of degree adverbs finds a parallel in Italian. The anaphoric *così* is appropriate in the exclamative context (12a); the nonanaphoric *molto* is not (12b):

(12) (a) *Non ci posso credere che*
        not it can.1SG believe.INF that
        sia così imbecille.
        is.SBJ.3SG so stupid
        'I can't believe he's so stupid!'
    (b) **Non ci posso credere che*
        not it can.1SG believe.INF that
        sia molto imbecille.
        is-SBJ.3SG very stupid
        ??'I can't believe he's very stupid!'

The fact that exclamatives in English and Italian (as well as other languages to be discussed in section 4) use anaphoric degree adverbs like *so* and *così* makes sense on the assumption that the scalar proposition expressed in the exclamation is presupposed. The use of an anaphoric adverb like *so* relies upon the hearer's ability to recover the relevant scale from the context.

2.4. Speech act function

An exclamation counts as an assertion that the degree in question is higher than the speaker would generally expect. The speaker's affective stance toward the propositional content can be overtly expressed by a negated epistemic predicator like *I can't believe* or by an interjection denoting the speaker's surprised affect. However, the speaker's affective stance is not necessarily encoded at the lexico-grammatical level. For example, in (8), an isolated-NP exclamative, the speaker's affective stance is not lexically expressed. In such cases we can say that the speaker's affective stance can be inferred by the hearer from the semiotic value conventionally attached to the form employed.

3. The exclamative sentence type

In this section, we will pull together the semantic and pragmatic properties which were attributed to exclamations in section 2, while introducing an additional property, which is closely related to the presuppositional property discussed in section 2.3: **referent identifiability**. We will view these properties as defining a **sentence type** – a conventional pairing of form and function. The formal expression of this sentence type is not specified, since, as we have seen, there is a many-to-one mapping of form to function. Instead, we will posit only a constraint on realization: all semantico-pragmatic components of the exclamative sentence type receive formal expression. Certain of these components can be realized through metonymic construal (a construal associated with hidden exclamatives) or through a type of pragmatic construal similar to that found in instances of null complementation (Fillmore 1986, Kay & Fillmore 1998).

The semantico-pragmatic features shared by exclamatives are summarized in (13):

(13) (a) Presupposed open proposition (with a degree as the variable);
    (b) Expression of commitment to a particular scalar extent;
    (c) Expression of affective stance toward the scalar extent;
    (d) Person deixis (judge is the speaker by default);
    (e) Identifiability of the referent of whom the scalar property is predicated.

As stated in (13e), the entity of whom the scalar property is predicated must be identifiable. An identifiable referent is one for which a shared representation exists in the minds of speaker and hearer at speech time (Lambrecht 1994). Identifiable referents surface as definite NPs or, if activated in discourse, pronominal NPs. Notice, for example, the anomaly of the sentences in (14):

(14) (a) **What a nice cake no one ate!*
    (b) ?*I can't believe how much a guy spent!*
    (c) ??*Someone is so messy.*

The identifiability constraint exemplified in (14) can be motivated by reference to the requirement of pragmatic presupposition. If a proposition is presupposed, then its arguments are necessarily identifiable to both speaker and hearer.

4. The cross-linguistic expression of exclamative meaning

Exclamative constructions are characterized by the following formal features: co-occurrence with interjections, complementation structures involving factive epistemic matrix verbs, topic constructions, anaphoric degree adverbs, question words, NP complements, ellipsis with NPs, and inversion.

4.1. Co-occurrence with interjections

The close relationship between interjections and exclamation was brought out in section 2. Those interjections which convey surprise typically co-occur with exclamative constructions. Some of these interjections are invocations; others, like *wow* in English and *aman* in Turkish, have no recognizable source. Examples are given for English, German, French, Italian, Turkish and Mandarin:

(15) *Jesus, what a mess!*

(16) *Mein Gott, ist es heiss!*
 'My God, is it hot!'

(17) *Qu'est-ce qu'il est con, sainte vierge!*
 — Reiser, *Les Oreilles Rouges*
 'Holy virgin, what a fool he is!'

(18) *Mamma, quante ore ho speso in vano!*
 'Mamma, how many hours I have spent in vain!'

(19) Turkish
 Aman, bu ne sicak!
 INTERJ this how heat!
 'Wow, it's so hot!'

(20) Mandarin
 Nàme guì ya!
 that.much expensive INTERJ
 'Wow, so expensive!'

4.2. Subordination to factive epistemic verbs

Both Grimshaw (1979) and Milner (1978) differentiate between main-clause exclamatives, like (21), and constructions containing exclamative complements, like (22):

(21) *Qu'est-ce qui est devenu de notre ville!*
 'What's become for our city!'

(22) *C'est incroyable qu'est-ce qui est devenu de notre ville!*
 'It's incredible what has become of our city.'

As Grimshaw points out, the matrix verbs and adjectives which appear in sentences like (22), which Milner refers to as **indirect exclamatives**, are necessarily factive, i.e., they presuppose the truth of their complements. These verbs and adjectives also presuppose a norm with which the outcome or situation at issue is implicitly compared. The adjectives in this class may appear in **right-dislocation structures** like (22), in which there is a referential pronominal subject with which the postverbal clause corefers (→ Art. 80), or in **extraposition structures**, which lack a referential subject. Exclamative constructions involving extraposition are exemplified in (23–26) for English, Italian, Croatian and Palestinian Arabic, respectively:

(23) *It's amazing how much noise they make.*

(24) *È pazzesco quanto rumore fanno.*
 'It's amazing how much noise they make.'

(25) Croatian
 Za ne-vjerovati je koliko
 to NEG-believe.INF is.3SG how.much
 je potrošila.
 is.3SG spend.PAP.SG.F
 'It's unbelievable how much she spent.'

(26) Palestinian Arabic
 Mish maʕʔuul addaysh
 not reasonable how.much
 dafʕat.
 paid.3SG.F
 'It's amazing how much she paid.'

In such constructions, the matrix adjective denotes the property of causing disbelief, for the speaker and for people in general. The generic interpretation is possible because the identity of the judge is not overtly specified.

Adjectives may also appear in constructions containing a referential subject denoting the source of the noncanonicity judgement. An example is given for English in (27) and for Setswana in (28):

(27) *I'm amazed at how much time it took.*

(28) Setswana
Ke makatswa ke gore o
I amazed by that she
dirisitse bokae
used how.much
'I'm amazed at how much she spent.'

Exclamatives with cognizer subjects also commonly contain matrix predicators headed by verbs. The lexical verb is typically a negated form of the verb which means *believe*. This verb may also be accompanied by a modal element denoting ability, in which case it is the expression of ability which is negated. Examples are given in (29–34) for Italian, Turkish, Malay, German, Setswana and Mandarin:

(29) *Non ci posso credere*
Not it can.1SG believe.INF
che hai speso così tanto.
that has.3SG spent that that.much
'I can't believe that she spent that much.'

(30) Turkish
Nereye kadar yüzmüşşün ki
where extent swam.2SG EXCL
inanmtyorum
believe NEG.PRES.1SG
'I don't believe how far you swam!'

(31) Malay
Saya tak percaya siapa yang
I not believe who RM
bercakap.
spoke
'I don't believe who spoke up!'

(32) *Ich kann nicht glauben, wer sich zu Wort gemeldet hat.*
'I can't believe who spoke up.'

(33) Setswana
Ga ke dumele se re se boneng
NEG I believe RP we OM found.
'I don't believe what we found!'

(34) Mandarin
(Wǒ) jiǎnzhí bù gǎn xiāng xìn
(I) simply not dare believe
tā doū nàme dà le!
3SG even that.much big PERF
'I simply can't believe that he's so big now!'

The indirect exclamative has a strong semantico-pragmatic motivation. Since the assertion of surprise is an essential condition upon the exclamative speech act, and since no language lacks for psychological predicates denoting disbelief or the property of inducing disbelief, it is natural that languages should use such predicates in complementation structures denoting the speaker's affective stance toward a scalar proposition. The subordinating predicator merely expresses the otherwise implicit affective stance of the speaker.

4.3. Topic constructions

Lambrecht (1994) and Lambrecht & Michaelis (1998) distinguish between two kinds of **pragmatic presupposition**, which correspond to different kinds of assumptions a speaker may have concerning the addressee's state of mind at the time of an utterance: **knowledge** and **topicality** presuppositions. Knowledge presuppositions concern the assumed knowledge state of a hearer at the time of utterance; they are what linguists typically have in mind when they use the term *(pragmatic) presupposition*. They are manifested in the complements of factive verbs, in sentential subjects, in various constructions involving open propositions, in definite descriptions, etc. According to our analysis of the exclamative sentence type, the propositional content of exclamations is knowledge presupposed. Topicality presuppositions concern the assumed statuses of referents as topics of current interest in the discourse.

In accordance with Lambrecht (1994), we can define a topic as a referent (an entity or proposition) which the speaker assumes to be a relatively predictable argument of predications in the conversation. Topic constructions, like left dislocation and right dislocation, differ according to whether the referent in question is an **established topic**. Lambrecht observes that the referents of right-dislocated topic expressions, which he refers to as **antitopics**, tend to be more established as topics than those of topicalized and left-dislocated topic expressions, which, as observed by Prince (1981), are often contrastive (→ Art. 80). An important prosodic characteristic of antitopics is that they are pronounced with a low pitch accent characteristic of established topics (Pierrehumbert & Hirschberg 1990). Examples of right dislocation and left dislocation are given in (35–36). Sentence accents (high pitch accents) are marked by small caps:

(35) (a) *She's pretty SHARP, my mom.*
(b) *That's certainly a SHAME, that he's not willing to discuss it.*

(36) (a) *The FIRST one, I'm not so SURE about it.*
(b) *That there's LIABILITY, this seems OBVIOUS.*

The (a) examples involve topical entities, while the (b) examples involve topical propositions. Topical propositions, and their syntactic encoding, will be of interest to us here.

We have said that the propositional content of exclamations is knowledge presupposed. That is, e. g., an open proposition of the form 'It's hot to some degree' is taken for granted by a speaker who employs the exclamative form *It's so hot!* A knowledge presupposed proposition may be either topical or nontopical. Some exclamative constructions treat the scalar propositions which they presuppose as topical. Such exclamations often take the form of right-dislocation structures. Examples are given for French and Italian in (37–38); the resumptive pronouns are in boldface:

(37) *C'est incroyable comment elle nous traite.*
'It's incredible how she treats us.'

(38) *Non **ci** posso credere che*
Not it can.1SG believe.INF that
hai speso cosí tanto.
has.3SG spent that that.much
'I can't believe that she spent that much.'

Related to (37–38) is an English exclamative construction which, although lacking the resumptive pronoun characteristic of right dislocation, features a rightward declarative clause pronounced with the low pitch accent characteristic of antitopics. This construction, exemplified in (39), is referred to by Michaelis & Lambrecht (1996a) as the **antitopic exclamative**:

(39) (a) *GOD it's hot out there.*
(b) *My GOODNESS you're late.*

In this construction, a clause-initial interjection which denotes the epistemic stance receives the sole sentence accent. The clause following the interjection does not contain a degree adverb, but this clause must express a scalar proposition, as shown by the ill formedness of (40):

(40) *GOD *that's an even number.*

Topic expressions used to express exclamative meaning may also take the form of **unlinked topics**. Unlinked topics, described by Aissen (1992) for Tzotzil and Lambrecht (1994) for English and French, are leftward topic expressions which lack a syntactic relationship to a clause that predicates something relative to that topic. An example of an unlinked topic is given in (41):

(41) *Most cities, you can't walk alone at night.*

There is an exclamative construction of Turkish which appears to instantiate an unlinked topic construction. An example is given in (42):

(42) Turkish
Nereye kadar-yüzmüşşün ki
where extent swam.2SG EXCL
gözlerime inanmtyorum
eyes.my believe.NEG.PRES.1SG
'How far you swam! I don't believe my eyes.'

While the translation of (42) uses two separate clauses, one to express the topical proposition and the other to express the speaker's epistemic stance, the Turkish construction does not reflect this division. Instead, one can analyze the scalar proposition as an unlinked topic, and the following clause as providing additional information about this topic (i. e., expressing the speaker's attitude toward this proposition).

Exclamative constructions which invoke right-dislocated and unlinked topics are strongly motivated in terms of the exclamative sentence type, which involves knowledge presupposition of a scalar proposition. Since knowledge presupposed propositions, like identifiable entities, are often topical, it makes sense that some exclamative constructions in a language should additionally express the topic status of the proposition which they presuppose.

4.4. Anaphoric degree adverbs

We will use the general label *anaphoric* as a cover term for both cataphoric and anaphoric uses of words like *so*, on the assumption that both anaphoric and cataphoric uses involve a word whose interpretation requires the hearer to find an appropriate reference point in the conversational context. In section 2.3., we also distinguished between anaphoric degree adverbs, like *so* and *cosí*, which are generally found in exclamations, and nonanaphoric degree adverbs like *very* and *molto*, which are not involved in the expression of exclamative meaning.

Using as a diagnostic of anaphoricity the ability of a degree word to appear in anaphoric contexts like the correlative resultant-state construction exemplified in (15), we find that when languages use degree words other than question words in exclamative constructions, these are anaphoric degree words analogous to *so* (in English and German), Italian *cosi*, and French *tellement*. Examples of anaphoric degree words in exclamative contexts, and in the diagnostic resultant-state context, are given in (43–44) for Malay, in (45–46) for Croatian, and in (47–48) for Turkish:

(43) *Saya tidak percaya banyak*
    I   NEG believe much
    sangat duit dia dah guna.
    so   money s/he past use
    'I can't believe she spent so much.'

(44) *Cuaca panas sangat sampai*
    weather hot   so   until
    saya hampir pengsan.
    I   almost faint
    'It was so hot I almost fainted.'

(45) *Tako je   vruće.*
    So is.3SG hot
    'It's so hot!'

(46) *Bilo   je   tako vruće da*
    be.PAP.SG.N is.3SG so   hot   that
    sam   se   skoro onesvjestila.
    is.1SG REFL almost faint.PaP.SG.F
    'It was so hot I almost fainted.'

(47) *Öyle zenga   ki!*
    so   rich.3SG.PRES EXCL
    'He is so rich!'

(48) *Öyle zengin   ki,   yat   bile*
    so   rich.3SG.PST result yacht even
    aldi.
    buy.PST.3SG
    'He was so rich that he even bought a yacht.'

As we noted in section 2.3, the prevalence of anaphoric degree words in exclamatives can be explained on the assumption that the scalar proposition expressed in the exclamation is presupposed. If a speaker in using an exclamative construct like *He is so rich* is invoking a knowledge presupposition of the form 'He is rich to some extent', then an anaphoric degree adverb like *so* can then be used to refer to that point on a scale of wealth.

4.5. Information-question form

Perhaps the most prevalent source, cross linguistically, of degree words in exclamations is the set of question words. Sadock & Zwicky (1985) observe this tendency, and ascribe it to the fact that both exclamatives and interrogatives are nonassertoric. Given this commonality, they say, it stands to reason that the two sentence types should share formal features. However, it is not the class of interrogative constructions per se whose properties (whatever they might be) are found in exclamatives. The interrogative type which exclamations most closely resemble typologically is the information (or 'wh') question. In exclamatives like the Vietnamese example in (49), we see a structural relationship with information questions, in that an argument, determiner, or adjunct role is filled by an (in situ) question word (which is sometimes, as in Vietnamese, identical to the set of indefinites):

(49) Vietnamese
    Ở   đó   có   bao nhiêu là
    be.at there have how-many INTS
    người!
    people
    'There are so many people there!'

(50) Vietnamese
    Ở   đó   có   bao nhiêu người?
    be.at there have how-many people
    'How many people are there?'

While (49–50) show that exclamatives and information questions may look alike, constructions which instantiate the two sentence types have distinct formal markings. For example, nonsubject information questions feature subject-auxiliary inversion in English, while *wh*-exclamatives lack inversion. Intonational distinctions between exclamations and information questions are also obvious in English, where question-word exclamations feature a tune distinct from the H* L L% pattern which Pierrehumbert & Hirschberg (1990) identify with declaratives and *wh*-questions. Exclamations are also characterized by exclamative markers, like the intensifying postmodifier *là* in Vietnamese (exemplified in (49)), and the postclausal exclamative particle *ki* in Turkish, exemplified in (47). Further, the syntactic behavior of question words may differ in the two classes of constructions. In English, e.g., the modifier *what* may precede an indefinite NP in an exclamative (*What a sad story!*) but not in an information question (**What a sad story did you read?*). Hence, while exclamations may owe aspects of their form to information questions, their formal properties are determined by exclamative constructions.

The idiomatic nature of question-form exclamations is also evident when we look at their **external syntax and semantics** (i.e., their behavior as complements). Milner's label *indirect exclamative* suggests an analogy between exclamative complement clauses and indirect questions — an analogy which appears to have been overstated. An indirect question, as in the boldfaced portion of (51), does not have the illocutionary force of the corresponding direct question. Sentence (51) is a declarative, and not a question. By contrast, an indirect exclamative, as in the boldfaced portion of (52), has the same force that its complement clause would if it were used as a matrix exclamative. Both (52) and its complement clause count as exclamations:

(51)   *I know **who left**.*

(52)   *I can't believe **how few people really care**.*

Why does the complement of (52) represent the same kind of speech act as (52)? The answer is straightforward when we recall that aspects of the exclamative speech-act scenario (like the source of the noncanonicity judgement) may be recovered pragmatically rather than directly encoded. Matrix exclamatives, such as question-form exclamatives and anaphoric degree exclamations, require the interpreter to recover the affective stance appropriate to the semantico-pragmatic model which these constructions instantiate: the exclamative sentence type.

One puzzle that arises here is the following. As Elliott (1974: 236–237) and McCawley (1988: 717) have observed, not all question-form exclamatives which serve as indirect exclamatives are equally able to serve as matrix exclamatives. In English, the only indirect exclamatives which correspond to well-formed matrix exclamatives are *wh*-clauses introduced by the degree word *how*. Other *wh*-clauses cannot stand alone as matrix exclamatives. Well-formed indirect exclamatives are given in the (a)-sentences of (53–55), with corresponding anomalous matrix exclamatives in the (b)-sentences:

(53)   (a) *You won't believe who they hired.*
        (b) *?Who they hired!*

(54)   (a) *I can't believe where they go!*
        (b) *?Where they go!*

(55)   (a) *I'm amazed at what we found.*
        (b) *?What we found!*

One likely source of the grammaticality facts evidenced in (53–55) is this: the *wh*-complements in these examples do not intrinsically invoke a property scale. The person uttering (53a) invokes a presupposed proposition 'They hired someone'. This proposition does not obviously evoke a scale. Nevertheless, the sentence is not easily taken to mean: 'They hired a certain person, and this surprises me'. Instead, the sentence does seem to evoke a scale. In accordance with Fillmore & Kay & O'Connor 1988, we assume that individuals are assigned positions on scales. Sentence (53a) presupposes or rather creates the presupposition that the person hired deserves to be ranked on the scale of incompetence. The sentence asserts that this ranking is remarkably high. The fact that (53a) can be construed as presupposing a propositional function of the form 'The person they hired is at some point on the incompetence scale' is a fact about constructional meaning, and the way in which constructions can impose meaning on their lexico-grammatical 'fillers': the *wh*-clause receives the appropriate scalar interpretation only in the context of the indirect-exclamative construction. When used as a matrix exclamation, as in (53b), the *wh*-clause lacks the syntactic context needed to force the scalar interpretation.

How-clauses in English are unique not only in their ability to serve as matrix exclamatives, but also in their ability to yield a **committed** reading (Cruse 1986) in nonexclamative factive contexts like (56):

(56)   *I realize how hard you tried.* (→ you tried hard)

Other *wh*-clauses, like *Where you are*, since they do not evoke a scale, cannot be said to be commited with regard to a scalar degree in factive contexts (like *I realize where you are*). Hence, in English, the ability to yield a commited reading in factive contexts may be the property which enables *how* clauses to serve as matrix exclamatives.

The constraint exemplified in (53–55) is not universal. There are languages which allow matrix exclamatives like those in the (b)-sentences of (53–55). As shown in (57), Italian is among these languages, as is Turkish, as shown in (58–59):

(57)   *Dove si   arrampicano, questi*
        Where they climb.3PL   these
        ragazzi!
        boys
        'The places they climb, these boys!'

(58) Turkish
Kimleri   gördük,   (kim)!
who.PL.OBJ saw.PST.1PL who
'The people we saw!'

(59) Turkish
Neler   bulduk,   (neler)!
what.PL   find.PST.1PL. what.PL
'The things we found!'

The English translations of (57–59) employ definite NPs, and thus represent hidden exclamatives of the type to be discussed in sections 4.6.–4.7.

The widespread use of question forms in exclamations, both direct and indirect, has a straightforward semantico-pragmatic basis. It has long been maintained by a variety of scholars that an information question presupposes a propositional function in which the argument, adjunct or modifier encoded by the question words is represented as a variable (Jackendoff 1972, Prince 1986, Rooth 1992, Raymond & Homer 1996, Lambrecht 1994, Lambrecht & Michaelis 1998). Thus, for example, the open proposition presupposed by (60a) is (60b):

(60) (a) *How much did he spend?*
(b) He spent x amount

As we have seen in sections 2 and 3, it is reasonable to propose that an exclamation of the form *I can't believe how much he spent* or *How much he spent!* also presupposes (60b). Exclamations and questions differ with regard to what is asserted. In using (60a), the speaker asserts the desire to know where the spending ranks on a numerical scale (Lambrecht & Michaelis 1998). In using an exclamative like *How much he spent!*, the speaker asserts that the spending ranks high on that numerical scale. However, both speech acts have the same pragmatic starting point: the speaker takes for granted, and presumes that the hearer is willing to take for granted, the proposition in (60b).

Since exclamations and information questions have identical presuppositional structure, it makes sense that this shared pragmatic feature should be reflected in a formal overlap between these two sentence types.

4.6. NP Complements

The tendency to use hidden exclamatives as exclamative complements is widespread. Examples are given for English, French, Italian, German, Setswana and Turkish in (99–104), respectively:

(61) *Everyone's afraid that the next cutback will involve them. You wouldn't believe the bickering that goes on!*
— 'For Better or for Worse' 8/5/94

(62) *C'est incroyable le bruit qu'ils font.*
'It's incredible the noise they make.'

(63) *È pazzesco il rumore che fanno.*
'It's incredible the noise they make.'

(64) *Unfassbar, der Krach, den sie machen.*
'Unimaginable, the noise that they make.'

(65) Swetswana
Ga ke dumele ka moo a
NEG I believe CLF way she
dirisang   madi ka teng
uses.PROG   money PRT PRT
'I don't believe the way she spends money.'

(66) Turkish
Yaptıklari   gürültü
make.PST.RP.PL.OBJ noise.OBJ
inanmtyorum!
believe.NEG.PRS.1SG
'I can't believe the noise they make.'

Each of these NP complements is readily translatable by a question-form complement introduced by *how much*. It is not, e.g., the noise itself that engenders disbelief, but the duration or amplitude of the noise. Hence, Michaelis & Lambrecht (1996a, 1996b) claim that these NPs refer metonymically to a point on a scale. The metonymic target is often indeterminate, since a sentence like *I can't believe the people you know* may be used to invoke the number, the variety, or the peculiarity of the people in question. In typically requiring context for recovery of the appropriate scale, hidden-exclamative complements resemble question-form complements like that in (53a), which require the hearer to invoke an appropriate scale on which to rank the person in question.

An interpretively vague nominal head which frequently appears in hidden exclamatives is one denoting manner, as in the Setswana sentence (65), or the English sentence in (67):

(67)   *I can't believe the way they treat us.*

The hidden exclamative in (67) has the same indeterminacy as the question-form complement in (68):

(68)   *I can't believe how she treats us.*

Both (67) and (68) are indeterminate as to whether the relevant scale for treatment is cruelty, condescension, etc.

The use of a NP to denote a scalar degree is motivated in terms of semantico-pragmatic properties of the exclamative sentence type. The proposition presupposed by an exclamation refers to a scalar extent. A scalar extent is something which can be indexed, as we noted in the discussion of anaphoric degree expressions in section 4.4. Something which can be indexed counts as referential, i.e., as an entity. Since nouns prototypically refer to entities (Croft 1990: 64−154), it stands to reason that a noun should be used to refer to a scalar extent in a construction which serves to comment on that extent.

The particular use of *definite* NPs in exclamative contexts (in those languages which express definiteness) can be motivated by reference to the presupposed status of the open proposition denoted by the NP. If a sentence like (61) presupposes a proposition like 'There is some degree of bickering', then this degree is also mutually identifiable to speaker and hearer. The claim that factivity motivates the definiteness of hidden exclamatives is substantiated by the use of definite NPs in nonexclamative factive contexts, as in (69):

(69)   *I regret the trouble we caused.*

Since it contains a factive matrix verb, sentence (69) can be seen as presupposing a proposition of the form 'We caused some degree of trouble'. The presupposed status of this proposition can then also be seen as rendering this degree identifiable. Referent identifiability has already been mentioned as a semantico-pragmatic constraint on exclamatory statements (13e). The statement in (13e) pertained to the entities of which scalar properties, like that of spending a large amount of money, are predicated. In this section, however, we see that identifiability is a property that we can use to characterize two referents in an exclamation: the described entity and the degree. Insofar as this is the case, exclamations are double predications: they not only predicate a scalar property of a given referent, but also predicate a property (that of violating expectation) of a degree.

4.7. Free NPs

The exclamative use of a free NP is exemplified in (8) for English. The free-NP type of exclamation is exemplified for French, German, Turkish, Setswana and Korean in (70−74):

(70)   *Le bruit qu'ils font!*
         'The noise they make!'

(71)   *Der Krach, den manche Leute machen!*
         'The noise that some people make!'

(72)   Turkish
         Gittikleri   yerler!
         go.PST.RP.PL.OBJ place.PL
         'The places they go!'

(73)   Setswana
         Mo.dumo   o   ba o dirang!
         CLF.noise RP   they OM make.PROG
         'The noise they make!'

(74)   Korean
         Ah,   cheo sori!
         INTERJ the sound
         'The noise!'

While English and German generally require that isolated-NP exclamatives contain a relative clause, French does not, as seen in the following attested example:

(75)   [Child looking at a man's large stomach.] ***Le bide!*** [...] *Le gros bide comme ça!* [gestures]. [...] *Le plus gros bide de l'année.*
         − Reiser, *Les Oreilles Rouges*
         'The stomach [on this guy]! A stomach like *this*! [gestures] The biggest stomach of the year!'

The motivation for the exclamative use of free NPs is the same as that brought out in the discussion of matrix exclamations which contain question words and anaphoric degree words. Exclamative constructions, like other expressive forms, need not overtly specify the speaker's affective stance toward the content encoded. This stance can be inferred from the speaker's choice of an exclamative form.

4.8. Inversion

A minor pattern instantiated by matrix exclamative constructions is the inversion of subject and finite verb, discussed by McCawley (1973) for English and exemplified for English and German in (76−77), respectively:

(76)   *The narrative is pretty jerky, but, man, can this kid direct second unit!*
         − *Time* 5/19/97

(77)   *Hast du Glück gehabt!*
         'Did you luck out!'

Both McCawley (1988) and Sadock & Zwicky (1985) have related the use of inversion here to the use of inversion in interrogative contexts. The use of the inversion pattern in both interrogative and exclamative contexts is motivated for these theorists insofar as both of these sentence types express nondeclarative speech acts. If we focus only on the use of inversion in **yes-no questions**, the adduced motivation seems valid: only yes-no questions share with inversion exclamatives the property of using inversion as the sole syntactic feature which marks a deviation from declarative syntax. Yes-no questions deviate from the declarative prototype in that their content is not asserted. Similarly, exclamatives, as discussed in section 2, do not assert their propositional content, but rather presuppose it.

5. Conclusion

As Bybee & Perkins & Pagliuca (1995: 3) argue, explanation in linguistics requires one not merely to describe the functions associated with a given construction, but also to address the question of why that form has the functions it does. This question can be answered in both a synchronic model, which concerns the way in which grammatical structures are motivated via relations of association (formal and semantic overlap), and a diachronic model, which concerns patterns in the semantic extension of forms. This typological survey has shown that exclamations are characterized across languages by several recurrent formal features – most saliently, the presence of information-question forms and anaphoric degree adverbs. Appeal to semantico-pragmatic features of the exclamative sentence type has enabled us to show why these grammatical forms are used to express noncanonicity judgements which involve semantic scales.

6. References

Aissen, Judith. 1992. "Topic and focus in Mayan". *Languages* 60: 48–80.

Austin, John L. 1962. *How to do things with words.* Oxford: Clarendon Press.

Bybee, Joan & Perkins, Revere & Pagliuca, William. 1994. *The evolution of grammar: Tense, aspect and modality in the languages of the world.* Chicago: Chicago University Press.

Croft, William. 1990. *Typology and universals.* Cambridge: Cambridge University Press.

Cruse, D. A. 1986. *Lexical semantics.* Cambridge: Cambridge University Press.

Ehlich, Konrad. 1986. *Interjektionen.* Tübingen: Niemeyer.

Elliott, Dale E. 1974. "Toward a grammar of exclamations". *Foundations of Language* 11: 231–46.

Fillmore, Charles. 1982. "Toward a descriptive framework for spatial deixis". In: Jarvella, Robert J. & Klein, Wolfgang (eds.). *Speech, place and action.* London: Wiley, 31–59.

–. 1986. "Pragmatically controlled zero anaphora". *Berkeley Linguistics Society* 12: 95–107.

Fillmore, Charles & Kay, Paul & O'Connor, Mary C. 1988. "Regularity and idiomaticity in grammatical constructions". *Language* 64: 501–538.

Geis, Michael L. 1995. *Speech acts and conversational interaction.* Cambridge: Cambridge University Press.

Goldberg, Adele. 1995. *Constructions: A construction grammar approach to argument structure.* Chicago: University of Chicago Press.

Grimshaw, Jane. 1979. "Complement selection and the lexicon". *Linguistic Inquiry* 10: 279–326.

Hoeksema, Jacob & Napoli, Donna Jo. 1993. "Paratactic and subordinative *so*". *Journal of Linguistics* 29: 391–314.

Jackendoff, Ray. 1972. *Semantic interpretation in generative grammar.* Cambridge, MA: MIT Press.

Kay, Paul & Fillmore, Charles. 1998. *Construction grammar.* Stanford: Stanford University Press.

Lambrecht, Knud. 1994. *Information structure and sentence form.* Cambridge: Cambridge University Press.

–. 1996. "On the formal and functional relationship between topics and vocatives: Evidence from French". In: Goldberg, Adele (ed.). *Conceptual structure, discourse and language.* Stanford: CSLI, 267–288.

– & Michaelis, Laura. 1998. "On sentence accent in information questions". *Linguistics and Philosophy* 21: 477–544.

Makkai, Adam. 1985. "Where do exclamations come from?" In: Makkai, Adam & Melby, Alan K. (eds.). *Linguistics and philosophy: essays in honor of Rulon S. Wells.* Amsterdam: Benjamins, 445–472.

McCawley, James D. 1988. *The syntactic phenomena of English*, 2. Chicago: University of Chicago Press.

McCawley, Noriko, 1973. "Boy, is syntax easy!" *Chicago Linguistics Society* 9: 369–377.

Michaelis, Laura. 1994a. "A case of constructional polysemy in Latin". *Studies in Language* 18: 45–70.

Michaelis, Laura. 1994b. "Expectation contravention and use ambiguity: The Vietnamese connective *cũng*". *Journal of Pragmatics* 21: 1–36.

Michaelis, Laura & Lambrecht, Knud. 1996a. "Toward a construction-based model of language function: The case of nominal extraposition". *Language* 72: 215–247.

—. 1996b. "The exclamative sentence type in English". In: Goldberg, Adele (ed.). *Conceptual structure, discourse and language*. Stanford: CSLI, 375–390.

Milner, Jean-Claude. 1978. *De la syntaxe à l'interpretation*. Paris: Seuil.

Morel, Mary-Annick. 1995. "L'Intonation exclamative dans l'oral spontane". *Faits de Langues* 6: 63–70.

Pierrehumbert, Janet B. & Hirschberg, Julia. 1990. "The meaning of intonational contours in the interpretation of discourse". In: Cohen, Philip & Morgan, Jerrold & Pollack, Martha (eds.). *Intentions in communication*. Cambridge, MA: MIT Press, 271–311.

Prince, Ellen. 1981. "Topicalization, focus movement and Yiddish movement: A pragmatic differentiation". *Berkeley Linguistics Society* 7: 249–264.

Prince, Ellen. 1986. "On the syntactic marking of presupposed open propositions". *Chicago Linguistics Society* 22: 208–222.

Raymond, William R. & Homer, Kristin. 1996. "The interaction of pragmatic roles and thematic structure in the selection of question form". *Berkeley Linguistics Society* 22: 316–327.

Rooth, Mats. 1992. "A theory of focus interpretation". *Natural Language Semantics* 1: 75–116.

Sadock, Jerrold, & Zwicky, Arnold. 1985. "Speech act distinctions in syntax". In: Shopen, Timothy (ed.). *Language typology and syntactic description*, 1. Cambridge: Cambridge University Press, 155–196.

Searle, John R. 1979. *Expression and meaning*. Cambridge: Cambridge University Press.

Slobin, Dan & Aksu, Ayhan. 1982. "Tense, aspect and modality in the use of the Turkish evidential". In: Hopper, Paul J. (ed.). *Tense aspect: Between semantics and pragmatics*. Amsterdam: Benjamins, 185–200.

Zwicky, Arnold. 1995. "Exceptional degree markers: A puzzle in internal and external syntax". *Ohio State University working papers in linguistics* 47: 111–23.

Laura A. Michaelis, University of Colorado, Boulder (USA)

80. Dislocation

1. Definition and terminology
2. Dislocation and superficially similar constructions
3. The structure of dislocation sentences
4. The grammatical status of dislocated constituents
5. Discourse functions of Left-Dislocation and Right-Dislocation
6. Special abbreviations
7. References

1. Definition and terminology

A **dislocation** construction (also called **detachment** construction) is a sentence structure in which a referential constituent which could function as an argument or adjunct within a predicate-argument structure occurs instead outside the boundaries of the clause containing the predicate, either to its left (**left-dislocation**, henceforth **LD**) or to its right (**right-dislocation**, henceforth **RD**). The role of the denotatum of the dislocated constituent as an argument or adjunct of the predicate is represented within the clause by a pronominal element which is construed as coreferential with the dislocated phrase. Typically, the dislocated phrase is marked with special prosodic features.

The above definition involves four criteria: (i) extra-clausal position of a constituent, (ii) possible alternative intra-clausal position, (iii) pronominal coindexation, (iv) special prosody. These four criteria apply in prototypical instances. However, there are many instances in which one or more of them fail to apply. Only criterion (i) is a necessary (though not sufficient) condition for a sentence construction to qualify as an instance of dislocation. Our definition will be modified as we go along.

Examples (1a) and (2a) are attested instances of LD and RD in English, followed by their canonical (i.e. non-dislocated) counterparts in (1b) and (2b). The dislocated constituents are enclosed in square brackets, for easy recognition. The coreference relation between the dislocated constituent and the intraclausal pronominal element is indicated by subscripts. Following a common orthographic practice, the clause boundary is signalled by a comma; this comma does not indicate a pause. The small capitals indicate the location of the main sentence accent, or **focus accent**:

(1) LEFT-DISLOCATION:
 (a) *[That Chris]$_i$, he$_i$ sleeps* LATE, *yeah.*
 (b) *That Chris sleeps* LATE, *yeah.*

(2) RIGHT-DISLOCATION:
 (a) *She$_i$'s a smart* COOKIE, *[that Diana]$_i$.*
 (Ward & Birner 1996)
 (b) *That Diana is a smart* COOKIE.

The left-dislocated — but not the right-dislocated — constituent may also be prosodically prominent, a possibility which we ignore for the moment. Dislocation sentences have the same semantic structure, or the same truth conditions, as their canonical counterparts; however, they are subject to different appropriateness conditions, i.e. they do not appear in the same discourse environments.

The basic structure of LD and RD sentences is represented in (3), where XP is the dislocated constituent and pro the anaphoric or cataphoric pronominal element; as before, subscripts indicate the coreference relation between this pronominal element and the dislocated XP:

(3)
LEFT-DISLOCATION: XP$_i$ $_S$[... pro$_i$ ...]
RIGHT-DISLOCATION: $_S$[... pro$_i$ ...] XP$_i$

(A more complete representation will be provided in § 4.2.6.) The pro$_i$ element in (3) is often referred to as "resumptive" pronoun in the literature. In the present analysis, it will be called **pronominal**. The pronominal can be a syntactically free personal pronoun, a syntactically bound atonic pronominal morpheme (a so-called "clitic"), an inflectional affix, or a null element (→ Art. 56). Under certain conditions, the pronominal can also be a possessive pronoun or affix (cf. items (41) and (42)).

Item (4) contains an RD sentence from a popular French comic book (*Astérix*), followed by its English, German, Russian, Italian, and Turkish equivalents:

(4) (a) *Ils$_i$ sont fous, [ces Romains]$_i$.*
 they are crazy these Romans
 (b) *They$_i$ are crazy, [these Romans]$_i$.*
 (c) *Die$_i$ spinnen, [diese Römer]$_i$.*
 they are.crazy these Romans
 (d) *Oni$_i$ s uma sošli, [èti Rimljane]$_i$.*
 they of mind went these Romans
 (e) *Son-o$_i$ pazzi, [questi Romani]$_i$.*
 be-3.PL crazy these Romans.

(f) *ø$_i$ deli, [bu Romi-lar]$_i$.*
 crazy these Roman-PL

In (4a), the pronominal is a bound atonic pronoun; in (b), (c), (d) it is a free pronoun; in (e) it is an inflectional suffix; and in (f) it is phonologically unrealized. (5) contains the corresponding LD sentences (the demonstrative determiner is changed into the definite article for reasons of naturalness):

(5) (a) *[Les Romains]$_i$, ils$_i$ sont fous.*
 (b) *[The Romans]$_i$, they$_i$ are crazy.*
 (c) *[Die Römer]$_i$, die$_i$ spinnen.*
 (d) *[Rimljane]$_i$, oni$_i$ s uma sošli.*
 (e) *[I Romani]$_i$, son-o$_i$ pazz-i.*
 (f) *[Romi-lar]$_i$, ø$_i$ deli.*

The structural similarity among the sentences in (4) and (5) is evident. As we will see, dislocation constructions can be identified in most, if not all, languages of the world, independently of language type and genetic affiliation.

The present analysis assumes a monostratal, i.e. non-transformational, syntactic framework, of the type represented by Lexical-Functional Grammar (LFG), Head-driven Phrase Structure Grammar (HPSG), Construction Grammar (CG), or Role and Reference Grammar (RRG). Dislocation structures will thus not be analyzed as involving movement of a constituent from a basic (canonical) to a derived (dislocated) position. Consequently, the analysis will not appeal to "empty categories" or "traces". The term *dislocation*, which suggests syntactic movement, is used for convenience only. Instead of *dislocation* (or *detachment*), various alternative terms have been used in the literature. The left-dislocated constituent has been referred to as "theme" (Dik 1980, Moutaouakil 1989), "topic" (Lambrecht 1981, 1994), "link" (Vallduví 1992), and for certain instances "nominativus pendens" (classical grammar). The right-dislocated constituent has been called "tail" (Dik 1978, Moutaouakil 1989, Vallduví 1992), "antitopic" (Chafe 1976, Lambrecht 1981, 1994), "post-predicate constituent" (Erguvanli 1984), "mubtada? mu?ahhar" (Arabic grammar), and "defocused NP". These terms are generally used to refer both to the position and to the function of the dislocated constituent. To refer to dislocation as a type of construction we find the traditional terms "epexegesis" (classical grammar), "inverted word order" (Chinese grammar, cf. Chao 1978), "devrik cümle" (Turkish grammar), and

"Loslösung" (Paul 1920). In the present analysis, left-dislocated and right-dislocated constituents will be labelled **TOP** (topic, following Chomsky 1977) and **ANTITOP** (antitopic) constituents respectively. The syntactic position or slot in which these constituents occur will be referred to as **TOP position** and **ANTITOP position**.

2. Dislocation and superficially similar constructions

LD must be distinguished from the so-called **Topicalization** construction. Topicalization resembles LD in that it involves a referential constituent in non-canonical initial position. But while in LD this constituent occurs in the extra-clausal TOP position, the "topicalized" phrase occurs in the so-called pre-clausal COMP (complementizer) or WH-position, where it preserves its syntactic and semantic role as a complement of the verb (→ Art. 104). The English sentence in (6b) and its German equivalent in (7b) are instances of Topicalization; the topicalized NP is in square brackets and the underlined "gap" indicates the position which the NP would occupy in the corresponding canonical sentence (cf. (6a) and (7a)). (6c) and (7c) contain the corresponding LD sentences:

(6) (a) *I saw [this movie] when I was a kid.*
 (b) *[This movie] I saw __ when I was a kid.*
 (c) *[This movie]$_i$, I saw it$_i$ when I was a kid.*

(7) (a) *Ich sah [diesen Film], als ich*
    I saw this.ACC film when I
    ein Kind war.
    a child was
 (b) *[Diesen Film] sah ich __, als*
    this.ACC film saw I when
    ich ein Kind war.
    I a child was
 (c) *[Diesen Film]$_i$, den$_i$ sah ich,*
    this.ACC film it.ACC saw I
    als ich ein Kind war.
    when I a child was

In languages which do not freely permit the null-instantiation of definite direct objects, like English or German, the difference between LD and Topicalization is reflected in the fact that a dislocated element can always be omitted without causing structural ill-formedness of the remaining sentence while a topicalized phrase cannot. Compare the (b) and (c) sentences in (6) and (7) with those in (6′) and (7′), where the bracketed constituents have been omitted:

(6′)(b) **I saw __ when I was a kid.*
  (c) *I saw it when I was a kid.*

(7′)(b) **Ich sah __, als ich ein Kind war.*
  (c) *Den sah ich, als ich ein Kind war.*

In German, the positional difference between a topicalized and a TOP NP is indicated also by the position of the finite verb. It is well-known that in German main clauses the finite verb occupies the second constituent position (the so-called V-2 constraint). The fact that the verb immediately follows the topicalized NP in (7b) is therefore evidence that this NP is the first constituent in the clause; and the fact that the TOP NP in (7c) is followed by a constituent other than the verb shows that it must be external to the clause.

That a topicalized constituent does not occur in the same syntactic position as a TOP constituent is further demonstrated by the (b) sentences in (6″) and (7″), in which the topicalized element has been extracted out of an adverbial clause:

(6″)(a) *When I saw [this movie] I was a kid.*
  (b) **[This movie], when I saw __ I was a kid.*
  (c) *[This movie]$_i$, when I saw it$_i$ I was a kid.*

(7″)(a) *Als ich [diesen Film] sah, war ich ein Kind.*
  (b) **[Diesen Film], als ich __ sah, war ich ein Kind.*
  (c) *[Dieser Film]$_i$, als ich den$_i$ sah, war ich ein Kind.*

(For the difference in case marking between *diesen Film* and *dieser Film* in (7″) see § 4.2.3.). The Topicalization structures are ungrammatical because the COMP position in which the topicalized NP must occur is filled with the WH-word *when* (*als*), thus preventing the topicalized NP from functioning as the object of the verb *see*. The LD structures, on the other hand, are grammatical because the object requirement of the verb is satisfied by the pronominal argument, the dislocated NP occurring in TOP position, which precedesd the COMP slot.

Another sentence type with which LD should not be confused is the so-called **Focus-Movement** (or **Focus-Preposing**) construction (see Prince 1981, Ward 1988 for English, Stempel 1981 for French; → Art. 46, 81). Attested examples are given in (8). Small caps indicate the fronted focal constituent. As in (6) and (7), the "gap" indicates the position which the focussed NP would occupy in the corresponding canonical sentence:

(8) (a) FIFTY SIX HUNDRED DOLLARS *we raised __ yesterday.*
  (b) French (Stempel 1981)
   L'AMOUR *elle appelle ça __.*
   'LOVE she calls it.'
  (c) Spanish (Silva-Corvalán 1983)
   SEIS PUNTOS *me hicieron __!*
   'SIX STITCHES they gave me!'
  (d) Finnish (Vilkuna 1989)
   TÄMÄN *minä otan __.*
   this.ACC I take
   'THIS I take.'

Focus-Movement resembles Topicalization (and differs from LD) syntactically in that the initial constituent occurs in COMP position, hence functions as a complement of the verb. However, it differs from Topicalization prosodically, in that the initial constituent is necessarily the sole point of prosodic prominence in the sentence (marking the proposition minus the fronted object as discourse-active and pragmatically presupposed). Moreover, unlike Topicalization, a Focus-Movement sentence cannot be converted into LD by filling the "gap" with its ungrammatical counterpart in (8'a):

(8') (a) *fifty six hundred dollars we raised them yesterday.*

Pragmatically, focus-movement differs both from Topicalization and from LD in that the initial constituent does not have a topic but a focus relation to the proposition.

Just as LD must be distinguished from Topicalization and Focus-Movement, RD must be distinguished from the so-called **Clitic-Doubling** construction, in which a subject or object argument is represented within the same predicate-argument structure both by an atonic pronominal and a tonic lexical or pronominal NP. Compare the Spanish and French clitic-doubling sentences in (9a) and (10a) and their RD counterparts in (9b) and (10b):

(9) (a) *Le di un beso a* MARÍA.
   to.her I.gave a kiss to Maria.
   'I gave a kiss to MARIA.'
  (b) *Le$_i$ di un* BESO, *[a María]$_i$.*
   'I gave her a KISS, Maria. / I gave Maria a KISS.'

(10) (a) *Elle est venue* ELLE.
   she is come she
   'SHE came.'
  (b) *Elle$_i$ est* VENUE, *[elle]$_i$.*
   'She CAME (her).'

The (a) sentences differ from their RD counterparts in that the relevant NP occurs in argument position and has a focus relation to the proposition, hence is necessarily accented (Lambrecht 1994, and → Art. 81). For example (9a) could serve as a reply to the question "Who did you give a kiss?", and (10a) could answer the question "Who came?" In contrast, (9b) and (10b) could not answer these WH-questions (cf. § 5.1.). In the RD sentences, the right clause boundary is indicated by the focus accent and the ANTITOP constituents are marked as non-focal via deaccentuation.

Related to Clitic-Doubling is the so-called **Extraposition** construction, in which a subject or object constituent is "extraposed" to the end of the clause while its canonical argument position is filled by a dummy pronominal element like English *it*. The extraposed constituent is typically a complement clause, as in (11) (a) and (b), but it can also be an indirect interrogative, as in (c), or even a nominal, as in the so-called "Nominal Extraposition" construction in (d) (Michaelis & Lambrecht 1996; → Art. 79); the extraposed constituents are bracketed:

(11) (a) *It surprises me [that she is still* HUNGRY*].*
  (b) *I find it surprising [that she is still* HUNGRY*].*
  (c) *It doesn't make any difference [what we* SAY*].*
  (d) *It's amazing [the* DIFFERENCE*]!*

Like Clitic-Doubling, Extraposition differs crucially from RD in that the extraposed constituent is an intra-clausal argument, which has a focus rather than topic relation to the proposition, hence is necessarily accented. The difference is shown also in the fact that the Extraposition sentences do not have LD counterparts. Compare e. g. (11a/b) with the ungrammatical versions in (11'):

(11') (a) **[That she is still hungry], it surprises me.*
  (b) **[That she is still hungry], I find it surprising.*

If the sentences in (11) were instances of RD, we would expect the corresponding LD sentences in (11') to be grammatical.

Finally, RD must be distinguished from certain **subject-inversion** constructions in which a subject occurs at the end rather than the beginning of a clause. Compare the Italian and French inversion sentences in (12a) and (13a) with the superficially similar RD sentences in (12b) and (13b):

(12) (a) *È$_i$ arrivata$_i$* MARIA$_i$.
is arrived.FEM Maria
'MARIA arrived.'

(b) *E$_i$ ARRIVATA$_i$, [Maria]$_i$.*
'She ARRIVED, Maria.'

(13) (a) *Il est arrivé deux* FEMMES.
it is arrived two women
'Two WOMEN arrived. / There arrived two WOMEN.'

(b) *Elles$_i$ sont* ARRIVÉES,
they.FEM are arrived.FEM.PL
[les deux femmes]$_i$
the two women
'They ARRIVED, the two women.'

As with Extraposition, in the inversion structures in (12a) and (13a) the inverted subject is necessarily accented, while in the RD structures in (12b) and (13b) it is necessarily unaccented (cf. 5.2.). While the Italian sentences differ only prosodically from each other, the French sentences differ both prosodically and morphosyntactically. In the inversion sentence in (13a), the subject pronoun is the neuter *il* (relating this construction to Extraposition), which does not trigger agreement on the past participle. In the RD sentence (13b), however, the pronominal is fully referential and does trigger both gender and number agreement.

3. The structure of dislocation sentences

3.1. Grammatical functions of the pronominal

The coindexed pronominals in dislocation sentences can have various grammatical functions. Most commonly they are **subjects**, as in (14) and (15):

(14) Norwegian (Fretheim 1995)
Han$_i$ bare lo, [ambassadøren]$_i$
'He just laughed, the ambassador.'

(15) Indonesian (Li & Thompson 1976)
[Ibu anak itu]$_i$, dia$_i$ membeli
mother child that she buy
sepatu.
shoe
'That child's mother, she bought shoes.'

In the Finnish example (16), what would be a subject in English appears in the adessive case triggered by the predicate *be* ("x BE-AT y" corresponding semantically to "y HAVE x"):

(16) Finnish (Vilkuna 1989)
***Sillä$_i$** ei ole kotia, [sillä*
it.ADE not is home.PAR it.ADE
ihmisellä]$_i$
person.ADE
'She has no home, that person.'

Sentences in which the dislocated element is coindexed with an **object** pronominal were given in (6c) and (7c) above. (17) contains further (attested) English examples, involving a direct object and an object of a preposition, respectively; (18) shows their (slightly modified) RD counterparts:

(17) (a) *Well, [this one book]$_i$, I read it$_i$ when I was a* KID. (Prince 1984)
(b) *[That hailstorm we had the other week]$_i$, I was the only one* PREPARED *for it$_i$.*

(18) (a) *I read it$_i$ when I was a* KID, *[this book]$_i$.*
(b) *I was the only one* PREPARED *for it$_i$ [that hailstorm]$_i$.*

Concerning RD examples like those in (18), it should be observed that languages like English often prefer to leave the relevant NPs **in situ** and to mark their special pragmatic status by **deaccenting** (Ladd 1978) them. Thus in the absence of discourse context, English speakers often prefer canonical sentences with deaccented object NPs to their dislocated counterparts. Compare the RD sentences in (18) with the canonical versions in (18'):

(18') (a) *I read [this book] when I was a* KID.
(b) *I was the only one* PREPARED *for [that hailstorm].*

In languages with flexible sentence accent (like English or German) deaccentuation often has the function served by syntactic detachment in other languages (cf. Lambrecht 1994, Vallduví 1995). In the English translations of RD examples from other languages we will therefore sometimes use structures with non-dislocated deaccented object constituents, for reasons of naturalness.

The Russian, Hebrew, and Spanish sentences in (19) through (21) are further examples of RD and LD involving direct-object pronominals:

(19) Ja ne ljublju ix$_i$,
I not like them.ACC
[policejskix]$_i$.
cops.ACC
'I don't LIKE (them,) the cops.'

(20) Ani lo ohev otam$_i$, [et
I not like them.ACC DO
ha-šotrim]$_i$.
the-cops
'I don't LIKE (them,) the cops.'

(21) (Silva-Corvalán, 1983)
Porque [esa monja]$_i$, la$_i$
because that nun her.ACC
adorabamos.
we.adored.
'Because that nun, we ADORED her.'

The coindexed pronominal may also be an **oblique object**, as in the Catalan and French RD and LD sentences in (22) and (23), involving locative complements:

(22) Catalan (Valldduví 1995)
(a) Hi$_i$ ficarem el GANIVET,
there we.will.put the knife
[al calaix]$_i$.
in.the drawer
'We will put the KNIFE (there,) in the drawer.'
(b) [Al calaix]$_i$, hi$_i$ ficarem el GANIVET.
'(In) the drawer, we'll put the KNIFE there.'

(23) French (Lambrecht 1981)
(a) Il faut y$_i$ aller quand il
it is.necessary there to.go when it
fait chaud, [à la plage]$_i$.
makes warm, to the beach
'You gotta go to the beach when it's WARM.'
(b) [La plage]$_i$, il faut y$_i$ aller quand il fait chaud.
'The beach, you gotta go there when it's WARM.'

The Catalan and French locatives *hi* and *y* are bound preverbal pronominals (so-called "proclitics"). (For the lack of a preposition in the French TOP phrase in (23b) see § 4.2.3.).

Finally, the pronominal may function as an **adjunct** rather than an argument represented in the predicate's valence. A well-known French example is (24), from a traditional song; (25) is an attested German example:

(24) [Sur le pont d'Avignon]$_i$, on
on the bridge of Avignon one
y$_i$ danse tout en rond.
there dances all in round
'On the Avignon bridge, people dance all around.'

(25) [In Ostdeutschland]$_i$ da$_i$ ist ein
in East-Germany there is one
Fünftel der Leute arbeitslos.
fifth of.the people unemployed
'In Eastern Germany, one fifth of the people are unemployed.'

In (24) and (25), the locative prepositional phrases in TOP position are coindexed with the atonic pronominals *y/da*. Another example involving an adjunct pronominal is (26), from the Bantu language Chicheŵa (SM stands for "subject marker" and the numeral 3 for the gender class of the noun):

(26) Chicheŵa (Bresnan & Mchombo 1987)
fisi a-na-pít-á nawó$_i$ ku
hyena SM-PST-go-IND with.it.3 to
msika, [mkángó uwu]$_i$.
market lion.3 this
'The hyena went with it to the market, this lion.'

In (26), the right-dislocated NP *mkángó uwu* is coindexed with the comitative adjunct pronominal *nawó* 'with it'.

3.2. Types of pronominals

So far, we have cited examples in which the dislocated TOP or ANTITOP constituents are coindexed with personal pronouns, whether morpho-syntactically free or bound. As noted earlier, the pronominal can also be an **inflectional affix**, as e.g. in Romance, Bantu, or Semitic languages. Recall that in the present article such inflectional affixes are included under the general cover term *pronominal*. Italian examples of RD and LD with inflectionally expressed pronominals were shown in (4e) and (5e). (27) is another Romance example:

(27) Occitan (Sauzet 1989)
(a) [Lo libre de Joan]$_i$, es$_i$
the book of John is.3.SG
interessant.
interesting
'John's book, it is interesting.'
(b) Es$_i$ interessant, [lo libre de Joan]$_i$.
'It is interesting, John's book.'

In the Italian sentences in (4) and (5), the dislocated phrase *questi Romani* is coindexed with the verbal suffix *-o*, which codes person and number. In the Occitan (27), the dislocated phrase *lo libre de Joan* is coindexed with the third person singular verb form *es*, in which stem and person marker are fused.

Examples like (4/5e) or (27) raise the theoretical issue of the categorization of inflectional affixes as either purely syntactic **agreement markers** or as **anaphoric pronominals**. Indeed, if LD exampes like (5e) or (27a) are analyzed as involving subject-agreement morphemes, such sentences will be potentially indistinguishable from the corresponding canonical sentences in which the relevant NPs occupy subject position. It is beyond the scope of the present article to enter the debate over this theoretical issue (cf. Jelinek 1984 and Bresnan & Mchombo 1987).

In some languages, both subjects and objects may be marked inflectionally on the verb, as e.g. in Chicheŵa (SM stands for "subject marker", OM for "object marker"):

(28) Chicheŵa (Bresnan & Mchombo 1987)
 (a) *[Njûchi]$_i$,   zi$_i$-ná-wá$_j$-lúm-a*
  bees   SM-PST-OM-bite-IND
  [alenje]$_j$
  hunters
  'The bees (they) BIT (them) the hunters.'
 (b) *[Alenje]$_j$, zi$_i$-ná-wá$_j$-lúma, [njûchi]$_i$*
  'The hunters, they BIT them, the bees.'

In (28), the subject marker *zi-* and the object marker *-wá-* agree in person, number, and gender class with the constituents *njûchi* and *alenje* in TOP or ANTITOP position. Notice that (28b) cannot mean that the hunters bit the bees, because the object marker is unambiguously coindexed with the NP *alenje* via its gender class. Inflectional subject and object coindexation is found also in Classical Arabic:

(29) Classical Arabic (Moutaouakil 1989)
 (a) *[Halidun], qabaltuhu*
  Halid.NOM met.1SG.3SG.ACC
  l-yawma
  the-day.ACC
  'Halid, I met him TODAY.'
 (b) *qabaltuhu l-yawma, [Halidun].*
  'I met him TODAY, Halid. / I met Halid TODAY.'

As in Chichŵa, both the subject and the object are marked on the verb; but unlike Chicheŵa, the dislocated NP is itself case-marked in Arabic (cf. § 4.2.3.).

In addition to pronouns and inflectional morphemes, the pronominal in LD or RD can also be a **null element**. This type of dislocation structure is prevalent in languages like Chinese, Lahu, Japanese, or Turkish, which, unlike English, freely permit the null instantiation of arguments denoting specific definite referents. Turkish examples of coindexation with a null subject were shown in (4f) and (5f). (30) contains additional Turkish examples involving null-instantiated objects. (30a) illustrates the canonical verb-final structure and (30b/c) two possible RD versions. For easy recognition, the null-instantiated complement is indicated by the symbol "ø":

(30) Turkish (Erguvanli 1984)
 (a) *Adam taŝ-i   oglan-a at-ti*
  man stone-ACC boy-DAT throw-PST
  'The man threw the STONE at the BOY.'
 (b) *Adam ø$_i$ oglan-a at-ti,*
  man   boy-DAT throw-PST
  [taŝ-i]$_i$.
  stone-ACC
  'The man threw it at the BOY, the stone.'
 (c) *Adam taŝ-i   ø$_i$ at-ti,*
  man stone-ACC throw-PST
  [oglan-a]$_i$.
  boy-DAT
  'The man threw the STONE at the boy.'

In the canonical structure in (30a), the theme (accusative) and goal (dative) arguments of the verb *throw* appear in preverbal object position, where they have a focus relation to the predicate. In (b) and (c), the NPs corresponding to the theme and the goal argument respectively appear in ANTITOP position. We know that these NPs are right-dislocated because in strict V-final languages like Turkish the verb indicates the right clause boundary.

(31) contains analogous examples from another strict V-final language, Japanese:

(31) Japanese (Kuno 1978)
 (a) *Kimi wa kono hon o   yonda?*
  you TOP this book ACC read
  'Have you read this BOOK?'
 (b) *Kimi wa ø$_i$ yonda, [kono hon o]$_i$?*
  'Have you READ (it,) this book?'
 (c) *ø$_i$ø$_j$ yonda, [kimi wa]$_i$ [kono hon o]$_j$?*
  'Have you READ (it,), you, this book?'

(31a) shows the canonical verb-final structure, with the agent and the theme argument in preverbal position. In (31b) the constituent corresponding to the theme, and in (31c) those corresponding to the agent and the theme, appear in ANTITOP position, leaving the corresponding preverbal argument slots unfilled. The gloss of (31c) is somewhat unnatural because English does not right-dislocate pronouns as freely as Japanese (but cf. (69) below). Example (32) illustrates coindexation of an ANTITOP phrase with a null pronominal in Mandarin Chinese:

(32) Mandarin (Guo 1997)
 tè nán ø$_i$ zhǎo, [wǒ zhèige]$_i$.
 very difficult find my this
 'It is very difficult to find, this (thing) of mine.'

As in the previous examples, the NP (*wǒ zhèige*) is marked syntactically, via word order, as right-dislocated; the direct-object argument of the verb *find* is left unexpressed.

Dislocation with null-instantiated pronominals is found also in the familiar European languages, such as Portuguese (e.g. Raposo 1986) or spoken French (Lambrecht & Lemoine 1996). Since in these languages object pronouns are normally expressed overtly, instances of LD with null pronominals are easily confused with Topicalization (cf. (6) and (7) above). Consider the French sentences in (33):

(33) (a) *[Les cacahuètes]$_i$, j$_j$'aime* BIEN *ø$_i$, [moi]$_j$.*
  the peanuts I like well
  me
  'Peanuts, I LIKE (them), me.'
 (b) *J'aime* BIEN *ø.*
  'I LIKE them.'
 (c) *[Les cacahuètes]$_i$, [moi]$_j$, j$_j$'aime* BIEN *ø$_i$.*

Given the well-formedness of (33b), (33a) can be analyzed as an instance of LD with an understood direct-object pronominal. That this is indeed the correct analysis is demonstrated by (33c), in which the initial NP *les cacahuètes* is separated from the clause by another dislocated NP (*moi*), which is coindexed with the overt pronominal subject *je*. By the same token, sentence (34a) below must be analyzed as an instance of RD with an understood object pronominal and with the final NP in ANTITOP position, rather than as a canonical sentence with an unaccented direct-object NP (as in the English gloss):

(34) (a) *J'aime* BIEN *ø$_i$, [les cacahuètes]$_i$.*
  'I LIKE peanuts.'
 (b) *J$_j$'aime* BIEN *ø$_i$, moi$_j$, [les cacahuètes]$_i$.*

The occurrence of the pronominal ANTITOP NP *moi* before *les cacahuètes* in (34b) is proof that the latter NP must also be in right-detached position.

While the pronominals in dislocation sentences may be free pronouns (English, Hebrew, Norwegian), morphologically bound atonic pronouns (Catalan, French), inflectional morphemes (Italian or Chicheŵa), or null elements (Turkish, Japanese, French), they may not belong to the set of **independent** or **tonic** pronoun forms, in those languages which possess two morphosyntactically distinct pronoun series. Consider e.g. the Chicheŵa sentences in (35):

(35) Chicheŵa (Bresnan & Mchombo 1987)
 (a) *[Mkángó uwu]$_i$ fîsi*
  lion.3 this hyena
  a-ná-ú$_i$-dy-a.
  SM-PST-OM.3-eat-IND
  'This lion, the hyena ate it'.
 (b) **?[Mkángó uwu]$_i$ fîsi*
  lion.3 this hyena
  a-ná-dy-á îwo$_i$.
  SM-PST-eat-IND it.3
  'This lion, the hyena ate it.'

Sentence (35b) is of doubtful grammaticality because the anaphoric pronominal *îwo* 'it' belongs to an independent pronoun set, rather than to the set of incorporated pronouns of which the object marker -ú- in (35a) is a member. The cross-linguistic generalization seems to be that whenever a morphosyntactically bound pronoun form is available in a language, a free pronominal form may not be used in a dislocation construction. As argued by Bresnan & Mchombo (1987), this constraint is explained by the different discourse functions which the two pronoun series serve in a language (cf. § 5.1.).

3.3. Unlinked topics

The dislocation type in which an element in TOP position is coindexed with a null pronominal must be distinguished from the LD construction in which a constituent appears in TOP position without any anaphoric link to an (overt or covert) intra-clausal argument or adjunct. This construction is a common feature of so-called "topic-prominent" languages (Li & Thompson 1976), like Chinese or Lahu. Topic-prominent languages are languages in which the topic-comment sentence type is more dominant than the subject-predicate type found in "subject-prominent" languages like English or French. The difference between the subject-predicate and the topic-comment type is illustrated by Li & Thompson with the following English example:

(36) (a) *John   hit Mary.*
        Subject Predicate
    (b) *As for education,*
        Topic
        John prefers Bertrand Russell's ideas.
        Comment

According to Li & Thompson, in subject-prominent languages the basic sentence structure is like that in (36a), whereas in topic-prominent languages it is more like that in (36b).

What distinguishes the type in (36b) from that in (36a) is that in the former the TOP constituent has no semantic or syntactic relation to the predicate. The TOP phrase *as for education* in (36b) does not satisfy a valence requirement of the verb *prefer*. Nor is this phrase a possible adjunct to that predicate. Unlike time, place, or manner adjuncts, which may occur in various positions in the sentence, the *as-for* phrase can only occur in pre-sentential position. The interpretive link between the TOP element and the following clause is purely pragmatic: it indicates a kind of **relevance** relation between the TOP entity and the proposition (see Dik 1978, Gundel 1988, Lambrecht 1994). Following Lambrecht (1994), we will call the TOP element in (36b) **unlinked** and we will call the entire construction the **unlinked-TOP construction**. Alternative labels for unlinked topics found in the literature are "détachées sans rappel" (Fradin 1990) and "absolute Rahmensetzung" (Stark 1997). Notice that corresponding to the unlinked-TOP construction there is no unlinked-ANTITOP construction (cf. § 4.2.4. below).

In (36b), the unlinked-TOP constituent is introduced by the prepositional marker *as for*. In spontaneous speech, such markers are generally absent. Though unacceptable in standard English, structures involving bare unlinked-TOP NPs are common in oral discourse. Attested examples are given in (37):

(37) (a) (In a discussion about how to grow flowers:)
        [Tulips], do you have to plant new bulbs every year?
    (b) A: *In Christianity, do you have to be a member of a religion in order to go to heaven?*
        B: *[The Baptists], you gotta be Baptist.*
    (c) A: *If you suffer from the heat here, you must have hated it in Austin.*
        B: *[Austin], at least you can sit near the AC.*

It should be noted that markers like *as for* in (36b) (whose function is that of indicating a topic shift) are appropriate only in a subset of the discourse environments which call for the use of an unlinked-topic construction.

Attested spoken French examples are shown in (38). As in English, unlinked-TOP sentences are considered substandard in French:

(38) (a) (Blanche-Benveniste 1981)
        [Mon premier mari], on avait une voiture puis une moto.
        'My first husband, we had a car then a motorcycle.'
    (b) (François 1974)
        [La mer], tu vois de l'eau.
        'The ocean, you see water.'
    (c) (Barnes 1985)
        Le métro, avec la Carte Orange, tu vas n'importe où.
        'The Metro, with the Orange Pass, you go anywhere you want.'

Corpus work on spoken French (Barnes 1985, Lambrecht 1987, Stark 1997) reveals that unlinked-TOP constructions are very common in unmonitored oral discourse in French. According to Barnes, such constructions account for 10% of the total number of LDs in her corpus.

A subtype of the unlinked-TOP construction is the one often (misleadingly) referred to as the "Double-Subject construction". In this type, the unlinked TOP constituent is followed by another nominal, which functions as the semantic (and sometimes syntactic) subject of the following predicate. (39) contains three examples:

(39) (a) Mandarin (Li & Thompson 1976)
        [*Nèige shù*] *yèzi   dà*
        that   tree leaves big
        'That tree, the leaves are big.'

(b) Japanese (Li & Thompson 1976)
   [Sakana wa] tai   ga
   fish   TOP red.snapper SUBJ
   oisii.
   delicious
   'Fish, red snapper is delicious.'
(c) Classical Arabic (Moutaouakil 1989)
   [L-lahmu], r-ritlu   bi
   the-meat.NOM the-pound.NOM with
   ᶜshrina   dirhaman.
   twenty.GEN dirham.ACC
   'Meat, the pound costs 20 dirhams.'

In (39), the semantic relation between the unlinked-TOP entity and the following NP is that between a semantic **frame** (Fillmore 1985) and an element of that frame. The Double-Subject type occurs also in English. (40) is an attested example, embedded in a minimal discourse context:

(40)   That's not the typical family anymore. [**The typical family today**], **the husband and the wife** both work.

As in (39), the subject denotatum in (40) (*the husband and the wife*) is linked to that of the topic (*the typical family today*) via a semantic frame relation.

Perhaps more common and better known, though still substandard, are Double-Subject sentences in which the topic and the subject stand in a **possessive** relation to each other. In such cases, the possessive determiner of the subject serves as an anaphoric link to the TOP NP. (41) shows an English and a French example (from Prince 1984 and Lambrecht 1981 respectively):

(41) (a) And [*this guy*]$_i$, *his*$_i$ *fishing pole fell down in the water.*
    (b) [*Napoléon*]$_i$, *sa*$_i$ *campagne de 1813 est très contestée.*
       'Napoleon, his 1813 campaign is quite contested.'

In these sentences, the unlinked TOP NPs (*this guy* and *Napoléon*) are coindexed with the possessive determiners (*his* and *sa*) of the following subject NPs. (42) and (43) are Indonesian and Arabic examples of the same construction type. In these languages, the possessor relation is not expressed by a possessive determiner but by a pronominal suffix on the possessed noun. (42a) contrasts with (16), repeated here for easy comparison as (42b), in which the possessor and the possessed NP form a single complex NP in TOP position:

(42) Indonesian (Li & Thompson 1976)
(a) [*Anak itu*]$_i$, *ibu-nja*$_i$ *membeli sepatu.*
   child that mother-POSS buy
   shoe
   'That child, his mother bought shoes.'
(b) [*Ibu   anak itu*]$_i$, *dia*$_i$ *membeli sepatu.*
   mother child that she buy
   shoe
   'That child's mother, she bought shoes.'

(43)   Classical Arabic (Moutaouakil 1989)
   [*Zaydun*]$_i$, *ʾabuhu*$_i$
   Zayd.NOM   father.NOM.3SG.GEN
   maridun.
   ill.NOM
   'Zayd, his father is ill. / Zayd's father is ill.'

(43) is perhaps better analyzed as involving two consecutive TOP phrases, with the subject argument of the predicate *ill* coded in null form (see examples (30) through (35) and § 3.4.).

The existence of the unlinked-TOP construction raises again the issue of the definitional criteria for dislocation. As mentioned in § 1., the term 'dislocation' naturally suggests the notion of a sentence element appearing in a derived ('abnormal') rather than a basic ('normal') position. It is this derivational notion that our criteria (ii) (possible alternative canonical position) and (iii) (pronominal representation) were meant to capture. It is clear that unlinked-TOP phrases do not satisfy these criteria since there is no possible alternative canonical position which they could occupy. As a corollary, there is also no possible intra-clausal anaphoric pronominal to represent them (cf. § 4.2.4.).

A similar problem of definition arises with **adverbial phrases** in TOP or ANTITOP position. Adverbial phrases differ from unlinked topics in that they do satisfy criterion (ii): they may occur both in dislocated and non-dislocated position. However when dislocated, they do not require the presence of an anaphoric or cataphoric pronominal element (even though such an element may sometimes occur, as examples (24) through (26) show). Herein they differ from prototypical dislocation sentences. Even though unlinked topics and dislocated adverbials do not satisfy all four criteria, they nevertheless satisfy the necessary condition of extra-clausal position, without which there would be no concept of dislocation.

3.4. Multiple dislocations

A common cross-linguistic phenomenon is the occurrence of more than one dislocated constituent in TOP or ANTITOP position. For example, next to the Catalan dislocation sentences in (22) (repeated here as (44a/b)), where *al calaix* is in TOP/ANTITOP and *el ganivet* in focus position, we also find the sentences in (44c/d), where *el ganivet* and *al calaix* occur both either in TOP or in ANTITOP position:

(44) Catalan (Valldují 1995)
  (a) *Hi$_i$ ficarem el GANIVET,*
     there we.will.put the knife
     [al calaix]$_i$.
     in i.the drawer
     'We will put the KNIFE (there,) in the drawer.'
  (b) *[Al calaix]$_i$, hi$_i$ ficarem el GANIVET.*
     '(In) the drawer, we'll put the KNIFE there.'
  (c) *[El ganivet]$_i$ [al calaix]$_j$, l$_i$'hi$_j$ FICAREM.*
  (d) *L$_i$'hi$_j$ FICAREM, [el ganivet]$_i$ [al calaix]$_j$.*

Similarly, next to the Chicheŵa sentence in (28a) above (repeated here as (45a)), we find the versions in (45b/c), where the NPs *njûchi* 'the bees' and *alenje* 'the Hunters' occur both either in TOP or in ANTITOP position:

(45) (a) *[njûchi]$_i$, zi$_i$-ná-wá$_j$-lúm-a,*
     bees SM-PST-OM-bite-INDIC
     [alenje]$_j$
     hunters
     'The bees (they) BIT (them) the hunters.'
  (b) *[Njûchi]$_i$ [alenje]$_j$, zi$_i$-ná-wá$_j$-luma.*
     'The bees, the hunters, they BIT them.'
  (c) *Zi$_i$-ná-wáj-luma, [njûchi]$_i$ [alenje]$_j$.*
     'They BIT them, the bees, the hunters.'

The same situation obtains in Turkish. Next to the RD sentences in (30b/c) (repeated as (46a/b)), we find the versions in (46c/d), with two nominal phrases in ANTITOP position:

(46) (a) *Adam oglan-a atti, [taŝ-i].*
     man boy-DAT threw stone-acc
     'The man threw it at the BOY, the stone.'
  (b) *Adam taŝ-i atti, [oglan-a].*
     man stone-ACC threw boy-DAT
     'The man threw the STONE at the boy.'
  (c) *Adam atti, [oglan-a] [taŝ-i].*
     man threw boy-DAT stone-ACC
     'The man THREW it at the boy, the stone.'
  (d) *taŝ-i at-ti, [oglan-a] [adam].*
     stone-ACC threw boy-DAT man
     'He threw the STONE at the boy, the man.'

Compare also the Japanese structure in (31c) above. It is also possible to find the TOP position occupied by one unlinked and one linked topic NP, as in the French example in (47) (cf. also the Arabic ex. (43) above):

(47) Spoken French (Lambrecht 1981)
    [Mon frère]$_i$ [sa$_i$ voiture]$_j$, elle$_j$
    my brother his car.FEM she
    est complètement foutue.
    is completely broken
    'My brother's car is totally wrecked.'

The question arises as to how many phrases may cooccur in TOP or ANTITOP position. Lambrecht (1981) argues that, in French at least, no more than two dislocated phrases may cooccur in the same position. Consider the examples in (48):

(48) Spoken French (Lambrecht 1981)
  (a) *[Moi] [ton frère], je le lui donnerai, [le livre].*
     'Me, your brother, I'll give it to him, the book.'
  (b) *[Moi] [le livre], je le lui donnerai, [à ton frère].*
  (c) *[Ton frère] [le livre], je le lui donnerai, [moi].*
  (d) ?*[Moi] [ton frère] [le livre], je le lui donnerai.*
  (e) ?*Je le lui donnerai, [moi] [à ton frère] [le livre].*

Among the various possible permutations in (48), (a) through (c) are acceptable, but (d) and (e) seem of diminished acceptability. Lambrecht (1994) suggests a processing explanation for the acceptability differences in (48): since the proposition expressed by a dislocation sentence is to be construed as conveying information about the referent of the TOP/ANTITOP constituent, the interpretation of such a sentence becomes increasingly difficult if the proposition is to be construed as being about several topics at the same time.

The difference is, however, a matter of degree, and under appropriate discourse circumstances sentences with more than two TOP or ANTITOP phrases may well constitute acceptable utterances. Hewitt (1979) cites the following sentence from Abkhaz:

(49)   Abkhaz (Hewitt 1979)
       [a-xàc'a]$_i$ [a-ph°ǝs]$_j$
       ART-man   ART-woman
       [a-s°q°'ǝ]$_k$, ø$_k$-lǝ$_j$-y$_i$-te-yt'
       ART-book   it-to.her-he-gave-TNS
       'The man gave the book to the woman.'

It is revealing to compare (49) with its (slightly modified) spoken French equivalent in (49'); to emphasize the formal similarity with (49), the morphologically bound status of the pronouns in the French verb complex is indicated by hyphens:

(49') *[L'homme]$_i$ [cette femme-là]$_j$*
       the man   that woman-there
       [mon livre]$_k$, il$_i$-le$_k$-lui$_j$-a-donné.
       my book   he-it.to.her-has-given
       'The man he GAVE my book to that woman.'

Though perhaps pragmatically unusual, (49') is nevertheless a grammatically well-formed spoken French sentence. The striking structural similarity between (49) and (49') confirms the observation, made early on by Vendryès (1914), that modern spoken French is typologically close to certain polysynthetic languages (Vendryès compares French to the Amerindian language Chinook).

A peculiar kind of multiple dislocation, which has not been generally recognized as such in the literature, is the construction sometimes referred to as 'Mad-Magazine sentence' in US linguistics (Akmajian 1984). In this construction, which is attested across languages (see Lambrecht 1990 for French and German), the TOP position is always filled by two constituents, one corresponding to an argument, the other to the predicate of a canonical sentence. Two English examples are given in (50):

(50) (a) *What, [[me] [worry]]? (Never!)*
      (b) *[[John] [a doctor]]? (Sure!)*

As argued in Lambrecht (1990), the Mad-Magazine construction is best analyzed as a special kind of LD whose two dislocated elements stand in a (pragmatically presupposed) predicate-argument relation to each other and whose clausal portion may remain unexpressed. Consider the variants of (50) in (50'), where the sarcastic comments "Never" and "Sure!" have been replaced by complete clauses:

(50') (a) *[[Me] [worry]]$_i$, that$_i$'s ridiculous!*
      (b) *[[John] [a doctor]]$_i$, I don't believe it$_i$!*

In these variants, the comment portion is a clause containing an anaphoric pronominal which refers to the presupposed proposition expressed by the predicate-argument structure denoted by the two TOP denotata. What distinguishes the Mad-Magazine type from other dislocation sentences is its conventional association with a specific kind of speech act: an incredulous comment on a previously mentioned proposition. It is this conventionality of the form-function association in this construction that makes it possible to omit overt expression of the incredulous comment.

3.5. Syntactic categories of dislocated constituents

Languages differ with respect to the types of constituents that may occur in dislocated position. While English seems relatively conservative, a language like modern French permits a remarkable variety of dislocated categories, including expressions at the subphrasal level. As the vast majority of the examples in this article demonstrate, by far the most commonly found category is the **noun phrase** (NP). Less common are **prepositional phrases** (PP). One example is (22) (Catalan), repeated here as (51), which contains a PP in TOP or ANTITOP position:

(51) (a) *Hi$_i$ ficarem el GANIVET, [al calaix]$_i$.*
          'We will put the KNIFE (there,) in the drawer.'
      (b) *[Al calaix]$_i$, hi$_i$ ficarem el GANIVET.*
          '(In) the drawer, we'll put the KNIFE there.'

An attested Spanish example of a PP in TOP position is (52):

(52)   Spanish (Silva-Corvalán 1983)
       [A todo el curso]$_i$, le$_i$
       to all the class it.DAT
       gustaba una monja que se fue.
       pleased a nun that REFL went
       'The whole class liked a nun who left.'

In the attested French example in (53), the ANTITOP PP has a partitive function:

(53) Il y   en$_i$ a   qui ne   sont
      it there of.3P   has who NEG are
      pas mal, [de ces hommes
      NEG bad   of   those men
      qu'on voit dans la rue]$_i$.
      that one sees in   the street
      'Some of them aren't bad, those men you see in the street.'

In French, PPs, though common in ANTITOP position, rarely occur in TOP position (see 4.1.). Two attested French examples of left-dislocated PPs are shown in (54):

(54) (a) Mais [après tout] [en
         but after all   in
         vacances]$_i$, j'y$_i$ vais
         vacations   I there go
         quand même.
         nevertheless
         'But after all, I DO take vacations.'
    (b) [Avec Michel]$_i$, on$_i$ est allé
         with Michel   we   is gone
         au   cinéma.
         to.the cinema
         'Michel and I, we went to the movies.'

The prepositions in (54) are necessary because they add a special meaning to the NP. *En vacances* in (a) is a fixed expression and *avec Michel* in (b) does not mean 'with Michel' but 'Michel and I' (justifying the coindexation of the TOP phrase with the pronominal *on* 'we'). Item (55) contains a French example involving an **adverbial phrase** (AdvP) in ANTITOP position:

(55)   J'y$_i$ ai   passé de bonnes
       I there have   spent of good
       vacances, [là-bas]$_i$.
       vacations over.there
       'I spend good VACATIONS there.'

Such examples are relatively rare because dislocated AdvPs are usually not coindexed with pronominals. Of course, dislocated adverbials occur commonly without pronominal coindexation.

Somewhat special is the case of dislocated **adjective phrases** (APs). In English, APs cannot be dislocated because English does not allow coindexation between adjectives and pronouns. Fronted APs in English are topicalized, not dislocated, as demonstrated by the contrasts in (56):

(56) (a) [Rich]$_i$ he is NOT ø$_i$.
    (b) *[Rich]$_i$, if he is NOT ø$_i$, she will not marry him.
    (c) *He is NOT ø$_i$, I think, [rich]$_i$.

(56a) is grammatical because the adjective *rich* is in COMP position, as required for Topicalization (cf. § 2.). (56b) is ungrammatical because the adjective does not occur in COMP but in TOP position. (56c) shows the same constraint for APs in ANTITOP position.

Structures equivalent to those in (56b/c) are well-formed in languages like French, where coindexation between APs and pronouns is a grammatical option. The French versions of (56a/b/c) are shown in (57):

(57) (a) [Riche]$_i$, il ne l$_i$'est pas.
    (b) [Riche]$_i$, s'il ne l$_i$'est pas, elle ne l'épousera pas.
    (c) Il ne l$_i$'est pas, je crois, [riche]$_i$.

An attested French example is shown in (58), embedded in a minimal discourse context:

(58)   Il a pas l'air d'être satisfait du tout.
       Il l$_i$'est tellement peu, [satisfait]$_i$,
       qu'il appuie sur la sonnerie.
       'He doesn't look satisfied at all. He is SO LITTLE satisfied that he rings the bell.'

In addition to nominal, prepositional, adverbial, and adjectival phrases, we also find **verb-headed phrases** (VPs) in dislocated position. (59) illustrates the occurrence of **nonfinite VPs**:

(59) (a) [To speak French]$_i$, everyone knows it$_i$'s not EASY.
    (b) Everyone knows it$_i$'s not EASY, [to speak French]$_i$.

(60) contains two attested French examples:

(60) (a) Je suis pas voleuse mais je verrais mes gosses qu'ils ont faim peut-être que je le$_i$ ferais, [de voler]$_i$. (Gadet 1989)
         'I'm not a thief, but I'd see my kids that they're hungry maybe I'd do it, steal.'
    (b) [De lui parler doucement]$_i$, ça$_i$ la$_j$ ramollissait, [la tigresse]$_j$.
        'Speaking gently to her (that) SOFTENED (her) the tigress.'

(60a) shows a right-dislocated infinitival VP coindexed with an object pronominal. (60b) also has an NP in ANTITOP position, in addition to the infinitival VP in TOP position.

The set of verb-headed dislocated phrases contains various kinds of finite **complement clauses**. A common type is the category [COMP + S] illustrated in (61):

(61) (a) *It$_i$'s a SHAME, [that you're not coming tonight]$_i$.*
    (b) *[That you're not coming tonight]$_i$, I can't BELIEVE it$_i$.*

Recall that left-dislocation of a complement clause, as shown in (61a), is to be distinguished from the superficially similar Extraposition construction discussed in § 2. (examples (11a/b)). (62) illustrates complement-clause dislocation in Classical Arabic:

(62)   Classical Arabic (Moutaouakil 1989)
    [ʔan tanjaha   fi l-imtihani]$_i$,
    that succeed.2SG in the-exam.GEN
    dalika ma$_i$ la sakka   fihi.
    this   that NEG doubt.ACC in.3.SG
    'That you will pass the exam noone doubts (it).'

In some languages, a dislocated phrase may correspond to a **non-maximal** phrasal constituent in canonical position. In particular, we find dislocated constituents which would be of category N rather than NP if they were to appear in a canonical sentence. French and Italian examples of N-dislocation are shown in (63) and (64). For easy comparison, the dislocation structures are preceded by their canonical counterparts, with the relevant NP argument in square brackets (the clumsy gloss of (63c) is meant to parallel as much as possible the French structure):

(63) (a) *Je mets   [quelle ROBE]?*
       I put.on which dress
       'Which DRESS am I going to wear?'
    (b) *Je mets LAQUELLE$_i$, [de robe]$_i$?*
       I put.on which.one of dress
       'WHICH dress am I going to WEAR?'
    (c) *[De robe]$_i$, je mets laquelle$_i$?* (Gadet 1989)
       'As for a DRESS, which one am I going to WEAR?'

(64) (a) *Adesso faccio scorrere [il tuo*
       now   I.make run   the your
       BAGNETTO].
       bath
       'Now I'll run your BATH.'

(b) *Adesso faccio scorrere il TUO$_i$,*
    now   I.make run   the your
    [di bagnetto]$_i$.
    of bath
    'Now I'll run YOUR bath.'

Since dislocation involves association of the dislocated phrase with a grammatically complete sentence, for N-dislocation to be possible, the constituent remaining in canonical position must be a well-formed NP. This explains the change of the French interrogative determiner *quelle* in (63a) into the pronominal form *laquelle*. Without this change, (63b/c) would be ungrammatical (compare **De robe, je mets quelle?* / **Je mets QUELLE, de robe?*).

Notice that both in French and in Italian the dislocated N is not bare put preceded by a preposition, resulting in a phrase of the form [*de* N] or [*di* N]. This kind of phrase may not occur in canonical position:

(63b′) **Je mets [quelle de ROBE]?*

(64a′) **Faccio scorrere [il tuo di BAGNETTO].*

The sequence *de* + N is a highly specialized piece of syntax, which exists for the purpose of N-dislocation alone. (65) illustrates various French structures involving right-dislocated [*de N*]:

(65) CANONICAL   RIGHT-DISLOCATED

(a) *J'ai [une CASSEROLE].*   *J'en ai UNE, [de casserole].*
    'I have a POT.'   'I HAVE a pot.'
(b) *C'est [la bonne CASSEROLE].*   *C'est la BONNE, [de casserole].*
    'It's the good POT.'   'It's the GOOD pot.'
(c) *J'ai [une CASSÉE].*   *J'en ai UNE, [de cassée].*
    'I have one that's BROKEN.'   'I have ONE that's broken.'
(d) *C'est [ma VOITURE].*   *C'est la MIENNE, [de voiture].*
    'It's my CAR.'   'It's MY car.'

Item (66) shows N-dislocation in Turkish. To emphasize the similarity in patterning, the Turkish structure in (b) is followed by its (spoken) French counterpart in (c):

(66)   Turkish (Erguvanli 1984)
    (a) *[Siz-in seyahat-iniz] nasil geĉ-ti?*
       you-GEN trip-POSS2PL how pass-PST
       'How did your TRIP go?'
    (b) *[Siz-in] nasil geĉ-ti,*
       you-GEN how pass-PST
       [seyahat-iniz]?
       trip-POSS.2.PL
       'How did YOUR trip go?'

(c) *[Le vôtre]* comment il s'est passé, *[de voyage]*?

In Turkish, the dislocated N is a maximal phrasal projection, hence does not require an adpositional element like French *de*.

An unusual kind of dislocation construction, which is very common in spoken French, involves extraction of a noun from a **predicate NP** (see Lambrecht 1996b for a detailed description). This construction is illustrated in the two attested sentences (67b) and (68b). The dislocation structures are again paired with their canonical counterparts for easy comparison; the canonical NP arguments are enclosed in square brackets (notice that (68b) involves multiple dislocation):

(67) (a) *C'est pas [une histoire* MARRANTE*].*
'This isn't a funny STORY.'
(b) *C'est pas* MARRANT$_i$, *[comme*
it is not funny as
histoire]$_i$.
story
'This isn't a FUNNY story.'

(68) (a) *C$_i$'est [un appareil* CHER*], [ça]$_i$.*
'That's an expensive CAMERA.'
(b) *C$_i$'est* CHER$_j$, *[comme*
it is expensive as
appareil]$_j$ [ça]$_i$.
camera that
'That's an EXPENSIVE camera.'
(c) *C$_j$'est* CHER$_j$, *[ça]$_i$, [comme appareil]$_j$.*

The word-order variant in (68c) demonstrates that the constituent [*comme appareil*] is indeed in ANTITOP position. The distinctive property of this French construction is that the dislocated N is linked to a predicate adjective instead of a pronominal argument. The construction has the effect of splitting up the content of an indefinite predicate NP in such a way that the noun is separated from the adjective which modifies it. Instead of the indefinite determiner (*un, une*), the dislocated N is preceded by *comme*, resulting in a constituent of the form [*comme* N]. As in the case of [*de* N] above, the phrase [*comme* N] may not occur in canonical position:

(67b′) **C'est pas [comme histoire marrante].*
(68b′) **C'est [comme appareil cher], ça.*

In addition to phrases headed by nouns, prepositions, adjectives, and verbs, it is very common for **pronouns** to occur in TOP and ANTITOP position. Attested English examples are given in (69):

(69) (a) *Lotta guys don't* ASK. *[ME]$_i$, I$_i$* ASK.
(b) (About cooking sweet potatoes.)
They$_i$ take a long TIME, *[them]$_i$.*

Notice the non-nominative form of the dislocated pronouns in these sentences (cf. § 4.1.). Items (70) through (75) provide a cross-linguistic sample of sentences with pronouns in TOP or ANTITOP position:

(70) Norwegian (Fretheim 1995)
Den$_i$ har et siksakband over
it has a zigzag band over
ryggen, [den]$_i$.
back it
'It [a kind of snake] has a zigzag band down its back, it.'

(71) Mandarin Chinese (Guo 1997)
ø$_i$ cǎi wǒ jiǎ o le, [nǐ]$_i$
step my foot PERF you
'You stepped on my foot, you.'

(72) Tzotzil (Mayan) (Aissen 1992)
Pero [li vo'on-e]$_i$, mu xixanav$_i$.
but DET I-ENC NEG I.walk
'But me, I don't walk.'

In (72), the morpheme *-e* glossed as ENC is an enclitic found obligatorily affixed to topic phrases in Tzotzil.

(73) Turkish (Zimmer 1986)
Ogrenci degil-im$_i$ ki [ben]$_i$.
student not-cop.1sg particle I
'But I'm not a student, me.'

While the English gloss of (73) may sound unnatural, its French equivalent in (73′) is perfectly idiomatic:

(73′) *Mais je$_i$ ne suis pas étudiant, [moi]$_i$.*

It is also common for a pronoun to cooccur with a lexical phrase in TOP or ANTITOP position, as in the Japanese sentence (31c), repeated below as (74):

(74) Japanese (Kuno 1978)
ø$_i$ ø$_j$ yonda, [kimi wa]$_i$ [kono
read you TOP this
hon o]$_j$?
book ACC
'Have you READ it, you, this book?'

In some languages, the pronominal and the nominal constituent cooccurring in dislocated position may refer to the same entity.

This is shown in the attested French examples in (75):

(75) (a) *[Tarzan]$_i$ [lui]$_i$, il$_i$ taillait ses calebards dans des panthères.*
'Tarzan, him, he cut his pants out of panther skins.'
(b) *[La bière]$_i$ [ça]$_i$, j'aime pas ø$_i$.*
'Beer, that I don't like.'

We will return to the phenomenon of pronoun dislocation in the analysis of the pragmatics of dislocation in § 5.

Finally, it is necessary to mention the common ocurrence of **vocative phrases** in TOP or ANTITOP position. By "vocative", we do not mean a morphological case form (although such a case form may occur) but a sentence constituent whose function is to call the attention of an addressee to a given proposition. Examples are the expressions *waiter* and *ma'am* in (76):

(76) (a) *[Waiter], there's a fly in my soup!*
(b) *May I help you$_i$, [ma'am]$_i$?*

Dislocated vocatives may be unlinked, as in (76a), or linked to a pronominal argument, as in (76b). English examples of linked vocative phrases are shown in (77):

(77) (a) *[Mary]$_i$, I love you$_i$.*
(b) *I love you$_i$ too, [John]$_i$.*

Given the optional pronominal linking of vocatives, sentences in which the pronominal is not in the first or second person are often ambiguous between a vocative and a topic reading:

(78) (a) *[Mary]$_{i,j}$, she$_j$ loves you$_i$.*
(b) *He$_i$ loves you$_j$, [John]$_{i,j}$.*

In (78), the dislocated proper noun can be coindexed either with the second-person pronoun *you*, in which case it is interpreted vocatively, or with the third-person pronoun *she/he*, in which case it is interpreted as a topic. (79) shows dislocated vocative phrases in Mandarin Chinese:

(79) Mandarin Chinese (Guo 1997)
(a) *[shushu], [zhèi jiǎndāo]$_i$,*
uncle this scissors
zěnme ø$_i$ liǎng bàn le?
how-come two half PERF
'Uncle, this pair of scissors, how come it is in two pieces?'
(b) *wǒ qù mǎi fàn qù, [bàbà].*
i go buy meal go dad
'I'm going to buy dinner, dad.'

In (79a) the unlinked vocative cooccurs with a linked topic in TOP position, confirming the syntactic similarity between the two categories. (80) illustrates vocative dislocation in classical Arabic (Moutaouakil 1989):

(80) (a) *[Ya Halidu], qtarib.*
O Halid.NOM approach
'Halid, come nearer.'
(b) *Hana waqtu n-nawmi,*
arrived time.NOM the-sleep.GEN
[ʔayyuha l-ʔatfalu].
o the-children.NOM
'Now is the time to sleep, children.'

In Classical Arabic, the vocative noun is in the nominative case and is typically preceded by a marker such as *ya* or *ʔayyuha*. As argued in Lambrecht (1996a), the fact that vocatives and topics appear in the same extra-clausal positions is motivated by a fundamental functional similarity between the two categories. In both, a pragmatically accessible discourse entity is associated with a proposition via a pragmatic relevance link (cf. § 5.1. below).

4. The syntactic status of dislocated constituents

The preceding sections were based on certain assumptions concerning the syntactic status of constituents in TOP and ANTITOP position. The purpose of the present section is to provide grammatical evidence supporting these assumptions. We will first analyze those properties which are common to all dislocated phrases (§ 4.1.). Then we will emphasize a number of differences between LD and RD (§ 4.2.).

4.1. Clause-external position of TOP and ANTITOP phrases

The most important property of dislocated phrases, expressed in criteron (i) of the definition in § 1., is their status as **extra-clausal** constituents, i. e. as constituents which do not partake in the semantic and syntactic dependency relations between predicates and their arguments. As a consequence of this independence, dislocated constituents are by definition **optional** sentence elements, in the sense that their omission from a sentence never causes structural or semantic unacceptability. This does not entail, of course, that their presence is optional also from a communicative point of view.

The property of optionality brings up the relationship between the category of dislocated constituents and the category **adjunct**, which is often defined in terms of optionality. It is important to acknowledge that the two categories are not coextensive: unlike TOP and ANTITOP phrases, adjuncts may occur in various sentence positions and they may have either a topic or a focus relation to a proposition. The term *adjunct*, like *argument* or *complement*, refers to a grammatical or semantic **relation** between a denotatum and a predication. In contrast, the term *dislocated phrase* refers to a constituent in a specific syntactic **position**, and this position indicates not a semantic or syntactic but a **pragmatic** relation to a predication. Strictly speaking, the notions *adjunct* and *dislocated phrase* are mutually exclusive. The category of TOP and ANTITOP phrases cannot be subsumed under the category *adjunct* but must be recognized as a formal and grammatical category of its own.

Some formal evidence for extraclausality of dislocated constituents was presented in the comparison between LD and Topicalization in § 2. Another type of evidence can be found in their position relative to other sentence elements which themselves are clause-external, such as certain **discourse particles**. Consider these Amerindian examples:

(81)   Caddo (Chafe 1976)
        [saʔuʔúš]ᵢ **bahʔna** sinátti ʔ
        Ms. Owl   it.is.said then
        tučátʔi.hahwahᵢ.
        she.spilled.it
        'Ms. Owl, they say, she spilled it.'

(82)   Seneca (Chafe 1976)
        káeoʔta **nae·**   hayáe-ʔthakᵢ ...
        gun   indeed he.used.to.use
        [nê-kê· ne ʔô-kweh]ᵢ.
        this   person
        'He used to use a gun, this person.'

As Chafe observes, in (81) the presence of the discourse particle *bahʔna* between the sentence-initial NP and the clause indicates that the NP is not a regular subject but what he calls a "premature subject" (i. e. a TOP constituent). Similarly, in (82) the final NP is marked as being in post-clausal (i. e. ANTITOP) position via a preceding "hesitation" (Chafe 1976: 53). The same phenomenon can be observed in a language like Catalan (Valluduví 1995). (83) is a variant of (44) above:

(83) (a) *Ficarem (*xec) el ganivet (*xec) al* CALAIX, *xec.*
        'We will put the knife in the drawer, man.'
    (b) *[El ganivet]ᵢ xec, elᵢ ficarem al* CALAIX.
        'The knife, man, we'll put it in the drawer.'
    (c) *Elᵢ ficarem al* CALAIX, *xec, [el ganivet]ᵢ.*
        'We'll put it in the drawer, man, the knife.'

In Catalan, the discourse particle *xec* may not occur clause-internally, as (83a) shows. Consequently, the occurrence of the dislocated NP *el ganivet* before this particle (TOP position) or after it (ANTITOP position) is evidence that this NP is itself clause-external.

The clause-external status of dislocated phrases is manifested also in their position relative to **focus** elements in the sentence (→ Art. 81, 104). Since focal denotata are by definition communicatively indispensable elements of propositions, and since propositions are expressed in clauses, focus constituents by necessity occur **clause-internally** (cf. Lambrecht 1994). TOP constituents must therefore **precede**, and ANTITOP constituents must **follow**, focus elements.

For RD, this sequencing constraint can be illustrated with the following examples, where small caps indicate the last element of the focus denotatum:

(84)   French (Lambrecht 1996a)
    (a) *Elleᵢ ne m'a pas rendu mon* ARGENT, *[Nicole]ᵢ.*
        'She didn't give me my money back, Nicole'
    (b) **Elleᵢ ne m'a pas rendu, [Nicole]ᵢ mon* ARGENT.

(85) (a) *Ilᵢ a vendu sa maison à* PROFIT, *[Jean]ᵢ.*
        'He sold his house at a profit, Jean.'
    (b) **Ilᵢ a vendu sa maison, [Jean]ᵢ, à* PROFIT.

The ANTITOP NPs in (84) and (85) cannot occur before the clause-final focus elements. In the case of LD, the relative position of dislocated and focus elements can be observed in sentence structures in which a focal element occurs in clause-initial rather than clause-final position. One such structure is the **Focus-Movement** construction illustrated in example (8). Consider the variants of (8a/b) in (86) and (87):

(86) (a) *[My friends]ᵢ*, FIFTY SIX HUNDRED DOLLARS theyᵢ raised.
(b) *FIFTY SIX HUNDRED DOLLARS *[my friends]ᵢ* theyᵢ raised.

(87) (a) *[Marie]ᵢ*, *l'AMOUR* elleᵢ appelle ça.
'Marie, LOVE she calls it.'
(b) **L'AMOUR* *[Marie]ᵢ* elleᵢ appelle ça.

The (b) versions are ill-formed because a TOP element may not follow a focus element in COMP position.

Another relevant structure are **information questions** with fronted question words (for justification of the focus status of question words cf. Lambrecht & Michaelis 1998). An example is the Chinese sentence (79a), repeated here as (88):

(88)   *[shushu]*, *[zhèi jiǎndāo]ᵢ*,
     uncle   this   scissors
     zěnme ∅ᵢ *liǎng bàn le?*
     how-come   two   half PERF
     'Uncle, this pair of scissors, how come it is in two pieces?'

In (88), the fact that the vocative and the topic NP precede the focal question expression *zěnme* 'how come' indicates that they must be in TOP position. The same argument can be made for the corresponding sentence in English:

(88′) (a) *Uncle, [this pair of scissors]ᵢ, how come itᵢ is in two pieces?*
(b) **Uncle, how come [this pair of scissors]ᵢ itᵢ is in two pieces?*
(c) *Uncle, how come this pair of scissors is in two pieces?*

As the (b) version shows, the dislocated NP cannot follow the question expression *how come*. If it does, the NP must be a regular subject, as in (c).

The same constraint holds of **interrogative particles** in yes-no questions. Since what is being questioned is a proposition, expressed in a clause, and since dislocated elements are extraclausal, a TOP element must precede a question particle. Consider the Arabic sentence in (89a) and its French equivalent in (89′a) (the French question expression *est-ce que* functions as a single word):

(89)   Classical Arabic (Moutaouakil 1989)
(a) *[Zaydun], ʾa najaha*
     Zayd.NOM   Q   succeeded
     masruʿuhu?
     plan.NOM-3sGEN
     'Zayd, did his plan come off?'
(b) **ʾa [Zaydun] najaha masruʿuhu?*

(89′) (a) *[Zayd]*, *est-ce que* son plan a
     Zayd   Q   his plan has
     réussi?
     succeeded
(b) **Est-ce que [Zayd], son plan a réussi?*

The ungrammaticality of the (b) sentences is due to the fact that the TOP expression follows rather precedes the Q markers.

An analogous argument can be made concerning the respective position of dislocated elements and **negative particles**. Since topics are by definition outside the scope of negation (cf. Lambrecht 1994), clause-initial negative particles must follow TOP phrases. Consider the Mayan sentences in (90):

(90)   Mayan (Aissen 1992)
(a) *[A li vo'ot-e]ᵢ mi **mu***
     TOP DET you-ENC   Q   NEG
     k'usi xana'ᵢ un?
     what you.know ENC
     'You, don't you know anything?'
(b) *Pero [li vo'on-e]ᵢ, **mu***
     but   DET I-ENC   NEG
     xixanavᵢ.   (= ex. (72))
     I. walk
     'But me, I don't walk.'

It would be ungrammatical to invert the positions of the TOP and the negative particles in these sentences.

The fact that a dislocated element is not part of a clausal predicate-argument structure also explains why, under appropriate discourse circumstances, the same constituent may occur both in TOP and in ANTITOP position. Attested examples from French and Chinese are (91) and (92):

(91)   *[Moiᵢ], jeᵢ fais pas tout le travail tout seul, [moi]ᵢ.*
'Me, I don't do all the work all by myself, me.'

(92)   Mandarin Chinese (Guo 1997)
shu shu, [zhèi jiǎndao]ᵢ zěnme ∅ᵢ
uncle   this   scissors   how-come
liǎng bàn le, [zhèi jiǎndao]ᵢ?
two   half PERF this   scissors
'Uncle, this pair of scissors, how come it is in two pieces, this pair of scissors?'

If the dislocated phrases were arguments or adjuncts in a predication, their double occurrence would violate a fundamental semantic well-formedness condition, i.e. that the same theta role may not be filled twice in a single predication.

In § 3.4., we saw that it is possible for more than one constituent to occur in TOP or ANTITOP position. One of the clearest indicators of the relational independence of dislocated constituents is the fact that in languages with otherwise rigid word order multiple dislocated constituents can be **ordered freely** with respect to one another. For example, in addition to the French multiple-dislocation example in (48a), repeated as (93a), we also find the variants in (93) (b), (c), and (d):

(93) (a) *[Ton frère] [le livre], je le lui donnerai, [moi]*.
'Your brother, the book, I'll give it to him, me.'
(b) *[Le livre] [ton frère], je le lui donnerai, [moi]*.
(c) *[Moi], je le lui donnerai, [le livre] [à ton frère]*.
(d) *[Moi], je le lui donnerai, [à ton frère] [le livre]*.
(e) *Je donnerai le livre à ton frère*.
'I will give the book to your brother.'
(f) **Je donnerai à ton frère le livre*.

While in dislocated position all possible permutations are grammatical, inside the clause the respective order of complements is fixed, as the contrast between (e) and (f) shows.

The same positional freedom of dislocated phrases is observable in Catalan, Chicheŵa, and Turkish:

(94) Catalan (Vallduví 1995; cf. (44))
(a) *[El ganivet] [al calaix], l'hi* FI-CAREM.
'The knife, in the drawer, we'll put it there.'
(b) *[Al calaix] [el ganivet], l'hi* FI-CAREM.
(c) *L'hi* FICAREM, *[el ganivet] [al calaix]*.
(d) *L'hi* FICAREM, *[al calaix] [el ganivet]*.

(95) Chicheŵa (Bresnan & Mchombo 1987; cf. (45))
(a) *[Njûchi] [alenje] zi-ná-wá-luma*.
'The bees, the hunters, they BIT them.'
(b) *[Alenje] [njûchi] zi-ná-wá-luma*.
(c) *Zi-ná-wá-luma [njûchi] [alenje]*.
(d) *Zi-ná-wá-luma [alenje] [njûchi]*.

(96) Turkish (Erguvanli 1984; cf. (46))
(a) *Adam atti, [oglan-a] [taŝ-i]*.
'The man THREW it at the boy, the stone.'
(b) *Adam atti, [taŝ-i] [oglan-a]*.

In all of these languages, all possible permutations within the TOP and ANTITOP position are grammatical. Notice, however, that the respective order of linked and unlinked TOP phrases is fixed: the unlinked TOP is always first in a sequence of TOP constituents (Hanson 1987).

4.2. Differences between LD and RD

In the preceding section we have established the syntactic status of dislocated constituents as clause-external elements, accounting for their omissibility, their position relative to other elements, and their positional freedom with respect to one another. It is now necessary to mention certain differences between LD and RD concerning the degree of autonomy shown by the dislocated phrase with respect to the associated clause. Cross-linguistically, ANTITOP elements are more tightly connected with the predicate-argument structure of the clause than TOP elements (cf. Lambrecht 1981, Ziv 1994). As a result, LD and RD obey different constraints on **locality, embeddability, case marking, anaphoric linking**, and **prosody**.

4.2.1. Locality

A constituent in TOP position can occur at an indefinite remove from the clause containing the anaphoric pronominal, and this clause can be at an arbitrary depth of embedding:

(97) (a) *[Mary]$_i$, it's obvious that she$_i$'s going to be mad at her brother*.
(b) *[John]$_i$, the books that he$_i$ reads are all in French*.
(c) *[Those kids]$_i$, to put them$_i$ to bed is really impossible for the parents*.

The pronominal associated with the TOP phrase occurs within a complement clause, a relative clause, and an infinitival complement. An ANTITOP constituent, however, must be **adjacent** to the clause containing the pronominal:

(98) (a) *That she$_i$'s going to be mad, [Mary]$_i$, is obvious*.
(a') **That she$_i$'s going to be mad at her brother is obvious, [Mary]$_i$*.
(b) *The books that he$_i$ reads, [John]$_i$, are all in French*.
(b') **The books that he$_i$ reads are all in French, [John]$_i$*.
(c) *To put them$_i$ to bed, [those kids]$_i$, is really impossible for the parents*.
(c') *?To put them$_i$ to bed is really impossible for the parents. [those kids]$_i$*.

In each of the primed sentences the ANTI-TOP NP is not directly adjoined to the clause containing the pronominal but to a clause following it, which is higher in the tree structure. The syntactic constraint operating in the starred sentences has been referred to as "Right-Roof" constraint (Ross 1983). The effect of this constraint in RD sentences is discussed in Lambrecht (1981) for French and in Bresnan & Mchombo (1987) for Chichewa.

The Right-Roof constraint does not hold for verb-final languages like Japanese or Turkish. For example in Japanese, ANTITOP elements associated with subordinate clauses must appear after the main verb (Kuno 1978). (99a) shows the canonical version, (99b) its dislocated counterpart:

(99) (a) *Kimi (wa) kono-aida ano*
you TOP other day that
***resutoran de** nani o tabeta ka*
restaurant at what ACC ate Q
oboete iru?
remembering are
'Do you remember what we ate at that restaurant the other day?'

(b) *Nani o tabeta ka oboete*
what ACC ate Q remembering
iru, [kimi] [kono-aida] [ano
are you other day that
resutoran de]?
restaurant at
'Do you remember what we ate there, you, the other day, at the restaurant?'

In (99b), both the topic of the main clause (*kimi* 'you') and the temporal and locative adjuncts (*kono-aida* 'the other day', *ano resutoran de* 'at that restaurant') associated with the indirect interrogative clause are appended in absolute sentence-final position after the main verb. No ANTITOP constituent associated with a subordinate clause may be directly appended to that clause:

(100) (a) *Kimi Taroo ga* **Hanako to**
you Taroo NOM Hanako WITH
kekkonsita koto sitte iru?
married that knowing are
'Do you know that Taroo married Hanako?'

(b) *Kimi Taroo ga ø_i kekkonsita*
you Taroo NOM married
koto sitte iru, [Hanako to]_i?
that knowing are Hanako with
'Do you know that Taroo married her, Hanako?'

(c) **Kimi Taroo ga ø_i kekkonsita, [Hanako to]_i, koto sitte iru?*

(100c) is ill-formed because the phrase *Hanako to* 'with Hanako' appears after the verb of the embedded clause rather than after the main verb, as it does in (b).

4.2.2. Embeddability

LD is a so-called "main-clause phenomenon", i.e. TOP constituents cannot freely occur within subordinate clauses (cf. Givón 1976, Lambrecht 1981):

(101) (a) *[John]_i, I wrote him_i a letter last week.*
(b) *?I believe that [John]_i, I wrote him_i a letter last week.*
(c) *??When [John]_i, I wrote him_i a letter last week, he was happy.*
(d) **The letter which [John]_i, I wrote him_i last week got lost.*

(101) shows a cline of acceptability depending on whether the subordinate clause containing the TOP phrase is a complement clause (as in (b)), an adverbial clause (as in (c)), or a relative clause (as in (d)). No such constraint holds for RD:

(101′) (a) *I wrote him_i a letter last week, [John]_i.*
(b) *I believe that I_i wrote him a letter last week, [John]_i.*
(c) *When I wrote him a letter last week. [John]_i, he was happy.*
(d) *The letter which I wrote him_i last week, [John]_i, got lost.*

Analogous facts have been reported for French (Lambrecht 1981), Turkish (Erguvanli 1984), Chichewa (Bresnan & Mchombo 1987), and Classical Arabic (Moutaouakil 1989). As argued in Givón (1976) and Lambrecht (1981, 1996a), the acceptability cline in (101) has a pragmatic explanation: the degree of unacceptability correlates with the degree to which the proposition expressed by the embedded clause is pragmatically presupposed. The propositions expressed in relative-clauses (so-called "Islands") being most strongly presupposed, such clauses are most reluctant to accept TOP constituents.

4.2.3. Case Marking

Given their relationally independent status, TOP elements need not, and often cannot, have the same **case** as their coindexed pronominals. This is not true of ANTITOP constituents. Consider the contrasts in these German and Russian examples:

(102) (a) *[Dieser Film]$_i$, als ich den$_i$*
this.NOM film when I it.ACC
sah, war ich ein Kind.
saw was I a.NOM child
'This film, when I SAW it I was a child.'

(b) *Als ich den$_i$ sah, [diesen Film]$_i$, war ich ein Kind.*
when I it.ACC saw this.ACC film was I a.NOM child
'When I SAW this film, I was a child.'

(c) **Als ich den$_i$ sah, [dieser Film]$_i$, war ich ein Kind.*

(103) (a) *[Volodja]$_i$, ona emu$_i$ napisala.*
Volodja.NOM she he.DAT wrote
'Volod, she wrote him.'

(b) *Ona napisala emu$_i$, [Volode]$_i$.*
she wrote he.DAT Volodja.DAT
'She wrote him, Volod.'

(c) **Ona napisala emu$_i$, [Volodja]$_i$.*

In both languages, the ANTITOP phrase must have the same case as the cataphoric pronominal, hence the ungrammaticality of the (c) sentences. The TOP phrase, however, appears in the nominative, independently of the case of the pronominal argument. This non-agreeing nominative case is referred to as **nominativus pendens** ('hanging nominative') in classical grammar. The constraint holds also for **prepositionial case marking**, as e. g. in Occitan:

(104) (a) *Lo cinema i vau sovent.*
the cinema there I.go often
'The movies, I go there often.'

(b) *I vau sovent, al cinema.*
there I.go often, to.the cinema,
'I go there often, to the movies.'

(c) **I vau sovent, lo cinema.*

See also the French examples in (23) above.

An apparent exception to the case-marking difference between TOP and ANTITOP phrases is (69), repeated here as (105):

(105) (a) *Lotta guys don't ask. [ME]$_i$, I$_i$ ASK.*
(b) *They$_i$ take a long TIME, [them]$_i$.*

In (105) the subject pronominals are in the nominative case (*I, they*), but both the TOP and the ANTITOP pronouns are in the non-nominative (accusative) case. (105) does not constitute a counterexample because in English the non-nominative form is the unmarked case form for pronouns: it is used whenever the pronoun is not a subject. An other apparent counterexample is the Chiceŵa sentence (106a):

(106) Chiceŵa (Bresnan & Mchombo 1987)
a. *ndi-na-pít-á nawó ku msika,*
I-REC.PST-go-IND with.it.3 to market
[mkángó uwu]
lion.3 this
'I went with it to market, this lion.'

b. **ndi-na-pít-á ndi iwó ku*
I-REC.PST-go-IND with it.3 to
msika, [mkángó uwu]
market lion.3 this
'I went with it to market, this lion.'

The ANTITOP phrase *mkángó uwu* lacks a preposition corresponding to English *with*. The apparent exception is explained by the fact that *nawó* is not a prepositional phrase but a "contracted prepositional pronoun" (Bresnan & Mchombo). As (106b) shows, the independent PP *ndi iwó* may not occur in the same construction.

4.2.4. Pronominal coindexation

Another major difference between LD and RD is that ANTITOP phrases (except adverbials) must be coindexed with intra-clausel pronominals: ANTITOP phrases cannot be **unlinked**. For example, corresponding to the unlinked-TOP sentences in (38a), (40), or (41), repeated in (107) through (109), we do not find the corresponding unlinked ANTITOP sentences:

(107) (a) *[Mon premier mari], on avait une voiture puis une moto.*
(b) **On avait une voiture puis une moto, [mon premier mari].*

(108) (a) *[The typical family today], the husband and the wife both work.*
(b) **The husband and the wife both work, [the typical family today].*

(109) (a) *And [this guy]$_i$, his$_i$ fishing pole fell down in the water.*
(b) **And his$_i$ fishing pole fell down in the water, [this guy]$_i$.*

Example (110) illustrates the same constraint in Arabic (cf. 39c)):

(110) (a) *[L-lahmu], r-ritlu bi*
the-meat.NOM the-pound.NOM with
ʿshrina dirhaman.
twenty-gen dirham.ACC
'Meat costs 20 dirhams the pound.'

(b) **r-ritlu bi ʿshrina dirhaman, [l-lahmu].*

The unlinked topic NP *l-lahmu* 'meat' cannot appear in ANTITOP position. The fact that ANTITOP phrases cannot be unlinked confirms our earlier observation that unlinked topics do not belong to the same syntactic category as adjunct phrases. For example, if the unlinked ANTITOP phrase *the typical family today* in (108b) were replaced by an adverbial, say *nowadays*, the sentence would become perfectly acceptable (*The husband and the wife both WORK, nowadays*).

Notice that the constraint against unlinked ANTITOP phrases does not pertain to sentences in which a coindexed pronominal is phononogically **null** (§ 3.2.). In fact, null instantiation of pronouns applies more freely in RD than in LD. For example, in some languages a coindexed subject pronoun may (under certain conditions) be omitted in the case of RD, but not of LD. This is shown in (111):

(111) French (Lambrecht 1996a)
    (a) *ø$_i$ mérite des* BAFFES, *[ce petit con]$_i$*.
    'Deserves a slap in the face, this little jerk.'
    (b) **[Ce petit con]$_i$, ø$_i$ mérite des* BAFFES.

In fact, in certain copular RD sentences both the subject pronominal and the copula may be omitted; however this is impossible in TOP sentences:

(112) (a) *ø$_i$ ø bizarre, [ce truc]$_i$.* [= *Il est bizarre, ce truc.*]
    'Strange, that thing.'
    (b) **[Ce truc]$_i$, ø$_i$ ø bizarre.*

(113) is an example of the same elliptical RD construction in Finnish:

(113) Finnish (Vilkuna 1989)
    ø$_i$ ø NÄTTI TYTTÖ, *[tuo Mikon*
        pretty girl   that Mikko.gen
    morsian]$_i$.
    fiancée
    'Pretty girl, that fiancée of Mikko's.'

The construction also exists in English, witness the naturalness of the glosses of (112) and (113).

4.2.5. Prosody

Finally, there is a clear **prosodic** difference between TOP and ANTITOP phrases. While the former necessarily have a degree of prosodic **prominence**, the latter are always **unaccented**. Looking at our cross-linguistic sample of RD sentences in (4), we notice in all six languages a clear intonation drop from the prosodically prominent clause-final focus constituent to the ANTITOP phrase following it. In the corresponding TOP sentences in (5), however, no clear difference in relative prominence is perceived between the TOP phrase and the following comment clause. (Of course TOP phrases may be more or less prominent, depending on the speech situation.) Lack of prosodic prominence on ANTITOP constituents has been observed for Turkish (Erguvanli 1984), Chinese (Guo 1997), French (Lambrecht 1981, Ashby 1994), and Norwegian (Fretheim 1995).

The perception of greater prosodic prominence of TOP constituents is consistent with the different syntactic status of the two types. It is known that degrees of relative prominence are perceived within syntactic units (Ladd 1978). Inasmuch as TOP phrases are syntactically independent, they also constitute independent phonological units; as such they necessarily have a degree of prosodic prominence. On the other hand, since ANTITOP phrases are syntactically connected with syntactic units containing focus elements, their relatively deaccented status is clearly perceived. The intonation drop between a focus and an ANTITOP phrase has often been described as a **pause**. However, pauses are a necessary feature neither of TOP nor of ANTITOP constituents (cf. 5.2.).

4.2.6. Summary

The various structural differences between LD and RD described in this section indicate that while both TOP and ANTITOP phrases are clause-external elements, the former exhibit a much higher degree of grammatical autonomy than the latter. The syntactic status of ANTITOP phrases is in between that of fully integrated arguments (subjects, objects, obliques) and fully independent TOP phrases (cf. Ziv 1994).

The observation concerning the semantic and syntactic independence of TOP phrases from the following predication leads us to a further revision of the definition of LD given in § 1. The coreference relation between a TOP phrase and a pronominal, which has generally been taken as criterial, turns out to be an epiphenomenon. Coreference in LD is not governed syntactically or semantically but is one of pragmatic construal alone. It follows that the coreference relation is always **cancellable**. For example in our paradigm example (5), the TOP NP and the pronominal may or may not have the same referent:

(114) (a) *[The Romans]$_i$, they$_i$ are crazy.*
(b) *[The Romans]$_i$, they$_j$ are crazy.*

It is possible to construe the TOP NP and the pronoun as disjoint in reference, although the coreference reading is strongly preferred in the absence of a discourse context (we can imagine (114b) in a context like "My parents don't care much for Italians in general, but the Romans, they are crazy, they absolutely love them"). Thus, from a strictly grammatical point of view, all TOP phrases are unlinked.

The syntactic structure of dislocation sentences is schematically represented in (115). This representation replaces the one in (3), which did not account for the hierarchical difference between LD and RD:

(115)
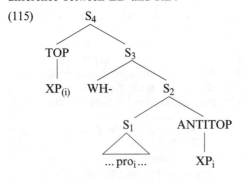

S_1 is the obligatory clausal core which contains the (possibly null) coindexed pronominal and whose proposition expresses the focal information of the sentence. S_2 is the sentential unit made up of S_1 and the sister-adjoined ANTITOP constituent to its right. S_3 is the sentential unit consisting of S_2 and the WH- (or COMP) slot found in languages with leftward WH-movement. This WH-slot may sometimes contain the focus instead of S_1. S_4 is the overall unit consisting of S_3 and the TOP slot to its left (the subscript on the TOP XP is in parentheses because of the occurrence of unlinked topics). Some researchers (e. g. Ziv 1994) insist on the non-sentential status of S_4 and prefer referring to it as a discourse unit rather than a sentence.

5. Discourse functions of Left-Dislocation and Right-Dislocation

5.1. Dislocation as topic-marking

There is a general consensus in the literature on dislocation that LD and RD are **topic-marking** constructions, i.e. grammatical constructions which serve to mark a constituent as denoting the **topic** (or **theme**) with respect to which a given sentence expresses a relevant **comment** (Dik 1978, Gundel 1988, Lambrecht 1994 and many others). Some researchers (e. g. Prince 1984, Ward 1988, Ward & Birner 1994) avoid the relational category *topic* and analyze LD and RD instead in terms of the pragmatic salience of the TOP and ANTITOP denotata alone. The categories **topic** and **comment** are defined in (116) (from Gundel 1988):

(116) Definition of Topic and Comment (Gundel 1988):
An entity, E, is the topic of a sentence, S, iff in using S the speaker intends to increase the addressee's knowledge about, request information about, or otherwise get the addressee to act with respect to E.
A predication, P, is the comment of a sentence, S, iff in using S the speaker intends P to be assessed relative to the topic of S.

Topic thus involves a relation of **aboutness** between an entity and a predication relative to a given discourse context (→ Art. 46, 104).

The topic of a predication contrasts with its **focus**. The focus is that element of a proposition whose occurrence makes it possible for a sentence to convey **new information** (Lambrecht 1994). Since TOP and ANTITOP phrases have a topic-relation to the predication, they are necessarily **non-focal** sentence elements. This can be verified by looking at the kinds of questions to which dislocation sentences may serve as appropriate replies. For example, our model sentence (1a), repeated in simplified form as (117c), could serve as a reply to the WH-question in (a) but not in (b):

(117) (a) *How long does Chris sleep in the morning?*
(b) *Who sleeps late in the morning?*
(c) *[That Chris]$_i$, he$_i$ sleeps LATE.*
(d) *That CHRIS does.*

Utterance (c) is a possible reply to (a) because the information requested via the WH-expression *how long* is provided by the focus expression *LATE*. However, (c) is not a possible reply to (b) because the topical nature of the NP *that Chris* prevents it from being construed as providing the information requested via the WH-word *who*. An appropriate reply to (b) would require a non-dislocated sentence like (d), whose subject can function as a focus.

For an entity to be construable as a topic in the sense of (116), and for a predication to be interpretable as a comment about this topic, a hearer must already have some mental representation of the entity prior to the act of predication, i.e. the referent of the topic expression must be **identifiable** for the hearer. One cannot assess a predication relative to a given topic unless one knows what the topic entity is (Lambrecht 1994). This cognitive identifiability constraint has consequences for the semantic interpretation of topic expressions. Consider the Japanese sentence in (118) (from Gundel 1988):

(118) *Neko wa kingyo o ijitte.*
cat TOP goldfish OBJ play.with
'The/*A cat is playing with the/a goldfish.'

While the object NP in (118) can receive either a definite or an indefinite interpretation, the TOP NP can only be construed as definite, i.e. as having a referent that is uniquely identifiable by the hearer. In languages which have a grammatical category of **definiteness**, a TOP or ANTITOP constituent must therefore be a **definite** expression, or else it must be capable of a **generic** interpretation. Consider the contrasts in (119):

(119) French (Lambrecht 1981)
(a) *[Un garçon]$_i$, il$_i$ attend devant la porte.
'A boy he is waiting outside the door.'
(b) [Un garçon]$_i$, ça$_i$ n'attend pas devant la porte, ça entre.
'A boy doesn't wait outside the door, he enters.'

(119a) is unacceptable because the TOP constituent is an indefinite NP with a specific unidentifiable referent. (119b) is acceptable because here the NP has a generic reading (triggered by the use of the pronominal *ça* instead of *il*). (120) and (121) illustrate the definiteness constraint in Turkish and Arabic:

(120) Turkish (Erguvanli 1984)
(a) *Adam-in oda-sin-da* **bir**
man-GEN room-POSS3-LOC one
lamba yani-yor-du.
lamp burn-PROG-PST
'A lamp was burning in the man's room.'
(b) **Adam-in oda-sin-da yani-yor-du,* [bir lamba].
It was burning in the man's room, a lamp.'

(121) Classical Arabic (Moutaouakil 1989)
(a) *[r-rajulu]$_i$, qara?tu*
the-man.NOM read.1SG
kitabahu$_i$.
book.ACC.3MS.GEN
'The man, I read his book.'
(b) *[rajulun]$_i$, qara?tu kitabahu$_i$.
'A man, I read his book.'

In Turkish and Arabic, as in French, the starred sentences are ill-formed because the dislocated constituents are grammatically marked as having unidentifiable referents.

For a dislocation construction to be used appropriately, a second pragmatic condition must be met. In order to be able to construe a denotatum as the topic of a predication the hearer must take it to be a center of present concern in the discourse, i.e. its topic role must be to some degree expectable at the time of utterance (Lambrecht 1994). A TOP or ANTITOP referent must therefore not only be identifiable but it must also have a degree of **salience** or **topicality** in the present discourse. This explains the oddness of (122b/c) compared to (122a) (the # sign indicates discourse-inappropriateness):

(122) (a) *Hi John. Guess what. I saw your* SISTER *last night.*
(b) #*Hi John. Guess what. Your sister, I* SAW *her last night.*
(c) #*Hi John. Guess what. I* SAW *her last night, your sister.*

Assuming that the addressee's sister is not an expectable topic at utterance time, the use of a dislocation construction is inappropriate. In Prince's (1992) terms, a topic referent must not only be "hearer-old", i.e. identifiable by the hearer at utterance time, but "discourse-old", i.e. it must have been in one way or another evoked in prior discourse or in the extra-linguistic context.

The topicality condition on the referents of dislocated NPs is illustrated in this Turkish RD example (Erguvanli 1984):

(123) A: *Nese Abla-yla görüs-tü-k.*
Nese Abla-with see-PST-1PL
'We saw Nese Abla.'
B: *Nasil bul-du-n, [Nese-Abla-yi],*
how find-PST-2SG Nese Abla-ACC
ihtiyarla-mis mi?
age-PST Q.ENGL
'How did you FIND (her,) Nese Abla, has she aged?'

A: *Yoo, ben cok iyi bul-du-m,*
   no   I   very well find-PST-1SG
   [Nese Abla-yi].
   Nese Abla-ACC
   'Not at all, I found Nese Abla very WELL.'

In A's first utterance, the new discourse referent 'Nese Abla' is introduced in preverbal position, which is the position for focus arguments in V-final languages (the fact that the NP also happens to be sentence-initial is coincidental). Use of a dislocation construction would have been as inappropriate here as it was in (122). However, once the referent 'Nese Abla' has been established as a potential topic for further commentary, dislocation becomes appropriate, if not obligatory. This basic topicality constraint on the referents of dislocated constituents is a well-established cross-linguistic fact. For example, the French translation of (123) in (123') has the same distribution of canonical vs. dislocated structures:

(123') A: *On a vu Nese Abla.*
          #*[Nese Abla], on l'a vue.*
       B: *Comment tu l'as trouvée, [Nese Abla]? Elle a vieilli?*
          #*Comment tu as trouve Nese Abla? Elle a vieilli?*
       A: *Pas du tout, je l'ai trouvée très bien, [Nese Abla].*
          #*Pas du tout, j'ai trouvé Nese Abla très bien.*

In A's first turn, canonical syntax is required and RD is unacceptable. After that, RD becomes appropriate and canonical syntax is (more or less) unacceptable.

5.2. Functional differences between Left-Dislocation and Right-Dislocation

Having established the basic discourse function of dislocation, we must now analyze the factors that govern a speaker's choice of LD vs. RD. This choice can be explained on the basis of a universal **iconic ordering principle** (Lambrecht 1996a). According to this principle, TOP vs. ANTITOP position of a topic expression correlates with the relative pragmatic salience of the topic referent at utterance time: while the order topic-comment signals **announcement** or **establishment** of a new topic relation between a referent and a predication, the order comment-topic signals **continuation** or **maintenance** of an already established relation.

The difference between topic-announcement and topic-continuation is illustrated in the following attested example from spoken French (Lambrecht 1987):

(124) Husband and wife at dinner table; H. looks at food on his plate:
H: *Ça n'a pas de* GOÛT, *ce poulet.*
   'It has no taste, this chicken.'
   #CE POULET, *ça n'a pas de* GOÛT.
W: *Le* VEAU, *c'est* PIRE.
   'Veal (it) is worse.'
   ##*C'est* PIRE, *le veau.*

In the husband's remark, RD is appropriate because the chicken on the plate counts as an already ratified topic of conversation, given its pragmatic salience in the discourse setting. (Across languages, RD frequently occurs in such deictic contexts.) Use of the topic-establishing LD device would have been less appropriate (though not necessarily unacceptable). In the wife's reply, the topic is shifted from the specific chicken on the plate to the generic topic *veal*. Since this new topic is not yet established in the discourse, use of the topic-maintaining RD device would be highly inappropriate. Any topic being overtly or implicitly **contrasted** with some possible alternative requires LD coding.

Notice that announcing a **new topic** for some predication via LD is not equivalent to introducing a **new referent** into a discourse. As we saw, for a predication to be construed as a comment about an entity, this entity must be discourse-salient, i.e. it must already be a potential topic. In the wife's reply in (124), the discourse referent 'veal', while not overtly established, is nevertheless inferrable as a potential topic by virtue of belonging to the semantic frame 'meat' which was evoked by the husband's utterance. Without this possibility of frame inference, use of a dislocation would have been inappropriate.

In some languages, the pragmatic difference between announcing vs. maintaining a topic referent has consequences for the choice between two types of coindexed pronominal. For example, German has two sets of third-person personal pronouns, which are distinguished by the presence or absence of an initial [d-] (*er, sie, es* vs. *der, die, das*). Pronouns of the *er*-set are used when the referent is an established topic, while those of the *der*-set occur when the topic relation between the referent and the predication is not yet ratified. Thus in anaphoric contexts such as that in (125), only a pronoun from the *er*-series may occur (Lambrecht 1994):

(125) Wenn {er$_i$/der$_j$} isst, macht {er$_i$/*der$_i$} so komische Geräusche.
'When he eats, he makes funny noises.'

Once the entity has been referred to with *er*, it cannot be referred to anaphorically with *der*. Now consider the data in (126):

(126) (a) *[Die Müllers], {die$_i$/*sie$_i$} wohnen im dritten Stock.*
'The Müllers, they live on the third floor.'
(b) *{Die$_i$/sie$_i$} wohnen im dritten Stock, [die Müllers]$_i$.*

In accordance with our general iconic principle, LD in German requires a coindexed pronominal of the *der*-series. The use of *die* over *sie* in (126a) is a consequence of the fact that LD is used for topics which are not yet established in the discourse.

The fundamental functional difference between topic announcement and topic continuation is directly reflected in the grammatical differences between LD and RD mentioned in § 4.2. First, it is reflected in the different constraints on **locality** (§ 4.2.1.). Cognitively, it is relatively easy to store an announced referent in short-term memory until a piece of information relevant to this referent is provided. Utterance of the clause containing the relevant piece of information can therefore be delayed. It is much more difficult to store a piece of information in short-term memory without knowing the referent with respect to which the information is being conveyed. One cannot evaluate a property unless one can identify the entity to which the property is being attributed. It is therefore necessary for the ANTITOP expression to immediately follow the clause containing the coindexed pronominal.

The same line of reasoning holds for the difference in **embeddability** (§ 4.2.2.). It is well-known that the propositions expressed in subordinate clauses tend to be pragmatically **presupposed** rather than **asserted**, with restrictive relative clauses being the most strongly presupposed kind. Since the function of LD is to announce a not yet discourse-presupposed topic referent, association of a TOP constituent with a clause whose proposition is pragmatically presupposed results in a clash between conflicting presuppositions. In the case of RD, no such clash arises. Since the ANTITOP referent is marked as already established, or presupposed, in the discourse, is association with a presupposed proposition is felicitous.

Essentially the same kind of explanation is available to account for the difference in **case-marking** (§ 4.2.3.). Since in RD the predicate-argument structure of the proposition is already established by the time the ANTITOP constituent is processed, it is impossible to construe the semantic role of the topic denotatum without making reference to the role of the case-marked pronominal cataphor. In LD, on the other hand, the semantic role of the topic denotatum is not predetermined by an already processed predicate-argument structure. Therefore the case form of the TOP NP is independent of that of the anaphoric pronominal. For the same processing reason, pronominal **coindexation** (§ 4.2.4.) is obligatory in RD but not in LD: ANTITOP phrases may not be unlinked because it is difficult to construe a proposition as being about a referent if the clause expressing the proposition has already been processed without such construal. Finally, the difference in **prosody** (§ 4.2.5.) between TOP and ANTITOP phrases is explainable in essentially the same terms: referential constituents are unaccented just in case the pragmatic relation between the referent and the proposition is already ratified at utterance time, as it is in RD (cf. Lambrecht 1994 and Lambrecht & Michaelis 1998). Since in LD this relation is not yet ratified, the TOP constituent is accented.

In defining the appropriateness conditions for LD and RD it is important to draw a conceptual distinction between the **topic role** of the TOP/ANTITOP referent and the cognitive **accessibility state** of the representation of the referent in the minds of the interlocutors at given points in the discourse. While different accessibility states can influence the choice of LD vs. RD, accessibility is only a necessary precondition for use of a dislocation construction; it is not the factor determining this choice. A referent with the same accessibility state may receive either LD or RD coding, depending on the degree of topicality it has in the discourse situation. This is particularly obvious in the case of **dislocated pronouns** (cf. § 3.5.). Since use of a pronoun signals a speaker's assumption that a referent is already highly accessible in the hearer's short-term memory (or can be pragmatically accommodated as such), the occurrence of dislocated pronouns in either ANTITOP or TOP position is evidence that the choice of one over the other is in principle independent of the relative accessibility state of the topic referent. Let us look again at the examples in (69), repeated here as (127):

(127) (a) *Lotta guys don't ASK. [ME]$_i$, I$_i$ ASK.*
 (b) (In conversation about how to cook sweet potatoes)
 They$_i$ take a long TIME, [them]$_i$.

The choice of the TOP position for the pronoun *ME* in (a) does not signal that the referent of the pronoun is less accessible than that of the pronoun *them* in (b). Indeed the referent of *ME*, i.e. the speaker, is by definition highly accessible. Rather LD coding in (a) is motivated by the fact that the topic of the predication 'I ask' is not the same as that of the preceding predication, hence that the topic role of 'me' needs to be established.

What is, then, the motivating factor for RD coding of the pronoun *them* in (127b)? Since the referent of this pronoun was expressed in the form of the unaccented pronominal *they* in the immediately preceding clause, repetition of the pronoun in ANTITOP position may seem redundant and communicatively inefficient. In fact, this apparent inefficiency characterizes all instances of RD, since in all cases a referent is first coded in pronominal form before it is expressed in ANTITOP position. In order to understand the discourse motivation for RD, it is useful to recall the similarity between topics and **vocatives** (§ 3.5.). Given the intuitive notion of vocatives as "calling forms" (Latin *vocativus casus*, 'calling case') used to draw an addressee's attention to some state of affairs, utterance of a vocative phrase **after** the sentence expressing the proposition to which the addressee's attention is being drawn seems illogical. Our intuition tells us, however, that there is nothing illogical in this strategy: the ANTITOP vocative serves to secure the continued attention of an addressee, i.e. to maintain a given relation between a referent and a proposition. This is not to say that in all instances of RD the referent of the ANTITOP phrase can be determined by the hearer on the basis of the intra-clausal pronominal alone. Various factors can make it necessary to code the topic referent both pronominally and in full lexical form. For example, RD coding may be required in the case of cooccurrence of two topics in the same proposition. In order to keep the two referents apart, they must each be lexically specified in ANTITOP position.

The occurrence of unaccented pronouns in ANTITOP position allows us to discard a common explanation for the phenomenon of RD (e.g. Hyman 1975, Dik 1978, Moutaouakil 1989). According to this explanation, RD expresses an **afterthought**, i.e. it serves as a **repair** mechanism used to provide a more explicit referential expression in a situation where use of a pronoun is judged to be insufficient for the hearer to identify the intended referent. The frequent and fully conventionalized use of unaccented pronouns in ANTITOP position clearly runs counter to this interpretation. An example of an afterthought sentence is given in (128) (from Ziv 1994):

(128) *I met him, your brother, I mean, two weeks ago.*

As Ziv (1994) observes, afterthought expressions differ from ANTITOP phrases in that they constitute separate intonation units; as such they are necessarily accented and preceded by a pause. ANTITOP phrases, on the other hand, form a single intonation contour with the preceding clause: they are unaccented and not preceded by a pause. Experimental evidence for a phonological distinction between afterthought and RD is provided by Ashby (1994) for French and by Fretheim (1995) for Norwegian. Another argument in favor of the distinction is provided by the frequent cooccurrence of illocutionary markers like *I mean* in (128), which explicitly signal the repair function of the afterthought expression. A Turkish example involving such a marker is shown in (129):

(129) Turkish (Erguvanli 1984)
 Koja-si **sey-de** *calis-iyor*
 husband-POSS3 thing-LOC work-PROG
 farbika-da
 factory-LOC
 'Her husband works at the whatchamacallit, the factory.'

The expression *sey-de* in the preverbal focus position functions as a kind of placeholder, making it possible for the speaker to produce the previously unavailable referential expression *farbika-da* after the sentence is completed.

6. Special abbreviations

ACC accusative
ADE adessive
ANTITOP antitopic (right-dislocated position or constituent)

COMP	complementizer
DO	direct object
ENC	enclitic
IND	indicative
LD	Left-Dislocation
RD	Right-Dislocation
SM	subject marker
OM	object marker
Q	question marker
PAR	paressive
PERF	perfective
PST	past
REFL	reflexive
TOP	topic (left-dislocated position or constituent)

7. References

Aissen, Judith L. 1992. "Topic and focus in Mayan." *Language* 68, 1: 43–80.

Akmajian, Adrian. 1984. "Sentence types and the form-function fit." *Natural Language and Linguistic Theory*, 2, 1: 1–23.

Ashby, William J. 1994. "An acoustic profile of right-dislocations in French." *French Language Studies* 4: 127–145.

Barnes, Betsy. 1985. *The pragmatics of Left Detachment in standard spoken French*. Amsterdam: John Benjamins.

Blanche-Benveniste, Claire. 1981. "La complémentation verbale: valence, rection, et associés." *Recherches sur la Français Parlé*, 3: 57–98. Aix-en-Provence: Publications Université de Provence.

Bresnan, Joan & Mchombo, Sam A. 1987. "Topic, pronoun, and agreement in Chicheŵa." *Language* 63, 4: 741–782.

Chafe, Wallace. 1976. "Givenness, contrastiveness, definiteness, subjects, topics and point of view." In: Li, Charles. (ed.). *Subject and topic*. New York: Academic Publishers, 25–56.

Chomsky, Noam. 1977. "On WH-Movement." In Culicover, Peter, Wasow, Thomas & Akmajian, Adrian (eds.) *Formal syntax*. New York: Academic Press, 71–132.

Daneš, Frantisek. 1966. "A three-level approach to syntax." In: *Travaux linguistiques de Prague*, vol. 1 (*L'école de Prague d'aujourd'hui*). Paris: Kliencksieck, 225–240.

Dik, Simon C. 1978. *Functional grammar*. Amsterdam: North Holland.

Erguvanli, Eser. 1984. *The function of word order in Turkish grammar*. (University of California Publications in Linguistics, vol. 106.) Berkeley, Los Angeles: UC Press.

Fillmore, Charles, J. 1985. "Frames and the semantics of understanding." *Quaderni di Semantica* VI, 2: 222–254.

Fradin, Bernard. 1990. "Approche des constructions à détachement. Inventaire." *Revue Romane* 52 1: 3–34.

François, Denise. 1974. *Français parlé. Analyse des unités phoniques et significatives d'un corpus recueilli dans la région parisienne*. 2 vols. Paris: S.E.L.A.F.

Fretheim, Thorstein. 1995. "Why right-dislocated phrases are not afterthoughts." *Nordic Journal of Linguistics*, 18: 31–54.

Gadet, Françoise. 1989. *Le français ordinaire*. Paris: Armand Colin.

Givón, Talmy. 1976. "Topic, pronoun and grammatical agreement." In: Li, Charles (ed.), *Subject and Topic*. New York: Academic Press, 149–188.

Gundel, Jeanette K. 1988. "Universals of Topic-Comment Structure." In: Hammond, Michael, Moravcsik, Edith & Wirth, Jessica (eds.), *Studies in Linguistic Typology*. Amsterdam/Philadelphia: John Benjamins, 209–239.

Guo, Jiansheng. 1997. "Right dislocation or right location? The "afterthought" phenomenon in Mandarin Chinese and markers of speakers' intentions." (Symposium Series of the Institute of History and Philology. Academia Sinica, Number 2.) *Chinese language and linguistics III: Morphology and lexicon*. Taipei, Taiwan: Academia Sinica, 237–276.

Hanson, Kristin. 1987. "Topic constructions in French: Some comparisons with Chicheŵa." *Berkeley Linguistic Society* 13: 105–116.

Hyman, Larry. 1975. "On the change from SOV to SVO: Evidence from Niger-Congo." In: Charles Li (ed.), *Word order and word order change*. Austin: University of Texas Press, 113–147.

Hewitt, Brian G. 1979. *Abkhaz*. (Lingua Descriptive Series, 2.) Amsterdam: North Holland.

Jelinek, Eloise. 1984. "Empty categories, case, and configurationality." *Natural Language and Linguistic Theory* 2: 39–76.

Kuno, Susumu. 1978. "Japanese: a characteristic OV language." In: Lehmann, Winfried (ed.), *Syntactic typology. Studies in the phenomenology of language*. Austin: University of Texas Press, 57–138.

Ladd, Robert D, Jr. 1978. *The structure of intonational meaning. Evidence from English*. Bloomington: Indiana University Press.

Lambrecht, Knud. 1981. *Topic, antitopic and verb-agreement in non-standard French*. Amsterdam: Benjamins.

Lambrecht, Knud. 1987. "On the status of SVO sentences in French discourse." In: Tomlin, Russell (ed.). *Coherence and grounding in discourse*. Amsterdam: Benjamins, 217–262.

Lambrecht, Knud. 1990. "What me worry? – 'Mad Magazine sentences revisited." *Berkeley Linguistics Society*, 16: 215–228.

Lambrecht, Knud. 1994. *Information structure and sentence form. Topic, focus, and the mental represen-*

tations of discourse referents. (Cambridge Studies in Linguistics, vol. 71.) Cambridge: Cambridge University Press.

Lambrecht, Knud. 1996a. "On the formal and functional relationship between topics and vocatives. Evidence from French." In: Golberg, Adele (ed.), *Conceptual Structure, Discourse, and Language.* Stanford: CSLI, 267−288.

Lambrecht, Knud. 1996b. "Compositional vs. constructional meaning: the case of French *comme* N." *Semantics and Linguistic Theory* (SALT), 5. Cornell University, 186−203.

Lambrecht, Knud & Lemoine, Kevin. 1996. "Vers une grammaire des compléments d'objet zéro en français parlé." In: Chuquet, Jean & Fryd, Marc (eds.), *Absence de marques et représentation de l'absence.* Travaux Linguistiques du CerLiCO, 9. Rennes: Presses Universitaires de Rennes, 279−310.

Lambrecht, Knud & Michaelis, Laura A. 1998. "Sentence accent in information questions: Default and projection." *Linguistics & Philosophy,* 21, 5: 477−544.

Li, Charles & Thompson, Sandra A. 1976. "Subject and topic: A new typology of language." In: Li, Charles (ed.), *Subject and topic.* New York: Academic Press, 457−490.

Michaelis, Laura A. & Lambrecht, Knud. 1996. "Toward a construction-based theory of language function: The case of Nominal Extraposition." *Language* 72:2: 215−247.

Moutaouakil, Ahmed. 1989. *Pragmatic functions in a grammar of Arabic.* Dordrecht: Foris.

Müller-Hauser, Marie-Louise. 1943. *La mise en relief d'une idée en français moderne.* Geneva: Droz, Zürich: Eugen Rentsch.

Paul, Hermann. 1920 (1975). *Prinzipien der Sprachgeschichte.* Tübingen: Max Niemeyer Verlag.

Prince, Ellen. 1981. "Topicalization, focus movement and Yiddish movement: a pragmatic differentiation." *Berkeley Linguistics Society* 7: 249−264.

Prince, Ellen F. 1984. "Topicalization and left-dislocation: A functional analysis." In: White, Sheila J. & Teller, Virginia (eds), *Discourses in reading and linguistics.* Annals of the New York Academy of Sciences, vol. 433. New York: The New York Academy of Sciences, 213−225.

Prince, Ellen F. 1992. "The ZPG letter: subjects, definiteness, and information-status." In: Mann, William C. & Thompson, Sandra A. (eds), *Discourse description. Diverse linguistic analyses of a fund-raising text.* Amsterdam: John Benjamins, 295−325.

Raposo, Eduardo. 1986. "On the null object in European Portuguese." In: Osvaldo Jaeggli & Silva-Corvalán, Carmen (eds), *Studies in Romance Linguistics.* Dordrecht/Riverton: Foris Publications, 373−390.

Ross, John R. 1983. *Infinite syntax!* Norwood, New Jersey: Ablex Publishing Corporation.

Sauzet, Patrick. 1989. "Topicalisation et prolepse en occitan", in Rouveret, Alain et Sauzet, Patrick (eds.), *La structure de la proposition dans les langues romanes. Revue des Langues Romanes,* 93−2: 235−273.

Silva-Corvalán, Carmen. 1983. "On the interaction of word order and intonation: some OV constructions in Spanish." In: Andreu, Flora-Klein (ed.), *Discourse perspectives on syntax.* New York: Academic Press: 117−140.

Stark, Elisabeth. 1997. *Voranstellungsstrukturen und "topic"-Markierung im Französischen.* (Romanica Monacensia, vol. 51.) Tübingen: Gunter Narr Verlag.

Stempel, Wolf-Dieter. 1981. "L'amour elle appelle ça − L'amour tu ne connais pas." In: Rohrer, Christian (ed.), *Studia linguistica in honorem Eugenio Coseriu.* Vol. 4, *Grammatik.* Berlin: de Gruyter, 351−367.

Vallduví, Enric. 1992. *The informational component.* New York: Garland.

Vallduví, Enric. 1995. "Structural properties of information packaging in Catalan." In: É. Kiss, Katalin (ed.) *Discourse configurational languages.* New York, Oxford: Oxford University Press, 122−152.

Vendryès, Joseph. 1914 (1968). *Le Langage. Introduction linguistique à l'histoire.* Paris: Editions Albin Michel.

Vilkuna, Maria. 1989. *Free word order in Finnish. Its syntax and discourse functions.* Helsinki: Suomalaisen Kirjallisuuden Seura.

Ward, Gregory L. 1988. *The semantics and pragmatics of preposing.* New York: Garland.

Ward, Gregory & Betty Birner. 1996. "On the discourse function of Rightward Movement in English." In: Goldberg, Adele (ed.), *Conceptual Structure, Discourse, and Language.* Stanford: CSLI, 463−480.

Zimmer, Karl. 1986. "On the function of post-predicate subject pronouns in Turkish." In: Koç, Ayhan A. & Erguvanli, Eser (eds.), *Proceedings of the Turkish Linguistics Conference,* August 1984. Istanbul: Bogazici University Publications, 195−206.

Ziv, Yael. 1994. "Left and Right Dislocations: Discourse functions and anaphora." *Journal of Pragmatics* 22: 629−645.

Knud Lambrecht, University of Texas, Austin

81. Focus constructions

1. The notion of focus construction
2. The grammatical structure of focus constructions
3. Focus marking and the grammaticalization of focus constructions
4. References

1. The notion of focus construction

1.1. Two types of focus construction

The term focus construction (FC) is often used in discussions of syntactic aspects of information structure, especially where languages of the discourse configurational type (→ Art. 104) are concerned, but it can also be found in works on the typology of grammar, such as Givón (1990, esp. ch. 16) or Dik (1997). The use of the term varies, but it always denotes a type of sentence that serves to promote a specified constituent, its focus, to a position of particular prominence by setting it off from the rest of the sentence in one way or another.

There is a growing consensus among students of information structure that two types of focus must be distinguished in terms of form and interpretation: presentational focus (or information focus, focus of assertion, rheme, usually wide focus) refers to a constituent which must be interpreted as new, or context-incrementing information, whereas contrastive focus (or identificational focus, operator focus, usually narrow focus) denotes a constituent that identifies a subset within a set of contextually given alternatives. In keeping with this we have to distinguish presentational focus constructions (PFC) and contrastive focus constructions (CFC). The difference between the two constructional types lies in the interpretation of their focussed constituents, but it also affects the interpretation of the rest of the sentence. In a CFC, the non-focal part of the sentence, the focus frame or background, has the status of a contextually salient open proposition against whose alternative substitution instances the focussed sentence is evaluated. The particular effect that a CFC may have on the context is subject to a limited amount of variation across languages (Kiss 1998). In contrast to this, focal prominence in a PFC always highlights a term introducing a new entity into discourse, but without the implication that the rest of the sentence is given (Rochemont 1986: n. 121, p. 199).

1.1.1. Contrastive focus constructions

In CFCs prominence can be achieved through various types of syntactic strategies, such as clefting or displacement of the focus to the periphery of the sentence or into the vicinity of the verb. (1) and (2) show similar **cleft constructions** in English and Aghem, (3) is a Japanese pseudo-cleft.

(1) It was [$_F$ John] that ate the apple.

(2) Aghem (Bantu, Watters 1979: 168)
á mɔ̀ lɔ́ [$_F$ bá'tóm wíl] ɔ́ ò
DS P$_1$ COP chief this REL he
mɔ̀ búɔ
P$_2$ come
'It was the chief who came'
DS = summary subject; P$_1$, P$_2$ = tense markers

(3) Kiyoko ga katta no wa
Kiyoko NOM buy.PAST NOM TOP
[$_F$ sono hon] da
the book COP
'It was the book that Kiyoko bought.'

Different types of **displacement** are exemplified in (4)−(10), illustrating the most common focus positions found in natural languages: focus in initial position, which is very frequent, in (4)−(7), focus in final position, which is very rare, in (8), focus in preverbal position in (9) and focus in postverbal position in (10), which occurs in many languages.

(4) Standard Arabic (Ouhalla 1993: 277)
[$_F$ riwaayt-an] ʔallaf -at
novel-ACC write (PERF)-3F
Zaynab-u (laa qasiidat-an)
Zaynab-NOM (not poem-ACC)
'It is a novel Zaynab has written (not a poem)'

(5) Gungbe (Gbe language, Kwa group; Aboh 1999: 258)
[$_F$ wémà lɔ́] wɛ̀ Sɛ́ná xìá
book DET FOC Sena read.PERF
'It was the book that Sena read'

(6) Babine-Witsuwit'en (Athabaskan; Denham 1997: 63)
[$_F$ George] 'en Lillian yunt'iy'
George FOC Lillian 3s-like-3s
'It's George that Lillian likes.'

(7) Maasai (Nilotic; Creider 1989: 109)
[_F olpayian] a-yiolo enkitok
man   1s-know woman
na-ta-dua
REL-PAST-see
'It is the man that I know the woman that saw.'

(8) Podoko (Hadic; Tuller 1992: 319)
dək pe mənai [_F amnai]
built new house chief
'THE CHIEF built the new house.'

(9) Hungarian (Horvath 1995: 31)
[_F az újságot]   dobtam el
The newspaper-ACC threw-I away
'I threw away THE NEWSPAPER.'

(10) Kimatuumbi (Bantu; Odden 1984: 291 f.)
 (a) Ųkųmų́ akatae namánị?
    Ukumu 3s.cut.NF what?
    'What was Ukumu cutting?'
 (b) Ųkųmų́ akatae [_F kaámba]
    Ukumu 3s.cut.NF rope
    'Ukumu was cutting ROPE.'

All of the above constructions isolate a narrowly focussed constituent in a specified syntactic position. As (10) shows, this position is shared by foci and interrogative phrases in Kimatuumbi. This parallelism between focus and WH is extremely common and can be found in all languages in (4)−(10) with the possible exception of Babine-Witsuwit'en, where fronted foci and WH-phrases co-occur in a limited number of cases.

Constituent questions and FCs may not only target the same syntactic position but usually also share other characteristics, in particular **island constraints.** Islands are specified syntactic configurations which block unbounded extractions, such as WH-movement. In the framework of generative grammar it is customary to distinguish between 'strong' and 'weak' islands, both of which are interpreted as evidence for syntactic movement (Cinque 1990). A so-called Complex NP, as in (11), is a strong island which disallows any kind of WH-extraction. Weak islands, on the other hand, show markedness effects only with certain WH-adverbials. An example of the latter type is negation, which only induces a selective effect, as shown in (12).

(11) *What/*When did John hear the news that Bill [_VP ate ___]?

(12) (a) Who did/didn't Bill [_VP invite ___]?
    (b) How well did/*didn't John [_VP behave ___]?

In Hungarian WH-movement targets the preverbal focus position and shows island effects (Horvath 1986, Kiss 1987). A stress-focussed constituent, however, has no effect on grammaticality as long as it occurs within an island, such as a Complex NP, but it causes a violation when it is extracted and displaced to the preverbal focus positions, as the following examples show (Horvath 1986: 100 f.):

(13) (a) Kati hallotta a hírt
    Cathy heard the news.ACC
    hogy Attila [_F a földrengéstöl]
    that Attila the earthquake-from
    félt
    feared
   (b) *Kati [_F a földrengéstöl]
    Cathy the earthquake-from
    hallotta a hírt hogy Attila
    heard the news.ACC that Attila
    félt
    feared
    'Cathy heard the news that Attila had been afraid of the EARTHQUAKE.'

Constituent questions and FCs in Standard Arabic and Gungbe are also sensitive to island constraints, but this is obviously not true for Maasai, as (7) shows. In (7), a focussed constituent appears in initial position, but is linked to a gap inside a relative clause. This type of configuration is acceptable in Maasai focus constructions, but causes a strong violation in WH-questions. Other (including weak) islands can be violated in WH-questions as well. Nilotic languages seem to show a considerable amount of variation in their tolerance to island configurations (Creider 1989). Other languages appear to be completely liberal in this respect. Both Akan (Kwa; cf. Saah 1999) and Tuki (Bantu; cf. Biloa 1995) have WH- and FCs which freely violate island constraints. In FCs like (1)−(10), the highlighting effect, though carried by syntactic form, is usually reinforced through additional coding devices, such as particles, inflectional morphology, or prosodic features, which may combine in various ways. Since **prosodic prominence** is perhaps the most frequently encountered focussing device, its relationship to focus has frequently been claimed to be universal (cf. Roberts

1998: 147). In languages where displacement in FCs affects bare foci, such as in Hungarian, prosodic prominence occurs as a supporting factor. In intonational languages, prosodic prominence is marked by a pitch accent, but an intricate relationship between focus and suprasegmentals has also been claimed for tone languages. Makua, for instance, a close relative of Kimatuumbi, also has the type of postverbal focus position shown in (10). Makua nouns have a high tone when unfocussed or in citation form, but shift to a low tone in focus position and a few other contexts (Stucky 1979: 369f.). Similar tonal shifts and other types of evidence for closer ties between focus and tonal structure have been reported for a number of languages (Bearth 1980). With particular reference to Bantu, however, Hyman (1999) argues that the relationship between focus and tonal structures is indirect.

Languages like Gungbe, Babine-Witsuwit'en and many others mark the constituent-in-focus position by means of **'pure' focus particles** (König 1991: 28), i.e. particles that associate with focus, but lack lexical content. Akan and some languages related to it also use their focus particles to mark cleft foci (Ameka 1992). It should be noted that at least some languages that combine a displacement strategy with focus-marking particles have been claimed to have FCs whose foci lack prosodic prominence (cf., Aboh 1999: 258; Derbyshire 1985: 146). Similar claims have been made for some languages with cleft-based focus constructions (Harries-Delisle 1978: 471 ff.).

(10) exhibits a focussed object in the **postverbal focus position** of Kimatuumbi, which is also the landing site of WH-movement. Focussed subjects and adverbials also occur in this position. Such displacement of a focussed argument, however, is accompanied by a morphological effect in Kimatuumbi, which has a number of **tense forms** that occur only with specific focus-background structures: in (10) the 'noun-focal progressive tense' shows the verbal stem -kata with the subject prefix a- and the noun-focal suffix -e directly attached to it. The noun-focal tense form also co-occurs with a WH-constituent, as shown in (10a). In addition, Kimatuumbi also has 'verb-focal' tenses which are selected when the verb is focussed, but are excluded when a noun phrase is questioned or modified by a lexical focus particle such as tú 'only'. Similar verb forms can be observed in Makua and in many other African languages (cf. Hyman & Watters 1984). Some other languages have also been said to mark the presence or absence of focus on the nominal head of a term. In Aghem, which is known to have an unusually complex focus marking system, nouns occur in a prefixed form when out of focus. In (14a) the nominal occurs in a prefixed form in postverbal focus position, followed by the focus marker nò. In (14b) the focus position is occupied by an adverbial and in (14c) the focus marker nò is placed after the verb, focussing the lexical content of the verb. In both cases the object term shows the suffixed out-of-focus form. In imperatives, however, a focussed object occurs in the suffixed form and is followed by nô, cf. (14d). (Cf. Hyman & Watters 1979: 235 ff.)

(14) (a) m̀ mɔ́ zɨ̀ [$_F$ kɨ́-bɛ́ nò] né
I PAST eat PFX-fufu FOC today
'I ate FUFU today.'
(b) m̀ mɔ́ zɨ̀ [$_F$ né] bɛ́-'kɔ́
I PAST eat today fufu-SFX
'I ate fufu TODAY.'
(c) m̀ mɔ́ [$_F$ zɨ̀ nô] bɛ́-'kɔ́ né
I PAST eat FOC fufu-SFX today
'I ATE fufu today.' (i.e., didn't cook fufu today)
(d) zɨ̀ [$_F$ bɛ́-'kɔ́ nô]
eat fufu-SFX FOC
'Eat FUFU!'

While the literature on FCs provides us with a wealth of information about their syntactic, morphological and phonological properties, discussions of the interpretation of CFCs are rarely explicit enough to allow us to derive firm conclusions. More often than not, the authors suggest an exclusively contrastive interpretation in the sense defined above, but there seem to be exceptions (cf., e.g., Odden 1984: 282). For this reason the term CFC has occasionally been criticized as inappropriate or misleading (cf., e.g., Ouhalla 1999 with reference to Moutaouakil 1989). In typological studies and in the analysis of the information structure of non-Indoeuropean – in particular African – languages the term 'focus construction' primarily stands for constructions with a contrastive reading.

1.1.2. Presentational focus constructions

The other important use of the term 'focus construction' originated in the attempts to analyze certain stylistically marked types of English sentences within a principle-based theory of universal grammar, in order to derive their 'stylistic' properties from a syntactic theory of focus structure. A major contribution to this effort was made in Rochemont & Culicover (1990), where the term 'focus construction' refers to English sentences like the following:

(15) (a) *A young man stepped into her room [F with long hair]*
 (b) *She invited a young man to her party [F with long hair]*

(16) *Into her room stepped [F a young man with long hair]*

(17) *There stepped into her room [F a young man with long hair]*

(18) *She invited to her party [F a young man with long hair]*

(15a) and (15b) illustrate the extraposition of adjuncts from noun phrases occupying external and internal argument positions. (16) exemplifies the stylistic inversion construction, (17) the Presentational THERE construction, and (18) the Heavy NP Shift construction. In each case the bracketed constituent is assumed to have undergone a process of **rightward displacement** to a position where the displaced item shows an obligatory focus effect. In (15a) and (15b) the focus effect on the extraposed modifier depends on the focussed status of its head. Rochemont (1986) distinguishes the constructions in (15)−(18) from constructions with a contrastive interpretation. He formulates both a Contrastive Focus Principle, which assigns a contrastive reading to the focus position of a set of constructions essentially equivalent to the CFCs discussed above, and a Constructional Focus Principle, which assigns a presentational reading to the elements occupying focus positions in (15)−(18). Rochemont & Culicover (1990) propose a generalized Focus Principle, which is meant to cover all types of focus positions, thereby avoiding making specific assumptions on interpretational differences. The position of Rochemont (1986), however, is more compatible with the results of typological work on presentational constructions than the generalized account represented by Rochemont and Culicover, which tries to abstract away from the distinction between contrastive and presentational cases. A subset of the construction types in (15)−(16), in particular inversions and expletive constructions, have been intensively studied in typological work under such labels as **'presentative movement'**, 'participant introduction' and 'topic continuity'. The term 'presentative' was first introduced by Hetzron (1971) in a study of the correlation between the sentence final position of a term, in particular the subject, and its availablility for further reference in subsequent discourse, i. e. its 'cataphoric persistence', in Givón's terms (cf. Givón 1983). Hetzron (1975) presented a wide range of crosslinguistic data to support his claim that there is a tendency to move 'new' and 'persistent' participants to a sentence-final or 'later than usual' position. Another often discussed aspect of presentative constructions comes under the heading of 'eventiveness': although a narrow focus reading may be required by specific contexts, such as in a question/answer pair (cf. § 1.2.), the context-changing effect of a presentative construction in Hetzron's sense is not limited to the introduction of a new participant; rather it makes an entire new event or situation available to the context. The event-introducing, episodic character of a presentative sentence corresponds to a wide-focus reading.

The idea that the focus effect on the constituents in sentences like (15)−(18) must be correlated with their appearance in a universally specifiable syntactic position seems to have arisen in Rochemont (1986) and Culicover and Wilkins (1984). Rochemont and Culicover's (1990) attempt to unify all types of focus position under a single criterion is based on Rochemont's (1986) Cleft Focus Principle, which stipulates that a cleft focus phrase occurs in a position that is governed by a head (such as the copula *be* in English clefts) which does not theta-mark it. The Cleft Focus Principle allows for parametric variation: in languages like English, where the governing head can only be the copula, the CFC is a cleft construction; the other alternative is a Hungarian-type CFC, which occurs in languages where the governing head can be any verb. Problematic under this approach, as Rochemont realizes, are languages like Aghem, which have both types of CFC. Rochemont and Culicover (1990) try to show that an appropriate revision of the Cleft Focus Principle can also accommodate the presentational cases. Such a unified characterization of all focus positions is perhaps desirable in principle; it does not, however, preclude the possibility that focus positions may arise in different syntactic configurations with different effects on interpretation.

Although the interpretation of sentences like (15)−(18) and similar constructions in other languages is still a matter of debate, the results obtained both in typological work on cross-linguistic tendencies in word-order variation and in discourse-function studies on stylistically marked constructions in individual languages, in particular English, support the conclusion that presentational and contrastive focus positions differ not only in interpretation but also in syntactic form. The construction types exemplified by the English sentences in (15)−(18) have not received an equal amount of attention in crosslinguistic discourse function studies. Inversion constructions, however, occupy a central position in Hetzron's work on 'presentative movement'. In (19) and (20), (a) represents the unmarked case; the inverted order in (b) marks the 'presented' element − the displaced subject − as the most important piece of information by raising its anaphoric persistence. In a strictly verb-final language such as Japanese the position targeted by 'presentative movement' is preverbal (cf. also Birner & Ward (1998: 261) on Farsi).

Hungarian:
(19) (a) *A lány ott ült a szobában*
         The girl there sat the room-in
         'The girl was sitting in the room'
     (b) *A szobában ott ült a lány*
         The room-in there sat the girl
         'The girl was sitting in the room'

Japanese:
(20) (a) *Otoko wa uchi ni iru*
         man   TOP house LOC is
     (b) *Uchi ni otoko ga iru*
         house LOC man   NOM is
         'The man is in the house'

Herring & Paolillo (1995) discuss data from Tamil and Sinhala and suggest a functional differentiation between pre- and postverbal presentational constructions. Postverbal presentation is claimed to be characteristic of the introduction of new referents and other entities central to the narrative plot. Preverbal presentation is assumed to have less persistent effects on discourse reference. Whether this type of phenomenon is related to the type of presentative constructions familiar from English, such as the Presentational THERE construction or Heavy NP Shift, must

remain an open question. The post-predicate position of subjects and objects in English presentative constructions is reminiscent of Herring & Paolillo's 'post presentation'.

The phenomenon observed by Hetzron occurs in many typologically diverse and unrelated languages, but the tendency to displace focussed material to the right is by no means universal (cf. Tomlin & Rhodes (1992) on Ojibwa; Payne (1990: 237 ff.) on Yagua; on 'decreasing communicative dynamism' in Gavião (Tupi) cf. Stute (1986) and in Xavante (Gê) cf. Burgess (1986); cf. also Herring (1990) on VSO languages). Furthermore, empirical work on stylistic inversion in English discourse has shown that this construction is used to introduce not only 'persistent' but also ephemeral participants. Birner (1996) even claims that an inverted subject does not always introduce a new participant. The same seems to be true for inversion constructions in a number of other languages. In many cases the postposed constituent represents discourse-familiar information, but the preposed constituent cannot represent less familiar information than the postposed subject. This seems to show that more fine-grained distinctions in term of information states are necessary to describe the discourse functions of postposing constructions. Prince (1992) argues for a subdivision of the traditional distinction between 'new' and 'old' information in terms of what is 'new' (or 'old') relative to the hearer or the discourse. Comparative work on postposing has only recently begun, but it has already been established that several types of postposing constructions can be crosslinguistically identified (Ward 1999; Birner & Ward 1996; cf. also Sasse 1995 for a typological survey of verb-subject order.) Similar observations may apply to the other, even less well-studied sentence types that would have to be subsumed under the label of PFC.

An even more neglected aspect of PFCs is **grammatical weight sensitivity**. Two of the constructions in (15)−(18), namely the Presentational THERE construction and the Heavy NP Shift construction, are weight sensitive in the sense that the acceptability of such a sentence increases with the 'heaviness', i.e. length or complexity, of the postposed constituent (cf. Rochemont & Culicover 1990: 156 f. on the Heaviness Effect). Besides that, the heaviness of the postposed constituent seems to have an effect on the contextual salience of the 'presented' participant. Comparative investigations on grammatical weight have been impeded by the fact that none of the various concepts of weight that have been proposed to date has proven satisfactory. In fact, it may be necessary to develop different notions of weight with respect to the facilitation of production and parsing (cf. Wasow 1997). Weight-sensitive PFCs are only rarely discussed in the typological literature. One of the better-known cases is the expletive *waxaa*-construction in Somali (Cushitic, SOV), identified as a case of 'cataphoric focalization' by Svolacchia, Mereu & Puglielli (1995: 75 ff.), following Hetzron (1971). (But cf. Saeed 1984: 42 ff. for an alternative analysis.) Characteristically, *waxaa*-sentences present 'heavy constituents'. (Svolacchia, Mereu & Puglielli 1995: 76)

(21) *waxaan doonaya shaah, caano iyo*
      EXPL-I   want   tea   milk and
      sonkor
      sugar
      'I want TEA, MILK AND SUGAR'

Although PFCs are perhaps primarily used to introduce or reintroduce focussed participants, this function does not induce the kind of sharp split between a focus and a background that is characteristic of CFCs. Although focus on the displaced constituents in (15)−(18) above may be narrow, a wide-focus reading is also possible. In this case, the entire sentence associates with the focus particle.

(22) *Out of the gate even trundled a small tank*

(23) *Behind the bailiff even stood a police officer*

Many students of information structure have observed that the highlighting of the participant is accompanied by a weakening of the force of the predicate, which tends to be interpreted as merely denoting the 'emergence' (Hetzron 1975) or 'existence/appearance on the scene' (Firbas 1975) of the participant presented. This is stronger in cases like (17) and (18), an observation which accords with the proposal that the presentative effect of weight-sensitive postposing constructions should actually be accounted for in terms of 'light verb phrase preposing' around the 'presented' constituent (cf. Drubig 1992). The introduction of a new event or situation is the central function of the **thetic sentence** (→ Art. 104) or sentence-focus construction, another type of PFC, whose great importance for the typology of focus and information structure was first demonstrated in Sasse (1987). The event-reporting character of thetic sentences is responsible for a number of specific discourse functions, which are comprehensively discussed and illustrated with particular reference to VS order in Sasse (1995). (24)−(27) are typical examples of thetic sentences. According to Sasse, thetic sentences may open episodes, specify sudden interruptions, or furnish explanations.

(24) *THE DOOR was even open.*

(25) *MY CAR broke down.*

(26) *MANY CHILDREN died.*

(27) *There were SOME CHILDREN in his garden.*

Each sentence in (24)−(27) has a prominent subject projecting focus over the entire sentence, which may associate with a focus particle as shown in (24). Furthermore, each such sentence has a predicate denoting a temporary or 'stage-level' property as defined in Kratzer (1995). And finally, as Milsark (1974) has shown, quantifiers in thetic sentences have a 'weak' or cardinal reading. This is true for *many* in (26), which means 'a multitude of', as well as for *some* in (27), which means 'a number greater than one'. An interesting study of the typology of subject-prominence marking in thetic sentences is Lambrecht & Polinsky (1997), which builds on the results of Sasse (1987). Like presentative all-focus sentences, thetic constructions have been claimed to have an 'eventive' interpretation. The predicate of a thetic sentence is either an episodic verb, typically one with the argument structure of an unaccusative (but cf. Drubig (1992) and Sasse (1995:6) on 'reinterpretation') or a predicate (AP, PP) denoting a stage-level property (Kratzer 1995). For all predicates occurring in sentences with a thetic interpretation we must assume that they have, in addition to their participant argument structure, a spatio-temporal argument, called 'l(ocation)' in Kratzer (1995) and 'stage' in Erteschik-Shir (1997). The situation-specific event-reporting interpretation of thetic as well as presentative sentences suggests that the spatio-temporal argument plays the role of a topic ('stage topic' in Erteschik-Shir's terms) in such sentences. According to this view, an 'eventive' sentence is 'about' the contextually specified space/time at which the reported event takes place (→ Art. 104).

The affirmation of a thetic sentence binds its speaker to an existential commitment (Ladusaw 2000). Asserting a sentence such as (25) directly commits the speaker to the existence of a particular eventuality, but only indirectly to the existence of a specific car. In contrast to the 'presented' argument in a presentative construction, the subject term of a thetic sentence is not, or is not necessarily, 'cataphoric' or 'persistent'. This is the reason why the discourse functions described by Sasse (1995) depend on the type of impact that the newly introduced eventuality may have on the context. Participants tend to be ephemeral and are, in fact, nonexistent in the case of meteorological reports, which are another common type of thetic sentence. The subject of a thetic sentence may initiate a topic chain in the subsequent discourse, but when this happens, it is a strictly epiphenomenal effect, not induced by syntactic form as in the case of a presentative construction. Unlike items undergoing 'presentative movement' the participant in a thetic sentence, if there is one, tends to have a subordinate, event dependent status. In some languages the difference between event-dependent (or 'nonsingulative') and individuated (or 'persistent') participants is marked in morphosyntactic form (cf. Hetzron 1975: 372f. and Givón 1978).

In Hungarian, objects show the following contrasts (Hetzron 1975: 372ff.)

(28) (a) *A fiú levelet ír*
   The boy letter-ACC writes
   'The boy is writing a letter' [= 'is busy letter-writing']
(b) *A fiú ír egy levelet*
   The boy writes a letter-ACC
   'The boy is writing a [specific] letter'
(c) *A fiú írja a levelet*
   The boy writes the letter-ACC
   'The boy is writing the letter.'

In (28a) the object, which appears in its nonsingulative bare form, is incorporated into the verb, forming a complex verbal unit 'letter-writing'. It carries main stress, but does not have the narrow-focus reading of sentences like (13a) in § 1.1.1. Focus in this case is projected over the entire predicate (cf. Komlósy 1986: 217f.). As Hetzron notes, the use of the incorporated articleless form of the noun does not lead to the establishment of a discourse referent and is, in fact, compatible with a context in which a referent has already been introduced. According to Komlósy (1986), a proper name in preverbal position cannot be incorporated and can only have a narrow focus reading. (28b), on the other hand, shows an indefinite noun phrase *in situ*, which is, in Hetzron's terms, [+ individual] as well as [+ presentative], and therefore serves to introduce a new participant. The definite form of the noun phrase *in situ* in (28c) is accompanied by verbal object agreement. It implies hearer familiarity in the sense of Prince (1992).

1.1.3. Summary

Summarizing we may say that there are two types of FC which must be distinguished. A CFC isolates narrowly focussed arguments or adjuncts in specific syntactic positions, which, in the majority of cases, are also targeted by WH-movement. Like a WH-phrase, the displaced focus functions as an operator and binds a variable. In most cases, it binds a gap under standard locality conditions, but in some languages a resumptive pronoun, which is free of locality restrictions and may be enclosed in syntactic islands. As an alternative to displacement, languages may also use clefting as a focus-marking strategy. The interpretation of such constructions is predominantly contrastive. In contrast to this, a PFC is a wide-focus construction with an event-introducing function. A subtype of PFC, the 'presentative construction', has the additional function of marking 'cataphoric' participants by means of postposing. In contrast to the syntactic movement in CFCs, displacement in presentative PFCs is local and unrelated to WH-movement. Presentative PFCs show a tendency to be weight-sensitive.

1.2. Completive Focus Constructions

The claim that the contrastive/presentational dichotomy exhausts the range of possible types of foci is at variance with a more extended taxonomy originally proposed by Dik et al. (1981) (cf. also Dik 1997: 330ff.), which has played a role in typological studies on focus (cf. Payne 1990: 198ff.). The authors propose the following classification (cf. (29)):

(29)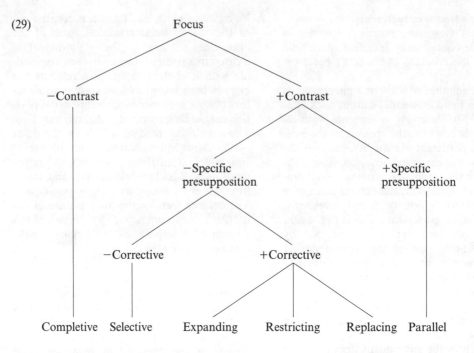

(30)–(35) exemplify the types of focus in (29):

(30) Completive Focus:
A: *What did John buy?*
Presupposition: John bought x;
x = __
B: *John bought COFFEE*

(31) Selective Focus:
A: *Did John buy coffee or rice?*
Presupposition: John bought x; x = coffee or x = rice
B: *He bought COFFEE, not RICE*

(32) Expanding Focus:
Presupposition of
A: John bought x; x = coffee
B: (a) *John not only bought COFFEE, he also bought RICE*
(b) *Yes, but he also bought RICE*

(33) Restricting Focus:
Presupposition of
A: John bought x; x = coffee and rice
B: (a) *No, he didn't buy RICE, he only bought COFFEE*
(b) *No, he only bought COFFEE*

(34) Replacing Focus:
A: *John went to London*
B: (a) *No, he didn't go to LONDON (he went to NEW YORK)*
(b) *No, he went to NEW YORK (he didn't go to LONDON)*

(35) Parallel Focus:
A: *I know that John and Peter bought a Volkswagen and a Toyota. But who bought what?*
B: *JOHN bought a TOYOTA, and PETER a VOLKSWAGEN*

As shown in (32)–(34), the difference in interpretation between the three types of focus marked "+ Corrective" in (29) is due to the different particles they are associated with: (32) and (33) correspond to the focus particles *also/too* and *only*, respectively, and (34) to replacive polarity. The remaining three types of focus are related to question/answer (Q/A) contexts: Selective Focus occurs in answers to alternative questions, Completive Focus in answers to single WH-questions, and Parallel Focus in pair-list answers to multiple WH-questions. In the taxonomy of Dik et al., Completive Focus is not associated with any specific presupposition, hence close to the category of presentational focus discussed in § 1.1.2. The constituent corresponding to the WH-phrase of an interrogative sentence is necessarily focussed. The answer may be either a focus or a constituent containing a focus, or else a sentence that contains the focussed constituent and is a redundant echo (or near echo) of the question. If the answering term is a focus, it may just fill in a blank; if it contains a focus, it presupposes a more highly structured multiple choice context and excludes alternatives (Kuno 1982). In many languages, WH-questions requiring an answer with a contrastive focus have a grammatical form that distinguishes them from 'neutral' information questions, which are answered by constituents or sentences with a presentational focus structure. Hajičová (1983: 88 ff.) observes that a focal accent on a WH-phrase in English induces a contrastive focus effect on a question, which also affects its answer potential. Thus, a negative answer, as in (37), appears to be less acceptable when the WH-phrase is focussed (36b) than when it is not. (Cf. Bartels 1997, ch. 6, for a discussion of the intonational properties of focussed questions in English).

(36)   (a) *Who came to the MEETING?*
       (b) *WHO came to the meeting?* (= Who was it who came to the meeting?)

(37)   *Nobody*

As shown in (36)–(37), a focussed WH-phrase presupposes a non-empty set of alternative answers. The evidence for such a distinction is even stronger in those languages that have syntactically distinct contrastive and 'neutral' WH-questions. In Akan, a neutral WH-question corresponds to a neutral answer, as in (38), and a focussed question to a focussed sentential answer (A_1) or a focussed constituent answer (A_2), as shown in (39). In (39), the focus particle *à* occurs only in term answers, while *nà* marks foci in full sentences (tones omitted in examples).

(38) Q: *Ama rehwehwɛ   hena?*
        Ama is-looking-for who?
        'Who is Ama looking for?'
     A: *(Ama rehwehwɛ) Kofi*

(39) Q: *HENA na   Ama rehwehwɛ?*
        who   FOC Ama is-looking-for
        'Who is it that Ama is looking for?'
     A_1: *KOFI na *(Ama rehwehwɛ)*
            Kofi FOC Ama is-looking-for
     A_2: *KOFI a (*Ama rehwehwɛ)*
            '(It is) KOFI (that Ama is looking for)'

Chinese, which has WH *in situ*, is another language showing this effect. According to Hoh & Chiang (1990) WH-phrases in neutral questions are *in situ* (40), but in a focussed question the WH-phrase moves to an initial position, where it is preceded by the focus particle *shi* (41). This latter type of question requires an answer in which the focussed term is in initial position and also preceded by *shi* (cf. Hoh & Chiang 1990: 48):

(40) Q: *ni   kanjian shenme dongxi diao*
        you see   what   thing fall
        dao wuding le?
        onto roof   ASP
        'What did you see fall on the roof?'

(41) Q: *shi shenme dongxi$_i$ ni kanjian t_i*
        FOC what   thing   you see
        diao dao wuding le?
        fall onto roof   ASP
        'What was it that you saw fall on the roof?'
     A: *shi shuzhi$_i$ wo kanjian t_i diao dao*
        FOC branch   I see   fall onto
        wuding le
        roof   ASP
        'I saw A BRANCH fall on the roof'

The fact that many languages have different WH-questions for neutral and focussed questions suggests that the classification of FCs in (29) is probably not adequate. As we have already seen, a question has a focus structure in its own right, which may be either presentational or contrastive. The information structure of the answer must correspond to that of the question. In languages where focus requires a particular morphosyntactic representation, the form of the WH-question often unambiguously indicates the information-structural status of the syntactic position targeted by the WH-operator.

From this we may draw the conclusion that Q/A pairs must perhaps be recognized as the instantiation of a particular type of gap-filling or 'completive' FC (cf. Brennan 1996 for a similar interpretation of questions). The constituent filling the gap may be either a presentational or a contrastive focus, depending on the specific information structure associated with the question. A question represents a particular type of completive FC consisting of an open proposition with one or more variables licensed by a WH-operator, and a syntactically disconnected structure, the answer, which supplies the constituent(s) filling the gap(s) in the open proposition. In order to derive a proposition with a context-changing effect, question and answer (filler and gap) must be connected. This would mean that 'completive focus' would have to be cross-classified in the feature framework used in the taxonomy proposed by Dik et al. 1981 (cf. (42)):

(42)

	− contrast	+ contrast
− completive	presentational focus (spontaneous)	contrastive focus (spontaneous)
+ completive	presentational focus (induced by a question)	contrastive focus (induced by a question)

Beyond that, the term 'completive FC', under the interpretation it is given here, might apply to all constructions with a discontinuous information structure. The defining feature of a completive FC in this sense is syntactic disconnectedness. Q/A pairs are only the most prominent example of this type of FC. Perhaps cleft constructions, which Carlson (1983) insightfully characterizes as a type of self-answered question, would have to be recognized as a kind of 'completive FC' too. In Q/A pairs focus and open proposition occur in separate speech acts, while in clefts they are linked by the predication relation.

This interpretation of the focus properties of WH-questions and cleft constructions, if correct, would add information structure as one more item to the long list of 'connectedness phenomena' that have been observed in such constructions (cf. Higgins 1979). Typical examples of connectedness effects found in WH-cleft sentences are shown in (43)−(44).

(43)   What John found in the drawer was a picture of himself.

(44)   *What he$_i$ misses is John's$_i$ wife.

(43) and (44) illustrate the phenomenon of binding connectivity, the most common type of connectedness effect. In (43) an anaphor occurs in the focus constituent of a cleft construction, which is coindexed with − but not c-commanded by − the antecedent contained in the cleft clause. In (44), the focus constituent is a referring expression causing a violation of a binding principle which requires that a lexical noun phrase be free, although the pronoun with which it is coindexed is contained in the cleft clause, from where it cannot bind its antecedent. In each case the constituent in the post-copular focus position acts as if it occupied the syntactic position bound by the WH-operator in the cleft clause. In order to account for such connectedness effects, Heycock & Kroch (1999) propose Reconstruction of the focus constituent at a post-LF level, whereas Kiss (1998) and Meinunger (1998) stipulate a derivational relationship between clefts and focus-fronting constructions (→ Art. 104).

The most important advantage of a Reconstruction analysis of cleft constructions is that it can be extended to Q/A pairs, which also show connectedness effects.

(45) Q: *What did John find in the drawer?*
     A: *A picture of himself*

The fact that both the term answers to WH-questions and the focus constituents of cleft constructions show similar connectedness effects is perhaps indicative of a deeper relationship between completive FCs. The great typological importance of the relationship between cleft constructions and focus-fronting constructions that motivated the 'reductive' proposals of Kiss (1998) and Meinunger (1998) will be discussed in § 2. and § 3.

2. The grammatical structure of focus constructions

2.1. Focus operator constructions

The term 'focus construction' originated in descriptive and typological work, primarily on African languages in the 1970s (cf. e. g. Takizala, 1972, Epée 1975 and others) partially under the influence of Schachter (1973), one of the first attempts to study FCs from a typological perspective. Schachter's approach was based on the theory of generative grammar, which made major contributions to the study of focus and the typology of FCs (Cf. Rebuschi & Tuller (1999a) for an overview of the study of focus in the generative tradition.). In generative approaches focus is interpreted as a syntactic feature (Jackendoff 1972), which either induces focus projection, i. e. the percolation of the focus feature over increasingly larger constituents (wide focus), or drives displacement (narrow focus). An important step was taken by Chomsky (1977: 203 f.), who showed that a narrow focus *in situ* in an English sentence like (46) must be analyzed as a quantifier-like operator, which is raised at the level of Logical Form (LF) by movement to a specified position in the periphery of the sentence.

(46)   *Bill's mother likes JOHN*

(47)   [FOCUS$_i$] [... x$_i$ ...]

Evidence for (47) is the so-called Weak Crossover Effect (WCO), a decrease in grammaticality derived from the following restriction (cf. Chomsky 1976: 201):

(48)   A variable cannot be the antecedent of a pronoun to its left

The focussed example in (49a) shows a WCO effect, in contrast to (49b). It can be analyzed as a violation of (48) if we assume that its representation at LF is as shown in (50).

(49)   (a) *His$_i$ mother likes JOHN$_i$*
       (b) *His$_i$ mother LIKES John$_i$*

(50)   [JOHN$_i$] [his$_i$ mother likes t$_i$]

Alternatively one might assume that focus *in situ* does not move but is coindexed with its scope-taking position. Guéron (1980) was first to point out that under a presentational interpretation the configuration in (49a) cannot arise, since a new information focus cannot be preceded by a coindexed pronoun. The alternative would be a contrastive interpretation, but even this possibility has come under criticism (cf. Vallduví 1992: 119 ff. for a resumé of critical objections and Williams 1997 for a more recent attack). This suggests that WCO effects do not provide a reliable basis for the claim that focus *in situ* is quantificational. There is, however, an additional sort of evidence, which seems to support the conclusion that focus *in situ* is not insensitive to locality restrictions. As we have seen in § 1.1.1., the displacement of focussed phrases in 'focus moving' languages is subject to island constraints when the focus binds a gap in its base position. If it could be shown that focus *in situ* is sensitive to similar restrictions, then this would amount to an additional argument for covert movement, provided that island constraints can be assumed to also restrict LF movement. Relevant here are replacive constructions, in which alternatives excluded by the focussed item are overtly identified (cf. Drubig 1994):

(51)   *John invited [the girl who knew [JANE]] to his party, not JENNIFER*

In (51), the bracketed focus is contained in a Complex NP. The fact that *JENNIFER* is understood not as an alternative to JANE, but to the Complex NP *the girl who knew JANE*, seems to support the conclusion that focus *in situ* is indeed sensitive to syntactic islands: if a focus is contained in an island, the entire island is interpreted as an internally complex focus — a 'focus phrase' according to Drubig (1994) — and presumably undergoes movement at LF. In focus-moving languages such as Hungarian, focus-phrase effects can be observed in overt syntax. If the argument that focus *in situ* raises at LF is valid, it has important consequences for a typology of information structure, because it implies that perhaps all languages have CFCs of the type found in focus-moving languages and that overt and covert displacement of focus must be understood as parametric instantiations of the same universal type of CFC. Brody (1990) shows that the target position of overt focus movement in Hungarian cannot be adjoined to IP or CP, and postulates the existence of a presumably universal functional projection FocP, to which narrow foci and presumably also WH-phrases must move in order to enter into a specifier-head relation, as shown in (52):

(52)   [Marí [$_{FocP}$ JÁNOST$_i$
       Mari   Janos-ACC
       [$_{Foc}$ látta$_j$] t$_j$ t$_i$]]
       saw...
       'Mari saw JANOS'

In order to be well formed, a CFC has to meet the condition in (53), which was first envisaged in Brody (1990), but is quoted here in a revised version based on a similar criterion proposed in Rizzi (1990: 378).

(53)   Focus Criterion
       a. A [+F] XP must be in a specifier-head configuration with a [+F] head.
       b. A [+F] head must be in a specifier-head configuration with a [+F] XP

In Hungarian, verbs can also be focussed.

(54)   *Mari LÀTTA Jánost   a*
       Mari saw   Janos-ACC the
       kertben
       garden-in
       'Mary SAW Janos in the garden'

In (54) the position where a focussed phrase would have to occur is empty, which shows that verbs in Foc° cannot be focussed simultaneously with phrases in SpecFocP, a fact which Brody tries to account for by assuming that the verb moves to the head of FocP to pass its own focus feature to the phrase in the specifier. This would account for the verb second effects in CFCs in Hungarian and other languages with verb-related focus positions, such as Basque.

The Focus Criterion (53) can then be subsumed under a generalized principle which specifies that not only focus, but all sorts of operators, including, e. g., WH-phrases and negative phrases, must be licensed in the type of configuration shown in (52). The parametrization of this principle, which is assumed to operate at the level of Phonetic Form (PF) in 'focus prominent' languages (→ Art. 104) and, presumably, at LF in languages with focus *in situ*, is parallel to the parametrization of WH-movement. A related approach is presented by Rizzi (1997), who argues that CP must be split into a number of component projections and that FocP is located between the force and finiteness components of CP (cf. Puskas 2000: ch. 2 for an analysis of Hungarian focus within Rizzi's framework). Aboh (1999) proposes that the pure focus particle accompanying the focus in CFCs in Gungbe and other languages should be analyzed as the spell-out of Foc° in Rizzi's sense. A similar proposal is made in Green (1997), a minimalist approach to Hausa CFCs based on Brody's theory.

Another important question discussed in recent work on CFCs concerns the identity and featural context of FocP, in addition to the question of its varying location within the functional structure of clauses, which may also have to be understood as a function of parametric choice. Some authors, among them Ouhalla (1999), view FocP as a general functional projection that accommodates all operators which "express information over and above the propositional content of the sentence" (p. 339), including modality and WH-phrases, besides focus. Some authors try to reduce FocPs to an independently necessary functional projection, a strategy that appears to be mandatory under the minimalist perspective now favored by generative approaches. Focussing on languages with pre- or postverbal focus positions, Kenesei (1993) locates the equivalent of Brody's FocP within the INFL range and tentatively suggests TenseP as a candidate, which allows him to account for the pre/postverbal dichotomy (cf. Hungarian vs. Aghem and perhaps other languages) in terms of feature strength (cf. Green 1997: 59 ff. for a critical reaction).

An important question raised by the FocP approach concerns the assumed operator status of focussed constituents. Unlike WH-phrases or negative quantifiers, bare foci do not appear to be accompanied by anything that could be interpreted as a reflection of their quantificational properties. Some linguists have hinted at the possibility of a 'silent only', an invisible operator, binding bare foci (Lasnik & Stowell 1991: 716, cf. also Rebuschi & Tuller 1999: 8 f.). Others suggest that FocP should be identified with Laka's (1990) polarity projection (cf., e. g., Piñon 1993 or Drubig 1994), where not only [+F] but also some operator features are checked, but none of the proposals have been worked out in sufficient detail. The way focus is interpreted in some of these syntactic approaches bears a certain similarity to the 'relational' theory of focus originally proposed by Jacobs (1984). Under the relational approach, focus is necessarily bound and semantically affected by certain operators, such as negation or illocutionary force (cf. Moser 1992 for a discussion and extension of Jacobs' theory).

The existence of languages which have both a sentence peripheral and a VP peripheral focus position may indicate that some languages use two instances of FocP, one in the COMP and the other in the INFL range, perhaps associated with different interpretations. Whether this is true for Kanakuru (Chadic), which has both initial and postverbal focus, remains an open question (cf. Tuller 1992: 325; Newman 1974). Green (1997) tries to show that the pre- and postverbal focus positions in some Chadic languages can also be analyzed as sentence peripheral (cf. Horvath 1995 for a critical view of FocP and Green 1997 for a reply).

2.2. Cleft constructions as focus operator constructions

A number of approaches to CFCs try to extend the FocP hypothesis to the analysis of cleft constructions. The grammatical structure of this type of sentence is an unsolved problem, but there is general agreement that the subordinate clause of a cleft construction must be analyzed as a relative clause. The sentences (55), (56) and (2) (repeated as (57)) conform to the pattern in (58).

(55)   *It was [$_F$ John] that Mary loved*

(56) Irish (McCloskey 1979)
 Is é [$_F$ Seán] aL thigeann'
 COP him Sean COMP comes
 nabhaile
 home
 'It's Sean that comes home'

(57) Aghem (Bantu, Watters 1979: 168)
 à mɔ̀ lɔ̀ [$_F$ bàʔtóm wíl] á ò
 DS P$_1$ COP chief this REL he
 mɔ̀ búɔ
 P$_2$ come
 'It was the chief who came'

(58) (Expletive) – Copula – Focus – CP

The most important question is the relationship between Focus and CP in (58). Under the more traditional 'predicative' approach to cleft constructions, the cleft clause is analyzed as a relative clause, i.e. an open proposition with a silent operator binding its variable that allows the cleft clause to function as a predicate. Hence, the analysis of (55) can be represented as in (59).

(59) It was [$_{PredP}$ John Pred° [$_{CP}$ OP$_i$ [$_C$ that] Mary loved t$_i$]]

According to Browning (1987: 60ff.), the predicative component of (59) is a CP small clause, which we assume is headed by the predication operator Pred°, a semantic element that is responsible for the predicational nature of any predicate (cf. Bowers 1993: 647). (59) is in accordance with the analysis of cleft constructions as a predicational type of completive FC (§ 1.2.). Cleft sentences in other languages, such as (56) and (57), would have to be accounted for in the same way.

An alternative approach to clefts based on a raising analysis of relative clauses is suggested in Kayne (1994). Under Kayne's analysis, relative clauses are the complements of determiners. The constituent functioning as the head is base generated within the relative clause and raised to a non-argument position in its periphery:

(60) [$_{DP}$ the [$_{CP}$ picture$_i$ [that [$_{IP}$ Bill saw t$_i$]]]]

This approach suggests a straightforward answer to the question of what the structure of a cleft construction is like: just as an attributive relative clause is analysed as a complement of D°, its predicative counterpart in a cleft construction is analyzed as a complement of the copula (Kayne 1994: 153). The structure of (55) would then be (61). Since CP in (61) is a complement rather than a relative, the categories that may undergo raising are not identical.

(61) It Past [$_{VP}$ be [$_{CP}$ John$_i$ [that [$_{IP}$ Mary invited t$_i$]]]]

One of the advantages that a raising analysis may claim over predication-based approaches is that 'connectedness effects' can be derived in a simple manner.

Kayne's analysis is reminiscent of an earlier proposal by Schachter (1973). One problem that such an analysis is confronted with is the focus effect that occurs in clefts but not in relatives. Schachter's suggestion that a relative clause as such is some kind of FC, which was later echoed in a number of studies (Odden 1984: 294; Green 1997) appears unmotivated. A possible way out is suggested by Kiss (1998) (cf. also Meinunger 1998). Kiss stipulates that the head of FocP selects not only IP but also CP. A cleft construction can then be viewed as a CFC with a FocP selecting CP instead of IP. The head of FocP is occupied by the copula, a verbal expletive under Kiss's analysis. This allows Kiss to account for cleft FCs in English and focus fronting in Hungarian on a unified basis (→ Art. 104).

(62) [$_{CP}$ [$_{IP}$ it was$_i$ [$_{FocP}$ John$_j$ t$_i$ [$_{CP}$ t$_j$ that [$_{IP}$ Mary invited t$_j$]]]]]

In (62), the cleft focus is extracted from the position in CP in which it originates and is raised to SpecFocP to check its focus feature.

Beyond the necessity to derive the focus effect, this additional step in the derivation may also be necessary to account for cleft constructions in SOV languages such as Japanese. Kayne's (1994) approach is based on a restrictive theory of phrase structure in which the relation between hierarchy and linear order is inflexible: heads universally precede their complements. In languages with head final order, such as Japanese, complements are presumably displaced to specifier positions higher in the functional hierarchy than their heads. Relative clause constructions in Japanese, which are prenominal, are derived from the configuration in (60) by displacement of IP to SpecDP. Japanese cleft constructions, however, display an order which suggests that focus is extracted first; then the remnant CP undergoes obligatory topicalization and moves to a higher position (cf. Matsuda 1997: 173 ff. on the type-shifting character of this topicalization). The resulting structure is at least compatible with a FocP analysis along the lines of Kiss (1998) and Meinunger (1998).

(63) (a) [$_{CPi}$ *Boku ga kono tokei o t$_j$*
          I   NOM this watch ACC
  katta no] wa [$_{PPj}$ *Pari de]
  buy-PAST NO TOP   Paris LOC
  da*
  COP
  'It was in Paris that I bought this watch'
 (b) [$_{TopP}$ CP$_i$ *wa* [$_{FocP}$ PP$_j$ *da* t$_i$]]

The raising analysis of relative clauses offers a natural account for the relation between head-external and so-called 'head-internal' or 'circumnominal' relative clauses (Dik 1997: 65 ff.), which occur primarily in SOV languages (Cole 1987). This has important consequences for the typology of CFCs. Under the raising approach, circumnominal relatives turn out to be the *in situ* counterpart of the more familiar *ex situ* relative shown in languages like English. If we assume that any universally available strategy for relative clause formation can be exploited in cleft constructions (cf. Harris & Campbell 1995: 153), we are led to expect that there must also be circumnominal cleft constructions. The so-called *noda*-construction in Japanese has been analyzed as an example of this type of 'cleft *in situ*' construction (Schaffar 2000).

(64)   [*Kono tokei o*   [$_F$ *Pari de]*
       This watch ACC   Paris LOC
   katta no] da
   buy-PAST NO COP
   'I bought this watch IN PARIS'

In (64) the clause is accompanied by the nominalizing particle *no* and precedes the copula. Under the FocP hypothesis this position is arguably identical to SpecFocP. The fact that *noda*-constructions display 'focus phrase effects' (cf. Schaffar 2000) is in accordance with such an analysis.

Another type of cleft construction which may have to be analyzed along the same lines is the so-called 'inferential construction' shown in (65).

(65) (a) *It was just that it was raining*
 (b) *It is not that I don't love you*

English inferentials have the appearance of cleft constructions whose focus is the entire *that*-clause and whose cleft clause is missing. The clausal component of an inferential always contains a focus, often in a 'projecting' position. According to Delahunty (1995) the discourse function of such a construction is to indicate that the focussed clause must be understood as an interpretation of the local context, which is affirmed, denied or questioned by the inferential. In some languages inferentials are marked by focus particles (cf. Bearth 1999 on the use of *nà* in Akan and similar particles in other African languages). The Japanese inferential clefts turn out to be *noda*-constructions (Kuno 1973, Schaffar 2000).

(66) *Kibun ga warui no desu ka?*
   feeling NOM bad-is NO COP Q
   'Is it that you don't feel well?'

In (66) the entire cleft clause appears to be focussed. The same could be said about the English sentences in (65). This assumption would account for the fact that the whole clause is affected by negation or affirmation in such constructions.

2.3. The demarking of focus

While clefts function as CFCs in a wide range of languages (cf. Harries-Delisle 1978), many languages have cleft constructions with discourse functions that are incompatible with a contrastive interpretation. The best known case is perhaps French, which has both copula-supported and reduced clefts with a thetic interpretation as noted by Sasse (1987), who lists a number of other languages with similar phenomena. In (67) the cleft focus is not narrow but projects wide focus.

(67) *C'est* [$_F$ *ma mére] qui est morte*
   It's   my   mother who is dead
   'My mother is dead'

With reference to English, Hetzron (1975: 359 ff.) observes that pseudo-clefts can have a 'cataphoric' or 'presentative' reading under certain conditions.

(68) *What I saw was the pink elephant*

(68) is by no means contrastive when used in a narrative report. Another type of cleft construction with a non-contrastive reading is the 'stressed presupposition *it*-cleft' discussed in Prince (1978). A necessary prerequisite for this type of use of (68) seems to be a context in which the presupposition expressed in the cleft clause is trivialized, as Hetzron demonstrates. This phenomenon, which is context dependent in English but appears to play a greater role in many other

languages, is indicative of an important general process called '**demarking**' in Dik (1997a: 325 ff.): FCs, in particular clefts, may lose their contrastive force and are then reduced to a presentational interpretation. Demarking plays a great role in the historical development of cleft focus constructions into presentational focus constructions (§ 3. below), a process which may also be responsible for the fact that clefting is cross-linguistically one of the more important coding strategies for subject prominence in thetic sentences (cf. Sasse 1987). Wide-focus effects can also be observed in connection with predicate-clefting constructions in creole languages and in West African (cf. Larson & Lefebvre 1991: 250 ff. on Haitian Creole and Dekydtspotter 1995: 36 ff. on Yoruba).

Demarking may not only affect clefts but also focus-operator constructions. A number of languages, among them Italian and Hebrew (Belletti and Shlonsky 1995; Samek-Ludovici 1996), are claimed to have FocP constructions which have undergone a demarking process resulting in a FC with a presentational reading (cf. also Ordóñez 1997 on other Romance languages).

2.4. Cleft-based focus constructions

While many languages have focus-fronting constructions displaying the characteristic properties of A-bar movement, such as island sensitivity and WCO effects, some languages discussed in the literature do not conform to this pattern. In such languages a narrow focus with a contrastive reading regularly occurs in a left-peripheral position. The position in the sentence which the focussed category binds, however, is not occupied by a gap, but by a resumptive pronoun, which in some languages may be phonetically empty under certain conditions. Furthermore, this type of FC may not only violate locality conditions, as was shown in § 1.1.1.; it also lacks WCO effects. WH-questions often have the same properties in such languages, as the following sentences (Akan; tones omitted) show.

(69) *Adaka$_i$ bɛn na wo nim*
    box   which FOC you know
    [$_{DP}$ onipa [$_{CP}$ a [$_{IP}$ ɔ
       person   REL   (s)he
    rehwehwɛ   e$_i$]] no]
    is-looking-for (it)   the
    'Which box$_i$ do you know the person who is looking for (it$_i$)?'

(70) *Adaka$_i$ no na wo nim*
    box   this FOC you know
    [$_{DP}$ onipa [$_{CP}$ a [$_{IP}$ ɔ
       person   REL   (s)he
    rehwehwɛ   e$_i$]] no]
    is-looking-for(it)   the
    'This box$_i$ you know the person who is looking for (it$_i$)'

(69) is a focussed question, which has a focussed answer in Akan, as shown in § 1.2. (70) is a possible answer to (69). Both WH-phrase and focus occupy the sentence-initial focus position, and both are accompanied by the obligatory focus particle *nà*. Both the WH-phrase in (69) and the focus in (70) bind an argument position embedded in a complex NP. As Saah (1988, 1994) has shown, empty categories in sentences like (69) and (70) must be analyzed as null resumptive pronouns. Pronouns with inanimate antecedents are always empty, but when the antecedent is animate, the resumptive pronoun has phonetic content, as (71) shows. This type of pronominal variation is very common in West African languages (Ameka 1992), but it also occurs in Bantu (cf. Biloa 1995 on Tuki).

(71) *ɔbaa$_i$ no na me huu no$_i$*
    WOMAN the FOC I saw (her)
    'It was the woman I saw (her)'

(71) shows that resumptive pronouns in Akan are not restricted to island configurations. In Akan this turns out to be true for all types of constructions where such pronouns occur, in particular CFCs, WH-questions and relative clauses. Besides arguments, adjuncts may also be focussed and placed in initial position under locality conditions, but there are no pronominal copies (Ameka 1992: 17). Similar observations have been made in other African languages, e. g., in Bantu languages such as Tuki (Biloa 1995) or Duala (Epée 1976), but also in Cushitic (cf. Saeed 1984 and Svolacchia, Mereu and Puglielli 1995 on Somali). Akan and Tuki appear to use rather similar strategies in the formation of long dependencies in WH-questions, CFCs and relative clauses. Other languages show similarities between CFCs and relative clauses, but lack the expected parallels between CFCs and WH-questions. As noted in § 1.1., CFCs and relative clauses in Maasai and other Nilotic languages violate Subjacency, while WH-questions respect island constraints.

Since CFCs and focussed WH-questions in Akan and other languages of this type depend on resumptive pronouns, they cannot be derived by means of A-bar movement. As a matter of fact, we have good reason to assume that the pronominal nature of the binding relation indicates an underlying resumptive relative-clause construction. From this we may conclude that there is evidence for two distinct types of focus (and focussed WH-) constructions:

(72) Focus Constructions
   (a) Type I: Focus operator construction
       Focus$_i$ ... t$_i$ ...
       ↑_____|

   (b) Type II: Resumptive Focus Construction
       Focus$_i$ [$_{CP}$ ...pronoun$_i$ ...]
       |_____↑

In Type I constructions, focus is an operator undergoing A-bar movement (overt in Hungarian, covert in English) under standard locality restrictions, accompanied by WCO effects. In Type II constructions, on the other hand, focus appears to be base generated in the focus position, from where it binds a resumptive pronoun, which presumably is embedded in a relative clause. This binding relationship cannot be construed as movement, since no locality effects are observed and the position of the variable is not occupied by a trace. Type II also does not show WCO effects. As the comparative literature on FCs since Schachter (1973) has demonstrated, the evidence for a deeper relationship between relative clauses and Type II constructions goes well beyond the distribution of resumptive pronouns and includes a large number of morphosyntactic parallels, ranging from "relative tense" to auxiliaries, forms of negation, complementizers and many others (§ 3.1.). A particularly rich selection of such phenomena has been attested in African languages. Tuller (1986: 106) mentions Chadic languages, such as Kanakuru and Tera, as well as Fula (West Atlantic), More (Gur), Zulu and Kikuyu (both Bantu). Non-African languages quoted by Clements (1985) include Jacaltec, Chippewa, Malagasy and Telugu. Some authors, in particular Saah (1988, 1994) for Akan as well as Biloa (1995) for Tuki, try to circumvent the problem of resumption by means of an analysis in which both contrastive foci and focussed WH-phrases are base generated in SpecCP (73). Binding is established through coindexation with a resumptive pronoun *in situ*. Resumptive construal, which amounts to a violation of Chomsky's (1982: 59 f.) proposal to constrain Free Indexing to argument positions, is justified as an alternative to the movement account of A-bar binding (cf. Goodluck, Saah & Stojanović 1995).

(73) (a) [$_{CP}$ WH-operator$_i$ [$_C$ na] IP[...
         pro$_i$ / no$_i$...]]
    (b) [$_{CP}$ Adaka$_i$ no [$_C$ na] [me huui
         box   the FOC   I   saw
         pro$_i$]]
         (it)
         'It was THE BOX that I saw'

One of the shortcomings of this approach is that it has nothing to say on the suggestive parallels between CFCs, WH-questions and relative clauses that can be observed in languages with resumptive FCs of Type II. An alternative proposal could depart from a more explanatory theory of resumptive pronouns proposed in Demirdache (1997). According to this approach, resumptive pronouns are relative WH-pronouns *in situ*. Like interrogative WH-pronouns *in situ*, resumptive pronouns are turned into variable-binding operators at LF. For reasons outlined in Demirdache (1997), the resulting operator-variable configurations in relative clauses are not subject to standard locality restrictions. Under this proposal, the type of resumptive WH-questions we find in Akan must be analyzed as interrogative cleft constructions of a particular type. Hence, focussed WH-questions in Akan and presumably also in other languages with Type II WH- and focus constructions would have the analysis shown in (74). In (74) the focus particle *na* is analyzed as a complementizer, as suggested in (73).

(74) [$_{CP}$ Hena$_i$ [$_{CP}$Spec [na]] [ne$_i$
     who   C°   his/her
     maame dɔ   no$_i$]]
     mother loves him/her
     'Who does his/her mother love (him/her)?'

A CFC in Akan would then be the equivalent of (74) with a lexical focus phrase occupying the cleft focus position. This analysis seems superior to (73 b), because it accounts for the similarities observed by Schachter in a natural way: CFCs and focussed WH-questions show structural parallels with relative clauses because they are cleft constructions, whose predicative component is a relative clause.

In contrast to the more familiar type of clefts, the construction underlying (74) lacks a copula. Cleft constructions of this type can be found in a number of languages. According to McCloskey (1979), Irish has two different cleft constructions: 'full clefts', which represent the familiar type of copula construction, and copula-free 'reduced clefts', as shown in (75).

(75) Seán Bán aL   d'inis an sceál
      Seán Bán COMP told   the story
      dom
      to me
      'It was Seán Bán who told me the story'

Type II languages, in particular Akan, are not the only languages with cleft-based WH-questions. Cheng (1991) examines WH-fronting in three 'optional WH-fronting languages', Bahasa Indonesia, Egyptian Arabic and Palauan, which are similar to Akan in one respect: they have WH-phrases in a fronted position, in addition to WH *in situ*. (76) is an Indonesian WH-cleft construction, as analyzed in Cheng (1991: 68), which requires a null operator binding a trace under standard locality conditions. Since the quantifier in (76) also binds a pronoun not c-commanded by its trace, the presence of this pronoun induces a WCO effect.

(76) *[$_{CP}$ Siapa$_i$ [$_{CP}$ Op$_i$ [yang]
         who$_i$ C°
      [$_{IP}$ dosen-nya$_i$ suka t$_i$]]]
         professor-his   like
      'Who$_i$ does his$_i$ professor like?'

In contrast to this, the Akan counterpart of this construction, shown in (74), contains a resumptive pronoun, i.e., a relative operator *in situ*. Due to this fact, it shows neither WCO nor island effects.

Cheng's 'optional fronting languages', in particular Bahasa Indonesia, also have Type II FCs that are very similar to those found in Akan or Tuki, but lack resumptive pronouns. In the Indonesian example (77), the focus position preceding the complementizer (or focus particle) *yang* is occupied by a Complex NP functioning as a 'focus phrase' of the type discussed in § 2.1. above (Soemarmo 1971: 67).

(77) [Anak yang lewat TADI PAGI]
      child that passed this morning
      yang   membeli sepatu
      that/FOC bought shoes
      'It was the child that passed THIS MORNING that bought the shoes.'

The important difference between Type II constructions in Akan or Tuki and their counterparts in languages like Bahasa Indonesia lies in their behavior with respect to locality restrictions. While a Type II construction in Bahasa Indonesia involves an empty operator moving at PF under standard locality conditions, foci in the focus positions of Type II constructions in Akan and Tuki are linked to resumptive pronouns, which may be embedded in islands of various types. With reference to (69) and (70) it was argued that such Subjacency effects are unexpected under an approach that tries to account for this type of construction on the basis of Type I constructions. The reduced cleft analysis of Type II constructions combined with Demirdache's analysis of resumption as relativization *in situ* suggests a straightforward solution to the apparent dilemma. Since resumptive pronouns undergo covert movement, their distribution is parallel to the distribution of WH-phrases and foci *in situ*: Both resumptive pronouns and WH or focus *in situ* are licit in positions from which traces at PF (gaps) are excluded. We may account for this by saying that each sentence in which a link between a focussed constituent and a resumptive pronoun is supported across an island involves 'pied piping' of the entire island to the SpecCP of the relative clause functioning as the predicate of the Type II focus construction (cf. Drubig 1994 on pied-piping effects). This shows that the crucial differences between Type I and Type II constructions can be derived from the relative clauses underlying cleft-based Type II FCs.

3. Focus marking and the grammaticalization of focus constructions

3.1. Focus-marking phenomena

The most prominent work on morphological focus-marking systems, their genesis and their development have been written on the basis of data from African languages (Heine & Reh 1984; Hyman & Watters 1984). In this overview it will be shown that the existence of morphological focus-marking phenomena is not restricted to this linguistic area, but rather can be found in many Asian and some European languages as well. Many scholars have noticed that these systems developed out of cleft or relative constructions, and the particular properties were interpreted as stages of a grammaticalization process (Heine & Reh 1984; Harris & Campbell 1995).

Apart from accent marking strategies, many languages have morphological means to mark information structure. The morphological marking can affect the focussed constituent itself (primarily by means of nominal particles attached to the focussed constituent) or the verb (in-focus and out-of-focus verb forms). However, in many languages we find a connection between both strategies (nominal particles that trigger specific verb forms, agreement phenomena between nominal particles and verb forms). These morphological phenomena vary in many different respects: The obligatoriness of marking in a given language and the exact meaning of the marking can be different from language to language. Polarity, aspect and tense forms are affected in a different way within one language.

3.1.1. Marking of the focussed constituent

As mentioned in § 1.1., there are many languages that have special particles to mark foci. Boni, a language of the Sam family, has a special morpheme for the marking of focus. The following discussion is based on Sasse (1981) and Heine & Reh (1984: 169). A sentence like (78) expresses a wide information focus (neutral focus, according to Sasse's terminology). If the focus particle, -é for a verbal argument (79) or á- for the predicate (80) is attached to a constituent, this constituent will be the focus of the sentence.

(78) *an biyóo ajık-a*
      I   water drink
      'I drink water.'

(79) *an biyóo-é ajık-a*
      I   water   drink
      'I drink WATER.'

(80) *an biyóo á-ajık-a*
      I   water drink
      'I DRINK water.'

Both focus markers can be traced back to the copula *-ahei*, which was weakened to á- or -é.

In Chinese we find the particle *shi* which precedes focussed constituents, whether nominal or verbal. (81) without the particle is a neutral sentence with wide information focus. In (82) the focus particle marks the time adverb as focus, and in (83) the verb itself is focussed.

(81) *wo zuotian kan le zhe ben*
      I   yesterday read PERF this CLASS
      shu.
      book
      'I read this book yesterday.'

(82) *wo shi zuotian kan le zhe*
      I   FOC yesterday read PERF this
      ben shu.
      CLASS book
      'It was yesterday that I read this book.'

(83) *wo zuotian shi kan le zhe*
      I   yesterday FOC read PERF this
      ben shu.
      CLASS book
      'I read this book yesterday. (I did not buy it.)

Just as in Boni, the Chinese focus marker can be reconstructed as the copula *shi*. This is a very general tendency across many (but not all) languages. The verbal origin of the focus particle can explain why in some languages there are traces of agreement connected with this marking strategy (Cf. Kazenin 1999; to appear).

3.1.2. Marking on the verb
(of the background)

In some languages, not the focus itself is marked, but the verb form shows different morphological properties depending on the information structure. The terminology is very diverse and often misleading, but the rough lines can be summarized in the following way: Many languages have different verb forms for main clauses and embedded clauses.

Chin, a Tibeto-Burman language spoken in northern Burma, distinguishes between so-called primary and secondary verb stems. The following data and their interpretation is taken from Osborne (1975: 71 ff.). The primary stem is used in matrix sentences such as (84), whereas the secondary stem appears in various types of embedded clause, such as relative clauses, conditional clauses, nominalizations or temporal clauses as in (85). Note, that the only difference between the stems is the tone.

(84) *qaársâ   kaqéey* (primary stem)
      Chicken-meat I-eat
      'I ate the chicken.'

(85) *thiqsí qaqĕey hnû (qaq), ...*
      poison he-eat after at
      'After he took the poison, ...'

A sentence with the main verb in its primary stem form (84) expresses a neutral information focus answering the question "What happened?", or a focus on the verb alone answering the question "Did you throw out the chicken?".

However, there are sentences in which the main verb appears in its secondary stem, such as (86). This sentence is used as an answer to questions like "Did you eat the fish?", where the focus lies on the object only.

(86) qaársâ
      Chicken-meat
      kaqěey (secondary stem)
      I-eat
      'I ate the chicken.'

In African languages the distinction between matrix verb form (main clauses tense) and embedded verb forms (relative tense) is a widespread phenomenon (Cf. § 1.1.1. on noun- and verb-focal suffixes in Kimatuumbi). The use of these different forms for the expression of information structure has also been documented for many other languages over a vast area. Since the main clause tense forms as in (84) express a focus reading including the verb, this form is also called the *in-focus form* whereas the relative tense form in (86), which expresses a focus on a constituent elsewhere in the sentence, is called the *out-of-focus form*.

3.1.3. Combination of
       the two marking strategies

In most of the languages with morphological focus marking, the marking of the focussed constituent and of the verb cooccur in one sentence. The following data on Akan are taken from Schachter (1973). As in the examples from Chin, Akan marks the difference between the in-focus form and the out-of-focus form with a tone difference. (87) expresses a wide information focus. In a relative clause, the tone on the subordinated verb changes to a high tone, as shown in (88), and it is this verb form that occurs in sentences like (89), in which one constituent is marked as a focus with the focus particle *nà* for constituent focus.

(87) mìhúù àbòfrá
      saw   child
      'I saw a child.'

(88) àbòfrá áà míhúù nó
      child that saw   him
      'a child that I saw'

(89) àbòfrá nà míhúù nó
      child FOC saw   him
      'It's a child that I saw.'

Another example of this connection from a different linguistic area is Sinhala (Sumangala 1992; Gair & Sumangala 1991). In Sinhala, the finite verb form ending in *-a* can be distinguished from a nominalized form ending in *-e*. A sentence with a wide information focus, such as (90), takes the finite ending, whereas the emphatic particle *tamayi* and other particles require the nominalized verb form *-e*, as shown in (91).

(90) *Siri waduwædə keruwa*
      Siri woodworking did-A
      'Siri did woodworking.'

(91) *Siri waduwædə tamayi keruwe*
      Siri woodworking   did-E
      'Siri did WOODWORKING.'

The distinction between in-focus verb forms and out-of-focus forms, clear though it may appear, is easily mixed up with another morphological distinction on the verb. In some languages, verb morphemes mark a focus on the truth value, the aspect or tense of the action ('auxiliary focus'; cf. Hyman & Watters 1984). The following treatment of the Aghem data is taken from Hyman & Watters (1984). Example (92) expresses a wide information focus reading, including the object. In (93), the object is marked with the particle *nò* as a contrastive focus. In (94) the time adverb occurs in a marked position after the verb and is interpreted as a contrastive focus. Note that neither in (93) nor in (94) does the verb form or the tense morpheme change. What changes, however, is the marking of the object itself. In (92) and (93), where the object is in focus, it occurs in a focus-marked prefixed form. In (94), where it represents old information, it occurs in its suffixed, defocussed form.

(92) ḿ mɔ́ zɨ̀ kɨ́-bɛ́ nɛ́
      I P1 eat fufu today
      'I ate fufu today.'

(93) ḿ mɔ́ zɨ̀ kɨ́-bɛ́ nò nɛ́
      I P1 eat fufu FOC today
      'I ate FUFU today.'

(94) ḿ mɔ́ zɨ̀ nɛ́   bɛ́-'kɔ́
      I P1 eat today fufu
      'I ate fufu TODAY.'

However, there is a special morphologically marked variant of the tense particle, which occurs in (95). With this variant, the sentence is interpreted with a focus on the truth value or on the time information of the sentence, like its English translation, with emphatic stress on periphrastic *do*.

(95) m̀ máà zɨ bɛ́-'kɔ́ nɛ́
I P1 eat fufu today
'I DID eat fufu today.'

Because of this interpretation, Hyman & Watters (1984) interpreted *máà* as a focussed variant of the plain form in (92)−(94), calling it 'auxiliary focus'. In their typological overview, they treat examples of auxiliary focus as an instance of the in-focus vs. out-of-focus distinction that we discussed on the basis of data from of Chin, Akan and Sinhala.

However, syntactically and morphologically this form has a very different significance. Contrary to the in-focus form in Chin, Sinhala or Akan, *máà* does not mark a neutral finite sentence conveying an information focus. Morphologically it is often constructed with the out-of-focus form, an additional morpheme (Hyman & Watters 1984: 252), which we take as an indication that it should rather be treated in analogy with the predicate-marking particles of Boni or Chinese. Heine & Reh (1984: 168) reconstruct the predicate focus marker in Rendille from the structure copula + subordinate predicate.

3.2. Problems for typological description / parameters of typological variation

The morphological connection between out-of-focus verb forms and complementation as well as the connection between focus-marking particles and copula morphemes has led to an analysis that derives these forms of morphological focus marking from cleft or relative constructions. Prominent examples are the analysis of Kihung'an by Takizala (1972) and Givón (1979) and the typological work by Heine & Reh (1984). In Kihung'an a sentence like (96) may have a neutral wide focus interpretation. In (97), where the tone on the object changes to a high tone, the object is interpreted as the focus of the sentence. Although both sentences seem to be identical in every other respect, Takizala was able to show that the verb in (97) shares some properties with a verb in a relative clause, as in (98), or in clefts such as (99) or (100). Apart from its particular interaction with negation, one such property is that verbs in FCs as well as in clefts cannot incorporate an object clitic such as *ki*.

(96) Kìpés ká-(ki)-swíím-ín kìt
Kipese PA-buy-past chair
zòòn.
yesterday
'Kipese bought a chair yesterday.'

(97) Kìpès ká-(*ki)-swíím-ín kít
Kipese PA-buy-past chair
zóónó.
yesterday
'Kipese bought a CHAIR yesterday.'

(98) kít ki a-(*ki)-swíím-ín Kìpès
chair pro PA-it-buy-past Kipes
zòòn.
yesterday
'The chair that Kipese bought yesterday.'

(99) kwe kít Kìpès ka-(*ki)-swíím-ín
it's chair Kipes PA-it-buy-past
zóónó.
yesterday
'It's a chair that Kipese bought yesterday.'

(100) kiim ki a-(*ki)-swíím-ín Kìpès
thing pro PA-it-buy-past Kipes
zòòn kwe kít
yesterday is chair
'What Kipese bought yesterday is a chair.'

Another example of the morphological connection between focus and cleft sentences can be found in the Efik examples in (101)−(103) taken from Hyman & Watters (1984). The out-of-focus verb form occurring in case of a narrow focus on the object, as in (102), is the same as the one occurring in sentences like (103) with a morphologically marked focus in sentence initial position, which resembles a cleft sentence.

(101) e-tìm a-mà ɔ-bɔ́b
Etim he-pst he-built (+foc verb form)
à-kam-ba u-fɔ́k
big house
'Etim BUILT A BIG HOUSE.'

(102) e-tìm ɔ-kɔ-bɔ̀b
Etim he-pst-built (−foc verb form)
à-kam-ba u-fɔ́k.
big house
'Etim built A BIG HOUSE.'

(103) à-kam-ba u-fɔ́k kɛ e-tìm
big house FOC Etim
ɔ-kɔ-bɔ́b
he-pst-built (−foc verb form)
'It's a house that Etim built.'

The parallelism between the morphology in focus and cleft constructions is a rather ubiquitous phenomenon which led to the hypothesis that the focus morphology in general can be derived from cleft structures of the form (104). The morphological and syntactic differences, however, were explained as grammaticalization processes that reduced the original cleft structure to a more fixed pattern, including phonological fusion and attrition of certain morphemes, as well as deletion processes.

(104) [$_F$NP] be [background CP]

3.2.1. Morphological problems

There are several problems with the exact analysis of the focus-marking strategies as well as with the exact morphological development. As we will show later, it is not the case that the focus-marking particles are invariably derived from copulas, as the scheme might suggest. Another problematic point is the exact analysis of the out-of-focus verb form. Takizala (1972) and Givón (1979) derive it from relative clauses, whereas Schachter (1973) and Heine & Reh (1984) insist on a difference between constructions derived from relative clauses and other constructions.

3.2.2. Syntactic problems: The obligatoriness of marking

Heine & Reh notice that focus morphology differs in terms of obligatoriness. While in Boni, which was cited in (78)−(80), the marking is optional, in Rendille as well as in Somali the marking is obligatory. Unlike the Boni example in (78), in Somali a sentence without a focus marker, as shown in (105), is ungrammatical. Our analysis is based on data from Livnat (1983) and Svolacchia, Mereu & Puglielli (1995).

(105)   *Cali moos cunay
         Ali   banana ate

(106)   [$_F$ Cali baa] moos cunay.
         Ali   FOC   banana ate
         'It is Ali that ate the banana.'

(107)   Cali [$_F$ moos baa-uu] cunay.
         Ali   banana FOC-CLITIC ate
         'It is the banana that Ali ate.'

(108)   Cali moos [$_F$ waa-uu cunay.]
         Ali   banana FOC-CLITIC ate
         'It is eating that Ali did with the banana.'

Both forms of the focus marker, baa for term focus and waa for predicate focus, can be reconstructed as eroded copula morphemes. But apart from the focus readings that are given as translation in (106)−(108), we have shown above that the syntactic behavior of the morphological focus markers is equivalent to the neutral sentence accent in so far as it projects focus and receives a wide information focus reading. In Somali, we find a copula-derived focus particle in every sentence. However, there also are languages which obligatorily mark the verb with an out-of-focus form. In the Bearnais dialect of French, every main clause is marked with a so-called enunciative morpheme que that can be reconstructed as a complementizer que (Wüest 1985, Joly 1976).

3.2.3. Obligatoriness of marking due to the argument structure of the verb, tense, aspect and polarity

The obligatoriness of focus marking does not necessarily affect the entire morphological or syntactical marking system of a language. Some languages can be analyzed as occupying an intermediate position between optional and obligatory focus marking. In Nupe, sentences with intransitive verbs are obligatorily focus marked, whereas in sentences with transitive verbs focus marking is optional (Heine & Reh 1984). For other languages it has been shown that specific tense and aspect forms as well as instantiations of polarity do not show the in-focus vs. out-of-focus distinction.

There are two cases to be distinguished: Sometimes these exceptional tense, aspect or polarity forms do not show any in-focus vs. out-of-focus distinction and occur in the in-focus form only. This means that sentences with these forms are always morphologically marked for a neutral wide focus. This often occurs in future tenses in contrast to past tenses. From this phenomenon we have to distinguish exceptional tense, aspect and polarity forms that are always marked for focus in the sense of Hyman & Watters' idea of auxiliary focus. These forms are derived from the subordinate out-of-focus verb form plus focus marker. According to Sasse (1981), every negative sentence in Boni shows obligatory focus marking. In affirmative sentences, on the other hand, we find a contrast between sentence patterns with and without morphological focus marking. This morphological appearance led to the assumption that negative polarity and other tense and aspect forms that show the same behavior are inherently or intrinsically marked for focus for semantic or functional reasons (Marchese 1983, Givón 1979, Hyman 1979).

The Aghem examples (95), repeated here as (109), and (110) are taken from Hyman (1979). Hyman & Watters (1984) analyze the verb form in (109) as a variant with the interpretation of focus on the truth value. They argue for this interpretation because the object can only occur in its defocussed form. In negative sentences, however, the object also obligatorily appears in its defocussed form, which leads to the analysis that negative verb forms invariantly mark focus on the truth value as well.

(109) m̀ máà zɨ̀   bɛ́-'kɔ́   nɛ́
       I P1 eat fufu   today
       'I DID eat fufu today.'

(110) ŋ kâ zɨ̀ bɛ́-'kɔ́   nɛ́
       I NEG ate fufu:OUT-OF-FOC today
       'I didn't eat fufu today.'

3.2.4. Historical perspective

What is noteworthy in connection with the obligatoriness of marking is the interpretation of a given FC. In languages with optional focus marking the FC is clearly marked and the focus-marked constituent tends to be interpreted as a narrow focus, possibly with a contrastive interpretation. That is the case for Chinese, Boni, Sinhala, Akan and Kihung'an. In Somali, Bearnais and other languages with obligatory focus marking, however, the marking of one constituent or of the verb form is not necessarily interpreted as a case of narrow focus marking. In these constructions, the focus-marking morphology has actually lost its capacity to mark focus.

It has been repeatedly noticed that the development of focus marking systems follows a directional path of grammaticalization. On the basis of Takizala's (1972) analysis of Kihung'an, Givón (1979) sketched the following steps of development: Starting from a paratactic construction with a headed, non-restrictive relative clause, the relative clause first loses its relative pronoun, then the copula is lost, and finally the marked word order is adapted to the unmarked word order of the sentence. (Cf. (99) and (97), repeated here as (111) and (112).)

(111) kwe kít   Kìpès ka-(*ki)-swíím-ín
       it's chair Kipes PA-it-buy-past
       zóónó.
       yesterday
       'It's a chair that Kipese bought yesterday.'

(112) Kìpès ká-(*ki)-swíím-ín kít
       Kipese PA-buy-past   chair
       zóónó.
       yesterday
       'Kipese bought a CHAIR yesterday.'

The historical development of clefts into focus marking systems seems to be a prototypical grammaticalization path that can also be discovered in many other languages of Africa (Heine & Reh 1984), but also in many non-African languages such as Breton (Harris & Campbell 1995) or Malayalam (Comrie 1995).

From a more syntactical perspective, Harris and Campbell (1995) showed that a central step of this development is the transition from biclausal to monoclausal structures. In the historical development of Breton cleft sentences such as (113), the copula has been eroded and no longer occurs in the modern focus sentences such as (114). Harris and Campbell's analysis shows that this morphological erosion and grammaticalization step had a fundamental syntactic effect on the sentence structure.

(113) Ar vugale eo [$_{S'}$ Op$_i$ [$_S$ a
       the children Copula   that
       lenne t$_i$ al levrioù]]
       read   the books
       'It is the children that read the books.'

(114) Ar vugale$_i$ [$_S$ a   lenne t$_i$ al
       the children   that read   the
       levrioù]
       books
       'The CHILDREN read the books.'

A similar idea is pursued in Comrie's (1995) analysis of Malayalam and in many different recent studies of various African languages. The basic idea that focus morphology is derived from cleft constructions seems to be generally accepted, whereas the starting point of the development, the syntactic properties of the different intermediate steps, and the exact morphological development remain controversial.

4. References

Aboh, Enoch Oladé. 1999. *From the syntax of Gungbe to the grammar of Gungbe*. Ph.D. Diss., Université de Genève, Geneva.

Ameka, Felix. 1992. "Focus constructions in Ewe and Akan: A comparative perspective". In: Collins, Chris & Manfredi, Victor (eds.). *Proceedings of the*

Kwa comparative syntax workshop. (MIT Working Papers in Linguistic, 17.) Cambridge, MA, 1–25.

Bartels, Christine. 1997. *Towards a compositional interpretation of English statement and question intonation.* Ph.D. Diss., University of Massachusetts, Amherst, MA.

Bearth, Thomas. 1980. "Is there a universal correlation between pitch and information value?" In: Brettschneider, Gunter & Lehmann, Christian (eds.). *Wege zur Universalienforschung: Sprachwissenschaftliche Beiträge zum 60. Geburtstag von Hansjakob Seiler.* Tübingen: Gunther Narr Verlag, 124–130.

Bearth, Thomas. 1999. "The inferential gap condition". *Pragmatics* 9.2: 249–288.

Belletti, Adriana & Shlonsky, Ur. 1995. "The order of verbal complements: A comparative study". *Natural Language and Linguistic Theory* 13.3: 489–526.

Biloa, Edmund. 1995. *Functional categories and the syntax of focus in Tuki.* Munich: LINCOM Europe.

Birner, Betty J. 1996. *The discourse functions of inversion in English.* New York: Garland Publishing Inc.

Birner, Betty J. & Ward, Gregory. 1996. "A cross-linguistic study of postposing in discourse". *Language and Speech 39, Special issue on discourse, syntax and information*: 111–140.

Birner, Betty J. & Ward, Gregory. 1998. *Information status and noncanonical word order in English.* (Studies in Language Companion Series, 40.) Amsterdam: Benjamins.

Bowers, John. 1993. "The syntax of predication". *Linguistic Inquiry* 24: 591–656.

Brennan, Virginia. 1996. "Questions in discourse". In: Camacho, José & Choueiri, Lina & Watanabe, Maki (eds.). *The proceedings of the fourteenth west coast conference on formal linguistics.* Stanford, CA, 33–46.

Brody, Michael. 1990. "Remarks on the order of elements in the Hungarian focus field". In: Kenesei, István & Pléh, Csaba (eds.). *Approaches to Hungarian. Vol. 3: Structures and Arguments.* Szeged: JATE, 95–121.

Browning, Marguerite. 1987. *Null operator constructions.* Ph.D. Diss., MIT, Cambridge, MA.

Burgess, Eunice. 1986. "Focus and topic in Xavante". In: Grimes, Joseph E. (ed.). 27–41.

Carlson, Lauri. 1983. *Dialogue games: An approach to discourse anaphora.* Dordrecht: Reidel.

Cheng, Lisa Lai-Shen. 1991. *On the typology of Wh-Questions.* Ph.D. Diss., MIT, Cambridge, MA.

Chomsky, Noam. 1977. "Conditions on rules of grammar". In: Chomsky, Noam. *Essays on form and interpretation.* Amsterdam: North-Holland, 163–210.

Chomsky, Noam. 1982. *Some concepts and consequences of the theory of government and binding.* Cambridge, MA: MIT Press.

Cinque, Guglielmo. 1990. *Types of A-bar dependencies.* Cambridge, MA: MIT Press.

Clements, George N. 1985. "Binding domains in Kikuyu". *Studies in the Linguistic Sciences* 14.2: 37–56.

Cole, Peter. 1987. "The structure of internally headed relative clauses". *Natural Language and Linguistic Theory* 5: 277–302.

Comrie, Bernard. 1995. "Focus in Malayalam: Synchrony and diachrony". *Journal of Asian and African Studies* 48–49: 577–603.

Creider, Chet A. 1989. *The syntax of the Nilotic languages.* Berlin: Dietrich Reimers.

Culicover, Peter W. & Wilkins, Wendy K. 1984. *Locality in linguistic theory.* Orlando: Academic Press.

Dekydtspotter, Laurent Pierre Aimé. 1995. *Null operator-variable structures, predication and the interpretive interface.* Ph.D. Diss., Cornell University, Ithaca, NY.

Delahunty, Gerald P. 1995. "The inferential construction". *Pragmatics* 5.3: 341–364.

Demirdache, Hamida K. 1997. "Dislocation, resumption and weakest crossover". In: Anagnostopoulou, Eleni & Riemsdijk, Henk van & Zwarts, Frans (eds.). *Materials on left dislocation.* Amsterdam: Benjamins, 193–231.

Denham, Kristin E. 1997. *A minimalist account of optional WH-movement.* Ph.D. Diss., University of Washington, Seattle.

Derbyshire, Desmond C. 1985. *Hixkaryana and linguistic typology.* (Summer Institute of Linguistics Publications in Linguistics, 76.) Dallas, TX: University of Texas at Arlington.

Dik, Simon C. et al. 1981. "On the typology of focus phenomena". In: Hoekstra, Teun (ed.). *Perspectives on functional grammar.* Dordrecht: Foris, 41–74.

Dik, Simon. 1997. *The theory of functional grammar*, vol.1: *The structure of the clause,* 2 ed., ed. by Hengveld, Kees. Berlin: Mouton de Gruyter.

Drubig, H. Bernhard. 1992. "Zur Frage der grammatischen Repräsentation thetischer und kategorischer Sätze". In: Jacobs, Joachim (ed.). *Informationsstruktur und Grammatik.* (Linguistische Berichte, Sonderheft 4.) Opladen: Westdeutscher Verlag, 142–195.

Drubig, H. Bernhard. 1994. *Island constraints and the syntactic nature of focus and association with focus.* (Arbeitsberichte des Sonderfoschungsbereiches 340, Nr. 51.) Tübingen: University of Tübingen.

Epée, Roger. 1975. "The case for a focus position in Duala". In: Herbert, Robert K. (ed.). *Proceed-*

ings of the sixth conference on African linguistics, held at the Ohio State University, Columbus, april 12–13, 1975. (Working Papers in Linguistics, 20.) Columbus, Ohio, 210–226.

Epée, Roger. 1976. *Generative syntactic studies in Duala*. Ph.D. Diss., Cornell University, Ithaca, NY.

Erteschik-Shir, Nomi. 1997. *The dynamics of focus structure*. Cambridge: Cambridge University Press.

Gair, James W. & Sumangala, Lelwala. 1991. "What to focus in Sinhala". In: Westphal, Germán & Ao, Benjamin & Chae, Hee-Rahk (eds.). *ESCOL '91: Proceedings of the eighth eastern states conference on linguistics*. Columbus, Ohio, 93–108.

Givón, Talmy. 1978. "Definiteness and referentiality". In: Greenberg, Joseph (ed.). *Universals of human language*. (Vol. 4: Syntax.) Stanford, CA: Stanford University Press, 291–330.

Givón, Talmy. 1983. "Topic continuity in discourse: An introduction". In: Givón, Talmy (ed.). *Topic continuity in discourse: A quantitative cross-language study*. Amsterdam: Benjamins, 1–41.

Givón, Talmy. 1990. *Syntax: A functional typological introduction*. Amsterdam: Benjamins.

Goodluck, Helen & Saah, Kofi K. & Stojanović, Danijela. 1995. "On the default mechanism of interrogative binding". *Canadian Journal of Linguistics* 40: 377–404.

Green, Melanie. 1997. *Focus and copula constructions in Hausa*. Ph.D. Diss., School of Oriental and African Studies, University of London, London.

Grimes, Joseph E. 1986. *Sentence initial devices*. Dallas, TX: Summer Institute of Linguistics.

Guéron, J. 1980. "On the syntax and semantics of PP extraposition". *Linguistic Inquiry* 11: 637–678.

Hajičová, Eva. 1983. "On some aspects of presuppositions of questions". In: Kiefer, Ferenc (ed.). *Questions and Answers*. Dordrecht: Reidel, 85–96.

Harries-Delisle, Helga. 1978. "Contrastive emphasis and cleft sentences". In: Greenberg, Joseph H. (ed.). *Universals of human language*. (Vol. 4: Syntax.) Stanford, CA: Stanford University Press, 419–486.

Harris, Alice C. & Campbell, Lyle. 1995. *Historical syntax in cross-linguistic perspective*. Cambridge: Cambridge University Press.

Heine, Bernd & Reh, Mechthild. 1984. *Grammaticalization and reanalysis in African languages*. Hamburg: Buske.

Herring, Susan C. 1990. "Information structure as a consequence of word order type". In: Hall, Kira et al. (eds.). *Proceedings of the Sixteenth Annual Meeting of the Berkeley Linguistics Society, February 16–19, 1990*. Berkeley, CA, 163–174.

Herring, Susan C. & Paolillo, John C. 1995. "Focus position in SOV languages". In: Downing, Pamela & Noonan, Michael (eds.). *Word order in discourse*. (Typological Studies in Language, 30.) Amsterdam: Benjamins, 163–198.

Hetzron, Robert. 1971. "Presentative function and presentative movement". *Studies in African Linguistics. Supplement 2: Papers from the second conference on African linguistics UCLA, March 26–27. 1971*: 79–105.

Hetzron, Robert. 1975. "The presentative movement: Or why the ideal word order is V. S. O P". In: Li, Charles N. (ed.). *Word order and word order change*. Austin, TX: University of Texas Press, 345–388.

Heycock, Caroline & Kroch, Anthony S. 1999. "Pseudocleft connectivity: Implications for the LF interface level". *Linguistic Inquiry* 30.3: 365–397.

Higgins, Robert F. 1979. *The pseudocleft construction in English*. New York: Garland Publishing Inc.

Hoh, Pau-San & Chiang, Wen-yu. 1990. "A focus account of moved Wh-phrases at S-Structure in Chinese". *Lingua* 81: 47–73.

Horváth, Julia. 1986. *FOCUS in the theory of grammar and the syntax of Hungarian*. Dordrecht: Foris.

Horváth, Julia. 1995. "Structural focus, structural case, and the notion of feature-assignment". In: Kiss, Katalin É. (ed.). *Discourse configurational languages*. Oxford: Oxford University Press, 28–64.

Hyman, Larry M. (ed.). 1979. *Aghem grammatical structure*. (Southern California Occasional Papers in Linguistics, 7.) Los Angeles, CA.: Southern California University.

Hyman, Larry M. & Watters, John R. 1984. "Auxiliary focus". *Studies in African Linguistics* 15.3: 233–273.

Hyman, Larry. 1999. "The interaction between focus and tone in Bantu". In: Rebuschi, Georges & Tuller, Laurice (eds.). Amsterdam: Benjamins, 151–177.

Jackendoff, Ray S. 1972. *Semantic interpretation in generative grammar*. Cambridge, MA: MIT Press.

Jacobs, Joachim. 1984. "Funktionale Satzperspektive und Illokutionssemantik". *Linguistische Berichte* 91: 25–58.

Joly, André. 1976. "QUE et les autres morphèmes énonciatifs du bérnais: essay de psychosystematique". In: Boudreault, Marcel & Möhren, Frankwald (eds.). *Actes du XIIIe congrès international de linguistique et philologie romanes*. Québec, 441–433.

Kayne, Richard S. 1994. *The antisymmetry of syntax*. Cambridge, MA: MIT Press.

Kazenin, Konstantin I. 1999. "Fokusnaja konstrukcija (Focus construction)". In: Kibrik, Alexandr E. (ed.). *Elementy cachurskogo jazyka v tipologičeskom osveščenii (Elements of Tsakhhur grammar in typological perspective)*. Moscow: Nasledie, 452–456.

Kazenin, Konstantin I. to appear. "Focus in Daghestani and word order typology". *Linguistic Typology*.

Kenesei, Istvan. 1993. *A minimalist approach to the syntax of focus*. Unpublished manuscript, University of Szeged, Szeged.

É. Kiss, Katalin. 1987. *Configurationality in Hungarian*. Budapest: Akadémiai Kiadó.

É. Kiss, Katalin. 1998. "Identificational focus versus information focus". *Language* 74: 245–273.

Komlósy, Andrés. 1986. "Focussing on focus in Hungarian". In: Abraham, Werner & Meij, Sjaak de (eds.). *Topic, focus, and configurationality: Papers from the 6th Groningen grammar talks, Groningen 1984*. (Linguistik Aktuell, 4.) Amsterdam: Benjamins, 215–226.

König, Ekkehard. 1991. *The meaning of focus particles: A comparative perspective*. London: Routledge.

Kratzer, Angelika. 1995. "Stage and individual level predicates". In: Carlson, Gregory & Pelletier, Francis Jeffrey (eds.). *The Generic Book*. Chicago: University of Chicago Press, 125–175.

Kuno, Susumu. 1973. *The structure of the Japanese language*. Cambridge, M. A.: MIT Press.

Kuno, Susumu. 1982. "The focus of the question and the focus of the answer". In: Schneider, Robinson & Tuite, Kevin & Chametzky, Robert (eds.). *Papers from the parasession on nondeclaratives*. Chicago, IL, 134–157.

Ladusaw, William A. 2000. "Thetic and categorical, stage and individual, weak and strong". In: Horn, Laurence & Kato, Yasuhiko (eds.). *Negation and polarity: Syntactic and semantic perspectives*. Oxford: Oxford University Press, 232–242.

Laka Mugarza, Miren Itziar. 1990. *Negation in syntax: On the nature of functional categories and projections*. Ph.D. Diss., MIT, Cambridge, MA.

Lambrecht, Knud & Polinsky, Maria. 1997. "Typological variation in sentence-focus constructions". In: Singer, Kora & Eggert, Randall & Anderson, Gregory (eds.). *CLS 33: Papers from the panels on linguistic ideology in contact, universal grammar, parameters and typology, the perception of speech and other acoustic signals*. Chicago, IL, 189–206.

Larson, Richard K. & Lefebvre, Claire. 1991. "Predicate clefting in Haitian creole". In: Sherer, Tim (ed.). *Proceedings of the Northeast Linguistics Society, 21*. Amherst, MA, 247–261.

Lasnik, Howard & Stowell, Tim. 1991. "Weakest crossover". *Linguistic Inquiry* 22.4: 687–720.

Livnat, Michal Allon. 1983. "The indicator particle baa in Somali". *Studies in the Linguistic Sciences* 13.1: 89–132.

Marchese, Lynell. 1983. "On assertive focus and the inherent focus nature of negatives and imperatives: Evidence from Kru". *Journal of African Languages and Linguistics* 5: 115–129.

Matsuda, Yuki. 1997. *Representation of focus and presupposition in Japanese*. Ph.D. Diss., University of Southern California, Los Angeles, CA.

McCloskey, James. 1979. *Transformational syntax and model theoretic semantics: A case study in modern Irish*. Dordrecht: Reidel.

Meinunger, André. 1998. "A monoclausal structure for (pseudo-)cleft sentences". In: Tamanji, Pius N. & Kusumoto, Kiyomi (eds.). *Proceedings of the North East Linguistic Society, 28, vol. 1: Papers from the main session*. Amherst, MA, 283–298.

Milsark, Gary. 1974. *Existential sentences in English*. Ph.D. Diss., M.I.T., Cambridge, MA.

Moser, Margaret Gamble. 1992. *The negation relation: Semantic and pragmatic aspects of a relational analysis of sentential negation*. Ph.D. Diss., University of Pensylvania, Philadelphia, PA.

Moutaouakil, Ahmed. 1989. *Pragmatic functions in a functional grammar of Arabic*. Dordrecht: Foris.

Newman, Paul. 1974. *The Kanakuru language*. Leeds: Institute of Modern English Language Studies, University of Leeds.

Odden, David. 1984. "Formal correlates of focusing in Kimatuumbi". *Studies in African Linguistics* 15.3: 225–299.

Ordóñez, Francisco. 1997. *Word order and clause structure in Spanish and other Romance languages*. Ph.D. Diss., City University of New York, New York.

Osborne, Andrea Gail. 1975. *A transformational analysis of tone in the verb system of Zahao (Laizo)*. Ph.D. Diss., Cornell University, Ithaca, NY.

Ouhalla, Jamal. 1993. "Focus in Standard Arabic". *Linguistics in Potsdam* 1: 65–92.

Ouhalla, Jamal. 1999. "Focus and Arabic clefts". In: Rebuschi, Georges & Tuller, Laurice (eds.). Amsterdam: Benjamins, 335–359.

Payne, Doris L. 1990. *The pragmatics of word order: Typological dimensions of verb initial languages*. (Empirical Approaches to Language Typology, 7.) Berlin: Mouton de Gruyter.

Piñon, Christopher. 1993. "Sigma P and Hungarian". In: Mead, Jonathan (ed.). *The proceedings of the eleventh west coast conference on formal linguistics*. Stanford, CA, 388–404.

Prince, Ellen F. 1978. "A comparison of Wh-Clefts and It-Clefts in discourse". *Language* 54: 883–906.

Prince, Ellen F. 1992. "The ZPG letter: Subjects, definiteness and information-status". In: Mann, William C. & Thompson, Sandra A. (eds.). *Discourse description: Diverse linguistic analyses of a fund-raising text*. (Pragmatics & Beyond, New Series, 16.) Amsterdam: Benjamins, 295–325.

Puskás, Genoveva. 2000. *Word order in Hungarian: The syntax of A'-positions*. (Linguistics Today, 33.) Amsterdam: Benjamins.

Rebuschi, Georges & Tuller, Laurice. 1999. "The grammar of focus: An introduction". In: Rebuschi, Georges & Tuller, Laurice (eds.). 1−22.

Rebuschi, Georges & Tuller, Laurice (eds.). 1999. *The grammar of focus*. Amsterdam: Benjamins.

Rizzi, Luigi. 1990. "Speculations on verb second". In: Mascaró, Joan & Nespor, Marina (eds.). *Grammar in Progress: GLOW essays for Henk van Riemsdijk*. Dordrecht: Foris, 375−386.

Rizzi, Luigi. 1997. "The fine structure of the left periphery". In: Haegeman, Liliane (ed.). *Elements of grammar: Handbook of generative syntax*. Dordrecht: Kluwer, 281−337.

Roberts, Craige. 1998. "Focus, the flow of information, and universal grammar". In: Culicover, Peter W. & McNally, Louise (eds.). *The limits of syntax*. (Syntax and Semantics, 29.) San Diego, CA: Academic Press, 109−160.

Rochemont, Michael S. 1986. *Focus in generative grammar*. Amsterdam: Benjamins.

Rochemont, Michael S., Peter W. Culicover. 1990. *English focus constructions and the theory of grammar*. Cambridge: Cambridge University Press.

Saah, Kofi K. 1988. "Wh-Questions in Akan". *Journal of West African Languages* 18.1: 17−28.

Saah, Kofi K. 1992. "Null Object Constructions in Akan". In: Collins, Chris & Manfredi, Victor (eds.). *Proceedings of the Kwa comparative syntax Workshop, MIT 1992*. (MIT Working Papers in Linguistics, 17.) Cambridge, MA: MIT, 219−244.

Saah, Kofi Korankye. 1994. *Studies in Akan syntax, acquisition, and sentence processing*. Ph.D. Diss., University of Ottawa, Ottawa, Ontario.

Saeed, John Ibrahim. 1984. *The syntax of focus and topic in Somali*. (Cushitic Language Studies, 3.) Hamburg: Buske.

Samek-Ludovici, Vieri. 1996. *Constraints on subjects: An optimality theoretic analysis*. Ph.D. Diss., The State University of New Jersey, Brunswick, N. J.

Sasse, Hans-Jürgen. 1981. "'Basic Word Order' and functional sentence perspective in Boni". *Folia Linguistica* 15.3−4: 253−290.

Sasse, Hans-Jürgen. 1987. "The thetic/categorial distinction revisited". *Linguistics* 25: 511−580.

Sasse, Hans-Jürgen. 1995. "'Theticity' and VS order: A case study". In: Matras, Yaron & Sasse, Hans-Jürgen (eds.). *Verb-subject order and theticity in European languages*. (Sprachtypologie und Universalienforschung, 48: 1/2.) Berlin, 3−31.

Schachter, Paul. 1973. "Focus and relativization". *Language* 49.1: 19−46.

Schaffar, Wolfram. 2000. *Fokuskonstruktionen im japanischen Sprachraum. Eine synchrone, diachrone und typologische Analyse zirkumnominaler Spaltsätze*. Ph.D. Diss., University of Tübingen, Tübingen.

Soemarmo. 1971. *Subject, predicate, focus-presupposition, and topic-comment in Bahasa Indonesia and Javanese*. Ph.D. Diss., University of California, Los Angeles, CA.

Stucky, Susan U. 1979. "Focus of contrast aspects in Makua: Syntactic and semantic evidence". In: Chiarelli, Christine et al. (eds.). *Proceedings of the fifth annual meeting of the Berkeley Linguistics Society, 17−18 february, 1979*. Berkeley, CA: University of California, 362−372.

Stute, Horst. 1986. "Constituent order, cohesion, and staging in Gaviao". In: Grimes, Joseph E. (ed.). 7−25.

Sumangala, Lelwala. 1992. *Long-distance dependencies in Sinhala: The syntax of focus and Wh-questions*. Ph.D. Diss., Cornell University, Ithaca, NY.

Svolacchia, Marco & Mereu, Lunella & Puglielli, Annarita. 1995. "Aspects of discourse configurationality in Somali". In: É. Kiss, Katalin (ed.). 65−98.

Takizala, Alexis. 1972. "Focus and relativization: The case of Kihung'an". In: Kimball, John P. (ed.). *Syntax and semantics 2*. New York: Seminar Press, 123−148.

Tomlin, Russell S. & Rhodes, Richard. 1992. "Information distribution in Ojibwa". In: Payne, Doris L. (ed.). *Pragmatics of word order flexibility*. (Typological Studies in Language, 22.) Amsterdam: Benjamins, 117−135.

Tuller, Laurice. 1986. *Bijective relations in universal grammar and the syntax of Hausa*. Ph.D. Diss., University of California at Los Angeles, Los Angeles, CA.

Tuller, Laurice. 1992. "The syntax of postverbal focus constructions in Chadic". *Natural Language and Linguistic Theory* 10.2: 303−334.

Vallduví, Enric. 1992. *The informational component*. New York: Garland Publishing Inc.

Ward, Gregory. 1999. "A comparison of postposed subjects in English and Italian". In: Kamio, Akio & Takami, Ken-ichi (eds.). *Function and structure: In honor of Susumo Kumo*. Amsterdam: Benjamins, 3−21.

Wasow, Thomas. 1997. "Remarks on grammatical weight". *Language Variation and Change* 9.1: 81−105.

Watters, J. 1979. "Focus in Aghem". In: Hyman, Larry (ed.). 137−197.

Williams, Edwin. 1997. "Blocking and anaphora". *Linguistic Inquiry* 28.4: 577−628.

Wüest, Jakob. 1985. "Les énonciatifs gascond et la théorie de l'énonciation". In: Kristol, Andreas M. & Wüest, Jakob T. (eds.). *Drin de tot: Travaux de sociolinguistique et de dialectologie béarnaises*. Bern: Lang, 285−307.

H. B. Drubig/W. Schaffar,
Universität Tübingen (Deutschland)

82. Noun phrase coordination

1. Definition of the domain
2. Variation within the Coordinate Strategy
3. Variation within the Comitative Strategy
4. AND-languages and WITH-languages
5. Shift of WITH into AND
6. References

1. Definition of the domain

In Stassen (2000), a study which is based on a sample of 270 languages, the cross-linguistic domain of noun phrase coordination (and, by implication, the content of the data base for a typological investigation of this domain) is defined by the following set of semantic and formal restrictions:

(1) A sentence contains a case of noun phrase coordination if
   (a) it describes a single occurrence of an event (action, state, process, etc.), and if
   (b) this event is predicated simultaneously of two (and no more) participant referents, which are conceived of as separate individuals.

This definition rules out a number of construction types. First, it excludes sentences with dual, plural, or collective subjects, such as "They left" or "The two men left", from the data base, as such sentences do not encode the two participant referents as separate individuals. Secondly, the definition stipulates that a clausal or sentential conjunction such as "John left and Mary left" will be left outside of the data base, since such sentences do not necessarily describe a single event. Finally, sentences with more than two participants, such as "John, Bill, Harry, and Susan left", are ruled out by definition (1). As a result, the data base does not include noun phrase coordinations which have an enumerative "etcetera" reading. It can be observed that, in some languages, such enumerations exhibit special formal properties which are absent from the encoding of 'participant pairs'. An example is the Amazonian language Andoke, in which 'two participant' constructions consist in the juxtaposition of two NPs. In enumerations, however, all NPs in the series obligatorily receive the marker -añe:

(2) Andoke (Macro-Carib, Witotoan): (Witte 1977: 281)

(a) *Ñe   ni -pita   ni -θ*
   be.PST her-aunt her-sister
   'It was her aunt and her sister'
(b) (Landaburu 1979: 153)
   koata-añe-ʌ
   guacure-ENUM-NHNL
   tasumí-ẽñe-i   tami-ẽñe-i
   caimito-ENUM-NHNL raisin-ENUM-NHNL
   tomi   -ẽñe-i   siõkɔ̃
   pineapple-ENUM-NHNL all
   'guacures, caimitos, raisins, pineapples ...'

Furthermore, in many languages the use of the coordinating particle is different if more than two participants are involved. English, for example, has the possibility to restrict the use of the conjunctor *and* in enumerations to the last member of the series, while the other NPs are juxtaposed. This juxtapositional strategy is not an option for a 'two participant' sentence. In short, there is reason to assume that noun phrase coordination with three or more members form a special case, which, in regard to the typology of noun phrase coordination, can be viewed as a concomitant phenomenon.

Definition (1) effectively restricts the domain of noun phrase coordination to two encoding strategies. which are opposed to each other in a number of respects. The first of these strategies, which is illustrated in the English sentence.

(3) English
    John and Mary left

can be called the **Coordinate Strategy**. A fundamental formal characteristic of this strategy is that it encodes the two participants in the construction by way of noun phrases with equal structural rank. Thus, the two NPs involved are not differentiated as to syntactic function; they have the same thematic role, and in languages in which such NPs receive case marking they will both have the same case. Typically, though not necessarily, the two NPs in such constructions can be seen to form a constituent, viz., a coordinate (Plural or Dual) NP. As a result of this, they typically govern dual or plural number agreement on predicates, if they have a grammatical function for which this agreement is defined. Furthermore, the two NPs are commonly subject to the Coordinated Structure Constraint as formulated in Ross (1967), which forbids NP-extraction from such constructions:

(4) English
(a) *Who did you see and Mary?
(b) *The woman that I saw and Mary ...

The second encoding strategy for noun phrase coordination, which is illustrated by the sentences in (5), can be called the **Comitative Strategy**.

(5) English
(a) *John left with Mary*
(b) *Mary left with John*

Under the Comitative Strategy, the two participants in the event are morphosyntactically encoded as noun phrases of unequal structural rank. While one of the noun phrases can take any case role, the other noun phrase is invariably encoded as the head of an oblique NP. A prototypical characteristic of comitative structures is that the two noun phrases involved are not part of the same constituent. As a result, they typically do not force dual or plural agreement on predicates, and neither of the two NPs is subject to restrictions on extraction rules as defined by the Coordinate Structure Constraint.

2. Variation within the Coordinate Strategy

Within the Coordinate Strategy, it is possible to subcategorize coordinate NP-structures on the basis of the linking device which they employ. As we have seen in the example from Andoke (cf. (2a)), there are languages with **juxtaposition** or **zero-marking** of such structures. Traditionally, the term **asyndeton** is employed to refer to such constructions. Quite a few languages can be shown to have this encoding possibility as at least one of their options, but closer inspection reveals that asyndetic NP-coordination is nonetheless a minor strategy. For one thing, obligatory use of this variant is very rare. This option can be documented in only a few languages, among which no significant areal cohesion can be defined. An example is:

(6) Awtuw (Papuan, Sepik) (Feldman 1986: 110)
Yowmən Yawur du -k -puy -ey
Y. Y. DUR-IMPF -hit -IMPF
'Yowmen and Yawur are hitting (someone)'

In general, zero-marked NP-coordinations vary with an encoding which features one or more overt linking particles. In such cases, the zero option often performs a specific, restricted, function: it is used either in 'list-like' enumerations, or in the encoding of NP-pairs which habitually go together and can be said to form some conventionalized whole or "conceptual unit" (Mithun 1988: 332). Thus, pairs like 'husband and wife', 'boys and girls', 'horses and cattle', 'bow and arrows', or 'gold and silver' are more likely to be encoded by zero-marking than other, less predictable NP-coordinations. An example in which asyndetic NP-coordination is limited in this fashion is:

(7) Mandarin (Sino-Tibetan, Sinitic) (Mullie 1947: 232)
(a) *Zjé yué*
sun moon
'sun and moon'
(b) (Li & Thompson 1981: 657)
Lù Wényì gēn wǒ
L. W. and/with I
'Lu Wenyi and I'

Zero-marked NP-coordinations appear to be absent from Africa and from at least the western part of Europe. In all other parts of the world it must have been an old encoding option. However, the general trend all over the world is that zero-coordination tends to be marginalized into specific functions or is replaced altogether by overt marking strategies. Mithun (1988: 353–357) suggests that this development, which can be attested for NP-coordination and clausal coordination alike, has its source in the global increase in literacy. While the zero-strategy, which is basically intonational, is functionally quite well adapted to spoken language, written language requires a more overt formal marking of syntactic relations.

Overtly marked NP-coordinations can be subcategorized further on the basis of two interacting formal parameters. First, the number of coordinate particles involved gives rise to a distinction between **monosyndeton** (in which only one marker is present in the construction) and **polysyndeton** (in which both noun phrases in the structure have their linking particle). Furthermore, the structural position of the marker or markers may differ from type to type. Among the logical possibilities yielded by combining these two parameters, by far the most prominent option turns out to be the use of a **medial con-**

nective. In this case, we have one single linking morpheme, which is placed between the two NPs in the construction. For some languages which employ this option, it can be argued that the medial connective has greater structural cohesion with the second NP than with the first, or vice versa. Ross (1967) and Dik (1968) demonstrate that English *and*, as illustrated in (3), is in construction with the second NP, rather than with the first NP or with both NPs. However, it must be stressed that this difference in structural cohesion does not lead to a difference in structural rank for the two NPs in the English construction. In other words, *and* is not a subordinating item in English.

Monosyndetic NP-coordination by means of a medial connective can be encountered all over the globe. In some areas, notably Sub-Saharan Africa, the strategy has a minor distribution, but there is hardly any major linguistic area in which it is lacking totally. In comparison to medial monosyndeton, other overt coordinate strategies are fairly rare. All strategies at issue feature postposition or suffixation of the connective item or items. Among these options, polysyndeton appears to be the most popular. The strategy can be found in a number of unconnected linguistic areas such as the Caucasus, northeastern Africa, Australia and New Guinea, Southern India and northeastern Asia. In addition, we find isolated examples in the Americas, in West Africa, and in Burma. A randomly chosen example of the strategy is:

(8) Tamil (Dravidian) (Asher 1982: 69)
 Akkaa -vum taŋkacci -yum
 elder sister -and younger sister -and
 'Elder sister and younger sister'

Monosyndetic postposing of coordination markers may in principle take two different forms, depending on whether the item is postposed to the first or to the second NP in the coordination. Both types of construction occur in at least some languages, but their frequency is low. Moreover, the languages which present one (or both) of these options typically also allow a construction of the polysyndetic type, so that these monosyndetic constructions are best regarded as variants in which one of the markers in the polysyndetic construction can be optionally deleted. Given this, it will be clear that the two monosyndetic variants occur in roughly the same areas as have been listed for the polysyndetic construction. An example of the 'first-NP' subtype is Beja (North-East Africa), while the 'second-NP' subtype is illustrated by NP-coordinations from Tubu (Sahara).

(9) Beja (Nilo-Saharan, Cushitic) (Reinisch 1893: 195)
 (a) *Aní-wå barŭk-wå*
 1SG-and 2SG-and
 'you and I'
 (b) *Mēk-wå lagá*
 donkey-and calf
 'a donkey and a calf'

(10) Tubu (Nilo-Saharan, Saharan) (Lukas 1953: 166)
 (a) *Tûrku ye mɔlɔfûr ye*
 jackal and hyena and
 'the jackal and the hyena'
 (b) *Wúdɛn arkɔ́ ye*
 antilope goat and
 'the antilope and the goat'

Monosyndetic preposing on the first NP is not attested at all in the sample used in Stassen (2000). That is, there do not seem to be languages which conform to the AND-NP NP scheme. Monosyndetic preposing on the second NP can of course be claimed to exist in those languages in which the medial connective seems to be in construction with the second NP; thus, English would be a case in point. For a number of such languages, there is a polysyndetic preposed variant of the type AND-NP AND-NP. This variant, which can, among others, be attested in various languages of Europe, usually has an emphatic or contrastive function: the English *both ... and* construction is a fairly representative instance of this strategy. However, languages in which this preposed polysyndeton is the only option do not seem to occur.

It is highly probable that the variation encountered in the Coordinate Strategy is at least partially correlated with word order options. According to Stassen (2000), the two correlations formulated in (11) receive substantial empirical support:

(11) Word order correlations for Coordinate NP-types:
 (a) If a language has a (monosyndetically or polysyndetically) post-posed coordination marker, then that language is verb-final.
 (b) If a language is verb-initial, and if it has an overtly marked coordinate strategy for noun phrases, that strategy will involve a medial connective.

Furthermore, it is almost certain that the typological variation in the Coordinate Strategy has a diachronic dimension. Mithun (1988) shows that NP-coordinators derive from various sources by way of a process of grammaticalization. In particular, she mentions NP-coordinators which have their origin in grammaticalized comitative markers ('with'), or in grammaticalized sentence adverbials with the original meaning "also, too, as well", or "furthermore, then, moreover". To this list several other diachronic possibilities can be added. In some languages a coordinating particle for noun phrases clearly arises from a numeral such as 'two', 'both' or 'all', which is grammaticalized to a greater or lesser degree. A concentration of these cases is found in the Australian-Papuan area, but incidental instances are attested for other areas as well. Related to this 'numeral' strategy is a 'pronominal' strategy, in which dual or plural personal pronouns are gradually grammaticalized into coordinative markers for noun phrases. A further source for noun phrase coordinators lies in non-finite forms of verbs meaning "to be" or "to exist"; for example, the item *mi-cha* "and" in Choctaw is a participial or switch-referential form of the verb *mi* "to be" (Nicklas 1972: 257). Finally, there are a few cases where the NP-coordinator seems to be a specialization of the function of a general focus-marking particle. Examples of languages in which these various origins for coordinate items are illustrated include:

(12) Aranda (Australian, Pama-Nyungan) (Strehlow 1944: 208)
Ara aranga tara
red kangaroo euro two
'the red kangaroo and the euro'

(13) Waropen (Austronesian, New Guinean) (Held 1942: 90)
Mangha kisi bingha
man 3DU woman
'the man and the woman'

(14) Choctaw (Muskogean) (Nicklas 1972: 257)
Ano micha sashki
1SG be.DS my.mother
'my mother and I'

(15) Manam (Austronesian, Melanesia) (Lichtenberk 1983: 365, 483)
(a) Moáne-be áine di-púra
man-and woman 3PL-arrive
'the man and the woman arrived'
(b) Wabubu-ló-be i -púra
night -at-FOC 3SG-come
'It was at night that he came'.

It can be concluded, then, that the sources of coordinative elements for noun phrases are heterogeneous. It is reasonable to assume that these different origins may still have their bearing on the synchronic status of coordinate markers in individual languages, and that the syntactic behaviour of such markers is still to a certain degree influenced by formal properties of their source-items.

3. Variation within the Comitative Strategy

In contrast to the Coordinate Strategy, the Comitative Strategy is much more formally uniform across languages. In the overwhelming majority of languages, the Comitative Strategy manifests itself by way of an oblique marker 'with' on one of the participant noun phrases. If the language has a coordinate NP-strategy as well, the comitative marker is, in the typical case, not identical to the item used as an NP-coordinator. Depending on general morphosyntactic features of the language the comitative marker may take the form of an adposition or an affix. Although 'dependent marking' (Nichols 1986) is the predominant encoding option in comitative constructions, there are some languages which deviate from this pattern. A 'head-marking' strategy, in which the comitative marker is incorporated into the predicate, is encountered in languages of the North-West Caucasus:

(16) Ubykh (North-West Caucasian) (Dumézil 1931: 17)
yô a-u -ji-k'ä-φa
2SG 3SG-2SG -with-come-PF
'He came with you'.

In some cases, this incorporation leads to transitivization of the predicate, so that the 'comitative' NP takes on the syntactic status of a direct object. Assorted american languages present this option.

(17) Ona-Šelknám (Chon) (Tonelli 1926: 58)
Kokóš telken okel-enen
K. boys with-go
'Kokóš goes with the boys'.

That comitative constructions are liable to turn into (or, alternatively, may have their source in) transitive patterns is manifested even more explicitly in languages where the comitative NP is constructed as the direct object of a verb 'to accompany/to have/to hold/to take/to follow' in a serializiation construction. Obviously, such cases will be found in areas where verb serialilzation is rampant anyway. Thus, West Africa, Eastern Austronesia, and Sino-Tibetan are the places to search for this phenomenon. An example is:

(18)   Igbo (Niger-Kordofanian, Kwa) (Welmers 1973: 369)
       Há sò   anyị gá
       they accompany.STAT us   go to
       -á   'Ábá
       -NARR A.
       'They went to Aba with us'.

4. AND-languages and WITH-languages

The distinction between the Coordinate Strategy and the Comitative Strategy can be put to use in the assessment of the typological status of the sampled languages in regard to the encoding of the defined domain. A first observation to make is that, with only a few exceptions, all languages in the sample appear to have the possibility to employ the Comitative Strategy. Thus, having a comitative strategy does not constitute an interesting cross-linguistic parameter. What is interesting is the fact that a number of languages appear to use this comitative strategy as the only way to encode the domain. That is, in these languages the only way to encode the situation in which a single event is ascribed simultaneously to two different participants is to use a non-balanced, non-constituent, construal of the two NPs involved: coordination of noun phrases, in the structural sense, is not an option. Languages of this type will be called WITH-languages. A randomly chosen example is:

(19)   Samoan (Austronesian, Polynesian) (Marsack 1975: 119)
       o io'o 'a'ai Mana ma   Ioane i
       PROG eat M.   and/with I.   at
       fa'i
       banana.
       'Mary and John are eating bananas/ Mary is eating bananas with John'.

Opposed to WITH-languages, there are, of course, many languages like English, in which there is a clear differentiation between the comitative and the coordinative encoding of the domain. Such languages will be called AND-languages.

Stassen (2000) suggests that the dichotomy between WITH-encoding and AND-encoding may cluster with other typological parameters, such as the obligatory marking of tense-distinctions and the morphological marking of agents vs. patients. Also, the distinction between the two language types has clear areal features. AND-languages appear to be concentrated in two large linguistic areas. The first of these 'mega-areas' comprises what is called the Old World in Nichols (1992). It includes all the languages of Europe, Central Asia and Siberia; in the North-East, it also includes some, though not all, of the Austronesian languages of the Philippines. To the south-east, the area stretches as far as India. Finally, it includes the Middle East and Northern Africa. The major language phylums found in the area are Indo-European, Uralic, Altaic, Dravidian, Semitic, and Kartvelian. Moreover, AND-status can be argued for a number of isolate languages in the area, such as Basque, Ket, and Burushaski. The only cases of doubt are the North-West Caucasian languages and the Daghestanian languages; both Caucasian language groups seem to deviate from the straightforward AND-status of Old World languages to a certain extent.

A second mega-area of AND-languages is formed by (most of the) languages of Australia and New Guinea. Especially along the coast-lines of both islands, where Austronesian influence is notable, there are a number of counter-examples, but the central highlands of New Guinea and the bulk of the Australian mainland contain almost uniform AND-encoding.

Outside of these two main AND-areas, AND-encoding can be found in several other places, in particular in the Americas, but the distribution of these AND-languages seems to be rather whimsical. Perhaps the best case for a third AND-area can be made for the languages of the southern part of Central America and the eastern part of South America. This area, which one might call Meso-Andean America, comprises part of the Uto-Aztecan languages of Mexico the Oto-Manguean languages of southern Mexico and Honduras, the Chibchan languages of El Salvador, Nicaragua, Costa Rica, and Panama, and the languages of the Andes.

Large, unbroken, concentrations of WITH-languages are encountered in Africa, Asia, and the Americas. With the possible exception of Khoisan, all the languages of Africa in and below the Sahara exhibit (some degree of) WITH-encoding. A second WITH-area is made up of East and South-East Asia (including Tibet, China, Korea, and Japan) and the islands of Indonesia, Melanesia and Polynesia. On the American continent, WITH-status is normal for at least the Far North (Alaska, Canada), and the Deep South (non-Andean South America).

5. Shift of WITH into AND

Although both for WITH-languages and for AND-languages clear, 'pure' instances can be found, the typological status of these two types is probably not equally well-established. First, there is a marked difference of frequency between the two types: there are roughly twice as many AND-languages as there are WITH-languages. Secondly, there is a notable discrepancy in the stability of the types. In general, AND-languages can be said to be stable diachronically and 'pure' in their synchronic state: there is a sharp delineation of the two available strategies. On the other hand, 'pure' instances of WITH-languages are relatively rare. For a considerable number of such languages, some process of "diachronic drift" of the comitative encoding can be attested. The general outcome of this process in all relevant languages is that it effectuates a shift from a monolithical encoding of the domain towards a dualism of encoding. To put it in rather informal and anthropomorphic terms: WITH-languages do not have a coordinate strategy, but they would like to have one. To this end, they tend to differentiate the structural features of the comitative strategy, by changing one or more features of that strategy towards the features of the coordinate strategy. In this way, the language acquires a two-strategy encoding of the domain, in which one of the strategies is still purely comitative, while the other is some hybrid between the comitative and the coordinate strategy.

The "shift" of the comitative strategy in WITH-languages is a gradual process. Moreover, the structural features which are changed in the course of this process are different for various groups of WITH-languages. In structural terms, the grammaticalization of a comitative encoding pattern into a 'coordination-like' construction prototypically involves the creation of a single constituent, in which both the 'with'-phrase and the non-comitative NP are included, and in which the two NPs gradually come to be regarded as being of equal structural rank. However, there are several routes by which this end result can come about. In some cases, the creation of a coordinate NP involves 'movement' of the 'with'-NP from its canonical position in the sentence. In others, differentiation in verb agreement (mainly between singular and dual/plural) may be the main formal manifestation of the process. Still other WITH-languages signal the creation of a coordinate NP-structure by "doubling' the comitative marker in coordinations, thereby overtly indicating the equality in rank of the two NPs; and there are, of course, various conceivable combinations of these structural processes. In the end, however, all these languages come to exhibit a split between the two strategies in all relevant features except the lexical linking item. Thus, these mixed WITH-languages evolve towards AND-status. Indeed, one might call them AND-languages, if it were not for the fact that the particle employed in their coordinate NP-structure is still lexically identical to their comitative marker. Examples in which these various paths of WITH-drift are illustrated include:

(20) Babungo (Niger-Kordofanian, Bantoid) (Schaub 1985: 87)
 (a) *Làmbí gə̀ táa yìwìŋ ghɔ́ Ndùlá*
  L. go.PERF to market with N.
  'Lambi went to the market with Ndula'.
 (b) *Làmbí ghɔ́ Ndùlá gə̀ táa yìwìŋ*
  L. and/with N. go.PF to market
  'Lambi and Ndula went to the market'.

(21) Tolai (Austronesian, Melanesian) (Mosel 1984: 176)
 (a) *Nam ra tutana i ga rovoi ma ra pap*
  DEM ART man 3SG PF hunt with ART dog
  'That man went hunting with his dog'.
 (b) *Telengai dir rovoi ma ra pap*
  T. 2DU hung and/with ART dog
  'Telengai and his dog went hunting'

(22) Japanese (Altaic, isolate) (Kuno 1973: 103, 112)
 (a) *John ga Mary to benkyoosita*
  J. SBJ M. with studied
  'John studied with Mary'.
 (b) *John to Mary to Tom to ga kita*
  J. with M. with T. with SBJ came
  'John, Mary and Tom came'.

In addition of this gradual drifting of comitatives into coordinations, there are also cases of erstwhile WITH-languages which, over time, have developed an independent and separate coordinate construction. Such a process may, for example, have taken place in Celtic. While in Old Irish the comitative marker *co* could also be employed as a medial connective, later forms of Celtic have reserved the coordinating function for specialized linking particles, such as *agus* in Scottish Gaelic.

(23) Old Irish (Indo-European, Celtic) (Dottin 1913: 90)
  (a) *Luid   co   n -a   muintir*
      go.3SG.PRET with the -his family
      'He went with his family'.
  (b) *Lá   co   n   -óidche*
      day and/with ART -night
      'day and night'

(24) Scottish Gaelic (Indo-European, Celtic) (Mackinnon 1977: 16)
  Bha   Calum agus Mairi ag
  be.PRET C.   and M.   at
  obair
  work.VN
  'Calum and Mary were working'.

Stassen (2000) suggests that the 'drive' in WITH-languages to create a coordinate structure may be explained in terms of iconicity (see Haiman 1980). Acquiring a separate coordinate construction might enable these languages to encode the two participants in the construction as being of equal structural rank, which would then formally mirror the fact that, semantically, these two participants have equal function in any form of noun phrase coordination.

6. References

Asher, R. E. 1982. *Tamil*. Amsterdam: North-Holland.

Dik, Simon C. 1968. *Coordination*. Amsterdam: North-Holland.

Dottin, G. 1913. *Manuel d'irlandais moyen*. Paris: Champion.

Dumézil, Georges. 1931. *La langue des oubykhs*. Paris: Librairie ancienne Honor, Champion.

Feldman, H. 1986. *A grammar of Awtuw*. Canberra: The Australian National University.

Haiman, John. 1980. "The iconicity of grammar". *Language* 56: 515–540.

Held, G. J. 1942. *Grammatica van het Waropensch (Nederlandsch Noord Nieuw-Guinea)*. The Hague: Martinus Nijhoff.

Kuno, S. 1973. *The structure of the Japanese language*. Cambridge, Mass.: MIT Press.

Landaburu, J. 1979. *La langue des Andoke*. Paris: SELAF.

Li, Charles N. & Thompson, Sandra A. 1981. *Mandarin Chinese: a functional reference grammar*. Berkeley etc.: University of California Press.

Lichtenberk, F. 1983. *A grammar of Manam*. Honolulu: University Press of Hawaii.

Lukas, J. 1953. *Die Sprache der Tubu in der zentralen Sahara*. Berlin: Akademie Verlag.

Mackinnon, R. 1977. *Teach yourself Gaelic*. London: Hodder & Stoughton.

Marsack, C. C. 1975. *Teach yourself Samoan*. London: Hodder & Stoughton.

Mithun, Marianne. 1988. "The grammaticalization of coordination". In: Haiman, J. & Thompson, S. A. (eds.). Clause combining in grammar and discourse, 331–359. Amsterdam: Benjamins.

Mosel, Ulrike. 1984. *Tolai syntax and its historical development*. Canberra: Australian National University.

Mullie, J. L. M. 1947. *Korte Chinese spraakkunst van de gesproken taal (Noord-Pekinees dialect)*. The Hague: Martinus Nijhoff.

Nicklas, N. T. D. 1974. *The elements of Choctaw*. University of Michigan/Ph. D. Diss.

Nichols, Johanna. 1986. "Head-marking and dependent-marking grammar". *Language* 62: 56–119.

Nichols, Johanna. 1992. *Linguistic diversity in space and time*. Chicago: University of Chicago Press.

Reinisch, L. 1893. *Die Bedauye-Sprache in Nord-Ost Afrika*. Vienna: Tempsky.

Ross, John R. 1967. *Constraints on variables in syntax*. Bloomington: Indiana University Linguistics Club.

Schaub, W. 1985. *Babungo*. London: Croom Helm.

Stassen, Leon. 2000. "AND-languages and WITH-languages". Linguistic Typology 4-1: 1–54.

Strehlow, T. G. H. 1944. *Aranda phonetics and grammar*. Sydney: Australian National Research Council.

Tonelli, D. A. 1926. *Grammatica e glossario della lingua degli Ona-Šelknám della Terra del Fuoco*. Torino: Società Editrice Internazionale.

Welmers, William E. 1973. *African language structures*. Berkeley: University of California Press.

Witte, P. 1977. "Function of the Andoke copulative in discourse & sentence structure". In: Longacre, R. E. (ed.). *Discourse Grammar*, Part 3, 253–288. Danas: Summer Institute of Linguistics.

Leon Stassen, Nijmegen
(The Netherlands)

83. Converbs

1. Definition and delimitation
2. Types of converbal constructions
3. Semantic and pragmatic functions
4. Grammaticalization of converbs
5. Areal and etymological considerations
6. Correlating properties
7. Special abbreviations
8. References

1. Definition and delimitation

1.1. Definition

The term converb was coined in Altaic linguistics (Ramstedt 1903: 55) and is roughly synonymous with such terms as verbal adverb, adverbial/conjunctive participle, gerund (in the sense of the ablativus modi of the Latin gerund), depričastie (Russian), gérondif (French), sentence equivalent (Finnish), and absolutive (Indo-Aryan).

The following prototypical definition of the converb has been suggested by Martin Haspelmath: "a non-finite verb form whose main function is to mark adverbial subordination. Another way of putting it is that converbs are verbal adverbs, just like participles are verbal adjectives." (Haspelmath 1995: 3) E.g.

(1) English (Quirk & al. 1972: 763)
The manager APPROACHED us,
The manager approached us
SMIL-ING.
SMIL-ING.

(2) French (Halmøy 1982: 8)
Le plombier siffle en
the plumber whistles CONV
travaill-ant.
work-CONV
'The plumber whistles while working.'

(3) Basque (Saltarelli 1988: 55)
Lan-a egi-n-az
work-ABS do-PFV-MOD/INSTR (=CONV)
irabaz-ten d-a
earn-HAB 3ABS-PRES(-AUX1)
diru-a ez alferkeria-n
money-ABS NEG sloth-LOC
ego-n-az.
be-PFV-MOD/INSTR (=CONV)
'Money is earned by working, not by being lazy.'

(5) Dogon (Plungian 1995: 37)
Kɔrɔ gé mɔgɔ-gu wo
pumpkin DEF wash-DUR (=CONV) she
wɔ-gu, yeŋ sɔgri-i-Ø.
be: PRES-SIM thus make.noise-AOR-3SG
'When washing the pumpkin, she made a noise.'

(6) Classical Tibetan (Tikkanen 1987: 316)
Nam laŋ-nas soŋ.
night rise:PFV-ABL (=CONV) go:PFV
'When the night had risen, he went.'

(7) Indonesian (Kwee 1976: 103)
Se-tiba di rumah, saya masuk
CONV-come in house I enter
ke kamar saya.
to room I
'Coming home, I went to my room.'

(8) Ancash Quechua (Cole 1983: 2)
Lima-ta chaa-ri-r,
Lima-ACC arrive-after-SS (=CONV)
rikaari-shaq amigu-u-ta.
see-FUT friend-my-ACC
'After arriving in Lima, I will see my friend.'

A broader definition has been proposed by Nedjalkov (1995: 97): "As a first approximation we can define a converb as a verb form which depends syntactically on another verb form, but is not its syntactic actant, i.e. does not realize its semantic valencies."

This definition imposes no restriction on finiteness. Accordingly, a converb could be inflected for the subject (and possibly other arguments), such as the so called subordinative or participial moods or nominalized (declined) conjugated forms of Eskimo, Basque, Ket, Circassian, and many other languages.

(9) West Greenlandic (Fortescue 1984: 57)
Aallar-sima-til-lusi
leave-PFV-CAUS.MOOD-(1SG).2PL.CONT.MOOD
Kaali uqaluup-para.
Kaali speak.with-1SG.3SG.IND
'While you were away I spoke with Kaali.'

(10) Basque (Saltarelli 1988: 45)
Odol-a
blood-ABS
d-a-ri-o-la
3ABS-PRES-flow-3SG.DAT-MANNER
etorr-i d-a ume-a
come-PFV 3ABS-PRES-(AUX1) child-ABS
ikastola-tik.
school-ABL
'The child has come from school bleeding.'

The point is that the opposition finite/non-finite reflects a scale of desentialization or deranking of predicates, starting with the gradual loss of or constraints on the specification for subject (and possibly other arguments), mood, tense and aspect, often combined with a change of category status (nominalization, adverbialization) or the use of a special subordinative conjugational form (Stassen 1985: 76 ff.; Lehmann 1988: 193 ff.; Koptjevskaja-Tamm 1994: 1245 ff.). Inevitably there will then be forms which could be classified as either converbs or finite dependent or subordinative verb forms, according to the analysis or depending upon where we draw the line between finite and non-finite forms. The traditional line runs between forms expressing and forms not expressing the person-number of the subject. Of course, a language may have no finite forms according to this definition, or it may have no non-finite forms. However, non-finite forms are sometimes allowed to take possessive markers, which show agreement with the (notional) subject (e. g. Finnish, 29). But if non-finiteness is seen to exclude the possibility of subject agreement with regular subject markers, it may be that forms of the same paradigm must be assigned different finiteness status. For example, in Burushaski the primary converb takes finite subject markers with certain, mostly non-volitional, intransitive verbs, but not with most other verbs. In Evenki (Manchu-Tungusic), on the other hand, some tense forms take possessive subject suffixes like converbs and nominals (Nedjalkov 1995: 443–446; Haspelmath 1995: 6 f.).

A strange hybrid formation is found in Kurukh (North Dravidian), where the anterior converb is really a finite, inflected verb form to which a converb marker borrowed from Sadri/Sadani (Central Indo-Aryan) has been added.

(11)   Kurukh (Dube 1983: 6)
Sipaahi-r asan bar-c-ar kii
soldier-PL thither come-PAST-3PL CONV
nerr-an piṭi-y-ar cic-c-ar.
snake-ACC kill-PAST-3PL give-PAST-3PL
'The soldiers came there and killed the snake.'

At least in some cases it could then be expedient to introduce a distinction between conjugated (9–10) and non-conjugated converbs (1–8). The label 'non-finite' could still be maintained, given that the forms in question lack expression or implication of mood and are hence unable to function as (prototypical) independent predicates. However, the restriction against expression of the absolute tense cannot be made criterial. Some languages, including Korean and some Papuan languages, have converbs that inflect for the absolute as well as relative tense.

Returning to Haspelmath's definition, there is also the question of 'adverbial subordination'. Although converbs in European languages often express adverbial modification, in many cases the same converb may serve not only as an adverbial modifier, but also as a marker of conjoining or sequencing events in a so-called clause chain, or there may be converbs specialized for this function (copulative/coordinative or narrative converbs).

(12)   English (Haiman 1985: 196)
Leaving her children, she fled for safety.
(= She left her children and fled for safety.)

(13)   Japanese (Martin 1975: 479)
Sono miti o hidari e it-te,
that road OBJ left to go-CONV
tukiatat-te, migi e ore-te
reach.end-CONV right to turn-CONV
massugu oide nasai!
straight go IMP!
'Go to the left on that street, and when you get (having got) to the end of it, turn right and go straight ahead!'

Finally, there is the question of subordination. Converbal clauses often do show characteristics of subordination, such as centre-embedding, extraposition, extraction, backwards pronominal anaphora and control, as well as focusing. Yet many converbs lack signs of subordination. For example, the Hindi-Urdu anterior-modal converb, which has all the other features of subordination, cannot be focused (asserted, negated or questioned) per se, i. e. on its interpropositional (interclausal semantic) relation, except in its reading as a manner adverbial:

(14)   Hindi (Davison 1981: 109)
??Kyaa vah doost-õ̃ see
Q s/he friend-OBL.PL with
mil-kar deer see aa-y-aa?
meet-CONV lateness with come-PAST-MSG
'Did he come late [because of] having met his friends?'

(15)   Hindi (Davison 1981: 113)
       ??*Vah caay pii-kar   nahĩĩ*
       s/he tea   drink-CONV not
       jaa-ee-g-aa.
       go-2/3SG-FUT-MSG
       'He will not go having drunk tea.'
       (= *Vah caay piine ke baad nahĩĩ jaaeegaa* '... after drinking tea'.)

Contrary to what has been suggested, this restriction does not follow simply from the asyndetic link or semantically vague relationship to the main clause. Compare the preceding examples with the roughly synonymous Burushaski anterior converb:

(16)   Burushaski (Tikkanen 1995: 524, fn. 23)
       Shugúlo-ting ṭhúmuk
       friend-PL   encounter
       n-ú-man   iné
       CONV-3HPL-become s/he
       i-kháran-im-i-a?
       3SG-be.late-PRET-3SG-Q
       'Was he late [because of] having met his friends?'

Haiman (1985: 197) makes a distinction between subordination and incorporation (converbal clauses being instances of the latter: S2[...[S1]...]S2), but this does not explain the problem with the Hindi-Urdu converb (cf. also Haspelmath 1995: 48, fn. 3). The latter are simply not fully integrated in the scope of the main clause. Lack of integration is also manifested by postposed English converbal clauses, which become odd when questioned or negated

(17) (a) *The headmaster resigned in September, wishing (= because he wished) to devote all his time to his book. / leaving (= and left) for America.*
     (b) ?*Did the headmaster resign in September, wishing.../leaving...?*
     (c) ?*The headmaster did not resign in September, wishing... / leaving...*

By contrast, many Asian languages have converbal clauses that are integrated in the main clause under both the adverbial and, alternative, non-adverbial (coordinate-like) reading. In the former case the converbal clause is focusable, in the latter case it shares operators with the main clause (question, negation, illocutionary force).

(18)   Japanese (Martin 1975: 485 f.)
       Kare ni   at-te   sore o
       he   DAT meet-CONV that OBJ
       tutae-nakat-ta
       tell-NEG-PAST
       Lit. 'Having met him, I did not tell him that'
   (i) 'I met him, but I did not tell him that' ((CONV) MV)NEG
   (ii) 'I told him that, but not when I met him' (CONV (MV))NEG
   (iii) 'I did not meet him nor did I tell him that' ((CONV) (MV))NEG

In some instances, languages or systems have been seen to undergo change in this respect. The Turkish anterior/terminal converb in *-ıp* could not copy the negation of the main verb during older stages of the language, but in Modern Turkish it can (Schulz 1978: 128).

(19)   Turkish (Johanson 1995: 338)
       Ev-e   gel-ıp
       hom-DAT come-CONV
       el-ler-in-i
       hand-PL-POSS.3SG-ACC
       yıka-ma-d-ı.
       wash-NEG-TRM.PAST-3SG
       'He did not come home and [did not] wash his hands.'

In order to restrict the scope of the negation to the main clause, a particle such as *de* 'and; also' can be used. In this way the Turkish converb is similar to the Sanskrit anterior converb, but contrasts with the Tamil anterior converb, which even during its oldest known stage could share the main verb negation.

(20)   Old Tamil (Tikkanen 1987: 32)
       Nilan toṭ-ṭup   puk-ā-ar...
       earth dig-CONV enter-NEG-3PL
       'He cannot have dug up and entered the earth.'

In conclusion we may say that Haspelmath's prototypical definition goes a long way, but cannot cover all forms that have been labelled converbs in the literature. To subsume all the forms usually labelled as converbs, we would have to make provisions for non-finiteness, variation in scope behaviour and copulative converbs, i.e. converbs specifically used in clause chains. At this point, however, converbs start to merge with other dependent verb forms.

1.2. Delimitation from other forms

Converbs are formally and functionally closely related to participles (verbal adjectives), infinitives, and verbal nouns or gerunds (in the sense of the English gerund). They may, however, be multifunctional, overlapping with other forms, most typically participles and infinitives (Nedjalkov 1995: 104 ff.; König & van der Auwera 1990: 346 ff.).

(21) English (Quirk & al. 1972: 763)
I caught the boy smoking a cigar = 'I caught the boy while I was smoking a cigar' (supplementive clause = converb)
'I caught the boy in the act of smoking a cigar' (verb complementation = participle in object nexus)
'I caught the boy who was smoking a cigar' (postmodification)

Converbs can often be paraphrased or translated by conjunct and copredicative participles. They differ from the latter in not agreeing adjectivally with their (implicit) subjects in gender, number and case. In spite of adjectival agreement, conjunct participles tend to have adverbial or appositive function.

(22) Lithunian (Nedjalkov 1995: 105)
Tėvas parūk-ęs
father smoke-PCPL:MSG
(rūky-dam-as)   išėjo   iš
smoke-SEMIPCPL-MSG went.out from
kambario.
room
'Father, having smoked (smoking), went out of the room.'

(23) Vedic Sanskrit (Tikkanen 1987: 109)
Vṛtrám   ja-ghan-vā́m
Vrtra-ACC RED-kill-PCPL.PFV:MSG.NOM
ápa tád   va-vā́r-a
off it: NOM-ACC RED-cover-3SG.PERF.ACT
'Having killed Vritra, he uncovered it'. Cf.:

(24) *Yó   ha-tvā́   [á]hi-m*
who-MSG.NOM kill-CONV dragon-ACC
á-ri-ṇā-t   saptá síndhūn
PAST-release-9-3SG seven river:PL.ACC
'He who killed the dragon and released the seven rivers'

Number and gender agreement is, nevertheless, found in the Classical Arabic converb, which is formally the petrified accusative of the active participle:

(25) Classical Arabic
Ta-ḍārab-nā
REC-strike:REC.PFV-1PL
wāqif-ai-ni
stand:PCPL-DU-ACC/GEN (=CONV)
'We were hitting each other (while) standing.'

A problem may arise where participles do not inflect, as in English. The indeterminate cases must then be solved on the basis of the primary function as deduced from frequency.

It may be more difficult to draw a line between converbs and various clause chaining forms, such as medial verbs (→ Art. 100). The term (chain-)medial verb was coined in Papuan linguistics, but it has also been applied to similar verb forms in Australian and other languages, although their position need not be medial (Foley 1986: 176). Medial verbs tend to copy the sentential operators (question, negation, mood, tense-aspect) of the main clause of the clause chain. In this sense they do not, however, differ from many converbs in their clause chaining function (cf. 13).

(26) Tonkawa (Foley & Van Valin 1984: 258)
Tekekeʔe:k šʔa:pa-ta
in.that.bush hide-MEDIAL.SS
ke-yaše-w!
1SG.U-watch-IMP
'Hide in that bush and watch me!'

However, more so than converbs, medial verbs tend to manifest agreement with subjects (when non-coreferential) and to lack the formal characteristics of subordination. Haspelmath (1995: 20−27) has argued that while prototypical converbal clauses are subordinate (in the sense of 'embedded' or 'incorporated'), prototypical medial clauses in clause chaining constructions are cosubordinate (in the sense of Foley & Van Valin 1984: 242), i.e. dependent (distributionally and for certain grammatical categories such as mood and tense-aspect) but not embedded (as constituents of the main clause; cf. Halliday's (1985: 219) distinction between rank shifted and hypotactic clauses).

The distinction between medial verbs and converbs need not be clear-cut, however. Just as many converbs have alternative or primary clause chaining function and syntax, many medial verbs (and other clause chaining forms) have an alternative adverbial function, although their syntax may remain the same. In the case of the Japanese *te*-converb, however, it may have adverbial meaning and subordinate syntax when sharing subject or topic with the main clause. However, if it has an independent subject, it cannot occur inside the main clause as a genuine subordinate (embedded) clause (contrast 27a and 27b).

(27) Japanese (Kuno 1973: 207)
(a) *John ga uwagi o nui-de*
John SUBJ jacket OBJ strip-CONV
Mary wa hangaa ni kake-ta.
Mary TOP hanger on hang-PAST
'When John took off his jacket, Mary hung it on the hanger.'
(b) **Mary wa [John ga...]...*
Mary TOP John SUBJ
'Mary, when John took off his jacket, hung it on the hanger.'

Converbs and medial verbs differ from coordinate clauses in being at least distributionally dependent, but resemble the latter in their tendency to coreference and dependence on sentential operators (cf. conjunction reduction). (→ Art. 82)

A widespread phenomenon relevant not only to various subordinate and non-finite, but also to some coordinate structures, is that of switch reference (→ Art. 84). This is essentially the formal marking on the verb of a switch in subject or agent by a morpheme which usually carries other meanings in addition (cf. Stirling 1993: 1, etc.).

(28) Amele (Van Valin 1993: 103, Roberts 1988: 62, ex. 13a)
Ho busale-ce-b dana age
pig run.out-DS-3SG man 3PL
qo-ig-a fo?
hit-3PL-TPAST Q
'Did the pig run out and did the men kill it?'

As can be seen from example (28), switch reference may occur with subject markers. Switch reference is especially common and pervasive in North American, Papuan and Australian languages, and is inextricably linked with the expression of various interpropositional relations in clause linkage (mainly conjoining in Papuan, chiefly adverbial in North American languages). In fact, many switch reference forms are converbs. (But clearly, there are also non-converbal forms for marking referential (dis)continuity, and converbs that say nothing about reference.) Similarly, many prototypical converbs display switch reference, having coreferential forms agreeing with the subject and non-coreferential forms not agreeing with the subject and/or occurring with an independent (notional) subject (cf. section 2.1.).

Finnish
(29) *Kuul-tua-an tämä-n hän*
hear-CONV-3SG this-ACC s/he
ilahtu-i.
be.pleased-PAST(3SG)
'When s/he$_i$ heard this, s/he$_i$ was pleased.'

(30) *Opettaja-n kuul-tua tämä-n*
teacher-GEN hear-CONV this-ACC
nous-i meteli.
arise-PAST(3SG) noise
'When the teacher heard this, there was a racket.'

In many cases coreferential converbs and conjunct participles are in this way suppletive forms of participles in absolute constructions.

Medial verbs have their mirror image in the so-called consecutive or narrative tenses (Dahl 1985: 113 f.) of many African languages (e. g. Swahili) with VO order (and posterior clause chaining). However, the latter forms tend to take finite subject markers even when coreferential.

(31) Swahili (Masica 1976: 125)
Ni-li-kwenda soko-ni
1SG-PAST-go market-LOC
ni-ka-rudi.
1SG-KA-return
'I went to the market and came back.'

Finally, converbs may be compared with serial verbs, which, nevertheless, crucially lack the formal asymmetry between the conjoined verbs or verb phrases (→ Art. 106; Bisang 1995: 137 ff.).

(32) Chinese (Bisang 1995: 146)
Ni gui-xia-lai qiu
you kneel-go.down-come beg
Zhangsan.
Zhangsan.
'You knelt down in order to beg Z.' (purpose)
'You knelt down and then begged Z.' (consecutive action)
'You knelt down begging Z.' (simultaneous action)
'You knelt down and begged Z.' (alternating action)

Occasionally one finds the term serial verb used for forms which contain aspect or other markers, and which may hence be classified as converbs (cf. 5.).

(33) Chinese (Li & Thompson 1981: 225)
Ta neng qi zhe ma she jian.
s/he can ride DUR horse shoot arrow
'S/He can shoot an arrow while riding a horse.'

Converbs are syntactically differentiated from absolute participles, such as are found in the older Indo-European languages and some Australian languages. What characterizes absolute participles is that they are syntactically detached from the main clause, construed on the basis of an ungoverned case, and, typically, independent of the main clause subject:

(34) Latin
Haec sol-e ori-ent-e
these sun-ABL rise-PTCP.PRES-ABL
facta sunt.
done are
'This happened when the sun was rising.'

Converbs and infinitives are also syntactically distinct categories. They may, however, overlap in some functions, such as the purposive and as an adverbal complement. Some languages, such as Chukchi, Ket (Yeniseian), and Tamil (Dravidian) have combined infinitive-converbs (in Tamil such forms must have independent subjects to receive converbal interpretation).

(35) Tamil (Lehmann 1989: 261)
Kumaar tuuṅk-a Raajaa
Kumar sleep-INF Raja
paṭi-tt-aaṉ.
study-PAST-3SGM
'When/While Kumar was sleeping, Raja studied.'

2. Types of converbal constructions

2.1. Subject expression and control

Converbs may or may not take subject markers and/or an explicit subject, or the notional subject is in an oblique form. If the subject is unexpressed, it tends to be coreferential with the subject or some other semantically or pragmatically salient participant of the governing clause or speech event. Other control-conditioning factors include selectional restrictions and proximity.

When the converb has an explicit subject or pivot, the latter is usually not controlled by the subject or pivot of the main clause, although in many cases it may be coreferential with some other participant. (The complex subject rules for English converbs have been outlined by Kortmann 1991: 102 ff.; 1995: 206 ff.)

In Burushaski, which has ergative morphology, the shared 'subject' (head-marked on the verb) may be construed with either the main (or following) verb or converb. In the latter case, the converb is not embedded in the main clause.

(36) Burushaski
In(-e) nu-qás ásimi.
s/he(-ERG) CONV-laugh he.told.me
[In nuqás] [Ø ásimi] / [Ine [nuqás] ásimi]
'He laughed and said to me. / He said to me laughing.'

As mentioned above (§ 1.1.), converbs often display switch reference. In accordance with a theory advanced by Stassen (1985: 84 ff.), different- or open-subject converbs presuppose same-subject converbs.

In Chechen (North-east Caucasian), it is claimed that the different-subject converb shows independent reference (i. e. may under certain conditions be used with same subjects), carries temporal meaning and takes full valence, while the same-subject converb shows dependent reference, lacks temporal meaning of its own, and lacks one valence place (Nichols 1983: 39).

(37) Chechen (Nichols 1983: 27)
Cuo: iza äl-ča,
he:ERG this:NOM say-DS.CONV
a:rave:lira.
went.out
'Having said this, s/he went out.'
'She said this and Ø/he went out.'

Of particular interest are the rules that determine DS vs. SS converbs in cases of partial or overlapping coreference, impersonal constructions and other problematic cases. Typically the SS converb covers cases of partial coreference, where the main clause subject is properly included in the converb subject or stands in a part-whole relationship to it. Yet prescriptive grammars often criticize constructions where the implicit subject of the (coreferential) converb must be recovered from an oblique case NP in the main clause (e. g. genitive, dative, accusative, etc.):

(38) Russian (Rappaport 1984: 50)
Gulja-ja po gorodu, menja
walk-CONV along town:DAT I:ACC
vstreti-l staryj znakomyj.
meet-PAST:MSG old acquaintance
'(While [I was]) walking around the city, an old acquaintance met me.'

An interesting case is Tuva (Turkic), where the DS converb is (uniquely or preferably) used even when the main clause subject is referentially part of the converb subject. Yet when one subject is implicit and personal and the other one is a non-coreferential full NP, or when one subject is a natural factor or element and the other is inanimate, either the DS or SS converb may be used (Bergelson & Kibrik 1995: 378−394).

(39) Tuva (Bergelson & Kibrik 1995: 387)
Xlebti xoorajda bižir-arga /
bread town bake-DS /
bižir-gaš, beer onu mašina
bake-SS hither it car
söört-üp tur-ar.
bring-CONV AUX-IMPF
'They bake the bread in the town, and the car brings it here.'

If the converb subject is an impersonal zero, it is treated as a non-subject, and the DS converb is chosen:

(40) Tuva (ibid.)
Karaŋgila-j beerge (*ber-geš),
get.dark-CONV AUX:DS AUX-SS
soo-j ber-gen.
get.cold-CONV AUX-PFV,VBL.N
'It grew dark and it became cold.'

Some languages, including Finnish and Hungarian, do not even readily allow the converb with weather and other impersonal subjects.

(41) Finnish
*Sade-ttua-an / ?Sata-en
rain-CONV.ANT-3SG / rain-CONV.SIM
myrskys-i.
storm-PAST(3SG)
'It rained and stormed.'

The conclusion drawn by Bergelson & Kibrik (1995: 391) from the Tuva switch-reference system is that "[...] same-subject dependent clauses naturally imply a greater connectedness of events than the different-subject clauses. In connected discourse the form that expresses greater connectedness has communicative priority. This also explains the fact that in cases of deviation from the prototypical referential relations between clauses (i. e. from coreference) it is always the same-subject forms that expand into the domain of the different-subject forms, but never the other way round." And: "Presumably, [...] switch-reference first emerges in constructions where the type of coreference is least predictable from the semantic nature of the interclausal link itself" (id.: 405). In their study of switch reference, Haiman & Munro (1983: xiv) reach a conclusion suggesting that no language with simultaneous converbs exclude same-subject converbs. These findings are reaffirmed by Stirling's (1993) analysis of switch reference, according to which DS forms may indicate a switch not only in the subject/pivot/topic, but in any of the eventualities (incl. time, agentivity, etc.). This might explain why DS forms are often indifferent to coreference, while SS forms show at least some continuity of eventualities.

2.2. Syntagmatic properties

The converb with its possibly restricted number of complements and modifiers is mostly asyndetically linked as a unit to the controlling clause at the sentence or (extended) verb phrase level, preceding, following or incorporated into the controlling clause. The clause order, when not fixed, is largely determined by semantic and discourse pragmatic considerations, such as temporal and logical iconicity (which can be overridden by connectives and factors of relative tense and aspect) and/or information flow (e. g. preposed "guidepost" vs. postposed "afterthought").

A fundamental semantico-syntactic distinction, marked at least prosodically, is that between detached (autonomous, non-restrictive) and non-detached (non-autonomus) converbal clauses. This distinction has far-reaching implications at all levels and has been analyzed in detail for Russian by Rappaport (1984) and for Sanskrit by Tikkanen (1987). Autonomy is reflected in clause expansion, free subject and temporal deixis, aspectual autonomy, presuppositional opacity, focus restrictions, and semantic versatility.

(42) Russian (Rappaport 1984: 119−120)
 (a) /*Alik xodit po ulice*
    Alik walks along street
    spotykajas'./
    stumble:IMPF:CONV
    'Alik is walking along the street stumbling.' (non-detached)
 (b) /*Vitja stoit v koridore /*
    Vitja stands in corridor
    robeja. /
    feel.timid:IMPF:CONV
    'Vitja is standing in the corridor, feeling timid.' (detached)

König (1995: 89 f.) has pointed out that non-detached converbs in English tend to rely more on the presence of (semantic) connectives than do their Russian and French counterparts.

Converbal clauses cannot usually be coordinated with finite clauses. In many languages they can, however, be coordinated with adpositional and adverbial phrases of similar semantic function. In many languages they can also be headed by various conjunctions and connectives which may alter their meaning (or merely mark the clause juncture), and they may take operators and focus particles. The position of operators and focus particles determines their scope.

(43) Turkish (Johanson 1995: 333)
 (a) *Otur-up mu konuş-t-ular?*
  sit-CONV Q speak-TRM.PAST-3PL
  'Did they speak (while they were) sitting?'
 (b) ≠ *Oturup konştular mı?*
  'Did they sit down and speak?'

In Slavonic languages other than Russian there is a tendency for converbs to become more and more restricted with respect to the connectives, particles and syntagms they can combine with (Růžička 1978: 237).

3. Semantic and pragmatic functions

3.1. Relative tense (dependent taxis)

Converbs frequently display a formal opposition between simultaneous or unmarked and (basically) anterior forms, sometimes also posterior forms. In some languages finer temporal-aspectual distinctions are found. Some languages, such as Korean, are peculiar in allowing converbs to be combined with absolute tense suffixes (Račkov 1958: 44).

(44) Korean (Nedjalkov 1995: 126)
 Cwungkwuk-uy conthap-ul
 China-GEN pagoda-ACC
 mopangha-yessu-myense piektol
 copy-PAST-CONV brick
 taisin-ey tor-ul
 instead-DAT stone-ACC
 sayongha-yess-ki ...
 use-PAST-INF
 'Copying the Chinese pagodas, they used stone instead of brick ...'

Not infrequently anterior converbs are derived from simultaneous converbs by an auxiliary or they contain some indication of perfective aspect.

3.2. Semantic typology of converbs

In languages that rely heavily on converbs, such as Korean (more than 40 forms), there are often distinct converbs for different semantic relations, such as addition, alternation, sequence, time, manner, cause, reason, purpose, consequence, condition, concession, antithesis, etc. Converbs that have only one or two meanings of the adverbial type have been called specialized converbs (Nedjalkov 1995: 106−107).

In the following examples from Japanese, the specialized converb in *-tara* takes either conditional meaning with a non-past tense verb or temporal meaning with a past tense verb.

(45) Japanese (Kuno 1973: 177)
 (a) *John ga ki-tara boku wa*
  John SUBJ come-CONV I TOP
  kaeru
  return
  'If John has come, I will leave.'
 (b) *John ga ki-tara Mary wa*
  John SUBJ come-CONV Mary TOP
  kaet-ta.
  return-PAST
  'When John came, Mary returned.'

Converbs that are specialized for non-adverbial, conjoining, function often occur concatenated in strings. They are sometimes called copulative converbs in Uralic and Altaic linguistics. Nedjalkov uses the term narrative or coordinative converb (Nedjalkov 1995: 109). It should be stressed that these converbs are by no means restricted to narrative discourse, as they may often share any sentential operators (cf. (13)).

Typical converbs, especially in European languages, are, however, rather vague about their semantic value, being able to combine both adverbial and non-adverbial meanings, varying from language to language. Converbs that can take three or more adverbial meanings have been labelled contextual converbs (Nedjalkov 1995: 106 ff.). Their interpretation depends on co(n)textual factors, such as tense, aspect, Aktionsart, mood, word order, quantifiers, connectives, focus particles, idiosyncratic restrictions, and world knowledge. E. g., the conditional reading of a converbal clause in English requires the predicate to be a stage-level predicate and the main clause to have a non-factual interpretation (Stump 1985; König 1995: 79 ff.).

(46) English (König 1995: 81)
 (a) *Wearing his new outfit, John would fool anyone.*
 (b) *Being a master of disguise, John would fool anyone.*

Depending on the requirements with regard to background knowledge, there is a scale of informativeness for interpropositional relations, running from addition, accompanying circumstances, concomitance, and specification via manner to temporality, causality, instrument, condition, contrast and concession (Kortmann 1991: 124; 1995: 223). For instance, the temporal interpretation is possible for example (47b) only in an elaborate context, e. g. a professional singer, who even shaves while singing (König 1995: 85).

(47) French (Halmøy 1982: 286)
(a) *Je chante en me ras-ant.*
   I sing CONV myself shave-CONV
   'I sing (while) shaving.'
(b) *Je me rase en chant-ant.*
   I myself shave CONV sing-CONV
   'I shave singing.'

A more general parameter is that of semantic restrictiveness. Although expressing anteriority or some other temporal relation, a converbal clause need not stipulate a truth condition for the proposition of the main clause. Restrictive converbal clauses are non-detached, whereas non-restrictive ones are detached in languages that make this distinction (cf. 42, Rappaport 1984: 196). Restrictiveness is also connected with focusability: only restrictive converbal clauses can be focused. The focused status of the converb in (48) is clear from the final detached position of the preverb.

(48) Hungarian (Haiman 1985: 208)
Meghökken-ve áll-t-am meg.
be.amazed-CONV stop-PAST-1SG PREV
'It was in amazement that I stopped.'

Converbal clauses also carry certain pragmatic or discourse functional values which correlate with genre or discourse type. For instance, the English detached participle or converb, typically has a so-called 'depictive value' in narrative discourse, where it cannot easily be paraphrased by coordinate or subordinate clauses (Thompson 1983: 56).

In European languages converbs often have a backgrounding function (→ Art. 46), being pragmatically presupposed. On the other hand, the preferred use of converbs over coordinate and subordinate finite clauses in expressing the sequence or overlap of tightly linked events in especially literary narrative and expository discourse can also be seen as an iconic device to achieve compactness, co-hesion or vagueness (cf. Haiman 1985: 229; → Art. 47).

Specialized adverbial and contextual converbs can usually be negated in the same way as other non-finite forms, or they may have special, occasionally suppletive, negative forms.

(49) Finnish
Näke-mä-ttä ei voi
see-INF-ABESS (=CONV.NEG) not can
uskoa.
believe
'One cannot believe without seeing.'

Converbs are often ambivalent as to voice. Only in some languages do we find specifically passive converbs of the type 'being made', 'having been made'.

4. Grammaticalization of converbs

Not infrequently converbs are employed as (semantic) main verbs in periphrastic constructions expressing aspect or tense, or with an applicative function.

(50) Balti (Read 1934: 39)
Nga si rben yod.
I ERG write:CONV AUX
'I am writing (continually).'

Converbs may become adpositions (e. g. 'concerning', 'holding' = 'with'), conjunctions (e. g. 'considering', 'being'), and quotative markers (e. g. 'saying').

(51) Mundari (Tikkanen 1987: 312)
senog-jan men-te
go-COMPL.FIN say-ABL/INSTR (=CONV)
rag-tan-a-e.
weep-DEF.PRES-FIN-3SG.SUBJ
'... because (lit. 'saying') he went, he is weeping.'

Occasionally converbs turn up in lexicalized nominal compounds, etc.

(52) Hungarian (de Groot 1995: 290)
nyit-va-tart-ás
open-CONV-keep-NZN
'opening hours'

5. Areal and etymological considerations

Converbs are found widely in Eurasia (excl. parts of east and south-east Asia) and in the north-eastern part of Africa, less widely (or less prototypically) in the Americas, and sporadically (or less unambiguously) elsewhere. In particular, there are diverse subzones with regard to types and uses of converbs (cf. Masica 1976: Chapter 4; → Art. 109). In south and central Asia as well as in Japanese, the most frequent converbs are basically anterior and tend to carry various adverbial meanings (incl. manner) as well as a conjoining function ('and then'). In Europe, the most frequent converbs are simultaneous or temporally unmarked and carry mainly adverbial meanings. They are not normally used for sequencing actions, except in certain narrative styles or without assertive force. In some languages, such as German, converbal clauses tend, in addition, to be very short.

As regards formation, converbs in Indo-European languages are mostly derived from participles that have become indeclinable, but in the older or conservative Indo-European languages (Sanskrit, Ancient Greek, Latin, Lithuanian, Tocharian) we also find (petrified) cases of action nominals or verbal adverbs derived by adverbial suffixes (cf. Homeric Greek: *-don, dēn, -da, -ti*). In some languages converbs are formed periphrastically, e. g. French *en* + *-ant/ent*.

In Uralic, "Altaic" (Turkic, Mongolic, Tungusic), Yeniseian and many Tibeto-Burman languages, the converbs are often derived from petrified or specialized uses of cases of verbal nouns, or from aspect stems. In Dravidian and Japanese they are typically bare or enlarged verb stems with or without tense or aspect markers, thus also in South Munda. In Indonesian the simultaneous converb is derived by attaching the prefix *se-*, related to the quantifier 'one; same'.

In many converb-prominent languages, at least some converbs are etymologically opaque. For example, in Burushaski the anterior coreferential converb is formed with the opaque confix or prefix *n- (-n)* from the aorist stem, while the non-coreferential and other converbs are petrified cases of verbal nouns and participles. The etymology of the Turkish converb in *-ıp* is still open to debate.

6. Correlating properties

Languages which make abundant use of converbs have often been observed to exhibit a basic OV word order (favouring anterior clause chaining). Perhaps a more diagnostic, if obvious, feature is that they have restrictions on finiteness in clause linkage. In extreme cases, as in various degrees approximated by Japanese, Korean, Dravidian and "Altaic", a sentence can only have a single finite verb form, which is maximally specified for person, tense and mood. Dependent predications must then be expressed by reduced or deranked clauses (→ Art. 45, 100).

7. Special abbreviations

ABESS	abessive
ANT	anterior
CONT	contemporative
DS	different subject
FIN	finitizer
H	human
HAB	habitual
MOD	modal (case)
NPT	non-past
NZN	nominalization
PCL	particle
PREV	preverb
Q	question marker
REC	reciprocal
RED	reduplication
SEQ	sequential
SIM	simultaneous
SS	same subject
TPAST	today's past
TPL	temporal
TRM	terminal
U	undergoer

8. References

Bergelson, Mira B. & Kibrik, Andrej, A. 1995. "The system of switch-reference in Tuva: Converbal and masdar-case forms." In: Haspelmath & König (eds.), 373–414.

Bisang, Walter. 1995. "Verb serialization and converbs – differences and similarities." In: Haspelmath & König (eds.), 137–188.

Cole, Peter. 1983. "Switch reference in two Quechua languages." In: Haiman & Munro (eds.), 1–15.

Dahl, Östen. 1985. *Tense and aspect systems*. Oxford: Blackwell.

Davison, Alice. 1981. "Syntactic and semantic indeterminacy resolved: A mostly pragmatic analysis for the Hindi conjunctive participle." In: Cole, P. (ed.), *Radical pragmatics*. New York: Academic Press, 101–128.

Dube, K. C. (chief editor) 1983. *Ādibhāratī Bhāg 2. Kuṛukẖ-Hindī*. Bhopāl: Ādimjāti Anusandhān evam Vikās Saṃsthā.

Foley, William A. 1986. *The Papuan languages of New Guinea*. Cambridge: Cambridge University Press.

Foley, William A. & Van Valin, Robert D. Jr. 1984. *Functional syntax and universal grammar*. (Cambridge Studies in Linguistics, 38.) Cambridge: Cambridge University Press.

Fortescue, Michael. 1984. *West Greenlandic*. (Croom Helm Descriptive Grammars.) London: Croom Helm.

Groot, Casper de. 1995. "The Hungarian converb or adverbial participle in *-val-ve*." In: Haspelmath & König (eds.), 283–311.

Haiman, John. 1985. *Natural syntax. Iconicity and erosion*. (Cambridge Studies in Linguistics, 44.) Cambridge: Cambridge University Press.

Haiman, John & Munro, Pamela (eds.) 1983. *Switch reference and universal grammar*. (Typological Studies in Language, 2.) Amsterdam: Benjamins.

Halliday, M. A. K. 1985. *An introduction to functional grammar*. London: Edward Arnold.

Halmøy, Jane-Odile. 1982. *Le gérondif. Eléments pour une description syntaxique et sémantique*. Université de Trondheim.

Haspelmath, Martin. 1995. "The converb as a cross-linguistically valid category." In: Haspelmath & König (eds.), 1–55.

Haspelmath, Martin & König, Ekkehard (eds.) 1995. *Converbs in cross-linguistic perspective. Structure and meaning of adverbial verb forms – adverbial participles, gerunds*. (Empirical Approaches to Language Typology, 13.). Berlin/New York: Mouton de Gruyter.

Johanson, Lars. 1995. "On Turkic converb clauses." In: Haspelmath & König (eds.), 313–347.

König, Ekkehard. 1995. "The meaning of converb constructions." In: Haspelmath & König (eds.), 57–95.

König, Ekkehard & van der Auwera, Johan. 1990. "Adverbial participles, gerunds and absolute constructions in the languages of Europe." In: Bechert, Johannes et al. (eds.). *Towards a typology of European languages*. (Empirical Approaches to Language Typology, 8.) Berlin/New York: Mouton de Gruyter, 337–355.

Koptjevskaja-Tamm, Maria. 1994. "Finiteness." In: Asher, R. E. (ed.). *The encyclopedia of language and linguistics*. Oxford: Pergamon Press, 1244–1248.

Kortmann, Bernd. 1991. *Free adjuncts and absolutes in English: Problems of control and interpretation*. London/New York: Routledge.

–. 1995. "Adverbial participial clauses in English." In: Haspelmath & König (eds.), 189–237.

Kuno, Susumu 1973. *The structure of the Japanese language*. Cambridge, Massachusetts: MIT Press.

Kwee, John B. 1976. *Indonesian*. (Teach Yourself Books.) Second edition. Sevenoaks: Hodder & Stoughton.

Lehmann, Christian. 1988. "Towards a typology of clause linkage." In Haiman & Munro (eds.), 181–225.

Lehmann, Thomas. 1989. *A grammar of Modern Tamil*. Pondicherry : Institute of Linguistics and Culture.

Li, Charles N. & Thompson, Sandra. 1981. *Mandarin Chinese: a functional reference grammar*. Berkeley: University of California Press.

Martin, Samuel E. 1975.*A reference grammar of Japanese*. New Haven: Yale University Press.

Masica, Colin P. 1976. *Defining a linguistic area: South Asia*. Chicago/London: University of Chicago Press.

Nedjalkov, Vladimir P. 1995. "Some typological parameters of converbs." In: Haspelmath & König (eds.), 97–136.

Nichols, Johanna. 1983. "The Chechen verb forms in *-na* and *-ča*: Switch reference and temporal deixis." *Studia Caucasica* 5: 17–44.

Plungian, Vladimir. 1995. *Dogon*. (Languages of the World/Materials 64.) Münchzen/Newcastle.

Quirk, R. & Greenbaum, S. & Leech, G. & Svartvik, J. 1972. *A grammar of contemporary English*. London: Longman.

Račkov, Gennadij E. 1958. "Vremena deepričastij pervoj i vtoroj grupp v sovremennom korejskom jazyke." Učenye zapiski LGU, 236. Leningrad.

Ramstedt, Gustav J. 1903. *Über die Konjugation des Khalkha-Mongolischen*. (Mémoires de la Société Finno-Ougrienne, 19.) Helsingfors.

Rappaport, Gilbert C. 1984. *Grammatical function and syntactic structure: The adverbial participle of Russian*. Columbus, Ohio: OH Slavica Publishers (UCLA Slavic Studies 9).

Read, A. F. C. 1934. *Balti Grammar*. (James G. Forlong Fund, vol. XV.) London: The Royal Asiatic Society.

Roberts, John 1988. "Amele Switch-Reference and the Theory of Grammar." *Linguistic Inquiry* 19: 45–64.

Růžička, Rudolph. 1978. "Erkundungen für eine Typologie der syntaktischen und semantischen Strukturen der Gerundien (Adverbialpartizipien) in modernen slawischen Literatursprachen." *Zeitschrift für Slawistik* 23: 229–244.

Saltarelli, Mario. 1988. *Basque*. (Croom Helm Descriptive Grammar Series.) London/New York/ Sydney: Croom Helm.

Schulz, Peter. 1978. *Verbalnomina und Konverbia als adverbiale Ergänzungen im Alttürkischen*. Diss. Frankfurt am Main.

Stassen, Leon. 1985. *Comparison and universal grammar*. Oxford: Blackwell.

Stirling, Lesley. 1993. *Switch-reference and discourse representation*. (Cambridge Studies in Linguistics, 63.) Cambridge: Cambridge University Press.

Stump, Gregory T. 1985. *The semantic variability of absolute constructions*. Dordrecht: Reidel.

Thompson, Sandra A. 1983. "Grammar and discourse: The English detached participial clause." In: Klein-Andreu, F. (ed.), *Discourse perspectives on syntax*. New York: Academic Press, 43−65.

Tikkanen, Bertil. 1987. *The Sanskrit gerund: A synchronic, diachronic and typological analysis.* (Studia Orientalia, 62.) Helsinki: Finnish Oriental Society.

−. 1995. "Burushaski converbs in their South and Central Asian areal context." In: Haspelmath & König (eds.), 487−528.

Van Valin, Robert D. Jr. 1993. "A synopsis of Role and Reference Grammar." In: Van Valin, R. (ed.), *Advances in Role and Reference Grammar*. (Current issues in Linguistic Theory, 82.) Amsterdam/Philadelphia: Benjamins, 1−164.

Bertil Tikkanen, Helsinki
(Finland)

84. Reference maintenance in discourse

1. Preliminaries
2. Terminology
3. Two types of linguistic devices employed in reference maintenance
4. Primary referential devices: theory and typology
5. A typology of subsidiary referential devices
6. Pronominal systems
7. Other aspects of reference maintenance in discourse
8. Syntactic anaphora
9. Locative and temporal reference and predicate anaphora
10. Special abbreviations
11. References

1. Preliminaries

When people talk, they constantly mention various specific entities, such as:

(1) (i) participants of the current speech act (expressions such as *I, you*)
 (ii) other persons (*Mary, she*)
 (iii) living beings and objects (*the cat, that car, my hand, the cloud*)
 (iv) abstract notions conceptualized as objects (*the Great French Revolution, my salary*)
 (v) locations in space (*right here, on the Red Square*)
 (vi) moments in time (*tonight, on New Year's eve*)

Entities of category (i) constitute a very special type, due to their centrality in linguistic communication. Linguistic elements coding that kind of entities are among those called **deictics** (→ Art. 44 and 56). Entities of categories (v) and (vi) are also frequently deictic since human orientation in space and time is egocentric: locations and times are understood in relation to where and when the speaker (and/or the addressee) currently is. Some notes on (v) and (vi) will be made in § 9. below. This article (§§ 2.−8.) is primarily concerned with the entities of categories (ii), (iii), with occasional mentions of category (iv). It should be noted that reference to entities (ii), (iii) can also be deictic. For example, if a police officer says to his subordinate, gesturally pointing at a suspect, *Get him*, such usage of the pronoun should be considered deictic (non-anaphoric; see below). On the difference between deictic and anaphoric use of pronouns see, e. g., Lyons (1977: 673) and Ehlich (1982).

Mentioning entities is traditionally called **referring**, or **reference**. The entity being referred to is called **referent**. Sometimes referents are said to be entities in real world, but that approach creates many unnecessary problems with imaginary entities, like unicorns. So it is less problematic to understand referents as entities in the language users' minds. Referents are mentioned by means of various kinds of **referential expressions**. Grammatically, referential expressions are **nominal elements** − most typically, **noun phrases** (NPs), such as:

(2) (a) proper names
 (b) common nouns (with or without modifiers), or descriptions
 (c) pronouns
 (d) zero forms

A cover term for proper names and common nouns (with or without modifiers) is **full noun**

phrase (full NP). Besides the types of specific referents, listed above, there are various other kinds of entities that can be spoken of in human discourse, e. g. generics; the corresponding NPs are generally called **non-referential** (cf. Art. 39). These will not be a matter of discussion in the present article.

A fundamental and universal property of human discourse is that one and the same referent recurs as the discourse unfolds. Say, if we have a tale about Hansel and Gretel, there will be multiple mentions of these referents in the tale. Dozens of other referents will be mentioned more than once, too. (Usually there are some specific referents that do not recur.)

Evidently, when the speaker needs to mention referent X in a **non-introductory** way, s/he should be able to let the addressee know that referent X is identical to the one that is already known to the addressee. Consider the following simple constructed example.

(3)   *John$_i$ was sitting at the table. He$_i$ was daydreaming about the weekend.*

How does the speaker ensure that the pronoun *he* in the second sentence is understood as referring to the referent 'John'? However straightforward this process may seem at first blush, it is in fact far from trivial and involves many complex aspects. There are many different ways to talk about this phenomenon, relying on different metaphors; they are discussed in § 2.

2. Terminology

Under the view of text as a static object, linguists frequently say that the pronoun *he* in (3) is **coreferential** with *John* of the first sentence. Sometimes one talks about **coindexation**; note that the two NPs in (3) have the same subscript index "i".

Frequently it is said that *he* in (3) is an **anaphoric pronoun**, or an **anaphor** (in a non-generative-grammar usage of the term). The notion of **anaphora** (< Greek 'carrying back') suggests that the pronoun *he* refers back to the point in the preceding stretch of discourse where the clue to its reference is found. That clue is an NP with a presumably clearer and more straightforward reference. Such an NP is called the **antecedent** of the anaphoric pronoun. The notion of anaphora implicitly presupposes that the addressee makes a search procedure in the overt form of the preceding discourse, in order to find the antecedent and the referent. Such a hypothesis has not been proved and some psycholinguists have attempted to disprove it. The term "anaphora" is ambiguous insofar as it may be confined to pronouns and zero expressions only, or it may be applied to all forms of referent mention (in the latter case one would distinguish pronominal anaphora, zero anaphora, and full NP anaphora). For a useful overview of approaches to anaphora see Huang 2000.

According to a more dynamic view of discourse, the addressee does not simply search for an antecedent in the overt text structure when s/he faces an anaphoric pronoun, but rather keeps track of the referents mentioned in the discourse, and thus identifies the referents of incoming NPs. In this framework, linguists often speak about **referent-tracking** (see e. g. Foley & Van Valin 1984: Ch. 7).

Finally, there can be a dynamic view adopting not the addressee's but the speaker's perspective. Here what is central is not the addressee's tracking procedures but the speaker's strategies ensuring that referent identity is properly expressed. Under this approach, one sometimes talks about **maintenance of reference,** or **reference maintenance** (Marslen-Wilson & Levy & Tyler 1982). In this article we will stick to the speaker-oriented approach, since it is the speaker who is responsible for the shape of discourse. Often we will be using a less metaphorical terminology and talk about **referential choice** (following e. g. Clancy 1980) in discourse. When the speaker needs to mention a referent, s/he can choose among the repertoire of language-specific devices. For example, in English this repertoire comprises, in the first place, full NPs and independent pronouns. A number of other terms for the process of referent mentioning have been used in the literature such as **management of reference** (Tomlin & Pu 1991).

It should be stressed that referential choice is among the most fundamental skills of language users. About every third word in discourse (sometimes even more than that) is dependent on the process of referential choice. Clearly, linguistic communication would never be possible without this faculty. An account of referential devices is an essential part of a full description of any language, as necessary as the inventory of tenses or the rules of relative clause formation. Authors of descriptive grammars have recently started to acknowledge this fact, and sections on referential devices, as well as other discourse phenomena, are becoming rightful constituents of language descriptions; for a recent example see A. E. Kibrik (ed.) 1998. For a fieldwork-oriented methodology designed for describing referential devices of a language, see Levinsohn 1994.

3. Two types of linguistic devices employed in reference maintenance

When referring, speakers concurrently use two fundamental types of linguistic devices which are frequently confused but need to be distinguished. The first kind of devices, here called **primary referential devices**, are nominal elements themselves; they are the units that perform reference per se. Primary referential devices will be discussed in § 4. it will be argued that the choice between various referential devices is governed by the degree of the referent's activation in the working memory. Consider the following example where there are two referents mentioned by pronouns in the same clause.

(4) $John_i$ was sitting at the table. Suddenly a $girl_j$ approached him_i...
  (a) He_i yelled at her_j.
  (b) She_j yelled at him_i.

In both (4a) and (4b) there is a pair of referents playing the roles of participants in a two-place situation; in each case it is quite clear which referent plays which role. Therefore, in this particular context the conditions for using both pronouns are satisfied. Now consider another example, minimally different from (4).

(5) $John_i$ was sitting at the table. Suddenly a boy_j approached him_i...
  (a) $^?He_i$ yelled at him_j.
  (b) $^?He_j$ yelled at him_i.

Here (5a−b) appears unintelligible. Apparently the only difference from (4) is that both referents are of the same gender and the pronouns that can be used to refer to them are identical. Thus, the category of gender is an intrinsic component of referential choice in English. For example, the gender difference makes it possible to use pronouns in (4), while a better way to express the contents of (5a) would be the use of a full NP:

(5'a) $John_i$ yelled at him_j

Various linguistic devices which, like English gender, help to discriminate between two or more concurrently activated referents, are here called **subsidiary referential devices**. They do not perform reference themselves but are essential for the process of referential choice. Subsidiary devices will be considered in § 5.

4. Primary referential devices: theory and typology

4.1. Formal types of referential expressions

There are two fundamental types of primary referential devices: NPs that are lexically full (proper names and common nouns), and NPs that are **reduced** to a certain extent, to use the terminology of Bergelson & Kibrik (1980), or **attenuated**, to use the term of Chafe (1994). Anaphoric pronouns discussed above are an example of reduction, both semantic and phonological. The maximal degree of reduction is the zero expression of a participant, as in the second clause in the coordinate structure (6):

(6) $John_i$ was sitting at the table and $Ø_i$ daydreaming about the weekend.

A variety of alternative terms have been applied to the opposition of full and reduced referential expressions, e. g. strong vs. weak (Payne 1993). Givón (1983: 18), in a highly influential article, proposed a scale of "phonological size" comprising the following positions:

(7) (a) Ø
  (b) unstressed pronoun
  (c) stressed pronoun
  (d) full NPs

Full NPs are a very heterogeneous class, and the ways they are used present many challenges to the study of referential choice in discourse. But the fact is that full NPs are used both for introductory and non-introductory reference. In what follows we concentrate on the reduced referential expressions − those that are specialized in the lexicon and in morphosyntax for anaphoric reference, or reference under high activation.

Abstracting from the issue of accentuation, one should distinguish three formal types of reduced referential expressions found in languages of the world:

(8) (i) independent pronouns, such as English *he*
  (ii) bound pronouns − affixes or clitics − attached to the head constituent (typically the verb)
  (iii) zero forms

Type (i) is familiar and does not require much commentary. The standard grammatical theory has been based on languages employing this type of reduced referential expressions as the default option.

4.2. Bound pronouns

Type (ii) — bound pronouns — has been widely recognized as a type of genuinely referring units only recently (Kumaxov 1974, Van Valin 1977, 1985, Jelinek 1984, Mithun 1986), although Boas (1911) and even DuPonceau (1819) already wrote about pronouns incorporated into the verb (→ Art. 56). Consider the following example:

(9) Abkhaz (North-West Caucasian, or Abkhaz-Adyghean)
 i-l=z-i=c-sə-rgəlojt'
 3NH.NOM-3F.OBL=for-3M.OBL=with-1SG.ERG-build
 'I am building it (e. g., the house) for her together with him'

This example demonstrates four participants of a situation whose referential as well as case/role properties are indicated inside the inflected verb form. Such bound elements are indeed referential pronouns rather than agreement markers since full NPs are not obligatory elements of the clause in languages like Abkhaz (see Kumaxov 1974, Van Valin 1985). Consider an excerpt from an Abkhaz folk tale "The father's will" about an old man who had four sons (with a semi-literal translation, in a phonemic transcription):

(10)(a) *i-kuraxy   d-nejxyan,*
  his$_i$-old.age he$_i$ [=old man]-was,
 (b) *apsra d-analaga,*
  die he$_i$-when.started
 (c) *i-čk$_o$'ənc°a d-rə-pxyan,*
  his$_i$-sons$_j$ he$_i$-them$_j$-called,
 (d) *j-aajn,*
  they$_j$-came,
 (e) *adc'a   r-i-tejt'*
  the task them$_j$-he$_i$-gave
 'He was in his old age, and when he started dying, he called his sons, and they came, and he gave them a task'

In (10), there are multiple cases in which an argument of a clause is represented solely by a pronominal element affixed to the verb. If a full NP is there, as e. g. 'his sons' in (10c), it is in a loose "adjunct" (or "apposition") relation with the pronominal morpheme of the verb, in fact, in a sort of anaphoric relation. After Jelinek (1984) languages of this type have been often termed **pronominal argument languages**, as opposed to nominal argument languages like English (→ Art. 103). In pronominal argument languages, it is bound pronominal morphemes of the verb, rather than optional independent NPs, that function as arguments of the predication. The theoretical issue of whether and when bound pronouns can indeed be claimed to be full-fledged verb arguments, and how clearly they can be distinguished from plain agreement, cannot be considered as resolved; many arguments in favor of treating a particular language as a pronominal argument language are language-specific.

Chafe (1994: Ch. 12), looking at the pronominal argument language Seneca (Iroquoian), emphasized that in languages of this type the use of pronouns does not depend on activation of the referent: it suffices for a referent to be a core argument of the clause in order to be coded by a pronoun. In this respect bound pronouns are very different from independent pronouns alternating with full NPs. Even though bound pronouns are an analog of unstressed independent pronouns in languages like English, the very technique of morphological coding inside the inflected verb form has important morphosyntactic consequences. For example, since each participant is obligatorily represented in the clause by means of a bound pronoun, such languages typically do not use the headed strategy of relativization; rather they treat the whole relative clause as an adjunct to the bound pronoun on the main verb (see Kibrik 1992b). The employment of bound pronouns (or head-marking at the clause level, see next paragraph) is among the most basic properties of a language and imposes severe restrictions on its other characteristics.

Nichols (1986, 1992), interested in different aspects of essentially the same phenomenon, proposed the typological parameter "head marking vs. dependent marking" of predicate-argument relations (→ Art. 102). Nichols' consistently head marking languages, in fact, coincide with languages with bound pronouns. She found that some geographical areas are particularly disposed to head-marking, and these are, first and foremost, the Americas (see Mithun 1999). For example, consistently head-marking language families in North America include a majority of the biggest families, such as Eskimo-Aleut, Athabaskan, Algonquian, Iroquoian, Siouan, Salishan, Mayan, and others. Other areas abundantly representing the head-marking pattern include New Guinea, as well as some parts of western Oceania, of Australia (non-Pama-Nyungan languages of Arnhem Land), of Eastern Asia (especially Ainu), and of Africa (particularly the Bantu languages). Abkhaz, inmidst mostly dependent-marking language families of Europe and Western Asia (marking roles by means of nominal cases), is an utter geographical exception.

Studies exploring reference maintenance in languages with bound pronouns include Thompson (1989), Payne (1993), Heath (1983), Chafe (1994: Ch. 12), Chafe (ed.) (1990).

In languages with bound pronouns there still exist independent pronouns, but they are used in marked circumstances. The most typical ones are the NP coordination context (like *she and John*), as well as intensification and contrastiveness (like *he himself, he rather than someone else*); see Schwartz (1986); Payne (1993: Ch. 7).

4.3. Zero referential forms

The third formal type of reduced referential expressions, mentioned in (8) above, is so-called zero anaphora. Referential zero is of course not a real linguistic unit but the absence of a formal unit at the spot where some referent is clearly being mentioned. Consider example (11):

(11)   spoken Japanese (Clancy & Downing 1987: 18)
   (a) ... *de   yukichan$_i$ ga*⟨...⟩ *onigiri*
       ... and Yukichan SUBJ   onigiri
       o   tsukutteimasu
       DO   is.making
   (b) ... *de   kondo   Ø$_i$ kore o*
       and this time   this DO
       nanka-... iremono   ni
       sort-of   CONTAINER LOC
       tsumemashite ⟨...⟩
       is.packing
   (c) *Ø$_i$ dekakete*
       going.out
   (d) *Ø$_i$ iku wake desu.* ⟨...⟩
       go NOM COP
   (e) ... *de Ø$_i$ onigiri o* ⟨...⟩ *toridashite,*
       and   onigiri DO   taking.out
   (f) *Ø$_i$ hoobarinagara*
       while.cramming.into.mouth
   (g) *Ø$_i$ kooen ni ikimasu.*
       park to goes
   'And Yukichan is making onigiri ⟨...⟩ and then she packs them ⟨...⟩, walks out and goes ⟨...⟩. She takes an onigiri and, cramming it into her mouth, goes to the park'

Dominance of zero anaphora in a language has less obvious implications for other properties of the relevant language, compared to bound pronouns. The best known examples of zero anaphora languages are Japanese (Hinds ed. 1978) and Chinese (Tao 1996) — languages that have been in extensive contact but are genetically unrelated and typologically radically different. However, zero anaphora is particularly typical of East and South-East Asia, and West Africa, and these are two areas where the isolating morphological type is highly common; there may be a connection between zero anaphora and isolation. Gundel (1980) attempted to connect zero anaphora with "topic-prominence" (Li & Thompson 1976; → Art. 104), another typical feature of East and South-East Asia; see also § 5.2. In the languages of East and South-East Asia usage of zero anaphora is virtually unconstrained in respect to syntactic position; some other languages use zero anaphora only in certain positions (cf. § 8.). For example, some Romance and Slavic languages consistently use zero anaphora in the subject position, while employing pronominal clitics or independent pronouns in other positions. Some kind of zero anaphora is found in almost any language.

Since zero units are by definition invisible, one may wonder in some cases where to posit them — for example, there can be a choice between an "independent" and a "bound zero". Such decisions are usually made on systemic grounds. For instance, in Abkhaz some pronominal morphemes are zero, and by analogy with non-zero morphemes they are usually considered zero affixes.

4.4. Explanation of referential choice

What does referential choice depend on? A simple experimentation with actual discourse examples demonstrates that the choice between various referential options is far from arbitrary or "stylistic", and it is by no means the case that an anaphoric pronoun can always be replaced by a full NP and vice versa. There is considerable agreement in modern functional and typological linguistics that referential choice is cognitively determined and is ultimately related to the state of the speaker's and/or addressee's knowledge and mind in general. Givón (1983) proposed the notion of **topic continuity,** or **accessibility**. He postulated an important iconicity principle: the more continuous/accessible a topic (i.e., referent) is, the less linguistic material is used to code it (that is, pronouns and zero expressions); and vice versa, discontinuous/inaccessible referents require heavier coding (full NPs) (1983: 17–18). A similar approach was proposed by Ariel (1988, 1990) who distinguished markers of high accessibility (zero expressions and pronouns), mid-accessibility (demonstratives) and low accessibility (nouns) (1988: 77–81). In other works referential choice was more directly related to cognitive concepts. Chafe (1987, 1994) proposed that attenuated referential forms (such as unstressed pronouns) are used when the referent is **given**, or already **active** in the addressee's **consciousness**. Kibrik (1987a) tried to relate anaphoric reference to the speaker's **attention focus**. Givón (1995: 380–384) reinterpreted his earlier findings in terms of **attentional activation** and **search and retrieval operations**. Gundel & Hedberg & Zacharski (1993) suggested a **givenness hierarchy**, ranging between being in focus (anaphoric pronouns), through being activated and familiar (demonstratives), to being "type identifiable" (indefinite NPs). Tomlin & Pu (1991) and Kibrik (1996) explored the cognitive basis of referential choice and concluded that it is what is known in the cognitive psychological literature as **working memory** (Baddeley 1986); reduced referential forms are used if the referent is **activated** in working memory. The role of memory in reference is also emphasized by Cornish (1999).

Most of the cited work is typological in its nature, or typologically oriented. For example, Gundel & Hedberg & Zacharski (1993) compare givenness hierarchies in five languages. One interesting result of the authors' text counts (p. 291–292) is that in each language there are two polar, and by far the most common referential types: on the one hand, plain definite NPs (in all languages), on the other – third person pronouns (English, Russian), zero expression (Japanese), or a combination of third person pronoun and zero (Spanish, Chinese). Other referential types are incomparably less common.

Van Hoek (1997) and Langacker (1996) propose an approach to anaphora that is also termed "cognitive" but is different methodologically from the cognitive approaches discussed above (still it is probably compatible with them). There are some alternatives to cognitive explanations of referential choice in discourse. For example, Levinson (1987) and Huang (1994) treat anaphora in terms of Gricean pragmatics. Fox (1987a), Geluykens (1994), Tao (1996) studied anaphora in terms of the sociological approach known as Conversation Analysis.

4.5. Activation factors

What makes referents active, or focused, or accessible? A variety of discourse-based and other factors contributing to activation have been proposed in the literature. Among the most influential proposals was Givón's (1983: 13) measurement of **referential linear distance** back to the nearest antecedent, expressed in the number of clauses (see also Clancy 1980). If the referent has been mentioned one or two clauses back, it is likely to be highly accessible or activated and, as a consequence, to be referred to by a reduced expression. If linear distance is greater, the referent's activation is low. Consider an extract from Fazil' Iskander's story "Stalin and Vuchetich":

(12) Russian
 (a) *I vdrug lico* **Stalina**
  And suddenly, [the] face of.Stalin
  mgnovenno iskazilos' gnevom
  instantly got distorted with.anger
  i nenavist'ju.
  and hatred.
 (b) **On** *stal strašen.*
  He grew horrifying.
 (c) *Vučetič pomertvel,*
  Vuchetich turned.numb,
 (d)   *ne v silax osoznat',*
  [being] unable to.realize
 (e) *čem razgneval* **Stalina.**
  with.what [he] angered Stalin.

The referent 'Stalin' in clause (b) has linear distance of 1 since this referent has also been mentioned in the previous clause. The referent 'Stalin' in clause (e) has linear distance of 3. One can observe the corresponding difference in coding: pronoun *on* in (b) and full NP *Stalina* in (e). If such dependency is systematic, one can conclude that the factor of linear distance may indeed be involved in the process of referential choice.

Other authors proposed different measurements of distance. Ariel (1988) measured linear distance in terms of sentences, rather than clauses. Fox (1987a) indicated that in many cases it is not linear but rather **hierarchical** discourse structure that is relevant for identifying the antecedent. Not infrequently linear and hierarchical distance may be different. For example, when there is quoted conversation in a narrative, making referential choice after the quotation depends on the antecedent that appeared before the quotation; in such cases linear distance may be very large but hierarchical distance very small. Fox employed a theory of hierarchical discourse structure, Rhetorical Structure Theory (for the most recent version see Mann & Matthiessen & Thompson 1992). Still another important distance factor is **episodic**, or **paragraph, boundary** − see Marslen-Wilson & Levy & Tyler 1982, Fox 1987b, Tomlin 1987. These authors emphasized the paragraph boundary as the major factor influencing referential choice and suggested that reduced reference essentially occurs within one paragraph, and when the antecedent is across the paragraph boundary, a full NP is likely to be used. Distance factors are the most powerful ones; the notion of distance is even used as the basis for metaphorical terminology: Payne (1993) distinguishes between short-range and long-range coding devices (essentially, reduced and full referential expressions).

Besides distance to the antecedent, properties of the antecedent itself constitute another group of activation factors. It has long been known that **grammatical subjects** are better antecedents of pronouns and anaphoric zeroes than non-subjects. Consider the following constructed two-sentence example:

(13) Russian
  (a) ***Maša*** *razgovarivala s Tanej.*
     Masha was.talking with Tanya.
  (b) ***Ona*** *byla odeta v krasnoe*
     She was dressed in [a] red
     plat'e.
     dress.

Although there are two referents mentioned in clause (a), the pronoun *ona* in (b) refers clearly to the referent 'Masha' which was coded as grammatical subject in (a). As is well known, the notion of grammatical subject is not applicable to all languages (→ Art. 101). More elementary pragmatic and semantic notions, such as clause topic and Actor, may be relevant in addition to or instead of subject, in certain contexts and in certain languages. Even in Russian − a language with a clearly defined grammatical subject − dative Actors of experiential verbs (such as 'be cold', 'like') can be almost as good antecedents of pronouns as prototypical subjects in the nominative case. Tomlin (1995) experimentally demonstrated that in a number of languages, including English, Mandarin Chinese, Burmese (Tibeto-Burman), and Indonesian (Austronesian) the cognitive status of **focal attention** underlies the choice of subject. Thus, there is a tendency that what is focally attended in clause n becomes activated in working memory in clause $n+1$. In more traditional terms, theme/topic of clause n becomes given/old information in clause $n+1$.

In addition to factors related to the antecedent, there are activation factors of inherent properties of the referent. Some referents get activated more easily, and, as a result, are better suited for reduced mention. **Animate**, and especially human, referents, are much more frequently referred to with reduced forms; for example, in a sample of Russian discourse 78% of anaphoric third person pronouns had a human referent (Kibrik 1996: 266). A less permanent but also quite stable property of a referent is **protagonisthood**, or centrality (see Grimes 1978; Taylor 1994). Referents that are particularly important for the present discourse get activated more easily. On criteria and measurements of centrality see Givón (1990: 907−909).

A number of other factors potentially affecting activation and, as a result, referential choice, have been proposed in the literature; see, e. g., Payne (1993: Ch. 4, 5). However, the factors discussed above probably constitute the core of the cross-linguistically most important activation factors. In different languages, of course, the weight of different factors is different. Givón (ed. 1983) is a collection of papers applying one and the same methodology to a number of typologically and genetically diverse languages, including Spanish, Japanese, Hebrew, Ute (Uto-Aztecan), Chamorro (Austronesian), and others; other cross-linguistic data can be found in Hinds (1978), Chafe (1990), Fox (1996), Fretheim & Gundel (1996). How do different factors interact with each other? Kibrik (1996, 1999) attempted to design a numerical system modelling the interplay of all relevant factors and predicting, rather than post-hoc commenting, referential choices in a sample of discourse.

5. A typology of subsidiary referential devices

5.1. The notion of referential conflict

As was demonstrated in § 3., subsidiary referential devices serve to distinguish between more than one simultaneously activated referents. Such situations are far from infrequent in natural discourse. Provided that reduced referential devices are semantically incomplete, they have a very broad domain of reference. Therefore, a pronoun or zero can be attributed by the addressee to a referent different from the one meant by the speaker (but being equally activated). This existence of more than one possible candidate for the referent of a referential expression is called here **referential conflict** (otherwise it has been called ambiguity). The speaker should anticipate and preclude referential conflicts. The radical way to preclude a referential conflict (henceforth: RC) is to use a full NP. Natural languages, however, possess a broad repertoire of devices allowing one to stick to a reduced referential expression and still guarantee that the referent is recovered correctly. These devices are exactly what is called here subsidiary referential devices.

Heath (1975) was probably the first to observe that very different lexico-grammatical devices can be employed for the same purpose of telling apart two or more confusable referents. He further illustrated this point with data from Nunggubuyu (Northern Territory, Australia; Heath 1983) — a language that uses a fairly complex noun class system for the same purpose of "referential tracking" for which other languages use the morphosyntactic device of switch-reference (see § 5.4. below). Foley & Van Valin 1984: Ch. 7 and Van Valin 1987 proposed a comprehensive typology of subsidiary referential devices; that typology was inductive and therefore non-exhaustive but it is much used in the following discussion. Comrie (1989) and Kibrik (1991) further developed the typology or lexico-grammatical devices contributing to RC resolution, or **removal**.

It is essential to recognize RC as an important component of the system of referential choice, and, at the same time, as a component separate from activation factors. Both of these points have been questioned in the literature. For example, Chafe (1990) suggested that ambiguity does not exist in real languages, but only in the imagination of "exocultural" linguists. But consider examples (4) and (5) above. The difference in acceptability of (4a, b) and (5a, b) is due precisely to the fact that in the first case RC is removed by gender, and in the second case it is not. Therefore, gender does participate in the reference maintenance process and can be given the status of a referential device. Another group of authors (Givón 1983: 14, Ariel 1988: 28, Payne 1993: 89, Gernsbacher 1990) suggested (in their respective terminologies) that RC is among the activation factors and that a mention of an intervening referent inhibits the previously activated referent. Consider, however, examples (4) and (5) once again. Suppose that the use of the pronoun he_i in (5a) is unfavorable due to the fact that the intervening referent 'the boy' has inhibited the activation of the referent 'John'. Then in (4a) the intervening referent 'the girl' must have equally inhibited 'John' which apparently did not happen. Therefore, RC is a component of the system of referential choice which is separate from the operation of activation factors like those discussed in § 4.5. RC can rule out reduced referential expressions that are perfectly acceptable from the viewpoint of activation; but RC does not inhibit activation.

5.2. Conventional vs. ad hoc subsidiary referential devices

In the English examples (4) and (5) above, a RC was created by the concurrent activation of two referents. In (4), however, RC was further removed by the grammatical category of gender typical of English third person pronouns. In (5), RC was not removed, since both referents were masculine, and the pronominal references turned out to be unacceptable. Compare that example with the following where both referents are again masculine:

(14) $John_i$ *was sitting at the table. Suddenly a baby* boy_j *crawled up to* him_i.
   (a) *He_i lifted him_j.*
   (b) *$^{??}He_j$ lifted him_i.*

In (14) RC is again removed, but due to a totally different mechanism: semantic **compatibility** with the context of the clause. In (14a−b) the verb *lifted* has certain selective restrictions on it arguments. A speaker of English knows that this action can be done by a heavier agent to a smaller and lighter patient. Therefore, the reference as in (b) is ruled out. Subsidiary referential devices fall into two main types: **conventional**, or lexico-grammatical, devices, like gender, and **ad hoc** devices, based on semantic compatibility with the clause context. Foley & Van Valin (1984: Ch. 7), Van Valin (1987) termed the latter type "inference system" and "pragmatic system" thus emphasizing that not only semantics but a wider array of encyclopedic information is important for this type of RC removal. However, all these kinds of information are ultimately conveyed by the semantics of the clause in which the reduced referential device occurs. Van Valin (1987) observed that the ad hoc RC removal system is used in any language but is particularly important in the languages of East and Southeast Asia, including Japanese, Chinese, Thai. Van Valin also suggested that this phenomenon typically cooccurs with zero anaphora. Consider the following example:

(15) Mandarin Chinese (Li & Thompson 1979: 318, cited from Van Valin 1987: 520−521)
   (a) *Wáng-Miǎn$_i$ dé-le qián,*
       get-PERF money
       Ø$_i$ mǎi-le hǎo dōngxi,
       buy-PERF good things
       Ø$_i$ xiàojing Ø$_i$ mǔqin.
       filial   mother
   (b) *Yí chuán Ø liǎng, liǎng*
       one pass.on.to two two
       chuán Ø sān.
       pass.on.to three
   (c) *Zhū-Chàn yí xiàn dōu*
       whole county all
       xiǎode Ø$_i$ shì yíge huà
       know   is a paint
       méi-gú-huā-huì de míngbǐ
       flower-and-plant REL famous.painter
   (d) *Ø Zhēng-zhe lái-mǎi Ø.*
       fight-PROG come-buy
   (e) *Ø$_i$ dào-le shíqī-bā suì...*
       reach-PERF seventeen-eighteen year
   '(a) Wang-Mian got some money, [he] bought some good things to be filial to [his] mother. (b) One person told [that] to two, two people told [that] to three. (c) The whole county of Zhu-Chan knew that [he] was a famous painter of flowers and plants. (d) [People from the county] were fighting to buy [his paintings]. (e) As [he] reached seventeen−eighteen ...'

In example (15) there are multiple zero references; those referring to the protagonist are marked with the "i" subscript index; in sentences (b) and (d) three other referents are coded with zeroes. But still in (c) and even in (e) the protagonist referent is activated enough to be mentioned with zero, despite the existence of several competing referents. In languages like Mandarin the ad hoc system of RC removal operates on a larger scale than that in European languages; Mandarin probably has no conventional RC removing devices.

Conventional RC removing devices are all based on one general principle: they somehow **classify** referents that are currently activated. In the case of gender, such classification as based on **stable**, or permanent, properties of the referent and/or the corresponding NP. Other classifications are based on the **current**, or variable, properties of the referent (like e.g. being the subject of the preceding clause). These two types of referent classification, serving as RC removing devices, are considered below one at a time (for a fuller account see Kibrik 1991).

5.3. Stable classifications

Stable classifications fall into two main kinds: absolute and relative (i.e. hierarchies). **Absolute** classifications represented on pronouns are widely known as **noun classes**, or genders; for an overview see Corbett (1991). Noun classes are typical of Europe, the northern Caucasus, the Near East, most of Africa, New Guinea, some parts of Australia and the New World. The operation of the noun class distinctions marked on independent pronouns has been illustrated with English genders in examples (4), (5) above. One of the world's most extensive noun class systems is found in Pulaar-Fulfulde (= Fula) − this language has over 20 noun classes (Koval' 1997); the employment of Pulaar-Fulfulde noun classes for reference maintenance in discourse has been considered in Kibrik (1991, 1992a). Noun classes can be marked on bound pronouns in head-marking languages. The Abkhaz example (10) provides an illustration (in Abkhaz, number is a part of the noun class category; in the singular, masculine, feminine, and nonhuman are distinguished); see Heath (1983) on a similar system in Nunggubuyu. Some languages have a kind of noun/referent classification system built into the **verbal lexical semantics**. The best known example is Athabaskan languages of North America which have whole series of verb stems with the same meaning, with the only difference that they apply to distinct classes of referents (animate, round, flat, plural, etc.). Consider the following example:

(16) Navajo, Athabaskan (Bernice Casaus, p.c.)
   (a) *shidą́ą́dii yiníł'į̇*
       for.some.time 3NOM.looked

(b) *ńt'éé' 'ayęęzhii yęę ła'*
    then egg   that one
    nááhidees'náá'   jiní.
    again.3NOM.moved they.say
(c) *ła' 'éí t'óó t'áákǫ́ǫ́ t'óó*
    one that just right.there just
    doo-naha'náóó,   t'óó
    without-movement just
    si'ą̨́   jiní.
    3NOM.round.object.sits they.say
(d) *'áádóó shį̨́į̨́ t'óó yik'i*
    then   maybe just 3OBL.upon
    nááneezdá.
    again.3NOM.animate.sat

'(a) For some time she [= the female eagle] was watching. (b) Then that egg moved again, they say. (c) The one that was without movement, it was just sitting there. (d) Then she sat upon them again.'

In this extract two classificatory verb stems, both translating in their respective contexts as 'sit', are used: -*'ą́*, referring to arguments of roundish shape, and -*dá*, applicable only to animate referents. These roots alone are capable of removing RC, and such situations are quite common in Navajo. Besides independent and bound pronouns and verb roots, stable absolute classification can be marked on special constituents, known as **classifiers**; on usage of classifiers as referential devices see Downing (1986) and Aikhenvald (2000: 329 ff.). Classifiers are particularly typical of languages of East Asia, South-East Asia and Australia.

Stable **relative** classifications are **hierarchies** of referents according to a certain semantic or pragmatic parameter. One kind of hierarchy is the **activity**/agentivity hierarchy like the one discovered in Navajo by Hale (1973).

(17) Navajo, Athabaskan (Martha Austin, p. c.)
      shimásání   tł'ízí
      my.grandmother   goat
      yi-ł-deezdéel-go
      3ACC.AG>PAT-with-caught-SUBORD
      bi-yaa-haalwod
      3OBL.LOC>AG-under-3NOM.raced.away
      'When my grandmother caught the goat, it raced away from her'

In this example, the first clause has overt NPs indicating the participants. The verb has the *yi*- third person prefix (in the accusative position) that indicates, to put it most simply, that a more inherently active referent (human) acts upon a less active referent (animal). The second clause is again two-place, but has no overt NPs. Here the third person prefix *bi*- is used (in the oblique position). The prefix *bi*- suggests that the agent of the clause is less inherently active than the second participant. Thus the reference of the two pronominal elements in the clause is established: it is the goat that races away from the grandmother, rather than vice versa.

A totally different kind of hierarchy is based on the pragmatic status of relative social position. Such hierarchies are known as **honorific** and are particularly typical of languages of Far East and South-East Asia. For example, in Vietnamese (Lý Toǎn Thang, p. c.) referents that are comparable to or lower than the speaker in social status can be referred to by means of the third person pronoun *nó* whereas the polite way to mention referents like e. g. the speaker's father in an anaphoric context is, literally, 'my father' or 'that old man'. Therefore, if there is a RC between two referents with different social status in respect of the speaker, a usage of the pronoun can rule out one of those referents. For some further information on honorific distinctions in pronouns see Head (1978).

5.4. Current classifications

Stable classifications rely on fairly permanent properties of referents or corresponding NPs. Current classifications, by contrast, rely on context-dependent, fluid properties of referents, such as: being the protagonist or non-protagonist of the present discourse; being more or less activated at the present moment in discourse; being the subject or non-subject of the previous clause, etc. The range of such current properties is so great that it can be only partially illustrated below. Another crucial parameter in the typology of current classifications is, as in the case of stable absolute classifications, the type of constituent it is marked on: independent pronoun vs. bound pronoun vs. verbal categories vs. special auxiliary constituent. Examples of each of these loci of marking will be presented below.

The best known examples of current classifications marked on independent pronouns are so-called **logophoric** pronouns first identified in Africa by Hagège (1974) and Clements (1975). Classical logophoric pronouns appear in complement clauses embedded in matrix verbs of speech and thought. Logophoric pronouns are a special type of third person pronouns employed when a referent spoken of in the complement clause is identical with the subject of speech/thought; in the case of non-coreference plain third person pronouns are used:

(18) Angas, Western Chadic (Burquest 1986: 92)
Músá$_i$ lə̄ tènē ɗyí$_i$/kə́$_j$ mét
'Musa$_i$ said that he$_i$/he$_j$ will.go
kàsúwá
to.the.market'

Frequently the term "logophoric" is used not in the classical sense, but in an extended meaning, e. g. referring to any specialized pronoun appearing in any kind of dependent clause and indicating coreference with an argument of the main clause. Logophoric pronouns are an areal feature of West and Central Africa, see various articles in Wiesemann (ed. 1986). Similar pronouns are found elsewhere, e. g. in Nakh-Daghestanian languages (A. E. Kibrik 1977: 316−317, Testelec & Toldova 1998) and languages of Amazonia (Wiesemann 1986). In some other languages the system is reversed: a marked pronoun indicates **non-**coreference with the subject of the previous clause; this is how the Russian pronoun *tot* is used, opposed to the plain third person pronoun *on* (see Kibrik 1987b). In many languages current classifications are not restricted to tight syntactic contexts but operate on a discourse basis and differentiate more and less activated referents; this is again particularly common in West Africa (Bergelson 1988, Kibrik 1991: 78−81).

Among the current classifications marked on bound pronouns, the most widely known example is the opposition of **proximate** vs. **obviative** of the Algonquian languages of North America. Various terms have been used to define the proximate, such as "discourse topic", "focalized object", "point of view" etc. (see Russell 1996 for a discussion), but in most cases that referent is proximate which is most activated in the speaker's mind at the present moment; to all other referents the obviative status is attributed. Assignment of referents to the proximate vs. obviative status is done by explicit suffixes on the corresponding nouns; thereafter, reference is performed by pronominal suffixes on the verb. Actor proximates and obviatives are represented by overt pronominal suffixes while transitive patients remain unexpressed on the verb:

(19) Plains Cree, Algonquian (Bloomfield 1930; cited from Foley & Van Valin 1984: 337)
(a) kiskēyim-ēw   ayahciyiniw-a.
    know-DIR-3PROX$_i$ Blackfoot$_j$-OBV
(b) ēkwa   o-paskisikan pīhtāsō-w;
    and.then his$_i$-gun   load-3PROX$_i$
(c) mōskīstaw-ē-w
    attack-DIR-3PROX$_i$
(d) ē-pimisini-yit
    CONJ-lie-3OBV$_j$
'(a) He$_i$ knew him$_j$ for a Blackfoot. (b) Then he$_i$ loaded his$_i$ gun (c) and attacked him$_j$ (d) as he$_j$ lay on the ground'

North American languages, typically representing pronominal arguments, frequently employ current systems of referent classifications marked on pronominal affixes; such systems vary greatly in their basis of classification. For example, Central Yup'ik Eskimo (see e. g. Woodbury 1983) has a more grammaticalized system than Algonquian; in Eskimo plain third person and "reflexive third person" (analogue of proximate, but used in dependent clauses only) are distinguished. A system much less grammaticalized than in Algonquian is found in some Athabaskan languages (see e. g. Thompson 1989), where third and so-called fourth persons are distinguished.

Current classifications marked on specifically verbal morphemes has been known since Jacobsen (1967) as **switch-reference**. The canonical switch-reference system is based on a verbal inflectional category consisting of two morphemes: same-subject (SS) and different-subject (DS). The subject of the current clause is compared to the subject of a controlling clause (normally, preceding and/or being the main clause with respect to the current clause) as being either identical or different. Once the subject of the controlling clause is known, the SS marker on the verb of the current clause suffices to identify the referent; no further nominal or pronominal material is needed. Furthermore, even the DS marker can be enough to identify the referent of the clause subject: if there are two activated referents, and one of them is the subject of the controlling clause, then only the other one can be the referent in question. The following excerpt is preceded by a description of actions of the khan's wife:

(20) Tuva (Turkic)
(a) *demgi ool*$_b$ *ilbi-zi-bile   kör-üp*
    that.very boy magic-3-with see-CONV
    olur-arga,
    AUX-DS
(b) Ø$_w$ *xaan-niŋ*$_k$ *baarinda končug*
        khan-GEN   in.front.of very
    eki šinar-lig čem-i-n   sal-gaš,
    good quality-with food-3-ACC put-SS
(c) Ø$_w$ *ool-duŋ*$_b$ *baarinda miriŋaj*
        boy-GEN   in.front.of even
    xoran xolaan čem-i-n   sal-ip
    poison mixed food-3-ACC put-CONV
    boop-tur.
    be.CONV-COP
'(a) As that boy saw with his magic, (b) she put a very good food in front of the khan, (c) [and] put food mixed with real poison in front of the boy.'

The DS marker in clause (a) indicates that the subject of the following clause (on which (a) is dependent) is different from that of (a); therefore, it should be another referent activated at this point, namely 'the khan's wife' who has been spoken of before. The SS marker on the final verb in (b) signals that the subject of (b) and the subject of the main clause (c) are coreferential. Frequently switch-reference is found in languages that have the property of clause-chaining, that is, use long sequences of non-finite clauses where in other languages several finite sentences would be found (→ Art. 100).

Originally thought to be an exotic device of some native American languages, switch-reference turned out to be among the most common subsidiary referential devices; see Haiman & Munro (ed. 1983), Wiesemann (ed. 1986), Stirling (1993). Switch-reference systems are found in languages of all continents, but are especially typical of those languages that have a clearly defined syntactic subject. Some authors have mentioned complications with a strictly syntactic definition of switch-reference. Bergelson & Kibrik (1987), (1995) and Wilkins (1988) pointed to deviations from precise identity between referents. Mithun (1993) suggested that in many cases it may be clause connectedness rather than coreference that is coded by SS markers. Even if the latter is true, the referential function of switch-reference may be a distinct side effect of connectedness marking.

Switch-reference-type categories marked not on verbs but on auxiliary constituents are reported in West Africa (Carlson 1987) and Amazonia (Wiesemann 1986: 377, Popovich 1986).

As was pointed out above, various stable and current classifications of referents are very different in their nature but are cofunctional in a way: they all contribute to resolution of possible referential conflicts. Nevertheless, some languages, like Mandarin Chinese, seem not to employ any of the conventional RC removing devices, while others use an abundance of them. For example, Mundani (Western Grassfields Bantu, Cameroon), has noun class distinctions in pronouns, special logophoric pronouns, and switch-reference marked by verbal prefixes (Parker 1986); this phenomenon calls for an adequate interpretation.

6. Pronominal systems

Pronouns are among the central types of primary referential devices. Furthermore, as has been shown in § 5., they are the most common locus of marking subsidiary referential devices. Thus a typology of pronominal systems is most intimately related to the topic of the present article. However, since this article deals, first and foremost, with the dynamic process of reference maintenance in discourse, the static typology of pronominal systems will be only briefly considered here (→ Art. 56). Useful accounts of the typology of pronominal systems include Majtinskaja (1969), Krupa (1976), Ingram (1978), Sokolovskaja (1980), Jacobsen (1980). An invaluable source of data on the topic is the collection Wiesemann (ed.) 1986, containing detailed accounts of exotic pronominal systems in many individual languages (especially of South America, Africa, and Oceania), and typological articles. For example, Hutchisson (1986) reports a unique system with five numbers in Sursurunga (Patpatar Austronesian, Papua New Guinea): singular, dual, trial, quadral, plural. According to Simons (1986), To'aba'ita (Oceanic Austronesian, Solomon Islands) has a system of over 100 pronominal forms (in particular, aspect is marked on subject pronouns). In Xerente (Jê, Brazil) nominative pronouns are the locus of marking evidentiality, aspect, and intensiveness of action (Popovich 1986: 366).

7. Other aspects of reference maintenance in discourse

Reference in discourse can be approached from different viewpoints. The approach mostly employed above is oriented to the current state of the speech participant's mind: at any given time some referents are more activated in it, and some are less. In the course of time, various referents pass through it, like through a stage. On the other hand, reference can be viewed from the perspective of specific referents. On this approach, several phases can be distinguished in the "discourse life" of each referent: introduction, or gradual activation; maintenance in the activated state; deactivation; reactivation; addition of a referent to the set of activated referents; union of two activated referents into one single whole (like *he met her;* ***they*** *talked for an hour*); fragmentation — the reverse process. Languages tend to use specific devices for each of these phases; introductory activation, for example, frequently takes two mentions before the referent gets maximally activated; reactivation can be performed by one mention. For some case studies see Kibrik (1992a), Noonan (1992: Ch. 10).

Givón (1995) proposes still another approach: from the viewpoint of the addressee of discourse, various referential devices "cue" certain mental operations ensuring discourse coherence, e. g.:

(21) (after Givón 1995: 383)
 (a) if ZERO/ ⇒ continue current acti-
     PRONOUN   vation
 (b) if FULL NP ⇒ (i) defer activation
                     decision
                 (ii) determine refer-
                     ent's importance
 (c) if UNIM- ⇒ (i) do not activate
     PORTANT
                 (ii) continue current
                     activation
 (d) if IMPOR- ⇒ deactivate the cur-
     TANT   rent active node
                  etc.

Such generalizations are assumed to be universally applicable since they rely on the most general, culture-independent concept of how human cognition works.

Dependency between referential processes and discourse **register, genre, and type** have recently started to attract the attention of researchers. The collection Fox (1996) about anaphora contains a number of articles looking at referential processes in specific discourse types in various languages. Examples of explicit comparisons of referential strategies in various discourse registers and types include Fox (1987a), Biber (1991), Toole (1996).

An important issue in discourse reference is what is sometimes called perspective taking (perspectivization) or **subjectivity**. To give a primitive example, the same referent, depending on the speaker's identity and viewpoint, can be called *I, his wife, my wife, my mom, that heavenly creature*, etc. This referential phenomenon is a part of more general phenomenon: it is an inherent property of human discourse that information can be presented from different perspectives, esp. those associated with different individuals. This issue has been recognized for a long time as being of prime importance for literary studies, since fiction frequently is a combination of different "voices" belonging to the author, different characters, etc. Now it is recognized that perspective taking is as crucial for ordinary conversations as for literary texts. There is a huge amount of research on this topic; selected references include Vološinov (1929: Ch. 3), Arutjunova (1992), Chafe (1994), a number of chapters in Duchan & Bruder & Hewitt (ed. 1995), Green (1995), Padučeva (1996: Part II).

In the discussion in § 2.−5. the identity of different mentions of the referent was usually implied. Reality sometimes deviates from this prototype; for example, there may be no actual antecedent in discourse but the referent of the anaphoric expression is inferred. In such cases one talks about **indirect anaphora**; see Epstein (1999) and references therein.

8. Syntactic anaphora

Historically the study of reference started in linguistics from occurrences of anaphoric expressions that are syntactically induced, as in the following examples:

(22) (a) *Joseph and **his** brothers*
 (b) *Joseph insulted **his** brothers*
 (c) *Joseph said that **he** saw a dream*
 (d) *Father loved Joseph and Ø always praised **him***

In examples (22) the occurrences of anaphoric expressions share three properties: (i) they are obligatory, that is, the anaphoric expression cannot be replaced by a full NP without changing reference; e. g. *Joseph insulted Joseph's brothers* most likely would imply two different people called Joseph; (ii) the anaphoric expression and the antecedent appear in one and the same sentence; (iii) such occurrences are explicable in syntactic terms, that is, certain structural relations between the target syntactic position and the antecedent position are sufficient for using an anphoric expression; in (22b), for example, the subject of a clause controls pronominalization of its object's possessor, while in (22d) subject and object positions are controlled by parallel positions in the linearly preceding conjoined clause. All work on reference done within the generative and other formal frameworks, and most of that done in the logical framework (with the partial exception of the so-called Discourse Representation Theory, see Groenendijk & de Jongh & Stokhof (1987), Kamp & Reyle (1993)), deal with syntactic anaphora. (There is vast literature on reference in both the generative and the logical traditions; see surveys in Freidin (1992: Ch. 7) and Padučeva (1985: Part 2), respectively.) Referential phenomena discussed in §§ 2.−5., by contrast, deal mostly with reference in discourse, irrespective of sentence boundaries and syntactic contexts. (For this reason no attention was given here to prototypically clause-internal coreference devices, such as reflexives.) Syntactic anaphora is a subcase of discourse anaphora, and syntactic rules are derivative of discourse strategies. For example, studies of syntactic anaphora usually emphasize the role of antecedent subjecthood. In the generative tradition, a huge literature on so-called c-command grew out from the observation that subjects of main clauses are better antecedents than other syntactic positions. This fact is merely a syntactic reflection of a more general fact that using a referent in the subject position (grammaticalization of attention focus) causes further activation of the referent, and thus its reduced mention subsequently.

Nevertheless, in many cases it is useful to state simple rules for intrasentential anaphora in syntactic terms. For example, English in general is not very much of a zero anaphora language, but in (22d) a zero referential form is used. (In certain theoretical approaches, a distinction between zero anaphora and ellipsis is made, and this particular case could be considered ellipsis, but for the present discussion that distinction is irrelevant.) Most languages use a zero form to express the commonality of an argument (in this case, subject) of two conjoined clauses. In fact, the existence of restrictions on the kinds of deletable arguments are among the main tests for the relevance of the notion of syntactic subject in a language. In English, only subjects can be deleted in coordinate constructions. Objects can be "shared" only if both verbs precede the object full NP: *Father loved and always praised Joseph*. In many other languages, such restrictions are not imposed on zero anaphora in conjoined clauses, e. g.:

(23) Svan, Kartvelian
 bäč$_i$ žixojäx č'q'int'-s$_j$ i Ø$_i$
 rock fell boy-DAT and
 čwadgär Ø$_j$
 killed
 'The rock fell on the boy and killed him'

There is a typological scale of languages, one pole of which includes languages like English with very constrained argument deletion in coordinate constructions, whereas the other pole includes languages with extensive use of zero anaphora and absolutely no restrictions on argument deletion. Svan is in fact in the middle of such scale.

9. Locative and temporal reference and predicate anaphora

As was pointed out in § 1., reference to living beings and objects does not exhaust all kinds of reference to specific entities, even though it is the central and the best studied form of reference. At least two other types need to be recognized: reference to places and reference to times. No extensive discussion of these large topics will be presented here, only some brief orientation will be given.

Reference to places (= spatial/local/locative reference) cannot be discretely and objectively distinguished from reference to objects; cf. a chain of referents that take different positions on the axis of size: *this pen − this table − this room − this building − this town − this country*. Each of these entities can be conceptualized as either an object or a location depending on the speaker's goals, even though smaller entities are inherently more inclined to be objects while larger entities are more likely to be mentioned as locations. Thus locative reference is the closest to the object reference considered above. Locative reference has been explored in: several contributions to Jarvella & Klein (1982), Givón (1995: 364−367), Zubin & Hewitt (1995) (→ Art. 43, 44).

Reference to times (temporal reference) can also be viewed as a subtype of reference to objects, since moments and intervals of time can be conceptualized as objects. Such occurrences of temporal reference interact in a complex way with verbal categories of aspect and tense (→ Art. 42, 59). Some issues of temporal reference in sentence and discourse are considered in Partee (1984), Bulygina & Šmelev (1992), Klein (1994), Givón (1995: 367–372), Almeida (1995), Arutjunova & Janko (eds. 1997).

Questions of reference are frequently subsumed in the literature in a more general domain of discourse **coherence**, or **connectedness** (→ Art. 47). Givón (1990: 896) distinguished four types of coherence: referential, temporal, spatial (= local, locative), and event coherence. The three first phenomena have been considered above. An analog from the area of event coherence would be identification of events by means of semantically reduced verbs, such as *do* or *happen*. For example:

(24) *Not everybody congratulated John. Sam **did**, but Mary **didn't**.*

This phenomenon has been sometimes called **predicate anaphora** or VP anaphora. On predicate anaphora and other peculiar types of reference see Asher 1993 and references therein.

Acknowledgements

Research underlying this article was supported by a R. C. Hunt grant #5577 of the Wenner-Gren Foundation for Anthropological Research, and by grant #98-06-80442 of the Russian Foundation for Basic Research. The author is very grateful to both organizations for their support.

10. Special abbreviations

AG	agent
CONJ	conjunct mode
COP	copula
DIR	direct
DS	different-subject
NH	non-human
OBV	obviative
PROX	proximate
PAT	patient
RC	referential conflict
SS	same-subject
SUBORD	subordinating affix

11. References

Aikhenvald, Aleksandra Y. 2000. *Classifiers. A typology of noun categorization devices*. Oxford: Oxford University Press.

Almeida, Michael J. 1995. "Time in narrative". In: Duchan & Bruder & Hewitt (eds.), 159–190.

Ariel, Mira. 1988. "Referring and accessibility". *Journal of Linguistics* 24: 65–87.

Ariel, Mira. 1990. *Accessing noun phrase antecedents*. London: Routledge.

Arutjunova, Nina D. 1992. "Dialogičeskaja modal'nost' i javlenie citacii" [The dialogic modality and the phenomenon of citation]. In: Bulygina (ed.), 52–78.

Arutjunova, Nina D. & Janko, Tat'jana E. (eds.) 1997. *Jazyk i vremja* [Language and time]. Moscow: Indrik.

Asher, Nicholas. 1993. *Reference to abstract objects*. Dordrecht: Kluwer.

Baddeley, Alan. 1986. *Working memory*. Oxford: Clarendon Press.

Bergelson, Mira B. 1988. "Mestoimennye anaforičeskie sredstva jazyka bamana" [Pronominal anaphoric devices in Bamana]. In: Ajxenval'd, A. Ju (ed.) *Tezisy konferencii aspirantov i molodyx sotrudnikov. Jazykoznanie*. Moscow: IV AN SSSR, 13–16.

Bergelson, Mira B. & Kibrik, Aleksandr E. 1980. "K voprosu ob obščej teorii jazykovoj redukcii" [Toward the general theory of linguistic reduction]. In: Narin'jani, Aleksandr S. (ed.) *Formal'noe opisanie struktury estestvennogo jazyka* [Formal description of the structure of natural language]. Novosibirsk: VC SO AN SSSR, 147–161.

Bergelson, Mira B. & Kibrik, Andrej A. 1987. "Sistema pereključenija referencii v tuvinskom jazyke" [The system of switch-reference in Tuva]. *Sovetskaja tjurkologija* 1987.2: 16–32; 1987.4: 30–45.

Bergelson, Mira B. & Kibrik, Andrej A. 1995. "The system of switch-reference in Tuva: Converbal and masdar-case forms". In: Haspelmath, Martin & König, Ekkehard (eds.). *Converbs in cross-linguistic perspective*. Berlin: Mouton de Gruyter, 373–414.

Biber, Douglas. 1991. *Using computer-based corpora to analyze the referential strategies of spoken and written texts*. Preprint paper for the Nobel Symposium on Corpus linguistics. Stockholm.

Bloomfield, Leonard. 1930. *Sacred stories of Sweet Grass Cree*. Bulletin 60, Anthropological series II. Ottawa: National Museum of Canada.

Boas, Franz. 1911/1964. *Introduction to the Handbook of American Indian Languages*. Washington, D. C.: Bureau of American Ethnology, 1–83.

Bulygina, Tat'jana V. & Šmelev, Aleksej D. 1992. "Temporal'nyj dejksis. Obščie zamečanija" [Temporal deixis. General remarks]. In: Bulygina (ed.), 236–243.

Bulygina, Tat'jana V. (ed.) 1992. *Čelovečeskij faktor v jazyke. Kommunikacija. Modal'nost'. Dejksis.* [The human factor in language. Communication. Modality. Deixis.] Moscow: Nauka.

Burquest, Donald. 1986. "The pronoun system of some Chadic languages". In: Wiesemann (ed.), 71–101.

Carlson, Robert. 1987. "Narrative connectives in Sùpyìré". In: Tomlin, Russell (ed.) *Coherence and grounding in discourse.* Amsterdam: Benjamins, 1–19.

Chafe, Wallace. 1987. "Cognitive constraints on information flow". In: Tomlin, Russell (ed.) *Coherence and grounding in discourse.* Amsterdam: Benjamins, 21–52.

Chafe, Wallace. 1990. Introduction. In: Chafe (ed.), 313–316.

Chafe, Wallace. (ed.) 1990. Special issue on third-person reference in discourse. *International Journal of American Linguistics* 56.3.

Chafe, Wallace. 1994. *Discourse, consciousness, and time. The flow and displacement of conscious experience in speaking and writing.* Chicago: University of Chicago Press.

Clancy, Patricia. 1980. "Referential choice in English and Japanese narrative". In: Chafe, Wallace (ed.) *The pear stories. Cognitive, cultural, and linguistic aspects of narrative production.* Norwood, NJ: Ablex, 127–202.

Clancy, Patricia M. & Downing, Pamela. 1987. "The use of *Wa* as a cohesion marker in Japanese oral narratives". In: Hinds, John & Maynard, Senko K. & Iwasaki, Shoichi (eds.). *Perspectives on topicalization: The case of Japanese 'wa'.* Amsterdam, 3–56.

Clements, George N. 1975. "The logophoric pronoun in Ewe". *Journal of West African Languages* 10: 142–177.

Comrie, Bernard. 1989. "Some general properties of reference-tracking systems". In: Doug Arnold et al. (eds.) *Essays on grammatical theory and universal grammar,* 37–51. Oxford: Clarendon.

Corbett, Greville. 1991. *Gender.* Cambridge: Cambridge University Press.

Cornish, Francis. 1999. *Anaphora, discourse, and understanding.* Oxford: Clarendon Press.

Downing, Pamela. 1986. "The anaphoric use of classifiers in Japanese". In: Craig, Colette G. (ed.) *Noun classes and categorization.* Amsterdam: Benjamins, 345–375.

Duchan, Judith & Bruder, Gail & Hewitt, Lynne. (eds.) 1995. *Deixis in narrative. A cognitive science perspective.* Hillsdale, NJ: Erlbaum.

DuPonceau, Peter S. 1819. "Report of the Historical and Literary Committee to the American Philosophical Society". *Transactions of the Historical and Literary Committee of the American Philosophical Society.* Vol. 1.

Ehlich, Konrad. 1982. "Anaphora and deixis: same, similar, or different?" In: Jarvella & Klein (eds.), 315–338.

Epstein, Richard. 1999. "Roles, frames, and definiteness". In: van Hoek, Karen & Kibrik, Andrej A. & Noordman, Leo (eds.) *Discourse in cognitive linguistics.* Amsterdam: Benjamins, 53–75.

Foley, William A. & Van Valin, Robert D. Jr. 1984. *Functional syntax and universal grammar.* Cambridge: Cambridge University Press.

Fox, Barbara. 1987a. *Discourse structure and anaphora in written and conversational English.* Cambridge: Cambridge University Press.

Fox, Barbara. 1987b. "Anaphora in popular written English narratives". In: Tomlin, Russell (ed.) *Coherence and grounding in discourse.* Amsterdam: Benjamins, 157–174.

Fox, Barbara. (ed.) 1996. *Studies in anaphora.* (Typological Studies in Language, vol. 33.) Amsterdam: Benjamins.

Freidin, Robert. 1992. *Foundations of generative syntax.* Cambridge, MA: MIT Press.

Fretheim, Thorstein & Gundel, Jeanette K. (eds.) 1996. *Reference and referent accessibility.* Amsterdam: Benjamins.

Geluykens, Ronald. 1994. *The pragmatics of discourse anaphora in English: Evidence from conversational repair.*

Gernsbacher, Morton Ann. 1990. *Language comprehension as structure building.* Hillsdale, NJ: Erlbaum.

Givón, T. 1983. "Topic continuity in discourse: An introduction". In: Givón T. (ed.), 1–42.

Givón, T. (ed.) 1983. *Topic continuity in discourse: A quantitative cross-language study.* (Typological Studies in Language, vol. 3) Amsterdam: Benjamins.

Givón, T. 1990. *Syntax: A functional-typological introduction.* Vol. 2. Amsterdam: Benjamins.

Givón, T. 1995. *Functionalism and grammar.* Amsterdam: Benjamins.

Green, Keith (ed.) 1995. *New essays on deixis: Discourse, narrative, literature.* Amsterdam: Rodopi.

Grimes, Joseph (ed.) 1978. *Papers in discourse.* Arlington: SIL.

Groenendijk, Jeroen & de Jongh, Dick & Stokhof, Martin (eds.) 1987. *Studies in Discourse Representation Theory and the Theory of Generalized Quantifiers.* Dordrecht: Foris.

Gundel, Jeanette K. 1980. "Zero NP-anaphora in Russian: A case of topic-prominence". In: Kreiman, Jody & Ojeda, Almerindo (eds.) *Papers from the parasession on pronouns and anaphora, Chicago Linguistic Society.* Chicago: CLS, 139–146.

Gundel, Jeanette K. & Hedberg, Nancy & Zacharski, Ron. 1993. "Cognitive status and the form of referring expressions in discourse". *Language* 69: 274–307.

Hagège, Claude. 1974. "Les pronoms logophoriques". *Bulletin de la Société de linguistique de Paris* 69: 287–310.

Haiman, John & Munro, Pamela (eds.) 1983. *Switch-reference and universal grammar*. Amsterdam: Benjamins.

Hale, Kenneth. 1973. "A note on subject-object inversion in Navajo". In: Kachru, Braj et al. (eds.) *Papers in linguistics in honor of Henry and Renee Kahane*. Urbana: University of Illinois Press, 300–309.

Head, B. F. 1978. "Respect degrees in pronominal reference". In: Greenberg, Joseph H. (ed.) *Universals of human language. Vol. 3: Word structure*. Stanford: Stanford University Press, 151–212.

Heath, Jeffrey. 1975. "Some functional relationships in grammar". *Language* 51: 89–104.

Heath, Jeffrey. 1983. "Referential tracking in Nunggubuyu". In: Haiman & Munro (eds.), 129–150.

Hinds, John (ed.) 1978. *Anaphora in discourse*. Edmonton: Linguistic Research Inc.

Huang, Yan. 1994. *The syntax and semantics of anaphora*. Cambridge: Cambridge University Press.

Huang, Yan. 2000. *Anaphora. A cross-linguistic approach*. Oxford: Oxford University Press.

Hutchisson, Don. 1986. "Sursurunga pronouns and the special use of quadral numbers". In: Wiesemann (ed.), 1–20.

Ingram, David. 1978. "Typology and universals of personal pronouns". In: Greenberg, Joseph H. (ed.) *Universals of human language. Vol. 3: Word structure*. Stanford: Stanford University Press, 213–247.

Jacobsen, William. 1967. "Switch-reference in Hokan-Coahuiltecan". In: Hymes, Dell & Bittle, W. (eds.). *Studies in Southwestern ethnolinguistics: Meaning and history in the languages of the American Southwest*. The Hague: Mouton, 238–263.

Jacobsen, William. 1980. "Inclusive/exclusive: A diffused pronominal category in native western North America". In: Kreiman, Jody & Ojeda, Almerindo (eds.) *Papers from the parasession on pronouns and anaphora, Chicago Linguistic Society*. Chicago: CLS, 204–227.

Jarvella, Robert J. & Klein, Wolfgang. (eds.) 1982. *Speech, place, and action. Studies in deixis and related topics*. Chichester: Wiley.

Jelinek, Eloise, 1984. "Empty categories, case, and cofigurationality." *Natural Language and Linguistic Theory* 2: 39–76.

Kamp, Hans & Reyle, U. 1993. *From discourse to logic*. Dordrecht: Reidel.

Kibrik, Aleksandr E. 1977. *Opyt strukturnogo opisanija arčinskogo jazyka. Vol. 2: Taksonomičeskaja grammatika*. [An experimental structural description of Archi. Vol. 2: The taxonomic grammar.] Moscow: Izdatel'stvo Moskovskogo Universiteta.

Kibrik, Aleksandr E. (ed.) 1998. *Èlementy caxurskogo jazyka v tipologičeskom osveščenii* [Elements of Tsakhur: A typological perspective]. Moscow: Nasledie.

Kibrik, Andrej A. 1987a. "Fokusirovanie vnimanija i mestoimenno-anaforičeskaja nominacija" [Focusing of attention and pronominal anaphora]. *Voprosy jazykoznanija* 1987.3: 79–90.

Kibrik, Andrej A. 1987b. "Mexanizmy ustranenija referencial'nogo konflikta" [Mechanisms of referential conflict removal]. In: Kibrik, Aleksandr E. & Narin'jani, Aleksandr S. (eds.). *Modelirovanie jazykovoj dejatel'nosti v intellektual'nyx sistemax* [Modelling linguistic activity in intellectual systems]. Moscow: Nauka, 128–145.

Kibrik, Andrej A. 1991. "Maintenance of reference in sentence and discourse". In: Lehmann, Winfred P. & Hewitt, Helen-Jo J. (eds.) *Language typology*. Amsterdam: Benjamins, 57–84.

Kibrik, Andrej A. 1992a. "Dynamics of attention focus in narrative discourse: The Pulaar case". *Languages of the World* 4: 4–11.

Kibrik, Andrej A. 1992b. "Relativization in polysynthetic languages". *International Journal of American Linguistics* 58: 135–156.

Kibrik, Andrej A. 1996. "Anaphora in Russian narrative prose: A cognitive account". In: Fox, Barbara A. (ed.), 255–304.

Kibrik, Andrej A. 1999. "Reference and working memory: Cognitive inferences from discourse observations". In: van Hoek, Karen & Kibrik, Andrej A. & Noordman, Leo. *Discourse studies in cognitive linguistics*. Amsterdam: Benjamins, 29–52.

Klein, Wolfgang. 1994. *Time in language*. London: Routledge.

Koval', Antonina I. 1997. "Imennye kategorii v pular-ful'ful'de" [Nominal categories in Pulaar-Fulfulde]. In: Vinogradov, Viktor A. (ed.) *Osnovy afrikanskogo jazykoznanija. Imennye kategorii*. [Fundamentals of African linguistics. Nominal categories.] Moscow: Aspekt Press, 92–220.

Krupa, Viktor. 1976. "A semantic typology of personal pronouns". *Asian and African Studies* 12: 149–155.

Kumaxov, Muxaddin A. 1974. "O strukture predloženija v jazykax polisintetičeskogo tipa" [On sentence structure in polysynthetic languages]. In: *Universalii i tipologičeskie issledovanija*. [Universals and typological studies.] Moscow: Nauka, 125–134.

Langacker, Ronald. 1996. "Conceptual grouping and pronominal anaphora". In: Fox, Barbara A. (ed.), 333–378.

Levinsohn, Stephen H. 1994. "Field procedures for the analysis of participant reference in a monologue discourse". In: Levinsohn, Stephen H. (ed.). *Discourse features of ten languages of West-Central Africa.* Dallas: SIL and University of Texas at Arlington, 109—124.

Levinson, Stephen C. 1987. "Pragmatics and the grammar of anaphora: a partial pragmatic reduction of Binding and Control phenomena". *Journal of Linguistics* 23: 379—434.

Li, Charles & Thompson, Sandra A. 1976. "Subject and topic: a new typology of languages". In: Li, Charles (ed.) *Subject and topic.* New York: Academic Press, 457—489.

Li, Charles & Thompson, Sandra A. 1979. "Third-person pronouns and zero anaphora in Chinese discourse". In: Givón T. (ed.) *Discourse and syntax.* New York: Academic Press, 311—335.

Lyons, John. 1977. *Semantics.* 2 vols. Cambridge: Cambridge University Press.

Majtinskaja, K. E. 1969. *Mestoimenija v jazykax raznyx sistem.* [Pronouns in languages of different types.] Moscow: Nauka.

Mann, William C. & Matthiessen, Christian M. I. M. & Thompson, Sandra A. 1992. "Rhetorical Structure Theory and text analysis". In: Mann, William C. & Thompson, Sandra A. (eds.) *Discourse description: Diverse linguistic analyses of a fund-raising text.* Amsterdam: Benjamins, 39—78.

Marslen-Wilson, William & Levy, Elena & Tyler, Lorraine K. 1982. "Producing interpretable discourse: The establishment and maintenance of reference". In: Jarvella & Klein (eds.), 339—378.

Mithun, Marianne. 1986. "Disagreement: The case of pronominal affixex and nouns". In: *Proceedings of the Georgetown University Round Table Conference on language and linguistics.* Washington, D.C.: Georgetown University Press, 50—66.

Mithun, Marianne. 1993. "Switch-reference: Clause combining in Central Pomo". *International Journal of American Linguistics* 59: 119—136.

Mithun, Marianne. 1999. *The languages of native North America.* Cambridge: Cambridge University Press.

Nichols, Johanna. 1986. "Head-marking and depending-marking grammar". *Language* 62: 56—119.

Nichols, Johanna. 1992. *Linguistic diversity in space and time.* Chicago: University of Chicago Press.

Noonan, Michael. 1992. *A grammar of Lango.* Berlin: Mouton de Gruyter.

Padučeva, Elena V. 1985. *Vyskazyvanie i ego sootnesennost' s dejstvitel'nost'ju.* [The utterance and its relation to reality.] Moscow: Nauka.

Padučeva, Elena V. 1996. *Semantičeskie issledovanija.* [Semantic studies.] Moscow: Škola "Jazyki russkoj kul'tury".

Parker, Elisabeth. 1986. "Mundani pronouns". In: Wiesemann (ed.), 131—165.

Partee, Barbara H. 1984. "Nominal and temporal anaphora". *Linguistics and Philosophy* 7.3: 243—286.

Payne, Thomas E. 1993. *The twins stories. Participant coding in Yagua narrative.* Berkeley: University of California Press.

Popovich, Harold. 1986. "The nominal reference system of Maxakalí". In: Wiesemann (ed.), 351—358.

Russell, Kevin, 1996. "Does obviation mark point of view?" In: Nichols, John D. & Ogg, Argen C. *Nikotwâsik iskwâhtêm, pâskihtêpayih! Studies in honor of H. C. Wolfart. Algonquian and Iroquoian Linguistics, Memoir 13.* Winnipeg, 367—382.

Schwartz, Linda. 1986. "The function of free pronouns". In: Wiesemann (ed.), 405—436.

Simons, L. 1986. "The pronouns of To'aba'ita (Solomon Islands)". In: Wiesemann (ed.), 21—35.

Sokolovskaja, Natal'ja K. 1980. "Nekotorye semantičeskie universalii v sisteme ličnyx metoimenij" [Some semantic universals in the system of personal pronouns]. In: *Teorija i tipologija mestoimenij.* [Theory and typology of pronouns.] Moscow: Nauka, 84—103.

Stirling, Leslie. 1993. *Switch-reference and discourse representation.* Cambridge: Cambridge University Press.

Tao, Liang. 1996. "Topic discontinuity and zero anaphora in Chinese discourse: Cognitive strategies in discourse processing". In: Fox (ed.), 487—514.

Taylor, Carolyn P. 1994. "Participant reference in Nɔmaandɛ narrative discourse". In: Levinsohn, Stephen H. (ed.). *Discourse features of ten languages of West-Central Africa.* Dallas: SIL and University of Texas at Arlington, 91—108.

Testelec, Jakov G. & Toldova, Svetlana Ju. "Vozvratnye mestoimenija v dagestanskix jazykax i tipologija vozvratnosti" [Reflexive pronouns in the Dagestanian languages and the typology of reflexives]. *Voprosy jazykoznanija* 1998.4: 35—57.

Thompson, Chad. 1989. *Voice and obviation in Athabaskan and other languages.* Ph. D. dissertation. Eugene: University of Oregon.

Tomlin, Russell. 1987. "Linguistic reflections of cognitive events". In: Tomlin, Russell (ed.) *Coherence and grounding in discourse.* Amsterdam: Benjamins, 455—79.

Tomlin, Russell. 1995. "Focal attention, voice, and word order: An experimental, cross-linguistic study". In: Downing, Pamela & Noonan, Michael (eds.) *Word order in discourse.* Amsterdam: Benjamins, 517—554.

Tomlin, Russell & Pu, Ming-Ming. 1991. "The management of reference in Mandarin discourse". *Cognitive Linguistics* 2: 65—93.

Toole, Janine. 1996. "The effect of genre on referential choice." In: Fretheim & Gundel (eds.), 263—290.

van Hoek, Karen. 1997. *Anaphora and conceptual structure*. Chicago: University of Chicago Press.

Van Valin, Robert D. Jr. 1977. *Aspects of Lakhota syntax*. Ph. D. diss. Berkeley: University of California.

Van Valin, Robert D. Jr. 1985. "Case marking and the structure of the Lakhota clause". In: Nichols, Johanna & Woodbury, Anthony (eds.) *Grammar inside and outside the clause*. Cambridge: Cambridge University Press, 363–413.

Van Valin, Robert D. Jr. 1987. "Aspects of the interaction of syntax and pragmatics: Discourse coreference mechanisms and the typology of grammatical systems". In: Verschueren J. & Bertuccelli-Papi M. (eds.) *The pragmatic perspective: selected papers from the 1985 International Pragmatics Conference*. Amsterdam: Benjamins, 513–531.

Vološinov, V. N. 1929. *Marksizm i filosofija jazyka*. [Marxism and the philosophy of language.] Leningrad: Priboj.

Wiesemann, Ursula. 1986. "Grammaticalized coreference". In: Wiesemann (ed.), 437–463.

Wiesemann, Ursula. (ed.) 1986. *Pronominal systems*. Tübingen: Narr.

Wilkins, David. 1988. "Switch-reference in Mparntwe Arrernte (Aranda): Form, function, and problems of identity". In: Austin, Peter (ed.) *Complex sentence constructions in Australian languages*. Amsterdam: Benjamins, 141–176.

Woodbury, Anthony. 1983. "Switch-reference, syntactic organization, and rhetorical structure in Central Yup'ik Eskimo". In: Haiman & Munro (eds.), 291–316.

Zubin, David & Duchan, Lynne E. 1995. "The deictic center: A theory of deixis in narrative". In: Duchan et al. (eds.), 129–158.

*Andrej A. Kibrik, Institute of Linguistics,
Russian Academy of Sciences,
Moscow (Russia)*

XI. Lexical typology
Lexikalische Typologie
La typologie lexicale

85. Lexical typology from a cognitive and linguistic point of view

1. Is there such a thing as lexical typology?
2. Parameters of lexical typology
3. Onomasiological perspective: paradigmatic axis: hierarchical aspect
4. Onomasiological perspective: paradigmatic axis: motivational aspect
5. Onomasiological perspective: syntagmatic axis
6. Semasiological perspective
7. Concluding remarks
8. References

1. Is there such a thing as lexical typology?

In 1957, Joseph H. Greenberg enumerated the following six classes of linguistic typologies: "phonologic, morphologic, syntactic, those pertaining to canonic form [i.e. word classes, phonemic morpheme structures etc.], semantic, and symbolic [including onomatopoeia etc.]" (71). Morphological, syntactic, and even phonological typology is well established (→ Art. 48−84; 94−98). By 'semantic', Greenberg clearly means 'lexical-semantic', but we may wonder if a (lexical-)semantic typology exists at all, because the lexicon seems to be too full of interlingual diversity and of idiosyncrasies to lend itself to systematic typological studies.

As soon as 1953, Ullmann had sketched "a linguistic typology based on semantic features" (1953: 237), a proposal he took up again in his fundamental 1963 article on "Semantic universals" (²1966), putting forward "[...] four [...] features [...] − motivation, generic *versus* specific terms, polysemy, and homonymy −" that "may, if studied on a suitable scale, yield criteria for linguistic typology" (237f.; for the application of these criteria see sections 4., 3.2.1./3., 6.1., and 6.2.).

Less optimistic, the Praguian typologist Vladimír Skalička claims "dass es nicht möglich ist, die Verschiedenheiten des Wortschatzes mit den typologischen Methoden zu beschreiben" (1965: 152). Interestingly, though, what he underlines is not the above-mentioned too great diversity, but the too great similarity of languages, that he takes for granted on onomasiological grounds: "Für jede Sprache gibt es dieselbe Aussenwelt und so auch dieselbe Basis des Wortschatzes. [...] Die Unterschiede in der Konstruktion [sc. der lexikalischen Systeme] unterliegen unbedeutenden Schwankungen, die mit Hilfe der Statistik behandelt werden können" (1965: 157; this opinion does not prevent Skalička from furnishing several excellent examples for what will be discussed in 3.3.1., 4.4.2., and 6.1.).

As to the tension between lexical diversity and similarity, a potential new stimulus for typology could have been simply the reorientation of language typology towards language universals research (cf. Greenberg 1966b, with substantial clues for lexical typology: esp. 100−111; cf. also Lehrer 1974: 150−172; see below 3.2.2.). Still, it is symptomatic that lexical typology received important inspirations especially from the "safe" borderland between grammatical typology and lexicology (cf. Plank 1984; Müller-Gotama 1992; Lehmann 1990; Rijkhoff 2000; Antinucci 1977; Geisler 1988; Bossong 1998; Lyons 1967; Hengeveld 1992; Heine 1997; Feuillet 1998; see below 5.1./2.). Undeniably, a further, though limited, encouragement for lexical typologists came from Cognitive Semantics (cf. Talmy 1985 and 1991; see below 5.2.1.). Yet, lexical-typological studies remained *disiecta membra*.

So, in 1992 Lehrer still deplored (249f.) that lexical typology was not mentioned in the two recent linguistic encyclopedias Crystal 1987 and Newmeyer 1988. The same holds for Glück 1993. Similarly, a few years ago,

König (1996: 48) and Lang (1996: 314) found lexical typology still in its infancy.

We should not neglect, however, the less spectacular contributions of (even traditional) contrastive and structural linguistics and of anthropology to lexical typology (see also below 3.2.1., 3.3.3., 4.4.2., 5.1., 5.2., and 6.). After all, a first — at that time up-to-date — synthesis of what could be called 'lexical typology' was written, not surprisingly, from the point of view of contrastive linguistics (Schepping 1985).

In order to systematize relevant problems and achievements, we first have to define the central task of lexical typology and then relate it to essential aspects of human language and of language studies. As Lehrer puts it, lexical typology is concerned with "the characteristic ways in which language [...] packages semantic material into words" (1992: 249). More precisely, problems of lexical typology are only a subset of the problems linked to the universal of 'discursivity', as defined by Oesterreicher: "In meinen Augen ist die Diskursivität insofern als der für jede ernstzunehmende typologische Forschung unverzichtbare Grundbegriff zu betrachten, als mit ihm notwendig die Betrachtung der Prinzipien der *Verknüpfung* von Inhaltsprozessen mit Ausdrucksprozessen gefordert ist, als mit ihm die Zeichenbildung auf allen relevanten Ebenen der sprachlichen Strukturierung ins Zentrum rückt" (1989: 241 f.). In the realm of lexical typology, the connection between content (i. e. conceptual) processes and expression processes is always considered **in relation to the linguistic unit of the lexeme** — in a positive and in a negative sense: languages also can diverge in that one of them uses a particular, single lexeme where the other uses a more complex word, a lexeme belonging to another part of speech, a sequence of lexemes, etc. (see 4.4.2., 5.). The problems of lexical typology, then, can be systematized with respect to current parameters of linguistic investigation (s. section 2., Figure 85.1).

Quite in Ullmann's tradition, this article will not deal with "the semantics of so-called 'form-words' — pronouns, articles, conjunctions, prepositions, etc. — which, though they behave like words in some respects, have a purely grammatical function and do not therefore belong to the lexical system of a language" (1966: 219).

2. Parameters of lexical typology

Universals and typology are currently regarded as complementary. Nevertheless, two different emphases have to be distinguished: first of all, comparative semanticists can search mainly for substantial lexical universals without denying divergences in detail (cf. already Ullmann 1966: 249 f., and especially Anna Wierzbicka's works as, e. g. 1996; 1999; Goddard/Wierzbicka 1994; → Art. 87); secondly — and that will be the concern of the present article —, they can note the lexical differences, reveal typological similarities and alliances and finally search for underlying general principles and relational, often implicational, universals (as for the importance of implicational universals, cf. Greenberg et al. 1966, xix f.; Coseriu 1975; Croft 1990: 44—63; with special regard to lexical typology: Ullmann 1966: 220).

Any contrastive and typological study of languages presupposes a *tertium comparationis*. When the linguistic objects under examination are signifying units, i. e. signs (lexemes or grammemes), it is difficult to find a *tertium* based on the *signifiant* and to carry out a semasiological-typological investigation. In opposition to this, it is natural to take semantic, conceptual *tertia* and to conduct the investigation from an onomasiological perspective (for a sound 'noematic' methodology in terms of *Außereinzelsprachlichkeit*, cf. Heger 1990/91). As shown in Figure 85.1, lexical typology, too, will be implemented primarily from an onomasiological perspective (3., 4., and 5.), whereas semasiological considerations will be of minor importance in this field, though not totally absent (6.). The onomasiological perspective will be subdivided according to the distinction between the paradigmatic and the syntagmatic axis (for further subdivisions, see the sections indicated in Figure 85.1). In theory, the synchrony-diachrony dichotomy could apply as well, but the present article will be limited to synchronic issues, though diachronic implications will emerge repeatedly.

As for the 'cognitive' approach, the ultimate three cognitive relations underlying all semantic relations and patterns in the lexicon are the associative relations of 'contiguity', 'similarity', and 'contrast' (cf. Jakobson 1956; Raible 1981; Koch 1991: 284; 1999a: 140 ff.; 2001a; Blank 1997: 131—156). Starting with these primitives, we can generate all the other cognitively fundamental principles: 'frame'

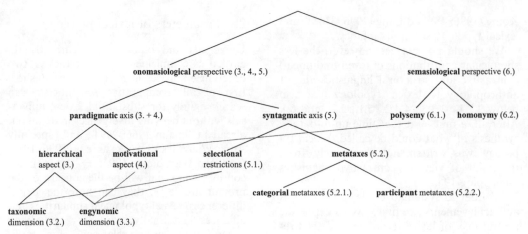

Fig. 85.1: Parameters of lexical typology

and 'prototype' (for these two concepts, cf. e. g. Fillmore 1975; 1985; Rosch 1978; Taylor 1995: 38−92; Kleiber 1990; Barsalou 1992; Ungerer/Schmid 1996: 1−113, 205 ff.; Koch 1996; 1999 a; see also below 3.1., (ii)); 'metaphor' (cf. Bühler 1965: 342−350; Black 1977; Lakoff/Johnson 1980; Koch 1994), and 'taxonomy' (see below 3.1., (i)).

3. Onomasiological perspective: paradigmatic axis: hierarchical aspect

Without doubt, the richest domain of lexical typology is the onomasiological investigation on the paradigmatic axis, which is concerned with the organizational principles of conceptual material with respect to single lexical units. We have to distinguish between the hierarchical aspect (3.) and the motivational aspect (4.). The hierarchical aspect consists in exploring how the cognitive "material" is organized with respect to conceptual hierarchies.

3.1. Types of conceptual hierarchies

To obtain valid observations in this field, we have to strictly distinguish between two fundamental hierarchical dimensions: taxonomic hierarchies and relations (i) and engynomic hierarchies and relations (ii).

(i) As shown in Figure 85.2, taxonomic relations are: (a) relations of conceptual inclusion between a superordinate concept and subordinate concepts (e. g. between TREE on the one hand and OAK, FIR, or APPLE-TREE on the other, the latter belonging to different particular frames); (b) relations of co-taxonomic similarity between subordinate concepts of the same superordinate concept (e. g. between OAK and FIR, OAK and APPLE-TREE etc.). In view of the fact that prototype theory severely criticizes traditional logical-taxonomic semantics (cf. Taylor 1995: 22−58; Kleiber 1990: 21−117), it has to be stressed that even prototype theory − especially with regard to basic levels and 'folk taxonomies' − rests on the principle of taxonomy as such (even though in an attenuated and "chastened" form). Taxonomic hierarchies in this sense undeniably constitute one basic dimension of onomasiological-paradigmatic lexical typology (see 3.2.). In the following, I call the conceptual complex corresponding to a taxonomic hierarchy '(taxonomic) field'.

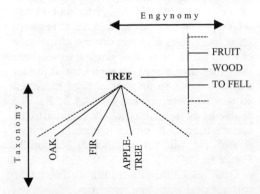

Fig. 85.2: Taxonomy and engynomy (example TREE)

(ii) The term 'engynomy' derives from Anc. Gr. ἐγγύς 'near, close' (cf. τὸ σύνεγγυς 'the contiguous (thing)' in Aristotle, De memoria et reminiscentia, 451b: 18−22). As exempli-

Table 85.1: SIBLING section of the KINSHIP field

Malay	[born of the same parents] *saudara*							
E.	[female] *sister*				[male] *brother*			
Hung.	*nővér*				*fivér*			
	[elder] *néne*		[younger] *hug*		[younger] *öcs*		[elder] *bátya*	
Malay	*kakak*		*adik*				*abang*	
Jap.	[own] *ane*	[other's] *imōto*	[own] *onēsan*	[other's] *imōtosan*	[own] *ōtōto*	[other's] *ōtōtosan*	[own] *ani*	[other's] *onīsan*

fied in Figure 85.2, engynomic relations are: (a) contiguity relations between a conceptual/perceptual frame and its elements (e. g. between TREE on the one hand and FRUIT, WOOD, or TO FELL on the other); (b) contiguity relations between elements of the same frame (e. g. between FRUIT and WOOD, WOOD and TO FELL etc.; these examples show that TOTUM-PARS relations and PARS-PARS relations, i.e. 'partonomies', are only one type of engynomic relations). Engynomic relations in this sense constitute another basic dimension of onomasiological-paradigmatic lexical typology (see 3.3.). In the following, I call '(engynomic) domain' the conceptual complex corresponding to an engynomic hierarchy (cf. Koch 1998: 120 ff.; 1999a: 144−153; 2001b).

(Note, with respect to Cruse 1986: 136−180, that 'taxonomy' here includes natural kinds as well as nominal kinds and that 'engynomy' comprises much more than 'meronomy/partonomy').

3.2. Taxonomic dimension

When describing the taxonomic dimension, lexical typology can naturally take advantage of the experiences of Structural Semantics and Componential Analysis, as developed in the European linguistic tradition since the 1830s (Trier 1931; Hjelmslev 1957; Pottier 1964; Greimas 1966; Coseriu/Geckeler 1981; cf. also Schepping 1985: 185). An emblematic example of relevant "structurations" differing between languages is the taxonomic field of KINSHIP (see the SIBLING section of this field represented for some languages in Table 85.1; cf. Steinthal/Misteli 1893: 1 f.; Hjelmslev 1957: 104; Ullmann 1966: 251 f.; Baldinger 1984: 83). 'Structuration' in this sense means 'taxonomic organization' of lexical units (for the examples in Tables 85.1 and 85.2, cf. Koch 1998: 114 f.; 2000: 101 f.).

3.2.1. Taxonomic interlingual divergence patterns

We can establish a systematics of interlingual divergence patterns in the taxonomic organization of lexical units. According to a first pattern (TAXOα), one language type A and another language type B disagree by choosing, within a given taxonomic hierarchy, different levels of abstraction to organize conceptual material, i. e., type B is taxonomically more fine-grained than type A (cf. Ullmann 1966: 227 ff.; Schwarze 1983: 204): e. g., type A = Malay *saudara* (but see below for more details) vs. type B = E. *sister/brother*; or type A = English vs. type B = Jap. *ane/imōto/ onēsan/*etc., as illustrated in Table 85.1; (cf. Table 85.2: type A = English, German, Rumanian etc. vs. type B = Latin, French, ... Hopi, ..., Swahili; as to the differences within type B, see pattern TAXOγ below):

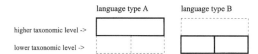

Fig. 85.3: Taxonomic interlingual divergence pattern TAXOα

According to a second pattern (TAXOβ), one language type A may lexicalize at the same time two (or more) different taxonomic levels, whereas another language type B displays only one — either the more fine-grained or the less fine-grained type (e. g., type A = Hung. *nővér/fivér* and *néne/hug/bátya/öcs* vs. type B₁ = E. *sister/brother*, as illustrated in Table 85.1; note that Hung. *nővér* and *fivér* are neologisms of about 1840):

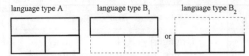

Fig. 85.4: Taxonomic interlingual divergence pattern TAXOβ

The divergence pattern TAXOβ can apply recursively. According to Table 1, Malay is type A in comparison to English. However, E. *brother/sister* corresponds to type B₁ with respect to Malay *kakak/adik/abang*, but to type B₂ with respect to Malay *saudara*.

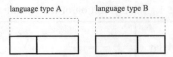

Fig. 85.5: Taxonomic interlingual divergence pattern TAXOγ

According to a more intricate taxonomic interlingual divergence pattern (TAXOγ: Figure 85.5), one language type A and another language type B — both equally fine-grained — disagree by organizing conceptual material differently at the s a m e level of abstraction of a taxonomic hierarchy (e. g. Latin vs. French, Ital., etc. vs. Hopi, Guaraní vs. Swahili according to Table 85.2).

So far, taxonomic interlingual divergence was a matter of lexical invariance and differentiation at distinct levels of abstraction (in

Table 85.2: HAIR (cf. also Geckeler 1993: 162; Koch, P., 2000: 102)

	→ HEAD	→ BEARD	→ HUMAN BODY	→ ANIMAL
E.	*hair*			
Germ.	*Haar*			
Rum.	*păr*			
Russ.	*vólos*			
Bret.	*bleven*			
Arab.	*šaʿra*			
Itza (Maya)	*tzo'otz(el)*			
Basque	*ile/bilo* (dialectal variants)			
Lat.	*capillus*		*pilus*	
Fr.	*cheveu*		*poil*	
Ital..	*capello*		*pelo*	
Hung.	*hajszál*		*szőrszál*	
Turk.	*saç*		*kıl*	
Jap.	*kami (no ke)*		*ke*	
Hopi	*höömi*	*sowitsmi*	*pöhö*	
Guaraní	*avalacärague*	*tendîvá*	*tagué*	
Swah.	*unywele*	*udevu*	*laika*	*nyoya/unyoya*

pattern TAXOα, e. g., type A displays lexical invariance at one level, whereas the fine-grained type B displays differentiation at the next lower level, etc.). In these cases, it is sound to interpret lexical invariance not as polysemy but, like Structural Semantics would do, as monosemy (thus, for E. *sister* in Table 85.1 we would not postulate two senses 'elder female sibling' and 'younger female sibling', but only one sense 'female sibling'). There is also a type of lexical invariance that covers two levels of abstraction in a taxonomic hierarchy, as with B_1 in language type B in Figure 85.6:

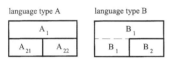

Fig. 85.6: Taxonomic interlingual divergence pattern TAXOδ

In the taxonomic field HUMAN BEING, for instance, English is a type B language with B_1 = *man* (expressing the concepts HUMAN BEING as well as MALE HUMAN BEING) and B_2 = *woman*, in contrast to German as a type A language with A_1 = *Mensch*, A_{21} = *Mann*, and A_{22} = *Frau*. In this taxonomic field, other type B languages are especially Romance languages, except Rumanian (e. g. Fr. B_1 = *homme;* B_2 = *femme*). Other type A languages are: Mod.Gr. A_1 = *ánθropos*, A_{21} = *ándras*, A_{22} = *jinéka*; Lat. A_1 = *homo*, A_{21} = *vir*, A_{22} = *mulier*; Rum. A_1 = *om*, A_{21} = *bărbat*, A_{22} = *femeie*; Russ. A_1 = *čelov'ék*, A_{21} = *mužčina*, A_{22} = *žénščina*; Hung. A_1 = *ember*, A_{21} = *férfi*, A_{22} = *nő, asszony*; Turk. A_1 = *insan, adam*, A_{21} = *erkek*, A_{22} = *kadın*; Arab. A_1 = *ʔinsān*, A_{21} = *raǧul*, A_{22} = *ʔimraʔa* (cf. also, for other concepts, Schwarze 1983, 206 f.).

A pattern somewhat analogous to Figure 85.6 occurs in "culinary" verb semantics (cf. Lehrer 1974, 155—167):

Type A languages are, for instance: English (A_1 = *to cook*; A_{21} = *to boil*); French (A_1 = *cuire*; A_{21} = *(faire) bouillir*); Persian (A_1 = *poxtæn*; A_{21} = *jusandæn*); Japanese (A_1 = *ryōri-suru, nitaki*; A_{21} = *niru*); Navaho (A_1 = *chiʼyáán 'alnééhgo*; A_{21} = *shibéezhgo*). Type B languages are, for instance: German (B_1 = *kochen*); Polish (B_1 = *gotawać*); Yoruba (B_1 = *sè*). Chinese, e. g., is mixed (A_1/B_1 = *peng-jen*; A_{21} = *chǔ*).

To summarize, language type A in Figures 85.6 and 85.7 is characterized by a 'vertical lexical differentiation' A_1/A_{21}, whereas language type B shows a 'vertical polysemy' (Gévaudan, ms.) in B_1. In the field of culinary verb semantics, vertical polysemy is clearly motivated by the prototypical status of PREPARING FOOD FOR MEALS BY HEAT WITH WATER = BOILING within the taxonomy PREPARING FOOD FOR MEALS BY HEAT (due perhaps to the highly cultural character of BOILING, doubly mediated by water and by the recipient: cf. Lévi-Strauss 1964: 21—24). Nevertheless, the analysis in terms of polysemy of B_1 surely is preferable to the structuralist analysis in terms of monosemy of B_1, based on an 'inclusive opposition' between the unmarked lexeme B_1 (meaning '(male) human being') and the marked lexeme B_2 (meaning 'female human being') (cf. Coseriu/Geckeler 1981, 57 n. 103). Indeed, we can distinguish, even within the paradigmatic lexical organization of a type B language system, two senses of B_1 bound together with two different series of oppositions (cf., e. g., E. *man* /vs./ *animal, plant* etc. on the one hand and *man* /vs./ *woman, child* etc. on the other; Germ. *kochen* /vs./ *backen, brauen* etc. and *kochen* /vs./ *braten, grillen* etc.).

3.2.2. Universals and hierarchies

The taxonomic interlingual divergence patterns discussed in 3.2.1. are of a very general, undoubtedly universal nature and independent of particular taxonomic fields. The question is whether we can formulate less abstract generalizations concerning individual taxo-

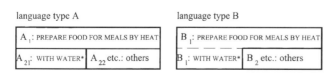

* or WATER-BASED LIQUID (WINE, STOCK, MILK ...)

Fig. 85.7: Vertical lexical differenciation vs. vertical polysemy in culinary verb semantics

nomic fields. In this respect, Structuralism was rather inclined to stress the idiosyncrasies of lexicalization in particular languages (cf. esp. Hjelmslev 1957; Coseriu/Geckeler 1981: 21−27). It is obvious that this point agrees largely with Wilhelm v. Humboldt's concept of *innere Sprachform* (Humboldt 1979: 463 ff.; cf. Trabant 2000) and with elements of the Whorfian Hypothesis (Whorf 1956). It is undeniable that the individual "fingerprint" of any particular language has to be respected as a product of historical and cultural circumstances in its own right (cf. also Lehrer 1974: 169 f.; publications of the last few years have given a fresh impulse to discussions on linguistic relativity: cf. Gumperz/Levinson 1996; Niemeier/Dirven 2000; Pütz/Verspoor 2000). Nevertheless, cautious − often implicational − generalizations are not impossible and do not necessarily contradict language diversity in the realm of the lexicon.

In particular, interesting generalizations have been formulated for kinship terms, for colour terms, for culinary terms verb semantics, and for dimension terms.

The more or less fine-grained character of taxonomic distinctions seems to depend, interlingually and intralingually, at least in part on: 1° factual universals, 2° implicational distance hierarchies, and 3° implicational markedness hierarchies (note that for the sake of terminological precision we have to distinguish taxonomic and engynomic 'hierarchies' as relational principles from 'implicational hierarchies' as assessment principles; in 2° and 3° in the following, we are concerned with implicational hierarchies in relation to taxonomic hierarchies).

1° Factual universals. Kroeber (1909) reduced the hundreds or thousands of conceivable relationships in the taxonomic field of kinship concepts to eight fundamental underlying dimensions: 1. *generation*; 2. *consanguineal vs. affinal*; 3. lineal or collateral; 4. *sex of relative*; 5. sex of connecting relative; 6. sex of speaker; 7. age in generation; 8. condition of life of connecting relative. Kroeber already identified two language types in relation to these dimensions: the "European" type (represented by English) expressing a smaller number of dimensions, but more completely (i. e. in larger parts of the kinship vocabulary) vs. the "American Indian" type expressing a greater number of dimensions, but less completely (i. e. only in part of the kinship vocabulary so that the number of kinship lexemes is not necessarily superior to the number found in European languages).

Three of the above-cited dimensions (the italicized ones), however, seem to be universal according to Greenberg (1966: 110), which only means that they are present at least at some point of the lexical kinship term systems of all languages. Thus, with respect to (4.) 'sex of relative', Bavenda has only one lexeme for the second ascending generation (*makhulu* 'grandparent'), but two for the first ascending generation (*khotsi* 'father' and *mme* 'mother'). "It is indeed a probable 'factual universal' that all systems distinguish male and female parent by separate terms [...]" (op. cit.: 101).

2° Implicational distance hierarchies. The eight dimensions of kinship term systems mentioned above (1°) provide, among other things, a rationale for measuring distances between positions in a taxonomy. These distances can in turn account for the taxonomically more or less fine-grained lexicalization in different languages. Greenberg (1966b: 108−110) pointed out that kinship relationships differing in two dimensions are jointly lexicalized with less probability than those differing in only one dimension. The section GRANDPARENT, for instance, is quadripartite with respect to the dimensions (4.) sex of relative and (5.) sex of connecting relative (FATHER'S FATHER − MOTHER'S FATHER − FATHER'S MOTHER − MOTHER'S MOTHER). But of the fifteen theoretically possible lexicalization types, only three are really common: the coarse-grained type with only one overall word (e. g. the already cited Bavenda *makhulu*), the two-word English type (*grandfather/grandmother*, indifferent to dimension (5.)), and the fine-grained four-word type (e. g. Swed. *farfar/morfar/farmor/mormor*). Except for the overall type, all those logically possible types that would jointly lexicalize FATHER'S FATHER and MOTHER'S MOTHER, differing in two dimensions, do not occur, and types that jointly lexicalize MOTHER'S FATHER and FATHER'S MOTHER, differing in two dimensions as well, do not occur or are rather rare.

3° Implicational markedness hierarchies. For kinship relationships Greenberg established the following hypothetical markedness hierarchy (confirmed also by text frequencies of kinship terms):

(1) FIRST ASCENDING GENERATION
 < EGO'S GENERATION/FIRST DESCENDING GENERATION
 < SECOND ASCENDING GENERATION
 < SECOND DESCENDING GENERATION
 < THIRD ASCENDING GENERATION
 < THIRD DESCENDING GENERATION

Since a taxonomically more fine-grained structure is less probable (though not impossible) with more marked relationships, this hierarchy would also account, e. g., for the Bavenda data presented in 1° (since FIRST ASCENDING GENERATION < SECOND ASCENDING GENERATION). Likewise, it would be fully compatible with the following universal formulated by Greenberg (1966: 107): "distinction of sex [sc. of relative] in the second descending generation implies the same distinction in the second ascending generation, but not vice versa" (since SECOND ASCENDING GENERATION < SECOND DESCENDING GENERATION). Indeed, of the four types logically possible, only three occur: a type without any sex distinction in both generations (e. g. Amharic *ayat*, Rotuman *ma'piŋ*), the English type (*grandfather/grandmother/grandson/granddaughter*) and a third type, represented, e. g., by Logoli with *guga* 'grandfather'/*guku* 'grandmother'/*omwitjuxulu* 'grandchild'.

According to the structuralist view, colour terms were considered an outstanding example of arbitrary, language-particular (taxonomic) categorization (cf. Hjelmslev 1957; curiously enough, it is the field of colour that proved to be inaccessible to a non-trivial description in terms of structuralist distinctive features: cf. Jackendoff 1983: 113). Ullmann, however, already observed: "These differences are highly significant, but it would be equally interesting to know whether there are any elements common to all classifications of colors, any distinctions which have to be expressed everywhere" (1966: 251). Indeed, Berlin/Kay (1969), insisting on the notion of 'focal colour', achieved to set up an implicational hierarchy of (basic) focal colours. Surely, some of Berlin/Kay's data and conclusions had to be revised (cf. an overview in Taylor 1995: 10–13; cf. also Schepping 1985: 186–188); in particular the two anthropologists had underestimated the importance of (taxonomic) differentiation. Nevertheless, it seems possible to establish the following type of a universal implicational hierarchy of taxonomic distinctions underlying the diversity of language-particular basic colour term systems:

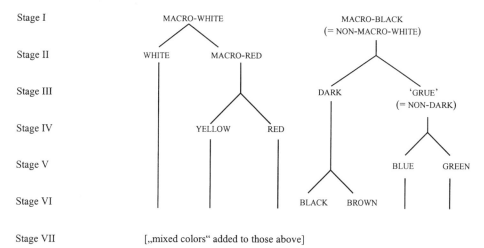

Fig. 85.8: Implicational hierarchy of taxonomic distinctions for basic colours (after Wierzbicka 1990: 144 f.)

If a language has colour differentiation corresponding to a stage *n*, we can predict that it will also possess all the differentiations corresponding to the stages $x < n$ (according to certain authors, however, stage IV may optionally be prior to stage III). Whereas Kay/McDaniel (1978) attribute the progressive differentiation of colour terms to neurophysiological processes in the perception of colour, Wierzbicka (1990) relates it to a number of universal 'environmental concepts' corresponding to prototypical supports of colours in human experience: DAYLIGHT (→ WHITE), NIGHTTIME (→ MACRO-BLACK), FIRE (→ [MACRO-]RED), SKY (→ BLUE) etc. (interestingly, she in this way integrates an engynomic component into the foundations of an implicational hierarchy for taxonomic distinctions).

Another conceptual field that — at least at the top of the taxonomic hierarchy — may be governed by certain implicational markedness hierarchies is that of culinary verb semantics (cf. Figure 85.7), for which Lehrer (1974: 164–167) proposed some tentative implications: (i) "In general, if a language has at least two cooking words that contrast, one [i.e. A_{21} or B_1] will be used for boiling" (this is valid also for languages like Jacaltec or Ge where A_1 is lacking); (ii) "if a language has three or more cooking words, in addition to a term for boiling [i.e. A_{21} or B_1], the non-boiling domain [i.e. A_{22} or B_2 etc.] will be subdivided"; etc. Highly relevant parameters seem to be, for instance, the result of the cooking process and, related to this, the differences between cooking in water and in fat, between direct and indirect heat, etc.

Basic dimension terms, one of the earliest fields of application for Structural Semantics (cf. Greimas 1966c: 31–36), have been submitted to typological studies by Ewald Lang during the last decade (cf. e.g. Lang 1996). Besides the prominence of the vertical axis – a factual universal (1°) determined by gravity and the upright walk of man – he distinguishes a proportion-based strategy of lexicalization on the one hand, and an observer-based strategy on the other.

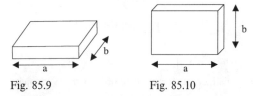

Fig. 85.9   Fig. 85.10

Being a prototypical representative of the proportion-based type, Chinese gives priority to the maximal (most extended) axis *a* and unitarily denominates it *cháng* in Figure 85.9 as well as in Figure 85.10. Axis *b* then, remaining just as a transversal in relation to *a*, is denominated *kuān* in Figure 85.9, whereas the corresponding term in Figure 85.10 is *gāo* because of the prominence of the vertical axis *b*. Korean, an observer-based language (albeit with some exceptions), denominates the axis (*a* or *b*) that coincides with the observer axis in Figure 85.9 and 85.10 *selo*, and the axis (*a* or *b*) transversal to the observer axis *kalo* (*nophi* being an alternative for *b* in Figure 85.10 – independently of the observer – due to the prominence of the vertical axis). Despite some divergences in detail, English and German agree in that they have a mixed strategy: proportion-based for Figure 85.9 (*a* = E. *long*, Germ. *lang*; *b* = E. *wide*, Germ. *breit*), observer-based for Figure 85.10 (*a* = E. *wide*, Germ. *breit* or E. *long*, Germ. *lang*, depending on the position of the observer; because of the prominence of the vertical axis, *b* always = E. *high*, Germ. *hoch*). Further refinements of the parameters involved seem to reveal a scalar lexical typology (from proportion-based to observer-based; cf. Lang 1996: 344–348):

(2)   Chinese – Russian – Polish – Slovak – German – Korean

Another well-known example of taxonomic, typological differences in the lexicon is the dyad of verbs for COMING and GOING (cf. for German vs. Spanish: Heger 1966, 168f.; for English: Fillmore 1966). In this field, Ricca (1993) establishes a typology for 20 European languages with respect to deixis, *Aktionsart*, and mode. A first group of 'fully deictic languages' concentrated around the Mediterranean and in the Balkans (Table 85.3, A) displays a lexical split corresponding to the contrast between a CENTRIPETAL movement (towards the *hic et nunc* of the speaker: e.g. Span. *venir*) and a CENTRIFUGAL movement (away from the *hic et nunc* of the speaker: e.g. Span. *ir*). In a second, central and northern group of 'mainly deictic languages' (Table 85.3, B), the lexical split still corresponds prototypically to CENTRIFUGAL vs. CENTRIPETAL movement, but it is often counterbalanced by *Aktionsart* factors (e.g. E. *to come* vs. *to go*). In a third, northeastern group of 'non-deictic languages' (Table 85.3, C), there is no lexical split on deictic grounds (e.g. Russ. *idtí*).

Table 85.3: Typology of movement verbs in European languages (after Ricca 1993)

A fully deictic	B mainly deictic	A non-deictic
Portuguese	Serbo-Croatian	Czech
Spanish	Slovenian	Polish
Italian	German	Ukrainian
Albanian	French	Russian
Modern Greek	Dutch	Lithuanian
Hungarian	English	
Finnish	Danish	
	Swedish	

Within these groups, there are further differentiations. For instance, Portuguese and Spanish are particularly restrictive, excluding any use of the centripetal verb with a SECOND PERSON GOAL.

3.2.3. Levels of abstraction

A major issue in prototype theory is the discovery of salience effects in the vertical dimension of (folk) taxonomies: the 'basic level' of categorization, e. g. BIRD, is cognitively more salient than the 'superordinate level', e. g. ANIMAL, and the 'subordinate level', e. g. ROBIN (cf. Berlin 1978; Rosch 1978; Taylor 1995: 46−51; Kleiber 1990: 78−91; Ungerer/Schmid 1996: 60−109). The taxonomic dimension of lexical typology seems to be an ideal testing ground for basic-level theory.

As is well-known, the morphosyntactic features of superordinate level terms are frequently, though not necessarily, somewhat deviant (cf. also Mihatsch 2000): e. g. E. *furniture*, Germ. *Möbel* (uncountable; but cf. Fr. *un meuble*); Germ. *Geschwister* (plurale tantum; but cf. E. *sibling*). Subordinate level terms, in turn, are often, though not necessarily, compounds whose head is the corresponding basic level term: e. g. Aguaruna (Ecuador) basic: *ipák* 'achiote (*Bixa orellana*)'; subordinate: *beeŋ ipák* 'kidney achiote', *čamíŋ ipák* 'yellow achiote', *hémpe ipák* 'hummingbird achiote', *šiŋ ipák* 'genuine achiote' (Berlin 1978: 20). From here a connection leads to the motivational aspect of lexical typology (4.3.1./2.).

The salience and unmarkedness of the basic level could suggest that the choice of levels of abstraction in lexicalization is cross-linguistically determined by an implicational hierarchy: if in a given language the super-/subordinate level is lexicalized, the basic level is lexicalized as well, but not vice versa. This seems to be confirmed by several data (cf. Taylor 1995: 49 f.), though a large cross-linguistic study is still lacking. All languages seem to have, for instance, at least some 'basic' colour terms (3.2.2., 3°), but many − perhaps all? − of them do not have a superordinate term. In German, neither *farbig* 'coloured' (excluding BLACK, WHITE, and GREY) nor *bunt* 'colourful, multicoloured' serves this purpose. In the field of kinship terms, English has the basic level terms *sister* and *brother* as well as the superordinate term *sibling*, whereas French has only the basic level terms *sœur* and *frère*, but no superordinate term (and, therefore, has to resort to the syntagmatic expression *frères et sœurs*). Looking to the opposite end of the hierarchy, German, for instance, has the basic level term *Pferd* 'horse' as well as the subordinate level terms *Schimmel* 'white horse', *Rappe* 'black horse', *Fuchs* 'sorrel' etc., whereas Latin possesses only the basic level term *equus* (and has to recur to syntagmatic expressions: *equus albus/niger/russeus/* etc.).

Yet, things are surely more complicated, given the interlingual divergence patterns TAXOα and TAXOβ (3.2.1.). First of all, there are methodological problems with basic level. Apart from its presumable context-dependence (cf. Kleiber 1994), the basic level cannot always easily be assigned to empirical cross-linguistic lexical material. For instance, we may wonder which one of the five taxonomically different types visible in Table 85.2 lexicalizes just the basic level: English/German etc.? Latin? French/Italian etc.? Hopi/Guaraní? or Swahili? Even for BIRD, one of the favorite examples of prototype theory, we have to cope with awkward cases: Macedo-rumanian, e. g., has nothing but a lexeme *pul'* 'little bird' (Coseriu 1990: 279; cf. also Albrecht 1995: 26 f.). Still greater problems arise when we consider colour terms of older European languages, like Latin, which does not possess terms for WHITE, BLACK, BLUE etc., but only lexemes like *albus* 'mat white', *candidus* 'brilliant white', *ater* 'mat black', *niger* 'shiny black', *caeruleus* 'deep-blue, blackish-blue' etc. (cf. André 1949; Coseriu 1964: 158).

One could think of situating the basic level on varying levels of abstraction, depending on the language and the conceptual field under examination. Such a solution, however, would rule out basic level as a typological *tertium* in favour of relative levels of abstraction. But there is also a factual limit to the solution of varying "basic levels". For a long time, anthropologists, psychologists, philosophers, and linguists have been raising the problem of the level of abstraction aimed at in the languages of "primitive" cultures. The Bushman language, for instance, possesses several terms for different types of eating, but no general lexeme for EATING: //kà:ŋ 'to eat raw meat'; /ùŋ 'to eat marrow'; !kuŋ 'to eat fat'; *m* 'to eat fruits'; similarly, it has many terms for different fruits, e. g. /gara 'fruit of the kareeboom', but no general lexeme for FRUIT (Stopa 1968: 134). Even if there may have been misinterpretations of linguistic material (cf. Hill 1952), the evidence is overwhelming: we note "l'absence à peu près complète de termes génériques, correspondant aux idées proprement générales, et [...] l'extraordinaire abondance des termes spécifiques, c'est-à-dire désignant des êtres ou objets dont une image particulière et précise se dessine quand on les nomme" (Lévy-Bruhl 1922, 190; cf. also Cassirer 1953: 262—264; Ullmann 1953: 231 f.; 1966: 228—230; Gipper 1972: 92 f.; Schepping 1985: 189 f.). If we let vary the basic level to the extent that it covers even such specific terms, the concept of basic level itself would break down. If, on the contrary, we were to maintain it on a constant level of abstraction, it would yield an overtly ethnocentric cognitive standard with respect to the data of "primitive" languages.

Undoubtedly all these embarrassing examples reveal that the choice of different levels of abstraction in different languages constitutes a highly relevant lexical-typological parameter. But instead of being related to a constant, universal basic level, it should be regarded as an indicator of different 'cognitive styles' in the sense of Hymes (1961). As to the preference for specific terms, it can probably be explained as a characteristic of archaic, oral societies (cf. also Kalmár 1985; meanwhile, several authors have tried to relate the whole Whorfian Hopi/SAE opposition to that between oral and literate cultures: Goody/Watt 1968: 64 f.; Assmann/Assmann 1983: 268; cf. also Ong 1982: 49—57, 174 f.).

Of course, this area of investigation is never immune to misconceptions. Looking to the opposite end of the taxonomic hierarchy, we come across discussions like the one on the "abstract" character of French, as opposed especially to German (cf. Bally 1965: 346 ff., 369; Malblanc 1968: 286; Vinay/Darbelnet 1964: 207; Ullmann 1969: 316; 1966: 227 f.). A meticulous examination of current arguments (Albrecht 1970; 1995) and a confrontation with the taxonomic framework of 3.2.1. reveal, in some cases, the choice of a more abstract taxonomic level in French than in German (cf. Fr. *mettre* 'to put' vs. Germ. *stellen, legen, setzen, stecken, hängen* etc.), but the opposite constellation is not nonexistent (cf. Germ. *Straße* vs. Fr. *rue* 'street'/*route* 'road'); on the other hand, many of the phenomena usually cited concern totally different aspects of lexical typology (engynomy: 3.3.1.; motivation: 4.2.; 4.4.2./3.; metataxis: 5.2.1.; polysemy: 6.1.; homonymy: 6.2.). Apart from this, the confusion of typically French and general Romance characteristics, of language system and discourse traditions, etc., have led in part to erroneous conclusions.

3.3. Engynomic dimension

Unlike the taxonomic dimension, the engynomic one has been neglected for a long time in lexicological studies. When Structural Semantics did deal with engynomic problems, linguists tended to confuse them with taxonomic problems, as our examples will show. Meanwhile, frame theory and studies in partonomies, as components of Cognitive Semantics, have provided us with the necessary prerequisites to put engynomic phenomena in their right place.

In the lexicalization of certain engynomic domains (frames and their elements), critical points seem to come up that compel languages to make typologically relevant decisions. An emblematic example of relevant 'shapings' differing between languages is the engynomic domain of BODY PARTS (cf. Schepping 1985: 185 f.). 'Shaping' in this sense refers to the 'engynomic organization' of lexical units (and should not be confused with — taxonomic — 'structuration': cf. 3.2.).

3.3.1. Engynomic interlingual divergence patterns

Similarly as in the taxonomic dimension, we can establish a systematics of interlingual divergence patterns in the engynomic organization of lexical units, as well. Despite vague analogies to some taxonomic interlingual divergence patterns presented in 3.2.1., the different character of the two types of hierarchies should be stressed.

According to the first engynomic interlingual divergence pattern (ENGYα), one language type A and another language type B disagree by organizing conceptual material differently within the same frame, i.e., generally, by delimitating the parts of a whole differently (there is a rough analogy to patterns TAXOα as well as TAXOγ, since in the case of ENGYα the qualitative aspect of delimitation of parts cannot necessarily be separated from the quantitative aspect of number of parts):

language type A   language type B

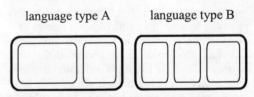

Fig. 85.11: Engynomic interlingual divergence pattern ENGYα

We find particularly salient divergences in the domain of DAY(-TIME). For instance, languages splitting the DAY according to the position of the sun (e.g. Germ. *Nachmittag* and Tuscan Ital. *pomeriggio* TIME (ROUGHLY) FOLLOWING THE PEAK OF SUN'S ALTITUDE) contrast with languages splitting the DAY at the hour of lunch (e. g. Span. *tarde* and Sard. *sero* TIME FOLLOWING LUNCH, which, especially in Spain, can be rather late) (for further interesting aspects, cf. Sobrero 1978: 140–143; Geckeler 1993: 162).

According to a second pattern (ENGYβ), one language type A may lexicalize more different hierarchical levels than another language type B within the same engynomic domain (the analogy to the taxonomic pattern TAXOβ is very vague):

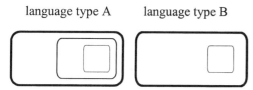

Fig. 85.12: Engynomic interlingual divergence pattern ENGYβ

Thus, for the UPPER and the LOWER LIMB in the domain BODY, type A would correspond to languages that distinguish, among others, the three engynomic (and partonomic) levels ARM – HAND – FINGER and LEG – FOOT – TOE respectively: e. g. Germ. *Arm – Hand – Finger* and *Bein – Fuß – Zeh* (other languages of this type are English, French, Spanish, Urdu, Chinese, Thai, Navaho, Eskimo etc.). Type B, on the other hand, would correspond to languages that distinguish only the two partonomic levels ARM + HAND – FINGER and LEG + FOOT – TOE respectively: e. g. Swahili *mkono* 'arm and hand' – *kidole (cha mkono)* 'finger' and *mguu* 'leg and foot' – *kidole (cha mguu)* 'toe' (before borrowing *futi* from Engl. *foot*); other languages of this type are, e. g., Ibo-Nigerian, Chirah-mbwa, Kewa, and Tzeltal (cf. Brown 1976: 406, 413, 416).

Whereas the aforementioned patterns represent divergences concerning distinct elements of frames or distinct hierarchical levels, the following involve the absence or presence of polysemy between different elements or levels (which is also relevant under the motivational aspect: 4.3.1./2.). According to a pattern ENGYγ, for instance, one language type B unites two contiguous elements of the same frame in a polysemous lexical unit, whereas type A does not:

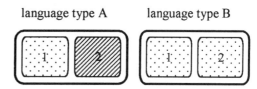

Fig. 85.13: Engynomic interlingual divergence pattern ENGYγ

This can be exemplified by the two concepts 1 = SUN and 2 = DAYLIGHT TIME: They are separately lexicalized (type A), e. g., in E. 1: *sun* / 2: *day*; Germ. 1: *Sonne* / 2: *Tag*; Swed. 1: *sol* / 2: *dag*; Fr. 1: *soleil* / 2: *jour*; Russ. 1: *sólnc'e* / 2: *d'en'l*; Finn. 1: *aurinko* / 2: *päivä*; Pers. 1: *āftāb* / 2: *rūz*; they are united in polysemy (type B: 1+2), e. g., in Hung. *nap*; Mordv. *či*; Jap. *hi*; Chin. *rì* (cf. also Skalička 1965: 156).

The engynomic interlingual divergence pattern ENGYδ is based on the absence vs. presence of polysemy involving different hierarchical levels (for an engynomic and typological reassessment of the examples discussed in connection with Figures 85.14 and 85.15 and with Table 85.4, that have often been erroneously discussed on a par with taxonomic problems, cf. Koch 1998: 114–122; 2000: 102–104):

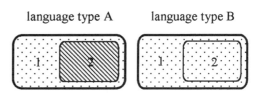

Fig. 85.14: Engynomic interlingual divergence pattern ENGYδ

A particularly relevant example (already noted by Saussure 1916, 160) is the treatment of 1 = ANIMAL concepts (= frame) and the corresponding 2 = MEAT concepts (= element) in different languages. For several, though not all, animals, English behaves according to type A (1: *cow, pig, sheep, calf* / 2: *beef, pork, mutton, veal*), whereas French and Italian, e. g., belong to the polysemy type B (Fr. 1+2: *bœuf* etc., Ital. 1+2: *manzo* etc.). Pattern ENGYδ can also apply alternatively to different hierarchical levels within the same frame, as is shown by the famous example of FOREST/WOODS – TREE – WOOD (cf. Hjelmslev 1957: 104 f.; also Geckeler 1993: 163):

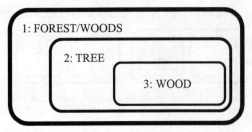

Fig. 85.15: Frame FOREST/WOODS − TREE − WOOD

With respect to this conceptual material, we have essentially three types of languages with respect to the engynomic dimension. Type A possesses three different lexemes, as exemplified here by Latin; type B has a (metonymic) polysemy FOREST/WOODS − WOOD, as here exemplified by French; type C, exemplified by Russian, has a (metonymic) polysemy TREE − WOOD (the possibility of a triple metonymic polysemy, as in Oir. *fid* − and marginal even there − seems to be rather rare):

above type B, Fr. 1: *bois* vs. *forêt*; Hjelmslev 1957: 104 f., just mixes up all these taxonomic and engynomic interlingual divergences).

A final engynomic interlingual divergence pattern ENGYε (somewhat analogous to pattern TAXOα, with which it actually has been erroneously confused) is as follows:

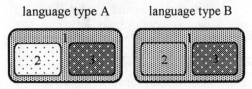

Fig. 85.16: Engynomic interlingual divergence pattern ENGYε

A striking example is the treatment of 1 = DAY (24 HOURS), 2 = DAYLIGHT TIME, and 3 = NIGHT in different languages. Type A languages have separate words for all three concepts: e. g. Swed. 1: *dygn* / 2: *dagn* / 3: *natt*;

Table 85.4: Lexicalization types in the frame FOREST/WOODS − TREE − WOOD

		1: FOREST/WOODS	3: WOOD	2: TREE
Type A	three different lexemes	Lat. *silva*	Lat. *lignum*	Lat. *arbor*
Type B	polysemy 1−3	Fr. *bois*	Fr. *bois*	Fr. *arbre*
Type C	polysemy 2−3	Russ. *l'es*	Russ. *d'er'evo*	Russ. *d'er'evo*

Other examples are: (type A:) Germ. 1: *Wald* / 2: *Holz* / 3: *Baum*; Czech 1: *les* / 2: *dřevo* / 3: *strom*; Mod.Gr. 1: *ðásos* / 2: *ksílo* / 3: *ðéndro*; Turk. 1: *koru* / 2: *odun* / 3: *ağaç*; Chin. 1: *sēnlín* / 2: *shù* / 3: *mù(-cái, -tou)*; (type B:) Bret. 1+3: *koad* / 2: *gwezenn* (as for English *woods*, cf. 4.4.3.); (type C): Dan. 1: *skov* / 2+3: *træ*; Srb.-Cr. 1: *šuma* / 2+3: *drvo*; Lith. 1: *girė* / 2+3: *medis*; Lett. 1: *mežs* / 2+3: *kuoks*; Hung. 1: *erdő* / 2+3: *fa*; Finn. 1: *metsä* / 2+3: *puu*; Swah. 1: *msitu* / 2+3: *mti*; Jap. 1: *mori* / 2+3: *ki* (it would be interesting to visualize the obvious arealtypological clusters in a map; according to Witkowski et al. 1981, ca. two-thirds of a sample of 66 languages all over the world belong to type C). Of course, these engynomic patterns are not affected by supplementary taxonomic divergences of the type TAXOα (cf., within the above type A, e. g. Span. 1: *bosque* vs. *selva* vs. *monte* / 2: *madera* / 3: *árbol* or Arab. 1: *γāba* vs. *ḥarağ* / 2: *šağar* / 3: *xašab*; within the

Russ. 1: *sutky* / 2: *d'en'* / 3: *noč*; Pers. 1: *šebanerūz* / 2: *rūz* / 3: *šab*; Arab. 1: *jaum* / 2: *nahār* / 3: *laila*; Finn. 1: *vuorokausi* / 2: *päivä* / 3: *yö*; Mordv. 1: *či-ve* / 2: *či* / 3: *ve*. Type B languages connect 1 and 2 in a metonymical polysemy: e. g. E. 1+2: *day* / 3: *night*; Germ. 1+2: *Tag* / 3: *Nacht*; Fr. 1+2: *jour* / 3: *night* (and similarly other Romance languages); Mod.Gr. 1+2: *(i)mera* / 3: *nixta*; Turk. 1+2: *gün* / 3: *gece*; Hung. 1+2: *nap* / 3: *éj(szaka)*; Jap. 1+2: *hi* (2 also: *hiru*) / 3: *yoru*; Chin. 1+2: *rì* (1 also: *rìzi* or *tiān*; 2 also: *báitiān*) / 3: *yè* (cf. also Skalička 1965,156). The metonymic polysemy of type B clearly is due to the salience of DAYLIGHT TIME within the frame DAY (24 HOURS).

3.3.2. Universals and hierarchies

The engynomic interlingual divergence patterns discussed in 3.3.1. are of a very general, undoubtedly universal nature and independent of particular engynomic domains. As with taxonomic fields, the question is whether we can formulate less abstract generalizations concerning individual engynomic domains. Since Structuralism, in the final analysis, does not have the power to describe non-taxonomic relations (cf. Koch 1998), the relevant investigations into this area have been conducted instead from an anthropological point of view, venturing cautious — and here, too, often implicational — generalizations and respecting nevertheless the individual "fingerprints" of the particular languages.

It is in the domain of body parts that major achievements have been obtained. Universals of engynomic labeling for this domain include, among others, the following (cf. Brown 1976; Andersen 1978: 352; Wilkins 1996; considerations including other motivational aspects than polysemy would have to be treated in the framework delineated in 4.3.):

① The concepts BODY, HEAD, EYE, NOSE, and MOUTH are labeled in all languages (HEAD always as an immediate part of BODY).
② The concepts FINGER and TOE as well as FINGERNAIL and TOENAIL (or simply NAIL) are always labeled.
③ A concept ARM or ARM+HAND is always labeled (cf. also 3.3.3.).
④ Labeling of a concept HAND presupposes labeling of a concept ARM (but not vice versa). Labeling of a concept FOOT presupposes labeling of a concept LEG or at least LOWER LEG (but not vice versa).

and so on.

Unfortunately, the reliability of the data supporting the cited investigations is not guaranteed in all cases, even for very common languages. Thus, in Andersen (1978: 358) German is mentioned as a language 1° having an ARM-HAND-polysemy like Russian (*ruka*; cf. 3.3.3.), which is not at all the case (cf. Germ. *Arm* vs. *Hand*), and 2° having a LEG-FOOT-polysemy like Irish (*cos*), which holds only for southern dialects, but not for German *tout court* (strangely enough, the striking example Russ. *nogá* 'leg; foot' is not mentioned in this context). Thus, data will have to be checked by future research, and, above all, similar investigations into other important engynomic domains would be desirable.

The purely engynomic universals just mentioned are not to be confused with those universals concerning taxonomic relations w i t h i n an engynomy (cf. Brown 1976: 405; Andersen 1978: 352):

⑤ Labeling of LEG (+FOOT) presupposes a separate term for ARM (+HAND).
⑥ If both HAND and FOOT are labeled, they are labeled differently (in contrast to other symmetrical parts of upper and lower body).

3.3.3. Levels of depth

The different levels of abstraction we can distinguish in the taxonomic dimension (cf. 3.2.3.) seem to have in the engynomic dimension as a kind of analogon the so called 'levels of depth', especially in partonomies. But the analogy is rather limited. Whereas we can face the question of taxonomic levels of abstraction as a general problem independent of the taxonomic field under examination, the quality and the number of levels of depth seems to depend entirely on the specific engynomic (partonomic) domain considered.

Once again, this has been systematically and cross-linguistically exemplified for body-part terminology (cf. for the following: Liston 1972; Brown 1976; Andersen 1978; as for the reliability of the data used, cf. 3.3.2.). It could be shown here that, just like taxonomic levels of abstraction, partonomic levels of depth, together with salience effects, impinge upon motivational aspects of lexical typology (cf. 4.3.):

① All immediate parts of the whole (BODY) are usually expressed through simple (or at least opaque) lexical items: the universally labeled HEAD and ARM (+HAND) (with the one exception Finn. *kasivarsi*, literally 'hand handle', containing *käsi* 'hand'); if labeled, also LEG (+FOOT) (cf. 3.3.3., ① and ③).
② The less immediate body parts EYE and MOUTH, as universally labeled (3.3.2., ①), as well as FACE and EAR are usually expressed through simple lexical items.
③ The less immediate body parts HAND and FOOT, if labeled, are usually expressed through simple lexical items.
④ The even less immediate, universally labeled body parts FINGER and TOE, if they are not both endowed with two entirely separate, simple lexical items (e. g. Germ. *Finger/Zehe*; Fr. *doigt/orteil*), are expressed through one lexical element appearing either as a simple lexical item or, especially if contextually necessary, as head of a complex lexical item, containing as modifier an expression for FOOT alone (e. g. Fr. *doigt/doigt de pied*; Span. *dedo/*

dedo (del pie); Srb.-Cr. *prst/prst (na nozi)*) or for HAND and FOOT (e. g. Chin. *shŏuzhĭ/jiăozhĭ*; Huastec *tihaš in k'ubak/tihaš in akan*) – but never for HAND alone. Note that these observations concern the taxonomic organization within an engynomy, just like those made in 3.3.2., ⑤ and ⑥. and so on.

Partonomic levels are by no means universally organized. According to Liston and Andersen, the concept EAR, for instance, shows up expressed by *ninri* at level 3 in Quechua (attached to the higher levels 2 FACE – 1 HEAD – 0 BODY), by *šutšun* at level 2 in Huastec (attached to levels 1 HEAD – 0 BODY), and by *uho* at level 3 in Serbo-Croatian (attached to levels 2 NON-FACE – 1 HEAD – 0 BODY). The concept HAND appears, expressed by *maki* at level 3 in Quechua (attached to the higher levels 2 FINGER TO ELBOW – 1 ARM – 0 BODY), by *k'ubak* at level 3 in Huastec (but this time as a concept parallel to 3 ARM, both being attached to levels 2 BACK – 1 TRUNK – 0 BODY), and only provisionally expressed by *šaka* 'fist' at level 2 in Serbo-Croatian (attached to levels 1 HAND+ARM – 0 BODY). Despite such divergences, "human anatomical partonomies rarely exceed five hierarchical levels in depth [...] and never exceed six hierarchical levels" (Brown 1976: 404).

In view of the existence of languages, however, where one and the same word covers, for instance, ARM and HAND (and/or likewise for LEG and FOOT), we may ask for the criteria permitting us to determine which levels of such a partonomy are really labeled and which are not. Why should we consider, for instance, as Brown does, Russ. *ruká* as a polysemous word labeling ARM as well as HAND (and likewise for *nogá* with respect to LEG and FOOT; cf. language type B of pattern ENGYδ in Figure 14), while he considers (traditional) Swahili *mkono* or *mguu* as monosemic words labeling only ARM+HAND or LEG+FOOT respectively (example already cited above to illustrate type B of pattern ENGYβ in Figure 12)? As Brown (1976: 407, 415) puts it, speakers of a language with the monosemic solution would regard, e. g., FINGERNAIL/TOENAIL as part of ARM/LEG, whereas speakers of a language with the polysemous solution would not (perhaps because they see HAND/FOOT as "connected to" rather than as "part of" ARM/LEG). Certainly these quite hypothetical issues have to be further corroborated.

4. Onomasiological perspective: paradigmatic axis: motivational aspect

Ferdinand de Saussure, the modern exponent of the arbitrariness of the linguistic sign, nevertheless admitted: "Le principe fondamental de l'arbitraire du signe n'empêche pas de distinguer dans chaque langue ce qui est radicalement arbitraire, c'est-à-dire immotivé, de ce qui ne l'est relativement" (1916: 180). In a quasi typological perspective, he distinguishes 'langues lexicologiques', where the non-motivatedness reaches its maximum, from 'langues grammaticales', where it drops to a minimum (op. cit., 183).

Ullmann (1966: 221 f.) considers the existence of both opaque (i. e. non-motivated) and transparent (motivated) words a semantic universal. He further systematizes linguistic motivation by discriminating phonetic motivation (in onomatopoeic words like E. *sizzle*, *boom*, etc.), morphological motivation (in cases of word formation like E. *think|er*, *arm|chair*, etc.), and semantic motivation (in cases of metaphor like E. *bonnet* 'cover of a motor-car engine', *pivot* 'that on which anything depends', etc.). Even though these three types of motivation seem to be of undeniable (lexical-)typological interest, they cannot be considered to be on a par. Note, for instance, that 'morphological motivation' insists on formal properties of words, whereas 'semantic motivation' (in the sense of 'metaphorical motivation') highlights cognitive relations.

4.1. The motivational "square"

To give a more systematic account of motivation, one has to start from the basic constellation represented in Figure 85.17 (cf. also Rettich 1981; Lakoff 1987: 96, 346 f., 448 f., 537–540, and passim): a lexical item L_1 (lexeme, word, idiom) expressing a concept C_1, is motivated with respect to a lexical item L_2 expressing a concept C_2, if there is a cognitively relevant relation between C_1 and C_2, paralleled by a recognizable formal relation between the *signifiants* of L_1 and L_2: e. g. L_1 = E. *bank|er*/L_2 = E. *bank*.

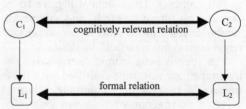

Fig. 85.17: "Motivational square"

The edges of this basic square can undergo different reductions and modifications (see below 4.2., Figure 85.18, 4.3.1., 4.4.2., 4.4.3.).

4.2. Onomatopoeic motivation

In 'primary' onomatopoeia, the square of Figure 85.17 shrinks essentially to the edge L_1-C_1 or rather to L_1-A_1, where A_1 is an acoustic phenomenon (Figure 85.18). Disregarding for the moment the content of the brackets, we can say that L_1 is directly connected with A_1 by a relation of phonological similarity (iconicity), as e. g. in E. *to snore* (Bühler 1965: 208, calls this type "erscheinungstreu"; for onomatopoeia in general, cf. French 1976; Jakobson/Waugh 1979: 182 ff.; Groß 1988; Sharp/Warren 1994; Bredin 1996):

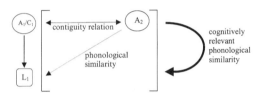

Fig. 85.18: Modified "motivational square" for onomatopoeia

A more complex, but very frequent case can be illustrated by L_1 = E. *cuckoo* that designates a non-acoustic concept C_1 standing in a relation of contiguity to the acoustic phenomenon A_2 [in brackets]. It is only due to this motivation that L_1 is phonologically similar to A_2.

'Secondary' onomatopoeias, like L_1 = Ital. *piccolo*, that do not designate an acoustic phenomenon, but a concept C_1 belonging to another perceptual domain can be explained in two different ways: either like *snore* (assuming an immediate synesthetic similarity relation between L_1 and C_1; Bühler, loc. cit., calls this type "relationstreu" or "gestalttreu") or like *cuckoo* (claiming that speakers designate C_1 by choosing a lexical item L_1 phonetically similar to an imaginary acoustic phenomenon A_2 [in brackets], which is in turn contiguous to C_1: small objects, for instance, are supposed to utter high-pitched sounds like [i]; cf. Pesot 1980: 15).

It is well-known that despite divergences and arbitrary choices in detail (cf. Saussure 1916, 101 f.) there are often clear phonetic "family resemblances" between onomatopoeias in different languages (cf. Ullmann 1966: 224–226): e. g. E. *to snore*, Fr. *ronfler*, Span. *roncar*, Ital. *russare*, Germ. *schnarchen*, Russ. *chrapet'*, Mod.Gr. *ruxalízo*, Hung. *horkolni*, Turk. *horlamak*, Arab. *šaxara*, etc. Even in secondary onomatopoeias, we observe amazing parallels, due probably to converging gestalt perception: e. g. E. *little*, Fr. *petit*, Span. *pequeño*, Ital. *piccolo*, Germ. *klein*, Mod.Gr. *mikrós*, Hung. *kis, kicsi*, Turk. *küçük*, Arab. *saγīr*, Chin. *xiǎo*, etc. (but cf. also E. *small*, Russ. *mal'en'kij*).

It is open to argument whether the frequency of (primary or secondary) onomatopoeias can be a criterion of lexical-typological characterization. In comparison to German and English, French is said to be poor in onomatopoeic words, but other Romance languages seem to be even poorer (cf. Bally 1965: §§ 197 ff., 568; Ullmann 1969: 131; Albrecht 1970: 16, 118–123). In Tamil, "onomatopoeic words [...] are so numerous [...] that they fill an entire dictionary" (Steever 1987: 743). Yoruba displays particularly interesting devices for building up secondary onomatopoeias, especially through reduplication (cf. Pulleyblank 1987: 981 f.).

A more systematic contrastive investigation into a larger language sample is still desirable.

4.3. A three-dimensional model of linguistic motivation

Starting from our basic motivational "square" in Figure 85.17, we have to specify the formal as well as the cognitive relations involved in order to get typologically relevant parameters.

4.3.1. The formal dimension of motivation (transparency)

We can describe the relation between the *signifiants* of L_1 and L_2 in terms of formal contiguity as well as formal similarity. Formal contiguity is here to be understood as a relation of part (L_2) to whole (L_1). This kind of formal contiguity presupposes, in turn, some kind of formal similarity − going in the ideal case until total identity − between L_2 and the corresponding portion of the *signifiant* of L_1, since total formal dissimilarity (as e. g. between L_1 = E. *dairy* and L_2 = *milk*) produces total opacity. There are different types of formal (part-whole) contiguity between L_1 and L_2, among others:

(a) idioms, as e. g. L_1 = E. *to lend a [helping] hand*;

(b) compounds, as e. g. L_1 = E. *post-card*, or lexicalized syntagms, as e. g. L_1 = E. *red wine* (cf. Gévaudan 1999);
(c) derivatives, as e. g. L_1 = E. *bank|er*;
(d) grammatical category alternation, as e. g. L_1 = E. *to shade*;
(e) polysemy, as e. g. in E. *jet* 'nozzle, spout, pipe' and 'stream of water, gas, etc.'.

Derivatives (c) correspond to the basic situation represented in Figure 85.17, where L_2 (e. g. *bank*) constitutes only one, albeit central, part of the whole L_1 (*bank|er*).

On the one hand, this situation can become more complex, when L_2 is duplicated. E.g., in compounds (b) like L_1 *post-card* with L_{21} *card* and L_{22} *post*, each L_2 part covers a considerably smaller portion of L_1 (and similarly for lexicalized syntagms like L_1 *red wine*, with L_{21} *wine* and L_{22} *red*). The same holds for idioms (a), where this is even applied recursively: e. g. first L_1 *helping hand*, with L_{21} *hand* L_{22} and *helping*, and, second, L_1' *to lend a helping hand*, with L_{21}' *to lend* and L_{22}' *a helping hand*.

On the other hand, the basic situation of Figure 85.17 can be radicalized, as in grammatical category alternations (d): e. g. L_1 *to shade* with L_2 *shade*, where the "part" L_2 is even congruent with the "whole" L_1 and where L_2 is very similar to L_1, though not totally identical (notwithstanding the identity in external shape, there is a difference in grammatical category: L_1 = verb/L_2 = noun; besides word class alternation, there also exist, for instance, number alternation and, in languages other than English, gender alternation: see below 4.4.5.).

Ultimately, the most radical − and simple − solution is polysemy (e) as in *jet*, which can be interpreted as if the edge $L_1 - L_2$ in Figure 85.17 has shrunk to a vertex $L_{1=2}$ corresponding to a single lexical expression for both C_1 and C_2 (which are cognitively related to each other). In a certain sense, the aspect of transparency here becomes trivial, because we have the extreme case of part-whole identity $L_1 = L_2$ and at the same time maximal similarity, i. e. identity of L_1 and L_2.

The formal types of relations discussed in this section correspond to the vertical dimension in Table 85.6. The first line labeled 'formal identity' (00−01 etc.) represents the case $L_{1=2}$, i.e. polysemy. The above list (a)−(e) is far from being complete, since there are many other formal-motivational devices existing in the world's languages (see below 4.4.1.). But despite formal differences in detail, all the relevant lexical devices can supposedly be assigned to positions on the universal continuum that goes from polysemy to relatively complex lexical items such as compounds or idioms (cf. also Figure 85.19).

4.3.2. The cognitive dimension of motivation

As to the relation $C_1 - C_2$ in Figure 85.17, we can specify it in terms of the cognitive-associative relations already mentioned in section 2. and completed in 3.1. Before presenting the entire cross-classification of the formal and the cognitive relations in Table 85.6 below, the cognitive relations are illustrated in Table 85.5, in order to save space, only by (English) examples of the formal types of polysemy (□ 00−01 − etc.) and of suffixation (□ 80−81 − etc.).

The cognitive relations listed in Table 85.5 are necessarily universal, and together with the types of formal relations discussed in 4.3.1, they yield a typologically relevant cross-classification, as represented in Table 85.6, where the cognitive relations correspond to the horizontal dimension (cf. Koch, P., 2000; this is the synchronic adaptation of a systematics originally developed for diachronic lexicology; for the overall systematics and the underlying cognitive relations, cf. Blank 1996; 1997: 157−344; 1998; 2001; in press a and b; Koch 1994; 1996; 1999a; 2001a and b; Gévaudan 1999; in press; cf. also Gauger 1971: 60−134; Guilbert 1975; Schifko 1979).

On the basis of Table 85.6, Ullmann's distinction between 'morphological' and 'semantic' motivation turns out to correspond not to a clear-cut opposition between disjunct motivational devices, but to two cross-classified dimensions of the motivation problem in general: vertical axis = formal 'morphological' dimension (4.3.1.) and horizontal axis = cognitive 'semantic' dimension (4.3.2.).

Note that, as far as the formal relation of polysemy is concerned, there are inevitable intersections with the hierarchical aspect already considered: □ 04/05 (taxonomic super-/subordination) represents the phenomenon of vertical polysemy discussed in 3.2.1., pattern ΤΑΧΟδ (type E. *man* or Germ. *kochen*); □ 01 (contiguity) represents all the phenomena of metonymic polysemy discussed in 3.3.1. (Figures 85.13, 85.14, and 85.16, always type B; Table 85.4, types B and C).

It goes without saying that in the complex types of motivation like composition or idi-

Table 85.5: Cognitive relations, illustrated by polysemy and suffixation

cognitive relation	L_1	C_1	square □ in Table 85.6	L_2	C_2	formal relation
conceptual identity	logically incompatible ...		00	... with polysemy		polysemy
	E. *freedom*	STATE OF BEING FREE	80	*free*	STATE OF BEING FREE	suffixation
contiguity	E. *jet*	NOZZLE, SPOUT	01	*jet* = L_1	STREAM OF WATER, GAS ...	polysemy
	E. *banker*	ONE WHO KEEPS ESTABLISHMENT C_2	81	*bank*	ESTABLISHMT. FOR CUSTODY OF MONEY	suffixation
metaphorical similarity	E. *to grasp*	TO COMPREHEND	02	*to grasp* = L_1	TO SEIZE AND HOLD	polysemy
	E. *midget*	VERY SMALL PERSON	82	*midge*	GNAT-LIKE FLY	suffixation
co-taxonomic similarity	E. *fir*	PINE	03	*fir* = L_1	ABIES	polysemy
	E. *bullock*	CASTRATED MALE OF OX	83	*bull*	UNCASTRATED MALE OF OX	suffixation
taxonomic super-ordination	E. *man*	HUMAN BEING	04	*man* = L_1	MALE HUMAN BEING	polysemy
	?	?	84	?	?	suffixation
taxonomic sub-ordination	E. *man*	MALE HUMAN BEING	05	*man* = L_1	HUMAN BEING	polysemy
	E. *booklet*	LITTE C_2	85	*book*	MAJOR BOUND PUBLICATION	suffixation
co-taxonomic contrast	E. *bad* (slang)	EXCELLENT	06	*bad* = L_1	BAD	polysemy
	E. *uncertain*	NOT CERTAIN	86	*certain*	CERTAIN	suffixation
A very rare eighth type of cognitive relation, conceptual or antiphrastic contrast (cf. Blank 1997, 220-225), is neglected here						

oms (cf. 4.3.1.) L_2 and the formal relations, but also C_2 and the cognitive relations, are duplicated, as e. g. in E. L_1 *coffee break* / C_1 BREAK FOR HAVING COFFEE with L_{21} *break* / C_{21} SPELL OF RECREATION and L_{22} *coffee* / C_{22} DRINK MADE FROM POWDER OF COFFEE-BEANS, where the head L_{21}/C_{21} corresponds to square 105 and the modifier L_{22}/C_{22} to □ 101 in Table 85.6.

4.3.3. The stratificational dimension of motivation

Lexical borrowing is an omnipresent diachronic process in all languages (cf. Hock 1991: 380−425; Trask 1996: 17−30; Campbell 1998: 57−78; for a comprehensive classification that can be mapped onto Table 85.6: Kiesler 1993). As a result, the lexicon of any language displays an internal stratification as to the origin of its lexical material. This 'stratificational' aspect (stratum 1 vs. stratum 2 and so on) corresponds to the front-back dimension in Table 85.6. On the synchronic level and in the present context, this aspect is relevant only inasmuch as determinate lexical items are "felt" as belonging to different strata of the lexicon. Typological implications of the stratificational dimension will become clear in 4.4.3.

4.4. Possible typological applications

The lexical-typological relevance of the motivational grid in Table 85.6 can be illustrated by a choice of possible applications.

4.4.1. Inventory of formal relations

Whereas the horizontal dimension in Table 85.6 constitutes a closed set of universal cognitive relations, the vertical dimension has to account for the great variety of morpholexical devices fulfilling lexical motivation tasks in the world's languages. In the present open-ended version of Table 85.6, this variety is already adumbrated. Besides the universal phenomenon of polysemy (= formal identity), the list contains, first, the current devices of average European languages (present, though, even in other language types): number alternation (□ 30−31−etc.), word class alternation (□ 70−71−etc.; but see below), suffixation (□ 80−81 etc.), prefixation (□ 90−91− etc.), composition (□ 100−101−etc.), lexi-

Table 85.6: Linguistic motivation – a tree-dimensional grid
(the numbers 00, 01, 02, etc., 10, 11, 12, etc. etc. are purely arbitrary and only serve as means for identifying the different squares that are referred to by □ + number in the following)

stratum n →	absence of motivation	motivation	conceptual identity	contiguity	metaphorical similarity	taxonomic similarity
stratum 1		formal identity	00	01	02	03

		conceptual identity	contiguity	metaphorical similarity	taxonomic similarity	taxonomic superordination	taxonomic subordination	co-taxonomic contrast
absence of motivation	motivation							
	formal identity	00	01	02	03	04	05	06
	tone alternation	10	11	12	13	14	15	16
	reduplication	20	21	22	23	24	25	26
	number alternation	30	31	32	33	34	35	36
	gender alternation	40	41	42	43	44	45	46
	voice alternation	50	51	52	53	54	55	56
	stem alternation	60	61	62	63	64	65	66
	word-class flexibility/alternation	70	71	72	73	74	75	76
	suffixation	80	81	82	83	84	85	86
	prefixation	90	91	92	93	94	95	96
	composition	100	101	102	103	104	105	106
	serial verb	110	111	112	113	114	115	116
	lexical. syntagm	120	121	122	123	124	125	126
	idiom	130	131	132	133	134	135	136
	...	...	...	...	...	...	...	...
	...	...	...	...	...	...	...	...

calized syntagms (□ 120−121−etc.), and idioms (□ 130−131−etc.). The list contains, second, less current (or less obvious) devices of average European languages: e. g. gender alternation (□ 40−41−etc.; see below 4.4.5.); voice alternation (□ 50−51−etc.; e. g. Anc.Gr. L_1 *gameîsthai* / C_1 TO MARRY (AGENT = BRIDE) with L_2 *gameîn* / C_2 TO MARRY (AGENT = BRIDEGROOM), example corresponding to □ 41, because involving different perspectives within one frame). The list contains, third, devices typical of certain non-European languages: tone alternation (□ 10−11−etc.; e. g. Lahu (Tibeto-Burman) L_1 *cā* / C_1 TO FEED with respect to L_2 *câ* / C_2 TO EAT, example corresponding to □ 11); reduplication (□ 20−21−etc.; e. g. Yoruba L_1 *lílọ* (deverbal nominal form) with L_2 *lọ* (verb) / $C_1 = C_2$ = ACTION OF GO, corresponding to □ 20); stem alternation (□ 60−61−etc.; e. g. Arab. L_1 *ʾatˤama* (stem IV) / C_1 TO FEED with L_2 *taˤima* (stem I) / C_2 TO TASTE, TRY, corresponding to □ 61); serial verb (□ 110−111−etc.; e. g. Yoruba L_1 *gbé ... wá* / C_1 TO BRING with L_{21} *gbé* / C_{21} TO CARRY and L_{22} *wá* / C_{22} TO COME, where both components correspond to □ 111). But the open list of formal devices in Table 85.6 still has to be completed in order to have an inventory of all the formal devices fulfilling lexical motivation tasks.

In addition, the typologically different shapings of the very general categories appearing in the vertical dimension of Table 85.6 would have to be worked out, as a few examples will show. □ 70−71−etc. comprise word-class flexibility of multifunctional lexemes in languages without inflexion (e. g. Chin. *shàng* 'upper', 'to mount', and 'on'; Hait. Creole *chita* 'to sit down', 'the sitting', and 'stagnant') as well as competing word-class alternation devices in languages with rich inflexion: e. g. alternation through replacement of word-class specific bound grammemes as in Ital. *invit*o 'invitation' with respect to *invit*are 'to invite' (□ 71) vs. alternation with unchanged word-class specific bound grammemes as in Ital. *(l')avere* 'credit' with respect to *avere* 'to have' (□ 71) (English is rather near the word-class flexible type: e. g. *open* 'not closed', 'make/became open', and 'open air, space'; cf. also Vogel 1996). − Phrasal verbs as E. *to go up* could be associated to idioms (□ 130−131−etc.), but in some languages they optionally look like a kind of prefixation (□ 90−91−etc.): cf. Germ. *wenn er ihn herüber|lockt* 'if he lures him to come over', but: *er lockt ihn herüber* 'he lures him to come over'; Hung. *elfutott*, but also *futott el* 's/he ran away'. − Lexicalized syntagms (□ 120−121−etc.) comprise typically Romance prepositional phrases as Fr. *livre de poche* 'paperback' (C_{21} BOOK = □ 105; C_{22} POCKET = □ 101) as well as, for instance, Persian *ezāfe* constructions (e. g. Pers. *kise-ye pul* 'purse': C_{21} BAG = □ 105; C_{22} MONEY = □ 101). − Besides the widespread binominal compounds such as E. *coffee break* or Fr. *pause café* (differing only by the opposite modifier-head order), the formal type 'composition' (□ 100−101−etc.) also includes, among others, the typically Romance verb-noun-compounds (e. g. Fr. *ouvre-boîte*, Span. *abre|latas* etc. 'tin opener': cf. for alternative analyses within the framework of Table 85.6: Blank 1998: 21; Gévaudan 1999: 22).

4.4.2. Non-motivatedness, explicitness of transparency and preferences for formal types of motivation

A rather traditional issue is the study of language specific preferences (or non-preferences) for motivation and, within motivation, for different formal types of transparency relations $L_1−L_2$, independently of underlying cognitive relations: "The proportion of opaque and transparent terms, and the relative frequency of the various forms of motivation, may provide valuable criteria for linguistic typology" (Ullmann 1966: 222; for what follows, cf. op. cit., 222−224, 228; Ullmann 1953; 1969: 127−131, 316; Bally 1965: 341−359; Skalička 1965: 155 f.; Malblanc 1968; Vinay/Darbelnet 1964; Schepping 1985: 189; a critical survey in Blumenthal 1997: 107−111). Composition, for instance, is present in principle in Germanic as well as in Romance languages: e. g. E. *sleeping car* and Germ. *Schlaf|wagen* as well as Fr. *wagon-lit*, Span. *coche cama*, or Ital. *vagone letto* (□ 101 (modifier) + 105 (head) in Table 85.6, in Romance typically, though not generally, opposite order; cf. also the especially Romance verb-noun compound mentioned in 4.4.1.). Nevertheless, it has been stressed frequently enough that German possesses many motivated words (compounds or at least derivatives), whose French equivalents display no synchronic motivation at all or less motivation, whereas other Romance languages and English occupy a somewhat intermediate position: e. g. Germ. *Kaffee|kanne* or E. *coffee|pot* (□ 101 (modifier) + 105 (head)) vs. Fr. *cafet|ière*, Span. *cafet|era*, Ital. *caffett|iera*, or Rum. *cafetieră* (□ 81); Germ. *Finger|hut* (□ 101 (modifier) + 105 (head)) vs. Span. *de|dal*, Ital. *dit|ale*, or Rum. *deget|ar* (□ 81) vs. E. *thimble*, Fr. *dé* (no synchronic motivation); cf. also examples from other languages: Finn. *ava|in* 'key' (□ 81), Arab. *mi|ftāḥun* 'key', Hausa *má|buḋ|i* 'key' (□ 91), derived respectively from Finn. *avata*, Arab. *fataḥa*, Hausa *buḋa*, all 'to close' or 'to open', vs. E. *key*, Fr. *clé*, Span. *llave*, Ital. *chiave*, or Rum. *cheie* (no motivation; for Germ. *Schlüssel*, see 4.4.3. below). On the other hand, French (and other Romance languages, but sometimes also English), makes use of even more explicit formal devices than German: e. g. Fr. *agence de voyage*, Sp. *agencia de viajes*, or Ital. *agenzia di viaggi* (□ 125 (head) + 121 (modifier)) vs. E. *travel agency* or Germ. *Reise|büro* (□ 101 (modifier) + 105 (head)); Fr. *année universitaire*, Sp. *año académico*, Ital. *anno accademico*, or E. *academic year* (□ 125 (head) + 121 (modifier), in English opposite order) vs. Germ. *Studien|jahr* (□ 101 (modifier) + 105 (head)).

These considerations involve the factors of formal (part-whole) contiguity and formal similarity already touched in 4.3.1. We can establish a continuum of degrees of 'explicitness' within transparency, going from absence of motivation via total formal identity (polysemy; cf. also 6.1.) and formal part-whole identity with more or less formal dissimilarity of the wholes (tone alternation, category alternation) to more and more marked part-whole differentiation (derivation, composition, idioms):

In addition to degrees of explicitness, based on formal part-whole contiguities and formal similarity between whole lexical items (Figure 85.19), we have to specify degrees of congruence within transparency, based on degrees of formal similarity between parts of

− ← ──────────────────────────────────── → +

no motivation/ transparency	polysemy = formal identity	tone alternation	number gender voice alternation	reduplication stem alternation	derivation: suffixation prefixation	composition serial verb	lexicalized syntagm	idiom
∅	01-02-...	10-11-...	30-31-...	20-21-...	80-81-...	100-101-...	120-121-	130-131-
			40-41-...	60-61-...	90-91-...	110-111-...	...	...
			50-51-...					

word class flexibility/alternation

70-71-...

Fig. 85.19: Degrees of explicitness in transparency (numbers referring to squares □ in Table 85.6)

To get valuable typological insights, contrastive observations concerning motivational explicitness would have to be consolidated by large scale investigations broadened in at least two directions: 1° considering a large range of concepts of different domains, and 2° investigating a greater sample of languages. As for point 2°, we can expect typical preferences (and quasi-equivalences) according to different phonological, morphological or syntactic language types, as for instance: tone alternation in tone languages vs. polysemy, voice alternation, derivation, etc. in other languages; gender alternation in languages with extensive gender systems (s. below 4.4.5.) vs. polysemy, nominal derivation, etc. in other languages; stem alternation in Semitic languages vs. polysemy, voice alternation, derivation, etc. in other languages; serial verbs in languages like Hindi, Yoruba, Chinese, Creoles, etc. vs. verbal derivation etc. in other languages, and so on.

4.4.3. Congruence and stratification

The existence of a cognitive relation between two concepts C_1 and C_2 does by no means imply that there actually is an observable formal relation L_1-L_2. In fact, the edge corresponding to the latter relation in Figure 85.17 can be totally lacking, as, for instance, in E. L_1 *journey* / L_2 *to travel* (C_1-C_2 = identity), E. L_1 *dairy* / L_2 *milk*, already cited in 4.3.1. (C_1-C_2 = contiguity), or E. L_1 *queen* / L_2 *king* (C_1-C_2 = taxonomic similarity). In such cases, there is no explicit formal relation at all between L_1 and L_2, i.e. total opacity.

lexical items (cf. the scale of 'diagrammaticity' presented in Dressler 1985: 130 f.). Since congruence presupposes at least minimal explicitness (i.e., polysemy which necessarily achieves maximal congruence), the two continua are organized in the following way:

There are combinations of different degrees of explicitness with different degrees of congruence. A word like Germ. L_1 *Schlüssel* C_1 KEY, belonging theoretically into □ 81 in Table 85.6, has medium explicitness, but clearly reduced congruence with respect to L_2 *schließen* C_2 TO CLOSE (as opposed to totally non-explicit E. *key* on the one hand and to medium-explicit and congruent Hausa *mábuḍi* on the other hand: cf. 4.4.2). Cases of lexical suppletion correspond to non-congruence: e.g. Fr. L_1 *vitesse* C_1 QUALITY OF BEING FAST, medium-explicit (□ 80), but non-congruent in relation to L_2 *rapide* $C_{1=2}$ QUALITY OF BEING FAST (as opposed to totally non-explicit E. L_1 *speed* in relation to L_2 *fast* on the one hand and to medium-explicit and congruent Ital. L_1 *velocità* in relation to L_2 *veloce* on the other hand).

The presence of more or less congruent motivated lexical items in a given language is an important feature for lexical typology. Languages with strong allomorphic tendencies necessarily reduce lexical congruence: e.g. Anc.Gr. L_1 *pístis* C_1 FAITH (□ 80) in relation to L_2 *peíthesthai* C_1 TO TRUST. But as can be seen from the example of root inflection, congruence depends not only on formal similarity, but also on the vitality of the morph(on)ological patterns concerned. In

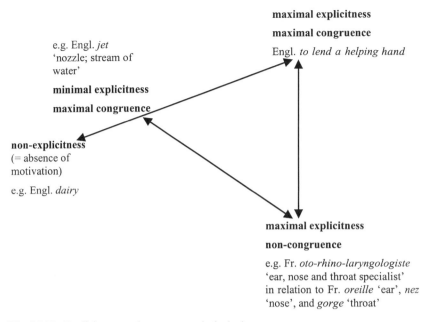

Fig. 85.20: Explicitness and congruence in lexical transparency

Arabic, with its full-fledged root-and-pattern system, cases of root inflection, like L_1 *qāri'* C_1 READER □ 71 in relation to L_2 *qara'a* C_1 TO READ, are highly regular and, hence, transparent; in German, they are still supported by – limited – analogical series (e. g. L_1 *Flug* C_1 FLIGHT □ 70 with L_2 *fliegen* C_1 TO FLY; cf. *Schub*, *Guss*, *Genuss*, etc.), and in English much less so (e. g. L_1 *song* □ 70/71 with L_2 *to sing*).

Note that reduced formal congruence absolutely has to be distinguished from obscured cognitive motivation resulting from semantic change either in L_1 or in L_2 (e. g. Ital. L_1 *calzolaio* C_1 SHOEMAKER with L_2 *calza* C_2 SHOE, but today C_2' STOCKING, C_2 being expressed now by *scarpa*). Since semantic change is omnipresent in all languages, these facts hardly yield a basis for synchronic lexical typology.

On the contrary, a fundamental factor involved in motivational congruence is the third, stratificational dimension of the onomasiological grid in Table 85.6. At first sight, the non-autochthonous character (and origin) of lexical items is a purely diachronic issue. On the synchronic level, these facts seem to be relevant only inasmuch as in a given language, certain components of the lexicon keep a "foreign" aspect, due to non-autochthonous phonological shape, accentuation, inflection, etc. (e. g. latinisms, grecisms, gallicisms, anglicisms, etc. in Modern German; gallicisms, anglicisms, etc. in Spanish, Italian etc.; but even in English, which easily integrates foreign lexical elements, there are the so-called 'hard words'). From the perspective of lexical motivation, however, it is much less the "foreign" aspect of a lexical item than, more generally, the degree of motivational congruence that counts. So, the problem arises in every language containing different strata in its lexicon, even if these are perfectly integrated in the synchronic consciousness of the speakers, as, e. g., Germanic, French, and Latin elements in English; inherited and 'learned' Latin elements in all the Romance languages; Romance, Slavonic, and other strata in Rumanian; Turkic and Arabic elements in Turkish; Iranian and Arabic elements in Persian; *wago* (Japanese) and *kango* (Sino-Japanese) in Japanese; etc. For our purpose, then, it will be sufficient to distinguish merely different 'strata' in the third dimension of Table 85.6 without specifying their (non-)autochthonous status. If the lexicon of a given language contains (at least) two deeply rooted different strata that affect motivation processes in the lexicon, it can be assigned to a "two-storeyed" language type ("langue à deux étages"; cf. Gauger 1971: 168; Ullmann 1966: 223 f.; 1969: 128–131; Albrecht 1970: 28–30. 215–220; Jespersen 1905: 46, 132; Blumenthal 1997: 108; see also above the end of 3.2.3.). In Japanese, for instance, L_1 *suibun* C_1 MOISTURE contains a modifier L_{22} *sui* (□ 101) borrowed from Chin. *shui* WATER and totally non-congruent with Japanese *mizu* C_{22} (COLD) WATER. Similarly, Turk. L_1 *inşaat* C_1 CONSTRUCTION WORK (originating from Arab. *inšāāt*) is non-congruent with L_2 *kurmak* C_2 TO BUILD. Due to the massive presence of — originally learned — latinisms in the lexicon, Romance languages as well as English belong to a similar lexical language type: cf. e. g. L_1 Fr. *urbain* Span. *urbano* Ital. *urbano* E. *urbain* C_1 RELATED TO THE TOWN/CITY □ 81 (borrowed from Lat. *urbanus*), lacking any congruence with respect to Fr. *ville* Span. *ciudad* Ital. *città* E. *town, city* C_2 TOWN/CITY. Unlike in English, the degree of congruence in Romance languages often depends on the relative impact of sound change on present-day *signifiants*, which is particularly drastic in French: cf., e. g., L_1 Fr. *maturité* C_1 RIPENESS/MATURITY □ 80 (borrowed from Lat. *maturitas*), showing only weak congruence with respect to Fr. *mûr* C_2 RIPE/MATURE vs. L_1 Span. *madurez* Ital. *maturità* with L_2 Span. *maduro* Ital. *maturo*.

In this way, the languages just cited are opposed to a language type favouring motivational relations within one and the same stratum of the lexicon: cf., e. g., Finn. *laki* 'law', *laillinen* 'legal', *laillisuus* 'legality', etc.; Hung. *tudomány* 'science', *tudományos* 'scientific', *tudományosság* 'scientific character', etc. (cf. Sauvageot 1964, 63–66).

4.4.4. From cognitive to formal relations

One of the heuristic assets of the three-dimensional grid in Table 85.6 for lexical typology is the possibility of observing the assignment of formal relations to cognitive relations and vice versa. Starting from a specific cognitive relation between two given (types of) concepts C_1-C_2, we can distinguish different lexical types according to the formal relation L_1-L_2 expressing C_1-C_2 (for the opposite direction see below 4.4.5.). A striking example of the interlingual cognitive equivalence of different formal motivation devices, akin to Fr. *bois* (Table 85.4, language type B FOREST/WOODS – WOOD, characterized by a metonymic polysemy = □ 01 in Table 85.6), is, cognitively speaking, the English solution *woods – wood*, as based on contiguity. It is quite analogous, except that it is realized by number alternation on the formal level (□ 31).

On a large scale, equivalences of this kind can be illustrated here by the cognitive contiguity relation between TREE and FRUIT concepts (cf. Koch 1999c). If the FRUIT concept (C_2) is more salient than the TREE concept (C_1), it is the expression for the latter, L_1, that is almost universally motivated by the expression for the former, L_2 (e. g. E. L_1 *pear-tree* with L_{22} *pear*), or at least, the motivation between the two lexical items is reciprocal (e. g. Ital. *pera* and *pero*). In a sample of 26 European and non-European languages, we find for a salient FRUIT concept C_2, like PEAR, DATE, or MANGO, the following formal types of transparency for expressing the contiguous TREE concept C_1.

This example shows that the different formal realization of one and the same cognitive relation is an interesting onomasiological parameter for lexical typology (having more space, we could visualize the obvious arealtypological clusters in a map).

4.4.5. From formal to cognitive relations

Conversely, we can also start from a specific formal relation L_1-L_2 and determine the different cognitive relations C_1-C_2 that can be expressed through L_1-L_2 in different languages. This can be illustrated here by the formal relation of gender alternation (taking 'gender' not in the narrow sense typical, e. g., of Indo-European and Semitic languages, but including extensive noun class systems found in the majority of Niger-Congo languages; cf. Corbett 1991; Aikhenvald 2000). It is obvious that Swahili, for instance, employs gender (i. e. noun-class) alternation for expressing in a productive way a wide range of cognitive relations (the FRUIT–TREE programme with alternation between classes 3/4 and 5/6, exemplified in Table 85.7, type B, being only one of the examples for the relation of contiguity).

As Table 85.8 shows, Italian, too, surprisingly exploits gender alternation in a somewhat similar way (cf. Koch, P., 2000: 107). To be sure, Italian gender alternation is limited to bilateral correspondences within a two-gender system, whereas Swahili displays multilateral correspondences between its numerous noun classes, and, moreover, gender alternation is less productive in Italian than in Swahili. Nevertheless, even in Italian it still functions as a motivational device with possible extensions to new applications (e. g. to new, exotic fruits like BANANA, in Table 85.8; or, for instance, in *pillolo* PILL FOR MEN in relation to *pillola* PILL FOR WOMEN). From the

Table 85.7: Transparency types for the contiguity relation C_1 TREE–C_2 FRUIT

		C_1 PEAR-TREE (et al.)	C_2/C_{22} PEAR (et al.)
type A	metonymic **polysemy** (□ 01)	Sard.I *pira* Russ. *gruša* Czech *hruška*	*pira* *gruša* *hruška*
type B	gender alternation* (□ 41)	Ital. *pero*, m. Rum. *păr*, m. Lat. *pirum*, n. Anc.Gr. *ápion*, n. Swah. *mtende*, class 3/4 [DATE-PALM]	*pera*, f. *pară*, f. *pirus*, f. *ápios*, f. *tende*, class 5/6 [DATE]
type C	suffixation (□ 81)	Fr. *poirier* Span. *peral** Port. *pereira* Cat. *perer(a)* Czech II *hruše* Mod.Gr. *axlaðjá, apiðjá*	*poire* *pera* *pera* *pera* *hruška* *axláði, apíði*
type D	composition (□ 101)	**modifier + head:** E. *pear-tree* Germ. *Birnbaum* Swed. *päronträd* Ndl. *pereboom* Hung. *körtefa* Jap. *nashinoki* Chin. *lí shù* **head + modifier:** Breton. *gwez-pér* Guadel.-Creole *pyé-mango* [MANGO TREE]	*pear* *Birne* *päron* *peer* *körte* *nashi* *lí* *pér* *mango* [MANGO]
type E	lexicalized syntagm (□ 121)	**modifier + head:** Turk. *armut ağaci* **head + modifier:** Sard. II *arbore de pira* Pers. *deraxt-e golābi* Arab. *šağara al-kummaθrai*	*armut* *pira* *golābi* *kummaθrai*

* But cf. Span. L₁ *manzano* with L₂ *manzana* (= type B)

		C_1 PEAR	C_2 PEAR TREE
Special case with opposite motivation:			
	suffixation (□ 81)	Pol. *gruszka*	*grusza*

typological point of view, this issue is highly relevant. The world's languages can be subdivided into those who possess a morphological gender/noun-class system and those who do not (such as, e. g., English, Persian, Turkish, Chinese, Japanese etc.; cf. Aikhenvald 2000: 77–80). The former group can, in turn, be subdivided into a subgroup that makes use of gender alternation as a device for lexical motivation (as Swahili and other affiliated languages, Italian and other Romance languages like Spanish, etc.) and a subgroup that, although possessing gender (French, German, etc.), does not.

Analogous considerations could be made for all the other formal motivation devices in order to reveal their cognitive "load" in different languages or language types.

Table 85.8: Gender alternation as a formal motivation device: examples from Swahili and Italian

	Swah.	Ital.
contiguity (□ 41)	*mtende*, 3/4 DATE-PALM – *tende* 5/6 DATE *mti*, 3/4 TREE – *kiti*, 7/8 WOODEN STOOL *mkó*, 1/2 DIRTY PERSON – *ukó*, 11/10 DIRTINESS *mzazi*, 1/2 PARENT – *uzazi*, 11/10 BIRTH etc.	*banano* m. BANANA TREE – *banana* f. BANANA *gobbo* m. HUNCHBACK (PERSON) – *gobba* f. HUNCHBACK *canapo* m. ROPE – *canapa* f. HEMP *pendolo* m. PENDULUM – *pendola* f. PENDULUM CLOCK etc.
metaphorical similarity (□ 42)	*mkomo*, 3/4 HAND – *komo*, 5/6 YOUNG WILLOW SHOOT *mkomo*, 3/4 HAND – *ukomo*, 11/10 YOUNG PUMPKIN SHOOT etc.	*foglio* m. SHEET OF PAPER – *foglia* f. LEAF *fronte* m. FRONT – *fronte* f. FOREHEAD *midollo* m. MARROW – *midolla* f. SOFT INNER PART OF BREAD etc.
taxonomic similarity (□ 43)		*pozzo* m. WELL – *pozza* f. PUDDLE *fiasco* m. BIG-BELLIED FLASK – *fiasca* f. FLAT FLASK etc.
taxonomic super-/subordination (□ 44/45)	*mtoto*, 1/2 CHILD – *kitoto*, 7/8 BABY *mlima*, 3/4 MOUNTAIN – *kilima*, 7/8 HILL *udole*, 11/10 FINGER – *kidole*, 7/8 LITTLE FINGER *mtu*, 1/2 MAN – *jitu*, 5/6 GIANT *mto*, 3/4 RIVER – *jito*, 5/6 LARGE RIVER *nyoka*, 9/10 SNAKE – *joka*, 5/6 GIANT BOA/PYTHON etc.	*legno* m. WOOD – *legna* f. FIREWOOD *pezzo* m. PIECE – *pezza* f. PIECE OF CLOTH *tavolo* m. TABLE – *tavola* f. TABLE FOR DINING *fosso* m. DITCH – *fossa* f. PIT etc.

Prima facie, these are semasiological considerations (from form to cognitive relation), but they result from general onomasiological considerations concerning the three-dimensional grid as a whole, and in the final analysis, they yield onomasiological insights about the formal devices that a given language (type) productively exploits for realizing transparency motivated by cognitive connections on the conceptual/perceptual level.

4.4.6. Designation strategies as typological features

The vertical and the horizontal dimension of the onomasiological grid in Table 85.6 also can serve as a measure for designation strategies in different languages with respect to a given (class of) concept(s). In the – restricted – language sample presented in Table 85.9, e.g., we find for the concept MOTORCAR, apart from the absence of motivation (A), essentially two fundamental motivational strategies: taxonomic subordination (C) and contiguity (D, with different subtypes and sub-subtypes), strategy B (taxonomic similarity) being marginal in this sample (diachronically – but no more synchronically – it can be reduced to C). It does not matter that both strategy C and D can be realized by different formal devices (C: □ 05, 105: D: □ 01, 71, 101).

Virtually, the onomasiological grid in Table 85.6 can help us to discover general abstract preferences of designation for given (classes of) concept(s). For example, there seems to be a high probability that the two concepts TO RENT (REAL ESTATE) and TO LET FOR RENT (REAL ESTATE) are expressed in a way that reflects their profound reciprocal cognitive connection: polysemy (□ 01) Fr. *louer*, Span. *alquilar*, Ital. *affittare*, Port. *alugar*, Rum. *a închiria*, Mod.Gr. *enikjázo*, Turk. *kiralamak*; voice alternation (□ 51) Anc.Gr. *misthûsthai* – *misthûn*; stem alternation (□ 61) Arab. *ʾistaʾǧara* (stem X) – *ʾaǧǧara* (stem II) / *ʾāǧǧara* (stem IV); suffixation (□ 81) Swah. *-pangal-kodi* – *-pangishal-kodi-sha*; parallel suffixation derived from some

Table 85.9: Designation strategies and subtypes for the concept MOTORCAR

	designation strategy	L₁ expressing C₁ MOTORCAR		L₂ expressing C₂
A	absence of (synchronic) motivation	Germ. *Auto* Swed. *bil* Hung. *autó* Turk. *oto*		(cf. 4.4.3)
B	taxonomic similarity	Span. *coche*	03	= L₂ *coche* C₂ CARRIAGE
C	taxonomic subordination	E. *car* Fr. *voiture* Port. *carro* Hung. *kocsi* Chin. *qìchē* (head)	05 05 05 05 105	= L₂ *car* C₂ VEHICLE = L₂ *voiture* C₂ VEHICLE = L₂ *carro* C₂ VEHICLE = L₂ *kocsi* C₂ VEHICLE L₂₁ *chē* C₂₁ VEHICLE
D1	contiguity with part	Ital. *macchina* Rum. *maşină* Russ. *mašina* Jap. *kuruma*	01 01 01 01	= L₂ *macchina* C₂ MACHINE = L₂ *maşină* C₂ MACHINE = L₂ *mašina* C₂ MACHINE = L₂ *kuruma* C₂ WHEEL
D2	contiguity with power	Chin. *qìchē* (modifier) Mod. Gr. *aftokínito* (modifier)	101 101	L₂₂ *qì* C₂ STEAM L₂₂ *aftó* C₂ SELF
D3	contiguity with process	Arab. *sajjāra* Mod.Gr. *aftokínito* (head)	71 71	L₂ *sajjār* C₂ IN PERCEPTUAL MOTION L₂₁ *kínito* C₂ MOVED (deriving via 81 from *kinó* TO MOVE)

hypothetical basic form (□ 81) Jap. *kariru − kasu*; prefixation/phrasal verb (□ 91/131) Am. E. *to rent − to rent out*; Swed. *hyra − hyra ut*, Germ. *mieten − vermieten*; serial verb (□ 111) Chin. *zū − chūzū*; idiom (□ 131) Hung. *bérbe venni − bérbe adni* (without motivation: E. *to rent − to let*, Russ. *snimát' − sdavát' vnájem*; and Hung. *(ki)bérelni − kiadni*). Even if the formal motivational devices used may considerably vary in formal details, the underlying cognitive relation is, of course, contiguity in all these cases (two different perspectives within the same frame; cf. Koch 1991: 296f.; 2001b; Blank 1997: 272−275, 393; Waltereit 1998: 76−79).

4.4.7. A heuristic grid

We have to bear in mind that not all the theoretical combinations represented in Table 85.6 are necessarily realized in any of the world's languages. In this sense, Table 85.6 offers an interesting heuristic grid for the search of lexical universals: what are the theoretical combinations that occur in all languages? which are those that do not occur in any language of the world? and why? This can be discussed here only in a highly tentative way with the help of a few examples.

Since polysemy is a universal phenomenon, all the combinations □ 01−02−etc. surely will be found in all languages. In contrast to this, word-class flexibility/alternation is by nature unsuitable for cognitive relations tied to a constant word class (similarity, taxonomic relations, contrast), and it is therefore restricted to the cognitive relations of identity and contiguity: cf. Fr. L₁ *le dîner* C₁ SUPPER □ 70 with L₂ *dîner* C₂ TO TAKE SUPPER; Fr. L₁ *le savoir* C₁ SUM OF WHAT IS KNOWN □ 71 with L₂ *savoir* C₂ TO KNOW; Fr. L₁ *voyager* C₁ TO

TRAVEL □ 70 with L₂ *voyage* C₂ JOURNEY; Fr. L₁ *pomper* C₁ TO PUMP □ 71 with L₂ *pompe* C₂ PUMP. A final example: it would be interesting to explore the range of cognitive relations covered, for instance, by stem alternation. Since the typically three-consonantal Arabic roots seem to be made for seizing conceptual frames (cf. the stimulating remarks in Bühler 1965, 221), it goes without saying that stem alternation can express contiguity relations within frames: e. g. Arab. L₁ *ʔinkasara* (stem VII) C₁ TO BREAK (INCHOATIVE) □ 61 with L₂ *kasara* (stem I) C₁ TO BREAK (CAUSATIVE). At least taxonomic subordination is likewise possible: e. g. Arab. L₁ *kassara* (stem II) C₁ TO SMASH (= a special manner of breaking) □ 65 with L₂ *kasara* (see above).

By examining in this way all the combinations conceived in Table 85.6, we will achieve a better understanding of the possibilities and limitations of human language in expressing concepts through motivational devices.

5. Onomasiological perspective: syntagmatic axis

If paradigmatic lexical typology deals with problems of packaging conceptual material into single lexical items according to hierarchical (3.) and motivational (4.) principles, syntagmatic lexical typology has to cope with the problems that arise from packaging conceptual material into sequences of lexical items.

5.1. Selectional restrictions

The problem of selectional restrictions has been attracting linguists' attention at least since Porzig's discovery of 'wesenhafte Bedeutungsbeziehungen' in 1934. It has been studied within the generative paradigm (Chomsky 1965: 75–100, 106–111; McCawley 1968: 132–135; Bierwisch 1970; also Lehrer 1974: 173–184) as well as in valency theory (Helbig 1969) and in structural semantics (Coseriu 1967; Coseriu/Geckeler 1981: 63). Coseriu has rightly insisted on distinguishing linguistic 'lexical solidarities' from restrictions due to our encyclopedic knowledge. An interesting aspect for lexical typology, however, is the fact that even language-specific selection restrictions typically seem to recur in particular conceptual spheres. Some of these are, for instance, HORSE (3), HAIR (4), and NOSE (5) (cf. also Bally 1965, § 206):

(3) E. *sorrel*, Fr. *alezan*, Span. *alazán*, Ital. *sauro/baio*, Rum. *roib* (HORSE: SORREL)

(4) (a) E. *fair*, Germ. *blond*, Fr. *blond*, Span. *rubio*, Ital. *biondo*, Lat. *falvus*, Mod. Gr. *ksanθós*, Hung. *szőke*, Arab. *ʔašqar* (HUMAN HAIR: FAIR)

(b) Fr. *roux*, Russ. *rýžij* (HUMAN HAIR: RED)

(5) (a) E. *aquiline*, Fr. *aquilin*, Span. *aguileño*, Ital. *adunco*, Rum. *acvilin* (HUMAN NOSE: AQUILINE)

(b) Fr. *camus*, Ital. *camuso* (HUMAN NOSE: SQUAT)

(c) E. *snub* (HUMAN NOSE: SHORT AND TURNED-UP)

As indicated by the dotted lines in Figure 85.1, the syntagmatic problem of selectional restrictions is interwoven with the taxonomic as well as the engynomic hierarchical aspect of the paradigmatic axis. Taxonomically speaking, lexical items for particularly fine-grained concepts (SORREL, FAIR (HAIR), etc.) are selected by virtue of the hierarchy of the selecting concepts (taxonomy: HORSE (3); engynomy: HUMAN HAIR (4), HUMAN NOSE (5)). It is probably not by mere chance that in all these cases there is some connection with the anthropologically fundamental engynomy of BODY PARTS (cf. 3.3.2./3.; even the HORSE taxonomy is subspecified in terms of the body part HAIR).

Müller-Gotama (1992) presents an interesting case of lexical-typological divergence in verb-object collocations with an EFFECTED OBJECT in English, Indonesian, German, Korean, and Russian (Table 85.10). The more specific verb, depending on the taxonomy of EFFECTED OBJECTS, is always acceptable in all five languages (except *kkomay* in Korean), but the possibility of replacing it with an all-purpose verb declines going from English (with a minimal restriction) to Russian (with maximal restrictions). According to Müller-Gotama, this scale of increasing lexical specificity parallels the scale of semantic transparency in grammar in the languages under consideration (as opposed to tendencies of grammaticization).

Indeed, English (but also French) and German seem to differ systematically on the level of 'semantic agreement' (Plank 1984) between verbs and their objects (cf. also König 1996: 49 f.):

(6) (a) *to put on one's glasses*   *mettre ses lunettes*   *die Brille aufsetzen*
    (b) *to put on one's jacket*   *mettre son veston*   *das Jackett anziehen*
    (c) *to put on a tie*   *mettre une cravatte*   *eine Krawatte umbinden*
    (d) *to put on a ring*   *mettre un anneau*   *einen Ring anstecken*

There can be no doubt: "Selektionsbeschränkungen [gehören] unbedingt zu den relevanten Parametern einer 'lexical typology'" (Lang 1996: 348; cf. also Schepping 1985: 190).

5.2. Metataxes

The examples presented in 5.1. have shown interlingual lexical divergences emerging as syntagmatic constraints, without, however, affecting the syntactic categories and functions of the lexical items concerned: the selectional restrictions held between adjective and noun, between verb and object, etc. But lexical typology must also account for divergences involving the packaging of conceptual material into categories and functions within the sentence. From a primarily syntactic perspective, interlingual divergences of this kind have been discussed by Lucien Tesnière under the heading 'metataxis' (Fr. *métataxe*; cf. Koch in press): "Toute langue établit entre les **catégories de la pensée** et les **catégories grammaticales** qui les expriment, certaines correspondances qui lui sont propres. [...] Mais, toutes les langues ne faisant pas forcément appel à la même catégorie grammaticale pour exprimer la même catégorie de la pensée, il en résulte que la traduction d'une langue dans une autre nécessite quelquefois l'appel à une catégorie grammaticale différente. C'est la forme la plus simple de la métataxe" (Tesnière 1959: 284). Even if many metataxes are only of syntactic interest, the cognitive implications discoverable in this quotation foreshadow the possible relevance of metataxes for contrastive lexicology and lexical typology. Indeed, the divergent categorial processing of the conceptual material is an important issue for lexical typology (5.2.1.). Since the verb constitutes at the same time the syntactic pivot and the most complex lexical item of the sentence, the divergent functional organization of its participants is also highly relevant for lexical typology (5.2.2.).

5.2.1. Categorial metataxes

Categorial interlingual divergences with lexical relevance have been described for several conceptual fields and domains: PROPERTY, ASPECT, STATE CHANGE, REALIZATION OF ACTION, ACTION CORRELATING, MOTION, and PART OF SPACE (cf. Talmy 1985; 1991; Lehmann 1990). This will be illustrated here by examples for PROPERTY and MOTION.

Depending on the language type, PROPERTIES are expressed typically through adjectives

Table 85.10: Lexical specificity with EFFECTED OBJECTS

EFFECTED OBJECT	E.	Indon.	Germ.	Kor.	Russ.
	all-purpose verb: *make*	all-purpose verb: *buat*	all-purpose verb: *machen*	all-purpose verb: *mantul*	all-purpose verb not used
DRESS	+/*sew*	+/*jahit*	+/*nähen*	+/(*kkomay*_AFF)	*/*šit'*
BREAD	+/*bake*	+/*panggang*	+/*backen*	+/*kwup*	*/*peč'*
TEA	+/*brew*	+/*masak*	+/*kochen*	*/*kkulhi*	*/*varit'*
ROPE	+/*weave*	+/*tenun*	+/*weben*	+/*cca*	*/*vit'*
NEST	+/*weave*	+/*bangun*	+/*bauen*	+/*tul*	*/*vit'*
ROAD	+/*lay*	+/*bangun*	?/*bauen*	+/*noh*	*/*proložit'*
HOUSE	?/*build*	??/*bangun*	?/*bauen*	*/*cis*	*/*stroit'*

+/ = all-purpose verb possible;   ?/, ??/ = all-purpose verb more or less problematic
*/ = all-purpose verb not permitted;   AFF = usable only with AFFECTED OBJECT

(type A), by stative verbs (type B), or by abstract nouns (type C), respectively (there are also mixed types; cf. in general Dixon 1977):

Table 85.11: Expression of PROPERTIES (after Lehmann 1990, 171)

	type A e. g. English	Type B e. g. Turkana	type C e. g. Tamil
attribute	adjective	relativized stative verb	adjective derived from abstract noun
predicative	adjective + copula	stative verb	abstract noun (or derivative)
noun	abstract noun derived from adjective	abstract noun derived from stative verb	abstract noun

In type B languages, PROPERTY concepts can be attributed only by relativization of the corresponding stative verb (7); in languages of type C, they are attributed, except for very few primary adjectives, by derivation of an adjective from the corresponding abstract noun (8):

(7) Turkana
 e-kìle
 M SG-man(NOM)
 lɔ-a-mɔn-a-n
 REL M SG-3 SG-mean-STAT-SG
 'mean man'

(8) Tamil
 ganam-uḷḷa manusan
 weight-y man
 'heavy man'

Rijkhoff (2000) points out that a language can have a major class of adjectives necessarily characterized by the feature [−Shape] only if it has first order nouns characterized by the feature [+Shape] (singular object nouns, set nouns).

Categorial metataxes often produce a kind of syntactic "recasting" (Fr. *chassé-croisé*). This has been studied for MOTION verbs in French, German, and English at least since Charles Bally ([4]1965: 349 f.; Malblanc 1968: 66−70, 92−94, 161−165; Vinay/Darbelnet 1964: 58, 105−107; Wandruszka 1969: 460−469; Schwarze 1983: 205 f.; Schepping 1985: 191; Blumenthal 1997: 11, 70 f.; in terms of syntactic metataxis: Tesnière 1959: 307−310). Within the cognitive paradigm, Talmy (1985; 1991) describes the structure of a MOTION event-frame as consisting of a FIGURE (the moving object), a MOTION, a PATH, a MANNER, and a GROUND (a point or zone of reference for the moving object). As illustrated in Figure 85.21, we can distinguish, with respect to the central component PATH, two language types: (A) 'satellite-framed' languages that render PATH by a 'satellite', i. e. an adverb, a preposition, a verbal prefix, etc., and (B) 'verb-framed' languages that express PATH through the verb (cf. also König 1996: 48 f.; Ungerer/Schmid 1996: 233−246).

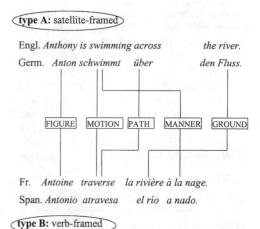

Fig. 85.21: Satellite-framing and verb-framing in a MOTION frame-event (taking up a traditional example from Tesnière 1959: 310; representation after Ungerer/Schmid 1996: 238)

According to Talmy, the satellite-framed type A includes most Indo-European (except Romance) and the Finno-Ugric languages as well as Chinese, Ojibwa, and Warlpiri, whereas the verb-framed type B includes Romance, Semitic, Polynesian, most Bantu, and most Mayan languages as well as Japanese, Tamil, Nez Perce, and Caddo (for Italian as a mixed language, cf. Koch, P., 2000: 108 f.; for Atsugewi as belonging to a third type that conflates FIGURE in the MOTION verb, cf. Talmy 1985: 73 f.). Note that the two types A and B in Figure 85.21 are not totally symmetrical.

In fact, on the cognitive level PATH is indispensable for a MOTION event-frame (except for a few very general verbs like E. *to go*), and on the syntactic level the verb is indispensable for the sentence. So, satellite-framed languages always h a v e to express MOTION and MANNER (conflated in the verb), as well as PATH. In contrast to this, verb-framed languages h a v e to express only MOTION and PATH (conflated in the verb), whereas MANNER is optional. In a strong context (e. g., a very deep river), Fr. *Antoine traverse la rivière*/Span. *Antonio atravesa el río* would be sufficient, and adding the MANNER expression might be rather clumsy (cf. also Slobin 2000). From the taxonomic point of view (3.2.), verb-framed MOTION expressions without MANNER specification belong to a hierarchically higher level, i. e. they are more "abstract" (s. the end of 3.2.3.).

5.2.2. Participant metataxes

Due to the central role of the verb in valency theory, Tesnière (1959: 286—299) takes a particular interest in metataxis affecting the realization of verbal participants (*interversion des actants*). (9 a/b) is a striking example of what he calls *interversion double des actants*, as the subject (S) and the indirect object (IO) of the French verb *manquer* correspond to the direct object (DO) and to the subject of the English verb *to miss* respectively:

(9) (a) E. *I*$_S$ *miss you*$_{DO}$.
    (b) Fr. *Vous*$_S$ *me*$_{IO}$ *manquez*.

But whereas according to Tesnière "il s'agit d'exprimer une idée sémantiquement identique par une phrase structuralement différente" (1959: 284), a more sophisticated approach to clause structure reveals that syntactic form and conceptual categories interact in a more intricate way that is highly significant from the typological point of view. There is considerable agreement among linguists as to a stratification of clause structure that comprises at least three levels with non-univocal, but prototypical correspondence patterns: (i) (formal) syntactic structure, (ii) semantic role structure, and (iii) informational structure (cf., e. g., Daneš 1964; Halliday 1970; Dik 1979: 13 f.; Koch 1981: 36—52; Lazard 1981; Givón 1984: 30—36; Oesterreicher 1991: 349—361). So, it is natural to conceive a likewise stratified model of participant metataxes on the (i) syntactic level, on the (ii) semantic-role level, and/or on the (iii) informational level (cf. Koch 1995; in press, section 4.3.2.). In view of the fact that every verbal lexical item *per se* bears a specific — unmarked — informational profile triggering a specific syntactic coding of the participants (cf. Oesterreicher 1991: 353—357), participant metataxes affecting (also) levels (ii) and/or (iii) are of immediate interest for lexical typology.

This can be illustrated, for instance, by psych-verbs that are characterized by the semantic roles of EXPERIENCER and EXPERIENCED. Since neither the EXPERENCIER role nor the EXPERIENCED role is particularly salient on an AGENT-PATIENT continuum (Dowty 1991), psych-verb concepts have reduced semantic transitivity in the sense of Hopper/Thompson (1980), and the syntactic options of different languages depend on informational and lexical factors. We can establish a semantic continuum of the following kind:

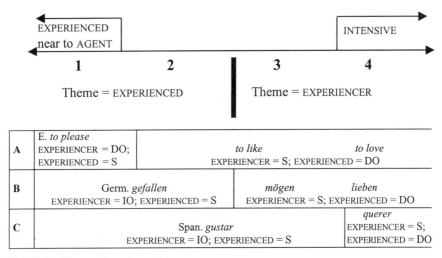

Fig. 85.22: The psych-verb continuum

The interlingual divergences concern not only the more or less transitive syntactic coding of the psych relation, but also lexical split within the whole area 1–4 (cf. Antinucci 1977: 90–92; Geisler 1988; Whitley 1995; Bossong 1998; Koch, I., 2000: 261–283, 294; Koch, P., 2000: 109–111; 2001 c). Languages with high subject prominence (cf. Sasse 1982), like English (A), tend to cover not only the thematic EXPERIENCER (zone 3), but also the thematic EXPERIENCED (zone 2) with one transitive verb (*to like*) that — in the unmarked case — has a thematic EXPERIENCER subject (indeed, E. *please*, used with EXPERIENCED subject, is rather unpopular and almost limited to zone 1: cf. the famous Chomskyan sentence *John is eager to please*; Fr. *plaire* is still more vital, but transitive *aimer* is penetrating into zone 2 as well). Languages with low subject prominence, like Spanish and many other Romance languages (C), tend to cover not only zone 2, but also zone 3 with one non-transitive verb (*gustar*) that has an EXPERIENCER subject (the transitivity split involving a lexical split with *querer* occurs only in zone 4). Interestingly, the overall non-transitive verb regularly renders a thematic EXPERIENCED (zone 2: Span. *Esta cerveza me gusta*. 'I LIKE this beer') as well as a thematic EXPERIENCER (zone 3: *Me gusta la cerveza*. 'I like beer'). A compromise type is realized in German (B), where it is the transition from EXPERIENCED subject to EXPERIENCER subject that triggers a transitivity split together with a lexical split (between *gefallen* and *mögen*; a variant is found in Portuguese, where non-transitive *agradar* with EXPERIENCED subject in zone 1 and 2 is opposed to non-transitive *gostar de* with EXPERIENCER subject, but prepositional EXPERIENCED, covering zone 3 and part of 4). A complete typological picture would have to include other solutions available in the world's languages, as double nominative (for EXPERIENCER and EXPERIENCED) in Jap. *suki*, impersonal constructions (e. g. — marginally — with Rum. *a plăcea* and Anc.Fr. *plaire*), or 'auto-conversion' in polysemous overall verbs with two opposite informational perspectives and valency orientations (e. g. E. *to please s. o.* vs. *Go as you please*; Fr. *répugner à qn.* 'to disgust s. o.' vs. *répugner à qc.* 'to detest s.th.'; with interesting diachronic implications: cf. Koch 1991: 296 ff.; 2001: 73–77; Blank 1997: 276–278; Waltereit 1998: 75–83).

Similar considerations, involving additional taxonomic, engynomic, and motivational problems, could be applied to interactions between the conceptual domains of POSSESSION, LOCATION, and EXISTENCE (cf. Lyons 1967; Clark 1978; Koch 1993; 1999 b; Hengeveld 1992: 73–126; Heine 1997; Feuillet 1998).

6. Semasiological perspective

As already pointed out in section 2., lexical typology is mainly onomasiological. Even the apparently semasiological step from formal to cognitive relations in motivation (4.4.5.) is ancillary to overriding onomasiological questions. Nevertheless, there remain at least two semasiological issues to be discussed in lexical typology: these are the lexical phenomena of polysemy (6.1.) and homonymy (6.2.) that are definable only from the point of view of the *signifiant*.

6.1. Quantitative aspects of polysemy

Qualitative aspects of polysemy are to be treated from an onomasiological perspective in terms of hierarchy (3.2.1., Figure 85.6; 3.3.1., Figures 85.13, 85.14, 85.16) and motivation (4.3.1., passim). If, on the contrary, polysemy is seen as a quantitative feature of language, it has to be treated as a semasiological problem, i. e. from the point of view of the *signifiant* of $L_{1=2}$ (cf. 4.3.1).

Bally (1965, § 569) claims that French is a language that favours lexical polysemy as a motivational device (cf. also Ullmann 1966: 232; Blumenthal 1997: 108). Indeed, it is easy to demonstrate correspondences between polysemous French words and more explicit German word formations: e. g. Fr. *livrer* 'to deliver (merchandise); to cater for; to extradite' vs. Germ. *liefern* 'to deliver', *be|liefern* 'to cater for', *aus|liefern* 'to extradite' (cf. also Fr. *louer* vs. Germ. *mieten*, *ver|mieten* in 4.4.6.). Bally explains the French preference for polysemy by hinting at the tendency towards non-motivation (cf. 4.4.2.), as he believes opacity to stimulate proliferation of senses in a given lexical item (in contrast to a transparent lexical item that is more strongly linked to its "etymological" meaning). This purely semasiological argument ignores the fact that from an onomasiological perspective, polysemy, just like word formation, is itself a motivational device (cf. 4.3.1. above). The real difference resides in the degree of explicitness, which often actually seems to be reduced in French (cf. 4.4.2.). But since explicitness is reduced in other Romance languages and in English as well, we should expect a high polysemy rate in these languages, too. In fact, Skalička (1965: 156) deduces an equally strong tendency towards polysemy from the 'isolating' character of not only French, but also English (for the special sense of 'isolating' in his typological construct, cf. Skalička 1966).

All in all, without statistical evaluation of a large language sample and a wide range of concepts, "it would be difficult to prove that semantic motivation [i. e. polysemy], by metaphor or other means, has greatly benefited by the decline of composition and derivation" (Ullmann 1966: 224) in French or in English (all the more so, as these languages make ample use of latinisms as a supplementary stratum: 4.4.3.; cf. Ullmann 1969: 131).

6.2. Quantitative aspects of homonymy

It goes without saying that the homonymy rate of a given language is a remarkable semasiological feature for lexical typology (cf. Ullmann 1966: 235 ff.). Chinese represents a particularly striking case in point: cf. $lǐ_1$ 'ritual, ceremony; politeness'; $lǐ_2$ 'lining'; $lǐ_3$ 'neighbourhood; (home) village'; $lǐ_4$ 'in; inner'; $lǐ_5$ 'texture, grain; law, reason, truth; science; to administer, to conduct; to prepare, to arrange'; $lǐ_6$ 'vulgar'; $lǐ_7$ 'river carp' (these are homophones, but not homographs; note that tone paronyms like *lí* and *lì* are not included in the above list!). Another language with a high homonymy (i. e. homophony) rate is French: cf. *cinq* /sɛ̃/$_1$ 'five'; *ceint* /sɛ̃/$_2$ 'girt'; *seing* /sɛ̃/$_3$ 'signature'; *sein* /sɛ̃/$_4$ 'bosom'; *sain* /sɛ̃/$_5$ 'sound; healthy'; *saint* /sɛ̃/$_6$ 'holy'.

7. Concluding remarks

The material presented in this article has repeatedly confirmed Ullmann's statement: "Even languages belonging to the same family and culture will sometimes show remarkable discrepancies" (1966: 252). This means that conversely, the lexical-typological alliances are often independent of genetic and areal connections. Their base must be, instead, of a more general kind.

At first glance, examples of lexical typology may seem somewhat anecdotal. On closer inspection, however, most of the onomasiological examples recurring in the literature turn out to belong to anthropologically fundamental conceptual fields and domains: KINSHIP, HUMAN BODY, HUMAN BEING, PREPARATION OF FOOD, COLOUR, DIMENSIONS, MOTION, DAY AND NIGHT, FOREST – TREE – WOOD – FRUIT, ANIMALS AND MEAT, SOUNDS, MAKING OF OBJECTS, PUTTING ON OBJECTS, PROPERTIES, PSYCHOLOGICAL ATTITUDES, etc. Furthermore, very general cognitive and formal constants in lexical semantics can be highlighted: prototypes (including implicational hierarchies), frames, cognitive relations as represented in Table 85.6, taxonomic and engynomic interlingual divergence patterns, polysemy, explicitness and congruence in transparency, selection restrictions, categorial metataxes, participant metataxes, etc. Very much like grammatical typology, lexical typology has to deal with recurrent designation problems, and despite the great lexical variety in the world's languages, the number of possible solutions does not seem to be unlimited when viewed from a cognitive perspective.

8. References

Aikhenvald, Alexandra Y. (2000): *Classifiers. A Typology of Noun Categorization Devices.* Oxford.

Albrecht, Jörn (1970): *Le français langue abstraite?* (= Tübinger Beiträge zur Linguistik 10). Tübingen.

Albrecht, Jörn (1995): "Le français langue abstraite?" Neue Antworten auf eine alte Frage aus der Sicht der Prototypensemantik. In: Hoinkes, Ulrich (ed.), *Panorama der Lexikalischen Semantik. Thematische Festschrift aus Anlaß des 60. Geburtstags von Horst Geckeler* (= Tübinger Beiträge zur Linguistik 412). Tübingen, 23–40.

Andersen, Elaine S. (1978): "Lexical universals of body-part terminology." In: Greenberg et al. 1978, vol. III, 335–368.

André, Jacques (1949): *Etude sur les termes de couleur dans la langue latine* (= Etudes et Commentaires 7). Paris.

Antinucci, Francesco (1977): *Fondamenti di una teoria tipologica del linguaggio* (= Studi linguistici e semiologici 7). Bologna.

Assmann, Aleida/Assmann, Jan (1983): "Schrift und Gedächtnis." In: ead./id./Hardmeier, Christof (eds.), *Schrift und Gedächtnis. Beiträge zu einer Archäologie der literarischen Kommunikation.* München, 265–284.

Baldinger, Kurt (1984): *Vers une sémantique moderne* (= Bibliothèque française et romane a, 46). Paris.

Bally, Charles (⁴1965): *Linguistique générale et linguistique française.* Bern.

Barsalou, Lawrence W. (1992): "Frames, concepts, and conceptual fields." In: Lehrer, Adrienne/Kittay, Eva F. (eds.), *Frames, Fields, and Contrasts. New Essays on Semantic and Lexical Organization.* Hillsdale, NJ/ London, 21–74.

Berlin, Brent/Kay, Paul (1969): *Basic Color Terms. Their Universality and Evolution*. Berkeley/Los Angeles.

Berlin, Brent (1978): "Ethnobiological classification." In: Rosch/Lloyd 1978, 9–26.

Bierwisch, Manfred (1970): "Selektionsbeschränkungen und Voraussetzungen." In: *Linguistische Arbeitsberichte* 3, 8–22.

Black, Max (1977): "More about metaphor." In: *Dialectica* 31, 431–457.

Blank, Andreas (1996): *"Tyson est aux anges* – Zur Semantik französischer Funktionsverbgefüge." In: *Zeitschrift für französische Sprache und Literatur* 106, 113–130.

Blank, Andreas (1997): *Prinzipien des lexikalischen Bedeutungswandels am Beispiel der romanischen Sprachen* (= Beihefte zur Zeitschrift für Romanische Philologie 285). Tübingen.

Blank, Andreas (1998): "Kognitive italienische Wortbildungslehre." In: *Italienische Studien* 19, 5–27.

Blank, Andreas (2001): "Pour une approche cognitive du changement sémantique lexical: aspect sémasiologique." In: François 2001.

Blank, Andreas (in press a): "Words and concepts in time: towards diachronic cognitive onomasiology." In: Schwarze, Christoph/Eckardt, Regine (eds.), *Words in Time*.

Blank, Andreas (in press b): "Polysemy in the lexicon." In: Nerlich, Brigitte et al. (eds.), *Polysemy*.

Blumenthal, Peter ([2]1997): *Sprachvergleich Deutsch – Französisch* (= Romanistische Arbeitshefte 29). Tübingen.

Bossong, Georg (1998): "Le marquage de l'expérient dans les langues d'Europe." In: Feuillet 1998 a, 259–294.

Bredin, Hugh (1996): "Onomatopoeia as a figure and a linguistic principle." In: *New Literary History* 27, 555–569.

Brown, Cecil H. (1976): "General principles of human anatomical partonomy and speculations on the growth of partonomic nomenclature." In: *American Ethnologist* 3, 400–424.

Bühler, Karl ([2]1965): *Sprachtheorie. Die Darstellungsfunktion der Sprache*. Stuttgart.

Campbell, Lyle (1998): *Historical Linguistics. An Introduction*. Edinburgh.

Cassirer, Ernst ([2]1953): "Philosophie der symbolischen Formen." In: *Die Sprache*. Darmstadt.

Chomsky, Noam (1965): *Aspects of the Theory of Syntax*. Cambridge, Mass.

Clark, Eve V. (1978): "Locationals: existential, locative, and possession constructions." In: Greenberg et al. 1978, vol. IV, 85–126.

Comrie, Bernard (eds.) (1987): *The World's Major Languages*. New York/Oxford.

Corbett, Greville G. (1991): *Gender*. Cambridge etc.

Coseriu, Eugenio (1964): "Pour une sémantique diachronique structurale." In: *Travaux de Linguistique et de Littérature* 2/1, 139–186.

Coseriu, Eugenio (1967): "Lexikalische Solidaritäten." In: *Poetica* 1, 293–303.

Coseriu, Eugenio (1975): "Die sprachlichen (und die anderen) Universalien." In: Schlieben-Lange, Brigitte (ed.), *Sprachtheorie*. Hamburg, 127–161.

Coseriu, Eugenio (1990): "Semántica estructural y semántica 'cognitiva'." In: Profesor Francisco Marsá. *Jornadas de Filología* (= Col·lecció Homenatges 4). Barcelona, 239–282.

Coseriu, Eugenio/Geckeler, Horst (1981): *Trends in Structural Semantics* (= Tübinger Beiträge zur Linguistik 158). Tübingen.

Croft, William (1990): *Typology and Universals*. Cambridge.

Cruse, D. Alan (1986): *Lexical Semantics*. Cambridge etc.

Crystal, David (ed.) (1987): *The Cambridge Encyclopedia of Language*. Cambridge.

Daneš, František (1964): "A three-level approach to syntax." In: *Travaux linguistiques de Prague* 1, 225–240.

Dik, Simon C. ([2]1979): *Functional Grammar* (= North-Holland Linguistic Series 37). Amsterdam etc.

Dixon, Robert M. W. (1977): "Where have all the adjectives gone?" In: *Studies in Language* 1, 19–80.

Dressler, Wolfgang U. (1985): "On the predictiveness of Natural Morphology." In: *Journal of Linguistics* 21, 321–337.

Dowty, David (1991): "Thematic proto-roles and argument selection". In: *Language* 67, 547–619.

Feuillet, Jack (ed.) (1998 a): "Actance et Valence dans les Langues de l'Europe" (= Empirical Approaches to Language Typology EUROTYP 20–2). Berlin/New York.

Feuillet, Jack (1998 b): "Typologie de 'être' et phrases essives." In: Feuillet 1998 a, 663–751.

Fillmore, Charles J. (1966): "Deictic categories in the semantics of *come*." In: *Foundations of Language* 2, 219–227.

Fillmore, Charles J. (1975): "An alternative to checklist theories of meaning." In: *Proceedings of the Annual Meeting of the Berkeley Linguistic Society* 1, 123–131.

Fillmore, Charles J. (1985): "Frames and the semantics of understanding." In: *Quaderni di Semantica* 6, 222–254.

François, Jacques (ed.)(2001): *Mémoire 2000 de la Société de Linguistique de Paris*. Leuven.

French, Patrice L. (1976): "Toward an explanation of phonetic symbolism." In: *Word* 28, 305–322.

Gauger, Hans-Martin (1971): *Durchsichtige Wörter. Zur Theorie der Wortbildung*. Heidelberg.

Geckeler, Horst (1993): "Wortschatzstrukturen des Französischen und des Spanischen in kontrastiver Sicht." In: Rovere/Wotjak 1993, 155−165.

Geisler, Hans (1988): "Das Verhältnis von semantischer und syntaktischer Transitivität im Französischen." In: *Romanistisches Jahrbuch* 39, 22−35.

Gévaudan, Paul (1999): "Semantische Relationen in nominalen und adjektivischen Kompositionen und Syntagmen." In: *Philologie im Netz (PhiN)* 9, 11−34.

Gévaudan, Paul (in press): "Lexikalische Filiation. Eine diachronische Synthese aus Onomasiologie und Semasiologie." In: Blank, Andreas/Koch, Peter (eds.), *Kognitive romanische Onomasiologie und Semasiologie.* Tübingen.

Gévaudan, Paul (ms.): *Taxonomic semantic change and vertical polysemy.*

Gipper, Helmut (1972): *Gibt es ein sprachliches Relativitätsprinzip? Untersuchungen zur Sapir-Whorf-Hypothese.* Frankfurt a. M.

Givón, Talmy (1984): *Syntax. A Functional-Typological Introduction.* Vol. 1. Amsterdam/Philadelphia.

Glück, Helmut (ed.) (1993): *Metzler Lexikon Sprache.* Stuttgart/Weimar.

Goddard, Cliff/Wierzbicka, Anna (eds.) (1994): *Semantic and Lexical Universals. Theory and Empirical Findings* (= Studies in Language Companion Series 25). Amsterdam/Philadelphia.

Goody, Jack/Watt, Ian (1968): "The consequences of literacy." In: Goody, Jack (ed.), *Literacy in Traditional Societies.* Cambridge, 27−68.

Greenberg, Joseph H. (1957): "The nature and uses of linguistic typologies." In: *International Journal of American Linguistics* 23, 68−77.

Greenberg, Joseph H. (ed.) (^{2}1966a): *Universals of Language.* Cambridge, Mass./London.

Greenberg, Joseph H. (1966b): "Language universals." In: Sebeok, Thomas A. (ed.), *Current Trends in Linguistics. III: Theoretical Foundation.* Den Haag/Paris, 61−112.

Greenberg, Joseph H./Osgood, Charles E./Jenkins, James J. (1966): "Memorandum concerning language universals." In: Greenberg 1966a, xv−xxvii.

Greenberg, Joseph H./Ferguson, Charles A./Moravcsik, Edith A. (eds.) (1978): *Universals of Human Language.* 4 vol. Stanford.

Greimas, Algirdas-Julien (1966): *Sémantique structurale.* Paris.

Groß, Michael (1988): *Zur linguistischen Problematisierung des Onomatopoetischen* (= Forum Phoneticum 42). Hamburg.

Guilbert, Louis (1975): *La créativité lexicale.* Paris.

Gumperz, John J./Levinson, Stephen C. (eds.) (1996): *Rethinking Linguistic Relativity* (= Studies in the Social and Cultural Foundations of Language 17). Cambridge etc.

Halliday, Michael A. K. (1970): "Language structure and language function." In: Lyons, John (ed.), *New Horizons in Linguistics,* Harmondsworth, 140−165.

Heger, Klaus (1966): "Valenz, Diathese und Kasus." In: *Zeitschrift für Romanische Philologie* 82, 138−170.

Heger, Klaus (1990/91): "Noeme als Tertia Comparationis im Sprachvergleich." In: *Vox Romanica* 49/50, 6−30.

Helbig, Gerhard (1969): "Valenz, Tiefenstruktur und Semantik." In: *Glottodidactica* 3/4, 11−46.

Heine, Bernd (1997): *Possession. Cognitive Sources, Forces, and Grammaticalization* (= Cambridge Studies in Linguistics 83). Cambridge.

Hengeveld, Kees (1992): *Non-verbal Predication. Theory, Typology, Diachrony* (= Functional Grammar Series 15). Berlin/New York.

Hill, Archibal A. (1952): "A note on primitive languages." In: *International Journal of American Linguistics* 18, 172−177.

Hjelmslev, Louis (1957): "Pour une sémantique structurale." In: id., *Essais linguistiques.* København ^{2}1970, 96−112.

Hock, Hans Henrich (^{2}1991): *Principles of Historical Linguistics.* Berlin/New York.

Hopper, Paul, J./Thompson, Sandra A. (1980): "Transitivity in Grammar and Discourse." In: *Language* 56, 251−299.

Humboldt Wilhelm v. (1979): *Werke in fünf Bänden. III: Schriften zur Sprachphilosophie.* Darmstadt.

Hymes, Dell H. (1961): "On typology of cognitive styles in language." In: *Anthropological Linguistics* 3, 22−51.

Jackendoff, Ray (1983): *Semantics and Cognition* (= Current Studies in Linguistics Series 8). Cambridge, Mass./London.

Jakobson, Roman (1956): "Two aspects of language and two types of aphasic disturbances." In: id./Halle, Morris, *Fundamentals of Language.* Den Haag/Paris 1971, 67−96.

Jakobson, Roman/Waugh, Linda R. (1979): *The Sound Shape of Language.* Brighton.

Jespersen, Otto (1905): *Growth and Structure of the English Language.* Leipzig.

Kalmár, Ivan (1985): "Are there really no primitive languages?" In: Olson, David R./Torrance, Nancy/Hildyard, Angela (eds.), *Literacy, Language, and Learning. The Nature and Consequences of Reading and Writing.* Cambridge, 148−166.

Kay, Paul/McDaniel, Chad K. (1978): "The linguistic significance of the meanings of basic color terms." In: *Language* 54, 610−646.

Kiesler, Reinhard (1993): "La tipología de los préstamos lingüísticos: no solo un problema de terminología." In: *Zeitschrift für Romanische Philologie* 109, 505−525.

Kleiber, Georges (1990): *La sémantique du prototype. Catégories et sens lexical.* Paris.

Kleiber, Georges (1994): "Lexique et cognition: Y a-t-il des *termes* de base?" In: *Rivista di Linguistica* 6, 237–266.

Koch, Ildikó (2000): *Die Metataxe im deutsch-italienischen Sprachvergleich. Eine Studie der verbbedingten Abweichungen im Satzbau* (= Studia Romanica et Linguistca 29). Frankfurt am Main etc.

Koch, Peter (1981): *Verb · Valenz · Verfügung. Zur Satzsemantik und Valenz französischer Verben am Beispiel der Verfügungs-Verben* (= Reihe Siegen 32). Heidelberg.

Koch, Peter (1991): "Semantische Valenz, Polysemie und Bedeutungswandel bei romanischen Verben." In: Koch/Krefeld 1991, 279–306.

Koch, Peter (1993): "Haben und Sein im romanisch-deutschen und im innerromanischen Sprachvergleich." In: Rovere/Wotjak 1993, 177–189.

Koch, Peter (1994): "Gedanken zur Metapher – und zu ihrer Alltäglichkeit." In: Sabban, Annette/Schmitt, Christian (eds.), *Sprachlicher Alltag. Linguistik – Rhetorik – Literaturwissenschaft. Festschrift für Wolf-Dieter Stempel.* Tübingen, 201–225.

Koch, Peter (1995): "Aktantielle 'Metataxe' und Informationsstruktur in der romanischen Verblexik (Französisch/Italienisch/Spanisch im Vergleich)." In: Dahmen, Wolfgang et al. (eds.), *Konvergenz und Divergenz in romanischen Sprachen. Romanistisches Kolloquium VIII* (Tübinger Beiträge zur Linguistik 396), 115–137.

Koch, Peter (1996): "La sémantique du prototype: sémasiologie ou onomasiologie?" In: *Zeitschrift für französische Sprache und Literatur* 106, 223–240.

Koch, Peter (1998): "Saussures *mouton* und Hjelmslevs *træ*: zwei Schulbeispiele zwischen Semstruktur und Polysemie." In: Werner, Edeltraud/Liver, Ricarda/Stork, Yvonne/Nicklaus, Martina (eds.), *et multum et multa. Festschrift für Peter Wunderli zum 60. Geburtstag.* Tübingen, 113–136.

Koch, Peter (1999a): "Frame and Contiguity. On the cognitive bases of metonymy and certain types of word formation." In: Panther, Klaus-Uwe/Radden, Günter (eds.), *Metonymy in Language and Thought* (= Human Cognitive Processing 4). Amsterdam/Philadelphia, 139–167.

Koch, Peter (1999b): "Cognitive aspects of semantic change and polysemy: the semantic space HAVE/BE." In: Blank, Andreas/Koch, Peter (eds.) (1999), *Historical Semantics and Cognition* (= Cognitive Linguistics Research 13). Berlin/New York, 279–305.

Koch, Peter (1999c): "Tree and fruit. A cognitive-onomasiological approach." In: *Studi Italiani di Linguistica Teorica e Applicata* 28, 331–347.

Koch, Peter (2000): "Indirizzi cognitivi per una tipologia lessicale dell'italiano." In: *Italienische Studien* 21, 99–117.

Koch, Peter (2001a): "Pour une approche cognitive du changement sémantique lexical: aspect onomasiologique." In: *François 2001.*

Koch, Peter (2001b): "Metonymy: unity in diversity." In: *Journal of Historical Pragmatics* 2/2.

Koch, Peter (2001c): *"As you like it.* Les métataxes actantielles entre Expérient et Phénomène." In: Schøsler, Lene (ed.), *La Valence, Perspective Romane et Diachronique.* (= Beihefte zur Zeitschrift für französische Sprache und Literatur 30). Stuttgart, 59–81.

Koch, Peter (in press): "Metataxe bei Lucien Tesnière." In: Ágel, Vilmos et al. (eds.), *Dependenz und Valenz. Ein internationales Handbuch zeitgenössischer Forschung.* Berlin/New York.

Koch, Peter/Krefeld, Thomas (Hgg.) (1991): *Connexiones Romanicae. Dependenz und Valenz in romanischen Sprachen* (= Linguistische Arbeiten 268). Tübingen.

König, Ekkehard (1996): "Kontrastive Grammatik und Typologie." In: Lang/Zifonun 1996, 31–54.

Kroeber, Alfred L. (1909): "Classificatory systems of relationship." In: *Journal of the Royal Anthropological Institute* 39, 77–84.

Lakoff, George (1987): *Women, Fire, and Dangerous Things. What Categories Reveal about the Mind.* Chicago/London 1987.

Lakoff, George/Johnson, Mark (1980): *Metaphors We Live By.* Chicago.

Lang, Ewald (1996): "Lexikalisierung und Wortfeldstruktur – typologisch betrachtet." In: Lang/Zifonun 1996, 312–355.

Lang, Ewald/Zifonun, Gisela (eds.) (1996): *Deutsch – typologisch. Jahrbuch 1995 des Instituts für Deutsche Sprache.* Berlin/New York.

Lazard, Gilbert (1981): "Les structures de la phrase." In: *Compréhension du langage* (= Collection "Linguistique" 12). Paris, 43–45.

Lehmann, Christian (1990): "Towards lexical typology." In: Croft, William/Denning, Keith/Kemmer, Suzanne (eds.), *Studies in Typology and Diachrony. Papers presented to Joseph H. Greenberg on his 75th birthday* (= Typolological Studies in Language 20). Amsterdam/Philadelphia, 161–185.

Lehrer, Adrienne (1974): *Semantic Fields and Lexical Structure* (= North-Holland Linguistics Series 11). Amsterdam etc.

Lehrer, Adrienne (1992): "A theory of vocabulary structure: Retrospectives and prospectives." In: Pütz, Manfred (ed.), *Thirty Years of Linguistic Evolution. Studies in Honour of René Dirven on the Occasion of his Sixtieth Birthday.* Philadelphia/Amsterdam, 243–256.

Lévi-Strauss, Claude (1964): "Le triangle culinaire." In: L'Arc 26, 19–29.

Lévy-Bruhl, Lucien ([7]1922): *Les fonctions mentales dans les sociétés inférieures.* Paris.

Lyons, John (1967): "A note on possessive, existential and locative sentences." In: *Foundations of Language* 3, 390–396.

Malblanc, Alfred (⁴1968): *Stylistique comparée du français et de l'allemand. Essai de représentation linguistique comparée et Etude de traduction* (= Bibliothèque de stylistique comparée 2). Paris.

McCawley, James D. (1968): "The role of semantics in a grammar." In: Bach, Emmon/Harms, Robert T. (eds.), *Universals in Linguistic Theory.* New York, 125–169.

Mihatsch, Wiltrud (2000): "La relation partie-tout aux confins de l'hyponymie." In: *Scolia* 12, 237–258.

Müller-Gotama, Franz (1992): "Towards a semantic typology of language." In: Kefer, Michel/van der Auwera, Johan (eds.), *Meaning and Grammar. Cross-Linguistic Perspectives* (= Empirical Approaches to Language Typology 10). Berlin/New York, 137–178.

Newmeyer, Frederick (ed.) (1988): *Language. The Cambridge Survey.* 4 Vols. Cambridge.

Niemeier, Susanne/Dirven, René (eds.) (2000): *Evidence for Linguistic Relativity* (= Current Issues in Linguistic Theory 198). Amsterdam/Philadelphia.

Oesterreicher, Wulf (1989): "'Konsistenz' als typologisches Kriterium?" In: Raible, Wolfgang (ed.), *Romanistik, Sprachtypologie und Universalienforschung* (Tübinger Beiträge zur Linguistik 332). Tübingen, 223–262.

Oesterreicher, Wulf (1991): "Verbvalenz und Informationsstruktur." In: Koch/Krefeld 1991, 349–384.

Ong, Walter J. (1982): *Orality and Literacy. The Technologizing of the Word.* London/New York.

Pesot, Jürgen (1980): "Ikonismus in der Phonologie." In: *Zeitschrift für Semiotik* 2, 7–18.

Plank, Frans (1984): "Verbs and objects in semantic agreement." In: *Journal of Semantics* 3, 305–360.

Porzig, Walter (1934): "Wesenhafte Bedeutungsbeziehungen." In: *Beiträge zur deutschen Sprache und Literatur* 58, 70–97.

Pottier, Bernard (1964): "Vers une sémantique moderne." In: *Travaux de Linguistique et de Littérature* 2/1, 107–137.

Pütz, Martin/Verspoor, Marjolijn H. (eds.) (2000): *Explorations in Linguistic Relativity* (= Current Issues in Linguistic Theory 199). Amsterdam/Philadelphia.

Pulleyblank, Douglas (1987): "Yoruba." In: Comrie 1987, 971–990.

Raible, Wolfgang (1981): "Von der Allgegenwart des Gegensinns (und einiger anderer Relationen). Strategien zur Einordnung semantischer Information." In: *Zeitschrift für Romanische Philologie* 97, 1–40.

Rettich, Wolfgang (1981): *Sprachliche Motivation. Zeichenrelationen von Lautform und Bedeutung am Beispiel französischer Lexikoneinheiten* (= Studia Romanica et Linguistica 12). Frankfurt am Main/Bern.

Ricca, Davide (1993): *I verbi deittici di movimento in Europa: una ricerca interlinguistica* (= Pubblicazioni della Facoltà di Lettere e Filosofia dell'Università di Pavia 70). Firenze.

Rijkhoff, Jan (2000): "When can a language have adjectives? An implicational universal." In: Vogel, Petra M./Comrie, Bernard (eds.), *Approaches to the Typology of Word Classes* (= Empirical Approaches to Language Typology 23). Berlin/New York, 217–257.

Rosch, Eleanor (1978): "Principles of categorization." In: Rosch/Lloyd 1978, 27–48.

Rosch, Eleanor/Lloyd, Barbara B. (eds.) (1978): *Cognition and Categorization.* Hillsdale, N. J.

Rovere, Giovanni/Wotjak, Gerd (eds.) (1993): *Studien zum romanisch-deutschen Sprachvergleich* (= Linguistische Arbeiten 297). Tübingen.

Sasse, Hans-Jürgen (1982): "Subjektprominenz." In: Heinz, Sieglinde/Wandruszka, Ulrich (eds.): *Fakten und Theorien. Festschrift für Helmut Stimm* (= Tübinger Beiträge zur Linguistik 191), 511–580.

Saussure, Ferdinand de (1916): *Cours de linguistique générale,* Paris.

Sauvageot, Aurélien (1964): *Portrait du vocabulaire français.* Paris.

Schepping, Marie-Theres (1985): "Das Lexikon im Sprachvergleich." In: Schwarze, Christoph/Wunderlich, Dieter (eds.), *Handbuch der Lexikologie.* Königstein, Ts., 184–195.

Schifko, Peter (1979): "Die Metonymie als universales sprachliches Strukturprinzip." In: *Grazer Linguistische Studien* 10, 240–264.

Schwarze, Christoph (1983): "Une typologie des contrastes lexicaux." In: Faust, Manfred et al. (eds.), *Allgemeine Sprachwissenschaft, Sprachtypologie und Textlinguistik. Festschrift für Peter Hartmann* (Tübinger Beiträge zur Linguistik 215). Tübingen, 199–211.

Sharp, Harriet/Warren, Beatrice (1994): "The semantics of onomatopoeic words." In: *Folia Linguistica* 28, 437–447.

Skalička, Vladimír (1965): "Wortschatz und Typologie." In: *Asian and African Studies* 1, 152–157.

Skalička, Vladimír (1966): "Ein "typologisches Konstrukt"." In: *Travaux linguistiques de Prague* 2, 157–163.

Slobin, Dan I. (2000): "Verbalized events. A Dynamic Approach to Linguistic Relativity and Determinism." In: Niemeier/Dirven 2000, 107–138.

Sobrero, Alberto A. (1978): *I padroni della lingua. Profilo sociolinguistico della lingua italiana.* Napoli.

Steever, Sanford B. (1987): "Tamil and the Dravidian languages." In: Comrie 1987, 725–746.

Steinthal, Heyman/Misteli, Franz (²1893): *Abriß der Sprachwissenschaft. II: Charakteristik der hauptsächlichsten Typen des Sprachbaus.* Berlin.

Stopa, Roman (1968): "Kann man eine Brücke schlagen zwischen der Kommunikation der Primaten und derjenigen der Urmenschen?" In: *Homo* 19, 129–136.

Talmy, Leonard (1985): "Lexicalization patterns: semantic structure in lexical forms." In: Shopen, Timothy (Hg.), *Language Typology and Syntactic Description. III: Grammatical Categories and the Lexicon.* Cambridge, 57–149.

Talmy, Leonard (1991): "Path to realization: a typology of event conflation." In: *Proceedings of the Annual Meetings of the Berkeley Linguistics Society* 17, 480–519.

Taylor, John R. (^{2}1995): *Linguistic Categorization. Prototypes in Linguistic Theory.* Oxford.

Tesnière, Lucien (1959): *Eléments de syntaxe structurale.* Paris.

Trabant, Jürgen (2000): "How relativistic are Humboldt's "Weltansichten"?" In: Pütz/Verspoor 2000, 25–44.

Trask, R. L. (1996): *Historical Linguistics.* London.

Trier, Jost (1931): *Der deutsche Wortschatz im Sinnbezirk des Verstandes. Die Geschichte eines sprachlichen Feldes. I: Von den Anfängen bis zum Beginn des 13. Jahrhunderts.* Heidelberg.

Ullmann, Stephen (1953): "Descriptive semantics and linguistic typology." In: *Word* 9, 225–240.

Ullmann, Stephen (^{2}1966): Semantic universals. In: Greenberg 1966a, 217–262.

Ullmann, Stephen (^{4}1969): *Précis de sémantique française* (= Bibliotheca Romanica I, 9). Bern.

Ungerer, Friedrich/Schmid, Hans-Jörg (1996): *An Introduction to Cognitive Linguistics.* London/New York.

Vinay, Jean-Paul/Darbelnet, Jean (1964): *Stylistique comparée du français et de l'anglais. Méthode de traduction* (= Bibliothèque de stylistique comparée 1). Paris.

Vogel, Petra Maria (1996): *Wortarten und Wortartenwechsel. Zu Konversion und verwandten Erscheinungen im Deutschen und in anderen Sprachen* (= Studia Linguistica Germanica, 39). Berlin/New York.

Waltereit, Richard (1998): *Metonymie und Grammatik. Kontiguitätsphänomene in der französischen Satzsemantik* (= Linguistische Arbeiten 385). Tübingen.

Wandruszka, Mario (1969): *Sprachen vergleichbar und unvergleichlich.* München.

Whorf, Benjamin L. (1956): *Language, Thought, and Reality. Selected Writings of Benjamin Lee Whorf.* Cambridge, Mass.

Whitley, Stanley M. (1995): "*Gustar* and other psych verbs." A problem in transitivy. In: *Hispania* 78, 573–585.

Wierzbicka, Anna (1990): "The meaning of color terms: semantics, culture, and cognition." In: *Cognitive Linguistics* 1, 99–150.

Wierzbicka, Anna (1996): *Semantic. Primes and Universals.* Oxford/New York.

Wierzbicka, Anna (1999): *Emotions across Languages and Cultures. Diversity and Universals.* Cambridge.

Wilkins, David P. (1996): "Natural tendencies of semantic change and the search for cognates." In: Durie, Mark/Ross, Malcolm (eds.), *The Comparative Method Reviewed.* Oxford, 264–304.

Witkowski, Stanley R./Brown, Cecil H./Chase, Paul K. (1981): "Where do tree terms come from?" In: *Man* (n.s.) 16, 1–14.

Peter Koch, Universität Tübingen (Germany)

86. Lexical typology from an anthropological point of view

1. Introduction
2. Polysemy and overt marking
3. Cultural and social correlates
4. A survey of universal tendencies
5. Implications for the study of language change
6. Lexical acculturation and universal tendencies
7. Absolute lexical universals
8. Lexical typology and linguistic areas
9. References

1. Introduction

Anthropologists have undertaken substantial work on lexical typology most of which is little known to linguists. The modern era of this research began with the publication of Berlin & Kay's (1969) well-known book treating basic color terms (→ Art. 90). Since 1969, two other books dealing with aspects of lexical typology have been published: Greenberg's (1978) edited compilation in the series *Universals of Human Language* entitled *Word Structure* (Volume 3), and my (Brown 1984) *Language and Living Things* treating cross-language lexical uniformities in the folk classification and naming of plants and animals. In addition to these books, numerous articles have appeared. In this essay I review only works published since 1980. For a general overview of earlier literature, readers are directed to Witkowski & Brown (1978) and Brown & Witkowski (1980). (The basic cross-language findings of my 1984 book [see above] are also outlined in these two surveys.)

Anthropologists have been primarily concerned with how lexical typology contributes to the study of lexical universals. This has often involved, as in the examples of Berlin & Kay (1969) and Brown (1984), implicational relationships and their pertinence for ascertaining cross-language regularities in the growth and development of the lexicon. A diachronic perspective on lexical universals continues to dominate anthropological orientation. For the most part, lexical typologies revealed by anthropological study attest to universal tendencies in language rather than to universals of an absolute nature. Anthropologists have been particularly interested in the development of explanatory frameworks to account for universal tendencies, especially those involving changes in the lexicon correlated with social and cultural phenomena (cf. Brunel 1987). In addition to concern with lexical universals, anthropological investigation has focused on lexical typology as it pertains to areal linguistics (→ Art. 105–110).

2. Polysemy and overt marking

Many of the universal tendencies entailing the lexicon uncovered since 1980 involve polysemy and overt marking. For example, approximately two-thirds of the languages of the world polysemously designate 'wood' and 'tree' by using a single term to denote both of these related referents (Witkowski & Brown & Chase 1981), and slightly over one-third merge 'hand' and 'arm' under a single term resulting in polysemy (Witkowski & Brown 1985). Related referents are also repeatedly found to be nomenclaturally linked by overt marking across languages. For example, of the large number of languages nomenclaturally associating 'eye' and 'face' (see below), approximately 60 percent do so through overt marking constructions such as 'background of eye' in reference to face, and 'seed of face' in reference to eye (Brown & Witkowski 1983).

Polysemy plays an important role in lexical change. The development of polysemy is a common means whereby languages encode new referents or alter the encoding of existing ones (Brown & Witkowski 1983). Typically this involves extending a word for one referent to another when the two referents are in some manner perceptually and/or conceptually related to one another (cf. Brown 1979; Casagrande & Hale 1967; Lyons 1963, 1977). For example, 'tree' is conceptually related to 'wood' through the association 'source of', trees are the source of wood. Typically, development of polysemy entails extending a term for a high salience referent (e. g., 'wood') to a related referent that initially is low in salience (e. g., 'tree') (see below for discussion).

Referent salience relates to two factors, natural salience and cultural importance. Some things are naturally salient for humans because our species is innately predisposed in some manner to perceive them as *standing out* or, in other words, as especially attention-getting or fetching, for example, by having a bright color or large size (Berlin 1992; Berlin & Boster & O'Neill 1981; Hunn 1976, 1977). Others may be salient because they are culturally important (useful) in some way. Both natural salience and cultural importance can combine to contribute to the overall salience of a referent.

Overt marking is another common way in which related referents can be nomenclaturally connected. This involves a base term, such as Indonesian *kaju* 'wood,' united with a modifier (overt mark) such as Indonesian *pohon* 'origin,' creating a complex expression such as *pohon kaju* as a label for 'tree.' This construction nomenclaturally relates two referents, i. e., 'wood' and 'tree,' which are connected through the relation 'source of.'

Overt marking often develops from polysemy. This occurs when the salience value of one or both of polysemously linked referents changes radically for some reason. For example, across languages the development of 'wood'/'tree' polysemy is invariably the result of extending a term for high salience 'wood' to lower salience 'tree.' An increase in the salience value of 'tree' over time may lead to loss of polysemy through development of overt marking (Witkowski & Brown & Chase 1981). This involves uniting the polysemous based term ('wood'/'tree') with an overt mark (e. g., 'origin'), thus creating a complex expression (e. g., 'origin' + 'wood'/'tree') as a label for 'tree.'

Overt marking of the acquired referent may at first be optional; that is, the base (polysemous) term can be used to denote the acquired referent with or without the overt mark (modifier). Further increases in the salience of the acquired referent can lead to obligatory overt marking, whereby the base term becomes restricted in meaning to its original referent ('wood') and polysemy is totally lost. In such a case, the referent labeled through overt marking ('tree') is still less salient than its original partner in polysemy ('wood'), but not nearly as low in salience as when polysemy originally developed. Moreover, should the overtly marked referent increase in salience to the extent that it equals or surpasses the salience of its partner referent, overt marking is lost and the two referents become labeled by separate, unrelated terms.

Overt marking can also develop when one referent of a polysemous pair decreases in salience and the other increases. For example, when imported sheep were first encountered by Tzotzil (Mayan) speakers in highland Chiapas, Mexico, they referred to these creatures through use of their term (X) for the highly salient native deer (Witkowski & Brown 1983). As sheep increased in economic importance, an overt marking construction developed for them involving the base term (X) and a modifier, i.e., 'cotton' + X. While sheep were increasing in cultural importance, the native deer, for several reasons, decreased in significance. As a result, an overt marking construction, 'wild' + X, developed as a label for deer, creating an instance of *double overt marking*. Double overt marking exists when a language lacks polysemy, but nomenclaturally relates two referents through two obligatory overt marking constructions involving the same base element, e.g., 'cotton' + X = sheep *and* 'wild' + X = deer, where X is the term which originally denoted only deer.

An almost identical development took place in a neighboring Mayan language, Tzeltal (Berlin 1972). This language at first referred to newly encountered sheep through use of the expression 'cotton deer.' Later the original 'deer' term was used in an unmodified form to refer to sheep while deer became designated through an overt marking construction based on the 'sheep' term, i.e., 'wild sheep.' Such lexical changes are known as *marking reversals* (Witkowski & Brown 1983). These are typically observed in the context of cultural processes such as innovation, invention, or interaction between markedly different cultures, as with Old World influence on New World groups (Witkowski & Brown 1983: 571; Brown 1996a).

3. Cultural and social correlates

Nomenclatural developments entailing polysemy and overt marking are often correlated with cultural and social factors. For example, a strong positive correlation exists between societal complexity and the occurrence of 'wood'/'tree' polysemy (Witkowski & Brown & Chase 1981). Speakers of languages polysemously uniting 'wood' and 'tree' usually live in small-scale, traditional societies while speakers of languages separating them usually live in large nation states. Since the general thrust of societal development over the past several millennia has been from small- to large-scale configurations, it follows that many languages spoken in large-scale societies now having separate words for 'tree' and 'wood,' at some point in the past had both meanings united under a single term. For instance, the contemporary English word *tree* designated both 'tree' and 'wood' in Old English (*trēow*) and in Middle English (*tre*). The modern word has lost the latter meaning, which is now carried solely by *wood*. *Wood*, in turn, can be traced to Old English *wudu* and Middle English *wode*, both of which denoted 'woods, forest, wood' (cf. Buck 1949). Loss of 'wood'/'tree' polysemy in English, then, involved deletion of the 'wood' referent in response to a competing word for 'wood' and retention of the old term as a label for 'tree' alone.

Loss of 'wood'/'tree' polysemy may trace to two specific changes associated with increases in societal complexity: (1) a shift in basic naming level for biological organisms, and (2) advances in woodworking technology (Witkowski & Brown & Chase 1981).

The *basic naming level* in folk biological taxonomies is that at which the most salient categories are found (cf. Rosch et al. 1976; Dougherty 1978). In small-scale societies, this tends to be exclusively the generic level of naming (English examples of generic categories are *oak, ivy, robin, trout*). On the other hand, in folk taxonomies of people living in large national societies, life-form categories (e.g., English *tree, bird, fish*) are often highly salient as well and thus tend to comprise a component of the basic naming level (Dougherty 1978; Brown 1984). Thus, in the shift from small- to large-scale societal organization there tends to be an accompanying augmentation in the importance of life-form classes. The salience of 'tree' and other life-form is typically significantly enhanced. When 'tree' becomes just as salient as 'wood,' the two referents tend to become separately labeled if previously united in polysemy.

An additional factor contributing to lexical segregation of 'wood' and 'tree' may be elaboration of woodworking technology (Segall et al. 1966). In small-scale societies, woodworking seldom involves radical alteration in tree products. Branches, logs, sticks, and the like rarely require extensive modification for the construction of shelters, or for use as firewood or as tools. On the other hand, in large-scale societies, manipulation by woodworking specialists occurs to such an extent that the appearance of wood is often only remotely suggestive of its affinity with trees in the wild. Of course, wood in small-scale societies can at times be greatly altered, for example, in mask carving. It seems likely, however, that many more instances of radical alteration occur in large societies, and this wide perceptual distance between living trees and many of the wooden products of modern urban peoples contributes to 'wood'/'tree' nomenclatural separation.

4. A survey of universal tendencies

The following is a review of cross-language lexical uniformities, many of which entail polysemy and overt marking, uncovered by anthropologists since around 1980. In some instances these, like the 'wood'/'tree' example cited above, show associations with social/cultural phenomena.

A cross-language survey of 118 languages, which are largely discontinuously distributed across genetic and geographic boundaries, shows that 49 languages, or 42 percent of the sample, link 'eye' and 'face' either through polysemy or overt marking (Brown & Witkowski 1983). This suggests that nomenclatural association of 'eye' and 'face' often has developed through independent invention. Brown & Witkowski (1983) assemble several lines of evidence showing that terms for naturally salient 'eye' typically expand to less salient 'face.' In addition, there is a strong relationship between societal scale and labels for 'eye' and 'face': languages nomenclaturally linking these referents tend to be associated with small-scale societies, and those separating them, with large-scale groupings.

The nomenclatural uncoupling of 'eye' and 'face' in large societies may be due to an augmentation in cultural activities associated with facial appearance such as special cleansing, hair removal, and decoration. Increase in societal scale may encourage elaboration of these activities through innovations such as the looking glass and development of fine control over color through special techniques of dyeing, painting, staining, and powdering. Increase in cosmetic activity may elevate the cultural importance of face as a distinct body part. With the heightened importance of the face, a tendency develops to label this body part with a term separate from and unrelated to eye.

Among the 118 languages surveyed by Brown & Witkowski (1983), 21 (18 percent) nomenclaturally unite the referents 'seed' and 'fruit.' For the most part, distribution of languages with this nomenclatural equation is discontinuous across language boundaries suggesting its frequent independent invention. Several types of evidence are assembled (Brown & Witkowski 1983) showing that the union of 'seed' and 'fruit' typically develops through the referential expansion of a term for salient 'seed' to less salient 'fruit.' Also, a reasonably strong association exists between societal scale and labels for 'seed' and 'fruit': languages nomenclaturally relating these referents are typically spoken in small-scale societies, while those separating them are found among large-scale groups. The nomenclatural separation of 'seed' and 'fruit' is possibly linked to the enhanced cultural importance and consequent increase in salience of fruit as a foodstuff category in large-scale societies, possibly related to the availability of a wide range of individual fruits due to elaborate marketing, storage, and transport facilities.

In a survey of 109 globally distributed languages, Witkowski and Brown (1985) find that the referents 'hand' and 'arm' are nomenclaturally linked in 57 languages, among which 50 show 'hand'/'arm' polysemy (46 percent). Similarly, 49 languages nomenclaturally equate 'foot' and 'leg,' wherein 42 of these show 'foot'/'leg' polysemy (39 percent). Lexical marking and other evidence indicate that direction of polysemy development typically involves a distal to proximal expansion: a term for salient 'hand' expanding to less salient 'arm' and a word for salient 'foot' extending to less salient 'leg.' While there appears to be no association between limb terminology and societal scale, there is, however, a correlation with environment. Speakers of languages showing limb polysemy typically inhabit warm zones near the equator while those lacking it commonly live in cold regions away from the equator. This suggests that individual limb parts are more salient, and thus more frequently given distinct labels by speakers inhabiting cold climatic zones compared to those of warm ones.

Environmental influence on limb part salience is almost certainly mediated by cultural factors. The existence of tailored clothing covering the limbs and associated gear such as gloves, mittens, socks, shoes, and boots, constitutes a plausible intervening cultural variable. Activities involving the manufacture, wear, and care of limb apparel would greatly increase appropriate cultural occasions for referring to limb parts, thus increasing the frequency of use and salience of these referents, and the likelihood of their acquiring distinct labels. Thus, in nonequatorial zones where cold wheather encourages limb covering and limb parts tend to be highly salient referents for humans, 'hand'/'arm' and 'foot'/'leg' polysemy are less common and individual limb parts tend to be labeled with separate terms. On the other hand, limb parts are less salient and limb polysemy is more common in languages spoken in equatorial regions.

Chiara (1986) investigated the regular nomenclatural association of 'wind' and 'air.' In a survey of 60 languages, she found that these referents are nomenclaturally linked in 28 or 47 percent of those surveyed. Linkage in all cases is through polysemy. In an expanded treatment of this relationship involving a survey of 221 globally distributed languages, I have found that 80 languages or 36 percent nomenclaturally relate 'wind' and 'air' (Brown 1989a). I encountered six languages of these 80 which relate the two referents through overt marking, e. g., Czech's 'wind' term which is literally 'flow air.'

Of the two referents, 'wind' is clearly initially high in salience while 'air' is low, at least when first lexically encoded through polysemy. Distribution of terms for these referents across the 221 languages bears this out. A term for 'wind' occurs in all 221 languages, strongly suggesting that the lexical encoding of 'wind' is an *absolute universal* of language (see section 7). On the other hand, a large number of languages, 84 or 38 percent, totally lack a term for 'air' (polysemous or otherwise). This is not surprising since 'air' is a concept of considerable sophistication whose realization is connected with relatively recent advances in medical, meteorological, navigational, and architectural understanding (Chiara 1986). Consequently, direction of polysemy development involving 'wind' and 'air' has universally entailed expansion of a term for the former high-salience referent to the latter initially low-salience referent.

Cardinal directions, like 'air,' are concepts associated with technological achievements. Cardinal direction terms are also, for the most part, relatively recent additions to lexicons of the world's languages (Brown 1983). Technological advances accompanying increases in societal scale such as ocean-going vessels, the compass, maps, clocks, mathematics, and so on, obviously have contributed significantly to this development (cf. Taylor 1957). The typical recency of cardinal direction terms is attested by their usual etymological transparency revealed through polysemy, overt marking, and descriptive labels. The latter often involve universal tendencies in lexical growth.

Cardinal direction terms have been investigated through a survey of 127 globally distributed languages (Brown 1983). The four cardinal directions are found to be regularly nomenclaturally associated with other concepts in polysemy, overt marking, and descriptive labels: (1) 'east' with the rising of the sun in 58 languages, (2) 'west' with the setting of the sun in 59 languages, (3) 'south' with a celestial body or event in 13 languages (e. g., 'where the sun is at midday'), (4) 'north' with a celestial body or event in eight languages, (5) 'north' with wind or a wind from a particular direction (e. g., 'north wind') in 17 languages, (6) 'south' with wind or a wind from a particular direction (e. g., 'south wind') in 15 languages, (7) all cardinal directions with temperature, weather, or season in 15 languages, (8) all cardinal directions with other more general directions such as up, down, below, down, under, etc., in 27 languages, (9) 'east,' 'north,' and 'south' with the left and/or right sides of the human body in six languages, (10) all cardinal directions with the direction of flowing water (e. g., up river, upstream, downstream, etc.) in eight languages, (11) all cardinal directions with environment-specific features (e. g., at the pines, rocky place, etc.) in 12 languages.

Not all languages have cardinal direction terms, and languages that do have these terms do not always possess words for all four directional concepts. The distribution of these items works out implicationally (Brown 1983). For example, of the 28 languages of the sample having from one to three of the four cardinal direction terms, 24 show terms for 'east' and/or 'west' while only 14 have terms for 'north' and/or 'south.' Thus, languages having 'north' and/or 'south' typically have 'east' and/or 'west' but not vice versa.

These implicational associations indicate a universal tendency for both 'east' and 'west' to be lexically encoded before languages add a term for either 'north' or 'south,' a finding which may reflect the relatively greater importance of the rising and setting sun for humans compared to the sun at its zenith.

Widmann (1987) has undertaken a cross-language survey of terms entailing the polysemous relationships of three chronological concepts, 'daytime,' 'nighttime,' and '24-hour period.' For example, in English the term *day* denotes both 'day-time' and '24-hour-period.' Among the 180 globally distributed languages considered by her, the following frequently occurring polysemies are in evidence: (1) 'daytime' and '24-hour period' in 23 percent, (2) 'daytime,' '24-hour period,' and 'sun' (triple polysemy) in 17 percent, (3) 'daytime' and 'sun' in 17 percent, (4) 'nighttime' and 'darkness' in 16 percent, (5) 'daytime' and 'light' in 12 percent, (6) '24-hour period' and 'sleep' in nine percent, (7) '24-hour period' and 'time' in seven percent, (8) '24-hour period' and 'sun' in six percent, (9) 'daytime' and '24-hour period,' and 'time' in six percent, and (10) 'nighttime' and '24-hour period' in four percent.

Reoccurring examples of overt marking and polysemy frequently entail function words, i.e., words whose meanings reside primarily in their application, and only secondarily, if at all, involve reference to some person, object, concept, event, process, or activity. I (Brown 1985) have comparatively investigated a special class of such words known as deictics, which are used to bring attention to things either in the actual spatiotemporal context in which language is being used or in some way embedded in ongoing discourse. Some deictics serve to identify the spatial or temporal aspects of a language use situation. For example, English *I/you, this/that, here/there*, and *now/then* have such an application. In other instances, a deictic may simply call attention to an entity whose existence has been previously established in discourse, for example, English *that, the, he, she*, and *it*.

Evidence is assembled from 129 globally distributed languages showing universal tendencies in ways in which deictic functions are nomenclaturally related (Brown 1985). The following is a summary of functions frequently associated through polysemy and/or overt marking: (1) 'this' with 'here' in 68 of the 129 languages, (2) 'that' with 'there' in 80 languages, (3) 'this' and/or 'that' (neutral demonstratives) with 'here' and/or 'there' in 10 languages, (4) 'that' with third person pronouns ('he', 'she', and 'it') in 50 languages, (5) 'this' with third person pronouns in 22 languages, (6) neutral demonstratives with third person pronouns in five languages, (7) 'this' with 'now' in 33 languages, (8) 'this' with 'then' in 36 languages, (9) neutral demonstratives with 'now' in six languages, (10) neutral demonstratives with 'then' in three languages, (11) 'here' with 'now' in 27 languages, (12) 'there' with 'then' in 22 languages, (13) 'this' with 'the' in 12 languages, (14) 'that' with 'the' in 25 languages, and (15) third person pronouns with 'the' in 22 languages.

Lexical marking evidence and evidence from historical-comparative linguistics attest to regular directions of polysemy development involving deictics (Brown 1985). For example, terms for 'this' tend to absorb functions denoted by 'the,' 'here,' and 'now' and by personal pronouns. In some distances, paths of polysemy development appear to be bidirectional. For example, while 'this' terms clearly become extended to 'the,' 'the' terms may also expand to 'this' (Brown 1985: 305). In other cases, paths are strictly unidirectional, for instance, words for 'this' tend to extend to 'here,' but 'here' terms do not expand to 'this.'

Figurative language for body parts is a rich source of examples of universal tendencies involving the lexical component of language (Brown & Witkowski 1981). Metaphor-like expressions often gain currency in languages as stable nonliteral names for parts of the body. For example, many languages equate the pupil of the eye with a human being or a human-like object, usually small in size, through use of established figurative expressions translating literally as 'baby of eye,' 'girl of eye' or 'doll of eye' — for instance, Spanish *niña del ojo* (literally, 'the small girl of the eye') (cf. Tagliavini 1949). An alternative, nonfigurative way of naming this part would involve an expression such as 'small black spot of eye'. (English *pupil*, of course, means both 'young student' and 'pupil of the eye.' The term and its meanings were borrowed from Latin through French. Although contemporary speakers do not usually think of the two meanings as connected, perhaps when the borrowing from French took place, the expression 'pupil of the eye' was still alive as a metaphor.)

Brown & Witkowski (1981) document the occurrence of the 'pupil' metaphor and several others in 118 globally distributed languages. The 'pupil' metaphor is found in 25 of these. Also widespread are figurative labels for fingers and toes based on terms for people, usually kinsmen. The basic design of the metaphor identifies the thumb and big toe by use of a term for an older, ascending generation relative, usually a parent (mother or father), while the remaining digits (fingers and toes) are labeled by terms for younger relatives, usually offspring (son or daughter). This lexical metaphor occurs in 42 of the languages sampled. Muscle and muscular parts of the body are often named through use of terms for various small creatures, e.g., the Chrau (Vietnam) word for 'biceps,' which is literally 'rat of arm.' Mice and rats predominate among animals entering into this metaphor, with other small mammals occurring next most frequently, followed by creatures such as toads and lizards. This metaphor is found in 23 of the surveyed languages (English *muscle* ultimately traces to a small animal/muscle equation: namely, Latin *musculus*, which translates literally as 'little mouse.'). Finally, the naming of testicle is based on terms for 'egg' in 21 of the surveyed languages.

Figurative labels for body parts are built on perceived similarities and associations between body parts and other things in the physical world. In some cases, these are more or less self-evident, e.g., 'egg'/'testicle'. In other cases, they are less so, e.g., 'small girl'/'pupil of the eye' and 'mother'/'thumb.' Even the latter equations, however, are built on physical bases. Thus, for example, 'small girl of the eye' for pupil probably draws on the physical association of the pupil with the minute human image reflected in the center of the eye. The association of mother with thumb and children with fingers draws on the observation that mother and children form a natural group as do thumb and fingers. In these groupings, mothers stand out from children as thumbs do from fingers. Muscular body parts are characterized by their ability to move rapidly by contraction and relaxation independently of one another. Human muscles as individual parts of the body are also relatively small. Few things in the physical world, other than small creatures such as mice, rabbits, frogs, and lizards, have enough in common with muscular body parts to enter into reasonable figurative labels for them.

These animals hop and scurry in a manner reminiscent of muscles that move by tensing and relaxing. Muscles move as if they were small creatures beneath the skin (Brown & Witkowski 1981).

5. Implications for the study of language change

Knowledge of especially likely lexical change paths (e.g., small creature to muscular body part or mother to thumb) could be very useful for comparative-historical investigation of language. Studies reported here indicate that it is possible to produce a thesaurus of regular semantic change paths. Such a compendium would be extremely helpful to historical linguists in making judgments of cognation when linguistic forms are phonologically similar but appear to have unrelated, radically different referents. It would provide as well important constraints on semantic reconstruction in historical linguistics comparable to those that presently guide phonological reconstruction (cf. Blank 1997). It would have the additional advantage of providing a basis for formulating regularities and testing theories of general lexical change processes. A more thorough understanding of these processes has the potential to contribute to a deeper knowledge of human cognition.

6. Lexical acculturation and universal tendencies

Lexical acculturation refers to how languages lexically adjust to new objects or concepts encountered as a result of contact (Brown 1999). The naming of introduced objects and concepts is a source of much lexical regularity across languages.

While languages have occasionally independently developed a concept of a cycle of time shorter than a lunar month and longer than a day, the concept 'week' (especially the seven-day week) has, for the most part, diffused to the world's languages from an Occidental source (Brown 1987; Zerubavel 1985). I have investigated the lexical acculturation of 'week' through a survey of 176 globally distributed languages (Brown 1987). Forty languages or 28 percent of the sample altogether lack terms for 'week'. Thirty-six, or 21 percent, have borrowed 'week' labels from other languages, for the largest part from Western tongues such as English, Spanish,

Portuguese, and French. By far, most languages of the sample (71 or 40 percent) have developed a label for 'week' by extending a term for a specific day of the week, usually Sunday, to the concept of the seven-day cycle. This is attested by polysemy and overt marking constructions in which 'Sunday' (or some other weekday) and 'week' are nomenclaturally linked.

Terms for a day of the week extended to 'week' are sometimes European language loans (Brown 1987). For example, Northern Tiwa (New Mexico) used the word *tumîgu* to denote 'week.' This is Northern Tiwa's version of the Spanish word for 'Sunday', *domingo*. In addition, *tumîgu* is polysemous, denoting 'Sunday' as well as 'week.' In this case, direction of polysemy development is unambiguous: a borrowed term for 'Sunday' has been expanded in reference to 'week.'

Upon encountering the Western concept 'Sunday,' rather than borrowing a term for it as Northern Tiwa has done, some languages innovated their own 'Sunday' labels, which they subsequently expanded to 'week' (Brown 1987; Brown 1989c). For example, the 'Sunday'/'week' label in Mikasuki, a language of Florida, is literally 'holy day.' Similarly, Waorani, a South American Indian language, has a 'Sunday'/'week' label translating literally as 'God's day.' A total of 17 languages of the 71 linking a specific day of the week and 'week' have innovated terms for 'Sunday,' which subsequently developed as labels for 'week' through polysemy or overt marking. These languages offer additional evidence of the priority of 'Sunday' in the nomenclatural relating of 'Sunday' and 'week.'

Nomenclatural evidence assembled in Brown (1987) indicates that, when lexically acculturated, 'Sunday' typically has been considerably more salient for people than 'week.' Zerubavel's (1985: 115–116) discussion of a *pulsating week* is enlightening here. When the Western week was first adopted by non-Western groups, its most immediate and notable effect must have been a feeling of the *beat* of the pulsating week – an awareness that the week alternated between several days of ordinary activity and a single day of special activity, i.e., Sunday. In short, the importance of the week initially related not so much to its existence as a seven-day time unit, but rather to the fact that every seven days something exceptional happened. Consequently, the week itself was defined by the occurrence of Sunday and this phenomenon has often been realized in the naming of the seven-day cycle.

I have recently undertaken a study of lexical acculturation entailing a survey of words for 77 items of Occidental culture (e. g., chicken, horse, apple, rice, scissors, soap, and Saturday) in the vocabularies of 292 Native American languages and dialects spoken from the Arctic Circle to Tierra del Fuego (Brown 1994, 1995, 1996b, 1999). A major finding is that geographically and genetically unrelated languages of Amerindians have strongly tended to develop semantically similar native labels for objects and concepts introduced by European intruders.

For example, Native American languages have commonly used a borrowed European-language term for a specific currency denomination (e. g., English *dollar* or Spanish *peso*) as a label for money in general. Of 183 language cases of the sample showing analyzable native terms for 'money', 81, or 44 percent, have extended European currency words to 'money' (referentially expanded European loans are considered *native terms* in my study [Brown 1999]). (In contrast, only 30 of the 263 language cases for which some term for 'money' is recorded have simply borrowed European words for the item, e. g., English *money* or Spanish *dinero*.) Languages extending borrowed European currency words to money in general are spoken in North, Central, and South America. While diffusion almost certainly accounts for part of this feature's distribution, it is unlikely that borrowing could explain it all. Clearly, there is a strong inclination for Amerindian languages to develop terms for 'money' independently through referential extension of borrowed European terms. This is probably a universal naming tendency. (I hesitate to assert definitively that any naming inclination is universal until the feature is determined to occur in languages other than those spoken in the New World.)

Of the 77 items of acculturation employed in the study, 37 are found to be associated with what I call *strong* naming tendencies across Native American languages. A strong naming tendency is considered to exist when an acculturated item is labeled by semantically similar native terms in at least 50 percent of the language cases for which analyzable native words for the item have been identified. For example, 'clock' shows semantically similar native terms in 109 of the 131 language cases manifesting analyzable native labels for the item, yielding a *naming tendency* percentage of 83. All of the 109 similar labels for 'clock' have in common the use of a constituent element that denotes 'sun' or the closely semantically allied referent, 'day' (see above discussion), e.g., Chaque (South America) 'sun to measure' and Tunica (North America) 'day counter'.

Commonly occurring native terms for some of the 37 items of acculturation showing strong naming tendencies are as follows: 'hard milk' = CHEESE, 'female horse' = MARE, 'milk fat' = BUTTER, 'small cow' = CALF, 'little horse' = COLT, 'fire maker' = MATCH, 'eating place' = TABLE, 'buying house' = STORE, 'round beans' = PEAS, 'day three' = WEDNESDAY, 'flat wood' = BOARD, 'reading house' = SCHOOL, 'leaf water' = TEA, 'sweet salt' = SUGAR, 'washing thing' = SOAP, 'black water' = COFFEE, 'digging thing' = SHOVEL, 'rolling wood' = WAGON, 'stinking onion' = GARLIC, 'sour orange' = LEMON, 'opening thing' = KEY, 'sewing thing' = NEEDLE, 'fastening thing' = BUTTON, 'male chicken' = ROOSTER, 'hair cutter' = SCISSORS.

While not prominent on the list of items associated with strong naming tendencies, introduced living things, especially animals, tend to be given native terms which designate similar organisms indigenous to the New World. For example, 'cow' is not included on the list because it does not demonstrate a naming tendency percentage of 50 or greater. The highest percentage associated with 'cow' is 33 (31/95). This number relates to the nomenclatural equating of 'cow' with the native bison. Other equations for 'cow' include 'cow' = 'tapir' at 8 percent, 'cow' = 'deer' at 7 percent, 'cow' = 'caribou' at 5 percent, 'cow' = 'moose' at 4 percent, 'cow' = 'elk' at 3 percent, and 'cow' = 'dog' and 'cow' = 'musk ox' at 1 percent each.

The naming of introduced living things by Amerindians has commonly involved associating biological things to be named with perceptually similar living things native to their habitats. The introduced organism is assigned a name already given to a living thing it most closely resembles among all living things labeled in a language, i.e., the *closest analog*. When the closest analog turns out to be the same (or very similar) for speakers of different languages, semantically similar names will emerge in those languages for the same imported biological entity. Under this interpretation, the more often speakers of different languages have closest analogs in common, the more frequently the introduced organism will show semantically similar labels across languages.

As noted above, among all New World creatures the bison is most commonly nomenclaturally associated with the introduced cow in Native American languages. Scientifically, cow and bison are closely related, both belonging to the same family, Bovidae, within the order Artiodactyla. Thus, nomenclatural evidence suggesting bison to be the closest analog for cow for numerous Amerindian groups is not surprising. That a relatively low naming tendency percentage (i.e., 33 percent) is associated with 'bison'/'cow' almost certainly reflects the fact that bison do not occur widely in the Americas (at least relatively speaking): these creatures are limited to North America, excluding the Arctic and most of Mexico. If bison were more broadly distributed, a naming tendency percentage greater than 33 would be expected.

Other analogs of cow — i.e., tapir, deer, caribou, moose, elk, dog, and musk ox (see above) — are nomenclaturally linked to cow at percentages less than nine. With the possible exception of the musk ox, none of these analogs resemble cow as closely as bison — if scientific classification can be taken as a reasonably good guide to perceptual similarity (but see Brown 1992). In most New World localities in which bison and one or more of the other creatures are cohabitants, bison constitutes the closest analog to cow. Consequently, words for bison have displayed a reasonably strong tendency to be used in reference to cow in languages spoken in such localities. Words for tapir, deer, caribou, mouse, elk and dog appear to have been referentially extended to cow in localities in which, for whatever reasons, these animals were not competing with bison for the title of cow's closest analog (Brown 1999).

As a member of the family Bovidae, musk ox would compete with bison as cow's closest analog. However, the native musk ox and bison do not live in the same regions of North America, so that such a head-to-head competition has probably never actually taken place. That a substantially greater naming tendency percentage pertains to 'bison'/'cow' (33 percent) compared to 'musk ox' (1 percent) simply reflects musk ox's drastically smaller geographic range (i.e., Arctic regions of North America) compared to that of bison.

7. Absolute lexical universals

Are there any objects or concepts that are lexically encoded in all human languages? In other words, are there any absolute lexical universals of language? As mentioned above, a term for 'wind' is found in all 221 languages surveyed for words for 'wind' and 'air' (Brown 1989a), suggesting that 'wind' is lexically encoded in all languages. Berlin & Kay's (1969) survey of 98 languages indicates that both 'black' and 'white' may be absolute lexical universals; however, 'white' is now in question since some so-called 'white' terms are actually focused in red rather than white (cf. Witkowski & Brown 1977). My impression after years of surveying large numbers of languages for various lexical items is that absolute lexical universals are not especially common.

Anna Wierzbicka in numerous publications (e.g., 1972, 1996) has devoted nearly three decades to fleshing out semantic primes or primitives of meaning. For her, meaning is defined as unique and culture-specific configurations of universal semantic primitives: "To state the meaning of a word is to reveal the configuration of simple concepts encoded in it ..." (1996: 212). Semantic analysis is all about "ways of saying the same thing in other words" where those "other words" are semantic primes that cannot themselves be defined (1996: 107). Such basic meanings are presumed innate to the human species and, consequently, universally known to humans. For the purposes at hand, Wierzbicka's most important claim is that semantic primes are denoted by words in all languages and, hence, are absolute lexical universals.

Originally fourteen primitives were posited (see Wierzbicka 1972), of which ten have survived to this time. As of 1994, the list had grown to 37 (see Goddard & Wierzbicka 1994), and by 1996 (Wierzbicka 1996), to a whopping 55. Examples of currently recognized semantic primes include items such as I, PEOPLE, SAY, BIG, ABOVE, PART (OF), IF, SOME, SEE, MOVE, MAYBE, and WORD.

About ten years ago, Wierzbicka (1989) challenged those interested in semantic primitives to undertake cross-language research to show empirically that proposed meaning primes are lexical universals. Only recently, however, has she made some strides along these lines herself with the publication of an edited book entitled *Semantic and Lexical Universals* (Goddard & Wierzbicka 1994). In chapters of the latter, authors discuss the lexical occurrence, or non-occurrence, of proposed semantic primes respectively in 16 languages studied in considerable depth by each scholar. While an admirable effort, conclusions of this study with respect to the lexical universality of specific primes should not be readily embraced due to the small sample of languages surveyed.

To my knowledge, I am the only one to take up Wierzbicka's challenge by surveying a large number of globally distributed languages for words for proposed semantic primes (Brown 1989b). Seven primitives were investigated in 50 languages. The former include KNOW, PLACE (SOMEWHERE), SAY, SOMETHING (THING), THINK, TIME (WHEN), and WANT. The cross-language data assembled unambiguously show that PLACE (SOMEWHERE) and SOMETHING (THING) are *not* absolute lexical universals. Data suggest that the remaining primes all may be absolute lexical universals, but some are more likely to be so than others. It is highly probably that SAY is lexically encoded in all languages. It is probable, but not highly so, that WANT is an absolute lexical universal. KNOW, THINK, and TIME (WHEN) are all possible, but not probable, absolute universals.

8. Lexical typology and linguistic areas

Specific semantic equations (realized lexically) are frequently found to show regional clustering or, in other words, to occur in several or more languages of a single world area. When the distribution of these is not accountable either to genetic relationship of languages, to universal tendencies, or to coincidence, they are indicative of a *linguistic area*. A linguistic area is apparent when geographically contiguous languages, some of which are not genetically related to one another, share linguistic features, and when feature sharing is largely explained by areal diffusion (i.e., borrowing). (See Campbell & Kaufman & Smith Stark [1986] for a detailed background discussion of linguistic area.)

Campbell & Kaufman & Smith Stark (1986) have assembled evidence showing that Mesoamerica constitutes a linguistic area. Mesoamerica is a culture region of Middle America stretching from Central Mexico to northern Central America. Included among their evidence are examples of lexical formulae that occur over and over again in Mesoamerican languages (i.e., calques or loan translations). In a more recent treatment, Smith Stark (1994) has expanded investigation of Mesoamerica-specific calques, identifying fifteen that meet the criteria of features defining a linguistic area. These include the following lexical relationships: 'head (of leg)' = 'knee', 'deer snake' = 'boa,' '(rock) ashes' = 'lime (stone),' 'neck (of hand)' = 'wrist', 'stone/bone (of bird)' = 'egg,' 'road (of blood)' = 'vein,' 'grindstone' = 'molar,' 'edge' = 'mouth,' 'poor' = 'widow,' = 'orphan,' 'awake' = 'alive,' 'God excrement' = 'silver/gold,' 'find/meet' = 'marry,' 'water-mountain' = 'town,' 'mother (of hand)' = 'thumb,' 'child (of hand)' = 'finger.'

Of these fifteen, as Smith Stark (1994: 40) notes, the last two treating digits of the hand are problematic as features of a Mesoamerican linguistic area since, as Brown & Witkowski (1981, and see above) have shown, these occur in many languages of the world in addition to those of Mesoamerica. However, as Smith Stark also mentions, the Mesoamerican rate for these features is still considerably higher than the global rate reported by Brown & Witkowski, indicating that these may nonetheless constitute diffused features of the area.

When regionally shared lexical traits in Amerindian languages are names for objects and concepts introduced by Europeans, linguistic areas are post-contact developments. I have compiled lexical evidence attesting to five major post-contact linguistic areas in the Americas, including the Southeastern United States, the Pacific Northwest, Andean South America, Mesoamerica, and Tropical Forest South America (Brown 1999).

The nature of post-contact linguistic areas can be illustrated through reference to data from languages of the Southeastern United States (Brown 1996a, 1999). Nineteen languages of the area, including 13 from five different genetic groupings, five language isolates, and a pidgin (Mobilian Jargon), show semantically similar native names for items introduced by Europeans. These include words for 'peach' based on terms for the native plum, words for 'pig' based on the opossum, terms for 'sheep' based on rabbit, words for 'monkey' based on raccoon, and others. The mentioned calques all have in common the fact that they occur frequently across Southeastern languages and infrequently, if at all, in other languages of the world, strongly indicating their diffusion across languages of the area.

Robust distributional evidence indicates that, in all five post-contact linguistic areas, lingua francas have been instrumental in the spread of widely shared lexical features. For example, the major lingua franca of the Southeastern United States, Mobilian Jargon (now extinct), shows all diffused lexical traits pertaining to languages of the region (see above), while other area languages only sporadically demonstrate them. If Mobilian Jargon were largely responsible for areal diffusion of these traits, all, or at least very nearly all, traits should pertain to its lexicon. On the other hand, this should not necessarily be so of recipient languages of the region. I have compiled comparable evidence showing that Chinook Jargon, Peruvian Quechua, Nahuatl, and Tupí (with Guaraní), all lingua francas, have similarly influenced development of post-contact linguistic areas respectively in the Pacific Northwest, in Andean South America, in Mesoamerica, and in Tropical Forest South America (Brown 1999).

9. References

Berlin, Brent. 1972. "Speculations on the growth of ethnobotanical nomenclature." *Language in Society* 1: 51–86.

Berlin, Brent. 1992. *Ethnobiological classification*. Princeton, New Jersey: Princeton University Press.

Berlin, Brent & Boster, James Shilts & O'Neill, John P. 1981. "The perceptual bases of ethnobiological classification: Evidence from Aguaruna Jívaro ornithology." *Journal of Ethnobiology* 1: 95–108.

Berlin, Brent & Kay, Paul. 1969. *Basic color terms: Their universality and evolution*. Berkeley: University of California Press.

Blank, Andreas. 1997. *Prinzipien des lexikalischen Bedeutungswandels in den romanischen Sprachen*. Tübingen: Niemeyer.

Brown, Cecil H. 1979. "A theory of lexical change (with examples from folk biology, human anatomical partonomy and other domains)." *Anthropological linguistics* 21: 257–276.

Brown, Cecil H. 1983. "Where do cardinal direction terms come from?" *Anthropological Linguistics* 25: 121–161.

Brown, Cecil H. 1984. *Language and living things: Uniformities in folk classification and naming*. New Brunswick, New Jersey: Rutgers University Press.

Brown, Cecil H. 1985. "Polysemy, overt marking, and function words." *Language Sciences* 7: 283–332.

Brown, Cecil H. 1987. "La polysémie, l'attribution d'une marque et le concept 'semaine'." *Recherches Amérindiennes au Québec* 17: 37–50.

Brown, Cecil H. 1989a. "Universal constraints on polysemy and overt marking." *Quaderni di Semantica* 10: 33–50.

Brown, Cecil H. 1989b. "Lexical universals and semantic primitives." *Quaderni di Semantica* 10: 279–295.

Brown, Cecil H. 1989c. "Naming the days of the week: A cross-language study of lexical acculturation." *Current Anthropology* 30: 536–550.

Brown, Cecil H. 1992. "British names for American birds." *Journal of Linguistic Anthropology* 2: 30–50.

Brown, Cecil H. 1994. "Lexical acculturation in Native American languages." *Current Anthropology* 35: 95–117.

Brown, Cecil H. 1995. "Lexical acculturation and ethnobiology: Utilitarism versus intellectualism." *Journal of Linguistic Anthropology* 5: 51–64.

Brown, Cecil H. 1996a. "A widespread marking reversal in languages of the Southeastern United States." *Anthropological Linguistics* 38: 439–460.

Brown, Cecil H. 1996b. "Lexical acculturation, areal diffusion, lingua francas, and bilingualism." *Language in Society* 25: 261–282.

Brown, Cecil H. 1999. *Lexical acculturation in Native American languages*. New York: Oxford University Press.

Brown, Cecil H. & Witkowski, Stanley R. 1980. "Language universals." *Toward Explaining Human Culture: A Critical Review of the Findings of Worldwide Cross-cultural Research*. (Authors of the rest of the book, David Levinson and Martin J. Malone). New Haven, Connecticut: HRAF Press, 359–384.

Brown, Cecil H. & Witkowski, Stanley R. 1981. "Figurative language in a universalist perspective." *American Ethnologist* 8: 596–615.

Brown, Cecil H. & Witkowski, Stanley R. 1983. "Polysemy, lexical change, and cultural importance." *Man* 18: 72–89.

Brunel, Gilles. 1987. "L'enfant de l'œil: La contribution de Brown à l'ethnoscience." *Recherches Amérindiennes au Québec* 17: 51–57.

Buck, Carl Darling. 1949. *A dictionary of selected synonyms in the principal Indo-European languages*. Chicago: University of Chicago Press.

Campbell, Lyle & Kaufman, Terrence & Smith Stark, Thomas C. 1986. "Meso-America as a linguistic area". *Language* 62: 530–570.

Casagrande, Joseph B. & Hale, Kenneth. 1967. Semantic relationships in Papago folk definitions. In: Hymes, Dell H. (ed.). *Studies in Southwestern ethnolinguistics*. The Hague: Mouton, 165–193.

Chiara, Maria. 1986. *Polysemy, overt marking, and atmospheric features: The development of a lexical domain*. (unpublished M. A. thesis) Northern Illinois University.

Dougherty, Janet W. D. 1978. "Salience and relativity in classification." *American Ethnologist* 5: 66–80.

Goddard, Cliff & Wierzbicka, Anna (eds.). 1994. *Semantic and lexical universals: Theory and empirical findings*. Amsterdam & Philadelphia: Benjamins.

Greenberg, Joseph H. (ed.). 1978. *Universals of human language, Volume 3, Word structure*. Stanford, California: University Press.

Hunn, Eugene. 1976. "Toward a perceptual model of folk biological classification." *American Ethnologist* 3: 508–524.

Hunn, Eugene. 1977. *Tzeltal folk zoology: The classification of discontinuities in nature*. New York: Academic Press.

Lyons, John. 1963. *Structural semantics*. Oxford: Blackwell.

Lyons, John. 1977. *Semantics. Volume 1*. London: Cambridge University Press.

Rosch, Eleanor & Mervis, Carolyn B. & Gray, Wayne D. & Johnson, David M. & Boyes-Braem, Penny. 1976. "Basic objects in natural categories." *Cognitive Psychology* 8: 382–439.

Segall, Marshall H. & Campbell, Donald T. & Herskovits, Melville J. 1966. *The influence of culture on visual perception*. Indianapolis: Bobbs-Merril Co.

Smith Stark, Thomas C. 1994. "Mesoamerican calques." In: MacKay, Carolyn & Vázquez, Verónica (eds.). *Investigationes Lingüísticas en Mesoamérica*. México: Universidad Nacional Autonoma de Mexico, 15–50.

Tagliavini, Carlo. 1949. "Di alcune denominazioni della 'pupilla'." *Annali dell' Instituto Universitario di Napoli* 3: 341–378.

Taylor, E. G. R. 1957. *The haven-finding art: A history of navigation from Odysseus to Captain Cook*. New York.

Widmann, Angelika. 1987. *'Daytime,' 'nighttime' and '24-hour-period' terms: A cross-linguistic study of polysemies*. (unpublished M. A. thesis) Northern Illinois University.

Wierzbicka, Anna. 1972. *Semantic primitives*. Linguistische Forschungen. No. 22. Frankfurt: Athenäum.

Wierzbicka, Anna. 1989. "Semantic primitives and lexical universals." *Quaderni di Semantica* 10: 103–121.

Wierzbicka, Anna. 1996. *Semantics: Primes and universals*. Oxford & New York: Oxford University Press.

Witkowski, Stanley R. & Brown, Cecil H. 1977. "An explanation of color nomenclature universals." *American Anthropologist* 79: 50–57.

Witkowski, Stanley R. & Brown, Cecil H. 1978. "Lexical universals." *Annual Review of Anthropology* 7: 427–451.

Witkowski, Stanley R. & Brown, Cecil H. 1983. "Marking-reversals and cultural importance." *Language* 59: 569–582.

Witkowski, Stanley R. & Brown, Cecil H. 1985. "Climate, clothing, and body-part nomenclature." *Ethnology* 24: 197–214.

Witkowski, Stanley R. & Brown, Cecil H. & Chase, Paul K. 1981. "Where do tree terms come from?" *Man* 16: 1–14.

Zerubavel, Eviatar. 1985. *The seven day circle: The history and meaning of the week*. New York: Free Press.

Cecil H. Brown, Dept. of Anthropology, Northern Illinois University (USA)

87. Universal units in the lexicon

1. Introduction
2. A partial review of proposed universal lexical units
3. Conclusions
4. References

1. Introduction

1.1. Definitions and overview

Cruse (1986: 77–78) defines a "lexical unit" as the pairing of a single specifiable sense (meaning) with a lexical form; see also Mel'čuk (1989). The concept is not to be identified either with "lexeme" (a family of lexical units) or with "lexical form" (a family of word forms which differ only in respect of inflection). A polysemous word is a lexeme which consists of more than one lexical unit. A lexical form need not be formally monomorphemic: it may be a compound or derived word or a phraseme.

This focus of this article is the question: Are there any universal lexical units? Or, more precisely: Are there any meanings which exist as the senses of lexical units in all languages? For terminological brevity, I will refer to meanings which (putatively) satisfy this description as "universally lexicalised meanings", or, more simply as "lexical universals".

One issue which immediately arises is what standard of precision it is reasonable to adopt. In discussions of lexical universals there is a tendency to speak at a level of approximate, rather than precise, semantic identity. For example, it is sometimes said, in the wake of Berlin and Kay (1969), that all languages have words for 'black' and 'white', but this statement is at best valid only at an approximate level because in languages with only a small number of abstract colour words, the words which cover black and white also cover many other hues.

Many suggestions about approximate lexical universals are closely linked with proposals, scattered throughout the anthropological literature, about cultural universals. Brown (1991) is a useful summary. Aside from various universals concerning language, he nominates things like: use of non-verbal communication, making of tools and shelter, use of fire, some form of marriage, a system of kinship, sexual regulations and standards of sexual modesty, division of labour, some system of "law" and sanctions, some standards of etiquette and hospitality, some concept of personal belongings, religious or supernatural beliefs, rituals, bodily adornment, medicines and healing practices, dancing and music, aesthetic standards, and many others. Ideas about approximate lexical universals also come from generalisations about the physical environment, and from inherent properties and capabilities of the human body.

To deal adequately with a reasonable sample of possible approximate lexical universals would be impossible here. Furthermore, precise lexical universals (if they exist) are surely more interesting than approximate ones. Limitations of space also preclude consideration here of implicational universals among lexical units, cf. Brown (1984, 1989), Witkowski and Brown (1978). For these reasons, this article will focus on the search for precise, and absolute, lexical universals.

The search for universal lexical units obviously presupposes that we have a principled and practical method of semantic description. Here we adopt reductive paraphrase in natural language as the basic method of specifying meanings. That is, a "meaning" of an expression will be regarded as a paraphrase, framed in semantically simpler terms than the original expression, which is substitutable without change of meaning into all contexts in which the original expression can be used.

This is the foundational postulate of the "natural semantic metalanguage" (NSM) approach to semantic analysis, originated by Anna Wierzbicka (1992, 1996, among other works; Goddard 1998). It is also followed, broadly speaking, by the Meaning-Text Model of Igor Mel'čuk and colleagues (cf. Mel'čuk 1988, 1989). The postulate implies the existence, in all languages, of a finite set of indefinable expressions (words, bound morphemes, phrasemes). The meanings of these indefinable expressions, which represent the terminal elements of language-internal semantic analysis, are known as "semantic primes". About 60 semantic primes have been proposed (Wierzbicka 1996). They are listed in § 1.2. below.

Wierzbicka and colleagues hypothesise that the semantic primes of all languages coincide. This is the strongest claim about universally lexicalised meanings to be found in the contemporary linguistic literature. Even if one grants that semantic primes have the best claim to being universals, however, it does not follow that they are the only possible lexical universals. There may be certain complex meanings which represent universals of human experience, and are thus plausible candidates for lexicalisation in all languages. The 50 or so proposed lexical universals considered in this article are about evenly divided between primes and non-primes.

So far as data is concerned, it is unfortunately not possible to rely on conventional dictionaries, because they do not meet the necessary standards of language-internal semantic analysis. In particular, they generally do not characterise semantic invariants of meaning in a clear or accurate (i. e. predictive) fashion, nor do they distinguish adequately between polysemy and semantic generality. These criticisms apply even to major monolingual dictionaries of English and other European languages, let alone to dictionaries of "out of the way" indigenous languages. Before reliable conclusions about lexical universals can be drawn, it is fundamental that polysemy be recognised as appropriate, and distinguished from semantic generality, because otherwise we cannot even establish the number and nature of lexical units belonging to each lexeme.

It is not possible here to discuss criteria for recognising polysemy, except to say that we here adopt the traditional "definitional" approach; i. e. an expression has a single meaning if and only if it is possible to formulate a single reductive paraphrase explication which is predictive of its full range of distribution. An expression is polysemous if this is not possible, and two (or more) distinct explications are required. Formal indications of polysemy include the putatively distinct meanings having different syntactic properties, or having different antonyms, or only one of the senses participating in a derivational process (cf. Apresjan 1992; Mel'čuk 1988; Wierzbicka 1996: 242−44, 270−74).

Given the unsuitability of data from dictionaries, it may be asked whether any real progress can be made on identifying universally lexicalised meanings. If we confine ourselves to high quality information, we will not be able to sample more than a small fraction of the 5,000 or so languages of the world. It turns out, however, that this limitation is not as profound as it seems, because most proposed lexical universals fail even on a small sample of geographically dispersed languages. The sample used in this article consists mainly of languages which I know personally or have been able to discuss with native speakers or colleagues who have done intensive semantic-lexicographical research: Yankunytjatjara, Malay, Cantonese, Kalam, Japanese, Polish and Russian. They represent six language families (Pama-Nyungan, Austronesian, Sinitic, Papuan, Japanese, Indo-European).

1.2. Divergent approaches: Swadesh, Wierzbicka, and Brown

It is interesting to contrast Morris Swadesh's (1972) list of 100 "basic vocabulary" items with Anna Wierzbicka's (1996) list of 55-odd "semantic primes". The purposes and origins of these two lists are, of course, very different. Swadesh was chiefly interested in identifying a sample of stable, widely lexicalised meanings which could be used for the purposes of lexicostatistical analysis. His approach was purely pragmatic and inductive. He adjusted his initial hypotheses several times as a result of pretesting before proposing the 100-items listed in Table 87.1. Swadesh describes these items as designating "universal and simple things, qualities, and activities, which depend to the least possible degree on the particular environment and cultural state of the group". They include "pronouns, some quantitative concepts, parts and simple activities of the body, movements, and some general qualities of size, colour, and so on" (Swadesh 1972: 275). Swadesh recognised that languages may not have precise semantic equivalents to these items.

Table 87.1: 100-item Basic Vocabulary List (Swadesh 1972)

I, you, we, this, that, who, what, not, all, many, one, two, big, long, small, woman, man, person, fish, bird, dog, louse, tree, seed, leaf, root, bark, skin, flesh, blood, bone, grease, egg, horn, tail, feather, hair, ear, eye, nose, mouth, tongue, claw, foot, knee, hand, belly, neck, breasts, heart, liver, drink, eat, bite, see, hear, know, sleep, kill, die, swim, fly, walk, come, lie, sit, stand, give, say, sun, moon, star, water, rain, stone, sand, earth, cloud, smoke, fire, ash, burn, path, mountain, red, green, yellow, white, black, night, hot, cold, full, new, good, round, dry, name

Swadesh does not ascribe any significance to the ordering of the list, but to some extent it must reflect a hypothesis about the durability and universality of the items. It can be no coincidence that almost all of the first dozen-and-a-half prove to be relatively strong candidates as universally lexicalised meanings. Surprisingly, in view of their different origins, most of the early Swadesh items also occur on Wierzbicka's list of proposed universal semantic primes.

Wierzbicka's proposals differ from those of Swadesh in that they are derived entirely from semantic analysis. The items listed in Table 87.2 are, according to Wierzbicka (1996), meanings which are both incapable of any further (non-circular) definition, and essential for adequate paraphrase analysis of the lexicon at large. It is claimed that every one of the proposed semantic primes exists as the meaning of a lexical unit in all languages. Furthermore, the claim is that the meaning correspondence across languages is not merely approximate, but precise.

The "double-barrelled" items in Table 87.2, such as *something/thing*, *someone/person*, and *when/time*, indicate meanings which, in English, are expressed by means of variant forms ("allolexes") in different grammatical contexts (Wierzbicka 1997: 26−27). *Something*

Table 87.2: Proposed semantic primes (Wierzbicka 1996)

Substantives: *I, you, someone/person, people; something/thing*
Determiners: *this, the same, other*
Quantifiers: *one, two, same, all, many/much*
Attributes: *good, bad, big, small*
Mental predicates: *think, know, want, feel, see, hear*
Speech: *say, word*
Actions, events, movements: *do, happen, move*
Existence: *there is*
Life and death: *live, die*
Time: *when/time, now, before, after, a long time, a short time, for some time*
Space: *where/place, here, above, below; far, near; side, inside*
Logical concepts: *not, maybe, can, because, if*
Intensifier, augmentor: *very, more*
Taxonomy, partonomy: *kind of, part of*
Similarity: *like*

and *thing*, for example, express the same meaning except that *something* cannot be used in combination with a specifier; compare (a) *something happened*, (b) *the same thing happened again*, (c) *I don't know when this thing happened*. Note also that several more terms are under consideration as possible semantic primes, including *body, true, touch,* and *have*.

The list in Table 87.2 is not sufficient in itself to identify the intended meanings, because many of these English expressions are polysemous. Each prime is also provided with a set of "canonical contexts"; that is, a set of sentences exemplifying its characteristic grammatical (combinatorial) contexts. For example, to ascertain which sense of English *know* is intended as a prime one can refer to canonical contexts such as *I don't know where he is* and *This person knows something about you*. (Note that equivalents of semantic primes may have different morphosyntactic characteristics, and hence belong to different "parts of speech", in different languages, without this necessarily disturbing their canonical combinatorial properties.)

The claim that semantic primes are universal has been empirically investigated in a collection of studies published as *Semantic and Lexical Universals* (Goddard & Wierzbicka (eds.) 1994). In these studies, contributors investigated whether 39 proposed semantic primes (the full number at that time) were to be found "embodied", as it were, in lexical units in a varied range of languages. The sample was typologically and genetically diverse, containing only one European language, French. The other languages were: Acehnese (Indonesia), Arrernte, Kayardild and Yankunytjatjara (Australia), Ewe (Ghana), Japanese, Longgu (Solomon Islands), Kalam and Mangap-Mbula (Papua New Guinea), Mandarin Chinese, three Misumalpan languages (Nicaragua), Samoan, and Thai. Subsequent work (Goddard (ed.) 1997) has examined aspects of the combinatorial syntax of primes in Japanese, Longgu, French, and Hawaiian Creole English. A set of comprehensive studies of Lao, Malay, Mandarin Chinese, Polish, and Spanish is underway (Goddard and Wierzbicka (eds.) In press).

Finally, mention should be made of the cross-linguistic lexical surveys of Cecil Brown, Stanley Witkowski, and colleagues (Witkowski and Brown 1978; Brown 1984, 1989). Inspired by the work of Berlin and Kay (1969) these scholars have mounted a series of studies into regularities in body-part nomenclature, folk biology, weather terminology, and various other lexical fields (→ Art. 85, 86). The relevance of these surveys to the existence of precise lexical universals is, however, rather limited; firstly, by the fact that the investigators were primarily interested in finding implicational universals of lexical field structure, rather than precise lexical universals, and secondly, by their reliance on data from bilingual dictionaries, which, as noted earlier, is generally not of a suitable semantic standard to support the identification of precise lexical universals.

2. A partial review of proposed universal lexical units

We can now undertake a review of proposed universally lexicalised meanings, including both proposed semantic primes and other, non-prime, meanings such as those identified by the work of Swadesh and others. It is impossible, in the space available, to attempt a comprehensive coverage so we will confine ourselves to a selection of substantives, quantifiers, attributes, and predicates.

2.1.1. Substantives

Typologists take for granted the universality of the singular pronouns 'I' and 'you'. The only substantial issue concerns languages like Thai and Japanese which have several different pronouns in each category, the choice between them signalling some kind of interpersonal message to do with solidarity, social distance, or the like. This has been discussed by Diller (1994) and Onishi (1994), who both conclude that, initial impressions notwithstanding, it is possible to identify primary, semantically unmarked equivalents for 'I' and 'you' in Thai and Japanese, respectively. It is sometimes claimed that English *you* is indeterminate as to number, but in reality the word is polysemous between *you(SG)* and *you(PL)*, as shown by the contrast between the reflexives *yourself* and *yourselves*.

All – or nearly all – languages appear to have separate words for 'someone' and 'something' (cf. Goddard and Wierzbicka (eds.) 1994; Haspelmath 1997). Sometimes the same words are also used as interrogatives and/or "knowledge complements", (i. e. in constructions like *I don't know who did it* or *I know what happened*), as with Acehnese *soe* 'who/someone' and *peue* 'what/something' (Durie et al. 1994). More commonly, one set of forms is morphologically basic and the others are built upon it. In some polysynthetic languages, the equivalents of 'something' and 'someone' are bound morphemes, as, for example, in Koasati (Louisiana) in which the relevant forms are *na:si-* and *a:ti-*, respectively (Kimball 1985: 106, 135−9).

In some languages the meanings 'someone' and 'other' are expressed by the same lexeme, but because their syntactic properties are so different ('someone' being a substantive and 'other' a specifier) it is usually straightforward to establish polysemy on language-internal grounds. For example, Yankunytjatjara *kutjupa* means 'other' when it is adnominal, as in a phrase like *kungka kutjupa* 'another woman', and 'someone' when it is the head of an NP in its own right, as in (1).

(1) *Kutjupa-ngku katingu.*
 someone-ERG take:PAST
 'Someone took (it)'.

It might be thought that the latter usage is elliptical, with an implied head noun such as *anangu* 'people/person', but this analysis is not viable since *kutjupa(ngku)* 'someone' can be used to refer to non-human beings, such as the Christian God, who could never be referred to as an *anangu* '(human) person'.

2.1.2. Relational substantives

Linguists seem to agree that partonomic relationships are fundamental to the vocabulary structure of languages, but although 'part (of)' is postulated to be a semantic prime there are languages which do not have a unique lexeme for this meaning. Typically, in such cases, the meaning 'part (of)' is expressed by means of the word for 'something', 'thing', or 'what', used in a grammatical construction associated with "possession". This can be illustrated from Mbula (Austronesian, Papua New Guinea).

(2) Mbula (Bugenhagen In press)
ti tomtom na koroŋŋa-nda
we person given thing-our
boozo, kumbu-ndu nama-nda ...
many leg-our head-our
'We people, our parts are many: legs, heads, ...'

Presumably, it is no coincidence that 'part' is sometimes expressed by means of the same lexeme as 'something'. A part of something is itself a 'something'. One might even call 'part' a "relational substantive".

As with partonomy, so with taxonomy. Linguists and cognitive anthropologists seem to agree that taxonomy is a basic principle of lexical organisation, especially in the realm of living things (cf. Berlin 1992) (→ Art. 86). All languages have hierarchies of designations which specify that certain individually named animals and plants are 'kinds' of some higher level "life forms"; e.g. a *sparrow* is a kind of *bird*, an *oak* is a kind of *tree*. But there is less agreement about whether all languages contain a lexical unit which can articulate the nature of this arrangement.

All languages examined in Goddard and Wierzbicka ((eds.) 1994) do contain a lexical unit meaning 'kind (of)', but in several languages this unit belonged to a polysemous lexeme. For example, in Yankunytjatjara 'kind of' is expressed by the lexeme *ini* which can also mean 'name'. For example:

(3) Yankunytjatjara (Goddard 1994)
wayuṯa kuka ini kutjupa
possum meat name(=kind) other
'The possum is another kind of meat-animal'.

In Kayardild, 'kind' is expressed by *minyi*, which can also mean 'colour' (Evans 1994).

2.1.3. Human classification and relationships

It seems that all languages have a lexical item one of whose meanings corresponds to that of English *people* in non-specific uses like 'people think ...', 'people say ...', and so on.

In European languages this word is often a collective term, unrelated to the word for an individual human being; for example, French *les gens*, Russian *ljudi*. In languages without obligatory number marking, the term for 'people' can usually be used to refer to a single individual. This is the case, for example, with Japanese *hito*, Yankunytjatjara *anangu*, and Malay *orang*.

In some languages the term for 'people' is formally complex, e.g. Kalam *bin-b* (lit. 'man-woman') (Pawley 1993). Sometimes the expression for 'people' appears to be a pluralised version of the term for 'someone'; for example, Mbula *zin tomtom* (lit. PL marker + 'someone'). The Mbula expression is not semantically the sum of its parts, however, because *tomtom* 'someone' can refer to beings other than humans, whereas *zin tomtom* cannot.

'Man' and 'woman' are not proposed semantic primes, but they nevertheless have some claim to being universal meanings. It is true that often their nearest equivalents can be conflated with "social" information (e.g. rank or age-level), but it can often be shown that such lexemes are polysemous, with both general and specific meanings. In Pitjantjatjara, for example, there are two words for 'woman', *kungka* and *minyma*, the distinction being based on the age and associated seniority of the individual. Further, *wati* 'man' normally refers only to initiated men. However, it is arguable that in both cases there is polysemy, with *wati* and *minyma* also having more general meanings as 'man' and 'woman', respectively (cf. Goddard 1996). One piece of evidence for this conclusion is that the words *wati* and *minyma* are used when it is necessary to speak about men and women in general, without regard to their social status (for example, to discuss sexually transmitted diseases or to discuss ritual or economic division of labour). Both words are also routinely used about non-Aboriginal men and women.

A potential counter-example of a different kind is found in Japanese, where instead of single words for 'man' and 'woman' there are phrasemes of the form 'male person' and 'female person': *otoko no hito* and *onna no hito*. Normally, however, these Japanese expressions are not used to refer to children, and as far as I know, they have the same referential range as English *man* and *woman*. Until and unless some specific differences are identified, the claim that 'man' and 'woman' are lexical universals remains viable. Cantonese at first appears to have similar "phrasemic" equivalents to 'man' and 'woman' but on closer examination there is evidence that the forms are lexical compounds. For example, in *léuih-yán* 'woman' (lit. 'female person') the second morpheme *yán* has rising tone, but as a separate word *yàhn* has low-falling tone. This kind of tone change indicates that the combination has been lexicalised (Matthews and Yip 1994: 26).

'Child' is not a viable universal meaning for at least two reasons, both of which can be illustrated from Spanish. First, in some languages there is no gender-neutral term answering to 'child'; Spanish *niño* and *niña* designate a male child and a female child, respectively. Second, there may be several terms corresponding to 'child' depending on the age of the individual. Spanish *niño* and *niña* are appropriate only to young children (including babies). After about 11 or 12 years of age, the words *muchacho* and *muchacha*, roughly 'boy' and 'girl', are called for.

Kinship is probably the most intensively studied of all cultural phenomena. According to most experts, the biological link between mother and child provides an essential "linking principle" in all kin systems, raising the question of whether 'mother' could be a universally lexicalised meaning. The proposal is not necessarily upset by the existence of "classificatory" kin terminology because there may be language-internal grounds for recognising polysemy in such languages (cf. Wierzbicka 1992).

To illustrate the kind of evidence and arguments involved, consider Yankunytjatjara *ngunytju*, which can be used not only for one's mother but also for one's mother's sisters and mother's female cousins (among others). There are arguments for recognising two lexical units: *ngunytju*$_1$ 'mother', and an extended sense *ngunytju*$_2$. First, the expression *ngunytju mula* (*mula* 'true') can only refer to one's biological mother; if *ngunytju* did not have a distinct sense as "biological *ngunytju*" it is hard to see how *ngunytju mula* could have this sense. Second, unlike other kin terms, *ngunytju* is routinely used about animals, where there is no question of classificatory extension and where the biological basis for the usage seems particularly clear.

In other languages, there may be additional reasons for favouring a polysemy analysis. For example, Dyirbal not only has the word *yabu* for 'mother' (including classificatory mother), it also has *jarraga* for non-classificatory mothers (Dixon 1989). Walmajarri not only has *ngamaji* for 'mother' (including classificatory mother), it also has *kumpurru* 'foster-mother', *parnmarn* 'a man's actual mother-in-law', and *karntiya* 'a woman's actual son-in-law' (Richards & Hudson 1990). If the concept of 'mother' (i. e. biological mother) is salient enough to figure as a semantic component of other words, this suggests at least that it is likely to exist as the meaning of a lexical unit in its own right.

We can say then that 'mother', in its biological sense, has a reasonable claim to the status of a universally lexicalised meaning. Wierzbicka (1992) contends that the same logic applies to 'father', but this conclusion does not seem as secure, mainly because the role of "father" is more open to social factors than that of 'mother' (cf. Foley 1997: 133–4).

2.1.4. The natural world

Research on ethnobiological nomenclature has shown that certain "life-form" terms ('tree', 'bird', and 'fish') are extremely common, if not absolutely universal (Brown 1984, Berlin 1992). At best, however, these meanings can lay claim to the status of approximate lexical universals. English, for example, recognises several botanical life-form words (*tree*, *bush*, *vine*, etc.), with the result that English *tree* is much narrower in its referential range than the nearest term in a language with fewer life-form categories, such as Yankunytjatjara, whose main botanical life-form *punu* takes in trees, bushes, vines, grasses and fungi. *Punu* can be glossed as 'living thing which grows out of the ground', whereas English *tree* includes this component plus the specification that the thing in question have a 'trunk'. Clearly the semantic match between *punu* and *tree* is not precise. Similar facts to those which disqualify 'tree' as a precise lexical universal also apply to 'bird' and to 'fish'.

Surprising as it may seem to speakers of European languages, 'water' is probably not a lexical universal. Japanese has two words (*mizu* and *yu*) for 'water', with *yu* (often with honorific prefix *o-*) being reserved for hot water (Suzuki 1978: 51–52). *Mizu* cannot be used about hot water, and combining the adjective *atsui* 'hot' with *mizu* sounds unnatural (Suzuki calls it "self-contradictory"), though there is no such restriction in relation to other liquids, e. g. *atsui miruku* 'hot milk'. These facts imply that *mizu* and *yu* have a reference to "temperature" built into their meanings. There are also languages like Yimas (Foley 1997: 35) which have no word reserved for water alone: Yimas *arm* 'liquid' includes petrol and kerosene in addition to water.

The claim that 'fire' is a universal lexicalised meaning seems quite plausible; however, Russian may present a counter-example. As well as *ogon'*, normally glossed as 'fire', Russian has another common word *kostër*, for a fire which is lit outside usually for the purpose of keeping people warm. The significant fact is that a *kostër* cannot be referred to, in Russian, as an *ogon'* (or as a kind of *ogon'*), though it would definitely qualify as a *fire* in English.

Foley (1997: 35) hypothesis that a noun corresponding to 'rock' is "a predetermined category" in the vocabularies of all languages, but this contention does not hold up if we understand it to mean that all languages have a lexical unit meaning precisely the same as English *rock*. Polish *skała*, for example, is normally glossed as 'rock' but it is quite different to English *rock*. *Skała* is used for big rocks set into the ground, and could not be used to refer to a rock the size of (say) a loaf of bread.

As for 'day' and 'night', it is necessary to indicate which senses of these words are intended as possible universal meanings. In some languages, separate words are used for the "ambient condition" vs. "unit of time" senses; for example, Yankunytjatjara *ka̲la̲la* 'by day, in the daylight', *tji̲ntu (kutjara)* '(two) days'; Malay *siang* 'by day', *(dua) hari* 'two days'. It seems that the "unit" sense of 'day' is more likely to be a universal than the ambient sense. I am not aware of any counter-example.

There are languages in which the word closest in meaning to 'night' is not normally used in a "unit" sense. For example, in Polish it would sound very odd to say the equivalent of 'three nights'. This suggests that if 'night' is to have any claim to being a lexical universal, it is in the "ambient" sense of the word (e.g. in a phrase like 'at night'). Polish, however, can be used to furnish counter-evidence to this proposal. The key fact is that Polish *wieczór* (roughly) 'evening' differs from its nearest English counterpart in being viewed as the last part of the day (rather than the first part of the night, like English *evening*). Hence Polish *noc* (roughly) 'night' doesn't start till *wieczór* is over; in other words, *noc* starts later than English *night*. Differences like this suggest that 'night' is not a precise lexical universal.

2.2. Attributes

Terms for the semantic primes 'good' and 'bad' appear to exist in all languages (Goddard & Wierzbicka (eds.) 1994; cf. Dixon 1982). It appears possible in all languages to express meanings involving 'good' and 'bad' in both attributive and in predicative frames; i.e. to say the equivalents of things like 'do something good/bad' and 'be good/bad'.

It must be acknowledged, however, that expressions for 'good' and 'bad' do not have exactly the same range of uses in different languages. Obviously, one source of such disparities is simply that different cultures regard different things as good and bad (and for different reasons). But not all differences can be explained in this way. In particular, there are idiosyncratic restrictions on combinations of these terms with semantically complex words, e.g. in French one can speak of *mauvais temps* 'bad weather', but not of *bon temps 'good weather'.

Terms for 'big' and 'small' also appear to exist in all languages (Goddard & Wierzbicka (eds.) 1994; cf. Dixon 1982) (→ Art. 91). In some languages, the term for 'big' shares a form with 'much/many' or with 'very'; but in these cases the existence of different grammatical properties makes it necessary to recognise polysemy.

A non-prime "attributive" meaning with some claim to universal status is 'old'. Dixon (1982) has claimed that all languages have at least one "age" term, and given the social significance of old people in most societies, it might be thought that 'old' is the best candidate for a lexical universal of "age". Presumably the meaning is quite simple: to say that someone 'is old' is to say that this person has 'lived for a long time'. However, in some cultures age-standing is conflated with other social meanings, particularly gender and seniority, and there may be no lexeme meaning simply 'old'. For example, in Yankunytjatjara to speak of an 'old' man one uses the term *tjilpi*, whereas to speak of an 'old' woman one uses the term *wampa*. There is no single term which can be used "generically", as it were, to refer to 'old people'. One has to say 'old men (and) old women' or 'grandparents (and) grandmothers'. This implies that 'old' is not a lexical universal.

2.3. Quantifiers

No convincing counter-examples have been reported to the claim that 'one' and 'two' are lexical universals, providing one is prepared to recognise that they may have different morphosyntactic properties (i.e. belong to different word-classes) in different languages. For example, in Samoan numbers are formally verbs, so that to say 'two men', for example, one says, in effect, 'man being-two'. It also has to be recognised that a language's having terms for 'one' and 'two' does not necessarily mean that the speakers of the language employ these words for "counting". Many cultures lack the institution of serial counting ('one, two, three, four, ...'), and some have no words for numbers higher than three or four.

It seems likely that all languages have at least one word with the meaning 'many' and/or 'much'. An unresolved question is whether these are properly regarded as separate meanings, as suggested by the existence of distinct words in English and many other languages (e.g. Thai *lă:y* 'many', *mâ:k* 'much'), or whether they are contextual variants of a single meaning, as suggested by the fact that in many other languages a single word is used in both functions (for example, Mandarin *xǔduō*, Arrernte *arunthe*, French *beaucoup*).

There are also languages in which there are overlaps in form, but not complete identity. For example, in German *viele* is 'many' (*viele Leute* 'many people') but *viel* is 'much' (*viel Bier* 'much beer'); the two words also have different case-marking patterns. Another possibility is for there to be a single form, but one which manifests slightly different combinatorial syntax depending in its meaning. For example, Malay *banyak* can be combined with *sangat* 'very' when it means 'many' (*sangat banyak kucing* 'very many cats'), but not when it means 'much' (**sangat banyak air* 'very much water'). Overall, the evidence suggests that 'many' and 'much' should be regarded as separate meanings.

Despite various claims that certain "primitive" languages lack the resources for making "absolute generalisations", no reputable linguistic description has reported a language which lacks an equivalent for 'all'. It is clear, however, that words for 'all' can vary in their syntax from language to language. In particular, in some languages 'all' has an "adverbial" syntax, i.e. it does not combine directly with nouns (→ Art. 92). For example, Japanese *minna* 'all' is a verbal modifier (Onishi 1994); Mandarin Chinese *dōu* 'all' is an adverb (Chappell 1994).

2.4. Predicates

2.4.1. Events and actions

Most complex events are easily disconfirmed as lexical universals. For example, 'break' and 'hit' have no hope of attaining this status because many languages lexically distinguish different kinds of breaking and hitting. The most plausible candidates for universal "event" meanings are more general in nature; specifically, the proposed semantic primes 'happen' and 'do'. It appears that both meanings have a strong claim to universality, once various instances of polysemy are properly understood.

In many languages, e.g. Mbula, Ewe, and French, the word for 'happen' has secondary meanings 'appear' or 'arrive'. This is not difficult to understand once we see that 'appearing' and 'arriving' both involve something 'happening in a place', after which something or someone is in the place in question.

Another polysemy which recurs sporadically around the world is between 'happen' and 'do'. For example, in Kalam a single stem *g-* expresses both meanings (and also 'feel', see below). There are contexts in which *g-* can only mean 'happen', as in (a), contexts where it can only mean 'do', as in (b), and contexts like (c), which are ambiguous.

(4) Kalam (Pawley 1994: 408, 396, 408)
 (a) *Mñab nb ak ned wagn ak*
  country such this first origin the
  g gek mñab Aytol-jl
  happen it-happened country Aytol-jl
  'The place where this originally happened was at Aytol-jl'.
 (b) *Gos etp agi ap*
  thought what having.thought come
  kun gpan?
  such you.did
  'What where you thinking that you came and did that?'
 (c) *Tap etp gp?*
  thing what happen/do.3SG.PERF
  'What's happened?' Or: 'What has he done?'

A crucial analytical question is whether it is possible to sustain a monosemy interpretation of the Kalam data. The problem for such an interpretation is that if *g-* had a unitary meaning in (a) and (b) — a "Kalam-specific" meaning which cannot be stated in English — then (c) cannot be ambiguous after all, which seems unlikely in the light of Pawley's description.

Focusing now on 'do', it can be observed that a great many languages either have a unique lexeme for this meaning or a lexeme which is polysemous between 'do' and 'make'. To be sure, there are complications in some languages. Aside from polysemy between 'do' and 'happen' (as in Kalam), polysemy between 'do' and 'say' is not uncommon. For example, Samoan *fai* can mean either 'do' or 'say', but the two lexical units have different morphosyntactic properties (Mosel 1994). *Fai* 'say' is a non-ergative verb, selecting an absolutive subject, whereas *fai* 'do' selects an ergative subject. As well, *fai* 'do' often occurs in the so-called long (suffixed) form *fai = a*, which is usual when an ergative verb is preceded by a pronoun, even when *fai* 'do' is used in a non-transitive frame, for example to say 'Who did it?'.

Two non-prime meanings with some claim to universality are 'make' and 'give'. Humans being quintessentially "tool-making" creatures, it might be conjectured that all languages would have a lexical unit corresponding to 'make'. I know of no counter-example to this proposal.

It is well-known that in many languages from around the world one uses the same lexeme for both 'do' and 'make' (e.g. Malay *buat*, Yankunytjatjara *palyani*, Miskuti *daukaia*, Arrernte *mpware-*, Kalam *g-*), but it seems likely that there are language-internal grounds for positing polysemy in such cases. For example, the meaning 'make' (but not 'do') will be compatible with a "material source" argument (i.e. one could ask the equivalent of: 'What did you make it from?'). Also, native speakers clearly recognise that some sentences, e.g. those of the form 'What did you do/make?', are ambiguous between the two meanings.

Polysemy between 'do' and 'make' makes sense given that the meaning of 'make' involves 'do' along with other elements. Specifically, 'making' something (Y) involves purposefully 'doing something' with some material with a certain goal in mind, which can be roughly stated as: 'if I do this, there will be a Y here; I want this'.

In a broad sense, 'giving' has a good claim to being a universal of human behaviour. Lists of basic vocabulary almost always include 'give', and the word is one of the first verbs to be acquired by young children (cf. Newman 1996). Dixon (1982) includes 'giving' as one of his fundamental "semantic types", implying that every language has at least one "verb of giving".

Though Dixon's claim seems entirely plausible, it does not follow that every language has a "verb of giving" with exact semantic counterparts in all other languages. One factor which might suggest otherwise is the familiar fact that 'giving' can be construed either from the point of the recipient or of the thing transferred, as in the English constructions *X gave person-Y thing-Z* vs. *X gave thing-Z to person-Y*. Many languages allow both types of construction, but there are also languages in which only one of the construction types is found. For example, Ojibwa and Tzotzil only have the "thing as direct object" pattern, whereas Maori and French only have the "recipient as direct object" pattern (Dryer 1986). If one were to assume that these different construction types express different construals, these facts would militate against the universality of any single 'give' meaning. Admittedly, such an assumption would require independent justification. At the moment, then, the situation with 'give' is unclear, though it is highly likely to be, at least, an approximate lexical universal.

2.4.2. Motion

Though linguists generally assume that "motion" is a universal linguistic category, it is unlikely that any complex verb of motion will be a true lexical universal, given that languages differ greatly in the pattern by which semantic specifications of other kinds (e.g. manner, means, path) are conflated with motion (Talmy 1985). If any motion verb is a viable lexical universal, the best candidate is probably the simplest motion verb of all, namely, 'move' (Wierzbicka 1996).

Given that 'move' is not the kind of word which normally figures in basic vocabulary lists, it is surprising that there is often no difficulty in finding equivalents to it in languages from around the world (in canonical contexts such as 'something moved in the bushes' or 'I was so cold/frightened, I couldn't move'). For example, Malay *bergerak*, Yankunytjatjara *yurinyi*, Kalam *am-*. On the other hand, some languages reportedly distinguish between moving-without-change-of-location and moving-with-change-of-location. For example, Lao has *nêng³* 'move (not from place to place)' and *ñaaj⁴* 'move from place to place' (Enfield In press). Reports of this kind challenge the universal status of 'move'.

'Go' is not viable as a universally lexicalised meaning. Even within Europe, there are languages which do not have exact semantic equivalents for 'go'. For example, German has two everyday words for "translational motion": *gehen* (roughly), 'go on foot' and *fahren* 'go, not on foot' (e.g. in a vehicle). In the broader sample of languages, the non-viability of 'go' is even more apparent (cf. Wilkins and Hill 1996).

2.4.3. Cognition

The semantic prime 'know' is found in canonical contexts such as: (a) *I don't know where he is*, (b) *She knows you said something about her*. 'Know' in this sense (German *wissen*, French *savoir*, Malay *tahu*, Polish *wiedziec*') has a strong claim to being a universally lexicalised meaning. In some languages, the relevant expression is formally complex, but not in ways which challenge the semantic integrity of the meaning 'know' itself. For example, Japanese *sitte iru* 'know' consists of the verb *siru* with the linking suffix *-te* and the auxiliary *iru*. Since *siru* by itself means 'learn, come to know' it might be thought that *sit-te iru* means 'be in the state of having come to know', but resultative readings of this kind are possible only in highly specific contexts. Usually *sitte iru* simply indicates a state. The best interpretation is therefore that *sitte iru* is polysemous, with its stative meaning being fully equivalent to 'know' (Onishi 1994: 368).

It is sometimes claimed that certain little-studied languages do not draw a distinction between mental predicates like 'think' and 'know', and perceptual ones like 'hear', but where data is available this claim turns out to be a confusion based on failure to understand polysemy. Just as French *entendre* has two distinct meanings ('hear' and 'understand'), so Yankunytjatjara *kulini* does double duty for both 'think' and 'hear'. The two senses can be differentiated on language-internal grounds, since each has a distinct syntactic frame from which the other is excluded (Goddard 1991; cf. Evans and Wilkins 2000).

As for 'want', evidence assembled in the studies in Goddard and Wierzbicka ((eds.) 1994), and subsequently in Harkins (1995), strongly suggests that 'want' is a universally lexicalised meaning. This fact is, however, frequently obscured by language-specific patterns of polysemy which mean that the lexemes in question do not have identical ranges of use. For example, Yankunytjatjara *mukuringanyi* 'want' has a broader range of use than English *want*, because *mukuringanyi* can also mean 'like, be fond of (a person)' (Goddard 1991). Similarly, Spanish *querer* not only has the meaning 'want', but also a secondary meaning 'love, like (a person)'. Polysemy between 'want' and 'seek' is fairly common, being found, for example, in Ewe (Ameka 1994).

Some languages use distinct lexical forms for 'want' in different syntactic contexts. For example, the Japanese desiderative suffix *-tai* is the normal equivalent of 'want' in an "equi" complement clause, which has an embedded structure. With non-equi complement clauses, however, 'want' is expressed by a distinct adjectival word *hosii* and the complement clause is marked by the subordinating suffix *-te* (Onishi 1997).

(5) Japanese
   (a) *Ore wa soko no iki-tai.*
       I TOP [there LOC go]-want
      'I want to go there.'
   (b) *Ore wa sore oki-te   hosii.*
       I TOP that happen-CONJ want
      'I want that to happen.'

Despite the different allolexes, and the different syntactic structures, there seems to be no specifiable semantic difference between *-tai* and *hosii*, so that they have to be analysed as members of the same lexical unit.

2.4.4. Sensations and emotions

The semantic prime 'feel' is neutral to the distinction between emotion and sensation. Emotion terms are constructed by combining 'feel' with cognitive predicates such as 'think' and 'want', and other elements such as 'good' and 'bad'. Sensation terms involve similar components as well as the prime 'body'.

Perhaps because of its frequent semantic compounding, lexemes for 'feel' are often polysemous and/or formally complex. For example, English *feel* can convey not only the primitive meaning, but also a "touch-related" meaning (e.g. *She felt his pulse*), and, in a different syntactic frame, a "cognitive" meaning (e.g. *He felt it was wrong*). To illustrate some of the formal complexities, consider the following three formations: (a) *dhäkay-ŋänha* 'taste-hear' (Yolngu Matha, Australia); (b) *huu.sùk* 'know-[unknown root]' (Lao); (c) *se sese le-lãme* 'hear feeling in-body' (Ewe).

In some languages 'feel' is expressed by a lexical unit of a lexeme which also expresses 'happen' and/or 'do'. This is common in the languages of Papua New Guinea. The meaning 'feel' is, however, usually associated with a distinctive grammatical construction. In Kalam, for example, when g- expresses the meaning 'feel' it is found in a distinctive experiencer construction, in which the verb takes 3SG marking and the experiencer appears as a noun or free pronoun with objective case-marking; for example, *Yp tep gp* (lit. me good it-feels) 'I feel good'. In various languages the lexeme for 'feel' is identical to a body-part word such as 'liver', 'heart', or 'stomach'. For example, in Yankunytjatjara to say 'I feel good' one says *Ngayulu tjuni palya* (lit. I stomach good). Sentences like this have often been interpreted as "figurative", and no doubt in some languages they are figurative — when there is another language-internal way of stating the "literal" meaning; but in Yankunytjatjara locutions with *tjuni* are the plainest and simplest way of expressing the meaning 'feel'.

Coming now to complex meanings based on 'feel', it seems obvious that all languages must have words to refer to the kinds of sensations indicated by English *hot* and *cold*. But this does not necessarily mean that all languages have lexical units with precisely the same meanings as these English words, especially once we take into account that English draws a distinction between *hot* and *warm* (if something is *warm*, it is not *hot*). In languages which lack this distinction, the nearest equivalent to 'hot' has a broader range (e. g. Yankunytjatjara *waru* 'hot, warm'). Even in languages which do draw distinctions close to those of English, the match-up need not to be exact. For example, in German the shift between *warm* and *heiss* takes place further up the temperature scale than in English.

"Basic tastes" like 'sweet', 'bitter', 'sour', and 'salty' may have some claim to universal status, on account of the fact that "receptor cells" for these tastes are localised in particular regions of the human tongue. The best candidate is probably 'sweet', given that sweet foods are supposed to be universally valued by human beings, but it can be ruled out as a precise lexical universal on the evidence of Cantonese and Japanese. The nearest Cantonese equivalent *tihm* can be used not only about sweet food, but about other nice-tasting food and drinks generally. The nearest Japanese equivalent *amai* can be used not only about sweet tastes but also about "bland" tastes (Backhouse 1994). There is little chance that any of the other "tastes" are lexical universals, given that 'bitter', 'sour' and other "bad tastes" are all covered by one word *kumarlpa* in Warlpiri (Laughren and Hale 1997).

Moving now to emotions, there is a school of thought in psychology, associated primarily with Paul Ekman (e. g. 1992, 1993), which holds that there is a small set of physiologically in-built "basic emotions", such as fear, anger, sadness, disgust, surprise, and joy. It is often claimed, in connection with this proposal, that all (or most) languages have words for these basic emotions.

However, a substantial body of anthropological and semantic evidence indicates that at best there is only an approximate match across languages between the meanings of basic emotion terms (cf. Russell 1991; Wierzbicka 1986, 1992; Goddard 1997). Some of them are known to have no equivalents, not even near-equivalents, in particular languages; for example, Yankunytjatjara has no near-equivalent to 'disgust', Tahitian has no near-equivalent to 'sadness'. In other cases, it can be demonstrated that an apparent equivalence is only approximate. This is easiest in languages which have more than one near-equivalent for a particular putative basic emotion, e. g. Yankunytjatjara *pikaringanyi* and *mirpanarinyi* for 'angry'; Malay *terkejut* and *terperanjat* for 'surprise', German *Angst* and *Furcht* for 'fear'. Even when there is a single near-equivalent, semantic differences can often be detected; for example, it can be shown that Russian *grust'* is not precisely identical with *sadness*, that Italian *rabbia* is not precisely identical to *anger*, that Malay *malu* is not precisely identical to *ashamed*, and so on.

2.4.5. Bodily postures and activities

'Sit' is not a universal lexical unit, if only because in some languages the verb which covers sitting (in the English sense) also covers squatting on one's haunches (without the bottom touching the ground). This applies to the Lao word *nang¹* and the Tagalog word *upo*. In the case of Lao, squatting is probably the prototypical "sitting" position.

The universal status of 'stand' can probably be disconfirmed on the basis of European (Romance) languages. In French, for example, there are two expressions which are near-equivalents to English *be standing*, both based on the adverb *debout* 'being upright'. The expression *être debout* 'be *debout*' merely describes one's position, whereas the more common expression *se tenir debout* '(lit.) RE-FLEX hold *debout*' conveys the idea of an activity (something akin to "holding" or maintaining a posture). It seems that either French expression conveys a slightly different meaning to that conveyed by English verb *stand*.

Aside from postures, the most plausible candidates for universals in the domain of body actions are probably 'eat' and 'drink', but their claim to universal status is doubtful. Some languages do not have separate words for 'eat' and 'drink'; for example, Kalam *ñŋ-*, Yimas *am-*, Warlpiri *ngarni* can all be glossed 'ingest, consume' (Pawley 1993; Foley 1997; Laughren and Hale 1997). In some cases these languages have phrasemes roughly corresponding to 'eat' and 'drink'; e.g. Kalam *tap ñŋ-* 'food consume' (Pawley 1993: 107). But the Kalam phraseme does not mean precisely the same as English *eat*₂ if only because *eat* can be used about ingesting solids other than food (e.g. *The baby was eating sand*).

Even when a language has a word which is usually glossed as 'drink', the semantic correspondence need not be precise. For example, Japanese *nomu* can be used not only about drinking water, tea, coffee, etc. but also for swallowing solid terms items such as pins and rings, and for smoking a cigarette. Suzuki (1978: 17–19) argues that *nomu* means 'to introduce something into one's body without chewing it'. He also notes that rice is normally something to *taberu* 'eat', but if a fish bone is stuck in someone's throat, one says in Japanese, "You should *nomu* some rice".

3. Conclusions

As stated at the onset, it is impossible to proclaim with absolute certainty that any meaning is universally attested as the meaning of a lexical unit in all languages. The sample of languages on which we are able to obtain information and analysis of the necessary quality is too small. This does not mean, however, that we reach the end of this survey without any firm conclusions.

First, we can observe that even a small sample of languages shows that only a very small set of meanings have any chance at all of being universals. Many impressionistically "basic" items of English vocabulary (such as *go*, *water*, and *eat*) lack precise equivalents in other languages.

Second, it emerges very clearly that the best candidates for the status of universal meanings are overwhelmingly to be found within the set of proposed semantic primes. To see this, consider the fact that of the 25 or so NON-prime candidates for universal status reviewed in this article, only the following seem to have much hope: 'man', 'woman', 'mother', 'day', and 'make'.

Furthermore, the universality of any non-prime meaning is always compromised by its semantic complexity. There is always the possibility that apparent equivalents in different languages may differ slightly in their underlying semantics. Indeed, it might seem unlikely that ANY complex meaning — not matter how solidly based in human experience it may appear — will be present in precisely the same shape (i.e. identical in every single detail) in all languages.

On the other hand, of the 25 or so prime meanings we have considered, all 25 are strong candidates for universal status. Constraints of space have prevented us from canvassing the entire inventory of 55-odd primes. Aside from various predicates we have not examined (including *say, see, hear, there is, have, live, die*), there are entire "mini-domains" of temporal, spatial, and "logical" meanings we have left untouched (see Table 87.2). Though it is too early to be conclusive, sufficient cross-linguistic evidence is available to indicate that all or most of them are plausible lexical universals, cf. Goddard and Wierzbicka ((eds.) In Press).

With new research attention being focused on the question of semantic universals, and more and better descriptive accounts of languages now becoming available, it is not too much to hope that the next decade may see the establishment of a comprehensive inventory of universally lexicalised meanings. Needless to say, aside from its inherent interest, establishing the scope and nature of semantic universals is of fundamental theoretical importance to lexical typology, lexicology, and semantic methodology in general.

4. References

Ameka, Felix. 1994. "Ewe". In: Goddard, Cliff & Wierzbicka, Anna (eds.). *Semantic and Lexical Universals-Theory and Empirical Findings*. Amsterdam: Benjamins, 57–86.

Apresjan, Yuri D. 1992 [1974] *Lexical Semantics: User's Guide to Contemporary Russian Vocabulary*. Ann Arbor: Karoma.

Backhouse, Anthony E. 1994. *The Lexical Field of Taste: A Semantic Study of Japanese Taste Terms*. Cambridge: Cambridge University Press.

Berlin, Brent. 1992. *Ethnobiological Classification*. Princeton, NJ: Princeton University Press.

Berlin, Brent and Kay, Paul. 1969. *Basic Color Terms: Their Universality and Evolution*. Berkeley & Los Angeles: University of California Press.

Brown, Cecil H. 1984. *Language and Living Things*. New Brunswick, NJ: Rutgers University Press.

—. 1989. "Universal constraints on polysemy and overt marking". *Quaderni di Semantica* 10.1: 33–50.

Brown, Donald E. 1991. *Human Universals*. Philadelphia: Temple University Press.

Bugenhagen, Robert A. In press. The syntax of semantic primitives in Mangaaba-Mbula. In: Goddard, Cliff & Wierzbicka, Anna (eds.). *Meaning and Universal Grammar*. Amsterdam: Benjamins.

Chappell, Hillary. 1994. "Mandarin semantic primitives". In: Goddard, Cliff & Wierzbicka, Anna (eds.). *Semantic and Lexical Universals-Theory and Empirical Findings*. Benjamins, 109–147.

Cruse, D. A. 1986. *Lexical Semantics*. Cambridge: Cambridge University Press.

Diller, Anthony. 1994. "Thai". In: Goddard, Cliff & Wierzbicka, Anna (eds.). *Semantic and Lexical Universals-Theory and Empirical Findings*. Amsterdam: Benjamins, 149–170.

Dixon, R. M.W. 1982. *Where Have All the Adjectives Gone? and other essays in Semantics and Syntax*. Berlin: Mouton de Gruyter.

—. 1989. "The Dyirbal kinship system". *Oceania* 59: 245–68.

Dryer, Matthew S. 1986. "Primary objects, secondary objects, and antidative". *Language* 62: 808–845.

Durie, Mark. 1985. *A Grammar of Acehnese*. Dordrecht: Foris.

—, Daud, Bukhari and Hasan, Mawardi. 1994. "Acehnese". In: Goddard, Cliff & Wierzbicka, Anna (eds.). *Semantic and Lexical Universals-Theory and Empirical Findings*. Amsterdam: Benjamins, 171–201.

Ekman, Paul. 1992. "An argument for basic emotions". *Cognition and Emotion* 6.3/4: 169–200.

—. 1993. "Facial expression and emotion". *American Psychologist* 48.4: 384–392.

Enfield, N. T. In press. "Combinatoric properties of Natural Semantic Metalanguage expressions in Lao". In: Goddard, Cliff & Wierzbicka, Anna (eds.). *Meaning and Universal Grammar*. Amsterdam: Benjamins.

Evans, Nicholas. 1994. "Kayardild". In: Goddard, Cliff & Wierzbicka, Anna (eds.). *Semantic and Lexical Universals-Theory and Empirical Findings*. Amsterdam: Benjamins, 203–228.

Evans, Nicholas and Wilkins, David P. 2000. "In the mind's ear: The semantic extensions of perception verbs in Australian languages." *Language* 76.3: 516–592.

Foley, William A. 1997. *Anthropological Linguistics*. Oxford: Blackwell.

Goddard, Cliff. 1991. "Testing the translatability of semantic primitives into an Australian Aboriginal language". *Anthropological Linguistics* 33.1: 31–56.

—. 1994. "Lexical primitives in Yankunytjatjara". In: Goddard, Cliff & Wierzbicka, Anna (eds.). *Semantic and Lexical Universals-Theory and Empirical Findings*. Amsterdam: Benjamins, 229–262.

—. 1996. *Pitjantjatjara/Yankunytjatjara to English Dictionary* [Revised 2nd edition]. Alice Springs: IAD Aress.

—. 1997. "Contrastive semantics and cultural psychology. 'Surprise' in Malay and English". *Culture & Psychology* 3.2: 153–181.

—. 1998. *Semantic Analysis: A Practical Introduction*. Oxford: Oxford University Press.

Goddard, Cliff (ed.) 1997. *Studies in the Syntax of Universal Semantic Primitives*. Special Issue of *Language Sciences* 19.3

Goddard, Cliff & Anna Wierzbicka (eds.). 1994. *Semantic and Lexical Universals-Theory and Empirical Findings*. Amsterdam: Benjamins.

Goddard, Cliff & Anna Wierzbicka (eds.). In press. *Meaning and Universal Grammar*. Amsterdam: Benjamins.

Harkins, Jean. 1995. *Desire in Language and Thought: A Cross-linguistic and Cross-cultural Study*. PhD thesis. The Australian National University.

Haspelmath, Martin. 1997. *Indefinite Pronouns*. Oxford: Clarendon Press.

Kimball, Geoffrey David. 1985. *A Descriptive Grammar of Koasiati*. PhD dissertation. Tulane University.

Laughren, Mary & Hale, Kenneth. 1997. *Warlpiri Dictionary*. Electronic version. Department of English and Linguistics, University of Queensland.

Matthews, Stephen and Yip, Virginia. 1994. *Cantonese: A Comprehensive Grammar*. London: Routledge.

Mel'čuk, Igor A. 1988. "Semantic description of lexical units in an explanatory combinatorial dictionary: Basic principles and heuristic criteria". *International Journal of Lexicography* 1.3: 165–188.

—. 1989. "Semantic primitives from the viewpoint of the Meaning-Text linguistic theory". *Quaderni di Semantica* 10.1: 65–102.

Mosel, Ulrike. 1994. "Samoan". In: Goddard, Cliff & Wierzbicka, Anna (eds.). *Semantic and Lexical Universals-Theory and Empirical Findings*. Amsterdam: Benjamins, 331–360.

Newman, John. 1996. *Give. A Cognitive Linguistic Study*. Berlin: Mouton de Gruyter.

Onishi, Masayuki. 1994. "Semantic primitives in Japanese". In: Goddard, Cliff & Wierzbicka, Anna (eds.). *Semantic and Lexical Universals-Theory and Empirical Findings*. Amsterdam: Benjamins, 361–386.

–. 1997. "The grammar of mental predicates in Japanese". *Language Sciences* 19.3: 219–233.

Pawley, Andrew. 1993. "A language which defies description by ordinary means". In: W. A. Foley (ed.). *The Role of Theory in Language Description*. Berlin: Mouton de Gruyter, 88–129.

–. 1994. "Kalam exponents of lexical and semantic primitives". In: Goddard, Cliff & Wierzbicka, Anna (eds.). *Semantic and Lexical Universals-Theory and Empirical Findings*. Amsterdam: Benjamins, 387–422.

Richards, Eirlys & Hudson, Joyce. 1990. *Walmajarri-English Dictionary*. Darwin: Summer Institute of Linguistics.

Russell, James A. 1991. "Culture and the categorization of emotions". *Psychological Bulletin* 110.3: 426–450.

Suzuki, Takao. 1978. *Japanese and the Japanese: Words in Culture*. Tokyo: Kodansha International Ltd.

Swadesh, Morris. 1971. "What is glottochronology?" In: J. Sherzer (ed.). *The Origin and Diversification of Languages*. Chicago: Aldine, Atherton, 271–292.

Talmy, Leonard. 1985. "Lexicalization patterns: Semantic structure in lexical forms". In: Shopen, Timothy (ed.). *Language Typology and Syntactic Description, Vol. III*. Cambridge: Cambridge University Press, 57–149.

Wierzbicka, Anna. 1986. "Human emotions: Universal or culture-specific?" *American Anthropologist* 88.3: 584–594.

–. 1992. *Semantics, Culture, and Cognition*. Oxford: Oxford University Press.

–. 1996. *Semantics, Primes and Universals*. Oxford: Oxford University Press.

Wilkins, David P. & Hill, Deborah. 1995. "When 'go' means 'come': Questioning the basicness of basic motion verbs". *Cognitive Linguistics* 6.2/3: 209–259.

Witkowski, Stanley R. & Brown, Cecil H. 1978. "Lexical universals". *Annual Review of Anthropology* 7: 427–452.

Cliff Goddard, University of New England (Australia)

88. Kin terms in grammar

1. Terms and concepts
2. Earlier research
3. Special abbreviations
4. References

1. Terms and concepts

1.1. Some basic terminology with regards to kinship

Kin relations can be described by **kin types**. A kin type is an arbitrarily detailed description of a certain kind of kin relation. For instance, we may say that all relatives of the same generation constitute a single kin type. We can also be more specific and say that siblings constitute one kin type and cousins another. Of course, we may be even more detailed and say that father's brother's son, father's brother's daughter, father's sister's son, father's sister's daughter, etc, all constitute different kin types. Depending on how detailed one is in a specific case, a kin term may cover many kin types, or vice versa.

The technical term **consanguineal kinship** refers to kinship established biogenetically; i.e. consanguineal kinsmen are those related by blood. The term **affinal kinship**, on the other hand, refers to kinship established through marital ties – not only between a husband and wife but also between a person and the consanguineal relatives of that person's spouse.

Collateral kinship involves sibling ties, while **lineal kinship** does not. For instance, a person is related to his/her father, daughter or grandparents by means of lineal kinship, but to his/her sister, uncle (parent's sibling) or cousin (parent's sibling's off-spring) by means of collateral kinship. Sometimes however, especially in the anthropological literature, siblings are classified as lineal relatives. Related to the concept of collateral kinship are the concepts of **parallel kinship** and **cross kinship**. Parallel kinship involves sibling ties where the siblings in question are of the same sex, while cross kinship involves sibling ties where the siblings are of opposite sex. A parallel cousin, for instance, is either father's brother's off-spring or mother's sister's off-spring, while a cross cousin is either father's sister's off-spring or mother's brother's off-spring. Sometimes the concept of parallel kinship is expanded to include lineal kin terms, where the same-sex tie is a lineal one rather than a collateral one, and thus the terms *paternal grandfather* (father's father) and *maternal grandmother* (mother's mother) may count as kin terms expressing parallel kinship.

1.2. Reference versus predication of kin terms

Kin terms may be used in different ways. They may be said to have a **referential use** when referring to kinsmen, like in *I saw your uncle today*, or they may be said to have a **predicative use** when predicating a kin type of a kinsman or group of kinsmen, such as in *She is my sister*. A special kind of referential function is found when kin terms are used to address a kinsman or a group of kinsmen directly with the intention to bring him or them into the speech situation. They are known as **vocatively used** kin terms, or simply as kin terms of address. Kin terms with a vocative use fall outside the syntactic structure of a clause, as exemplified by a sentence like *Mom, I have to go now*. Non-vocative referential uses may be called designative uses (cf. Chao 1956), but usually they are simply termed referential uses (without including vocatives). I will adhere to the latter convention in this paper since it is an established use.

The distinction between referential and vocative uses of kin terms is the one traditionally made in the anthropological and linguistic literature, while predicative uses are commonly ignored (one exception being Dahl & Koptjevskaja-Tamm (forthcoming)).

1.3. Referents and anchors

Since kin terms relate persons or groups of people to other persons or groups of people by means of kinship, they are inherently relational. They relate the **referent** of the term to what will here be called the **anchor** (following Dahl & Koptjevskaja-Tamm (forthcoming)), i.e. the person, or group of people, from whose perspective the kinship relation is calculated. If I say something like *My niece won the race*, my niece is the referent while I am the anchor, as indicated by the first person possessive pronoun *my*.

The anchor of kinship relations is usually called 'ego' (se e.g. Keesing, 1975) or 'propositus' (Evans 2000) by anthropologists. In the linguistic literature, the term 'relatum' is also in use (Amith & Smith-Stark, 1994). While 'anchor', 'relatum', and 'propositus' may have a broader linguistic use, also labelling other relational entities than entities of kin relations (for example the possessor in possessive constructions in general), 'ego' is used exclusively in descriptions of kin relations.

The notion of anchor is particularly clear for referential and vocative uses of kin terms, since they in most cases have clear-cut referents who can be related to clear-cut anchors. Kin terms used predicatively do not have referents and anchors in the same sense, since they predicate a kin type rather than refer to a kinsman. But in most cases with kin terms used predicatively, the referent of the constituent that assumes the kin type expressed by the predicate may also be seen in a wider perspective as the referent, not of the kin term itself but of the kin relation expressed by it. Likewise, the constituent that assumes the anchor role may be seen as the anchor. Thus, in *Tim is Henry's uncle*, Tim is the referent and Henry is the anchor of the kin relation expressed by the kin term *uncle*.

In many languages the anchors of referential and vocative kin terms do not have to be explicitly indicated by means of lexical items or grammatical markers. Anchors of kin terms used this way may thus be called **implicit anchors** as opposed to anchors overtly expressed, which may be called **explicit anchors** (Dahl & Koptjevskaja-Tamm, forthcoming).

Kin terms with implicit anchors may be used on their own as **bare nouns** without any determiners (i.e. articles, demonstratives or possessive pronouns) or lexical modifiers, or they may be used in combination with various determiners (and optionally also with lexical modifiers) in full NPs which, however, make no reference to an anchor. An example of the first case is presented by the clause *I will ask dad*, where *dad* appears as a bare noun, and an example of the second case is presented by the clause *The proud father smoked his cigar*, where *father* appears as the head of a definite NP. Kin terms with implicit anchors may also lack determiners while they are still combined with lexical modifiers, as exemplified by the clause *Take care, dear son*, where *son* appears without any determiner but is modified by *dear*. Such kin terms end up somewhere between bare nouns and full-fledged NPs (since they are not bare but still lack determiners).

We may also make another distinction with regard to implicit anchors. In some cases their identity may be, and must be for the expression to be understood correctly, inferred from the context and situation in which the utterance in question occurs. We may call this kind of implicit anchors **contextual anchors**. As an example we may give the clause *Mom went shopping*, where the anchor of *mom* must be inferred from the context for the clause to be understood. In other cases, the identity of the anchor is of no importance in contrast to the quality of the kin type denoted by the kin term in question. As with contextual anchors, the identity of these anchors may be inferred from the context, but in contrast to contextual anchors it is not a necessity for the expression to be understood correctly. I shall call this latter kind of implicit anchors **out-of-focus anchors**. As an example we may give the clause *The mothers went shopping*, where for the NP *the mothers* the quality of motherhood is in focus, while the identity of the anchor is not. In English, kin terms used as bare nouns have contextual anchors, while kin terms in NPs including determiners without reference to an anchor have out-of-focus anchors (cf. the English examples with *dad* and *the proud father* above), but this division need not be so consistent in other languages, cf. the Samoan example below.

(1) Samoan (Polynesian, Austronesian)
    Mo le   uso   peleina
    for SPEC.SG sister sweet
    'for my dear sister' (lit. '...the dear sister')

Also for kin terms used predicatively, there may be a lack of explicit anchors, as in the clause *He has become a father*. In this clause the subject, *he*, assumes the referent role of the kin relation predicated, while there is no constituent that assumes the anchor role. Since it is not necessary to know the identity of the anchor for the expression to be understood correctly, we may also talk about out-of-focus anchors in such cases.

In some languages it is possible to use kin terms as modifiers of nouns and verbs in the way exemplified for Samoan below.

(2) Samoan (Polynesian, Austronesian)
   (a) *'au   uso*
       team   same.sex.sibling
       'sibling team' or 'team of siblings'

   (b) *fai   āvā*
       do   wife
       'be married' (said of a man)

In these cases, it is not transparent how to make out the identity of anchors or even referents of the kin terms, since they are non-specific and merely indicate that the event expressed by the verb or the entity referred to by the noun generally involves the kin type denoted by the kin term in question. In line with the definition given above, we may also consider the anchors to be out-of-focus anchors in such cases.

1.4. Grammatic versus semantic person

Grammatically, we can distinguish between first person, expressed by first person pronouns, second person, expressed by second person pronouns, and third person, expressed by third person pronouns or nouns. Semantically, we can say that the speaker is first person, the one spoken to is second person, and the one spoken about is third person. Thus, we may distinguish **grammatical person** from **semantic person**. Normally, grammatical and semantic person coincide, so that one speaks of oneself in the first person, etc. However, one may also speak of oneself in third person, like in the clause *Do you want to sit with daddy [speaker] when he is eating*. In this case, *daddy* is a noun – third person grammatically – but refers to the speaker – first person semantically. Also, *he* in the subclause – a third person pronoun – refers to the speaker – first person semantically.

The distinction between grammatical and semantic person is not traditionally made, but may be useful in determining the identity of referents and anchors in such cases as exemplified by the clause above.

1.5. Some further taxonomy of kin terms

With respect to the generation affiliation of the referent and anchor, we may distinguish between ascending, descending and horizontal kin terms (Dahl & Koptjevskaja-Tamm, forthcoming). **Ascending kin terms** are terms like 'father', 'grandmother' and 'uncle', whose referents belong to a generation (one step or more) above the generation of the anchor; **descending kin terms** are terms like *daughter, niece* and *grandson*, whose referents belong to a generation (one step or more) below the generation of the anchor; while **horizontal kin terms** are terms like *brother, sister* and *cousin*, where the referent and anchor belong to the same generation. Note that these labels are not applicable to collective terms, like *family*, which may refer to people from generations both above and below the anchor, or certain reciprocal terms spanning more than one generation, like *wawu* in the Australian language Ilgar, which is used by grandparents for their grandchildren as well as by grandchildren for their grandparents.

Terms that have their basic use within the kinship system of a language, i.e. that refer relationally to kinsmen, may be called **proper kin terms**. In English, terms like *mother, father, brother* and *sister*, etc, are proper kin terms. In addition to these, there are terms in many languages that have one use within the kinship system referring relationally to kinsmen, and another, typically non-relational but at least equally basic, use outside the kinship system. Such terms may be called **improper kin terms**. As examples we can take the English terms *child* and *old man*, which may refer to a son or daughter, and to a father respectively, but also to young humans, and to an aged male human, respectively. Sometimes, improper kin terms are merely metaphoric extensions of originally non-relational terms, as is the case with *old man*. In other cases, the two uses of an improper kin term are both equally established, the term *child* being an example. The kin term use of such terms, however, may also originally have come about as metaphoric extensions of non-relational terms. Proper kin terms may also be metaphorically extended. For instance, the English term *father* may refer to a catholic priest, or to the Christian god, in addition to its basic reference to a kinsman. The terms 'proper and improper kin terms' were first introduced by Dahl & Koptjevskaja-Tamm (forthcoming).

We may define **simple kin terms** as those describing a kin relation between two people by involving reference to only one kinsman. Simple kin terms may be monomorphemic, like the term *mother*, or multimorphemic, like *grandmother*. A kin relation between two people may also be described by explicitly linking a number of kinsmen to each other. In such cases we may talk about **analytic kin circumlocutions**. Quite obviously, *uncle* is a simple kin term, while *cousin of my mother* is an analytic kin circumlocution in English. What is a simple kin term in one language may of course not necessarily be a simple kin term in another language. Some kin terms in some languages may also end up somewhere in between simple kin terms and analytic kin circumlocutions. The Swedish kin term *farmor*, 'paternal grandmother', illustrates this point. Since *far* means father and *mor* mother, the term literally means 'father-mother' and thus links a person to his/her grandmother via his/her father. For this reason it could be called an analytic kin circumlocution. But since juxtaposition is not the normal strategy for creating genitive expressions in Swedish, and since *farmor* is used as one conceptual unit, the term could also be thought of as a simple kin term (although it is bimorphemic rather than mono-morphemic).

2. Earlier research

Kin terms and kinship systems have been studied in both linguistics and anthropology. While the latter discipline has a long tradition in the field, spanning at least three centuries, kin term studies seem to have been taken up in linguistics quite recently, in fact only during the last century. The linguistic study of kin terms has mainly been concerned with the semantics of kin terms — a heritage from anthropology — and, with few exceptions, only briefly with their grammatical properties.

2.1. Kinship terminologies

Different cultures and languages employ different kinship terminologies. They differ with respect to which specific kin terms they include and how kinsmen are grouped together and labelled with different kin terms. For instance, while English has one term *cousin* (parent's siblings off-spring), another language may separate different kinds of cousins, e.g. maternal from paternal cousins, or female from male cousins, etc.

Kinship terminologies of the languages of the world can be grouped into different types. The set of types may differ from one typology to another depending on the criteria by which the types are defined. Below is an outline of the typologies for kinship terminologies most frequently referred to in the anthropological literature.

Morgan (1870) [quoted in Schusky 1983] distinguished between only two types; 'descriptive' and 'classificatory' terminologies. Descriptive terminologies are those that separate certain collateral relations, for instance those that employ different kin terms for father and paternal uncle (like English), while classificatory terminologies are those that do not make such distinctions.

Lowie (1928) recognised four types of terminologies; 'generational', 'lineal', 'bifurcate merging', and 'bifurcate collateral'. These are based on either the female or the male relatives of the first ascending generation. Using the male relatives, Lowie's (1928) typology can be described in the following way: (i) generational terminologies employ one and the same kin term for father, father's brother and mother's brother; (ii) lineal terminologies employ one term for father and another for father's brother and mother's brother (as in English); (iii) bifurcate merging terminologies have one and the same term for father and father's brother and another for mother's brother; and (iv) bifurcate collateral terminologies employ three different kin terms for these three kin types. (A fifth type, noted by Murdock (1947), is logically possible, but not found in any language, viz. a type where there is one term for father's brother and another for father and mother's brother.)

Murdock (1949), concentrating on the terms for cousins and siblings, presented a further detailed typology of kinship terminologies, which is perhaps the one most frequently used in the anthropological literature today. His six types are called 'Hawaiian', 'Eskimo', 'Sudanese', 'Iroquois', 'Crow', and 'Omaha'. The Hawaiian type has the same terms for cousins as for siblings; the Eskimo type has different terms for siblings and cousins (as in English); the Sudanese type separates siblings from cousins and distinguishes among some different cousin types (viz. cross cousins versus parallel cousins, and paternal cousins versus maternal ones); the Iroquois type equates parallel cousins with siblings but separates these from cross cousins; the Crow type is like the Iroquois type with regards to siblings and cousins, but is different in that it also equates maternal cross cousins with brother's children, thus skewing generations; the Omaha type is a mirror image of the Crow type, since it equates paternal cross cousins with sister's children.

More detailed kinship typologies for specific parts of the kin term lexicon (e. g. typologies for sibling terminologies, grandparental terminologies, etc.) have also been developed (see for example Murdock, 1970).

2.2. The semantics of kin terms and componential analysis

The main interest for the anthropologist with regard to kin terms is the cultural and sociological aspect of kinship, i. e. how kin relations determine the interactions between individuals, and groups of individuals, in a certain culture. Kroeber (1909), a distinguished anthropologist, however, was of the opinion that kinship terminologies were primarily a linguistic phenomenon, which should be analysed by linguistic methods, and he seems to have been the first one to look at kin terms from a linguistic point of view. His interest was in the categories of meaning that underlie the relations expressed by kin terms in various languages. He distinguished between eight underlying categories with relevance for kin relations, and argued that kinship terminologies and the meaning of kin terms could be analysed through these categories. His eight categories were: (1) difference in generation between the anchor and referent, (2) age difference within a generation between the anchor and referent, (3) sex of referent, (4) sex of speaker, (5) sex of connecting relative (e. g. female for maternal grandfather), (6) condition of connecting relative (e. g. living or dead), (7) consanguineal versus affinal kinship, and (8) collateral versus lineal kinship. (In some instances, Kroeber's (1909) terminology have been altered as to conform to the terminology used here.)

Kroeber's (1909) article was an early precursor of a discipline that would develop later, namely that of componential analysis (Lounsbury 1956; Goodenough 1956; Wallace & Atkins 1960; Romney & d'Andrade 1964). Componential analysis is the semantic study of kin terms (and also other areas of the vocabulary of a language) by which meaning is analysed in terms of atomic components in such a way that, for every term, different values are given to a group of semantic features (also known as dimensions). Semantic features thus correspond to what Kroeber (1909) called categories. Both anthropologists and linguists have been concerned with kin terms and componential analysis, and as for linguistics, this is probably the field of study where kin terms and kinship have received the most thorough treatment. Among more recent work on componential analysis and kin terms, Pericliev & Valdes-Perez (1998) can be mentioned. The authors present a computer program designed to find the simplest componential analysis, with a minimal number of semantic features, for any given kinship terminology.

Other papers dealing, in part or wholly, with kin term semantics, though not within the frame work of componential analysis are

Hale (1982), Laughren (1982) and Merlan & Heath (1982) — all in a collection (Heath & Merlan & Rumsey 1982) on linguistic aspects of kinship in Australian aboriginal languages.

2.3. Markedness theory applied to kin terms and kinship terminologies

Some studies of kin terms and kinship terminologies have also been carried out within markedness theory.

Greenberg (1966) presents evidence for the existence of markedness hierarchies among kin terms. As in other markedness hierarchies, kin term hierarchies of markedness may be determined by various criteria, such as structure (the marked category often has overt phonetic expression where the unmarked category is indicated by zero), defective paradigms (the unmarked category tends to have more distinctions than the marked category, e. g. a distinction between male and female, making the marked category defective in the paradigm), and frequency (the unmarked category occurs more frequently than the marked one). Using these criteria on kin terms from about 120 languages, Greenberg (1966) finds a number of universal hierarchies among kin terms, of which the following are examples (with illustrations in English):

— Consanguineal kin terms are unmarked as against affinal kin terms (e. g. *father-in-law* has phonetic expression where *father* has none).
— Ascending kin terms are unmarked as against descending kin terms of equal genealogical distance from the anchor (e. g. *mother* is normally more frequent in texts than *daughter*).
— Lineal kin terms are unmarked as against collateral kin terms (e. g. *cousin* lacks a distinction in gender while all English lineal kin terms have such a distinction).
— Kin terms denoting kin types of generations more remote from the anchor are marked as against kin terms denoting kin types of generations less remote from the anchor (e. g. *grandfather* has phonetic expression where *father* has none).

In another article Greenberg (1980) emphasises the relevance of markedness theory and language universals in explaining the design of kinship terminologies in different languages.

Nerlove & Romney (1967) investigate sibling terminologies cross-linguistically, and find that out of 4140 logically possible ways to asign kin terms to the eight kin types older or younger brother or sister of male or female (with one and the same term for all of them as one extreme and eight different terms as the other extreme) only 12 account for as many as 87% (214/245) of the terminologies in their sample. These 12 ways of assigning sibling kin terms are illustrated in table 88.1 below, where kin terms are symbolised by capital letters followed by a specification of the kin type they include.

Table 88.1: Common ways of assigning kin terms to sibling types crosslinguistically

DIVISION OF SIBLING TERMS	NUMBER OF TERMINOLOGIES
A: sibling	14
A: brother B: sister	21
A: elder brother B: younger brother C: sister	3
A: elder sibling B: younger sibling	21
A: elder brother B: elder sister C: younger sibling	38
A: elder brother B: younger brother C: elder sister D: younger sister	78
A: parallel sibling B: cross sibling	6
A: parallel sibling B: cross brother C: cross sister	6
A: cross sibling B: parallel brother C: parallel sister	6
A: parallel brother B. parallel sister C: cross brother D: cross sister	5
A: elder parallel sibling B: younger parallel sibling C: cross sibling	9
A: elder parallel sibling B: younger parallel sibling C: cross brother D: cross sister	7
Total	**214**

(Derived from figure 1 and table 2 in Nerlove & Romney (1967: 182−183))

Nerlove & Romney (1967) argue that the 12 ways of assigning sibling terms illustrated in the table above are a priori more likely to occur than any other ways of assigning such terms. They base their arguments on certain anthropological assumptions and factors relating to cognitive economy.

2.4. Cross-linguistic phonetic similarities between parental kin terms

The tendency for different languages separated both genetically and areally to develop phonetically similar words for mother and father on the basis of nursery forms (i. e. forms used by, and in conversation with, children) has been noticed in many studies of child language. Lewis (1951), for instance, claims that the mother is usually named with an "m-form" and the father with a "p-, b-, t- or d-form". This tendency was investigated statistically by Murdoch (1959) in a study that shows that cross-linguistically the words for mother tend to involve nasal bilabials or nasal dentals, typically [m] or [n], combined with low vowels, typically [a] or [ə], while the words for father tend to involve non-nasal dentals or bilabials, [p], [b], [f], [t], [d], etc., combined with low vowels. Specifically, out of the 210 terms for mother in his sample that combined any bilabials or dentals with low vowels in the first syllable of their root, 170 — i. e. 81% — were nasals, and out of the 306 terms for father that combined any bilabials or dentals with low vowels in the first syllable of their root, 257 — i. e. 84% — were non-nasals.

Murdock's (1959) results are analysed and commented by Jakobson (1962) who argues that the earliest meaningful units emerging in infant speech are based on the polarity between the maximal energy output of low vowels and the maximal reduction in energy output caused by consonants formed with complete oral closure, i. e. stops and nasals. Since the most important entities in the infants world are its mother and father, it will apply its first meaningful words to them. The Proto-Indo-European *mātēr, 'mother', and *pətēr, 'father', are presumed to have developed this way from mā- and pə- combined with the suffix -tēr, 'father', are presumed to have developed this way from mā- and pə- combined with the suffix -tēr, used for various kin terms.

Jakobson (1962) explains the fact that nasals dominate in the terms for mother by referring to breast feeding: "Often the sucking activities of a child are accompanied by a slight nasal murmur [...] Later this phonatory reaction to nursing is reproduced as an anticipatory signal at the mere sight of food and finally as a manifestation of a desire to eat, or more generally, as an expression of discontent and impatient longing for missing food or absent nurser, and any ungranted wish" (Jakobson 1962: 542). Since the infant's longings are normally addressed to its mother initially, these nasal interjections will gradually turn into a kin term meaning 'mother'. Parental kin terms developed from nursery words are sometimes taken up in the inventory of kin terms and frequently coexist with other established terms, which in turn may also have originally developed from nursery terms but undergone phonetic and morphological change. This may have been the case in French where the forms *maman*, 'mom', and *papa*, 'dad', coexist with the older forms *mère*, 'mother', and *père*, 'father'. Other sources from which kin terms are renewed are slang forms, terms of endearment (often diminutives), and loans from other languages. Examples of the last mentioned case are found in the Germanic and Slavic languages where the terms for mother and father have been loaned from French and coexist with older form; thus English *mama/mom* and *mother*, and *papa/pa* and *father*.

2.5. Speech act studies of kin terms

Kin terms have also been dealt with in studies on communication and speech acts within the interdisciplinary fields of pragmatics and sociolinguistics.

Perhaps one of the first studies in this area is a paper by Stanner (1937) dedicated to the question of how different linguistic forms — like kin terms, personal names, nick names, signs, etc. — can be used for addressing and referring to persons among Australian aboriginies in his area of field work (which was northwestern Northern Territory, Australia). Another similar study was carried out by Chao (1956), who investigated kinship terms, titles, proper names, and pronouns as means of address in Chinese.

The collection of articles on Australian aboriginal languages edited by Health & Merlan & Rumsey (1982) also includes some studies on pragmatics and the social functions of kin terms in conversation, e. g. Merlan (1982), Rumsey (1982) and Sutton (1982). Other relatively recent investigations include Mufwene (1988), who studies the honorific and endearing usage of kin terms for both kin and non-kin in Kituba (a creole spoken in Zaire, Africa), Wu (1990), who investigates patterns of vocative kin term usage for non-kin in Chinese and the restrictions of such usage, and Choi (1997), who writes about the use of kin terms instead of personal pronouns (between kinsmen as well as non-kin) in Korean and Bulgarian.

2.6. Grammatical properties of kin terms

With few exceptions, the grammatical properties of kin terms have been only briefly touched upon in the literature, either as supplementary information in anthropological or pragmatic/semantic studies on kin terms, or in linguistic studies on possession where kin terms are mentioned as a group of NPs that, when expressing the possessee, show up in inalienable possessive constructions in many languages, i.e. constructions which are commonly described as involving an inherent or natural bond between the possessor and the possessee (cf. example (3a)), as opposed to alienable possessive constructions where no such bond exists (cf. example (3b)).

(3) Maltese (Semitic) (Dahl & Koptjevskaja-Tamm, 1998: 38)
 (a) INALIENABLE
  bin is-sultān
  son DEF-king
  'the king's son'
 (b) ALIENABLE
  is-siġġu ta' Pietru
  DEF-chair of Peter
  'Peter's chair'

Some of the investigations that do focus on grammatical aspects of kin terms and the influence of kinship on grammatical systems will be presented below.

Some studies – e.g. Hale (1966), Schebeck (1973), Hercus & White (1973), Alpher (1982) and Koch (1982) – have drawn attention to the intricate pronominal systems of some Australian aboriginal languages, which encode certain kinship-related information. A feature often present in (some or all of) the dual and plural personal pronouns of these languages is the information whether all the referents of the pronoun in question are included in the same set of alternate generations or if any of the referents are included in a different set of alternate generations. People included in the same set of alternate generations either belong to the same generation, like cousins, or to two (or more) different generations separated by an even number of generations, like a grandparent and his or her grandchild. People included in different sets of alternate generations belong to two (or more) different generations separated by an odd number of generations, like a mother and daughter, or a great-grandparent and his or her great-grandchildren. If this system is carried out consistently, as, for instance, in the Australian languages Lardil, spoken in Queensland, Australia (Hale 1966), and Dalabon, spoken in Northern Territory, Australia (Alpher 1982), dual and/or plural pronouns will have two forms throughout the pronominal system, the choice between which depends on the relative alternate generations of the referents included in the pronominal form in question. For illustration, the Lardil system is outlined in table 88.2 below.

Table 88.2: Lardil non-singular pronouns

		same alternate generations	different alternate generations
dual	1 in	ŋakuri	ŋakuni
	1 ex	ɲari	ɲa·nki
	2	kiri	ɲi·nki
	3	piri	ɲi·nki
plural	1 in	ŋakuli	ŋakulmu
	1 ex	ɲali	ɲalmu
	2	kili	kilmu
	3	pili	pilmu

(Hale, 1966: 320)

Some languages also include in (some or all of) their dual and plural pronominal forms information on whether all the referents are members of the same patri- or matriline or if any of them are included in a different line, and thus extend the number of pronominal forms further. Examples of such languages are Lower Aranda, spoken in Northern Territory (Hale, 1966), and Kaytej also spoken in Northern Territory (Koch 1982). A somewhat different variant of a pronominal system encoding kinship information is found in Adnjamathanha, a language spoken in South Australia (Schebeck 1973; Hercus & White 1973), where there are ten series of personal pronouns, the use of which depends on the kinship relations both between the speaker and the referent(s), and between the referents internally.

Another interesting study focusing on kinship in grammar is a study by Evans (2000) that treats a special set of kin terms used as verbs in some Australian aboriginal and American Indian languages. These verbs have the meaning 'be K to', 'have as K', 'call a K', or 'consider as a K' (where K represents the kin type expressed by a particular kin term). He gives a thorough presentation of how such kin verbs work in the closely related Australian languages Ilgar and Iwaidja spoken in Northern Territory, and goes on to make a comparison with the usage of kin verbs in some American Indian languages of the Iroquoian family, spoken in western USA and Canada, the Yuman subfamily, spoken in Mexico and south western USA, and the Uto-Aztecan family, spoken in south western USA and Central America, as well as with a few Australian languages of Northern Territory of the Gunwinyuguan family. He also compares kin verbs with other verbs and finds that they share different grammatical properties, such as availability for tense/aspect/mode-marking (TAM) and subject/object-affixation etc, to varying degrees in the different languages under consideration.

It is interesting to see that in most of the languages in this study both kin verbs and kin nouns may have both a referential and a predicative use. Verbs (with affixes for subject and object) may have a referential use through the means of headless relative clauses; for instance, roughly like English *[the one such that] she mothers me*. This is illustrated for Ilgar in example (4).

(4) Ilgar (Iwaidjan, Australian) (Evans 2000: 120-1)
yi-ŋa-yalma-ŋ
3.SG.M.ABS-3.SG.F.ERG-search.for-NPAST
ɹaga
DEM
yiɲ-i-maga-n
3.SG.F.ABS-3.SG.M.ERG-be.husband.to-NPAST
'She is looking for her husband'
(lit.: 'She is looking for that (one such that) he is husband to her')

Evans (2000) finds five basic factors governing the choice between kin verbs and kin nouns in expressing kin relations. These are reviewed below (in a different order than in Evans' paper).

(i) PERSON VALUE: Certain person combinations between the anchor and the referent trigger the use of either kin nouns or kin verbs in some languages, so that verbal constructions are used or preferred with one set of combinations, while nominal constructions are used or preferred with others. In Central Guerrero Nahuatl (Uto-Aztecan), for instance, a verb-like construction is normally used when an anchor in the first or second person or the third person definite is combined with a referent in the first or second person. A nominal construction is used in all other cases.

(ii) ADDRESS VS REFERENCE: It seems that kin verbs used referentially are not completely equivalent to NPs since they do not, in general, also have a vocative use. Nouns, being morphologically simpler, are usually preferred over verbs in address.

(iii) KIN TYPE: Kin verbs do not usually cover all the kin types denoted by nominal terms in a language with kin verbs. The kin type one wants to designate, then, may obviously be a deciding factor in the choice between nominal and verbal kin terms.

(iv) ACTUAL VS CLASSIFICATORY KIN: Languages that classify everyone in the known social universe with different kin terms according to various criteria (like many Australian languages do) seem to use verbs (if they employ kin verbs) rather than nouns to emphasise actual kin rather than classificatory kin.

(v) EXTRA SEMANTICS: Either kin term nouns or kin term verbs may carry semantic information in addition to the information that simply describes a kinship relation. In Huichol (Uto-Aztecan), for instance, a predication involving a kin term noun carries the meaning 'be K', while a predication involving a kin term verb has the meaning 'consider as K' or 'look upon as K'. The use of kin verbs in Huichol, then, indicates that the social context in a certain situation provides reasons for equating with kinship a certain relation which is perhaps not (or not yet) a kinship relation.

Dahl & Koptjevskaja-Tamm (forthcoming) is perhaps the first attempt to make a systematic treatment of the general grammatical properties of kin terms. The authors' concern, however, is solely on kin terms as nouns. They go through a number of grammatical properties that in many languages set kin terms apart from other nouns. They note that kin terms are not usually, and in some languages cannot be, combined with definite articles or other determiners. This often leads to a bare noun use of kin terms, similar to the use of proper names in many languages. In such cases kin terms are normally treated, morphosyntactically, as definite and/or specific, though they do not carry a definite or specific marker (or any other determiner). Example (5) illustrates this point for Hungarian.

(5) Hungarian (Uralic) (Beáta Megyesi, personal communication)
 (a) *Lát-om   apu-t*
     see-1.SG.S/DEF.O father-ACC
     'I see (my) father.'
 (b) *Lát-om   a   cicá-t*
     see-1.SG.S/DEF.O DEF cat-ACC
     'I see the cat.'

Note that the verb in both (a) and (b) appear in the definite object conjugation though only *cicá-*, 'cat', and not *apu-*, 'father', is preceded by a definite article.

Dahl and Koptjevskaja-Tamm present further similarities between kin terms and proper names. These include (i) their plural formation; both kin terms and proper names often either lack a plural or have the same special plural markers, (ii) their use as possessors in possessive constructions; both kin terms and proper names sometimes make use of the same special possessive marker, or as possessors occupy the same position in syntax different from that of other possessor nouns, and (iii) their use with proprial articles (i.e. markers used in some languages primarily with proper names); the use of these may often include both proper names and kin terms. These properties shared between proper names and kin terms may arise in different ways. With proprial articles, kin terms and proper names form the core of lexemes for which the article is targeted, whereas with definite articles, kin terms and proper names usually seem to be some of the last nouns to be affected by a grammaticalization process spreading the use of definite articles.

Dahl and Koptjevskaja-Tamm also discuss some properties of kin terms as possessees, i.e. heads of possessive constructions. As already mentioned, kin terms as possessees are commonly used in inalienable possessive constructions cross-linguistically. Dahl and Koptjevskaja-Tamm argue that the split between alienable and inalienable possessive constructions may be "the result of a grammaticalization process by which a younger and expanding possessive construction is encroaching on the territory of an older one", often leaving kin terms, especially those frequently used, as one of the last lexical domains affected by the process. Thus, in a particular language, the new construction will be an alienable construction while the old one will be an inalienable construction. In the final stages of such a grammaticalization process there may be a split among the kin terms so that some frequently used terms evoke (older) inalienable constructions while other kin terms evoke (younger) alienable constructions. This point is also discussed (and in more detail) in Dahl & Koptjevskaja-Tamm (1998).

Dahl and Koptjevskaja-Tamm also argue that a kin term is more likely to appear in an inalienable possessive construction, and also to be used as a proper-name-like bare noun, under certain conditions, viz. (A) if it denotes an ascending relation (father rather than son), or (B) if it has a unique referent within a family (father rather than uncle), or (c) if the distance between anchor and referent is no more than one generation (father rather than grandfather). These conditions make up what they call the 'parental prototype', shaping the contour of grammatical properties with kin terms in the world's languages. It is interesting to note that the conditions of Dahl's and Koptjevskaja-Tamm's parental prototype all correspond (wholly or partially) to kin term markedness hierarchies suggested by Greenberg (1966); namely the following: an ascending kin term is unmarked as against a descending kin term of equal genealogical distance from the anchor (corresponding to condition A); a kin term denoting lineal kinship is unmarked as against one denoting collateral kinship (corresponding to condition B); and a kin term denoting a kin type of a generation more remote from the anchor is marked as against a kin term denoting a kin type of a generation less remote from the anchor (corresponding to condition C).

3. Abbreviations

Abbreviations not found in the general list of abbreviations are listed below.

1	first person
3	third person
ex	exclusive
in	inclusive
K	kin type
NPAST	non-past
O	object
S	subject
SPEC	specific

4. References

Alpher, Barry. 1982. "Dalabon dual-subject prefixes, kinship categories, and generation skewing". In: Heath, Jeffrey & Merlan, Francesca & Rumsey, Alan (eds.). *The languages of kinship in aboriginal Australia*, pp 19–30. Sydney. The University of Sydney.

Amith, Jonathan D. & Smith-Stark, Thomas C. 1994. "Predicate nominal and transitive verbal expressions of interpersonal relations". *Linguistics*, vol 32, pp 511–547.

Chao, Yuen Ren. 1956. "Chinese terms of address". *Language*, vol 32, pp 217–241.

Choi, Gwon Jin. 1997. "Viewpoint shifting in Korean and Bulgarian: the use of kinship terms". *Pragmatics*, vol 7, pp 389–395.

Dahl, Östen & Koptjevskaja-Tamm, Maria. 1998. "Alienability splits and the grammaticalization of possessive constructions". In: Haukioja, Timo (ed.). *Papers from the 16th Scandinavian conference of Linguistics*, pp 38–49. Turku. Åbo Akademis tryckeri.

Dahl, Östen & Koptjevskaja-Tamm, Maria. Forthcoming. "Kinship in grammar". To appear in: Herslund, Michael (ed.). *Dimensions of possession*. Amsterdam & Philadelphia. John Benjamins.

Evans, Nicholas. 2000. "Kinship verbs". In: Vogel, Petra Maria & Comrie, Bernard (eds.). *Approaches to the Typology of Word Classes*, pp 103–172. Berlin & New York. Mouton de Gruyter.

Goodenough, Ward C. 1956. "Componential analysis and the study of meaning". *Language*, vol 32, pp 195–216.

Greenberg, Joseph H. 1966. *Language universals*. (Janua Linguarum, Series Minor, no 59.). The Hague. Mouton.

Greenberg, Joseph H. 1980. "Universals of kinship terminology". In: Maquet, Jacques (ed.). *On linguistic anthropology: Essays in honor of Harry Hoijer*, pp 9–32. Malibu. Udena Publications.

Hale, Kenneth. 1966. "Kinship reflections in syntax: Some Australian languages". *Word*, vol 22, pp 318–24.

Hale, Kenneth. 1982. "The logic of Damin kinship terminology". In: Heath, Jeffrey & Merlan, Francesca & Rumsey, Alan (eds.). *The languages of kinship in aboriginal Australia*, pp 31–37. Sydney. The University of Sydney.

Heath, Jeffrey & Merlan, Francesca & Rumsey Alan (eds.). 1982. *Languages of kinship in Aboriginal Australia*. (Oceania Linguistic Monographs, no 24.). Sydney. University of Sydney.

Hercus, Luise A. & White, Isobel M. 1973. "Perception of kinship structure reflected in the Adnjamathanha pronouns". In: Schebeck, Bernhard & Hercus, Luise A. & White, Isobel M. (contributors). *Papers in Australian linguistics: no 6*. Canberra. Australian National University Press.

Jakobson, Roman. 1962. "Why 'mama' and 'papa'?". In: Jakobsson, Roman (ed.). *Phonological studies*, pp 538–545. (Selected writings, vol 2). The Hague. Mouton.

Keesing, Roger M. 1975. *Kin groups and social structure*. New York. Holt, Rinehart and Winston, Inc.

Koch, Harold J. 1982. "Kinship categories in Kaytej pronouns". In: Heath, Jeffrey & Merlan, Francesca & Rumsey, Alan (eds.). *The languages of kinship in aboriginal Australia*, pp 64–71. Sydney. The University of Sydney.

Kroeber, Alfred. 1909. "Classificatory systems of relationship". *Journal of the Royal Anthropological Institute of Great Britain and Ireland*, vol 39, pp 77–84.

Laughren, Mary. 1982. "Warlpiri kinship". In: Heath, Jeffrey & Merlan, Francesca & Rumsey, Alan (eds.). *The languages of kinship in aboriginal Australia*, pp 72–85. Sydney. The University of Sydney.

Lewis, Morris M. 1951 (1936). *Infant speech*. London. Routledge & Kegan Paul.

Lounsbury, Floyd G. 1956. "A semantic analysis of the Pawnee kinship usage". *Language*, vol 32, pp 158–194.

Lowie, Robert H. 1928. "A note on relationship terminologies". *American Anthropologist*, vol 30, pp 263–268.

Nerlove, Sarah & Romney, Kimball. 1967. "Sibling terminology and cross-sex behaviour". *American Anthropologist*, vol 69, pp 179–187.

Merlan, Francesca. 1982. "'Egocentric' and 'altercentric' usage of kin terms in Maŋarayi". In: Heath, Jeffrey & Merlan, Francesca & Rumsey, Alan (eds.). *The languages of kinship in aboriginal Australia*, pp 125–140. Sydney. The University of Sydney.

Merlan, Francesca & Heath, Jeffrey. 1982. "Dyadic kinship terms". In: Heath, Jeffrey & Merlan, Francesca & Rumsey, Alan (eds.). *The languages of kinship in aboriginal Australia*, pp 107–124. Sydney. The University of Sydney.

Morgan, Lewis H. 1870. *Systems of consanguinity and affinity*. (Smithsonian Institution Contributions to Knowledge, vol 17, no 218.). Washington. Smithsonian Institution.

Mufwene, Salikoko S. 1988. "The pragmatics of kinship terms in Kituba". *Multilingua*, vol 7, pp 441–453.

Murdock, George P. 1947. "Bifurcate merging". *American Anthropologist*, vol 49, pp 59–69.

Murdock, George P. 1949. *Social structure*. New York. Macmillan.

Murdock, George P. 1959. "Cross-language parallels in parental kin terms". *Anthropological linguistics*, vol 1, pp 1–5.

Murdock, George P. 1970. "Kin term patterns and their distribution". *Ethnology*, vol 9, pp 165–207.

Pericliev, Vladimir & Valdes-Perez, Raul E. 1998. "Automatic componential analysis of kinship semantics with a proposed structural solution of multiple solutions". *Anthropological Linguistics*, vol 40, pp 272–317.

Romney, Kimball & d'Andrade, Roy G. 1964. "Cognitive aspects of English kin terms". *American Anthropologist*, vol 66, no 3, part 2, pp 146–170.

Rumsey, Alan. 1982. "Gun-Gunma: An Australian aboriginal avoidance language and its social functions". In: Heath, Jeffrey & Merlan, Francesca & Rumsey, Alan (eds.). *The languages of kinship in aboriginal Australia*, pp 160–181. Sydney. The University of Sydney.

Schebeck, Bernhard. 1973. "The Adnjamathanha personal pronoun and the 'Wailpi kinship system'". In: Schebeck, Bernhard & Hercus, Luise A. & White, Isobel M. (contributors). *Papers in Australian linguistics: no 6*. Canberra. Australian National University Press.

Schusky, Ernest L. 1983 (second edition). *Manual for kinship analysis*. Lanham & New York & London. University Press of America.

Stanner, W. E. H. 1937. "Aboriginal modes of address and reference in the north-west of the Northern Teritory". *Oceania*, vol 7, pp 300–315.

Sutton, Peter. 1982. "Personal power, kin classification and speech ettiquette in aboriginal Australia". In: Heath, Jeffrey & Merlan, Francesca & Rumsey, Alan (eds.). *The languages of kinship in aboriginal Australia*, pp 182–200. Sydney. The University of Sydney.

Wallace, Anthony F. C. & Atkins, John. 1960. "The meaning of kinship terms" *American Anthropologist*, vol 62, pp 58–80.

Wu, Yongyi. 1990. "The usage of kinship address forms amongst non-kin in Mandarin Chinese: the extension of family solidarity". *Australian Journal of Linguistics*, vol 10, pp 61–88.

*Niklas Jonsson, Department of Linguistics,
University of Stockholm (Sweden)*

89. Derivation

1. Introduction
2. The limits of derivation
3. Morphological processes
4. The semantics of derivation
5. References

1. Introduction

Derivation has not attracted sustained interest in typologically oriented research. At most, information on derivation in handbooks of typology concerns specific phenomena in comparatively few languages (Shopen (ed.) 1985). The same applies to the treatment of typological aspects in general works on morphology (Matthews 1991, Bauer 1988, Anderson 1992, Spencer 1991, Carstairs-McCarthy 1992, *Yearbook of Morphology*). Only few studies apply to derivation the cross-linguistic sampling techniques that have proven so useful in research on universals (Bybee 1985, Cutler, Hawkins & Gilligan 1985), and they are incomparably more concerned with "grammatical" morphology (inflection) than with its lexical counterpart. On the other hand, considerable attentions has been devoted to theoretical issues such as the place of derivation in the architecture of grammar, the nature and properties of derivational rules, and possible universal constraints on such rules (see Hammond & Noonan (eds.) 1988, Anderson 1992, Carstairs-McCarthy 1992, Spencer 1991, Everaert et al. (eds.) 1988, Aronoff (ed.) 1992, Buszard-Welcher et al. (eds.) 1992). Although this discussion has been carried on mainly on the basis of the best described among the Indo-European languages, it has also stimulated in-depth treatment of some phenomena in more exotic languages. In fact, in this field there is more than the usual imbalance favoring theory building over large-scale cross-linguistic comparison. This state of affairs is not surprising, given the formidable difficulties posed by derivation even at the most elementary descriptive level. This is only mentioned here as a *caveat* concerning the limitations of this article. Empirical coverage of derivation in reference works on morphology is not very wide (an exception is Mel'čuk 1993–94), and many experts in the field are aware of the "Eurocentricity of the morphological research tradition" (Muysken 1986: 629, cf. also Scalise 1988: 564).

2. The limits of derivation

Derivation comprises patterns of morphologically encoded lexical relations that are in principle productive and thus constitute a central resource for enlarging the lexical inventory of a language. However, there are several open issues concerning the boundaries between derivation and other systematic lexical relations, other word-formation processes, and, most pervasively, inflectional morphology.

2.1. Derivation and inflection

It is somewhat of an irony that the best known universal generalizations concerning derivation, Greenberg's Universals 28 ("If both the derivation and the inflection follow the root, or they both precede the root, the derivation is always between the root and the inflection") and 29 ("If a language has inflection, it always has derivation") (Greenberg 1963: 90), hinge upon the distinction between derivation and inflection, since this distinction has proven particularly elusive, and some researchers express misgivings as to its universal validity (cf. Behrens 1996: 60–61). The conceptual core of the distinction is clear enough and it is best captured in the so-called "split-morphology"-hypothesis (Anderson 1992, Perlmutter 1988). From a formal standpoint, one can distinguish between morphological processes expressing morphological category-values or properties (Matthews 1991: 39–40) that form part of the syntactic vocabulary for the language in question, and morphological processes that alter in manifold ways the inherent properties of lexical items without involving their appearance in particular syntactic structures. The former constitute the domain of inflection: they define "the form taken by words as a consequence of the syntactic structure in which they appear" (Anderson 1992: 184) and have word-forms as their output. The latter constitute the domain of derivation: they specify systematic form-meaning relations among lexical items and have lexemes as their output. From a functional standpoint, inflection corresponds to morphology in the service of phrase and sentence building, whereas derivation corresponds to morphology in the service of lexical structuring and lexical creation. The appeal of this conceptualization is great, since it projects the traditional lexicon-syntax distinction onto the domain of morphology and offers a principled explanation for Universal 28 (derivation being always "closer" to the root than inflection because it is pre-syntactic). It is however diminished in practice by the fact that its application in descriptive practice presupposes two quite formidable tasks. The first is to decide for any particular language what is the exact vocabulary of its syntax, or, if one adopts a universalistic view of syntax, what is the repertoire of "functional categories"; the second is that of deciding on the identity conditions for lexemes in a language. The split-morphology hypothesis has been called into question with counterexamples that involve inflected forms or even syntactic phrases as bases of derivational processes (cf. Kageyama (1982: 252) on Japanese, and Booij (1996), Rainer (1996) on "inflection inside derivation" in Dutch and Ibero-Romance). However, counterexamples are exceptional and cluster around easily circumscribed cases (Dressler 1988), so that the No-Phrase-, No-Inflection-Constraint on derivational bases associated with the split-morphology hypothesis seems robust enough as a tendency (cf. also Baker (1988: 27–29) for strong evidence in this sense from the lack of internal inflection in incorporation → Art. 53).

In actual practice, linguists resort to a wide array of criteria in order to ascertain the inflectional or derivational status of morphological processes, and the idea that inflection and derivation form a continuum (Bybee 1985, Dressler 1989, Haspelmath 1996) has found many followers. A survey of these criteria provides some insight into the characteristic properties of lexical morphology.

Derivation, in contrast to inflection, is not obligatory (Plank 1981: 20, Bybee 1985, Anderson 1985: 30, Melč'uk 1993–94: I, 299). Since no morphosyntactic environment requires the expression of a particular derivational category, derivatives can, as a corollary, be replaced by simple (monomorphematic) words (Matthews 1991: 50, Bybee 1985: 81–3, Dressler 1989). However, the applicability of this criterion presupposes that no total suppletive relations (like between *bad* and *worse*) exist in the domain of derivation (Aronoff 1976: 2, but see Dressler 1989 and § 4.3).

Derivation does not necessarily come in paradigms, i.e. in tightly organized sets of contrasting forms, none of which is semantically or functionally presupposed by the others (Matthews 1991, Dressler 1989, Mel'čuk 1993–94: I, 289). As a consequence of the lack of paradigmatic organization, derivation is less prone to analogical leveling (Plank 1981: 30, Dressler 1989) and to selection of competing forms in standardization processes (since variants can always give rise to secondary lexical differentiation). The more agglutinating character of derivational morphology (Bybee 1985, Dressler 1987: 120) may be linked to the fact that the "cumulative" morphs which are typical of fusional morphology (→ Art. 49) can only be recognized as such in paradigmatics sets (Anderson 1985: 38−9). On the other hand, derivation is in principle directional, not only from the formal, but also from the functional point of view (a derived lexeme presupposes the lexeme it is derived from). Directionality in inflectional morphological processes is, to a great extent, a matter of economy of description, and it becomes largely irrelevant in the absence of formal clues (Matthews 1991: 138−9). In the case of derivation, ascertaining the orientation of the process is never irrelevant, since it has consequences for the semantics of the forms involved. It is true that the functional orientation of derivation can easily be assimilated to the distribution of markedness values among the members of an inflectional category (→ Art. 32), but the relationship between a primary and a secondary lexeme is qualitatively distinct from that between the unmarked and the marked member(s) of a paradigm. Even in the case of derivational relationships expressed by processes such as introflection (→ Art. 50), which are formally non-directional, it is possible to identify a semantically basic form (so that Classical Arabic *ka:tab* 'write to someone', *xa:šan* 'treat harshly' are considered to be secondary with respect to *katab* 'write', *xašun* 'be harsh', cf. Anderson (1985: 35)).

Inflection and derivation relate differently to word class-systems. While the distribution of inflectional categories helps define word classes, derivational processes often change the word class of a lexeme (Scalise 1988, Dressler 1989). They may also apply to lexemes of different word classes (cf. Plank 1981: 52−5 on Germ. *-er* in the derivation of deverbal and denominal agents, such as in *lehren* 'teach' > *Lehrer* 'teacher' vs. *Garten* 'garden' > *Gärtner* 'gardener'; Anderson 1985: 30 on derivational aspectual and number affixes in Kʷakʷ'ala, and Bybee 1985: 161 on derivational temporal affixes attaching to verbs and nouns in Kwakiutl), thus contradicting the Unitary Basis Hypothesis (according to which the domain on which a derivational rule operates should be categorially homogeneous, cf. Aronoff 1976, Corbin 1991: 21). However, the statistical validity of this hypothesis remains to be ascertained.

Derivational processes are typically cumulative, in the sense that a derivative can be the basis for further derivation, and they show some degree of recursiveness (Scalise 1988: 570−1). The limits to recursiveness in derivation can be accounted for in a principled way, either because of the incompatibility of a derivational category with lexical items of the same category (thus, it would make little sense to derive an abstract noun from an abstract noun, as in *assiduitiness) or by some version of the *horror aequi* constraint that explains truncations (cf. § 3.3). Recursiveness is quite usual in the domain of evaluative derivation (cf. Span. *chiqu-it-it-ito* 'very very tiny', ital. *panc-in-ino* 'little belly', or with different affixes, *poch-ett-ino* 'a tiny bit', cf. Dressler/Merlini-Barbaresi 1994: 99−100). It is reported to occur quite freely in Manipuri (Tibeto-Burman) as an intensifying device with prospective markers (cf. *saw-rò-rò-rò-ni* 'is certainly going to be angry, from *saw-* 'angry' (Chelliah 1992: 293)). Apart from "intensifying" contexts, recursiveness occurs in Turkish causatives, with different affixes (cf. *öl-dür-t-tü* 'caused to cause to die', from *öl-* 'die' (Comrie 1985b: 324)), and quite commonly in prefixation (cf. Germ. *über-über-morgen* 'the day after the day after tomorrow'. Span. *pos-posmodemo* 'postpostmodern', Engl. *meta-meta-theoretical*). Although derivation expressed by introflection is claimed to be characteristically non-cumulative by Anderson (1985: 37), Kilani-Schoch & Dressler (1984: 55−6) assume some amount of cumulativeness (in the form of derivational chains) for Classical Arabic. The cumulative nature of derivation manifests itself in the fact that the order of derivational affixes reflects the order of semantic operations, whereas the order of inflectional affixes is fixed and/or semantically irrelevant (Scalise 1988: 571, 577−9). Thus, Span. *sombr-er-illo* 'small hat' contrasts with *sombr-ill-ero* 'vendor of parasols', both from *sombra* 'shadow'. Examples of this sort are much less marginal in languages with a highly polysynthetic or agglutinative morphology (see Anderson 1985: 33 on the contrast between the Kʷakʷ'ala sequences *-exsd* + *-amas* 'cause to want', as in *ne'nakʷ'exsdamas* 'cause to want to go home', and *-amas* + *-exsd* 'want to cause', as in *q'aqoλamadzexsd* 'want to teach', as well as Muysken 1988: 278 on Quechua). Chelliah (1992: 292) has emphasized the relevance of ordering principles for distinguishing between derivational and inflectional morphology in languages where most other criteria fail to apply. It is very likely that these languages exhibit a third type of formative apart from the derivational and inflectional ones, which has been described as "internal syntax" by De Reuse (1992: 164−172). As he points out, the number of possible sequences of such elements in Eskimo is too high for them to be plausible candidates for lexical storage. A similar class of syntactic affixes occurring between derivation an inflection is assumed by Muysken (1988: 265) for Cuzco Quechua.

The most widely invoked characteristic of derivation is its irregularity (cf. Plank 1981). There are two apparently interrelated sides to this question. On the one hand, irregularity can be conceived of as a conflict between the fact that derivation is a system of processes for creating complex units and the fact that these complex units are lexemes, so that they typically end up as members of a structural inventory, the lexicon. This side of the question is associated to the issues of the restricted productivity of derivational processes and of the restricted semantic compositionality of its products. On the other hand, irregularity manifests itself at the level of form-meaning solidarities as many-to-many correlations of sometimes maddening complexity. Although defectivity, semantic idiosyncrasy and non-unique form-meaning associations are not unknown in inflection, the sheer degree they attain in derivation makes them seem something qualitatively different, so that some researchers take them as clues for the derivational status of some processes (Bybee 1985: 147, Haspelmath 1996, Comrie 1985b: 311−2, Dressler 1987, 1989, Mel'čuk 1993−94: I, 290−294). The manifold factors that play a role in restricting the productivity of a derivational process (so that either few derivatives are attested or new derivatives are judged unacceptable by speakers) make it difficult to define the domain of a derivational rule. Furthermore, the fact that the semantics of attested derivatives is usually only partly compositional, since derivatives, as lexemes, tend to acquire some degree of autonomy from their bases and from the process they instantiate, is an obstacle to ascertaining the exact semantic operation(s) associated with a particular morphological process. As for form-meaning relations, derivation is largely characterized by putatively identical meaning categories exhibiting polymorphous expressions (Mel'čuk 1993−94: I, 294, Dressler 1989: 6) and by identical formal processes expressing different meaning categories (Zwanenburg 1996). Since cases of complementary distribution among competing formal processes are almost never absolute, it is difficult to identify allomorphy, except when allomorphs differ minimally in phonological shape and their distribution is phonologically determined (cf. Matthews 1984: 91−92). It is equally difficult to distinguish genuine homonymy among derivational categories from motivated semantic variation (polysemy) (cf. § 4.4). This is part of the reason why some researchers plead for a separate treatment of form and meaning as the only way to a coherent description of derivation (Coseriu 1977, Beard 1990, 1993).

It is widely assumed that there are substantial differences between derivational and inflectional meanings. Derivational meanings are said to be more concrete than inflectional meanings (Dressler 1989; Mel'čuk 1993−94: I, 294), and derivational processes are assumed to produce more important alterations in the semantics of the items they apply to than inflectional processes (Bybee 1985, Dressler 1989, Scalise 1988). However, the concrete-abstract distinction is not an obvious one, and certainly not one that could be easily operationalized. It seems to be the case that inflectional meanings are abstract in so far as they are determined by systems of contrasts and much less so by properties of denotata, whereas derivational meanings can be more easily linked to properties of denotata and are therefore more autonomous, more "substantial". Nonetheless, the perceived concreteness of derivational meanings could be simply an effect of analogical lexicalization patterns (cf. § 4.1). As a correlate to concreteness, it is sometimes assumed that derivational categories show wider cross-linguistic variation and are therefore more language-specific than inflectional categories (Cutler, Hawkins & Gilligan 1985: 736; Dressler 1989). In any case, we have known at least since the pioneering work of Sapir (1921, cf. also Plank 1981: 16−20, Anderson 1992: 325−334) that it is not possible to decide on the inflectional or derivational status of a category on the grounds of meaning alone: a "derivational concept" in a language, which only plays a role in lexical extension, may be an inflectional category in another (a "concrete-relational concept" that plays a role in phrase and sentence building).

Morphological processes whose derivational status is problematic typically exhibit conflicting properties. The most widely discussed boundary cases are: (i) those that do not change the word class, have some effect on the combinatorial properties of the items in question, express distinctions that are quite pervasive for the language, but show a high degree of irregularity in form/meaning relations as well as lexicalization and restrictions on productivity, as in Slavic aspectual morphology (Comrie 1985b: 310−311, Mel'čuk 1993−94: II, 95−98); (ii) those that do not change the word class, have little or no effect on the combinatorial properties of the items in question, but are at the same time very regular and productive, e. g. diminutive formation in Spanish, Italian or Polish; (iii) those that are highly regular and transparent, although they change the word class and seem to exhibit a syntactically determined distribution, e. g. English nominalizations in *-ing* (Comrie & Thompson 1985: 359), or adverb formation in *-ly*. Interestingly enough, highly regular and productive processes of type (ii) and (iii) tend to close derivational chains, not permitting further derivation (Bybee 1985: 97).

As for diachronic links between inflection and derivation, both processes leading to the creation of inflectional material from derivation and also their reverse (derivational material arising from inflection) are known to occur. Thus, Comrie (1985a) describes how several forms of the Chukchi verb paradigm arise from a reanalysis of derivation, the agreement marker for 1st person singular objects *ine-/ena-* being originally an antipassive derivational marker, the imperfect prefix *n-* arising from the derivation of deverbal adjectives, etc.. Mithun (1988) and Langdon (1992) describe how derivational distributive markers on verbs give rise to derivational plurality markers on nouns, and finally (under the heavy influence of English) to the creation of an inflectional plural in some North-American languages. Material of inflectional origin seems to be integrated in derivation mostly as part of a more complex process. Thus, the Latin neuter plural ending *-a* was reinterpreted as a collective marker in Romance, but it only survived in its new derivational function as part of a suffix, as in Span. *osa-menta* 'skeleton', *arbol-eda* 'group of trees, wood', Ital. *pin-eta* 'pine wood', *ferra-glia* 'scrapmetal' (cf. Lüdtke 1996: 243−4). Inflectional elements that become entrapped in derivation, such as genitive and plural markers in German or Dutch (cf. Germ. *wolke-n-los* 'cloudness', *zweifel-s-frei* 'doubtless', Dutch *held-en-dom* 'heroism', *leerling-en-dom* 'set of pupils' (Booij 1996)), or the feminine marker in Romance adverb formation (cf. Spanish *calm-a-mente* 'calmly') tend to end up as interfixes or stem extensions (cf. § 3.3).

2.2. Derivation, conversion and compounding

The distinction between derivation and inflection is one of function in the overall organization of the language. But derivation also has to be distinguished from other lexical relations and processes that share with it a common functional basis while differing from it in their formal properties. Whereas derivation primarily involves the creation of lexemes on the basis of morphological processes that operate on single lexemes (and on their exponents), conversion is characterized by the absence of overt morphological processes and compounding by the fact that two lexemes are involved in the process. In the case of conversion, the main problem is that of deciding where the threshold lies that should lead us to recognize two different lexemes, as opposed to different senses or uses of the same lexeme. In the case of compounding, problems may arise as to the lexematic or affixal status of one of the units involved in a concatenation. In practice, it is normally assumed that a change of word class, especially if it is accompanied by a major change in inflectional categories, as in N > V or V > N shifts, is a sufficient condition for establishing two distinct lexemes. This is the basis for ascribing conversion *qua* word-class-change to the domain of derivation. By contrast, some systematic and oriented meaning shifts that affect the combinatorial possibilites of a lexeme without altering its inflectional class, e. g. mass-count alternations in the nominal domain or valency changes in the verbal domain, are held to be extensions of meaning within one and the same lexeme (Don 1993: 186−188). This way of seeing things might tell us more about the traditional prominence assigned to word classes than about the optimal treatment of morphologically unmarked systematic lexical relations (cf. Behrens 1996, but see also § 3.2).

The problem of the lexematic or affixal status of some of the units involved in a concatenation is both a distributional and a semantic one. Distributionally, an affix is traditionally defined as a bound form belonging to a restricted inventory; semantically, it is best understood as the exponent of a complex operation on a lexeme. However, there are bound forms that seem to contribute a lexematic content to a construction, as well as freely occurring forms without a clearly lexematic content. Some of the incorporation processes that are typical of polysynthetic languages exemplify the first case. So, for instance, the incorporating verbal element -*si*- 'get' in Eskimo (cf. *sapangar-si-voq* 'he bought beads', with *sapangaq* 'bead' as incorporated noun) is a bound form, whereas in Tzotzil, bound nominal elements like -*van*- 'person' trigger incorporation (cf. Baker 1988: 15—17), and Kʷakʷ'ala exhibits bound forms corresponding to most major body parts that are obligatorily incorporated (Anderson 1985: 27). Thus, incorporation cuts across the composition-derivation distinction (cf. Bybee 1985: 106—107, Anderson 1985: 25—33). As to formatives that have freely occurring counterparts but do not qualify automatically as lexemes, we have, on the one hand, the case of adpositional or adverbial particles that play a role both in phrase and in lexeme formation, mostly as prefixes, e. g. Germ. *gegen* 'against' (cf. *gegen mich* 'against me' vs. *Gegenteil* 'opposite, contrary'), *vor* 'before' (cf. *vor ihm* 'before him', *vorkommen* 'happen') (cf. Malkiel 1978: 127). On the other hand, we have lexemes belonging to major lexical categories that are being grammaticalized as derivational affixes by a well documented diachronic process in which derivational patterns emerge from series of compounds (or of set phrases that have been subject to univerbation). So, for instance, the status of Germ. *frei* 'free', *voll* 'full', *arm* 'poor' in *risikofrei* 'free from risk, unrisky', *angstvoll* 'fearful', *gefühlsarm* 'showing little feeling, insensitive', is doubtful (cf. Olsen 1986 and Becker 1990: 100). In such cases, affixal status only becomes certain when the corresponding lexeme disappears (as in the case of the nominal etymon of Germ. -*heit*) or when a clear semantic and/or formal split intervenes that disrupts the etymological connection (as in the case of Engl. *full* vs. -*ful*, or Span. *mente* 'mind', vs. the adverbial suffix -*mente*).

3. Morphological processes

Since the problem of distinguishing between derivation and inflection arises precisely because the formal means for expressing both are largely the same (Mel'čuk 1993—94: I, 297), I will only insist on those aspects of morphological processes that might show some particular link to derivation (→ Art. 49, 50, 52).

The overwhelming predominance of two operations, prefixation and suffixation, in the best described derivational systems, is usually explained in terms of its semiotic naturalness (transparency and diagrammaticity, cf. Dressler 1985, 1987). Other additive operations, such as infixation and circumfixation, are much rarer. Considerable effort has been invested into trying to analyze away some Romance "parasynthetic" pattern which might arguably represent cases of circumfixation, such as French *introniser* 'enthrone' from *trône* 'throne', *encablure* 'cable's length' from *cable* 'cable', *prerévolutionnaire* 'prerevolutionary' from *révolution* 'revolution' (Corbin 1987: 121—139). The reasons that militate against a circumfix analysis of such cases are not necessarily valid for other processes in other languages (e. g. in the case of the Indonesian nominalizing circumfix *ke-* ... -*an* occurring in *bisa* 'able' > *kebisaan* 'capability', *tidak mampu* 'not be able' > *ketidakmampuan* 'impotence', (Anderson 1992: 53)). It is important to notice that reluctance to admit operations of discontinuous affixation on theoretical grounds might act as a hindrance to ascertaining how rare these operations actually are in the languages of the world.

Modulating and replacing operations, such as apophonic processes (Dressler 1987: 108), consonantal changes (e. g. the substitution of a homorganic nasal for an initial consonant in Javanese denominal verbs, as in *pistul* 'gun' > *mistul* 'to shoot with a gun', *tilpun* 'phone' > *nilpun* 'to phone', cf. Becker 1990: 102), and the even rarer use of metathesis as a derivational marker (Kilani-Schoch & Dressler 1984, 1986), are seldom the sole exponent of a derivational process, they are typically unproductive, and they are known to arise from the morphologization of phonetic or phonological rules (Becker 1990: 84—87, Anderson 1992: 345—346).

3.1. Predominantly derivational morphological processes

An almost unexplored question concerns the existence of morphological processes that are exclusively or predominantly attested in derivation. An obvious candidate is conversion, which by definition is not inflectional. It is admittedly difficult to speak of a formal operation on a stem in cases such as Engl. *break*~V~ > *break*~N~, Germ. *Knie* 'knee' > *knien* 'kneel', or French *aveugle*~A~ 'blind' > *aveugle*~N~ 'blind person', so that treating conversion as a morphological process might seem a misleading way of speaking (Becker 1990: 92). But conversion of nouns and adjectives to verbs involves the selection of a thematic vowel (cf. Latin *albus* 'white' > *alb-e-re* 'to be/look white', *servus* 'slave' > *serv-i-re* 'serve') in languages such as Latin and Romance, and conversion of verbs to nouns sometimes requires the addition of a final vowel (cf. Span. *avanzar* 'go forward' > *avance* 'advance', *avanzo* 'budget', Cat. *dubtar* 'doubt~V~' > *dubte* 'doubt~N~'). If we assume that both thematic vowels and adaptive final vowels are empty morphs and not suffixes, (Malkiel 1978: 130, 142−3, Lüdtke 1996: 254, 261−2), then these languages show that at least some cases of conversion involve stem adaptation processes that legitimately belong to morphology.

Interestingly enough, some of the more exotic, non-concatenating morphological processes are reported to occur more frequently in derivation. Such is the case of infixation, as exemplified by the Span. diminutive *-it-* (*azúcar* 'sugar' > *azuqu-it-ar*) or by the Quileute approximate *-yV-* (*t'lè'x* 'stiff' > *t'le-yé-x* 'rather stiff', cf. Ultan 1975: 178). In Bybee's sample, infixation appears to be exclusively derivational (Bybee 1985: 97), and it is characterized as serving predominantly derivational functions by Ultan (1975), who analyzed infixes in some 70 languages. Reduplication is also more frequently derivational than inflectional for Bybee (1985: 97); most of the meaning categories found to be expressed by reduplication in Moravcsik (1978: 316 ff.), over and above those she explicitly regards as derivational, can be surmised to be derivational rather than relational or concrete-relational concepts.

As for subtractive processes, Anderson (1992: 65−6) cites only one case of a clearly inflectional subtractive process (Danish imperative formation), all the others being either clearly or possibly derivational. Although subtraction in the form of clipping, as in Engl. *Josephine* > *Jo, condominium* > *condo* or Span. *colegio* 'school' > *cole, milicia* 'military service' > *mili* is seldom treated as a standard case of derivation, because it seems to alter only the lexeme-exponent (cf. Marchand 1969: 441), the connotations conveyed by such formations (familiar register, affective attitude) are not very far from those conveyed by affective affixation, as becomes particularly evident when they are used in hypocoristics (cf. Dressler 1987).

A somewhat weaker connection seems to relate introflection and prefixation with derivation. In fact, the introflective patterns characteristic of Semitic morphology exist side by side with affixational patterns, but the latter are more often than not inflectional, so that the most of the burden of lexical morphology falls on introflection (Malkiel 1978, Anderson 1985: 34 ff., Ultan 1975: 169, Kilani-Schoch & Dressler 1984). As for prefixation, Cutler, Hawkins & Gilligan (1985), who have found it to be significantly less frequent than suffixation, insist on the scarcity of languages with inflectional prefixes (1985: 747), so that the question arises as to the extent to which the skewing in favor of suffixation is maintained in lexical morphology (→ Art. 52).

Although it is tempting to link the higher frequency of infixation and introflection in derivation with Greenberg's Universal 28 (cf. § 2.1.) and with Bybee's correlation between morphotactic closeness and semantic relevance (1985) (cf. Ultan 1975: 169), the overall pattern can be due to a much more trivial fact of statistical distribution. Since languages tend to have more derivational than inflectional processes, and there are languages that have derivation but lack inflection, the less frequently occurring morphological processes stand more chances of being found among the more numerous derivational processes than elsewhere.

3.2. Characteristic morphological phenomena

Some morphological phenomena concerning redundant or void affixation and the distribution of affixes are, to my knowledge, only reported to exist in connection with derivation. Redundant or void affixation can be exemplified by interfixes and by the void application of an affix to a stem that already expresses the semantic category associated with the affix. Interfixes are known to play an important role in suffixal derivation and in composition in languages with a rich fusional morphology, such as the Romance or the Slavic languages (Malkiel 1966, Dressler 1986). They are morphs that regularly intervene between stems and derivational suffixes or between two stems in composition, are not associated with any particular semantic or grammatical value, and are very often optional, as for instance the morph *-et-* in Span *lam-et-ón* or the morph *-s-* in Germ. *Verfassung-s-treue*. They can be used for secondary lexical differentiation, and in many cases they seem to ensure the recognizability of the stem (Dressler 1986). Although their diachronic origins are manifold, they always seem to involve processes of reanalysis and analogical extension (Malkiel 1966). As for the void application of an affix, it can be exemplified by the addition of the German agentive suffix *-er* to morphologically simple nouns denoting agents, such as in *Bäck* 'baker' > *Bäcker, Dolmetsch* 'interpreter' > *Dolmetscher* (Dressler 1987: 110), or by the addition of French *-ier*, a suffix which is regularly used to obtain names of plants and trees from their fruits and flowers, to nouns denoting plants and trees (as in *magnolia* 'magnolia' > *magnolier* or *peuplier* 'poplar' from Lat. *populus*). Corbin (1987: 134−137, 1991: 14, 22) has devoted some attention to this phenomenon, which she describes as "paradigmatic integration".

As for phenomena of affix distribution that seem to be characteristic of derivation, two of them, namely truncation and potentiation of affixes are intimately related to the cumulative nature of derivation. In truncation, a part of the stem of which the affix is attached is erased, so that affixation becomes in these cases a subtractive-additive operation. More often than not, the erased part of the stem coincides with a derivational affix (as in German *zimperlich* 'prim' > *Zimperling* 'prim person', *Zauberer* 'magician' > *Zauberin* 'female magician') or with an indicator of lexical category (as in Engl. *evacuate* > *evacuee, assduous* > *assiduity*) (Aronoff 1976, Plank 1981: 203 ff.). The existence of truncation processes is an unquestionable fact. They seem to arise mainly in two situations, namely to avoid repetition of identical phonetic sequences (haplology) or in connection with the borrowing of derivational subsystems (Plank 1981). However, there is no agreement on the conditions under which it is analytically sound to assume truncation processes in a description. While some researchers tend to resort quite freely to this assumption, and are thus able to obtain more regular form-meaning patterns in derivation (cf. Corbin (1987, 1991)), others warn of the circularity effects that can arise from the unrestricted assumption of truncation, especially when it is used to weaken apparent counterexamples to purported general principles or constraints on derivation (Plank 1981).

As for affix potentiation, some derivational affixes feed the domain of application of other affixes (and, correspondingly, bleed that of functionally related ones, if they exist). Thus, Engl. *-ize* "feeds" the nominalizing suffix *-tion*, and is "fed" by *-al*. This leads to some characteristic suffixal chains, which are diachronically apt to blend into a single suffix (e. g. in the Romance followers of Lat. *-arius*, which combined with the followers of *-ia* to give French *-erie*, Span. *-ería*, etc. (Malkiel 1966, Lüdtke, 1996: 256)), but can also extend to sets of prefixes and suffixes (as in English verbs prefixed by *en-* or *be-*, which are nominalized by means of *-ment* to the exclusion of other suffixes (*endear* > *endearment, bewilder* > *bewilderment*).

Finally, derivational morphological processes seem to be sensitive to some sort of stratification of the lexicon in etymological layers of native and non-native items. The best studied examples are, of course, the learned/popular stratification of the Romance languages and the Latinate vs. Germanic stratification of English. In both cases, the preferred distribution of stems and affixes (popular/native affixes can apply both to popular/native and to learned/borrowed stems, whereas learned/borrowed affixes tend to associate exclusively with learned/borrowed stems, cf. Plank 1981: 129 ff., Corbin 1987: 90 ff.) is obviously a consequence of the borrowing of entire lexical patterns and of the lesser or greater success of the affixes in transcending these original patterns. A different type of stratum sensitivity is found in Japanese, for which Kageyama (1982: 227−231) reports of a negative prefix *hu-* that only attaches to native and Sino-Japanese bases, to the exclusion of foreign ones (*hu-too* 'unjust' vs. **huriaru* 'unreal'), as well as of a noun-forming suffix *-sei* which requires its base to be nonactive (i. e. foreign or Sino-Japanese, cf. *arukaru-sei* 'alcalinity' vs **otoko-sei* 'male').

4. The semantics of derivation

I make the possibly controversial assumption that those syntactic aspects which undoubtedly play a major role in derivation, namely lexical category and argument structure, legitimately belong to the semantics of lexical items. For reasons of space, little attention will be devoted to the discussion of the relation between syntax and derivation in recent generative linguistics. Since existing works on theoretical morphology offer excellent surveys of these questions (cf. in particular Spencer 1991, Carstairs-McCarthy 1992), to do otherwise would amount to duplicating already existing syntheses in a unsatisfactorily abbreviated form. It is common to deplore the lack of attention devoted to lexical-semantic matters in current mainstream linguistics, and Carstairs-McCarthy (1992: 7, 97, 118 and passim) is right in pointing to the need for more sophisticated theories of meaning relationships and possible meanings of derived words. However, there exist some richer traditions outside the mainstream, so that there is fortunately more to report on this topic than might appear at first sight.

4.1. Derivational sense and lexicon sense

First and foremost, there is widespread consensus on the fact that two levels of meaning have to be distinguished when describing the semantics of (established or actualized) derived lexemes: the meaning they possess qua actual lexemes or lexicon sense, and the meaning they possess qua derived lexemes, or derivational sense. Whereas, the lexicon-sense is primarily given and can be determined by whatever relations also determine the meaning of non-derived lexical items, including denotation, the derivational sense is exclusively determined by the relation of the lexeme to its base. If one accepts that this relation is to be captured by the semantic operation associated with the derivational process, then derivational sense turns out to be *per definitionem* compositional and predictable (Lüdtke 1978: 14−18, Laca 1986: 129−140, Corbin 1991). Notice that the distinction between lexicon-sense and derivational sense is implicit in the notion of lexicalisation: derived words are said to be lexicalised or opaque when their lexicon-sense deviates considerably from their derivational or "expected" sense. However, there is much less agreement on the definition of derivational senses, in particular in how general or how specific the semantic operations linking bases and derived lexemes should be. Derivational senses are usually apprehended by means of paraphrastic formulae that contain a variable for the base and express the semantic relationship between series of pairs of derivationally related lexemes, such as 'capable of being V-ed' for rendering the series *break* > *breakable, eat > edible, formulate > formulable*, etc., or 'similar to N' for the series *film > filmy, ice > icy, rust > rusty*, etc. But neither the formulae nor the series they should account for are given in advance. The lack of consensus on this matter is particularly prejudicial when we try to ascertain the extent to which derivational categories vary across languages. So, for instances, if one assumes, on the basis of the series *Darwin > Darwinism, Marx > Marxism*, etc. that the semantic operation associated with English *-ism* creates denotations for systems of belief or theories, this is clearly a language-specific category (cf. Aronoff 1984). But if one enlarges the series to include also *Maloprop > malapropism, cannibal > cannibalism* and decides that the semantic operation creates denotations for an activity characteristically related to the base (or for the results of such an activity), then the category will be found to recur in quite a number of unrelated languages. In fact, when one compares semantic descriptions of derivational categories such as "agent noun" and "causative", on the one hand, and "hide or fur of an animal Y" (reported by Mel'čuk 1993−94: II, 380 for Even, as in *korovas* from *korova* 'cow', *camakas* from *camak* 'marmot', etc.) or "small specialized restaurant where food of type Y is served" (which would account for the meaning of Russ. *blinnaja* 'crêperie' from *blin* 'crêpe' or *buterbrodnaja* 'sandwich shop' from *buterbrod* 'sandwich', cf. Mel'čuk 1993−94: II, 381−2) on the other hand, the suspicion arises that the descriptions have been carried out on two completely different levels of abstraction. The notion of a regular lexicalisation pattern, as something different from the semantic operation defining a derivational category, might be helpful for coming to grips with the fact that derivatives tend to cluster in denotational groups, while maintaining at the same time that the semantic operations in derivation are more general than these patterns (Lüdtke 1978: 16, Laca 1986: 140−147). In a seminal, if sketchy, discussion of the semantics of derivation, Aronoff (1984: 48) delineates the following position: "derivation may make reference to all syntactically motivated categories of a language, including major lexical categories such as noun, verb, and adjective, and their subcategories, such as transitive and intransitive; thematic relations such as agent, patient, and instrument; and syntactico-semantic selectional categories like mass, count, animate, and inanimate. According to this view, derivational semantics should still be relatively free from the real world that the semantics of individual members of major lexical categories must cope with". Although Aronoff goes on to dismiss this position as "disconfirmed by inexorable fact", a case can be made for treating the more culture-specific, denotation-oriented aspects of the semantics of derived lexemes in terms of regular lexicalisation patterns.

4.2. Taxonomies of derivational categories

Since the traditional classification of derivational patterns in homogeneous (word-class maintaining) and heterogeneous (word-class changing) ones, there has been no dearth of universal taxonomies ("typologies") of derivational categories. These taxonomies are universal in the sense that they are based on complementary alternatives and thus purport to exhaust the field of what is possible. But they are only very weakly predictive, and the only constraints they impose on the notion "possible derivational category" arise from the criteria which are held to be taxonomically relevant (plus the very general assumption that the structures or processes involved are binary). Some of these taxonomies take into account the lexical category of the base and that of the derivative (Leumann 1944/1973, Zwanenburg 1996). Others operate with very general denotational categories that are more or less directly linked to basic grammatical concepts, such as the Modifier-Head or the Predicate-Argument distinction (Dokulil 1968, Mel'čuk 1993−94: II, 314−387). It is apparent that lexical category systems, as well as some version of categorial semantics, and the sorted ontology of natural languages it should cope with, play an absolutely central role in the classification of derivational categories. In this sense, it is to be hoped that the study of the semantics of derivation should profit from the interest in sortal approaches to ontology developed in the field of formal semantics in recent years.

Although the relationship between the lexicon and syntax, and especially the underlying conception of syntax remain quite unexplicit in his approach, the semantic typology of word-formation processes due to Coseriu (1977) deserves special mention, because it claims to have a grammatical foundation. Coseriu's views on derivation show some affinity with those of Beard (1990), inasmuch as both assume that there is an analogy between the features and relations that are relevant to derivation and those that are relevant in the morphosyntactic organisation of a language. Coseriu distinguishes between modification, development and prolexematic composition. The latter involves a second, "pronominal" element that entertains a (para-)grammatical relation to the base. It comprises mainly processes that can be described as argument-linking or incorporation in the case of bases with a clear argument structure (as in deverbal agent or patient nominalizations), together with various processes whose results are similar to nominal compounds, except for the fact that the modified element or "head" is not a nominal lexeme, but an abstract categorial value (in fact a general substitute for first order entities, as in Span. *jardín* 'garden' > *jardinero* 'gardener', *avispa* 'wasp' > *avispero* 'wasp nest/hive' *jazmín* 'jasmine' (flower)' > *jazminero* 'jasmine shrub'). The distinction between modification and development is based on a contrast between inactual (or inherent) and actual (or relational) grammatical functions (while also reflecting the traditional contrast between homogeneous and heterogenous derivation).

4.3. Derivation and lexical structure

The overall view of derivation associated with Coseriu's typology is similar to the position sketched by Aronoff (cf. § 4.1.): the semantics of derivation mirrors to a greater or lesser extent the semantics of grammar (cf. also Lüdtke 1996: 238). This contrasts with the view expressed by Bybee (1985: 83), according to whom derivational relationships mirror semantic relationships between morphologically unrelated lexical items. Bybee's view relies on the perceived semantic analogies between pairs such as *happy − sad* and *happy − unhappy, freeze − thaw* and *freeze − unfreeze, fly − flyer* and *fly − pilot*, etc. It is certainly true that these analogies have been unsufficiently explored (cf. Carstairs-McCarthy 1992: 47 ff., 187 ff.). However, it should be borne in mind that derivational relationships are characteristically oriented, so that they involve a basis or primary item and a derived or secondary item, and that they are best conceived of as injections from a basis domain on a range (Anderson 1992: 189), thus excluding one-to-many or many-to-one mappings. Even if a case can be made for the orientation of some semantic relationships between morphologically unrelated items, a clear orientation seems to be the exception rather than the rule in this domain. It arises first and foremost in cases of encapsulation (i.e. in pairs such as *die – kill, foot – kick*), as well as in cases involving general or local markedness considerations, e.g. in the oppositions between male and female or adult and young representatives of a species, or in polar oppositions between "positive" and "negative" terms (cf. Cruse 1986: 246–257). Notice, furthermore, that encapsulations usually involve series of nearly synonymous lexemes (*kick* entertains essentially the same relation with *foot* as with *hoof*, and not only *kill*, but also *do in, eliminate, liquidate* are lexical causatives to *die*). Thus, derivational relationships mirror only a small and atypical subset of lexical relationships (precisely those that some morphologists are tempted to classify as "total-suppletive" derivational relationships).

There is a further interesting issue concerning the relation between derivation and lexical organization that has not, to my knowledge, been explored at all. The theory of categorisation developed in prototype semantics distinguishes three levels of categorisation: an optimal or basic level organised around "information-rich bundles of co-occurring perceptual and functional attributes", a more abstract superordinate level and a more specific subordinate level (Rosch et al. 1976: 382). These levels are defined by psycholinguistic criteria. Although there is probably some relevant correlation between derivational expression and the non-basic-level status of a category, no studies seem to have been devoted to this question.

4.4. Regular polysemy

The study of semantics of derivation is considerably complicated by the fact that form/meaning relations in this domain seem to be characteristically irregular (see § 2.1.). Against this background, it is particularly important to recognize patterns of regular polysemy and to offer some explanatory account for their existence. More often than not, a given morphological process in a given language expresses several different semantic operations or, equivalently, is associated with several different semantic categories. This one-to-many relationship is, however, seldom isolated: it often recurs in other morphological processes, either in the same language, or in other languages, or both intra- and cross-linguistically. Obviously, frequently recurring patterns are not plausible cases of fortuitous homonymy among categories. Like polysemy in general, regular polysemy in derivation can be tackled with two different strategies, the "common denominator" strategy, in which a general undertermined sense is posited to which the more specific distinct senses relate as further specified variants, and the "structured constellation" approach, in which different senses on a similar level of specificity are linked to each other by chains of motivating relationships, possibly organized around one or more "central" links. Although this is by no means necessary, common denominator approaches tend to assume that the undetermined senses posited are to some extent arbitrary and language-specific, whereas structured constellation approaches rely on purportedly universal cognitive links. Different cases of regular polysemy seem more or less amenable to one or the other strategy.

As far as nominalization is concerned, most morphological processes used for deriving abstract nominalizations (roughly, names of events, states or properties) can also give rise sporadically to agentive, instrumental, manner, locative, and objective nominalizations (cf. French *diriger* 'lead, direct' > *direction* 'action of directing, leading' and also 'person(s) responsible for management', 'steering mechanism in a car', 'management offices', etc.). In the theory of abstract nominalizations developed by Lüdtke (1978), these semantic extensions can be understood as a result of underdetermination: since in abstract nominalizations no argument is linked ("topicalised", in the terminology Lüdtke has adopted from Marchand (1969)), they are in principle compatible with further semantic specialization involving the linking of an argument or adjunct. On the other hand, agent nominalizations that very often coincide formally with instrument nominalizations are known to coincide with locative nominalizations. Some researchers have advanced a common denominator solution for this type of polysemy, associating the agent-instrument ambiguity to the neutralization of the thematic rules of agent and instrument either in the subject position of an active verb (Laca 1986) or in the case-marking of instruments and agent-phrases in passive sentences (Beard 1990). The formal coincidence of instrument and locative nouns can, in turn, be reduced to a general category of mediation or finality (Serbat 1975). Other researchers tend to insist on the cognitive links between agents and instruments, on the one hand, and between (some) instruments and (some) places (the role of the simultaneously instrumental and local conceptualization of "containers" as a possible source is certainly not to be dismissed), and resort to explanations in terms of semantic or lexical extension (see Dressler 1980, Booij 1986). I do not think that current evidence justifies a decision as to the correct treatment of this phenomenon. But it should be stressed that Beard's Unitary Grammatical Function Hypothesis (i.e., that there is a universal set of grammatical functions constraining both derivation and inflection), together with his Parallel Polysemy Corollary (that a set of grammatical functions marked by a single category in inflection will be marked by some single affix in derivation more often than would be expected from chance, cf. Beard 1990) has an explanatory power and a degree of falsifiability that cognitive extension models lack. If the corollary or some version of it stands up to wider empirical testing, we will have learnt something very central as to the semantics of derivation.

Regular polysemy that cuts across the main types of derivational categories is a problem for all of the classifications discussed above, since it shows that some clusters of semantic operations are orthogonal to the classification. Some of these cases of regular polysemy can be related to specific properties of the grammatical organization of the language in which they appear. In languages with a high degree of permeability between the lexical categories N and A, such as the Romance languages, prolexematic composition will very often coincide in its expression with development: whole series of relational adjectives will be nominalized, "incorporating" a variable for the elliptic noun they determine, and some derived nouns will acquire adjectival uses, with categorially ambiguous suffixes as a typical result (cf. French -ier, from Lat. -arius, an originally adjectival suffix that derives both denominal adjectives and nouns, -(at)eur, from Lat. -tor, an originally nominal suffix that derives both nouns and adjectives, Span. -ista, an originally agentive nominal suffix that occasionally derives relational adjectives).

Other cases occur frequently enough cross-linguistically to justify the search for a general explanation. Examples are the coincidence in the expression of denominal collective nouns and abstract nominalizations denoting a social status or function, or the use of primarily evaluative affixation (diminutives, augmentatives, pejoratives) for deriving agent or instrument nouns, well attested in the Romance and Germanic languages, but documented also for Mandarin Chinese (Jurafsky 1996: 553). In recent years, there has been an upsurge in research that combines an interest in the semantics of derivation with the treatment of evidence from other than the best described European languages (see Beard 1990, 1993, Zwanenburg 1996). In this context, Jurafsky's study on the semantics of the diminutive in over 60 languages (Jurafsky 1996) deserves special mention on account of its empirical coverage and of the issues raised, which also involve semantic reconstruction. Quite independently of the accuracy of his "radial category" model (a version of the cognitive extension approach), it is to be expected that future progress in our understanding of the semantics of derivation will proceed along similar paths.

5. References

Anderson, Stephen R. 1985. "Typological distinctions in word formation". In: Shopen, Timothy (ed.): 3–56.

Anderson, Stephen R. 1992. *A-Morphous Morphology*. Cambridge, University Press.

Aronoff, Mark. 1976. *Word formation in generative grammar*. Cambridge/MA, MIT Press.

Aronoff, Mark. 1984. "Word formation and lexical semantics". *Quaderni di Semantica* V,I: 45–50.

Aronoff, Mark (ed.) 1992. *Morphology now*. Albany, SUNY Press.

Baker, Mark. 1988. "Morphology and syntax: an interlocking dependence". In: Everaert, Martin (ed.): 9–31.

Bauer, Laurie. 1988. *Introducing linguistic morphology*. Edinburgh. Edinburgh Univ. Press.

Beard, Robert. 1990. "The nature and origins of derivational polysemy". *Lingua* 81: 101–140.

Beard, Robert. 1993. "Simultaneous dual derivation in word formation". *Language* 69,4: 716–741.

Becker, Thomas. 1990. *Analogie und morphologische Theorie*. Munich, Fink.

Behrens, Leila. 1996. "Lexical rules cross-cutting inflection and derivation". *Acta Linguistica Hungarica* 43: 33–65.

Booij, G. 1979. "Semantic regularities in word formation". *Linguistics* 17: 985–1001.

Booij, Gerd & van Marle, Jaap (eds.) 1996. *Yearbook of Morphology 1995*. Dordrecht, Kluwer.

Booij, Gerd. 1996. "Inherent versus contextual inflection and the split morphology hypothesis". In: Booij, Gerd & van Marle, Jaap (eds.): 1–16.

Buszard-Welcher, Laura et al. (eds.) 1992. *Proceedings of the 18th annual meeting of the Berkeley Linguistics Society. General session and parasession on the place of morphology in grammar*. Berkeley: BLS.

Bybee, Joan. 1985. *Morphology. A study of the relation between meaning and form*. Amsterdam, Benjamins.

Carstairs-McCarthy, Andrew. 1992. *Current morphology*. London, Routledge.

Chelliah, Shobhana. 1992. "Pretty derivational morphemes all in a row". In: Buszard-Welcher, Laura et al. (eds.): 287−297.

Comrie, Bernard. 1985a. "Derivation, inflection, and semantic change in the development of the Chukchi verb paradigm". In: Fisiak, J. (ed.), 1985: 85−96.

Comrie, Bernard. 1985b. "Causative verb formation and other verb-deriving morphology". In: Shopen, Timothy (ed.): 309−348.

Comrie, Bernhard & Thompson, Sandra. 1985. 'Lexical nominalization". In: Shopen, Timothy (ed.): 349−399.

Corbin, Danielle. 1987. *Morphologie dérivationnelle et structuration du lexique*. Tübingen, Niemeyer.

Corbin, Danielle. 1991. "Introduction. La formation des mots: structures et interprétations". *Lexique* 10: 7−30.

Coseriu, Eugenio. 1977. "Inhaltliche Wortbildungslehre". In: Brekle, Herbert & Kastovsky, Dieter (eds.) *Perspektiven der Wortbildungsforschung*. Bonn, Bouvier: 48−61.

Cruse, D. A. 1986. *Lexical semantics*. Cambridge, University Press.

Cutler, Anne & Hawkins, John & Gilligan, Gary. 1985. "The suffixing preference: a processing explanation". *Linguistics* 23: 723−758.

De Reuse, Willem. 1992. "The role of internal syntax in the historical morphology of Eskimo". In: Aronoff, Mark (ed.): 164−178.

DiSciullo, Anna M. & Williams, Edwin. 1987. *On the definition of word*. Cambridge/MA, MIT Press.

Dokulil, Miklos. 1968. "Zur Theorie der Wortbildung". *Wissenschaftliche Zeitschrift der Karl-Marx-Universität Leipzig* 17: 203−211.

Don, Jan. 1993. *Morphological conversion*. Utrecht, Rijksuniversiteit Utrecht.

Dressler, Wolfgang. 1980. "Universalien von Agens-Wortbildungen". In: Brettschneider, G. & Lehmann, Christian (eds.) *Wege zur Universalienforschung (Festschrift H. Seiler)*. Tübingen, Narr: 110−114.

Dressler, Wolfgang. 1985. "Suppletion in word formation". In: Fisiak, Jacek (ed.) 1985: 97−112.

Dressler, Wolfgang. 1986. "Forma y función de los interfijos". *Revista Española de Lingüística* 16: 381−395.

Dressler, Wolfgang. 1987. "Word formation (WF) as a part of natural morphology". In: Dressler, Wolfgang et al. *Leitmotifs in natural morphology*. Amsterdam, Benjamins: 99−126.

Dressler, Wolfgang. 1988. "Preferences vs. strict universals in morphology: word-based rules". In: Hammond, Michael/Noonan, Michael (eds.): 143−153.

Dressler, Wolfgang. 1989. "Prototypical differences between inflection and derivation". *Zeitschrift für Sprachwissenschaft und Kommunikationsforschung* 42: 3−10.

Dressler, Wolfgang & Merlini-Barbaresi, Lavinia. 1994. *Morphopragmatics. Diminutives and intensifiers in Italian, German and other languages*. Berlin, Mouton-de Gruyter.

Everaert, Martin et al. (ed.) 1988. *Morphology and modularity. In honor of Henk Schultink*. Dordrecht, Foris.

Fisiak, Jacek (ed.). 1985. *Historical semantics and historical word formation*. Berlin.

Greenberg, Joseph. 1963. "Some universals of grammar, with particular reference to the order of meaningful elements". In: Greenberg, Joseph (ed.) *Universals of language*. Cambridge/MA, MIT Press: 58−90.

Greenberg, Joseph et al. (eds.) 1978. *Universals of human language. Vol. III: Word structure*. Stanford/CA, University Press.

Hammond, Michael & Noonan, Michael (eds.) 1988. *Theoretical morphology. Approaches in modern linguistics*. New York, Academic Press.

Haspelmath, Martin. 1996. "Word-class changing inflection and morphological theory". In: Booij, Gerd & van Marle, Jaap (eds.): 43−66.

Jurafsky, Dan. 1996. "Universal tendencies in the semantics of the diminutive". *Language* 72,3: 533−578.

Kageyama, Taro. 1982. "Word formation in Japanese". *Lingua* 57: 215−258.

Kilani-Schoch, Marianne & Dressler, Wolfgang. 1984. "Natural morphology and Classical vs. Tunisian Arabic". *Wiener Linguistische Gazette* 33/34: 51−68.

Kilani-Schoch, Marianne & Dressler, Wolfgang. 1986. "Metathèse et conversion morphologique en arabe tunisien". *Zeitschrift für Phonetik, Sprachwissenschaft und Kommunikationsforschung* 39: 61−75.

Laca, Brenda. 1986. *Die Wortbildung als Grammatik des Wortschatzes*. Tübingen, Narr.

Langdon, Margaret. 1992. "Yuman plurals: from derivation to inflection to noun agreement". *International Journal of American Linguistics* 58: 405−424.

Leumann, Manu. 1944/1973. "Gruppierungen und Funktionen der Wortbildsuffixe des Lateins". In: Strunk, Karl (ed.) *Probleme der lateinischen Grammatik*. Darmstadt, Wissenschaftliche Buchgesellschaft: 131−161.

Lin, Yen-Hwei. 1993. "Degenerate affixes and templatic constraints: rhyme change in Chinese". *Language* 69,4: 649–682.

Lüdtke, Jens. 1978. *Prädikative Nominalisierungen mit Suffixen im Französischen, Katalanischen und Spanischen*. Tübingen, Niemeyer.

Lüdtke, Jens. 1996. "Gemeinromanische Tendenzen IV. Wortbildungslehre". In: Holtus, Günther et al. (eds.) *Lexikon der Romanistischen Linguistik. Vol. II, I: Latein und Romanisch*. Tübingen, Niemeyer: 235–272.

Malkiel, Yakov. 1966. "Genetic analysis of word formation". In: Sebeok, Thomas (ed.) *Current trends in linguistics. Vol. III: Theoretical foundations*. The Hague, Mouton: 305–364.

Malkiel, Yakov. 1978. "Derivational categories". In: Greenberg, Joseph et al. (eds.): 126–149.

Marchand, Hans. 1969. *The categories and types of present-day English word-formation*. 2nd ed. Munich, Beck.

Matthews, Peter. 1984. "Word formation and meaning". *Quaderni di Semantica* V,1: 85–92.

Matthews, Peter. 1991. *Morphology*. 2nd. ed. Cambridge, Cambridge University Press.

Mel'čuk, Igor. 1993–94. *Cours de morphologie générale. Vol. I: Introduction et première partie: Le mot. Vol. II: Deuxième partie: Significations morphologiques*. Montréal. Presses de l'Université – CNRS Editions.

Mithun, Marianne. 1988. "Lexical categories and the evolution of number marking". In: Hammond, Michael & Noonan, Michael (eds.): 211–233.

Moravcsik, Edith. 1978. "Reduplicative constructions". In: Greenberg, Joseph et al. (eds.): 297–334.

Muysken, Pieter. 1986. "Approaches to affix order". *Linguistics* 24: 629–643.

Muysken, Pieter. 1988. "Affix order and interpretation: Quechua". In: Everaert, Martin et al. (eds.): 259–279.

Olsen, Susan. 1986. "Argument linking and unproduktive Reihen bei deutschen Adjektivkomposita". *Zeitschrift für Sprachwissenschaft* 5: 5–24.

Perlmutter. David. 1988. "The split morphology hypothesis: evidence from Yiddish". In: Hammond, Michael & Noonan, Michael (eds.): 79–100.

Plank, Frans. 1981. *Morphologische (Ir-)regularitäten. Aspekte der Wortstrukturtheorie*. Tübingen, Narr.

Rainer, Franz. 1996. "Inflection inside derivation: evidence from Spanish and Portuguese". In: Booij, Gerd & van Marle, Jaap (eds.): 83–92.

Rosch, Eleanor et al. 1976. "Basic objects in natural categories". *Cognitive Psychology* 8: 382–436.

Sapir, Edward. 1921. *Language*. New York. Harcourt Brace.

Scalise, Sergio. 1988. "Inflection and derivation". *Linguistics* 26: 561–581.

Serbat, Guy. 1975. *Les dérivés dénominaux latins à suffixe médiatif*. Paris, Belles Lettres.

Shopen, Timothy (ed.) 1985. *Language typology and syntactic description. Vol. III. Grammatical categories and the lexicon*. Cambridge, University Press.

Spencer, Andrew. 1991. *Morphological theory: an introduction to word structure in generative grammar*. Oxford & Cambridge, Blackwell.

Ultan, Russell. 1975. "Infixes and their origins". In: Seiler, Hansjakob (ed.) *Linguistic Workshop*. Munich, Fink: 158–205.

Zwanenburg, Wiecher. 1996. "Catégories lexicales et structure conceptuelle en morphologie". In: Blumenthal, Peter et al. (eds.) *Lexikalische Analyse romanischer Sprachen*. Tübingen, Niemeyer: 157–163.

Brenda Laca, Université des Sciences Humaines de Strasbourg (France)

90. Color terms

1. Color ethnography
2. Universals
3. Types of relation between categories
4. Types of relation within categories
5. References

1. Color ethnography

Between 1879 and 1905, scholars from ophthalmology, biology, philology, and anthropology classfied systems of color naming among peoples throughout the world (Herne 1954: 9–19; Parsons 1915: 145–51). They reported languages that named all color with only two terms, as if everything were red or black. When a language used additional color terms, red, black, and white were always named; a term for green predicted a term for yellow, while both were predicted by a term for blue (red black < white < yellow < green < blue). The relations suggested color terms everywhere evolved in one order. A long debate ensued about whether the sequence implied stages in the evolution of language or unequal visual abilities (cf. MacLaury 1997a: 15−18). The psychologist Woodworth (1910: 179) conducted a perceptual test with 300 tribal peoples assembled from around the world at the 1904 St. Louis Fair, and he reviewed earlier studies. He settled the debate in favor of language by concluding "the color sense is probably very much the same all over the world." Woodworth, thus, opened the gate to Franz Boas, his colleague at Columbia University. Boas (1910: 377) issued his first proclamation of linguistic relativity, citing as support the naming of yellow-with-green by a single term in certain languages *versus* the singular naming of green-with-blue in others. As linguistic relativity hardened into doctrine over the next fifty years, descriptions of color naming fostered that framework (e. g., Geddes 1946: 35; Ray 1953: 103; cf. MacLaury 1997a: 18−20; 2000: 252−60). Color-term typology was almost forgotten.

Berlin & Kay (1969: 1−14), aiming to confute the excessive relativism, revived the evolutionary typology of years past, but they added precision. After collecting 98 studies and word lists, they found regularities indeed pertain among **basic color terms** (BCTs), those that speakers easily recall and commonly apply with simplest morphology in all situations without including the meanings within ranges of other color terms. Depending on the language, BCTs will number from two to eleven. But regardless of the number in a particular language, its speakers will *focus* (i. e., choose a best example for) each BCT on precisely one among eleven narrowly confined areas in a standard array of color stimuli, only 30% of 329 Munsell chips. Further, Berlin & Kay refined the earlier predictions of color-term co-occurrence into an implicational evolutionary order of seven stages, shown in Fig. 90.1a. Universal foci of BCTs implied that color perception is unevenly constituted with a few percepts purer than the many others. Both this and the evolutionary order presupposed a panhuman perceptual determinant: All people see color in the same way and name what they see as the functional need arises.

Berlin & Kay's 1969 sequence, like those that preceded, treated its typological stages as a naming of points, such as white, black,

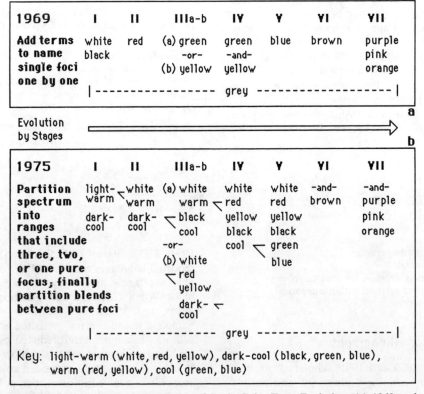

Fig. 90.1: Berlin and Kay's Sequences of Basic Color-Term Evolution, (a) 1969 and (b) 1975.

red, etc., which left the margins of color-term ranges to assume any extent or configuration. Such allowed Berlin & Kay to ignore the distinction, say, between a black range that includes dark red and a black range that excludes red entirely, a difference that may reflect varying interests in brightness *versus* hue perception (Conklin 1973: 937). However, new fieldwork revealed seven color-term systems that each, at a different stage, partitioned all Munsell color chips between the hues expected to receive foci, which suggested the systems named hue rather than brightness (cited in MacLaury 1997a: 23). The data motivated Berlin & Kay (Berlin & Berlin 1975: 84−5; Kay 1975: 258−9) to revise their evolutionary sequence to accomodate exhaustive partition at each of its stages and to commit the sequence to exclusively hue naming, as shown in Fig. 90.1b with the broadest categories defined in its key: *light-warm*, *dark-cool*, *warm*, and *cool*. Hue naming has never been shown to devolve, as Kristol (1980: 143) tried to show by arguing Roman scribes named Stage V while Italian peasants in the 1920s named Stage IV (Probably the peasants did not descend from the scribes).

Kay & MacDaniel (1978: 639) adapted a minor revision of this 1975 hue sequence to a fuzzy-set formalism, justifying the model with available understanding of primate visual physiology. Although since 1978 physiological knowledge has changed, most vision researchers still believe, as they did then, that humans perceive white and black as extremes of brightness and see four unique hues as purest red, yellow, green, and blue (cf. Saunders & van Brakel 1997: 213); red-green and yellow-blue are opponent pairs, each of whose two colors cannot be viewed at the same place and time. The unique hues span the gamut of light to dark but each is seen with a maximally vivid point in its span, that is, the reddest red, yellowest yellow, greenest green, or bluest blue. In the fuzzy model, Stages I through V progressively partition these six point-like sensations, whereby composite basic categories comprise the fuzzy unions of three or two points and primary basic categories comprise single points as fuzzy identities. Stages VI and VII derive basic categories from fuzzy intersections within certain pairs of points: brown (yellow + black), purple (red + blue), pink (red + white), orange (red + yellow), and grey (white + black). Kay & McDaniel intended the calculus to address gradation of color-term meanings, to integrate expected foci with vague margins, to incorporate a neural model, and to distinguish types of hue terms as **composite**, **primary**, or **derived**. This typology remains very useful, whithersoever go fuzzy sets.

The 1975 sequence does not address all hue naming. As will be shown, the 1969 order alone constrains color-term typology in two sequences recently identified. Apparently, this original formulation plumbs a deep-seated tendency to favor primary and derived color perception in the order expressed by Fig. 90.1a. Further evidence lies in studies of preverbal infant response to primary hue (Jones-Molfese 1977; Staples 1932; Valentine 1914), child color-term acquisition (Arnaud 1986; Mills 1976), and adult salience ranking (Bolton 1978; Morgan and Corbett 1989). Salience tests are suited to experiments, such as asking subjects to list terms in free recall (Pollnac 1975: table 1), measuring substitution of terms across separate naming tasks (Uchikawa and Boynton 1987), and timing latency of response (Johnson 1986). Salience is also tested against phonemic length of color terms (Durbin 1972), number of connotations per color term (Williams, Morland, and Underwood 1970; Crisp and Chang 1987), number of qualifiers per term (Corbett and Morgan 1988: 38), and frequency of terms in literature (McManus 1983). Resultant rankings are statistically assessed against the 1969 sequence by the Spearman rank order correlation, as, for example, Hays et al. (1972) find correlations ranging from .76 to .96 in English, Spanish, French, German, Russian Rumanian, and Hebrew literature. However, weaker correlations appear among compilations tabulated without intent to compare results with the Berlin-Kay order: (1) Pratt (1898: table I) tallies color terms of 17 English poets from Langland (1332−1400) to Keats (1795−1821), showing GN 1113 > W 1092 > BK 924 > R 752 > BU 651 [> GY 553] > PL 317 > Y 203 > BN 191 > O 7 > PK 5; (2) Arias Abellán (1994) counts color terms of Roman authors Cato, Varro, Columella, Pliny, and Paladius in agricultural and encyclopedic writings, revealing W 325 > BK 260 > GN 157 [> GY 60] > R 55 > Y 11; (3) Kober (1932) does likewise of Greek poets from Homer through those of the Alexandrian Age, finding BK $\mu\varepsilon\lambda\alpha\varsigma$ 552 > W $\lambda\varepsilon\upsilon\kappa\acute{o}\varsigma$ 463 [> GY $\gamma\lambda\alpha\upsilon\kappa\acute{o}\varsigma$ 177] Y $\xi\alpha\upsilon\theta\acute{o}\varsigma$ 168 > BU $\kappa\upsilon\alpha\nu\alpha\iota\gamma\iota\varsigma$ 159 > PL $\pi o\rho\varphi\upsilon\rho\varepsilon\acute{o}\varsigma$ 138 > GN $\chi\lambda\omega\rho\acute{o}\varsigma$ 115 > R $\varepsilon\rho\upsilon\theta\rho\acute{o}\varsigma$ 87 > BN $\alpha\iota\theta o\psi$ 46. The English sums from Pratt are restricted to only terms that today are basic; Latin sums from Arias Abellán include all major terms that name each elemental color, for example, of *ruber* 24, *rufus* 26, *russeus* 3, and *rubeus* 2 as names of red; the Greek sums include only the most prevalent name of each color, some of which have several names. While any of these strategies could be invalid, use of alternative strategies do not change the relations. Price's (1883: 10) percentages of color terms from only Vergil stray even farther from predictions than do the ratios of Arias Abellán; however, McCrea (1884: 193) in Ovid's work finds R *ruber* 81 > GN *viridis* 66 > Y *flavus* 51 > BU *caeruleus* 50. Wallace's (1927: 66−67, tables a−c) proportions from only *The Iliad* and *The Odyssey* match those of Kober. Dik (1989: 31) shows Dutch color-term frequencies with Y less used than BU or BN, Kreig (1979: 433) Old English frequencies with R second to only W and GN dead last after Y, BN, PL, and BU. The above-mentioned genre of studies involving infants, children, and adults show equivalently mixed correlations. But despite such grounds for caution, the three synopses by, respectively, Hays et al., Bolton, and McManus together suggest that primary and derived color perceptions are universally lined up as Berlin & Kay (1969) extrapolated, which is consistent with the role of this order in newly found types − to be discussed as sequences 5 and 6.

Three surveys collected unprecedented data and, in the process, improved typology, theory, and descriptive method. In 1976−78, Berlin & Kay conducted the World Color Survey (WCS) in collaboration with missionary W. R. Merrifield of the Summer Institute of Linguistics. Its members used Munsell chips to collect data in 110 minor and tribal languages in 22 countries of the Americas, Africa, Asia, Australia, and the Philippines, usually 25 interviews per language (Merrified 1992: 164). In 1979−81, MacLaury followed with an in-depth regional complement, the Mesoamerican Color Survey (MCS), mainly in Mexico and Guatemala (1986a: 5−11; 1997a: 395−407). After pooling MCS and WCS data, coverage of Mesoamerica included 898 interviews in 116 languages. A survey in the Pacific Northwest (PNCS) covered four Salish languages and sampled others (cited in § 3.4). The WCS recorded data as each informant named 330 Munsell chips one by one in random order and selected foci of the names from an organized array of the chips. Adopting these methods, the MCS further collected qualifiers and added an independent mapping procedure by which an informant placed grains of rice on chips of the array to cover the range of each term volunteered during mapping. Prompts, such as "Put rice on more of X-term," elicited broad mappings, often in steps corresponding to repeated prompts. Two arrays of identical chips were used − one green-centered, the other red-centered − which prevented the artificial breaks of the array from influencing mappings. Analyses were based on correspondence between head lexemes and qualifiers, foci, mappings, and their steps, not on anyone sort of data (cf. MacLaury 1997a: 76−85). Mappings will not be shown herein, although they contribute immensely to interpretation of data and to typology.

Fig. 90.2 displays the naming ranges and foci of a German speaker, which are derandomized in the format of a green-centered array. The figure exemplifies graphics and pro-

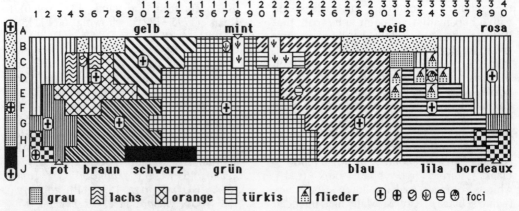

Fig. 90.2: Hochdeutsch, f 24, Friedstadt, Schleswig-Holstein, Germany, 1998.

vides the reader with a specimen against which to interpret examples of color naming in unfamiliar languages. This system is much like those used by other dialects and languages of western Europe (MacLaury 1986a, Appendix I: 1−11). Each row-column intersection represents one chip. The figure depicts light to dark from top to bottom through rows (A−J at left, otherwise B−I), rainbow hues from left to right across columns 1−40. Hues are saturated to the maximum attainable with 1976 pigments (specified in MacLaury 1997a: 11). The left column represents desaturated chips from white through shades of grey to black. The informant named the chips with 16 terms, of which *weiß, schwarz, rot, grün, gelb, blau, braun, lila, rosa, orange*, and *grau* are basic, others secondary. Distinctive hatching marks the chips named by each term. The focus of every BCT corresponds to its naming range and, thus, is marked as a cross in an oval, large or small. Only the focus of secondary *bordeaux* so corresponds on chip I1, while other secondary foci do not. Noncorrespondence of a focus and name is common, especially when ranges overlap. Such a focus is shown as an oval marked by the hatching of its term, as is the focus of *lachs* C5, *mint* B17, *türkis* E23, and *flieder* D34. Foci in the unnumbered left column are encoded in text by Ø, as with AØ, FØ, and JØ for *weiß, grau*, and *schwarz*. Gender and age are abbreviated, for example, f 24. In 90.5−11 and in text, specimens in the WCS database are referenced by language and number, for example, Tlapanec WCS 5 and 7.

2. Universals

Every person applies a singular cognitive dynamic to a highly specific perceptual infrastructure. Their interaction propels change in the direction symbolized by arrows in the typology of 90.3. The specifics of perception determine details of types.

2.1. Cognition

Any pair of separate senses, say green and blue, are to an extent similar and, to a reciprocal extent, different. An individual can emphasize the perceived similarity or the perceived difference, establishing a tension between the strengths at which he recognizes each perception. Speakers of a language can share this cognition. Over time such people can shift the balance, say, favoring difference progressively while deemphasizing similarity. A people would be motivated to increasingly attend to difference by the amount of novelty that impinges on them from external sources, such as population pressure, diminishing resources, increasing hardship, culture contact, globalization, and much more, and they would be so motivated by the rate at which novelty impinges. Their progressive favoring of differentiation would help them survive in circumstances that demand continual analysis, a cognitive adaptation that is straightforwardly evolutionary. Development of vocabulary to communicate such elaboration of view, too, would be adaptive. Probably the world has seldom become simpler and easier for people to live in, and, accordingly, the shift of emphasis between similarity and difference usually and everywhere has advanced in favor of differentiation, however slow the movement. But certainly the pace has quickened in recent times for everyone, even people formerly insulated from the worldly mainstream. Within the model to be used here, this global shift of attention from similarity to difference is the propelling force of color-term evolution. However, change throughout a domain of categories follows from change within each of them. Therein, recognitions of similarity and difference do not magically combine with color perception to constitute a category. We shall now and then draw upon vantage theory, an account of the integrative process by which a human agent actively coordinates attention to similarity and difference with selected color perceptions to construct a category as a point of view (MacLaury 1997a: 109−218). This process, too, is in theory universal.

2.2. Perception

Universals of the color sense consist of (1) light *versus* dark and four unique hues, (2) six purest point sensations of white, black, red, green, yellow, and blue, (3) distinct perceptual distances between these points, (4) primacy of red, (5) cardinal opposition between red and green, (6) complexities of hue between pure points, (7) complexities of desaturated color, (8) brightness-sensitive rods on the periphery of the retina and wavelength-sensitive cones in its center that absorb different ratios of light when an individual dilates or focuses concentration, (9) effects of light and dark on discrimination. MacLaury (1997b: 202) tests the importance to color naming of (1) and (2) by compiling all 15,186 singular foci (chosen on only one chip or on nonadjacent chips) collected by the WCS, disregarding the type of color category each focused term names. The histogram shows stepped ascents to apexes in Munsell columns 1, 9, 17, 29, those whose pigments most resemble the unique hues, with deepest troughs at 5, 14, 23, and 37. The 6 noncontiguous densest clusters on single chips — by far the densest — occur at AØ (white), JØ (black), G1 (red), C9 (yellow), F17 (green), and F29 (blue), the purest points. In addition to these plurality peaks, the stepped contour of the distribution suggests that most foci are placed, at least, in reference to the favored columns, if not, in all likelihood, to the colors at peaks: The unique hues and pure points are critical to the meaning of most color terms in the WCS. This experiment replicates with enhanced quantification the pattern Berlin & Kay (1969: 9) diagrammed of normalized BCT foci from twenty languages. Boynton & Olson (1987: 102—3) simulate (3) by quantifying overlapping use of neighboring terms within the quadrangular geometry of the Optical Society of America color solid. For example, they compute green and blue to be very close to each other, yellow and green a little farther apart, yellow and red considerably farther apart, and red and blue hugely separate. MacLaury (1997a: 88, 92—3) summarizes independent findings of the same relative distances. Perceptual universals (6) through (9) are elaborated in §§ 3.1—3., while (4) and (5) pertain to processes treated elsewhere (1997a, index: 608).

3. Types of relation between categories

MacLaury (1992: 160) proposed separate evolutionary sequences that differentiate BCTs of hue from BCTs of brightness but allow the latter to transform into the former: Figures 90.3—4 refine that scheme into four sequences and add sequences 5—6. The figures will guide discussion of types in §§ 3.1.—6., which treat, respectively, sequences 1—6. On the right of 90.3., cross-reference to 90.5—11 matches horizontally the sequences they exemplify. Because 90.3. cannot convey all relations in its two dimensions, 90.4 depicts a third dimension as a circle around which sequence numbers are positioned, clockwise in

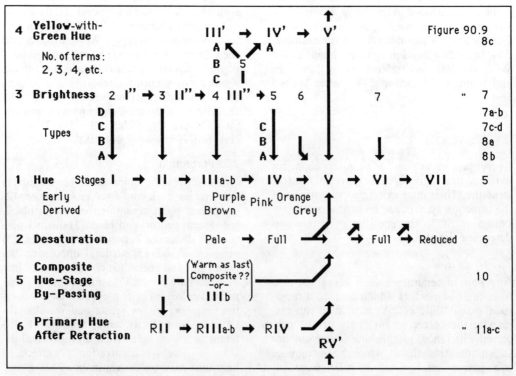

Fig. 90.3: Typological Sequences 1—6 of Basic Color-Term Evolution.

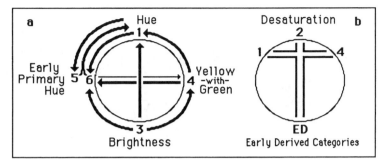

Fig. 90.4: Relations between Sequences: (a) Transformation, (b) Coevolution.

(a) as 1, 4, 3, 5 and 6, or in (b) as 1, 2, 4, and Early Derived Categories. Part (a) shows directions in which one sequence may convert into another, while (b) shows coevolution of sequences affirmed in single systems. Kay, Berlin & Merrifield (1991: 19), Kay, Berlin & Maffi et al. (1997: 30−2), and Kay & Maffi (1999: 748−57) have thrice revised their multilineal typology, whose argumentation differs from that adopted here.

3.1. Hue

In 90.3, sequence 1 copies Berlin & Kay's 1975 hue sequence (Fig. 90.1b). Most latter-day languages represent at least one of these seven types, with variation between types occurring in many (Kay 1975: 263). Hue naming predominates in most populations. Its commonality justifies posing sequence 1 as the core of color-term typology for contemporary languages. Sequence 1 is driven forward by the application of cognition to perception, characterized in § 2.1 and § 2.2 (1−3). At Stage I, people name hue with only two terms because they attend very strongly to similarity. But as they attend more to difference, they separately name the pure color points, first separating points that differ most and last separating points that differ least. For example, red and yellow are named separately before Stage IV, wherein green and blue are still named as one category (cf. 90.1b). Unequal perceptual differences could have no bearing on color-term evolution if people did not engage them with specifically that cognition. Fig. 90.5 exemplifies each stage of sequence 1 with a specimen. All were elicited with Munsell chips, except that of (a) Lani, which was elicited with Nick Hale's replica: the Lani speaker named chips one by one along the rows through a chip-size aperture, producing a quadrangular contour (MacLaury 1997a: Hale plate, 12, 51). Otherwise, the Lani ranges might have appeared scrambled, as with specimens (b−d). Specimens (e−h) at late stages show less scrambling. At Stage VII, a Finnish speaker has not named pink apart from red, using one BCT fewer than the German speaker. Stage VII incorporates purple, pink, orange, and grey in any order, which can be incomplete. Specimens (a−h) were picked for typological purity; thus, unlike the German specimen, they lack secondary terms.

The five derived BCTs name color between pure points that are perceptually the most distinct from each other, such as red and blue, red and yellow, red and white, or black and white, not between points that are perceptually the most similar, such as green and blue or green and yellow (cf. § 2.2 [3]); brown, which occurs between black and yellow, is named with a BCT for this reason, but also for its complexity as a desaturated hue (§ 2.2 [6−7]). Thus, in Berlin & Kay's 1975 hue sequence − herein, sequence 1 − brown is named at Stage VI. Commonly, one or a few BCTs among brown, purple, pink, orange, and grey are named in a system that otherwise would count as a pure Stage IIIa or pure Stage IV, especially in the latter (MacLaury 1997a: 55, 58, 103, 167, 245, 262, 269). In 90.3., these BCTs are indicated as Early Derived in conjunction with sequence 1, and they are ordered as they most often appear in systems collected by the MCS (MacLaury & Stewart 1984: 5−7). Early Derived BCTs are so common that pure Stage V and Stage VI are very rare; if we take naming data by themselves, only three pure examples of Stage V appear in the WCS, one in the PNCS (Mac Laury 1986b: 101), and none in the MCS. Specimen (g) is one of the two Munsell recordings of pure Stage VI. The literature portrays whole languages representing Stage V or Stage VI, such as Southeast

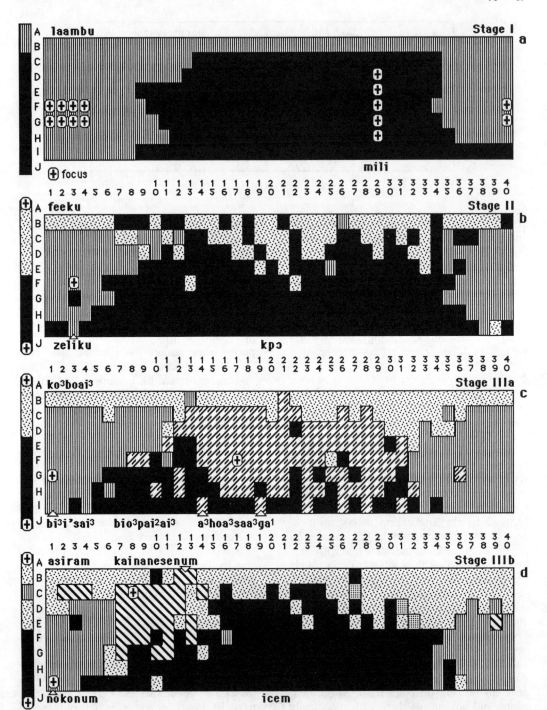

Fig. 90.5: Sequence 1, Hue: (a) Lani (Danian), Yugwa, Karbaga, Jayawi Jaya (The Grand Valley), Irian Jaya, m 50, 1992 (Wesly Dale); (b) Bété (Niger-Kordofanian), Sieqduekou, West Central Department, Ivory Coast, f 75, 1978; (c) Múra Pirahá (isolate), Rio Maici, Amazonas, Brazil, m 40, 1977; (d) Kwerba (Trans-New Guinea), Aurime, Upper Tor River, Irian Jaya, f 25, 1978; (b–d WCS 7, 18, 4)

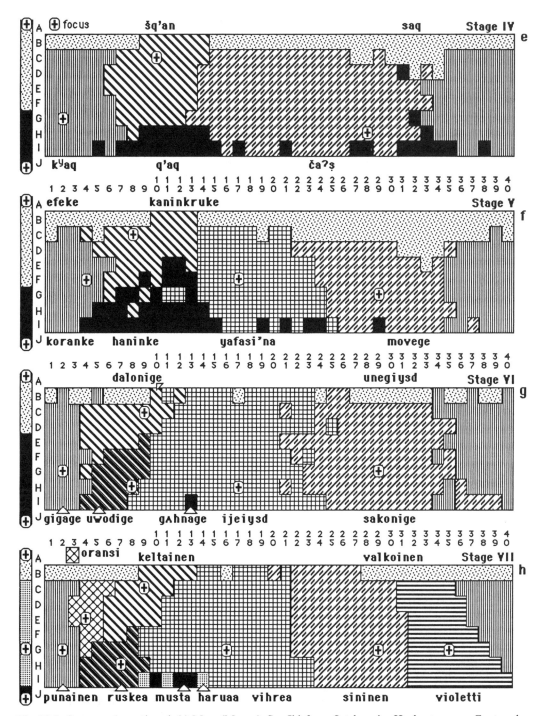

Fig. 90.5: Sequence 1, continued: (e) Mam (Mayan), San Ildefonso Ixtahuacán, Huehuetenango, Guatemala, f 56, 1980; (f) Kamano (Trans-New Guinea), Kanampa, E. Highlands, Papua New Guinea, m 38, 1977 (WCS 20); (g) Cherokee (Iroquoian), Locust Grove, Oklahoma, USA; (h) Finnish (Urgo-Finic), Lapendranta, Kymenlaani, Finland (Monica Heller).

Asian Yao (Thongkum 1992: 8−9) or Patagonian Tsoneca (Musters 1897: 321), but such summaries might oversimplify. Berlin & Kay's (1969: 83−90) conception of Stage V and Stage VI, too, is based on summary reports, save a contested interview in Mandarin (125; Lü 1997: 4). More fieldwork and study are needed because many apparent Early Derived terms might be identified as secondary if they were mapped (e.g., MacLaury 1997a: 102). WCS and MCS data suggest the full complement of five derived BCTs consolidates long after Stage V emerges, regardless of whether its emergence is accompanied by some of the derived BCTs. Figure 90.4b indicates Early Derived BCTs also coevolve with sequence 4: in 90.9c, brown accompanies yellow-with-green; in 90.8b−c, *tsipi* 'purple' coincides with composite categories and even precedes brown ([b] represents sequence 1, [c] sequence 4). Finally, the forward thrust of BCT evolution is rendering very rare the basic two-term system (MacLaury 1997: 49−52 re available data). Only languages in the Central Highlands of Irian Jaya are known to name hue at Stage I. Although red-black hue systems are called light-warm *versus* dark-cool, it would match our few data to call them warm-light (red, yellow, white) *versus* cool-dark (blue, green, black): foci can be red *versus* blue, as in 90.5a (cf. MacLaury 1997a: 502n11 re Hittite).

3.2. Desaturation

About half of all languages at Stages IV through VI − give or take derived terms − name a core of desaturated color that includes and exceeds the narrow range of grey. The breadth of this term protrudes through the surface of the Munsell array in least saturated areas of brown, lavender, beige, and pale. Even the German specimen shows slight desaturation naming by applying *grau* to C31−32 near *flieder*. Fig. 90.6 shows desaturation terms with typological differences among them, *kimaaxxaat* in Seri and *lopoban* in Colorado. They represent Stage IV in specimens (a−c) with (d) of special interest at almost Stage V. Naming of desaturated color is usually accompanied by brightness recognition, which occasions speakers of one or another language to vary the desaturated range between light and dark, even white versus black (e.g., Tlapanec WCS 5 *vs* 7). Specimen (a) manifests a strong example focused in middle brightness grey at EØ. Specimen (b) concentrates the range at lower brightness, focused in brown at H6−7. Specimen (c) directs the meaning to high brightness, focusing the term in lavender at C29. As shown in 90.3, sequence 2, the desaturation term may retain its range through Stage VI, although diagonal arrows depict that at any stage it can retract to become grey or brown of sequence 1. By Stage VII, if the term has not transformed to grey or brown, it will become secondary, as apparently has Irish English *dun*. When, as in Colorado, most speakers concentrate the desaturation term on high brightness, some may convert it to a BCT naming blue; we see this change between specimen (c), focus C29, and specimen (d), focus F29 (cf. Hinde 1901: 49, 57, 66, 74). Colorado speaker (d) is evolving a Stage V system through a different route than has Kamanokafe speaker (f) in 90.5; thus, different arrows point toward Stage V in 90.3. Sequence 2 coevolves with sequence 1 or 4, as shown in 90.4b. In 90.9c, slight application of a desaturation term, *mamát*, participates in sequence 4. The desaturation terms in 90.6 are BCTs, even though their ranges vary more than do ranges of hue terms and terms for black or white. The fixed locations of pure points stabilize such ranges, whereas desaturated color is complex and assorted with nothing pure about it, as specified in § 2.2 (7). One might speculate that a desaturation term names a residual category of nondescript color, an amorphous conceptual void. However, Greenfeld (1986: 909) asked Apache speakers to map their desaturated *libaah* (cf. MacLaury 1997a: 56). They placed rice on grey, brown, lavender, beige, and pale, with those priorities, demonstrating internal structure.

3.3. Brightness

Certain color terms appear to have little relation to hue or desaturation because they span most of the Munsell array, as do those in Fig. 90.7. Possibly, they name a level of lightness or degree of brightness, or they might name a combination of the latter with extremes of saturation. We do not know what quality of the light sense interests people who name color chips in this way because no researcher has tried to find out. Some evidence suggests these terms name brightness (MacLaury 1997a: 49−52); at least, "brightness term" is a convenient appellation. As argued elsewhere (MacLaury 1992: 150−62; 1997a: 69−72), brightness terms may transform into hue terms, which is further implied in 90.8.

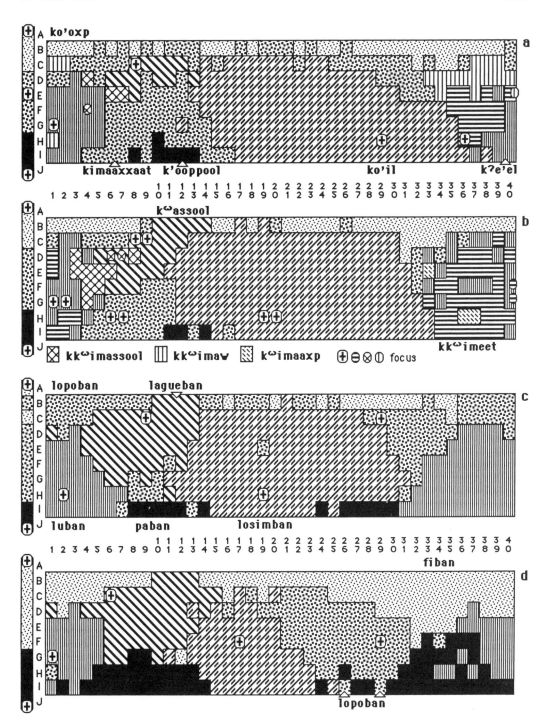

Fig. 90.6: Sequence 2, Desaturation: (a–b) Seri (Hokan), Desemboque, Sonora, Mexico, f 26 and f 38, 1978; (c–d) Colorado (Chibchan), Santo Domingo de los Colorados, Ecuador, m 22 and f 41, 1979; (WCS 5, 17, 3, 24).

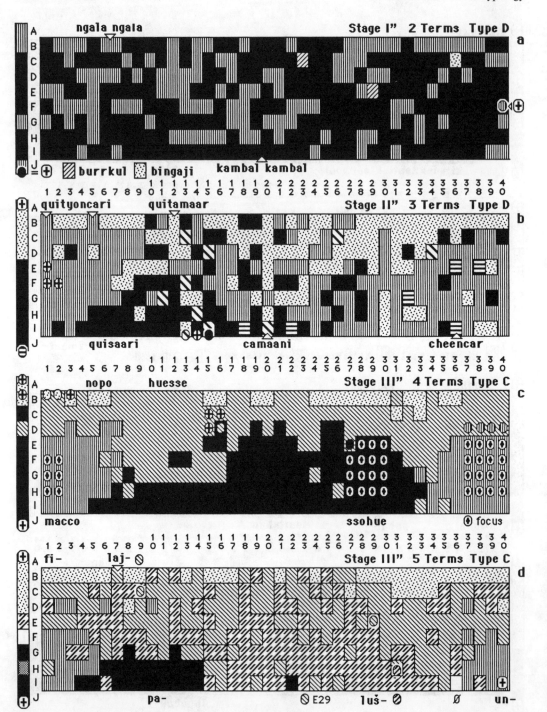

Fig. 90. 7: Sequence 3, Brightness: (a) Kuku Yalanji (Australian), Bloomfield River, Queensland, m 55, 1978; (b) Ucalyali Campa (Arawakan), Mencoriari, Loreto, Peru, m 15, 1978; (c) Culina (Arawakan), San Bernardo, Rio Alto Purús, Ucayali, Peru, f 38, 1977; (d) Cayapa (Chibchan), Esmeraldas, Ecuador, f 28, 1978; (WCS 18, 14, 8, 6).

Evidence of change from brightness to hue is seen in Agta of the Philippines (1997a: 72), wherein the merger toward hue is accompanied by addition of loanwords and increase of null responses. There is no support in any language of the reverse merger from hue to brightness. Peralta (1980: 53), who describes brightness naming in Philippine I'waak, attributes its difference from hue naming to the absence of pressure on such people as the I'waak to routinely concentrate on detail in daily life. That is, the I'waak concentrate on special domains, such as plants, but do not concentrate as a general and constant strategy under such impingements as enumarated in § 2.1, as would urban people. In keeping with § 2.2 (8), concentration changes the shape of the eye such as to direct more light particles into the fovea centralis, a maximally sensitive pit in the center of the retina where most wavelength receptive cones are lodged; cones transduce to hue perception. Rods are distributed in the retinal periphery, from which concentration substracts light; rods transduce to brightness perception. Attention to difference is a function of concentration that, too, directs light into the fovea. When people differentiate as a routine, they convert the meanings of color terms from brightness to hue.

In 90.3, sequence 3 represents the development of brightness naming in increments of 2, 3, 4, and 5 terms per system, exemplified, respectively, by specimens (a), (b), (c), and (d) in Fig. 90.7. Specimen (c) shows four separately named basic categories, the maximum observed in any brightness system. Specimen (d) also includes four categories, although one of them is named with two coextensive terms. MacLaury (1992: 156 top) depicts a system in Bolivian Chacobo that names three brightness categories with four terms, two of them coextensive. It is very hard and often impossible to identify the BCT in a coextensive brightness pair using only Munsell chips. Conversely, in specimen (a), we must guess that the two major terms name separate categories, commingled as they are. In the abstract, then, brightness terms name Stage I″ of two categories, Stage II″ of three categories, and Stage III″ of four categories, but the types may involve more major terms than categories. The number of terms, rather than the stage they name, may have the greatest effect or even the only effect on sequences 1 and 4 when types therein descend from types in sequence 3, as diagrammed in 90.3 by vertical arrows. Thus, sequence 3 is expressed in reference to numbers of major terms as well as to stages of BCTs.

Any brightness term is typed according to how much it appears to have transformed to a hue term: a term of Type D names only brightness, Type C more brightness than hue, Type B more hue than brightness, and Type A only hue (Vantage theory models Type C and Type B as hierarchical arrangements of brightness and hue recognitions on which equal emphases are impossible [for motivations see MacLaury 1992: 149]). Each type of term manifests subtypes, for example, across roughly middle brightness specimen (c) names a predominantly light category, specimen (d) a very broad category, although both represent Type C. Although the typology principally applies to any term by itself, an individual's system of terms can be assigned to one of the types according to an average among its terms. Specimens (a) and (b) are systemically Type D because each term that is focused in red (F40 or E1+F1−2) crosses the spectrum, as do their other terms. But specimens (c) and (d) are systemically Type C because their red-focused terms (D−H37−40 +F−H1−3 or I40) are curtailed such as to apparently name hue. Only their other terms act like they name brightness. In 90.8, specimen (a) is systemically Type B because, not only is its red-focused term (G1) curtailed, but its coextensive middle brightness terms (F14 and G18) show more separation than do those of specimen (d) of Type C in Fig. 90.7. In Fig. 90.8, specimens (b) and (c) represent Type A, completed transformations to hue naming. The systemic type may be expressed after the stage and number of terms, for example, in 90.7, specimen (c) is Stage III″ 4 Terms Type C. A few Stage III″ systems are named with more than five terms, as among those of Australian Murrinh-Patha in the WCS. The present typology classifies all 25 specimens of this notorious challenge (cf. Kay and Maffi 1999: 754−5). Although sequence 3 specifies no more than five terms, Murrinh-Patha surpasses this limit by adding triple coextension and by combining brightness terms and hue terms in Type B. Some systems of Type B can be further specified by suffixing in brackets the hue stage toward which they seem to be developing, for example, Murrinh-Patha (WCS 19) Stage III″ 5 Terms Type B [IV] or abbreviated (10) III″ 7 B [IV′].

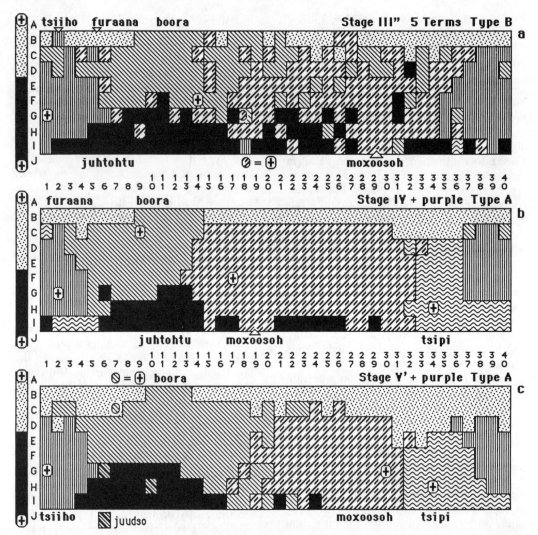

Fig. 90.8: Sequence 3 Merging to Sequences 1 and 4, Brightness Transforming to Hue: Ocaina (Witoan), Rio Yaguasyacu, Loreto, Peru, 1977, (a) Puca Urgillo f 65, (b–c) Puerto Isango, m 21 and m 29, (WCS 16, 7, 12).

3.4. Yellow-with-Green Hue

Sequence 4 consists only of Stages III′, IV′, and V′. Its diagnostic BCT names all hues of yellow and green and only those. Possible earlier stages of sequence 4 are reported in Chukchi of Siberia and Nuba of Sudan (Almquist 1883: 47; Faris 1972: 59), of which measurement is lacking. Lévi-Strauss (1948: 117) describes Stages III″ and V′ among Nambikwara dialects. Dictionaries, letters (cf. Kay 1975: 260–61n), and sundry passages report yellow-with-green terms far and wide. But the only Munsell attestations come from Kwakwala and Cree (cf. § 3.6.), Ocaina (e. g., Fig. 90.8c), and the PNCS (MacLaury 1986b: 102–12; 1987: 108–9; 1989: 1–5, 7–10; MacLaury & Galloway 1988: 1–5; Galloway 1993: 663). Sequence 4 is based on PNCS Salish data: Stage III′ names white, black, warm, cool, yellow-with-green; Stage IV′ white, black, red, cool, yellow-with green; Stage V′ white, black, red, blue, yellow-with-green. Each stage is named with five terms: warm and cool shrink, respectively, to red and blue, moving the sequence through Stages III′ and IV′ into V′. Naming separately either yellow or green converts Stage V′ to Stage V, as is recorded, respectively, among speakers of Sechelt and Lillooet (MacLaury 1991: 33; 2000: 256–8). Figure 90.9 exemplifies sequence 4. In (a), a Lillooet speaker representing Stage III′ names a warm

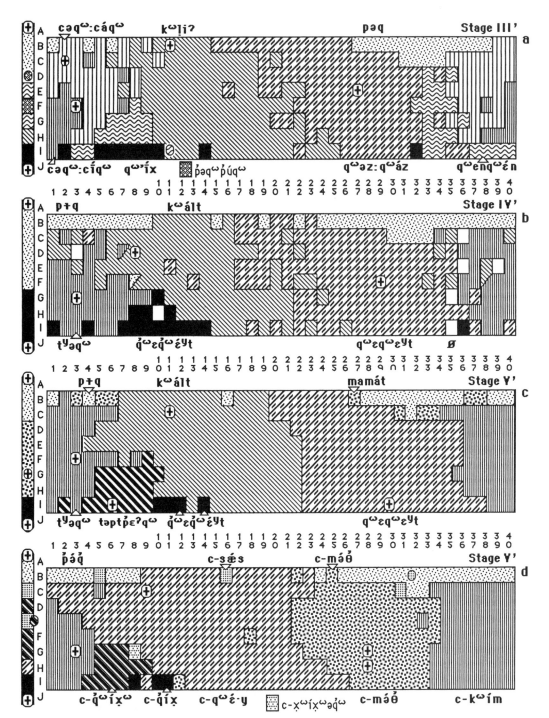

Fig. 90.9: Sequence 4, Yellow-with-Green Hue: (a) Lillooet (Interior Salish), Mt. Currie, B. C., Canada, m 73, 1988; (b–c) Shuswap (Interior Salish), B. C., Canada, 1985, (b) Sugar Cane Reserve, m 73 and (c) Alkalai Lake, f 45; (d) Halkomelem (Coast Salish), Tait Dialect, Chawutnel, f 60±, 1987.

category with a pair of terms that are centrally and peripherally focused (F3, C2) and related to each other by ablaut. The red-focused warm range beyond elemental yellow (C9) is attested at C10; the blue-focused cool range beyond elemental green (F17) is attested at E16. The yellow-with-green range covers both C9 and F17. In (b) and (c), respectively, naming data show Stages IV' and V', lacking evidence for the warm category in (b) and for both the warm and the cool category in (c). Throughout the world and in accord with § 2.2 (3), sequence 1 is far more common than sequence 4 because green is a little more similar to blue than to yellow. But, given this perception, it remains unexplained why even a few languages categorize yellow-with-green at Stage V' after their separate category of green-with-blue has retracted to only blue. Kay & Maffi (1999: 753) proclaim "The Yellow/Green Mystery Resolved," but they essentially mean just that Stage III" merges into either sequence 1 or 4.

Kinkade (1988: 448) traces the origin of Salishan yellow-with-green to a yellow-green-blue brightness category in Proto-Salishan, hypothetically *Stage III" (of which Sechelt retains living remnants [MacLaury 1991: 33–37]). He considers evidence such as the cognates in 90.9: (a) Lillooet $q^{\omega}əz{:}q^{\omega}áz$ 'cool', (b–c) Shuswap $q^{\omega}εq^{\omega}ε^{y}t$ 'cool' or 'blue', and (d) Halkomelem $c\text{-}q^{\omega}έ{\cdot}y$ 'yellow-with-green'; or (a) Lillooet $k^{\omega}liʔ$ 'yellow-with-green' and (b–c) Shuswap $k^{\omega}ált$ 'yellow-with-green'. It appears that Lillooet and Shuswap, both Interior Salish languages, derived their current systems from coextensive naming of yellow-green-blue brightness of the kind seen in Cayapa of 90.7d and Ocaina of 90.8a: the ranges of $k^{\omega}liʔ$ and $k^{\omega}ált$ retracted to yellow-with-green, those of $q^{\omega}əz{:}q^{\omega}áz$ and $q^{\omega}εq^{\omega}ε^{y}t$ to cool (a–b) or, finally, to blue (c). But (d) suggests that Halkomelem, a Cost Salish language, converted its sole yellow-green-blue brightness cognate, $c\text{-}q^{\omega}έ{\cdot}y$, to name latter-day yellow-with-green in mirror opposition to the green-with-blue meaning that Lillooet and Shuswap assigned $q^{\omega}əz{:}q^{\omega}áz$ and $q^{\omega}εq^{\omega}ε^{y}t$. Conversely, Halkolemem names blue with $c\text{-}máθ̂$, which is cognate with the Shuswap desaturation term, $mamát$ (c). Perhaps Halkomelem derived the blue meaning from a desaturation meaning, as did the Colorado speaker in 90.6d. The descent of sequence 4 from sequence 3 may take more than one route of lexicalization, either beginning with coextensive naming of yellow-green-blue brightness or by adopting en route the fifth term from a different source. In Fig. 90.3, the transition between sequences affords both options. The Y-shape of this path, however, means merely that warm may or may not contract to only red before sequence 4 is established as a development of Type A hue categories, thus starting at either Stage III' or Stage IV'.

3.5. Composite Hue-Stage By-Passing

In most languages, secondary terms anticipate the next stages of evolution, as secondary cool at Stage II might anticipate Stage IIIa (MacLaury 1997a: 4.3–10) and certainly would foretell Stage IV. Rarely, a language will add to Stage II three salient secondary terms for, respectively, yellow, green, and blue. In such a case, if the warm category retracts to red, the yellow term will become basic, creating Stage IIIb. Then, if the dark-cool category retracts to black, both the green term and the blue term will become basic, thus skipping Stage IV and moving directly to Stage V. This likely scenario is foreshadowed in Fig. 90.10 by data from Vagla. Mapping data might clarify to what extent, if any, the scenario has actually progressed. Without mappings, we cannot preclude a second scenario in which dark-cool will contract to black before warm retracts to red, as occurs in sequence 1 at Stage IIIa. If this common event were to occur in Vagla, warm would persist as the last composite category, an extreme violation of Berlin and Kay's enduring predictions (cf. 90.1b). A third scenario is that warm and dark-cool will contract simultaneously, fostering a detour around both designs of Stage IIIa–b as well as around Stage IV. In 90.3, sequence 5 includes the three possibilities, with parentheses representing the by-pass of both Warm as the Last Composite Category and Stage IIIb. In any case, Stage IV will be skipped and, thus, is absent from sequence 5. In Vagla, Stage II may persist for all current speakers. The secondary terms have salient ranges for only some speakers while the terms remain descriptive phrases. Likely, these would simplify if they became basic, perhaps to *sasao*, *koriihuu*, and *burgu* — transparent BCTS like English *orange*. Levinson (2000) describes such simplification among phrasal color terms that become basic in Yélîdnye under other conditions (described in § 3.6). Although sequence 5 seems to project the probable future of Vagla and its neighbors (Dyi-

90. Color terms

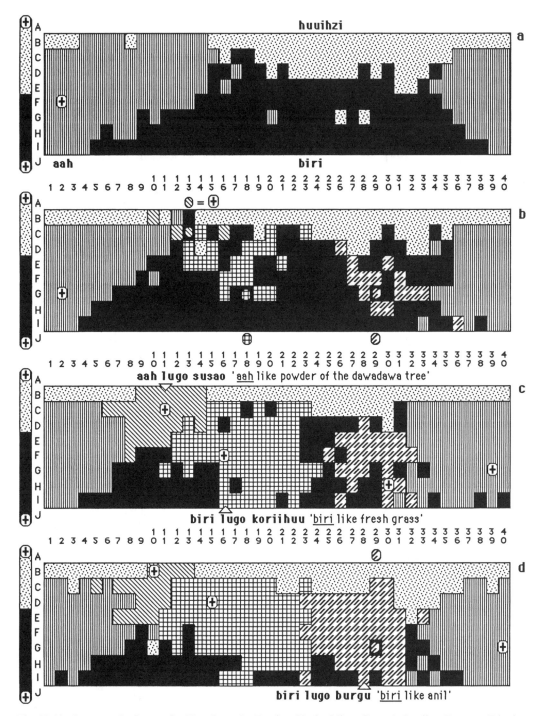

Fig. 90.10: Sequence 5, Composite Hue-Stage By-Passing: Vagla (Niger-Congo), Jentilpe, Damago District, Ghana, 1978; m 30, f 11, f 20, m 16 (WCS 10, 2, 24, 15; Marjorie L. Crouch, letter 1995).

mini [WCS], Mo [p. c. M. Crouch], and Tera [Newman 1964: 44−45]), no evidence from our sparse surveys proves that sequence 5 has anywhere transpired on the basic level.

3.6. Naming of Primary Hue after Retraction

Sequence 6 evolves after speakers of a language discontinue the manner in which their forebears named color. They retract the broad ranges of early-stage BCTs so as to apply each term to only one of the pure perceptions described in § 2.2 (2). They leave many or even most colors unnamed, including some of the pure points. Such is documented by the WCS in Malayo-Polynesian Ifugao on Luzon and in Algonquian Micmac and Cree of Canada, by the MCS in Uto-Aztecan Tepecano and in Mayan Quiché of Choiquimula and Cakchiquel of Panajabal (MacLaury 1997a: 226, 229−30, 270−1), by the PNCS in Salishan Samish and Sechelt (MacLaury 1991: 32−7), and by Saunders (1992: 147−50) in Wakashan Kwakwala on Vancouver Island. When any such language remains viable, a subsequent generation renames one by one each neglected pure point with a primary BCT. On the whole, speakers do not rename the points as yellow *versus* green-with-blue of Stage IV (Fig. 90.5e), as yellow-with-green *versus* blue of Stage V' (Fig. 90.9c), or as all of yellow-green-blue together, as in Stage III" (Fig. 90.7d, cf. MacLaury 1992: 151). Rather, the stages of sequence 6 are those proposed by Berlin & Kay in 1969, here in Fig. 90.1a.

Sequence 6 pertains to the stabilization of BCTs. Like lexical innovation in other domains (e. g., flying machine, aircraft, aeroplane/airplane, plane), phrases, metonyms, and alternative forms may abound until a single, simple term gains unanimous acceptance at each pure point. Meanwhile, none of the competing lexemes qualify as a BCT. Snow (1971: 387) reports this process in Samoan of Polynesia, whose speakers vary among animate and inanimate terms for green, are settling for the inanimate term as a BCT, and name blue metonymically but decidedly as "color of the deepest part of the sea" (cf. Vagla phrases, Fig. 90.10). Beaglehole (1939: 171) reports of Polynesian Tongan "There is no specific colour-name for blue and possibly none for green ... Their difficulty, they said, was simply one of finding words," and he translates their descriptive phrases. In Fig. 90.3, sequence 6 is depicted by prefixing R (for "retraction") to stage numbers. Excluding unattested Stage RI (white, black), three stages are so far attested: Stage RII (white, black, red), Stage RIIIa−b (add [a] green or [b] yellow), and Stage RIV (add green and yellow). Naming blue with a BCT converts sequence 6 to Stage V of sequence 1.

Levinson (2000; cf. Kay & Maffi 1999: 751−3) finds Stages RII, RIIIa, RIV, and V with Munsell interviews of eight Yélîdnye speakers on Rossell Island, Papua New Guinea. Yélîdnye is stabilizing new names for primary green, yellow, and blue, in that order, adding them to old names for white, black, and red, whose ranges apparently have retracted. The sample is too small and too young to assess whether any speaker names Stage II or Stage II'. In Ifugao, sequence 6 unfolds through Stages RII, RIIIb, RIV, and V, part of which appears in Fig. 90.11 a−c. The figure emphasizes retraction. Specimen (a) shows partial retraction within a Stage II" 3-Term Type C system. Specimen (b) shows full retraction, creating Stage RII of only white, black, and red. Specimen (c) represents the result of sequence 6, after three more primary BCTs have been stabilized. In other WCS data, Ifugao speakers all name white, black, and red, and, among them, 3 name only yellow, Stage RIIIb; 12 name yellow *versus* green, Stage RIV; 5 name yellow, green, and blue, Stage V. They vary lexically by naming yellow with either of 4 terms, green with either of 2 terms, and blue with either of 2 terms, but most employ the BCTs of (c). However, in addition to naming white, black, and red, 2 speakers name yellow *versus* green-with-blue, Stage IV; one names yellow-with-green *versus* green-with-blue, Stage IV'. Figure 90.4a covers possible conversions from sequence 6 to sequence 1, but only a thin arrow represents conversion from sequence 6 to sequence 4 because solely this Ifugao speaker attests to it. In Yélîdnye and Ifugao, sequence 6 probably started earlier than it did in the other languages that show retraction. Figure 90.4a allows as well such later retraction of ranges that were in either sequence 3 or sequence 1 before retraction. The latest possible retraction of a composite range occurs at Stage IV: cool retracts to green while blue is left unnamed, Stage RIV, as in Tepecano and Panajabal Cakchiquel. Kwakwala leaves yellow unnamed but separately names green versus blue, which descends from sequence 4 as RV'. In Fig. 90.3, RV' exits the diagram at top and re-enters at

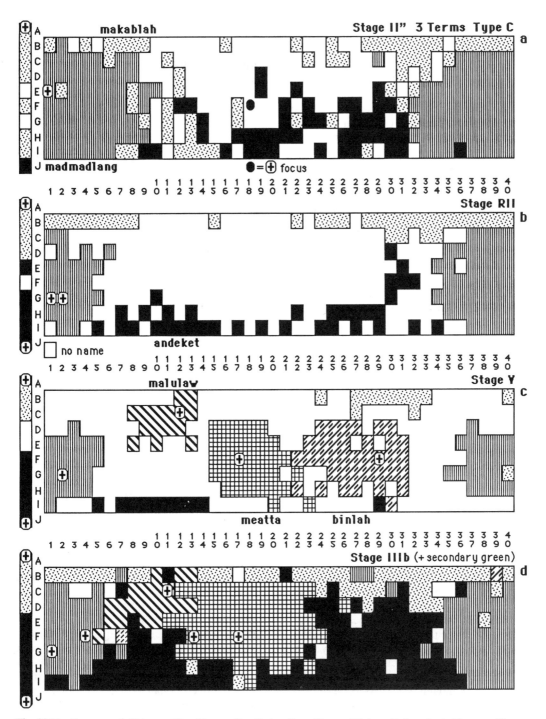

Fig. 90.11: Sequence 6, Primary Hue Stages after Retraction: Ifugao (Malayo-Polynesian), Nayapo, Ifugao Province, Luzon, The Philippines, (a–d) f 55, m 30, m 23, m 27, 1978 (WCS 11, 18, 14, 16).

bottom. The last Samish speaker left yellow unnamed but named cool, RIV'.

How do we know a language has retracted its ranges? For example, we could suppose Maori and Bellonese (Colenso 1882: 73; Kuschel and Monberg 1974: 220) independently extended their color-term ranges to Stage II from a curtailed condition in Proto-Polynesian while Samoan and Tongan remained unchanged until they recently named with BCTs hues they had earlier named with ad hoc phrases. A hypothesis of primordially deficient BCTs is shielded from falsification because it is often impossible to determine what occurred in prehistory. Of the dozen stunted cases, Samoan, Tongan, Yélîdnye, and Samish occur on small islands, Ifugao and Kwakwala on large islands. Sechelt, Kwakwala, Micmac, and Cree persist in situations of English-dominant bilingualism and acculturation. The Samish and Tepecano systems were elicited from sole surviving speakers. Panajabal Cakchiquel and Chiquimula Quiché show independent signs of strong attention to difference that exceed those found by the MCS in other Mayan languages. Such corollaries suggest that exceptional events have fostered exceptional color naming. Deficiency of BCTs is not proposed within the main lines of typological development, nor is the absence of BCTs proposed as an ancient condition that proceeded any of the sequences. This stance contrasts with that of Kay (1999; Kay & Maffi 1999: 744−5), who says nothing about retraction while entertaining a typological role for systems not fully partitioned by BCTs.

3.7. Controversial types

Certain types of color categories have been widely acclaimed to be basic even though they may never become so. For example, speakers of some languages appear to thwart Stage IV by naming only primary green rather than green-with-blue, while they name blue with their black-focused term. In Fig. 90.11d, an Ifugao speaker would accomplish this by not having retracted his range of dark-cool (cf. Fig. 90.10c). Because no researcher has collected mappings of such a system, we do not know whether the range of green is encompassed by the dark-cool category. Such would make the green term nonbasic and, thus, ineligible for inclusion in a typology of BCTs. Further, in every language whose widespread use of such a green term is confirmed with Munsell-chip naming, at least as many speakers apply the term to green-with-blue as to only green, as do, for example, Induna speakers of Papua New Guinea (MacLaury 1997a: 60). This fluctuation suggests the green term is becoming a basic cool term but is still secondary for those who curtail its range. Bartlett (1928: 37), too, reports this flux, while Rivers (1901: 48) presents its extremes as separate types. Because there are many reports like these, the system represented by Ifugao specimen (d) is pointedly recognized here. But it is provisionally typed as Stage IIIb plus a secondary term naming green. This typology differs from the three proposed by Kay and colleagues (cited in § 3), wherein they, like Rivers, consider any such system to constitute a distinct type.

Fig. 90.12 represents three controversial types. In (a), a Ukrainian speaker saliently names light blue *blakytnyy*. This usage is like that of *goluboj*, the renown Russian name of light blue, which linguists and psychologists have deemed to be basic after performing experiments that measure salience (e. g., Corbett and Morgan 1988: 55; Frumkina and Mikhejev 1996: 94; reviewed by Paramei 1999). But Taylor, Mondry, and MacLaury (1997: 424−7) show with mappings that *goluboj* is secondary because its range, depending on the speaker, is either included by the range of basic *sinij* 'blue' or is the lesser ("recessive") member of a coextensive relation; this light secondary range is pulling away from its basic blue partner in a dynamic whose formal properties we model with vantage theory. The satellite relation of *goluboj* to *sinij* would be neither apparent in results of salience tests nor explicable by other accounts of categorization. So the controvery will persist. This Ukrainian subject mapped *blakytnyy* and *syniy* separately, which implies both are basic (not diagrammed). But she is a tetralingual professor who might be inclined to consciously separate her concepts. Nevertheless, she mapped *salatovyy* as a subset of *zelenyy*, implying her notions of *syniy* and *blakytnyy* are more separated. Unlike the German specimen, this Ukranian system strongly emphasizes contrast of light *versus* dark, which further complicates the question of how many color categories a worldly individual will be predisposed to regard as basic.

Wierzbicka (1990: 112) notes "the relation between basic and non-basic color terms is not always clear-cut," intuiting from her native Polish that *niebieski* 'blue' is more basic than *granatowy* 'dark blue'. This problem of

90. Color terms

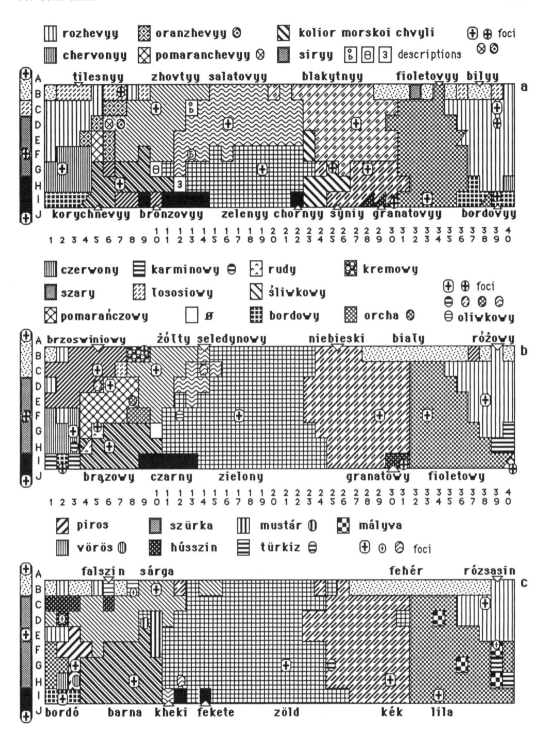

Fig. 90.12: Controversies: (a) Ukranian blue vs. light blue, Ternopil, Ukraine, f 28, 1997; (b) Polish blue vs. dark blue, Tarnów, Poland, f 23, 1997; (c) Hungarian red vs. dark red, Budapest, Hungary, f 22, 1992.

degree shows up in (b), wherein *granatowy* names only two chips and is focused on one of them at I31. In another task (not diagrammed), the subject reserved precisely and exclusively that chip for her mapping of *granatowy*, which shows the term is indeed small in range but, like a well-behaved BCT, is independent of other ranges. How small is too small to be basic? Berlin & Kay (1969: 5−7) characterized the concept with criteria that do not involve size, wisely no doubt.

Other researchers argue that Hungarian has two basic red terms, *piros* and *vörös* (e. g., Moss 1988: 168−9), with the debate spanning a century of Hungarian literature (MacLaury, Almási, and Kövecses 1997: 78−79). One of our explorations appears in (c), which shows that *vörös* is not only small in range but is encompassed at its focus (H3) by the term that dominates it, *piros*. This resembles the behavior of most German secondary color terms but is unlike Polish *granatowy*. As the literature attests, the salience of *vörös* resides in its strong association with sinister passion, which elevates its cultural importance. Such criteria lie outside the basic color-term tradition.

4. Types of relation within categories

The kinds of dynamic processes and resulting semantics within single color categories are as extensive as the types expounded in §§ 3−6. The following highlights this typology as it is developed and supported in MacLaury (1997*a*, index). (1) Two or more terms may name one hue category from different slants, as is suggested by their distinct foci and different sizes of ranges. They may bear a relation of near synonymy, coextention, or inclusion, each type showing greater distance between foci and larger difference in size between ranges. The asymmetry, which is called the dominant-recessive pattern, is addressed by vantage theory. (2) Some cool categories skew toward one hue as they divide, leaving the disfavored hue to be designated by a newly coined name. In terms of vantage theory, the vantage point is said to be placed closest to the favored hue. Such a category is called the hue-stressing type. But another type of cool category seems to behave erratically: it may be named on one hue, mapped on the other, and focused anywhere. Different speakers vary wildly from each other. When the category divides, both hues are named by new terms while the original cool term drops out of use. The seemingly erratic behavior is called crossover, the categories "crossover categories." They are also called relation-stressing categories because, in theory, the vantage point situates closer to the emphases on similarity and difference that bind and juxtapose the hues than to the hues themselves, making the separate identity of each hue less important to the viewer. But crossover is orderly and not at all erratic, which is shown by coextensive terms that cross over: the dominant-recessive pattern persists among their naming ranges, mappings, and foci, despite the impression of chaos. Crossover reflects a coherent native view on categorizing color that is almost unfathomable to a speaker of a foreign language, such as German or English, who stresses hue rather than relations between hues. (3) Speakers of one language may focus the cool category with a different pattern than do speakers of another language, for example, with a single focus in green, a single focus in blue, a single focus in either green or blue but never in both, dual foci with one on each hue but with green chosen first, or triple foci placed in the order of blue, green, and turquoise. These diverse but culturally shared patterns are explained in terms of the degree of removal to which people place a vantage point when categorizing, which produces the gamut of outlooks from subjective sumersion in immediate acts to detached reflectivity on one's own process of thinking. (4) Color qualifiers may differentiate dark from light parts of a category (Lewitz 1974: 157), its center from its periphery (Schaefer 1983: 170−78), patchwork partitions within it (Ducatez 1980: 159−71), or its intergradation with neighboring ranges (Meunier 1979: 162). A language may exploit any one, two, or three of these types (MacLaury 1986a: Appendix I, 2−12; MacLaury 1997a: 79, 84, 165, 224, 248, 325−8), or rarely all four (Colenso 1882: 73−74; Fischer 1965: 142−228; MacLaury & Galloway 1988: 3−17). Coupling of color terms with other sensory meaning has scarcely been explored (Bricker 1999). The foregoing selects typological observations from the 100 that are indexed.

5. Literature

Almqvist, Ernst B. 1883. "Studien über den Farbensinn der Tschuktschen". In: *Die wissenschaftlichen Ergebnisse der Vega-Expedition*, vol. I, A von Nordenskiöld (ed.), 42−9. Leipzig: Brockhaus.

Arias Abellán, Carmen. 1994. *Estructura Semántica de los Adjectivos de Color en los Tratadistas Latinos de Agricultura y parte de la Enciclopedia de Plinio*. Seville: University of Seville.

Arnaud, Jacqueline. 1986. "Les couleurs errantes chez Khair Eddine." *Littérature Orale Arabo-Berbère* 16–17 (1985: 86): 179–93.

Bartlett, Harley H. 1928. "Color nomenclature in Batak and Malay." *Papers of the Michigan Academy of Sciences, Arts, and Letters* 10: 1–52.

Beaglehole, Ernest. 1939. "Tongan color-vision". *Man* 39: 170–2.

Berlin, Brent & Berlin, Elois Ann. 1975. "Aguaruna color categories". *American Ethnologist* 2: 61–87.

Berlin, Brent & Kay, Paul. 1969. *Basic Color Terms: Their University and Evolution*. Berkeley/Los Angeles: University of California Press.

Boas, Franz. 1910. "Psychological problems in anthropology". *Journal of Psychology* 21: 371–84.

Bolton, Ralph. 1978. "Black, white, and red all over: The riddle of color term salience." *Ethnology* 17: 287–311.

Boynton, Robert M. & Olson, Conrad X. 1987. "Locating basic colors in the OSA space." *Color Research and Application* 12: 94–105.

Bricker, Victoria R. 1999. "Color and texture in the Maya language of Yucatan." *Anthropological Linguistics* 41: 283–307.

Colenso, William. 1882. "On the fine perception of colours possessed by the ancient Maoris." *Transactions and Proceedings of the New Zealand Institute* 14: 49–76.

Conklin, Harold C. 1973. "Color categorization" (review of Berlin & Kay 1969). *American Anthropologist* 75: 931–42.

Corbett, Greville C. & Morgan, Gerry. 1988. "Colour terms in Russian: reflections of typological constraints in a single language." *Journal of Linguistics* 24: 31–64.

Crisp, Peter & Chang, Zhang Yan. 1987. "Patterns of connotation in Chinese and English colour terms." *Chinese University Education Journal* 15: 50–59.

Dik, Simon C. 1989. *The Theory of Functional Grammar*, Part I: *The Structure of the Clause*. Dordrecht/Providence: Foris.

Ducatez, Guy & Jacky. 1980. "Formation des dénominations de couleur et de luminosité en arabe classique et pre-classique: essai de périodisation selon un approach linguistique et anthropologique." *Peuples Méditerréens* 10: 139–72.

Durbin, Marshall. 1972. "Basic-terms – off color?" *Semiotica* 4: 257–88.

Faris, James C. 1972. *Nuba Personal Art*. Toronto: University of Toronto Press.

Fischer, Wolfdietrich. 1965. *Farb- und Formbezeichnungen in der Sprache der altarabischen Dichtung*. Wiesbaden: Otto Harrassowitz.

Frumkina, Rebecca M. & Mikhejev, Alexei V. 1996. *Meaning and Categorization*. New York: Nova Science Publishers.

Galloway, Brent D. 1993. *A Grammar of Upriver Halkomelem*. University of California Publications in Linguistics 96. Berkeley/Los Angeles: University of California Press.

Geddes, W. R. 1946. "The color sense of Fijian natives." *British Journal of Psychology* (General) 37: 30–6.

Greenfeld, Philip J. 1986. "What is grey, brown, and sometimes purple: the range of 'wild card' color terms." *American Anthropologist* 88: 908–16.

Hays, David G., Margolis, Enid, Narroll, Raoul & Perkins, Dale R. 1972. "Color term salience." *American Anthropologist* 74: 1107–21.

Herne, Alf A. Gunnar. 1954. *Die slavischen Farbenbenennungen: Eine semasiologische etymologische Untersuchung*. Uppsala: Almquist and Wiksells.

Hinde, Hildegarde B. 1901. *The Masai Language: Grammatical Notes together with a Vocabulary*. Cambridge: University Press.

Johnson, Eric G. 1986. "The role of bilingualism in color naming." *Psychologia* 29: 156–64.

Jones-Molfese, Victoria J. 1977. "Responses of neonates to colored stimuli." *Child Development* 48: 1092–94.

Kay, Paul. 1975. "Synchronic variability and diachronic change in basic color terms." *Journal of Language in Society* 4: 257–70.

–. 1999. "The emergence of basic color lexicons hypothesis." In *The Language of Color in the Mediterranean*, 76–90, Alexander Borg, ed. Stockholm: Almqvist & Wiksell International.

Kay, Paul & McDaniel, Chad K. 1978. "The linguistic significance of basic color terms." *Language* 54: 610–46.

Kay, Paul, Berlin, Brent & Merrifield, William R. 1991. "Biocultural implications of systems of color naming." *Journal of Linguistic Anthropology* 1: 12–25.

Kay, Paul, Berlin, Brent, Maffi, Luisa & Merrifield, William R. 1997. "Color naming across languages." In: *Color Categories in Thought and Language*, Clyde L. Hardin & Luisa Maffi (eds), 21–56. Cambridge/New York/Melbourne: Cambridge University Press.

Kay, Paul & Maffi, Luisa. 1999. "Color appearance and the emergence and evolution of basic color lexicons." *American Anthropologist* 101: 743–60.

Kinkade, M. Dale 1988. "Proto-Salish color." In *In Honor o Mary Haas*, W. Shipley, ed., 443–446. Berlin: Mouton de Gruyter.

Kober, Alice E. 1932. *The Use of Color Terms in the Greek Poets: Including all the Poets from Homer to 146 B. C. Expect the Epigrammatists*. Geneva, N. Y.: W. F. Humphrey.

Kreig, Martha F. 1979. "The Influence of French color vocabulary on Middle English." *Michigan Academician: Papers of the Michigan Academy of Science, Arts, and Letters* 11(4): 431–37.

Kristol, Andrés M. 1980. "Color systems in Southern Italy: a case of regression." *Language* 56: 137–47.

Kuschel, Rolf & Monberg, Toren. 1974. "'We don't talk much about colour here': a study of colour semantics on Bellona Island." *Man* 9: 213–42.

Levinson, Stephen C. 2000. "Yélîdnye and the theory of basic color terms." *Journal of Linguistic Anthropology* 10: 1–53.

Lévi-Strauss, Claud. 1948. La vie familiale et sociale des indiens Namibikwara. *Journal de la Société des Américanistes de Paris* n. s. 37: 1–131.

Lewitz, Saveros. 1974. "Recherches sur le vocabulaire cambodgien: du vieux khmer au khmer moderne." *Journal Asiatique* 262 (1–2): 143–70.

Lü, Ching-Fu. 1997. "Basic Mandarin color terms." *Color Research and Application* 22: 4–10.

McCrea, Nelson G. 1884. "Ovid's use of colour and of colour-terms." In *Classical Studies in Honour of Henry Brisler*, 180–94, ed. anonymous. New York/London: MacMillan.

MacLaury, Robert E. 1986a. *Color in Mesoamerica*, vol. I. *A Theory of Composite Categorization*. Berkeley: University of California doctoral dissertation in anthropology.

–. 1986b. "Color categorization in Shuswap, Chilcotin, Haisla, and Makah." *Working Papers of the 21st International Conference on Salish and Neighboring Languages*, 100–22. Seattle: University of Washington.

–. 1987. "Color-category evolution and Shuswap yellow-with-green." *American Anthropologist* 89: 107–24.

–. 1989. *Lillooet Color Categories Based on Munsell Stimuli*. The Jacobs Fund Collection, Archives of the University of Washington Library, Seattle.

–. 1991. "Exotic color categories: linguistic relativity to what extent?" *Journal of Linguistic Anthropology* 1: 26–51.

–. 1992. "From brightness to hue: an explanatory model of color-category evolution." *Current Anthropology* 33: 137–86.

–. 1997a. *Color and Cognition in Mesoamerica: Constructing Categories as Vantages*. Austin: University of Texas Press.

–. 1997b. "Ethnographic evidence of unique hues and elemental colors." *Behavioral and Brain Sciences* 20: 202–3.

–. 2000. "Linguistic relativity and the plasticity of categorization: universalism in a new key." In: *Explorations in Linguistic Relativity*, 251–93, M. Pütz & M. H. Verspoor, eds. Amsterdam/Philadelphia: John Benjamins.

MacLaury, Robert E., Almási, Judit & Kövecses, Zoltán. 1997. "Hungarian *piros* and *vörös*: color from points of view." *Semiotica* 114–1/2: 67–81.

MacLaury, Robert E. & Galloway, Brent D. 1988. "Color categories and color qualifiers in Halkomelem, Samish, Lushootseed, Nooksack, and Yakima." *Working Papers of the 23rd Conference on Salish and Neighboring Languages*. Eugene: University of Oregon.

MacLaury, Robert E. & Stewart, Stephen O. 1984. "Simultaneous sequences of basic color-category evolution." Paper at the 83rd Annual Meeting of the American Anthropological Association, Denver (available from author).

McManus, I. C. 1983. "Basic color terms in literature." *Language and Speech* 26, Part 3: 247–52.

Merrifield, William R. 1992. Comment on MacLaury 1992 with detail on the WCS database. *Current Anthropology* 33: 164–5.

Meunier, Annie. 1979. "Some remarks on French colour adjectives." *Journal of Linguistic Calculus* 1979 (1–2): 148–65 (from French in 1975 *Annales de l'Université Toulouse-Le Mirail*, n. s. 11[5]: 37–61).

Mills, Carl. 1976. "Universality and variation in the acquisition of semantic categories: English color terms." In *Language Use and the Uses of Language*, 197–204, eds. R. W. Shuy and A. Shnukal. Washington, D. C.: Georgetown University Press.

Morgan, Gerry, & Corbett, Greville. 1989. "Russian colour term salience." *Russian Linguistics* 13: 125–41.

Moss, A. E. 1988. "Russian blues and purples: a tentative hypothesis." *Quinquereme* 11: 164–77.

Musters, George C. 1897. *At Home with the Patagonians*. London: John Murray.

Newman, Paul. 1964. "A word list of Tera." *Journal of West African Languages* (1(2): 33–50.

Paramei, Galina. 1999. "One basic or two: A rhapsody in blue." *Behavioral and Brain Sciences* 22: 967.

Parsons, John H. 1915. *An Introduction to the Study of Colour Vision*. Cambridge: Cambridge University Press.

Peralta, Jesus T. 1980. "Perception of color categories: a view from I'wak." *Philippine Sociological Review* 28 (1–4): 51–9.

Pollnac, Richard B. 1975. "Intra-cultural variability in the structure of the subjective color lexicon in Buganda." *American Ethnologist* 2: 89–110.

Pratt, Alice E. 1898. *The Use of Color in the Verse of the English Romantic Poets*. Chicago: University of Chicago Press.

Price, Thomas R. 1883. "The color-system of Vergil." *American Journal of Philology* 4 (whole 13): 1–20.

Ray, Verne F. 1953. "Human color perception and behavioral response." *New York Academy of Sciences*, ser. 2, 16: 98–104.

Rivers, William H. R. 1901. "Primitive color vision." *Popular Science Monthly* 59: 44–58.

Saunders, Barbara A. C. 1992. *The Invention of Basic Colour Terms*. Utrecht: ISOR, University of Utrecht.

Saunders, Barbara A. C. & van Brakel, Jap. 1997. Are there nontrivial constraints on colour categorization? *Behavioral and Brain Sciences* 20: 167–228.

Schaefer, Ronald P. 1983. "The synchronic behavior of basic color terms in Tswana and its diachronic implications". *Studies in African Linguistics* 14: 159–94.

Snow, David L. 1971. "Samoan color terminology." *Anthropological Linguistics* 13(8): 385–90.

Staples, Ruthl 1932. "The responses of infants to color." *Journal of Experimental Psychology* 15: 119–41.

Taylor, John R., Mondry, Henrietta, & MacLaury, Robert E. 1997. "A cognitive ceiling of eleven basic color terms." Appendix IV of MacLaury 1997a, 419–29.

Thongkum, Theraphan L. 1992. *Khamriak si nai phasa Yao (Mian)* [Color terms in Yao]. Bangkok: Rongphim, Chulalongkorn University.

Uchikawa, Keiji, & Boynton, Robert M. 1987. "Categorical color perception of Japanese observers: Comparison with that of Americans." *Vision Research* 27: 1825–1833.

Valentine, C. W. 1914. "The colour perception and colour preferences of an infant durings its fourth and eighth months." *British Journal of Psychology* 6: 363–86.

Wallace, Florence E. 1927. "Color in Homer and in ancient art: preliminary studies." *Smith College Classical Studies* 9, eds. J. H. Caverno and F. A. Gragg. Northampton, Mass.: Smith College.

Wierzbicka, Anna. 1990. "The meaning of color terms: semantics, culture, and cognition". *Cognitive Linguistics* 1: 99–150.

Williams, John E., Morland, J. Kenneth & Underwood, Walter L. 1970. "Connotations of color names in the United States, Europe, and Asia." *Journal of Social Psychology* 82: 3–14.

Woodworth, Robert S. 1910. "Racial differences in mental traits." *Science* 31: 171–186.

Robert E. MacLaury,
University of Pennsylvania, U.S.A.

91. Spatial dimension terms

1. Defining the domain: phenomena and problems
2. The semantics of Dimension Assignment
3. The lexical field of SDTs: a typological approach
4. Conclusions and extensions
5. Symbols
6. References

1. Defining the domain: phenomena and problems

To assign a dimension to some (concrete or abstract) object x is to locate it on a scale that draws on a category feature F for the class X of objects to which x is taken to belong. A dimension of x thus covers the range of values that x may assume w.r.t. F. Dimension assignment (for short: DA) thus amounts to submitting (tokens of) categorized objects to comparison, gradation and measurement and putting the outcome into words. As a cognitive operation, DA is practically unlimited. Progress in science heavily relies on creating new dimensions and on defining complex units with artificial names to measure them.

The specific linguistic aspect of DA, however, is a more limited one. Confining ourselves to the basic domain of space, we will concentrate on a small subset of the core lexicon, viz. the spatial dimensional terms (henceforth: SDTs), which according to the common view show the following characteristics:

(1) (a) SDTs make reference to spatial dimensions like height, length, width, depth, thickness, size, volume, distance.
(b) SDTs come as [+N αV], typically in pairs of polar antonyms, furnished with morphosyntactic features that enable them to combine with measure phrases and to enter the grammar of gradation and comparison (see (2) in § 2.2.). These features are crucial to separate SDTs from mere shape terms like *round, oval, flat, square, circle* etc.

The morphosyntax and semantics of gradation and comparison, which prototypically involve SDTs, have gained much attention (→ Art. 75) – as there are striking differences in the way languages encode comparative constructions, which call for a typological approach. In contrast to this, the lexical field of SDTs as stated in (1a) seemingly lacks overt symptoms of cross-linguistic variation.

In what way (1a) might be defended as capturing universal features of DA remains to be seen, of course. Nevertheless, the substance of (1a) has not been questioned on practical grounds (looking up (1a) in any bilingual dictionary will not reveal interesting differences) nor seriously been challenged by empirical findings (to the extent that languages have been carefully examined wrt. SDTs). Until recently, the main concern of the literature on SDTs has been with language-particular aspects on a descriptive level, the major issue being to point out facets of polysemy (cf. Dervillez-Bastuji 1982, Durrell 1981, 1988a, b, Hlebec 1983, 1986, Lafrenz 1983, Robering 2001, Spang-Hanssen 1990, 1993a, b, Svorou 1987, Togeby 1978, Vandeloise 1988, 1992, 1993, Wurzel 1987, Zhurinskij 1971).

Another reason for taking the universality for granted is the widely held view that our spatial concepts more or less directly originate in the human perceptual endowment. An early guideline for determining the stock and structure of SDT claims that "the dimensions languages pick out are just those dimensions the human perceptual apparatus is tuned to pick out" (cf. Clark 1973, Clark & Clark 1977). True as this may be, it cannot be the whole story.

In the meantime, as space has become the favourite playground for cognitive studies (→ Art. 43, 44, 58, 86), we have come to know that there is more to DA than just naming perception-based axes, planes, extensions etc. or projecting top-bottom, front-rear, left-right sides from some observer-based body schema (cf. Herskovits 1986) onto spatial objects. A series of studies devoted to SDTs (Bierwisch & Lang (eds.) 1989; Lang 1990a, b; Lang, Carstensen & Simmons 1991) has (i) presented a sizeable body of facts which indicate that there is no short cut from spatial perception to the way language structures space for DA, but rather an indirect, conceptually mediated and controlled relationship; and (ii) developed a notional and representational framework to cope with the grammar of DA in a comprehensive way.

Though drawing on German and English data, the studies mentioned may serve as a key to address typological issues from a new perspective. Their data base was compiled by a series of elicitation tests (naming object extents, guessing objects via SDT combinations) which are now being extended to cross-linguistic data collection − cf. § 3. The exhaustivity of the data base and the consistency of the analysis proposed have been checked by a PROLOG implementation (Lang, Carstensen & Simmons 1991). Most promising, however, is what the semantic approach offers by way of revealing hitherto unnoticed aspects of DA that are subject to typological variation − just below the surface of cross-linguistic similarities in the field of SDTs stated in (1a). Hence the focus is on the intersection of semantics and typology.

The article is organized as follows: § 2. outlines the above mentioned approach, guided by an overall picture (Fig. 91.1) and a "catalogus mundi" of spatial objects (Fig. 91.2). Controversies among competing models as represented by e.g. Landau & Jackendoff (1993); Jackendoff (1996) vs. Dirven & Taylor (1988) vs. Bierwisch & Lang (1989) will be backgrounded here, though not ignored. § 3 examines the lexical field of SDTs by specifying which term is based on which frame of reference, the major distinction being that of proportion- vs. observer-basedness of the items at issue. This is done by means of data from a small sample of languages with the aim of setting out a typology that draws on the scope of lexical coverage and selectional restrictions of SDTs as items of a correspondingly partitioned field. § 4 lists some conclusions and suggests some extensions by raising topics for further research. It should be noted that the typological study of SDT semantics, compared to that of e.g. number names, kinship and colour terms, is still in its infancy. The data base available, though covering a number of Asian, Caucasian and Finno-Ugric languages, still suffers from an Indo-European bias. The monograph by Stolz (1996) deserves special mention as it has tested, enriched, and largely corroborated the approach proposed here in field work on Yucatec Maya.

2. The semantics of Dimension Assignment

2.1. Blueprint of the architecture

Guided by the question "What turns a feature in object perception into a dimension term in language?", the framework adopted here proposes a modular approach (Fig.

91.1) which assumes three levels on which spatial features relevant to DA have to be accounted for.

The **perceptual** level is involved as the source that provides the sort of sensory input (from vision and other senses), which DA draws on, albeit in a selective way.

The **conceptual** level serves as a filter system by means of which perceptual distinctions are categorized to the extent that is needed for the naive physics which underlies our everyday knowledge of space.

The **semantic** level accounts for the way in which conceptually approved features of DA are encoded in lexical items, which in turn instantiate morpho-syntactic categories.

The interconnection of these levels is brought about by the following components:

(I) **Gestalt and Position features.**
DA is basically organized not by a single body schema but by two interacting frames of reference called "Inherent Proportion Schema" (IPS — yielding proportion-based gestalt features) and "Primary Perceptual Space" (PPS — yielding position features). Each of these is rooted in the human perceptual endowment; both of them consist of a system of axes which, differing in origin as well as nature, provide the conceptual features that DA operates on (see Fig. 91.1 below; for details see § 3).

(II) **Parameters.**
DA rests on a small set of Dimension Assignment Parameters (DAPs) which — emerging from IPS and PPS in (I) — occur in two representational formats: (a) as entries of Object Schemata (that is, as conceptual instantiations of DAPs; written in plain style — cf. Fig. 91.2 in § 2.4); (b) as part of the lexical meanings of SDTs and of object names (written in SMALL CAPS — see § 2.2). The stock of these parameters provides a notional system

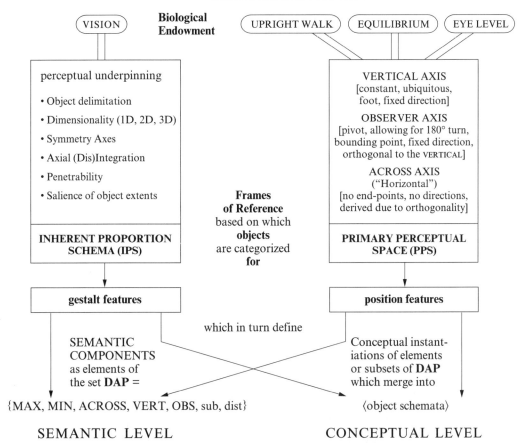

Fig. 91.1: Cognitive components involved in DA to spatial objects

on which the search for universals and typological variation in the domain of SDTs can be based as well as a notational tool to establish semantic distinctions far more precisely than would be possible on the basis of English glosses taken from (1a).

(III) Conceptual-Semantic Interfaces.
DA involves a set of devices that account for the differentiation between, as well as the interaction of, non-linguistic conceptual **world knowledge** and language-bound **word knowledge** as regards the way in which conceptually categorized objects (see Fig. 91.2) are subject to "primary" (Fig. 91.2, left side) and/or "contextually induced" DA (Fig. 91.2, right side) by means of SDTs.

2.2. Dimension Assignment Parameters (DAPs)

2.2.1. Introduction

DAPs are the stuff which the lexical meanings of SDTs are made of. Note that the elements listed below as SEMANTIC COMPONENTS of SDTs (Small Caps) form but a proper subset of the spatial features defined by PPS and IPS. In other words, only a subset of the conceptually approved features occurring in OS (see left column in Fig. 91.2 below) also occur as lexically encoded conditions. This reflects the basic idea that DA rests on designating certain specified object extents as spatial dimensions.

Taken as semantic components, the elements of the set {DAP} are not mere labels but theoretical constructs having a clear-cut interpretation as parts of more complex representations that − e. g. for adjectival SDTs − have the general format (cf. Bierwisch & Lang 1989) shown in (2).

(2) $\lambda c \: \lambda x \: [\text{QUANT} \: [\mathbf{d} \: x] = [v \pm c]]$

As DA crucially involves gradation and comparison (→ Art. 75), the quantitative comparison component QUANT is included in all DTs to account for a scaling operation which assigns a scalar value composed of a comparison value **v** and a difference value **c** to some spatial object **x** with regard to a dimension $\mathbf{d} \in \{\text{DAP}\}$; '+' and '−' account for polarity within antonym pairs. Though (2) offers many aspects that invite typological considerations, we will focus on $\mathbf{d} \in \{\text{DAP}\}$, which for a particular SDT gets instantiated by one of the components listed in (a)−(e) below.

2.2.2. Inventory

The DAPs are defined by the following conditions they lexically encode into SDTs.

(a) MAX identifies the maximal extent of some object x, provided there is exactly one maximal extent available.
(b) VERT identifies an extent of some object x as the one that is aligned with the Vertical axis of the primary perceptual space (PPS).
(c) OBS identifies an extent of some object x as the one that is aligned with the Observer axis of the primary perceptual space (PPS).
(d) ACROSS identifies an extent of some object x as the one that is orthogonal to MAX, VERT, or OBS
(e) MIN identifies a minor extent of a 3D object x which is not identifiable by MAX or ACROSS.

Besides those DAPs that are overtly lexicalized in SDTs, there are some more (among them Sub and Dist − cf. Fig. 91.1) that are covertly involved as features of selectional restrictions associated with certain SDTs. To round up the inventory of DAPs, there are three comments to be made.

First, a further candidate as a DAP, viz. the holistically assigned parameter SIZE (involved in SDTs like *big, large, groß* − cf. Lang (1989: chap. 5)), has been omitted here as it meets the criteria in (1b) only in part.

Second, MIN as proposed here meets criticisms by Vandeloise (1993), Weydt & Schlieben-Lange (1995, 1998), and Stolz (1996) of what was subsumed under SUB in Lang (1989). Terms like *thick, dick, épais* or *gros*, based on which the parameter SUB was postulated, are not to be taken as proper SDTs, as Weydt & Schlieben-Lange (1998) have pointed out. Now MIN is reduced to delimiting a proportion-based scope of variation, the lexical coverage of which draws on some typological features to be established in § 3. This is in line with the observation that in some languages MIN terms (*thick-thin, dick-dünn*) extend to "substance"-related dimensions outside IPS like density or consistency (*thick forest, ~ cream, ~ fogs*), whereas in other languages terms which encode MIN as IPS-related feature and terms which encode features of other domains are clearly differentiated − for typological considerations see § 4.1. The third comment, being the most important one, deserves a paragraph of its own.

2.3. The ACROSS parameter as a source of variation

The list above can be partitioned as follows: MAX and MIN, which refer to gestalt properties, clearly emerge from the inherent proportion schema (IPS), while VERT and OBS which assign position properties to objects, clearly emerge from the primary perceptual space (PPS). ACROSS, however, has a share in both. In fact, the parameter ACROSS serves as a **stop-gap** in two respects: (i) within both of IPS and PPS, (ii) between IPS and PPS.

Within IPS, ACROSS supplements the parameters MAX and MIN in that it is assigned to an extent **d** to which neither of these applies; within PPS, ACROSS covers the horizontal in that it defines an axial extent **d** to which neither VERT nor OBS apply. This is the reason why ACROSS picks out some object extent **d** only in relation to some other extent **d′** that is identifiable by one of the other major DAPs. We may conceive of this as a type of selectional restriction that an ACROSS term imposes on the object it is to apply to. As an example, the dimension part of English *wide-narrow* is represented as in (3), which states that ACROSS is orthogonal to **d′**, with **d′** being one of the following: Max, Vert or Obs.

(3) (a) ... [**d′** ⊥ ACROSS x] ...;
    (b) **d′** ∈ {Max, Vert, Obs}

(3a) accounts for the inherently relational nature of ACROSS (= stop-gap in the sense of (i) above), while (3b) specifies the range of the values **d′** may assume for the language at issue (= stop-gap in the sense of (ii) above) — for ample illustrations see § 3. Put in familiar semantic terminology, (3a) represents the **lexical meaning** of *wide* as an element of the field, (3b) the **selectional restrictions** that *wide* imposes on the object it is to apply to — see Fig. 91.3 below. Now, ACROSS reveals a domain of variation, and due to this it provides a major source of ambiguity within, and typological variation between, languages — details in § 3.2.

2.4. Conceptual Compatibility

Dimension assignment to spatial objects rests on the joint outgrowth of the two categorization grids IPS and PPS. This approach suitably accounts for the fact that there are various cases in which a given object extent is not identified by a single parameter but by a combination of parameters from both grids. Such combinations occur on the Semantic as well as on the Conceptual Level, as the following examples illustrate.

Semantically, the English adjective *tall* comprises a combination of MAX and VERT, though not as a symmetric conjunction. The extent referred to by *tall* is identified as the object's maximal extent, which is furthermore specified as being aligned to the Vertical. This amounts to representing the relevant part of *tall* as MAX | VERT (read as: MAX, further specified by VERT; by convention, the specificatory parameter is placed to the right of the one to be specified). This is substantiated by the fact that the antonym of *tall* is *short* (a MAX term) and not the VERT term *low* (the lexical antonym of the VERT term *high*).

Conceptually, the combination Max | Vert occurs in the Object Schemata of trees and towers (see object class VI-v1 in Fig. 91.2 below). These objects have a **canonical orientation** w.r.t. verticality, which is bound to their maximal axis. Besides occurring as conceptually fixed combinations, parameter combinations can also result from **contextual specification**. So for poles (see class VI in Fig. 91.2), the entry Max suffices to assign e.g. *the pole is 3 m long* a regular interpretation — MAX from *long* and Max from the OS for poles simply match. However, the interpretation of e.g. *the pole is 3m tall / high*, which contains a MAX | VERT term (*tall*) or a VERT term (*high*), provides a contextually induced verticality feature which results in a complex entry Max | Vert. This is how a gestalt property (Max) of some object x is turned via contextual specification into a position property (Max | Vert) of x. Fig. 91.2 presents a *catalogus mundi* that emerges from categorizing objects by their spatial properties that are relevant to DA.

Now, the fundamental claim regarding DA is this: on the conceptual level, both the full range of **possible objects** as represented in OS (Fig. 91.2, left side) and the scope of **admissible DA** (primary or contextually induced) that can apply to them (Fig. 91.2, right side) are determined by a small set of **compatibility conditions** that specify what axial properties may combine. On the lexical level, these act as constraints on lexicalization by determining which combinations of DAPs can be packaged into a SDT, and which cannot. For details see Lang (1989), here I list the major results only. Given the definitions of the DAPs in 2.2., we obtain the following admissible combinations (listed as OS entries in plain style):

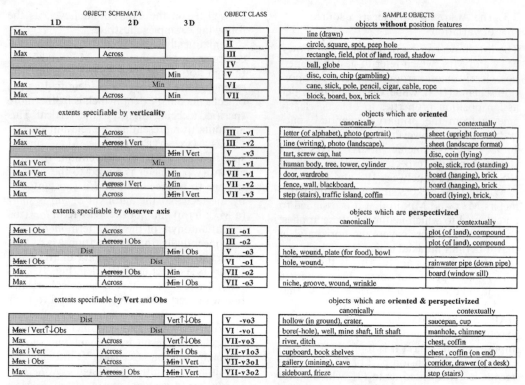

Fig. 91.2: Catalogue of spatial objects sorted according to accessibility to DA parameters
Notes on Fig. 91.2:
The object schemata (OS) shown at the left side represent spatial objects categorized by, and reduced to, the features that are conceptually relevant to DA. The columns contain features that can be assigned to the 1st, 2nd, and 3rd object extents; white cells represent disintegrated axes, shaded cells integrated ones. The latter normally are not accessible to SDTs.
Object classes I–VII are exclusively defined by proportion-based IPS features. Regarding primary DA, they thus form the basic inventory of object classes. Subclasses emerge when the classes III–VII are furnished with position features from PPS, the combinatorics of which defines subclasses III-v1–VII-v3o2.
Note that the OS of these subclasses are listed as admissible feature combinations − regardless of whether they are brought about via primary (e.g. "canonical") DA or via "contextually induced orientation or perspectivization" (cf. sample objects).
In combinations of the form X | Y, the basic feature is on the left side, the specificatory one on the right side; crossed out features indicate relabelling − for details see (20) in § 3.3.

(4) (a) single parameters:
  Max, Min, Across, Vert, Obs;
(b) combinations (based on compatible axial properties):
  Max | Vert, Min | Vert, Across | Vert
  Max | Obs, Min | Obs, Across | Obs
  Max | Across,
  Vert ↑↓ Obs

Due to the specific properties of the Observer axis (pivot allowing for a 180° turn in either of two planes), the combinations of Vert and Obs deserve some comment. PPS defines orthogonality between the Vertical and the Observer axis (= Vert ⊥ Obs) as the default case. Specificatory use of Obs w.r.t. Vert is restricted to looking at a vertical extent in the opposite direction (= Vert ↑↓ Obs; see object subclasses V-vo3–VII-v3o2 in Fig. 91.2). The combination Vert ↑↑ Obs, where the Vertical and the Observer axis run in the same direction (at 0°), is perceptually quite common but, interestingly, does not constitute a conceptually relevant parameter for DA.

2.5. Selectional restrictions

SDTs as lexical items are sensitive to the spatial properties of the object x they are to be applied to. Conditions of this sort can be subsumed under the classical notion of "selectional restriction". The fact that each DAP encoded in a particular SDT is associated with certain selectional restrictions (cf. (5) below) has consequences for lexical packaging and for the structure of the field. The examples in (6), as well as the data presented in § 3, show that while covering the same DAP, languages may differ w.r.t. the selectional restrictions the SDT in question imposes on the objects it is being applied to. It seems reasonable to divide selectional restrictions found with SDTs into two types. The first type is rooted in the perception-based features of the particular DAP and thus may be taken to be valid cross-linguistically. (5) illustrates this type with the dimensionality criterion:

(5) MAX terms may apply to
            1D, 2D, or 3D objects
     VERT and ACROSS terms require
            2D or 3D objects
     Some OBS terms require   3D objects

The other kind of selectional restriction shows up in restrictions that certain SDTs of the field impose on the objects they apply to, and can be language-particular (6a) or typologically defining (6b):

(6) (a) Both being ACROSS terms, Germ. *breit* requires an object of at least 2D, *weit* one of 3D, while Engl. *wide* vs. *broad* behave like *breit* and *weit* respectively, contrary to what the lexical relationships suggest ("false friends").
    (b) In proportion-based languages, OBS terms are restricted to hollow (parts of) objects and cover Vert ⊥ Obs as the default case − for details see § 3.4.

2.6. Conditions on lexicalization

The restrictions on possible combinations of DAPs shown in (4) have far-reaching implications w.r.t. universals and typological variation in the realm of SDTs. The assumption that the avoidance of word-internal contradictions is a decisive factor in lexical packaging suggests (7) as a (presumably universal) **constraint on SDT lexicalization**:

(7) Only admissible combinations of DAPs are lexicalized, that is, there are no lexical items covering simultaneous reference to axes identifiable by parameter combinations like Max | Min or Vert ↑↑ Obs.

In addition, (7) predicts that DAPs that draw on mutually exclusive axial properties are lexicalized separately − that is, if reference to Max and to Min is included in a lexical field of SDTs, the terms drawing on them are lexically distinct. Furthermore, the observations on the stop-gap nature of the parameter ACROSS (see 2.3.) suggest that axial salience has an impact on lexicalization. So (8) seems to be a reasonable claim about minimal distinctness within a lexical field of SDTs:

(8) Reference to the most salient axes of both IPS and PPS is lexicalized separately, that is, in a lexical field of SDTs, there are at least distinct items for MAX and non-MAX (usually differentiated into ACROSS and MIN) and for VERT and OBS.

Note that (8), taken as a claim about minimal distinctness, is not at variance with the fact that e. g. English lexicalizes VERT (*high-low*), MAX (*long-short*) and MAX | VERT (*tall*) separately, nor with the fact that some languages encode OBS (orthogonal to the Vertical) and VERT ↑↓ OBS into distinct SDTs, e. g. Korean *selo* vs. *kiphi* (see §§ 3.2, 3.4).

3. The lexical field of SDTs: a typological approach

3.1. Mismatches and polysemy

Languages dispose of an inventory of SDTs which, though limited in number, form a lexical field that at any rate is richer and more complex than would be needed simply to provide distinct labels for the three axes of a Cartesian system of coordinates. This is clear evidence that Dimension Assignment involves several sources, e. g. IPS and PPS. On the other hand, we observe that none of the languages of our sample exhausts the repertoire of admissable combinations of DAPs listed in (4) above by distinct lexical items. Rather, the average repertoire of SDTs ranges between 7−10 (disregarding antonyms), which indicates a DAP ⇒ SDT mismatch.

As a consequence, we should expect various possible partitions of the set {DAP} as regards the scope of **lexical coverage**. In fact, as will be shown in the following, languages do vary with regard to these partitions. We enter the field of typology by embarking on a search for recurrent patterns and principles to explain this variation. While looking from

DAPs to SDTs is one part of the task ahead, the other part emerges from the "notorious polysemy" observed with SDTs, which yields evidence for a SDT ⇒ DAP mismatch (cf. Lafrenz 1983, Spang-Hanssen 1990, 1993a, b; Vandeloise 1988, 1992; Dirven & Taylor 1988).

Constancy of the perceptual features of a given object, say its spatial extents, does not necessarily imply constancy in selecting the SDT to name the object's dimensions, and vice versa. So what we face is a many-to-many mapping relation between SDTs and object extents. Taking the lexicalization and interpretation of the stop-gap parameter ACROSS as starting point, we will show step by step that typological variation w.r.t. DA is not so much due to differences in the inventory of items as to differences in the selectional restrictions the items are associated with. This will reveal the hidden field structure of SDTs. Besides the ACROSS terms (§ 3.2), there are two sources for typological variation: (i) the role of verticality assignment in mediating between proportion-based and observer-based DA (§ 3.3.), (ii) the scope of reference and lexical coverage of the OBS terms (§ 3.4.).

3.2. The role of the ACROSS terms

For convenience, the particular issues will be introduced by means of English data and then assessed by contrasting them with Mandarin and Korean data. As will become clear, each of the three languages chosen represents a different type within the typology to be established in this section. In order to illustrate all facets of meaning and reference involved in DA, the data sets in (9)−(11) are examined in detail and in parallel. Furthermore, to gain a better understanding, the polysemy problem will be decomposed into aspects concerning referential ambiguity, contextual specification, and inferences (3.2.1.−2.), which are easier to pin down in terms of the semantics adopted here.

The settings were chosen to examine the way DA works in different languages when an object with constant extents − a wooden board sized 1 m × 0.30 m × 0.03 m − is integrated into a given spatial configuration. While setting I presents the board as a freely movable object, settings II and III show it as part of the surrounding space with position features. The purpose of the naming task was to retrace to what extent and in what way changes in the settings are reflected in overt differences w.r.t. the choice and interpretation of SDTs.

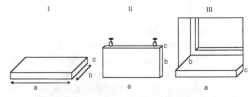

Fig. 91.3: Wooden board in various spatial settings

(9) ENGLISH
a = long   a = wide / long   a = wide / long
b = wide   b = high /*wide   b = deep
c = thick   c = thick   c = thick

(10) MANDARIN (predicative form)
a = cháng   a = cháng /*kuān   a = cháng /*kuān
b = kuān   b = gāo   b = kuān /*shēn
c = hòu   c = hòu   c = hòu

(11) KOREAN (nominal form)
A a = selo   a = selo   a = selo
   b = kalo   b = nophi / kalo   b = kalo
   c = kulki   c = kulki   c = kulki
B a = kalo   a = kalo   a = kalo
   b = selo   b = selo / nophi   b = selo
   c = kulki   c = kulki   c = kulki
C a = kili   a = kili /*phok   a = kili /*phok
   b = phok   b = nophi   b = phok / kiphi
   c = kulki   c = kulki   c = kulki

3.2.1. Referential ambiguity

ENGLISH. Regarding reference, only the coupling of extent **c** and *thick* is constant — cf. (9-I) vs. (9-II) and (9-III). Looking from extents to SDT we observe that extent **a** can be referred to by *long* or *wide*, extent **b** by *wide, high, deep*; looking from SDT to extents we observe that *long, high*, and *deep* are unambiguous as to which extent they refer to (at least within the SDT combinations applied to the board), whereas the SDT *wide* can refer to **a** or **b**. This last aspect will be called the "referential ambiguity" of a SDT. In order to spell out what has been claimed about the stop-gap nature of the ACROSS term in § 2.3, let us examine the distribution of English *wide* in (9) a bit more closely.

First note that in isolation (i. e. divorced from any situational or linguistic context) an English sentence like (9′) is ambiguous (or rather unspecified) as to which extent of the board *wide / in width* refer to:

(9′)   *The board is 50 cm wide / in width.*

This fact is captured by the analysis of *wide* in (3a) ... [**d′** ⊥ ACROSS x]..., whereby the selectional restriction (3b) requires the variable **d′** to be instantiated by one of the values {Max, Vert, Obs}. As (9′) does not deliver any of these values, the variable **d′** is left unspecified, which in turn leaves the reference of *wide / in width* in (9′) unspecified. Due to (3b) **d′** ∈ {Max, Vert, Obs}, the English ACROSS term participates in both IPS and PPS, which in turn provides the source for its referential ambiguity out of context. We may call this the **mixed** solution of anchoring the ACROSS term (see scores in columns 1−3 in Fig. 91.6).

MANDARIN. Concerning the reference of the ACROSS term, the picture offered by (10) is entirely different. We observe that extent **a** is constantly labeled by the MAX term *cháng*, while extent **b** in (10-I) and (10-III) is reserved for the ACROSS term *kuān*. This suggests that the Mandarin ACROSS term, if analyzed according to (3a) as [**d′** ⊥ ACROSS x], is selectionally confined to **d′** = {Max}. This analysis is supported by the way it accounts for other facts we obtain from (10).

First, it correctly predicts that − in contrast to English (9′) − a Mandarin sentence like (10′) is not ambiguous as to which extent of the board *kuān* is meant to refer to. (That the translation needs to be commented on proves that using English SDTs from (1a) to gloss those of other languages simply misses the point, see also (11′) below.)

(10′)   *Zhè kuài mùbǎn kuān*
        This CL   board   Max ⊥ Across
        wǔshí límǐ
        50   cm
        'This board is 50 cm wide / in width'
        [i. e. in its *secondary* extent!]

Second, the analysis proposed explains why Mandarin *kuān* does not display any referential shift and why extent **a**, being the supplier of **d′** = {Max}, is unavailable to *kuān* (indicated by *kuān in (10-II, III)). Besides capturing the distribution data and the non-ambiguity of *kuān*, the analysis settles a central issue of how the lexical field of SDTs may be partitioned. It reveals that in Mandarin the ACROSS term, due to **d′** = {Max}, is fixed to a proportion relation between IPS parameters and is hence exhaustively determined within this frame of reference. Let's call this the **proportion-based** anchoring of the ACROSS term (see columns (1−3) in Fig. 91.6).

KOREAN. First note that the lexical field of Korean SDTs contains a subset which includes the MAX term *kili* and the Max ⊥ ACROSS term *phok*, which closely resemble Mandarin *cháng* and *kuān*, respectively − see (11-C). As this data set − except (11-C-III-b) − patterns exactly like the Mandarin data set in (10), we will not pursue it further. In addition, there is another subset of SDTs, which Zubin & Choi (1984: 337) describe thus: "the spatial terms *kalo* and *selo* [...] pick out the edges of a surface which are *across* and *in line with* the observer's visual field, respectively, with no regard for the relative extension of these edges." Having been submitted to elicitation tests, the two SDTs (quoted here in their basic form) show the distribution set down in (11-A) and (11-B), respectively. To make the data more comprehensible, hints on the respective positions taken by the subjects have been added.

Worth noting is the complementary distribution of *kalo* − *selo* w.r.t. the extents **a** and **b** within, as well as between, the data sets (11-A) and (11-B). Rephrased in our jargon, this means: *kalo* is to be analysed as an ACROSS term [**d′** ⊥ ACROSS x] whose instantiation is fixed to **d′** = {Obs}, whereas *selo* is to be analysed as pure OBS term without further ado. Interestingly, the two subsets, i. e. proportion-based *kili* − *phok* and observer-based *selo* − *kalo* never co-occur in a SDT combination but are kept strictly disjoint. The same holds for Japanese proportion-based *nagai* [MAX] – *haba* [Max ⊥ ACROSS] and observer-based *tate* [OBS] – *yoko* [Obs ⊥ ACROSS], respectively.

As any instantiation of OBS, by the very nature of this parameter, is situation-dependent, the analysis proposed accounts for the distribution data in (11-A, 11-B). As to referential ambiguity, it predicts that an attempt to translate (9′) or (10′), neither of which has a single counterpart in Korean, will yield a twin result (11′):

(11′)   *Ku-nelphanci-nun selo-ka* /
        DET.board.TOP   OBS.SUBJ /
        kalo-ka   50cm ita.
        Obs ⊥ ACR.SUBJ 50 cm DECL
        'This board is 50 cm wide (in this view ☺) / 50 cm wide (in this view ☻)'

The reason is obvious: being correlatively based on OBS, both *kalo* and *selo* are ambiguous (or unspecified) as regards reference to extent **a** or **b**, as long as they are presented without contextual cues for deciding whether (☺ = A) or (☻ = B) applies.

To sum up, the Korean ACROSS term *kalo*, due to **d′** = {Obs}, is fixed to correlate with values provided by the OBS term *selo*, hence both terms are exhaustively determined within PPS. This explains the complementarity of the Mandarin data in (10) and the Korean data in (11-A, 11-B). Moreover, it provides the second clear-cut option for partitioning the lexical field of SDTs. We will call this the **observer-based** anchoring of the ACROSS term. For ease of exposition, the relevant aspects of the lexical field will be classified as following either the **proportion-based (P)** or the **observer-based (O) strategy** for field partitioning, the final score is given in Fig. 91.6 in § 3.5.

As an interim balance, the analyses of the ACROSS terms in (12) below represent the three basic solutions to the stop-gap problem raised by the inherent relationality of this parameter: **P**-fixed, **O**-fixed, and **P/O**-mixed.

(12)   ACROSS term: (i) invariant part: ... [**d′** ⊥ ACROSS x] ...
       (ii) varying part: selectional restrictions on **d′**

Options for (ii)	language type	languages exemplifying (ii)
(a) **d′** = {Max}	**P**-fixed	Chin. *kuān*, Mongol. *örgön*
		Kor. *phok*, Jap. *haba*
(b) **d′** = {Obs}	**O**-fixed	Kor. *kalo*, Jap. *yoko*
(c) **d′** ∈ {Max, Vert, Obs}	**P/O**-mixed	Germanic *bred*, *breit* etc. Engl. *wide*; Romance *larg-* Finn. *leveys*, Hung. *széles*, Turk. *geniş*, Georg. *sigane*
(d) **d′** ∈ {Max, Vert}	[see (21, 22)]	Russ. *shirokij*, Bulg. *širok*, Yucatec *kóoch*
(e) **d′** ∈ {Max, Obs}	[see (23, 24)]	Pol. *szeroky*, Slovak *široký*, Vietn. *rộng*

The **P/O**-mixed type also includes languages with the subsidiary choices (d) **d′** ∈ {Max, Vert} or (e) **d′** ∈ {Vert, Obs}, which will be discussed in § 3.3.

3.2.2. Contextual specification and inferencing

The analysis in the previous section has shown why the ACROSS terms in the languages of the two fixed types are not available for the sort of referential shift we observe with English *wide* in (9′). We now resume this issue by asking: what enables English *wide* to shift between extent **b** and extent **a** – cf. (9-I) vs. (9-II, III) – while maintaining unique reference? Spelling out how the referential uniqueness of *wide* in (9) is brought about demonstrates directly how the analysis proposed in (12c) works.

In (9-I) *wide* assumes the specification Max ⊥ Across, the value **d′** = Max being provided by extent **a**, hence *wide* refers to extent **b**; in (9-II) *wide* assumes the specification Vert ⊥ Across, the value **d′** = Vert being provided by extent **b**, hence *wide* refers to extent **a**; in (9-III) *wide* assumes the specification Obs ⊥ Across, the value **d′** = Obs being provided by extent **b**, hence *wide* refers to extent **a** again. Retracing the way in which the reference of *wide* is computed in (9-I–III) makes us aware of three interesting consequences of (12) that shed more light on the way Dimension Assignment works.

First, the **equivalence of situational and verbal context cues**. Recall that the data in (9)−(11) were collected in tests where subjects presented with (pictures of) objects in various spatial settings had to name object extents. Now, the conditions, which were presented to the subjects by means of non-verbal contextual settings, can just as well be obtained from the linguistic context. The sentences in (13) provide exactly the same contextual information as the spatial settings I−III. (Crossed out features indicate that a given object extent is being relabelled, e.g. *wide* ⇒ *high*).

(13) (a) *The board is long & wide enough*
    d′ = Max, **d** = Max ⊥ Across
    as in (9-I)
  (b) *The board is wide & high enough*
    d′ = Vert, **d** = ~~Max~~ | Vert ⊥ Across
    as in (9-II)
  (c) *The board is wide & deep enough*
    d′ = Obs, **d** = ~~Max~~ | Obs ⊥ Across
    as in (9-III)

This not only shows *that*, but also *how*, a **P/O**-mixed type language like English makes use of both strategies that are at its disposal. What is excluded is simultaneous use in one and the same construction: **The board is 1 m wide and 30 cm wide* is clearly out (informants sometimes used *wide* with the same object twice − though, of course, accompanied by distinguishing gestures). The unacceptability of such constructions follows from a general homogeneity condition on coordinate structures, which for Dimension Assignment narrows down to this:

(14) **Uniqueness constraint**:
    In an instance of naming distinct axial extents **a, b, c** of some object x by enumeration, one and the same SDT may apply only once.

Next, the **IPS-PPS asymmetry**. In a sense, the Across terms of fixed type languages come with their contextual specifications built-in, which has implications for the relation between lexical coverage and primary vs. contextually induced DA. The **P**-fixed Across terms, i.e. those for which **d′** = {Max}, are available for primary DA only − cf. Mandarin in (10). The **O**-fixed Across terms, i.e. those for which **d′** = {Obs}, make any occurrence of the term into an instance of contextually induced DA − cf. Korean in (11-A, 11-B). This asymmetry between the two fixed type languages is but one facet of the issue. The Across terms of **P/O**-mixed type languages trigger an interplay of primary and contextually induced DA, which also reflects the asymmetry of IPS and PPS. This is shown by taking another look at the English data in (9).

Note how (9-I−III) integrate the object at issue stepwise into the surrounding space. In (9-I), the SDTs (including *wide*) refer to the gestalt properties of the board per se, that is, as a freely movable object (class VII in Fig. 91.2), whose primary DA is fully covered by IPS. In (9-II) *high* and *wide*, in (9-III) *deep* and *wide*, refer to position properties of the board via contextually induced DA. As regards the Across term *wide*, the move from (9-I) to (9-III) reflects the order of selecting Max, Vert, or Obs as the appropriate value with which to instantiate **d′**. Conceptually, proportion-based gestalt properties of objects can be turned into position properties − but not vice versa. The IPS-PPS asymmetry is pervasive in DA, for a final balance see § 4.

Finally, **inferences**. The SDT combinations in (9-II) and (9-III) are bound to the respective settings, yet they are optional. We may apply the primary DA (9-I) also to setting II or III thereby ignoring the position features of the given object. Semantically, this implies that − given the options available to English as a **P/O**-mixed type language − (9-I) can be validly inferred from (9-II) and from (9-III) − but not vice versa:

(15) (a) *The board is 1 m wide, 30 cm deep* →
    The board is 1 m long, 30 cm wide
  (b) *The board is 1 m wide, 30 cm high* →
    The board is 1 m long, 30 cm wide
  (c) *The board is 1 m long, 30 cm wide* |→
    The board is 1 m wide, 30 cm high

The inferences are based on **de-specification**, that is, by removing the contextually induced features of the given object in order to obtain its primary DA (cf. the subclasses of VII vs. the major class VII and the sample objects in the right column in Fig. 91.2).

As predicted by (12a, b) and spelled out in the asymmetry discussion above, the **P**-fixed type languages disallow inference patterns like (15) because their Across terms are bound to primary DA. Applied to (10), the inference patterns of **P**-fixed Mandarin are complementary to those in (15), as shown in (16):

(16) (a) *Zhè kuài mùbǎn kuān 1 m, *shēn 30 cm* |→ ... *cháng 1 m, kuān 30 cm*
(b) *Zhè kuài mùbǎn *kuān 1 m, gāo 30 cm* |→ ... *cháng 1 m, kuān 30 cm*
(c) *Zhè kuài mùbǎn cháng 1 m, gāo 30 cm* → ... *cháng 1 m, kuān 30 cm*

As predicted by (12b) and confirmed by the data in (10-III), Mandarin lacks the premises needed to turn (16a, b) into valid inferences: the SDT *kuān*, being lexically fixed to refer to Max ⊥ Across, does not provide any specifications that could be despecified. However, Mandarin allows the inference in (16c), that draws on replacing the contextually induced VERT term *gāo* with the **P**-fixed ACROSS term *kuān* (cf. 3.3.).

What about Korean? In view of the two subgroups of SDTs — the **P**-fixed *kili-phok* in (11-C), and the **O**-fixed *selo-kalo* in (11-A, B) — there is a way to mimic the pattern of **P/O**-mixed type languages by inferring (11-C) from (11-A) or (11-B). So (17) is valid along the lines of de-specification. (I will leave it at giving glosses).

(17) *Ku-nelphanci-nun kalo-ka 1 m, selo-ka 0.3 m ita.* [**O**-fixed set]
DET.board.TOP Obs ⊥ Across-axis.SUBJ 1 m, OBS-axis.SUBJ 0.3 m DECL
→ *Ku-nelphanci-nun kili-ka 1 m, phoki 0.3 m ita.* [**P**-fixed set]
DET.board.TOP MAX-axis.SUBJ 1 m, Max ⊥ ACROSS-axis 0.3 m DECL

To sum up: the semantic analysis of the ACROSS terms in (12), which draws on distinct selectional restrictions, is confirmed by correspondingly distinct inferential behaviour and other ramifications they have in the realm of DA. The **fixed** type languages stand out for having ACROSS terms that uniquely and disjointly cover one of the basic choices to affiliate the ACROSS axis to — either IPS or PPS. The **P/O**-mixed type languages stand out for having ACROSS terms which offer the choice between IPS and PPS conflated on the same lexical item — which causes these to be referentially ambiguous. This is, in a nutshell, what makes the ACROSS terms anchor points of field partition.

3.3. The role of the VERT terms

With respect to setting II, all data sets in (9)−(11), regardless of type, allow extent **b** of the board to be named by a VERT term (Engl. *high, tall*, Mandarin *gāo*, Korean *nophi*), which is another significant fact for the partition of the lexical field we are developing. No doubt, VERT is a PPS parameter and hence refers to position features of the object it applies to. However, the fact that, in setting II, the VERT term can occur "across the board" in all types listed in (12) indicates that verticality assignment is somehow independent of the rest. Actually, being the dominant axis of our spatial orientation, the Vertical is privileged in DA. A plausible way to spell this out is a preference rule like (18), which marks another facet of the IPS-PPS asymmetry:

(18) The Vertical prevails:
If a non-minimal object extent **d** coincides with the Vertical of PPS, then this coincidence — regardless of being primary or contextually induced — makes a VERT term the preferent choice to name **d**.

Based on the evidence of some 40 languages, (18) seems to capture the autonomy which verticality assignment enjoys in DA. What matters from a typological perspective is the interplay of maximality and verticality assignment. If maximality and verticality are assigned to distinct extents of an object, there are two possibilities. The first, which follows from (12) for **fixed** type languages, is (19):

(19) The VERT term occurs in accordance with (18) but does not interfere with the application of the MAX term or the ACROSS term to the other extents of the object at issue.

This is what we observe in setting II with Mandarin in (10), Korean in (11-C) as specimens of the **P**-fixed type (12a), but also with Korean in (11-A, B) as an example of the **O**-fixed type (12b). Hence, in fixed type languages verticality assignment leaves the basic options for the other dimensions untouched, and this is what (19) states as a corollary of (12). For **P/O**-mixed type languages, there is another, more subtle, option to realize maximality and verticality assignment on the same object:

(20) The occurrence of the VERT term causes (or at least allows) the maximal extent of the object x to be named by the ACROSS term, provided it has a suitable specification for **d'**. (The relabelling operation is represented as M̶a̶x̶ | **d'** ⊥ Across.)

This is what we observe with the **P/O**-mixed type languages in (12c), illustrated by English in (9-II), where **a** = *wide* instantiates M̶a̶x̶ | Vert ⊥ Across. So (20) describes the effect of verticality assignment on the selection of the Across term and the fixing of its reference.

Now, beyond addressing the languages listed in (12c), the operation (20) acts as a litmus test, in that it divides P/O-mixed languages whose range of selecting **d′** is smaller than that of (12c) into subtypes. The first relevant subtype (= 12d) is illustrated by the Russian and Bulgarian data in (21) and (22), which both have Across terms restricted to **d′** ∈ {Max, Vert}. The settings I–III are as in (9); extent **c**, being irrelevant here, is omitted; for clarity, glosses in the notation developed in this chapter are added.

Vert}, is confirmed. Moreover, the analysis accounts for the minimal difference between these languages and Mandarin in (10-II), for which we assumed **d′** = {Max}. In Russian or Bulgarian, Vert delivers an additional value, viz. **d′** = Vert ⊥ Across, to instantiate the Across term, thereby triggering the relabelling operation (20). Note that the relabelling of extent **a** in (21) and (22) is optional, so these languages may either stick to proportion-basedness by (19) or use a positional specification by (20). They get the mark **P/O** for (19) and a **P** mark for (20), see Fig. 91.6 in § 3.5.

The catalytic role of the Vert parameter gets confirmed by the other subtype of **P/O**-

(21) RUSSIAN (nominal form)

I	II	III
a = *dlina*	a = *dlina* / *shirina*	a = *dlina* / **shirina*
Max | Max	Max | Max	Max | Max
	/ M̶a̶x̶ | **Vert** ⊥ Across	/***Obs** ⊥ Across
b = *shirina*	b = *vysota*	b = *shirina* / **glubina*
Max ⊥ Across	**Vert**	**Max** ⊥ Across / ***Obs**

(22) BULGARIAN (nominal form)

a = *dâlžina*	a = *širina* / *dâlžina*	a = *dâlžina* / **širina*
Max | Max	M̶a̶x̶ | **Vert** ⊥ Across	Max | Max
	/ Max | Max	/***Obs** ⊥ Across
b = *širina*	b = *visočina* / **širina*	b = *širina* / ø / **dâlbočina*
Max ⊥ Across	**Vert** / ***Max** ⊥ Across	**Max** ⊥ Across / ø / ***Obs**

The typologically relevant distribution facts are: (i) in setting II, the maximal extent **a** may be relabelled by the Across term, as the Vert term for **b** provides a suitable instance

mixed languages (12e), whose Across terms are restricted to **d′** ∈ {Max, Obs}. They are exemplified by Polish and Vietnamese data in (23) and (24), respectively.

(23) POLISH (adjectival form)

I	II	III
a = *długi*	a = *szeroki* / **długi*	a = *szeroki* / **długi*
Max | Max	M̶a̶x̶ | **Vert** ⊥ Across	M̶a̶x̶ |**Obs** ⊥ Across
	/ *Max | Max	/ *Max | Max
b = *szeroki*	b = *wysoki*	b = *głęboki*
Max ⊥ Across	**Vert**	**Obs**

(24) VIETNAMESE (predicative form)

a = *dài*	a = *dài*	a = *rộng* / **dài*
Max | Max	Max | Max	M̶a̶x̶ | **Obs** ⊥ Across
		/ *Max | Max
b = *rộng*	b = *cao*	b = *sâu*
Max ⊥ Across	**Vert**	**Obs**

on which to hook it; (ii) in setting III, the maximal extent **a** may not be relabelled by the Across term. There is no provider for a suitable instance on which to hook it: **b** is not available to an Obs term. Hence, the restriction posited for these languages, **d′** ∈ {Max,

Both Polish in (23-III) – in contrast with its Slavic cognates in (21) and (22) – and Vietnamese in (24-III) – in contrast with Mandarin – allow for **b** to be named by an Obs term. Given this, these languages have an additional instance for **d′** on which to hook the

Across term, i.e. Obs ⊥ Across, which in turn triggers an **O**-based relabelling operation in setting III. The occurrence of the Vert term and the Obs term in II and III render the relabelling of the maximal axis in III obligatory, so these languages get an **O** mark for (19) and (20).

To summarize: Languages which keep maximality and verticality assignment apart in the form of disjointly distributed lexical items – cf. (19) can be thought of as pursuing the fixed basic options w.r.t. proportion- or observer-basedness. An interference of maximality and verticality assignment with the choice of SDTs involved – cf. (20) – is symptomatic of **P/O**-mixed languages and provides – depending on the range of values for **d'** – another reflection of the **P-O** dichotomy. In view of the operation (20), the role of the Vert parameter might be considered as that of a catalyst, which neatly fits with the autonomy claim in (18). Drawing on the role of the Vert terms, the data in (21–24) illustrate gradual moves from **P** to **O** among cognate languages. The typology established in §§ 3.2, 3.3 is corroborated by the role of the Obs terms, to which we now turn.

3.4. The role of the Obs terms

The typology expounded so far by examining the behaviour of the Across and the Vert terms is confirmed by three observations on the semantics of the Obs terms that reveal the close interconnection of the latter with the former.

3.4.1. Selectional restrictions

In **P**-based languages (including **P**-fixed Mandarin or Mongolian, but also Russian, Bulgarian or Yucatec, that is, all those with more **P** marks than **O** marks in Fig. 91.6), the Obs terms are selectionally restricted to apply to hollow (parts of) objects. In these languages, the Obs terms – often obscuringly glossed as "deep" – draw on a specific gestalt-property of the objects concerned. Here some form of cavity is the basis of Dimension Assignment and the observer-axis plays the role of specifying the way in which the cavity is assigned a dimensionable extent. This in turn makes the combination Vert ↑↓ Obs, which is the canonical DA of e.g. hollows in the ground, into a standard case to be covered by these Obs terms. This explains why Obs terms in **P**-based languages apply only as primary DA.

In **O**-fixed type languages like Korean and Japanese, we find – as with the Across terms discussed in § 3.2 – two lexically disjoint subsets of Obs terms: (i) Kor. *kiphi*, Jap. *fukai*; (ii) Kor. *selo*, Jap. *tate*. Distinct from the former, Obs terms like (ii) involve an observer (normally in upright posture) as the source of DA in that his/her line of sight provides the axis along which an object's extent is identified and dimensionized. This explains why Obs terms of this sort can apply as primary or as contextually induced DA.

3.4.2. Lexical coverage

In **P/O**-mixed languages the following picture emerges: correlating with the **P** and **O** marks for the Across and Vert terms (cf. Fig. 91.6), the Obs terms show a gradual transition from **P**-basedness, i.e. being selectionally restricted to hollow objects, to **O**-basedness by stepwise loosening this selectional restriction. The Obs term in a **P/O**-mixed language is definitely freed from **P**-based selectional restrictions, if the Across term includes Obs as a value to instantiate **d'** with – cf. (12c–e). Parallel to this the Obs terms become applicable to a wider range of objects thus eventually covering both Vert ↑↓ Obs and Vert ⊥ Obs. The **final stage** seems to be reached when the Obs term in a **P/O**-mixed language may apply to an extent of an (actually 2D) object as in Fig. 91.4.

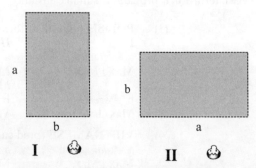

Fig. 91.4: Plot of land, a = 20 m, b = 10 m

Korean and Japanese apply the **O**-fixed SDTs *seloltate* to **a** in I and to **b** in II (and *kalolyoko* to **b** in I and to **a** in II) thus illustrating paragon cases of Obs terms covering Vert ⊥ Obs. **P**-based languages predictably name **a** and **b** in both settings by terms covering Max and Max ⊥ Across, respectively. Some (not all) **P/O**-mixed type languages have reached the stage where their Obs terms may apply to **a** in setting I and **b** in setting II, the other extent being named by an Across term instantiating Obs ⊥ Across. This holds for the languages with an **O** mark in columns 5 & 6 in Fig. 91.6, including Slovak, French, German. The bulk of mixed type languages, however, spreads over intermediate stages which lead to a more fine-grained typology. A closer look at two samples will make this clear.

The Obs terms in **P**-based languages lexically cover the parameter combination Vert ↑↓ Obs as the default case of primary DA to hollow objects. In those **P/O**-mixed type languages that rank high on the **O**-scale, e. g. the Germanic languages with Obs terms of the *deep-tief-djup* etc. variety, the combination Vert ↑↓ Obs may also result from contextually induced DA – viz. by alternating Vert terms and Obs terms on the same extent, cf. *This saucepan is too high* (Vert) *to fit into the shelf but not deep enough* (Vert | Vert ↑↓ Obs) *to fry the turkey in it* and the data in (26–27) below.

Slavic languages, having Obs terms of the common-slavonic *glubokij, dâlbok, hlboký* etc. variety, illustrate distinct stages of this gradual transition. Russian, Byelorussian and Bulgarian have Across terms restricted to **d′** = {Max, Vert}, cf. (12d), and get a **P** mark for (20). In parallel with this, their Obs terms bear the **P**-based selectional restriction to hollow objects – cf. (21–22). Polish, Czech or Slovak, however, parallel with having Across terms whose instantiation includes **d′** = Obs, cf. (12e), and getting an **O** mark for (20), have Obs terms that are selectionally less restricted and thus available for contextually induced DA applicable to non-hollow objects.

The typologically distinctive behaviour of the Obs terms can best be illustrated by the data collected in connection with the staircase setting in Fig. 91.5. The object in question (a stair) has a canonical orientation (a Vert term is obligatory) and allows for contextually induced perspectivization by Obs terms. To elicit the latter, subjects were prompted to respond twice, while imagining themselves (i) going upstairs, (ii) going downstairs. Parallel with the basic options w.r.t. the Across terms in (12), languages differ in allowing or disallowing distinct sets of primary DA (upward) and contextually induced DA (downward).

(25) **P-based languages**
   (a) MANDARIN   a = *gāo*   Vert
                           b = *cháng*   Max
                           c = *kuān*   Max ⊥ Across
   (b) KOREAN   a = *nophi*   Vert
      (**P**-fixed set)   b = *kili*   Max
                           c = *phok*   Max ⊥ Across
   (c) RUSSIAN   a = *vysokij*   Vert
                           b = *dlinnyj*   Max
                           c = *shirokij/*glubokij*   Max ⊥ Across/*Obs

(26) **KOREAN (O-fixed set)**

   I **(upstairs)**   II **(downstairs)**
   a = *nophi*   Vert   a = *kiphi*   V̶e̶r̶t̶ | Vert ↑↓ Obs
   b = *kalo*   Obs ⊥ Across   b = *kalo*   Obs ⊥ Across
   c = *selo*   Obs   c = *selo*   Obs

(27) **P/O-mixed type languages**
   (a) POLISH
      a = *wysoki*   Vert   a = *głęboki*   V̶e̶r̶t̶ | Vert ↑↓ Obs
      b = *długi*   Max   b = *długi*   Max
      c = *szeroki*   Max ⊥ Across   c = *szeroki*   Max ⊥ Across
   (b) SLOVAK
      a = *vysoký*   Vert   a = *hlboký*   V̶e̶r̶t̶ | Vert ↑↓ Obs
      b = *dlhý/široký*   Max   b = *dlhý*   Max
                             M̶a̶x̶ | Vert ⊥ Across
      c = *široký/hlboký*   Max ⊥ Across/Obs   c = *široký*   Max ⊥ Across

(c) GERMAN (also Dutch, Afrikaans, English, Swedish etc.)
   a = *hoch*   VERT   a = *tief/hoch*   ~~Vert~~ | Vert ↑↓ Obs/VERT
   b = *breit*   ~~Max~~ | Vert ⊥ Across   b = *breit*   ~~Max~~ | Vert ⊥ Across
   c = *tief*   OBS   c = ???

(d) ITALIAN (also French, Spanish, Portuguese etc.)
   a = *alto*   VERT   a = *alto/profondo* VERT
                                                                       ~~Vert~~ | Vert ↑↓ Obs
   b = *largo*   ~~Max~~ | Vert ⊥ Across   b = *largo*   ~~Max~~ | Vert ⊥ Across
   c = *profondo*   OBS   c = *profondo???/*
                                                      largo???/lungo???

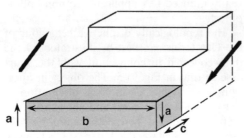

Fig. 91.5: The staircase setting

As regards the behaviour of OBS terms, the data in (25–27) reproduce the typology developed so far on the basis of the catalytic role of the VERT terms in (19, 20) and the semantics of the ACROSS terms in (12).

In **P**-based languages, illustrated in (25), only the primary DA applies. As a stair is not a concave object, the selectionally restricted OBS terms cannot apply, contextually induced perspectivization is excluded anyway. In **O**-fixed type languages, exemplified by Korean in (26), contextually induced perspectivization is operative with properly disjoint OBS terms, viz. *selo* (covering Vert ⊥ Obs for extent **b**) and *kiphi* (realizing the downward specification ~~Vert~~ | Vert ↑↓ Obs on extent **a**).

In the **P/O**-mixed type languages Polish and Slovak in (27a, b), we observe distinct phases of loosening the selectional restriction associated with the OBS term, with both languages deviating from their **P**-based cognate Russian in (25). Two points are of special interest: (i) the move from **P** to **O** starts with the extension of the use of the OBS term to contextually induced DA, while the core meaning reserved for primary DA to hollow objects remains unchanged; (ii) the conditions under which the OBS term refers to Vert ⊥ Obs or to Vert ↑↓ Obs are directly linked with specific instantiations of the ACROSS terms.

If the OBS term applies to Vert ↑↓ Obs specifying VERT on extent **a**, the rest of the DA sticks to **P**-basedness, allowing the ACROSS term to be instantiated by d' = Max only – cf. extents **b** (Max) and **c** (Max ⊥ Across) in the Polish and Slovak data sets. If the OBS term applies to Vert ⊥ Obs, the ACROSS term is instantiated by d' = Vert – cf. the Slovak set in (26b). Note that the correlation is fixed, but applying the OBS term to Vert⊥Obs is optional – cf. the **P-O** scores in Fig. 91.6.

In the Germanic and Romance languages, exemplified by (27c–d), the VERT term – as predicted by (20) – obligatorily causes the relabelling of extent **b** by ~~Max~~ | d' ⊥ Across, d' = Vert or d' = Obs – see both DA sets in (27c). At the same time, we observe a **designation gap** w.r.t. extent **c** in the downward set. A closer look at the data reveals why this is so.

(i) If, for instance, *tief* is used to realize the optional VERT – OBS alternation on extent **a** and *breit* is fixed for extent **b** by (20), then extent **c** poses a naming problem. Applying *tief* to it (as in the upward set I) or applying *breit* twice would violate the Uniqueness constraint (14), while applying *lang* would contradict the built-in maximality feature. Almost all informants who chose set II showed themselves baffled, some attempted escape manoeuvres by naming **c** = *schmal* (antonym of *breit*) or **c** = *wide* (adding "in this direction ✓ [gesture]") or by filling in **c** = *long??/ lungo??*. Based on (14) and (20), such gap-creating conflicts are predictable within the analysis of SDTs proposed, so the baffled reaction of the informants can be taken as confirming support.

(ii) In addition, informants who did not make use of option (i) but retained *hoch/alto* and *breit/largo* for **a** and **b**, respectively, refused to apply *tief/profondo* to extent **c** when asked to imagine themselves going downstairs. This reaction reveals a peculiar feature of OBS terms, to which we now turn.

3.4.3. Antonymy

The two basic claims made above were that (i) OBS terms in **P**-based languages are gestalt-related, are selectionally restricted to hollow objects, and cover Vert ↑↓ Obs as default case of primary DA, while (ii) OBS terms in (fixed or mixed) **O**-based languages are observer-related, are selectionally less restricted, and cover Vert ⊥ Obs as default case of contextually induced perpectivization. These claims are supported by observations on antonym formation.

The general finding is that OBS terms – compared with other SDTs – show a remarkable deficit of regular polar lexical antonyms. In fact, in the strict sense defined by (1b) – which involves the forming of semantically equivalent converses like (i) *A is 30 cm longer than B* ≡ (ii) *B is 30 cm shorter than A* – **none** of the OBS terms in our sample comes with a regular polar lexical antonym.

However, there are partial antonyms to OBS terms whose distribution confirms the distinction claimed in (i) and (ii). What emerges from the data across all languages in the sample can be summarized as follows:

(28) Lexical antonyms of OBS terms
  (a) are confined to object classes with Vert ↑↓ Obs as primary DA
  (b) are loaded with additional class-specific selectional restrictions
  (c) do not allow for regular converses with the OBS term.

So partial antonyms to OBS terms like Mandarin *qiăn* (: *shēn*), Japanese *asai* (: *fukai*), Korean *yalda* (: *kiphi*), are confined to hollows in the ground, preferably waters; the Chinese characters for *shēn – qiăn* both have the radical "water" and are used as Kanji/ Hantsa characters for the corresponding Japanese/Korean term pairs. Likewise, Yucatec *hayáam* (: *táam*) – cf. Stolz (1996: 226 f.), Russian *melkij* (: *glubinnyj*), English *shallow* (: *deep*), German *flach* (: *tief*) are confined to hollows in the ground, German *seicht* (: *tief*) to waters. None of these can take a measure phrase and form a regular converse – cf. [*The left river arm is*] *10 m deeper/*shallower/ *seichter/*flacher* [*than the right one*]. In short: if OBS terms happen to have lexical antonyms, the latter turn out to be shape terms in the sense of (1b) that become involved with the field of SDTs by way of suppletion. All this supports claim (i); claim (ii) is indirectly confirmed by the finding (29):

(29) OBS terms covering Vert⊥Obs do not have lexical antonyms at all.

This predictably holds for **O**-fixed Korean *selo* or Japanese *tate* – cf. 3.4.1. But informants of **P/O**-mixed languages also, when asked to rename the upward set I in Fig. 91.5 by matching opposite terms, unanimously resorted to negating the OBS term: **c** = *not/less deep, pas/peu profond, neje hlboký, nicht/ weniger tief* etc. and rejected **shallow, *plat, *flach* etc., i.e. the terms defined in (28) as partial antonyms to **P**-based OBS terms. Stolz (1996: 223) states that for Yucatec "uses of *táam* "deep" in which the observer axis is at an angle of 90° to the Vertical are much contested, and no lexical antonym of *táam* can be used", while uses of *táam* for containers with Vert ↑↓ Obs allow for antonyms of the type described in (28).

3.4.4. Part – whole inferences

The staircase setting may also serve as a diagnostic for inferences that draw on DA inheritance from parts to wholes and vice versa. So subjects were asked (a) to name the extents of the first step (shaded), (b) to name the extents of the staircase as a whole. The results obtained from the data include the following:

As may be expected from the properties of this PPS axis (cf. Fig. 91.1) and the prevailing role of the VERT terms put down in (18), verticality assignment is both part-whole and whole-part inheritable independently of differences among languages in other respects:

(30) (a) *The height of the staircase is composed of the heights of the steps*
  (b) *Die Höhe der Treppe ergibt sich aus den Höhen der Stufen* [German]
  (c) *Vysota lestnicy sootvetstvuyet summe vysoty stupenej* [Russian]
  (d) *Wysokość schodów wynika z wysokości schodków* [Polish]
  (e) *Výška schodišťa sa skladá zo sučtu výšiek schodov* [Slovak]
  (f) *Zhěng gè tái-jiē de gāo-dù shì*
      staircase.DE   height is
      gè jí gāo-dù zhī hé [Mandarin]
      steps height.ZHI sum

Given the part-whole structure of a staircase, we would expect differences in the DA that draws on MAX and ACROSS terms. As can be deduced from Fig. 91.6, the **P** and **O** marks for (19) and (20) determine, whether or not in the given language the DA for extent **b** is inheritable from the steps to the staircase. **O** marks for (19) and (20) warrant the part-whole inheritability of Across terms covering Vert ⊥ Across − see English and German in (31), **P**-based options, however, make a change of terms obligatory − see the Russian and Mandarin data in (31). West-Slavonic Polish and Slovak are in between.

(31) (a) *The width of the steps is equal to the width of the staircase*
 (b) *Die Breite der Stufen ist gleich der Breite der Treppe* [German]
 (c) *Dľžkalšírka schodov udáva šírku schodišťa* [Slovak]
 (d) *Długość schodków odpowiada szerokości schodów* [Polish]
 (e) *Dlina stupenej sootvetstvuyet shirine lestnicy* [Russian]
 (f) *Dì yī jì de cháng-dù dĕngyú*
  1st step.DE length (Max) equal
  zhĕng gè tái-jiē de kuān-dù
  staircase.DE width (Max ⊥ Across)
  [Mandarin]

As regards the part-whole inheritability of DA realized by Obs terms, the distinctions set up in 3.4.2. and 3.4.3. are confirmed. If an Obs term occurs with extent **a** in the downward set, covering ~~Vert~~ | Vert ↑↓ Obs, informants attest part-whole inheritance under the proviso that the staircase in question is one that leads into the cellar. With this proviso, the data in (32) follow from what has been established so far:

(32) (a) *The depth of the staircase is composed of the depths of the stairs*
 (b) *Die Tiefe der Treppe ergibt sich aus den Tiefen der Stufen* [German]
 (c) *Hľbka schodišťa sa skladá zo sučtu hl'bok schodov* [Slovak]
 (d) *Głębokość schodów wynika z głębokości schodków* [Polish]
 (e) **Glubina lestnicy sootvetstvuyet summe glubiny stupenej* [Russian]
 (f) **Zhĕng gè tái-jiē de shēn-dù shì*
  staircase.DE depth is
  gè ji shēn-dù zhī hé [Mandarin]
  steps depth.ZHI sum

If an Obs term occurs with extent **c** in the upward set, covering Vert ⊥ Obs, as exemplified by Slovak and Germanic and Romance languages in the sample − cf. (27b−d), informants reject part-whole inheritance. So the inferential behaviour, which separates Obs terms covering Vert ↑↓ Obs from those covering Vert ⊥ Obs, matches the distinction discussed in 3.4.3. of having (partial) antonyms vs. lacking antonyms.

In view of the **P-O** typology established so far we obtain the follwoing parallels between the Obs terms and the Across terms: (i) Both are non-ambiguous if they are referentially and selectionally fixed to parameters within the same frame of reference: in **P**-based languages Obs and Across are anchored in IPS (Mandarin, Russian, Yucatec), in **O**-fixed languages (Korean, Japanese) there are − in addition to **P**-based terms − Obs and Across terms that are solely anchored in PPS. (ii) Ambiguity arises in **P/O**-mixed languages to the extent that the selection restrictions associated with Across and Obs terms additionally involve PPS. This arises when Across terms have the additional option to select also values from PPS (**d'** = Vert, **d'** = Obs) and when at the same time Obs terms relax their (IPS-related) restriction to hollow objects and become applicable to object extents identifiable by the observer-axis of PPS.

3.5. Interim Balance

The scores for **P** and **O** marks extracted from the data are summarized in Fig. 91.6 below. The headings of the columns repeat the criteria involved and refer to the relevant paragraphs in this text. The grey middle bar roughly marks the border between **P**-based and **O**-based languages, the bold frames partition the sample into **P**-fixed, **P/O**-mixed, and **O**-fixed languages. Of course, the scale is not just a matter of counting **P**s and **O**s, but rather of implications between basic options (bold-faced). So the marks in columns 1 or 2, together with those in 5, imply the respective marks for the other criteria: e. g. the marks in column 5 entail those in 3 and 4, and are in turn presupposed by those in 6. The correlation of Obs and Across terms is reflected by non-contradicting marks in columns 5, 4, and 3. The marks assigned to Yucatec are based on data by Stolz (1996).

4. Conclusions and extensions

4.1. Frames of Reference

Having examined the features of **P**- and **O**-based partition of the lexical field of SDTs in detail, we now take a step back to see what general patterns emerge while keeping in mind the distinct levels on which spatial features prove to be relevant to DA (cf. § 2.1). First recall the delimitation of the topic.

Languages	1: Relationship Max term: Across term, see (12)	2: Relationship Obs term: Across term, see (12)	3: Relationship Vert term: Across term, see (19)	4: Relationship Vert term: Max term, see (20)	5: Selectional restrictions on Obs term, see 3.4.1	6: Obs term alternates with Vert term on **d**, see 3.4.1
Mandarin, Mongolian	P		P	P	P	
Korean C, Japanese C	P		P	P	P	P
Russ., Bulg., Yucatec, Mod. Greek	P	P	P/O	P	P	P
Finnish, Hungarian	P	O	P/O	O	P/O	P
Polish, Vietnam.	P	O	O	O	P/O	P
Italian, French	P	O	O	O	O	P/O
English, Dutch	P	O	P/O	O	O	O
German, Slovak	P	O	O	O	O	O
Korean A, B; Japan. A, B	O	O	O	O	O	

Fig. 91.6: Proportion-based (P) vs. observer-based (O) options in the lexical field of SDTs

SDTs, as assumed here, consist of a constant part and a varying part. The constant part, by virtue of which an item belongs to the lexical field of SDTs, is defined by the category features listed in (1) and the semantic structure shown in (2) and (3). The varying part is defined by parameters (DAPs) taken from two frames of reference, which instantiate the dimensional component of SDTs and thus specify what is particular to a given item in relation to the rest of the field. This definition, while being restrictive w.r.t. the category features of SDTs, still allows for a range of possible mappings between DAPs and SDTs. Data illustrating various types of such mappings have been amply discussed in § 3.

Next, the two frames of reference, IPS and PPS (Fig. 91.1), provide the DAPs that are relevant to our conceptual knowledge of spatial objects (represented as Object Schemata in Fig. 91.2), whereby only a certain subset of the DAPs occur as lexicalized dimension components in SDTs, the rest figuring in one way or another as part of the selectional restrictions associated with SDTs (see §§ 2.2.2., 3.2.–3.5.).

Finally, recall the claim that DA in natural languages is realized by partial mappings between two levels, viz. the (non-linguistic) level of spatial concepts organized in Object Schemata, and the (linguistically determined) level of semantic components lexicalized in SDTs. It is the relative autonomy of these levels that allows for variation in the mapping relations between the frames of reference and the spatial lexicon in natural languages. In this view, the field of SDTs focussed on in this article is but one of the domains at issue.

We will briefly summarize the typological pattern that emerges in the domain of DA (4.1.1.) and then look at some adjacent lexical fields (4.1.2.), which also involve IPS or PPS, but package the parameters in lexical items that categorially differ from SDTs.

4.1.1. The interaction of IPS and PPS in DA

As shown in § 3, the partition of the lexical field of SDTs crucially depends on the semantics of the ACROSS and OBS terms and their interrelation with Maximality and Verticality assignment. The range of options that emerges has been scored by means of marks for **P**-basedness and **O**-basedness in Fig. 91.6. Appropriately regrouped, the information in Fig. 91.6 will reveal the typologically relevant partitions of the lexical field. What emerges is the pattern shown in Fig. 91.7.

The distinction **fixed** vs. **mixed** refers to relevant types of mapping relations between DAPs and SDTs in a given field, including the lexical coverage and the referential (non-)ambiguity of the ACROSS and OBS terms involved. So a language is of the **fixed** type if the **P**-based and the **O**-based features listed above are realized by disjoint subsets of SDTs in the field, which allows for two subtypes. A language is **P-fixed** if the lexical field (except VERT) is exhausted by SDTs that realize **P**-based features only — e. g. Mandarin, Mongolian. A language is **O-fixed** if **P**-based features and **O**-based features are allocated to disjoint subsets of the SDTs in the field — e. g. Korean, Japanese. Fixedness entails referential non-ambiguity (cf. §§ 3.2., 3.4.).

A language is **P/O-mixed** if **O**-based features are realized by SDTs that also realize **P**-based features — as holds for the majority of the sample. The SDTs concerned show these characteristics: being able to cover **P**- and **O**-based features correlates with (i) being referentially ambiguous (in isolation), (ii) switching between primary and contextually induced DA, and (iii) being selectionally less restricted than the ACROSS or OBS term counterparts in fixed languages.

The interaction of the two frames of reference in DA is pervaded by what was called in § 3.2.2 the IPS-PPS asymmetry. The priority of IPS over PPS is certainly rooted in the conceptual basis of DA: dimensioning a spatial object x presupposes the availability of gestalt-properties of x to be picked out and submitted to comparison, gradation and measurement. This explains why none of the languages examined so far can do without IPS. But interestingly, none of the languages rests on IPS alone — all include terms that refer to the Vertical (cf. § 3.3), thus unavoidably inducing PPS parameters in DA.

	P-fixed	
	P-based	O-based
ACROSS term selectionally restricted to **d'** = Max	yes	no
OBS term selectionally restricted to hollow objects	yes	no
VERT term interferes with the application of MAX, ACROSS, OBS to x	no	yes
ACROSS term and OBS term can realize only primary DA	yes	no
MIN terms lexically differentiated within IPS and beyond	yes	no
	P-based	O-based
	O-fixed	

(P/O-mixed spans the combined region)

Fig. 91.7: A typology of SDT field structures

The IPS-PPS asymmetry is a decisive ingredient of the typology in Fig. 91.7, its effects show up on all levels of DA. On the conceptual level, the asymmetry is reflected in the stock of parameter combinations in (4); it underlies the object categorization shown in Fig. 91.2, above all the division into classes I–VII and their subclasses III-v1–VII-v3o2. Semantically, it reappears as a factor behind the differentiation of, and the inferences between, "primary" and "contextually induced" DA, as shown by the way Across terms with lexically fixed values (**P**-fixed- vs. **O**-fixed) affect DA; it also shows up in the way contextual specification works in **P/O**-mixed type languages (cf. § 3.2). Lexically, it is reflected in asymmetric antonym formation with SDTs (cf. § 2.4 for *tall-short*, § 3.4 for Obs terms; for details, see Lang 1993). Finally, this asymmetry is what determines the gradual transition from **P**-basedness to **O**-basedness we observe with Obs terms (cf. § 3.4). Whether or not the conceptual IPS-PPS asymmetry also acts as a compass for diachronic change will be taken up briefly in § 4.2.

4.1.2. Extension to other lexical domains

The typology developed here invites the search for further correlations. One such concerns the lexical differentiation of Min terms. The sample of languages examined so far strongly suggests the following generalization:

(33) **P**-based languages have a richer subfield of Min terms differentiating object extents within IPS, **O**-based languages of the **P/O**-mixed type have a poor subfield of Min terms that typically overlap with other frames of reference.

What in **O**-based English is covered by *thick – thin*, gets differentiated in **P**-based Mandarin or Russian into (i) a number of gestalt-related SDTs, including *cū – xí / tuchnyj – xudoshchavyj* (for integrated axes), *hòu – bó / tolstyj – tonkij* (for disintegrated axes), *pàng – shòu /* (for body volume), and (ii) terms that clearly refer to other domains like density (of parts within a whole) *mì – xì / gustoj – redkij* or consistency (of liquids) *nóng – xì / plotnyj – zhidkij*.

Lexicalization facts such as these lend support to the more general claim that DA is basically confined to axial reference as defined by IPS and PPS. Based on this, the items in a given lexical field divide into genuine SDTs and terms that indicate an overlap with a third frame of reference. The stock of IPS terms (Max, Across), for instance, is supplemented by terms that draw on another spatial frame of reference, e. g. geometric shape, or even on other domains of object categorization. Cases in point are the Min terms (see (33) and § 2.2.2), the antonyms of Obs terms (see § 3.4.3), and presumably the Size terms (omitted here).

Other types of overlap are exemplified by lexical fields which are adjacent to SDTs in that they also draw on PPS parameters but have them packaged in morphosyntactic categories that differ from those assumed for SDTs in (1). An example that immediately comes to mind is what is known in the literature as "positional" or "distance use" of Vert, Obs, and Across terms, as illustrated in (34):

(34) (a) *The windows are (2 m) high* [ambiguous]
 (b) *The windows are 2 m in height* [dimensional use]
 (c) *The windows are at a height of 2 m* [distance use]

In view of English or German data like (34a), it is commonly assumed that one and the same Vert term occurs in two "distinct uses", corresponding to paraphrases like (34b, c). However, relying on languages with a poor morphology in [+N αV] predication obscures the fact that in other languages the so-called distance use of PPS terms is linked with robust morphosyntactic effects at the sentence level. (35) presents a small sample of annotated data from languages in which the counterparts of (34a) show SDTs (a) to be clearly separated from distance terms (b).

(35) French
 (a) *Les fenêtres sont hautes* [number + gender agreement]
 (b) *Les fenêtres sont haut* [no agreement features]

 Spanish
 (a) *Las ventanas son altas* [*ser*-copula, number + gender agreement]
 (b) *Las ventanas están alto* [*estar*-copula, no agreement]

 Hungarian
 (a) *Az asztal 2 m magas* [no copula]
 (b) *Az asztal 2 m magasan van* [local *van*-copula]

MANDARIN
(a) *Chuānghù 2 mǐ gāo* [no copula]
(b) *Chuānghù lídì 2 mǐ gāo* [local copula]

The data suggest that while SDTs behave like standard primary predicates, distance terms carry the syntactic marks of secondary predication. There is another less known but widespread fact that supports this correlation. Adjectival SDTs and distance terms are both restricted w.r.t. adverbial marking. While SDTs allow for e. g. *-ly, -ment* etc. only in non-spatial metaphoric use (*highly appreciate, deeply regret; hautement alouer, profondément déplorer*), distance terms do not take adverbial markings at all — cf. *we are flying rather high(*ly)/nous volons très haut(*ement)/vogliamo alto (*altamente); he is diving deep(*ly), il plonge profond(*ément)*. This confirms that distance terms are closely related to SDTs semantically but differ from them syntactically.

Considerations such as these invite further typological studies that focus on how one and the same set of semantic components is submitted to categorially distinct types of lexical packaging. In addition to distance terms, the field of local adpositions needs to be examined in this respect. The analysis of this part of the spatial lexicon has invoked a number of additional frames of reference, e. g. the absolute, the relative, and the intrinsic system of spatial orientation, and to corresponding typologies drawing on these (see Levinson 1995). It would be a rewarding endeavour to investigate to what extent adherence to **P**- or **O**-basedness in DA correlates with, say, preference for the intrinsic or relative frame of reference in spatial orientation.

4.2. Theoretical issues

Besides suggesting extensions that could contribute to a more complete picture of the spatial lexicon on the descriptive level, the approach presented here raises some issues that call for solutions on the explanatory level. It suffices here to address two such issues.

4.2.1. Unravelling binarism

The study of SDTs has played a significant part in the history of lexical semantics, not least in being a permanent source for revisions in theory and methodology. Of special interest is the role of binarity in semantics in comparison to, say, syntax and phonology, and the light it has shed on the make-up of semantic representations.

It was the analysis of SDTs in Bierwisch & Lang (1989) that proved the binary features of classical structural semantics (Greimas 1966, Bierwisch 1967) to be inadequate. The main reason for banning binarity from the realm of semantic features is that Minus-values of features induce unresolvable inconsistencies in hierarchies.

Binarity was also an issue of semantic decision making applied to the field of SDTs. There have been several attempts (Miller & Johnson-Laird 1976, Spang-Hanssen & Erlandsen 1988, Weydt & Schlieben-Lange 1995, 1998) to algorithmize DA by a sequence of binary decisions on assigning SDTs to object extents. None of these attempts has succeeded, and there is a principled reason for this. The facts presented in § 3 should suffice to show that the grammar of DA cannot be captured by merely enumerating combinations and variations of SDTs, because the latter have also to be specified as representing "primary" or "contextual induced" DA w.r.t. classes of objects. Otherwise crucial facts like (non-)ambiguity or inference relations remain unaccounted for, let alone the full range of admissible combinations. So DA seems to resist rule-based or even algorithmized approaches and to favour constraint-based approaches of the sort roughly outlined in §§ 2 and 3.

Nevertheless, the role of binarism in DA remains an intriguing problem. The present approach suggests that this issue should be approached from a modular perspective, that is, binary decisions should be viewed as applying stepwise not to a list of items but to arrays of parameters organized in what we call frames of reference. Further research will show to what extent DA (including the asymmetries summarized in § 4.1.1) is related to binarism.

4.2.2. Going into Depth

The observations on Obs terms made in § 3.4 suggest at least two topics for further research. First consider the finding that **P/O**-mixed languages present the overall picture of a transition from **P**-basedness to **O**-basedness (cf. Fig. 91.6), the crucial point being the gradual relaxation of the selectional restriction of the Obs terms involved. This observation fits in with the idea that the IPS-PPS asymmetry pervades DA as a whole. The questions that need to be answered are (i) how is this transition brought about and (ii) does it reflect the direction of diachronic changes in the field of SDTs?

There are two sources from which answers might be obtained: etymology and language contact. The fact that e. g. Slavic and Germanic languages differ in the number of **O**-marks (see Fig. 91.6) seems to be rooted in the etymology of the respective OBS terms. The common Slavonic root *glub-* traces back to Gr. *glýphō* '(to) carve', *glyphís* 'cavity', Lat. *glubo* '(to) peel', OHG *klioban*, Sax. *cliofan* 'to split', 'to cleave' and has survived in modern Germanic *cleft*, *Kluft* etc. Whatever changes are involved, the common feature of all these cognate words is to make reference to an object feature ⟨hollow⟩, which is the source of what we today observe as the selectional restriction of Russ. *glubokij* etc. The common Germanic root **deup-a*, Got. *diup*, Sax. *deop*, Dutch *diep*, Germ. *tief*, Swed. *djup* etc. is allied to the verbs *to dip* and *to dive*, Germ. *tauchen*, *taufen*, whose radical sense is 'to thrust' or 'to plunge'. The common feature of these cognate words is to make reference to an activity of a (human) agent (w.r.t. the spatial environment) that is being guided by the agent's gaze of sight. This fits in with the observation that in modern Germanic languages OBS terms lack the selectional restriction to hollow bodies and are thus enabled to cover Vert ⊥ Obs. Needless to say, these are but preliminary speculations.

The fact that the **O**-marks of e. g. Polish and Slovak deviate from those of Russian and approach those of German (cf. Fig. 91.6) is suggestive of interference. West Slavonic languages have been in close contact with German for centuries. What is remarkable is the subtlety of the influence: it relaxes the selectional restriction of the common Slavonic OBS term, thereby making it applicable to Vert ⊥ Obs. Stolz (1996: 224) considers a similar case by assessing the extended use which the **P**-based Yucatec OBS term *táam* has acquired under the influence of **O**-based Spanish, and my Vietnamese informants attribute the deviance of Vietn. *sâu* from cognate Mandarin *shēn* to the influence of French.

The other intriguing fact about OBS terms is the finding that none of the languages under review has a clear-cut lexical polar antonym of **O**-based OBS terms. The search for an explanation for this cross-linguistically robust fact will probably take us back to the conceptual or even the perceptual basics of DA. Let's go into depth more deeply.

5. Symbols

x / y	x and y are alternatives in the given context
x | y	x is specified by y
x ⊥ y	x and y are orthogonal to each other
x ↑↓ y	x and y are at an angle of 180°, with x, y ∈ {DAP}
X | Y	term X is replaced with/overwritten by term Y
x → y	x entails y/y can be validly inferred from x
x ↦ y	x does not entail y/y cannot be validly inferred from x, with x, y assertions

6. References

Bierwisch, Manfred. 1967. "Some semantic universals of German adjectivals". *Foundations of Language* 3.1: 1–36.

Bierwisch, Manfred. 1989. "The Semantics of Gradation". In: Bierwisch, Manfred & Lang, Ewald (eds.) *Dimensional Adjectives: Grammatical Structure and Conceptual Interpretation.* Berlin etc., 71–261.

Bierwisch, Manfred & Lang, Ewald (eds.) 1989. *Dimensional Adjectives: Grammatical Structure and Conceptual Interpretation.* Berlin etc.

Bierwisch, Manfred & Lang, Ewald. 1989. "Somewhat Longer – Much Deeper – Further and Further. Epilogue to the Dimension Adjective Project". In: Bierwisch, Manfred & Lang, Ewald (eds.). *Dimensional Adjectives: Grammatical Structure and Conceptual Interpretation.* Berlin etc., 471–514.

Clark, Herbert H. 1973. "Space, time, semantics, and the child". In: Moore, Terry (ed.). *Cognitive Development and the acquisition of language.* New York, 27–63.

Clark, Herbert H. & Clark, Eve V. 1977. *Psychology and Language. An Introduction to Psycholinguistics.* New York.

Dervillez-Bastuji, Jacqueline. 1982. *Structure des relations spatiales dans quelques langues naturelles.* Genève/Paris.

Dirven, René & Taylor, John R. 1988. "The Conceptualisation of Vertical Space in English: The Case of Tall". In: Rudzka-Ostyn, Brygida (ed.). *Topics in Cognitive Linguistics.* Amsterdam/Philadelphia, 379–402.

Durell, Martin. 1981. "Contrasting the lexis of English and German". In: Russ, Charles V. J. (ed.). *Contrastive Aspects of English and German.* Heidelberg, 35–54.

Durell, Martin. 1988a. "Zu einigen deutschen und englischen Dimensionsadjektiven. Eine vergleichende Analyse". In: Munske, Horst H. et al. (eds.). *Deutscher Wortschatz. Lexikologische Studien*. Berlin/New York, 93–115.

Durell, Martin. 1988b. "Some problems of contrastive lexical semantics". In: Hüllen, Werner & Schulze, Rainer (eds.). *Understanding the Lexicon. Meaning, Sense and World Knowledge in Lexical Semantics*. Tübingen, 230–241.

Greimas, Algirdas J. 1966. *Sémantique Structurale*. Paris.

Herskovits, Annette. 1986. *Language and cognition. An interdisciplinary study of the prepositions in English*. Cambridge, UK.

Hlebec, Boris. 1983. "A Lexico-semantic Study of English One-dimension Adjectives". *Anali filoloshkog fakulteta* [Beograd] 15: 243–280.

Hlebec, Boris. 1986. "Sources of Shared Polysemy in English Spatial Adjectives". *Studia Anglica Posnaniensia* 18: 205–222.

Jackendoff, Ray. 1996. "The architecture of the linguistic-spatial interface". In: Bloom, P. et al. (eds.). *Language and Space*. Cambridge/MA, 1–30.

Landau, Barbara & Jackendoff, Ray. 1993. "What" and "where" in spatial language and spatial cognition. *Behavioral and Brain Sciences* 16: 217–238.

Lafrenz, Peter G. 1983. *Zu den semantischen Strukturen der Dimensionsadjektive in der deutschen Gegenwartssprache*. Göteborg.

Lang, Ewald. 1989. "The Semantics of Dimensional Designation of Spatial Objects". In: Bierwisch, Manfred & Lang, Ewald (eds.). *Dimensional Adjectives: Grammatical Structure and Conceptual Interpretation*, Berlin etc., 243–417.

Lang, Ewald. 1990a. "Primary Perceptual Space and Inherent Proportion Schema". *Journal of Semantics* 7.2: 121–141.

Lang, Ewald. 1990b. "Sprachkenntnis, Objektwissen und räumliches Schließen". *Zeitschrift für Linguistik und Literaturwissenschaft* 78: 59–97.

Lang, Ewald. 1993. "The meaning of German projective prepositions: a two-level approach". In: Zelinsky-Wibbelt, Cornelia (ed.). *The Semantics of Prepositions. From Mental Processing to Natural Language Processing*. Berlin/New York, 249–291.

Lang, Ewald. 1995. "Das Spektrum der Antonymie. Semantische und konzeptuelle Strukturen im Lexikon und ihre Darstellung im Wörterbuch". In: Harras, Gisela (ed.). *Die Ordnung der Wörter*. (IdS-Jahrbuch 1993) Berlin/New York, 30–98.

Lang, Ewald, Carstensen, Kai-Uwe, Simmons, Geoffrey. 1991. *Modelling Spatial Knowledge on a Linguistic Basis. Theory – Prototype – Integration*. (Lecture Notes in Artificial Intelligence, 481) Berlin etc.

Levinson, Stephen. 1995. "Frames of reference and Molyneux's question: cross-linguistic evidence". In: Bloom, Paul et al. (eds.). *Language and Space*. Cambridge/MA, 109–169.

Miller, George A. & Johnson-Laird, Philip N. 1976. *Language and Perception*. Cambridge/UK.

Robering, Klaus. 2002. "Dimensionsadjektive". In: Cruse, D. Alan et al. (eds.) *Lexikologie – Lexicology*. (HSK). Berlin/New York.

Spang-Hanssen, Ebbe. 1990. "La sémantique des adjectifs spatiaux". *Revue Romane* 25: 292–309.

Spang-Hanssen, Ebbe. 1993a. "Naming the dimensions of a spatial object". In: Darski, Józef & Vetulani, Zygmunt (eds.). *Sprache – Kommunikation – Informatik*. (Linguistische Arbeiten, 293) Tübingen, 195–200.

Spang-Hanssen, Ebbe. 1993b. "Géométrie et fonctionnalité dans la description des adjectifs de dimension". *Cahiers de Grammaire* 18: 93–107.

Spang-Hanssen, Ebbe & Erlandsen, Jens. 1988. "Om at få en datamat til at forstå rumlige adjektiver." *SAML* 13: 7–23.

Stolz, Christel. 1996. *Spatial Dimensions and Orientation of Objects in Yucatec Maya*. (Bochum-Essener Beiträge zur Sprachwandelforschung, 29) Bochum.

Svorou, Soteria. 1987. "The semantics of spatial extension terms in Modern Greek". *Buffalo Working Papers in Linguistics* 87.1: 56–112.

Togeby, Ole. 1978. "Er planken høj eller lang"? In: Gregersen, Kirsten (ed.). *Papers from the 4th Scandinavian Conference of Linguistics*. Odense, 317–322.

Vandeloise, Claude. 1988. "Length, Width and Potential Passing". In: Rudzka-Ostyn, Brygida (ed.) *Topics in Cognitive Linguistics*. Amsterdam, 403–427.

Vandeloise, Claude. 1992. "Les adjectifs de dimension". *Cahiers de Lexicologie et Lexicographie* 61.2: 85–110.

Vandeloise, Claude. 1993. "The role of resistance in the meanings of thickness". *Leuvense Bijdragen* 82.1: 29–47.

Weydt, Harald & Schlieben-Lange, Brigitte. 1995. "*Hoch – tief – niedrig*. Primäre und metaphorische Bedeutungen von antonymischen Adjektiven". In: Hoinkes, U. (ed.). *Panorama der lexikalischen Semantik*. Tübingen, 715–743.

Weydt, Harald & Schlieben-Lange, Brigitte. 1998. "The meaning of dimensional adjectives. Discovering the semantic process". *Lexicology* 4.2: 199–236.

Wurzel, Wolfgang U. 1987. "Zur Morphologie der Dimensionsadjektive". In: Bierwisch, Manfred & Lang, Ewald (eds.). *Grammatische und konzeptuelle Aspekte von Dimensionsadjektiven*. Berlin, 459–516.

Zhurinskij, Andrej N. 1971. "O semanticheskoj strukture prostranstvennyx prilagatel'nyx" [On the semantics of spatial adjectives]. In: *Semanticheskaja struktura slova*. Moscow, 96–124.

Zubin, David A. & Choi, Soonja (1984). "Orientation and gestalt: Conceptual organizing principles in the lexicalization of space". CLS-20. *Parasession on lexical semantics*. Chicago, 333–345.

Zubin, David A. & Svorou, Soteria (1984). "Perceptual schemata in the spatial lexicon: A cross-linguistic study". CLS-20. *Parasession on lexical semantics*. Chicago, 346–358.

Ewald Lang, Humboldt University (Berlin)
& Centre for General Linguistics (ZAS)
(Germany)

92. Quantifiers

1. Introduction
2. Internal typologies
3. External typologies
4. Delimitation of quantification
5. Special abbreviations
6. References

1. Introduction

Quantifiers are free-standing expressions whose meanings involve the notion of quantity, such as English *three, several, numerous, most, every, one hundred and twenty three, all but seventeen*, and so forth.

The basic semantic structure of quantification is bipartite, consisting of the quantifier itself plus the expression that it quantifies. For example, in a sentence such as *Three boys have come*, *three* is the quantifier, and *boys* the quantified expression.

Quantification has traditionally been of great interest to semanticists, logicians and philosophers of language, due at least in part to the perceived 'logical' or 'mathematical' nature of the meanings involved. As such, it is striking to observe how such basic and seemingly immutable meanings may, in different languages, be expressed with very different morphosyntactic strategies, exhibiting a great degree of cross-linguistic variation.

Typologies of quantification are of two fundamental kinds. **Internal** typologies are concerned with the quantifiers themselves, their internal morphosyntactic structure and their basic semantic properties. In contrast, **external** typologies are concerned with the quantifiers in context, that is to say, the syntactic and semantic relationships between the quantifiers and the quantified expressions and/or the remainder of the sentences in which they occur.

2. Internal typologies

Internal typologies of quantification make reference to a variety of fundamental morphosyntactic and semantic properties.

2.1. Mass and count quantifiers

One of the most basic distinctions is between **mass** and **count** quantifiers (Pelletier ed. 1979, Allan 1980, Higginbotham 1995, Gil 1996). Mass quantifiers constitute expressions which denote an undifferentiated homogeneous mass; for example, English *much* is a mass quantifier, because it forms expressions such as *much water, much cake*. In contrast, count quantifiers constitute expressions which refer to one or more countable units of characteristic size and shape; for example, English *many* is a count quantifier, because it forms expressions such as *many boys, many cakes*. Whereas many quantifiers belong to just one of the two types, mass or count, some quantifiers are undifferentiated with respect to the mass/count distinction, and may appear in expressions of either kind. For example, English *all* is undifferentiated with regard to the mass/count distinction, because it may occur in expressions such as *all the water, all the cake*, denoting a mass, and also in expressions such as *all the boys, all the cakes*, referring to countable units. In general, as suggested by the English examples, the mass/count distinction is reflected in the lexical inventories of quantifiers in different languages.

An interesting case is that of the so-called classifier languages, many of which are located in the East Asian linguistic region (Craig ed. 1986, Downing 1996, Aikhenvald 2000). In such languages, many or all of the count quantifiers cannot occur in immediate construction with the noun that they quantify; instead, the quantifier must occur in construction with a special form known as a **classifier**, and the quantifier-plus-classifier constituent may then occur in construction with the noun. For example, in Mandarin, *sān* 'three' cannot occur directly with *huā* 'flower'; instead, a classifier must also be present, such as *zhī*, forming the expression *sān zhī huā* 'three flowers'. Typically, the classifier makes reference to various characteristics — size, shape, function, and so forth — of the quantified noun; for example, the classifier *zhī* typically picks out elongated objects, such as flowers, pencils, sticks, and so forth. Accordingly, different nouns often require different classifiers; for example, round objects such as balls and apples cannot occur with the classifier *zhī*. However, in some cases, different classifiers may occur with the same noun, sometimes resulting in subtle differences in meaning. For example, with flowers, whereas *sān zhī huā* conjures up an image of three flowers on their stalks, *sān duǒ huā*, with a classifier for round objects, focuses in on the actual florescences, to the exclusion of the stalks.

In general, classifier languages are ones in which an NP consisting entirely of a bare noun may be understood as either mass or count, and as either singular or plural (Gil 1987). For example, in Mandarin, in the sentence *Tā chī píngguǒ* 'He ate apple', the NP *píngguǒ* 'apple' may be understood as 'apple' (mass), 'an apple' (singular), or 'some apples' (plural). This cross-linguistic generalization has lead to a widespread belief that in such languages, the classifier is needed in order to individuate the noun and provide the necessary units to facilitate quantification (Thompson 1965, Quine 1969, Stein 1981, Link 1991). Thus, according to this view, the Mandarin *sān píngguǒ is semantically ill-formed for the same reason that the English **three water(s)* is: just as English *water* requires an explicit measure noun before it can be quantified, as in *three glasses/ounces/drops of water*, so Mandarin *píngguǒ* requires a classifier before it can be successfully enumerated, as in *sān gè píngguǒ*.

However, this explanation for the occurrence of classifiers is belied by a variety of additional facts. Unlike English *water*, the Mandarin noun *píngguǒ* does indeed come with a conventional unit of enumeration, namely the individual round fruit that one can hold in one's hand — and therefore does not need a classifier in order to be counted.

Evidence for this is provided by size and shape adjectives: whereas in English, constructions such as *big water* are bizarre, in Mandarin, constructions such as *dà píngguǒ* 'big apple' are syntactically well-formed, and understood in the same way as their English counterparts. A further argument against this explanation is provided by the existence of languages in which, like in Mandarin and other classifier languages, an NP consisting entirely of a bare noun may be understood as either mass or count, and as either singular or plural — but in which there are no numeral classifiers. For example, in Tagalog, in the sentence *Kumain siya ng mansana* 'He ate apple', *mansana* 'apple' may be understood as 'apple' (mass), 'an apple' (singular), or 'some apples' (plural); however, it does not require a classifier in order to occur with a numeral, as in *tatlong mansana* 'three apples'. Thus, the obligatory occurrence of classifiers in classifier languages has no straightforward semantic explanation; in the absence of any better-motivated account, it must accordingly be viewed as just another arbitrary conventionalized fact about the grammars of the languages in question.

2.2. Existential and universal quantifiers

Of particular interest to logicians are the **existential** and **universal** quantifiers (Vendler 1967, Givón 1981, Heim 1982, Gil 1995). Existential quantifiers, such as English *some* and *a(n)*, form expressions denoting at least a minimal, non-zero amount or number of the quantified expression, for example *some water, a boy*. Universal quantifiers, such as English *all* and *every*, form expressions referring to an exhaustive amount or number of the quantified expression, for example *all the water, every boy*. Existential and universal quantifiers are semantically related to each other through negation by means of the classical 'square of opposition': thus, in English, *Not a boy came* is equivalent to *All the boys did not come*, and *Not all the boys came* is equivalent to *A boy did not come*.

Given the importance of existential and universal quantifiers in mathematical logic, it is worthy of note how relatively unimportant these quantifiers are within the grammatical systems of languages. It is indeed not all that common to find a single form, in any language, whose interpretation corresponds precisely and unproblematically to either the existential or the universal quantifier. Moreover, there is probably no language in which expressions of existential and universal quantification constitute a natural grammatical class to the exclusion of other expressions.

Existential quantification, in many languages, is inextricably intertwined with singular number and/or indefiniteness: in some cases they are expressed identically, while in other cases they are expressed by means of the same marker occurring in different constructions, or by means of similar though not identical markers. For example, in English, *some* also expresses indefiniteness, while *a(n)* is the singular indefinite article, and is historically derived from the numeral *one*. In Modern Hebrew, the existential quantifier *eḥad* is the numeral 'one'; moreover, in its unstressed form it marks an NP as indefinite but specific. In Turkish, as well, the existential quantifier *bir* is the numeral 'one'; here too the same form may double as a marker of indefiniteness, but with different syntactic behaviour: as a numeral, it occurs, like other numerals, at the front of the NP, however as an indefinite article it may occur within the NP, immediately in front of the final head noun.

In other cases, though, existential quantification is expressed via various alternative and quite different strategies. One such strategy is that of an existential predicate. For example, in the Tagalog sentence *May binasa ako* 'I read something', *May* is an existential predicate which takes as its argument the form *binasa* 'read', which is inflected for voice (patient-topic) and aspect (perfective); literally, *May binasa* means 'There exists a thing-that-was-read'. This whole construction is then predicated of the topic pronoun *ako* 'I', in what is essentially a possessive construction, 'I have a thing-that-was-read': replace *binasa* with *libro* 'book', and *May libro ako* means 'I have a book'.

Universal quantification, too, is expressed in a variety of different ways across languages. Some languages, such as English, do have dedicated universal quantifiers, that is to say, words such as *all* and *every* whose primary or exclusive function is the expression of universal quantification. However, many other languages lack such words, instead making use of more complex circumlocutions if and when the expressive need arises. For example, in the Australian language Warlpiri, the same word, *panu*, can mean either 'all' or 'many', depending on context (Bittner and Hale 1995); while in another Australian language Mayali, the same form *djarrk-* 'all' bears the additional meaning of 'acting together, at same place and time' (Evans 1995). Indeed, many languages with universal quantifiers often also choose to make use of various periphrastic devices instead of using a universal quantifier. For example, in English, instead of *Eat all*, one can use the verb-plus-particle construction *Eat up*; similarly, in Riau Indonesian, instead of *Makan semua* 'eat all', one would be more likely to say *Makan habis* 'eat finish'.

A particularly interesting case is provided by the distributive key universal quantifiers (see § 3.4), those which mean 'every' (Gil 1995). Whereas in English, *every* is a simple lexical item, in many other languages, there is no simple world for 'every'; instead, the meaning is conveyed by various kinds of periphrasis. In some languages, 'every' consists of the same lexical item as 'all' but in a different morphosyntactic construction, typically involving singular rather than plural number marking. For example, in Maltese, *kull raġel* 'every man' is formed from the universal quantifier *kull* in construction with the singular noun *raġel*, while *kull l-irġiel* 'all the men' is formed from the same quantifier in construction with the plural (and definite) noun *l-irġiel*. In other languages, 'every' is expressed by a distributive share form of the numeral 'one'. For example, in Maricopa, *šentxper-* 'every' is formed from *šent-* 'one' by suffixation of the distributive marker *-xper*. Finally, in many languages, 'every' is expressed by some combination of a determiner, typically interrogative, and/or a focus particle (König 1991, Gil 1994, Haspelmath 1997). For example, in Galilean Arabic, *ayy raajil* 'every/any man' is formed from the interrogative determiner *ayy* 'which'; in Hungarian, *minden ember* 'every man' is formed from the focus particle *mind* 'also' (plus adverbial suffix); while in Malayalam, *eetə manuṣyanum* 'every/any man' is formed from the interrogative determiner *eetə* 'which' plus the focus particle *-um* suffixed to the noun.

The diversity of morphosyntactic expression of existential and universal quantifiers across the world's languages suggests that, although greatly valued by logicians, they may not be endowed with privileged status vis à vis the structure of language.

2.3. Numerals

'In between' the existential and the universal quantifiers lie a variety of **mid-range** quantifiers, such as, in English, *few, several, many, most*, and so forth. Among the mid-range quantifiers, a particularly privileged category is that of **cardinal numerals** − quantifiers which refer to natural numbers, for example *one, two, thirteen, one hundred and twenty seven* (Brandt Corstius ed. 1968, Menninger 1969, Hurford 1975, Greenberg 1978).

Languages differ with respect to their inventory of numerals, and with regard to their internal structure. At one end of the spectrum there are languages with very impoverished means of counting. For example, in Minor Mlabri, a hunter-gatherer language of Southeast Asia, *bɛɛr* 'two', is the highest numeral that can occur in attributive position; for, say, 'three pieces', a periphrastic construction is required: *bɛɛr ləbo? hlooj*, literally 'two piece odd' (Rischel 1995). At the other end of the spectrum there are languages which, by exploiting the recursive nature of syntax, are capable of expressing essentially any natural number − for example, in English, by stacked occurrences of the highest commonly used numeral, *trillion*.

Like other expressions, numerals may be characterized in terms of their internal structure as lexical and monomorphemic, for example English *three*, Russian *sorok* 'forty', Indian English *crore* 'ten million'; lexical and polymorphemic, for example Selepet (a language of New Guinea) *bâtnobot* 'hand.side' for 'five' (McElhanon 1972), English *seventeen*, Nepali *bayaasi* 'two.eighty' for 'eighty two'; phrasal, for example Selepet *nobolân yâhâp* 'side.LOC two' for 'seven'; Igbo *ìrí là asáà* 'ten and seven' for 'seventeen' (Swift, Ahaghotu and Ugorji 1962), English *one hundred and twenty seven*; or discontinuous, for example Minor Mlabri *bɜɜr __ hlooj* 'two __ odd' for 'three' (above), Igbo *óhu __ nì irí* 'twenty __ and ten' for 'thirty', Biblical Hebrew *meʔɔ __ wəʕɛśrim __ wəšɛḇaʕ __* 'hundred __ and.twenty __ and.seven.F' for 'one hundred and twenty seven' (Genesis 23: 1), in the latter case the quantified noun being repeated after each numerical expression.

Complex phrasal numerals often make use of syntactic patterns available elsewhere in the language; however, in addition, they sometimes exhibit unique structural features not found in other grammatical domains. The most characteristic feature of numeral systems is the use of a *base* for counting, usually ten, but occasionally some other number. For example, the English numeral *one hundred and twenty seven* makes use of the base ten, via the formula $1 \cdot 10^2 + 2 \cdot 10^1 + 7 \cdot 10^0$. In contrast, the French numeral *six cents quatre-vingt dix-sept* 'six hundred and ninety seven' mixes bases ten and twenty, in accordance with the formula $6 \cdot 10^2 + 4 \cdot 20^1 + 1 \cdot 10^1 + 7 \cdot 10^0$. As suggested by the preceding examples, complex numerals are typically formed from a sequence of constituent numerals, or addends, of decreasing size; each addend combining a power of the base with a simple numeral multiplier.

In some cases, however, variations on the theme may be observed. In certain limited instances, a smaller addend may precede a larger one. For example, in the German *zwei-hundert-drei-und-vierzig* 'two.hundred-three-and-forty' for 'two hundred and forty three', the smaller addend *drei* 'three' precedes the larger one *vierzig* 'forty'; similarly, in the Biblical Hebrew *šiša wəšiḇʕim ɛlɛp waḥăměš meʔɔt* 'six.M and.seventy thousand and.five.F hundred.PL.F' for 'seventy six thousand five hundred', the smaller addend *šiša* 'six (thousand)' precedes the larger one *šiḇʕim* 'seventy (thousand)' (Numbers 26: 22). An additional complication is the occasional phenomenon of overcounting, whereby a constituent may be subtracted rather than added. For example, in the Latin *duo-de-sexaginta* 'two-from-sixty' for 'fifty eight', two is subtracted from sixty; similarly, in the Ainu *wan e re hotne* 'ten from three twenty' for 'fifty', ten is subtracted from sixty (Menninger 1969). Yet another source of cross-linguistic variation is provided by the interpretation of addends in which the base is not overtly expressed. For example, whereas in English, in a numeral such as *two thousand and five*, the last addend is interpreted as 'five units', or simply 'five', in the corresponding Vietnamese numeral *hai nghìn năm*, the last addend is understood as multiplying the next smallest power of the base, in the case at hand hundreds − accordingly, the complex numeral is assigned the interpretation 'two thousand five hundred'.

2.4. Other internal typologies

Quantifiers are sometimes classified as either **strong** (alternatively referred to as **definite**) or **weak (indefinite)** (Milsark 1977, Plank 1992, de Hoop 1995). Strong quantifiers, such as English *all* and *most*, are inherently definite in their meaning, whereas weak quantifiers, such as English *some* and *three*, are not. Strong and weak quantifiers often exhibit different syntactic behaviour; for example, strong quantifiers are typically awkward or ungrammatical in existential sentences, e. g. *?There is all the water on the floor.*

Some further semantic distinctions are captured by the categories of **increasing** (alternatively referred to as **upward entailing**) and **decreasing** (or **downward entailing**) (Barwise and Cooper 1981, Keenan and Stavi 1986). A quantifier is increasing if a sentence containing it would be logically true in a situation in which the amount or number of quantified expressions involved is *larger* than that explicitly stipulated by the quantifier. For example, English *at least three* is upward entailing, because a sentence such as *At least three boys have come* would be true in a situation where four, five, or any larger number of boys had come. Conversely, a quantifier is decreasing if a sentence containing it would be logically true in a situation in which the amount or number of quantified expressions involved is *smaller* than that explicitly stipulated by the quantifier. For example, English *at most three* is downward entailing, because a sentence such as *At most three boys have come* would be true in a situation where two, one, or no boys at all had come. Other quantifiers, such as English *exactly three*, are neither increasing nor decreasing.

An interesting problem is posed by simple monomorphemic quantifiers such as *three*. At first blush, such quantifiers appear to be neither increasing nor decreasing: if somebody says *There are three cats on the bed*, the mental picture that is conjured up is, of course, one of three cats, not two, or four, or any other number. However, a moment's reflection will reveal an important asymmetry. If in fact there are exactly two cats on the bed, then the above sentence is clearly false. In contrast, if there are exactly four cats on the bed, then, in most contexts, the above sentence would obviously be misleading and inappropriate – but it would not, strictly speaking, be false. Thus, while the pragmatic appropriateness conditions of *three* resemble those of *exactly three*, the actual truth conditions of *three* are identical to those of *at least three*. Hence, *three* is, in fact, increasing.

In general, almost all monomorphemic quantifiers in English are increasing; the only two exceptions are *no* and *few*, which are decreasing. In general, across languages, increasing quantifiers are more common, and of simpler morphosyntactic structure, than non-increasing ones. In particular, it is probably true that in all languages, simple numerals are increasing; non-increasing numerals are derived from their increasing counterparts by periphrasis, as in English, or by various morphological devices. For example, in Maricopa, non-increasing non-decreasing numerals are formed by suffixation of *-xot^y*, eg. *xmokxot^y-* 'exactly three' from *xmok-* 'three', while in Tagalog, they are formed by initial CV-reduplication, eg. *tatatlo* 'only three' from *tatlo* 'three'.

3. External typologies

External typologies of quantification make reference to the morphosyntactic and semantic relationships which obtain between the quantifiers and the quantified expressions and/or the remainder of the sentences in which they occur.

3.1. Nominal and verbal quantification

One basic semantic typology relates to the category of the quantified expression; specifically, whether it is of a nominal or verbal nature (Langacker 1987, Gil 1993). Consider the following two sentences from Georgian:

(1) Georgian
 (a) *samma bavšvma imɣera*
  three.ERG boy.ERG PFV.sing.3.SG
  'Three boys sang'
 (b) *zviadma samjer imɣera*
  Zviad.ERG three.time PFV.sing.3.SG
  'Zviad sang three times'

In (1a) the numeral *samma* quantifies a noun, *bavšvma*; this sentence accordingly illustrates **nominal quantification**. In contrast, in (1b) the numeral *samjer* quantifies a verb, *imɣera*; this sentence accordingly instantiates **verbal quantification**.

The Georgian sentences underscore the fundamental similarity between nominal and verbal quantification. Obvious, but still worth noting, is the fact that in both cases, the same quantifier stem, *sam-* 'three', is used. Moreover, in both cases, the quantifier takes a suffix: whereas in (1a) the suffix is a case marker, the ergative *-ma*, in (1b) it is the suffix *-jer*, which, although not strictly speaking a case marker, occurs in the morphological slot characteristic of such markers. Finally, in both cases, the quantifier precedes the quantified expression, though in both cases some freedom of word order is permitted. Thus, the two Georgian constructions appear to be formally parallel.

However, turning to their English glosses, a somewhat different picture emerges. First, whereas in the gloss to (1a) *three* occurs in immediate construction with *boys*, in the gloss to (1b) *three* must first take the expression *times* before it can occur with *sang*. Secondly, whereas in the gloss to (1a) *three* governs the noun grammatically, assigning it the plural suffix *-s*, in the gloss to (1b) no such relationship is evident. Thirdly, whereas in the gloss to (1a) *three* is tightly bound to *boys*, in the gloss to (1b) *three times* is more loosely bound to *sang*, and in fact can be moved away, for example to the beginning of the sentence. Facts such as these point towards the existence of an important distinction between nominal and verbal quantification — further suggesting that of these two types, the latter is more highly marked. Perhaps it is for this reason that, to date, almost all studies of quantification are exclusively concerned with quantification of the nominal variety — a situation which future research may hopefully redress.

In addition to nominal and verbal quantification, various other kinds of quantification may occur, though with considerably less frequency. For example, constructions such as *three-coloured, many sided*, and so forth, may be considered to provide examples of adjectival quantification.

3.2. Continuous and discontinuous quantification

A distinct albeit related syntactic typology pertains to the position of the quantifier with respect to the quantified expression; specifically, whether or not the two form a continuous constituent (Capell 1969, Lewis 1975, Gil 1993, Bach et al. eds. 1995). Sentences (2)−(5) below all instantiate nominal quantification, in which a numeral quantifies an expression referring to an apple; however, each of the examples exhibits a different syntactic configuration:

(2) Modern Hebrew
 raiti [šloša tapuhim]
 see.PAST.1.SG three.M apple.PL.M
 'I saw three apples'

(3) Tagalog
 Tatlo [ang nakita
 three TOP PAT.TOP.PFV.see
 kong mansana]
 DIR.1.SG.LIG apple
 'I saw three apples' ('The apples seen by me were three')

(4) Kutenai (Matthew Dryer, p. c.)
 hu [qaɬsaɬ wu:kati] kanusnana
 1.SG three.PRV see.IND apple
 'I saw three apples' ('I three-saw apples')

(5) Japanese
 Watasi wa ringo o sanko
 1.SG TOP apple ACC three.CLF
 mita
 see.PFV
 'I saw three apples' ('I saw apples threely')

In Modern Hebrew, in (2), as in its English gloss, the quantifier groups with the quantified expression, *šloša tapuhim*, to the exclusion of the remainder of the sentence; in Tagalog, in (3), the quantifier *tatlo* stands alone as a sister to the remainder of the sentence, which forms a constituent; in Kutenai, in (4), the quantifier occurs in construction with the verb, *qaɬsaɬ wu:kati*, to the exclusion of the remainder of the sentence, while in Japanese, in (5), the quantifier *sanko* is a sentential adverb not forming an obvious constituent with any part of the remainder of the sentence.

Constructions (2) and (3) exemplify **continuous quantification**, in which the quantifier and the quantified expression form a constituent. Hebrew (2) provides a prototypical example of continuous quantification, in which the quantifier occupies the slot of a determiner, adjective, or other attributive expression, occurring in construction with the quantified noun to form a Noun Phase. A rather different kind of continuous quantification is exemplified in Tagalog (3): here, the quantified expression is actually the phrasal *ang nakita kong mansana* 'apples seen by me', which then constitutes the argument of the predicative quantifier *tatlo* 'three'.

In contrast, constructions (4) and (5) exemplify **discontinuous quantification**, in which the quantifier occurs apart from the quantified expression. In Kutenai, in (4), the numeral *qaɬsa* 'three' is suffixed with *-ɬ*, marking it as a preverb, in construction with the following verb *wu:kati* 'see'. And in Japanese, in (5), the numeral-plus-classifier expression *sanko* 'three' is a sentential adverb: although it is adjacent to the NP *ringo o* 'apple', the position of the phrase-final accusative marker *o* shows that the quantifier is not actually part of the NP.

Since in (4) and (5) the quantifier belongs with the noun semantically, some analyses of discontinuous quantification consider the quantifier to have undergone "movement", or to have "floated" away from its proper place. Whatever the merits of such analyses in particular instances, it should be noted that constructions such as these are cross-linguistically widespread, providing the unmarked strategy for the expression of quantification in many languages; accordingly, their distribution provides no support for their characterization as derivative in any sense.

Occasionally (see Bach et al. eds. 1995), constructions such as in (2) are referred to as *determiner quantification*, as distinct from *adverbial quantification* in (4) and (5); however, this terminology is inappropriate for a number of reasons. First, not all NP-internal quantifiers are determiners – see § 3.3.2 below. Secondly, the constructions in (4) and (5) are as distinct from each other as each is from (2), and only (5) contains a quantifier in what appears to be an adverbial position.

Examples (2)–(5) above illustrate the distinction between continuous and discontinuous quantification with respect to nominal quantification. In principle, a similar distinction may also be drawn with respect to verbal quantification. Specifically, one may distinguish between continuous verbal quantification, in which a quantifier occurs in construction with the verb it quantifies, and discontinuous verbal quantification, in which a quantifier occurs apart from the verb it quantifies.

In fact, however, the range of constructions with which verbal quantification is expressed would appear to be rather limited. In particular, whereas instances of nominal quantifiers occurring on a verb, as in Kutenai (2) above, are relatively common, there are few, if any, clear-cut instances of the mirror-image phenomenon, that of verbal quantification occurring on a noun. One marginal instance of this is perhaps provided by English constructions such as *an occasional sailor walked by*. To the extent that this sentence may be considered to be a paraphrase of *A sailor walked by occasionally*, the expression *occasional* may be viewed as quantifying the verbal expression *walked by*, while actually occurring apart from the verb, within the NP *an occasional sailor*.

3.3. Quantifier as a grammatical category

Quantifier is primarily a semantic category: an expression is a quantifier only if it bears certain meaning properties. One of the most striking characteristics of quantifiers is the absence of any distinctive shared formal morphosyntactic features, which might justify the positing of a corresponding grammatical category of quantifier. Within languages, different quantifiers often display different grammatical properties. And across languages, the 'same' quantifier may exhibit different morphosyntactic behaviour as well. Thus, in terms of their formal properties, quantifiers constitute a heterogeneous collection, exhibiting a great amount of morphological and syntactic diversity.

The formal heterogeneity of quantifiers may be illustrated by an examination of their ability to occur in referential, attributive, and predicative positions, without recourse to any additional overt grammatical markers, such as classifiers, nominalizers, ligatures, copulas, as shown in Table 92.1.

As suggested in Table 92.1, all of the eight logically possible combinations are instantiated by different quantifiers in different languages. Language-internal variation is illustrated by English *every* vs. *three*. In referential position, only *three* can occur, eg. *I saw *every/three*; in attributive position both can occur, eg. *I saw every apple/three apples*, and in predicative position neither can occur, eg. *The apples *every/*three*. And variation across languages is exemplified by the different forms all meaning 'three'. At one extreme, the Hokkien sa^{44} 'three' can never occur without a classifier, while at the other extreme, the Riau Indonesian *tiga* 'three'

Table 92.1: Quantifiers in referential, attributive and predicative positions

	Hokkien Chinese sa^{44} 'three'	Maricopa *xmok* 'three'	English *every*	Abkhaz *x-* 'three'	Thai *săam* 'three'	Tagalog *tatlo* 'three'	English *three*	Riau Indonesian *tiga* 'three'
referential	–	–	–	–	√	√	√	√
attributive	–	–	√	√	–	–	√	√
predicative	–	√	–	√	–	√	–	√

can occur in referential, attributive, and predicative positions without any additional grammatical markers whatsoever.

3.3.1. Quantifiers within languages

There is probably no language within which there is a formal grammatical category consisting exactly of all quantifiers but no other expressions. Rather, in most or all languages, different quantifiers exhibit different arrays of grammatical properties, some grouping together with expressions belonging to one category, others patterning together with expressions belonging to some other category, yet others exhibiting idiosyncratic morphological or syntactic behaviour.

One of the ways in which quantifiers may differ from each other within languages is with respect to the continuous/discontinuous dichotomy (§ 3.2 above). For example, in English, nominal quantifiers typically occur NP internally; however, some but not all quantifiers may also occur in adverbial position, as evidenced by contrasts such as *The boys have all/each come* vs. **The boys have every/three come*. In a more extreme case, in Mayali, there are two largely distinct classes of nominal quantifiers, one occurring NP internally, the other occurring either adverbially or in immediate construction with the verb − for example NP-internal *rouk* 'all' vs. verbal proclitic *djarrk-* 'all' (Evans 1995).

Even the well-defined set of NP-internal quantifiers may exhibit diverse grammatical properties. This is illustrated in Table 92.2, for English, with respect to three arbitrarily chosen diagnostic criteria, namely, whether a quantifier Q can occur in NPs of the following forms: (a) *my Q N*; (b) *not Q N*; and (c) *Q three N*.

As shown in Table 92.2, each of the eight logically possible combinations is attested by at least one NP-internal quantifier in English; in other words, these three diagnostics define eight subclasses of NP-internal quantifiers, each with distinct syntactic behaviour. As indicated in the bottom row of Table 92.2, three of these eight subclasses coincide with other categories of nominal modifiers: the subclass containing *some* resembles nominal possessors such as *Bill's*, the subclass exemplified with *all* shares properties with demonstratives such as *these*, and the subclass instantiated by *occasional* exhibits similar behaviour to that of adjectives such as *big*. (Of course, this is an artifact of the diagnostics chosen: other diagnostics may suggest a different picture.) What this shows, then, is that there is no sense in which one can talk of a viable grammatical category of quantifier in English.

Indeed, even the semantically well-defined subcategory of numerals often fails to exhibit uniform grammatical behaviour. One cross-linguistically widespread pattern is that whereby lower numerals tend to resemble adjectives, while higher numerals tend to pattern together with nouns (Greenberg 1978). Such a pattern is illustrated below in Modern Hebrew:

(6)   Modern Hebrew
  (a) *talmid   tov*
      student.M.SG good.M.SG
      'good student'
  (b) *talmid   eħad*
      student.M.SG one.M.SG
      'one student'
  (c) *šney   talmidim*
      two.M student.M.PL
      'two students'
  (d) *šloša talmidim*
      three.M student.M.PL
      'three students'
  (e) *ʕasara talmidim*
      ten.M   student.M.PL
      'ten students'

Table 92.2: Grammatical properties of NP-internal quantifiers in English

Q	most	some	much	all	four	occasional	many	every
(a) *my Q N*	−	−	−	−	√	√	√	√
(b) *not Q N*	−	−	√	√	−	−	√	√
(c) *Q three N*	−	√	−	√	−	√	−	√
other expressions		Bill's		these		big		

(f) *mea   talmidim*
    hundred student.M.PL
    'a hundred students'
(g) *revavat   talmidim*
    ten.thousand.CONSTR.SG.F student.M.PL
    'ten thousand students'
(h) *knufiyat   talmidim*
    gang.CONSTR.SG.F student.M.PL
    'a gang of students'

Example (6) shows how the same noun occurs in construction with an adjective in (6a), another noun in (6h), and an ascending sequence of numerals in (6b)–(6g): as the numerals get larger, they become less like the adjective in (6a) and more like the noun in (6h). The relevant morphological and syntactic properties are summarized in Table 92.3:

matical features one-by-one: (i) The numeral 'one' follows the noun, like adjectives; higher numerals precede the noun, like nominal heads. (ii) When the NP is definite, the proclitic definite marker *ha-* precedes both the noun and the numeral 'one', *hatalmid haehad* 'the one student', like it does with adjectives, *hatalmid hatov* 'the good student'; however, with higher numerals, the proclitic definite marker occurs only on the second element, *šney hatalmidim* 'the two students', as is the case with noun-noun constructions, *knufiyat hatalmidim* 'the gang of students'. (iii) The numeral 'one' agrees with the head noun in number – both may take the masculine plural suffix -*im*, as in *talmidim ahadim* 'several students', just like *talmidim tovim* 'good students'; in contrast, higher numerals, like no-

Table 92.3: Grammatical properties of NP-internal numerals in Hebrew

Q		good	1	2	3	10	100	10000	gang
(i)	Q follows N	√	√	–	–	–	–	–	–
(ii)	Q, N both marked for definiteness	√	√	–	–	–	–	–	–
(iii)	Q agrees with N in number	√	√	–	–	–	–	–	–
(iv)	Q in construct state when definite	–	–	–	√	√	√	√	√
(v)	Q has inherent number	–	–	–	–	√	√	√	√
(vi)	Q agrees with N in gender	√	√	√	√	√	–	–	–
(vii)	Q has inherent gender	–	–	–	–	–	–	√	√
(viii)	Q in construct state invariably	–	–	–	–	–	–	√	√

In Table 92.3, columns represent the variable element, and rows the relevant properties (with *Q* standing for the variable element and *N* for the noun); the jagged line descending from upper left to lower right separates adjective-like behaviour, to the left, from noun-like behaviour, to the right.

As evident from Table 92.3, the numeral *ehad* 'one' behaves like the adjective *tov* 'good' with respect to all of the specified grammatical features, whereas the numeral *revava* 'ten thousand' patterns with the noun *knufiya* 'gang' with respect to the same grammatical features; intermediate numerals exhibit some adjectival-like features and some noun-like features. Going through the gram-

minal heads, do not agree with the second element in number. (iv) When the NP is definite, the lower numerals 'one' and 'two' remain uninflected, like adjectives; however, numerals from 'three' up occur in the construct state, marked with the suffix -*t*, *šlošet hatalmidim* 'the three students', like nominal heads, *knufiyat hatalmidim* 'the gang of students' – but see item (viii) below. (v) Numerals below ten do not possess inherent number, as is the case for adjectives in attributive position; however, 'ten', 'hundred' and so forth do possess inherent number, that is to say, they may, independently of the quantified noun, be either singular, or plural, as in *ʕasarot talmidim* 'tens of students', thereby resembling nominal heads, as in *knufiyot talmidim* 'gangs of students'. (vi) Numerals up to and including 'ten' agree with their quantified nouns in gender, and may be marked as feminine, as in *ʕeser talmidot* 'ten (female) students', in this respect resembling adjectives, as in *talmida tova* 'good (female) student; in contrast, 'hundred' and higher numerals do not agree with their quantified nouns in gender, thereby resembling head nouns. (vii) Most numerals, like adjectives, do not have inherent gender; however, the highest numeral, *revava* 'ten thousand', is inherently feminine, as evidenced by the fact that the NP *revavat talmidim*, if in subject position, will trigger feminine verbal agreement, even though the quantified noun *talmidim* is masculine – in this respect 'ten thousand' resembles head nouns such as *knufiya* 'gang', also inherently feminine. (viii) Lower numerals and adjectives never occur in the construct state, and numerals from 'three' to 'thousand' occur in the construct state only when the NP is definite; however, 'ten thousand', when in attributive position, always occurs in the construct state, regardless of whether the NP is definite or indefinite – in this respect too, 'ten thousand' resembles a head noun.

3.3.2. Quantifiers across languages

Across languages, quantifiers with the same meaning often exhibit quite different morphological and syntactic behaviour.

Examples (2)–(5) above showed how the numeral 'three', as a nominal quantifier, may occur, in different languages, in a variety of different constructions, exhibiting continuous and discontinuous quantification of various kinds. Even if attention is restricted to the most well-known type, that of continuous NP-internal quantification, as in (2), a great amount of cross-linguistic variation may be observed. In particular, in different languages, nominal quantifiers in attributive NP-internal position may resemble, to various degrees, nouns, adjectives, and/or verbs.

The grammatical patterning of quantifiers in attributive position may be illustrated by a comparison of attributive constructions involving a typical quantifier, the numeral 'three', with attributive constructions containing prototypical nominal, adjectival and verbal modifiers, involving, respectively, a possessor, e.g. 'John's', a colour term, e.g. 'red', and an event term, e.g. 'that John bought'. Such a comparison, for fourteen different languages, is presented in examples (7)–(20) below. For each language, the numeral-noun construction is provided; next, in those cases where one or more of the other attributive constructions are formally identical to the numeral-noun construction, they too are given. (To conserve space, attributive constructions that are not formally identical to the numeral-noun construction are not shown.)

(7) English
Three apples

(8) Russian
tri   jabloka
three apple.GEN.SG
'three apples'

(9) Yukaghir (Elena Maslova, p.c.)
jan   oqill'aa
three.LNK perch
'three perch'

(10) Balinese
salak (a)tetelu
salak (3.)ASSOC.three
'three salak'

(11) Mandarin Chinese
sān ge píngguǒ
three CLF apple
'three apples'

(12) Vietnamese
ba   quä táo
three CLF apple
'three apples'

(13) Modern Hebrew
šloša tapuħim
three.M apple.PL.M
'three apples'

(14) White Hmong (Martha Ratliff, p.c.)
(a) *peb lub txiv duaj*
three CLF fruit peach
'three peaches'
(b) *Txoov lub txiv duaj*
Dzong CLF fruit peach
'Dzong's peach'

(15) Hungarian
(a) *három alma*
three   apple
'three apples'
(b) *piros alma*
red   apple
'red apple'

(16) Singlish
  (a) three   apple
  (b) John   apple
  (c) red   apple

(17) Tagalog
  (a) *tatlong mangga*
      three.LIG mango
      'three mangoes'
  (b) *pulang mangga*
      red.LIG mango
      'red mango'
      pula na mangga
      red LIG mango
      'red mango'
  (c) *binili   ni   Jojong*
      PAT.TOP.PFV.buy PERS.DIR Jojo.LIG
      mangga
      mango
      'mango that Jojo bought'
      binili   ni   Jojo na
      ⟨PAT.TOP.PFV⟩buy PERS.DIR Jojo LIG
      mangga
      mango
      'mango that Jojo bought'

(18) Volga Tatar
  (a) *öš   alma*
      three   apple
      'three apples'
      öš   danœ alma
      three   CLF   apple
      'three apples'
  (b) *kəzəl alma*
      red   apple
      'red apple'
  (c) *tahir algan   alma*
      Tahir   buy.PRTC apple
      'apple that Tahir bought'

(19) Cantonese Chinese
  (a) *saam⁵⁵   go³³ piŋ¹¹-guo³⁵*
      three   CLF   apple
      'three apples'
  (b) *a³³-faay⁵⁵   go³³ piŋ¹¹-guo³⁵*
      Ah Fai   CLF   apple
      'Ah Fai's apple'
  (c) *ʔhooŋ²² go³³ piŋ¹¹-guo³⁵*
      red   CLF   apple
      'red apple'
  (d) *a³³-faay⁵⁵ maai¹³ go³³ piŋ¹¹-guo³⁵*
      Ah Fay   buy   CLF   apple
      'apple that Ah Fai bought'

(20) Hokkien Chinese
  (a) *si²¹⁻⁵³ e²⁴⁻²² pʰeŋ²⁴⁻²²-ko⁵³*
      four   ASSOC   apple
      'four apples'
      si²¹⁻⁵³ liap⁴⁻²¹ pʰeŋ²⁴⁻²²-ko⁵³
      four   CLF   apple
      'four apples'
  (b) *a⁴⁴⁽⁻⁴⁴⁾-beŋ²⁴ e²⁴⁻²² pʰeŋ²⁴⁻²²-ko⁵³*
      Ah Beng   ASSOC   apple
      'Ah Beng's apple'
  (c) *aŋ²⁴ e²⁴⁻²² pʰeŋ²⁴⁻²²-ko⁵³*
      red   ASSOC   apple
      'red apple'
  (d) *a⁴⁴⁽⁻⁴⁴⁾-beŋ²⁴ bue⁵³ e²⁴⁻²²*
      Ah Beng   buy   ASSOC
      pʰeŋ²⁴⁻²²-ko⁵³
      apple
      'apple that Ah Beng bought'

The grammatical patterning of numeral-noun constructions evidenced in the above examples is summarized in Table 92.4.

In Table 92.4, columns represent grammatical constructions involving, from left to right, an attributive numeral followed by prototypical attributive nouns, adjectives and verbs; while rows represent languages. Within individual cells, letters *A* and *B* denote distinct numeral-noun constructions (*A'* denotes a morphophonemic variant of *A*); the letter *x* denotes any number of other grammatical constructions not associated with numerals; shadings indicate the degree to which other constructions resemble the numeral-noun construction.

In the first seven languages, the numeral-noun construction is formally distinct from each of the other three constructions. In English, the numeral-noun construction is the only one in which the attributive expression assigns grammatical number to the head noun; moreover, each of the other three constructions possesses its own characteristic morphosyntactic features setting it apart from the others. In Russian, the numeral-noun construction is the only one in which the attributive expression assigns genitive singular case to the head noun — this is true for the numerals 'two', 'three' and 'four'. In Yukaghir, the numeral-noun construction is the only one in which the attributive expression is marked with the linker *-n*. In Balinese, the numeral-noun construction is the only one in which the attributive expression undergoes initial CV-reduplication, and is optionally marked with the prefix *a-*. In Mandarin, the numeral-noun construction is the only one in which a classifier is present. In Vietnamese, the numeral-noun construction is the only one of the form *attributive − classifier − head*: in other constructions, either there is no classi-

Table 92.4: Grammatical properties of NP-internal numerals across languages

language	numeral	possessor	colour	event
English	A	x	x	x
Russian	A	x	x	x
Yukaghir	A	x	x	x
Balinese	A	x	x	x
Mandarin Chinese	A	x	x	x
Vietnamese	A	x	x	x
Modern Hebrew	A	x	x	x
White Hmong	A	A x	x	x
Hungarian	A	x	A	x
Singlish	A	A x	A x	x
Tagalog	A	x	AA' x	AA' x
Volga Tatar	AB	x	A	A x
Cantonese Chinese	A	A x	A x	A x
Hokkien Chinese	AB	A' x	A' x	A' x

fier, or, if there is, the order of the three elements is different and/or additional grammatical markers are present. And in Modern Hebrew, the numeral-noun construction is the only one in which the attributive expression precedes the head noun.

Thus, in all of these languages, the numeral-noun construction is formally distinct from noun-noun, adjective-noun and verb-noun constructions. These examples accordingly illustrate the distinctive nature of the morphology and syntax of quantification. Note, however, that in each of these seven languages, the numeral-noun construction is, in addition, formally distinct from that in each of the remaining six languages (except for Mandarin and Vietnamese, which share the same *numeral − classifier − noun* construction). This variety underscores the heterogeneous nature of the morphology and syntax of quantification.

In the second set of seven languages, a somewhat different picture presents itself: here, the numeral-noun construction is formally identical to at least one of the other three constructions under consideration. In White Hmong, numerals must occur in construction with a classifier, and possessors may also occur with a classifier in the same construction; however, possessors may also occur without a classifier, and colour and event terms may only occur without a classifier. In Hungarian, numerals and colour terms both occur in bare construction with the noun; whereas possessors and event terms require additional overt construction markers. In Singlish (also known as Colloquial Singapore English), numerals may only occur in bare construction with the noun, while possessors and colour terms may also occur in the same bare construction; however, possessors and colour terms may also occur in constructions requiring additional overt markers, and event terms may only occur in other overtly marked constructions. In Tagalog, numerals occur only in a construction of the form *attributive − ligature − head*; while colour and event terms may also occur in the same construction; however, for colour and event terms an alternative *head − ligature − attributive* order is also possible, while for possessors a different grammatical marker is employed. (A further minor difference between numerals, on the one hand, and colour and event terms, on the other, pertains to a morphophonemic rule changing the form of the ligature from *na* to *-ng* if the preceding word ends in a vowel: this rule is obligatory for numerals but optional for colour and event terms.) In Volga Tatar, numerals may occur either in bare construction with the noun, a construction shared also by colour and event terms, or with a classifier, a construction which is unique to numerals; however, possessors occur only in a construction involving a different grammatical marker. In Cantonese, numerals, possessors, colour terms and event terms may all occur in a construction of the form *attributive − classifier − head* (though this construction is disfavoured for colour terms); however, for possessors, colour terms and event terms, a variety of other construction types are also available. Finally, in Hokkien, numerals, possessors, colour terms and event terms may all occur in a construction of the form *attributive − e^{24}-head*; however, numerals alone may also occur in a construction involving a classifier, while various more complex constructions are available for possessors, colour terms and event terms. (Again, a further minor difference between numerals and other attributive expressions in the *attributive − e^{24}-head* construction pertains to patterns of tone sandhi, indicated in (20) with the symbol '>': while a numeral preceding the marker e^{24} is subject to tone sandhi, other attributive expressions preceding e^{24} do not undergo tone sandhi.)

Thus, in each of the latter seven languages, the numeral-noun construction is formally identical, or nearly identical, to one or more of the other attributive-noun constructions. This formal coalescence is at its greatest in the two Chinese languages, Cantonese and Hokkien, where the same grammatical markers may be used for numerals, possessors, colour terms, and event terms, when occurring in attributive position. These patterns of macrofunctionality suggest that in the languages in question, numerals, or quantifiers in general, do not constitute a grammatical category to the exclusion of various other, non-quantificational expressions. Again, though, the specific patterns differ greatly from language to language, thereby highlighting once more the non-unitary nature of the morphosyntax of quantification, and the absence of a coherent cross-linguistically consistent grammatical category of quantifier.

In summary, then, each of the fourteen NP-internal attributive numerals in (7)−(20) exhibits a different array of morphological and syntactic properties − thereby belying the common but facile characterization of such quantifiers as 'determiners'.

3.4. Scope and distributivity

When two quantified expressions are present in the same construction, a variety of semantic relations may obtain between the two expressions (Jackendoff 1972, Gil 1982b, Aoun and Li 1993). The English sentence in (21), containing two numerically quantified NPs, may, at least potentially, be interpreted in any or all of the four ways indicated below:

(21)   English
       Three boys saw two girls
  (a) 'Each of three boys saw each of two girls'
       not scope differentiated:
       strong symmetric
  (b) 'Three boys saw two girls between them'
       not scope differentiated:
       weak symmetric
  (c) 'Three boys saw two girls each'
       scope differentiated:
       wide scope for *three boys*
       distributive key: *three boys*;
       distributive share: *two girls*
  (d) 'Two girls were seen by three boys each'
       scope differentiated:
       wide scope for *two girls*
       distributive key: *two girls*;
       distributive share: *three boys*

Interpretations (21a) and (21b) both involve a single set of three boys and a single set of two girls: each of the two NPs has independent reference. These interpretations are accordingly characterized as **non-scope-differentiated**, or **symmetric**. Interpretations (21c) and (21d) present a more complex picture. In (21c) there is a single set of three boys; however, each of the three boys is associated with a different set of two girls. Thus, while the subject NP has independent reference, the direct-object NP is referentially dependent on the subject NP. In this interpretation, then, the subject NP has *scope* over the direct-object NP. More precisely, the two NPs are in a relationship of **distributivity**, with the subject NP as **distributive key**, and the direct-object NP as **distributive share**. In (21d), a mirror-image situation obtains. Here, there is a single set of two girls; however, each of the two girls is associated with a different set of three boys. Accordingly, while the direct-object NP has independent reference, the subject NP is referentially dependent on the direct-object NP; the direct-object NP has scope over the subject NP. Here too then, a relation of distributivity obtains; this time, though, it is the direct object NP which is the distributive key and the subject NP which is the distributive share.

The above four interpretations are not equally readily available for speakers of English. Specifically, the symmetric interpretations (21a) and (21b) are more easily available than the asymmetric interpretations (21c) and (21d). Moreover, between the latter two interpretations, (21c) with wide scope for the subject NP, is more readily available than (21d) with wide scope for the direct-object NP. These preferences are not accidental; rather, they are particular consequences of more general principles governing the assignment of quantifier scope across languages.

In general, NPs that are syntactically, semantically and/or pragmatically prominent tend to have wider scope than NPs that are less prominent. In many languages, such prominence is translated into a grammatical relations hierarchy, with subjects at the top, and direct objects at the bottom of the hierarchy. It is this hierarchy which, in English, accounts for the preference for interpretation (21c), with wide scope for the subject NP, over (21d), with wide scope for the direct object NP. However, in languages with different clause structures, different hierarchies may underlie quantifier scope preferences. Consider the closest equivalent of sentence (21) in Tagalog:

(22) Tagalog
Nakakita   ng dalawang babae
ACT.TOP.PFV.see DIR TWO.LIG girl
ang tatlong lalaki
TOP three.LIG boy
'Three boys saw two girls.'

In the above sentence, there is an opposite (albeit weak) preference for interpretation (21d) over (21c). In Tagalog, it has been suggested by several scholars that the traditional grammatical relations of subject and direct object are not viable. Unsurprisingly, then, in Tagalog quantifier scope appears to be governed by a different, thematic role hierarchy, with patients tending to have wider scope than actors, regardless of their grammatical function in the clause.

A second, more general principle governing the assignment of quantifier scope is that symmetric/non-scope-differentiated interpretations are preferred over their asymmetric/scope differentiated counterparts. It is this general principle which accounts for the preference of interpretations (21a) and (21b) over (21c) and (21d) for sentence (21) in English. In fact, in many other languages, this principle applies with even greater force. Consider the closest equivalent of sentence (21) in Bengali:

(23) Bengali
tinṭi   čʰēlē   duṭi   mēyēkē
three.CLF boy.NOM two.CLF girl.ACC
dēkʰēčʰil
see.PFV
'Three boys saw two girls.'

In (23), only the symmetric interpretations, those in (21a) and (21b), are available; the asymmetric interpretations indicated in (21c) and (21d) are not just dispreferred but completely unavailable.

It should be noted that in order to appreciate the extent to which symmetric interpretations are preferred over their asymmetric counterparts, it is necessary to examine sentences containing numerical or other midrange quantifiers. If, instead, existential or universal quantifiers are chosen, then the distinction between symmetric and asymmetric interpretations collapses, partially or completely. For example, in many languages, a sentence such as *All the boys saw a girl* may be understood as involving a single unique girl. In principle, such an interpretation may be analyzed either as a symmetric interpretation in which both NPs independently refer, or as an asymmetric interpretation with wide scope for the NP *a girl*. Unfortunately, in much current work in formal syntax and semantics, it is the latter analysis that is unquestioningly chosen, even though, in the absence of evidence to the contrary, the former analysis is more consistent with the general preference for symmetric interpretations over their asymmetric counterparts.

Given the general preference for symmetric interpretations, languages generally have at their disposal various lexical and morphosyntactic devices whose function is to induce the more marked asymmetric interpretations, when these are required (Ioup 1975, Choe 1987, Gil 1992, Evans 1995). Consider the following English sentences:

(24) English
(a) *All* the boys carried three suitcases
(b) *Every* boy carried three suitcases

Sentences (24a) and (24b) differ in the lexical choice of quantifier within the subject NP. Whereas in (24a), with *all*, a variety of scope relationships may obtain between the two NPs, and the number of suitcases may vary between three in total and three per boy, in (24b), with *every*, the subject NP has scope over the direct object NP, and the suitcases number three per boy. Whereas *all*, like *three*, is a simple quantifier, *every* is a **scopal quantifier**, that is to say, a quantifier endowed with an additional denotational component, one that forces a particular scope relationship to obtain between the NP in which it occurs, and some other expression. In particular, it is a **distributive-key quantifier**, inducing a relationship of distributivity, in which the NP containing the quantifier in question is the distributive key, or element with wide scope.

Many languages, like English, have distinct lexical items for simple and distributive-key universal quantifiers, for example Turkish *bütün* 'all' vs. *her* 'every'. Tagalog *lahat* 'all' vs. *bawat* 'every' (Gil 1995, Haspelmath 1995). However, evidence from other languages suggests that of these two kinds of quantifiers, the distributive key universal quantifiers are more highly marked than their simple counterparts. Thus, in some languages, distributive-key universal quantifiers are derived from their simple counterparts via morphological processes. For example, in Georgian, *q'oveli* 'every' is derived from *q'vela* 'all' by intercolation of vowel *-o-*; and in Lakhota, *iyohila* 'every', is derived from *iyuha* 'all' by suffixation of *-la* (Leonard Faltz, p.c.). However, in no languages are simple universal quantifiers derived from distributive key ones via opposite morphological processes. Also, in some languages, there are simple universal quantifiers but no distributive-key ones, for example White Hmong *txhua* 'all' (Martha Ratliff, p.c.): Yukaghir *jawnom* 'all' (Elena Maslova, p.c.). But in no languages are there distributive key universal quantifiers but no simple ones.

A different kind of scopal quantifier is exemplified by the following pair of Turkish sentences:

(25) Turkish
(a) *Çocuklar üç bavul taşıdı*
child.PL three suitcase carry.PFV.3.SG
'The children carried three suitcases'
(b) *Çocuklar üçer bavul taşıdı*
child.PL three.DIST.SHARE suitcase carry.PFV.3.SG
(i) 'The children carried three suitcases each'
(ii) 'The children carried the suitcases three by three'

Sentences (25a) and (25b) differ only in the form of the numeral within the direct-object NP. Sentence (25a) contains a simple numeral, *üç* 'three', and is ambiguous in roughly the same ways as its English gloss. In contrast, sentence (25b) contains the same numeral plus the suffix *-er*, whose effect is to mark the numeral *üçer* and the NP containing it as **distributive share**. The ambiguity exhibited by sentence (25b) results from different expressions being selected as the distributive key counterpart. Under interpretation (25b/i), the subject NP *çocuklar* 'children' is chosen as distributive key: the suitcases accordingly number three per child. Under interpretation (25b/ii), the verb *taşıdı* 'carried' is chosen as distributive key: here the suitcases accordingly number three per carrying.

Cross-linguistically, distributive-share numerals are formed by a variety of formal processes (Gil 1982a, Choe 1987, Link 1991). As in the above Turkish example, they are often formed by affixation, for example Tagalog *tigtatlo* from *tatlo* 'three', Maricopa *xmokxper-* from *xmok-* 'three'. In many other cases, with iconic motivation, they are formed by reduplication, for example Gã *etẽẽtẽ* from *etẽ* 'three', Bengali *tin-tin* from *tin* 'three'. In yet other cases they are formed by periphrasis, for example Rumanian *cîte trei* from *trei* 'three', Russian *po tri* from *tri* 'three'. And occasionally they are formed by suppletion, as in Latin *terni* from *tres* 'three', Malayalam *ooŕoo* from *oŕu* 'one'.

Distributive-share numerals are of two main varieties: NP-internal, as in the above Turkish example, and adverbial. NP-internal distributive-share numerals are widespread but not universal: many languages, including English, Modern Hebrew and Vietnamese, are lacking in such forms. In contrast, adverbial distributive-share numerals are present in most or all languages; English 'three by three', occurring in one of the glosses to (25b) above, is an example of such a form. In languages with both adverbial and NP-internal distributive-share numerals, the two types may be of identical form, as for example in Japanese and Riau Indonesian, or they may be different. For example, in Turkish, adverbial distributive-share numerals are formed from their NP-internal counterparts by reduplication, eg. *üçer üçer* from *üçer*.

Cross-linguistically, NP-internal distributive-share numerals generally give rise to ambiguities similar to those exemplified above for Turkish. In contrast, adverbial distributive-share numerals tend to permit a more limited range of interpretations; typically selecting a verb or VP as distributive key, while not allowing an NP as distributive key. Thus, for example, in English, *three by three* can select a VP but not an NP as distributive-key — this is why a sentence containing *three by three* is appropriate as a gloss for exactly one of the two possible interpretations of Turkish sentence (25b) above.

In conjunction, sentences (24) and (25) exemplify the two most common types of scopal quantifiers, and in doing so underscore an important asymmetry between the two. Distributive-key quantifiers are generally universal, as is English *every* and its counterparts in other languages: distributive-key quantifiers that are not universal are either rare or non-existent. In contrast, distributive-share quantifiers are most commonly numeral; other distributive-share quantifiers are much less common. More specifically, if a language possesses non-numeral distributive-share quantifiers then it also possesses numeral distributive-share quantifiers, but not vice versa. Accordingly, in some languages all distributive-share quantifiers are numerals, for example English, with *three by three* from *three* but no *many by many from *many*, and Turkish, with *üçer* from *üc* 'three' but no *çokar from *çok* 'many'; while in other languages there are distributive-share numerals alongside other distributive-share quantifiers, for example Maricopa, with *xmokxper-* from *xmok-* 'three' and also *pal^{y}xper-*, from *pal^y-* 'many', and Georgian, with *sam-sami* from *sami* 'three' and also *bevr-bevri* from *bevri* 'many' (Gil 1988).

4. Delimitation of quantification

The discussion in the preceding sections was based on a bipartite definition of quantifiers as 'free-standing expressions' whose meanings 'involve the notion of quantity'. Like many similar definitions, this one is useful, but not unproblematical. Specifically, in addition to prototypical quantifiers such as those discussed above, there are numerous expressions and construction types for which it is difficult to adjudicate whether or not they may appropriately be characterized as quantificational.

4.1. Formal delimitation

The first part of the definition is formal: in order for an expression to be considered as a quantifier, it must be free standing — a word or a phrase, rather than an affix or some other bound morphological unit. Accordingly, various kinds of clitics, particles, and other intermediate units smaller than words but larger than affixes may provide borderline cases straddling the boundary between what is a quantifier and what is not.

For example, whereas English *all* is clearly an independent word and hence a quantifier, the Ngizim form *-naa*, with similar meaning, is clearly a suffix, attaching to verbs, such as *masənaa* 'buy.all' (Russ Schuh, p. c.). Consider, however, the English particle *up*, as in *buy up*. While its meaning clearly involves the notion of quantity, in terms of its form it exhibits some properties of an independent word but other properties of a bound form. Thus, its characterization as a quantifier is somewhat indeterminate.

The distinction between free and bound forms is what underlies the distinction between quantification and the semantically-related grammatical category of *number*. Specifically, whereas quantifiers are free standing, number markers are bound forms. Thus, for example, in the Malay/Indonesian *dua istana* 'two palace' for 'two palaces', *dua* 'two' is free standing and hence a quantifier, specifically a numeral; whereas in the Upper Sorbian *hrodaj* 'palace.DU', *-aj* 'DU' is a suffix and therefore a number marker, namely a dual (Stone 1993). Similarly, in an expression such as the English *three cats, three* is an independent word, and hence a quantifier, while *-s* is a suffix, and therefore a number marker.

However, in some instances it may be difficult to adjucate whether a form associated with a quantificational meaning is free or bound, and hence whether it constitutes an instance of quantification or of number. One typical case is provided by markers of plurality, as for example Tagalog *mga* 'PL', written as a separate word, but with phonological properties of a proclitic. Another common case is that of numerals which form compounds with the expressions that they quantify, for example Abkhaz *x-* 'three' as in *xaç°ak'* 'three.apple.INDEF' or 'three apples', and Yinhawangka *-kutharra* 'two' as in *ngunhakutharra* 'that.two' or 'that two' (Alan Dench, p. c.).

In order to determine whether forms such as these are quantifiers or number markers, it may be necessary to make use of additional diagnostic criteria distinguishing quantifiers from number markers. These might include the following: (a) paradigmatic variety: languages usually have many quantifiers, but at most a very few distinct categories of number − often just singular and plural; (b) productivity: quantifiers tend to combine regularly with their quantified expressions, whereas number markers often exhibit idiosyncratic behavior, e. g. English *goats* vs. **sheeps*; (c) agreement: quantifiers rarely occur in repetitive redundant constructions, but number markers do so commonly, in patterns of number agreement, e. g. Modern Hebrew *tapuḣim yerukim* 'apple.PL.M green.PL.M' for 'green apples'; and (d) government: when quantifiers and number markers cooccur, this is typically the result of a process of government, whereby a particular quantifier assigns a specific number to the quantified nouns, as in the English *three cats*, where the quantifier *three* assigns plural number marking *-s* to the noun *cat*.

4.2. Semantic delimitation

The second part of the definition of quantifier is the obvious semantic condition: its meaning must involve the notion of quantity. While in many instances this is quite straightforward, in other cases, quantificational meanings may shade off gradually into other kinds of meanings not generally considered to be quantificational.

One class of expressions related in meaning to nominal quantifiers are those denoting size and other scalar properties. In English, pairs of adjectives such as *big/small, long/short, heavy/light* parallel pairs of quantifiers such as *many/a few, much/little*; thus, *a big house*, with size adjective *big*, is one which occupies *much space*, with quantifier *much*. Occasionally, indeed, quantifiers are formed from the corresponding size expressions. For example, in English, *a little* is formed from size adjective *little*; similarly, Minangkabau *saketek* 'a little' from 'one.little', and Lao *nɔ́y naŋ* 'a little' from 'little one'. And, at the other end of the scale, Quebec French *gros gros* 'a lot' from *gros* 'big' (Pierre Larrivee, p. c.), and Aradhin Christian Aramaic *ra:ba* 'very much' and 'big' (Bob Hoberman, p. c.). However, for the most part, languages keep the expression of quantification formally distinct from that of other scalar properties: even when the forms are similar, the constructions into which they enter are often different. Thus, in English, constituency distinguishes the quantificational structure *[a little] cake* from the size adjective expression *a [little cake]*.

Corresponding to the relationship between nominal quantifiers and scalar properties is that between verbal quantifiers and aspect. In English, the construction exemplified by *cried and cried* or *hit him and hit him* may be characterized as aspectual, involving categories such as durative or iterative; however, it may also be considered to be quantificational − as suggested by the possible paraphrases: *cried for a lot of time*, with quantifier *a lot*, or *hit him many times*, with quantifier *many*. In many languages, identical or similar forms often appear to function both as quantifiers and as aspect markers. Several examples can be adduced from colloquial dialects of Malay/Indonesian. In Riau Indonesian, the form *habis* 'finish' (see § 2.2) may function as a universal quantifier, in constructions such as *makan habis* 'eat up' or 'eat all'; however, the same form, in a different order, may also function as a marker of perfective aspect, for example *habis makan* 'finish eating' or 'have eaten'. In Jakarta Indonesian, the form *lagi* has a range of quantificational meanings, including 'more', as in *makan lagi* 'eat more'; however, in a different order, it is interpreted as a marker of progressive aspect, as in *lagi makan* 'is eating'. And in Kuala Lumpur Malay, the form *tengah* 'middle' forms the basis for the quantificational expression *setengah* 'one.middle' or 'a half', as in *makan setengah* 'eat half'; but again, in a different order, it is understood as a marker of progressive aspect, as in *tengah makan* 'is eating'. Examples such as these underscore the affinity between quantification and aspect; however, at the same time, the different word orders suggest that these two categories need to be kept distinct.

More generally, different quantifiers in different languages may be related to an extremely broad range of non-quantificational concepts, synchronically and/or diachronically (Evans 1995, Haspelmath 1995). Consider, for example, the Modern Hebrew universal quantifier *kol* 'all'. Synchronically it is clearly monomorphemic; however, in its diachronic origins, it reflects an ancient biconsonantal root morpheme *k-l*. Such roots form the basis of much of the Afroasiatic lexicon; however, in the Semitic family, the biconsonantal roots are often expanded into tri-consonantal ones, by the addition of a third root consonant. Resulting from this historical process, and also from the synchronic processes of word formation in Modern Hebrew, is a large family of words, all containing reflexes of the original root morpheme *k-l*, and all connected via a semantic network based on the related concepts of ability, containment, consumption, exhaustiveness, and the like. Some members of this family include verbal forms such as *yaxal* 'be able to' (from root *y-k-l*); *axal* 'eat', *ikel* 'consume' (*ʔ-k-l*); *ʕikel* 'digest' (*ʕ-k-l*); *kala* 'end', 'cease to exist'; *kila* 'finish', 'exterminate' (*k-l-y*); *kala* 'imprison' (*k-l-ʔ*); *kal* 'measure', *hexil* 'contain' (*k-w-l*); *kiyel* 'calibrate' (*k-y-l*); *kalal* 'include', *hixlil* 'generalize', *šixlel* 'improve' (*k-l-l*); and *kilkel* 'support', 'provide for' (*k-l-k-l*); and also related nominal forms such as *oxel* 'food'; *kli* 'utensil'; *kila* 'bed curtain'; *meyxal* 'container'; *heyxal* 'palace'; *mixlala* 'college'; *makolet* 'grocery store'; *kele* 'jail'; *klal* 'rule'; *kilayon* 'extermination'; *yexolet* 'ability'; *kalkala* 'economy' and many others. (Note that in many of the above examples, *k* is reflected by its allophone *x*.) Although many of these concepts, such as 'eat' and 'food', are by no stretch of the imagination quantificational, others, such as those meaning 'finish' or 'extermination', bear a closer relationship to quantification, thereby suggesting possible paths of grammaticalization along which a non-quantificational expression might develop, over time, into a quantificational one.

A somewhat different problem facing the delimitation of the notion of quantification is posed by various portmanteau expressions, in which a single morpheme or word combines two denotational components, one quantificational, the other not. For example, English forms such as *triplet, trio, trinity, triptych* and *triangle* all combine one meaning component shared by the numeral 'three' with another, more idiosyncratic, non-quantificational denotational component. Similar but more systematic examples are provided by various alternative non-cardinal numeral series, such as **ordinals**, e. g. English *third, fourth, fifth*, etc.; **collectives**, e. g. English *threesome, foursome, fivesome*, etc.; and others. In 'numeral classifier' languages, the numeral-plus-classifier constituent, e. g. Mandarin *sān zhī, sān duǒ* (§ 2.1), constitutes a portmanteau expression combining reference to a number with reference to a property of the quantified expression. In many other languages, a numeral may combine with a variety of markers expressing categories such as voice, tense, aspect and the like; for example, in Modern Hebrew, *šilašti* combines the numeral root *š-l-š* 'three' with the derivationial morphology of a transitive verbal *binyan* plus inflections for past tense and first person singular, to mean 'I tripled'; similarly, in Tagalog, the form *pakipagtatluhin* combines the numeral *tatlo* 'three' with markers of politeness *paki-*, indirect action *pag-* and patient-topic imperative *-in*, resulting in an expression meaning 'Please let be three'. Indeed, the concepts that can be formally combined with numerals are extremely variegated. For example, in Kutenai, the form *qałsakxni* combines the numeral *qałsa* 'three' with the suffix *-kx* 'do with the mouth' and the indicative suffix *-ni* — resulting in a portmanteau expression meaning 'eat three' (Matthew Dryer, p. c.).

Yet another problem is presented by constructions in which a quantificational meaning emerges from the combination of a particular lexical item with a particular structural configuration. For example, English verbs such as *gather* and *assemble* impose a quantificational interpretation on one of their nominal arguments, namely that it be plural. (The argument in question is either the subject, if the verb is used intransitively, or the direct object, if it is used transitively.) An near-mirror image phenomenon occurs in NP-internal constructions in some dialects of Malay/Indonesian. In Malay and Indonesian, NPs consisting of bare nouns, such as *kucing* 'cat(s)', are unmarked for number, as are demonstratives such as *itu* 'that', 'those'. Not surprisingly, in Standard Malay and Indonesian, the collocation of a noun and a demonstrative is similarly unmarked for number: *kucing itu* can be understood either as singular 'that cat' or plural 'those cats'. However, in some dialects, including the mesolectal varieties of Kuala Lumpur and Singapore, NPs such as *kucing itu* can be understood only as singular, not as plural. (In order to say 'those cats', the noun would have to be overtly marked as plural, by means of reduplication: *kucing-kucing itu*.) In those dialects, then, the demonstrative form, although unmarked for number itself, imposes a singular interpretation on the noun that it modifies. Accordingly, this particular quantificational meaning arises out of a particular lexical item occurring in a particular syntactic environment.

5. Special abbreviations

ACT	actor
ASSOC	associative
CLF	classifier
CONSTR	construct state
DIR	direct case
LIG	ligature
LNK	linker
PAT	patient
PERS	personal

6. References

Aikhenvald, Alexandra Y. 2000. *Classifiers: A typology of noun categorization devices.* Oxford: Oxford University Press.

Allan, Keith. 1980. "Nouns and countability". *Language* 56: 541–567.

Aoun, Joseph & Yen-hui Audrey Li. 1993. *The syntax of scope*, Linguistic Inquiry Monograph 21. Cambridge: MIT Press.

Bach, Emmon, Eloise Jelinek, Angelika Kratzer, & Barbara H. Partee (eds.) 1995. *Quantification in natural languages.* Dordrecht: Kluwer Academic Publishers.

Barwise, Jonh & Cooper, Robin. 1981. "Generalized quantifiers and natural language". *Linguistics and Philosophy* 4: 159–219.

Bittner, Maria & Hale, Ken. 1995. "Remarks on definiteness in Warlpiri". In: E. Bach, E. Jelinek, A. Kratzer, and B. H. Partee (eds.) *Quantification in natural languages.* Dordrecht: Kluwer Academic Publishers, 81–105.

Brandt Corstius, Hugo (ed.) 1968. *Grammars for number names.* Dordrecht: Reidel.

Capell, Arthur. 1969. *A survey of New Guinea languages.* Sydney: Sydney University Press.

Choe, Jae-Woong. 1987. *Anti-quantifiers and a theory of distributivity.* PhD Dissertation, University of Massachusetts, Amherst.

Craig, Colette (ed.) 1986. *Noun classes and categorization*, Typological Studies in Language 7. Amsterdam: John Benjamins.

Downing, Pamela. 1996. *Numeral classifier systems: The case of Japanese,* Studies in Grammar and Discourse, Volume 4. Amsterdam: John Benjamins.

Evans, Nick. 1995. "A-quantifiers and scope in Mayali". In: E. Bach, E. Jelinek, A. Kratzer, & B.H. Partee (eds.), *Quantification in natural languages.* Dordrecht: Kluwer Academic Publishers, 207–270.

Gil, David. 1982a. *Distributive numerals.* PhD Dissertation, University of California, Los Angeles.

Gil, David. 1982b. "Quantifier scope, linguistic variation, and natural language semantics". *Linguistics and Philosophy* 5: 421–472.

Gil, David. 1987. "Definiteness, noun-phrase configurationality, and the count-mass distinction". In: E. J. Reuland & A. G. B. ter Meulen (eds.), *The representation of (in)definiteness.* Cambridge: MIT Press, 254–269.

Gil, David. 1988. "Georgian reduplication and the domain of distributivity". *Linguistics* 26: 1039–1065.

Gil, David. 1992. "Scopal quantifiers: Some universals of lexical effability". In: M. Kefer & J. van der Auwera (eds.), *Meaning and grammar, Cross-linguistic perspectives.* Berlin: Mouton de Gruyter, 303–345.

Gil, David. 1993. "Nominal and verbal quantification". *Sprachtypologie und Universalienforschung* 46: 275–317.

Gil, David. 1994. "Conjunctive operators: A unified semantic analysis". In: P. Bosch & R. van der Sandt (eds.), *Focus and Natural Language Processing,* Volume 2, Semantics, Proceedings of a Conference in Celebration of the 10th Anniversary of the Journal of Semantics, 12th–15th June, 1994, Hotel Schloß Wolfsbrunnen, Meinhard-Schwebda, Germany, Working Papers of the Institute for Logic and Linguistics, Working Paper 7, ISSN 0946-7521, IBM TR-80.94-007, 311–322.

Gil, David. 1995. "Universal quantifiers and distributivity". In: E. Bach, E. Jelinek, A. Kratzer, & B. H. Partee (eds.), *Quantification in natural languages.* Dordrecht: Kluwer Academic Publishers, 321–362.

Gil, David. 1996. "Maltese 'collective nouns': A typological perspective". *Rivista di Linguistica* 8: 53–87.

Givón, Talmy. 1981. "On the development of the numeral 'one' as an indefinite marker". *Folia Linguistica Historica* 2: 35–53.

Greenberg, Joseph H. 1978. "Generalizations about numeral systems". In: J. H. Greenberg (ed.), *Universals of human language, Volume 3, Word structure.* Stanford: Stanford University Press, 249–295.

Haspelmath, Martin. 1995. "Diachronic sources of 'all' and 'every'". In: E. Bach, E. Jelinek, A. Kratzer, & B. H. Partee (eds.) *Quantification in natural languages.* Dordrecht: Kluwer Academic Publishers, 363–382.

Haspelmath, Martin. 1997. *Indefinite pronouns.* Oxford: Oxford University Press.

Heim, Irene. 1982. *The semantics of definite and In:definite noun phrases.* PhD Dissertation, University of Massachusetts, Amherst.

Higginbotham, James. 1995. "Mass and count quantifiers". In: E. Bach, E. Jelinek, A. Kratzer, & B. H. Partee (eds.) *Quantification in natural languages.* Dordrecht: Kluwer Academic Publishers, 383–419.

Hoop, Helen de. 1995. "On the characterization of the weak-strong distinction". In: E. Bach, E. Jelinek, A. Kratzer, & B. H. Partee (eds.) *Quantification in natural languages.* Dordrecht: Kluwer Academic Publishers, 421–450.

Hurford, James R. 1975. *The linguistic study of numerals.* Cambridge: Cambridge University Press.

Ioup, Georgette. 1975. "Some universals of quantifier scope". In: J. Kimball (ed.), Syntax and Semantics 4. Bloomington: Indiana University Press, 37–58.

Jackendoff, Ray S. 1972. *Semantic interpretation in generative grammar.* Cambridge: MIT Press.

Keenan, Edward L. & Stavi, Jonathan. 1986. "A semantic characterization of natural language determiners". *Linguistic and Philosophy* 9: 253–326.

König, Ekkehard. 1991. *The meaning of focus particles, A comparative perspective.* London and New York: Routledge.

Langacker, Ronald W. 1987. "Nouns and verbs". *Language* 63: 53–94.

Lewis, David. 1975. "Adverbs of quantification". In: E. Keenan (ed.), *Formal semantics of natural language.* Cambridge: Cambridge University Press, 3–15.

Link, Godehard. 1991. "Quantity and number". In: D. Zaefferer (ed.), *Semantic universals and universal semantics.* Berlin: Foris Press, 133–149.

McElhanon, K. A. 1972. *Selepet grammar, Part I, From root to phrase,* Pacific Linguistics, Series B – No. 21. Canberra: The Australian National University.

Menninger, Karl. 1969. *Number words and number symbols*, translated from German by Paul Broneer. Cambridge: MIT Press.

Milsark, G. 1977. "Toward an explanation of certain peculiarities in the existential construction in English". *Linguistic Analysis* 3: 1–30.

Pelletier, Francis Jeffry (ed.) 1979. *Mass terms: Some philosophical problems.* Dordrecht: Synthese Language Library, Reidel.

Plank, Frans. 1992. "Possessives and the distinction between determiners and modifiers". *Journal of Linguistics* 28, 453–468.

Quine, Willard van Orman. 1969. "Ontological relativity". In: *Ontological Relativity and Other Essays.* New York: Columbia University Press, 26–68.

Rischel, Jørgen. 1995. *Minor Mlabri, A hunter-gatherer language of Northern Indochina.* Copenhagen: Museum Tusculanum Press.

Swift, L. B., A. Ahaghotu & E. Ugorji. 1962. *Igbo Basic Course.* Washington: Foreign Service Institute. Department of State.

Stein, Mark J. 1981. *Quantification in Thai.* PhD Dissertation. Amherst: University of Massachusetts.

Stone, Gerald. 1993. "Sorbian (Upper and Lower)". in B. Comrie & G. G. Corbett (eds.), The Slavonic Languages. London: Routledge, 593–685.

Thompson, Laurence C. 1965. *A Vietnamese Grammar.* Seattle: University of Washington Press.

Vendler, Z. 1967. *Linguistics and Philosophy.* Ithica: Cornell University Press.

David Gil, Max-Planck-Institut für evolutionäre Anthropologie, Leipzig (Germany)

93. Verbs of perception

1. The general structure of the field
2. Lexical typological markedness and the sense-modality hierarchy
3. Realizations of the sense-modality hierarchy
4. Languages with restricted sets of simple verbs
5. The place of perception verbs in lexicon and grammar
6. How explain the sense-modality hierarchy?
7. Conclusion
8. References

1. The general structure of the semantic field

The primary function of perception in humans is to recognize and identify objects and events and their spatial and temporal arrangements and to provide the environmental input for the construction of a model or cognitive representation of the external world. Most of the complex sets of neural recodings at various levels that take place after light, sound or other stimuli strike a receptor and finally contribute to our experience of the external world proceed at levels below consciousness. Objects and events are often experienced as if they could be accessed directly without the mediation of the senses. In a language such as English, situations can be reported linguistically without indicating the perceptual sources of the information: *A bull came running from behind the bushes at the other side of the field* or *An ant is creeping up my leg.* The prototypical function of verbs of perception such as *see*, *hear* and *feel* is to indicate the sense modality and the experiencer which is the source of the information. *Charlie could hear a bull coming* or *I can feel an ant creeping up my leg*.

Verbs of perception form a restricted part of several broader systems of linguistic expressions both of information sources (e. g. verbs of Verbal communication and verbs of Cognition) and of expressions connected to specific sense modalities (e. g. adjectives describing qualities of color, taste, etc.). In spite of this, it is interesting to single out the verbs of perception for a general typological study, since they form a relatively clearly structured lexical semantic field in which it is possible to identify a small set of 15 basic meanings (set out in Table 93.1) which represent the basic structure of the field in a satisfactory way even if all such demarcations entail a certain degree of arbitrariness. (Apart from terminological differences, the analysis is in accordance with Rogers 1971, 1972, 1974. It is further motivated in Viberg 1984. Cf. more recently, Heid coord. 1996.)

As verbs in general, the verbs belonging to the field of perception can be described semantically with respect to one set of field-specific components and to a number of general field-independent components shared by several or all verbal semantic fields.

The *sense modalities* represent the primary field-dependent semantic parameter. The following analysis will deal with the five modalities sight, hearing, touch, taste and smell, which are our primary sources for direct information about the external environment. Even if it is possible to use physical perception verbs to report (relatively) pure sensations (*I can see a light, I heard a noise*), these verbs usually refer to much more complex phenomena which require a great amount of cognitive interpretation. The phenomena that are identified range from physical events

Table 93.1. The verbs of perception

	EXPERIENCER-BASED		PHENOMENON-BASED
	ACTIVITY	EXPERIENCE	
S I G H T	Peter was looking/looked at the birds.	Peter saw the birds.	Peter looked happy.
H E A R	Peter was listening/listened to the radio.	Peter heard the radio.	Peter sounded sad.
T O U C H	Peter felt the cloth /to see how soft it was/	Peter felt a stone under his foot.	The cloth felt soft.
T A S T E	Peter tasted the food /to see if he could eat it/	Peter tasted garlic in the soup.	The soup tasted good/bad/of garlic.
S M E L L	Peter smelled the food /to see if he could eat it/	Peter smelled garlic in the soup.	The soup smelled good/bad/of garlic.

(*Peter heard the tree fall*) to physical objects (*Peter saw a tooth-pick*) and substances (*Peter tasted honey in the warm milk*). In addition to perception verbs proper, ordinary language has words for Pain (*hurt, ache*) and Physiological conditions (of the body) such as hunger, thirst and alertness/fatigue. Pain can provide information about the environment but verbs like *ache* and *hurt* only report a localized sensation (*My finger hurts*).

Within psychology, the classification is partly different from ordinary language. In addition to sight and hearing, Schiffman (1994) recognizes the skin senses (touch and pressure, temperature, pain), the chemical senses (taste, smell) as well as the body senses (kinaesthesis concerned with the body's own limb movements and the vestibular sense resposible primarly for balance and the general orientation of the body). The body senses usually operate below consciousness. Ordinary language has terms only for malfunctions such as giddiness and motion sickness.

There are also two sets of contrasts serving to distinguish verbs of perception which cut across all the semantic fields of verbs and thus represent field-independent semantic dimensions. One has to do with the selection of subject or topic and accounts for contrasts such as *Peter looked at me* vs. *Peter looked happy to me*. The other one has to do with the dynamic system and accounts for contrasts such as *Peter looked at me* vs. *Peter saw me*. *Subject/Topic-selection* refers to the choice of grammatical subject or topic among the semantic case roles associated with the verb. With respect to this system, perception verbs behave like mental verbs in general. Typically, one of the arguments of a mental verb is an Experiencer and very often, there are pairs of mental verbs, which contrast with respect to subject-selection (Viberg 1984; cf. flip-flop, psych-movement etc.). Experiencer-based verbs take as their subject the Experiencer, i.e. the individual who experiences a mental process. Phenomenon-based verbs take the Phenomenon that gives rise to the mental experience as subject.

Another system that cuts across all verbal semantic fields is **the dynamic system**, which covers lexical aspect (event structure), causativity and agentivity. (Only the characteristics relevant for the present analysis will be sketched.) Verbs can either designate a state (no change) or a change, for example *know* (State) – *realize* (Change) or *have, own* (State) – *get, lose* (Change). Changes can either be inchoatives, which means they are pure changes without any indication of the cause, or causatives, which indicate a cause. The verbs in the central column of Table 93.1 which are called Experiences and represent the most typical verbs of perception are states or inchoatives. Activity (the leftmost column) refers to a process which is non-resultative (unbounded): *The butler looked through the key hole but could not see anything*. A further difference is that activities are controlled (intentional), whereas experiences are uncontrolled. It would, for example, be rather impolite to say *Could you repeat that? I was not listening*, whereas *I didn't hear* would be a natural excuse, since *hear* refers to a situation that cannot be controlled. There are also test frames such as __ *in order to* and *persuade X to* __. It is possible to say *Bill persuaded Peter to listen* but not *Bill persuaded Peter to hear*. In terms of case grammar, activities have an Agent, which experiences do not. (The analysis allows double case roles, which explains why activities are said to have an Experiencer similar to experiences.)

From a functional point of view, both the experience and the activity are realized by clauses with non-prototypical transitivity. The subject of the experience is non-agentive (involuntary, out of control), whereas the activity describes a non-resultative event. Formally this is reflected in the case-marking system in many languages and/or in the use of an adposition in combination with the object of the activity (*Look at the bird* etc.).

In Axvax, an ergative North-West Caucasian language (Kibrik 1985), the Experiencer of 'see' is encoded in the dative and the Phenomenon in the nominative, whereas the Agent of 'look' is marked either with the ergative or the nominative and the Phenomenon with an oblique case:

(1) wašoLa jaše   harig$_o$ari
     boy.DAT girl.NOM   saw
     The boy saw the girl.

(2) ⎧ wašode ⎫   jašoga harig$_o$ari
     ⎪ boy.ERG ⎪   girl.OBL saw
     ⎨ waša   ⎬
     ⎩ boy.NOM ⎭
     The boy looked at the girl.

In these examples, 'look' and 'see' are realized as separate roots. In languages which do not have a lexical contrast between activity and experience in a certain sense modality, a case shift of this type may be the major overt marker of this contrast.

It is relatively common that languages mark the subject of mental verbs with another case than the one that is used with canonical physical actions. This is characteristic of Indo-Aryan and Dravidian languages of South Asia, in which the dative (or experiencer) subject often appears with mental verbs. It tends to appear instead of an ordinary subject primarily with verbs describing an uncontrolled mental process or a mental state, although the pattern is never completely regular but rather subjected to a certain randomness (see the studies in Verma & Mohanan, 1990, and the introduction to that volume).

2. Lexical typological markedness and the sense-modality hierarchy

There is great variation between languages with respect to the number of basic perception verbs that can be found. In spite of that, it can be shown that there are strong restrictions on the possible patterns of lexicalization. The restrictions can be captured in a lexicalization hierarchy similar to the hierarchies presented for colour terms (Berlin & Kay 1969, Hardin & Maffi 1997) and folk biological life-forms (Brown 1977, 1979).

In the following, it will be shown how the fifteen meanings illustrated in Table 93.1 are realized in various languages with particular focus on the extent to which the experiences are expressed in the various sense modalities. As a point of departure, I will use my own crosslinguistic study of perception verbs (Viberg 1984). The markedness hierarchy presented in that paper was based on data from approximately 50 languages. Apart from a number of complications, the hierarchy can be stated as in Table 93.2.

Table 93.2: The sense-modality hierarchy for perception verbs

SIGHT	> HEARING	>	TOUCH TASTE SMELL

The hierarchy is based on the markedness criteria originally presented in the classical study by Greenberg (1966). In a review of a number of studies in this tradition, Croft (1990) concludes that the criteria suggested for markedness can be reduced to three general categories: 1) Structural (number of morphemes to express the exponents), 2) Behavioral (with respect to inflections and number of syntactic environments), 3) Frequency (a) Textual (in individual languages) and (b) Crosslinguistic (number of languages in which an exponent is found). All of these criteria were used in some form in the study. In addition, the hierarchy restricts the patterns of polysemy that are possible. A verb whose prototypical meaning is related to a certain modality can extend its meaning to cover more marked modalities, but the opposite is not possible. This is similar to the semantic paths that are discussed in works on grammaticalization (e. g. Bybee, Perkins & Pagliuca 1994). At the end of the paper, it will also be shown how the hierarchy is reflected in data from language acquisition.

3. Realizations of the sense-modality hierarchy

English represents the type of language where all sense modalities are distinguished with separate verbs. In this section, data from languages representing other possibilities will be exemplified. Primarily, data from languages not included in the earlier study will be presented.

3.1. Djaru

In the majority of languages, 'see' and 'hear' are lexicalized as separate verbs. Languages in which 'hear' is realized as an extended sense of 'see' have, however, been clearly documented in several continents. Unfortunately, I have not been able to collect data concerning the complete set of realizations of the 15 meanings in the basic system as set out in Table 93.1. Several Pama-Nyungan languages in Australia such as Djaru spoken in Kimberley, Western Australia are of this type (data compiled from various examples in Tsunoda 1981). In this language, 'see' is realized as the simple verb root ɲaŋ-, while 'hear' is realized with the same root together with an extension which indicates the non-prototypical sense modality.

(3) ɲumbir-u mawun ɲaŋ-an
woman-ERG man see-PRES
A woman sees a man.

(4) ɲumbir-u mawun buṟa ɲaŋ-an
woman-ERG man hearing see-PRES
A woman hears a man.

(5) mawun-du ŋa-la jambagina-wu
man-ERG C-3SG.DAT child-DAT
buṟa ɲaŋ-an
hearing see-PRES
A man tries to listen to a child.
(p. 150)

(C = catalyst, a base for bound pronouns with different forms in declarative and non-declarative sentences which generally occurs in the second position of the sentence)

Examples of other Pama-Nyungan languages, where 'see' dominates 'hear' are Warlpiri (Hale 1971: 478), Guugu Yimidhirr (Haviland 1979) and Ngankikurungkurr (Hoddinott & Kofod 1988). Some examples of languages where 'see' dominates 'hear' are clearly attested also from other areas than Australia. One such case is Caddo (Caddoan family), currently spoken by a few old people in Oklahoma. According to Wallace Chafe (personal communication), there seems to be no distinction between activity and experience in this language. The verbal stem *-yibah* means 'look at, see' and is used also in *-bak-yibah* 'listen to, hear' and *-ka-yibah* 'taste', where *-bak-* means 'sound' and *-ka-* has an unclear etymology. The verb stems for touch and smell do not contain the element *-yibah*. In Lezgian (North-East Caucasian), 'see' is lexicalized as a simple verbal root *akun*, whereas 'hear' is lexicalized as two words *wan atun*, which literally means 'voice come' (Martin Haspelmath, personal communication. See also Haspelmath 1993). According to my criteria, 'see' is dominant with respect to 'hear' also in Tariana (an Arawak language, Brazil). According to Wierzbicka (1996, note 8 p. 80), who bases her analysis on a personal communication from Sasha Aikhenvald, 'the same verb is used for SEE and HEAR, but in the HEAR sense it requires an object which implies an "auditory" object ('words', 'sounds', 'language', etc.)'. It is typically the more marked meaning that requires an additional element (overt marking) to be expressed in an unambiguous way.

As will be discussed at the end of this paper, the verbs of perception have a tendency to extend their meaning to cover purely cognitive meanings such as 'know', 'understand' and 'think'. In spite of the fact that 'hear' is more marked than 'see' among the verbs of perception in many Australian languages, cognitive predicates are in general related to hearing rather than sight, as is common among European languages. In Djaru, the words *bina* and *binari*, which are etymologically derived from 'ear', form the core of verbal expressions like *bina juŋ* etymol. 'ear' + 'give' = 'teach' (p. 95) and the expression for 'know' ('ear stay'), 'learn' and 'teach' ('ear give'). The reflexive of *buṟa ɲaŋ-* 'hear' means 'think about' (p. 155).

The ear is regarded as the seat of intelligence and memory, while the belly is regarded as the seat of emotions. The expression 'having ears' means 'wise' and 'without ears' means 'unwise'. The expression 'having a good belly' usually corresponds to 'happy', while 'bad belly' corresponds to 'unhappy' (p. 7).

(6) ŋad,u ŋa-ŋa munda gida
1SG C-1SG.NOM belly good
ɲinaŋ-an
stay-PRES
'I feel good in the belly'/'I am happy'

3.2. Setswana

Setswana, a southern Bantu language spoken in Botswana, represents a type which seems to be particularly frequent among African languages. Among the experiences, there is a basic verb meaning 'see' and a second one which covers the other sense modalities and tends to have the default interpretation 'hear'. The data from Setswana are based on translations of close equivalents to the English sentences in Table 93.1 carried out by five native speakers (students of the University of Gaborone).

The data clearly show that 'see' is represented by a separate verb *bona*, while the rest of the experiences share one verb *utlwa*. The status of *utlwa* is not as clear, but my interpretation is that 'hear' is the prototypical meaning of this verb and the other uses represent extended senses. For Setswana, this claim is based primarily on intuitive statements of the informants such as giving 'hear' as a translation when asked to translate the word from *utlwa* taken in isolation. In several other languages, where 'hear' is extended, the verb is combined with a noun in the non-prototypical sense modalities. In Luo (Western Nilotic, Kenya), for example, the verb *winjo* 'hear' is extended to *winjo ndhadu* (lit. 'hear taste$_N$') and *winjo tik* (lit. 'hear smell$_N$') as translations of the English verbs *taste* and *smell* in their uses as experiences.

There are also languages where 'see', 'hear' and 'feel' are realized as separate verbs but 'feel' is extended to 'taste' and 'smell' (as ex-

93. Verbs of perception

Table 93.3. The verbs of perception in Setswana (Bantu, Botswana)

	ACTIVITY	EXPERIENCE	PHENOMENON-BASED
SIGHT	leba	bona	lebega
HEAR	reetsa	utlwa	utlwala
TOUCH	utlwa *or* tshwara	utlwa	utlwala
TASTE	utlwa (*or* leka 'try')	utlwa	utlwala
SMELL	nkga (*or* dupa)	utlwa	nkga

-ala 'neuter' Cole (1955) § 11.20 (p. 197)

periences). A clear example of this is found in Swedish. The experiences are realized as: *se* 'see', *höra* 'hear' *känna* 'feel' and *känna smaken* 'taste' (lit. 'feel the taste') and *känna lukten* 'smell' (lit. 'feel the smell'). A similar system is found in several Slavonic languages (Russian, Polish, Serbo-Croat) and in Hungarian. Even in this case, there is a tendency towards areal clustering.

3.3. Inuit

Inuit (Eskimo-Aleut) represents a rather common pattern for the modalities taste and smell. As experiences, these two modalities are realized with a common verb root *nai-*. Taste and smell share exponents even in phenomenon-based expressions, but in this case another characteristic of these sense modalities appears in Inuit. Evaluation is obligatorily expressed as a choice between *mamar-* 'taste/smell good' and *mamai-* 'taste/smell bad'. The complete set of basic perception verbs is shown in Table 93.4.

It seems as if 'taste' is the unmarked sense modality for the phenomenon-based stems *mamar-* 'taste/smell good' and *mamai-* 'taste/smell bad', since when 'smell' is intended, a more marked construction is required (IND = Indicative):

(7) *nigi mamar-tu-viniq*
 food -IND-IndefPAST
 The food tasted good.

(8) *nigi mamar-tu-viniq*
 nair-sugu
 smell-INDAttributive
 The food smelled good.

The lexical incorporation of evaluation in the modalities taste and smell has parallels in several other languages. In Oromo (a Cushitic language), which distinguishes taste and

Table 93.4. The verbs of perception in Inuit ugausingit (Nouveau-Quebec)

	ACTIVITY	EXPERIENCE	PHENOMENON-BASED
S I G H T	taku-naa- see-CAUS	taku- see	guna-
H E A R	tusa-aju- hear-CONTINUOUS	tusar- hear	guna-
T O U C H	attui- touch	ippigussuttu- notice	(Paraphrase)
T A S T E	uqummia- keep in one's mouth	nai- perceive smell or taste	mamar- taste/smell good
S M E L L	nai-gasuk- smell-try		mamai- taste/smell bad

smell lexically, there are separate roots both for 'taste = good' and 'taste = bad' and for 'smell = good' and 'smell = bad' but no roots with neutral evaluation. There is also a tendency for verbal roots meaning 'smell' and 'taste' to have a default evaluation. In Swedish, for example, the verb *lukta* 'smell' can be freely combined with adverbs meaning good or bad: *det luktar gott/illa* 'it smells good/bad', but if the verb is used without any modification a negative evaluation is strongly suggested: *Han luktar* 'He smells (understood: bad)'. Similarly, 'taste' tends to have a positive default interpretation (cf. the adjectives *smelly* and *tasty* in English and extended uses such as *taste freedom* and *smell treason*).

3.4. Abkhaz

In Abkhaz, a West Caucasian language, 'see' and 'hear' are represented by separate roots, whereas touch and taste are realized by the same root and smell is realized as an extended use of 'hear' *fẁᵒə ha* 'smell_N hear'. The complete basic system is shown in Table 93.5.

The extension of 'hear' to 'smell' as an experience has a parallel in several other language. It is found also in Russian, Persian and Yoruba.

Even if it has only been possible to show data from a few languages, the patterns shown above have parallels in several other languages described in the earlier study. In addition to the markedness hierarchy presented in Table 93.2, it seems to be possible to say something about relationships between the three most marked modalities smell, taste and touch. There appears to be a close relationship between either smell and taste or between taste and touch. Each of these pairs has a tendency to be realized in the same verb root, even if it has not been possible in most cases to establish whether one of the modalities in these two pairs should be regarded as more basic or prototypical. (The distinc-

Table 93.5. The verbs of perception in Abkhaz (West Caucasian)

	ACTIVITY	EXPERIENCE	PHENOMENON-BASED
SIGHT	pšə	ba	-šºa qa 'apparent be'
HEAR	ʒərw̋º	ha	ʒərw̋º 'listen' (in paraphrase)
TOUCH	-s- 'hit'	nər	ba 'see' (in paraphrase)
TASTE	gºa + ta try (<heart give)	nər	g˜ama ma taste have
SMELL	fw̋ºəgºa + ta smell_N try	fw̋ºə ha smell_N hear	fw̋ºə ma smell have

tion may also be neutralized.) These semantic relationships, which are symbolized with double-headed arrows in Table 93.6, appear to be rather natural. Taste and smell are both involved in examining food and share a strong evaluative component. Even for speakers of languages such as English, where these senses are realized as distinct verbs, it is difficult to separate the qualities of these two senses. Many of the qualities of food that are registered by the olfactory receptors are experienced as 'taste'. The relationship between taste and touch is probably motivated by the similarities between the activities of tasting and touching (indicated as + contact in the table). If you taste something, you touch it with your tongue and lips. As an activity, 'taste' is realized by the same word as 'kiss' in some languages.

The relationships shown between smell, taste and touch in Table 93.6 represent a weaker generalization than the markedness relations shown in Table 93.2, since they are bidirectional. The modalities that are ordered in the markendess hierarchy can only enter into unidirectional semantic relationships, i.e. semantic extensions always go from the least to the more marked modalities. This is symbolized with single-headed arrows in the table. In principle, sight and hearing can be

Table 93.6. Semantic relatedness between experiences in different sense modalities

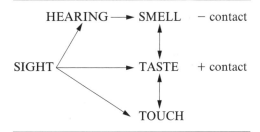

extended to all modalities lower in the hierarchy, but it appears as if certain extensions are more frequent than others. In particular, 'hear' is extended exclusively to 'smell' in a number of languages as mentioned above. An explanation for this might be that hearing and smell are both primarily used to perceive stimuli from a distance (-contact). The arrangement of the arrows in the table are meant to show that 'hear' can extend to 'taste' and 'touch' only if it also extends to 'smell'. Similarly, 'see' does not seem to extend to 'smell' without also extending to some other modality. The generalizations in Table 93.6 are more tentative than the markeness hierarchy presented in 93.2, which is supported by several other types of criteria than the patterns of semantic extension.

4. Languages with restricted sets of simple verbs

Before we move on to attempts to explain the major predictions of the sense-modality hierarchy, it must be emphasized that there are languages in which no sense modality is clearly realized as a simple perception verb. Even if they appear to be few in number, the existence of such languages clearly shows that there is no absolute universal such as: All languages have at least one verb of perception meaning 'see'. On the other hand, however, this is a very strong and well documented tendency and those few languages that have been found to lack even 'see' are characterized by an extremely small number of simple verbs. Of course, it would be possible to say that the languages lacking any verb marked for a single sense modality fall outside the scope of the hierarchy, but even if that sounds smart, that would really mean begging the question. Unless the number of such languages is small, the hierarchy would lose in predictive power, since it would not predict anything for the languages outside its scope. The strongest, empirically based version would thus state that there is a very strong tendency for languages to have at least 'see' and that the further elaboration of the field follows the restrictions laid down in the hierarchy with the caveat that the internal relationships between the three most marked modalities touch, taste and smell are not as well documented as the first steps of the hierarchy.

4.1. Ngarinjin

The most reduced system in terms of simple verbs has been found in Ngarinjin, a non-Pama-Nyungan Australian language spoken in Northern Kimberley. In this language, there are only around a dozen simple verbs which are frequent. All other simple verbs appear to be very infrequent. What is particularly illuminating is that one of these simple verbs belong to one of the mental fields, which thus lack unmarked verbs in Ngarinjin. (see Viberg 1994, based on Capell 1976 and Coate & Oates 1970). In other languages, the unmarked status of concrete physical verbs with respect to mental verbs is reflected in the strong tendency of polysemy to extend from concrete verbs into various mental fields. The simple concrete verb -o:- when used by itself means 'strike/hit':

(9)   *a-ŋ-o:-n*
       him-I-hit-PRES-IND
       I hit him.

Together with a particle, which originally meant 'light', this single verb can form a compound verb meaning 'see':

(10)   *aṟi woŋaj maṟa nj-Ø-o:-ni*
        man woman light her-he-hit-PAST.IND
        The man saw the woman.

Often as in this case, the meaning can be varied by using one of the other simple verbs:

(11)   *maṟa a-ŋ-ela-n*
        light him-I-hold-PRES.IND
        I hold him with light./I watch him.

Other perception verbs are formed by combining a simple verb with some other particle:

(12)   *windjaŋun ŋalug wurumaṇ*
        fire   smell   it.she.took
        She smelt the fire.

Complex verbs like these have relatively straightforward parallels in European languages in several cases, such as *cast one's eye over, cast a glance at* or *have a taste, have a smell*, the major difference being the extent to which Ngarinjin has to exploit such possibilities.

4.2. Kobon

Kobon is a Papuan language spoken in the Madang province, Papua New Guinea. The data in Table 93.7 are based on translated sentences provided by John Davies, who has published a detailed grammar of the language (Davies 1981). All realizations of the fifteen meanings except two are built around the verb root *nöŋ*, which also is used to express various cognitive meanings. As can be observed, most of the fifteen meanings can be distinguished by the addition of various particles or by verb serialization. In many cases, these extra markers are optional, however.

The mental predicates of Kalam, which is the only close relative of Kobon, have been described by Pawley (1994) and appear to have a very similar structure. Kalam has the cognate verb root *nŋ-*, which in various contexts may be glossed as 'know, think, see, hear, feel, remember, understand' etc. It is thus a very general concept, covering many types of mental processes. This verb also occurs in a number of lexicalized phrases with a more specific meaning such as *wdn nŋ-* 'see' (lit. 'eye perceive'), *d nŋ-* 'feel (by touching)' ('touch perceive'), *ñb nŋ-* 'taste' ('consume perceive'), *pug nŋ-* 'smell' ('sniff perceive') and even *gos nŋ-* ('thought perceive').

5. The place of perception verbs in lexicon and grammar

5.1. *See* as a nuclear verb

The verb lexicon is characterized in many (probably all) languages by a skewed frequency distribution between a small number of basic verbs and a large number of much less frequent non-basic verbs. Languages like Ngarinjin and Kobon or Kalam represent only the most pronounced manifestations of this tendency. Although there are around 10 000 verbs in Swedish, the 20 most frequent verbs in written Swedish cover 46% of the occurrences of verbs in running text. Similar proportions are found in other languages for

Table 93.7. The verbs of perception in Kobon

	ACTIVITY	EXPERIENCE	PHENOMENON-BASED
SIGHT	nöŋ mid	nöŋ	nöŋ[1]
HEAR	(apdi) nöŋ mid	(apdi) nöŋ	(apdi) nöŋ[1]
TOUCH	ud nöŋ[2] take hold of	nöŋ	ud nöŋ[1]
TASTE	ñiŋ nöŋ eat	ñiŋ nöŋ eat	dö g- (Positive evaluation) dö g-ag- (Neg. eval.)
SMELL	ud nöŋ[2] take hold of	(haɫiŋ) nöŋ smell_N	haɫiŋ au smell_N come

[1] Observer must be overtly expressed [2] In combination with expression of purpose

which statistics are available. Some of these verbs are grammatical such as the copula and modal verbs, but in addition, a number of basic verbs with a lexical meaning are found in this frequency range.

One important characteristic of verbal semantic fields in European languages that seems to reflect a universal tendency is that they are organized around one or two **nuclear verbs**, which are typologically unmarked and tend to have the same basic meaning in a wide range of languages. Some of the most important of the nuclear verbs have meanings such as 'go' (field: Motion), 'make' (Production), 'give', 'take' (Possession), 'say' (Verbal communication), 'see' (Perception), 'know', 'think' (Cognition). With only a few exceptions, verbs with these meanings turned out to occur among the 20 most frequent verbs in 11 European languages according to frequency dictionaries, which in general were based on 1 million running words (Viberg 1993). In all the 11 languages, 'see' was the most frequent verb of perception. 'See' is thus unmarked both with respect to textual frequency in individual languages with many perception verbs (e. g. English) and in terms of crosslinguistic frequency.

In languages such as Ngarinjin and Djaru with a restricted (less than 50) number of simple verbs there is a tendency for semantic equivalents to the nuclear verbs to be found with the exception of the cognitive ones ('know', 'think'), which are usually realized as complex verbs. The dominant position of 'see' in the markedness hierarchy for perception verbs seems to have parallels in other basic verbal semantic fields, even if this is a topic that requires much further work.

The present study has been concerned with *lexical universals*, a term which I would like to reserve for *patterns of realization* of lexical semantic notions, in particular as reflected in various aspects of markedness. This approach is different from (but not necessarily incompatible with) the approach taken by Anna Wierzbicka, who, in my view, is concerned primarily with *conceptual (or semantic) universals*. Wierzbicka has developed a series of primitives forming the Natural Semantic Metalanguage, whose basic purpose is to establish a minimal set of lexical concepts which can serve to paraphrase all the words in any human language. In an earlier version, 4 of the 37 primitives were mental predicates (Wierzbicka 1992): THINK, KNOW, FEEL, WANT. In Wierzbicka (1996), SEE and HEAR are added as primitives to this list. Obviously, HEAR and in particular FEEL have a much more marked realization than SEE in many languages, but Wierzbicka has been more concerned to show that the primitives can in principle be expressed, with a phrase or in some cases by using one word in separate constructions. This would indicate that a particular concept is valid, even if it is not clearly lexicalized.

5.2. Cognitive and other extended senses of perception verbs

Like verbs in general, the verbs of perception have a tendency to extend their meaning. Metaphorically based extensions in Indo-European languages are described in Sweetser (1990). In particular, the verbs of perception have a tendency to extend their meaning into the neighboring field of cognition and to cover meanings such as 'know' and 'think'. In many Indo-European languages, the word for 'know' can be traced to the IE root *weid- 'see'. The extension probably originated with the perfective form *woida 'have seen'. This meaning was then transferred to other tenses. Alternatively, it could form the basis of a separate conjugation (Buck 1949: 1209). The extension seems to be based on inference (what you have seen, you know) and semantic bleaching (neutralization of the sense modality and the source of knowledge in general). The extension 'see' > 'know' is also common in non-Indo-European languages, but it is far from universal. The conception that the ear is the seat of thinking and intelligence that was mentioned above in connection with Djaru is common in Australian aboriginal culture (Dixon 1980: 112) and as could be seen in Djaru such beliefs tend to be reflected in the internal structure of mental verbs.

The extension may even start from 'taste'. The Latin verb *sapere* was primarily associated with taste but could also be used with the meanings 'know', 'be wise' probably based on the association between taste and fine discrimination. In Spanish, the verb *saber* 'know' is still used also with the meaning 'taste' but in French *savoir*, 'know' is established as the only basic meaning. Classen (1993), in her anthropologically oriented work on the symbolic associations of the senses across cultures, gives several striking examples of how cultures can contrast with regard to which sense is given special prominence in the system of cultural beliefs. For example, smell holds a central position in the cosmology of the speakers of Onge in the little Andaman islands in the bay of Bengal.

Extensions of meaning can result in grammaticalization, but the development into a grammatical marker seems to be relatively restricted even for 'see'. It can develop into a morphological evidential marker (Willett 1988). At least in one case, 'see' has also developed into a copula, namely in Kpelle (Welmers 1973: 315–317). This is worth mentioning primarily because this seems to be part of a more general path. A semantically related verb 'find', is used as an existential copula in a number of languages such as Swedish, Turkish and Arabic. In Papuan languages, the verb meaning 'see' is used with certain very characteristic grammatical functions. The use of 'see' in constructions where it means 'try' is 'almost universal' (Foley 1986: 152). 'See' (and 'seek') is one of the sources of verbs meaning 'try' also in European languages (Buck 1949).

5.3. Argument structure and complementation

The tendency for perception verbs to take dative or other types of obliquely marked subjects in languages that have such structures has already been commented on. Verbs of perception can take a wide range of objects and of sentential complements in English and this seems to represent a general tendency across languages for the most unmarked perception verbs. Dik & Hengeveld (1991) provide data from a number of languages to show that formal contrasts between each of the following four functional types of complements can be found at least in some languages through varying means such as contrasting construction types or contrasting complementizers:

Immediate perception of individual
I saw your brother last night.

Immediate perception of state of affairs
I saw him walk down the street.

Mental perception of propositional content
I saw that Mary had been crying.

Reception of the propositional content of a speech act
I heard from John/saw in the newspaper that Peter had been fighting.

Immediate or **direct perception** as it will be called here involves cognitive interpretation minimally and requires simultaneity between the perceptual event and the perceived situation. It is even possible to construct sentences of this type where the perception is at odds with the cognitive interpretation: *I could see pink elephants dancing in the room even though I faintly realized there weren't any.* Mental or **indirect perception** usually involves inference and a certain amount of cognitive interpretation.

5.4. Lexicon and grammar of perception verbs in language acquisition

The sense-modality hierarchy is also reflected in acquisitional data. The visual verbs appear before the other verbs of perception in first language acquisition and can often be found already at the one-word stage, even if they initially have a deictic function (e. g. Edwards & Goodwin 1986). Bloom (1991) has shown how sentential complements (that-S and WH-S) first appear in English child language following a very small number of verbs consisting of the visual verbs *look* and *see* in addition to the cognitive verbs *know* and *think*. Parallel data have been presented for Swedish child language by Lundin (1987). In second language acquisition with restricted input, it has been found both for Swedish and for German that learners have a tendency to use the verb meaning 'look' (Swed. *titta*, Germ. *gucken*) very frequently and even to overextend its use ('I could look that he was sleeping'). The learners use a visual verb but not the most unmarked one in the target language. The explanation for this seems to be input salience and the more concrete meaning of 'look' which can more easily be deduced from the situation to which the utterance refers (Viberg 1993). One of the more striking reflections of the unmarked status of visual verbs comes from a study of the language acquisition of a blind child by Landau & Gleitman (1985). The earliest and most frequent perception verbs for this child were *look* and *see*. Similar to sighted children, the blind child used these verbs with respect to her dominant sense modality about haptic exploration and perception when referring to her own experience ('explore by hand', 'perceive by hand'). She also had a remarkably good understanding of what these verbs meant for sighted persons and had a good grasp of what was involved in visual perception at a distance and across barriers, for example. Syntactic evidence and high frequency of occurrence in the input were found to be important for this achievement.

5.5. Evidentiality and the Reliability hierarchy

There is a close relationship between certain central uses of perception verbs and morphological evidential markers, which indicate the source and reliability of knowledge. In languages which have developed such systems, there are often particular markers for visual evidence and sometimes even a special marker for auditory evidence or a more general marker indicating evidence based on any other sense modality than vision. (See the studies in Chafe & Nichols 1986). The evidentials tend to form a hierarchy. Oswalt (1986) presents the following hierarchy for Kashaya, a Pomo language from California with one of the most discriminating systems:

Performative > Factual-Visual > Auditory > Inferential > Quotative

Performative which represents the most reliable type of evidence is based on the speaker's own actions. Next comes the marker indicating knowledge based on what the speaker can see or has seen, which also is the marker of facts that are common knowledge. Auditory represents knowledge the speaker has because he could hear but did not see the action, whereas Inferential represents inferences based on what the speaker could perceive directly. The least reliable type of evidence is the Quotative which is based on what other people have said. As Oswalt remarks, the hierarchy is probably universal at the conceptual level and reflected even in languages lacking morphological markers of evidentiality.

In languages which do not have morphological evidential markers, similar contrasts can be expressed with perception verbs and the verbal communication verb 'say'. Such verbs form the sources for grammaticalized evidential markers in some languages. In Maricopa, a Yuman language spoken in Arizona, the evidential markers are derived from verbs meaning 'see', 'hear' and 'say' (Gordon 1986). Inferential perceptual evidence can be signaled syntactically in many languages through the choice of sentential complements related to indirect perception. As demonstrated in Table 93.8, there seems to be a general reliability hierarchy underlying the use of both perception verbs and evidential markers. Perceptual verbs cover the portion involving direct and indirect perception.

One reason why 'see' is less marked than 'hear' is that visual evidence is invoked more frequently than auditory when both are at hand, since visual evidence tends to be more reliable. An utterance such as *I heard Harry entering the room* in most situations invites the inference that I did not see him.

6. How explain the sense-modality hierarchy?

The dominance of vision among the sense modalities is well-established within cognitive psychology and neuropsychology. Psychologists have estimated that around 80% of perception is accounted for by vision (Dodwell 1994). A very large part of the primate neocortex is devoted to the processing of visual information (Goodale 1995).

Psychologists have also devised a great variety of experiments where a conflict is created between two senses. There is a strong tendency for vision to dominate over both hearing and touch according to Smyth's (1984) survey of experimental studies where the relationship between various sensory inputs were manipulated. For example, subjects instructed to respond as quickly as possible to either a light or a tone were not aware

Table 93.8. The reliability hierarchy

MOST RELIABLE			→ LEAST RELIABLE
Participation →	*Direct perception* →	*Indirect perception* →	*Quotation*
What you have done yourself (and experienced with all your senses)	What you have experienced with your own senses	What you have inferred based on sensory evidence	What you have heard from others
	Visual > Auditory > Other		

that they had heard a tone when the two types of stimuli were presented simultaneously on some occasions. In other experiments where a light source and a sound source were moved apart, vision dominated hearing. Sound seemed to come from a visible source even when the situation had been manipulated in such a way that the sound came from some other direction out of sight.

Rock (1975) accounts for a number of experiments showing that vision dominates over touch when conflicting information is provided simultaneously to these two senses. In particular the judgment of the site and shape of tangible concrete objects were studied. In one study, a 1-inch square was observed through a reduction lens that made it appear half its real size. At the same time, subjects could feel the square from below with their fingers through a thin cloth so that the hand could not be seen. The domination of vision was so strong that subjects did not experience any conflict but rather felt the size to be in accordance with the visual impression. Conflicting information concerning shape was studied by letting subjects run their hand along a straight rod, while they could simultaneously see it through a lens that made it look curved. Even in this case, vision dominated to such an extent that the rod felt curved. Experiments were also run with long exposure time (up to 30 minutes) showing that the domination of vision persisted under these conditions. The perception of touch under certain conditions was modified even when the subjects no longer could see the objects but could only touch them.

Even if vision, ironically, was not reliable in these manipulated situations, these demonstrations highlight to what extent human perceivers rely on visual information and under normal conditions this is a successful strategy. The unmarked status of visual verbs is a reflection of this preference.

7. Conclusion

There is a great variation among languages with respect to how many sense modalities are expressed as simple perception verbs. All values between 0 and 5 have been attested, even if most languages tend to have at least 'see'. In spite of this variation, there are strong restrictions on the patterns of lexicalization and of polysemy that tend to occur across languages and these restrictions can be expressed as a markedness hierarchy, which is reflected in a number of ways, in particular with respect to the most unmarked, nuclear verb. Compared to other verbs of perception:

- 'see' is lexicalized as a simple verb in most languages
- 'see' has higher textual frequency (attested for European languages)
- 'see' shows greater morphological and syntactic flexibility (see Viberg 1984 for some discussion)
- 'see' is dominant in patterns of polysemy and has a tendency to extend unidirectionally to other sense modalities than sight
- 'see' has a greater tendency to be grammaticalized (relatively weak in comparison to nuclear verbs in general)
- 'see' (or visual verbs) are acquired early in first and second language acquisition

Such strong patterning is not the rule, but is, however, also found for the nuclear verbs within other basic verbal semantic fields. The reason why these patterns are so strong for 'see' is the dominance of the visual modality in human perception and the obvious relationship between visual perception and the eye. The uniformity of these patterns can be compared to the greater variation crosslinguistically with respect to the development of basic cognitive verbs such as 'know', 'think', 'remember' and 'forget'. These verbs tend to be related to certain body parts (the 'seat' of the faculty) and/or to certain sense modalities, but, as we have seen, cultural beliefs can vary widely on this point as they also do for emotions. The modern, Western 'theory of mind' both in its lay and scientific versions is based on culturally transmitted beliefs rather than common experience and direct observation and is the result of many reinterpretations through history. The basic cognitive verbs also appear later in (English) first language acquisition than the visual verbs, which is related to the fact that 'the concept of mind' is much harder to grasp for the child than the most obvious aspects of perception. Certain basic cognitive experiences such as forgetting and remembering things seem, however, to be shared by humans in general and can probably be expressed in some way in all languages. It is primarily the underlying model that is subject to cultural variation, but this is often reflected in the lexicalization even of the most basic cognitive verbs.

After the submission of the final version of this article in 1997, a very interesting article on verbs of perception in Australian languages has been published by Evans & Wilkins (2000).

Acknowledgement

This work has been carried out within the project Crosslinguistic Lexicology (Swed. Tvärspråklig lexikologi) financially supported by the Swedish Research Council for the Humanities and Social Sciences.

8. References

Berlin, Brent & Kay, Paul. 1969. *Basic color terms.* Berkeley: University of California Press.

Bloom, Lois. 1991. *Language development from two to three.* Cambridge: Cambridge University Press.

Brown, Cecil H. 1977. "Folk botanical life-forms: Their universality and growth". *American Anthropologist 79.* pp. 317–342.

–. 1979. "Folk zoological life-forms: Their universality and growth." *American Anthropologist 81.* pp. 791–817.

Buck, Carl Darling. 1949. *A dictionary of selected synonyms in the principal Indo-European languages.* Chicago: The University of Chicago Press.

Bybee, Joan, Perkins, Revere & Pagliuca, William. 1994. *The evolution of grammar.* Chicago: University of Chicago Press.

Capell, Arthur. 1976. "Ngarinjin." In: Dixon, Robert Malcolm Ward (ed.). *Grammatical categories in Australian languages.* (Linguistic Series No. 22. Australian Institute of Aboriginal Studies. Canberra.) New Jersey: Humanities Press. pp. 625–29.

Chafe, Wallace & Nichols, Johanna (eds.). 1986. *Evidentiality: The linguistic coding of epistemology.* Norwood/New Jersey: Ablex.

Classen, Constance. 1993. *Worlds of sense: exploring the senses in history and across cultures.* London & New York: Routledge.

Coate, H. J. & Oates, Lynette F. 1970. *A grammar of Ngarinjin, Western Australia.* (Australian Aboriginal Studies 25.) Canberra: Australian Institute of Aboriginal Studies.

Cole, Desmond T. 1955. *An introduction to Tswana grammar.* Cape Town: Longman Penguin Southern Africa.

Colman, Andrew (ed.). 1994. *Companion encyclopedia of psychology. Vol. 1.* London & New York: Routledge.

Croft, William. 1990. *Typology and universals.* Cambridge: Cambridge University Press.

Davies, John. 1981. *Kobon.* (Lingua Descriptive Studies.) Amsterdam: North-Holland.

Dik, Simon & Hengeveld, Kees. 1991. "The hierarchical structure of the clause and the typology of perception-verb complements." *Linguistics 29,* 231–259.

Dixon, Robert Malcolm Ward. 1980. *The Languages of Australia.* Cambridge: Cambridge University Press.

Dodwell, Peter. 1994. "Fundamental processes in vision." In: Colman (ed.). pp. 155–177.

Edwards, D. & Goodwin, R. 1986. "Action words and pragmatic function in early language." In: Kuczaj, Stan & Barrett, Martyn (eds.). *The development of word meaning.* New York: Springer-Verlag.

Evans, Nicholas & Wilkins, David. 2000. "In the mind's ear: the semantic extensions of perception verbs in Australian languages." *Language 76: 3,* 546–592.

Foley, William. 1986. *The Papuan Languages of New Guinea.* Cambridge: Cambridge University Press.

Goddard, Cliff & Wierzbicka, Anna (eds.). 1994. *Semantic and Lexical Universals. Theory and empirical findings.* Ansterdam/Philadelphia: John Benjamins.

Goodale, Melvyn Alan. 1995. "The cortical organization of visual perception and visuomotor control." In: Kosslyn, Stephen & Osherson, Daniel (eds.). *An invitation to cognitive science. Vol. 2. Visual cognition.* Cambridge/Mass.: The MIT Press. pp. 167–213.

Gordon, Lynn. 1986. "The development of evidentials in Maricopa." In: Chafe & Nichols. (eds.). pp. 75–88.

Greenberg, Joseph. 1966. *Language universals with special reference to feature hierarchies.* (Janua Linguarum. Series minor LIX.) The Hague: Mouton.

Hale, Kenneth 1971. "A note on a Walbiri tradition of antonymy." In: Danny Steinberg & Leon Jakobovits. (eds.). *Semantics.* Cambridge: Cambridge University Press.

Hardin, Clyde L. & Maffi, Luisa (eds.). 1997. *Color categories in thought and language.* Cambridge: Cambridge University Press.

Haspelmath, Martin. 1993. *A grammar of Lezgian.* Berlin: Mouton.

Heid, Ulrich Coordinator. 1996. With S. Atkins, G. Bès, N. Calzolari, O. Corrazari, C. Fillmore, K. Krüger, S. Schwenger & M. Vliegen. A lexicographic and formal description of the lexical classes of perception and speech act verbs. Deliverable S-III-1 of DELIS.

Hoddinott, William G. & Kofod, Frances M. 1988. *The Ngankikurungkurr language (Daly river area, Northern territory).* (Pacific Linguistics. Series D – No. 77.) Canberra.

Kibrik, A. E. 1985. "Toward a typology of ergativity." In: Nichols, Johanna & Woodbury, Anthony (eds.). *Grammar inside and outside the clause.* Cambridge: Cambridge University Press, pp. 268–323.

Landau, Barbara & Gleitman, Lila R. 1985. *Language and experience. Evidence from the blind child.* Cambridge/Mass.: Harvard University Press.

Lundin, Barbro. 1987. *Bisatser i små barns språk. En analys av fem barns första bisatser.* (Lundastudier i nordisk språkvetenskap A 39.) Lund: Lund University Press.

Oswalt, Robert L. 1986. "The evidential system of Kashaya." In: Chafe & Nichols. (eds.), pp. 29–45.

Pawley, Andrew. 1994. "Kalam exponents of lexical and semantic primitives." In: Goddard & Wierzbicka. (eds.), pp. 387–421.

Rock, Irvin. 1975. *An introduction to perception.* New York: Macmillan Publishing Co.

Rogers, Andy. 1971. "Three kinds of physical perception verbs." *Papers presented at the 7th meeting of the Chicago Linguistic Society.*

–. 1972. "Another look at flip perception verbs." *Papers presented at the 8th meeting of the Chicago Linguistic Society.*

–. 1974. *Physical perception verbs in English. A study in lexical relatedness.* (Unpublished Ph. D. dissertation, University of California, Los Angeles.) London: University Microfilms International.

Schiffman, Harvey Richard 1994. "The skin, body and chemical senses." In: Colman (ed.), pp. 224–250.

Smyth, Mary M. 1984. "Perception and action." In: Smyth, Mary M. & Wing, Alan M. (eds.). *The psychology of human movement.* London: Academic Press. pp. 119–152.

Sweetser, Eve. 1990. *From etymology to pragmatics: metaphorical and cultural aspects of language.* Cambridge: Cambridge University Press.

Tsunoda, Tasaku. 1981. *The Djaru language of Kimberley, Western Australia.* (Pacific Linguistics Ser. B. No. 78.) Canberra.

Verma, Manindra & Mohanan, Karavannur Puthanvettil (eds.). 1990. *Experiencer subjects in South Asian Languages.* Stanford University: The Center for the Study of Language and Information.

Viberg, Åke. 1984. "The verbs of perception: a typological study." *Linguistics 21*: 123–162.

–. 1993. "Crosslinguistic perspectives on lexical organization and lexical progression." In: Hyltenstam, Kenneth & Viberg, Åke (eds.). *Progression and regression in language.* Cambridge: Cambridge University Press. pp. 340–385.

–. 1994. "Vocabularies." In: Ahlgren, Inger & Hyltenstam, Kenneth (eds.). *Bilingualism in deaf education.* Hamburg: Signum-Verlag, pp. 169–199.

Welmers, William E. 1973. *African language structures.* Berkeley: University of California Press.

Wierzbicka, Anna. 1972. *Semantic primitives.* Frankfurt: Athenäum.

–. 1992. "The search for universal semantic primitives." In: Pütz, Martin (ed.). *Thirty years of linguistic evolution.* Amsterdam: John Benjamins. pp. 215–242.

–. 1996. *Semantics. Primes and universals.* Oxford: Oxford University Press.

Willett, Thomas. 1988. "A cross-linguistic survey of the grammaticalization of evidentiality." *Studies in Language* 12, 51–97.

Åke Viberg, Uppsala University (Sweden)

XII. Phonology-based typology
Typologie auf phonologischer Basis
Typologie du domaine phonologique

94. Silbenstruktur

1. Einleitung
2. Basiseigenschaften, prosodische Eigenschaften
3. Typologie der Lautverbindungen
4. Typologie des Silbengewichts
5. Silbenstrukturmodelle
6. Probleme
7. Ausblick
8. Abkürzungen
9. Zitierte Literatur

1. Einleitung

Trotz bedeutender phonetisch orientierter Abhandlungen zur Silbe um die Jahrhundertwende (vgl. Sievers 1901, Jespersen 1920) beklagt noch Eduard Hermann (1923: 1), dass dem Silbenbau von den Sprachforschern bis dato noch nie im Zusammenhang Beachtung geschenkt und in keinem der bekannten Handbücher ein besonderes Kapitel gewidmet worden sei. Das Interesse an einer näheren Untersuchung der Silbenstruktur ist allerdings gerade in den letzten drei Jahrzehnten sprunghaft gestiegen. Lag das Augenmerk anfangs primär auf einzelsprachlichen Untersuchungen, wuchs mit der Zeit das theoretische und typologische Interesse an der äußeren und inneren Struktur von Silben derart, dass eine Behandlung der Silbenstruktur aus rezenteren Abhandlungen nicht mehr wegzudenken ist.

Die gerade aus phonologischer Sicht kaum haltbare Negation der Entität Silbe, wie sie die aufkommende generative Schule im Zuge von Chomsky & Halle (1968) propagierte, stellt sich aus der Retrospektive in diesem Zusammenhang eher als Impetus der Silben(struktur)forschung denn als retardierendes Momentum dar.

Der Begriff Silbenstruktur setzt mindestens drei Punkte voraus: a) Die Existenz von Silben, b) eine äußere Struktur der Silben, d. h. unter anderem Klarheit über ihre Grenzen und c) eine innere Struktur der Silben. Dieser Artikel beschränkt sich unter Ausklammerung der Frage, ob es Silben gibt und wie diese sich definieren lassen, auf die beiden letzten Punkte, also die äußere und innere Struktur von Silben. Allerdings sei bemerkt, dass ein Teil der Evidenz, die im folgenden angeführt wird, auch eine Rolle bei Versuchen spielt, die Silbe zu definieren (vgl. hierzu Blevins 1995 und die dort zitierte Literatur).

Nach dem folgenden Abschnitt, der der Einführung und Charakterisierung von Grundbegriffen dient, wird in § 3. das Verhältnis von Einzellaut und Silbe näher beleuchtet. § 4. erörtert die Abhängigkeit der Akzentsysteme von strukturellen Eigenschaften von Silben. Auf die innere (Konstituenten-)Struktur der Silbe wird in § 5. eingegangen, während § 6. auf Problembereiche hinweist, die sich im Rahmen der Silbenstrukturforschung ergeben.

2. Basiseigenschaften, prosodische Eigenschaften

Nach Blevins (1995: 206 f.) sind (phonologische) Silben strukturelle Einheiten, die für phonologische Segmentketten eine melodische Organisation bereitstellen, wobei diese melodische Organisation vor allem auf der Sonorität der phonologischen Einzelsegmente beruht. Sonorität lasse sich definieren als die relative Lautheit eines phonologischen Segments (vgl. § 3.1.).

Die Vorstellung, dass sich Silben als Konkatenationen von Einzellauten beschreiben lassen, hat ihren Ursprung in der Antike. Nach Aristoteles (vgl. Steinthal 1890: 259) ist die Silbe im Gegensatz zum Elementarlaut zerlegbar. Nach Dionysios Thrax ist die Silbe eine Zusammenfassung von Konsonanten mit einem Vokal oder mit Vokalen unter einem Ton und einem Atem (Steinthal 1891: 203).

Die Grundlage dieser Auffassung ist in der stark alphabetischen Orientierung der griechischen Lautlehre zu suchen. Zwar ist nach Aristoteles der Elementarlaut nicht etwas unmittelbar Gegebenes, sondern vielmehr, da er sich erst aus einer künstlichen Zerlegung ergibt, ein den zusammengesetzten Gebilden zugrundeliegendes Urelement. Wichtig ist jedoch vor allem seine Unzerlegbarkeit. Die Silbe sei zwar in einem bestimmten Sinne auch unzerlegbar, aber auf eine andere Art und Weise. Während der Laut überhaupt nicht zerlegbar sei (oder doch nur in Bestandteile gleicher Artbeschaffenheit), könne die Silbe zerlegt werden, wenn auch nur unter Zerstörung ihrer Artbeschaffenheit. Die hier spürbare Zurückhaltung Aristoteles' im Hinblick auf die Zerlegbarkeit der Silbe tritt im weiteren Verlauf der Sprachwissenschaft immer stärker in den Hintergrund. Wichtig in diesem Zusammenhang ist jedoch nicht die Entwicklung der Silbenauffassungen (vgl. dazu Laziczius 1961: 156−193, Jensen 1963), sondern die daraus resultierende Folgerung, wonach eine Silbe vor allem eine Folge von Lauten sei.

Dem steht die in diesem Artikel vertretene Sicht gegenüber, dass der Zusammenhang zwischen der Silbe und den Lauten durchaus komplexer zu verstehen ist.

Die Silbe wird hier als ein Grundkonzept geführt, für das sich a) elementare und b) prosodische Eigenschaften angeben lassen. Dabei wird wohlgemerkt nicht vorausgesetzt, dass diese angegebenen Eigenschaften in ihrer Kombination die Grundkategorie Silbe ERSCHÖPFEND beschreiben. Die **elementaren Eigenschaften** der Silbe bilden ihre **Basis**. Sie enthält alle segmentalen Informationen, z. B. Einzellaute in Theorien, die diese als Grundkategorien führen und auf die wir uns im folgenden beschränken werden. Über die Basis hinaus kommen der Silbe **prosodische Eigenschaften** zu, die sich in strukturelle, tonale und ballistische (wie Silbenschnitt, stød, kontrollierte vs. ballistische Silben) einteilen lassen. Zu den strukturellen Eigenschaften ist zunächst die Position eines Zentrums der Silbe, des **Nukleus** oder **Kerns**, zu zählen. Ausgehend von dieser Strukturposition lässt sich der Bereich der Silbe, die dem Nukleus vorausgeht, als **Kopf** (engl. *head*), der dem Nukleus folgende als **Koda** (engl. *coda*) identifizieren. Für die Verbindung von Nukleus und Koda ist der Begriff **Reim** (engl. *rhyme, rime*) geläufig, während Kopf und Nukleus den **Körper** einer Silbe bilden. Die **Schale** einer Silbe besteht unter Ausschluss des Nukleus aus Kopf und Koda.

(1)

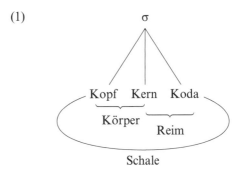

Eine Silbe mit leerer Koda heißt **offen**, sonst **geschlossen**. Eine Silbe mit leerem Kopf (d. h. mit silbeninitialem Nukleus) heißt **nackt**, sonst **bedeckt**.

Eigenschaften wie Vokal- oder Konsonantenharmonie werden hier nicht als Eigenschaften von Silben, sondern von Wörtern klassifiziert.

3. Typologie der Lautverbindungen

Als eine der zentralen Aufgaben der Silbenstrukturforschung ist die Klärung des Verhältnisses zwischen den als Grundkategorien zu führenden Entitäten Einzellaut und Silbe zu nennen. Darunter fällt nicht nur die Affiliation von Einzellauten zu Silben, sondern auch das Verhältnis der Einzellaute zueinander. Ein Beispiel für ein solches relationales Konzept für Einzellaute ist das der Sonorität bzw. Konsonantischen Stärke (vgl. § 3.1.), das im allgemeinen ohne Rekurs auf die Silbe eingeführt wird. In § 3.2. wird auf die Typologie der Relationen von Lauten innerhalb von Silben, in § 3.3. auf das Verhältnis von Lauten eingegangen, die unterschiedlichen Silben zugerechnet werden. Der Abschnitt schließt mit Bemerkungen zum syllabischen Wortbau (§ 3.4.).

3.1. Das Konzept der Sonorität/ Konsonantischen Stärke

Jede phonologische Theorie, die Sprachlaute als Grundkategorien führt, muss sich der Frage widmen, warum bestimmte Abfolgen und Kombinationen von Lauten in den Sprachen der Welt präferiert sind, d. h. unter anderem häufiger als andere vorkommen. So ist z. B. die tautosyllabische Abfolge Plosiv −

Liquid − Vokal eine durchaus übliche Kombination von zwei Konsonanten + Vokal (z. B. im Deutschen/Englischen), während die Abfolge Liquid − Plosiv − Vokal nur in wenigen Sprachen (z. B. im Russischen) eine zulässige Verbindung von Sprachlauten in ein und derselben Silbe ist. Um derartige Beobachtungen zu beschreiben und in eine möglichst allgemeine Form zu bringen, bedient man sich üblicherweise eines relationalen Konzepts, das unter Bezeichnungen wie *Sonorität* oder *Konsonantische Stärke* geläufig ist (zur Geschichte des Sonoritätskonzepts vgl. Murray 1988 und Ohala 1990).

(2) Skala der Sonorität/ Konsonantischen Stärke
 ↑ *zunehmende Konsonantische Stärke*
 stimmlose Plosive
 stimmhafte Plosive
 stimmlose Frikative
 stimmhafte Frikative
 Nasale
 laterale Liquide (*l*-Laute)
 zentrale Liquide (*r*-Laute)
 hohe Vokale
 mittlere Vokale
 tiefe Vokale
 ↓ *zunehmende Sonorität*

Ziel einer solchen Relationalisierung ist es, die Tendenz von Lautklassen zur Nah- bzw. Fernstellung gegenüber dem Silbenkern zu explizieren: Elemente von Lautklassen, die auf der Sonoritätsskala der Klasse der Vokale am nächsten liegen, haben demnach eine größere Tendenz, nah am Silbenkern zu stehen, als Elemente von solchen, die auf der Sonoritätsskala weiter von der Klasse der Vokale entfernt sind. Die oben angeführte Präferenz für die Abfolge Plosiv-Liquid-Vokal lässt sich mit Hilfe des Sonoritätskonzepts beschreiben als Ausdruck der im Vergleich zu den Plosiven größeren Tendenz von Liquiden, nah am vokalischen Silbenkern zu stehen.

Blevins (1995: 210) formuliert die durch das Sonoritätskonzept ausgedrückte Tendenz wie folgt (zum Begriff des Sonoritätsplateaus siehe § 6.2.):

(3) Sonority Sequencing Generalization (SSG) nach Blevins (1995)
 Between any member of a syllable and the syllable peak, a sonority rise or plateau must occur.

Die in der Literatur vorgeschlagenen Sonoritätsskalen (vgl. u. a. Sievers 1901; Jespersen 1920; Hooper 1972; Hankamer & Aissen 1974; Ladefoged 1982; Murray & Vennemann 1983; Steriade 1984; Vennemann 1988a; Clements 1990; Blevins 1995; Zec 1995a) unterscheiden sich zum einen bezüglich der Zahl der Abstufungen, die vorgenommen werden, zum anderen bezüglich der Klasseneinteilung.

Greenbergs typologische Untersuchung von 1978 kann die Gültigkeit einer Abfolgetendenz wie in (3) nur zum Teil bestätigen. So setzt die Existenz einer wortinitialen Abfolge Liquid + Plosiv die Existenz der unmarkierteren Abfolge Obstruent + Liquid voraus (1978: 257), und Spiegelbildliches gilt auch für die wortfinale Position (Plosiv + Liquid lässt auf Liquid + Plosiv schließen). Die Tendenz zur unmarkierten Serialisierung gemäß der Sonoritätsskala wird aber häufig durchbrochen, worauf in § 6.2. und § 6.3. noch einmal eingegangen wird; daher kann (3), wenn überhaupt, so nur als Präferenzgesetz verstanden werden. Auf der Basis der Daten von Greenberg lässt sich jedoch zumindest die Unmarkiertheit der Abfolge in (4) feststellen.

(4) Obstruent/Nasal − Liquid − Halbvokal − Vokal − Halbvokal − Liquid − Nasal/Obstruent

Kontrovers diskutiert wird die Frage, ob und wie die in der phonologischen Sonoritätshierarchie ausgedrückten Präferenzen phonetisch oder anderweitig motiviert (und damit in einem stärkeren Sinn erklärt) werden können (vgl. insbesondere die kritischen Bemerkungen in Ohala 1990). Als phonetische Korrelate wurden vor allem artikulatorische (Vokaltraktöffnung) und akustische Parameter (Lautheit) vorgeschlagen, aber auch solche psychoakustischer Art (vgl. Pompino-Marschall 1990, 1993).

Das Konzept der Sonorität erlaubt eine prägnante Formulierung von Präferenzgesetzen zur Silbenstruktur, wie dies im folgenden anhand einiger ausgewählter Beispiele illustriert wird.

Präferenzgesetze sind dabei als graduierende Qualitätsfeststellungen aufgefasst. Die Konzeption ist eine Generalisierung der Jakobsonschen (Un-)Markiertheitsauffassung: Statt mit dem Gegensatzpaar 'Unmarkiert': 'Markiert' arbeitet sie mit der Graduierung 'Umso weniger markiert, je' bzw. 'Umso stärker präferiert, je', oder einfach 'Umso besser, je'. Im einzelnen sind die graduierenden Qualitätsfeststellungen anhand der Jakobsonschen Kriterien (Jakobson 1941) zu begründen: Eine sprachliche Eigenschaft ist umso besser, je verbreiteter sie in den Sprachen der Welt ist; wie Jakobson gezeigt hat, stimmt dieses Kriterium weitgehend mit dem anderen überein, von Kindern im Erstspracherwerb umso früher gelernt zu werden, sowie mit dem weiteren, im aphatischen Sprachverlust umso länger erhalten zu bleiben. (Diese drei Kriterien sind im dreiteiligen Titel von Jakobson 1941 angesprochen.)

Diese Konzeption lässt sich auf alle Bereiche des Sprachbaus und der Sprachverwendung (ferner auch auf andere in der menschlichen Natur begründete kulturelle Systeme und ihre Verwendung) anwenden. Jakobsons ursprüngliche Demonstrationsdomäne waren die Sprachlautinventare (Phonemsysteme). Spielarten des Ansatzes liegen der sogenannten Natürlichen Phonologie, Morphologie und Syntax zugrunde. Hier wird die Konzeption im Anschluss an Vennemann (1988a) auf den Bau der Silben und Silbenfolgen sowie auf die syllabische Organisation von Wörtern angewendet. Die Illustration stützt sich dabei wie in anderen Domänen auch auf die folgende Verallgemeinerung, die zum Ausdruck bringt, dass Sprachsysteme auf jedem Parameter, der mehrere Einstellungen erlaubt, der Tendenz nach optimiert sind, nämlich insofern, als sie im allgemeinen nicht irgendwelche schlechten Strukturen auf einem Parameter aufweisen, ohne zugleich alle besseren Strukturen desselben Parameters ebenfalls aufzuweisen. Dies ist in der folgenden Synchronischen Maxime zum Ausdruck gebracht:

SYNCHRONISCHE MAXIME: Ein Sprachsystem enthält im allgemeinen mit einer auf einem bestimmten Parameter konstruierbaren Struktur auch alle auf demselben Parameter konstruierbaren besseren Strukturen.

Die Relativierung durch „im allgemeinen" ist nötig, da gelegentlich durch parameterübergreifenden Sprachwandel oder durch Sprachkontakt auf Parametern „Löcher" entstehen können. Aber im allgemeinen sind Parameter dicht besetzt, und zwar stets am „besseren" Ende des Parameters, bei der Spitze des Qualitätspfeils. Das wiederum hat seinen Grund darin, dass systemimmanenter, also nicht durch Sprachkontakt induzierter Sprachwandel stets die schlechtesten Strukturen auf einem Parameter zuerst trifft, im Einklang mit der Diachronischen Maxime:

DIACHRONISCHE MAXIME: Die Tendenz zur Veränderung einer Struktur auf einem Parameter ist umso stärker, je schlechter die Struktur auf dem Parameter ist.

Dies lässt sich folgendermaßen grafisch verdeutlichen (Abb. 1):

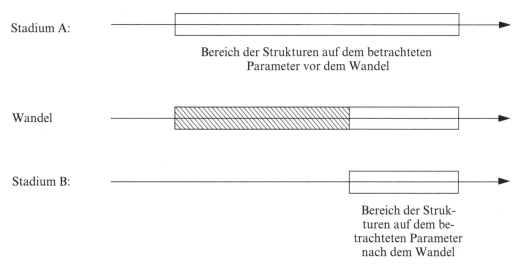

Abb. 1: SCHEMATISCHE DARSTELLUNG ZUR NATUR DES STRUKTURELLEN SPRACHWANDELS

Es folgt, dass aller Sprachwandel (zumindest aller systemimmanente Sprachwandel, aber für anders verursachten Wandel gilt das ebenso) meliorativ ist: Sprachwandel ist Sprachverbesserung (so der Titel von Vennemann 1989). Dieses natürlichkeitstheoretische Prinzip spielt auch in der sogenannten Optimalitätstheorie eine zentrale Rolle, vgl. hierzu Prince & Smolensky (1993) sowie die zusammenfassende Darstellung mit zahlreichen weiteren Literaturhinweisen in Kager (1999), dort zu den hier behandelten Parametern vor allem die Kapitel 3 „Syllable structure and economy", 4 „Metrical structure and parallelism" und 5 „Correspondence in reduplication". Elegant in der Darstellung und durch den Versuch einer konsequenten Integrierung natürlichkeitstheoretischer Gesichtspunkte in die grammatische Beschreibung selbst (wie versuchsweise bereits in Kapitel 9 von Chomsky & Halle 1968), trägt dieser Ansatz allerdings zum inhaltlichen Verständnis der Probleme wenig bei. Insbesondere bleibt er in der Erfassung der Silbenstruktur hinter dem schon Erreichten zurück, indem es ihm z. B. nicht gelingt, das graduierende Konzept des 'je besser, desto X' zu akkommodieren, etwa dort, wo X auf eine Skala der Konsonantischen Stärke (bzw. Sonorität) Bezug nimmt.

Aus Platzgründen behandeln wir nur das erste der folgenden Gesetze einigermaßen ausführlich, die übrigen mit knapper Illustration.

3.2. Intrasyllabische Relationen

Über den Bau einzelner Silben liegen schon lange zahlreiche Einzelergebnisse vor. Die wichtigste empirische Erhebung ist Greenberg (1978). Wir orientieren uns hier an den graduierenden Generalisierungen der Präferenzgesetze für Silbenstruktur in Vennemann (1988a). Wie man sehen wird, fallen die Gesetze unter die Verallgemeinerung, dass eine Silbe umso besser gebaut ist, je monotoner sie ist, wobei Monotonie definiert ist als ununterbrochener Abfall der Konsonantischen Stärke im Körper und ununterbrochener Anstieg der Konsonantischen Stärke im Reim; vgl. auch oben (3). Zusammen bringen die Gesetze ferner zum Ausdruck, dass die optimale Silbe einen einzigen starken Konsonanten im Kopf, einen weiten Vokal im Nukleus und eine leere Koda hat, wie z. B. *pa* und *ta*, auch *ma*.

3.2.1. Kopfgesetz

KOPFGESETZ: Ein Silbenkopf ist umso besser,

(a) je näher die Anzahl seiner Sprachlaute bei Eins liegt,
(b) je größer die Konsonantische Stärke seines ersten Sprachlauts ist und
(c) je schärfer die Konsonantische Stärke vom ersten Sprachlaut auf den folgenden Nukleus zu abfällt.

Zu (a): Silben mit Köpfen, deren Kardinalität kleiner als 1, also 0 ist, d. h. Silben mit leeren Köpfen sind ungünstig. Das erkennt man daran, dass es keine Sprachen gibt, die ausschließlich Silben mit leeren Köpfen hätten, umgekehrt aber durchaus Sprachen, die keine Silben mit leeren Köpfen zulassen. Ein Beispiel hierfür ist das Tolowa (Athabaskisch), das die Silbentypen CVV, CCVV, CVC, CCVC, CCVCC, CVCC und − selten − CV erlaubt, aber nicht VV, VC und VCC (Collins 1989). S. u. § 3.2.3. zu einer systematischen Ausnahme.

Im Standarddeutschen norddeutscher Aussprache werden leere Köpfe von Erstsilben und von Akzentsilben mit dem Glottalverschluß besetzt, z. B. *chaotisch* [kʰa.'ʔo.tʰɪʃ] (aber *Chaos* ['kʰa.ɔs]), *Aorta* [ʔa.'ʔɔr.tʰa]. Doch ist die Abneigung gegen leere Köpfe nicht sonderlich groß, denn es gibt durchaus Sprachen, in denen zahlreiche Wörter nackte Silben, also Silben mit leeren Köpfen haben; z. B. beginnt im Baskischen ungefähr die Hälfte der Wörter mit Vokal. Allerdings brauchen nackte Silben nicht überall im Wort die gleiche Rolle zu spielen; viele Sprachen haben z. B. spezielle Regeln für den Hiat, siehe § 3.3.2..

Umgekehrt sind auch Silbenköpfe mit einer Kardinalität über Eins ungünstig, und zwar umso mehr, je größer die Zahl der Kopfsprachlaute ist. Das erkennt man daran, dass für ein und dieselbe Sprache (1) mit den nicht-leeren Köpfen einer bestimmten Länge immer auch nicht-leere Köpfe jeder geringeren Länge vorkommen, (2) eine obere Kopflängengrenze gilt und (3) die Beschränkungen mit zunehmender Kopflänge zunehmen. Zum Beispiel erlaubt das Standarddeutsche nichtleere Köpfe mit 1, 2 und 3, aber nicht mit mehr Sprachlauten und erfüllt damit die ersten beiden Punkte. Dass es auch den dritten erfüllt, erkennt man, wenn man prüft, zu welchen Zweierfolgen auch die Umkehrfolge erlaubt ist (nicht z. B. zu allen Gruppen aus Obstruent und Resonant, also etwa *kr*-, aber **rk*-; *ʃm*-, aber **mʃ*-), und wenn man sich ferner vergegenwärtigt, dass mit den ca. 20 möglichen Kopfsprachlauten nicht etwa 20 × 20 × 20, also 8.000 Kopfdreiergruppen erlaubt sind, sondern nur 4, nämlich *ʃpr-, ʃpl-, ʃtr-, skr-* (*springen, Splitter, streng, Skrupel*), dazu in einigen wenig integrierten Lehnwörtern *skl-* (*Sklerose*) und vielleicht *str-* (*Strip*); ob *pfr-, pfl-, tsv-* zu zählen sind, hängt von der Wertung der Affrikaten [pᶠ], [tˢ] ab.

Im Sprachwandel erkennt man diesen Teil des Kopfgesetzes in der häufigen Verkürzung der Silbenköpfe. Zum Beispiel erlaubte das Altindische (Vedisch und Sanskrit) Silbenköpfe der Länge 3, aber das mittelindische

Prakrit nur maximal solche der Länge 1. Komplexe Köpfe wurden innerhalb weniger Jahrhunderte durch verschiedene Sprachwandel systematisch auf 1 gekürzt. Das Umgekehrte, eine systematische Verlängerung der Köpfe, scheint es nicht zu geben; scheinbare Fälle von Kopfverlängerung haben immer einen spezifischen Grund, der nicht eigentlich mit der Silbenstruktur zu tun hat. Zum Beispiel behebt die Epenthese *sr* > *str* im Vorgermanischen die schlechte Sprechbarkeit der Konsonantengruppe, die dann aber auch nicht auf Köpfe beschränkt zu sein braucht: urgerm. ⁺*strauma-z*, anord. *straumr*, mhd. *stroum* 'Fluß', mit regionaler Monophthongierung nhd. *Strom*, auch lett. *strauma*, russ. *struya* 'Strom', aber ohne Epenthese aind. *srávati* '(er) fließt', griech. *rheûma* 'Strömung, Strom', *rhé(v)ein*, *rheîn* 'fließen' (wie im *pánta rheî* 'alles fließt' des Heraklit), *rhó(v)os* 'Strömung, Flut', air. *srúaim* (auch *strúaim*) 'Bach' sowie, mit anderer Lösung des *sr*-Problems, air. *sruth*, aber mkymr. *frut*, nkymr. *ffrwd* 'Bach'; aber eben auch urgerm. ⁺*swester-* (< uridg. ⁺*swesr-*), nhd. *Schwester*, anord. *systir*, aksl. *sestra*, vgl. aind. *svásar-*, lat. *soror* (mit Rhotazismus) usw. Natürlich entstehen komplexe Silbenköpfe auch neu durch Synkope, aber deren Motivation ist erkennbar nicht silbenphonetisch, sondern wortkürzend.

Zu (b): In vielen Sprachen sind Köpfe, die nur die konsonantisch schwächsten Sprachlaute enthalten, ausgeschlossen, z. B. alle Vokale wie im Standarddeutschen. Die Tendenz zum starken Anlaut zeigt sich besonders am Wortanfang, da ihr im Wortinnern die Tendenz zur assimilatorischen Konsonantenschwächung entgegenwirkt. Im Spanischen können im Wortinnern /r/ und /r/ (dort -r- bzw. -rr- geschrieben) Silbenköpfe bilden, am Wortanfang nur /r/ (dort r- geschrieben): *pero* 'aber', *perro* 'Hund', aber nur *rojo* /roxo/ 'rot'. Viele Sprachen erlauben im wortinitialen Kopf nur stimmlose, keine stimmhaften Frikative (z. B. das Altenglische), oder sie aspirieren dort ihre Plosive (z. B. das Neuenglische).

Zu (c): Im Standarddeutschen sind starke Konsonanten (Obstruenten) im Kopf vor Resonanten erlaubt, schwache (Resonanten) nicht, und zwar auch dann nicht, wenn sie relativ stärker sind: *Knie*, *Platz*, *blank*, *groß*, *frei*, *schmal*, *Schnee*, *schlimm*, *schräg*, aber *⁺mn-*, *⁺ml-*, *⁺mr-*, *⁺nl-*, *⁺nr-*, *⁺lr-*.

Auch /h/ erweist sich hiernach als schwacher Konsonant: *⁺hn-* usw. Historisch leitet sich dieser Konsonant durch allgemeine Schwächung aus urgerm. ⁺/x/ her, gemäß der Urgermanischen (Ersten) Lautverschiebung aus uridg. ⁺/k/. Im Zuge der Schwächung ging er im Silbenkopf vor Konsonant in den germanischen Sprachen verloren. Nur im Isländischen hält er sich noch (*hníga* 'fallen, sich beugen („neigen")', *hlaupa* 'rennen, springen („laufen")', *hringur* 'Ring', *hvítur* 'weiß'). Im Englischen geht /h/ lektal (Cockney) als Phonem bereits vor Vokal verloren, während es sich umgekehrt regional vor /w/ noch hält: *white* mit /hw-/. Im Isländischen ist gerade diese Gruppe durch die generelle Stärkung von /w/ zu /v/ gefährdet; soweit sich /w/ nicht genau in dieser Position der Stärkung widersetzt, wird umgekehrt /h/ zu /k/ gestärkt, um ein hinreichendes Gefälle im Kopf zu bewahren: /hv-/ > /kv-/, z. B. in *hvítur*.

Instruktiv ist auch das bekannte Beispiel des anlautenden /k/ (ähnlich auch /g/) im Englischen. Altenglisch hatte wie das heutige Deutsch die Verbindungen *kn-*, *kl-*, *kr-*, *kw-*, *kV-*. Im Mittelenglischen wurde die schlechteste dieser Verbindungen instabil; das /k/ ging verloren, während das Schriftbild es noch anzeigt: *knee* 'Knie'. Auf der verbleibenden Skala, *kl-*, *kr-*, *kw-*, *kV-* ist nunmehr *kl-* die schlechteste Verbindung, und theoriegemäß ist sie derzeit regional unter Beschuss. Die besseren Verbindungen (mit dem schwächeren Hangkonsonanten) sind indessen überall völlig intakt; *kr-* und *kw-* können erst fallen, nachdem außer *kn-* auch *kl-* beseitigt ist, und zwar wird *kr-* früher instabil werden als *kw-*, es sei denn, /w/ würde wie im Isländischen und Deutschen zu /v/ gestärkt. (zu den englischen Entwicklungen vgl. Lutz 1991).

Statt zum Verlust — oder zur Stärkung — eines ersten Kopfsprachlauts kann es auch zur Schwächung des zweiten kommen. Zum Beispiel haben die romanischen Sprachen Kopfgruppen aus Obstruent plus Liquida geerbt, nachdem Gruppen aus Obstruent plus Nasal schon im Lateinischen verlorengegangen waren:

```
*KN-   Kl-   Kr-
——+——+——+——→  zunehmende
                Kopfqualität
```

In mehreren Sprachen wurden die nunmehr schlechtesten Gruppen instabil, die aus Obstruent und *l*. Zum Beispiel wandelte sich im Portugiesischen in einer ersten Welle *l* nach stimmlosem Obstruenten in den palatalen Halbvokal, woraufhin sich die Gruppe allmählich in den stimmlosen alveopalatalen Frikativ *ch* /ʃ/ entwickelte: lat. *plumbum* 'Blei', *clavis* 'Schlüssel', *flamma* 'Flamme' > port. *chumbo, chave, chama*. In einer zweiten Welle wandelte sich *l* nach stimmhaftem Plosiv sowie — in neu in die Sprache gelangten Wörtern — nach stimmlosem Obstruenten in *r*; man vergleiche span. *blanco* 'weiß', *obligar* 'verpflichten', *regla* 'Regel', *plancha* 'Brett', *clavo* 'Nagel', *flota* 'Flotte' mit port. *branco, obrigar, regra, prancha, cravo, frota*. Das Ziel dieser Entwicklung war das folgende verbesserte System, das freilich durch neue Entlehnungen, auch Doppelentlehnungen, immer wieder gestört wird (z. B. *flauta* neben *frauta* 'Flöte'):

```
*KN-  *Kl-   Kr-
 ├─────┼─────┼──────>  zunehmende
                       Kopfqualität
```

Köpfe aus Obstruent plus *r* sind bisher überall stabil; sie sind ja zum Teil sogar das Ziel des Abbaus der *l*-Gruppen (vgl. zu den Kopfgruppen Vennemann 1989: 17−21 [1993: 326−330]).

3.2.2. Kodagesetz

KODAGESETZ: Eine Silbenkoda ist umso besser,

(a) je näher die Anzahl ihrer Sprachlaute bei Null liegt,
(b) je geringer die Konsonantische Stärke ihres letzten Sprachlauts ist und
(c) je schärfer die Konsonantische Stärke vom letzten Sprachlaut auf den vorangehenden Nukleus zu abfällt.

Zu (a) und (c): Im Sanskrit werden wortfinale Kodas von außen nach innen gekürzt, bis höchstens noch der innerste Konsonant übrig ist: *adan* 'essend', für *ad-ant-s* (vgl. lat. *edēns* für *ed-ent-s*, Akk. *edentem*). Die einzigen Ausnahmen bilden die Gruppen aus /r/ und Plosiv, also gerade diejenigen mit dem steilstmöglichen Anstieg in der Koda: *āvart* '(er) drehte', *amārṭ* '(er) wischte', *vark* '(er) bog'.

Zu (b): Nach der Durchführung von Klingenhebens Gesetz, dem zufolge in der Koda alle lingualen Konsonanten zu /r/ und alle labialen und velaren Konsonanten zu /w/ wurden, erlaubte das Hausa nur noch diese beiden schwächsten Konsonanten in der Koda: ⁺*ma.za.ma.za* 'sehr schnell (redupl.)' > ⁺*maz.ma.za* > *mar.ma.za*; ⁺*ma.kaf.ni.ya* 'eine blinde' > *ma.kaw.ni.ya* (zu *ma.kā.fo* 'ein blinder'); ⁺*hag.ni* 'linke Seite' > *haw.ni* (zu *ba.ha.go* 'ein linkshändiger') usw. (Klingenheben 1928).

3.2.3. Nukleusgesetz

NUKLEUSGESETZ: Ein Silbennukleus ist umso besser,

(a) je näher die Anzahl seiner Sprachlaute bei Eins liegt und
(b) je geringer die Konsonantische Stärke seiner Sprachlaute ist.

Zu (a): Mit Nuklei einer bestimmten Länge (> 1) hat eine Sprache immer auch Nuklei jeder geringeren Länge (≥ 1); und die Obergrenze ist in allen Sprachen niedrig (≤ 3); Monophthonge kommen in allen Sprachen vor, Diphthonge nicht, und Triphthonge sind selten (z. B. im Portugiesischen). Diachronisch zeigt sich die Präferenz in den ständig spontan auftretenden Monophthongierungen; Diphthongierungen treten hingegen nie spontan auf, sondern sind immer durch Zwänge des jeweiligen Systems motiviert.

Zu (b): Niedrige Vokale eignen sich nur als Nuklei (auch, aber nicht gut, als Abglitt von Diphthongen). Je höher ein Vokal, desto mehr tendiert er zur Marginalisierung, vor allem in der Nachbarschaft von anderen Sprachlauten, die sich ebenfalls als Nuklei eignen. Konsonanten eignen sich wenig als Nuklei, und zwar umso weniger, je konsonantischer sie sind. Dies zeigt sich darin, dass nur wenige Sprachen konsonantische Nuklei haben, und dann in aller Regel kontinuierliche Abschnitte am vokalischeren Ende der Skala der Konsonantischen Stärke, also etwa nur *r* (wie das Kroatische, z. B. *Krk* (eine Adria-Insel)) oder *r* und *l* (wie das Sanskrit), oder diese und dazu die Nasale (so ja auch das Standarddeutsche in unakzentuierten Silben: *Becher, Sattel, diesen, diesem*). S. u. § 6.3.

KOROLLAR ZUM NUKLEUSGESETZ: Die Schale einer Silbe unterliegt umso eher gewissen Einschränkungen, je größer die Konsonantische Stärke in ihrem Nukleus ist.

Das Korollar erklärt sich dadurch, dass Kopf- und Kodagesetz nicht mehr leicht in allen Punkten zu erfüllen sind, wenn der Nukleus mit einem starken Sprachlaut besetzt ist; wenn etwa in einer standarddeutschen Lautgeste der Nukleus /s/ enthält, schränkt die Beachtung des Monotonieprinzips die Schale auf Plosive ein, *pst*. So erklärt sich denn auch die einzige Ausnahme zur Regularität der Kopfbesetzung im Tolowa (vgl. § 3.2.1.), dass nämlich ein mit /n/ besetzter Nukleus überhaupt keine Schalenbesetzung erlaubt.

3.3. Intersyllabische Relationen

Sprachen können sich nicht nur nach dem Bau einzelner Silben, sondern auch nach der Weise unterscheiden, wie sich Silben − etwa beim Aufbau der phonologischen Form der Wörter − miteinander verbinden. Eine fruchtbare Forschungsrichtung hat sich an der Frage entwickelt, wie sich Sprachlaute innerhalb einer Sprachlautfolge auf Silben verteilen.

Die bekannteste Antwort auf diese Frage ist das Prinzip der Kopfmaximierung (*maximal onset principle, CV-rule, onset-first principle, left-precedence principle,* vgl. z. B. Varma 1961; Allen 1951; Bell 1977; Selkirk 1982; Clements 1990). Dieses Prinzip ist, jedenfalls wenn man es als universelle Regel des Sprachbaus auffasst, falsch. Das sieht man leicht daran, dass verschiedene Sprachen − sogar ein und dieselbe Sprache auf verschiedenen Stufen ihrer Entwicklung − dieselbe Sprachlautfolge verschieden syllabieren können.

Die letztere Erscheinung kennt man bereits seit der Antike, da unterschiedliche Syllabierungen bei Gruppen aus Obstruent M plus Resonant L − die Alten sprachen von *Muta* bzw. *Liquida*, vgl. auch Vennemann (1987) − zwischen Vokalen, VMLV, bei kurzem Erstvokal den Dichtern der quantitierenden antiken Sprachen Probleme schufen, indem die durch phonologischen Sprachwandel entstandene Syllabierung V$MLV eine kurze und damit leichte, die traditionelle Syllabierung VM$LV eine lange und damit schwere Erstsilbe induzierte (vgl. zur Terminologie Vennemann 1995), wobei gemäß dem Prinzip der Auflösung (lat. *resolutio*) eine schwere Silbe metrisch (übrigens auch phonologisch) zwei leichten Silben gleichgalt (Allen 1970, 1973, 1974). Die Alten fanden sogar einen Terminus für die Kürzung einer Silbe mit kurzem Nukleus durch Tautosyllabierung der Gruppe *Muta cum Liquida* in der Folgesilbe, den Begriff der Korreption (vgl. *correptio Attica* im klassischen Griechisch bei Allen 1973: 211, danach *correptio Argentea* im Gotischen bei Vennemann 1987. Auch die Ausprägungen der antiken Sprachen ohne Korreption, in denen also ML heterosyllabiert wird (M$L), haben ML-Verbindungen im Wortanlaut, z. B. im älteren Griechisch *kr-* in *krókos* 'Krokus', gleichwohl $k^s r$ in *pikrós* [pik.rós] 'scharf' (Allen 1974: 101 f.). Das Prinzip der Kopfmaximierung würde hier [pi.krós] fordern.

Nicht einmal als Ausdruck einer universellen Tendenz lässt sich ein Prinzip der Kopfmaximierung aufrechterhalten. Denn es wäre zwar die Korreption im Einklang mit ihm, nicht aber die ebenfalls vorkommende Produktion (Längung, *productio*) wie im späten Latein, z. B. klass.-lat. *integrum* ['in.te.grum] 'ganz, heil (Nom./Akk. Sg. N.)', mit leichter Pänultima und deshalb Antepänultimalakzent, aber spätlat. *integro* [in.'teg.ro], vgl. port. *inteiro* [in.'tei.ru], span. *entero* [en.'te.ro], ital. *intero* [in.'te:.ro].

Seit der Thematisierung solcher Probleme bei Vennemann (1972), Murray & Vennemann (1982, 1983), Lutz (1985, 1986), Clements (1990), Vennemann (1987, 1988a: 40−55) − seit (1982) unter dem Stichwort „Silbenkontakt" (womit die Verbindung zweier Sprachlaute A und B an der Silbengrenze, A$B, bezeichnet ist) − ist klar, dass die Syllabierung ein graduierender Parameter ist, der in starkem Maße von der relativen Konsonantischen Stärke der beteiligten Sprachlaute abhängt. Zum Beispiel werden im Färöischen Muta und Liquida durchweg in der Zweitsilbe tautosyllabiert (nur *tl* ist hiervon wie in vielen anderen Sprachen ausgenommen), aber im nah verwandten Isländischen gilt Tautosyllabierung nur bei Fortis-Obstruenten M und nur für L = *r*, nicht für L = *l*; vielmehr gilt im Isländischen V$MLV für Fortis-M und L = *r* (und = *v* und *j*, die als ehemalige Halbvokale als noch schwächer denn *r* gelten), aber VM$LV für L = *l* und für alle stärkeren Konsonanten, und für Lenis-M (und alle schwächeren Erstkonsonanten) ausnahmslos. Übrigens ist die Tautosyllabierung stets zweifelsfrei an der Dehnung in offener Tonsilbe zu erkennen, umgekehrt die Heterosyllabierung an der Kürzung. Diese Neuverteilung der Länge betrifft alle alten Kurzvokale, Langvokale und Diphthonge (vgl. zur differentiellen Syllabierung im Isländischen und Färöischen Vennemann 1972, 1978).

Sprachen können sich ferner danach unterscheiden, wie die Syllabierung mit anderen prosodischen Eigenschaften zusammenhängt, etwa mit dem Akzent oder mit der Position im Wort (§ 3.4.).

3.3.1. Silbenkontaktgesetz

SILBENKONTAKTGESETZ: Ein Silbenkontakt ist umso besser, je größer die Stärkedifferenz zwischen dem zweiten und dem ersten Sprachlaut ist.

Illustrierungen des Gesetzes finden sich bereits im vorstehenden Abschnitt. Die isländische Tautosyllabierung V$MLV bei Fortis-M, d. i. M = /p t k s/, und L = /r v j/ (wo /v/

und /j/ aus den entsprechenden Halbvokalen hervorgegangen sind) vermeidet die Kontaktbildung, M^{S}L, genau bei den zwölf ungünstigsten Fällen, in denen die im Kontaktgesetz angesprochene Stärkedifferenz am kleinsten ist, nämlich sogar negativ. Das zeigt sich besonders klar, wenn man die Konsonanten wie in (5) auf einer numerisch interpretierten partiellen Stärkeskala anordnet (Vennemann 1972: 6).

(5)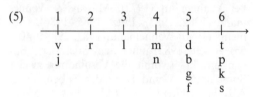

Wir können dann sagen: Zwei Konsonanten A und B bilden im Isländischen nur dann einen Kontakt A^{S}B, wenn die kritische Stärkedifferenz, ks(B) − ks(A), größer als oder gleich −3 ist. Dies ist z. B. bei /pl/ der Fall: ks(/l/) − ks(/p/) = −3; deshalb ist *epli* 'Apfel' syllabisch /ep.li/, erkennbar am kurzen Tonvokal, dazu an der Präaspiration des Fortisplosivs: ['ɛʰp.lɪ]. Aber es ist nicht der Fall bei /pr/: ks(/r/) − ks(/p/) = −4; deshalb ist *skopra* 'rollen' syllabisch /sko.pra/, erkennbar am gedehnten Tonvokal, dazu an der Postaspiration des Fortisplosivs: ['skɔːpʰra].

Wie auch die anderen Präferenzgesetze manifestiert sich das Kontaktgesetz in Sprachveränderungen, die bessere Kontakte herbeiführen. Unter den einschlägigen Mechanismen finden sich die folgenden (Vennemann 1988a):

(6)
1. Tautosyllabierung: A^{S}B → ^{S}AB
2. Gemination: A^{S}B → A^{S}AB
3. Kalibration: A^{S}B → A^{S}C, wo ks(C) > ks(B)
4. Kontaktepenthese: A^{S}B → A^{S}CB, wo ks(C) > ks(A)
5. Kontaktanaptyxe: A^{S}B → AV^{S}B, mit einem Vokal V
6. Kontaktmetathese: A^{S}B → B^{S}A, wo ks(A) > ks(B)

Illustrationen:

(7) 1. aisl. *sköp.ra* > nisl. *skó.pra* 'rollen' (s. o.)
2. urgerm. $^+ap.lV$- > westg. $^+ap.plV$- (engl. *apple*, dt. *Apfel*)
3. mhd. *var.we* > nhd. *Far.be*
4. westg. $^+a.li.ra$ > $^+al.ra$ > $^+al.dra$ > engl. *alder*, dt. *Eller*
5. ahd. *zes.wa* > *ze.sa.wa* 'rechte Hand', got. *taihswo*
6. span./frz. *sa.ble* → bask. *sab.le* > *sal.be* 'Sand', Sidamo (Kuschitisch):
has-némmo → *han.sémmo* 'wir suchen'
hab-némmo → *ham.bémmo* 'wir vergessen'
gud-nónni → *gun.dónni* 'sie beendeten'
duk-nánni → *duŋ.kánni* 'sie tragen'

3.3.2. Hiatgesetz

HIATGESETZ: Ein Hiat ist disfavorisiert, und zwar umso mehr, je geringer die Zahl der Merkmale ist, in denen sich die beiden Hiatvokale unterscheiden, aber auch desto mehr, je besser sich einer der sich berührenden Vokale zum Gleitlaut eignet.

Da ein Hiat als Berührung zweier Nuklei (meistens zweier nuklearer Vokale) bzw. einer offenen und einer nackten Silbe definiert ist, lässt schon das Kopfgesetz, das durch Teil (a) nackte Silben disfavorisiert, erwarten, dass dies auch für Hiate gilt. Tatsächlich finden sich teils dieselben Mechanismen, die leere Köpfe beseitigen, auch im Hiat am Werk, teils kommen weitere Mechanismen zur Anwendung. Zu letzteren gehört die Gewinnung eines Gleitlauts aus der vokalischen Umgebung, z. B. im Italienischen, wo der Gleitlaut sogar zum Obstruenten gestärkt erscheint:

(8)   *Ge.nu.a* > *Ge.no.va*
ru.i.na > *ro.vi.na* 'Ruine'
ma.te.ri.a.le > $^+ma.dri.a.le$ > *ma.dri.ga.le* 'Madrigal'

Es gehört dazu auch die Verschmelzung zweier Vokale identischer Qualität in einen, wobei in Quantitätssprachen stets ein Langvokal resultiert, z. B. im Sanskrit (im Sandhi):

(9)   *na asti* → *nāsti* 'er-ist nicht'
tat.ra ā.sīt → *tat.rā.sīt* 'da war-er'
dē.vī i.va → *dē.vī.va* 'wie eine-Göttin'
sā.dhu uk.tam → *sā.dhūk.tam* 'wohl gesprochen'
kartṛ ṛju → *kartṝju* 'richtig handelnd'

Ferner gehört dazu die Halbvokalisierung (Marginalisierung) eines der beiden sich berührenden Vokale (Nuklei), vgl. wiederum im Sanskrit:

(10) *dē.vī ā.ha* → *dē.vyā.ha* 'die-Göttin sprach'
pi.ba.tu au.ṣa.dham → *pi.ba.tvau.ṣa.dham* 'er-trinke die-Medizin!'
kar.tṛ as.ti → *kar.tras.ti* 'er-ist tätig'

Gegebenenfalls bilden sich dabei Diphthonge, die ihrerseits der Monophthongierung unterliegen können, wie ebenfalls im Sanskrit, wo die Sandhiregeln die Tautosyllabierung der Nuklei und eine vorgeschichtliche Monophthongierung von ⁺ai und ⁺au widerspiegeln:

(11) a, ā + i, ī → ē: vi.nā īr.ṣya.yā → vi.nēr.ṣya.yā 'ohne Eifersucht'
a, ā + u, ū → ō: sā u.vā.ca → sō.vā.ca 'sie sprach'
a, ā + ṛ → ar: ya.thā ṛ.ṣiḥ → ya.thar.ṣiḥ 'wie ein-Seher'

Ein häufig angewandtes elementares Mittel der Hiatbeseitigung ist schließlich die (regressive oder progressive) Elision. Die folgende Elisionsregel für Präfixe im Kinyarwanda (Kenia) ist regressiv:

(12) a + V → V (ausgenommen ist V = i im Nominalsystem)
aba + ami → abami 'Könige'
aka + obo → akobo 'Loch'
aza + oga → azoga 'er wird schwimmen'
ara + emera → aremera 'er glaubt'
aza + imuka → azimuka 'er wird bewegen'
ara + iga → ariga 'er studiert'

Bei Nominalpräfixen findet sich stattdessen Verschmelzung:

(13) aba + iza → abeza 'gute (Plur.)'
ama + inʸo → amenʸo 'Zähne'
aka + ibo → akʸebo 'Korb' (mit Palatalisierung des k vor e)

Die folgende Elisionsregel des Sandhi im Sanskrit ist progressiv:

(14) ē + a → ē: tē api → tē.pi 'diese sogar'
ō + a → ō: pra.bhō a.tra → pra.bhō.tra 'du-Mächtiger hier'

Dass Hiate disfavorisiert sind, sieht man auch daran, dass es Sprachen gibt, in denen sie gar nicht erlaubt sind (nach Bell & Hooper (1978: 8) sind sie nur in etwa der Hälfte der Sprachen der Welt zugelassen), selbst wenn sie ansonsten, nämlich als Erstsilben, nackte Silben zulassen, wie z. B. das Tamazight, ein Zweig des Berberischen (Saib 1978: 96):

(15) /in-na#as/ → [innayas] 'he told him'

3.3.3. Initialgesetz

INITIALGESETZ: Wortmediale Silbenköpfe sind umso besser, je weniger sie sich von wortinitialen Silbenköpfen unterscheiden.

Im Lateinischen sind alle wortmedialen Silbenköpfe auch am Wortanfang erlaubt, aber nicht umgekehrt. Nur am Wortanfang kommt nämlich s- als Präpendix vor: *speciēs* 'Ansicht', *stella* 'Stern', *scola* 'Schule'. Im Wortinnern werden die Gruppen heterosyllabiert, z. B. ist *pestis* 'Pest' syllabisch /pes.tis/, mit trotz Kurzvokal schwerer Erstsilbe (Allen 1973: 137).

Oft ist zu beobachten, dass Gruppen, die — sei es durch interne Prozesse, sei es durch Entlehnung — im Wortinnern entstehen, keine Köpfe bilden, die am Wortanfang verboten sind. So führt die Synkope der Mittelsilben in den folgenden Verbformen (1. P. Sing. Präs.) in süd- und norddeutscher Aussprache zu geringfügig unterschiedlichen Ergebnissen:

(16)   süddeutsch norddeutsch
po.pe.le   *po.ple*   *po.ple*
rä.ke.le   *rä.kle*   *rä.kle*
ver.ei.te.le   *ver.ei.tle*   ***ver.eit.le***
ho.be.le   *ho.ble*   *ho.ble*
re.ge.le   *re.gle*   *re.gle*
ra.de.le   *ra.dle*   ***rad.le***

Bei Verben mit suffixoidem *r* statt *l* ist hingegen das Ergebnis einheitlich (auch im Norddeutschen *ze.te.re* → *ze.tre*, *ha.de.re* → *ha.dre*). Die norddeutschen Syllabierungen -*eit.le* und *rad.le*, letztere erkennbar an der Auslautverhärtung, [raːt.lə], der zufolge Obstruenten in der Koda stimmlos zu sein haben (Vennemann 1972: 12 f., 1978: 178—180), hat ihren Grund offensichtlich darin, dass von allen Gruppen aus Plosiv und Liquida genau die Gruppen aus dentalem Plosiv (*t*, *d*) und lateraler Liquida (*l*) im Wortanlaut ausgeschlossen sind. Vgl. im Englischen *a.tro.cious* : *At.lan.tic*, *a.droit* : *ad.lib*, *ar.thritis* : *ath.lete* und weiter zur Problematik solcher Gruppen Vennemann (1978: 184, Fn. 9).

3.3.4. Finalgesetz

FINALGESETZ: Wortmediale Silbenkodas sind umso besser, je weniger sie sich von wortfinalen Silbenkodas unterscheiden.

Dieses Gegenstück zum Initialgesetz entfaltet nur eine schwache Wirkung; tatsächlich haben viele Sprachen Beschränkungen für wortfinale Kodas, die im Wortinnern nicht gelten. Doch gibt es durchaus den Fall, dass ein wortinterner Prozess nur durch Vergleich mit dem Wortende verständlich wird.

Im Sanskrit, in dem es Tendenzen zur Gemination von Kodaplosiven im Wortinnern gibt, findet sich auch die Gemination von Kopfplosiven im Wortinnern (Varma 1961):

(17) mār.gam → mārg.gam 'das Wild betreffend'
var.gam → varg.gam 'Abwehrer, Abschnitt'
dīr.gha- → dīrg.gha- 'weit, lang'
ar.kaḥ → ark.kaḥ 'Sonne'
ār.ta → ārt.ta 'betroffen'
has.ta- → hast.ta- 'Hand'
puṣ.ṭa- → puṣṭ.ṭa- 'reichlich'
a.vas.kan.da- → a.vask.kan.da- 'Angriff'

An dieser Gemination nehmen als auslösende Kodakonsonanten nur *r* und *s/ṣ* teil — gerade die beiden Konsonanten, die auch im freien Wortauslaut (*in pausa*) nicht erlaubt sind. Genau so ist das Problem auch bei Varma (1961: 62−64, 75) aufgefasst.

3.4. Zum syllabischen Wortbau

In der Erforschung und Diskussion der Silbenstruktur stand lange Zeit die Einzelsilbe im Mittelpunkt. Das hatte und hat durchaus eine gewisse Berechtigung, wie auch die Einrichtung des obigen § 3.2. zeigt. Doch gibt es hierzu auch Relativierungen, und zwar in zwei Richtungen. Einerseits wird erwogen, inwieweit die Einzelsilbe auf elementarere Kategorien zurückgeführt werden kann (Bell 1977, 1978, Vennemann 1988b, 1994, Restle 1998). Dies ist eine Frage der theoretischen Phonologie. Andererseits gibt es Überlegungen, inwieweit die Silbe im Zusammenhang mit anderen Kategorien erforscht werden muss, insbesondere der des Wortes und der dieses mitkonstituierenden Prosodien (Vennemann 1974; Auer 1994), hier vor allem des Wortakzents, der allein eine umfangreiche typologisch-sprachvergleichende Forschung hervorgerufen hat (vgl. z. B. Hyman 1977; Liberman & Prince 1977; Halle & Vergnaud 1987; Hayes 1995; Kager 1995; Halle & Idsardi 1995). Diesen die Einzelsilbe übergreifenden Zusammenhängen ist zum Teil bereits durch die Einrichtung des § 3.3. Rechnung getragen, und verschiedentlich wurde in den vorstehenden Abschnitten darauf hingewiesen, dass sich Sprachen erheblich im Verhältnis ihrer Silben zur Position im Wort unterscheiden können. Weiteres sei hier an einigen charakteristischen Beispielen demonstriert.

3.4.1. Syllabierung und Akzent

Ist zwar ein einfaches Kopfmaximierungsprinzip nicht korrekt (vgl. oben § 3.3.), so lassen sich doch Bedingungen angeben, unter denen eine Syllabierung als relativ gut zu gelten hat. Der graduierende und multipel bedingte Charakter der Syllabierung wurde bezeichnenderweise zuerst in der historischen Phonologie, nämlich der Erforschung syllabierungssensitiver handschriftlicher Worttrennungen am Zeilenende deutlich (Lutz 1985, 1986). Hier kann nur knapp das Ergebnis jener Untersuchungen zusammengefasst werden (nach Vennemann 1988a: 58−64).

DEFINITION DER REIMATTRAKTIVITÄT: Die Reimattraktivität einer Silbe ist ihre Fähigkeit, den Anlaut der Folgesilbe zu sich zu ziehen (d. h., mit ihm als Verlängerung ihres Reims wieder eine Silbe zu bilden).

DEFINITION DER KÖRPERATTRAKTIVITÄT: Die Körperattraktivität einer Sprachlautfolge ist ihre Fähigkeit, den Auslaut der vorausgehenden Silbe zu sich zu ziehen (d. h. mit ihm als Verlängerung ihres Körpers wieder eine Silbe zu bilden).

REIMATTRAKTIVITÄTSGESETZ: Die Reimattraktivität einer Silbe ist umso größer (d. h. eine Heterosyllabierung in sie hinein ist umso besser),

(a) je stärker sie relativ zur Folgesilbe akzentuiert ist,
(b) je kürzer ihr Reim ist und
(c) je geringer die konsonantische Stärke in ihm ist, insbesondere im Auslaut.

KOPFATTRAKTIVITÄTSGESETZ: Die Körperattraktivität einer Silbe ist umso größer (d. h. eine Heterosyllabierung in sie hinein ist umso besser),

(a) je stärker sie relativ zur vorausgehenden Silbe akzentuiert ist,
(b) je kürzer ihr Körper ist und
(c) je geringer die konsonantische Stärke in ihm ist, insbesondere im Anlaut.

DEFINITION DES KONTAKTBETTS: Sei A$^\$$B der Silbenkontakt einer Silbenfolge $S_1.S_2$. Das Resultat der Verkürzung des Reims von S_1 um seinen Auslaut (den Kontaktsprachlaut A) heißt die An-Silbe des Kontakts; das Resultat der Verkürzung des Körpers von S_2 um seinen Anlaut (den Kontaktsprachlaut B) heißt die Ab-Silbe des Kontakts. Die Folge aus seiner An-Silbe und seiner Ab-Silbe heißt das Bett des Kontakts.

KONTAKTEINBETTUNG: Ein Silbenkontakt A$^\$$B ist umso besser eingebettet (d. h. das Bett des Kontakts ist umso besser), je größer die Reimattraktivität seiner An-Silbe und die Körperattraktivität seiner Ab-Silbe ist.

ALLGEMEINES SYLLABIERUNGSGESETZ (LUTZ' GESETZ): Eine Syllabierung ist umso besser,

(a) je besser der resultierende Silbenkontakt ist und
(b) je besser dieser Silbenkontakt eingebettet ist.

Die Richtigkeit dieser Bewertungen lässt sich an Lutz' Zahlen unmittelbar ablesen.

Zum Beispiel sagt das Gesetz für eine gegebene Gruppe, etwa *dr*, dass zwischen einer akzentuierten und einer unakzentuierten Silbe ein Kontakt *d.r* besser ist als zwischen zwei unakzentuierten Silben; tatsächlich ist in den altenglischen Handschriften das (abgerundete) Verhältnis der Trennschreibungen von *d* und *r* (*d/r*) zu den Zusammenschreibungen auf der nächsten Zeile (*/dr*) im ersteren Fall 12:1, im letzteren 1:4.

Ferner sagt das Gesetz, dass bei gegebener Gruppe, etwa *pr*, zwischen akzentuierter Erstsilbe und unakzentuierter Zweitsilbe die Kontaktbildung *p.r* nach Kurzvokal besser ist als nach Langvokal; tatsächlich ist das Verhältnis von *p/r* zu */pr* nach Kurzvokal 1:1, nach Langvokal 1:5.

Schließlich sagt das Gesetz, dass ein Hangkonsonant unmittelbar vor dem Kontakt diesen schlecht macht, und zwar umso mehr, je stärker dieser Hangkonsonant ist. Tatsächlich steigt das Verhältnis von *d/r* zu */dr*, das bei Abwesenheit eines Hangkonsonanten (*Vd/r*, *V/dr*) ungefähr 1:1 ist, bei vorhandenem C (*Cd/r*, *C/dr*) folgendermaßen an: für C = *r* 1:1,5, für C = *l* 1:6, für C = *n* 1:12, für C = *d* (Geminate, also *dd/r* zu *d/dr*) 1:24.

3.4.2. Silbenbau und Akzent

Die Zusammenhänge zwischen Silbenbau und Akzent sind vielfältig, aber alle scheinen einem übergreifenden Präferenzgesetz zu genügen (vgl. ähnlich Vennemann 1988a: 58):

AKZENTSILBENGESETZ: Silbenstrukturkomplexitäten sind umso weniger disfavorisiert, je mehr rhythmische Prominenz auf einer Silbe liegt.

Das Gesetz manifestiert sich am deutlichsten, wo sich Silbenstrukturbeschränkungen kategorisch mit dem Wortakzent verbinden. Zum Beispiel wurden im Isländischen in unakzentuierten Silben Quantitäts- und Chromatizitätsunterschiede bei den Vokalen eingeebnet, bis nur die drei Kurzvokale *i/e*, *a*, *u/o* (heute [ɪ, a, ʏ]) übrig blieben, während in Akzentsilben ca. 22 Kurz-, Lang- und Diphthongphoneme kontrastierten; im Mittelhochdeutschen führte der entsprechende Prozess bis zur gänzlichen Neutralisation in [ə] (sog. Vokalreduktion).

Manche strukturelle Veränderung, die früher pauschal in Kategorien wie Dissimilation, Haplologie oder Metathese eingeordnet wurden, erweist sich nunmehr als subtile Implementation des Akzentsilbengesetzes. So liegt in der im brasilianischen Portugiesisch zu hörenden Aussprache *problema* [pu.'βre.mə] außer der oben in § 3.2.1. besprochenen Kopfverbesserung *ble* > *bre* dissimilatorische Haplologie der ersten Liquida vor. Warum der ersten? Das Gesetz beantwortet diese Frage.

In span. *pe.'ri.c(u)lu* > *pe.'li.gro* 'Gefahr', *mi.'ra.c(u)lu* > *mi.'la.gro* 'Wunder', *pa.'ra.b(o)la* > *pa.'la.bra* 'Wort' liegt sicherlich Liquidenmetathese vor. Warum aber wird nicht umgekehrt *si.mu.'la.cro* 'Trugbild' zu *si.mu.'ra.clo*? Auch hier gibt das Akzentsilbengesetz zusammen mit dem Kopfgesetz die Antwort: *Cl*-Köpfe sind schlechter als *Cr*-Köpfe, erst recht in unakzentuierten Silben. Man wird aus einem solchen Silbenkopf *l* gegen *r* nicht herein-, sondern nur hinaustauschen.

Sehr verbreitet ist im Italienischen die Hangversetzung der Liquiden (diese und zahlreiche weitere Beispiele bei Rohlfs (1972: §§ 322–323), sortiert und interpretiert bei Vennemann (1997: 316–318)):

(18) (ältere Schriftsprache 'stru.po < 'stu.-pro 'Schändung', 'dren.to < 'den.tro 'innerhalb'
Schriftsprache 'fia.ba < ⁺'fla.ba < 'fa.b(u)la 'Märchen'
altit. ca.'pres.to < ca.'pes.tro 'Seil'
im Dialekt von Marken 'cra.pa < 'ca.pra 'Ziege'
von Rovigo 'cio.pa < 'clo.pa 'Paar' < 'co.p(u)la 'Band'
von Kalabrien 'prub.bi.cu < 'plub.-bi.cu < 'pub.bli.co < 'pub.li.co, lat. *publicus* 'öffentlich'

Wie man sieht, wandert die Liquida vom Kopfhang einer unakzentuierten zum Kopfhang einer akzentuierten Silbe. Allerdings ist die Wanderung zugleich eine nach vorn, und tatsächlich mag eine zweite Tendenz im Spiel sein (Vennemann 1997: 318):

FRÜHSILBENGESETZ: Silbenstrukturkomplexitäten sind umso weniger disfavorisiert, je früher im Wort die Silbe liegt.

Als Grenzfall gilt die Bevorzugung der Erstsilbe (Erstsilbengesetz). In wieweit diese Tendenz universell ist oder aber auf trochäische Sprachen beschränkt ist, während vielleicht für jambische Sprachen ein entsprechendes Spätsilbengesetz (mit Letztsilbenfavorisierung) gilt, ist noch zu untersuchen. – Jedenfalls finden sich in den Dialekten Italiens die folgenden Hangversetzungen:

(19) Kalabrisch *cra.'pes.tu* < *ca.'pes.tro* 'Seil', *fri.'nes.ta* < *fi.'nes.tra* 'Fenster'
Sizilianisch *tri.'a.tu* < *te.'a.tro* 'Theater'
Toskanisch *pra.'do.ne* < *pa.'dro.ne* 'Herr', *crom.'pa.re* < *com.'pra.re* 'kaufen', *drot.'ti.na* < *dot.'tri.na* 'Doktrin'
Altligurisch *cras.'ta.o* < *cas.'tra.to* 'kastriert'
Mailändisch *dro.vá* < *a.do.pe.'ra.re* 'gebrauchen'
Kalabrisch *chium.'pi.re* 'reifen' < ⁺*clum.'pi.re* < *com.'ple.re* 'füllen'
Verbreitet im Süden: *fri.'va.ru* (lat. *februārius*, it. *febbraio*) 'Februar'

Eine Bewegung in der umgekehrten Richtung wird von Rohlfs als Ausnahme angesehen; sein einziges Beispiel ist altpadov. *pà.tri.ga* < *'pra.ti.ca* (griech.-lat. *practicus*).

3.4.3. Silbenstruktur und Rhythmus

Der Satzrhythmus bildet seine eigene Typologie (→ Art. 99). Hier sei lediglich darauf hingewiesen, dass mit den Rhythmustypen auch Silbenbaupräferenzen korrelieren.

RHYTHMUSGESETZ: Silbenstrukturkomplexitäten sind umso weniger favorisiert, je kleiner die rhythmuskonstituierende Einheit ist.

Zum Beispiel hat das Englische, das als prototypische „akzentzählende" Sprache gilt, eine reiche Silbenstruktur, mit Hangbesetzung in Kopf und Koda, Ambisyllabizität, und Appendices an beiden Worträndern und sogar im Wortinnern. Das Spanische, das als prototypische „silbenzählende" Sprache gilt, hat maximale Silbenbasen der Gestalt CCVC, wobei Kopfhang und Koda starken Einschränkungen unterliegen, und es hat keine Ambisyllabizität und keine Appendices; der einzige lateinische Appendix, präpendikales *s-*, wurde und wird durch Prosthesis beseitigt, z. B. *sco.la* > *es.cue.la* 'Schule', *spatha* > *es.pa.da* 'Schwert', *Estocolmo*. Das Japanische, eine „morenzählende" Sprache, reiht morische Einheiten der Gestalt CV, V und VC aneinander, wobei Koda-C auf den „Mora-Nasal" und den „Mora-Obstruenten" (einen mit dem obstruentischen C der folgenden Moraeinheit identischen Obstruenten, der Fall der Geminate) beschränkt ist; Ambisyllabizität und Appendices gibt es nicht.

4. Typologie des Silbengewichts

4.1. Binäre Silbengewichtssysteme

Das klassische Konzept des Silbengewichts fußt auf der Beobachtung, dass bestimmte Typen von Silben aufgrund ihrer strukturellen Eigenschaften den Wortakzent auf sich ziehen, während andere Typen den Akzent entweder nicht anziehen oder ihn gar abstoßen, indem sie überhaupt nicht betonbar sind. Für die daraus resultierende Dichotomie sind die Termini **schwere Silben**, d. h. solche, die den Akzent auf sich ziehen, und **leichte Silben** üblich.

Das Phänomen lässt sich gut am Wortakzent des Lateinischen zeigen. Die vorletzte Silbe (Pänultima) enthält den Hauptakzent dann, wenn sie entweder durch einen Konsonanten geschlossen ist (vgl. (21 c)) oder einen Langvokal oder Diphthong enthält (vgl. (21a−b)). Eine Pänultima mit einem monophthongischen Kurzvokal in offener Silbe (vgl. (21d)) wird nicht akzentuiert. Wenn man Silben mit den akzentattrahierenden Eigenschaften (Langvokal, Diphthong, postnuklearer Konsonant) unter dem Terminus schwere Silbe zusammenfasst, lässt sich für das Lateinische die Akzentregel in (20) aufstellen.

(20) Akzentregel des Lateinischen
Der Akzent von drei- und mehrsilbigen Wörtern liegt auf der Pänultima, falls diese schwer ist, sonst auf der Antepänultima. Bei Zwei- und Einsilbern fällt er auf die vorderste Silbe.

Unter der Voraussetzung, dass der Akzent vom Ende des Wortes her einen geeigneten Landeplatz sucht, nie aber die letzte Silbe treffen kann (mit Ausnahme von einsilbigen Wörtern), „lassen" also leichte Silben (im Fall des Lateinischen offene Silben mit kurzem Monophthong) und nur diese den Akzent bis zur Antepänultima „durch".

(21) a) *re.gí.na* b) *collaúdat*

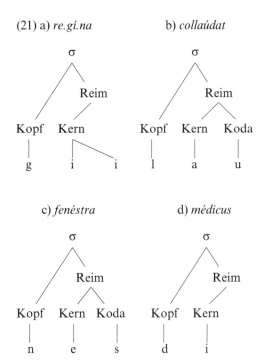

c) *fenéstra* d) *médicus*

(22') a) b) c) d)

(23') a) b) c) d)

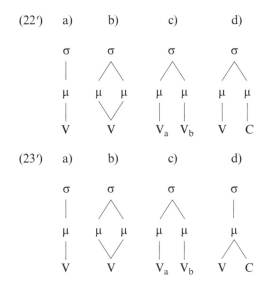

In dieser Repräsentationsform kommt unmittelbar zum Ausdruck, dass ein einfacher postnuklearer Konsonant in (22'd) zum Silbengewicht beiträgt, indem er von einer eigenen Moraeinheit dominiert wird, in (23'd) jedoch nicht.

Die Situation kompliziert sich allerdings zusätzlich dadurch, dass es Mischtypen zwischen (22) und (23) zu geben scheint, bei denen manche CVC-Strukturen schwer, andere aber leicht sind. Einen solchen Fall nimmt Hayes (1995: 242 ff., 302) für das zentralalaskische Yupik an, indem er geschlossene Silben mit Kurzvokal am Wortanfang als schwer, sonst als leicht bewertet.

Die bisher beschriebenen Silbengewichtssysteme legen nahe, dass Langvokale eine

Es ist jedoch wichtig festzuhalten, dass die akzentattrahierenden strukturellen Eigenschaften sprachspezifisch sind. Neben dem weitverbreiteten Silbengewichtssystem, das im Lateinischen wirkt (vgl. (22)), ist vor allem das in (23) beschriebene Gewichtssystem zu nennen, wie es z. B. dem Malayalam (Dravidisch, vgl. Mohanan 1986; Broselow et al. 1997), Cahuilla (Utoaztekisch, vgl. Seiler 1977) und Wargamay (Pama-Nyungan, vgl. Dixon 1981) zu eigen ist.

(22) Leichte Silbe   Schwere Silbe   (C_0 = null oder mehr Konsonanten)
     C_0V $C_0V_aV_aC_0$ (langer Monophthong)
                     $C_0V_aV_bC_0$ ((langer) Diphthong)
                     C_0VC_1 (C_1 = ein oder mehr Konsonanten)

(23) Leichte Silbe   Schwere Silbe   (C_0 = null oder mehr Konsonanten)
     C_0VC_0 $C_0V_aV_aC_0$ (langer Monophthong)
                     $C_0V_aV_bC_0$ ((langer) Diphthong)

In dem in (23) beschriebenen System besteht im Gegensatz zu Sprachen wie dem Lateinischen keine metrische Äquivalenz zwischen den (Teil-)Strukturen VC und VV. Letztere lassen sich (unter Vernachlässigung der silbengewichtsinsensitiven Bestandteile der Silbe) in einer moraischen Notation in Abhängigkeit vom Silbengewicht wie folgt darstellen, wobei leichte Silben als einmorig, schwere als (mindestens) zweimorig gekennzeichnet sind:

Silbe universell schwer machen, während postnukleare Konsonanten nur in einem Teil der gewichtssensitiven Sprachen zum Silbengewicht beitragen. Die Gültigkeit eines solchen potentiellen Universales könnte jedoch zumindest von zwei eng verwandten Sprachen, dem Holländischen und dem Deutschen, in Frage gestellt werden. Unabhängig voneinander fordern Lahiri & Koreman (1988) und Kager (1989) für das Holländische und Vennemann (1990) für das Deutsche, dass geschlossene Silben und diphthongische Silben in diesen Sprachen als schwer zu werten sind, während offene Silben, deren Vokal unter Akzent immer lang realisiert wird, als leicht gelten müssen. Das Universale kann jedoch beibehalten werden, falls man für das Deutsche und Holländische den phonetischen Kontrast zwischen langen und kurzen Vokalen auf eine phonologische Silbenschnittopposition zurückführt und damit keine phonologische Quantitätsopposition annehmen muss. Eine auf der Silbenschnittkorrelation basierende Definition des Silbengewichts im Deutschen ist in (24) zu finden.

(24) Silbengewicht im Deutschen
Eine Vollsilbe heißt leicht im Standarddeutschen, wenn sie offen, monophthongisch und sanft geschnitten ist; sonst schwer.

Wertet man durch scharfen Schnitt ambisyllabisch geschlossene und diphthongische Silben als geschlossen, kann man auch die folgende alternative Formulierung wählen:

(24′) Silbengewicht im Deutschen
Im Standarddeutschen sind offene Silben leicht, geschlossene Silben schwer.

Die Richtigkeit dieser Einteilung erweist sich darin, dass Antepänultima-Akzent auf *Kakadu* möglich (und richtig) ist, auf *Veranda, Suleika* und *Marokko* nicht (standarddeutsche Pänultimaregel).

4.2. Ternäre und multiple Gewichtssysteme

Für manche Sprachen erscheint es sinnvoll, die oben beschriebene Zweigliedrigkeit des Silbengewichtssystems zu erweitern. So weist das Hindi (Kelkar 1968; Hayes 1995) das in (25) charakterisierte dreistufige Gewichtssystem auf. Enthält ein Wort eine überschwere Silbe, so wird diese betont, bei mehreren überschweren Silben die am weitesten rechts stehende, sofern sie nicht die letzte Silbe ist (vgl. (26 a)). Wenn keine der Silben überschwer ist, erhält die am weitesten rechts stehende schwere Silbe den Akzent, sofern sie nicht die letzte Silbe ist. Eine schwere Ultima erhält den Akzent nur, wenn sie die einzige schwere Silbe des Wortes ist (vgl. (26 b)). Bei einer Relationierung überschwer > schwer > leicht lässt sich die Akzentregel des Hindi wie in (27) formulieren.

(25) Ternäres Silbengewicht des Hindi
überschwer $C_0V{:}C, C_0VCC$
schwer $C_0V{:}, C_0VC$
leicht C_0V

(26) Hindi (Hayes 1995: 276 ff., Daten aus Kelkar 1968: 27−29)
a) *á:zmā:ja:h, a:zmaá:nja:h, musalmá:n*
b) *ruká:ya:, qísmat, rupiá:*
c) *samíti*

(27) Akzentregel des Hindi
Der Wortakzent liegt auf der Silbe mit dem höchsten Silbengewicht. Im Falle eines Gleichstands wird die letzte der schwersten Silben akzentuiert, nicht aber die Ultima.

Die Basis der bisher angeführten Silbengewichtssysteme sind silbenstrukturelle Unterscheidungen (verzweigender Nukleus, verzweigender Reim). Die physische Realisierung ist dabei ikonisch zur Terminologie: schwere Silben verfügen über ein „Mehr" an Substanz im Silbenreim. Für eine begrenzte Anzahl von Sprachen wurden jedoch auch Silbengewichtsdistinktionen vorgeschlagen, die zusätzlich zu silbenstrukturellen auf qualitativen Unterscheidungen von Silbenbestandteilen aufbauen.

Ein solches elaboriertes Silbengewichtssystem wurde z. B. für das Pirahã (Mura, Nordwest-Brasilien) von Everett & Everett (1984), Davis (1988a, b) und Hayes (1995) vorgeschlagen. Das Pirahã unterscheidet demnach nicht nur zwischen fünf Gewichtsabstufungen, sondern es bezieht auch den Faktor der segmentalen, in diesem Fall konsonantischen Qualität in die Hierarchie des Silbengewichts ein:

(28) Fünfgliedriges Silbengewicht des Pirahã (nach Hayes 1995: 286, T = stimmloser Konsonant, D = stimmhafter Konsonant)
***** $TV{:}C_0$
**** $DV{:}C_0$
*** $V{:}C_0$
** TV
* DV

(29) Akzentregel des Pirahã
Der Akzent liegt auf der schwersten der drei letzten Silben eines Wortes. Im Falle eines Gleichstands wird die letzte akzentuiert.

(30) Akzentdaten zum Pirahã (Davis 1988b: 2)
kái.bai   'species of monkey'
bii.sái   'red'
ʔá.ba.gi   'toucan'
ʔa.ba.pá   Eigenname

Als Beispiel für ein vierstufiges (Payne 1990) bzw. dreistufiges (Hayes 1995) Gewichtssystem, das auf vokalischen Qualitätsunterschieden beruht, kann das peruanische Asheninca (Arawakisch) dienen:

(31) Dreigliedriges Silbengewicht des Asheninca (nach Hayes 1995: 288 ff., N = Nasal)
    ***   CVV
    **   C*a*, C*o*, C*e*, C*i*N,
    *   C*i*

Allerdings kann eine gewisse Skepsis an der Gültigkeit der in diesem Abschnitt angeführten Gewichtssysteme nicht ausbleiben. Zum einen sind sie überaus selten, zum anderen gestaltet sich in vielen dieser Fälle die Formulierung von Akzentregeln selbst mit der Annahme derart ungewöhnlicher Silbengewichtssysteme durchaus schwierig.

4.3. Prominenz

Daten wie die des eben erwähnten Pirahã und des Asheninca illustrieren, dass es neben den klassischen strukturellen Eigenschaften wie Vokalquantität oder Verzweigung des Silbenreims noch andere akzentattrahierende Eigenschaften gibt, die insbesondere im qualitativen und tonalen Bereich zu finden sind. So zieht im Golin (Chimbu, Neuguinea) die letzte Silbe mit einem Hochton den Wortakzent auf sich (Bunn & Bunn 1970).

Da solche Eigenschaften wie Töne in einem sogenannten moraischen Silbenstrukturmodell (siehe § 5.) nicht auf derselben Ebene repräsentiert werden wie die klassischen akzentattrahierenden Eigenschaften, prägte Hayes (1995: 270 ff.) den Begriff der Prominenz (vgl. auch die Modifikationen in Goedemans 1998, Abschnitt 4.5. und 5.). Die Unterscheidung von Silbenquantität und Prominenz ist somit theorieabhängig und nur in moraischen Beschreibungsansätzen nötig.

Zu ebenso theorieabhängigen Diskussionen führt die Frage, ob nur bestimmte Bereiche einer Silbe zum Gewicht bzw. zur Prominenz beitragen können, oder alle (vgl. auch S. 1327). So werden potentielle Akzentsysteme, die auf die strukturelle (oder qualitative) Beschaffenheit des Silbenkopfes/Anfangsrandes Bezug nehmen (vgl. z. B. auch (28) oben), von Hayes (1995) und Goedemans (1998) grundsätzlich als Prominenzsysteme und nicht als Gewichtssysteme geführt, da sich eine solche offensichtlich strukturelle Unterscheidung in dem von diesen Autoren verwendeten moraischen Modell nicht als solche akkommodieren lässt.

Unter dem Aspekt der Erhöhung der Komplexität einer allgemeinen Akzenttheorie, die durch die Annahme von multiplen Silbengewichten und von Prominenz entsteht, verwundert es nicht, dass in einigen dieser Fälle alternative Analysen vorgeschlagen wurden, die dies zu vermeiden suchen. Das lässt sich an der Analyse des Akzentsystems des Mathimathi (alias Madimadi, Pama-Nyungan) illustrieren.

(32) Akzentregel des Mathimathi
Der Akzent liegt in zweisilbigen Wörtern auf der ersten Silbe. In drei- und mehrsilbigen Wörtern wird die zweite Silbe betont, wenn diese schwer ist (verzweigender Nukleus oder postvokalischer Konsonant) oder wenn die erste Silbe leicht ist und gleichzeitig die zweite Silbe mit einem koronalen Konsonanten beginnt. Ansonsten wird die Erstsilbe betont.

Während Davis (1988b: 4 ff.) die Akzentregel in (32) vorschlägt, kann Gahl (1996) zeigen, dass sich das Phänomen durch die morphologische Charakteristik des Mathimathi erklären lässt, indem sich die bestehende Korrelation zwischen Zweitsilbenbetonung und koronalen Konsonanten durch stammfinale Betonung und durch ein Vorherrschen von pränuklearen koronalen Konsonanten in Finalsilben von Stämmen ergibt.

Es bleibt daher abzuwarten, ob eine Reanalyse der anderen typologisch markierten Gewichtssysteme es ermöglichen wird, Silbengewichtsdistinktionen auf eine silbenstrukturell basierte Zweistufigkeit zu beschränken.

4.4. Extrametrikalität

Eine wichtige Eigenschaft des in § 4.1. illustrierten Wortakzents des Lateinischen ist, dass (abgesehen von Monosyllaben) die letzte Silbe eines Wortes nie betont ist, selbst wenn sie nach geltenden Silbengewichtsdefinitionen schwer oder überschwer ist. Dieses Phänomen lässt sich dadurch beschreiben, dass man Ultimae als extrametrisch klassifiziert und auf der verbleibenden Basis von rechts nach links moraische Trochäen aufbaut (vgl. Hayes 1995: 91 f.). Der Akzent trifft dann im Lateinischen die vorletzte Mora eines Wortes (wobei Kurzvokale und postnukleare Konsonanten als einmorig, Langvokale und Diphthonge als zweimorig definiert werden). Die

Annahme von silbischer Extrametrikalität ist allerdings in vielen Fällen nur durch die in manchen Theorien selbst auferlegte Beschränkung motiviert, dass Füße maximal binär sein sollten. Zum anderen muss Extrametrikalität für den Fall ausgeschlossen werden, dass sie den gesamten Anwendungsbereich einer Regel trifft, da sonst z. B. einsilbige Wörter im Lateinischen gar nicht akzentuiert werden dürften.

Neben der syllabischen Extrametrikalität wurden für viele andere Entitäten mit Konstituentenstatus (Segment, Fuß, phonologisches Wort, Affix) ähnliche Konzepte vorgeschlagen. Das Instrument der Extrametrikalität (vgl. Liberman & Prince 1977; Hayes 1979; Roca 1992) lässt sich somit allgemeiner als das Verbergen phonologischer Konstituenten zum Zwecke einer einfacheren Anwendung von phonologischen Regeln charakterisieren.

Das Phänomen der segmentalen Extrametrikalität lässt sich gut am Estnischen zeigen. Während wortinitiale und mediale CVC-Strukturen schwer sind, verhalten sie sich wortfinal wie leichte CV-Strukturen, indem sie notwendigerweise unbetont sind:

(33) Silbengewicht im Estnischen (Prince 1980: 530 f.)

	nichtfinal	final
leicht	CV	CV, CVC
schwer	CV:	CV:
	CVC	CV:(:)C
	CV:(:)C(C)	CVC(:)C

Unter der Annahme, dass wortfinale Konsonanten im Estnischen nicht für das Silbengewicht und damit die Akzentzuweisung sichtbar sind, d. h. extrametrisch sind, kann das Silbengewicht nichtfinaler und finaler Silben gleich behandelt werden (CV-Strukturen sind leicht, alle anderen schwer).

Da das Konzept der Extrametrikalität die Erzeugungs- und Beschreibungskapazität einer Theorie stark erhöht, wurden Beschränkungen dieses Instruments vorgeschlagen, deren wichtigste die Beschränkung auf den rechten oder linken Rand der Domäne der anzuwendenden Regel ist (z. B. den rechten oder linken Rand eines Wortes für den Wortakzent). Zudem muss darauf hingewiesen werden, dass das Ausblenden von phonologischer Basisinformation oft als kontraintuitiv bewertet wird. Eine Zusammenfassung von Argumenten, die trotz dieser Nachteile für die Annahme von Extrametrikalität sprechen, bietet Hayes (1995: 58 ff.).

5. Silbenstrukturmodelle

Die in der heutigen Forschung so wichtige Teilung der Silbe in verschiedene subsyllabische Konstituenten ist eine relativ rezente Erscheinung. Einer der ersten Vorschläge stammt von Pike & Pike (1947), die terminologisch zwischen einem Silbenrand (*margin*) und dem Silbennukleus trennen. Hockett führt 1955 die Teilung in Kopf (*onset*), Nukleus (*peak*) und Koda (*coda*) ein, die er im intervokalischen Bereich durch das *interlude* ergänzt.

Durch Gruppierung dieser bereits in § 2. eingeführten Grundkonstituenten entstehen die unter den Begriffen Silbenkörper, Silbenreim und Silbenschale geläufigen Einheiten. Diese bilden die Grundlage für die in Abbildung (34) illustrierten hierarchischen Silbenmodelle. Sie stehen im Kontrast mit flachen Silbenstrukturen (vgl. (1)), wie sie etwa von Kahn (1980), Clements & Keyser (1983), Davis (1982) und Noske (1993) vertreten werden.

(34) Hierarchische Silbenmodelle
 a) *Reimstruktur* b) *Körperstruktur*

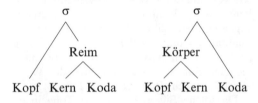

 c) *Schalenstruktur* d) *Überlappungsstruktur*

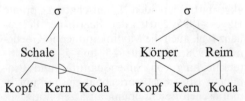

Für jedes der oben angeführten Silbenmodelle kann Evidenz angeführt werden, die es als (zur Beschreibung der phonologischen Daten) besonders geeignet erscheinen lassen. Darunter fallen insbesondere phonotaktische Beschränkungen zwischen Kopf/Kern/Koda und die Beschreibung des Wortakzents, aber auch andere Phänomene, die sich auf subsyllabische Einheiten beziehen lassen, wie Reduplikationen und Versprecher (vgl. Berg 1989; Picard 1992).

Donegan & Stampe (1978), Davis (1988a) und insbesondere Vennemann (1988b) haben darauf hingewiesen, dass die Frage, welches Silbenmodell das beste sei, kaum befriedigend zu beantworten ist. Angemessener erscheint die Fragestellung, welches der vorgeschlagenen Modelle für die Beschreibung bestimmter Daten geeigneter ist.

Für die Reimstruktur (vgl. neben vielen anderen Kuryłowicz 1948; Anderson 1969: Fudge 1969; Selkirk 1982; Treiman & Kessler 1995) spricht, dass die weitaus meisten Akzentregeln sensitiv für die interne Struktur des Reims sind.

So ziehen im Lateinischen diejenigen Silben den Akzent auf sich, deren Reim direkt oder indirekt verzweigt (vgl. (21)). Dies setzt allerdings voraus, dass man Langvokale parallel zu Diphthongen als Abfolge zweier kurzer Vokale repräsentiert. Demgegenüber sind leichte Silben durch einen nichtverzweigenden Reim gekennzeichnet. Kopfkonsonanten haben im Lateinischen keinen Einfluss auf das Silbengewicht und damit auf die Akzentzuweisung.

Als Beispiel für eine phonotaktische Beschränkung, die für das Reimmodell spricht, kann die Beschränkung des Neuhochdeutschen angeführt werden, dass eine hauptbetonte offene Silbe einen langen, gespannten Vokal oder einen Diphthong aufweisen muss. Diese Beschränkung gilt aber nicht für qua Ambisyllabizität geschlossene Silben, so dass wiederum von einer Äquivalenz von V_aV_a, V_aV_b und VC ausgegangen werden muss, die sich am elegantesten als obligatorische Verzweigung des Silbenreims beschreiben lässt.

Daneben spricht die Häufigkeit des Endreims in der Dichtung (Gleichheit/Ähnlichkeit des Silbenreims) für eine auf dem Reimmodell aufbauende Silbenstruktur.

Der Phänomenbereich der kompensatorischen Dehnung (z. B. lateinisch *kasnus > ka:nus, vgl. Ingria 1980; Hayes 1989 und Bickmore 1995 für weitere Beispiele) bietet sich prima facie zur Untermauerung hierarchischer Silbenmodelle an, ist jedoch nicht auf den Silbenreim beschränkt (vgl. griechisch *odwos > o:dos, *selasna: > lesbisch selanna — ionisch selɛ:nɛ:) und scheidet daher zur Stützung aus.

Evidenz für die Angemessenheit des Körpermodells hat insbesondere Stuart Davis (1982, 1988a, b) in die Diskussion eingebracht. So führt er das zentralaustralische Aranda mit einer Akzentregel an, der zufolge Wörter, deren erste Silbe nackt ist (d. h. mit dem Nukleus beginnen), auf der zweiten Silbe betont werden, während bedeckte erste Silben den Akzent auf sich ziehen.

Zwar könnte gegen dieses Argument eingewendet werden, dass sich die Akzentregel im Aranda auch als Besetztheit vs. Nichtbesetztheit des Silbenkopfes beschreiben ließe (statt über die Verzweigung des Silbenkörpers). Dieser Einwand greift jedoch in gleichem Maße für die akzentologische Reimevidenz, die sich ja ebenfalls mit ausschließlichem Rekurs auf Silbennukleus und Silbenkoda beschreiben ließe. Ähnliche silbenkopfsensitive Akzentregeln wurden für das australische Mathimathi (vgl. (32)), Pirahã (vgl. (28)–(30)) und das Italienische (Davis 1990) vorgeschlagen.

Silbenstrukturellen Beschränkungen wie denen des Deutschen, dass jede betonte Silbe mit einem Konsonanten beginnen muss, kann auch mit der Annahme von obligatorisch verzweigenden Silbenkörpern Rechnung getragen werden. Dies würde wiederum das Körpermodell stützen.

Für die Körperstruktur und die Schalenstruktur wurden auch die poetische Assonanz bzw. Alliteration und Schussreim als Evidenz angeführt.

Das Überlappungsstrukturmodell, bei dem der Silbenkern sowohl zum initialen Silbenanstieg als auch zum finalen Silbenabfall gerechnet wird, wurde vor allem von Donegan & Stampe (1978) als Reaktion auf die oben angesprochene Widersprüchlichkeit der Evidenz zur internen Struktur der Silbe vertreten.

Eine binäre Silbenstruktur propagieren auch Vennemann (1994) und Restle (1998), beide allerdings ohne die für Donegan und Stampe (1978) typische Überlappung. Das Crescendo-Descrescendo-Modell von Vennemann (1994) zeichnet sich durch eine variable Assoziation des Nukleus entweder nur mit dem Crescendo oder sowohl mit Crescendo als auch Decrescendo zur Beschreibung von Silbenschnittkontrasten aus, während Restle (1998) unterschiedliche Grade der Verbindung der Silbenbestandteile Öffnung und Schließung annimmt.

Reduplikationsphänomene stützen eher die erhöhte Flexibilität des Überlappungsmodells, der flachen Silbenstruktur oder des Körpermodells als die des Reimmodells. Abgesehen vom trivialen Fall, dass die gesamte Basis verdoppelt wird, werden entweder körperbezogene Einheiten redupliziert oder aber Teile der Basis, die in keinem der geläufigen Modelle Konstituentenstatus besitzen. So wird bei der präfigierenden CV-Reduplikation des Ilokano (Hayes & Abad 1989) der Körper der ersten Silbe der Basis verdoppelt:

(35) liŋʔét 'Schweiß'
      si-liliŋʔét 'mit Schweiß bedeckt'

Die verbleibenden Reduplikationstypen werden meist durch komplexe Transformationen abgeleitet (vgl. McCarthy & Prince 1995). So erstreckt sich das verdoppelte Material in (36) (präfigierende CVC-Reduplikation im Ilokano) auf den Konsonanten, der auf den Nukleus der ersten Silbe folgt — unabhängig davon, ob er gängigen Silbenstrukturtheorien zufolge zum Reim der ersten oder zum Kopf der zweiten Silbe der Basis zu zählen ist. Die Daten zur VC-Reduplikation (hier in (37) anhand des Tzeltal (Berlin 1963) illustriert) stellen die Silbenstrukturmodelle vor ähnliche Probleme. Restle (1999) begegnet diesen Schwierigkeiten durch eine Weiterentwicklung des Überlappungsmodells.

(36) **kal**kaldíŋ 'Ziege' **kal**kaldíŋ 'Ziegen'
      púsa 'Katze' **pus**púsa 'Katzen'

(37) -nitan 'es schieben'
      -nititan 'es auf einer gekrümmten Bahn schnell schieben'

Trotz dieser uneinheitlichen Evidenz hat sich in der Literatur vor allem das Reimmodell durchgesetzt und zu zahlreichen Fortentwicklungen geführt. Zu letzteren zählen z. B. Kiparskys (1981) metrisches Silbenstrukturmodell, Hymans (1985) moraisches Modell, das von Hayes (1989) verfeinert wurde, und das Modell der Rektionsphonologie von Kaye, Lowenstamm & Vergnaud (1990).

Das metrische Modell der Silbe stellt das Verhältnis der Elemente der Silbe zueinander in binär verzweigenden Bäumen dar (vgl. Abbildung (38)). Das Konzept der Sonorität begegnet hier als intrasyllabisches Gegenstück zur (suprasyllabischen) Rhythmusstruktur.

(38) Dt. *Freund*

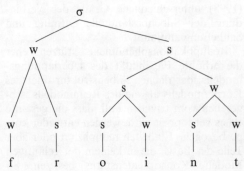

Zentral für das moraische Modell (einen Überblick bieten u. a. Broselow 1995, Bickmore 1995 und Zec 1995b) ist die Annahme, dass die Mora neben ihrer ursprünglichen Funktion als Gewichtseinheit gleichzeitig als primitive subsyllabische Konstituente fungiert.

(39) (a) Lat. *fenéstra* 'Fenster'

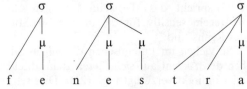

(b) Lat. *adaéquō* 'ich mache gleich'

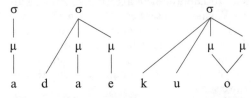

Die Kopf/Reim-Asymmetrie kommt dadurch zum Ausdruck, dass nur im Silbenreim befindliche Elemente von Moren dominiert sein können, während Elemente des Silbenkopfs direkt vom Silbenknoten dominiert werden.

Die Rektionsphonologie verzichtet zwar darauf, die Silbe als Grundkategorie zu führen (Brockhaus 1995: 201 f.), stellt aber Silbenkopf und Silbenreim (mit dem Nukleus als Regens) zur Verfügung, vgl. Abbildung (40) (nach Brockhaus 1995: 198, wobei R = Reim, O = Kopf, N = Kern):

(40) Engl. *foster* '(Kind etc.) aufziehen'

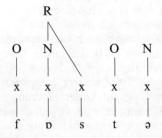

6. Probleme

6.1. Ambisyllabizität

Bisher wurde stillschweigend vorausgesetzt, dass die Grenze zwischen zwei adjazenten Silben mit einer Segmentgrenze übereinstimmt. Es lassen sich jedoch einige Argumente gegen die Universalität dieser Annahme anführen.

So verbietet das Deutsche betonte Kurzvokale in offener Silbe, vgl. (41) und die ähnlich gearteten Daten aus dem Englischen in (42).

(41) (a) *Kitt   Tüll   Mull   Fell   komm   fäll(e)   Löß   Bach*
         [kʰɪtʰ] [tʰʏl] [mʊl]   [fɛl]   [kʰɔm] [fɛl]   [lœs] [bax]
     (b) *Knie   früh   Kuh   Fee   Po   jäh   Bö   nah*
         [kʰniː] [fryː] [kʰuː] [feː]   [pʰoː] [jɛː]   [bøː] [naː]
     (c) *[kʰnɪ] *[frʏ] *[kʰʊ] *[fɛ]   *[pʰɔ] *[jɛ]   *[bœ] *[na]

(42) (a) *kit   pot   cat*
         [kʰɪt]   [pʰɒt] [kʰæt]
     (b) *[kʰɪ]   *[pʰɒ] *[kʰæ]

Wortintern gibt es im Deutschen aber Kurzvokale, auf die nur ein einziger intervokalischer Konsonant folgt, vgl. (43).

(43) *Mitte   Böller   Wasser*
     [mɪtʰə]   [bœlɐ]   [vasɐ]

Da im Deutschen (wie in den meisten Sprachen der Welt) zumindest eine sehr starke Tendenz besteht, dass ein einzelner intervokalische Konsonant den Silbenkopf der zweiten Silbe bildet, ist die gegenteilige Annahme, dass die hervorgehobenen Konsonanten in (43) exklusiv zur ersten Silbe zu rechnen sind, unbefriedigend. Um nun weder die Verallgemeinerung aufgeben zu müssen, dass betonte Silben mit kurzem Monophthong geschlossen sein müssen, noch die, dass einzelne intervokalische Konsonanten zum Kopf der zweiten Silbe zu rechnen sind, wurde vorgeschlagen, derartige Elemente als sowohl zur Koda der ersten Silbe als auch zum Kopf der zweiten Silbe gehörig zu analysieren (vgl. (44)). Für solche doppelt assoziierten Laute sind die Begriffe *ambisyllabisches Segment*, *Silbengelenk* (Vennemann 1982: 269 f.) und engl. *interlude* (Hockett 1955: 52) geläufig.

(44) *Mitte*

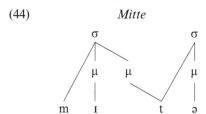

Zu erwähnen ist, dass sich solche ambisyllabischen Repräsentationen mit dem Sprachgefühl vieler Sprecher decken, die gerade in diesen Fällen über keine klare und präzise Intuition bezüglich der Position der Silbengrenze verfügen.

Obwohl die Erweiterung von Silbenstrukturtheorien um das Konzept der Ambisyllabizität viele Vertreter hat (u. a. Sievers 1901: 209; Jespersen 1920: 202 f.; Hockett 1955: 52; Anderson & Jones 1974: 5; Kahn 1980; Vennemann 1982: 269 ff.; Clements & Keyser 1983: 3 f.; Anderson & Durand 1986: 14), wird sie von manchen Autoren als unnötige Schwächung dieser Theorien verstanden (vgl. Haugen 1956; Kiparsky 1979; Selkirk 1982; Borowsky 1984; Harris & Kaye 1990). Als Alternative zur Ambisyllabizität wird in generativ orientierten Silbentheorien das Instrument der Resyllabierung angeboten.

6.2. Appendices

Das in § 3.1 als Tendenz formulierte Prinzip Sievers (1901: 204), wonach die Sonoritätsskala Ausdruck für die relative Nähe zum Silbennukleus ist, führt zu streng monotonen, d. h. bezüglich der Sonorität kontinuierlich Laut für Laut zunehmenden bzw. abnehmenden Silbenkörpern bzw. Silbenreimen. Nach Sievers (1901: 198) führt die entsprechende Erwartungshaltung des Hörers dazu, dass Minima der Sonorität als Silbengrenzen interpretiert werden.

Nun gibt es aber eine Fülle von Gegenevidenz gegen ein solches Prinzip, wie Sievers selbst und viele andere Autoren nach ihm bemerkt haben (vgl. Vennemann 1982; Clements 1990). (45) bietet einige ausgewählte Illustrationen für lokale Sonoritätsmaxima, die nicht den Status eines Silbenkerns besitzen. Der komplementäre Fall, dass ein Silbenkern nicht zugleich ein lokales Sonoritätsmaximum darstellt, wird in § 6.3. behandelt.

(45)
Deutsch: *Sport* [ʃpɔrtʰ], *Raps* [raps],
              Obst [ʔoːpstʰ], *Akt* [ʔaktʰ]
Englisch: *skew* [skjuː] 'schief', *lapse*
              [læps] 'Fehler'
Französisch: *stage* [staʒ] 'Praktikum',
              temple [tãpl] 'Tempel'
Russisch: *rta* 'Mund (gen.)',
              lba 'Stirn (gen.)'
Totonac   [spúun] 'Vogel', [lmáan]
(MacKay 1994): 'lang', [tíks] 'gut'

Seri   *stak* 'Bimsstein', *ka:txk*
(Marlett 1988):   'Heuschrecke'
Wiyot   *šbót* 'Bogen', *hátb* 'Süden',
(Teeter 1964):   *bótks* 'Feind'

Abfolgen von Lauten gleicher Sonorität (z. B. Plosiv + Plosiv, vgl. engl. *fact* [fækt]) werden auch als Sonoritätsplateaus bezeichnet. Die in (3) gegebene Präferenz trägt solchen Plateaus dadurch Rechnung, dass sie neben einem kontinuierlichen Sonoritätsanstieg/-abfall auch gleichbleibende Sonorität benachbarter Laute zulässt. Demnach werden nur noch Fälle, in denen lokalen Sonoritätsmaxima kein Silbenstatus zukommt, als Ausnahmen zum Sonoritätsprinzip klassifiziert.

Die in (45) hervorgehobenen Laute sind jeweils sonorer als ihre Umgebung (vgl. die zwei zusätzlichen Sonoritätsmaxima in (46)), sollten daher nach dem Sonoritätsprinzip als Silbenkerne fungieren. Angesichts der Divergenz zwischen dem qua Sonorität zu erwartetem, faktisch aber (zumindest aufgrund der metrischen Evidenz) nicht gegebenen Silbigkeitsstatus dieser Segmente prägte Sievers (1901: 205 f.) den Begriff *Nebensilbe*. Vennemann (1982: 298) verwendet den Begriff *Appendix*, was die terminologische Unterscheidung von silbeninitialen (Präpendix) und silbenfinalen (Suppendix) Erweiterungen des streng monotonen Teils von Silben erleichtert.

(46)   Deutsch *(des) Herbsts*

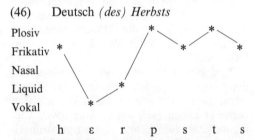

Appendices können sich sprachgeschichtlich durchaus wieder zu eigenen Silben entwickeln (vgl. spätlat. *schola* [skɔ.la] > spanisch [es.-kue.la] und § 3.2.1.), sie können jedoch auch ganz abgebaut werden (vgl. frz. *table* [ta.blə] > [tabl] > umgangssprachlich [tab]).

Donegan & Stampe (1978: 32) nehmen an, dass nichtsilbische Sonoritätsmaxima auf Phoneme begrenzt sind, die eine gewisse intrinsische Unabhängigkeit (qua deutlicher Hörbarkeit) aufweisen, wozu die Autoren Sonoranten und insbesondere das häufig als Appendix auftretende [s] zählen. Sievers (1901: 205 f.) vertritt die gegenteilige Auffassung, dass [s] gerade „wegen der geringen Schallfülle der hier auftretenden stimmlosen Geräuschlaute" als Appendix geeignet ist. Universalphonologisch sind allerdings wohl nur unreduzierte Vollvokale von Appendices ausgeschlossen.

6.3. Silbische Konsonanten

Das Sonoritätskonzept weist in Kombination mit dem in § 3.2.3. formulierten Nukleusgesetz Vokale als präferierte Silbennuklei qua maximaler Sonorität aus. Weniger präferierte (konsonantische) Nuklei hingegen sind nicht zwangsläufig lokale Sonoritätsmaxima, wie die Beispiele der silbischen Konsonanten in (47) zeigen.

(47)
Deutsch: *sollen* [zɔln̩] (vs. *Solln* [zɔln]),
                harren [harn̩] (vs. *Harn* [harn])
Englisch: *castle* [kʰasl̩] 'Burg'
Bella Coola: *stp* [s̩.t̩ʰ.p̩ʰ] 'Muttermal',
                q̓psttx̣ [q̓̍.ps̩.t̩ʰ.tx̣] 'probiere es'
                (Hoard 1978: 68)
Columbia: *nm̓m̓ə́l̓* [n̩.m̩̓.m̓ə́l̓] 'lauwarm'
                (Hoard 1978: 63)
Berberisch: *tftktst, tfktstt* [tf̩.tk̩.tst̩ tf̩k.tst̩t]
                'du hast es verstaucht (fem.) und dann hergegeben' (Bagemihl 1991: 593)
Kammu: *tk̩.lòk* 'Nacken', *t̩.klə́:ŋ* '(Ortsname)' (Svantesson 1994: 267)

Insbesondere die silbischen Obstruenten, wie sie für einige Salish-Sprachen (z. B. das Bella Coola, vgl. Hoard 1978; Bagemihl 1991), kaukasische Sprachen (z. B. das Abchasische und Georgische, vgl. Kuipers 1976; Anderson 1978), Mon-Khmer-Sprachen (z. B. das eben erwähnte Kammu, vgl. Sloan 1988; Svantesson 1994) und das Berberische (Dell & Elmedlaoui 1988) angenommen werden, sind typologisch auf zweierlei Weise ungewöhnlich. Zum einen stellen die obstruentischen Nuklei nach der phonologischen Sonoritätsskala keine lokalen Maxima dar und scheinen daher Sievers Perzeptionsthese zu widersprechen, nach der (nur) lokale Sonoritätsmaxima den perzeptiven Silbigkeitsstatus hervorrufen. Zum anderen sind obstruentische Nuklei nach dem Nukleusgesetz stark dispräferiert.

Die vokallosen Silben des Bella Coola wurden von Hockett (1955: 57) dadurch beschrieben, dass er eine leere Silbenkernposition ansetzte. Eine solche Analyse kann jedoch den Silbigkeitsstatus dieser Strukturen nur stipulieren, nicht aber aus der Sonoritätsstruktur ableiten. Hoard (1978) geht wie Bell (1978) demgegenüber phonetisch in jedem

Fall von einer Gipfelbildung aus, indem er die silbischen Obstruenten als komplexe Segmente in Anlehnung an Affrikaten versteht, bei denen eine Zunahme bzw. Abnahme der Sonorität zumindest im Fall der silbischen Plosive durch die Abfolge von Verschluss und Sprengung plus Aspiration gewährleistet ist. Bagemihl (1991) plädiert auf der Grundlage von Daten zur Reduplikation für einen nichtsyllabischen Status dieser Obstruenten (vgl. das unsilbifizierte /st'/ in (48)). Der einzige Unterschied zu typologisch weniger ungewöhnlichen Sprachen sei der Umstand, dass unsilbifizierte Laute nicht im Ableitungs-Prozess getilgt würden (cf. (48)):

kation nicht berücksichtigen Obstruenten als silbisch zu analysieren und die Reduplikation auf Silben mit steigender Sonorität zu beschränken. Eine klarere, bisher jedoch fehlende Evidenz für den Silbigkeitsstatus solcher Obstruenten könnte eine Untersuchung ihres metrischen Verhaltens bringen; hier liegt eine Forschungsaufgabe.

Die Quelle von silbischen Konsonanten liegt nach Bell (1978: 165 ff.) in den allermeisten Fällen im Ausfall eines Vokals (vgl. ahd. *leffil* > mhd. *leffel* > nhd. *Löffel* [lœfl̩]) oder dem Übergang eines hohen Vokals zu einer konsonantischen Artikulation (vgl. kŋ̍ < kũ im Yoruba).

(48) Bagemihl (1991: 615 f.): *st̓q̓ʷlus* → *st̓q̓ʷlq̓ʷlus-i* 'black bear snare' → diminutiv

Gegen eine solche Analyse spricht jedoch die mangelnde Berücksichtigung der Parallelität der fraglichen Strukturen (C̥) des Bella Coola mit denen (CV̥) verwandter Sprachen, vgl. Bagemihls (1991: 643) eigenes Beispiel: Oowekyala [t̓xt̓kʷs] 'fish hawk' vs. Heiltsuk [t̓ixtʊ́kʷʊs]. Die bei den fraglichen Strukturen häufige Alternation zwischen langsamerer (ohne Vokal) und schnellerer Aussprache (mit Reduktionsvokal) (vgl. z. B. Kammu *tk̓.lòk* [tk̓.lòk] ~ [tək̓.lòk] (Svantesson 1994: 267) müsste in einer an Bagemihl angelehnten Analyse nicht nur als Verschiebung der Nukleusposition, sondern als Unterschied in der Anzahl der Silben − ein- vs. zweisilbig − beschrieben werden. Die Fähigkeit von /k/, als Tonträger zu fungieren, spricht also zumindest im Kammu klar gegen eine solche Beschreibung.

Im übrigen ist schon theoretisch gar nicht zu erwarten, dass Reduplikationsdaten Aufschluß über die Silbenstruktur der Reduplikationsbasis und damit über den Silbigkeitsstatus einzelner Segmente innerhalb der Basis liefern können. Das sieht man bereits daran, dass einer der häufigeren Reduplikationstypen, die CVC-Reduplikation, vgl. (36), einen postvokalischen Konsonanten unabhängig davon verdoppelt, ob er zur selben Silbe gehört wie der mitkopierte Vokal, oder nicht. Derlei Kritik trägt Broselows Vorschlag (1995: 203) Rechnung, die von der Redupli-

Das Phänomen silbischer Konsonanten tritt bevorzugt in schwach- oder unbetonter Umgebung auf. Dieser Umstand und die eben angesprochenen Bedingungen ihrer Entstehung erklären, warum die Komplexität der Köpfe und Kodas von Silben ohne vokalischen Nukleus immer geringer oder gleich der Komplexität der Köpfe und Kodas von Silben mit vokalischem Nukleus ist (vgl. Bell 1978: 163).

Die Distribution der silbischen Obstruenten lässt sich nur zum Teil auf das Sonoritätskonzept zurückführen. Zwar sind silbische Sonoranten deutlich gegenüber silbischen Obstruenten präferiert, z. B. gibt es deutlich mehr Sprachen, die nur silbische Sonoranten zulassen, aber keine silbischen Obstruenten, als Sprachen, die nur silbische Obstruenten zulassen, aber keine silbische Sonoranten. Bell (1978: 158) nennt als Beispiel für den letzteren Sprachtypus u. a. das Chipaya (Uru-Chipaya, Maya, Bolivien), das nach Olson (1967: 302) nur vokalische und sibilantische Nuklei zulässt. Allerdings erweist sich die Abgrenzung silbischer Obstruenten von entsprechenden silbenappendikalen Elementen unter Ermangelung von metrischer Evidenz als durchaus schwierig. So spricht im Chipaya nach Olson vor allem die rhythmische Äquivalenz von Formen wie *at.ñi.ki.ča* 'er ist üblicherweise in der Lage, so wird gesagt' vs.

at.ṣ̌.ki.ča 'er ist in der Lage, so wird gesagt' für eine silbische Wertung dieser Elemente.

Auch innerhalb der Klasse der Obstruenten lässt sich feststellen, dass die Existenz silbischer Plosive in einer Sprache die Existenz silbischer Frikative voraussetzt. Eine ähnlich starke Präferenz gilt für die silbischen Plosive, indem stimmlose silbische Plosive stimmhafte Pendants voraussetzen.

Auf der anderen Seite sind in der Klasse der Sonoranten deutlich die Nasale und nicht etwa die sonoreren Liquiden als konsonantische Nuklei präferiert (vgl. Bell 1978: 169). Eine Erklärung dieser gegen die Sonoritätshierarchie laufenden Präferenz steht noch aus.

7. Ausblick

Dieser Artikel versucht deutlich zu machen, dass der Bereich der Silbenstrukturforschung eine Reihe von Parametern für Typologien bietet. An verschiedenen Stellen wurde bereits auf Zusammenhänge mit anderen Typologien hingewiesen. Die Beschreibung der großen Zusammenhänge steht allerdings noch aus. Gerade deshalb stellt die typologische Erforschung der Silbenstruktur der Sprachen der Welt ein überaus fruchtbares und attraktives Gebiet für weitergehende Untersuchungen dar.

8. Abkürzungen

ahd.	althochdeutsch
aind.	altindisch
air.	altirisch
aisl.	altisländisch
akk.	akkadisch
aksl.	altkirchenslawisch
altit.	altitalienisch
altpad.	altpadovanisch
anord.	altnordisch
dt.	deutsch
engl.	englisch
Fn.	Fußnote
frz.	französisch
got.	gotisch
griech.	griechisch
lat.	lateinisch
lett.	lettisch
mhd.	mittelhochdeutsch
mkymr.	mittelkymrisch
nhd.	neuhochdeutsch
nisl.	neuisländisch
nkymr.	neukymrisch
port.	portugiesisch
russ.	russisch
sog.	sogenannte
span.	spanisch
spätlat.	spätlateinisch
urgerm.	urgermanisch
uridg.	urindogermanisch
westg.	westgermanisch

9. Zitierte Literatur

Allen, William Sidney. 1951. *Phonetics in Ancient India.* London: Oxford University Press.

Allen, William Sidney. ²1974. *Vox Graeca: A guide to the pronunciation of Classical Greek.* Cambridge: Cambridge University Press. [¹1968].

Allen, William Sidney. 1970. *Vox Latina: A guide to the pronunciation of Classical Latin.* Cambridge: Cambridge University Press.

Allen, William Sidney. 1973. *Accent and rhythm: Prosodic features of Latin and Greek: A study in theory and reconstruction.* Cambridge: Cambridge University Press.

Anderson, John. 1969. „Syllabic or non-syllabic phonology". *Journal of Linguistics* 5: 136−143.

Anderson, John & Jones, Ch. 1974. „Three theses concerning phonological representations". *Journal of Linguistics* 10: 1−26.

Anderson, John & Durand, Jacques. 1986. „Dependency phonology". In: Jacques Durand. *Dependency and non-linear phonology.* London: Croom Helm, 1−54.

Anderson, Stephen R. 1978. „Syllables, segments and the Northwest Caucasian languages". In: Bell & Hooper (eds.), 47−58.

Auer, Peter. 1994. „Einige Argumente gegen die Silbe als universale prosodische Hauptkategorie." In: Ramers, Karl Heinz et al. (eds.). *Universelle phonologische Strukturen und Prozesse* (= Linguistische Arbeiten 310). Tübingen: Niemeyer, 55−78.

Bagemihl, Bruce. 1991. „Syllable structure in Bella Coola". *Linguistic Inquiry* 22: 589−646.

Bell, Alan. 1977. „The distributional syllable." In: Juilland, Alphonse (ed.). *Linguistic studies offered to Joseph Greenberg on the occasion of his sixtieth birthday.* Saratoga/Kalifornien: Anma Libri, 249−262.

Bell, Alan. 1978. Syllabic consonants. In: Greenberg, Joseph H. (ed.). *Universals of human language. Volume 2: Phonology.* Stanford/Kalifornien: Stanford University Press, 153−201.

Bell, Alan. 1979. „The Syllable as constituent versus organizational unit" In: Clyne, R. P. et al. (eds.). *The Elements. A Parasession on Linguistic Units and Levels.* Chicago: Chicago Linguistic Society, 11−20.

Bell, Alan & Bybee Hooper, Joan (eds.). 1978. *Syllables and segments.* Amsterdam: North-Holland Publishing Company.

Bell, Alan & Bybee Hooper, Joan. 1978. „Issues and evidence in syllabic phonology". In: Bell & Hooper (eds.), 3–22.

Berlin, Brent. 1963. „Some semantic features of reduplication in Tzeltal". *International Journal of American Linguistics* 29: 211–218.

Berg, Thomas. 1989. „Intersegmental cohesiveness". *Folia Linguistica* 23: 245–280.

Bickmore, Lee S. 1995. „Accounting for compensatory lengthening in the CV and moraic frameworks". In: Durand & Katamba (eds.), 119–148.

Blevins, Juliette. 1995. „The syllable in phonological theory". In: Goldsmith (ed.), 206–244.

Borowsky, Toni. 1984. „On resyllabification in English". In: M. Cobler, M & MacKaye, S. & Westcoat, M. T. (eds.). *Proceedings of the West Coast Conference on Formal Linguistics 3.* Stanford/Kalifornien: Stanford Linguistics Association, 1–5.

Brockhaus, Wiebke 1995. „Skeletal and suprasegmental structure within government phonology". In: Durand & Katamba (eds.), 180–221.

Broselow, Ellen. 1995. „Skeletal positions and moras". In: Goldsmith (ed.), 175–205.

Broselow, Ellen & Chen, Su-I & Huffman, Marie. 1997. „Syllable weight: convergence of phonology and phonetics". *Phonology* 14: 47–82.

Bunn, Gordon & Bunn, Ruth. 1970. „Golin Phonology". *Pacific Linguistics* A23. Canberra: Australian National University, 1–7.

Chomsky, Noam & Halle, Morris. 1968. *The sound pattern of English.* New York: Harper & Row.

Clements, G. N. & Keyser, S. Jay. 1983. *CV Phonology: A Generative Theory of the Syllable.* Cambridge/MA: MIT Press.

Clements, G. N. 1990. „The role of the sonority cycle in core syllabification". In: Beckman, Mary E. & Kingston, John (eds.). 1990. *Papers in Laboratory Phonology I. Between the Grammar and Physics of Speech.* Cambridge: Cambridge University Press, 283–333.

Collins, James. 1989. „Nasalization, lengthening, and phonological rhyme in Tolowa". *International Journal of American Linguistics* 55: 326–340.

Davis, Stuart. 1982. „Rhyme, or Reason? A Look at syllable-internal constituents". In: Maccaulay, Monica et al. (eds.). *Proceedings of the Annual Meeting of the Berkeley Linguistic Society* 8. Berkeley: Berkeley Linguistics Society, 525–532.

Davis, Stuart. 1988 a. *Topics in syllable geometry.* New York: Garland.

Davis, Stuart. 1988 b. „Syllable onsets as a factor in stress rules". *Phonology* 5: 1–19.

Davis, Stuart. 1990. „The onset as a constituent of the syllable: evidence from Italian." In: Ziolkowski, Michael et al. (eds.). *Papers from the 26th regional meeting of the Chicago Linguistic Society. Volume 2: Parasession on the syllable in phonetics & phonology (= CLS 26).* Chicago: Chicago Linguistic Society, 71–79.

Dell, F. & Elmedlaoui, M. 1988. „Syllabic consonants in Berber: Some new evidence." *Journal of African languages and linguistics* 7: 105–130.

Dixon, Robert M. W. 1981: „Wargamay". In: Dixon, R. M. W. & Blake, Barry (eds.). *Handbook of Australian languages. Volume 2.* Amsterdam: John Benjamins, 1–144.

Donegan, Patricia J. & Stampe, David. 1978. „The syllable in phonological and prosodic structure". In: Bell & Hooper (eds.), 25–34.

Durand, Jaques & Francis Katamba (eds.). 1995. *Frontiers of Phonology: Atoms, Structures, Derivations.* London: Longman.

Everett, D. & Everett, K. 1984. „Syllable onsets and stress placement in Pirahã". In: M. Cobler, M. & MacKaye, S. & Westcoat, M. (eds.). *Proceedings of the West Coast Conference on Formal Linguistics* 3. Stanford/Kalifornien: Stanford Linguistics Association, 105–116.

Fudge, Erik C. 1969. „Syllables". *Journal of Linguistics* 5: 253–287.

Gahl, Susanne. 1996. „Syllable onsets as a factor in stress rules: the case of Mathimathi revisited". *Phonology* 13: 329–344.

Goedemans, Rob. 1998. *Weightless segments: A phonetic and phonological study concerning the metrical irrelevance of syllable onsets.* The Hague: Holland Academic Graphics.

Goldsmith, John A. (ed.) 1995. *The handbook of phonological theory.* Cambridge/MA: Blackwell.

Greenberg, Joseph H. 1978. „Some generalizations concerning initial and final consonant clusters". In: Greenberg, Joseph H. (ed.). *Universals of human language. Volume 2. Phonology.* Stanford/Kalifornien: Stanford University Press, 243–279.

Halle, Morris & Idsardi, William. 1995. „General properties of stress and metrical structure." In: Goldsmith, John A. (ed.). *The handbook of phonological theory.* Cambridge/MA: Blackwell, 403–443.

Halle, Morris & Vergnaud, Jean-Roger. 1987. *An essay on stress.* Cambridge/MA: MIT Press.

Hankamer, Jorge & Aissen, Judith. 1974. „The Sonority Hierarchy". In: Bruck, A & Fox, R. A. & LaGaly, M. W. (eds.). *Papers from the parasession on Natural Phonology (=CLS 10).* Chicago: Chicago Linguistic Society, 131–145.

Harris, John & Kaye, Jonathan. 1990. „A tale of two cities: London glottalling and New York City tapping". *The Linguistic Review* 7: 251–274.

Haugen, Einar. 1956. „The syllable in linguistic description". In: Halle, M. & Lunt, H. & McLean, H. (eds.). *For Roman Jakobson.* Den Haag: Mouton, 213–221.

Hayes, Bruce. 1979. „Extrametricality". *MIT Working Papers in Linguistics 1*: 77–86.

Hayes, Bruce. 1989. „Compensatory lengthening in Moraic Phonology". *Linguistic Inquiry* 20: 253–306.

Hayes, Bruce. 1995. *Metrical stress theory. Principles and case studies.* Chicago: The University of Chicago Press.

Hayes, Bruce & Abad, May. 1989. „Reduplication and syllabification in Ilokano". *Lingua* 77: 331–374.

Hercus, L. 1969. *The languages of Victoria: a late survey.* Canberra: Australian Institute of Aboriginal Studies.

Hermann, Eduard. 1923. *Silbenbildung im Griechischen und in den andern indogermanischen Sprachen.* Göttingen. [Nachdruck Göttingen: Vanderhoeck & Ruprecht 1978].

Hoard, James E. 1978. „Syllabification in Northwest Indian languages, with remarks on the nature of syllabic stops and affricates". In: Bell & Hooper (eds.), 59–72.

Hockett, Charles. 1955. *A manual of phonology.* (= International Journal of Linguistics Monograph Series 21, Memoir 11). Bloomington/Indiana: University of Chicago Press.

Hooper, Joan. 1972. „The syllable in phonological theory". *Language* 48: 525–540.

Hyman, Larry (ed.). 1977. *Studies in stress and accent.* Los Angeles. (= *Southern California occasional papers in Linguistics* 4).

Hyman, Larry. 1985. *A theory of phonological weight.* Dordrecht: Foris.

Ingria, Robert. 1980. „Compensatory Lengthening as a Metrical Phenomenon". *Linguistic Inquiry* 11: 465–495.

Jakobson, Roman. 1941. *Kindersprache, Aphasie und allgemeine Lautgesetze.* Uppsala. [Wiederabdruck in: R. Jakobson. 1962: *Selected writings I: Phonological studies.* Den Haag: Mouton, 328–401].

Jensen, M. Kloster. 1963. „Die Silbe in der Phonetik und Phonemik". *Phonetica* 9: 17–38.

Jespersen, Otto. ³1920. *Lehrbuch der Phonetik.* Leipzig: Teubner.

Kager, René. 1989. *A metrical theory of stress and destressing in English and Dutch.* Dordrecht: Foris.

Kager, René. 1995. „A metrical theory of word stress." In: Goldsmith (ed.), 367–402.

Kager, René. 1999. *Optimality Theory.* Cambridge: Cambridge University Press.

Kahn, Daniel. 1980. *Syllable-based generalizations in English phonology.* New York: Garland Press.

Kaye, Jonathan & Lowenstamm, Jean & Vergnaud, Jean-Roger. 1985. „The internal structure of phonological elements: a theory of charm and government". *Phonology* 2: 305–328.

Kaye, Jonathan & Lowenstamm, Jean & Vergnaud, Jean-Roger. 1990. „Constituent structure and government in phonology". *Phonology* 7: 193–231.

Kelkar, Ashok Ramchandra. 1968. *Studies in Hindi-Urdu I. Introduction and word phonology.* Poona: Deccan College, Postgraduate and Research Institute.

Kiparsky, Paul. 1979. „Metrical structure assignment is cyclic". *Linguistic Inquiry* 10: 421–441.

Kiparsky, Paul. 1981. „Remarks on the metrical structure of the syllable". In: Dressler, W. & Pfeiffer, O. & Rennison, J. (eds.). *Phonologica 1980. Akten der Vierten internationalen Phonologie-Tagung.* Innsbruck: Institut für Sprachwissenschaft Innsbruck, 245–256.

Klingenheben, August. 1928. „Die Silbenauslautgesetze des Hausa", *Zeitschrift für Eingeborenensprachen* 18: 272–297.

Kuipers, A. H. 1976. „Typologically salient features of some Northwest Caucasian languages". *Studia Caucasica* 3: 101–127.

Kuryłowicz, Jerzy. 1948. „Contribution à la théorie de la syllabe". *Biuletyn Polskiego Towarzystwa Jezykoznawczego* 8: 80–114. [Nachdruck in Jerzy Kuryłowicz ²1973. *Esquisses linguistiques I (= International library of general linguistics, 16.1).* München: Fink, 193–220].

Ladefoged, Peter. 1982. *A course in phonetics.* New York: Harcourt Brace Jovanovich.

Lahiri, Aditi & Koreman, Jacques. 1988. „Syllable weight and quantity in Dutch". In: Borer, H. (ed.). *Proceedings of the West Coast Conference on Formal Linguistics* 7. Stanford: Stanford Linguistic Association, 217–228.

Laziczius, Julius. 1961. *Lehrbuch der Phonetik.* Berlin: Akademie-Verlag.

Liberman, Mark & Prince, Alan S. 1977. „On stress and linguistic rhythm". *Linguistic Inquiry* 8: 249–336.

Lutz, Angelika. 1985. „Die Worttrennung am Zeilenende in altenglischen Handschriften: Phonologische Betrachtungen zu Dieter Wetzels gleichnamigem Buch". *Indogermanische Forschungen* 90: 227–238.

Lutz, Angelika. 1986. „The syllabic basis of word division in Old English manuscripts". *English Studies* 67: 193–210.

Lutz, Angelika. 1991. *Phonotaktisch gesteuerte Konsonantenveränderungen in der Geschichte des Englischen* (= Linguistische Arbeiten, 272). Tübingen: Niemeyer.

MacKay, Carolyn J. 1994. „A sketch of Misantla Totonac phonology". *International Journal of American Linguistics* 60: 369–419.

Marlett, Stephen A. 1988. „The syllable structure of Seri". *International Journal of American Linguistics* 54: 245–278.

McCarthy, John J. & Prince, Alan S. 1995. „Prosodic morphology". In: Goldsmith (ed.), 318–366.

Mohanan, K. P. 1986. *The theory of lexical phonology*. Dordrecht: Reidel.

Murray, Robert. 1988. *Phonological strength and early Germanic syllable structure*. München: Fink.

Murray, Robert & Vennemann, Theo. 1982. „Syllable contact change in Germanic, Greek and Sidamo". *Klagenfurter Beiträge zur Sprachwissenschaft* 8: 321–349.

Murray, Robert & Vennemann, Theo. 1983. „Sound change and syllable structure [: Problems] in Germanic phonology". *Language* 59: 514–528.

Newman, Paul. 1972. „Syllable weight as a phonological variable". *Studies in African linguistics* 3: 301–323.

Noske, Roland. 1993. *A theory of syllabification and segmental alternation. With studies on the phonology of French, German, Tonkawa and Yawelmani*. Tübingen: Niemeyer.

Ohala, John J. 1990. „Alternatives to the sonority hierarchy for explaining segmental sequential constraints". In: Ziolkowsky, M. et al. (eds.). *Papers from the 26th regional meeting of the Chicago Linguistic Society. Bd. 2. The parasession on the syllable in phonetics and phonology*. Chicago: Chicago Linguistic Society, 319–338.

Olson, Ronald D. 1967. „The syllable in Chipaya". *International Journal of American Linguistics* 33. 300–304.

Payne, Judith. 1990. „Asheninca stress patterns". In: Payne, Doris L. (ed.). *Amazonian linguistics*. Austin: University of Texas Press, 185–209.

Picard, Marc. 1992: „Syllable structure, sonority and speech errors: a critical assessment". *Folia Linguistica* 26: 453–465.

Pike, Kenneth & Pike, Evelyn G. 1947. „Immediate constituents in Mazatec Syllables". *International Journal of American Linguistics* 13: 78–91.

Pompino-Marschall, Bernd. 1990. *Die Silbenprosodie. Ein elementarer Aspekt der Wahrnehmung von Sprachrhythmus und Sprechtempo*. Tübingen: Niemeyer.

Pompino-Marschall, Bernd. 1993. „Die Silbe im Deutschen – gesprochen, geschrieben, beschrieben". In: Baurmann, J. & Günther, H. & Knopp, U. (eds.). *Homo Scribens. Perspektiven der Schriftlichkeitsforschung*. Tübingen: Niemeyer, 43–65.

Prince, Alan. 1980. „A metrical theory of Estonian Quantity". *Linguistic Inquiry* II: 511–562.

Prince, Alan S. & Smolensky, Paul 1993. „Optimality Theory: constraint interaction in generative grammar". Ms. Rutgers University: New Brunswick.

Restle, David. 1998. „Silbenschnitt – Quantität – Kopplung. Zur Geschichte, Charakterisierung und Repräsentation der Anschlussprosodie unter dem Blickwinkel einer Oszillationssilbentheorie". Unveröffentlichte Dissertation, Universität München, Institut für Deutsche Philologie.

Restle, David. 1999. „Reduplication as pure constituent copying. In defense of the syllable against the phonemic melody". In: Rennison, John & Kühnhammer, Klaus (eds.): *Phonologica 1996: Syllables!? Proceedings of the Eighth International Phonology Meeting Vienna, 1996*. Den Haag: Holland Academic Graphics.

Roca, Iggy. 1992. „Constraining extrametricality". In: Dressler, Wolfgang et al. (eds.) *Phonologica 1988. Proceedings of the 6th International Phonology Meeting*. Cambridge: Cambridge University Press.

Rohlfs, Gerhard. 1949: *Historische Grammatik der italienischen Sprache und ihrer Mundarten* (Bibliotheca Romanica, 5). 3 Bde. Bd. I: Lautlehre (2. unveränderte Aufl. 1972.). Bern: Francke.

Saib, Jilali. 1978. „Segment organization and the syllable in Tamazight Berber". In: Bell & Hooper (eds.), 92–104.

Seiler, Hansjakob. 1977. *Cahuilla grammar*. Banning, Kalifornien: Malki Museum Press.

Selkirk, Elizabeth. 1982. „Syllables". In : van der Hulst, Harry & Smith, Norval (eds.). *The structure of phonological representations, Bd. 2*. Dordrecht: Foris, 337–383.

Sievers, Eduard. ^{5}1901. *Grundzüge der Phonetik zur Einführung in das Studium der Lautlehre der indogermanischen Sprachen*. Leipzig: Breitkopf & Härtel. [Nachdruck Hildesheim. 1976].

Sloan, K. 1988. „Bare-consonant reduplication: Implications for a prosodic theory of reduplication". In: Borer, H. (ed.). *Proceedings of the West Coast Conference on Formal Linguistics 7*. Stanford: Stanford Linguistic Association, 319–330.

Steinthal, Heymann. ^{2}1890. *Geschichte der Sprachwissenschaft bei den Griechen und Römern mit besonderer Rücksicht auf die Logik. Erster Teil*. Berlin: Dümmler.

Steinthal, Heymann. ^{2}1891. *Geschichte der Sprachwissenschaft bei den Griechen und Römern mit besonderer Rücksicht auf die Logik. Zweiter Teil*. Berlin: Dümmler.

Steriade, Donca. 1984. „On the major class features and syllable theory". Aronoff, M. & Oehrle, R. (eds.). *Language sound structure*. Cambridge/MA: MIT Press, 107–136.

Svantesson, Jan-Olof. 1994. „Syllable constituents in Kammu reduplication". In: Dressler, Wolfgang U. et al. (eds.). *Phonologica 1992. Proceedings of the 7th International Phonology Meeting*. Turin: Rosenberg & Sellier, 265–274.

Teeter, Karl V. 1964. *The Wiyot language*. Berkeley: University of California Press. *(=University of California Publications in Linguistics 37)*.

Treiman, Rebecca & Kessler, Brett. 1995. „In defense of an onset-rime syllable structure for English". *Language and Speech* 38: 127–142.

Varma, Siddheshwar. 1961. *Critical studies in the phonetic observations of Indian grammarians*. Delhi: Munshi Ram Manohar Lal. [Nachdruck der Originalausgabe London. 1929].

Vennemann, Theo. 1972. „On the theory of syllabic phonology", *Linguistische Berichte* 18: 1—18.

Vennemann, Theo. 1974. „Words and syllables in natural generative grammar." In: Bruck, Anthony et al. (eds.). *Papers from the Parasession on Natural Phonology*. Chicago: Chicago Linguistic Society, 346—374.

Vennemann, Theo. 1978. „Universal syllabic phonology". *Theoretical Linguistics* 5: 175—215.

Vennemann, Theo. 1982. „Zur Silbenstruktur der deutschen Standardsprache". In: Vennemann, Theo (ed.). *Silben, Segmente, Akzente*. Tübingen: Niemeyer, 261—305.

Vennemann, Theo. 1987. „Muta cum Liquida: Worttrennung und Syllabierung im Gotischen", *Zeitschrift für deutsches Altertum und deutsche Literatur* 116: 165—204.

Vennemann, Theo. 1988a. *Preference laws for syllable structure and the explanation of sound change. With special reference to German, Germanic, Italian, and Latin*. Berlin: Mouton.

Vennemann, Theo. 1988b. „The Rule Dependence of Syllable Structure". In: Duncan-Rose, Caroline & Vennemann, Theo (eds.). *On Language. Rhetorica Phonologica Syntactica. A Festschrift for Robert P. Stockwell from his Friends and Colleagues*. London: Routledge, 257—283.

Vennemann, Theo. 1989. „Language change as language improvement". In: Orioles, Vincenzo (ed.). *Modelli esplicativi della diacronia linguistica: Atti del Convegno della Società Italiana di Glottologia, Pavia, 15—17 settembre 1988*. Pisa. 11—35. [Nachdruck in: Jones, Charles (ed.) 1993. *Historical linguistics: Problems and perspectives*. London: Longman, 319—344.].

Vennemann, Theo. 1990. „Syllable structure and simplex accent in Modern Standard German". In: Ziolkowsky, M. et al. (eds.): *Papers from the 26th regional meeting of the Chicago Linguistic Society. Bd. 2. The parasession on the syllable in phonetics and phonology*. Chicago: Chicago Linguistic Society, 399—412.

Vennemann, Theo. 1994. „Universelle Nuklearphonologie mit epiphänomenaler Silbenstruktur", In: Ramers, Karl Heinz et al. (eds.). *Universelle phonologische Strukturen und Prozesse*. Tübingen: Niemeyer, 7—54.

Vennemann, Theo. 1995. „Der Zusammenbruch der Quantität im Spätmittelalter und sein Einfluss auf die Metrik". In: Fix, Hans (ed.). *Quantitätsproblematik und Metrik (Amsterdamer Beiträge zur Älteren Germanistik 42)*. Amsterdam: Rodopi, 185—223.

Vennemann, Theo. 1997. „The Development of Reduplicating Verbs in Germanic." In: Rauch, Irmengard & Carr, Gerald F. (eds.). *Insights in Germanic linguistics II: Classic and contemporary (Trends in Linguistics, Studies and Monographs, 94)*. Berlin: Mouton de Gruyter, 297—336.

Zec, Draga. 1995a. „Sonority constraints on syllable structure". *Phonology* 12: 85—129.

Zec, Draga. 1995b. „The role of moraic structure in the distribution of segments within syllables. In: Durand & Katamba (ed.), 149—179.

David Restle, München (Deutschland)
Theo Vennemann, München (Deutschland)

95. Phonologische Prozesse

1. Der deskriptive Horizont
2. Die sprachtheoretische Erschließung
3. Der typologische Ertrag
4. Präliminarien eines typologisch brauchbaren Prozessbegriffs
5. Zitierte Literatur

1. Der deskriptive Horizont

Die Beschreibung der lautlichen Organisation natürlicher Sprachen hat in den letzten dreißig Jahren große Fortschritte gemacht; dafür ist nicht zuletzt die Konzentration des Forschungsinteresses auf drei Bereiche verantwortlich, die in der klassischen Phonologie Prager Provenienz stiefmütterlich behandelt wurden:

— die Variation, d. h. die Allophonie, und ihre Konditionierung,
— die phonische Struktur syntagmatischer Einheiten wie der Silbe und des Worts;
— die prosodische, insbesondere die rhythmische Organisation der Signifikanten.

Zum Schlüsselbegriff, unter dem die unterschiedlichen Verfahren der Lautvariation, der Lautlinearisierung und ihrer suprasegmentalen Integration zusammengefasst werden, avancierte der Begriff 'Prozeß' (bzw. 'Regel'), 'Prozessphonologie' wird deshalb nicht selten als Oberbegriff für ganz verschiedene Ansätze gebraucht (vgl. § 2.). Eine maximalistische Definition gibt Ferguson: „The notion of 'phonological process' will be understood in this paper in the very broad sense of any relation between two sounds (or stretches of sound, or components of sound) which may be regarded as the one sound 'becoming' the other under specifiable (or conjecturable) conditions, on other words any relation which may be represented by the formula

X → Y/Z

read X becomes Y under conditions Z, where X and Y represent sounds of human language." (Ferguson 1978: 405)

In ihrer nicht zu überbietenden Allgemeinheit erlaubt diese Bestimmung immerhin, den empirischen Horizont abzustecken; sie umfasst sowohl Erscheinungen des Sprachwandels ('Lautgesetze'), des Spracherwerbs bzw. -verlusts und der synchronen Variation (vgl. ebd.: 406, Anm. 2) als auch sprachkontaktbedingte Transferenzen.

Zwar bietet Fergusons Prozessbegriff keine unmittelbare Hilfe bei der Typisierung der zahlreichen Prozesse, er zeigt jedoch, dass entsprechende Bemühungen bei den lautlichen Phänomenen einerseits und ihren Konditionierungen andererseits ansetzen müssen.

1.1. Lautliche Effekte

Das lautliche Ergebnis phonologischer Prozesse kann sich in segmentaler Variation − in Form von unterschiedlichen Merkmalspezifikationen, von Tilgungen (vgl. Mayerthaler 1982), von Epenthesen und von Metathesen (vgl. Ultan 1978, Geisler 1994) − und/oder in suprasegmentaler Variation − etwa in Form von Akzentverlagerungen, von Rhythmuswechseln oder von Resyllabierungen − manifestieren.

Die segmentalen Prozesse lassen sich je nach den implizierten Merkmalen und den Phonemklassenwechseln, die sie bewirken, differenziert subklassifizieren; so spricht man z. B. von Lenisierungen (Geisler 1992), Diphthongierungen und Monophthongierungen, Spirantisierungen, Assibilierungen, Palatalisierungen (vgl. Bhat 1978), Velarisierungen, Labialisierungen, Nasalierungen (vgl. Mayerthaler 1975; Ruhlen 1978), Aspiration (vgl. Hurch 1988), Rhotazismen bzw. Vokalisierungen, Konsonantisierungen usw.

Bei den genannten segmentalen Prozessen ist weiterhin zu berücksichtigen, wie sie sich in den syntagmatischen Kontext einfügen; wenn die Variation in der Übernahme mindestens eines in der phonematischen Umgebung vorhandenen Merkmals besteht, liegt eine Assimilation vor, wenn die Variation durch Hinzufügung umgebungsfremder Merkmale erfolgt, spricht man dagegen von Dissimilation.

1.2. Konditionierung

Mit dem syntagmatischen Kontext ist bereits die Frage der Konditionierungen angesprochen; hier sind segmentale und suprasegmentale Erscheinungen phänomenal nicht selten miteinander verflochten. Wenn dies der Fall ist, dann sind die segmentalen Erscheinungen stets suprasegmental konditioniert; so verlangen beispielsweise Akzentuierungsregeln, die mit dem Wechsel der Tonstelle einhergehen, oft auch Segmentsubstitutionen (z. B. das sog. Vernersche Gesetz, oder Variationen des Typs engl. *electric* [i'lɛktrik] vs. *electricity* [ilɛk'trisiti]) usw.

Wir können überhaupt festhalten: Die Analyse der Prozesskonditionierung muß in jedem Fall von syntagmatisch komplexeren Strukturen ausgehen; je nach Sprache kommen phonologische Silben-, Wort- oder Phrasenstrukturregeln in Frage, die lautlich (d. h. rhythmisch, akzentuell, tonal und intonatorisch), aber auch semiotisch (eben in der Art der bedeutungstragenden Einheit wie Monem, Wort etc.) fundiert sein können.

2. Die sprachtheoretische Erschließung

Nun erweist sich der für die linguistische Erschließung der genannten Verfahren (und für eine mögliche Typologisierung der betroffenen Sprachen) grundlegende Begriff des Prozesses als in hohem Maße theorieabhängig; die verschiedenen einschlägigen Forschungsrichtungen, also die 'generative' Phonologie (vgl. Chomsky & Halle 1968), die 'natürliche' Phonologie (vgl. Stampe 1979), die 'natürliche generative' Phonologie (vgl. Hooper 1976), die 'atomare' Phonologie' (Dinnsen & Eckman 1977; Dinnsen 1979a), die 'lexikalische' Phonologie (Mohanan 1986), die 'autosegmentale' Phonologie (Goldsmith 1976), die 'metrische' Phonologie (Nespor 1993: 149−185) sowie die 'Silbenphonologie' (Vogel 1982) divergieren untereinander beträchtlich. Tiefgreifend sind vor allem auch die Divergenzen zwischen diesen 'neueren Entwicklungen' (vgl. Vennemann 1986) einerseits und der 'klassischen' Phonologie Prager Provenienz andererseits. Sie sind nämlich so grundlegend, dass man sich fragt, ob das gemeinsame Etikett der 'Phonologie' überhaupt noch gerechtfertigt ist; in gewisser Hinsicht ist es sogar irreführend, da es nicht vorhandene substanzielle Gemeinsamkeiten suggeriert.

Trubetzkoy hat 'seine' Wissenschaft folgendermaßen bestimmt: „Die Phonologie hat zu untersuchen, welche Lautunterschiede in der betreffenden Sprache mit Bedeutungsunterschieden verbunden sind, wie sich die Unterscheidungselemente (oder Male) zueinander verhalten und nach welchen Regeln sie miteinander zu Wörtern (bzw. Sätzen) kombiniert werden dürfen" (^{3}1958: 14).

Die Phonologie wurde, mit anderen Worten, als einzelsprachlich und segmentbasiert konzipiert; das Maß aller phonologischen Dinge ist die Distinktivität. Auf diesen gemeinsamen Nenner (die Analyse der einzelsprachlich-systemischen Organisation minimaler distinktiver Einheiten) lassen sich die genannten neueren Methoden nicht mehr bringen.

Freilich liegt ihnen auch kein positiv gemeinsames Programm zugrunde; sie teilen allenfalls ihren universalistischen Erklärungsanspruch sowie eine starke Neigung zu physiologischer Fundierung: die neuere Phonologie, auch die amerikanische, knüpft nicht selten an lautphysiologisch ausgerichtete Überlegungen der vorstrukturalistischen (europäischen) Phonetik an (vgl. etwa den Verweis des Amerikaners James Foley 1977: 53 auf den europäischen Junggrammatiker Maurice Grammont). Manche Richtungen, vor allem in der natürlichen Phonologie, laufen geradezu Gefahr, die Phonologie in einer allgemeinen Phonetik 'aufzulösen'.

Diese beiden allgemeinen Prinzipien, der Universalismus und der Physiologismus, sind insofern von grundsätzlicher Bedeutung, als sie die Bedeutung der – *per definitionem* – einzelsprachlichen Phoneme in beträchtlichem Maße relativieren.

Einige divergierende sprachtheoretische Grundannahmen, an die der Prozessbegriff oft geknüpft wird, werden im folgenden kurz präsentiert.

2.1.1. Generativismus

Die stark rezipierte und für weite Teile der Forschung maßgebliche Grundlegung der generativen Phonologie von Chomsky & Halle (1968) verzichtet explizit auf den Phonembegriff (11). Radikal aufgewertet wird dagegen der Status der in der Tat universalen phonologischen Merkmale (64 f.). 'Phonological representations' in diesem Sinne sind syntagmatische Kombinationen von paradigmatischen Merkmalsbündeln ('units', die jedoch nicht unbedingt den Phonemen entsprechen); so ist beispielsweise [$_V$s*ng]$_V$ die phonologische Repräsentation der Vergangenheitsform von engl. *sing*, wobei der Asterisk für die 'phonological rule' steht, welche engl. /sɪŋ/ in /sæŋ/ überführt. Phonologische Regeln leiten also aus diesen hochabstrakten phonologischen Repräsentationen die jeweiligen phonetischen Korrelate ab (65). Man beachte, dass die phonologische Repräsentation nicht als Beschreibungsmodell, sondern als reale Instanz des Sprechens vorausgesetzt wird (so auch Dressler 1985: 26).

In der Konzeption der generativen Phonologie, die zumindest im angloamerikanischen Raum einen Paradigmenwechsel nach sich gezogen hat, wird der Begriff der phonologischen Regel in zweifacher Hinsicht überdehnt und letztlich trivialisiert. Zunächst wird jede phonetische Repräsentation durch phonologische Regeln aus ihrer zugrundeliegenden ('underlying') phonologischen Repräsentation abgeleitet, auch dann, wenn keinerlei Variation bzw. Restriktion impliziert ist; also z. B. auch die Realisierung von phonetischem [sɪŋ] aus zugrundeliegendem phonologischen /sɪŋ/. Sodann werden eindeutig morphologische Regeln, wie etwa die Bildungstypen der starken engl. Vergangenheitsformen, unter denselben Regeltyp subsumiert. Die Phonologie wird hier der Morphologie untergeordnet und verliert so ihre sprachtheoretische Autonomie (so auch Vennemann 1986: 11 f.).

2.1.2. Natürlichkeit

Als produktiv und für die Entwicklung des Prozess- und Regelbegriffs entscheidend erwiesen sich der von Chomsky & Halle ausführlich diskutierte (aus der Prager Tradition stammende) Begriff der Markiertheit sowie das von Chomsky & Halle noch eher beiläufig gebrauchte Konzept der Natürlichkeit. Beide wurden in der sog. 'natürlichen' Phonologie systematisch entwickelt (vgl. kritisch Anderson 1981). Man vergleiche etwa die programmatische Definition, die Stampe vorschlägt: „A phonological process is a mental operation that applies in speech to substitute, for a class of sounds or sound sequences presenting a specific common difficulty to the speech capacity of the individual, an alternative class identical but lacking the difficult property. For example, voiced stops are relatively difficult to articulate because their characteristic obstruction of the nose and mouth impedes the air stream on which the glottal vibration of voicing depends. There is a phonological process which avoids this difficulty simply by substituting voiceless stops for voiced; it is observable in the speech of many young children and in the pronunciation of voiced stops by speakers of languages which lack them – Hawaiian, for example. There are other processes which offer means of avoiding the difficulty without giving up voice: these include (pre)nasalization, which relieves it through the mouth; and implosion, which relieves it by lowering the glottis and increasing the size of the supra-glottal cavity." (Stampe 1973: 1)

Den trotz seiner Unschärfe zentralen Begriff der *difficulty* hat vor allem Mayerthaler (1982: 226–231) durch ein ganzes Bündel ausdrücklich lautphysiologisch (225) fundierter Markiertheitsrelationen zu operationalisieren versucht; dabei sind die prozessualen Markiertheitsrelationen den silbenpositionalen und segmentalen hierarchisch übergeordnet. Im einzelnen formuliert Mayerthaler zehn durchgängig hierarchisierte unmarkierte bzw. natürliche 'Regelpaare'; es gilt: Regel 1 ist unmarkierter als Regel 2, Regel 2 unmarkierter als Regel 3 usw. Dem hohen Anspruch auf universale Gültigkeit kann dieser Katalog jedoch kaum entsprechen; die Regelanordnung und -auswahl sind dezisionistisch (wieso wird die Nasalisierungsregel R1 als Grundregel gesetzt, wieso gibt es keine Lenisierungsregel etc.?) und einzelnen Regeln (so R2) fehlt es durchaus an Evidenz.

Dressler (1977: 30) schlägt vor, alle natürlichen phonologischen Regeln alternativ entweder in Assimilationen in Form von Kürzungen, Schwächungen (z. B. R1 und R2), Zentralisierungen, Tilgungen (z. B. R3 und R4) und Verschmelzungen oder aber in Dissimilationen in Form von Diphthongierungen, Epenthesen, Längungen und Stärkungen (z. B. R5–R10) einzuteilen.

Die radikale Hinwendung zum Physiologismus hat schwerwiegende Weiterungen. Zunächst wird es notwendig, die spezifisch einzelsprachlichen Verfahren der Variation, die ja oft gerade nicht im genannten Sinn 'vereinfachend' sind, klar von den universalen Prozessen zu trennen. Stampe unterscheidet beide Begriffe auch terminologisch: „In this discussion it is essential that the distinction between innate phonological processes and acquired phonological 'rules', like that governing the k/s alternation in English, be kept firmly in mind, for these two classes of constraints have quite different characteristics" (Stampe 1973: 46). Dieser Unterschied sei – so Stampe – „an absolute one, a distinction between constraints which the speaker brings to the language and constraints which the language brings to the speaker, whose distinct origins are reflected in their distinct roles in speech production" (Stampe 1973: 47).

Diese universalen phonologischen Prozesse bilden den eigentlichen Gegenstand der Phonologie (vgl. Dressler 1984: 30; Hurch 1988: 8); die natürliche Phonologie ist deshalb keine einzelsprachliche Disziplin.

Natürliche Prozesse (Dressler spricht von *process types*) werden gewöhnlich durch ein-

Tabelle 95.1: Unmarkierte (natürliche) Regeln (nach Mayerthaler 1982: 230; verbale Formulierung vom Verf.)

R1) $V \rightarrow [+\text{nasal}] / \_[C +\text{nasal}]$
Vokale werden vor Nasalkonsonant nasaliert.

R2) $V \rightarrow [+\text{nasal}] / \_\#$
Wortauslautende Vokale werden nasaliert.

R3) $C \rightarrow \emptyset / \_C$
Vor Konsonant werden Konsonanten getilgt.

R4) $C \rightarrow \emptyset / \_V$
Vor Vokal werden Konsonanten getilgt.

R5) $[V +\text{hoch}] \rightarrow G / \_V$
Vor Vokal werden geschlossene Vokale zu Gleitlauten (Halbvokalen).

R6) $V \rightarrow G / \_V$
Vor Vokal werden Vokale zu Gleitlauten (Halbvokalen).

R7) $\emptyset \rightarrow ə / [+\text{obstr}]L\_\#$
Im Wortauslaut wird an eine Obstruent-Liquid-Verbindung ein Schwa angehängt.

R8) $\emptyset \rightarrow C / [+\text{obstr}]L\_\#$
Im Wortauslaut wird an eine Obstruent-Liquid-Verbindung ein Konsonant angehängt.

R9) $[+\text{obstr}] \rightarrow [-\text{sth}] / \_\$$
Vor der Silbengrenze werden Obstruenten stimmlos.

R10) $[+\text{obstr}] \rightarrow [-\text{sth}] / \_V$
Vor Vokal werden Obstruenten stimmlos.

zelsprachliche Regeln mehr oder weniger stark, in Extremfällen völlig, eingeschränkt. Ein häufig angeführtes Beispiel ist die sog. Auslautverhärtung, d. h. die Neutralisierung der Stimmhaftigkeitskorrelation (durch Generalisierung der stimmlosen Konsonanten); während im Dt. alle Obstruenten in der Silbenkoda stimmlos werden (R8 in Tabelle 1; z. B. [-s] in [haʊs] und [haʊstə] vs. [-z] in [hɔizɐ] *Häuser* und [haʊzn] *hausen*), sind im Türkischen nur Okklusive und Affrikaten in dieser Position betroffen; noch weiter wird der Prozess im Russischen, Polnischen, Bretonischen und Albanischen unterdrückt, wo Auslautverhärtung nur am Wortende eintritt (vgl. Dressler 1985: 59); völlige Unterdrückung charakterisiert beispielsweise das moderne Standardfranzösische oder das Rumänische.

Die einzelsprachlichen Regeln haben (in nicht isolierenden Sprachen) deshalb eine klare Affinität zur Morphologie; anders gesagt: Regeln morphonologischer Variation lassen sich nicht selten als grammatikalisierte phonologische Prozesse deuten; so etwa der dt. Umlaut von [aʊ] → [ɔi] im genannten Beispiel [haʊs] vs. [hɔizɐ], der die morphologische Pluralisierung durch *-er* kosignalisiert (zum Verhältnis von phonologischen und morphonologischen Verfahren vgl. Dressler 1985: 57 ff.).

Die sprachtheoretisch wichtige, auch in anderen Bereichen der Linguistik (wie der Syntax und der Mündlichkeitsforschung) grundlegende Dichotomie ist empirisch schwer abzusichern; Indizien für die Natürlichkeit im genannten Sinn bietet vor allem die sog. externe Evidenz, d. h. frequente Belege in Spracherwerb, Sprachabbau und Fehlleistungen, im Sprachwandel, in der Behandlung von Entlehnungen usw.; interne Indizien sind die höhere Frequenz, Generalisierungen bei Neutralisierung und analogischem Wandel und die weniger eingeschränkte Distribution (vgl. Dressler 1984: 47 ff.; Mayerthaler 1982: 216 ff.).

Vor allem die folgenden Unterschiede fallen ins Auge: Prozesse (Dressler 1984: 37 f.) sind ausnahmslos, Regeln implizieren Unregelmäßigkeiten. Ein gutes Beispiel für die Komplexität einzelsprachlicher Regelsysteme gibt das bereits genannte dt. Suffix *-er* [ɐ], das unter bestimmten morpho-lexikalischen Bedingungen (im Plural) „in der Regel", d. h. in der Mehrzahl seiner Okkurrenzen, die Substitution nicht-palater Tonvokale durch palatale auslöst (vgl. etwa [a] → [ɛ] in *Rand* → *Ränder*, *Band* → *Bänder* etc.). Diese Regel greift jedoch weder in allen Pluralformen (vgl. *der Kater* vs. *die Kater*), noch ist dieses Suffix im Verbund mit dem (nurmehr) sogenannten Umlaut im Singular grundsätzlich ausgeschlossen (vgl. *der Städter* vs. *die Städter*); im übrigen schließt singularisches *-er* keineswegs eine andere morphologische Pluralmarkierung aus (vgl. *die Klammer* vs. *die Klammern*). Deshalb gilt, daß die Flexionsklasse die morphonologische Regel konditioniert (und nicht umgekehrt).

Prozesse sind produktiv, Regeln nicht. Der Ablaut im Deutschen ist zweifellos eine (morphologische) Regel, da Neologismen und Lehnintegrate unmöglich nach diesem Typ flektieren (vgl. *gelten*, *galt*, *gegolten* vs. *checken*, *checkte*, *gecheckt* (nicht **chack*, **gechocken*).

Prozesse begegnen in jedem Fall in Versprechern, Regeln nicht unbedingt. Prozesse erweisen sich im aphatischen Sprachabbau als stabiler.

Da die Gültigkeit der natürlichen Regeln unabhängig von allen einzelsprachlichen Einschränkungen ('inhibitions'), denen sie unterliegt, vorausgesetzt wird, liefert die natürliche Phonologie letztlich ein Modell der Performanz (und nicht der Kompetenz; Dressler 1984: 45).

Methodologisch problematisch bleibt die notgedrungen zirkuläre Vorgehensweise: „We cannot determine what the natural rules are until we have some well-developed concept of naturalness, but we cannot develop a concept of naturalness until we have the empirical input, i. e., the corpus of natural rules" (Hooper 1976: 134).

Es kommt hinzu, dass kontrastiv breit angelegte Bestandsaufnahmen phonologischer Prozesse (die man etwa im Überblick von Maddieson 1984 über die Phoneminventare vergleichen könnte) bisher nicht erstellt wurden. 'Naturalness' als inhärente Qualität mancher − und nur mancher − Prozesse kann deshalb wohl nicht mehr sein als eine intuitiv einleuchtende, heuristisch nützliche Annahme.

Von der 'natürlichen generativen Phonologie' wurde deshalb der Vorschlag gemacht, allen beobachtbaren phonologischen Prozessen denselben, gleichermaßen natürlichen Status zuzusprechen (vgl. Hooper 1976: 133 ff.). „If we predict that all surface-true, phonetically conditioned rules are 'natural', then we have a body of data on which to base a substantive concept of naturalness. Of course, the hypothesis would not be worth much if it did not have some a priori plausibility, but it does. First, the great majority of P-rules in any language DO have obvious and well-known phonetic explanations, so it is not a great leap to claim that they all do if such explanations could be developed. Second, we assume that all linguistic phenomena have some raison d'être and that there is no reason to have a P-rule if it does not optimize the phonetic string in some way" (Hooper 1976).

2.2. Kommunikativ-semiotischer Funktionalismus

Nun kann die Natürlichkeit phonologischer Regeln nicht nur durch die physiologischen Grundlagen des Sprechens fundiert werden: auch die kommunikativen Rollen sowie die mit der Produktion und Rezeption jeweils verbundenen kognitiven Korrelate zählen in ihrer Universalität grundsätzlich zu den natürlichen Voraussetzungen.

Dressler entwickelt daher in der Nachfolge von Donegan und Stampe eine Zweiteilung in verdeutlichende, hörerorientierte und entdeutlichende, sprecherorientierte phonologische Prozesse: „Processes optimizing perception are called fortition or dissimilatory (≈ strengthening) processes; those contributing to ease of articulation are called lenition or assimilatory (≈ weakening) processes. This bipartition ties up with what is widely held to be the main function of phonology in language: to make language pronounceable and perceivable (or more precisely: the outputs/elements of lexicon and grammar). The bipartition of processes can be refined in the following way: [...] Processes serving optimal perception should be better named foregrounding processes, e. g., vowel lengthening. The antagonist function is backgrounding, e. g. vowel shortening. This is a secondary function" (Dressler 1985: 44; vgl. auch den von Back 1991 eingeführten Unterschied zwischen semiotisch relevanten ('kommunikationstaktischen') Prozessen auf der einen Seite und semiotisch irrelevanten Harmonisierungen auf der anderen Seite).

Problematisch erscheint nun an der Dresslerschen Konzeption weniger die Proliferation der Terminologie als vielmehr die ganz unterschiedliche Perspektivierung mit ihrer wenig einsichtigen Begrifflichkeit; es ist nämlich durchaus unklar, was 'gestärkt'/'geschwächt' bzw. 'verdeutlicht'/'entdeutlicht' wird und wie beide Parameter mit dem 'Hören' und 'Sprechen' korreliert sind. Die drei angeführten Dichotomien bedürfen deshalb eines kurzen Kommentars.

2.2.1. 'Stärkende' vs. 'schwächende Prozesse'

Die Opposition 'Stärkung' vs. 'Schwächung' (bzw. *fortition* vs. *lenition* usw.) ist ausschließlich in phonischer Perspektive sinnvoll und zwar im Blick auf Stärkehierarchien, die auf dem für die lautliche Organisation fundamentalen Kontrast zwischen 'vokalischen' und 'konsonantischen' Segmenten, letztlich also zwischen dem Öffnen und Schließen des Mundes, beruhen; die meist alternativ, gelegentlich auch komplementär (vgl. Geisler 1992) angewandten Kriterien sind die Obstruktion und die Sonorität (vgl. den Überblick in Hooper 1976: 195−207). Genauer ist zwischen „genetischer" und „positionsbedingter" Stärke zu unterscheiden (vgl. Geisler 1992: 24−37), wobei die einzelsprachlich-systemischen Verhältnisse zu berücksichtigen sind: Auch ein aus universaler Perspektive als genetisch und positionsbedingt stark einzuschätzender Laut (bzw. eine Lautklasse), wie z. B. ein initialer Okklusiv, kann sich einzelsprachlich als schwach erweisen (dazu Krefeld 1994). Gestärkt oder geschwächt wird der vokalische bzw. konsonantische Charakter eines Lautes in einer bestimmten Umgebung; die minimale Umgebung, in der sich dergleichen Prozesse manifestieren können, ist die in der Silbenphonologie und neben dem Fuß auch in der metrischen Phonologie zur Basiseinheit phonologischer Deskription avancierte Silbe. Gemessen am Kriterium des maximalen Kontrastes ist die optimale Silbe also K[onsonant]V[okal]; in der Tat wird diese, wie es scheint, universale Silbe von vielen Sprachen als einzige zugelassen. Komplexere Baupläne unterliegen dagegen mehr oder weniger ausgeprägten Restriktionen (vgl. Vennemann 1988).

2.2.2. 'Verdeutlichende' vs. 'entdeutlichende' Prozesse

Die Opposition 'Verdeutlichung' vs. 'Entdeutlichung' setzt dagegen eine semiotische Perspektive voraus. 'Deutlichkeit' ist ein wahrnehmungspsychologisches Prädikat und bezieht sich auf die Perzeption der Signifikanten; es meint, genauer gesagt, die Zuverlässigkeit, mit der das Signifikat eines spezifischen Signifikanten erkannt wird. Der maximale Grad an Deutlichkeit ist erreicht, wenn das gesamte Distinktionspotential des Signifikanten ausgeschöpft wird, d.h. wenn die Summe aller das jeweilige phonologische Zeichen definierenden Oppositionen perzipierbar ist; 'Entdeutlichung' tritt bei einem Verlust an Distinktivität ein. Eine 'Verdeutlichung', die einen Zuwachs an Distinktivität (und eine Vermehrung der Minimalpaare) voraussetzt, kann es jedoch strenggenommen gar nicht geben: Jede entstehende Variation impliziert Entdeutlichung, da sie immer auf Kosten der perzeptiven Konstanz des variierenden Zeichens geht (und im übrigen stets die Möglichkeit von Homonymenkonflikten birgt). Der Begriff 'Verdeutlichung' ist kontradiktorisch und allenfalls, cum grano salis, in Bezug auf solche Prozesse gerechtfertigt, die ein neues, spezifisches Segment mit sich bringen, das unabhängig vom jeweiligen Prozess nicht existiert. (Im übrigen betreffen alle Veränderungen des Segmentinventars ausschließlich die Ebene der einzelsprachlichen Organisation; ob universale Prozesse zu einer 'Verdeutlichung' im Sinne Dresslers führen, liegt also ebenso ausschließlich in der Natur der betroffenen einzelsprachlichen Systeme — und gerade nicht in der Natur der auf sie einwirkenden universalen Prozesse).

Der Versuch, die Phonologie semiotisch zu fundieren, ist zweifellos richtungsweisend; in der einseitigen Bindung der Verdeutlichungs-/Entdeutlichungsdichotomie an den phonematischen Distinktionsbegriff erweist sich die Dresslersche Konzeption jedoch m. E. als wenig realistisch und reduktionistisch.

Die semiotische Grundlage einer 'natürlichen' Phonologie ist erst dann verläßlich, wenn sie sich in erster Linie auf die in der natürlichen Kommunikation ausgetauschten semiotischen Einheiten, d.h. auf die Zeichen, stützt. Die Intention der Kommunikanten richtet sich auf die (Re-)Produktion und die Perzeption (d.h. das Wiedererkennen) von Signifikanten. Die Phoneme sind dagegen normalerweise keine intentionalen Größen ('sound intentions'), wie Dressler (1984: 32) in der Nachfolge Baudouin de Courtenays definiert. Sie können freilich sekundär, auf einer metasprachlichen Ebene, jederzeit dazu erhoben werden. Das geschieht quasi automatisch, wenn die Wahrnehmung der geäußerten Signifikanten auf Grund bruchstückhafter Realisierung, auf Grund von Nebengeräuschen usw. problematisch ist, und die Situation Mehrdeutigkeiten erlaubt. Erschwerte Kommunikationsbedingungen dieser Art führen zu besonders klarer Artikulation, — oft auch deshalb, weil der Adressat sich durch Rückfrage versichert ('Was hast du gesagt, *bekleidet* oder *begleitet?*'). Die phonematische Struktur bildet also gewissermaßen ein zweites Sicherheitsnetz der Kommunikation (vgl. Krefeld 1998: 137—144, in Anlehnung an Karl Bühler).

Damit wurde bereits die dritte bei der Typisierung phonologischer Prozesse häufig bemühte Dichotomie berührt.

2.2.3. 'Sprecher-' vs. 'hörerorientierte' Prozesse

Das Verhältnis zwischen 'sprecher-' und 'hörerorientierten' Prozessen wird als konfliktuell aufgefaßt, da beide Gruppen antagonistischen Prinzipien untergeordnet sind; während hörerfreundliche Verfahren die perzeptive Klarheit garantieren (oder gar optimieren), stehen die hörerunfreundlichen Verfahren im Zeichen der artikulatorischen Bequemlichkeit. In welchem Maß nun der eine bzw. der andere Typ das Sprechen beeinflusst, hängt in hohem Maße von der Formalität der Sprechsituation ab. Es gilt: je formeller, desto hörerbezogener und 'deutlicher' (vgl. Dressler 1984: 33; 1985: 44 ff.).

Nun deutete sich in der Diskussion der 'Verdeutlichungs-/Entdeutlichungsdichotomie' bereits an, wie gering der Kenntnisstand in Sachen Sprachperzeption (noch) ist. In der Tat gibt es Indizien dafür, daß die Gleichsetzung von 'Sprecher' und 'Produktion' auf der einen Seite und diejenige von 'Hörer' und 'Perzeption' auf der anderen Seite sowie die antagonistische Gegenüberstellung 'Sprecher'/'Produktion' vs. 'Hörer'/Perzeption' womöglich in eine falsche Richtung weisen (Krefeld 1998). Zumindest zwei Aspekte dürfen nicht übersehen werden:

(1) Der Sprecher hört sich selbst reden, ist also — gerade im physiologischen Verständnis — immer auch Hörer; der Hörer dagegen spricht geradezu mit, während er hört; ein deutliches Anzeichen sind die häufig beobachtbaren Lippenbewegungen des Hörers;
(2) Sprechen und Hören haben eine gemeinsame Basis, die auch prozedural greifbar sein sollte: die 'Abrufung' memorisierter Einheiten. Vieles spricht dafür, dass auch die 'Suche' nach der passenden Einheit in der Produktion nicht nur von inhaltlichen und intentionalen, sondern auch von formalen Faktoren, von der Gestalt abhängt.

Phonologische Prozesse betreffen also neben der Phonation und der Audition auch die Memoration. Neben der artikulatorischen

Bequemlichkeit (bzw. der mutmaßlichen Trägheit der entsprechenden Organe) und dem auditiven Distinktionsbedürfnis muß auch mit der mnemotechnischen Präferenz bestimmter Gestaltungsweisen als Quelle phonologischer Prozesse gerechnet werden. Etwa die unterschiedliche 'Anfälligkeit' der Laute für metathetische Prozesse, speziell die „disproportional high and (widespread) frequency of occurrence of liquids in metathesis" (Ultan 1978: 375) könnte damit zusammenhängen.

Die Liquiden sind nämlich insofern Konsonanten besonderer Art, als sie — neben der typisch konsonantischen Eigenschaft der Silbenrandbildung — dank ihrer ausgeprägten Sonorität einerseits eine hohe Affinität zum Silbenkern besitzen (vgl. die silbischen Liquide), andererseits jedoch im Unterschied zu den anderen silbenkernfähigen Sonoranten (wie etwa den Nasalen) auch privilegierte Begleiter von Obstruenten im Silbenkopf sind (sog. *muta cum liquida*-Verbindungen). Die Liquide können deshalb bei der Memorisierung von Signifikanten nicht auf quasi selbstverständliche Art und Weise mit einer spezifischen Linearisierung und Positionierung innerhalb der Silbe (oder komplexer Einheiten) assoziiert werden.

3. Der typologische Ertrag

Im Bereich der phonologischen Typologie, insbesondere im Blick auf die integrative Zusammenführung phonologischer und morphosyntaktischer Parameter ist noch viel Arbeit zu leisten. Als fruchtbar hat sich in dieser übergreifenden typologischen Perspektive die auf Pike (1945) zurückgehende Konzeption einer rythmischen Alternative erwiesen, gemäß der Sprachen entweder silbenisochron ('syllable timed') oder akzentisochron ('stress timed') organisiert seien (→ Art. 99).

Obwohl sich echte Isochronie auf der Ebene der Produktion im strengen physikalisch-meßtechnischen Sinn nicht nachweisen läßt, spielen isochrone rhythmische Muster bei der Perzeption eine wichtige Rolle (vgl. Auer & Uhmann 1988, 254 f.). Die Annahme alternativer Rhythmisierung, die sich, wie Auer & Uhmann zeigen, auch kontinual auffassen läßt, ist jedoch typologisch nicht zuletzt deshalb nützlich, weil sowohl die 'prototypische' Akzentisochronie als auch die 'prototypische' Silbenisochronie jeweils mit einer ganzen Reihe phonologischer Prozesse in Verbindung gebracht werden, die in der Tat oft kopräsent begegnen. In gewisser Hinsicht sind die beiden Rhythmisierungsprinzipien deshalb nicht mehr (und nicht weniger) als nützliche Etikettierungen (vgl. Auer & Uhmann 1988: 244) der folgenden Bündel von lautlichen Prinzipien (nach Auer 1993; eine ganz ähnliche Aufstellung gibt Mayerthaler 1982: 231 aus markiertheitstheoretischer Sicht); cf. Tabelle 95.2.

Gelegentlich werden rhythmisch/prosodisch basierte Konzeptionen mit 'holistisch'-typologischem Anspruch formuliert; d. h., es werden nicht nur segmentale Prozesstypen mit suprasegmentalen verknüpft, sondern beide werden zudem mit der morphosyntaktischen Organisation der jeweiligen Einzelsprache bzw. des jeweiligen Typs korreliert.

Viel Beachtung fand der Vergleich zweier genetisch eng verwandter, jedoch typologisch völlig divergenter austroasiatischer Sprachfamilien (Munda und Mon-Khmer) von Patricia Donegan und David Stampe (1983). Die Tabelle 95.3. gibt einen Überblick (Donegan & Stampe 1983: 337).

Tabelle 95.2.

Silbenrhythmus	Akzentrhythmus
— keine Reduktion unbetonter Silben und Vokale	— Reduktion unbetonter Silben und Vokale
— keine zentralisierten und/oder stimmlosen Vokale	— zentralisierte und/oder stimmlose Vokale
— einfache Silbenstruktur	— komplexe Silbenstruktur
— Vokalharmonie	— keine Vokalharmonie
— Tonoppositionen auch in unbetonten Silben	— keine Tonoppositionen in unbetonten Silben
— weniger starke Prominenz der Tonsilbe	— starke Prominenz der Tonsilbe
— freie Tonsilbe	— Tonsilbe festgelegt

Tabelle 95.3.

	MUNDA	MON-KHMER
Phrase Accent:	Falling (initial)	Rising (final)
Word Order:	Variable – SOV, AN NA, Postpositional	Rigid – SVO, Prepositional
Syntax:	Case, Verb Agreement	Analytic
Word Canon:	Dactylic,	Trochaic, Iambic, Monosyllabic
Morphology:	Agglutinative, Suffixing, Polysynthetic	Fusional, Prefixing or Isolating
Timing:	Isosyllabic, Isomoric	Isoaccentual
Syllable Canon:	(C)V(C)	(C)V or (C)(C)V́(C)(C)
Consonantism:	Stable, Geminate Clusters	Shifting, Tonogenetic, Non-Geminate Clusters
Tone/Register:	Level Tone (Korku Only)	Contour Tones/Register
Vocalism:	Stable, Monophthongal, Harmonic	Shifting, Diphthongal, Reductive

Die von den Autoren an die erste Stelle gesetzte Opposition zwischen initialem und finalem Satzakzent ist auch die hierarchisch wichtigste, „because *accent is the only factor pervading all the levels of language*, and the only factor capable of explaining the specific typological tendencies at each level in evolutions such as those of Munda and Mon Khmer" (340; Hervorhebung im Text). Wie man sieht, wird dem Satzakzent die 'Erklärung' aller typologisch relevanten Faktoren (Wortstellung, Kongruenz, Rhythmus, Silbenstruktur) zugemutet; dazu zählen auch segmentale Prozesse wie die Vokalharmonie und -reduktion, vokalischer und konsonantischer Wechsel usw. Vielversprechend ist die rhythmustypologisch basierte Rekonstruktion von Klitisierungsprozessen im europäischen Portugiesischen und deren Abbau im Brasilianischen (vgl. Reich 2000).

Frans Plank hat gezeigt, daß die holistische Hoffnung, eine typologisch stichhaltige Kovariation zwischen der phonologischen Ebene auf der einen Seite und der morphologisch/syntaktischen Ebene auf der anderen festzustellen, die Sprachwissenschaft seit je begleitet hat (1998: 223); seine Zusammenstellung zeigt aber auch, wie sehr sich die bisher vertretenen Positionen widersprechen: „the likeliest candidates for true cross-level links would be agglutination/flection, and perhaps morpheme and word size in morphology, constituent order in syntax, and segment inventories, phonotactics, vowel harmony processes, and rhythm in phonology. For all these parameters it is yet to be seen whether frequency of mention will be confirmed by the sounder evidence of reasonable cross-linguistic samples" (224).

4. Präliminarien eines typologisch brauchbaren Prozessbegriffs

Nach dem kurzen, weder vollständigen noch objektiven *tour d'horizon* stellt sich nun die Gretchenfrage, welche Prozesse in welcher theoretischen Modellierung überhaupt typologisch relevant sind. Eine mögliche Antwort sollte den folgenden Punkten Rechnung tragen:

(1) Es ist sinnvoll, die Existenz einer eigenständigen phonologischen Organisationsebene anzunehmen (wobei 'eigenständig' nicht gleichbedeutend ist mit völlig autonom). Der Gegenstandsbereich der Phonologie darf deshalb nicht zwischen einzelsprachlicher Morphologie und außer(einzel)sprachlicher Lautphysiologie aufgeteilt werden. Vielmehr ist es das Ziel der Typologie, übereinzelsprachliche Verallgemeinerungen aus einzelsprachlich beobachtbaren Prozessen abzuleiten.

(2) Sinnvoll ist nur ein Regelbegriff à la Ferguson (vgl. § 1.), der sich auf die Beschreibung oberflächlich evidenter Variationen und Bindungen beschränkt. Jeder typologisch relevante segmentale Prozess ist somit phonotaktisch konditioniert; die Annahme kontextfreier Prozesse ist (einzelsprachlich) phonologisch unnötig und daher (übereinzelsprachlich) typologisch irrelevant.

(3) Daraus ergibt sich nun weiterhin das methodische Prinzip, alle diachronen Prozesse auf eine 'synchrone Prozessbasis' zurückzuführen (Back 1991).

(4) Das Einzelsegment (Phonem) ist eine notwendige phonologische Domäne; sie ist jedoch für die einzelsprachliche und für die typologisch ausgerichtete phonologische Be-

schreibung in keinem Fall hinreichend. Vielmehr ist es notwendig, die segmentalen 'Kohäsionsregeln' (*bonding rules*) herauszuarbeiten (vgl. Vennemann 1988: 273 ff.).
(5) Die Kontexte, über denen die Kohäsionsregeln operieren, konstituieren die in der jeweiligen Einzelsprache und im zugehörigen Typ relevanten phonologischen Domänen; es kann sich dabei um Silben, um phonologische Wörter, um phonologische Füße und um phonologische Phrasen handeln. Keine dieser 'kohäsiven' Domänen ist notwendigerweise als phonologisch relevant anzusehen.
(6) Alle regelhaft beschreibbaren phonologischen Domänen sind perzeptiv von grundlegender Bedeutung; sie bilden wiederholbare und ablösbare Gestalten der Sprachwahrnehmung. Wahrnehmung ist aber primär keine negative Perzeption von distinktiven Unterschieden, sondern positive Identifikation von Inhalten. Die Wahrnehmungsgestalten müssen — mit anderen Worten — an die Ebene der Signifikate angebunden werden. In dieser Perspektive lassen sich phonologische Prozesse als gestaltbildende Verfahren deuten, die in einzelsprach- bzw. sprachtypspezifischer Weise die Konstanz und Prägnanz der Lexeme, Wörter und Phrasen steuern. So manifestiert sich etwa in Prozessen wie Harmonisierungen, Nasalierungen, grammatischem Wechsel, tonalen Konstellationen usw. eine Schärfung der Wortprägnanz, die deutlich auf Kosten der Lexem- und Wortkonstanz geht; prägnante rhythmische Phrasenstrukturen, wie sie etwa in durchgängiger jambischer Oxytonie und/oder in Sandhiregeln zum Ausdruck kommen, schwächen dagegen sowohl Prägnanz als auch Konstanz der Lexeme und der Wörter.

Zentral für die Entwicklung einer phonologischen Typologie, oder besser gesagt der phonologischen Komponente einer umfassenden Sprachtypologie, ist jedoch weniger die (m. E. vielsprechende) Orientierung an der Gestalttheorie, als vielmehr die Einsicht, daß die deskriptive Zusammenstellung phonologischer Prozesse und ihrer rein phonologischen Implikationen noch keine tragfähige Basis für typologisch relevante Verallgemeinerungen abgibt.

5. Zitierte Literatur

Abercrombie, David. 1967. *Elements of general phonetics*. Edinburgh: Edinburgh University Press.

Andersen, Henning (ed.). 1986. *Sandhi phenomena in the languages of Europe*. Berlin: Mouton de Gruyter.

Anderson, Stephen R. 1981. „Why phonology isn't natural". *Linguistic Inquiry* 12: 493—539.

Auer, Peter & Uhmann, Susanne. 1988. „Silben- und akzentzählende Sprachen. Literaturüberblick und Diskussion". *Zeitschrift für Sprachwissenschaft* 7: 214—259.

Auer, Peter. 1993. *Is a rhythm-based typology possible? A study on the role of prosody in phonological typology*. Universität Konstanz: KontRi Working Paper No. 21.

Back, Michael. 1991. *Die synchrone Prozeßbasis des natürlichen Lautwandels*. (= ZDL; Beiheft 71) Stuttgart: Steiner.

Basbøll, Hans. 1979. „Phonology". *Proceedings of the 9th International Congress of Phonetic Sciences* 9.1: 103—132.

Bell, Alan. 1978. „Syllabic consonants". In: Greenberg 1978: 153—201.

Bhat, D. N. S. 1978. „A general study of palatalization". In: Greenberg 1978: 47—92.

Chomsky, Noam & Halle, Morris. 1968. *The sound pattern of English*. New York etc.: Harper & Row.

Dinnsen, Daniel & Eckman, Fred R. 1976. „The atomic character of phonological processes". In: Dressler & Pfeiffer (eds.): *Phonologica 1976. Akten der dritten Internationalen Phonologie-Tagung. Wien, 1.—4. September 1976*, Innsbruck, 133—139.

Dinnsen, Daniel (ed.). 1979. *Current approaches to phonological theory*. Bloomington: University Press.

Dinnsen, Daniel. 1979. „Atomic phonology". In: Dinnsen 1979: 31—49.

Dinnsen, Daniel. 1983. „On the phonetics of phonological neutralization". In: *Proceedings of the 13. International Congress of Linguistics*, 1294.

Donegan, Patricia & Stampe, David. 1983. „Rhythm and the holistic organization of language structure". In: Richardson, John F. & Marks, Mitchell & Chukerman, Amy. *The interplay of phonology, morphology and syntax*, Chicago: Chicago Linguistic Society, 337—353.

Dressler, Wolfgang U. & Pfeiffer, Oskar E. (eds.) 1977. *Phonologica 1976. Akten der dritten Internationalen Phonologie-Tagung. Wien, 1.—4. September 1976*. Innsbruck: Becvar (= Innsbrucker Beiträge zur Sprachwissenschaft 19).

Dressler, Wolfgang U. 1977. *Grundfragen der Morphonologie*. Wien: Verlag der österreichischen Akademie der Wissenschaften (= Sitzungsberichte der philosophisch-historischen Klasse 315).

Dressler, Wolfgang U. (ed.). 1981. *Phonologica*. Innsbruck: Becvar (= Innsbrucker Beiträge zur Sprachwissenschaft 36).

Dressler, Wolfgang U. 1984. „Explaining natural phonology". *Phonology Yearbook* 1: 29—51.

Dressler, Wolfgang U. 1985. *Morphonology: the dynamics of derivation*. Ann Arbor: Karona.

Duncan-Rose, Caroline & Fisiak, Jacek & Vennemann, Theo (eds.). 1988. *Rhetorica, Phonologica, Syntactica: a Festschrift for Robert P. Stockwell.* London & New York: Routledge.

Ferguson, Charles. 1978. „Phonological processes". In: Greenberg 1978, 403–443.

Foley, James. 1977. *Foundations of theoretical phonology.* Cambridge etc.: Cambridge University Press.

Geisler, Hans. 1992. *Akzent und Lautwandel in der Romania* (= Romanica Monacensia 38) Tübingen: Narr.

Geisler, Hans. 1994. „Metathese im Sardischen". *Vox Romanica* 53: 106–137.

Goldsmith, John. 1979. „The aims of autosegmental phonology". In: Dinnsen 1979, 202–222.

Goldsmith, John. 1979. *Autosegmental phonology.* New York & London: Garland.

Goldsmith, John. 1982. „Accent systems". In: van der Hulst & Smith 1982, 47–65.

Goldsmith, John. 1990. *Autosegmental and metrical phonology.* Oxford & Cambridge (Mass.): Blackwell.

Goldsmith, John (ed.). 1995. *The handbook of phonological theory.* Oxford: Blackwell.

Greenberg, Joseph H. (ed.). 1978. *Universals of human language.* Vol. 2. *Phonology.* Stanford: Stanford University Press.

Harlig, Jeffrey & Bardovi-Harlig, Kathleen. 1988. „Accentuation typology, word order, and theme-rheme structure". In: Hammond, Michael et al. (eds.). *Studies in syntactic typology.* Amsterdam: Benjamins, 125–146.

Hayes, Bruce. 1984. „The phonology of rhythm in English". *Linguistic Inquiry* 15: 33–74.

Hayes, Bruce. 1995. *Metrical stress theory: principles and case studies,* Chicago: Chicago University Press.

Hooper, Joan Bybee. 1976. *An introduction to natural generative phonology.* New York: Academy Press.

Houlihan, Kathleen & Iverson, Gregory K. 1977. „Phonological markedness and neutralization rules". *Minnesota working papers in linguistics and philosophy of language* 4: 45–58.

Hurch, Bernd. 1988. *Über Aspiration: ein Kapitel aus der natürlichen Phonologie.* Tübingen: Narr.

Hyman, Larry M. 1978. „Word demarcation". In: Greenberg 1978, 443–470.

Kleinhenz, Ursula. 1996. „Zur Typologie phonologischer Domänen". In: Lang, Ewald & Zifonun, Gisela (eds.). *Deutsch – typologisch.* (= Jahrbuch 1995 des IdS). Berlin/New York: de Gruyter, 569–584.

Kloeke, Wus van Lessen. 1982. *Deutsche Phonologie und Morphologie.* Tübingen: Niemeyer (= Linguistische Arbeiten 117).

Krefeld, Thomas. 1994. „Rezension von H. Geisler 1992". *RJb* 45: 184–188.

Krefeld, Thomas. 1998. *Wortgestalt und Vokalsystem in der Italoromania. Plädoyer für eine gestaltphonologische Rekonstruktion des romanischen Vokalismus.* Kiel: Westensee.

Kučera, H. 1973. „Language variability, rule interdependency, and the grammar of Czech". *Linguistic Inquiry* 4: 499–521.

Ladefoged, Peter & Maddieson, Ian. 1996. *The sounds of the world's languages.* Oxford: Blackwell.

Leben, William. 1982. „Metrical or Autosegmental". In: van der Hulst & Smith 1982, 177–191.

Liberman, Mark. 1979. *The intonational system of English.* New York/London: Garland.

Linell, Per. 1977. „Morphonology as part of morphology". In: Dressler, Wolfgang U. & Pfeiffer (eds.) 1977, 9–21.

Linell, Per. 1979. „Evidence for a functionally-based typology of phonological rules". In: *Communication and cognition* 12.1: 53–106.

Maddieson, Ian. 1978. „Universals of tone". In: Greenberg 1978, 335–367.

Maddieson, Ian. 1984. *Pattern of sounds.* Cambridge etc.: Cambridge University Press.

Mayerthaler, Eva. 1982. *Unbetonter Vokalismus und Silbenstruktur im Romanischen: Beiträge zu einer dynamischen Prozeßtypologie.* Tübingen: Narr.

Mayerthaler, Willi. 1975. „Gibt es eine universelle Nasalierungsregel?". In: Dressler, Wolfgang & Mareš, František V. (eds.). *Phonologica 1972. Akten der zweiten Internationalen Phonologie-Tagung. Wien, 5.–8. September 1972.* München/Salzburg: Fink.

Mayerthaler, Willi. 1982. *Morphologische Natürlichkeit.* Wiesbaden: Athenaion.

Mayerthaler, Willi. 1982a. „Markiertheit in der Phonologie". In: Vennemann, Theo (ed.). *Silben, Segmente, Akzente.* Tübingen: Niemeyer, 205–246.

Mohanan, K. P. 1986. *The theory of lexical phonology.* Dordrecht u. a.: Reidel.

Nespor, Marina & Vogel, Irene. 1982. „Prosodic domains of external sandhi rules". In: van der Hulst & Smith 1982, 225–257.

Nespor, Marina. 1993. *Fonologia.* Bologna: Il Mulino.

Pike, Kenneth. 1945. *The intonation of American English.* Ann Arbor: University of Michigan Press.

Plank, Frans. 1998. „The co-variation of phonology with morphology and syntax: A hopeful history". In: *Linguistic Typology* 2, 195–230.

Reich, Uli. 2000. *Freie Pronomina, Verbalklitika und Nullobjekte im Spielraum diskursiver Variation des Portugiesischen in São Paulo.* Diss. München (erscheint in: Romanica Monacensia).

Ruhlen, Merrit. 1978. „Nasal vowels". In: Greenberg 1978, 203–241.

Ruhlen, Merrit. 1987. *A guide to the languages of the world*. Stanford: Stanford University Press.

Schane, Sanford A. 1973. *Generative phonology*. Englewood Cliffs.

Skalička, Vladimir. 1979. *Typologische Studien*. Braunschweig/Wiesbaden: Vieweg.

Sommerstein, Alan H. 1977. *Modern phonology*. London: Arnold.

Stampe, David. 1979. *A dissertation on Natural Phonology*. New York & London: Garland.

Trubetzkoy, Nikolaj S. ³1958. *Grundzüge der Phonologie*. Göttingen: Vandenhoek & Rupprecht.

Ultan, Russel. 1978. „A typological view of metathesis". In: Greenberg 1978, 367–402.

van der Hulst, Harry & Smith, Norval. 1982. „ An overview of accent and metrical phonology". In: van der Hulst & Smith (eds.) 1982, 1–45.

van der Hulst, Harry & Smith, Norval (eds.). 1982. *The structure of phonological representation*. Dordrecht: Foris Publ.

Vennemann, Theo. 1971. „The phonology of Gothic vowels". *Language* 47: 90–132.

Vennemann, Theo. 1972. „Phonetic detail in assimilation: Problems in Germanic phonology". *Language* 48: 863–892.

Vennemann, Theo. 1986. *Neuere Entwicklungen in der Phonologie*, Berlin etc.: de Gruyter.

Vennemann, Theo. 1988. „The rule dependence of syllable structure". In: Duncan-Rose, Caroline & Fisiak, Jacek & Vennemann, Theo (eds.). *Rhetorica, Phonologica, Syntactica: A Festschrift for Robert P. Stockwell*, London & New York: Routledge, 257–283.

Vihman, Marilyn M. 1978. „Consonant harmony: its scope and function in child language". In: Greenberg 1978, 281–335.

Vogel, Irene. 1982. *La sillaba come unità fonologica*. Bologna: Zanichelli.

Thomas Krefeld, München (Deutschland)

96. Metrical patterns

1. Introduction
2. The syllable as a constituent
3. The foot
4. Typology and metrical structures
5. Universals, implications and correlations
6. Conclusion
7. References

1. Introduction

Metrical patterns in languages are obtained by combining various elements of prosodic structure: syllables and their constituents, feet, and other higher level organisational units like prosodic words, phrases and so on. Within a given metrical organisation, a particular constituent may be the most prominent. This relative prominence is marked by stress, which is the central theme of this article. Stress, under this conception, is not merely a phonetic feature, but is the means of marking relative prominence within various organisational groupings of metrical units (cf. Liberman 1975; see the articles by Kager, and Halle & Idsardi in Goldsmith 1995 for surveys of different metrical theories of stress). In order to establish stress patterns, we first discuss how different metrical constituents are relevant for the phonological systems as a whole. Since the covariation of linguistic variables is fundamental to language typology (cf. Plank 1997), our goal is not merely to list the observed metrical patterns, but also to examine possible relationships between the different patterns.

To this end we will focus on 'metrical coherence' from two perspectives and address the following questions. First, we ask whether a given metrical constituent varies in its properties within a single language. For instance, the metrical constituent 'foot' is generally used to account for word stress. However, there may be other processes which are sensitive to foot structure. If so, one would like to know if foot types vary for different processes within a given language, or whether with respect to a given metrical constituent, the system is coherent (Dresher & Lahiri 1991). The second issue is whether the type of stress a language has can predict the properties of its metrical constituents. This particular perspective has not been an issue in the phonological descriptions of metrical patterns, but is extensively discussed in typological literature on the covariation of stress with the nature of syllables, headedness of phrasal stress and such (cf. Donegan & Stampe 1983; Gil 1986). Thus, we begin by motivating syllables and feet as necessary metrical constituents in the description of phonological systems. For each of the constituents we provide evidence from segmental processes as well as for stress, and then move on to issues on metrical coherence and covariation of metrical units, which are rather crucial for typological research.

2. The Syllable as a constituent

In this section, we first review the syllable's status in phonology before discussing the role of the syllable in the assignment of stress. The syllable has traditionally been assumed to consist of an onset followed by a rhyme which is divided into a nucleus and a coda. The nucleus is the obligatory and most important part of the syllable, while the onset and coda are optional. The most frequent syllable inventory in natural language consists of the following: V, CV, VC, CVC (see Blevins 1995 for a survey). The more complex syllable inventories arise from including more segmental material in the onset and the coda, and even the nucleus can be branching. Complex onsets and codas are generally governed by the *Sonority Scale* which states that onset consonants increase in sonority and codas decrease in their sonority (cf. Clements & Hume 1995). The accepted sonority scale in terms of rising sonority is obstruents < nasals < liquids < glides < vowels.

The notions 'closed' and 'open' syllables play an important role in phonology. Closed

(2) Resyllabification in German
glau**b**   [p]   glau**b**-en   [b]
Ta**g**   [k]   Ta**g**-e   [g]

syllables are those which are closed by a coda consonant, while open syllables end in a vowel (long or short) or a diphthong. To decide whether medial consonants are part of onsets or codas, the principle of maximisation of the onset is often invoked. That is, when there is more than one intervocalic consonant, whether all of them are part of the onset of the second syllable, depends on whether the language permits 'maximising the onset' based on sonority principles. Phonological processes can help determine whether consonants fall in the coda or not. This is illustrated with an example from German which has a process of syllable final devoicing. The data are from Vennemann (1972). German has a rule of syncopation which follows for the following types of alternations.

(1) Syncope and syllable final devoicing in German
Standard German
             'flirt'   'sail'   'go by bicycle'
Infinitive   li:bəl+n   ze:gəl+n   ra:dəl+n
1SG.IND.PRES li:bl+ə   ze:gl+ə   ra:dl+ə
Standard German, Northern pronunciation
              li:bl+ə   ze:gl+ə   ra:tl+ə

After syncopation, the consonant clusters that are created are not equally accepted as onsets in the Standard German as compared to the Northern pronunciation. In Standard German, the sequence [dl] is accepted as a syllable onset, and the maximisation of onset prevents the [d] being in the coda. Hence, coda-devoicing does not apply. In contrast, the Northern pronunciation which allows [bl] and [gl] clusters, permits maximisation of consonants in these cases, but prevents [dl] from being part of an onset. As a result, coda-devoicing applies and the surface form is [ra:t.lə] rather than *[ra:.dlə].

Maximisation of the onset is closely related to the notion of a core syllable, or a CV syllable. There is a general tendency to avoid onsetless syllables such that in most if not all languages, a VCV string is syllabified as [V.CV]. Resyllabification to prevent onsetless syllables is central to the analysis of German devoicing as well (cf. Rubach 1990, Giegerich 1992). The following alternations are relevant.

glau**b**-lich   [p/b]   'believe' 2SG IMP./INF./ADJ.
tä**g**-lich   [k/g]   'day' SG./PL./ADV.

As we have seen before, coda devoicing makes the word final consonants in the first column voiceless. A suffix vowel is added to the words in the second column. Here the medial sequence VCV is syllabified as [V.CV] forcing the medial consonant to be an onset, thereby blocking coda devoicing. Oddly enough, when the suffix begins with a sonorant consonant, and although the obstruent + liquid is a possible onset (as we saw in the previous example), resyllabification can be blocked for certain speakers and coda devoicing applies. Obviously, for those speakers who devoice the obstruents, resyllabification is sensitive to certain morphemes even if allowable onsets may arise. However, the crucial point is that when a suffix with an initial vowel follows, resyllabification is obligatory since German always requires a syllable with an onset.

Words or syllables without a surface consonant are always preceded by a glottal stop: cf. *Atmen* [ʔatmən] 'breathing', *abteilen* [ʔaptailən] 'to separate', *mitarbeiten* [mɪtʔarbaitən] 'to cooperate' etc. For some speakers the glottal stop insertion is restricted to stressed syllables; hence, *Theater* [tʰeʔáːtɐ]) 'theatre', but *Bebauung* [bebáʊʊŋ] 'building development', and not [bebáʊʔʊŋ].

2.1. Preferred syllable structure

Once we accept the fact that languages have preferred syllable structures, any deviation from these preferences are repaired. Strategies for repairing them can differ. For instance, if affixation leads to unacceptable syllables, either epenthesis or syncope are invoked to maintain the preferred structures. In a language like Koryak (a Paleosiberian language spoken in Kamchatka; Spencer 1996: 63–64), the most complex syllable structure permitted is CVC. Hence any affixation which leads to complex structures is resolved by schwa epenthesis.

(3)   Koryak schwa epenthesis
       Verb root /pŋlo/ 'ask'
       Prefixes: *t-* 1SG.SUBJ. *mt-* 1PL.SUBJ.,
       na- 3PL.SUBJ.
(a) t-pŋlo-n   təp.ŋə.lon   'I asked him'
(b) mt-pŋlo-n   mət.pəŋ.lon   'we asked him'
(c) na-pŋlo-n   nap.ŋə.lon   'they asked him'

If the segments are syllabified from left to right obeying the preferred CVC syllabic template, then the introduction of the schwa is entirely predictable. If we did not assume that epenthesis was syllable based, it would not be possible to account for the difference between the schwa insertions in the verb root in (3a) and (3b): *pŋəl* vs. *pəŋl*.

Epenthesis is one of the most frequent ways to resolve unwanted clusters and to obtain a preferred syllable template. Related languages often exhibit a difference in the acceptance of initial and final clusters. A striking example comes from certain final liquid + obstruent clusters in Germanic languages. English and German allow [l + obstruent] clusters in words like *milk* or *Milch*, but Dutch disallows such clusters and introduces a schwa as in *melək*.

Along with epenthesis, deletion is another means for cluster simplification. In Bengali, the present indicative ending begins with a geminate affricate -*tʃtʃʰ* which is degeminated when added to a verb root ending in a consonant (Fitzpatrick-Cole 1994, 1996; Lahiri 2000).

(4)   Bengali degemination as cluster simplification
(a) ʃu-lam   ʃu-tʃtʃʰi   'sleep 1PAST/ 1PRESENT'
(b) boʃ-lam   boʃ-tʃʰi *boʃ-tʃtʃʰi 'sit 1PAST/ 1PRESENT'

Bengali does not allow coda clusters. Since a geminate consonant belongs to the coda of one syllable and the onset of the following syllable, if the preceding syllable ends in a consonant, the geminate introduces a coda cluster and is degeminated to fit the syllable template of the language.

Thus, both deletions and insertions are frequently found in languages, and almost always in the context of repairing an unacceptable syllable. Preference for syllable types, and hence repairs, is usually restricted to the lexical level. In the postlexical level, there is more variation. The last example of degemination can also be viewed as shortening, and as we will see in § 2.3., lengthening and shortening phenomena are also linked to syllable structure. However, in these cases it is the weight of the syllable which plays a crucial role.

2.2. Syllable quantity and weight

One view of representing syllable weight is by using moras. The moraic theory of representation views moras as phonological positions which come between prosody and segments (rooted in the feature tree). Long and short vowels, and long and short consonants (i.e. geminate and single consonants) are differentiated by their moraic representation. Moraic representations in (5) are based on Hayes (1989).

(5)   Moraic representations

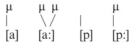

Short vowels have one mora, long vowels have two moras, a single consonant has no moras, and a geminate consonant comes with one mora. A single consonant is not assigned a mora in the lexical representation. It may or may not be assigned a mora depending on whether it is in the coda and whether the language treats closed syllables as heavy. If the coda is counted as heavy, then weight-by-position assigns a mora to the coda consonant. Geminates, on the other hand, are part of the onset of a syllable, but must close the preceding syllable as well, automatically adding weight to this syllable. (A problem arises in languages where geminates do not contribute to weight but long vowels do; see Lahiri & Koreman (1988), Hayes (1989), Kager (1989) for further discussion.) Hypothetical syllabifications are given below.

(6)   Syllable structure assignment
      [oka]   [okta]   [okka]   [o:ka]

```
μ  μ      μ  μ      μ μ μ     μ μ  μ
|  |      |  \      | | |      \/  |
o  k a    o k t a   o  k  a    o   k a

σ    σ    σ    σ    σ    σ     σ    σ
|    |    \    /    |    \     ∧    |
μ    μ    μ   μ     μ μ μ      μ μ  μ
|    |    |   \     | \ |       \/  |
o    k a  o k t a   o  k  a    o    k a

σ   σ     σ    σ    σ    σ     σ    σ
|  /|    /|    |\   / \  |     ∧    ∧
μ / μ    μ μ / μ    μ μ/ μ     μ μ / μ
| / |    | | /\     | \/ |      \/ /|
o  k a   o k t a    o  k  a    o   k a
```

Just as languages often try to preserve preferred syllable structures, we often find processes which attempt to maintain the weight of a syllable. Bimoraic syllables are heavy, irrespective of whether they are closed syllables (the coda consonant adding weight to the syllable), or whether they have a long vowel. However, not all languages necessarily consider closed syllables to be heavy. Languages tend to avoid trimoraic syllables although they do exist. Further consequences of syllable weight will be discussed when we consider stress.

2.3. Compensatory lengthening

Similar to deletions and insertions, shortening and lengthening processes are closely related to the syllable. A frequent process of lengthening is compensatory lengthening, where the loss of a segment is compensated by lengthening an adjacent segment. This can be accomplished by total assimilation or by vowel lengthening. For instance, in Bengali an [r] followed by a coronal consonant is optionally deleted and the consonant becomes a geminate (Hayes & Lahiri 1991). The assimilation can apply within words, across morphemes, as well as across words, the constraint being that the [rC] sequence must belong to a single phonological phrase. Some examples are given in (7).

(7)   Bengali total assimilation
pɔrda   pɔd:a   'curtain'
por-tam   pot:am   'wear-1SG.PAST HABITUAL'
gʰɔr dʒamaɪ gʰɔdʒ:amaɪ 'house son-in-law; son-in-law who lives in the house of his in-laws'

Other common instances of compensatory lengthening involve the loss of a coda consonant which leads to the lengthening of the preceding vowel. We find this in Old English with the loss of a coda nasal. If we compare the words for *five* and *tooth* in Old High German, Old English and their modern descendants, we find the pattern in (8). Since ungrammatical forms are marked elsewhere with an asterisk, the Proto-Germanic reconstructed forms will be indicated with the sign †.

(8)   Compensatory lengthening in Germanic

German	OHG	English	OE	Proto-Germanic
fünf	fimf, fumf	five	fīf	†fimfi
Gans	gans	goose	gōs	†gans

The Proto-Germanic words had a short vowel followed by a nasal consonant. The nasal has been retained in German and the vowels are still short. The loss of the nasal in English, however, has led to long vowels (which were later sometimes diphthongised) – an instance of compensatory lengthening which we can represent in a nonlinear fashion. In (9a), V and N represent any vowel or a nasal. Since long vowels are bimoraic, delinking after the loss of the nasal and reassociation, gives us the desired result. In (9b), the same effect is realised for the [r] deletion and concomitant gemination in Bengali, except that only a single mora is involved. Here the mora, which was originally linked to the [r] in the coda, is then linked to onset consonant (represented by C) in the next syllable, thus creating a geminate.

(9)   Compensatory Lengthening as spreading
      (a) Germanic

```
μ  μ         μ μ
|  |    →    \/
V  N         V̄
```

(b) Bengali

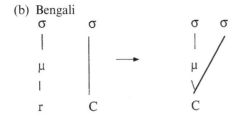

It is worth noting that when the loss of the consonant in such circumstances is closely linked with vowel lengthening, it is invariably confined to a particular syllable position, and a similar loss elsewhere in the phonology of a language will not show any concomitant lengthening. For instance, in Old English the [n] sometimes disappeared between consonants: OE *elboga* beside *elnboga* 'elbow'; OE *sæterdæg* beside *sæterndæg* 'saturday'.

(10) Loss of nasal in Old English not leading to compensatory lengthening
Compensatory lengthening as spreading onto a free mora

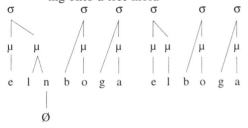

In (10) the deleted [n] is not immediately preceded by a vowel. It is in a branching coda, sharing the mora with another consonant. The loss of the nasal does not free the mora of the coda and therefore there is no spreading and no lengthening. Thus, compensatory lengthening can be viewed as maintaining the weight of a syllable.

2.4. Ambisyllabicity

The notion of ambisyllabicity has been used in two ways: as an environment for syllable-based processes and as a means of providing a coda to add weight to a syllable. The most frequently discussed phenomena where ambisyllabicity plays a role are aspiration and flapping in English (cf. Kahn 1976; Gussenhoven 1986). Both processes are governed by surface syllable structure, and hence are stress-sensitive. The ambisyllabicity results from the attraction of the first consonantal onset of an unstressed syllable to form a coda of the preceding syllable. This consonant then becomes ambisyllabic, since it belongs both to the onset and the coda of two syllables.

The usual onset and coda constraints of the language apply. This procedure leading to ambisyllabicity is labelled as Extended Right Capture in Gussenhoven (1986: 130), the formulation of which is based on two different processes in Kahn (1976).

(11) Ambisyllabicity
Extended Right Capture

σ   σ
|╲ ╲   ╱╱|
X   C C$_0$ V
             |
         [-stress]

Ambisyllabicity accounts for a number of postlexical phonological rules of American English like flapping, aspiration, glottalization etc. Flapping weakens coronal stops [t, d] to a flap [ɾ] when they are ambisyllabic. This accounts for why the coronal stops in *later, shouting, matter* are subject to flapping, while those in *latex, bait, tail* are not. In the latter set of words, the stops are either followed by a stressed syllable (cf. *látèx*), are only in the coda (cf. *bait*), or only in the onset (cf. *tail*), and hence none of them are ambisyllabic. Similarly, aspiration is also subject to ambisyllabicity. Aspiration of voiceless stops in American English occurs when in absolute syllable onset position, and ambisyllabic consonants cannot be aspirated. This is different in British English where absolute onset position is not required for aspiration. Thus, words like *happy*, where the medial consonant is ambisyllabic, may be aspirated in British English, but never in American English. However, British English also requires ambisyllabicity as a structural possibility, since rules like weakening (which 'weaken the oral closure of obstruents' in fast informal speech, Gussenhoven 1986: 125–6) can operate on the output of aspirated consonants. However, weakening only operates on ambisyllabic aspirated consonants, and those that are in absolute onset position are exempt.

As we mentioned above, ambisyllabicity has also been argued to play a role in assigning syllable weight (cf. van der Hulst 1985 and Lahiri & Koreman 1988 for Dutch; Ghini 2001 for Miogliola, a northern Italian dialect). Under these analyses, ambisyllabicity not only allows a consonant to be part of an onset in one syllable and a coda in the other, the coda consonant also projects a mora. The representation would look as follows:

(12) Ambisyllabicity and weight

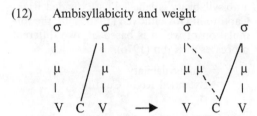

After ambisyllabicity, the phonological representation is identical to that of a geminate. However, in languages in which ambisyllabicity is invoked for syllable weight, there are no contrastive geminates (cf. also Borowsky, Itô & Mester 1984). Whether one could then assume that all such ambisyllabic consonants could be treated as geminates is a much debated topic.

The notion of ambisyllabicity has not found favour with many researchers particularly because of the dual linking of a single consonant to two syllables (Kiparsky 1979; see also Blevins 1995 for a discussion). However, the arguments in Gussenhoven (1986) are very persuasive and since dual linking has to be permitted for geminate consonants that in itself is not a sufficient argument against ambisyllabicity.

So far we have focused on two different aspects of syllable structure: syllable as a context for phonological rules and strategies to maintain preferred syllable structure and syllable weight. We now move on to discuss the role of syllable weight and its interaction with metrical stress.

3. The foot

A fundamental insight in metrical theory is that syllable weight plays a crucial role in stress assignment. As we mentioned above, the weight of a syllable usually depends on whether it has a long bimoraic vowel or whether the coda of a closed syllable contributes a mora to the syllable. Vowel quality is never taken into account where syllable weight is concerned. It would be very odd indeed, if for instance, all front vowels were treated as heavy while other vowels including long vowels were light. However, syllables are not sufficient to account for stress assignment in languages of the world. Recent theories of metrical stress argue that the foot, which is a constituent built on groups of syllables, accounts for stress. In general, syllables are considered to be grouped into metrical feet consisting of strong and weak syllables. The feet differ in terms of whether the head of the foot, i.e. the stressed position, occurs at the left or right edge. A left headed foot is known as a trochee, and a right headed foot is an iamb. We will not however, begin with the assumption that syllable weight and feet are crucial elements in stress assignment. Instead, with examples from two languages, we will trace step-by-step the motivations for assuming (a) syllables are a necessary constituent for assigning stress, (b) syllables are not enough to account for universal stress systems, (c) a fixed inventory of foot types built on syllables can delimit all stress patterns and (d) the weight of syllables play a role in building feet.

3.1. Are syllables necessary for stress?

Chomsky & Halle (1968) accounted for English stress using only a linear sequence of consonants and vowels, ignoring any hierarchical constituent like the syllable. However, referring only to a linear sequence is not enough. Let us consider the facts of the well known Latin stress rule, which has been discussed in metrical terms for a long time. The length of a vowel is indicated with a macron.

(13) Latin stress
    3rd vowel   2nd vowel
    from end   from end
    mínimus   reféctus   incŭdis
    múrmuris   volúptas   relătus
    exístimo   dēléctat   inimĭcus
    adsimíliter   excérpsit   refĕcit

If asked which vowels are stressed without taking recourse to syllables, one would come up with the rule in (14):

(14) Latin stress rule based on vowels
  (i) If the penultimate vowel is long, it is stressed.
  (ii) If the penultimate vowel is followed by two consonants, it is stressed.
  (iii) Else, the antepenultimate vowel is stressed.

Such a rule, however, would cause problems for the following words.

(15) Problem cases
    3rd from left Expected 2nd from left
    ténebras   *tenébras
    vólucres   *volúcres
    mániplis   *maníplis
    látebras   *latébras

If we take the second part of the stress rule which says that if the second to last vowel is followed by two consonants it should be stressed, we have incorrect results. The solution lies in the evidence from syllabification following the sonority hierarchy. The above words are syllabified as [te.ne.bras], [vo.lu.cres], [ma.ni.plis] and [la.te.bras], as against [re.fec.tus], [vo.lup.tas] etc. Thus, the stress rule can be simplified as follows: If the penultimate syllable has a short vowel with no coda then the antepenultimate syllable bears the main stress; otherwise the penultimate syllable is stressed.

This description is very characteristic of stress rules. Syllables with long vowels or with a coda consonant pattern together. And now we come to syllable weight. As we have seen before, this division is descriptively characterised as heavy syllables versus light syllables. The Latin stress rule can then be stated as:

(16) Latin stress rule in terms of syllable weight
  (i) If the penultimate syllable is heavy, it is stressed.
  (ii) Else, the antepenultimate syllable is stressed.

3.2. Are syllables enough for stress?

So far we have seen that a linear string of consonants and vowels is not enough to account for stress. Instead we require the notion of syllables, and particularly syllable weight. But is syllable weight enough to capture stress facts of various languages? That is, is it always the case that stress assignment can be characterised in terms of heavy and light syllables? The answer is no. Let us look at a more complicated case – Creek, a Muskogean language. The data in this paper comes from Haas (1977). Haas describes Creek as having tonal accent, which falls on a 'key syllable' (p. 195). There can be more than one 'key' syllable, each one being 'one step lower than the preceding' one (p. 196). The tones themselves can be level, falling or rising. Assuming that the key syllables are the prominent syllables indicating main and secondary stresses, Creek provides us with a rich source of data. Further data is given in Hayes (1995: 64–65). Consider the following facts:

(17) Creek data (length is indicated with the diacritic [:])
  pocóswa 'axe'
  cofí 'rabbit'
  acolakí 'old timers, elders'
  osáhwa 'crow'
  ahicitá 'one to look after'
  cá:lo 'trout'
  sókca 'sack'
  famí:ca 'canteloupe'

If we assume that all consonant clusters are broken up into onset and coda, and that closed syllables are heavy, Creek stress can be described as follows:

(18) Creek stress – first approximation
  (i) If the penultimate syllable is heavy, it is stressed.
  (ii) Else, the last syllable is stressed.

So far, the Creek data look quite similar to Latin, the only difference being that in Creek if the penult is not heavy the last syllable is stressed. Now let us consider a few more words.

(19) Further data in Creek
  ifóci 'puppy'
  imahicíta 'one to look after for (someone)'
  itiwanayipíta 'to tie each other'
  acahaŋkatíta 'one to count me'

In the above words, the penultimate syllable is light, but nevertheless it is stressed. According to our preceding assumption, the last syllable should have borne stress. Perhaps we can salvage the analysis by the following statement:

(20) Creek stress – second approximation
  (i) If the penultimate syllable is heavy, it is stressed.
  (ii) If the penultimate syllable is light, stress the final or penultimate whichever is even-numbered, counting left to right.

Unfortunately this does not solve the problem. Consider the following words:

(21) More data from Creek
  aktopá 'bridge'
  wa:kocí 'calf'
  hoktakí 'women'
  iŋkosapitá 'one to implore'

Clearly, our previous rules will not suffice. In all the words, the penult is light, but the syllable that is stressed is not even-numbered counting left-to-right. What we need to do is not to start counting from the beginning of the word, but from the rightmost heavy syllable. The stress rule could then be described as follows:

(22) Creek stress – third approximation
  (i) If the penultimate syllable is heavy, it is stressed.
  (ii) If not, examine the maximum string of light syllables at the end of the word.
  (iii) Within this string, stress the rightmost even-numbered syllable counting left-to-right.

We go through two examples following the steps elaborated above.

(23) Deriving Creek stress – third approximation
  iŋkosapitá   acahaŋkatíta
  (i)   –   –
  (ii) iŋ (ko sa pi ta)   acahaŋ (ka ti ta)
  (iii)   *   *
       1 2 3 4   1 2 3
       iŋ (ko sa pi tá)   acahaŋ (ka tí ta)

This description is not particularly illuminating. Clearly we are missing a generalisation. If the penult is not heavy, it is not syllable counting that gives us the right answer, but some constituent which groups syllables together. Such a constituent in poetic meter is known as a foot, and in the next section we discuss the universal inventory of feet that have been suggested for natural language.

3.3. Inventory of feet

Hayes (1995) argues that there are three basic foot types used in linguistic systems universally: a syllabic trochee, a moraic trochee, and an iamb. The syllabic trochee groups any two syllables together regardless of their weight. A moraic trochee and an iamb are weight sensitive. These three foot types are given below. The foot is demarcated between parentheses and the strong and weak branches are indicated by a [x] and a dot [.] respectively.

(24) Trochees and Iambs
  (a) Syllabic trochee (weight insensitive)
      (x .)
       σ σ
  (b) Moraic trochee: left headed (constructed over two light syllables or one heavy syllable)
      (x .)   (x)
       σ σ   σ
       | | /\
       μ μ   μμ
  (c) Iamb: right headed (construed over two light syllables, a light plus a heavy syllable, or one heavy syllable)
      (. x) (. x) (x)
       σ σ   σ σ   σ
       | | | /\   /\
       μ μ   μ μμ   μμ

Although the moraic trochee and the iamb are both weight sensitive (i.e. the weak branch cannot be heavier than the strong branch), under Hayes' analysis these two feet are asymmetric. Under this system, an iamb may have a [L(ight) H(eavy)] sequence, but a trochee is not permitted to have a branching head. The way stress assignment works is as follows. A string of syllables are parsed into feet going from left-to-right or right-to-left. The last foot on the left or the right is assigned main stress: End Rule (left/right). Thus, main stress is always at an edge of a word, edge being defined by foot structure and not by syllables or vowels. To assign stress, we therefore require the following parameters:

(25) Stress assignment
  (a) Foot type
  (b) Direction of parsing
  (c) End Rule

We illustrate this first with the most straightforward foot type, namely the syllabic trochee, which is weight insensitive. The syllabic trochee groups syllables together regardless of their internal structure. The analysis is from Hayes (1995: 62–63).

(26) Syllabic trochee (Pintupi, a Pama-Nyungan language of Australia)
  Foot construction: Left to Right
  Main stress: End Rule Left (indicated with X)
  (X   )   (X   )   (X   )   (X   )
  (x .)(x .)   (x .)(x .)   (x .)(x .)(x .)   (x .)(x .)(x .)
   σ σ σ σ   σ σ σ σ σ   σ σ σ σ σ σ   σ σ σ σ σ σ σ
   máɭawàna   púɭiŋkàlatʲu   tʲámulìmpatʲùŋku   tíɭiriŋulámpatʲu
   'through from behind' 'we (sat) on the hill' 'our relation' 'the fire for our benefit flared up'

Let us now turn back to Creek and investigate which of the foot types would be appropriate to account for the entire set of data. Clearly syllable weight plays a role since the penultimate syllable is stressed only when it is heavy. The End Rule appears to be on the right, since stress falls always towards the right edge of the word. Now we need to determine the direction of parsing and whether the foot type is a moraic trochee or an iamb. The syllabic trochee cannot be considered since it is quantity insensitive. The decision is not a difficult one since in our third approximation we saw that when a sequence of light syllables occur at the end of a word, the rightmost even numbered syllable can get stressed. As a result final light syllables may bear stress and this is not possible for a trochee. Thus, if the foot inventory is indeed sufficient, then the foot type must be an iamb.

The final decision regarding stress assignment must be the direction of parsing. Again in the last approximation, if the penult was not stressed, the grouping of syllables into a larger constituent began after the last heavy syllable. Hence, the parsing must be from left-to-right. Following Hayes (1995), applying these parameters to Creek we obtain the following structures:

not exist for footing and, therefore, not for stress. Thus, there are four parameters to be taken into account: foot type, extrametricality, direction of foot parsing and the end rule. In the two following examples taken from Hayes (1995) we see instantiations of the moraic trochee with and without extrametricality (cf. (28)).

This brings us back to Latin stress. Recall that in Latin, stress fell on the penultimate syllable if it was heavy. Otherwise the antepenultimate syllable bore stress regardless of weight. We can now analyse Latin in the following way (cf. (29)).

The moraic trochee along with the extrametricality does away with the oddity of the syllable based description which required that syllable weight was responsible for attracting stress on to the penultimate syllable but not for the antepenultimate syllable. The antepenult could be stressed regardless of syllable weight; it depended on the lack of weight of the penult. In the foot based analysis, the explanation rests on the fact that the antepenult and the penult together can make up a single foot if both are light.

The inventory given above excludes the possibility of asymmetric moraic trochees which are the mirror images of iambs. How-

(27) Stress assignment in Creek: final version
Syllable weight: Long vowels and closed syllables are heavy
Foot type: Iamb
Foot construction: Left to Right
Main stress: End Rule Right

```
( X)   ( X )        (     X)        (   X  )         ( X  )
(. x)  (. x)        (. x)(. x)      (. x)(. x)       (. x)
μ μ    μ μ μ μ      μ μ μ μ         μ μ μ μ μ        μ μμ μ
co fí  i f ó c i    a co la kí      i mahi cí ta     fa mí: ca

(    X)             (       X)        (   X  )
(x)(. x)            (x)(. x)(. x)     (. x)(x) (. x)
μμ μ μ              μμ μ μ μ μ        μ μ μμ μ μ μ
wa: ko cí           iŋ ko sa pi tá    a ca haŋ katí ta
```

Thus, although syllables may provide an adequate description for stress patterns in some languages, they are not sufficient to account for the complicated systems like Creek. Once we introduce a larger constituent grouping syllables together into feet, the analysis of the stress pattern becomes very simple.

In addition to the three basic foot templates, it is necessary to invoke the notion of extrametricality to understand some other stress patterns. Syllables or segments (usually consonants) at right edges are often extrametrical; that is, they behave as if they do

ever, others like Dresher & Lahiri (1991), Lahiri & Dresher (1999, for Germanic), Jacobs (1989, 2000, for Latin), Kager (1989, for English) have claimed that asymmetric trochees incorporating [H L] sequences are necessary as well. For instance in Latin, using an asymmetric trochee would mean that words like *murmuris* would be parsed into feet as ([mur. mu] ⟨ris⟩). The traditional trochee is, in fact, asymmetric (cf. Hayes 1981). Although we are not in a position here to exhaustively compare these various proposals, while discussing the foot based phonological

(28) Moraic trochees with and without extrametricality
Moraic trochee (with extrametricality)
Cairene Arabic (No classical words are considered)
Syllable weight: Long vowels and closed syllables are heavy
Extrametricality: Final consonant of a word (indicated by ⟨ ⟩)
Direction of Parsing: Left to Right
Main stress: End Rule Right

(X)   (X)   (X)   (X)   (X)   (X)
(x)   (x)   (x)   (x)   (x) (x.)   (x .)(x .)
μμ μ   μ μμ   μ μμ   μ μμ μ   μ μμ μ μ   μ μ μ μ
be:tá⟨k⟩   gató: katáb⟨t⟩ mudárri⟨s⟩   mudarrísi⟨t⟩   katabítu
'your (M.SG.) house cake'   'I wrote'   'teacher'   'teacher (f. construct)' 'she wrote it (M.)'

Moraic trochee (Wargamay: Pama-Nyungan language of Australia)
Syllable weight: Long vowels are heavy
Direction of parsing: Right to Left
Main stress: End Rule Left

(X)   (X   )   (X)   (X   )
(x)   (x .)(x .)   (x .)   (x .) (x .)
μμ μ   μ μ μ μ   μ μ μ   μ μ μ μ μ
mú:ba   gíɟawùlu   gagára   ɟuɾágaymìri
'stone fish'   'freshwater jewfish' 'dilly bag'   'Niagara-Vale-from'

(29) Latin stress revisited
Syllable weight: Long vowels and closed syllables are heavy
Extrametricality: Final syllable
Direction of Parsing: Right to Left
Main stress: End Rule Right

(X   )   (X   )   (X   )   (X   )
 (x)   (x) (x)   (x .)   (x)
μ μμ μμ   μμ μμ μμ   μ μ μμ   μμ μ μμ
re féc ⟨tus⟩   dē léc ⟨tat⟩   vó lu ⟨cres⟩   múr mu ⟨ris⟩

(30) Constraining gemination in OE
Gemination blocked:
(x   .)   (x   .)
([μμ] μ)   [μμμ] μ   ([μ μ] μ)   [μ μμ] μ
H   L   L L L
wī tje > *wītte   æ þe lje > *æ þel le
'punishment DAT. SG.'   'noble DAT. SG.'

Gemination permitted
(x   .)   (x) (x   .)   (x   )   (x   .)
([μμ] μ) μ   ([μμ]) ([μμ] μ)   ([μ μ])   ([μμ] μ)
H L L   H H L   L L   H L
wē ste nje   >   wē sten ne   cy nje   >   cyn ne
'desert DAT. SG.'   'race DAT. SG.'

processes, we will draw on evidence from segmental rules and stress in Germanic to provide support for asymmetric trochees.

3.5. Foot-based phonological processes

Phonological processes can be sensitive to the foot. The foot relevant for Germanic was a resolved moraic trochee, which is essentially an asymmetric trochee, where the head must branch. An example of a foot based process is West Germanic gemination, which is simply a process by which all consonants are doubled when followed by a front glide /j/. It is constrained only when the head becomes trimoraic. The following Old English nouns illustrate gemination, where the head of the foot is circumscribed by square brackets (cf. (30)).

The form *wītte is impossible because the head cannot be trimoraic. Similarly, *æþelle is disallowed because the weak branch of the head is strengthened and again the head becomes trimoraic. Not just strengthening processes, but deletions can also be sensitive to foot structure. For instance, high vowels in Old English were deleted in the weak branch of a foot (Dresher & Lahiri 1991). In the following examples the underlined vowels are deleted (cf. (31)).

The [u] in *lofu* is not deleted because it is within the head. In contrast, in *wordu* and *færeldu*, the [u] is in the weak branch of the foot, and hence is deleted. Note that a trimoraic head in *færeld* is permitted because there was no choice to begin with. However, a process like gemination is prohibited from creating one as we saw in the case of *æþelle. The foot also accounts for stress: the head of the foot in each word bears main stress.

3.6. Minimal word and the foot

The phonological word is the next constituent above the foot. Just like the syllable and the foot, most languages adhere to constraints which try to maintain a 'minimal word'. Most languages have a minimal word requirement which is closely related to a foot. The minimal word must be at least a foot, or two syllables, or bimoraic, or some other prosodic constraint. Our interest here is primarily on the correlation between minimal word requirements and metrical coherence. We will, therefore, briefly illustrate the role of the minimal word in prosodic phonology and morphology.

Vowels are often lengthened to meet a minimal word requirement. In Bengali, for instance, a vowel in a monosyllabic word is always lengthened unless the vowel nucleus has a diphthong (Fitzpatrick-Cole 1994).

(32) Vowel lengthening in Bengali
a. tʃɑ: 'want, ask for 2P.FAMILIAR IMPERATIVE / tea'
b. tʃɑ+i > tʃɑi   'want, ask for +1P. PRESENT'
c. tʃɑ:=i   'tea=ONLY'
d. nɑ:k   'nose'
e. nɑk+i   'nose+ADJECTIVAL SUFFIX / nasal'
f. nɑ:k=i   'nose=ONLY'

The morpheme /tʃa/ can be both a verb root 'to want' or the noun 'tea'. The '+' boundary indicates a suffix while the '=' sign marks a clitic. The different suffixation and cliticised forms show the vowel length alternation. It should be noted that Bengali does not have contrastive vowel length. At first glance the lengthening of the vowel in (32 c, f) seems to be a counterexample to the minimal word requirement. In fact, (32e) shows that a derived word which is disyllabic does not lengthen a vowel similar to the monosyllabic word in (32b). However, the final vowel in (32f) is not a suffix but a clitic, just as in (32c). Clitics are added to a word and hence, the minimal word requirement must be met before the clitic is added. We see a difference in (32b) and (32c) where the former is a suffixed word and the resulting diphthong satisfies the minimal word requirement. In (32c), however, the final vowel is a clitic and again, the initial vowel is lengthened.

(31)   Foot based syncope in OE

(X)	(X)	X)	(X)
(x .)	(x .)	(x .)	(x .)
([μμ] μ) μ	([μμ] μ)	([μ μμ] μ)	([μμ] μ) μ
H L L	H L	L H L	H L L
hēa fu̱ de	wor du̱	fæ rel du̱	clī we nu
hēafde	*word*	*færeld*	*clīwenu*
'head'	'word'	'journey'	'ball of thread, clew'
DAT. SG.	NOM.PL.	NOM.PL.	NOM. PL.
(X)	(X)	(X)	(X)
(x .) (x)	(x .)	(x)	(x)
([μμ] μ) [μμ]	([μ μ] μ)	([μ μ])	([μ μμ])
H L H	L L L	L L	L H
hēa fu̱ des	we ru du̱	lo fu	su num
hēafdes	*werud*	*lofu*	*sunum*
'head'	'troop'	'praise'	'son'
GEN.SG.	NOM.PL.	NOM.PL.	DAT.PL.

These facts are not unusual. Many languages, including Germanic languages like English, Dutch and German, also have minimal word requirements. No content word of these languages can end with a single lax vowel: *[sɪ] or *[bɛ] would be completely impossible words in these languages. They should either have a long vowel as in *sea/see* [si:], or should be closed as in *sit* [sɪt]. The research of McCarthy & Prince (1990) demonstrates that the minimal word plays an important role in the prosodic morphology of languages. In their discussion of this phenomenon in Arabic, they give examples of a small number of nouns (usually related to body parts and kinship terms) which disobey the bimoraic, minimal word requirement (final consonants are extrametrical and hence do not count for weight): [ʔab] 'father', [ʔax] 'brother' etc. However, when these nouns serve as the basis of regular word formation processes, they acquire an extra consonant, thus fulfilling the minimality requirement: [ʔab] 'father', but [ʔabaw-iy] 'paternal'; cf. [maṣr] 'Egypt', [maṣr-iy] 'Egyptian'.

Minimal word requirements are also often reflected in blocking the application of rules that may shorten a word beyond the minimum. For instance, Lardil has a disyllabic word minimum. Apocope applies freely to trisyllabic or longer stems, but it is blocked in disyllables since it would shorten a word beyond the acceptable minimal word requirement (Kenstowicz 1994). In the following examples we see that the final stem vowel is always deleted in the uninflected form, except in the last two words which are disyllabic.

(33) Lardil apocope

uninflected	inflected	gloss
yalul	yalulu-n	'flame'
mayar	mayara-n	'rainbow'
karikar	karikari-n	'butterfish'
mela	mela-n	'sea'
wiṭe	wiṭe-n	'inferior'

Minimality constraints can also add a mora or a syllable when the base has less than the weight required to satisfy the minimum word requirements. Such a process is also evident in Lardil (Kenstowicz 1994).

(34) Addition of a mora in Lardil

uninflected	inflected	gloss
kentapal	kentapal-in	'dugong'
yaraman	yaraman-in	'horse'
yaka	yak-in	'fish'
ṭera	ṭer-in	'thigh'

In the last two examples, the base forms are not disyllabic since the suffixation shows that they are consonant final stems (cf. the examples above). However, to meet the minimal word requirement, a final vowel is added to the base stem or the uninflected form to ensure that it surfaces as disyllabic.

3.7. The foot and typological premises

How do the above analyses fit into the usual typological premises made when referring to stress? We have argued that stress is not a feature on a vowel, but rather is the linguistic manifestation of rhythmic structure. As such, although one could state that a given syllable in a word bears the main stress, this is not the best way to account for stress rules. An alternative and better way is to construe stress placement as the parsing of a word into metrical feet. This does not preclude the possibility that there are languages with fixed main stress either on the initial syllable or on the final syllable. Out of 300 languages, Hyman (1977) noted that 114 languages have initial stress, 97 final stress, 77 penultimate stress and only 12 have stress on the second syllable. Such a statement, however, says nothing about how secondary stress could work. Under a metrical foot analysis, a language with final syllable stress could easily have either a moraic trochee or an iamb, if all final syllables happened to be heavy and parsing was from right to left. Predictions for secondary stress, however, would be different. Consider the following hypothetical example.

(35) Final syllable stress: iamb or trochee?
Parsing Right to Left, Moraic trochee, End Rule Right
(X)
 (x)(x .) (x)   (x)
 σ̆ σ̄ σ̆ σ̆ σ̄ σ̆ σ̄
Parsing Right to Left, Iamb, End Rule Right
(X)
(. x)   (. x)(. x)
σ̆ σ̄ σ̆ σ̆ σ̄ σ̆ σ̄

The final syllable obtains stress in both instances. But parsing into metrical feet predicts that the third syllable from the beginning could bear secondary stress only if the foot is a moraic trochee, and not if it is an iamb. Thus, broad typological statements such as main stress is final, can be misleading. This does not mean that stress cannot be fixed regardless of the type of syllable. Usually this happens if stress, or rather the metrical parameters, are in some way morphologically governed. For instance, with English productive affixation like *béautiful*, stress is insensitive to rhythmic patterns. Stress falls on the antepenultimate syllable because it happens to be the initial syllable of the stem. Another way of looking at it is that in derived adjectives the final syllable is extrametrical. Morphological effects of stress can be also found when certain suffixes always bear stress as in German *-ier*, (e. g. *Juwelíer*), or English *-ee*, (e. g. *devotée*). However, even with morphologically stress, the window within which stress falls is usually constrained. Hence, when typological correlations are drawn with respect to stress, it is worthwhile to be more precise about the rhythmic organisation and the type of foot. We will discuss this in more detail in § 4.

In this section, we have covered a wide range of facts involving metrical structures. We have briefly discussed various phonological processes sensitive to metrical structure, including shortening and lengthening processes, segmental alternations, repair strategies for preferred syllables, etc. The central goal was to show that along with stress assignment, phonological rules do not only operate in local segmental contexts, but that hierarchical structures like syllables and feet also constrain representations and processes.

4. Typology and Metrical Structures

Having established the necessity for metrical constituents like syllables and feet, we are now in a position to address issues of typological implications. In the preceding sections, we outlined different types of syllable structures and feet which languages appear to have. We have not discussed, however, any particular correlations between such structures nor any possible relationship between the existence of different types of metrical structures within a given language. For instance, is it possible that all types of feet co-exist in a single language? Would it be possible to infer the preferred syllable structure of a language if its type of foot is known? Are there any implications to be drawn from preferred metrical structures of language and the types of rules that are permitted? Such questions are rarely if at all addressed within phonology. We will draw attention to three possible typologically interesting issues: (a) the relevance of metrical constituents outside phonology, (b) the coherence of metrical units within a given language, and (c) correlations drawn between metrical constituents and other phonological and morphological patterns.

4.1. Metrical constituents outside phonology

Research in prosodic morphology (cf. McCarthy & Prince 1986, 1993) indicates that metrical categories required in phonology are the same that are necessary for morphological processes like reduplication. Typologically, therefore, the implication is that if a new category is found to be necessary to describe either stress or any other phonological process, it ought to be found relevant for a morphological process as well. The following two examples support the view that both syllables and feet are relevant for morphology.

In Mokilese, the progressive is expressed by a form of reduplication (Harrison & Albert 1976; McCarthy & Prince 1986). Samples of the data are given below.

(36)   Mokilese progressive
    a. pɔ.dok   **pɔd**-pɔ.dok   'plant'
    b. pa   **paa**-pa   'weave'
        di.ar   **dii**-di.ar   'find'
    c. sɔɔ.rɔk   **sɔɔ**-sɔɔ.rɔk   'tear'
        caak   **caa**-caak   'bend'
    d. an.dip   **an.d**-an.dip   'spit'
        o.nop   **on.n**-o.nop   'prepare'

At first glance, it seems as if the progressive is formed by some sort of a prefix which is equivalent to a syllable. However, the nature of the syllable differs for each word type. The reduplication is essentially the prefixation of a bimoraic syllable [$\sigma_{\mu\mu}$]. In (36a) the initial syllable of the stem is monomoraic and hence the following onset is included to form the prefix. In (36b), where the stem is monosyllabic or where the second syllable has no consonantal onset, the vowel is lengthened to satisfy the bimoraic requirement. In (36c) the bimoraic requirement is met by simply taking the initial long vowel. The most interesting case is (36d) where [an] or [on] would surely have met the bimoraic requirement. However, the output form would then have been *[on-onop], which would then be syllabified as *[o.no.nop] and the initial prefix would be monomoraic. Thus, the constraint is that the morphological prefix must be an entire bimoraic syllable, and simultaneously the onset of the next syllable must be maximised. For the latter, if the stem begins with a vowel, either the onset of the second syllable is used even if it has to be doubled.

In the next example we see that a morphological process can be sensitive to a foot. The data is from Ulwa (McCarthy & Prince 1990).

(37)   Ulwa construct state (3 SG. POSSESSED)
    a. kii   (kii)-ka   'stone'
       bas   (bas)-ka   'hair'
       sana   (sana)-ka   'deer'
       sapaa   (sapaa)-ka   'forehead'
       amak   (amak)-ka   'bee'
    b. suulu   (suu)-ka-lu   'dog'
       baskarna   (bas)-ka-karna   'comb'
       siwanak   (siwa)-ka-nak   'root'
       anaalaaka   (anaa)-ka-laaka   'chin'
       karasmak   (karas)-ka-mak   'knee'

The data in (a) is straightforward — a suffix [ka] is added to the stem. However, the data in (b) shows that the [ka] behaves like an infix and the way in which the stem is divided up appears to be different in each case. In the first two examples, the [ka] is added to the first syllable, while in the others it is added after two syllables. If we compare the two sets, we can see that [ka] is added after two syllables only when the first syllable is light and the second is heavy or light — [a.nɑɑ] — but not, when the first syllable is heavy and the second is light as in [suu.lu]. Thus, it is not a syllable which is the relevant constituent but a foot and a typical iamb [$\sigma_\mu \sigma_{\mu\mu}$]. The morphological process is thus the following: add the suffix [ka] to the leftmost iambic foot.

Thus, the metrical constituents including syllables, feet and minimal word that are used for the description of stress and are sensitive to other phonological processes are argued to be the same for morphological processes. The obvious question that now comes to mind is whether within a given language, the same metrical constituent is used both for stress and other phonological processes, and in addition whether morphology and phonology share precisely the same type of constituent as well. We now turn to these issues.

4.2. Metrical coherence

Typically languages adhere to the same foot for stress as well as for other phonological processes. A language following such a principle would be judged as being metrically coherent and arguably such a language would also be easier to learn (cf. Dresher & Lahiri 1991). One could also extend the principle of metrical coherence to morphology as well. As Hayes (1995) points out, usually in any given language, the kind of foot used for stress is the same as that used in morphology. We will address this issue first from a purely phonological perspective and then briefly address the notion of coherence within prosodic phonology and morphology.

4.2.1. Coherence in stress and phonological processes

There is nothing discussed in the earlier sections that suggests that metrical coherence is a must or even preferred. One could imagine that metrical structures are counting devices such that one type of foot is used for stress and another could be used as the context for other phonological rules. For instance, Keyser and O'Neill (1976) suggested that in Old English, stress required an initial quantity insensitive left-headed foot while a quantity sensitive right-headed iamb was necessary to account for the rule of high vowel deletion, where R = rhyme

(38)   Feet in Old English following Keyser and O'Neill
    a. Word stress: left-headed unbounded foot

    b. High vowel deletion: following a right-headed quantity sensitive foot in an open syllable

Under such an analysis, headedness is completely arbitrary. For the purposes of stress, the left head of a foot is the strongest, while for syncope, the right head of the foot is strong. However, such a system would be incredibly difficult for the language learner to acquire. As shown in § 3.5., this analysis is not the only one that could account for the data. Germanic is essentially metrically coherent, and both stress and deletion of high vowels can be accounted for by a single foot type. Other languages have similar properties. One example is Unami, an Eastern Algonquian language described in Hayes (1995: 211−213) based on Goddard (1979). Hayes argues that stress in Unami is accounted for by forming iambs left to right with foot extrametricality and End Rule Right. Moreover, voiceless consonants other than [h] are geminated after a strong vowel which would be the head of a foot.

(39) Unami stress and gemination
```
         ( X)
         (.  x) ⟨(.  x)⟩
         nə mə t əme:        'I follow a trail'
       →
         ( X)
         (.  x) ⟨(.  x)⟩
         nə mə tt əme:
         Compare /mətəme:w/ → [mətə́me:(w)]
         'he follows a trail'
```

In general, phonological rules sensitive to foot structure are usually deletion, weakening or strengthening processes as we have seen in earlier sections. In most instances, they apply to either repair metrical structures or are invoked to build preferred structures. Therefore it is not surprising that the foot required for stress and other phonological processes would be the same. What is more interesting is the notion of metrical coherence outside phonology to which we turn next.

4.2.2. Metrical coherence and morphology

As we mentioned earlier, the set of metrical constituents that are relevant for phonology are the same that are used in prosodic morphology. For instance, often, suffix allomorphy is governed by a metrical unit. In Dutch, the nominalising suffix {-aar} adds only to bisyllabic verbs, while {-er} is added to monosyllabic verbs: *luister* 'to listen' > *luister-aar* 'listener'; *bel* 'to ring' > *bell-er* 'ringer'. Booij (1997) argues that the underlying reason for this allomorphy is to maintain a proper trochee on the surface. The form **luisterer* would not form a proper trochee while *luisteraar* ends up as two acceptable feet.

Our interest here is whether the type of foot necessary for a language's morphological system is the same as that required for stress. That is, can we extend the notion of metrical coherence to morphology as well. It appears that almost always the foot used for stress is the same as that used for prosodic morphology. One example is Manam (Austronesian language, spoken in New Guinea). The description of stress is given in Kenstowicz (1994: 614, 659) and the morphological process of reduplication is described in McCarthy & Prince (1986: 39).

(40) Manam Stress and Reduplication
a. mó.tu   'island'
    ma.nám   'Manam island'
    wa.rí.ge   'rope'
    ma.la.bóŋ   'flying fox'
    ʔi-po.a.sa.gé.na   'we are tired'
b. láʔo   laʔo- láʔo   'go'
    moíta   mo-ita-íta   'knife'
    malabóŋ   mala-bom-bóŋ   'flying fox'

Stress is assigned by a moraic trochee parsed from right to left. The reduplication also clearly refers to the same foot. However, there is nothing inherent about metrical structures that requires the same foot to be used for phonology and morphology. One glaring counterexample in the literature is Axininca Campa. While stress is iambic (Payne 1981; Spring 1990a; McCarthy & Prince 1993), there is disagreement in the literature about the foot type(s) needed for morphology (Spring 1990a, 1990b; McCarthy & Prince 1993). For instance, Spring (1990b) claims that while the foot necessary for genitive allomorphy is the moraic trochee, the foot for verb reduplication is the iamb.

However, other analyses of Axininca Campa suggest that the situation is not as complicated as suggested by Spring. While the distinctive base of both genitive allomorphy and reduplication is characterised by a bimoraic foot, the reduplicant is a different constituent with a strong tendency towards disyllabicity. Metrical coherence may be maintained for Axininca Campa if the bimoraic foot is regarded as 'minimal iamb', while the disyllabic foot is considered to be a 'maximal iamb'. Only a small sample of the crucial data is presented to show the analysis (cf. (41)).

The descriptive generalisation for the genitive allomorphy is that if the stem contains only two moras, the suffix /ni/ is taken, otherwise the suffix is /ti/. This led Spring (1990b) to suggest that the genitive allomorphy was sensitive to a trochee. However, a bimoraic foot could be both a trochee as well as an iamb, the difference being the headedness. Since there is no evidence of headedness in this context, the analysis could just as well be that if the foot is a minimal iamb, the suffix is /ni/. The verb reduplication is more straightforwardly an iamb. If the non-prefixed stem is a single syllable, the reduplication includes the prefix. That the reduplicant

(41) Axininca Campa
   a. Stress (following McCarthy & Prince 1993, Spring 1990a, 1990b): Iamb, Left to Right, Final light syllable extrametrical.
   (ki.mí).ta.⟨ka⟩   'maybe'
   (o.cí).(to.mó).⟨ko⟩   'monkey'
   (i.ráa).(wa.ná).⟨ti⟩   'su caoba'
   b. Genitive allomorphy (data Spring 1990a)
   /sima/   no-sima-ni   'my fish'
   /mii/   no-mii-ni   'my otter'
   /sawoo/   no-sawoo-ti   'my cane'
   /maini/   no-maini-ti   'my bear'
   /cokori/   no-cokori-ti   'my armadillo'
   c. Verb reduplication-prefixed pattern (Payne 1981)
   /kiNtʰa/   noŋ - kintʰa - kintʰa   'tell'
   /kawosi/   noŋ - kawosi - kawosi   'bathe'
   /naa/   no - naa - nonaa   'chew'
   /na/   no - na - nona   'carry'
   /osaNpi/   n - osampi - sampi   'ask'
   /apii/   n - apii - napii   'repeat'

is a canonical iamb is seen in the last example. Normally, the stem initial vowel is not reduplicated as in [n-osampi-sampi]. However, when the stem itself is disyllabic as in /apii/, the reduplication does not ignore the initial vowel. The reduplicated form is [n-apii-napii] and not *[n-apii-pii] showing that there is strong preference to have a canonical iamb if possible (Black 1991; Loewe 1996).

Thus, even in a complex set of interactions as in Axininca Campa, there is no clear evidence that entirely different feet are required for morphology and phonology. Since in most instances, morphology requires either a disyllabic or bimoraic foot with no clear headedness preferences, or just a minimal word (cf. § 3.6.), the stress facts do not clash with morphological processes (cf. McCarthy & Prince 1990 for various examples). It seems, therefore, that metrical coherence can be extended to morphology as well.

5. Universals, implications and correlations

In the typological literature, little has been said concerning the details of metrical constituents and implications thereof. The focus of attention has been either to associate morphological types like agglutination vs. flection with stress-timing or syllable-timing, or with general rhythmic patterns like iambic and trochaic with possible syllable types and types of clusters. For example, Lehmann (1973, 1978) claims that agglutinating languages correlate with simple syllable structure, pitch accent and mora-counting, while flective languages have complex syllable structures, stress accent with reduction of unstressed syllables, and syllable-counting. Plank (1998) provides a detailed account of the various attempts in the literature to draw correlations within phonological constituents as well as between phonological and morphological categories. The results are highly unsatisfactory, and as Plank points out, often contradictory. Our interest here is primarily on metrical constituents and we will discuss briefly some of the proposals put forward in the literature.

Donegan & Stampe (1983) argue that rhythmic properties determine different morphological types and syntactic word order. The central notion is that since accent is the only factor which is pervasive through all levels of language, it is the only meaningful determinant in connecting the different levels of language. For instance, there is a direct relationship between word order and phrasal accent. In a sentence, the operand or head is given information, while the operator or modifier is asserted and hence bears the main accent, regardless of the relative order of the two parts. They make a very strong claim that rising (final) vs. falling (initial) phrase accent is the primary variable and that operand/operator order follows from it. In fact, primary phrase accent determines more than just word order: syllable and word canons, phonological segments, as well as timing are closely related. For instance, initial phrase accent correlates with trochaic word accent, syllable-timing or mora-timing, a preference for (C)V(C) syllables and geminate clusters. Final phrase accent and iambic word accent goes hand in hand with stress-timed languages, with (C)V or (C)(C)V(Glide)(C) syllables and non-geminate clusters. The trochaic pattern goes with agglutinative morphology while the iambic pattern goes with more flective morphology.

Gil's approach to prosodic typology is also based on rhythm (Gil 1986), but it seems to make somewhat opposite predictions. Although Gil agrees with Donegan & Stampe that trochaic rhythm patterns with syllable timed languages and iambic rhythm with stress timed languages, he supports the view that agglutinative languages prefer iambic rhythm, are stress timed, have a high consonant-vowel ratio, and have a simple syllable structure. In contrast, flective languages prefer trochaic rhythm, are syllable-timed, have complex syllable structure, and have a low consonant-vowel ratio. Thus, the correlation between agglutinative/flective morphology with trochaic/iambic rhythm is the opposite. Gil (1987) however, lays less emphasis on the typological prominence of phrasal rhythm, since, he states, most languages tend to have iambic patterns on the phrase and clause level. What he had in mind is perhaps that an intonation phrase is invariably divided up into HEAD+NUCLEUS where the nucleus contains the most important information (cf. Hayes & Lahiri 1991). However, it is not the case that within the nucleus, languages always prefer iambic patterns. Banking on the difference between iambic and trochaic rhythm within phonological phrases, Nespor, Guasti & Christophe (1996) argue that language learners correlate this difference with the branching nature of syntax. Thus, a trochaic rhythm correlates with left-branching structures and an iambic rhythm with right-branching structures. The syntactic branchingness correlates with heaviness. Crucially, the authors make no attempt to link word stress with phrasal stress, the former being an independent variable.

In sum, in the attempts to draw correlations between rhythm (which is of interest to us since it is related to metrical structures) and other phonological, morphological, and syntactic structures, there are two major approaches. First, a correlation is established between phrasal rhythm and syntactic structure (Donegan & Stampe 1983, Nespor, Guasti & Christophe 1996), but Gil (1987) views phrasal rhythm as not being a dependable variable to support typology. The difference between Donegan & Stampe and Nespor et al. is that the former connect phrasal rhythm with word rhythm, while for the latter word stress is an independent variable.

Second, a correlation is made between word rhythm and other phonological constituents like syllable structure, stress/syllable timing, and morphological structure. Here, as we mentioned earlier, Donegan & Stampe, and Gil sometimes make opposite predictions. For instance, Donegan & Stampe associate iambic rhythm with complex syllable structure while Gil has it the other way around. Other authors who have attempted these correlations do not always agree either (see Plank 1998: 216 for details). What then do these typological correlations mean? We will concentrate on the correlations drawn on the basis of word rhythm since this has been the primary focus in this paper.

The authors (Donegan & Stampe, and Gil) are basing their hypotheses and analyses on samples of data from which they have observed certain patterns. But the conclusions do not appear to be based on detailed properties of metrical constituents as we have discussed so far. It is true that if a language prefers an iambic foot, it is almost certain that it would have long vowels since an iamb is by nature asymmetric in quantity. However, there is nothing to prevent a language from preferring an iambic foot where the quantity is determined solely on the basis of closed vs. open syllables. But more important, preferring an iambic word rhythm, does not necessarily mean that the language prefers stress to be at the right edge of a word, which is what the correlations seem to imply. Whether the right or the left edge of a word bears main stress depends on the End Rule and not only on the foot type. Consider once again a hypothetical example.

(42)   Iambs: End Rule Right/Left
       Language A
       Parsing Right to Left, Iamb, End Rule Right
       (X)
       (. x)   (. x)(. x)
       ŏ ō ŏ ŏ ō ŏ ō
       Language B
       Parsing Right to Left, Iamb, End Rule Left
       (X   )
       (. x)   (. x)(. x)
       ŏ ō ŏ ŏ ō ŏ ō

If each parsing represented a language, then for the given sequences of light and heavy syllables, in Language A the main stress would fall on the word final syllable, while in Language B, main stress would fall on the second syllable of the word. Although these are hypothetical examples, they are by no means exceptional. Consider the examples given in (28). Both Cairene Arabic and Wargamay have a moraic trochee, but the direction of parsing as well as the End Rule are different. As a result, although two and three syllable words look very similar for stress assignment, four syllable words are different. We repeat the crucial examples here.

(43) Moraic trochees in Cairene and Wargamay
Cairene Arabic: Parsing Left-to-Right, End Rule Right
(X   )   (X   )
(x)   (x .)(x .)
μμ μ   μ μ μ μ
be:tá⟨k⟩   katabítu
your (M.SG.) house   she wrote it (M.)
Wargamay: Parsing Right to Left, End Rule Left
(X   )   (X   )   (X)
(x)   (x .)(x .)   (x .)
μμ μ   μ μ μ μ   μ μμ
mú:ba   gíɟawùlu   gagára
stone fish   freshwater   dilly bag
               jewfish

Cairene tends to have main stress towards the end of a word (*katabítu*), while Wargamay has stress at the beginning of the word (*gíɟawulu*).

Thus, before we attempt to establish correlations between word rhythm and other phonological constituents, we have to first establish whether we are dealing with iambic/trochaic feet or whether we are referring to merely word edges. Since we are dealing with foot type, direction of parsing, End Rule (plus extrametricality) as parameters for assigning stress, any correlation concerning word rhythm could refer to all of them collectively or any one of them individually.

What types of correlations and implications can we then draw given what we know about metrical patterns? One sort of correlation could be connected with metrical coherence. If languages prefer to stick to a given type of foot for stress, phonological processes as well as morphology, one might think that various types of rules would conspire to achieve a preferred foot. Thus, if the language requires iambs for stress, then vowel lengthening or gemination rules would apply to convert a minimal iamb $[\sigma_\mu \sigma_\mu]$ to a canonical one $[\sigma_\mu \sigma_{\mu\mu}]$. Such iambic lengthening examples are frequently mentioned in Hayes (1995). Similarly, as we saw in § 2., epenthesis or deletion processes are often invoked to obtain preferred syllable structures. One could construct a set of strategies that correlate with preferred metrical structures as in (44).

(44) Correlations of preferred metrical structures and repair strategies

Preferred structures	Strategies
(a) Languages prefer open syllables	coda deletion, vowel epenthesis
(b) Languages prefer closed syllables	apocope or syncope; no coda deletion, vowel epenthesis
(c) Iamb	Iambic lengthening
(d) Moraic trochee	Trochaic shortening
(e) Minimal Word	Vowel lengthening, epenthesis

Unfortunately, a constant problem in phonology is that surface output forms can easily be opaque with respect to the metrical structures of the language. Thus, just as iambic lengthening is frequent, deletion of unstressed syllables are equally frequent, reducing a disyllabic iamb $[\sigma_\mu \sigma_{\mu\mu}]$ to a monosyllabic one $[\sigma_{\mu\mu}]$. This type of opacity has been addressed repeatedly throughout the history of generative phonology.

In recent research, opacity is elegantly captured in terms of constraint interaction within the framework of Optimality Theory (OT, cf. Prince & Smolensky 1993; McCarthy & Prince 1995; for a recent survey, see Kager 1999). In OT, the explanatory burden is shifted from processes to output candidates. The central claim is that universal grammar is made up of a set of constraints, all of which are available to a given language. The grammar generates a potentially infinite set of output candidates for each input, which are then evaluated based on the constraint system of the language. The candidate which best fits the constraint system is the victor. Languages differ in the way the constraints are ranked. For our purposes, since constraints are violable and can easily conflict, one of the most interesting consequences is that an output form need not conform to all the constraints of the language. Let us consider some of the preferences stated in (44) and examine how they can conflict. A language could have the following preferences translated into constraints:

(45)   Possible ranked constraints
   a. Last syllable cannot be stressed.
   b. Foot is not right-headed; i.e. it is iambic.
   c. Main stressed foot aligns with the right edge of a word.

The constraints (a) and (c) are in direct conflict. Constraint (c) says that the head of the foot should coincide with the right edge of the word. Since the foot is an iamb, the last syllable stress seems to be preferred. However, there is a direct conflict with (a) which says right syllables must not be stressed. In (46) we provide two possible candidates given the above ranking.

(46)   Possible candidates
   i. (. x)(. x)(. x)
       σ̆ σ̄ σ̆ σ̄ σ̆ σ̄
   ii. (. x)(. x)
  ☞   σ̆ σ̄ σ̆ σ̄ σ̆ σ̄

Since (43a) is ranked above (43c), the last constraint will lose out and (46 ii) would be the preferred candidate. The output is then opaque to the fact that the head of the foot should preferably line up with the right edge of the word.

What would this mean for the possible typological correlations suggested in (44)? Given that preferences and constraints can be conflicting which predicts that the output may be opaque, we can only state the correlations we have as preferences and not absolute. Obviously, the preferences remain as open questions.

6. Conclusion

In this article, we have established that there are systematic organising principles which construct metrical patterns in natural languages. These organising principles combine various units of prosodic structure like syllables and feet. There is a limited inventory of syllable and foot types for all languages. Stress, which marks relative prominence within metrical constituents, is a result of various independent parameters including the type of foot and the edge of a word and direction of parsing.

Metrical constituents are however, not only relevant for stress but for other phonological and morphological phenomena. We have argued that typologically, languages adhere to metrical coherence within both the phonological and morphological systems of a given language. However, when it comes to drawing correlations between metrical structure and other aspects of phonology and morphology, the typological literature is somewhat uncertain in drawing any conclusions. Part of the reason is that only fixed templatic structures have been taken into account and metrical patterns are not viewed as organising principles of grammatical systems. However, since we do have a well understood set of metrical patterns and are aware of possible processes and constraints, future research will undoubtedly try to lay out meaningful typological implications in this area.

7. References

Black, Andrew. 1991. "The optimal iambic foot and reduplication in Axininca Campa". In: *Phonology at Santa Cruz* 2: 1–18.

Blevins, Juliette. 1995. "The Syllable in Phonological Theory". In: Goldsmith, John (ed.), 206–244.

Booij, Geert. 1979. "Allomorphy and autonomy of morphology". *Folia Linguistica* 31: 25–56.

Borowsky, Toni & Itô, Junko & Mester, Armin. 1984. "The formal representation of ambisyllabicity: evidence from Danish". *North Eastern Linguistic Society* 14: 34–48.

Chomsky, Noam & Halle, Morris. 1968. *The sound pattern of English.* New York: Harper and Row.

Clements, G. Nick & Hume, Elizabeth V. 1995. "The internal organisation of speech sounds". In: Goldsmith, John (ed.), 245–306.

Donegan, Patricia J. & Stampe, David. 1983. "Rhythm and the holistic organisation of language structure". In: Richardson, John F. & Marks, Mitchell & Chuckerman, Amy (eds.), *Papers from the Parasession on the Interplay of Phonology, Morphology and Syntax,* 337–353. Chicago: Chicago Linguistic Society.

Dresher, B. Elan & Lahiri, Aditi. 1991. "The Germanic Foot: Metrical coherence in Old English". *Linguistic Inquiry* 22: 251–286.

Eisenberg, Peter & Ramers, Karl Heinz & Vater, Heinz (eds.). 1992. "Silbenphonologie des Deutschen". *Studien zur deutschen Grammatik* 42. Tübingen: Gunter Narr Verlag.

Fitzpatrick-Cole, Jennifer. 1994. *The prosodic domain hierarchy in reduplication.* PhD dissertation, Stanford University.

Fitzpatrick-Cole, Jennifer. 1996. "Reduplication meets the phonological phrase in Bengali". *The Linguistic Review* 13: 305–356.

Ghini, Mirco. 2001. *Asymmetries in the phonology of Miogliola*. (Studies in Generative Grammar.) Berlin: Mouton de Gruyter.

Giegerich, Hans. 1992. "Onset maximisation in German: the case against resyllabification rules". In: Eisenberg, Peter & Ramers, Karl Heinz & Vater, Heinz (eds.), *Silbenphonologie des Deutschen*, 134–171.

Gil, David. 1986. "A prosodic typology of language". *Folia Linguistica* 20: 165–231.

Gil, David. 1987. "On the scope of grammatic theory". In: Modgil, Sohan & Modgil, Cecilia (eds.), *Noam Chomsky: Consensus and Controversy*, 119–141. Barcombe: Falmer Press.

Goddard, Ives. 1979. *Delaware Verbal Morphology*. New York: Garland publishing.

Goldsmith, John (ed.). 1995. *The Handbook of Phonological Theory*. Oxford: Blackwell.

Greenberg, Joseph H. & Kashube, Dorothea. 1976. "Word prosodic systems: A preliminary report". *Working Papers on Language Universals* 20: 1–18.

Gussenhoven, Carlos. 1986. "English plosive allophones and ambisyllabicity". *Gramma*. 10.2: 119–141.

Haas, Mary. 1977. "Tonal accent in Creek". In: Hyman, Larry (ed.) *Studies in stress and accent. Southern California Occasional papers in Linguistics* 4, 195–208. Los Angeles: University of Southern California, Department of Linguistics.

Halle, Morris & Idsardi, William. 1995. "General properties of stress and metrical structure". In Goldsmith, John (ed.), 403–443.

Harrison, Sheldon P. & Albert, Salich Y. 1976. *Mokilese Reference Grammar*. Honolulu: University of Hawaii Press.

Hayes, Bruce. 1981. *A metrical theory of stress rules*. Cambridge, Mass.: MIT PhD dissertation. Distributed by Indiana University Linguistics Club and published by Garland Press in 1985.

Hayes, Bruce. 1989. "Compensatory lengthening in moraic phonology". *Linguistic Inquiry*, 20: 253–306.

Hayes, Bruce. 1995. *Metrical Stress Theory: Principles and Case Studies*. Chicago: University of Chicago Press.

Hayes, Bruce & Lahiri, Aditi. 1991. "Bengali intonational phonology". *Natural Language and Linguistic Theory* 9: 47–96.

Hulst, van der, Harry. 1984. *Syllable structure and stress in Dutch*. Dordrecht: Foris.

Hulst, van der, Harry. 1985. "Ambisyllabicity in Dutch". In: Bennis, Hans & Beukma, Frits (eds.) *Linguistics in the Netherlands*. Dordrecht: Foris.

Hyman, Larry M. 1997. "On the nature of linguistic stress". In: Hyman, Larry M. (ed.) *Studies in Stress and Accent. Southern California Occasional Papers in Linguistics*. 4: 37–82.

Jacobs, Haike. 1989. *Historical studies in the nonlinear phonology of French*. PhD dissertation, University of Nijmegen.

Jacobs, Haike. 2000. "The revenge of the uneven trochee: Latin main stress, metrical constituency, stress-related phenomena and OT". In Lahiri, Aditi (ed.). 333–352.

Kager, René. 1989. *A metrical theory of stress and destressing in English and Dutch*. Linguistic models 14, Dordrecht: Foris.

Kager, René. 1995. "The metrical theory of word stress". In: Goldsmith, John (ed.), p. 367–402.

Kager, René. 1999. *Optimality Theory*. Cambridge: Cambridge University Press.

Kahn, David. 1976. *Syllable-based generalizations in English phonology*. Cambridge, Mass.: MIT PhD dissertation. Distributed by Indiana University Linguistics Club.

Kenstowicz, Michael. 1994. *Phonology and generative grammar*. Oxford: Blackwell.

Keyser, Samual J. & O'Neill, Wayne. 1976. *Rule generalization and optionality in language change*. Dordrecht: Foris.

Kiparsky, Paul. 1979. "Metrical structure is cyclic". *Linguistic Inquiry* 10: 421–441.

Lahiri, Aditi (ed.). 2000. *Analogy, Levelling, Markedness: Principles of change in phonology and morphology*. Berlin: Mouton de Gruyter.

Lahiri, Aditi. 2000. "Hierarchical restructuring in the creation of verbal morphology in Bengali and Germanic: evidence from phonology". In: Lahiri, Aditi (ed.), 71–123.

Lahiri, Aditi & Dresher, B. Elan. 1999. "Open syllable lengthening in West Germanic". *Language* 75: 678–719.

Lahiri, Aditi & Koreman, Jacques. 1988. "Syllable weight and quantity in Dutch". *West Coast Conference on Formal Linguistics* 7: 217–228.

Lahiri, Aditi & Riad, Tomas & Jacobs, Haike. 1999. "Diachrony". In: van der Hulst, Harry (ed.) *Word Prosodic Systems in the Languages of Europe*, 335–422. Berlin: Mouton de Gruyter.

Lehmann, Winfred. 1973. "A structural principle of language and its implications". *Language* 49: 47–66.

Lehmann, Winfred P. 1978. "Conclusion: Towards an understanding of the profound unity underlying languages". In: Lehmann, Winfred P. (ed.) *Syntactic Typology: Studies in the Phenomenology of Language*, 395–432. Austin: University of Texas Press.

Liberman, Mark. 1975. *The intonational system of English*. Cambridge, Mass.: MIT PhD dissertation. Distributed by Indiana University Linguistics Club.

Loewe, Martha. 1996. *Prosodic structures*. MA thesis, University of Konstanz.

McCarthy, John & Prince, Alan. 1986. "Prosodic Morphology". Manuscript, University of Massachusetts, Amherst and Brandeis University.

McCarthy, John & Prince, Alan. 1990. "Foot and Word in Prosodic Morphology: the Arabic broken plurals". *Natural Language and Linguistic Theory* 8: 209–282.

McCarthy, John J. & Prince, Alan. 1993. "Generalized alignment". *Yearbook of Morphology*, 79–153.

McCarthy, John J. & Prince, Alan. 1995. "Prosodic Morphology". In: Goldsmith, John (ed.), 318–366.

Nespor, Marina & Guasti, Therese & Christophe, Anne. 1996. "Selecting word order: the rhythmic activation principle". In: Kleinhenz, Ursula (ed.) *Interfaces in Phonology. Studia Grammatica* 41, 1–26. Berlin: Akademie-Verlag.

Payne, David. 1981. *The phonology and morphology of Axininca Campa*. Publication of the Summer Institute of Linguistics and the University of Texas at Arlington.

Plank, Frans. 1997. "Linguistic Typology: introducing a new journal". *Linguistic Typology*, 1, 1–3.

Plank, Frans. 1998. "The covariation of phonology with morphology and syntax". *Linguistic Typology*, 2, 195–230.

Prince, Alan & Smolensky, Paul. 1993. "Optimality theory: Constraint interaction in generative grammar". Manuscript, Rutgers University and University of Colorado at Boulder.

Rubach, Jerzy. 1990. "Final devoicing and cyclic syllabification in German". *Linguistic Inquiry* 21: 79–94.

Spencer, Andrew. 1996. *Phonology*. Oxford: Blackwell.

Spring, Cari. 1990a. *Implications of Axininca Campa for Prosodic Morphology and Reduplication*. PhD dissertation, University of Arizona, Tucson.

Spring, Cari. 1990b. "How many Feet per Language?" In: *The Proceedings of the Ninth West Coast Conference on Formal Linguistics*, 493–508.

Vennemann, Theo. 1972. "On the theory of syllabic phonology". *Linguistische Berichte* 18: 1–19.

Aditi Lahiri, University of Konstanz (Germany)

97. Tone systems

1. Defining "tone"
2. Typologizing tone systems by phonological contrasts
3. Typologizing tone systems by function
4. Typologizing tone systems by tone rules
5. Tone and/or accent
6. Tone-marking conventions
7. References

1. Defining "tone"

Within the phonological realm, few typological issues have generated as much discussion (and controversy) as the issue of tone. It is generally assumed that as many as half of the world's languages are "tonal". While most language families in the world have one or more tonal offsprings, including those in North and South America, Europe, and Oceania, languages with fully developed tone systems are highly concentrated in Subsaharan Africa, Southeast Asia, and Mexico. Beyond these generalities, the typological study of tone systems has at times faltered on the very basic question of what constitutes a "tone" and hence a "tone system". Welmers' (1959, 1973) definition is as good as most: "A tone language is a language in which both pitch phonemes and segmental phonemes enter into the composition of at least some morphemes." Thus, tone is clearly indicated in the case of such pairs as Pawaian [Oceanic] sú 'tooth' and sù 'road' and Mende [Sierra Leone] pélé 'house' and bèlè 'trousers' (see § 6. for tone-marking conventions). While Pike (1948) had suggested that a tone language has "contrastive, but relative pitch on each syllable", Welmers improves on this definition by recognizing the existence of toneless morphemes, especially grammatical morphemes which take their tone from the surrounding context. If we reinterpret Welmers in modern terms to mean that the pitch phonemes must be presented in "the underlying representations of at least some morphemes", this will allow for the Mende toneless postpositions -hu 'in' and -ma 'on', which copy their tone from the preceding nominal, e.g. pélé-hú, pélé-má; bèlè-hù, bèlè-mà. It is also possible for lexical morphemes to be underlyingly toneless. Hyman (1981) has analyzed tone in Somali as being largely predictable on the basis of morphological features. Thus, in the case of one declension class, masculine nouns such as *ínan* 'boy, son', *náʕas* 'stupid man' and *náil* 'male lamb' receive a penultimate H tone (the remaining "toneless" vowels being realized with lower pitch), while the corresponding feminine nouns *inán* 'girl, daughter', *naʕás* 'stupid woman' and *naíl* 'female lamb' receive a final H tone. It is thus possible to say that nouns such as /inan/ 'boy' [m.] and /inan/ 'girl' [f.] are both underlyingly toneless lexical morphemes which receive their predictable H tones by morphological rule: penultimate H if masculine, final H if feminine. Somali at the same time vindicates the view of the morpheme as a realizational process or rule (cf. Anderson 1992) and shows that a morpheme, so-defined, need not involve segmental phonemes at all. In fact, as subject, nouns in this declension undergo a subtractive process which produces toneless lexical morphemes on the surface, e.g. *inan wáa dhaʕay* 'a boy fell', *inan-i wáa dhaʕday* 'a girl fell'. These sentences with the verb focus indicator *wáa* show that verbs may also be toneless in Somali.

In Somali, a word can have a H only on its penultimate or final vowel − or it may be toneless. Consequently, I propose that the final definition of tone be as follows: "A language with tone is one in which an indication of pitch enters into the lexical realization of at least some morphemes." The wording in this definition intentionally bypasses a problem which could arise if we required the pitch feature or features to be present lexically. Although I now reject the analysis, Hyman (1981) did not directly assign H tones to nouns such as *ínan* and *inán*, but rather diacritic accents (marked by *): *ǐnan and in*̌an. If H pitch is assigned at the phrase level (i.e. **postlexically**) to each vowel carrying an asterisk, there will be no "lexical tone" per se. However, these asterisks are merely global markers of tone features and nothing else. In cases where such asterisks exclusively constitute "an indication of pitch" (as also in Goldsmith's 1984 treatment of Tonga [Bantu]), an author's notational preference for diacritics should not − and by the above definition does not − affect the classification of a system as tonal vs. non-tonal (cf. Pulleyblank's 1986 strictly tonal analysis of Tonga). Finally, the definition requires a "lexical realization" so as to rule out intonational pitch features (and boundary tones) which one might wish to consider as morphemes. Since these come in at the phrase level, e.g. in English (Pierrehumbert 1980), most pitch phenomena associated with intonation will not in themselves qualify a system as "tonal".

2. Typologizing tone systems by phonological contrasts

Limiting ourselves to languages whose pitch phenomena meet the definition in § 1., we can now turn to typologizing tone systems. The first issue is to determine what the proper tone-bearing unit (TBU) is in each system. In Somali, where there is one tone per TBU, it is clearly the vowel (or **vocalic mora**). Thus, the assignment of a penultimate H to masculine nouns results in a rising tone in *qaálin* 'young male camel' (cf. *qaalín* 'young female camel') vs. a falling tone in *ʕeesáan* 'young he-goat' (cf. *ʕeesaán* 'young she-goat'). However, in other languages with a vowel length opposition the syllable has sometimes been said to be the TBU, e.g. Kikuyu, Hausa. In languages lacking a length or syllable weight distinction, each syllable is one mora, and one can often speak of either as the TBU. Finally, in Chinese and other Asian languages, where lexical morphemes and words tend to be monosyllabic, tones have normally been seen to be the property of syllables (cf. examples in next paragraph).

A common way of typologizing tone systems is by the nature and number of tonal oppositions contained within them. Pike (1948) proposed an early typological distinction between **contour** vs. **register** tone systems. Contour tone systems, typically found in Asia, have a preponderance of modulated or contour tones, with a pitch rise and/or fall occurring within the TBU on which they are realized. Chinese dialects all have this character. Thus, of the four full tones of Standard Mandarin, three have an underlying contour: ma^{35} 'hemp', ma^{214} 'horse' and ma^{51} 'scold' (see § 6. for tone marking). The remaining full tone, illustrated by ma^{55} 'mother', is a level tone, not a contour. Similarly, three of the five **non-stopped** syllables of Lahu [Tibeto-Burman] involve contours, e.g. ca^{45} 'boil', ca^{54} 'eat' and ca^{21} 'paddy' vs. ca^{33} 'seek' and ca^{11} 'feed'. What makes such tonal contours seem so "basic" in Chinese and Southeast Asian languages is that they typically cannot be broken down into independently occurring level tones. Thus, there is no phonemic 11, 22 or 33 tone in Standard

Mandarin, nor is there a 22, 44 or 55 tone in Lahu. (Lahu does have two stopped tones, realized as 4 and 2, e. g. *caʔ⁴* 'string', *caʔ²* 'push', which can be interpreted as shortened, stopped variants of 45 and 21, respectively.)

This situation contrasts with the typical **register** tonal type found throughout Africa, the Americas, Oceania, and elsewhere. In these languages the basic unit is the tone **level**. Depending on the language, there may be two, three or four levels contrasting on the surface:

H, L	H, M, L	H, M, 'M, L
e. g. Suena	e. g. Cemuhi	e. g. Chatino
[New Guinea]	[Oceanic]	[Mexico]
dzá 'Areca nut'	*tíí* 'destroy'	*kú* 'I eat'
dzà 'mushroom'	*tīī* 'harvest'	*kū* 'I grind'
	tìì 'write'	*k˺u* 'sweet potato'
		kṵ̀ 'dove'

In so-called register tone systems, contour tones may be totally absent, or where they occur, they can typically be analyzed as combinations of independently occurring level tones. Thus, when Etsako [Nigeria] /ówà/ 'house' is reduplicated as /ówà òwà/ 'every house', the /a/ is deleted before /o/ and the L and H tones combine to create a LH rising tone in the surface realization [ówǒwà]. Similarly, when /ítúɔ̀/ 'underneath' is realized as [ìtwɔ̂] by gliding of /u/ to [w], its H tone combines with the L of /ɔ/ to derive a HL falling tone. This difference in compositionality has prompted Yip (1989) to refer to the Asian-type complex tone as a true **contour** vs. the African-type as a **tone cluster**. Contours in Yip's sense are like complex segments (e. g. kʷ, ᵐb, aⁱ), while clusters are like segmental sequences (e. g. kw, mb, ai etc.). A different **tonal geometry** is, thus, proposed to account for the general intuition that Asian tonal contours function more as units than do African rising or falling tones. (For further generalizations concerning surface tonal inventories, see Maddieson 1978.)

A recurrent issue in the study of tone is the problem of generalizing beyond specific analyses. For example, although there have been occasional claims of five contrasting levels, e. g. Trique [Mexico] (Longacre 1952, Hollenbach 1988), Ticuna [Brazil] (Anderson 1966), Usila Chinantec [Mexico] (Skinner 1962), Dan [Liberia/Ivory Coast] (Bearth & Zemp 1967), some of these are open to reinterpretation. In Copola Trique, the highest two tones actually rise in pitch, although Hollenbach (1988) prefers to view them as phonological level tones. This raises the question of whether the number of contrastive levels should be established at the underlying or phonetic level — or somewhere in between. Besides Trique there are other cases where a phonetic contour is said to function as a level tone. For example, although Thai is often cited as having H, M and L tone, e. g. *kháá* 'to trade', *khāā* 'be lodged, stuck', *khàà* 'galanga', what is labeled "H tone" actually exhibits a modulation of 453, i. e. high to highest and down to mid. This Thai triplet contrasts with two true contours, e. g. *khǎà* 'to trade' (rising-falling) and *khâá* 'leg' (falling-rising).

Another typological distinction proposed by Welmers and applied to the **register** type systems of Africa and Mexico, is that between **discrete** vs. **terrace-level** tone systems. Discrete systems are those within which the individual tones maintain a relatively fixed pitch range throughout an utterance. In the Haya [Bantu] utterance [bákàbónà kátò] 'they saw Kato', there is little if any perceptible change in the alternating H and L pitches from beginning to end. In a terrace-level system, the realization of the same tones can be quite different depending on where they occur in an utterance. Thus, in the Igbo [Nigeria] utterance *ọ́ nà ázà ụ́lọ̀* 'he is sweeping the house', the alternating H's and L's gradually descend. The result is a **downdrifting** or **automatic downstepping** of tone which can be represented numerically as 1-3-2-4-3-5, where 1 = the highest pitch. As indicated, it is possible for a later H to be at the same (and ultimately lower) level as an earlier L, e. g. the H of *ụ́lọ̀* and the L of *nà*.

The presence vs. absence of automatic downstep in Igbo vs. Haya can be seen as an intonational difference which, in some languages, is restricted to declarative utterances (and hence suspended in interrogatives, e. g. in Twi [Ghana]). The same cannot be said about phonemic or **non-automatic downstep**. In the simplest case the lowering of a H tone is conditioned by a L tone which has been dislodged from its TBU. For example, the vowel [ɔ] in the Twi input /mé ɔ̀bó/ 'my stone' is frequently deleted. While there is a dialectal variant [mê bó], where the L of /ɔ̀/ has been reassigned to the preceding vowel to create a HL falling tone on [mê], the more widespread realization is [mé ˈbó], where ˈ indicates a drop in pitch conditioned by the

L of the deleted [ɔ]. Phonetically, the downstepped ꜜH typically drops the same interval from a preceding H tone as would a M tone, i. e., the sequence H-ꜜH is often phonetically identical to H-M. The differences are systemic: ꜜH still acts like a H tone in that it establishes a ceiling for subsequent H tones, which will be realized on the same level. M tone, on the other hand, does not exert this ceiling effect. Thus, H-ꜜH-H is pronounced [⁻⁻⁻], while H-M-H is pronounced [⁻⁻⁻]. Since ꜜH does not constitute a "new" tonal entity per se, but rather a lowered "old" one, downstepping can be iterative — and, in principle, infinitely recursive. Thus, in the Dschang dialect of Bamileke [Cameroon], /séŋ è séŋ/ 'bird of bird' is realized [séŋ ꜜséŋ] by the same process as in Twi, and /séŋ è séŋ è séŋ è séŋ/ 'bird of bird of bird of bird' is realized [séŋ ꜜséŋ ꜜséŋ ꜜséŋ], with each ꜜH realized on a lower pitch level. In addition to ꜜH, ꜜL is also attested in Dschang, and ꜜM occurs in Ngamambo [Cameroon]. Such downsteps are widespread in Africa and also in Mexico. In Coatzospan Mixtec [Mexico], ꜜH is not synchronically predictable from the elision or assimilation of L tone vowels, but can still be analyzed as an underlyingly unlinked or **floating** L tone which triggers downstep. Thus, H morphemes such as /túʔtú`/ 'paper', which have this L, condition a following downstep, while others which lack the floating L, e. g. /kúʔcí/ 'pig'. Thus compare túʔtú ꜜkúʔsì-ŏ 'we will bury paper' vs. kúʔcí kúʔsì-ŏ 'we will bury a pig'. Downstep is recursive in this language as well: dió-kó ꜜtúʔtú ꜜlúʔkú 'I want crazy paper'.

Whether all tone systems fall neatly into the above categories or not, in many languages the surface or output tones may be quite different from the underlying or input tones. This is true even about the number of levels itself. For example, Hyman (1986) shows that the four different level tones (H, M, ꜜM, L) which occur in Ngamambo are readily derived from an underlying binary opposition of /H/ vs. /L/. As in segmental morphophonemics, complex statements or rules are often required to account for the different realizations of the same morphemes in different contexts. As an illustration, consider the H-Ø-H underlying representation of /ó-mu-tí/ 'tree' in Haya, which consists of the root -tí, the toneless noun class prefix mu-, and the augment prefix ó-. As the following examples show, this word can occur with all eight possible combinations of H and L tones on its three TBU's:

L-H-L : *omúti*   'tree'
L-H-H : *omútí % Káto* 'a tree, Kato'
H-H-L : *okubón. ómúti* 'to see a tree'
H-H-H : *okubón. ómúti % Káto* 'to see a tree, Kato'
L-L-H : *omutí gwange* 'my tree'
H-L-H : *okubón. ómutí gwange* 'to see my tree'
L-L-L : *omuti gwa Káto* 'Kato's tree'
H-L-L : *okubón. ómuti gwa Káto* 'to see Kato's tree'

In these examples, the period (.) marks the elision of the final -a of the verb *okubóna* 'to see'. *Káto* a personal name, used vocatively in the second and fourth examples, where % marks a phrase boundary.

In Chinese languages tonal alternations across words known as **tone sandhi** may condition the replacement of one tonal configuration (level tone or contour) by another. An example of this comes from Xiamen (Chen 1987, 2000), which has five **free** and two **stopped** syllables. Whenever these tones appear non-finally within a syntactically defined **tone group**, they undergo the following indicated alternations (cf. Table 97.1.):

As seen from these examples, the distribution of individual tones may be severely constrained by context. In Xiamen the tonal contour 24 only appears in non-sandhi contexts, which supports the indicated direction of derivation (isolation tone → contextual tone, rather than contextual tone → isolation tone).

Table 97.1

*p'ang*⁴⁴	'fragrant'	→	*p'ang*²² *tsui*⁵³	'fragrant water (perfume)'
*we*²⁴	'shoe'	→	*we*²² *tua*²¹	'shoe laces'
*pih*²²	'ailment'	→	*pih*²¹ *lang*²⁴	'sick person'
*tsu'*²¹	'house'	→	*ts'u*⁵³ *ting*⁵³	'roof top'
*hai*⁵³	'ocean'	→	*hai*⁴⁴ *kih*²⁴	'ocean front'
*lip*⁴	'entry'	→	*lip*²¹ *k'ao*⁵³	'entry point; import'
*bat*³²	'know'	→	*bat*⁴ *li*²²	'know characters (literate)'

Table 97.2

a. monosyllabic	:	H	L		
b. bisyllabic	:	H-n	n-H		
		L-n	n-L		
c. trisyllabic	:	H-n-n	n-H-n	n-n-H	
		L-n-n	n-L-n	n-n-L	
d. quadrisyllabique	:	H-n-n-n	n-H-n-n	n-n-H-n	n-n-n-H
		L-n-n-n	n-L-n-n	n-n-L-n	n-n-n-L

Table 97.3

'to drop'	'to ask'	
ku-lagaz-a	*ku-lombéz-a*	(without derivational suffixes)
ku-lagaz-il-a	*ku-lombez-íl-a*	'... for (someone)'
ku-lagaz-an-a	*ku-lombez-án-a*	'... each other'
ku-lagaz-il-an-a	*ku-lombez-il-án-a*	'... for each other'

Such distributional constraints may come into play at all levels of analysis.

Whether the TBU is the mora or the syllable, and whether the system has downstep or not, there can be significant phonological and morphological constraints on the distribution of tones, either underlyingly or on the surface. In many languages tonal oppositions are restricted to occurring on a stressed syllable. This is the case in Fasu [New Guinea] (May & Loweke 1964), where H and L contrast on the stressed syllable of a word, nonstressed syllables carrying a predictable neutral pitch. This thus produces the tonal distribution given in Table 97.2.

Other examples of the dependency of tone on stress come from Copala Trique [Mexico] (Hollenbach 1988), where tone initially links to the stressed final syllable, or in Isthmus Zapotec (Mock 1988), where tone is initially associated to the stressed initial syllable.

The tendency for tones to gravitate to metrically strong positions has been dubbed the **Tone to Accent Attraction Condition** by Goldsmith (1987). Many cases can be cited from Eastern Bantu languages which frequently impose a penultimate stress over the word or phrase. As an example, the infinitive forms given in Table 97.3 show two possible tone patterns on verbs in Chizigula [Bantu].

All of the morphemes in forms for 'to drop', including the root *-lagaz-* are underlyingly toneless, realized with L pitch on the surface. In the case of 'to ask', Kenstowicz (1989) sets up the root *-lombez-* with an underlying H tone which migrates to the metrically strong penultimate position.

Among other phonological conditions on tonal distribution is the frequent prohibition against a H tone appearing on a vowel that is adjacent to pause. Returning to Haya, the final H of /ó-mu-tí/ 'tree' spreads onto the penultimate vowel at the end of an assertive phrase (%), e.g. *okubón. ómútí % káto* 'to see a tree, Kato'. It is then lowered before pause, e.g. *okubón. ómúti* 'to see a tree'. As seen in the isolation form o̱múti, Haya also lowers the H of a post-pausal vowel. While many languages lower H to L when pause-adjacent, others lower H to M, e.g. Kukuya [Bantu] (before pause) and Kom [Cameroon] (after pause). Another environment where H tone may be dispreferred is domain-internally. In Kukuya, for instance, CVCVCV stems with a HL or LH **melody** are predictably mapped as H-L-L and L-L-H, respectively, rather than H-H-L or L-H-H, as if the internal syllable constituted a **prosodic trough** that disprefers H tone.

A final phonological condition on tone of considerable importance is the interaction between tone and non-tonal (typically laryngeal) features. In Kanakuru [Nigeria], the tone of verbs is partially predictable from the initial consonant (Newman 1972): If the verb begins with a voiceless or glottalized consonant (e.g. implosive), it will have L-H tone, e.g. *tùpé* 'send', *ɓùlí* 'write'. On the other hand, if a verb begins with a voiced obstruent, it will have H-L tone, e.g. *dápè* 'collect', gɔ́mì 'fill'. Verbs which begin with a sonorant consonant or vowel can have either tone pattern: màànέ 'return (sth.)' vs. múúlè 'smooth (sth.)', àɗέ 'eat' vs. átè 'dip out'. In Nupe [Nigeria] the H of a L-H sequence will become a rising tone if the intermediate consonant is voiced, but not if it is voiceless: /èbá/ → [èbǎ] 'is sour', /èwá/ → [èwǎ] 'wants'; but: /èpá/ → [èpá] 'is peeling'. On the other hand, Yoruba effects this same alternation without regard to the nature of the intervening consonant. As an option, then, the intrinsic pitch depressing effect of voiced obstruents may be phonologized onto a following tone. Ultimately, a voiced obstruent may forbid the occurrence of a phonetic H on the next vowel, as in Ikalanga [Bantu]. A voiceless obstruent, on the other hand, may have a pitch-elevating effect on the following vowel, while sonorants, including vowels, are neutral, i. e. they exert no intrinsic effect on pitch. Other laryngeal articulations and phonation types may also come into play or even be part of the definition of a tone, e. g. the low creaky tone of Vietnamese. The historical introduction of tone into a language, or **tonogenesis** (Matisoff 1973), may in fact be traced to earlier laryngeal articulations on consonants in Asia and elsewhere. The glottal stop plays an important role in this regard in Mixtecan languages. In Acatlán Mixtec [Mexico], the loss of an historical glottal stop is reflected synchronically by the **upstepping** of a following tone. Such cases of **upstep** are quite rare, but apparently can have the same recursive effect as in the case of downstep. Thus, the utterance nūkíni↑té↑sí↑ʔí↑dá 'if he will shoot the animal day after tomorrow' is realized on six pitch levels.

3. Typologizing tone systems by function

In addition to these phonological conditions on tone, there may be grammatical ones. First, tones may be distributed by grammatical category. In Mpi, nouns and verbs belong to three non-intersecting tone classes: sí 'four', sī 'a color', sì 'blood' vs. sǐ 'to be putrid', sí 'to roll', sî 'to die'. In the Fe'fe' dialect of Bamileke [Cameroon], H tone is found only on grammatical morphemes (e. g. demonstrative lá) or as a derived output in specific grammatical constructions, e. g. mōh 'fire' + mūū 'child' → móh mūū 'fire of child'. In addition, tone sequences can be restricted also by grammatical category. Thus in Acatlán Mixtec, where most lexical morphemes are bisyllabic, underlying M-H is limited to nouns while underlying H-M is limited to verbs (cf. ᵐbēlú 'hat' vs. ⁿzíʔī 'entering').

In different languages tone is put to quite different functions. The basic dichotomy is between lexical and grammatical tone. From the examples cited it is clear that tone frequently distinguishes lexical morphemes. Grammatical morphemes also may differ only in tone, e. g. Aghem [Cameroon] à 'with' vs. â 'to/for'. Tone may be involved in the inflectional morphology of the nominal or verbal paradigms of a language. Besides marking gender in Somali, tone figures in the expression of number in Noni [Cameroon] (e. g. bwě 'dog', pl. bwé) and case in Maasai [Eastern Sudanic], e. g. ɔ̀kítèŋ 'ox [nom.]' vs. ɔ̀kítéŋ 'ox [abs.]'. It also marks tense in Bukusu [Bantu], e. g. xwaalímile 'we have just cultivated' vs. xwaalímile 'we cultivated' (earlier today). Tone may also be used in the derivational morphology, e. g. in nominalizations: Lendu [Congo/Uganda] ɓó 'give' vs. ɓò 'gift', dhù 'insult [v.]' vs. dhú 'insult [n.]'. In Tibetan the following verbs become causative by raising the initial part of a tonal contour: $\textit{ɲɛ}^{14}$ 'sleep' → $\textit{ɲɛ}^{44}$ 'make sleep'; $\textit{phap}^{13}$ 'descend' → $\textit{pap}^{53}$ 'make descend'; $\textit{sum}^{15}$ 'be firm' → $\textit{tsum}^{54}$ 'make firm'. While the balance between lexical vs. grammatical use of tone varies across languages, most tone systems probably involve some of each. Thus, even in Chinese, where there are few grammatical affixes, for example, a high-pitched suffix in Cantonese which adds a H suffixal floating tone to a preceding non-high tone as an expression of endearment or familiarity, e. g. a^{33} $\textit{ts'an}^{31}$ + ^{5} → a^{33} $\textit{ts'an}^{35}$ 'ol' Chen'.

The realization of tone can be affected by the syntax. While there are construction-specific tonal effects, the realization of specific tones is commonly conditioned by their position within prosodic domains: the prosodic word, the prosodic phrase, the intonational phrase, and the utterance. Examples we have already seen include the lowering of H tone before pause in Haya and the sandhi effects on the seven tones of Xiamen. The tone sandhi in Xiamen can be seen as the reduction of all but the final full tone in a tone group, which in turn is defined by the syntax. The reverse situation is found in Shanghai, where all but the first tone is reduced in a tone group, e. g. in compounds. Thus note the loss of lexical tones on all but the first morpheme in the forms of Table 97.4., provided by Eric Zee (personal communication, 1987):

Table 97.4.

ɕɪŋ				→	ɕɪŋ	'new'
HL					/\	
					H L	
ɕɪŋ	vəŋ			→	ɕɪŋ vəŋ	'news'
HL	LH				| |	
					H L	
ɕɪŋ	vəŋ	tɕia		→	ɕɪŋ vəŋ tɕia	'new reporting circle'
HL	LH	MH			| \/	
					H L	
ɕɪŋ	ɕɪŋ	vəŋ	tɕi tsɛ	→	ɕɪŋ ɕɪŋ vəŋ tɕi tsɛ	'new news reporter'
HL	HL	LH	MH MH		| \\//	
					H L	

As seen, only the HL contour of the first morpheme remains and is mapped onto the entire compound.

In other cases it may be the head of a construction that undergoes tone reduction. Thus, in Haya, a noun stem loses its H tone when followed by a H tone possessor, e. g. *omukóno* 'arm', *omukono gwa Káto* 'Kato's arm'. In the same language many verb forms lose their H tones when followed by a complement, e. g. *abóna* 'he sees', *abona Káto* 'he sees Kato'. In other cases, instead of tone reduction per se, there will be a tonal interaction between a head word and its complement. One such case is H tone plateauing whereby L's are raised between H's, e. g. Luganda [àlàbà] 'he sees' + [kàtàmbâ] (a name) → [àlábá kátámbâ] 'he sees Katamba'. In some languages tonal interaction between a verb and its complement may depend on focus. Thus compare the following two sentences from Cibemba [Bantu]:

nga mwaatóba úmutóndó, twáákuláatápíla múnsupa
'if you break the pot, we will have to use a calabash to draw water'

nga mwaatóba úmutóndó, bálééisaafúlwá
'if you break the pot, they will get angry'

In the first example, focus is on the pot, the verb is out of focus, and the if-clause constitutes a single tone group. In the second example, focus is on the whole action represented by the proposition, rather than on any subconstituent within it. As a result, the verb is part of the focus and there is a prosodic break before the object, which in this case allows the last H (on [tó]) to spread onto the final mora [ba].

As seen, the tones of a language can be influenced by phrasing, which in turn may be determined by the syntax and focus system. The realization of tone can also be affected by boundary tones which enter at the phrase level. The toneless word *omulimi̱* 'farmer' in Kinande [Bantu] is realized as a sequence of L tones in phrase-internal position. However, it also has the following realizations:

[òmùlímí̱]   [òmùlímì̱]   [òmùlímí̱]
H%   H%L//   H%H//
→   →   →

In these examples H% represents a phrase-final boundary H tone, while L// and H// are intonational boundary tones, marking declarative and interrogative (and list) intonations, respectively. As seen, these tones link right-to-left: Since all daughters of a sentence S are marked off as phonological phrases, the first form (L-L-L-H) will occur when 'farmer' appears as subject of the sentence. The second form (L-L-H-L) is how 'farmer' appears in isolation, or at the end of an intonational phrase marked by declarative intonation. The third form (L-L-H-H) appears intonational phrase-finally with either interrogative or list intonation. While H%, L// and H// do not meet the technical definition for (lexical) tone which was offered in § 1., they potentially interact with lexical tones (cf. Pierrehumbert & Beckman's 1989 treatment of Tokyo Japanese).

4. Typologizing tone systems by tone rules

A number of authors have sought to characterize tone systems by the types of rules contained within them. Hyman & Schuh (1974) and Schuh (1978) attempt to catalogue the different kind of rules that tones may undergo. African tone systems are well-known for their assimilatory rules of raising, lowering, and spreading. Such rules are much more marginal in Asian languages. This observation prompts Chen (1992) to propose a basic typological split: Asian languages tend to respect Chen's principle of "territorial integrity", by which is meant that a tone of one TBU does not spread onto the TBU of another tone. That is, the tones of one morpheme do not combine with the tones of another. That is, we rarely find developments whereby an underlying sequence /55 + 11/ is realized as [55 + 51] by spreading of the 5 tone from the first to second TBU. Instead, the normal situation is one of tone replacement (e.g. of one tonal configuration by another, as we saw in Xiamen), or of tone reduction, as in the neutral tone of Standard Mandarin. A major exception is seen in the Wu dialects of Chinese. As illustrated above from Shanghai, the tones of an initial TBU may spread over a prescribed domain, e.g. in compounds. However, as Chen points out, a prerequisite to such spreading of tone is that the original tones are reduced (deleted). The order of derivation is thus for the tones to be deleted from all but the first element in a tone group, whose tones are subsequently redistributed.

Turning to the assimilatory rules of other tone systems, it is convenient to distinguish between vertical and horizontal assimilations. In a vertical assimilation, a tone is raised or lowered in the environment of a higher or lower tone. The sequence L-H is particularly vulnerable to vertical assimilation. In Kom [Cameroon], both *mó* 'lake' and *bzɨ* 'goat' are pronounced with H tone in isolation. However, in the phrase *mó ò bzɨ* 'lake of goat', the H of 'goat' is lowered to M after a L. In neighboring Mbui, however, L-H is instead modified by raising the L to M: /nì-bɨ́ɨ/ → [nī-bɨ́ɨ] 'breast'. In a horizontal assimilation, a tone spreads onto a neighboring TBU. Spreading of the first tone of /L-H/ and /H-L/ to the right frequently results in LH and HL contour tones, e.g. Yoruba /iwé/ → [iwě] 'paper', Aboh Igbo /únò/ → [únô] 'house'. In other cases the tone of the targeted TBU is lost, e.g. Aghem [Cameroon] /kɨ́-fú/ 'rat' + /kɨ̀-mɔ̀ʔ/ 'one' → [kɨ́fú kɨ́-mɔ̀ʔ] 'one rat'. In some cases there is evidence of a two step assimilation + contour simplification: A LH or HL contour is produced by L- and H- spreading, respectively whose endpoint is subsequently **absorbed** into a following like tone, i.e. L-H-H → L-LH-H → L-L-H and H-L-L → H-HL-L → H-H-L.

Hyman & Schuh (1974) note two important tendencies in horizontal tonal assimilations. First, left-to-right tone spreading is more prevalent than right-to-left. The latter, when occurring, is often restricted, sometimes motivated by an attraction to a metrically strong position (e.g. the spreading of phrase-final H to phrase-penultimate position in Haya). Second, tone-spreading first affects maximally different tone levels rather than tones which are closer in pitch. Thus, Yoruba /L-H/ and /H-L/ are realized [L-LH] and [H-HL], respectively, while the sequences L-M, M-L, M-H and H-M do not undergo tone spreading.

In some cases it is difficult to determine whether a process should be analyzed as vertical or horizontal assimilation − and, if the latter, whether the spreading is from left-to-right or right-to-left. This problem sometimes arises in languages that have tone plateauing: the raising of L (or unmarked) TBU's to H when these occur between H's. In Kihunde [Bantu] H-L-H is realized as H-H-H, where only a single L TBU can be affected, while H plateauing can occur across any number of non-H TBU's in Luganda: /né mutunda-bitabo waa katambá/ → [né mútúndá-bítábó wáá kátámbâ], 'with Katamba's book-seller' (H is realized as a HL falling tone before pause). While Asian tones are claimed to exhibit fewer assimilatory processes than African tone systems, this "minimizing of ups and downs" also occurs in Chinese. As seen in the following example, Standard Mandarin 35 optionally becomes 55 after a 5-final tone (when it is itself followed by another full tone): $tuŋ^{55}$ nan^{35} $fəŋ^{55}$ ~ $tuŋ^{55}$ nan^{55} $fəŋ^{55}$ 'southeast wind'. A corresponding change of a 53 tone to 55 occurs in Cantonese when followed by a 5-initial tone. These Cantonese and Mandarin alternations can be described by the same process: 3 → 5 / 5 __ 5. But is this a vertical or horizontal assimilation? If the latter, is it the 5 of the first TBU that spreads, or the 5 of the second?

As with plateauing, tone-spreading can be **bounded** or **unbounded**. That is, a tone can spread once (e.g. to the right), or it can keep going until it reaches the edgemost TBU of the domain. In addition, the same language can have more than one spreading rule, such that a H tone can spread once by one rule and then again by another. One language, Ikalanga, has been claimed to have three H tone spreading rules which apply cumulatively, each one operating within a different domain: the prosodic stem, the phonological phrase, the utterance.

In some languages, rather than observing the multiple representation of a tone by means of tone spreading, the underlying tone is realized once, but on a different TBU. The same bounded vs. unbounded opposition applies. The following examples show the realization of the H of the verb root -lúm- 'bite' as its infinitive is pronounced in context in two Bantu languages:

Kinande /eri-lúm-a/ → erí-luma 'to bite'
Bukusu /xúu-lúm-a/ → xúu-lumá 'to bite'

As seen, the H of -lúm- is anticipated onto the infinitive prefix eri- in Kinande, but shifts to the -a suffix in Bukusu. As with the directionality of spreading, shifting to the right is much more frequent than shifting to the left. Cases where a single H is unambiguously anticipated over an unbounded string of toneless vowels are rare, perhaps the best examples being suffixal H tones that are attracted to the second mora of a verb stem, e.g. Luganda /gulirira + H/ → [gùlírìrà] 'bribe'. On the other hand, the rightward long-distance shifting of H is common, as noted already in Chizigula, e.g. /ku-lómbez-il-an-a/ → ku-lombez-il-án-a 'to ask for each other'. Similarly, in Chichewa, a root H shifts to the final mora. Thus, /khúlulukir-a/ 'pardon!' is realized khululukir-á in context. It is likely that anticipation and shifting rules begin as spreading rules, such that Chizigula ku-lombez-il-án-a would once have been pronounced [kù-lómbéz-íl-án-à].

Though somewhat less frequent than assimilation, tones may undergo dissimilatory processes. While the sequence L-H frequently undergoes vertical assimilation to L-M or M-H, as indicated above, the opposite sequence H-L is often subject to vertical **dissimilation**. In Engenni [Nigeria], a H TBU is raised when followed by L. Thus compare the following utterances:

mì mọ́ní wọ̣ 'I saw you'
ị̀ꜛkpílàmá nụ́ 'as for snail'
mì mọ́ ꜛwọ́bhẹ̀ẹ̀ 'I did see you'
ị̀ꜛkpílàꜛmá nà 'the snail'

Similarly, in Bariba [Benin/Togo], H is raised to a top tone (ꜛH) and M is raised to H before L:

ná tású dūūrā 'I planted yams'
gònā 'guinea fowl'
ná táꜛsú dùùrè 'I plant yams'
gòná yèní 'that guinea fowl'

One might identify such cases of tone raising with upstep, although only one additional level ("top") is acquired by this process. This dissimilatory effect applying to a higher tone followed by a lower one, although not always noted, is probably more frequent than generally acknowledged. In fact, although rarely if ever transcribed, tone raising may also affect a whole sequence of H tones in anticipation of a downstepped H tone, e.g. in Luganda: àbásíbá Kígùndú 'they who tie up Kigundu' vs. tèꜛbásíbá ꜛKígùndú 'they do not tie up Kigundu'. In these examples there is a step up of 1 pitch level in the initial sequence [àbá] vs. a step up of 2 pitch levels in [tèꜛbá]. By raising H tones in this way, more tonal space is created for the downsteps that may occur later.

Other dissimilatory processes are more sporadic and open to interpretation. Leben (1971) claims that in Hausa a word-final L-L sequence dissimilates to L-H if the final L is on a long vowel, e.g. /káràntàa/ → [káràntáá] 'reading'. Another example is the change of a sequence of 214 + 214 tones to 35 + 214 in Standard Mandarin, e.g. /lɑu^{214} li^{214}/ → [lɑu^{35} li^{214}] 'old Li'. Noting that the 4 of the 214 tone is frequently absent, Cheng (1973) analyzes this tone as /L/ and proposes the dissimilatory rule: L → LH / __ L (where LH = the 35 tone). Since 214 is realized as 21 before the three other tones of Mandarin (i.e. before 55, 35 and 51), the situation is reminiscent of what has been called **polar** tone in African languages. In this latter case an affix takes the opposite tone of the immediately adjacent tone of the base. An example is the verbal noun prefix in Igbo, e.g. à-gá 'going' vs. á-zà 'sweeping'.

Finally, it is possible to typologize tone systems not only by the phonological rules that affect underlying tones, but also by morphological tone assignment rules. For example, Odden (1988, 1995) surveys morphologically predictable tone in a range of Bantu languages which, depending on tense, aspect, etc., may assign a H tone to the first, second, third or even fourth mora of a verb stem (or some combination of these). In at least one language, Kirundi [Bantu], a morphological H may be assigned to every other vowel within the relevant domain. Thus, the word *ku-há-bi-mú-ku-sáb-ir-a* 'to ask him for them for you there' arguably has only one underlying H tone repeated as an alternating pattern.

Comparing this section to preceding discussion, we can summarize as follows: Some tone systems have natural assimilatory and dissimilatory tone rules that affect tones in context, while others have more arbitrary morphotonemics. Still others have relatively inert tones, i.e. tones which are not subject to tone sandhi at all. In general, Asian languages, which have a preponderance of contour tones, tend not to have such assimilatory rules, but we have seen exceptions in both Cantonese and Standard Mandarin.

5. Tone and/or accent

With the above parameters of tone systems established, we can now consider the most pressing typological issue: whether all languages that have lexical tone in the sense of the above definition are in fact "tone languages". Past typologies have divided prosodic systems either into two or three types. An old – and clearly inadequate – view is that prosodic systems fall into two types: those which have stress vs. those which have tone. We now know that stress and tone are not mutually exclusive, a point that was most forcefully argued by Kenneth Pike and his colleagues, particularly those working in Mexico. In fact, languages from all areas of the globe have been analyzed with both stress and tone (cf. the sketch of Fasu in § 2.). Another view is that languages fall into three types: tone, stress, and **pitch-accent**. The last category has included the Scandinavian languages (with their Accent 1 and Accent 2), Serbo-Croatian, Mohawk, Fasu and others which have both well-defined stress systems as well as lexical pitch phenomena. The term **pitch-accent** has however also been applied to languages such as Somali and Tokyo Japanese. These languages differ from Swedish, Fasu etc. in lacking a clearly defined stress system that exists independently of tone. On the other hand, they differ from other two-tone systems in that the distribution of H and L tones is highly constrained. In Tokyo Japanese, words will either have a HL melody or will be all H in pitch. Thus, rather than having eight contrasting tone patterns of H's and L's on trisyllabic words in Tokyo Japanese (2 × 2 × 2), only the following four lexical tone patterns are distinguished:

inoti 'life'   kokŏro 'heart'
ínòtì   kókórò
[ĭnòtʃi]   [kòkórò]
atamǎ 'head'   miyako 'capital city'
átámá   míyákó
[àtámá]   [mìyákó]

(The phonetic transcriptions in brackets show the effects of phrase-level initial-lowering.) As McCawley (1968), Haraguchi (1977) and others have shown, the lexical pitch contour of Tokyo words can be accounted for by the placement of a single mark per word, e.g. a diacritic accent (*). In this analysis, asterisked and all preceding vowels carry H tone, while any subsequent vowels are realized as L. In the case of *atamǎ* 'head', whose last vowel is asterisked, the drop from H to L will only be realized if an enclitic, e.g. nominative = *ga*, is added: *atamǎ = ga* [àtámá = ŋà]. In the case of *miyako* 'capital city', which lacks an asterisk, = *ga* will be realized without a drop, i.e. [mìyákó = ŋá]. Since there can be at most one drop from H to L per domain, just as other languages have at most one primary stress per domain, it has been tempting to view Japanese tone as an accentual phenomenon. However, unlike stress, which may have multiple effects on a phonological system, the proposed diacritic accent serves only a tonal function. It is thus possible to follow Archangeli & Pulleyblank (1984), Poser (1984), Pierrehumbert & Beckman (1989) and others and analyze Tokyo Japanese in strictly tonal terms, e.g. with a prelinked H taking the place of the asterisk. Because of the paucity of tonal features in underlying representations, Tokyo Japanese might therefore be viewed as a **restricted tone system** (Voorhoeve 1973, Schadeberg 1973). However, we know that a continuum exists between the full marking of tone on every underlying TBU vs. the potential lack of underlying tone marking in Somali. The distinction between full vs. restricted tone systems may therefore not be a principled one.

As mentioned, tone is often contrasted with stress in typologizing prosodic systems. If stress is defined as the presence of metrical structure at the lexical (e.g. word) level, four logical tone-stress types ought to be attested:

Type 1: [+tone, −stress] e.g. Yoruba, Igbo
Type 2: [−tone, +stress] e.g. English, Russian
Type 3: [−tone, −stress] e.g. Korean, Berber, Gafat [Ethiopia]

Type 4: [+tone, +stress] e.g. Fasu, Swedish, Palantla Chinantec [Mexico]

Type 1 is unambiguously referred to as a "tone language" while type 2 is a "stress language". Type 3 lacks both lexical tone and stress, instead assigning prosody at the phrase level. As seen, type 4 groups together languages which have both tone and stress. Although these are commonly referred to as "pitch-accent" or "tonal accent" systems, note that Somali and Tokyo Japanese – to which these terms have also been applied – are not included. (They are instead tone systems whose tones are severely restricted in terms of distribution.) Although clumped together as "pitch-accent languages", it is easy to see that this label is not a coherent one. Rather, "pitch-accent" merely refers to the residue that obtains once the easily definable languages have been assigned to types 1, 2 and 3.

What I believe is needed is a parametric approach to prosodic typology with two "prototype" systems: (i) a type 1 tone system exclusively with lexical pitch features vs. a type 2 stress system exclusively with lexical metrical structure. The prototypical properties are enumerated below for each type. In doing this typology, I follow McCawley's (1968, 1970) basic insight: Tone is like segmental features; stress is unlike segmental features. The idea is that languages may choose from either the prototypical tonal or prototypical stress properties – and they may mix properties, in which case the resulting prosodic system will be a hybrid that does not fall neatly into a "type". It is this "mixing" of properties that allows some stress systems to have a tonal component and causes some tone systems to seem "accentual".

I divide up these properties into eight categories:

(1) Prototypical distribution
(a) Tone: **free**.
Multiple identical (or non-identical) tones may occur within the same word, and toneless words are also possible. Tones may be subject to various distributional constraints, e.g. no word-final H, no LH rising tones, no two H tones in sequence, etc. However, these restrictions are "non-essential" to the definition of a tone system.
(b) Stress: **culminative**
There can be only one primary stress per word. Lexically, stressless words are excluded, although a word's stress may undergo reduction in a phrasal context. Clash resolution may be invoked to avoid contiguous or closely spaced stresses.

(2) Prototypical lexical domain
(a) Tone: **morpheme.**
Like other phonological features, tones are properties of morphemes. A morpheme may carry one or another tonal feature or may be toneless.
(b) Stress: **word**.
Although placement and other properties may be partially determined by morphological composition and morpheme identities (e.g. root vs. affix), stress is a property of words. While there may be stressless grammatical morphemes, including stress-less clitics (which escape the lexicon), lexical morphemes prototypically undergo lexical stress assignment.

(3) Prototypical function
(a) Tone: **distinctive.**
Tones consist of distinctive features which enter into a **paradigmatic** relationship with each other. In a prototypical tone system, one asks what the distinctive tone is of each TBU. That is, one **identifies** each tone. Thus, a H tone contrasts with a L tone in exactly the same fashion as a high vowel contrasts with a low vowel: F_o and F_1 are scalar, but each tone or vowel height is a discrete unit in terms of phonological function.
(b) Stress: **demarcative**.
Stress results from imposing metrical structure at the edge of a constituent. It is thus primordially **syntagmatic**: In a prototypical stress system, one asks for each domain where the stress or stresses are. That is, one **locates** each stress. In this sense stress is different from any other phonological property. While many languages have **free** or distinctive stress, the prototypical function of stress is **demarcation**, i.e. the marking the edges of words and other domains.

(4) Prototypical realization
(a) Tone: F_o.
Tone is realized prototypically through pitch (F_o). Other features entering into the composition of a tone (e.g. phonation types, duration) are not prototypical. The tone-bearing unit is prototypically the syllabic segment, e.g. vowel or mora. Assigning tone by syllable is a secondary option.
(b) Stress: **complex**.
Early studies showing that pitch, duration and/or intensity correlated with primary stress overemphasized the effects of intonation,

which is often assigned with respect to stress placement. Unlike tone, stress has no inherent phonetic correlates. It is instead defined as an abstract metrical structure whose realization may involve the intonational features of pitch, duration and/or intensity — or may be known simply by its effect on the segmental phonology. The stress-bearing unit is the syllable. Any metrical structure built up out of units smaller than the syllable, e. g. the mora, should not be viewed as stress.

(5) Prototypical effect on phonology
(a) Tone: **self-contained**.
Tones affect tones. Tones are not expected to affect consonants or vowels or cause any of the mutations affiliated with stress (see next paragraph). Where a tone appears to have such an effect, more is involved than pitch features.
(b) Stress: **non-contained**.
The presence vs. absence of stress can affect virtually any aspect of the segmental or tonal phonology. Consonants are strengthened (e. g. aspirated, affricated, geminated) under stress and weakened (e. g. deaspirated, voiced, spirantized) under stresslessness. Stressed vowels are lengthened and/or diphthongized, while unstressed vowels become peripheral [i, u, a] or are centralized, e. g. to schwa. Tones may be attracted to stressed positions, and level tones can be converted to contours under stress.

(6) Prototypical effect of phonology on it
(a) Tone: **affected by consonant types**.
Tones are affected by consonant types, e. g. voiced obstruents are tone-depressors, while voiceless obstruents are tone-elevators. Sonorant consonants have no intrinsic effect on tones and, like vowels, are free to accept any tone, if syllabic. Voice quality, glottal stop and /h/ have all played an important diachronic role in the genesis and evolution of tone. Tones rarely interact with vowel quality, though they can be sensitive to moraic structure.
(b) Stress: **affected by syllable weight**.
Stress is affected by syllable weight and is hence often restricted to long vowel or closed syllables. Stress may thus be quantity-sensitive, but is prototypically not affected by the featural make-up of individual segments, e. g. whether a consonant is voiced. Stress may pass over syllables which have a reduced vowel not because of its quality, but because of its lack of quantity. Diachronically stress does not originate from the intrinsic properties of segments. Rather, stress appears to result from the generalization of intonational effects at domain edges, via boundary narrowing, or from the phonologization of the root-affix contrast.

(7) Prototypical interaction with grammar
(a) Tone: **compositionial**.
The tones of complex words and phrases are prototypically determined in a compositional manner, where each tone inputs the rule system. The appearance of tonal morphemes which cause alternations may be conditioned by the grammar, just as segmental affixes and clitics often are. There is no necessary direct conditioning of tonal outputs by the grammar. Where this does occur, e. g. when tone is affected by phrase structure or by focus structure, this is a secondary or non-essential property. Similarly, languages with contrastive tone often lack discrete intonational (e. g. boundary) tones, although intonational factors may influence the phonetic realization of pitch and pitch intervals.
(b) Stress: **integrated**.
Stress is highly integrated into the grammatical system of languages. Sentence accent is often determined by phrase structure and focus and serves as input to the assignment of intonational features and melodies.

(8) Prototypical rule types
(a) Tone: **similar to segmental rules**.
Tones are affected by the same kind of assimilatory and dissimilatory rules to which segmental features are submitted. Prototypically these rules apply locally, i. e. between adjacent TBU's. Like certain other **prosodies** (e. g. nasalization, vowel harmony), they may become generalized to apply iteratively or at a distance. A process such as Meeussen's Rule, whereby a H is lost when immediately following another H, can be viewed as dissimilation, rather than a metrically-based clash resolution.
(b) Stress: **different from segmental rules**.
Stress does not show assimilatory properties, because it is not a feature. Stress rules frequently refer to the initial building of metrical structure followed by its modification (e. g. retraction to avoid clash) or potential destructuring. Stress is, thus, necessarily **hierarchical**, with weaker stresses subordinated to stronger ones.

The above eight properties are designed to give a framework within which a tone and/or stress system can be evaluated for its distance from two end points: the prototypical tone system and the prototypical stress system. There are doubtless other ways this could be done and other generalizations to be uncovered. The basic idea underlying this typology is that as tone becomes less **paradigmatic** and more **syntagmatic**, it takes on more of an accentual character. The most paradigmatic tone systems are those in which words tend to be monosyllabic, e. g. Chinese, Kru [Liberia/Ivory Coast] etc. A highly paradigmatic tone system exhibits multiple tone levels which often interact with consonant types. At the other end, tone in highly agglutinative languages such as in the Bantu and Athabaskan families is much more syntagmatic. These languages rarely show more than two pitch levels and often have one active and one default tone (e. g. active H in Chizigula, active L in Dogrib). While languages with two tones (H and L) show the full range of morphological types (isolating, agglutinative, inflectional), what appears to be missing is a highly agglutinative language with H, M and L tones which combine in a paradigmatic and compositional way to define most or all of the logical possibilities. In other words, a highly developed paradigmatic system of tonal oppositions appears not to be very compatible with a highly developed syntagmatic system of agglutinative morphology.

6. Tone-marking conventions

In this chapter tones are generally marked as follows: (´) H(igh), (¯) M(id), (') 'M (lower mid), (`) L(ow), (ˇ) LH rising, (ˆ) HL falling, (ꜜ) downstep. Vowels which lack an accent are pronounced L, e. g. in Somali, Haya etc., where L is the underspecified or **default** tone. In the case of Chinese and Southeast Asian languages, I have maintained the tradition of referring to tones by integers, where 5 = the highest pitch and 1 = lowest pitch. The indication of a H tone as 55 rather than 5 is a convention by which at least two tones are indicated on non-stopped syllables (i. e. those which are not closed by an oral stop), which have greater duration than stopped syllables.

7. References

Anderson, Lambert. 1966. "The structure and distribution of Ticuna independent clauses". *Linguistics* 20: 5–30.

Anderson, Stephen R. 1992. *Amorphous morphology*. Cambridge: Cambridge University Press.

Bearth, Thomas & Zemp, Hugo. 1967. "The phonology of Dan (Santa)". *Journal of African Languages* 6: 9–29.

Chen, Matthew. 1987. "The syntax of Xiamen tone sandhi". *Phonology [Yearbook]* 4: 109–150.

Chen, Matthew. 1992. "Tone rule typology". In: Buszard-Welcher, Laura et al (eds.). *Proceedings of the 18th Annual Meeting of the Berkeley Linguistics Society*, Special Session on *The Typology of Tone Languages*, 54–66.

Chen, Matthew. 2000. *Tone sandhi*. Cambridge: Cambridge University Press.

Cheng, Chinchuan. 1973. *A synchronic phonology of Mandarin Chinese*. The Hague: Mouton.

Goldsmith, John. 1984. "Tone and accent in Tonga". In: Clements, George N. & Goldsmith, John (eds.). *Autosegmental studies in Bantu tone*. Dordrecht: Foris, 19–52.

Goldsmith, John. 1987. "Tone and accent and getting the two together". *Proceedings of the 13th Annual Meeting of the Berkeley Linguistics Society*, 88–104.

Haraguchi, Shosuke. 1977. *The tone pattern of Japanese: an autosegmental theory of tonology*. Tokyo: Kaitakusha.

Hollenbach, Barbara E. 1988. "The asymmetrical distribution of tone in Copala Trique". In: van der Hulst, Harry & Smith, Norval (eds.). *Autosegmental studies on pitch accent*. Dordrecht: Foris, 167–182.

Hyman, Larry M. 1981. "Tonal accent in Somali". *Studies in African Linguistics* 12: 169–203.

Hyman, Larry M. 1986. "The representation of multiple tone heights". In: Logers, Koen, van der Hulst, Harry & Mous, Maarten (eds.). *The phonological representation of suprasegmentals: Studies on African languages offered to John M. Stewart on his 60th birthday*. Dordrecht: Foris Publications, 109–152.

Hyman, Larry M. & Russell G. Schuh. 1974. "Universals of tone rules: evidence from West Africa". *Linguistic Inquiry* 5: 81–115.

Kenstowicz, Michael. 1989. "Accent and tone in Kizigua – a Bantu language". In: Bertinetto, Pier Marco & Loporcaro, M. (eds.). *Certamen Phonologicum* I.

Leben, William. R. 1971. "The morphophonemics of tone in Hausa". In: Kim, Chin-Wu & Stahlke, Herbert (eds.). *Papers in African Linguistics*. Edmonton: Linguistic Research, Inc., 201–218.

Longacre, Robert E. 1952. "Five phonemic pitch levels in Trique". *Acta Linguistica* 7: 62–82.

Maddieson, Ian. 1978. "Universals of tone". In: Greenberg, Joseph H. (ed.). *Universals of human language*. Stanford: Stanford University Press, vol. 2, 335–366.

Matisoff, James A. 1973. "Tonogenesis in Southeast Asia". In: Hyman, Larry M. (ed.), *Consonant types and tone* (Southern California Occasional Papers in Linguistics, 3). Los Angeles: University of Southern California, 71–96.

May, Jean & Loeweke, Eunice. 1964. "The phonological hierarchy in Fasu". *Anthropological Linguistics* 7.5: 89–97.

McCawley, James D. 1968. *The phonological component of a grammar of Japanese*. The Hague: Mouton.

McCawley, James D. 1970. "Some tonal systems that come close to being pitchaccent systems but don't quite make it". *Proceedings of the Sixth Regional Meeting of the Chicago Linguistics Society*, 526–532.

Mock, Carol C. 1988. "Pitch accent and stress in Isthmus Zapotec". In: van der Hulst, Harry & Smith, Norval (eds.). *Autosegmental studies on pitch accent*. Dordrecht: Foris, 197–223.

Newman, Paul. 1972. "Syllable weight as a phonological variable". *Studies in African Linguistics* 3: 301–323.

Odden, David. 1988. "Predictable tone systems in Bantu". In: van der Hulst, Harry & Smith, Norval (eds.). *Autosegmental studies on pitch accent*. Dordrecht: Foris, 225–251.

Odden, David. 1995. "Tone: African languages". In: Goldsmith, John (ed.). *The Handbook of Phonological Theory*. Oxford: Basil Blackwell, 444–475.

Pierrehumbert, Janet B. 1987. *The phonetics and phonology of English intonation*. Bloomington: Indiana University Linguistics Club (Ph.D. Dissertation, M.I.T., 1980).

Pierrehumbert, Janet B. & Beckman, Mary E. 1989. *Japanese tone structure*. Cambridge, Mass.: M.I.T. Press.

Pike, Kenneth L. 1948. *Tone languages*. Ann Arbor: University of Michigan Press.

Poser, William J. 1984. *The phonetics and phonology of tone and intonation in Japanese*. Ph.D. Dissertation, M.I.T.

Pulleyblank, Douglas. 1986. *Tone in lexical phonology*. Dordrecht: Kluwer.

Schadeberg, Thilo C. 1973. "Kinga, a restricted tone system". *Studies in African Linguistics* 4: 23–47.

Schuh, Russell G. 1978. "Tone rules". In Fromkin, Victoria A. (ed.). *Tone: a linguistic survey*. New York: Academic Press, 221–256.

Skinner, Leo E. 1962. "Usila Chinantec syllable structure". *International Journal of American Linguistics* 28: 251–255.

Voorhoeve, Jan. 1973. "Safwa as a restricted tone language". *Studies in African Linguistics* 4: 1–22.

Welmers, William E. 1959. "Tonemics, morphotonemics, and tonal morphemes". *General Linguistics* 4: 1–9.

Welmers, William E. 1973. *African language structures*. Berkeley: University of California Press.

Yip, Moira. 1989. "Contour tones". *Phonology* 6: 149–174.

Larry M. Hyman, University of California, Berkeley (USA)

98. Intonation

1. Introduction
2. Intonational universals
3. Intonational typology
4. Intonational phonetics
5. References

1. Introduction

Intonation occupies a somewhat unusual place in any discussion of language universals and language typology. In dealing with most aspects of language one takes for granted that languages differ: what typology is about — and in a sense what linguistics is about — is identifying the patterns of similarities amid the differences. But this basic assumption does not necessarily hold for intonation. A great deal of influential research — for example, the work of Bolinger (e. g., 1978, 1989), Lieberman (1967), and Fujisaki (e. g. 1983) — is based on what will be referred to here as the *universalist* approach to intonation. In this view, intonation is essentially peripheral to language. It reflects a pre-linguistic communicative code, and/or it depends on physical properties of the speech production mechanism. The important features of intonation are actually the same in all languages; any observable differences are merely conventionalized variations on the universal themes, and therefore any typological generalizations we may find will be different in kind from those that can be drawn about phonology or syntax. In recent years the universalist view has lost some ground to what we might call the *phonological* approach, based on the work of Bruce (1977), Pierrehumbert (1980), Beckman (1986) and others. As we shall see in § 2.3., this approach treats intonation as part of phonology, and as such is compatible with the idea that normal typological generalizations about intonation may be possible. Nevertheless, the universalist view still thrives, and one important task in writing about intonational universals and intonational typology is to do justice to both points of view.

Section 2 of this article presents the undisputed cross-language similarities of intonation first (§ 2.1.), together with a universalist interpretation (§ 2.2.) and a critical evaluation of that interpretation (§ 2.3.). Section 3 then summarizes three aspects of intonation — melody (§ 3.1.), sentence-stress (§ 3.2.), and phrasing (§ 3.3.) — that differ across languages in a way that reflects possible typological dimensions. Finally, § 4. briefly discusses several dimensions of what we might call the phonetic typology of intonation.

2. Intonational universals

2.1. Substantive universals

The most basic use of intonation is to divide the stream of speech into chunks, which we will refer to here as intonational phrases or IPs. (The term IP is used in a pretheoretical way, to refer to intonationally defined subunits of utterances, and should not necessarily be identified with e.g. the intonation phrase of Nespor & Vogel 1986 or Pierrehumbert & Beckman 1988; see § 3.2.3., for further discussion). The existence of IPs — and hence IP boundaries — provides the basis for many of the cross-linguistic generalizations emphasized by universalists. These generalizations focus on overall pitch trends across IPs and on pitch movements at the ends of IPs. The most important observations are the following: (1) pitch tends to decline from the beginning of an IP to the end, a tendency known as declination (Pike 1945, Cohen & 't Hart 1967, Cooper & Sorensen 1981, Ladd 1984); (2) the beginning of an IP may be marked by a local sharp rise in pitch or "reset" (Brown, Currie & Kenworthy 1980, 't Hart, Collier & Cohen 1990); (3) in IPs that are utterance-final and/or in statements, there may be a local drop in pitch at the end of the IP in addition to any overall declination spanning the IP as a whole (Lieberman 1967, Liberman & Pierrehumbert 1984); (4) in IPs that are in questions and/or not utterance-final, declination may be moderated, suspended or even reversed, i.e. the overall trend may be less steeply declining, level, or even slightly rising (Thorsen [Grønnum] 1980, Lindau 1986); (5) in addition to exhibiting reduced declination, non-final and interrogative IPs may also have a local rise in pitch at the end, or at least have no local drop (Lieberman 1967). The validity of these observations, as general tendencies, is not in doubt.

The other basic use of intonation is to signal local prominence or emphasis. In a great many languages, particular syllables or words can be picked out from the stream of speech by some combination of increased loudness and/or duration, greater force and/or precision of articulation, and pitch movement and/or widened pitch range. In many languages these features are put to use in the unquestionably linguistic phenomenon of "stress" or "accent", but even in languages which do not seem to have stress or accent, and in languages where pitch is lexically specified ("tone languages" and "pitch accent languages") it is still possible to identify intonational cues to local prominence or emphasis. For example, in both Chinese (Gårding 1987) and Japanese (Pierrehumbert & Beckman 1988), pitch is lexically specified, but local emphasis can be signalled by a local widening of the overall pitch range.

2.2. Universalist interpretations

Two types of explanation have been offered for the substantive universals just sketched. The more common of the two, which we might call the biomechanical view, emphasizes the universal physical characteristics of the speech production mechanism. The mechanisms of speech obviously require speakers to stop talking every so often to breathe, which results naturally in the division of speech into IPs (indeed, Lieberman (1967) and others refer to IPs as "breath groups"). At the same time, the cognitive mechanisms of speech seem to operate in terms of meaningful constituents of some sort, and in all languages, so far as is known, there is a tendency for IP boundaries to correspond with the boundaries between such constituents. Universalists emphasize the naturalness of the correspondence between breath pauses and constituent boundaries (but see further § 3.3.). The physical mechanisms of speech also require the expenditure of breath, which may lower subglottal pressure, which in turn may manifest itself as lower fundamental frequency and hence declination across the IP.

The release of subglottal pressure at the end of phonation naturally creates a sharp drop in pitch at the end of the IP. The combination of natural tendencies to declination and final pitch drop leads to a universal association between low pitch and finality or completeness. Given that association, an IP that ends without a pitch drop will sound incomplete; this incompleteness may then signal either that the speaker has not finished talking (high pitch for continuation), or that the speaker's utterance needs to be completed by an utterance of the addressee's (high pitch for interrogation). As for local prominence, local rises in pitch can be explained in terms of momentary increases in subglottal pressure, force of articulation, etc., which will perturb the overall trends across the IP but will not otherwise affect them. Explanations along these general lines have a long history (e.g. Lieberman 1967, Vaissière 1983).

Besides the biomechanical view, intonational universals have also been explained with reference to universal sound symbolism. This view is strongly identified with Bolinger's work (e.g. 1978, 1989) and has been developed by e.g. Cruttenden (1981). Rather than emphasizing the mechanisms of speech production, this view posits the existence of a universal, prelinguistic "meaning" of high and low pitch, part of a universal code for signalling states of the organism. High pitch signals interest, tension, incompleteness, etc., while low pitch signals resolution, completeness, and rest. This view is not necessarily incompatible with the biomechanical view, but at the very least it emphasizes different aspects of the problem. For example, in the sound symbolic view, the high pitch that begins an IP bears some semiotic relation to the high pitch that signals local emphasis, even though they may be produced by different mechanisms. Mention should also be made of the difficulty of describing sound symbolic meanings, which makes it difficult to evaluate competing hypotheses. For example, Ohala (1982) has also proposed that there is a universal pitch code − universal to all mammals, in fact − based on the metaphor of high pitch for smallness and submissiveness and low pitch for bigness and dominance. It is not clear whether Ohala's proposal is compatible with Bolinger's.

The universalist view, and in particular the biomechanical version of it, often goes hand in hand with what Ladd (1983, 1996) has called the *overlay* model of intonation. In the overlay view, contours result from the interaction of two components, which (following Fujisaki) we will refer to as the *phrase component* and the *accent component*. The details differ from one description to another, but in general the idea is that the phrase component gives an overall characterization of the trend of pitch across an IP − gradually declining, level, etc. − while the accent component (which can be extended to model lexical tone in languages like Chinese) generates local pitch movements that are superimposed on the phrase-level trend. The two broad types of intonational universals (IP-related and prominence-related) thus correspond to two distinct aspects of speech production. However, the overlay model is logically distinct from the universalist view, and some proponents of overlay models emphasize their language-specific application (e.g. Grønnum 1995, Möbius, Pätzold & Hess, 1993).

2.3. A phonological interpretation

To some extent, the question of whether intonation is basically universal (with minor variations) or basically language-specific (with many broad cross-language similarities) is not an empirical question but a matter of emphasis. However, one important argument against the universalist approach is that it is effectively unfalsifiable. A concrete example will make this clear. Under many circumstances, yes/no questions in many languages of Eastern Europe (e.g. Greek, Hungarian) end with a sharply rising-falling pitch movement spanning the last two or three syllables. This contour sounds to speakers of many Western European languages (e.g. English, Italian) like an emphatic *declarative* contour. That is, there is no simple cross-linguistic interpretability of pitch contours, which is what the strongest version of the universalist theory would lead us to expect. The universalist generalizations are broad enough to accommodate this kind of cross-linguistic fact: the Eastern European question contour can be treated as a combination of rising or high pitch for question and a sentence-final fall that signals the end of the utterance, while the Western European emphatic declarative contour can be treated as an example of high pitch for emphasis and sentence-final fall for finality. But the very ability to accommodate this kind of cross-linguistic ambiguity severely limits the predictive power of the theory.

As noted in the introduction (§ 1.), a good deal of recent work on intonation has replaced the universalist view — and the overlay model — with an explicitly phonological approach that Ladd (1996) refers to as the "autosegmental/metrical" theory. In this theory, a pitch contour in any language is treated as a sequence of tones, some of which are related to local prominences (or in the case of "tone languages", to individual lexical items), and others of which are related to IP boundaries. The inventory of possible tones, and the question of whether tones are lexically or intonationally specified, is part of the phonology of a language; the details of the association between tones and segmentals are governed by prosodic structures that are in part language-specific.

A central feature of the autosegmental/metrical approach is that the phonological elements of which pitch contours consist are *local* "events", not global shapes or slopes. Overall trends across IPs (e.g. gradual lowering of pitch) are mostly modelled as the result of repeated local effects (e.g. repeated downstepping of accents in succession). There is some instrumental evidence for this sequential view of overall trends (e.g. Liberman & Pierrehumbert 1984), and there is more general evidence for the view that IP edges may be locally marked by tones. Even in traditional works that assume the overlay view, it has been noted that in some tone languages (such as Chinese [Chang 1958] or Thai [Abramson 1962]) sentence-level intonational meanings are conveyed by modifications of the *last* lexical tone in a phrase or utterance. This is easily modelled as the local effect of an additional "boundary tone" associated with the final syllable.

3. Intonational typology

We now turn to the aspects of cross-linguistic intonational variation that appear to be of typological interest. There are three such aspects, which we refer to here as *melodic*, *accentual*, and *prosodic*.

3.1. Melodic typology

3.1.1. Lexical vs. intonational

As is well known, pitch features in "tone languages" are specified lexically. Such lexically assigned pitch features are not a part of intonation, and are not treated here (→ Art. 97). However, the interaction of lexical and intonational features appears to be of typological interest. As we saw in § 2.3., Chinese and Thai appear to have lexical tones on most syllables and, in addition, intonational boundary tones at the ends of IPs. However, as noted by Ladd (1996: 149) there are some tone languages (e.g. Yoruba) that seem to have only lexical tones, and no boundary tones at all. Further combinations of lexical and intonational tones may be found in so-called "pitch accent" languages: in Tokyo Japanese, the accent tones are lexical but the boundary tones intonational (Pierrehumbert & Beckman 1988); in several European pitch accent languages it appears that some accent tones are lexical while other accent tones, like boundary tones, are intonational (Gussenhoven & Bruce 1999). The foregoing list is merely suggestive of the typological possibilities, which so far remain almost entirely unexplored.

3.1.2. Intonational melodic features

Concentrating only on languages without lexically specified pitch ("intonation languages"), we may observe melodic differences of several types. First, languages may use "the same" tune in different ways. For example, the English rising nuclear tune is widely used in both questions and statements in North America, Australia, and New Zealand, but is largely restricted to echo or confirmation questions in most British varieties (Cruttenden 1994, Ladd 1996). Second, languages may use different tunes for the same basic function (e.g. the difference in basic yes/no question intonation discussed in § 2.3.). Third, some languages (e.g. many European languages) seem to have a greater variety of possible tunes than others (e.g. Indonesian, Odé and van Heuven 1994). None of these differences lead to clear typological generalizations in our present limited state of knowledge. However, the phonological approach acknowledges the existence of the differences, and does not attempt to reduce them all to variations on the same universal pattern. Research is now being devoted to issues that had previously escaped notice (such as the precise alignment of pitch targets relative to the segmental string, e.g. Prieto, van Santen & Hirschberg 1995; Arvaniti, Ladd & Mennen 1998; Ladd, Mennen & Schepman 2000). There is growing evidence of systematic cross-linguistic differences of intonation.

One such difference involves the treatment of *tonal crowding*. This arises particularly in the case of accented phrase-final monosyllables; in e.g. *Did she buy a car?*, the pitch on *car* may be required to rise and then fall and then rise again. In some languages (e.g. English) all the specified pitch movements in such cases are normally realized fully. In others there are various ways of dealing with tonal crowding that avoid multiple pitch movements on a single syllable. For example, in Greek, pitch movements may begin earlier and the pitch range may be compressed (Arvaniti, Ladd, and Mennen, 1998); in Hungarian, the pitch movement may simply be truncated (Ladd 1996). The typological distinction between "truncation" and "compression" is explored by Grønnum (1991).

3.2. Accentual typology
3.2.1. Lexical vs. intonational

As with melodic features, it is necessary to distinguish between word-level (lexical) accentual properties and sentence-level (intonational) ones. Word-level accent, or word-stress, has always been a topic of importance within generative phonology and is the subject of a large literature. Some of this literature is explicitly typological, e.g. Halle & Vergnaud's attempt (1987) at a principles-and-parameters description of possible word-stress systems (see also Hayes 1995, and for a rather different approach Guierre 1979). Word-stress is treated separately in this handbook (→ Art. 96) and is not discussed further here. The rest of this section deals with sentence-level accent, or sentence-stress.

3.2.2. Cross-linguistic differences of sentence-stress

We begin with the universalist position that sentence-stress, as part of intonation, is essentially the same in all languages. In this view, individual words are rendered prominent − made to stand out phonetically in some way from their context − in order to "highlight" them, to signal their importance or salience in the discourse. This view is espoused by Bolinger (e.g. 1972, 1986) and by quite a number of other broadly "functionalist" researchers. If we accept this view, then there can be no meaningful typology of sentence-stress.

However, a number of recent works have identified ways in which sentence-stress appears to differ cross-linguistically. A case in point involves *deaccenting*: Ladd (1990, 1996), Vallduví (1992), Cruttenden (1993), and Zubizarreta (1998) have all presented evidence that languages systematically differ in the extent to which sentence-stress occurs on repeated or contextually given words (i.e. the extent to which repeated or contextually given words are "deaccented"). For example, in English the repeated *have* would be daccented as in (1a), and the form with both occurrences of *have* accented (1b) is very odd. Exactly the reverse is true in the structurally parallel Italian sentences (2a) and (2b).

(1) a. Better to HAVE one than NOT to have one.
  b. *Better to HAVE one than not to HAVE one.

(2) a. *Meglio AVERne che NON averne.
  b. Meglio AVERne che non AVERne.

On the basis of such differences, Vallduví (1992) proposes the existence of a typological parameter [plastic]: in [+ plastic] languages like English, the accentual pattern can be molded to express information structure, whereas in [− plastic] languages like Catalan or Italian, the accentual pattern is fixed and the job of expressing information structure falls to syntax. Related ideas are explored by Zubizarreta (1998), although her formal analysis is rather different.

Another apparent difference between languages involves sentence-stress in questions. Ladd (1990, 1996) has drawn attention to the fact that in some languages, including English, French, and German, sentence-stress in questions does not differ from that in statements: to the extent that the most prominent word is the rightmost content word in statements, the same is true in questions, both yes/no questions and question-word (WH) questions. In other languages, including Greek, Hungarian, and Russian, questions and statements differ: yes/no questions have sentence stress on the finite verb, while WH-questions have sentence stress on the WH-word. This can be seen in the contrast between the English examples in (3) and the closely parallel Greek equivalents in (4).

(3) *Statement*: He bought CHOCOLATES.
  Yes/No question: Did he buy CHOCOLATES?
  WH-question: Where are the CHOCOLATES?

(4) *Statement*: Agorase SOKOLATES.
  Yes/No question: AGORASE sokolates?
  WH-question: PU ine i sokolates?

Ladd suggests that, cross-linguistically, questions may either exhibit the sentence stress pattern of statements (as in English), or else consistently diverge from the statement pattern (as in Greek), but it may also be that sentence-stress patterns in yes/no questions and WH-questions vary independently. In any case this is a rich potential field of typological research. The reader is referred to Ladd (1996) for more discussion of various aspects of sentence-stress typology.

3.2.3. Phonological or syntactic typology of sentence-stress?

The cross-linguistic differences just discussed are very much *sui generis*: there is no obvious way in which a tendency to deaccenting can be related to other aspects of a language's phonology, nor any obvious link between sentence-stress patterns and the syntax of questions. In the long run this is surely unsatisfactory. If there are typological patterns to sentence-stress, it seems likely that they will be part of a larger typological picture. However, attempts to relate sentence-stress to other aspects of phonology or syntax are still very preliminary.

One such attempt is the work of Halle & Vergnaud (1987), who explicitly treat the location of sentence-stress (prominence within the IP) as a phonological matter, like the location of word-stress (prominence within the foot or phonological word). In Halle & Vergnaud's terms, IPs, like feet or phonological words, are either "right-headed" or "left-headed". (The most prominent element within a prosodic domain is its phonological "head"). The parameters of variation posited to account for word-stress (left-headed vs. right-headed, bounded feet vs. unbounded feet, etc.) apply at the level of sentence-stress as well. Among other things, this view predicts that some languages typically have prosodic prominence on the last (rightmost) word of an IP while others have it on the first (leftmost).

On the face of it, Halle & Vergnaud's claim seems implausible, because, as Cinque (1993) points out, it predicts typological variety in sentence-stress systems of a sort that does not appear to be attested. Concretely, in many languages the greatest prominence seems to occur at the right end of the IP. This was the essence of Chomsky & Halle's Nuclear Stress Rule for English (1968), and Cinque himself espouses a modified version of this claim as valid for all languages. (Specifically, Cinque says that sentence-stress goes on the most deeply-embedded terminal node of the syntactic tree; superficial differences between languages reflect syntactic differences, not sentence-stress differences as such.). Yet a prediction very much like Halle & Vergnaud's is made, on rather different grounds, by Nespor & Vogel (1986), who claim that relative prominence within the IP (their "phonological phrase") is a function of syntactic headedness. Specifically, they state that syntactically head-final languages are phonologically left-headed (i. e. have greatest prominence at the beginning), while syntactically head-initial languages are phonologically right-headed (i. e. have greatest prominence at the end). They provide a variety of examples that seem to support their claim.

It is beyond the scope of this article — and beyond the scope of our present knowledge — to evaluate these competing views. However, it is worth noting that they may be partially reconciled by assuming that there are actually two different levels of IP. Many proposals have been made over the years distinguishing what we might call "major IPs" from "minor IPs", with a major IP consisting of one or more minor IPs. The currently most influential version of this idea is Beckman & Pierrehumbert's (1986) distinction between *intonation phrases* (major) and *intermediate phrases* (minor). It seems accurate to state that Nespor & Vogel, and perhaps also Halle & Vergnaud, are primarily concerned with differences at the level of the minor IP, which correspond roughly to syntactic "maximal projections" (noun phrases, prepositional phrases, etc.). Cinque's claims, on the other hand, apply mainly to major IPs, which tend to correspond to whole sentences and parenthetical phrases, and which probably do tend to have their greatest prominence on the right.

Examples from Hungarian are relevant to the points just raised. Hungarian is strongly left-headed phonologically: words have fixed stress on the first syllable, and at least certain kinds of phrases, such as adjective-noun phrases, are left-headed as well.

(5)   NEHÉZ nyelv "difficult language"
        [no contrast implied on *nehéz* "difficult"]

The similarity of word-stress and phrase-stress patterns appears to provide evidence for Halle & Vergnaud's assumption that "stress" is a unified phenomenon, whether at the word level or higher. At the same time, the stress pattern in (5) may also support Nespor & Vogel's claim about the relation between syntactic and phonological headedness, since Hungarian is generally head-final syntactically. However, at the level of the major IP (e.g. long noun phrase or whole sentence), there are plenty of cases where even Hungarian is right-headed, such as long number phrases, discussed by Varga (1998):

(6) KÉTszáz "two hundred"
kétszáz HÁROM "two hundred three"

There are also, of course, other languages where adjective-noun phrases do not so obviously support the preliminary typological claims. English has both left-headed and right-headed aspects to its word-stress rules, so it is at best unclear what Halle & Vergnaud would predict for adjective-noun phrases like *difficult language*. Nespor & Vogel would apparently wrongly predict stress on the adjective, since adjective-noun phrases are head-final in English. Clearly, much research remains to be done.

3.3. Prosodic typology

3.3.1. Syntax-prosody mapping

The term "prosodic" typology is used here to refer to differences in the way prosodic structure is related to morphosyntactic structure. As noted in § 2.2. above, universalist descriptions emphasize the naturalness of the association between IP boundaries and morphosyntactic constituent boundaries. The empirical reality appears much messier. For example, there are many well-known cases in which IP boundaries seem to "come in the wrong place", such as the English children's verse *The House that Jack built*:

(7) This is the dog | that chased the cat | that killed the rat | that ate the malt | that lay in the house that Jack built.

As noted by Chomsky & Halle (1968: 371 f.), the IP boundaries (indicated by |) interrupt the repeatedly right-branching noun phrases. The existence of such syntax-prosody "mismatches" has been the subject of a great deal of theoretical research since the 1970s (e.g. Langendoen 1975, Nespor & Vogel 1986). One contribution to this line of research, that of Steedman (1991, 2000), argues that the problem is not a matter of syntax-prosody mapping at all, but that the complications reside rather in the mapping from semantics to syntax, and in the nature of syntactic structure itself. Most other researchers, however, continue to treat this as a problem of the "interface" between syntax and phonology, and there has been a considerable amount of explicitly typological work on the topic within the generative principles-and-parameters approach.

In an influential article, Selkirk (1986) proposed that languages vary systematically in (a) whether they locate IP boundaries relative to the left or right edges of syntactic constituents, and (b) which constituents are relevant for IP boundary placement. In the case of *The House that Jack built*, one could say that an IP boundary is placed at the right edge of every syntactic maximal projection; the choice of right edges and maximal projections is a typological generalization about English, and the claim would be that other languages could make different choices. Selkirk's proposal has spawned much descriptive work on a variety of languages (e.g. Rice 1987 on Slave, Chen 1987 on Xiamen Chinese), and has more recently been recast in terms of Optimality Theory (Selkirk 1995, Truckenbrodt 1999), using the notion of "generalized alignment" constraints (McCarthy & Prince 1993).

Again, note that the distinction between "major IPs" and "minor IPs" (§ 3.2.4.) may help to reconcile this typological work with the universalist assumption of a natural connection between syntactic constituent boundaries and IP boundaries. Minor IPs, which are the focus of much of the work based on Selkirk, may show considerable cross-linguistic difference, while major IPs may more consistently correspond to whole sentences and parenthetical phrases.

3.3.2. Sentence-stress and phrasing

It has been observed by Venditti, Jun, & Beckman (1996) that Japanese and Korean exhibit a prosodic phenomenon that is comparable pragmatically, but not phonologically, to English deaccenting (§ 3.2.2.). Contexts which would lead to deaccenting or other sentence-stress shifts in English often lead to what Venditti et al. term *dephrasing* in Japanese and Korean: two content words which would normally each comprise separate prosodic words or "accentual phrases" are combined into a single phrase. This is seen in the following example from Korean (Venditti et al. 1996: 307):

(7) {kwijəun} {maŋatʃi} "cute colt" [two phrases, pragmatically neutral]
{kwijəun maŋatʃi} "CUTE colt" [one phrase, focus on adjective]

One of the words in the combined phrase corresponds to the deaccented word in English, but it is not possible to analyze the Korean data as involving "deaccenting", because accent is lexically assigned. As Ladd (1996) notes, this correspondence between deaccenting and dephrasing suggests that sentence-stress in English and similar languages is not primarily a matter of the location of pitch accents, but more generally a matter of relative prominence within prosodic structure. This possibility needs to be kept in mind in investigating typology, because it may mean that what we are calling "accentual typology" and "prosodic typology" are simply two different facets of the same basic phenomenon. Once again, this is a fertile field for future research.

4. Intonational phonetics

This section briefly discusses several dimensions of cross-linguistic variation regarding the phonetic realization of intonational features and categories. These are roughly analogous to segmental phonetic differences like whether languages have vowel reduction in unstressed syllables, or whether they have retroflex stops (or clicks, or front rounded vowels). It is possible that variation on these points is systematic, but little definite is known, and the following typological remarks must be regarded as speculative. A further topic that fits naturally in this section, the distinction between stress-timed and syllable-timed rhythm, is discussed separately in Art. 99.

4.1. Declination

While declination is apparently a universal tendency, the details certainly vary from language to language. Two possible dimensions of variation should be noted. First, it may be useful to think of the extent to which declination is "phonologized" in any given language. Many languages have rules of *downstep*, which cause a given tone to be realized at a lower pitch than a previous occurrence of the same tone. These rules are well attested in the lexical tone languages of Africa (e.g. Clements 1979) and in Japanese (Kubozono 1989), and are argued by many to apply in the European languages as well (Pierrehumbert 1980, Grice 1995). Second, it seems likely that languages differ in how much the overall amount of declination is to be explained by downstep and similar phonological rules, and how much is truly gradual background declination that is part of the overall phonetic shape of an IP. It has been suggested that some languages, especially languages with three or more lexical level tone phonemes, limit background declination severely (e.g. Yoruba, Connell and Ladd 1990).

4.2. Overall pitch range

The term "overall pitch range" can be defined quantitatively in a number of partially contradictory ways; because of this, and because of the conspicuous differences of pitch range between male and female speakers or between "lively" and "monotonous" speakers, it is difficult to make valid statements about pitch range in cross-language perspective. However, impressionistic evidence suggests that *ceteris paribus* speakers of some languages habitually use a wider or higher range than speakers of other languages. For example, the data in Connell and Ladd's study of Yoruba showed that two of the three male speakers used a pitch range comparable to that of the one female speaker, and very much higher than ranges typically reported for male speakers of European languages. It is tempting to speculate that this may be related to Yoruba's use of lexically specified level tone, but other explanations are at least as plausible. In particular, cultural explanations related to gender differences are almost certainly relevant to many such cases, if not to Yoruba itself: it is known that some cultures place a greater value than others on low male voices or high female voices (e.g. Scherer, London & Wolf 1973 on American vs. German; Bezooijen 1995 on Dutch vs. Japanese). In our present state of knowledge it is impossible to assess the respective roles of phonological and cultural factors in cross-language pitch range differences.

4.3. Dynamic vs. melodic accent

Beckman (1986), basing herself on a careful experimental comparison of Japanese and English, shows that the traditional distinction between dynamic and melodic accent has a considerable basis in acoustic reality. In particular, she shows that there is a useful distinction to be drawn between "stress" and "non-stress" accent: in "non-stress" languages (like Japanese) accent is signalled almost exclusively by pitch, and features related to force of articulation (duration, intensity, spectral differences, etc.) are virtually absent; in "stress" languages (like English), duration, intensity, and spectral differences are important concomitants of the pitch features that signal accent, and may even signal accent on their own (i.e. in the absence of pitch cues) in some contexts. Work on Dutch by Sluijter & van Heuven (1996) appears to confirm this view, though there is considerable disagreement about the details (cf. Campbell & Beckman 1997).

For typological purposes, the only important addendum to Beckman's claim is the one made by Ladd (1996). Ladd points out that Beckman's choice of English and Japanese as examples may give rise to the impression that "stress" languages have only intonationally specified pitch features (cf. § 3.1.), while pitch features in "non-stress" languages are lexically specified. The two typological dimensions are actually independent. Both Swedish and Chinese have (in rather different ways) lexically specified pitch features, but both are also widely said to have stress. Other languages (such as Bengali and Indonesian) certainly have intonationally specified pitch features, and probably have lexical accent (in the sense that some syllable in each word is designated the bearer of any intonational pitch prominence), but do not appear to make any use of stress in Beckman's or Sluijter and van Heuven's sense. Again, this is a rich potential field for typological research.

5. References

Abramson, Arthur (1962). The vowels and tones of standard Thai: Acoustical measurements and experiments. *International Journal of American Linguistics* 28, No. 2 part 3.

Arvaniti, Amalia & Ladd, D. Robert & Mennen, Ineke (1998). Stability of tonal alignment: the case of Greek prenuclear accents. *Journal of Phonetics* 26, 3–25.

Beckman, Mary E. (1986). *Stress and Non-Stress Accent*. (Netherlands Phonetic Archives 7). Dordrecht: Foris Publications.

Beckman, Mary E. & Pierrehumbert, Janet B. (1986). Intonational Structure in English and Japanese. *Phonology Yearbook* 3, 255–310.

Bezooijen, Renée van (1995). Sociocultural aspects of pitch differences between Japanese and Dutch women. *Language and Speech* 38, 253–265.

Bolinger, Dwight (1972). Accent is predictable (If your're a mind-reader). *Language* 48, 633–644.

Bolinger, Dwight (1978). Intonation across languages. In J. Greenberg (ed.) *Universals of Human Language Volume 2: Phonology*. Stanford: Stanford University Press, pp. 471–524.

Bolinger, Dwight (1986). *Intonation and its Parts*. Stanford: Stanford University Press.

Bolinger, Dwight (1989). *Intonation and its Uses*. Stanford: Stanford University Press.

Brown, Gillian & Currie, Karen & Kenworthy, Joanne (1980). *Questions of intonation*. London: Croom Helm.

Bruce, Gösta (1977). *Swedish Word Accents in Sentence Perspective*. Lund: Gleerup.

Campbell, W. N. & Beckman, Mary E. (1997). Stress, prominence, and spectral tilt. In A. Botinis, G. Kouroupetroglou, and G. Carayiannis (eds.), *Intonation: Theory, Models and Applications*. European Speech Communication Association.

Chang, Nien-Chuang (1958). Tones and Intonation in the Chengtu Dialect (Szechuan, China). *Phonetica* 2, 59–84. Reprinted in D. Bolinger (ed.), *Intonation* (Penguin Books, 1972), pp. 391–413.

Chen, Matthew (1987). The syntax of Xiamen tone sandhi. *Phonology Yearbook* 4, 109–149.

Cinque, Guglielmo (1993). A null theory of phrase and compound stress. *Linguistic Inquiry* 24, 239–297.

Chomsky, Noam & Halle, Morris (1968). *The Sound Pattern of English*. New York: Harper and Row.

Clements, G. N. (1979). The description of terrace-level tone languages. *Language* 55, 536–558.

Cohen, Antonie & 't Hart, Johan (1967). The anatomy of intonation. *Lingua* 19, 177–192.

Connell, Bruce & Ladd, D. Robert (1990). Aspects of pitch realisation in Yoruba. *Phonology* 7, 1–30.

Cooper, William & Sorensen, John (1981). *Fundamental Frequency in Sentence Production*. Heidelberg: Springer.

Cruttenden, Alan (1981). Falls and rises: Meanings and universals. *Journal of Linguistics* 17, 77–91.

Cruttenden, Alan (1993). The de-accenting and re-accenting of repeated lexical items. *Lund University Working Papers in Linguistics and Phonetics* 41, 16–19.

Cruttenden, Alan (1994). Rises in English. In J. Windsor Lewis (ed.), *Studies in General and English Phonetics: Essays in Honour of Professor J. D. O'Connor*. (London: Routledge), pp. 155–173.

Fujisaki, Hiroya (1983). Dynamic characteristics of voice fundamental frequency in speech and singing. In: Peter F. MacNeilage (ed.), *The Production of Speech* (New York: Springer), pp. 39–55.

Gårding, Eva (1987). Speech act and tonal pattern in standard Chinese: constancy and variation. *Phonetica* 44, 13–29.

Grice, Martine (1995). Leading tones and downstep in English. *Phonology* 12, 183–233.

Grønnum, Nina (1991). Prosodic parameters in a variety of regional Danish standard languages, with a view towards Swedish and German. *Phonetica* 47, 188–214.

Grønnum, Nina (1995). Superposition and subordination in intonation: A non-linear approach. *Proceedings of the 13th International Congress of Phonetics Sciences, Stockholm*, vol. 2, pp. 124–131.

Guierre, Lionel (1979). *Essai sur l'accentuation en anglais contemporain*. Université de Paris VII.

Gussenhoven, Carlos & Bruce, Gösta (1999). Word prosody and intonation. In H. van der Hulst (ed.), *Word Prosodic Systems in the Languages of Europe* (Berlin: Mouton de Gruyter), pp. 233–271.

Halle, Morris, & Vergnaud, Jean-Roger (1987). *An Essay on Stress*. Cambridge MA: MIT Press.

't Hart, J., Collier, René, & Cohen, A. (1990). *A perceptual study of intonation: An experimental-phonetic approach*. Cambridge: Cambridge University Press.

Hayes, Bruce (1995). *Metrical Stress Theory: Principles and Case Studies*. Chicago: University of Chicago Press.

Kubozono, Haruo (1989). Syntactic and rhythmic effects on downstep in Japanese. *Phonology* 6, 39–67.

Ladd, D. Robert (1984). Declination: a review and some hypotheses. *Phonology Yearbook* 1, 53–74.

Ladd, D. Robert (1990). Intonation: emotion vs. grammar (Review article on Bolinger 1989). *Language* 66, 806–816.

Ladd, D. Robert (1996). *Intonational Phonology*. Cambridge: Cambridge University Press.

Ladd, D. Robert & Mennen, Ineke & Schepman, Astrid (2000). Phonological conditioning of peak alignment in rising pitch accents in Dutch. *Journal of the Acoustical Society of America* 107, 2685–2969.

Langendoen, D. Terence (1975). Finite-state parsing of phrase-structure languages and the status of readjustment rules in the grammar. *Linguistic Inquiry* 6, 533–554.

Liberman, Mark & Pierrehumbert, Janet (1984). Intonational invariance under changes in pitch range and length. In M. Aronoff and R. Oerhle (eds.) *Language Sound Structure* (Cambridge MA: MIT Press), pp. 157–233.

Lieberman, Philip (1967). *Intonation, Perception, and Language*. Cambridge MA: MIT Press.

Lindau, Mona (1986). Testing the Model of Intonation in a Tone Language. *Journal of the Acoustical Society of America* 80, 757–764.

McCarthy, John & Prince, Alan (1993). Generalized alignment. In G. Booij & J. van Marle (eds.), *Yearbook of Morphology 1993*, pp. 79–153.

Möbius, Bernd & Pätzold, Matthias, & Hess, Wolfgang (1993). Analysis and synthesis of German F0 contours by means of Fujisaki's model. *Speech Communication* 13, 53–61.

Nespor, Marina, & Vogel, Irene (1986). *Prosodic Phonology*. Dordrecht: Foris Publications.

Odé, Cecilia, & van Heuven, Vincent J. (eds.) (1994). *Experimental Studies of Indonesian Prosody*. University of Leiden.

Ohala, J. J. (1982). Cross-language use of pitch: An ethnological view. *Phonetica* 40, 1–18.

Pierrehumbert, Janet (1980). *The Phonology and Phonetics of English Intonation*. PhD Dissertation, Massachusetts Institute of Technology.

Pierrehumbert, Janet & Beckman, Mary (1988). *Japanese Tone Structure*. Cambridge MA: MIT Press.

Pike, Kenneth L. (1945). *The Intonation of American English*. Ann Arbor: Univ. of Michigan Press.

Prieto, Pilar, van Santen, Jan & Hirschberg, Julia (1995). Tonal alignment patterns in Spanish. *Journal of Phonetics* 23, 429–451.

Rice, Keren (1987). On defining the intonational phrase: evidence from Slave. *Phonology Yearbook* 4, 37–60.

Scherer, K. R., London, H., & Wolf, J. J. (1973). The voice of confidence: paralinguistic cues and audience evaluation. *Journal of Research in Personality* 7, 31–44.

Selkirk, Elisabeth O. (1986). On derived domains in sentence phonology. *Phonoloy Yearbook* 3, 371–405.

Selkirk, Elisabeth O. (1995). Sentence prosody: Intonation, stress, and phrasing. In J. Goldsmith (ed.) *The Handbook of Phonological Theory* (Oxford: Blackwell), pp. 550–569.

Sluijter, Agaath, & van Heuven, Vincent (1996). Spectral balance as an acoustic correlate of linguistic stress. *Journal of the Acoustical Society of America* 100, 2471–2485.

Steedman, Mark (1991). Structure and intonation. *Language* 67, 260–296.

Steedman, Mark (2000). Information Structure and the Syntax-Phonology Interface. *Linguistic Inquiry* 31, 649–689.

Thorsen, Nina (1980). A study of the perception of sentence in intonation: Evidence from Danish. *Journal of the Acoustical Society of America* 67, 1014–1030.

Truckenbrodt, Hubert (1999). On the relation between syntactic phrases and phonological phrases. *Linguistic Inquiry* 30, 219–255.

Vaissière, Jacqueline (1983). Language-independent prosodic features. In A. Cutler & D. R. Ladd (eds.), *Prosody: Models and Measurements* (Heidelberg: Springer), pp. 53–66.

Vallduví, Enric (1992). *The Informational Component*. New York and London: Garland Press.

Varga, László (1998). Rhythmical variation in Hungarian. *Phonology* 15, 227–266.

Venditti, Jennifer, Jun, Sun-Ah & Beckman, Mary E. (1996). Prosodic cues to syntactic and other linguistic structures in Japanese, Korean, and English. In James L. Morgan & Katherine Demuth (eds.), *Signal to Syntax: Bootstrapping from Speech to Grammar in Early Acquisition* (Hillsdale NJ: Lawrence Erlbaum), pp. 287–311.

Zubizarreta, Maria Luisa (1998). *Prosody, Focus, and Word Order*. Cambridge MA: MIT Press.

D. Robert Ladd, University of Edinburgh (Great Britain)

XIII. Salient typological parameters
Typologisch besonders markante Parameter
Paramètres typologiques particulièrement saillants

99. Silben- und akzentzählende Sprachen

1. Allgemeines
2. Die phonetischen Grundlagen
3. Multifaktorielle Ansätze in der Phonetik
4. Typologien prosodischer Konstituenten
5. Einige phonologische Eigenschaften von Wort- und Silbensprachen
6. Gesamteinschätzung
7. Zitierte Literatur

1. Allgemeines

Die Unterscheidung zwischen silben- und akzentzählenden Sprachen (*syllable- and stress-timed languages*) stammt aus der Phonetik und kann dort auf eine umfangreiche Forschungstradition zurückblicken. Im vorliegenden Artikel wird diese Forschungstradition nur insofern dargestellt, als sie für die phonologische Sprachtyplogie Konsequenzen hatte. Die Dichotomie „silben- vs. akzentzählend" wird also als ein prosodischer Klassifikationsparameter für die Sprachen der Welt angesehen, der sich in eine Reihe mit Parametern wie Akzent- vs. Tonsprachen (vgl. Art. 97), Silben- und Morensprachen (vgl. unten), Sprachen mit jambischen vs. trochäischen Akzentsystemen (vgl. Art. 96), etc. stellen lässt. Im Gegensatz zu diesen ist aber für die Dichotomie „silben- vs. akzentzählend" verschiedentlich beansprucht wurden, dass sie stark prädiktiven Wert für andere phonologische Eigenschaften von Einzelsprachen hat, mithin also über die reine Klassifikation hinausgehend als Grundlage einer typologischen Unterscheidung dienen kann. Ob dies tatsächlich der Fall ist, soll hier aufgrund der vorliegenden Forschungsergebnisse diskutiert werden. Von ihrer Art her stehen prosodisch basierte Systeme für phonologische Typologien inventarbezogenen gegenüber; Vertreter prosodisch basierter Systeme machen geltend, dass sich inventarbezogene phonologische Typologien nur relativ schlecht mit anderen phonologischen oder gar grammatischen Eigenschaften der klassifizierten Sprachen korrelieren lassen, insbesondere mit phonologischen Prozessen.

2. Die phonetischen Grundlagen

Die Unterscheidung zwischen akzent- und silbenzählenden Sprachen wird im allgemeinen auf Pike (1945: 35 f.) zurückgeführt. In einer einflußreichen Formulierung fasst sie der Phonetiker Abercrombie später (1967: 96 f.) folgendermaßen zusammen:

„As far as is known, every language in the world is spoken with one kind of rhythm or with the other. In the one kind, known as a syllable-timed rhythm, the periodic recurrence of movement is supplied by the syllable-producing process; the chest pulses, and hence the syllables, recur at equal invervals of time − they are isochronous. [...] In the other kind, known as a stress-timed rhythm, the periodic recurrence is supplied by the stress-producing process: the stress-pulses, and hence the stressed syllables, are isochronous. [...] When one of the two series of pulses is in isochronous succession, the other will not be. Thus in a syllable-timed rhythm, the stress-pulses are unevenly spaced, and in a stress-timed rhythm the chest-pulses are unevenly spaced."

Diese sog. *Isochroniehypothese* unterstellt also in den akzentzählenden Sprachen die Identität der zeitlichen Intervalle von einem Akzent zum nächsten (innerhalb des [phonetischen] Fußes), während in den silbenzählenden Sprachen die zeitlichen Intervalle von einem Silbenbeginn (oder Silbengipfel) zum nächsten gleich sein sollen. In dieser Form dürfte die Isochroniehypothese jedoch nach dem heutigen Stand der phonetischen Forschung nicht haltbar sein (vgl. u. a. die Überblicksartikel von Auer & Uhmann 1988; Bertinetto 1989; Couper-Kuhlen 1993: 5−36; den Os 1983; Lehiste 1977; Roach 1982); die

Isochronie der rhythmischen Füße (*stress-to-stress intervals*) in sog. akzentzählenden Sprachen (wie Englisch, Holländisch, Portugiesisch, Deutsch, Russisch, Arabisch, etc.) ist nicht eindeutig im physikalischen Signal nachweisbar, Isochronie der Silben in sog. silbenzählenden Sprachen (wie dem Italienischen, Spanischen, Telugu, Yoruba, etc.) liegt ziemlich sicher nicht vor.

Es gibt verschiedene phonetische Versuche, die Isochroniehypothese trotzdem zu retten; der aussichtsreichste davon verlagert die Isochronie vom Schallereignis in seine Wahrnehmung durch die Sprachbenutzer und versucht durch komplizierte intervenierende Faktorenkonstellationen die Divergenzen zwischen Wahrnehmung und Sprachsignal zu erklären (vgl. Donovan & Darwin 1979; Darwin & Donovan 1980; Pompino-Marschall 1990). Diese Versuche werden hier ebenso wenig referiert wie die zahlreichen methodischen Probleme, die die bisherige experimentelle Forschung zur Isochronie behindert haben (etwa die häufige Verwendung von „reiterant speech" – also Kunstsilben – in der Laborforschung). Ebenfalls nicht berücksichtigt wird die Forschung zu interaktiven Aspekten von Sprachrhythmus als Signalisierungsresource in natürlichen Interaktionen (vgl. dazu Auer & Couper-Kuhlen & Müller 1998).

3. Multifaktorielle Ansätze in der Phonetik

Interessanter für die Sprachtypologie ist der Versuch verschiedener Phonetiker und Phonetikerinnen, die Unterscheidung zwischen silben- und akzentzählenden Sprachen zwar beizubehalten, jedoch von der eindimensionalen Fixierung auf reine Dauerstrukturen zu lösen und stattdessen die Wahrnehmung der unterschiedlichen Rhythmus-Typen als Folge einer jeweils unterschiedlichen *Konstellation* phonetischer Faktoren zu sehen. Diesen Versuchen liegt die Überlegung zugrunde, daß Isochronie im oben definierten Sinn ja nur denkbar ist, wenn in den akzent- und silbenzählenden Sprachen unterschiedliche Kompensationseffekte eintreten: nur in akzentzählenden Sprachen ist zu erwarten, dass bei variierender interner Struktur der Füße die Silben um so mehr komprimiert werden, je mehr solche Silben in einem Fuß Platz finden müssen. In silbenzählenden Sprachen ist ein solcher zeitlicher Komprimierungseffekt im Fuß nicht notwendig, dafür aber im Inneren der Silbe zu erwarten, und zwar in Abhängigkeit von ihrer strukturellen Komplexität: die Dauer der Silben kann nur dann konstant gehalten werden, wenn in komplexeren Silben zeitliche Dauerreduktion eintritt. (Logischerweise ergibt sich daraus, dass – anders als von Abercrombie postuliert – neben akzentzählenden und silbenzählenden Sprachen ein dritter Typ möglich ist, in dem weder auf der einen noch auf der anderen Ebene Komprimierung stattfindet. Dieser Typ rhythmisiert möglicherweise auf einer kleineren prosodischen Ebene als der der Silbe, nämlich auf der Morenebene. Vgl. zum Japanischen als potentiell morenmetrisierter Sprache u. a. Hoequist 1983, Nagano-Madsen 1992.)

Die multifaktorielle Herangehensweise hat allerdings weniger die faktische Variation der Dauerparameter auf der Silben- oder Fußebene im Auge als die verschiedenen phonetischen Prozesse, die der Teleologie der Akzent- vs. Silbenmetrisierung dienen und die zeitliche Komprimierung im genannten Sinn erst möglich machen. Eine solche Verlagerung des Forschungsinteresses ist schon in Pikes ursprünglicher Formulierung der Isochroniehypothese angelegt, wenn er auf das „crushing of syllables", „abbreviations – in which syllables may be omitted entirely" und „the obscuring of vowels" hinweist, die im Englischen als akzentzählender Sprache dem Ziel dienen, die Fußdauer konstant zu halten.

In der moderneren experimentalphonetischen Literatur ist tatsächlich nachgewiesen worden, dass in („akzentzählenden") Sprachen wie dem Schwedischen, Holländischen oder Deutschen ein deutlicher Komprimierungseffekt in Abhängigkeit von der Anzahl der Silben im Fuß eintritt, auch wenn dieser Effekt nicht stark genug ist, um die Fußdauer – im Sinne Abercrombies – völlig konstant zu halten. Dieser Komprimierungseffekt fehlt hingegen in („silbenzählenden") Sprachen wie dem Italienischen. Genauere Untersuchungen zeigen außerdem, dass der Komprimierungseffekt nicht nur die unbetonten, sondern (aus phonologischer Sicht überraschend) auch die akzentuierten Silben erfasst (vgl. u. a. Lindblom/Rapp 1973; Marotta 1985; Farnetani/Kori 1990; den Os 1988; für das Deutsche Kohler 1983). Verschiedene weitere Details der Komprimierungseffekte, die auch für die phonologische Beschreibung relevant sind (etwa die Frage der antizipatorischen Komprimierung; vgl. Fowler 1981, 1983) sind aber noch ungeklärt. Ingesamt scheint die phonetische Forschungslage die Meinung Bertinettos (1989: 123) zu unterstützen, dass sich die Unterscheidung zwischen silben- und akzentzählenden Sprachen eher als eine zwischen prinzipiell zeitlich kompensierenden und prinzipiell nicht-kompensierenden verstehen lässt, wobei die kompensierenden Sprachen sowohl innerhalb des Fußes als auch innerhalb der Silbe die Zeitdauer kompensieren. Es sind dies die „akzentzählenden" Sprachen im Sinne Pikes oder Abercrombies, während die „silbenzählenden" Sprachen nur geringe oder gar keine Dauerkompensationen vornehmen.

Weitere Korrelate des akzentzählenden Rhythmustyps, die in der phonetischen Literatur vorgeschlagen worden sind, umfassen: (a) die qualitative (im Gegensatz zur rein quantitativen) Reduktion nicht-akzentuierter Silben (Delattre 1969), (b) die stärkere qualitative und quantitative Reduktion der nicht-akzentuierten Vokale bei höherer Sprechgeschwindigkeit (Fletcher 1987), (c) unklare Beurteilung der Silbengrenzen und der Anzahl der Silben im Wort durch Laienbeurteiler, (d) die Tendenz der Akzentsilben, bei insgesamt variabler Silbifizierung den Anstieg oder Abfall nicht-betonter Silben an sich zu ziehen (Bailey 1980; so wird aus engl. Wis&con&sin in schnellerem Tempo Wi&scon&sin, etc. [& = Silbengrenze]), (e) phonetische Realisierung des Akzents durch Tonhöhenbewegungen (*pitch accents*).

Wenn man einer solchen Argumentationsweise folgt, wird die Unterscheidung zwischen silben- und akzentzählenden Sprachen von einer dichotomischen zu einer skalaren. Es zeigt sich freilich auch, dass die Beschränkung der Konstellationen von Parametern, die die jeweiligen Rhythmustypen dann prototypisch repräsentieren, auf phonetische (und mit experimentalphonetischen Methoden nachweisbare) Merkmale kaum mehr sinnvoll ist. Vielmehr wird oft angenommen, „that the rhythmic differences we feel to exist between languages such as English and Spanish are more a result of *phonological, phonetic, lexical, and syntactic* facts about that language than any attempt on the part of the speaker to equalize interstress or intersyllable intervals" (Dauer 1983: 55; Herv. P. A.). Dies ist auch plausibel, denn die Voraussetzungen zur Dauerkompensation in einer Sprache umfassen offensichtlich neben rein phonetischen auch phonologische Faktoren wie etwa die Phonologie des Nebenakzentvokalismus. Damit wird die Grenze zur Phonologie/Linguistik überschritten und die Unterscheidung zwischen silben- und akzentzählenden Sprachen zu einem Parameter, der für die Sprachtypologie unmittelbar relevant ist.

Zugleich stellt sich aber die Frage, welcher phonologische Parameter zum Zentrum der Typologie gemacht werden soll, wenn der ursprünglich verwendete Parameter der Dauerkonstanz auf Fuß- vs. Silbenebene einerseits wegen seiner rein phonetischen Natur, andererseits wegen der nur geringen empirischen Unterstützung, die er bisher erfahren hat, aufgegeben werden muß. Die beim augenblicklichen Stand der Forschung wohl attraktivste Antwort auf diese Frage lautet, dass dieser Parameter die Festlegung der prosodischen Grundeinheit in einer Hierarchie prosodischer Konstituenten (von der More bis zur Intonationskontur/*intonation unit*) sein sollte (vgl. zu solchen Hierarchien Nespor & Vogel 1986). Fällt diese Wahl zum Beispiel auf die Silbe, wäre von einer *Silbensprache* zu sprechen, fällt er auf das phonologische Wort, sprechen wir von einer *Wortsprache*. Man kann hier also von *Typologien auf der Basis prosodischer Konstituenten* sprechen (denen Typologien gegenüberstehen, die bestimmte prosodische Verfahren oder Prozesse wie Akzent oder Ton zum zentralen Parameter erheben).

4. Typologien auf der Basis prosodischer Konstituenten

4.1. Trubetzkoys Silben- vs. Morensprachen

Damit lässt sich die phonologische Typologie an Ansätze anschließen, die schon vor der phonetischen Isochroniehypothese im Sinne von Pike in der Linguistik eine Rolle gespielt haben, und zwar insbesondere in der Prager Schule und ihrem Umfeld. Der wichtigste davon geht auf Trubetzkoy zurück (1939/1952: 169 ff.), der Silben- und Morensprachen unterscheidet. Morensprachen werden als solche definiert, in denen die Gleichung V: = VV oder VC gilt (wobei C auch ein nicht-silbischer Vokal/*glide* sein kann). In solchen Sprachen können prosodische Phänomene wie Akzent (Slovenisch), *stød* (Dänisch) oder Ton (Efik) auf jede der beiden Moren fallen, oder die beiden Moren sind zumindest im Rahmen der Akzentzuweisung getrennt zu zählen (klass. Latein). Hingegen gilt für Silbensprachen wie Deutsch, Englisch oder Holländisch, dass in ihnen „die prosodischen Einheiten immer mit den Silben zusammenfallen" (Trubetzkoy 1939/1952: 174). Der Unterscheidung zwischen Moren- und Silbensprachen ordnet Trubetzkoy zumindest eine weitere prosodische Eigenschaft von Sprachen kategorisch zu, nämlich die Differenzierung der prosodischen Grundeinheiten („Prosodeme") entweder durch Intensität (Silbensprachen) oder durch Tonhöhe (Morensprachen). (Zu den letzteren gehören sowohl Tonsprachen im heutigen Sinn als auch Sprachen mit „musikalischem Akzent"). Prosodemeigenschaften können ausschließlich distinktiv sein (dann werden sie in jedem Prosodem unterschieden) oder zusätzlich kulminativ (dann wird ein Prosodem über die anderen im Wort hervorgehoben). Ob sich die Unterscheidung zwischen Moren- und Silbensprachen typologisch, d. h. prädiktiv einsetzen läßt, wird von Trubetzkoy nicht diskutiert; sein Vorgehen scheint jedoch eher auf eine klassifikatorische Verwendung des Begriffpaars hinzudeuten.

Einen ähnlichen Gedanken (aber aus einem anderen Blickwinkel) formuliert Jakobson (1931) in seiner Diskussion der „polytonischen" Sprachen (i. e., solchen mit musikalischem Akzent). Wie bei Trubetzkoy müssen sie (a) morenzählend sein, also ein- und zweimorige Vokale unterscheiden, (b) die zweimorige Betonung kann auf zwei kurze Silben 'gespreizt' werden, (c) nur in den betonten Silben gilt der phonemische Unterschied zwischen verschiedenen Tonverläufen und (d) kurze Vokale können nicht zugleich nach den Merkmalen Betonung („Tonstufenkorrelation") und Tonverlauf („Tonverlaufkorrelation") unterschieden werden. Bei den „monotonischen" Sprachen (i. e., solchen mit „Druckakzent") gibt es hingegen nach Jakobson keine phonemische Quantitätsunterscheidung. (Entsprechend ist für ihn das deutsche Vokalsystem durch die Silbenanschlußkorrelation, nicht durch die Quantitätskorrelation differenziert.)

4.2. Pulgrams *nexus*- und *cursus*-Sprachen

Trubetzkoy erwähnt ebenfalls, dass sich Sprachen dadurch unterscheiden, ob prosodische Kategorien mit morphologischen zusammenfallen (z. B. jedes grammatische Affix auch mit einer eindeutig begrenzten Silbe). Diese Idee ist von anderen Autoren aufgegriffen worden (vgl. etwa Holm 1990); sie hat vor allem bei Pulgram (1970) zu einem ausgearbeiteten typologischen „Vorschlag" geführt. Zentral für Pulgrams Ansatz ist die Frage, wie sich (phonologische) Wörter in höhere prosodische Einheiten einfügen, die man als phonologische Phrasen (*nexus*) und Intonationskonturen (*cursus*) bezeichnen könnte. Es sind drei Fälle zu unterscheiden. Zum einen ist es möglich (nach Pulgram aber kaum empirisch belegt), dass das phonologische Wort weder segmentale noch suprasegmentale Eigenschaften verliert, wenn es sich in größere Einheiten integriert. Wesentlich häufiger ist der zweite Fall, nämlich, dass zumindest in manchen *nexus* phonologische Wortgrenzen (bzw. teils auch suprasegmentale Merkmale) getilgt werden: der *nexus* insgesamt verhält sich wie das einzelne Wort (z. B. hat er nur einen Akzent). In einer *nexus*-Sprache kommen also phonologische Wörter alleine oder in *nexus*-Verbindungen vor, die Integration von *nexus* in größere Einheiten (Intonationskonturen) hat aber keine Auswirkungen. Der dritte Fall sind *cursus*-Sprachen, in denen auch auf dieser Ebene die segmentalen und/oder suprasegmentalen Eigenschaften der tieferen prosodischen Kategorien getilgt werden. Aus der Tatsache, dass Pulgram zum Beispiel das Französische als *cursus*-Sprache, das Italienische hingegen als *nexus*-Sprache bezeichnet, wird bereits ersichtlich, dass dieser „typologische Vorschlag" zu anderen Ergebnissen führt als die klassische Isochroniehypothese vorhersagen würde, aber auch zu anderen als Trubetzkoys Unterscheidung zwischen Moren- und Silbensprachen.

4.3. Donegan & Stampes Wort- und Silbenrhythmus

Möglicherweise am ergiebigsten für die phonologische Sprachtypologie ist ein Vorschlag von Donegan & Stampe (1983), der anhand der Munda- und Mon-Khmer-Sprachfamilien exemplifiziert wird. Die Autoren ordnen ihren beiden Typen — Wortrhythmus und Silbenrhythmus — die folgenden Paare von Eigenschaften zu, die auch in die Inventartypologie, in die Grammatik, in die Diachronie und in die Künste ausgreifen: (a) die Lage des Satzakzents (*phrasal accent*) — final vs. initial, (b) die Lage des Wortakzents (rechts vs. links), (c) die Richtung der Klitisierung (Proklise vs. Enklise), (d) der Isochronietyp (akzentmetrisierend vs. silben- oder morenmetrisierend), (e) Wortlänge (kurz vs. lang), (f) Konturtöne/*voice registers* vs. einfache (*level*) (oder gar keine) Töne, (g) Reim vs. Alliteration in der Dichtung, (h) rigide vs. freie Wortstellung, (i) SVO vs. SOV, (j) analytischer Sprachbau vs. Kasus- und Kongruenzsystem, (k) „fusional", präfigierende oder isolierende vs. agglutinierende Tendenz in der Morphologie. Außerdem haben die folgenden phonologischen Eigenschaften nur in einem Rhythmustyp Platz: (1) Vokalreduktion in unbetonten Silben nur bei Wortrhythmus, (m) Vokalharmonie nur bei Silbenrhythmus, (n) ungespannte Akzentvokale und Diphthongierung nur bei Wortrhythmus, (o) Nasalierung und Verlust silbenauslautender Nasale nur im Silbenrhythmus, (p) hintere ungerundete und/oder zentrale Vokale nur bei Wortrhythmus, (q) explosionslose Plosive (*unreleased stops*) als Grenzmarkierung des Worts nur bei Wortrhythmus, (r) „liaison" nur bei Silbenrhythmus, (s) unterschiedliche Komplexität der Silbenstruktur nur bei Wortrhythmus, (t) Tilgung anakrustischer Silben und Aphaerese mit resultierenden Anlautkonsonantenverbindungen nur bei Wortrhythmus, (u) Geminaten nur bei Silbenrhythmus, (v) Stimmhaftigkeitsopposition bei Plosiven nur bei Silbenrhythmus, (w) Assimilationen/Dissimilationen, Aspiration und Stimmhaftigkeitsverlust in Konsonantenverbindungen nur bei Wortrhythmus.

Da die Typologie von Donegan & Stampe nicht im Detail ausgearbeitet ist und die meisten der unterstellten Merkmale der beiden Typen nur ansatzweise diskutiert werden, lässt sich eine abschließende Bewertung nicht ohne umfangreiche empirische Überprüfungen geben. Es ist aber recht wahrscheinlich, dass dieser Vorschlag zu stark von den spezifischen Struktureigenschaften der genannten südostasiatischen Sprachgruppen (bzw. deren v. a. untersuchten Vertretern, nämlich den Einzelsprachen Sora und Khmer) geprägt ist, als dass er sich generalisieren ließe (vgl. Auer 1993: 15 ff.).

5. Einige phonologische Eigenschaften von Wort- und Silbensprachen

In diesem Abschnitt werden einige aussichtsreiche Kandidaten für die phonologischen Eigenschaften von Wort- und Silbensprachen aufgeführt und ihr Bezug auf den Grundparameter – phonologisches Wort vs. Silbe als zentrale prosodische Kategorie – hergestellt. Die Diskussion eines möglichen Zusammenhangs zu nicht-phonologischen Eigenschaften der Sprachen unterbleibt aus Platzgründen. Sie müsste unter anderem den Zusammenhang zwischen Silbengliederung und morphologischer Struktur explizieren, der in einer Silbensprache isomorph sein sollte (d. h. z. B., dass Affixe immer mindestens Silbenstatus haben), während dies in Wortsprachen, die die Silbe weniger vor Veränderungen durch morphologische Prozesse schützen, nicht der Fall ist; von dort wäre der Zusammenhang zwischen Wort- und Silbensprachen einerseits, und der traditionellen typologischen Unterscheidung zwischen agglutinierenden und flektierenden Sprachen andererseits zu diskutieren; (→ Art. 49).

– *Wortakzent.* Von den (im Sinne Trubetzkoys) kulminativen und deliminativen Funktionen der Phonologie, die naturgemäß bei einer an prosodischen Kategorien orientierten Typologie im Mittelpunkt des Interesses stehen, ist vielleicht die wichtigste die gipfelbildende Hervorhebung einer und nur einer Silbe (oder More) über alle anderen innerhalb einer Einheit in der Größenordnung des phonologischen Wortes. Diese Funktion ist typisch für Wortsprachen; sie kann sowohl durch dynamischen wie durch musikalischen Akzent erfüllt werden. (Sowohl in einem wie auch im anderen Fall kann die gipfelbildende Hervorhebung, sei es durch die Lage im Wort, sei es durch das realisierte Tonmuster, zugleich zur kulminativen auch distinktive Funktion haben, also lexikalisch oder grammatisch ausgenützt werden.) Im besten Fall einer Wortsprache (Prototyp) haben alle phonologischen Wörter einen und nur einen phonetisch deutlich realisierten und durch einfache und eindeutige Regeln zu bestimmenden Akzent. Im entgegengesetzten Fall einer reinen Silbensprache (Prototyp) wird die Akzentuierung nicht auf der Ebene des phonologischen Wortes, sondern der der phonologischen Phrase („cursus" im Sinne Pulgrams) phonetisch geregelt (meist in Form eines konstanten initialen oder finalen Phrasenakzents); das Gewicht der Einzelsilben in der Phrase kann zudem durch ein phonetisches Alternanzprinzip bestimmt sein, sie hängt aber nicht von Information aus der Wortebene ab. (Von den indoeuropäischen Sprachen in Europa, die meist recht eindeutige Wortakzentsprachen sind, scheint lediglich das Französische keinen Wortakzent zu haben (vgl. Wenk & Wioland 1982)). Außerhalb des (indo)europäischen Sprachraums sind Sprachen ohne Wortakzent jedoch durchaus häufig; vgl. z. B. Eskimo, Fiji, Vietnamesisch, Yoruba, Mundari u. a. Es ist zu berücksichtigen, dass zwischen den beiden Prototypen zahlreiche Zwischenformen möglich sind, etwa Sprachen, die nicht allen Wörtern Akzent zuweisen (Japanisch, mit musikalischem Akzent).

— *rhythmische Adaptionsprozesse ('beat retraction, iambic reversal'*, etc.). Die Rolle des Akzents in einer Sprache ist eng verbunden mit dem Aufbau rhythmischer Strukturen auf der Wortebene. Dabei gelten — vermutlich universale — Euphonieprinzipien, die die Alternanz zwischen hervorgehobenen und nicht hervorgehobenen "Prosodemen" (im Sinne Trubetzkoys) regeln und auf die optimale rhythmische Struktur einer regelmäßigen Alternanz hinarbeiten. Dazu gehören u. a. Akzentverlagerungsregeln wie die bekannte *iambic reversal*-Regeln etwa im Englischen oder (bedingt) im Deutschen (vgl. *ein 'himmelblaues 'Ehebett* vs. *das 'Ehebett ist himmel'blau*), die Zusammenstöße von rhythmischen Schlägen (*beat clashes*) — wie in *himmel'blaues 'Ehebett* — vermeiden helfen. Nespor & Vogel (1989) vermuten, dass solche rhythmisch bedingten Prozesse in Silbensprachen wie dem Italienischen auf einer niedrigeren Ebene operieren (also schon bei Akzentzusammenstößen auf der Silbenebene wirksam werden und dort z. B. Prozesse wie das *raddoppiamento sintattico* auslösen), während sie in Wortsprachen (in ihrem Beispiel Neugriechisch, aber auch Englisch oder Deutsch wären einschlägig) auf einer höheren Ebene (der des Fußes) operieren. (So kann im genannten Beispiel auch die intervenierende Schwa-Silbe — *'blaues 'ehe-* — den *beat clash* nicht aufhalten.)

— *Silbenstruktur*. Die Silbenstrukturregeln (vgl. dazu Art. 94) einer typischen Silbensprache lassen sich ohne Rekurs auf die Position der Silbe im Wort formulieren; sie gelten für alle Silben gleichermaßen. Hingegen sind die Silbenstrukturregeln einer typischen Wortsprache von der Stellung der Silbe im Wort abhängig. Insbesondere unterscheiden sich Akzentsilben von nicht-akzentuierten Silben und Silben, deren Rand mit dem Wortrand zusammenfällt, von solchen im Wortinneren: sowohl Wortrandsilben als auch Akzentsilben weisen komplexere Ränder auf als die sonstigen Silben. Wortsprachen weichen aus diesem Grund mehr als Silbensprachen von der Teleologie der optimalen Silbe (vgl. Vennemann 1988) ab (Auer 1994), denn in ihnen wird diese Tendenz zur CV-Silbe von Präferenzregeln für optimale Wörter überlagert. Sprache mit positionsunabhängigen Silbenstrukturen haben hingegen insgesamt eine geringere Silbenkomplexität und kommen dem Ideal des *maximal onset* (Maximierung des Silbenanstiegs) besonders nah. Statistische Untersuchungen zu sog. silbenzählenden Sprachen (Französisch, Spanisch, Italienisch) belegen diese Tendenz (vgl. Dauer 1983: 56; Brakel 1985).

— *Vokalismus im Haupt- und Nebenakzent*. Wenn eine Wortsprache einen gipfelbildenden Akzent hat, tendiert sie typischerweise dazu, nicht-akzentuierte Silben zu reduzieren. Diese Reduzierung kann phonemisch sein; dies bedeutet, daß sich das Vokalsystem im Haupt- und Nebenakzent unterscheidet, und zwar zu Lasten der Komplexität des letzteren (vgl. etwa Bolinger 1981 für das Amerikanische Englisch). U. a. entfallen im Nebenakzent von typischen Wortsprachen die in der Akzentposition gegebenenfalls relevanten Oppositionen zwischen langen und kurzen Vokalen. (So lässt etwa die Hokan-Sprache Diegueño in nicht-akzentuierter Position keine Langvokale und in den nicht-akzentuierten Silben nach dem Wortakzent zusätzlich keine Diphthonge zu; Langdon 1970.) Andererseits kann die Differenz zwischen Haupt- und Nebentonvokalismus auch phonetisch sein (bzw. interpretiert werden). In diesem Sinn bedeutet Reduktion nicht unbedingt den Verlust phonemischer Oppositionen, sondern lediglich eine deutliche Zentralisierung und teils auch Entstimmhaftung der Nebentonvokale (vgl. Delattre 1969: 308; Brakel 1985 zur Entspannung von Nebentonvokalen in einigen europäischen Sprachen; diese Entspannung geht auch immer mit Zentralisierung einher).

— *Vokaltilgungen und epenthetische Vokale/ Konsonanten*. Vokaltilgungen kommen sowohl in Wort- wie auch Silbensprachen vor, jedoch ist ihr Charakter völlig unterschiedlich. In Wortsprachen sind sie die Extremform der Reduktion von Nebentonsilben; als Konsequenzen entstehen komplexe Konsonantenverbindungen am Wortrand, die entweder die Komplexität der Akzentsilbe oder die der Wortrandsilben erhöhen. (Ein typisches diachrones Beispiel ist die Abschwächung der Nebentonsilben im Deutschen; vgl. etwa germ. **harbista-* > ahd. *her&bis&to* > mhd. *her&best* > nhd. *herbst*.) Hingegen dienen Vokalelisionen in Silbensprachen meist dazu, die optimale CV-Silbenstruktur auch über morphologische und syntaktische Operationen hinweg zu bewahren und so gerade komplexe Konsonanten- oder Vokalverbindungen zu vermeiden. (Solche „Tilgungen" sind oft morphonologisch geregelt. Man vergleiche etwa die typischen Alternanten des

Italienischen beim Artikel: *uno anno > un' anno* 'ein Jahr'; *la altra > l'altra* 'die andere' zur Vermeidung von Vokalsequenzen, oder lat. *ille > lo specchio* 'der Spiegel' statt sonst *il* zur Vermeidung von Konsonantenclustern.)

Vokalepenthesen/-epithesen treten in Silbensprachen auf, um komplexe Silbenränder zu vermeiden (vgl. türkisch *bur&n + u* 'Nase' (POSS.) aber *bu&run* (NOM.) − und nicht etwa einsilbig mit komplexem Rand *burn.) Besonders typisch ist die Verbreitung der Epenthesen bei der Integration von Entlehnungen aus Wortsprachen wie Englisch oder Russisch. Zusätzlich optimieren Silbensprachen ihre Silbenstruktur auch durch die Epenthese von Konsonanten in Vokalsequenzen (vgl. etwa türkisch *ev + i* 'das Haus' (AKK.), aber *baba + i > babayı* 'den Vater (AKK.)'.) Damit werden die einzelnen Silben geschützt und eine Verschmelzung des anstiegslosen Vokals mit dem Vokal der offenen vorausgehenden Silbe vermieden; es kommt zu keiner Diphthongierung.

− *wortbezogene phonologische Prozesse.* Damit sind phonologische Prozesse gemeint, die nur in einer bestimmten Position im phonologischen Wort (initial, medial oder final) auftreten und die nicht akzentabhängig sind. Initial und final haben diese Prozesse demarkative Funktion. Es kann sich dabei phonologisch gesehen um Neutralisierungen handeln (wie etwa bei der wortfinalen Auslautverhärtung im Usbekischen, Türkischen oder Russischen). Oft sind die wortfinalen und medialen Prozesse aber einfach phonetische Schwächungen (etwa: nicht-explodierende Plosive/ *unreleased stops* am Wortende in der Papua-Sprache Asmat; Voorhoeve 1980; mediale Schwächung der Plosive in fast allen deutschen Dialekten; Auer 1998). Wortinitial sind Aspiration und Insertion eines Glottalverschlusses vor Vokal verbreitete deliminative Techniken; wesentlich seltener, aber ebenfalls deliminativ zusätzlich zu ihrer grammatischen Funktion, sind die bekannten keltischen Anlautmutationen.

− *silbenbezogene phonologische Prozesse.* Ein typisches Beispiel sind *liaison* und *enchaînement* im Französischen, also Resilbifizierung über morphologische und syntaktische Grenzen hinweg. Ebenfalls typisch sind Prozesse, die regelmäßig Phoneme im Silbenanstieg oder -abfall erfassen; vgl. etwa die zahlreichen Schwächungsprozesse in der koreanischen Silben-Coda, wie der silbeninitial distinktiven Lenes, Fortes und aspirierten Plosive ebenso wie der Affrikaten und des /h/, die silbenauslautend zu einer einzigen Serie nicht-explodierender Lenisverschlüsse neutralisiert werden (Kim-Renaud 1978).

Ein besonderer Fall eines silbenbezogenen Prozesses, der schon die Grenze der Phonologie zur Morphologie überschreitet, ist die Reduplikation (mit nicht nur expressiver Funktion), wie sie in zahlreichen Sprachen (etwa: Mandarin, Hausa, Yoruba, Vietnamesisch) anzutreffen ist. Sie beruht in der Regel auf der erkennbaren Wiederholung einer Silbe und ist daher auf eine relativ ähnliche Struktur der Silben im Wort angewiesen, wie sie nur in einer Silbensprache zu erreichen ist.

− *Assimilationen.* Kontaktassimilationen von Konsonanten innerhalb des Wortes sind natürlich nur dann in einer Sprache von Bedeutung, wenn dort Konsonantenverbindungen zugelassen sind. Während dies in einer optimalen CV-Sprache grundsätzlich vermieden wird, steigt die Frequenz von zwischenkonsonantischen Assimilationen evidenterweise mit den in Wortsprachen typischen Konsonantenverbindungen am Silben- bzw. Wortrand an: sie sind somit ein sekundäres (indirektes) Merkmal von Wortsprachen. Vollständige Assimilationen in tautosilbischen Verbindungen führen allerdings zu einer Vereinfachung der Silbenstruktur und damit vom Prototyp der Wortsprache weg. Vollständige Assimilationen über Silbengrenzen führen hingegen oft zur Entstehung von Geminaten, die die Silbenstruktur unverändert lassen und daher für Silbensprachen typisch sind.

− *Geminaten/Ambisilbizität.* Als Folge der klar artikulierten Silbenstruktur sind in Silbensprachen keine ambisilbischen Elemente zu erwarten; ihnen entsprechen dort oft Geminaten (vgl. den entsprechenden Übergang Ahd. zu Mhd.).

− *Ton.* Tonhöhenverlaufsoppositionen auf Silben oder Moren können kulminative Funktion haben und dann ein Merkmal von Wortsprachen sein (vgl. oben, „musikalischer Akzent"). In einer echten Tonsprache ist die Tonhöhenverlaufsopposition jedoch nicht gipfelbildend, weil sie auf mehreren oder allen „Prosodemen" im Wort auftreten kann. Echte Tonsprachen sind also Silbensprachen. Dies korreliert mit der Tatsache, dass tontragende Silben i. d. R. nicht reduziert werden können. (Kommen in einer Sprache − wie etwa dem Mandarin − auch reduzierte Silben vor, so sind sie zugleich nicht tontragend.)

− *Vokalharmonie.* Dieses morphonologische Verfahren ist schwer einzuordnen, weil es sowohl Beziehungen zu Wortsprachen wie auch zu Silbensprachen aufweist. Einerseits hat Vokalharmonie deutlich deliminative Funktion; auch ist das Vokalsystem der harmonierenden Silben strukturell reduziert. Andererseits setzt die Kopie bestimmter Vokalmerkmale voraus, dass in allen Silben des Wortes Vokale phonetisch gesehen annähernd gleich realisiert werden können. Dies lässt Vokalharmonie eher als Eigenschaft von Silbensprachen erscheinen.

6. Gesamteinschätzung

Die genauere Untersuchung der typologischen Hypothese Silben- vs. Wortsprachen steht noch aus; sie erfordert neben der eingehenden Untersuchung von Einzelsprachen in ihrer gesamten Erscheinungsbreite (nicht nur der kodifizierten Standardsprache) und unter Einschluß rhythmisch bedingter phonologischer Prozesse auch die empirische Überprüfung der oben skizzierten Korrelationen zwischen einzelnen Merkmalen von Einzelphonologien. In Auer (1993) werden in einem Pilot-Sample 34 genetisch und areal verschiedenen Sprachen miteinander verglichen und einige Korrelationen — teils allerdings nur in schwacher, quantitativer Form — bestätigt. (So zum Beispiel die negativen Korrelationen zwischen Ton und Silbenkomplexität, Wortakzent, Vokalreduktion im Nebenakzent und wortbezogenen Prozessen, oder die positiven zwischen Silbenkomplexität bzw. wortbezogenen Prozessen und Vokalreduktion im Nebenakzent, zwischen Silbenkomplexität und wortbezogenen Prozessen oder zwischen fehlendem Wortakzent und einfacher Silbenstruktur.) Notwendig sind jedoch weitaus größere Stichproben.

Ingesamt zeichnet sich ab, dass die Unterscheidung zwischen silben- und akzentzählenden Sprachen vermutlich nur in einer multifaktoriellen Form empirisch überlebensfähig ist; genau in dieser Form wird sie jedoch auch für die Sprachtypologie relevant. Im Vergleich zu früheren Formulierungen der Hypothese etwa bei Abercombie wird man außerdem nicht mehr davon ausgehen können, daß Sprachen entweder dem einen oder dem anderen Typ angehören; vielmehr sind vielerlei Zwischenstufen möglich. Schließlich dürfte sich die überragende Bedeutung, die in der Isochroniehypothese dem Wortakzent zukommt, durch die weitere Forschung deutlich relativieren; seine zentrale Stellung könnte ein Konstrukt europäischen (oder sogar eurozentrischen) linguistischen Denkens sein, dass sich innerhalb vor allem in einigen europäischen Sprachen (allen voran dem Englischen) bestätigt.

7. Zitierte Literatur

Abercrombie, David. 1967. *Elements of general phonetics*. Edinburg: University Press.

Auer, Peter. 1993. *Is a rhythm-based typology possible? A study on the role of prosody in phonological typology.* = KontRI Arbeitspapier Nr. 21, Universität Konstanz, Fachgruppe Sprchwissenschaft.

Auer, Peter. 1994. „Einige Argumente gegen die Silbe als universale phonologische Hauptkategorie." In Ramers, Karl-Heinz & Heinz Vater & Henning Wode (Hrsg.), *Universale phonologische Strukturen und Prozesse*. Tübingen: Niemeyer, S. 55—78.

Auer, Peter. 1998. „Variabilität der intervokalischen Position in deutschen Trochäen". In Butt, Matthias & Fuhrhop, Nanna (eds.) *Wortphonologie des Deutschen*. (Sonderheft „Germanistik" Heft 141—142). S. 304—333.

Auer, Peter & Couper-Kuhlen, Elizabeth & Müller, Frank. 1998. *Language in time. The rhythm and tempo of verbal interaction*. New York: Oxford University Press.

Auer, Peter & Uhmann, Susanne. 1988. „Silben- und akzentzählende Sprachen". *Zeitschrift für Sprachwissenschaft* 7, 2: 214—259.

Bailey, Charles-James. 1980. „Evidence for variable syllabic boundaries in English". In: Waugh, Linda R. & van Schooneveld, Cornelis H. (eds.) *The melody of language*. Baltimore: University Park Press, 25—39.

Bertinetto, Pier Marco. 1989. „Reflections on the dichotomy 'stress' — vs. 'syllable-timing' ". *Revue de phonétique appliquée* 91—93: 99—130.

Bolinger, Dwight L. 1981. *Two kinds of vowels, two kinds of rhythm*. Bloomington: Indiana University Linguistics Club.

Brakel, Arthur. 1985. „Towards a morphological approach to the study of linguistic rhythm. *Chicago Linguistic Society* 21, 1: 15—25.

Couper-Kuhlen, Elizabeth. 1993. *English speech rhythm*. Amsterdam: Benjamins.

Darwin, C. J. & Donovan, A. 1980. „Perceptual studies of speech rhythm: isochrony and intonation". In: Simon, J. C. (ed.). *Proceedings of the NATO-ASI on spoken language generation and understanding*. Dordrecht: Foris, 77—95.

Dauer, R. M. 1983. „Stress-timing and syllable-timing reanalysed". *Journal of Phonetics* 11: 51—62.

Delattre, Pierre. 1969. „An accoustic and articulatory study of vowel reduction in four languages". *International Review of Applied Linguistics*: 295—325.

den Os, Els. 1983. „Stress-timed and syllable-timed languages". *Progress Report* 8, Institute of Phonetics, University of Utrecht, 12−23.

den Os, Els. 1988. *Rhythm and tempo of Dutch and Italian.* Promotionsschrift, Univ. Utrecht.

Donegan, Patricia J. & Stampe, David. 1983. „Rhythm and the holistic organization of language structure". *Papers from the Parasession on the Interplay of Phonology, Morphology and Syntax, Chicago Linguistics Society,* 337−53.

Donovan, A. & Darwin, C. J. 1979. "The perceived rhythm of speech". *Proceedings of the Ninth International Congress of the Phonetic Sciences.* Vol. II, Copenhagen, 268−274.

Farnetani, Edda & Kori, Shiro. 1990. „Rhythmic structure in Italian noun phrases: A study on vowel durations". *Phonetica* 47: 50−65.

Fletcher, Janet. 1987. „Some micro-effects of tempo changes on timing in French". *Proceedings of the 11th International Congress of the Phonetic Sciences,* Vol. 3, Tallinn: Academy of Sciences of the Estonian S. S. R., Institute of Language and Literature, 129−133.

Fowler, Carol A. 1981. „A relationship between coarticulation and compensatory shortening". *Phonetica* 38: 35−50.

Fowler, Carol A. 1983. „Converging sources of evidence on spoken and perceived rhythms and speech: cyclic production of vowels in monosyllabic stress feet". *Journal of Experimental Psychology, General,* 112: 386−412.

Hoequist, Charles Jr. 1983. „Syllable duration in stress-, syllable- and mora-timed languages". *Phonetica* 40: 203−237.

Holm, Catherine. 1990. „Le cadre des changements phonétiques dans les languages romanes. Mot et 'syntagme phonétique' ". In: Andersen, Henning & Koerner, Konrad (eds.). *Historical Linguistics 1987.* Amsterdam: Benjamins, 231−243.

Jakobson, Roman. 1931. „Die Betonung und ihre Rolle in der Wort- und Syntagmaphonologie". *Travaux du cercle linguistique de Prague* IV (wieder in: *Selected Writings* Band I, The Hague: Mouton. S. 117−136.)

Kim-Renaud, Young-Key. 1978. „The syllable in Korean phonology". In: Chin-Woo, Kim (ed.). *Papers in Korean Linguistics.* Columbia, S. C.: Hornbeam Press, 85−98.

Kohler, Klaus J. 1983. Stress-timing and speech rate in German. In: *Arbeitsberichte des Instituts für Phonetik der Universität Kiel* (AIPUK), Nr. 20. 55−97.

Langdon, Margaret. 1970. *A Grammar of Diegueño. The Mesa Grande Dialect.* Berkeley, etc.: University of California Press.

Lehiste, Ilse. 1977. „Isochrony reconsidered". *Journal of Phonetics* 5: 253−63.

Lindblom, Björn & Rapp, Karin. 1973. *Some temporal regularities of spoken Swedish* = *Papers from the Institute of Linguistics, University of Stockholm,* No. 21.

Marotta, Giovanni. 1985. *Modelli e misure ritmiche: la durata vocalica in italiano.* Bologna: Zanichelli.

Nagano-Madsen, Yasuko. 1992. *Mora and prosodic coordination. A phonetic study of Japanese, Eskimo and Yoruba.* Lund: University Press.

Nespor, Marina & Vogel, Irene. 1979. „Clash avoidance in Italian". *Linguistic Inquiry* 14: 19−100.

Nespor, Marina & Vogel, Irene. 1986. *Prosodic phonology.* Dordrecht: Foris.

Nespor, Marina & Vogel, Irene. 1989. „On clashes and lapses". *Phonology* 6: 69−116.

Pike, Kenneth. 1945. *The intonation of American English.* Ann Arbor: University of Michigan Press.

Pompino-Marschall, Bernd. 1990. *Die Silbenprosodie. Ein elementarer Aspekt der Wahrnehmung von Sprachrhythmus und Sprechtempo.* Tübingen: Niemeyer.

Pulgram, Ernst. 1970. *Syllable, word, nexus, cursus.* The Hague: Mouton.

Roach, Peter. 1982. „On the distinction between stress-timed and syllable-timed languages". In: Crystal, David (ed.). *Linguistic controversies.* London: E. Arnold, 73−79.

Trubetzkoy, Nikolaus. 1939 (3. Aufl. 1952). *Grundzüge der Phonologie.* Göttingen: Vandenhoeck und Ruprecht.

Vennemann, Theo. 1988. *Preference laws for syllable structure.* Berlin: Mouton de Gruyter.

Voorhoeve, Clemens L. 1980. *The Asmat languages of Irian Jaya.* Canberra: Australian National University.

Wenk, B. & Wioland, François. 1982. „Is French really syllable-timed?" *Journal of Phonetics* 10: 193−216.

Peter Auer, Freiburg i. Br. (Deutschland)

100. Finite vs. non finite languages

1. Introduction
2. Finiteness as a scalar phenomenon
3. The concept of obligatoriness and the creation of the finite/non finite distinction
4. Finite vs. non finite in Formal linguistics
5. Conclusion
6. References

1. Introduction

The finite vs. non finite distinction goes back to the Greek and Latin tradition which is based on verb morphology. From the description of the Classical languages this distinction was transferred to traditional grammatical descriptions of other languages. According to this tradition, there are finite verbal forms which are 'limited' (from the Latin past participle of the perfect *finitus* 'limited') e. g. by person, number, and tense and non finite verbal forms such as infinitives and participles which do not have these limiting features. From the point of view of language typology, such a definition is too language-specific to provide a particularly useful basis for cross-linguistic comparison.

In modern linguistics there is a general agreement in functionalism as well as in formalism that the opposition of finite vs. non finite is a property of the clause. Moreover, finiteness belongs to the grammar of interclausal connectivity. In the context of functional grammar, finiteness has been described from the point of view of scalarity and from the point of view of obligatoriness. The scalar approach will be described in § 2. The concept of obligatoriness will be presented in § 3. The obligatoriness of some particular operators forms the basis for finite/non finite asymmetries which can be used for establishing different types of finiteness. It is thus in § 3. where the distinction between finite and non finite languages and their areal distribution in Eurasia will be discussed.

In his article on complementation, Noonan (1985: 57) defines infinitives as "verb-like entities that do not bear syntactic relations to their notional subjects; i. e. their subjects do not take nominative case marking or condition verb agreement (where otherwise appropriate for subjects), nor are they marked in the associative (genitive) case. The notional subjects of infinitives are typically equi-deleted ..., raised ..., or made objects of adpositions". Noonan's definition more or less covers in functional terms what Principles & Parameters treats as non-finiteness with more formal rigour. The crucial criterion for the finite/non finite distinction in Principles & Parameters is the existence of Tense or AGR as part of IP. The formal treatment of finiteness will be discussed in § 4. A short conclusion in § 5. will be presented at the end of this article. This conclusion briefly discusses the hypothesis that obligatority may be the crucial factor for the emergence of a finite/non finite distinction in general.

2. Finiteness as a scalar phenomenon

The most detailed study on finiteness as a scalar phenomenon seems to be the one presented by Givón (1990: 852−891). He points out the following four characteristics of the finite/non finite distinction (Givón 1990: 853):

- "*Clausal domain*: Finiteness is a property of the *clause* (rather than of the verb).
- *Complexity and scalarity*: Finiteness is a complex, multifeatured, *scalar* grammatical metaphenomenon (rather than a single, discrete, binary feature).
- *Coding function*: Finiteness is the systematic grammatical means used to express the degree of integration of a clause into its immediate clausal environment. The *syntactic dependence* of the clause − i. e. its finiteness − is thus used to code *thematic dependence* of an event/state on its discourse context.
- *Scope of dependency*: While some clause-dependencies (such as V-complements, sentential subjects or REL-clauses) may be expressed in terms of purely *syntactic* relations, clausal dependency − like event integration − is ultimately a matter of *discourse coherence*. Syntactic dependencies are but a restricted subset of discourse-pragmatic dependency."

Givón (1990: 853) presents the following "main syntactic features" which determine the degree of finiteness of a given clause in comparison to a "prototype transitive main clause":

- Tense-aspect-modality (TAM)
- Pronominal ('grammatical') agreement
- Nominalizing affixes
- Case marking of the subject and object
- Articles, determiners

Each of these features and its impact on finiteness will be discussed below. I shall also present some implicational-hierarchic scales to show how these features are correlated. TAM and pronominal agreement are treated as inflectional categories by Givón (1990). We shall see below that TAM also can create a finite/non finite distinction if it is not expressed by inflection (cf. example (4) from Supyire). Finally, I would like to add a sixth feature dealing with pragmatics, i. e. topic.

In the context of verbal inflection and TAM, Givón (1990: 854) presents two scales:

(1) *Scale of finiteness of tense-aspect-modality*:
more finite > less finite
terminated > non-terminated
realis > irrealis
punctual > durative
in-sequence > anterior

(2) *Finiteness ranking of tense-aspect-modality*:
most finite: Tense
Modality
Aspect
least finite: Negation

An example for (1) is the subjunctive (cf. below) which in most cases denotes some modality of irrealis or intention. Subjunctives predominantly cannot be uttered independently.

An example for (2) is the use of the conjunctive in Classical Greek. In this form, which is used overwhelmingly in dependent clauses, tense distinction is lost whereas aspectual distinction between present and aorist is preserved.

Noonan (1985: 57) presents another inflection-based scale which is not limited to TAM and does not mention negation. He suggests the following four degrees.

(3) 1. full range of tenses
2. past vs. non-past
3. aspect
4. voice, transitivity, causative, desiderative, object agreement

The further to the bottom "an item is on this scale, the less likely it is to be coded on a non-indicative complement" (Noonan 1985: 57), where "indicative" means "the form that most closely resembles declarative main clauses" (Noonan 1985: 51).

As is well-known, categories of tense-aspect are not necessarily expressed inflectionally. Nevertheless, they can be employed for marking different degrees of finiteness. This is shown by examples from various African languages collected by Carlson (1992). In Supyire (Senufo), the narrative/subjunctive auxiliary *sí* can be combined only with the auxiliary encoding imperfective aspect, whereas the other auxiliaries "exhibit a greater freedom of co-occurrence with each other" (Carlson 1992: 80). A similar situation seems to exist in Bambara, where the auxiliary *ka* which is used in many non finite contexts cannot co-occur with any auxiliary marking tense-aspect (Carlson 1992: 80). The following example of a purpose clause is from Supyire. The same auxiliary *sí* is also used with conditionals and sequentials (sequence of events in the order of their temporal development).

(4) *Pi na wyīge tùrù sí*
they PROG hole.DEF dig.IPV SUBJ
lvɔhɔ ta.
water get
'They are digging the hole in order to get water.' (Carlson 1992: 61)

Apart from the reduction of tense-aspect marking in non finite contexts, differences in agreement marking are the second inflectional criterion for distinguishing finite and non finite clauses. Thus, a reduction of the finite agreement pattern can often be observed in less finite clauses.

For languages in which agreement is linked to nominative case, Givón (1990: 857) presents the following prediction: "if no subject agreement exists, an overt subject in a less-finite clause is not marked as nominative".

Nominalization is particularly interesting, because it is itself a scalar phenomenon. In Lehmann (1988) it is situated within the continuum of desentientialization from clause to noun. This continuum is part of the overall continuum from elaboration to compression which determines the degree of interrelatedness between two clauses. The most basic distinction is the one between lexical nominalizations and fully productive processes of nominalization. In English we find lexical nominalizations such as *arrival* in *Her early arrival was a surprise* (Givón 1990: 507) or more productive forms such as *for to* nominalizations, *to* infinitives and the *-ing* form (the examples are from Givón 1990, 507):

(5) *For him to arrive early would be a mistake.*

(6) *To arrive early would be a mistake.*

(7) *Arriving early was not what she had in mind.*

In English only lexical nominalizations can co-occur with a large range of determiners (cf. (8) below from Givón 1990, 507). This does not only demonstrate that English lexical nominalizations show the highest degree of nounhood, it is also an indicator of their low degree of finiteness.

(8) a. *The arrival of the Argonauts was unexpected.*
    b. *This early arrival of his is unexpected.*
    c. *Early arrival of most guests is anticipated.*

In languages such as English or Georgian (cf. (9), for details cf. Hewitt 1987, 15—7; Vamling 1989, 35 f., 100 ff.) participants of nominalized clauses change case marking.

(9)   burt-is   da-gor-eb-a   bavšv-is   mier
      ball-GEN   roll.NML   child-GEN by
      'the rolling of the ball by the child'
      (Vamling 1989: 101)

In other languages such as Mongolian, verbal nouns can occur in relative constructions, in embedding, in adverbial clauses if followed by a case marker and in finite clauses. In the following example from Classical Mongolian (Poppe 1974: 178) we find the verbal noun of the future in an adverbial function with case marking of the participants being identical to case marking in a matrix clause:

(10) manu   nökör   ire-kü-dür   bida
      our   friend   come-VN.FUT-LOC   we
      bügüde mašida   bayas-ba.
      all   very   glad-PST
      'When our friend came, all of us were very glad.'

Differences in the case marking of subject and object between a prototypically finite clause and a less finite clause are well attested. If the above example (9) from Georgian is transformed into a matrix clause the subject is in the nominative (with present tense-forms), ergative (with aorist tense-forms) or in the accusative (with perfect-tense forms) whereas the object would be in the accusative (with present tense-forms), the absolutive (with aorist tense-forms) or in the nominative (with perfect-tense forms). Similarly, Mongolian subjects can occur in the nominative, the genitive and the accusative in the context of verbal nouns. In finite clauses, they can only occur in the nominative. The other participants, however, do not deviate in case marking from finite clauses.

The role of articles and determiners is already discussed above in the context of nominalization. Highly nominalized verbs can co-occur with determiners. This is at the same time an indicator of their low degree of finiteness.

As pointed out above, the occurrence of topic markers is a further indicator of finiteness which is not mentioned by Givón. This can be illustrated by the Japanese topic marker *wa*, whose use is limited to the matrix clause:

(11) a. *Hanako ga shin-da koto o*
        Hanako SBJ die-PST thing ACC
        shira-nakat-ta.
        know-NEG-PST
        'X did not know that Hanako died.'
     b. *Hanako wa shin-da koto o*
        Hanako TOP die-PST thing ACC
        shira-nakat-ta.
        know-NEG-PST
        'Hanako did not know that X died'
        (Shibatani 1990: 272)

In (11 a), Hanako is marked by the subject marker *ga*. For that reason, it belongs to the verb of the dependent clause with the verb *shinda* 'died'. In (11 b) Hanako is marked as topic. Therefore, it must belong to the matrix clause whose verb is *shiranakatta* 'didn't know'. Since only fully finite clauses which can occur independently are supposed to be marked for pragmatic features, it comes as no surprise if dependent clauses cannot be marked for such features as e. g. topic.

With regard to major verb-form categories, Givón (1990: 854) presents the following hierarchical scale (on this scale also cf. Palmer 1986, 162).

(12) most finite: Indicative
                      Subjunctive/Modal
                      Participial
                      Infinitive
      least finite: Nominal

Subjunctives tend to use the same case marking as in finite clauses and they tend to show verb agreement in languages in which the matrix verb also shows agreement. For reasons such as these subjunctives are treated as finite in traditional grammar. Nevertheless, the pattern of tense-aspect marking in subjunctives is considerably reduced in comparison to the pattern of indicatives. Thus Bemba (Bantu) shows a distinction of twenty-four tense-aspect categories in the indicative and only five tense-aspect categories in its two types of subjunctives (Givón 1990: 855; Givón 1972). In most languages, subjunctives occur mainly in dependent clauses although they can occur marginally in matrix clauses such as Greek *iōmen* / Latin *eamus* 'let's go!' or in (13 b) from French:

(13) a. *Dieu vous bénit* (INDIC).
    'God blesses you.'
  b. *Dieu vous bénisse* (SUBJ).
    'May God bless you!'

As in the above example (13), most subjunctives have modal meaning. Thus we often find more specific terms such as optative, irrealis, potential, etc. in grammars of individual languages. The Georgian optative is used to express wishes and orders, mostly after matrix verbs belonging to this semantic field (14). In some rare instances, we even find the Georgian optative in a matrix clause (15):

(14) *Is cdilob-s, rom gaaķetes*
    3s try-PRS.3s that do.OPT.3s
    qvelaper-i ķarg-ad.
    everything good-ADV
    'He tries to do everything well.'
    (Tschenkéli 1958: 176)

(15) *Mţer-i moķvdes.*
    enemy-ABS die.OPT.3s
    'May the enemy die!' (Vogt 1971: 196)

In Written Arabic the conjunctive is obligatory after some conjunctions such as *li-* 'in order to', *kay* or *likay* 'in order to'. With some other conjunctions such as the complementizer *'an* 'that' and *ḥattā* 'until' it occurs if an intention or a potential consequence is implied, otherwise we find the perfect or the imperfect (Fischer 1972: 97). In the following example with an adverbial clause introduced by the purpose marker *kay* the conjunctive is obligatory:

(16) *ya-tūq-u   qalb-ī   'ilay-kum*
    3s-long-IPF:3s heart-POSS:1s for-2p
    kay   yu-lāqiy-a-kum.
    so.that 3s-meet-CONJ-2s
    'My heart longs to meet with you.'
    (Fischer 1972: 197)

Participials can take tense-aspect distinctions and negation, but they show no pronominal agreement. Other types of agreement such as gender and number are well possible as is shown by the following example from Spanish, in which the Participle (*terminad-a*) is marked by the feminine agreement suffix *-a* because *la recreación* 'the break' is feminine.

(17) *Termina-da la recreación, se continuaron las clases.*
    'After the break has finished, classes went on.'

In many languages participles are case marked in the context of adverbial subordination. Georgian is such a language as is illustrated by the following example with the future participle in the adverbial case denoting purpose:

(18) *çavedi   ţqe-ši   datv-is*
    go.AOR.1s forest-to bear-GEN
    mosaķlav-ad.
    kill.PART.FUT-ADV
    'I went into the woods to kill a bear.'

Infinitives show still further reduction of inflectional categories. European infinitives are generally used in complement clauses and in purpose clauses. Furthermore, the infinitival subject is generally left implicit and is controlled by an argument of the main clause (Haspelmath 1989).

The role of nominals with regard to finiteness has already been discussed above. The above hierarchical scale on major verb-form categories (12) can also be analysed in the framework of nominalization which is a good indicator of finiteness. There is a decrease of nominality from participles to infinitives to nominals. Thus, scale (12) seems to be correct only if we understand "nominals" in the sense of "lexicalized nominalizations".

Another indicator of finiteness apart from nominalization is thematic coherence or thematic continuity. Givón (1990: 875) presents the following predictions:

(19) a. "Clauses that involve higher *referential continuity* tend to receive *less-finite* marking".
  b. "Clauses that involve higher *sequential action continuity* tend to receive *less finite* marking".
  c. "Clauses that involve higher *tense-aspect-modal continuity* tend to receive *less finite* marking".

To conclude this section, I would like to present Hengeveld's (1998) study on the correlation between semantic types of adverbial clauses and their degree of dependence. In this study, the expression format to be compared with semantic types is the form the verb takes in subordinate vs. main clause constructions. In order to avoid any formal classification — which entails the problem of defining "finiteness" cross-linguistically — Hengeveld takes the functional perspective in which "verb forms are classified in terms of the syntactic functions they may fulfil within a language". Thus, Hengeveld uses the terms "independent" if a "verb form is one which may be used in main clauses" and "dependent" if a "verb form is one which is used in subordinate constructions only" (Hengeveld 1998: 339).

Hengeveld's analysis is based on a sample of 45 European languages for which he presents four hierarchies. The first parameter deals with entity types. According to Lyons (1977: 442–447) and Dik (1989: 1997) linguistic units may refer to entities of five different types. To the zero order belong properties or relations. First order entities are individuals. They are evaluated in terms of existence. This order is of no relevance within the context of adverbial subordination, since it is limited to noun phrases. Second order entities denote states of affairs and can be evaluated in terms of their reality. Third order entities refer to propositional contents which can be evaluated in terms of truth. Finally, speech acts are fourth order entities. They can be evaluated in terms of informativeness.

The four entity types showing up in the form of adverbial clauses are linked to the following semantic relations:

– *Zero order:*
  Means
– *Second order:*
  Cause, simultaneity, addition, anteriority, potential circumstance, purpose, unreal circumstance, negative circumstance
– *Third order:*
  Reason, concession, potential condition, unreal condition
– *Fourth order:*
  Explanation

With regard to entity types, Hengeveld (1998: 359) presents the following hierarchy:

(20) *Entity Type Hierarchy*
  zero order > second order > third order > fourth order
  dependent V form > ind. V form

This hierarchy reads as follows: "If a language uses a dependent verb form for the expression of an adverbial clause designating an entity of a certain order, then it will also use a dependent form for the expression of adverbial clauses designating entities of lower orders, and vice-versa for independent verb forms" (Hengeveld 1998: 359).

The second parameter is time dependency, which applies only to second order entity types. This parameter is based on the question whether an adverbial clause depends on the matrix clause with regard to time reference or not. The third parameter is factuality, the fourth and last parameter is presupposedness. For each of these parameters, Hengeveld presents a hierarchy constraining the verbal form (dependent vs. independent) by which a certain semantic relation is expressed.

(21) *Time-Dependency Hierarchy*
  dependent time reference > independent time reference
  dependent V form > ind. V form
  (Hengeveld 1998: 377)

(22) *Factuality Hierarchy*
  factual > nonfactual
  dependent V form > ind. V form
  (Hengeveld 1998: 365)

(23) *Presupposedness Hierarchy*
  presupposed > nonpresupposed
  dependent V form > ind. V form
  (Hengeveld 1998: 353, 371)

Hengeveld's four hierarchies certainly apply to European languages which generally seem to make a morphological distinction between dependent and independent verb forms. Nevertheless, there are languages (cf. § 3. and § 4.) in which there is no such morphological distinction.

3. The concept of obligatoriness and the creation of the finite/non finite distinction

In this section I would like to develop a concept which is sufficiently independent of the idiosyncrasies of individual languages to cover all the phenomena which are otherwise treated under the heading of finite vs. non finite. This concept is more general than the finite vs. non finite distinction usually discussed in the context of European languages. Thus it may turn out to be more adequate cross-linguistically. On the other hand it is mainly based on the morphology of verbs and may need further elaborations with regard to syntax and pragmatics, although the concept of obligatority to be discussed below is certainly not limited to morphologically marked categories.

The two basic notions of my concept are obligatoriness and asymmetry (Bisang 1995: 1998 a). In East and Southeast Asian languages such as Chinese, Vietnamese and Thai no grammatical category (e. g. tense-aspect, number) has to be marked obligatorily. For that reason, these languages are characterized as indeterminate in Bisang (1992, 1998a, b). In a given pragmatic situation the utterance of a mere concept in the case of a noun or the utterance of a mere state of affairs in the case of a verb without any further indications can be informative enough. In such languages it is possible to infer "that if X is not present, not-X is meant, which creates a zero and thus an obligatory category" (Bybee 1997: 34). Further below I shall try to show that the existence or non existence of obligatory categories has important consequences for the type of clause combining a language belongs to.

Languages with no obligatory categories cannot develop any asymmetry between finite and non finite clauses, since asymmetry can be produced only by leaving out some categories in the subordinate form that are compulsory in the main clause form or by adding information to the subordinate form which is not necessary in the main clause form. Departing from the point of view of the verb form in the function of a main clause I shall call the former type of asymmetry "minus-asymmetry" and the latter type "plus-asymmetry".

In Bisang (1995, 1998a) I developed the concept of asymmetry in the context of converbs, i. e. verb forms that are specialized for combining clauses sequentially or adverbially (Haspelmath 1995 and V. Nedjalkov 1995 do not include sequentiality in their definition), but cannot form a sentence on their own, i. e. they cannot occur as main predicates of independent clauses. Converbs are characteristic for one particular type of clause combining (converb type, cf. below).

The categories which can produce asymmetry are operators in the sense of Dik's (1989, 1997) π_1 to π_4 or in the sense of Role & Reference Grammar (Van Valin 1993, Van Valin & LaPolla 1997), markers denoting reference tracking (also cf. Bickel 1991 on "Fährtenlegen"), case markers and markers specialized for expressing dependence. These categories are combined in the following way to the above two types of asymmetry:

Minus-asymmetry
— tense
— declarative marker
— person

Plus-asymmetry
— marker of subordination
— case
— person

Forms which exclusively mark clause combining such as markers of sequentiality or of adverbial subordination need a special treatment. If they are combined with the omission of a category which is obligatory in the verb form of the main clause I shall subsume them under the heading of minus-asymmetry (cf. (24) from Japanese). If they are added to a form which could otherwise also occur in the function of a main clause I shall treat them as a case of plus-asymmetry (cf. example (29) on Camling).

Minus-asymmetry with regard to tense can be illustrated by Japanese converb forms. In this language, the only forms which are clearly non finite as well as dependent in the sense that they cannot occur alone in a main clause are converb forms. They exclusively occur in subordinate functions. In turn, the only forms which are clearly finite as well as independent are honorative forms because they exclusively occur in main clause functions. The only grammatical form that must obligatorily be marked in a verb form that can be uttered independently is tense (present, past, and — more rarely — imperative and voluntative/dubitative). This category is missing in all the Japanese converb forms. In (24), the present tense of the three actions in a sequence only becomes visible at the very end of the sentence with the last verbal form. The converb form in (25) contains a considerable lot of different TAM markers, the only marker which is lacking and which cannot occur in this form is the tense marker.

(24) *Koobe e it-te, tomodachi ni*
Koobe DIR go-CONV friends DAT
at-te, issho-ni tabe-masu.
meet-CONV together-DAT eat-PRS.HON
'[I] go to Kobe, meet my friend, and [we] eat together.' (Hinds 1986: 85)

(25) *yame-sase-rare-taku-nakere-ba,*
quit-CAUS-PASS-VOL-NEG-CONV
yoku hatarai-te kudasai.
well work-CONV please
'If [you] don't want to be dismissed, do your work.'

Minus-asymmetry with regard to the declarative marker can be illustrated by Abkhaz. Finite forms are characterized by the suffixes *-(y)t'* or *-n* (the only exception being Future I in *-p'*, cf. Hewitt 1987). These suffixes are missing or replaced by *-z* in non finite forms. Thus we find the suffix *-(y)t'* in the finite verb form of example (26 a) and no marking of finiteness in (26 b, c). Simultaneity is marked by the suffix *-anǝ-*, which occurs between the prefix marking object agreement (S, O) and the prefix marking subject agreement (A) (cf. example (26 b)). The concept of 'before' is marked by the suffix *-àa-nʒa* (cf. example (26 c)).

(26) a. *dǝ-z-ba-yt'*.
   3s.OBJ-1s.SBJ-see-AOR.FIN
   'I saw him.'
   b. *d-anǝ̀-z-ba   a-š°q°'ǝ̀*
   3s.OBJ-when-1s.SBJ-see the-book
   (ø-)lǝ̀-s-ta-yt'.
   3s.OBJ-3sf.IO-2s.SBJ-give-AOR
   'When I saw her, I gave her the book.' (Hewitt 1987: 138)
   c. *wǝy dǝ-z-b(a)-àa-nʒa*
   he   3s.OBJ-1s.SBJ-see-before
   'Before I saw him [, they took him out of hospital].' (Hewitt 1987: 168)

Minus-asymmetry with regard to person is attested in some Turkish converbs such as those in *-ip* and *-erek*. Another example is Iatmul (Papua language of New Guinea) with regard to dependent-coordinate forms:

(27) *Vɨ-laa   ya-wun.*
   see-CONV come-1s
   'Having seen it I come.' (Staalsen 1972)

Plus-asymmetry with regard to markers of subordination can again be illustrated by Iatmul. The form to be discussed in this context is the conditional form in *-an* which is fully marked for person (and tense):

(28) *Gay-at yi-ka   waala kla-laa*
   house-to go-CONV dog   get-CONV
   ya-d-ey-an   di-gat vɨ-kiyo-wun.
   come-3s-FUT-COND he-for see-FUT-1s
   'If he comes after he has gone to the house and got the dog, I will see him.' (Staalsen 1972: 176)

In a considerable number of languages case markers are affixed to a finite form. An example for such an instance of plus-asymmetry with regard to case markers is Camling (Kiranti, Tibeto-Burman). In the following example we find the ablative marker *-daka* in the context of clause combining:

(29) *Uileko tyiso mi-riŋa-daka*
   earlier thus 3p.SBJ-say-ABL
   i-ma-ŋo   parne khu-lai-ŋo.
   give-INF-EMPH must 1s-DAT-EMPH
   'As/after they had said so before, they had to give her to him.' (Ebert 1993: 94)

Examples for plus-asymmetry with regard to person can be found in Fore and Hua (two Papuan languages of New Guinea; on Hua cf. Haiman 1980, on Fore cf. Scott 1978). The following example is from Fore. Like Hua, this language does not only mark the subject of the predicate, it also marks the subject of the next predicate (anticipatory subject, cf. below on switch-reference):

(30) *Kaná-uʔ-ki-na*
   come-2s.AG.PST-DEP-3s.AG
   a-ka-ʔtá-i-e.
   3s.UG-see-PST-3s.AG-DECL
   'You came and he saw it.' (Scott 1978)

Asymmetry is crucial for switch-reference. My argumentation is based on Haiman (1983) who deals with Papuan languages of New Guinea. Since most of these languages are SOV, the finite verb occurs at the end of a clause or of a chain of clauses. I shall call this form in accordance with Haiman "final verb". Other verbal forms which are dependent on the final verb occur in front of it. I shall call them again in accordance with Haiman "medial verbs". Both English terms are presumably borrowed from Pilhofer's (1933) German terms of "Satzinnenform" vs. "Satzendform".

Both verb forms, the medial form and the final form, can be marked for person. To distinguish the two types of person, i. e. the two different sets of markers to express this category, Haiman (1983: 107) proposes the following symbolization:

(31)   Final verb = Verb + person
       Medial verb = Verb + PERSON

This model leads Haiman (1983: 108) to the following idealized pattern with regard to medial verbs:

(32)   DS = Verb + PERSON
       SS = Verb + ø

If a medial verb is same subject (SS) or same agent (SA), there is — theoretically speaking

– no actual need to mark person, since it will be marked on the final verb. For that reason, same subject medial verbs sometimes follow the principle of minus-asymmetry in the above pattern (31). In the case of different subject medial verbs (DS) or different agent medial verbs, however, asymmetry is kept up by the fact that the person markers of the medial form are from a different set than the person markers of the final form. In most cases, however, there are additional asymmetries such as markers of sequentiality or simultaneity in the case of plus-asymmetry, or the absence of a tense marker in the case of minus-asymmetry. The only exceptions based entirely on the 'PERSON' vs. 'person' distinction seem to be Ono (Finisterre-Huon Superstock) and Kewa (33). Ono seems to be the only language which fully follows the above pattern (31). Kewa shows additional markers of simultaneity and sequentiality in the case of same subject which are replaced by a PERSON marker in the case of different subject:

(33) Kewa (Haiman 1983: 109)
 a. *Epo la-ri epa-wa.*
   whistle say-SIM.SS come-1s
   'I came whistling.'
 b. *Epo la-a epa-wa*
   whistle say-SEQ.SS come-1s
   'I whistled and then I came.'
 c. *Epo la-na epa-wa.*
   whistle say-3s.PERSON come-1s
   'He whistled and I came.'

At a further degree of elaboration, medial forms are not only marked for their own subject, but also for the subject or agent of the following clause. The above example (30) is an illustration to this type of switch-reference with anticipatory subject.

In all the examples quoted so far, the finite form occurred at the end of the sentence. The mirror image of this situation is also well attested (cf. e. g. Givón 1990: 891). Longacre (1972; 1990: 88) calls this phenomenon "consecutive tense". In Bambara, the finite form is at the beginning of the clause, the dependent forms, which are marked by the auxiliary *ka*, follow after it. The direction from finite to non finite clauses seems to be particularly well represented in Africa. All the examples analysed by Carlson (1992) follow this pattern. Another African language, in which sequentiality is expressed morphologically by the prefix *-ka-* is Swahili as illustrated in the following example:

(34) *Tu-li-kwenda mji-ni*
   1p-PST-go village-LOC
   tu-ka-mw-ona Ali, tu-ka-sema
   1p-KA-3s-see Ali 1p-KA-speak
   na-ye, tu-ka-ondoka, tu-ka-rudi
   with-3s 1p-KA-come.away 1p-KA-return
   kwe-tu.
   LOC.CLASS-our
   'We went to the village and saw Ali and spoke with him, and came away and returned to our home.' (Perrott 1950: 51)

The direction from finite to non finite seems to be somehow linked to VO languages ("VO clause-chaining" in terms of Givón 1990: 891; Givón discusses American languages such as Miskitu and Chuave), the opposite direction from non finite to finite occurs in OV languages ("OV clause-chaining").

In Bisang (1998 a) I present three different types of clause combining based on the occurrence of the following four techniques:

– converbs
– adverbial subordinators
– verb serialization
– relativization/nominalization

The three types of clause combining are:

– European type
– Eurasian or converb type
– Far East or verb serialization type.

The European type can be characterized by the abundant use of adverbial subordinators and of infinitives, verbal nouns and wh-clauses (nominalization). Furthermore, there is a limited set of non finite verbal forms which are, in some languages, also used as participles (i. e., attributively) or as verbal nouns/infinitives (i. e., nominally). These forms can be treated as converbs. If they also display the function of participles or verbal nouns/infinitives, they are called "non strict converbs" (I. Nedjalkov 1998; e. g. the *-ing* form in English). Verb serialization is of almost no relevance in this type.

In the Eurasian or converb type (with languages such as Turkish, Mongolian, Dravidian, Japanese, Korean) clause combining is reflected by asymmetry in the morphological form of the verb. This can be realized either by converbs which are used exclusively for clause combining ("strict converbs" in terms of I. Nedjalkov 1998) or by various forms of verbal nouns or masdar forms. The number of adverbial subordinators is relatively small.

Very often, adverbial subordinators are grammaticalized converbs or verbal nouns or they are borrowed from other languages (e. g. Arabic or Persian which do not belong to the converb type). Verb serialization is again very marginal in this type.

Languages belonging to the Far East type (e. g. Chinese, Thai, Vietnamese, Cambodian, Hmong) are generally characterized by their high degree of indeterminateness, i. e. by the lack of obligatory grammatical categories. Languages of this type combine clauses by verb serialization, free adverbial subordinators and syntactic constructions of nominalization. Verb serialization is defined as follows: "Verb serialization is the unmarked juxtaposition of two or more verbs or verbal phrases (with or without actor and/or undergoer), each of which would also be able to form a sentence on its own." (Bisang forth., also cf. my older definition in Bisang 1992: 9). In the context of clause combining, verb serialization is to be understood in a broad sense in which clauses are merely juxtaposed without any further marking such as in the following two examples from Modern Standard Chinese. The semantic relation between the two clauses can only be inferred from context.

(35) *Nĭ guì-xià-lái   qíu*
you kneel-go.down-come beg
Zhāngsān.
Zhangsan
Purpose: 'You knelt down in order to beg Zhangsan.'
Consecutive Action: 'You knelt down and then begged Zhangsan.'
Simultaneous Action: 'You knelt down begging Zhangsan.'
Alternating Action: 'You knelt down and begged Zhangsan.' (Li & Thompson 1973: 98)

(36) *Rén bú fàn wǒ, wǒ bú*
people NEG attack I(we) I(we) NEG
fàn rén.
attack people
'We will not attack unless we are attacked.' / 'If we are not attacked, we shall not attack.'

The status of adverbial subordinators is different in the Far East type of languages from those in European type languages inasmuch as they do not need to be mentioned obligatorily (cf. the above examples (35) and (36); also cf. Bisang 1998a). In Far East-type languages nominalization is realized by grammaticalized head nouns which are determined by a relative clause. A very common construction for expressing simultaneity is based on a grammaticalized noun with the meaning 'time' to which a clause is attributed.

The distinction between languages which allow asymmetries and languages which do not yields the Far East type on the one hand and the European and the Eurasian type on the other hand. Thus, languages belonging to the Far East type may be called "non finite languages" (in the sense that they are neutral to the finite/non finite distinction) on the basis of their lack of obligatory categories, i. e. their indeterminateness. Similarly, languages belonging to the latter two types may be called "finite languages" (in the sense that the finite/non finite distinction is possible). Within the finite languages, there seem to be languages who consistently show morphological asymmetry between independent and dependent clauses. This seems to be the case with Eurasian type languages. In European languages, however, there is no consistency with regard to morphological asymmetry. Of course, there are infinitives, verbal nouns, participles and converbs which clearly are not marked for all the categories required in matrix clauses in European languages as well. But there are many other constructions in which the same verbal form can be used in the dependent clause as well as in the matrix clause. Moreover, we find subjunctives which show no asymmetry, but are primarily used in dependent clauses. Thus, from the point of view of consistency with regard to asymmetry, we may draw the following continuum which also represents the degree of consistency with which the finite/non finite distinction is at work in the three types of clause combining.

Far East	European	Eurasian
no asymmetry	→	consistent asymmetry

The above typology of finite vs. non finite languages is mainly based on morphology, although obligatoriness and the potential of building up asymmetry is not limited to morphology as we have seen above e. g. in the context of example (4) from Supyire. As we shall see in the next section, the finite/non finite distinction is also attested syntactically at least in some of the languages in which it is not visible morphologically.

4. Finite vs. non finite in Formal Linguistics

As pointed out in § 1., Tense or AGR in IP are crucial for the finite/non finite distinction (cf. George & Kornfilt 1981 for tests based on agreement and tense). I shall first discuss AGR and empty pronouns (*pro* and PRO). Later, I shall look at Tense (T).

According to the description of Plag (1993), Sranan (English based Creole spoken in Surinam) is a clear instance of a language in which the finite/non finite distinction is visible only from the point of view of syntax. Plag's analysis of Sranan is based on the standard assumption of Principles & Parameters that empty subjects can be either *pro* or PRO. *pro* is the subject of a final clause and it is licenced by a finite INFL. PRO is always in an ungoverned position, where it is not assigned case, and it must be the subject of a non finite clause. The phenomenon analysed by Plag in this framework is the complementizer *fu* (Engl.: *for*). Apart from its function as a preposition, *fu* occurs in two different functions. In overt type clauses, i.e. in clauses with an overt subject as in (37), and in the empty subject type (cf. (38) below).

(37) *Mi winsi fu a kon tamara.*
 I want CPL he come tomorrow
 'I want him to come tomorrow.' (Plag 1993: 101)

In overt type clauses, the subject is nominative-marked. As for the empty subject type, Plag shows by the following sentences that the empty subject in question is a PRO (Plag 1993: 117). The sentences of this example and their interpretation is parallel to Kouwenberg (1990) on Papiamentu *pa*.

(38) a. *Amba$_i$ taki bun fu Pieter$_j$*
 Amba praise PREP Pieter
 fu PRO$_i$/pro$_i$ kisi na moni.
 CPL get ART money
 'Amba praised Pieter in order to get the money.'
 b. *Amba$_i$ taki bun fu Pieter$_j$ fu*
 Amba praise PREP Pieter CPL
 a$_{i/j/k}$ kisi na moni.
 he get.the.money
 c. **Amba$_i$ taki bun fu Pieter$_j$*
 fu pro$_{j/k}$ kisi na moni.

In the above example, we have a subject control structure, i.e. the reference of the empty subject is controlled by the matrix verb. As we can see from (38 b), the overt embedded pronoun, i.e. *a* 'he' in this case, can refer to either participants of the matrix clause or even to a sentence-external participant, whereas the empty pronoun must refer to the subject of the matrix clause (cf. the ungrammaticality of (38 c)). The control structures in (38 a) provides good evidence for the existence of PRO, i.e. for the non finiteness of empty subject type *fu* clauses in Sranan (Plag 1993: 117). Plag (1993, 118–119) presents further evidence for this analysis from long distance binding and split antecedents which I shall not discuss in the present paper. Plag's analysis of Sranan data shows that it is possible to distinguish meaningfully between finite vs. non finite languages in spite of the absence of any morphological indication. In this sense he goes beyond Mufwene & Dijkhoff (1989: 300) who recognize the importance of syntax for the finite/non finite distinction but do not apply it to languages without any verbal morphology.

One of the terms in which C.-T. J. Huang (1984, 1989) discusses the question of finite vs. non finite in Chinese is *pro*/PRO. He defines *pro*/PRO as an empty category of which *pro* and PRO are two variants. If the clause is assumed to be finite, a zero anaphor occurring in subject position can be interpreted either as an A-bound variable or as a *pro*. If the clause is assumed to be non finite, the zero anaphor occurring in subject position is a PRO. Since there are serious objections against such an analysis raised by Y. Huang (1994: 24–57), I shall not discuss this topic in the present paper any further. I would only like to briefly quote Y. Huang's (1994: 57) conclusions to present the opposite position to C.-T. J. Huang: "I have demonstrated that (i) PRO as defined by Chomsky cannot occur in Chinese, since there are only finite clauses in the language; (ii) *pro* as defined by Chomsky cannot occur in Chinese, either, since the question of how it is locally identified in the language remains unknown ..." (Y. Huang 1994: 57).

In most recent approaches to the question of finite vs. non finite, Tense seems to be crucial (also see the important role of Tense for building up asymmetry in § 3.). Thus, Shlonsky (1997: 6) on Semitic languages assumes that a full clause must contain a TP. Moreover, he sees a dependence between TP and CP. For him, "there is an obvious sense in which T and C (or one of the heads within the CP layer) are related. For example, the choice of complementizer is determined in part by the finiteness of the clause" (Shlonsky

1997: 6). On the same page, Shlonsky also proposes to look at the relationship between C^0 and T^0 in terms of selection: "a nonfinite C^0 selects or subcategorizes for a nonfinite T^0 and a finite C^0 takes a finite T^0 complement." Such an approach can also integrate subjunctives as they occur e. g. in Arabic (cf. example (16)) into the finite/non finite discussion. On this basis, "the essential difference between full and small (or reduced) clauses is that the former are CPs, and are hence endowed with a TP projection, while the latter are clausal chunks that may vary in size — that is, in the number of functional projections they include — but they crucially lack TP and hence CP" (Shlonsky 1997: 6).

According to Li (1990: 17), who follows C.-T. J. Huang in this respect, it is necessary to distinguish tensed clauses from infinitives in Chinese even if there is no clear morphological distinction between finite and non finite clauses in this language. Only the subject position of finite clauses can have overt lexical NP's, whereas infinitives cannot. Thus the subject position of infinitives is a caseless position. Li (1990: 17–24) tries to show that finite and non finite clauses behave differently (1) in the realization of aspect, (2) in the licensing of negative polarity items by negation and (3) in the occurrence relation between certain time adverbials and aspect markers. Li relates these differences in behaviour to the claim that finite clauses but not infinitives can have tense. I shall briefly illustrate Li's first and Li's third test. The first test is based on two different types of verbs, i. e. *persuade*-type verbs (39 a, b) and *tell*-type verbs (39 c, d):

(39)   Chinese (Li 1990: 19–20)
   a. *Wǒ quàn tā jiè guo yān,*
      I   persuade he stop TAM cigarette
      kěshi tā bù kěn jiè.
      but he NEG will stop
      'I persuaded him to stop smoking but he will not stop.'
   b. *Wǒ bī tā chī yào, kěshi tā*
      I force he eat medicine but he
      bù kěn chī.
      NEG will eat
      'I forced him to take medicine but he will not.'
   c. **Wǒ gàosu tā tāmen jiè guo*
      I tell he they stop TAM
      yān, kěshi tāmen bù kěn jiè.
      cigarette but.they.would.not.stop
      'I told him that they stopped smoking but they would not stop (smoking).'
   d. *Wǒ gàosu tā tāmen jiè yān.*
      I tell he they stop cigarette
      Tāmen dōu bú zài chōuyān le.
      they all NEG again smoke PF
      'I told him that they stopped smoking. They never smoked again.'

In examples (39 a) and (39 b) the use of the experiential marker *guo* does not necessarily refer to the dependent clause where it actually appears. It only denotes that the act of persuasion or forcing has taken place before. For that reason, it is absolutely normal to state that the causee did not want to do what he was called to do by the subject of the matrix clause. In (39 c) and (39 d), however, in which the matrix verb is a *tell*-type verb, the aspect marker *guo* can only refer to the embedded clause. For that reason, (39 c) is not possible because the 'but'-clause implies that the aspect marker *guo* refers to the *tell*-verb in the matrix position. (39 d) is possible, because the second clause refers to the aspect marking of the clause embedded to *gàosu* 'tell'. Thus "the cross-clausal aspectual relation is possible with sentences containing *persuade*-type verbs but impossible with sentences containing *tell*-type verbs" (Li 1990: 20). Consequently, *persuade*-verbs typically take non finite clauses as their complements, whereas *tell*-type verbs take finite clauses with their own tense marking.

The problem with Li's argumentation may be that it is — according to Y. Huang (1994: 256) — "empirically wrong". In the following example, we find a perfective aspect marker with the verb *hē* 'drink'. This verb occurs within a clause embedded to a *persuade-type* verb which is supposed to be non finite and thus should not have a tense marker.

(40)   *Māma bī   Xiǎomíng [ø hē-le*
      Mum force Xiaoming   drink-PFV
      tāng].
      soup
      'Mum forced Xiaoming to drink soup.' (Y. Huang 1992: 252)

Of course, aspect is not tense. For that reason, Y. Huang's argument based on aspect (and on another example not quoted here with mood) may turn out to be not quite pertinent. In some further examples, Li (1990: 22) explicitly states that future markers, i. e. real tense markers, cannot occur in non finite clauses, i. e. in clauses whose matrix verb is a *persuade*-type verb:

(41) *Wŏ quàn/bī   tā [huí lái].
     I   persuade/force he will come

From this we may conclude that the finite/non finite distinction only holds with regard to tense but not with regard to aspect and mood. This conclusion depends on the interpretation of the semantics of *huí* and *yào*, which are both exclusively tense markers denoting future according to Li (1990: 21–22). However, if we look at the careful semantic analysis of *huí* and *yào* by Alleton (1984) these two markers are far from denoting future tense exclusively. This finding would leave us then with the conclusion that there is no marker which strictly and exclusively marks tense in Modern Standard Chinese.

Even if we may not be able to stipulate a grammatical category strictly and exclusively referring to tense, the other two tests presented by Li (1990) show that there seems to be some difference between *persuade*-type and *tell*-type verbs. I shall only present one of these tests which refers to the co-occurrence relation between certain time adverbials such as *cóngqián* 'before' and certain aspect markers such as the experiential marker *guo*.

(42) Chinese (Li 1990: 19)
  a. *Wŏ cóngqián gàosu tā [nĭ lái
      I   before   tell   he you come
     guo zhèr].
     TAM here
  b. Wŏ cóngqián qĭng tā [chī-guo
     I   before   invite he eat-TAM
     fàn].
     meal
     'I invited him to eat before.'

In contrast to (42a), where the matrix verb is a *tell*-verb, it is possible in (42b) with a *persuade*-verb to have the time adverbial in the matrix clause and the aspect marker correlating with it in the embedded clause. Thus there is a difference between *tell*-type verbs and *persuade*-type verbs along the line of finite vs. non finite. But, as we can see from (42b), clauses embedded to *persuade*-type verbs can have their own TAM marker.

In the above discussion, Sranan seems to represent a language where the finite/non finite distinction is clearly visible even if there is no morphological marking. The case of Chinese seems to be less clear. Even the existence of tense in its strict sense seems to be farely questionable. There are some cases as illustrated by (42) and the licensing of negative polarity items by negation which show that there may be some distinction along the lines of finite vs. non finite also in Chinese. But this evidence is far less consistent than the one in Sranan.

5. Conclusion

In § 2., finiteness was introduced as a scalar phenomenon. In § 3., it was described in a more general way from the point of view of obligatoriness and asymmetry. In this context the emphasis was clearly on morphology although I pointed out that syntactic phenomena are not excluded from building up asymmetry. § 4. finally concentrated on purely syntactic evidence for a distinction between finite and non finite. That there are languages in which this distinction is based exclusively on syntax seems to be attested by languages such as Sranan. What may turn out to be crucial for Sranan to keep up with this distinction may be the obligatoriness of the subject constituent in an independent utterance. If this were true then Sranan has the possibility to build up a minus-asymmetry with regard to person between finite and non finite clauses. In Chinese, there is no such obligatority. Neither the subject is obligatory nor is tense(-aspect-mood). Of course, the existence of a TP is not based on the obligatority of T, but the fact that T does not have to occur if the context is clear enough may yield the consequence that it is not reliable enough for the finite/non finite distinction to develop quite clearly. If this is true, obligatoriness may turn out to be the crucial factor for describing finiteness in general, be it morphological or syntactical. It is needless to say that this is a matter of further research.

6. References

Alleton, Viviane. 1984. *Les auxiliaires de mode en chinois contemporain.* Paris: Édition de la maison des sciences de l'homme.

Bickel, Balthasar. 1991. *Typologische Grundlagen der Satzverkettung. Ein Beitrag zur allgemeinen Grammatik der Satzverbindung und des Fährtenlegens.* Zürich: Universität Zürich.

Bisang, Walter. 1992. *Das Verb im Chinesischen, Hmong, Vietnamesischen, Thai und Khmer (Vergleichende Grammatik im Rahmen der Verbserialisierung, der Grammatikalisierung und der Attraktorpositionen).* Tübingen: Narr.

Bisang, Walter. 1995. "Verb serialization and converbs – differences and similarities." In: Haspelmath, Martin and Ekkehard König. eds. *Converbs in cross-linguistic perspective,* 137–188. Berlin: Mouton de Gruyter.

Bisang, Walter. 1996. "Areal typology and grammaticalization: Processes of grammaticalization based on nouns and verbs in East and mainland South East Asian languages". *Studies in Language,* 20.3, 519–597.

Bisang, Walter. 1998a. "The view from the far East. Comments on seven thematic areas". In: Van der Auwera, Johan with Dónall P. Ó. Baoill. eds. *Adverbial constructions in the languages of Europe,* 641–812. Berlin: Mouton de Gruyter.

Bisang, Walter. 1998b. "Verb serialization and attractor positions: Constructions and their potential impact on language change and language contact." In: Kulikov, Leonid & Vater, Heinz. eds. *Typology of verbal categories, Papers presented to Vladimir Nedjalkov on the occasion of his 70th birthday,* 255–271. Tübingen: Niemeyer.

Bisang, Walter. to appear. "Areality, grammaticalization and language typology. On the explanatory power of functional criteria and the status of Universal Grammar", in: Bisang, Walter. ed. *Aspects of language typology and universals.* Berlin: Akademie-Verlag.

Bybee, Joan. 1997. "Semantic aspects of morphological typology." In: Bybee, Joan, John Haiman and Sandra A. Thompson, eds. *Essays on language function and language type.* Amsterdam/Philadelphia: Benjamins.

Carlson, Robert. 1992. "Narrative, subjunctive, and finiteness." *Journal of African Languages and Linguistics* 13, 59–85.

Dik, Simon C. 1989. *The theory of functional grammar, Part I: The structure of the clause.* Dordrecht: Foris.

Dik, Simon. 1997. *The Theory of Functional Grammar. Part 1: The Structure of the Clause (TGF 1).* Ed. by Hengeveld, Kees. Berlin & New York: Mouton de Gruyter.

Ebert, Karen H. 1993. "Kiranti subordination in the South Asian areal context." In: Ebert, Karen H. ed. *Studies in clause linkage, Papers from the First Köln–Zürich Workshop,* 83–110. Zürich: Arbeiten des Seminars für Allgemeine Sprachwissenschaft, Nr. 12.

Fischer, Wolfdietrich. 1972. *Grammatik des klassischen Arabisch.* Wiesbaden: Harrassowitz.

George, L. and Kornfilt, J. 1981. "Finiteness and boundedness in Turkish." In: Henry, F. ed. *Binding and filtering,* 105–127. London: Croom Helm.

Givón, Talmy. 1972. *Studies in ChiBemba and Bantu grammar. Studies in African Linguistics,* Supplement 3.

Givón, Talmy. 1990. *Syntax. A functional-typological introduction, Vol. II.* Amsterdam/Philadelphia: Benjamins.

Haiman, John. 1980. *HUA: A Papua language of the Eastern Highlands of New Guinea.* Amsterdam: Benjamins.

Haiman, John. 1983. "On some origins of switch-reference marking." In: Haiman, John and Pamela Munro. eds. *Switch-Reference and universal grammar,* 105–128. Amsterdam/Philadelphia: Benjamins.

Haspelmath, Martin. 1989. "From purposive to infinitive – a universal path of grammaticization." *Folia Linguistica Historica* 10, 287–310.

Haspelmath, Martin. 1995. "The converb as a cross-linguistically valid category." In: Haspelmath, Martin and Ekkehard König. eds. *Converbs in cross-linguistic perspective,* 1–55. Berlin: Mouton de Gruyter.

Hengeveld, Kees. 1998. "Adverbial clauses in the languages of Europe." In: Van der Auwera, Johan in collaboration with Dónall P. Ó Baoill. eds. *Adverbial constructions in the languages of Europe,* 335–419. Berlin: Mouton de Gruyter.

Hewitt, B. G. 1987. *The typology of subordination in Georgian and Abkhaz.* Berlin/New York/Amsterdam: Mouton de Gruyter.

Hinds, John. 1986. *Japanese.* London/New York: Routledge.

Huang, C. T. James. 1984. "On the distribution and reference of empty pronouns." *Linguistic Inquiry* 15, 531–574.

Huang, C. T. James. 1989. "Pro-drop in Chinese: a generalized control theory", in: Jaeggli, O. A. and K. F. Safir. eds. *The syntax and pragmatics of anaphora,* 185–214. Dordrecht: Kluwer.

Huang, Yan. 1992. "Review of: Li, Audrey Yen-hui. 1990. Order and constituency in Mandarin Chinese. Dordrecht: Kluwer." In: *Journal of Linguistics* 28, 251–256.

Huang, Yan. 1994. *The syntax and pragmatics of anaphora.* Cambridge: Cambridge University Press.

Kouwenberg, Silvia. 1990. "Complementizer *pa,* the finiteness of its complements and some remarks on empty categories in Papiamento." *Journal of Pidgin and Creole Languages* 5.1, 39–51.

Lehmann, Christian. 1988. "Towards a typology of clause linkage." In: Haiman, John and Sandra A. Thompson. eds. *Clause combining in grammar and discourse,* 181–225. Amsterdam/Philadelphia: Benjamins.

Li, Charles N. and Sandra A. Thompson. 1973. "Serial verb constructions in Mandarin Chinese: Subordination or co-ordination?" In: *Chicago Linguistic Society* 9, 96–103.

Li, Yen-Hui Audrey. 1990. *Order and constituency in Mandarin Chinese.* Dordrecht: Kluwer.

Longacre, Robert E. 1972. *Hierarchy and universality of discourse constituents in New Guinea languages: Discussion.* Washington: Georgetown University Press.

Longacre, Robert E. 1990. "Storyline concerns and word order typology in East and West Africa." *Studies in African Linguistics, Supplement, 10*.

Lyons, John. 1977. *Semantics*. 2 Vols. Cambridge: Cambridge University Press.

Mufwene, Salikoko & Martha Dijkhoff. 1989. "On the so-called 'infinitive' in Atlantic Creoles." *Lingua* 77, 297−330.

Nedjalkov, Igor. 1998. "Converbs in the languages of Europe." In: Van der Auwera, Johan in collaboration with Dónall P. Ó Baoill. eds. *Adverbial constructions in the languages of Europe*, 421−455. Berlin: Mouton de Gruyter.

Nedjalkov, Vladimir. 1995. "Some typological parameters of converbs." In: Haspelmath, Martin and Ekkehard König. eds. *Converbs in cross-linguistic perspective*, 97−136. Berlin: Mouton de Gruyter.

Noonan, Michael. 1985. "Complementation." In: Noonan, Michael. ed. *Language typology and syntactic description, Vol. II. Complex constructions*, 42−140. Cambridge: Cambridge University Press.

Palmer, F. R. 1986. *Mood and modality*. Cambridge: Cambridge University Press.

Perrott, D. V. 1950. *Swahili*. Kent: Hodder & Stoughton.

Pilhofer, Georg. 1933. *Grammatik der Kâte-Sprache in Neuguinea*. Berlin: Reimer.

Plag, Ingo. 1993. *Sentential complementation in Sranan*. Tübingen: Niemeyer.

Poppe, Nicholas. 1974. *Grammar of Written Mongolian*. Wiesbaden: Harrassowitz.

Scott, G. 1978. *The Fore language of Papua New Guinea*. (Pacific Linguistics, B. 47). Canberra: Australian National University.

Shibatani, Masayoshi. 1990. *The languages of Japan*. Cambridge: Cambridge University Press.

Shlonsky, Ur. 1997. *Clause structure and word order in Hebrew and Arabic. An essay in comparative Semitic syntax*. New York/Oxford: Oxford University Press.

Staalsen, P. 1972. "Clause relationships in Iatmul." In: *Pacific Linguistics*, A. 31: 45−69.

Tschenkéli, Kita. 1958. *Einführung in die georgische Sprache, Band I*. Zürich: Amirani Verlag.

Vamling, Karina. 1989. *Complementation in Georgian*. Lund: Lund University Press.

Van Valin, Robert D. Jr. 1993. "A synopsis of Role and Reference Grammar." In: Van Valin, Robert D. Jr. ed. *Role and Reference Grammar*, 1−164. Amsterdam, Philadelphia: Benjamins.

Van Valin, Robert D. Jr. & LaPolla, Randy. 1997. *Syntax: structure, meaning and function*. Cambridge: Cambridge University Press.

Vogt, Hans. 1971. *Grammaire de la langue géorgienne*. Oslo: Universitetsforlaget.

Walter Bisang, Mainz (Germany)

101. Subject-oriented vs. subjectless languages

1. Introduction
2. The semantics of syntactic relations
3. Languages with cumulative packaging of NPs
4. Mono-pivotal (role-dominated) languages
5. Multi-pivotal subjectless languages
6. Pivotless languages
7. Subject-oriented languages
8. Subject-oriented and subjectless languages in diachronic perspective
9. References

1. Introduction

In the majority of contemporary syntactic theories, we still see the dominance of the assumption inherited from traditional grammar that subject-object relations are universal. And indeed, for the syntactic systems of European languages, which have been the empirical basis of the theory of grammar, the notions of subject and object are the most fundamental ones, and all the major syntactic phenomena and processes are described in these terms (cf. Lazard 1997). First, the core arguments of the predicate are distinguished by typical formal coding. Thus, in case-marking languages (e. g. Latin, German, Russian), the subject is normally expressed by the nominative case, and the (direct) object is expressed by the accusative case. In English, subject and object are kept distinct by their position with respect to the verb (the subject is preverbal, the object postverbal). Besides, in the clause the subject NP controls verbal agreement. Second, the subject and the object are different in the way they participate in syntactic processes (passivization, reflexivization, sentence coordination, switch-reference, serialization, in forming complex-predicate constructions of various kinds). These processes themselves are of course described in terms of syntactic relations.

However, for many other languages the application of these notions leads to a large number of problems, especially the problem of identifying the subject and the object in basic sentences (on basic sentences, see Keenan 1976: 307−309). Thus, for more than a hundred years linguists have been discussing which NP is the subject in an ergative construction. Even non-ergative languages have been discovered in which the use of the notions of subject and object is no less problematic. As a result, the universality of the subject has been repeatedly questioned in recent times (cf., e.g., Li & Thompson 1976, Schachter 1976, 1977, Van Valin 1977, 1981, Kibrik 1979, Durie 1987, 1988).

The arguments against the universality of the subject are very convincing. It thus has to be recognized that besides languages with subject-object relations (called **subject-oriented** languages here for brevity), there are languages in which clause structure is not determined by subject-object relations (these languages will be called **subjectless** languages). Given this, we are confronted with at least the following questions:

− What are the functional equivalents of subject-object relations in subjectless languages?
− What is the space of typological possibilities concerning the parameter of subjectless vs. subject-oriented languages?
− What is the diachronic relation between subject-oriented and subjectless languages?

Historically, the discovery of subjectless languages was made inductively, because in the dominant theory the assumption that subject-oriented languages are universal was not questioned, and it was only under the weight of the contradictory evidence from newly described languages that this assumption was gradually revised. In this article, however, I have chosen a different order of presentation: First I will demonstrate deductively, starting out from the properties of subject-oriented languages, that the existence of subjectless languages must also be recognized, and then I will show that this hypothesis is confirmed by empirical evidence from concrete languages.

2. The semantics of syntactic relations

In languages that are indisputably subject-oriented, it is usually not difficult to describe the subject in formal terms. However, practice shows that it is impossible to answer the question "What does the subject mean?", i.e. to give it a semantic interpretation in terms of necessary and sufficient content features. This does not mean that a subject NP has no semantic characteristics of its own. The most important ones are as follows.

First of all, the NPs of a clause have so-called role meanings. Role meanings concern the semantics of the extralinguistic situation that is described by the clause, and more specifically the categorization of its participant types. Thus, in sentence (1)

(1)   *Mother washed the linen.*

the roles of the event participants are contrasted in a clear fashion: The subject *mother* has the semantic role of agent, and the object *linen* has the semantic role of patient. Moreover, there is not a single agentive verb in which the roles can be expressed in an inverted way, since the agent can never occupy the direct-object position. However, one cannot claim that the subject and the object are directly correlated with the agent and patient roles. We can also have sentence (2)

(2)   *The linen was washed by mother.*

where the patient is found in the subject position. In sentence (3),

(3)   *Who do you see?*

the experiencer *you* is in the subject position, and the stimulus *who* is in object position. I will call the semantic domain to which these meanings belong the **role dimension**.

Thus, there is an indisputable correlation between semantic roles and syntactic relations, but this correlation is not one-to-one. Syntactic relations also correlate with discourse-pragmatic characteristics of noun phrases which are determined by an NP's place in the information flow of the discourse (called "flow characteristics" here): Whether it is the starting point of an utterance, whether it conveys old or new information, whether it is in the focus of attention, in the focus of empathy, etc. (→ Art. 46). I will call this semantic domain the **flow dimension**. Thus, often the subject is the topic, and the object (together with the verb) is the comment of an utterance. But this is by no means always the case. For instance, in introductory utterances like (4) there is no topical constituent, but a subject is present.

(4) Russian
Žili-byli starik so staruxoj.
lived-was old.man with old.woman
'There were once an old man and an old woman.'

There are also correlations between syntactic relations and other semantic dimensions, for instance, the deictic and the referential dimensions. In the prototypical case the meanings of the **deictic dimension** correlate the utterance with the coordinates of the speech act, and in particular they mark those situation participants which are simultaneously speech act participants (→ Art. 44). The influence of the deictic dimension on the choice of the of syntactic positions of NP's is seen in the fact that those NP's that denote speech act participants (speaker and hearer) have a tendency to occupy a core syntactic position (preferably the subject position) in the clause.

The meanings of the **referential dimension** contribute to the identification or formation of correct NP referents by the hearer. The referential dimension concerns, among others, the fact that the subject designates a definite referent more often than the direct object, and that the subject usually carries with it an existence presupposition and is referentially autonomous, i.e. it exists independently of the described situation. These and other semantic correlations with the subject relation are described in Keenan (1976).

In the typological literature it is often observed that the subject represents a grammaticalized expression of the combination of role, flow and referential properties of NPs (cf., e.g., Dik 1978, Comrie 1981, Andrews 1985). In European languages, the unmarked characteristics of the subject are agent (in the role dimension), topic (in the discourse dimension), and definite referent (in the referential dimension), although concrete utterances allow all kinds of deviations from this prototypical situation. These deviations are possible because the subject-object relations are an abstract way of ranking **core** NPs, contrasting a central core NP and non-central core NPs, where the first rank (subject) is not rigidly linked to any concrete meaning, but signals maximal prominence of the argument along several semantic parameters that are relevant for the speech act.

The division into core and periphery in the proposition and the ranking of core arguments follows certain rules, which involve diverse semantic properties of NPs. Lack of space does not allow us to go into any detail. In non-core (or **peripheral**) NPs (also called obliques), the relation between the formal expression and the semantic roles is usually more direct (English uses various kinds of prepositional phrases), though depending on the speaker's communicative goals a peripheral argument may also be promoted into a core position. Thus, in (5) the instrumental argument is shifted into the subject position, and the agent is removed from the set of semantic argument positions of the verb *open*.

(5) *The key opened the door.*

(Note that there is usually no change of the coding of peripheral arguments when their peripheral status is preserved.)

Thus, in subject-object languages there is a mechanism of highlighting one or two core argument positions within a proposition, which are a **cumulative** means of expressing the meanings of more than one dimension, primarily the role and flow dimensions. (It is possible that some languages also have a third core argument — the indirect object, which is represented, for instance, by the addressee in the three-place verb 'give' and by the experiencer in two-place verbs like 'see', 'love'. The indirect object occupies an intermediate position between typical core arguments and typical peripheral arguments. However, this is irrelevant for what follows.)

A dimension that is grammaticalized within a language and in whose terms NPs may be characterized will be called **pivot**. Thus, subject-object languages, in which the specification of NPs depends on different semantic dimensions, can be regarded as **multi-pivotal** languages.

3. Languages without cumulative packaging of NPs

If we interpret the essence of subject-object relations in this way, it becomes clear that there are no logical grounds to postulate that every language must necessarily use precisely this packaging technique for a predicate's argument, although it is well-motivated from the communicative point of view: Usually there are not more than one or two NPs present within a clause, and this technique allows a language to avoid an explicit coding of different semantic properties of arguments, making use of the minimal number of syntactically distinguishable positions (like subject and object). In contrast to subject-oriented languages, a subjectless language is one that does not make use of the technique of cumulative coding of semantic characteristics of NPs.

But what are the functional equivalents of subject-object relations in subjectless languages? Of course, these are the same concepts that are coded cumulatively by means of syntactic relations in subject-oriented languages. As was noted above, subject-oriented languages code at least the role and flow parameters of NPs in a cumulative way. These semantic dimensions are the most basic ones for a language. We can postulate the following **Hierarchy of Semantic Dimensions**.

role < flow < deictic/referential < others

It is concepts of these dimensions that contribute the most to choosing the subject NP. Every concrete language individually tends to grammaticalize one or more semantic dimensions and their conceptual categorization, but this hierarchy predicts that

- if the concepts of the deictic dimension are grammaticalized, then the concepts of the flow and role dimensions are grammaticalized;
- if the concepts of the flow dimensions are grammaticalized, then the concepts of the role dimensions are grammaticalized;
- if the concepts of the role dimension are not grammaticalized, then the concepts of the other dimensions are not grammaticalized either.

Subjectless languages which grammaticalize concepts of several dimensions in their arguments (multi-pivotal languages) differ from subject-oriented languages only in that the corresponding concepts are coded immediately by means of the **separatist**, rather than the **cumulative** technique (cf. Plank (1991) for this use of the terms *cumulative* ('several meanings expressed simultaneously in one form') and *separatist* ('each meaning expressed by a separate form')). An example of such a language, according to Schachter 1976, 1977, is Tagalog (see further § 5.).

Languages which are oriented toward only one dimension (called mono-pivotal languages below), have to be **role-dominated languages**, following the Hierarchy of Semantic Dimensions. One can assume that there are also **pivotless** languages, which do not ascribe any additional semantic characteristics to NPs.

How does this hypothetical picture relate to the observed situation in languages? Let us consider first languages that are candidates for mono-pivotal languages, then multi-pivotal languages, and finally pivotless languages.

4. Mono-pivotal (role-dominated) languages

4.1. Ergative role-dominated languages

The clearest representatives of mono-pivotal languages are the Daghestanian languages of the northeastern Caucasus. Despite considerable structural differences among them and their different position on the scale from mono-pivotal to multi-pivotal languages, they show a number of fundamental features of role-dominated languages with an **ergative pattern** of argument alignment, where semantically transitive verbs (in the sense of Hopper & Thompson 1980) code the patient in the same way as the argument of a one-place verb (with the unmarked case, the nominative), and the agent with a marked case (the ergative). For example:

(6) Archi (Daghestanian)
 (a) *dija   w-akdi.*
  father.1CL.NOM 1CL-go.away.PAST
  'Father went away.'
 (b) *buwa-mu   dija*
  mother-ERG father.1CL.NOM
  o-w-ka.
  1CL-bring.PAST
  'Mother brought father.'

The NP *dija* in (6a–b) has the form of the unmarked case (nominative), and the agentive NP 'mother' in (6b) is in the ergative. Besides, the verb agrees in class and number with the nominative argument (the noun 'father' belongs to the 1st class of male persons and controls verbal agreements: the marker of the 1st class is -*w*-).

The case coding is highly sensitive to the role characteristics of arguments. First, the nominative NP is not such a semantic "wastebasket" as the subject position in Indo-European languages. It can be related to the **hyperrole Absolutive** (a metonymic extension of the role of the transitive patient), the "immediate, nearest, most involved or affected participant of the situation" (Kibrik 1997: 292). Second, this hyperrole contrasts with the **hyperrole Agentive**, the "most Cause (Agent)-like participant of a multi-participant event" (Kibrik 1997: 289). The Daghestanian languages show a remarkably narrow interpretation of the hyperrole Agentive. In particular, the experiencer is not subsumed under this hyperrole and has a special coding (by means of the dative, a locative case, or a special experiencer case, the affective). For example:

(7) Archi (Daghestanian)
 buwamu-s dija w-aku.
 mother-DAT father.1CL.NOM 1CL-see.PAST
 'Mother saw father.'

This kind of role coding by means of case marking is not a quirk of the nominal morphology, but reflects profound syntactic properties of these languages. The choice of the case coding is generally completely motivated by the (hyper-)role characteristics of the arguments and consequently cannot be changed without changing the role characteristics of the arguments. This explains the non-existence of syntactic voice transformations like the passive in Indo-European languages and the antipassive in Dyirbal, and the irrelevance of many subject-oriented restrictions on the syntactic structure of the sentence (cf. below).

It must be noted that we sometimes observe deviations from these principles in role-dominated languages, but on closer inspection they turn out to be superficial: They can be explained either historically, or they have an additional semantic motivation. Due to lack of space we cannot discuss these cases in detail, so a few examples must suffice.

In some languages, for instance in Bezhta, there is an analog of the antipassive, but it is motivated semantically, not syntactically like the Dyirbal antipassive (for which see § 7.):

(8) Bezhta (Daghestanian)
 (a) *is-t'i ɬi RarLol-ca.*
  brother-ERG water.NOM boil-PRES
  'The brother is boiling water.'
 (b) *is ɬi-d*
  brother.NOM water-INSTR
  RarLol-da:-c.
  boil-ANTIPASS-PRES
  'The brother boils water.'

The verb in the antipassive (marker *-da:-*) denotes a non-referential (habitual, regular, characteristic) situation, and the patient, if it is present in the clause, is also used non-referentially, denoting a class of objects, not a concrete object. The antipassive derivation in Bezhta is not connected with any syntactic processes (like clause coordination, complementation, etc.), i.e. the antipassive in Bezhta is the result of a process of word-formation which turns a transitive verb with two core arguments into an intransitive verb with a single (agentive) core argument, which is completely regularly coded as nominative.

In a number of languages there is a causative derivation, which adds an agentive argument to the verb. Remarkably, causativization in Archi is possible only with one-place verbs and those two-place verbs that do not have an Agentive argument. For instance, pairs like the following are possible (causatives are formed analytically by means of the verb *as* 'do'):

marc' (X_{NOM})   'X is clean'
marc' as (A_{ERG}, X_{NOM})   'A cleans X'
baqI'as (X_{NOM})   'X returns'
baqI'as as (A_{ERG}, X_{NOM}) 'A returns X'
jaqI'an (E_{DAT}, X_{NOM})   'E understands X'
jaqI'an as (A_{ERG}, E_{DAT}, 'A explains X to E'
X_{NOM})

Verbs like 'beat', 'build', 'sew' with the case frame (A_{ERG}, X_{NOM}) do not form causative correlates with the meaning 'A_1 causes A_2 to build X', because this would result in two ergative-marked Agentives in the clause, and one of them would have to be marked differently. An analogous restriction on causativization is found in Lak.

In Khvarshi, there is an interesting process of agentivization which changes the role meaning of the argument that is involved in this process:

(9) Khvarshi (Daghestanian)
 (a) *uža-l dac šut'un.*
  boy-DAT lesson.NOM forget
  'The boy forgot the lesson.'
 (b) *uža dac šut-Xi.*
  boy.ERG lesson.NOM forget-AG
  'The boy forgot the lesson and it was his fault.'

As (9a) shows, the verb 'forget' has an experiencer argument in the dative. But when the participant is responsible for having forgotten the lesson, then the marker of agentivization *-Xi* is added to the verb and the corresponding noun receives the case of the Agentive, the ergative.

(10) Khvarshi
 (a) *dijo t'uqI liti.*
  I.GEN knife.NOM get.lost
  'My knife got lost.'

(b) *de   t'uqI   lit-Xi.*
    I.ERG knife.NOM get.lost-AG
    'I lost my knife and it was my fault.'

In (10), the possessor of the noun 'knife' is in the genitive. But if the possessor participant bears the responsibility for the event, then the corresponding argument is raised from the NP and receives ergative case marking and the agentivization marker is added to the verb.

(11) Khvarshi
  (a) *is   di-qol   uni.*
      brother.NOM I-POST.LAT speak
      'Brother spoke with me.'
  (b) *de   is   un-Xi.*
      I.ERG brother.NOM speak-AG
      'I made brother speak.'

In (11) we see two perspectives in which the situation of speaking may be seen. In (11a) there is one core argument ('brother') in the nominative and one peripheral argument ('I'). If the latter is regarded as an agentive participant of the event which acts on the second participant ('brother'), then the corresponding argument is coded by the ergative.

In Godoberi, a variable interpretation of the hyperrole Absolutive has been attested (see Andrej Kibrik 1996: 127):

(12) Godoberi (Daghestanian)
  (a) *ilu-di   (hanq'u-č'u)   čarta*
      mother-ERG house-CONT.ESS clay.NOM
      b-uša.
      3-smear.PAST
      'Mother smeared the clay on the house.'
  (b) *ilu-di   hanq'u   (čarta-di)*
      mother-ERG house.NOM clay-ERG
      b-uša.
      3-smear.PAST
      'Mother smeared the house with clay.'

The three-place verb 'smear' has arguments with the roles agent, means, and place, the first of which is uniquely interpreted as Agentive, and there is no obvious candidate for the Absolutive hyperrole (such as an argument with the patient role). Therefore both variants are possible, depending on the construal of the event: The Absolutive hyperrole can be assigned either to the means argument (cf. 12a) or to the place argument (cf. 12b). This phenomenon is semantic in nature, not syntactic, as in the case of *load*-type predicates in English.

It is interesting to note that in Daghestanian languages multi-predicate constructions with coreferential arguments have a tendency not to distinguish the status of core arguments. For instance, in Archi we have the following:

(13) Archi
  (a) *w-ez$_i$ Ø$_i$ w-irX$_o$mu-s   L'an-ši*
      1-I.DAT   [NOM.1   1-work-INF]   want-GER
      w-i.
      1-AUX.
      'I want to work.'
  (b) *ez$_i$ Ø$_i$ pult'u šubu-s   L'an-ši*
      4.I.DAT [ERG   coat.4 buy-INF] want-GER
      i.
      4.AUX
      'I want to buy a coat.'
  (c) *w-ez$_i$ buwa-mu   Ø$_i$*
      1-I.DAT   [mother-ERG 1.NOM
      w-irk̄u-s   L'an-ši   w-i.
      1-search-INF] want-GER 1-AUX
      'I want mother to look for me.'

The dependent clause in (13a) has a single argument which is coreferential with the NP argument of the main verb 'want', and this argument is omitted. In (13b), the omitted argument is an Agentive in the ergative, and in (13c), it is an Absolutive in the nominative. Thus, the rule for infinitival complementation is neutral with respect to the role characteristics of the omitted arguments.

A neutral strategy is preferably chosen in clause chaining, too. For instance:

(14) Lak (Daghestanian)
  (a) *Ø$_i$ na   awīunu,*
      [ERG   I.NOM   beat.CONV]
      lawgun-di   g$_o$a$_i$.
      go.away.PAST-3 P   he.NOM
      'He beat me and went away.'
  (b) *g$_o$a-nal Ø$_i$ awīunu,*
      [he-ERG   NOM   beat.CONV]
      lawgu-ra   na$_i$.
      go.away.PAST-1P   I.NOM
      'He beat me and I went away.'

The argument of the converbal construction which is coreferential with the sole argument of the main clause is omitted irrespective of its role.

Some languages admit a neutral strategy even in the context of reflexivization, which is held to follow the accusative control pattern universally (cf. Dixon 1994: 138). For instance:

(15) Dargwa, Chiragh dialect (Daghestanian)
  (a) *it-i   čej   iXIib.*
      he-ERG self.NOM take.care.past

(b) it   čine   iẌIib.
    he.NOM self.ERG take.care.past
    'He took care of himself.'

Both the ergative and the nominative argument can occur as controller or as target of reflexivization.

Thus, we see that in role-dominated languages there is no syntactic reason for singling out a subject NP with syntactic properties that the other NPs lack.

4.2. Active role-dominated languages

Role languages need not necessarily follow the ergative alignment pattern (just as ergative alignment in a language does not imply that it is a role-dominated language – compare Dyirbal, which is syntactically ergative). As was shown convincingly by Durie 1987, 1988, Acehnese (an Austronesian language of Sumatra) is an **active** role-dominated language. The coding of NP arguments distinguishes the hyperroles of Actor and Undergoer, as they are discussed in Van Valin's and Foley's work (Foley & Van Valin 1984, Foley 1993, Van Valin 1993). The coding of Actor and Undergoer in Acehnese is shown in (16).

(16) Acehnese (Austronesian; Durie 1987: 369)
 (a) *geu-jak gopnyan.*
     (s)he-go (s)he
     '(S)he goes.'
 (b) *gopnyan rhet(-geuh).*
     (s)he   fall(-(s)he)
     '(S)he falls.'
 (c) *gopnyan geu-mat lon.*
     (s)he   (s)he-hold I
     '(S)he holds me.'

The prefix *geu-* in (16 a) is controlled by the Actor with the one-place verb 'go', and the optional suffix *-geuh* is controlled by the Undergoer with the one-place verb 'fall'. These same markers code the Actor and the Undergoer with the transitive verb 'hold' (the suffixal Undergoer marker appears only in special circumstances). The syntactic behavior of the Actor and the Undergoer in Acehnese does not justify setting up a level of subject-object relations either (for a detailed analysis confirming this view, see Durie's work cited above, as well as Van Valin 1993: 51–56).

4.3. Accusative role-dominated languages

Due to their superficial similarity with the Indo-European language type, many languages with accusative alignment have been described inadequately, and this makes it difficult to find documented examples of semantically accusative languages. However, according to Andrej Kibrik's data, Navajo is a language of this type (cf. Kibrik 1997: 298–299). The verbal cross-reference markers in Navajo show accusative alignment, contrasting the hyperroles **Principal** and **Patientive**. An **accusative** role-dominated language, in contrast to accusative subject-oriented languages, features a single hyperrole that combines the argument of a one-place verb and the agent-like argument of a two-place verb – "the *main* participant, the 'hero' of the situation, who is *primarily* responsible for the fact that this situation takes place" (Kibrik 1997: 292), and not the syntactic subject position, which only in the prototypical situations has this role characteristic. In Navajo, the accusative coding strictly follows the role characteristics of the arguments and is not connected to the syntactic environment.

Thus, among the attested role-dominated languages we have ergative, active and accusative languages, in which the arguments are marked in accordance with the semantic hyperroles of the verbs' participants. In these languages, the role dimension is decisive for marking and distinguishing NP functions in the clause.

Following the Hierarchy of Semantic Dimensions, the existence of mono-pivotal flow-dominated, deixis-dominated, and reference-dominated languages is impossible or unlikely. An exception would be Lisu according to the description of Li & Thompson 1976. In this language, the argument roles are not distinguished, but there is a grammaticalized topic, i. e. a category of the flow dimension.

5. Multi-pivotal subjectless languages

In addition to grammaticalizing concepts of the role dimension, multi-pivotal subjectless languages also have grammaticalized concepts of the flow dimension, as well as other dimensions in accordance with the Hierarchy of Semantic Dimensions. With respect to the role characteristics, they do not contribute anything radically new, compared with mono-pivotal role-dominated languages. They, too, can be semantically ergative, active, or accusative. What is essential is that the characteristics of other dimensions can vary considerably. Unfortunately, there exists so far no typology of the concepts of the flow and deictic dimensions, and this has negative repercussions not only on the general theory, but also on descriptions of individual languages, which lack an appropriate metalanguage for representing the data.

Thanks to Schachter's (1976, 1977) detailed description of the relevant aspects of Tagalog, we can get an idea of a multi-pivotal subjectless language with accusative alignment of roles and an independent mechanism of coding the characteristics of the flow dimension, which consists in the marking of a topic. The semantic roles are generally expressed by prenominal particles, and the topic NP is marked by the prenominal particle *ang*, which makes it necessary to express the role of the topic morphologically on the verb. According to Schachter, Tagalog is functionally quite similar to subject-oriented languages, but it shows separatist coding of role and flow characteristics.

Tsakhur, a Daghestanian language, combines the traditional ergative role orientation with an independent marking of another flow concept: focus.

(17) Tsakhur (Daghestanian)
 (a) *maIhamad-e: Xaw*
    Muhammad-ERG house.IV.NOM
    alja?a-wo=d.
    build-COP=IV
    'Muhammad is building a house.'
 (b) *maIhamad-e: Xaw-wo=d*
    Muhammad-ERG house.IV.NOM
    alja?a.
    build-COP=IV
    'Muhammad is building A HOUSE (not a bridge, etc.).'
 (c) *maIhamad-e:-wo=d Xaw*
    Muhammad-ERG house.IV.NOM
    alja?a.
    build-COP=IV
    'MUHAMMAD (not Ali, etc.) is building a house.'

The ergative role coding is preserved in all three sentences in (17), but besides this, the copula can attach enclitically to the focused NP.

As has become clear from examining many language descriptions in the present framework, there exists a fairly great diversity of combinations of role concepts with concepts of other dimensions (see Kibrik 1997 for more details). Unfortunately, this is often not realized by authors of descriptive grammars, so that it is often difficult, if not altogether impossible, to discern the real type of the language under the mask of the subject-object terminology. This is ironic, because the true nature of the concepts of the various dimensions is considerably more transparent in multi-pivotal subjectless languages than in subject-oriented languages, which due to an unfortunate historical accident have served as the starting point for the formulation and the development of linguistic theory.

6. Pivotless languages

The pioneering work of David Gil (Gil 1994) has demonstrated the possibility of a subjectless language which does not grammaticalize the concepts of any semantic dimension at all. According to Gil's description, in Riau Indonesian (spoken in Sumatra and adjacent islands opposite Singapore) there is no marking of the role characteristics of core NPs, or of any other concepts of the semantic dimensions. Of course, in this language there are no grounds for setting up subject-object relations.

(18) Riau Indonesian (Gil 1994)
 (a) *David takot saya.*
    you=David fear I:SG
    'You [i.e. David] frightened me.'
 (b) *Saya takot ini.*
    I:SG fear that
    'I'm frightened by that.'
 (c) *Masok putih, masok putih, masok*
    enter white enter white enter
    putih.
    white
    [playing billiards] 'The white one is going in, the white one is going in, the white one is going in.'
 (d) *Gidi saya kuning lagi.*
    tooth I:SG yellow CONJ
    'My teeth are still yellow.'

(18a−b) show that the arguments of the verb 'fear' may appear in either order. Moreover, each of these sentences is ambiguous. (18a) can also mean 'I frightened you', and (18b) can mean 'I frightened that'. As (18c−d) show, word order is free with one-place verbs, too. There are no morphological markers of the semantic or syntactic status of NPs.

7. Subject-oriented languages

It is not difficult to see that subject-oriented languages differ from multi-pivotal subjectless languages primarily in the formal aspects − in showing cumulative coding of concepts from different semantic dimensions. They can be just as diverse as mono-pivotal subjectless languages.

The Indo-European standard exemplifies the type of the flow/role-dominated language with accusative role alignment (syntactically accusative languages). In this type, the semantic hyperrole Principal is the basis for the subject. Dyirbal differs from the Indo-European languages only in showing ergative alignment (as a syntactically ergative language). In this language, the semantic hyperrole Absolutive is the basis of the subject.

(19) Dyirbal
(a) ba-ji yar^{y}a banin^{y}u.
    CL-NOM.I man.NOM come
    'Man came/is coming.'
(b) ba-la-n d^{y}ugumbil ba-ŋgu-l
    CL-NOM-II woman.NOM CL-ERG-I
    yar^{y}a-ŋgu balgan.
    man-ERG hit
    'Man hit/is hitting woman.'
(c) ba-yi yar^{y}a ba-gu-n
    CL-NOM.I man.NOM CL-DAT-II
    d^{y}ugumbi-lgu balgal-ŋa-n^{y}u.
    woman-DAT hit-ANTIPASS-TENSE
    'Man hit woman.'

The sole argument of the intransitive verb in (19 a) and the patient of the transitive verb in (19 b) show a common marking in the nominative, and the Agentive of the transitive verb in (19 b) is marked as ergative. However, the transitive verb can appear in the antipassive (marker -ŋa- in (19 c)), where the Agentive is in the nominative, and the Absolutive in the dative. The Dyirbal antipassive is radically different from the Daghestanian antipassive in that it has specific syntactic functions. In clause coordination, coreferential NPs must be in the nominative, and the second NP is omitted. Therefore antipassivization is required if one of the coreferential NPs is an Agentive NP. This is illustrated in (20).

(20) Dyirbal
(a) [ba-yi yar^{y}a$_i$ banin^{y}u] [Ø$_i$
    CL-NOM.I man.NOM come   NOM
    ba-ŋgu-n dyugumbi-r^{y}u balgan].
    CL-ERG-II woman-ERG hit
    'Man came here and was hit by woman.'
(b) [ba-yi yar^{y}a$_i$ banin^{y}u] [Ø$_i$
    CL-NOM.I man.NOM come   nom
    bagun dyugumbil-gu
    CL.DAT.II woman-DAT
    balgal-ŋa-n^{y}u].
    hit-ANTIPASS-TENSE
    'Man came here and hit woman.'

Analogous processes can be found also in the formation of other multi-predicate structures. Therefore the nominative in Dyirbal is not associated with a fixed semantic role, and marks the NP with the highest syntactic rank, i. e. in essence it is a subject marker.

Strange as it may seem, it turns out that subject-oriented languages are at present not better known than subjectless languages because previous descriptions are based on the wrong presupposition that the organizing principles of predicate-argument structure invariably follow the Indo-European model.

Thus, the space of typological possibilities of subjectless and subject-oriented languages is enormous, and at present we can discern only its broad outlines. We have yet to discover the existence of various implicational universals which put restrictions on the logically possible combinations of characteristics from the various semantic dimensions and their cumulative realization in the subject-object pattern.

It is possible to formulate several statistical correlations between the syntactic types of languages and the morphosyntactic means that serve to code the corresponding features of NPs. Thus, pivotless languages prefer isolating morphology with weakly developed analytic structures and free word order; subjectless languages prefer agglutinating morphology and free word order; and subject-oriented languages usually have flective morphology or fixed word order. Although there are not yet any systematic cross-linguistic studies that confirm these hypotheses, they follow naturally from the present theoretical framework and should be taken into account in future empirical work.

It is also possible to formulate several more specific correlations. The role characteristics are preferably marked by means of nominal surface cases or verbal affixes. The deictic meanings have a tendency to be expressed by means of cross-reference markers. The flow properties are preferably coded by word order and/or by analytic means: function words or particles. The referential characteristics are generally expressed by articles or particles. These correspondences are not fixed, but they can be used as empirical clues for identifying languages of the corresponding types.

Subject-oriented languages usually have highly developed means (especially voices) for promoting arguments into privileged core positions and for demoting their status, while subjectless languages lack such syntactic properties: They only display means for increasing/decreasing the verbal valence, especially for transitivization or intransitivization of the verb, and also for changing the role meanings of arguments.

It needs to be kept in mind that the sharp distinctions drawn in this article between cumulative and separatist coding, between subject-oriented and subjectless languages, and between mono-pivotal and multi-pivotal languages is primarily intended to facilitate understanding and does not reflect the reality of languages. These contrasts represent extreme meanings on the corresponding scales of cumulativity, subject-orientation and pivotness, and in reality we are faced with a continuous set of transitional types, in accordance with the real diversity of natural languages and the multiplicity of their historical states.

8. Subject-oriented and subjectless languages in diachronic perspective

We still have to answer the last question asked at the beginning of this article: What are the possible diachronic paths of change of linguistic types? Are all logically possible paths of transition from one language type to another likely? Since it is even more difficult to gather relevant diachronic data from a wide variety of languages, any answer to these questions must remain speculative at this stage. However, the theoretical ideas laid out in this article have natural diachronic implications. Starting from the principle of unidirectionality and cyclicity of language change, and omitting possible paths of change within a type, I propose the schema in Fig. 101.1 as a hypothesis:

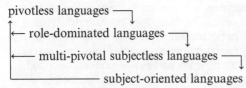

Figure 101.1: Diachonic paths of change in linguistic type

This schema claims that the original state of the diachronic cycle is the pivotless language. The diachronic development is directed from the pivotless type to the (mono-pivotal) role-dominated type, from this to the multi-pivotal subjectless type and, finally, to the subject-oriented type. In principle the diachronic cycle can be interrupted at any stage, returning to the original pivotless state, but the reverse development (for instance, from a multi-pivotal subjectless language to a role-dominated language, or from a subject-oriented language to a role-dominated or multi-pivotal subjectless language) is impossible.

Judging by the typological characterization of several language families, at least several stages of this cycle are very stable. Thus, the Daghestanian languages clearly form a typological unity, which was inherited from the common Daghestanian language state, whose age is estimated at roughly 5000—6000 years by data from recent Daghestanian historical-comparative research (Starostin & Nikolaev 1994). In some languages we see concepts of the flow dimensions being grammaticalized, i. e. we have a transition from a mono-pivotal to a multi-pivotal role-dominated language, but there are no signs yet of these languages moving toward the subject-oriented stage.

It would appear that particularly important for the stability of a linguistic type is its internal structure. Thus, accusative role-dominated languages have more chances of becoming subject-oriented than ergative or active languages, because the semantic hyperrole Principal is in harmony with the flow characteristic of the topic. In fact, the majority of subject-oriented languages are accusative, and subject-oriented ergative languages are found only sporadically. So far no subject-oriented active languages have been attested, and apparently this is not accidental. The active alignment singles out two core roles of equal status, and this contradicts the idea of ranking that is at the basis of the subject-object pattern. It cannot be excluded that the transition to the subject-oriented stage requires additional internal reorganization and a change in role type.

We may assume that a more careful study of the languages that are currently described as subject-oriented will reveal many of them to be somewhere on the borderline between subject-oriented languages and subjectless languages, or to be subjectless languages after all (note that practically all languages which are regarded as subjectless in this article have been described as standard subject-oriented languages).

Acknowledgement

This work was supported by a grant from the Russian Foundation of Basic Research (RFFI), project 98−06−80458.

9. References

Andrews, Avery. 1985. "The major functions of the noun phrase". In: Shopen, Timothy (ed.). *Language typology and syntactic description*, vol. 1. Cambridge: Cambridge University Press, 62–154.

Comrie, Bernard. 1981. *Language universals and linguistic typology.* Chicago: The University of Chicago Press.

Dik, Simon C. 1978. *Functional Grammar.* Dordrecht: Foris.

Dixon, R. M. W. 1994. *Ergativity.* Cambridge: Cambridge University Press.

Durie, Mark. 1987. "Grammatical relations in Acehnese." *Studies in Language* 11: 365–399.

Durie, Mark. 1988. "Preferred argument structure in an active language: Arguments against the category 'Intransitive subject'". *Lingua* 74: 1–25.

Foley, William A. 1993. "The conceptual basis of grammatical relations". In: Foley, William A. (ed.) *The role of theory in language description.* Berlin: Mouton de Gruyter, 131–174.

Foley, William A. & Van Valin, Robert D. 1984. Functional syntax and universal grammar. Cambridge: Cambridge University Press.

Gil, David. 1994. "The structure of Riau Indonesian". *Nordic Journal of Linguistics* 17: 179–200.

Hopper, Paul & Thompson, Sandra A. 1980. "Transitivity in grammar and discourse". *Language* 56: 251–299.

Keenan, Edward. 1976. "Towards a universal definition of 'subject'". In: Li, Charles (ed.). Subject and topic. New York: Academic Press, 303–333.

Kibrik, Aleksandr E. 1979. "Canonical ergativity and Daghestan languages". In: Plank, Frans (ed.) *Ergativity: Towards a theory of grammatical relations.* New York: Academic Press, 61–77.

Kibrik, Aleksandr E. 1997: "Beyond subject and object: Toward a comprehensive relational typology". *Linguistic Typology* 1.3: 279–346.

Kibrik, Andrej. 1996. "Transitivity in lexicon and grammar". In: Kibrik, Alexandr (ed.) *Godoberi.* (Lincom Studies in Caucasian Linguistics, 2.) Munich: Lincom Europa, 108–143.

Lazard, Gilbert. 1997. "*Ergativity,* by R. M. W. Dixon". *Linguistic Typology* 1: 243–268. [Review article on Dixon 1994].

Li, Charles & Thompson, Sandra A. 1976. "Subject and topic: A new typology of language". In: Li, Charles (ed.). *Subject and topic.* New York: Academic Press, 457–489.

Plank, Frans. 1991. "Of abundance and scantiness in inflection: A typological prelude." In: Plank, Frans (ed.). *Paradigms: The economy of inflection.* Berlin: Mouton de Gruyter, 1–39.

Schachter, Paul. 1976. "The subject in Philippine languages: topic, ctor, actor-topic, or none of the above." In: Li, Charles (ed.). *Subject and topic.* New York: Academic Press, 491–518.

Schachter, Paul. 1977. "Reference-related and role-related properties of subjects." In: Cole, Peter & Sadock, Jerrold M. (eds.). Grammatical relations. (Syntax and Semantics, 8.) New York: Academic Press, 279–306.

Starostin, Sergej & Nikolaev, Sergej. 1994. *Etymological dictionary of North Caucasian languages.* Moscow.

Van Valin, Robert D. 1977. "Ergativity and universality of subjects". *Chicago Linguistic Society* 13: 689–706.

Van Valin, Robert D. 1981. "Grammatical relations in ergative languages." *Studies in Language* 5: 261–394.

Van Valin, Robert D. 1993. "A synopsis of Role and Reference Grammar". In: Van Valin, Robert D. (ed.). *Advances in Role and Reference Grammar.* Amsterdam: Benjamins, 1–164.

Aleksandr E. Kibrik, Moscow (Russia)

102. Head-marking vs. dependent-marking languages

1. Introduction
2. Basic notions
3. Some head-marking and dependent-marking patterns
4. Applicability and distribution
5. Correlations with other typological parameters
6. Correlations with grammatical categories
7. Relevance for historical and theoretical linguistics
8. References

1. Introduction

The head- and dependent-marking parameter is a morphological-structural parameter which allows languages to be classified according to their head-marking and dependent-marking characteristics. Phrases, clauses, and complex sentences are grammatical units which are assumed to be hierarchically organized as constituents consisting of elements functioning as heads and other elements functioning as their dependents. Dependency relations within constituents on all levels of grammar can be marked morphologically either on the head element or on the dependent element. The central hypothesis of the head- and dependent-marking parameter, originally developed and introduced by Johanna Nichols (1986) and further elaborated in Nichols (1992), is the idea that languages tend to mark dependency relations consistently either on the head element or on a dependent element of their respective constituents. This means that languages can be classified according to these two marking types — predominantly head-marking and predominantly dependent-marking — with a significant clustering around these polar types.

In addition, Nichols contends that these morphological-structural characteristics are typologically important grammatical features of a language, because they can be shown within her analytic framework to enter into many correlations with other typological features such as word order type, alignment type, and certain grammatical categories. Furthermore, it is hypothesized that the head- and dependent-marking characteristics are diachronically the most conservative and stable features of a language so that they can serve as a tool to generate reasonable and substantial hypotheses about the genetic and areal relatedness of a language or group of languages reaching a time depth which transcends the limits of the traditional historical-comparative method.

The head- and dependent-marking parameter offers many ideas, claims and hypotheses relevant for linguistic typology, historical linguistics, grammaticalization theory, language contact, and grammatical theory. The implications for the different fields of linguistic research are far from being fully explored and understood. The innovative character of this concept is reflected in the reactions of the linguistic community; silence paired with skepticism prevailed in the beginning (e. g. Croft's influential book on language typology and universals did not even mention this concept; cf. Croft 1990). Some linguists began to integrate this concept in their research (e. g. Bresnan & Mchombo 1987, Van Valin 1987) and later, the reviews of Nichols' book (1992) were overwhelmingly positive (cf. Blake 1993, Haspelmath 1993, Dahl 1994, Niepokuj 1994). They collectively emphasized the new perspectives in linguistic research which were opened by the introduction and data-intensive typological exploitation of this concept. Although it is Nichols' merit to have demonstrated the importance of the head- and dependent-marking concept for linguistic typology, it was T. Milewski who originally had established this typological parameter (cf. Milewski 1950). Milewski distinguished between **concentric** versus **eccentric** languages which corresponds to Nichols' head- and dependent-marking classification. Languages were termed **concentric** by Milewski when they dominantly indicate the syntactic relation on the governing element of a constituent. Accordingly, languages were termed **eccentric** when they mark the existence of a syntactic relation on the governed element(s) of a constituent (see also Lehmann (1983) for a general discussion of the head- and dependent-marking concept with a different terminology and a brief mention of Milewski's concentric vs. eccentric typology).

Criticism was expressed by historical linguists about Nichols' diachronic research based on the head- and dependent-parameter (e. g. Greenberg 1993).

The following sections will provide an introduction into the basic notions of this parameter (§ 2.), and will give some illustrative examples for head- and dependent-marking patterns (§ 3.). In (§ 4.) problems and limitations regarding the cross-linguistic application of this parameter and the overall distribution of head- and dependent-marking patterns will be presented. The following two sections, (§§ 5.–6.), present some results of the correlation of head- and dependent-marking patterns with other already established typological parameters such as word order and alignment, and (§ 7.) will give some indications how this parameter can be relevant for historical and theoretical linguistics.

2. Basic notions

The head- and dependent-marking parameter is built on two theoretically independent concepts, **headedness** and **morphological marking**. The concept of **headedness** was developed and employed in different structuralist approaches to syntax. The framework of dependency grammar (cf. Tesnière 1966, Mel'čuk 1988, etc.) is, in particular, the theoretical background for Nichols' notion of **head**. Headedness is not directly or overtly given in the linguistic data, but can be determined by various independent criteria and operations (cf. e.g. Zwicky 1985, Corbett et al. 1994). The head of a given construction is "the word which determines the syntactic type of the entire constituent and hence the privileges of occurrence and syntactic distribution of the constituent. If there is any government (by which I mean requirement of one word in a particular grammatical function by another) within the constituent, it is the head that governs the dependent" (Nichols 1992: 46). The most important constituent types with their respective head and dependent relations which were chosen for the broad data-intensive typological study in Nichols (1986) and with some modifications in Nichols (1992) are shown in Table 1.

The other central concept is that of overt **morphological marking** of syntactic relations, i.e. an affix or some other morphological means signals the presence of a dependency relation and the kind of this relation either on the head or the dependent of a constituent. Nichols distinguishes three different ways in which morphological means indicate the kind of syntactic relation, but only two of them are relevant for the intended typological parameter. On the one hand, affixes may **index** certain properties of either the head or the dependent on the other corre-

Table 102.1: Constituent types and head/dependent relations

Constituent	Head	Dependent
Noun phrase	possessed noun	possessor
	noun	modifying adjective
	adposition	object of adposition
Clause	predicate/verb	arguments/adjuncts
	auxiliary verb	lexical/main verb
Sentence	main-clause predicate	subordinate clause

sponding constituent. For instance, the inflection of verbs in many Indo-European languages indexes the person/number categories of the subject (dependent) on the head of the clause (verb), and, similarly, the inflection of the attributive adjective in some Indo-European languages indexes gender/number categories of the head noun on the dependent (attributive adjective) of such a construction. This indexing function of morphology coincides broadly with what is traditionally called agreement.

The other way affixes may indicate the presence of a syntactic relation is by directly **coding** this relation. Ergative, nominative, accusative, and dative case forms directly code a syntactic relation such as subject, direct object and so on, of the (dependent) noun they are attached to. The same is true for the Indo-European verb inflection which signals that the dependent noun stands in a particular relation to the head (verb), namely in a subject relation.

The central criterion according to which the head- and dependent-marking parameter classifies languages is the locus of morphological marking of syntactic relations within a constituent. Morphological markers of various types — affixes, clitics, ablaut and other form changing mechanisms — can be located on the head word, the dependent word, on both or on neither. Constructions are **head-marking** if these markers are attached to the head word, they are **dependent-marking** if they are attached to the dependent word, and they are **double-marking** if markers are located on both head and dependent words of a construction. In order to further clarify what is meant with head-marking and dependent-marking constructions, some illustrative examples will be given in the next section.

3. Some head-marking and dependent-marking patterns

On the phrase level, there are at least three different types of syntactic relations which are cross-linguistically significant enough to serve as a basis for comparison, the possessive construction, the noun plus attributive ajective NP, and the adpositional phrase.

A possessive construction is dependent-marking, if the noun or pronoun referring to the **possessor** is morphologically marked while the noun reffering to the **possessum** ("thing possessed") remains unmarked. The possessum is generally assumed to be the head of a possessive construction. Compare the examples from German, a predominantly dependent-marking language, in (1 a−b). The head constituents in these and all the following examples are represented in bold letters.

(1) (a) German
    das **Haus** des Vater-s
    the.NOM house the.GEN father-GEN
    'father's house'
(b) sein **Haus**
    3SG.POSS house
    'his house'

The possessor noun *Vater* 'father' in (1 a) is marked by a genitive case which identifies the kind of syntactic relation which holds between *Haus* 'house' and *Vater*. In (1 b) the possessor ist referred to by a 3rd person pronoun which marks the possessive relation not by a case suffix but simply by its membership to the paradigm of possessive pronouns which are in opposition to other personal pronouns in German. In both examples, the head noun *Haus*, which refers to the possessum, remains unmarked.

Possessive constructions are head-marked, if the head noun − the possessum − bears the morphological marker indicating the possessive relation. Compare the examples (2 a−b) from Abkhaz, a Northwest Caucasian language which shows thorough head-marking characteristics.

(2) (a) Abkhaz (Hewitt 1979: 116)
    sarà sə-y°nə
    1SG 1SG-house
    'my house'

(b) à-č'k°'ən yə-**y°nə**
    ART-boy 3SG-house
    'the boy's house'

The head noun *y°nə* 'house' in (2 a) and (2 b) is marked by a bound pronoun which − in this context − indicates the possessive relation and refers to the possessor of this relation. Similar ways to express possession can be found in Mayan languages and many North American Indian languages.

The differences between head-marking and dependent-marking adpositional phrases parallel the ones found in possessive constructions. The adposition is assumed to be the head of an adpositional phrase which governs its object noun or pronoun which, consequently, counts as the dependent of such a construction. Compare the examples in (3 a−b).

(3) (a) Russian
    s brat-om
    with brother-INSTR
    'with (my, one's) brother'
(b) Tzutujil Mayan (Dayley 1985: 152)
    r-**umaal** jar aachi
    3AG-cause the man
    'because of, by the man'

The prepositional phrase in (3 a) is dependent-marking, because the object noun which is governed by the preposition *s* 'with' receives the case marker required for this kind of syntactic relation. Other prepositions in Russian govern different cases. The marking type of this construction would be the same if the object noun were replaced by a pronoun. The adpositional phrase in (3 b) is head-marked, because the adposition − the head of the construction − is marked by a 3rd person bound pronoun which cross-references the object noun of the construction.

Noun phrases consisting of a head noun and a modifying adjective (dependent) are − if there is any relation marking morphology − preferably marked on the dependent. The adjective receives the morphological marker of the relation, and agrees in gender, number, or case with the governing noun. It is typologically very significant that it is difficult to find any example for an adjective plus noun pattern which is head-marked. This fact indicates that such noun phrases strongly prefer dependent-marking patterns which seems to be a trait of this constituent type itself. Shuswap, a Salish language of the Northwest Pacific coast may serve as an example of this rare pattern. It has a special relative case prefix *t-* which is used to indicate the attributive relation on the head noun of the construction (cf. Kuipers 1974: 78).

The head-marked constructions in (2 a−b) and (3 b) have in common that the dependent nouns or pronouns which are cross-referenced, or indexed, on the respective head by a bound pronoun are optional, i. e. these constructions would be complete and perfect grammatical expressions, if the dependent nouns or pronouns were left out. This is not the case with the corresponding dependent-marked construction in (1 a−b) and (3 a). The constructions as such would be no longer existent, or would be simply ungrammatical, if the dependent nouns/pronouns were omitted.

Languages which show dependent-marking constructions on the clause-level usually have case marking systems. Nouns or pronouns representing the core arguments of the clause are the dependents of the verbal head of the clause. They are morphologically marked by case forms which indicate the presence of a dependency relation and, in addition, code the sort of syntactic relation between these constituents. The case marking of the core arguments is governed by the verbal head of the clause. Compare the example in (4) from Chechen, a Northeast Caucasian language of the Nakh group, which has strong dependent-marking characteristics.

(4) Chechen (Nichols 1986: 61)
    da:-s   wo'a-na   urs-Ø   tü:xira
    father-ERG son-DAT knife-ABS struck
    'The father stabbed the son.' (lit. 'father struck son with knife')

All three nominal arguments in (4) are marked by different case forms − ergative, dative, and absolutive. The verbal head *tü:xira* 'struck' shows no marking of syntactic relations at all, which holds for the majority of verbs in Chechen. There is a minor group of verbs which have a morphological slot for prefixes which agree in gender and number with the absolutive marked noun. This is the only head-marking trait to be found in Chechen.

An example for a head-marking construction on the clause level is given in (5).

(5) Abkhaz (Hewitt 1979: 36)
    a-xàc'a   a-pℏ°ǝs   a-š°q°'ǝ
    the-man   the-woman the-book
    Ø-lc̣-y-te-yt'
    it-to.her-he-gave-FINITE
    'The man gave the woman the book.'

In Abkhaz, the verb has maximally three slots for bound pronouns which refer to the core arguments of a transitive clause. The bound pronouns index the syntactic relations of the clause. The type of syntactic relation is morphologically encoded by the order of pronominal affixes on the verb. Nouns in Abkhaz are generally caseless. They are cross-referenced by the bound pronouns on the verb according to person, number, and gender. Their syntactic status is very different from the one nouns have in dependent-marked clauses. Lexical NPs in Abkhaz are optional. They can be omitted and usually are omitted in discourse as long as the reference of the bound pronouns is recoverable for the addressee. This means that the person-marked finite verb in Abkhaz represents a complete and fully grammatical clause. The appositional status of NPs in Abkhaz can be found in many other non-European languages and may be viewed as a defining feature, among others, of polysynthetic languages. The so-called "one-word-sentence" in polysynthetic languages and their major structural difference compared to the familiar Indo-European languages was already observed by Frans Boas in his famous Introduction to the *Handbook of American Indian Languages* (Boas 1911).

4. Applicability and distribution

4.1. Other marking patterns

The head- vs. dependent-marking parameter is designed to classify all constructions which show a morphological marking of the dependency relation either on the head or on the dependent(s) of a constituent. Morphological marking includes all types of form changing of either the head word or the dependent words. Therefore, all grammatical constructions which employ alternative means such as juxtaposition, word order, free function words, and relation marking clitics whose host is neither the head nor the dependent word fall out of the head- and dependent-marking classification. Nearly every language shows one of these marking techniques either as a minor or as a major pattern on one of the different constituent levels. For instance, the expression of possession by juxtaposition or compounding can be found in various languages, compare the examples in (6 a−c).

(6) (a) Chitimacha (Swadesh 1946: 327)
'iš **hana**
I house
'my house'
(b) Thai (Hudak 1990: 770)
năŋsŭ dèk
book child
'the child's book'
(c) **dèk** săam khon
child three classifier
'three children'

In Chitimacha, a now extinct language isolate of Louisiana, possessive relations are predominantly expressed by juxtaposition, with the possessor (dependent) preceding the possessum (head), no matter whether the possessor is expressed by a noun or a pronoun. There is no morphological marking of possessive or attributive relations at all. The same is true for Thai, a language of the Kam-Tai family in Southeast Asia. The possessive relation as well as the attribute relation (compare the examples in (6 b–c)) are expressed by word order with the head noun always preceding the dependent(s). The possessive construction in (6 b) would be the same if the dependent noun *dèk* 'child' were replaced by a pronoun. There is an alternative way to express (6 b) with a function word *khɔ̌ɔŋ* between possessum and possessor, which roughly corresponds to English *of*. In a strict sense, the possessive constructions with *khɔ̌ɔŋ* 'of' can not be considered as dependent-marking because it is not a morphological marker attached to the dependent word. The same problem arises with English *of* in *the house of the ancestors* where *of* cannot be counted as a morphological dependent-marker.

On the clause level, a similar problem emerges for the application of the head- and dependent-marking parameter with respect to relation-marking clitics – pronominal clitics – which are located in a special syntactic position not necessarily close to the head or in the preferred position of the nominal dependent(s). These pronominal clitics are dependents and show case distinctions, which qualifies them for the classification as dependent-marking. On the other hand, pronominal clitics tend to cluster in a rigid order in second position often directly preceding the main verb which brings them close to a head-marking construction, although they are not yet pronominal affixes. The peculiarities of pronominal clitics – e. g. in French, Serbo-Croatian, or Uto-Aztecan languages – cause some uncertainty in the application of the head- and dependent-parameter, which leads Nichols to introduce a third category besides head-marking and dependent-marking, namely **free** or **floated** marking (cf. Nichols 1992: 55–57). This third category is a kind of "waste basket" for all constructions involving pronominal clitics and relation marking particles which cannot be classified as head- or dependent-marking even if these criteria are applied in a less strict way.

Further problems with respect to the application of the head- and dependent-marking parameter cannot – because of lack of space – be treated in detail here, but should at least be mentioned briefly.

One of the points of departure of the whole head- and dependent-marking typology is the assumption that constituent structures on the phrase or clause level are basically the same but realized in a variety of different ways. This background assumption seems to be natural from the point of view of European languages which are dominantly dependent-marking. It turns out, however, that it is sometimes hard to identify adpositional phrases particularly in strong head-marking languages. The reason is that these languages lack European-style adpositions but employ **relational nouns** which are inflected with pronouns belonging to the possessive or object series of bound pronouns. The whole construction looks then more like a possessive construction (cf. Nichols 1992: 58). Other languages – particularly in New Guinea – use so-called **serial verbs** instead of adpositions, so that the resulting construction closely resembles a verbal phrase.

A similar problem arises with respect to attributive adjectives. Many languages – this is not restricted to radically head-marking languages – lack this lexical category, but express adjectival concepts by means of **inactive** or **stative verbs** or by nouns. The resulting attributive constructions look then more like simple predications in the first case, and like possessive constructions in the latter case.

Both problems indicate that the underlying model of the clause as a hierarchical structure of constituents with clearly identifiable dependency relations is not – especially with respect to head-marking languages – a firm ground for cross-linguistic comparison as it was expected. It seems to be the case that not all syntactic relations which were chosen as a universal set of dependency relations for cross-linguistic comparison in this study do occur in all languages. The problems with constituent structure and dependency relations as well as with their respective morphological marking are much more complicated with respect to the sentence level, i. e. the relations between main and subordinate clauses, relative clauses, causative constructions etc. Therefore, head-marking and dependent-marking strategies on the sentence level are not systematically surveyed in Nichols' typology.

4.2. Cross-linguistic distribution of head- and dependent-marking patterns

Nichols has examined the typological distributions of head- and dependent-marking patterns in a huge number of sample languages, 60 languages in her initial study (cf. Nichols 1986) and 174 languages in the book (cf. Nichols 1992), which were chosen according to their geographical distribution (**areas, macroareas**) and their genetic affiliation (**families, stocks**; for details of sampling cf. Nichols 1992: Ch 1.4.). Some of the results can be summarized as follows:

(a) Head- and dependent-marking features in each of the examined constituent types (i. e. the possessive NP, the adjective plus noun NP, the adpositional phrase, the clause, and the sum of possessive NP + adjective plus noun NP + clause) have approximately equal frequencies throughout the whole sample which means that there is no universally preferred marking type. But, with respect to areas, the head-marking patterns are preferred over dependent-marking patterns throughout the New World (North America, Mesoamerica, South America), while dependent-marking patterns are preferred in the Old World (Africa, Ancient Near East, Northern Eurasia, South and Southeast Asia). There is no significant preference in the Pacific Area (Oceania, New Guinea, Australia).
(b) The classification of languages according to their overall head-marking and dependent-marking properties — the sum of the marking properties of the single constituents in a particular language — reveals significant peaks around the two polar types, i. e. dominantly head-marking and dominantly dependent-marking. This is important evidence for the hypothesis that languages tend to be consistent with respect to the marking patterns they choose (cf. Nichols 1986: 70; 1992: 72 f.). In addition, Nichols makes the observation that the clustering of languages around the strong head-marking type is more compact than the clustering of languages around the dependent-marking type. The languages between the extreme types show to various degrees **split marking patterns** or **double marking patterns**. Double marking patterns means that a certain construction is head- and dependent-marked at the same time; e. g. pronominal cross-referencing of nominal arguments on the verbal head plus case marking of the nouns at the same time. Split marking means that a certain marking type is not employed throughout a certain constituent type; e. g. an adpositional phrase may be head-marked if the object of the adposition is a pronoun, but dependent-marked with a noun.
(c) Two implicational statements can be formulated regarding the distribution of head- and dependent-marked patterns across the different constituent levels within a language: (1) "If a language has major, salient head-marking morphology anywhere, it will have it at the clause level," and (2) "If a language has dependent-marking morphology at the clause level, it will have it at the phrase level." (Nichols 1986: 75).
(d) Many split-marking phenomena in the examined languages have to do with the different behavior of nouns and pronouns. There is a clear preference for possessive constructions and adpositional phrases to be head-marked if the respective dependents (i. e. possessor, object of adposition) are pronouns, while nouns show preferably dependent-marking patterns.

5. Correlations with other typological parameters

The distribution of head- and dependent-marking patterns shows some significant correlations with other typological parameters such as **word order types** (→ Art. 64) and **alignment types** which have already been established as important syntactic features of languages in the literature.

In relational typology, three major alignment types such as accusative, ergative, and stative-active are distinguished according to the marking patterns of the core arguments of a clause. Accusative alignment means that the transitive object/undergoer receives a special marking and therefore contrasts with the transitive subject/actor which is marked the same way as the intransitive subject, often by a nominative case. The accusative marking pattern, as well as the other alignment types, can be identified on various parts of speech such as nouns, pronouns, and verbs. Languages can employ distinct patterns, e. g. with nouns and pronouns, which results in the well-known split-marking systems such as split ergativity (cf. Silverstein 1976, DeLancey 1981). The accusative alignment seems to be the most frequent and unmarked type which is also reflected with respect to the distribution of head- and dependent-marking types. The numbers of head-marking, double-marking, and dependent-marking languages among the languages with dominantly accusative alignment are approximately the same (cf. Nichols 1992: 101). This means that accusative alignment is equally possible with head-marking, double-marking, and dependent-marking languages.

The correlation with ergative alignment, however, reveals a remarkable preference for dependent-marking patterns (cf. Nichols 1992: 101). Ergative alignment means that the subject/actor of a transitive clause is marked differently and contrasts with the transitive object/undergoer and intransitive subject which are both marked the same way, usually by an absolutive case. The majority of ergative languages in Nichols' sample are dependent-marking, which means that ergative alignment strongly prefers case marking.

Head-marking, on the other hand, is strongly associated with the stative-active alignment type (cf. Nichols 1992: 101). Stative-active alignment means that there is a marking split with respect to the intransitive subject. The intransitive subject, which is semantically the instigator of an action, is coded the same way as the subject/actor of a transitive clause, and the transitive object/undergoer is treated the same way as the intransitive subject which is involved in an uncontrolled state or process. The semantically determined coding of the core arguments of an intransitive or transitive clause in an active language is usually coupled with a rigid verb classification. The fact that these languages prefer head-marking patterns, i. e. the verb as the locus of the main syntactic information, is therefore functionally well motivated. There are, however, also dependent-marking or double-marking languages which exhibit stative-active coding patterns (e. g. Batsbi, Northeast Caucasian; cf. Holisky 1987).

The results of the statistical correlation of the head-, double-, and dependent-marking languages with the various word order types such as verb-initial, verb-medial, and verb-final types are less significant and convincing than the results of the correlation with the alignment types. Nevertheless, some interesting trends can be identified. First of all, SOV word order is by far the most dominant and prevailing basic word order type on nearly all continents (for some critical remarks regarding the assignment of word order types to Australian languages in Nichols' sample, see Blake 1993: 52). The data in Nichols (1992: 105 f.) show first of all the tendency for verb-medial and verb-final word order types to prefer dependent-marking patterns. Secondly the number of verb-initial languages is especially high for head-marking languages, while there are only very few verb-initial dependent-marking languages.

Nichols offers some functional explanations for the association of verb-initial word order with head-marking and the fact that the lack of basic word order is frequently found in head-marking languages. The lack of a basic word order is motivated by the appositional status of lexical NPs in strong head-marking languages. The grammaticalization of verb-initial order is explained with the principle that the main syntactic relations of a clause should be set up at the beginning of the clause. Head-marking languages indicate these relations on the verb, which explains the clustering of head-marking with the verb-initial order type. The same principle could motivate the preference of dependent-marking languages for verb-medial and verb-final order types. In these languages, the principal syntactic relations are marked on the noun or pronoun arguments of the clause which then tend to precede the verb (cf. Nichols 1992: 108 f.).

6. Correlations with grammatical categories

The most important result of the statistical correlation of various grammatical categories such as **inalienable possession, inclusive/exclusive** distinctions in the 1st person plural pronouns, **gender, noun classes, plural neutralization, non-finite** verb forms, and the use of **adpositions** with the various typological parameters discussed above (head- and dependent-marking, word order and alignment) is that **geography**, i. e. the geographical distribution of the categories over large areas, and head- and dependent-marking are the main limiting and predicting factors for the occurrence of these categories.

The occurrence of a distinction, for instance, between alienable and inalienable possession is exclusively bound to the head-marking patterns, i. e. either the language belongs to the overall head-marking type or there is a split-marking pattern, which always entails that the inalienable possession is represented by the head-marking construction. It seems that it is not possible for this category to be expressed by two different case forms, e. g. two different genitive cases. The often stated iconic motivation for the expression of inalienable possession (see e. g. Haiman 1980) seems to be secondary. The other predicting factor is geographical distribution. But this is secondary too. The almost complete lack of the alienable/inalienable distinctions in the Old World and the increasing frequency of occurrence of this distinction if one moves east to the New World seems to be an epiphenomenon of the general cline between the Old World and the New World with respect to the frequency of head-marking language types. For the other grammatical categories mentioned above, geographical distribution over large areas is the major predicting factor. If some typological parameter plays a role regarding the distribution then it is the head- and dependent-marking parameter, but only as a secondary factor. The inclusive/exclusive distinction is solely determined by geography.

7. Relevance for historical and theoretical linguistics

Head- and dependent-marking patterns are comparatively stable structural features of a language and language family. Language families tend to be very consistent with respect to their morphological marking type (head-, dependent-, double-, and split-marking). This means that the head- and dependent-marking parameter can be used as a hypothesis-generating tool in historical linguistics with respect to the relatedness of languages. It is not possible to state positively the genetic relatedness of adjacent languages, but, if there are sharp contrasts with respect to the morphological marking type between a particular language and the languages within a proposed language family, this can be taken as negative evidence for the assumed genetic relationship. Migration of people − i. e. non-relatedness − may be the reason for this otherwise unlikely contrast. If there are significant deviations from the average morphological marking type of a language family, this is due to areal influences (cf. Nichols 1986: 98).

The stability of the overall morphological marking type does not mean that there are no historical changes from one marking pattern to the other. With respect to such historical processes, Nichols formulates two principles which are highly relevant to grammaticalization theory. The first principle is that of **headward migration**, which allows a clear prediction about the historical behavior of function words, particles, and affixal morphology and gives an idea of how head-marking patterns emerge: "If any adposition or piece of affixal morphology moves, it will go from the dependent to the head of the constituent, not vice versa" (Nichols 1986: 84). The other principle is that of **reduction** − i. e. the reduction of whole words to affixes via cliticization − and **boundary shift**. Reduction is an analog of headward migration in that the original dependents get cliticized and eventually become markers of their head. Boundary shift means that constituents merge in the course of grammaticalization and that their former constituent boundaries disappear or move elsewhere; e. g. in the historical process of the development of case affixes, postpositions often are reduced and finally become case markers on their former dependent; the constituent boundary between the former constituents was collapsed with the constituent boundary of the NP. It is only via boundary shift that new dependent-marking morphology emerges (cf. Nichols 1986: 88).

One of the main merits of the introduction of the head- vs. dependent-marking parameter is to have brought the already well-known structural features of head-marking languages into a broad comparative perspective with the more familiar structural features of dependent-marking languages. It has become increasingly clear that grammatical theories which have based their central theoretical assumptions on the features of dependent-marking languages, e. g. the concept of government, fail to give satisfying accounts of head-marking languages (cf. Van Valin 1987).

8. References

Blake, B. J. 1993. "Review of Johanna Nichols, *Linguistic diversity in space and time.* Chicago: The University of Chicago Press, 1992." *Languages of the World* 6: 50−53.

Boas, Franz. 1911. "Introduction". In: Boas, F. (ed.) *Handbook of American Indian Languages*, Bulletin 40, Part I, Bureau of American Ethology. Washington DC: Government Printing Office, 1–83.

Bresnan, Joan & Sam A. Mchombo. 1987. "Topic, pronoun, and agreement in Chicheŵa". *Language* 63,4: 741–782.

Corbett, Greville C. et al. (eds.) 1994. *Heads in grammatical theory.* Cambridge: Cambridge University Press.

Croft, William. 1990. *Typology and universals.* Cambridge: Cambridge University Press.

Dahl, Östen. 1994. "Review of Johanna Nichols, *Linguistic diversity in space and time.* Chicago: The University of Chicago Press, 1992". *Sprachtypologie und Universalienforschung* 47,4: 375–379.

Dayley, Jon P. 1985. *Tzutujil Grammar* (University of California Publications in Linguistics 107). Berkeley: University of California Press.

DeLancey, Scott. 1981. "An interpretation of split ergativity and related patterns". *Language* 57: 626–657.

Greenberg, Joseph. 1993. "Review of Johanna Nichols, *Linguistic diversity in space and time.* Chicago: The University of Chicago Press, 1992". *Current Anthropology* 34,4: 503–505.

Haiman, Johan. 1980. "The iconicity of grammar: isomorphism and motivation". *Language* 54: 565–89.

Haspelmath, Martin. 1993. "Review of Johanna Nichols, *Linguistic diversity in space and time.* Chicago: The University of Chicago Press, 1992". *Journal of Linguistics* 29: 494–500.

Hewitt, B. G. 1979. *Abkhaz* (Lingua Descriptive Series 2). Amsterdam: North-Holland.

Holisky, Dee A. 1987. "The case of the intransitive subject in Tsova-Tush (Bats)." *Lingua* 71: 103–32.

Hudak, Thomas J. 1990. "Thai". In: Comrie, B. (ed.) *The world's major languages.* Oxford: Oxford University Press, 757–77.

Kuipers, Aert H. 1974. *The Shuswap language: Grammar, texts, dictionary.* (Janua linguarum, Series practica 225). The Hague: Mouton.

LaPolla, Randy. 1989. "Verb agreement, head-marking vs. dependent-marking, and the 'deconstruction' of Tibeto-Burman morpho-syntax". *Berkeley Linguistic Society* 15: 356–66.

Lehmann, Christian. 1983. "Rektion und syntaktische Relationen". *Folia Linguistica* 17: 339–378.

Mel'čuk, Igor. 1988. *Dependency syntax.* Albany: SUNY Press.

Milewski, Tadeusz. 1950. "La structure de la phrase dans les langues indigènes de l'Amérique du Nord". *Lingua Posnaniensis* 2: 162–207. (also in: Milewski, T. 1967. *Études typologiques sur le langues indigènes de l'Amerique.* Kraków: Polska Akademia Nauk, 70–101.)

Nichols, Johanna. 1986. "Head-marking and dependent-marking grammar". *Language* 62,1: 56–119.

Nichols, Johanna. 1992. *Linguistic diversity in space and time.* Chicago and London: The University of Chicago Press.

Niepokuj, Mary. 1994. "Review of Johanna Nichols, *Linguistic diversity in time and space.* Chicago: University of Chicago Press, 1992." *Diachronica* XI: 1, 120–125.

Silverstein, Michael. 1976. "Hierarchy of features and ergativity" in: Dixon, R. W. M. (ed.) *Grammatical categories in Australian languages,* Canberra (Australian Institute of Aboriginal Studies), 112–171.

Swadesh, Morris. 1946. "Chitimacha". In: Hoijer, Harry (ed.). *Linguistic structures of Native America* (Viking Fund Publications in Anthropology 6). New York: Viking Fund, 312–326.

Tesnière, Lucien. 1966. *Éléments de syntaxe structurale.* Paris: Klincksieck.

Van Valin, Robert D., Jr. 1987. "The role of government in the grammar of head marking languages". *International Journal of American Linguistics* 53,4: 371–97.

Zwicky, Arnold M. 1985. "Heads". *Journal of Linguistics* 21: 1–29.

Johannes Helmbrecht, Erfurt (Germany)

103. Configurationality and polysynthesis

1. Configurational and nonconfigurational languages
2. Theories of nonconfigurationality
3. Types of nonconfigurationality
4. Polysynthesis and nonconfigurationality
5. Special abbreviations
6. References

1. Configurational and nonconfigurational languages

English and French are prototypical **configurational** languages, in the sense that arguments with grammatical functions like subject and object consistently appear in particular phrase structure configurations. Virtually every English clause must have some kind of syntactically expressed subject, and clauses with transitive verbs must have syntactically expressed objects as well. The nearly-obligatory subject comes before the verb and any auxiliaries, whereas the direct object comes immediately after the verb:

(1)   *Pine Martens (should) climb trees.*

Furthermore, the object and the verb constitute a phrasal unit that does not include the subject, as shown by traditional phrase structures tests, such as VP-ellipsis, VP-pronominalization, and VP-fronting. Thus, objects are the only NPs that are immediately contained in the verb phrase in English, whereas subjects are the only NPs that appear outside the verb phrase in simple English sentences.

(2)
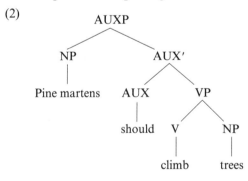

This strict correspondence between traditional grammatical functions and phrase structure positions opens up the possibility of taking a reductive approach to the grammatical functions, in which terms like "subject" and "object" are eliminated from grammatical theory in favor of terms like "NP outside the VP" and "NP that is immediately contained in VP". Syntactic and semantic conditions can then be written in such a way that they are sensitive to these phrase structure relationships, in order to capture the various other distinctive properties of subjects and objects. Historically, this is the approach that has been taken in most narrowly Chomskyan work over the past thirty years or so. When it is followed to its logical conclusion, phrase structure relationships become central to nearly all syntactic phenomena.

However, not all languages seem to attach the same importance to observable phrase structure configurations. In many — perhaps even most — languages, subjects and objects cannot be identified by word order and simple constituency tests in any straightforward way. Kenneth Hale has played a leading role in bringing this issue to attention, illustrating its dynamics from his extensive work on the Australian language Warlpiri, which presents an extreme case of a language of this kind. Hale (1983) shows that in Warlpiri any word order of the subject, verb, and object is possible, as long as the auxiliary is in the second position of the clause. Thus, the sentences in (3) are possible and are considered equivalent apart from matters of focus and emphasis.

(3) (a) Warlpiri (Simpson 1983: 140)
    Kurdu-ngku ka-ju   nya-nyi ngaju.
    child-ERG   PRES-1sO see-NPST I (ABS)
    'The child sees me.'
  (b) *Kurdu-ngku ka-ju ngaju nya-nyi.*
  (c) *Nya-nyi ka-ju kurdu-ngku ngaju.*
  (d) *Ngaju ka-ju nya-nyi kurdu-ngku.*
  (e) *Ngaju ka-ju kurdu-ngku nya-nyi.*
  (f) *Nya-nyi ka-ju ngaju kurdu-ngku.*

Sometimes more than one word can appear before the auxiliary, as long as those words form a noun phrase or similar constituent. However, the verb and its object never form a constituent in this sense, regardless of whether the object or the verb comes first:

(4)   Warlpiri (Simpson 1983: 141)
    *Ngaju nya-nyi ka-ju
    I(ABS) see-NPST PRES-1sO
    kurdu-ngku.
    child-ERG
    'The child sees me.'

Hale (1983: 7) also shows that either the subject or the object or both can be omitted. When this happens, the "missing" arguments of the verb are interpreted as pronominals:

(5) (a) *Ngarrka-ngku ka panti-rni.*
man-ERG AUX spear-NONPAST
'The man is spearing it.'
(b) *Wawirri ka panti-rni.*
kangaroo AUX spear-NONPAST
'He/she is spearing the kangaroo.'
(c) *Panti-rni ka.*
spear-NONPAST AUX
'He/she is spearing it.'

Finally, Warlpiri has the striking feature of allowing **discontinuous constituents** − multiple expressions of a single argument that do not form a phrase but rather are scattered throughout the clause. (6) is a relatively simple example (Simpson 1991: 257), where the sentence-initial noun and the sentence-final adjective work together to characterize the agent argument of the transitive verb.

(6) *Kurdu-jarra-ngku ka-pala maliki*
child-DU-ERG PRES-3dS dog
wajilipi-nyi wita-jarra-rlu.
chase-NPST small-DU-ERG
'Two small children are chasing the dog.'

Overall, one gets the impression that Warlpiri does not care much about syntactic phrases, since it puts no requirements on their presence, their position, or their integrity. Jiwarli, a related Australian language, may be an even more extreme case. Since it does not have second position clitics and full case concord is required among all nominals that characterize the same argument whether they are contiguous or not, there is no clear evidence that two words *ever* form a phrase in that language (Peter Austin, personal communication; see also Heath (1986) for Nunggubuyu).

More generally, the term "nonconfigurational" is used in two senses in the literature, which are sometimes confused. In the narrow sense, a nonconfigurational language is one that has the same characteristic cluster of features as Hale describes for Warlpiri, as outlined above. In a broader sense, languages with a reasonable number of similar properties, or indeed any language in which it seems difficult or inappropriate to use phrase structure to distinguish grammatical functions, can be called nonconfigurational. (Thus, even languages with strict Verb-Subject-Object order, like Irish, have been called nonconfigurational because of the difficulty of finding a constituent that contains the verb and the object but not the subject, although this is not common practice now.) The class of languages that have been considered nonconfigurational includes most Australian languages (Warlpiri, Dyirbal, Nunggubuyu, Jiwarli, etc.); various American Indian languages, including Salish, Uto-Aztecan (Jelinek 1984), Muskogean, Iroquoian (Baker 1996), Algonquian (Reinholtz and Russell 1994), Lakhota (Van Valin 1985), and Klamath/Sahaptian; certain South American languages, notably Quechua (Lefebvre & Muysken 1988); various New Guinea languages, such as Alamblak and Yimas (Foley 1991); South Asian languages such as Malayalam (Mohanan 1982); Hungarian (Kiss 1987 and many articles in Abraham & de Meij 1986), Japanese (Farmer 1984), and perhaps even German (see Abraham & de Meij (1986) and Webelhuth (1992) for review of the controversy), among others (see also the articles in Marácz & Muysken 1989).

2. Theories of nonconfigurationality

Hale himself proposed that the various nonconfigurational features of Warlpiri and similar languages could be traced to a single theoretical source − a **parameter** in the Chomskyan sense (→ Art. 24). He assumed that two kinds of representations exist in general: a **Phrase Structure** (PS) that represents surface constituency and a **Lexical Structure** (LS) that expresses argumenthood relationships. LS always has a rigid, hierarchical nature, where the number of arguments that a given predicate takes is fixed, and some of those arguments are marked as being more prominent than others. (This is broadly comparable to use of thematic role hierarchies and similar devices in other frameworks.) Certain important similarities between configurational and non-configurational languages can be captured by virtue of their similar LS representations. For example, in Warlpiri objects can be reflexive anaphors dependent on the subject for their reference, whereas subjects cannot be reflexive anaphors dependent on the object, just as in English (Hale 1983: 43). This is attributed to the fact that in both languages the subject is more prominent than the object at LS.

(7) (a) *Kurdu-jarra-rlu ka-pala-nyanu*
child-DU-ERG PRES-3 dS-REFL.O
para-rni.
strike-NPST
'The two children are striking themselves/each other.'
(b) #*Ngarrka ka-nyanu-Ø nya-nyi.*
man(ABS) PRES-REFL.S-3sO see-NPST
'*Heself$_i$ sees the man$_i$.' (OK as: 'He sees himself as a man.')

Hale gives a similar account of the fact that subjects of nonfinite clauses are required to be identical in reference to designated arguments of the main clause in both Warlpiri and English.

The differences between configurational and nonconfigurational languages, on the other hand, center around PS. In configurational languages like English, PS is required to have the same basic geometry as LS (stated in terms of Chomsky's Projection Principle). As a result, there must be one and only one NP for each logical argument of the verb, and that NP must be in the phrase structure position that corresponds to its relative prominence with respect to other arguments (e. g., subjects must be higher than objects). In contrast, no such homomorphism between LS and PS is required in Warlpiri. The two structures are only linked together by a loose relationship of "co-indexing", guided by the case-markings of the nominals. PS may not have a nominal corresponding to an LS argument, giving the effect of pronoun-drop. On the other hand, PS may have two or more distinct nominals corresponding to a single LS argument; this gives the effect of a discontinuous dependency. Finally, there are no syntactic constraints on where an NP needs to be in PS in order to correspond to a particular argument in LS; this gives free word order and the apparent absence of a VP. In this way, Hale achieves a unified analysis of the various aspects of nonconfigurationality. Thus an example like (6) with *maliki* 'dog' omitted would have the representations in (8) on his view:

(8) PS:

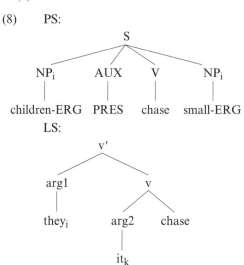

Hale also derives certain other features of Warlpiri from his proposal, such as the fact that it does not have any near equivalents of passive or raising, and the fact that it does not use place-holder pronouns like the *it* in *It rains*.

Hale's original ideas about nonconfigurationality have been developed in the subsequent literature in two distinct ways. The first approach emphasizes his distinction between LS and PS, building the whole conception of grammar around the idea that linguistic structure should be factored into different, nonhomomorphic types of representation in this way. This route has been taken by Lexical Functional Grammarians (Bresnan 1982, Mohanan 1982, Simpson 1991, Austin and Bresnan 1996). They identify Hale's LS with their "functional structure" and Hale's PS with their "constituent structure" — levels of analysis that they take to be independently motivated by various grammatical and psycholinguistic concerns.

The other line of research stemming from Hale's work was initiated by Jelinek (1984), who proposes the so-called **Pronominal Argument Hypothesis** (PAH). Jelinek begins with the observation that Warlpiri clauses do in fact contain elements that behave more like English-style subject and object arguments: namely the pronominal clitics attached to the second-position auxiliary. In contrast to the independent NPs, there is one and only one such clitic for each argument-slot of the verb. Furthermore, these clitics are in fixed positions, with the subject clitic preceding the object clitic. Thus, Jelinek proposes that the clitic pronouns are in fact the true arguments of the verb in Warlpiri, whereas case-marked nominals function as adverbial or dislocated elements loosely attached to the clause. On these assumptions, the structure of (8) would be something like (9):

(9)

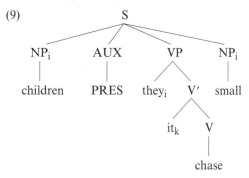

(9) can be thought of as a collapsing of Hale's LS and PS into a single, unified level of rep-

resentation, with the node labeled VP equivalent to Hale's LS and the VP-external structure equal to Hale's PS. Jelinek also accounts for the peculiar split ergativity found in Warlpiri in these terms: the pronominal clitics show a "normal" nominative/accusative pattern because they are the true arguments; independent NPs are free to have an ergative/absolutive pattern that does not correspond to the functions of subject and object in a simple one-to-one fashion because they are not the true subjects and objects.

Jelinek's PAH is attractive in that it achieves a unification of Hale's formal/generative research on nonconfigurational languages with a much older tradition of work on Native American languages, traceable back to Humboldt's early discussion of Nahuatl. Essentially the same idea has also been adopted more or less independently in many nongenerative approaches that do not have historical commitments to the centrality of phrase structure. For example, Mithun (1987: 232−25) invokes this idea in her discussion of free word order in Cayuga, Ngandi and Coos, and Van Valin (1985) develops essentially the same view in some detail in his analysis of Lakhota within Role and Reference Grammar. Van Valin's discussion is particularly notable, because his version of the PAH aspires to account not only for basic facts about the optionality of NPs in Lakhota and their freedom of order, but also for non-English-like patterns of coreference among arguments of different clauses. (However, some of these patterns appear to be rather particular to Lakhota, and not characteristic of the type. Note that Mithun (1987: 324−25) takes a more configurational view of Lakhota.)

If the PAH is correct, there should be other implications, which are explored by Baker (1991, 1996). In particular, the presence of the pronominal arguments should influence the interpretation of NPs in certain ways that go beyond the basic configurationality parameter, making those NPs act rather like the dislocated phrases found in Indo-European languages (→ Art. 80). For example, nonconfigurational languages should not have non-referential quantified expressions that are identical to *everyone* and *nobody* in English, since such nonreferential elements are very limited in their ability to antecede pronouns. Rather, nonconfigurational languages should only have elements like *all of them* and *anybody* in the scope of clausal negation. This prediction is true, at least for the best studied nonconfigurational languages, including Mohawk, Warlpiri, and Cree (Reinholtz and Russell 1994) (→ Art. 92).

(10) Mohawk (Baker, 1996: 55)
*Akwéku wa'-t-ha-[a]hsΛ"tho-'.
all FACT-DUP-MpS-cry-PUNC
'Everybody cried.' (OK with plural agreement, as 'All of them cried.')

Similar considerations also account for the absence of reflexive NPs like *herself*, of NPs with an English-like article system (→ Art. 64), and of unnominalized clausal complements (→ Art. 74) in nonconfigurational languages. Since each of these categories is something other than a fully referential noun phrase, they cannot be licensed in the clause by virtue of being coreferential with a pronominal argument (Baker 1996: ch. 2).

Jelinek's hypothesis that the overt NP in a sentence like (11) is not an object but rather an adjunct NP that is coreferential with the true (pronominal) object also accounts for the fact that the pronominal subject can be coreferential with the possessor of the object. In configurational languages like English, this kind of coreference is impossible: the subject is more prominent than the object, and hence cannot be referentially dependent on it. However, this condition does not apply in Mohawk, because the nominal containing the antecedent is not the grammatical object (Baker 1996: § 2.1.1.).

(11) Wa'-t-há-ya'k-e' [$_{NP}$ ne thíkΛ
FACT-DUP-1ss-break-PUNC NE that
Sak raó-[a]'share'].
Sak MSP-knife
'He broke that knife of Sak's.' (the breaker can be Sak)

Similar facts have been adduced for Lakhota, Cree, Nahuatl, and Southern Tiwa. (However, Warlpiri differs from Mohawk in this regard; see § 3.)

In summary, the PAH brings together the generative and functional/descriptivist traditions, and it sheds light both on basic facts of word order and more subtle matters of quantification and coreference. Thus, it has earned the status of being the standard view of nonconfigurationality − although plenty of controversies and unresolved problems remain.

3. Types of nonconfigurationality

A glance at the list in § 1. of languages that have been called nonconfigurational shows that these languages are far from a homogenous group in other typological respects. For example, the list includes both pure **head-marking** languages (Mohawk) and pure **dependent-marking** languages (Jiwarli) (→ Art. 102), as well as languages with both kinds of morphological resources. Similarly, the list includes both languages where word order seems entirely undefined (Warlpiri, Mohawk) and languages that seem to be of a fairly standard head-final type, in the sense of Greenberg's work (→ Art. 23) (Malayalam, Japanese, Lakhota). Given this, it is natural to ask whether the configurationality/nonconfigurationality distinction is an independent factor in linguistic typology, or whether there are important interactions between configurationality and other typological distinctions.

While this question is just starting to crystallize as a research topic, the rudimentary results available so far suggest that there are indeed interactions. Indeed, nonconfigurationality seems to take on somewhat different guises in different language types. Warlpiri by itself is not very revealing, since in addition to the full range of nonconfigurational characteristics it has both head-marking and dependent-marking resources in its morphosyntax. However, there seems to be an implicational hierarchy among Hale's various nonconfigurationality features, with discontinuous expressions implying widespread omission of pronouns, and widespread omission of pronouns implying free word order and lack of a VP, but not vice versa. Thus, Mohawk has very free word order and widespread null anaphora, but it does not allow discontinuous nominal expressions nearly as freely as Warlpiri does (Baker 1996: ch. 4):

(12) (a) Warlpiri (Kenneth Hale, p. c.)
  Kuyu Ø-rna luwa-rnu wawirri.
  animal PERF-1ss shoot-past kangaroo
  'I shot a kangaroo.'
 (b) Mohawk (Baker 1996: 140)
  ?* *KΛ'tsu ne auhá'a*
   fish   NE most
  te-wak-éka'-s rababhót.
  CIS-1so-like-HAB bullhead
  'I like bullhead fish the best.'

Many languages seem to be like Mohawk in this respect, judging largely from the silence of many grammars on this topic (see also Van Valin (1985) on Lakhota). On the other hand, there seem to be languages with a degree of free word order but without pronoun-drop or discontinuous constituents; German and perhaps Japanese are examples. If this is accurate, then we have the following implicational hierarchy:

(13) | | Discont. Const. > | Pronoun Drop > | Free Word Order |
|---|---|---|---|
| (Warlpiri) | YES | YES | YES |
| (Mohawk) | NO | YES | YES |
| (German) | NO | NO | YES |

Now it seems that other pure head marking languages like Nahuatl and Lakhota fall with Mohawk in the middle group; in order to get discontinuous constituents, some dependent-marking seems also to be necessary (Jiwarli, Nez Perce, Quechua). On the other hand, the least nonconfigurational languages are also the ones with the clearest attributes of a head-final language.

The PAH gives some provisional understanding as to why this might be the case. On this view, pronoun-drop lies at the heart of nonconfigurationality: verbs are inherently associated with pronominal arguments, so additional NPs are never required. Free word order follows more or less immediately from this, as the result of the option of adjoining coreferential NPs to the clause to increase its descriptive content. However, the possibility of discontinuous constituents does *not* follow automatically: notice that dislocation constructions in English and other familiar languages allow no more than one additional nominal to be coreferent with a pronominal argument (Baker 1996: 139). Thus, (14) is possible with either of the boldface NPs omitted, but not with both present:

(14) **The kangaroo**, I think that, **the animal**, John shot it.

Thus, Mohawk turns out to be the type of nonconfigurationality most naturally expected.

If this is correct, then a language must have some additional property beyond basic nonconfigurationality in order to make full-scale, Australian-style discontinuous constituents possible. One plausible suggestion is that a particular kind of case marking is required (Austin and Bresnan 1996); this allows one to recognize the different parts of what is interpreted as a single nominal by the fact that all the parts bear the same case. However, this may not be enough, since even languages with a decent amount of case marking do not necessarily allow free discontinuous constituents.

Another salient feature of the Australian languages is that they typically have no (or almost no) distinction between the categories of noun and adjective (→ Art. 40). In this respect, they differ not only from configurational English, which has a distinct category of adjective, but also from nonconfigurational languages like Mohawk, where adjectives are subsumed to verbs, not nouns. Now adjectives can be used more easily as predicates than true nouns can be, as shown by the English contrast in (15):

(15)   *I never saw Reagan angry/*president.*

Thus, it could be that the adjective-noun neutralization that happens in Warlpiri makes it relatively easy for members of that category to be used predicatively. This opens up a new way for nominals to be added to a clause in languages like Warlpiri that is not available in languages like Mohawk: they can be predicated of the pronominal argument instead of being in a dislocation relationship to it (see Speas 1990: 165−172). This additional option makes discontinuous constituents possible. Indeed, Bhat (1994) and Baker (2000) claim that discontinuous constituents are possible only in languages with no more than a weak N/A contrast; in addition to the Australian languages, other languages of this type include Quechua (Lefebvre & Muysken 1988: 162−65), Yimas (Foley 1991: 180−91, 369−76), Sanskrit (and perhaps Latin?) (Bhat 1994) and languages of the Klamath/Sahaptian family (Barker 1964: 338−39).

This difference in the status of "extra" nominals in Warlpiri and Mohawk may also be detectable in other ways. For example, it may explain the fact that coreference between the understood subject and the possessor of the object is fine in the Mohawk example in (11), but not in its Warlpiri equivalent (Simpson 1991: 176−83); see Baker (2000) for some discussion.

What then does this view imply about putatively nonconfigurational laguages that do not even allow free pronoun-drop, such as German? Clearly the PAH is not very plausible for such languages. However, this is as it should be, since their similarity to the nonconfigurational prototype is also the most tenuous. Their principal nonconfigurational property is their free word order, and even this is rather limited, in that the languages have clear head-final properties and an "unmarked" subject-object-verb word order is often discernible. Thus, it is reasonable to say that these languages are not nonconfigurational at all in the theoretically and typologically most interesting sense of the term. Rather, they seem to have a configurational structure, plus they allow some degree of relatively superficial rearrangement (often called **scrambling**) conditioned by pragmatic factors. This has become the standard generative view for the best studied languages of the type: Japanese, German, and Hindi.

This view can be corroborated by more subtle, interpretative facts of these languages as well. For example, nonreferential NPs like quantifiers and reflexives are possible in these languages, unlike in Mohawk and Warlpiri (compare (10)):

(16)   Hindi
       Sab-ko   uskii bahin pyaar
       everyone-ACC his   sister love
       kartii thi.
       do-F   be-F
       'His sister loved everyone.'

This helps to confirm that the PAH does not apply to languages of this type.

Jelinek's PAH has been challenged directly by Austin and Bresnan (1996). The focus of their criticism is that the PAH puts too much weight on the presence of the clitic pronouns on the verb or auxiliary in a language like Warlpiri. Austin and Bresnan investigate two situations where these clitic elements are not found: nonfinite clauses in Warlpiri, and main clauses in the related language Jiwarli. They show that in both contexts all the canonical features of nonconfigurationality still hold, even though there are no pronominal affixes to be the arguments. They conclude from this that the PAH approach to nonconfigurationality is inadequately general.

However, this criticism only counts against the most literal (and most common) implementation of Jelinek's proposal: the one in which the affixes on the verb or auxiliary really are the arguments. The comparative Australian data does not challenge the more fundamental insight that the free pronoun-drop property is at the heart of all the major nonconfigurationality phenomena. Thus, one can maintain the claim that the arguments of the verb are always pronouns (not full NPs) in these languages, even though those arguments may have no phonological expression.

The existence of clitic elements on the verb might promote the possibility of null pronouns, but they are not needed in order to have null pronouns; this is known apart from all considerations of nonconfigurationality by the fact that one can omit pronouns in uninflected configurational languages like Chinese (→ Art. 101).

4. Polysynthesis and nonconfigurationality

One additional matter of typology is worthy of special discussion: namely the connection between polysynthesis and nonconfigurationality. **Polysynthesis** is a term with its origins in the 19th century, and was used in the morphologically-based typologies of Boas and Sapir (→ Art. 20). Informally speaking, polysynthetic languages are those with a large amount of grammatical information coded on the main word of a constituent (particularly the verb), such that that word is the functional equivalent of an entire sentence in a language like English. These languages are head-marking languages par excellence, with extensive pronominal/agreement morphology; they also have other ways of elaborating the basic verb, such as incorporated nouns, (→ Art. 53), causative affixes (→ Art. 66), benefactive applicative markers, and other such derivational processes. Given this, it is reasonable to ask whether there is any interesting interaction between the polysynthetic/nonpolysynthetic distinction and the configurational/nonconfigurational distinction. Impressionistically, it seems likely that there would be, since the morphological elaboration of words that one finds in polysynthetic languages might render superfluous and thus come at the expense of phrasal groupings in a language like English (Mithun 1987: 323–24). Moreover, some of the canonical polysynthetic languages, such as Mohawk and Yimas, are clearly nonconfigurational as well. At the other extreme, the most notorious isolating languages (English, Chinese, Yoruba) are also some of the most clearly configurational.

In order to explore this relationship productively, one must sharpen the notion of what it is for a language to be polysynthetic. The informal idea that a language is polysynthetic if it has lots of verbal morphology is probably too vague and general to be very useful typologically, since languages can be morphologically complex in different ways. Thus, Baker (1996) proposes to take the existence of noun incorporation as a productive and discourse-relevant grammatical option (→ Art. 53) to be a central characterizing feature of polysynthesis. (17) shows a simple example of the noun incorporation alternation in Mohawk:

(17) (a) *Wa'-k-hnínu-'   ne ka-nákt-a'.*
FACT-1ss-buy-PUNC NE NSS-bed-NSF
'I bought the/a bed.'
(b) *Wa'-ke-nakt-a-hnínu-'.*
FACT-1ss-bed-Ø-buy-PUNC
'I bought the/a bed.'

This construction is somewhat rare crosslinguistically, and seems to be found only in a relatively homogenous set of languages. In particular, all languages that have discourse-active noun incorporation also have rather complete sets of pronominal/agreement markers for subjects, objects, and indirect objects (Mithun 1984: 859). Moreover, these pronominal/agreement markers are generally obligatory. For example, it is impossible in noun incorporating languages like Mohawk or Nahuatl to omit object markers, even though this is possible in languages like Chichewa or Yimas (morphologically complex head-marking languages that do not have noun incorporation).

(18) Mohawk (Baker 1996: 21)
*Sak (shako/*ra)-núhwe'-s ne*
Sak (MSS.FSO/MSS)-like-HAB NE
Uwári.
Mary
'Sak likes Mary.'

Similarly, Mohawk and Nahuatl have no nonfinite forms that allow one to suppress subject agreement, although Chichewa and Yimas (and Warlpiri) do.

(19) Mohawk (Baker 1996: 473)
K-atenyʌt-ha'
1ss-try-HAB
*(au-s-a-ke)-'sere-ht-aserúni-'.
OPT-ITER-1ss-car-NOML-fix-PUNC
'I am trying to fix the car.'

Languages with noun incorporation also generally have causatives, applicatives, and other such elements, although there is some variation on this point. Baker (1996) concludes that the existence of noun incorporation in a language is actually one reflection of a deep commitment on the part of a language to use head-marking techniques to express argument structure relationships, not merely as a preferred option, but as a grammatical requirement. He states the condition as follows:

(20) The Polysynthesis Parameter:
Every argument of a head must be related to a morpheme in the word that contains that head.

From this one can derive an implicational universal, such that languages that are polysynthetic (in this sense) are also nonconfigurational in the Hale/Jelinek sense. The steps in the derivation are as follows: One calls a language polysynthetic if it has lots of incorporation. A language has lots of incorporation only if it is strongly biased toward head-marking. However, incorporation itself can never express all the arguments of every predicate: agentive subjects and goal phrases are generally unincorporable, for example. Therefore, to express its commitment to head-marking, the language will have to have pronominal/agreement elements as well. These then count as the syntactic arguments of the head, as in Jelinek's view. The result is that independent noun phrases will be optional, have freedom as to where they are placed, and act like dislocated elements syntactically. (In addition, they may or may not have discontinuous constituents, depending on the case-marking properties and category inventory, as discussed above: Nunggubuyu does; Mohawk does not.) This prediction seems to be correct: Baker (1996) shows that all of the languages that have type III or IV (discourse-relevant) noun incorporation in the typology of Mithun (1984) are also nonconfigurational, including at least the Northern Iroquoian languages, the Caddoan languages, the Tanoan languages, Nahuatl (at least classical), the Gunwinjguan languages in Australia, and Chukchee/Koryak. (Baker's generalization has been challenged for Ainu, and for one modern variety of Nahuatl. It may be relevant that both of these languages have been strongly influenced by a nonpolysynthetic, configurational language spoken by a dominating culture (Japanese and Spanish). Indeed, their configurational properties match those of the contact language.)

Van Valin (1985: 406) makes the stronger claim that all head-marking languages are nonconfigurational, not just the polysynthetic ones. However, this is probably going too far. Some languages have pronominal/agreement affixes as an option, rather than as a requirement. Some of these languages show configurational properties, at least when the head-marking is omitted. For example, the Bantu language Chichewa behaves like a rather normal Subject-Verb-Object language when "object prefixes" are omitted (Bresnan and Mchombo 1987), whereas the Northern Athapaskan Slave behaves like a rather normal head-final language under the same conditions (Rice 1989). This is true in spite of the fact that the languages as a whole clearly count as head-marking.

While the implicational universal that discourse-relevant noun incorporation implies nonconfigurationality is encouraging, there is still much to be done in this area. It will no doubt prove useful to define other senses of "polysynthetic" that will bear on the general issue. For example, there are some languages that do not qualify as polysynthetic in Baker's incorporation-oriented sense, but are polysynthetic in the informal sense. Many of these seem to be nonconfigurational as well: Yimas, Quechua, and Inuktitut are salient examples; see particularly Foley (1991) on Yimas. On the other hand, Bach's (1993) work on Haisla and other languages of the American Northwest suggest that there is another, very different kind of polysynthesis that is oriented toward the expression of modification relationships, rather than the expression of argument relationships (as in Mohawk). Since morphology is not oriented toward argument relationships in these languages, it is perfectly consistent with their basic genius not to have pronominal/agreement markers. Then Jelinek's PAH does not apply, and one expects them to be relatively configurational. Indeed, Bach shows that Haisla is not a PAH language, and it has a Verb-Subject-Object syntax. Therefore, it is probably too crude to say that polysynthesis implies nonconfigurationality; rather, some types of polysynthesis imply some types of nonconfigurationality. What exactly the types are, and how they can be recognized reliably are matters of ongoing research.

5. Special abbreviations

Nonstandard abbreviations used:

CIS	cislocative
DUP	duplicative
FACT	Factual mood
HAB	habitual aspect
ITER	Iterative
LS	Lexical Structure
NOML	nominalizer

NPST	nonpast
NSF	nominal suffix
OPT	optative
PAH	Pronominal Argument Hypothesis
PS	Phrase Structure
PUNC	punctual aspect

6. References

Abraham, Werner & Meij, Sjaak de (eds.). 1986. *Topic, focus, and configurationality.* Amsterdam: Benjamins.

Austin, Peter & Bresnan, Joan. 1996. "Nonconfigurationality in Australian aboriginal languages". *Natural Language and Linguistic Theory* 14: 215–268.

Bach, Emmon. 1993. "On the semantics of polysynthesis". *Berkeley Linguistics Society* 19: 361–368.

Baker, Mark. 1991. "On some subject/object non-asymmetries in Mohawk". *Natural Language and Linguistic Theory* 9: 537–576.

Baker, Mark. 1996. *The polysynthesis parameter.* New York: Oxford University Press.

Baker, Mark. 2000. "The natures of nonconfigurationality". In: Baltin, Mark & Collins, Chris (eds.). *The handbook of contemporary syntactic theory.* Oxford: Blackwell.

Barker, M. A. R. 1964. *Klamath grammar.* Berkeley: University of California Press.

Bhat, D. N. S. 1994. *The adjectival category: criteria for differentiation and identification.* Amsterdam: John Benjamins.

Bresnan, Joan. 1982. "Control and complementation". In: Bresnan, Joan (ed.). *The mental representation of grammatical relations.* Cambridge/MA: MIT Press, 282–390.

Bresnan, Joan & Mchombo, Sam. 1987. "Topic, pronoun, and agreement in Chichewa". *Language* 63: 741–782.

Farmer, Ann. 1984. *Modularity in syntax.* Cambridge/MA: MIT Press.

Foley, William. 1991. *The Yimas language of New Guinea.* Stanford/CA: Stanford University Press.

Hale, Kenneth. 1983. "Warlpiri and the grammar of nonconfigurational languages". *Natural Language and Linguistic Theory* 1: 5–49.

Heath, Jeffrey. 1986. "Syntactic and lexical aspects of nonconfigurationality in Nunggubuyu (Australia)". *Natural Language and Linguistic Theory* 4: 375–408.

Jelinek, Eloise. 1984. "Empty categories, case, and configurationality". *Natural Language and Linguistic Theory* 2: 39–76.

Kiss, Katalin. 1987. *Configurationality in Hungarian.* Dordrecht: Reidel.

Lefebvre, Claire & Muysken, Pieter. 1988. *Mixed categories: nominalizations in Quechua.* Dordrecht: Kluwer.

Marácz, László & Muysken, Pieter (eds.). 1989. *Configurationality: the typology of asymmetries.* Dordrecht: Foris.

Mithun, Marianne. 1984. "The evolution of noun incorporation". *Language* 60: 847–893.

Mithun, Marianne. 1987. "Is basic word order universal?" In: Tomlin, Richard (ed.). *Coherence and grounding in discourse.* Amsterdam: John Benjamins, 281–328.

Mohanan, K. P. 1982. "Grammatical relations and clause structure in Malayalam". In: Bresnan, Joan (ed.). *The mental representation of grammatical relations.* Cambridge/MA: MIT Press, 504–589.

Reinholtz, Charlotte & Russell, Kevin. 1994. "Quantified NPs in pronominal argument languages: evidence from Swampy Cree". *North Eastern Linguistics Society* 25: 389–403.

Rice, Keren. 1989. *A grammar of Slave.* Berlin: Mouton de Gruyter.

Simpson, Jane. 1983. *Aspects of Warlpiri morphology and syntax.* Ph. D. dissertation, MIT.

Simpson, Jane. 1991. *Warlpiri morpho-syntax: a lexicalist approach.* Dordrecht: Kluwer.

Speas, Margaret. 1990. *Phrase structure in natural language.* Dordrecht: Kluwer.

Van Valin, Robert. 1985. "Case marking and the structure of the Lakhota clause". In: Nichols, Johanna & Woodbury, Anthony (eds.). *Grammar inside and outside the clause.* Cambridge: Cambridge University Press, 363–413.

Webelhuth, Gert. 1992. *Principles and parameters of syntactic saturation.* New York: Oxford University Press.

Mark C. Baker, Rutgers University (USA)

104. Discourse configurationality

1. The notion of discourse configurationality
2. Topic-prominence
3. Focus prominence
4. References

1. The notion of discourse configurationality

The idea that in some — or perhaps all — languages sentence structure is motivated by discourse-semantic considerations emerged in the 19th century in the work of Weil (1844), Brassai (1860–65), and Gabelentz (1869; 1875), and became a central research topic for two generations of the Prague School — see Mathesius (1929), Sgall & Hajičova (1973), and Daneš (1974), among others. At the same time, the formal approaches to language description, particularly the early generative school of linguistics, considered such discourse-semantic functions as topic and focus matters of pragmatics, and took no interest in them. Later, however, when the generative approach was extended to languages other than English, it became obvious that languages in which the discourse-semantic functions topic and focus are associated with distinguished structural positions of the sentence are common on all continents and in all language families. In Europe, Basque (de Rijk 1978, Ortiz de Urbina 1991), Catalan (Vallduví 1992a), Hungarian (Horvath 1986, É. Kiss 1987), Bulgarian (Rudin 1986), Russian (King 1995), Greek (Tsimpli 1994), Finnish (Vilkuna 1989), Rumanian (Ulrich 1985), Turkish (Erguvanli 1984), and Armenian (Comrie 1984) were the first languages to be identified as discourse-configurational. From Asia, Nepali (Wallace 1985), Hindi (Gambhir 1981), and Korean (Choe 1989), among others, have been reported in the literature to be discourse-configurational. Japanese (Kuroda 1972–73, Kuno 1973), and in some accounts Chinese have been claimed to be topic-prominent. African languages described as discourse-configurational include, among others, Somali (Lecarme 1991, Svolacchia/Mereu/Puglielli 1994), the Chadic languages (Tuller 1992, Horvath 1994), the Bantu languages Aghem and Kikuyu (Watters 1979, Clements 1984), Yoruba (Awobuluyi 1978) and Arabic (Ouhalla 1994). Of the American Indian languages, Haida (Enrico 1986), Omaha (Rudin 1990–91), the Mayan languages (Aissen 1991), and Quechua (Muysken 1994) have been argued to be discourse-configurational. According to evidence presented in Schachter (1973), the Austronesian Ilonggo may also belong to this language type.

We call a language discourse-configurational if it links either or both of the discourse-semantic functions topic and focus to particular structural positions. Languages which encode the topic function structurally are topic-prominent; those which encode the focus function structurally are focus prominent. Most of the above-mentioned languages are both topic- and focus-prominent.

2. Topic-prominence

It is a wide-spread assumption going back to Li & Thompson (1976) that languages can be classified according to whether their sentence structure primarily encodes the topic-predicate, or the grammatical subject-predicate dichotomy. This assumption will be the starting point of the present typological survey, as well, in § 2.5.. It will be argued, however, that the language type in which the basic sentence structure expresses the subject–predicate dichotomy is very much underrepresented among the languages of the world; most languages are topic-prominent. Consequently, it is more meaningful to classify languages according to what subtype of topic-prominence they represent; what constraints on topic selection they observe. The various subtypes of topic prominent languages will be identified in § 2.6.. Preparing the typological discussion, § 2.1. will introduce the discourse semantic function 'topic', 2.2. will examine its syntactic realization, 2.3. will discuss the notion of contrastive topic and its special properties, whereas 2.4. will analyze the distribution of topic in the various logical types of sentences.

2.1. The notion of topic

It has been regarded as a basic fact of language that sentences typically fall into two main parts. The first one foregrounds an entity, that which the sentence will be about, and the second one predicates something about this entity. The part to be predicated about, i.e., the subject of predication, used to be — and still often is — identified with the grammatical subject, but this has turned out to be a false generalization. On the one hand, in many languages a sentence can just as well make a statement about the referent of a non-subject argument. E. g.

(1) Hungarian
Jánost elütötte a vonat
John.ACC ran.over the train.NOM
'John was run over by the train.'

On the other hand, certain types of subjects (e. g. non-specific indefinites) cannot be predicated about. Thus the following sentence is not a statement about a sparrow:

(2) *There is a sparrow on every branch of this tree.*

Such facts have lead to the conclusion that the notion of 'grammatical subject' and the notion of 'subject of predication' have to be divorced — even if the two functions are often associated with one and the same constituent. To avoid a confusion, the subject of predication is now generally referred to by the term 'topic'. The most frequent carrier of the topic function is, indeed, the grammatical subject — but this is so only because a human topic is preferred to a non-human one, and a subject more often has the feature human than a non-subject. In the case of verbs taking a non-human theme subject and a human experiencer dative (e. g. *jemandem passiert etwas*), the dative will be the unmarked topic.

If the first part of the structural dichotomy that makes up a sentence is associated with the topic function, then many languages previously seen as displaying a free word order turn out to have an invariant topic-VP structure. These languages are free only in as much as they allow the subject of predication to be selected from among the arguments of the predicate freely, with no restriction on its grammatical function or case.

2.2. The syntactic properties of topic

The discourse-semantic function of the topic is to foreground an entity already present in the domain or the universe of discourse as the subject that will be predicated about. Entities count as present in the domain of discourse if they have been referred to previously (cf. (3a)), or they are concomitants of entities/events referred to previously (cf. (3b)), or they are physically present in the discourse situation (cf. (3c)), etc. An entity counts as present in the universe of discourse if its referent (or at least the existence of its referent) is known to the participants of the discourse (cf. (3d)).

(3) (a) *Suddenly, there appeared a man and a woman.* **The man** *wore a uniform.*
(b) *His concert was a great success.* **The tickets** *sold out in advance.*
(c) **This chair** *is broken.*
(d) **The Earth** *is overpopulated.*

Since the topic refers to an entity whose existence has been previously established, it must be represented by a specific NP in the sense of Enç (1991). Specific NPs include names, personal pronouns (4a), definite NPs (4b), and generic NPs (names of kinds according to Carlson (1978)) (cf. (4c)), as well as indefinites which refer to the referent of a subset of a previously introduced set — (4d).

(4) (a) **Fido/it** *is chewing a bone.*
(b) **The dogs** *are chewing bones.*
(c) **Dogs** *like bones.*
(d) *He has half a dozen cats and dogs.* **A dog** *bit me when I visited him.*

A non-specific indefinite NP, introducing a new discourse referent, cannot function as a topic. The following two discourse fragments contain the same indefinite NP, first in a context requiring a non-specific interpretation (5a), and then in a context allowing a specific (partitive) interpretation (5b). The indefinite can be formulated as a topic only in the case of (5b):

(5) Italian
(a) *(I was travelling alone, but then)*
è salita sull'autobus una ragazza.
is got on.the bus a girl
'A girl got on the bus.'
(b) *(Students were waiting at the bus-stop.)*
Una ragazza è salita sull'autobus.
'A girl got on the bus.'

It is now generally assumed in Chomskyan syntactic theory that all the arguments of a verb, including the grammatical subject, are generated inside the VP, and the argument selected to function as the topic is extracted from the VP by a movement transformation. The resulting structure, consisting of a maximal projection with an empty argument position, and a constituent c-commanding it and binding its empty argument position — see (6) — is non-distinct from the syntactic (primary) predication structure identified in Williams (1980). That is, the discourse-semantic topic—predicate dichotomy is the function of the syntactic primary predication structure.

(6)
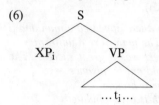

The VP in (6) means an extended verb projection, which includes the verb-related tense and agreement projections, as well as the predicate operators, among them negation, and in some languages, the focus.

In a variant of this structure, represented e. g. by Greek (Tsimpli 1994), the VP-internal argument position bound by the topic is filled by a resumptive pronoun.

Many languages, e. g. Catalan (Vallduví 1992a) or Hungarian (É. Kiss 1987: 76) allow the repeated application of topic movement, which results in a multiple topic construction. For example:

(7) Hungarian
 (a) *János Marit* [VP *meg hívta*]
  John.NOM Mary.ACC PREV invited
  'Mary, John invited.'
 (b) *Marit János* [VP *meg hívta*]
  'Mary, John invited.'

As shown by (7 a, b), the topics are usually interchangeable, and the order of topic constituents has no consequence for the interpretation of the sentence; hence the intuition is that such sentences do not involve a topic-predicate structure embedded into another one, but involve a single predication about two (or more) participants of a given event.

The question arises what clues we have to determine if an argument is in the extended VP projection, or occupies a VP-external topic slot. A cross-linguistically wide-spread (perhaps universal) clue is the position of sentence adverbials such as *probably, in my opinion*, or *luckily*. They are never internal to the predicate; hence, when in sentence-internal position, they are located between the topic and the predicate:

(8) German
 (a) *weil die Ameisen **ja doch** einen*
  because the ants indeed a
  Postbeamten gebissen haben
  postmaster bitten have
  'because the ants indeed bit a postmaster.'

 (b) *weil den Postbeamten **ja doch***
  because the postmaster-ACC indeed
  Ameisen gebissen haben
  ants bitten have
  'because the postmaster was indeed bitten by ants'

For further German examples, see Diesing (1992) and Kratzer (1989). Hungarian and English examples can be found below under (18)—(20), and (23), respectively.

In some languages, e. g. Korean (cf. Choe 1989), Quechua (Muysken 1994), and Japanese (Kuroda 1972—73), the topic is marked by a morpheme. In other languages, e. g. in Hungarian, sentence structure can be identified primarily on the basis of stress: the first obligatory stress, which is also the heaviest in the clause, falls on the initial constituent of the predicate (É. Kiss 1987: 43).

Sentence adverbials which do not bind an argument position in the predicate phrase, e. g. speaker-oriented adverbials, although VP-external, naturally do not qualify for the topic role. As for adverbials of place and time, if they are allowed to constitute optional arguments of the verb, they can be analyzed as topics, which is not contrary to intuition.

2.3. Contrastive topic

It has been found in various languages, e. g. Japanese (Kuno 1973: 37, 44—45), German (Büring 1995), or Hungarian (É. Kiss 1987: 81—88) — that a constituent unsuitable for the role of topic (e. g. a quantifier, a non-specific NP, or a predicative adjective) can also appear in VP-external position if it is pronounced with a contrastive intonation. E. g.

(9) Hungarian
 Szép nem vagyok.
 beautiful not am.I
 'Beautiful, I am not.'

It is not obvious that this type of constituent, called contrastive topic by Szabolcsi (1981), Lambrecht (1994), Molnár (1998), etc., or I-topic (Jacobs 1996), or S-topic (Büring 1995), indeed represents a sub-type of topic in the syntactic and the discourse-semantic sense; e. g. Selkirk (1984), and Krifka (1998) consider it a type of focus. (For a comprehensive analysis of the conflicting views, see Molnár (1998).) Assuming that a contrastive topic is a topic, it is presumably the contrast implied by prosody that makes it qualify for topichood also when it is represented by an inherently non-specific, possibly even non-individual-denoting constituent. When a constituent is set into a contrast, its referent is seen as an individual, a member of a set of comparable, distinct entities. Furthermore, the fact that it is understood to represent a subset of a set of entities present in the domain of discourse also makes it [+specific] (assuming the specificity theory of Enç (1991)). In the case of (9), for example, *szép* 'beautiful' pronounced with a rising intonation is understood as an attractive human quality set into contrast with other attractive human qualities. That is, (9) means:

(9) '(As opposed to other attractive qualities,) the quality of beauty I do not possess.'

A quantifier such as *every student*, or *somebody*, when pronounced with the rising contour of a contrastive topic, can have narrow scope with respect to a subsequent operator. E. g.

(10) German
Mindestens ein Student hat jeden
at.least one student has every
Roman gelesen.
novel read
'Every novel was read by at least one student.'

For alternative explanations of this phenomenon, see Büring (1995), and Krifka (1998).

2.4. Categorical and thetic judgements

Not all sentences contain a topic even in a topic-prominent language, because not all sentences express predication about an individual. According to the logical theory of Marty (1918, 1965), adopted in linguistics by Kuroda (1972−73), judgements fall into two types: categorical and thetic judgements. Categorical judgements consist of two acts: the act of recognition of that which is to be made the subject of predication, and the act of affirming or denying what is expressed by the predicate about the subject. Thetic judgements consist of a single act: the act of the recognition of the material of a judgement (cf. Kuroda 1972−73: 154). It is only categorical judgements which are realized linguistically in the form of a topic-predicate structure in topic-prominent languages; sentences corresponding to thetic judgements consist of a mere predicate.

Thetic judgements, formulated as topicless sentences, include impersonal and existential sentences (11)−(12), and may include other types of sentences with a non-specific subject (13), as well.

Hungarian
(11) (a) *Havazik.*
snows
'It is snowing.'
(b) *Fontos, hogy idejében induljunk.*
important that in.time we.leave
'It is important that we leave in time.'

(12) *Van egy macska a háztetőn.*
is a cat on.the roof
'There is a cat on the roof.'

(13) *Alakult egy énekkar*
formed a choir
az iskolánkban.
in.our.school
'A choir was formed in our school.'

A sentence is necessarily topicless only if it does not contain any specific, topicalizable argument. If its subject is non-specific, but it has e. g. a specific locative, in many languages it can be formulated as a statement about that argument, i. e., as a categorical judgement expressed in the form of a topic-predicate structure:

(14) Hungarian
Az iskolánkban alakult egy
in.our.school formed a
énekkar.
choir
'In our school, a choir was formed.'

Predicates may select the specificity feature of their arguments, and through this they may be predestined to occur only in one or the other of the two sentence types. Thus predicates which assert the existence, the availability, or the coming into being of their subject (such as *be, be available, arise, be formed* − but not the emphatic *exist*) do not allow their subject to be expressed by a specific NP carrying an existential presupposition − cf. Szabolcsi (1986) − presumably because the existence of a constituent cannot be simultaneously asserted and presupposed. This type of verb can only occur in a thetic, topicless sentence − unless it also has a topicalizable argument, e. g. a locative.

Marty and Kuroda did not consider thetic sentences which contain a specific grammatical subject inside the VP. This sentence type exists in many languages. As Calabrese (1992) pointed out, a specific grammatical subject can remain VP-internal if it refers to an individual which is known both to the speaker and the listener, but is newly introduced into the domain of discourse:

(15) Költöznek a   fecskék.
      migrate   the swallows
      'Swallows are migrating.'

(16) Megérkezett a nagynéném
      arrived   my.aunt
      Bécsből.
      from.Vienna
      'My aunt has arrived from Vienna.'

Stative/individual-level predicates select a [+specific] subject − see É. Kiss (1997). This fact in itself would not prevent them from occurring in thetic sentences of the type illustrated in (15)−(16) − still, they cannot have all their arguments in the VP. In other words, sentences with a stative predicate must have a topic-predicate structure:

(17) Hungarian
      ??Gyűlölte Jánost   Mari.
        hated   John.ACC Mary.NOM
      'Mary hated John.'

The ungrammaticality of (17) will fall out if we make the following two assumptions: (i) Following Davidson (1967) and Kratzer (1989), we attribute to action/stage-level predicates an invisible event argument. (ii) We assume that both categorical and thetic judgements express predication; merely thetic judgements predicate about the invisible event argument of their verb: a variable bound deictically or anaphorically, corresponding to 'here and now', or 'there and then'. Under these assumptions, stative/individual-level predicates do not occur in thetic sentences because they have no event argument to predicate about. For an alternative account, see Diesing (1992).

Although judgements with a universal subject were classified by Marty as thetic, Kuroda (1972−73) found that in Japanese they pattern with categorical judgements. In fact, if categorical judgements express predication about a specific individual, then a universal sentence cannot represent a categorical judgement, and if thetic judgements express predication about 'here and now', or 'there and then', then many universal sentences (those of the *All men are mortal* type) cannot represent thetic judgements, either. Accordingly, in Hungarian, a universally quantified grammatical subject is neither in topic position, nor in VP-internal position, but occupies a special operator position preceding the VP and the focus, reserved for distributive quantifiers. Compare the following three Hungarian sentences:

(18) A macskánk valószínűleg szereti
      our.cat   probably   likes
      a halat.
      the fish
      'Our cat probably likes fish.'

(19) (a) *Minden macska valószínűleg
         every cat   probably
         szereti a   halat.
         likes   the fish
         'Every cat probably likes fish.'

     (b) Valószínűleg minden macska szereti
         a halat.
         'Probably every cat likes fish.'

(20) Valószínűleg nyávog egy macska
      probably   mews   a   cat
      a háztetőn.
      on.the.roof
      'Probably a cat is mewing on the roof.'

The specific subject in (18) precedes the sentence adverbial marking the boundary between the topic and the predicate; the universal subject in (19 b) follows it but precedes the verb; whereas the non-specific subject in (20) follows both the sentence adverbial and the verb. Vallduví (1992 b) reports a quantifier position from Catalan.

It is not only universally quantified sentences that do not fit naturally either into the class of categorical judgements or into the class of thetic judgements; imperatives, questions, and sentences containing a focus operator represent a similar problem. The syntactic realization of quantificational sentences depends on whether the given language has its focus and quantifier positions at the head of the VP, or at the head of the clause. In the former case, a quantificational structure can − but need not − be preceded by a topic, and in the latter case, it can − but need not − embed a topic-predicate structure; the presence or absence of a topic does not change the discourse-semantic value of the sentence. This confirms that quantificational sentences are neither categorical, nor thetic, but represent a third type in syntax, too.

A reason why the differentiation of the quantificational sentence type is essential is that the constraints on the specificity feature of the subject, resulting in different subject positions, e.g. that requiring that an existential predicate have a non-specific subject, or that requiring that a stative predicate have a specific subject, are neutralized in quantificational sentences (cf. Alberti (1997)). Compare the following sentences:

(21) Hungarian
 (a) *Van a könyv az asztalon.
   is the book on.the.table
   'There is the book on the table.'
 (b) *Az asztalon van a könyv.
   'On the table is the book.'
 (c) AZ ASZTALON van a könyv.
   'It is ON THE TABLE where the book is.'

The existential *van* 'is' does not tolerate a specific subject whether it occurs in a thetic (21a) or in a categorical (21b) sentence; but it is perfectly grammatical with a specific subject in a focus structure. If no quantificational sentence types are acknowledged, no reliable generalizations concerning the correlation of predicate type, argument specificity, and argument position can be obtained.

In sum: sentences form three logical-semantic (or discourse-semantic) types. They can be categorical, expressing predication about a specific individual; they can be thetic, expressing predication about an empty event variable bound by the situation or by the context; and they can be quantificational, expressing e.g. universal quantification, focusing, or interrogation. The topic function is the function of the subject of predication in categorical sentences.

2.5. Topic-prominence versus subject-prominence

Languages can be classified typologically on the basis of how closely they reflect the discourse-semantic structure of their sentences in syntax. First it seemed that the basis of typological classification should be whether a language chooses to encode the grammatical subject−grammatical predicate articulation, or the topic−comment articulation in the syntactic structure. In an influential paper, Li and Thompson (1976) classified languages into a subject-prominent and a topic-prominent type on the basis of this criterion. (They also established a class of 'both subject- and topic-prominent' languages, which express both relations by different constructions, and a class of 'neither subject- nor topic-prominent' languages, which encode neither relation syntactically.)

Li and Thompson compiled a set of properties which allegedly distinguish topic-prominent languages from subject-prominent ones. For example, topic-prominent languages have no dummy subject, whereas subject-prominent languages have one; topic-prominent languages have no passive (or have it only marginally), whereas subject-prominent languages have one; in topic-prominent languages topic controls coreference, while in subject-prominent languages the subject controls it; in topic-prominent languages there is a double-subject construction like the Japanese (22), whereas in subject-prominent languages there is none, etc.

(22) *Sakana wa tai   ga*
   fish TOP red.snapper NOM
   oisii.
   delicious
   'As for fish, red snapper is delicious.'

Since, however, Li and Thompson did not offer an explicit definition of topic-prominence, the relation between topic-prominence and these properties remained accidental. A further problem inherent in their classification was that they did not recognize that a VP-external specific subject is also an instance of topic − thus they concluded that in subject-prominent languages like English topicalization is rare and marked. The case of English is now seen differently. In English, topic-selection is constrained: a specific subject must always function as a topic.

Sasse (1987) reinterpreted the typological difference that Li and Thompson noticed between English and Chinese. He claims that Chinese differs from English in as much as it expresses the difference between categorical and thetic utterances syntactically. In his view, a language is topic-prominent if it formulates categorical judgements as primary predication structures, and thetic judgements as mere predicate phrases. In subject-prominent languages, the difference between categorical and thetic judgements is not reflected in syntax; both types of utterances share the same grammatical subject−grammatical predicate structure. In this language type the non-topic (or in a different terminology, non-thematic) subjects of thetic sentences are "dethematized" only by phonological means.

A recent survey of 35 European languages (by É. Kiss 1997) has shown, however, that the subject-prominent language type of Sasse (1987) may not exist at all. Non-specific subjects have to remain inside the (extended) VP-projection in practically all languages examined — including English. There is ample empirical evidence indicating that specific and non-specific subjects occupy different positions in the English sentence, as well. It is only non-specific subjects that stand in Spec,IP (the extended VP-projection); specific subjects are extracted into an IP-external position — undergoing topic movement. The evidence for the two subject positions is of the following type (cf. É. Kiss (1996)):

(i) Only a specific subject can precede a sentence-adverbial without a comma intonation (cf. (23 a)); a non-specific subject must follow (cf. (23 b)):

(23) (a) *John luckily was born on time.*
(b) *??A baby luckily was born to them.*
cf. (c) *Luckily a baby was born to them.*

(ii) Specific subjects precede negation; non-specific subjects follow it:

(24) (a) *John was not born on time.*
(b) **A baby was not born.*
(c) *Not a baby was born.*

(iii) A sentence with a non-specific subject cannot undergo VP-deletion. This falls out if VP-deletion is the deletion of the extended VP-projection, which also includes the non-specific subject, but excludes the specific one. Cf.

(25) (a) *John was born on time, and Peter was, too.*
(b) **A girl was born, and then a boy was, too.*

(iv) An *only* or *even* preceding a non-specific subject can include the whole sentence in its scope (cf. (26a)). An *only* preceding a specific subject, on the other hand, only has scope over the subject (cf. (26b)). This, again, falls out if the maximal scope of *only* and *even* extends over the IP, which includes the non-specific subject, but excludes the specific one.

(26) (a) *Only a baby was born.*
(nothing else happened.)
(b) *Only John was born on time.*
*(*nothing else happened.)*

These facts, characteristic of all the languages examined in É. Kiss (1997) except three, make the existence of the subject-prominent language type highly questionable. The three languages not belonging to the topic-prominent type according to the criterion of Sasse (1987) are neither topic-prominent, nor subject-prominent: they are the VSO Irish, Welsh, and Scottish Gaelic (in Breton the VSO structure can be freely subjected to topicalization). According to McCloskey (1991) and Tallerman (1997), the VSO sentence of Celtic languages is an IP derived by verb movement into I; so in these languages the syntactic structure of sentences corresponds to the logical structure of thetic judgements; there is no visible topic movement in categorical sentences.

2.6. Parameters of topic prominence

Even though the majority of languages belong to the same topic-prominent type, they vary along various minor parameters. They differ in the position of the grammatical subject within the extended verb-projection. Some languages, like Hungarian, allow the subject to remain in its base-generated argument position (cf. (15–16)); others, like English, require it to move into a non-argument position within the extended verb-projection. This difference must derive from a difference in case assignment; in English nominative assignment is obviously associated with a fixed position.

Whereas in most languages there is no syntactic indication of an empty topic position in thetic sentences, some languages fill it with an expletive. In the European sample examined, these languages were the verb second languages, as well as English, which has also retained some 'residual verb second' features from its past. For example:

(27) Swedish
Det står en katt vid dörren.
there stands a cat at the.door

The topic can be morphologically marked; e.g. there is a topic marker in Japanese, Korean (Choe 1989) and Quechua (Muysken 1994).

The majority of the European languages allow more than one topic in a clause. A multiple topic construction is naturally incompatible with verb second, and is also excluded in Estonian, Finnish, Breton (cf. É. Kiss 1997), or Korean (cf. Choe 1989).

In multiple topic constructions, the order of topics may be free, as in Spanish — see (28), or may be fixed, as in English — see the English equivalents of (28).

(28) (a) *A Juan, Maria llegó a*
to Juan, Maria got to
conocer-lo el año pasado.
know-him the year last
'John, Mary got to know last year.'

(b) *Maria, a Juan, llegó a conocer-lo el año pasado.*
'John, Mary got to know last year.'

In Somali, the topics can be preceded, followed or interrupted by a focus (Svolacchia/Mereu/Puglielli 1994).

In some languages, e.g. Greek (Tsimpli 1994), Catalan (Vallduví 1992a), Somali, Korean (Choe 1989), Haida (Enrico 1986), Tzotzil, and Jacaltec (Aissen 1991), the topic binds a resumptive pronoun in the VP. In Bulgarian, the use of a resumptive pronoun is optional (cf. Rudin 1986). In the Romance languages, a resumptive pronoun coindexed with the topic may be obligatory, optional, or excluded, depending on many factors. In Greek, the relation between the topic and the resumptive pronoun in argument position observes Subjacency (cf. Tsimpli 1994) – hence there is no reason to discard the movement analysis of topicalization. In Korean, Jakaltak, Tzotzil, and Haida, on the other hand, there are no Subjacency effects, and the occurrence of topic is limited in embedded contexts, which argues for the base-generation of the topic outside the VP.

Most of the European languages examined (except the Caucasian group) allow topic movement into a superordinate clause:

(29) Spanish (É. Kiss 1997)
A Juan, dudo que lo conozca
to John doubt-I that him knows
María.
Maria
'John, I doubt that Mary knows.'

The topic constituent must – or at least can – bear the case assigned to the empty argument or resumptive pronoun coindexed with it. At the same time, some languages, e.g. Greek, Italian, or Russian, also allow a *nominativus pendens*, i.e., a topic in the nominative case. Compare the two Greek alternatives:

(30) Greek (Tsimpli 1994: 180)
(a) *Tus fitités, óli i kathijités*
the.ACC students all the lecturers
tus-ipostirízun.
them-support.3PL
'All lecturers support the students.'
(b) *I fitités, óli i kathijités*
the.NOM students all the lecturers
tus-ipostirízun.
them-support.3PL
'All lecturers support the students.'

3. Focus prominence

3.1. The notion of focus

Languages differ not only in the way in which they encode in syntax the logical structure of utterances expressing predication; they also differ in the way in which they encode the logical structure of utterances expressing various types of quantification, among them focusing.

The term 'focus' is used in at least two meanings in the linguistic literature. On the one hand, it denotes a sentence constituent expressing exhaustive identification, and on the other hand, it denotes the section of the sentence which carries new, non-presupposed information. We will distinguish the two notions by calling the former identificational focus, and the latter, information focus. It is identificational focus that has syntactic, and hence, typological relevance. A language is focus-prominent if it expresses identificational focus by a particular structural relation.

An identificational focus identifies a proper subset of a set of contextually or situationally given elements as such for which the action or state described in the sentence exclusively holds. For example:

(31) Hungarian
János MARIT hívta meg
John Mary.ACC invited PREV
vacsorára.
to.dinner
'It was Mary that John invited for dinner.'

The sentence expresses that of a set of potential candidates present in the domain of discourse, it is true of Mary and no one else that John invited her for dinner.

The feature content of identificational focus is subject to parametric variation: in some languages, e.g. Arabic, Rumanian, Italian, Catalan, or Greek, it also includes the feature [+contrastive], in addition to [+exhaustive]. In such languages, an identifying focus can only be used if the identification operation is performed on a closed set of entities which are known to the participants of discourse. In this case, the exhaustive identification of the subset of entities for which the sentence holds goes together with the exhaustive identification of the subset for which the sentence does not hold – hence the contrastive effect.

Thus if in Arabic the question *What did Zayd drink* is answered by the sentence *Zayd drank tea*, as in (32), *tea* cannot be formulated as an identificational focus, because the context, i.e., the question, does not provide a closed set of alternative drinks; hence the identification of tea as such that Zayd drank it does not exclude specific beverages that he did not drink. Thus *tea* must be an in-situ information focus in the answer.

(32)   Arabic (Ouhalla 1994: 66)
   (a) *maaðaa šariba Zaydun?*
       'What did Zayd drink?'
   (b) *šariba Zayd-un šaay-an*
       drank Zayd-NOM tea-ACC
       'Zayd drank tea.'
   (c) **Šaay-an šariba Zayd-un*
       tea-ACC drank Zayd-NOM
       'It was tea that Zayd drank.'

(c) is used when the context or situation clearly determines a closed set of alternatives for Zayd to choose from, e.g.:

(33)   *Šaay-an šariba Zayd-un laa*
       tea-ACC drank Zayd-NOM not
       'asiir-an
       juice-ACC
       'It was tea that Zayd drank, not juice.'

For a formal semantic theory of identificational focus, see Szabolcsi (1994). The general semantic theories of focus, which do not make a clear distinction between identificational focus and information focus, include the 'structured meaning' theory elaborated by von Stechow (1981; 1991), Jacobs (1983), and Krifka (1992), among others. In this approach, the focus feature of a constituent induces the partitioning of the semantic representation of the sentence into a focus part and a background/presupposition part. For instance, the focus structure in (34a) determines the structured meaning in (34b):

(34)   (a) I introduced BILL to Sue.
       (b) ⟨λx[introduced I x to Sue], Bill⟩

(34b) expresses that the individual who has the property of having been introduced to Sue by me is Bill.

In the theory of Rooth (1985), the focus is assumed to generate a set of alternatives. Thus the sentence *JOHN won*, when used in a situation involving, say five competitors (John, Bill, Peter, George, and Sam), expresses that the alternatives exist: *John won, Bill won, Peter won, George won,* and *Sam won.* In this theory, exhaustiveness must be expressed by some additional device – e.g. by an explicit *only.*

Meaningful generalizations about the syntactic realization of focus can only be obtained if identificational focus is consistently distinguished from information focus. To facilitate this, we confront the properties of the two focus types.

3.2. Identificational focus versus information focus

The differences between identificational focus and information focus will be illustrated by comparing English cleft constructions with English foci in situ. Both Rooth (1996) and É. Kiss (1998) claim that the English cleft construction represents an identificational focus. An English emphatic focus in situ, on the other hand, exemplifies an information focus. Even if it can be attributed an identificational meaning in some cases, its 'information focus' interpretation can never be excluded.

Identificational foci and information foci differ in the following respects:

(i) Whereas identificational focus expresses exhaustive identification, information focus merely marks the non-presupposed nature of the information it carries:

(35)   (a) *It was a coffee that I ordered.*
       (b) *I ordered a COFFEE.*

(35a), containing an identificational focus, evokes a set of relevant items which the speaker could have ordered, and states that of these items it is true only of a coffee (and nothing else) that the speaker ordered it. (35b), containing an information focus, on the other hand, merely states that the speaker ordered a coffee, without evoking and excluding alternatives, i.e., without suggesting that the speaker ordered nothing else.

(ii) Universal quantifiers, or *even* phrases cannot function as identifying foci. Information focus, on the other hand, does not involve any distributional restrictions. Cf.

(36)   (a) **It was everybody/even Mary that John invited.*
       (b) *John invited EVERYBODY/EVEN MARY.*

The impossibility of a universal quantifier or *even* phrase in the role of an identificational focus follows from the fact that an identificational focus identifies the **proper** subset of a set of alternatives; i.e., the identifying operator performs not only the identification of a subset, but also the exclusion of the conplementary subset. In the case of a universal quantifier or an *even*, the exclusion element of the operation is absent.

(iii) An identificational focus (more precisely, the identifying operator whose value it represents) is an operator with scope, which enters into scope relation with other operators.

(37) *It is always Mary that every boy wants to dance with.*
'On every occasion, it is true of Mary and no one else of the girls present that every boy wants to dance with her.'

In (37), exhaustive identification is in the scope of the universal quantifier *always*, and has scope over the universal quantifier *every boy*. An information focus, e.g. that in (38), on the other hand, does not have scope; on the contrary, it represents the nuclear scope of the universal quantifier, with the presupposed part of the sentence moved into the restrictor of the quantifier:

(38) *Every boy wanted to dance with* MARY.
'For every x, x a boy and x wanted to dance with someone, x wanted to dance with Mary.'

(iv) The identificational focus occupies a scope position also in syntax — either visibly, or in the logical form; information focus, on the other hand, is in situ (unless moved for an independent reason). This has been demonstrated by all the examples discussed in section 3.

According to a widely accepted proposal of Brody (1990, 1995), identificational focus undergoes focus movement, the landing site of which is the specifier position of a focus projection, called FP (focus phrase). F, the head of FP, is an abstract functional head, which must be lexicalized by the verb in some languages. This is the case e.g. in Hungarian, where the F head is filled by verb movement into it. The complement of F is the sentence part over which the identificational focus takes scope.

Consider the structure of a Hungarian identificational focus construction:

(39)
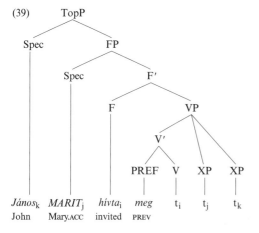

The identificational focus undergoes operator movement into an A' position, e.g. Spec,IP, or Spec,CP, also in the alternative syntactic analyses of focus by Tuller (1992), and Horvath (1994).

(v) Since the identificational focus is subject to operator movement, it must be a maximal projection whose movement does not violate Subjacency. Information focus, on the other hand, can be either smaller or larger than a maximal projection.

It has been debated what constitutes the focus in sentences of the following type:

(40) *Was it* BERGER'*s car that was the fastest?*

In (40) *BERGER* represents the non-presupposed part, but this only means that *Berger* is the information focus. The identification (and the concomitant exclusion) operation is performed on a set of cars; hence the subset of this set selected by the identificational focus must refer to a car, too. Consequently, the identification focus of the question extends over the maximal NP *Berger's car.* This is confirmed by the fact that the sentence can be answered as follows:

(41) *No, it was a Ferrari (that was the fastest).*

3.3. Parameters of focus prominence

Focus prominence, i.e., the expression of identificational focus in an invariant structural position, must be fairly common in the languages of the world. Of a sample of 35 European languages, 27 were found to be focus-prominent (cf. É. Kiss 1997). In that sample, practically all European languages with no structural focus belong to one group: the Germanic family. The lack of structural focus may be questionable even in the case of some of the Germanic languages. If Rooth (1996) and É. Kiss (1998) are right in claiming that the identificational focus in English is the cleft constituent, and if É. Kiss (1998) is right in claiming that the English cleft construction is an FP, then English is also a language with structural focus; merely, in English the F head takes a CP complement instead of a VP. Since the IP and CP boundaries block verb movement into F, F is lexicalized by the dummy *be.* Spec,FP is filled by movement or by base-generation, in which case the CP-internal argument position is occupied by a WH-pronoun. That is:

(42)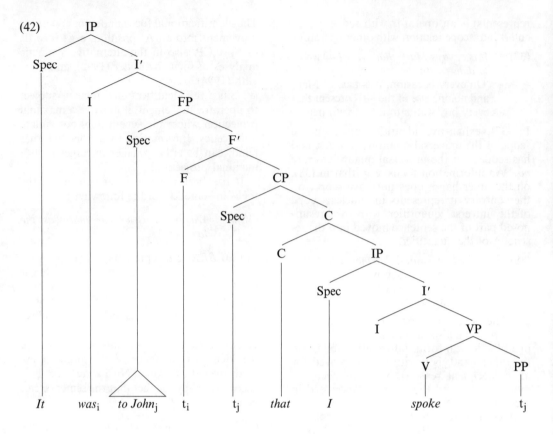

Under this analysis English is also focus-prominent, because it expresses identificational focus by a structural relation. At the same time, the identificational focus may also remain in situ in English — at least when its identificational operator role is overtly indicated e. g. by the particle *only*. (*Only* serves to add an evaluative component to the identificational operator.) There are also further significant differences between English and e. g. Greek, Hungarian, or Somali with respect to focus-prominence: a focus construction is comparatively rare and marked in English; whereas it is very common e. g. in Greek and Hungarian. In Somali, every sentence must have a focus (cf. Svolacchia/Mereu/Puglielli 1994).

Brody (1995) argues that all languages have a focus projection; what is subject to parametric variation is whether focus movement into Spec,FP takes place in visible syntax or in LF. In some languages, e. g. Rumanian, Italian, or Catalan, syntactic focus movement is optional; it can be postponed until LF (cf. É. Kiss 1998). In others, like Greek or Hungarian, it must take place in syntax.

The identificational focus has a morphological marker e. g. in Kikuyu (cf. Clements 1984), Somali (Svolacchia/Mereu/Puglielli 1994), Quechua (Muysken 1994), Haida (Enrico 1986), or Korean (Choe 1989). In Arabic, if the focus is morphologically marked, it need not undergo visible focus movement; if it is not, it has to land in Spec,FP (cf. Ouhalla 1994).

In Somali and Quechua, and certain Haida dialects, the focus is restricted to matrix, or tensed, clauses. In Greek, only one focus per complex sentence is allowed. It can be either in the matrix or in an embedded clause, but it must have matrix scope in either case (cf. Tsimpli 1994). Many languages allow long focus movement. E. g.:

(43) Hungarian
  Jánost$_i$ szeretném, ha
  John.ACC I.would.like if
  meghívnánk t$_i$.
  we.invited
  'It is John that I would be glad if we invited.'

In exactly two thirds of the focus-prominent languages of the European sample of É. Kiss

(1997), the focus is immediately preverbal; in one third, it is clause-initial. The Bantu language Aghem and some Chadic languages, e. g. Western Bade have been reported to have an immediately postverbal identificational focus (see Watters (1979) on Aghem, Tuller (1992) on Chadic, and Horvath (1994) on both). The identificational focus is claimed by Tuller and Horvath to be external to the VP in this case, too; merely, the verb leaves the VP, and crossing the focus, it adjoins to Inflection. The Chadic languages Kanakuru, Tangele and Ngizim can have their focus either in postverbal or in clause-initial position.

The interrogative WH-operator appears to share the position of identificational focus in all the languages described in the literature. This is as predicted by Horvath (1986), according to whom a WH-phrase can only function as an interrogative operator if it has a [+focus] feature.

In sum: the configurational encoding of the topic function and the configurational encoding of the focus function are characteristic of sets of languages of a different order. Most languages (perhaps all that are not V-initial) associate the topic function with a pre-VP constituent. They only differ along minor parameters of topic-prominence, involving, among others, restrictions on the case, syntactic category, number, and relative order of topics. On the other hand, languages genuinely differ in whether or not they express identificational focus in a particular structural position. Languages belonging to the focus-prominent type can also be further subdivided — e. g. according to the semantic feature content of their focus, as well as its syntactic properties, e. g. clause-initial or preverbal position.

4. References

Aissen, Judith. 1991. "Topic and focus in Mayan". *Language* 68: 43–80.

Alberti, Gábor. 1997. "Restrictions on the degree of referentiality of arguments in Hungarian sentences". *Acta Linguistica Hungarica* 44.3–4.

Awobuluyi, O. 1978. "Focus constructions as noun phrases". *Linguistic Analysis* 4: 93–114.

Brassai, Sámuel. 1860–65. "A magyar mondat." *Magyar Akadémiai Értesítő. A Nyelv- és Széptudományi Osztály Közlönye* 1: 179–399; 3: 3–128; 173–409.

Brody, Michael. 1990. "Some remarks on the focus field in Hungarian". *University College London Working Papers in Linguistics* 2: 201–226.

Brody, Michael. 1995. "Focus and checking theory". In: Kenesei, István (ed.). *Approaches to Hungarian V. Levels and Structures*. Szeged: JATE, 29–44.

Büring, Daniel. 1995. "The great scope inversion conspiracy". *Linguistics and Philosophy* 20: 175–194.

Calabrese, Andrea. 1992. "Some remarks on focus and logical structures in Italian". *Harvard Working Papers in Linguistics* I: 91–127.

Carlson, Gregory. 1978. *References to kinds in English*. New York: Garland Publishers.

Choe, Hyon-Sook. 1989. "Restructuring parameters and scrambling in Korean and Hungarian". In: Marácz, László & Muysken, Pieter (eds.). *Configurationality*. Dordrecht: Foris, 267–292.

Clements, G. N. 1984. "Binding domains in Kikuyu". *Studies in the Linguistic Sciences* 14.2: 37–57.

Comrie, Bernard. 1984. "Some properties of focus in Modern Eastern Armenian". *Annual of Armenian Linguistics* 5: 1–21.

Daneš, Frantisek (ed.). 1974. *Papers on functional sentence perspective*. Prague: Academia.

Davidson, Donald. 1967. "The logical form of action sentences". In: Rescher, N. (ed.). *The logic of decision and action*. Pittsburgh: Univ. of Pittsburgh Press, 81–95.

Diesing, Molly. 1992. *Indefinites*. Cambridge/MA: MIT Press.

Enç, Mürvet. 1991. "The semantics of specificity". *Linguistic Inquiry* 22: 1–25.

Enrico, John. 1986. "Word order, focus and topic in Haida". *International Journal of American Linguistics* 52: 91–123.

Erguvanli, E. E. 1984. *The function of word order in Turkish grammar*. Berkeley: University of California Press.

Gabelentz, Georg von der. 1869. "Ideen zu einer vergleichenden Syntax — Wort und Satzstellung". *Zeitschrift für Völkerpsychologie und Sprachwissenschaft* 6: 376–384.

Gabelentz, Georg von der. 1875. "Weiteres zur vergleichenden Syntax". *Zeitschrift für Völkerpsychologie und Sprachwissenschaft* 8: 129–165.

Gambhir, V. 1981. *Syntactic restrictions and discourse functions of word order in Standard Hindi*. [Ph.D. dissertation], University of Pennsylvania.

Horvath, Julia. 1986. *FOCUS in the theory of grammar and the syntax of Hungarian*. Dordrecht: Foris.

Horvath, Julia. 1994. "Structural focus, structural case, and the notion of feature assignment". In: É. Kiss, Katalin (ed.). *Discourse-configurational languages*. Oxford: Oxford University Press, 28–64.

Jacobs, Joachim. 1983. *Fokus und Skalen. Zur Syntax und Semantik der Gradpartikeln im Deutschen.* Tübingen: Niemeyer.

Jacobs, Joachim. 1996. "Bemerkungen zur I-Topikalisierung". *Sprache und Pragmatik* 41: 1–48. Lund.

King, Tracy H. 1995. *Configuring topic and focus in Russian.* Stanford: CSLI Publications.

É. Kiss, Katalin. 1987. *Configurationality in Hungarian.* Dordrecht: Reidel.

É. Kiss, Katalin. 1996. "Two subject positions in English". *The Linguistic Review* 13.2: 119–142.

É. Kiss, Katalin. 1997. "Discourse-configurationality in the languages of Europe". In: Siewierska, Anna (ed.). *Constituent order in the languages of Europe.* Berlin: Mouton.

É. Kiss, Katalin. 1998. "Identificational focus versus information focus". *Language* 75.2.

Kratzer, Angelika. 1995. "Stage and individual level predicates". In: Carlson, Gregory N. and Pelletier, Francis J. (eds.) *The Generic Book.* Chicago: The University of Chicago Press, 125–175.

Krifka, Manfred. 1992. "A framework for focus-sensitive quantification". In: Barker, Carl & Dowty, David (eds.). *SALT II. Proceedings from the second conference on semantics and linguistic theory.* (Working Papers in Linguistics 40.) Columbus, 215–236.

Krifka, Manfred. 1998. "Scope inversion under the rise-fall contour in German." *Linguistic Inquiry* 29: 75–112.

Kuno, Susumu. 1973. *The structure of the Japanese language.* Cambridge/MA: MIT Press.

Kuroda, Sige-Yuki. 1972–73. "The categorical and the thetic judgment". *Foundations of Language* 9: 153–185.

Lambrecht, K. 1994. *Information structure and sentence form.* Cambridge: Cambridge University Press.

Lecarme, Jacqueline. 1991. "Focus en Somali: syntaxe et interpretation". *Linquistique Africaine* 7.

Li, Charles N. & Thompson, Sandra A. 1976. "Subject and topic: a new typology of language". In: Li, Charles N. (ed.). *Subject and topic.* New York: Academic Press, 457–490.

Marty, Anton 1918. *Gesammelte Schriften,* II. Band, 1. Abteilung. Halle: Niemeyer.

Marty, Anton. 1965. *Psyche und Sprachstruktur.* Bern: Francke.

Mathesius, Vilém. 1929. "Zur Satzperspektive im modernen Englisch". *Archiv für die neueren Sprachen und Literaturen* 155: 202–210.

McCloskey, James. 1991. "Clause structure, ellipsis and proper government in Irish". *Lingua* 85: 259–302.

Molnár, Valéria. 1998. "Topic in focus". *Acta Linguistica Hungarica* 45: 89–166.

Muysken, Pieter. 1994. "Focus in Quechua". In: É. Kiss, Katalin (ed.). *Discourse-configurational languages.* Oxford: Oxford University Press, 375–393.

Ortiz de Urbina, Jon. 1991. *Parameters in the grammar of Basque.* Dordrecht: Foris.

Ortiz de Urbina, Jon. 1993. "Residual verb second and verb first in Basque". In: É. Kiss, Katalin (ed.). *Discourse-configurational languages.* Oxford: Oxford University Press, 99–121.

Ouhalla, Jamal. 1994. "Focus in standard Arabic". *Linguistics in Potsdam* 1: 65–92.

Rijk, R. P. G. de. 1978. "Topic fronting, focus positioning and the nature of the verb phrase in Basque". In: Jansen, Frank (ed.). *Studies on fronting.* Lisse: Peter de Ridder Press.

Rooth, Mats. 1985. *Association with focus.* [Ph.D. dissertation, University of Massachusetts, Amherst].

Rooth, Mats. (1996). "Focus". In: Lappin, Shalom (ed.). *The handbook of contemporary semantic theory.* Oxford: Blackwell.

Rudin, Catherine. 1986. *Aspects of Bulgarian syntax: Complementizers and Wh constructions.* Columbus, Ohio: Slavica Publishers.

Rudin, Catherine. 1990–91. "Topic and Focus in Bulgarian". *Acta Linguistica Hungarica* 40: 429–448.

Sasse, Hans-Jürgen. 1987. "The thetic/categorical distinction revisited". *Linguistics* 25: 511–580.

Schachter, Paul. 1973. "Focus and relativization". *Language* 49: 19–46.

Selkirk, Elisabeth. 1984. *Phonology and syntax. The relation between sound and structure.* Cambridge/MA.

Sgall, Peter & Hajičova, Eva. 1973. *Topic, focus and generative semantics.* Kronberg/Taunus: Scriptor Verlag.

Stechow, Arnim von. 1981. "Topic, focus, and relevance". In: Klein, Wolfgang & Levelt, W. (eds.). *Crossing the boundaries in linguistics.* Dordrecht: Reidel, 95–130.

Stechow, Arnim von. 1991. "Current issues in the theory of focus". In: Stechow, Arnim von & Wunderlich, Dieter (eds.). *Semantics. An international handbook of contemporary research.* Berlin: de Gruyter, 804–825.

Svolacchia, Marco & Mereu, Lunella & Puglielli, Annarita. 1994. "Aspects of discourse configurationality in Somali". In: É. Kiss, Katalin (ed.). *Discourse configurational languages.* Oxford: Oxford University Press, 65–98.

Szabolcsi, Anna. 1981. "The semantics of topic-focus articulation". In: Jan Groenendijk et al. (eds.). *Formal methods in the study of language.* Amsterdam, 513–541.

Szabolcsi, Anna. 1986. "From the Definiteness Effect to Lexical Integrity". In: Abraham, Werner &

Meij, Sjaak de (eds.). *Topic, focus and configurationality*. Amsterdam: Benjamins, 321–348.

Szabolcsi, Anna. 1994. "All quantifiers are not equal: the case of focus". *Acta Linguistica Hungarica* 42.3–2: 171–187.

Tallerman, Maggie. 1997. "Celtic word order: some theoretical issues". In: Siewierska, Anna (ed.). *Constituent order in the languages of Europe*. Berlin: Mouton, 599–648.

Tsimpli, Ianthi Maria. 1994. "Focussing in Modern Greek". In: É. Kiss, Katalin (ed.). *Discourse-configurational languages*. Oxford: Oxford University Press, 176–206.

Tuller, Laurice. 1992. "The syntax of postverbal focus constructions in Chadic". *Natural Language and Linguistic Theory* 10: 303–334.

Ulrich, Miorita. 1985. *Thetisch und kategorisch. Funktionen der Anordnung von Satzkonstituenten am Beispiel des Rumänischen und anderer Sprachen*. Tübingen: Narr.

Vallduví, Enric. 1992a. *The informational component*. New York: Garland Publishers.

Vallduví, Enric. 1992b. "A preverbal landing site for quantificational operators". *Catalan Working Papers in Linguistics (CWPL)* 1992. 319–343.

Vallduví, Enric. 1993. "Catalan as VOS: Evidence from information packaging". In: W. J. Ashby et al. (eds.). *Linguistic perspectives in the romance languages*. Amsterdam: Benjamins, 335–350.

Vilkuna, Maria 1989. *Free word order in Finnish*. Helsinki: Suomalaisen Kirjallisuuden Seura.

Wallace, W. D. 1985. *Subjects and subjecthood in Nepali*. [Ph.D. dissertation.] University of Illinois, Urbana-Champaign.

Watters, J. 1979. "Focus in Aghem". In: Hyman, L. (ed.). *Aghem grammatical structure. Southern California Occasional Papers in Linguistics* 7.

Weil, Henri. 1844. *De l'ordre des mots dans les langues anciennes comparées aux langues modernes*. Paris: Joubert.

Williams, Edwin. 1980. "Predication". *Linguistic Inquiry* 11: 203–238.

Katalin É. Kiss,
Research Institute for Linguistics,
Hungarian Academy of Sciences (Hungary)

XIV. Typological characterization of language families and linguistic areas
Typologische Charakterisierung von Sprachfamilien und Sprachbünden
La caractéristique typologique de familles et d'aires linguistiques

105. Principles of areal typology

1. Introduction
2. Critique of the notion of Sprachbund
3. Migration and language shift
4. Convenient fictions of areal linguistics and areal typology
5. Areal typology and the science of geography
6. Areal linguistics and sampling
7. Sample areas
8. The areal distribution of some major typological features
9. Are statistical universals historical accidents?
10. The areal dimension of grammaticalization
11. References

1. Introduction

Areal typology is not among the traditional divisions of linguistics. Yet, areal linguistics, on one hand, and language typology, on the other, have had close ties for a long time. The original motivation of both was the insufficiency of the genetic Stammbaum model for the study of relationships between languages. Thus, areal linguistics is traditionally concerned with similarities between geographically contiguous languages, in particular when they cannot be ascribed to a common protolanguage, and the identification of so-called **Sprachbünde** (plural of German *Sprachbund*, literally 'language union') or as they are often referred to in English, **linguistic areas**. Similarly, the aim of typology has been understood as the establishment of a taxonomy of languages based on grammatical and phonological features, independent of genetic relationships. To the extent that typologically interesting features are not evenly spread geographically but tend to cluster in specific areas, there is an obvious overlap in interests between the two fields. However, there is a difference in focus, in that the primary object to be identified and characterized in areal linguistics is the linguistic area, whereas in typology, the basic units are the features or properties that characterize individual languages. Consequently, areal typology would study the geographical distribution of such features, rather than the characteristics of individual areas. This implies that, as Johanna Nichols stresses in her important 1992 monograph, diversity is as essential as similarity. Thus, areal patterns are of interest irrespective of whether they can be described in terms of linguistic areas in the traditional sense. Indeed, as we shall see, the concept of "area" itself receives a somewhat different interpretation within areal typology than in traditional areal linguistics. A further consequence of the difference in focus is that inspiration for areal typology will come as much from the fields of dialectology and sociolinguistics as from areal linguistics understood as the study of Sprachbünde. (For an alternative understanding of the term "areal linguistics" relevant to this statement, see the discussion of the Italian neolinguistic school and its notion of *linguistica spaziale* in Art. 106.)

Areal typology, then, is the study of patterns in the areal distribution of typologically relevant features of languages. It is both descriptive and explanatory; that is, it looks both at the patterns themselves and the processes that give rise to them. In other words, areal typology has both a synchronic and a diachronic side. As a not fully established discipline, areal typology is still searching for its

2. Critique of the notion of Sprachbund

As noted in § 1., areal linguistics was originally inspired by the insufficiency of genetic relationships as an explanation for similarities between languages, in particular, by the recognition of grammatical and phonological similarities which were due to language contact. Thus, the notion of Sprachbund (the term is usually ascribed to Trubetzkoy) was introduced as a characterization primarily of groups of languages which are genetically unrelated or at least not very closely related but which still share salient traits. (Although Trubetzkoy (1928) does not say so explicitly, it mentions the lack of shared core vocabulary as a positive criterion for a Sprachbund.) More recent definitions of "areal linguistics" and "linguistic area" still reflect this emphasis. For instance, Emeneau (1980: 124) defines "linguistic area" as "an area which includes languages belonging to more than one family but showing traits in common which are found not to belong to the other members of (at least) one of the families". Masica (1992) while finding this definition too restricted and not applicable e. g. to the classical Balkan Sprachbund (→ Art. 108) still defines "areal linguistics" as "the study of resemblances among languages based on geographic rather than genetic relationships". Campbell (1994: 1471) says that "'areal linguistics' deals with the diffusion of structural features across linguistic boundaries" and that the members of a linguistic area are "either unrelated or from different subgroups of a language family". Thus, the role of areal linguistics still seems to be to care of what is left unexplained by "genetic" historical linguistics − when "inheritance" has done its job we look at "diffusion" to account for the remaining similarities.

However, putting diffusion against inheritance leads us astray. If diffusion is defined as a spread of an innovation from one location to another, this is part and parcel of virtually every process of linguistic change. The restriction to diffusion "across linguistic boundaries" is potentially vacuous, in that linguistic boundaries which are not the result of migration have to be the outer limits of earlier processes of diffusion, and any more significant change has to cross at least some of these. To avoid vacuity, one would have to define a minimum height of the boundaries to be crossed, and there seems to be no non-arbitrary way of doing so. It may be conjectured that there is a correlation between the height of a linguistic boundary and the probability that a certain change will cross it. Thus, the spread of a linguistic feature from one language to another is of course in a sense more spectacular if the languages are unrelated. On the other hand, if we look at things from the point of view of typology, restricting attention to this tip of the iceberg is wholly unmotivated and indeed counterproductive in that it leaves most of the areal patterning unaccounted for. In fact, traits shared by the members of a language family are frequently due not to inheritance from a common proto-language but to later diffusion processes. More often than not, such processes do not cover the whole territory of the family at the same time as they may well spill over into non-related languages in the area.

Another problematic aspect of areal linguistics in the traditional sense is its unresolved relationship to the synchrony-diachrony distinction. More specifically, it is not clear if one is studying linguistic change, or rather, the result of change. For instance, while Campbell (1994) sees areal linguistics as the study of the diffusion of structural features; Campbell, Kaufman, & Smith-Stark (1986) give the same characterization of the field except that they say that the object of study is "the result of the diffusion of structural features".

As already mentioned, traditional areal linguistics focuses on similarity rather than diversity. At the same time, it is acknowledged that not all cases of similarities between languages are relevant: linguistic areas are deemed to be interesting only to the extent that the similarities between the languages are not trivial. That is, the finding that two languages share a certain feature is not interesting as long as we have not found a sufficient number of languages that do not share the feature in question. In other words, the study of non-trivial similarities between languages presupposes an understanding of linguistic diversity.

Furthermore, the null assumption cannot always be one of diversity, as the case of historical linguistics illustrates. Understood as comparative linguistics in the sense this term obtained in the 19th century, historical linguistics does explain similarities between languages by postulating a common origin of them. But understood as the theory of language change, historical linguistics tries to explain how and why two subsequent synchronic states of a language come to be different. In the latter case, it is diversity rather than similarity that has to be explained. Likewise, the study of social and geographic variation in synchronic linguistics has to take uniformity between dialects as the null hypothesis.

One of the most prominent types of areal pattern is the **centre-periphery** pattern, which is typically the result of a spread of innovations from a cultural, economic and/or political centre. Such a spread is often incomplete in that it leaves some less accessible areas untouched and/or that the innovations are only partially implemented in some locations. This kind of pattern is well known from dialectology (→ Art. 106) and the general study of innovations in social science. From the synchronic point of view, the result is often a set of non-contiguous residual areas in which the previous state of the language (with respect to the particular innovation(s)) is preserved. (It should be noted that the residual areas are not always located at the geographic periphery, they may as well be less accessible locations in the middle of the area.) For a concrete example, consider the virtual disappearance of the nominal case inflections in the Scandinavian languages in the Middle Ages, which was implemented in the standard varieties but never reached Iceland, the Faroes, and several dialects in mainland Scandinavia, which now form a kind of quasi-Sprachbund, defined off the agenda by traditional areal linguistics, but certainly important for typology. It should be noted that a centre-periphery pattern may arise not only from the diffusion of individual linguistic traits but also from wholesale language shift and migration (see also below).

Discussions of linguistic areas in the literature have been rather heavily influenced by the traditional paradigm example, the Balkan Sprachbund, characterized by Thomason & Kaufman (1988: 95) as being "without asymmetric dominance relations or large-scale shifts, and with multilateral rather than one-way bi- and multi-lingualism". The term "Sprachbund" also in itself suggests a symmetric relationship between the member languages. One sometimes even sees this mentioned as a definitional criterion. It is obvious that this would exclude a very large part of all contact relationships between languages, since some kind of asymmetry is very often involved. On the other hand, long-term multilateral symmetric contact situations do occur in various parts of the world, as noted by Thomason & Kaufman, and may well exhibit particular patterns. For instance, New Guinea is often mentioned as an area in which strong areal influence between languages is an obstacle to the identification of genetic relationships.

On a more fundamental level, it may be noted that the traditional division of labour between genetic and areal explanations presupposes a previous understanding of the nature of genetic and non-genetic relationships that does not necessarily exist.

In the end, we are led to the following more far-going question about the notion of area: to what extent do areas in typology have a reality of their own and to what extent are they just convenient ways of summarizing certain phenomena? At the most basic level, linguistic contact relationships are binary: one language influences another. An area is then simply the sum of many such binary relationships. But such an area need not display shared features in the classical sense — that is features that characterize all the languages within the area and which define a clear boundary to the rest of the world. Like a classical dialect continuum, in which any two adjacent dialects are mutually comprehensible but pairs whose members are farther apart are not, we may travel in an area without passing any sharp boundaries and still find that there are none of the properties left that we found at the point of departure. Map 105.1, adapted from van der Auwera (1998), shows what typically happens when a larger number of features are mapped. It also Illustrates the use of **isopleths** — lines showing the geographical distribution of languages which share the same number (not necessarily the same subset) of some set of features. In this case, the features pertain to tense and aspect and the area is what van der Auwera calls "the Charlemagne area" in Europe.

3. Migration and language shift

The migration of speakers is an important factor in the creation of areal patterns which is not on the agenda of traditional areal linguistics but which is impossible to neglect

105. Principles of areal typology

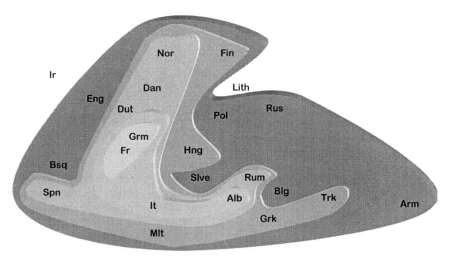

Map 105.1: The "Charlemagne area" in Europe (Auwera 1998)

for the typologist. The resettlement of a part of a speech community from one location to another extends the geographical domain of their language and consequently of all its features. Simultaneously, it cuts the original speech community in two and thus creates the preconditions for a (wholly or partially) separate linguistic development, but also for external influence through contacts with new neighbors.

It is obvious that the present distribution of language families on earth reflects the history of the original expansion of humankind and the subsequent migrations of larger and smaller groups of people. But also the distribution of typological features is at least partially a result of the same processes, as has been argued particularly in Nichols (1992).

Migrations may complicate the internal relationships in a language family, in that languages that move away from their closest relatives are less likely to adopt innovations that spread within the family. Thus, the Germanic languages spoken on islands in the Atlantic – Icelandic, Faroese, English – have been partially insulated against changes that have spread in mainland Europe.

Migrations may also obscure the result of earlier areal influence, in various ways. A language may retain properties characteristic of an area from which its speakers have been removed for a long time. Neighboring languages may become non-contiguous through the intrusion of a foreign group, making it impossible to talk of a language area according to many current definitions which make contiguity a necessary condition. A similar split-up of an earlier coherent area may also arise through external influence. Consider e. g. the contacts between the Baltic and Balto-Fennic languages, which have given rise to a number of shared features, some of which have disappeared from Estonian under the influence of Germanic (Koptjevskaja-Tamm & Wälchli, forthcoming), leaving behind a non-contiguous area consisting of Finnish, Latvian and Lithuanian.

Language shift (more precisely, the non-transmission of a language to the next generation in a speech community) is another phenomenon that influences the areal distribution of linguistic features. It creates a logical difficulty for the application of the notion of diffusion. Commonly, when one group of people adopt the language of another group, there is some interference from their old language – this is referred to as substratum influence. The resulting language thus contains elements from both input languages, although in the normal situation the bulk comes from the newly adopted language. The question is now what is diffused. From the geographical point of view, it looks as if the features of the new language have been spread in the sense that they show up in a place where they were not represented before; in traditional areal linguistics, on the other hand, one would probably rather say that it is the substratum features that have jumped the linguistic boundary between the two languages. The problem becomes acute when there is no clear asymmetry between the input languages, as in the so far relatively few cases of bona fide mixed languages.

4. Convenient fictions of areal linguistics and areal typology

Almost by definition, areal linguistics neglects the social dimension of language diversity. More generally, the whole notion of "areal phenomena" as well as the idea of drawing language maps, build on the convenient fiction that each language has a specific location in space, that no more than one language is spoken in each place, and that language contact takes place between adjacent languages. However, language contacts typically occur in densely populated places where speakers of many languages live together and bi- and multilingualism is common. In addition, many languages have a widely scattered distribution, and via the medium of writing, languages may influence each other over long distances in space and time. Yiddish illustrates all these points: with its pre-war speakers spread and mixed with other groups all over Eastern Europe it creates almost insurmountable problems for constructors of typological maps; in addition to being influenced by the surrounding Slavic languages, the Hebrew adstratum is also evident. In modern times, some of the strongest and most obvious cases of linguistic influence is found in colonial or post-colonial situations, most often between European and non-European languages. Languages such as English and French are of course ubiquitous, but there are also cases like Dutch, which has been present in places as different as South Africa, Indonesia, Suriname and the Caribbean. Assuming that we may find traces of Dutch influence on languages in all these locations, we would thus obtain a "linguistic area" of a rather peculiar kind. In general, the European expansion has wrought havoc in the linguistic world-map; in describing the distribution of the world's languages one often conveniently pretends that the Europeans were never there.

5. Areal typology and the science of geography

Although there is an obvious relationship between areal linguistics and the science of geography, areal linguistics in the traditional (narrow) sense is not equal to the intersection of linguistics and geography. For the latter, the term "geolinguistics" is sometimes used. It is perhaps symptomatic that there are no cross-references between the two articles "Areal linguistics" and "Geography and Language" in Asher (1994).

In areal typology, geography provides various types of background factors that may help explaining areal patterns on different levels. Some features of physical geography relatively obviously influence the linguistic diversity of a given area; mountainous areas tend to be populated by small, relatively isolated communities with ensuing high diversity, while large plains are more likely to show little diversity and few sharp linguistic boundaries. The distinction between residual zones and spread zones made in Nichols (1992) builds on these and similar observations.

Intuitively, a spread zone is an area in which languages tend to spread quickly and repeatedly (typically, areas consisting of large plains or navigable seas), and a residual zone is one where languages tend to remain basically undisturbed in the same place over long periods (for example, mountainous areas). As illustrative examples, Nichols gives the Eurasian steppe (basically, present-day Ukraine, Southern Russia and Kazakhstan) and the Caucasus, as traditionally defined. Table 1 is a condensation of Nichols's account of the main differences between the two types of zones. In her material, Nichols identifies the following spread zones: Ancient Near East, Europe, Central Australia, Interior North America, Mesoamerica. The residual zones are: Ethiopia & Kenya, Caucasus, North Asia Coast, Northern Australia, California (cf. Table 105.1):

Physical geography and the distribution of languages and linguistic features are of course mediated by factors to do with human ecology and economy. The fact that one finds exceptionally large speech communities and thus little linguistic diversity in regions with a prevailing monsoon climate is readily explainable by the extreme population density characteristic of rice-cultivating areas. Certain types of economic activity, such as fishing, tend to give rise to small and tight communities, which in their turn are the most favourable setting for the development of separate language varieties. Animal husbandry favours nomadic life-styles and thus tends to be accompanied by the spread of languages over large areas etc.

There is a relationship, although it is not clear in details, between the size of speech communities and what Nichols (1990) calls

Table 105.1: Properties of spread zones and residual zones.

	Spread zones	Residual zones
Genetic density	Low	High
Structural diversity	Low	High
Depth of language families	Shallow	Deep
Spread and succession of languages	Rapid	None
Innovation pattern	Classic dialect-geographic area with innovating centre and conservative periphery	No clear centre of innovation
Long-term net increase in diversity	No	Yes
Lingua franca	The spreading language	None

"density of lineages", that is, the number of language families in a given area. Nichols finds the following parameters to be correlated with density of lineages (high density going with the first member of the pair), assuming that they are reducible to the cultural factor of economic scale:

(i) low vs. high latitudes
(ii) coastal vs. island areas
(iii) high vs. low precipitation
(iv) mountains vs. plains
(v) "colonized" areas (i. e. the New World) vs. the Old World

As a note of caution, it should be added that it is not obvious how density of lineages should be calculated, in particular how it relates to population density. It is reasonable to assume that even under Paleolithic conditions there would be significant differences in population density between, say, Alaska and Mesoamerica, making it rather difficult to compare the number of families per thousand square kilometers.

6. Areal linguistics and sampling

6.1. Sampling of languages

A linguistic theory should describe and explain the properties of human languages, both in terms of absolute generalizations and statistical tendencies. We should therefore not be content with a report of what happens to be the case but should look for the essential rather than the accidental properties of human language. These considerations must also guide typological research. One of the most important methodological issues for typology is thus how to draw valid conclusions from the apparent patterns of cross-linguistic data. The observation that many typologically interesting properties have an areally skewed distribution makes the areal dimension essential in typology and brings the question of representativeness of samples to the fore (→ Art. 33). However, it is important to realize that the principles of sampling that apply on the global level do not necessarily carry over to areal sampling, as we shall see in this section.

The first obvious methodological consideration is that a generalization about human languages should not build on a database which is areally biased. It is easy to find examples in the linguistic literature of statements that violate this principle. In fact, it has traditionally been rare for a linguist to have any explicit samples at all; scholars have simply generalized out from the languages they happen to know something about, a practice which mostly automatically leads to eurocentrism. Even those scholars who have been aware of the problem have often been content with considering a few token non-European languages. In recent years, most linguists working in the typological research tradition try to base themselves on as broad databases as possible, and freedom from areal and genetic bias is an explicit goal. But there are many stumbling-stones here.

In early discussions of language sampling, it was assumed that an ideal sample should reflect the areal and genetic make-up of the languages of the world. Thus, Bell (1978) suggested that each language family should have the same percentage of the languages in a sample as it has in the languages of the world. To take an example, since the Bantu languages make up about eight per cent of all existing languages, they should also provide eight per cent of the members of the sample. However, as among others Dryer (1989) emphasizes, the fact that there are so many Bantu languages is a historical accident which should not be allowed to influence our view of what human languages are like. For instance, it turns out that about 40 per cent of all SVO languages in the world belong to the Niger-Congo family (where the Bantu languages are the largest group), a fact which significantly raises the global incidence of SVO word order. More recent typological samples have therefore been constructed with the aim of not allowing more than one member from each genetic grouping (at some predefined level) (e. g. Nichols 1992, Bybee et al. 1994) or have taken those groupings rather than individual languages as the units to be sampled (e. g. Dryer 1989). In addition, one also sometimes strives to maximize the geographic distance between the languages in the sample (or with Perkins (1992), choose the languages from different cultural areas).

This is all laudable if the aim is to make global generalizations about typologically interesting properties, as free from biases of any kind. But by minimizing the probability that the languages in the sample have influenced each other, one makes those areal patterns that are the concern of areal typology invisible.

The role of the attempts to avoid genetic bias in samples is even trickier. Partly, they enhance the effect of maximizing geographical distance — it is reasonable to assume that genetic and geographical distance are relatively strongly correlated. But the fact that pairs of closely related languages are excluded from typological samples also means that areal influence between related languages will not be visible in the sample. In this sense, typology has inherited the tendency of traditional areal linguistics to treat areal phenomena as complementary to genetic relationships.

A further consequence of the sampling method is that geographical areas will be unevenly represented due to differences in genetic diversity. The general importance of such differences is one of the points made in Nichols (1992). She thus notes the high density of genetic groupings on the west coast of North America, the southeastern United States, Mesoamerica, New Guinea and northern Australia. However, she does not discuss explicitly the consequent under-representation of some relatively large areas such as Africa south of the Equator, which is almost a white spot on her map, the reason being that it is inhabited mainly by speakers of the large Bantu grouping, mentioned above as a problem for typological sampling. From giving Bantu languages a twelfth of the whole sample, typologists have now landed at the other extreme, usually letting it be represented by a single language.

There are two obvious parameters in characterizing a geographical area that are of relevance to the study of areal linguistic influence: density of population and genetic diversity. Restricting oneself to a binary division of each, we obtain four types of areas:

- densely populated areas with high genetic diversity,
- genetically homogeneous densely populated ares,
- sparsely populated areas with high genetic diversity
- genetically homogeneous sparsely populated areas.

The currently popular principles of typological sampling, as we can see, will not do justice to (b) and (d). The bottom line is that areal typology needs somewhat different sampling methods, which are more suited to revealing local patterns.

6.2. Sampling of features

While the problem of finding a representative sample of languages has been discussed fairly extensively in the literature, the orthogonal question of sampling of features has hardly been touched upon at all. Yet, it is essential to any investigation that purports to estimate the similarity between languages. In particular, in judging the extent of areal influence within a set of languages, the results may come out very differently depending on how the features to be compared are chosen. In traditional areal linguistics, there is hardly any sampling in the proper sense, since the aim is normally to test a hypothesis about the existence of a linguistic area, and the investigator chooses whatever features seem to confirm the hypothesis. A goal of future research is to find a way of measuring the overall structural similarity of arbitrary language pairs as a basis for areal studies.

7. Sample areas

An obvious method of checking whether a statistical generalization about languages is influenced by areal skewing is to divide up the global sample into areally defined sub-samples. The null hypothesis here is that the incidence of the various properties involved in the generalization will not differ significantly from area to area. For this to work, one must of course first define a set of areas. It should be emphasized that the "sample areas" talked about here are rather different from the "linguistic areas" in traditional areal linguistics, as is the motivation for postulating them. Rather than demand that the languages in an area should share properties in a non-trivial way, that is, exhibit the effects of having influenced each other or together been influenced by a third source, sample constructors usually want the properties found in one area not to be influenced by whatever properties are found in other areas. Thus, external independence rather than internal similarity is the goal. However, to what extent such independence is at all possible is not clear, and it may not even be necessary if the method of areal sub-samples is seen only as a safeguard against blatant areal skewings in the material and as a way of spotting clusterings of properties.

The move from the global sample to areal sub-samples is more problematic than is often assumed. The problems start when we take the percentages of languages in an areal sample not only as a check of the corresponding global data but as an indication of characteristics of that particular area. This implies, to start with, that the criteria for representativeness that have been applied at the global level cannot be transferred to the individual areas. One immediate problem is that a typological sample that contains a satisfactory number of languages overall may be just too small to ensure reliability on the areal level. Enlarging the sample is a problematic undertaking for several reasons. To start with, it may be difficult for purely practical reasons: there may not be a sufficient number of well-described languages. But one also runs into problems of more fundamental nature. It is not at all clear what a "representative" sample of the languages in a geographical area should look like, if the idea makes sense in the first place. We may return to the problem of Sub-Saharan Africa (here conveniently define as Africa south of 5° N), which was already mentioned above a couple of times. In Bybee et al. (1994) this area is represented by two languages, in Nichols (1992) by eight languages, out of which three are Khoisan, three Nilo-Saharan, one Afro-Asiatic and one Niger-Congo. Geographically, two of the Khoisan languages are situated at the south-west corner of the area, all the others are sitting up at the opposite north-east corner. There is thus an enormous uncovered area in between, mainly consisting of Niger-Congo (mostly Bantu) languages. This is not really a case of bad choice but rather a consequence of the current principles of sampling, and it is fairly obvious that any meaningful extension of this sample must violate them by adding a significant number of relatively closely related Niger-Congo languages. But any judgment of the incidence of typological properties in the area will be heavily dependent on the size of this addition. One such property is basic word order − as we saw above, the dominant order in the Niger-Congo group is SVO, which is found only in two of the eight sub-Saharan languages in Nichols's sample.

A related problem is the following: An area with the typical centre-periphery structure will often exhibit the greatest genetic diversity in the peripheral parts, which will be "residual zones" in the sense defined above. This means that an areal sample that aims at genetic representativeness will over-represent those parts and under-represent the more homogeneous centre. It also means that minor adjustments in the ways the borders of an area are defined may have rather dramatic consequences for such a sample. We find a typical case of such a situation in Europe, where the inclusion of the Caucasus changes the character of the area in many important ways.

The above considerations, then, put into doubt the possibility of applying meaningfully the notion of representativeness to areal samples, and indeed, the meaningfulness of making quantitative statements about the occurrence of linguistic properties within an area. This applies not only to simple percentages and the like but also to properties depending on them such as "areal consistency" (Nichols 1992, Chapter 5). This again raises the question about the reality of linguistic areas (see § 2).

8. The areal distribution of some major typological features

8.1. Basic word order

Basic word order, a central concern to 20th century language typology, is also one of the phenomena which has been best studied from the areal point of view. Tables 105.2−105.3

show the distribution of basic word orders over continent-size samples areas in the samples of Dryer (1989) and Nichols (1992).

Dryer's counts are based on numbers of language families ("genera") in which the respective word orders appear; Nichols's sample consists of individual languages. Nichols's figures include languages with object-subject order; Dryer's do not. Also, the divisions into areas do not coincide. The figures are therefore not entirely comparable. However, they show the same tendencies. Verb-final languages (mainly SOV) are universally the dominant group. Verb-medial (mainly SVO) languages are much more common in the Old World (Africa and Eurasia) and verb-initial languages (with VSO languages as the largest group) show up mainly in North America. These figures already support an underlying asymmetry between the word orders in that non-verb-final word order is in some sense a special or "marked" choice, a fact reflected in its more concentrated distribution, which is further reinforced if we look at Map 105.2 which shows the distribution in Nichols's sample of the three word-order types.

We can see that there are indeed heavy local concentrations of verb-medial languages in Europe, Africa, Australia and verb-initial languages in North America. It may be noted that this uneven distribution within the large areas (referred to by Nichols as "macro-areas") speaks against the possibility of interpreting the percentages in Table 105.3 meaningfully as properties of the areas as wholes. The concentrations are most clearly defined in the case of verb-initial-languages. Due to the high genetic diversity of Northern America (particularly its western part), the contours of the continent are clearly discernible in Map 105.2. What we see is that two separate areas, one around the border between the U.S. and Canada, and one in Mesoamerica, account for 13 verb-initial languages, that is, 62 per cent of the total number of such languages in the sample. We should not forget at this point, however, that many local concentrations of verb-initial languages are just too small to be visible in a sample like that of Nichols. Thus, neither the Celtic nor the Semitic VSO languages show up there.

The relative order of subject and object is not discussed by Dryer and Nichols. However, it is fairly clear that the distribution of OS order is even more strongly areally skewed. One of the areas where OS order shows up coincides with the verb initial area in Mesoamerica. Out ot the 30 OS languages

Table 105.2: Distribution of basic word orders according to Dryer (1989)

	Africa	Eurasia	Australia–New Guinea	North-America	South-America	Total
Number of genera containing SOV lgs	22	26	19	26	18	111
Number of genera containing SVO lgs	21	19	6	6	5	57
Number of genera containing VSO lgs	5	3	0	12	2	22
Total no. of genera	45	52	30	60	31	218
Perc. SOV genera	49%	50%	63%	43%	58%	51%
Perc. SVO genera	47%	37%	20%	10%	16%	26%
Perc. VSO genera	11%	6%	0%	20%	6%	10%

Table 105.3: Distribution of basic word orders according to Nichols (1992)

	Old World	Pacific	New World	Total
Verb-final order	31	20	27	111
Verb-medial order	15	9	5	57
Verb-initial	2	2	17	22
Total no. of languages	55	49	69	174
Perc. verb-final languages	56%	41%	39%	64%
Perc. verb-medial languages	27%	18%	7%	33%
Perc. verb-initial languages	4%	4%	25%	13%

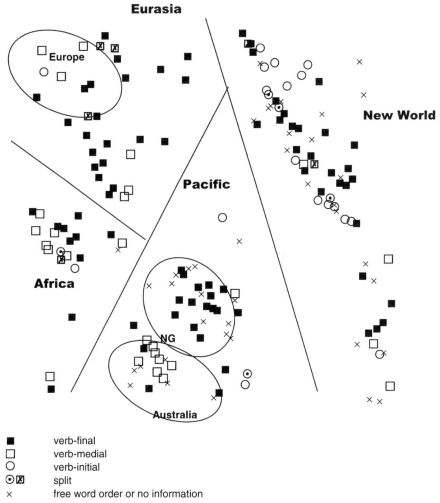

Map 105.2: Distribution of basic word order types in Nichols's (1992) sample.

listed in Pullum (1980), twelve are spoken in Mexiko and/or Guatemala.

As an example of a somewhat more complex parameter, consider the relationship between object-verb and adjective-noun word order discussed by Dryer (1989). Dryer notes that the widely assumed preference for adjectives to precede nouns in OV languages does not hold globally but only as an areal trend in Eurasia. More precisely, there is "an area that extends from Turkey to Japan, and from south India to northern Russia to Siberia", where almost all SOV languages have adjective-noun order.

8.2. Ergativity

Another major focus of typological research is what Nichols (1992) calls "alignment", that is, the choice between case marking principles such as accusative and ergative case marking and analogous distinctions with respect to agreement and other syntactic phenomena. To simplify, we shall only consider what Nichols calls "dominant ergative alignment", that is, a reasonably consistent identification of intransitive subjects and transitive objects. Table 105.4 shows the distribution of dominant ergative alignment in Nichols's macro-areas.

Again, the macro-area breakdown reveals that the distribution is indeed skewed, the percentages varying from 10 to 32. Among the smaller areas defined by Nichols, we find that Australia has the highest concentration, with 8 of 19 dominantly ergative languages, and that there are two entirely ergative-free areas, Africa and Eastern North America. Like in the case of basic word order, how-

Table 105.4: Distribution of ergative alignment in Nichols's sample

Macro-area	Dominant ergative alignment	Total no. of languages in sample
Old World	9 (16%)	55
Pacific	16 (32%)	49
New World	7 (10%)	69
Entire sample	32 (18%)	174

ever, visual inspection of the map may be more revealing than the area statistics. In Map 105.3, we see that 14 out of the 32 ergative languages are found in Australia and New Guinea, and that they seem to belong to one or possibly two fairly contiguous areas. The bulk of the rest are also found in relatively clear clusters in Eurasia and North America. This distribution indeed seems to confirm the hypothesis of ergative alignment as a special or marked construction type. The map also reveals stative-active alignment as another such type.

8.3. Tense and aspect

Tense and aspect systems are significantly less well mapped than the more traditional typological parameters. This section builds on an analysis presented in Dahl (1995) of the data presented in Bybee et al. (1994). As shown in Bybee (1985), Dahl (1985) and Bybee & Dahl (1989), there is cross-linguistic consistency in the ways tense and aspect categories are expressed grammatically. Only a very limited set of distinctions, or in Bybee and Dahl's terminology, gram types, are regularly marked inflectionally (rather than by periphrastic means), the most important being (in traditional terms) past tenses (nor-

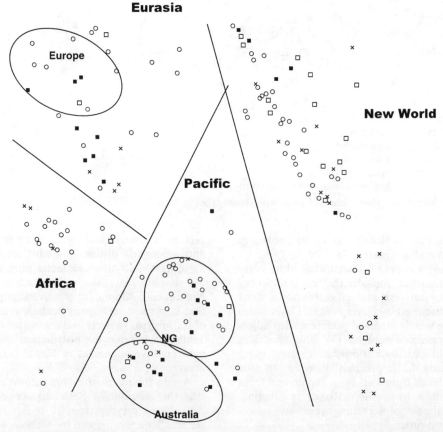

Map 105.3: Distribution of Alignment types in Nichols's (1992) sample.

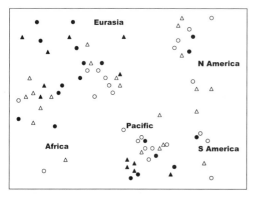

Symbol	Past (incl. past imperfectives and remoteness markings)	Perfective/ imperfective
▲	+	+
●	+	−
△	−	+
○	−	−

Map 105.4: Distribution of pasts and perfective/imperfectives in the GRAMCATS sample.

mally opposed to unmarked non-past or present tenses) and perfective and imperfective aspect (treated together in the following discussion). The distribution of these gram types is heavily areally skewed, which can be clearly seen by plotting the languages in the sample in spite of its rather restricted size (75 languages), as Map 105.4 shows. It may be seen that all the four logically possible combinations of gram types are represented by local concentrations; this contradicts the common idea of complementarity between tense and aspect markings.

One of the more salient concentrations in Map 105.4 is the group of languages in south (actually southeastern) Eurasia in which neither pasts nor perfective:imperfective markings show up. There is an obvious relationship here to the traditional typological parameter of degree of syntheticity: the concentration by and large coincides with the area in South-East Asia in which isolating languages are the dominating type. The lack of exponents of those gram-types that are commonly expressed inflectionally is congruent with the general lack of inflectional categories in those languages.

9. Are statistical universals historical accidents?

One important lesson of areal typology is that it is imperative to realize that the set of all existing languages may in fact be a rather skewed sample of the population we are ultimately after − the set of all possible languages. In other words, statistical generalizations about human languages may be partly due to historical accidents. Consider for instance the distribution of verb-initial languages as discussed in § 8.1. Suppose that the American continents had never been populated, all other things remaining the same (if that is imaginable). Then the percentage of verb-initial languages in a sample like that of Nichols would drop from 12% to 4%. Assuming another possible world, where the Pacific were a typological twin copy of the Americas, we would instead have 21 per cent verb-initial languages.

Dryer (1989) argues that it is at least in principle possible that the statistical preference for SOV word order is a result of inheritance (i.e. "Proto-World" as a SOV language) and diffusion. He notes, however, that observations about correlations of parameters cannot be explained in this way. Discussing the low frequency of OS languages, Pullum (1981) argues that "no one has any idea to what extent the history of the human race has skewed the distribution of constituent-order types of skewing the distribution of people" and that "the statistical problem of determining whether OS languages are rarer than they ought to be ... is impossibly intractable". In spite of the obvious difficulties, this conclusion seems overly pessimistic, at least if taken as a general statement about the impossibility of using distributional facts as evidence for universal preferences. Even for a more common word order, such as verb-initial order, it seems intuitively unlikely in view of its concentration to a few areas that the global percentage is due to a historical accident and that there is thus no preference against this order. Such a statement should of course be backed up by a statistical argument, a difficult but hopefully not an impossible task, which should be a challenge for future typological research. One heuristic guide is the comparison of samples like that of Tomlin (1982), which represent areas and families in proportion to their size, and those of Dryer (1989) and Nichols (1992). Since the latter were constructed to avoid over-representing any individual area or family, they should be more immune to the effects of historical accidents such as the expansion of Indo-European or Niger-Congo. Taking verb-initial order as an example, it makes up 12 per cent of Tomlin's sample and 13 per cent of Nichols's. If the markedness of verb-initial order were just apparent, we would expect the latter figure to be perceptibly larger. In fact, in the case of SVO order, which has a much lower incidence in Dryer's and Nichols's samples than in Tomlin's, the comparison suggests that it is the absence of a preference that is a historical accident rather than the other way round.

10. The areal dimension of grammaticalization

In § 8., we saw how one can go from statistics about large geographical areas to the identification of smaller areas as "hotbeds" for various typological phenomena. A further zooming-in gives a possibility of seeing the synchronic traces of specific diffusion processes. Grammaticalization processes are no exception from the general principles of diffusion of linguistic innovations. The gradual character of grammaticalization as a diachronic process is reflected in synchronic patterns of different kinds. Thus, a grammatical construction or morpheme tends to be obligatory in the central (prototypical, focal) uses and optional in the peripheral ones, with sinking propensity of use as we go outwards. This makes it possible to talk of **grammaticalization clines**, that is, ordered sets of contexts along which the frequency of grammatical constructions and forms decreases monotonically. Such clines may of course involve several dimensions, and most probably do in the majority of cases. The cline may also be interpreted diachronically, as the path in "grammatical space" along which the grammaticalization process has proceeded. But to the extent that this process spreads in physical space outwards from a centre of innovation, the propensity to use a construction or morpheme in a certain context will decrease as we move away from that centre. As a real life example we may take the development of

Table 105.5: Number of *passato prossimo* responses and corresponding percentages for the Perfect questionnaire

Semantic functions	North	Centre	South	Sicily	Sardinia	row total
a. inclusivity	30 100%	30 100%	30 100%	10 100%	10 100%	110 100%
b. Speech Time-oriented adverbs	90 100%	87 96.5%	83 92%	29 96.5%	30 100%	319 97%
c. persistent result	206 98%	200 95%	181 86%	67 95.5%	70 100%	724 94%
d. experientiality	86 95.5%	89 99%	82 91%	28 93.5%	28 93.5%	313 95%
PERFECTAL FUNCTIONS (a−d)	412 98%	406 96.5%	376 89.5%	134 95.5%	138 98.5%	1466 95%
e. personal narration	209 69.5%	166(*) 55.5%	74 24.5%	53* 53%	78 78%	580 53%
f. impersonal narration	66* 55%	37 31%	27 22.5%	13 32.5%	25* 62.5%	168 38%
g. historical narration	7 23.5%	2 6.5%	6 20%	1 10%	2(*) 20%	18 16.5%
NARRATIVE FUNCTIONS (e−g)	282 62.5%	205(*) 45.4%	107 23.5%	67* 44.5%	105 70%	766 46%
column total	694 79.5%	518 70%	483 55.5%	201 63.5%	243 84%	

perfects into perfectives, as exemplified by the various Romance languages in which a Compound Past (*passé composé, passato prossimo*) has taken over or is taking over the domain of use of the Simple Past (*passé simple, passato remoto*). The development in Italian is studied in some detail in Squartini & Bertinetto (2000). A questionnaire (see Lindstedt 2000) was given to Italian informants from different parts of Italy. The numbers and percentages of *passato prossimo* responses are shown in Table 105.5.

For the three peninsular regions, we obtain a fairly smooth cline: the use goes from 100 per cent for the typical perfectal contexts to figures close to zero in the least favorable contexts – historical narration – in the South. Sicily and Sardinia, though, display a stronger influence from the northern centre of innovation than their geographical positions would suggest, showing that the relationship between physical space and spread of innovations is not always straightforward. (All the figures pertain to regional varieties of Standard Italian rather than local vernaculars (*dialetti*).)

Looking at the synchronic distribution of various grammatical phenomena as the results of grammaticalization processes, a conclusion that is hard to avoid is that grammaticalization is highly contagious. In other words, while the chance that a certain morpheme or construction in a language will undergo a particular kind of grammaticalization is on the whole rather small, the probability increases dramatically if a neighbouring language undergoes the process in question. In the majority of all such cases, the languages involved are more or less closely related, but if the external conditions are the right ones, also totally unrelated languages may be affected.

In Dahl (2000b), the term "gram family" is proposed for grams with related functions and diachronic sources that show up in genetically and/or geographically related groups of languages, in other words, what can be assumed to be the result of one process of diffusion. To take one example, constructions formed with a verb meaning 'to go', with uses sometimes referred to as "prospective", show up in a number of languages in Western Europe, both in the Germanic and the Romance group. Map 105.5, adapted from Dahl (2000b), shows schematically this and some other major "gram families" in Europe which

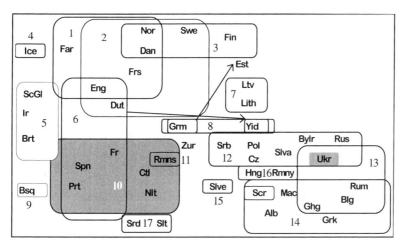

Map 105.5: Major "gram families" with future time reference in Europe (excl. Caucasus) (Dahl 2000b)
Numbered areas denote: 1. North European de-volitive construction; 2. Germanic de-obligative 'shall'; 3. Scandinavian de-venitive construction; 4. Icelandic de-obligative; 5. Celtic inflectional future; 6. West-European de-andative construction; 7. Baltic inflectional future; 8. Circum-Baltic 'become' future; 9. Basque de-obligative futures; 10. Romance inflectional future; 11. Romansh de-venitive construction; 12. North Slavic copular imperfective future; 13. Balkan de-obligative construction (incl. Ukrainian inflectional imperfective future); 14. Balkan de-volitive construction; 15. Slovenian copular construction; 16. Hungarian-Romani 'take' construction; 17. South Italian de-obligative future.
Shaded areas denote inflectional futures.

have in common that they mark future time reference. The map is an illustration of the intricate patterns that the result from diffusion processes. Note that it is very seldom that the borders of gram families coincide with those of a language family, and that several of the former cross the borders between the latter.

11. References

Asher, R. E. (ed.). 1994. *The Encyclopedia of Language and Linguistics*. Oxford: Pergamon Press.

Bell, Alan. 1978. "Language samples". In: Greenberg, Joseph (ed.). *Universals of human language. Vol. 1. Method and theory*, 123–156. Stanford: Stanford University Press.

Bybee, Joan L. 1985. *Morphology: a study of the relation between meaning and form*. Amsterdam, John Benjamins.

Bybee, John & Dahl, Östen. 1989. "The creation of tense and aspect systems in the languages of the world". *Studies in Language* 13: 51–103.

Bybee, John & Perkins, Revere & Pagliuca, William. 1994. *Evolution of grammar: The Grammaticization of Tense, Aspect and Modality in the Languages of the World*. Chicago, University of Chicago Press.

Campbell, Lyle. 1994. "Grammar: Typological and Areal Issues". In: Asher, R. E. (ed.), *The Encyclopedia of Language and Linguistics*, Vol. 3., 1471–1474.

Campbell, Lyle, Kaufman, Terrence & Smith-Stark, Thomas C. 1986. "Meso-America as a linguistic area". *Language* 62: 530–70.

Dahl, Östen. 1985. *Tense and Aspect Systems*. Oxford: Blackwell.

Dahl, Östen. 1995. "Areal tendencies in tense-aspect systems". In: Bertinetto, Pier Marco & Bianchi, Valentina & Dahl, Östen & Squartini, Mario (eds.). *Temporal Reference, Aspect and Actionality*. Vol. 2: Typological perspectives, 11–28. Torino: Rosenberg & Sellier.

Dahl, Östen. 2000a. *Tense and Aspect in the Languages of Europe*. Berlin: Mouton de Gruyter.

Dahl, Östen. 2000b. "The Grammar of Future Time Reference in European languages". In: Dahl (2000a). 309–328.

Dryer, Matthew. 1989. "Large linguistic areas and language sampling". *Studies in Language* 62: 808–45.

Emeneau, Murray B. 1980. *Language and Linguistic Area*. Stanford: Stanford University Press.

Koptjevskaja-Tamm, Maria & Wälchli, Bernhard. Forthcoming. "Circum-Baltic languages: An area-typological approach". In: Dahl, Östen & Koptjevskaja-Tamm, Maria (eds.). *The Circum-Baltic Languages: Typology and Contacts*.

Lindstedt, Jouko. 2000. "The Perfect – Aspectual, Temporal and Evidential". In: Dahl (2000a). 365–383.

Masica, Colin P. 1976. *Defining a Linguistic Area: South Asia*. Chicago: University of Chicago Press.

Masica, Colin P. 1992. "Areal linguistics". In: Bright, William (ed.). *International Encyclopedia of Linguistics, Vol. 1*, 108–112. Oxford: Oxford University Press.

Nichols, Johanna. 1990. "Linguistic diversity and the first settlement of the New World". *Language* 66: 475–521.

Nichols, Johanna. 1992. *Linguistic Diversity in Space and Time*. Chicago and London, The University of Chicago Press.

Perkins, Revere D. 1992. "Deixis, grammar, and culture". *Typological studies in language* 24. Amsterdam & Philadelphia: Benjamins.

Pullum, Geoffrey. 1981. "Languages with object before subject: a comment and a catalogue". *Linguistics* 19: 147–155.

Squartini, Mario & Bertinetto, Pier Marco. 2000. "The Simple and Compound Past in Romance languages". In: Dahl (2000a). 403–440.

Thomason, Sarah Grey & Kaufman, Terrence. 1988. *Language contact, creolization and genetic linguistics*. Berkeley: Univ. of California Press.

Tomlin, Russell. 1982. *Basic Constituent Orders: Functional Principles*. London: Croom Helm.

Trubetzkoy, Nikolay. 1928. "Proposition 16". In: *Actes du premier congrès international de linguistes*, 17–18. Leiden: Sijthoff.

van der Auwera, Johan. 1998. *Adverbial Constructions in the Languages of Europe*. Berlin: Mouton de Gruyter.

Östen Dahl, Stockholm (Sweden)

106. Arealtypologie und Dialektologie

1. Einleitung
2. Datengewinnung („Sampling") in Arealtypologie und Sprachgeographie
3. Partikuläre Datenauswertung
4. Globale Datenauswertung
5. Zusammenfassung und Perspektiven
6. Zitierte Literatur

1. Einleitung

Das Generalmotto dieses Beitrags lautet: was können Arealtypologie und **Dialektologie** inhaltlich, methodisch und wissenschaftsgeschichtlich voneinander lernen? Dabei soll unter **Dialektologie** ihre raumbezogene Spielart verstanden werden, die genauer mit **Sprachgeographie**, **Geolinguistik**, **géographie linguistique** etc. bezeichnet wird. Bekanntlich unterscheidet sich die **Sprachgeographie** von der **Dialektologie** durch die konsequente Berücksichtigung der Verteilung sprachlicher Merkmale im Raum, worunter eine größere Anzahl von geographisch möglichst kompakt liegenden Ortschaften (Meßpunkten etc.) zu verstehen ist. Die von der Sprachgeographie – und auch von der Arealtypologie – konsequent und systematisch zuerst erhobenen und danach untersuchten Daten haben demnach die Struktur einer zweidimensionalen Matrix – **N** mal **p** –, wobei **N** für eine beliebig große Anzahl von Meßpunkten und **p** für eine beliebig große Anzahl von sprachlichen Merkmalen steht. Die Konfiguration **N** mal **p** (siehe Figur 106.1) ist sowohl für die in der modernen Arealtypologie – etwa im Rahmen des europäischen Typologie-Projekts EUROTYP (cf. z. B. van der Auwera (ed.) 1998) – üblichen „Samples" (Stichproben) als auch für die wichtigsten Datenkorpora der Sprachgeographie – die Sprachatlanten – konstitutiv und bezeichnend.

Im Rahmen der Neueren Philologien wurden seit deren Begründung sehr elaborierte sprachgeographische Erfahrungen gemacht, wobei jene der Romanistik und der Germanistik ohne jeden Zweifel am ausgeprägtesten sind. Die Erträge der anglistischen, slavistischen (etc.) Sprachgeographie sind dagegen jüngeren Datums, beruhen auf einer kürzeren Erfahrung mit der Sprachatlasarbeit und haben sowohl auf ihre Mutterphilologien als auch auf die Allgemeine Linguistik einen vergleichsweise geringeren Einfluß ausgeübt (cf. dazu Pop 1950, HSK 1 und die Sprachgeographie-Kapitel der beiden Handbücher LGL und LRL).

Im wissenschaftshistorischen Rückblick und im wissenschaftssystematischen Vergleich zeigt sich, daß viele der im Rahmen der romanistischen und germanistischen Sprachgeographie zum Thema Datengewinnung, Datenauswertung und Dateninterpretation gemachten Erfahrungen und auch die darüber durchgeführten Diskussionen für die moderne Areal-

MERKMALSBEZOGENE TYPOLOGIE

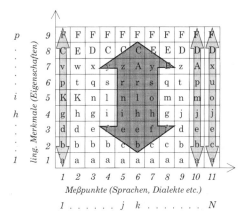

RAUMBEZOGENE TYPOLOGIE

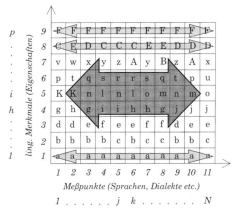

Figur 106.1: Schema einer merkmals- und einer raumbezogenen Typologie
Kleine Pfeile: partikuläre Auswertung der Merkmals- bzw. Meßpunktvektoren
Große Pfeile: globale Auswertung der Merkmals- bzw. Meßpunktvektoren
a...z; A...F: linguistische Merkmale (auf nominalem Skalenniveau)

typologie überaus bedeutsam sein können. Überhaupt habe ich nach Einsicht wichtiger arealtypologischer Texte (exemplarisch z. B.: Simpson 1994) der letzten zwei Jahrzehnte den Eindruck gewonnen, daß von den beiden hier zur Diskussion stehenden Disziplinen — Arealtypologie und Sprachgeographie — es aus vorwiegend wissenschaftshistorischen Gründen eher die erstere ist, die aus einem wechselseitigen Lernprozeß Vorteil und Nutzen ziehen könnte.

Einen besonderen Hinweis verdient in diesem Kontext noch die Kategorie des (geographisch-natürlichen) Raumes, der nach Kant nicht nur — gemeinsam mit der Zeit — ein elementares A priori darstellt, sondern auch eine für jedes menschliche Tun und Handeln eminent wichtige Dimension ist. Damit liegt es im Interesse aller mit humanen (und auch biologischen) Objekten und Problemen befaßten Wissenschaften, eine der Wirksamkeit des Raumes auf die von ihnen untersuchten Objekte gewidmete Subdisziplin auszubilden. Bei weitem nicht nur in der Geographie hat sich die Stichhaltigkeit des nunmehr bald drei Jahrhunderte alten Diktums von Gottfried Wilhelm Leibniz (1646—1716) bewahrheitet, demzufolge der Raum den Ordnungsrahmen für die Koexistenz synchron bestehender Objekte ergebe: „Spatium est ordo coexistendi seu ordo existendi inter ea quae sunt simul." (G. W. Leibniz, Initia rerum mathematicarum metaphysica III, 1715). Daraus folgt, daß alle mit der Dimension des Raumes befaßten Human- und Biowissenschaften ein prinzipielles Interesse daran haben sollten, ihre raumspezifischen Erfahrungen hinsichtlich Empirie, Methoden, Hypothesen oder Theorien im interdisziplinären Dialog auszutauschen.

2. Datengewinnung („Sampling") in Arealtypologie und Sprachgeographie

Beiden ist ein genuin komparatistisches Interesse gemeinsam. Während in der Sprachgeographie das über **p** Merkmale und **N** Meßpunkte definierte Untersuchungs-Relativ unterhalb der Ebene dessen liegt, was gemeinhin eine „historische Sprache" genannt wird, umfaßt das Erkenntnisinteresse der Arealtypologie in der Regel eine größere Anzahl „historischer Sprachen" in ihrer diasystematischen Gesamtheit, welche zudem genetisch gar nicht verwandt sein müssen: cf. dazu die Liste von 40 bzw. 100 Sprachen bei Haspelmath 1997: 18—19. Dieser prinzipielle Unterschied, in dem sich auch die verschiedenen Erkenntnisinteressen der beiden Disziplinen widerspiegeln, hat aber auch empirische Konsequenzen, die im Umgang mit den beiden Sorten von Datensätzen (bzw. N mal p dimensionierten Relativen) deutlich zu Buche schlagen und damit im interdisziplinären Dialog Schwierigkeiten bereiten können (→ Art. 105).

Wenn man annimmt, daß eine sprachgeographische Untersuchung (mit entsprechender Feldarbeit oder analoger Datenbereitstellung) dazu dient, in der Realität existierende geolinguistisch relevante Ähnlichkeiten (Konvergenzen) oder Unähnlichkeiten (Divergenzen), die durch spontane Genese, Diffusion oder sonstige Kontaktprozesse entstanden sein können, hinreichend genau abzubilden bzw. empirisch zu erfassen — damit diese solcherart linguistisch beschrieben und im besten Fall erklärt werden können —, so ist es ohne weiteres einleuchtend, daß ein derartiges Unterfangen dann bessere Chancen auf ein erfolgreiches Gelingen hat, wenn — unter der Annahme einer kontinuierlichen Siedlungsdichte — der mittlere Abstand der explorierten (oder dokumentierten) Merkmale zwischen 5 und 10 Kilometern (betrifft die Sprachgeographie) liegt, als wenn er zwischen 500 und 1000 Kilometern (betrifft die Arealtypologie) beträgt. Damit ist das Problem der Maschendichte des Untersuchungsnetzes angerissen, dem in der empirischen Sozialforschung mutatis mutandis jenes der **Repräsentativität** einer Stichprobe entspricht. Aus der empirischen Sozialforschung ist ferner die Problematik der **Validität** der zu erhebenden bzw. erhobenen Daten bekannt, worunter — stets bezogen auf einen explizit vorliegenden Erhebungsplan — die innere Konsistenz bzw. Schlüssigkeit der gesammelten Daten zu verstehen ist. So ist die Erhebung verschiedener Realisationen eines einfachen postnominalen Relativsatzes (z. B. „[...] die Frau, die das Kind getreten hatte"; Beispiel nach Lehmann 1984: 73) in verschiedenen deutschen Dialektgebieten bestimmt einfacher (und werden die dabei registrierbaren Antworten deutlich interkomparabler und damit valider sein), als dies beim schon zitierten 100-Sprachen-Sample von Haspelmath (1997: 19) der Fall wäre, welches Sprachen aus allen fünf Erdteilen umfaßt.

Ein wesentlicher Punkt ist ferner, daß sowohl die Erstellung von Fragebüchern bzw.

die Auswahl der Meßpunkte im Rahmen der Sprachgeographie als auch jene der in der modernen Arealtypologie üblichen Samples von einer a priori vorhandenen Forschungstheorie geleitet werden müssen. Damit ist die im Rahmen der modernen Arealtypologie für die Definition der **N** Meßpunkte und **p** Merkmale verwendete theoretische Vorarbeit (cf. z. B. Rijkhoff et alii 1993) durchaus mit jener vergleichbar, die für die 40 Prüf-Sätze des „**Deutschen Sprachatlasses**" (DSA) von Georg Wenker oder für das Questionnaire des „**Atlas linguistique de la France**" (ALF) von Jules Gilliéron und für die Fixierung der jeweiligen Meßpunkt-Netze geleistet worden war. Bei DSA und ALF hatten Georg Wenker und Jules Gilliéron, die beiden Sprachatlasautoren, – stets mit Blick auf die damals anstehenden Fragestellungen der historischen Laut- und Formenlehre des Deutschen bzw. des Galloromanischen sowie auf die onomasiologische Gliederung der beiden Sprachräume – ihre Fragen (Stimuli etc.) sehr genau ausgewählt und an die jeweils in Aussicht genommenen Explorationsmodalitäten (DSA: Erhebung durch Korrespondenz; ALF: Erhebung durch direkte Feldenquete) angepaßt (cf. Pop 1926 und die Kapitel IV und V in Besch et al. 1982–83).

Überhaupt lassen sich an der Genese von DSA und ALF, den wissenschaftshistorisch wichtigsten und inhaltlich bis heute lehrreichsten Sprachatlanten überhaupt, all jene Probleme in exemplarischer Form aufzeigen, die sowohl beim sprachgeographischen wie beim arealtypologischen Sampling auftreten können. Dabei muß auch eine völlig unwissenschaftliche Kategorie, die der **Machbarkeit**, erwähnt werden. Selbstverständlich ist es wünschenswert, alles über alle Sprachen dieser Welt oder – im Falle einer einzelsprachlichen Sprachgeographie – alles über alle Ortsdialekte einer historischen Einzelsprache zu erkunden bzw. zu wissen. Doch muß solches aus einsichtigen Gründen ein unrealisierbarer, frommer Wunsch bleiben. Daher ist eine Beschränkung auf **Stichproben** angezeigt, wobei man sich – eher noch als Sprachgeograph denn als Arealtypologe – die im Rahmen der empirischen Sozialforschung an Tausenden von Beispielsfällen erhärtete Erfahrung zunutze machen kann, daß die Grundstrukturen bestimmter sozial (und damit auch räumlich) verteilter Phänomene bereits durch die Untersuchung relativ kleiner Stichproben hinreichend genau abgebildet bzw. erkannt werden können. Zur Zeit von Georg Wenker (1852–1911) und Jules Gilliéron (1854–1926) gab es die moderne Stichprobentheorie noch nicht. Als sich Georg Wenker um das Jahr 1875 dafür entschied, zunächst in der Rheinprovinz und danach im ganzen Deutschen Reich anhand seiner 40 Sätze einen Sprachatlas zu machen, schien es ihm – offenbar mit Blick auf die für ihn selbstverständliche „preußische Disziplin" – durchaus „machbar" zu sein, diese Exploration im **Korrespondenzweg** in **allen** existierenden Gemeinden durchzuführen. Er verzichtete damit auf eine Stichprobenziehung (und auf die Vorteile einer direkten Enquete) und griff solcherart auf die Gesamtpopulation zu.

Der Franzose bzw. Welschschweizer Jules Gilliéron hatte bei seinen Planungen für den ALF durchaus die Gesamtanzahl aller Gemeinden Frankreichs vor Augen – die damals rund 36 000 betrug –, entschied sich aber – wohl mit Blick auf die Kosten der Exploration im Feld und vor allem der späteren Publikation der Daten – für eine stichprobenartige Erhebung von nur 638 Ortsdialekten im Wege der direkten Feldenquete.

Zu einer Gegenüberstellung von DSA und ALF hinsichtlich ihrer „Operationalität" siehe Tabelle 106.1.

Aus dieser Vergleichstabelle ersieht man, daß – alles in allem genommen – der ALF die „vernünftigere Lösung" darstellt: er hat zwar ein weitmaschigeres Netz, dafür aber deutlich mehr Atlaskarten, die zudem die Originaldaten in Lautschrift enthalten. Diese vermitteln zwar – wie das von germanistischer Seite immer wieder kritisiert wird – keinen karthographischen Sofortüberblick, lassen aber eine **multiple** Auswertung mittels (entsprechend einzufärbender) „stummer Karten" zu, die im Rahmen der Romanistik sofort nach Erscheinen des ersten ALF-Faszikels im Jahr 1902 begonnen hat und mit immer neuen Fragestellungen bis heute andauert.

Die deutsche Tradition der Gesamtexploration im Korrespondenzweg hat im „Deutschen Wortatlas" (DWA) von Walter Mitzka (1888–1976) (rund 48 000 Meßpunkte, ca. 200 Karten, Publikation: 1951–1980) ihre Fortsetzung gefunden. Die französische Tradition des ALF wurde in einer ganz Frankreich abdeckenden Serie von engmaschigeren Regionalatlanten (publiziert größtenteils zwischen 1950 und 1985) fortgeführt (zu einer Übersicht cf. Goebl 1992b). Dabei hat sich allerdings gezeigt, daß die Variabilität der solcherart erhobenen Daten trotz des gegenüber dem ALF deutlich dichteren Meßpunkte-

Tabelle 106.1: Vergleich wichtiger Kenndaten der Sprachatlanten DSA („Deutscher Sprachatlas") und ALF („Atlas linguistique de la France").

	DSA	ALF
1 Anzahl der Meßpunkte	ca. 52.800	638
2 Anzahl der publizierten Atlaskarten	128	1421 (Serie A)
3 Erhebungszeitraum	1876−1939	1897−1901
4 Explorationsprinzip	Korrespondenz	direkte Feldenquete
5 Erscheinungszeitraum	1927−56	1902−1909
6 Neudruck	nein	ja
7 Formatgröße	großformatige Faltkarten	in Folio-Bänden
8 Prinzip der Kartenerstellung	Punktsymbolkarte	Volltextkarten (in Lautschrift)
9 Originaldaten zur Gänze veröffentlicht	nein	ja
10 Auswertung der Atlaskarten durch die Atlasbenutzer	durch Punktsymbolkodierung sehr eingeschränkt	sehr vielfältig (Verwendung von „stummen Karten")

Netzes nicht wesentlich gestiegen ist. Man kann darin eine späte Bestätigung des von Jules Gilliéron − wahrscheinlich intuitiv − beachteten Stichprobenprinzips sehen.

Ein weiterer Unterschied, dessen forschungsgeschichtliche und -praktische Relevanz viel zuwenig beachtet wird, besteht in der Präsentation der Daten von DSA und ALF. Während der Leser/Benutzer beim DSA nach einem bestimmten Prinzip symbolkodierte Karten vorfindet und damit keinen direkten Zugriff auf die Originaldaten (mehr) hat, muß der Benutzer des ALF bei der Lektüre jeder einzelnen Atlaskarte zunächst einen eigenen Kodierungs-Standpunkt definieren, um aus den Originaldaten selektiv den ihn speziell interessierenden geolinguistischen Aspekt herauszufiltern. Damit kann einer ALF-Karte eine im Prinzip **offene Anzahl** von „Arbeitskarten" entnommen werden, die − jede für sich genommen − den heuristischen Status einer DSA-Karte hat. Man erkennt daraus die verfahrenstechnische Beengtheit des − angesichts der riesigen Meßpunkt-Menge allerdings unvermeidbaren − DSA-Kartierungs-Prinzips und − umgekehrt − die prozedurale Elastizität des ALF-Prinzips, das überdies − von ganz wenigen Ausnahmen abgesehen − bis heute in der Romanistik vorherrschend geblieben ist.

Bei den Sprachatlanten der „zweiten Generation" − d. h. bei den in den letzten 30−40 Jahren initiierten Regionalatlanten vorwiegend der Romanistik und Germanistik − hätte das Problem der Fragebogenerstellung gegenüber dem DSA und dem ALF in sprachtheoretisch innovativerer Form gelöst werden können. Allerdings war das Augenmerk der Promotoren der Atlanten der zweiten Generation dominant darauf gerichtet, einem allgemein im Zug der Modernisierung vermuteten Dialektrückgang nachzugehen, so daß die letztendlich fixierten Dimensionen der betreffenden Sprachatlanten zwei Maximen gehorchten: 1. dichteres Meßpunktnetz als früher, 2. Fragebuch möglichst ähnlich oder vergleichbar mit vorhergehenden Erhebungen. In Einzelfällen gab es auch Bemühungen (z. B. beim Mittelrheinischen Sprachatlas MRhSA, oder beim Uruguay-Atlas ADDU) zusätzlich zur diatopischen auch die diastratische Dimension miteinzubeziehen und der in den Fragebüchern oft vernachlässigten Syntax mehr Raum zu gewähren.

Neuerdings ist es im Zuge der fortschreitenden Implementierung von EDV zur Produktion von auf genuinen Datenbanken beruhenden Sprachatlanten gekommen (z. B. Sprachatlas von Bayerisch-Schwaben SBS oder Ladinienatlas ALD), was der Auswertung der betreffenden Datenmatrizen ganz neue Dimensionen eröffnen wird. Es existieren auch schon „sprechende Sprachatlanten", wobei die dazugehörenden Datenbanken zu jedem in Transkription notierten Einzelbeleg den entsprechenden im Feld erhobenen mündlichen Reflex enthalten.

3. Partikuläre Datenauswertung

Sprachatlasdaten sind Massendaten. Die Struktur der Datenmatrix (N mal **p**: siehe Figur 1) erlaubt beim raumbezogenen, typologischen (bzw. klassifikatorischen) Arbeiten prinzipiell eine Auswertung **einzelner** Merkmalsvektoren (bzw. Atlaskarten) oder eine **mehrere** Atlaskarten einbeziehende Datenauswertung. Man muß demnach zwischen einer „partikulären" und einer „globalen" Datenauswertung (vgl. Abschnitt 4.) unterscheiden. Diese zwei Forschungsorientierungen implizieren in methodologischer Hinsicht eine korrekte Bemeisterung der Dimensionen des **Besonderen** und des **Allgemeinen** und auch von **Induktion** und **Deduktion**. Damit verbunden ist ebenso ein korrekter Umgang mit **Allgemein**begriffen wie „**Typ, Dialekt, Dialektgruppe, Sprachgruppe**" etc. und mit **Partikulär**begriffen wie „**sprachliches Merkmal, Isoglosse, Areal**" etc.

Allerdings wird in der Arealtypologie der Terminus „Areal" meistens als **Allgemein**begriff verwendet und bezeichnet dabei die Verschnittmenge mehrerer Strate (= Verbreitungsgebiete einzelner Sprachmerkmale). Doch kommt daneben auch die Verwendung als **Partikulär**begriff vor, worauf Masica 1971: 5 explizit hinweist. In der Dialektometrie ist für die Bezeichnung signifikanter Raumaggregate quantitativen Zuschnitts seit einiger Zeit der Terminus „Chorem" üblich, der gut in das in der Linguistik übliche Terminologie-Schema nach dem Vorbild von Phon**etik**/Phon**emik** etc. passt.

Diese Problematik kommt überdies nicht nur im Rahmen der Sprachgeographie vor, sondern auch überall dort, wo matrizenartig angelegte Datenbasen (Schema **N** mal **p**: siehe Figur 1) zur Verfügung stehen, das heißt in allen Humanwissenschaften mit räumlich stratifizierten Massendaten. Im wissenschaftshistorischen Rückblick ist festzustellen, daß es in Sprachgeographie beim methodisch korrekten Umgang mit den Dimensionen des Besonderen und des Allgemeinen bis heute eigentlich immer gehapert hat. So beruht die weiter unten (Abschnitt 3.3.) beschriebene Diskussion um die **Existenz von Dialekten** und die **Arealnormativik** von M. Bartoli (Abschnitt 3.4.) auf diesem Defizit. Aus **wissenschaftsvergleichender** Perspektive ist zweierlei festzustellen: 1.) daß das angezeigte Defizit Teil eines gewaltigen Forschungsdilemmas ist, das sich vom „Großen Universalienstreit" des Hoch- und Spätmittelalters bis zur „Konstruktivismus-Problematik" des 20. Jhs. erstreckt (cf. Stegmüller 1978); 2.) daß zwar zahlreiche Wissenschaften von dieser Problematik betroffen waren, aber nur selten versucht wurde, diese durch wissenschaftstheoretische Reflexionen und/oder interdisziplinäre Vergleiche zu lösen. Exemplarisch dafür ist die Selbstbesinnung der Geographie in den 70-er Jahren (cf. Hard 1973).

3.1. Sprachatlaskarten und Mustererkennung

Eine der ersten elementaren Erfahrungen der Autoren und Benutzer von DSA und ALF bestand in der Feststellung der keineswegs chaotischen, sondern wohlgeordneten Gliederung von Sprachatlaskarten. Daraus ergab sich die Notwendigkeit, die vorgefundenen Ordnungsmuster zu interpretieren und zu erklären. In kartographisch-heuristischer Hinsicht diente dazu die Analyse von **Flächen** (Arealen, Strukturen etc.) und der diese **umschließenden Linien** (Isoglossen). Die Meßpunktedichte war bei DSA und ALF jedenfalls immer hinreichend groß, um in den bei der Kartenanalyse herauspräparierten Raumstrukturen allgemein bekannte Ordnungsmuster wie „**Trichter, Staffel, Fächer, Insel, Halbinsel, Durchbruch, Horst, Scholle**" etc. erkennen zu können. Die Betrachter solcher Konfigurationen wurden sozusagen intuitiv veranlaßt, diese als Resultate räumlicher Diffusionsprozesse einfacher oder — was noch häufiger der Fall war — höchst komplexer Art zu interpretieren. Damit kam sofort eine **diachrone** Komponente mit ins Spiel, die bis heute in der (partikulären und globalen) Interpretation von Sprachatlasdaten ihre volle Gültigkeit bewahrt hat.

Eine weitere Elementarerfahrung der Benutzer von DSA und ALF war, daß die Raumgliederungen thematisch eng verwandter Karten wider Erwarten — wobei diese Vorerwartung auf der junggrammatischen Idee der Regelhaftigkeit von Lautgesetzen beruhte — sehr oft deutlich voneinander divergierten. So hatten im DSA die Isoglossen zwischen den Typen **machen** und **maken** (auf der Karte „machen") einerseits und andererseits zwischen den Typen **ich** und **ik** (auf der Karte „ich") wider Erwarten streckenweise einen deutlich anderen Verlauf. Analoges fiel auch auf den Karten des ALF sofort nach Erscheinen von dessen erstem Faszikel (im Jahr 1902) auf. Man hätte nun erwarten können, daß sich aus dieser empirischen Evidenz zwei zueinander komplementäre Forschungsrichtungen entwickeln würden: eine auf die Beschreibung und Erklärung **einzelner** Laut- und Worttypen (hier **machen, maken, ich** oder **ik** betreffend) abzielende **Partikulär**forschung und eine auf die Herausarbeitung **räumlicher Großtrends** (i. e. räumlicher **Typen**) abzielende

Globalforschung. Tatsächlich ist es aber sehr rasch zu einer massiven Konzentrierung auf die Partikulärforschung gekommen, wobei die in deren Rahmen erarbeiteten Resultate und Erkenntnisse ohne jeden Zweifel überaus wertvoll waren und dies noch immer sind. Dagegen wurde die Globalforschung eigenartigerweise weitgehend vernachlässigt bzw. ihre Sinnhaftigkeit und Berechtigung in Einzelfällen sogar explizit geleugnet. Konkreter Ausdruck dieser forschungsgeschichtlich bemerkenswerten Situation sind der inhaltlich bis auf Jacob Grimm zurückverfolgbare Satz „Jedes Wort hat seine eigene Geschichte" (cf. Christmann 1971) und der im letzten Viertel des 19. Jhs. in Frankreich ausgebrochene Streit um die Existenz von Dialekten (vgl. Abschnitt 3.3.).

3.2. Raum und Zeit auf Sprachatlaskarten

Rasch wurde bei der Analyse einzelner Sprachatlaskarten auch klar, daß die auf den Atlaskarten diatopisch miteinander konkurrierenden Einzelformen (phonetischer, morphologischer und lexikalischer Art) auch sprachhistorisch deutlich voneinander differieren konnten. Eine derartige Differenzierung konnte dort umso besser analysiert werden, wo zur Interpretation der Sprachatlasdaten zusätzlich kleinräumig gegliederte diachrone Informationen (betreffend Mittelalter und frühe Neuzeit) herangezogen werden konnten (cf. dazu exemplarisch Jaberg 1908). Es stellte sich heraus, daß **ältere** Formen sehr oft in **peripheren** Zonen des Untersuchungsgebietes auftraten, daß **geomorphologisch** (wie Gebirge) oder **politisch** (wie Diözesen, Herzogtümer etc.) in besonderer Weise konfigurierte Gebiete häufig ältere oder regional speziell markierte Formen konservierten, oder daß es Irradiationszentren für sprachliche Innovationen gab, von denen diachron jüngere Formen **radial** bzw. **wellenartig** diffundiert wurden, sei es bis zum Auftreffen auf ein markantes Hindernis (z. B. auf eine Konkurrenzform), sei es ungehindert bis zum Kartenrand. Analoge, wenn auch meist nicht so detaillierte Erfahrungen wurden in Anthropologie, Ethnographie, Ethnologie, Geographie und Biologie (Fauna, Flora) gemacht. Aus dem Bereich der Anthropologie stammt das Schlagwort von der „Age-and-area-hypothesis" (Willis 1922), welches das Problem der deutlich vorhandenen Beziehung zwischen der aktuellen räumlichen Lage und dem effektiven Alter eines durch Diffusion verbreiteten Phänomens (Merkmals, Features etc.) prägnant zusammenfaßt.

Dabei kann — je nach Einzellage — das geringer verbreitete Phänomen deutlich älter als das häufiger auftretende Phänomen sein (Reliktlage eines im Verschwinden begriffenen Stratums) oder auch umgekehrt (Persistenz des älteren und meistverbreiteten Typs gegenüber einem jüngeren — fallweise auch hochsprachlich gestützten — Konkurrenten). Auf jeden Fall kann hier den räumlich komplementären Straten auch ein entsprechendes Alter zugeschrieben werden. Raum und Zeit korrelieren also miteinander: ob positiv oder negativ bzw. in welchem Ausmaß, muß von Fall zu Fall ermittelt werden. Generell gültige Gesetze, wie sie Bartoli vermutete, gibt es dazu allerdings nicht.

3.3. Graziadio Isaia Ascoli, Paul Meyer und Gaston Paris: der Streit um die Existenz von Dialekten

Fast alle einschlägigen germanistischen sowie romanistischen Hand- und Fachbücher der Dialektologie berichten über diesen Streit, allerdings meist aus zweiter Hand. Immerhin ist solcherart das Problem allgemein bekannt geworden. Die wesentlichsten Marksteine dieses romanistischen Disputs liegen zwischen 1875 und 1888, betreffen also eine Zeit, zu der es in der Romanistik noch keine (echten) Sprachatlanten gab. Die Protagonisten sind einerseits Graziadio Isaia Ascoli (1829—1907), ein vorwiegend durch Selbststudium zu einem weitläufig gebildeten Universalgelehrten herangereifter Sprachforscher mitteleuropäischen Zuschnitts, und andererseits die beiden hochrenommierten (nord)französischen Philologen Paul Meyer (1840—1917) und Gaston Paris (1859—1903). Der Streit entzündet sich an einer 1874 publizierten Schrift Ascolis namens „Schizzi franco-provenzali", in der Ascoli unter impliziter Anwendung von damals (und auch heute noch) in der Biologie üblichen Klassifikationsverfahren einen geolinguistischen Typ — einen „Geotyp" — namens „franco-provenzale" aus der Taufe hob und in methodisch sehr korrekter Weise als Verschnittmenge einer bestimmten Anzahl explizit genannter sprachlicher Merkmale definierte. Ascoli stützte sich dabei datenseitig auf Wörterbücher und Ortsmonographien. Paul Meyer bestritt in seiner 1875 dazu erschienenen Besprechung prinzipiell die Möglichkeit einer gruppen- und typenbildenden Klassifikation von sprachgeographischen Daten, vorwiegend mit dem

Argument, daß die den betreffenden Dialekt (bzw. Geotyp) konstituierenden sprachlichen Merkmale keine koinzidenten Verbreitungsareale hätten und sich solcherart keine **klar ausgeprägten** bzw. **deutlich sichtbaren** Grenzen ergäben. Man begegnet diesem Argument, das Ascoli in seiner Replik von 1876 treffend widerlegen sollte, eigentlich bis heute immer wieder. Ich habe es in früheren Schriften als „Merkmalsillusion" (bzw. als „typological fallacy", „mirage caractérologique") bezeichnet. Die Replik auf P. Meyer ist – leider – Ascolis einzige Stellungnahme in dieser Causa geblieben. Sie ist argumentativ konzis und gedanklich überaus dicht. Die Zentralpassage lautet: „[...] il distintivo necessario del determinato tipo sta appunto nella simultanea presenza o nella particolar combinazione di quei caratteri." (Ascoli 1876: 387) (cf. dazu die wissenschaftshistorische Aufarbeitung in Goebl 1990). Aus der Konfrontation Ascoli–Meyer wurde deutlich, daß letzterem die Methoden und Zielsetzungen jeglichen Klassifizierens und Typisierens fremd (bzw. sogar unheimlich) waren. Rückblickend empfiehlt es sich, zur Bezeichnung dieser Divergenzen die Termini „typophil" (für Ascoli) und „typophob" (für Meyer und Paris) zu benutzen.

1888 wurde der Diskussionskomplex, der zwischenzeitlich zu einem innerfranzösischen Streit zwischen (typophilen) Regionalisten (aus Okzitanien, der Normandie und Lothringen) und (typophoben) Zentralisten (P. Meyer, J. Gilliéron – dem späteren Autor des ALF) geworden war, durch eine eklatant typophobe Stellungnahme von G. Paris kräftig angeheizt, in der die alten Argumente P. Meyers mit stark auf die innere sprachliche (bzw. sprachpolitische!) Einheitlichkeit Frankreichs abzielenden Gedanken vermengt wurden. Eigenartigerweise geriet aber diese Stellungnahme von G. Paris zur Initialzündung für das Anlaufen der Vorarbeiten zum ALF. Bereits kurze Zeit später erschienen zwei den ganzen Disput kritisch beleuchtende Zusammenfassungen (Horning 1893 und Gauchat 1903), denen wohl die Bekanntheit dieser Debatten auch außerhalb der Romanistik zu verdanken ist. Beide Autoren vertraten eher typhophile Ansichten, gingen aber dem eigentlichen Problem – nämlich jenem von Klassifikation und Typologie in den Human- und Biowissenschaften – nicht explizit auf den Grund. Dieses methodische bzw. auch methodologisch-erkenntnistheoretische Defizit ist trotz der im Rahmen der Dialektometrie versuchten Aufholarbeit eigentlich bis heute nicht ausgeräumt worden.

Einer der tiefgreifendsten Mängel bestand darin, daß zwei wesentliche methodische Prinzipien von typhober Seite nicht (an)erkannt wurden: 1.) daß die räumliche Erstreckung **einzelner Sprachmerkmale** erkenntnistheoretisch auf der Ebene des **Besonderen** liegt, während die räumliche Erstreckung eines **Typs** (Dialekts, Geotyps etc.) auf jener des **Allgemeinen** angesiedelt ist; 2.) daß die räumliche Erstreckung eines **einzelnen Sprachmerkmals** einem **qualitativen** Begriff entspricht, während die räumliche Erstreckung eines **Typs** (Dialekts, Geotyps etc.) einem **quantitativen** Begriff gleichkommt. Damit ist überdies der Gegensatz zwischen **mono-** und **poly**thetischer Klassifikation angesprochen (cf. dazu Altmann & Lehfeldt 1973: 27).

3.4. Matteo Bartoli und die „Arealnormen"

Die fraglichen Normen gehen auf zwei Texte Bartolis aus dem Jahr 1925 (Bartoli 1925 und Bertoni & Bartoli 1925) zurück und hatten bzw. haben vermöge ihrer ab initio inhärenten Defizite stets eine nur sehr beschränkte Relevanz. Daß sie dennoch auch außerhalb der Romanistik – wenigstens namentlich – relativ gut bekannt sind und oft zitiert werden, hat sicher damit zu tun, daß Bartolis Normen-Programm Teil einer größeren Attacke gegen die Indogermanistik war, der Bartoli den pompösen Namen „Neolinguistica" gegeben hat. Unter Norm versteht er eine gesetzesähnliche Relation zwischen der **diachronen** Ausprägung (**älter/archaischer – jünger/innovativer**) eines sprachlichen Merkmals und dessen **arealer** Verbreitung (**lateral – zentral, größer – kleiner**). In den Texten Bartolis und seiner Anhänger (v. a. Bonfante 1970) werden sowohl die diachronen als auch die sprachgeographischen Aspekte der diskutierten Merkmale in erstaunlich oberflächlicher Art abgehandelt. Zum einen kommt dabei weder die gerade in der Romanistik der 20-er Jahre bereits sehr hoch entwickelte Einzelwortgeschichte zum Tragen, noch werden zum anderen die damals tongebenden romanistischen Sprachatlanten (ALF und AIS) benützt. In sprachgeographischer Hinsicht verwendet Bartoli nur allergröbste Unterteilungen der Romania („Iberia, Gallia, Italia, Dazia"; vereinzelt fügt er Regionen wie „Portogallo, Castiglia, Catalogna, Sardegna, Toscana, Ladinia" etc. dazu). In keiner seiner neolinguistischen Schriften befindet sich zudem auch nur eine einzige Karte! Die trotz dieser erstaunlichen Grobkörnigkeit nach 1945 immer komplexer werdenden areologischen Aussagen Bartolis (er spricht zuletzt von den folgenden Arealen: „isoliertes, Seiten-, diskontinuierliches, hufeisenförmiges, ringförmiges, größeres, späteres, untergehendes Areal"; cf. Weinhold 1985) verbleiben weitgehend ohne empirische Deckung. Nur illustrationshalber seien hier die in Bertoni & Bartoli 1925 enthaltenen fünf Grundnormen zitiert.

1) Von zwei (oder mehreren) semantisch älteren Bezeichnungstypen ist der ältere in der „area più isolata" erhalten.
2) Wenn von zwei Bezeichnungstypen sich einer an der Peripherie („in aree laterali") und einer im Zentrum befindet, so ist in der Regel („di norma") jener der Peripherie der ältere.
3) Wenn das gesamte Untersuchungsgebiet in eine „area maggiore" (mit Bezeichnungstyp 1) und eine „area minore" (mit Bezeichnungstyp 2) zerfällt, so bewahrt in der Regel die „area maggiore" den älteren Bezeichnungstyp.
4) Bartoli unterscheidet früher („area anteriore") und später („area seriore") romanisierte Zonen und postuliert als normal, daß älteres Wortgut sich in der „area seriore" befindet (vor allem, weil in der „area anteriore" nachrückende Innovationen sich nicht bis zur „area seriore" ausbreiten konnten).
5) Wenn von zwei Bezeichnungstypen einer im Lauf der Sprachgeschichte überhaupt verschwindet und nur der andere überlebt, so ist/war in der Regel („di norma") der verschwundene Bezeichnungstyp der ältere.

Sogar die von Bartoli selbst dazu angeführten Beispiele zeigen die Widersprüchlich- und Brüchigkeit seiner „Normen" auf. Im großen und ganzen stellen die Normen Bartolis eine empirisch und methodisch auf wenig soliden Beinen stehende Kasuistik dar. Die daran geübte Kritik (cf. Hall 1946 und die zahlreichen Refutationen von Mańczak, 1965—1994) erfolgte zu Recht. In einer detaillierten wissenschaftshistorischen Aufarbeitung des Gesamtkomplexes (Weinhold 1985) konnte gezeigt werden, daß das Problem des Ineinandergreifens von Diachronie und Diatopie im Sinne der Age-and-area hypothesis (Willis 1922) viel treffender durch eine sorgfältige Analyse der jeweiligen Diffusionsbedingungen bearbeitet werden kann, wobei der Autor auf analoge Beispiele aus der Human- und Kulturgeographie (vor allem Frankreichs) hinweist.

4. Globale Datenauswertung

Unter einer als „global" bezeichneten Datenauswertung ist jede mehr als einen Merkmalsvektor (einer **N** mal **p** messenden Datenmatrix: siehe Figur 1) einbeziehende Auswertung von Sprachatlasdaten zu verstehen. Das damit verbundene Forschungsinteresse ist primär **induktiv** und bezweckt — freilich in sehr variablem Umfang — die Erkennung von in den Sprachatlasdaten **tiefer** verborgenen Mustern und Strukturen aller Art. Wissenschaftshistorisch spannt sich dabei ein weiter Bogen von einfachen **Dichtekarten** (erzeugt durch die Superposition von mehreren Verteilungsarealen) und **Isoglossensynthesen** (generiert durch die Superposition von mehreren dieses Verteilungsareal umgebenden Grenzlinien bzw. Isoglossen) bis zur modernen Dialektometrie. Wiewohl heute erwiesen ist, daß bei der globalen Datenauswertung der Rekurs auf die zwei einschlägigen Hilfswissenschaften „**Kartographie**" und „**Numerische Klassifikation**" (auch „Numerische Taxonomie, Taxometrie" etc. genannt) unverzichtbar ist, wurde bei der Erstellung von Dichtekarten und Isoglossensynthesen von Germanisten, Romanisten und Anglisten bis in die 70-er Jahre weitgehend unfachmännisch und unreflektiert zu Werk gegangen. Ähnliche Tendenzen scheinen auch in der modernen Arealtypologie vorzuliegen. Für die Isoglossenproblematik ist allerdings bereits vor dem Erscheinen von DSA und ALF eine brillante Ausnahme anzumerken: die vom Germanisten (und auch Romanisten) Karl Haag im Jahr 1898 zur geordneten Isoglossensynthese vorgeschlagene Polygonisierung des Meßpunktenetzes nach der — wie es in der Mathematik traditionellerweise heisst — **Delauny-Voronoi**-Methode, wofür in Karto- und Geographie der Terminus **Thiessen**-Methode üblich ist. Vor allem die Germanisten haben sich immer wieder der Haagschen Polygonisierung — freilich oft mehr implizit als explizit — bedient (z. B. in den Monographieserien „Deutsche Dialektgeographie" und „Mitteldeutsche Studien"). Klassische Beispiele für Methode, Kartierungstechnik und Heuristik bieten in diesem Zusammenhang Jaberg 1908 und Rosenqvist 1919 (Isoglossensynthesen), ferner Jaberg 1936 (Dichtekarten) sowie auch

106. Arealtypologie und Dialektologie

Ettmayer 1924 (Isoglossensynthesen). Überdies wird in Ettmayers ansonsten sehr akkurat gearbeitetem Kartenteil deutlich, welche heuristischen Mängel bei der Nichtanwendung der Haagschen Polygonisierung entstehen können. Zu einer forschungsgeschichtlichen Aufarbeitung des Begriffs- und Methodenkomplexes der „Isoglosse" cf. Händler & Wiegand (1982).

Beim Einsatz von Dichtekarten (Arealsuperpositionen) und Isoglossensynthesen muß man sich zweierlei vor Augen halten: 1.) daß beide primär **quantitative** Informationen enthalten, 2.) daß jedem der beiden Kartentypen ein exakt zu definierendes **Kartenthema** (in der Form eines **idealen quantitativen Begriffes**) zugrunde liegt, das an den verschiedenen Meßpunkten des Untersuchungsfeldes in (mindestens ordinal, meist aber metrisch) abgestufter Intensität auftritt.

4.1. Von der arealen Exploration zur arealen Klassifikation (Typologie) in der Sprachgeographie

Dichtekarten und Isoglossensynthesen dienen in der Regel nur dazu, in sprachgeographischen (und auch arealtypologischen) Datensätzen eine erste, sehr selektive Ordnungssuche vorzunehmen bzw. eher an der Oberfläche liegende Ordnungsstrukturen sichtbar zu machen. Dieser mehr von spontaner Forschungsintuition als von systematischer Methodik gesteuerte Vorgang sei hier „**Exploration**" genannt. Davon zu unterscheiden ist der Vorgang der „**Klassifikation**" (bzw. Typenfindung oder Typologie), der − wie in vielen Human-, Bio- und Naturwissenschaften seit geraumer Zeit üblich − sich dem Problem der zielbewußten Auffindung von in den Sprachatlasdaten enthaltenen bzw. verborgenen Ordnungsmustern bzw. -strukturen (Geotypen) systematisch stellt. Dabei ergibt sich die Möglichkeit, ein und demselben Datensatz durch variable Klassifikationsfragen und durch dementsprechend vielfältige Klassifikationsmethoden eine (theoretisch unbegrenzte) Vielzahl von Ordnungsmustern zu entnehmen, die wiederum speziellen Fragestellungen (bzw. Hypothesen oder Theorien) dienlich sind. Daraus wird deutlich, daß hier eine „**erkenntnistheoretische Spirale**" zwischen „**Induktion**" und „**Deduktion**" in Gang gebracht werden kann, und zwar dergestalt, daß nach jedem Klassifikationsvorgang (durch Induktion) unser Kenntnisstand über den erforschten Datensatz deutlich verbessert wird. Dabei erfährt unser diesbezügliches theoretisches A priori (durch Deduktion) eine fortlaufende Optimierung. Diese Leistung wird eigentlich erst von der modernen Dialektometrie erbracht (cf. dazu Goebl 1984 passim (Romanistik) und Schiltz 1996 (Germanistik)).

4.2. Einige dialektometrische Fallbeispiele

Die Karten 1−6 dienen nur dazu, auf die im Rahmen der modernen Dialektometrie vorhandenen Möglichkeiten exemplarisch hinzuweisen. Der Leser benötigt für das korrekte Verständnis der hier gezeigten Karten hinreichend genaue Informationen zu den analysierten Datensätzen, den eingesetzten kartographischen Verfahren und den verwendeten numerisch-klassifikatorischen (bzw. taxometrischen) Methoden. Es werden Beispiele aus drei Datensätzen gezeigt: zwei davon enthalten **neuzeitliche** (aus AIS und CLAE) und einer **mittelalterliche** (aus Dees 1980: 13. Jahrhundert) Daten.

4.2.1. Übersicht über die benutzten Datensätze (AIS, CLAE und Dees 1980)

Siehe dazu die Tabelle 106.2.

Zu beachten ist, daß dialektometrisch verwertbare Datenmatrizen nur durch eine adäquate Kodierung aus bereits vorhandenen Quellen (Sprachatlanten) gewonnen werden können. Dabei entspricht diese Kodierung einem komplexen Meßvorgang. Ein entscheidendes Kriterium ist die Anzahl der in die Kodierung einbeziehbaren Meßpunkte und Merkmale (Atlaskarten). Sie sollte in beiden Fällen „möglichst groß" (d. h. mehrere Hundertschaften umfassen) und trotzdem „operationell" (d. h. EDV-technisch und kartographisch gut handhabbar) sein. Allerdings sind, wie entsprechende dialektometrische Erfahrungen gezeigt haben (Goebl 1985), gute Resultate auch schon bei nur mehrere Dutzend Meßpunkte umfassenden Datensätzen möglich.

4.2.2. Kartographische Konventionen

Die numerische Variation der zu visualisierenden Häufigkeitsverteilungen wird mittels spezieller Intervallalgorithmen (MINMWMAX, MEDMW) auf einer sechs Raster- bzw. Schraffurstufen umfassenden Signaturenskala abgebildet. Die Verwendung von nach dem Sonnenspektrum geordneten Farben (blau bis rot) wäre natürlich um vieles besser. Die verwendete Anzahl der Wertstufen (hier: 6) wurde in der Fachkartographie ausgiebig getestet und soll daher nicht weiter diskutiert

Tabelle 106.2: Vergleich wichtiger Kenndaten des Sprachatlasses AIS sowie der Datensätze CLAE und Dees 1980.

	AIS (Italien und Südschweiz)	CLAE (England)	Dees 1980 (Nordfrankreich)
1 Datenquelle	Sprachatlas AIS vol. I, II und IV	Sprachatlas SED bzw. CLAE	3300 mittelalterliche Urkunden
2 Explorationsmodus	direkte Feldenquete	direkte Feldenquete	philolog. Textexhaustion
3 Zeitliche Gültigkeit der Daten	1919–1926	1948–1961	13. Jahrhundert
4 Art der Meßpunkte	kleinere Ortschaften und Städte	kleinere Ortschaften	mittelalt. Schreibzentren bzw. Kanzleien
5 Art der Merkmale der Quellen	lautschriftlich fixierte Antworten der Gewährsleute	lautschriftlich fixierte Antworten der Gewährsleute	Schreibformen in mittelalterl. Urkunden
6 Anzahl der Meßpunkte	250 AIS-Meßpunkte + 1 Kunstpunkt (Standarditalienisch)	313 SED- bzw. CLAE-Meßpunkte + 1 Kunstpunkt (Standardenglisch)	85 Schreibzentren
7 Anzahl der kodierten Merkmale	696	597	119 (Vokalismus) bzw. 66 (Konsonantismus)
8 Grammatische Kategorie der kodierten Merkmale	lexikalisch, morphologisch	lexikalisch, morphologisch und syntaktisch	phonetisch (Vokalismus, Konsonantismus)
9 Anzahl der kodierten Einzelformen (Taxate)	4836	7101	119 bzw. 66
10 Kodierung vorgenommen durch	Goebl	Team des CLAE	Dees
11 Meßtheoretisches Niveau der kodierten Merkmale	nominal (polytom)	nominal (polytom)	nominal (binär)
12 Mehrfachbelege pro Meßpunkte und Atlaskarte	nein	ja	nein

werden. Die Obergrenze der Wertstufe 3 entspricht überall dem arithmetischen Mittel der betreffenden Häufigkeitsverteilungen, welche überdies zur raschen statistischen Analyse in der rechten unteren Ecke der betreffenden Karten mittels Histogrammen visualisiert wurden. Dazu und zu weiteren hier nicht angesprochenen Problemen cf. Goebl (1984 I: 90–98). Die Karten 106.1–6 wurden dankenswerterweise von G. Schiltz (Basel) produziert.

4.2.3. Taxometrische Konventionen

Die Karten 106.1–4 stellen Ähnlichkeitsmessungen dar. Dabei wird – stets anhand eines genau festgelegten Index bzw. Maßes – die (quantitative) Ähnlichkeit von N – 1 Meßpunktvektoren zum Merkmalsvektor eines vorher festzulegenden Prüfbezugspunktes gemessen. Das hier durchgängig verwendete Ähnlichkeitsmaß ist der „Relative Identitätswert" (RIW) oder „Relative Identity Value" (RIV): cf. dazu Goebl 1984 I: 74–78. Das Sigel RIVs verweist auf eine von G. Schlitz definierte Spielart des RIW/RIV, die bei Datenmatrixen mit Mehrfachbelegen zur Anwendung kommt (cf. Schlitz 1997: 664). Das den Karten 106.5–6 zugrunde liegende Meßmoment ist dagegen komplexer: cf. dazu unter Abschnitt 4.2.4.2.

4.2.4. Interpretationen der Karten 106.1–6

4.2.4.1. Interpretationen der Karten 106.1–4
Die Karten 106.1–4 veranschaulichen den eindeutig mit der räumlichen Entfernung zusammenhängenden Abfall der linguistischen

106. Arealtypologie und Dialektologie

Ähnlichkeit eines Prüfbezugspunktes zum Rest des Untersuchungsgebietes. Dabei kann die Lage des Prüfbezugspunktes (überall weiß belassen) in Analogie zum Gipfel eines rundum mehr oder weniger gleichmäßig abfallenden Gebirges gesehen werden. Auf Karte 106.1 (England) ist dieser Abfall — abgesehen von näher zu erklärenden Ausreißern in Wertklasse 4 rund um London — von Nord nach Südwest (Cornwall) weitgehend kontinuerlich. Auf Karte 106.2 (Italien) ist der Messwertabfall nach Norden (Graubünden) um vieles abrupter als nach Westen, Süden und Osten. Um den Prüfbezugspunkt bildet sich in der Regel eine kleinere Zone größter Affinität (in Wertklasse 6) aus, die die Reichweite des lokalen Subdialekts markiert. Dabei ist zu beachten, daß das Kartenthema quantitativ ausgeprägt ist und die Grenzen zwischen den einzelnen Wertstufen nicht mit Isoglossenbündeln bzw. mit Dialektgrenzen im üblichen Sinn verwechselt werden dürfen.

Jede Ähnlichkeitskarte enthält ein spezielles Raumprofil (in der Form eines Geotyps), das sich beim Wandel des Prüfbezugspunktes mehr oder weniger stark verändert. An dieses Phänomen können weitere typodiagnostische Meßmomente angebunden werden. Aus geolinguistischer Perspektive dienen Ähnlichkeitskarten zu folgenden Zwecken: Eruierung der Stellung eines Ortsidioms inmitten seines Umfeldes; Prüfung der typologischen Homogenität bzw. der diffusorischen Durchlässigkeit des Untersuchungsnetzes von variablen Standpunkten aus; Feststellung der Relation zwischen der naturräumlichen Entfernung (in km) und der geolinguistischen Ähnlichkeit: siehe dazu auch Figur 106.2. Zu weiteren Details cf. Goebl (1984 I: 100−110).

Genuin statistische Tests anhand verschiedener Datensätze haben zudem die folgenden Regularitäten gezeigt: bei zufallsgesteuerter Merkmalsauswahl werden bereits anhand von rund einem Drittel der Totalkorpora diesel-

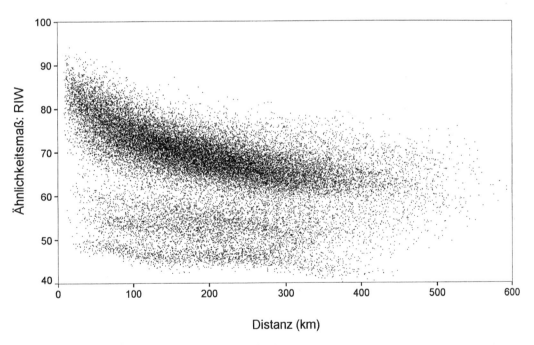

Gesamtkorpus: 251 Meßpunkte (31.375 RI-Werte)

Figur 106.2: Relation zwischen linguistischer Ähnlichkeit und geographischer Distanz
Quelle: AIS; Bände I, II und IV
Daten: 251 Meßpunkte, 696 Merkmalsvektoren
Ähnlichkeitsmessung: Relativer Identitätswert (RIW)
Kommentar: Die kartierten 31.375 RI-Werte bilden grosso modo drei Punktwolken: Eine kompakte (oben) und zwei diffuse (unten). Die kompakte Wolke entsteht aus den genuin italienischen Anteilen des Untersuchungsnetzes, die beiden diffusen Wolken verweisen auf die frankoprovenzalischen und rätoromanischen Anteile desselben. Die Zahl 31.375 ergibt sich aus der Formel N/2 · (N-1) bei N = 251. Die quantitative Konsistenz der Relation zwischen Ähnlichkeit und Entfernung ist deutlich erkennbar.

ben Resultate wie anhand der Totalkorpora selber sichtbar. Die taxometrisch ermittelten Raummuster sind also redundant in den Daten verteilt bzw. sehr tief in diese eingeschnitten. Auch bei der rein **qualitativen** Manipulation an den Merkmalsvektoren zeigt sich − entsprechende Mindestmengen bei den Atlaskarten vorausgesetzt −, daß **phonetisch**, **lexikalisch** oder **morphosyntaktisch** relevante Subkorpora einander sehr ähnliche geotypologische Resultate liefern: vergleiche dazu die Karten 106.3 (**Vokalismus**) und 106.4 (**Konsonantismus**), die diesen Sachverhalt anhand mittelalterlicher Materialien deutlich aufzeigen. Auch hier entsteht der Eindruck, daß in den Datensätzen fest bzw. **tief verankerte** Regularitäten vorliegen, wofür allerdings eine erschöpfende Erklärung bis heute noch aussteht: cf. dazu auch Goebl 1984 I: 197−219.

4.2.4.2. Interpretation der Karten 5−6

Den Karten 106.5 und 106.6 liegt ein taxometrisches Meßmoment zugrunde, das aus einer kommunikationstheoretischen Überlegung zu den bei der Ähnlichkeitsmessung anfallenden Häufigkeitsverteilungen abgeleitet wurde. Bei der Analyse solcher Ähnlichkeitsverteilungen konnte festgestellt werden, daß deren Symmetrie großregional dergestalt schwankt, daß **asymmetrische** Verteilungen in − im weitesten Sinn − eher **peripheren** Gebieten auftreten, während **symmetrische** Verteilungen eher in **zentral** gelegenen Zonen vorkommen. Die Figur 106.3 zeigt das schematische Aussehen zweier solcher Verteilungen: links sieht man eine asymmetrische Verteilung (mit einem bündnerromanischen Prüfbezugspunkt), rechts eine sehr symmetrische Verteilung (mit einem nordlombardischen Prüfbezugspunkt).

Die Symmetrie der Verteilungen wird unter anderem dadurch bestimmt, wieviel Prozent der Ähnlichkeitsmeßwerte zu beiden Seiten des arithmetischen Mittels (MW) liegen. Dabei kann der zwischen Mittelwert und Maximalwert (welcher der größten Ähnlichkeit zum jeweiligen Prüfbezugspunkt entspricht) liegenden Meßwertmenge eine besondere kommunikative bzw. interaktive „Güte" zugemessen werden. Immerhin werden dadurch jene Merkmalskomponenten erfasst, über die der betreffende Vektor überdurchschnittlich gut mit dem Rest des Untersuchungsnetzes „verkehrt" bzw. „interagiert". Eine taxometrische bzw. statistische Modellierung dieser Idee verweist auf die „Schiefe" (Definition und Formel in allen Statistikhandbüchern und bei Goebl 1984 I: 150−154 bzw. 1982a: 44−46 und Goebl & Schiltz 1997: 17).

Tatsächlich zeigen die kartographischen Synopsen von jeweils N Schiefewerten ausnahmslos sehr klar strukturierte Kartenbilder. Die in Wertklasse 1 figurierenden Polygone markieren Zonen **hohen kommunikativen Austausches** bzw. **Kontakts** innerhalb des Gesamtnetzes, während die in Wertklasse 6 aufscheinenden Polygone Gebieten großer Konservativität bzw. extremer Abgeschiedenheit (stets innerhalb des vorliegenden Gesamtnetzes) entsprechen. Auf Karte 106.5 (England) bilden die Polygone einen grosso modo von Oxford ausstrahlenden **Stern**, der den Süden Englands dominiert. Auf Karte 106.6 (Italien) bilden die Polygone in Wert-

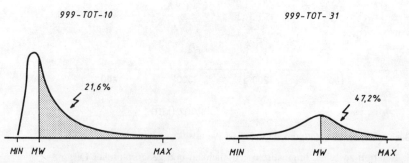

Figur 106.3: Relativer Anteil der Meßpunkte mit überdurchschnittlichen Ähnlichkeitswerten (nach RIW) bei verschiedenen Ähnlichkeitsverteilungen.
MIN − Minimalwert
MW − arithmetisches Mittel
MAX − Maximalwert
Anzahl der Ähnlichkeitswerte in beiden Fällen: 250
Links: Ähnlichkeitsverteilung zum AIS-Meßpunkt 10 (Camischolas, Graubünden)
Rechts: Ähnlichkeitsverteilung zum AIS-Meßpunkt 31 (Osco, Tessin)

klasse 1 eine **Zange**, deren Schenkel entlang des Apennin und der Etsch verlaufen. In beiden Fällen werden damit historisch und linguistisch überaus bedeutsame Übergangs-, Interaktions- und Austauschräume markiert, die sehr vielfältig interpretiert werden können. Ähnliches gilt für die in Wertklasse 6 rubrizierten Randgebiete, deren Lateralität aus historischer und linguistischer Sicht ebenso gut bekannt ist. Bemerkenswert ist nun in beiden Fällen, daß anhand derselben Daten durchgeführte dialektometrische Isoglossensynthesen eine deutliche Koinzidenz von dicken Isoglossenbündeln einerseits (wodurch **Abgrenzung** markiert wird) und den eben erwähnten Polygonen in Wertklasse 1 andererseits (womit **Kommunikation** verbunden ist) zeigen. Damit kommt die in vielen Geowissenschaften immer wieder evozierte **Doppelnatur** von Grenz- und Übergangsgebieten (hinsichtlich **Abgrenzung** versus **Interaktion**) deutlich zum Vorschein. Zu weiteren Vertiefungen cf. Goebl 1992a: 448−450; 1993a: 52−53; 1993b: 289−291. Neben der **Schiefe** können noch zahlreiche **andere statistische Parameter** der Ähnlichkeitsverteilungen zur geolinguistischen Mustererkennung und -analyse benützt werden.

4.2.5. Dendrographische Dialektometrie und Lexikostatistik

Die baumgenerierende (dendrographische) Klassifikation mittels hierarchisch-agglomerativer Verfahren figuriert heute standardmäßig in allen taxometrischen Handbüchern (z. B. Bock 1974 oder Sneath & Sokal 1973). Diese Verfahren lassen sich − wie zahlreiche Anwendungsfälle deutlich gezeigt haben (cf. Goebl 1982a: 785−787; 1992a: 453−454; 1993a: 58−68; 1993b: 292−292 und 1997) − sehr gut auch auf sprachgeographische Datensätze anwenden. Dabei fallen jeweils ein **Baum** und dessen **räumliche Umlegung** an. Die Strukturen des Baumes (in der Form einer Hierarchie von „Dendremen") und jene der räumlichen Umlegung (in der Form eines Mosaiks von das Gesamtnetz fugenlos abdeckenden „Choremen"; Terminus bei den Geographen entlehnt; cf. Brunet 1987: 190, 211) sind klassifikatorisch überdies interessant und haben sowohl **diachrone** wie **synchrone** Relevanz. Sie gestatten es nämlich, in der Zeit abgelaufene Sprachausgliederungsprozesse modellhaft nachzuvollziehen, wie das auch in der **Lexikostatistik** − freilich anhand viel kleinerer Datensätze − versucht wird. Dabei ist anzumerken, daß zwischen Dialektometrie und Lexikostatistik enge datenseitige und methodische Affinitäten bestehen, die allerdings von der Fachwelt bislang weitgehend unbemerkt geblieben sind. In beiden Fällen werden zwischen Meßpunktvektoren mehr oder weniger regelhaft existierende quantitative Relationen zur Erstellung klassifikatorisch und heuristisch relevanter Schemata (vor allem von Bäumen) benutzt. In der Lexikostatistik betreffen diese quantitativen Relationen **diachron** unterschiedene Meßpunktvektoren (vermittels der „lexicon replacement rate"), in der Dialektometrie **diatopisch** unterschiedene Meßpunktevektoren (vermittels verschiedener Ähnlichkeitsmaße). Gerade für die moderne Arealtypologie scheint diese sowohl diachrone als auch diatopische Dimensionen einbeziehende Methode vielversprechend zu sein. In den frühen 90-er Jahren hat überdies die Lexikostatistik methodisch den Anschluß an die Numerische Klassifikation gefunden, so dass Dialektometrie und Lexikostatistik auch hier konform gehen (cf. Dyen & Kruskal & Black 1992). Außerdem ist die zwischen Lexikostatistik und **moderner Humangenetik** seit langer Zeit bestehende Schiene konsequent ausgebaut worden (cf. z. B. Cavalli-Sforza & Wang 1996). Damit kann heute von einem weitgehenden Methodenparallelismus zwischen Lexikostatistik, Dialektometrie und der raumbezogenen Human- bzw. Populationsgenetik gesprochen werden (cf. dazu beispielsweise Sokal 1991, Ruhlen 1994 und Goebl 1996). Dieser Gleichschritt betrifft weitgehend auch das Erkenntnisinteresse dieser drei Disziplinen.

5. Zusammenfassung und Perspektiven

Wenn van der Auwera (1998: 20) in der Einleitung zu seinem Sammelband über europäische Adverbialkonstruktionen mit Blick auf die geodiagnostischen Möglichkeiten der Dialektometrie und auf die „Qualität" der in der modernen Arealtypologie verwendeten Daten schreibt, daß „the data simply are not good and large enough to take dialectometric work worthwhile", so muß ich dem als in diesem Zitat angesprochener Dialektometer zweierlei entgegenhalten: 1.) Zum einen hat sich die Arealtypologie noch lange nicht alle Erfahrungen der prädialektometrischen Sprachgeographie zunutze gemacht: dies betrifft sowohl die Datenspezifik als auch alle mit der Auswertung der Daten verbundenen begrifflichen, methodischen und technischen Aspekte. 2.) Zum anderen liegen innerhalb der Dialektometrie und in deren methodischem Umfeld sehr ermutigende Erfahrungen mit gut brauchbaren quantitativen bzw. taxometrischen Explorationen und Klassifikationen vor, die anhand von Datensätzen durchgeführt worden sind, welche jenen der Arealtypologie modernen Zuschnitts sehr ähnlich sind. Vonseiten der Arealtypologie müßte der „Sprung ins (kalte?) Wasser der Taxo- oder Dialektometrie" simpel und einfach einmal gewagt werden. Vor allem im überschaubaren Bereich der Sprachen eines Kontinents (etwa in Europa im Rahmen des eingangs zitierten Projekts EUROTYP) wären derartige Einstiegserfahrungen empfehlenswert. Auch die von Genetikern (um R. R. Sokal oder L. L. Cavalli-Sforza) mit kontinent- und sogar weltweiten Datensätzen (stets **genetischer** und **linguistischer** Art) gemachten Klassifikationserfahrungen stellen eine zusätzliche Ermutigung dar. Die Arealität sprachlicher Merkmale ist ohne jeden Zweifel ein überaus komplexes Phänomen und Problem zugleich. „Area is therefore an important dimension of linguistic features generally. It is an integral bit of information about them that should not be neglected, even though – and indeed partly because – its ultimate significance may not be fully understood." (Masica 1971: 170). Dieser Feststellung, der inhaltlich auch jeder Sprachgeograph (sowie jeder mit Raumaspekten befaßte Human- und Biowissenschaftler) beipflichten kann, müßten allerdings im Rahmen der modernen Typologie die entsprechenden methodischen Konsequenzen folgen. Die oft gemachte Feststellung des „area character"(s) bestimmter linguistischer Merkmale (hier: Ramat & Bernini 1990: 34) oder die Vermutung, daß „language phenomena exist as geographical continua and that the transitions between different geographical areas correspond to transitions between different geotypes of those phenomena" (Bechert 1990: 115) weisen in dieselbe Richtung, obwohl sie aus sprachgeographischer Sicht ganz elementare – sit venia verbo – Selbstverständlichkeiten sind. Auch die derzeit im Rahmen einfacher explorativer Methoden (hier: Arealsuperpositionen in der Form von Dichtekarten) gewonnenen globalen Erkenntnisse (z. B. der „Charlemagne-Sprachbund": cf. van der Auwera 1998b: 271 f. und Haspelmath 1998: 814 ff.) stellen Ermutigungen dar, die auch von der Warte des daten- und methodenspezifischen Erfahrungshorizonts der Sprachgeographie überaus plausibel sind. Vonseiten der modernen Arealtypologie müßten die Generierung und Auswertung entsprechender Datensätze (mit mehreren Dutzend Sprachen und ebenso vielen Merkmalen) organisiert und dabei auch dafür Sorge getragen werden, daß mehrere solche Datensätze in weiterer Folge meßpunkt- und vor allem merkmalsseitig kombiniert werden können. Allerdings wäre bei diesem Vorgang bereits die volle Assistenz- bzw. Berücksichtigung der Dialektometrie notwendig, um die mit einer eventuellen „Wiedererfindung des Rades" verbundenen Risiken und Verzögerungen zu vermeiden.

6. Literatur

ADDU: Thun, Harald et alii (eds.). *El Atlas lingüístico diatópico y diastrático del Uruguay.* Kiel, Montevideo (in Vorbereitung).

AIS: Jaberg, Karl & Jud, Jakob (eds.). 1928–1940. *Sprach- und Sachatlas Italiens und der Südschweiz.* Zofingen: Ringier. 8 Bände (Neudruck 1971: Nendeln: Kraus).

ALD: Goebl, Hans et alii (eds.). 1998. *Atlante linguistico del ladino dolomitico e dei dialetti limitrofi* – 1a parte. *Sprachatlas des Dolomitenladinischen und angrenzender Dialekte* (7 Bände) – 1. Teil. Wiesbaden: L. Reichert.

ALF: Gilliéron, Jules & Edmont, Edmond (eds.). 1902–1910. *Atlas linguistique de la France.* Paris (Champion). 9 Bände (Neudruck 1971. Bologna: Forni).

Altmann, Gabriel & Lehfeldt, Werner. 1973. *Allgemeine Sprachtypologie. Prinzipien und Meßverfahren.* München: Fink.

Ascoli, Graziadio Isaia. 1874. „Schizzi francoprovenzali". *Archivio glottologico italiano* 3 [1878]: 61–120.

Ascoli, Graziadio Isaia. 1876. „P. Meyer e il francoprovenzale". *Archivio glottologico italiano* 2: 385–395.

Bartoli, Matteo. 1925. *Introduzione alla neolinguistica. Principi, scopi, metodi.* Genf: Olschki.

Bechert, Johannes. 1990. „The structure of the noun in European languages". In: Bechert/Bernini/Buridant (eds.), 115–140.

Bechert, Johannes & Bernini, Giuliano & Buridant, Claude (eds.). 1990. *Toward a typology of European languages.* Berlin, New York: de Gruyter.

Bertoni, Giulio & Bartoli, Matteo. 1925. *Breviario di neolinguistica.* Modena: Società tipografica modenese.

Besch, Werner & Knoop, Ulrich & Putschke, Wolfgang & Wiegand, Herbert Ernst (eds.). 1982–1983. *Dialektologie. Ein Handbuch zur deutschen und allgemeinen Dialektforschung.* 2 Bände. Berlin, New York: de Gruyter.

Bock, Hans Hermann. 1974. *Automatische Klassifikation. Theoretische und praktische Methoden zur Gruppierung und Strukturierung von Daten (Cluster-Analyse).* Göttingen: Vandenhoeck & Ruprecht.

Bonfante, Giuliano. 1970. *La dottrina neolinguistica. Teoria e pràtica.* Turin: Giappichelli.

Brunet, Roger. 1987. *La carte. Mode d'emploi.* Paris: Fayard.

Cavalli-Sforza, Luca, L. & Wang, William S.-Y. 1986. „Spatial distance and lexical replacement". *Language* 62: 38–55.

Christmann, Hans Helmut. 1971. „Lautgesetze und Wortgeschichte. Zu dem Satz „Jedes Wort hat seine eigene Geschichte" ". In: Coseriu, Eugenio & Stempel, Wolf-Dieter (eds.). *Sprache und Geschichte. Festschrift für Harri Meier zum 65. Geburtstag.*, München: Fink, 111–124.

CLAE: Viereck, Wolfgang & Ramisch, Heinrich (eds.). 1991, 1997. *The Computer Developed Linguistic Atlas of England.* 2 Bände. Tübingen: Niemeyer.

Dees, Anthonij. 1980. *Atlas des formes et des constructions des chartes françaises du 13ᵉ siècle.* Tübingen: Niemeyer.

DSA: *Deutscher Sprachatlas* aufgrund des von Georg Wenker begründeten Sprachatlas des Deutschen Reiches in vereinfachter Form begonnen von Ferdinand Wrede, fortgesetzt von Walther Mitzka und Bernhard Martin. 1927–1956. Marburg/Lahn: Elwert. 23 Lieferungen mit 128 Karten.

DWA: *Deutscher Wortatlas* von Walther Mitzka & Ludwig Erich Schmidt & Rainer Hildebrandt. 1951–1980. Gießen: Schmitz. 22 Bände.

Dyen, Isidore & Kruskal, Joseph B. & Black, Paul. 1992. *An Indoeuropean classification: A lexicostatistical experiment.* Philadelphia (Transactions of the American Philosophical Society, 82/5).

Ettmayer, Karl von. 1924. *Über das Wesen der Dialektbildung erläutert an den Dialekten Frankreichs.* Wien (Denkschriften der Akademie der Wissenschaften in Wien, phil.-hist. Klasse, Band 66/3).

Gauchat, Louis. 1903. „Gibt es Mundartgrenzen?". *Archiv für das Studium der neueren Sprachen und Literaturen* 111: 365–403.

Goebl, Hans. 1982a. *Dialektometrie. Prinzipien und Methoden des Einsatzes der Numerischen Taxonomie im Bereich der Dialektgeographie.* Wien (Denkschriften der Österreichischen Akademie der Wissenschaften, phil.-hist. Klasse, Band 157).

Goebl, Hans. 1982b. „Ansätze zu einer computativen Dialektometrie". In: Besch et al. (eds.) 1982–83, Band 1: 778–792.

Goebl, Hans. 1984. *Dialektometrische Studien. Anhand italoromanischer, rätoromanischer und galloromanischer Sprachmaterialien aus AIS und ALF.* 3 Bände. Tübingen: Niemeyer.

Goebl, Hans. 1985. „Coup d'œil dialectométrique sur les *Tableaux phonétiques des patois suisses romands (TPPSR)*". *Vox romanica* 44: 189–233.

Goebl, Hans. 1990. „Ma il distintivo necessario del determinato tipo sta appunto nella simultanea presenza o nella particolar combinazione di quei caratteri". Methodische und wissenschaftsgeschichtliche Bemerkungen zum Diskussionskomplex „unità ladina". *Ladinia* 14: 219–257.

Goebl, Hans. 1992a. „Problèmes et méthodes de la dialectométrie actuelle (avec application à l'AIS)". In: Euskaltzaindia/Académie de la langue basque (ed.). *Nazioarteko dialektologia biltzarra. Agiriak/Actes du Congrès international de dialectologie.* Bilbo/Bilbao: Euskaltzaindia, 429–475.

Goebl, Hans. 1992b. „Die Sprachatlanten der europäischen Romania. Entstehung, Struktur und Aufbau sowie ihre Leistung für die Wort- und Sachforschung". In: Beitl, Klaus & Chiva, Isac & Kausel, Eva (eds.). *Wörter und Sachen. Österreichische und deutsche Beiträge zur Ethnographie und Dialektologie Frankreichs. Ein französisch-deutsch-österreichisches Projekt.* Wien (Sitzungsberichte der Österreichischen Akademie der Wissenschaften, phil.-hist. Klasse, Band 586): 249–287.

Goebl, Hans. 1993a. „Probleme und Methoden der Dialektometrie: Geolinguistik in globaler Perspektive". In: Viereck, Wolfgang (ed.). *Verhandlungen des internationalen Dialektologenkongresses in Bamberg 1990.* Stuttgart: Steiner, Band I: 37–81.

Goebl, Hans. 1993b. „Dialectometry. A short overview of the principles and practice of quantitative classification of linguistic atlas data". In: Köhler, Reinhard & Rieger Burkhard (eds.). *Contributions to quantitative linguistics.* Dordrecht: Kluwer, 277–315.

Goebl, Hans. 1996. „La convergence entre les fragmentations géo-linguistique et géo-génétique de l'Italie du Nord". *Revue de linguistique romane* 60, 25–49.

Goebl, Hans. 1997. „Some dendrographic classifications of the data of CLAE 1 and CLAE 2". In: CLAE 2: 23–32.

Goebl, Hans & Schiltz, Guillaume. 1997. „A dialectometrical compilation of CLAE 1 and CLAE 2. Isoglosses and Dialect Integration". In: CLAE 2: 13–21.

Haag, Karl. 1898. *Die Mundarten des oberen Neckar- und Donaulandes (Schwäbisch-alemannisches Grenzgebiet: Baarmundarten).* Reutlingen: Hutzler (Beilage zum Programm der königlichen Realanstalt zu Reutlingen).

Händler, Harald & Wiegand, Herbert Ernst. 1982. „Das Konzept der Isoglosse: methodische und terminologische Probleme". In: Besch et al. (eds.) 1982–83, Band 1: 501–527.

Hall, Robert A. jr. 1946. „Bartoli's 'Neolinguistica'". *Language* 22: 273−283.

Hard, Gerhard. 1973. *Die Geographie. Eine wissenschaftstheoretische Einführung*. Berlin, New York: de Gruyter.

Haspelmath, Martin. 1997. *Indefinite pronouns*. Oxford: Oxford University Press.

Haspelmath, Martin. 1998. „How young is Standard Average European?". In: Ramat, Paolo (ed.). *Areal Typology*, special issue of *Language Sciences* 20.3: 271−287.

Horning, Adolf. 1893. „Über Dialektgrenzen im Romanischen". *Zeitschrift für Romanische Philologie* 17: 160−187, auch in: Spitzer, Leo (ed.). 1930 *Meisterwerke der romanischen Sprachwissenschaft*, München: Hueber, Band 2: 264−298.

Jaberg, Karl. 1908. *Sprachgeographie: Beitrag zum Verständnis des Atlas linguistique de la France*. Aarau: Sauerländer.

Jaberg, Karl. 1936. *Aspects géographiques du langage*. Paris: Droz.

Lehmann, Christian. 1984. *Der Relativsatz*. Tübingen: Niemeyer.

LGL: Althaus, Hans Peter & Henne, Helmut & Wiegand, Herbert Ernst (eds.). 1980[2]. *Lexikon der Germanistischen Linguistik*. Tübingen: Niemeyer.

LRL: Holtus, Günther & Metzeltin, Michael & Schmitt, Christian (eds.). 1988 f. *Lexikon der Romanistischen Linguistik*. Tübingen: Niemeyer.

Mańczak, Witold. 1965. „La nature des archaïsmes des aires latérales". *Lingua* 13: 177−184.

Mańczak, Witold. 1994. „Les zones latérales sont-elles plus archaïques que les zones centrales?". *Folia linguistica historica* 15: 125−130.

Masica, Colin P. 1971. *Defining a linguistic area: South Asia*. Chicago, London: University of Chicago Press.

Meyer, Paul. 1875. Besprechung zu: Ascoli 1873. *Romania* 4: 293−296.

MRhSA: Bellmann, Günter & Herrgen, Joachim & Schmidt, Jürgen (eds.). 1994 f. *Mittelrheinischer Sprachatlas*. Tübingen: Niemeyer.

Pop, Sever. 1926. *Buts et méthodes des enquêtes dialectales*. Paris: Gamber.

Pop, Sever. 1950. *La dialectologie. Aperçu historique et méthodes d'enquêtes linguistiques*. 2 Bände Louvain, Gembloux: Chez l'auteur, Duculot.

Ramat, Paolo & Bernini, Giuliano. 1990. „Area influence versus typological drift in Western Europe: the Case of Negation". In: Bechert/Bernini/Buridant (eds.), 26−46.

Rijkhoff, Jan et alii. 1993. „A method of language sampling". *Studies in Language* 17: 169−203.

Rosenqvist, Arvid. 1919. „Limites administratives et division dialectale de la France". *Neuphilologische Mitteilungen* 20: 87−119.

Ruhlen, Merritt. 1994. *On the origin of languages. Studies in linguistic taxonomy*. Stanford: Stanford University Press.

SBS: König, Werner (ed.). *Bayerischer Sprachatlas. Sprachatlas von Bayerisch-Schwaben*, 1996 f. Heidelberg: Winter.

SED: Orton, Harold & Halliday, Wilfrid J. (eds.). 1962−1971. *Survey of English Dialects*. 13 Bände. Leeds: Croom Helm. (Neudruck 1998: London: Routledge).

Schiltz, Guillaume. 1996. *Der Dialektometrische Atlas von Südwest-Baden (DASB). Konzepte eines dialektometrischen Informationssystems*. 4 Bände. Marburg: Elwert.

Schiltz, Guillaume. 1997. „Current trends in dialectometry: the handling of synonym feature realizations." In: Klar, R. & Opitz, Otto (ed.). *Classification and knowledge organization*. Berlin, Heidelberg, New York: Springer, 661−668.

Simpson, J. M. Y. 1994. „Areal linguistics". In: Asher, R. E. & Simpson, J. M. Y. (eds.). *The Encyclopedia of Language and Linguistics*. Oxford, New York, Seoul, Tokyo: Pergamon Press, Band I, 206−212.

Sneath, Peter, H. A. & Sokal, Robert R. 1973. *Numerical taxonomy. The principles and practice of numerical classification*. San Francisco: Freeman.

Sokal, Robert R. 1991. „Ancient movement patterns determine modern genetic variances in Europe". *Human Biology* 63: 589−606.

Stegmüller, Wolfgang (ed.). 1978. *Das Universalienproblem*. Darmstadt: Wissenschaftliche Buchgesellschaft.

van der Auwera, Johan. 1998a. „Introduction". In: van der Auwera 1998, 1−23.

van der Auwera, Johan. 1998b. „Conclusion". In: van der Auwera 1998, 813−36.

van der Auwera, Johan (ed.). 1998. *Adverbial constructions in the languages of Europe*. Berlin, New York: de Gruyter.

Weinhold, Norbert. 1985. *Sprachgeographische Distribution und chronologische Schichtung. Untersuchungen zu M. Bartoli und neueren geographischen Theorien*. Hamburg: Buske.

Willis, John. Christopher. 1922. *Age and area. A study in geographical distribution and origin of species*. Cambridge: Cambridge University Press, (Neudruck 1970: Amsterdam: Ascher).

Hans Goebl, Salzburg (Österreich)

106. Arealtypologie und Dialektologie

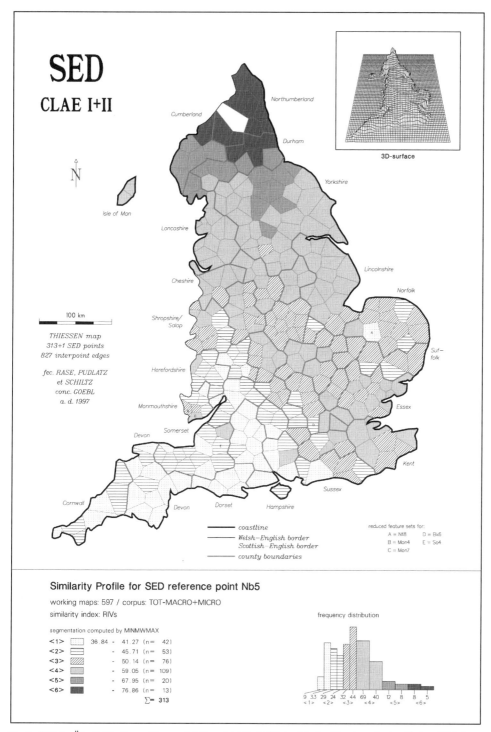

Karte 106.1: Ähnlichkeitsprofil zum Meßpunkt Nb 7 (Haltwhistle, Northumberland) des SED bzw. des CLAE

Korpus: 597 Merkmalsvektoren bzw. „working maps" (Lexikon und Morphosyntax)
314 Meßpunkte nach SED bzw. CLAE

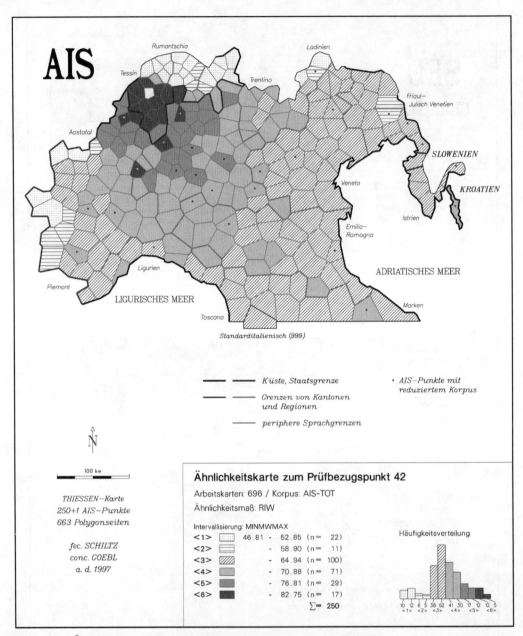

Karte 106.2: Ähnlichkeitsprofil zum Meßpunkt 42 (Sonogno, Tessin) des AIS
Korpus: Merkmalsvektoren bzw. „Arbeitskarten" (Lexikon und Morphologie)
251 Meßpunkte nach AIS

106. Arealtypologie und Dialektologie

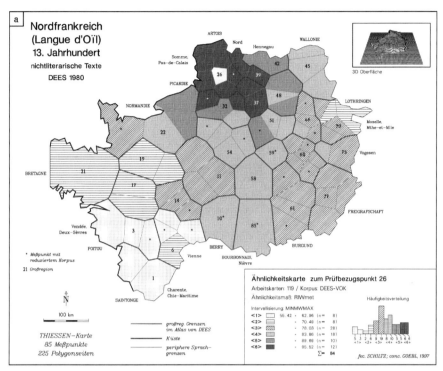

Karte 106.3: Ähnlichkeitsprofil zum Meßpunkt 26 (Somme, Pas-de-Calais) des Atlas von Dees 1980
Korpus: 119 Merkmalsvektoren bzw. „Arbeitskarten" (Phonetik: Vokalismus)
      85 Meßpunkte nach Dees 1980

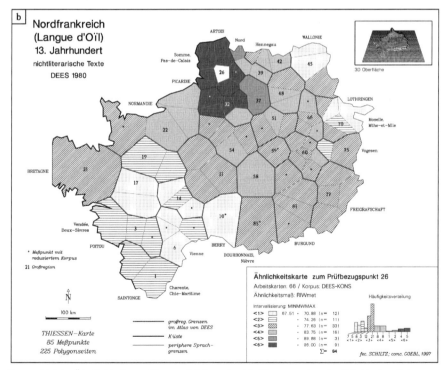

Karte 106.4: Ähnlichkeitsprofil zum Meßpunkt 26 (Somme, Pas-de-Calais) des Atlas von Dees 1980
Korpus: 66 Merkmalsvektoren bzw. „Arbeitskarten" (Phonetik: Konsonantismus)
      85 Meßpunkte nach Dees 1980

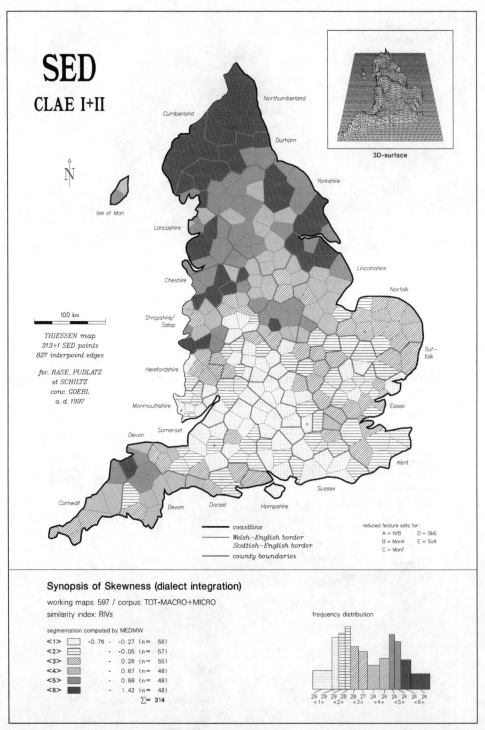

Karte 106.5: Choroplethenprofil der Synopse der Schiefen von 314 Ähnlichkeitsverteilungen
Korpus: 597 Merkmalsvektoren bzw. „working maps" (Lexikon und Morphosyntax)
314 Meßpunkte nach SED bzw. CLAE

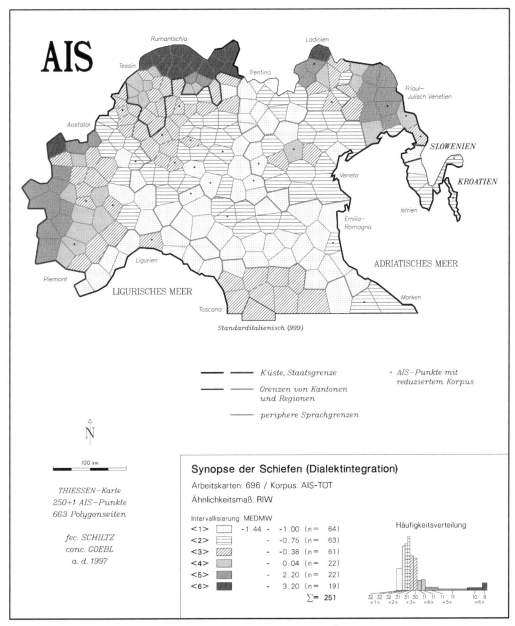

Karte 106.6: Choroplethenprofil der Synopse der Schiefen von 251 Ähnlichkeitsverteilungen
Korpus: 696 Merkmalsvektoren bzw. „Arbeitskarten" (Lexikon und Morphologie)
251 Meßpunkte nach AIS

107. The European linguistic area: Standard Average European

1. Introduction
2. The major SAE features
3. Some further likely SAE features
4. Degrees of membership in SAE
5. How did SAE come into being?
6. Abbreviations of language names
7. References

1. Introduction

This article summarizes some of the main pieces of evidence for a linguistic area (or *Sprachbund*) in Europe that comprises the Romance, Germanic and Balto-Slavic languages, the Balkan languages, and more marginally also the westernmost Finno-Ugrian languages (these will be called *core European languages* in this article). This linguistic area is sometimes called **Standard Average European** (abbreviated SAE), following Whorf (1941) [1956: 138]. The existence of this linguistic area is a relatively new insight (cf. Bechert et al. 1990, Bernini & Ramat 1996, Haspelmath 1998, van der Auwera 1998, König & Haspelmath 1999).

While the close syntactic parallels among the Balkan languages have struck linguists since the 19th century and the existence of a Balkan *Sprachbund* has been universally accepted, the European linguistic area has long been overlooked. This may at first appear surprising, because the members of the *Sprachbund* are among the best studied languages of the world. However, it is easy to understand why linguists have been slow to appreciate the significance of the similarities among the core European languages: Since most comparative linguists know these languages particularly well, they have tended to see non-European languages as special and unusual, and the similarities among the European languages have not seemed surprising. Thus, it was only toward the end of the 20th century, as more and more had become known about the grammatical properties of the languages of the rest of the world, that linguists realized how peculiar the core European languages are in some ways when seen in the world-wide context. From this perspective, Standard Average European may even appear as an "exotic language" (Dahl 1990).

A linguistic area can be recognized when a number of geographically contiguous languages share structural features which cannot be due to retention from a common proto-language and which give these languages a profile that makes them stand out among the surrounding languages. There is thus no minimum number of languages that a linguistic area comprises (*pace* Stolz 2001a). In principle, there could be a linguistic area consisting of just two languages (though this would be rather uninteresting), and there are also very large (continent-sized) linguistic areas (Dryer 1989a). Likewise, there is no minimum number of structural features that the languages must share in order to qualify as a *Sprachbund*. For instance, Jakobson (1931) establishes his "Eurasian linguistic area" on the basis of just two phonological features, but of course an area that shares more features is more interesting. As will be shown below, Standard Average European languages share over a dozen highly characteristic features, so we are dealing with a very interesting *Sprachbund*.

A linguistic area is particularly striking when it comprises languages from genealogically unrelated languages (like the South Asian linguistic area (→ Art. 109), or the Mesoamerican linguistic area (→ Art. 110)), but this is not a necessary feature of a *Sprachbund*. The Balkan languages are all Indo-European, but they are from different families within Indo-European (Romance, Slavic, Greek, Albanian), and not all languages of these families belong to the Balkan linguistic area, so nobody questions the validity of the Balkan *Sprachbund* (→ Art. 108). In the case of SAE, three entire branches of Indo-European (Romance, Germanic and Balto-Slavic) belong to the linguistic area. However, here too it is clear that we are not dealing with a genealogical grouping, because nobody ever proposed a branch of Indo-European that consists of precisely these three families. On the contrary, Indo-Europeanists typically assume a particularly close genealogical relationship between Italic and Celtic (and sometimes even an Italo-Celtic protolanguage), but Romance (the sole descendant of Italic) is inside SAE, while the Celtic languages do not belong to SAE. And since so much is known about the grammatical properties that Proto-Indo-European must have possessed, it is fairly easy to test whether an SAE feature is an Indo-Europeanism or not. As was shown in Haspelmath (1998), most of the characteristic SAE features (also called **Europeanisms** here) are not Indo-Europeanisms but later common innovations.

Thus, what needs to be shown in order to demonstrate that a structural feature is a Europeanism is

(i) that the great majority of core European languages possesses it;
(ii) that the geographically adjacent languages lack it (i.e. Celtic in the west, Turkic, eastern Uralic, Abkhaz-Adyghean and Nakh-Daghestanian in the east, and perhaps Afro-Asiatic in the south);
(iii) that the eastern Indo-European languages lack it (Armenian, Iranian, Indic); and
(iv) that this feature is not found in the majority of the world's languages.

Particularly the last point is not easy to demonstrate for many features because there are still far too few representative world-wide studies of grammatical structures, so to the extent that our knowledge about the world's languages is incomplete and biased, we cannot be sure about the European linguistic area. In this article, I will cite whatever information is available, and sometimes I will have to resort to impressionistic observations.

The designation "core European language" for members of SAE is deliberately vague, because the European linguistic area does not have sharp boundaries. It seems possible to identify a nucleus consisting of continental West Germanic languages (e.g. Dutch, German) and Gallo-Romance (e.g. French, Occitan, northern Italo-Romance). For this set of languages, van der Auwera (1998a: 824) proposes the name **Charlemagne Sprachbund**. Of the other languages, those which are geographically further from this center also seem to share significantly fewer SAE features, i.e. Ibero-Romance, insular Scandinavian (Icelandic and Faroese), East Slavic (Russian, Ukrainian, Belorussian) and Baltic. Even English, a West Germanic language, is clearly not within the nucleus. Of the non-Indo-European languages of Europe, the western Uralic languages (i.e. Hungarian and Balto-Finnic) are at least marginal members of Standard Average European; they are in many ways strikingly different from eastern Uralic. Maltese also exhibits a number of Europeanisms not shared by other Arabic varieties, but Basque seems to show very few of them. Somewhat further to the east, Georgian in the southern Caucasus (and perhaps the other Kartvelian languages) shares a surprising number of features with the core European languages. These impressionistic statements should eventually be quantified, but since it is not clear how much weight should be attached to each feature, this is not straightforward.

All of the features discussed below are syntactic, or concern the existence of certain morphosyntactic categories. I am not aware of any phonological properties characteristic of the core European languages (cf. Jakobson 1931: 182: "do six por ne udalos' najti ni odnogo obščeevropejskogo ... položitel'nogo fonologičeskogo priznaka [so far not a single Europe-wide positive phonological feature has been found]"). Perhaps phonologists have not looked hard enough, but at least one major recent study of word prosody in European languages has not found any phonological evidence for Standard Average European (van der Hulst et al. 1999, especially Maps 1–4) (but cf. Pisani 1969). A few generalizations are discussed by Ternes (1998), but he finds that in most respects European languages are unremarkable from a world-wide perspective. Perhaps the only features worth mentioning are the relatively large vowel inventories (no 3-vowel or 4-vowel inventories) and the relatively common consonant clusters (no restriction to CV syllables). In these respects, European languages are not average, but they are by no means extreme either.

2. The major Standard Average European features

In this section I will discuss a dozen grammatical features that are characteristic of the core European languages and that together define the SAE *Sprachbund*. In each case I will briefly define the feature and give a few examples from SAE languages. Then a name map, which indicates the approximate location of languages by the arrangement of (abbreviated) language names, shows the distribution of the various feature values within Europe. In each case it can be observed that the nuclear SAE languages are within the SAE isogloss, and that the marginal languages tend to be outside the isogloss to a greater or lesser extent. (Part of the material presented here was already included in Haspelmath 1998.)

2.1. Definite and indefinite articles

Both a definite and an indefinite article (e. g. English *the book/a book*; → Art. 62) exist in all Romance and almost all Germanic languages plus some of the Balkan languages (Modern Greek, perhaps Albanian and Bulgarian), but not outside Standard Average European. To be sure, their forms and syntactic behavior show considerable diversity (see Nocentini 1996 for an overview), but their very existence is characteristic enough. The distribution of articles in European languages is shown in Map 107.1. (Abbreviations of language names are given in the Appendix.)

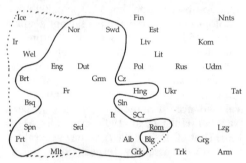

—— definite and indefinite article present
- - - - only definite article present

Map 107.1: Definite and indefinite article

In large parts of eastern Europe there are no articles at all (East Slavic, West Slavic, Finno-Ugrian other than Hungarian, Turkic, Nakh-Daghestanian, Kartvelian). Some neighboring non-SAE languages do have definite articles (e. g. Celtic, Semitic, Abkhaz, Mordvin), and Turkish has an indefinite article, but no neighboring non-SAE language has both definite and indefinite articles. The only exception among Germanic languages, Icelandic (which only has definite articles like nearby Celtic), is also the most peripheral Germanic language geographically. We can also be certain that the existence of definite and indefinite articles is not an Indo-Europeanism: The Iranian and Indic languages have generally lacked articles throughout their history.

World-wide, articles are not nearly as common as in Europe: According to Dryer's (1989b: 85) findings, "it appears that about a third of the languages of the world employ articles" (125 out of a sample of about 400 languages). Only 31 languages of those in Dryer's sample (i. e. less than 8%) have both definite and indefinite articles.

2.2. Relative clauses with relative pronouns

The type of relative clause found in languages such as German, French or Russian seems to be unique to Standard Average European languages. It is characterized by the following four features: The relative clause is postnominal, there is an inflecting relative pronoun, this pronoun introduces the relative clause, and the relative pronoun functions as a resumptive, i. e. it signals the head's role within the relative clause (cf. Lehmann 1984: 103–109, Comrie 1998). In English, a relative construction like *the suspicious woman whom I described* also displays all these features. Furthermore, in most SAE languages the relative pronoun is based on an interrogative pronoun (this is true of all Romance, all Slavic and some Germanic languages, Modern Greek, as well as Hungarian and Georgian). (Languages like German, whose relative pronoun is based on a demonstrative, or Finnish, which has a special relative pronoun, are not common.) The geographical distribution of the relative pronoun strategy is shown in Map 107.2.

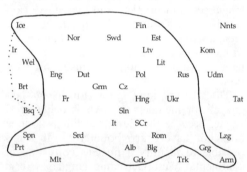

—— relative clause with introducing relative pronoun
- - - - only particle relative clause

Map 107.2: Two relative clause types in Europe

The only other type that is widespread in Europe is the postnominal relative clause introduced by a relative particle (Lehmann 1984: 85–87), which often occurs in the same language beside the resumptive relative pronoun type just described (an English example would be *the radio that I bought*). Particle relatives of this type exist in most Slavic and Romance languages, as well as in Scandinavian languages and Modern Greek, but also in Welsh and Irish (Lehmann 1984: 88–90). The relative particle is sometimes difficult to distinguish from a degenerate resumptive pronoun, and in many European languages it developed from a relative pronoun through the gradual loss of inflectional distinctions. However, this also means that the relative clause loses its specifically European flavor, because particle relatives are also attested widely elsewhere in the world (e. g. in Persian, Modern Hebrew, Nahuatl, Indonesian, Yoruba, and Thai, cf. Lehmann 1984: 85– 97).

However, the relative pronoun strategy clearly is typically European. It is not found in the eastern Indo-European languages, and as Comrie (1998: 61) notes, "relative clauses formed using the relative pronoun strategy are quite exceptional outside Europe, except as a recent result of the influence of European languages ... The relative pronoun strategy thus seems to be a remarkable areal typological feature of European languages, especially the standard written languages".

2.3. 'Have'-perfect

Another well-known feature typical of SAE languages is the (transitive) perfect formed by 'have' plus a passive participle (e. g. English *I have written*, Swedish *jag har skrivit*, Spanish *he escrito*; → Art. 59). A perfect of this kind exists in all Romance and Germanic languages plus some of the Balkan languages (Albanian, Modern Greek, Macedonian), and also in Czech (Garvin 1949: 84). These perfects do not all mean the same thing, because they are at different stages in the grammaticalization process: in French and German, the perfect can be used as a normal perfective past, including the function of a narrative tense, while in Spanish, English and Swedish the perfect has a distinct present-anterior meaning. What is important here is that they all must have had basically the same meaning when they were first created. The geographical distribution of 'have'-perfects in Europe is shown in Map 107.3.

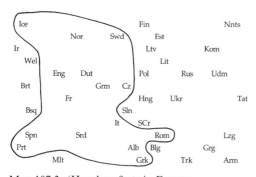

Map 107.3: 'Have'-perfects in Europe

In contrast to the languages just mentioned, in Slavic, Finno-Ugrian and Armenian the perfect is usually based on a participial construction with an active participle and a copula (e. g. Finnish *ole-n saa-nut* [be-1SG receive-PTCP] 'I have received'). Hungarian seems to lack a perfect completely. In some Nakh-Daghestanian languages (e. g. Lezgian and Godoberi), the perfect is formed on the basis of the past converb plus the copula. Georgian comes closest to the SAE prototype in that its transitive perfect is based on a passive participle, but this is combined with the copula rather than the transitive verb 'have', so that the perfect has a quasi-passive structure, with the agent in the dative case ('The letter is-written to-me', rather than 'I have-written the letter'). In Welsh, the perfect is formed with the preposition *wedi* 'after' ('She is after selling the house' for 'She has sold the house'). The eastern Indo-European languages also lack a 'have'-perfect (for instance, both Persian and Hindi/Urdu have a perfect based on a participle plus the copula, somewhat like Slavic and Armenian).

Dahl (1995, 1996: 365), taking a global perspective, notes that the 'have'-perfect is almost exclusively found in Europe. Now one might object that this is not a primitive feature of European languages. Many languages do not use a transitive 'have'-verb for indicating predicative possession at all, and it has in fact been suggested that the very existence of a transitive verb of predicative possession is a Europeanism (e. g. Lazard 1990: 246–47; Benveniste 1960 [1966: 195]: "L'expression la plus courante du rapport indiqué dans nos langues par *avoir* s'énonce à l'inverse par *être à* ... Telle est la situation dans la majorité des langues.") The restriction of a 'have'-perfect to Europe would then be just a consequence of this (cf. Dahl 1990: 7). However, so far no published research has documented an areal restriction for 'have' verbs. From Heine's (1997: 47–50, 240–44) survey of predicative possessive constructions, not much support can be drawn for such a claim. Still, this is an interesting idea to be addressed by further research. If 'have'-verbs turn out to be typical of Europe, that would fit with the tendency of European languages to have nominative experiencers in experiential verbs (see the next section).

2.4. Nominative experiencers

There are two ways of expressing experiencer arguments of verbs of sensation, emotion, cognition and perception: The experiencer may be assimilated to agents and coded as a nominative subject (e. g. *I like it*), or it may be assimilated to a patient or goal, so that the stimulus argument is coded as the nominative subject (e. g. *It pleases me*). In Bossong's (1998) typology, the first type is called *generalizing*, and the second type is called *inverting*. Bossong studies the expression of ten common experiential predicates in 40 European languages. He computes the relation between inverting predicates and generalizing predicates, arriving at figures between 0.0 for English (where all predicates are generalizing) and 5.0 for Lezgian (where all predicates are inverting). By arbitrarily dividing the languages into those showing predominant generalization (ratios between 0.0 and 0.8) and those showing predominant inversion (ratios between 0.8 and 5.0), we arrive at the geographical pattern shown in Map 107.4.

European is fairly clear: Indic languages are well-known for their "dative subjects" of experiencer verbs, so again the feature is not genetic (see also Masica 1976, especially Map 6, for the areal distribution of dative subjects in Eurasia and northern Africa). (See Haspelmath 2001 for more discussion of experiential predicates in European languages.)

2.5. Participial passive

Standard Average European languages typically have a canonical passive construction (→ Art. 67) formed with a passive participle plus an intransitive copula-like verb ('be', 'become', or the like). In this passive the original direct object becomes the subject and the original subject may be omitted, but it may also be expressed as an adverbial agent phrase. Such constructions occur in all Romance and Germanic languages, but also in

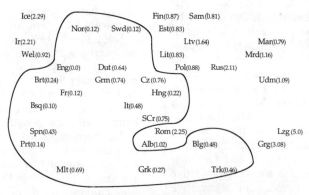

Map 107.4: Predominant generalization (center) vs. inversion (periphery)

Thus, Bossong's study basically confirms earlier claims (Lazard 1990: 246−47, Dahl 1990: 7) that the generalizing type is characteristic of SAE, although some of the figures are perhaps a bit surprising (e. g. the fact that Hungarian turns out to be more SAE than German or Dutch, and the inclusion of Turkish, but not Romanian or Albanian, with respect to this feature). It is not possible to explain everything here, but we evidently have before us a fairly typical SAE pattern with French and English at the center, Celtic (plus Icelandic this time) at the western margin, Balto-Slavic, Finno-Ugrian and Caucasian at the eastern margin, and fairly gradual transitions within the macro-areas. No systematic world-wide studies have been made, but at least the behavior of eastern Indo-

all Slavic (including East Slavic) and Balkan languages, as well as in Irish. The geographical distribution of such participial passives is shown in Map 107.5.

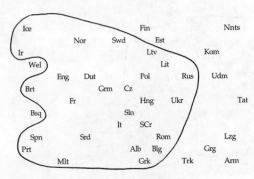

Map 107.5: Participial passives in Europe

No passives exist in Nakh-Daghestanian and in Hungarian, and passives of different formal types are found in Turkic, Georgian, and Armenian (stem suffix), in Basque, and in Celtic (cf. the Welsh 'get'-passive: 'Terry got his hitting by a snowball' for 'Terry got hit by a snowball'). Finnish and Irish have passives of a different syntactic type: In this construction, only the subject is backgrounded, while the direct object remains in its place.

Participial passives are very rare in languages other than Standard Average European. In Haspelmath (1990) I surveyed a world-wide sample of eighty languages and found that a passive exists only in the minority of the languages (thirty-one). Of these thirty-one languages, only four have a passive formed from a participle plus an intransitive auxiliary, and two of them are European languages (Latin and Danish). The most common formal type of passive is the stem suffix (found in twenty-five languages). Syntactically, the possibility of an adverbial agent phrase is also by no means universal, but it is characteristic of SAE languages (Lazard 1990: 246).

It must be admitted that the SAE status of this feature is less evident than that of the first two features because the eastern Indo-European languages also tend to have passives of this type. In fact, in my 1990 study, the two non-European languages with participle-auxiliary passives were Baluchi (an Iranian language) and Maithili (an Indic language). Thus, one might say that this feature is an Indo-European genealogical feature. However, at least the Celtic languages and Armenian, two non-SAE branches of Indo-European, do not have such passives, and Maltese is a non-Indo-European language with such a passive (calqued from Italian).

2.6. Anticausative prominence

There are three ways in which languages can express inchoative-causative alternations such as 'get lost/lose', 'break (intr.)/break (tr.)', 'rise/raise'. One is by means of a causative derivation (→ Art. 66), i.e. a derived verb based on the inchoative member of the alternation, e.g. Mongolian *xajl-uul-* 'melt (tr.)', from *xajl-* 'melt (intr.)'. The second is by means of an anticausative derivation, i.e. a derived verb based on the causative member, e.g. Russian *izmenit'-sja* 'change (intr.)', from *izmenit'* 'change (tr.)'. (The third type, in which neither member is derived from the other, i.e. *non-directed* alternations, will not be considered further here.) In Haspelmath (1993), I examined 31 verb pairs in 21 languages and found that languages differ greatly in the way inchoative-causative pairs are expressed: Some languages are *anticausative-prominent*, preferring anticausatives to causatives, while others are *causative-prominent*. It turns out that anticausative-prominence is a characteristic feature of SAE. In my sample, German, French, Romanian, Russian, Modern Greek and Lithuanian show the highest percentages of anticausative verb pairs (between 100% and 74% of all pairs that do not belong to the third, non-directed, type). The percentage in the European languages of my sample are shown in Map 107.6.

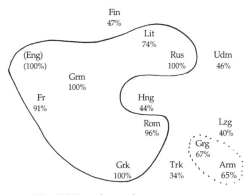

——— 70–100% anticausatives
- - - - 50–70% anticausatives

Map 107.6: Percentage of anticausative pairs

By contrast, Asian languages show much lower percentages of anticausatives, preferring causatives instead (e.g. Indonesian: 0%, Mongolian: 11%, Turkish: 34%, Hindi/Urdu 35%, Lezgian: 40%). An intermediate position is occupied by the Finno-Ugrian languages of eastern Europe (Finnish 47%, Udmurt 46%, Hungarian 44%) as well as Georgian (68%) and Armenian (65%). In a study involving more languages from Asia, Africa and Europe but less language-particular detail, Masica (1976) found a clear distinctive pattern for Europe: few causatives, heavy reliance on anticausatives (see especially his Maps 2 and 3). In a recent worldwide study of 18 verbs from 80 languages, Nichols et al. (to appear) report that in inchoative-causative pairs involving inanimate participants (i.e. the most typical subtype), the causative is generally favored worldwide and is strongly disfavored only in Europe.

Anticausative-prominence is not an Indo-Europeanism: Older Indo-European had a productive causative formation, which lost its productivity in the European branches, but continued to be productive in eastern Indo-European (cf. the low figure of 35% anticausatives in Hindi/Urdu).

2.7. Dative external possessors

In König & Haspelmath (1998) and Haspelmath (1999), we studied the distribution of external possessors in thirty European languages (→ Art. 73). We found three main language types in Europe: (i) those with dative external possessors, e. g. German *Die Mutter wäscht dem Kind die Haare* 'The mother is washing the child's hair', (ii) those with locative external possessors, e. g. Swedish *Någon bröt armen på honom* 'Someone broke his arm (lit. on him)', and (iii) those that lack external possessors and must express possessors NP-internally, e. g. English. The SAE feature, external possessors in the dative, is found in Romance, Continental West Germanic, Balto-Slavic, Hungarian and Balkan languages (Greek, Albanian). North Germanic and Balto-Finnic languages have locative external possessors, i. e. they are somewhat peripheral SAE languages with respect to this feature. The geographical distribution is shown in Map 107.7.

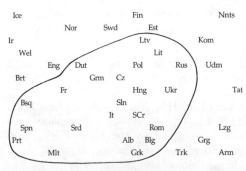

Map 107.7: Dative external possessor

In the far west (Welsh, Breton, English) and in the southeast (Turkish, Lezgian) of Europe there are languages which do not have external possessors at all. The eastern Indo-European languages Kurdish, Persian and Hindi/Urdu also belong to this type. Outside Europe a fourth type enjoys considerable popularity: the "relation-usurping" type, where he possessor "usurps" the syntactic relation of the possessum (e. g. Chichewa, a Bantu language, has 'The hyena ate the hare the fish' for 'The hyena ate the hare's fish'). This type is not found in Europe at all. Conversely, dative external possessors seem to be very rare outside Europe (the only case I am aware of is Ewe, cf. Ameka 1996), so this is a very robust example of an SAE feature.

2.8. Negative pronouns and lack of verbal negation

The areal distribution of negation in Europe has been studied in detail by Bernini & Ramat (1996) (see also Ramat & Bernini 1990). Here I will single out just one aspect of negation, the cooccurrence of verbal negation with negative indefinite pronouns. I distinguish two main types: (i) V + NI (verb + negative indefinite), e. g. German *Niemand kommt* 'nobody comes', and (ii) NV + NI (negated verb + negative indefinite), e. g. Modern Greek *Kanénas dhen érxete* 'nobody (lit. not) comes'. A third, mixed type might be distinguished in which verbal negation cooccurs with negative indefinites only when the indefinite follows the verb but not when it precedes it, e. g. Italian *Nessuno viene* 'nobody comes', but *Non ho visto nessuno* 'Not I have seen nobody'. For our purposes we can classify this type as a subtype of (i), V + NI.

The Standard Average European type is V + NI (cf. Bernini & Ramat 1996: 184, Haspelmath 1997: 202). It is found in French (if we disregard the particle *ne*), Occitan and all Germanic languages, as well as (in the mixed variety) in Ibero- and Italo-Romance and Albanian (but not in Romanian or other Balkan languages). The geographical distribution of the types is shown on Map 107.8.

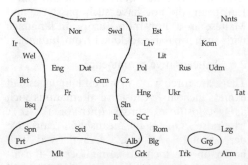

Map 107.8: Languages lacking verbal negation with a negative indefinite

All the eastern European languages (Balto-Slavic, Finno-Ugrian, Turkic, Nakh-Daghestanian) with the exception of Georgian, and the Celtic languages in the west show the NV + NI type. This type is also that of the eastern Indo-European languages (Iranian and Indic), as well as that of the clear majority of the world's languages: Kahrel (1996) has studied negation in a representative worldwide sample of 40 languages and found only five languages with V + NI negative patterns, one of which is the SAE language Dutch (the other four are Mangarayi (Australia), Evenki, Chukchi (Siberia), and Nama (southern Africa)), as against 41 NV + NI patterns, and seven others. I found a very similar pattern in my (non-representative) sample of 40 languages (Haspelmath 1997: 202).

2.9. Particles in comparative constructions

Comparative constructions were investigated by Stassen (1985) in a world-wide study of 19 languages (→ Art. 75). Stassen distinguishes six main ways in which the standard of comparison may be expressed: Three kinds of locative comparatives ('bigger from X', 'bigger to X', 'bigger at X'), the exceed comparative ('Y is big exceeding X'), the conjoined comparative ('Y is big, X is little'), and the particle comparative ('bigger than X'). The particle in this latter type is often related to a relative pronoun (cf. English *than/that*, Latin *quam/qui*), and the case marking of the standard is not influenced by the particle (so that it is possible to distinguish 'I love you more than she' from 'I love you more than her').

As Heine (1994) notes, the six types are not evenly distributed among the languages of the world. Of the 18 particle comparatives in Stassen's sample, 13 are in Europe, and of the 17 European languages in the sample, 13 have a particle comparative. The distribution within Europe again conforms to our expectations: Particle comparatives are found in Germanic, Romance, Balto-Slavic, the Balkans, Hungarian, Finnish and Basque, so this is the SAE type. The distribution is shown in Map 107.9.

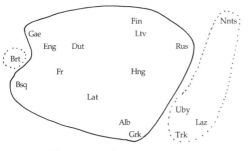

——— particle comparative
- - - - locative comparative

Map 107.9: Comparative types in Europe

The locative comparatives are all at the western fringe (Breton) or the eastern fringe of Europe (Finnish, Russian, Nenets, Ubykh, Turkish, Laz). The other two types do not exist at all in Europe — the exceed comparative is found particularly in Africa, and the conjoined comparative occurs only in the Americas and Oceania.

2.10. Relative-based equative constructions

Comparison of equality (equative constructions) is discussed less often than comparison of inequality, and nobody has undertaken a study of equatives on a world-wide scale. Still, there are good reasons to think that equative constructions provide evidence for Standard Average European (Haspelmath & Buchholz 1998). In Europe, many languages have an equative construction that is based on an adverbial relative-clause construction. For example, Catalan has *tan Z com X* 'as Z as X' (where Z is the adjective and X is the standard). Catalan *com* is an adverbial relative pronoun, and *tan* is a correlative demonstrative. A very similar construction is found elsewhere in Romance (Portuguese *tão Z como X*, Occitan *tan Z coma X*), in Germanic (German *so Z wie X*), in Slavic (Czech *tak Z jako X*, Russian *tak(oj) že Z kak X*), in Romani (*kade Z sar X*), in Hungarian (*olyan Z mint X*), in Finnish (*niin Z kuin X*), and in Georgian (*isetive Z rogorc X*). In the English construction, the relative-clause origin of *as* is not fully transparent synchronically, but diachronically *as* derives from a demonstrative (*eall swa* > *all so*) that was also used as a relative pronoun. In some Balkan languages, the correlative demonstrative is not used (e.g. Bulgarian *xubava kato tebe* 'as pretty as you'), but the standard marker is clearly of relative-pronoun origin. (There is probably some connection between the relative-pronoun origin of equative markers and the relative-pronoun origin of comparative standard markers that we saw in § 2.9.).

Non-SAE languages have quite different equative constructions. Many SOV languages in eastern Europe have a special equative standard marker (Lezgian *x̂iz*, Kalmyk *šing*; also Basque *bezain* and Maltese *daqs*), and the Celtic languages have a special (non-demonstrative) marker on the adjective (e.g. Irish *chomh Z le X* 'EQUATIVE Z with X'). In the Scandinavian languages, the word 'equally' is used on the adjective (e.g. Swedish *lika Z som X* 'equally Z as X'). The distribution of the relative-based equative construction in Europe is shown in Map 107.10, following Haspelmath & Buchholz (1998: 297).

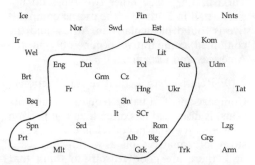

Map 107.10: Relative-based equative-constructions

Impressionalistically, relative-based equatives seem to be rare in the world's languages, and the eastern Indo-European languages do not seem to use them in general (however, a counterexample is Punjabi).

2.11. Subject person affixes as strict agreement markers

The majority of the world's languages have bound person markers on the verb that cross-refer to the verb's subject (or agent). When these subject affixes cooccur with overt subject NPs (full NPs or independent subject pronouns), they are called *agreement markers*. However, in most languages they can occur on their own and need not cooccur with overt subject NPs. For example, in the Bulgarian phrase *vie rabotite* 'you (pl.) work', we see the subject suffix *-ite* (2nd person plural) cooccurring with the independent subject pronoun *vie* 'you (pl.)', showing that *-ite* is an agreement marker. But in Bulgarian it is equally possible and probably more common to say just *rabotite* 'you (pl.) work', i.e. the subject suffix can have a referential function on its own. In German, by contrast, this is not possible: 'you work' is *ihr arbeit-et*. Since the agreement suffix *-et* does not have such an independent referential function, the subject pronoun *ihr* cannot be omitted. Languages like German are often called "non-pro-drop languages", and languages like Bulgarian are called "pro-drop languages"; better terms would be "strict-agreement languages" vs. "referential-agreement languages".

It has sometimes been thought that strict agreement, as exhibited by German, English, and French, is the norm and that referential agreement is somehow special. But in fact, referential agreement is far more widespread in the world's languages, and strict subject agreement is characteristic of a few European languages, some of which happen to be well-known. In her world-wide sample of 272 languages, Siewierska (1999) finds only two strict-agreement languages, Dutch (an SAE language) and Vanimo (a Papuan language of New Guinea). Siewierska further notes that outside of Europe, she is aware of only two additional strict-agreement languages that are not in her sample (Anejom and Labu, two Oceanic languages). Gilligan (1987) reached a similar conclusion on the basis of a sample of 100 languages. The distribution of strict subject agreement markers in some European languages is shown in Map 107.11.

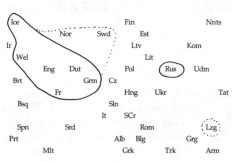

—— languages with strict subject agreement
---- languages with obligatory subject pronouns, lacking verb agreement

Map 107.11: Obligatory subject pronouns

The map shows two non-contiguous areas in which subject agreement suffixes cannot have a referential function: Germanic and Gallo-Romance languages with Welsh on the one hand, and Russian on the other. Perhaps only the western European area should be thought of as being relevant for SAE; in Russian, past-tense verbs do not have subject person affixes, so Russian is not a very good example of a strict-agreement language. In the eastern Nordic languages (Norwegian, Swedish, Danish), the subject pronouns are obligatory as they are in English, German or Icelandic, but the languages have lost agreement distinctions on the verb entirely (cf. Swedish *jag biter/du biter/han biter* 'I/you/he bite(s)', Icelandic *ég bít/þú bítur/hann bítur*). These languages are thus "non-pro-drop" in a sense, but they are not strict-agreement languages. English is approaching this type, as the only remnant of subject agreement is the 3rd person singular present-tense suffix *-s*. (There are also some languages of this type in the eastern Caucasus, and indeed in many other parts of the world, but they may never have had subject person agreement marking.)

2.12. Intensifier-reflexive differentiation

Intensifiers are words like English *self*, German *selbst*, French *même* and Russian *sam* that characterize a noun phrase referent as central as opposed to an implicit or explicit periphery (e.g. *The Pope himself gave us an audience*, i.e. not just the cardinals (→ Art. 57; König & Siemund 1999). In many languages, the intensifier expression is also used as a reflexive pronoun, for instance in Persian (*xod-aš* 'himself': *Hušang xod-aš* 'Hushang himself', and *Hušang xodaš-rā did* [Hushang self-ACC saw] 'Hushang saw himself'). However, a feature that is typical of SAE languages is the differentiation of reflexive pronouns and intensifiers (König & Haspelmath 1999). For instance, German has *sich* (reflexive) vs. *selbst* (intensifier), Russian has *sebja* vs. *sam*, Italian has *si* vs. *stesso*, Greek has *eaftó* vs. *ídhjos*. Map 107.12 shows the languages in Europe with special reflexive pronouns that are not identical to intensifiers.

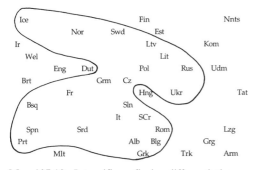

Map 107.12: Intensifier-reflexive differentiation

Intensifier-reflexive differentiation is not an Indo-Europeanism, because eastern Indo-European languages have the same expression for intensifiers and reflexives (e.g. Persian *xod-aš*, Hindi *aap*). There are no published world-wide studies yet, but it seems that non-differentiation is very common around the world, and while differentiation is also found elsewhere, it is not found in areas immediately adjacent to European languages.

3. Some further likely SAE features

In this section, I will mention a few features which are less well-documented than those in § 2, or whose geographical distribution is less striking, but which nevertheless seem good candidates for Europeanisms. No maps will be given for these features, and the evidence will be summarized only briefly.

3.1. Verb fronting in polar interrogatives

In the large majority of languages, polar interrogatives are marked by interrogative intonation or an interrogative particle or both (→ Art. 77). In his sample of 79 languages, Ultan (1978) found only seven languages showing the alternative strategy of verb fronting (often called "subject-verb inversion"). Of these, six are European (English, French, Romanian, Russian, Hungarian, Finnish; the seventh language is Malay), so that the SAE status of verb fronting seems beyond doubt. In fact, the large majority of Germanic, Romance and Slavic languages (plus Modern Greek) appear to have verb fronting in polar questions in one form or another. The three European languages for which Ultan explicitly reports that no verb fronting occurs are peripheral: Basque, Gaelic and Lithuanian. Furthermore, SAE languages are characterized by the absence of an interrogative particle. In Ultan's data, the nine European languages exhibiting a particle in polar questions are all peripheral to a greater or lesser extent: Basque, Irish, Scottish Gaelic, Albanian, Hungarian, Lithuanian, Russian, Finnish, Turkish (and I can add Nakh-Daghestanian). Verb fronting in polar questions was suggested as a Europeanism already by Beckman (1934) (cf. Dahl 1990).

3.2. Comparative marking of adjectives

Most European languages have special forms for adjectives occurring in comparative constructions. For instance, English uses the suffix *-er* in this way (*The dog is bigg-er than the cat*). Such an inflectional marker of adjectives is not common in the world's languages outside of Europe. Some languages use some kind of adverbial particle modifying the adjective ('more'), but perhaps the most common type is represented by Japanese, where the comparative semantics is carried by the standard marker alone (e.g. *inu-ga neko yori ookii* [dog-SUBJ cat from big] 'the dog is bigger than the cat').

Special comparative forms are found in all Germanic, Balto-Slavic and Balkan languages (with the exception of Romanian and Albanian), and most Romance languages preserve at least four suppletive forms (e.g.

Italian *maggiore* 'bigger', *minore* 'smaller', *peggiore* 'worse', *migliore* 'better'). Comparative forms also exist in Basque (e. g. *haundi-ago* 'bigg-er'), Hungarian (*nagy-obb* 'bigg-er'), Finnish (*iso-mpi* 'bigg-er'), and other Finno-Ugrian languages.

Comparative forms are not completely unknown outside of Europe. Arabic has a special comparative form (e. g. *ʔakbar* 'bigger', from *kabiir* 'big'), but it is unique among Afro-Asiatic languages in this respect. Old Indo-Iranian languages had comparative forms, and the modern Iranian languages have preserved them to some extent (e. g. Persian *-tær*, Zaza *-êr*). But further east, in modern Indic, the comparative does not exist anymore, and languages like Hindi-Urdu and Bengali use a construction analogous to the Japanese example just cited. Similarly, in the Uralic languages, the further east we go, the fewer comparatives we find. For instance, Khanty (a Finno-Ugrian language spoken in western Siberia, i. e. outside of Europe) does have a comparative form in *-sək* (e. g. *jam-sək* 'better'), which is used when no standard is present. But in a complete comparative construction, no marking is found on the adjective (e. g. *naŋ ke:se:-n e:welt jam* [you knife-2SG from good] 'better than your knife', Nikolaeva 1999: 21).

Thus, although this feature is not confined to Europe, it is typical of a SAE feature in that it is robustly present in western Indo-European and Uralic languages, but gets rarer the further east we go in these families.

3.3. "A and-B" conjunction

The feature discussed in this section is less distinctive than the others mentioned so far, but I hope to show that it is not at all devoid of interest. Stassen (2000) offers the first world-wide typological study of NP conjunction strategies, based on a sample of 260 languages (→ Art. 82). He distinguishes two basic types, *and*-languages (using a symmetric particle) and *with*-languages (using an asymmetric comitative marker). Two thirds of Stassen's sample languages are *and*-languages, and since SAE clearly belongs to this type, too, it is not a very distinctive property. *And*-languages cover all of northern Eurasia, South Asia, the Middle East and northern Africa, Australia, New Guinea, and parts of Central and South America. *With*-languages are encountered in sub-Saharan Africa, East and Southeast Asia, the islands of Oceania, and large areas of North and South America.

However, within the *and*-languages there are several sub-types according to the position of the particle, which we may call "A and-B", "A-and B", "A-and B-and", and "A B-and" (of the remaining logical possibilities, "and-A B" seems to be inexistent, and "and-A and-B" occurs only as a secondary pattern). Most European languages, and in particular all SAE languages, belong to the sub-type "A and-B". The types "A-and B-and" and "A-and B" are found in some languages of the Caucasus and in some Turkic languages, as well as scattered throughout northern Eurasia and South Asia (e. g. in Abkhaz, Archi, Persian, Sinhalese, Tamil, Burmese, Korean according to Stassen; Stassen also points out that there is a correlation with verb-final word order here). Furthermore, some peripheral European languages make restricted use of the *with*-strategy (e. g. Russian *my s toboj* 'I and you', lit. 'we with you', and also Old Irish, Lithuanian, Polish and Hungarian, according to Stassen). Taken together, these data do show that belonging to the "A and-B" type is not a trivial feature of the SAE linguistic area.

3.4. Comitative-instrumental syncretism

In all SAE languages, the preposition that expresses accompaniment (= comitative) also serves to express the instrument role (e. g. English *with*: *with her husband/with the hammer*). Such languages are said to exhibit comitative-instrumental syncretism. Stolz (1996) studied comitative and instrumental markers in a world-wide sample of 323 languages and found that this kind of syncretism is typical of Europe. Non-European languages more commonly possess separate markers for these two semantic roles (e. g. Swahili *na* 'with (comitative)', *kwa* 'with (instrumental)'. As Table 107.1 shows, about two thirds of Stolz's sample languages are non-syncretic, and only one quarter is syncretic. (The remaining languages belong to a mixed type, which I ignore here for the sake of simplicity; thus, the percentages do not add up to 100%.)

Two areas diverge significantly from the general trend: Oceania has far less syncretism than the world average, and Europe has far more syncretism than the world average. When we look at the pattern within Europe, it becomes even clearer that we are dealing with an SAE feature (as Stolz recognizes, cf. 1996: 120). Of the 16 non-syncretic languages in Europe, 10 are Caucasian languages, i. e. they are clearly outside of SAE, and one is

Table 107.1: Comitative-instrumental: Syncretic and non-syncretic languages

	syncretic (e.g. English)		non-syncretic (e.g. Swahili)	
	languages	percentage	languages	percentage
Europe	25	49%	16	31%
Africa	20	31%	38	58%
Americas	16	21%	54	69%
Asia	12	18%	47	71%
Oceania	6	10%	54	86%
World	79	24%	209	65%

only politically, not anthropologically, in Europe (Greenlandic). Four of the remaining five languages are also otherwise not typical instances of SAE (Basque, Finnish, Maltese, Mari). And when we look at the 38 Indo-European languages in Stolz's sample, we see that syncretism cannot be regarded as an Indo-Europeanism: Of the eight Indo-European languages not spoken in Europe, only three show syncretism, while five show non-syncretism. Thus, in Asia Indo-European languages behave like Asian languages, and there is no general pattern for Indo-European.

3.5. Suppletive second ordinal

Most languages have a suppletive form of the ordinal numeral 'first', i.e. a form not derived from the cardinal numeral 'one'. An example is German, where '1st' is *erster* (unrelated to *eins* '1'), contrasting with other ordinals such as *zweiter* '2nd' (cf. *zwei* '2'), *vierter* '4th' (cf. *vier* '4'), and so on. In Stolz's (2001b) study of 100 languages world-wide, there are 95 languages with special ordinal numerals, and of these, 78 have a suppletive word for 'first'. Thus, languages that say (literally) 'oneth' for '1st' are not common. However, the same sample has only 22 languages in which the word for '2nd', too, is suppletive and not derived from '2' (e.g. English *second*). Thus, most languages have (literally) 'twoth' for '2nd'. The 22 languages that have a suppletive '2nd' word are heavily concentrated in Europe: 17 are European languages, and this type is clearly the majority within Europe (which is represented by 27 languages in Stolz's sample). Of the 10 European languages that do not have a suppletive second ordinal, six are clearly outside SAE (Basque, Turkish, Armenian, Georgian, Lezgian, Greenlandic). Among SAE languages, only some Balkan languages (Romanian, Albanian, Romani) and German lack a suppletive second ordinal.

This is clearly a very marginal feature in grammar, but it is intriguing that it should show such a clear geographical distribution.

3.6. Some other characteristics of SAE

The features examined so far present the most striking evidence for Standard Average European, but there are probably many more features that will turn out to be characteristic of the core European languages in one way or another. In this subsection, several such candidates will be mentioned briefly. The first few features in the following list are purely negative: At first glance, this may seem odd, but of course the lack of a category that is widespread elsewhere is no less significant than the presence of a category that is rare elsewhere.

(i) Lack of an alienable/inalienable opposition in adnominal possession (→ Art. 72). In Nichols's (1992) world-wide sample, almost half of the languages show such an opposition, but no European language does (1992: 123). More generally, this opposition is rarer in the Old World and common in the New World, but in Europe it is even less common than in Africa and Asia.

(ii) Lack of an inclusive/exclusive opposition in first person non-singular pronouns. Again, this opposition is commonest in the New World and in the Pacific region, but in Europe it is even rarer than in Africa and Asia, as was shown by Nichols (1992: 123).

(iii) Lack of reduplicating constructions. I have no systematic evidence to back up the claim that this is a characteristic feature of European languages, but reduplication is so common across languages that its almost total absence in the core European languages becomes striking. (Interestingly, reduplication existed in older Indo-European languages at least in one construction, the perfect, but even here it was lost entirely by the Middle Ages.)

(iv) Discourse pragmatic notions such as topic and focus are expressed primarily by sentence stress and word order differences (Lazard 1998: 116). Only the Celtic languages and French give a very prominent role to clefting, and particles marking discourse pragmatic notions are virtually unknown.

(v) SVO basic word order at the level of the clause. This feature is of course found elsewhere in the world, but in Europe it correlates particularly well with the other SAE features. The Celtic languages in the west have VSO order (except for Breton, which is also otherwise more SAE than Irish and Welsh), and the eastern languages have SOV word order. Interestingly, Balto-Finnic (Finnish, Estonian, etc.) and (less unequivocally) Hungarian have SVO word order, whereas the eastern Uralic languages have SOV. Similarly, the eastern Indo-European languages tend to show SOV word order. (See Dryer 1998 for more on word order in the languages of Europe.)

(vi) European languages tend to have just one converb (→ Art. 83) (cf. Nedjalkov 1998). For instance, Romance languages have the *gerundio/gérondif*, English has the *-ing*-form, and Slavic and Balkan languages have their adverbial participle. The Celtic languages in the west completely lack such a form, and the languages east of SAE tend to have more than one converb. Otherwise the core European languages tend to have adverbial conjunctions (→ Art. 63) to make adverbial clauses. According to Kortmann (1997: 344), they have "a large, semantically highly differentiated inventory of free adverbial subordinators placed in clause-initial position". More generally, they tend to have finite rather than non-finite subordinate strategies (→ Art. 100), though a multi-purpose infinitive usually exists (except for the Balkan languages).

(vii) European languages usually have a special construction for negative coordination, e. g. English *neither A nor B*, Italian *né A né B*, Russian *ni A ni B*, Dutch *noch A noch B*, Hungarian *sem A sem B*. Again, no worldwide study has been published, but such a negative coordinating construction is rarely reported from languages outside Europe (cf. Haspelmath to appear).

(viii) SAE languages have a large number of characteristic properties in the area of phasal adverbials (expressions like *already, still, no longer, not yet*) (van der Auwera 1998b). These are rather well documented, but for the detail I have to refer the reader to van der Auwera's thorough study.

(ix) "Preterite decay": the loss of the old preterite and its replacement by the former present perfect. This is a change that occurred in the last millenium in French, German and northern Italian, as well as in some other adjacent European languages (cf. Thieroff 2000: 285). Its distribution is far narrower than that of the other Europeanisms, but it is the only feature of those studied by Thieroff whose geography comes close to Standard Average European (cf. also Abraham 1999).

Quite a few additional features have been mentioned in the earlier literature as characteristic of SAE, but earlier authors have sometimes neglected to make sure that a proposed Europeanism is not also common elsewhere in the world. Most of Whorf's original examples of SAE features seem to be of this kind. For instance, he notes that in contrast to SAE, Hopi lacks "imaginary plurals" (such as 'ten days', according to Whorf a "metaphorical aggregate"). But of course, we have no evidence that such plurals of time-span nouns are in any way characteristic of European languages. It may well be that they are common throughout the world. (To give Whorf his due, it must be added that he was not interested in demonstrating that SAE languages form a *Sprachbund*. He just used this term as a convenient abbreviation for "English and other European languages likely to be known to the reader", without necessarily implying that these languages are an exclusive club.)

4. Degrees of membership in SAE

Membership in a *Sprachbund* is typically a matter of degree. Usually there is a core of languages that clearly belong to the *Sprachbund*, and a periphery of surrounding languages that share features of the linguistic area to a greater or lesser extent.

In order to quantify the degrees of membership in SAE, a simple procedure suggests itself that was first applied to areal typology by van der Auwera (1998a). In addition to individual maps in which the lines denote isoglosses (as in Maps 107.1–12), we can combine different features in a single map and show the number of isoglosses shared by the language. Map 107.13 shows such a "cluster map" in which the lines stand for "quantified isoglosses" (or "isopleths"). The map combines nine features of § 2.: definite and indefinite articles, relative clauses with relative pronouns, 'have'-perfect, participial passive, dative external possessors, negative pronouns and lack of verbal negation, relative-based equative constructions, subject person affixes as strict agreement markers, and intensifier-reflexive differentiation. The languages in the nucleus (French and German) show the SAE value in all nine of these features. The languages in the next layer (Dutch, other Romance, Albanian) show eight features, the next layer (English, Greek, Romanian) shows seven features, and so on. In this map, the resulting picture is actually very clear, because the SAE area with at least five SAE features stands out from the remaining languages, which have at most two SAE features.

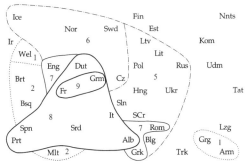

Map 107.13: A cluster map combining nine features

Such cluster maps are thus a fairly direct representation of degrees of membership in a linguistic area. But of course, the cluster map directly reflects the choice of features that are combined, and this choice is always somewhat arbitrary. Of the twelve features in § 2, only nine were selected here because information on the other three was incomplete. Ideally, the features of § 3 should have been added, too. But it seems to me that the main results of Map 107.13 would not be changed (this map can also be compared to the very similar map in van der Auwera (1998a: 823), which combines five adverbial features or feature clusters). The most striking features of Map 107.13 are:

(a) The nucleus of Standard Average European is formed by French and German (a finding that led van der Auwera (1998a: 824) to propose the term *Charlemagne Sprachbund* for the nuclear area of SAE). In view of the historical role played by speakers of these two languages both in the early medieval history of continental Europe and in the very recent attempt at European unification, this is of course an extremely intriguing result.

(b) The southern European languages (both Romance and Balkan languages) are at least as close, if not closer to the nucleus than the northern languages and English. This means that it is misleading to call SAE features "Western European features", as is sometimes done. It is true that the Slavic languages in the east lack many SAE features, but the Balkan languages are generally more SAE than Slavic, although they are not western European.

(c) England stands somewhat apart from the European nucleus (as noted also by van der Auwera 1998a: 823), although it is closely related genealogically to German and has been thoroughly influenced by French. Since English is currently the dominant language throughout the world, it is worth pointing out its somewhat marginal status among its European sister languages.

It is important to keep in mind that the features on which Map 107.13 is based have not been selected randomly and are thus by no means representative of the morphosyntactic features of European languages. They were included precisely because they were known to show a distribution that supports the SAE hypothesis. Thus, no claim is made that all (or even the majority of) features will show a similar distribution. It is perfectly possible that we will some day discover another *Sprachbund*, based on a different set of features, that has Russian at its core and extends all the way to western Siberia in the east and central Asia in the south, but within Europe comprises only the Slavic, Balkan, and Scandinavian languages. This area would overlap with SAE, but it would not contradict it. Thus, a language may in principle belong to different linguistic areas, and different linguistic areas may coexist "on top of" each other. Since areal typology is only in its infancy, we do not know how common such situations are, but nothing in the logic of a *Sprachbund* implies that the world should be exhaustively divisible into non-overlapping *Sprachbünde*.

In fact, a number of smaller linguistic areas within Europe have been proposed in the literature (apart from the Balkan area, whose importance is not doubted by anyone),

e. g. by Lewy (1942), Wagner (1959), Décsy (1973), Haarmann (1976), and Ureland (1985) (cf. also Wintschalek 1993 on a Volga-Kama area). Currently the most thoroughly studied areas are the Circum-Baltic area (cf. Stolz 1991, Dahl & Koptjevskaja-Tamm (eds.) 2001) and the Mediterranean area (cf. Cristofaro & Putzu (eds.) 2000). However, no strong claims about a Circum-Baltic or a Mediterranean linguistic area seem to have been made as a result of these studies.

5. How did SAE come into being?

Linguistic areas arise through language contact, but precisely which contact situation gave rise to Standard Average European is not immediately clear. And what is the source of the various Europeanisms: Who borrowed from whom? A full discussion of the sociohistorical, cultural and sociolinguistic issues is beyond the scope of this article, so I will restrict myself here to mentioning just five possibilities:

(i) retention of Proto-Indo-European structures and assimilation of some non-Indo-European languages to Indo-European language structure;
(ii) influence from a common substratum of a pre-Indo-European population in Europe;
(iii) contacts during the great transformations at the transition from late antiquity to the early Middle Ages in Europe;
(iv) the official language (Latin) and the common European culture of the Middle Ages;
(v) the common European culture of modern times, from the Renaissance to the Enlightenment.

The fifth possibility must be rejected because a time depth of 300–500 years is not sufficient to account for grammatical commonalities of the kind discussed above. If lexical similarities between the European languages are discussed — for instance neoclassical compounding (*socio-/paleo-/ortho-/demo-, -graphy/-logy/-cracy*, etc.) or idiomatic structure (e. g. *ivory tower/torre d'avorio/Elfenbeinturm, as poor as a church mouse/pauvre comme un rat d'église/arm wie eine Kirchenmaus*) — then the last several centuries are the appropriate time frame for explaining the historical links, but the basic syntactic structures common to SAE languages must be older.

The first possibility must be rejected because the great majority of Europeanisms are innovations with respect to Proto-Indo-European. For instance, as far as we know, Proto-Indo-European did not have articles, a 'have'-perfect, "A and-B" conjunction, strict subject agreement, particle comparatives, or relative clauses with relative pronouns (cf. Lehmann 1974, Haspelmath 1998). With respect to Proto-Indo-European, and also with respect to the oldest Indo-European languages attested in Europe (Ancient Greek, Old Latin, Gothic), Standard Average European is clearly an innovation.

The second possibility, a pre-Indo-European substratum in Europe causing the SAE features, would be extremely difficult to demonstrate, but it might be worth pursuing. It is intriguing to note that the geographical space occupied by SAE languages coincides fairly precisely with the area of the Old European hydronymy, i. e. the homogeneous layer of river names discovered by Hans Krahe (see Vennemann 1994 for recent discussion). Vennemann (1994) proposes that these Old European hydronyms were not coined by an early prehistoric Indo-European population, but by a pre-Indo-European people which he calls Vasconic (the only surviving Vasconic language being Basque). Furthermore, the Old European hydronymy is hardly attested in the British Isles, where the Celtic languages are spoken, i. e. they could not have been influenced by the Vasconic substratum. This is in perfect harmony with the well-motivated hypothesis that the Celtic languages acquired some of their striking features from a different substratum related to the Afro-Asiatic languages (Pokorny 1927–30, Gensler 1993).

The main argument against the substratum view is that the SAE features seem to be gaining ground too late for a pre-Indo-European substratum to have caused them. Some SAE features appear only in the first millenium CE, but also the earlier features usually come fairly late, so that the earliest records of Indo-European-languages in Europe still show traces of the Proto-Indo-European patterns (e. g. causatives, relative clauses, locative comparative, "A B-and" conjunction). If these SAE features were caused by a substratum, then we should have much more evidence of the population speaking this substratum language. Moreover, a Vasconic substratum can hardly account for the SAE features because modern Basque is in most relevant ways very much unlike the SAE languages.

Of the remaining two possibilities, we can probably exclude option (iv) (the influence of Latin in the Middle Ages), because most SAE features were absent in Latin and developed only in the Romance languages. There are only two features for which Latin influence is a likely factor: negation and relative pronouns. In the case of these two features, the standard languages sometimes show deviations from the vernacular dialects, so at least the written standard languages may have been influenced by Latin, the European written language par excellence for many centuries. Thus, non-standard English has constructions like *I won't do nothing* ('I won't do anything'), and similarly in non-standard German and French (cf. Haspelmath 1997: 205). Analogously, Latin-type relative pronouns occur widely in the standard languages of Europe, but vernacular speech often prefers relative particles (Lehmann 1984: 88, 109). However, Latin probably only helped to reinforce these structures in those languages where they existed already independently as variants.

Thus, we are left with option (iii), the time of the great migrations at the transition between antiquity and the Middle Ages. This seems to be the appropriate time frame at least for articles, the 'have'-perfect, the participial passive, anticausatives, negative indefinites, nominative experiencers and verb fronting. The rise of these constructions can be observed only with difficulty because they were by and large absent in the written classical languages but seem to be well in place once the vernacular languages appear in the written record toward the end of the first millennium CE (cf. also Fehling 1980). This hypothesis derives some further plausibility from the fact that language contact must have been particularly intensive and effective during the great migrations, and in the case of French and northern Italian we have ample records of the lexical effects of these contacts. However, it is not so easy to fit features such as particle comparatives, „A and-B" conjunction and relative pronouns into this picture, because these features seem to have developed around the middle of the first millenium BC or even earlier (cf. Haspelmath 1998). Of course, we must always reckon with the possibility (or even likelihood) that different SAE features are due to different historical circumstances, and the correct picture is likely to be much more complicated than we can imagine at the moment, let alone discuss in this article.

6. Abbreviations of language names

Alb	Albanian
Arm	Armenian
Blg	Bulgarian
Brt	Breton
Bsq	Basque
Cz	Czech
Dut	Dutch
Eng	English
Est	Estonian
Fin	Finnish
Fr	French
Gae	Scots Gaelic
Grg	Georgian
Grk	Greek
Grm	German
Hng	Hungarian
Ice	Icelandic
Ir	Irish
It	Italian
Kom	Komi
Lat	Latin
Laz	Laz
Lit	Lithunian
Ltv	Latvian
Lzg	Lezgian
Mar	Mari
Mlt	Maltese
Mrd	Mordvin
Nnts	Nenets
Nor	Norwegian
Pol	Polish
Prt	Portuguese
Rom	Romanian
Rus	Russian
SAE	Standard Average European
Sam	Saami
SCr	Serbian/Croatian
Sln	Slovene
Spn	Spanish
Srd	Sardinian
Swd	Swedish
Tat	Tatar
Trk	Turkish
Uby	Ubykh
Udm	Udmurt
Ukr	Ukrainian
Wel	Welsh

7. References

Abraham, Werner. 1999. "Preterite decay as a European areal phenomenon". *Folia Linguistica* 33.1: 11–18.

Ameka, Felix. 1996. "Body parts in Ewe grammar". In: Chappell, Hilary & McGregor, William (eds.). *The grammar of inalienability: A typological perspective on body part terms and the part-whole relation*. Berlin: Mouton de Gruyter, 783−840.

Bechert, Johannes & Bernini, Giuliano & Buridant, Claude (eds.). 1990. *Toward a typology of European languages*. (Empirical Approaches to Language Typology, 8.) Berlin: Mouton de Gruyter.

Beckman, Natanael. 1934. *Västeuropeisk syntax: Några nybildningar i nordiska och andra västeuropeiska språk*. [West European syntax: Some innovative constructions in the Nordic and other West European languages.] Göteborg: Göteborgs högskolas årsskrift.

Benveniste, Émile. 1960. "'Être' et 'avoir' dans leurs fonctions linguistiques". *Bulletin de la Societé de linguistique de Paris* 55: 113−134. (Reprinted in: Benveniste, Émile. 1966. *Problèmes de linguistique générale*. Paris: Gallimard, 187−207.)

Bernini, Giuliano & Ramat, Paolo. 1996. *Negative sentences in the languages of Europe: A typological approach*. (Empirical Approaches to Language Typology, 16.) Berlin: Mouton de Gruyter.

Bossong, Georg. 1998. "Le marquage de l'expérient dans les langues d'Europe". In: Feuillet (ed.), 259−294.

Comrie, Bernard. 1998. "Rethinking the typology of relative clauses". *Language Design* 1: 59−86.

Cristofaro, Sonia & Putzu, Ignazio (eds.) 2000. *Languages in the Mediterranean area: typology and convergence*. Milan: Franco Angeli.

Dahl, Östen. 1990. "Standard Average European as an exotic language". In: Bechert et al. (eds.), 3−8.

Dahl, Östen. 1995. "Areal tendencies in tense-aspect systems." In: Bertinetto, Pier Marco & Bianchi, Valentina & Dahl, Östen & Squartini, Mario (eds.) *Temporal reference, aspect and actionality*, vol. 2: *Typological perspectives*. Turin: Rosenberg & Sellier, 11−28.

Dahl, Östen. 1996. "Das Tempussystem des Deutschen im typologischen Vergleich." In: Lang, Ewald & Zifonun, Gisela (eds.). *Deutsch − typologisch*, Berlin: de Gruyter, 359−368.

Dahl, Östen (ed.). 2000. *Tense and aspect in the languages of Europe*. (Empirical Approaches to Language Typology-EUROTYP, 20−6.) Berlin: Mouton de Gruyter.

Dahl, Östen & Koptjevskaja-Tamm, Maria (eds.) (2001) *Circum-Baltic languages*. Vol 1−2. Amsterdam: Benjamins.

Décsy, Gyula. 1973. *Die linguistische Struktur Europas*. Wiesbaden: Harrassowitz.

Dryer, Matthew. 1989a. "Large linguistic areas and language sampling". *Studies in Language* 13: 257−92.

Dryer, Matthew. 1989b. "Article-noun order". *Chicago Linguistic Society* 25: 83−97.

Dryer, Matthew. 1998. "Aspects of word order in the languages of Europe". In: Siewierska, Anna (ed.) *Constituent order in the languages of Europe*. Berlin: Mouton de Gruyter, 283−319.

Fehling, Detlev. 1980. "The origins of European syntax". *Folia Linguistica Historica*, 1: 353−387.

Feuillet, Jack (ed.). 1998. *Actance et valence dans les langues d'Europe*. (Empirical Approaches to Language Typology-EUROTYP, 20−2.) Berlin: Mouton de Gruyter.

Garvin, Paul. 1949. "Standard Average European and Czech". *Studia Linguistica* 3: 65−85.

Gensler, Orin D. 1993. *A typological evaluation of Celtic/Hamito-Semitic syntactic parallels*. Ph. D. dissertation, University of California at Berkeley.

Gilligan, Gary M. 1987. *A cross-linguistic approach to the pro-drop parameter*. Ph. D. dissertation, USC.

Haarmann, Harald. 1976. *Aspekte der Arealtypologie: Die Problematik der europäischen Sprachbünde*. Tübingen: Narr.

Haspelmath, Martin. 1990. "The grammaticization of passive morphology". *Studies in Language*, 14.1: 25−71.

Haspelmath, Martin. 1993. "More on the typology of inchoative/causative verb alternations". In: Comrie, Bernard & Polinsky, Maria (eds.). *Causatives and transitivy*. Amsterdam: Benjamins, 87−120.

Haspelmath, Martin. 1997. *Indefinite pronouns*. Oxford: Oxford University Press.

Haspelmath, Martin. 1998. "How young is Standard Average European?" *Language Sciences* 20: 271−87.

Haspelmath, Martin. 1999. "External possession in an European areal perspective". In: Payne, Doris L. & Barshi, Immanuel (eds.) *External possession*. (Typological Studies in Language, 39.) Amsterdam: Benjamins, 109−135.

Haspelmath, Martin. 2001. "Non-canonical marking of core arguments in European languages". In: Aikhenvald, Alexandra & Dixon, R. M. W. (eds.) *Non-canonical subjects and objects*. (Typological Studies in Language) Amsterdam: Benjamins.

Haspelmath, Martin. To appear. "Coordination". In: Shopen, Timothy (ed.) *Language typology and linguistic description*. 2nd ed. Cambridge: Cambridge University Press.

Haspelmath, Martin & Buchholz, Oda. 1998. "Equative and similative constructions in the languages of Europe". In: van der Auwera (ed.), 277−334.

Heine, Bernd. 1994. "Areal influence on grammaticalization". In: Pütz, Martin (ed.) *Language contact and language conflict*. Amsterdam: Benjamins, 55−68.

Heine, Bernd. 1997. *Possession: Cognitive sources, forces, and grammaticalization*. Cambridge: Cambridge University Press.

Jakobson, Roman. 1931. "K xarakteristike evrazijskogo jazykovogo sojuza". [Characterizing the Eurasian linguistic area.] Reprinted in: Jakobson,

Roman. 1971. *Selected writings, vol. I*. The Hague: Mouton, 144–201.

Kahrel, Peter. 1996. *Aspects of negation*. Ph. D. dissertation: University of Amsterdam.

König, Ekkehard & Haspelmath, Martin. 1998. "Les constructions à possesseur externe dans les langues d'Europe". In: Feuillet (ed.), 525–606.

König, Ekkehard & Haspelmath, Martin. 1999. "Der europäische Sprachbund". In: Reiter, Norbert (ed.). *Eurolinguistik*. Wiesbaden: Harrassowitz, 111–127.

König, Ekkehard & Siemund, Peter. 1999. "Intensifiers and reflexives: a typological perspective." In: Frajzyngier, Zygmunt & Curl, Traci S. (eds.) *Reflexives: Forms and functions* (Typological studies in language, 40.). Amsterdam: Benjamins, 41–74.

Kortmann, Bernd. 1997. *Adverbial subordination: A typology and history of adverbial subordinators based on European languages*. Berlin: Mouton de Gruyter.

Lazard, Gilbert. 1990. "Caractéristique actancielles de l'"européen moyen type'." In: Bechert et al. (eds.), 241–53.

Lazard, Gilbert. 1998. „Définition des actants dans les langues européennes". In: Feuillet (ed.), 11–146.

Lehmann, Christian. 1984. *Der Relativsatz*. Tübingen: Narr.

Lehmann, Winfred P. 1974. *Proto-Indo-European syntax*. Austin: University of Texas Press.

Lewy, Ernst. 1942. *Der Bau der europäischen Sprachen*. (Proceedings of the Royal Irish Academy, Vol. 48). Dublin: Hodges & Figgis.

Masica, Colin P. 1976. *Defining a linguistic area*. Chicago: University of Chicago Press.

Nedjalkov, Igor' V. 1998. "Converbs in the languages of Europe". In: van der Auwera (ed.), 421–455.

Nichols, Johanna. 1992. *Linguistic diversity in space and time*. Chicago: The University of Chicago Press.

Nichols, Johanna & Peterson, David A. & Barnes, Jonathan (to appear). "Causativizing and decausativizing languages". Ms., University of California, Berkeley,

Nikolaeva, Irina. 1999. *Ostyak*. Munich: Lincom Europa.

Nocentini, Alberto. 1996. "Tipologia e genesi dell'articolo nelle lingue europee". *Archivio Glottologico Italiano* 81.1: 3–44.

Pisani, Vittore. 1969. "Tipi d'accento nelle lingue dell'Europa". In: *Actes du Xe Congres International des Linguistes, Bucuresti*, vol. II, 57–60. Bucuresti.

Pokorny, Julius. 1927–30. "Das nicht-indogermanische Substrat im Irischen". *Zeitschrift für celtische Philologie* 16: 95–144, 231–266, 363–394; 17: 373–388; 18: 233–248.

Ramat, Paolo & Bernini, Giuliano. 1990. "Area influence versus typological drift in Western Europe: the case of negation". In: Bechert et al. (eds.), 25–46.

Siewierska, Anna. 1999. "From anaphoric pronoun to grammatical agreement marker: Why objects don't make it". *Folia Linguistica* 33.1–2: 225–51.

Stassen, Leon. 1985. *Comparison and universal grammar*. Oxford: Blackwell.

Stassen, Leon. 2000. "AND-languages and WITH-languages". *Linguistic Typology* 4.1: 1–54.

Stolz, Thomas. 1991. *Sprachbund im Baltikum? Estnisch und Lettisch im Zentrum einer sprachlichen Konvergenzlandschaft*. Bochum: Brockmeyer.

Stolz, Thomas. 1996. "Some instruments are really good companions – some are not: On syncretism and the typology of instrumentals and comitatives". *Theoretical Linguistics* 23.1–2: 113–200.

Stolz, Thomas. 2001a. "No Sprachbund beyond this line! On the age-old discussion on how to define a linguistic area". *Sprachtypologie und Universalienforschung* 54.

Stolz, Thomas. 2001b. "Ordinalia – Linguistisches Neuland: Ein Typologenblick auf die Beziehung zwischen Kardinalia und Ordinalia und die Sonderstellung von EINS und ERSTER". In: Igla, Birgit & Stolz, Thomas (eds.) *Was ich noch sagen wollte ... Festschrift für Norbert Boretzky zu seinem 65. Geburtstag*. Berlin: Akademie-Verlag.

Ternes, Elmar. 1998. "Lauttypologie der Sprachen Europas". In: Boeder, Winfried & Schroeder, Christoph & Wagner, Karl Heinz & Wildgen, Wolfgang (eds.) *Sprache in Raum und Zeit: In memoriam Johannes Bechert. Band 2*. Tübingen: Narr, 139–152.

Thieroff, Rolf. 2000. "On the areal distribution of tense-aspect categories in Europe". In: Dahl (ed.), 265–305.

Ultan, Russell. 1978. "Some general characteristics of interrogative systems". In: Greenberg, Joseph H. (ed.) *Universals of human language, vol. 4*. Stanford: Stanford University Press, 211–248.

Ureland, P. Sture. 1985. "Sprachkontakt und Glottogenese in Europa". In: P. Sture Ureland (ed.) *Entstehung von Sprachen und Völkern: Glotto- und ethnogenetische Aspekte europäischer Sprachen*. Tübingen: Niemeyer, 7–43.

van der Auwera, Johan. 1998a. "Conclusion". In: van der Auwera (ed.), 813–36.

van der Auwera, Johan. 1998b. "Phasal adverbials in the languages of Europe". In: van der Auwera (ed.), 25–145.

van der Auwera, Johan (ed.). 1998. *Adverbial constructions in the languages of Europe*. (Empirical Approaches to Language Typology-EUROTYP, 20–3.) Berlin: Mouton de Gruyter.

van der Hulst, Harry & Hendriks, Bernadet & van de Weijer, Jeroen. 1999. "A survey of word prosodic systems of European languages". In: van der Hulst, Harry (ed.) *Word prosodic systems in the languages of Europe.* (Empirical Approaches to Language Typology-EUROTYP, 20–4.) Berlin: Mouton de Gruyter, 425–475.

Vennemann, Theo. 1994. "Linguistic reconstruction in the context of European prehistory". *Transactions of the Philological Society* 92: 213–282.

Wagner, Heinrich. 1959. *Das Verbum in den Sprachen der britischen Inseln: ein Beitrag zur geographischen Typologie des Verbums.* Tübingen: Niemeyer.

Whorf, Benjamin Lee. 1941. "The relation of habitual thought and behavior to language". In: Spier, Leslie (ed.) *Language, culture, and personality: Essays in memory of Edward Sapir.* Menasha, Wis.: Sapir Memorial Publication Fund, 75–93. [Reprinted in Whorf (1956), 134–159.]

Whorf, Benjamin Lee. 1956. *Language, thought, and reality: Selected writings of Benjamin Lee Whorf.* Edited by John B. Carroll, Cambridge/MA: MIT Press.

Wintschalek, Walter. 1993. *Die Areallinguistik am Beispiel syntaktischer Übereinstimmungen im Wolga-Kama-Areal.* (Studia Uralica, 7.) Wiesbaden: Harrassowitz.

Martin Haspelmath, MPI Leipzig
(Deutschland)

108. Aire linguistique balkanique

1. Généralités
2. Phonologie
3. Système verbal
4. Système nominal
5. Autres unités
6. Relations phrastiques
7. Subordination
8. Références

1. Généralités

La linguistique balkanique est une discipline relativement récente, bien que la découverte de traits communs entre les langues balkaniques remonte à la première moitié du XIXe siècle. Les spécialistes (Asenova 1979: 5–45; Schaller 1975: 37–45) s'accordent à diviser l'histoire de la discipline en trois périodes: une période *préliminaire*, où l'on cherche à expliquer les traits communs par l'influence du substrat, une période *classique* où la linguistique balkanique acquiert ses lettres de noblesse grâce à la publication en 1930 de *Linguistique balkanique. Problèmes et résultats* de Sandfeld, qui représente la première synthèse complète, et une période *moderne*, marquée par le polycentrisme et l'internationalisation des recherches (nombreuses revues spécifiques et organisation de congrès).

La linguistique balkanique ne consiste pas à juxtaposer des descriptions de langues diverses dont le seul lien serait la contiguïté géographique: il faut que ces langues forment une « union linguistique » (*Sprachbund*). Même si certaines voix s'élèvent encore pour nier la réalité de l'union balkanique (Andriotis & Kourmoulis 1968), la plupart des linguistes sont convaincus de son existence. En effet, les traits communs sont trop nombreux pour qu'ils soient le fruit du hasard. Il est vrai que les spécialistes discutent encore de la notion de « balkanisme », que l'on définira ici comme un trait typologique propre à au moins trois langues de l'union. Ce trait n'a pas besoin d'être unique en son genre (ainsi, l'article défini postposé existe dans les langues scandinaves, le « redoublement » de l'objet se retrouve dans les langues romanes); il doit être le résultat d'une convergence qui aboutit à un résultat identique ou quasi identique, alors qu'il n'existait pas à des stades plus anciens.

Les tâches de la linguistique balkanique sont consignées dans l'histoire de la discipline. Elles ont un triple aspect: synchronique (description) panchronique (extension) et diachronique (formation et évolution). Bien que l'essentiel du travail descriptif semble avoir été acompli (la monographie de Sandfeld a éte complétée, souvent améliorée, par des centaines d'articles et d'études de détail qui ont permis d'accroître et d'approfondir les données), il reste toujours beaucoup à faire. L'étude de l'extension des balkanismes nécessite le recours à la géographie linguistique (ou linguistique aréale) pour déterminer avec exactitude le lieu d'apparition de chaque balkanisme et son extension réelle sur le terrain. Enfin, la perspective diachronique n'est jamais perdue de vue par les balkanologues, malgré les nombreuses difficultés auxquelles ils sont confrontés, faute de documents écrits. Trois aspects sont à prendre en considération: 1) La genèse de l'union linguistique balkanique; 2) La genèse des balkanismes; 3)

Les problèmes liés au substrat, à l'adstrat et, éventuellement, au superstrat. Ces aspects sont étroitement solidaires et ne sont pas séparés dans le raisonnement, car il est vraisemblable, sinon certain, que plusieurs phénomènes ont joué dans le processus complexe de formation des traits communs. Les recherches actuelles s'orientent plutôt sur l'effet de symbiose. Pour que des langues différentes présentent de si nombreuses concordances, il faut qu'elles aient été longtemps en contact. Cela suppose de nombreux déplacements à l'intérieur de l'espace balkanique.

On fait la différence (Schaller 1975: 29) entre la conception géographique (*Sprachen des Balkans* « langues des Balkans » = ensemble des langues parlées dans la péninsule balkanique) et la conception linguistique (*Balkansprachen* « langues balkaniques » = langues qui présentent un certain nombre de traits communs). Les langues qui présentent le plus grand nombre de traits communs sont l'albanais (avec ses deux grands dialectes, le guègue au Nord et le tosque au Sud), le bulgare, le macédonien et le roumain (avec ses quatre dialectes: daco-roumain ou roumain proprement dit; aroumain; mégléno-roumain et istro-roumain, disparu). Puis vient le grec qui ne connaît pas certains balkanismes. Le serbe est touché par quelques phénomènes, mais il n'appartient pas *stricto sensu* à l'union. Le romani, langue parlée par les Tziganes, montre également un certain nombre de traits « balkaniques ». Quant au turc, il est exclu, bien que son rôle lexical ait été important.

2. Phonologie

2.1. Système vocalique

Il y a cinq voyelles de base qui se retrouvent dans toutes les langues balkaniques: *i/u, e/o* et *a*. Les moyennes sont toujours réalisées ouvertes sous l'accent, soit [ɛ] et [ɔ]. Certaines langues ne possèdent que ce système: c'est le cas du grec moderne et du macédonien littéraire. Mais deux phénomènes beaucoup plus rares peuvent être considérés comme des balkanismes. D'une part, l'existence d'une voyelle centrale en bulgare (*ă*), en albanais (*ë*) et en roumain (*ă*), dont la réalisation est proche de [ə]: alb. *bënë* « ils firent », bulg. *vărxăt* « le sommet », roum. *casă* « maison ». Ce phonème apparaît aussi bien en syllabe accentuée qu'en syllabe inaccentuée. C'est sans doute ce trait qui est le plus frappant. On a cherché l'origine de cette voyelle dans le substrat. Ainsi, Rosetti (1985: 189) pense qu'elle est un héritage du daco-mésien. Poghirc (1983: 81–85), étudiant les hésitations graphiques *a/e* en thrace, conclut à l'existence d'une voyelle centrale moyenne dans cette langue. Il est possible d'envisager une évolution spécifique en roumain et en albanais, car la concordance d'origine est frappante. Les conditions d'apparition du *ă* en bulgare sont différentes, puisque cette voyelle ne provient pas de *a*, mais de la vocalisation du grandier (*ŭ*) en position forte ou de la dénasalisation de la voyelle nasale *ǫ*, ce qui rend la concordance encore plus remarquable. Le bulgare et le roumain se rejoignent sur deux points: la voyelle centrale [ă] peut apparaître en toute position, sauf à l'initiale où elle est pratiquement exclue. D'autre part, les phonèmes /a/ et /ă/ ne peuvent s'opposer qu'en syllabe accentuée.

Le second phénomène est la « réduction vocalique ». En roumain, dans les dialectes bulgares orientaux et dans les parlers septentrionaux de la Grèce, les voyelles moyennes *e*, *o* (et *a*, sauf dans les dialectes grecs) se confondent en syllabe inaccentuée avec les voyelles fermées correspondantes *i* et *u* (et *ă* en roumain et en bulgare). Le roumain note l'alternance graphiquement: *pot* « je peux »/ *putem* « nous pouvons »; *cad* « je tombe »/ *cădem* « nous tombons ». En bulgare oriental, *detéto* « l'enfant » est réalisé [di'tɛtu]. Il est à noter que le bulgare littéraire confond /a/ et /ă/ en syllabe inaccentuée, comme les dialectes orientaux, mais que la réduction de /ɛ/ et de /ɔ/ va moins loin. Enfin, Thumb (1910: 6) cite les formes suivantes dans les dialectes du Nord de la Grèce: [pi'ði] = grec standard *peðí* « enfant »; [kirði'menus] = *kerðeménos* « gagné »; ['fitrosi] = *fítrose* « grandit, poussa ».

Si l'on compare les différents systèmes vocaliques des langues balkaniques, on s'aperçoit qu'on peut établir un type moyen possédant six phonèmes et représenté par le bulgare:

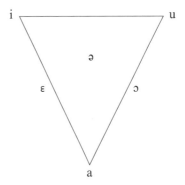

D'un côté, on a les systèmes du grec et du macédonien qui ont cinq phonèmes (le /ă/ est absent); de l'autre côté, on a les systèmes de l'albanais et du roumain à sept phonèmes (l'albanais a une palatale arrondie /y/ en plus, tandis que le roumain possède, en plus des six voyelles citées, un /ɨ/, voyelle centrale fermée, correspondant au turc ı et au russe ы, qu'il note î ou â).

2.2. Système consonantique

La plupart des spécialistes émettent des réserves sur l'existence de balkanismes dans le consonantisme (Ivić 1968: 133−141, Schaller 1975: 132). Cependant, Georgiev (1968: 10) note que «l'articulation de la plupart des consonnes est identique [...]» et Simeonov (1977) a pu proposer des faisceaux de corrélations.

2.2.1. On trouve partout les occlusives p/b, t/d, k/g, les constrictives f/z, les nasales m, n, les liquides l et r (apical), la semi-consonne j. Il n'y a là rien d'original, sinon peut-être la sonorisation de p, t, k après nasale en grec, en aroumain et en albanais (Sandfeld 1930: 102). On notera aussi l'absence de la semi-consonne /w/ dans toutes les langues balkaniques.

2.2.2. Plus originale est l'existence d'une corrélation sifflantes ~ chuintantes dans l'ordre des occlusives et des affriquées:

/s/ ~ /z/   /š/ ~ /ž/
/c/ ~ /dz/   /č/ ~ /dž/

Elle n'existe pas en grec où il n'y a pas de chuintantes (du moins dans la langue littéraire), mais elle est présente en serbo-croate et en turc. Comme l'écrit Ivić (1968: 139): «Il y a pourtant une singularité du consonantisme commune à presque tous les dialectes des langues balkaniques. C'est l'existence d'au moins deux membres de la triade [c č ć]». Il s'agit donc bien d'un balkanisme.

2.2.3. Les langues balkaniques ont toutes, en plus des vélaires dures /k/ et /g/, des vélaires molles /k'/ ([c]) et /g'/ ([ɟ]). Ce sont partout des phonèmes autonomes. L'opposition dure/molle est neutralisée en bulgare, en grec et en roumain en faveur de la molle devant voyelle palatale. On ne peut, dans cet inventaire, oublier le turc qui présente k et g mouillés devant voyelle palatale, ainsi que devant les voyelles longues (d'origine arabe ou persane) â, î, û. Les vélaires molles k', g' du bulgare et du macédonien apparaissant devant voyelle vélaire ne se trouvent d'ailleurs que dans les emprunts au turc.

2.2.4. Ivić (1968: 139) écrit que «la plupart des idiomes balkaniques ont un [h] (ou un [x]), mais il y a assez de dialectes [...] sans un phonème de ce genre». Toutes les langues littéraires, en tout cas, possèdent cette constrictive, qui a toujours au moins deux réalisations: une du type [ç] devant voyelle palatale et une du type [x] devant voyelle vélaire, mais se rapprochant plus de la laryngale [h] que du *ach-Laut* de l'allemand.

2.2.5. Les géminées sont dans l'ensemble très rares dans les langues balkaniques: on ne les trouve qu'à la frontière morphématique. En grec commun, il y a toujours simplification de deux consonnes identiques.

2.2.6. Le grec, l'albanais et l'aroumain (sous l'influence du grec) possèdent deux constrictives interdentales: [θ] (noté *th* en albanais) et [ð] (noté *dh* en albanais).

Si l'on fait abstraction de l'absence de chuintantes en grec démotique et de la présence d'interdentales en albanais et en grec, ainsi que d'un /γ/ dans cette dernière langue, on peut reconstituer un archétype du consonantisme balkanique qui a la forme suivante:

OCCLUSIVES	/p/	/t/	/k'/	/k/
	/b/	/d/	/g'/	/g/
CONSTRICTIVES	/f/	/s/	/š/	/h, ç, x/
	/v/	/z/	/ž/	
AFFRIQUÉES		/c/	/č/	
		/dz/	/dž/	
NASALES	/m/	/n, ŋ/		
LIQUIDES	/l/	/r/		
SEMI-CONSONNE			/j/	

2.3. Système accentuel

2.3.1. L'accent est partout de type dynamique (accent dit «d'intensité»). Dans les langues qui constituent l'union *stricto sensu*, il n'y a pas de tons.

2.3.2. L'accent est mobile, sauf en macédonien littéraire où il s'est fixé sur l'antépénultième. Mais même dans cette langue, il y a des exceptions. L'accent a une valeur culminative. Sa place peut être distinctive, en particulier dans les paradigmes: bulg. *četé* «il lit»/*čéte* «il lut», grec *aγapá* «il aime»/*aγápa* «aime!», roum. *súnă* «il sonne»/*sună* «il sonna », alb. *njerí* « homme »/*njérëz* « hommes ». Mais c'est surtout pour distinguer des termes qui seraient homophones que la place de l'accent joue un rôle important: bulg. *závet* « abri »/*zavét* « précepte »; grec *jéros* « vieillard »/*jerós* « robuste »; alb. *bári* « l'herbe »/*barí* « berger », macéd. *kraváta* « cravate »/*krávata* « la vache ».

2.3.3. Le trait commun le plus prégnant est sans doute la tendance générale des langues balkaniques à restreindre la liberté accentuelle dans les paradigmes et en cela, le macédonien est précurseur de ce que pourrait être la situation future des autres langues. Ainsi, en bulgare, l'accent ne se déplace jamais dans un temps donné. Depuis toujours, le grec connaît la loi dite de « limitation » qui interdit à l'accent de remonter au-delà de la troisième syllabe à partir de la fin (de la deuxième si la voyelle de la syllabe finale est une ancienne longue). Cette loi s'applique toujours en grec moderne. En roumain, l'accent frappe toujours la même syllabe du radical dans la flexion nominale. L'albanais a régularisé dans une large mesure la place de l'accent. Il est donc possible, dans de nombreux cas, de prévoir la place de l'accent quand on connaît la forme de base. Par contre, il n'est normalement pas possible de prévoir sa place dans ladite forme de base.

3. Système verbal

Dans l'ensemble, les langues balkaniques possèdent des systèmes verbaux complexes, riches en formes et en oppositions. La morphologie verbale s'organise autour de deux thèmes en albanais, bulgaro-macédonien et grec: celui du présent et de l'aoriste. Les choses sont plus simples en roumain, mais pour quelques verbes irréguliers, il est nécessaire de connaître aussi le thème de l'infinitif-présent et celui du passé simple-participe passé.

Toutes les langues balkaniques connaissent des oppositions d'aspect, de temps et de mode. Le médio-passif n'a d'expression synthétique qu'en grec et en albanais.

3.1. Oppositions aspectuelles

Toutes les langues balkaniques possèdent l'opposition d'accomplissement. Si l'on représente le procès par un segment AB, c'est le point B, marquant l'achèvement du procès, qui constitue la charnière du système: soit on est avant, soit on est après ce point B.

L'accompli a toujours une expression périphrastique (si l'on excepte le cas curieux du plus-que-parfait roumain, héritier du subjonctif plus-que-parfait latin, que est de type synthétique) reposant sur une structure auxiliaire + participe. L'auxiliaire choisi est « avoir » en albanais, grec et roumain et le participe est de type « passé passif » (le grec ayant une autre possibilité): alb. *ka larë* « il a lavé », roum. *a jurat* « il a juré », grec *to éxo akúsi* (ancien infinitif aoriste) et *to éxo akusméno* (participe passif variable), la seconde forme étant plus rare, « je l'ai entendu ». Le macédonien utilise soit la périphrase constituée de « avoir » (*imam*) et du participe passé passif au neutre invariable (*imam noseno* « j'ai porté »), soit la périphrase constituée de « être » et du participe parfait en -*l* (*sum nosel*). Seule cette construction, héritée du vieux bulgare qui n'en connaît pas d'autre, est grammaticalisée en bulgare littéraire (*az săm nosil*), mais la périphrase avec « avoir » se trouve dans certains dialectes, et elle est attestée dans la langue littéraire (Georgiev 1976).

Si l'on compare la situation actuelle à l'état ancien, on remarque que le grec ancien et le latin avaient des parfaits (et tous les temps de l'accompli, du moins à l'actif) synthétiques, et il est vraisemblable que le proto-albanais ne devait pas avoir de parfait périphrastique. Seul le vieux slave l'atteste, avec une formation unique dans les langues indo-européennes puisque les rapports sont inversés: auxiliaire « être » + participe actif, ce qui donne comme sens premier « je suis ayant porté ».

Une autre convergence est l'existence d'un imparfait opposé à un aoriste. Même si cette opposition est limitée à la langue écrite en roumain (et également en serbo-croate), elle est généralisée dans l'aire balkanique. Là encore, ce n'est pas un phénomène exceptionnel en soi. Mais il faut noter la conservation en slave balkanique de ces deux temps qui ont disparu des autres langues slaves à l'exception du sorabe. Le creuset balkanique pourrait bien expliquer ce maintien.

Il existe également une remarquable convergence du grec et du bulgaro-macédonien dans l'opposition entre l'imperfectif et le perfectif slaves d'une part, entre le continu et le momentané grecs (appelés d'ailleurs imperfectif et perfectif par Joseph & Philippaki-Warburton 1987) d'autre part. Elle se vérifie jusque dans l'identité des contextes, à savoir en subordonnée après *da*/*na*, au futur et à l'impératif. Le momentané du grec et le perfectiv slave ne s'emploient au présent que s'ils sont accompagnés d'une « particule », soit de futur (bulg. *šte*, grec *θa*) soit de « subjonctif » (bulg. *da*, grec *na*). En ce qui concerne les temps du passé, l'imparfait grec est formé sur le radical du continu (*éferne* « il portait ») et l'aoriste sur le radical du momentané (*éfere* « il porta »). C'est exactement la situation du macédonien où l'imparfait est toujours imperfectif et l'aoriste perfectif. Le bulgare montre le même type d'affinités, mais il n'y a pas ce type de servitude grammaticale, puisqu'il existe des imparfaits perfectifs qui sont malgré tout peu fréquents.

3.2. Oppositions temporelles

Les temps peuvent être regroupés en deux systèmes: ceux qui se rattachent morphologiquement au présent (valeur de *non-distanciation*) et ceux qui se rattachent au passé (*distanciation*). À l'intérieur de chaque système, on a une double opposition d'accomplissement (non-accompli/accompli) et de repère temporel (centre/ultérieur), ce qui donne une double opposition binaire présent/parfait et futur/futur antérieur dans la non-distanciation, imparfait/plus-que-parfait, et futur-conditionnel/futur-conditionnel antérieur (sauf en roumain, où le conditionnel n'a pas cette valeur). Il y a une opposition supplémentaire (imparfait/aoriste) à l'intérieur du centre. Les formes du centre, non marquées, peuvent s'employer avec la valeur d'ultérieur si elles sont accompagnées d'un circonstant temporel indiquant la postériorité. Les divers futurs antérieurs sont rares, sauf avec une valeur modalisatrice: les langues utilisent plutôt les formes de parfait avec circonstant.

S'il y a un balkanisme qui est reconnu de longue date, c'est bien la formation du futur avec l'auxiliaire (conjugué ou figé) « vouloir ». On a tant écrit sur cette question (voir par ex. le développement que lui consacre Asenova 1989: 155–172) qu'on peut considérer que les faits sont maintenant bien établis. Le futur balkanique représente à l'origine une périphrase du type « je veux que j'écrive = je veux écrire > j'écrirai »: grec *θe na γráfo > θa γráfo*, bulg. *šta da piša > šte piša* (macéd. *k'e pišam*), alb. *do të shkruaj* et aussi *do shkruaj*, roum. *o să scriu* et aroum. *va scriu*. On a donc non seulement le même type de formation avec « vouloir », mais aussi la même évolution: figement de l'auxiliaire à une forme invariable qui devient un morphème temporel et disparition (en grec et en bulgaro-macédonien, mais non en daco-roumain) de la conjonction. Ce balkanisme a touché aussi le serbo-croate qui forme son futur avec le verbe *htjeti* « vouloir » conjugué + infinitif en *-ti* (*ću raditi* « je ferai ») ou avec la forme abrégée de l'infinitif (sans *-ti*) suivie de « vouloir » conjugué (*radiću*).

Dans certaines langues existent d'autres expressions du futur; le roumain en compte quatre: *voi, vei, va* (« vouloir » conjugué) + infinitif, *oi, ei, a* (< *voi, vei, va*) + infinitif, *o* + *să* + présent du subjonctif (*o* provient aussi de « vouloir »), et enfin une formation avec « avoir » conjugué (*am, ai, are*) + *să* + présent du subjonctif. La périphrase avec « avoir » se retrouve dans d'autres langues: elle est grammaticalisée dans le futur négatif bulgare *njama da piša* « je n'écrirai pas » (avec *njama* invariable); en guègue, on a *kam me punue* « je travaillerai » (*kam* « avoir » + infinitif). Il semble maintenant bien établi que le point de départ de la périphrase avec « vouloir » est à chercher en grec. Il y a à la fois l'extension géographique du phénomène et son ancienneté: *θélo* + infinitif est attesté dès les premiers siècles de notre ère, et la combinaison *θe na gráfo* apparaît en grec médiéval (Sandfeld 1930: 182). Le bulgare, le roumain et l'albanais, qui ont à l'origine la même structure, l'ont certainement calquée sur le grec. Quant à la périphrase avec « avoir », elle fait songer au futur des langues romanes, et il est fort possible que le point de départ soit à chercher dans le latin balkanique.

Le futur de distanciation (*futurum præteriti*) montre un incontestable parallélisme dans sa formation, bien que les types soient plus variés. Il y a la solution bulgare qui consiste à utiliser l'imparfait conjugué de l'auxiliaire « vouloir »: *štjax da četa* « je lirais », *šteše da četeš* « tu lirais » (c'était également la solution grecque jusqu'au XVIIe s.); la solution roumaine (étant bien entendu que le futur simple serait possible, car il n'y a pas de concordance des temps) est proche: c'est l'auxiliaire « avoir » qui est conjugué, « vouloir » étant dans ce cas totalement impossible. Il y a d'autre part les solutions de l'albanais, du grec et du macédonien qui consistent à conjuguer l'imparfait du verbe et à garder la forme invariable de l'auxiliaire du futur: grec *θa éferne* « il porterait », alb. *do të punoja* « je travaillerais », mac. *k'e vlezeše* « il entrerait ».

Les langues balkaniques (à l'exception du roumain) sont parmi les langues qui ont le mieux conservé l'opposition entre l'aoriste et le parfait. On signalera une convergence en albanais, bulgaro-macédonien et grec sur une valeur particulière de l'aoriste: dans un registre familier, lié à l'émotivité, ce dernier peut avoir une valeur de futur immédiat: le locuteur est tellement sûr du résultat qu'il considère l'action déjà faite alors qu'elle n'a pas encore eu lieu (Feuillet 1986: 65): alb. *Ika unë! Do të shkoj të pres babanë* «Je vais y aller! Je veux aller attendre papa!»; bulg. *Na pomošt, bratja, zaginax!* «À l'aide, mes frères, je vais périr!»; grec: *éftasa* «j'arrive à l'instant!». Asenova (1989: 208−209) ajoute que le passé simple roumain peut également avoir, bien que rarement, cette valeur: *Eu mă cam duséi* «Je suis presque parti = Voilà, je vais partir maintenant». En aroumain, cet emploi est régulier.

La principale différence entre l'aoriste et le parfait (qui est le temps marqué) tient à l'attitude du locuteur devant un fait situé objectivement dans un moment antérieur à celui de l'énonciation. S'il est localisé avec précision et considéré comme relégué dans le passé, on se sert de l'aoriste. Mais s'il garde un lien avec le présent (au sens large du terme), c'est-à-dire avec l'actualité du locuteur, on utilise le parfait qui sert essentiellement à *réactualiser* un événement que le locuteur considère comme important au moment où il élabore son message. En d'autres termes, l'aoriste et le parfait rendent la différence entre un passé coupé objectivement du présent et un passé continuant d'agir dans le présent, donc réintégré. On peut classer ainsi les valeurs du parfait: *indétermination* (le parfait présente un caractère plus général que l'aoriste), *affectivité* (on trouve toute une gamme de nuances: amertume, déception, reproche, indignation. Dans tous les cas, le locuteur souligne qu'il est touché par l'événement); *valeur conclusive* (le parfait est le temps du bilan: il est utilisé pour tirer des conclusions ou jeter un regard rétrospectif sur ce qui a été fait).

Dans toute l'aire où l'opposition aoriste/parfait est vivante, l'aoriste domine très largement. La situation du roumain n'en apparaît que plus curieuse.

3.3. Oppositions modales

D'un point de vue morphologique, la situation des modes apparaît extrêmement variée dans les langues balkaniques. Il y a partout un impératif réduit aux deuxièmes personnes et un conditionnel; en albanais un optatif, en albanais et en bulgaro-macédonien un admiratif, en bulgaro-macédonien un mode spécial qui a reçu plusieurs dénominations: non-testimonial, renarratif, médiatif, imperceptif.

Malgré cette situation qui semble très variée, les domaines où l'on constate des convergences sont nombreux. Ainsi, l'emploi de la négation pour la défense entraîne souvent des changements par rapport à la forme affirmative. En roumain, on n'emploie pas l'impératif négatif dans la langue soignée, on le remplace par l'infinitif: *nu jura!* «ne jure pas!» (par opposition à *jură* «jure!»). En bulgare, il est impossible d'employer l'aspect perfectif. En grec, il est impossible de nier directement l'impératif, quelle que soit la négation.

En grec et en slave, il n'y a plus ou pas de subjonctif formellement distinct. L'albanais et le roumain l'ont confondu avec l'indicatif, sauf à deux personnes (2e−3e du singulier en albanais, 3es en roumain). Malgré ces données morphologiques différentes, il y a une convergence très frappante: toutes les langues se sont recréé un substitut de subjonctif en se servant de la même conjonction qui sert à introduire la subordonnée remplaçant l'infinitif, à savoir alb. *të*, bulg. *da*, grec *na*, roum. *să*. L'emploi du subjonctif seul en albanais et en roumain est devenu très rare: en albanais, dans la langue familière avec la négation *mos*; et en roumain dans des expressions figées (Lombard 1974: 130): *fie-i țărâna ușoară* «que la terre lui soit légère!», *fie ce-o fi!* «advienne que pourra!»

On peut souligner l'identité générale des valeurs sémantiques véhiculées par le subjonctif dans les langues balkaniques. Il y a d'abord l'expression du souhait (optatif) et de l'ordre (jussif). En effet, aux personnes manquantes de l'impératif, on utilise le subjonctif: alb. (Boissin 1975: 296): *le të udhëtojmë* «voyageons»; bulg. *da pukne!* «qu'il crève!», *da vărvim!* «marchons!»; grec (Mackridge 1985: 283): *o Jórγos na érθi sto tiléfono!* «que Georges vienne au téléphone!» D'autres valeurs, en revanche, sont plus rares, comme le *suppositif* (dans les langues balkaniques, il y a équivalence sémantique entre la conditionnelle à l'indicatif introduite par «si» et le subjonctif ou son substitut: alb. *në*, bulg. *ako*, grec *an*, roum. *dacă* + indicatif. Cela correspond exactement au type français *S'il vient maintenant, tout est perdu = Qu'il vienne maintenant et tout est perdu*), le *dubitatif*, comme dans alb. *të jëtë gjallë vallë?* «est-il vraiment vivant?», bulg. *toj da băde bogat?* «lui, être riche?»; grec *ti na jíni?* «que faire?», roum. *să plec sau să rămîn?* «dois-je partir ou rester?».

L'opposition fonctionne également dans le cadre d'une subordonnée: bulg. *tărsja čovek, kojto ima pari* « je cherche un homme qui a de l'argent » opposé à *kojto da ima pari* « qui ait de l'argent »; roum. *caut o casă care îmi convine* « je cherche une maison qui me convient »/*care să-mi convină* « qui me convienne »; grec *θέlo mja δaktiloγráfo pu kséri angliká* « je veux une dactylo qui sait l'anglais »/*pu na kséri* « qui sache »; alb. (Buchholz & Fiedler 1987: 135): *Atë trim që të njohë këtë se ç'gjë është, e kam për të marrë për burrë* « Le brave qui sache ce que c'est, je le prendrai pour mari »/*që njeh* « qui sait ».

L'albanais est la seule langue balkanique moderne à posséder un optatif qui exprime le « souhait » ou la malédiction: *ardhtë kjo ditë!* « puisse ce jour arriver! ». Ce mode peut également apparaître en subordonnée avec sa valeur propre (surtout après *që*) et s'employer après *në* pour exprimer la condition: *në daç, thirrmë* « si tu veux, appelle-moi ».

L'hypothétique, qui est toujours en rapport morphologique avec les temps du passé, est une virtualité de distanciation. Les langues balkaniques offrent de grandes similitudes dans la formation et l'emploi de ces formes modales. Ainsi, le futur de distanciation (sauf en roumain) sert normalement de mode hypothétique. Mais il y a également des formations spécifiques. La particularité des langues balkaniques est de n'opposer à l'indicatif qu'une seule autre valeur, qui réunit l'irréel dans sa totalité. Autrement dit, sans circonstant de temps explicite, on peut rendre la construction imparfait dans la protase, conditionnel présent dans l'apodose par l'imparfait ou le plus-que-parfait dans la protase et le conditionnel présent ou accompli dans l'apodose. Ce fait n'est pas aussi net en roumain, qui dispose d'un conditionnel présent et d'un conditionnel passé (accompli) s'utilisant aussi bien dans la protase que dans l'apodose, mais il peut remplacer le conditionnel passé par un imparfait: *Dacă aş fi putut veneam* ou *Dacă puteam veneam* « Si j'avais pu, je serais venu » (Baciu 1978: 95). On peut en conclure qu'à quelques nuances près, les langues balkaniques opposent à l'indicatif une virtualité de distanciation qui couvre tout le spectre du potentiel et de l'irréel.

Le mode « admiratif » n'apparaît qu'en albanais et en bulgaro-macédonien. Il marque avant tout la surprise du locuteur devant une situation ou un fait inattendus. En albanais, le système, qui est formé au présent et à l'imparfait par inversion de la périphrase d'accompli, c'est-à-dire participe (amputé de sa finale) + auxiliaire « avoir » au présent ou à l'imparfait (*jam larë* « j'ai lavé » > *(u) lakam*; *isha larë* « j'avais lavé » > *lakësha*), est richement développé. En bulgare, on se sert du participe parfait sans auxiliaire aux troisièmes personnes, avec auxiliaire aux autres personnes: *Čorbadži, ti si imal lepa devojka, mašalla!* (Vazov) « Čorbadži, tu as une belle fille, bravo! ».

Le bulgaro-macédonien et le turc ont en commun de posséder des formes verbales spéciales que le locuteur-narrateur utilise lorsqu'il n'a pas été témoin des faits qu'il rapporte (d'où le nom de « non-testimonial » qu'on donne souvent à ce mode). Il y a une convergence typologique entre le turc et le bulgaro-macédonien dans les emplois des formes non-testimoniales. On les trouve: dans l'Histoire et les contes populaires (avec les mêmes exceptions: on n'emploie pas les formes non-testimoniales quand il s'agit de la Parole divine (Bible ou Coran); d'autre part, on peut utiliser les temps de l'indicatif quand il s'agit d'événements historiques bien connus); dans le discours rapporté; avec valeur inférentielle (réflexion ou raisonnement sur des situations non observées). Dans tous les cas, le mode non-testimonial est le signal explicite que le message n'est pas livré directement et que sa vérité n'est pas garantie.

4. Système nominal

4.1. Genre et nombre

À l'exception du roumain qui ne se distingue pas sur ce point des autres langues romanes, les langues balkaniques ont conservé les trois genres masculin/féminin/neutre de l'indo-européen. Cependant, le neutre est en recul en albanais, puisqu'il n'y a plus que quinze substantifs non dérivés qui le présentent encore dans la langue littéraire (cinq le sont obligatoirement selon la norme).

Un trait commun à l'albanais et au roumain est l'existence d'un nombre important d'ambigènes, c'est-à-dire de noms masculins au singulier et féminins au pluriel. Les grammairiens roumains présentent ces substantifs comme des neutres, parce que beaucoup de ces ambigènes proviennent de neutres latins à pluriel en *-a* et en *-ora*, mais synchroniquement, cette dénomination est inexacte, puisque les déterminants et les adjectifs accompagnant le nom n'ont pas de forme spéciale. Au point de vue sémantique, ces ambigènes ne désignent jamais des êtres animés en albanais et très rarement en roumain (*animal* « animal », *macrou* « maquereau », *neam* « peuple », *personaj* « personnage »). L'albanais et le roumain ont également en commun le fait de se servir des formes féminines des pronoms pour exprimer le neutre: ainsi, roum. *asta* signifie « celle-là et « cela », *una* « une » et « une chose », *alta* « une autre » et « une autre chose » (Sandfeld 1930: 132—133).

Toutes les langues balkaniques connaissent une opposition de nombre singulier/pluriel. Les morphèmes de pluriel sont nombreux, mais Georgiev (1968: 10) a fait remarquer qu'« en grec, bulgare et roumain, le (nominatif) pluriel masculin se termine en -*i*: grec -οι = *i*, bulg. -*i*, roum. -*i*, -*ĭ*. Le -*ĭ* roumain (c'est-à-dire la palatalisation de la consonne précédente) est un développement récent de -*i* dont on trouve la correspondance exacte en albanais ». La fréquence du morphème -*i* est effectivement frappante. On peut ajouter qu'il est le morphème unique des féminins en bulgare et qu'il est répandu en roumain avec les féminins en -*e*: *floare*/*flori* « fleurs ». D'autre part, le morphème -*i* de pluriel est caractéristique des polysyllabes masculins (et d'une trentaine de monosyllabes, dont tous les noms de peuples), -*ove* étant celui des monosyllabes. On signalera enfin la bonne conservation du morphème -*a* dans les pluriels neutres en bulgaro-macédonien, en grec et en albanais (sous la forme -(*ë*)*ra*). Il est difficile malgré toutes ces concordances de parler de vrais balkanismes. Ce serait plutôt une ressemblance dans la gestion de l'héritage commun.

4.2. Cas

Les langues balkaniques ont conservé un certain nombre de morphèmes casuels, mais on constate de nombreux phénomènes de syncrétisme qui montrent un recul général des déclinaisons et un développement de l'analytisme. Si l'on excepte le vocatif, la situation est la suivante: le bulgaro-macédonien n'a plus de déclinaison; le roumain oppose d'une part le nominatif-accusatif, et d'autre part le datif-génitif; le grec a un nominatif, un accusatif et un génitif-datif; l'albanais a un nominatif, un accusatif, un génitif-datif et un ablatif. Le vocatif est encore vivant en bulgaro-macédonien, en grec (seulement avec les masculins en -*os*) et en roumain (le vocatif masculin en -*e* pourrait à la rigueur s'expliquer par le latin (*dominus*/*domine* « seigneur »), mais le vocatif féminin en -*o*, qui n'existe pas en latin, ne peut être qu'un emprunt au slave). Il y a quelques exemples de vocatif en albanais, mais uniquement avec des noms de parenté et assimilés: *bir*/*biro* « (mon) fils », *nënë*/*nëno* (*nënë*) « maman », *shok*/*shoko* « camarade ». Sans qu'on puisse prétendre que la présence d'un vocatif est un balkanisme, il convient cependant de mettre en évidence la conservation de ce cas, qui est justement le seul du bulgaro-macédonien. Cela peut s'expliquer par sa position marginale dans la flexion, encore que les langues choisissent plutôt la solution contraire.

Le nombre d'oppositions morphologiques à l'intérieur des déclinaisons est d'une manière générale en recul dans toutes les langues balkaniques, car les phénomènes de syncrétisme sont nombreux. En roumain, la flexion des substantifs est bien malade, puisque les masculins et les pluriels ne se déclinent pas. Seuls les féminins, à quelques exceptions près, ont un génitif-datif différent du nominatif-accusatif, qui a la même forme que celle du pluriel: *casă*/GD *casei* « maison », *inimă*/*inimii* « cœur », *vulpe*/*vulpii* « renard ». Cependant, comme les articles (défini et indéfini) ont des formes différentes au NA et au GD, il se maintient dans l'ensemble une opposition binaire au sing. et au plur. En grec, on a la plupart du temps seulement deux formes distinctes au singulier et au pluriel. En dehors du type en -*os*, les masculins opposent au singulier un nominatif en -*s* à une forme unique sans -*s*. En revanche, les féminins et les neutres opposent, aussi bien au singulier qu'au pluriel, une forme de NVA à une forme de génitif. Les morphèmes sont dans l'ensemble peu nombreux. Seuls les masculins en -*os* gardent (en plus du vocatif sg. en -*e*) trois formes casuelles différentes au sing. et au pl. Mais (et en cela le grec rejoint le roumain et l'albanais), l'article défini a des formes différentes au nominatif, à l'accusatif et au génitif masculin et féminin, et le neutre deux formes distinctes (NA et G) aux deux nombres. La forme de génitif pluriel est commune aux trois genres. En albanais, on constate aussi de nombreux phénomènes de syncrétisme. À la déclination non articulée, on a deux formes au singulier: NA et GD; au pluriel, on a trois formes: NA, GD (en -*ve* à tous les genres) et ablatif (en -*sh* partout), mais cette forme peut être remplacée par celle de GD. Cela donne donc finalement une opposition binaire aux deux nombres. À la déclinaison articulée, la forme d'accusatif sg. en -*n* est différente de celle du nominatif au masculin et au féminin;

en revanche, l'ablatif n'a pas de forme particulière.

Il est difficile de prétendre que la régression des déclinaisons est un fait typiquement balkanique. Néanmoins, la réduction à une opposition binaire dans la plupart des types (le slave balkanique étant exclu) est une convergence intéressante, d'autant plus qu'elle s'accompagne de deux autres phénomènes: les oppositions sont plus nombreuses à la forme déterminée; la confusion presque généralisée du nominatif et de l'accusatif au substantif n'est pas trop gênante en grec et en albanais, car la distinction est assurée à l'article. Cependant, elle a certainement eu comme conséquence une rigidité plus grande de l'ordre sujet − objet, car il est important, surtout si les deux actants principaux sont des humains, de distinguer l'agent et le patient sémantiques. Il faut y voir aussi l'origine lointaine du fameux « redoublement de l'objet » (pour transcender l'ordre SVO) et également du marquage différentiel de l'objet en roumain.

La confusion du génitif et du datif a toujours été considéré comme un balkanisme primaire. C'est un phénomène ancien: il remonte en grec aux premiers siècles de l'ère chrétienne, et il est antérieur aux premiers textes albanais et roumains. En vieux bulgare, il y a de nombreux exemples, à l'intérieur du groupe nominal, où le génitif et le datif semblent interchangeables sans différence apparente de sens. Morphologiquement, c'est le génitif qui élimine le datif en grec; en roumain, c'est le datif qui a évincé le génitif; il a dû en être de même en bulgare, étant donné la plus longue conservation du morphème de datif. En albanais, la genèse est plus curieuse: au singulier, c'est le datif qui a évincé l'ancienne forme de génitif, alors qu'au pluriel, c'est le génitif qui s'est imposé au détriment du datif. Mais le résultat est le même: dans toutes les langues balkaniques, les deux cas ne sont plus distincts.

Cette confusion morphologique, déjà remarquable et unique en son genre, se double d'une identité des fonctions remplies par cette forme de génitif-datif. En effet, on exprime le complément de possession (complément adnominal au génitif) et le complément d'attribution (objet II) de la même manière: alb. *libri i mësuesit* « le livre de l'instituteur »; *i jap librin mësuesit* « je donne le livre à l'instituteur »; bulg. *knigata na deteto* « le livre de l'enfant »; *davam knigata na deteto* « je donne le livre à l'enfant »; grec *to vivlío tu maθití* « le livre de l'enfant »; *o patéras δiní to vivlío tu maθití* « le père donne le livre à l'enfant »; roum. *cartea copilului* « le livre de l'enfant »; *i-a dat cartea copilului* « il a donné le livre à l'enfant ».

En bulgare, c'est la même préposition *na* qui apparaît dans les deux structures. En daco-roumain et en aroumain, c'est la préposition *a, ad* d'origine dative qui peut exprimer la relation adnominale, ce qui prouve la suprématie du datif sur le génitif (Asenova 1989: 60). Ce phénomène est à mettre en parallèle avec l'emploi des pronoms personnels inaccentués au datif pour exprimer la possession: Sandfeld traite d'ailleurs les deux faits ensemble.

4.3. Déterminants

4.3.1. Article défini

S'il est un domaine où la réflexion s'est particulièrement exercée, c'est bien celui de l'article défini, considéré depuis longtemps comme une preuve de l'étroitesse des liens entre les différentes langues balkaniques et donc comme un balkanisme fondamental. Le bulgare n'a d'article défini que postposé. En macédonien (et dans certains dialectes bulgares, comme ceux des Rhodopes), cet article a trois formes, liées à la position dans l'espace: *-t* (non-marqué), *-s* (ou *-v*) pour l'objet rapproché, *-n* pour l'objet éloigné. L'albanais a un article postposé et un article appelé souvent « copulatif ». Le grec a un article antéposé et un article copulatif. Le roumain a un article postposé et deux articles antéposés, appelés respectivement « possessif » et « démonstratif ».

Il y a accord d'emploi en bulgare, albanais et roumain lorsque le noyau nominal déterminé est seul: l'article postposé est obligatoire. Lorsqu'il est accompagné d'un adjectif, c'est le premier constituant qui prend l'article en bulgare et en roumain; pour des raisons de contrainte syntaxique (l'adjectif précédant toujours le substantif), ce sera l'adjectif en bulgare (*novijat teatăr* « le nouveau théâtre »), mais ce peut être l'adjectif ou le substantif en roumain (*teatrul nou* ou *noul teatru*). La marque de détermination ne peut être répétée que dans le cas de la coordination de deux adjectifs (bulg. *novijat i važnijat teatăr*, roum. *noul şi importantul teatru* « le nouveau et important théâtre »). Si les adjectifs sont juxtaposés, on ne répète pas la marque de la détermination en bulgare (*novijat xubav teatăr* « le nouveau beau théâtre »); en roumain, le deuxième adjectif doit être obligatoirement postposé, et il est relié au reste par l'article «démonstratif»: *vinul alb cel nou și sec* «le vin blanc nouveau et sec». En albanais, l'adjectif est normalement postposé: en ce cas, il est obligatoirement relié au substantif (déterminé) par l'article copulatif: Nom, sg. *guri i bardhë*, acc. sg. *gurin e bardhë* «la pierre blanche»; s'il est antéposé, il est précédé de l'article copulatif, et il prend lui-même l'article postposé tandis que le noyau nominal reste invariable: Nom. sg. *i mjeri burrë*, Obl. sg. *të mjerit burrë* «le pauvre homme», NA pl. *të mjerëve burra*, Obl. *të mjerëvet burra*. On voit donc qu'il y a double détermination. Cela s'explique par le fait que l'adjectif étant toujours accompagné, en fonction épithétique, de l'article copulatif, il faut marquer quelque part la définitude.

L'origine de la postposition de l'article n'a pas reçu de solution unanimement acceptée. Il s'agit sans doute d'un phénomène d'adstrat, et non de substrat. Mais on ne peut pas savoir quelle est la langue de départ qui a innové ou même s'il n'y a pas eu en différents points de l'aire une structure de ce type qui a fait son apparition. Le bulgare semble avoir subi dans ce domaine l'influence du roumain, mais entre l'albanais et le roumain, il est impossible de trancher.

L'albanais, le grec et le roumain ont, comme il a été dit, des articles antéposés. Quand le substantif est accompagné d'un adjectif, le grec peut dire soit *to kaló peðí* «le bon garçon» (ordre normal non marqué), soit *to peðí to kaló* (ordre plus marqué, insistant sur la qualité). Cette construction n'est plus possible avec un complément adnominal. Une des particularités de l'albanais est d'utiliser l'article copulatif pour former certains adjectifs, comme *i mirë* «bon» (par opposition à *mirë* «bien»), *i bardhë* «blanc»; *i vjetër* «vieux». Il détermine obligatoirement les adjectifs ordinaux et surtout, il est obligatoire pour exprimer la relation adnominale (ou «génitivale»): *guri i murit* «la pierre du mur», *ca gurë të malit* «des pierres de la montagne» (Boissoin 1975: 89). En roumain, les articles antéposés ont reçu le nom de «possessifs» et de «démonstratifs». Le premier est en *a-*, le second en *ce-*. *Al* est employé avec les possessifs et les ordinaux à partir de «deuxième», tandis que *cel* est employé avec les expressions de qualité (adjectif qualificatif, participe à valeur adjectivale, groupe préposition + substantif) et avec les nombres cardinaux et ordinaux: *cel bătrân* «le vieux», *cel iubit* «le bien aimé» (Lombard 1974: 191–192). Tous les spécialistes ont noté le parallélisme des structures entre l'albanais et le roumain. En effet, on peut dire en roumain *omul bun* ou *omul cel bun* «l'homme bon», et *drumul de piatră* ou *drumul (a) cel (a) de piatră* «le chemin de pierre», les secondes constructions correspondant exactement aux constructions albanaises *njeru i mirë* et *guri i murit* «la pierre du mur» (et aussi en grec en qui concerne l'adjectif). L'article copulatif est utilisé dans les deux langues avec les possessifs (roum. *al meu* «le mien», alb. *e mi*) et les ordinaux.

L'article défini a beaucoup d'emplois qui se recoupent d'une langue à l'autre. Voici quelques remarques d'ordre général:

a) L'article est régulierement employé dans un sens générique: alb. *Hekuri është një metal i fortë* «Le fer est un métal solide», *Mizat bëjnë pjesë në klasën e insekteve* «Les mouches appartiennent à la classe des insectes»; bulg. *Prilepăt e bozajnik* «La chauve-souris est un mammifère», grec *To áloγo íne oréo zóo* «Le cheval est un bel animal», pl. *Ta áloγa íne oréa zóa* «Les chevaux sont de beaux animaux»; roum. *Vă plac romanele?* «Vous aimez les romans?»

b) L'article défini est employé avec un nom apposé à un pronom: bulg. *Nie, bălgarite*, «Nous, Bulgares», roum. *noi, românii* «nous, Roumains», alb. *ju zengjinët* «vous les riches».

c) Les compléments de temps sont normalement articulés: bulg. *večerta* «le soir», *esenta* «en automne», alb. *ditën*, *natën*, roum. *ziua, noaptea* «le jour, la nuit», grec *ti nixta* «la nuit».

Le partitif est exprimé par l'article ø partout.

On emploie en albanais comme en roumain l'article défini après «comme»: alb. *Luftuam si burrat*, roum. *Ne-am bătut ca leii* «Nous avons combattu en hommes».

4.3.2. Démonstratifs

Si l'on excepte le macédonien littéraire et les parlers bulgares des Rhodopes, on constate que les démonstratifs balkaniques reposent sur une opposition proximal/distal: alb. *ky/ai*, *ay*, bulg. *tozi/onzi*, grec *aftós/(e)kínos*, roum. *acest/acel*. Cette convergence est d'autant plus remarquable que dans les langues dont on peut suivre l'histoire (grec, vieux, bulgare, latin), les demonstratifs reposaient à date ancienne sur une opposition ternaire liées aux personnes. Le phénomène atteint plus généralement l'expression de la deixis. En bulgare, le distal peut prendre le sens de « autre, opposé » (*na onja svjat* « dans l'autre monde »), emploi qui se retrouve en albanais et en roumain, sans doute sous l'influence du slave (Sandfeld 1930: 158): alb. *ajo dunja* « id. », roum. *de cealaltă parte rîului*, alb. *matanë lumit* « de l'autre côté de la rivière ».

La combinaison de l'article et du démonstratif révèle un dégradé à trois degrés: en grec, l'article est toujours obligatoire avec le démonstratif, en albanais et en roumain, l'article est facultatif; en slave balkanique, il y a incompatibilité entre l'article et le démonstratif.

4.3.3. Interrogatifs

Un des traits remarquables des langues balkaniques est l'existence de deux interrogatifs là où, par exemple, le français (*quel*), l'anglais (*which*) ou l'allemand (*welcher*) n'en ont qu'un. La différence est claire: l'un interroge sur l'identité, l'autre sur la qualité attribuable à l'objet référé. Elle peut être illustrée de la manière suivante: grec: *pjo vivlío θélis?/ti vivlío θélis?*; bulg. *koja kniga iskaš?/kakva kniga iskaš?*; alb. *cilin libër do?/ç' libër do?*; roum. *care carte vrei?/ce carte vrei?* « Quel livre veux-tu? ». Avec le premier interrogatif, on interroge, comme on l'a dit, sur l'identité: Lequel, parmi ces livres, de ces livres, désires-tu?; avec le second interrogatif, le sens est: Quel genre de livre, quelles sont les qualités que doit posséder le livre que tu veux? Seul l'interrogatif qui interroge sur la qualité peut s'employer comme exclamatif: alb. *ç' natë e bukur!* « quelle belle nuit! », bulg. *kakăv čovek!*, roum. *ce om!* « quel homme! », grec *ti zésti!* « quelle chaleur! ».

4.3.4. Numéraux

Alors que le numéral « un » connaît des oppositions de genre, on a au maximum deux formes distinctes de 2 à 4, et une seule forme à partir de 5 (on exclut ici les numéraux « mille », « million », « milliard » traités comme des substantifs). Le trait commun dégagé ne concerne que le nominatif-accusatif.

Les numéraux sont surtout cités en linguistique balkanique pour l'identité de leur formation de « onze » à « dix-neuf ». En effet, sauf en grec, la structure est « un (deux, trois, etc.) sur dix »:

11: bulg. *edinnadeset*, alb. *njëmbëdhjetë*, roum. *unsprezece*
12: bulg. *dvanadeset*, alb. *dymbëdhjetë*, roum. *doisprezece*

Le grec a une formation différente: pour 11 et 12, il a « un-dix » (*éndeka*) et « deux-dix » (*δόδeka* pour *δíoδeka*), et de 13 à 19, il a « dix-trois » (*δekatrís*), dix-quatre », etc.

Comme cette formation se trouve dans toutes les langues slaves (ainsi qu'en lette), il y a tout lieu de penser que ce balkanisme est d'origine slave. Cette hypothèse est confirmée par la présence en hongrois d'une construction du même type.

4.3.5. Possessifs

Les possessifs des langues balkaniques présentent des traits communs qui font partie du catalogue classique des balkanismes primaires. Le plus connu est l'emploi des pronoms enclitiques comme possessifs: bulg. *kăštata mu* « sa maison », macéd. *glasot mu* « sa voix », grec *to spíti mu* « ma maison », roum. *păru-mi* « ma chevelure » (Schaller 1975: 165). L'albanais ne connaît cette possibilité qu'aux troisièmes personnes: *libri i tij* « son livre (à lui) », *libri i saj* « son livre (à elle) », *libri i tyre* « leur livre » (avec article de connexion obligatoire). Sandfeld (1930: 189) fait remarquer aussi que dans les cas où le substantif est précédé d'un adjectif, le possessif se place entre l'adjectif et le substantif, sauf en albanais: roum. *umilul tău sclav* « ton humble esclave », grec *i meγáli sas aδelfí* « votre grande sœur », bulg. *malkata ti sestra* « ta petite sœur ». Enfin, il note que dans toutes les langues balkaniques, on peut aussi marquer la possession en faisant précéder le verbe par un pronom personnel datif atone. Il existe d'autres concordances. On a d'abord un clivage entre le grec, qui ne peut exprimer le possessif qu'à l'aide du pronom personnel au GD (enclitique), le bulgare et le roumain qui disposent à la fois de pronoms personnels enclitiques et de « vrais » possessifs, c'est-à-dire des déterminants variables, et l'albanais qui possède un système mixte constitué de vrais possessifs pour les premières et deuxièmes personnes et de pronoms courts pour les troisièmes (c'est en fait aussi la situation du roumain moderne où les formes enclitiques ne sont courantes qu'aux 3es personnes). Le possessif ne peut normalement pas occuper la position initiale dans un groupe nominal. La règle est absolue pour le grec, elle l'est pratiquement toujours pour l'albanais et le roumain; en bulgare, la règle est absolue pour les pronoms personnels enclitiques, mais ne vaut pas pour les vrais possessifs qui sont en tête du groupe à la forme articulée: *kăštata mi* « mai maison », mais *mojata kăšta*. L'omission de l'article n'est pas due au hasard: on la constate en albanais, bulgare et roumain avec un sous-système lexical particulier; celui des noms de parenté. Le bulgare dit obligatoirement *bašta mi* « mon père », *majka ti* « ta mère », *dăšterija mi* « ma fille » (mais curieusement *sinăt mi* « mon fils », avec article, comme le roumain *fiul*). L'albanais, de la même manière, n'a pas d'article, mais de plus antépose le possessif variable: *im vëlla* « mon frère », *ime më* « ma mère », *im kunat* « mon beau-frère [frère du mari] ». Cependant, la plupart de ces noms peuvent avoir aussi le possessif postposé: *gjyshja ime* « ma grand-mère » à côté de *ime gjyshe, gjyshi yt* « ton grand-père » à côté de *yt gjysh*, mais obligatoirement *im shoq* « mon époux », *ime më* « ma mère ». Le roumain dira de même, dans la langue parlée ou populaire: *taică-meu* « mon père », *maică-ta* « ta mère », *frate-meu* « mon frère », *soră-ta* « ta sœur ». Dans un langage plus châtié, on préfère la construction avec l'article: *tatăl meu* « mon père », *mama ta*. Il est à noter aussi que le bulgare emploie l'article défini si le possessif est de forme adjectivale (plus rare): *mojat bašta* « mon père », *tvojata majka* « ta mère ». Pour ces trois langues, cette particularité ne vaut qu'au singulier.

5. Autres unités

5.1. Groupes pronominaux

À quelques exceptions près, les pronoms ont les mêmes formes que les déterminants. Seuls les pronoms personnels présentent des particularités. En effet, les langues balkaniques possèdent deux séries de pronoms personnels: une série dite « tonique » (ou « accentuée ») comprenant les pronoms libres, susceptibles d'élargissements (appositions ou relatives), et une série dite « atone » (ou « inaccentuée ») constituée de pronoms clitiques (dits aussi « conjoints ») ou plutôt d'indices pronominaux. L'opposition ne joue pas au nominatif, mais uniquement à l'accusatif et au datif.

Les figures phoniques sont très proches. Georgiev (1968: 10) écrit par exemple que « les formes du datif-génitif et de l'accusatif du pronom personnel de la première personne [sont] presque identiques: grec *ména mu*, bulg. *mene mi*, roum. *mie mie*; grec *ména me*, bulg. *mene me*, roum. *mine mă* ». Poghirc (1977: 86) a fait remarquer que l'existence d'une particule déictique *-ne* qui apparaît surtout à l'accusatif des pronoms personnels balkaniques (roum. *mine*, alb. *mua* < *mene, grec *(e)ména*, bulg. *mene* et qui a donné naissance à un système d'oppositions avec les formes inaccentuées sans *-ne* pourrait être d'origine substratique. En effet, l'existence du phénomène en grec ancien et la présence de *-ne, -n* après pronom dans les inscriptions thraces semblent fournir des preuves solides.

Aux troisièmes personnes (qui sont d'anciens démonstratifs), toutes les langues balkaniques distinguent les genres (sauf au pluriel en bulgare), mais, là aussi, il y a de nombreux cas de syncrétisme. Les oppositions dans le système des clitiques sont souvent réduites à peu de choses.

Le roumain et l'albanais emploient les formes féminines des pronoms personnels au sens neutre (Sandfeld 1930: 132): roum. *o cunosc* « je la connais » et *o ştiu* « je le sais »; alb. *i tha këto* « il lui a dit cela ».

Voici quelques remarques complémentaires sur les pronoms personnels.

a) L'utilisation de pronoms libres en début de phrase entraîne pratiquement toujours la présence simultanée et contiguë de pronoms conjoints. Au départ, il s'agit d'un phénomène de thématisation qui s'est banalisé au point de ne plus exprimer que le thème sans intention de mise en relief: alb. *mua më duket*, bulg. *mene mi se struva*, grec *eména mu fénete*, roum. *mie mi se pare* « il me semble ».

b) Les langues balkaniques ayant bien conservé les désinences personnelles au verbe, elles n'ont normalement pas besoin d'utiliser les formes de nominatif des pronoms personnels s'il n'y a pas mise en relief particulière.

Domi (1975) a fait remarquer qu'il n'existe pas dans les langues balkaniques de mot spécial pour « on ». On utilise soit la troisième personne du pluriel, soit la deuxième du singulier, soit un pronom indéfini (« quelqu'un ») ou un substantif signifiant « homme » (qui est à l'origine du franç. *on* ou de l'allem. *man*): alb. *nuk të pyeste njeri* « on ne demanderait pas »; grec *borí kanís na pi* « on peut dire », bulg. *čovek ne znae nikoga kakvo može da se sluči* « on ne sait jamais ce qui peut arriver »; roum. *omul se deprinde cu orice* « on s'habitue à tout ». On peut ajouter les formes médio-passives du grec et de l'albanais et la tournure réfléchie en bulgare et en roumain.

c) Schaller (1975: 167−168) signale qu'en grec et en slave balkanique, on utilise le pronom atone après « voici » et « voilà »: grec *na me* « me voici », bulg. *eto go, eto gi* « le voici, les voilà », macéd. et serbo-cr. *evo me* « me voici ».

5.2. Adjectifs

La morphologie adjectivale reflète le genre et le nombre du substantif. De nombreux phénomènes de syncrétisme limitent la variabilité de l'adjectif.

La formation de type analytique des degrés de comparaison dans toutes les langues balkaniques est considérée depuis toujours comme un balkanisme. Effectivement, les quatre langues concordent pour utiliser une sorte de préfixe avec le sens de « (le) plus » :

	albanais	bulgare	grec	roumain
comparatif	më	po-	pjo	mai
superlatif	më (+article)	naj-	o pjo	cel mai

Exemples:
- alb. *i bukur* « beau » / *më i bukur* / *më i bukuri*.
- bulg. *dobăr* « bon » / *po-dobăr* / *naj-dobăr*.
- grec *psilós* « haut » / *pjo psilós* / *o pjo psilós*
- roum. *bun* « bon » / *mai bun* / *cel mai bun*.

Seul le grec conserve encore quelques comparatifs et superlatifs formés à l'aide d'un suffixe et quelques formes irrégulières, comme *kalós* « bon »/*kalíteros* « meilleur »/*áristos* « le meilleur », mais la construction analytique reste possible.

Cette formation représente un type nouveau: le grec ancien, le latin et le vieux bulgare (tout comme les langues slaves modernes en dehors de l'aire bulgaro-macédonienne) ne connaissent que des degrés de comparaison formés de manière snythétique. La convergence des langues balkaniques n'en est que plus frappante. L'origine de ce balkanisme semble être romane.

Les langues balkaniques s'accordent également pour employer une préposition de valeur ablative (à côté d'une conjonction ayant le sens de « que ») comme complément du comparatif: alb. *Liria është më e bukur nga* [synonyme de *prej*] *e motra* « Liria est plus belle que sa sœur », bulg. *Toj e po-goljam ot mene* « Il est plus grand que moi », grec *meɣalíteros apó sas* « plus âgé que vous », roum. *a lucrat mai mult de oră* « il a travaillé plus d'une heure ». La construction roumaine est cependant rare s'il ne s'agit pas de numéraux: on emploie normalement *decât* (*a lucrat mai mult decât mine* « il a travaillé plus que moi ») où l'on reconnaît le *de* ablatif.

5.3. Groupes adverbiaux

On se contentera de quelques remarques sur leur formation. La manière la plus économique de former des adverbes est de combiner les différents interrogatifs avec des racines pronominales: elle est très bien attestée dans les langues balkaniques, ce qui permet d'obtenir un système cohérent.

Sandfeld (1930: 191–192) a fait remarquer que les langues balkaniques avaient perdu la distinction entre *ubi* « où » (locatif = lieu où l'on est) et *quō* « où » (directif = lieu où l'on va) et qu'elles utilisaient le même interrogatif: alb. *ku*, bulg. *kăde*, grec *pu*, roum. *unde*. Ainsi, bulg. *kăde živee/otiva?*, roum. *unde locuiește/se duce?*, grec *pu káθete/pijéni*, alb. *ku banon/vete?* « où habite-t-il/va-t-il? ». Parallèlement, il n'existe pas d'opposition entre *ibi* (locatif) et *eo* (directif) « ici » ou entre *foris* et *foras* « dehors ». Comme l'opposition locatif/directif existait en vieux bulgare (*kŭde/kamo*), en grec ancien (ποῦ/ποῖ) et en latin, il s'agit d'un balkanisme général. Le système de la deixis, comme pour les pronoms, s'est réduit à une opposition binaire proximal/distal.

Pour former des adverbes de manière, on se sert des adjectifs exprimant la qualité. Les langues balkaniques ont choisi une forme de l'adjectif et l'ont figée. Ainsi, le slave se sert normalement de la forme neutre de l'adjectif qualitatif (bulg. *tărpelivo* « patiemment », à partir de l'adjectif *tărpeliv*, fém. *tărpeliva*); le grec se sert parfois du neutre singulier de l'adjectif, mais il utilise avant tout le neutre pluriel, sans limitation: *oréa* « parfaitement » (*oréos* « beau »), *efxárista* « agréablement » (*efxáristos* « agréable »). Le roumain utilise la forme du masculin de l'adjectif: *merge încet* « il marche lentement » (*încet* signifie aussi bien « lent » que « lentement »), *cântă frumos* « il chante joliment (= bien) ». L'albanais utilise également l'adjectif comme adverbe, mais dans ce cas, l'article de connexion n'apparaîtra jamais: *ëmbël* « agréablement », *qartë* « clairement ».

La formation d'adverbes de manière (et autres) par redoublement est fréquent (Domi 1975): alb. *kështu e kështu* « ainsi (et ainsi) », *vetëm e vetëm* « purement et simplement », bulg. *koga i koga* « quelquefois », *samo i samo* « à tout prix », grec *siɣá-siɣá* « doucement », *póte-póte* « de temps en temps », roum. *când și când* « id. », *numai și numai* « simplement ». Il s'agit en fait du phénomène plus général de la réduplication expressive.

Toutes les langues balkaniques utilisent le coordonnant « et » dans le sens de « aussi, également »: alb. *edhe ti* « toi aussi », grec *ki o Pávlos* « Paul aussi » bulg. *i az*, roum. *și mie* « moi aussi », *aveți și un cîine* « vous avec aussi un chien », *vin și eu cu tine* « je viens moi aussi avec toi ».

6. Relations phrastiques

6.1. Types de phrases

6.1.1. Phrases sans actants

Bien que les langues balkaniques soient normalement des langues à servitude subjectale, il existe des structures sans sujet. Avec les verbes dits «météorologiques», il y a figement à la 3ᵉ personne du singulier (avec indice pronominal intégré), et la phrase ne peut contenir que des circonstants: gr. *vréxi* «il pleut», *xjonízi* «il neige», roum. *plouă* «il pleut», *ninge* «il neige», alb. *bubullin* «il tonne», *rigon* «il bruine», bulg. *gărmi* «il tonne», *rămi* «il bruine».

6.1.2. Constructions avec «être»

La copule s'emploie à tous les temps et à toutes les personnes. Elle n'est omise régulièrement que dans les exclamatives avec adjectif: grec *tí oréo!*, bulg. *če xubavo!*, roum. *ce frumos(e)!* «que c'est beau!»

On n'utilise jamais de pronom «vide» avec «être» accompagné d'un adjectif ou d'un substantif désignant un phénomène naturel: bg. *studeno/gorešto e* «il fait froid/chaud» (litter. froid/chaud (Nt) est), roum. *e soare* «il fait du soleil», alb. *është natë* 'c'est la nuit».

Le bulgare et le roumain présentent la même structure que l'allemand *mir ist kalt* «à moi est froid = j'ai froid» (bg. *studeno mi e*, roum. *mi-e frig*; cf. *frică mi-e* «j'ai peur», *mi-e foame* «j'ai faim»), alors que l'albanais emploie *kam* «avoir»: *unë kam ftohtë/ngrohtë* «j'ai froid/chaud».

En ce qui concerne le prédicat d'existence, le roumain (uniquement) et le grec (à côté d'autres possibilités) utilisent «être» (variable en nombre) avec le sens de «il y a»: roum. *pe masă sunt flori*, grec *íne lulúðja sto trapézi* «il y a des fleurs sur la table». Les autres langues se servent de la 3ᵉ singulier du présent du verbe «avoir»: grec *éxi*, alb. *ka*, bg. *ima*; le roumain peut employer aussi *are* (3ᵉ singulier du présent du verbe *avea* «avoir»), mais uniquement avec la négation.

Toutes les langues balkaniques utilisent «être» + datif-génitif (préposition *na* en bulgare) pour exprimer la possession: roum. *Al cui e copilul ăsta?*, bg. *na kogo e tova dete?* grec *Pjanú íne to peðí aftó?* «A qui est cet enfant?»; alb. *I kujt është ky libër?* «A qui est ce livre?», *shtëpia është e atit* «la maison est au père». Mais elles possèdent toutes également un verbe «avoir».

6.1.3. Passif

On a une nette césure dans les langues balkaniques entre le grec et l'albanais d'une part, qui possèdent des formes médio-passives synthétiques aux temps simples, le bulgare et le roumain d'autre part, qui se servent de l'auxiliaire «être» et du participe passé passif, et plus souvent encore de la forme réfléchie. Le complément d'agent est peu utilisé dans l'ensemble.

Il y a une vaste concordance dans les valeurs des formes médio-passives: outre le passif, elles expriment le réfléchi (gr *dínume* «je m'habille», *skotónume* «je me tue») et le moyen. Sur ce dernier point, les langues balkaniques se rejoignent avec des moyens différents (formes médio-passives pour le grec et l'albanais, emploi du réfléchi en bulgare et en roumain). Voici quelques exemples particulièrement nets: gr. *fovúme*, alb. *druhem*, bg. *boja se*, roum. *a se teme* «craindre»; gr. *epanérxome*, alb. *kthehet*, bg. *vrăštam se*, roum. *se întoarce* «revenir, rentrer»; gr. *iperifanévome*, alb. *krenohet*, bg. *gordeja se* «être fier», roum. *pattіsn a se îndoiește*, bg. *sămnjavam se* «douter»; etc.

En grec comme en albanais, on trouve à la fois des verbes qui ont un sens différent à l'actif et au médio-passif, et des verbes qui ne s'emploient qu'au médio-passif. D'autres valeurs du passif et du réfléchi se retrouvent dans toutes les langues balkaniques. Par exemple, l'emploi de la 3ᵉ singulier avec le sens de «on»: gr. *aftós akújete* «on parle de lui»; *léjete óti*, alb. *thuhet që*, roum. *se zice, se spune că*, bg. *kazva se če* «on dit que»; alb. *dihet* «on sait», *flitet* «on parle». En dehors du grec qui ne connaît pas ce type, le passif (ou réfléchi) impersonnel est très répandu dans les autres langues: alb. *Këtu flihet deri në orën dhjetë* «Ici se dort = on dort jusqu'à dix heures» (bg. *Tuk se spi do deset časa*), roum. *Magazinul se deschide la ora opt* «Le magasin (s')ouvre à huit heures». Enfin, le passif ou le réfléchi peuvent avoir une valeur modale de possibilité: alb. *Kjo nuk hahet* «Cela ne se mange pas» (cf. bg. *Tova ne se jade*); grec *trójete* «cela se mange» et «cela peut se manger = c'est mangeable», *jínete* «ça arrive» et «ça peut arriver» (bg *slučva se*).

On peut donc parler pour toutes les langues balkaniques d'une voix passive (grec, albanais) et d'une voix réfléchie à valeur passive (bulgare, roumain), plus courante que le passif proprement dit, avec une large concordance des valeurs.

6.2. Relations internes

6.2.1. Fonctions actancielles

Dans les phrases uniactancielles, l'actant unique est au nominatif (grec, roumain, albanais) ou au *casus generalis* (bulgaro-macédonien); c'est le sujet qui impose l'accord au verbe. L'actant est à l'accusatif avec «il y a». En dehors des constructions avec «être», il n'y a pas réellement de verbes uniactanciels présentant un membre au datif. On trouve en revanche des emplois de verbes (passifs en albanais, réfléchis en bulgare) avec pronom personnel au datif avec le sens de «avoir envie de»: alb. *më flihet*, bulg. *spi mi se* «j'ai envie de dormir»; *më rrihet* «j'ai envie de m'asseoir»; bg. *ne mu se jade* «il n'a pas envie de manger». Dans toutes les langues balkaniques, le verbe «devoir» ne s'emploie qu'à la troisième personne du singulier (cf. fr. *il faut*). Il est suivi d'une subordonnée, mais il peut également avoir un membre au datif dans le sens de «il me faut, j'ai besoin»: bg. *trjabva da si otida* «je dois m'en aller», *trjabva mi njakakăv săvet* «j'ai besoin d'un conseil»; alb. *duhet të nisem nesër* «je dois partir demain».

Dans les phrases biactancielles, la marque privilégiée de la relation objectale est l'accusatif (ou «complément direct»). On constate en grec une large extension de ce cas là où d'autres langues ont d'autres constructions: *vlápto* «nuire à», *zilévo* «être jaloux de», *voïthó* «aider», *diathéto* «disposer de», *zitó* «demander qn», *onirévome* «rêver de», *pistévo* «croire [qn]», etc. L'emploi de l'accusatif ne va pas aussi loin dans les autres langues balkaniques, mais il est incontestable que la construction prototypique gagne du terrain. La plus grande originalité est le marquage différentiel de l'objet en roumain à l'aide de la préposition *pe*.

Dans les structures triactancielles, le schéma de loin le plus répandu est celui qui implique un accusatif et un datif. Le double accusatif est peu répandu, mais les verbes concernés concordent. Le roumain a exactement le même inventaire que l'allemand: *a costa* «coûter», *a întreba* «demander, questionner», *a ruga* «demander, prier», *a învăța* «apprendre, enseigner». En grec, on a également *rotó* «demander, questionner», *didásko, mathéno* «apprendre» (accusatif ou datif de la personne) et quelques autres. La construction est plus rare en albanais: *porosis* «charger qn de qc», *mësoj* «apprendre, enseigner», *pyes* «demander qc à qn», et l'accusatif de la chose doit toujours être indéterminé. En bulgare, la construction ne se trouve qu'avec le verbe *pitam* «demander», à la condition que l'objet désignant la chose soit un pronom (sinon, il faut *za*): *Šte te pitam nešto* «Je vais te demander quelque chose».

6.2.2. Fonctions adnominales

On a depuis longtemps répertorié le phénomène de confusion du génitif et du datif, c'est-à-dire l'identité des moyens pour exprimer la fonction d'objet II et la fonction adnominale de possession. Mais la situation est plus contrastée qu'on ne l'imagine au premier abord. Le grec privilégie le génitif seul, sans préposition, pour un grand nombre de valeurs (possession, qualité, origine, etc.), ainsi que l'albanais, mais toujours avec l'article de connexion. À l'autre extrémité, le bulgare, qui a perdu les cas, se sert de la préposition *na* qui a également de nombreuses valeurs. Entre ces deux pôles, le roumain semble connaître une vaste gamme de possibilités: génitif-datif seul (*casa tatălui* «la maison du père»; *dar patriei* «don à la patrie»), préposition *lui* (*pentru numele lui Dumnezeu* «au nom de Dieu»), préposition *de* (*fiul de văduvă* et *fiul văduvei* «le fils d'une veuve»), relateur *a* (*plecarea a toată lumea* «le départ de tout le monde»). Mais en fait, les moyens de marquage sont plus ou moins en distribution complémentaire.

6.2.3. Fonctions circonstancielles

Les langues balkaniques montrent de remarquables concordances dans l'emploi des prépositions: d'une manière générale, si l'on divise les circonstants qui s'ordonnent par rapport au procès en circonstants d'amont, d'aval et de concomitance, on constate que les langues balkaniques utilisent les mêmes prépositions pour les domaines spatial, temporel et notionnel: grec *apó*, alb. *prej*, bulg. *ot*, roum. *de*; grec et alb. *me*, roum. *cu*, bulg. *s*; grec *ja*, alb. *për*, roum. *pentru*, bulg. *za*.

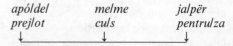

| *apó/del* | *me/me* | *ja/për* |
| *prej/ot* | *cu/s* | *pentru/za* |

Les prépositions d'amont expriment dans toutes les langues balkaniques l'origine spatiale («(à partir) de»), temporelle («depuis»), la cause, l'agent au passif, le complément de matière (dans l'unité nominale) et le partitif, surtout après pronom. Les prépositions liées au centre marquent la manière, l'instrument, le moyen, le comitatif et le sociatif (« avec »). Celles d'aval expriment le but, le bénéficiaire et, d'une manière générale, l'entité terminale (« pour »).

6.3. Ordre des mots

D'une manière générale, les langues balkaniques montrent une grande souplesse dans l'agencement des constituants. Même si l'ordre non marqué est SVO, on trouve très fréquemment des séquences différentes. Les servitudes positionnelles sont rares: elles concernent surtout les enclitiques (pronoms atones, marquants temporels et modaux, négation) qui se situent d'une manière générale en tête de phrase ou le plus près possible du début de la phrase. Le bulgare littéraire est la seule langue où les pronoms atones doivent être couverts par un autre élément: alb. *e shikoni* « vous le regardez », *i fola* « je lui parlai »; macéd. *gi gledam* « je les regarde », *im rekov da dojdat* « je leur ai dit de venir »; grec *to vlépo* « je le vois », *sas milúme* « nous vous parlons »; roum. *mă vede* « il me voit », *vă vorbește* « je vous parle ». Il en est de même aux temps composés formés avec l'auxiliaire « avoir ». Le roumain connaît cependant une exception avec le pronom féminin *o* qui se place après le participe: *am căutat-o* « je l'ai cherchée », *aș fi căutat-o* « je l'aurais cherchée ». Le pronom court au datif précède celui à l'accusatif: alb. *ma dha* « il me le donna » (*ma* est la contraction de *më* + *ë*); bulg. *az mu go/gi dadox* « je le/les lui ai donné(s) »; grec *su ti δíno* « je te la donne », *mu to les* « tu me le dis »; roum. *i le-am dat* « je les leur ai données », *ni-i dai* « tu nous les donnes ».

Les langues balkaniques se rejoignent également dans l'agencement des pronoms conjoints avec les diverses « particules ». Ainsi, les pronoms conjoints se placent entre le marquant de futur et de subjonctif, excluant alors la présence de tout groupe nominal ou de tout pronom sujet. Le roumain fait exception pour le futur formé avec l'infinitif. Alb. *Nuk ju kisha vëllezër, po tani e tutje do të ju kem* « vous n'étiez pas mes frères, mais vous le serez », *do të ta (= të + e) jap* « je te le donnerai », *mund të më marrësh vesh* « tu peux me comprendre »; bulg. *šte ti kaža nešto* « je te dirai quelque chose », *iskam da ti go dam* « je veux te le donner »; grec *θa sas tus δíxome* « nous vous les montrerons », *fovúme na tis to po* « je crains de le lui dire (= à elle) »; roum. *o să te văd* « je te verrai » (mais *te voi vedea*, avec pronom précédant l'auxiliaire), *vreau să mă vadă* « je veux qu'il me voie ».

Enfin, il y a une complète convergence en ce qui concerne la négation; elle précède toujours les marquants temporels et les pronoms conjoints: alb. *s'i ndihmon* « il ne l'aide pas », *s'do t'ia ketë dhënë* « il ne le lui aura pas donné »; bulg. *ne mu gi dadox* « je ne les lui ai pas donnés », *ne šte ti go kaža* « je ne te le dirai pas », grec *δe mu to ípes* « tu ne me l'as pas dit », *δe θa tus ti δósis* « tu ne la leur donneras pas », roum. *nu mi-o dă* « il ne me la donne pas », *n-o să ti-o dau* « je ne te la donnerai pas » (le premier *o* est l'auxiliaire du futur, le second le pronom personnel), mais *nu ți-oi da-o*.

6.3.1. Ordre sujet/verbe

La loi fondamentale est celle de la progression informative, c'est-à-dire que les éléments lourds ont tendance à se situer à la fin de la phrase. Dans une phrase uniactancielle, si le sujet est rhématique, il se placera après le verbe. Les langues balkaniques n'ont pas besoin d'un pronom « postiche » (comme le français *il* ou l'allemand *es*) pour couvrir le verbe. Cette construction se rencontre pratiquement toujours avec les verbes événementiels, les verbes impliquant un phénomène météorologique ou ceux qui ont une charge sémantique faible (comme « être » ou « avoir »): bulg. *Dojde esen* « Arriva l'automne », *Mina vreme* « Le temps passa », *vali dăžd* « il pleut »; alb. *Ndodhi një aksident* « Il s'est produit un accident », *U bë heshtje* « Il se fit silence », *bie borë* « il neige »; grec *Vrískondan ki Élines ekí?* « Y avait-il aussi des Grecs là-bas? », *Jínonde δjapraɣmatéfsis* « Des négociations ont lieu », *Sisoréftikan polá xjónja* « Une neige épaisse s'est amoncelée »; roum. *nu se întîmplă niciodată nimic* « il ne se passe jamais rien », *Ziua cernuse o ploaie măruntă* « Pendant la journée, il était tombé une pluie fine ».

6.3.2. « Redoublement de l'objet »

Une des principales raisons de la souplesse syntaxique des langues balkaniques est la possibilité qu'elles ont d'extraposer l'objet I ou l'objet II et de le rappeler dans le rhème par un pronom court. C'est une manière de transcender l'ordre trop rigide SVO. Le bulgare, qui a perdu les marques casuelles, montre la même souplesse que les autres langues balkaniques: quand le sujet et l'objet ont la même forme et qu'ils désignent des animés, on peut malgré tout mettre l'objet en tête avec rappel obligatoire par le pronom clitique:

(1) Bulgare
Marija ja   običa Ivan
Maria la:ACC aime Ivan
« Ivan aime Maria; Maria, Ivan l'aime ».

La première position de l'objet dans la phrase sert aussi bien à thématiser qu'à focaliser ce membre fonctionnel: c'est en ce cas la prosodie qui sert à distinguer les deux types, l'accent focalisateur étant exclusif. Le rappel du membre extraposé par un pronom court, s'il est fréquent, n'est pas toujours obligatoire, et la situation varie selon les langues. Voici un aperçu:

a) Les langues balkaniques n'ont pas de structures de rappel avec le nominatif (du type *Mon père, il travaille beaucoup*), car il n'y a pas à ce cas de double série pronominale.
b) L'utilisation du pronom court est aussi courante dans le cas où l'objet est support (en tête de phrase) que dans celui où il est report.

(2) Roumain
  (a) *pe   vecin l-am văzut*
      PREP voisin le-ai vu
      « Le voisin, je l'ai vu ».
  (b) *l-am văzut pe   vecin*
      l'ai vu   PREP voisin
      « Je l'ai vu (ou j'ai vu) le voisin ».

(3) Grec
  (a) *ti María δen tin   íδa*
      ART Marie NEG pron.3 SG.ACC vis
      akómi
      encore
      « Marie, je ne l'ai pas encore vue ».
  (b) *δen tin   íδa akómi ti*
      NEG PRON.3 SG.ACC vis encore ART
      María
      Marie
      « Je ne l'ai pas encore vue, Marie ».

Il en est de même en bulgare et en albanais.
c) Les servitudes varient selon les langues. En albanais, le pronom court du datif est toujours obligatoire si la phrase contient un groupe nominal en fonction d'objet II.

(4) Albanais
    i   dhashë sqarime
    PRON.3e SG.DAT donnai explications
    një student-i
    un étudiant-DAT
    « J'ai donné des explications à un étudiant ».

On notera que le roumain anticipe également le complément au datif, mais ce n'est pas cependant une servitude.

(9) Roumain
    mi-a   dat şi
    PRON.1 SG.DAT (court) -a donné aussi
    mie o carte
    à.moi un livre
    « A moi aussi, il m'a donné un livre ».

En bulgare, le « redoublement » est très fréquent, mais il n'est réellement obligatoire que si les fonctions sujet et objet I peuvent être confondues. Le grec présente à peu près la même situation. Dans les langues balkaniques, il y a un lien incontestable entre thématisation (définie) et emploi proleptique du pronom court. En roumain, il est impossible d'employer le pronom court si l'objet est indéterminé. Dans les autres langues, la reprise pronominale est rare. En macédonien, la norme veut qu'un objet défini soit toujours repris par un pronom court, toute transgression étant ressentie comme grossière. Ce n'est pas le cas en bulgare littéraire. On notera la très haute fréquence − qui devient à la limite une servitude (c'est le cas en albanais s'il n'y a pas contraste) − de la succession pronom long + pronom court: grec *eména me vlépi*/alb. *mua më sheh*/bulg. *mene me viždal* roum. *pe mine mă vede* « moi me (il) voit = Moi, il me voit ».

On constate également qu'on n'utilise généralement pas le pronom proleptique si l'objet initial est mis en relief (contraste, emphase, focalisation). La loi est stricte en albanais: si l'objet est rhème ou s'il appartient au rhème et porte l'accent principal, il n'est pas repris par le pronom. Cette loi n'est plus absolue en bulgare contemporain. Il en est de même en roumain.

7. Subordination

On ne peut proposer une étude complète de la subordination, et l'on signalera simplement les phénomènes marquants.

7.1. Complétives

Le trait commun remarquable de toutes les langues balkaniques est de posséder un système de complétives tout à fait semblable. La cause première est bien évidemment la disparation complète ou partielle de l'infinitif et son remplacement par le subjonctif. Cette disparition a entraîné la création d'un double système de subordonnants selon que la complétive a valeur « subjonctive » ou non: alb. *tëlqë*, bulg. *dalčě*, grec *nalóti*, roum. *sălcă*. Les emplois de la conjonction subjonctive correspondent dans l'ensemble aux emplois de l'infinitif ou du subjonctif français: modalités de nécessité, possibilité et volonté; procès non encore réalisé, c'est-à-dire simplement conçu: on trouvera tous les verbes de volonté, d'intention, de désir, d'attente; avec les verbes exprimant divers sentiments ayant normalement une connotation négative: hésitation, crainte, honte; avec les verbes de commandement, de prière, d'invitation, de conseil, c'est-à-dire le désir que soit accomplie une action; avec les verbes de phase (« commencer », « continuer », poursuivre », « achever ») et divers autres. On doit distinguer les servitudes grammaticales, comme après les types qu'on vient d'énumérer, et les cas où la concurrence joue avec l'indicatif. Ainsi, on emploiera la conjonction subjonctive si « penser » ou « dire » expriment respectivement les sens de « envisager » et de « commander »: alb. *Mendoni se ai mund ta bëjë?* « Pensez-vous qu'il puisse le faire? », bulg. *Kazax im, če šte trăgvat* « Je leur ai dit qu'ils allaient partir »/*Kazax im da trăgvat* « Je leur ai dit de partir », *Mislja, če postăpva v njakoi kursove* « Je pense qu'il suit quelques cours »/*Mislja da postăpja v njakoi kursove* « Je pense suivre quelques cours ». La présence de la négation entraîne souvent l'utilisation du subjonctif: alb. (Buchholz & Fiedler 1987: 137): *Se nuk di të kem të bëj me ty?* « Je ne sache pas que j'ai quelque chose à faire avec toi »; bulg. *Ne mi kaza da go e viždal* « Il ne m'a pas dit qu'il l'ait vu » (mais *Ne mi kaza, če go e viždal* « Il ne m'a pas dit qu'il l'avait vu ») »; roum. *cred că e bolnav* « je crois qu'il est malade », mais *nu cred să fie bolnav* « je ne crois pas qu'il soit malade ». On oppose également de manière générale ce qui est considéré comme sûr (indicatif) et ce qui est considéré comme incertain ou douteux: roum. (Lombard 1974: 282): *regret că e bolnav* « je regrette qu'il soit malade », mais *aş regreta să fie bolnav* (ou plutôt *să îl ştiu bolnav*) « je regretterais qu'il soit malade ».

7.2. Relatives

Toutes les langues balkaniques ont la particularité de posséder des relatifs variables, qui ont une morphologie de type pronominal, et un ou plusieurs relatifs invariables. Le trait commun, sûrement d'origine grecque, est l'existence d'un relatif d'origine spatiale (sauf en roumain): grec *pu*, bulg. *kădeto*, alb. *tek*, mais surtout *që* (comparable à l'anglais *that*). Il est assez fréquent que le pronom personnel à la forme courte rappelle la fonction du relatif (quand il n'est pas sujet), mais ce n'est pas une obligation: bulg. *Ključăt e pod onaja ploča, deto ja znaeš* « La clé est sous cette dalle que tu connais », grec *o ánθropos pu tu δánisa ta leftá íne o θíos mu* « l'homme à qui j'ai prêté l'argent est mon oncle ».

7.3. Subordonnées circonstancielles

a) Dans les langues balkaniques, les subordonnées à sens spatial ou temporel utilisent comme conjonctions les interrogatifs. Le bulgare présente un phénomène particulier (et cela est valable pour tout le système): il distingue, à une ou deux exceptions près, l'interrogatif de la conjonction en ajoutant à cette dernière un *-to* postposé: *koga* (interrogatif)/*kogato* (conjonction) « quand »; *zašto* « pourquoi? »/*zaštoto* « parce que », *kak* « comment? »/*kakto* « comme ».

Sandfeld (1930: 137) signale un balkanisme intéressant. En albanais, la conjonction *sa* « combien, tant que » s'emploie très fréquemment comme conjonction temporelle: *sa vate ne ura* « quand il arriva au pont ». Le roumain présente le même emploi de *cât*: *cât a sosit* « quand il est arrivé » (la phrase est cependant refusée par les roumanophones). Il en est de même pour le macédonien *kolkoto* et le grec *óso*: *i vasílisa óson íγlepe tin omorfián tis kóris* « quand la reine vit la beauté de sa fille ».

b) La conjonction exprimant la concession peut se former à l'aide d'une préposition signifiant « malgré » et du subordonnant extensif « que »: alb. *me ghithë + se > megjithëse*), bulg. *văpreki če*, grec *me ólon óti > molonóti*, roum. *cu toate că*. Plus frappant est la présence de « tout » dans les formations prépositionnelles et conjonctionnelles en rapport avec la préposition « avec » (alb. *me*, grec *me*, roum. *cu*); en bulgare, on a *pri* qui peut marquer l'accompagnement de circonstances: *pri vse če*. Cela correspond exactement à allem. *bei*. Un autre trait commun est l'utilisation du coordonnant « et » dans la constitution de la conjonction: alb. *edhe (p)se*, grec *an ke*, roum. *deşi, totuşi* et bulg. *makar i da*. On voit nettement que la formation correspond à « même si ». Sandfeld (1930: 108) note qu'en grec une concessive est fréquemment formée avec une expression signifiant « et laisse que cela soit » et correspondant à « même si »: *Θié mu, δos m'éna peδí, ki' as íne ke misó* « Seigneur, donne-moi un enfant, et laisse que cela soit (= même si c'est) un demi-enfant ». Il en est de même en aroumain: *Doamne, ună feată, ş'las s'hibă şună Dafnă* « Donne-moi,

Seigneur, une fille, même si c'est un laurier», en alb. *dëftomë mua, pa letë vdesësh ti* «dis-le moi, même si tu en meurs» et en macédonien *Ej Gospodi! daj-mi edno momiče, ta pak makari lamija neka da e* «Ô Seigneur, donne-moi une fille, même si c'est un monstre».

c) On a une formation semblable de la conjonction de but en bulgare, grec et roumain que se retrouve d'ailleurs en français: bulg. *za da*, grec *ja na*, roum. *pentru ca să* «pour que». L'albanais connaît également cette formation, mais avec les formes impersonnelles: *për të* + participe. Dans toutes les langues balkaniques, on peut simplement se servir du marquant de subjonctif pour exprimer le but après les verbes de mouvement: alb. *Erdha (që) të them të vërtetën* «Je suis venu (pour) te dire la vérité», bulg. *Otidox da go vidja* «Je suis allé (pour) le voir», grec *píje na féri neró* «elle partit (pour) chercher de l'eau», roum. *a venti să te întrebe ceva* «il est venu (pour) te demander quelque chose».

8. Références

Andriotis, N. P. & Kourmoulis G. 1968. «Questions de la linguistique balkanique et l'apport de la langue grecque», in *Actes ...*, 21−30.

Asenova, Petja. 1979. «Aperçu historique des études dans le domaine de la linguistique balkanique», *Balkansko ezikoznanie*, XXII, 1, 5−45.

Asenova, Petja. 1989. *Balkansko ezikoznanie*, Sofia: Nauka i izkustvo.

Baciu, Ioan. 1978. *Précis de grammaire roumaine*, Lyon: L'Hermès.

Boissin, Henri. 1975. *Grammaire de l'albanais moderne*, Paris: Chez l'auteur.

Buchholz, Oda & Fiedler, Wilfried. 1987. *Albanische Grammatik*, Leipzig: Verlag Enzyklopädie.

Domi, Mahir. 1975. «Considérations sur les traits communs ou parallèls de l'albanais avec les autres langues balkaniques et sur leur étude», *Studia Albanica*, XII, 1, 81−91.

Feuillet, Jack. 1986. *La linguistique balkanique*, N° 10 des *Cahiers balkaniques*, Paris: Publications Langues O'.

Georgiev, Vladimir, Gălăbov, Ivan & Zaimov, Jordan (rédacteurs). 1968. *Actes du premier congrès international des études balkaniques et sud-est européennes*, vol. VI, Sofia: Académie Bulgare des Sciences.

Georgiev, Vladimir. 1968. «Le problème de l'union linguistique balkanique», *Actes ...*, 7−19.

Georgiev, Valdimir. 1976. «Văznikvane na novi složni glagolni formi săs spomagatelen glagol *imam*» in Pašov & Nicolova, 294−311.

Ivić, Pavel. 1968. «Liens phonologiques entre les langues balkaniques», *Actes ...*, 133−141.

Joseph, Brian & Philippaki-Warburton, Irene. 1987. *Modern Greek*, London: Croom Helm.

Lombard, Alf. 1974. *La langue roumaine*, Paris: Klincksieck.

Mackridge, Peter. 1985. *The modern Greek Language*, Oxford: Oxford University Press.

Pašov, Petăr & Nicolova, Ruselina. 1976. *Pomagalo po bălgarska morfologija. Glagol*, Sofia: Nauka i izkustvo.

Poghirc, Cicerone. 1977. «L'apport des substrats antiques à l'union linguistique balkanique», *Balkansko ezikoznanie*, XX, 1−2, 85−86.

Poghirc, Cicerone. 1983. *Philologica et Linguistica*, Bochum: Brockmeyer.

Reiter, Norbert. 1994. *Grundzüge der Balkanologie*, Wiesbaden: Harrassowitz.

Rossetti, Alexandru. 1985. *La linguistique balkanique*, București: Editura Univers.

Sandfeld, Kristian. 1930. *Linguistique balkanique. Problèmes et résultats.* Paris: Klincksieck.

Schaller, Helmut. 1975. *Die Balkansprachen*, Heidelberg: Carl Winter.

Simeonov, Boris. 1977. «Obščie čerty fonologičeskix sistem balkanskix jazykov», *Balkansko ezikoznanie*, XX, 1−2, 53−59.

Thumb, Albert. 1910. *Handbuch der neugriechischen Volkssprache*, Straßburg: Truebner.

Jack Feuillet, Nantes (France)

109. Südasien als Sprachbund

1. Einleitung
2. Areale Charakteristika
3. Methodische Probleme
4. Die Frage der Abgrenzung
5. Fazit
6. Spezielle Abkürzungen
7. Zitierte Literatur

1. Einleitung

In Südasien werden rund 450 Sprachen gesprochen, die − wenn man von den isolierten Nahali und Burushaski absieht − zu vier verschiedenen Sprachfamilien gehören. Eine genauere Zahl der Sprachen lässt sich nicht angeben, da zum einen die Zählung stark differiert, zum anderen die Abgrenzung des Areals. Bei Emeneau (1956, 1971) war noch die Rede von einem „Indian Linguistic Area". Dieser Begriff wurde später aus politischen Gründen aufgegeben. Geographisch gesehen zählen zu Südasien die Länder Pakistan, Indien, Nepal, Bhutan, Bangladesch und Sri Lanka. Sprachen Nepals oder Bhutans werden allerdings ebenso selten in die areallinguistische Diskussion einbezogen wie die tibeto-burmanischen Sprachen im Nordosten Indiens.

Was die Anzahl der Sprecher betrifft, bilden die indoarischen (iar.) Sprachen die größte Gruppe (78%), gefolgt von den Sprechern dravidischer (drav.) Sprachen (20%). Die Sprecher der tibetoburmanischen (tb.) und der austroasiatischen Munda-Sprachen (mu.) machen zusammen also nicht mehr als 2% aus. Die drav. Sprachen bilden ein relativ kompaktes Areal, das die Südspitze des Subkontinents abdeckt. Einzelne drav. Einsprengsel in Bihar (Kurukh, Malto) und Pakistan (Brahui) zeugen von der früher ausgedehnteren Verbreitung dieser Sprachgruppe. Die Munda-Sprachen bilden Inseln vor allem in den Staaten Bihar und Orissa. Die nächstverwandte Sprache ist das Khasi in Assam, das ebenfalls zur austroasiatischen Familie gehört. Tb. Sprachen sind an den nordwestlichen bis nordöstlichen Rändern des südasiatischen Areals zu finden. Sie bilden nach der Zahl der Sprachen die größte Gruppe und weisen die größte strukturelle Verschiedenheit auf.

Aufgrund der Vielfalt der beteiligten Sprachen bietet Südasien ein äußerst interessantes Gebiet für Untersuchungen der Verbreitung sprachlicher Strukturen über genetische Grenzen hinweg. In der Literatur zur Areallinguistik Südasiens werden die Sprachen allerdings eher nach der Zahl ihrer Sprecher berücksichtigt als nach linguistischer Diversität. Vermeer (1969) z. B. widmet 120 Seiten den iar., 49 den drav. und 16 den mu. Sprachen; tb. Sprachen kommen gar nicht vor. Im Wesentlichen werden in der Literatur gemeinsame Merkmale zwischen iar. und drav. Sprachen behandelt, mit gelegentlichen Hinweisen auf Munda. Dies ist z. T. bedingt durch Beschreibungsdefizite in Bezug auf die kleineren Sprachen, von denen viele noch immer nach dem „Linguistic Survey of India" (Grierson 1903−1928) zitiert werden. Das Anliegen der meisten Forscher ist jedoch erklärtermaßen, den Prozeß der „Indisierung" der iar. Sprachen, möglicherweise unter drav. Einfluss, zu klären.

Neben dem Balkan gilt Südasien als ein klassisches Beispiel für einen Sprachbund. Schon den Sprachwissenschaftlern des 19. Jhs. fiel auf, dass die iar. Sprachen mit den drav. gemeinsame Züge aufweisen. Die Frage einer möglichen Übernahme retroflexer Konsonanten aus dem Drav. ins Sanskrit wurde eingehend erörtert. Caldwell (1956: 55) erwähnt darüberhinaus die oblique Form der Nomina, an die im Singular und Plural die gleichen Kasussuffixe angehängt werden, die Unterscheidung inklusiver und exklusiver Pronomina, die Stellung der modifizierenden Attribute vor dem Kopf, die Verwendung von Postpositionen statt (wie sonst im Indoeuropäischen) Präpositionen. Einen drav. Einfluss hält er jedoch, wie die meisten Indologen und Sanskritisten nach ihm, für nicht wahrscheinlich.

Die fundiertere Diskussion bei Bloch (1934) geht ebenfalls von der Fragestellung aus, ob das Iar. strukturelle Merkmale aus dem Drav. entlehnt haben könnte. Blochs Liste enthält u. a. die retroflexen Konsonanten, Echowörter, das Fehlen von Präfixen, die Verwendung von Konverben (bei ihm wie allgemein in der Indologie „Absolutiv" genannt) und die partizipiale Form von Relativsätzen. Sein erklärtes Ziel ist es, die Zahl der postulierten Entlehnungen zu minimieren, und er kommt dementsprechend zu dem Fazit: „Ainsi donc, si profondes qu'aient été les influences locales, elles n'ont pas conduit l'aryen de l'Inde ... à se différencier forte-

ment des autres langues indo-européennes."
(1934: 330).

Die Linguistik Südasiens erhielt neue Impulse durch Emeneau, der den Begriff Sprachbund („linguistic area") auf Südasien anwandte und zu einem ganz anderen Ergebnis kommt als Bloch: „Certainly the end result of the borrowings is that the languages of the two families, Indo-Aryan and Dravidian, seem in many respects more akin to one another than Indo-Aryan does to the other Indo-European languages" (1980 [1956]: 119−120). Emeneau kommt das Verdienst zu, eine Brücke zwischen der Dravidologie und der Indologie geschlagen zu haben. Er brachte eine Reihe neuer Merkmale in die Diskussion ein, die er anhand umfangreichen Materials vor allem auch kleinerer drav. Sprachen untersuchte.

Den ersten umfassenden Versuch einer präzisen Definition des südasiatischen Sprachbundes und seiner Begrenzung nach außen hin unternahm Masica (1976). Sein Buch gilt heute als Standardwerk zum Sprachbund Südasien (s. § 3.4.).

Ich werde im Folgenden die wichtigsten Merkmale aus dem Katalog der arealen Charakteristika vorstellen und danach einige methodologische Probleme sowie die Frage der Abgrenzung des Sprachbundes diskutieren.

2. Areale Charakteristika

2.1. Retroflexe Konsonanten

Alle Sprachen im Zentrum des südasiatischen Areals haben retroflexe Verschlusslaute in Opposition zu dentalen (Ramanujan & Masica 1969). Viele westliche iar. Sprachen, aber auch Oriya, haben ausser der Unterscheidung t : ṭ und d : ḍ auch phonemisches ṇ und ḷ, wie die meisten drav. Sprachen. In den Sprachen des Nordostens (z. B. Naga-Sprachen (tb.), Khasi (austroas.), Assamesisch (iar.)) findet man keine solchen Oppositionen. Der mögliche drav. Ursprung der retroflexen Konsonanten wurde rund hundert Jahre lang heftig diskutiert, von Sanskritisten und Indogermanisten jedoch immer wieder abgelehnt. Erst Kuiper (1967) belegte in einer sorgfältigen Untersuchung plausibel die Rolle eines drav. Substrats bei der Ausbildung der retroflexen Phoneme, indem er deren graduelle Zunahme in den aufeinanderfolgenden Büchern der Rigveda nachwies. Auch die retroflexen Konsonanten in den Munda-Sprachen müssen auf ein drav. Vorbild zurückgehen.

2.2. Morphologische Kausative

Morphologische Kausativbildungen finden wir überall in Südasien. Während jedoch die Sprachen im größten Teil des Subkontinents Suffixe verwenden, werden im Osten Kausative vermehrt mithilfe von Präfixen gebildet. In den austroasiatischen Sprachen sowie in den tb. Sprachen des Nordostens ist dies das normale Verfahren, z. B. Kharia (mu.) ñog/ob-ñog, Mundari (mu.) jom/a-jom, und Sora (mu.) jum/a-jumjum 'essen/füttern'; Khasi tip/pn-tip 'wissen/informieren', iap/pn-iap 'sterben/töten', Mao Naga (tb.) apo/so-pho 'durchbrechen (itr./tr.)', ako/so-kho 'zerbrechen' (itr./tr.).

Eine Reihe von Sprachen haben darüberhinaus sekundäre Kausativierungen: Malayalam (drav.) oṭi-/oṭi-kk-/oṭi-ppi-kk- 'brechen (itr./tr.); brechen lassen'; Kaschmiri (iar.) con/caavun/caavinaavun 'trinken; zu trinken geben; zu trinken geben lassen'; Marathi (iar.) bas-/basaw-/basawaw- 'sich setzen; setzen; sich setzen lassen'. Emeneau (1980 [1971]: 174) vermutet aufgrund der Chronologie in iar. Sprachen, dass in der zweifachen Kausativformation Konvergenz mit dem Drav. vorliegt. Nach Masica (1976: 57, 101) sind die Sprachen im Osten von den sekundären Kausativierungen ausgeschlossen. Ein kursorischer Blick durch Grammatiken kleinerer Sprachen fördert aber auf Anhieb eine Reihe solcher Bildungen in Sprachen dieses Gebiets zutage, z. B. Mikir (tb.) mē-/pe-mē-/pa-pe-mē- 'gut sein/verbessern/verbessern lassen', thì-/pe-thì-/pa-pe-thì- 'sterben/töten/töten lassen'; Limbu (tb.) thang-/thakt-/thangs- 'heraufkommen/-bringen/heraufbringen lassen'. Diese können weder vom Drav. noch vom Iar. beeinflusst sein; sekundäre Kausativbildungen kommen in den benachbarten iar. Sprachen Assamesisch, Bengali und Nepali nicht vor.

2.3. OV-Wortstellung

Die Sprachen Südasiens von Pakistan bis Assam haben Verbendstellung (s. Beispiele in § 2.4.). Die einzigen Ausnahmen bilden das Kaschmiri (iar.) im Nordwesten und das Khasi (austroas.) im Nordosten, die beide (S)VO haben. Bei der Stellung der Modifikatoren finden sich allerdings gewisse Unterschiede. In den meisten nordöstlichen Sprachen (einschliesslich Bengali und Assamesisch) kann das Zahlwort dem Nomen folgen. Die tb. Sprachen dieser Region haben Adjektive und/oder Demonstrativa nach dem Nomen (Nocte, Lhota, Manipuri, Mizo). In

Munda-Sprachen steht bei Inkorporierung das Objekt nach dem Verb und reflektiert damit die ältere austroasiatische Wortstellung.

2.4. Konverben

Als arealtypisches Merkmal wird in der Literatur stets das sequentielle Konverb („conjunctive participle", „Absolutiv") angeführt. Dieses verbindet aufeinanderfolgende Handlungen, die oft zu einer langen Kette gereiht werden können.

(1) Koḍava (drav.)
ava visha iṭṭ-ë seebï
sie Gift geb.PFV-PTCP Apfel
paṇṇï-na tind-itï
Frucht-ACC ess.PFV-CONV
cattï-pooc-i.
sterb.PFV-geh.PFV-3
'Sie aß den vergifteten Apfel und starb.'

(2) Nepali (iar.)
ma bas-era euṭa kitāp paḍ-chu.
ich sitz-CONV ein Buch les-FUT:1s
'Ich werde mich hinsetzen und ein Buch lesen.'

(3) Santali (mu.) (McPhail 1953: 77)
oṛak'-khon naheɛl hatao-kate ona
Haus-ABL Pflug nimm-CONV DEM
agua-ñ-ma.
bring-1SG.OBJ-IMP
'Nimm den Pflug vom Haus und bring ihn mir.'

(4) Newari (tb.)
ji-gu la dæ:-k-aa
ich-NOML Fleisch koch-CAUS-CONV
sɔkɔsi-nõ nɔ-i.
alle-ERG ess-FUT.DISJUNKT
'Sie werden mein Fleisch kochen und alle werden essen.'

(Beispiele ohne Quellenangabe stammen aus meinem eigenen Material.) Satz (1) zeigt über die konverbale Verbindung hinaus die Relativsatzeinbettung mithilfe eines Partizips, die von manchen Autoren als eigenes areales Merkmal angeführt wird (Bloch 1934, Emeneau 1956), aber meist mit Konverben einhergeht. Das sequentielle Konverb ist nur eines von verschiedenen Möglichkeiten der konverbalen Satzverbindung. In den drav. und tb. Sprachen haben Nebensätze typischerweise nonfinite Form und sind dem Hauptsatz vorangestellt. Ein längerer Satz mit mehreren Einbettungen hat nur ein finites Verb am Satzende.

Nonfinite Nebensätze sind, wie die Beispiele (1) bis (4) zeigen, in allen vier Sprachfamilien zu finden. Es muss hinzugefügt werden, dass eindeutig konverbale Formen in tb. Sprachen des Nordostens und in einigen Munda-Sprachen nur beschränkt zu finden sind (vgl. Ebert 1993). Die iar. Sprachen haben häufig Nebensätze mit einer einleitenden Konjunktion und einem finiten Verb. Insgesamt weisen die Nebensatzkonstruktionen in den Sprachen Südasiens eine große Bandbreite verschiedener Typen auf (vgl. Masica 1991: 401–402).

2.5. Explikatorverben

Südasiatische Sprachen bilden Verbkomplexe („compound verbs") bestehend aus einer nonfiniten Form des Inhaltsverbs (V1) gefolgt von einem finiten Zweitverb (V2), das verschiedene Funktionen übernehmen kann. In der Literatur werden diese Zweitverben u. a. „explicator verb", „vector verb", „aspectivizer", „verbal specifier" genannt. Die fortlaufende Suche nach einer geeigneten Bezeichnung spiegelt die vielfältigen, nicht leicht unter einen Hut zu bringenden Funktionen des V2. Oft telisiert das V2 ein atelisches oder aktional nicht spezifiziertes V1. Manche V2 atelisieren jedoch oder sind als Progressivmarkierung grammatikalisiert; andere drücken phasenspezifizierende Bedeutungen aus (z. B. inchoativ, kontinuativ), oder sie geben der Aussage eine emotive Komponente. Aus den vielen Möglichkeiten führe ich hier nur ein paar zur Illustration an: Tamil (drav.) *uṭantu pooyirru* '(es) ging kaputt' mit V2 *poo* 'gehen', *katavai tirantu koṭuttan* '(er) öffnete die Tür für jem.' mit V2 *koṭu* 'geben'; Marathi (iar.) *ṭakun dilaa* '(er) warf weg' mit V2 *di* 'geben', *phaaṛun ṭaaklaa* '(er) zerriss' mit V2 *ṭaak* 'werfen'.

Ähnliche Verbindungen finden sich über den ganzen Subkontinent verbreitet. In der Regel hat das Inhaltsverb wie in den obigen Beispielen die Form des sequentiellen Konverbs. In manchen Sprachen steht der einfache Stamm von V1, z. B. Maithili (iar.) *kha lelah* '(er) aß es auf' mit V2 *le* 'nehmen', *uiṭh gelah* '(er) wachte auf' mit V2 *ge* 'gehen'; Koḍava (dr.) verwendet den perfektiven Stamm (vgl. Beispiel (1)).

Nach Masica (1976: 146–147) haben die in den verschiedenen Sprachen als V2 verwendeten Verben oft eine ähnliche Semantik; als Vollverben bedeuten sie z. B. 'gehen', 'kommen', 'werfen', 'setzen'. Es gibt jedoch viele einzelsprachliche Besonderheiten, und das einzige übereinstimmende Merkmal scheint die nonfinite Form von V1 zu sein. Die Munda-Sprachen fügen sich überhaupt nicht in ein gängiges Muster. Masicas Liste der Explikatorverben nennt für Santali, der einzigen berücksichtigten Munda-Sprache, nur die Verben *jom* 'essen' und *goṭ* 'pflücken'. Für beide sind Entsprechungen aus iar. oder drav. Sprachen nicht bekannt. Die Verhältnisse sind ähnlich in anderen Munda-Sprachen, aber auch im norddrav. Kurukh, wo wir ungewöhnliche Explikatorverben wie *biʔ* 'kochen', *kuʔn* 'auf die Hüfte setzen' finden. Zudem passen die Verbverbindungen in manchen Munda-Sprachen, im Kurukh wie auch in den Kiranti-Sprachen (tb.) noch nicht einmal der Bildung nach zum südasiatischen Typus. Sie setzen sich aus zwei flektierten Verben zusammen, z. B. Parengi (mu.) *silay-ing ta'y-ing* (näh-1s V2:geb-1s) 'näh für mich!', Camling (tb.) *sip-ung-pid-ung* (dass.).

Eine vergleichende Untersuchung der Verbverbindungen unter Einbeziehung der Semantik steht noch aus. Sogar für die einzelnen Sprachen sind die Funktionen meist alles andere als klar.

2.6. „Dativ-Subjekt"

Gefühle, kognitive Zustände, aber auch Verpflichtung und Fähigkeit werden typischerweise mithilfe einer Dativkonstruktion ausgedrückt:

(5) Tamil (drav.)
ena-kku kuḷirā irukkutu.
er-DAT kalt sein.PRES.NEUT
'Ihm ist kalt.'

(6) Hindi (iar.) (Masica 1991: 347)
bacce-ko ṭhaṇḍ lag rahī hai.
Kind-DAT Kälte befall- PROG ist
'Dem Kind ist kalt.'

(7) Mundari (mu.) (Abbi 1990: 258)
əiyā-ke bubu mena.
ich-DAT Fieber ist
'Ich habe Fieber.'

(8) Newari (tb.)
ji-tɔ sekɔ̃ cal-ɔ.
ich-DAT Erkältung nehm-PRET.DISJUNKT
'Ich habe mich erkältet.'

Inwieweit die Dativkonstituente Subjekteigenschaften hat, ist umstritten und auch von Sprache zu Sprache unterschiedlich (vgl. Aufsätze in Verma (ed.) 1976, Verma & Mohanan (eds.) 1990). Manche Autoren sprechen daher lieber von der Dativkonstruktion oder vom Experiencer-Subjekt.

Besondere Experiencer-Konstruktionen finden sich in allen vier Sprachfamilien, wie die Beispiele (5) bis (8) zeigen; sie werden aber nach Osten hin seltener. Im Munda sind sie weniger ausgeprägt als im Iar. und Drav., und in den östlichen tb. Sprachen sowie im Khasi (austroas.) wurden keine solchen Konstruktionen gefunden (Abbi 1990: 260). Bengali verwendet häufig Genitiv statt Dativ: *taar* (er.GEN) *ṭhaṇḍa lag-lo* 'ihm ist kalt'.

2.7. Oblique Stämme

Dieses Merkmal, das schon Caldwell (1856) erwähnt, wird in der Literatur zu Südasien kaum behandelt. Es ist jedoch, da typologisch recht ungewöhnlich, von hoher arealer Signifikanz. In drav. und iar. Sprachen werden alle oder einige Kasussuffixe nicht (oder nicht bei allen Nomina) an die Nennform angefügt, sondern an einen obliquen Stamm. Bei Pronomina ist dieses Phänomen üblich (und dies wird häufig in arealer Literatur vermerkt), jedoch ist es auch bei Nomina weitverbreitet; z. B. Koḍava (drav.) *mara* 'Baum', obliquer Stamm: *maratï*, Akkusativ: *mara-tï-na*; Hindi (iar.) *kamraa* 'Zimmer', obliquer Stamm: *kamre*, Lokativ *kamre-mẽ*. Die Verhältnisse im Munda liegen insofern etwas anders, als Postpositionen auf einen Genitiv (*-a, -naa*) folgen, z. B. Juang: *selog-a-ta* 'von dem Hund weg', Sora: *ḍumbaa-naa-mang* 'vor dem Tänzer', und ähnlich im Newari (tb.): *kɔlaa* 'Ehefrau', Genitiv: *kɔla-ya*, Dativ: *kɔla-ya-tɔ*. Hier könnten einfach Genitivkonstruktionen der Art *in front of* vorliegen. Man könnte sie aber auch als „gropings in the direction of the pan-Indian scheme" (Masica 1994: 197) interpretieren.

Aus tb. Sprachen weiter östlich sind keine Entsprechungen bekannt. Bengali und Assamesisch haben nur für Pronomina einen obliquen Stamm. Da oblique Stämme im Drav. seit frühester Zeit belegt sind, könnte hiermit ein weiteres Beispiel für eine Nachahmung drav. Muster in iar. Sprachen vorliegen.

2.8. Zitierpartikel

Kuiper (1967) fügt der Liste der potentiellen arealen Merkmale ein weiteres hinzu, nämlich die Übereinstimmung in der Verwendung zwischen dem Sanskrit Wörtchen *iti* 'so' und der tamilischen Reportpartikel *ena, enru* (eigentlich 'gesagt habend'). *iti* rückt im Laufe der Entwicklung immer mehr vom Anfang an das Ende eines Zitats und übernimmt nach und nach alle Funktionen von *ena, enru*. Kuipers These der Übernahme einer drav. Struktur ins Sanskrit ist im Allgemeinen akzeptiert worden (für eine kritische Einschätzung s. jedoch Hock (1982)). Nun ist die Redeeinbettung mit einer Partikel, insbesondere mit Partikeln der Bedeutung 'sagen' oder 'gesagt habend', und deren Entwicklung zu kausalen und konditionalen Subordinatoren so universell verbreitet, dass sie in einzelnen südasiatischen Sprachen unabhängig voneinander entstanden sein kann. Die bei Kuiper skizzierte historische Entwicklung von *iti* wäre nur dann interessant, wenn sie zusammen mit *ena, enru* eine typologische Besonderheit aufwiese. Kuiper nennt ein Detail, das es erlaube, aus einer Analogie in einer modernen Munda-Sprache auf prähistorische iar. Entwicklung zu schliessen: Santali *mente* 'gesagt habend' wird wie *iti* und *enra* mit onomatopoetischen Ausdrücken verwendet. Der argumentative Wert dieser Parallele ist nicht klar, da über diese spezielle Verwendung aus der typologischen Literatur und aus Grammatiken nichts zu erfahren ist. Eine andere, anscheinend neuere Entwicklung ist jedoch auf Südasien beschränkt, nämlich die Verwendung einer Ableitung aus dem Verb 'sagen' zum Ausdruck des Komparativs (Ebert 1991: 87). Wie weit diese Konstruktion in Südasien verbreitet ist, ist noch ungewiß. Außer im Newari (tb.) und im Nepali (iar.) ist sie nach Saxena (1995: 359) auch im Telugu belegt. Diese spezielle Entwicklung ist in der Literatur zum Sprachbund Südasien nicht erwähnt.

2.9. Echowörter

Die drei zentralen Sprachfamilien verfügen über eine Wortkonstruktion, in denen ein Morphem der Struktur CVX wiederholt wird, wobei CV durch eine bestimmte Silbe (im Drav. oft *ki-, gi-*) oder C durch einen bestimmten Konsonanten ersetzt wird und der Rest des Wortes ein 'Echo' bildet. Die Bedeutung entspricht dem umgangssprachlichen deutschen 'und so', z. B. Tamil *kudirai-gidirai* 'Pferde und so'. Emeneau (1980 [1956]: 114) vermutet, die iar. Sprachen hätten die Echoformen entlehnt, da sie sonst im Indoeuropäischen nicht vorkämen (vgl. jedoch Bildungen wie *Kuddel-Muddel, schicki-micki*). Echowörter sind in ganz Südasien vor allem im mündlichen Stil verbreitet, und eine ursprüngliche Gebersprache lässt sich nicht feststellen. Die Untersuchung der Bildungselemente ergibt jedoch ein areales Muster (vgl. Karte in Trivedi 1990: 80−81): Im Norden zieht sich ein Streifen mit dem Bildungselement *s-* von Westen nach Osten. Südwestlich schließt sich zunächst ein Gebiet mit *w-* an, und in Gujerat und Maharashtra überwiegt dann *b-*. Der drav. Süden hat ausschließlich *k-, g-*. In Orissa und Westbengalen finden wir *p-, ph-*, während der Nordosten neben *s-* vor allem *ṭ-, t-* verwendet. In einzelnen Gegenden kommt verstreut auch *m-* vor. Das Muster der Echobildungen ist unabhängig von genetischen Grenzen, vgl. z. B. Oriya (iar.) *iskul-phiskul* 'Schule und so', *cinī-phinī* 'Zucker und so' mit Ho (mu.) *oe-poe* 'Vögel und so', *ɔpis-pɔpis* 'Büro und so'; Bengali (iar.) *ghusur-ṭusur* 'Schweine und so', *sināte-ṭināte* 'baden und so' mit Nocte (tb.) *san-ṭan* 'Sonne und so', *se-ṭe* 'singen und so' und Santali (mu.) *bɔkɔp-ṭɔkɔp* 'Brüder und so'.

2.10. Andere Merkmale

Eine Reihe anderer Merkmale sind von einzelnen Autoren vorgeschlagen und meist wieder verworfen worden, z. B. aspirierte Konsonanten, nasalierte Vokale, negative Konjugation, ergative Konstruktion, Klassifikatoren, das Fehlen von Präfixen, das Fehlen eines Verbs für 'haben'. Eine ziemlich vollständige Liste mit einer Bewertung gibt Masica (1976: 187−190). Für etwa die Hälfte der Merkmale kommt er zu dem Ergebnis, dass sie nicht arealdefinierend sind. Bei anderen bleibt ein Fragezeichen. Die Unsicherheit in der Beurteilung ergibt sich z. T. aus mangelnden Daten, z. T. durch das Fehlen eines gültigen Kriteriums dafür, was arealdefinierend ist.

3. Methodische Probleme

3.1. Was macht einen Sprachbund aus?

Als minimale Voraussetzung für einen Sprachbund kann Emeneaus Definition gelten: „This term 'linguistic area' may be defined as meaning an area which includes languages belonging to more than one family but showing traits in common which are found not to belong to the other members of (at least) one of the families" (Emeneau 1980 [1956]: 124). In einem einleitenden Artikel zu gesammelten Aufsätzen nennt Emeneau zwei weitergehende methodologische Prinzipien: Zunächst muss ein typologisches Merkmal als panindisch und nicht außerindisch definiert werden. Wenn mehrere solcher Merkmale etabliert sind und ihre Grenzen ungefähr in einem Isoglossenbündel zusammenlaufen, kann ein Sprachbund als etabliert gelten (1980: 2). Im zweiten Schritt gilt es, den Ursprung der arealen Merkmale und ihre Verbreitung durch die einzelnen Sprachen aufzuzeigen. Wenn ein gemeinsames Merkmal für die Protosprache X rekonstruiert werden kann, muss sie in die Sprache oder Sprachgruppe Y entlehnt worden sein.

Allerdings nehmen es die meisten Autoren, Emeneau selber eingeschlossen, mit diesen Prinzipien nicht so genau. Ob ein Merkmal panindisch ist, wird selten geprüft. Man begnügt sich in der Regel mit einer Reihe von Belegen aus iar. und drav. Sprachen. Wenn dann noch ein paralleles Beispiel in einer Munda-Sprache aufgespürt werden kann, gilt die areale Diffusion als gesichert. Ein mögliches Vorkommen außerhalb der Grenzen Südasiens, obwohl manchmal vermerkt, scheint nicht zu stören. Emeneau verwirft allerdings das von ihm selber früher vorgeschlagene Merkmal der Numeralklassifikatoren aufgrund ihres häufigen Vorkommens in Südost-Asien: „it fails lamentably in demonstrating that India is a linguistic area and may be interpreted as showing that there are linguistic traits that occur in common in India and the rest of Asia." (1980 [1965]: 131).

Isoglossenbündel wurden nie nachgewiesen: „Unfortunately I know of no demonstration of such a bundling of isoglosses. In fact, when in the earlier paper I treated India as a linguistic area, I made no attempt to demonstrate a bundling of isoglosses, but rather discussed a number of traits that cross family boundaries in India and I was concerned as regards one or two of them to demonstrate the 'Indianization' of Indo-Aryan, i. e. to demonstrate that Indo-Aryan at various periods shows traits that originated in Dravidian and spread over more or less wide Indo-Aryan territories." (Emeneau 1980 [1965]: 128).

Bei den meisten Autoren steht das zweite (historische) Prinzip im Vordergrund. Die Diskussion geht im Wesentlichen darum, ob etwas aus dem Drav. entlehnt sein kann oder nicht. Das obige Zitat kann hier stellvertretend stehen.

Einigkeit besteht inzwischen wohl darüber, dass Isoglossenbündelung keine Bedingung für einen Sprachbund sein kann (vgl. Campbell et al. 1986: 561−562). Die Beschränkung eines Merkmals auf das zu definierende Gebiet kann für Südasien ebenfalls nicht aufrechterhalten werden, da die meisten der angeblich arealen Merkmale auch für altaische Sprachen typisch sind (s. § 3.4.).

Die arealdefinierenden Merkmale müssen unabhängig voneinander sein und eine zufällige Konvergenz muss ausgeschlossen werden. Eine areale Hypothese kann erhärtet werden, wenn es gelingt zu zeigen, dass ein Merkmal sich von einem Zentrum aus verbreitet hat. Dies kann durch historische und/ oder quantitative Untersuchungen geschehen.

3.2. Historische Evidenz

Die genauesten sprachhistorischen Untersuchungen liegen, bedingt durch das Interesse der Indologie am Sanskrit und an der Frage nach den Gründen oder Quellen der „Indisierung" der iar. Sprachen, für die frühesten Überlieferungen vor. Als vorbildlich gilt der bereits zitierte Aufsatz Kuipers (1967) zur Entwicklung der retroflexen Konsonanten, des Konverbs und der Zitierpartikel *íti*. Allgemeine Zustimmung fand auch Emeneaus Untersuchung (1974) zur Sanskrit-Partikel *api* 'auch, sogar'. Diese hat im klassischen Sanskrit, wie das entsprechende *-um* im klassischen Tamil, fünf Funktionen: 1. ist sie eine additive Fokusmarkierung, 2. wird sie im Sinne von 'und' verwendet, 3. markiert sie konzessive Nebensätze, 4. verbindet sie sich mit Fragewörtern zu Indefinitpronomina, und 5. kann sie im Zusammenhang mit Zahlwörtern Totalität anzeigen. Emeneau geht die Quellen zu iar. und drav. Sprachen durch und kommt zu dem Schluss, dass die fünf Verwendungen in allen Untergruppen des Drav. zu finden sind. Andererseits stellt er fest, dass die einheitliche Markierung der fünf Funktionen nur in wenigen modernen iar. Sprachen (Marathi, Oriya) gegeben ist. Da *-um* mit den fünf Funktionen für Protodrav. rekonstruiert werden kann, aber nicht alle Funktionen in vedischen und frühen Sanskrittexten zu finden sind, folgert Emeneau, dass das Sanskrit die Funktionen von *api* in Analogie zu Tamil *-um* ausgebaut hat. Darüberhinaus formuliert er vorsichtig die Vermutung, dass die Auflösung der Einheit in den iar. Sprachen stattfand, als sie den Kontakt mit dem Drav. verloren (Emeneau 1980 [1974]: 218). Eventuelle Parallelen in mu. und tb. Sprachen werden nicht angeführt. *api/-um* ist eines der wenigen Charakteristika, die in Masicas Übersicht (1976: 187−190) als uneingeschränkt arealdefinierend bewertet werden. Hier gilt also die Wahrscheinlichkeit der Übernahme einer Verwendung vom Drav. ins Iar. vor ca. 2500 Jahren als ausreichend, um ein Phänomen als arealdefinierend zu bewerten, obwohl die Übernahme offensichtlich zeitlich sehr begrenzt war und z. T. wieder rückgängig gemacht wurde. Nicht unwichtig ist in diesem Zusammenhang auch, dass das Zusammenkommen zumindest der ersten vier Funktionen typologisch alles andere als eine Seltenheit ist. Über die fünfte, die Verbindung mit Zahlwörtern, ist in Grammatiken wenig zu erfahren (vgl. auch Emeneau 1980 [1974]: 202), und es bleibt zu untersuchen, ob damit eine südasiatische Besonderheit vorliegt. Sie wäre dann aber immer noch räumlich und zeitlich beschränkt und keineswegs panindisch.

Die Literatur zum Sprachbund Südasien besteht über weite Strecken aus solchen Untersuchungen der Entwicklung von Gemeinsamkeiten zwischen Iar. und Drav. in den frühesten Quellen.

Den sprachhistorischen Untersuchungen sind natürlich dadurch Grenzen gesetzt, dass sie sich auf das beschränken müssen, was Eingang in die Schriftnorm gefunden hat — und die Gelehrten waren in Südasien immer extrem puristisch. Die Umgangssprache hat sich daher zu allen Zeiten stark von der Schriftsprache unterschieden (De Silva 1974: 60—68), und die Entlehnungen sind vermutlich im Gesprochenen viel stärker gewesen, als historische Quellen belegen können. Studien der gegenwärtigen Situation zeigen, dass es in begrenzten Räumen zu einer fast totalen Konvergenz kommen kann. Gumperz & Wilson (1971) demonstrieren in ihrer Studie zur Kontaktsituation in Kupwar an der Grenze zwischen Maharashtra und Karnataka, dass die Grammatiken der dort gesprochenen Varianten des Kannada, Marathi und Urdu mit einem einzigen Regelapparat beschrieben werden können.

In den urbanen Zentren haben sich stark vereinfachte Verkehrssprachen entwickelt, die z. T. Züge eines Pidgin tragen, wie das Kalkutta-Hindustani (Chatterji 1931) oder das Hindi-Urdu in Bombay (Apte 1974). Im Nordosten dient das auf dem Assamesischen basierende Naga Pidgin („Nagamese") als Verkehrssprache zwischen den Nagavölkern. Es wird auch in einer Reihe von offiziellen Situationen verwendet, so in der gesetzgebenden Staatsversammlung und in Schulen und Universitäten, um die nicht verstandenen englischen Texte zu erklären (Shapiro & Schiffman 1983: 210, Sreedhar 1985: 25). Für die ursprünglich tibeto-burmanischen Kacharis, die im 19. Jh. ihre Sprache durch Assamesisch ersetzten, ist inzwischen Nagamese zur Muttersprache geworden. Sadari, ein auf dem Hindi basierendes Pidgin, wurde in den 50er Jahren zur identitätsstiftenden Sprache für Gruppen, die ihre angestammten drav. und mu. Sprachen aufgegeben haben (Sreedhar 1985: 21—22). Im Zuge mehrfacher Überlagerungen und mehrfachen Sprachwechsels mit langen Phasen der partiellen Zwei- oder Mehrsprachigkeit dürfte es immer wieder zur Ausbildung von vereinfachten Verkehrssprachen gekommen sein, die sich dann sekundär wieder an sanskritische Normen anglichen. Ein etwas spekulatives, aber nicht unwahrscheinliches Pidginisierungsszenario entwirft Southworth (1971) für das frühe Marathi.

Über die Geschichte der tb. und der mu. Sprachen ist fast nichts bekannt. Masica (1976: 8) verweist als nahe Verwandte mit langer Schrifttradition auf Tibetisch und Khmer. Jedoch ist Tibetisch nur entfernt mit den tb. Sprachen Südasiens verwandt und kann über deren Entwicklung kaum Aufschluss geben. Aus synchronen Daten und unserem spärlichen Wissen aus der Geschichtsschreibung sind Rückschlüsse über die Entwicklung der Sprachen im Osten des Subkontinents nur sehr begrenzt möglich. Wir wissen, dass die tb. und mu. Sprachen einmal eine sehr viel weitere Verbreitung hatten, und dass Sprecher iar. Sprachen im Nordosten lange in der Minderheit waren. Das Assamesische z. B. ist in der Formationsperiode, als sein Zentrum noch weiter westlich lag, stark von austroasiatischen Sprachen beeinflusst worden (Kakati 1941: 34—38). In großen Teilen Orissas haben sich drav. und mu. Sprachen über lange Zeiträume bis in die Gegenwart gegenseitig beeinflusst. Teilweise hat es mehrfache Überlagerungen gegeben: „Shifts in language have not been uncommon in South Asia, and in some cases seem to have occurred more than once., e. g., from Munda to Dravidian to Indo-Aryan, or from Mon-Khmer to Tibeto-Burman to Indo-Aryan. We see clearly only the most recent phases. Although hints of earlier phases are often still embedded in the language, inferences remain largely speculative." (Masica 1991: 42). Die Diffusion ging nicht immer einförmig in die gleiche Richtung. Das Nepali z. B. scheint zunächst viel von den tb. Sprachen der Umgebung aufgenommen zu haben, während jetzt eine massive Entlehnung in umgekehrter Richtung zu verzeichnen ist.

3.3. Frequenz eines Merkmals

Hook (1987) zeigt, wie mit einer quantitativen Analyse areale Diffusion nachgewiesen werden kann. Die Auswertung einer Fragebogenaktion ergab, dass westlich des Indus in allen erfassten Orten die Nebensätze nachgestellt wurden, während südlich von Goa alle vorangestellt wurden. Die Zahl der vorangestellten Nebensätze nimmt mit der Entfernung vom drav. Modell kontinuierlich ab. Dass diese Stellung in OV-Sprachen typologisch wahrscheinlich ist, erweist sich damit für die areale Frage als ebenso irrelevant wie die Tatsache, dass sie auch in Zentralasien vorherrscht.

Southworth (1974) wertet Texte in modernen iar. Sprachen im Hinblick auf die Häufigkeit retroflexer Konsonanten aus. Ihre Frequenz nimmt von West nach Ost graduell ab. Während in Texten in den westlichen iar. Sprachen Marathi, Gujarati und Panjabi die Verteilung dentaler und retroflexer Konsonanten mit 3 : 1 der in drav. Sprachen entspricht, liegt sie im Bengali bei 12 : 1 (1974: 212). Southworth vergleicht diesen Befund mit dem Vorkommen der Numeralklassifikatoren. Diese bilden einen festen Bestandteil des Assamesischen, Bengali, Maithili und Oriya, kommen in westlichen iar. Sprachen dagegen höchst spärlich vor. Gleichzeitig wird nach Osten hin das grammatische Genus der iar. Sprachen reduziert, zunächst von einem Drei-Genus- auf ein Zwei-Genus-System (Hindi, Bhojpuri); im Bengali und Assamesischen fehlt es gänzlich. Southworth interpretiert die areale Verteilung der retroflexen Konsonanten und der Klassifikatoren als Evidenz für ein überwiegend drav. Substrat im Westen, mit dem Zentrum in der Indusebene, und ein überwiegend tb. Substrat im Gangesdelta.

Das Problem der quantitativen Auswertung ist, dass man aus einer negativen Korrelation wenig schliessen kann. Sie ist also nur geeignet, um eine Hypothese zu untermauern, für die noch weitere Evidenz vorliegt. Hook (1977) versuchte durch eine quantitative Analyse der Frage nach dem Ursprung der Explikatorverben auf den Grund zu gehen. Die Auszählung ergab die grösste Häufigkeit solcher Verbverbindungen im Nordwesten und im Hindi sowie eine starke Abnahme nach Süden hin. Hook schliesst daraus, dass die Konstruktion nicht aus dem Drav. übernommen sein kann, wobei er von der Voraussetzung ausgeht, dass die heutige Frequenz ein direktes Abbild der Verteilung vor 1500−2500 Jahren ist (1977: 344). Hooks Fazit, dass die Verbverbindungen in den iar. Sprachen unabhängig entstanden sind, mag faktisch richtig sein − ähnliche Arten von Verbverbindungen sind aus vielen Sprachen der Welt bekannt − jedoch geht dies nicht aus seiner Untersuchung hervor.

3.4. Isoglossen

Den ersten Versuch, dialektologische Methoden systematisch auf die südasiatische Sprachbundfrage anzuwenden, unternimmt Masica (1976). Er untersucht die folgenden fünf Merkmale auf ihr Vorkommen im gesamten eurasiatischen Raum und auch darüber hinaus: morphologische Kausativformen, Wortstellung, Konverben, Explikatorverben und die Dativkonstruktion. Die aus seiner Untersuchung resultierenden Isoglossen für OV-Wortstellung und Konverben fallen über weite Strecken zusammen und umschliessen fast ganz Asien mit Ausnahme des Südostens (s. Karte in Masica 1976: 181). Die Linie der Explikator-Verben schliesst Tibet und Persien aus, die der sekundären Kausativierungen auch den östlichen Teil Indiens. Alle vier Merkmale sind auch für die altaischen Sprachen typisch. Lediglich die Dativkonstruktion erweist sich als eine Besonderheit Südasiens; sie findet sich erst im Kaukasus und in Teilen Europas wieder. Die Isoglossen in Masicas Karten demonstrieren sehr eindrücklich ein indo-altaisches Areal. Dort, wo sie auseinanderklaffen, zeigen sie nach Masica Übergangszonen an (1976: 170). In Bezug auf Südasien sind sie jedoch weniger aussagekräftig.

Eine entscheidende Frage ist, was eine Isoglosse abbilden sollte, das äußerste Vorkommen einer Konstruktion oder die Grenze des Gebiets, in dem Entlehnung stattgefunden hat. Masica wendet das erste Prinzip an, jedoch scheint das zweite areallinguistisch relevanter. Masicas Karte zeigt z. B., dass die Dativkonstruktion bis in den äußersten Nordosten Indiens hinein belegt ist. Sie zeigt nicht, dass sie hier nur im Iar. vorkommt und dass die zahlreichen kleineren Völker der Region sie nicht übernommen haben (vgl. § 2.6.). In einer areallinguistischen Auswertung wäre ebenso zu berücksichtigen, dass sie in Munda-Sprachen selten ist. Das grobe Verfahren der Kartierung mithilfe des binären Prinzips kann die graduellen Übergänge nicht erfassen (s. dazu auch Masica selbst (1976: 172)). Ebenfalls nicht dargestellt werden unterschiedliche Formen der Kodierung. Wenn im Westen Kausativformen ausschließlich mithilfe von Suffixen gebildet werden, im Osten z. T. (oder auch mehrheitlich?) durch

Präfixe (vgl. § 2.2.), so ist das areal relevant, kommt jedoch durch Masicas Isoglossen nicht zum Ausdruck.

4. Die Frage der Abgrenzung

Masicas Ziel war es, die Grenzen des südasiatischen Sprachbundes zu definieren. Dass dies nur teilweise gelungen ist, liegt daran, dass zu wenig Merkmale und zu wenig Sprachen berücksichtigt wurden. Ich beschränke mich im Folgenden auf Beobachtungen zu den Sprachen im Osten des Subkontinents.

In Masicas Übersichtskarten gehört ganz Indien zum südasiatischen Sprachbund. Die Merkmale OV-Wortstellung, Konverben, Explikator-Verben und Dativ-Konstruktion sind bis in die äußersten Winkel hinein vorhanden. Lediglich für das Merkmal der sekundären Kausativierungen verläuft die Linie weiter westlich, etwa entlang dem 84. Längengrad. Diese Linie ist in der Tat bedeutsam, jedoch ist sie ironischerweise gerade in Bezug auf das Merkmal, das sie bei Masica abbilden soll, nicht haltbar. Sekundäre Kausativierungen gibt es, wie in § 2.2. gezeigt wurde, östlich und westlich davon.

Östlich des 84. Längengrads kann man zwei Zonen unterscheiden: a) die Kontaktzone zwischen Munda, Drav. und Tb., die von Ostnepal über Bihar nach Orissa verläuft, und b) den Nordosten, der vor allem tb. Gebiet ist. Die über hundert Sprachen dieses Gebiets werden in der arealen Literatur mangelhaft bzw. gar nicht berücksichtigt. Die Charakteristika des südasiatischen Sprachbundes sind hier, wenn wir von den zwei großen iar. Sprachen Bengali und Assamesisch absehen, nur selten zu finden. Zwar weisen die Sprachen beider Zonen (ausser Khasi) OV-Wortstellung auf, aber bei der Stellung der Determinatoren finden wir oft den Modifikator nach dem Nomen. Die Frage, ob die nordöstlichen bzw. östlichen Sprachen Konverben haben, ist nicht immer einfach zu beantworten. In einigen Sprachen liegt eindeutig eine nonfinite Form vor, da die Finitheitsmarkierung fehlt (Garo, Mao Naga, Athpare (tb.), Santali (mu.)). Bei anderen ist die Reduzierung des Verbs vor dem sequentiellen Subordinator optional. So kann z. B. im Mikir (tb.) das reihende Suffix -si entweder an den Stamm oder an ein Verb mit Tempusmarkierung — was einem finiten Verb entspricht — angehängt werden (Grüßner 1978: 101−102). Sprachen des Raumes Ostnepal-Orissa zeichnen sich durch äusserst komplexe Verbmorphologie aus, die sie auch in der Subordination meist beibehalten (vgl. Ebert 1993).

Dieselbe unklare Situation liegt bei den Verbalkomplexen vor. Viele Sprachen reihen einfach Stämme aneinander, andere verbinden zwei voll flektierte Verben (vgl. § 2.5.). Wollen wir „compound verb" nach der Morphologie definieren, nämlich so, dass ein finites Explikatorverb einem nonfiniten Inhaltsverb folgt, ergibt sich für den Osten des Subkontinents ein eher negatives Bild. Die Semantik der Verbverbindung ist noch heterogener und eignet sich daher noch weniger für einen arealen Vergleich.

Die beiden spezifisch südasiatischen Merkmale, Dativkonstruktion und retroflexe Konsonanten, finden wir im Nordosten nicht. Dagegen weisen verschiedene Charakteristika dieser Sprachen nach Südostasien, z. B. glottalisierte Konsonanten, Präfixe zur Kausativmarkierung, Numeralklassifikatoren. Insgesamt rechtfertigen es die Befunde nicht, den Nordosten als Teil des südasiatischen Sprachbundes anzusehen. Das Gebiet zwischen dem 84. und dem 88. Längengrad bildet eine Übergangszone. Hier scheint sich in jahrtausendelangen Kontakten zwischen Drav., Mu. und Tb. ein eigenes Areal herausgebildet zu haben (vgl. Ebert 1993), in dem wiederum mehrere Subareale unterschieden werden können, z. B. Jharkhand (Abbi 1995) und die Khondmals (Steever 1986).

5. Fazit

Versuche, den südasiatischen Sprachbund exakt zu definieren und seine Grenzen zu bestimmen, sind bisher nicht sehr erfolgreich verlaufen. Dies ist nicht verwunderlich, denn „Sprachbund situations are notoriously messy" (Thomason & Kaufman 1988: 95). Eine klare Definition ist noch nicht einmal für die vergleichsweise einfache Situation auf dem Balkan gelungen. Südasien hat ein Vielfaches an Sprachen und an typologischer Verschiedenheit aufzuweisen. Viele der Sprachen sind nicht beschrieben, und über die Geschichte der meisten ist so gut wie nichts bekannt.

Verschiedene zur Definition eines Sprachbundes vorgeschlagene Kriterien erwiesen sich als nur bedingt brauchbar. Offenbar kann eine Sprachbundhypothese nur durch kumulative Evidenz erhärtet werden.

In Südasien haben sich ohne Zweifel verschiedene grammatische Konstruktionen und phonologische Merkmale über genetische Grenzen hinweg ausgebreitet. Wenn man davon ausgeht, dass der Nordosten Indiens nicht zum Sprachbund gehört, sind zumindest zwei Merkmale in den drei zentralen Familien Südasiens verbreitet, nämlich die Dativkonstruktion und die retroflexen Konsonanten. Wichtig ist, dass diese Merkmale unabhängig voneinander sind und in den altaischen Sprachen nicht vorkommen. Weniger aussagekräftig sind Konverben und die OV-Wortstellung, da sie auch für den altaischen Bereich typisch sind. Eine ganze Reihe weiterer Merkmale, z. B. Form und Semantik der „compound verbs" oder die Muster der Echobildungen haben sich über Teilzonen verbreitet. Wenn man noch die Übereinstimmungen in der Semantik und Idiomatik, wozu kaum Untersuchungen vorliegen, hinzunimmt, verdichtet sich das Bild eines Kulturraumes, in dem sich Sprachen über jahrtausendelange intensive Kontakte aneinander angeglichen haben.

6. Abkürzungen

austroas. austroasiatisch
drav. dravidisch
iar. indoarisch
mu. Munda
tb. tibetoburmanisch

7. Zitierte Literatur

Abbi, Anvita. 1990. „Experiential constructions and the 'subjecthood' of the experiencer NPs in South Asian languages." In: Verma & Mohanan (eds.), 253−265.

− 1995. „Morphological change in tribal languages of Central India." *Journal of Dravidic Studies* 5.1: 1−9.

Apte, Mahadev L. 1974. „Pidginization of a lingua franca: A linguistic analysis of Hindi-Urdu spoken in Bombay." In: Southworth & Apte (eds.), 21−41.

Bloch, Jules. 1934. *L'indo-aryen, du Véda aux temps modernes.* Paris: Adrien-Maisonneuve.

Caldwell, Robert. 1961 [1856]. *A comparative grammar of the Dravidian or South-Indian family of languages.* Wiederabdruck Madras: University of Madras.

Campbell, Lyle, Kaufman, Terrence & Smith-Stark, Thomas C. 1986. „Meso-America as a linguistic area." *Language* 62: 530−70.

Chatterji, S. K. 1931. „Calcutta Hindustani − a study of a jargon dialect." *Indian Linguistics* 1: 177−234.

De Silva, M. W. Sugathapala. 1974. „Convergence in diglossia: the Sinhalese situation." In: Southworth & Apte (eds.), 60−91.

Ebert, Karen H. 1991. „Vom verbum dicendi zur Konjunktion − Ein Kapitel universaler Grammatikentwicklung." In: Bisang, Walter & Rinderknecht, Peter (eds.). *Von Europa bis Ozeanien − Von der Antonymie zum Relativsatz.* Zürich: ASAS Verlag, 77−95.

− 1993. „Kiranti subordination in the South Asian areal context." In: Karen H. Ebert (ed.). *Studies in clause linkage.* Zürich: ASAS Verlag, 83−110.

Emeneau, Murray B. 1956. „India as a linguistic area." *Language* 32.1: 3−16 [auch in Emeneau 1980, 1−18].

− 1965. „India and linguistic areas." *India and Historical Grammar.* Annamalai University, Department of Linguistics Publication No. 5, 25−75 [auch in Emeneau 1980, 126−166].

− 1971. „Dravidian and Indo-Aryan: The Indian linguistic area." In: Sjoberg, Andrea F. (ed.) *Symposium on Dravidian Civilization.* Austin: Jenkins [auch in Emeneau 1980, 167−196].

− 1974. „The Indian linguistic area revisited." In: Southworth & Apte (eds.), 92−134 [auch in Emeneau 1980, 197−249].

− 1980. *Language and Linguistic Area. Essays by Murray B. Emeneau.* Stanford: University Press.

Grierson, George A. (ed.) 1903−1928. *Linguistic Survey of India* (11 Bde.). Delhi: Motilal Banarsidass.

Grüßner, Karl-Heinz. 1978. *Arleng Arlam − die Sprache der Mikir.* Wiesbaden: Steiner.

Gumperz, John J. & Wilson, Robert. 1971. „Convergence and creolization: a case from the Indo-Aryan/Dravidian border." In: Hymes (ed.), 151−167.

Hock, Hans Henrich. 1982. „The Sanskrit quotative: a historical and comparative study." *Studies in the Linguistic Sciences* 12.2: 39−85.

Hook, Peter E. 1977. „The distribution of the compound verb in the languages of North India and the question of its origin." *International Journal of Dravidian Linguistics* 6.2: 336−351.

− 1987. „Linguistic areas: getting at the grain of history." In: Cardona, George & Zide, Norman (eds.). *Festschrift for Henry Hoenigswald.* Tübingen: Narr, 155−68.

Hymes, Dell (ed.) 1971. *Pidginization and creolization of languages.* Cambridge: Cambridge University Press.

Kakati, Banikanta. 1941. *Assamese, its formation and development.* Gauhati: Narayani Handiqui Historical Institute.

Krishnamurti, Bh. (ed.) 1986. *South Asian languages. Structure, convergence and diglossia.* Delhi: Motilal Banarsidass.

Kuiper, F. B. J. 1967. „The genesis of a linguistic area." *Indo-Iranian Journal* 10: 81−102.

Masica, Colin P. 1976. *Defining a linguistic area: South Asia.* Chicago: The University of Chicago Press.

− 1991. *The Indo-Aryan languages.* Cambridge: Cambridge University Press.

− 1994. „Some new perspectives on South Asia as a linguistic area." In: Davison, Alice & Smith, Frederick M. (eds.) *Papers from the fifteenth South Asian Language Analysis Roundtable Conference 1993.* Iowa: University of Iowa, 187−200.

McPhail, R. M. 1953: *An introduction to Santali.* Calcutta: Firma KLM Private Limited.

Ramanujan, A. K. & Masica, Colin. 1969. „Toward a phonological typology of the Indian linguistic area." In: Thomas E. Sebeok (ed.) *Current Trends in Linguistics*, Vol. 5: Linguistics in South Asia, 543−577.

Saxena, Anju. 1995. „Unidirectional grammaticalization: Diachronic and cross-linguistic evidence." *Sprachtypologie und Universalienforschung* 48: 350−372.

Shapiro, Michael & Schiffman, Harold F. 1983. *Language and Society in South Asia.* Dordrecht: Foris Publications.

Southworth, Franklin C. 1971. „Detecting prior creolization. An analysis of the historical origins of Marathi." In: Hymes (ed.), 255−73.

− 1974. „Linguistic stratigraphy in North India." In: Southworth & Apte (eds.), 201−223.

− & Apte, Mahadev L. (eds.) 1974. *Contact and convergence in South Asian languages* (= International Journal of Dravidian Linguistics 3/1; special issue).

Sreedhar, M. V. 1985. *Standardized grammar of Naga Pidgin.* Mysore: Central Institute of Indian Languages.

Steever, Sanford B. 1986. „Morphological Convergence in the Khondmals: (Pro)nominal Incorporation." In: Krishnamurti (ed.), 270−85.

Thomason, Sara Grey & Kaufman, Terrence. 1988. *Language Contact, creolization, and genetic linguistics.* Berkeley: University of California Press.

Trivedi, G. M. 1990. „Echo formation." In: Krishan, Shree (ed.) *Linguistic traits across language boundaries.* Calcutta: Anthropological Survey of India, 51−82.

Verma, Manindra K. (ed.) 1976. *The notion of subject in South Asian languages.* Madison: University of Wisconsin.

Verma, Manindra K. & Mohanan, K. P. (eds.) 1990. *Experiencer subjects in South Asian languages.* Stanford: Stanford University.

Vermeer, Hans J. 1969. *Untersuchungen zum Bau Zentral-Süd-Asiatischer Sprachen (Ein Beitrag zur Sprachbundfrage).* Heidelberg: J. Groos.

Karen H. Ebert, Zürich (Schweiz)

110. Mesoamerica as a linguistic area

1. Mesoamerica
2. History
3. Size and make-up
4. Features
5. Origins
6. Conclusion
7. References

1. Mesoamerica

According to the definition put forward by Kirchhoff (1943), Mesoamerica constitutes an area in which cultural, economic, and social similarities of quite a variety of indigenous ethnic groups are so numerous that it seems legitimate to speak of a cultural area distinct from neighbouring areas. Roughly, this Mesoamerican cultural area corresponds to a region south of a line cutting from east to west across the territory of the modern Mexican states of Veracruz, San Luís Potosí, Guanajuato, Guerrero, Zacatecas, and Nayarit, while the southern borderline of Mesoamerica runs north to south from the Caribbean coast of Honduras through Nicaragua to the Pacific coast of Costa Rica. Thus, Mesoamerica includes most of modern Mexico, Guatemala, Belize, El Salvador, the western half of Honduras, the western coastal region of Nicaragua, and the northwest of Costa Rica (Prem 1989: 3). Most of the cultural traits which are said to be characteristic of Mesoamerica date back to the millennia of the preconquest era during which the succession of different politically, economically, and culturally dominant and expansive groups − such as, e.g., the Olmecs and the Toltecs − contributed to the widespread diffusion and assimilation of certain cultural features among the early Mesoamericans. Such features are, e. g., technological innovations, architectural styles, religious beliefs and rites, cosmological patterns, calendaric systems, etc.

In the first place, the bulk of the evidence which speaks in favour of the Mesoamerican cultural area stems from disciplines like pre-Columbian archaeology, prehistory, ethnography, and anthropology. In contradistinction to the role played by non-linguistic facts in Mesoamericanist research, it took some time before the lexical and structural similarities of many indigenous languages spoken in Mesoamerica eventually became a major focus of interest. Besides, notwithstanding the almost unanimous acceptance of Mesoamerica as a cultural area of long standing, not every scholar agrees with the *Sprachbund* hypothesis which views the common features of Mesoamerican languages as by-products of the age-long cultural contacts in the area.

2. History

As early as the 1820s, Wilhelm von Humboldt was among the first linguists to speculate about the "grosse Gleichmässigkeit" and "auffallende (...) Aehnlichkeit der Amerikanischen Sprachen" (Trabant 1994: 16) without trying to explain their structural affinities as instances of a distant genetic relationship. However, almost 140 years had to pass before the first serious attempt at developing a research-programme for the description and analysis of the common traits of Mesoamerican languages was actually made by Hasler (1959). Prior to his programmatic sketch of Mesoamerican linguistics, only the two volumes by W. Lehmann (1920) are worth mentioning. As a matter of fact, their focus is on the languages of Central America. Yet, W. Lehmann does not only survey the languages spoken from Costa Rica down south to Panama, but also adds hypotheses about apparent structural and lexical similarities that link Central American languages to South American and Mesoamerican languages. Up until W. Lehmann's contribution, Mesoamerican linguistics had been mainly concerned with inventorying the languages of Mexico and Central America with a view to classifying them according to genetic principles (Pimentel 1862/65, Thomas & Swanton 1911). Sherzer (1976: 1−10), Suárez (1983: 1−10), and Liedtke (1991: 103−109) adequately summarize the early period of research. It turns out that leading figures of early Amerindian linguistics such as, e. g., Franz Boas, Alfred L. Kroeber, Ronald Dixon, and Edward Sapir discussed areal diffusion of structural features as an alternative explanation of linguistic similarities as opposed to genetic relationship. The culmination of this discussion is Kroeber's (1939) monograph on cultural areas in North America.

Symptomatic of the subsequent lack of interest in questions of areal typology which prevailed for much of the time in Amerindian linguistics is the fact that the linguistic volumes of the monumental Handbook of Middle American Indians (Wauchope & McQuown 1967, Reifler Bricker & Edmonson 1984) are exclusively concerned with descriptive sketches of individual languages. There are no hints at possible areal convergence phenomena.

Starting from the early 1970s, areal-typology gained more attention in Amerindian linguistics − with the notable exception of South American Indian languages though. Areal-typological features of the languages spoken north of Mesoamerica have been discussed in some detail by Darnell & Sherzer (1971), Bright & Sherzer (1976), and Sherzer (1973, 1976). Much at the same time, areal-typological research of Mesoamerican languages gradually began to take shape. Obviously, Mesoamericanists benefitted quite a lot from the discussion of areal-typological phenomena in North-American Indian languages. Liedtke (1991: 103−118) presents a useful sketch of the history of areal-typological research in Amerindian linguistics.

In their publications, Lyle Campbell (1979) and Terrence Kaufman (1973) − also jointly Campbell & Kaufman (1980, 1983) − prepared the ground for the central ideas presented in their seminal paper on Mesoamerica as a linguistic area (Campbell et al. 1986). While much of the previous research can be characterized as "circumstantialist" (Campbell et al. 1986: 534), Campbell et al. (1986) present the first systematic collection and evaluation of Mesoamerican areal features. The only book-length documentation and analysis of these and additional features is Yasugi (1995).

Campbell et al. (1986: 563) claim Mesoamerica "to be among the very strongest (cases of linguistic areas) that are known" and quite a few linguists readily share their point of view (Ligorred 1992: 80). However, their views have not gone unchallenged. Hamp (1979) is of the opinion that Mesoamerica is rather an agglomeration of several autonomous *Sprachbünde* of smaller size and not a homogenous large-scale linguistic area. Moreover, Jorge A. Suárez (1983: 160−161) explicitly rejects the idea of a pre-Columbian *Sprachbund* in Mesoamerica. In what follows, his criticism and alternative suggestions will be presented together with the principal hypotheses formulated by the proponents of the *Sprachbund* approach.

3. Size and make-up

At present, some 7.5−10 million native speakers of Amerindian languages are estimated to live in Mesoamerica (Ligorred 1992: 224). Indigenous languages seem to have the strongest position in Guatemala, where roughly 50% of the population speak an Amerindian language as first language. Recently, four of the major Guatemalan Mayan languages have been recognized as co-official languages. However, many of the languages actually spoken in Mexico or elsewhere in Mesoamerica are in fact endangered languages. Since the time of the Spanish conquest several languages − exactly 11 according to Suárez (1983: xvi−xvii) or 29 including some unnamed Central American languages according to Ligorred (1992: 224) − have become extinct even though, in the ongoing discussion of Mesoamerican areal features, they are usually treated on a par with the nowadays obsolete classical written languages (Colonial or Classical Náhuatl, Yucatec Maya, Quiché, etc.) and present-day languages. Accordingly, when it comes to discussing features of the Mesoamerican *Sprachbund* or linguistic area, considerations of synchronousness hardly seem to matter.

Thomason & Kaufman (1988: 95) characterize most *Sprachbund* situations as being "notoriously messy". With regard to the Mesoamerican area, the situation is not much different either. In order to get a better grip on the distinctive properties of Mesoamerican languages, some of the descriptive studies disregard the boundaries of Mesoamerica and include languages spoken outside the area under scrutiny for the purpose of contrasting Mesoamerican and non-Mesoamerican structural features. Thus, it is quite common to find members of the Mesoamerican area proper and Central American languages treated together under the heading of Middle American languages (Kaufman 1973, Campbell 1979, Ligorred 1992, Yasugi 1995). At least equally often, Mexican languages − be they members of the Mesoamerican area or not − receive separate treatment as if constituting an areal type in its own right (Escalante Hernández 1977). North-American Indian languages are sometimes included in the group of what Campbell et al. (1986: 536) call "control languages" (Yasugi 1995).

Discounting Greenberg's (1987) much disputed Amerind hypothesis which is too difficult to accomodate within an areal-typological approach, we can distinguish several genetically unrelated language-families within the boundaries of Mesoamerica. The exact number of Mesoamerican languages varies slightly from source to source: Suárez (1983: xvi−xvii) counts 14 families with a total of 89 languages − half a dozen of which actually "are outside Mesoamerica" (Suárez 1983: xvii), Campbell et al. (1986: 540−542) have 10 families and isolates with 70 languages instead, and Yasugi's (1995: 6−9) inventory is up to 17 families with 174 languages of which only about 15 and 80, respectively, can be regarded as properly belonging to the Mesoamerican area. Ligorred (1992: 91) calculates some 123 languages for the whole of Mexico and Central America together. However, according to Grimes (1996: 76), in Mexico alone, there are about 295 languages. Doubtlessly, the region with the highest degree of linguistic diversity in Mesoamerica is the Mexican state of Oaxaca in which at least 14 indigenous languages of different genetic affiliation have been reported (Muntzel & Pérez González 1987: 580, 592−595).

Irrespective of the remaining statistical uncertainties, members of the following language families appear in the inventories of or are discussed as potential Mesoamerican languages in at least one of the pertinent publications (language family names according to Suárez (1983), geographical order from north to south): Uto-Aztecan, Totonac-Tepehua, Otomanguean, Tarascan, Cuitlatec, Tequistlatec-Jicaque, Huave, Mixe-Zoque, Mayan, Xinca, Lenca, Chibcha, Arahuacan, and Misumalpan. Still, there is some disagreement among specialists as to the inclusion of several Uto-Aztecan languages such as, e.g., those of the Corachol branch, and especially of the southernmost language families, i.e. Lenca, Chibcha, Arahuacan, and Misumalpan. Partly, this can be explained by the fact that Suárez (1983) and Campbell et al. (1986) locate the boundaries of Mesoamerica in different places. In contradistinction to Suárez (1983) and Smailus (1990: 270), whose version of linguistic Mesoamerica seems to be even more extended, Campbell et al. (1986) exclude some regions in the north of Mexico and much of Honduras and Nicaragua from Mesoamerica. The northern boundary they suggest seems to be more in line with the general opinion based on the concept of Mesoamerica as a cultural area. As to the question of the southern boundary, however, it is too hard to determine which of the two alternative suggestions is the more likely one because, from the geographical point of view, the differences appear to be negligible.

Moreover, the issue of where to draw the boundaries of Mesoamerica seems to lose much of its importance if one abandons the strictly static perspective. Owing to the possibility that migrations and other socio-historical events may have repeatedly changed the linguistic composition and geography of Mesoamerica in prehistoric times, Suárez (1983: 152–153) adopts a more flexible point of view which allows him to take into account languages spoken outside of his maximalist version of present-day Mesoamerica, such as, e.g., the Chibchan language Paya in north-eastern Honduras.

Anyway, it is an undisputable fact for the great majority of language families that all of their members are exclusively spoken in Mesoamerica, no matter which of the alternative definitions one choses. On the other hand, it is equally clear that the Uto-Aztecan language family reaches far beyond any of the northern boundaries proposed for Mesoamerica. Only if one accepts Suárez's interpretation, could two more language families come into play which are predominantly spoken outside of Mesoamerica, viz. Arahuacan and Chibcha. Most of their linguistic relatives are to be found in South America. While Chibchan and Misumalpan languages are claimed to belong to a cultural "transition zone" (Suárez 1983: 11–13), which, to Suárez' mind, justifies their inclusion in a description of Mesoamerican languages, Suárez, for various reasons, does not consider Arahuacan a similar case.

Of course, it cannot be denied that the definition of the boundaries of Mesoamerica heavily bears upon the central issue of the *Sprachbund* hypothesis. The more extended the area and the higher the number of languages to be compared, the less likely are sufficient structural affinities between the languages under scrutiny. Not surprisingly, Suárez (1983) and Campbell et al. (1986) favour two rather different readings of the term Mesoamerican language: For Suárez, independent of structural characteristics, any indigenous language that once was or has been spoken in the area is, in principle, a Mesoamerican language. Note, however, that Suárez (1983: 13) does not hesitate to skip the Arahuacan language Garífuna (Black Carib) spoken in Belize and Honduras "because it belongs to a South American linguistic family and (...) represents a late arrival (early eighteenth century) to the area." For Campbell et al. (1986), the attribute Mesoamerican is exclusively reserved for those languages of the area which share at least some of a set of features, i.e. not every language spoken in Mesoamerica forms necessarily part of the *Sprachbund*.

4. Features

Campbell et al. (1986: 530–536) painstakingly discuss the methodological and theoretical problems of defining a *Sprachbund* or linguistic area (→ Art. 105). In addition, they review most of the relevant literature on this controversial issue published before the mid 1980s. Since many of the previous claims that certain clusters of languages represent a *Sprachbund* or an area of linguistic convergence have been heavily criticized for apparent lack of convincing evidence, the major concern of Campbell et al. (1986: 536–537) is to present absolutely watertight proof for their *Sprachbund* hypothesis. This preoccupation with sound evidence compels them to take "the strongest critical stance" by discarding those features which (a) are also found in neighbouring areas, or, (b) have only a limited or local distribution among Mesoamerican languages, or, even more crucially, (c) "may easily develop independently in language" (Campbell et al. 1986: 537). Thus, for purely methodological reasons, their focus is on exclusive peculiarities of Mesoamerican languages. However, the authors rightfully add that there is further supporting evidence which cannot meet the rather strict criteria but should nevertheless be taken into account. Consequently, the catalogue of Mesoamerican areal features is divided into two categories of traits: Category I (cf. § 4.1.) comprises those traits which are assumed to be exclusive Mesoamericanisms, while category II (cf. § 4.2.) includes some of those features which are especially strong in Mesoamerica but recur also outside the area.

4.1. Exclusive traits

The review of the supposedly exclusive traits of Mesoamerican languages, however, demonstrates that none of the features can actually pass the test faultlessly. Campbell et al. (1986: 537) tacitly acknowledge this partial failure. Especially their criterion (c) proves to be the most difficult to fulfill, especially because the proponents fail to define what is meant by "easily". Notwithstanding the impossibility of identifying exclusive Mesoamericanisms, the evidence accumulated so far is indeed indicative of a linguistic area.

Instead of simply replicating the original evidence adduced by Campbell et al. (1986), we exemplify every single candidate for the status of areal feature by data drawn on languages representing three of the major language families of Mesoamerica, viz. Uto-Aztecan, Otomanguean, and Mayan. Owing to the fact that not every individual member of these language families still preserves each of the features under scrutiny, it is necessary every once in a while to have recourse to the classical written languages of the early colonial period or to more conservative modern dialects/varieties.

Furthermore, we do not look into the areal distribution of loan translations and semantic calques. Some of the 13 cases mentioned by Campbell et al. (1986: 553−555) involve metaphorical extensions of body-part terms such as, e.g., 'lip' being used to designate 'rim' as in Classical Náhuatl *tēntli* 'lip = rim', Tzotzil *ti'(il)* 'lip = rim, edge, border' (de León 1992: 583−584). Others are of a different nature. It cannot be denied that the existence of loan translations and semantic calques indeed lends credibility to the hypothesis that there have been contacts between the Mesoamerican languages. However, neither the absolute number of reported cases nor their distribution among the Mesoamerican languages is impressive enough to call for a detailed discussion together with other features. One may also dispute that some of the calques fulfill the criteria (b) and (c).

On top of that, Yasugi (1995: 133−151) elaborates on patterns of syncretism in pronominal systems (→ Art. 56). However, his findings do not support the idea that there really are pan-Mesoamerican features (Yasugi 1995: 148−149). Thus, we do not touch on this subject-matter in the present text.

4.1.1. Nominal possession

Genitival constructions ("nominal possession" in the terms of Campbell et al. 1986: 545) (→ Art. 72) have the following structure in the majority of Mesoamerican languages (with N1 representing the possessum and N2 the possessor): POSS-N1 N2, i.e. there is an affix − almost exclusively a prefix − on the possessum noun cross-referencing the possessor. The order of possessor and possessum noun may be inverted, though possessum preceding possessor is the most common linearization. Determiners such as, e.g., definite articles may occur in between the two nouns.

Examples (1)−(3) from three genetically unrelated modern Mesoamerican languages − Uto-Aztecan Náhuatl, Mayan Ch'ol, and Otomanguean Otomí − confirm that such head-marking genitival constructions are indeed common in the area.

(1) Náhuatl (Wohlgemuth 1981: 117)
¿*tē   in   i-tōcā   in   tāga'?*
what ART POSS.3-name ART man
'What is the man's name?'

(2) Ch'ol (Warkentin & Scott 1980: 26)
i   tyaq'uin   i   yalobil
POSS.3 money   POSS.3 son
c-amigo
POSS.1SG-friend
'the money of my friend's son'

(3) Otomí (Voigtlander & Echegoyen 1985: 64)
rá   ngu   ra   Xuua
POSS.3 house he Juan
'Juan's house'

This type of construction is reported for the oldest recorded documents of the classical written languages of Mesoamerica (Smailus 1989: 112). In Classical Náhuatl, discontinuous constituency occurred frequently with possessum noun and possessor noun (Launey 1981: 92).

Campbell et al. (1986: 545) claim that the Mesoamerican style genitival constructions are absent from most of their control languages. Moreover, Náhuatl behaves differently from its Uto-Aztecan relatives outside Mesoamerica. It should not go unmentioned, though, that Nichols' (1992: 69−72) statistics suggest that head-marking structures are found all over the place in the Americas — with dependent-marking being extremely rare in Mesoamerica. Clearly, genitival constructions similar to the ones typically employed by Mesoamerican languages are also known from other continents, though not from the North American and Central American control languages (Campbell et al. 1986: 545 footnote 5).

4.1.2. Relational nouns

Another widespread feature among Mesoamerican languages is the use of relational nouns for functions that roughly correspond to those fulfilled by adpositions in the familiar European languages (Campbell et al. 1986: 545–546) (→ Art. 55). Very frequently, body-part terms — among others — are used in a construction of the genitival type exemplified by (1)–(3) (Yasugi (1995: 124) seems to be somewhat surprised to find the two constructions to be identical). In such cases, the noun designating a body-part functions as the possessum and, consequently, carries the possessor prefix, as in Náhuatl (4).

(4) Náhuatl (Wohlgemuth 1981: 133–136)
ijti- 'belly' >   i-y-ijti-co
                  POSS.3-y-belly-LOC
                  'in him'
īx- 'face' >   i-y-īx-taj
                  POSS.3-y-face-LOC
                  'in front of him'
tepotz- 'shoulder' >   no-tepotz-taj
                       POSS.1SG-shoulder-LOC
                       'behind me'
tzīn- 'posterior' >   i-tzīn-tan
                      POSS.3-posterior-LOC
                      'at his feet, under him'
nacas- 'ear' >   i-nacas-tan
                  POSS.3-ear-LOC
                  'at his side'

In Náhuatl, we find a variety of possible locative affixes on the possessed body-part terms (-co, -taj, -tan, and many more), a fact that probably indicates that, prior to recruiting relational nouns via grammaticalization, Proto-Náhuatl possessed a postpositional system similar to morphological case distinctions (Campbell et al. 1986: 546). In Ch'ol, body-part terms are part of a prepositional phrase headed by the general (desemanticized) preposition ti. This preposition coalesces regularly with the possessor morpheme i' 'his, her, their' yielding the form ti' 'in, on, at his, her, their', cf. (5).

(5) Ch'ol (Warkentin & Scott 1980: 98)
pam 'face' >   t-i' pam mesa
                  LOC-POSS.3 face table
                  'on the table'
pat 'shoulder' > t-i' pat mesa
                  LOC-POSS.3 shoulder table
                  'behind the table'
t'ejl 'side' >   t-i' t'ejl mesa
                  LOC-POSS.3 side table
                  'at the side of the table'
oc 'foot' >   t-i' yoc mesa
                  LOC-POSS.3 foot table
                  'at the foot of the table'
mal 'inside' >   t-i' mal otyot
                  LOC-POSS.3 inside house
                  'in the house'

Slightly less often, the body-part term appears without any possessor morpheme. It is not always easy to determine whether a former possessor prefix was lost in the course of language history or whether it has never been there at all. In Zapotec, relational noun and dependent noun are juxtaposed with the relational noun obligatorily occurring to the left of the dependent, cf. (6). The same linearization holds good for Náhuatl and Ch'ol and, of course, for genitival constructions in these languages as well. In Zapotec, no other devices with locative functions such as, e. g., adpositions or case markers, are used alongside relational nouns.

(6) Zapotec (Butler 1988: 235)
lao 'face' >   lao yo
                  face earth
                  'on the ground'
cožə' 'shoulder' > cožə' ya'an
                   shoulder mountain
                   'behind the mountain'
le'e 'belly' >   le'e yɨšən'
                  belly paper
                  'on the paper'
xan 'posterior' > xan mesən'
                  posterior table
                  'under the table'
cho'a 'mouth' >   cho'a bentan
                  mouth window
                  'on the window'

For Yucatec Maya, a situation is reported that might reflect a transition from the Ch'ol type system to the one represented by Zapotec (Goldap 1992: 615–618): Most of the complex adpositions involving relational nouns require the general locative preposition *ti'* – a cognate of Ch'ol *ti-*, and some in addition require the possessor morpheme *u* and/or a relational suffix *-Vl*, but *ich(il)* 'in' < *ich* 'eye, face' is used in the Zapotecan way, i. e. bearing neither preposition nor possessor morpheme (which, however, has been the case since the earliest records (Smailus 1989: 151)). Thus, it can be stated that the morphosyntax of relational nouns is not completely homogeneous in Mesoamerica.

Though there are actually hints suggesting that relational nouns could pass as innovations in Náhuatl (and in some Uto-Aztecan languages of the northern transition zone), relational noun constructions have been documented since the very earliest written records of Mesoamerican languages (Launey 1981: 229–230, Dürr 1988: 57–60, Smailus 1989: 154–155).

Like genitive constructions, relational nouns can hardly be considered an exclusive trait of Mesoamerican languages. Campbell et al. (1986: 546) claim, however, that relational nouns are absent from most of the control languages on the northern and southern borders of Mesoamerica. On the status of grammaticalized body-part terms as potential Mesoamericanisms, cf. § 4.2..

4.1.3. Vigesimal numeral system

According to Campbell et al. (1986: 546) one especially strong areal feature is the almost exceptionless existence of vigesimal numeral systems in Mesoamerican languages (→ Art. 92). Further relevant data are discussed in Yasugi (1995: 77–105). For many of the modern indigenous languages, however, the loss of the traditional numeral system – rapidly ongoing or already completed – can be observed. It is quite common to find Amerindian numerals above 3, 4, or 5 giving way to those derived from Spanish (Yasugi 1995: 91), as is the case with the dialect of Náhuatl spoken at Mecayapan (Wohlgemuth 1981: 60). Classical Náhuatl, however, had a system based on 5 and 20 (combined quinary and vigesimal), cf. (7).

(7) Classical Náhuatl (Launey 1981: 65, 239–240)

1 *cē*	11 *màtlāctli oncē*	30 *cempōhualli ommàtlāctli*
2 *ōme*	12 *màtlāctli omōme*	40 *ōmpōhualli*
3 *ēyi*	13 *màtlāctli omēyi*	50 *ōmpōhualli ommàtlāctli*
4 *nāhui*	14 *màtlāctli onnāhui*	60 *ēpōhualli*
5 *mācuilli*	15 *caxtōlli*	70 *ēpōhualli ommàtlāctli*
6 *chiuccē*	16 *caxtōlli oncē*	80 *nāuhpōhualli*
7 *chicōme*	17 *caxtōlli omōme*	90 *nāuhpōhualli ommàtlāctli*
8 *chicuēyi*	18 *caxtōlli omēyi*	100 *mācuilpōhualli*
9 *chiucnāhui*	19 *caxtōlli onnāhui*	110 *mācuilpōhualli ommàtlāctli*
10 *màtlāctli*	20 *cempōhualli*	120 *chiucuacempōhualli*

Numerals above the bases 5, 10, and 15, etc. are formed by addition (5 + 1, 10 + 1, 15 + 1). 40, 60, 80, 100, 120, etc. are expressed by multiplications of the base 20, intermediate decades are formed by addition (20 + 10, 40 + 10, 60 + 10, etc.). Above 20, the next base numeral is *tzontli* '400'.

In Ch'ol, there is no quinary element in the numeral system, which rather appears to be a combination of decimal and vigesimal principles. The numerals below 20 and the intermediate numerals quoted in (8) contain the general classifier *-p'ej* 'piece'.

(8) Ch'ol (Warkentin & Scott 1980: 107–108)

1 *jump'ej*	11 *junlujump'ej*	30 *lujump'ej i cha'c'al*
2 *cha'p'ej*	12 *lajchʌmp'ej*	40 *cha'c'al*
3 *uxp'ej*	13 *uxlujump'ej*	50 *lujump'ej i yuxc'al*
4 *chʌmp'ej*	14 *chʌnlujump'ej*	60 *uxc'al*
5 *jo'p'ej*	15 *jo'lujump'ej*	70 *lujump'ej i chʌnc'al*
6 *wʌcp'ej*	16 *wʌclujump'ej*	80 *chʌnc'al*
7 *wucp'ej*	17 *wuclujump'ej*	90 *lujump'ej i jo'c'al*
8 *waxʌcp'ej*	18 *waxʌclujump'ej*	100 *jo'c'al*
9 *bolomp'ej*	19 *bolonlujump'ej*	110 *lujump'ej i wʌcc'al*
10 *lujump'ej*	20 *junc'al*	120 *wʌcc'al*

Numerals above 10 are again formed by addition (= overcounting) (1 + 10, 2 + 10, etc.). As in Classical Náhuatl, the numerals for 40, 60, 80, 100, 120, etc. are construed as multiples of 20. For the intermediate values, however, the orientation of the numerals changes to the next highest multiple of 20 (= undercounting) (21 = '1 towards 40', 41 = '1 towards 60', etc.). Above 20, the next base numeral is *jumbac'* '400'.

As to the numeral system used in Zapotec, it has to be mentioned that quinary, decimal, and vigesimal features co-occur, cf. (9).

(9)   Zapotec (Butler 1988: 211–212)
1 *to*   11 *šnej*   30 *šichoa*
2 *chopə*   12 *šižin̪*   40 *choa*
3 *šon̪ə*   13 *ši'in̪*   50 *šiyon*
4 *tap*   14 *žda'*   60 *gyon*
5 *gueyə'*   15 *šino'*   70 *gyonši*
6 *xop*   16 *ši'into*   80 *taplalj*
7 *gažə*   17 *ši'inchopə* 90 *taplaljši*
8 *xon'*   18 *ši'inšon̪ə*   100 *gueyə'əlalj*
9 *ga*   19 *tgualj*   110 *to gueyoa ši*
10 *ši*   20 *galjə*   120 *xoplalj*

From 1–10, the system looks ordinarily decimal. However, numerals 16–18 are formed by additions to a base 15 (15 + 1, 15 + 2, 15 + 3), while 19 is formed by subtraction from the base 20 (1 − 20). 80, 100, 120, etc. are again treated as multiples of the base 20 (4 × 20, 5 × 20, 6 × 20, etc.), whereas the numerals for 40 and 60 are etymologically independent of the base 20. As reported for Ch'ol, intermediate numerals are oriented towards the next highest multiple of 20 (30 = '10 towards 40', 50 = '10 towards 60', from 61 onwards with inverted order). In present-day Zapotec, the Spanish loanword *tmil* '1000' is the next highest base numeral.

Obviously, the numeral systems do not entirely follow the same pattern. Typically, Mesoamerican vigesimal features are combined with features of other systems (Yasugi 1995: 103). The admixture of decimal and the absence of quinary features possibly points at diachronic layering, i.e. the higher-level vigesimal structure could be interpreted as an innovation in at least some of the Mesoamerican languages. Yasugi (1995: 89), therefore, is of the opinion that, in preconquest times, the vigesimal system spread by diffusion through Mesoamerica, eventually crossing the borders to neighbouring areas. Before this spread took place, quite a variety of numerical systems were used in Mesoamerica.

Again, vigesimal systems do not really qualify as an absolutely exclusive Mesoamericanism. Already prestructuralists like Friedrich A. Pott (1868: 29–109) and Wilhelm Schmidt (1926: 357–380) have demonstrated that vigesimal systems have a relatively wide distribution over the globe − though more restricted as opposed to decimal systems − and that they abound in the Americas. Campbell et al. (1986: 546), however, claim that the majority of control languages do not share this feature with languages of Mesoamerica proper.

4.1.4. Word order

In comparison to the other Mesoamerican features presented so far, basic word order is discussed more extensively by Campbell et al. (1986: 547–548) (→ Art. 64), because they have to come to terms with some supposed cases of counterevidence. Their conclusion is that Mesoamerican languages in their entirety disfavour verb-final basic word order. This observation really seems to hold good for the vast majority of Mesoamerican languages though, for quite a few of them, there are competing suggestions as to the basic word order. Split word order is not rare either (11 or 13 reported cases in Yasugi (1995: 123)).

As in the case of numeral systems, it can be suspected that Spanish influence has brought about some changes in the neutral order of constituents in quite a few Mesoamerican languages. As a matter of fact, the erstwhile verb-initial structure of Classical Náhuatl − as in (10) − has been superseded by a new neutral word order of the SVO-type in many Uto-Aztecan languages in modern Mesoamerica. Admittedly, word order was extremely free in the early documented history of the written language (Launey 1981: 40).

(10)   Classical Náhuatl (Launey 1981: 40)
        qui-cua   in   pilli   in   nacatl
        OBJ.3-eat ART child:ABS ART meat:ABS
        'The child is eating the meat.'

Verb-initial structures are also typical of Mayan and Otomanguean languages with both VOS and VSO being reported for individual members of both language families (though others have experienced contact-induced word-order change to SVO under the impact of Spanish). The Guatemalan Mayan language Mam (11) and Zapotec (12) are representative of the VSO-languages.

(11)   Mam (England 1990: 237)
        nnok ky-kin xjaal jun wech
        ASP 3PL-see people one jaguar
        'The people are watching a jaguar.'

(12)   Zapotec (Butler 1988: 171)
        che'ej   cabeyən' nis
        DUR:drink horse   water
        'The horse is drinking water.'

Pipil, the southernmost Uto-Aztecan language spoken in El Salvador and a near relative of Classical Náhuatl, cf. (10), seems to have acquired basic VOS word order via contact with neighbouring Mayan and Lencan languages (Campbell 1985: 103), cf. (13).

(13) Pipil (Campbell 1985: 103)
ki-miktih ne wa:kax ne ta:kat
OBJ.3-kill ART COW ART man:ABS
'The man killed the cow.'

In Nichols' (1992: 94) sample, Mesoamerican languages display predominantly verb-initial basic word order. Nevertheless, there are also SVO-languages in Mesoamerica though their status is not always clear. However, Mazatec is often classified as being basically SVO (Campbell et al. 1986: 547, Yasugi 1995: 121), but the descriptions at hand clearly indicate that it rather belongs to the VSO-languages instead (Jamieson 1988: 18). Suárez (1983: 97) claims that both SVO and VSO occur in Mazatec. Totonac, which has variable word order according to Suárez (1983: 95) and is left unspecified for word oder in Campbell et al. (1986: 556–557), counts among the SVO-languages in Yasugi (1995: 121). An example which shows neutral SVO-order is (14).

(14) Totonac (Levy 1990: 111)
Juan maq-ni:-lh kin-chichi
Juan CAUS-die-PFV POSS.1SG-dog
'Juan killed my dog.'

For Proto-Náhuatl, the basic word order SOV has been reconstructed (Steele 1976). Thus, it seems that the once predominant verb-inital structures of Classical Náhuatl were indeed innovations. For other languages (especially of the Mixe-Zoque family), there are also residual characteristics of an earlier SOV-order which seems to have given way to VOS or SVO (Campbell et al. 1986: 547–548).

Irrespective of the problems connected with the identification of basic word-order types, Suárez (1983: 96), Campbell et al. (1986: 548), and Yasugi (1995: 120) actually do agree on one point: With the exception of Chichimec (Otomanguean), none of the Mesoamerican languages proper belongs to the SOV-languages which seem to be more frequent – even abundant – among the control languages (18 of 19 SOV-languages in Yasugi (1995: 123, 131) are control languages). Yasugi (1995: 158) even redefines the borders of Mesoamerica by excluding Chichimec from the area. In addition, the exclusion of V from the final position in basic word order seems to be a feature that has spread within Mesoamerica via diffusion. The spread hypothesis is also supported by residual typological features at the phrase level which point to a former SOV-word order in a number of Mesoamerican languages (Yasugi 1995: 124–130).

Clear cases of V-medial languages are a minority among Mesoamerican languages, while V-initial languages are the locally unmarked case: In Yasugi's (1995: 123) sample, there are 20 SVO-languages as opposed to 20 VSO-languages and 17 VOS-languages, i.e. V-initial languages outnumber V-medial languages by a ratio of almost 2:1.

Interestingly, outside of Mesoamerica and Oceania, verb-initial basic word order is relatively rare. In a global perspective (and within the Americas), verb-final basic word order is the unmarked case (Nichols 1992: 94). The areal character of the Mesoamerican preference, in this case, is rather obvious. It still remains remarkably pronounced if we add verb-medial basic word order to the list.

4.2. Noteworthy preferences

The cases presented in § 4.1. are convincing insofar as their proponents are able to prove that these features are not shared by the languages spoken in the neighbouring areas. Therefore, the most useful of the criteria employed by Campbell et al. (1986) is (a). However, it can by no means be completely ruled out that structures which are found in Mesoamerica but not in the immediately neighbouring areas might easily develop elsewhere.

On much the same grounds, Campbell et al. (1986: 544) do not consider phonological phenomena to be exclusive areal features. Yasugi (1995: 11–75) proves them right because he fails to identify any really pan-Mesoamerican properties in the realm of phonology. Owing to violations of at least one of the criteria (a)–(c) (cf. beginning of § 4.), Campbell et al. (1986: 548–553), at first, exclude several other features from the list of possible Mesoamericanisms mentioned in the extant literature (unless otherwise stated, examples are from Classical Náhuatl):

(i) absence of switch-reference (→ Art. 84)

(15) *qui-'toa in Pedro in ca*
OBJ.3-say ART Pedro ART ASSERTION
huāl-lā-z
hither-go-FUT
'Pedro$_i$ says that he$_{i/j}$ (= himself or some other 3rd person) will come here' (Launey 1981: 293)

(ii) intimate possession (→ Art. 72)

(16) in   no-nac
      ART   POSS.1SG-meat
      'my meat (to eat)'

(17) in   no-naca-yo
      ART   POSS.1Sg-meat-INALIENABLE
      'my flesh' (Launey 1981: 100)

(iii) locatives derived from body-parts (cf. (4)−(6))

(iv) absolutive affixes

(18) naca-tl
      meat-ABS
      'meat' (Launey 1981: 24)

(v) absence/limited occurrence of plural markers on nouns (→ Art. 61)

(19) cal-li
      house-ABS
      'house(s)'

(20) tlāca-tl   tlāca-ᴬ
      man-ABS.SG man-ABS.PL
      'man ≠ men' (Launey 1981: 28−29)

(vi) numeral classifiers (→ Art. 92)

(21) on-te-tl   cal-li
      two-stone.CLASSIFIER-ABS house-ABS
      'two houses' (Launey 1981: 69)

(vii) noun incorporation (→ Art. 53)

(22) ni-naca-cua
      1SG-meat-eat
      'I (usually) eat meat' (Launey 1981: 166)

(viii) body-part incorporation (→ Art. 53)

(23) ni-mitz-mā-tēn-namiqui
      1SG-OBJ.2SG-hand-lip-meet
      'I kiss your hands, lit. I meet your hands with my lips' (Launey 1981: 168)

(ix) directional affixes

(24) ni-mitz-on-itta
      1SG-OBJ.2SG-thither-see
      'I am going to visit you there'

(25) ni-mitz-huāl-itta
      1SG-OBJ.2SG-hither-see
      'I am going to visit you here' (Launey 1981: 61)

(x) verbal aspect (→ Art. 59)

(26) Yucatec Maya (C. Lehmann 1990: 41)
      k-in   tàa-s-k-o'b
      IMPF-1SG   come-CAUS-TR.IMPF-3PL
      'I (will) bring them'

(27) Yucatec Maya (C. Lehmann 1990: 41)
      t-in   tàa-s-h-o'b
      PFV-1SG   come-CAUS-TR.PFV-3PL
      'I (have) brought them'

(xi) inclusive vs. exclusive 1st person plural (→ Art. 56)

(28) Mazatec (Jamieson 1988: 46)
      niji 'we (exclusive)' vs. naja 'we (inclusive)'

(xii) zero copula

(29) ca   cual-li   in   cal-li
      ASSERTION   good-ABS   ART house-ABS
      'the house is good' (Launey 1981: 54)

(xiii) pronominal copular constructions

(30) ni-mexìca-tl
      1SG-Mexican-ABS
      'I am a Mexican' (Launey 1981: 30)

(xiv) absence of a verb 'to have' (→ Art. 71)

(31) ni-cal-ê
      1SG-house-POSS
      'I have got a house, lit. I am a house-owner' (Launey 1981: 102)

Inevitably, one starts to feel uncomfortable with the impact exercised by the overrigid methodology which requires that so many phenomena be left out of account. Not surprisingly, in the last chapters of their article, Campbell et al. (1986: 558) abandon the restrictive methodology and claim that at least the features (iii), (v), (vi), (xi), and (xiii) are to some extent peculiar to Mesoamerica (as well as, to their minds, final devoicing of sonorants, voicing of obstruents after nasals, stress on vowels before final consonant or single consonant + vowel, retroflex fricatives/affricates).

De León & Levinson (1992: 527) criticize Campbell et al. (1986) for overlooking that some of the features they claim to be exclusive Mesoamericanisms are actually tightly connected not only to one another but also to some of the features which had to be discounted as areal phenomena for methodological reasons. According to de León & Levinson (1992: 527−528), pace Suárez (1983: 161), genitival constructions, relational nouns, quite a few of the semantic calques, locatives derived from body parts, noun incorporation − and more specifically − body-part incorporation, shape-oriented numeral classifiers, and directional affixes are interconnected phenomena all of which are indicative of the typical Mesoamerican "preoccupation with space and shape" (→ Art. 43).

Much in the same vein, Levinson & Haviland (1994: 613) claim that with regard to space and shape, "(e)ven when universal tendencies are properly taken into account, the Mesoamerican pattern seems distinctive." Hollenbach (1990: 295) is equally positive that "(t)he extensive use of body-part nouns to express relations is an areal feature of Mesoamerica". Likewise, MacLaury (1989: 153) concludes that irrespective of minor differences in the use actually made of body-part terms as space relators in languages such as, e. g., Zapotec, Mixtec, and Trique, body-part derivations share enough traits to be "diagnostic of the Mesoamerican diffusion area".

Recruiting body-part nouns for the purpose of expressing grammatical and/or spatial relations, of course, is a universal phenomenon. In fact, it is the paradigm case of grammaticalization (→ Art. 113) (Heine & Claudi & Hünnemeyer 1991: 123−147). Not surprisingly, the use of body-part nouns designating the belly in order to express a relation covered by the English prepositions *in, into, within* is not confined to Mesoamerican languages. Rather, it shows up in languages from almost every other part of the world (T. Stolz 1992: 175−178). With the exception of African languages (Heine & Claudi & Hünnemeyer 1991: 126), however, the grammaticalization process BELLY > IN(TO) seems to be relatively frequent only in Mesoamerica, while many − though not all − Amerindian languages outside the area, at least on superficial inspection, seem to prefer other body-part terms to encode an inessive/illative relation (T. Stolz 1992: 175). Thus, there is good reason to consider Mesoamerica an area in which a certain set of universally possible grammaticalization processes have been activated preferentially (cf. Heine (1994) for the notion of *grammaticalization area*).

Levinson (1994: 810−812) does not subscribe to the metaphorization hypothesis put forward by cognitive semanticists. Yet, he admits that "(b)ody-part metaphors are a Mesoamerican areal feature central to spatial description in many of the languages of the region" (Levinson 1994: 839). What strikes him most is the fact that many Mesoamerican languages "of unrelated stock utilize a similar core set of body-part terms OFTEN WITH ALMOST EXACTLY THE SAME SHAPE APPLICATIONS" (Levinson 1994: 839, original caps). Levinson (1994: 839) regards these grammaticalized body-part terms as semantic calques "based on high-prestige languages during various periods of imperial extension". Note that Classical Náhuatl, one of the potential high-prestige languages, is notorious for the extensive use of body-part terminology for the purpose of creating new lexical expressions for concepts (López Austin 1989). This leads us to the question of how the areal features have come into being.

5. Origins

Suárez (1983) is rather sceptical as to the validity of the *Sprachbund* hypothesis. To his mind, "the proposal does not seem to be supported by the facts" (Suárez 1983: 160). He does not accept any of the features as evidence for a pre-Columbian *Spachbund* because he believes them to be purely coincidental (Suárez 1983: 161). Instead he sides with Diebold (1962: 49), who claimed that "since (…) the intrusion (of Spanish) to the Americas (…) it has created in Mexico a single great *Sprachbund* characterized by Spanish-derived affinities evinced by the various Indian languages spoken there, as a result of their common tradition of contact with and interference from Spanish." Before the arrival of Spanish, Mexico constituted "a linguistically diverse area". Accordingly, Suárez (1983: 161) states that "Mesoamerica as a linguistic area is the result of the influence of Spanish on the native languages".

It is an indisputable fact that Hispanicization has yielded similar results in quite a few Mesoamerican languages either via grammatical calques or overt grammatical borrowing (Suárez 1983: 135−137). It is equally true that some contacts of Mesoamerican languages were made possible only by the officialization and subsequent propagation of the so-called "lenguas generales" i. e. co-official languages of indigenous stock in a given Spanish vice-royalty (or other colonial territory). (Suárez 1983: 155−156, Miller 1990). However, it remains doubtful whether a sufficient number of the striking similarities of Mesoamerican languages could be attributed to Hispanicization or even to chance. As for overt grammatical borrowings − and maybe not only for them −, Mesoamerica is not much different from other areas which have shared the same superstrate. We find exactly the same grammatical Hispanisms in Mesoamerican, Central American, South American, and Austronesian languages (C. Stolz & T. Stolz 1998). Thus, Mesoamerica would form part of a larger circum-Pacific linguistic area created by Spanish contact-influence.

This more extended and more recent linguistic area does not necessarily force us to abandon the idea of a pre-Columbian *Sprachbund*. Indeed, Mesoamerican languages also display similarities among each other that they do not share with languages from South America or the Philippines. These Mesoamerican features point at a source different from and older than Hispanicization.

First of all, there is evidence for contacts between individual Mesoamerican languages without any interference from Spanish (Suárez 1983: 154−159, McQuown 1990), though Suárez (1983: 158−159) emphasizes that pre-conquest linguistic contacts occurred at best sporadically and only concerned the upper classes of indigenous societies.

The opposite view is held by Yasugi (1995: 157), who tries to reconstruct the cultural prehistory by way of evaluating areal-typological features of present-day Mesoamerican languages. According to Suárez (1983: 156−157), overt borrowings are relatively rare or at times rather doubtful, whereas Campbell et al. (1986: 558) are of a completely different opinion: to their minds, loanwords are rather numerous in Mesoamerica. Avoiding the still unsolved problem of loanwords, Yasugi (1995: 159) presents the spread of the vigesimal numeral system (cf. § 4.1.3.) as evidence for the possibility that abstract principles may be borrowed without any accompanying material being borrowed. He discusses two possible scenarios for the origin and subsequent spread of the vigesimal system (Yasugi 1995: 156−159). In both cases, the hypothesized origin of the vigesimal system is identical with the origin of the conventionalized representation of numerical values in the traditional pre-conquest writing systems. The so-called bar-and-dot notation is very common in Mesoamerica. Yasugi (1995: 156) claims that the source from where the vigesimal system must have spread was an Otomanguean language, for the languages which are spoken nearest to the oldest archaeological documents (500 B.C.−A.D. 900) with inscriptions in the bar-and-dot notation at Monte Albán, Oaxaca, belong to the Otomanguean family. The inscriptions of Monte Albán are considered to reflect proto-Zapotecan grammar (Yasugi 1995: 158). Moreover, the reconstructed relative order of numeral and noun in proto-Otomanguean is said to correspond closely to the order of glyphs in the earliest inscriptions, viz. NOUN BEFORE NUMERAL. Note, however, that in modern Otomanguean languages, the order NUMERAL BEFORE NOUN is the rule, while in other grammatical subsystems the order HEAD BEFORE MODIFIER prevails. In addition, Yasugi (1995: 157−158) speculates about Mixe-Zoquean languages (Olmec) as an alternative to the assumed Otomanguean origin of vigesimal systems. The Mixe-Zoquean origin would precede the Monte Albán inscriptions. This alternative is based on the fact that, in modern Mixe-Zoquean languages, both linearizations are possible i.e. there is free variation of the orders NOUN BEFORE NUMERAL and NUMERAL BEFORE NOUN. Yasugi (1995: 158) suggests that NOUN BEFORE NUMERAL should be interpreted as the older order. If so, the proto-Mixe-Zoquean order is in line with the bar-and-dot notation and glyphs of the Monte Albán inscriptions.

However, it is hardly likely that Mixe-Zoquean languages are responsible for the majority of areal features ascribed to Mesoamerican languages. Some features seem to indicate an Otomanguean source (Yasugi 1995: 159). In other cases, the best we can do is to identify those languages which have acquired the features via language contact (Yasugi 1995: 160). Historically, the Mesoamerican area has been shaped by several waves of innovations etc. from different centers of hegemony. The same holds good for the linguistic aspects: the linguistic area is not the result of diffusion from one single source, rather several such sources, located in different places, succeeded one another and exerted influence to different degrees over only partially overlapping regions.

6. Conclusion

Many aspects of the Mesoamerican *Sprachbund* are still controversial. There are quite a lot of hypotheses which need more convincing substantialization. In addition, there are also quite a few phenomena which possibly have a special Mesoamerican touch but remain to be investigated. Among these, we find dimensional adjectives (→ Art. 91) (C. Stolz 1996), comparative constructions (→ Art. 75) (C. Stolz & T. Stolz 1995), basic colour terms (→ Art. 90) (Manrique Castañeda 1988: 94−

101), and tendential omnipredicativity (→ Art. 39) (Launey 1994) worth studying in some detail. Further study is also needed for the "sprechbund" postulated by Campbell et al. (1986: 558). The *sprechbund* involves pragmatics, discourse organization, and communicative styles common to many Mesoamerican language communities (→ Art. 36).

In view of the criticism by Suárez (1983: 161), to whom the supposed Mesoamericanisms turn out to be pan-Amerindianisms, it seems appropriate to continue to apply criterion (a) of the methodology proposed by Campbell et al. (1986). If it is indeed possible to demonstrate that features which abound in a certain region become noticeably infrequent at its margins and/or beyond, then this is proof enough of an areal preference (we are still awaiting such a proof for many of the phenomena associated with the Mesoamerican preoccupation with shape and space). There is no need to prove that such an areal preference is unique. If it is likewise possible to show that some of the genetically unrelated languages in a certain region share features that are absent from their nearest relatives outside the area, then this is indicative of areal convergence (T. Stolz 1991: 101–105). Ultimately, Campbell et al. (1986: 558) also favour this less rigid approach to identifying areal traits.

7. References

Bright, William & Sherzer, Joel. 1976. "Areal phenomena in North American Indian linguistics." In: Bright, William (ed.). *Variation and change in language.* Stanford: University of Stanford Press, 228–268.

Butler, H., Inez M. 1988. *Gramática Zapoteca. Zapoteco de Yatzachi el Bajo.* (Serie gramáticas de lenguas indígenas de México 4). México: Instituto Lingüístico de Verano.

Campbell, Lyle. 1979. "Middle American languages." In: Campbell, Lyle & Mithun, Marianne (eds.). *The languages of native America: Historical and comparative assessment.* Austin, London: University of Texas Press, 902–1000.

Campbell, Lyle. 1985. *The Pipil language of El Salvador* (Mouton Grammar Library 1). Berlin, etc.: Mouton Publishers.

Campbell, Lyle & Kaufman, Terrence. 1980. "On Mesoamerican linguistics." *American Anthropologist* 82: 850–857.

Campbell, Lyle & Kaufman, Terrence. 1983. "Mesoamerican historical linguistics and distant genetic relationship: getting it straight." *American Anthropologist* 85: 362–372.

Campbell, Lyle & Kaufman, Terrence. 1990. "Lingüística mayance: ¿dónde nos encontramos ahora?". In: England, Nora C. & Elliott Stephen R. (eds.). 1990. *Lecturas sobre la lingüística maya.* La Antigua Guatemala: Centro de Investigación Regionales de Mesoamérica, 51–58.

Campbell, Lyle & Kaufman, Terrence & Smith-Stark, Thomas C. 1986. "Meso-America as a linguistic area." *Language* 62.3: 530–570.

Darnell, Regna & Sherzer, Joel. 1971. "Areal linguistic studies in North America: a historical perspective." *International Journal of American Linguistics* 37: 20–28.

De León, Lourdes. 1992. "Body parts and location in Tzotzil: a case of grammaticalization." *Zeitschrift für Phonetik, Sprachwissenschaft und Kommunikationsforschung* 45.6: 570–589.

De León, Lourdes & Levinson, Stephen C. 1992. "Introduction: Spatial description in Mesoamerican languages." *Zeitschrift für Phonetik, Sprachwissenschaft und Kommunikationsforschung* 45.6: 527–529.

Diebold jr., A. Richard. 1962. "A laboratory for language contact." *Anthropological Linguistics* 4.1: 41–51.

Dürr, Michael. 1988. "Reference to space in colonial Quiché." *Función* 8: 47–78.

England, Nora C. 1990. "El Mam: semejanzas y diferencias regionales." In: England, Nora C. & Elliott, Stephen R. (eds.). 1990. *Lecturas sobre la lingüística maya.* La Antigua Guatemala: Centro de Investigación Regionales de Mesoamérica, 221–252.

Escalante Hernández, Roberto. 1975. "Tipología de las lenguas de México." In: Arana de Swadesh, Evangelina (ed.). *Las lenguas de México I.* México: Instituto Nacional de Antropología e Historia, 91–127.

Goldap, Christel. 1991. *Lokale Relationen im Yukatekischen.* (Continuum 8). Frankfurt a. M., etc.: Peter Lang.

Goldap, Christel. 1992. "Morphology and semantics of Yucatec space relators." *Zeitschrift für Phonetik, Sprachwissenschaft und Kommunikationsforschung* 45.6: 612–625.

Greenberg, Joseph H. 1987. *Language in the Americas.* Stanford: Stanford University Press.

Grimes, Barbara F. (ed.). 1996. *Ethnologue. Languages of the World.* Dallas: Summer Institute of Linguistics.

Hamp, Eric P. 1979. "A glance from here on." In: Campbell, Lyle & Mithun, Marianne (eds.). *The languages of native America: historical and comparative assessment.* Austin, etc.: University of Texas Press, 1001–1016.

Hasler, Juan A. 1959. "Una lingüística meso-americana." *La Palabra y el Hombre* 12: 535–547.

Heine, Bernd. 1994. "Areal influence on grammaticalization." In: Pütz, Martin (ed.). *Language Contact – Language Conflict.* Amsterdam: John Benjamins, 55–68.

Heine, Bernd & Claudi, Ulrike & Hünnemeyer, Friederike. 1991. *Grammaticalization. A conceptual framework.* Chicago, etc.: The University of Chicago Press.

Hollenbach, Barbara E. 1990. "Semantic and syntactic extensions of Copala Trique body-part nouns." In: Garza Cuarón, Beatriz & Levy, Paulette (eds.). 1990. *Homenaje a Jorge A. Suárez. Lingüística indoamericana e hispánica.* (Estudios de lingüística y literatura 18). México: El Colegio de México, 275–296.

Jamieson, Carole. 1988. *Gramática Mazateca del municipio de Chiquihuitlan, Oaxaca.* (Gramáticas de lenguas indígenas de México 7). México: Instituto Lingüístico de Verano.

Kaufman, Terrence. 1973. "Areal linguistics and Middle America." In: Sebeok, Thomas (ed.). *Current trends in linguistics 11.* The Hague: Mouton, 459–483.

Kirchhoff, Paul. 1943. "Mesoamérica: sus límites geográficos, composición étnica y carácteres culturales." *Acta Americana* 1: 92–107.

Kroeber, Alfred L. 1939. *Cultural and natural areas of native North America.* (University of California Publications in American Archaeology and Ethnology 38). Berkeley: University of California Press.

Launey, Michel. 1981. *Introduction à la langue et à la littérature aztèques. Tome I:* Grammaire. Paris: L'Harmattan.

Launey, Michel. 1994. *Une grammaire omniprédicative. Essai sur la morphosyntaxe du nahuatl classique.* Paris: CNRS Éditions.

Lehmann, Christian. 1990. "Yukatekisch." *Zeitschrift für Sprachwissenschaft* 9: 28–51.

Lehmann, Walter. 1920. *Zentral-Amerika. Erster Teil: Die Sprachen Zentral-Amerikas in ihren Beziehungen zueinander sowie zu Süd-Amerika und Mexiko.* 2 vols. Berlin: Dietrich Reimer.

Levinson, Stephen C. 1994. "Vision, shape, and linguistic description: Tzeltal body-part terminology and object description." *Linguistics* 32.4/5: 791–855.

Levinson, Stephen C. & Haviland, John. 1994. "Introduction: Spatial conceptualization in Mayan languages." *Linguistics* 32.4/5: 613–622.

Levy, Paulette. 1990. *Totonaco de Papantla, Veracruz.* (Archivo de Lenguas Indígenas de México 15). México: Colegio de México.

Liedtke, Stefan. 1991. *Indianersprachen. Sprachvergleich und Klassifizierung. Eine ethnolinguistische Einführung in die Grundlagen und Methoden.* Hamburg: Helmut Buske.

Ligorred, Francesc. 1992. *Lenguas indígenas de México y Centroamérica (de los jeroglíficos al siglo XXI).* (Colecciones MAPFRE 1492, V-5). Madrid: MAPFRE.

López Austin, Alfredo. 1989. *Cuerpo humano e ideología. Las concepciones de los antiguos nahuas* (Serie antropológica 39). México: Universidad Nacional Autónoma de México.

MacLaury, Robert. 1989. "Zapotec body-part locatives: prototypes and metaphoric extensions." *International Journal of American Linguistics* 55.2: 119–154.

Manrique Castañeda, Leonardo. 1988. *Atlas cultural de México: Lingüística.* México: Instituto Nacional de Antropología e Historia.

McQuown, Norman A. 1990 "Relaciones históricas del huasteco con los idiomas y las culturas adyacentes." In: Garza Cuarón, Beatriz & Levy, Paulette (eds.). 1990. *Homenaje a Jorge A. Suárez. Lingüística indoamericana e hispánica.* (Estudios de lingüística y literatura 18). México: Colegio de México, 347–350.

Miller, Wick R. 1990. "Early Spanish and Aztec loan words in the indigenous languages of Northwest Mexico." In: Garza Cuarón, Beatriz & Levy, Paulette (eds.). 1990. *Homenaje a Jorge A. Suárez. Lingüística indoamericana e hispánica.* (Estudios de lingüística y literatura 18). México: Colegio de México, 351–365.

Muntzel, Martha C. & Pérez González, Benjamín. 1987. "México: Panorama general de las lenguas indígenas." *América Indígena* 47.4: 572–605.

Nichols, Johanna. 1992. *Linguistic diversity in space and time.* Chicago, etc.: The University of Chicago Press.

Pimentel, D. Francisco. 1862/65. *Cuadro descriptivo y comparativo de las Lenguas Indígenas de México.* 2 vols. México: Epstein.

Pott, Friedrich A. 1868. *Die Sprachverschiedenheit in Europa an den Zahlwörtern nachgewiesen. Sowie: Die quinäre und vigesimale Zählmethode.* Halle: Waisenhaus.

Prem, Hanns J. 1989. *Geschichte Alt-Amerikas.* (Oldenbourg Grundriß der Geschichte 23). München: Oldenbourg.

Reifler Bricker, Victoria & Edmonson, Munro S. (eds.). 1984. *Handbook of Middle American Indians. Supplement II: Linguistics.* Austin: University of Texas Press.

Schmidt, Wilhelm. 1926. *Die Sprachfamilien und Sprachenkreise der Erde.* Heidelberg: Carl Winter.

Sherzer, Joel. 1973. "Areal linguistics in North America." In: Sebeok, Thomas (ed.). *Current trends in linguistics 10.* The Hague: Mouton, 749–795.

Sherzer, Joel. 1976. *An areal-typological study of American Indian languages north of Mexico.* (North-Holland linguistic series 20). Amsterdam: North-Holland.

Smailus, Ortwin. 1989. *Gramática del Maya Yucateco colonial.* (Wayasbah-Publication 8). Hamburg: WAYASBAH.

Smailus, Ortwin. 1990. "Sprachen." In: Köhler, Ulrich (ed.). 1990. *Alt-Amerikanistik. Eine Einführung in die Hochkulturen Mittel- und Südamerikas.* (Ethnologische Paperbacks). Berlin: Dietrich Reimer, 255–273.

Steele, Susan. 1976. "A law of order: word order change in Classical Aztec." *International Journal of American Linguistics* 42: 31–45.

Stolz, Christel. 1996. *Spatial dimensions and orientation of objects in Yucatec Maya.* (Bochum-Essener Beiträge zur Sprachwandelforschung 29). Bochum: Norbert Brockmeyer.

Stolz, Christel & Stolz, Thomas. 1995. "Spanisch-Amerindischer Sprachkontakt: Die Hispanisierung mesoamerikanischer Komparationsstrukturen." *Iberoamericana* 58/59.2/3: 5–42.

Stolz, Christel & Stolz, Thomas. 1998. "Universelle Hispanismen? Von Manila über Lima bis Mexiko und zurück: Muster bei der Entlehnung spanischer Funktionswörter in die indigenen Sprachen Amerikas und Austronesiens." *Orbis* 39: 1–77.

Stolz, Thomas. 1991. *Sprachbund im Baltikum? Estnisch und Lettisch im Zentrum einer sprachlichen Konvergenzlandschaft.* (Bochum-Essener Beiträge zur Sprachwandelforschung 13). Bochum: Norbert Brockmeyer.

Stolz, Thomas. 1992. "On turning bellies into locatives. Mesoamerican, universal, or both?" *Papiere zur Linguistik* 47.2: 1–25.

Suárez, Jorge A. 1983. *The Mesoamerican Indian languages.* (Cambridge Language Surveys). Cambridge, etc.: Cambridge University Press.

Thomas, Cyrus & Swanton, John R. 1911. *Indian languages of Mexico and Central America.* (Smithsonian Institution. Bureau of American Ethnology, Bulletin 44). Seattle: Bureau of American Ethnology.

Thomason, Sarah Grey & Kaufman, Terrence. 1988. *Language contact, creolization, and genetic linguistics.* Berkeley: University of California Press.

Trabant, Jürgen. 1994. "Ein weites Feld: Les langues du nouveau continent." In: Zimmermann, Klaus & Trabant, Jürgen & Mueller-Vollmer, Kurt (eds.). *Wilhelm von Humboldt und die amerikanischen Sprachen. Internationales Symposium des Ibero-Amerikanischen Instituts PK 24.–26. September 1992 in Berlin.* (Humboldt-Studien). Paderborn: Friedrich Schöningh, 11–26.

Voigtlander, Katherine & Echegoyen, Artemisa. 1985. *Luces contemporáneas del otomí. Gramática del otomí de la sierra* (Serie Gramáticas de lenguas indígenas de México 1). México: Instituto Lingüístico de Verano.

Warkentin, Viola & Scott, Ruby. 1980. *Gramática Ch'ol* (Serie Gramáticas de lenguas indígenas de México 3). México: Instituto Lingüístico de Verano.

Wauchope, Robert & McQuown, Norman A. (eds.). 1967. *Handbook of Middle American Indians. V: Linguistics.* Austin: University of Texas Press.

Wohlgemuth, Carl. 1981. *Gramática náhuatl del municipio de Mecayapan, Veracruz.* (Serie Gramáticas de lenguas indígenas de México 5). México: Instituto Lingüístico de Verano.

Yasugi, Yoshiho. 1995. *Native Middle American languages. An areal-typological perspective.* (Senri Ethological Studies 39). Osaka: National Museum of Ethnology.

Christel Stolz and Thomas Stolz,
Bremen (Germany)

XV. Diachronic aspects of language types and linguistic universals
Diachronische Aspekte von Sprachtypologie und Universalienforschung
Aspects diachroniques de la recherche typologique et universaliste

111. Historizität − Sprachvariation, Sprachverschiedenheit, Sprachwandel

1. Historizität: sprachtheoretische und wissenschaftstheoretische Vorbemerkungen
2. Dimensionen der Historizität
3. Sprachvariation: Varietäten und Diskurstraditionen
4. Sprachverschiedenheit: Idiome, Sprachen, Sprachgruppen, Sprachtypen
5. Sprachwandel: Innovationen, Übernahmen, Bahnen grammatischen und lexikalischen Wandels
6. Historizität als Herausforderung
7. Zitierte Literatur

1. Historizität: sprachtheoretische und wissenschaftstheoretische Vorbemerkungen

1.1. Historizität und Geschichtlichkeit

Wenn die Ausdrücke 'Historizität' oder 'Geschichtlichkeit' im Zusammenhang mit Sprachen und Diskursen verwendet werden, denkt man in der Regel an Sprachgeschichte und Sprachwandel oder an Veränderungen in Diskursformen, Gattungssystemen, Stilen usw. Ein derartiger Zuschnitt der Begriffsbedeutung von 'Historizität' hin auf eine von vornherein schon in Relation zur sogenannten Synchronie definierte 'Diachronie' greift aber deshalb zu kurz, weil er den geschichtlichen Charakter des in Frage stehenden Gegenstandsbereichs als Ganzem schon in bestimmte wissenschaftlich-disziplinäre Forschungszusammenhänge rückt, also mit Partialisierungen oder Formalobjekten operiert, die je schon Resultate einer bloß 'regionalen' Methodologie sind. Aus diesem Grunde ist daran zu erinnern, daß eine *Sprachtheorie* als regulative, am Begriff der Sprache orientierte Konzeptualisierung *vor* allen derartigen Partialisierungen steht (vgl. Coseriu 1973; Oesterreicher 1979: 224−315, auch 1975).

'Historizität' ist als auf Sprache bezogene Grundkategorie deshalb keineswegs einfach mit der Prozessualität sprachhistorischer Veränderungen zu identifizieren, weil 'Geschichtlichkeit' als Bestimmung, die die Seinsweise der *menschlichen Grundstellung* konstituiert (vgl. Gadamer 1986: 1496; Gehlen 1971), auch für die Seinsform der menschlichen Sprache Gültigkeit besitzt. Sprachtheoretisch muß 'Historizität' daher als essentielles Universale verstanden werden, das aus dem Begriff der menschlichen Sprache folgt (→ Art. 1, § 4.4; vgl. Coseriu 1974 und 1980; Oesterreicher 1983; auch v. Polenz 1984). In dieser Hinsicht steht die 'Historizität' der menschlichen Sprache in einem Konstitutionszusammenhang mit den anderen generisch-essentiellen sprachlichen Universalien, nämlich mit der 'Semantizität', der 'Alterität', der 'Kreativität', der 'Exteriorität' und der 'Diskursivität' (vgl. Coseriu 1974; Oesterreicher 1988).

Dabei sind die 'Exteriorität' und 'Semantizität' auf die Zeichenhaftigkeit bezogen, bei der es um die sich in sinnlich wahrnehmbaren, medial phonischen oder graphischen Formen manifestierende Bedeutungshaftigkeit der Sprache geht. Mit 'Alterität' ist die Tatsache gemeint, daß Sprache immer ein *alter ego* voraussetzt; es geht dabei also um die generelle 'Verstehenszumutung' sprachlicher Kommunikation (vgl. Orth 1967) und die sich daraus ergebende Intersubjektivität, Regularität und Stabilität sprachlicher Formen und Bedeutungsgebungen. Mit der 'Kreativität' wird demgegenüber Bezug genommen auf die aktiv-reflexiven Vermittlungsleistungen, die in Sprechen und Sprache je schon dadurch manifest sind, daß Sprachen im Gebrauch jeweils fortgebildet werden. Die 'Historizität' ist gewissermaßen Produkt aus den Kennzeichen der Alterität und der Kreativität, so wie die Exteriorität sich aus der Semantizität und Alterität ableiten läßt. Unter 'Diskursivität' ist schließlich die Synchronisierung von auf dem Prinzip der Linearisierung beruhenden ausdrucksbezogenen Prozessen und Gestalten (Exteriorität) mit Inhaltsformen (Semantizität) zu verstehen, die auf den unterschiedlichen Ebenen der Sprachzeichenbildung — also von der Morphemkombination bis hin zum Text — jeweils notwendig ist. In diesem Gesamtzusammenhang läßt sich ein Sprachbegriff entwickeln, der als solcher aber natürlich nicht einfach Gegenstand einer Einzelwissenschaft werden kann (→ Art. 1; vgl. Oesterreicher 1979 und 1988; auch Hockett 1966).

'Historizität' — verstanden als eine dieser essentiellen Grundbestimmungen des Sprachlichen — weist Aspekte auf, die entfaltet werden sollen. Zuvor sei jedoch eine kurze Bemerkung zur Geschichte der Sprachreflexion eingerückt.

Exkurs zur Geschichte der Sprachreflexion: Der Blick in die Geschichte der Sprachreflexion zeigt, daß Aspekte der 'Semantizität' und 'Exteriorität' ebenso wie der 'Alterität' schon früh ins Blickfeld der Betrachter gerückt sind. Diese Aspekte sind in der Sprachbetrachtung, nicht nur im Abendland, vor allem in der Beschäftigung mit Texten schon früh fruchtbar gemacht worden — man denke nur an die antiken, vor allem die alexandrinischen Grammatiker, den 'Paradigma'-Begriff und die Diskussionen zwischen Analogisten und Anomalisten, aber auch die arabische, indische und chinesische Grammatiktradition (vgl. vor allem Auroux (ed.) 1989: Kap. III–VI; Auroux et al. (eds.) 2000: Kap. I–XII).

Dies gilt nicht in gleicher Weise für die 'stärkere' sprachliche Differenzerfahrungen voraussetzenden Aspekte der 'Diskursivität', die einzelsprachlich zwar etwa schon in Paraphrasebeziehungen wahrgenommen werden kann, aber natürlich vor allem vom Vergleich unterschiedlicher Varietäten und Sprachen befördert wird. Die Wahrnehmung von unterschiedlichen Formen der Differenz im Sprachlichen liegt letztlich auch den mit den Begriffen 'Kreativität' und 'Historizität' gemeinten Sachkomplexen und ihrer reflexiven Verarbeitung zugrunde: Während aber Aspekte der 'Kreativität' immerhin in rhetorisch-poetologischen Diskursen schon früh begrifflich gefaßt wurden, gilt es ausdrücklich festzuhalten, daß die Einsicht in die Geschichtlichkeit von Sprache — also nicht nur die Wahrnehmung von Veränderung, sondern auch die Anerkennung des fundamental geschichtlichen Charakters von Sprache — relativ spät erfolgt ist. Nach wichtigen Vorstufen vor allem in Renaissance und Aufklärung mit 'prozessual', 'genetisch' oder 'evolutionär' zu nennenden Konzeptionen (→ Art. 16, 19; vgl. Droixhe 1978; Formigari 1972 und 1990; Bossong 1990; Auroux (ed.) 1992 und Auroux et al. (eds.) 2000: Kap. XXII; auch Arens 1969) bricht sich diese Einsicht bekanntlich endgültig Bahn im Denken des Historismus (vgl. Koselleck 1992), dem wir nicht zufällig auch die Konstituierung der Sprachbetrachtung als 'Wissenschaft', ihre Institutionalisierung als 'wissenschaftliche Disziplin' zu Beginn des 19. Jhs. verdanken; die Entstehung der Sprachwissenschaft ist mit den Namen August Wilhelm Schlegel, Franz Bopp, Rasmus Rask, Jacob Grimm und vor allem Wilhelm von Humboldt verbunden (vgl. Formigari 1977; Gauger et al. 1981: 19–28; Oesterreicher 1983, 1994 und 2000; Auroux (ed.) 2000; vgl. auch Foucault 1966: 13 f.).

1.2. Historizität vs. Synchronie und Diachronie

Wie schon angedeutet, wäre es kurzschlüssig, die Einsicht in die Historizität der menschlichen Sprache einfach mit sprachlicher 'Veränderung' und 'Prozessualität' in den verschiedenen Domänen des Sprachlichen zu identifizieren. Dies hieße nämlich, einen umfassenden sprachtheoretischen Standpunkt zugunsten einer schon disziplinär-formierten, partialisierten Sicht von sprachlichen Gesamtverhältnissen aufzugeben.

Die sprachtheoretische Forderung nach einer Berücksichtigung der 'Historizität' der Sprache darf aber auch nicht einfach mit der bekannten Position von Hermann Paul identifiziert werden, dessen berühmtes Diktum eine zu apodiktische und übertreibende Festlegung enthält: „Es ist eingewendet, daß es noch eine andere wissenschaftliche Betrachtung gäbe, als die geschichtliche. Ich muß das in Abrede stellen [...] ich wüßte überhaupt nicht, wie man mit Erfolg über eine Sprache reflektieren könnte, ohne daß man etwas darüber ermittelt, wie sie geschichtlich geworden ist" (Paul 1920: 20; vgl. Coseriu 1980).

Abstand zu nehmen gilt es auf *dieser* sprachtheoretischen Argumentationsebene vor allem von der vorschnell-unreflektierten, häufig nur forschungsstrategisch begründeten 'Aufteilung' des Sprachlichen in Synchronie und Diachronie; wenn man bei dieser Aufteilung *einsetzt*, gibt es synchronisch ja nur noch einzelsprachliche Unterschiede, die dann — im Wechsel der Perspektive — diachronisch unter Umständen als Etappen eines Sprachwandels interpretiert werden können (vgl. Knoop 1975; Mattheier 1984b; Jäger 1998).

Historizität manifestiert sich aber gerade nicht nur in Erscheinungen, die im linguistisch-disziplinären Forschungsbereich der Diachronie und im sogenannten Sprachwandel unbestritten besonders eindrücklich greifbar sind. Sie kommt in sprachtheoretischer Sicht vielmehr schon in klar der sogenannten Synchronie zuzurechnenden Gegebenheiten zum Ausdruck, die als solche nicht durch Prozessualität definiert sind. Hierbei handelt es sich erstens um die *Sprachvariation* und zweitens um die *Sprachverschiedenheit*, die in sprachtheoretischer Sicht beide notwendige und zentrale Bestimmungsstücke des historischen Charakters von Sprachlichem sind (vgl. Oesterreicher 1983: 170—178).

Die Sprachverschiedenheit kann man insofern als *externen* Aspekt der sprachlichen Historizität begreifen, als damit die bekannte Tatsache angesprochen ist, daß die menschliche Sprache eigentlich immer nur im Plural existiert, daß zum Sprachbegriff notwendig eine Pluralität von Sprachen und Idiomen gehört. Daß wir es immer nur mit Sprachen als historischen Techniken des Sprechens, also mit verschiedenen Idiomen und Sprachen zu tun haben, ist das eine. Zum anderen, und dies ist der *interne* Aspekt der Historizität, sind diese Idiome und Sprachen als historische Techniken — gewissermaßen in der Innensicht — selbst immer durch Varianz, durch Sprachvariation gekennzeichnet. Es wird sich zeigen, daß *Sprachverschiedenheit* und *Sprachvariation* gerade keine 'unterschiedlichen Realitäten' sind; sie beruhen als Aspekte der Historizität auf einer fundamentalen, aber trotzdem unterschiedlich zu konzipierenden Differenzerfahrung von Sprachlichem (vgl. 4.1.).

1.3. Sprachbewußtsein, Sprachreflexion, Sprachforschung:
Stufen der Erkenntnis von Sprachlichem

Wie auch immer die Objektebene im Bereich des Sprachlichen bestimmt wird, unstrittig ist jedenfalls, daß es — nach der bloßen Alltagserfahrung des Sprachlichen im jeweiligen Vollzug mit dem entsprechenden *Sprachbewußtsein* — letztlich gerade die ebenfalls noch alltagsweltlich bestimmte Wahrnehmung von Auffälligkeit, Differenz und sprachlicher Veränderung ist, die die Erkenntnis von Sprachlichem vorantreibt. Diese Wahrnehmungen führen bei Individuen und bei Gruppen von Sprechern zu erfahrungsinduzierten Konzeptualisierungen von Sprachlichem (vgl. Luckmann 1973 und 1980; Graumann 1966 und 1972). Diese Ebene eines schon von vornherein reflexiv gewendeten Wissens ist nicht nur Grundlage aller alltagsweltlich verankerten, mehr oder minder 'systematischen' *Sprachreflexion*, sie ist letztlich auch Fundament jeglicher *Sprachforschung als wissenschaftlicher Erkenntnis* der menschlichen Sprache, die übrigens, was häufig vergessen wird, gerade nicht ausschließlich in der *Sprachwissenschaft* oder *Linguistik* verfolgt und gewonnen wird, sondern auch in anderen, etwa soziologischen, pädagogischen, psychologischen, biologischen oder medizinischen Forschungskontexten zu wichtigen Ergebnissen führt; insofern ist die Definition der Sprachwissenschaft als 'Wissenschaft von der Sprache' unzutreffend (→ Art. 3—11; 35; vgl. Orth 1970; Oesterreicher 1979: 257—297; vgl. 2. und 6.).

Auch wenn wissenschaftliche Erkenntnis also auf den angedeuteten Wahrnehmungs- und Erfahrungskontexten basiert, so besitzt sie im Vergleich mit diesen Wissensbeständen und Erkenntnisformen doch grundsätzlich eine andere Qualität, einen anderen Status: Wahrnehmungs- und erfahrungsbezogene *Daten* werden in der wissenschaftlichen Betrachtung zu *Fakten*, und dies geschieht, wie man noch heute gerne sagt, eben 'im Lichte von Theorien'. Dies soll heißen, daß beim Aufbau wissenschaftlicher Erkenntnis unvermeidlich theoretische Konzepte im Spiel sind, wobei ihre Datenbasis, ihre abstraktive Ausrichtung und ihr Abstraktionsgrad bezüglich der Gegenstandsbestimmungen sowie die sie fundierenden Erkenntnisinteressen und Fragehorizonte jeweils zu analysieren sind (vgl. Habermas 1968; Oesterreicher 1979; → Art. 1, § 3.). Diese den linguistischen Erkenntnisaufbau je schon steuernden und strukturierenden konzeptuellen Zusammenhänge sind auch für die synchronischen *und* diachronischen Aspekte der Sprachtypologie und der Universalienforschung insofern fundamental, als diese Aspekte, wie vermittelt auch immer, auf linguistisch 'konstruierte' Faktenkonfigurationen rekurrieren müssen, die als solche letztlich *alle* Ausfluß und Kennzeichen der Historizität von Sprache sind. Sie müssen, in sprachtheoretischer Hinsicht, als solche kenntlich gemacht werden (→ Art. 1 und 2).

1.4. Zur Notwendigkeit eines neuen Darstellungsrahmens

Für die angedeutete Fragestellung sei ein Rahmen entwickelt, der es — ausgehend von der Sprachvariation und der Sprachverschiedenheit als Ausprägungen von Historizität — erlaubt, die Datenbasis, die Abstraktionswege der Gegenstandsbestimmungen und die Abstraktionsgrade der linguistischen Begriffsbildungen, die Daten-Bearbeitung, Daten-Transformation und linguistische Faktenformierung sowie die damit gegebenen Implikate wissenschaftlicher Erkenntnisbemühungen zu markieren. Insbesondere kann in einem solchen Rahmen auch typologische und universalienbezogene sprachwissenschaftliche Erkenntnis in ihrem Status und ihrer Reichweite sprach- und wissenschaftstheoretisch korrekt beurteilt werden.

Es wird sich zeigen, daß derartige Überlegungen dazu beizutragen vermögen, gewisse in der *Sprachwissenschaft* verbreitete Fehleinschätzungen zu vermeiden:

- Einmal lassen sich theoretische Ansätze und Forschungen, die von interessierter Seite gerne pauschal als luftige Theoriekonstruktionen diskreditiert werden, durch die Nachzeichnung und Überprüfung des ihnen zugrundeliegenden komplexen Erkenntnisaufbaus legitimieren (gegebenenfalls natürlich auch kritisieren).
- Sodann können in dieser Perspektivierung Leistung *und* Grenzen sogenannter empirienaher Forschungsansätze realistischer eingeschätzt werden, die sich in der Regel einfach damit begnügen, selbstbewußt auf die Verläßlichkeit einer methodologisch nicht eigens hinterfragten Datenbasis zu pochen.
- Eine derartige Überprüfung kann die Partialisierungen bestimmen, die einer disziplinär-forschungsstrategischen Formierung des Gesamtgegenstands Sprache entsprechen und häufig isoliert und verabsolutierend gesetzt werden; in einem zweiten Schritt lassen diese sich gegebenenfalls in ihrer Komplementarität erkennen.

Nach der Klärung dieser Zusammenhänge lassen sich die Anschluß- und Schnittflächen markieren, die universalistisch und typologisch dimensionierte Fragestellungen und Lösungsvorschläge verbinden; damit wird es auch möglich zu zeigen, wie sich diese beiden Fragestellungen gegenseitig stützen und letztlich bedingen (→ Art. 1; vgl. Beiträge in Raible (ed.) 1989). Vor allem aber müssen diese beiden Fragerichtungen hin auf andere linguistische Domänen in der synchronischen und diachronischen Linguistik geöffnet werden. Und dabei reicht es nicht aus, das Verhältnis von synchronischen und diachronischen Fragestellungen nur abgrenzend zu kennzeichnen, diese Forschungsfelder als bloße Juxtaposition zu verstehen.

Vielmehr gilt es einerseits schon in einer *systematischen* Perspektive, den Zusammenhang der typologischen und universalistischen Fragen möglichst mit Sprachbeschreibungen in Bezug zu setzen bzw. zu fragen, wie die sprachlichen Größen und Konzepte mit denen in der typologischen Betrachtung gearbeitet wird, aus Sprachbeschreibungen und den diese fundierenden Kontexten entwickelt wurden bzw. mit diesen relationiert sind. Man denke etwa an einen Begriff wie '(Grund-)Satzgliedstellung' oder die Formulierung eines implikativen Universale des Typs 'wenn A, dann B'.

Andererseits sind im Bereich *diachronischen* Fragens mit den Motivationen für sprachliche Innovationen und mit den für die Übernahmen der Innovationen verantwortlichen Einbettungen der Prozeßverläufe in soziokulturelle, varietäten- und kontaktlinguistische sowie diskurspragmatische Kontexte schon *sprachwandelrelevante Problemfelder* benannt, die bei der universalistischen und typologischen Faktenformierung und den entsprechenden Konzeptualisierungen keineswegs ausgeblendet werden dürfen. Diese Problemzusammenhänge sollten gerade von bestimmten Richtungen der sogenannten kognitiven Linguistik und der Prototypentheorie, der Grammatikalisierungsforschung, den Theorien zum Sprachwandel, aber auch von Forschungen zu Themen wie dem typologischen Wandel oder dem 'Sprachentod' berücksichtigt werden (→ Art. 1; → Art. 115, 116, 117 und 118; vgl. Ammon et al. (eds.) 1987/1988).

Für die Bearbeitung der angesprochenen Aufgaben benötigen wir daher einen begrifflichen Aufriß, der im folgenden Kapitel gegeben wird.

2. Dimensionen der Historizität

2.1. Die Ebenen-Trias: Sprechtätigkeit – Sprachen und Diskurstraditionen – Diskurse

Die skizzierten essentiellen Universalien 'Semantizität', 'Alterität', 'Kreativität', 'Historizität', 'Exteriorität' und 'Diskursivität' (1.1.) sind durch Aspekte des Sprachlichen zu ergänzen, die als Statuskennzeichnungen für die den genannten Universalien entsprechenden sprachlichen Gegebenheiten fungieren und gewissermaßen zu ihnen querliegen. Diese Aspekte sind insofern selbst wiederum als universelle Bestimmungsstücke zu betrachten, als Sprachliches je schon diese Perspektivierungen aufweist, und damit auch dementsprechend betrachtet werden kann. Diese Aspekte, die sich auf drei Ebenen des Sprachlichen manifestieren, müssen analytisch strikt geschieden werden. Sie sollen ausgehend von einer knappen 'Definition' der menschlichen Sprache verständlich gemacht werden, die Eugenio Coseriu gegeben hat:

„El lenguaje es una actividad humana *universal* que se realiza *individualmente*, pero siempre según técnicas *históricamente* determinadas [...] En el lenguaje se pueden, por tanto, distinguir tres niveles: uno *universal*, otro *histórico* y otro *individual* [...]" (Coseriu 1981b: 269 f.).

Schon an dieser Stelle sei darauf hingewiesen, daß diese Ebenen mit ihren spezifischen Faktenkonfigurationen jeweils eine gewisse Autonomie besitzen, also keinesfalls aufeinander reduzierbar sind. Im konkreten Sprechen sind sie jeweils unauflöslich *gleichzeitig* gegeben. Sprachtheoretisch können sie im Sinne einer *sukzessiven Determination des Sprachlichen* verstanden werden, die von *allgemeinsten Bestimmungen des Sprechens über Determinanten der historischen Ebene bis hin zum individuellen, aktuellen, einmaligen Diskurs* führt. Schematisch kann dies folgendermaßen dargestellt werden:

Universelle Ebene:	Sprechtätigkeit	
	↓	↓
Historische Ebene:	Einzelsprache	Diskurstraditionen
	↓	↓
Aktuelle Ebene:	Diskurs/Text	

Fig. 111.1: Die Ebenen-Trias

2.2. Die universelle Ebene: Sprechtätigkeit

Der Begriff der menschlichen Sprechtätigkeit bezieht sich auf allgemeine, und das heißt zwar *entwicklungsgeschichtlich* (phylo- und ontogenetisch), aber natürlich gerade nicht *historisch* fundierbare *Sprechleistungen*, die beim Sprechen, Hören, Schreiben und Lesen in den Sprachen zum Einsatz kommen: Es sind dies Leistungen wie 'Referentialisierung', 'Prädizierung', 'Lokalisierung', 'Temporalisierung', 'Kontextualisierung', 'Finalisierung' usw. (vgl. Schlieben-Lange 1983: 13–25; Oesterreicher 1988; vgl. auch Raible 1999). Diese auf fundamentale kognitive, semiotisch-kommunikativ relevante Fähigkeiten und übereinzelsprachliche Verbalisierungsstrategien bezogenen Aspekte der Sprechtätigkeit – etwas als etwas erkennen und benennen, etwas über etwas aussagen, einen Sachverhalt zeitlich einordnen, Sachverhalte und kommunikative Größen lokalisieren, Sachverhalte gewichten und sie diskursiv ordnen, bestimmte Sprechakte vollziehen, Diskursen Zwecke einschreiben usw. – kovariieren zwar mit außersprachlichen Kommunikationsbedingungen, die ihrerseits historisch spezifizierbar sind; auch müssen diese Leistungen als Sprechregeln im Spracherwerb von den Sprechern der verschiedensten Sprachen durchaus sukzessive aufgebaut werden; sie bleiben als Sprechleistungen aber trotzdem universell, und das heißt: sie sind als solche nicht historisierbar (→ Art. 1 und einige Art. in Abschnitt VII).

Auch ohne die Sprache zu erkennen, wissen wir normalerweise, daß jemand spricht; auf die Sprechtätigkeit, und nicht auf die Einzelsprache, nehmen wir Bezug, wenn wir sagen, ein Kind spricht noch nicht; Kinder und auch Erwachsene müssen Typen der Kontextnutzung im Feld der personalen, zeitlichen und räumlichen (→ Art. 35, 42, 43 und 44), aber auch innerdiskursiven Beziehungen erlernen (→ Art. 45, 46 und 47); Sprecher machen diesbezüglich 'Fehler', und selbstverständlich gibt es Fälle, in denen die Sprechleistungen systematisch pathologisch deformiert sind, jemand also überhaupt nicht oder nicht mehr 'richtig' sprechen kann (→ Art. 9). In allen diesen Fällen beziehen wir uns eindeutig gerade auf das universelle Sprechenkönnen, die Sprechtätigkeit. Man kann in diesem Zusammenhang die lateinischen Ausdrücke *latine loqui, graece loqui* 'auf lateinische, griechische Art sprechen' erwähnen, in denen — im Unterschied zu Formulierungen wie *deutsch sprechen, parler français* usw. — die Universalität des Sprechens im Verb und die dafür dienstbar gemachte historische Sprachtechnik durch die Adverbien *latine* und *graece* besonders schön zum Ausdruck kommen.

Festzuhalten ist also: Obschon sich Sprechen immer nur als Sprechen in bestimmten Situationen und mit Sprachtechniken zeigt und die Kommunikationsbedingungen, auf die das Sprechen dabei — etwa mit unterschiedlichen Formen der Referentialisierung, Prädizierung oder Kontextnutzung — reagiert, systematisch variieren können, ist die Sprechtätigkeit von diesen Größen unabhängig. Die Betrachtung des Sprechens als Vollzug zielt auf dieser Ebene immer auf universelle Aspekte des Sprachlichen, die durchaus *Regelhaftigkeiten* aufweisen, die jedoch nicht die Form *historischer Sprachregeln oder Diskursnormen* aufweisen (vgl. Koch 1988 und 1997a). Die Universalität der Sprechtätigkeit und der Sprechregeln, die sich im angedeuteten Sinn aber gerade nicht durch *Gleichförmigkeit* auszeichnen, konstituiert gewissermaßen die Einheit des Sprachlichen.

Es soll schon hier darauf verwiesen werden, daß bestimmte synchronische und diachronische Fragestellungen, Konzeptualisierungen und Lösungsvorschläge in der neuesten, vor allem kognitionswissenschaftlich orientierten Linguistik — ohne daß dies immer gesehen würde und die notwendigen theoretischen Konsequenzen gezogen würden — teilweise auf dieser Ebene allgemeiner Sprechleistungen und deren Regularitäten angesiedelt sind (vgl. 5. und 6.).

Es ist, so denke ich, deutlich geworden, daß das Sprechen ganz und gar in die Vollzüge des *menschlichen Gesamtleistungsaufbaus* (Arnold Gehlen) eingebettet ist, der bekanntlich volitional-motivationale, affektive und kognitive, aber etwa auch artikulatorisch-motorische, auditive und visuelle Komponenten umfaßt (vgl. Gehlen 1971: 46— 73). Diese Komponenten können auf keinen Fall einfach als sprachlich bezeichnet werden; das Sprechen ist hier also ausdrücklich als nur sprach*bezogen* zu qualifizieren. Diese Feststellung macht verständlich, warum die Sprachwissenschaft — im Unterschied zur Erforschung historischer Sprachen, die ja das ureigenste Gebiet der Linguistik darstellt (vgl. 2.3.1.) — auf der universellen Ebene des Sprechens in ihren Forschungsbemühungen naturgemäß auf eine Zusammenarbeit angewiesen ist mit Wissenschaften wie Phonetik und Physiologie, Biologie, Kognitionswissenschaft und Psychologie, Kommunikationswissenschaft, Soziologie und Wissenssoziologie, Semiotik, Logik, Anthropologie usw. (vgl. Oesterreicher 1979; Koch 1997a: 56; → Art. 3—11).

2.3. Die historische Ebene: Sprachen und Diskurstraditionen

Im Unterschied zu den unter 2.2. angeführten Sprechleistungen, die zwar erlernt werden müssen und in der konkreten Applikation beträchtlich variieren, als universelle Sprechtätigkeitsaspekte aber *nicht* dem historischen Wandel unterliegen, sind die Sprachen oder Idiome, allerdings zusammen mit den Diskurstraditionen, jeweils als Resultate *kontingenter* einzelsprachlicher und diskursiver Entwicklungen mit ihren Elementen, Regeln und Normen *per definitionem* historisch fortbildbar, also geschichtlicher Veränderung unterworfen.

Auf dieser Ebene gilt es, die lakonische Coseriusche Kennzeichnung aus 2.1. ergänzend, zwischen *zwei* historischen Regelzusammenhängen oder Techniken zu unterscheiden, die dem Sprechen 'nachgeordnet' sind, im Sprechen 'genutzt' werden. Sprechen heißt einmal nach und mit den Regeln einer Einzelsprache, eines Dialekts usw. sprechen; darüber hinaus folgen wir notwendig immer auch Modellen der Diskursgestaltung, den sogenannten Diskursregeln und Diskursnormen, die keineswegs nur für einzelne Sprachen Gültigkeit besitzen. Diese Modelle regeln nicht allein die Art der Informationsverarbeitung, sondern selegieren bekanntlich gleichzeitig auch bestimmte Sprach- und Ausdrucksformen. Aus diesem Grund sind die Diskurstraditionen — man spricht hier auch von Textsorten, Textmodellen, Gattungen und Stilen — von vornherein in die Betrachtung mit einzubeziehen (vgl. Schlieben-Lange 1983: 26−28 und Kap. 6 und 7; Koch 1987 und 1997a; Oesterreicher 1997; → Art. 1, § 1; Art. 36).

Die Historizität manifestiert sich gerade auf dieser Ebene in der Vielfalt von geschichtlichen Ausprägungen der Techniken des Sprechens in Sprachen und in Diskurstraditionen.

2.3.1. Sprachtechniken

Die Sprachen als historische Techniken 'im Dienste' des Sprechens sind durch unterschiedliche einzelsprachliche, varietätenlinguistisch zu spezifizierende phonetisch-phonologische, morphosyntaktische und lexikalische, auch transphrastische Regel- und Normkomplexe definiert; diese 'bedienen' ihrerseits die schon angesprochenen kommunikativ-funktionell variablen Kommunikationsbedingungen und -kontexte. Alle diese Sprachregeln und Sprachnormen müssen innerhalb des durch das Sprechen universell vorgegebenen Rahmens als *historisch kontingent* betrachtet werden.

Es ist also diese Ebene, auf der historische Formen der sprachlichen Verschiedenheit manifest werden können; im Unterschied zur universellen Ebene interessiert auf der historischen Ebene nämlich gerade, *wann, wo, wie* und *in welcher Form* Sprachliches *historisch Gestalt annimmt* − und dies impliziert natürlich auch die Frage, wie unterschiedliche historische Sprachgestalten produziert werden (vgl. 2.4. und 5.).

Unterschiede in der historischen Sprachtechnik sind anzutreffen in allen Domänen des Sprachlichen. Und es gilt dabei − so sei vorläufig formuliert −, Sprachvarietäten als unterschiedliche Techniken innerhalb einer Sprache oder eines Idioms zu lokalisieren (vgl. 3.); andererseits beziehen sich natürlich auch die Ausprägungen der Sprachverschiedenheit auf historische Techniken (vgl. 4.).

Wichtig ist die Tatsache, daß die Differenzqualitäten dieser Gestaltungen, die oben *Sprachvariation* und *Sprachverschiedenheit* genannt wurden, eigentlich zusammengehören. Gerade wenn man die Schwierigkeiten einer Abgrenzung von Sprachen untereinander und die von Sprachen und Dialekten usw. ernst nimmt (vgl. Coseriu 1981c/1988a und 1988b; Oesterreicher 1995a), wird die *Spannung von Sprachverschiedenheit und Sprachvariation* besonders deutlich: Es handelt sich nämlich um ein *'innen-'* und *'außen'-perspek*-*tivisches*, zusätzlich noch *hierarchiestufenbezogenes Verhältnis* (vgl. 4.1.).

Dies leuchtet unmittelbar ein, wenn man beachtet, daß auf der historischen Ebene der sprachlichen Techniken ganz unterschiedliche Fokussierungen notwendig sind und wie gestaffelt hierbei Konzepte und Regeltypen angesetzt werden müssen. Völlig legitim sind in diesem Bereich nämlich synchronische und diachronische Fragen nach individuell-idiolektalen, nach varietätenlinguistischen, einzelsprachbezogenen, kontrastiv-linguistischen, sprachvergleichenden und kontaktlinguistischen, sprachgruppenbezogenen und eben auch typologischen Regularitäten, die jeweils ihre unverwechselbaren Fragehorizonte besitzen und durch spezifische Fragestellungen weiter aufgefächert werden.

Dieser Punkt ist auch für die Sprachtypologie entscheidend, die zwar gerade nicht einfach induktiv in mehrstufigen Abstraktionsschritten entwickelt werden kann, sondern ihre *tertia* − dies wird noch beschrieben werden − ganz anders gewinnt, nämlich durch den Zugriff auf universell definierte Funktionszusammenhänge im Bereich der mit Sprachen zu erbringenden Sprechleistungen. Trotzdem sind die von ihr verarbeiteten und angeführten sprachlichen Fakten, die ja jeweils aus Daten *empirischer* Corpus-Materialien zu entwickeln sind, in ihrem Status sorgfältig zu überprüfen. In diesem Sinne hat auch die auf Sprachverschiedenheit bezogene Typologie, wie abstrakt ihre Positionen auch formuliert und wie universalistisch ihre *tertia* auch angesetzt sein mögen, durchaus auf der historischen Ebene der Sprachen ihren systematischen Ort. Anders ausgedrückt: Selbst bei den höchsten Stufen der typologischen Qualifizierung ist Sprachverschiedenheit noch als Resultat historisch-kontingenter Prozesse präsent, und diese Prozesse gilt es kenntlich zu machen (→ Art. 1 und 2).

Festzuhalten ist an dieser Stelle die Tatsache, daß es sich bei dem sich auf historische Sprachtechniken beziehenden Forschungsbereich gewissermaßen um das *Herzstück der Sprachwissenschaft* handelt: Es gibt *keine* andere wissenschaftliche Disziplin, deren Erkenntnisziel die Analyse und Beschreibung von Sprachen als historischen Techniken wäre; als genuin sprachwissenschaftliche Gegenstände des Forschens, als linguistische Formalobjekte 'gehören' diese damit allein der Sprachwissenschaft (vgl. Oesterreicher 1979: 257−297).

2.3.2. Diskurstraditionen

Die über einzelne Sprachgemeinschaften hinausgehenden, nicht mehr einzelsprachlich zu fassenden Traditionen des Sprechens sind natürlich ebenfalls der historischen Ebene der Betrachtung zuzuordnen. Sie werden hier 'Diskurstraditionen' genannt. Die diskurstraditionelle Perspektivierung gilt der Beschäftigung mit den sprachlichen Aspekten von Textsorten, Gattungen, Stilen, rhetorischen Genera, Gesprächsformen, historischen Ausformungen von Sprechakten usw., denen als wiederholbaren kommunikativen Handlungsschemata und Diskursmodellen eigene Normen und Regeln zugeordnet werden müssen (vgl. Schlieben-Lange 1983: 26−28 und Kap. 6 und 7; Koch 1987 und 1997a; Oesterreicher 1997; → Art. 36). Diskurstraditionen, die jeweils ihren spezifischen 'Sitz im Leben' haben und damit auch die unterschiedlichsten semiotischen Modi und Funktionszusammenhänge zu aktualisieren vermögen, sind logischerweise nicht mehr allein sprachlicher Natur; entsprechend sind sie − wie schon die Sprechtätigkeit − als 'nur' sprach*bezogen* zu charakterisieren (vgl. Coseriu 1981a: 153; Raible 1980 und 1983; Oesterreicher 1988: 362 ff. und 380 f.; Koch 1997a: 49 ff.).

Die Sprechtätigkeit kann sich ohne diskurstraditionelle und einzelsprachliche historische Vorgaben *nicht* in einem konkreten Diskurs manifestieren. Diskursnormen und Diskursregeln sind in *allen* Äußerungen, also nicht nur in literarischen Diskursformen, notwendig vorausgesetzt und präsent (vgl. Schlieben-Lange 1983; Koch 1987; Oesterreicher 1997).

Zu betonen ist allerdings, daß diese historischen Traditionen des Sprechens von vornherein kommunikativ-konzeptionell geprägt sind, also durch bestimmte Konfigurationen von Kommunikationsbedingungen und entsprechende Verbalisierungsstrategien determiniert werden. Dadurch ist Diskurstraditionen je schon ein konzeptionelles Profil eingeschrieben, das diesen pragmatischen und verbalisierungsbezogenen Bedingungen entspricht (vgl. 3.3.). Wenn wir bestimmte Gattungen und Textsorten betrachten, wird auch deutlich, daß diese Profile keineswegs einheitlich sind, sondern durchaus Formen der sprachlichen und argumentativen Varianz definitorisch einfordern können; Diskurstypen sind häufig konstitutiv direkt 'komposit', das heißt, in ihnen können regelmäßig expositorische, argumentative oder narrative Diskursteile kombiniert erscheinen (vgl. Stempel 1972; vgl. auch Brandt & Rosengren 1992 und Brinker 1992).

Es wäre im Sinne einer Präzisierung der Ausführungen in 2.2. interessant, die für bestimmte Diskurstraditionen als Kristallisationen von kommunikativen Parameterwerten geforderten Sprechleistungen *und* den historischen Charakter der Diskurstraditionen genauer nachzuzeichnen. Dies könnte geschehen einerseits durch eine universalistisch gerichtete Betrachtung ihres Erwerbs und ihrer kommunikativen Leistungen sowie andererseits durch die historisch gerichtete Beschreibung ihrer Entstehung, ihres Wandels durch Ausdifferenzierung, Mischung und Konvergenz, ihrer Verbreitung und ihres Absterbens (vgl. Koch 1997a: 59−70; Oesterreicher 1997).

Bei den sprachbezogenen diskurstraditionellen Fragestellungen kommt naturgemäß einer Kooperation mit anderen Disziplinen wiederum größte Bedeutung zu, in diesem Falle etwa mit Literaturwissenschaft und -geschichte, mit Theologie, Rhetorik, Musikologie, Kunstgeschichte, Diplomatik, Rechtswissenschaft, Geschichtswissenschaft, Rechts- und Kirchengeschichte usw.; diese Disziplinen sind spezialisiert auf die Untersuchung der in den verschiedensten Bereichen der Gesellschaft funktionierenden Textsorten und Gattungstraditionen (vgl. Koch 1997a: 56; auch Krefeld 1985).

Schließlich sei hier nochmals auf den fundamentalen Zusammenhang hingewiesen, der zwischen Diskurstraditionen als historischen Formen der kommunikativen Wirklichkeitsbewältigung und Sinngebung sowie bestimmten Varietäten als einzelsprachlich gegebenen Techniken des Sprechens besteht (vgl. Koch & Oesterreicher 1985, 1990 und 1994). Affinitäten zwischen Diskurstraditionen und Varietätenwahl müssen gerade auch auf der historischen Ebene der Sprachbetrachtung zu einer möglichst engen Zusammenarbeit von Textsortenlinguistik und Varietätenlinguistik führen, wobei − nicht allein für die diachronische Sprachwissenschaft − das dornige Problem darin besteht, daß der Varietätenraum einer historischen Sprache im Prinzip allein durch die Erfassung aller möglichen Diskurstraditionen und der entsprechenden Äußerungstypen korrekt beschreibbar ist (vgl. 3.2. und 3.3.; Oesterreicher et al. (eds.) 1998; Schmidt-Riese 1997; Jacob & Kabatek (eds.) 2001).

Um die linguistische Relevanz des skizzierten Problemkomplexes weiter zu untermauern, seien einige Fragestellungen angeführt, die noch genauer zu betrachten sein werden: Diskurstraditionelle Parameter und Kanäle sind nämlich nicht allein für einzelsprachliche *Ausbauprozesse* und *kontaktlinguistische Szenarien* entscheidend, es ist außerdem kaum möglich, *Lexikalisierungs-* und *Grammatikalisierungsprozesse*, ja *Sprachwandelprozesse* überhaupt korrekt zu konzeptualisieren, wenn auf der historischen Betrachtungsebene die Diskurstraditionen ausgeklammert werden (vgl. 5.; → Art. 1, § 1).

2.4. Die aktuelle Ebene: Diskurse

Auf der individuellen Ebene des Diskurses geht es schließlich um aktuelle, medial phonisch oder graphisch realisierte Äußerungen unterschiedlichster Extension und unterschiedlichsten konzeptionellen Zuschnitts. Die Realisierungsformen reichen von sogenannten Einwortsätzen bis zu umfänglichsten Druckerzeugnissen und von sehr informellen bis hin zu höchst elaborierten Diskursen (vgl. 3.3. [3]). Die Äußerungen liefern das konkrete Material, auf das sich unsere sprachwissenschaftlichen Beobachtungen – auch diejenigen, die mit dem Sprechen oder den Diskurstraditionen zu tun haben – letztlich alle beziehen (vgl. aber 3.4.).

Äußerungen weisen bekanntlich eine beachtliche interne Variationsbreite auf; genannt seien hier die folgenden *Typen von Varianz*: Ausdrucksmodulationen wie Lautstärke oder Sprechgeschwindigkeit, Artikulationsgenauigkeit, Einsatz von Varietäten und Sprachmischung, 'Fehler' und bewußte Regelverletzungen, spontane Innovationen, 'Zitate', spezifische Diskursstrategien usw.

Entscheidend ist, daß *Äußerungen jeweils als ein einmaliges Ganzes mit einem historischen Zeitpunkt und dessen kommunikativen sachlichen und personalen Bedingungen 'synchronisiert' sind. Aus diesem Grunde unterliegen Äußerungen auch nicht dem historischen Wandel*. Die provokant-paradoxe Formulierung, die Eugenio Coseriu einmal wählte, „Linguistic change does not exist" (1983), ist gerade auf die Ebene der Diskurse zu beziehen. Im Sprechen, im aktuellen Funktionieren der Sprache kann eine Sprachtechnik zwar durchaus 'abweichend' und 'innovativ' verwendet werden; diese sprachtheoretische, gewissermaßen humboldtianische Sicht des Sprechens, die sich in der Tat aus den im individuellen Sprechen jeweils erforderlichen Vermittlungsleistungen ergibt und die dem Universale der Kreativität und der dieser impliziten Reflexivität des Sprachgebrauchs entspricht, darf aber keinesfalls einfach mit 'Sprachwandel' identifiziert werden (vgl. Coseriu 1973; Oesterreicher 1999 und 2001a).

Die an sich richtige Redeweise, daß Sprachen im jeweiligen Sprechen 'fortgebildet' werden, erfordert also durchaus noch begriffliche Distinktionen; hier sind vor allem Begriffe wie 'Innovation', 'Motivation', 'Übernahme', 'Wandel' usw. zu betrachten, deren Bedeutung und Reichweite durch eine Lokalisierung und Statuskennzeichnung im skizzierten Ebenenmodell gut erfaßt werden kann (vgl. 5.).

Diskurse sind und bleiben allein *Voraussetzung* für eine linguistische Bestimmung der Historizität der jeweiligen Sprachtechnik, sie *konstituieren* diese aber noch keineswegs. Diese vielleicht überraschende Feststellung wird in ihrer Bedeutung klarer, wenn wir andere Diskurs- und Textwissenschaften und ihre jeweiligen Erkenntnisziele mit dem zentralen sprachwissenschaftlichen Erkenntnisinteresse vergleichen. Die *Einmaligkeit des individuellen Diskurses*, die etwa für die Literaturwissenschaft, die Theologie usw. erstes Erkenntnisziel sein muß – an das dann selbstverständlich weitere werk- und autorenbezogene, produktions- und rezeptionspragmatische, 'intertextuelle' oder gattungstheoretische Fragestellungen angeschlossen werden können –, ist für die Sprachwissenschaft grundsätzlich nie *Gegenstand* der wissenschaftlichen Betrachtung.

Der individuelle Diskurs mit seinem Datenbestand – wie ernsthaft und intensiv er linguistisch auch immer befragt wird – repräsentiert für die Sprachwissenschaft allein *Materialien für eine zu erschließende oder Belege für eine schon erschlossene historische Technik*. Sprachliche Techniken stehen, gewissermaßen als eine 'höhere Wirklichkeit' hinter den Diskursen, als solche können sie dem Linguisten im aktuellen Diskurs oder Text daher grundsätzlich nie direkt und unvermittelt entgegentreten (vgl. Koch & Oesterreicher 1990 und 1996; Jacob & Kabatek 2001; Oesterreicher 2001a).

Der individuelle Diskurs, in dem der oben angesprochene Prozeß der sukzessiven Determination des Sprechens seinen Abschluß findet, muß als ein Geschehen begriffen werden, bei dem immer sprachliche und nichtsprachliche Vollzüge synthetisiert werden. In jedem Diskurs liegt ein „diskursives Ensemble" (Reich 2002: Kap. 2.1.) vor, das – abgekürzt gesprochen – Sprache, Wissen und Situation „diskursiv klammert" und das damit notwendig in den verschiedensten 'Richtungen' offen bleibt (vgl. auch Caron 1983).

Diesen dynamisch-offenen Aspekt, der nach der Durchmusterung der verschiedenen Ebenen deutlicher konturiert werden kann, hebt auch François Rastier hervor, wenn er betont:

„Le langage est simplement un lieu privilégié de l'activité interprétative que nous déployons pour constituer et modifier notre entour. En d'autres termes, le langage est une partie du monde où nous vivons. Apprendre une langue, ce n'est pas régler des paramètres, c'est s'y adapter [...] Elle exige une activité interprétative spécifique et prolongée [...] Formations culturelles, les performances linguistiques et sémiotiques composent le milieu où s'opère la socialisation, par le partage parfois polémique des objectivités et des valeurs. Le langage est une partie commune de l'entour, et c'est ainsi que l'on peut comprendre l'hypothèse que les normes linguistiques sont tout à la fois l'effet et la cause du lien social dans sa forme juridique et politique. Qu'on se serve du langage et des autres systèmes sémiotiques à des fins de représentation ou de communication ne suffit pas à les transformer en instruments dédiés à ces usages voir configurés par eux. Les usages ludiques ou esthétiques, à vocation hédonique, sont aussi universellement attestés" (Rastier 1997: 77).

3. Sprachvariation: Varietäten und Diskurstraditionen

3.1. Diskurse und Varianz

Die aktuelle Ebene des Diskurses ist für die Linguistik deshalb so bedeutsam, weil allein im Diskurs die empirischen Daten für die Untersuchung von Sprachlichem gegeben sind, weil letztlich alle Erkenntnis von Sprachlichem auf der Wahrnehmung und der Erfahrung von individuellen Diskursen aufruht. Wie schon diskutiert, darf dies aber nicht mißverstanden werden: Die Realität des Diskurses ist nicht die ganze sprachliche Wirklichkeit, denn auch die skizzierten historischen Sprachtechniken und Diskurstraditionen zusammen mit den Aspekten der Sprechtätigkeit gehören — allerdings in jeweils spezifischer Weise — zur Wirklichkeit des Sprachlichen.

Ein aktueller Diskurs — so ist definiert worden — ist eine Art von Totalität, die sprachliche und sehr viele nichtsprachliche Aspekte aufweist. Das genannte *diskursive Ensemble*, das in diskursiver Klammerung alle diese Aspekte verbindet, geht über die spezifisch linguistischen Gegenstandsbestimmungen und die linguistische Beobachtung weit hinaus. *Aus diesem Grund darf der linguistische Begriff des Corpus nicht einfach mit dem Diskurs identifiziert werden, Diskurse sind nur in einem ganz bestimmten Sinne Corpora.*

Dies liegt, erstens, an der Tatsache, daß das linguistische Interesse an den medial phonisch und graphisch realisierten Diskursen und ihrer aktuellen Gesamtfunktionalität notwendig eingeschränkt ist: Die Linguistik interessiert sich am Diskurs bekanntlich nicht für alle Aspekte des Diskursiven, sondern eben nur für das, was sprachwissenschaftlich, und das heißt: als rekurrentes Phänomen, über die bloße Aktualität und Individualität des Diskurses hinaus als Sprachregel und Sprachnorm überindividuelle, generalisierbare Geltung besitzt.

Dies impliziert, zweitens, *daß ein linguistisches Corpus selbst kein diskursives Phänomen mehr ist*, sondern eine für bestimmte Zwecke — für synchronische oder diachronische phonetische, morphosyntaktische, lexikalische, textlinguistische und semantisch-pragmatische Fragestellungen — zugerichtete Unternehmung; ein Corpus ist mithin notwendig 'theorieabhängig' aufbereitetes Sprachmaterial. (vgl. 3.4.; Koch & Oesterreicher 1990: 25—30; Stubbs 1996, bes. 230—234; → Art. 1, § 3).

Der Nichtunterscheidung von Diskurs und Corpus entspricht eine generelle Konfusion, der zahlreiche Arbeiten aus dem Bereich der zur Zeit aktuellen '*Variations*linguistik' unterliegen. Sehr häufig verbergen sich unter diesem Etikett Arbeiten aus dem Dunstkreis einer bloß interpretierenden, vage pragmatisch orientierten Diskurs- und Konversationsanalyse oder Textforschung. Diese Forschungen sind nicht zu kritisieren, solange sie sich nicht eigentlich linguistisch verstehen, sondern kommunikationspraktische, pädagogische, psychologische oder ideologiekritische Interessenorientierungen verfolgen. Sobald sich solche Forschung jedoch als *linguistisch* versteht, dabei aber nur die Diskurs- und Textbefunde im jeweiligen kommunikativen und sozialen Kontext interpretierend nachzeichnet und es bei der Konstatierung der sprachlichen Varianz und ihren diskursiv-textuellen Funktionen beläßt, ergeben sich methodische Probleme:

— In die jeweiligen Diskursinterpretationen fließen massiv und unreflektiert linguistische Konzepte ein, die aus den unterschiedlichsten methodisch-theoretischen Zusammenhängen stammen; diese Posi-

tionen sind eklektizistisch, und außerdem atomistisch, insofern ein theoretischer Zusammenhang fehlt, der die betrachteten Daten überhaupt erst zusammenzuschließen könnte. Derartige Untersuchungen verbleiben auf der individuellen Ebene des Diskurses und praktizieren eine 'offene Texthermeneutik'.
- Die nicht unberechtigte Abneigung gegen allzu 'systematische', 'schematische', 'strukturalistische' Modellierungen etablierter linguistischer Richtungen sollte zur Diskussion der Angemessenheit varietätenlinguistischer Modellierungen führen (vgl. Lieb 1998), nicht jedoch zur Rechtfertigung intuitivistischer Arbeitsweisen und zu dezisionistischen Setzungen.

Eine derartige *Variations*linguistik ist somit Produkt eines Mißverständnisses. Die Anerkennung der Tatsache, daß Sprachvariation existiert, ist im Blick auf die neuere Linguistikgeschichte natürlich durchaus erfreulich zu nennen; es darf jedoch nicht bei dieser Feststellung bleiben, denn die Weigerung, Varianz begrifflich zu verarbeiten, würde den sprachwissenschaftlichen Erkenntnisverzicht zum Programm erheben. Auch der Gebrauch der Bezeichnung *Variationslinguistik* sollte daher vermieden werden (vgl. Ammon et al. (eds.) 1998; Lieb 1998).

3.2. Zur Modellierung von Sprachvariation

Empirische Diskursmaterialien sind notwendig zu transzendieren, sie müssen in varietätenlinguistisch und diskurstraditionell gerichteten *wissenschaftlichen Beschreibungen* überhaupt erst zu sprachlichen Fakten formiert werden, sie müssen also von der aktuellen Diskursebene auf die Ebene der historischen sprachlichen Techniken und des diesen entsprechenden kommunikativ-geteilten Regel- und Norm-Wissens der Sprecher 'angehoben' werden. Diese Forderung gilt übrigens gleichermaßen für die synchronische und die diachronische Sprachforschung, da — wie schon verschiedentlich gesagt — Diskursbefunde und Beschreibungen von Sprachregeln und Techniken ganz prinzipiell nicht zur Deckung gebracht werden können. Dies bedeutet auch, daß das letztlich *interpretative Element* ('im Lichte von Theorien'), das in der Applikation der theoretisch-methodischen Vorgaben des Linguisten liegt, immer präsent ist.

Schon im Rahmen des europäischen Strukturalismus gab es Bemühungen, die Sprachvariation und die linguistische Varietätenproblematik zu thematisieren; an sie konnten spätere Forschungen durchaus anschließen (vgl. Albrecht 2000; Koch & Oesterreicher 1990: 12—24). Auch wenn diese Versuche letztlich dazu gedacht waren, die bei der Konstruktion homogener sprachlicher Strukturen (Saussure, Chomsky) störende Varianz gerade auszuschalten, sie 'unschädlich' zu machen, ist doch festzuhalten, daß damit eben die *Existenz* der Sprachvariation, die mithin auch für den Begriff der historischen Sprache als eines *Diasystems* bzw. als einer *Architektur* diasystematischer Unterschiede konstitutiv ist, anerkannt wurde. Einer strukturierenden Systematisierung zugänglich sind — nach klassisch strukturalistischer Überzeugung — allerdings allein homogene, in sich einheitliche sprachliche Varietätendimensionen. Eugenio Coseriu spricht hier von „notwendigen Vorunterscheidungen", die *vor* einer strukturellen Analyse und Darstellung bezüglich des sprachlichen Materials vorgenommen werden müssen (Geckeler 1971: 179—191). Man muß aber wohl richtiger von *Idealisierungen* der sprachlichen Datenbasis sprechen, womit die methodologisch unvermeidlichen disziplinären Partialisierungen wissenschaftstheoretisch insofern präziser benannt sind, als zugleich Richtung und Grad der abstrahierenden Modellierungen als Probleme in den Blick rücken.

An dieser Stelle ist vor allem der Begriff des *Varietätenraums* in die Diskussion einzubeziehen; er zielt auf die Gesamtheit der in der Architektur einer historischen Einzelsprache gegebenen unterschiedlichen Sprachformen. Ein Varietätenraum *kann* auch mit einem *Kommunikationsraum* zusammenfallen. Der Begriff des Kommunikationsraums ist gerade deshalb so wichtig, weil er es erlaubt, die in einem, etwa staatlich-national, aber auch klein- oder großräumiger definierten Territorium koexistierenden verschiedenen Sprachen und Idiome zu betrachten (vgl. Oesterreicher 1995a; Koch & Oesterreicher 1996 und 2001).

In der angelsächsischen Tradition spricht man bezüglich der Varietäten von *dialects* und *social dialects*, die als *varieties according to users* bezeichnet werden, sodann von *varieties according to use*, die den sogenannten *registers* bzw. *styles* entsprechen (vgl. Halliday 1978; Quirk et al. (eds.) 1985; Biber 1988 und 1995; Ammon et al. (eds.) 1987: Kap. III). Durchaus vergleichbare Unterscheidungen trifft die von Coseriu vorgeschlagene

Modellierung der Architektur, bei der die folgenden Varietätendimensionen vorgeschlagen werden (vgl. Coseriu 1988a und 1988b): Die sprachlichen Unterschiede im Raum werden als *diatopisch*, die Unterschiede hinsichtlich der gesellschaftlichen Schichten oder Gruppen werden als *diastratisch* und die Unterschiede bezüglich bestimmter 'Sprachstile', die auf verschiedene Kommunikations- und Sprechsituationen reagieren bzw. in diesen angemessen sind, werden als *diaphasisch* bezeichnet.

Entscheidend ist übrigens ein Punkt, der häufig nicht beachtet wird und in der Redeweise von 'Varietätendimensionen' oder *social dialects* überspielt wird: allein ein Dialekt ist eine 'vollständige' Sprache, insofern er selbst wieder 'Variation' impliziert (vgl. 4.1.); die diastratischen und diaphasischen Unterschiede werden – terminologisch 'unsauber' – zwar auch 'Varietäten' genannt, sie besitzen diesbezüglich jedoch einen anderen Status (vgl. Coseriu 1988b).

Coserius Sicht der Varietäten enthielt von Anfang an einen außerordentlich wichtigen Gedanken, der zwar immer wieder zitiert, aber überraschenderweise weder von Coseriu selbst noch von anderen systematisch fruchtbar gemacht worden ist. Die skizzierten Varietätendimensionen, die intern skaliert sind (also stark, schwach oder nicht diatopisch markiert, diastratisch oder diaphasisch sehr niedrig bis sehr hoch markiert), stehen nicht einfach nebeneinander, sondern weisen ganz bestimmte *Affinitäten* zueinander auf, die zu einem in der Reihenfolge *Diatopik > Diastratik > Diaphasik* gerichteten Funktionieren der entsprechenden Sprachmittel führen. In den Worten von Coseriu: „un dialecto puede funcionar como nivel y como estilo de lengua, y un nivel también como estilo de lengua, pero no al revés" (Coseriu 1981c: 21). Bestimmte diatopisch markierte sprachliche Erscheinungen können also sekundär so verwendet werden, *als ob* sie diastratisch markiert wären; primär oder sekundär diastratisch markierte Erscheinungen funktionieren unter Umständen wie genuin diaphasisch markierte Elemente. Diese Dynamik innerhalb der Architektur kann man als *Varietätenkette* bezeichnen (vgl. Koch & Oesterreicher 1990: 14; Oesterreicher 1995a: 4–6). Der Begriff 'Dynamik' darf allerdings nicht diachronisch verstanden werden, denn bei der Varietätenkette handelt es sich um ein rein synchronisch faßbares Phänomen, also um ein das pure Funktionieren unserer Sprachen kennzeichnendes Faktum.

Daß derartige Prozesse des 'Wanderns' im Varietätenraum in dem Augenblick diachronisch relevant werden, wenn eine Erscheinung ihre ursprüngliche Markierung verliert und definitiv in einer neuen Varietät 'heimisch' wird, also eine Markierungsveränderung *qua* Sprachwandel eingetreten ist, versteht sich von selbst (vgl. unten 5.4.).

Architektur und Varietätenkette lassen sich etwa folgendermaßen veranschaulichen:

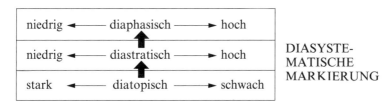

DIASYSTEMATISCHE MARKIERUNG

Fig. 111.2: Die drei Dimensionen der Sprachvariation

3.3. 'Kommunikative Nähe' und 'kommunikative Distanz' als Bezugsrahmen für Varietäten und Diskurstraditionen

Die in 3.2. vorgestellten varietätenlinguistischen Konzeptualisierungen sind in einem entscheidenden Punkt unvollständig und auch begrifflich ungenau. Daher soll hier eine Präzisierung geliefert werden.

Durch die Einbeziehung der Mündlichkeits- und Schriftlichkeitsproblematik hat die Varietätenlinguistik in letzter Zeit eine neue Qualität gewonnen. Zentrale Begriffe sollen kurz in Erinnerung gerufen werden (vgl. Günther & Ludwig 1994; Koch 1997c; Koch & Oesterreicher 1985, 1990, 1994 und 2001).

Einmal sind bezüglich aller Sprachvarietäten bloß *mediale Fragen* der sprachlichen Realisierung strikt von den *konzeptionellen Fakten* zu trennen, die sich auf den sprachlichen Duktus, also auf Grade der Formalität und Elaboriertheit von Äußerungen beziehen. Auch dort, wo diese *terminologische* Unterscheidung nicht bekannt ist oder nicht beachtet wird, werden die angesprochenen *begriffli-*

chen Entitäten unter Umständen trotzdem mehr oder weniger klar unterschieden. Man vergleiche etwa Kollokationen von Termini, die sich — ohne Unterschied — gerade auf die beiden genannten Bereiche beziehen: ital. *parlato scritto, parlato parlato, scritto parlato, scritto scritto* oder span. *oral escrito* usw. (vgl. Nencioni 1976; Cano Aguilar 1996; Koch 1999a).

Konzeptionelle Fakten werden in der Linguistik gelegentlich in ganz verschiedenen Zusammenhängen unter Bezeichnungen wie etwa *formell* vs. *informell, elaborierter* und *restringierter Kode*, auch *pragmatischer* vs. *syntaktischer Modus* usw. behandelt (vgl. etwa Chafe 1985; Givón 1979 usw.). Man kann hier auch genauer von Sprachformen der *kommunikativen Nähe* und der *kommunikativen Distanz* sprechen (vgl. Koch & Oesterreicher 1985, 1990 und 1994). Die prinzipielle Unabhängigkeit der Aspekte *Medium* und *Konzeption* bedeutet gerade nicht, daß es zwischen beiden nicht im einzelnen wichtige Affinitäten und interessante Wechselwirkungen gibt, die gerade auch historische Fragen betreffen (vgl. Koch & Oesterreicher 2001: 3. und 4.).

Während bei den medialen Problemen die *Dichotomie* zwischen phonischer vs. graphischer Realisierung fundamental ist — hier bietet sich die terminologische Festlegung *phonischer Kode* vs. *graphischer Kode* (frz. *code phonique* und *code graphique* usw.) an —, müssen wir bei den konzeptionellen Fakten von einem *Kontinuum* zwischen zwei Polen von sprachlichen Ausprägungen ausgehen, die in unseren Schriftkulturen am besten als *gesprochen/Mündlichkeit* vs. *geschrieben/Schriftlichkeit* (frz. *écrit/parlé*, span. *hablado/escrito*, ital. *parlato/scritto*) bzw. *nähesprachlich* vs. *distanzsprachlich* bezeichnet werden. Zwischen den 'extremen' konzeptionellen Ausprägungen des *Gesprochenen* und *Geschriebenen* bzw. der *Nähe-* und *Distanzsprache* gibt es Abstufungen, Zwischenformen.

Dies läßt sich an den konzeptionellen Abstufungen verdeutlichen, die die folgenden Diskurstraditionen und ihre sprachlichen Gestaltungen kennzeichnen (vgl. besonders Koch & Oesterreicher 1990 und 2001):

(a) spontane Unterhaltung zweier Freunde
(b) Telephongespräch zweier Freunde
(c) Privatbrief eines guten Freundes
(d) Vorstellungsgespräch
(e) Presse-Interview
(f) Predigt
(g) wissenschaftlicher Vortrag
(h) Leitartikel
(i) Gesetzestext

Die Unabhängigkeit der konzeptionellen Fakten von den medialen Verhältnissen läßt sich deutlich zeigen etwa an (g), wo eine konzeptionell klar distanzsprachliche, elaborierte Diskursgestaltung in phonischer Realisierung vorliegt, oder etwa an (c), wo eine klar nähesprachliche, informelle Konzeption in graphischer Form erscheint. Trotzdem gilt natürlich, daß die phonische Realisierung durchaus nicht zufällig eine Affinität zur nähegeprägten, informellen Konzeption (oder konzeptionellen Mündlichkeit) besitzt und die graphische Realisierung eine besonders enge Beziehung zur distanzgeprägten, elaborierten Konzeption (oder konzeptionellen Schriftlichkeit) aufweist.

Es sei daran erinnert, daß sich die Notwendigkeit einer strikten Unterscheidung von Medium und Konzeption gerade in den Fällen deutlich zeigt, in denen eine Gesellschaft über gar kein graphisches Medium zur Aufzeichnung von Sprachlichem verfügt. Die in einer derartigen Gesellschaft — hier spricht man auch von *primärer Mündlichkeit* (vgl. Ong 1982) — allein phonisch realisierten Diskurse weisen aber notwendig ebenfalls ein beachtliches konzeptionelles Profil auf.

Die die angeführten konzeptionellen Fakten bestimmenden Kommunikationsbedingungen wurden in anderer Perspektivierung schon häufig beschrieben, sie brauchen daher nicht eigens diskutiert zu werden (vgl. Steger et al. 1974; Henne & Rehbock 1995). Man vergleiche die folgende, keineswegs exhaustive Liste von für das konzeptionelle Kontinuum einschlägigen Kommunikationsbedingungen:

(1) private vs. öffentliche Kommunikation (1')
(2) bekannte vs. unbekannte Kommunikationspartner (2')
(3) starke vs. schwache emotionale Beteiligung (3')
(4) maximale vs. minimale Handlungs- und Situations-Verankerung (4')
(5) maximale vs. minimale referenzielle Verankerung (5')
(6) raum-zeitliche Kopräsenz vs. raum-zeitliche Trennung (6')
(7) intensive vs. minimale Kooperation (7')
(8) Dialog vs. Monolog (8')
(9) Spontaneität vs. Reflektiertheit (9')

(10) thematische Freiheit vs. thematische Fixierung (10')
usw.

Die Parameterwertkombination (1)–(10) definiert eine extreme konzeptionelle Ausprägung, die *kommunikative Nähe* oder *konzeptionelle Mündlichkeit* genannt werden soll; sie kommt, wie schon angeführt, etwa in einem lockeren, freundschaftlichen Gespräch zum Ausdruck, in dem sprachliche Mittel und diskursive Strategien verwendet werden, die man entsprechend extrem 'nähesprachlich' nennen kann. Die Parameterwertkombination (1')–(10') stellt hingegen die andere extreme Ausprägung dar, die *kommunikative Distanz oder konzeptionelle Schriftlichkeit* heißen soll; sie prägt sich beispielsweise in einem Gesetzestext aus, der in seinem sprachlichen Duktus und seiner diskursiven Elaboriertheit extrem 'distanzsprachlich' genannt werden soll. Alle Dimensionen oder Parameter sind aber, wenn man von der Dimension 6/6' absieht, selbst *intern gradierbar*, was am Beispiel der Parameterwerte in Fig. 111.3 veranschaulicht werden kann. Das Diagramm repräsentiert idealtypisch ein 'Vorstellungsgespräch', das sich als Diskurstyp durch eine Kombination von nähesprachlichen mit bestimmten distanzsprachlichen kommunikativen Kennzeichen definieren läßt und für das die Gesamtqualifikation 'gemäßigt distanzsprachlich' wohl angemessen ist (vgl. Koch & Oesterreicher 2001).

Diese kurze Andeutung des Zusammenhangs zwischen dem Grad der sprachlich-konzeptionellen Elaboration und entsprechenden Diskurstraditionen muß an dieser Stelle genügen; er macht auch nochmals

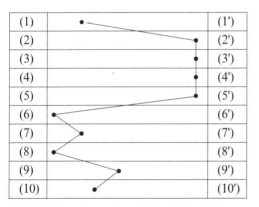

Fig. 111.3: Das konzeptionelle Profil einer Diskurstradition

deutlich, inwiefern nicht Mediales die entscheidende Rolle spielt, sondern die konzeptionelle Ausprägung des jeweiligen Kommunikationstyps fundamental ist.

Das kommunikative Kontinuum ist letztlich anthropologisch, genauer: sprach- und kommunikationstheoretisch fundiert; die Definition des Kontinuums impliziert damit je schon pragmatische, soziolinguistische und psycholinguistische Forschungshorizonte. Die sprachliche Kommunikation definierenden Parameter, die zwar 'universalistisch' zu konzipieren sind, müssen aber natürlich jeweils historisch konkretisiert werden; dies wird besonders deutlich bei Parametern wie 'Öffentlichkeit', 'Emotion' usw., deren Bewertung und deren Stellenwert im „Kommunikationshaushalt" unterschiedlicher Gesellschaften beträchtlich variiert (vgl. Luckmann 1997).

Entscheidend ist die durch die Parametrisierung ermöglichte Perspektivierung eines konzeptionell-kommunikativen Gesamtraums, in dem *Diskurstraditionen als Kristallisationen von Redekonstellationen* ihre Wirksamkeit entfalten. Daß es hierbei Affinitäten bestimmter universeller Verbalisierungsverfahren und einzelsprachlicher Techniken sowie Varietäten zu Diskurstraditionen und Textsorten gibt, die bestimmte sprachliche Züge *fordern*, andere aber *ausfiltern*, ist natürliche Konsequenz des konzeptionellen Kontinuums (vgl. 2.3.2.; Schlieben-Lange 1983; Luckmann 1997; Koch 1997a; Oesterreicher 1997).

Durch die vorgetragene Sicht der Dinge ergibt sich eine weitere äußerst wichtige Unterscheidung. Im Rahmen einer synchronischen Varietätenlinguistik gilt es nämlich, 'bloß' historisch-kontingente einzelsprachliche Varietätenstrukturen – also eigentlich alle diasystematischen Fakten der Einzelsprache – strikt von den universell motivierten, aber auf unterschiedliche Verbalisierungstypen bezogenen sprachlichen Verfahren zu unterscheiden (vgl. 2.1.), die ihrerseits mit den konzeptionell-diskurstraditionellen Rahmenbedingungen in Beziehung stehen (vgl. Koch & Oesterreicher 1990: 6–16 und 1994: 589–591, 594–596). Letztere besitzen zwar einen einzelsprachlichen Ausdruck, als textpragmatische, syntaktische und semantische Erscheinungen haben sie jedoch einen anderen Status als die genuin einzelsprachlichen diasystematisch markierten Strukturen. Derartige Fakten der Sprachvariation müssen einer Dimension der Sprachvarietät zugeordnet werden, die sich allein aus dem Nähe-Distanz-Kontinuum ergibt. Nach dieser Dimension richten sich — und dies ist der entscheidende Punkt — alle anderen Varietäten letztlich aus (vgl. Oesterreicher 1988: 376–378; Koch & Oesterreicher 1990: 13–15). Diese Phänomene sind nichts anderes als die bekannten *universalen Merkmale* gesprochener beziehungsweise geschriebener Sprache (vgl. auch Schlieben-Lange 1983: 46 ff.; Chafe 1985; Halliday 1985).

Als textuell-pragmatische, syntaktische und lexikalisch-semantische Aspekte der Nähesprache wären also die sprachlichen Verfahren und Techniken zu nennen, die auf Situationseinbettung, geringe Planung, Dialogizität, Emotionalität usw. zugeschnitten sind: Gliederungssignale, *turn-taking*-Signale, Sprecher- und Hörer-Signale, *hesitation phenomena*, Korrektursignale, Interjektionen und Abtönungsverfahren usw.; nicht-satzförmige Äußerungen, Kongruenzschwächen, Fehlstarts, Anakoluthe, Nachträge, Segmentierungserscheinungen und andere Lockerungen der syntaktischen Integration usw.; Präsentative und *passe-partout*-Konstruktionen, geringe Variation in der Wortwahl, allerdings beachtlicher lexikalischer Reichtum in durch Emotionalität gekennzeichneten Sinnbezirken usw. (vgl. Hofmann 1951; Koch & Oesterreicher 1990: 50–126; Koch 1995a; Stark 1997).

Aspekte der Distanzsprache, die situationsentbunden, stark geplant, eher monologisch und schwach emotional geprägt ist, sind Phänomene wie explizite Textgliederungssignale, fast ausschließlich mit sprachlichen Mitteln hergestellte Textkohärenz, eine durchstrukturierte semantische Progression, planungsintensive Textphorik usw.; syntaktische Wohlgeformtheit im kompakten Satzformat, Differenzierung von Präpositionen und hypotaktischen Konjunktionen, strikte Regularisierung des Tempus- und Modusgebrauchs, Intensivierung von Subordination und Hypotaxe usw.; verfeinerte lexikalische Paradigmen, Intensivierung der Wortbildung und Entlehnung, Nutzung von Abstraktionsmöglichkeiten und konsequenten Begriffshierarchien, hohe *type-token*-Relation usw. (vgl. Stempel 1964; Bossong 1979: 165–196; Raible 1992a: 78–111, 160–166).

Diese dem Nähe-Distanz-Kontinuum folgenden und durch dieses motivierten Regularitäten entsprechen in der Einzelsprache mithin *universalen Merkmalen*. Sie dürfen in ihrem Status nicht verwechselt und vermischt werden mit den *einzelsprachlichen Merkmalen* der Nähe und Distanz, die im Unterschied zu den erstgenannten eben als synchronisch vorliegendes Resultat historisch-kontingenter Prozesse der Sprachentwicklung zu gelten haben. Die einzelsprachlichen Merkmale sind in der beschriebenen Diasystematik greifbar. Einzelsprachliche Merkmale sind also aufzusuchen in den in der Einzelsprache existierenden zahlreichen deskriptiven Normgefügen und ihren phonetisch-phonologischen, morphosyntaktischen und lexikalischen Ausprägungen (vgl. 3.2.; Koch & Oesterreicher 1990, 1994 und 2001).

Diese die konzeptionelle Mündlichkeit *und* Schriftlichkeit kennzeichnenden einzelsprachlichen und universalen Merkmale der Variation können in ihrem unterschiedlichen Status im folgenden Schaubild zum Ausdruck gebracht werden:

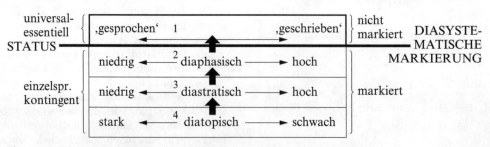

Fig. 111.4: Dimensionen der Sprachvariation I

Die komplexen Verhältnisse, die bestimmte Sprachen, etwa das Französische, im Bereich bestimmter historisch-kontingenter Erscheinungen aufweisen und die dazu führen, daß diese Erscheinungen nicht mehr der Diaphasik zugeordnet werden können (vgl. vor allem Koch 1999), erfordern eine Erweiterung des Schemas; so können etwa der nfrz. Aussprachetyp *quat'* oder *tab'* (für *quatre, table*), ein *ça* (statt *cela*), die Negation allein mit *pas* (statt *ne pas*), das Fehlen des *subjonctif imparfait* usw. nicht mehr diasystematisch als registermarkiert angesehen werden; diese Erscheinungen funktionieren wie die wirklich universalen Merkmale 'gesprochener' Sprache; sie werden daher in einer Dimension 1b 'untergebracht' (vgl. hierzu Koch & Oesterreicher 1990 und 1994; Oesterreicher 1988, 1995a und 2001b; zur Diaphasik vgl. Koch 1999a; auch Gadet 1998b); damit wird die Modellierung in Fig. 111.5 notwendig.

sinnig ist, weil die Kompetenz eines Individuums in diesem Sinne nicht nur nicht beschreibbar ist, sondern auch gar nicht interessieren würde. Das *sprechende Subjekt* ist allein interessant in dem, was es mit anderen Sprechern teilt, was von anderen Sprechern verstanden wird; in diesem Sinne ist das sprechende Subjekt *wirklich* in der alteritätsbezogenen Projektion der Gegenseitigkeit von

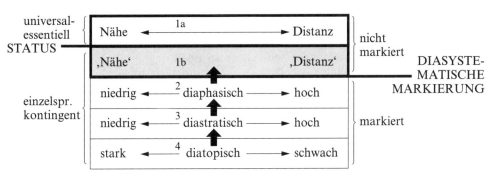

Fig. 111.5: Dimensionen der Sprachvariation II

Es kann nicht überraschen, daß in der hier vertretenen Sicht der Dinge eine Varietätenlinguistik in noch näher zu bestimmendem Sinne ebenfalls als 'Herzstück' der diachronischen Sprachwissenschaft zu gelten hat (vgl. 5.4.).

Daß die skizzierten kommunikativ-konzeptionellen Zusammenhänge gerade auch Konsequenzen für die Unterscheidung von *Sprachverschiedenheit* und *Sprachvariation* haben, wird in 4.1. diskutiert.

3.4. Corpora und Diskurstraditionen

Varietäten können nicht, wie dies oft noch heute in bestimmten Richtungen der Soziolinguistik geschieht, allein mit Hilfe von sprach- und diskursexternen Kriterien und Parametern bestimmt werden; derartige Kriterien sind etwa: 'Alter', 'Generation', 'Religion', 'Ethnizität', 'Schicht', 'Gruppe', 'Schulbildung', 'Beruf', 'soziales Netzwerk' usw. (vgl. Croft 2000: 166ff.; Ammon et al. (eds.) 1987: Kap. II). Es ist vielmehr zu berücksichtigen, daß Sprecher und Sprechergruppen über eine *plurale Kompetenz* verfügen, die diskurstraditionell aufgefächert ist; und dies gilt gerade nicht allein — wie häufig behauptet wird — für die sogenannten Sprachregister oder die diaphasische Varietätendimension, sondern eben auch schon für 'reine' Dialektsprecher.

Dies bedeutet gleichzeitig, daß eine strikt ideolektale Kompetenzbeschreibung widder-

Verstehenserwartungen in seinem Diskurs, es verwirklicht sich in den Sprachregeln und Sprachnormen sowie in den Diskurstraditionen, an denen es teilhat und die es, sie fortbildend, gebraucht: *La langue — c'est les autres* gilt also auch dort, wo innovativer Sprachgebrauch und schöpferische Sprechleistungen vorliegen und zu Sprachwandel führen; genau in diesem Sinne — dies ist oben schon kurz angedeutet worden (vgl. 2.4.) — sind Diskurse ja der Ort von Innovationen und *ad-hoc*-Bildungen, die im Abschnitt zum Sprachwandel genauer betrachtet werden (vgl. 5.4.).

Das diskurstraditionelle und diskursvariationelle Problem ist für die derzeit so erfolgreiche *Corpuslinguistik* von großer Bedeutung (vgl. Biber 1990; Beiträge in Svartvik (ed.) 1992). Es zeigt sich nämlich immer deutlicher, daß mit der Vergrößerung der angelegten Corpora und mit der Multiplikation der Datenmengen nichts erreicht wird, wenn diese nicht begleitet werden von einer sorgfältig diskurstraditionellen Bestimmung und Interpretation des im Corpus verarbeiteten Materials. Konzeptionell breit gestreute Corpora sind zwar eine notwendige, aber keineswegs hinreichende Bedingung für eine fruchtbare Bearbeitung varietätenlinguistischer Fragen: die Aussagekraft eines Corpus oder einer Corpusfamilie hängt auch ab von der Sichtbarmachung der im ursprünglichen Profil der Diskurse realisierten Konzeption, die systematisch getrennte Erhebungen notwendig macht.

Die Einsicht in den Zusammenhang von sprachlichen Formen und diskurstraditioneller Bindung der Corpora führt auch dazu, zwei 'klassische' Forderungen der Corpuslinguistik zu relativieren, die gelegentlich direkt als Erkenntnishindernis betrachtet werden müssen; es geht um die 'ritualisierte' Forderung nach Authentizität sowie die Hinweise auf die Gefahr einer Verfälschung von Ergebnissen (*Beobachter-Paradoxon*) (vgl. Reich 2001).

Zu Recht werden bei Okkurrenzen teilweise systematisch sogenannte A-Daten („actual, authentic, attested data"), M-Daten („modified data") und I-Daten („invented, intuitive, introspective data") unterschieden (Stubbs 1996: 4). Dies ist jedoch nur die Hälfte des Problems. Es ist – und Varietätenlinguisten wissen dies seit längerem – unter Umständen notwendig, *Corpora zu konstruieren*. Für eine Untersuchung bestimmter Probleme und Phänomene, die in 'normalen' Kommunikationskontexten, gerade auch in stark nähesprachlicher und dialogisch geprägter Kommunikation, *nicht* erscheinen, muß der Linguist gezielt *Kontexte und Kommunikationsbedingungen konfigurieren*, in denen Informanten dann sprachlich agieren: „Durch gezielte Beeinflussung des diskursiven Ensembles 'fangen' solche Diskursspiele Okkurrenzen, statt auf sie zu warten" (Reich 2001). Derartige 'Manipulationen' erlauben es überhaupt erst, Okkurrenzen bestimmter sprachlicher Erscheinungen in repräsentativer Menge und mit der notwendigen Trennschärfe zu elizitieren (vgl. Reich 2002, der dieses Problem für seine Untersuchung der sogenannten Null-Objekte im brasilianischen Portugiesisch überzeugend beschreibt und löst).

Diese Problemzusammenhänge sind, teilweise etwas anders akzentuiert, besonders auch bei der Erstellung und Beurteilung diachronischer Corpora zu reflektieren, die – zumindest für die europäischen Kultursprachen – in jüngster Zeit in großer Zahl entwickelt werden, wobei allerdings bei der Erstellung teilweise überraschend nachlässig zu Werke gegangen wird (vgl. dazu etwa Lenker 2000). Vorgängig zu leistende Reflexionsschritte werden einfach 'übersprungen'.

Es geht nämlich, erstens, darum, in schriftlich überlieferten Textexemplaren die epochenbezogenen Kennzeichnungen von konzeptionellen Profilen der Diskurstraditionen und Textsorten vorzunehmen, was bekanntlich durch eine Reihe von Faktoren nicht unerheblich erschwert wird: So stellt etwa das Fehlen autoritativer Textzeugen für die chronologische Bestimmung und auch die sogenannte *mouvance du texte* (Paul Zumthor) ein Problem dar; aber auch Fragen der Interpretation der kommunikativen Kontexte, also der am Diskursgeschehen ursprünglich beteiligten nicht-sprachlichen semiotischen Kodes, sind solche Schwierigkeiten (vgl. dazu Oesterreicher 1998; vgl. auch Zumthor 1985 und 1987; Cerquiglini 1981 und 1989; Fleischman 1990).

Erforderlich ist aber, zweitens, auch die systematische Nachzeichnung und Erkenntnis des auf der *Zeitachse* sich vollziehenden historischen Wandels von Gattungen und Textsorten, der sich häufig hinter gleichbleibenden Gattungsbezeichnungen und Namensidentitäten von Textsorten verbirgt (vgl. Frank 1997); ein bloßes 'Zusammenschieben' von äußerlich ähnlichen, aber nicht qualifizierten Texten führt nicht weiter. Nur sorgfältige serielle Analysen können dieses Problem entschärfen (vgl. Selig 1992: 1−19; Jacob 1994 und 2001; Koch 1987 und 1997a; Oesterreicher 1995b, 1997, 1998 und 1999; vgl. auch Beiträge zum Spanischen in Jacob & Kabatek (eds.) 2001).

Kurz: Die Repräsentativität der als Corpora der Varietätenbestimmung zugrundegelegten Diskurse und Texte ist also für synchronische und diachronische Diskurs- und Textbetrachtungen gleichermaßen ein methodologisches Problem, das zusammen mit der unaufhebbaren Differenz von belegten Sprachformen und der 'generalisierten' Realität sprachlicher Techniken mit einer bloßen Steigerung von Textmengen nicht gelöst werden kann.

4. Sprachverschiedenheit: Idiome, Sprachen, Sprachgruppen, Sprachtypen

4.1. Sprachvariation und Sprachverschiedenheit

In 1.2. ist betont worden, daß *Sprachvariation* und *Sprachverschiedenheit* als interne und externe Aspekte der Historizität von Sprache in einem engen Verhältnis zueinander stehen und eigentlich dieselbe Realität darstellen. Dieser Gedanke kann jetzt vertieft werden.

Die Sprachvariation und die Sprachverschiedenheit sind als 'innen- und außenperspektivisch' und gleichzeitig als 'hierarchiestufenbezogen' bezeichnet worden (vgl. 2.3.1.). Zwischen beiden Perspektivierungen gibt es nicht nur bezüglich der Hierarchiestufenbezogenheit entscheidende Unterschiede, die die Sprachverschiedenheit als eine 'eingeschränktere Kategorie' klar von der Sprachvariation unterscheiden. Ob also eine diatopische Varietät, etwa ein primärer Dialekt, auf weitere interne Varianz hin untersucht wird oder ob die Varietäten einer historischen Einzelsprache zur Debatte stehen, in beiden Fällen liegt die erste Perspektivierung vor, weil — definitorisch — konzeptionelle und diskursvariationelle Fakten eine Rolle spielen und berücksichtigt werden müssen; *dieselben Größen*, nämlich Dialekte und Einzelsprachen, können gleichzeitig aber 'außenperspektivisch' gegen andere, hierarchisch nicht notwendig gleichartige Größen gesetzt werden, womit die zweite Perspektivierung appliziert wird: Auf die Möglichkeit der Verbindung der sprachlichen Differenzen mit kommunikativ-konzeptionellen und diskurspragmatischen Fakten wird dabei grundsätzlich verzichtet (vgl. 4.2.).

Mit anderen Worten: Aus den Überlegungen zum Nähe-Distanz-Kontinuum, auf das hin sich die einzelnen Varietätendimensionen mit ihren Varietäten ausrichten, geht hervor, daß der Variationsaspekt der zu diesen Varietäten führt, immer auf anthropologische und sprachtheoretisch-kommunikative, mithin konzeptionelle und diskurspragmatische Zusammenhänge bezogen bleibt, die mit universalistisch zu fundierenden Kommunikationsbedingungen und Verbalisierungsstrategien zu tun haben.

Demgegenüber löst sich die Betrachtung der Sprachverschiedenheit — dem Variationsaspekt ganz anders verbunden — dadurch von derartigen Zusammenhängen, daß sie gerade den systemischen, sprachtechnikbezogenen Strukturaspekt von Idiomen, Sprachen usw. in den Mittelpunkt rückt. Es geht, gerade nicht mehr kommunikativ-konzeptionell orientiert, um den reinen 'außen-perspektivischen' Vergleich von Struktureigenschaften sprachlicher Techniken. Sprachverschiedenheit ist mithin ausschließlich im Bereich der Sprachtechniken auf der historischen Ebene zentriert.

Bei der 'innenperspektivisch' auf kommunikativ-diskurspragmatische Fakten bezogenen Sprachvariation stellt eine historische Einzelsprache prinzipiell die höchste Abstraktionsstufe dar, die noch mit einem konzeptionell konstituierten Sprach- und Sprecherbewußtsein 'versehen' ist (vgl. Heger 1989b). Insofern ist es gerade nicht mehr sinnvoll, etwa die romanischen Sprachen oder in einem Sprachbund zusammengeschlossene Sprachen oder gar typologische Gruppierungen von Sprachen im Sinne des Begriffs 'Sprachvariation' zu qualifizieren. Eine derartige Einschränkung entfällt beim Konzept der Sprachverschiedenheit: In der Außenperspektivierung lassen sich nämlich *alle* historischen sprachlichen Gestaltungen und Techniken, welcher Extension oder Hierarchiestufe auch immer, miteinander kontrastierend vergleichen — mehr noch: alle Sprachformen, welche Herkunft und Ausprägung sie auch besitzen mögen, alle Zeiten und Zeiträume, alle Räume und Raumteile, sogar 'konstruierte', 'künstliche' Sprachen *können* in der Perspektivierung 'Sprachverschiedenheit' angegangen werden.

Diese Unterscheidungen machen weiterhin verständlich, daß die Sprachvariation als Problem auf allen Ebenen des Sprachlichen Relevanz beanspruchen kann; demgegenüber ergibt die Anwendung des Begriffs der Sprachverschiedenheit im Bereich der Sprechtätigkeit und des aktuellen Diskurses ebenso wie im Bereich der Diskurstraditionen eigentlich keinen Sinn (vgl. 2.).

Das schließt nicht aus, daß in ganz anderen, nämlich *sekundären* Perspektivierungen — die interessanterweise gerade auch das Verhältnis zwischen dem Varietätenraum einer Einzelsprache und dem möglicherweise 'mehrsprachig besetzten' Kommunikationsraum betreffen — konzeptionell durchaus relevante Fragen auch bezüglich der Sprachverschiedenheit gestellt werden können. So kann man etwa fragen: „Welche kognitiven Prozesse werden im *code-switching* aktiviert? An welchen Stellen der syntaktisch-semantischen Struktur findet der *switch* statt?", „Wie erklärt sich die Tatsache, daß auf der Iberischen Halbinsel im Mittelalter verschiedene Idiome — Kastilisch und Gallego — für verschiedene literarische Gattungen verwendet wurden?" oder „Welche Positionen besetzen unterschiedliche Sprachen in einem gegebenen Kommunikationsraum, wie werden sie eingesetzt?" usw. (vgl. Lüdtke 1988). Es ist offensichtlich, daß hier sekundär wiederum konzeptionelle, für ein Sprecherbewußtsein und für eine Sprachgemeinschaft bzw. eine

Kommunikationsgemeinschaft relevante Problemstellungen zur Debatte stehen.

Schließlich ist ausdrücklich auch noch einmal auf den *Zeitfaktor* und das *Raumkriterium* hinzuweisen: Sprachvariation impliziert einen Ort und Gleichzeitigkeit (oder zumindest raum-zeitliche Kontiguität); bei der Sprachverschiedenheit sind diesbezüglich prinzipiell keinerlei Einschränkungen auszumachen. Dies bedeutet, auch wenn die Sprachverschiedenheit als Aspekt der externen Historizität gelten muß, daß die genannten Kennzeichnungen kontrastierend zu den die Sprachvariation konstituierenden kommunikativ-konzeptionellen Zusammenhängen ausdrücklich anzuerkennen sind.

Sprachvariation und *Sprachverschiedenheit* − beide konstituiert durch 'Differenzqualitäten' von Sprachlichem − sollten wegen der unterschiedlichen Implikationen ihrer Fragerichtung begrifflich in der beschriebenen Weise konzipiert und auch terminologisch unterschieden werden.

4.2. Im Feld der Sprachverschiedenheit

Wie schon betont, sind einer die Sprachverschiedenheit in den unterschiedlichsten Bereichen der Sprachtechnik aufsuchenden Forschung (fast) keine Grenzen gesetzt. Aus diesem Grund sind die folgenden Hinweise höchst selektiv und punktuell. Zuerst sei ausdrücklich darauf hingewiesen, daß − obschon dies häufig unbeachtet bleibt und durch intuitive Setzungen und pragmatisch motivierte Entscheide überspielt wird − *jede* Feststellung von Sprachverschiedenheit und *jeder* Vergleich letztlich ein *tertium comparationis* voraussetzt.

So können nicht nur phonologische Systeme oder Teilsysteme beschrieben und verglichen werden (in unterschiedlichen Sprachen oder innerhalb einer historischen Sprache), sondern auch ganz bestimmte nichtfunktionelle lautliche Realisierungen betrachtet werden. Für letztere kann man kontrastierend etwa die Reichweite von Aussprachemodulationen zusammenstellen (Varianz eines alemannischen [a] im Vergleich zu einem schwäbischen [a]) oder aber Norm-Realisierungen beschreiben: Während also etwa frz. und ital. /e/ und /ɛ/ phonematisch sind, gibt es span. allein nicht-phonematische, allerdings 'normale' Realisierungen [e] (in *pero* 'aber') und [ɛ] (in *perro* 'Hund') ('Norm' im Sinne Coserius). Die vergleichbaren Lautsubstanzen umfassen so 'exotische' Laute wie die afrikanischen Schnalze (Khoisan-Sprachen in Namibia, Botswana, Südafrika und Tansania), den im Walisischen/Kymrischen existierenden lateral kontaminierten Kakuminallaut (Retroflex) etwa in den Ortsbezeichnungen *Llandudno, Llanberis* usw. (*llan* = 'Kirchspiel') oder aber verbreitete Phänomene wie die Assibilierung von ⟨rr⟩ und ⟨tr⟩ (*carro, cuatro*) in einigen Varietäten des amerikanischen Spanisch.

Die Besonderheiten der Vergangenheitstempora des Deutschen können differenziell beschrieben werden, ohne daß auf die konzeptionellen Implikationen des süddeutschen Verlusts des Präteritums eingegangen werden müßte. Ebenso kann das System der lateinischen Tempora gesamthaft mit den in den romanischen Sprachen 'bewahrten' und den neu entwickelten Tempuskategorien verglichen werden. Und für die Vergangenheitstempora würde dann der Vergleich des Spanischen, des Französischen und des Italienischen in der Perspektive der Sprachverschiedenheit es erlauben, die funktionelle und gebrauchsstatistische Stabilität der drei Vergangenheitsformen Imperfekt, Perfekt und zusammengesetztes Perfekt für das Spanische zu konstatieren; bekanntlich gibt es die drei Tempora ebenfalls im frz. Standard, nicht jedoch im *français parlé*, wo das *passé simple* fehlt; im italienischen Sprachraum ist die Situation insofern besonders interessant, als in den norditalienischen und den süditalienischen Varietäten jeweils unterschiedliche Reduktionen auf nur zwei Tempora vorgenommen werden usw. Alle diese Phänomene können − wie schon betont − ohne die geringste Bezugnahme auf die in der Regel vorhandenen massiven konzeptionell-varietätenlinguistischen Implikationen 'außenperspektivisch' differenziell-systemisch beschrieben werden.

Auf der Zeitachse kann die Sprachverschiedenheit in der Kontinuität aufeinanderfolgender Epochen und Etappen der Sprachen und ihrer Varietäten festgestellt werden, es sind aber auch Zeitsprünge möglich, etwa drei 'Schnitte' des Typs *Latein − Altfranzösisch − Neufranzösisch*. Gerade derartige Zusammenrückungen (auch wenn sie genealogisch motiviert sind) zeigen ganz klar, daß die der Konfrontierung jeweils zugrundegelegte Sprachtechnik oder Varietät − dies sei nochmals ausdrücklich wiederholt − immer schon eine methodisch idealisierte, ja 'purgierte' linguistische Größe ist; diese bezieht sich weder auf die Gesamtheit der zum anvisierten Zeitpunkt existierenden Varietäten und Normen der genannten Idiome (vgl. 3.2. und 3.3.), noch darf sie einfach mit bestimmten Diskursvorkommen identifiziert werden (vgl. 3.4.). Alle diese Gesichtspunkte sind natürlich auch bei den geläufigen, abkürzend gebrauchten Ausdrücken für die sogenannten Sprachfamilien (also 'die romanischen Sprachen', 'die slavischen Sprachen' usw.) präsent zu halten (→ Art. 120, 121, 122 usw.).

Was nun die räumlichen Koordinaten eines Vergleichs angeht, so können die Differenzqualitäten von zwei im Schwarzwald gelegenen Nachbardörfern, deren Dialekte kontrastiert werden, bis hin zur arealtypologischen und sprachbundbezogenen Charakterisierung von Sprachen im Blick auf Unterschiede (und Gemeinsamkeiten) behandelt werden (→ Art. 105, 106, 107, 108, 109 und 110).

Auch wenn bei den bisher angeführten Beispielen noch raum-zeitliche Bezüge sichtbar werden (Nachbarschaft, Genealogie usw.), so sind derartige Beziehungen keineswegs notwendig: Zur Illustration eines Sprachtyps können die unterschiedlichsten Idiome aus allen Räumen und (dokumentierten) Zeiten angeführt werden; umgekehrt lassen sich Typdifferenzen ebenso belegen.

Für die hier entwickelte Argumentation und ihre 'innen'- und 'außenperspektivische' Sicht interessant sind aber auch weniger naheliegende, aber trotzdem auf Sprachverschiedenheit bezogene Problemkonstellationen. Während die Diglossie-Situation gerade in varietätenbezogen-konzeptioneller Hinsicht interessiert (vgl. Ferguson 1959), führt die sogenannte *Plurizentrik* von Sprachkulturen zu wichtigen Formen und Aspekten der Sprachverschiedenheit, die deskriptiv, soziolinguistisch und sprachpolitisch von großer Bedeutung sind: Es geht darum, daß bestimmte historische Sprachen (das Englische, das Portugiesische, das Spanische usw.) *Regionalstandards* besitzen, die als Referenzvarietäten selber wiederum die entsprechenden Varietätenräume strukturieren; es wäre also kurzsichtig, hier einfach von diatopischer Variation — im oben (3.2. und 3.3.) diskutierten Sinne — zu sprechen (vgl. Oesterreicher 2001b). Selbstverständlich können auch die Ausbaugrade von Idiomen 'außenperspektivisch'-kontrastiv als Phänomene der Sprachverschiedenheit behandelt werden (vgl. Kloss 1978). In 4.1. ist schon erläutert worden, daß Mehrsprachigkeit in einem gegebenen Kommunikationsraum als Sprachverschiedenheit gerade sekundär in konzeptioneller Hinsicht große Bedeutung gewinnt, weil in diesen Fällen klare funktionelle Verteilungen auf im Nähe-Distanz-Kontinuum etablierte Domänen vorliegen. Auch die durch Sprachkontakt bedingten Resultate sprachlichen Wandels (vgl. 5.4.) können in der Perspektive der Sprachverschiedenheit angegangen werden; Beispiele wären hier die historischen Konstellationen im mittelalterlichen Spanien (Muslime, arabischer Einfluß, Veränderungen im Wortschatz usw.), sodann die auch durch den Kontakt mit der indianischen Bevölkerung sowie den spanischen Kolonisatoren nachfolgenden Immigranten entstandenen Differenzen zwischen amerikanischem und europäischem Spanisch (vgl. Plurizentrik *und* die jeweils zugeordneten Varietäten Hispanoamerikas) oder auch die unterschiedliche Aufnahmebereitschaft für Anglizismen in europäischen Sprachen. Material zu derartigen Problemen enthalten sprachgeschichtliche Darstellungen wie Durante 1981; Cano Aguilar 1982; Bruni 1984; Balibar 1985; Banniard 1992 usw. Genannt seien auch noch die Problemkreise Kreolisierung (→ Art. 116) und Pidginisierung (→ Art. 117), aber auch der 'Sprachentod', bei denen neben den soziolinguistisch interessanten konzeptionellen Fakten natürlich auch sprachverschiedenheitszentrierte Fragestellungen möglich und häufig sind (→ Art. 118; auch 119).

In einer ganz anderen, nämlich wissenschaftssystematischen Perspektive kann man schließlich auf die mit Sprachverschiedenheit verbundenen Formen und Fragestellungen der sogenannten Angewandten Linguistik verweisen, die sich in Interessenorientierungen wie dem Dolmetschen und Übersetzen, der Fremdsprachendidaktik, der Kontrastiven Linguistik usw. manifestiert.

4.3. Sprachverschiedenheit,
Sprachtypologie, Universalienforschung

Für eine Bestimmung der Sprachverschiedenheit sind, wie schon angedeutet, die aus den Universalien 'Semantizität', 'Alterität', 'Exteriorität' und 'Diskursivität' resultierenden Kriterien bedeutsam, die es erlauben, *alle* festgestellten Differenzqualitäten von Sprachlichem zu bestimmen und damit die Relationen der in Frage stehenden Fakten zu etablieren.

Auf der Ebene einer *typologischen* Betrachtung (→ Art. 1 und 2) ist es deshalb ganz unvermeidlich, die *tertia* eines möglichen Vergleichs auf den verschiedenen Ebenen des Sprachlichen *ausdrücklich* zu markieren, weil hier einfach pragmatische oder intuitive Setzungen nicht mehr 'funktionieren'.

Die in jedem semiotischen System gegebene Verbindung von Semantizität und Exteriorität kann 'Konnektivität' genannt werden. Die Zeichenfunktion in der Sprache kann damit genauer als Vermittlung und 'Synthetisierung' von Semantizitätstypen und sprachlichen Exterioritätsgestaltungen gefaßt werden, die – im Unterschied zu anderen semiotischen Systemen – durch die notwendig *zeitliche* Bestimmtheit der produktions- und rezeptionsbezogenen Prozesse ihre spezifische auf 'Linearität' bezogene Ausprägung erhält. Die 'Diskursivität' als spezifische Form der sprachlichen Semiosis (vgl. 1.1.) entspricht daher einem *konnektiven essentiellen Universale*. Gerade dieses Universale zeigt im Vergleich mit der Konnektivität anderer semiotischer Systeme – bildende Kunst, Musik, Architektur, Film usw. – besonders eindrücklich die *differentia specifica* der menschlichen Sprache (→ Art. 1; vgl. auch Oesterreicher 1988 und 1989: 239–242).

Für die typologische Forschung ist die *Diskursivität* insofern als unverzichtbarer Grundbegriff anzusehen, als mit ihm notwendig die Betrachtung der Prinzipien der Verknüpfung von Inhaltsprozessen mit Ausdrucksprozessen auf der Zeitlinie gefordert ist; die Diskursivität ermöglicht mithin *tertia* des Vergleichs auf allen Ebenen der Strukturierung der *Sprachzeichenbildung*. Man darf sich dabei nicht dadurch irritieren lassen, daß die diskursivitätsrelevanten Phänomene traditionell zur Lexikologie, Wortbildung, Morphologie, Morphosyntax und Syntax sowie zur transphrastischen Grammatik gezählt werden. Von der Hierarchiestufe der Monemkombination über die anderen Ebenen der möglichen einzelsprachlichen Strukturierung (Wort, Syntagma, Proposition, Satz) bis hin zu den noch einzelsprachlichen Regularitäten der Textkonstitution (vgl. Coseriu 1981a; Oesterreicher 1996a und 1996b) sind hierbei *alle* Zuordnungsregularitäten von Semantischem und Ausdrucksstrukturellem zu betrachten. So geht es in dieser für die Sprachtypologie zentralen Perspektive beispielsweise um den Ausdruck von 'Wortklassen', um Polyfunktionalität und Polymorphie, um Besonderheiten diskontinuierlicher Elemente, um Wortbildungsverfahren, um analytische und synthetische Verfahren, um den Ausdruckstyp von grammatischer Markierung, um Translationstypen, um Redundanz- und Implikationsverhältnisse, um Segmentierungserscheinungen, um Prä- und Postdetermination, um den Ausdruck der Fundamentalrelation sowie der semantischen Rollen und pragmatischen Kategorien, um die Gestaltung semantischer Isotopien und informationsstruktureller Profile sowie um kataphorische und anaphorische Beziehungen in Satz und Text. An allen diesen Erscheinungen (und vielen mehr) ist die einzelsprachlich und sprachgruppenspezifisch je unterschiedliche Synthetisierung von Inhaltsstrukturen und Ausdrucksgestaltungen nachzuzeichnen (vgl. als Hintergrund für diese Konzeption auch die „Théorie des trois points de vue" von Claude Hagège 1982: 207–233).

Es sei angemerkt, daß nach dieser auf der Zeichenfunktion basierenden Bestimmung die Untersuchung phonetisch-phonologischer Zusammenhänge, die zwar wichtige klassifikatorische Ergebnisse zeitigen kann, deshalb grundsätzlich aus dem Bereich *typologischer* Forschung ausgeschlossen werden muß, weil hierbei kein konnektives *tertium* etabliert werden kann. Phonetisch-phonologische Verhältnisse werden allerdings typologisch dann relevant, wenn sie, über die bloße Signifikantenkonstruktion hinaus, Konsequenzen für die Sprachzeichenbildung besitzen. Dies ist selbstverständlich immer dort der Fall, wo Lautsysteme, morphonologische Prozesse oder silbenstrukturelle, akzentuelle oder intonatorische Gegebenheiten Wirkungen auf die Sprachzeichenbildung haben (→ Art. in Kap. XII).

Es ist hier nicht der Ort, Formen und Positionen der modernen Sprachtypologie zu diskutieren, die als *holistische* oder *whole-system*-Typologien ganz anderen Ansprüchen genügen müssen als die *partiellen* Typologien/Teiltypologien, die als alternative Organisationsschemata und Lösungsstrategien für sprachliche Teilaufgaben höchst unterschiedliche Reichweiten und Erklärungsansprüche besitzen (→ Art. 1, 2, 23–28; vgl. auch Comrie 1981; Raible (ed.) 1989; Heger 1989a; Croft 1990; Oesterreicher & Raible 1993; Ramat 1984; Jacob 2002). Hier ist dann auch der Gedanke einer *Korrelation* unterschiedlicher sprachlicher Eigenschaften wichtig, der sich als außerordentlich fruchtbar erweist (vgl. Jacob 2002: 1.3. und 1.4.; Körner 1987; Oesterreicher 1996a). Insgesamt kann der von Georg von der Gabelentz formulierte Wunsch in der Forschung aber wohl allein als regulative Idee, nicht jedoch als konkretes Forschungsziel der Sprachtypologie gelten: „Aber welcher Gewinn wäre es auch, wenn wir einer Sprache auf den Kopf zusagen dürften: Du hast das und das Einzelmerkmal, folglich hast du die und die weiteren Eigenschaften und den und den Gesammtcharakter!" (Gabelentz 1901: 481).

Abschließend sei jedoch noch eine Einschätzung der 'empirischen Universalienforschung' gegeben, anläßlich derer auch eine Reihe von grundsätzlichen Fragen bezüglich der Sprachtypologie diskutiert werden kann. Bei dieser Richtung handelt es sich um einen für die Sprachtypologie besonders wichtigen Ansatz, der gerade auch für die historische Sprachforschung fruchtbar gemacht wird (vgl. Bossong 1982; es sind vor allem die zahlreichen von Georg Bossong und Bernard Comrie seit 1987 im Verlag de Gruyter in der Reihe *Empirical Approaches to Language Typology* publizierten Bände zu nennen).

Die Unterscheidung von 'essentiellen', 'empirischen' und 'möglichen' Universalien zielt bekanntlich auf den unterschiedlichen *Status* der jeweils in Frage stehenden Fakten (vgl. Coseriu 1974; Seiler (ed.) 1978). 'Empirisch' sagt damit gerade nichts darüber aus, *wie* die entsprechenden Fakten gewonnen wurden, sondern eben nur, *daß* sie im Vergleich zu den essentiellen, deduktiv aus dem Sprachbegriff gewonnenen, und solchen, die semiotisch möglich sind (also auch die beiden genannten), aus einer empirisch genannten Materialbasis stammen. Nach den Bemerkungen zu den komplexen und unterschiedlich gerichteten Idealisierungs- und Abstraktionsprozessen, die überhaupt erst zur möglichen Kennzeichnung und Zuordnung von Sprachen und Sprachgruppen als Vertreter dieses oder jenes Typs führen, ist evident, daß der Ausduck 'empirische Universalien' in diesem Forschungszusammenhang eine Bedeutung besitzt, die sowohl die sogenannten *near universals* oder *universal tendencies* als auch die sogenannten *implikativen* oder *relationalen* Universalien des Typs *'given x, we always find y'* abdeckt (→ Art. 23). Gerade letztere betreffen auch Unterschiede zwischen den Sprachen (vgl. Jacob 2002: 1.4.).

Bei den typologischen Kennzeichnungen von Idiomen, Sprachen und Sprachgruppen beispielsweise bezüglich der Aktantenmarkierung, besonders der differenziellen Objektmarkierung (→ Art. 65), der Verfahren zum Ausdruck der Diathesen (→ Art. 66, 67, 68), der Satzverknüpfung (→ Art. 45 und 74), der aspektualitäts-, modalitäts- und temporalitätsbezogenen Kategorisierungen (→ Art. 42, 59, 60), der Verfahren der Serialisierung (→ Art. 64) usw. gilt es – und dieser Punkt wird von Typologen leider häufig nicht genügend herausgestellt – immer in Erinnerung zu behalten (vgl. 4.2.), daß eine bestimmte deskriptive Norm (neben anderen) Grundlage der Beschreibung war, daß allein unmarkierte Verfahren (neben zahlreichen markierten) ausgewählt wurden, daß der Zeitfaktor (und seine synchronischen Effekte) unberücksichtigt blieb, daß auch im Bereich diskurspragmatischer Kriterien maximale 'Abwahlen' vorgenommen wurden usw.

Damit ist klar, daß eigentlich alle in 2.3. und 3. beschriebenen, die Vielfalt sprachlicher Fakten konstituierenden konkreteren Bedingungszusammenhänge der Sprachvariation idealisierend und abstrahierend ausgeblendet sind.

Diese Tatsache wird von sprachwissenschaftlichen Traditionalisten gerne als Argument dafür benutzt, typologischen und empirisch-universalistischen Forschungen rundweg ihren Wert abzusprechen: Es handle sich nur um luftige wissenschaftliche Konstruktionen, um blutleere Erfindungen und windige Setzungen; besonders beliebt ist außerdem die Behauptung, daß die Typologen ihr Wissen über die Sprachen ja nur aus Grammatiken und Wörterbüchern beziehen würden und den ganzen Reichtum der sprachlichen Ausdrucksmittel der angeführten Sprachen nicht richtig beurteilen könnten, daß es sich also letztlich um bloße Spekulation handle.

Es braucht hier nicht bestritten zu werden, daß es – wie überall – auch in der typologischen Forschung gelegentlich unerfreuliche Übertreibungen gibt; man vergleiche diesbezüglich etwa die Diskussion um die Möglichkeit sogenannter globaler Typologien, den sogenannten *drift* und die 'Konsistenz'-These in der *word-order-typology* (→ Art. 64; Oesterreicher 1989); auch sind gelegentlich durchaus sachlich fragwürdige Entscheide bezüglich des angeführten Belegmaterials zu monieren (vor allem bei 'exotischen' Sprachen).

Mit allem Nachdruck sei deshalb festgestellt, daß derartige Vorwürfe völlig am Kern der Sache vorbei gehen: Das methodische Vorgehen der Sprachtypologie ist nämlich nicht nur völlig *gerechtfertigt*, insofern diese überhaupt erst *nach* den beschriebenen hierarchiebezogenen Abstraktions- und Idealisierungsschritten den ihrer Fragestellung angemessenen Ort im Gesamtraum linguistischer Forschung findet. Diese Forschungsrichtung ist auch *notwendig*, um tatsächlich mögliche Strukturen der Sprachen der Welt in den zeichenbezogenen Bereichen in ihrem ganzen ausdrucksbezogenen und funktionellen Reichtum in den Blick zu bekommen (→ Art. in den Kap. VIII, IX, X sowie XI; Comrie 1981 und 1987; Croft 1990; auch Oesterreicher & Raible 1993; Jacob 2002).

Gerade die Universalität des Sprechens und die allgemeinen Kennzeichen der Sprechtätigkeit, die den Rahmen für die Leistungen 'abstecken', die von einzelnen Sprachen mit ihren jeweiligen Techniken und Funktionsgestaltungen zu 'erbringen' sind, erweisen die Typologie *als 'rangstufenhöchste' Teildisziplin einer Linguistik der historischen Sprachtechniken* (vgl. 2.3.). Sprachtypologie ist dabei aber gleichzeitig notwendig angewiesen auf eine Universalienforschung, die — im Konzert mit den in 2.2. angeführten Disziplinen — ein Panorama dieser allgemeinen, *universellen Sprechleistungen* vorgeben kann (→ Art. 1; Seiler (ed.) 1978; Raible (ed.) 1989). *Sprachtypologie ist also eingespannt in diesen doppelten Bezug.* Es wäre absurd, von dieser Forschungsrichtung einen Typ von 'historischer' Konkretion einfordern zu wollen, den sie nicht geben kann und nicht zu geben braucht.

Diese Sachlage schließt nicht aus, daß man durchaus verlangen muß, daß die sprachtypologische Forschung über ihre Optionen und die skizzierten methodisch notwendigen 'Ausblendungen' und 'Idealisierungen' Rechenschaft zu geben vermag. Es sei nicht verschwiegen, daß die Typologie in der letzten Zeit gerade den angesprochenen sprechtätigkeitsbezogenen, universalistischen Bezug besonders 'stark' macht und daß sie die Problematik der für ihren Faktenbestand konstitutiven Idealisierungs- und Abstraktionsschritte — wenn überhaupt — sehr zögerlich angeht (vgl. 6.). Dies ist gerade auch für den sogenannten typologischen Wandel von großer Bedeutung, dessen abstraktionsstufenbezogene Differenzen zu Sprachwandelphänomenen des in 5. beschriebenen Typs ebenfalls immer bewußt bleiben sollten (→ Art. 114 und 115; Art. 120−125).

Exkurs zur Geschichte der Sprachreflexion:
Es ist in unserem Zusammenhang interessant (vgl. auch 6.), daß in der Geschichte der vorwissenschaftlichen Sprachbetrachtung die in der europäischen Neuzeit immer drängendere Frage nach einer befriedigenden Einschätzung der Sprachvariation und der Sprachverschiedenheit (und ihrer Gründe) ganz bezeichnende Reaktionen hervorruft.

Die Sprachvariation, vor allem in Form der dialektalen Varianz, aber auch der niedrig markierten diastratischen und diaphasischen Varietäten, wird verteufelt und mit den Mitteln einer strikten präskriptiven Normativität eliminiert (vgl. Oesterreicher 1983 und 2000).

Was die Sprachverschiedenheit angeht, die sich nach der sukzessiven 'Nobilitierung' der europäischen Volkssprachen und der europäischen kolonialen Expansion als Fragestellung natürlich aufdrängt, so kann man sagen, daß ihr zu Geschichtlichkeit und Historisierung drängendes Problempotential gerade in der neuen und erfolgversprechenden Form der Sprachbetrachtung, die schon früh als 'Typologie' bezeichnet wird (→ Art. 19; vgl. auch Droixhe 1978: 315−320), zur 'Stillstellung' eben dieses in der Sprachvielfalt liegenden Potentials eingesetzt wurde. In diesem Sinne hat man die typologische Betrachtung von Sprachen in der französischen Aufklärung, etwa in der großen Enzyklopädie, zu Recht als das letzte Bollwerk eines Denkens herausgestellt, das Sprachverschiedenheit 'nur' typologisch verarbeiten kann und das sich mit dieser Ausrichtung gleichzeitig — natürlich unbewußt — verzweifelt gegen die Anerkennung der sich massiv vorbereitenden 'romantischen' Einsicht in den historischen Charakter von Sprache und Sprachlichem wehrt, für den Sprachvariation und Sprachverschiedenheit zentrale Postulate sind (vgl. Monreal-Wickert 1977; Droixhe 1978; Oesterreicher 1983, 1994 und 2000; zu den 'exotischen' Sprachen und der sogenannten Missionarslinguistik, vgl. Oesterreicher & Schmidt-Riese 1999; Auroux et al. (eds.) 2000: Kap. XX).

5. Sprachwandel: Innovationen, Übernahmen, Bahnen grammatischen und lexikalischen Wandels

5.1. 'Traditionelle' und 'moderne' diachronische Linguistik

Es ist betont worden, daß die Historizität des Sprachlichen sich naturgemäß besonders auffällig und eindrucksvoll in den Veränderungen sprachlicher Erscheinungen der unterschiedlichen Bereiche der Einzelsprachen manifestiert. So sind lautliche, morphologische, syntaktische und lexikalische Sprachwandelprozesse ausgezeichnete Themen einer diachronisch orientierten Sprachwissenschaft, in der traditionell die entsprechenden sprachlichen und diskurstraditionellen Veränderungen beschrieben werden, also diese 'Historizität' von Sprachen und Texten thematisch wird. Gegenüber der traditionellen diachronischen Sprachwissenschaft, die ihre Ergebnisse in Historischen Grammatiken, Sprachgeschichten, etymologischen und wortgeschichtlichen Darstellungen und Wörterbüchern usw. darstellt, gibt es eine neuere Ausrichtung der diachronischen Linguistik, die zur Zeit Hochkonjunktur hat. Eine vom Leerlauf und den schwindelerregenden Verfallszeiten vor allem generativer Theorieansätze frustrierte linguistische Öffentlichkeit begrüßt die Arbeit dieser 'historischen Sprachwissenschaft' heute fast durchweg als erfreuliche, neue Wertschätzung 'historischer Themen'. Dieser neueren Ausrichtung ist es sogar gelungen, eine sehr präzise arbeitende diachronische Soziolinguistik in den Hintergrund treten zu lassen (vgl. Ammon et al. (eds.) 1988: Kap. XII; vgl. auch McMahon 1994: 200–313).

Die neue 'historische Linguistik' zeigt sich in zwei eng miteinander zusammenhängenden Formen, nämlich der *Theorie des Sprachwandels* und der sogenannten *Grammatikalisierungsforschung*. Diese Ansätze öffnen sich in Richtung auf allgemein kybernetische, biologistische und vor allem kognitivistische Theoriezusammenhänge. Insgesamt dominieren diese beiden Forschungsrichtungen die aktuelle 'theoriebewußte' diachronische Diskussion. Leistung und Grenzen dieser Linguistik und ihrer Denkfiguren sollen im Blick auf die 'Historizitäts'-Frage überprüft werden.

5.2. Aspekte von Theorien des Sprachwandels

Es werden hier exemplarisch Grundgedanken besprochen, die einige der Sprachwandeltheorien kennzeichnen und die wichtige Gesichtspunkte der Gesamtdiskussion zum Ausdruck bringen (vgl. allgemein Mattheier 1984a; Labov 1994; McMahon 1994; Campbell 1998; Fritz 1998b; Haas 1998; Leiss 1998b).

Seit den 80er-Jahren gibt es das von Helmut Lüdtke entwickelte und sukzessive präzisierte Kreislaufmodell des Sprachwandels, das als „periphrasis-fusion-erosion cycle" (Croft 2000: 156–165; Hopper & Traugott 1993: 87 ff.) inzwischen auch in die angelsächsische Linguistik Eingang gefunden hat. Lüdtke beruft sich in seinem Modell ausdrücklich auf kybernetisch-homöostatische Modellvorstellungen (vgl. Lüdtke 1980a und 1980b). Rudi Keller hat dieses Kreislaufmodell in sein bekanntes Buch *Sprachwandel. Von der unsichtbaren Hand in der Sprache* (²1994) aufgenommen und die Diskussion weitergeführt:

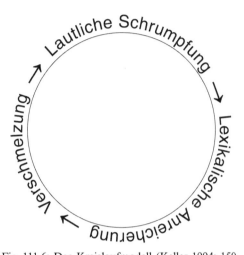

Fig. 111.6: Das Kreislaufmodell (Keller 1994: 150, nach Lüdtke 1980a und b)

Die im Kreismodell visualisierte Auffassung des Sprachwandels geht aus von lexikalisch bzw. grammatisch komplexen Konstruktionen, die dann durch Verschmelzung ihre Autonomie verlieren; die Fusionsprodukte unterliegen dann der lautlichen Reduktion:

„The result of each phase in the cycle creates the conditions for the next phase of the change [...] As erosion proceeds, the need not to be misunderstood may assert itself, and the periphrasis – fusion – erosion cycle may repeat itself for the particular function in question [...] PERIPHRASIS [...] is the recruitment of a new, periphrastic construction for a particular function" (Croft 2000: 159).

In seiner zwingenden Abfolge von Ursache und Wirkung scheint dieses Modell durch eine Vielzahl von historischen Belegen bestätigt zu sein, so beispielsweise beim 'Ersatz' des mittelfranzösischen *moult* durch *bel cop* 'guter Schlag', 'guter Schluck' (> nfrz. *beaucoup*) (vgl. Baldinger 1959). Mit der Entwicklung von lat. *multum* über altfrz. *molt* zu mfrz. *moult* [mu] läßt sich die lautliche Reduktion (*erosion*) hervorragend belegen; die Erosion läßt die Wortform sogar mit einer Reihe anderer frz. Wörter homophon werden, was die Distinktivität des Wortsignifikanten empfindlich reduziert:

frz. *moult* [mu] 'viel'
　　mou [mu] 'weich'
　　mou [mu] 'Lunge (Schlachtvieh)'
　　moue [mu] 'Schmollmund, Flunsch'
　　moût [mu] 'Most'

Bei dieser Sachlage scheint sich der 'Ersatz' von *moult* durch *bel cop* von selbst zu ergeben. Allerdings enthält eine solche, auf den ersten Blick bestechende Interpretation zwei Denkfehler: Zum einen wird eine Relationierung zweier voneinander durchaus unabhängiger Prozesse – *erosion* und *periphrasis* – vorgenommen, die die angebliche 'Kreisbewegung' ermöglichen soll: *erosion* als Bedingung für die Periphrase. Tatsächlich aber – und dies kann nur eine historische und varietätenlinguistisch gerichtete Betrachtung zeigen – ist es notwendig so, daß die 'Periphrase', die unabhängig von der 'Erosion' entstanden ist, in einer Varietät der Sprache schon vorher existiert, also eine gewisse Zeit schon eine – zuerst einmal diasystematisch markierte – 'Konkurrenzform' darstellt:

kierte' Elemente bestimmte semantisch ausgezeichnete Wortformen 'umgeben' (vgl. auch Baldinger 1958; Stefenelli 2000), läßt sich auf den grammatischen Bereich übertragen; direkt als *Trabantenkonstruktionen* können nämlich die hier zur Debatte stehenden, varietätenlinguistisch fundamentalen grammatischen Verhältnisse bezeichnet werden – *bel cop* neben *moult* oder *cantare habeo/debeo/volo, habeo ad cantare* neben *cantabo* usw. (vgl. Koch & Oesterreicher 1996: 88).

Am Beispiel des eben zitierten romanischen Futurs kann man auch den zweiten kritischen Punkt aufzeigen. Den periphrastischen Neubildungen, die mit den 'alten' synthetischen Futurformen *koexistieren*, entsprechen zunächst durchaus *funktionelle Differenzen*. Die Identifikation von Formen und Funktionen im Rahmen von Kreisläufen angeblich 'feststehender', 'gleichbleibender' grammatischer Kategorien („the periphrasis – fusion – erosion cycle may repeat itself for *the particular function in question*", Croft

lat.	afrz.	mfrz.	nfrz.
multum 'viel'	> *molt* 'viel' *bel cop* 'schöner Schlag'	> [mu] 'viel' > 'viel'	... > *beaucoup* 'viel'

Fig. 111.7: *multum, molt, moult, bel cop, beaucoup*

Der 'Kreislauf' muß also an der Stelle der Innovation und Übernahme von *bel cop* 'unterbrochen' werden, wodurch sich – wenn man denn den Prozeß graphisch veranschaulichen will – etwa das Schema in Fig. 111.8 ergibt.

Der Einwand ist keineswegs auf dieses Beispiel für einen lexikalischen Sprachwandel beschränkt (vgl. Beispiele in Blank 1997; Fritz 1998a). An den Ausgangspunkten der sog. romanischen Futurbildung des Typs *cantare habeo/debeo/volo, habeo ad cantare* usw. oder den periphrastischen Neubildungen des Typs nfrz. *je vais chanter*, span. *voy a cantar* usw. ließen sich die entsprechenden grammatischen Prozesse und Konstellationen ebenso schlagend nachweisen (vgl. Fleischman 1982; auch Beiträge in Harris & Ramat (eds.) 1987; Oesterreicher 1996a).

Wichtige Aspekte des Problems von Ursache und Wirkung bei der Ersetzung im Sprachwandel waren bereits Gegenstand einer Methodendiskussion zwischen Jules Gilliéron und Walther von Wartburg. Wartburgs suggestiver Begriff der *Trabantenwörter* (Wartburg 1943/1970: 146), die als 'mar-

2000: 159; Hervorhebung W. Oe.) erweist sich als vorschnell. Krefeld zeigt dies am Bei-

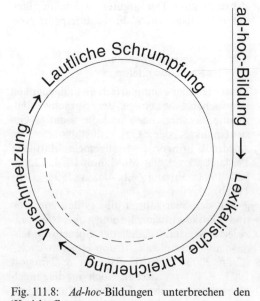

Fig. 111.8: *Ad-hoc*-Bildungen unterbrechen den 'Kreislauf'

spiel der romanischen Adverbbildung, wo eben nicht die Rede davon sein kann, daß die koexistierenden 'alten' und 'neuen' Wortformen und Konstruktionen funktionell einfach identisch sind (vgl. Krefeld 1999a; vgl. auch 5.3.).

Die Zweifel an dem Kreislaufmodell mit seiner Ursache-Wirkung-Kette bestätigen bezüglich der Entstehung der Periphrasen und der 'eindimensionalen' Annahme von funktionaler Kontinuität gerade auch solche Fälle, in denen ältere Formen nicht durch die neuen, periphrastischen Formen abgelöst werden, sondern in 'spezialisierten' Funktionen erhalten bleiben. Ältere und neuere Formen 'teilen sich' Funktionsbereiche und bilden teilweise ausgesprochen stabile Paradigmata aus. Für die romanischen Sprachen sind hier vor allem die Vergangenheitstempora zu nennen, in denen eine derartige stabile Koexistenz des synthetischen und periphrastischen Perfekts besteht (vgl. Fleischman 1983; weitere Beispiele in Oesterreicher 1996a und 1996b; auch Agard 1984, II; vgl. auch Leiss 1998b).

5.3. Das Konzept der Grammatikalisierung

Die bekannte Formulierung von Antoine Meillet, der von „le passage d'un mot autonome au rôle d'élément grammatical" (Meillet 1912: 131) spricht, ist der gern zitierte Ausgangspunkt für die Grammatikalisierungsforschung geworden. In ihr wurde eine ganze Reihe von interessanten Fragen aufgeworfen, und mit neuen Konzepten zur Analyse und Beschreibung konnte die ursprüngliche Fragestellung entscheidend vertieft und präzisiert werden. Neben der Sprachtypologie bildet sie das zweite, diachrone 'Standbein' der sogenannten Funktionalen Grammatik. Allgemein gesprochen liegt die grundlegende Fragestellung der Grammatikalisierungstheorie vor allem in der Aufdeckung der *kognitiven und kommunikativ-semiotischen* Grundlagen von Sprachsystemen, die sich gerade auch in Prozessen des Sprachwandels ausprägen (→ Art. 1, § 5.3; → Art. 113; vgl. vor allem Lehmann 1985 und 1995; Sweetser 1988; Traugott 1988 und 1995; Haspelmath 1990 und 1998; Heine et al. 1991; Traugott & König 1991; Hopper & Traugott 1993; Stolz 1994; Bybee et al. 1994; Diewald 1997; Langacker 1999; Lang & Neumann-Holzschuh (eds.) 1999).

Die oben skizzierte Modellierung des Sprachwandels berührt sich naturgemäß eng mit Grundannahmen der sogenannten Grammatikalisierungsforschung, die den Prozeß der Innovation beim grammatischen Wandel mit Hilfe einer Reihe von lautlichen, prosodischen, morphologischen, syntaktischen und 'funktionalen' Parametern beschreibt. Für die Grammatikalisierungsprozesse ergibt sich vor allem durch die systematische Berücksichtigung der paradigmatischen und syntagmatischen Bezüge der in Frage stehenden sprachlichen Elemente eine komplexe und sehr präzise Klassifikation und Bestimmung der Verlaufsform der Prozesse.

Die Dimensionen der Grammatikalisierung, die von Christian Lehmann ebenfalls schon in den frühen 80er Jahren zusammengestellt wurden und weithin Zustimmung gefunden haben (Lehmann 1982/1995 und 1985), lassen sich in einem Schema folgendermaßen veranschaulichen:

	paradigmatic	syntagmatic
weight	integrity	structural scope
cohesion	paradigmaticity	bondedness
variability	paradigmatic variability	syntagmatic variability

Fig. 111.9: Grammatikalisierungsparameter (nach Lehmann 1995: 123)

Jeder dieser sechs Dimensionen können zusammen mit dem ihr zugehörigen 'Prozeß' genauer die folgenden, den Kriterien 'schwach' bis 'stark grammatikalisiert' entsprechenden Parameterwerte zugeordnet werden (vgl. auch die Referate in McMahon 1994: 160−173 und Croft 2000: 156−165; siehe Fig. 111.10, S. 1580).

Die vorgeschlagenen Korrelationen können an der schon erwähnten romanischen Adverbbildung veranschaulicht werden (vgl. Krefeld 1999a: 113−119). Bekannt ist die beträchtliche Polymorphie der Ableitungsmuster der Adverb-Kategorie im Lateinischen (vgl. die Typen *recte, cito; breviter; funditus* 'von Grund auf'; *statim, ordinatim, olim; multum, tantum, quantum; plus, magis* usw.). Die bis auf das Kriterium 'obligatorification' maximal grammatikalisierten Adverbialmarker besitzen eine nur minimale Bildungstransparenz. Im Laufe des auch typologisch massiven Wandels des Lateinischen zu den romanischen Sprachen sind alle diese Ableitungsprogramme geschwunden. Schon im Latein Ver-

parameter	weak grammaticalization	process	strong grammaticalization
integrity	bundle of semantic features; possibly polysyllabic	attrition →	few semantic features oligo- or monosegmental
paradigmaticity	item participates loosely in semantic fields	paradigmaticization →	small, tightly integrated paradigm
paradigmatic variability	free choice of items according to communicative intentions	obligatorification →	choice systematically constrained, use largely obligatory
structural scope	item relates to constituent of arbitrary complexity	condensation →	item modifies word or stem
bondedness	item is independently juxtaposed	coalescence →	item is affix or even phonological feature of carrier
syntagmatic variability	item can be shifted around freely	fixation →	item occupies fixed slot

Fig. 111.10: Korrelation der Grammatikalisierungsparameter (nach Lehmann 1995: 164)

gils, dann auch bei Cicero usw. finden sich Kollokationen des Typs *furiata mente – simulata mente – percussa mente – tota mente – sana mente*, aus denen schließlich ein Adverbial-Konstruktionstyp entsteht, der über Fügungsfreiheiten und Zwischenstufen (die teilweise noch heute in der Iberoromania existieren) schließlich zur Affixkonstruktion wurde.

Wie schon beim Kreislaufmodell des Sprachwandels wird bei diesem Gesamtprozeß in der Regel Kategorienkonstanz vorausgesetzt (vgl. etwa Hopper & Traugott 1993: 130 ff.). Differenzierter interpretiert hier Lehmann. Er spricht einerseits von dem für den Grammatikalisierungsprozeß entscheidenden Aspekt der *innovation*; er betrifft die Frage der Funktionalisierung von ursprünglich freien Konstruktionen, etwa *clara mente*, für einen bestimmten grammatisch-kategorialen Zusammenhang; dieser manifestiert sich dann etwa in den romanischen Adverbien frz. *clairement*, span. *claramente*, ital. *chiaramente* (vgl. Lehmann 1995: 20). In einer ganz anderen Perspektivierung, Lehmann spricht von *renovation*, rückt ein ital. *chiaramente* in einen funktionellen Zusammenhang ein, der im Lateinischen durch *clare* zum Ausdruck kommt. Anders ausgedrückt: *chiaramente* setzt zwar *clara mente* fort, es entspricht aber funktionell einem lat. *clare*. Allein die Lehmannsche *innovation* betrifft dabei die am skizzierten Grammatikalisierungsvorgang beteiligten Elemente.

Mit dieser wichtigen Unterscheidung läßt sich im Prinzip die Koexistenz *und* funktionelle Nicht-Identität der älteren und neueren Formen (vgl. 5.2.) postulieren und, davon unabhängig, der Grammatikalisierungsvorgang beschreiben.

Neuerdings wird von verschiedener Seite kritisiert, daß der Grammatikalisierungsprozeß aber letztlich zu 'unsemantisch' konzipiert und zu abstrakt allein auf kategoriale Veränderungen bezogen ist (vgl. Detges 1999). Dies wird belegt mit den 'klassischen' Beispielen, bei denen die abstrakten funktional-kategorialen Veränderungen im Mittelpunkt des Interesses stehen (vgl. etwa die Liste aus Haspelmath 1998: 157):

a. full verb > auxiliary > tense/aspect/mood affix
b. verb > adposition
c. noun > adposition
d. adposition > case affix
e. adposition > subordinator
f. emphatic personal pronoun > clitic pronoun > agreement affix
g. cleft sentence marker > highlighter
h. noun > classifier
i. verb > classifier
j. demonstrative > article > gender/class marker

k. demonstrative or article > complementizer or relativizer
l. collective noun > plural affix
m. numeral 'one' > indefinite article
n. numerals 'two' or 'three' > dual/paucal/plural number affix

Die dabei zwar häufig beschriebenen semantischen Veränderungen, die diesen grammatischen Wandelprozessen zugrunde liegen, werden in der Tat jeweils nur sehr abstrakt thematisch. Vor allem bleiben bei der qualitativen Beschreibung des Wandels, ganz unabhängig von den angedeuteten morphosyntaktischen oder semantischen Gewichtungen, Fragen offen.

In der Regel wird Grammatikalisierung nämlich als *kontinuierlicher Prozeß* aufgefaßt: kontinuierlicher Verlust von Eigengewicht bei Morphemen, kontinuierlicher Verlust von spezifischen Bedeutungsaspekten (*bleaching*) bzw. kontinuierlicher Übergang von einem Bedeutungsbereich zu einem anderen, etwa von 'Modalität' zu Zeitdeixis, von 'Raum' zu Zeitdeixis, von 'Zeit' zu 'Kausalität' oder 'Konditionalität', von räumlichen Beziehungen zu Partizipationsbeziehungen, von 'Quantität' zu 'Definitheit' usw. (vgl. Sweetser 1988; Detges 1999). Die Grammatikalisierungsforschung bemüht sich dabei jeweils um die Ermittlung der *universellen* „Kanäle" (Lehmann 1995: 24 ff.) oder „Pfade" (Bybee et al. 1994: 14 ff.), auf denen sich grammatische Morpheme, Kategorien oder Paradigmen aus meist lexikalischen Ausgangsformen bilden (vgl. auch Croft 1995). Beliebt ist auch die 'Methode' der 'Kartierung' semantischer Felder (*semantic mapping*), mit der sich der Prozeß der Grammatikalisierung als metonymischer Übergang von einem Bereich zu einem benachbarten darstellen läßt, und die in idealer Weise den kognitivistischen Interessen der Grammatikalisierungsforschung entgegenkommt (zu den kognitivistischen, auch prototypikalitätstheoretischen Grundlagen, vgl. Lakoff 1987; Langacker 1991; Taylor 1995; Raible 1996a und 1996b; Geeraerts 1997; Lakoff & Johnson 1999; zurückhaltend Rastier 1997 und 1999; auch Coseriu 1990).

So wichtig die angesprochenen Aspekte auch sind, sie vermögen die *Motivation* für die Entstehung der betrachteten sprachlichen Prozesse nicht eigentlich plausibel zu machen. Ein ähnlicher Vorwurf wird neuerdings auch gegen die im Kontext der Grammatikalisierungsforschung entstandenen Studien zur sogenannten Reanalyse erhoben. Diese wird von Ronald W. Langacker ja definiert als „change in the structure of an expression or class of expressions that does not involve any immediate or intrinsic modification of its surface manifestation" (Langacker 1977: 58; vgl. Lang & Neumann-Holzschuh 1999).

Es ist hier nicht der Ort, die Diskussion um Grammatikalisierung und Reanalyse nachzuzeichnen (vgl. Beiträge in Lang & Neumann-Holzschuh (eds.) 1999; vgl. auch Giacalone Ramat & Hopper (eds.) 1998). Hingewiesen werden muß jedoch auf die Tatsache, daß die angedeutete fast ausschließlich morphologisch-syntaktische und funktional-kategoriale Perspektivierung der skizzierten Prozesse inzwischen Konkurrenz durch Arbeiten bekommen hat, die ausdrücklich semantisch-pragmatische Motivationen für diese Prozesse in Betracht ziehen.

Diese 'Umwertung', die an der Reanalyse angedeutet werden soll, stellt mit guten Argumenten zwei Grundpositionen der gängigen Reanalyse-Forschung (vgl. Haspelmath 1998) in Frage: Erstens, Reanalyse setzt nicht eine syntaktische Ambiguität der Ausgangsstruktur voraus, sondern diese Ambiguität ist schon Resultat einer 'neuen' semantisch-pragmatischen Interpretation der gegebenen Grundstruktur; die „Semantik der neuen Struktur [ist] in der alten schon angelegt", die neue Lesart „aktiviert ein in der alten angelegtes Inferenzpotential" (Waltereit 1999: 21). Zweitens wird damit gleichzeitig die gängige Behauptung *ad absurdum* geführt, daß Reanalysen Folge von spracherwerbbezogenen 'Übertragungsfehlern', sogenannten *misacquisitions*, sind; Reanalysen werden vielmehr als hörerseitige Neuerungen faßbar, deren kommunikativer Wert unbestreitbar ist.

Die neuen Lesarten sind zuerst einmal 'nur' Inferenzen (vgl. Caron 1983: passim; Brown & Yule 1983: bes. Kap. 2 und 7; Sperber & Wilson 1986: 65−117); der diesen Prozessen zugrundeliegende semantische Mechanismus beruht auf 'Weltwissen', genauer: auf Kontiguitätsrelationen zwischen Sachverhalten. Kontiguitäten sind manifest in Erfahrungs- und Handlungszusammenhängen, die die kognitive Semantik diskutiert unter Bezeichnungen wie *frames* und *scripts*, auch 'Szenarien', 'Schemata' und 'mentale Modelle' (vgl. Brown & Yule 1983: 236−256). Wie der Ausdruck 'sachliche Nähe' schon zeigt, gibt es hierbei Grade der Erwartbarkeit, die jeweils plausibilisiert und deren lexikalische *und* grammatische Konsequenzen genau zu bestimmen sind.

Dies bedeutet, daß es dieser Position außerdem gelingt, Grammatik *und* Lexikon zusammen in den Blick zu nehmen (vgl. Waltereit 1999: bes. 25—27; Blank 1997: 119— 125; vgl. auch Fritz 1998b).

Diese Interpretationen, die den Innovationsprozeß von rein strukturellen und kategorialen auf semantisch-pragmatische kognitive Prozesse verschieben, ließen sich gerade auch auf die Lehmannsche *renovation* übertragen. Die beschriebenen Positionen bieten nämlich auch für das sprachwandeltheoretisch zentrale Problem der *Usualisierung*, also der *Übernahme und Verbreitung von Innovationen*, durch die grundsätzliche *frame*-Orientierung überzeugende sprach- und kommunikationstheoretische Argumente (vgl. 5.4.).

Wichtig ist aber auch der *qualitative Wechsel*, der mit dem skizzierten Funktionswandel einhergeht. Grammatikalisierung, also das Entstehen einer grammatischen Kategorie, eines grammatischen Morphemparadigmas oder einer grammatischen Regel im Sinne der Lehmannschen *innovation*, stellt nämlich immer einen *Wechsel in der Natur der beteiligten Kategorien*, somit eine echte *Diskontinuität*, einen *Ebenensprung* dar.

Um noch einmal das Beispiel des *romanischen Futurs* zu bemühen: Wenn sich eine modale Periphrase zur temporalen Endung grammatikalisiert, so ist dies nicht nur einfach der Wechsel zwischen zwei 'benachbarten', also *kontingenten semantischen Konzepten*. Es handelt sich dabei *auch* um den Übergang von der Ebene *pragmatisch-interaktionaler Kategorien* zu einer Ebene rein *zeitlogischer Kategorien*. Ähnliches ist etwa bei der *Satzgliedstellung* zu beobachten, deren Regularitäten etwa im Französischen — anders als im Lateinischen oder in romanischen Nachbarsprachen — von einer ursprünglich *diskurspragmatischen Funktion* (Markierung von Thema und Rhema) auf die *Ebene der Syntax im engeren Sinne* (Markierung von Subjekt und direktem Objekt) 'verschoben' wurden (vgl. Bossong 1982).

Die Frage des Ebenenwechsels ist in der Grammatikalisierungsforschung durchaus diskutiert worden, zumeist unter der einprägsamen, jedoch zu einfachen Formel „from discourse to syntax" (vgl. vor allem Givón 1979). Vor allem die Vieldeutigkeit des Ausdrucks 'Pragmatik' hat aber die Diskussion dieser Übergänge massiv verunklart — bis hin zum polemisch formulierten Gegenpostulat der 'Pragmatik' als Endpunkt der grammatischen Entwicklung (vgl. die Diskussion in Heine et al. 1991: Kap. 8; Traugott & König 1991; Langacker 1999; vgl. auch Sweetser 1990). In diesem Sachbereich besteht weiter entschieden Klärungsbedarf. Ähnlich unscharf und uneinheitlich ist übrigens auch das Konzept der *subjectification*, mit dem der qualitative Wandel in der Natur der Kategorien beschrieben werden soll (vgl. zuletzt Langacker 1999; Traugott 1999).

5.4. Innovationen und der historische Ort des Sprachwandels

Wie schon im Zusammenhang mit der Besprechung der Entstehung und der Funktionen von Periphrasen und Trabantenwörtern/ -konstruktionen angedeutet wurde, leidet die gängige Grammatikalisierungsforschung an einer Nichtberücksichtigung beziehungsweise an einer zu stark homogenisierenden Sicht und Darstellung sprachexterner Aspekte des grammatischen Wandels, die sich letztlich aus ihrer *universalistischen Interessenorientierung* herleitet. Diese 'Ferne' zur Ebene der historischen Sprachtechniken zeigt sich vor allem an der Tatsache, daß die Kategorien *Diskurstradition*, *Varietätenraum* und *Kommunikationsraum* ignoriert werden und sprachgeschichtliche Zusammenhänge völlig ausgeblendet sind (vgl. 2.3., 3.2. und 3.3.; vgl. auch Leiss 1998a; Oesterreicher 2001a).

Die Grammatikalisierungstheorie geht also bis heute von einem weitgehend eindimensionalen Sprachbegriff aus; die entscheidende Rolle des Nebeneinanders verschiedener *Sprachvarietäten* und *Diskurstraditionen* bzw. *Kommunikationsmodi* wird nicht berücksichtigt. Dies ist insofern erstaunlich, als eine varietätenlinguistische Sicht schon angelegt ist in zwei stillschweigenden Grundannahmen, von denen nicht nur in der traditionellen Sprachwandelforschung ganz selbstverständlich ausgegangen wird: Einmal wird ja gerne hervorgehoben, daß die *gesprochene Sprache* der wichtigste Bereich sprachlicher Innovation, ja der 'Motor' der Sprachentwicklung sei (vgl. Frei 1929/1971: 31 ff.; Harris 1978: 15; Hock 1991: 466f.; kritisch Gadet 1998a und Koch & Oesterreicher 1996). Zweitens ist evident, daß auch der mit der Entwicklung zur Schriftsprache jeweils gegebene *Ausbauprozeß* mit Notwendigkeit grammatische Veränderungen besonders stark und signifikant befördert (vgl. Kloss 1978; Raible 1992a und

1998; Koch & Oesterreicher 1994; Beiträge in Jacob & Kabatek (eds.) 2001).

Bezüglich der Ausbauproblematik gibt es immerhin eine Reihe von einschlägigen Arbeiten, die sich mit der Entwicklung von 'Grammatik' im Prozeß der Verschriftlichung, gerade auch von Kreolsprachen, beschäftigen (vgl. etwa Michaelis 1994; Ludwig 1996; Kriegel 1996; auch Raible 1992a). Bisher ausgesprochen wenig entwickelt ist das Problem der Rolle des *Sprachkontakts* beim grammatischen Wandel (vgl. immerhin einzelne Beiträge in Fisiak 1995).

Alle diese kritischen Punkte erfordern nicht nur eine überzeugendere sprachtheoretische Fundierung, insbesondere im Bereich der kommunikativ-verstehenstheoretischen Aspekte, sondern vor allem eine Verbesserung der 'empirischen Methodik': Sprachliche Formen müssen in *Texten* aufgesucht werden (vgl. 3.4.); auch in der Grammatikalisierungsforschung müssen die beschriebenen Formen von der *Diskurspragmatik* der jeweiligen Textsorten her interpretiert werden (vgl. 3.4.; vgl. allgemein Ehlich 1991).

Gerade wenn man den mit dem Universale 'Kreativität' umrissenen Problembereich reflexiver sprachlicher Vermittlungsleistungen ins Auge faßt und sodann den im Universale 'Alterität' zentrierten interaktiv-kommunikativen Bereich fokussiert, der mit den – von der Grammatikalisierungsforschung ignorierten – varietäten- und kontaktlinguistischen, diskurstraditionellen und diskurspragmatischen Fragestellungen angesprochen wurde, sind sprachtheoretisch zwei Prozesse sichtbar, die wiederum Coseriu (schon 1953) klar zum Ausdruck gebracht hat. Das folgende Zitat bezeichnet genau den Punkt, an dem in einer historischen Einzelsprache, genauer: in einer ihrer Varietäten – also nicht nur in einem bloß individuellen Diskurs oder Text – etwas Neues entsteht, nämlich *Sprachwandel* geschieht; Coseriu betont zu Recht:

„El *cambio lingüístico* ('cambio en la lengua') es la difusión o generalización de una innovación, o sea, necesariamente, una serie de adopciones sucesivas. Es decir que, en último análisis, todo cambio es originariamente una adopción" (Coseriu 1973, 79 f.).

Ausgehend von dieser wichtigen Feststellung, die den Unterschied zwischen *Innovation/Neuerung/Schöpfung* usw. und *Sprachwandel/Übernahme/Verbreitung/Adoption* usw. markiert, kann überhaupt erst die varietäten- und diskurslinguistisch entscheidende Fragestellung diskutiert werden. Sie macht im Vergleich auch noch einmal deutlich, inwiefern weite Teile der aktuellen diachronischen Linguistik dieser Unterscheidung nicht die notwendige Beachtung schenken und an einem so verstandenen Sprachwandel überraschenderweise auch nicht interessiert sind; diese Richtungen fokussieren in einer universalistischen, kognitivistisch-motivationalen Interessenorientierung gerade den Problemkomplex der Innovation in einer klar sprechtätigkeitsbezogenen Perspektivierung: Das Interesse dieser Forschung gilt mithin fast ausschließlich den sprachlichen Neuerungen zugrundeliegenden abstrakten Motivationen und von den Sprechern jeweils eingesetzten universellen kognitiven Strategien und ihren sprachlichen Resultaten, wobei sowohl der lexikalische Bereich als auch der Bereich der Grammatik auf diese Weise behandelt werden (vgl. → Art. 112 und 113; auch Art. 85 und 86).

Wenn man die Coseriusche Feststellung ernst nimmt, dann ist zuerst einmal der Begriff der *Innovation* zu radikalisieren. Er muß nämlich *alle* auf reflexiven Sprachvollzügen beruhenden Formen der in Diskursen wahrnehmbaren Neuerungen oder *ad-hoc*-Formulierungen erfassen. Als Innovationen sind damit aber nicht nur *im Diskurs/Text* erscheinende, mehr oder minder gewagte Schöpfungen oder dort vorgenommene ausdrucks- oder inhaltsbezogene *Veränderungen* gegebener einzelsprachlicher Elemente und Einheiten anzusprechen (Laute, Grammeme und Lexeme sowie komplexe Sprachzeichenbildungen), sondern eben auch die Verwendung eines normalerweise in einer bestimmten Varietät und in bestimmten diskursiven Kontexten existierenden Elements in einem neuen Kontext wie auch der nur kontaktlinguistisch zu beschreibende Einsatz 'fremdsprachlicher' Elemente oder Konstruktionstypen in der Formulierungsaufgabe des konkreten Verbalisierungsvorgangs. Mit diesen Innovationen, die selbstverständlich ganz unterschiedlich motiviert sein können, werden *pragmatische Äußerungsabsichten* mit Hilfe der Sprache von den Sprechern ad hoc realisiert. *Es geht den Sprechern dabei gerade nicht darum, die Sprache zu verändern, einen Sprachwandel zu induzieren.* Tatsache ist auch, daß wohl die allermeisten Innovationen *keine* Chance haben, in die Sprache 'übernommen' zu werden, und das heißt, einen *Sprachwandel* zu bewirken.

Erst in einem zweiten Schritt geht es also um die *Generalisierung* von Innovationen, also um die Tatsache, daß diese sich aus ihren *ad-hoc*-Kontexten und ihrer *ad-hoc*-Verwendung lösen und – in der Regel natürlich zunächst kleinräumig und sprechergruppen-, varietäten- und textsortenbezogen – zu *Sprachregeln* werden. Dieser Schritt, also das, was man auch *Übernahme* nennt, ist entscheidend: Hier erst geschieht *Sprachwandel*.

Der Analyse und Beschreibung dieser *Übernahmen*, seien sie bezogen auf Neuschöpfungen, Markierungsveränderungen oder Entlehnungen, ist bislang allein in der diachronischen Soziolinguistik die nötige Aufmerksamkeit geschenkt worden ('klassisch' ist Labov 1975; vgl. auch die Übersichten in McMahon 1994: 200–313; auch Ammon et al. (eds.) 1988: Kap. XII). In diesem Kontext wichtig sind auch die allerdings mit anderer Interessenorientierung entwickelten, nämlich Bewußtheit und Wahrnehmung von Wandel betreffenden Labovschen soziolinguistischen Konzepte *change from above* und *change from below*, die sich aber indirekt auch auf die Veränderungen im Varietätenraum einer Sprache und damit verbundene Markierungsschübe beziehen lassen (vgl. Labov 1994: bes. 78, 155–158). Die in soziolinguistischen Arbeiten eingesetzten Instrumente können jedoch insofern nicht immer überzeugen, als in der Regel zu stark auf sprachexterne Kriterien und Parametrisierungen rekurriert wird. Die Diskussion der diskurstraditionellen Zusammenhänge sowie der diesen affinen Varietäten mit ihrem jeweiligen historischen Innovationspotential und mit der sie kennzeichnenden 'Übernahme-Bereitschaft' kommt dabei meist zu kurz (vgl. Koch & Oesterreicher 1996).

Es reicht also nicht aus, einfach den strukturellen Bildungstyp und die semantisch-kognitiven 'Bahnen des Wandels' nachzuzeichnen und dann das leicht nachprüfbare Resultat, also die Existenz einer Form und Funktion in einer Varietät oder Sprache als 'Beleg' für Sprachwandel anzuführen. Historische Erkenntnis muß in jedem Fall nach dem Ort und dem Zeitpunkt der Übernahme von Innovationen und Veränderungen in einem Idiom fragen, sie muß also den *konkreten Zeitkern* von sprachlichen Erscheinungen freilegen. Dieser Zeitkern ist ein theoretisches Konzept, das nichts mit der Suche nach Erstbelegen zu tun hat, sondern mit der Zuordnung solcher Erscheinungen zu Sprachtechniken und mit ihrer Einordnung in Diskurstraditionen (vgl. 2.4. und 3.4. bzw. 2.3. und 3.2. und 3.3.).

An einem einfachen Beispieltyp, der gerne und ausführlich in der Grammatikalisierungsforschung besprochen wird, sei dieser Problemkomplex veranschaulicht. Es geht um einen 'klassischen' Grammatikalisierungspfad – die Entstehung von Präpositionen und Konjunktionen aus Partizipien (vgl. Kortmann 1997).

Für das Französische wird hier gerne *pendant* 'während' angeführt, das sich in der Tat vom Vollverb mit seinem Partizip über die Adjektivstufe zum grammatischen Element, zur Präposition entwickelt hat (vgl. König & Kortmann 1992). Kurt Baldinger (1993: 6) macht jedoch mit Recht darauf aufmerksam, daß eine derartige Feststellung, die die universalistischen und kognitivistischen Interessen einer bestimmten diachronischen Linguistik 'bedient', zwar nicht 'falsch', aber eben ungenügend ist. Die *historische Erkenntnis* dieses Sprachwandels muß nämlich auch Hinweise darauf enthalten, daß hier ein absolutes Partizip nach lateinisch-juristischem Vorbild (*pendens*) in Fügungen wie *le siège pendant, le temps pendant* usw. – gerade nicht zufällig – im 14. Jahrhundert in die französische 'Gemeinsprache' übernommen wird. „Im Falle *pendant* hätten wir es mit einem Übergang von der (juristischen) Fachsprache in die Allgemeinsprache zu tun." Und weiter: „Nur die Sprachhistoriker können übrigens (in diesem Fall) diesen Sachverhalt historisch aufdecken" (Baldinger 1993: 6; vgl. auch Reichmann 1998; weitere Beispiele → Art. 45, § 3.2.3. und § 6).

Das Beispiel kann uns zeigen, was Sprachwandel als historisches Phänomen *nicht* ist. Er unterscheidet sich von bloß diskursrelevanter Innovation oder Veränderung; andererseits ist Sprachwandel mehr, als in den abstrakten, ort- und zeitlosen Kreislauf-, Grammatikalisierungs- und Reanalyse-Modellen dargestellt ist. Die Überlegungen zeigen:

Sprachwandel kann sinnvoll allein radikal historisch, also diskursbezogen varietätenlinguistisch und kontaktlinguistisch konzipiert werden. Kognitivistisch-grammatikalisierungstheoretisch dimensionierte Erklärungsmuster sind in ihrer Ort- und Zeitlosigkeit deshalb nur bedingt brauchbar, weil Sprachwandel auch nicht ohne 'echte', das heißt von *sprechenden Subjekten produzierte Diskurse* konzipiert werden kann, von denen ausgehend historische Erkenntnis des Sprachlichen allein gewonnen werden kann (vgl. Oesterreicher 2001a; auch Steger 1998; Schank 1984).

Bei aller Kritik an den Schwachpunkten der beschriebenen Sprachwandeltheorien und Grammatikalisierungsmodellierungen kappt ein sprachtheoretisch fundierter linguistischer Begriff des Sprachwandels keineswegs die Bezüge zu den angesprochenen kognitionswissenschaftlichen und grammatikalisierungstheoretischen Fragestellungen. Denn diese müssen und können als wertvolle Konzeptualisierungen, die universelle Aspekte des Sprachlichen modellieren, in jedem Falle in die linguistische Betrachtung einbezogen werden – allerdings immer mit der Maßgabe, daß sie sich einer historischen Konkretisierung und Komplettierung öffnen.

6. Historizität als Herausforderung

Historizität ist nicht mit Diachronie zu identifizieren, und die verschiedenen Aspekte des Sprachlichen, die unterschieden wurden, sind natürlich nicht deshalb so strikt getrennt worden, um das Phänomen Sprache 'aufzulösen'. Ganz im Gegenteil: Die analytische Scheidung der Aspekte in einer sprachtheoretisch verantworteten Gesamtperspektivierung kann im Rahmen der Linguistik die Berechtigung der Vielfalt von Forschungsbemühungen verdeutlichen und diese miteinander in Bezug setzen. Dadurch erhält, erstens, die sprachwissenschaftliche Forschung in dem Sinne neue Impulse, daß die unterschiedlichen, sich ergänzenden linguistischen Ansätze in ihrer Komplementarität erkannt werden. Zum zweiten geht es auch darum, die spezifische Stellung der Linguistik und ihre Anschlußflächen im interdisziplinären Konzert der Sprachforschung zu klären. Die *Bedeutung* und *Strahlkraft des Gesamtphänomens 'menschliche Sprache'* kann nur dadurch wirklich erfaßt werden, daß – um mit Wilhelm von Humboldt zu sprechen – einmal die tätigkeitsbezogenen Aspekte der Sprache des Menschengeschlechts, sodann die historischen Sprachen und Diskurstraditionen sowie schließlich die individuellen sprachlichen Kommunikationsakte als eine *große Einheit* in den Blick rücken. Dabei sind die anvisierten *sciences du langage* aber keinesfalls als die 'indische Nacht' zu verstehen, in der alle Kühe schwarz sind; die Aufgabe der *sciences du langage* ist es gerade, in einer rationalen Rekonstruktion, die Verschiedenheit der Aspekte in ihrer Einheit herauszustellen.

Wenn man nun die Präsenz der skizzierten Fragestellungen – gerade was das Konzept der Historizität angeht – in der linguistischen Forschung überprüft, so stellt man eine erstaunliche Koinzidenz fest.

Dabei geht es gerade nicht um die mathematisch-logisch oder anders formallinguistisch zugerichtete linguistische Forschung. Gemeint ist vielmehr der massive 'Auszug' der Forschung aus dem historischen Zentralbereich linguistischer Erkenntnisinteressen: Forschungsbemühungen auf der *universellen* und der *aktuellen* Ebene des Sprachlichen haben nämlich gerade mit solchen Themen Hochkonjunktur, die an sich historisch konstituierte Gegenstände und historisch gerichtete Fragen betreffen.

Diese Feststellung ist kein Vorwurf an die Adresse qualifizierter Diskursanalysen in pragmatischer Absicht oder der attraktiven, erfolg- und ertragreichen Forschungsfelder 'Typologie' und 'Universalienforschung'; diese Forschungsfelder sind sprachtheoretisch und wissenschaftssystematisch natürlich grundsätzlich notwendig. Andererseits muß man aber einräumen, daß auch Sprachtypologie und Universalienforschung – dies ist wohl deutlich geworden – nicht ganz unschuldig sind an der Schwächung und Abwertung des Historischen in der aktuellen Sprachwissenschaft. Und dies einfach deshalb, weil beide Richtungen es versäumt haben, ihre Standorte sprachtheoretisch und wissenschaftssystematisch zu reflektieren und diejenigen Fragestellungen herauszuarbeiten und zu valorisieren, bei denen ihre Forschung mit der historischen Ebene und ihren Problemkomplexen in Kontakt steht.

Gerade diejenigen Fragestellungen, die neben den wichtigen soziolinguistischen Ansätzen die deutlichsten Anschlußflächen zur konkreten Historizität der Sprache und des Sprachlichen aufweisen, also etwa die Grammatikalisierungs- und Reanalyse-Forschung oder die Sprachwandeltheorien, sind inzwischen aus dem historischen Kernbereich der Sprachwissenschaft 'ausgewandert'; sie haben auch ihre Herkunft und die sie fundierenden Zusammenhänge erfolgreich verdrängt. Dies zeigen vor allem die von diesen Richtungen akzeptierten Leitwissenschaften Biologie, Kybernetik, 'Kognitionswissenschaft'. Forschungsrichtungen, deren Anliegen es gerade *auch* sein müßte, *historische Formen des Sprachwandels universalistisch zu fundamentieren und für linguistische Untersuchungen historisch verortete Diskurse fruchtbar zu machen*, zeigen sich an wirklich historischen Fragestellungen uninteressiert; beide begnügen sich leichtfertig und unreflektiert mit *Surrogaten der Historizität des Sprachlichen.*

Daß dieses durchaus nicht so sein muß, zeigen aus dem Bereich der kognitionswissenschaftlich orientierten Linguistik etwa bestimmte Arbeiten von Elizabeth Closs Traugott (1999), Louis Goossens (1999) und anderen, in denen die historische Textbasis *nicht* aufgegeben ist und die jeweils interessierenden Phänomene ausgehend von Texten und Corpora historisch verankert werden.

Es ist sicherlich nicht zufällig (vgl. Heger 1989a; Oesterreicher & Raible 1993; Jacob 2002), daß Versuche, die modernen kognitionswissenschaftlichen, typologischen und empirisch-universalistischen Forschungsansätze mit sprachhistorischen und sogar mit sprachgeschichtlichen Fragestellungen zu verbinden, besonders in der Romanistik verbreitet und ertragreich sind (vgl. vor allem Baldinger 1993; Bossong 1982; Blank 1997; Blank & Koch (eds.) 1999; Detges 1999; Fleischman 1982, 1983 und 1991; Harris 1978; Heger 1989a; Jacob 1994 und 1995; Jacob & Kabatek 2001; Koch 1995b, 1997b und 2001; Koch & Oesterreicher 1996; Krefeld 1999a und 1999b; Lang & Neumann-Holzschuh (eds.) 1999; Ludwig 1996; Lüdtke 1964, 1999a, 1999b und 2001; Mair 1992; Raible (ed.) 1989, 1992a und 1992b; Schmidt-Riese 1998; Selig 1992; Stark 1999; Stehl (ed.) 2001; Waltereit 1998 und 1999; Wanner 1987). Dies liegt nicht zuletzt auch an der Tatsache, daß den Romanisten teilweise ganz hervorragende Materialien zur Verfügung stehen, die von der 'klassischen' Historischen Grammatik und Etymologie – teilweise von 'Altmeistern' – erarbeitet wurden.

In diesen Kontext gehören auch die Bemühungen der Tübinger Arbeitsgruppe *Dictionnaire étymologique et cognitif des langues romanes* (DECOLAR), die im Grunde einer häufig als anekdotisch und intuitivistisch kritisierten etymologischen Forschung eine Art universalistische Fundamentierung geben: Es soll ein Typ traditioneller historischer Erkenntnis derart neu bestimmt werden, daß er auch den Ansprüchen einer modernen linguistischen Theorie- und Methodendiskussion genügen kann (vgl. Blank et al. 2000; auch Koch 1997b und 2001).

Die beschriebene Abwendung vom Historischen ist auch deshalb inakzeptabel, weil die skizzierten Forschungsrichtungen, die alle ihre relative Berechtigung haben, sich bezüglich ihres theoretischen Status dezisionistisch abschirmen, diesen also weder wissenschaftstheoretisch und wissenschaftssystematisch noch sprachtheoretisch in Frage stellen. Andere historische Forschungen und ihre Interessenorientierungen werden nicht wahrgenommen und in dogmatischer Überheblichkeit kurzerhand mit dem durchaus auch existierenden reinen Sammeln von sprachlichen Daten einer überkommenen diachronischen Forschung identifiziert.

Es ist nicht ganz falsch, von einem – ich will hier das harte Wort gebrauchen – Erkenntnisverzicht im Bereich zentraler linguistischer Forschungsziele zu sprechen. Dieser Vorwurf ist keine wohlfeile Wissenschafts- oder Kulturkritik. Denn immerhin sei bedacht, daß von den kritisierten Forschungsansätzen die Prinzipien historischen Denkens *und* die Problemstellungen historischen Forschens beiseite gelassen werden.

Wohlgemerkt, es geht nicht um die heutige *Form der Disziplin Sprachwissenschaft*, also diejenige, die wir seit langem kennen. Sie ist als historisches Phänomen selbst dem Wandel unterworfen, und es ist sicher möglich, die Sprachbetrachtung im Sinne des französischen Begriffs der *sciences du langage*, also einer *umfassenden Sprachforschung*, zu transformieren (vgl. 1.3.; vgl. Auroux 1989: 13 f.). Trotzdem muß klargestellt werden, daß auch in einem derartigen, sicherlich institutionell und forschungsstrategisch neu ausgerichteten Disziplinenverbund die Berechtigung und Notwendigkeit historischen Fragens und historischer Erkenntnis *neben* anderen Forschungsinteressen gerechtfertigt bleibt – und dies *nicht* aus Nostalgie oder Wissenschaftskonservatismus, sondern weil es *Gegenstandskonstitution und Seinsweise des Phänomens 'menschliche Sprache'* erfordern.

7. Zitierte Literatur

Agard, Frederick B. 1984. *A Course in Romance Linguistics*. 2 vols. Washington, D. C.: Georgetown University Press.

Albrecht, Jörn. ²2000. *Europäischer Strukturalismus: ein forschungsgeschichtlicher Überblick*. (UTB, 1487.) Tübingen: Francke.

Albrecht, Jörn & Lüdtke, Jens & Thun, Harald. (eds.) 1988. *Energeia und Ergon. Sprachliche Variation, Sprachgeschichte, Sprachtypologie. Studia in honorem Eugenio Coseriu*. 3 vols. Tübingen: Narr.

Ammon, Ulrich & Dittmar, Norbert & Mattheier, Klaus J. (eds.) 1987/1988. *Sociolinguistics/Soziolinguistik. An International Handbook of the Science of Language and Society/Ein internationales Handbuch zur Wissenschaft von Sprache und Gesellschaft.*

2 vols. (HSK, 3.1. und 3.2.) Berlin & New York: de Gruyter.

Ammon, Ulrich & Mattheier, Klaus J. & Nelde, Peter H. (eds.) 1998. *Variationslinguistik/Linguistics of variation/La linguistique variationnelle.* (sociolinguistica, 12.) Tübingen: Niemeyer.

Arens, Hans. ²1969. *Sprachwissenschaft. Der Gang ihrer Entwicklung von der Antike bis zur Gegenwart.* (Orbis Academicus, I/6.) Freiburg & München: Karl Alber.

Auroux, Sylvain. 1989. „Introduction". In: id. (ed.), 13−37.

Auroux, Sylvain. (ed.) 1989/1992/2000. *Histoire des idées linguistiques.* 3 vols. (Philosophie et langage) Liège & Sprimont: Mardaga.

Auroux, Sylvain & Koerner, E. F. K. & Niederehe, Hans-Josef & Versteegh, Kees (eds.) 2000. *History of the Language Sciences/Geschichte der Sprachwissenschaften/Histoire des sciences du langage. An International Handbook on the Evolution of the Study of Language from the Beginnings to the Present/Ein internationales Handbuch zur Entwicklung der Sprachforschung von den Anfängen bis zur Gegenwart/Manuel international sur l'évolution de l'étude du langage des origines à nos jours.* Vol. 1. (HSK, 18.1.) Berlin & New York: de Gruyter.

Bailey, Charles-James N. 1980. „Old and New Views on Language History and Language Relationship". In: Lüdtke (ed.) 1980, 139−181.

Baldinger, Kurt. 1958. „Vom Affektwort zum Normalwort. Das Bedeutungsfeld von agask. *trebalh* 'Plage, Arbeit'". In: Keller, Hans-Erich (ed.). *Etymologica. Walther v. Wartburg zum 70. Geburtstag.* Tübingen: Niemeyer, 59−93.

Baldinger, Kurt. 1959. „Le remplacement de 'moult' par 'beaucoup'. A propos des bases méthodologiques d'un dictionnaire du moyen français". *Cahiers de l'Association Internationale des Etudes françaises* 11: 233−264 (jetzt auch in: id. 1990. *Die Faszination der Sprachwissenschaft. Ausgewählte Aufsätze zum 70. Geburtstag.* Tübingen: Niemeyer, 355−389).

Baldinger, Kurt. 1993. „Ist die unsichtbare Hand wirklich unsichtbar? Kritische Betrachtungen zum Bedeutungswandel". In: Schmidt-Radefeldt & Harder (eds.) 1993, 1−8.

Balibar, Renée. 1985. *L'institution du français. Essai sur le colinguisme des Carolingiens à la République.* Paris: PUF.

Banniard, Michel. 1992. *Viva voce. Communication écrite et communication orale du IVᵉ au IXᵉ siècle en Occident latin.* (Collection des études augustiniennes; Série Moyen-Âge et temps modernes, 25.) Paris: Institut des Études Augustiniennes.

Barra Jover, Mario. 2001. „Corpus diacrónico, constatación e inducción". In: Jacob & Kabatek (eds.) 2001, 177−197.

Besch, Werner & Reichmann, Oskar & Sonderegger, Stefan (eds.) 1984. *Sprachgeschichte. Ein Handbuch zur Geschichte der deutschen Sprache und ihrer Erforschung.* Vol. 1. (HSK, 2.1.) Berlin & New York: de Gruyter.

Besch, Werner & Betten, Anne & Reichmann, Oskar & Sonderegger, Stefan (eds.) ²1998. *Sprachgeschichte. Ein Handbuch zur Geschichte der deutschen Sprache und ihrer Erforschung.* Vol. 1. (HSK, 2.1.) Berlin & New York: de Gruyter.

Biber, Douglas. 1988. *Variation across Speech and Writing.* Cambridge: Cambridge UP.

Biber, Douglas. 1990. „Methodological issues regarding corpus-based analyses of linguistic variation". *Literary and Linguistic Computing* 5/4: 257−269.

Biber, Douglas. 1995. *Dimensions of register variation: a cross-linguistic comparison.* Cambridge: Cambridge UP.

Blank, Andreas. 1997. *Prinzipien des lexikalischen Bedeutungswandels am Beispiel der romanischen Sprachen.* (Beihefte zur Zeitschrift für Romanische Philologie, 285.) Tübingen: Niemeyer.

Blank, Andreas & Koch, Peter (eds.) 1999. *Historical Semantics and Cognition.* (Cognitive Linguistics Research, 13.) Berlin & New York: Mouton de Gruyter.

Blank, Andreas & Gévaudan, Paul & Koch, Peter. 2000. „Onomasiologie, sémasiologie et l'étymologie des langues romanes: Esquisse d'un projet". In: Englebert, Annick (ed.). *Actes du XXIIe Congrès International de Linguistique et de Philologie Romanes.* Vol. 4. Tübingen: Niemeyer, 103−114.

Bossong, Georg. 1979. *Probleme der Übersetzung wissenschaftlicher Werke aus dem Arabischen in das Altspanische zur Zeit Alfons des Weisen.* (Beihefte zur Zeitschrift für Romanische Philologie, 169.) Tübingen: Niemeyer.

Bossong, Georg. 1982. „Historische Sprachwissenschaft und empirische Universalienforschung". *Romanistisches Jahrbuch* 33: 17−51.

Bossong, Georg. 1990. *Sprachwissenschaft und Sprachphilosophie in der Romania. Von den Anfängen bis August Wilhelm Schlegel.* (TBL, 339.) Tübingen: Narr.

Brandt, Margareta & Rosengren, Inger. 1992. „Zur Illokutionsstruktur von Texten". *Zeitschrift für Literaturwissenschaft und Linguistik* 86: 9−51.

Brinker, Klaus. ³1992. *Linguistische Textanalyse. Eine Einleitung in Grundbegriffe und Methoden.* Berlin: Schmidt.

Brinker, Klaus & Antos, Gerd & Heinemann, Wolfgang & Sager, Sven F. (eds.) 2000. *Text- und Gesprächslinguistik/Linguistics of Text and Conversation.* (HSK, 16.1.) Berlin & New York: de Gruyter.

Brown, Gillian & Yule, George. 1983. *Discourse Analysis.* (Cambridge Textbooks in Linguistics.) Cambridge: Cambridge UP.

Bruni, Francesco. 1984. *L'italiano. Elementi di storia della lingua e della cultura.* Turin: UTET.

Bybee, Joan L. & Perkins, Revere D. & Pagliuca, William. 1994. *The Evolution of Grammar. Tense, Aspect, and Modality in the Languages of the World.* Chicago & London: University of Chicago Press.

Campbell, Lyle. 1998. *Historical Linguistics. An Introduction.* Edinburgh: Edinburgh UP.

Cano Aguilar, Rafael. ²1982. *El español a través de los tiempos.* Madrid: Arco Libros.

Cano Aguilar, Rafael. 1996. „Lenguaje 'espontáneo' y retórica epistolar en cartas de emigrantes españoles a Indias". In: Kotschi, Thomas & Oesterreicher, Wulf & Zimmerman (eds.). *El español hablado y la cultura oral en España e Hispanoamérica.* Frankfurt a. M/Madrid: Vervuert/Iberoamericana, 375–404.

Carapezza, Marco & Gambarara, Daniele & Lo Piparo, Franco (eds.) 1997. *Linguaggio e cognizione. Atti del XXVIII Congresso della Società di linguistica italiana. Palermo, 27–29 ottobre 1994.* (Società di Linguistica Italiana, 37.) Rom: Bulzoni.

Caron, Jean. 1983. *Les régulations du discours. Psycholinguistique et pragmatique du langage.* Paris: PUF.

Cerquiglini, Bernard. 1981. *La parole médiévale. Discours, syntaxe, texte.* Paris: Éd. Minuit.

Cerquiglini, Bernard. 1989. *Éloge de la variante.* Paris: Éd. du Seuil.

Chafe, Wallace L. 1985. „Linguistic differences produced by differences between speaking and writing". In: Olson, David R. et. al. (eds.). *Literacy, Language, and Learning. The Nature and Consequences of Reading and Writing.* Cambridge etc.: Cambridge UP, 105–123.

Cherubim, Dieter (ed.) 1975. *Sprachwandel. Reader zur diachronischen Sprachwissenschaft.* Berlin & New York: de Gruyter.

Comrie, Bernard. 1981. *Language universals and linguistic typology.* Oxford: Blackwell.

Comrie, Bernard. 1987. *The world's major languages.* New York etc.: Oxford UP.

Coseriu, Eugenio. ²1973. *Sincronía, diacronía e historia: el problema del cambio lingüístico.* (BRH; II, 193.) Madrid: Gredos (¹1958 Montevideo: Universidad de Montevideo; deutsche Übersetzung: *Synchronie, Diachronie und Geschichte. Das Problem des Sprachwandels.* München: Fink 1974).

Coseriu, Eugenio. 1974. „Les universaux linguistiques (et les autres)". In: *Proceedings of the Eleventh International Congress of Linguists.* Vol. 1. Bologna: Il Mulino, 47–73 (deutsche Übersetzung: „Die sprachlichen (und die anderen) Universalien". In: Schlieben-Lange (ed.) 1975, 127–161).

Coseriu, Eugenio. 1980. „Vom Primat der Geschichte". *Sprachwissenschaft* 5: 125–145.

Coseriu, Eugenio. ²1981a. *Textlinguistik. Eine Einführung.* Hrsg. und bearbeitet von Jörn Albrecht. Tübingen: Narr.

Coseriu, Eugenio. 1981b. *Introducción a la lingüística.* Madrid: Gredos.

Coseriu, Eugenio. 1981c. „Los conceptos de 'dialecto', 'nivel' y 'estilo de lengua' y el sentido de la dialectología". *Lingüística Española Actual* 3: 1–32.

Coseriu, Eugenio. 1983. „Linguistic Change does not exist". *Linguistica nuova ed antica. Rivista di linguistica classica medievale e moderna* (Galatina Congedo Editore) 1: 51–63.

Coseriu, Eugenio. 1988a. „Die Begriffe 'Dialekt', 'Niveau' und 'Sprachstil' und der eigentliche Sinn der Dialektologie (1981)". In: Albrecht et al. (eds.) 1988. Vol. 1, 15–43.

Coseriu, Eugenio. 1988b. „'Historische Sprache' und 'Dialekt' (1980)". In: Albrecht et al. (eds.) 1988. Vol. 1, 45–61.

Coseriu, Eugenio. 1988c. „Der romanische Sprachtyp. Versuch einer neuen Typologisierung der romanischen Sprachen (1971)". In: Albrecht et al. (eds.) 1988. Vol. 1, 207–224.

Coseriu, Eugenio. 1990. „Semántica estructural y semántica 'cognitiva'". In: Alvar, Manuel et al. (eds.). *Profesor Francisco Marsá: Jornadas de Filología.* (Colleció homenatges, 4.) Barcelona: Publicacions Universitat de Barcelona, 239–282.

Croft, William. 1990. *Typology and universals.* (Cambridge Textbooks in Linguistics) Cambridge etc.: Cambridge UP.

Croft, William. 1995. „Autonomy and functionalist linguistics". *Language* 71: 490–532.

Croft, William. 2000. *Explaining Language Change. An Evolutionary Approach.* (Longman Linguistics Library) Harlow: Pearson Education.

Detges, Ulrich. 1999. „Wie entsteht Grammatik? Kognitive und pragmatische Determinanten der Grammatikalisierung von Tempusmarkern". In: Lang/Neumann-Holzschuh (eds.) 1999, 31–52.

Detges, Ulrich. 2001. *Grammatikalisierung. Eine kognitiv-pragmatische Theorie, dargestellt am Beispiel romanischer und anderer Sprachen.* Tübingen: Niemeyer.

Diewald, Gabriele. 1997. *Grammatikalisierung. Eine Einführung in Sein und Werden grammatischer Formen.* Tübingen: Niemeyer.

Dik, Simon C. 1978. *Functional grammar.* Amsterdam & New York & Oxford: North Holland.

Droixhe, Daniel. 1978. *La linguistique et l'appel de l'histoire (1600–1800). Rationalisme et révolutions positivistes.* (Langue et Cultures, 10.) Genf: Droz.

Durante, Marcello. 1981. *Dal latino all'italiano moderno.* Bologna: Zanichelli.

Eberenz, Rolf. 2001. „Los *regimientos de peste* a fines de la Edad Media: configuración de un nuevo género textual". In: Jacob & Kabatek (eds.) 2001, 79–96.

Ehler, Christine & Schaefer, Ursula (eds.) 1998. *Verschriftung und Verschriftlichung. Aspekte des*

Medienwechsels in verschiedenen Kulturen und Epochen. (ScriptOralia, 94.) Tübingen: Narr.

Ehlich, Konrad. 1991. „Funktional-pragmatische Kommunikationsanalyse − Ziele und Verfahren". In: Flader, Dieter. (ed.). *Verbale Kommunikation. Studien zur Emiprie und Methodologie der Pragmatik.* Stuttgart: Metzler, 127−143.

Ferguson, Charles. 1959. „Diglossia". *Word* 15: 325−340.

Fisiak, Jacek (ed.) 1995. *Linguistic Change under Contact Conditions.* Berlin & New York: Mouton de Gruyter.

Fleischman, Suzanne. 1982. *The future in thought and language. Diachronic evidence from Romance.* (Cambridge Studies in Linguistics, 36.) Cambridge etc.: Cambridge UP.

Fleischman, Suzanne. 1983. „From pragmatics to grammar. Diachronic reflections on complex pasts and futures in Romance". *Lingua* 60: 183−214.

Fleischman, Suzanne. 1990. „Philology, Linguistics, and the Discourse of Medieval Text". *Speculum* 65: 19−37.

Fleischman, Suzanne. 1991. *Discourse pragmatics and the verb: evidence from Romance.* London etc.: Routledge.

Formigari, Lia. 1972. *Linguistica e antropologia nel secondo Settecento.* (Biblioteca di filosofia moderna, 3.) Messina: La Libra.

Formigari, Lia. 1977. *La logica del pensiero vivente. Il linguaggio nella filosofia della Romantik.* Bari: Laterza.

Formigari, Lia. 1990. *L'esperienza e il segno. La filosofia del linguaggio tra Illuminismo e Restaurazione.* Rom: Editori Riuniti.

Foucault, Michel. 1966. *Les mots et les choses.* Paris: Gallimard.

Frank, Barbara. 1997. „'Innensicht' und 'Außensicht'. Zur Analyse mittelalterlicher volkssprachlicher Gattungsbezeichnungen". In: Frank et al. (eds.) 1997, 117−136.

Frank, Barbara & Haye, Thomas & Tophinke, Doris. (eds.) 1997. *Gattungen mittelalterlicher Schriftlichkeit.* (ScriptOralia, 99.) Tübingen: Narr.

Frei, Henri. 1971. *La grammaire des fautes.* Genève: Slatkine Reprints Paris (Original: 1929 Paris & Genf).

Fritz, Gerd. 1998a. *Historische Semantik.* Stuttgart & Weimar: Metzler.

Fritz, Gerd. 1998b. „Ansätze zu einer Theorie des Sprachwandels auf lexikalischer Ebene". In: Besch et al. (eds.) ^{2}1998, 860−874.

Gabelentz, Georg v. d. 1901/^{2}1969. *Die Sprachwissenschaft, ihre Aufgaben, Methoden und bisherigen Ergebnisse.* Nachdruck Tübingen: Narr.

Gadamer, Hans-Georg. ^{3}1986. „Geschichtlichkeit". In: Galling, Kurt et al. (eds.). *Religion in Geschichte und Gegenwart.* Handwörterbuch für Theologie und Religionswissenschaft.* Vol. 2. Tübingen: Mohr, 1496−1498.

Gadet, Françoise. 1998a. „Le 'français avancé' à l'épreuve de ses données". In: Bilger, Mireille & van den Eynde, Karel & Gadet, Françoise (eds.). *Analyse linguistique et approches de l'oral.* Leuven & Paris: Peeters, 59−68.

Gadet, Françoise. 1998b. „'Cette dimension de la variation que l'on ne sait nommer'". In: Ammon et al. (eds.) 1998, 53−71.

Gauger, Hans-Martin & Oesterreicher, Wulf & Windisch, Rudolf. 1981. *Einführung in die romanische Sprachwissenschaft.* (Die Romanistik. Einführung in Gegenstand, Methoden und Ergebnisse ihrer Teildisziplinen) Darmstadt: Wissenschaftliche Buchgesellschaft.

Geckeler, Horst. 1971. *Zur Wortfelddiskussion. Untersuchungen zur Gliederung des Wortfeldes 'alt-jung-neu' im heutigen Französischen.* (Internationale Bibliothek für Allgemeine Linguistik, 7.) München: Fink.

Geeraerts, Dirk. 1997. *Diachronic Prototype Semantics. A Contribution to Historical Lexicology.* Oxford: Clarendon Press.

Gehlen, Arnold. ^{9}1971. *Der Mensch. Seine Natur und seine Stellung in der Welt.* Frankfurt a.M.: Athenäum.

Giacalone Ramat, Anna & Hopper, Paul J. (eds.) 1998. *The Limits of Grammaticalization.* Amsterdam/New York: Benjamins.

Givón, Talmy. 1979. *On understanding grammar.* (Perspectives in neurolinguistics and psycholinguistics.) New York: Academic Press.

Givón, Talmy. 1984/1990. *Syntax. A Functional-typological introduction.* 2 vols. Amsterdam etc.: Benjamins.

Givón, Talmy. 1995. *Functionalism and Grammar.* Amsterdam & Philadelphia: Benjamins.

Goossens, Louis. 1999. „Metonymic bridges in modal shifts". In: Panther, Klaus Uwe & Radden, Günter (eds.). *Metonymy in language and thought.* (Human Cognitive Processing, 4.) Amsterdam & Philadelphia: Benjamins, 193−210.

Graumann, Carl F. 1966. „Bewußtsein und Bewußtheit. Probleme und Befunde der psychologischen Bewußtseinsforschung". In: id. (ed.). *Handbuch der Psychologie.* Vol. 1/1. Göttingen: Hogrefe, 79−127.

Graumann, Carl F. 1972. „Interaktion und Kommunikation". In: id. (ed.). *Handbuch der Psychologie.* Vol. 7/2. Göttingen: Hogrefe, 1109−1262.

Greenberg, Joseph H. ^{2}1966. „Some Universals of Grammar with Particular Reference to the Order of meaningful Elements". In: id. (ed.). *Universals of Language.* Cambridge, MA: M.I.T. Press, 73−113.

Günther, Hartmut & Ludwig, Otto (eds.) 1994. *Schrift und Schriftlichkeit/Writing and Its Use. Ein interdisziplinäres Handbuch internationaler For-*

schung/An Interdisciplinary Handbook of International Research. (HSK, 10.1.) Berlin & New York: de Gruyter.

Haas, Walter. 1998. „Ansätze zu einer Theorie des Sprachwandels auf lautlicher Ebene". In: Besch et al. (eds.) ²1998, 836–850.

Habermas, Jürgen. 1968. *Erkenntnis und Interesse*. Frankfurt a. M.: Suhrkamp.

Hagège, Claude. 1982. *La structure des langues*. Paris: PUF.

Halliday, Michael A. K. 1978. *Language as social semiotic: the social interpretation of language and meaning*. London: Edward Arnold.

Halliday, Michael A. K. 1985. *Spoken and Written Language*. Geelong: Deakin University Press.

Harris, Martin B. 1978. *The Evolution of French Syntax: A Comparative Approach*. London & New York: Longman.

Harris, Martin B. & Ramat, Paolo (ed.) 1987. *Historical Development of Auxiliaries*. (Trends in Linguistics, 35.) Berlin & New York: Mouton de Gruyter.

Harris, Alice & Campbell, Lyle. 1995. *Historical Syntax in cross-linguistic perspective*. Cambridge: Cambridge UP.

Haspelmath, Martin. 1990. „The grammaticalization of passive morphology". *Studies in Language* 14: 25–72.

Haspelmath, Martin. 1998. „Does grammaticalization need reanalysis?". *Studies in Language* 22: 49–85.

Heger, Klaus. 1989a. „Grundsätzliche Überlegungen zum Thema 'Romanistik, Sprachtypologie und Universalienforschung'". In: Raible, Wolfgang (ed.) 1989, 263–270.

Heger, Klaus. 1989b. „Zur plurizentrischen Sprachkultur". *Zeitschrift für germanistische Linguistik* 17: 226–228.

Heine, Bernd & Claudi, Ulrike & Hünnemeyer, Friederike. 1991. *Grammaticalization. A Conceptual Framework*. Chicago & London: University of Chicago Press.

Henne, Helmut & Rehbock, Helmut. ³1995. *Einführung in die Gesprächsanalyse*. Berlin & New York: de Gruyter.

Hock, Hans Heinrich. ²1991. *Principles of Historical Linguistics*. Berlin & New York: Mouton de Gruyter.

Hockett, Charles F. ²1966. „The Problem of Universals in Language". In: Greenberg, Joseph H. (ed.). *Universals of Language*. Cambridge, MA: M. I. T. Press, 1–29.

Hofmann, Johann Baptist. ³1951. *Lateinische Umgangssprache*. Heidelberg: Winter.

Hopper, Paul & Traugott, Elizabeth Closs. 1993. *Grammaticalization*. (Cambridge Textbooks in Linguistics.) Cambridge: Cambridge UP.

Ineichen, Gustav. ²1991. *Allgemeine Sprachtypologie. Ansätze und Methoden*. (Erträge der Forschung, 118.) Darmstadt: Wissenschaftliche Buchgesellschaft.

Jacob, Daniel. 1994. *Die Auxiliarisierung von habere und die Entstehung des romanischen periphrastischen Perfekts, dargestellt an der Entwicklung vom Latein zum Spanischen*. Habilitationsschrift Freiburg i. Br. (unveröffentlicht).

Jacob, Daniel. 1995. „Von der *Subjekt*-Relevanz zur Gegenwartsrelevanz: Gebrauch und Entwicklung der Perfektperiphrase *aver* + Partizip Perfekt Passiv im Altspanischen". *Romanistisches Jahrbuch* 46: 251–286.

Jacob, Daniel. 2001. „¿Representatividad lingüística o autonomía pragmática del texto antiguo? El ejemplo del pasado compuesto". In: Jacob & Kabatek (eds.) 2001, 153–176.

Jacob, Daniel. 2002. „Prinzipien der Typologie und der sprachinternen Klassifikation der romanischen Sprachen". In: Ernst, Gerhard et al. (eds.). *Romanische Sprachgeschichte. Ein internationales Handbuch zur Geschichte der romanischen Sprachen und ihrer Erforschung*. (HSK) Berlin/New York: de Gruyter (im Druck).

Jacob, Daniel & Kabatek, Johannes (eds.) 2001. *Lengua medieval y tradición discursivas en la Península Ibérica. Descripción gramatical – pragmática histórica – metodología*. (Lingüística Iberoamericana, 12.) Frankfurt a.M. & Madrid: Vervuert & Iberoamericana.

Jäger, Ludwig. 1998. „Das Verhältnis von Synchronie und Diachronie in der Sprachgeschichtsforschung". In: Besch et al. (ed.) ²1998, 816–824.

Kabatek, Johannes. 2001. „¿Cómo investigar las tradiciones discursivas medievales? El ejemplo de los textos jurídicos castellanos". In: Jacob & Kabatek (eds.) 2001, 97–132.

Keller, Rudi. 1993. „Zur Erklärungskraft der Natürlichkeitstheorie". In: Schmidt-Radefeldt & Harder (eds.) 1993, 109–117.

Keller, Rudi. ²1994. *Sprachwandel. Von der unsichtbaren Hand in der Sprache*. Tübingen: Francke.

Keller, Rudi. 1999. „Gibt es funktionale Erklärungen von Sprachwandel?". In: Kanngießer, Siegfried & Vogel, Petra M. (eds.). *Elemente des Sprachwandels*. Opladen & Wiesbaden: Westdeutscher Verlag, 36–47.

Kloss, Heinz. ²1978. *Die Entwicklung neuer germanischer Kultursprachen seit 1800*. Düsseldorf: Schwann.

Knoop, Ulrich. 1975. „Die Historizität der Sprache". In: Schlieben-Lange (ed.) 1975, 165–187.

Koch, Peter. 1987. *Distanz im Dictamen – Zur Schriftlichkeit und Pragmatik mittelalterlicher Brief- und Redemodelle in Italien*. Habilitationsschrift Freiburg i.Br. (unveröffentlicht).

Koch, Peter. 1988. „Norm und Sprache". In: Albrecht et al. (eds.) 1988, 327–354.

Koch, Peter. 1995 a. „Subordination, intégration syntaxique et 'oralité'". *Etudes romanes* 34: 13–42.

Koch, Peter. 1995 b. „Der Beitrag der Prototypentheorie zur Historischen Semantik: Eine kritische Bestandsaufnahme". *Romanistisches Jahrbuch* 46: 27–46.

Koch, Peter. 1997 a. „Diskurstraditionen: zu ihrem sprachtheoretischen Status und ihrer Dynamik". In: Frank & Haye & Tophinke (eds.) 1997, 43–79.

Koch, Peter. 1997 b. „La diacronia quale campo empirico della semantica cognitiva". In: Carapezza et al. (eds.) 1997, 225–246.

Koch, Peter. 1997 c. „Orality in literate cultures". In: Pontecorvo, Clotilde (ed.). *Writing Development. An Interdisciplinary View.* (Studies in Written Language and Literacy, 6.) Amsterdam & Philadelphia: Benjamins, 149–171.

Koch, Peter. 1999 a. „'Gesprochen/geschrieben' – eine eigene Varietätendimension?". In: Greiner, Norbert & Kornelius, Joachim & Rovere, Giovanni (eds.). *Texte und Kontexte in Sprachen und Kulturen. Festschrift für Jörn Albrecht.* Trier: WVT, 141–168.

Koch, Peter. 1999 b. „Frame and contiguity: On the cognitive bases of metonymy and certain types of word formation". In: Panther, Klaus-Uwe & Radden, Günter (eds.). *Metonymy in Language and Thought.* Amsterdam & Philadelphia: Benjamins, 139–167.

Koch, Peter. 2001. „Bedeutungswandel und Bezeichnungswandel", *Zeitschrift für Literaturwissenschaft und Linguistik* 121: 7–36

Koch, Peter & Krefeld, Thomas. (eds.) 1991. *Connexiones Romanicae. Dependenz und Valenz in romanischen Sprachen.* (Linguistische Arbeiten, 268.) Tübingen: Niemeyer.

Koch, Peter & Oesterreicher, Wulf. 1985. „Sprache der Nähe – Sprache der Distanz. Mündlichkeit und Schriftlichkeit im Spannungsfeld von Sprachtheorie und Sprachgeschichte". *Romanistisches Jahrbuch* 36: 15–34.

Koch, Peter & Oesterreicher, Wulf. 1990. *Gesprochene Sprache in der Romania: Französisch, Italienisch, Spanisch.* Tübingen: Niemeyer.

Koch, Peter & Oesterreicher, Wulf. 1994. „Schriftlichkeit und Sprache". In: Günter & Ludwig (eds.) 1994, 587–604.

Koch, Peter & Oesterreicher, Wulf. 1996. „Sprachwandel und expressive Mündlichkeit", *Zeitschrift für Literaturwissenschaft und Linguistik* 102: 64–96.

Koch, Peter & Oesterreicher, Wulf. 2001. „Gesprochene und geschriebene Sprache/Langage écrit et langage parlé". In: *LRL.* Vol. 1 (im Druck).

König, Ekkehard & Kortmann, Bernd. 1992. „Categorial reanalysis: the case of deverbal prepositions". *Linguistics* 30: 671–697.

Körner, Karl-Hermann. 1987. *Korrelative Sprachtypologie: Die zwei Typen romanischer Syntax.* Stuttgart: Steiner.

Kortmann, Bernd. 1997. *Adverbial subordination: a typology and history of adverbial subordinators based on European languages.* (Empirical approaches to language typology, 18.) Berlin etc.: Mouton de Gruyter.

Koselleck, Reinhart. ^{3}1992. „Geschichte, Historie". In: Brunner, Otto et al. (eds.). *Geschichtliche Grundbegriffe. Historisches Lexikon zur politisch-sozialen Sprache in Deutschland.* Vol. 1. Stuttgart: Klett-Cotta, 593–717.

Krefeld, Thomas. 1985. *Das französische Gerichtsurteil in linguistischer Sicht. Zwischen Fach- und Standessprache.* (studia romanica et linguistica, 17.) Frankfurt a. M.: Lang.

Krefeld, Thomas. 1999 a. „Agens mit Leib und Seele. Zur Grammatikalisierung romanischer Adverbbildungen". In: Lang & Neumann-Holzschuh (eds.) 1999, 111–127.

Krefeld, Thomas. 1999 b. „Cognitive ease and lexical borrowing: the recategorization of body parts in Romance". In: Blank & Koch (eds.) 1999, 259–277.

Kriegel, Sibylle. 1996. *Diathesen im Mauritius- und Seychellenkreol.* (ScriptOralia, 88.) Tübingen: Narr.

Labov, William. 1975. „Zum Mechanismus des Sprachwandels". In: Cherubim (ed.) 1975, 305–334.

Labov, William. 1994. *Principles of linguistic change.* Vol. 1: *Internal factors.* (Language in Society, 20.) Oxford & Cambridge MA: Blackwell.

Lakoff, George. 1987. *Women, Fire, and Dangerous Things. What Categories Reveal About the Mind.* Chicago: University of Chicago Press.

Lakoff, George & Johnson, Mark. 1999. *Philosophy in the Flesh. The Embodied Mind and Its Challenge to Western Thought.* New York: Basic Books.

Lang, Jürgen & Neumann-Holzschuh, Ingrid. 1999. „Reanalyse und Grammatikalisierung. Zur Einführung in diesen Band". In: Lang & Neumann-Holzschuh (eds.) 1999, 1–17.

Lang, Jürgen & Neumann-Holzschuh, Ingrid. (eds.) 1999. *Reanalyse und Grammatikalisierung in den romanischen Sprachen.* (Linguistische Arbeiten, 410.) Tübingen: Niemeyer.

Langacker, Ronald W. 1977. „Syntactic reanalysis". In: Li, Charles N. (ed.). *Mechanisms of syntactic change.* Austin: University of Texas Press, 57–139.

Langacker, Ronald W. 1991. *Concept, Image, and Symbol. The Cognitive Basis of Grammar.* (Cognitive Linguistics Research, 1.) Berlin & New York: Mouton de Gruyter.

Langacker, Ronald W. 1999. „Losing control: grammaticization, subjectification, and transparency". In: Blank & Koch (eds.) 1999, 147–175.

Lass, Roger. 1980. *On Explaining Language Change*. Cambridge: Cambridge UP.

Lass, Roger. 1997. *Historical Linguistics and Language Change*. Cambridge: Cambridge UP.

Lehmann, Christian. 1983. „The present state of linguistic typology". In: *Proceedings of the XIIIth International Congress of Linguists, August 29 − September 4, 1982, Tokyo*. Tokyo, 950−956.

Lehmann, Christian. 1984. *Der Relativsatz. Typologie seiner Strukturen − Theorie seiner Funktionen − Kompendium seiner Grammatik*. Tübingen: Narr.

Lehmann, Christian. 1985. „Grammaticalization: synchronic variation and diachronic change". *Lingua e Stile* 20: 303−318.

Lehmann, Christian. 1995. *Thoughts on grammaticalization. A programmatic sketch*. (LINCOM studies in theoretical linguistics, 1.) München: Lincom Europa; zuerst 1982 (akup, 48.) Köln: Universität Köln.

Leiss, Elisabeth. 1998a. „Über das Interesse der Grammatiktheorie an Sprachwandel und ihr Desinteresse an Sprachgeschichte". *ZAS Papers in Linguistics* 13: 196−211.

Leiss, Elisabeth. 1998b. „Ansätze zu einer Theorie des Sprachwandels auf morphologischer und syntaktischer Ebene". In: Besch et al. (eds.) 1998, 850−860.

Lenker, Ursula. 2000. „Rez. von Rissanen, Matti (ed.). *English in Transition: Corpus-based Studies in Linguistic variation and Genre Styles* und *Grammaticalization at Work: Studies of Long-term Developments in English*. Berlin & New York: de Gruyter 1997". *Anglia* 118: 103−109.

Lightfoot, David W. 1979. *Principles of diachronic syntax*. Cambridge: Cambridge UP.

Lieb, Hans-Heinrich. 1998. „Variationsforschung: grundlegende Begriffe und Konzeption". In: Ammon et al. (eds.) 1998, 1−21.

LRL = Holtus, Günter & Metzeltin, Michael & Schmitt, Christian. (eds.) 1990−2001. *Lexikon der Romanistischen Linguistik*. 7 vols. Tübingen: Niemeyer.

Luckmann, Thomas. 1973. „Aspekte einer Theorie der Sozialkommunikation". In: Althaus, Hans Peter & Henne, Helmut & Wiegand, Herbert Ernst (eds.). *Lexikon der germanistischen Linguistik*. Vol. 1. Tübingen: Niemeyer, 1−13.

Luckmann, Thomas. [2]1980. „Aspekte einer Theorie der Sozialkommunikation". In: Althaus, Hans Peter & Henne, Helmut & Wiegand, Herbert Ernst (eds.). *Lexikon der germanistischen Linguistik*. Tübingen: Niemeyer, 28−41.

Luckmann, Thomas. 1997. „Allgemeine Überlegungen zu kommunikativen Gattungen". In: Frank et al. (eds.) 1997, 11−17.

Ludwig, Ralph. 1996. *Kreolsprachen zwischen Mündlichkeit und Schriftlichkeit. Zur Syntax und Pragmatik atlantischer Kreolsprachen auf französischer Basis*. (ScriptOralia, 86.) Tübingen: Narr.

Lüdtke, Helmut. 1964. „Zur Entstehung romanischer Schriftsprachen". *Vox Romanica* 23: 3−21.

Lüdtke, Helmut. 1980a. „Sprachwandel als universales Phänomen". In: id. (ed.) 1980, 1−19.

Lüdtke, Helmut. 1980b. „Auf dem Weg zu einer Theorie des Sprachwandels". In: id. (ed.) 1980, 182−252.

Lüdtke, Helmut. 1999a. „Diachronic semantics: towards a unified theory of language change?". In: Blank & Koch (eds.) 1999, 49−60.

Lüdtke, Helmut. 1999b. „Sprache zwischen 'Chaos' und spontaner Ordnung". In: Stehl (ed.) 1999, 1−17.

Lüdtke, Helmut. 2001. „Von der historischen Grammatik zur Geschichte der Kommunikation". In: Stehl (ed.) 2001 (im Druck).

Lüdtke, Helmut. (ed.) 1980. *Kommunikationstheoretische Grundlagen des Sprachwandels*. Berlin & New York: Mouton de Gruyter.

Lüdtke, Jens. 1988. „Situations diglossiques, variétés et conscience linguistique". In: *Actes du XVIIIe Congrès International de Linguistique et de Philologie Romanes*. Vol. 5. Tübingen: Niemeyer, 121−128.

Lüdtke, Jens. 1994. „Diferenciación y nivelación del español en la expansión a Canarias y al caribe en el período de orígenes". In: id. (ed.). *El español de América en el siglo XVI*. Frankfurt a.M.: Vervuert, 39−56.

Lüdtke, Jens. 1998. „Español colonial y español peninsular. El problema de su historia común en los siglos XVI y XVII". In: Oesterreicher et al. (eds.) 1998, 13−36.

Maingueneau, Dominique. 1987. *Nouvelles tendances en analyse du discours*. (Langue − linguistique − communication.) Paris: Hachette.

Mair, Walter N. 1992. *Expressivität und Sprachwandel. Studien zur Rolle der 'Subjektivität' in der Entwicklung der romanischen Sprachen*. Frankfurt a. M.: Lang.

Mattheier, Klaus J. 1984a. „Allgemeine Aspekte einer Theorie des Sprachwandels". In: Besch et al. (eds.) 1984, 720−730.

Mattheier, Klaus J. 1984b. „Sprachwandel und Sprachvariation". In: Besch et al. (eds.) 1984, 768−779.

McMahon, April M. S. 1994. *Understanding language change*. Cambridge: Cambridge UP.

Meillet, Antoine. 1912. „L'évolution des formes grammaticales". In: id. *Linguistique historique et linguistique générale*. Paris: Champion, 131−148.

Michaelis, Susanne. 1994. *Komplexe Syntax im Seychellen-Kreol. Verknüpfung von Sachverhaltsdarstellungen zwischen Mündlichkeit und Schriftlichkeit*. (ScriptOralia, 49.) Tübingen: Narr.

Monreal-Wickert, Irene. 1977. *Die Sprachforschung der Aufklärung im Spiegel der großen französischen Enzyklopädie*. (lingua et traditio, 3.) Tübingen: Narr.

Nencioni, Giovanni. 1976. „Parlato-parlato, parlato-scritto, parlato-recitato". *Strumenti critici* 10: 1–56.

Oesterreicher, Wulf. 1975. „Sprachtheorie – Zur Problematik der Verwendung eines Terminus". In: Schlieben-Lange, Brigitte (ed.). *Sprachtheorie*. Hamburg: Hoffmann & Campe, 81–126.

Oesterreicher, Wulf. 1979. *Sprachtheorie und Theorie der Sprachwissenschaft*. Heidelberg: Winter.

Oesterreicher, Wulf. 1983. „'Historizität' und 'Variation' in der Sprachforschung der französischen Aufklärung – auch: ein Beitrag zur Entstehung der Sprachwissenschaft". In: Cerquiglini, Bernard & Gumbrecht, Hans Ulrich (eds.). *Der Diskurs der Literatur- und Sprachhistorie. Wissenschaftsgeschichte als Innovationsvorgabe*. (stw, 411.) Frankfurt a. M.: Suhrkamp, 167–205.

Oesterreicher, Wulf. 1988. „Sprechtätigkeit, Einzelsprache, Diskurs und vier Dimensionen der Sprachvarietät". In: Albrecht et al. (eds.) 1988. Vol. 2, 325–386.

Oesterreicher, Wulf. 1989. „'Konsistenz' als typologisches Kriterium?". In: Raible (ed.) 1989, 209–248.

Oesterreicher, Wulf. 1991. „Verbvalenz und Informationsstruktur". In: Koch & Krefeld (eds.) 1991, 349–384.

Oesterreicher, Wulf. 1994. „Sprachwissenschaft und Sprachphilosophie in der Romania". *Historiographia linguistica* 21: 157–171.

Oesterreicher, Wulf. 1995a. „Die Architektur romanischer Sprachen im Vergleich. Eine Programm-Skizze". In: Dahmen, Wolfgang et al. (eds.). *Konvergenz und Divergenz in den romanischen Sprachen. Romanistisches Kolloquium VIII*. Tübingen: Narr, 3–21.

Oesterreicher, Wulf. 1995b. „Blinde Flecken der historischen Wortforschung oder: Die Angst des Linguisten vor der Sprachvariation. Am Beispiel der Lexik des Spanischen in Amerika (16. Jahrhundert)". In: Hoinkes, Ulrich (ed.). *Panorama der lexikalischen Semantik. Thematische Festschrift aus Anlaß des 60. Geburtstags von Horst Geckeler*. Tübingen: Narr, 489–516.

Oesterreicher, Wulf. 1996a. „Gemeinromanische Tendenzen V: Morphosyntax". In: *LRL*. Vol. II/1, 273–309.

Oesterreicher, Wulf. 1996b. „Gemeinromanische Tendenzen VI: Syntax". In: *LRL*. Vol. II/1, 309–355.

Oesterreicher, Wulf. 1997. „Zur Fundierung von Diskurstraditionen". In: Frank et al. (eds.) 1997, 19–41.

Oesterreicher, Wulf. 1998. „*Textzentrierung* und *Rekontextualisierung*. Zwei Grundprobleme der diachronischen Sprach- und Textforschung". In: Ehler & Schaefer (eds.) 1998, 10–39.

Oesterreicher, Wulf. 1999. „*Ad-hoc*-Formulierungen als Herausforderung für Lexikologie und Lexikographie". In: Falkner, Wolfgang & Schmid, Hans-Jörg (eds.). *Words, lexemes, concepts – approaches to the lexicon. Studies in honor of Leonard Lipka*. Tübingen: Narr, 69–84.

Oesterreicher, Wulf. 2000. „L'étude des langues romanes". In: Auroux (ed.) 2000, 183–192.

Oesterreicher, Wulf. 2001a. „Sprachwandel, Varietätenwandel, Sprachgeschichte. Zu einem verdrängten Theoriezusammenhang". In: Schaefer, Ursula & Spielmann, Edda (eds.). *Varieties and Consequences of Orality and Literacy*. Tübingen: Narr, 217–248.

Oesterreicher, Wulf. 2001b. „Plurizentrische Sprachkulturen – der Varietätenraum des Spanischen". *Romanistisches Jahrbuch* 51 (im Druck).

Oesterreicher, Wulf & Raible, Wolfgang. 1993. „Présentation de la section". In: Hilty, Gerold (ed.). *Actes du XXe Congrès International de Linguistique et Philologie Romanes*. Vol. 3, IV: *Typologie des langues romanes*. Tübingen & Bern: Francke, 3–23.

Oesterreicher, Wulf & Schmidt-Riese, Roland. 1999. „Amerikanische Sprachenvielfalt und europäische Grammatiktradition. Missionarslinguistik im Epochenumbruch der Frühen Neuzeit". *Zeitschrift für Literaturwissenschaft und Linguistik* 116: 62–100.

Oesterreicher, Wulf & Stoll, Eva & Wesch, Andreas. (eds.) 1998. *Competencia escrita, tradiciones discursivas y variedades lingüísticas. Aspectos del español europeo y americano en los siglos XVI y XVII*. Tübingen: Narr.

Ong, Walter J. 1982. *Orality and literacy: the technologizing of the word*. (New accents.) London: Methuen.

Orth, Ernst W. 1967. *Bedeutung, Sinn, Gegenstand. Studien zur Sprachphilosophie E. Husserls und R. Hönigswalds*. Bonn: Bouvier.

Orth, Ernst W. 1970. „Grundlagen und Methodenprobleme der Sprachwissenschaft vom Standpunkt der Transzendental-Philosophie". *Linguistische Berichte* 5: 1–25.

Paul, Hermann. ^{5}1920. *Prinzipien der Sprachgeschichte*. Halle: Niemeyer (^{7}1966 Tübingen: Niemeyer).

Polenz, Peter v. 1984. „Die Geschichtlichkeit der Sprache und der Geschichtsbegriff der Sprachwissenschaft". In: Besch et al. (eds.) 1984, 1–8.

Quirk, Randolph & Greenbaum, Sidney & Leech, Geoffrey & Svartvik, Jan. (eds.) 1985. *A Comprehensive Grammar of Contemporary English*. London: Longman.

Raible, Wolfgang. 1980. „Was sind Gattungen? Eine Antwort aus semiotischer Sicht". *Poetica* 12: 320–349.

Raible, Wolfgang. 1983. „Vom Text und seinen vielen Vätern oder: Hermeneutik als Korrelat der Schriftkultur". In: Assmann, Aleida & Assmann, Jan & Hardmeier, Christof (eds.). *Schrift und Gedächtnis. Beiträge zur Archäologie der literarischen Kommunikation*. München: Fink, 20−23.

Raible, Wolfgang. 1992 a. *Junktion. Eine Dimension der Sprache und ihre Realisierungsformen zwischen Aggregation und Integration*. (Sitzungsberichte der Heidelberger Akademie der Wissenschaften; Philosophisch-Historische Klasse, 1992, 2.) Heidelberg: Winter.

Raible, Wolfgang. 1992 b. „The pitfalls of subordination. Subject and object clauses between Latin and Romance". In: Brogynanyi, Bela & Lipp, Reiner (eds.). *Historical Philology. Greek, Latin, and Romance. Papers in Honor of Oswald Szemerényi*. Amsterdam & Philadelphia: Benjamins, 299−337.

Raible, Wolfgang. 1993. *Sprachliche Texte − genetische Texte: Sprachwissenschaft und molekulare Genetik*. (Sitzungsberichte der Heidelberger Akademie der Wissenschaften; Schriften der Philosophisch-Historischen Klasse, 1993, 1.) Heidelberg: Winter.

Raible, Wolfgang. 1996 a. „Kognition und Sprachwandel". *Akademie-Journal* 1 (Heidelberg): 38−43.

Raible, Wolfgang. 1996 b. „Kognitive Grundlagen des Sprachwandels". In: Michaelis, Susanne & Thiele, Petra (eds.). *Grammatikalisierung in der Romania*. (Bochum-Essener Beiträge zur Sprachwandelforschung, 28.) Bochum: Brockmeyer, 61−80.

Raible, Wolfgang. 1998. „Die Anfänge der volkssprachlichen Schriftkultur in der Romania oder: Die Eroberung konzeptueller Räume". In: Ehler & Schaefer (eds.) 1998, 156−173.

Raible, Wolfgang. 1999. *Kognitive Aspekte des Schreibens*. (Sitzungsberichte der Heidelberger Akademie der Wissenschaften; Schriften der Philosophisch-Historischen Klasse, 1999, 14.) Heidelberg: Winter.

Raible, Wolfgang. (ed.) 1989. *Romanistik. Sprachtypologie und Universalienforschung*. (TBL, 332.) Tübingen: Narr.

Ramat, Paolo. 1984. *Linguistica tipologica*. Bologna: Il Mulino.

Rastier, François. 1997. „La sémiotique et les recherches cognitives. Une perspective herméneutique sur la médiation sémiotique". In: Carapezza et al. (eds.) 1997, 63−87.

Rastier, François. 1999. „Cognitive semantics and diachronic semantics: the values and evolution of classes". In: Blank & Koch (eds.) 1999, 109−144.

Reich, Ulrich. 2001. „Erhebung und Analyse von Corpora in diskursvariationeller Perspektive: Chancen und Probleme". In: Pusch, Claus D. & Raible, Wolfgang (eds.), *Romanistische Korpuslinguistik*. (ScriptOralia) Tübingen: Narr (im Druck).

Reich, Ulrich. 2002. *Freie Pronomina, Verbalklitika und Nullobjekte im Spielraum diskursiver Variation des Portugiesischen in São Paulo*. (Romanica Monacensia, 62.) Tübingen: Narr (im Druck).

Reichmann, Oskar. 1998. „Sprachgeschichte: Idee und Verwirklichung". In: Besch et al. (eds.) 1998, 1−41.

Schank, Gerd. 1984. „Ansätze zu einer Theorie des Sprachwandels auf der Grundlage von Textsorten". In: Besch et al. (eds.) 1984, 761−768.

Schlieben-Lange, Brigitte. ²1978. *Soziolinguistik. Eine Einführung*. (Urban-TB, 176.) Stuttgart: Kohlhammer.

Schlieben-Lange, Brigitte. ²1979. *Linguistische Pragmatik*. (Urban-TB, 198.) Stuttgart: Kohlhammer.

Schlieben-Lange, Brigitte. 1983. *Traditionen des Sprechens. Elemente einer pragmatischen Sprachgeschichtsschreibung*. Stuttgart: Kohlhammer.

Schlieben-Lange, Brigitte. 2000. *Idéologie: zur Rolle von Kategorisierungen im Wissenschaftsprozeß*. (Sitzungsberichte der Heidelberger Akademie der Wissenschaften, Schriften der Philosophisch-Historischen Klasse, 2000, 18.) Heidelberg: Winter.

Schlieben-Lange, Brigitte. (ed.) 1975. *Sprachtheorie*. Hamburg: Hoffmann und Campe.

Schmidt-Radefeldt, Jürgen & Harder, Andreas. (eds.) 1993. *Sprachwandel und Sprachgeschichte. Festschrift für Helmut Lüdtke zum 65. Geburtstag*. Tübingen: Narr.

Schmidt-Riese, Roland. 1997. „Schreibkompetenz, Diskurstradition und Varietätenwahl in der frühen Kolonialhistoriographie Hispanoamerikas". *Zeitschrift für Literaturwissenschaft und Linguistik* 108: 45−86.

Schmidt-Riese, Roland. 1998. *Reflexive Oberflächen im Spanischen*. (Romanica Monacensia, 55.) Tübingen: Narr.

Seiler, Hansjakob. (ed.) 1978. *Language Universals. Papers from the Conference held at Gummersbach/Cologne, Germany, October 3−8, 1976*. (TBL, 111.) Tübingen: Narr.

Selig, Maria. 1992. *Die Entwicklung der Nominaldeterminanten im Spätlatein. Romanischer Sprachwandel und lateinische Schriftlichkeit*. (ScriptOralia, 26.) Tübingen: Narr.

Sperber, Dan & Wilson, Deirdre. 1986. *Relevance. Communication and Cognition*. Oxford: Blackwell.

Stark, Elisabeth. 1997. *Voranstellungsstrukturen und 'topic'-Markierung im Französischen. Mit einem Ausblick auf das Italienische*. (Romanica Monacensia, 51.) Tübingen: Narr.

Stark, Elisabeth. 1999. „Französische Voranstellungsstrukturen − Grammatikalisierung oder universale Diskursstrategien?". In: Lang & Neumann-Holzschuh (eds.) 1999, 129−146.

Stefenelli, Arnulf. 2000. „Von der Prestigevariante zur Normalbezeichnung". In: Guille, Martine &

Kiesler, Reinhard (eds.). *Romania una et diversa. Philologische Studien für Theodor Berchem zum 65. Geburtstag.* Vol. 1. Tübingen: Narr, 341–353.

Steger, Hugo et al. 1974. „Redekonstellation, Redekonstellationstyp, Textexemplar, Textsorte im Rahmen eines Sprachverhaltensmodells. Begründung einer Forschungshypothese". In: *Gesprochene Sprache. Jahrbuch 1972 des Instituts für Deutsche Sprache.* Düsseldorf: Schwann, 39–97.

Steger, Hugo. 1998. „Sprachgeschichte als Geschichte der Textsorten, Kommunikationsbereiche und Semantiktypen". In: Besch et al. (eds.) 1998, 284–300.

Stehl, Thomas. (ed.) 1999. *Dialektgenerationen, Dialektfunktionen, Sprachwandel.* (TBL, 411.) Tübingen: Narr.

Stehl, Thomas (ed.) 2001. *Unsichtbare Hand und Sprecherwahl. Typologie und Prozesse des Sprachwandels in der Romania.* Tübingen: Narr (im Druck).

Stempel, Wolf-Dieter. 1964. *Untersuchungen zur Satzverknüpfung im Altfranzösischen.* Braunschweig: Westermann.

Stempel, Wolf-Dieter. 1972. „Gibt es Gattungen?". In: Gülich, Elisabeth & Raible, Wolfgang (eds.). *Textsorten. Differenzierungskriterien aus linguistischer Sicht.* Frankfurt a. M.: Athenäum, 175–179.

Stolz, Thomas. 1994. *Grammatikalisierung und Metaphorisierung.* (Bochum-Essener Beiträge zur Sprachwandelforschung, 23.) Bochum: Brockmeyer.

Strube, Gerhard et al. (eds.) 1996. *Wörterbuch der Kognitionswissenschaft.* Stuttgart: Klett-Cotta.

Stubbs, Michael. 1996. *Text and Corpus Analysis. Computer-assisted Studies of Language and Culture.* (Language in Society, 23.) Oxford: Blackwell.

Svartvik, Jan. (ed.) 1992. *Directions in Corpus Linguistics.* Berlin & New York: Mouton de Gruyter.

Sweetser, Eve. 1988. „Grammaticalization and semantic bleaching". *BLS* 14: 389–405.

Sweetser, Eve. 1990. *From Etymology to Pragmatics: Metaphorical and Cultural Aspects of Semantic Structure.* (Cambridge Studies in Linguistics, 54.) Cambridge: Cambridge UP.

Taylor, John. ²1995. *Linguistic Categorization.* Oxford: Clarendon Press.

Thomason, Sarah Grey. 1997. „A typology of contact languages". In: Spears, Arthur K. & Winford, Donald (eds.). *Pidgins and creoles: structure and status,* Amsterdam: Benjamins, 71–88.

Thomason, Sarah Grey & Kaufmann, Terrence. 1988. *Language contact, creolization, and genetic linguistics.* Berkeley: University of California Press.

Traugott, Elizabeth Closs. 1988. „Pragmatic strengthening and grammaticalization". *BLS* 14: 406–416.

Traugott, Elizabeth Closs. 1995. „Subjectification in grammaticalization". In: Stein, Dieter & Wright, Susan (eds.). *Subjectivity and subjectivisation in language. Linguistic perspectives.* Cambridge: Cambridge UP, 31–54.

Traugott, Elizabeth Closs. 1999. „The rhetoric of counter-expectation in semantic change: a study in subjectification". In: Blank & Koch (eds.) 1999, 177–196.

Traugott, Elizabeth Closs & König, Ekkehard. 1991. „The semantics-pragmatics of grammaticalization revisited". In: ead. & Heine, Bernd (eds.). *Approaches to Grammaticalization.* Vol. 1. Amsterdam: Benjamins, 189–218.

Vitale, Maurizio. ⁵1971. *La questione della lingua.* Palermo: Palumbo.

Waltereit, Richard. 1998. *Metonymie und Grammatik. Kontiguitätsphänomene in der französischen Satzsemantik.* (Linguistische Arbeiten, 385.) Tübingen: Niemeyer.

Waltereit, Richard. 1999. „Reanalyse als metonymischer Prozeß". In: Lang & Neumann-Holzschuh (eds.) 1999, 19–29.

Wanner, Dieter. 1987. *The Development of Romance Clitic Pronouns. From Latin to Old Romance.* Berlin & New York: Mouton de Gruyter.

Wartburg, Walther v. 1943/³1970. *Einführung in Problematik und Methodik der Sprachwissenschaft.* Tübingen: Niemeyer.

Zumthor, Paul. 1985. „Archaïsme et fiction: les plus anciens documents de la langue 'romane'". In: Auroux, Sylvain et al. (eds.). *La linguistique fantastique.* Paris: Joseph Clims & Denoël, 285–299.

Zumthor, Paul. 1987. *La lettre et la voix. De la 'littérature' médiévale.* Paris: Éd. du Seuil.

Wulf Oesterreicher, LMU München (Deutschland)

112. Pathways of lexicalization

1. Introduction
2. Lexical innovation and the types of conventionalization
3. Lexicalization and grammaticalization
4. Lexicalization as the conventionalization of complex words
5. Degrees of idiomaticity
6. Demotivation and formal reduction
7. Further pathways of lexicalization
8. Conclusion
9. References

1. Introduction

The term 'lexicalization', like most deverbal derivations, can denote a process as well as the result of this process. Furthermore, even the processual understanding of the word, which shares the fate of many linguistic terms, has more than one meaning (the same problem with grammaticalization is discussed in Lehmann 1995: 9ss.).

In structural and generative semantics, lexicalization is sometimes used in the sense of replacing an abstract semantic configuration (i.e. a sememe or a deep structure) by a lexeme (cf. e.g. Lyons 1977: I, 235s.; Kastovsky 1982: 268). In a wider understanding we could say that this way of using the term means that a concept is verbalized by lexical elements. The more common term for referring to this transformational process however is lexical insertion (cf. Katz 1972: 401—6; Fodor 1977: 155—60; Scalise 1990: 27), so that we may exclude it from discussion here.

This use excepted, the present article adopts an inclusive understanding of lexicalization, comprising all sorts of pathways by which new lexical or semantic material is conventionalized on the level of a "historical language" (cf. § 2.). Further developments of already lexicalized entities that change their status within the lexicon are also to be regarded as lexicalizations, so that we will come to four different but interdependent definitions of lexicalization (cf. below §§ 4.; 6.3.; 7.1.). First however, I will introduce different types of conventionalization of lexical entities (§ 2.) and contrast lexicalization with grammaticalization (§ 3.).

2. Lexical innovation and the types of conventionalization

2.1. Lexicalization deals with lexical change and conventionalization. According to Eugenio Coseriu (1958: 44s.), linguistic change can be described as a continuous series of adoptions of an individual innovation by other speakers. Conventionalization on the level of the lexicon concerns not only word formation and idioms, but also, to the same extent, semantic change, borrowings and some other types of lexical change (cf. below § 7.).

There are two major domains of conventionalized linguistic rules that should be strictly distinguished: the domain of "discourse traditions" and the level of "historical languages" (cf. Schlieben-Lange 1983; Koch 1988: 337—42; Koch 1997; Blank 1997: 114—19).

2.2. A discourse tradition (also called 'text tradition' in Schlieben-Lange 1983) is the inventory of the rules that are necessary for the production of certain culture-specific text types like minnesong, talk-show, the selling of used cars, etc. Text type rules do not normally coincide with a speech community, but are essentially linked to the text type in which they occur and to the users of this text type. A typical example from minnesong is the metaphorical use of words for SERVING in the sense of 'to love, to worship' (cf. Koch 1997: § 3.). All languages that were used for minnesong have verbalized this metaphor, but as a mere rule of poetic discourse and not as a language rule. It could thus not be used beyond this specific text type (or only as a 'quotation'). As a conventionalization that concerns such a discourse tradition is not a part of any language's lexicon I would prefer — instead of lexicalization — to call this type of adoption '*usualization*'.

2.3. The other type of conventionalization affects a diatopically or diastratically defined group of speakers (dialect, sociolect, technolect) or a certain style (familiar, vulgar, etc.). Whenever a group of speakers has adopted an innovation as a language rule, we can say that a lexicalization (on the level of the corresponding diasystem) has occurred, as in

(1) ENGLISH *to kick the bucket* 'to die'.

which is lexicalized in slang. Lexicalization can be preceded by usualization on the level of a discourse tradition, but may also occur independently. It can also (or subsequently) affect the standard level (if existing) or the whole speech community.

Semantic innovations on the basis of already lexicalized simple or complex words can take the same route from innovation via adoption by a defined group of speakers to unmarked polysemy for all speakers. The polysemy can be reduced by giving up the older or even the newly lexicalized meaning (cf. Blank 1997: 119−25). An explicit example is the following:

(2) EARLY MODERN FRENCH *déjeuner* 'to have breakfast' > MODERN FRENCH 'to have lunch' / FRENCH DIALECTS 'to have breakfast'.

The semantic innovation probably emerged in Parisian FRENCH and became directly lexicalized in standard FRENCH. Subsequently, the older meaning was dropped in Parisian and in standard FRENCH, but was kept in dialectal and regional uses of FRENCH which have never been affected by the innovation.

2.4. New word-formations, idioms, borrowings, metaphors or metonymies are produced every day without ever being lexicalized or usualized. If I call, e.g., a computer a *data factory*, this is clearly a metaphoric word-formation, but it is not conventionalized and probably never will be: it is simply an *innovation*, nothing more.

While *data factory* is rather unusual, a new metaphor like GERMAN *inhalieren* *'to understand' (lit. "to inhale") would be an innovation too, but it is sustained by analogous metaphors like GERMAN *fressen, schlucken, sich reinziehen* (cf. Keller 1995; 222s.). The image scheme or "conceptual metaphor" TO UNDERSTAND IS TO EAT being established, innovations of the kind stand good chances of being successful (cf. Lakoff & Johnson 1980; Liebert 1992). Keller (1995: 228) calls such metaphors "half-lexicalized". This is, however, a misleading use of the word, as a metaphor like GERMAN *inhalieren* *'to understand' does not belong, as far as I know, to the lexicon of any speaker of GERMAN. It is true, however, that the underlying scheme is familiar to GERMAN speakers and that the conventionalization of a scheme can further the lexicalization of innovations (cf. also Fritz, forthcoming, § 3.2.).

2.5. When can we say that an innovation has become lexicalized? The question is esp. important for lexicographers who have to decide if a new word or a new meaning is worth being listed in the dictionary (cf. Pawley 1986: 100ss.). Recent developments are difficult to judge: Will a creation like GERMAN *Diana-Effekt* (*Der Spiegel*, Sept. 22, 1997) become a language rule (in the sense of 'collective self-abandon to emotions') or will it remain an ephemeron? Temporal distance makes decisions easier, but to fully classify transparent formations in old texts remains difficult: GERMAN *Heiliger Geist* 'Holy Spirit' is clearly lexicalized, but we cannot be sure whether "Ther infangenēr is fona *heiligemo geiste*" in the OLD HIGH GERMAN creed ("Catechism of Weissenburg", ca. 790 AD; cf. Naumann & Betz 1967: 103s) was already a rule-based use or an innovative loan-translation of LATIN *spiritus sanctus*, nor can we say, in case it was already conventionalized, whether it was at the stage of a text type rule or already a language rule. Lexicalization and its different types of conventionalization, like most individual linguistic processes, is thus best stated *post festum*.

3. Lexicalization and grammaticalization

The parallelism holding between the terms 'lexicalization' and 'grammaticalization' gives rise to a comparison of the underlying processes. According to Lehmann (1989: 14s.), the main difference is as follows: grammaticalization transfers linguistic entities to grammar and thus changes a syntagm or word-form into a rule of grammar (e.g. the grammaticalization of LATIN INF + *habeo, habes* etc. as 'future'), whereas lexicalization brings linguistic entities into the lexicon and thus "individualizes" and "deregulates" them, e.g., by combining two morphemes (cf. below § 6.2.).

Both processes can be seen as "abductions" from discourse to either grammar or lexicon. There is, however, an important difference, insofar as grammaticalization transforms words into grammatical rules, while lexicalization transforms words into other words or even preserves them completely (cf. § 7.).

There exists, at least theoretically, the possibility of the "return" of a grammatical form to the lexicon; this, of course, would be a kind of "lexicalization". Lehmann (1995: 16−19), however, concludes his discussion of examples of "degrammaticalizations" with the statement that "no cogent examples of degrammaticalization have been found" (1995:

19). Grammaticalization is thus considered to be unidirectional. As a general rule, unidirectionality is also typical of lexicalization, but processes of remotivation or reanalysis do occur (cf. below §§ 6. and 7.).

4. Lexicalization as the conventionalization of complex words

4.1. The term 'lexicalization' is found most frequently in studies dealing with word-formation and idioms. For these lexical processes, a rather general definition of 'lexicalization' is given in Schwarze & Wunderlich (1985: 16): „[...] Lexikalisierung ist ein ständiger Prozeß: mögliche Wörter werden ins aktuale Lexikon übergeführt: Lexikalisierung ist oft (aber nicht immer) damit verbunden oder davon gefolgt, daß die komplexen Wörter idiosynkratische Eigenschaften annehmen, d. h. formal, semantisch oder phonologisch nicht mehr transparent sind." Similar definitions can be found in various studies (cf. Kastovsky 1982: 164s; Quirk & et al. 1985; 1525ss.; Pawley 1986: Günther 1987: 188s.; Lehmann 1989; Lutzeier 1995: 36s.).

The definition however encompasses different processes that should be treated separately (cf. also below §§ 5. and 6.), namely the conventionalization and the possible concomitant or subsequent processes. Thus, some authors introduce a distinction between *institutionalization*, i. e. the conventionalization of a complex word that has been created by a productive morphological process and which is semantically completely predictable from its constituents, and *lexicalization*, which describes the subsequent demotivation or idiomatization (cf. Bauer 1983: 48; 1988: 246s.; Matthews 1991: 100; Lipka 1977: 120s.; 1981: 155; 1990: 94ss.; cf. also Fleischer & Barz 1992: 15s.). According to this interpretation, ex. (3) is considered to be not lexicalized, while examples (4) are "lexicalizations" at a low level", because specific semantic features are added; still more idiomatic, and thus further lexicalized, is ex. (5) (Lipka 1977: 158; 1990: 97s.):

(3)   ENGLISH *musical theory* 'theory about music'.

(4) (a) *rattlesnake* 'pit viper having a rattle';
    (b) *crybaby* 'person who cries readily for very little reason'.

(5)   *wheelchair* 'chair mounted on large wheels for use by invalids'.

This view, however, causes severe problems which are raised by the idea of "complete predictability" and an improper use of 'idiomaticity': strictly speaking, the sense of a word-formation is never completely predictable from the meaning of its components (cf. also Quirk et al., 1526s.). The simple combination of the senses of two words by compounding would virtually lead to rather abstract meanings: a *wheelchair* then would be just a *chair* that is somehow determined by having a *wheel* (or maybe more). More precisely: a *rattlesnake* could, theoretically, also be a snake that eats rattles (cf. GERMAN *Ameisenbär* 'ant-eater') and a *musical theory* could be a theory that is sung or played. Speakers combined words because they want to refer to specific concepts; the sense of a word-formation product thus depends on what it usually refers to; it is induced from our encyclopaedic knowledge (cf. also "Stoffhilfen" in Bühler 1934/65: 169—72; "Kenntnis der Sachen" in Coseriu 1966/78: 206s.) and not systematically derivable from the meaning of its components (cf. also Fill 1980: 56ss.). As Coseriu puts it, "Wortbildungsprodukte enthalten immer mehr als ihre lexikalischen Grundlagen" (1977: 53), and are conventionalized on the level of what he calls the "norm" (for details cf. Coseriu 1952/75).

This means that, right from the start, the complex word *rattlesnake* was used to designate a certain reptile. In this so to speak "low idiomatic" sense, and only in this sense, it became conventionalized and has not undergone any semantic process since. The choice made out of the semantic potential of the two combined words can, therefore, by no means be described as adding up semantic features to a given meaning, simply because there was no one before. In this sense, ENGLISH *wheelchair* or *rattlesnake* cannot be said to be "more" lexicalized than ENGLISH *musical theory*: although the latter's meaning is surely easier to derive from its components, the senses of all three compounds have to be learned.

This holds true even more for ENGLISH *crybaby*, which designates any person that is likely to complain, not only babies and toddlers. This compound's sense is clearly metaphoric and thus 'idiomatic', but its idiomaticitiy has never changed after the complex word was created.

4.2. From a purely linguistic viewpoint predictability of derivation is even worse: FRENCH *pomm-ier* is an 'apple tree' while *beurr-ier* is a 'butter-dish' and *plomb-ier* is a 'plumber'; ITALIAN *pre-cedere* means 'to precede', *pre-vedere* 'to foresee' (i. e. "to see what will happen"). Language here only tells us that the derivation designates something or someone which has to do with the object designated by the simple lexeme (cf. already Paul 1880/1995: 90); the rest is determined by our encyclopaedic knowledge (there are neither butter trees nor lead trees) and by certain derivational programs ('name of fruit' + *-ier* = 'tree or bush') which are concretized on the level of the norm (cf. Gauger 1971: 45—59).

4.3. We can conclude that complex words are never fully predictable from their components and that their senses can be more or less idiomatic (cf. § 5.). Further semantic and formal developments should be considered separately (cf. §§ 6. and 7.). The distinction between institutionalization and lexicalization should therefore be dropped. Our first definition of lexicalization then reads as follows:

DEF₁: Lexicalization₁ is a process by which word-formations and other syntagmatic constructions become syntactically and semantically fixed entries of the mental lexicon. These entries are called 'complex words' (cf. also Pottier's "lexie"; 1974: 265ss.).

The semantic and syntactic fixation of a complex word can be tested (cf. the list of criteria in Pawley 1986: 104—12; cf. also § 4. and 5.): ENGLISH *bullet-hole* is a hole made by a bullet and not a hole for putting bullets in; ENGLISH *John kicked the bucket* 'John died' cannot be transformed into **The bucket was kicked by John*.

5. Degrees of idiomaticity

We have already noticed above that there are semantic differences between lexicalized compounds like ENGLISH *musical theory*, *wheelchair* or *crybaby*, and this was exactly what misled linguists to distinguish between non-idiomatized institutionalizations and idiomatized lexicalizations. In fact, all examples so far are consistent with DEF₁, but show *different degrees of idiomaticity*:

1. Ex. (3) is not idiomatic at all, insofar as it realizes one of the possible combinations of the literal readings of the combined words. How literal readings give rise to semantically totally different compounds is exemplified by the following three compounds with GERMAN *Kuchen*:

(6) (a) GERMAN *Apfelkuchen* 'apple pie';
    (b) *Rührkuchen* 'cake made of stirred dough';
    (c) *Hundekuchen* 'dog biscuit'.

Again, these examples show that the sense of complex words is not fully predictable from the meaning of their parts, but it is obvious that all three compounds are based on the usual meanings of the simple lexemes. The same type of low level idiomatization can be found in syntagmatic constructions and phrasemes:

(7) (a) SPANISH *lengua extranjera* 'foreign language';
    (b) PORTUGUESE *máquina de barbear* ('electric') shaver';

(8) (a) FRENCH *mettre en bouteilles* 'to bottle';
    (b) GERMAN *Rede und Antwort stehen* 'to give an account of'.

2. A second group of complex words shows more idiomaticity. The sense of the complex word is still based on the usual meanings of the simple lexemes, but on the referential level we find rather untypical, specialized representatives of the designated category: ENGLISH *wheelchair* is indeed a kind of *chair*, but rather peripheral compared with a prototypical *chair*. This referential deviation is mirrored by a semantically more detailed compound.

3. The third degree of idiomaticity concerns metonymic and metaphoric transpositions. In these cases, one component or the complex word as a whole has to be interpreted by establishing a conceptual contiguity or similarity as regards the literal reading.

Metonymy:

(9) (a) ENGLISH *redskin* 'American indian';
    (b) ITALIAN *alzare il gomito* 'to drink (a little bit to much)'.

Metaphor:

(10) (a) GERMAN *Marmorkuchen* 'marble cake';
    (b) ITALIAN *bocca di leone* 'snapdragon';

(c) FRENCH *mettre à l'alambic* 'to examine carefully' (lit. "to put into the still").

The examples cited above show different degrees of idiomaticity, but — and this is the important point — their respective idiomaticity was there right from the start and is not due to any further lexical process. On a scale of predictability, it is probably more difficult to derive the idiomatic formations from their components, whereas non-idiomatic complex words only offer a small number of possible interpretations; but all of them are *transparent*, insofar as their senses can be motivated by interpreting the components (for transparency in word-formation cf. Gauger 1971).

6. Demotivation and formal reduction

6.1. There are of course many complex words which, through the years, have become partially or totally opaque and thus are more or less demotivated (Günther 1987). Demotivation is a diachronic process and can affect both the semantic and the formal aspect of complex words.

6.1.1. The first reason for demotivation is the disuse and subsequent loss from the lexicon of one or more of the components; a formerly simple lexeme survives "frozen" inside a compound or an idiom, as GERMAN *-od* and ITALIAN *fio* in the following examples:

(11) (a) GERMAN *Kleinod* 'jewel, treasure';
    (b) ITALIAN *pagare il fio* 'to do penance for'.

Typical bound morphs of this type are the "berry-words" (e. g. GERMAN *Him-*, *Brom-*, ENGLISH *boysen-*, *whortle-*). Interpretations of the sense through the meanings of the components become speculative or impossible, because the defunct simple lexeme is, synchronically, "meaningless". Remotivation by interpreting the complex word is however possible (Lipka 1981: 123, n. 4; cf. also § 6.1.4.).

6.1.2. In a certain sense, the opposite happens when complex words remain entirely transparent on the level of their components, but have become, with time, semantically opaque as complex words:

(12) (a) ITALIAN *essere al verde* 'to be stony-broke' (lit. "to be at the green [part]");
    (b) FRENCH *construire des châteaux en Espagne* 'to build castles in the air' (lit. "to build castles in Spain").

In both cases, the semantic motivation has been lost: in (12a) the "green" was the usually green-coloured bottom of a candle (cf. GERMAN *abgebrannt sein*); "castles in Spain" refers to fiefs granted during the Reconquista, the conquest of which remained up to the vassal.

6.1.3. Lipka (1981: 127, 131; 1990: 97) points out that compounds like GERMAN *Handtuch* 'towel' (lit. *hand-cloth*) or ENGLISH *watchmaker* are demotivated, because nowadays they do not mean what an analysis of their components would suggest: a *watch-maker* is rather 'someone who sells and repairs watches' than a 'person who makes watches', and a *Handtuch* is also used to dry other parts of the body. In fact, these words have undergone semantic change, because they have been used to designate slightly different concepts (cf. Blank 1997: 347s.).

This kind of semantic demotivation can be observed at any time when complex words have been affected by semantic change and the older sense has disappeared. It often goes hand in hand with phonological, morphological and/or graphemic changes:

(13) (a) MIDDLE ENGLISH *holy day* 'religious feast' > MODERN ENGLISH *holiday* 'day off from work' > 'vacation';
    (b) MIDDLE HIGH GERMAN *Hôchgezîte* 'celebration' (lit. "high time") > MODERN GERMAN *Hochzeit* 'wedding' (cf. also §§ 6.2.1. and 7.2.);
    (c) MIDDLE FRENCH *desjeuner* 'to have the first meal of the day' (lit. "to defast") > MODERN FRENCH *déjeuner* 'to have lunch'.

6.1.4. In other cases, the complex words keep their meaning perfectly, but their components do not. This, once again, leads to demotivation of the complex words that have been created earlier:

(14) (a) OLD HIGH GERMAN *gift* 'gift' > 'poison', thus demotivated GERMAN *Mitgift* 'dowry';
    (b) MIDDLE HIGH GERMAN *vaz* 'vessel' > GERMAN *Fass* 'barrel', thus demotivated GERMAN *Tintenfass* 'inkpot', *Salzfass* 'salt-cellar'.

Semantic demotivation can be counterbalanced by semantic reanalysis (popular etymology): FRENCH *être à la discretion de qn.* 'to be at someone's discretion' is nowadays related to FRENCH *discretion* 'measurement, discretion' and not to the older meaning 'power of determination' (cf. Blank 1996: 127); OLD HIGH GERMAN **grasa-smucka* 'warbler' (lit. "grass-snuggler") has been interpreted since the early Middle Ages as a *grasa-mugga* > MODERN GERMAN *Grasmücke* (lit. "grass-fly"; cf. Wurzel, forthcoming).

6.1.5. A last type of semantic demotivation, which already touches upon grammar, is the loss of a morphological rule. Although the complex word remains virtually unchanged, if has become difficult to analyze by the speakers who use it:

(15) (a) LATIN *terrae motum* 'earthquake' > ITALIAN *terremoto*;
(b) FRENCH *fête-Dieu* 'Corpus Christi Day'.

In (15a), the LATIN construction NGEN-N has become opaque; ITALIAN *terre-* could be reanalyzed as a plural, but in any case, the word-formation rule is not productive anymore. The same holds true for (15b), which in OLD FRENCH was a compound of the type N-NOBL, replaced in MODERN FRENCH by N-PREP-N (*enfant de chœur*).

6.2. The specific word-formation rules of languages determine to a certain extent the disposition of complex words to fusion.

6.2.1. In CLASSICAL CHINESE, e. g., word-formation was mainly a matter of syntax, as special word-formation rules did not exist and fusion did not occur (Coulmas 1985: 256). Modern MANDARIN makes more use of word-formation, producing more and more polysyllabic words, but still prefers isolating devices such as compounding and reduplication and shows little inclination towards inflection (Li & Thompson 1987: 816ss.). In GERMAN, on the other hand, syntagmatic constructions tend to fuse more easily (cf. ex. 20 and 21), showing typical morphological markers such as "Fugenlaut" (16a) and the tendency towards inflection on the right (16b), which, in non-standard carieties, can even give rise to a "double" superlative (16c):

(16) (a) GERMAN *Hochzeitstag* 'wedding day';
(b) GERMAN *lange Weile*, > Langeweile 'boredom'; GEN: *der Langenweile* or *der Langeweile*;
(c) GERMAN (non-standard) *meistgelesenst* 'he most read-SUPERLATIVE'.

ROMANCE (and also ENGLISH) compounds often retain a certain formal independence. The typical seqeunce DETERMINATUM – DETERMINANS in ROMANCE languages requires inner reflection for plural marking, which keeps the complex character overt. PORTUGUESE even keeps inflection inside certain derivations (cf. Rainer 1995: 88s.):

(17) (a) ITALIAN *capostazione* 'stationmaster'; PL *capistazione*;
(b) SPANISH *coche-cama* 'sleeping-car'; PL *coches-cama*;
(c) PORTUGUESE *flor* 'flower' (PL *flores*) → *florzinha* 'little flower'; PL *florezinhas*.

Although the inclination towards fusion is less strong in ROMANCE languages, this process nevertheless occurs, as in the current ex. (18a), and can even lead to reduction of analyzability (18b):

(18) (a) ITALIAN *bassiriliev-i* or *bassoriliev-i*;
(b) ITALIAN *pom-i d'oro* > *pomidoro* > *pomodor-i*.

In languages where complex words remain morphologically autonomous, the flexibility in concrete utterances is higher: in ENGLISH *classical language teacher* the adjective determines the DETERMINANS of the complex word *language teacher*. This is impossible in German, where a **klassische(r) Sprach(en)-lehrer* would be, if at all possible, a "classical" teacher of languages (cf. Coulmas 1985: 256). On the other hand, relatively autonomous constructions remain semantically more transparent, and thus in FRENCH a construction like **poisson rouge blanc* 'white goldfish' is excluded, while GERMAN *weisser Goldfisch* is possible (but not **weisser goldener Fisch*).

6.2.2. Fusion and the reduction of inflection are typical signs of the "loss of structure" to which complex words can be subject to ("Strukturverlust", Coulmas 1985: 254ss.). This process concerns mainly word formation and syntagmatic constructions, and more rarely proper idioms, which are syntactically more or less fixed but keep a certain inner autonomy (cf. for details Coulmas 1985: 257ss.; Palm 1995: 29–36). Fusion often goes hand in hand with semantic demotivation. It starts with slight phonological changes ranging from the shift of the accent (19) to modifications of vowels (2) and complex phonetic reductions, leading straight to the effacement of the complex character of the construction in question (21) (cf. Lipka 1977; Coulmas 1985; Wurzel, forthcoming):

(19)　ENGLISH *White house* < *white hóuse*.

(20)　(a) ENGLISH *policeman* [pəˈliːsmən];
　　　(b) GERMAN *Hochzeit*, [ˈhɔxtsaIt].

(21)　(a) ENGLISH *forecastle* [fəʊksl];
　　　(b) GERMANIC **matiz-sahsa-* 'food-sword' > OLD HIGH GERMAN *mezzisahs* > MIDDLE HIGH GERMAN *mezzeres* > GERMAN *Messer* 'knife';
　　　(c) LATIN *avicellus* 'little bird' > VULGAR LATIN *aucellus* 'bird' > FRENCH *oiseau*, ITALIAN *uccello*, OCCITAN *aucèu*, CATALAN *ocell*, RHETO-ROMANSH *utschè*.

Morphophonemic fusion reduces simple lexemes in compounds to parts of simple lexemes, and simple lexemes and affixes in derivatives to parts of simple lexemes (21c). Graphetic fusion is always a reflex of morphosyntactic fusion, but sometimes graphetic conservatism perpetuates a former historical stage, and spelling pronunciation can even "restore" morphophonemic complexity (cf. Lipka 1977: 156):

(22)　ENGLISH *forehead* [ˈfɔrid] vs. [ˈfɔə-hed]

Reanalysis of complex words is not always successful, as shows FRENCH *il y a belle lurette* 'a long time ago', which originally was *il y a belle heurette* (lit. "a pretty little hour ago") in informal or dialectal pronunciation. *Lurette* is not a simple lexeme in French; the whole idiom is thus demotivated (cf. § 6.1.1.). Fusion can happen to all kinds of compounds, but it is particularly often observable in adverbs, conjunctions, prepositions and pronouns. By this means, expressive accumulations of lexemes are consequently reduced (for this "cybernetic" process cf. Lüdtke 1986; Koch & Oesterreicher 1996):

(23)　(a) LATIN **ho(c) die* > *hodie* 'today' > OLD FRENCH *hui*, ITALIAN *oggi*, SPANISH *hoy*, RUMENIAN *azi* etc.;
　　　(b) VULGAR LATIN **eccu tibi istu* lit. "this there with you" > ITALIAN *codesto* 'DEM 2ND PERSON';
　　　(c) SPANISH *vuestra merced* 'honorific salutation (lit. "your honour")' > *Usted* 'polite salutation'.

Syntagmatic constructions show a certain formal stability, but can also fuse, esp. in the case of semantic change (24a) and loss of expressivity (24b):

(24)　(a) OLD FRENCH *gens d'armes* 'soldiers' (*gendarme* SG 'knight serving to the king' > MODERN FRENCH 'policeman';
　　　(b) OLD FRENCH *au jour d'hui* 'on the day of today' > MODERN FRENCH *aujourd'hui* 'today'; that *aujourd'hui* is felt as an unanalyzed unit is shown by the fact that speakers of FRENCH frequently use *au jour d'aujourd'hui*.

Another case where fusion occurs is delocutive change of word class: a whole utterance is transformed into a more or less complex word expressing a contiguous concept (cf. Anscombre 1979; Koch 1993; cf. also § 7.4.):

(25)　(a) ITALIAN *all'arme!* 'to arms!' > *allarme* 'alert';
　　　(b) Pseudo FRENCH *m'aidez!* 'help me!' > ENGLISH *mayday* 'international distress signal' > 'ship/aircraft disaster';
　　　(c) FRENCH *fous le camp!* 'go away!' > FRENCH-based GUYANA-CREOLE *foukan* 'to go away'.

6.2.3. While fusion reduces complex words to simple lexemes, morphological reanalysis of compounds as affixes (esp. of whole series of partially isomorphic compounds) gives rise to new affixes which, in turn, become productive in derivation (cf. Lehmann 1989: 12; Posner 1996: 81ss.; Wurzel, forthcoming):

(26)　(a) OLD HIGH GERMAN *heit*, OLD ENGLISH *hād* 'person, rank, manner' > MIDDLE HIGH GERMAN *-heit*, MIDDLE ENGLISH *-hood* 'abstract, collective';
　　　(b) LATIN *mente* 'in that manner (ABL)' > VULGAR LATIN *-mente* 'ADV';
　　　(c) ENGLISH *gate* 'door' as in Watergate (hotel) > *-gate* 'political scandal or conspiration with involvement of the government' (*Irangate, filegate*, cf. also GERMAN *Waterkantgate*).

An interesting case of reanalysis is ENGLISH *hamburger* (steak) 'cooked patty of chopped beef between two halves of a bun', which has been interpreted as being a compound of ENGLISH *ham* 'meat of the rear quarters of a hog' + *burger* '?'. Subsequently, ENGLISH *burger* has become lexicalized in the sense 'cooked patty of sth. between two halves of a bun' and is found in compounds like ENGLISH *cheeseburger, pizzaburger*, GERMAN *Dönerburger, Ökoburger*, etc.

While in this last case a new simple lexeme was created, examples (26) do not so much concern the concrete compounds which comprise these words (unless we say that change from a compound to a derivative complex lexeme is a kind of lexicalization), but rather the turning of these words into affixes. On the theoretical ground of the "lexicalist hypothesis", according to which word-formation is excluded from grammar (cf. Chomsky 1970: 187−190; Bauer 1988: 125−49; Scalise 1990: 37−42), this process is another clear case of lexicalization. If, however, one prefers to see word-formation as the "grammaticalization of the lexicon" (Coseriu 1977: 54), the change of an autonomous word into an affix (and from free compounding into a rule-based process) is rather a kind of grammaticalization. Word-formation then is regarded as a device of one language's grammar which is used to enrich the lexicon.

6.3. Demotivation and the formal reduction of complex words are traditionally seen as processes of lexicalization. Since in § 4. we have defined lexicalization as the fixation of complex words on the level of the lexicon, one is tempted to describe in different terms the processes which happen to already lexicalized complex words. I will nevertheless opt for keeping the term 'lexicalization' for what has been described in this section, because, with every step they take towards the unmotivated simple lexeme, complex words achieve a different status in the lexicon. We can thus summarize this section in two more definitions:

DEF2: Lexicalization$_2$ is a process by which complex words formally or semantically loose their motivation.

DEF3: Lexicalization$_3$ is a process by which complex words become simple words.

The three types of lexicalization so far discussed are entirely compatible in the sense that DEF1 is implied in DEF2 and DEF3 and that the latter are interconnected: lexicalization$_2$ being possible without lexicalization$_3$, but lexicalization$_3$ entailing lexicalization$_2$ automatically. Reanalysis excluded, the processes described here are unidirectional, leading to the "prototype" of a lexicalized formation: the simple lexeme (Günther 1987: 188).

7. Further pathways of lexicalization

7.1. Lexicalization is mainly discussed in word-formation, and our DEF1 in § 4. reflects this tradition. But indeed, there is no plausible reason for this restriction (cf. also Quirk & al. 1985: 1530). In this section we will present other possibilities of expanding the lexicon (cf. also the "matrices lexicogéniques" in Tournier 1985: 47−51). All the following processes, as well as word-formation and idioms, fulfill the requirements of a more general definition:

DEF4: Lexicalization$_4$ is a process by which new linguistic entities, be it simple or complex words or just new senses, become conventionalized on the level of the lexicon.

7.2. In § 6.1.3. we saw that complex words can undergo semantic change and thus lose their motivation. Semantic change is not a matter of abrupt change, but obligatorily goes through a stage of polysemy (cf. Blank 1997: 406−24): we can be sure that, at a given period, MIDDLE HIGH GERMAN *hôchgezîte* meant 'celebration' and esp. 'wedding celebration', and that the wider sense fell into disuse in the course of time. Semantic change of complex words is quite common, and so is polysemy of complex words, as shows Lipka's example ENGLISH *reader* (1977: 158s.), which was first lexicalized with the deverbal sense of 'one who reads', and developed on this basis senses like 'one who reads aloud' (restriction of meaning), 'one who judges manuscripts for a publisher' (metonymy) or 'university teacher ranking between professor and lecturer' (metonymy). If we consider these further sense developments of overt compositions and derivations as lexicalizations too, there's only a small step to semantic change of simple lexemes:

(27) (a) ITALIAN *braccio* 'arm' > 'wing [!] of a building' (metaphor);
(b) LATIN *hostis* 'guest' > 'stranger' > 'enemy' > 'opposed army' (metonymies);
(c) VULGAR LATIN *hostis* 'opposed army' > OLD ITALIAN *oste*, OLD FRENCH *ost* 'army' (extension of meaning);

(d) OLD ENGLISH *steorfan* 'to die' > MODERN ENGLISH *to starve* 'to die of hunger' (restriction of meaning);
(e) GASCON *hasâ* 'pheasant' > 'rooster' (co-hyponymic transfer);
(f) HEBREW *berach* 'to bless' > 'to curse' (antiphrasis).

With regard to semantic change, the main difference between ENGLISH *reader* and ex. (27a) to (27f) is that newer meanings of a complex word loosen the relation to the simple lexeme(s) from which it originally derived, and thus reduce transparency (cf. DEF₂). On the other hand, the loss or reduction of motivation is "replaced" by a motivated associative link (similarity, contiguity or contrast) between the different senses of a word. These associative links make semantic change a very smart tool for expanding the lexicon, regardless of whether complex or simple words are involved (cf. the 'classical' studies of Bréal 1899; Nyrop 1913; Ullmann 1957; 1962; for an overview on semantic change and a detailed typology cf. Blank 1997).

A special "interface" between complex and simple lexemes is created by *lexical ellipsis*. Traditionally, ellipsis is interpreted as the formal reduction of a complex word (cf. Nyrop 1913: 58; Ullmann 1962: 222; Lipka 1981: 124) and should have been listed in § 6.2. This view involves a number of problems that cannot be discussed here (cf. Blank 1997: 286ss.). In my opinion, lexical ellipsis is rather a type of semantic innovation by which a simple lexeme that is part of a complex word is also used in the sense of this complex word. The simple lexeme in this new sense and the complex word are synonymous (cf. Blank 1997: 288–92):

(28) (a) LATE LATIN *solidus* 'massive' > FRENCH *sou*, ITALIAN *soldo* 'little, massive coin' (< LATE LATIN *solidus nummus*);
(b) GERMAN *Weizen* 'wheat' > 'beer made from barley and wheat' (< GERMAN *Weizenbier*).

7.3. *Conversion* or "*zero-derivation*" is a process by which a word is transferred into another word class without changing its formal aspect (cf. Marchand 1969: 359ss.; Quirk et al. 1985: 1558; Staib 1989: 19s.; Schpak-Dolt 1992: 60). It is, thus, an intermediate between word-formation and semantic change. Conversion seems to be especially productive in CREOLES and in languages tending to the agglutinating or to the isolating type where it is difficult to draw formal borderlins between word classes (cf. Skalička 1979: 336, 339s.):

(29) (a) ENGLISH *out* 'not in' (ADV) → *to out* 'to become known', 'to reveal the homosexuality of so.';
(b) CHINESE *shōu* 'to collect', 'to harvest' ('[the] harvest');
(c) FRENCH *voleur* 'thief' > MAURITIAN CREOLE *volor* 'to steal'.

The question is whether conversations are lexicalizations: According to Staib, they are mainly context phenomena which keep the semantic aspects of the word class they derive from (1989: 19s.). Lipka judges conversation an "extremely process [...] by which many new lexemes are formed" (1990: 85), but, according to his systematisation, these new lexemes are only "lexicalized" once they have undergone semantic change (cf. our criticism in § 4.1.). Indeed, I would opt for a case of lexicalization when a word is of common use in the function of another word class.

7.4. Another, less frequent type of lexicalization is based on delocutivity. The term "dérivation délocutive" was created by Benveniste (1966: 277–85) to explain cases like LATIN *salutare* 'to greet', which is not derived from the word *salus* 'health', but from the locution *salus!* 'hail!' (cf. also Conte 1984: 65ss.). Ascombre (1979) and Koch (1993) expanded the concept of delocutivy to semantic change where utterances are transformed metonymically into performatives (30a), and to a special case of categorical change (30b) which Koch, rather than "conversation", calls "delokutiver Kategoriensprung" (1993: 270ss.; cf. also our examples [25]):

(30) (a) OLD FRENCH *desfier* 'to break the vassals oath' > 'to defy';
(b) ITALIAN *non so che* 'I don't know" > *non so che* (also: *nonsoche*) 'sth. which is difficult to explain'.

Ex. (25) and (30b) are surely marginal phenomena, but they maybe represent the most typical case of "lexicalization" at all: the transforming of a speech act into a word.

7.5. Delocutive derivation should not be confused with onomatopeia. The difference is that an onomatopoetic word describes the sound: ENGLISH *to buzz* means 'to make a humming sound', while LATIN *salutare* means 'to say ‹salus!›' (Conte 1984: 66). Thus, onomatopeia is yet another way of expanding the lexicon. Words like ENGLISH *to buzz, bang*, GERMAN *brummen, Peng!* are formally motivated, but they are lexicalized differently from language to language, as shows the well-known example of the crowing of the rooster:

(31)   ENGLISH *cock-a-doodle-doo*, GERMAN *Kikeriki*, FRENCH *coquerico*, SPANISH *quiquiriqui*.

The examples are instructive in that they show traces of reanalysis: the ENGLISH and FRENCH word evoke BRITISH ENGLISH *cock* and FRENCH *coq*, and the GERMAN word evokes (dial.) *Gicker(l)*. These words, in turn, are probably derived from the rooster's crowing.

7.6. The fifth group of lexicalizations exceeding the traditional view is made up of formal changes other than sound change and of blendings. The first type, clipping, concerns not so much words but the deletion of one or more syllables of complex or just longer words (cf. Marchand 1969: 441−50; Tournier 1985: 304−8): speakers can clip the beginning (aphaeresis), the end (apocope) or even at both ends):

(32)   (a) FRENCH *marchand d'ail* > *chandail*; ITALIAN *violoncello* > *cello*;
       (b) GERMAN *Universität*, > *Uni*; FRENCH *faculté* > *fac*;
       (c) ENGLISH *influenza* > *flu*.

Clipping is more than just phonological reduction, it reduces words systematically; it is also different from ellipsis, because it creates a new word that is a synonym of its older parent. This becomes esp. evident in cases where clipped words are provided with a new suffix (for FRENCH cf. Kilani-Schoch & Dressler 1992):

(33)   (a) FRENCH *apéritif, intellectuel* > FRENCH (informal) *apér-o, intell-o*;
       (b) GERMAN *Bundeswehrsoldat, Student* > GERMAN (informal) *Bund-i, Stud-i*.

A special subtype of formal change is the reinterpretation of an article as a part of the word or, vice versa, of a part of the wird as a part of the article:

(34)   (a) ARABIC *al qāḍī* 'the judge' > SPANISH *(el) alcalde* 'major';
       (b) ROMANCE *l'Apulia* 'Apulia' > ITALIAN *(la) Puglia*.

The creation of a new word by reduction can also be effectuated by *acronymy* or "word-manufacturing" (Marchand 1969: 452ss.; for details cf. Tournier 1985: 308−12), but this process works on a completely different level: inventions, discoveries, new institutions and organizations are often named by combining the words expressing most important aspects of the new thing, such as e. g. ENGLISH *Acquired immune deficiency syndrome* or ITALIAN *Confederazione General dei Lavaratori*. Names like these are hardly ever get memorised and are usually reduced to abbreviations. The abbreviation or acronym can consequently be lexicalized as a simple word:

(35)   (a) ENGLISH *Acquired immune deficiency syndrome* > *Aids*;
       (b) ITALIAN *Confederazione Generale dei Lavoratori* > *Cgl* [tʃidʒi'ɛlːe].

In the latter case, a spelling pronunciation has to be chosen in order to respect phonotactic rules (cf. Schwarze 1988: 542s.). In recent years, one gets the impression that the invention of the acronym sometimes precedes the long name in order to avoid consonant clusters like in (35b) and to guarantee a motivated and suggetive acronym (cf. Geisler 1994: 109−14):

(36)   (a) *Erasmus* < *EuRopean community Action Scheme for the Mobility of University Students*;
       (b) ITALIAN *Fuori* < *Fronte Unitario Omosessuale Rivoluzionario Italiano*.

Acronyms like these are simple lexemes, but they are nevertheless motivated because they establish a contiguity which connects the denoted concept to something else: in (36a) to the historical prototype of a mobile European student, Erasmus of Rotterdam, and in (36b) to a program of homosexual self-manifestation (ITALIAN *fuori* 'out').

Another, even more subtle type of manufacturing a motivated word is *blending*, where parts of two words are combined in such a way that both words can be discerned (the most eloquent term for this process is FRENCH *mot-valise* "suitcase-word"). The new formation denotes a concept which combines aspects of both the simple lexemes that are blended, and is thus a rather playful type of compounding (for details cf. Windisch 1991):

(73)   (a) ENGLISH *motor + hotel → motel* 'roadside hotel typically having bedrooms with individual entrances and nearby parking space';

(b) FRENCH *français* + *anglais* → *franglais* 'usage of French with strong English influence'.

7.7. So far, most of the processes of lexicalization discussed have used domestic linguistic material. Yet, one of the most important sources for enriching the lexicon is *linguistic borrowing*, which is indeed an inappropriate term, because usually nothing is ever given back. According to Haugen (1950), we distinguish between *loanwords*, *loanblends* and *semantic loans*.

7.7.1. A loanword is the integral borrowing of a foreign word (cf. Betz 1949/65; Deroy 1980; Blank 1995). Formally, loanwords become more or less integrated into the borrowing language: phonologically (38a), morphologically (38b/c), graphematically (38d) and semantically (36e/f):

(38) (a) GERMAN *Führer* [ˈfyːʀɐ] > FRENCH *führrer* [fyˈʀœʀ];
(b) ARABIC *wa-šaʾ Allāh* > OLD SPANISH *ojalá* [oʃaˈla]; > MODERN SPANISH [oχaˈla]
(c) ENGLISH *to download, downloaded* > GERMAN (computerese) *downloaden, downgeloadet*;
(d) ENGLISH *computer* > ITALIAN *computer* → *computeristico, computerizzare* → *computerizzazione*;
(e) FRENCH *chauffeur* 'driver' > TURKISH *şoför*;
(f) SPANISH *sombrero* 'hat' > ENGLISH *sombrero* 'broad-brimmed, tall crowned hat' (restriction of meaning);
(g) ARABIC *al wazir* 'minister, governor' > SPANISH *alguacil* 'lower law-court official' > ITALIAN *aguzzino* 'slave driver, torturer' (popular etymology influenced by ITALIAN *aguzzare* 'to sharpen').

It should be noted that borrowing speech communities are only interested in one of the meanings of a polysemous loanword and lexicalize it with only the meaning: while ENGLISH *goal* means 'aim', 'end point of a race', 'pole marking such an end-point', 'area toward or into which players aim to score', 'the score', ITALIAN *goal* has only this last sense. The reason for this choice is that we do not really borrow words, but rather whole frames in which certain concepts play an important part.

7.7.2. *Loanblends* are borrowings that are partially translated into the borrowing language:

(39) (a) ENGLISH *compact disk player* > FRENCH *lecteur compact disque*;
(b) ENGLISH *to make a good job of it* > GERMAN *einen guten Job machen*.

7.7.3. *Semantic loans* (GERMAN "Lehnprägung") are normal processes of lexicalization as discussed here (word formation; semantic change, idioms), but which are initiated by foreign influence (cf. esp. Betz 1949/65; Höfler 1971; Blank 1995). Semantic loan is thus a very smart tool for naming imported concepts while avoiding the loanword:

(40) (a) ITALIAN *grattacielo*, FRENCH *gratte-ciel*, GERMAN *Wolkenkratzer*, (< ENGLISH *sky-scraper*);
(b) GERMAN *Geist* 'mind' > 'wit' (< FRENCH *esprit*);
(c) FRENCH *pas de problème*, ITALIAN *non c'è problema* (< ENGLISH *no problem*).

One notices that ITALIAN *grattacielo* and FRENCH *gratte-ciel* are word-for-word translations of ENGLISH *sky-scraper*, while in GERMAN *Wolkenkratzer* only the second part is identical ("Lehnübertragung" in Betz 1965): GERMAN *Wolke* 'cloud' is related to the concept SKY by contiguity (cf. Blank 1995: 43s.).

8. Conclusion

The term lexicalization has been wrongly restricted to the adoption of complex words into the lexicon (DEF₁). As showed in the last section, a whole bundle of lexical processes can be subsumed under this label, necessitating a wider definition (DEF₄ in section 7.1.). Lexicalization thus parallels grammaticalization on the level of the lexicon.

As a general diachronic device lexicalization affects all parts of the lexicon and establishes new linguistic material (either formal, semantic or both) as a language rule for a sociolinguistically defined group of speakers. It concerns, firstly, new complex words, borrowings, acronyms and delocutive formations; and secondly, the further development of already lexicalized material by semantic change, conversion, reinterpretation, formal reduction, fusion, loss of transparency, etc. (DEF₂ and DEF₃). The pathways of lexicalization turn out to be as multifaceted as the lexicon itself.

9. References

Anscombre, Jean-Claude. 1979. "Délocutivité benvenistienne, délocutivité généralisée et performativité". In: *Langue Française* 42: 69–84.

Bauer, Laurie. 1988. *Introducing linguistic morphology*. Edinburgh.

Benveniste, Emile. 1966. Problèmes de linguistique générale. Vol. 1. Paris.

Betz, Werner. 1949/65. *Deutsch und Lateinisch. Die Lehnbildungen der althochdeutschen Benediktinerregel*. Bonn.

Blank, Andreas. 1993. "Das verwaiste Wort. Zum Bedeutungswandel durch Volksetymologie". In: Foltys, Christian & Kotschi, Thomas (eds.). *Berliner romanistische Studien. Für Horst Ochse*. Berlin, 43–61.

Blank, Andreas. 1995. "Lexikalische Entlehnung – Sprachwandel – Sprachvergleich: Beispiele aus dem Computer-Wortschatz". In: Schmitt, Christian & Schweickard, Wolfgang (eds.). *Die romanischen Sprachen im Vergleich*. Bonn, 38–69.

Blank, Andreas. 1996. "Tyson est aux anges – Zur Semantik französischer Funktionsverbgefüge". In: *Zeitschrift für französische Sprache und Literatur* 106: 113–30.

Blank, Andreas. 1997. *Prinzipien des lexikalischen Bedeutungswandels am Beispiel der romanischen Sprachen*. Tübingen.

Bréal, Michel. 1899. *Essai de sémantique*. Paris.

Bühler, Karl. 1934/65. *Sprachtheorie. Die Darstellungsfunktion der Sprache*. Stuttgart: Gustav Fischer.

Chomsky, Noam. 1970. "Remarks on nominalization". In: Jacobs, Roderick A. & Rosenbaum, Peter S. (eds.). *Readings in English transformational grammar*. Waltham/MA: Ginn, 184–221.

Conte, Maria-Elisabeth. 1984. "Délocutivité, performativité, contreperformativité". In: Serbat, Guy (ed.). *Emile Benveniste aujourd'hui*. Paris, 65–76.

Coseriu, Eugenio. 1952/75. "System, Norm und Rede". In: id.: *Sprachtheorie und allgemeine Sprachwissenschaft*. Munich, 11–101 (Original: "Sistema, norma y habla". 1952).

Coseriu, Eugenio. 1966/78. "Einführung in die strukturelle Betrachtung des Wortschatzes". In: Geckeler, Horst (ed.). *Strukturelle Bedeutungslehre*. Darmstadt: Wissenschaftliche Buchgesellschaft, 193–238.

Coseriu, Eugenio. 1977. "Strukturelle Wortbildungslehre (am Beispiel des Typs coupe-papier)". In: Brekle, Herbert E. & Kastovsky, Dieter (eds.). *Perspektiven der Wortbildungsforschung*. Bonn.

Coulmas, Florian. 1985. "Lexikalisierung von Syntagmen". In: Schwarze & Wunderlich, 250–68.

Deroy, Louis. 1980. *L'emprunt linguistique*. Paris.

Fill, Alwin. 1980. *Wortdurchsichtigkeit im Englischen. Eine nicht-generative Studie morphosemantischer Strukturen*. Innsbruck.

Fleischer, Wolfgang & Barz, Irmhild. 1992. *Wortbildung der deutschen Gegenwartssprache*. Tübingen.

Fodor, Janet D. 1977. *Semantics. Theories of meaning in generative grammar*. New York.

Fritz, Gerd. forthcoming. "Ansätze zu einer Theorie des Sprachwandels auf lexikalischer Ebene". In: Betten, A. & al. (eds.). *Sprachgeschichte. Ein internationales Handbuch*. Berlin & New York: de Gruyter.

Gauger, Hans-Martin. 1971. *Durchsichtige Wörter. Zur Theorie der Wortbildung*. Heidelberg.

Geisler, Hans. 1994. "Che fine fanno i Bot? Anmerkungen zur Akronymenbildung im Italienischen". In: Sabban, Annette & Schmitt, Christian (eds.). *Sprachlicher Alltag. Linguistik – Rhetorik – Literaturwissenschaft. Festschrift Wolf-Dieter Stempel*. Tübingen, 97–117.

Günther, Hartmut. 1987. "Wortbildung, Syntax, be-Verben und das Lexikon". In: *Beiträge zur Geschichte der deutschen Sprache und Literatur* 109: 179–201.

Haugen, Einar. 1950. "The Analysis of Linguistic Borrowing". In: *Language* 26: 210–31.

Höfler, Manfred. 1971. "Das Problem der sprachlichen Entstehung". In: *Jahrbuch der Universität Düsseldorf* 1969/70: 58–67.

Kastovsky, Dieter. 1982. *Wortbildung und Semantik*. Düsseldorf, Bern, Munich.

Katz, Jerrold J. 1972. Semantic theory. New York etc.

Keller, Rudi. 1995. *Zeichentheorie. Zu einer Theorie semiotischen Wissens*. Tübingen.

Kilani-Schoch, Marianne & Dressler, Wolfgang Ulrich. 1992. "Prol-o. intell-o, gauch-o et les autres. Propriétés formelles de deux opérations du français parlé". In: *Romanistisches Jahrbuch* 43: 65–86.

Koch, Peter. 1988. "Norm und Sprache". In: Albrecht, Jörn & al. (eds.). *Energeia und Ergon. Sprachliche Variation – Sprachgeschichte – Sprachtypologie*. Vol. 2. Tübingen: Narr, 327–54.

Koch, Peter. 1993. "Kyenbé – Tyonbo: Wurzeln kreolischer Lexik". In: Foltys, Christian & Kotschi, Thomas (eds.). *Berliner romanistische Studien. Für Horst Ochse*. Berlin, 259–287.

Koch, Peter. 1994. "Gedanken zur Metapher – und zu ihrer Alltäglichkeit". In: Sabban, Annette & Schmitt, Christian (eds.). *Sprachlicher Alltag. Linguistik – Rhetorik – Literaturwissenschaft. Festschrift für Wolf-Dieter Stempel*. Tübingen, 201–225.

Koch, Peter. 1997. "Diskurstraditionen: zu ihrem sprachtheoretischen Status und ihrer Dynamik". In: Frank, Barbara & Haye, Thomas & Tophinke,

Doris (eds.). *Gattungen mittelalterlicher Schriftlichkeit*. (ScriptOralia 99.) Tübingen: Narr, 43−79.

Koch, Peter & Oesterreicher, Wulf. 1996. "Sprachwandel und expressive Mündlichkeit". In: *Zeitschrift für Linguistik und Literaturwissenschaft LiLi* 26: 64−96.

Lakoff, George & Johnson, Mark. 1980. *Metaphors We Live By* Chicago.

Lehmann, Christian. 1989. "Grammatikalisierung und Lexikalisierung". *Zeitschrift für Phonetik, Sprachwissenschaft und Kommunikationsforschung* 42: 11−19.

Lehmann, Christian. 1995. *Thoughts on grammaticalization*. München: Lincom Europa.

Li, Charles N. & Thompson, Sandra A. 1987. "Chinese". In: Comrie, Bernard (ed.). *The World's Major Languages*. London & Sydney, 811−33.

Liebert, Wolf-Andreas. 1992. *Metaphernbereiche der deutschen Alltagssprache. Kognitive Linguistik und die Perspektiven einer Kognitiven Lexikographie*. Frankfurt.

Lipka, Leonhard. 1977. "Lexikalisierung, Idiomatisierung und Hypostasierung als Probleme einer synchronischen Wortbildungslehre". In: Brekle, Herbert E. & Kastovsky, Dieter (eds.). *Perspektiven der Wortbildungsforschung*. Bonn, 155−64.

Lipka, Leonhard. 1981. "Lexikalisierung im Deutschen und Englischen". In: Lipka, Leonhard & Günther, Hartmut (eds.). *Wortbildung*. Darmstadt, 119−32.

Lipka, Leonhard. 1990. *An outline of English lexicology*. Tübingen.

Lüdtke, Helmut. 1986. "Esquisse d'une théorie du changement langagier". In: *La Linguistique* 22: 3−46.

Lutzeier, Peter. 1995. *Lexikologie. Ein Arbeitsbuch*. Tübingen.

Lyons, John. 1977. *Semantics* 2 vols. Cambridge.

Marchand, Hans. 1969. *The Categories and Types of Present-Day English Word-Formation*. München.

Matthews, Peter. 1991. *Morphology*. Cambridge.

Naumann, Hans & Betz, Werner. 1967. *Althochdeutsches Elementarbuch*. Berlin.

Nyrop, Kristoffer. 1913. *Grammaire historique de la langue française*. Vol. 4. "Sémantique". Copenhague.

Palm, Christine. 1995. *Phraseologie. Eine Einführung*. Tübingen.

Paul, Hermann. 1880/1995. *Prinzipien der Sprachgeschichte*. Tübingen.

Pawley, Andrew. 1986. "Lexicalization". In: Tannen, Deborah & Alatis, James E. (eds.). *Georgetown-University Round Table on Languages and Linguistics 1985*. Washington, 98−120.

Posner, Rebecca. 1996. *The Romance Languages*. Cambridge.

Pottier, Bernard. 1974. *Linguistique générale. Théorie et description*. Paris.

Quirk, Randolph & Greenbaum, Sidney & Leech, Geoffrey & Svartvik, Jan. 1985. *A Comprehensive Grammar of the English Language*. London & New York.

Rainer, Franz. 1995. "Inflection inside derivation: evidence from Spanish and Portuguese". *Yearbook of Morphology 1995*: 83−91.

Scalise, Sergio. 1990. *Morfologia e lessico. Una prospettiva generativista*. Bologna.

Schlieben-Lange, Brigitte. 1983. *Traditionen des Sprechens. Elemente einer pragmatischen Sprachgeschichtsschreibung*. Stuttgart: Kohlhammer.

Schpak-Dolt, Nikolaus. 1992. *Französische Morphologie*. Tübingen.

Schwarze, Christoph. 1988. *Grammatik der italienischen Sprache*. Tübingen.

Schwarze, Christoph & Wunderlich, Dieter (eds.). *Handbuch der Lexikologie*. Frankfurt.

Skalička, Vladimir. 1979. *Typlogische Studien*. Ed. by Peter Hartmann. Braunschweig & Wiesbaden: Westermann.

Staib, Bruno. 1989. "Typisierung und Hierarchisierung der sprachlichen Transposition". *Romanistisches Jahrbuch* 40: 15−25.

Stein, Peter. 1984. *Kreolisch und Französisch*. Tübingen: Niemeyer.

Tournier, Jean. 1985. *Introduction descriptive à la lexicogénétique de l'anglais contemporain*. Paris & Geneva.

Ullmann, Stephen. 1957. *Principles of Semantics*. Oxford: Blackwell & Glasgow: Jackson.

Ullmann, Stephen. 1962. *Semantics. An Introduction to the Science of Meaning*. Oxford.

Windisch, Rudolf. 1991. "Die Wortverschmelzung − ein 'abscheuliches Monstrum' der französischen und deutschen Wortbildung?". *Romanistisches Jahrbuch* 42: 34−51.

Wunderli, Peter. 1989. *Französische Lexikologie. Einführung in die Theorie und Geschichte des französischen Wortschatzes*. Tübingen.

Wurzel, Wolfgang Ullrich. forthcoming. *Zur Entwicklung von Wörtern im Lexikon*.

Andreas Blank (†), University of Marburg (Germany)

113. Les processus de grammaticalisation

1. Introduction
2. Les opérations conceptuelles
3. Les opérations formelles
4. Les points de départ et les points d'arrivée
5. Directionnalité de la grammaticalisation
6. Conclusion
7. Références

1. Introduction

On attribue l'invention du terme de *grammaticalisation* à un article d'Antoine Meillet (1912) qui l'oppose à l'analogie comme autre procédé par lequel les langues étendent leurs moyens d'expression. C'est surtout à partir des années 1970 que les linguistes ont commencé à exploiter la notion de grammaticalisation (cf. Givón 1971, Hagège 1975: 163, 173, 255). Le mouvement s'accentue durant les années 80, où paraissent des ouvrages, comme Lehmann 1982 ou Heine & Reh 1984. Les années 1990 voient une véritable floraison de travaux sur la grammaticalisation, dont Heine, Claudi & Hünnemeyer 1991a, Traugott & Heine 1991, Hagège 1993 et Hopper & Traugott 1993. Certains étudient la notion en relation avec celle d'iconicité (→ art. 30). Chez tous les auteurs, la grammaticalisation est définie à peu près de la même façon, comme le processus par lequel une unité lexicale d'une langue se développe, au cours du temps, en unité grammaticale, ou une unité grammaticale en unité plus grammaticale encore.

Le présent article se propose d'examiner la grammaticalisation en montrant quelles opérations elle met en jeu (§ 2.: Les opérations conceptuelles, § 3.: Les opérations formelles), à quoi elles aboutissent (§ 4.: Les points de départ et les points d'arrivées) et selon quelle direction elles se déroulent (§ 5.: Directionnalité de la grammaticalisation). A travers toutes ces étapes, il apparaîtra que l'étude des faits de grammaticalisation représente une contribution essentielle à la linguistique générale: ce qui est en cause, c'est l'évolution morphogénétique par laquelle les langues spécifient leur grammaire.

2. Les opérations conceptuelles

L'extension des moyens d'expression d'une langue peut être conçue comme un problème à résoudre, et dont la solution met d'abord en jeu des processus conceptuels (§ 2.1.). Mais il faut aussi tenir compte de l'implication personnelle des locuteurs (§ 2.2.). Enfin, l'étude des aspects conceptuels de la grammaticalisation ne doit pas faire oublier l'importance des aspects syntaxiques et contextuels (§ 2.3.).

2.1. Le problème linguistique et sa solution notionnelle

2.1.1. La grammaticalisation comme stratégie de réponse à un problème

Il peut être éclairant d'examiner les faits des langues dans le cadre de l'activité des locuteurs-auditeurs. Un problème essentiel pour les usagers humains des langues est évidemment celui de la structuration du message en une succession d'ensembles appelés phrases, dont l'organisation reflète et produit, à la fois, la grammaire de chaque langue. Ces phrases ne peuvent pas être constituées uniquement de ce que la tradition CHINOISE appelle les mots pleins, et la linguistique occidentale les lexèmes, à savoir les unités lexicales. Beaucoup de ces unités, n'ayant pas de rôle syntaxique en soi, ont besoin d'être reliées entre elles pour constituer des phrases acceptables, et ne peuvent l'être que grâce à la présence de l'autre grand type, les unités grammaticales ou morphèmes, que les locuteurs-auditeurs, pour résoudre le problème posé, doivent construire. Ils sont donc des constructeurs de langue (CLs). Or les CLs n'ont d'autres matériaux que les lexèmes eux-mêmes. Il leur faut donc fabriquer des morphèmes à partir de lexèmes, ce qui est la définition même de la grammaticalisation dans son aspect principal.

2.1.2. Les processus conceptuels sous-jacents à la grammaticalisation

Une aptitude mentale caractéristique de l'espèce humaine consiste à conceptualiser un objet ou un événement de nature plus abstraite ou à base non physique dans les termes d'un objet ou d'un événement de nature plus concrète ou à base physique. Or c'est ce qu'on observe dans bien des cas de grammaticalisation. Examinons trois exemples en KABIYÉ (langue NIGER-CONGO du Togo; cf. Heine, Claudi & Hünnemeyer 1991a: 148−150):

(1) pɛ-té   wɛ ɖéu
     3PL.POSS-maison est belle
     « leur maison est belle »

(2) maa-woki man-ɖani té
    1SG.NEG-aller 1SG.POSS-amie chez
    « Je ne vais pas chez ma petite amie »

(3) kólú té húyiŋ
    forgeron de sacs
    « les sacs du forgeron ».

Le contexte et la position dans lesquels apparaît *té* sont chaque fois différents: en (1), il est après un possessif et avant un verbe; en (2), il suit un nom et se trouve en fin d'énoncé; en (3), il est entre deux noms. Si à cette observation on ajoute les différences de sens, on établira que *té* en (1) est un nom, en (2) un relateur sous l'espèce d'une postposition directionnelle, et en (3) un joncteur (marque de détermination nominale).

Comment peut-on passer de l'un à l'autre de ces emplois? Pour rendre compte du passage de « maison » à « chez », on est conduit à supposer un processus d'abstraction métaphorique en vertu duquel un objet situé dans l'espace, ici une maison, en vient à référer à cet espace lui-même: une entité concrète devient le véhicule d'expression d'un domaine abstrait. Quant au passage de « maison » à l'abstrait « de », il implique que ce qui est situé dans le lieu où habite un individu appartient, de ce fait, à sa sphère de possession, avec l'intéressante réserve que ce lieu ne lui étant pas inhérent comme le sont les parties de son corps, l'emploi du nom de la maison en tant que marque du rapport de possession ne s'applique en KABIYÉ qu'à la possession aliénable, ainsi qu'il apparaît dans les deux exemples suivants:

(4) kólú té píya
    forgeron de enfants
    « les enfants du forgeron »

(5) kólú píya
    « les enfants du forgeron ».

Le FRANÇAIS ne marque pas ici la distinction, d'où l'identité de traduction de (4) et (5), mais en (5), sans joncteur, il s'agit bien des enfants du forgeron, c'est-à-dire de possession inaliénable, alors que (4) parle des enfants vivant dans une des cases du forgeron. Ainsi, malgré l'abstraction, le sens concret d'un mot dont les CLs se servent comme véhicule d'expression d'une notion abstraite ne disparaît pas totalement.

La conceptualisation de l'abstrait en termes de concret peut encore être illustrée par le passage du volitionnel au futur. On sait qu'un très grand nombre de langues, de l'ANGLAIS au CHINOIS en passant par des idiomes d'Europe, d'Afrique et d'Asie, expriment le futur au moyen d'un verbe « vouloir ». Comme un vouloir ne peut être qu'humain, s'il est attribué non à un agent humain conscient, mais à n'importe quelle entité non humaine inapte à une entreprise volontaire, le sens cesse d'être volitionnel, pour devenir épistémique: il s'agit alors d'une prédiction. L'étape suivante est celle d'une pure et simple expression du temps futur. On peut donc considérer qu'un trait de comportement typiquement humain, la volonté, se trouve utilisé, à travers les éléments linguistiques qui l'expriment, pour traduire une catégorie temporelle abstraite, le futur.

2.1.3. Les chaînes métaphoriques et le débat sur la métonymie

Il apparaît que les CLs déploient une remarquable créativité dans l'opération de grammaticalisation comme stratégie de solution d'un problème. Avant de la formaliser, considérons encore quatre exemples pris en ÉWÉ (langue NIGER-CONGO du Togo; cf. Heine, Claudi & Hünnemeyer 1991b: 161–164):

(6) é-pé megbé fá
    3SG-POSS dos être froid
    « il a froid au dos »

(7) xɔ-á megbé le nyúíé
    maison-DEF arrière être joli
    « l'arrière de la maison est joli »

(8) é le xɔ-á megbé
    3SG être maison DEF derrière
    « il est derrière la maison »

(9) é kú le é megbé
    3SG mourir être 3SG après
    « il est mort après lui ».

On voit qu'ici le dos, partie du corps en (6), est, par transfert métaphorique, pris comme vecteur d'expression de la notion de partie arrière d'un objet de l'espace en (7); une abstraction supplémentaire fait passer au sens purement spatial, et non plus objectal-spatial, de « derrière » en (8), et une autre produit le sens de succession temporelle d'« après » en (9). Le rapprochement des exemples (1), (2), (6), (7), (8) et (9) suggère d'établir, pour simuler les opérations mentales supposées ici, une chaîne de métaphorisation comme

(10) CORPS ∷ OBJET ∷ POSSESSION ∷ ESPACE ∷ TEMPS,

où le signe ∷ signifie « est ce dans les termes de quoi est interprété ». Il importe de souligner que ce cheminement du moins au plus abstrait est propre aux processus de grammaticalisation. Dans le lexique, on ne l'observe pas. Ainsi, alors que le SWAHILI *mbele* « poitrine, partie antérieure » est la source lexicale à partir de laquelle se forme un relateur locatif (statique) *mbele* « en face de » et un relateur temporel *mbele* « avant », illustrant pour l'avant corporel, spatial et temporel le processus d'abstraction formulé en (10) exactement comme les exemples (6), (7), (8) et (9) l'illustrent pour l'arrière, un sens lexical nouveau s'est dégagé à partir de *mbele*, et ce sens, loin d'être plus abstrait, pourrait plutôt paraître encore plus concret que celui de « partie antérieure », puisqu'il s'agit des organes sexuels mâles, non directement nommés car tabous (cf. Heine, Claudi & Hünnemeyer 1991a: 50).

Un débat s'est ouvert sur la question de savoir si les processus d'abstraction qu'on vient de présenter relèvent du seul domaine de la métaphore, et si la métonymie n'y aurait pas aussi sa part. L'opposition classique entre métaphore et métonymie remonte au moins à l'ouvrage de Jakobson et Halle (1956), qui présente la première comme un choix fonctionnant sur l'axe paparadigmatique et convoquant par analogie de perceptions un élément *in absentia*, alors que la seconde est une association entre éléments contigus *in praesentia*, et se déploie donc sur l'axe syntagmatique. Ces notions peuvent être utilisées dans l'étude de la grammaticalisation. Ainsi, nous savons que c'est une interprétation métaphorique du futur immédiat en termes de mouvement vers un point proche qui peut rendre compte de l'évolution de sens par laquelle le *va*, à contenu motionnel, de l'exemple (11), en est venu à servir de marqueur du futur comme dans l'exemple (12):

(11) *Jean va en ville*

(12) *Jean va partir.*

Or on se sert de ce même marqueur lorsque le sujet n'est pas comme en (12) un humain, d'où des énoncés tels que

(13) *la pluie va tomber,*

qui « viole » la logique, puisqu'« aller » est le fait d'un agent humain, non de la pluie; de même dans l'équivalent ANGLAIS:

(14) *the rain is going to come,*

qui n'a probablement pas pu s'employer avant le XVème siècle (cf. Jespersen 1911: 217). De plus, en (14), « aller » (*go*) et venir (*come*) coexistent sans mal. Cette possibilité d'employer ensemble deux mots dont les sens se contrediraient si tous deux étaient des lexèmes est l'indice sûr du changement de sens, dans ce contexte, de l'un d'eux, celui qui s'est grammaticalisé. C'est ce que l'on a appelé (Hagège 1993: 224) le *Principe de Contradiction Inaperçue* (PCI), utilisable comme critère de la grammaticalisation d'un des éléments des énoncés (15) et (16):

(15) *ʔom-t   nim-t*
INCH.1SG-PASSÉ dormir 1SG-PASSÉ
« je me suis endormi ».

En (15), exemple pris à L'ARABE ÉGYPTIEN, *ʔom-t*, première personne du singulier du passé du verbe *ʔâm* « se lever », sert d'auxiliaire de sens inchoatif, en vertu d'une démarche cognitive également illustrée dans beaucoup d'autres langues: l'acte concret de se lever est vu comme un *analogon* de la notion immatérielle de commencer. La preuve sémantique du fait que *ʔom-t* n'est plus ici un syntagme verbal « je me suis levé » est qu'il peut apparaître au voisinage immédiat d'un verbe signifiant « dormir », sens totalement contradictoire avec celui de « se lever », sans que cette contradiction soit aperçue ni qu'elle invalide l'énoncé. Le même phénomène s'observe en (16), exemple du dialecte mouroum du NGAMBAY-MOUNDOU, langue TCHADIQUE parlée au Tchad:

(16) *d'-ísī   d'-áo*
ils-PROGR ils-aller
« ils sont en train de partir ».

Dans cet énoncé, *ísī*, verbe signifiant « s'asseoir » dans son emploi lexématique, est employé comme auxiliaire marquant le progressif. Il est clair que cet emploi fait de *ísī* un élément de la grammaire, car si c'était un lexème, son sens d'« asseoir » produirait, avec le sens de *áo*, « aller », une contradiction assez forte pour invalider cet énoncé. Le Principe de Contradiction Inaperçue s'applique donc, et il y a bien ici transfert métaphorique du sens de s'asseoir » à celui de « être en train de »: la notion abstraite de progressivité est exprimée, comme dans beaucoup d'autres langues (dialectes ARABES, nombreux CRÉOLES etc.), par l'image concrète de s'asseoir, action dont le résultat est supposé durer au moins quelque temps.

Si l'on peut proposer une interprétation métaphorique des processus sémantico-cognitifs qui conduisent aux marqueurs de futur immédiat des exemples (12) à (14), au marqueur d'inchoatif de l'exemple (15) et au marqueur de progressif de l'exemple (16), cela n'exclut pas une interprétation métonymique. Ainsi, le passage, en (14), d'un verbe signifiant « aller » à un morphème de futur immédiat n'est pas simplement, dans l'absolu, celui d'un lexème à un morphème, un verbe *go*, par une métaphore liée à son sens spatial, s'auxiliarisant en indicateur d'imminence; ce qui est en question ici, c'est bien le syntagme entier *is going to*, et l'on ne saurait négliger le rôle joué par le phénomène purement contextuel de la congituïté entre *going* et *to*, morphème de sens final-directionnel (cf. Hopper & Traugott 1993: 81).

La même explication peut valoir pour la grammaticalisation du verbe « prendre ». Quand il produit une marque d'instrument, comme dans de nombreuses langues d'Asie du Sud-Eest (CHINOIS, THAI, etc.), ainsi que d'Afrique de l'Ouest (YORUBA OU AKAN), les incompatibilités sémantiques sont un indice de ce chargement. Soit, en YORUBA, les phrases

(17) *mo fi àdé gé igi*
      1SG prendre machette couper arbre
      « j'ai coupé l'arbre avec une machette »

(18) *mo fi ogbon gé igi*
      1SG prendre habilité couper arbre
      « j'ai coupé l'arbre avec habileté ».

Ici, le passage de « prendre », verbe de sens concret, à « se servir de », plus abstrait, et, dans le cadre syntaxique d'une structure sérielle (cf. 4.2.1.1.), au relateur instrumental « au moyen de », n'est pas remis en cause par des contraintes contextuelles: tout comme on prend une machette, la langue permet de dire qu'on « prend » l'habileté. Cependant, cette bizarrerie conceptuelle oblige à considérer, en vertu du *PCI*, que *fi* en (18) est, plutôt qu'un verbe, un relateur de manière 'avec'.

En revanche, quand « prendre » produit une marque de patient, si le sens du verbe en fonction de prédicat principal exclut une saisie préalable de l'objet qui correspond à ce patient, il sera impossible d'utiliser cette marque de patient. C'est ce que l'on observe en GÃ, parlé au Ghana, pour la marque *kè*, lorsque le prédicat est un verbe signifiant « voir », « pondre », ou toute autre opération qui, faisant affleurer à l'existence ou à la perception un certain objet, implique qu'on n'a pas pu commencer par prendre cet objet. De même, en MANDARIN moderne, on dit

(19) *tā bǎ zhèi běn shū mài le*
      3SG M.PATIENT DÉICT. CLASS livre vendre PASSÉ
      « il a vendu ce livre »,

mais on ne peut pas dire

(20) **tā bǎ zhei běn shū mǎi le*
      « il a acheté ce livre »,

car on sait que *bǎ*, aujourd'hui marque de patient en MANDARIN, était un verbe « prendre » en ANCIEN CHINOIS; or *mǎi* « acheter » suppose qu'on n'ait pas commencé par saisir ce qu'on achète (sans quoi, dans la logique de cette langue, on le posséderait déjà et n'aurait pas lieu de l'acheter), alors que *mài* « vendre » (étymologiquement son causatif avec changement tonal (« vendre » = « faire acheter »)) n'exclut pas que l'on prenne en main l'objet que l'on vend. Ainsi, l'évolution du sens de « prendre » vers l'emploi comme marque de patient suggère de poser une relation métonymique entre le fait de prendre et l'objet que l'on prend.

On peut dire, en conclusion de tout ce qu'on vient de voir, que la place prise dans la grammaticalisation par les processus de transfert métaphorique n'exclut pas les processus métonymiques. C'est le recours à une interprétation mettant en évidence une action conjuguée de l'un et de l'autre qui paraît le mieux rendre compte de cette opération complexe.

Encore est-il important d'ajouter que dans toute une partie des faits de grammaticalisation, cette association des deux modes d'explication ne peut même pas être envisagée: il s'agit des cas dans lesquels la source lexématique des morphèmes, essentiellement les relateurs, n'est pas nominale mais verbale; en effet, la formule (10) de passage métaphorique ne concerne que des notions statiques, principalement les objets et l'espace où ils se situent; mais quand la source des relateurs est verbale (cf. § 4.1.1.1.), le sens n'est plus statique, il est dynamique. Ce n'est donc pas par hasard que les exemples (17)−(19) ci-dessus, où l'on a vu que l'interprétation par la métaphore est inopérante à elle seule et que la métonymie doit être envisagée pour apporter un éclairage, contiennent des relateurs d'origine verbale.

2.2. L'implication personnelle des locuteurs-auditeurs

Les processus cognitifs par lesquels se caractérise l'activité des locuteurs face au problème à résoudre de la grammaticalisation n'épuisent pas la question traitée dans le présent article. Les CLs n'accomplissent pas d'opérations dans le vide. La relation interpersonnelle qui s'institue entre eux dans l'acte d'interlocution exerce un effet direct sur la négociation des sens. Le résultat de celle-ci est ici plus complexe qu'on ne l'a dit. Plusieurs auteurs, en effet, ont vu la grammaticalisation comme une « affaiblissement sémantique » (Guillaume 1964), un « affadissement sémantique » (Givón 1975), une « déplétion sémantique » (Lehmann 1982), une désémanticisation. Pour Heine & Reh, qui sont, à l'époque où paraît leur ouvrage (1984), parmi les tenants de cette dernière notion, les unités linguistiques, du fait de l'évolution en cause, perdent en complexité sémantique et en importance pragmatique.

En fait, s'il y a dans la grammaticalisation moins d'élaboration des sens d'origine que dans le changement lexical, il y a néanmoins apport d'un sens nouveau, celui-là même qu'on peut considérer comme un sens grammatical (Sweetser 1988: 392). En d'autres termes, si un sens est perdu, un autre est acquis. Il n'est pas vrai que, comme on aime à le répéter, la grammaticalisation aboutisse à des unités figées ou sans contenu. Il serait plus vrai de dire qu'elle aboutit à des unités spécialisées. En même temps, et sans contradiction, elle aboutit, au moins dans beaucoup de cas, à des unités de portée générale.

Les unités grammaticales telles que les relateurs, par exemple, sont spécialisées dans la mesure où elles fonctionnent comme des outils; elles sont le produit d'une généralisation dans la mesure où leur sens est en partie déterminé par le contexte. Ainsi, la préposition CHINOISE *yú*, historiquement issue d'un verbe qui signifiait « se référer à », peut, selon l'environnement dans lequel elle apparaît, prendre des sens comme « à », « dans », « vers », « en faveur de », « depuis », « contre », « avec », « en comparaison de », etc. (cf. Hagège, 1975: 152). Le morphème *r*, unique relateur du PALAU, langue AUSTRONÉSIENNE d'une île de Micronésie, est, comme l'implique à l'évidence cette situation, très fortement polysème (cf. Hagège 1986).

Ce que les CLs font donc quand ils constituent des mots grammaticaux à partir de mots lexicaux, c'est d'infléchir la langue selon les exigences de la transmission et de l'interprétation d'un message. Cet engagement personnel des locuteurs-auditeurs équivaut à un travail sur le sens qu'il faut considérer non comme une désémanticisation, mais plutôt comme une resémanticisation (cf. Hagège, 1993: 225).

C'est, dans ces conditions, un renforcement de l'implication des CLs qui se donne ici à observer. L'évolution des sens de certains conjonctifs fait bien apparaître que les inférences de ces éléments, bien qu'elles soient, au stade initial, purement conversationnelles, donc fortuites et liées à une situation particulière de communication, finissent par se conventionnaliser, devenant partie intégrante du sens desdits éléments. Traugott et König (1991: 194–195) donnent des illustrations claires de ce phénomène. Ainsi, alors que *since* revêt un pur sens temporel dans l'exemple (21):

(21) *I have done quite a bit of writing since we last met,*

il n'en va pas de même dans les exemples (22) et (23):

(22) *Since Susan left him, John has been very miserable*

(23) *Since you are not coming with me, I will have to go alone.*

En (22), qui représente une étape ultérieure du processus, le locuteur augmente la force informative de l'énoncé par le fait qu'il privilégie la relation entre *since Susan left* et *John has been very miserable*, et laisse entendre qu'il y avait une pertinence à mentionner ce fait d'apparence purement temporelle qu'est le départ de Susan, dans la mesure où, en réalité, il s'agissait, à la fois, d'événement antérieur et de cause. Ainsi, (22), énoncé où la relation de dépendance est polysémique, c'est-à-dire aussi bien causale que temporelle, laisse voir comment l'implication conversationnelle s'installe. En (23), représentant l'étape finale du processus, on n'a plus que le sens causal. Dans l'histoire de la langue ANGLAISE, c'est au XVème siècle que cette étape a été atteinte, mais l'évolution sémantique qui devait y conduire s'esquisse dès les textes de VIEIL-ANGLAIS qui s'échelonnent entre les IXème et XIème siècles.

Une évolution semblable s'est produite dans bien d'autres langues, comme l'atteste l'histoire de *puisque* et *du moment que* en FRANÇAIS, de *eftersom* en DANOIS, de *koska* en FINNOIS, de *paräst* en ESTONIEN, etc. L'implication personnelle des locuteurs-auditeurs semble apporter ici un éclairage utile, et il ne peut suffire de considérer, comme certains auteurs (cf. Heine, Claudi & Hünnemeyer 1991a: 75), que l'on a affaire à un passage métaphorique de la notion de temps à celle de cause, qui serait « plus abstraite ».

Un autre exemple est celui du passage d'un sens de concomitance à un sens de concessivité. Ainsi, l'ancêtre VIEIL ANGLAIS du *while* d'aujourd'hui, à savoir *hwile*, était le datif d'un mot signifiant « temps », et exprimait très exactement, précédé du démonstratif d'éloignement *tha*, également au datif, et du conjonctif *the* « que », la simultanéité, puisque l'ensemble signifiait « au moment où ». Au cours de l'évolution de la langue, ce sens purement temporel de simultanéité en vient à s'assortir d'inférences conversationnelles, parmi lesquelles celle qui, présentant comme une surprise une certain événement, a pour effet d'y greffer un sens nouveau, en sorte qu'il ne s'agit plus, simplement, du cadre dans lequel (signifié purement chronologique), mais de celui en dépit duquel, un certain événement survient.

L'exemple de *while* est loin d'être isolé. Le même mouvement qui conduit du sens de cooccurrence à celui d'opposition s'observe pour le FRANÇAIS *tandis que*, le TURC *iken*, l'INDONÉSIEN *sekali-pun* (= « à ce moment précis + même »), le JAPONAIS *nagara*, le HAWAIEN *oiai*, le HOPI *naama-hin* (= « ensemble + ainsi »), le QUILEUTE *-t'e*, etc. (cf. Traugott & König 1991: 199). Tous ces exemples font apparaître la façon dont un rapport de « simple » simultanéité chronologique est réinterprété, dans les circonstances concrètes de l'échange interlocutif, par adjonction de sens autres que temporels, liés aux présupposés, aux déductions, aux attentes du locuteur et de l'auditeur; → art. 63, fig. 63.1, 63.2; art. 45, § 4 et Table 45.2.

2.3. Les aspects syntaxiques et contextuels

Dans tout ce qui précède, on s'est efforcé de faire apparaître l'importance du problème notionnel que pose le processus de grammaticalisation, ainsi que celle de l'implication personnelle des locuteurs dans ce processus. Mais les données linguistiques sont beaucoup plus complexes et font intervenir tous à la fois beaucoup plus de paramètres que ne peut le laisser croire l'étude nécessairement décumulée qu'en présente l'exposé scientifique. En même temps qu'ils accomplissent des opérations qui relèvent de la métaphorisation, de la métonymisation, de l'inférence conversationnelle, les CLs construisent des phrases, et par là même les règles de leur construction, c'est-à-dire leur syntaxe. Considérons les phrases ÉWÉ (24) et (25):

(24) *xɔ-á   megbé le   nyúíé*
maison-DEF arrière être joli
« l'arrière de la maison est joli »

(25) *é   le   xɔ-á   megbé*
3SG être maison-DEF derrière
« il est derrière la maison ».

On a vu ci-dessus (§ 2.1.3.), à propos des énoncés (7) et (8), ici reproduits, qu'une chaîne de métaphorisation peut être posée, comme on l'a fait en (10), pour interpréter les processus sous-jacents aux opérations de grammaticalisation illustrées par ces énoncés. Cependant, en (25), il n'y a pas seulement interprétation de la position dans l'espace en termes de partie d'un objet occupant un certain emplacement. Si on raisonne dans un cadre uniquement sémantique et ne s'intéresse qu'aux opérations cognitives ici sous-jacentes, on ne peut pas expliquer comment il se fait que (25) ne signifie pas « il est l'arrière de la maison ». Pour rendre compte du fait que « l'arrière de la maison » ne désigne plus ici un object mais une circonstance, il faut reconnaître un phénomène syntaxique essentiel: *megbé* est devenu une marque locative, c'est-à-dire un outil grammatical régissant, pour les subordonner au prédicat verbal, des compléments spatiaux. En d'autres termes, *xɔ-á megbé* n'est plus un syntagme nominal ordinaire fonctionnant comme sujet ainsi qu'il l'est en (24), c'est-à-dire un actant, mais un circonstant. La relation de dépendance syntaxique qui s'instaure ainsi peut sans doute être elle-même interprétée en termes cognitifs, mais d'une part on ignore encore de quelle façon exactement, et d'autre part, cette relation demeure un phénomène nucléaire, qu'il est exclu de négliger dans l'étude de la grammaticalisation. Ces considérations reçoivent un appui supplémentaire si l'on examine les cas dans lesquels l'étroitesse du rapport de dépendance est encore plus clairement marquée. Ainsi, en SO, langue KULIAK du nord de l'Ouganda, on trouve les trois énoncés.

(26) *néké íca sú-o   sóg*
être 3SG arrière-ABL montagne

(27) *nékɛ íca sú-o sóg-o*

(28) *nékɛ íca sú sóg-o.*

Les auteurs qui les citent (Heine, Claudi & Hünnemeyer 1991a: 249), déclarent que ces énoncés signifient tous trois « il est derrière la montagne », mais ils sont surtout intéressés par les problèmes que leur paraît poser cette quasi-synonymie.

Or on remarque ici des différences intéressantes entre les types de relations syntaxiques illustrés par ces trois énoncés. En (26), le verbe *nékɛ*, qui gouverne dans cette langue un complément de lieu à l'ablatif, tient sous sa dépendance le syntagme nominal *sú-o sóg* « l'arrière de la montagne », référant à ce lieu où se trouve l'individu désigné par *íca* « il ». En (27), le mot *su*, tout en restant, comme l'indique le maintien de la marque d'ablatif, sous la dépendance de *nékɛ*, gouverne lui-même un complément de lieu à l'ablatif (on pourrait aussi considérer que *sóg-o* est à l'ablatif par attraction casuelle, mais le so ne semble pas connaître plus ce phénomène que les autres langues de la région et du groupe); cela signifie que *sú*, sans avoir un statut de relateur puisqu'il est lui-même suffixé d'un relateur *-o*, ne se comporte plus vis-à-vis de *sóg* comme une nominal déterminé par un autre nominal.

Enfin, en (28), *sú* est à considérer comme un relateur véritable: il n'est plus sous la dépendance du prédicat verbal *nékɛ* puisqu'il n'est plus marqué par un suffixe d'ablatif, et il régit lui-même le nom *sóg*; c'est donc cet ensemble, à savoir un syntagme à relateur, qui se trouve, en tant que tel, sous la dépendance du prédicat.

Ainsi, l'exploration des aspects conceptuels de la grammaticalisation conduit à faire également leur place aux opérations syntaxiques, qu'elles aient ou non elles-mêmes un sous-bassement cognitif décelable. La syntaxe s'inscrit à son tour dans le cadre plus général de l'organisation contextuelle. Par conséquent, étudier la grammaticalisation, c'est aussi prendre en considération l'importance du contexte. Un seul exemple suffira ici à la faire apparaître. En ÉWÉ (cf. Heine, Claudi & Hünnemeyer 1991a: 194−197), l'unité *kpɔ́* est, dans son emploi lexématique, un verbe « voir », ainsi qu'on le note en (29):

(29)   *e   kpɔ́ e   a*
       2SG voir 3SG MARQU. QUEST.
       « est-ce que tu l'as vu? ».

Mais *kpɔ́* connaît aussi un autre emploi comme marque de l'inattendu, après un verbe; c'est le cas en (30):

(30)   *e se e kpɔ́ a* (*se* = « entendre »)
       « as-tu vraiment entendu cela? »

Si *kpɔ́* était un verbe « voir » en (30), cet énoncé signifierait « as-tu entendu cela as-tu vu? », ce qui est ininterprétable. Pour comprendre comment *kpɔ́* en vient à prendre ce sens de marque de l'inattendu, examinons l'énoncé (31):

(31)   *Kofi á   vá   kpɔ́ a*
       K.   FUT venir voir MARQU. QUEST.
   (a) « Kofi viendra-t-il voir? »
   (b) « Kofi viendrait-il vraiment? »

On voit que (31) peut avoir deux sens: ou bien *kpɔ́* y est un verbe, la structure est sérielle (cf. § 4.1.1.1.), la marque de futur *á* s'appliquant aussi bien aux deux verbes en série, et le sens est alors celui donné en (a); ou bien *kpɔ́* est un morphème marquant l'inattendu, et le sens est alors celui que l'on a en (b). Ce sens, quand c'est lui qui est sélectionné, résulte de la pression du contexte. En effet, le témoignage de la perception visuelle étant tenu pour apte, par définition, à garantir la réalité des faits, le verbe « voir » employé dans le voisinage d'un autre verbe peut être utilisé par les locuteurs-auditeurs de l'ÉWÉ pour souligner que le procès dénoté par ce verbe a irréfutablement eu lieu, ce caractère irréfutable pouvant lui-même être présenté comme contraire à ce qui était attendu.

Tout ce qu'on vient de voir semble attester l'importance du lien que les aspects syntaxiques et contextuels du processus de grammaticalisation établissent avec ses aspects notionnels. C'est donc très naturellement que l'on est conduit à étudier maintenant la matière même sur laquelle sont fondées les règles de la syntaxe et plus généralement toutes les relations contextuelles, à savoir les formes linguistiques proprement dites. C'est à quoi sera consacrée la partie suivante du présent article.

3. Les opérations formelles

« Formelles » n'est pas à entendre ici au sens où l'on parle de linguistique formelle ou de forme des modèles scientifiques, mais en un sens presque opposé: il s'agit des opérations qui sont effectuées sur le matériau concret des langues, c'est-à-dire des phénomènes morphologiques précis qui sont les signes de la grammaticalisation. Cette dernière ne peut être posée définitivement comme telle que dans la mesure où on a établi des critères matériels précis permettant de décider s'il y a lieu ou non de parler de grammaticalisation.

Certains de ces critères sont classiques (§ 3.1.), d'autres sont moins souvent utilisés, mais importants aussi (§ 3.2.).

3.1. Les critères matériels classiques de grammaticalisation

3.1.1. Grammaticalisation et réanalyse

Il est utile de distinguer la grammaticalisation d'un autre processus avec lequel elle a bien des points communs, à savoir l'opération de réanalyse. Les auteurs qui critiquent leur fréquente confusion sont fondés à le faire. Cependant, on ne retiendra pas ici le critère donné par certains de ces auteurs (cf., par exemple, Heine & Reh 1984: 95 sqq.), à savoir que la grammaticalisation est unidirectionnelle alors que la réanalyse ne l'est pas nécessairement. Il existe, en effet, comme on le verra ci-dessous (cf. § 5.), des cas qui, bien qu'ils n'illustrent pas un processus d'inversion d'une direction, consistent en l'utilisation lexématique d'un morphème qui est lui-même le produit d'une grammaticalisation. La réanalyse a été définie (cf. Hagège 1993: 61−63) comme l'opération par laquelle les CLs remplacent une certaine analyse des unités syntaxiques par une nouvelle analyse, avec des marques diverses de nouvelles relations. La grammaticalisation, quant à elle, est un processus dynamique, dont le résultat est l'apparition de nouveaux morphèmes ou de nouvelles classes de morphèmes.

Une réanalyse peut évidemment conduire à une grammaticalisation, comme on le voit dans les langues sériantes où un des verbes en série peut être réanalysé comme relateur. Mais alors que, comme le montre cet exemple même, la réanalyse ne met pas en cause d'autre axe que l'axe syntagmatique, la grammaticalisation crée ou enrichit une classe de morphèmes. Elle intéresse donc aussi l'axe paradigmatique (ici le système morpho-syntaxique de la langue). Evidemment, une réanalyse est un cas de grammaticalisation lorsque la nouvelle répartition des fonctions affecte toutes les manifestations des unités qui les remplissent, et crée par là une nouvelle classe.

3.1.2. Les discriminants les plus courants

Les phénomènes formels, c'est-à-dire phonétiques et morphologiques, qui accompagnent la grammaticalisation d'un lexème en morphème, et qui peuvent donc être considérés comme les discriminants permettant de juger que ce processus a bien eu lieu, sont les suivants:

(1) la réduction phonique: perte totale ou partielle d'une syllabe, d'un phonème ou d'un trait pertinent, soit sans facteur conditionnant dans le contexte, soit par élision à une frontière;
(2) la réduction morphologique: disparition du marqueur ou des marqueurs qui jusque là contribuaient à l'identification du lexème comme tel;
(3) la fusion formelle: dans de nombreux cas, aucun élément ne peut être inséré entre la nouvelle unité résultant de la grammaticalisation et un élément contigu, avec lequel elle acquiert un nouveau type de relation;
(4) la fixation séquentielle: la nouvelle unité et l'élément contigu ne peuvent pas être permutés.
(5) la limitation des latitudes combinatoires par rapport à celles que possédait le lexème source;
(6) la spécialisation syntaxique: la nouvelle unité n'a pas, dans les phrases, les mêmes fonctions que sa source; ou bien elle n'apparaît que dans une de ces fonctions.

Le détail de tous ces critères est donné dans Hagège 1993: 195−198, auquel on renvoie, ne fournissant ici que des illustrations de certains points. En ÉWÉ, par exemple, *vá* « venir » donne un marqueur de futur *á* : le phonème initial, *v-*, a donc été perdu. En YUCATEC, ancienne langue maya du Yucatan (Mexique), un verbe donne une marque de temps, comme le fait apparaître la comparaison entre les deux énoncés suivants (cf. Lehmann 1993: 318):

(32) *le bèet-ik k-u*
DET faire-TRANS IMPERF-3SG
y-úuch-ul t-èech le he'l-o'
cela-arriver-INTR à-2SG DÉT DÉM-2DEIX
« C'est ce qui fait que cela t'arrive »

(33) *úuch-ts'iib-nak-en-e'*
PASSÉ LOINTAIN-écrire-SUJ-ABS.1sg-DÉCL
« J'ai écrit il y a longtemps ».

On voit tout de suite que le verbe *úuch* « arriver » (au sens de « se produire ») de l'énoncé (32) perd, quand il devient un marqueur de passé lointain en (33), aussi bien son sujet *y-* que son suffixe d'intransitif *-ul*; d'autre part, en (33), on ne peut ni permuter *úuch* et *ts'iib*, ni insérer le moindre autre élément entre eux. En d'autres termes, le traitement du *úuch* de (33) comme résultat de la grammaticalisation du *úuch* de (32) se fonde sur les critères de réduction morphologique, de fixation séquentielle et de fusion formelle.

Certains autres faits formels peuvent venir s'ajouter aux discriminants ci-dessus pour indiquer qu'un nouveau statut est en cause. L'un d'entre eux est si universellement présent dans les langues que, n'y prenant pas attention du fait de son apparition récurrente, on risquerait d'oublier son pouvoir distinctif. Il s'agit de l'intonation. Soit, par exemple, un énoncé YORUBA comme (34) (Hagège 1993: 197−198):

(34) mo ń-š'išẹ́   Òjó sì
      1SG PROGR-travailler O. se joindre
      ń-jẹ+un
      PROGR-manger+chose
      « je suis en train de travailler et Ojo est en train de manger »

Dans cet énoncé, *sì* est par son sens un coordonnant car l'énoncé ne signifie pas « je suis en train, de travailler, Ojo (m') a joint est en train de manger ». On pourrait objecter que ce n'est pas là un argument positif, et qu'en tout état de cause, il ne se fonde sur aucun fait formel, sinon peut-être que *sì* est à la forme aoriste nue et non à la forme progressive comme les deux autres verbes. Mais en réalité, il existe un critère décisif: la courbe intonative dans cet énoncé demeure au même niveau entre *š'išẹ́* et *Òjó*, ce qui indique que l'on a non pas deux phrases indépendantes, mais bien deux propositions au sein d'une même phrase. Un autre phénomène formel indique lui aussi que l'on a un énoncé complexe et un morphème qui le marque comme tel; considérons, en effet, l'exemple (35), emprunté à l'ÉWÉ (Hagège, *ibid.*):

(35) é súsú bé yē á-vá
      3SG penser (« dire » =) que LOG FUT-venir
      « il₁ pense qu'il₁ viendra ».

On peut poser que *bé*, qui est un verbe « dire » dans d'autres contextes, ne l'est pas ici, mais qu'il s'agit du conjonctif ouvreur de discours indirect. La raison n'en est pas seulement que quand on pense on ne parle pas, argument de bon sens qui n'est pas exploitable dans une démonstration linguistique, mais plutôt que *yē* est une forme spéciale, celle qui est couramment appelée *logophorique* depuis l'invention de ce terme par Hagège 1974: *yē* est la forme, distincte de *é*, qui renvoie au sujet d'un verbe déclaratif ou intellectuel quand celui-ci est suivi d'une proposition subordonnée indiquant ce qui est dit ou pensé. Il faut donc considérer *bé* comme un subordonnant « que », de même que dans beaucoup d'autres langues, notamment africaines, où il est issu de la grammaticalisation d'un verbe « dire ».

3.2. Autres critères

Trois autres critères peuvent être ajoutés aux précédents, qui, le cas échéant, y joignent leur pouvoir démonstratif. L'un concerne le degré d'occurrence des unités à l'étude, l'autre la cooccurrence en contiguïté sans exclusion, le troisième le degré de conscience chez les CLs.

3.2.1. Le degré d'occurrence

Si une unité linguistique apparaît dans deux contextes différents et si, au sein d'un texte assez long d'oralité ou d'écriture, elle apparaît beaucoup plus souvent dans l'un de ces contextes que dans l'autre, on doit considérer que cette différence de degré d'occurrence est l'indice d'une différence de statut. Ce critère vient confirmer les autres lorsque ces derniers s'appliquent. Lorsque tel n'est pas le cas, et en particulier quand l'unité à l'étude ne change pas de forme quel que soit son contexte d'occurrence, le fait qu'elle connaisse une plus grande fréquence dans un de ses contextes ne peut pas ne pas alerter. On sait, en effet, qu'il fait, pour faire un texte, plus d'éléments de liaison que d'éléments à relier: par exemple, les chances d'apparition du jonteur *de*, dans un texte quelconque en français, sont bien plus élevées que celles d'un nom ou d'un verbe particulier. Or les éléments de liaison figurent parmi les principaux morphèmes produits par la grammaticalisation des lexèmes.

3.2.2. La cooccurrence en contiguïté sans exclusion ou le principe de la Preuve par Anachronie

La grammaticalisation étant un processus dynamique (cf. § 5.), il arrive très souvent que, pour une même unité, le stade encore lexématique et le stade déjà grammaticalisé coexistent. On peut considérer qu'ils représentent deux états historiques différents, mais que la langue continue de posséder l'un et l'autre. Quand il arrive que les unités représentant ces deux stades apparaissent en contiguïté dans le même énoncé, on peut être certain que l'une des deux est le morphème produit par la grammaticalisation, car autrement, deux mots morphosyntaxiquement identiques seraient juxtaposés, ce que le système des langues exclut (on ne peut dire, par exemple, **où est le livre couteau?*). Ce critère de grammaticalisation peut être appelé *Preuve par Anachronie*, et illustré par les deux exemples suivants, pris l'un au JAPONAIS, l'autre au HINDI (cf. Hagège 1993: 200sq.):

(36) *kami o hikidashi ni*
papier ACC tiroir LOC
shimatte-shimatta
jeter-AUXIL.TERM.+PASSÉ
« il finit par jeter le papier au tiroir »

(37) *Râm-se le-lo* ɔr
R-ABL prendre-AUX.AVERS.+IMP et
Syam-ko de-do
S-DAT donner-AUX.BÉN.+IMP.
« prends-le à Ram et donne-le à Cham. »

On voit qu'en (36), l'auxiliaire de sens terminatif issu par grammaticalisation, en JAPONAIS, du verbe signifiant « fermer » ne peut être employé en contiguïté avec lui que parce qu'il s'agit aujourd'hui d'une unité de tout autre statut. C'est pour la même raison qu'en HINDI ([37]), l'auxiliaire aversif issu du verbe « prendre » et l'auxiliaire bénéfactif issu du verbe donner » peuvent être contigus aux verbes qui en sont respectivement les sources.

3.2.3. Le degré de conscience chez les locuteurs-auditeurs

Ce critère est évidemment celui qui s'applique le moins souvent, puisque, comme le montre le phénomène même étudié en 3.2.2., la conscience métalinguistique des CLs, qui existe dans le domaine du lexique, est beaucoup plus rare dans celui de la morphosyntaxe. On trouve pourtant quelques cas de conscience dans ce dernier domaine. Un exemple peut en être cité pour le JAPONAIS, tel du moins qu'il apparaît à travers une pratique qui est extérieure à la langue mais en atteste la conscience, à savoir l'écriture: le mot *koto* est écrit en caractères CHINOIS quand il signifie « chose, affaire », mais en syllabaire JAPONAIS (*hiragana*) quand il s'emploie comme conjonctif signifiant « (le fait) que »; de même, *miru, oku, shimau, kureru, morau* sont notés en caractères quand ils sont verbes aux sens respectifs de « voir », « mettre », « finir », « donner », « recevoir », et en syllabaire quand ils sont les auxiliaires valant, respectivement, « essayer de », « faire ... à l'avance », « finir par », « faire ... en faveur d'ego », « se faire ... ».

4. Les points de départ et les points d'arrivée

Les points de départ et les points d'arrivée du processus de grammaticalisation sont très variés. Pour éviter une énumération de catalogue, on peut les regrouper sous différents titres. Le premier concerne le type le plus connu de grammaticalisation, celui qui produit des morphèmes à partir de lexèmes (§ 4.1.). Mais il existe aussi un type d'évolution qui va du grammatical au plus grammatical encore (§ 4.2.).

4.1. La production de morphèmes à partir de lexèmes

Les points de départ, ici, sont les trois grandes catégories lexicales du nom, du verbe et de l'adverbe. Leurs issues étant assez dispersées, et certains points d'arrivée étant ceux que, à travers les langues, on voit le plus souvent se constituer à partir de sources variées, il paraît plus éclairant de se placer d'abord dans la perspective de ces points d'arrivée, et de revenir ensuite aux points de départ lexématiques pour examiner leurs issues moins courantes.

4.1.1. Les relateurs et leurs sources

Toutes les langues humaines ont besoin de relateurs, c'est-à-dire d'instruments qui ont pour fonction de relier une partie de la phrase à une autre en mettant la première dans la dépendance de la seconde. Dans les langues INDO-EUROPÉENNES, les principaux relateurs sont les prépositions, et, pour l'énoncé complexe, les conjonctions de subordination.

Il existe évidemment dans bien des langues des relateurs qui ont ce statut depuis les premiers temps attestés, et dont on ignore d'où ils viennent, si du moins on fait l'hypothèse que les relateurs, dans l'histoire des langues, sont seconds par rapport aux lexèmes, et diachroniquement issus d'eux. Mais très souvent aussi, on a des traces repérables de naissance de relateurs par grammaticalisation à partir de lexèmes. Ces derniers sont essentiellement les verbes, les noms et les adverbes.

4.1.1.1. Les relateurs de source verbale

Le cadre syntaxique dans lequel s'opère la grammaticalisation de verbes en relateurs est le plus souvent celui que l'on trouve dans les langues sériantes, c'est-à-dire les langues où deux ou plusieurs verbes, dont un au moins est transitif, peuvent apparaître en séries, le signe de cette cohésion syntaxique étant la non-répétition du sujet commun, ou des déterminants verbaux, sur chaque verbe. Soit la série verbale V1 + V2 + N ou V1 + N1 + V2 + N2 (où N vaut pour nom ou syntagme nominal): dans ce cadre, qui est celui des langues à séquence SVO, où le verbe transitif

113. Les processus de grammaticalisation

précède son objet, la position V1 ou V2 est celle où peut se dégager un relateur, et ce relateur sera donc une préposition, puisqu'il occupera la même position, avant son régime, que le verbe dont il est issu et qui était situé avant son objet. Les schémas correspondants peuvent être, par exemple, les suivants (où sont notés entre guillemets des sens, valables pour toute langue, et non des mots du FRANÇAIS):

(38) « parler » + « donner » + « homme » (= V1 + V2 + N)

(39) « porter » + « livre » + « donner » + « enfant » (= V1 + N1 + V2 + N2)

(40) « donner » + « lui » + « dire » + « parole » (*id.*).

Le verbe « donner » dégage une préposition attributive « à » en position V1 d'énoncés attestés dans des langues comme le CHINOIS, et qui suivent le schéma (40), équivalent au sens « lui parler », ou en position V2 d'énoncés attestés dans les CRÉOLES à base lexicale FRANÇAISE OU ANGLAISE, et qui suivent le schéma (39), équivalent au sens « apporter le livre à l'enfant », ou, si V1 est intransitif, le schéma (38), équivalent à « parler à l'homme ». S'il s'agit de langues à séquence SOV, où le verbe transitif suit son objet, on aura une série verbale N + V1 + V2 quand V2 est intransitif, ou, s'il ne l'est pas, N1 + V1 + N2 + V2: ici encore, la position V1 ou V2 est celle où peut se dégager un relateur, et cette fois, il s'agira d'une postposition, puisqu'il sera issu d'un verbe postposé à son objet. On aura donc des schémas comme

(41) « route » + « suivre » + « aller » (= N + V1 + V2)

(42) « femme » + « accompagner » + « ville » + « atteindre » (= N1 + V1 + N2 + V2).

Le verbe « suivre » donne naissance à une postposition sécutive « le long de » en position V1 de (41), qui équivaut à « aller le long de la route » et se réalise dans des langues comme l'UTE (Colorado); le verbe atteindre » dégage une postposition allative « vers » en position V2 de (42), lequel équivaut au sens « accompagner la femme vers la ville », et peut être illustré par des langues comme l'IJO (famille KWA, sud du Nigéria).

Pour qu'un verbe donne naissance à un relateur, il ne suffit pas qu'il apparaisse dans le cadre sériel qu'on vient de présenter. Il faut aussi que, par la généralité de son sens, il ait une certaine vocation à se grammaticaliser. A travers un grand nombre de langues, on constate que cinq zones sémantiques du lexique verbal sont celles qui fournissent le plus souvent des relateurs (cf. Hagège 1993: 211−212):

(1) la zone statique, où les évolutions sont « être dans » > « dans », « faire face à » > « en face de »;
(2) la zone des mouvements: « aller » > « à, vers », « atteindre » > « à, vers » (cf. (42)), « suivre » > « avec », « sortir de » > « (hors) de », « traverser » > « à travers, au moyen de »;
(3) la référence: « se rapporter à » > « quant à », « ressembler à » > « comme », « se conformer à > « selon », « comparer à » > « au regard de »;
(4) le groupe des verbes de sens dynamique dénotant l'effet d'une entité sur une autre: « utiliser » > « avec », « exclure » > « sans », « remplacer » > « au lieu de », « s'appuyer sur » > « sur la base de », « s'opposer » > « contre », « donner » > « à, pour » (cf. (38) à (40)), « entourer » > « autour de »;
(5) une zone où l'on trouve « prendre » donnant un marqueur de patient: c'est là un trait bien connu du CHINOIS (cf. exemple (19), également attesté en NITINAHT (langue WAKASH de la région de Vancouver), mais « prendre » est un verbe qui, du fait de la forte variété de ses sens, donne aussi d'autres catégories de relateurs, soit comitatifs, soit instrumentaux, ces deux issues étant illustrées par des langues africaines et CRÉOLES.

D'autres types de séries verbales sont ceux qui mettent en juxtaposition deux verbes déclaratifs ou conceptuels de sens voisins, dont l'un, introduisant un discours, devient un ouvreur de ce discours, équivalent au « que » du français, selon un modèle « dire » ou « penser » + « dire » > « dire que », attesté dans de nombreuses langues d'Afrique (cf. exemple ÉWÉ (35) ci-dessus en 3.1.2.), d'Amérique et d'Asie.

Outre les séries verbales, un autre cadre syntaxique de génération des relateurs à partir de verbes est celui des prédicats secondaires qu'on appelle converbes. Dans la mesure où le converbe exprime une subordination circonstancielle, il a vocation, quand le sens de l'élément nominal qu'il régit s'y prête, à produire, au cours de l'évolution des langues, les marques mêmes de cette subordination. Dans les langues INDO-EUROPÉENNES, OURALIENNES OU ALTAÏQUES, par exemple, les converbes devenus relateurs prennent la forme de participes, comme en FRANÇAIS *pendant*, *durant* (certains, comme *moyennant* ou *nonobstant*, n'ayant plus de verbe d'emploi lexématique encore vivant qui leur corresponde), etc., en ANGLAIS *considering* « étant donné », *following*, *barring*, *excepting*, *notwithstanding* « malgré » (ce dernier pouvant, tout comme *durant*, s'employer en postposition, par rémanence de la syntaxe ancienne, car le régi d'aujourd'hui est le nom sujet d'autrefois), etc., en RUSSE *blagodarja* « grâce à », *ne smotrja na* (litt. « ne regardant pas sur ») « malgré », *spustja* après », en HONGROIS *nézve* « du point de vue de », *fogva* « depuis », *mulva* (litt. « ayant passé ») « après, au bout de », en TURC *göre* selon » (de *gör(mek)* « voir »), *olarak* « en qualité de » (de *ol(mak)* « être »), en JAPONAIS *ni tsuite* (de *(X) ni tsuku* « être en rapport avec (X) ») et *megutte* (de *meguru* « tourner autour de »), l'un et l'autre signifiant « au sujet de » (cf. Hagège 1997).

4.1.1.2. Les relateurs de source nominale

Ici, le cadre syntaxique de production de relateurs est le syntagme nominal de détermination. C'est le nom déterminé qui constitue la source du relateur, ce qui est intéressant du point de vue de la relation entre syntaxe et sémantique: en effet, le nom déterminé était le centre du syntagme nominal, et il continue d'être régissant quand il devient relateur (le nom dominé par une préposition ou une postposition est le régime de cette dernière, qui le subordonne par là au prédicat), alors même qu'il n'est plus ici qu'un outil grammatical et qu'au contraire, l'ancien nom déterminant demeure un lexème. Si la langue connaît le type de séquence 'Nom déterminé + Nom déterminant', le relateur sera une préposition; si elle connaît l'ordre inverse, le relateur sera une postposition. On aura donc respectivement, pour prendre l'exemple du nom « tête » donnant le relateur « sur »,

(43) « tête » + « homme » > « sur l'homme »

(44) « homme » + « tête » > « sur l'homme ».

Le schéma (43) est illustré par le MBUM (cf. Hagège 1970) et de nombreuses autres langues africaines ayant la même organisation séquentielle du syntagme nominal, et le schéma (44) par le BAMBARA et de nombreuses autres langues africaines à séquence inverse de celle du MBUM. Par conséquent, tout comme les relateurs d'origine verbale, les relateurs d'origine nominale conservent la séquence des lexèmes dont ils sont les produits. Cette situation est tout à fait compréhensible, et il n'y a pas de raison pour que la grammaticalisation la remette en cause.

En ce qui concerne la morphologie des relateurs, les critères étudiés au § 3.1.2. s'appliquent à des degrés variables selon les langues. La réduction phonique et morphologique ainsi que la fusion formelle sont nettes, dans les langues à déclinaisons, chez les désinences que l'on peut rapporter à une origine nominale attestée ou restituable.

Elles sont beaucoup moins régulières dans les langues agglutinantes: ainsi, les postpositions *etew* « derrière », *mēǰ* « dans », *šurǰ* « autour de », *tak* « sous », *verǰ* « après », *vray* « sur » de l'ARMÉNIEN occidental moderne conservent l'article défini; en revanche, la postposition *râ* du PERSAN ne garde qu'une syllabe du nom *rādiy* « but, intention » du VIEUX-PERSE dont la grammaticalisation, il est vrai, a dû commencer en 600 avt J. C. ... D'autre part, il arrive souvent que les relateurs spatiaux d'origine nominale aient une forme complexe, celle d'un syntagme nominal où le nom-source est, si on pratique une analyse interne, le régi d'un relateur plus ancien dont l'origine n'est plus identifiable, le régi du relateur complexe lui-même lui étant relié par une marque de jonction telle que le FRANÇAIS *de* ou le JAPONAIS *no* : ces derniers apparaissent dans beaucoup de relateurs complexes, par exemple ces deux-ci, qui sont exactement symétriques, l'un traduisant l'autre en miroir: FRANÇAIS *à l'intérieur de*/JAPONAIS *no naka ni* (= « de intérieur à »).

Sémantiquement, les relateurs d'origine nominale appartiennent pour la plupart à la zone statique de l'espace où l'on se trouve, et proviennent, de façon assez naturelle si l'on adopte un cadre théorique anthropolinguistique (cf. Hagège 1993), des noms qui indiquent le plus adéquatement pour l'homme sa situation dans l'espace, à savoir ceux qui se réfèrent d'une part aux parties de son corps et d'autre part aux positions des objets par rapport à ce dernier. On peut donc, en étendant la notion flexionnelle de cas (*ptôsis*) à tous les types de relateurs quelle que soit leur forme, parler d'*anthropologie casuelle* (cf. Hagège 1982: 118), pour caractériser le système matriciel de formation des relateurs, tel qu'il est observable dans beaucoup de langues (notamment en Afrique et en Océanie), à partir de ces noms. Les principaux cheminements sont les suivants:

(45) Parties du corps
  « tête » > « sur »
  « pied » > « sous »
  « visage », > « devant »
  « front »,
  « dos » > « derrière »
  « flanc » > « à côté de »
  « estomac », > « dans »
  « ventre »

(46) Portions de l'espace
  « haut », > « au dessus de »
  « surface »
  « bas », « base » > « au dessous de »
  « arrière » > « derrière »
  « avant » > « devant »
  « milieu » > « parmi »
  « intervalle » > « entre ».

Il est intéressant de noter cependant que dans certaines sociétés pastorales, notamment d'Afrique de l'Ouest, les parties du corps auxquelles se réfère la désignation de portions de l'espace sont celles des animaux de bétail. Ainsi, en MASAI (langue nilotique du nord du Kénya et de la Tanzanie), *ɛn-dukúya* « tête » donne *dukúya* (avec perte du préfixe de classe) « devant »; en SOMALI, *dul* « dos » donne un relateur signifiant « sur ». Il est facile de voir que ces évolutions vers des sens spatiaux correspondent bien à la disposition des parties du corps d'un quadrupède, mais non d'un être humain. On peut pourtant considérer qu'indirectement, il s'agit toujours d'anthropologie casuelle, l'homme fabriquant ici une partie de ses outils linguistiques au moyen des noms de parties du corps d'animaux qu'il a intégrés à sa culture.

4.1.1.3. Les relateurs de source adverbiale

Les adverbes sont des sources assez naturelles de relateurs. Syntaxiquement, et aussi historiquement, de nombreux relateurs sont des adverbes transitivés. Un exemple suffira: F. de Saussure (1916: 247) mentionne l'évolution du GREC ARCHAÏQUE *óreos baínō káta* (montagne (GÉN) je ~ viens de ~ haut ~ en ~ bas) « je descends de la montagne », où *káta*, adverbe, ne fait qu'orienter le mouvement, au GREC CLASSIQUE *katà óreos baínō*, où *katà*, qui a subi un changement formel (tonal et accentuel), est régissant, c'est-à-dire est devenu un relateur « du haut de ». Cela dit, un lexème peut produire deux, ou plusieurs, morphèmes distincts, et une autre évolution également attestée a donné *katabaínō óreos*, où l'on trouve, issu du même adverbe, un préverbe directionnel *kata-*. On va justement étudier maintenant ce type de morphèmes.

4.1.2. Les verbants et leurs sources

On appelle ici *verbants*, en reprenant la terminologie de Hagège (1982: 75; 80 sqq.), les divers morphèmes qui gravitent dans la zone d'influence du verbe, et avec lesquels il constitue un syntagme verbal capable d'assumer la fonction prédicative. Les verbants prennent souvent la forme d'affixes, c'est-à-dire, selon les langues, préfixes, suffixes, infixes (ces derniers sont fréquents dans les langues des Philippines, par exemple) ou simulfixes (pour ce cas, cf., par exemple, le PALAU [Hagège 1986: 41−44, 59]).

Une source courante de verbants est constituée par les adverbes, comme on vient de le voir en 4.2.1.3. pour les verbants directionnels. On pourrait encore mentionner l'exemple du SOMALI, qui s'est constitué un *ventif* (marqueur de mouvement vers ego), le préfixe *soo-*, à partir de l'adverbe *soke* « à côté ». Des verbants temporels ont aussi une source adverbiale dans bien des langues, notamment les CRÉOLES (cf. Hagège 1993: 222 sq.): le PAPIAMENTU *lo*, du PORTUGAIS *logo* « tout de suite », le BICHELAMAR *bambae*, de l'ANGLAIS *by and by*, le MAURITIEN *pu*, du FRANÇAIS *pour* et le HAÏTIEN *ap*, du FRANÇAIS *après*, sont tous des marqueurs du futur ou de temps-aspects reliés au futur.

Dans tous ces cas, il ne s'agit pas d'évolution interne, puisque les sources se trouvent dans d'autres langues, dont les CRÉOLES sont issus. Mais on rencontre aussi des verbants temporels d'origine adverbiale dans les langues africaines: ainsi, les langues KRU (cf. Marchese 1978) possèdent des marqueurs de temps (passé, futur, etc.) qui proviennent d'adverbes désignant les divers moments mesurés par rapport à ego: « hier » donne le passé, « demain » le futur, etc. Divers critères phonologiques et distributionnels permettent d'attribuer le statut de verbants à ces unités, mais dans d'autres cas, comme ceux du SANGO, de L'AKA ou du BAKA (langues de République Centrafricaine), ces critères ne s'appliquent pas, et on doit considérer que ce sont des adverbes de plein statut qui indiquent le temps.

Cependant, ce sont les verbes qui sont la source prototypique de verbants. En effet, au contact d'autres verbes, certains verbes s'auxiliarisent, c'est-à-dire se spécialisent dans l'indication de divers aspects, diverses modalités et divers cadres temporels du procès. Les évolutions les plus courantes (cf. Hagège 1993: 217−222) produisent les morphèmes d'ingressif, résultatif, égressif, perfectif, progressif, habituel, exhaustif, réitératif, à partir, respectivement, des verbes signifiant « commencer », « devenir », « sortir », « arrêter », « rester », « être habitué », « dépasser », « retourner ». Le processus d'auxiliation qui donne ces verbants s'accompagne souvent d'altérations formelles (cf. exemples (32) et (33)), mais ce n'est pas toujours le cas, et l'on peut avoir à faire jouer d'autres critères (cf. (36) et (37)), car si l'auxiliaire peut être un élément de composé verbal, ou un affixe, il ne change pas toujours de forme pour autant, et peut même demeurer un verbe plein, juxtaposé ou coordonné au verbe principal. Celui-ci étant souvent alors réduit à une forme nue, on a une intéressante contradiction entre centralité syntaxique et primauté sémantique (cf. Hagège 1993: 48).

Le sens, enfin, n'est pas toujours aussi clairement déductible du verbal que dans les évolutions, vues ci-dessus, de « commencer » vers l'ingressif, etc.: en BIRMAN, « savoir » donne un habituel, en MOORÉ (Burkina), « être fatigué » donne un perfectif, en NEWARI (TIBÉTO-BIRMAN, Népal) le verbe « garder » donne un datif, un perfectif et un *médiaphorique* (cf., pour l'introduction de ce dernier terme, Hagège 1995), et en KURUKH, langue DRAVIDIENNE du Chota Nagpur, « cuire » donne une marque de surprise ...

4.1.3. Autres résultats de grammaticalisations

Sans entrer dans le détail des types moins courants dont traitent les ouvrages cités au § 7. Références, on rappellera que les noms donnent souvent des classificateurs (dans les langues à classes), mais aussi, tout comme les verbes (cf. ex. (35)), des conjonctifs (cf. FRANÇAIS *(le fait) que*), ainsi que des joncteurs (cf. ex. (3)−(5)), mais aussi des pronoms, soit réfléchis (« corps » ou « tête », etc. donnant « soi-même »), soit autres (nombreuses langues d'Asie du Sud-Est où « je » vient de « serviteur », « tu » de « seigneur », etc.).

4.2. La production de morphèmes à partir de morphèmes

Une unité grammaticale peut à son tour en générer une autre que est plus grammaticale encore. Ainsi, d'une désinence casuelle de sens plus concret peut en émerger une autre, plus abstraite: dans beaucoup de langues, le directionnel donne un datif, l'ablatif un génitif, le suressif un génitif (ex. BULGARE *na*). Par ailleurs, les déctiques sont souvent les sources des conjonctifs (ANGLAIS *I know that: « he came »* est l'origine de *I know that he came*), ou des copules (l'ARABE et le CHINOIS on traité comme sujet le thème d'une structure « X, cela Y », d'où « X est Y »), des articles, ou, aussi bien que ces derniers, des pronoms relatifs. Une relative « qui est à » a même donné, en HÉBREU ISRAÉLIEN, un joncteur possessif (*šel*).

La créativité des CLs produit même des marques de subordination à partir de structures syntaxiques réinterprétées. Ainsi, en RUSSE, *esli* « si » provient de *est' li* « existe-t-il (que) ... »: une question pose une prémisse, et appelle donc une apodose.

5. Directionnalité de la grammaticalisation

On observe dans beaucoup de langues une constante réalimentation du stock de morphèmes, en particulier les relateurs, à partir de lexèmes, et les classes « fermées » ne le sont pas tant, comme le dit la notion même de grammaticalisation. On ne connaît pas d'exemple de cheminement à rebours, par lequel une unité résultant d'un processus de grammaticalisation reviendrait au lexème qu'elle était, ou disparaîtrait en faveur des seuls emplois lexématiques quand ils se sont maintenus. C'est pourquoi on peut considérer la grammaticalisation comme unidirectionnelle. Mais cela ne signifie pas qu'un morphème ne puisse être lexématisé: FRANÇAIS *le pour et le contre*, ANGLAIS AMÉRICAIN *to up* « augmenter », *ade* (cf. *orange-ade*) « boisson de fruit », ESPAGNOL MEXICAIN *ate* (cf. *guayabate* « confiture de goyave ») « confiture », CHINOIS *sì huà* « les quatre -isations » (slogan politique), JAPONAIS parlé *nagara-zoku* (« pendant ~ que-gens ») « ceux qui regardent la télévision en faisant autre chose », etc. Dans tous ces cas, on voit que si la grammaticalisation d'une unité donnée est irréversible, la lexématisation de certains morphèmes n'est pas exclue quand elle possède une utilité. En outre, sur de longues périodes, des cycles s'observent (cf. Hagège 1993, chap. 5).

6. Conclusion

L'étude de la grammaticalisation n'est pas simplement un chapitre d'une recherche syntaxique de haute technicité. Elle ne peut, certes, être abordée sérieusement que moyennant un examen approfondi de faits précis des langues les plus diverses. Mais le cadre véritable dans lequel s'inscrit cet examen, c'est celui de la morphogenèse. Tout comme les espèces vivantes évoluent selon des mécanismes de plus en plus complexes adaptés au milieu, de même les langues, par l'action constante de leurs constructeurs humains, se façonnent les outils dont ces derniers ont besoin. Cette opération se déroule dans la chaîne, mais ses résultats concernent le système, de sorte que la grammaticalisation transcende la séparation de ces deux axes. C'est une entreprise humaine, largement, mais non totalement, inconsciente (cf. Hagège 1993), dont on peut beaucoup apprendre sur l'activité de construction intellectuelle de l'homme, en attendant qu'un jour, peut-être, on connaisse ses fondements neurologiques.

7. Références

Givón, Talmy. 1971. «Historical syntax and synchronic morphology: An archaelogist's field trip». *Chicago Linguistic Society* 7: 394–415.

Givón, Talmy. 1975. «Serial verbs and syntactic change: Niger-Congo». In: Li, Charles N. (ed.). *Word order and word order change*. Austin: University of Texas Press, 47–112.

Guillaume, Gustave. 1964. *Langage et science du langage*. Paris: Nizet.

Hagège, Claude. 1970. *La langue mbum de Nganha: Phonologie-Grammaire*. Paris: SELAF.

Hagège, Claude. 1974. «Les pronoms logophoriques». *BSL* 69.1: 287–310.

Hagège, Claude. 1975. *Le problème linguistique des prépositions et la solution chinoise*. Paris: Société de linguistique de Paris & Louvain: Peeters.

Hagège, Claude. 1982. *La structure des langues*. Paris: Presses Universitaires de France.

Hagège, Claude. 1986. *La langue palau. Une curiosité typologique*. München: Fink.

Hagège, Claude. 1993. *The Language Builder*. Amsterdam & Philadelphia: Benjamins.

Hagège, Claude. 1995. «Le rôle des médiaphoriques dans la langue et dans le discours». *BSL* 90.1: 1–19.

Hagège, Claude. 1997. Compte rendu de M. Haspelmath et E. König, eds. *Converbs in cross-linguistic perspective*. Berlin & New York: Mouton de Gruyter, 1995, *BSL* 96. 2: 94–110.

Heine, Bernd & Reh, Mechthild. 1984. *Grammaticalization and reanalysis in African languages*. Hamburg: Buske.

Heine, Bernd & Claudi, Ulrike & Hünnemeyer, Friederike. 1991a. *Grammaticalization: A conceptual framework*. Chicago: University of Chicago Press.

Heine, Bernd & Claudi, Ulrike & Hünnemeyer, Friederike. 1991b. «From cognition to grammar». In Traugott & Heine, I: 149–187.

Hopper, Paul J. & Traugott, Elizabeth C. 1993. (Cambridge textbooks in linguistics.) *Grammaticalization*. Cambridge: Cambridge University Press.

Jakobson, Roman & Halle, Morris. 1956. *Fundamentals of language*. 's Gravenhage: Mouton.

Jespersen, Otto. 1911. *A modern English grammar on historical principles*. Londres: Allen & Unwin.

Lehmann, Christian. 1982. *Thoughts on grammaticalization*. A programmatic sketch. Köln: Institut für Sprachwissenschaft.

Lehmann, Christian. 1993. «Theoretical implications of processes of grammaticalization», in Foley, William (ed.). *The role of theory in language description*. Berlin & New York: Mouton de Gruyter, 315–340.

Marchese, Lynell. 1978. «Le développement des auxiliaires dans les langues kru». *Annales de l'Université d'Abidjan*. 11.1: 121–131.

Meillet, Antoine. 1912. «L'évolution des formes grammaticales». *Scientia* 12.

Saussure, Ferdinand de. 1916. *Cours de linguistique générale*. Paris: Payot.

Sweetser, Eve E. 1988. «Grammaticalization and semantic bleaching». *Berkeley Linguistic Society* 14: 389–405.

Traugott, Elizabeth Closs & Heine, Bernd. 1991. *Approaches to grammaticalization* I–II. Amsterdam & Philadelphia: Benjamins.

Traugott, Elizabeth Closs & König, Ekkehard. 1991. «The semantics-pragmatics of grammaticalization revisited». In: Traugott & Heine I, 189–218.

Claude Hagège, Collège de France
(France)

114. Conceptions of typological change

1. Preliminaries
1. Morphology
2. Word and constituent order
3. Interrelations between morphology, linearization and syntactic rules
4. Realignments and typological cyclicity
5. Concluding remarks
6. References

1. Preliminaries

Typological change is naturally defined as change from one language type to another. The conception of language type underlying investigations of typological change may in principle be based on or at least take as its vantage point some particular aspect or level of language structure, or it may involve several, ideally all grammatical levels (phonology, morphology, syntax, the lexicon).

A well-known example of the uni-level approach in synchronic and diachronic typological studies is traditional morphological typology. In the seminal work of August Wilhelm von Schlegel (1818) the synthetic/analytic distinction was actually introduced to describe different historical stages within the systematic category of inflectional languages (Geckeler 1989; see § 2.).

More recently, word order typology of the kind initiated by Greenberg (1966) has made important contributions even in the domain of diachronic studies (see § 3.), and the basically typological distinction between configurational and non-configurational languages has also been viewed in a historical perspective (see § 4.).

The vast literature on the coding of syntactic relations, in particular, the nominative/accusative vs. ergative/absolutive or active/inactive types of marking, also comprises studies on presumed evolutionary links between different systems (see § 5.).

Multi-level typological approaches come in several varieties and seldom manifest themselves as all-embracing holistic descriptions. Eugenio Coseriu (1980), who takes his main inspiration from contrastive linguistics rather than from typology in the strict sense, is an example of the endeavour to subsume lexically and morphosyntactically disparate linguistic expressions under one common semantico-functional denominator without any attempt at integration into the overall grammatical system or the history of the languages in question.

The research on nominativity vs. ergativity alignments and on configurational vs. non-configurational languages acquires a multi-level orientation when the interrelations between morphological marking and syntactic rules are taken into account (cf. Anderson 1976, Askedal 1993).

The work of Vladimír Skalička (e. g. 1979a) is programmatically multi-level, or rather holistic, with its characteristic orientation towards establishing prototypical links between different grammatical levels, including even phonology (Skalička 1979c), which has tended to play a less prominent part in mainstream language typology (but cf. e. g. Lehmann 1978: 217—22, Roelcke 1997, Ch. 3). Winfred P. Lehmann, Vladimír Skalička and others have dealt with typological aspects of language change (e. g. Skalička 1979b, Gukhman 1986, Li (ed.) 1975, W. P. Lehmann 1995: 1122f., Greenberg 1995, Hawkins 1995). Typological studies have also made interesting contributions to linguistic reconstruction (Lehmann (ed.) 1991, Fisiak (ed.) 1997). A natural, but admittedly speculative extension of diachronic typology is the quest for principles of cyclicity in typological change (cf. § 5.).

2. Morphology

From a strictly synchronic point of view, a distinction can be made between morphological inflection and its absence, traditionally referred to by the terms *syntheticity* and *analyticity* or *isolation*. The typological canon of inflectional techniques occurring in natural languages comprises *agglutination, fusion, introflection* and *polysyntheticity*. (On the history and systematization of these concepts see Campbell 1995: 1144—46, Vennemann 1982; → art. 2.)

In the absence of inflection, the question is what coding techniques perform functions similar to those of inflectional morphology. Table 114.1 represents an amalgam — and a partial interpretation — of different terminological proposals made in the literature.

The terms in Table 114.1 are principally used to characterize word forms and constructions in individual languages. They are

Table 114.1: Main types of morphosyntactic techniques

main types of morphosyntactic techniques	
A. inflecting ('synthetic')	B. non-inflecting ('analytic')
a. agglutination b. fusion c. introflection d. polysyntheticity	a. ordering restrictions b. auxiliary words

secondarily (in a historical perspective originally) applied to give wholesale typological characterizations of language systems, hence the common classification into synthetic and analytic or isolating etc. languages according to what kind of morphosyntactic technique is considered to predominate. Typological change in the morphological domain is then naturally conceived of as replacement of one characteristic typological technique by another in particular constructions, or as crosscategorial change from one main type to another. In the latter case the term "typological shift" seems appropriate (Gukhman 1986).

Before turning to the diverse types of typological change in morphology, it should be noted that the classification as 'synthetic' or 'analytic' is only applicable to those parts of speech where inflection is a universally common option, i.e. mainly verbs, nouns (including pronouns) and adjectives.

Secondly, there is no a priori theoretical or empirical need to assume a general crosscategorial convergence principle to the effect that the various inflecting parts of speech (or constructions containing them) behave in a parallel typological fashion in situations of linguistic change. Hence a term like "split synthetic/analytic language" would seem empirically natural (but is hardly ever used).

It is a common assumption, for instance in traditional Indo-European linguistics (cf. Lehmann 1993: 151; 153−55), that agglutination gives rise to fusion (with the allomorphic variation characteristic of declensional classes as a residual problem to be separately accounted for). For instance, case endings may derive historically from local adverbs or postpositional particles. It should be noted that there also exists a different kind of agglutinating process where both elements are inflected.

One example of this kind of agglutination developing into (secondary) fusion is the suffixal 'definite article' in the Scandinavian languages. Its origin in sequences of a noun and a cliticized demonstrative pronoun is readily recognizable in OLD ICELANDIC. Here the pronoun by way of phonotactic adjustment has lost its initial *h*-, but the preceding noun and the cliticized pronoun retain independent inflection:

Table 114.2: Agglutination developing into secondary fusion

OLD ICELANDIC			MODERN NORWEGIAN
SgM	Nom	hestrinn	hesten
	Acc	hestinn	–
	Dat	hestinum	–
	Gen	hestsins	hestens

horse-DEF 'the horse

The original pattern of parallel inflection is still transparent in MODERN ICELANDIC and FAROESE. The MODERN MAINLAND SCANDINAVIAN LANGUAGES show no traces of parallel inflection (apart form fixed locutions like NORWEGIAN *havsens bunn* 'the bottom of the sea'). In these languages the original agglutinating structure with parallel inflection has yielded a suffixal fusional definiteness marker.

A similar instance from the domain of adjectives is the Baltic 'definite' and the corresponding SLAVIC 'long-form' (or 'complete') declination of adjectives which derive historically from combinations of an independently inflecting adjective and an agreeing agglutinated pronoun. The original state of parallel inflection is still easily recognizable in MODERN LITHUANIAN (Senn 1966: 163−69; 191 f.), whereas the corresponding SLAVIC forms have developed clear-cut fusional characteristics. Cf. the masculine singular forms in Table 114.3.

The three languages thus exhibit two different stages of a progressive diachronic typological change from fusional inflection very close to agglutination to morphologically rich fusion.

Table 114.3: Gradual disappearance of parallel inflection

SgM	LITHUANIAN:	RUSSIAN:	SORBIAN:
Nom	turtìngas + jìs = turtìngasis	staryj	dobry
Acc	turtìngą + jį̃ = turtìngajį̃	(starogo)	(dobreho)
Dat	turtìngam + jám = turtìngajam	staromu	dobremu
Gen	turtìngo + jõ = turtìngojo	starogo	dobreho
Instr	turtìngu + juõ = turtìnguoju	starym	dobrym
Loc	turtìngame + jamè = turtìngajame	starom	dobrym
	'rich'	'old'	'good'

Similar processes are assumed to occur with verbs also. A case in point is the classical theory that Indo-European personal endings arose through fusion of postposed pronouns with the verb stem, presumably after a stage of agglutination (cf. Campbell 1995: 1145; 1149; cf. also Comrie 1982, Mithun 1991).

In certain discussions of MODERN FRENCH verb morphology pronominal subjects and objects in front of the finite verb are taken as emergent examples of pre-specifying fusional structures of basically the same sort as traditional verb endings (Harris 1988: 231 f.). Another, more generally acknowledged example is the fusional merger of formerly syntagmatically independent forms of VULGAR LATIN 'habere' with a dependent infinitive, yielding new finite future forms in Romance languages (Posner 1996: 177−79).

The transition in the opposite direction from fusion to agglutination appears to occur more seldomly.

One instance is the development in a number of MODERN GERMANIC languages of the fusional genitive into an invariable *s*-suffix which is not only appended to nouns, i.e. nominal heads, but even to the last attributive constituent of a complex NP (ENGLISH *the Queen of England's castles*, NORWEGIAN *dronningen av Englands slott*). One might even surmise that ENGLISH with its morphophonologically highly transparent distribution of in particular *-(e)s* and *-(e)d* morphemes has in fact reached a stage where an agglutination analysis would seem appropriate in a large part of the morphology.

According to the terminological proposals summarized in Table 114.1, transition from syntheticity to analyticity in the strict sense ought to mean wholesale loss of inflection. (CHINESE is reputed to be a putative example of this.) However, loss of inflection may not be total but rather lead to a reduction of morphological oppositions (cf. Schlegel 1818). An example of reduced syntheticity is verb-inflection in the MODERN MAINLAND SCANDINAVIAN languages, where person, number and mood oppositions have been discarded altogether and finite verb marking consists in a simple present/preterite opposition.

In Table 114.1, ordering restrictions and auxiliary words are presented as coding techniques characteristic of the non-inflecting analytic type. Within a diachronic typological framework, the question arises to which extent such non-inflectional techniques have taken over the functions of previously existing inflectional means, or whether they supplement synthetic expressions still in existence.

Whereas OLD NORSE had a rich system of synthetic case marking both with pronouns and nouns, MODERN MAINLAND SCANDINAVIAN has only residual case marking in the shape of a subject/non-subject opposition with personal pronouns. When the categorially unrestricted first position of main declarative clauses is disregarded, the three basic syntactic categories subject, direct and indirect object occur in the fixed order Subj − IO − DO both with pronouns and full NPs; cf. the NORWEGIAN examples in (1), (2) and (3):

(1) Nå ga han (Subj) henne (IO)
 now gave he her
 den (DO).
 it
 'Now he gave it to her.'

(2) Nå ville den lille gutten (Subj)
 now would the small boy-DEF
 gi piken (IO) ballen (DO).
 give girl-DEF ball-DEF
 'Now the small boy wanted to give the girl the ball.'

In addition, semantically equivalent PPs are of frequent occurrence:

(3) *Nå ville den lille gutten (Subj)*
now would the small boy-DEF
gi ballen (DO) til den lille
give ball-DEF to the small
piken (PP).
girl-DEF
'Now the small boy wanted to give the ball to the small girl.'

Such PPs have not in general superseded NPs with IO function.

When compared with LATIN, FRENCH displays a similar, but not wholly identical state of affairs. With pronouns there is still, albeit residually, a morphological three-way distinction between nominative, accusative and dative, two distinct linearization patterns, but no possibility of functional word order variation. Full NPs have subject and DO function, and as the equivalent of pronominal IOs one finds non-pronominal PPs with the grammaticalized preposition *à*. The three categories occur in the fixed order Subj – DO – *à*-PP. Cf.:

(4) *Il* (Subj) *le* (DO) *lui* (IO) *a donné.*
Il (Subj) *me* (IO) *l'* (DO) *a donné.*
Le petit garçon (Subj) *l'* (DO) *a donné à la petite fille* (PP).

Clearly, synthetic case marking has been replaced by other, analytic means both in MODERN MAINLAND SCANDINAVIAN and in FRENCH, but there are interesting differences of detail regarding the extent to which these newer analytic means are exploited: one particular serialization pattern has been generalized in SCANDINAVIAN, and in FRENCH one particular preposition has been generalized with PPs that correspond functionally to IOs.

In the domain of verbs, auxiliary constructions are commonly considered in the context of increasing analyticity. A case in point is the competition between the simple preterite (or perfect) and the periphrastic perfect in MODERN GERMAN and FRENCH, resulting in the almost total replacement of the former synthetic form by the latter analytic formation in SOUTH GERMAN DIALECTS and in modern colloquial FRENCH.

Considering these developments it should, however, be kept in mind that the analytic formations in question contain a synthetic component in the shape of a finite verb (compare also the GERMAN *würde* construction as a substitute for the synthetic finite preterite subjunctive – *lebte/würde leben*, but also *gäbe/würde geben* –, which has a synthetic finite subjunctive form as one of its component parts).

In the case of adjectives, neutralization of endings and replacement of suffixal by lexical comparative formation are instances of transition from syntheticity to analyticity (or at least strong reduction of syntheticity). Again, MODERN ROMANCE and GERMANIC LANGUAGES provide well-known examples. In the case of adjective endings, ENGLISH has gone all the way, with MODERN DUTCH and WEST FRISIAN not lagging far behind. With regard to comparison of adjectives, MODERN FRENCH has only residual traces of former LATIN synthetic comparatives and superlatives (*meilleur, pire, pis*).

The question of the causality relation in the transition from syntheticity to analyticity is rather intricate. Loss of synthetic case-marking or other endings is traditionally often assumed to be caused by phonological and morphological attrition, giving rise to linearization restrictions as an alternative means of coding syntactic relations (cf. Campbell 1995: 1151; 1157 on the history of these views).

This conception seems to be based on the premiss that syntactic restructuring is the effect of morphological restructuring rather than vice versa. This is by no means self-evidently valid as a general principle of diachronic typological development, cf. Plank's (1980: 290) observation that there is "empirical evidence that quite generally suggests that analytic coding increases prior to morphological decay".

Besides, copious case marking and fixed word order co-exist in a number of languages, as for instance MODERN ICELANDIC, whose case morphology is richer than that of MODERN GERMAN, but whose word order in pertinent cases is normally just as fixed as in corresponding MODERN MAINLAND SCANDINAVIAN instances.

Hence, the possibility that loss of case marking may also be the outcome of deeper syntactic restructuring should not be dismissed out of hand (cf. Campbell 1995: 1152).

The causality question presents itself even more forcefully in connection with the development of auxiliaries. For instance, the loss of the simple preterite and its replacement by the periphrastic perfect in SOUTH GERMAN DIALECTS is commonly attributed to categorial homonymy due to phonological change (apocope) (cf. Lindgren 1957), but in the recent literature it has been argued that a functional explanation should be sought in the tense reference itself (Dentler 1997).

In the case of other instances of auxiliary development, the assumption of some sort of replacement function often seems very unlikely. SPANISH and BULGARIAN have a number of periphrastic verb constructions which do not replace simple synthetic forms but rather add to the expressive power of the over-all verb system (whereas in modern colloquial FRENCH periphrastic forms have to a large extent ousted simple forms).

A similar case is the proliferation in GERMAN in the course of the last few centuries of modal and passive auxiliary constructions which appears to be primarily a matter of semantic and structural differentiation (cf. e. g. Helbig & Buscha 1984: 122−27; 175 f.; 184−88).

As a result of this process the overall impression of the verb phrase of present-day GERMAN is one of structural and lexical analyticity, but again it should be kept in mind that this is combined with a fairly high degree of syntheticity in the maximally governing finite verb of the complex verb constructions in question.

Given GERMAN case marking, the development in this language of analytic verb phrases raises the question of cross-categorial convergence or divergence with regard to syntheticity and analyticity. One might naturally expect languages changing their main coding strategies from synthetic to analytic to do so in all main lexical categories, but this expectation is only partly borne out by the facts.

BULGARIAN (Gukhman 1986: 113) and SPANISH are examples of languages whose ancestors had highly synthetic nouns, verbs and adjectives. Both BULGARIAN and SPANISH have, however, retained a large number of synthetic verb forms while undergoing a radical change towards analyticity in the domain of nouns and adjectives with general loss of case inflection, but partial retention of number and gender marking.

This noun/verb asymmetry seems to be typical in the sense that the opposite tendency of changing from synthetic to analytic in the domain of verbs, but not in nouns, seems to occur more rarely. (As noted above, MODERN GERMAN is only an apparent counter-instance to this.)

The more typical West European scenario for typological change along the syntheticity/analyticity dimension is one where there has been, since the Middle Ages, a wholesale drift towards a more analytic mode of expression, but where synthetic techniques are still present to a varying extent.

For instance, ENGLISH is certainly analytic to a very high degree; cf. the complete loss of case marking with nouns and of adjective morphology, and the numerous constructions involving auxiliary words (auxiliary verbs for tense, passive, mood and modality, in the latter case with loss of regular verb inflection in *shall − should, may − might*, etc.; prepositional indicator of possession: *the lord of the land*; comparison of adjectives: *more/most sensible*).

However, ENGLISH is still an inflecting language; witness the use of agglutination (the -*s*-genitive), fusion (*ships, boys, horses*) and even introflection (the preterite and past participle of so-called strong or irregular verbs: *found*, and marginally in the plural of nouns: *man − men*).

In Germanic, the most radical move towards a wholesale analytic, isolating structure has been made in AFRIKAANS, where there are only a few isolated remnants of inflection left (Gukhman 1986: 116).

Synthetic marking may in principle follow two different patterns. It is either distributive in the sense that it affects all constituents of a construction on some level, or it may be selective, i.e., affecting only a subset of the constituents of a construction. Distributive marking is a well-known Indo-European characteristic, of which a full-fledged version is still found in the agreement rules of complex NPs in MODERN ROMANCE and SLAVIC, cf. for instance RUSSIAN (5):

(5) M.Sg. et-ot krasiv-yj star-yj dom
       'this beautiful old house'
   F.Sg. et-a krasiv-aja star-aja kniga
       'this beautiful old book'
   N.Sg. et-o krasiv-oje star-oje okno
       'this beautiful old window'

All the older GERMANIC LANGUAGES had essentially the same sort of system which has, however, in MODERN STANDARD GERMAN been replaced by what German linguists call "Monoflexion" (Ronneberger-Sibold 1997). In this case, inflectional categories pertaining to the whole NP are marked − selectively − on only one (6), (7) or two (8), (9) of the constituents of the complex NP:

(6)   *die Wünsche des neuen Kunden*
      ≠ *der neuen Kunden*

(7)   Sie wollte den jungen Mann unterstützen.
      ≠ Sie wollte dem jungen Mann helfen.

(8)   die Wünsche des jungen Mannes

(9)   mit den alten Männern

In GERMAN NPs, morphological change has thus led to economization of expression rather than to loss of morphological distinctions. This state of affairs contrasts with other European languages which have developed from morphologically rich syntheticity in the direction of analyticity through loss or at least reduction of morphology in the nominal as well as in other domains.

For instance, in MODERN ROMANCE and in MAINLAND SCANDINAVIAN languages case marking is generally lost in nouns and adjectives, but gender and number marking continues to exist with adjectives where it is marked on a distributive basis through agreement rules.

The interesting point is here that GERMAN has remained morphologically synthetic to a high degree, but has reshaped the agreement rules in accordance with a principle of marking economy, whereas ROMANCE and MAINLAND SCANDINAVIAN languages have, conversely, undergone a process of morphological loss resulting in increased analyticity while at the same time retaining agreement rules in their basically Indo-European format.

In connection with adjective agreement of the kind discussed here mention has to be made of the fact that GERMAN, although being more synthetic, has dispensed with agreement in predicative adjectives and in periphrastic passives (10), whereas more analytic MODERN ROMANCE languages and, among the Mainland Scandinavian languages, MODERN SWEDISH (11) and NEW-NORWEGIAN have retained both:

(10) Das Buch ist/Die Bücher sind teuer
      (non-inflecting adj.).
      Das Buch wurde/Die Bücher wurden verkauft
      (non-inflecting part., i.e. 'supine').

(11) Boken er dyr
      (inflecting adj., sg.).
      Böckerna er dyra
      (inflecting adj., pl.).
      Boken blev såld
      (inflecting part., sg.).
      Böckerna blev sålda
      (inflecting part., pl.).

At first glance it might seem tempting to consider GERMAN "Monoflexion", loss of predicative agreement and the change from participial agreement to non-agreeing verb-governed supine forms as stepping stones towards a greater degree of analyticity. However, in view of the over-all case-inflecting, SOV structure of MODERN GERMAN, the proper theoretical conclusion to be drawn is rather that the relationship between syntheticity and analyticity in typological change should not be associated too closely with some particular kind of marking rule.

When in a language or a subset of its constructions a non-inflecting analytic state has been reached, the question is to what extent the two characteristic techniques − ordering restrictions and auxiliary words − are brought into play. A case in point is the replacement of case-marked indirect objects by linearly fixed NPs and functionally equivalent PPs and the language-specific distribution of these two options as exemplified in (1)−(4).

One may also observe a variation of the two analytic techniques that goes well beyond basic grammatical relations. An interesting example of this is provided by the two neighbouring languages SWEDISH and NORWEGIAN, both of which derive from Proto-Scandinavian. Both languages have undergone the same development from a highly synthetic fusional structure to residually inflecting analyticity resulting in fixed ordering patterns showing only minor differences between the two languages. Still there is a general difference with regard to the use of auxiliary words of categorially diverse kinds (Askedal 1997). Consider for instance the cases listed in (12):

(12) (a) More periphrastic morphology in NORWEGIAN vs. more suffixal morphology in SWEDISH in the passive:
      NORWEGIAN Døren ble åpnet. vs. SWEDISH Dörren öppnades.
      'The door was opened.'
      (b) Obligatory perfect auxiliary in NORWEGIAN vs. optionality in subordinate clauses in SWEDISH:
      NORWEGIAN Jeg takker alle dem som har hjulpet meg i mitt arbeide, ... vs. SWEDISH Jag tackar alla dem som Ø hjälpt mig i mitt arbete, ...
      'I thank all those wo have assisted me in my work.'

(c) More widespread use of the infinitive particle with governed infinitives in NORWEGIAN than in SWEDISH:
NORWEGIAN *De hadde sluttet å diskutere marsjen.* vs. SWEDISH *De hade slutat Ø diskutera marschen.*
'They had stopped discussing the march.'

(d) Obligatory expletive subject in NORWEGIAN vs. occasional optionality in SWEDISH:
SWEDISH *Efter honom skulle Ø komma andra generationer.* vs. NORWEGIAN *Etter ham skulle det komme andre generasjoner.*
'After him new generations would come.'

In these cases restrictions on linear ordering (including linear adjacency requirements) would seem to be the systematically primary technique, on which auxiliary words are incremental.

3. Word and constituent order

It was realized by Greenberg (1966: 100 *et passim*) that a number of the categories entering into his implicational ordering rules were heads and modifiers in a variety of syntactic constructions, and that comparison of different constructions in individual languages revealed a significant amount of construction-internal linearization correspondence with regard to the relative position of head and modifier. In subsequent work by Vennemann (1974a) and Lehmann (1973) this gave rise to a more general Head/Modifier (or Operand/Operator, etc.) schema (cf. Strömsdörfer & Vennemann 1995a: 1040), where verbs, nouns, and prepositions are heads, and NPs, adjectives, genitives and PPs with different functions are modifiers (for a convenient more complete survey see Dryer 1995: 1052 f.):

(13) Postspecification (right-branching):
[Head [Modifier]]
Prespecification (left-branching):
[[Modifier]Head]

A corollary of this conception was the notion of linearization consistency vs. inconsistency, consistent languages being those with uniform pre- or postspecification of the head/modifier relation, and inconsistent languages those with a mixture of both linearizations (cf. Oesterreicher 1989, Dryer 1995: 1052 *et passim*).

From these deliberations there emerged a diachronic hypothesis to the effect that inconsistent languages might be expected to be undergoing — or to be likely candidates for — further change towards cross-categorially harmonious, uniform linearization of all head/modifier relationships.

A long-term process of this kind is observable throughout the history of ROMANCE from EARLY through CLASSICAL LATIN and to the modern languages, as prespecifying constructions with postpositions, clause-final verbs and prenominal adjectives were gradually replaced by their postspecifying counterparts (Lehmann 1995: 1119—21).

A process very similar in kind, but extending over a considerably shorter period of time is the series of syntactic changes that GERMAN underwent at the beginning of the NEW HIGH GERMAN (NHG) period and which yielded an increase and a structural stabilization of prespecifying modifiers (Lehmann 1971: 20 ff.; cf. also Hawkins 1983, Ch. 5):

(14) (a) Development of a number of postpositions (*dem Befehl zufolge*).
(b) Strengthening of verb-finality in subordinate clauses.
(c) Restricting inflecting determiners, possessives and attributive adjectives to prenominal position (MIDDLE HIGH GERMAN (MHG) *sîn bruoder* and *der bruoder sîn* vs. NHG German only *sein Bruder*).
(d) Restricting the modifiers of adjectives and participles to preadjectival/preparticipial position with subsequent extension of the use of such syntagmatically complex prenominal modifiers (cf. Schiller's mixed left- and right-branching *die aufgewälzten Berge zu des Ruhmes Sonnenhöhen* vs. MODERN GERMAN left-branching *die zu des Ruhmes Sonnenhöhen aufgewälzten Berge*).

Connected with such ordering changes is the general question whether one particular pair of modifier and head categories tend to play a leading role in short or long term developments of this kind. The investigations of Hawkins (1983) seem to imply that the linearization of adposition and dependent NP is the most reliable indicator of synchronic linear systematicity, but the very stability of this relation would seem to imply that it is less suitable as a predictor of linearization change.

The relation between verbal predicate and object is often taken to be basic due to its semantico-syntactic centrality and variability, and the constituents of other head/modifier pairs are then categorized as verb patterners and object patterners, respectively (Dryer 1995: 1052 *et passim*).

In the GERMAN case summarized in (14), this seems to make sense even from a diachronic point of view, but in a universal perspective the linearization of various kinds of heads and modifiers in relation to each other appears to be so multifarious (Dryer 1995: 1052 *et passim*), and the evidence for truly convincing causality chains in this domain so scanty, that universal conclusions about the leading role of verb-object linearization are hardly warranted.

The power of the principle of cross-categorially uniform linearization as a predictor of language change is limited by the fact that it is by definition based on the dependency − government or agreement − relation between head and modifier and does not take account of other functional aspects of linearization.

This would pose no theoretical problem were it not for the embarrassing empirical fact that most known languages appear to display "inconsistent" linearization. Moreover, most of these languages do not seem to be in a clearly "transitional" state but rather to remain fairly stable in their "inconsistent" condition. Besides, individual developments occur which run counter to the linearization preferences and tendencies otherwise observable.

This over-all picture calls for a broadening of the range of factors relevant for the understanding of linearization developments. First, it appears that the tendency towards cross-categorially uniform linearization may be counteracted by purely grammatical rules. The history of the attributive genitive in SCANDINAVIAN and GERMAN provides examples of this. In OLD NORSE, the attributive genitive is found in post- and in prespecifying position (*þræll konungs* 'the king's slave', *jarls sæti* 'the earl's seat').

Paradoxically, whereas MODERN NORWEGIAN has a clear majority of postspecifying constructions, the genitive has turned the other way around and has become stabilized as a prenominal modifier. The reason for this is presumably that the genitive has been integrated into the prespecifying determiner position (*denne/kongens gamle træll* 'this/the king's old slave', *dette/jarlens tapte sæte* 'this/the earl's lost seat').

In GERMAN, the opposite development has taken place. The MHG pre- or postspecifying genitive is in NHG normally postspecifying (MHG *aller slachte schande* − NHG *Schande aller Art*). This may be due to the fact that in NHG prenominal position is in principle reserved for inflecting agreeing modifiers (determiners, adjectives), whereas postnominal position is occupied by non-agreeing modifiers (genitive, PP, attributive clauses).

Second, general semantic tendencies may be at work. One may here refer to the ROMANCE difference between indexically or emotionally specifying prenominal adjectives and more objectively qualifying postnominal adjectives (*l'Ancien Régime* − *un livre ancien, ce fameux film* − *ce film fameux*; cf. Oesterreicher 1989: 248−53). The interesting point is that LATIN had no differentiation of this sort. Hence, the present linear "inconsistency" is caused by a semantically motivated deviation from a main trend towards postspecification.

Third, a typologically basic linearization pattern may be overruled by pragmatically conditioned ordering (which may then become grammaticalized). For instance, all MODERN GERMANIC languages have V/2 and V/1 main clauses, which in GERMAN, DUTCH and MODERN WEST FRISIAN contrast with the V/Last structure of subordinate clauses (Gerritsen 1984: 109 f. *et passim*):

(15)   *Er hat ein Auto gestohlen.* (V/2)
       Hat er ein Auto gestohlen? (V/1)
       Man fragt ihn, warum er ein Auto gestohlen hat. (V/Last)

The typological ordering paradox in these three languages is resolved if V/2 is recognized as a functionally independent marker of assertion (and constituent questions), and V/1 as a marker of sentence questions, these two orders being superimposed on the basic, pragmatically neutral V/Last pattern. This common areal characteristic of MODERN GERMANIC has in the course of the centuries been reinforced and stabilized independently of whatever changes may have taken place in subordinate clauses and in sequences containing non-finite verb forms.

It is commonly assumed that pragmatically conditioned ordering may not only be at variance with typologically basic serialization but may even in the course of time modify or supplant it, thereby effecting major typological change. Thus, frequent use of rhematizing or explicating afterthought constructions is supposed to have caused shifts from basic SOV to SVO (Hyman 1975). Similarly, frequent topicalization may be considered a cause of transition from VSO to SVO (or, at least in theory, OVS).

4. Interrelations between morphology, linearization and syntactic rules

In connection with typological change, different kinds of morphosyntactic rules have to be distinguished. In § 2. it was pointed out that in modern West European languages verb and, to a somewhat lesser extent, adjective morphology is more resistent to loss than is case marking with nouns. Agreement rules have on the whole proved comparatively stable despite the general drift towards more analytic, non-inflecting structures (cf. Plank 1980: 289), but individual languages differ with regard to what kind of agreement rules are retained as compared with the known LATIN and earlier GERMANIC state of affairs.

MODERN ROMANCE LANGUAGES have in general verb agreement (or distinctive verb endings which make pronominal subjects expendable) and adjective agreement within NPs as well as in predicative position.

Relatively analytic MODERN GERMANIC LANGUAGES display different morphological patterns. DUTCH and MODERN WEST FRISIAN have verb agreement and adjective agreement in NPs, but not in predicative position. ENGLISH has a small amount of verb agreement, but no adjective agreement whatsoever, whereas the MAINLAND SCANDINAVIAN languages have retained adjective agreement within the NP as well as in predicative position, but have discarded verb agreement.

These various developments show that agreement rules as a class do not necessarily develop along the same lines as syntactic rules operating on constituents representing syntactic relations on the clause level.

Within the latter class of rules, a distinction has to be made between relationally neutral rules and rules sensitive to syntactic relations. In general, topicalization belongs in the first category, whereas the rules involved in passive constructions are prototypical instances of the second category.

In typological synchronic and diachronic descriptions of relationally sensitive rules, the interrelations between morphology and syntax have to be taken into consideration. For instance, Greenberg's (1966: 96) Universal 41:

(16) "If in a language the verb follows both the nominal subject and nominal object as the dominant order, the language almost always has a case system."

posits a positive correlation between one specific ordering type (SOV) and one specific kind of marking of syntactic relations (case-marking).

This correlation may be subject to change, as evidenced by the development from OLD LATIN to MODERN ROMANCE which has led to a new correlation between SVO ordering and absence of morphological case marking with the majority of NPs.

The question naturally arises which one of the two individual typological changes — loss of case-marking or linear restructuring — is the cause of the other and hence of the two-level change involving both morphology and linearization. It has been proposed that the linearization change in question can be accounted for by phonological erosion of case endings in connection with Greenberg's Universal 41 quoted above, according to which OV and absence of morphological case is a non-favoured combination (Hawkins 1995: 1181; cf. also Hock & Joseph 1996: 210 for a formulation of the traditional view not invoking Greenbergian universals).

Thus, a fairly well-established universal generalization would in this case provide the methodological prerequisite for understanding possible "pathways" (Hawkins) of typological change.

Recent research seems, however, to indicate that changes of this kind can only be fully accounted for by investigating the interrelations between syntactic rules and different strategies for coding syntactic relations. Within a Neogrammarian framework where morphology is central and syntax peripheral, it seems natural to assume change, in particular loss, of morphology to be the cause of syntactic change. However, closer inspection of data from a number of languages seems to indicate that this traditional assumption need not be correct in all cases (as suggested already by Jespersen 1894: 361 f.).

Theoretically, the following scenarios may be envisaged concerning the relationship between morphology and syntactic rules:

Table 114.4: Types of relationship between morphology and syntactic rules

i.	presence of case marking	syntactic rules are restricted by morphological case
ii.	absence of case marking	syntactic rules are restricted by morphological case
iii.	presence of case marking	syntactic rules are not restricted by (one particular) morphological case
iv.	absence of case marking	syntactic rules are not restricted by morphological case

Scenario (i) is universally well-known. It is the traditional Indo-European system found in, e. g., MODERN SLAVIC languages and MODERN GERMAN, disallowing for instance the subjectivization of non-accusatives in the *werden* passive (17), and infinitive formation (18) and conjunction reduction (19) through deletion of non-nominatives:

(17) *Die Freunde halfen ihm* [D].
 Ihm [D] *wurde von den Freunden geholfen.*
 *Er [N] *wurde von den Freunden geholfen.*

(18) *Mir* [D] *fehlt das Geld* [N].
 *Ich hoffe, __ [D] *das Geld* [N] *nicht zu fehlen.*

(19) **Er* [N] *gilt als tüchtig, aber __* [D] *kommt die Hausarbeit* [N] *zu schwer vor.*
 Er gilt [N] *als tüchtig, aber ihm* [D] *kommt die Hausarbeit* [N] *zu schwer vor.*

As formulated in Table 114.4, scenario (ii) is clearly self-contradictory, but still there are cases on record which make sense when described in this way. For instance, MODERN DUTCH has lost all case oppositions in full NPs, and the opposition between the accusative and the dative in pronouns. In spite of this, formerly dative marked indirect objects are commonly not subjectivized in the passive, even when the direct object is elliptically left out (for details cf. Abraham 1983):

(20) *Ons werd opengedaan.* (Corresponding to GERMAN: *Uns wurde geöffnet.*)

Scenario (iii) represents the normal state of affairs in ergative languages, where the ergative with transitive and the absolutive with intransitive verbs usually have the same subject rule-properties (cf. Anderson 1976). Among the GERMANIC LANGUAGES, it is found in MODERN ICELANDIC and FAROESE, cf. GERMAN (18), (19) above and ICELANDIC (21), (22) (cf. Cole & al. 1980: 722−28):

(21) *Mig* [A] *vantar ekki peninga* [A].
 'I don't lack money.'
 Ég vonast til að __ [A] *vanta ekki peninga* [A].
 'I hope not to lack money.'

(22) *Honom* [D] *finst verkefnið* [N] *of þungt.*
 'He finds the homework too hard.'
 Hann [N] *segist vera duglegur, en __* [D] *finst verkefnið* [N] *of þungt.*
 'He considers himself able but finds the homework too hard.'

In FAROESE (but not in ICELANDIC) this even extends to subjectivization in the passive (Barnes & Weyhe 1994: 213) not possible in ICELANDIC or GERMAN:

(23) *Teir hjálptu honum* [D].
 (Cf. GERMAN: *Sie halfen ihm* [D].)
 Hann [N] *varð hjálptur.*
 (Cf. GERMAN: *Ihm* [D] *wurde geholfen.*)

In cases like (21), (22), dative, accusative and even genitive NPs exhibit the same rule properties as the nominative subjects whose linear distribution they share, and are therefore aptly dubbed "oblique subjects" in the current literature (Thráinsson 1994: 175−77, Barnes 1986).

Scenario (iv) is represented by such non-case languages as MODERN ENGLISH and NORWEGIAN which allow for the subjectivization of a variety of syntactic categories, including direct, indirect (24) and prepositional ("oblique") (25) objects, consider for instance:

(24) *He had been awarded a prestigious prize.*

(25) *The bed had not been slept in __.*

In the Germanic cases at hand, scenarios (ii)−(iv) are, as far as we can tell, the outcome of an original OLD GERMANIC case-marking and basically (S)OV system which conformed to scenario (i) in Table 114.4. From this the following more general conclusions seem to follow:

1. Trivially, VO structure and absence of case marking combines with morphologically unrestricted syntactic rules (ENGLISH, NORWEGIAN). Conversely, retention of case marking and OV structure combines with retention of the traditional LATIN type rule dependence on morphology (MODERN GERMAN).
2. Not so trivially, case marking may coexist with syntactic rules not being restricted by one particular morphological case. In Germanic this is attested in combination with fixed VO structure (ICELANDIC, FAROESE).
3. Conversely, generalization of morphologically unrestricted syntactic rules may not be carried through despite loss of morphological case marking. In Germanic this is attested in the case of former dative objects in combination with retention of OV structure (DUTCH and MODERN WEST FRISIAN).

The general conclusion appears to be that VO structure may favour morphologically unrestricted syntactic rules irrespective of loss or retention of morphological case marking.

At this point an important addition has to be made. Like MODERN MAINLAND SCANDINAVIAN and ENGLISH, but unlike MODERN GERMAN, the order of sentence elements in ICELANDIC and FAROESE is quite fixed. Hence one is led to assume that VO order also favours fixed element order on the clause level, and, concomitantly, a more strictly structured VP constituent than in OV languages where the preverbal domain is to a greater extent available for focusing and rhematizing functions.

Thus it would seem that, first, morphological loss is not a necessary condition for restructuring from OV to VO (cf. ICELANDIC and FAROESE).

Second, the observable interrelations with syntactic rules indicate that in the development of the Germanic languages the process of diachronic restructuring is one from lesser to stricter syntactic configurationality (cf. Fanselow 1987, Faarlund 1990; on the somewhat different notion of "focus configurationality" see Sasse 1995: 1071–74), with morphological case marking becoming less and topological coding of syntactic relations becoming more important. It is noteworthy that, according to Faarlund (1990: 83–110), OLD ICELANDIC displays a number of clearly non-configurational traits which contrast with the configurational syntactic behaviour illustrated in (21), (22).

Third, the above comparison of a number of GERMANIC LANGUAGES shows configurationality to be a gradient parameter, where gradience is explicable in terms of the number of syntactic rules for which either morphological or topological conditions apply; cf. the configurationality hierarchy in (26) (cf. Askedal 1993):

(26)   ENGLISH, MAINLAND SCANDINAVIAN > FAROESE > ICELANDIC > GERMAN

Topological configurationality is not restricted to, and may even not be most characteristically realized in clause level relationships. It is a common observation that word order freedom is in general less extensive within NPs and PPs than on the clause level (Hawkins 1983: 11 f.). The lack of agreement rules between the noun and attributive elements (determiners and adjectives) in MODERN ENGLISH NPs as compared with OLD and MIDDLE ENGLISH may be seen as an instance where the marking of NP-internal relationships by means of morphology has yielded completely to marking by configurational adjacency.

Such developments are presumably less natural when the attributive element is a noun or an NP, due to the need to distinguish nominal heads from nominal modifiers, but as Plank (1980: 297–301) has shown, typological change may have the effect that even NP-internal attributive relationships of this kind are coded without recourse to morphological marking.

The proper methodological conclusion appears to be that typological change in the linear domain should in principle be investigated in connection with both morphology and syntax, but without any bias in favour of morphological developments as primary causes. Due allowance has to be made for the fact that in a great number of cases syntactic change precedes morphological change (cf. Cole & al. 1980: 719; Estival & Myhill 1988: 463 ff.)

5. Realignments and typological cyclicity

The morphological marking of the primary arguments of intransitive and transitive verbs plays a prominent role in modern language typology. The subject of transitive verbs (S_{tr}), of intransitive verbs (S_{itr}) and the object of transitive verbs (O_{tr}) may theoretically be morphologically marked in five different ways (Comrie 1978: 330−34; art. 28; 37), to which a sixth type has to be added when a possible bifurcation with intransitive verbs (Type (v.) in (27), cf. Nichols 1990) is also taken into consideration:

(27) (i.) S_{itr}-specifying: $S_{itr} \neq S_{tr} = O_{tr}$
(ii.) Differential marking: $S_{tr} \neq S_{itr} \neq O_{tr}$
(iii.) Nominative/accusative (accusativity): $S_{tr} = S_{itr} \neq O_{tr}$
(iv.) Ergative/absolutive (ergativity): $S_{tr} \neq S_{itr} = O_{tr}$
(v.) Active/inactive (or stative) (activity): $S_{tr} = S_{itr/active} \neq S_{itr/inactive} = O_{tr}$
(vi.) Non-specifying: $S_{tr} = S_{itr} = O_{tr}$

Type (i.) is not known to exist empirically. Type (ii.), being redundant from a marking point of view, appears to be very rare. Type (vi.) is a possible formula for the absence of any kind of differential morphological marking, but does not exist as a syntactic type. For instance, MODERN ENGLISH and MAINLAND SCANDINAVIAN have only vestigial case marking with a few pronouns, but syntactically these languages are still manifestations af the accusativity type where the subject/object opposition is no longer realized morphologically, but configurationally in terms of ordering restrictions.

This leaves us with the three types (iii.), (iv.) and (v.) where the categories S_{tr}, S_{itr} and O_{tr} are aligned differently. Realignments are known or assumed to have occurred, for instance by extension of the ergative to S_{itr}, in which case accusativity results, or when the agent phrase of passives within a non-ergative pattern is extended to non-passive transitive verbs yielding ergativity (Plank 1985, Harris 1990).

In certain cases reasons may be found for positing an anterior activity phase, as in Schmidt's (1979) discussion of Indo-European as a possible candidate for a three-stage development from activity via ergativity to accusativity. This conception presupposes grammaticalization of relational functions. However, a still earlier stage may be envisaged where arguments were not ascribed to the predicate on the basis of grammatical valency requirements, but on a more direct semantic basis (cf. Sasse 1982: 279).

The twofold assumption that typological shifts of this kind are stages in a causality chain, and that the main grammatical techniques and strategies are finite in number, has led a number of researchers to propose various theories of typological cyclicity. Such theories are in general conjectural due to the fact that, as far as we can tell, no known languages or language families have been attested in all the stages required for completing a full cycle.

One such theory, whose general traits go back to Rasmus Rask and Wilhelm von Humboldt (cf. Campbell 1995: 1146) is basically morphological and concerned with the interplay between morphological techniques and phonetic developments. It assumes that agglutination develops into fusional inflectional morphology which again is lost by phonological attrition resulting in isolation. This last isolating stage is then the point of departure for the reintroduction of agglutination, at which point a new cycle has been triggered off. Cf. Table 114.5:

Table 114.5: Cyclical evolution based on the interplay between morphological techniques and phonological development

A. agglutination	→	B. fusional inflection
↑		↓
D. isolation	←	C. phonetic attrition

A more refined version, due to Vennemann (1974b, 371), takes into account syntactic and pragmatic factors as well. Cf. Table 114.6:

Table 114.6: Cyclical evolution taking into account syntactic and pragmatic factors

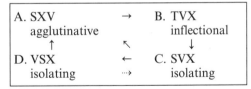

According to this model, a subject construction with O/XV order yields to a topicalization structure where the clause-internal verb is accorded some sort of demarcational function. In connection with the ensuing morphological change from inflection to isolation the theme position is resyntactizied as subject position. At this stage new agglutinative morphology may be developed, or verb order may change from its residual demarcational position to clause-initial.

As is evident from the diagram, this model is not strictly cyclical as the possibility of the reverse change form VSX to SVX is also reckoned with. The alleged demarcational function of the verb remains a moot point. Besides, the model does not explicitly take into consideration syntactic rules in a stricter sense.

A kind of pragmatico-syntactic cyclicity theory based on the grammaticalization of topics as subjects was devised by Li & Thompson (1976: 485). Cf. Table 114.7.

the former backgrounded passive agent in its new function as foregrounded active agent, and perhaps even leading to the loss of passive verb morphology.

Further development into a new nominative/accusative system is achieved by generalizing one common morphological marker for the subject of transitive and intransitive verbs (in accordance with the common distribution described by Anderson 1976 where the first, subject argument of transitive and intransitive verbs share syntactic rule properties):

Table 114.7: Cyclicity based on pragmatico-syntactic factors

A. *Topic* integration of topics into basic sentence structure	→	B. *Neither Subject nor Topic* increasing integration of the topic into the semantico-syntactic valency of the verb
↑		↓
D. *Both Subject and Topic* topics become less marked, more basic	←	C. *Subject* complete integration of the topic into the semantico-syntactic valency of the verb as a subject, marked topicalization structures

Table 114.8: Cyclicity based on semantico-syntactic factors

	A. nominative/accusative	
generalizing the agent phrase, foregrounding it, acquisition of syntactic subjecthood (loss of passive verb morphology)	↓ ↑	generalizing common marker to subjects of transitive and intransitive verbs due to shared syntactic subjecthood
	B. ergative/absolutive	

This approach is concerned with syntactic functions and lexical rules, but hardly with morphology in any principled way. (For further discussion and critical comments see Sasse 1995: 1068 f.)

The fourth approach is syntactico-semantical in character and relates to the coding and syntactic rule properties of subjects and objects. According to Estival & Myhill (1988: 445 *et passim*), deverbal passive constructions with their basis in a nominative/accusative system may develop into an ergative pattern and from there on into a new active construction within a nominative/accusative pattern. (The following is a simplified account intended to illustrate the main line of reasoning.)

The first stage is brought about by generalizing the agent phrase of the original passive and foregrounding it. This pragmatic reanalysis incurs a syntactic reanalysis consisting in transferring syntactic subject properties to

In this model, morphological case marking and the possession and acquisition of syntactic rule properties (syntactic subjecthood) are accorded primary importance. Linearization differences relating to the OV/VO opposition are absent. This is only natural, given the fact that really convincing examples of topologically, not morphologically coding ergative languages so far appear to be lacking (but cf. Plank 1985: 285).

These various conceptions of typological cyclicity may be assumed to comply with the general principle of "uniformitarianism" (Vennemann & Strömsdörfer 1995b: 1129; Hawkins 1995: 1178), i.e. the assumption that human languages have at all times past and present had a defining common structural core of systematic options.

On the other hand, the relationship between the cyclicity conceptions and the principle of "connectivity" (Vennemann & Strömsdörfer

1995b: 1129; 1131), i. e. that any type may change into any other type, appears to be rather problematic.

6. Concluding remarks

The admittedly controversial concept of inconsistency has above all played an important role in word order typology, but the above discussion has shown that it is highly relevant in other domains too, with regard to the syntheticity/analyticity distinction and the relationship between morphology and syntactic rules (cf. also the phenomenon of "split ergativity" and the fact that "syntactic ergativity" appears to be very rare).

There may well be system-internal tendencies to generalize analyticity or to favour one particular pattern of head/modifier linearization or to provide certain syntactic rules with a unitary relation to one particular case or one particular topological position, but such tendencies are evidently checked and balanced by, first, the system-internal interplay of the various components of the grammar and, second, functional, pragmatically motivated needs of expression.

These general considerations do not answer all questions pertaining to the motivation and causes of typological change. For instance, the question remains why certain types or groups of languages appear to be far more stable than others, cf. for instance the relatively stable agglutinative character of Turkic languages (→ art. 122) as against the multitude of structural upheavals within the Indo-European family in historical times.

Another vexing question is the influence of areal relations (→ art. 2, § 4. and section XIV in this volume). Here opinions range from the assertion that structure cannot be borrowed (cf. Campbell 1995: 1158) to the assumption that borrowing is the main and perhaps only cause of typological change (cf. Smith 1981). It is evident that these extreme positions are both wrong. (For a succinct survey of methodological problems pertaining to diachronic typology cf. Comrie 1983, Ch. 10.)

With regard to the possibilities of grammar-internal explanations for language change, there has been a remarkable upsurge in the interest in grammaticalization phenomena among typologists during the last couple of decades (cf. Croft 1990, Ch. 8.5; Traugott & Heine (ed.) 1991; → art. 113). Presumably there are two reasons for this. First, grammaticalization processes are linguistic changes which often give rise to new structures which may have typological effects. Second, grammaticalization processes often reflect needs of expression rather directly and are therefore a potential source of insight into the functional basis of typological structures.

7. References

Abraham, Werner. 1983: "Bemerkungen zum semantischen Transitivitätsbegriff". In: Askedal, John Ole et al. (eds.), *Festschrift für Laurits Saltveit zum 70. Geburtstag am 31. Dezember 1983*. Oslo etc.: Universitetsforlaget, 16–29.

Anderson, Stephen R. 1976. "On the notion of subject in ergative languages". In: Li, Charles N. (ed.), 1–24.

Askedal, John Ole. 1993. "Configurationality in language typology and diachronic syntax: Evidence from Germanic". *Norsk Lingvistisk Tidsskrift* 11.2: 125–34.

Askedal, John Ole. 1997. "Typological and Semiotic Aspects of Certain Morphosyntactic Differences Between Norwegian and Swedish." *Interdisciplinary Journal for Germanic Linguistics and Semiotic Analysis* 2.2: 187–220.

Barnes, Michael P. 1986. "Subject, Nominative and Oblique Case in Faroese". *Scripta Islandica* 37: 13–46.

Barnes, Michael P. & Weyhe, Eyvind. 1994. "Faroese". In: König, Ekkehard & Johan van der Auwera (eds.), 190–218.

Campbell, Lyle. 1995. "History of the Study of Historical Syntax". In: Jacobs, Joachim & al. (eds.), 1136–66.

Cole, Peter & Harbert, Wayne & Hermon, Gabriella & Sridhar, S.N. 1980. "The acquisition of subjecthood". *Language* 56.4: 719–43.

Comrie, Bernard. 1978. "Ergativity". In: Lehmann, Winfred P. (ed.), 329–94.

Comrie, Bernard. 1980. "Morphology and word order reconstruction: problems and prospects". In: Fisiak, Jacek (ed.), 83–96.

Comrie, Bernard. 1983. *Language Universals and Linguistic Typology. Syntax and Morphology.* Oxford: Blackwell.

Coseriu, Eugenio. 1980. "Partikeln und Sprachtypus. Zur strukturell-funktionellen Fragestellung in der Sprachtypologie". In: Brettschneider, Gunter & Lehmann, Christian (eds.), *Wege zur Universalienforschung. Sprachwissenschaftliche Beiträge zum 60. Geburtstag von Hansjakob Seiler*. Tübingen: Narr, 199–206.

Croft, William. 1990. *Typology and Universals*. Cambridge: Cambridge University Press.

Dentler, Sigrid. 1997. *Zur Perfekterneuerung im Mittelhochdeutschen. Die Erweiterung des zeitreferentiellen Funktionsbereichs von Perfektfügungen.* (Göteborger germanistische Forschungen, 37.) Göteborg: Acta Universitatis Gothoburgensis.

Dryer, Matthew S. 1995. "Word Order Typology". In: Jacobs, Joachim & al. (eds.), 1050−65.

Estival, Dominique & Myhill, John. 1988. "Formal and functional aspects of the development from passive to ergative systems". In: Shibatani, Masayoshi (ed.), *Passive and Voice.* (Typological Studies in Language, 16.) Amsterdam & Philadelphia: Benjamins, 441−91.

Faarlund, Jan Terje. 1990. *Syntactic Change. Toward a Theory of Historical Syntax.* (Trends in Linguistics. Studies and Monographs, 50.) The Hague: Mouton de Gruyter.

Fanselow, Gisbert. 1987. *Konfigurationalität. Untersuchungen zur Universalgrammatik am Beispiel des Deutschen.* (Studien zur deutschen Grammatik, 29.) Tübingen: Narr.

Fisiak, Jacek (ed.). 1980. *Historical Morphology.* (Trends in Linguistics. Studies and Monographs, 17.) The Hague etc.: Mouton.

Fisiak, Jacek (ed.). 1997. *Linguistic Reconstruction and Typology.* (Trends in Linguistics. Studies and Monographs, 96.) Berlin etc.: Mouton de Gruyter.

Geckeler, Horst. 1989. "'Alter Wein in neue Schläuche'. Überlegungen zur Nützlichkeit verworfener traditioneller Kategorien für die typologische Beschreibung romanischer Sprachen". In: Raible, Wolfgang (ed.), 163−90.

Gerritsen, Marinel. 1984. "Divergent word order developments in Germanic languages: A description and tentative explanation". In: Fisiak, Jacek (ed.). *Historical Syntax.* (Trends in Linguistics. Studies and Monographs, 23.) Berlin etc.: Mouton de Gruyter, 107−35.

Greenberg, Joseph H. 1966. "Some Universals of Grammar with Particular Reference to the Order of Meaningful Elements". In: Greenberg, Joseph H. (ed.), *Universals of Language*, 2nd Ed. Cambridge/MA & London: MIT Press, 73−113.

Greenberg, Joseph H. 1995: "The Diachronic Typological Approach to Language". In: Shibatani, Masayoshi & Bynon, Theodora (eds.), *Approaches to Language Typology.* Oxford: Clarendon, 145−66.

Gukhman, M.M. 1986. "On Typological Shift". In: Lehmann, Winfred P. (ed.), 111−21.

Harris, Alice C. 1990. "Alignment Typology and Diachronic Change". In: Lehmann, Winfred P. (ed.), 67−90.

Harris, Martin. 1988. "French". In: Harris, Martin & Vincent, Nigel (eds.), *The Romance Languages.* London: Routledge, 209−45.

Hawkins, John A. 1983. *Word Order Universals.* New York etc.: Academic Press.

Hawkins, John A. 1995. "Typology-based Research into Syntactic Change". In: Jacobs, Joachim & al. (eds.), 1176−83.

Heinz, Sieglinde & Wandruszka, Ulrich (eds.). 1982. *Fakten und Theorien. Beiträge zur romanischen und allgemeinen Sprachwissenschaft.* (Tübinger Beiträge zur Linguistik, 191.) Tübingen: Narr.

Helbig, Gerhard & Buscha, Joachim. 1984. *Deutsche Grammatik. Ein Handbuch für den Ausländerunterricht.* Leipzig: VEB Verlag Enzyklopädie.

Hock, Hans Henrich & Joseph, Brian. 1996. *Language History, Language Change, and Language Relationship. An Introduction to Historical and Comparative Linguistics.* (Trends in Linguistics. Studies and Monographs, 93.) Berlin etc.: Mouton de Gruyter.

Hyman, Larry. 1975. "On the Change from SOV to SVO: Evidence from Niger-Congo". In: Li, Charles N. (ed.), 113−47.

Jacobs, Joachim & von Stechow, Arnim & Sternefeld, Wolfgang & Vennemann, Theo (eds.). 1995. *Syntax. Ein internationales Handbuch zeitgenössischer Forschung.* 2. Halbband. (Handbücher zur Sprach- und Kommunikationswissenschaft, 9.2.) Berlin etc.: de Gruyter.

Jespersen, Otto. 1894. *Progress in language with special reference to English.* London: Swan Sonnenschein & Co.

Klimov, G.A. 1986. "On the Notion of Language Type". In: Lehmann, Winfred P. (ed.), 105−10.

König, Ekkehard & Johan van der Auwera (eds.). 1994. *The Germanic Languages.* London & New York: Routledge.

Lehmann, Winfred P. 1971. "On the rise of SOV patterns in New High German". In: Schweisthal, K. G. (ed.), *Grammatik Kybernetik Kommunikation.* Bonn: Dümmler, 19−24.

Lehmann, Winfred P. 1973. "A structural principle of language and its implications". *Language* 49.1: 47−66.

Lehmann, Winfred P. 1979. "English: A Characteristic SVO Language". In: Lehmann, Winfred P. (ed.), 169−222.

Lehmann, Winfred P. 1993. *Theoretical Bases of Indo-European Linguistics.* London & New York: Routledge.

Lehmann, Winfred P. 1995. "Objectives of a Theory of Syntactic Change". In: Jacobs, Joachim & al. (eds.), 1116−26.

Lehmann, Winfred P. (ed.) 1978. *Syntactic Typology. Studies in the Phenomenology of Language.* Austin/TX: University of Texas Press.

Lehmann, Winfred P. (ed.). 1986. *Language Typology 1985. Papers from the Linguistic Typology Symposium, Moscow, 9−13 December 1985.* (Amsterdam Studies in the Theory and History of Linguistic Science. S. IV: Current Issues in Linguistic Theory, 47.) Amsterdam & Philadelphia: Benjamins.

Lehmann, Winfred P. (ed.). 1990. *Language Typology 1987. Systematic Balance in Language. Papers from the Linguistic Typology Symposium, Berkeley, 1–3 December 1987.* (Amsterdam Studies in the Theory and History of Linguistic Science. S. IV: Current Issues in Linguistic Theory, 67.) Amsterdam & Philadelphia: Benjamins.

Lehmann, Winfred P. & Hewitt, Helen-Jo Jakusz (eds.). 1991. *Language Typology 1988. Typological Models in Reconstruction.* (Amsterdam Studies in the Theory and History of Linguistic Science. S. IV: Current Issues in Linguistic Theory, 81.) Amsterdam & Philadelphia: Benjamins.

Li, Charles N. (ed.). 1975. *Word Order and Word Order Change.* Austin/TX: University of Texas Press.

Li, Charles N. (ed.) 1976. *Subject and Topic.* New York etc.: Academic Press.

Li, Charles N. & Thompson, Sandra Annear. 1976. "Subject and Topic: A new typology of languages". In: Li, Charles N. (ed.), 457–89.

Lindgren, Kaj B. 1957. *Über den oberdeutschen Präteritumschwund.* (Annales Academiæ scientiarum fennicæ, Ser. B, 112,1). Helsinki: Academia Scientiarum Fennica.

Mithun, Marianne. 1991. "The Development of Bound Pronominal Paradigms". In: Lehmann, Winfred P. & Hewitt, Helen-Jo Jakusz (eds.), 85–104.

Nichols, Johanna. 1990. "Some preconditions and typical traits of the stative-active language type (with reference to Proto-Indo-European)". In: Lehmann, Winfred P. (ed.), 95–113.

Oesterreicher, Wulf. 1989. "'Konsistenz' als typologisches Kriterium?" In: Raible, Wolfgang (ed.), 223–62.

Plank, Frans. 1980. "Encoding grammatical relations: acceptable and unacceptable non-distinctness". In: Fisiak, Jacek (ed.), 289–325.

Plank, Frans. 1985. "The extended accusative/restricted nominative in perspective". In: Plank, Frans (ed.), *Relational Typology.* (Trends in Linguistics. Studies and Monographs, 28.) Berlin etc.: Mouton, 269–310.

Posner, Rebecca. 1996. *The Romance Languages.* (Cambridge language surveys.) Cambridge: Cambridge University Press.

Raible, Wolfgang (ed.). 1989. *Romanistik, Sprachtypologie und Universalienforschung. Beiträge zum Freiburger Romanistentag 1987.* (Tübinger Beiträge zur Linguistik, 332.) Tübingen: Narr.

Roelcke, Thorsten, 1997: *Sprachtypologie des Deutschen.* (Sammlung Göschen, 2812.) Berlin & New York: de Gruyter.

Ronneberger-Sibold, Elke. 1997. "Typology and the diachronic evolution of German morphosyntax". In: Fisiak, Jacek (ed.), 313–35.

Sasse, Hans-Jürgen. 1982. "Subjektprominenz". In: Heinz, Sieglinde & Wandruszka, Ulrich (eds.), 267–86.

Sasse, Hans-Jürgen. 1995. "Prominence Typology". In: Jacobs, Joachim & al. (eds.), 1065–75.

Schlegel, August Wilhelm von. 1818; [2]1971. *Observations sur la Langue et la Littérature Provençales.* Neudruck der ersten Ausgabe Paris 1818 herausgegeben mit einem Vorwort von Gunter Narr: "August Wilhelm Schlegel – ein Wegbereiter der Romanischen Philologie". (Tübinger Beiträge zur Linguistik, 7.) Tübingen: Narr.

Schmidt, Karl Horst. 1979. "Reconstructing Active and Ergative Stages of Pre-Indo-European". In: Plank, Frans (ed.), *Ergativity. Towards a Theory of Grammatical Relations.* London: Academic Press, 333–45.

Senn, Alfred. 1966. *Handbuch der litauischen Sprache.* Band 1: Grammatik. Heidelberg: Winter.

Skalička, Vladimír. 1979a. "Das Erscheinungsbild der Sprachtypen". In: Skalička, Vladimír 1979d: 21–58.

Skalička, Vladimír. 1979b. "Die Gesetzmäßigkeit in der Entwicklung der Sprache". In: Skalička, Vladimír 1979d: 263–79.

Skalička, Vladimír. 1979c. "Konsonantenkombinationen und linguistische Typologie". In: Skalička, Vladimír 1979d: 307–11.

Skalička, Vladimír. 1979d. *Typologische Studien.* Mit einem Beitrag von Petr Sgall. Herausgegeben von Peter Hartmann. (Schriften zur Linguistik, 11.) Braunschweig & Wiesbaden: Vieweg.

Smith, Neil. 1981. "Consistency, markedness and language change: on the notion 'consistent language'". *Journal of Linguistics* 17.1: 39–54.

Strömsdörfer, Christian & Vennemann, Theo. 1995a. "Ziele der syntaktischen Typologie". In: Jacobs, Joachim & al. (eds.), 1031–43.

Strömsdörfer, Christian & Vennemann, Theo. 1995b. "Das Verhältnis des Syntaxwandels zur Theorie der Sprachzustände". In: Jacobs, Joachim & al. (eds.), 1126–35.

Thráinsson, H. (1994): "Icelandic". In: König, Ekkehard & Johan van der Auwera (eds.), 142–89.

Traugott, Elizabeth Closs & Heine, Bernd (eds.). 1991. *Approaches to Grammaticalization.* Vol. 1: Focus on Theoretical and Methodological Issues. Vol. 2: Focus on Types of Grammatical Markers. (Typological Studies in Language, 19: 1–2.) Amsterdam & Philadelphia: Benjamins.

Vennemann, Theo. 1974a. "Analogy in generative grammar. The origin of word order". In: Heilmann, Luigi (ed.), *Proceedings of the 11th International Congress of Linguists, Bologna – Florence, Aug. 28–Sept. 2, 1972.* Bologna: Il Mulino.

Vennemann, Theo. 1974b. "Topics, subjects, and word order: From SXV to SVX via TVX". In. Anderson, John M. & Jones, Charles (eds.), *Historical Linguistics I. Syntax, morphology, internal and comparative reconstruction. Proceedings of the First International Conference on Historical Linguistics, Edinburgh 2nd–7th September 1973.* Amsterdam etc.: North Holland, 339–76.

Vennemann, Theo. 1982. "Isolation – Agglutination – Flexion". In: Heinz, Sieglinde & Wandruszka, Ulrich (eds.), 327–34.

John Ole Askedal
University of Oslo (Norway)

115. Contact-induced typological change

1. Introduction
2. When should we expect typological change as a result of contact?
3. What counts as typological change?
4. Immediate typological effects
5. Delayed typological effects
6. Is language mixing typological change?
7. Conclusion
8. References

1. Introduction

It is easy to show that contact-induced change can have a profound effect on the typological profile of the receiving language. Probably the most obvious examples, and also the ones that are easiest to find, are changes in basic sentential word order. These are especially striking because it is word order features that have attracted the most attention in the typological literature, starting with the famous 1963 article by Greenberg that moved typology into the mainstream of linguistic research. But word order features – or, more generally, morpheme order features – are by no means the only parts of language structure that have been transformed under the influence of other languages. Contact-induced changes have also affected the typological character of morphological, phonological, lexical semantic, and discourse systems in a wide variety of languages.

This article surveys contact-induced typological changes and shows where and how different degrees of change correlate with different social conditions. After some introductory comments on the contact conditions in which typological change is likely to happen (see § 2.) and on the problem of determining whether a given change is typologically significant or not (see § 3.), I will discuss and exemplify immediate typological effects (see § 4.) and delayed typological effects (see § 5.). Finally, I will consider the question of whether or not language mixing constitutes contact-induced typological change (see § 6.). The article ends with a brief conclusion (see § 7.).

2. When should we expect typological change as a result of contact?

The first step in discussing contact-induced typological change is to sketch the circumstances under which it is likely to occur. The crucial point – hardly an astonishing one – is that intense contact is more likely than casual contact to result in typological restructuring of the receiving language. The question of what counts as intense contact (an admittedly vague term) depends on the perspective: the expected results differ according to whether the situation is one of borrowing, where fluent speakers of the receiving language adopt features from the source language, or imperfect learning, where native speakers of the source language have learned the receiving language imperfectly and incorporate their learners' errors into their version of it. The latter type of situation usually, though not always, involves language shift; for convenience, I will refer to these as shift situations.

The expected linguistic results are as different as the processes: in *borrowing situations*, the first interference features to turn up in the receiving language are loanwords, followed (if contact becomes intense enough) by structural features, especially in the phonology and syntax. In *shift situations*, by contrast, the first interference comprises phonological and syntactic features, and sometimes there are very few loanwords at any stage.

Intensity of contact in a *borrowing situation* depends largely, though not entirely, on the level of bilingualism (number of bilinguals, degree of fluency) among borrowing-language speakers: more bilinguals, more intensity, more interference. If the level of bilingualism among borrowing-language speakers is low, then interference features are likely to be confined to loanwords and minor structural features that do not disrupt the typological patterns of the borrowing language. Only if there are many bilinguals, and great cultural pressure on borrowing-language speakers, are major typological changes likely to occur. But in addition, in borrowing situations the degree of typological distance between source language and receiving language influences the kinds of features that are likely to be transferred; so one sometimes finds typologically congruent interference features being transferred at relatively low levels of bilingualism.

Intensity of contact in a *shift situation* depends to a considerable extent, but also not entirely, on the numbers of shifting speakers compared to the numbers of target-language speakers: the larger the shifting group, the more interference features there are likely to be. In a shift situation, because interference features are introduced by the imperfect learners themselves, the very first interference features to appear in the receiving language are likely to be typologically disruptive, because the learners will carry over features from their native language and fail to learn certain features of the target language. Indeed, structural features shared by the source and receiving languages are less likely to present learning problems for the shifting speakers, so these target-language features are more likely to be learned correctly.

In shift situations, then, intense contact is not needed for typologically disruptive interference features to appear in individual learners' versions of a target language. But it is needed for such features to be incorporated in an integrated version of the target language that is spoken both by members of the shifting group and their descendants and by original target-language speakers and their descendants: unless there are a great many shifting speakers relative to the number of original target-language speakers, only a subset of the shifting speakers' errors are likely to be adopted by original target language speakers. Of course, it sometimes happens that shifting speakers remain a partially isolated subgroup of the target language speech community, without integrating into the larger community; in such cases their version of the target language may well retain most of the original shifting group's interference features.

This outline of the basic split between borrowing and shift situations, although it applies neatly in many cases of contact-induced change, is difficult or impossible to sort out for a sizable number of contact situations, in the absence of explicit social information about the nature of contact. One problem is that shift-induced interference and borrowing often occur in one and the same contact situation; another is that areal phenomena involving several languages may arise through a complex combination of processes, some involving imperfect learning and some involving borrowing.

But perhaps the most important caveat is that NECESSARY conditions for contact-induced change are by no means the same thing as SUFFICIENT conditions for change, especially in potential borrowing situations: sometimes, even in the most intense contact situations, with extensive bilingualism in (say) a minority group and with extreme cultural pressure, speakers of the minority language fail, or refuse, to borrow anything much from the dominant language. When deciding whether to expect typological change to result from contact, therefore, we must always keep in mind that our expectations may be disappointed, even when the basic social setting seems outwardly ideal. Speakers' attitudes are unpredictable, and attitudinal factors can and do play a major role in this domain.

3. What counts as typological change?

Before we can survey the kinds of typological change caused by language contact, we must identify the object of study. Clearly, not all contact-induced changes alter the typology of the receiving language. Some of them are typologically inert: either they fit neatly into the typological patterns of the reciving language, or they are too minor to constitute a significant typological change. A typical example is the introduction of a loanword like Persian *shah* into ENGLISH. The only segments that survive in the ENGLISH pronunciation, the [š] and the [a], already have close phonetic analogues in ENGLISH; and, though a word-final stressed [a] is unusual in an ENGLISH word, it does occur occasionally (e. g. in the colloquial address form *pa* for 'father'). Similarly, the borrowed word *asparagus* is too long for a native morpheme, but is phonologically ordinary for an ENGLISH word. And a great many other loanwords, such as *reindeer* and *animal*, don't clash even with minor phonotactic patterns.

A more interesting example is the GERMAN name *Bach*, which some ENGLISH speakers pronounce with a GERMAN dorso-uvular fricative [χ] instead of an anglicized [k]. The phone [χ] is foreign to ENGLISH, but it is confined to this one word, so its presence can hardly be said to have transformed ENGLISH phonology. And even if there were more examples of [χ], they would not disrupt the ENGLISH phonological system significantly, because the distinctive features specifying voicelessness and fricativeness are already needed to describe native ENGLISH consonant phonemes. Adding [χ] would necessitate no changes in the basic feature structure — only in the instantiation of the features in a previously unused combination.

Comparable examples can be found in the syntax, where an increase in the frequency of one of several possible word orders, under the influence of a language in which one of the patterns is basic, alters the overall word order typology only slightly. There are numerous examples of this sort in the literature. To mention just one, the Waikurúan language Kadiwéu of Brazil has quite free word order — OVS, VOS, SOV, OSV, VSO, and SVO word orders are all possible and well attested in the language. But Kadiwéu/Portuguese bilinguals tend to prefer SVO word order, which matches Portuguese (Sandalo 1995; and see, as prominent examples among many other sources, Pfaff 1979 and Silva-Corvalán 1994 for discussion of other instances in which bilinguals favor surface patterns that are common to both languages). If all the possible word orders continue to be used in such a case, the change in the frequency of use of one particular pattern has no drastic overall effect on the language.

Other contact-induced changes, of course, do have clear typological effects. The introduction into ENGLISH of FRENCH words like *very*, with initial voiced fricatives, contributed to the phonemicization of the formerly allophonic distinction between voiced and voiceless fricatives, though several internal changes also played a role in this process; and the very large number of FRENCH and Latin loanwords into Middle ENGLISH obscured and ultimately destroyed the inherited Germanic pattern of fixed initial stress.

The shift in Ethiopic Semitic languages from verb-initial to verb-final word order, together with other typical characteristics of verb-final syntax, also altered the languages' syntactic typology. The starting point was a typically Semitic structure with VSO sentential word order, auxiliary preceding main verb, and relative clause following head noun; after the Semitic languages of Ethiopia came under the influence of indigenous Cushitic languages, some of whose speakers shifted to Semitic, the pattern changed to SOV, main verb preceding auxiliary, and relative clause preceding head noun. (For a detailed discussion of this case, see especially Leslau 1945, 1952, but also Moreno 1948, Hetzron 1954, and Little 1974; → art. 124). In a related change, prepositional phrases were altered by the addition of postpositions, yielding a construction type Preposition-NP-Postposition — identical neither to the prepositional Semitic pattern nor to the postpositional Cushitic pattern, but rather a combination of the two. This same basic change can be seen also in the addition of a negative perfect suffix to a construction already containing a Semitic negative perfect prefix, resulting in a verb form with a negative perfect circumfix.

Nor were Cushitic-induced typological changes in the Semitic languages of Ethiopia confined to morpheme order features: the typical Semitic pattern in which coördination and subordination were expressed primarily by finite verbs in coördinate and subordinate clauses was replaced by typically Cushitic gerund constructions; the dual number was lost almost completely; a new labialized dorsal stop series was introduced; and the inherited Semitic pharyngealized emphatic consonants were replaced by glottalized consonants. In this case there is no doubt that significant typological change has occurred, and the link to contact — the imperfect learning of Semitic by shifting Cushitic speakers — is firmly established. This is the sort of case for which Malcolm Ross has proposed the label 'metatypy' (1996: 182).

It is easy, then, to identify clear cases on both sides of the typological change/no typological change boundary, but it's also necessary to recognize a large area in the middle where reasonable people might differ on the question of whether contact has resulted in significant typological change or not. Changes like the addition of a new phoneme /X/ in the GERMAN name *Bach* to some varieties of

ENGLISH and the increase in the frequency of SVO word order in Kadiwéu-Portuguese bilinguals' speech fall into the fuzzy boundary area. In the rest of this essay I will concentrate on clear cases of typological change through contact.

4. Immediate typological effects

The word 'immediate' in the title of this section is not meant to imply that any contact-induced change happens overnight, because no linguistic change is that abrupt. In real life, one or more speakers innovate, and those innovations spread through the innovators' speech and the community's speech in various ways and at various rates, with extensive variation in both individuals and the community as a whole during the process. The distinction I have in mind, in this section and the next, is rather different: some contact-induced changes, once implemented in an individual or a community, have an immediate typological effect (this section); others, though they may be typologically insignificant at first, trigger a sequence of internal changes that ultimately results in significant typological change (section 5).

Although the language contact literature is full of descriptions of changes in the most-studied linguistic subsystems, relatively little has been written about contact-induced changes in other areas, notably lexical semantics. It is possible, however, to find changes in the less-studied subsystems too; one example from lexical semantics is the restriction of feminine gender to human females in the dialect of the Indic language URDU that is spoken in Kupwar, under the influence of a Dravidian language, KANNADA.

Here are a few typical examples of immediate typological effects of contact-induced phonological changes. When, as a result of the influence of Caucasian languages, the Iranian language Ossetic acquired a new glottalized stop series (Comrie 1981: 167, 171), the typological structure of its consonant inventory was significantly altered. The merger of the two Greek interdental fricatives with other phonemes (e. g. dental stops) in Asia Minor Greek, a result of Turkish influence (Dawkins 1916: 44, 76, 77) sharply reduced the fricative inventory. Dramatic morphophonemic changes such as the loss of vowel harmony in some dialects of the Turkic language Uzbek, under the influence of the Iranian language Tadzhik (Comrie 1981: 51 f., 56), and the mirror-image development of partial vowel harmony in some dialects of Asia Minor Greek under Turkish influence (Dawkins 1916: 47, 68) are fairly easy to find in intimate contact situations. Contact can also cause changes in syllable structure constraints; an example is the loss of syllable-initial consonant clusters, apparently due to Kwakiutl (Wakashan) influence (Thompson 1979: 732), in the Salishan language Comox, a member of a family which otherwise boasts some of the most elaborate consonant clusters in the world.

Comparably dramatic immediate effects can be found in contact-induced changes in the morphology and syntax of a wide variety of languages, changes that bring about significant alterations in the grammar of particular subsystems. Examples are the development of agglutinative case + number suffixation on nouns in Asia Minor Greek through borrowing from Turkish, replacing inherited flexional Indo-European case/number inflection (Dawkins 1916: 114); the emergence of nine new agglutinative cases in Ossetic, under Caucasian influence (Comrie 1981: 171); possessive pronominal suffixes in the Dravidian language BRAHUI, through borrowing from the neighboring Iranian language BALOCHI or possibly from a northwestern Indic language (Emeneau 1980 [1962]: 60); conjugated negation via a suffix placed between the verb and the subject marker in the Indic language MARATHI (under Dravidian influence; Klaiman 1977: 311); the new inclusive/exclusive 'we' distinction in the URDU dialect spoken in Kupwar (via borrowing from KANNADA and/or MARATHI — Gumperz & Wilson 1971); loss of the inclusive/exclusive 'we' distinction in BRAHUI, under BALOCHI influence (Emeneau 1980 [1962]: 56); the partial loss of preverbs in a variety of American Hungarian, a complex change resulting in part from attrition processes in language death (→ art. 118) and in part from borrowing from ENGLISH (Fenyvesi 1994); the development of rigid SOV word order in the CHINESE language Wutun, under the influence of Anduo Tibetan (Li 1983: 32); the loss of gender agreement in noun modifiers in Kupwar dialects of MARATHI and URDU under the influence of KANNADA (Gumperz & Wilson 1971); and the development of numeral classifiers in the Dravidian languages Kui-Kuwi, Kurukh, and Malto under the influence of Bengali, Assamese, and other eastern Indic languages (Emeneau 1980 [1965]: 131).

The examples above are presented as a scattershot list, to provide a glimpse of the variety of contact-induced morphosyntactic changes in the world's languages. But plucking an instance here and an instance there from a given language may suggest — erroneously — that a typologically significant change might be isolated in the linguistic system of a particular language. Such isolation is unlikely: a language is much more likely to have undergone either a whole range of contact-induced typological changes in its various subsystems or none.

A more realistic balance can be found in any of a number of case studies of particular language contact situations — among them the studies from which the scattershot examples were drawn. Consider, to take just one instance, Ross's description (1996: 187–202) of two striking cases from Papua New Guinea: Takia and Maisin, two languages of the Western Oceanic branch of Austronesian which have undergone extensive interference from non-Austronesian languages of New Guinea. Among the interference features shared by Takia and Maisin are rigid verb-final word order in clauses, lack of articles, postpositions instead of prepositions, preposed instead of postposed possessor noun phrases, and 'chains of coordinate dependent clauses terminating with an independent clause' (p. 202). Maisin has several other Papuan features in addition to these, including a set of tense/aspect/mood markers that occur in the position (though not with the exact functions) of tense/aspect/mood markers in nearby non-Austronesian New Guinea languages (p. 196). Ross does not discuss changes in the phonology of Takia and Maisin, but in fact intense contact is likely to result in both phonological and morphosyntactic change; to give just one instance, note the extensive typological changes that took place in Asia Minor Greek under Turkish influence, as described in Dawkins 1916 (and, for a brief synopsis of this case, see the report in Thomason & Kaufman 1988).

It is possible that some of these changes, especially those in the morphology and syntax, were later stages in a chain reaction which, though originally set off by contact, proceeded by internally induced change later on. To decide whether they were immediate or delayed effects of contact, it would be necessary to know precisely which bits of the relevant linguistic structures are linked in such a way that a contact-induced change in one place might trigger an internal change in another. We already know about linkages in aspects of morpheme order, since certain patterns have been shown to co-occur in a nonrandom way; morpheme-order changes are therefore good candidates for delayed typological changes. But in most instances, because of the lack of ancient documentation, we do not know — even for this much-studied feature, much less for others — whether a set of morpheme-order changes happened more or less all at once (so that each change was a direct instance of interference) or in a chain reaction (so that only the first change in the chain was an immediate effect of language contact). This difficulty is easier to describe than to resolve, so I will leave it as a cautionary note and move on to a consideration of contact-induced changes that seem fairly clearly chained.

5. Delayed typological effects

Delayed typological effects occur when the first in a series of changes is typologically minor or irrelevant, but later changes in the series lead to significant typological change. That is, there is a snowball effect: the first change triggers the next, which triggers the next, and so forth. Assuming that only the initial change in the series is caused directly by contact, a question arises: how many of the changes in the series are contact-induced? Only the first one, or all the later ones as well? The answer to this question depends on one's definition of contact-induced change. Here is mine: a change is caused at least in part by language contact if it is less likely to have occurred outside a particular contact situation. Note that this definition includes both actual interference from one language into another and changes like attrition in language death, which are caused by contact but are not interference features per se. According to this definition, the entire series of changes in a chain reaction would be contact-induced, since none of them would have been as likely to occur outside the contact situation that caused the initial change.

One of the most common, or at least best-attested, contact-induced chain reactions concerns the syntactic expression of subordination. One typical set of changes took place in ASIATIC ESKIMO. The initial change, a direct influence from CHUKCHI, was the borrowing of conjunctions into ESKIMO (Menovščikov 1969: 124−30). Function words are frequently borrowed, and the conjunctions themselves would not disrupt the typology of clause combining. Later, however, as a result of this initial change, ESKIMO replaced native gerund and other non-finite verbal constructions with constructions of conjunction + finite clause. Similar change processes led to the development of finite subordinate clauses in BRAHUI, starting with a subordinating conjunction *ki* borrowed from BALOCHI (Emeneau 1980 [1962]: 59), and in Azerbaidzhani, in which inherited Turkic participial or gerund constructions were replaced by subordinating conjunctions and finite verbs (Comrie 1981: 84).

In the phonology, delayed typological change can be exemplified by at least one case of tonogenesis and one apparent case of its reverse. The process of tonogenesis in VIETNAMESE probably began − though precise documentation is lacking − with the introduction of large numbers of CHINESE loanwords during periods of very strong CHINESE influence on the culture and language of Vietnam. It's likely that these loanwords were nativized at first, entering the nontonal borrowing language without their tones and with segmental alterations as well to fit native (Pre-)VIETNAMESE phonological structure. But, as is typical with patterns of contact-induced change, an increase in bilingualism among borrowing-language speakers presumably led to the abandonment of nativization as a strategy, and new CHINESE loanwords would then be nativized less drastically or not at all − in particular, keeping their tones. The later changes which led to the emergence of VIETNAMESE as a full-blown tonal language were internal, involving consonant losses and mergers that left traces of the original consonant distinctions in (originally consonant-induced) pitch distinctions on the neighboring vowels. A similar change, but in reverse, may well have led to the loss of the tonal system of Swahili: masses of loanwords from the nontonal language Arabic into Swahili, which as a Bantu language would have inherited tones, would eventually have led to the abandonment of tones even in native Swahili words.

I know of a few other examples that seem to fit into this category of typological change through language contact, but clear examples of delayed typological effects are certainly less common than changes that seem to fit into the immediate category. As noted above, some changes that look as if they must have had immediate typological effects on the receiving language may in fact have had delayed effects instead − a chain reaction often can't be detected after the fact, given the lack of adequate documentation for the vast majority of linguistic changes, contact-induced as well as internally-motivated. The difficulty of establishing large numbers of examples, however, does not make the distinction between immediate and delayed effects trivial; a systematic search for new examples of delayed typological effects is likely to be fruitful.

6. Is language mixing typological change?

So far I have said nothing about the most striking of all typological effects of language contact − namely, the typology of mixed languages, which are usually or always typologically unlike all of their source languages. Mixed languages fall into three general categories (Thomason 1997): pidgins (→ art. 116), creoles (→ art. 117), and bilingual mixtures. Most pidgins and creoles draw their lexicon primarily from a single source language, the lexifier, and their grammars do not come from that source language or from any other single language; the grammar of a typical pidgin or creole is in fact quite different from the grammar of any of the source languages. Bilingual mixtures emerge, as the name suggests, in a context of bilingualism between two groups in contact, and several combinations of components are attested in the small set of well-understood cases: lexicon from one source and grammar from the other, as in the Media Lengua, a Spanish/Quechua mixture (Muysken 1997), or Ma'a, a Cushitic/Bantu mixture (Mous 1994); noun phrases from one language and verb phrases and sentential syntax from the other, as in Michif, a FRENCH/Cree mixture (Bakker & Papen 1997); lexicon and grammar mostly from one source but finite verb morphology from the other, as in MEDNYJ ALEUT, an Aleut/Russian mixture (Menovščikov 1969); and so forth.

It is easy to prove that mixed languages of all these types do not match any of their source languages typologically. In pidgins and creoles, which arise in a context where, and indeed usually because, there is insufficient mutual bi-/multilingualism, the phonology and morphosyntax are typically quite unlike those of the lexifier language (though not always, in the case of the phonology); they may be a better typological fit with the other source languages, but their relative (and often absolute) poverty in inflectional morphology distinguishes their typological profile sharply from those of many or most of their source languages.

Bilingual mixed languages, which arise from combining subsystems of two languages, show little or no distortion of material drawn from the source languages, but the structure as a whole does not match either source language. In MEDNYJ ALEUT, for instance, features of verb inflection such as preposed negation, gender in subject markers, and flexional morphology do not resemble Aleut structure at all, while other structural features, such as polysynthetic morphology (outside the finite verb morphology), ergative noun morphology, and dual inflection in nouns are typologically divergent from Russian. Similarly, Michif noun phrases have FRENCH phonological, morphological, and syntactic features — among them vowel nasalization, masculine/feminine gender agreement, and lexical adjectives — that do not fit Algonquian typology, while Michif verb phrases have Cree features like heavy agglutination, an animate/inanimate gender distinction, and obviative marking, which do not fit FRENCH typology.

The problem here, then, is not a question of whether or not language contact has led to the emergence of languages with typologically divergent structures, by comparison to their various source languages. Rather, the question is whether we are looking at language change in these cases: if the process by which mixed languages arise is not language change, then these are not cases of contact-induced typological CHANGE. For creoles, at least, the answer depends on which theory of creole genesis one adopts (focusing solely on creoles that arise without a well-established pidgin stage, as opposed to creoles that arise as nativizations of pre-existing pidgins): if one accepts the currently popular theory of gradual creolization, according to which each new contingent of imported slaves learned a variety of the lexifier language slightly more divergent from the lexifier language than the variety spoken by the immediately preceding contingent, then creolization is a process of repeated shift-induced interference — and therefore a process of language change. But if the competing theories of abrupt creolization are correct, so that creole genesis is a process of creation of a new language through a kind of negotiation among members of a new contact community, then characterizing it as a process of change from a previously existing language seems inappropriate. To make the issue even more complex, note that there is no reason to assume that all creoles arose in the same way, so that the gradualist hypothesis might well be valid for some but the abrupt hypothesis for others. One example of definitely abrupt creole genesis — because the original population was not added to — is Pitcairnese, which arose on Pitcairn Island after nine ENGLISH-speaking Bounty mutineers and sixteen Polynesians took refuge there in 1790.

As for pidgins, a theory of gradual emergence analogous to the gradualist hypothesis for creolization might be valid for some of them — specifically those which have their origins in a simplified foreigner-talk variety of the lexifier language, such as Hiri Motu (Dutton 1997) — but probably not for those pidgins which arose in new trade settings. In the case of abrupt pidgin genesis, the process again seems to be one of language creation rather than language change.

Bilingual mixed languages, finally, fall into two general categories. The one that is best understood includes Michif, Mednyj Aleut, and Media Lengua, among others, and comprises languages that arose abruptly as a marker of in-group identity. The genesis of these languages is not language change in any ordinary sense; instead, what happens is that bilingual speakers combine chunks of their two languages into a single speech form that serves some useful function in the community and therefore achieves some stability, being learned thereafter as a language by each new generation of speakers. Other bilingual mixtures, for instance Ma'a, apparently arose through gradual change, with incremental borrowing from another language that eventually overwhelms the native structures altogether. Mixed languages in this category are similar in their developmental process to creoles that arise through gradual incremental change: the end result is a mixed language that is typologically divergent from each of its source languages, but the process, at each step, is ordinary contact-induced language change.

The answer to the question of the status of mixed languages with respect to contact-induced change, then, appears to be this: the gradual development of a mixed language is unusual only in the extreme nature of the end state; the process, at every stage, is contact-induced typological change. But mixed languages — pidgins, creoles, and bilingual mixtures alike — that arise abruptly do not emerge through processes of language change at all, and they therefore are not appropriately characterized as examples of contact-induced typological change.

7. Conclusion

This article has attempted to answer the following two questions: what kinds of typological changes occur in contact situations, and under what circumstances are they likely to occur? An important theme, however, is the indeterminacy of many contact phenomena with respect to their typological impact. In particular, some contact-induced changes seem only marginally relevant to the receiving language's typological profile, so it's hard to decide whether they constitute typological change or not; and mixed languages, though certainly typologically divergent from all of their source languages, do not all arise through processes of change in a pre-existing language. One source of indeterminacy that has not been explored in any depth here is the problem of deciding whether a given change is contact-induced or not. The definition of contact-induced change given in section 5 covers cases of multiple causation, where there are both internal and external causes of a particular change, but even this inclusive definition does not solve the problem entirely. As in other areas of historical linguistics (and in historical sciences in general) our lack of complete and completely reliable historical information makes indeterminacy a constant companion.

8. References

Bakker, Peter & Papen, Robert. 1997. "Michif". In: Sarah G. Thomason (ed.). *Contact languages: a wider perspective*. Amsterdam & Philadelphia: Benjamins, 295−363.

Dawkins, R.M. 1916. *Modern Greek in Asia Minor: a study of the dialects of Sílli, Cappadocia, and Phárasa*. Cambridge: Cambridge University Press.

Comrie, Bernard. 1981. *The languages of the Soviet Union*. Cambridge: Cambridge University Press.

Dutton, Tom. 1997. "Hiri Motu". In: Sarah G. Thomason (ed.). *Contact languages: a wider perspective*. Amsterdam: John Benjamins, 9−41.

Emeneau, Murray B. 1980 [1962]. "Bilingualism and structural borrowing". In: Anwar Dil (ed.). *Language and linguistic area*. Stanford: Stanford University Press, 38−65. Reprinted from the *Proceedings of the American Philosophical Society* 106: 430−42 (1962).

Emeneau, Murray B. 1980 [1965]. "India and linguistic areas". In: Anwar Dil (ed.). *Language and linguistic area*. Stanford: Stanford University Press, 126−65. Reprinted from *India and historical grammar* (Annamalai University Department of Linguistics Publication No. 5.), 25−75 (1965).

Fenyvesi, Anna. 1994. *Language contact and language death in an immigrant language: The case of American Hungarian.* Pittsburgh, PA: University of Pittsburgh M.A. thesis.

Greenberg, Joseph H. 1963. "Some universals of grammar with particular reference to the order of meaningful elements". In: Joseph H. Greenberg (ed.). *Universals of Grammar*, Cambridge, MA: MIT Press, 58−90.

Gumperz, John J. & Wilson, Robert. 1971. "Convergence and creolization: a case from the Indo-Aryan/Dravidian border in India". In: Dell H. Hymes (ed.). *Pidginization and creolization of languages* Cambridge: Cambridge University Press, 151−67.

Hetzron, Robert. 1975. "Genetic classification and Ethiopian Semitic". In: Bynon, James & Bynon, Theodora (eds.). *Hamito-Semitica*. The Hague: Mouton, 103−27.

Leslau, Wolf. 1945. "The influence of Cushitic on the Semitic languages of Ethiopia: A problem of substratum". *Word* 1: 59−82.

Leslau, Wolf. 1952. "The influence of Sidamo on the Ethiopic languages of Gurage". *Language* 28: 63−81.

Li, Charles N. 1983. "Languages in contact in western China". *Papers in East Asian Languages* 1: 31−51.

Menovščikov, G. A. 1969. "O nekotoryx social'nyx aspektax 'evoljucii jazyka'". In: *Voprosy social'noj lingvistiki* Leningrad: Nauka, 110−34.

Moreno, Martino Mario. 1948. "L'azione del cuscito sul sistema morfologico delle lingue semitiche dell'Ethiopia". *Rassegna di Studi Etiopici* 7: 121−30.

Mous, Maarten. 1994. "Ma'a or Mbugu". In: Bakker, Peter & Mous, Maarten (eds.). *Mixed languages*. Amsterdam: Institute for Functional Research into Language and Language Use [IFOTT], University of Amsterdam, 175−200.

Muysken, Pieter. 1997. "Media Lengua". In: Sarah G. Thomason (ed.). *Contact languages: a wider perspective*. Amsterdam & Philadelphia: Benjamins, 365−426.

Pfaff, Carol W. 1979. "Constraints on language mixing: intrasentential code-switching and borrowing in Spanish/English". *Language* 55: 291–318.

Ross, Malcolm D. 1996. "Contact-induced change and the comparative method: cases from Papua New Guinea". In: Malcolm Ross and Mark Durie (eds.). *The comparative method reviewed: regularity and irregularity in language change*. Oxford: Oxford University Press, 180–217.

Sandalo, Filomena. 1995. *A grammar of Kadiwéu*. Pittsburgh, PA: University of Pittsburgh dissertation.

Silva-Corvalán, Carmen. 1994. *Language contact and change: Spanish in Los Angeles*. Oxford: Oxford University Press.

Thomason, Sarah Grey. 1997. "A typology of contact languages". In: Spears, Arthur K. & Winford, Donald (eds.). *Pidgins and creoles: structure and status*. Amsterdam: Benjamins, 71–88.

Thomason, Sarah Grey & Terrence Kaufman. 1988. *Language contact, creolization, and genetic linguistics*. Berkeley: University of California Press.

Thompson, Laurence C. 1979. "Salishan and the Northwest". In: Campbell, Lyle & Mithun, Marianne (eds.). *The languages of Native America: historical and comparative assessment*. Austin: University of Texas Press, 692–765.

Sarah Grey Thomason
University of Michigan (U.S.A)

116. Typology and universals of Pidginization

1. Definitions
2. Types of Pidgin universals
3. The history of the study of Pidgin
4. Current issues in Pidgin studies
5. Conclusions
6. References

1. Definitions

The label 'Pidgin' covers a wide range of phenomena differing both in structural complexity and in the range of their social functions. The failure by many past scholars to take into account such differences has reduced the importance of Pidgin studies to language typology and linguistic universals.

Pidgins by definition are second languages typically developed or learned by adults who do not share the same first language. Their structural complexity varies according to the range of communicative functions and discourse domains in which they are employed and their structural ability according to the extent of their institutionalization. One therefore needs to distinguish the following developmental stages

Table 116.1: Stages of Pidgin development

Jargon	less complex
Pidgin	↕
extended Pidgin	more complex

Developmental complexity interacts with a number of largely independent parameters that determine the degree to which Pidgins become codified or institutionalized. These include focusing and target-dependency.

By focusing one understands the acceptance by Pidgin users of agreed internal norms of pronunciation and grammar, by target-dependency their orientation towards external norms of the superimposed lexifier language: If these two parameters are incorporated, the resulting model becomes multidimensional and considerably more complex than a widely used two dimensional model represented in figure 116.2.

The revision of this model is necessitated by the fact that even relatively complex and extended Pidgins can exhibit a great deal of internal variation. Thus speakers of MOBILIAN JARGON (Drechsel 1997) have quite a variable lexicon. CHINOOK JARGON (a fairly complex Pidgin rather than a jargon) has been shown by Silverstein (1972) to have a multiple grammar and RUSSENORSK exhibits both lexical variation and never achieved syntactic stability "which might tempt one to write a grammar of RUSSENORSK without reference to the primary language" (Fox 1973: 41).

Jean Aitchison's study of TOK PISIN relativization (1983) shows several very different solutions employed by members of the same social network and similar observations can be made for most areas of core grammar of this language (Mühlhäusler 1985). This raises the problem as to the role a shared grammatical code plays in successful communication

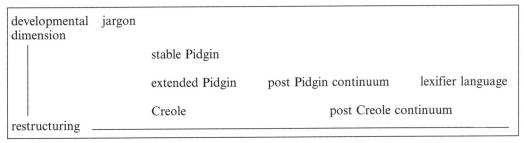

Figure 116.2: Current two-dimensional model of Pidgin development

(see Mühlhäusler 1992). Robert B. Le Page and Andrée Tabouret-Keller (1985) observed that the lack of agreed lexical and grammatical norms can persist into the Creole phase.

Focusing serves a range of meta-communicative functions such as expressing solidarity or shared identity; it is not a function of the speakers' having learnt the language as a second language after the critical learning age. Target-dependency is a parameter related to the physical ability as well as the psychological propensity of Pidgin speakers to orient their speech towards an external model: In classrooms L_2 learners are presented with and encouraged to emulate a target language. The degree to which they accept the norm of the target or fossilize at a pidginized interlanguage stage depends on their integrative motivation (see Schumann 1978). In naturalistic Pidgin development the matter is more complex. Whereas in some situations Pidgin speakers are under the impression that they are learning the other party's language (as when the Melanesians learning TOK PISIN which they called TOK WHITEMAN or English speakers learning MOBILIAN JARGON which they took for the Indian language), in other instances they have little desire to approximate a target (see Baker 1990) and yet in other instances access to a target language is not possible. This was the case when German became the official language of a number of PIDGIN ENGLISH speaking territories in the Pacific. The principle that input does not equate intake is very much involved in Pidgin development.

2. Types of Pidgin universals

The study of universal properties of Pidgin spans a considerable time and different scholars have meant a variety of things by this notion. There is least disagreement in their practice to focus on Greenberg's unrestricted independent universals and their neglect of implicational ones. However, there are considerable differences as to whether universals are seen to reflect biological aspects of human language or the pragmatic and functional practice in situations of maximum pressure for intercommunication. Nor is it clear whether the universals identified are universals of language mixing or language internal. There are also very considerable differences in the observational basis for past pronouncements on universals. The data available to most scholars are quite restricted, often second-hand and lacking situational information. Conspicuous by their absence are data for indigenous Pidgins other than a few (such as HIRI MOTU) that were triggered off by European colonization.

Most Pidgin scholars have focused on Greenberg type universals (universals of language) rather than Chomskyan (universals of formalization) universals. Derek Bickerton (1981) combines the practice of postulating Creole universals on the basis of a single language (HAWAIIAN CREOLE ENGLISH) with that of identifying substantive universals. While Bickerton devised his account for Creoles, his proposals have been widely used as diagnostic tools in Pidgin studies as well.

3. The history of the study of Pidgin

An account of the history of ideas about universals in Pidgin studies is made difficult by differences in the interpretation of this notion as well as additional terminological problems. The distinction between Pidgins as second languages and Creoles as naturalized first languages is relatively recent and earlier scholars often failed to make such a distinction. It is not always clear whether Francisco Adolfo Coelho comments on the universal properties of PORTUGUESE CREOLES (Coelho 1880/1967) or their predecessor Pidgins. Dirk

Christiaan Hesseling who worked on AFRIKAANS and NEGERHOLLANDS (1979) regarded the structural properties of Creole varieties of Dutch as the outcome of language independent modes of second language acquisition. In what he wrote around the turn of the 19th century on Pidgins and Creoles, Hugo Schuchardt focused on language mixing, whereas he admitted the operation of universal forces in his work on the LINGUA FRANCA and SARAMACCAN (1914). Structuralism which dominated Pidgin and Creole studies from the 1920s to the 1960s was inherently hostile to universalist explanations and similarities between Pidgins were explained in terms of common ancestry, an explanation which was reinforced by the concept of relexification (Voorhoeve 1973) which postulated changes in lexical forms with preservation of grammar.

Relexification was shown to offer at best a partial explanation for structural similarities among Pidgins by scholars working on indigenous Pidgins. Thus, Bernd Heine (1973, 1975) showed that African Pidgins that were quite unrelated to those based on European languages shared many commonalities with the latter.

From the early 1970s, the idea of universals was very much mainstream thinking. It is unsurprising that a number of scholars (Agheyisi 1971, Kay and Sankoff 1974, Mühlhäusler 1974, and Givón 1979) should come up independently with the suggestion that Pidgins are probably the universal base from which other languages can be derived by means of language-specific transformations. Whatever the limitations of this view, it certainly directed researchers to an inquiry into the common features of Pidgins, and thus indirectly promoted the study of non-European-based Pidgins and Creoles.

The main limitations of most approaches to Pidgin universals has been their being based on idealized atemporal descriptions, reflecting different and hence not comparable states of development. An external limitation which discouraged research into such universals is the fact that Pidgins were often learnt after puberty, i. e. at a stage in speakers' lives when access to universals allegedly was much reduced according to the prevailing critical threshold hypothesis.

The first limitation was overcome by the development of variation grammar (in particular DeCamp 1971 and Bailey 1973) with their implicational scales which allowed the description of longitudinal processes as well as "synchronic" variability. Implicational scales turned out to be powerful heuristic devices to the discovery of implicational universals.

The second limitation was set aside by a number of scholars looking at longitudinal trends in L_2 acquisition, in particular John H. Schumann (1978) and other inter-language researchers (Corder and Roulet (eds.) 1976) who demonstrated the systematic nature of second language acquisition. Their findings point to the ability of adults to engage in rule changing and rule creating creativity. This ability was demonstrated by the present author for TOK PISIN word formation (1979), pronoun development (1990), the development of number marking (1980a) and causativity (1980b) and by Gillian Sankoff and Penelope Brown (1976) for aspect and tense. A survey of these studies is given by Suzanne Romaine (1992). The findings for TOK PISIN suggest that grammatical development is largely independent of the speakers' first languages.

4. Current issues in Pidgin studies

4.1. General remarks

The fact that Pidgins contain grammatical constructions that are also found in other languages has prompted some researchers to dismiss Pidgin as a special type of language. The question as to their specific properties is better framed as "what type of grammar is not found in Pidgin?" and "what particular packages of constructions are unique to Pidgins?"

Regarding the first question, it is widely acknowledged that Pidgins by and large lack inflectional morphology, for most of them develop a very rudimentary derivational morphology, lack abnatural constructions such as passives and subordination (in particular multiple embedding) and typically lack abnatural sounds and sound sequences such as complex consonant clusters.

However, as Pidgins acquire greater complexity their naturalness tends to decrease. This is due to the fact that the initial favouring of strategies that optimize perception are gradually supplemented with strategies favouring optimalization of production, with inevitable conflicts between natural phonological and natural morphological strategies resulting. Compare:

Table 116.3: Naturalness bleaches in diachrony

(1) Early Tok Pisin	
mi-pela	'we' (exclusive)
yu-pela	'you'
em-pela	'they'
(2) Present day Tok Pisin	
mitla	'we' (exclusive)
yupla	'you'
ol	'they'

Early Pidgins tend to lack syntactic rules and word order is largely determined by discourse pragmatics. There is a pronounced tendency for SVO grammar to become dominant in later stages, even where such order is rare or absent in Pidgin users' first languages.

4.2. Towards a structural typology of pidgins

As yet there is no agreed typology of Pidgins. The criteria employed are structural, social, or a combination thereof. Next to that already mentioned typology based on degrees of complexity, Keith Whinnom (1971) introduced the structural distinctions between secondary and tertiary hybrids. The former, in his model, are the unstable multilingual idiolects found when speakers of one substratum language attempt to communicate with speakers of the superstratum, as in:

$$L_1 \times L_2$$
$$\downarrow$$
$$\text{unstable secondary hybrid H}$$

Figure 116.4: The emergence of unstable hybrids

More stable Pidgins proper or tertiary hybrids develop when speakers of the various unstable idiolects communicate with one another as shown in Figure 116.5:

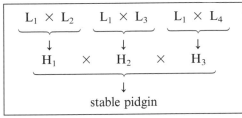

Figure 116.5: Development of a stable tertiary hybrid

Thus whilst in Western Australia an unstable secondary hybrid NYUNGAR Pidgin English was used between white settlers and the local Nyungar population (Mühlhäusler & McGregor 1996), a wide variety of language forms was encountered. When the Pidgin began to be used as a means of contact between Aboriginal people from different language backgrounds, on the prison island of Rottnest a more stable form of Pidgin crystallised (or jelled). Some observers have contrasted the instability of Pidgin in vertical (master/slave communication) and the stability of varieties involving horizontal (slave/slave) contact. Keith Whinnom's typology is an attempt to explain stability in terms of the absence of the superstrate model but whilst this absence contributes to stabilization, it is neither a sufficient nor a necessary component.

Similar to Whinnom's classification, but without the factors of social status differences, is the distinction between single-source and dual-source Pidgins. This distinction is based initially on the sources of the lexicon: Whereas most Pidgin Englishes have their very high (more than 90%) proportion of English based words, a language such as the Norwegian Russian contact language RUSSENORSK has a fifty-fifty lexicon: Trudgill (1996: 11) observes that the two types of Pidgin differ in their developmental potential. Single-source Pidgins can undergo very considerable development as in:

pre-Pidgin → Pidgin → Creole → post-Creole → vestigial post-Creole

Only two stages have been documented for dual-source Pidgins:

jargon → dual-source Pidgin

This differential development would seem to be due to social factors. Single-source Pidgins develop in non-egalitarian power situations whilst dual-source Pidgins are used among equals. Their function is to preserve the speakers' first languages rather than to acculturate them to the dominant culture. Dual-source Pidgins are very widely encountered in North America (see Drechsel 1997) and Melanesia (e. g. Laycock 1970 and Mühlhäusler et al. 1996). The hypothesis that dual-source Pidgins promote a common core grammar is not supported by available evidence. Structurally, they tend to exhibit the same simplifications and reductions encountered in single-sourced Pidgins.

In spite of the popular view that Pidgins are macaronic mixtures of numerous languages, no Pidgins exhibiting a lexicon of three or more languages to equal parts have been found — typically one or two languages account for the vast bulk of their vocabulary, unlike for instance, in certain invented auxiliary languages.

This suggests another basis for Pidgin typology: the degree to which they can be a deliberate invention. Whilst the majority of Pidgins develop spontaneously, there are a range of proposals for artificial Pidgins, for instance the colonial German developed by the German military during World War I (see Mühlhäusler 1984). Such invented Pidgins differ structurally from organically developed Pidgins. As they were never implemented, one can only speculate that they would have changed from languages defined by mathematical simplicity to Pidgins sensitive to naturalness considerations (→ art. 31).

4.3. Social typologies of pidgins

Attempts to identify different social types of Pidgins date to the 1930s when Ernst Schultze (1933) and John E. Reinecke (1937) applied criteria to a range of non-standard languages. Their respective classifications are:

Table 116.6: Ernst Schultze's classification

Type	Example
Colonial jargon	Afrikaans, Pennsylvania Dutch
Trade jargon	Chinook Jargon, Lingua Geral Brasilica
Languages of the study table	Esperanto
Slave's and servant's languages	Pidgin English

Table 116.7: John E. Reinecke's classification

Type	Example
Immigrant's mixed dialects	Imperfect acquisition of a new language by immigrants
Trade Pidgins	Chinese Pidgin English
Plantation Creole dialects	Jamaican Creole

A more recent proposal is that by Bickerton (1989: 16 ff.) who distinguishes:

Plantation — Fort — Maritime

Bickerton to some extent continues a tradition of classifying Pidgins according to domains, such as military Pidgins (Gebhard 1979), trade Pidgins or tourism Pidgins (Hinnenkamp 1982) but at this point it is far from clear how many different domains need to be distinguished and what structural consequences the use of Pidgins in different domains might have.

It has been known for some time that mission boarding schools can be a centre of creolization, with languages such as New Caledonian Tayo (a French Creole), Australian Northern Territory Kriol (an English Creole) and New Guinea Unserdeutsch (a German Creole) all developed in this context. Data from the investigation of the role played by Melanesian mission schools in Auckland and Norfolk Island shed light on the early development of Melanesian Pidgin English. They lend themselves to comparison with Pidgin German on mission stations in the German Pacific (Mühlhäusler 1984b).

Next to classification according to domain, a number of functional classifications have been devised. They are derived from the widely employed conduit model of commu-

Table 116.8: Language functions

Functions	Role in communication
Propositional	The message itself, the information exchanged, information
(referential)	whose truth value can be established
Directive	Getting things achieved, manipulation of others
Integrative	Creation of social bonds, use of language as an index of group membership
Expressive	Expression of own personal feelings towards the message or interlocutors
Phatic	Keeping open channels of communication, counteracting socially undesirable silence, creation of rituals
Metalinguistic	Use of language to discuss language
Poetic	Use of language to focus on the message for its own sake, to play with verbal material
Heuristic	Use of language for obtaining information

nication with its components of sender, message, channel, receiver etc. Roman Jakobson's assignment of a communicational function to each of these components results in Table 116.8.

Mühlhäusler (1997: 86) provides an attempt to relate these functions to the various developmental stages of Tok Pisin. Whilst it is difficult to generalize from the findings of one language it is clear that

a) Pidgins are functionally restricted
b) Pidgins form part of a speech repertoire in which there is a complementary distribution of functions (in stable social situations) or overlap and shift (in unstable or post-Pidgin situations).
c) The referential, directive and heuristic functions are the primary functions of Pidgins with the directive functions being particularly important in colonial context (see Sankoff 1980).

The Jakobson (1960) based model of language functions, because of its mechanistic view of communication is quite limited when meta-communicative functions of Pidgin such as the ones described by Emanuel J. Drechsel (1997) are to be accounted for, in particular the function of serving as a language of regional identity or that of a buffer between the first language of different groups of Pidgin users.

Most functional classifications have as their object European based plantation or colonial Pidgins. As the list of non-European Pidgin grows (see Wurm & Mühlhäusler & Tryon 1996) types of Pidgins are added which may necessitate a drastic reassessment of what has been said about Pidgins on the basis of limited information.

5. Conclusions

Any attempt to develop a typology of Pidgin is likely to suffer from a number of limitations:

a) a very uneven database
b) incomplete coverage
c) the arbitrariness of criteria chosen
d) the variability of structure, function and domain within single named Pidgin

Inasmuch as typology is seen as an aid to reconstruction or predicting language drift on the basis of existing salient properties, progress with Pidgin typology has been quite moderate and as more Pidgins become better known, the inadequacy of existing typologies is becoming evident. Existing criteria as applied to full languages because of their static nature and lack of attention to pragmatic factors are of relatively little help. For instance:

a) because of fluctuation in word order and rapid typological changes classifications such as osv or svo are of limited use;
b) morphological criteria need to be sensitive to the typological changes (from isolating to agglutinating to inflexional) that can occur in a couple of generations of Pidgin speakers;
c) semantactic categories such as ergativity or verb chaining are not shared by all Pidgin users. Certain Pidgins have multiple generative systems and it is often difficult to distinguish between idiolectal and socially agreed grammar.

The absence of abnatural grammar is greatest in tertiary hybrids (i.e. Pidgins used by speakers with little access to the original lexifier language).

As Pidgins are complexity-changing, the search for universals would need to focus on the implicational rather than absolute universals. It is hypothesized that Pidgin development is constrained by natural principles of the type more natural constructions (i.e. those that are easier to process) precede less natural ones. Moreover, when Pidgins are untargeted (see above § 1.), the order of their emergence is not determined by language specific parameters.

6. References

Agheyisi, Rebecca. 1971. "West African Pidgin English: simplification and simplicity". Unpublished PhD thesis, Stanford University.

Aitchison, Jean. 1983. "Social Networks and Urban New Guinea Pidgin (Tok Pisin)". *York Papers in Linguistics* 11: 9–18.

Bailey, Charles James Nice 1973. *Variation and linguistic theory*. Arlington/VA: Center for Applied Linguistics.

Baker, Philip. 1990. "Off Target". *Journal of Pidgin and Creole Languages* 5: 107–120.

Bickerton, Derek. 1981. *Roots of language*. Ann Arbor: Karoma.

Bickerton, Derek. 1989. "The lexical learning hypothesis and the Pidgin-Creole cycle". Pütz & Dirven (eds.), 11–31.

Coelho, Francisco Adolfo. 1880/1967. *Os Dialectos Românicos.* reprinted In: Morais-Barbosa, Jorge (ed.) *Estudos linguísticos crioulos.* Lisbon: Academia Internacional da Cultura Portuguesa.

Collinge, Neville E. (ed.) 1990. *An Encyclopedia of Language.* London: Routledge.

Corder, Stephen Pit & Roulet, Eddy (eds.) 1976. *The notions of simplification, interlanguages and Pidgins and their relation to second language pedagogy.* (Recueil de travaux/Univ. de Neuchâtel, Faculté des Lettres, 35.) Geneva: Droz.

DeCamp, David. 1971. "Toward a generative analysis of a post-creole speech continuum". Hymes (ed.), 349–370.

DeCamp, David & Hancock, Ian F. (eds.). 1974. *Pidgins and Creoles: current trends and prospects.* Washington/D.C.: Georgetown Univ. Press.

Drechsel, Emanuel J. 1997. *Mobilian Jargon. Linguistic and sociohistorical aspects of a native American pidgin.* (Oxford studies in language contact.) Oxford: Clarendon Press.

Edmondson, Jerold A., Feagin, Crawford & Mühlhäusler, Peter (eds.) 1990. *Development and Diversity. Language variation across time and space.* (Summer Institute of Linguistics and the University of Texas at Arlington publications in linguistics, 93.) Dallas/TX: Summer Institute of Linguistics.

Fox, James A. 1973. "Russenorsk: A study in language adaptivity". (Unpublished term paper, University of Chicago).

Gebhard, Jerry G. 1979. "Thai Adaptation of English Language Features: A study of Thai English". *Canberra: Pacific Linguistics (A-57)*, 201–216.

Givón, Talmy. 1979. "Prolegomena to any sane creology". In: Hancock (ed.), 3–36.

Hancock, Ian F. (ed.) 1979. *Readings in Creole Studies.* (Story-Scientia linguistics series, 2.) Ghent: Story-scientia.

Heine, Bernd. 1973. *Pidginsprachen im Bantubereich.* (Kölner Beitrage zur Afrikanistik, 3.) Berlin: Reimer.

Heine, Bernd. 1975. "Some generalizations of African-based Pidgins". Paper presented at the International Conference on Pidgins and Creoles, Honolulu.

Hesseling, Dirk Christiaan 1979. *On the origin and formation of Creoles. A miscellany of articles.* (ed. by Thomas C. Markey and T. Roberge). (Linguistica extranea: Studia, 4.) Ann Arbor: Karoma.

Hinnenkamp, Volker. 1982. *Foreigner Talk and Tarzanisch. Eine vergleichende Studie über die Sprechweise gegenüber Ausländern am Beispiel des Deutschen und des Türkischen.* Hamburg: Buske.

Hüllen, Werner (ed.) 1980. *Understanding Bilingualism.* (Forum linguisticum, 27.) Frankfurt: Lang.

Hymes, Dell (ed.) 1971. *Pidginization and Creolization of Languages.* London: Cambridge University Press.

Jahr, Ernst Håkon & Broch, Ingvild (eds.) 1996. *Language Contact in the Arctic. Northern pidgins and contact languages.* (Trends in linguistics: Studies and monographs, 88.) Berlin: Mouton de Gruyter.

Jakobson, Roman. 1960. "Linguistics and poetics". In: Sebeok (ed.), 350–377.

Kay, Paul & Sankoff, Gillian. 1974. "A Language-universals approach to Pidgins and Creoles". In: DeCamp & Hancock (eds.), 61–72.

Laycock, Donald C. 1970. "Language and thought in a polyglot island". *Hemisphere* 14,8: 11–15.

Laycock, Donald C. & Mühlhäusler, Peter. 1990. "Language Engineering: Special Languages". In: Collinge (ed.), 843–875.

Le Page, Robert B. & Tabouret-Keller, Andrée. 1985. *Acts of Identity: Creole-based approaches to language and ethnicity.* Cambridge: Cambridge University Press.

Mühlhäusler, Peter. 1974. *Pidginization and Simplification of Language.* Canberra: Pacific Linguistics B-26.

Mühlhäusler, Peter. 1979. *Growth and Structure of the Lexicon of New Guinea Pidgin.* Canberra: Pacific Linguistics C-52.

Mühlhäusler, Peter. 1980a. "The Development of the Category of Number in Tok Pisin". In: Muysken (ed.), 35–84.

Mühlhäusler, Peter. 1980b. "Phases in the Devellopment of Tok Pisin". In: Hüllen (ed.), 119–130.

Mühlhäusler, Peter. 1984 "Tracing the roots of Pidgin German". *Language and Communication* 4: 27–58.

Mühlhäusler, Peter. 1985. "Syntax of Tok Pisin". In: Wurm & Mühlhäusler (eds.), 341–421.

Mühlhäusler, Peter. 1990. "Towards an implicational analysis of pronouns development". In: Edmondson & al. (eds.), 351–370.

Mühlhäusler, Peter. 1992 "Redefining Creolistics". In: Wolf George (ed.) *New departures in linguistics.* New York: Garland, 193–98.

Mühlhäusler, Peter & Mcgregor, William. 1996. "Post-contact language of Western Australia". In: Wurm & Mühlhäusler & Tryon (eds.), 101–122.

Mühlhäusler, Peter & Dutton, Tom & Hovdhaugen, Even & Williams, Jeff. 1996. "Precolonial patterns of intercultural communication in the Pacific Islands". In: Wurm & Mühlhäusler & Tryon (eds.), 205–238.

Mühlhäusler, Peter. 1997. *Pidgin and Creole Linguistics.* London: Westminster University Press.

Muysken, Pieter (ed.) 1980. *Generative Studies on Creole Languages.* (Studies in generative grammar, 6.) Dordrecht: Foris.

Pütz, Martin (ed.) 1992. *Thirty years of linguistic evolution.* Amsterdam & Philadelphia: Benjamins.

Reinecke, John E. 1937. "Marginal Languages". Unpublished Phd thesis, Yale University.

Romaine, Suzanne (ed.) 1992. *Language, education and development. Urban and rural Tok Pisin in Papua New Guinea.* Oxford: Clarendon.

Sankoff, Gillian & Brown, Penelope. 1976. "On the origins of syntax in discourse: a case study of Tok Pisin relatives". *Language* 52: 631–666.

Sankoff, Gillian. 1980. "Variation Pidgins and Creoles". In: Valdman & Highfield (eds.), 139–165.

Schuchardt, Hugo. 1914. "Die Sprache der Saramakkaneger in Surinam". *Verhandelingen der Koninklijke Akademie van Wetenschappen te Amsterdam,* Afd. Letterkunde, Nieuwe Reeks, Deel XIV.6: iii–xxxv, 1–121.

Schultze, Ernst. 1933. "Sklaven und Dienersprachen". *Sociologus* 9: 378–418.

Schumann, John H. 1978. *The Pidginization Process. A model for second language acquisition.* (Series sociolinguistics.) Rowley/MA: Newbury House.

Sebeok, Thomas A. (ed.) 1960. *Style in language.* Cambridge/MA: MIT Press.

Silverstein, Michael. 1972. "Chinook Jargon: Language Contact and the Problem of Multi-level Generative Systems". *Language* 48: 378–406, 596–625.

Trudgill, Peter. 1996. "Dual-sourced Pidgins and reverse Creoloids: Northern perspectives on Language Contact". In: Jahr & Broch (eds.), 5–14.

Valdman, Albert & Highfield, Arnold (eds.) 1980. *Theoretical orientations in Creole studies.* New York: Academic Press.

Voorhoeve, Jan. 1973. "Historical and Linguistic Evidence in favour of the Relexification Theory in the formation of Creoles". *Language in Society* 2: 133–145.

Whinnom, Keith. 1971. "Linguistic hybridization and the 'special case' of Pidgins and Creoles". In: Hymes (ed.), 91–115.

Wurm, Stephen A. & Mühlhäusler, Peter (eds.) 1985. *Handbook of Tok Pisin (New Guinea Pidgin).* (Pacific Linguistics, C-70.) Canberra, A.C.T., Australia: Dept. of Linguistics, Research School of Pacific Studies, Australian National University.

Wurm, Stephen A., & Mühlhäusler Peter & Tryon, Darrell. (eds.) 1996. *Atlas of Languages of Intercultural Communication in the Pacific, Asia, and the Americas.* (Trends in linguistics: documentation, 13.) Berlin: Mouton de Gruyter.

Peter Mühlhäusler,
University of Adelaide (Australia)

117. Creolization

1. Introduction
2. Delimination and processes of genesis
3. Lexicon
4. Grammatical categories
5. Word order
6. Serial verbs and prepositions
7. Question words and reflexives
8. Absence of inflection, passives, and the subject
9. A creole type?
10. References

1. Introduction

While there has been a great deal of work on the grammatical features that creole languages share, little of this has actually tried to place the creole languages in a broader typological perspective. The present article will provide some of the building stones for such an enterprise.

The main purpose of this article will be to review a number of typological properties of creole languages: lexicon, categories, word order, serial verbs and prepositions, question words and reflexives, and finally the absence of inflection, passives, and the subject. First, however, I discuss the question of delimitation of the notion of 'creole languages' and the main processes of creole genesis.

2. Delimination and processes of genesis

I embark on the task of outlining some of the typological features of creoles aware of its limitations and risks. One of the problems lies in the definition of 'creole'. Languages called 'creoles' are spoken all over the world, and the field of creole studies has arisen and flourished because similarities have been observed between these different creoles (Bickerton 1981, 1984). Indeed, a number of similarities exist. However, it is not clear how superficial or fundamental such similarities are and whether they are so general that they can be taken to be a typologically defining characteristic of the creole languages. This article will try to contribute some data to this discussion, and I will return to it in § 9.

There are a number of prototypical creoles in the Carribean, including plantation creoles like HAITIAN, JAMAICAN Creole, NEGERHOLLANDS, and the Surinam creole language SRANAN. Also recognized as focal members of the set of creole languages are Maroon creoles such as SARAMACCAN (again Surinam) and PALENQUERO (near Cartagena in Colombia). All these languages emerged fairly rapidly, in the context of the African slave trade, associated with Europen plantation agriculture, in the period 1650–1750, and in areas with a large proportion of non-target language speakers in the overall population. Recruitment areas were mostly KWA (AKAN, FONGBE) and BANTU (KIKONGO) speaking.

Next to the core coup of proto-typical creoles, we find other sets of languages, which differ in one or more of these features: there are plantation creole languages that emerged in West Africa, the Indian Ocean, and the Pacific, rather than in the Carribean. Some of these involved African slaves with the same language backgrounds as those of the core creoles; others, such as HAWAIIAN CREOLE ENGLISH (HCE), involved speakers of very different languages, and of course, far removed from the Caribbean. TOK PISIN emerged in the 19th century on islands in the Pacific and eventually gelled as a creole in Papua New Guinea. BERBICE DUTCH Creole, to mention another case, conforms to all these criteria, but differs from the other Caribbean creoles in that only one African language appears to have played a major role: KALABARI IJAW. PAPIAMENTU arose fairly rapidly in a Caribbean setting among an African slave population, but whether this was primarily in a plantation setting and with a large proportion of non-target speakers is not so clear. SÃO TOMÉ PORTUGUESE CREOLE shares most of its features with the Caribbean creoles but emerged in an African rather than Caribbean setting. SESELWA, finally, shares some of its background with the Atlantic creoles and had demographic input from Atlantic slaves, but the Seychelles in the Indian Ocean also had a large influx of slaves from eastern Africa and Madagascar, as well as from South Asia in the later period.

The delimitation issue is a vexed one. We simply do not know which features of the creoles are due to universal processes of creolization and which to specific properties of all the languages involved.

A great deal has been written about the genesis of creole languages, some of it on the mark, some of it off the wall, some of it in

Table 117.1: Characteristics of some Creoles (*The genesis of BERBICE DUTCH may have taken slightly longer.)

	Caribbean	fairly rapidly	African slaves	European plantation setting	1650–1750	non-target
SRANAN	+	+	+	+	+	+
HCE	−	+	−	−	−	+
TOK PISIN	−	−	−	−	−	+
BERBICE	+	+*	+	+	+	+
PAPIAMENTU	+	+	±	+	+	+
SAO TOMÉ	−	+	+	+	+	−
SESELWA	−	±	±	+	+	−

part of right track (Arends & al. 1996, Mühlhäusler 1986; Romaine 1987; Sebba 1997). It is clear that we need a multidimensional model for creole genesis, in which at least the following specific processes interact with general properties of the human language faculty, and different linguistic traditions, African and European, were continued to different degrees. In the genesis of different creoles, the contribution of these various processes and components differs considerably. Also, the different processes frequently interact, either countering or reinforcing each other.

The first process is the simplification of the European target language input, due to accomodation by native speakers of these languages in contact settings, but most of all to second language learning strategies on the part of the slaves. This simplification is apparent in several ways. There is selective adoption of target language material: content words and phonetically strong forms are taken over, most morphological endings and (unstressed) preverbal clitics disappear. Syntactically, simplification is manifest in the loss of ordering possibilities. Creoles generally have much less variable word order than their European lexifier languages.

A second process concerns relexification of the structural patterns of the first language with words from the European colonial languages. This process is also referred to as intertwining (Bakker 1997), and is similar in its results to what is often termed native language transfer, conservation of L_1 patterns, and insertion or embedding of new vocabulary in a native matrix language structure (Myers-Scotton 1993).

The third major process involved in at least some cases of creole genesis is convergence between the patterns of the languages in contact. This process was referred to in terms of multi-level generative systems by Michael Silverstein (1972a, b) when he discussed the mutual adaptation of ENGLISH and CHINOOK in the emergence of CHINOOK JARGON. It has been taken up again by Kouwenberg (1992) in an analysis of the mutual adaptations of KALABARI IJAW and DUTCH to produce BERBICE DUTCH, a creole spoken in Guyana. The surface convergence is assumed to be based on comprimises between the categories of the different languages as well as between their word order patterns.

A final issue to be discussed in this context is the nature of pidgins, contact languages without native speakers. Often pidgins are taken to be unstructured and more simplified precursors of creoles, following the idea that pidgins and creoles are stages of the same 'cycle' of languages genesis. In fact, only a few of the pidgins actually documented fit into this scheme, particularly pidgins spoken in the Pacific. Most pidgins do not resemble prototypical creoles at all, but rather form a category of their own, with vocabulary and structural features taken from various languages involved in the contact. Prototypical creoles generally have most vocabulary items from one single source. By the same token, most Caribbean creoles have no documented pidgin source. Due to space limitations, I will not go into typological features of pidgins any further (→ art. 116).

3. Lexicon

Although a number of African and Amerindian etyma have survived in the Caribbean creole languages, the majority of the vocabulary items in the Caribbean creoles have a European source. Originally, this may have been quite a limited set. Norval Smith (personal communication) estimates the number of ENGLISH roots in SRANAN (ENGLISH was

SRANAN's original lexifier language) at around 700. Of course, this implies that there must have been rapid lexical expansion (Hancock 1980) in the early creoles to serve the needs of a full-fledged community language. In addition to borrowing, reduplication, and limited derivational affixation, two processes play a particularly important role in lexical expansion: multifunctional use of roots (also termed zero derivation; → art. 89) and phrasal compounding. Jan Voorhoeve (1981) gives a number of striking examples of multifunctional use in SRANAN:

Table 117.2: Multifunctional use in SRANAN (Voorhoeve 1981: 28)

siki	'sick'	doti	'dirty'
siki	'sickness'	doti	'dirt'
siki	'be sick'	doti	'be dirty'
siki	'make sick'	doti	'make dirty'

While here the etymological root is an adjective, there are also cases where a verb or noun is the etymological base, such as *bosro* 'brush' which can be both a noun and a transitive or intransitive verb.

Marta B. Dijkhof has carried out an extensive analysis of phrasal compounding in PAPIAMENTU, with examples such as:

Table 117.3: Phrasal compounding in PAPIAMENTU (Dijkhoff 1993)

palu di garganta	'neck bone' [stick of neck]
kabes di boto	'lift' [head of boat]
barba di yonkuman	'herb' [beard of a young man]

While these forms contain a *di* 'of' linking preposition, there is a different type of phrasal compound in SARAMACCAN, involving an agentive element *ma* (< ENGLISH *man*), best analyzed as a suffix:

Table 117.4: Phrasal compoundings in SARAMACCAN (Bakker & al. 1995: 173; Arends & al. 1995: 326)

pai ma	'pregnant woman' [bear man]
tja buka ma	'messenger' [carry mouth man]
pai ku mujee ma	'midwife' [bear with woman man]

4. Grammatical categories

With respect to the categorial inventory of creole languages, a number of issues come to the fore. The limited lexical inventory inherited from the European languages, coupled with the paucity of derivational affixes, lead to considerable multifunctionality. The first issue concerns the status of the preverbal Tense/Mood/Aspect (TMA-)markers. They can be related to different other categories. A typical first example concerns the status of elements like HAITIAN *pou* (< FRENCH *pour*), which can function as a preposition, complementizer, and mood marker:

(1)   HAITIAN (Koopman & Lefebvre 1980: 203)
        Pote sa pou mwen.
        carry this for me
        'Bring this for me.'

(2)   HAITIAN (Koopman & Lefebvre 1980: 209)
        Nou pa te pou wè sa.
        1PL NEG ANT MD see this
        'We did not have to see this.'

(3)   HAITIAN (Hall 1953: 192)
        Li pa-jam tro ta pou chen
        3SG NEG-ever too late for dog
        anraje.
        go.mad
        'It is never too late for a dog to go mad.'

Another categorial source for the preverbal markers are verbs, to be sure. One example was *te* in (2), etymologically related to FRENCH *était*. Another one is given with *wa* in the BERBICE DUTCH example (4):

(4)   BERBICE DUTCH Creole (Kouwenberg 1995: 82)
        èk wa jefi-a kali kali
        1SG ANT eat-DUR little little
        'I was eating very little.'

This example shows yet a third categorial source, which is much rarer in the Caribbean creoles, namely an affix, here durative *-a*. There are some affixal tense and aspect markers in the West-African Portuguese creoles, and PAPIAMENTU has *-ndo*, derived from SPANISH or PORTUGUESE gerundial *-ndo*, but these are the exceptions.

In addition to their categorial status, the TMA-markers raise complicated issues with respect to finiteness. PAPIAMENTU *ta* occurs in main clauses, but not with infinitives:

(5) PAPIAMENTU (fieldwork data)
 (a) *mi ta kome*
  1SG ASP eat
  'I eat/I am eating.'
 (b) *mi a ker kome*
  1SG PA want eat
  'I wanted to eat.'

However, clauses marked with *ta* such as *mi mes ta kanta na radio* 'myself singing on the radio' allow a reflexive anaphor in subject position, as in (6a), while true finite clauses introduced by *ku* 'that' do not, as in (6b):

(6) PAPIAMENTU (fieldwork data)
 (a) *Mi a tende mi mes ta kanta na radio.*
  1SG PA hear 1SG self ASP sing
  LOC radio.
  'I heard myself singing on the radio.'
 (b) **Mi a tende ku mi mes ta kanta na radio.*
  1SG PA hear that 1SG self ASP
  sing LOC radio
  'I heard that myself was singing on the radio.'

Similarly, the semantic scope of a negated universal quantifier can be wide in a clause marked with *ta*, as in (7a), but only narrow in a finite clause, as in (7b):

(7) PAPIAMENTU (fieldwork data)
 (a) *Mi ta mira [niun hende ta sali.]*
  1SG ASP see not.one person ASP
  leave
  'I see no one leaving.'
  (There is no one such that I see that person leaving.)
 (b) *Mi ta mira [ku niun hende ta sali].*
  1SG ASP see that not.one person
  ASP leave
  'I see that no one is leaving.'
  (I see that there is no one such that that person is leaving.)

Thus *ta* is similar to ENGLISH *-ing*. This is also clear from the fact that it can appear on the complement of aspectual verbs:

(8) PAPIAMENTU (Maurer 1988: 262)
 E-l-a kumisá a kome djente.
 3SG-EU-PA start ASP eat tooth
 'He started grinding his teeth.'

Again, preverbal *ta* resembles ENGLISH *-ing* here or SPANISH *-ndo*.

A second categorial issue concerns the potential distinction between the categories 'Adjective' and 'Verb'. In PAPIAMENTU, this distinction is transparent. Here we have a regular and invariant copula that precedes nonverbal predicates:

(9) PAPIAMENTU (fieldword data)
 Mi ta na kas.
 1SG COP LOC house
 'I am in the house.'

(10) *Mi ta Pedro.*
 1SG COP Pedro
 'I am Pedro.'

(11) *Mi ta grandi.*
 1SG COP big
 'I am tall.'

However, in many other creoles stative descriptive predicates can occur without a copula, casting doubt on the verb/adjective distinction. The following data are from SARAMACCAN:

(12) SARAMACCAN (Alleyne 1987)
 di mujee hanse
 DET woman beautiful
 'The woman is beautiful.'

(13) *di pasi limbo*
 DET path clear
 'The path is clear.'

In SARAMACCAN, there is a presentative copula *da*, and a form *de* used in locatives:

(14) *de da wanlo mii u mi*
 3PL COP some child GEN 1SG
 'They are some of my children.'

(15) *mi de a wosu aki*
 1SG COP LOC house here
 'I am in this house.'

Notice now that with reduplicated predicates *de* is obligatory:

(16) *mi de tjalitjali*
 1SG COP sad.REDUP
 'I am sad.'

This suggests that the non-reduplicated forms are true verbs, and the reduplicated forms derived adjectives. Often the reduplicated from has a derived, more specific meaning in SARAMACCAN, suggesting its lexicalized status:

(17) (a) *di mii bunu*
  DET child good
  'The child is good.'
 (b) *di mii de bunbunu*
  DET child COP good-REDUP
  'The child is fine.'

(18) (a) *a   satu*
    3SG salt
    'It has been salted.'
(b) *a de satusatu*
    3SG COP salt.REDUP
    'It is salty.'

The reduplicated forms can also occur in prenominal position:

(19) SARAMACCAN (Bakker 1987: 25)
    di lailai   goni
    DET load.REDUP gun
    'the loaded gun.'

(20) *di dɛɛ-dɛɛ   koosu*
    DET dry.REDUP cloth
    'the dried cloth'

A final categorial issue concerns the intricate relation between nouns and postpositions in several creole languages, such as SRANAN and BERBICE DUTCH. Consider the following data:

(21) SRANAN (Adamson and Smith 1995: 228)
    na fesi tapu a   skowtu-oso
    LOC face top DET police-house
    'in front of/above the police station'

(22) *na a   skowtu-oso fesi/tapu*
    LOC DET police-house face/top
    'at the front of/on top of the police station'

These two examples are not exactly synonymous: in (21) a more exact location is implied than in (22). This suggests that it has the more literal meaning associated with a noun; indeed it is a possessive construction. In (21) *fesi* and *tapu* function as pre-positions.

5. Word order

Most creole languages have fairly rigid word order:

(23) Subject / TMA elements / NEG / V / Indirect Object / Direct Object / Adverbial and Prepositional complements

Remarkable is the fact that in double object constructions the order almost invariably is IO−DO. This is not only the case with languages with ENGLISH- and DUTCH-derived lexicon, where we might expect this order given the European model:

(24) (a) NEGERHOLLANDS (Bruyn & al. 1999)
    ham a   gi   de man ši
    3SG ASP give DET man 3SG.POSS
    gout
    gold
    'He gave the man his gold.'

(b) SARAMACCAN (Bruyn & al. 1999)
    mi ke   pindja i   wan soni
    1SG want tell   2SG one think
    'I want to tell you something (in secret).'

It also holds in languages with a Romance-derived lexicon, such as PAPIAMENTU and HAITIAN Creole:

(25) (a) Papiamentu (fieldwork data)
    bo a   duna-mi e   buki
    2SG ASP give-1SG DET book
    'You have given me the book.'
(b) HAITIAN (Bruyn & al. 1999)
    li rakonte papa-li   istwa sa-a
    3SG tell   father-3SG story this
    'He told his father this story'.

In PAPIAMENTU the order of the two objects is not affected by the noun/pronoun distinction:

(26) PAPIAMENTU (fieldwork data)
    bo a duna mi ruman e
    2SG PA give 1SG 3SG
    'You gave my brother him/it.'

The rigid order can be modified by fronting various elements to initial position, often after a focus particle.

A very typical construction of the Atlantic creoles is predicate cleft. The verb focused on is repeated at the beginning of the clause, preceded by a focus particle which may be related to a copula:

(27) PAPIAMENTU (fieldword data)
    ta traha e   ta traha
    COP work 3SG ASP work
    'S/he is really working.'

What occurs in the fronted position is strictly limited. Starting from a simple case such as (28), it is impossible to make the fronted verb past with the particle *a* as in (29a), add an object pronoun (even a phonological clitic) to it as in (29b), or make the focus marker past, as in (29c). However, the focus marker can be negated, as in (29d).

(28) PAPIAMENTU (fieldwork data)
    ta duna m'a   duna-bo e   buki
    COP give 1SG-PA give-2SG DET book
    'I have really given you the book.'

(29) (a) **ta a duna duna-bo e   buki*
       COP PA 1SG-PA give-2SG DET book
(b) **ta dunabo   m'a   duna-bo e*
    COP give-2SG 1SG-PA give-2SG DET
    buki
    book

(c) *tabata duna mi tabata
    COP-PA give 1SG-PA give-2SG
    duna-bo e buki
    DET book
(d) no ta duna m'a duna-bo e
    NEG COP give 1SG-PA give-2SG DET
    buki
    book

While many Caribbean creoles have forms of predicate cleft, there are also some differences. One concerns the structural scope of the phenomenon. How far can the clefted predicate and the predicate in its canonical position be apart? So far, three patterns have been found:

(30) (a) unbounded   HAITIAN, West
                          African languages
     (b) clause-bound   PAPIAMENTU
     (c) across one   SRANAN,
         clause boundary SARAMACCAN

A second issue concerns the meaning of predicate cleft constructions. It can generally be used to mark predicate focus, as in the examples given. However, it is also used in concessives, factive clauses and adverbial clauses indicating circumstance. No thorough comparative work has been done in this area.

6. Serial verbs and prepositions

It is well-known that many Caribbean creoles have a rich inventory of serial verb constructions. The three examples listed here are typical, given in order of width of distribution in the Caribbean.

(31) PAPIAMENTU (fieldwork data)
     e-l-a bula bai
     3SG-EU-PA fly go
     'He flew away.'

(32) GUYANAIS (St. Jacques-Fauquenoy 1972: 54)
     li pote sa bay mo
     3SG bring that give 1SG
     'He brought that for me.'

(33) GULLAH (Turner 1974: 211)
     dèm go in tèk im go bak
     3PL go and take 3SG go back
     'They are going back with him.'

Adverbial directionals as in (31) are quite frequent (so frequent in fact that *bula bai* has been lexicalized as a compound verb), and there are a number of cases of benefactive series, as in (32). Finally, comitative and instrumental 'take' constructions as in (33) are not as frequent. There is a large literature on these serial verbs, both in terms of their syntactic structure and of their origin.

One issue that merits more comparative investigation is the possibility of marking the individual verbs in these constructions with tense, mood, and aspect particles. In all creoles the first verb can be marked with the full range of these particles, but in some creoles the other verbs cannot. Kouwenberg (1994) shows, however, that in BERBICE DUTCH several particles can be added to other verbs than the first in the string. Byrne (1987) has argued that in SARAMACCAN as well other verbs in the string can be marked with *bi* 'anterior tense' and *ta* 'durative'. However, this is only confirmed for *ta* in Veenstra (1997). In other Caribbean creoles, no tense or aspect marking of verbs other than the initial one has been reported.

Another area related to the expression of arguments where there is some variation among the creole languages is preposition stranding (compare: *the knife that he cut the bread with ...*). In JAMAICAN and NEGERHOLLANDS this is allowed. Consider the following NEGERHOLLANDS example in which *fa* is stranded:

(34) NEGERHOLLANDS (Bruyn & Veenstra 1993)
     Am ne kan fin it widi di
     3SG NEG can find out who DET
     skun hotu fa
     shoe belong of
     'He could not find out who the shoe belonged to.'

However, in SRANAN true prepositions such as *nanga* 'with' cannot be stranded:

(35) SRANAN (fieldwork data)
     *a nefi san a koti a brede
     DET knife that 3SG cut DET bread
     nanga ...
     with
     'the knife that he cut the bread with ...'

The situation in PAPIAMENTU represents a special case. Prepositions can occur in their original position with a pronoun representing the relativized element. A bare preposition is impossible:

(36) PAPIAMENTU (fieldword data)
     e kuchu ku e-l-a korta
     DET knife that 3SG-EU-PA cut
     e pan kuné/*ku ...
     DET bread with-3SG/with
     'the knife that he cut the bread with ...'

However, this pronoun obligatorily has the singular form, even if the relativized element is plural:

(37) e   kuchu-nan ku e-l-a
      DET knife-PL   that 3SG-EU-PA
      korta e pan
      cut   DET bread
      kuné/*kul/*ku nan ...
      with-3SG/with/with-3PL
      'the knives that he cut the bread with ...'

This suggests that the phenomenon here is not a true resumptive pronoun, but rather represents a marker indicating the position of the moved element. Thus we have three types of creoles with respect to preposition stranding:

(38) (a) stranding allowed: JAMAICAN, NEGERHOLLANDS
     (b) stranding not allowed: SARAMACCAN, SRANAN, HAITIAN
     (c) stranding with marking: PAPIAMENTU

7. Question words and reflexives

While many of the European content words have been transmitted to the creole languages more or less intact, function words are often completely new. One example of this are question words, which often consist of a question element (glossed Q below) and a general noun marking time, place, person, etc. Some examples are given below.

(39) (a) NEGERHOLLANDS
         wa tit
         Q   time
         'when'
     (b) SRANAN
         o   pe
         Q   place
         'where'
     (c) HAITIAN
         ki žan
         Q   genre
         'how'

However, we also find hybrid forms, as in (40a), synthetic forms, as in (40b), and forms with a more complex origin, as in (40c), which is based on a question word from the FONGBE languages.

(40) (a) JAMAICAN
         wen taym
         when time
         'when'
     (b) PAPIAMENTU
         ken
         'who'
     (c) SARAMACCAN
         andi
         'what'

In many creoles, reflexive pronouns are also compound forms, consisting of a pronoun and some other element, either an emphatic identifying form like 'self' or a body-part noun like 'head':

(41) (a) SRANAN
         mi srefi
         1SG self
         'myself'
     (b) HAITIAN
         tèt-li
         head-3SG
         'himself'

What is remarkable, however, is that sometimes a number of different elements compete, each with slightly different distributions (Carden & Stewart 1988). A typical example is PAPIAMENTU. The bare form *kurpa* 'body' is only used in fixed combinations with specific verbs:

(42) PAPIAMENTU
      kurpa (< PORTUGUESE corpo, SPANISH cuerpo 'body')
      lanta kurpa 'get up' (< SPANISH levantarSE)

More productive is the same form combined with a possessive pronoun:

(43) possessive + kurpa
      skonde su kurpa 'hide' (< SPANISH esconderSE)

This form is mostly used with verbs indicating a physical action, and could be interpreted in terms of a relation of inalienable possession between the antecedent and the anaphor.

Often we simply find a bare pronoun used in a reflexive construction:

(44) object pronoun
      sinti e tristi 'feel sad' (< SPANISH sentirSE)
      haña e 'find oneself' (< SPANISH hallarSE)

This possibility mostly occurs with non-physical inherently reflexive verbs, and with recently introduced polysyllabic 'learned' verbs of SPANISH origin. It may be that the bare pronoun here is indeed a postverbal clitic element.

Very productive is the combination possessive pronoun + *mes*:

(45) possessive pronoun + *mes*
      hasi su mes malu 'hurt oneself'
      (< SPANISH *hacerSE mal*)

This form competes with the body part reflexives and is the preferred form in ordinary non-physical reflexive predicates. With 'drown' and 'help' both *su mes* and *su kurpa* are allowed:

(46) *e-l-a   hoga   su   mes/su*
      3SG-EU-PA drown 3POSS SELF/3POSS
      kurpa na lama
      body LOC .sea
      'He has drowned himself in the sea.'

(47) *bo   a   yuda bo mes/bo kurpa*
      2SG PA help 2SG self/2SG body
      'You have helped yourself.'

With learned non-physical verbs such as *ekiboka* 'make a mistake' (< SPANISH *equivocarSE*) possessive + *mes* competes with the bare pronoun form:

(48) *m'a   ekiboka mi/mi   mes/*mi*
      1SG-PA mistake 1SG/1SG self/1SG
      kurpa
      body
      'I made a mistake.'

The distribution and behaviour of the reflexive forms in the different creole languages constitutes a very rich area of study (Déchaine and Manfredi 1994).

8. Absence of inflection, passives, and the subject

The general observation to be made with respect to creole morpho-syntax, of course, is that there is very little of any inflection, at least overt inflection. This is evident from many of the examples given so far. The following pairs illustrate this further. The (a) sentences are PAPIAMENTU examples already shown and the (b) sentences show the SPANISH (one of the source languages for PAPIAMENTU) equivalents. In the (b) sentences the elements that do not appear again in PAPIAMENTU are underlined:

(49) (a) PAPIAMENTU (fieldwork data)
          Mi ta mira [niun hende ta
          1SG ASP see not.one person ASP
          sali].
          leave
          'I see no one leaving.'
          [There is no one such that I see that person leaving.]

(b) SPANISH
    No veo   sali-r
    NEG see.PR.1SG leave-INF
    a nadie.
    DEF.AN.OB nobody
    'I see no one leaving.'

(50) (a) PAPIAMENTU (fieldword data)
         bo   a   duna-mi e   buki
         2SG ASP give-1SG DET book
         'You gave me the book.'
     (b) SPANISH
         me   diste   el   libro
         1SG-OB give.PA.2SG DET.MSG book

However, there are some syntactic patterns, e. g. in passive constructions, that suggest that verbs behave as if they were marked as passive participles. The following example is from HAITIAN:

(51) HAITIAN (Muysken and Veenstra 1995: 161)
      plen pa plen se-bay-li
      full NEG full FOC-give-3SG
      'Pregnant or not she must be given back to him.'

Here the verb *bay* 'give' is used in a passive sense, even if it has no marking for passive. A similar example from BERBICE DUTCH:

(52) BERBICE DUTCH (Kouwenberg 1995: 235)
      o   kor djas kèk hos di... kori
      3SG work just like how this made
      'It is made just like this one is made.'

Here the verb *kor(i)* 'made, worked' receives no passive marking.

In other creoles, the meaning of passive is conveyed by the use of an impersonal dummy subject:

(53) FA D'AMBU (Post 1995: 199)
      A   xa baya ba-tela
      3SG ASP dance dance-land
      na-name   tesyi
      DET-brother three
      'The traditional dances are danced by three friends.'

Here the lexical subject appears in the rightmost position as a further specification of the dummy grammatical subject.

The HAITIAN and BERBICE DUTCH examples suggest that with respect to passive, the creoles have a syntactic pattern corresponding to a language with passive inflection, while there is no overt marking present. A similar set of observations is made in Kriegel

(1996). The same issue can be raised with respect to the possibilities of null-subjects, one of the most complicated issues in creole typology. On the one hand, it is clear that PAPIAMENTU is not like SPANISH or PORTUGUESE in not allowing absent pronominal subjects in simple main clauses, (54b). Neither does it permit post-verbal subjects in simple sentences, (54c):

(54) PAPIAMENTU (fieldwork data)
  (a) *e ta kome*
     3SG ASP eat
     'He is eating.'
  (b) **ta kome*
     ASP eat
     (compare SPANISH *está comiendo*)
  (c) **ta kome Maria*
     ASP eat Maria
     (compare SPANISH *está comiendo María*)

Thus with respect to ordinary pronominal subject carrying person features, PAPIAMENTU patterns like ENGLISH. Null-subjects are ungrammatical. This is not unexpected since the language shows no morphological person marking anywhere in the verbal paradigm:

(55)   *mit ta kome*
     bo ta kome
     e ta kome
     nos ta kome
     boso(nan) ta kome
     nan ta kome

Empty subjects occur in PAPIAMENTU in a number of contexts, however. First of all, indefinite subjects can remain null:

(56) PAPIAMENTU (Muller, 1983)
  (a) *Ta bende flor.*
     ASP sell flower
     'Flowers are sold (here).'
  (b) *Tabata toka bon musika.*
     PA.ASP play good music
     'They played good music.'

That this possibility is limited to strictly generic contexts is shown by the ungrammaticality or unacceptability of (57a) and (57b):

(57) (a) **Ta bende e flor.*
     ASP sell DET flower
     'The flowers are sold (here).'
  (b) ? *Tabata toka e musika di Edgar Palm.*
     PA-ASP play DET music of Edgar Palm
     'They played the music of Edgar Palm.'

In addition, the occurrence of this type of pattern is limited to signs, announcements, etc. I take this empty subject to be a third person null pronoun, the interpretation of which is contextuality determined.

A second context for empty subjects is constituted by weather verbs. Here, no subject is possible:

(58) (a) *Tabata jobe*
     PA.ASP rain
     'It rained.'
  (b) **E tabata jobe*
     3SG PA.ASP rain
(59) (a) *Ta hasi kalor.*
     ASP make heat
     'It is not.'
  (b) **E ta hasi kalor.*
     ASP make heat

Third, non-argumental expletive subjects are null:

(60) *Tin baliamentu.*
     EXIST dance
     'There is a dance.'

(61) *No ta importami ni un bledu*
     NEG ASP matter not one bit
     'It does not matter a bit to me.'

(62) *Parse ku Maria ta kanta.*
     appear that Maria ASP sing
     'It appears that Mary is singing.'

The three clases of null subjects can occur in subordinate contexts as well.

We also find, in specific circumstances, cases of inversion. When there is a preposed locative or temporal phrase, it is possible to place the subject after the verb in PAPIAMENTU. Both (63a) and (63b) are grammatical:

(63) PAPIAMENTU (fieldwork data Tonjes Veenstra)
  (a) *Riba e isla aki un million hende ta biba*
     on DET island here one million people ASP live
     'On this island a million people live.'
  (b) *Riba e isla aki ta biba un million hende*
     on DET island here ASP live one million people
     'On this island live a million people.'

Consider now (64), however:

(64) ?? *Ta biba un million hende riba*
ASP live one million people on
e isla aki
DET island here
'Live a million people on this island.'

The subject postposing is only fully acceptable when there is a preposed locative or temporal expression.

The subject cannot intervene between a verb and its object, however, as in (65b). Neither can it follow the object, as in (65c):

(65) (a) *Den Mei hopi hende ta pasa*
in May many people ASP pass
eksamen
exam
'In May, many people pass their exams.'
(b) **Den Mei ta pasa hopi hende*
in May ASP pass many people
eksamen
exam
(c) **Den Mei ta pasa eksamen*
in May ASP pass exam
hopi hende.
many people

The postposed subject cannot be definite:

(66) **Riba e isla aki ta biba*
on DET island here ASP live
e homber
DET man
'On this island here lives the man.'

The sentences in (67b) and (68b) show that the subject follows both elements of the compound verb *bula bai* in (67b), but not of a true serial verb construction with *kore sali*, as in (68b). This parallels the possibilities in predicate cleft: both verbs in the compound *bula bai* can be fronted together in (67a), but not the combination *kore sali* in (68a):

(67) (a) *Ta bula bai nos ta bula bai*
COP fly go 1PL ASP fly go
Hulandes.
Holland
'We really fly to Holland.'
(b) *Den Yanuari ta bula bai hopi*
in January ASP fly go many
hende Korsow.
people Curaçao
'In January many people fly to Curaçao.'

(68) (a) **ta kore sali hopi hende kore*
COP run leave many people run
sali for di sino
leave out of cinema
'Many people really run away from a cinema.'
(b) **Den kaso di kandela ta kore*
in case of fire ASP run
sali hopi hende for di sino
leave many people out of cinema
'In case of fire many people run away from a cinema.'

These examples show the complexity of the null-subject issue and its interaction with other phenomenons. An in-depth study of null-subject phenomena in the creole languages has yet to be carried out, but there is considerable variation. HAITIAN resembles PAPIAMENTU (DeGraff 1993), while in SRANAN we find expletive *a* '3SG' in *a gersi dati* ... 'it seems that ...' MISKITO COAST CREOLE ENGLISH is reported to have frequent null-subjects.

9. A creole type?

In earlier work (Muysken 1988), I have denied the existence of a creole 'type' implied by Bickerton (1981, 1984), on the basis of the type of variation in grammatical structures encountered even in the proto-typical Caribbean creole languages. Recently John H. McWhorter (1998) has claimed that all creoles share three features not shared in that combination by other languages, allowing us to speak of creoles as a unique typological class, structurally distinguishable from other languages.

(69) (a) little or no inflectional affixation.
(b) little or no use of tone to lexically contrast monosyllables or encode syntax
(c) semantically regular derivational affixation

McWhorter's argument can be tackled in two ways: empirical and conceptual.

Let us take the claims one by one. There is no doubt that in many core creoles there is very little inflectional affixation. This is also to be expected since in the second language acquisition of the European colonial languages, part of the process of creole formation, inflection is often lost. However, the contributing superstrate and substrate languages were not very rich in their inflection either, and in several cases (BERBICE DUTCH Creole, PAPIAMENTU, CAPE VERDIAN) we do get some inflections. If we take creolization in typologically very different languages such as SHABA SWAHILI (de Rooij 1995) and Amazonian Ecuadorian QUECHUA (Muysken 2000), there is simplification and regularization of inflection, but not loss of inflection. The absence of inflection is the singlemost frequently noted supposed typological feature of the creoles, and indeed may be the way many people identify a language as a creole. However, it may be the unfortunate by-result, from a scholarly point of view, of the limited typological spread in the languages contributing to the proto-typical creoles. A final remark concerns the question of the overtness of inflection. As I showed with respect to passive and null-subjects, some creoles behave syntactically as if there is inflection present, even if this is not visible.

There is no space here to discuss McWhorter's claims concerning tone in creoles in depth. Jan Voorhoeve's well-known study on tone and grammar in SARAMACCAN (1961) and Rountree's (1972) follow up study, neither of which is cited by McWhorter (1998), argue that tonal contrasts play a central role in SARAMACCAN grammar. Raúl Römer (1992) documents a number of ways that the PAPIAMENTU lexicon and syntax depend on tonal contrasts. The role that tonal contrasts play in Caribbean creoles is not surprising given the importance of tone in West-African languages. The only reason, it appears, why McWhorter puts so much emphasis on tone is to maximize the differences between the creoles and languages like CHINESE, which shares many syntactic features with the Caribbean creoles.

The only detailed study of the derivational morphology of a Caribbean creole, finally, is Dijkhoff's (1993) work on PAPIAMENTU. It shows a very considerable amount of semantically non-transparent derivational morphology. Some examples:

(70)   PAPIAMENTU (Dijkhoff 1993)
        balia-mentu 'dance' [not: dancing]
        lubida-dó 'absent-minded' [not: forgetting]
        kabe'i boto 'prow; lift' [not: head of boat]

McWhorter assumes that derivational morphology in the creoles would be transparent because of their recent emergence. However, non-transparent meanings take a very short time to arise and gel in the lexicon, much shorter than the 300 years that we are dealing with in the case of the Caribbean creoles discussed here.

There are psycholinguistic and sociolinguistic universals underlying the processes I outlined above, that have played a role in creole genesis: simplification, relexification, and convergence. However, we are not yet at the point of understanding how these universals manifest themselves in the interaction of various typologically different language pairs.

10. References

Adamson, Lilian & Smith, Norval. 1995. "Sranan". In: Arends, Jacques & al. (eds.), 219–32.

Arends, Jacques & Muysken, Pieter & Smith, Norval (eds.). 1995. *Pidgins and creoles. An introduction.* (Creole language library.) Amsterdam & Philadelphia: Benjamins.

Arends, Jacques & Muysken, Pieter & Smith, Norval. 1995. "Conclusions". In: Arends, Jacques & al. (eds.), 319–30.

Bakker, Peter. 1997. *A language of our own. The genesis of Michif. The mixed Cree-French language of the Canadian Metis.* (Oxford studies in anthropological linguistics, 10.) New York & Oxford: Oxford Univ. Press.

Bakker, Peter & Smith, Norval & Veenstra, Tonjes. 1995. "Saramaccan". In: Arends, Jacques & al. (eds.), 165–79.

Bickerton, Derek. 1981. *Roots of Language.* Ann Arbour/MI: Karoma Publ.

Bickerton, Derek. 1984. "The language bioprogram hypothesis". *The Brain and Behavioral Sciences* 7: 123–221.

Bruyn, Adrienne & Muysken, Pieter & Verrips, Maaike. 1999. "Double object constructions in the creole languages: development and diachrony". In: DeGraff, Michel (ed.). *Creolization, language change, and language development.* (Learning, development and conceptual change.) Cambridge/MA: MIT Press, 329–74.

Byrne, Francis. 1987. *Grammatical relations in a radical creole. Verb complementation in Saramaccan.* (Creole language library, 3.) Amsterdam & Philadelphia: Benjamins.

DeGraff, Michel. 1993. "Is Haitian Creole a pro-drop language?" In: Byrne, Francis & Holm, John (eds.). *Atlantic meets Pacific. A global view of pidginization and creolization. Selected papers from the Society for Pidgin and Creole linguistics.* (Creole language library, 11.) Amsterdam & Philadelphia: Benjamins, 71–90.

Carden, Guy & Stewart, William A. 1988. "Binding Theory, Bioprogram, and Creolization: Evidence from Haitian Creole". *Journal of Pidgin and Creole Language* 3: 1–68.

Déchaine, Rose-Marie & Manfredi, Victor. 1994. "Binding domains in Haitian". *Natural Language and Linguistic Theory* 12: 203–58.

Dijkhoff, Marta B. 1993. *Papiamentu word formation. A case study of complex nouns and their relation to phrases and clauses.* Doctoral dissertation: University of Amsterdam.

Hall, Robert A. 1953. *Haitian Creole. Grammar, texts, vocabulary.* (Memoirs of the American Folklore Society, 43.) Philadelphia.

Hancock, Ian. 1980. "Lexical expansion in creole languages". In: Valdman, Albert & Highfield, Arnold (eds.). *Theoretical Orientations in Creole Studies. Proceedings of a Symposium on Theoretical Orientations in Creole Studies held at St. Thomas, U. S. Virgin Islands, March 28–April 1, 1979.* New York: Academic Press, 63–88.

Koopman, Hilda & Lefebvre, Claire. 1981. "Haitian Creole Pu". In: Muysken, Pieter (ed.). *Generative studies on creole languages.* (Studies in generative grammar, 6.) Dordrecht: Foris Publ., 25–34.

Kouwenberg, Silvia. 1987. "Papiamento complementizer PA, the finiteness of its complements, and some remarks on empty categories in Papiamentu". *Journal of Pidgin and Creole Languages* 5: 39–52.

Kouwenberg, Silvia. 1992. "From OV to VO. Linguistic negotation in the development of Berbice Dutch Creole". *Lingua* 88: 263–99.

Kouwenberg, Silvia. 1994. *A grammar of Berbice Dutch Creole.* (Mouton grammar library, 12.) Berlin & New York: Mouton de Gruyter.

Kouwenberg, Silvia. 1995. "Berbice Dutch". In: Arends, Jacques & al. (eds.), 233–46.

Kriegel, Sibylle. 1996. *Diathesen im Mauritius- und Seychellenkreol.* (ScriptOralia, 88) Tübingen: Narr.

Maurer, Philippe. 1988. *Les modifications temporelles et modales du verbe dans le papiamentu de Curaçao (Antilles Néerlandaises). Avec une anthologie et un vocabulaire papiamento-français.* (Kreolische Bibliothek, 9.) Hamburg: Buske.

MacWhorter, John H. 1998. "Identifying the creole prototype: Vindicating a typological class". *Language* 74: 788–818.

Muller, Enrique. 1983. "Some specific rules in Papiamentu syntax". In: *Papiamentu: Problems and Possibilities. Papers presented at the Conference on Papamentu, 4–6 june 1981.* Zutphen: Walburg Pers, 35–54.

Mühlhäusler, Peter. 1986. *Pidgins and creole linguistics.* (Language in society, 11.) Oxford: Blackwell.

Muysken, Pieter. 1978. "Three kinds of movement in Papiamentu". In: Jansen, Frank (ed.). *Studies on Fronting.* Lisse: De Ridder, 65–80.

Muysken, Pieter. 1988. "Are creoles a special type of language?". In: Newmeyer, Frederick (ed.). *Lingiustics: The Cambridge Survey II.* Cambridge: Cambridge Univ. Press, 285–302.

Muysken, Pieter. 2000. "Semantic transparency in Lowland Ecuadorian Quechua morphosyntax". *Linguistics* 38: 973–988.

Muysken, Pieter & Veenstra, Tonjes. 1995. "Haitian". In: Arends, Jacques & al. (eds.), 153–64.

Myers-Scotton, Carol. 1993. *Duelling languages. Grammatical structure in codeswitching.* Oxford: Clarendon Press.

Post, Marike. 1995. "Fa d'Ambu". In: Arends, Jacques & al. (eds.), 191–204.

Romaine, Suzanne. 1988. *Pidgin and creole languages.* (Longman linguistics library.) London: Longman.

Rooij, Vincent de. 1995. "Shava Swahili". In: Arends, Jacques & al. (eds.), 179–90.

Rountree, Catherine. 1972. "Saramaccan tone in relation to intonation and grammar". *Lingua* 29: 308–25.

Römer, Raúl G. 1991. *Studies in Papiamentu Tonology.* (Caribbean Culture Studies, 5.) Amsterdam: Amsterdam Centre for Caribbean Studies.

Saint Jacques Fauquenoy, Marguerite. 1972. *Analyse structurale du créole guyanais.* (Etudes linguistiques, 13.) Paris: Klinksieck.

Sebba, Mark. 1997. *Contact languages. Podgins and Creoles.* (Modern linguistics series.) Basingstoke: Macmillan.

Silverstein, Michael. 1972a, b. "Multilevel generative systems: the case of Chinook Jargon, I & II". *Language* 48, 137–85, 243–97.

Turner, Lorenzo D. 1974. *Africanism in the Gullah dialect.* Ann Arbor: Univ. of Michigan Press.

Veenstra, Tonjes. 1997. *Serial verbs in Saramaccan.* Doctoral dissertation, University of Amsterdam, HIL series.

Voorhoeve, Jan. 1961. "Le ton et la grammaire dans le Saramaccan". *Word* 17: 146–63.

Voorhoeve, Jan. 1981. "Multifunctionality as a derivational problem". In: Muysken, Pieter (ed.). *Generative studies on creole languages.* (Studies in generative grammar, 6.) Dordrecht: Foris Publ., 25–34.

Pieter Muysken,
Katholieke Universiteit Nijmegen
(The Netherlands)

118. Typological changes in language obsolescence

1. Introduction
2. Terminological prerequisites
3. Material loss: Simplification, reduction, and negative borrowing
4. Material gain: Borrowing of substance and patterns
5. Creative processes
6. Language intertwining
7. References

1. Introduction

When, in the course of language shift, an individual or a community abandon their native tongue and acquire a new one, this process is usually accompanied by particular changes in the language systems underlying the speech of the speakers of the abandoned language. These changes are often quite dramatic, resulting in a drastic reorganization of the fundamental principles of the grammar of the respective language vis-à-vis that which is considered the 'normal' grammar of this language.

The literature is full of descriptions of this kind of phenomena, which are traditionally deemed to be symptoms of 'atrophy', i.e. linguistic 'reductions' and 'simplifications' brought about by imperfect acquisition and limited opportunities of use, coupled with a lack of interest on the part of elder full speakers in maintaining their traditional linguistic norm (i.e. lack of 'correction'), and eventually leading to a general neglect for the 'cultivation' of the obsolescent language.

The negative flavour of loss and destruction is reflected in such frequently used terms as 'disintegration', 'decay', 'atrophy', and 'attrition' (cf. Lambert & Freed 1982, Weltens & al. 1986, Seliger & Vago 1991, and many others). While aspects of loss of linguistic skills and norms are certainly involved in such cases, we will see below that it is more than just low proficiency resulting in a 'broken' version of a once full-fledged language. At least two additional factors are found to be operative in the moulding of obsolescent language systems: contact-induced change and individual innovation (via grammaticalization, analogy, and invention of new patterns), both involving considerable achievements of linguistic creativity on the part of the speakers, not to mention the 'ludic potential', which plays a significant role under certain sociolinguistic circumstances.

Whether the traits under discussion here are justifiably considered 'typological' is a matter of the definition of 'typology'. At any rate they may be taken to define a specific type or several specific types of language systems that occur on the particular sociolinguistic conditions of language obsolescence. If it turned out that generalizations about the structure of obsolescent language systems could be made, it would be possible to posit a set of criteria for the identification of an obsolescent language system which could be helpful in manifold respects, be it as a descriptive grid for researchers in language death situations, as a guideline for the reconstruction of the historical development of languages, or as a set of criteria for the evaluation of material from a language for which only limited data is available (cf. Sasse 1992b).

Scholars working in the field of language death are generally pessimistic on the issue of universal generalizations about the structural make-up of obsolescent languages. This is reflected in a characteristic early passage by Jane Hill worth being quoted here: "An examination of UTO-AZTECAN contexts alone argues that there is not enough homogeneity in the process to justify the current emphasis on universals. Investigators of language death should be extremely suspicious of general claims about the presence or absence of particular linguistic processes in language death, since there seems to be no a priori reason for all these different situations to be accompanied by the same kinds of linguistic processes" (Hill 1983: 272).

This is certainly correct since – as often pointed out in the literature – it is the sociology and psychology behind the linguistic phenomena rather than the language system itself (not to mention its 'Universal Grammar' properties) that leads to the structural phenomena in question. Nevertheless, it is an observable fact that the general sociological and psychological background of language loss – despite all of its potential for individual developments in particular situations and the imponderables of human behaviour – leads to typologically very similar linguistic results in quite disparate cases all over the world.

This comes as no surprise. Regardless of individual political, social, or psychological peculiarities, which may result in typologically distinct manifestations of the general pattern (see below), someone who gradually replaces his/her language with a another lives in a specific sociolinguistically and psycholinguistically marked situation, which is not only different from that of the monolingual, but also from that of permanent well-balanced bilingualism. This situation often leads to a particular kind of in-group behaviour, in which the obsolescent language becomes a vehicle for special communicative purposes closely tied up with the desire of members of such a community to maintain and affirm their distinct identity to each other.

As a result of this extremely specific situation and its peculiar characteristics, certain marked linguistic patterns emerge which shape the systems into which the residual linguistic knowledge of the members of a dying speech community is moulded. It is these patterns, which are triggered by universals of human social and psychological behaviour rather than by universals of grammatical structure, that often make up the similarities between otherwise quite dissimilar cases.

2. Terminological prerequisites

Before we proceed, it is necessary to introduce a number of terminological distinctions for reference in the remainder of this article.

In terms of the languages used in a multilingual setting, we will distinguish between FIRST LANGUAGE (L_1) and SECOND LANGUAGE (L_2) on the one hand, and between PRIMARY LANGUAGE (PL) and SECONDARY LANGUAGE (SL) on the other. The distinction between L_1 and L_2 is one of order of language acquisition: L_1 is the language learned first, it is the medium in which primary socialization takes place. In certain totally bilingual situations it may be difficult to distinguish L_1 from L_2, given the fact that the child is regularly addressed in more than one language from the very outset. In such a situation, code-switching is acquired as an additional part of the bilingual's pragmatic competence (Meisel 1989).

By contrast, the distinction between PL and SL is one of proficiency; a speaker's PL is the language mastered with a higher degree of lexical, grammatical, and pragmatic competence. L_1 and PL on the one hand, and L_2 and SL on the other, may, but not necessarily do, coincide, depending on the individual conditions of language use. For example, a person may have been primarily socialized in language A but acquired a higher degree of competence in language B afterward by way of school education and/or daily interaction with monolingual speakers of B in a predominantly B-oriented community. We would then say that the pattern of this person is A = L_1/SL, B = L_2/PL.

In order to refer to the direction of contact-induced change, we will call the donor language from which a linguistic phenomenon is transferred the SOURCE LANGUAGE, and the recipient language to which it is transferred the REPLICA LANGUAGE. This pair of terms is not identical with the distinction between the two languages involved in a process of language shift, which will be called the RECESSIVE LANGUAGE and the DOMINANT LANGUAGE.

In terms of language acquisition, we will first distinguish between NORMAL LANGUAGE TRANSMISSION (NLT) and DISRUPTED LANGUAGE TRANSMISSION (DLT). NLT is defined as the regular passing-on from one generation to the next of what speakers consider to be one and the same language. This is normally achieved by the application of language transmission strategies, i.e. the entire array of techniques used by adults to assist their children in first language acquisition. In the case of DLT, this process is consciously and deliberately hindered. For further details of this distinction cf. Sasse 1992a; cf. also Thomason & Kaufman 1988. We will then distinguish between COMPLETE and INCOMPLETE ACQUISITION. Incomplete acquisition is often the result of DLT, given that the child acquires the language by simply being (more or less frequently) exposed to it rather than aided by a language-transmitting adult. Incomplete acquisition naturally results in a lower proficiency, though this is not the only source of limitations in language knowledge. Lower proficiency may also be the result of DESUETUDE, when a completely acquired L_1 falls into oblivion.

In terms of time-span covered by a process of language obsolescence we will distinguish between RADICAL DEATH (rapid language loss usually due to severe political repression) and GRADUAL DEATH (the loss of a language due to gradual shift to the dominant language in a language-contact situation). For a finer-grained typology of language death situations the reader is referred to the classical paper by Campbell & Muntzel (1989).

In terms of a typology of speakers in an obsolescent language setting, we will make a distinction between FULL SPEAKERS and SEMI-SPEAKERS. The latter term refers to 'imperfect' speakers found in situations of gradual death, not necessarily non-fluent speakers, but located somewhere on a continuum of proficiency characteristic of such situations. There is no prototypical semispeaker; rather, several types of semispeaker can be distinguished depending on their different acquisition histories. For a more detailed classification of semispeakers cf. Dorian 1977, Campbell & Muntzel 1989, Dressler 1991. A recessive language may be maintained by semispeakers over several generations. The semispeaker is thus distinguished from the TERMINAL SPEAKER (i.e. the last-generation speaker). Terminal speakers in radical death situations are often FORGETTERS (out of desuetude) rather than semispeakers.

Finally, we will introduce a number of terms for processes characteristically occurring in the situation of language obsolescence. First, we will distinguish between SIMPLIFICATION and REDUCTION. Simplification is the loss of formal complexity and redundancy, while reduction is the loss of essential or functionally necessary parts of the language.

Furthermore, we will distinguish between CONTACT-INDUCED CHANGES (externally induced changes) and INTERNALLY INDUCED changes. The necessity of this distinction for the understanding of the typological concomitants of L_1 attrition has often been pointed out (e.g. Campbell & Muntzel 1989, Seliger & Vago 1991, Sasse 1992b). Contact-induced changes are due to phenomena of transfer from L_2 as the dominant language into L_1 as the recessive language. In this case, L_1 acts as a replica language.

Three types of borrowing may be distinguished: BORROWING OF SUBSTANCE (transfer of overt markers), BORROWING OF PATTERNS (imitation of structural make-up), and NEGATIVE BORROWING (abandonment of structure and categories absent from the source language). In language obsolescence, such phenomena cannot be distinguished from the regular cases of borrowing in normal language contact situations except perhaps for their intensity; contact-induced changes usually being much more dynamic in moribund languages than in healthy ones.

3. Material loss: Simplification, reduction, and negative borrowing

As already noted in the introduction, the notion of 'loss' plays a dominant role in earlier work on obsolescent language systems. Trudgill (1977) makes extensive use of the notions of simplification and reduction, borrowed from Creolist terminology, in his discussion of ARVANITIKA, the obsolescent language of the descendants of mediaeval immigrants in Greece. He considers the speech forms used by ARVANITIKA semispeakers a 'creolization in reverse', i.e. something that starts out as a normal language, goes through a stage of creole-like simplification and reduction, and eventually disappears. Among the signs of simplification and reduction, he mentions loss of significant grammatical categories and syntactic structures (e.g. subordinative mechanisms), analytical tendency, agrammatism, and phonological and morphological instability.

Simplification has been widely discussed in relation to morphological attrition (Dorian 1978, Schmidt 1985, Dressler 1988), but also in relation to lexical shrinkage (cf. below). In morphosyntax, Ferguson (1982) distinguishes four main types of simplification: (1) polymorphemic expressions tend to become monomorphemic (loss of information is compensated by analytic constructions), (2) loss of function words, (3) highly fusional morphological systems are abandoned and replaced by isolation or agglutination, and (4) allomorphy and morphophonemic complexity is regularized.

For an early comprehensive summary of assumptions and hypotheses about the linguistic attributes of L_1 attrition cf. Sharwood Smith (1989), summarizing chiefly the works of Andersen (1982), Preston (1982), and Sharwood Smith (1983). A theoretical evaluation of linguistic aspects of L_1 attrition is also found in Seliger & Vago (1991). While the catalogs of features presented in these works are mainly based on sources dealing with L_1 loss in the emigration scenario, Campbell & Muntzel (1989) have presented evidence for typological changes in obsolescent varieties in the minority scenario, chiefly drawing on Mesoamerican languages. The results are strikingly similar.

Taken together with results from some well-investigated cases such as ARVANITIKA, EAST SUTHERLAND GAELIC (Dorian), DYIRBAL (Schmidt), BRETON (Dressler), NAHUATL (Hill), TIWI (Lee 1987), PENNSYLVANIA GERMAN (Van Ness 1990), KEMANT (Zelealem Leyew, forthcoming), and others, these studies appear to provide evidence for the universality of at least the following simplification tendencies:

(1) Loss of phonological distinctions. Especially low functional-load distinctions and contrasts non-occurring in the dominant language are abandoned (cf. Andersen 1982, Campbell & Muntzel 1989 for extensive general discussion; cf. Sasse 1985 for a detailed description of phonological loss in ARVANITIKA).
(2) Regularization of morphophonemics by analogical levelling. Almost all authors report on morphophonemic and morphological regularization: simplification of consonant mutation in BRETON (Dressler), EAST SUTHERLAND GAELIC (Dorian 1973, 1977, 1981 and later) and SHOSHONI (Miller 1971), regularization of consonant gradation in AMERICAN FINNISH (Campbell & Muntzel 1989), plural umlaut in ARVANITIKA (Sasse 1985), strong verbs in AMERICAN GERMAN (Seliger & Vago 1991), etc.
(3) Loss of function words. In attrited languages, function words are often omitted (e. g. copula, Ferguson 1982) or replaced by equivalents from the dominant language (ARVANITIKA semispeakers tend to replace almost all conjunctions and many prepositions with their GREEK equivalents).
(4) Analyticity. Complex synthetic constructions are replaced by analytic periphrastic constructions (e. g. inflected verb forms by support verb constructions as in TIWI (Lee 1987) or case forms by prepositional phrases as in AMERICAN RUSSIAN (Polinsky in press)).
(5) Isolation/agglutination. Extreme loss of morphology is almost always described for advanced attrition in cases where the language once had extensive inflectional paradigms. In TIWI, very little of the complex polysynthetic morphology has been retained. In the RUSSIAN and ARMENIAN of second and third-generation speakers in the U.S. and Canada, case inflection and verbal inflection for person tend to be minimized (Polinsky 1995, 1997, in press).
(6) Loss of syntactic complexity (e. g. subordination). This feature has become a stereotype ever since Hill (1973, on NAHUATL). It has been reported for almost all attrited varieties studied so far.
(7) Agrammatism. From ARVANITIKA semispeakers phrases such as *u sheh ti* 'I see you' (lit. 'I you-see you', for regular *të shoh*) have been recorded, combining both agrammatism and analyticity (use of independent pronouns instead of person-inflected verb form, wrong agreement). This is a common phenomenon in advanced attrition. Imperfect speakers often have a small inventory of residue word forms of a lexeme but are unable to master the entire paradigm. These residue forms are then inserted in an analytic construction like stems. Cf. CAYUGA (IROQUOIAN, Canada) (in a telephone conversation overheard August 1998): 'Evelyn gwęní:yo: gęh?' (lit. 'Evelyn am I a good speaker?', intended meaning: 'Is Evelyn a fluent speaker?').
(8) Phonological and grammatical instability (variability). Speakers of attrited varieties often show variation (both within the same speaker and across speakers) where there once was a categorial rule. For phonological variability in ARVANITIKA and KEMANT cf. Sasse (1992b). Instability is often rooted in a speaker's individual acquisition history.
(9) Reduction of vocabulary. This has been reported for all attrited languages and is a consequence of several converging factors in the situation of obsolescence: stylistic shrinkage, limited domains of use, limited exposure, imperfect acquisition, and perhaps others.
(10) Increase in lexical ambiguity. This feature was pointed out by many researchers on attrition in the past (cf. Sharwood Smith 1989 for a review). The availability of fewer items lead to extreme semantic extension of those that are retained so that one word may stand for a great variety of concepts where there once was differentiated vocabulary. Zelealem Leyew found this a significant concomitant of vocabulary loss in KEMANT; I have made similar observations in ARVANITIKA and CAYUGA.

Several items on this list are strongly reminiscent of a set of features usually said to be characteristic of aphasic speech. The relationship between language attrition and pathological speech has been addressed repeatedly (Menn (1989), Dressler (1991), Sasse (1992a & b), among others), but detailed research is yet to be carried out. Sasse's characterization of semispeaker speech as 'pathological' is perhaps too strong, given the innovative potential that has come to light recently (cf. the following sections).

Dressler compares features of semispeaker BRETON and aphasic varieties of the same language and points out that some of them are very similar, others less so. There are certainly some fundamental differences between semispeaker speech and aphasic speech. First, simplification in one area may lead to complication in another (Campbell & Muntzel 1989: 189), thus giving rise to structural reorganization, an option that remains inaccessible to the aphasic. An example is the reorganization of aspect stems in terminal CAYUGA, which are put together suppletively from different derivations (e. g. instead of the regular imperfective of the simplex still used by elder speakers, younger speakers may use the imperfective of the causative or the distributive, which results in entirely new, very complex, and sometimes individual morphological classes).

Furthermore, the only compensation strategy available to an aphasic patient is prevarication, while the bilingual with L_1 attrition is always able to draw on L_2.

This leads us to the question of contact-induced change and borrowing (→ 115). Are the typological changes observed in language obsolescence really always due to 'imperfectness'? It should not be overlooked that the vast majority of the available studies on L_1 attrition (both in the immigration and in the minority context) worked with ENGLISH as L_2, PL, dominant and source language. A good deal of the alleged analyticity and tendency toward isolation may be due to contact-induced influence in the form of negative borrowing from ENGLISH, as already pointed out by several authors.

By contrast, ASIA MINOR GREEK became agglutinative on the TURKISH model but does not show any tendency toward isolating structure even in its very final phase. ARVANITIKA, being in contact with inflectional GREEK, may show signs of agrammatism in its semispeaker varieties, but nevertheless remains inflectional. As for the loss of grammatical categories, the influence of negative borrowing must be taken into account carefully. The abandonment of grammatical categories in the replica language that the source language does not possess is a common phenomenon in language contact.

'Pathological' reduction can be accredited only to those cases where the source language provides comparable categories and yet their replica function is not exploited in the attrited language. It is only these cases that lead to severe expression deficits. Such reduction may indeed result in typologically very marked patterns in that there is loss of rudimentary means of expression to a degree considered 'illicit' in normal languages (e. g. zero negation, i. e. systematic ambiguity between affirmative and negative expressions with certain verbs in obsolescent BERBICE DUTCH (Silvia Kouwenberg, p. c.), or the total loss of aspect and tense distinction in certain forms of semispeaker ARVANITIKA reported by Trudgill (1977)). But such cases are apparently rare and do not normally occur when the language is still in use.

4. Material gain: Borrowing of substance and patterns

It is commonplace in the literature on language contact that the loss of existing categories and syntactic patterns is usually paralleled by the introduction of new categories and patterns in the replica language on the model of the source language, given the tendency for structural isomorphism between languages in contact. This is particularly the case when a recessive language is under extreme sociocultural pressure from a dominant one and collective bilingualism prevails for a sufficient period of time.

To cite just a few examples from my own experience (cf. Sasse 1971), several SEMITIC languages have independently developed a copula where there was once simple juxtaposition of subject and predicate nominal. ARABIC and NEO-ARAMAIC dialects in southeastern Turkey cliticize the copula to the predicate noun just as all the surrounding languages do. CYPRIOTE MARONITE ARABIC places it between the subject and the predicate noun after the model of GREEK (Newton 1964). In all known cases the copula is developed from the independent personal pronouns, exploiting an earlier (perhaps universal) practice of optionally using anaphoric pronouns in resumptive function as a pronominal copy of the topical subject (cf. ENGLISH *My father, he's an engineer*).

Moreover, the SEMITIC languages of Anatolia have developed an entire set of tense-aspect-mood prefixes parallel to that used by neighboring languages, in part borrowed, and in part developed from auxiliaries. KARAIM, an obsolescent Turkic language spoken in Poland and Lithuania, has acquired Balto-slavic syntax and gender markers. ASIA MINOR GREEK is often cited as one of the most spectacular examples of heavy contact-induced change after a long period of cultural oppression, which changed its entire morphological type from inflectional to agglutinative, including total restructuring of morphosyntactic categories and borrowing of grammatical morphemes (Thomason & Kaufman 1988).

Sharwood Smith (1989: 188−9) and Seliger & Vago (1991: 7 ff.) have pointed to the fact that phenomena very similar to those described for cases of prolonged language contact occur with bilingual individuals in the case of L_1 attrition. Imperfect speakers of immigrant languages in the U.S. copy rules for agreement, tag question, word order, and preposition stranding from ENGLISH. Schmidt (1985, 1991) shows that, among other things, word order, agreement, and subordinate clause structure are borrowed from ENGLISH into the semispeaker version of DYIRBAL, an obsolescent Australian language. Campbell & Muntzel (1989: 190−1) report that non-first generation speakers of AMERICAN FINNISH permit agentive phrases (on the model of the ENGLISH *by* phrases) with erstwhile impersonal verb constructions not allowing the specification of an agent in normal Finnish because they equate these constructions with the ENGLISH passive. Many obsolescent languages develop perfect systems for the morphological integration of loanwords from the dominant language (cf. Sasse 1992b: 69).

It should be added that in spite of all this borrowing of structure one sometimes finds astonishing resistance against foreign influence in certain specific areas. Not only are categories that are not matched in the dominant language often retained, but Nancy C. Dorian also reports that word-order control is remarkably intact among semispeakers of East Sutherland Gaelic, and Annette Schmidt states that in DYIRBAL the purposive inflection and the conjugation contrast are maintained. ARVANITIKA semispeakers often control the functional contrast between active and middle voice/passive surprisingly well, even though it is different from the comparable categories of GREEK; the Arvanitic pattern even persists into the GREEK varieties spoken by former ARVANITIKA speakers for at least one generation.

5. Creative processes

Among the factors that might conspire to facilitate or inhibit language loss Sharwood Smith (1983) mentions the 'ludic potential', i. e. the playing with language. Bilinguals very often enjoy the conscious manipulation of their bilingual resources, and particularly so when the recessive language takes on an in-group function.

Ample anecdotic evidence for this comes from my own experience with semispeakers of ARVANITIKA and AROMUNIAN in Greece during the sixties and seventies, when the languages were more widely used. On the occasion of family gatherings, drinking sessions, and similar in-group events, ARVANITIKA and AROMUNIAN semispeakers often displayed an incredible linguistic inventiveness drawing on traditional sources such as names, rhymes, conventional phraseology, and 'funny words' known as stereotypes in the community. Even children who were otherwise almost monolingual in GREEK appeared to enjoy the cozy in-group atmosphere created by the activation of the poetic and phatic potential of the recessive language and used to join in making up little 'maccaronic' stanzas, exploiting virtually everything their limited knowledge of the language made available to them. For further examples and considerations along these lines cf. Tsitsipis (1981, on ARVANITIKA).

While most of this 'ludic' manipulation of the language in the narrower sense is ad hoc, semispeakers who use the language more often than others frequently show a related but more stable type of inventiveness in that they compensate for gaps in their knowledge of the traditional system by inventing their own grammatical patterns to which they usually stick with great vigour throughout their lifetimes (cf. Dorian's publications for a number of examples).

Given the lack of normative correction, it is not unusual to observe the emergence, in a very short space of time, of a number of family, mini-group or even individual 'lects', leading to considerable grammatical divergence among the population of the entire group. For example, on the Six Nations Reserve in Ontario it has become commonplace that of the three dozen or so speakers of CAYUGA who still use the language on a more or less regular basis each one has his or her own dialect.

We therefore have to conclude that there is considerable creativity even in the final stage of a language's existence, resulting in entirely new individual grammatical patterns, provided that the language continues to be spoken by at least a small in-group with a separate identity.

The role of linguistic creativity in the situation of obsolescence is particularly stressed in Dorian (1999). For example, inherited derivational devices may be exploited to compensate for gaps in lexical knowledge. The young German-Hungarian bilinguals of Oberwart (Austria) draw on certain high-frequency word-formation processes to supply lexical innovations where conventional lexical items are missing from their repertoire (Gal 1989). Note that such a practice is likely to have been interpreted as a process of 'overgeneralization' (i. e. of 'attrition') by earlier researchers (see e. g. Preston 1982).

It is possible that the agglutinative character of the derivational suffixes of the HUNGARIAN verb facilitates their analogical extension, as Dorian suggests. Nevertheless, the same observations can be made in cases of highly fusional languages. Zelealem Leyew (forthcoming) reports similar phenomena for KEMANT, a recessive language of Ethiopia (side by side with immediate borrowing from AMHARIC, the dominant language). In addition, terminal speakers of CAYUGA are fairly versatile in combining derivational prefixes and suffixes with a small number of inherited stems and roots to create new words.

Creativity may go far beyond the extension of traditional material. Dorian (1999) mentions three as yet unpublished reports on innovative processes during language obsolescence, where new grammatical material has developed within only a few decades by means of re-analysis and rapid grammaticalization: (1) development of focus markers from erstwhile nominal case endings (JINGULU, Australia; data supplied by Rob Pensalfini); (2) unusually rapid grammaticalization of serial verbs (TARIANA, Brazil; data supplied by Sascha Aikhenvald); (3) emergence of an entire set of new verbal inflections for person via reanalysis of post-verbal clitic pronouns (POMATTERTITSCH, a German dialect in Northern Italy; data supplied by Silvia Dal Negro). Polinsky (in press) found that a new case system has developed in AMERICAN RUSSIAN by reinterpreting the accusative as a dative and using prepositional phrases for the rest of the oblique cases.

A further, though less spectacular, case from my own experience may be added. In a certain regional variant of ARVANITIKA, the endings of the 1st and 3rd persons singular present *-ënj* and *-ën* (but not that of the 2nd person *-ën*) − originally restricted to a certain verb class − have been extended to a great number of verbs, especially those with zero person endings and umlaut in the 2nd and 3rd persons. Thus, standard ARVANITIKA *marr/merr/merr* 'I/you/he-she-it take(s)' has become *marrënj/merr/merrën*. The result is a threefold distinction of person in the present singular, something which has never occurred in the recorded history of ALBANIAN and which runs counter to the tendencies of ALBANIAN as a whole. Note that *-ënj* and *-ën* were not originally inflectional endings for person, but stem-forming suffixes.

A further group of innovative processes that have been reported for the speech of semispeakers in different parts of the world may be subsumed under the general rubric of 'hypercorrection'. Campbell & Muntzel mention the 'overuse of typical phonemes' (1989: 188−9): 'things that are marked or 'exotic' from the point of view of the dominant language' are overgeneralized. The authors adduce examples from the Guatemalan language XINCA, where semispeakers use glottalized consonants with much greater frequency than appropriate for the healthy version of the same language.

According to traditional lore, this would again have to be taken as just another instance of imperfect learning. It is very clear, however, that hidden behind those 'hog-wild' overgeneralizations is the conscious attempt to preserve the distinct characteristics of the obsolescent language. During my research on ARVANITIKA in Boeotia, I have frequently observed that conservative ARVANITIKA semispeakers (especially those connected with culture-preserving activities such as folk singers, etc.), use [x] in front of e instead of the common [ç] which is adopted from the GREEK allophonic pattern (e. g. [xerə] 'time' for [çerə]). The reason for this is quite clear: the original sound, still remembered from the speech of very old speakers, was the frictionless glottal continuant [h], something which an L$_1$-GREEK-based speaker is not able to pronounce anymore. The choice falls on [x] because the occurrence of the allophone [ç] before front vowels is automatic in GREEK, hence the occurrence of [x] in this environment breaks the rules of GREEK phonology and is therefore suitable as a strong mark of un-GREEK phonology.

The phenomenon described is thus clearly an instance of re-introduction of a 'foreign' pattern into the phonology of ARVANITIKA after a phase of almost complete assimilation of the phonology of ARVANITIKA to the

GREEK phonological model during a stage where the language was still 'healthy' but subject to extensive language contact. (For a detailed account of the different stages of ARVANITIKA-GREEK phonological convergence cf. Sasse 1985.). This is a specific type of hypercorrection which can also be observed with certain semispeakers of CAYUGA who tend to overuse the nasalized ǫ instead of o because the former is considered characteristic of the language.

A closely related phenomenon at the morphological level is what I have termed 'phantasy morphology', i.e. the pleonastic use of suffixes considered 'typical' (cf. Sasse 1992b with examples from ARVANITIKA und KEMANT). All these phenomena must be regarded as counter-reactions against the influence of the dominant language in an attempt to preserve the 'distinctness' of the recessive language after heavy contact-induced change.

6. Language intertwining

From a typological point of view, the most spectacular outcome of language obsolescence is language intertwining, i.e. the emergence of 'mixed' languages, which combine entire subsystems from different languages and thus bring up the question of genetic affiliation.

Language intertwining has been the subject of much recent research (e.g. Bakker & Mous 1994, Thomason 1997). The commonest pattern is 'morphology (bound affixes as well as function words) from language A + vocabulary (content word stems) from language B' (MEDIA LENGUA: QUECHUA morphology + SPANISH vocabulary; MA'A or MBUGU: BANTU morphology + CUSHITIC (or otherwise non-BANTU) vocabulary; ANGLO-ROMANI: ENGLISH morphology + ROMANI vocabulary). Other subsystem divisions are also attested (MITCHIF: nouns from FRENCH, verbs from CREE; MEDNYJ (Copper Island) ALEUT: ALEUT vocabulary and noun morphology + RUSSIAN verb morphology). The following examples from ANGLO-ROMANI and MITCHIF may suffice here to demonstrate these types of mixture:

> ANGLO-ROMANI (ROMANI elements in italics):
> Once *apre* a *chairus* a *Rommany chal chor*ed a *rani chillico*
> 'Once upon a time a Romani fellow stole a lady bird (= turkey).' (Boretzky & Igla 1994: 50)

> MITCHIF (CREE elements in italics)
> *giː-ša:pu-st-a:na:n* lɨ rũ d
> 1PAST-pass-go-1pl.excl the circle of
> pɔrt *ši-piːstɪkweː-ja:hk*
> door COMP-enter-1pl.EXCL
> 'We walked through the archway to come in.' (Bakker & Papen 1996: 316)

The recent increase in the interest in language intertwining was stimulated by Thomason & Kaufman (1988), who claim that at least some of these cases can be explained as the result of the transfer (borrowing) of the complete morphology from the dominant language to the recessive language under heavy social pressure. A different interpretation (codeswitching with "flipping of the matrix language") was given by Myers-Scotton (1992 and later).

Both explanations have not gained great acceptance among specialists of mixed languages. All authors of the contributions to Bakker & Mous (1994) agree that these languages are neither the result of extensive morphological borrowing nor the result of codeswitching.

It stands to reason that none of these cases has developed by means of normal continuous language transmission. Rather, all of them are probably consciously developed ingroup languages, now or once spoken side by side with normal varieties of one of the two languages that have contributed to the mixture. GYPSY languages are in-group languages by definition. MITCHIF has a strong in-group character among the Métis (descendants of a Fench-Cree mixed population in the U.S. and Canada). Peter Bakker (1994: 28) explains the creation of MITCHIF as an attempt by people of mixed blood to form "a new group with a new identity". Evgenij Golovko (1994: 118) characterizes MEDNYJ ALEUT as a language game, a secret code, whose invention was guided by the "aspiration of a group of people for a separate identity".

We have to conclude, then, that the creation of mixed languages is a further extension of the ludic potential which the multilingual situation offers and which is particularly exploited to meet a want for an identity-marking in-group code. Language intertwining is not necessarily connected with obsolescence, but it may occur in such situations as an attempt of the moribund language community to preserve its linguistic identity by creating a phoenix from the ashes. In such cases language intertwining is an example of "language birth" as in the case of pidginization and creolization (Ferguson 1982), but typologically quite distinct from the latter.

7. References

Aikhenvald, Alexandra Y. Forthcoming. "Areal Typology and Grammaticalization: The Emergence of New Verbal Morphology in an Obsolescent Language". In: Gildea, Spike (ed.). *The Interference between Comparative Linguistics and Grmmaticalization Theory: Languages of the Americas.* Amsterdam: John Benjamins.

Andersen, Roger W. 1982. "Determining the Linguistic Attributes of Language Attrition". In: Lambert, R. & Freed, B. (eds.), 83–118.

Bakker, Peter. 1994. "Michif, the Cree-French Mixed Language of the Métis Buffalo Hunters in Canada". In: Bakker, Peter & Mous, Maarten (eds.), 13–33.

Bakker, Peter & Mous, Maarten (eds.). 1994. *Mixed Languages. 15 Case Studies in Language Intertwining.* (Studies in language and language use, 13.) Amsterdam: IFOTT.

Bakker, Peter & Papen, Robert A. 1996. "Michif: A Mixed Language Based on Cree and French". In: Thomason (ed.), 295–363.

Boretzky, Norbert & Igla, Birgit. 1994. "Romani Mixed Dialects". In: Bakker, Peter & Mous, Maarten (eds.), 35–68.

Brenzinger, Matthias (ed.). 1992. *Language Death. Factual and Theoretical Explorations with Special Reference to East Africa.* (Contributions to the sociology of language, 64.) Berlin/New York: Mouton de Gruyter.

Campbell, Lyle & Muntzel, Martha C. 1989. "The Structural Consequences of Language Death". In: Dorian, Nancy C. (ed.), 181–196.

Dal Negro, Silvia. 1998. "Spracherhaltung in der Beiz – Das Überleben von der Walsersprache zu Pomatt/Formazza". *Wir Walser* 36: 13–16.

Dorian, Nancy C. 1973. "Grammatical Change in a Dying Dialect". *Language* 49: 413–438.

Dorian, Nancy C. 1977. "The Problem of the Semi-Speaker in Language Death". In: Dressler, Wolfgang U.. & Wodak-Leodolter, Ruth (eds.). *Language Death* (= IJSL 12), 23–32.

Dorian, Nancy C. 1978. "The Fate of Morphological Complexity in Language Death". *Language* 54: 590–609.

Dorian, Nancy C. 1981. *Language Death: The Life Cycle of a Scottish Gaelic Dialect.* Philadelphia: Univ. of Pennsylvania Press.

Dorian, Nancy C. 1999. "The Study of Language Obsolescence: Stages, Surprises, and Challenges". To appear in: *Langues et Linguistique/Languages and Linguistics,* vol.1, no.2.

Dorian, Nancy C. (ed.). 1989. *Investigating Obsolescence. Studies in Language Contraction and Death.* (Studies in the Social and Cultural Foundations of language, 7.) Cambridge: Cambridge Univ. Press.

Dressler, Wolfgang U. 1972. "On the Phonology of Language Death". *Proceedings of the Chicago Linguistic Society* 8: 448–457.

Dressler, Wolfgang U. 1988. "Language Death". In: Newmeyer, Frederick J. (ed.). *Linguistics: The Cambridge Survey.* Vol. 4: Language: The Sociocultural Context. Cambridge: Cambridge Univ. Pr., 184–191.

Dressler, Wolfgang U. 1991. "The Sociolinguistic and Patholinguistic Attrition of Breton Phonology, Morphology, and Morphonology". In: Seliger, Herbert W. & Vago, Robert M. (eds.), 99–112.

Ferguson, Charles A. 1982. "Simplified Registers and Linguistic Theory". In: Obler, Loraine K. & Menn, Lise (eds.), *Exceptional Language and Linguistics.* (Perspectives in neurolinguistics, neuropsychology and psycholinguistics.) New York: Academic Pr., 49–68.

Gal, Susan. 1989. "Lexical Innovation and Loss: The Use and Value of Restricted Hungarian". In: Dorian, Nancy C. (ed.), 313–331.

Golovko, Evgenij V. 1994. "Copper Island Aleut". In: Bakker, Peter & Mous, Maarten (eds.), 113–121.

Hill, Jane H. 1973. "Subordinate Clause Density and Language Function". In: Corum, Claudia (ed.). *You Take the High Node and I'll Take the Low Node.* Chicago: Chicago Linguistic Society, 33–52.

Hill, Jane H. 1983. "Language Death in Uto-Aztecan". *International Journal of American Linguistics* 49: 258–276.

Hyltenstam, Kenneth & Obler, Loraine K. (eds.). 1989 *Bilingualism Across the Lifespan. Aspects of Acquisition, Maturity, and Loss.* Cambridge: Cambridge Univ. Press.

Lambert, Richard D. & Freed, Barbara F. (eds.). 1982. *The Loss of Language Skills.* Rowley/MA: Newbury House Publishers

Lee, Jennifer. 1987. *Tiwi Today: A Study of Language Change in a Contact Situation.* (= Pacific Linguistics Series C, No. 96.) Canberra: Dept. of Linguistics, ANU.

Meisel, Jürgen. 1989. "Early Differentiation of Languages in Bilingual Children". In: Hyltenstam, Kenneth & Obler, Loraine K. (eds.), 13–40.

Menn, Lise. 1989. "Some People Who Don't Talk Right: Universal and Particular in Child Language, Aphasia, and Language Obsolescence". In: Dorian, Nancy C. (ed.), 335–345.

Miller, W. 1971. "The Death of Language or Serendipity Among the Shoshoni". *Anthropological Linguistics* 13: 114–20.

Myers-Scotton, Carol. 1992. "Codeswitching as a Mechanism of Deep Borrowing, Language Shift, and Language Death". In: Brenzinger (ed.), 31–58.

Newton, Brian. 1964. An Arabic-Greek Dialect. In: Austerlitz, Robert (ed.). *Papers in Memory of George C. Pappageotes* (supplement to Word 20), 43–52.

Pensalfini, Rob. Forthcoming. "Case Suffixes as Discourse Markers in Jingulu." *Australian Journal of Linuistics.*

Polinsky, Maria. 1995. "Cross-Linguistic Parallels in Language Loss". *Southwest Journal of Linguistics* 14: 87–124.

Polinsky, Maria. 1997. "American Russian: Language Loss Meets Language Acquisition". In: Browne, Wayles et al. (eds.). *Annual workshop on Formal Approaches to Slavic Linguistics.* Ann Arbor: Michigan Slavic Publications, 370–407.

Polinsky, Maria. In press. "A Composite Linguistic Profile of a Speaker of Russian in the U.S." To appear in: Kagan, Olga & Rifkin, Benjamin (eds.), *Slavic Languages and Cultures: Toward the 21th Century.* Bloomington/IN.

Preston, D. 1982. "How to Lose a Language". *Interlanguage Studies Bulletin* 6.2: 64–87.

Sasse, Hans-Jürgen. 1971. *Linguistische Analyse des arabischen Dialekts der Mhallamiye in der Provinz Mardin (Südosttürkei).* Ph.D. Diss. München.

Sasse, Hans-Jürgen. 1985. "Sprachkontakt und Sprachwandel: Die Gräzisierung der albanischen Mundarten Griechenlands". *Papiere zur Linguistik* 32: 37–95.

Sasse, Hans-Jürgen. 1992a. "Theory of Language Death". In: Brenzinger, Matthias (ed.), 7–30.

Sasse. Hans-Jürgen 1992b. "Language Decay and Contact-Induced Change: Similarities and Differences". In: Brenzinger, Matthias (ed.), 59–80.

Schmidt, Annette. 1985. *Young People's Dyirbal. An Example of Language Death from Australia.* (Cambridge studies in linguistics: Suppl. vol.) Cambridge: Cambridge Univ. Press.

Schmidt, Annette. 1991. "Language Attrition in Boumaa Fijian and Dyirbal". In: Seliger & Vago (eds.), 113–124.

Seliger, Herbert W. & Vago, Robert M. 1991. "The Study of First Language Attrition: an Overview". In: Seliger, Herbert W. & Vago, Robert M. (eds.), 3–15.

Seliger, Herbert W. & Vago, Robert M. (eds.). 1991. *First Language Attrition.* Cambridge: Cambridge Univ. Press.

Sharwood Smith, Michael A. 1983. "On Explaining Language Loss". In: Felix, Sascha & Wode, Henning (eds.). *Language Development at the Crossroads.* (Tübinger Beiträge zur Linguistik.) Tübingen: Narr, 49–69.

Sharwood Smith, Michael A. 1989. "Crosslinguistic Influence in Language Loss". In: Hyltenstam, Kenneth & Obler, Loraine K. (eds.), 185–201.

Thomason, Sarah Grey (ed.). 1996. *Contact Languages. A Wider Perspective.* (Creole language library, 17.) Amsterdam & Philadelphia: Benjamins.

Thomason, Sarah Grey & Kaufman, Terrence. 1988. *Language Contact, Creolization, and Genetic Linguistics.* Berkeley: Univ. of California Press.

Trudgill, Peter. 1977. "Creolization in Reverse: Reduction and Simplification in the Albanian Dialects of Greece". *Transactions of the Philological Society* 1976-7: 32–50.

Tsitsipis, Lukas D. 1981. *Language Change and Language Death in Albanian Speech Communities in Greece: A Sociolinguistic Study.* Ph. D. Diss. University of Wisconsin-Madison.

Van Ness, Silke. 1990. *Changes in an Obsolescing Language: Pennsylvania German in West Virginia.* (Tübinger Beiträge zur Linguistik, 336.) Tübingen; Narr.

Weltens, Bert & de Bot, Kees & van Els, T. 1986. *Language Attrition in Progress.* (Studies on language acquisition, 2.) Dordrecht: Foris.

Zelealem Leyew. *Unpublished Kemant Materials.*

Hans-Jürgen Sasse,
University of Cologne (Germany)

119. 'Tote' Sprachen

1. Einteilungsprinzipien für die Sprachen der Welt
2. Der aktualgenetische Parameter
3. Geschichte der biologischen Metaphern für Sprachen
4. Traditionssprachen
5. Traditionssprachen unter aktualgenetischem Aspekt
6. Latein als lebende Sprache
7. Latein in der Kommunikationskrise
8. Latein als 'tote' Sprache
9. Namenkundliches
10. Griechisch als lebende und 'tote' Sprache
11. 'Tote' Sprache und moderne Wissenschaft
12. Zitierte Literatur

1. Einteilungsprinzipien für die Sprachen der Welt

Die Vielschichtigkeit dessen, was wir „eine Sprache" zu nennen gewohnt sind, und dazu die in der Welt vorfindliche Vielfalt an Sprachen erlauben eine Gliederung derselben nach mehreren möglichen Gesichtspunkten oder Parametern, wie etwa

- *quantitativ*: nach Sprecherzahl und Präsenz in der modernen Welt;
- *kulturell*: nach dem Grad des Ausbaus durch Verwendung zusätzlicher Medien (Pfeifen, Trommeln, Schrift) und der Intensität ihrer Nutzung;
- *kulturgeschichtlich*: nach dem diachronen Profil, d.h. der Länge ihrer geschichtlichen Überlieferung aufgrund von Schriftzeugnissen;
- *genealogisch*: nach ihrer Verwandtschaft aufgrund historisch bedingter Ähnlichkeiten;
- *typologisch*: nach ihren strukturellen Ähnlichkeiten und Unterschieden;
- *aktualgenetisch*: nach den Voraussetzungen ihres Seins, d.h. der Art ihres Zustandekommens.

In der zünftigen Linguistik herrschen das genealogische und das typologische Prinzip vor, und zwar ersteres im 19. und zu Beginn des 20. Jh.s, letzteres in der neueren Zeit. Das aktualgenetische Prinzip, das in diesem Artikel verwendet wird (vgl. § 2.), weist den Mangel auf, dass es den Einbezug subjektiver Gegebenheiten, nämlich Zufälle unseres Wissens bzw. Nichtwissens, erfordert, was seine Tragweite begrenzt. Es ist jedoch geeignet, die Besonderheiten herauszuheben, die die metaphorisch als 'tot' bezeichneten Sprachen charakterisieren.

2. Der aktualgenetische Parameter

Während sowohl die typologische als auch die genealogische Linguistik Sprachen in ihrer *Kannphase* untersucht, indem sie von Sprechern/Hörern ausgeht, die ihre Sprache bereits normal beherrschen, befaßt sich die aktualgenetische Linguistik ontogenetisch mit der *Lernphase*, d.h. mit der grundsätzlichen Erwerbsweise, die für die betreffende Sprache gilt, und phylogenetisch mit deren *Zustandekommen*, d.h. mit dem, was man (sei es als gewöhnlicher Sprachteilhaber, sei es als Linguist) über ihren „Lebenszyklus" weiß bzw. nicht weiß.

2.1. Beginn und Ende von Sprachen

Sprachen sind gekennzeichnet durch Kontinuität ihres Funktionierens als Kommunikationsverfahren über viele Generationen hinweg. Voraussetzung hierfür ist eine festgefügte Gemeinschaft von Sprechern/Hörern sowie darüber hinaus — angesichts begrenzter Lebenszeit des einzelnen Menschen — ständiger Vollzug individueller Spracherwerbsprozesse; wir haben dafür den Begriff *Stafettenkontinuität* (Lüdtke 1980: 4; 1997: 65). Die in die Sprachgemeinschaft hineinwachsenden Kinder haben das Bewusstsein, dieselbe Sprache zu sprechen wie ihre Eltern (und/oder sonstigen Bezugspersonen) sowie die Angehörigen ihrer *peer-group*. Die Stafettenkontinuität der Sprachen ist invariant nicht nur gegenüber den Lebensschicksalen (Geburt und Tod) der Individuen, sondern auch gegenüber Sprachwandel, d.h. allmählichen Strukturveränderungen des betreffenden Kommunikationsverfahrens, die wegen ihrer Langsamkeit und ihrer Geringfügigkeit im Vergleich zur Spannweite der Variation der Performanz des einzelnen Menschen (Lüdtke 1980: 184f.) selten direkt wahrgenommen werden. Stafettenkontinuität und das zeitgenössische Bewusstsein, dieselbe Sprache zu sprechen wie die jeweiligen älteren und jüngeren Sprachteilhaber, sind invariant sogar gegenüber historischen Änderungen des betreffenden Sprachnamens (z.B. Angelsächsisch/Mittelenglisch/Neuenglisch oder Latein/Italienisch);

diese beruhen auf kulturpolitischen Maßnahmen (unten §§ 8–9) oder Ereignissen und betreffen kulturelle Überformungen von Sprache, wie etwa Schrift, eventuell auch Standardisierungen der „verwalteten" Sprache und der öffentlichen Rede, lassen jedoch die Kontinuität der sprachlichen Alltagskommunikation unberührt.

Damit ist auch impliziert, dass „eine Sprache" im normalen, unmarkierten Fall keinen erleb- oder erkennbaren Anfang hat; sie ist eben – als in einer sich ständig reproduzierenden Gemeinschaft funktionierendes Kommunikationsverfahren – „immer schon da gewesen". Desgleichen lässt sich normalerweise auch kein Ende ausmachen: jede Sprache ist für sich genommen sozusagen auf immerwährendes Funktionieren angelegt. Sprachwandel (im Sinne allmählicher Strukturänderung) tut dabei nichts zur Sache, denn er belässt das sprachliche System in labilem Fließgleichgewicht (Homöorhese, vgl. Lüdtke 1980: 14 f.). Weder Beginn noch Ende zu haben, ist also im Kommunikationsgeschehen der Normalfall: wir sprechen hier metaphorisch von „lebenden" Sprachen. Daneben gibt es freilich Sonderfälle (vgl. § 2.2.–4.).

2.2. Aussterben („Sprachtod")

Bricht die Stafettenkontinuität einer lebenden Sprache ab, so sprechen wir vom Aussterben derselben (→ Art. 118). Ursache kann das physische Zugrundegehen der gesamten Sprachgemeinschaft sein (Katastrophen, Völkermord; vgl. Dressler 1988: 1551) oder aber der Kontakt mit einer expandierenden Sprache, der dazu führen kann, dass im Lauf der Zeit alle Sprecher/Hörer die zweite, weiter verbreitete und höher bewertete Sprache gelernt haben und nur diese an ihre Nachkommen weitergeben.

In der Praxis kann der Verzicht auf Weitergabe der sozial unterlegenen Sprache durchaus allmählich erfolgen, indem zwei oder gar mehrere Generationen diese zunächst immer unvollständiger erlernen (Dressler 1988: 1552–54) und immer weniger Anlass haben, sie zu verwenden, bis sie schließlich irgendwann ganz in Vergessenheit gerät. In dem Fall wird also das übliche Umschalten (e. *code-switching*) zwischen den beiden Sprachen immer seltener praktiziert. Etwas anders liegt der Sachverhalt bei Dia- oder Soziolekten, die so wenig vom überlegenen Sprachsystem abweichen, dass wechselseitige Verständlichkeit herrscht, also gar kein Umschalten nötig ist. In solchem Fall kann das unterliegende System sich in dem dominierenden allmählich auflösen (Lüdtke 1998b: 21–23).

In der oben geschilderten Weise der Nichtweitergabe an die Nachkommen sind in Europa zahlreiche Sprachen des römischen Reiches (u. a. Etruskisch, Oskisch-Umbrisch, Messapisch, Dakisch, Gallisch) vom Latein, andere vom Englischen (Kornisch) und Deutschen (Polabisch, Slovinzisch) verdrängt worden. Wir sprechen hier von ausgestorbenen (e. *extinct*) Sprachen (fr. *langues éteintes*), die mit den metaphorisch 'toten' (e. *'dead'*, fr. *'mortes'*) nicht verwechselt werden dürfen (siehe § 2.4).

Zu den Modalitäten des Aussterbens vgl. Dressler (1988: 1551–63 mit zahlreichen Literaturhinweisen).

2.3. Sprachbeginn

Wenn einerseits ab und an Sprachen durch Aussterben ihren Lebenszyklus beenden und andererseits keine Sprachen einen Anfang nehmen, d. h. neu zustande kommen, muß sich die sprachliche Vielfalt in der Welt irreversibel verringern. Auf den ersten Blick scheint das auch tatsächlich der Fall zu sein, denn im Pazifik, in Nordasien, Afrika und Amerika sind derzeit Tausende von Sprachen von baldigem Aussterben bedroht, und selbst in Europa scheint sich eine Entwicklung anzubahnen, die im Laufe des dritten Jahrtausends zur Verdrängung aller oder der meisten Sprachen durch das Englische führen kann; im Sprachverhalten der Menschen sowie in der Kulturpolitik sind die Weichen jedenfalls überwiegend in diese Richtung gestellt.

Diese Entwicklungsrichtung ist jedoch nicht als Universale vorgegeben, sondern sie beruht eindeutig auf der Industrialisierung. Für die Jahrtausende davor gilt sie nicht. Vielmehr führte die weiträumige Ausbreitung von Sprachen – in Europa Latein, Germanisch, Slavisch (vorher auch Keltisch) – immer zu deren Aufsplitterung in sich voneinander differenzierende Untermengen („Kladogenese"). Wenn beide Prozesse, Kladogenese und Aussterben, einander kompensierten, konnte die Zahl der Sprachen oszillierend in der gleichen Größenordnung verharren. Es brauchte also keinen Sprachbeginn zu geben; Differenzierung beinhaltet ja keinen Bruch der Stafettenkontinuität.

Dennoch verzeichnen wir Ausnahmen. Es sind dies zum einen Kreolsprachen, zum anderen (metaphorisch, und zwar mit einer sehr schlechten Metapher!) sogenannte 'tote'

Sprachen. Kreolsprachen (→ Art. 117) entstehen in einer „Stunde Null" der Sprachlosigkeit, d. h. des Fehlens einer gemeinsamen Sprache in einer plötzlich zusammengewürfelten Population unter bestimmten Rahmenbedingungen. Bei dieser Art von Sprachkontakt können die involvierten Sprachen je für sich in ihrer Stafettenkontinuität erhalten bleiben, indem nur ein Teil ihrer Sprecher von der Kommunikationskatastrophe betroffen wird, und es kann dennoch eine deutlich von den vorherigen verschiedene Drittsprache neu zustande kommen und in eigener Stafettenkontinuität weitergeführt werden. — Kreolsprachen sind also lebende Sprachen, bei denen wir zufällig von ihrem Beginn Kenntnis haben. Werden sie über viele Generationen tradiert, verlieren sich die für ihren Anfang typischen Eigenarten: sie normalisieren sich. Daher können wir gar nicht sagen, ob und gegebenenfalls welche für uns ganz unauffälligen lebenden Sprachen einmal als Kreolsprachen zustande gekommen sind.

2.4. 'Tote' Sprachen

Völlig anders verhält es sich mit den 'toten' Sprachen. Abgesehen davon, dass sie — den Kreolsprachen gleich — einen Beginn haben, unterscheiden sie sich radikal sowohl von den „normalen" lebenden und den Kreol- als auch von den ausgestorbenen Sprachen: sie sind in doppelter Hinsicht geplant, nämlich zum einen durch einen Willensakt, der sie zustande bringt, zum anderen durch einen Erwerbsprozess, der nicht spontan aufgrund eines angeborenen Dranges nach Eingliederung in die umgebende Gemeinschaft in der frühen Kindheit beginnt, sondern später einsetzt und auf rationaler Entscheidung beruht.

Bedeutsam ist außerdem die Rolle der Schrift: für die lebende Sprache ein kulturelles Akzidens, also nicht konstitutiv, ist Schrift für die 'tote' Sprache eine *condicio sine qua non*. Wenn wir von der doppelten Gegliedertheit der Sprache (fr. *double articulation du langage*) ausgehen, indem wir von „Etagen" sprechen: einer ersten, vorgeordneten, die aus Wortschatz und Grammatik besteht, und einer ihr nachgeordneten zweiten, der Lautung, so können wir bei Kultursprachen — lebenden ebenso wie 'toten' — eine zusätzliche Etage, nämlich Schrift ansetzen. Der typische Unterschied ist dann die Reihenfolge: während nämlich bei lebenden Sprachen die Schrift als nachgeordnete Instanz erscheint, als „dritte Etage", kehrt sich das Verhältnis bei der 'toten' Sprache um: das Schriftbild ist unmittelbar der ersten Etage (Wortschatz + Grammatik) zugeordnet und in seinem strukturellen Gehalt unverrückbar, wohingegen die Lautung dem Schriftbild nachgeordnet wird und — als sekundäres Artefakt — manipulierbar bleibt; m. a. W.: die Aussprache 'toter' Sprachen variiert nicht nur, sie kann auch per Dekret oder Übereinkunft „reformiert", d. h. willkürlich verändert werden. Schematisch lassen sich diese Zuordnungsverhältnisse wie folgt darstellen (mit Kursivdruck sind *Artefakte* bezeichnet):

Tabelle 119.1

Sprache	lebend	'tot'
1. Etage	{Grammatik+Wortschatz}	
2. Etage	Lautung	*Schriftbild*
3. Etage	*Schriftbild*	*Lautung*

Anhand eines konkreten Beispiels sei obiger Sachverhalt kurz illustriert. In Frankreich hat man es mit einer lebenden Sprache („Französisch") und einer 'toten' („Latein") zu tun. Für die Aussprache lateinischer Wörter gibt es (wie auch in den anderen europäischen Ländern) ein System von traditionellen Leseregeln (in Frankreich z. B. mit Endbetonung und Realisierung des Buchstabens U als /y/) und daneben ein mehr an internationalen Normen ausgerichtetes Verfahren. Das Nebeneinander von 'toter' und lebender Sprache stellt sich also wie folgt dar:

Tabelle 119.2

1. Etage	2. Etage	3. Etage
	→ CAPUT	→ /ka'pyt/ od. /'kaput/
	→ /tɛt/	→ TÊTE

Dem hier ikonisch suggerierten Begriff „Kopf" ist in der lebenden Sprache das durch den Erstspracherwerb natürlich gegebene Klangbild (Lautung /tɛt/) unverrückbar zugeordnet. In einer späteren Lernphase — als Schüler — erwirbt man dazu als Artefakt ein nachgeordnetes Buchstabenaggregat (tête). Bei der 'toten' Sprache hingegen hat es der Gymnasiast mit *zwei Artefakten* zu tun: der dem Begriff unmittelbar zugeordneten Graphie CAPUT und der dieser nachgeordneten Aussprache /ka'pyt/ oder /'kaput/.

Zu diesem systemlinguistischen Unterschied zwischen lebenden und 'toten' Sprachen gesellen sich freilich noch andere, nicht minder bedeutsame. In der primären Sozialisation durch Eltern und *peer-group* wächst man ungewollt und anfangs auch unbewusst in eine natürliche Gemeinschaft hinein und lernt spontanes Sprachverhalten. Demgegenüber bilden diejenigen, die heutzutage das Latein (in dessen verschiedensten Funktionen) handhaben, eher so etwas wie einen internationalen *Klub*, dem man sich aufgrund rationaler Entscheidung verbunden weiß. Hinzu kommt schließlich ein ontologisch bedeutsames Faktum: Eine lebende Sprache hat keine übergeordnete Instanz, durch die sie *instituiert* wird; sie ist dem Sprecher/Hörer immer schon vorgegeben, instituiert sich also selbst. Dagegen beruhen alle anderen in menschlichem Gebrauch befindlichen Zeichensysteme auf Fremdinstituierung, welche mittelbar oder unmittelbar immer durch Sprache erfolgt. Solche Fremdinstituierung gilt — wie überhaupt für gesteuert zu erlernende Fremdsprachen — auch für die 'toten' Sprachen. Ihr Erwerb setzt eine funktionierende lebende Sprache voraus. Damit rücken die real existierenden 'toten' Sprachen in die Nähe von sekundären Zeichensystemen (vgl. §§ 8.–11.).

Bevor wir diese Überlegungen weiterführen, sei hier ein Exkurs über das Zustandekommen des metaphorischen Begriffs 'tote' Sprache zwischengeschaltet.

3. Geschichte der biologischen Metaphern für Sprachen

Die Diskussion um die zwei Spracharten wird literarisch faßbar mit den Ausführungen Dante Alighieris in seinem Traktat über das Dichten in der Volkssprache (*De vulgari eloquentia* I,1, 2–3), wo es heißt:

... vulgarem locutionem appellamus eam qua infantes assefiunt ab assistentibus, cum primitus distinguere voces incipiunt; vel, quod brevius dici potest, vulgarem locutionem asserimus, quam sine omni regula nutricem imitantes accipimus. Est et inde alia locutio secundaria nobis, quam Romani gramaticam vocaverunt. Hanc quidem secundariam Greci habent et alii, sed non omnes: ad habitum vero huius pauci perveniunt, quia non nisi per spatium temporis et studii assiduitatem regulamur et doctrinamur in illa.

... Volkssprache nennen wir diejenige, welche die Kinder sich angewöhnen, sobald sie Wörter zu unterscheiden anfangen; oder kürzer gesagt: als Volkssprache bezeichnen wir diejenige, welche wir ohne Regel durch Nachahmung der Amme mitbekommen. Wir haben auch noch eine zweite Sprache, welche die Römer 'Grammatik' nannten. Solch eine zweite Sprache haben auch die Griechen sowie andere, jedoch nicht alle, denn zu ihrem Gebrauch gelangen nur wenige, weil man erst über eine lange Ausbildungszeit ihre Regeln erlernt.

Im 15. Jh. entbrennt dann ein Streit darüber, ob die alten Römer ähnlich wie die zeitgenössischen Toskaner ihre spontan erlernte Sprache nicht nur sprachen, sondern auch schrieben, oder ob sie – wie Dante ohne Überlegung angenommen hatte – zwei Sprachen besaßen, eine in früher Kindheit spontan und eine später schulmäßig erworbene, die als einzige geschrieben wurde. Im Rahmen der Diskussion, bei der es nicht zuletzt auch um die Verwendungsbereiche der beiden Sprachen („questione delle lingue"), Latein und Italienisch ging, hoben dann – wie Faithfull (1953: 280 ff.) darlegt – die Verfechter des Italienischen hervor, dass dieses die Sprache der Gegenwart, Latein hingegen die Sprache der Vergangenheit sei. Man begann in der Argumentation mit Metaphern zu operieren: die lateinische Sprache sei „tot und in den Büchern begraben" [*morta e sepolta ne' libri*], die italienische hingegen sei „lebendig" (*viva*), so 1540 Alessandro Citolini (vgl. Faithfull 1953: 281). Eine auf der Grundlage solcher Metaphorik aufgebaute, ansonsten aber durchaus vernünftige Klassifikation der damals in Italien bekannten vergangenen und gegenwärtigen Sprachen lieferte dann (vgl. Faithfull 1953: 286 f.) Benedetto Varchi in seinem *Ercolano* (zwischen 1560 und 1565, hier zitiert nach dem Mailänder Druck von 1804) I: 209–10 mit nachstehender Dreigliederung: *lingue vive* (=: die spontan erlernt werden) – *lingue mezze vive* (=: die zwar verwendet werden, jedoch nur gesteuert, mittels Büchern und/oder Unterricht gelernt werden können) – *lingue morte affatto* (=: die tatsächlich ausgestorben sind, d. h. entweder gar keine Texte hinterlassen haben oder solche, die man nicht entziffern könne; der Autor denkt hier an das Etruskische).

Mit einer solchen Einteilung, die dem Latein (und dem Altgriechischen) eine Sonderstellung zuerkannte, wäre die Argumentation wohl in rationalen Bahnen weiter gelaufen. Doch hat Varchis sachlich richtige Unterscheidung in der Folge keinen Anklang gefunden; vielmehr hat man die „halblebenden" und die „wirklich toten" in einen Topf geworfen. Und indem man nun alle Sprachen der Vergangenheit unterschiedslos als 'tot' bezeichnete, weil es vorrangig darum ging, die Besonderheit der *neueren* („lebenden") Sprachen hervorzukehren, leistete man der sich einschleichenden irrigen Meinung Vorschub, Latein sei *ausgestorben*, wo es doch in Wirklichkeit (nur eben unter anderen Namen) in Gestalt der „romanischen" Mundarten stafettenkontinuierlich bis heute fortlebt. Niemand wird wohl ernstlich behaupten, dass z. B. die Bewohner der Stadt Rom jemals Anlass gehabt hätten, ihre Sprache zugunsten einer anderen (vom wem zu übernehmenden?) aufzugeben.

4. Traditionssprachen

Es liegt nahe, bei vergleichender Betrachtung der mittelalterlichen und frühneuzeitlichen Kulturgeschichte verschiedener Völker Latein, Sanskrit und das vor-zionistische Hebräisch mit Rosén (1995: 58−61) unter einem Begriff „Traditionssprachen" zusammenzufassen. Alle drei haben nicht nur untereinander, sondern auch − das muss hinzugefügt werden − mit dem Griechischen (Kramer 1986: 135−209) und dem Arabischen gemeinsam (Versteegh 1986: 425), dass an ihnen als sprachlichen Trägern langfristige *Kulturüberlieferung* festgemacht worden ist. Nicht nur sind Großreligionen (Hinduismus, Judaismus, orthodoxes bzw. katholisches Christentum, Islam) mit der jeweiligen Traditionssprache verbunden, vielmehr dient diese gleichzeitig in hochgradig arbeitsteiligen, sozial differenzierten Gesellschaften auch der Bewahrung und Vermittlung weltlichen Sachwissens (Renou 1956: 86−132; Filliozat 1986; 20; Rosén 1995: 62−64; Sáenz-Badillos 1993: 202−09; Hunger 1978, I: 243 ff.; II: 87 ff.; Chejne 1969: 13−16 u. passim; Endress 1992: 3−152). Darüber hinaus fungieren sie − angesichts starker diatopischer Zersplitterung bei den Muttersprachen der betreffenden Bevölkerungen − als weiträumige *linguae francae* der jeweiligen Bildungseliten und in begrenztem Maße als Verkehrssprachen sowie schließlich *horribile dictu* gar als Instrumente sozialer Selektion in der Klassengesellschaft. − Traditionssprachen gründen sich auf ein kanonisches *Textkorpus*, dem ein hoher Wert beigemessen wird. Dieser beruht zunächst auf den in den Texten ausgedrückten Inhalten oder auch auf deren ästhetischer Gestaltung (stilistische Prägnanz, Versform) oder schließlich in der idealen Verbindung von beidem. Ist die Wertschätzung solcher Texte erst einmal im gesellschaftlichen Bewusstsein hergestellt, kann sie leicht auf deren sprachliche Form ausgedehnt werden; dadurch wird dann also auch diese überlieferungswürdig. Das aber tritt in dialektischen Gegensatz zum universal allgegenwärtigen, unausweichlichen, irreversiblen Sprachwandel (Lüdtke 1980: 9−14; 184−95; 205−22; 1986: 13−45; 1996: 531 f.; 537 f.; 1998a: 9−21), der von den Sprechern/Hörern ohne Absicht ständig vollzogen wird (Keller 1994: 25 ff.; 95 ff.; Lüdtke 1986: 6−7; 1996: 536; 1997: 71−81) und die ungewollte *Missachtung* tradierter Ausdrucksweisen einschließt. Aus geplantem Widerstand gegen ungeplanten Sprachwandel ergibt sich (in dialektischer Synthese) als *Novum* SPRACHLICHES TRADITIONSGUT, d. h. etwas, das aus dem unaufhaltsamen Strom des Sprachwandels künstlich herausgenommen wird. Es entsteht somit ein zusätzlicher Traditionsstrang.

Die Geschichte der verschiedenen Traditionssprachen unterscheidet sich in vielen Einzelheiten. Sollen nicht nur alte Texte überliefert, sondern zusätzlich weitere in der älteren sprachlichen Form produziert werden, kommt es über kurz oder lang zur Kodifizierung eben dieser Sprachform in Gestalt von Grammatiken (und dazu eventuell auch von Wörterbüchern). Erfolgt die Überlieferung weitgehend mündlich, wie es im alten Indien der Fall war (Masica 1991: 50−60), können die Einzelheiten der zu bewahrenden Aussprache numinosen Rang bekommen und zu einer ausgefeilten Theorie und Praxis der Phonetik Anlass geben, wie sie sich in der indischen Nagari-Schrift niederschlägt (Allen 1961: 6−8; 20 ff.; Filliozat 1986: 23). Anderwärts brauchte man die Aussprache nicht so wichtig zu nehmen: man überließ sie dem unmerklichen, ungewollten Wandel, sofern nicht irgendeine Katastrophe eintrat, wie das Aussterben des Hebräischen als spontan gesprochener Sprache (Sáenz-Badillos 1993: 112 f.; 128−35; 170 f.) oder die Kommunikationskrise im merovingischen Latein (s. u. § 7.).

5. Traditionssprachen unter aktualgenetischem Aspekt

Gemäss unseren obigen Ausführungen (vgl. § 4.) entstehen Traditionssprachen als (diastratisch/diaphasische) Register lebender Sprachen. Anders, d. h. mit Coseriu (1966: 192; 199−203 [1978: 215; 223−29]) ausgedrückt: es sind funktionelle innerhalb von historischen Sprachen: das biblische Hebräisch innerhalb der Spannweite, die von den Inschriften des ausgehenden −2. Jahrtausends bis zum heute gesprochenen Ivrit, der Staatssprache Israels, reicht; das (geschriebene und öffentlich gesprochene) Modernarabisch (Monteil 1960; 25−30) innerhalb eines historischen Komplexes, der sowohl die Sprachform des *Korans* und der *Hadith* als auch die heutigen Volksmundarten umfasst; die Werke Ciceros im Gesamtrahmen des lateinisch-romanischen Variationskontinuums, das vom Zwölftafelgesetz bis zu den heutigen romanischen Mundarten und Standardsprachen reicht; das Sanskrit innerhalb des Indoarischen; das klassische attisch-jonische Griechisch innerhalb der Spannweite vom Mykenischen bis zur modernen Dhimotikí und den griechischen Mundarten Apuliens und Kalabriens.

Im historisch einfachsten Fall behält die entstandene Traditionssprache den Status eines Registers einer lebenden Sprache; das gilt bekanntlich für Griechenland (Kramer 1986: 161 f. und passim; Hering 1987: 125) und die arabischen Länder (Monteil 1960: 25−30). Anders beim Hebräischen, dessen spontane mündliche Verwendung aufgrund stafettenkontinuierlicher Weitergabe gemäß der (laut Sáenz-Badillos 1993: 112 f.; 128−35; 170 f.) heute vorherrschenden Meinung im +2. Jh. aufgehört hat; hier wurde beim Aussterben der Spontansprache das traditionssprachliche Register in Form einer 'toten' Sprache fortgeführt, um dann schließlich um die Wende zum 20. Jh. in eine wieder entstehende lebende Sprache einzumünden (Sáenz-Badillos 1993: 269 ff.; Bar-Adon 1979: 19−25). Hingegen lebt das Indoarische bis heute stafettenkontinuierlich fort (Bloch 1934: 16−17; Masica 1991: 50−60); es hat sich in mehrere voneinander deutlich unterscheidbare Sprachen (allerdings mit Übergängen) aufgespalten, vergleichbar darin dem Latein-Romanischen. Die Verselbständigung des Sanskrit als 'tote' Sprache ist als solche evident; nur der Zeitpunkt dieses Vorgangs verliert sich im Dunkel mündlicher Überlieferung. Ganz ähnlich läge der Fall beim Latein, hätten wir nicht eine Reihe konvergierender Indizien, die uns den Prozess der Ablösung des traditionssprachlichen Registers aus dem Variationskontinuum deutlich werden lassen (vgl. § 6.).

6. Latein als lebende Sprache

Gegen −600 haben die Römer die (west)griechische Alphabetschrift wahrscheinlich durch etruskische Vermittlung kennen gelernt. Aber Schriftbesitz als solcher besagt noch nicht viel über Ausbau und Kulturniveau einer Sprache: Art und Umfang der Verwendung von Schrift ist entscheidend. So war es noch ein weiter Weg bis zu einer Traditionssprache Latein. Das Aufkommen einer lateinischen Literatur im −3. Jh. war immerhin ein erster Schritt in diese Richtung. Ein Jahrhundert später verzeichnen wir dann, was Horaz (Episteln 2.1.157) mit einem Hexameter-Vers treffend charakterisiert hat als „Graecia capta ferum victorem cepit et artes // intulit agresti Latio ..." [ein bezwungenes Griechenland bezwang den wilden Sieger und brachte die Künste in das bäurische Latium]. Doch auch der Prozess der Aneignung von Künsten und Wissenschaften brauchte seine Zeit: Rom hing noch geraume Weile am hellenischen Tropf, und Griechisch blieb für den Römer die Sprache der höheren Bildung.

Die ersten lateinischen Autoren, welche als den griechischen Vorgängern ebenbürtig erachtet wurden und deren Texte eine solche Wertschätzung erfuhren, dass sie von späteren Generationen als sprachliches Muster erwählt werden konnten, waren Cicero (106−43) und Vergil (70−19): ersterer für die Prosa, letzterer für die (Hexameter-)Dichtung. Beim Aufkommen einer Grammatiktradition (die dann für das ganze Mittelalter bestimmend werden sollte) im +4. Jh. mit Donat ist Vergil der mit Textbeispielen am meisten zitierte Autor (Holtz 1981: 118).

Den Anstoß für die Entstehung eines traditionssprachlichen Registers gab ein Lautwandel, der erhebliche morphologische Folgen nach sich zog: die Entnasalierung der (langen) Nasalvokale (die orthographisch im Wortauslaut durch -M gekennzeichnet waren). Bis dahin hatte man z. B. unterschieden zwischen

Tabelle 119.3

Nominativ	Ablativ	Akkusativ
AMICA /amīkā/	AMICA /amīkā/	AMICAM /amīkā̃/

Mit der Entnasalierung fielen die ehemals nasalen mit den gewöhnlichen, oralen Langvokalen zusammen; der Akkusativ, jetzt /amīkā/, war also nunmehr vom Ablativ /amīkā/ zwar weiterhin orthographisch, jedoch *nicht mehr hörbar* unterschieden. Der als Folge von Lautwandel in den Singularformen mehrerer

Deklinationsklassen (A/E/I/U) eingetretene Kasuszusammenfall wurde nicht etwa (was theoretisch durchaus denkbar gewesen wäre) durch Neubildungen nach der O-Deklination „repariert", vielmehr trat die Sprachgemeinschaft die „Flucht nach vorn" an, indem der Unterschied zwischen Akkusativ und Ablativ generell aufgehoben wurde. Von da an gab es im muttersprachlichen Latein nur noch fünf statt bisher sechs Kasus; Ablativ und Akkusativ waren zu einem einheitlichen „Objekts- und Präpositionskasus" vereinigt. Doch damit nicht genug: Nachdem IN CASA(M) unterschiedslos sowohl „in der Hütte" als auch „in die Hütte" bedeutete, schaffte man den formalen Unterschied zwischen Orts- und Richtungsbezeichnung völlig ab: statt QUO VADIS? und EO VADO konnte man nunmehr auch sagen: UBI VADIS? bzw. IBI VADO. Dieser Sprachgebrauch findet sich u. a. in den Inschriften von Pompeji, dessen Zerstörung durch den Ausbruch des Vesuvs im Jahre +79 uns einen *terminus ante quem* für den oben beschriebenen Sprachwandel liefert.

Die Gleichsetzung von Akkusativ und Ablativ liegt übrigens als einziger Kasuszusammenfall allen romanischen Mundarten zugrunde: nirgendwo finden wir Relikte der klassischen Unterscheidung; demgegenüber sind alle anderen Kasusunterschiede in der Romania entweder erhalten geblieben oder haben irgendwelche Spuren hinterlassen.

Für die Konstituierung einer lateinischen Traditionssprache können wir nachstehendes Szenario rekonstruieren: Die römische Bildungselite stand im +1. Jh. vor der Alternative, entweder − wie bisher − den „evolutionären Weg" (Kramer 1986: 205) zu gehen und den schriftlichen Sprachgebrauch am mündlichen auszurichten (wie es auch heutzutage in den meisten europäischen Sprachgemeinschaften üblich ist), d. h. dem natürlichen Sprachwandel ungeachtet aller Registerunterschiede auch beim Schreiben Rechnung zu tragen, oder aber: den schriftsprachlichen Gebrauch (und in Anlehnung daran auch den der öffentlichen Rede auf dem Forum) vom spontanen mündlichen *abzukoppeln*, also fortan zweierlei Grammatik (bei der Deklination fünf bzw. sechs Kasus) zu tradieren.

Wie wir wissen, wählte man letzteren Weg und begründete damit ein traditionssprachliches Register, einen neuen Traditionsstrang, nämlich eine besondere funktionelle Sprache innerhalb der historischen Sprache Latein. Damit waren die Weichen für die Zukunft gestellt. Als überlieferungswürdig geschätzt, ging das innerhalb der lebenden Sprache neu entstandene Register seinen Eigenweg: strenge Bewahrung des gesamten Flexionssystems und des Vokabulars unter Hinnahme einiger lexikalischer und syntaktischer Neuerungen. Dabei blieb die Verbindung mit dem spontanen, stafettenkontinuierlichen Traditionsstrang (der „Volkssprache") insofern gewahrt, als die Aussprache der Wörter über die Registerunterschiede hinweg identisch blieb. Man lernte als Elementarschüler also auch weiterhin, den in der frühen Kindheit spontan gelernten Lautungen − auch diatopischen Unterschieden zum Trotz − ein einheitliches, genormtes, tradiertes Schriftbild nachzuordnen und nicht etwa umgekehrt; also, um bei dem oben (§ 2.4.) gewählten Beispiel zu bleiben:

$$\text{👤} \rightarrow \left\{ \begin{array}{l} \text{/kaput/} \\ \text{/kapu/} \\ \text{/kabo/} \end{array} \right\} \rightarrow \text{caput}$$

Schema 119.4

Latein war und blieb also eine lebende Sprache, die lediglich ein traditionssprachliches Register hinzugewonnen hatte. Man war eben daran gewöhnt, ähnlich wie im heutigen Frankreich, wo sich ein spontaner *code parlé* vom in der Schule erworbenen *code écrit* abhebt, „dieselbe Sprache" mit zweierlei Grammatik zu sprechen (Koch/Oesterreicher 1990: 5−17). In Anlehnung an Fergusons Ausführungen (1959: 325 ff.; Lüdtke 1964: 205) könnte man hierfür den Ausdruck „interne Diglossie" verwenden, wenn der Diglossiebegriff nicht durch Fishman (1971: 286−88) in eine ganz andere Richtung umgebogen worden wäre, sodass bei Unkenntnis der Doppeldeutigkeit allzu leicht Verwirrung entsteht.

7. Latein in der Kommunikationskrise

In der Zeit zwischen dem ersten und dem achten Jahrhundert hat das Latein als lebende Sprache beträchtlichen Wandel erfahren, und zwar in allen Bereichen des Systems. Die meisten dieser Phänomene lassen sich mit den universalen Gesetzmässigkeiten des Sprachwandels (Lüdtke 1980: 9−14; 184−95; 205−22; 1986: 15−43; 1996: 531 f.; 537 f.; 1998a: 27−37) erklären und bedürfen keiner dilettantischen Substrat- oder Superstrat-Hypothesen. Abgesehen vom Lautwandel, der die Sprache als Gesamtheit, also unter Einschluss des traditionssprachlichen Registers, (§ 6.) betraf und unter anderem dazu führte, dass beim Zusammenfall von Lang- und Kurzvokalen („Quantitätenkollaps") die Grundlage der klassischen Versmetrik entschwand, sodass deren Fortführung nach 400 zu einer gelehrten Kunstübung verkam (Lüdtke 1991: 84−89), verschloss sich die Traditionssprache gegenüber nahezu allen entscheidenden Neuerungen der Spontansprache. So kam es zu dem Phänomen, das wir als DIACHRONISCHE SCHERE bezeichnen, d. h. einer als irreversibel hingenommenen stetigen Vergrösserung des Abstandes zwischen der Menge der stafettenkontinuierlich tradierten sprachlichen Mittel und der Menge der schulmäßig zu erlernenden Besonderheiten, deren Beherrschung für die Zugehörigkeit zur Bildungselite als unabdingbar angesehen wurde. Die diachronische Schere beinhaltete:

− für die Lernphase (s. § 2.) stetig anwachsenden Aufwand im muttersprachlichen Unterricht;
− für die Kannphase stetig zunehmende Fehlerquote bei der Produktion von Inschriften, Texten und öffentlicher Rede;
− in der „vertikalen" Kommunikation (d. h. im sprachlichen Verkehr zwischen Bildungselite und Volk), und zwar vor allem bei der Glaubensverkündung im christlich gewordenen Staat: immer größere Schwierigkeit, sich volksverständlich und dennoch grammatisch korrekt auszudrücken, ein Problem, worüber Augustin mehrfach klagt (*Enarratio in psalmum* XXXVI. III: 6; CXXIII: 8; CXXXVIII: 20; *De doctrina christiana* IV, x 24).

Zur diachronischen Schere kam im lebenden (Spät-)Latein noch ein zweiter irreversibel wirkender Faktor hinzu: die allmähliche DEGENERATION starrer phonographischer Zuordnungssysteme (Lüdtke 1993: 56−59). Wenn die tradierte Orthographie einer Sprache im Bewusstsein ihrer Sprecher/Hörer derartige Wertschätzung genießt (weil mit anderen Werten gekoppelt), dass ihre Reform undurchsetzbar wird, gerät sie auf die schiefe Bahn, weil nämlich die ihr zugeordnete Menge an Lautung gemäß einem universalen Gesetz (Lüdtke 1980: 11−14; 187−95; 1986: 14−23; 1996: 531; 1998a: 15−21) stetiger Schrumpfung unterliegt. Verkürzt und vereinfacht formuliert: Der lautliche Informationsgehalt der Wörter einer Sprache verringert sich unaufhaltsam, während gleichzeitig ihr graphischer Informationsgehalt unverändert bleiben kann (Lüdtke 2000: 27−31). Das verursacht Homonymien und führt zwangsläufig (falls keine Reformen stattfinden) dazu, dass manche Sätze der betreffenden Sprache nur noch als geschriebene verständlich sind, als gesprochene hingegen nicht mehr.

Ein französischer Pastor darf schreiben, aber nicht sagen: „Jésus est l'oint du Seigneur" [Jesus ist der Gesalbte des Herrn], weil seine Gläubigen statt *l'oint* wohl eher das gleichlautende *loin* („fern") verstehen würden; da er das wissen muss, beginge er Amtspflichtverletzung. Auch der Name des achten Monats (/u/) ist im Französischen „prekär": *août est un mois chaud* [August ist ein warmer Monat] als gesprochener Satz würde Ratlosigkeit hervorrufen, denn ein zu Beginn hörbares /uɛ … / wird natürlich als *où est …* (wo ist … ?) interpretiert. Zum Vergleich: der ähnlich gebaute Satz *janvier est un mois froid* [Januar ist ein kalter Monat] ist unanfechtbar. − Während wir es im Französischen (noch!) mit (leicht vermehrbaren) Einzelfällen zu tun haben, war die klassische chinesische Literatursprache, die erst in der Volksrepublik abgeschafft wurde und um die Mitte des 20. Jh.s an europäischen Universitäten noch als „das" Chinesische gelehrt wurde, so weit degeneriert (Fu 1997: 25−35; Lüdtke 2000: 31), dass ein geschriebener Text nicht laut vorgelesen werden konnte, wenn die Hörer ihn nicht gleichzeitig geschrieben vor Augen hatten. Yuen Ren Chao führt (1968: 120) als extremes Beispiel ein Gedicht mit sechs Zeilen zu je sechs Silben an, die allesamt /hsi/ lauten. Wer hintereinander 36 mal /hsi/ (wenngleich mit vier phonologisch relevanten Tönen) hört, versteht natürlich nichts.

Man stelle sich vor, das römische Reich bestünde bis heute und die Bewohner der gallischen Provinzen hätten nicht nur − wie es ja tatsächlich der Fall ist − ihre Spontansprache stafettenkontinuierlich bis heute fortgeführt, sondern dazu auch ihr traditionssprachliches Register von einst unverändert als solches beibehalten, also keinerlei Sprachreform durchgeführt: sie würden AUGUSTUM als /u/ aussprechen, AQUAM TIBI DABO [ich werde dir Wasser geben] als /otdu/, APIS EST HIC [die Biene ist hier] als /eɛi/ usw. Wir hätten dann in Frankreich (pardon: Gallien!) „chinesische" Verhältnisse.

Dieses Gedanken-Experiment dürfte klarstellen, dass die Grenze gesellschaftlich tolerierbarer Dysfunktionalität hier längst überschritten wäre. Reform war also unausweichlich; nur: *wer wo wann was für* Maßnahmen treffen würde, hätte natürlich kein „Vorwärtshistoriker" vorausahnen können.

8. Latein als 'tote' Sprache

Im Frankreich des 8. Jh.s war angesichts eines erheblich rascher (und vor allem mit viel stärkerer lautlicher Schrumpfung) als in den übrigen lateinischen Ländern verlaufenden Sprachwandels die sprachkulturelle Krise nicht mehr zu übersehen; die „Schmerzgrenze" war offensichtlich erreicht. Der Konflikt bestand in der Antithese zweier Werte: grammatische Korrektheit des Ausdrucks (im Sinne der traditionssprachlichen Norm) versus Erfolg der Kommunikation. Beides waren anzustrebende Ziele; eigentlich durfte keines von beiden als dem anderen nachrangig aufgegeben werden. Was also sollte geschehen, da die in Frankreich hergestellten Texte vor grammatischen Fehlern strotzten? Da das Bildungswesen ganz in Händen des Klerus lag, konnten Verstöße gegen grammatische Korrektheit nicht einfach als nebensächliche profane Angelegenheit abgetan werden, zumal sie nicht zuletzt auch sakrale Texte verunstalteten. Deshalb wurde in einer Reihe von Kapitularien Karls des Großen — wie Fleckenstein (1953: 49—53 und passim) ausführt — Ausmerzung von Fehlern in den vorhandenen und Sorgfalt in den zu schreibenden Texten angemahnt. Welchen Stellenwert man damals sprachlicher Korrektheit zuerkannte, möge nachstehender Satz aus der *Epistola de litteris colendis* zeigen (Monumenta Germaniae Historica. Legum Sectio II, Capitularia Regum Francorum, t. I, Hannover 1883, Nr. 29; 79): „... *qui Deo placere appetunt recte vivendo, ei etiam placere non negligant recte loquendo.*" [Wer bemüht ist, durch rechten Lebenswandel Gott zu gefallen, der solle auch nicht verabsäumen, ihm durch korrektes Schreiben und Sprechen zu gefallen.] Es ging um Bildungsreform, und die war für Karl den Großen ein Teil des Reformpakets, mit dem anstelle merovingischer Misswirtschaft karolingische Ordnung einkehren sollte.

Tatsache ist, dass vom ausgehenden 8. Jh. an die Texte korrekter werden. Tatsache ist außerdem, dass auf dem Konzil von Tours 813 die Bischöfe einstimmig beschlossen, die lateinischen Predigttexte sollten „offen in die (germanische oder romanische) Volkssprache 'übersetzt' werden, damit alle das Gesagte besser verstehen könnten": *ut easdem omelias quisque aperte transferre studeat in rusticam Romanam linguam aut Thiotiscam, quo facilius cuncti possint intellegere quae dicuntur* (Monumenta Germaniae Historica. Legum Sectio III, Concilia, t. II, Hannover 1906, Nr. 17, 288). Von romanischer Volkssprache war bis anhin noch nie die Rede gewesen.

Die Frage ist, wie die beiden obigen Tatsachen zusammenhängen. Was war geschehen? Wir können aufgrund der genannten und noch weiterer Indizien (Lüdtke 1991: 90—93) folgendes Szenario rekonstruieren:

Es muss realistischerweise mit Carl C. Rice (1902: 3; 7—9) und gegen W. Meyer-Lübke (1920: 120, § 99) davon ausgegangen werden, dass in merovingischer Zeit — ebenso wie vorher — beim Lesen geschriebener Texte die Wörter mit derselben Lautung versehen wurden wie beim spontanen Sprechen. Das ist eine Selbstverständlichkeit. Nur phonetisch Unbedarfte können auf die Idee kommen, Gebildete hätten in Vollzug befindlichen Lautwandel bemerkt und im Widerstand dagegen die Aussprache der Wörter unverändert bewahrt. Das widerspricht nahezu allem, was wir in heutigen Sprachen beobachten können. Lehrreich ist hier das Beispiel der Buchstabennamen, die oftmals sich nach denselben Lautgesetzen verändert haben wie die Alltagswörter (Lüdtke 1964: 14—15; 1968: 103—06) und im Englischen z. B. den *great vowel shift* mitmachen. Für das 7.—8. Jh. in Frankreich ergibt sich, dass die nachtonigen Vokale entweder zu einem einheitlichen /ə/ (schwa) eingeebnet wurden oder gar ganz entfielen und dass dadurch manche Kasusendungen mündlich nicht mehr unterscheidbar waren, woraus sich die zahlreichen einschlägigen Fehler erklären.

Wenn nun jemand auf die Idee kam, das Zuordnungsverhältnis zwischen Schriftbild und Lautung umzukehren, indem er das korrekte Schriftbild zur Richtschnur erhob und davon eine (künstlich zu schaffende) Lautung ableitete, dann konnte orthographische und grammatische Korrektheit erreicht werden. Das war nicht mehr und nicht weniger als — gemäß unserer eingangs (oben § 2.4.) gegebenen Definition — die Konversion des traditionssprachlichen Registers in eine 'tote' Sprache durch VORORDNUNG des Schriftbildes vor die Aussprache, die nunmehr als Artefakt neu geschaffen und schulmäßig tradiert werden musste. Damit wurde die Traditionssprache auch im Bewusstsein der Sprecher/Hörer von der Spontansprache abgekoppelt; sie war also nicht mehr Bestandteil der Muttersprache einer Gemeinschaft. Statt zweier Traditionsstränge (in einer und derselben Gesellschaft) gab es nunmehr deren drei:

Tabelle 119.5

SPONTAN-SPRACHE	SCHRIFT-SPRACHE	LESESPRACHE
Lautung	*Graphie*	*Graphophonie*

Für die Graphophonie, das „Lesen nach der Schrift", musste freilich erst ein praktikables Rezept gefunden werden. Wie es gelautet hat, können wir leicht rekonstruieren, da es bis heute in Frankreich befolgt wird. Gemäss der von den spätantiken Grammatikern überlieferten Formel *unicuique ... litterae accidunt tria: nomen ... figura ... potestas* (Isidor von Sevilla, *Etymologiae sive origines* I.IV, 16) wählte man für die Vokale A E I O U die Gleichsetzung von *nomen* und *potestas* (Lautwert), also /a/e/i/o/y/, für die Konsonanten die Verallgemeinerung derjenigen *potestas*, die sie im Wortanlaut hatten. In der Nordhälfte Frankreichs, wo in der Spontansprache alle Wörter auf dem letzten Vollvokal betont wurden, übertrug man dieses Prinzip der Endbetonung auf die neu zu lernende Graphophonie („Leseaussprache"); anderwärts war eine derart radikale Lösung nicht vonnöten (Lüdtke 1999: 46; 2000: 38−41).

Dieses leicht zu erlernende und zu handhabende Regelsystem musste freilich − wenn es einmal von Amts wegen in Kraft gesetzt war − mündlich verbreitet werden, da die lateinische Sprachgemeinschaft nicht über eine ausgefeilte Phonetik-Theorie und Praxis mit einschlägiger Terminologie verfügte.

Eine solche gab es dagegen im alten Indien (Pinault 1989: 304−13), und zwar offensichtlich ohne Stütze durch die Schrift. Der einschlägige Grundbegriff ist *akaṣara*, die 'Silbe', aufgefasst als „das, was nicht verloren gehen darf" und das deshalb durch ständiges Üben und Memorieren durch Generationen von Phonetikern weitergegeben wurde. Dazu passt, dass im alten Indien eine Analyse der Lautung in *distinktive Merkmale* selbständig entwickelt wurde, die in Europa unbekannt war und hier erst im frühen 19. Jh. als Folge der britischen Kolonialherrschaft und der dadurch bewirkten Kenntnis des Sanskrit importiert wurde.

Im mittelalterlichen Europa hingegen war Ausspracheregelung nur durch den Rekurs auf die Schrift möglich, und zwar in Form direkter Unterweisung von Mensch zu Mensch. Angesichts der geringen Zahl an Gebildeten und der Machtkonzentration am Hofe Karls des Großen (wo auch die Koryphäen der Geisteskultur sich aufhielten) war das offensichtlich machbar, wenngleich wir mit einer nicht unbeträchtlichen Diffusionszeit rechnen müssen. Da das Ergebnis der Sprachkulturreform (nämlich Latein als 'tote' Sprache) vorliegt und auch die Zeit ihrer Durchführung (Regierung Karls des Großen) erkennbar ist, bleibt die Frage nach ihrem Urheber. Unsere heiße Spur führt zu Alkuin (Fleckenstein 1953: 18−22; 54f.; 82; Lüdtke 1964: 20f.; Wright 1982: 104−13). Zwar liegt von ihm keine in moderner Terminologie formulierte Äußerung dergestalt vor, dass eine künstliche Leseaussprache einzuführen sei, doch kann man ein solches Prinzip implizit aus seiner Forderung ableiten, wonach die Wörter so auszusprechen seien, dass jeder Buchstabe mit seinem Lautwert (*sonus*) versehen werde: „*verba sint ... aequabiliter et leniter et clare pronunciata, ut suis quaeque litterae sonis enuntientur*" (in *De Rhetorica* 40; vgl. Halm 1863: 546). Angesichts der in der Spontansprache eingetretenen Nivellierung oder sogar des totalen Ausfalls der Nachtonvokale konnte die obige Forderung wohl als Abkehr von der Aussprachetradition vertreten werden. Dass Alkuin dabei eine Formulierung wählte, die in ihrem Schlussteil (*ut suis quaeque litterae sonis enuntientur*) über Julius Victor (vgl. Halm 1863: 441) auf Quintilians *Institutio oratoria* (I.11.4) zurückgeht, wie Banniard (1992: 363) zeigt, entspringt antiker und mittelalterlicher Traditionsbeflissenheit.

Die Instituierung des Lateins als 'tote' Sprache brachte allerdings einen gravierenden Nachteil mit sich, den Alkuin in seiner elitären Befangenheit (Banniard 1992: 334−47) offenbar übersehen (oder souverän ignoriert?) hatte: Das gemäß der (vom Papst angemahnten) *norma rectitudinis* gelehrt ausgesprochene, grammatisch korrekte und entsprechend auch stilistisch verfeinerte Latein war der breiten Masse der Gläubigen vielfach unverständlich. Das aber konnte vom Klerus nicht einfach hingenommen werden. Was die − laut Fleckenstein (1953: 119 Anm. 7) zwischen 780 und 800 erfolgten − angesichts der Autorität von König und Papst unangreifbaren Erlasse angerichtet hatten, musste in der Praxis irgendwie korrigiert werden. Da man wohl auch vorher beim Vorlesen von Texten schon mit improvisierten Verständnishilfen gearbeitet hatte, konnte man den hierfür opportunen Rückgriff auf volkssprachliche Register weiter ausbauen, ohne offen zu „zivilem Ungehorsam" aufrufen zu müssen. Nach Alkuins Tod 804 war schließlich auch daran zu denken, das „in rusticam Romanam linguam *transferre*" aus der Grauzone der Heimlichkeit herauszuholen und als OFFEN (*aperte*) zum Prinzip zu erheben. Es war also gewiss kein Zufall, dass das, was uns im nachhinein als zweiter Teil der Reform erscheint, 813 von einem Bischofskonzil und nicht vom (nunmehrigen) Kaiser ausging. Auch dass man die Übersetzung ins Deutsche (*in [linguam] Thiotiscam*), die doch seit Beginn der Mission unter Bonifacius unumgänglich gewesen sein muss, neben der umstrittenen, d.h. zuvor noch nicht autorisierten „Umsetzung" ins Romanische (was immer *transferre* in dieser Praxis im einzelnen bedeutet haben mag) ausdrücklich anführt, mag als stützende Begründung für die beschlossene Neuerung gedacht zu sehen sein.

Diese Interpretation der Fakten beinhaltet, dass die karolingische Reform kein geniales Werkstück aus einem Guss war, sondern viel eher auf *trial and error* gründete. Im übrigen konnte die Anerkennung der lebenden Volkssprache unter einem eigenen Namen neben dem nunmehr 'toten' Latein für die Durchsetzung der neuen Leseaussprache nur förderlich sein: erst jetzt war diese uneingeschränkt praktikabel.

9. Namenkundliches

Als Ableitungen von den Namen der Stadt (ROMA) und der Region (LATIUM) wurden die Adjektive ROMANUS und LATINUS als Bezeichnungen für die Sprache (LINGUA oder auch SERMO) — wie Richter (1979: 26−29), Kramer (1983: 81−8; 1998: 59−77; 91) und van Uytfanghe (1991: 115−17) gezeigt haben — ohne erkennbaren Unterschied verwendet. Das ändert sich im 9. Jh., indem allmählich dazu übergegangen wird, für die zur 'toten' gemachte Traditionssprache nur noch LATINUS bzw. adverbial LATINE (scil. LOQUI) zu gebrauchen. ROMANUS und seine Varianten (ROMANICE > *romantsch, romanz* u. ä., vgl. Kramer 1983: 88−94; 1998: 84−6; 143−62) werden dadurch frei zur Bezeichnung von Volkssprachen. Diese historische Namensverdoppelung hatte natürlich ursächlich nichts zu tun mit Wandel des Sprachsystems als Gegebenheit eines sprachgenealogischen Kontinuums. Sie findet auch — anders als der natürliche Sprachwandel — kein Gegenstück bei den anderen Sprachfamilien (Griechisch, Slavisch, Germanisch, Arabisch usw.). Im übrigen sind Sprachnamen Eigennamen: sie „tun nichts zur Sache", d.h. beinhalten nichts hinsichtlich der Beschaffenheit des bezeichneten Sprachsystems. Trotzdem kann der Wandel in der Namengebung leicht zu der irrigen Auffassung verleiten, jene oben genannten Sprachen seien „dieselben geblieben", Latein hingegen „zu etwas anderem geworden und hätte *deshalb* andere Namen bekommen", denn „Gewöhnlich glaubt der Mensch, wenn er nur Worte hört, es müsse sich dabei doch auch was denken lassen." (Goethe, *Faust* I: 2565): eine poetische Definition für Begriffsrealismus.

10. Griechisch als lebende und 'tote' Sprache

Während in Griechenland bis heute die antiken Texte mit der stafettenkontinuierlich entwickelten, spontan erworbenen Lautung versehen werden, also das traditionssprachliche Register („Altgriechisch") im Prinzip nach wie vor Bestandteil der lebenden Sprache ist (wie das geschriebene Latein bis zu Karl dem Großen, vgl. o. §§ 7−8.) und bis zur Sprachreform 1975 auch — wie Kramer 1986: 161 ff.) und Hering (1987: 125 f.) lehren — im Bildungswesen als solcher fungierte, hat im Abendland Erasmus 1528 mit seiner Schrift über die richtige Aussprache des Lateinischen und Griechischen (Kramer 1978: 108−19) eine neue Ära des Griechisch-Studiums inauguriert, indem er nach mittellateinischem Vorbild eine Graphophonie (s. § 8.) erfand, die sich ihrer Plausibilität wegen außerhalb Griechenlands durchgesetzt hat. Dadurch ist das Griechische (mit dem — expliziten oder impliziten − Zusatz „Alt-") als 'tote' Sprache instituiert, während es gleichzeitig in seiner Heimat als lebende fort existiert.

11. 'Tote' Sprache und moderne Wissenschaft

Außer ihrem rezeptiven Gebrauch in Form von Textlektüre und ihrem aktiven Gebrauch in Gestalt neu zu verfassender Texte bzw. als *linguae francae* können (lebende ebenso wie 'tote') Traditionssprachen auch als WORTMATERIAL-LIEFERANTEN für entstehende und/oder auszubauende neue Kultursprachen verwendet werden. Dieser sekundäre Gebrauch mag — historisch betrachtet − den primären ablösen, was gewöhnlich in Form zeitlicher Überlappung geschieht, d.h. die aktive Verwendung der betreffenden Traditionssprache geht im Lauf der Zeit mehr und mehr zurück, während gleichzeitig die „Steinbruch"-Funktion ihres Lexikons zunimmt. Das ist beim Sanskrit ebenso der Fall wie beim Latein: Sowohl die indoarischen als auch (wenngleich in nicht ganz so starkem Maße) die romanischen Sprachen (Lüdtke 1998: 500 ff.) weisen eine Fülle von Sanskrit- bzw. lateinischen Lehnwörtern (fr. *mots savants*, sanskr. *tatsama*) auf, die sich zumeist von den Erbwörtern (fr. *mots populaires*, sanskr. *tadbhava*) hinsichtlich ihrer graphischen und lautlichen Gestalt unterscheiden. Mit solchen *tatsamas* werden die terminologischen Ansprüche der modernen Welt befriedigt. Den zahlreichen *-graphia* und *-logia* im Westen entsprechen im (modernisierten) Sanskrit und von dorther in den neu-indoarischen Sprachen – und sogar mit offenbar ähnlich beliebiger Variation – die *-vidyā* und die *-śāstra*, freilich ohne direkten Abklatsch (z. B. heißt „Optik" *prakāśśāstra*, wörtlich 'Lichtkunde').

Die umgangssprachlichen Terminologien mögen in Einzelfällen irreführen; so ist die traditionelle indische Klassifikation ahistorisch, d. h sie berücksichtigt nur die äußere Form (Masica 1991: 64–67); danach wäre ital. port. katal. TERRA ein *tatsama*, weil es lat. TERRA unverändert entspricht. Andererseits haben manche ursprünglich gelehrten Entlehnungen aus dem Latein in romanischen Sprachen durchaus volkstümliche Konnotationen angenommen.

Bei den lebenden Traditionssprachen (Griechisch in Griechenland sowie Arabisch) ist der Vorgang der Übernahme innerhalb der historischen Sprache wenig spektakulär, weil hier weder Graphie noch Lautung chronologische Aufschlüsse geben: die Bezeichnungen für „Automobil" z. B., gr. *autokíneto,* ar. *sayyāra* (von der Wurzel *s-y-r* „fortbewegen") haben in *sprachlicher* Hinsicht nichts Modernes oder Antikes an sich. Das Hebräische andererseits fällt etwas aus dem Rahmen, indem es – obwohl doch Traditionssprache – für Begriffe der modernen Wissenschaft und Technik vielfach Anleihen bei anderen Sprachen gemacht hat (im Schulfächerkanon findet man u. a. *musika historiya fisika sport geografiya*). Das hängt natürlich damit zusammen, dass – wie Rosén (1995: 61) darlegt – die internationale Geltung des Hebräischen unter den jüdischen Schriftstellern sich in der Neuzeit lange auf den religiösen und jüdischrechtlichen Bereich beschränkte. Die Zukunft mag eine Umorientierung auf die typische semitische wurzel-interne Derivation (wie z. B. statt *filologiya: balšanut,* zu *lašon* 'Sprache', Wurzel *l-š-n*) bringen.

Im Hinblick auf ihre Funktion als lexikalische Reservoires für den Sprachausbau berühren sich 'tote' Sprachen mit LOGOGRAPHISCHEN (oder ideographischen) Schriftsystemen. Letztere (wie z. B. das chinesische) sind nämlich von vornherein *paradigmatische Wissenssysteme*, d. h. sie verkörpern sprachlich geformtes Weltwissen („gewortete Welt"), sind „syntaxneutral" (d. h. haben keine ihnen innewohnende Syntax) und sind nicht unbedingt an eine bestimmte Sprache gebunden: chinesische Logogramme werden auch in japanischem oder koreanischem Schriftkontext verwendet, und man verfügt über sie – ähnlich wie über den griechischen und den lateinischen Wortschatz – zwecks sprachlicher Bewältigung der modernen Wissenschaft und Technik (Miller 1980: 57, Neustupný 1978: 157). Wenn man nun andererseits Vollsprachen wie Latein, Griechisch, Sanskrit auf lexikalische Reservoirfunktion reduziert, werden sie ebenfalls zu paradigmatischen Wissenssystemen.

12. Zitierte Literatur

Allen, William Sidney. 1961. *Phonetics in ancient India*. (London oriental series/School of Oriental and African Studies, Univ. of London, 1.) Reprint. London: Oxford Univ. Press.

Banniard, Michel. 1992. VIVA VOCE. *Communication écrite et communication orale du IVe au IXe siècle en Occident latin*. (Collection des Etudes augustiniennes: Sér. Moyen-âge et temps modernes, 25.) Paris: Institut des Études Augustiniennes.

Bar-Adon, Aaron. ^{2}1979. *The Rise and Decline of a Dialect. A Study in the Revival of Modern Hebrew*. The Hague: Mouton.

Bloch, Jules. 1934. *L'indo-aryen du Véda aux temps modernes*. Paris: Maisonneuve.

Chao, Yuen Ren. 1968. *Language and Symbolic Systems*. Cambridge/GB: Univ. Press.

Chejne, Anwar G. 1969. *The Arabic Language. Its Role in History*. Minneapolis: University of Minnesota Press.

Coseriu, Eugeniu 1966 [1978]. „Structure lexicale et enseignement du vocabulaire". In: *Actes du premier colloque international de linguistique appliquée (26–31 octobre 1964, Nancy)*. Nancy: Annales de l'Est (Mémoire n°31), 175–217. Deutsch „Einführung in die strukturelle Betrachtung des Wortschatzes". In: Horst Geckeler (ed.). *Strukturelle Bedeutungslehre*. Darmstadt: Wissenschaftliche Buchgesellschaft, 193–238.

Dressler, Wolfgang. 1988. „Spracherhaltung – Sprachverfall – Sprachtod". In: Ammon, Ulrich & al. (eds.). *Sociolinguistics/Soziolinguistik. An International Handbook of the Science of Language and Society.* Vol. 3.2. Art. 170. Berlin: de Gruyter, 1551−63.

Endress, Gerhard. 1992. „Die [arabische] wissenschaftliche Literatur". In: Wolfdietrich Fischer (ed.). *Grundriss der arabischen Philologie.* Band III: Supplement. Wiesbaden: Reichert, 3−152.

Faithfull, R. Glynn. 1953. „The Concept of 'Living Language' in Cinquecento Vernacular Philology", *The Modern Language Review* 48: 278−292.

Ferguson, Charles A. (1959), „Diglossia", *Word* 15: 325−340.

Filliozat, Jean. 1986. „Le sanskrit et la culture générale du monde". In: Wolfgang Morgenroth, (ed.). *Sanskrit and world culture: proceedings of the 4th World Sanskrit Conference of the International Association of Sanskrit Studies, Weimar, May 23−30, 1979.* (Schriften zur Geschichte und Kultur des Alten Orients/Deutsche Akademie der Wissenschaften zu Berlin, Zentralinstitut für Alte Geschichte und Archäologie, 18) Berlin: Akademie-Verl., 17−28.

Fishman, Joshua A. (1971), „The Sociology of Language: An interdisciplinary Social Science Approach to Language in Society". In: Joshua Fishman (ed.). *Advances in the Sociology of Language.* Vol. 1. *Basic concepts, theories and problems: Alternative approaches* (Contributions to the sociology of language, 1.) The Hague: Mouton, 217−404.

Fleckenstein, Josef. 1953. *Die Bildungsreform Karls des Großen als Verwirklichung der Norma rectitudinis.* Bigge-Ruhr: Josef.

Fu, Jialing. 1997. *Sprache und Schrift für alle. Zur Linguistik und Soziologie der Reformprozesse im China des 20. Jahrhunderts.* (Arbeiten zur Sprachanalyse, 28.) Frankfurt/Main: Lang.

Halm, Carolus (1863) (ed.). *Rhetores Latini Minores.* Leipzig: Teubner.

Hering, Gunnar. 1987. „Die Auseinandersetzungen über die neugriechische Schriftsprache". In: Cazacu, Matei (ed.). *Sprachen und Nationen im Balkanraum: die historischen Bedingungen der Entstehung der heutigen Nationalsprachen.* (Slavistische Forschungen, 56.) Köln: Böhlau, 125−194.

Holtz, Louis. 1981. *Donat et la tradition de l'enseignement grammatical. Étude sur l'Ars Donati et sa diffusion (IV.−IX. siècle).* (Documents, études et répertoires.) Paris: CNRS.

Hunger, Herbert. 1978. *Die hochsprachliche profane Literatur der Byzantiner.* (Byzantinisches Handbuch; Teil 5, Bd. 1.) München: Beck.

Keller, Rudi. ²1994. *Sprachwandel. Von der unsichtbaren Hand in der Sprache.* (UTB für Wissenschaft: Uni-Taschenbücher, 1567.) Tübingen & Basel: Francke.

Koch, Peter & Oesterreicher, Wulf. 1990. *Gesprochene Sprache in der Romania: Französisch, Italienisch, Spanisch.* (Romanistische Arbeitshefte, 31.) Tübingen: Niemeyer.

Kramer, Johannes (ed.). 1978. *Desiderii Erasmi Roterodami De recta Latini Graecique sermonis pronuntiatione dialogus.* Desiderius Erasmus von Rotterdam, Dialog über die richtige Aussprache der lateinischen und griechischen Sprache. Als Lesetext herausgegeben, übersetzt und kommentiert. (Beiträge zur klassischen Philologie, 98.) Meisenheim am Glan: Hain.

Kramer, Johannes. 1983. „LINGUA LATINA, LINGUA ROMANA, ROMANICE, ROMANISCE. Studien zur Bezeichnung des Lateinischen und Romanischen", *Balkan-Archiv* 8: 81−94.

Kramer, Johannes. 1986. „Die griechische Sprache zwischen Tradition und Erneuerung", *Balkan-Archiv* 11: 121−209.

Kramer, Johannes. 1998. *Die Sprachbezeichnungen 'Latinus' und 'Romanus' im Lateinischen und Romanischen.* (Studienreihe Romania, 12.) Berlin: Erich Schmidt.

Lüdtke, Helmut. 1964. „Die Entstehung romanischer Schriftsprachen", *Vox Romanica* 23: 3−21.

Lüdtke, Helmut. 1968. „Ausbreitung der neuhochdeutschen Diphthongierung?", *Zeitschrift für Mundartforschung* 35: 97−109.

Lüdtke, Helmut 1980. (ed.). *Kommunikationstheoretische Grundlagen des Sprachwandels.* (Grundlagen der Kommunikation.) Berlin: de Gruyter.

Lüdtke, Helmut. 1986. „Esquisse d'une théorie du changement langagier". *La linguistique* 22.1: 3−46.

Lüdtke, Helmut. 1991. „Kontinuität und Innovation: zur Entstehung des Reimes in der abendländischen Dichtung". In: Tristram, Hildegard L.C. (ed.). *Metrik und Medienwechsel/Metrics and Media.* (ScriptOralia, 35.) Tübingen: Narr, 81−93.

Lüdtke, Helmut. 1993. „Theoretische und historische Bemerkungen zum Verhältnis von Mündlichkeit und Schriftlichkeit in der mittelalterlichen Romania". In: Werner, Otmar (ed.). *Probleme der Graphie.* (ScriptOralia, 57.) Tübingen: Narr, 53−61.

Lüdtke, Helmut. 1996. „Changement linguistique". In: Goebl, Hans & al. (eds.). *Kontaktlinguistik/ Contact Linguistics/Linguistique de contact.* (Handbücher der Sprach- und Kommunikationswissenschaft, 12.1.) Art. 65. Berlin: de Gruyter, 526−40.

Lüdtke, Helmut. 1997. „Sprachwandeltheorie: Erkenntnisse und Probleme". In: Huberty, Maren/ Perlick, Claudia (eds.). *Studia Historica Romanica in honorem Johannes Klare.* (Abhandlungen zur Sprache und Literatur, 90.) Bonn: Romanistischer Verlag, 61−83.

Lüdtke, Helmut. 1998. „Lateinisches Kultursuperstrat und Romanisch". In: *Lexikon der romanistischen Linguistik*, vol. VII, (Art. 481), 499−517.

Lüdtke, Helmut. 1998a. *El cambio lingüístico.* (Cuadernos de filología, 2.) Bellaterra: Universitat Autònoma de Barcelona.

Lüdtke, Helmut. 1998b. „Die Volkssprachen im mittelalterlichen und frühneuzeitlichen Europa (mit besonderer Berücksichtigung des Niederdeutschen)". In: *Niederdeutsches Jahrbuch* 121: 9−24.

Lüdtke, Helmut. 1999. „L'objectif visé par la réforme linguistique carolingienne". In: Petersmann, Hubert/Kettemann, Rudolf (eds.). *Latin vulgaire – latin tardif. Actes du Ve Colloque international sur le latin vulgaire et tardif (Heidelberg, 5–8 septembre 1997).* Heidelberg: Winter, 41–48.

Lüdtke, Helmut. 2000. „Latino vivo – Vernacolo – Lingua „morta". I precedenti dell'assetto linguistico culturale nell'Occidente (post)carolingio". In: Fusco, Fabiana/Orioles, Vincenzo/Parmeggiani, Alice (eds.). *Processi di convergenza e differenziazione nelle lingue dell'Europa medievale e moderna/Processes of Convergence and Differentiation in the Languages of Mediaeval and Modern Europe (Atti del Convegno Internazionale. Udine, 9–11 dicembre 1999).* Udine: Forum, 15–44.

Masica, Colin P. 1991. *The Indo-Aryan Languages.* (Cambridge language surveys.) Cambridge/GB: Cambridge Univ. Press.

Meyer-Lübke, Wilhelm. ³1920. *Einführung in das Studium der romanischen Sprachwissenschaft.* Heidelberg: Winter.

Monteil, Vincent. 1960. *L'arabe moderne.* (Études arabes et islamiques: Série 3, Études et documents.) Paris: Klincksieck.

Miller, Roy Andrew. 1980. *The Japanese Language.* (History and structure of languages.) Chicago: Univ. of Chicago Press.

Neustupný, J. V. 1978. *Post-Structural Approaches to Language. Language Theory in a Japanese Context.* Tokyo: Univ. of Tokyo Press.

Pinault, Georges-Jean. 1989. „Travaux à partir du corpus védique". In: Sylvain Auroux (ed.). *Histoire des idées linguistiques.* Vol. 1. Liège & Bruxelles: Mardaga, 303-330.

Renou, Louis. 1956. *Histoire de la langue sanskrite.* (Collection 'Les langues du monde', 10.) Lyon: IAC.

Rice, Carl C. 1902. The *Phonology of Gallic Clerical Latin After the Sixth Century.* Ph.D. Dissertation. Cambridge/MA.

Richter, Michael. 1979. „Latina lingua – sacra seu vulgaris?". In: Willem Lourdaux & Daniël Verhelst (eds.). *The Bible and Medieval Culture.* (Mediaevalia Lovaniensia: Ser. 1, 7.) Leuven: Presses Universitaires, 16–34.

Rosén, Haiim B. 1995. *Hebrew at the Crossroads of Cultures. From Outgoing Antiquity to the Middle Ages.* (Orbis: Supplementa, 3.) Leuven: Peeters.

Sáenz-Badillos, Angel. 1993. *A history of the Hebrew language.* (Historia de la lengua hebrea.) Cambridge/GB: Cambridge Univ. Press.

Uytfanghe, Marc van. 1991. „The consciousness of a linguistic dichotomy (Latin – Romance) in Carolingian Gaul: the contradictions of the sources and of their interpretation". In: Roger Wright (ed.). *Latin and the Romance Languages in the Early Middle Ages.* (Romance linguistics series.) London: Routledge, 114–29.

Versteegh, Kees. 1986. „Latinitas, Hellenismos, 'Arabiyya", *Historiographia Linguistica* XIII.2/3: 425–448.

Wright, Roger. 1982. *Late Latin and Early Romance in Spain and Carolingian France.* (Arca, 8.) Liverpool: Cairns.

Helmut Lüdtke, Universität Kiel (Deutschland)

120. From Latin to the Romance languages

1. General orientation
2. Selection of phenomena
3. Morphological shifts
4. Linearization in verb syntax
5. Linearization in non-verb syntax. Article
6. Univerbation. Future and conditional
7. Syntactic fixation
8. Special abbreviations
9. References

1. General orientation

The two poles of morphology and syntax represent two faces of one phenomenon: material substrate and an organizational superstructure. The syntactic dimension assures the productive combination of meaning and form. Morphology heavily depends in its development on the phonological foundation. A phonological modification, frequently also erosion, of existing morphological distinctions will provoke reorganization – reduction in scope, restoration, or new creation of categories and devices – or outright abandonment of existing functions. All of this can be observed very clearly in the transition from Latin to the Romance languages. The reorganization of Latin vowel quantities and qualities (Lausberg 1972) deeply affected the expressive potential of the existing inflectional endings. Later loss of some final consonants forced further reorganizations on the morphology. Morphological changes, such as the massive syncretism in case, gender and declension class, led to syntactic reorganizations.

The following considerations will start out from the morphological concreteness in a search for potential syntactic generalizations of the development. Phonological developments will only by mentioned where directly relevant to morphology and syntax. Syntactic change ranges over domains limited by semantic classifications and concretely staked out by lexical items: cf. the non-global behavior of bridge verbs with regard to clitic raising (→ § 7.2.3.). The present survey will thus focus on the surface of linguistic form, trying to establish common patterns across languages and through time. The accent lies on a coherent vision more than on enumerative completeness. While relevant scholarship informs the considerations, the essay does not try to provide a literature survey. Where the Romance languages impress by their considerable internal divergence and open-ended diachronic development, the Latin sketched here masks its underlying variety and difficult fluctuations between earlier and Classical Latin (cf. the entire Classicist tradition, linguistically elaborated e. g. in Pinkster 1990, much also in Calboli 1989), Vulgar Latin *lato sensu* (Coseriu 1954, Väänänen 1967, Pulgram 1950), Late Latin (E. Löfstedt 1959, B. Löfstedt 1961), Proto-Romance (Hall 1950, Dardel 1983), and Romance typology (Raible 1989). The occasional recourse to a construct of 'Medieval Romance' language, e. g. for what concerns clitic behavior, is a convenient way to refer to a common condition significantly informing the single-language diversity.

The syntactic framework used for the presentation is of minimal power, a default solution if the other dimensions, morphology, lexicon, and phonology, fail to yield an answer. The following dimensions are essential for syntactic description in this context:

(1) (a) precedence: /a > b/, e. g. *la maison*, not *maison la*
   (b) coherence, i.e. constituent formation /a − b | c/, with actual cohesion "−" and (relative) separation "|", e. g. *il ne-sait | rien*; or univerbation [NP [PARTICLE eccu] + [PRON illa]] > [NP = PRON quella]
   (c) dependency, or head and satellites: argumenthood and other lexical and structural subordinations, e. g. DO depending on V, or prep. *à* on predicate *penser*.
   (d) constructional identity: specific meaning associated with a given construction, e. g. /AUX(time x) + V$_{PPL}$/ having effect of "V in time previous to x", i. e. the compound anterior tense forms, e. g. *elles avaient dit*.

The constructs are transparent, simple, focused, and only minimally specific to syntactic problems not otherwise cognitively anchored. Two crucial additional dimensions are the lexical contribution of meaning, classificatory information, and other unpredictable, i.e. 'lexical' details, as well as the degree of implementation and grammaticalization of a mechanical device.

2. Selection of phenomena

The morphological and syntactic topics selected from the development of the Romance languages include the following:

(2) Linearization or the 'analytical' vector
   (a) Verb syntax (section 4): compound tenses; passive; and infinitival complementation
   (b) Non-verb syntax (section 5): article + N; preposition + NP (instead of case; and adverb + ADJ (gradation, quantification)

(3) Univerbation or the 'synthetic' vector (section 6): future and conditional

(4) Fixation or grammaticalization (section 7):
   (a) Rigid precendence and contiguity): /NEG > V/
   (b) Variable (contiguity): clitic formation and anchoring to Verb}
   (c) Major constituent arrangements (construction identity and typology): verb-position; verb second, displacements

None of the really new features of Romance — clitics, reorganized infinitival subordination, 'analytical' devolution of functions (compound tenses in particular; cf. Pinkster 1987) — come out of the nowhere. Latin had comparable trends and patterns, but not in the same kind of distribution or systematization. In view of the massive continuity amidst the clearly innovative features of Romance syntax, the typological split between Latin and Romance (excepting the later creole varieties) should not be deepened in the sense of a creolization hypothesis

(Thomason & Kaufman 1988, Dardel & Kok 1996).

The syntactic events and trends in (2) to (4) rest in part on the morphological developments summarized in section 3. Their relationship to syntax is usually quite evident with regard to considerable reductions and loss in nominal, pronominal, and adjectival inflection, but a relatively high degree of preservation in the verb. On a more impressionistic level, the salient phenomenological innovations of a Romance text compared to a Latin one fit into the observational categories of (5).

(5) (a) (object) clitic pronouns with V-anchoring
 (b) (in)definite articles
 (c) prepositional and positional signaling of argument function (using /V > DO/ and overt preposition marking for other arguments)
 (d) (post)initial V place in clause for a /(X) V Y Z/ pattern; (c) and (d) together yield the basic SVO appearance of most Romance languages
 (e) strict adjacency within simple constituents (anti-scrambling)
 (f) periphrastic nominal expressions (gradation, adverbs, etc.)
 (g) proliferation of different kinds of verbal periphrases
 (h) more clearly linear progression in processing order from left to right within an SVO pattern ("séquence progressive" of Bally 1944, but here not meant as an intrinsic merit of form).

At the same time, one could draw up a catalog of impressionistically stable surface features between Latin and Romance to anchor the genetic connection between the two chronological phases.

(6) (a) Pivotal role of verbal morphology for subject and tense, aspect, mood reference, with massive morphophonological continuity
 (b) Gender based subdivision of nominal elements in lexicon (with massive morphophonological continuity)
 (c) Continuity of syntactic procedures in principle, with clear differentiation in frequency and distribution.

An understanding of the development between Latin and the Romance languages requires a double perspective involving shape and analytical forces. A well rounded view is beyond the limits of this survey (still worthwhile Meyer-Lübke 1899; cf. Oesterreicher 1996a, b for a recent survey).

3. Morphological shifts

3.1. Nominal and adjectival morphology

3.1.1. Case

The five cases of Latin — nominative, genitive, dative, accusative, ablative (or six with the vocative) — suffered partial reduction in the entire Romania, and in most parts have resulted in a single caseless nominal-adjectival form for each number. The exceptions concern first Romanian, which still in its modern standard version maintains a suffix case distinction between a nom/acc (*casă* 'house', *cas-a* 'the house') and a dat/gen form (*case* 'of/for house', *case-i* 'of/for the house'; cf. below for the suffixal article). In addition, medieval Northern French and Occitan (as transmitted in their written versions) observed a different case reduction to a nominative ('cas sujet') vs. non-nominative ('cas régime') case form, e. g. OFr. (*li*) *mur-s* from Lat. (*illi*) *murus* vs. (*le*) *mur* '(the) wall' from (*illu*) *muru*, and imparisyllabic (*la*) *suer* < (*illa*) *s'oror* vs. (*la*) *serour* '(the) sister' < (*illa*) *sor'ore*. Parallel differentiations apply to plural forms. The general reconstruction of the reduction process assumes an intermediate three-case system of late spoken Latin (not documentable in the extant texts; cf. Väänänen 1967) from which both the Rumanian and the Galloromance systems could have descended. In a more elaborate, but also more controversial reconstruction, Dardel and Wüest (1993) postulate an early bifurcation of case-sensitive languages (Galloromance, Raetoromance, Dacororomance) vs. the others (Sardinian, Iberoromance, Italoromance) which would have dropped case inflection more or less in a single swoop. The complementary forces of phonological erosion (uncontested) and reduced functional rendition of inflectional case due to increasing use of prepositions (uncontested) have not been reconciled as to the primary cause of this reduction. Their cooperative effect, plus others (e. g. the modalities of the expansion of spoken Latin with concomitant imperfect learning results) will need to be recognized as contributing factors.

3.1.2. Gender and declension classes

While both of these (relatively) arbitrary subclassification devices of the lexicon constitute an important dimension of Latin-to-Romance continuity, they also underwent partial reductions of scope. The three Latin genders of masculine (*campus* 'field', *sol* 'sun'), feminine (*casa* 'hut', *pars* 'parte, side'), and neuter (*vinum* 'wine', *caput* 'head') generally continue as masculine, e. g. Span. *campo, sol, vino, cabo*) and feminine (Span. *casa, parte*). The neuter was absorbed into the masculine on the basis of phonological erosion and pre-existing formal affinities between masculine and neuter. The five Latin declension classes basically respond to different theme vowels: I in /a:/ for feminine, e. g. *casa, casa*, II in /u/ ~ /o:/ for masculine, neuter, e. g. *campus, campo, vinum, vino*, III in /Ø/ ~ /i/ ~ /e(:)/ for all genders, e. g. *sol ~ solis ~ solem ~ sole:s*, IV in /u(:)/ for masculine and neuter, e. g. *casus ~ casu:s* 'case', and V in /e:/ for feminine, e. g. *re:s* 'thing'. Inherent marginality in Latin and further phonological and morphological neutralizations brought these classes to a well demarcated set of three: the two vocalic types of Span. *casa* (FEM), *campo* (MASC), and the consonantal class with variable /e/, Span. *sol* (MASC), *cal* (FEM) 'gypsum', *puente* (MASC) 'bridge', *parte* (FEM) 'part'. Class IV coalesced with II (Span. *caso*), and class V with I (Span. *día*, but still MASC!). The local results do not always match this general pattern; yet the continuity, even though affected by lower-level adjustments, morphological analogies, and innovative solutions, remains clearly visible. The less convoluted adjectival situation in principle remains completely parallel to the nouns.

3.1.3. Maintenance of number

In all the case, gender, and morphological class reductions the semantically reinforced category of number is basically maintained. The singular-plural distinction now represents the bulk of Romance nominal inflection, unless there have been some secondary developments interfering with this segregation. Thus Span. and OFr. use /s/ as a plural marker: Span. *casa-s, campo-s, vino-s, sole-s, arte-s*, dialectally affected by variable phonetic elimination due to the orthogonal process of *s*-aspiration and/or deletion in coda position. Modern Fr. has lost this /s/ almost completely (except for *liaison*): [ry], [ã], [solɛj], etc. all SG = PL. A stable /s/ plural is still found in Port., Cat., Sard., Fr-Pr., Occ., and RRom./Dolomitic/Friulian. The so-called Eastern Romance languages (Italian and Romanian) exhibit vocalic marking for number due to the post-classical loss (and/or palatalization?) of final /s/: Ital. *campo – campi, casa – case, ponte – ponti*. The morphonological developments generally reinforce the syntactic agreement domain of number, while they eliminated case and some gender and inflection classes.

Overall, Latin nominal inflection has suffered heavy losses, but the remaining forms clearly continue their etymological base, even though sometime at a considerable distance.

3.2. Pronominal morphology

In principle, the personal pronouns form part of the nominal paradigm, and they largely follow its fate: reduction of case, reduction of gender, simplification of formal classifications, maintenance of number. The major difference concerns the multiple series coming out of the pronominal field: subject from nominative vs. object from accusative or dative; strong pronouns in NP function vs. clitics; cf. (7), (8).

(7) (a) subject, strong *moi, toi, lui, elle* (secondary from object series)
(b) subject, clitic *je, tu, il, elle* < *ego, tu, ille, illa*
(c) object, strong *moi, toi, lui, elle* < *me, te, *illui, illa*
(d) object, clitic *me, te, le, la, lui* < *me, te, illu, illa, *illui*

(8) (a) subject, strong *io, tu, egli, ella* (later: *lui, lei*) < *ego, tu, illi, illa*
(b) object, strong *me, te, lui., lei* < *me, te, *illui, *illei*

These three to four series originate from differential distribution of case forms combined with prosodic segregation according to the dynamic function of such pronouns (1st and 2nd persons) and deictics (3rd person) in the sentence context. The reduction in case forms affects the pronouns nearly as much as other nominals. While the subject form tended to be distinct at first, deriving from Latin nominatives (e. g. *ego* > Port. *eu*, Span. *yo*, Cat. *jo*, etc.) the pronominal and generally strong non-subject forms represent other cases (accusative for Ital. Fr. *me, moi* < *me*, perhaps dative for Span., Port. *mí, mim* < *mi(hi)*). In the clitics, generally only the 3rd person distinguishes DO from IO case (Latin acc. vs. dat./gen.): undifferentiated DO, IO for Span.

me, te, se, but distinct *lo, la* for clitic non-reflexive DO vs. *le* for IO. Only Romanian preserves the case distinction in the 1st and 2nd persons, in parallel with the general nominal paradigm of a nom/acc vs. dat/gen case inflection: *mă, te, se* for DO < *me, te, se* vs. *(î)mi, (î)ți, (î)și* for IO clitics fom *mi(hi), ti(bi), si(bi)*. The irregular gender, number, and case expression in Romance pronouns of all kinds is an inheritance of the Latin conditions combined with a number of unpredictable levellings and secondary differentiations; cf. any applicable handbook (e.g. Lausberg 1972: § 705−56). The pronouns cannot but follow suit and coalesce masculine and neuter, again in the form of the surviving masculine expressions. The only notable exceptions concern the neuter clitic pronouns of Cat., Occ. *ho, o* derived from an actual Latin neuter demonstrative HOC.

The generally surviving traits are thus number (SG, PL) and person (1, 2, 3); less so the case distinctions which may be have been coalesced early (clitics) or late (Fr. strong object pronouns >> strong subject pronouns). The origin of Romance pronouns are Latin pronouns (1, 2, 3 REFL) or pronominal deictics (3 non-REFL.). The Latin syntactic conditions and the morpholexical materials yield an almost faultless base for Romance pronominal manifestations. The pan-Romance formal innovation consists in the standardized morphological (and syntactic!) separation between strong and clitic pronouns, mainly for object function, sometimes also for the subject.

3.3. Verbal morphology

3.3.1. Passive

The inflectional passive/middle voice of Latin was replaced by a periphrastic arrangement. This auxiliated construction, ESSE plus past passive participle, e.g. *traditum est* 'it was/ has been reported', already had taken on the role of the perfective passive voice (perfect, pluperfect, futurum exactum, perfect and pluperfect subjunctive) yielding a ready model for expansion. The transition from anterior to simultaneous tense meaning with regard to the auxiliary verb was in part mediated by the resultative implications of an anterior passive action: it ends up in a subsequent state of affairs. The multiple transitions between action and state, previous occurrence and current situation provided the vehicle for the periphrasis (Span. *fue conde-* *corada* 'she was (not: she had been) honored') to constitute a new passive voice. However, formulaic passive expressions, especially with the rather highly marked 3 SG/PL endings in *-(n)tur*, continued in use for a long time. The typical periphrastic solution has the advantage of developing some of the many functions incorporated in the complex Latin verbal ending onto a different carrier, i.e. the famous 'analytical' tendency. In the same context, the gradual naturalization of the pronominal reflexive expression (Ital. *mi vesto ~ vestior* 'I get dressed'; *non ci salutiamo ~ non salutamur* 'we do not greet each other') hollowed out the inflectional middle/ passive which had doubled up as a reflexive and reciprocal device.

3.3.2. Future

The morphological expression of the future had a number of weak points in Latin, in addition to its falling prey to developing phonological mergers. Except for a sporadic *ero > jer, er* 'I will be' in Old French and Old Occitan, there are no direct Romance descendants of this tense. The replacement expressions derived from the modal connection of the future via a number of periphrases with *habere, debere, velle, venire*, but also *ire* and its replacements. These reached quite divergent degrees of amalgamation between the modal and the lexical infinitive; cf. below in section 6.

Further losses concern the synthetic perfect infinitive (*laudavisse*) which became periphrastic and the imperfect subjunctive (*laudarem*) replaced by the pluperfect form (*laudavissem*), eliminated from all Romance languages. The perfect subjunctive combined with the future perfect (*laudaverim* and *laudavero*) continues in older Spanish and modern Portuguese as a future subjunctive (Span. *hablare*), with a similar distribution for the pluperfect indicative (*laudaveram*) in the same function (Portuguese, dialectal and older Spanish), or as an irrealis or even past subjunctive (Spanish *hablara*).

The last categories of loss or limitation are clearly minor events in the overall Latin morphological panorama. The elimination of the passive formation, together with the introduction of compound anterior tenses, represents the more momentous effect of the transition into Romance, but still very far from jeopardizing the Latin verbal inflectional system in any serious way. The minor readjustment of the four conjugation classes (I: /a:/,

II: /eː/, III consonantal stem: /Ø, i, e(ː)/, III; *i*-stem: /i,e(ː)/, IV: /iː/) into three (/a/, /e/, /i/) seems to respond to the inevitable phonological difficulties in Spoken Latin with distinguishing II from III based on the current vocalic evolutions. The elimination of the old distinction between II and III, i. e. between /eː/ and /e/, is not even complete across the Romance languages. French, Occitan, Italian, and Romanian retain portions of distinction in different forms, mainly where the accent on the infinitive is concerned: Fr. *v'endre* vs. *val'oir* < *v'endere* III vs. *val'eːre* II. Only Romanian and Lombard dialects retain the stress differentiation in 1 PL pres.: Rom. *víndem* 'we sell' vs. *vedém* 'we see' < *v'endimus* vs. *vid'eːmus*. Overall, the Latin verbal system remained remarkably intact, with a high number of Latin forms yielding the appropriate etymological base for the Romance result.

The Romance languages can be viewed as direct, genetic descendants of the spoken forms of Latin. This is a crucial precondition for doing any serious syntactic interpretation.

4. Linearization in verb syntax

4.1. Analytic vs. synthetic

The development of the Romance languages from Latin cannot be equated with increasing analyticity, as has frequently been tried. In the overt linearization of previously inherent or inflectionally expressed functions, the new construction will be transparent within the contemporary grammar. Such an overt string may in turn lose transparency and produce new syncretisms and portmanteau events. This traditional tension between analytic and synthetic expression may ondulate through the history of a language without real predictability. At every speech phase there exists the option to update the transparency of a specific expression or construction, while other combinations become more grammaticalized. The typological divergence between the Romance future with the "synthetic" [$_V$ V_{inf} + AUX], e. g. Fr. (*elle*) *écrir* + *a*, and the 'analytical' compound tense formation [$_{V'}$ AUX + [$_V$ V_{ppl}]], e. g. (*elle*) *a écrit*, is a good example of the complications of this issue. The contrast between the devolutive trend in nominal inflection and the well-preserved inflectional richness in the verbal field is instructive. Each development should thus be viewed and evaluated in its own right.

4.2. Compound tenses

The formation of an entire series of compound tenses for anteriority is a clear-cut innovation extending a preexisting option in a natural way. The general Romance pattern /AUX + V_{ppl}/ possesses a constructional identity going beyond its simple string composition, since it puts the predicate V in a tense directly anterior to the one expressed by the auxiliary alone. So Ital. *abbiamo*$_{pres}$ *visto*$_{ppl}$ *un bel film* 'we have seen/we saw a nice movie' and *domani a questa ora sarà*$_{fut}$ *già partita*$_{ppl}$ 'tomorrow at this hour she will already have left' and *me n'ero*$_{impf}$ *andato*$_{ppl}$ *prima* 'I had gone away earlier' periphrastically modify the V with the help of an auxiliary. The origin of the anterior meaning of this construction can be found in the Latin perfective tense passives, e. g. *inventum est* 'it has been/it was found', and even more so in the deponentia, e. g. *mortua est* 'she has died' with its resultative overtone 'and thus she is now dead'. The participial form came to signal the past/anterior aspect, while the auxiliary tense retains tense reference within the domain of the simple tense. The combination yields the anterior tense, present vs. present perfect, imperfect/preterit vs. pluperfect, future/conditional vs. future/conditional perfect, and similarly for the subjunctives. The novelty of this construction with ESSE consists in its separation from the passive/middle voice meaning originally associated with the form, supported by the independent existence of the Latin deponentia with passive form, but non-passive meaning. The basic construction of the compound tense forms with relevant anterior meaning covers the entire Romània, pointing to its rather early creation in Late Latin/proto-Romance.

The choice of auxiliaries was originally pan-Romance in keeping with the double derivation of the Romance construction. The passive source contributed the auxiliary ESSE with subject agreement of the past participle, given the direct predication involved in this construction: *litterae*$_{NOM FEL PL}$ *scriptae*$_{NOM FEM PL}$ *sunt*$_{3 PL}$. The second source contained *habere* as a transitive verb supporting a secondary predication with the DO of *habere* plus the past participle, including formal agreement: *litteras*$_{ACC FEM PL}$ *scriptas*$_{ACC FEM PL}$ *habeo* "I have the letter (and it is) written" (Pinkster 1987). With a formulaic regularization of this construction, the meaning will easily slip into a direct predication with aspectual/temporal modification yielding a compound tense as applied to a transitive predicate. The two bases later on combined into a coherent construction with its own identity, claimed by some to be strongly influenced by spoken Greek in the late Empire (Coseriu 1977).

The choice between the auxiliaries *avere* and *essere* depends on a combined lexical and syntactic distribution: transitive Vs and most intransitives use *avere*, while the few 'unaccusative' and all reflexive predicates show *essere*. A frequent development modifying the auxiliary distribution shifts toward a greater importance of *habere*. Many languages have reached a stable uniformity of *habere*-only in their early modern versions: the three Iberoromance languages Portuguese (where *haver* has partially given way to *têr* < *tenere* 'to hold' in European Port.), Spanish, and Catalan, some Galloromance and Italoromance dialects, and Romanian. The single auxiliary solution is a clear indication that the compound tense pattern is a unified phenomenon, by extension also in the languages that still practice some choice (French, Occitan, Raetoromance, Sardinian, Italian). Parallel to the loss of overt auxiliary variation the agreement standard for the past particle reduces to invariability. ESSE requires obligatory subject agreement of the participle (*ils se sont trompés*), while direct object agreement with *habere* depends on the alternation of auxiliaries, and may be heavily restricted with regard to applicable structures. So modern French and Italian require or permit such agreement only with a preceding DO within the same clause (clitic or WH element), in Italian even restricted by grammatical person; cf. Fr. *il nous l_{FEM}' a écrite$_{FEM}$* vs. *il nous a écrit$_{MASC}$ cette lettre$_{FEM}$*.

4.3. Passive voice

The compound tenses are one of the two devolutions of the Latin passive expression in perfective tenses. The same Latin structure {AUX, PL} also serves the different function of the periphrastic Romance passive. The double charge of the Indo-European and Latin passive past participle permitted its divergent adaptation to passive and anterior tense meanings, in each case with singular concentration on one or the other of the coexisting features. The non-anterior reading of the passive is favored by the pragmatic ambiguity of anterior action and ensuing result, both tied to a cardinal time reference, e.g. anterior and cardinal present. The two {AUX, PPL} constructions of passive and compound tense may combine to yield an anterior tense passive: /AUX$_{AUX\ TNS}$ PPL$_{AUX\ PASS}$ PPL$_{LEX}$/, e.g. Span. *la publicación de la revista ha sido suprimida*, Ital. *la pubblicazione della rivista è stato cessata* 'the publication of the review has been suspended'. The two participial constructions cannot really enter into conflict due to the semantic restriction of passives to transitive predicates only.

4.4. Infinitival periphrasis

The proper field of free periphrastic creations in Romance concerns the infinitive. As in most other syntactic innovations, there exists an appreciable Latin foundation from which the Romance pattern directly derives. The Latin infinitive was a prime device for subordination in the typical format of the accusativus cum infinitivo (A.C.I.), a systematized version of exceptional case marking (ECM). The A.C.I. uses a lexical subject in the accusative *te* in combination with the infinitive: [$_S$ [$_S te_{ACC}$ *abisse*$_{INF}$ *hodie hinc*] *negas?*] (Plt.) 'do you deny (your) having today gone away from here?'

On the other hand, Classical Latin cannot use the infinitive introduced by a preposition, rather the gerundium or gerundivum. The prepositional infinitive appears starting in the 2nd c. CE as an extension of infinitival subordination. The reduction of the A.C.I. domain, the introduction of more verbs admitting a dependent infinitive under control, and the additional marking device of the complementizing preposition opened up a range of new construction options (Pinkster 1990, Raible 1992). All Romance languages thus inherited from Late Spoken Latin broad infinitival subordination options. As an extension of the Byzantine hegemony and reflected in the Balkan Sprachbund, Romanian and some Southern Italian dialects (parts of Calabria and the Salento), have reduced or lost the infinitive as a verbal form, leaving finite subordination as the only or at least strongly favored option.

The Romance schema generally contains the following infinitival subordination sectors. (a) Modal V + Ø + INF (*posse, debere, velle*): no complementizing particle; already standard in Latin; (b) aspectual V + (PREP) + INF (*ire, venire* 'begin', 'stop', 'repeat', 'be used to', etc.), as an innovation; causative V + INF, where Latin used finite subordination (*facere*) or also A.C.I. (*sinere*); (d) perception V + INF (*videre, audire, sentire*) instead of Lat. A.C.I. or present participle; this is a

Romance alternative using the gerund instead of the infinitive, with fine, but unstable semantic/pragmatic shading between the two). (e) Subject control verb + (PREP) + INF (*promittere*, ...), stemming from original A.C.I.; (f) object control verb + (PREP) + INF (*permittere, persuadere, iubere*) corresponding to a possible ambiguous structure between A.C.I. and control situation: *iubeo te abire* 'I order you that you should leave' vs. 'I give orders (to somebody) that you should leave'. (g) Other V with complements + (PREP) + INF with variable or no control of the subordinate subject; here group membership is open and varies across languages and time. The origin can be found in A.C.I. and also finite subordination. (h) Finally PREP + INF where various prepositions with adverbial function (*ad, de, in, cum, per, sine*) or adverbial prepositions (*post, ante*, ...) combine with the infinitive to yield non-finite adjunct clauses (time, manner, instrument, etc.); the Latin situation offered participial and finite subordination patterns.

This massive expansion of infinitial subordination is a rearrangement of the Latin options, but it was not triggered by any event in the morphological substrate. A.C.I. as ECM does not depend on the morphological expression of case, as English clearly shows (*she wants my brother to call her*). Rather, it seems to represent a formal syntactic shift driven by internal forces. The expansion is lexically and constructionally gradual; in many regards the modern Romance languages have not reached a formally clear-cut position. There is e. g. differential reaction to clitic climbing within the groups (b) and higher. In addition, differential rigidity of adjacency between the two verbs in (c) and (d) characterizes the various Romance languages. The historical trend is towards stricter adjacency, and a more systematic application for 'to cause' than 'to let', and more strictly adjacent with causatives (c) than with perception predicates (d); cf. **elle a fait Jean payer* vs. *elle a vu Jean partir*.

The major shift between Latin and Romance use of the subordinating infinitive concerns the systematic exploitation of the interpreted infinitival subject corresponding to a given context (infinitival control). Where Latin had the A.C.I. safeguard of overtly exposing the subject, the Romance pattern relies on its reconstructibility through subject or object control, based on semantico-pragmatic limitations. E. g. [SUBJ$_i$ *posse* [SUBJ$_j$ INF]] can only be interpreted if SUBJ$_j$ = SUBJ$_i$. Similar real-world restrictions limit the interpretations for *permittere* (object control) vs. *promittere* (subject control), etc. The utilization of the complementizing marker, i. e. the proposition introducing the infinitive depending on the lexical identity of the governing verb, does not become systematic. It changes through time without good motivation, it does not follow semantic or syntactic arrangements, and the different languages do not agree on the choice of a specific preposition for a given verb. Nevertheless, some preferences can be perceived, e. g. Ø for simplest modals, *a* for motion verbs and intension, *de* for separation, and as default preposition in Italian (but not in Spanish).

5. Linearization in Non-Verb Sytax. Article

The most profiled changed in NP syntax again concerns the linear stringing up of different functions. Case gave way to prepositional marking plus word order standardizations, and NP determinateness achieved visibility through the pan-Romance creation of a definite article.

Latin had no articles, either definite or indefinite. All the Romance languages have developed both of them in remarkably parallel formations, fully deployed already in the earliest Romance records. Two phenomena, a grammaticalized definite article, and a stable system of clitic object pronouns (cf. section 7.2.), identify an early text as Romance as opposed to belonging to the Latin domain. No Latin text, regardless of its pretended closeness to the spontaneous language, comes close to emulating the Romance article and clitic pronoun conditions.

The indefinite article is based on the progressively mechanized use of the numeral one, UNU/UNA, in part differentiated as an article by a clitic-specific special phonological derivation, e. g. Ital. full *una* and proclitic *na*, or *o* in Rom. from /ua/ and /una/ as opposed to the numeral *ună*.

Perhaps more interesting is the long-range morphological and functional debasing of the strong deictic *ill-* (distal demonstrative) to a true article. Its form is the cliticization (NP clisis, proclitic except for Romanian) of a demonstrative, passing from dynamically marked deixis to simple definiteness, and further down to the vague effect of a definite article. The dynamic/prosodic reduction brings with it a considerable phonological and morphological reduction, whereby the two-to-three syllable form — *ille, illu, illa, illoru* — is reduced to a single syllable, shedding the uninformative first stem syllable /il/, *lo/lu/le, la/le, lor*. Also, the long lateral consonant follows the development of the single lateral, usually /l/, rather than the geminate yielding /ʎ/. This presupposes degemination before palatalization of *-ll-*, effected by an early absorption into the string of the vowel-initial first syllable. Inevitably, the phonological development is exceptional to a certain degree. In Port. where intervocalic /l/ is generally lost while /ll/ is preserved as /l/, the article shows up as *o(s), a(s)*, with contextual variants /lo(s)/, /la(s)/ in Galician. The standard forms are thus similar to *il, lo, le* for MASC SG, *la, le* for FEM SG, *i, li, los, les* for MASC PL, and *le, las, les* for FEM PL with variants in determined phonological contexts (prevocalic, before /s+C/, etc.). Beyond some indication of the degree of definiteness, the article also signals the gender and number of the head noun in the privileged left-edge position in the NP.

Article development took place in the space of the relatively undocumented period of rapid typological change between the third and eight or ninth century. Anecdotal indications of this trend in the heavily purified Latin texts are not inconsiderable, but the degree of required interpretation removes these testimonies from the level of proof to that of suggestive hint. Consider in this context e.g. the "Gelenkspartikel" uniting N and appositive A as in *Macrobius ille Aegyptius* (Gamillscheg 1937), the many rather incongruent or superfluous uses of the demonstrative in texts such as the *Peregrinatio ad loca sancta* (4th c. CE) and the articloid appearances in a 7th c. maccaronic parody of the Lex Salica (Abel 1971, Selig 1992).

In addition to the standard result of a proclitic article, i.e. [$_{NP}$ ART [$_{N'}$ N]], Romanian developed an enclitic variety combining in its forms the definiteness indicator and, in addition to the standard gender and number features, also the remaining case markers for nom/acc. vs. gen/dat. Since morphological case in Romanian only shows up in the determiner (except for f SG gen/dat in certain declension classes), the arrangement [$_{NP}$ [$_{N'}$ N] + ART], e.g. *case-le noue* 'the new houses', comes close to a para-inflectional case/determiner system. The (marked) option of the article's post-adjectival positioning, as [$_{NP}$ [$_{N'}$ [$_{AP}$ ADJ] + ART N] *noue-le case*, indicates that linear precedence makes the article occupy a type of second position. Romanian also has recourse to a post-nominal uni-case 'genitive' or 'possessive' article. It introduces a NP complement in the genitive/dative case, *acțiuni* FEM PL NOM/ACC INDET *ale* FEM PL INV *Națiunilor* FEM PL GEN/DAT DET *Unite* FEM PL INDET 'the actions of the United Nations'. In addition Romanian knows an 'adjectival' or 'demonstrative' article determining and introducing a nominalized or otherwise prominent AP; this 'article' is preadjectival and inflects for case (*punctele cele negri și cele cenușii* 'the BLACK dots and the GREY ones'. In this situation Spanish can use the straight article forms (*los puntos negros y los grises*), while other languages have recourse to a demonstrative (Ital. *i punti neri e quelli grigi*; cf. Beyrer et al. 1987).

The Romance article derives in most languages from *ill-*. Modern Sardinian, Balearic and a handful of Catalan versions, and a few Occitan dialects still use articles representing Lat. *ips-* 'emphatic identity" with forms such as *es, su, sa, sus, sas*, etc. The medieval distribution shows considerably increased territory for *ips-*, mainly in the central Romance area The two bases were in competition within the rather amorphous Late Latin deictic system (Aebischer 1948, Selig 1992). None of the stabilized written Romance versions of the 12th and 13th c. belong to the *ips*-domain (notwithstanding the Sardinian written tradition with *(is)su, (is)sa*, etc. which started earlier and depended on different cultural conditions).

There is no question that one of the generally visible trends in the Romance evolution leads to the linear concatenation of generally free elements to express interdependent notions that Latin tried to comprise under inflection. The syntactic complexity is rather limited in the single phenomenon. Concatenation is sufficient to understand the relationship between the elements in the analytical expressions. The linearization in the verbal, nominal, and adjectival domains corresponds to a more transparent syntax. The intuitive difference between Latin and the Romance languages is a massive simplification of the morphology, and a 'straigthening out' of the syntax. Linearization of functions lies at the bottom of the clearly 'modern' cut of the Romance languages, even in their medieval varieties.

6. Univerbation.
Future and conditional

In necessary complementation of the linearizations explored in sections 4 and 5, the creation of the Romance languages also comprised new compositions taking a sequence of constituents beyond simple concatenation and making them into an opaque 'synthetic' unit.

Whatever the reason for the loss of the Latin future morphology, the concept continued to be expressible, even though essentially only by secondary predication (*habere* + gerundive for obligative modality), or by a modal periphrasis, e. g. INF + *debere, velle* (Pinkster 1987). The emphasis on the modal content of the future event, its possible, uncertain, anticipated, or forcible character, wore off the modality through extended use, letting the temporal value come to the fore again (Fleischman 1982). The first part of the development is thus another instance of linearization: [V, +fut]/future modality + lexical predicate/. So much is fully attested in Latin, starting at the latest with the familiar epistolary prose of Cicero, and continuing throughout the following less-than-formal tradition. The Romance results include four options: (i) continued compositional modal periphrasis, usually with *habere*, Span. *ha de ser verdad* 'it must be true'; (ii) specialized future formation between the lexical infinitive and special present tense forms of *habere*, with potential separation of the two parts by a clitic pronoun; e. g. OSpan. *dezir te hemos* 'we must tell you'; (iii) the same elements as in (ii), but fully amalgamated: Span. *te diremos* 'id.'; and (iv) a new linearizing periphrasis with a verb of motion, Span. *va a salir mañana* 'she will leave tomorrow'. The four classes also appear for the conditional (future of the past, and/or main clause irrealis tense) with the auxiliary in a past tense (preterit in Italian, imperfect otherwise). Options (i) to (iii) already characterize the medieval Romance language, where the 'analytical' or 'split' future (ii) is restricted to Iberoromance and Occitan. The univerbation (iii) results in an end-inflected future (or conditional) tense; any clitic will be external to this new nuclear form: (O) Span. *lo dirá*, (rarely, *dirá+lo*) 'id.'. Where the lexical verb takes on an irregular infinitive form (cf. *dir-* as compared to standard *dezir* for Medieval Castilian), this morphological irregularity only applies to the univerbated future/conditional. The 'split' future/conditional will always manifest the normal lexical format of the infinitive, *dezir lo ha*, not **dir lo ha*. The two future formations of Medieval Spanish (and the other languages concerned) are argued to be two distinct evolutionary strands (Company 1985—86). The special infinitival forms are a direct development of the new univerbated future tense (iii), in part motivated by the reduction of word stress on the infinitive, a kind of procliticization. Both constructions (ii) and (iii) are already dedicated as evidenced by the special derivation of the auxiliary forms: specially shortened clitic auxiliary forms of the present and imperfect (or preterit in Italian) of *habere*. In Span. the future 'endings' closely resemble the normal auxiliary verbs: inf. + {*(h)é, (h)as, (h)a; (h)emos/(av)emos, (av)edes/(hab)éis, (h)an*} for 1–3 SG; 1–3 PL; e. g. *hablar-é*, etc. But the conditional shows considerable discrepancies with the standard imperfect by suppressing the lexical stem entirely: *(hab)ía, (hab)íamos*, etc., e. g. *hablaría, hablaríamos*. Other languages (French, Italian) only document the newly univerbated version in their historical period. Here the new future/conditional left syntax completely behind since the earliest testimonies: cf. Fr. *(je) parler-ai, (nous) fer-ions,*, never **parler t'ai, *faire le ions*. The older modal periphrasis (i) of (Late) Latin, /*habere* + (*ad/de*) + INF/, in the more 'linear' sequence /modal + (complementizing PREP) + INF/: *aggio (a) cantá* (in part in NIt, S-Ital., Sard.), Port. *hei de cantar*. Romance type (i) /AUX + nonfinite V/ represents a syntactically open construction. Some languages, in particular Romanian, Surselvan, and Sardinian, actually never passed beyond this stage. Here we find only expressions with *habere, debere* (Sard.: *deppo kantari*), *velle* (Rom.: *voi cînta*), *venire ad* (Surselvan *jeu végnel a canta*) as modals. The so-called medieval Romance inverse conjugation (Lema & Rivero 1992) shows linear order as the univerbated solution, yet corresponds in meaning to the syntactically open modal periphrases of type (i): [v' [v nonfinite V]ᵢ[v' [AUX] Øᵢ]]. For Romanian, the "inverse conjugation" produces alternate forms (mainly of emphatic and dialectal use) with postposed auxiliary: *adormívom* "we will fall asleep", perhaps coming close to a type (ii) of the 'split' future. The reduction of syntax into more stable morphology in this future/conditional development underlines the different trends operative in the development of a language, producing an ondulating combination of linearization with univerbation.

7. Syntactic fixation

Components of a syntactic unit may retain their full independence and interchangeability with equivalent elements. Still, the two dimensions of linearization and adjacency can produce a rigid string format, e.g. concerning the article preceding its N'. Alternatively, they may lead to a variable, yet controlled, distribution, e.g. the pre- and postverbal occurrence of clitic pronouns. Finally, the surface appearance may correspond to a trend, without firm edges, as with most word order patterns for major constituents. Since new orderings are always local and constrained, there will be much interplay interplay between open and closed arrangements.

7.1. Rigid orderings

7.1.1. Negation in Latin

The negative particle NON, itself a result of pre-Latin *NE: ON- "NEG one") was only regulated by the semantic and prosodic constraints on Latin period construction. With the V in traditionally (but not unwavering) final position, negation usually was preverbal in a loose sense. It did not have a direct connection with the predicate, and it could take any constituent as its scope, usually signaled by their adjacency. *ego inquit non cotidie lavor* 'I, said he, do not bathe daily', NON can scope over *cotidie* or over the clause as a whole, i.e. being connected to the V in Romance terms. In *nec* (*nec* 'et non') *sane lavare potui* 'Nor could I possibly have bathed', the best interpretation gives negation clausal scope. The following example: *si non illam optime accepisset* 'if he had not generously taken her up' shows a presumably clitic negative particle in second position having clause scope (all examples from Petronius, *Cena Trimalchionis*, 42,1—7). In Romance, the negative particle usually derived from *non* has a firm preverbal position, separated from the V only by clitic object pronouns. The formula may thus be /NEG (cl*) V/ for a majority of the medieval and modern languages (Port., Span., Cat., Occ., Ital., Sard., Rom.), e.g. *se non l'avesse ricevuta con generosità* (cf. the last Latin example). However, French (and with it a number of Occitan dialects) practices a double negative exponence, a preverbal particle *ne* representing NON, plus a desemanticized postverbal element, standard *pas*, but also *point*, or any of the other lexical negations (*jamais, personne, rien, plus*); e.g. *s'il ne l'avait pas généreusement reçue*. Regardless of the position of the lexical negative element, the preverbal particle is required: *il n'a vu personne, personne n'est venu*. In spoken French, the double negative expression has been reduced to the essential portion, i.e. the lexical element *pas*, etc., with part phonological, part syntactic elimination of *ne*. In this way, French reached in its sponatenous modern version a post-verbal negative marking, with the fixed pattern of /(SUBJ CL) (*ne*) (OBJ CL) V *pas*/. There are further complications with the infinitive where *pas* may precede (*pour (ne) pas le faire*, but also *pour (ne) l'avoir pas su* with auxiliary V). Overall, the lexical origin of French negation produced an innovative postverbal arrangement. This situation, sometimes with different lexical materials (*punctum, *brik, non*, etc.), also characterizes Occitan, Northern Italian, Raetoromance, and even some Southern Italian dialects. Obligatorily in Surselvan, and variably in Surmeir, and in certain Northern Italian dialects again, negation may be purely postverbal, presumably after having gone through the French stages of evolution in the Jespersonian cycle: /NEG + V/ > /NEG + V + lex. NEG/ > /Ø + V + NEG/ (cf. Zanuttini 1997 on Romance negation in general.) Regardless of the verbal side it is on, the negative element is tied to the V as the semantic and syntactic point of the clause. Such negation is always interpreted as sentential in nature; the fixed place of the negative element(s) is a conventional solution protecting a potentially weak formal element from being overlooked. This is particularly important for negation which affects the meaning of the entire proposition.

7.1.2. Article

The Romance article precedes its N', except for Romanian; e.g. *l'ancien premier ministre*. Latin placed etymologically related demonstratives usually before the N, conforming to the SOV implication of /ADJ > N/. In addition to continuing the Latin situation, the Romance anteposition of the article is a functional choice for a language which does not have a regular final V typology. The left to right processing direction cannot but favor — even though not impose — the order in which the functional element precedes the lexical head. The debasing of the deictic to a simple article must have been enough to take it out of the expected reordering prediction /N > ADJ/ for the Romance SVO type and leave it prenominal as a determiner rather than adjective. The marked order /ADJ > N/ corresponds in Romance also to the marked class of very basic adjectives. (Fr. *bon, beau, grand, vieux, mauvais* etc.). The standard qualifying position for an adjective is postnominal, sometimes with possible contrast between the two arrangements. In Fr. *la blanche neige* vs. *le chocolat blanc*, where the inverse positions would carry specific implications, *la neige blanche* possibly in contrast to *la neige cendrée*, and *le blanc chocolat* as an expected form of chocolate. Given the less than determinate outcome of any such linearization, Romanian is providing the imaginable exception. The multilateral connections in the Balkan Sprachbund and the partial retention of inflectional case may have been catalytic or codetermining factors. Still, the postposition of the article does constitute one organic outcome of the Late Latin situation with double linearization options (→ § 5.).

The various linearizations in the verbal periphrases ended up in the fixed ordering of /AUX > V/ as discussed in 4.2., 4.3., 4.4. This is the logical and expected inversion compared with V final Latin, where the finite AUX counted as the real V, thus previously /V > AUX/. The result is however not uniform across constructions and periods. The univerbated future/conditional formations retain (or recreate?) the AUX-final pattern, somewhat in contradiction with regard to the remaining language. On the other hand, the compound tenses and the passive follow the expected Romance ordering. The modern languages have settled here on the invariable precedence of the auxiliary, with the exception of Sardinian (*kantau appo* 'I have sung/sang') and stylistically variable Romanian standard phenomena and dialectal presence. Yet in the medieval languages, the so-called inverted conjugation was quite frequently encountered, i.e. /V_{NONFIN} + AUX/, e.g. OSpan. *los que vencidos o ençerrados auedes* 'those which you have defeated or cornered' (13th c.). Sometimes there may even be intervening material, /V_{NONFIN} + X + AUX/, indicating thereby that the nonfinite V form had been preposed by some syntactic/stylistic device. The modern standard solution did not come into being out of necessity, but only as a secondary result of much more variable linguistic conditions.

The fixed orderings show a bundled consensus on a /modifier > head/ ordering, which thereby constitutes a defining Romance characteristic. But these are generalizations *post factum*, without predictive power, as the broader and narrower exceptions mentioned here clearly illustrate.

7.2. Variable order and adjacency

7.2.1. Clitics as a new category

Another innovation of the Romance languages is the creation of a class of homogeneous clitic object pronouns. The lexical material for the 3 PS pronouns is identical to the article coming from ILL-, and the applicable forms are also very close. Considerable energy has been spent on elucidating the synchronic functioning of clitics in modern as well as medieval Romance varieties. They represent a class of nearly homogeneous items for deictically lowest reference to internal argument functions (DO, IO). In the central Romance languages (Cat., Occ., Fr., Fr.-Pr., N-Ital, Ital., S-Ital., Sard.) two oblique relations (locative = *in, ad* + NP, and genitive/separative = *de* + NP) can be added. This set of pronouns is stable across the various languages and the centuries. The development concern first the transition from a non-descript Latin situation into the medieval Romance stable pattern. The transition took place in the absence of direct testimony, since the extant texts never record a spontaneous (very late) Latin. The clitics begin in full deployment with the first Romance texts.

Between the early texts and late medieval documentations, the clitic syntax undergoes some stabilization, even standardization depending on the writing tradition. The placement of these pronouns to the verb as anchor becomes regularized (actually, complicated in Spanish and Portguese with the 2P option), and their linearization before or after the anchor develops a stable syntactic reference frame. By the beginning of the modern linguistic phases — heralded by the advent of printing, the consumption of increasing amounts of written materials by a much enlarged readership, and the conscious preoccupation with using the vernacular language correctly, flexibly, and nobly —, the clitic pronoun system will have undergone a foundational change. The syntactic account of placement (anchoring) and linearization (proclisis, enclisis) gives way to a much flatter, morphological conception. The reanalysis is not yet complete, leaving remnants of the older situation partially intact, and thereby creating a complex phenomenon which still has not found a coherent formal analysis.

7.2.2. Clitic anchoring and linearization

A major consideration for clitics is their anchoring and linearization. In the modern languages anchoring is to the verb of the simple clause, {V, CL}, while linearization is guided by the finiteness of the verb form: either all linearizations are /CL + V/ (Fr. *Mona n'en sait rien, pour en savoir davantage*), or the nonfinite forms (and some imperatives) show /V_{NONFIN} + CL/ as opposed to the finite strings /CL + V_{FINITE}/ (Ital. *Mona non ne sa niente, per saperne di piú*). The unidirectional change from the medieval string based anchoring/linearization model is a considerable simplification of the syntactic aspects. The central portion of the medieval pattern is known as the Tobler-Mussafia condition (TM, Ramsden 1963) imposing a blockage against a clitic pronoun in clause-initial position: *[$_S$ CL-X ...]. This is a remnant of the earlier Wackernagel condition (W, Wackernagel 1892) in Latin, according to which clitic elements were preferentially found in sentential second position: [$_S$ X-CL...]. TM requires "Second Position" (2P) if the clitic would otherwise fall into initial position, but in contrast to W it does not force the clitic to show up in 2P in any other situation. The medieval Romance clitic can thus be found in 3rd, 4th or later positions in the clause. TM necessarily contains a high level of ambiguity in its application, since it relies on the left-edge condition of the simple clause. In actual practice there may be many competing loci for the beginning of a clause. If a subordinate clause precedes the main portion, finite or non-finite, even if it is only an extended adverbial expression, this clausal or phrasal element most of the time is counted as standing outside the simple clause: hence [$_{CP}$ X [$_{IP}$ V-CL...]. Several additional cases of serious ambiguity make TM less than transparent. TM was gradually abandoned, presumably on account of its insecure reconstruction in the context of much undecidable data; from the 13th c. on in French, and from the 14th/15th c. onward in most other languages, actual examples of absolute initial clitics can be found, directly negating the further absolute validity of TM.

The result of TM with a clause initial V is a syntactically conditioned variable clisis to its anchor. The surface data show a preponderance of postverbal occurrences due to the converging factors of early V position in the clause (1st or 2nd position), the frequent absence of any subject expression in these pro-drop languages, and the loose clause architecture which interprets anteposed elements in dislocated external positions rather than in the core clause.

As far as anchoring of the clitic is concerned, it stands in contiguity with the verb of its clause (but cf. the question of CR below in section 7.2.3.), some languages may show significant amounts of separation between the two terms. The clitic then comes to stand in an early clause position to the left of the V. This phenomenon, also called interpolation, characterizes certain aspects of Medieval Spanish and Portuguese, but is almost absent in the other Romance languages, including Catalan (Ramsden 1963; Fontana 1996). It reaches an apogee in the early 14th c. In Spanish, th 2P option is majorly reduced in the 15th c. and disappears from the language in the 16th c. (Wanner 1996), whereas in European Portuguese the medieval solution remains in effect up to this day (mostly north of Lisbon; also Galician; Progovac 1996). The central aspect of this medieval separation is the fact that it occurs practically only in subordinate clauses, where the clitic attaches leftward to the conjunction standing in first position. This 2P anchor is never more than an option; in each and every example, a VB based clitic position would be possible and can be documented in parallel examples, generally even in the same text. Much variation between enclisis and proclisis remains unaccounted for, eventually undermining the medieval system. The ensuing situation is clearly less syntactic and more morphologically driven (finiteness). The string conditions do no count any more, and clitics are found even in absolute initial position, depending on the pivotal verb of the clause.

7.2.3. Clitic raising (CR)

In combination with infinitival complementation, clitics also exhibit a displacement known as clitic raising (or climbing). An object clitic semantically connected to an embedded nonfinite form may show up as a dependent of the governing verb; Ital. *lo posso fare per domani* 'I can do it for tomorrow'. The clitic has been raised from the embedded to the higher clause, or it has 'climbed' the subordination slope by one step, from the clause defined by *fare* to the one containing *posso*. In Latin the word order patterns are too unconstrained for pinpointing a pronominal argument's position in the structure with certainty. There the closest to CR is the behavior of the subordinate pronominal subject accusative in the A.C.I. construction. It tends to be found at the left edge of the A.C.I., and with normative rightward extraposition of the A.C.I. the governing verb and this subject accusative tend to come in contact: *iubet te hinc abire* 'he orders you to go away from here'. This may indicate an early operation of CR mediated by subject-to-object raising (Wanner 1987). With the onset of the Romance documentation, CR actually represents the norm, compared to which the natural downstairs presence of object clitics in the common infinitival complementation structures is exceptional. CR is regulated by the class pertinence and lexical identity of the governing verb. The gradient of likelihood from high to low is: modal V > aspectual V > other complement V. This is additionally adjusted by the specific verb; e.g. Span. *me empiezan*/?*comienzan*/**inician a fastidiar* all 'they begin to bother me'. The difference between the medieval and the modern language is the broader applicability of CR earlier on. At least modern French since the later 17th c. has eliminated CR. The Romance varieties without a syntactically operative infinitive, Romanian and some S-Ital. dialects, cannot be considered at all in this context. In all other languages, some degree of CR is practiced, with considerable inter-speaker differences, and with marked stylistic preferences for limiting CR in more formal registers. Otherwise, the domain of CR is remarkably uniform across the applicable languages: modals are the mainstay of the phenomenon, with blurred profiles for the aspectuals, and only sporadic applicability for other predicates. The cross-linguistic stability points to the more systematic steering of this syntactic phenomenon through lexical semantics.

The structural correlations proposed to date cannot model the facts with sufficient accuracy without ad hoc interventions. If CR depends on the absence of an operative clause boundary between the infinitive and the governing V, it will be necessary to postulate double analyses for all these verbs, with controlling frequency measures added on top (semantic class, individual V). The strict implementation, whereby a combined-clause structure is said not to allow any intervening material has been shown to be wrong (Rizzi 1978). This is even more evident from the medieval languages where word order is less strictly controlled than in the standardized modern varieties. Any looser provision of structural variation becomes the equivalent of a fully learned data pattern. The more hopeful approach seems to be a conception of the construction as ambiguously interpretable: either as two-predicate configuration, focusing on the second of the two predicates ($-$CR), [$_S$... V_1 ... V_{INF} + CL ...]], or on the governing/conjugated V ($+$CR), [$_S$... CL + V_1 ... V_{INF} ...]]. The two perspectives are always present with a single structure not entailing a full-fledged two-clause analysis. The greater or lesser extent of manifest CR is then a function of stylistic choice and control by the individual speaker and the collective. The differences in written standards between the Middle Ages, and between early and later modernity may in this view be sufficient to explain the distributional frequency shifts observed throughout the Romance documentation.

8. Special Abbreviations

Cat.	Catalan
CR	Clitic raising
Fr.-Pr.	Franco-Provençal
Fr.	French
OFr.	Old French
Ital.	Italian
S-Ital.	Southern Italian
N-Ital.	Northern Italian
Lat.	Latin
Occ.	Occitan
Port.	Portuguese
OPort.	Old Portuguese
Rom.	Romanian
RRom.	Raetoromance
Sard.	Sardinian
Span.	Spanish
OSpan.	Old Spanish
2P	Second Position
TM	Tobler-Mussafia Law
W	Wackernagel Law

9. References

Abel, Fritz. 1971. *L'Adjectif démonstratif dans la langue de la Bible latine*. (*Zeitschrift für romanische Philologie*, Beiheft 125). Tübingen: Niemeyer.

Aebischer, Paul. 1948. "Contribution à la protohistoire des articles *ille* et *ipse* dans les langues romanes". *Cultura Neolatina* 8: 181–203.

Bally, Charles. ²1944. *Linguistique générale et linguistique française.* Berne: Francke.

Beyrer, Arthur & Bochmann, Klaus & Bronsert, Siegried. 1987. *Grammatik der rumänischen Sprache der Gegenwart.* Leipzig: Verlag Enzyklopädie Leipzig.

Calboli, Gualtiero (ed.). 1989. *Subordination and other topics in Latin.* Amsterdam: Benjamins.

Company Company, Concepción. 1985/86. "Los futuros en el español medieval: sus orígenes y su evolución". *Nueva Revista de Filología Hispánica* 43: 48–107.

Coseriu, Eugenio. 1954. *El llamado 'latín vulgar' y las primeras diferenciaciones romances.* Montevideo: Univ. de la República (also in Kontzi, Reinhold (ed.).).

Coseriu, Eugenio. 1977. "El aspecto verbal perifrástico en griego antiguo (y sus reflejos románicos)". In: Coseriu, Eugenio. *Estudios de lingüística románica.* Madrid: Gredos, 231–263.

Dardel, Robert de. 1983. *Esquisse structurale des subordonnants conjonctionnels en roman commun.* Geneva: Droz.

Dardel, Robert de & Kok, Ans de. 1996. *La Position des pronoms régimes atones – personnels et adverbiaux – en protoroman; avec une considération spéciale de ses prolongements en français.* Geneva: Droz.

Dardel, Robert de & Wüest, Jakob. 1993. "Les systèmes casuels du protoroman. Les deux cycles de simplification". *Vox Romanica* 52: 25–65.

Fleischman, Suzanne. 1982. *The future in thought and language.* Cambridge: Cambridge Univ. Press.

Fontana, Josep M. 1996. "Phonology and syntax in the interpretation of the Tobler-Mussafia Law". In: Halpern, Aaron L. & Zwicky, Arnold M. (eds.). *Approaching second. Second position clitics and related phenomena.* Stanford: Center for the Study of Language and Information, 41–83.

Gamillscheg, Ernst. 1937. "Zum romanischen Artikel und Possessivpronomen". In: Gamillscheg, Ernst. *Ausgewählte Aufsätze.* (*Zeitschrift für französische Sprache und Literatur*, Supplementheft 15) Jena: Gronau: 43–78.

Hall, Robert. 1950. "The reconstruction of Proto-Romance". *Language* 25: 1–14.

Hawkins, John A. 1983. *Word order universals.* New York: Academic Press.

Lausberg, Heinrich. 1972. *Romanische Sprachwissenschaft.* vol. 3: *Formenlehre.* (Sammlung Göschen) Berlin: Walter de Gruyter.

Lema, José & María Luisa Rivero. 1992. "Inverted conjugations and V-second effects in Romance". In: Laeufer, Christiane & Terrell A. Morgan (eds.). *Theoretical analyses in Romance Linguistics.* Amsterdam: Benjamins, 311–328.

Löfstedt, Bengt. 1961. *Studien über die Sprache der langobardischen Gesetze.* Stockholm: Almqvist & Wiksell.

Löfstedt, Einar. 1959. *Late Latin.* Oslo: Aschehoug & Co.

LRL = Holtus, Günter & Metzeltin, Michael & Schmitt, Christian (eds.) 1990–2001. *Lexikon der Romanistischen Linguistik.* 7 vols. Tübingen: Niemeyer.

Meyer-Lübke, Wilhelm. 1899. *Grammatik der romanischen Sprachen.* vol. 3: *Syntax.* Leipzig: Reisland.

Oesterreicher, Wulf. 1996a. "Gemeinromanische Tendenzen V: Morphosyntax". In: *LRL.* Vol. II/1, 273–309.

Oesterreicher, Wulf. 1996b. "Gemeinromanische Tendenzen VI: Syntax". In: *LRL.* Vol. II/1, 309–355.

Pinkster, Harm. 1987. "The strategy and chronology of future and perfect tense auxiliaries in Latin". In: Harris, Martin & Ramat, Paolo (eds.). *The historical development of auxiliaries.* Berlin: Mouton de Gruyter, 193–223.

Pinkster, Harm. 1990. *Latin syntax and semantics.* London: Routledge.

Progovac, Ljiljana. 1996. "Clitics in Serbian/Croatian: Comp as the second position". In: Halpern, Aaron L. & Zwicky, Arnold M. (eds.). *Approaching second. Second position clitics and related phenomena.* Stanford: Center for the Study of Language and Information, 411–428.

Pulgram, Ernst. 1950. "Spoken and written Latin". *Language* 26: 458–466.

Raible, Wolfgang. (ed.) 1989. *Romanistik. Sprachtypologie und Universalienforschung.* (TBL, 332.) Tübingen: Narr.

Raible, Wolfgang. 1992. "Pitfalls of subordination. Subject and object clauses between Latin and Romance". In: Brogyanyi, Bela & Lipp, Rainer (eds.). *Historical philology: Greek, Latin, and Romance.* Amsterdam: Benjamins, 299–337.

Ramsden, Herbert. 1963. *Weak-pronoun position in the early Romance languages.* Manchester Univ. Press.

Rizzi, Luigi. 1978. "A restructuring rule in Italian syntax". In: Keyser, J. S. (ed.). *Recent transformational studies in European languages.* Cambridge, MA: MIT Press, 113–158.

Selig, Maria. 1992. *Die Entwicklung der Nominaldeterminanten im Spätlatein. Romanischer Sprachwandel und lateinische Schriftlichkeit.* (ScriptOralia, 26.) Tübingen: Narr.

Thomason, Sarah G. & Kaufman, Terrence. 1988. *Language contact, creolization, and genetic linguistics.* Berkeley: Univ. of California Press.

Väänänen, Veikko. ²1967. *Introduction au latin vulgaire.* Paris: Klincksieck.

Wackernagel, Jacob. 1892. "Über ein Gesetz der indogermanischen Wortstellung". *Indogermanische Forschungen* 1: 333–436.

Wanner, Dieter. 1987. *The development of Romance clitic pronouns. From Latin to Old Romance.* (Empirical Approaches to Language Typology, 3.) Berlin: Mouton de Gruyter.

Wanner, Dieter. 1996. "Second position clitics in medieval Romance". In: Halpern, Aaron L. & Zwicky, Arnold M. (eds.). *Approaching second. Second position clitics and related phenomena.* Stanford: Center for the Study of Language and Information, 537–578.

Zanuttini, Raffaella. 1997. *Negation and clausal structure: a comparative study of Romance languages.* New York: Oxford Univ. Press.

Dieter Wanner, The Ohio State University (USA)

121. From Ancient Germanic to modern Germanic languages

1. The Germanic languages
2. Word order
3. Grammatical relations
4. Morphology
5. Phonology
6. Concluding remarks
7. References

1. The Germanic languages

The attested history of the Germanic languages can be conveniently divided into four periods: Ancient (2nd–6th century AD), Old (6th–11th c.), Middle (11th–16th c.), and Modern (16th c. to present). This periodization is of course a very rough one, and it may be more or less adequate for the history of individual languages.

Two languages or dialects are known from the ancient period, GOTHIC and ANCIENT NORDIC. The major source for GOTHIC is bishop Wulfila's Bible translation, made in South Eastern Europe in the 4th century. The GOTHIC language is now extinct, and has left no living descendents. The only existing documents in ANCIENT NORDIC are the runic inscriptions, mostly from Scandinavia. This material is very insufficient as a source for our knowledge of the ancient language, since it consists of a total of about 100 short epigraphic texts. There is also some controversy as to whether the language of the runic inscriptions from this period represents a common Northwest Germanic stage or a separate North Germanic variety (see Faarlund 2001 and the references there).

The old and middle stages of North Germanic (NORDIC) may be divided into two main dialect areas: East Nordic (OLD SWEDISH, OLD GUTNISH, and OLD DANISH) and West Nordic (OLD NORWEGIAN and OLD ICELANDIC). Old West Nordic is customarily referred to as OLD NORSE, which is the variety with the richest and most abundant literary sources. In this chapter, OLD NORSE material will be used to illustrate OLD NORDIC in general. Modern Nordic languages are represented by ICELANDIC, FAROESE, NORWEGIAN, SWEDISH, and DANISH. The latter three are very close morphologically and syntactically, and may be referred to collectively as mainland Scandinavian.

There is no attested common ancestor of the West Germanic languages. Old and middle versions of LOW GERMAN are usually called OLD and MIDDLE SAXON, and OLD DUTCH is sometimes referred to as OLD LOW FRANCONIAN. The oldest records in FRISIAN are from the late 13th century. Up till the mid 16th century this language is referred to as OLD FRISIAN. The modern West Germanic languages include GERMAN, YIDDISH, DUTCH, AFRIKAANS, FRISIAN, and ENGLISH.

2. Word order

It is generally difficult to make syntactic statements about the ancient period; Gothic texts are mainly translations, and it seems that the syntax of those texts is heavily influenced by the GREEK original. For ANCIENT NORDIC, the material is so limited that it can only serve as a weak support of syntactic hypotheses made on the basis of our knowledge of GERMANIC and INDO-EUROPEAN in general. Also for the old period, some of the languages are documented mainly through translations. This is above all true of OLD SAXON, OLD DUTCH, and OLD HIGH GERMAN.

Two word order systems relevant to the position of the verb will be dealt with here, the relative order of the main verb and its complements (OV vs. VO pattern), and the position of the finite verb in main clauses. Clearly these two systems may come into conflict with each other. The rules for the relative order of the verb and its complement may for example require the verb to be placed in final position, while the rules for the position of the finite verb may require it to be in second position in the sentence.

It is worth noting, however, that through their attested history the Germanic languages have had complex verb forms, consisting of an auxiliary and a main verb. The first system concerns the main verb, and the second the finite verb. In those cases where there is only one verb, that is when the main verb also is a finite verb, the tendency is for the principle of the position of the finite verb to overrule the principle for the order of verb and complement. The relative order of the verb and its complement should therefore be determined on the basis of sentences with a nonfinite main verb, or sentences without the verb second structure, such as subordinate clauses in some languages.

2.1. Order of verb and complement

The orders object-verb (OV) and verb-object (VO) are both represented as basic orders in Germanic. In addition, some languages show considerable variation in their VP internal order. ANCIENT GERMANIC was undoubtedly an OV language. Although the word order in the Gothic Bible in many cases was patterned on the GREEK original, some evidence of an indigenous OV pattern can be found whenever the GOTHIC text has a different syntactic construction from that of the GREEK original. Thus GREEK intransitive verbs are sometimes rendered by a predicate adjective followed by a copula, as in (1). OV order is also the most frequent pattern in the earliest runic inscriptions in ANCIENT NORDIC, (2).

(1) *siuk-s   ist*
     sick-NOM   be.PRES.3SG
     '(He) is sick'

(2) *ek   Hlewagasti-z   holt-ija-z*
     I.NOM Hlewagasti-NOM   Holt-of-M.NOM
     horn-a   tawido
     horn-ACC made
     'I, Hlewagasti of Holt, made the horn'
     (inscription from Gallehus, Denmark, 4th c.)

In OLD ENGLISH a variety of different word order patterns are found, with complements both preceding and following the verb, in both main and subordinate clauses. But on the basis of frequency and various syntactic properties, OLD ENGLISH is best analyzed as OV:

(3) *On   twæm   þingum   hæfde   God   þæs*
     on   two   things   had   God   this
     mannes   sawle   gegod-od
     man's   soul   endow-PTCP
     'God had endowed this man's soul with two things'
     (Kemenade 1994: 135).

MIDDLE DUTCH, MIDDLE LOW GERMAN, and MIDDLE HIGH GERMAN also exhibit quite a bit of variation in the order of the verb and its complement, but the unmarked pattern seems to be OV:

(4) MIDDLE DUTCH
     Spise,   die   sondere   lust   wert
     food   which   without   pleasure   is
     ghenom-en
     take-PTCP
     'Food which is taken without pleasure'
     (Burridge 1993: 77)

As we move into the modern period, the OV order becomes more and more frequent (Gerritsen 1980, Ebert 1980), to the point where MODERN GERMAN, DUTCH, and FRISIAN are predominantly OV languages.

(5) GERMAN
     Ich   habe   de-n   Kuchen   gegessen
     I.NOM have   the-ACC   cake   eaten
     'I have eaten the cake'

The general picture that can be drawn, then, for continental WEST GERMANIC is a continuous history of OV pattern, with varying frequency of *exbraciation* (the movement of an element to the right of the verb). It seemed that exbraciation increased during the old period, reached its summit in the late middle period, and then declined towards modern times.

Clearly, exbraciation may reach a critical point where it becomes so frequent that it leads to reanalysis: new generations of speakers may interpret the VO order as basic, rather than as a result of exbraciation (Faarlund 1985). This is what happened in MIDDLE ENGLISH, where the VO order became predominant during the 12th century, and gradually became the only possible one, as in MODERN ENGLISH.

In Nordic, the reanalysis may have taken place earlier. In OLD NORSE the VO order is the general one, but especially from the earlier period there are sentences which indicate an underlying OV pattern, (6). In later OLD NORSE texts this pattern has the character of a relic.

(6) *Vér viljum ekki lof hans heyr-a*
     we will not praise his hear-INF
     'We do not want to hear his praise'

As a result of the development sketched above, the modern Germanic languages belong to two distinct types in terms of the order of the verb and its complement: GERMAN, DUTCH, AFRIKAANS, and FRISIAN have OV as their unmarked order; ENGLISH, the NORDIC LANGUAGES, and YIDDISH are VO languages.

2.2. Position of the finite verb

Consistent with an OV pattern, finite verbs as well as non-finite verbs could be expected in final position. This pattern is found in GOTHIC and in ANCIENT NORDIC (cf. 2.1.). Also consistent with this pattern, a finite auxiliary may follow a non-finite main verb:

(7) GOTHIC
    þaruh sa andbahts meins wis-an
    there the servant mine be-INF
    hab-áiþ
    have-3SG
    'There shall my servant be'

(8) ANCIENT NORDIC
    hait-ina-z was
    call-PTCP-SG.M be.PRET.3SG
    '(He) was called'

Very early on, this pattern was replaced by another pattern caused by the verb-second rule (V2), which moves the finite verb to the second position of the sentence. In GOTHIC and ANCIENT NORDIC this seemed to be an optional rule, but at all later stages of GERMANIC (except MODERN ENGLISH) it is obligatory in main sentences (see, among others, examples (3), (5), (6)).

V2 is now one of the most prominent typological features of GERMANIC (see e. g. Haider & Prinzhorn 1986 and Haider et al. 1995 and the references there). V2 also applies in subordinate sentences in OLD NORSE, MODERN ICELANDIC, and YIDDISH; in the other languages it is restricted to main sentences. The actual mechanism underlying the introduction of V2 is uncertain. One hypothesis is that it is an effect of "Wackernagel's Law", by which an unstressed element is cliticized to the first autonomous word in the sentence. This rule may then first have affected auxiliaries only, then by extension all finite verbs (for details and arguments, cf. Faarlund 1990: 59 f.).

The position preceding the finite verb is a general topic position. The older stages of GERMANIC allow this position to be empty, thus having verb initial sentences:

(9) OLD ENGLISH
    Wæs Hæsten þa þær cumen mid
    was Hæsten then there come with
    his herge
    his army
    'Hæsten had then come there with his army'

Eventually structures with empty topic positions were grammaticalized as interrogatives, and every declarative main sentence required the topic position to be filled (see 3.6.). The most frequent occupant of the topic position is of course the subject. In ENGLISH, the order subject – verb was generalized in declarative sentences, so that the V2 pattern was replaced by a strict subject – verb pattern, which demotes the verb to third position when something other than the subject is fronted: *That cake I did not like.*

3. Grammatical relations

The GERMANIC languages have basically three kinds of morphosyntactic means of marking the arguments of the verb, case marking, verb agreement, and position. The relative importance of these means reflect the stage on a scale from a synthetic to an analytic linguistic type. At one end of the scale are languages with case marking of all major nominal categories, agreement marking in finite verbs for all person and number categories, and relatively free word order. At the other end are languages without case marking of most nominal categories, with very reduced or no verb agreement, and with a rather fixed word order. The GERMANIC languages are spread out along this scale. There is also a diachronic dimension to this distribution: all the ancient, old, and middle stages of GERMANIC are near the synthetic end, while the modern stages are spread out along the scale, with GERMAN and ICELANDIC still near the synthetic end, and ENGLISH and MAINLAND SCANDINAVIAN near the analytic end. There has thus been a typological drift through history, where the individual languages differ in terms of how far they have gone along the various parameters.

3.1. Case marking

All the ancient and old stages of GERMANIC have case marking of all major nominal categories. Subjects of finite verbs are in the nominative, and direct objects are mostly in the accusative. This system still exists in MODERN ICELANDIC, FAROESE, GERMAN and YIDDISH, see the GERMAN sentence (5).

In all the languages with this type of nominal case marking, certain verbs take their complement in the dative or the genitive. The origin of this lexical case marking is probably semantically determined. The dative expresses the recipient role, as in double object constructions, (10), but also in single object constructions, (11):

OLD NORSE

(10) Hon   skyldi bera   ǫl
      she.NOM should carry ale.ACC
      víking-um
      viking-PL.DAT
      'She was to bring ale to the vikings'

(11) Óláf-r   konung-r þakkaði henni
      Olaf-NOM king-NOM thanked her.DAT
      'King Olaf thanked her'

Being a syncretism of the INDO-EUROPEAN dative, instrumental, ablative and locative, the dative case in GERMANIC may also have these latter semantic functions.

The genitive was at one stage the case of a partitive or non-affected object:

OLD NORSE

(12) Hann   var ekki skald   ok
      he.NOM was not bard.NOM and
      hann   hafði þeir-rar   list-ar
      he.NOM had   that-PL.GEN skill-PL.GEN
      eigi fengit
      not   received
      'He was no bard, and he had not gotten any such skills'

(13) Heraðs-menn   leituðu henn-ar
      district-men.PL.NOM searched her-GEN
      'Men from the district searched for her'

In GERMAN there is a general tendency towards replacing the genitive with the accusative in object NPs, and in FAROESE the genitive has disappeared altogether in this function.

3.2. Position

All the GERMANIC languages observe certain constituent order constraints, and there is a preferred or stylistically neutral order of argument NPs. However, the languages with case marking enjoy a certain freedom of word order, depending on context and discourse functions.

In those languages that do not have a full nominal case system, subjects and objects are tied to specific positions relative to the verb(s), and can thus be identified by their position in the sentence. The subject most frequently comes first, and if something else precedes the finite verb in main sentences, the subject is normally first among the elements following the finite verb (or second among the elements preceding the finite verb in ENGLISH). Thus there are two possible subject positions:

(14) NORWEGIAN
  (a) Kona mi   har sett den filmen
      wife mine has seen that movie
      'My wife has seen that movie'
  (b) Den filmen har kona mi   sett
      that movie has wife mine seen
      'That movie my wife has seen'

The object has its unmarked position adjacent to the (position of the) non-finite verb. In YIDDISH, ENGLISH, and NORDIC this means immediately following the verb, in GERMAN, DUTCH, AFRIKAANS, and FRISIAN, immediately preceding the verb:

(15) (a) ENGLISH
          Bill has bought a car
      (b) DUTCH
          Wim heeft een auto gekocht
          Bill has a car bought

3.3. Verb agreement

With the exception of MAINLAND SCANDINAVIAN and AFRIKAANS, all the GERMANIC languages exhibit a certain degree of morphological marking of the verb in agreement with the subject. The agreement is for number and/or person. In languages with case marking, only nominative subjects can trigger verb agreement. If an NP in another case by certain criteria might be defined as the subject ("oblique subject", cf. 3.9.), it can never trigger verb agreement. It may also happen that a nominative subject fails to trigger agreement if it lacks typical subject properties, for example if it comes at the end of the sentence:

(16) OLD NORSE
Í þann tíma fann-st   í
in that time find.PRET.3SG-REFL in
Danmǫrk kvernstein-ar   tveir
Denmark millstone-PL.M.NOM two
'At that time there were two millstones in Denmark'

In MODERN ENGLISH, the verb agrees with the postverbal NP in existential sentences, *There are two people in the room*, and in GERMAN and DUTCH the verb may agree with a nominal predicate in the plural even if the subject is singular:

(17) GERMAN
Das sind schön-e Büch-er
that.SG be.3PL nice-PL book-PL
'Those are nice books'

3.4. Subjectless sentences

The GERMANIC languages can be divided into two groups depending on whether they have an obligatory subject requirement or not. In the old and middle stages, and in MODERN GERMAN, YIDDISH, ICELANDIC, and FAROESE (the languages with nominal case marking) there are various sentence types that do not need an overt grammatical subject. In the other modern languages every finite sentence (except imperative sentences) requires a grammatical subject in its surface manifestation.

The languages that do allow subjectless sentences, however, differ as to the extent and sentence types that allow it. The following is a sketchy survey of the development within GERMANIC, leaving details aside, and with the proviso that this part of the grammar is particularly problematic for languages where negative data are not available.

3.4.1. Pro-drop

Many languages outside the Germanic area allow a specific subject referent to be expressed through the verbal morphology only, by a process known as *pro-drop*. With the possible exception of YIDDISH, the GERMANIC languages do not seem to have been typical pro-drop languages during any part of their recorded history.

OLD NORSE and OLD and MIDDLE WEST GERMANIC normally have the subject pronoun expressed, (18), (19). However, if the subject has non-specific reference ('(some-)one' etc.), it can be represented by a null argument, (20).

(18) OLD NORSE
Haf-ið þit   verit hér um
have-2PL you.PL.NOM been here for
hríð
while
'You have already stayed here for some time'

(19) OLD ENGLISH
Þæt ic þas boc of   Ledenum
that I this book from Latin
gereorde to Engliscre spræce
language to English   tongue
awende
translate.1SG
'That I translate this book from Latin to English'

(20) OLD NORSE
Ekki sá   skip-it   fyrir
not see.PRET.3SG ship.ACC-DEF for
lauf-in-u
foliage-DEF-DAT
'One could not see the ship for the foliage'

Sentence (20) cannot be interpreted as 'He did not see the ship'. In the modern GERMANIC LANGUAGES such subjects are expressed by means of the 3rd person plural pronoun or by an indefinite pronoun derived from the numeral 'one' or the noun 'man':

(21) GERMAN
Man konnte das Schiff nicht sehen
one could the ship not see

3.4.2. Avalent verbs

Weather verbs and certain other verbs denoting natural processes usually take no arguments and assign no semantic roles. In the old and middle stages of GERMANIC, and in MODERN ICELANDIC, such sentences are subjectless:

(22) OLD NORSE
Gerði myrkt
made dark
'It got dark'

(23) ICELANDIC
Í gær   rigndi
yesterday rained
'Yesterday it rained'

Most MODERN GERMANIC languages now require a grammatical subject in this type of sentences, and use the neuter pronoun as an expletive subject:

(24) NORWEGIAN
Det vart   mørkt
it became dark

(25) GERMAN
   Es regnet
   it rains

3.4.3. Impersonal constructions

Sentences without a grammatical subject, but with semantic roles assigned to other argument phrases, are somewhat misleadingly referred to as 'impersonal constructions'. For lack of a better term, we will use it here, too, and include so-called impersonal passives. In the old and middle stages, and in MODERN GERMAN, ICELANDIC and FAROESE, such sentences may occur without a nominative subject:

(26) OLD NORSE
   Mun þik   kal-a
   FUT you.ACC cool-INF
   'You will be cold'

(27) GERMAN
   Gestern   wurde   getrunk-en
   yesterday PASS.3SG drink-PTCP
   'Yesterday there was drinking going on'

As the obligatory subject requirement took effect in all the languages except those just mentioned, these sentences were restructured. An oblique argument was replaced by a grammatical subject, compare (26) to the modern (28), and impersonal passives either disappeared (ENGLISH and YIDDISH), remained subjectless, (27) (GERMAN, ICELANDIC, FAROESE – but see 3.5.), or were equipped with an expletive subject, which is an unstressed version of either the neuter pronoun 'it/that', (29) (SWEDISH, NORWEGIAN) or of the adverb 'there', (30) (DANISH, DUTCH, FRISIAN):

(28) NORWEGIAN
   Du   vil frysa
   you.NOM will freeze
   'You will be cold'

(29) NORWEGIAN
   Det vart dans-a   til langt på
   it PASS dance-PTCP till far   on
   natt
   night
   'There was dancing going on until far into the night'

(30) FRISIAN
   Der   waard ta de nacht út
   there PASS till the night out
   dûns-e
   dance-PTCP
   (Same sense as (29))

3.5. Passive

The main syntactic operation of passivization common to all GERMANIC LANGUAGES consists of demoting the grammatical subject of the corresponding active sentence. This active subject then may or may not be added as an adjunct by means of a preposition. This is quite common in the modern languages (*The cake was eaten by my sister*), while in some of the older languages it seems to be limited to texts translated from LATIN.

As far as the subject of passive sentences is concerned, the GERMANIC LANGUAGES may again be divided into two groups. One group consists of languages with nominal case marking and which allow subjectless sentences. In these languages a passive sentence has a nominative subject only in those instances where the corresponding active sentence has an accusative direct object, as in (31 b), derived from (31 a). An object in any other case form in the corresponding active sentence remains in the same case in the passive, as the dative in (32), cf. (11), and the genitive in (33).

(31) OLD NORSE
   (a) *rak   hafr-a   heim*
       drive.PRET.3SG ram-PL.ACC home
   (b) *Senn vár-u   hafr-ar   heim*
       soon be.PRET-3PL ram-PL.NOM home
       rek-n-ir
       drive-PTCP-PL.M.NOM
       'Soon the rams were driven home'

(32) *Henni   var vel þakka-t*
    her.DAT was well thank-PTCP.NEUT.NOM
    'She was well thanked'

(33) *þá   er hefn-t*
    then is avenge-PTCP.NEUT.NOM
    fǫður
    father.GEN
    'Then the father was avanged'

This is the system found at all the old and middle stages, and in MODERN GERMAN, YIDDISH and ICELANDIC. In these languages, a distinction is made between structural and lexical case. Structural cases are nominative and accusative, lexical cases are dative, genitive, and accusative. The latter are assigned by lexical categories such as verbs, adjectives or prepositions, and cannot be changed through syntactic processes. Structural cases are assigned on the basis of their position in the sentence structure. An empty subject position in a passive sentence can be filled by another NP with a structural case. NPs with a lexical case cannot receive structural case in subject position, and they therefore remain in the same case form as in the active sentence.

In the MODERN GERMANIC LANGUAGES without case marking of nouns, direct and indirect objects, as well as the complements of certain prepositional phrases can become subjects in the passive: *She was given a reward; This bed has recently been slept in.* Thus it seems that at this stage the distinction between structural and lexical case has been abolished with the disappearance of the nominal case marking system. In SCANDINAVIAN, DUTCH, and FRISIAN, the subject position may also be filled by a dummy subject, leaving all objects in their original position:

(34) NORWEGIAN
 Det vart vis-t   oss eit brev
 it PASS show.PTCP us a letter
 'We were shown a letter'

This option is not available in ENGLISH. A blend of these two systems is found in FAROESE, where even a dative object may become nominative subject in the passive:

(35) (a) *Teir   fagnaðu honum væl*
      they.NOM received him.DAT well
   (b) *Han   var væl fagna-ð-ur*
      he.NOM was well receive-PTCP-M.NOM
      'He was well received'

3.6. Existential sentences

In GERMANIC as well as in most other languages there is a general tendency towards ordering the sentence elements in accordance with their role in the information flow; elements carrying given information tend to precede elements carrying new information. The means a given language has in order to comply with this general requirement, depends on its morphosyntactic type or typological class.

As already shown, the GERMANIC LANGUAGES differ as to their word order principles and morphological marking. At their earliest recorded stages, the word order of the GERMANIC LANGUAGES was relatively free. A subject carrying new information could come at the end of the sentence:

(36) OLD NORSE
 Var   þei-m   gef-in-n
 was.3SG them-DAT give-PTCP-M.NOM
 dagverð-r
 lunch-NOM
 'They were given lunch'

As is shown by (36), the preverbal position could be left empty in such cases. Eventually the verb first structure was grammaticalized as an interrogative structure. Consequently, declarative sentences with no thematic element to occupy the preverbal position, had to fill that position with something else. An expletive topic was therefore developed in all the GERMANIC LANGUAGES, starting with OLD ENGLISH. In the other languages it came later, mostly during the late middle period or at the transition from middle to modern. This expletive topic has the same origin as the expletive subject discussed in 3.4.1., either the neuter pronoun 'it/that' or the adverb 'there'. If some other element fills the first position, the expletive topic is not used:

(37) GERMAN
   (a) *Es lieg-en drei Büch-er auf dem*
      it lie-3PL three book-PL on the
      Tisch
      table
      'There are three books on the table'
   (b) *Auf dem Tisch lieg-en drei Büch-er*
      on the table lie-3PL three book-PL

In both cases, the NP is in the nominative case, and thus has the grammatical function of subject in the sentence. Besides GERMAN, this system still exists in YIDDISH, ICELANDIC, and FAROESE.

In the other languages, the expletive topic was reanalyzed as a subject. This is by no means surprising, since the first position in the sentence also is a typical subject position. MODERN ENGLISH, MAINLAND SCANDINAVIAN, DUTCH, AFRIKAANS, and FRISIAN all have an expletive subject used also in existential sentences. Since these languages no longer have a nominal case inflection, and since grammatical relations are defined by position, the postverbal NP in existential sentences can no longer be defined as a subject in these languages. In SCANDINAVIAN the postverbal NP has in fact most syntactic properties in common with a direct object. For one thing, it forms a constituent with the verb, as can be seen from topicalization. The highlighted part is a fronted VP including the NP:

(38) NORWEGIAN
 <u>*Kom folk*</u> *gjorde det heile*
 came people did it whole
 tid-a
 time-DEF
 'People were coming all the time'

3.7. Ergativity

The development of existential sentences described in 3.6. above has resulted in a new type of *ergative* constructions in MODERN GERMANIC. The sole argument of certain intransitive verbs has the same position and the same syntactic properties as the direct object of transitive verbs. Both sentences in (39) have a VP consisting of a verb followed by a complement NP and an adverbial:

(39) NORWEGIAN
(a) *Vi såg folk heile tid-a*
  we saw people whole time-DEF
  'We saw people all the time'
(b) *Det kom folk heile tida*
  it came people whole time-DEF
  'There came people all the time'

In MAINLAND SCANDINAVIAN, however, the class of verbs which can occur in this type of ergative constructions, exceeds the class of verbs that are usually considered unaccusative or ergative in other languages. A genuine intransitive verb, such as *arbeida* 'work', and even transitive verbs when used without an object, e.g. *eta* 'eat', can be used in ergative constructions:

NORWEGIAN
(40) *Det arbeider ein mann i hag-en*
  it works a man in garden-DEF
  'A man is working in the garden'

(41) *Det et mange turistar på denne restauranten*
  it eats many tourists in this restaurant
  'Many tourists eat in this restaurant'

3.8. Configurationality

As can be seen from this survey, it is not only case marking and freedom of word order which characterize two types of GERMANIC LANGUAGES. They differ also with regard to other morphosyntactic phenomena, such as the use of expletive subjects, promotion of NPs to subjecthood in passive sentences, and ergative constructions. There is thus no GERMANIC LANGUAGE with full case marking and expletive subjects in existential sentences. That would force the underlying subject to appear in an oblique case, e. g. the accusative. With the exception of MODERN FAROESE and some conservative MAINLAND SCANDINAVIAN dialects, which evidently are at a transitional stage, no GERMANIC LANGUAGE allows promotion of a lexically case marked NP to nominative subject in passive sentences. This kind of NP movement is permitted only for structurally case marked NPs, and can therefore affect other NPs than direct objects only in languages without case marking.

It is not likely that the differences between the two types are due to pure chance. A common underlying factor should be sought. Such a factor could be *configurationality*. It has been suggested (Hale 1983) that there is a typological distinction between configurational and non-configurational languages. The former have a strictly hierarchical sentence structure with binary branching. The latter may have a flatter structure with multiple branching in parts of its structure (Faarlund 1990, 1995). According to Hale 1983, who bases his hypothesis on the study of AUSTRALIAN LANGUAGES, non-configurational languages exhibit the following characteristics: 1) free word order; 2) elaborate case marking; 3) empty arguments; 4) discontinuous constituents.

The first three features have been shown to represent a difference between two types of GERMANIC LANGUAGES. As for discontinuity, there are various instances of discontinuous phrases in the old languages, which would be unacceptable in the modern varieties. The other syntactic differences that we have observed, follow from the ones just given: expletive subjects are used to avoid empty argument positions; the promotion of other NPs than direct objects to subject position in passive sentences is made possible by the lack of case marking, and is favored by the need to avoid empty subjects.

If the World's languages can vary along such a parameter, it is also likely that a language can shift from one value to the other. Then the morpho-syntactic differences which can be observed among the GERMANIC LANGUAGES can be explained as a variation along a configurationality dimension.

3.9. Oblique subjects

If a language moves towards a more configurational type without losing its nominal case morphology, a possible conflict may arise between case and position, in that a lexically case marked NP may be moved to a structural subject position. This is what seems to have happened in ICELANDIC. As mentioned above, ICELANDIC still has four cases, like the old GERMANIC LANGUAGES. But at the same time, ICELANDIC has a rather fixed word order, like the modern MAINLAND SCANDINA-

VIAN languages. Thus there is a fixed subject position immediately following the finite verb (for subjects that are not topicalized to the preverbal position), as in (42). In this position we may also find oblique NPs, (43). The verb *vanta* takes two accusative NPs, rather than a nominative and an accusative, and one of the accusatives behaves syntactically as a subject (for arguments, see Thráinsson 1994 with references); for example, it also serves as an antecedent of reflexives, (44); and it can cause deletion of an identical subject in a following conjunct, (45).

(42) hef-ur strák-ur-inn aldrei se-ð
 has boy-NOM-DEF never see-PTCP
 pening-a-na?
 money-PL.ACC-DEF
 'Has the boy never seen the money?'

(43) hefur strák-inn aldrei vanta-ð
 has boy.ACC-DEF never lack-PTCP
 peninga
 money-PL.ACC
 'Has the boy never lacked money?'

(44) Strák-in-n vantar pela-nn
 boy.ACC-DEF$_i$ lacks bottle.ACC-DEF
 sinn
 his.REFL$_i$
 'The boy lacks his bottle'

(45) Harald-i gleðj-a-st vel að
 Harold-DAT$_i$ rejoice-3SG-REFL well at
 Maríu og býð-ur henni
 Mary and —$_i$ invite-3SG her.DAT
 oft í bio
 often in movie
 'Harold likes Mary well and takes her often to the movies'

In languages that have lost their nominal case marking, these NPs would be unambiguous subjects, in ICELANDIC they are subjects in all respects except for their case marking (and their being unable to govern verb agreement, which is always restricted to the nominative).

4. Morphology

The ancient stages of GERMANIC are typical archaic INDO-EUROPEAN languages in that they have a rich inflexional morphology. Grammatical categories are to a large extent expressed by means of suffixation. Apart from the inherited *ablaut* system, there is little morphophonological variation. The complex morphophonology of later stages of GERMANIC is due to sound changes such as umlaut and syncope, which took place after 500 A.D. ANCIENT GERMANIC therefore has a more agglutinative character than its descendents.

4.1. Nominal system

4.1.1. Stem classes and gender

In PROTO-GERMANIC, nouns and adjectives belong to one of several declensional classes. The class is determined by the stem suffix. There are three types of stem suffixes: a vowel, a vowel + *n*, or zero (athematic stems). There are four different stem vowels: *a, ō, i, u.*

There are three genders, partly determined by the stem vowel: a-stems and an-stems are masculine or neuter; o-stems and on-stems are feminine; i-stems are masculine or feminine; u-stems are masculine, feminine, or neuter; athematic stems are masculine or feminine.

PROTO-GERMANIC must have had an agglutinative structure, where the root, the stem suffix and the number and case endings are added one to the other in that order. Through the history of GERMANIC, the agglutinative character was changed due to phonological development, the system of distinct stem classes was blurred, and gender became the predominant category. There is thus a tendency for inflexional suffixes in some languages to be generalized for each gender class rather than stem class. However, in most languages with a gender system, each gender may exhibit allomorphy in the plural formation, due to the original stem classes. Thus in MODERN NORWEGIAN, most masculine nouns form their plural with the suffix *-ar* from the old a-stems, which was the largest class of masculine nouns. The class of masculine nouns forming their plural with the suffix *-er* (< *-ir*) from the old i-stems has been gradually reduced through analogical pressure from the a-stems.

The stem suffix is followed by a suffix for number and case. As in other INDO-EUROPEAN languages, the two categories may be expressed by a single morpheme. The number/case morpheme varies according to gender and partly according to stem class. There is a singular/plural distinction, and at the ancient and old stages, at least four cases, nominative, accusative, dative, and genitive. Already at the ancient stage the stem vowel and the number/case ending may have coalesced, and the stem vowel is not identifiable as a separate segment in any of the attested GERMANIC languages.

4.1.2. Case

The oldest attested GERMANIC LANGUAGES have four distinct cases, plus possibly a separate vocative case in ANCIENT NORDIC and GOTHIC. An instrumental case exists in OLD WEST GERMANIC. The cases are expressed by inflectional endings originally added to the stem suffix in the singular and to the plural suffix in the plural. But already in prehistoric times, these suffixes merged into inflectional endings denoting number and case.

The primary function of the case system is to indicate the syntactic role of the NP, but on closer examination the Germanic case system turns out also to embody other functions and properties. In the following these functions and properties will be discussed and illustrated using data from OLD NORSE.

The nominative can only be used with finite verbs, and in the function of subject of the sentence it is neutral as to semantic role. The nominative is thus a *structural* case. The dative is primarily used to express the semantic role of recipient, as in (10) and (36) above. With adjectives, the dative expresses the experiencer, as in (46). But the dative is also used to express semantic roles that have their own cases in other INDO-EUROPEAN LANGUAGES, such as the instrumental, (47), the locative, (48), and the ablative, (49):

(46) *Mér   er   kal-t*
     me.DAT be.PRES.3SG cold-NEUT.NOM
     'I am cold'

(47) *þeim reið Goðgest-r konung-r*
     it.DAT rode Godgest-NOM king-NOM
     'King Godgest rode on it'

(48) *þá váru í Valland-i jarl-ar*
     then were in Valland-DAT earl-PL.NOM
     tveir
     two
     'Then there were two earls in Valland'

(49) *ofan frá fjǫll-u-num*
     down from mountain-PL.DAT-DEF
     'down from the mountains'

The GERMANIC dative is then first and foremost a *semantic* case, but rather than expressing one particular semantic role, it just indicates that the NP has some semantic role determined by the governing word (verb, adjective, or preposition).

The genitive is the only case that is used for adnominal NPs, such as possessors. This then is a structural genitive. Most of the prepositions that govern the genitive are historically derived from nouns, such as *til* 'to' (cf. GERMAN *Ziel* 'goal'). With verbs, the genitive basically has a partitive meaning, 'partitive' understood in a very wide sense. Besides the genuine partitive meaning which is found in NPs like 'all of us', and 'the king's head', it is extended to denote partial objects, as in 'provide some goods', 'try out (the effects of) a method', and by further extension to denote totally unaffected objects, in the sense that the referent of the NP is unaware of its role, as with verbs like 'desire', 'look for', 'wait for', 'miss', 'avenge', 'mention', etc. Cf. the examples (12) and (13). Note that 'partitive' is not the name of a semantic role assigned by a predicate word, it is rather a type of *reference*.

The accusative has a variety of functions. When governed by a preposition, it denotes direction and is thus semantic: *fara í land* 'travel/sail towards land'. It is also semantic when used in free adjuncts, *fara landveg* 'travel over land'. The accusative is the normal and unmarked case for direct objects, expressing a variety of roles depending on the meaning of the verb. These objects are converted into subjects in the passive, as in (31). The accusative is also used for the subject with non-finite verbs, viz. in accusative with infinitive constructions:

(50) *opt hefi ek heyrt yðr   þat*
     often have I heard you.PL.ACC that
     mæla
     say
     'I have often heard you say so'

There thus seems to be two types of accusatives in old GERMANIC languages, a semantic accusative and a structural accusative. (This division is purely synchronic, there is no indication of a historical syncretism as with the dative.)

The typical GERMANIC case system can now be described in the following matrix:

	Semantic	Referential	Structural
Dative	+	−	−
Genitive	−	+	+
Nominative	−	−	+
Accusative	+	−	+

In ENGLISH, DUTCH, AFRIKAANS, FRISIAN, and MAINLAND SCANDINAVIAN, the nominal case inflection has almost disappeared. A genitive suffix may still be in use, but only for determiners in NPs (*John's car*). This suffix is not a case ending, but a phrasal clitic, since it can be added to the last word of the phrase (*The queen of England's hat*). All the GERMANIC LANGUAGES do, however, maintain at least a two-way opposition between a nominative and an oblique form of personal pronouns. In some languages even this distinction is disappearing for certain person/number forms. Thus in certain varieties of NORWEGIAN there is no case distinction in the third person, and in AFRIKAANS there is no case distinction in the plural.

4.2. Verbal inflection

4.2.1. Conjugation classes

A typical feature of the Germanic languages is the distinction between *strong* and *weak* verbs. The distinction is made on the basis of the formation of the preterite and the past participle. The preterite of strong verbs is formed by changing the root vowel according to the inherited INDO-EUROPEAN ablaut system, as in MODERN ENGLISH *sing – sang – sung*. The original weak verbs are derived from nouns, adjectives or other verbs by means of a stem suffix, and their preterite is formed by adding a dental suffix to this derived stem. The stem suffixes are *-i-/-j-*, *-ō-*, *-ē-*, and *-nō-* (the last one in GOTHIC only). The preterite suffix is derived from *-dē/-dā*, probably a form of the verb 'do'.

PROTO-GERMANIC weak verbs then also must have had a clearly agglutinative structure, consisting of a root, a stem suffix, a tense suffix (in the preterite) which must have started out as a clitic, a modal suffix, and a number-person suffix. As in the nominal system, this agglutinative character was gradually diminished through a phonological reduction and merger of the individual morphemes.

The proportion of weak verbs has been growing at the cost of the strong verbs in most GERMANIC languages, both through analogical pressure and because the weak class has become the productive one, into which most new verbs are adopted.

4.2.2. Tense

GERMANIC has two inflectional tense forms attested at all historical stages: the present and the preterite. Future time reference is expressed by means of the present tense or by means of a verb meaning 'want', 'shall', 'become' or the like, taking the main verb in the infinitive as its complement. In addition there developed a perfect tense from the use of 'have' with a past participle form of transitive verbs. Originally the participle was an apposition to the direct object and agreed with it:

(51)   OLD NORSE
       mik   hefir Helgi hingat
       me.ACC   has   Helgi hither
       send-an
       send.PTCP-M.ACC
       'Helgi has sent me here'

Some of the verbs expressing future time reference, as well as 'have' (and 'be') expressing the perfect, were grammaticalized to become genuine auxiliary verbs in the modern languages. In ENGLISH this development has been carried to the point where the future auxiliaries *will* and *shall* no longer are verbs morphologically, and *be* is morphologically very deviant from other ENGLISH verbs. The grammaticalization of auxiliaries has not, however, been carried to the point where they have become affixes, which would have made the language more synthetic.

In some GERMANIC LANGUAGES (as in ROMANCE) the preterite form is being replaced by the perfect, as in GERMAN, where (52a) is being used more and more in stead of the more traditional (52b).

(52) (a) *Ich habe es gesehen*
          I   have it seen

      (b) *Ich sah es*
          I   saw it

In YIDDISH and AFRIKAANS the preterite is lost altogether. This is of course also a movement away from a synthetic type towards a more analytical type.

4.2.3. Modality

Proto-Germanic had three moods expressed through verbal inflection: indicative, subjunctive, and imperative. The inflectional subjunctive still exists in ICELANDIC and GERMAN. In the other languages the functions of the subjunctive have either been taken over by the indicative or by constructions with modal auxiliaries.

4.2.4. Voice

There are three types of passive constructions in GERMANIC. All the attested languages, past and present, may form the passive by means of an auxiliary ('be' or 'become') and the past participle of the main verb, as in *Mary was admired by everybody*. In addition, GOTHIC as the only GERMANIC LANGUAGE, retained the inflexional passive inherited from the INDO-EUROPEAN medio-passive: *nimada* is the 3rd person present passive of the verb *niman* 'take'. The modern NORDIC languages have developed a new inflexional passive by means of a suffix derived from a cliticized reflexive pronoun:

(53) NORWEGIAN
      Brev-et   må   send-a-st   i dag
      letter-DEF must send-INF-PASS today
      'The letter must be sent today'

4.2.5. Person and number

The finite verb in GERMANIC is generally inflected for person and number. There are three persons and two numbers, except that in GOTHIC there are also distinct forms for the 1st and 2nd person dual. The degree to which all persons and numbers are distinguished in the various tense and mood categories, differs between the languages and from one historical stage to another. The details are too complex to go into here, but if we look at the major, regular conjugation classes, we find the following general patterns.

The oldest and most conservative system has separate forms (with certain syncretisms) for each person and number in both present and preterite. This is the system found in GOTHIC, ANCIENT NORDIC and OLD NORSE. It has survived in MODERN ICELANDIC. The same full system also exists in all stages of HIGH GERMAN, and in OLD and MIDDLE DUTCH.

The earliest kind of simplification of this system consists in generalizing one form for the plural, with no person distinction. This is what we find in OLD and MIDDLE ENGLISH, OLD FRISIAN, and OLD SAXON, and in MODERN FAROESE. Another kind of simplification is giving up the person marking altogether in the preterite, keeping it only in the present. MODERN DUTCH and FRISIAN have person marking only in the present singular, but separate forms for the singular and the plural also in the preterite. ENGLISH regular verbs have a separate form only for the third person singular present. The simplest system is found in mainland Scandinavian and in AFRIKAANS, where person and number agreement has been given up entirely.

4.3. Drift

The morphological development of GERMANIC has been governed by two major trends, simplification and grammaticalization. The former has reduced the number of categories expressed by means of inflection, either by reducing or eliminating the categories themselves, as with nominal case and person/number inflection with verbs, or by replacing a morphological expression with a syntactic one, as with the modal system. This type of change is traditionally (since Sapir 1921) often referred to as *drift*, a drift from a synthetic to a more analytic linguistic type.

The other trend, grammaticalization, consists in a phonological and semantic reduction. This has primarily affected verbs that have been reduced to auxiliaries semantically, and in some cases to clitics phonologically, as in MODERN ENGLISH. Auxiliaries have never, however, developed into new verbal affixes, which would have meant a trend towards a more synthetic type. In fact, the auxiliary clitics in ENGLISH do not have the main verb as their host; they are enclitic on a preceding noun or pronoun: *You'd never do such a thing*.

5. Phonology

All the GERMANIC languages have undergone far-reaching sound changes, which have given each of them a phonological character distinct from that of their ancestors as well as from their contemporary cousins and from their non-Germanic neighbors. There are, however, certain phonological features shared by all the modern GERMANIC languages: a fixed stress pattern with a dynamic stress usually on the first syllable of the word; a rich vowel system but very few vowel contrasts in unstressed syllables; and a correlation between word accent and syllable quantity.

5.1. Accent

In PROTO-INDO-EUROPEAN, the word accent was variable, it could be carried by any type of syllable in the word. This situation lasted for some time into the PROTO-GERMANIC period, as can be seen from the effects of Verner's Law, whereby voicing of intervocalic consonants depend on the placement of the stress, cf. the contrast *was* – *were*. Early on, however, probably in pre-historic times, the accent was fixed on the first syllable of the word. And of the two INDO-EUROPEAN accent types, pitch accent and stress accent, the latter was generalized in Germanic. This change in the accentuation pattern had far-reaching consequences for the Germanic languages, first of all phonologically, but perhaps even morphologically and syntactically.

5.2. Vowel system

The vowel system of PROTO-GERMANIC was of a canonical INDO-EUROPEAN type. This is more or less what we find in GOTHIC and in ANCIENT NORDIC.

From its earliest history we find a differentiation in the vowel system of stressed and unstressed syllables. In unstressed syllables, the vowels were generally reduced. An early step towards such a merger was the loss of the opposition [+/− HIGH] with both front and back vowels in NORDIC, whereby the distinctions i/e and u/o were lost. OLD NORSE thus had three contrastive vowels in unstressed syllables, /i/, /u/, and /a/. By further reduction, many GERMANIC languages now have only one vowel in unstressed syllables of native words, the [ə]. These languages include DANISH, DUTCH, FRISIAN, and GERMAN. The final stage of reduction is total loss of unstressed vowels, as in originally open syllables in ENGLISH.

In stressed syllables the development was the opposite. New vowel phonemes were created through various phonological processes. Some of these processes were conditioned by the following syllable. Others by the accent itself. The most important one of the conditioned changes is the process of regressive assimilation known as *umlaut* or *mutation*. By this process the vowel of a stressed syllable adopts certain features from a vowel or a semivowel in an immediately following unstressed syllable. The most widespread umlaut phenomena in the attested history of GERMANIC are caused by an unstressed /i/ or /u/, hence the terms i-umlaut and u-umlaut. By i-umlaut the stressed vowel inherits the feature value [−BACK], and by u-umlaut it inherits [+ROUNDED]. As an illustration of the effects of umlaut, compare the GOTHIC forms with their OLD NORSE equivalents:

	GOTHIC	OLD NORSE	
i-umlaut:			
a > e	satjan	setja	'set'
o > ö	sokjan	søkja	'seek'
u > y	þugkjan	þykkja	'seem'
u-umlaut:			
a > ǫ	handum	hǫndum	'hands (dat)'
i > y	siggwan	syngva	'sing'

(⟨ǫ⟩ denotes a low, back, rounded vowel.) Initially, these new vowels were allophonic variants occurring in syllables preceding an unstressed *i* or *u*, but as the unstressed syllable in many cases would disappear, the umlauted variant was phonemicized, as in the OLD NORSE plural of *land*, which is *lǫnd* (<*[lǫndu]).

5.3. Syllable structure

The concentration of the stress on one particular syllable of the word made this syllable dominant in more than one way. We have already seen that it is qualitatively different from other syllables in that it has a larger vowel inventory. In most GERMANIC LANGUAGES it is also quantitatively dominant in that it is necessarily long. Precisely how to define a long syllable is problematic, and it may differ from one language to the next. Generally, however, there is a tendency through the history of GERMANIC to lengthen short vowels in open stressed syllables, as in DUTCH, where there is still a difference between singular forms of nouns with a closed syllable and a short vowel, *spel* 'game', and a plural form with an open syllable and a long vowel, *spele*. In other languages, e.g. Icelandic, a monosyllabic word with a historically short vowel followed by one consonant also counts as long, and had its vowel lengthened.

6. Concluding remarks

The differences between the GERMANIC languages can to a large extent be ascribed to their different stages on a continuous line of development. It may be a bold assumption that it all started with the fixation of the stress accent on the first syllable (perhaps under the influence of a non-INDO-EUROPEAN substratum?). The reduction of unstressed syllables then may have led to a reduction of the inflectional system, which again had certain syntactic consequences.

However this may have been, it is obvious that whatever change has taken place, and whatever the result, it is also conditioned by general typological patterns and constrained by general principles of Universal Grammar. What exactly those principles are, can only be revealed by further typological and diachronic research.

7. References

Burridge, Kate. 1993. *Syntactic Change in Germanic. Aspects of language change in Germanic with particular reference to Middle Dutch.* Amsterdam & Philadelphia: Benjamins.

Ebert, Robert P. 1980. "Social and stylistic variation in early new High German word order. The sentence frame ('Satzrahmen')." *Beiträge zur Geschichte der deutschen Sprache.* 102: 357–98.

Faarlund, Jan Terje. 1985. "Pragmatics in diachronic syntax." *Studies in Language.* 9: 361–93.

Faarlund, Jan Terje. 1990. *Syntactic Change. Toward a Theory of Historical Syntax.* (Trends in linguistics: Studies and monographs, 50.) Berlin & New York: Mouton de Gruyter.

Faarlund, Jan Terje. 1995. "Diachrony, typology, and universal grammar. From 'Classical' European to Modern Western European." In: *Papers from the 31st Annual Regional Meeting of the Chicago Linguistic Society.* Chicago: Chicago Linguistic Society, 153–70.

Faarlund, Jan Terje. 2001. "Early Northwest Germanic." In: Roger D. Woodard (ed.). *Encyclopedia of the World's Ancient Languages.* Cambridge: Cambridge University Press.

Gerritsen, Marinel. 1980. "An analysis of the rise of SOV patterns in Dutch." In: Traugott, Elizabeth Closs & Labrum, Rebecca & Shepherd, Susan (eds.). 1980. *Papers from the 4th International Conference on Historical Linguistics.* Amsterdam & Philadelphia: Benjamins, 123–36.

Haider, Hubert & Prinzhorn, Martin. 1986. *Verb second phenomena in Germanic.* Dordrecht & Riverton: Foris.

Haider, Hubert & Olsen, Susan & Vikner, Sten (eds.). 1995. *Studies in comparative Germanic syntax.* Dordrecht & Boston: Kluwer.

Hale, Kenneth. 1983. "Warlpiri and the grammar of non-configurational languages." *Natural Language & Linguistic Theory* 1: 5–47.

Kemenade, Ans van. 1994. "Old and Middle English." In: König, Ekkehard & van der Auwera, Johan (eds.). *The Germanic Languages.* London & New York: Routledge, 110–41.

Sapir, Edward. 1921. *Language. An introduction to the study of speech.* New York: Harcourt, Brace & company.

Thráinsson, Höskuldur. 1994. "Icelandic." In: König, Ekkehard & van der Auwera, Johan (eds.). *The Germanic Languages.* London, 142–89.

Jan Terje Faarlund, University of Oslo (Norway)

122. Vom Alttürkischen zu den modernen Türksprachen

1. Die Entwicklung des Türkischen
2. Phonologische Entwicklung
3. Morphologische Entwicklung
4. Syntaktische und morphosyntaktische Entwicklung
5. Lexikalische Entwicklung
6. Spezielle Abkürzungen
7. Zitierte Literatur

1. Die Entwicklung des Türkischen

Die einigermaßen überblickbare diachrone Entwicklung der türkischen Sprachen umspannt 1200 Jahre. Die erste dokumentierte Stufe ist die Sprache der ostalttürkischen Inschriften des 8. Jhs., oft einfach „Alttürkisch" genannt, obwohl sie nicht als Ahne aller heutigen Türksprachen gelten kann.

Die Türksprachen, die deutlich miteinander genetisch verwandt sind, weisen auch erhebliche Ähnlichkeiten in Phonologie, Morphologie und Syntax auf. Eine erste Divergenz erfolgte durch die frühe Abspaltung OGURISCHER („bulgarischer") Varietäten (heute durch das TSCHUWASCHISCHE im Wolga-Becken vertreten) vom Gemeintürkischen. Eine spätere Abspaltung des alttürkischen Arghu-Dialekts führte zur Entstehung des CHALADSCHISCHEN (in Zentral-Iran). Weitere Dialektspaltung und komplexe Kontaktprozesse führten zur Differenzierung des Gemeintürkischen in einen OGUSISCHEN, einen KIPTSCHAKISCHEN und einen UIGURISCHEN Zweig, die bei der späteren Verbreitung des Türkischen einer Aufteilung in sekundäre Zweige unterlagen.

Das TÜRKISCHE erwies sich früh als sehr expansiv. Durch die hohe Mobilität der Türkvölker verschoben sich ständig die Grenzen ihrer Sprachgebiete. Obwohl die vielen weiten Ausdehnungen ihrer Herrschaftsgebiete nicht immer zur Erweiterung des Sprachraums führten, hat das TÜRKISCHE insgesamt ein riesiges Territorium erobert. Der entscheidende Durchbruch in der Verbreitung erfolgte vom 13. Jh. an.

1.1. Einteilung, Periodisierung, Geltungsbereich

Die dynamische Geschichte der Türkvölker erschwert eine Klassifikation moderner Sprachen, die geographische und genetische Kriterien kombiniert. Sechs Hauptzweige, einige heterogenen Ursprungs, lassen sich unterscheiden:

(1) Der OGUSISCHE Südwestzweig umfaßt TÜRKEITÜRKISCH, ASERBAIDSCHANISCH, TÜRKMENISCH, GAGAUSISCH, CHORASSANTÜRKISCH sowie südogusische Dialekte in Iran (KASCHGAISCH, SONQORĪ, AYNALLU usw.) und Afghanistan (AFSCHARISCH).

(2) Der kiptschakische Nordwestzweig umfaßt KUMÜKISCH, KARATSCHAISCH, BALKARISCH, KRIMTATARISCH, KARAIMISCH, TATARISCH (KASANTATARISCH, MISCHÄRTATARISCH, westsibirische Dialekte), BASCHKIRISCH, KASACHISCH, KARAKALPAKISCH, KIPTSCHAK-USBEKISCH, NOGAISCH und modernes KIRGISISCH.

(3) Der uigurische Südostzweig umfaßt USBEKISCH (mit verschiedenen Dialekten), UIGURISCH, TARANTSCHI, „ostürkische" Dialekte (von KASCHGAR, JARKÄND, CHOTAN, KERYA, TSCHERTSCHEN, AKSU, KUTSCHA, TURFAN usw.) sowie die genetisch abweichenden GELBUIGURISCH und SALARISCH.

(4) Der sibirische Nordostzweig umfaßt JAKUTISCH (SAχA), DOLGANISCH, SAIANTÜRKISCH (TUWISCH, KARAGASSISCH/TOFA), JENISSEITÜRKISCH (CHAKASSISCH, SCHORISCH usw.), TSCHULYMTÜRKISCH, ALTAITÜRKISCH.

(5) Der ogurische Zweig wird vom TSCHUWASCHISCHEN vertreten.

(6) Der Arghu-Zweig wird vom CHALADSCHISCHEN vertreten.

Eine Periodisierung der Sprachentwicklung ist schwer, da die Quellen keine direkte Auskunft über gesprochene Sprachen geben und viele ältere Sprachen undokumentiert sind. Die Entwicklung der Schriftsprachen zerfällt in folgende Perioden:

(1) Eine alte Periode vom 8. bis zum 13. Jh. (Gabain 1974) umfaßt drei Stufen:
(A) OST-ALTTÜRKISCH, zuerst in Inschriften auf dem Gebiet der heutigen Mongolei belegt (Tekin 1968), mit Zügen eines noch nicht differenzierten Gemeintürkisch (Ogusisch-Kiptschakisch-Uigurisch).
(B) ALTUIGURISCH, bis zum 13. Jh. in mehreren Stufen entwickelt und in zahlreichen Handschriften belegt.
(C) KARACHANIDISCH, die erste islamischtürkische Schriftsprache, entwickelt im 11. Jh. in Ostturkestan, lexikalisch beeinflußt von ARABISCH und PERSISCH.

(2) Eine mittlere Periode vom 13. Jh. an umfaßt verschiedene regionale Schriftsprachen. Der ogurische Zweig ist in wolgabulgarischen Inschriften des 13. und 14. Jhs. vertreten. Die gemeintürkischen Varietäten, die als UIGURISCH, KIPTSCHAKISCH oder OGUSISCH bzw. als Mischungen davon bestimmt werden können, umfassen:
(A) CHORESMTÜRKISCH, eine Vorstufe des TSCHAGATAISCHEN, im 13. und 14. Jh. in der Goldenen Horde gebraucht.
(B) FRÜHTSCHAGATAISCH, im 15. und 16. Jh. im Reich der Timuriden gebraucht.
(C) KIPTSCHAKISCH vom 14. Jh. an.
(D) ALT-ANATOLISCHTÜRKISCH vom 13. Jh. an, in Osmanisch-Türkisch übergehend.
(E) TÜRKMENISCH, vom 14. Jh. an.
(F) ASERBAIDSCHANISCH, vom 15. Jh. an eigenständig entwickelt.

(3) Eine vormoderne Periode vom 16. Jh. an umfaßt Schriftsprachen, die durch regionale gesprochene Varietäten stärker beeinflußt sind:
(A) MITTEL- und SPÄTTSCHAGATAISCH, später in stärker örtlich geprägten Varietäten in Ostturkestan, im Wolga-Gebiet und auf der Krim.
(B) OSMANISCH (Mittel- und Spätosmanisch), zur führenden türkischen Schriftsprache entwickelt.
(C) MITTELASERBAIDSCHANISCH mit einer Blüteperiode vom 16. Jh. an.
(D) Schriftliche Formen kleinerer Kiptschaksprachen wie KARAIMISCH und ARMENO-KIPTSCHAKISCH.

(4) Die moderne Periode im 20. Jh. umfaßt 24 türkische Schriftsprachen.

Die meisten Schriftsprachen nach der alten Periode waren überregional. TSCHAGATAISCH hatte bis vor einem Jahrhundert einen enormen Geltungsbereich als Schriftsprache der west- und ostturkestanischen Türken, der Kasachen und Tataren. Die Herausbildung regionaler Varietäten begann in der zweiten Hälfte des 19. Jhs. mit Versuchen, „nationale" Schriftsprachen für Tataren, Usbeken,

Kasachen und Türkmenen zu schaffen. Dennoch hatten OSMANISCH, ASERBAIDSCHANISCH, USBEKISCH und TATARISCH noch große überregionale Geltung.

Im 20. Jh. entstanden viele neue Schriftsprachen. In der Türkei wurde OSMANISCH durch ein modernes TÜRKEITÜRKISCH ersetzt. In der Sowjetunion wurden die älteren Schriftsprachen auf „nationale" Gebiete beschränkt. Einige Sprachen, die bereits geschrieben worden waren, z. B. JAKUTISCH, TSCHUWASCHISCH, KASACHISCH und KUMÜKISCH, wurden weiterentwickelt. Eine Reihe neuer Schriftsprachen wurde in den 20er und 30er Jahren geschaffen: KIRGISISCH, BASCHKIRISCH, KARAKALPAKISCH, KARATSCHAISCH-BALKARISCH, NOGAISCH, TUWISCH, ALTAISCH (OIROTISCH), CHAKASSISCH und SCHORISCH. Eine sog. „neuuigurische" Sprache wurde zur Schriftsprache von Ostturkestan erklärt.

Übersichten über TÜRKSPRACHEN finden sich in Baskakov 1966, Comrie 1981, Deny et al. 1959, Johanson & Csató 1998, Menges 1995, historisch-komparative Darstellungen u. a. in Baskakov 1975, Doerfer 1971, 1990, Róna-Tas 1991, Ščerbak 1994, Tenišev 1984, 1988, Allgemeines zur türkeitürkischen Grammatik u. a. in Boeschoten & Verhoeven 1991, Hazai 1978, Johanson 1990, vergleiche mit dem Deutschen in Johanson & Rehbein 1999.

1.2. Typologische und genetische Verwandtschaft

Die genetische Verwandtschaft bedeutet, daß sich aufgrund gemeintürkischer und tschuwaschischer Daten eine hypothetische prototürkische Entwicklungsstufe rekonstruieren läßt. Das Verhältnis zwischen genetischer und typologischer Verwandtschaft ist noch unklar. Viele der den TÜRKSPRACHEN gemeinsamen wesentlichen Eigenschaften sind allen eurasischen Sprachen des altaischen und uralischen Typs gemein. Die Ähnlichkeit mit Sprachen wie MONGOLISCH, TUNGUSISCH, KOREANISCH und JAPANISCH hat bisher nicht ausgereicht, um die genetische Verwandtschaft des TÜRKISCHEN mit diesen Sprachen zu beweisen.

1.3. Typologischer Wandel

Insgesamt weisen die TÜRKSPRACHEN in ihrer bekannten Entwicklung einen erheblichen Wandel auf, der z. T. zum typologischen Wandel geführt hat. Die Darstellung der Veränderungen ist zum Teil problematisch. Ältere Entwicklungsstufen sind meist mangelhaft bekannt. Frühere Schriftsprachen weisen oft eine große Variation auf und spiegeln, auch wenn sie regionale Spezifika enthalten, die gesprochenen Varietäten nie wider. In traditionellen Interpretationen der verfügbaren Sprachdaten werden den älteren Entwicklungsstufen oft vereinfachte und zu moderne Strukturen unterstellt. Viele Aspekte des türkischen Strukturwandels bedürfen einer erneuten, unvoreingenommenen Analyse.

Das TÜRKISCHE weist schon in seiner ersten bekannten Form ein hohes Maß an Regelmäßigkeit und Einfachheit auf, eine Tendenz zum „Natürlichen" mit wenig markierten Strukturen. Diese Form mag bereits ein Ergebnis von nivellierender Koinebildung sein. Die weitgehende Einfachheit ist sicherlich ein Grund für die weite und schnelle Verbreitung türkischer Varietäten gewesen.

1.4. Ab- und Zunahme von Unterschieden

Die türkische Sprachfamilie gilt oft als ungewöhnlich homogen. Der Eindruck beruht z. T. auf ihrer Tendenz, Unregelmäßigkeiten durch Vereinheitlichungen immer wieder zu tilgen. Vor allem führte die Mongolenzeit, in der das TÜRKISCHE eine große Verbreitung erlangte, zu Mischung und Ausgleich bei den Sprachen der zentralen Gebiete. Die Sprachen der Randgebiete, auch z. B. TÜRKEITÜRKISCH, haben dagegen viele ältere Züge bewahrt. Stark nivellierende Kontaktgebiete waren etwa die Krim und die Amu Darya-Region. Manchmal ist der Einfluß einer TÜRKSPRACHE auf eine andere erheblich gewesen, z. B. der des TATARISCHEN auf das sehr unterschiedliche TSCHUWASCHISCHE. Das KIRGISISCHE mit seinen engen genetischen Beziehungen zum ALTAITÜRKISCHEN hat sich typlogisch dem KASACHISCHEN genähert.

Durch die politische Spaltung im 20. Jh. haben sich die TÜRKSPRACHEN wiederum mehr voneinander entfernt. Dies ist z. T. auch eine Folge von Sprachreformen. Das neue reformierte TÜRKEITÜRKISCH war außerhalb der Türkei schwer verständlich, die Sprachen der Sowjetunion unterlagen Veränderungen unter russischem Einfluß, und die Türksprachen Chinas, Irans und Afghanistans entwickelten sich in anderen Richtungen. Die Isolation führte zu neuen Unterschieden. Die Einführung unterschiedlicher Schriftsysteme für die einzelnen Sprachen machte auch viele tatsächliche Änderungen weniger sichtbar. Trotz entgegengesetzter Behauptungen ist die gegenseitige Verständlichkeit innerhalb der türkischen Familie als Ganzem ziemlich begrenzt.

1.5. Kontakte mit anderen Sprachen

Ein wesentlicher Teil der typologischen Divergenz in der türkischen Familie beruht auf vielfältigen Kontakten mit unterschiedlichen Sprachen wie IRANISCH, SLAVISCH, MONGOLISCH und URALISCH. Türksprachen bieten besonders reiche Daten für das Studium von Sprachkontakt.

Der fremde Einfluß auf das TÜRKISCHE ist verschiedener Art gewesen und hat unter unterschiedlichen realen, kulturellen und sozialen Bedingungen stattgefunden. Mal kopierten türkischsprachige Gruppen Elemente fremder Sprachen in ihre jeweiligen Varietäten; mal wechselten nicht türkischsprachige Gruppen zu TÜRKISCH über und übertrugen dabei als Substrateinfluß Züge der alten Muttersprache in ihre türkische Varietät. In beiden Fällen fand ein Kopieren von lexikalischen, lautlichen, morphologischen und syntaktischen Elementen statt, entweder global, indem die ganze Form und Funktion einer Struktur kopiert wurde, oder nur selektiv, indem eine ausgewählte Eigenschaft, z. B. ein Strukturmuster ohne fremde Morpheme nachgebildet wurde. Ein allmähliches Eindringen von Kopien fremder Einheiten, Strukturen und Kategorien hat in vielen Fällen einen erheblichen typologischen Wandel herbeigeführt (vgl. Johanson 1992a, 1993, 1998, 1999b, 1999c, Comrie 1995).

1.6. Arealtypologie

Die primären Zweige der Türksprachen unterlagen arealer Umgestaltung, besonders in Gebieten intensiver Berührung mit dem Persischen: Westturkestan, Iran und Afghanistan. Durch Konvergenz entstanden neue, genetisch relativ unabhängige arealtypologische Konfigurationen, wobei die zentralen Varietäten sich leichter beeinflussen ließen als die abgelegeneren. Im gewissen Sinne läßt sich sagen, daß einige Türksprachen einem westturkestanischen Sprachbund, andere einem Wolga-Kama-Sprachbund und wieder andere einem südsibirischen Sprachbund usw. angehören. Mit dem sog. Balkan-Sprachbund bestehen generell wenige Gemeinsamkeiten.

In bezug auf Wort- und Satzstruktur gehört TÜRKISCH einem großarealen mittel- und ostasiatischen „Bund" an und weist korrelative Eigenschaften auf, die für Sprachen des uralischen und altaischen Typs (einschließlich Koreanisch und Japanisch) charakteristisch sind.

1.7. Isolation und starker Fremdeinfluß

Türkische Randsprachen, die sich in relativer Isolation entwickeln, sind nicht nur konservativ, sondern erzeugen unter Fremdeinfluß oft auch wesentliche Neuerungen. Etliche Sprachen, die jahrhundertelang von den genetischen Zweigen, an denen sie einmal hingen, abgeschnitten waren, haben alte Züge bewahrt und in ihrer jeweiligen Umgebung neue Züge erworben. Von den in China gesprochenen Sprachen hat sich SALARISCH historisch von den Südwestsprachen entwickelt, während GELBUIGURISCH dem SAIANTÜRKISCHEN nahegestanden haben dürfte und die FU-YÜ-Sprache der Mandschurei, die als ein kirgisischer Dialekt gilt, mit dem JENISSEITÜRKISCHEN eng verwandt zu sein scheint. TSCHUWASCHISCH und CHALADSCHISCH weisen sehr spezifische archaische Züge und zugleich zahlreiche kontaktbedingte Neuerungen auf.

In einigen Sprachen hat ein massiver Fremdeinfluß zu beträchtlichen typologischen Veränderungen geführt. Eine mehr als tausendjährige Interaktion von IRANISCH und TÜRKISCH hat z. B. das USBEKISCHE tief beeinflußt. Auch der persische Einfluß auf türkische Dialekte in Iran und Afghanistan ist sehr intensiv. Besonders intensive und dauerhafte Kontakte haben Türksprachen erzeugt, deren Grammatik weitgehend nach nichttürkischen Mustern modelliert ist. Dies gilt z. B. dem slavisch beeinflußten KARAIMISCHEN und dem persisch beeinflußten KASCHGAISCHEN, deren Beispiele zeigen, daß unter extremen Bedingungen auch Strukturen kopiert werden, die typologisch im Widerspruch zur übrigen Sprachstruktur stehen (s. z. B. Csató 1996).

Gewisse Sprachen sind unter speziellen soziokommunikativen Bedingungen, vor allem Sprachwechsel, entstanden und sind von besonderer struktureller Diskontinuität geprägt. Viele ursprünglich nicht-türkischsprachige Gruppen, iranische, griechische, finnougrische, samojedische, jenisseische, tungusische und andere, haben Substrateinfluß auf türkische Varietäten ausgeübt. Extreme Formen von lexikalischem Substrateinfluß finden sich in Varietäten von Gruppen, die das grammatische System einer Türksprache angenommen und zugleich den Wortschatz ihrer ursprünglichen Sprache behalten haben. Ein Beispiel hierfür ist die Sprache der Äynu in Xinjiang, die einen vorwiegend persischen Wortschatz in einen UIGURISCHEN Basiscode kopiert haben. Die Sprache funktioniert als

Geheimsprache bei Besuchen außerhalb der Siedlungsorte. Im südlichen Zentralasien und in Anatolien leben ähnliche seßhaft gewordene Nomadengruppen, die eine örtliche türkische Morphosyntax mit einem Wortschatz teils persischen, teils unbekannten Ursprungs kombinieren.

1.8. Sprachentod

Mehrere kleinere Türksprachen, z. B. in Sibirien, sind in den letzten Jahrzehnten gestorben. Einige sind heute in ihrer Existenz stark gefährdet, und zwar durch Funktionsverluste, die den Willen zur Weitergabe der Sprache an die nächste Generation vermindert. Unmittelbar bedroht sind Fu-Yü und der Halič-Dialekt des KARAIMISCHEN, mittelfristig auch etliche Sprachen wie KARAGASSISCH, das litauische KARAIMISCH und die kleinen Türksprachen Irans. Vereinzelt werden Versuche unternommen, bedrohte Sprachen zu konsolidieren, etwa das SCHORISCHE in Südsibirien. Die bedrohten Sprachen zeigen alle durch fremde Struktureigenschaften bedingte typologische Veränderungen, jedoch kaum typische Verfallserscheinungen wie etwa stark strukturelle Vereinfachung.

2. Phonologische Entwicklung

2.1. Segmentinventare

2.1.1. Vokale

Viele heutige Türksprachen besitzen acht in bezug auf die Merkmale ±vorn, ±gerundet und ±hoch klassifizierbare Vokalphoneme: *a, ï, o, u, ä, i, ö, ü*. Die Situation im Ost-Alttürkischen war ähnlich. Kontrovers ist, ob die Distinktion *i : ï* fehlte, ob dem *ä* ein höheres *e* gegenüberstand und ob in nicht-ersten Silben reduzierte zentralisierte *schwa*-ähnliche Vokale (durch ° bezeichnet) vorkamen.

Es gab auch lange, eventuell als Diphthonge realisierte Vokalphoneme, *ā, ū* usw. Die entsprechenden Längedistinktionen sind nur im TÜRKMENISCHEN, JAKUTISCHEN und CHALADSCHISCHEN systematisch bewahrt, z. B. CHAL. *bᵘuz* 'kalt'. Im Stammauslaut sind ursprüngliche Langvokale heute allgemein als Kurzvokale bewahrt, z. B. *qara* 'schwarz', während alte Kurzvokale geschwunden sind, z. B. *är* 'Mann' < *ärä*. Alte Kurzvokale nichterster Silben wurden vor Konsonanten reduziert, z. B. *qar°n* 'Bauch', und schwanden vor vokalischem Suffixanlaut, z. B. *qarn-i* 'sein / ihr Bauch'.

Die Distinktion *ä : e*, die wohl ursprünglich eher eine Distinktion *ä : ā* war, ist nur in einigen modernen Sprachen z. B. ASERBAIDSCHANISCH, vorhanden.

Die Vokalentwicklung ist z. T. durch örtlichen Fremdeinfluß geprägt. Iranischer Einfluß hat die Realisationen des Merkmals ±vorn getrübt und bei den Distinktionen: *ä : a, ö : o, ü : u, i : ï* gewisser USBEKISCHER Dialekte zur Zentralisierung geführt. In gewissen Sprachen, vor allem UIGURISCH, ist der phonetische Unterschied *i : ï* schwach. Der Einfluß ist jedoch weniger tief als oft angenommen. Trotz phonetisch weniger klarer Realisationen wird die phonologische Distinktion ±vorn überall aufrechterhalten.

Unter iranischem Einfluß ist in mehreren Sprachen Rundung *a > å* erfolgt, z. B. USB. *åt*, CHAL. *håt* 'Pferd'. Eine ähnliche Rundung ist im Wolga-Gebiet zu beobachten: TAT., BASCHK. > *å*, TSCHUW. > *u*.

Typisch für das Wolga-Kama-Gebiet ist die systematische Erhöhung tiefer Vokale, *ä > i, o > u, ö > ü*, z. B. TAT., BASCHK. *kil-* 'kommen' (< *käl-*). Dafür sind hohe Vokale zentralisiert und gekürzt worden: TAT., BASCHK. *i > ĕ, ï > ă, u > ŏ, ü > ŏ*. Die Tendenz geht weiter in den reduzierten TSCHUWASCHISCHEN Vokalen *ă* und *ĕ*, z. B. *tăr-* 'stehen', *pĕr* 'eins' (TTÜ. *dur-, bir*). Obwohl beide Tendenzen phonetische Parallelen in FINNOUGRISCHEN Nachbarsprachen haben, sind sie in den Türksprachen intern phonologisch motiviert: die Zentralisierung und Kürzung hoher Vokale sicherten die durch die Erhöhung tiefer Vokale gefährdeten Distinktionen.

Auf IRANISCHEN Substrateinfluß mögen auch die regressiven Vokalassimilationen des UIGURISCHEN zurückgehen: die Erhöhung von *a* und *ä* zu *i* in offenen Silben, z. B. *balilar* 'Kinder' (*bala* 'Kind') und der Umlaut von *a* und *ä* zu *e* in unbetonten offenen Silben vor hohen ungerundeten Vokalen der nächsten Silbe, z. B. *balïq > belïq* 'Fisch'.

2.1.2. Konsonanten

Das OST-ALTTÜRKISCHE hatte vermutlich die Klusile *p, t, k, b, d* und *g* (z. T. positionsbedingt als Frikative realisiert), die Frikative *s, z* und *š*, die Affrikaten *č* und *ǰ* sowie die Sonoranten *r, l, m, n, ŋ* und *ń*. Frikative wie *f, v, ž, θ* und Affrikaten wie *ts, dz* fehlten und sind auch für spätere Türksprachen atypisch geblieben. Ausnahmen sind etwa *v* u. a. in TÜRKEITÜRKISCH und ASERBAIDSCHANISCH, *ž* u. a. in KASACHISCH und *θ* in BASCHKIRISCH und TÜRKMENISCH.

Im Anlaut fehlten gewisse Konsonanten, vor allem Sonoranten. Später ist *m-* in vielen Sprachen als Assimilationsprodukt von *b-* vor nasalen Konsonanten entstanden, z. B. *män* 'ich' < *bän*. In Südsibirien tritt auch *ń-* und *n-* auf. Außerdem fehlten wahrscheinlich *p-*, *d-*, *g-*, *ǰ-*, *z-* und *š-*. Ein älteres **p-* dürfte früh in *h-* übergegangen sein, das heute nur im CHALADSCHISCHEN regelmäßig bewahrt ist, z. B. *hadaq* 'Fuß'. Anlautende *k-* und *t-*Laute sind in den Südwestsprachen teils stimmlos geblieben, teils stimmhaft geworden. Obwohl auch SAIANTÜRKISCH sowohl *t-* wie *d-* aufweist, dürfte der Unterschied keine ältere Opposition *t-* : *d-* reflektieren. Sprachen der Kaukasusregion weisen stark aspirierte stimmlose Klusile und Glottalklusile auf, z. B. KRTSCH. *tʰapʰ-* 'finden'. Ähnliche Tendenzen finden sich in SALARISCH und GELBUIGURISCH. Südsibirische Sprachen und FU-YÜ weisen aspirierte anlautende Fortes *pʰ-*, *tʰ-*, *kʰ-* in Lehnwörtern auf.

Einem südwest- und südosttürkischen *y-*, z. B. TTÜ. *yol* 'Weg', entsprechen im Nordwesttürkischen *ǰ-* ~ *ž-*, z. B. KIRG. *ǰol*, KAS. *žol*, im Südsibirischen meist *č-*, im TSCHUWASCHISCHEN der palatalisierte Frikativ *ś-*, z. B. *śul*, und im Jakutischen *s-*, z. B. *suol*.

Andere erwähnenswerte Veränderungen sind der Übergang *č-* > *š-* in Sprachen des kasachischen Typs sowie die Entwicklungen *s-* > *h-* im Baschkirischen und *s-* > Ø im JAKUTISCHEN, z. B. *arï* 'Butter' (ttü. *sarï* 'gelb').

Die Lenes *b*, *d*, *g*, die bereits im Ost-Alttürkischen zur Spirantisierung neigten (Johanson 1979), sind später weiter geschwächt geworden. In einigen, vor allem OGUSISCHEN, Sprachen entwickelten sich die Fortes u. a. nach altem Langvokal zu sekundären Lenes, z. B. ASERBAIDSCHANISCH *od* 'Feuer', *od-u* 'sein Feuer'. In Nordwestsprachen wurden intervokalische *p-* und *k-*Laute regelmäßig stimmhaft, z. B. BASCHK. *hiqĕδ* 'acht' (TTÜ. *sekiz*). In Südsibirien wurde auch intervokalisches *-t-* stimmhaft, z. B. CHAK. *ada* 'Vater' (TTÜ. *ata*). Das SAITANTÜRKISCHE kann — trotz intervokalischer Sonorisierung und silbenfinaler Desonorisierung — starke Obstruenten durch Glottalisation kennzeichnen, z. B. TUW. *aʔt* 'Pferd' vs. *at* 'Name', *aʔd-ïm* 'mein Pferd', *ad-ïm* 'mein Name'. Auch wenn das Glottalelement auf fremdes Substrat zurückgehen mag, besitzt es hier eine intern motivierte Funktion als vorgreifendes Fortissignal (Johanson 1991: 84—98). SALARISCH und GELBUIGURISCH weisen ähnliche Signale auf.

OGURISCH unterscheidet sich vom Gemeintürkischen u. a. durch die Lautvertretungen *r* und *l* statt *z* and *š* in gewissen Wörtern, z. B. TSCHUW. *śěr* 'hundert', *śul* 'Jahr' (TTÜ. *yüz* 'hundert', *yaş* 'Alter'). Diese Erscheinungen werden von Altaisten und Nicht-Altaisten unterschiedlich erklärt.

2.2. Silbenstruktur

Das TÜRKISCHE weist bereits in seiner ersten bekannten Form eine einfache Silbenstruktur auf. Die Silbe besteht typisch aus dem Vokal mit einem vorangehenden und/oder folgenden Konsonanten, z. B. *qum-da* 'im Sand'. Vokalhiatus und initiale Konsonanten-Cluster werden vermieden. Erlaubt sind auslautende Cluster mit einem Nasal, Liquid oder Sibilanten, z. B. *türk* 'Türke'. Bei Kombination zweier Morphe können maximal drei Konsonanten aufeinander folgen, z. B. *dostlar* 'Freunde'. Unter Fremdeinfluß haben zumindest gewisse Soziolekte einige Restriktionen in bezug auf Konsonanten-Cluster überwunden.

Grundlegend ist die Distinktion zwischen vorderer und hinterer Artikulation. Schon die syllabische ost-alttürkische Kerbschrift unterscheidet deutlich vordere und hintere Silben. Jede Silbe wird als +vorn oder −vorn klassifiziert, und der vordere oder hintere Charakter wird oft durch sowohl Vokal- wie Konsonantensegmente signalisiert. So kann eine vordere Silbe als *kül* 'Asche' und ihr hinteres Gegenstück als *qul* 'Sklave' realisiert werden.

Es gibt viele Ausnahmen von dieser phonetischen Situation. Gewissen Konsonanten, in einigen Sprachen auch gewissen Vokalen, fehlen klar unterschiedene vordere und hintere Varianten. In Lehnwörtern könnten phonetisch vordere Vokale mit phonetisch hinteren Konsonanten vorkommen und umgekehrt, z. B. TTÜ. *kâr* [kʲa : r] 'Gewinn'. Dennoch wird die Silbe als Ganzes phonologisch als +vorn oder −vorn eingestuft, was die Wahl der angefügten Suffixvarianten bestimmt.

Die phonetischen Realisationen der vorderen und hinteren Segmente variieren stark. Östlichere Sprachen neigen bei den dorsalen Obstruenten *k* und *q* zum Unterschied velar : tiefvelar, westlichere Sprachen dagegen zum Unterschied palatal : velar. In gewissen Sprachen hat eine unter fremdem, meist iranischem oder slavischem Einfluß nach vorne verschobene Artikulationsbasis die phonetische Realisation der Konsonanten beeinflußt. Palatalisation vorderer Konsonanten ist typisch für GAGAUSISCH, TSCHUWASCHISCH, KARAIMISCH, ASERBAIDSCHANISCHE Dialekte usw. Hier kann die Distinktion palatalisiert : nicht palatalisiert die vordere oder hintere Qualität der Silbe signalisieren, z. B. KAR. m'en' 'ich'.

2.3. Anpassung von Lehnwörtern

Aus anderen Sprachen kopierte Lexeme werden meist phonologisch angepaßt und nach türkischen phonotaktischen Regeln umgestaltet. Fremde Segmente werden durch die als ihre nächsten Äquivalente aufgefaßten türkischen Segmente ersetzt, in Zentralasien etwa f durch p, χ durch q und h durch Ø, z. B. KIRG. payda 'Nutzen', qabar 'Botschaft', ar 'jeder' (TTÜ. fayda, haber, her). ARABISCHE Glottalklusile werden im TATARISCHEN und BASCHKIRISCHEN durch γ ersetzt, z. B. γömĕr, und schwinden meist in anderen Sprachen, z. B. TTÜ. ömür 'Leben'. Langvokale werden oft durch Kurzvokale ersetzt.

Unzulässige Konsonanten-Cluster werden oft durch prothetische, epenthetische, epithetische Vokale, Synkope, Apokope oder Metathese aufgelöst, z. B. TTÜ. gireyfurut 'Grapefruit', istasyon 'Bahnhof', KIRG. dos 'Freund', kum. fikru 'Gedanke', (TTÜ. dost, fikir). Wörter mit anlautenden Nasalen und Liquiden wurden früher oft mit prothetischen Vokalen versehen, z. B. KAS. orïs 'Russe'.

Fremde Silben werden, auch wenn sie keine intrasyllabische Harmonie aufweisen, gemäß der einheimischen Phonologie als +vorn und −vorn klassifiziert. Persische und russische Silben mit k und q werden oft als +vorn interpretiert. Ein deutsches k wird im TÜRKEITÜRKISCHEN oft als ein hinteres Segment beurteilt, da es weiter hinten als das türkeitürkische Gegenstück artikuliert wird. ARABISCHE und PERSISCHE Vokale werden in bezug auf die Distinktion ±vorn unterschiedlich wiedergegeben: AS. χäbär 'Botschaft', täräf 'side', TTÜ. haber, taraf usw.

Intersyllabische Harmonisierung gehört meist nicht zu den ersten Anpassungsmaßnahmen. USBEKISCH, UIGURISCH, ASERBAIDSCHANISCH und TÜRKEITÜRKISCH sind hier relativ zurückhaltend, z. B. TTÜ. günâh 'Sünde', während andere Sprachen konsequenter sind: TKM. günä, KIRG. künö.

In der sowjetischen Zeit galt es als ungehörig, jüngere Lehnwörter aus dem RUSSISCHEN phonologisch anzupassen.

2.4. Suffixphonologie

Durch Morphologisierung und Analogisierung sind gewisse morphologische Suffixalternationen entstanden.

Das OST-ALTTÜRKISCHE besaß einige auf alte Langvokale zurückgehende Suffixvokale: die ungerundeten a, ä, i, eventuell ï, und die gerundeten o, ö und/oder u, ü. Im Nicht-Auslaut erschien auch das auf ursprüngliche Kurzvokale zurückgehende Element °, das in phonetischer Hinsicht vermutlich ein schwa oder reduzierte Vokale (ă, ĕ usw.) darstellte.

Es gab vier Klassen von Suffixvokalen. Eine enthielt die tiefen Vokale a und ä, z. B. im Pluralsuffix -lAr. Die zweite enthielt einen hohen ungerundeten Vokal, z. B. im Verbalsuffix -miš. Die dritte enthielt gerundete Vokale, o, ö und/oder u, ü, z. B. im Verbalsuffix -dWk. Eine vierte Klasse enthielt °, z. B. im Passivsuffix -(°)l. Sie ist traditionell als ein Wechsel der Vollvokale ï, i, u, ü interpretiert worden, d. h. als die gleiche Alternation, die sich in den drei letzten Jahrhunderten im TÜRKEITÜRKISCHEN langsam herausgebildet hat.

2.4.1. Intersyllabische Lautharmonie

Die OST-ALTTÜRKISCHEN Suffixalternationen basierten z. T. auf intersyllabischer Lautharmonie. Die sog. Palatalharmonie ist eine systematische Neutralisation der phonologischen Distinktion ±vorn in Suffixsilben unter dem Einfluß einer vorangehenden Stammsilbe. Letztere bestimmt die Qualität eines folgenden harmonischen Suffixes in bezug auf vordere und hintere Artikulation. Obwohl sich die Harmonie meist am klarsten in der Wahl der Vokale manifestiert, betrifft sie die ganze Silbe. So weist das Dativsuffix in vielen Sprachen die Variation -kä, -gä, -qa, -γa auf.

Die Formen der intersyllabischen Harmonie variieren beträchtlich. Wenn die Harmonieregeln konsequent angewendet werden, schließen vordere und hintere Silben einander in Wortformen aus, z. B. TTÜ. ev-ler-im-e 'meinen Häusern', at-lar-ım-a 'meinen Pferden'. Oft besteht aber ein Widerspruch zwischen Stamm- und Suffixvokal, oder einer von ihnen ist phonetisch vage. In Lehnwörtern enthält eine vordere Stammsilbe oft einen hinteren Vokal und umgekehrt, z. B. TTÜ. rol-ler 'Rollen', harp-ler 'Kriege'. Dennoch funktioniert die Harmonie. So werden z. B. auch dort, wo keine Opposition i : ï besteht, lexikalische Stammsilben in bezug auf ±vorn kategorisiert. Auch nach dem neutralen i des modernen Uigurisch wird die Harmonie beobachtet. Hier ist die Kategorisierung lexikalisch bedingt: so wählt z. B. *iš* 'Arbeit' hintere Suffixe, z. B. *iš-lar* 'Arbeiten'.

Suffixe sind am Anfang ihrer Entwicklung unharmonisch, invariabel. Im OST-ALTTÜRKISCHEN war z. B. das Dativsuffix *-qa* ein hinteres Suffix, während das Possessivsuffix *-(s)i* ein vorderes Suffix war. Das erste uns bekannte TÜRKISCH weist also viele disharmonische Wortformen auf. Das OSMANISCHE behielt bis spät unharmonische Suffixe der *i*-Klasse. Heute ist z. B. standard-TTÜ. *-ken* 'während' noch invariabel, während mehrere Entsprechungen in Dialekten harmonisch geworden sind.

Die Harmonisierungsprozesse sind oft von Irregularitäten geprägt. Wie die OSMANISCHEN und ASERBAIDSCHANISCHEN Entwicklungen zeigen, können der Stufe der Vokalharmonie Indifferenzstufen vorangehen, auf denen phonetische Neutralvokale stehen (Johanson 1991, 26−70).

2.4.2. Labialharmonie

Die sog. Labialharmonie, die eher den Charakter einer Vokalassimilation hat, bedeutet Neutralisation der Distinktion ±gerundet im Vokal einer Suffixsilbe unter Einfluß des Vokals der Stammsilbe. Sie war im OST-ALTTÜRKISCHEN noch nicht entwickelt und ist auch in gewissen heutigen Sprachen, etwa im TATARISCHEN, nur schwach vorhanden. In der Regel hat sie sich jedoch zu einem gewissen Grad entwickelt und gewinnt immer noch an Boden.

In vielen Sprachen betrifft die Labialharmonie nur hohe Suffixvokale, was Suffixe mit vierfach wechselndem Vokal wie etwa im TÜRKEITÜRKISCHEN erzeugt, z. B. *kız-ım* 'mein Mädchen', *at-ım* 'mein Pferd', *el-im* 'meine Hand', *ip-im* 'mein Seil', *kuş-um* 'mein Vogel', *yol-um* 'mein Weg', *gül-üm* 'meine Rose', *göl-üm* 'mein See'. Die Etablierung von Palatal- und Labialharmonie hat in gewissen Sprachen zum Zusammenfall der drei Suffixklassen geführt, die im ALTTÜRKISCHEN hohe ungerundete Vokale, gerundete Vokale und Vokale des Typs ° enthielten. Die OSMANISCHE Entwicklung zu dieser neuen Klasse (*ï, i, u, ü*) war ein langer Prozeß, der nicht vor dem 18. Jh. abgeschlossen war. In etlichen Sprachen ist er noch nicht durchgeführt.

Sprachen wie etwa JAKUTISCH, KIRGISISCH, ALTAITÜRKISCH und TÜRKMENISCH gehen weiter und wenden die Labialharmonie auch auf Suffixe mit tiefen Suffixvokalen an, z. B. KIRG. *köl-lör-dö* 'in den Seen'. Damit werden bis zu vier Suffixvarianten möglich, z. B. JAK. *-lAr* in *aγa-lar* 'Väter', *oγo-lor* 'Kinder', *kihi-lär* 'Menschen', *börö-lör* 'Wölfe'. Auch andere Sprachen weisen ähnliche Tendenzen auf. In keiner Türksprache wird die Labialharmonie jedoch mit voller Konsequenz angewendet.

2.4.3. Konsonantenassimilationen

Die verbreitetste Konsonantenassimilation ist die progressive Desonorisierung anlautender Suffixkonsonanten nach stimmlosen Auslautkonsonanten, z. B. TTÜ. *at-ta* 'auf dem Pferd' < *at* 'Pferd' + *-DA*. Im OST-ALTTÜRKISCHEN war wegen des damals nur partiellen Schwundes kurzer auslautender Stammvokale dieser Assimilationstyp noch unüblich. So hatte z. B. das Lokalsuffix außer nach Sonoranten die Form *-δA* (Johanson 1979).

In Sprachen des aralokaspischen und sibirischen Gebiets sind auch Assimilationen üblich, die auf Kontakt stammauslautender Dentale, Nasale und Sibilanten mit suffixanlautenden Liquiden und Nasalen beruhen. Die Mehrzahl ist progressiv, z. B. TUW. *χol-dar* 'Hände', *nom-nar* 'Bücher'. Gewisse Sprachen weisen aber auch regressive Assimilationen auf, die auf den Stamm rückwirken (3.2.).

2.5. Prosodie

Prosodische Phänomene, u. a. Intonationsmuster, sind relativ wenig untersucht. Die türkischen Betonungssysteme sind durch komplexe Interaktion von Pitch-Akzent und expiratorischer Betonung geprägt. Ihre diachrone Entwicklung ist weitgehend unbekannt.

3. Morphologische Entwicklung

Die morphologische Struktur des TÜRKISCHEN ist relativ stabil geblieben. Oft finden sich jedoch funktionale Unterschiede zwischen etymologisch entsprechenden Formen. Die Hauptwortklassen sind Nominale (Substantive, Adjektive, Pronomina, Numeralia), Verbale und Indeklinabilien.

3.1. Morphologische Techniken

Als Ergebnis vielfältiger Grammatikalisierungsprozesse hat das TÜRKISCHE Wort eine hochgradig synthetische Struktur, d. h. kann eine hohe Anzahl gebundener Morpheme enthalten. Stark fremdbeeinflußte Randsprachen in China, Iran usw. weisen eine weniger komplexe Wortstruktur auf.

Die Wortstruktur ist auch agglutinativ im Sinne von Juxtaposition, einem niedrigen Fusionierungsgrad. Der Primärstamm bleibt meist intakt, und es besteht im wesentlichen Eins-zu-eins-Übereinstimmung zwischen grammatischen Kategorien und ihren Exponenten, z. B. KIRG. *üy-lör-öm-dö* (Haus-PL-1SGPOSS-LOC) 'in meinen Häusern'. Die Morpheme haben wenige, leicht abtrennbare, meist phonologisch vorhersagbare Varianten. Ausnahmen finden sich u. a. bei Pronominalstämmen, wo Introflexion in Form von Vokalalternationen vorkommt, z. B. *bän* 'ich', *baŋa* 'mir' (Dativ), bei den Allomorphen von Kausativsuffixen, z. B. TTÜ. *bil-dir-* 'wissen lassen', *anla-t-* 'verstehen lassen', und „Aorist"-Suffixen, z. B. TTÜ. *gel-ir* 'kommt', *gid-er* 'geht'. Ältere Sprachen weisen mehr Ausnahmen auf, während in jüngeren viele Vereinheitlichungen stattgefunden haben. Ausnahmen von der normalen Wortstruktur sind auch durch stark kontrahierte Verbalformen einiger Sprachen entstanden (3.2.).

TÜRKISCHE Affixe sind fast ausnahmslos Suffixe. Einige Elemente, die Primärstämmen vorangehen können, sind in Wirklichkeit Nomina, die als freie Formen vorkommen können, z. B. *ön* 'Vorderseite' in der TÜRKEITÜRKISCHEN Lehnübersetzung *ön-gör-* 'vorsehen'. Einige Sprachen haben jedoch unter Fremdeinfluß tatsächlich Präfixe entwickelt, z. B. USB. *nå-toɣri* 'unrichtig'.

Die Suffixe bilden Distributionsklassen je nach ihrer Fähigkeit, relative Positionen im Wort einzunehmen. Suffixe, die den Primärstamm modifizieren, stehen ihm am nächsten, d. h. Ableitungssuffixe gehen Flexionssuffixen voran. Jedes hinzugefügte Suffix neigt dazu, den ganzen vorangehenden Stamm zu modifizieren.

Morphologische Eigenschaften werden wegen der hochgradigen Synthese des TÜRKISCHEN Wortes relativ selten kopiert. Periphere Suffixe werden eher ersetzt als die dem Primärstamm am nächsten stehenden, z. B. aktionale und diathetische Verbalsuffixe. Vereinzelt sind fremde kombinatorische Muster kopiert worden. So gehen z. B. im TSCHUWASCHISCHEN die Possessivsuffixe den Pluralsuffixen voran, was gegen die TÜRKISCHE Norm verstößt.

3.2. Alternationen in Primärstämmen

Durch Lautveränderungen sind auch in Primärstämmen morphonologische Alternationen entstanden, die für agglutinative Sprachen untypische Unregelmäßigkeiten verursachen. Ein Beispiel ist das Auftreten sekundärer Lenisobstruenten (2.1.2.), die im Silbenauslaut stimmtonschwach und sonst stimmhaft sind, z. B. TKM. *git-* 'gehen', *gid-y̆är* 'geht'. Durch Umlaut entstehen UIGURISCHE Alternationen wie *baš* 'Kopf', *beš-im* 'mein Kopf'. Konsonantenveränderungen ergeben Fälle wie JAK. *as-* 'stechen', *Anyˇ-abïn* 'Ich steche', *bis-* 'schneiden', *Bïh-abïn* 'Ich schneide'. Regressive Assimilation führt zu Primärstammveränderungen wie JAK. *at* 'Pferd', *ak-ka* 'zum Pferd'. Durch Kontraktion entstehen Formen wie UIG. *qï-p* 'getanhabenderweise' (*qïl-* 'tun'). Kontraktionen und Assimilationen ergeben Fälle wie TUW. *saɣïn-* 'bedenken', *saqt-ïr* 'bedenkt'. Durch Kombination aktionaler und aspektueller Konstruktionen entstehen oft auch komplexe und kaum agglutinativ anmutende Formen wie USB. *Qil-yäppän* 'Ich tue (gerade)' < *qïl-a yat-ïp [tur-ur] men*.

3.3. Stammbildung

Seit den ersten bekannten Entwicklungsstufen des TÜRKISCHEN besteht ein scharfer Unterschied zwischen Nominal- und Verbalstämmen. Von primären Nominal- und Verbalstämmen werden sekundäre Nominal- und Verbalstämme gebildet. Die Stammbildungsprinzipien sind in allen bekannten Sprachen gleich geblieben, auch wenn die Suffixinventare stark fremdbeeinflußter Sprachen gewissen Reduktionstendenzen unterliegen.

3.4. Derivation

Zur Wortbildung in älteren Türksprachen, s. Berta 1996, Erdal 1991. Einige Sprachen haben gewisse die dem TÜRKISCHEN sonst fremde denominale Ableitungssuffixe kopiert, z. B. SLAVISCHE Feminsuffixe wie in TTÜ. *kral-içe* 'Königin', KAR. *karay-ka* 'Karaimin' oder ARABISCHE und RUSSISCHE Adjektivsuffixe wie OSM. *-î*, CHAK. *-nay*, *-skay*. Das TÜRKEITÜRKISCHE Adjektivsuffix *-(s)al* wurde als neologistischer Ersatz für *-ī* geschaffen, z. B. *din-sel* 'religiös' (*din-î*).

Eine große Rolle bei der Verbderivation spielen Kombinationen von Konverbformen mit darauf folgender Verbform, z. B. USB. *ål-ip kel-* ('genommenhabenderweise kommen') 'bringen'. Analytische Derivation denominaler Verbalstämme erfolgt mit Paraphrasen, die ein Proverb wie *et-*, *qïl-*, *yap-* 'tun' und ein inkorporiertes Nomen enthalten, z. B. TTÜ. *imza et-* 'unterschreiben' (synthetisch *imza-la-*). Mit dieser Methode sind aus fremdem Wortmaterial große Mengen TÜRKISCHER Verben gebildet worden.

3.5. Nominalflexion

Nominale nehmen in allen Türksprachen Numerus-, Possessiv- und Kasussuffixe an. Genusmarkierungen fehlen.

Das Pluralsuffix ist meist -*lAr* usw., z. B. TAT. *qolaq-lar* 'Ohren', im TSCHUWASCHISCHEN die Neuerung -*sem*. Im OST-ALTTÜRKISCHEN ist -*lAr* noch ein Kollektivsuffix unbekannter Etymologie (Pritsak 1963: 36).

Possessivsuffixe signalisieren Person und Numerus und weisen typischerweise die Formen -*(I)m*, -*(I)ŋ*, -*(s)I*, -*(I)mIz*, -*(I)ŋIz*, -*LArI* auf (mit dem Pluralelement -*Iz* in 1. und 2. P. Pl.).

Die Kasusformen sind relativ stabil geblieben. Heutige Sprachen besitzen außer dem suffixlosen Nominativ meist vier durch betonbare Suffixe ausgedrückte Grundkasus: Genitiv auf -*nIŋ* usw., Dativ auf -*GA* usw., Akkusativ auf -*NI* usw., Lokativ auf -*DA*, Ablativ auf -*DAn*.

Mehrere Abweichungen von diesem Schema sind zu verzeichnen. JAKUTISCH hat den Genitiv verloren. Verschmelzungen finden sich z. B. im TSCHUWASCHISCHEN Dativ-Akkusativ und im Genitiv-Akkusativ USBEKISCHER Dialekte, des KUMÜKISCHEN und des KARATSCHAISCH-BALKARISCHEN. Die Sprache der OST-ALTTÜRKISCHEN Inschriften hat ein Lokativ-Ablativ-Suffix, das später meist als Lokativsuffix, im JAKUTISCHEN aber als Partitivsuffix dient. Seine Ablativfunktion ist für das ältere OGUSISCH und das heutige CHALADSCHISCH typisch. Als chaladschisches Lokativsuffix dient wiederum -*čA*, das aus einem Äquativsuffix entwickelt sein mag.

Gewisse Sprachen besitzen periphere, durch unbetonbare Suffixe ausgedrückte Kasus, z. B. Äquativ ('wie'), Direktiv ('in Richtung auf'), Terminativ ('bis zu'), Komitativ ('zusammen mit'), Instrumental ('mittels'), Prodessiv ('für'), Komparativ ('als'). Einige dieser Marker sind eher Postpositionen, die Grundkasus regieren können. Etliche als Kasusmarker geltende OST-ALTTÜRKISCHE Suffixe sind unproduktiv und liegen nur in versteinerten adverbialen Relikten vor.

3.6. Pronominalflexion

ALTTÜRKISCHE Personal- und Demonstrativpronomina bilden eine morphologisch distinkte Subklasse mit besonderen obliquen Stämmen auf -*n*, z. B. *an*- für *ol* 'jener'. Die Personalpronomina *bän* 'ich' und *sän* 'du' gehen von **bi* und **si* aus und haben Pluralformen auf -*z*, *biz* 'wir', *siz* 'ihr'. Alte Spezifika der Pronominalflexion sind manchmal bewahrt, z. B. in TTÜ. *bana* 'mir', *sana* 'dir', und manchmal durch Regularisierungen verdrängt worden, z. B. USB. *men-gä*, *sen-gä*.

In den älteren Sprachen weisen Possessivsuffixe der 3. Person vor Kasussuffixen ein „pronominales *n*" auf, z. B. *atïŋa* 'seinem/ihrem Pferd'; der Akkusativ hat meist nur dieses Element als Endung. Es wurde z. T. schon im TSCHAGATAISCHEN aufgegeben und fehlt im heutigen UIGURISCH und USBEKISCH, z. B. USB. *åtigä* 'seinem/ihrem Pferd', *ånäsidä* 'bei seiner/ihrer Mutter' (TTÜ. *atına*, *annesinde*). Im JAKUTISCHEN bilden Nomina mit Possessiv- und Kasusmarkern spezielle, vom agglutinativen Prinzip recht abweichende Paradigmen.

Possessivpronomina stellen, wie im Balkan-Sprachbund, Genitivformen von Personal- und Demonstrativpronomina dar. Die Reflexivpronomina *kändi*, *öz*, *bot*, TSCHUW. *χa* usw. gehen, soweit etymologisierbar, auf Wörter für 'Inneres', 'Kern', 'Gestalt' zurück. Sie dienen oft als höfliche Personalpronomina der 3. Person, z. B. TTÜ. *kendisi* 'er/sie [in eigener Person]'. In der Regel besitzen Türksprachen aber nicht sehr elaborierte honorative Systeme der Anrede.

3.7. Personalsuffixe

Die Nominalmorphologie umfaßt als peripherstes Element kopulative Personalmarker, die als Subjektvertreter Person und Numerus des Erstaktanten ausdrücken. Kopulasätze der identifizierenden, attribuierenden und lokalisierenden nicht-verbalen Prädikation werden meist ohne Verben gebildet. Die Marker der 1. und 2. Person sind unbetonbare, aus Personalpronomina entwickelte Kopulaelemente, z. B. KIRG. *Qïrgïz-mïn* 'Ich bin Kirgise'. In der 3. Person fehlt oft eine Kopula, z. B. KAS. *Bolat žaqsï adam* 'Bolat ist ein guter Mann'. In einigen Sprachen werden unbetonbare Suffixe des Typs -*DIr* 'ist' < *turur* 'steht' verwendet. Im älteren Türkisch diente auch das Demonstrativpronomen der 3. Person *ol* als Kopula.

Die erwähnten Personalsuffixe erscheinen z. T. auch in der Verbalmorphologie, wo ein gewisser Synkretismus mit Possessivsuffixen festzustellen ist. Insgesamt herrschen auf dem Gebiet der Personalmarkierung recht große Unterschiede zwischen den heutigen Türksprachen.

3.8. Suffixe am Verb

Zahlreiche Modifikationen können am türkischen Verb realisiert werden: Aktionsart, Genus verbi, Possibilität, Negation, Aspekt,

Modus, Tempus, Person, Numerus, Interrogation usw., meist in dieser Reihenfolge. Lange Morphemsequenzen können somit erzeugt werden, z. B. TTÜ. *Kov-ala-n-ma-mış-tı-k* ('verfolgen' + Iterativ + Passiv + Negation + postterminaler Aspekt + Vergangenheit + 1. P. Pl.') 'Wir waren nicht verfolgt worden'. Die betreffenden Kategorien können so gut wie nie durch andere Mittel, etwa adverbiale Umschreibungen, realisiert werden.

Zu den Aktionsartsuffixen, die eine ausgedrückte Tätigkeit modifizieren, gehören Marker der Intensität, Frequentativität usw., z. B. KRIMTAT. *käs-kälä-* 'immer wieder schneiden'. Es gibt auch Desiderative und Similative wie in KARACHANIDISCH *kör-ügsä-* 'sehen wollen', *käl-imsin-* 'vorgeben zu kommen'. Suffixe dieses Typs sind aber in modernen Sprachen schwach vertreten.

Besser entwickelt sind analytische Methoden, bei denen ein Auxiliar die vorangehende Konverbform eines lexikalischen Verbs aktional modifiziert. Derartige Postverbien, die indoeuropäischen Präverbien entsprechen, tragen dazu bei, die Tätigkeit genauer zu beschreiben. Sie mögen eine Phase des lexikalischen Verbinhalts spezifizieren oder angeben, ob die Tätigkeit dauerhaft, momentan, wiederholt, ingressiv usw. ist, z. B. TTÜ. *yazıp dur-* ('schreibenderweise stehen') 'dauernd schreiben', USB. *yıγ-läb yubär-* ('weinenderweise senden') 'anfangen zu weinen'. Insbesondere dienen sie der Spezifikation von Transformativität und Nontransformativität (Schönig 1994), zwei für Aspektrealisationen grundlegenden semantischen Eigenschaften. Transformativa bezeichnen telische Tätigkeiten, die einen natürlichen Wendepunkt implizieren, und werden oft durch Verben wie 'senden' usw. spezifiziert. Nontransformativa, denen die erwähnte Eigenschaft fehlt, werden oft mit Verben wie 'stehen', 'liegen' usw. spezifiziert. Postverbien, oft irrtümlich „Aspektverben" genannt, sind in gewissen Sprachen, z. B. den südsibirischen, besonders gut entwickelt.

Was die Suffixe der Genera verbi betrifft, ist ihre Herkunft (vermutlich aus ehemaligen Hilfsverben) trotz einer Fülle von Spekulationen unbekannt. Für sie alle gilt, daß alternative analytische Konstruktionen mit Auxiliarverben fehlen.

Das häufigste Passivsuffix ist *-(I)l*, z. B. *ört-ül-* 'bedeckt werden'. Sog. Reflexivsuffixe des Typs *-(I)n* haben in älteren Sprachen oft mediale Bedeutung, z. B. *al-ïn-* 'für sich nehmen'. Zwischen Passiv- und Reflexivsuffixen bestehen enge Beziehungen und Verflechtungen. Beide drücken häufig antikausative Bedeutungen aus, und *-(I)n* ist in vielen Sprachen mehrdeutig, da es auch als Allomorph des Passivsuffixes auftritt, z. B. TTÜ. *tara-n-* 'gekämmt werden', 'sich kämmen'. Kausativsuffixe sind *-(I)r, -GUr, -(I)t, -DUr, -(I)z* usw., z. B. *öl-ür-* 'sterben lassen, töten', *ye-dür-* 'essen lassen, füttern'. Kooperativ-reziproke Suffixe, die Zusammenarbeit, Gegenseitigkeit oder Wettstreit von Partizipanten ausdrücken, haben meist die Form *-(I)š*, z. B. *kör-üš-* 'einander sehen'. Das OST-ALTTÜRKISCHE besitzt eine größere Anzahl Genera verbi-Suffixe, deren Funktionen noch nicht eindeutig feststehen.

Possibilitätsmarker sind postverbiale Marker aus Hilfsverben wie *bil-* 'wissen' und *al-* 'nehmen', z. B. KIRG. *ber-e al-* 'geben können'. Die meisten sind zu Suffixen geworden: TTÜ. *ver-ebil-* 'id.'.

Das verbale Negationssuffix weist vom Alttürkischen bis heute Formen wie *-MA* auf, z. B. TUW. *Käl-bä-diŋ* (komm-NEG-PRET-2SG) 'Du kamst nicht'.

3.8.1. Thematische Suffixe

Verbale Prädikate tragen thematische Suffixe, die Aspekt, Modus und Tempus ausdrücken. In syntaktischer Hinsicht sind sie oft, besonders in älteren Sprachen, vielseitig verwendbar: viele können sowohl finit, als Kern von Hauptsätzen, wie auch infinit, als Prädikatskern eingebetteter Sätze dienen. So dient etwa *-GAn* als Finitform, Verbalsubstantiv und Partizip, z. B. *käl-gän* 'ist gekommen', 'Kommen, Gekommensein', 'gekommen'. Die Bedeutungen einer Einheit in verschiedenen syntaktischen Funktionen können u. U. recht unterschiedlich sein. Viele moderne Sprachen haben relativ differenzierte Systeme entwickelt. In bezug auf finite und infinite Verwendung sind drei Kategorien von Suffixen zu unterscheiden: (1) nur infinit gebrauchte, (2) infinit und finit gebrauchte, (3) nur finit gebrauchte. Einheiten der Kategorie (1) können in die Kategorie (2) übergehen und dabei Einheiten der Kategorie (3) verdrängen. Übergänge in die Kategorie (3) sind nicht eindeutig belegt.

Türksprachen weisen meistens umfangreiche Inventare finiter thematischer Formen einfacher und komplexer Art auf.

3.8.2. Aspektotemporale Systeme

Gewisse Sprachen verfügen über sehr feinmaschige aspektotemporale Systeme. Die Hauptkategorien basieren immer auf drei

Aspektmarker-Typen, die unterschiedliche Perspektiven bieten, unter denen ein Ereignis relativ zu seinen Grenzen betrachtet werden kann:

(1) *Intraterminale* Einheiten wie Präsens- und Imperfektformen betrachten das Ereignis innerhalb seiner Grenzen, d. h. nach seinem Anfang und vor seinem Ende. Einige fokussieren näher auf den Befund am Blickpunkt, etwa im Sinne englischer Progressiva, z. B. USB. *kel-äyåtir* 'kommt gerade'. Andere, die weniger darauf fokussieren, werden für Ereignisse gebraucht, die eine allgemeinere Gültigkeit haben, z. B. KAS. *qus uš-adï* 'der Vogel fliegt'. Die intraterminale Fokalität kann relativ hoch, relativ niedrig oder nicht vorhanden sein. Es gibt auch entsprechende präteritale Einheiten, mehr oder weniger fokale Imperfekta.

(2) *Postterminale* Einheiten wie Perfekta und Konstativa betrachten das Ereignis nach seiner (mit dem aktionalen Inhalt wechselnden) relevanten Grenze. Einige fokussieren näher auf den Befund am Blickpunkt im Sinne von Stativa oder Resultativa, z. B. TTÜ. *öl-müş bulunuyor* ('ist im Zustand des Gestorbenseins') 'ist (gerade) gestorben'. Weniger fokale Einheiten ähneln Perfektformen, die die aktuelle Relevanz eines anterioren Ereignisses ausdrücken, z. B. KUM. *bar-γan* 'ist gegangen'. Auch hier kann die Fokalität relativ hoch, relativ niedrig oder nicht vorhanden sein. Entsprechende Plusquamperfekta drücken den postterminalen Aspekt in der Vergangenheit aus, z. B. KUM. *bar-γan edi* 'war gegangen'.

(3) *Terminale* Einheiten präsentieren das Ereignis direkt und als Ganzheit, indem sie das Erreichen seiner relevanten Grenze implizieren, z. B. das einfache Präteritum in USB. *yåz-di* 'schrieb'.

Die betreffenden GramMeme bilden in so gut wie allen Türksprachen rekurrente Aspekt-Tempus-Systeme (vgl. Johanson 1971, 1996a, 1998).

3.8.3. Aspekterneuerungen

Die Grammatikalisierungspfade aspektotemporaler Einheiten sind gut bekannt. Intra- wie Postterminalia neigen zur abnehmenden Fokalität, zur weniger engen Perspektive. So ist die Fokalität regelmäßig erneuert worden: die intraterminale durch neue hochfokale, „progressive" Präsens- und Imperfektformen, die postterminale durch neue hochfokale „Stativa" oder „Resultativa".

Das OST-ALTTÜRKISCHE Präsens („Aorist") auf *-(V)r* und das Imperfekt auf *-(V)r ärdi* waren Intraterminalia mit weitem Funktionsumfang. Später wurde, außer im JAKUTISCHEN, ihre Fokalität durch postverbiale Periphrasen mit Verben wie 'stehen', 'liegen', 'gehen' und 'sitzen' erneuert.

In Nordwest- und Südostsprachen dominiert das Muster *-A turur*, z. B. *yaz-a turur* ('steht schreibenderweise') 'ist am Schreiben' > 'schreibt'. Die Lautgestalt wurde später reduziert, z. B. KAS. *kel-edi* 'kommt', KUM. *bar-a* 'geht'. Entsprechende Imperfekta folgen dem Muster *-A tur-* + 'war'.

Südwestsprachen wählen *-A yorïr*, z. B. *yaz-a yorïr* ('geht schreibenderweise') 'ist am Schreiben' > 'schreibt'. Auch hier wurde die Lautform reduziert: TTÜ. *yaz-ıyor*, AS. *yaz-ïr*, TKM. *yaδ-yär*. Entsprechende Imperfekta folgen den Mustern *-A yorïr -* + 'war', z. B. TTÜ. *yaz-ıyor-du* 'schrieb (gerade)'.

Südsibirische Sprachen bevorzugen *-(I)p turur*, z. B. TUW. *kör-üp tur* 'sieht', Muster mit *yat-* 'liegen' usw.

Gewisse Sprachen erlebten eine zweite Erneuerung nach dem Muster *-A* oder *-(I)p* + Präsens von *tur-* 'stehen' oder *yat-* 'liegen', z. B. KRTSCH. *al-a-turadï* 'ist am Nehmen', KIRG. *oqu-p turat* 'ist am Lesen', UIG. *yez-iwatidu* 'ist am Schreiben'. Auch hier finden sich entsprechende, mit 'war' gebildete Imperfekta.

Die Fokalität der alten Postterminalia *-mIš* und *-GAn* wurde in gewissen Sprachen nach dem Muster *-(I)p turur* erneuert, z. B. *yaz-ïp turur* ('steht geschriebenhaberweise') 'ist im Zustand des Geschriebenhabens' > 'hat geschrieben'. Auch hier wurde die Lautgestalt reduziert, z. B. TKM. *yaδ-ïp-dïr*, AS. *yaz-ïb*. Die Form entwickelte sich später zum Perfekt ('hat geschrieben') und zum indirektiven Präteritum ('hat, wie sich herausstellt, geschrieben'). Gewisse Sprachen erlebten eine zweite Erneuerung nach dem Muster *-(I)p* + Präsens von *tur-* 'stehen', z. B. KRTSCH. *ket-ib tur-adï* 'ist gegangen', KUM. *gel-ip tur-a* 'ist gekommen'.

Alle Erneuerungen der Fokalität gehen von Postverbien aus. Einige Formen sind scheinbar identisch mit Formen der aktionalen Modifikation (Johanson 1995), werden aber durch spezifische Akzentkonturen davon unterschieden, z. B. NOG. *kel-é tur-adï* 'kommt' (durative Aktionsart + Präsens) : *kel-e tur-ádï* 'ist am Kommen' (hochfokales Präsens).

Der „Aorist" wurde durch den Fokalitätsschwund meist zu einer modalen Einheit, die Neigung, Disposition und Prospektivität ausdrückt, z. B. NOG. *ber-er* 'mag, wird, ist geneigt zu geben'. Das Suffix hat sich unterschiedlich entwickelt. Das im OST-ALTTÜRKISCHEN nach Vokalauslaut bewahrte *-yUr*, z. B. *bāš-lā-yur* 'führt an', wurde später kontrahiert, z. B. *bašlar*. Zu vermuten ist eine frühere ähnliche Entwicklung nach kurzen Vokalen, z. B. **atáyur > atar* 'wirft', **käliyur > kälir* 'kommt'. TÜRKEITÜRKISCH hat die Variation hoher und tiefer Vokale bewahrt: *at-ar, gel-ir*. TÜRKMENISCH hat das Suffix zu *-A(:)r* vereinheitlicht: *at-ar, gel-er*. Das ASERBAIDSCHANISCHE Einheitssuffix *-(y)Ar* unterscheidet sich vom Präsenssuffix *-(y)Ir* nur durch die Höhe des Vokals: *at-ar, gäl-är* (Präsens *at-ïr, gäl-ir*). Auch außerhalb der Südwestgruppe ist der Aoristvokal meist vereinheitlicht.

3.8.4. Modale Kategorien

Die Illokutionsmodi Imperativ und Optativ sind eng miteinander verbunden. Der Optativ tritt auch in ähnlichen Funktionen wie der Konditional auf. Die relevanten honorativen Ebenen der Imperative wechseln von Sprache zu Sprache. Nezessitativsuffixe drücken Obligativität und Desiderativität aus, z. B. TAT. *bar-asï* 'sollte gehen', AS. *gäl-mäli* 'sollte kommen'. Intentionalsuffixe drücken Absichten aus, z. B. UIG. *yaz-maqči* 'will schreiben'. Ältere Sprachen besitzen keine spezifischen Futursuffixe. Optative, Nezessitative und Aoriste üben auch prospektive Funktionen aus. Spätere Futursuffixe wie OSM. *-(y)AjAK* haben starke illokutivmodale Nuancen ('sollen' usw.).

Epistemische Modalitäten werden durch Indirektive und Präsumptive ausgedrückt. Die Indirektive sind evidentielle Kategorien, die ein Ereignis unter Bezugnahme auf seine Rezeption durch ein bewußtes Subjekt darstellen (s. Johanson & Utas 1999). Dieses wird nicht direkt, sondern als Ereignis einer Schlußfolgerung ('wie sich herausstellt', 'offensichtlich') darstellt. Die Quelle der Information mag Hörensagen, Inferenz aus Resultaten oder eigene Wahrnehmung sein. Postterminalia auf *-mIš* und *-(I)ptIr* neigen oft zur Indirektivität, z. B. TTÜ. *Ali gel-miş* 'Ali ist [wie ich schließe] gekommen', KAS. *bar-iptï*, JAK. *bar-bït* 'ist offenbar gegangen'. Es finden sich auch an Nominalstämme angefügte tempus-indifferente indirektive Kopularartikeln wie *emiš* und *ekän*, z. B. TTÜ. *Ali geliyormuş* 'Ali ist/war [wie ich schließe] am Kommen'. Die Partikel *ekän* kodiert meist 'wie sich herausstellt'.

Präsumptivmarker sind von *turur* 'steht' entwickelt, z. B. UIG. *yazγan-du* 'hat vermutlich geschrieben', TTÜ. *uyuyor-dur* 'schläft vermutlich'.

3.8.5. Personalsuffixe

Auch am finiten Verb sind die person- und numerusmarkierenden „Subjektvertreter" die peripherstens Elemente. In der 1. und 2. Person sind sie weitgehend identisch mit den an nicht-verbalen Prädikaten gebrauchten, z. B. KIRG. *Kele-biz* 'Wir kommen'. Die 3. Person ist meist unmarkiert. Das einfache Präteritum trägt betonbare Suffixe, die den Possessivsuffixen ähneln, z. B. USB. *Keldi-m* 'Ich kam'. Im Laufe der Sprachgeschichte ist ein erheblicher Synkretismus der Suffixtypen zu verzeichnen. In den TÜRKMENISCHEN, JAKUTISCHEN und SAIANTÜRKISCHEN Imperativsuffixen der 1. P. Pl. finden sich Spuren bzw. Ansätze einer Distinktion Inklusiv : Exklusiv.

In einigen Sprachen fehlen Personalsuffixe an bestimmten thematischen Stämmen, z. B. TKM. *Men geljek* 'Ich werde kommen', UIG. *Män yaz-γan* 'Ich habe geschrieben'. In den fremdbeeinflußten Randsprachen des chinesischen Gebiets ist dies die Regel, z. B. SALARISCH *Män kilär* 'Ich werde kommen', GELBUIGURISCH *Sän parar* 'Du wirst gehen'.

3.8.6. Infinite thematische Formen

Thematische Stämme infiniter Verbformen werden mit Suffixen der Nomina actionis sowie Partizipial- und Konverbsuffixen gebildet.

Nomen actionis-Suffixe sind etwa USB. *-Gän, -GänliK, -ädigän*, TTÜ. *-DIK, -(y)AcAK, -mA*, z. B. *al-dığ-ım* ('mein Nehmen'), '(die Tatsache,) daß ich genommen habe/nehme'.

Partizipien sind oft formal identisch mit den Nomina actionis, z. B. TTÜ. *al-dığ-ım* ('mein Nehmen') 'was ich genommen habe/nehme'. Die einzigen Vertreter des alten postterminalen Partizipialsuffixes („Perfekt-Partizips") *-mIš* sind heute TTÜ., AS. *-mIš* und JAK. *-BIT*, während sonst *-GAn* (vgl. SÜDWESTTÜRKISCH *-(y)An*) verwendet wird. Es finden sich auch intraterminale Partizipien („Präsens-Partizipien") verschiedener Fokalitätsgrade, z. B. KIRG. *oqu-p jatqan* '(gerade) lesend', prospektive Partizipien („Futur-Partizipien"), nezessitative Partizipien und „participia nondum facti", die noch nicht erfolgte Ereignisse bezeichnen, z. B. TUW. *käl-gäläk* 'noch nicht gekommen'.

Konverbmarker sind in allen bekannten Phasen des TÜRKISCHEN reichlich vorhanden. Dieser Reichtum ist ein großareales Phänomen mit seinem Zentrum in den ALTAISCHEN Sprachen. Die Formen sind meist syntaktisch monofunktional, d. h. dienen nur als Verbaladverbien. Einige Marker sind morphologisch unanalysierbar, z. B. USB. *yåz-gäč* 'geschriebenhabenderweise', andere komplex, auf Verbalnomina basierend und mit Kasus bzw. Postpositionen markiert, z. B. KIRG. *kel-gen-de* 'beim Kommen'.

Konverbmarker drücken verschiedene Relationen aspektueller, temporaler und anderer Art zum Inhalt des Matrixsatzes aus: Intraterminalität, Postterminalität, Terminalität, Anteriorität ('nachdem'), zeitliche Inklusion ('während'), Abtemporalität ('seitdem'), Limitation ('bis'), Grund ('weil'), Instrument ('dadurch, daß'), Zweck ('damit'), Übereinstimmung ('wie'), Ersatz ('statt'), Bedingung ('falls') usw. Alle Sprachen besitzen einen terminalen Konverbmarker, der gebraucht werden kann, ohne den Matrixsatz zu modifizieren: *-(I)p*, TTÜ. *-(y)Ip*, TSCHUW. *-sA*, JAK. *-(A)n*, z. B. TTÜ. *gid-ip* 'gehend (und ...)'.

Konditionalsätze basieren auf Suffixen des Typs *-sA* und Kopularpartikeln des Typs *esä* 'wenn ... ist'. Das vielleicht aus *sā-* 'rechnen' entwickelte *-sA* (OST-ATÜ. *-sa-r*) wird in älteren und einigen heutigen Sprachen auch temporal verwendet. Die Konditionalsysteme sind gut ausgestattet, um verschiedene Arten von Bedingung sowie aspektotemporale Unterschiede differenziert auszudrücken. Konzessive Konditionale entstehen durch Zusatz eines Elements 'auch', z. B. TTÜ. *gelse de* 'auch wenn er [usw.] kommen sollte'. Zu konditionalen Topik-Markern s. 4.9.

Nomina actionis und viele Partizipien tragen possessive Personalmarker, z. B. TTÜ. *gör-düǧ-üm* 'daß/was ich sehe/sah'. Auch Konditionalformen tragen Suffixe eines possessiven Typs, z. B. TTÜ. *gelse-m* 'wenn ich kommen sollte'. Komplexe Konverbformen enthalten oft Personalmarker, z. B. OST-ATÜ. *olor-duq-°m-a* 'als ich mich niederließ'. Dies gilt in der Regel nicht für einfache Formen. JAKUTISCHE Konverbformen enthalten jedoch, wohl unter TUNGUSISCHEM Einfluß, Personal- und Numerussuffixe, z. B. *bar-am-mïn* 'ich gegangenerweise'.

3.9. Freie grammatische Relatoren

Postpositionen bilden oft umfassende Systeme von grammatischen Relatoren, welche die durch die Kasus ausgedrückten relationalen Konzepte differenzieren. Einige, z. B. *bir-lä* 'mit', *soŋ-ra* 'nach', sind homonym mit Adverbien, die ihrerseits oft versteinerte Kasusformen, etwa Instrumentale und Direktive darstellen. Andere sind reanalysierte Konverbformen, z. B. USB. *kör-ä* 'gemäß' (*kör-* 'sehen'), *ål-ip* 'angefangen von' (*ål-* 'nehmen'). Viele regieren Kasus (Genitiv, Dativ, Ablativ), z. B. UIG. *biz-diŋ burun* 'vor uns' (Ablativ). Ein besonderer Typ basiert auf possessiv- und kasusmarkierten Substantiven, meist Raumsubstantiven, z. B. TTÜ. *ev(in) önünde* 'vor dem Haus' (3.10). Als Relatoren reanalysierte Konverbformen sind z. B. auch TTÜ. *olarak* ('seiend'), '(in der Eigenschaft) als' und *di-ye* ('sagend'), ein Junktor, der Äußerungen und Gedankeninhalte zitiert (4.11.3.2.).

3.10. Bildung postpositiver Marker

TÜRKISCHE postpositive Marker sind in systematischen Entwicklungsprozessen mit gut erkennbaren Einzelphasen entstanden. Analytische Konstruktionen haben sich durch Verschiebung der Wortgrenzen in synthetische entwickelt, d. h. durch Übergang von der Linksverzweigung im Satz zur Rechtsverzweigung im Wort.

Den Ausgangspunkt der Entwicklung eines Postpositionstyps bilden zwei durch Genitivkonstruktion verbundene Lexeme, z. B. *ev-in ön-ün-de* 'auf der Vorderseite des Hauses', wo *ön-ü* den Kopf des vorangehenden Substantivs darstellt. Durch Reanalyse wird es zum grammatischen Relator mit dem allgemeineren Inhalt 'vor', was eine Umkehrung der Modifikation bedeutet. Obwohl noch ein dekliniertes Substantiv, ist es nicht mehr ein von einem Genitivattribut *ev-in* modifiziertes Nominal. Junge Postpositionen wie *önünde* können immer noch frei, als Adverbialien, vorkommen. Später mag es möglich bzw. notwendig werden, das Genitivsuffix wegzulassen, z. B. *ev önünde*, oder die Postposition in einer lexikalisierten Kasusform zu verwenden, z. B. *hakkında* ('in seinem Recht') 'betreffend'.

Alte unanalysierbare Postpositionen wie *üčün* 'für' mögen ähnlichen Ursprungs sein. Sie haben eine Stufe erreicht, wo sie nicht mehr frei verwendet werden können, mögen aber immer noch Kasus regieren, z. B. TTÜ. *sen-in için* 'für dich' (Genitiv des Personalpronomens). Dieser Typ funktioniert als eine unbetonbare enklitische Partikel.

Der nächste Schritt mag die Entwicklung zu einem peripheren Kasussuffix sein, das zunächst unharmonisch ist und sich später dem

Stamm anpaßt. Auf dieser Übergangsstufe können freie und gebundene Varianten koexistieren, z. B. *ile* ~ *-(y)lA* in *uçak ile* ~ *uçakla* 'mit dem Flugzeug'. Auch andere Marker schwanken zwischen enklitischer Partikel und Suffix, z. B. Kopulamarker wie TTÜ. *idi* ~ *-(y)dI* 'war'. Die Prozesse sind im Prinzip unidirektional, obwohl nicht jedes konkrete Resultat der Internalisierung auf jeder Einzelstufe voraussagbar ist. Anders als OSM. *üčün* 'für' hat z. B. das moderne TTÜ. *için* keine suffigierte Variante.

Betonbarkeit verrät deutlicher als lautharmonische Anpassung das relativ hohe Alter eines Suffixes. Zu den unbetonbaren und vermutlich jüngeren Suffixen gehören pronominale Personalmarker des Typs *-mAn* < *bän* 'ich' und das unbetonbare Negationssuffix *-MA*.

Postverbien entstehen in ähnlichen Prozessen. In der Kombination *yaz-a tur-* 'schreibenderweise stehen' ist das Konverb ursprünglich dem zweiten Verb untergeordnet und modifiziert seinen Inhalt. Durch Grammatikalisierung erfolgt eine Umkehrung der Modifikation, so daß das zweite Verb das erste inhaltlich präzisiert: 'unaufhörlich schreiben'. Das Postverb kann auch mit dem Lexem verschmelzen, d. h. suffigiert werden, z. B. *yaz-adur-*. Es kann auch harmonisiert werden, z. B. TUW. *bižiwit-* 'durchlesen' < *bižip it-* (< 'schreibenderweise senden'). Einige Postverbkonstruktionen haben sich zu aspektotemporalen Kategorien weiterentwickelt (3.8.3.).

4. Syntaktische und morphosyntaktische Entwicklung

Der syntaktische Habitus der Türksprachen weist deutlich gemeinsame Züge auf. Die Entwicklung vieler Sprachen ist jedoch durch Fremdeinfluß bestimmt gewesen.

4.1. Methoden der Prädizierung

In bezug auf relationale Typologie sind alle bekannten Türksprachen akkusativisch. Finite Sätze sind optimal markiert in bezug auf Aspekt, Modus, Tempus, Personalreferenz und Illokution, und ihre Erstaktanten werden als Nominativsubjekte realisiert. Gewisse postterminale Partizipien und Verbaladjektive referieren aber bei Intransitiva auf non-agentivische Erstaktanten und bei Transitiva auf non-agentivische Zweitaktanten, z. B. TTÜ. *yan-ık* 'gebrannt' (*yan-* 'brennen'), *kes-ik* 'geschnitten' (*kes-* 'schneiden').

Die sprachliche Sachverhaltsdarstellung erfolgt mit Prädikatstypen verschiedener Art, die unterschiedliche Aktanzmuster vertreten und Komplementmarkierung mittels Kasussuffixe und Postpositionen verlangen. Der Genitiv, der Akkusativ und z. T. der Dativ erfüllen abstrakt-relationale Aufgaben. Dative haben auch lokale, direktive, allative und terminative Funktionen. In einigen sibirischen Sprachen versieht der Dativ auch Funktionen, die sonst für Lokative typisch sind, z. B. TUW. *Män Qïzïl-ɣa čurttap turɣan män* 'Ich habe in Kyzyl gelebt'. Lokative haben weite Bedeutungen des Raums und der Zeit ('in, auf, an, bei' usw.). Ablative bezeichnen Quelle, Weg, Grund, Mittel, Vergleichsbasis usw. ('von', 'aus', 'durch', 'entlang', 'wegen', 'als'). Äquative bezeichnen Ähnlichkeit ('wie') und haben auch mensurative und prosekutive Funktionen zur Angabe von Ausdehnung in Raum und Zeit. Oft dienen sie als allgemeine Adverbsuffixe. Andere Relationen werden durch zahlreiche Postpositionen mit spezifizierten Bedeutungen kodiert.

Zu den typologisch markanten syntaktischen Eigenschaften des TÜRKISCHEN gehört eine kopfmarkierende Struktur. Zwischen Dependens und Kopf in Nominalphrasen besteht keine Numerus- oder Kasuskongruenz. Obwohl bei belebten Subjektreferenten oft Numeruskongruenz zwischen Subjekt und Prädikatskern besteht, werden zwei eng benachbarte Pluralmarker vermieden, z. B. TTÜ. *Çocuklar geldi- (*ler)* '(Die) Kinder sind gekommen'. Bei unbelebten Subjektreferenten entfällt fast immer die Numeruskongruenz.

Türksprachen sind relativ inexplizit in bezug auf Partizipantenreferenz: Aktanten, auch Erstaktanten, bleiben unter bestimmten Bedingungen unausgedrückt. Semantisch leere syntaktische Platzhalter („dummies") entfallen. Diese Eigenschaften korrelieren mit der personalmarkierenden Verbflexion. Besonders oft weggelassen werden Konstituenten, die ein altes Texttopik vertreten. Anaphorische Pronomina können fehlen, wenn der Referent kontextuell identifizierbar ist. Die Verwendung und Auslassung von freien Possessivpronomina unterliegen wechselnden sprachspezifischen Regeln.

4.2. Diathetische Verhältnisse

Als Rest eines diathetisch weniger entwickelten Systems, das Aktantenrelationen weniger explizit markiert, finden sich im älteren TÜRKISCH aktivisch-unpersönliche Prädikationen wie *Alïn arslan tut-ar* (List-INSTR Löwe fang-AOR). 'Mit List fängt man Löwen').

Diese Muster sind in heutigen Sprachen selten. Geblieben ist die diathetische Indifferenz in einigen wenigen Finitformen, etwa im TÜRKEITÜRKISCHEN Nezessitativ, z. B. *Ne yapmalı?* (was tu-NEC) 'Was soll man tun?'. In gewissen infiniten Formen ist sie noch üblich. Prospektivpartizipien werden oft subjektlos-unpersönlich verwendet, z. B. TTÜ. *oku-yacak bir kitap* (les-PART ein Buch), BASCHK. *uqï-hï kitap* 'ein Buch zum Lesen'. Aktive Partizipien wie *-GAn* können auf andere Referenten als den Erstaktanten hinweisen, z. B. CHAK. *sa-γan inäk* ('melken-PART Kuh') 'die Kuh, die man gemolken hat'. Possessivsuffixe an derartigen Partizipien funktionieren in einer Weise, die an Ergativmarker erinnert: *kör-gän-im* ('sehen-PART-1POSS') 'was ich gesehen habe'.

Diathetische Beziehungen werden aber in der Regel durch Genus verbi-Suffixe ausgedrückt. Passiv- und Kausativmustern gemeinsam ist die Signalisierung von „Transzendenz": daß die Reichweite der Tätigkeit über den Bereich des Subjektsreferenten hinausgeht und daß dieser Ziel oder Quelle der Tätigkeit ist.

Bei Passivmustern ist der Erstaktant des entsprechenden Aktivmusters demoviert und braucht nicht ausgedrückt zu werden, z. B. TTÜ. *Buruda güzel yaşanıyor* (hier gut leb-PASS-PRES) 'Hier lebt sich's gut'. Wie bei den unpersönlichen Aktivkonstruktionen dient auch die Passivierung oft dazu, den Agens zu verdecken. Dieser kann aber bei Bedarf durch Postpositionen, OST-ATÜ. *üzä*, TTÜ. *tarafından*, USB. *tämänidän* usw. ausgedrückt werden. In Sprachen wie TSCHAGATAISCH, USBEKISCH und UIGURISCH können passive Verben auch mit akkusativmarkierten direkten Objekten auftreten, z. B. UIG. *Aš-ni ye-yil-gän* (Essen-ACC ess-PASS-PART) 'Das Essen wurde eingenommen'. Hier verdeckt das Passiv den Agens, während der Akkusativ das direkte Objekt topikalisiert.

Kausativsuffixe an Intransitiva erzeugen Transitiva, z. B. TTÜ. *Nuri, Ali'-yi öl-dür-dü* (Nuri Ali-ACC sterb-CAUS-PRET) 'Nuri tötete Ali'. Kausativsuffixe an Transitiva erzeugen Kausativmuster, in denen auch das direkte Objekt des entsprechenden nicht-kausativen Musters auftreten kann, z. B. *Nuri resm-i çek-tir-di* (Nuri Bild-ACC mach-CAUS-PRET) 'Nuri ließ das Bild machen'. Der veranlaßte Agens wird meist durch ein Dativkomplement ausgedrückt, z. B. *Nuri resm-i Ali'-ye çek-tir-di* (Nuri Bild-ACC Ali-DAT mach-CAUS-PRET) 'Nuri ließ Ali das Bild machen'.

In einigen Sprachen drücken Kausativa an Transitiva immer noch „Transzendenz" aus, indem sie auch implizieren können, daß der Erstaktant Patiens ist, z. B. TUW. *ölür-t-* 'töten lassen' ~ 'getötet werden' (*öl-ür-* 'töten'). Der Agens, der dem Erstaktanten des nicht-diathetischen Musters entspricht, steht im Dativ, z. B. *Xoy börü-γä čidir-t-kän* (Schaf Wolf-DAT fress-CAUS-PART) 'Das Schaf wurde vom Wolf gefressen'. „Reversive" Muster dieser Art, die in eurasischen Sprachen weit verbreitet sind, finden sich bereits im OST-ALTTÜRKISCHEN. Sie weisen eine Affinität sowohl zu permissiven Kausativkonstruktionen ('tun lassen') als auch zu Passivkonstruktionen ('getan werden') auf, sind aber mit keiner von ihnen identisch.

Sog. Reflexivsuffixe wie *-(I)n* geben an, daß die Tätigkeit nicht über den Bereich des Subjektreferenten hinausgeht, sondern immanent bleibt („Immanenz"). Der Erstaktant kann das Ziel der Tätigkeit sein ('reflexiv'), ihr Nutznießer ('medial') oder die Quelle einer Tätigkeit ohne ein spezifiziertes Ziel ('de-objektiv'), z. B. TUW. *bižittin-* (*biži-* 'schreiben') 'schreiben', 'für sich schreiben', 'geschrieben werden'. Reflexive Bedeutungen werden meist durch Reflexivpronomina ausgedrückt: TTÜ. *kendini öl-dür-* (sich-ACC sterb-CAUS) 'sich töten'.

Kooperativ-reziproke Suffixe dienen im KIRGISISCHEN dem Ausdruck von Mehrzahl in Verbparadigmen, z. B. *Qal-ïš-tï* 'Sie blieben' (TTÜ. *Kal-dı-lar*).

4.3. Adnominale Modifikation

Die Systeme von Demonstrativa variieren von Sprache zu Sprache, wobei drei- und mehrgliedrige Abstufungen dominieren, z. B. BASCHK. *bïl, ošo, šul*. Relevante Faktoren sind Auswahlmöglichkeit, Abstand und Sicherheit.

Allen Türksprachen fehlen definite Artikel, obwohl Demonstrativa und Possessivmarker eine ähnlich referenzspezifizierende Wirkung haben können, z. B. KIRG. *bār-ï* (all-3POSS) 'alles davon'.

Akkusativ- bzw. Genitivmarkierung in der Position unmittelbar vor dem Prädikatsverb kann eine spezifizierende Funktion ausüben. Diese Position erlaubt einen formalen Kontrast zwischen einem nontopikalen direkten Nominativobjekt und einem Akkusativobjekt, das Spezifität ausdrückt, z. B. TTÜ. *Ali (bir) resim çek-ti* (Ali [ein] Bild machen-PRET)

'Ali machte ein Bild/Bilder', *Ali, resmi çekti* (Ali Bild-ACC mach-PRET) 'Ali machte das Bild', *Ali, bir resmi çekti* (Ali ein Bild-ACC mach-PRET) 'Ali machte ein gewisses Bild'. Sind die Objekte vom Verb getrennt, so ist die Akkusativmarkierung meist obligatorisch und drückt die Spezifizität nicht explizit aus. Ähnliches gilt für Genitivsubjekte in Komplementsätzen (4.11.3.1.).

Der aus dem Numerale *bir* 'eins' entstandene indefinite Artikel wird in den Einzelsprachen mehr oder weniger häufig verwendet, am wenigsten dort, wo er noch eine stark individualisierende Funktion hat, z. B. TTÜ. *iyi bir at*, KIRG. *žaqšï at* 'ein gutes Pferd'.

4.4. Numerus

Pluralsuffixe signalisieren meist individuelle Vielzahl, z. B. TTÜ. *elma-lar* '(einzelne) Äpfel', TSCHUW. *pürt-sem* '(einzelne) Häuser'. Der Singular hat einen weiten, z. T. numerusindifferenten Gebrauch, der auch kollektive oder generische Referenz umfaßt, z. B. TTÜ. *Elma aldım* 'Ich kaufte einen Apfel/Äpfel'. Pluralsuffixe können auch dem Ausdruck von Respekt dienen, z. B. KAR. (Halič) *Bar-ad-lar* (geh-PRESS-PL) 'Er/sie geht'. Eine durch Zahlwörter und einige andere Quantoren ausgedrückte Vielzahl schließt meist kongruierende Pluralmarkierung aus, z. B. TTÜ. *iki at* 'zwei Pferde'. Nach Zahlwörtern werden oft Numeratoren gebraucht, z. B. KIRG. *dāna* 'Stück', USB. *båš* 'Kopf' (Tiere).

4.5. Numeralia

Moderne Türksprachen gebrauchen meist lexikalische Kardinalzahlen für die Zahlen 1−9, die Zehnerzahlen 10−90, 100 und 1000. Multiplikative Bildungen mit *ōn* 'zehn' usw., TTÜ. *doksan* '90', der die Zahlwörter 6−9 (*dokuz* '9' usw.) enthält, finden sich in den Zehnerzahlen 60−90, in einigen, vorwiegend südsibirischen Sprachen, auch in niedrigen Zehnerzahlen, z. B. TUW. *üžen* '30', FU-YÜ *durdïn* '40'. Die meisten Sprachen besitzen auch kollektive und distributive Numeralia.

Hunderte und Tausende werden multiplikativ ausgedrückt, z. B. TAT. *ikĕ yŏz mĕŋ* 'zweihundert tausend', die dazwischen liegenden Zahlen additiv, z. B. TTÜ. *on iki* ('zehn zwei') '12'. KARATSCHAISCH-BALKARISCH besitzt noch ein auf der Zähleinheit 20 basierendes Vigesimalsystem, z. B. *jïyïrma bile on* ('20 + 10') '30', *on jïyïrma* ('10 × 20') '200' (vgl. FRZ. *quatre-vingt*). Das CHALADSCHISCHE kennt Varianten wie *àkki ottuz* ('2 × 30') '60' und *üč hottuz u yirmi* ('3 × 30 + 20') '110'.

Das GELBUIGURISCHE bewahrt noch z. T. ein älteres System der Oberstufenzählung, das Einerzahlen mit der höheren Zehnerzahl kombiniert, z. B. *per otus* ('eins dreißig') '21'.

4.6. Komposition

Der dominante Typ von Nominalkomposita folgt dem Muster Nomen + Nomen + Possessivsuffix der 3. P., z. B. TTÜ. *el çanta-sı* 'Handtasche'. Anders als bei der Genitivkonstruktion kann kein Element zwischen die Nomina eingefügt werden. In älteren und neueren Sprachen finden sich viele Fälle ohne Possessivsuffix, z. B. KRTSCH. *alma terek* 'Apfelbaum'; vgl. den TÜRKEITÜRKISCHEN neologistischen Typ *budunbilim* ('Volk', 'Wissenschaft') 'Volkskunde'. Einige Sprachen haben PERSISCHE *izāfat*-Konstruktionen kopiert, z. B. OSM. *ilān-ï ašq* (Erklärung-MARKER Liebe) 'Liebeserklärung'. Das CHALADSCHISCHE kann damit sogar einheimische Nomina verbinden.

Identitätsattribution liegt vor, wenn zwei Nomina, die auf dieselbe Entität referieren, asyndetisch als Attribut + Kopf juxtaponiert werden, z. B. TTÜ. *kadın öğretmen* ('Frau', 'Lehrer') 'Lehrerin', *taş köprü* (Stein, 'Brücke') 'steinerne Brücke'. Einen anderen asyndetischen Typ bilden koordinative Synonym- oder Hyponymkomposita, z. B. OST-ATÜ. *iš küč* ('Arbeit, Kraft') 'Mühe', oft mit Alliteration und anderen Reimbildungen, z. B. TTÜ. *karıkoca* ('Ehefrau', 'Ehemann') 'Ehepaar'.

Verbalkomposition erfolgt mit Konverbkonstruktionen und Proverben (3.4.).

4.7. Einzelne morphosyntaktische Kategorien

Adnominale Possession wird meist durch Genitivkonstruktionen nach dem Muster [Possessor + Genitivsuffix] + [Possessum + Possessivsuffix] ausgedrückt, z. B. USB. *ådäm-niŋ üy-i* 'das Haus des Mannes'. Im JAKUTISCHEN fehlt das Genitivsuffix, z. B. *kihi jiä-tä* 'id.'. Existenzkonstruktionen werden in älteren wie neueren Sprachen mit Adjektiven der Typen *bar* 'vorhanden' und *yoq* 'nicht vorhanden' gebildet, wobei der Existens als Subjekt erscheint.

Prädikative Possession wird nach folgendem Muster gebildet: [Possessor + Genitivsuffix] + [Possessum + Possessivsuffix] + *bar*/*yoq*, z. B. USB. *Ådäm-niŋ pul-i bår* 'Der Mann hat Geld', UIG. *Qiz-niŋ dadi-si yoq* 'Das Mädchen hat keinen Vater'. Es finden sich auch Konstruktionen wie [Possessor +

Lokativsuffix] + Possessum + *bar/yoq*, z. B. KIRG. *Anda kitep bar* (er/sie-LOC Buch vorhanden) 'Er hat/sie hat Bücher'. In Infinitsätzen werden *bar* and *yoq* oft durch Verben wie *bol-* 'werden, sein' und *bol-ma-* ersetzt, z. B. TTÜ. *parası olmayan* (Geld-3POSS sei-NEG-PART) 'wer kein Geld hat'. Türksprachen Irans kennen auch den Typ Possessum + [*bar/yoq* + Possessivsuffix], z. B. CHAL. *Pul varïm* 'Ich habe Geld'. Der prädikativen Possession dienen auch Adjektive auf *-lIG* 'versehen mit' und *-sIz* 'ohne'.

Negation erfolgt durch das verbale Suffix *-MA* und negative Kopulapartikeln wie *ämäs, deyil* 'ist nicht', z. B. TTÜ. *fena değil* 'es ist nicht schlecht'. Kopulapartikeln dienen der Konstituentennegation, z. B. UIG. *Bešim ämäs, közüm aγïydu* 'Nicht mein Kopf, sondern meine Augen tun mir weh', und werden auch bei gewissen Finitformen jüngeren Alters gebraucht, z. B. TAT. *kiläčäk tügěl* 'wird nicht kommen'. TSCHUWASCHISCH verwendet, vielleicht unter Fremdeinfluß, ein präpositives *an* als Imperativnegation der 2. und 3. Person, z. B. *an kil* 'komm nicht!' (vgl. Menges 1995: 145).

Ja-Nein-Fragesätze werden durch Interrogativmarker gebildet, die nach der ganzen Prädikation oder nach der in Frage gestellten Konstituente stehen, z. B. TTÜ. *Ali bugün geliyor mu?* (Ali heute komm-PRES Q) 'Kommt Ali heute (oder tut er das nicht)?', *Ali mi bugün geliyor?* (Ali Q heute komm-PRES) 'Ist es Ali, der heute kommt (oder wer)?', *Ali bugün mü geliyor?* (Ali heute Q komm-PRES) 'Kommt Ali heute (oder wann)?'. Auch der Inhalt modifizierender Konverbformen kann so erfragt werden, z. B. *Ali gelince mi gittin?* 'Gingst du weg, als Ali kam (oder wann)?'. Die Plazierung relativ zu den Personalmarkern variiert von Sprache zu Sprache. Die Türksprachen Irans ersetzen unter PERSISCHEM Einfluß die Fragepartikel oft durch spezifische Intonationskonturen.

In Komparativkonstruktionen wird der Komparativgrad durch ein Ablativsuffix am Vergleichsmaßstab ausgedrückt, z. B. USB. *mendän yaχši* 'besser als ich'. Dem Adjektiv mag auch ein Wort für 'mehr' vorangehen oder ein Komparativsuffix nachgestellt werden, z. B. TTÜ. *daha iyi*, tat. *yaχšï-raq* 'besser'. JAKUTISCH kennt ein Komparativkasus auf *-nĀγAr*. Irantürkische Sprachen haben das PERSISCHE Komparativsuffix *-tar* kopiert. Superlative werden meist mittels Adverbien wie *eŋ* (TSCHUW. *či*) vor dem Adjektiv ausgedrückt, z. B. USB. *eŋ yaχši* 'am besten'.

In Äquativ- und Similativmustern wie 'A ist so groß wie B' und 'A singt wie B' wird der Vergleichsmaßstab durch Postpositionen oder Äquativsuffixe markiert, z. B. UIG. *qädär* 'so sehr', TAT. *kěběk* 'wie', USB. *-däy*.

4.8. Wortstellung

Türksprachen haben eine relativ stabile kopffinale Wortstellung im Sinne von SOV, AN, GN, NPostp. Eine übliche Reihenfolge in der Nominalphrase ist Demonstrativpronomen + Kardinalzahl + Adjektivattribut + Kopf, z. B. TTÜ. *bu üç mavi kuş* 'diese drei blauen Vögel'. Wo *bir* als indefiniter Artikel dient, tendiert es zur Position vor dem Kopf, z. B. USB. *kättä bir üy* 'ein großes Haus'.

Eine Plazierung von Konstituenten rechts vom Verb ist unter bestimmten pragmatischen Bedingungen in finiten, nicht aber in infiniten Sätzen zulässig. Postprädikative Elemente sind durch die ganze türkische Sprachgeschichte hindurch in geschriebenen Varietäten zu beobachten. Die postprädikative Position wird durch defokussierte Konstituenten, die oft schon aktivierte Topiks vertreten, propositionskommentierende Satzadverbialien, nachträgliche Gedanken usw. besetzt. Dagegen ist sie nicht für neue Information, Fragepronomina und -adverbien oder unmarkierte direkte Objekte mit spezifischer Referenz geeignet. Subjektpronomina in dieser Position können kein neues Texttopik einführen.

4.9. Informationsstruktur

Links vom Prädikatskern bestehen meist keine festgelegten syntaktischen Konfigurationen. Da die Relationen durch Kasusmarkierung klar sind, können Wortstellungsmodifikationen für die Informationsstrukturierung genutzt werden.

Die Anfangsposition ist der bevorzugte Platz des Satz-Topiks, in rhetorisch neutralen Sätzen identisch mit dem des Subjekts, z. B. TTÜ. *Ali resmi çekti* 'Ali machte das Bild'. Andere Konstituenten können topikalisiert werden, indem sie diesen Platz einnehmen, z. B. *Resmi Ali çekti* 'Das Bild machte Ali'. Ein direktes Objekt kann auch durch Passivierung topikalisiert werden, z. B. *Resim Ali tarafından çekildi* 'Das Bild wurde von Ali gemacht', was infolge der flexiblen Wortstellung selten erforderlich wird. Üblich sind auch aus Konditionalpartikeln entstandene nachgestellte Topikalisierungsmarker wie TTÜ. *ise*, TKM. *bolθa* ('wenn es ist'), z. B. TTÜ. *Ali ise resmi çekti* 'Was Ali betrifft, machte er das Bild'.

Die Position unmittelbar vor dem Prädikatskern, der Platz für unmarkierte direkte Objekte, dient auch dazu, andere Konstituenten zu fokussieren, z. B. das Subjekt in *Resmi Ali çekti* 'Es war Ali, der das Bild machte'. Dies ist also auch die natürliche Position für Fragepronomina und -adverbien, die neue Information erfragen, z. B. TAT. *Sin kĕmnĕ kürdĕŋ?* 'Wen hast du gesehen?'. Dieses Mittel ist üblicher als Fokusmarkierung durch Betonung. Eine andere Methode besteht in einem Spaltsatz, der einen Relativsatz als Subjekt mit dem zu fokussierenden Element als nominalem Prädikat kombiniert, z. B. *Resmi çeken Ali'ydi* ('Der das Bild Machende war Ali') 'Es war Ali, der das Bild machte'.

4.10. Kopierte Wortstellungsmuster

Wortstellungsmuster sind unter Fremdeinfluß häufig kopiert worden. Von den Sprachen, die unter dem stärksten Einfluß europäischer Sprachen standen, hat z. B. das KARAIMISCHE eine Wortstellung im Sinne von SVO, AN/NA, GN/NG, NPostp entwickelt. Derartige Veränderungen fangen oft bei Wortstellungen an, die unter bestimmten pragmatischen Bedingungen auch im TÜRKISCHEN möglich sind, und werden später verallgemeinert.

Kopiert wurden auch dem TÜRKISCHEN fremde iranische und slavische Präpositionen, die entweder als Postpositionen dienten oder aber präpositiv gebraucht, aber durch ein TÜRKISCHES postpositives Element, etwa ein Kasussuffix, syntaktisch verankert wurden, z. B. TTÜ. *ta Ankara'ya kadar* 'bis nach Ankara', AS. (Iran) *harij äz šähr-dä* 'außerhalb der Stadt'. In den am stärksten fremdbeeinflußten Sprachen können sie auch als echte Präpositionen vor einheimischen Wörtern stehen: CHAL. *bī sen* 'ohne dich'. Aus dem Slavischen kopierte KARAIMISCHE Präpositionen können sogar TÜRKISCHE Kasus regieren, z. B. KAR. (Halič) *do ceriw-ńi* (Akkusativ) 'vor dem Krieg'.

4.11. Junktion

Das TÜRKISCHE verfügt über ein breites Kontinuum der Satzverknüpfungstechniken, von der Juxtaposition bis zur Einverleibung von Sätzen als Satzglieder. Auffallend ist die geringe Zahl an einheimischen freien Junktoren (Johanson 1996b).

4.11.1. Koordination

Prädikationen von gleichem Status können asyndetisch, nur durch Juxtaposition und Intonation verbunden werden, z. B. TTÜ. *Geldim, gördüm, yendim* 'Ich kam, ich sah, ich siegte'. Der Koordination dienen interklausale Konjunktoren wie in USB. *keldi-dä, ketti* 'kam und ging'. Unter den möglichen Koordinationstilgungen finden sich Ellipsen wie TTÜ. *gelmiş ve gitmiş-tir* 'kam und ging', wo ein zu beiden Verbformen gehörendes Suffix nur am letzten Verb erscheint. Eine gewisse Aversion gegen 'und'-Koordination ist in vielen Sprachen bemerkbar. Konjunktoren mit Bedeutungen wie 'und', 'oder', 'aber', 'denn' stellen oft Kopien persischer, arabischer und russischer Konjunktionen dar, z. B. TTÜ. *ve* 'und', UIG. *pägat*, SCHOR. *no* 'aber'. Häufig kopiert werden Diskurskonjunktoren, die ganze Äußerungen einleiten und die pragmatische Organisation des Diskurses regeln, ohne die Struktur der verknüpften Sätze zu beeinflussen, z. B. KAR. *i* 'und', *bo* 'denn', GAG., SCHOR. *ili* 'oder', CHAK. *a* 'und, aber'. Der intraklausalen Verknüpfung dienen oft komitative Postpositionen, z. B. UIG. *ata bilän ana* 'Vater und Mutter', TTÜ. *karga ile tilki* 'die Krähe und der Fuchs'. Mit zunehmender Europäisierung vieler Türksprachen wird die Juxtaposition ohne syndetische Elemente wie 'und', 'oder' usw. weniger üblich.

4.11.2. Subordination

Das TÜRKISCHE bedient sich in der Hypotaxe infiniter Konstruktionen, in denen infinite thematische Suffixe als satzeinbettende Subjuktoren dienen. Die Einbettung ist rekursiv, indem Infinitsätze selber Infinitsätze als Satzglieder einverleiben. Infinitsätze können auch untereinander koordiniert werden.

Freie Subjunktoren spielen somit eine geringe Rolle. Sie sind nicht zu verwechseln mit Adjunktoren, konjunktionalen Adverbien, wie ALT-UIG. *anïn* 'deshalb', KAS. *sondïqtan* 'somit', die der syntaktischen Subordination unfähig sind. Viele Türksprachen haben aber fremde adverbiale Konjunktionen und Relativpronomina entlehnt oder ihre Funktionen auf einheimische (meist interrogative) Elemente kopiert, z. B. *qačan* 'wenn', *kim* 'wer, was, daß'. Diese Elemente verhalten sich in der TÜRKISCHEN Syntax jedoch oft anders als die unterordnenden Vorlagen der Gebersprachen. Vor allem sind die dadurch eingeführten Sätze meist nicht als postprädikative Konstituenten in den vorangehenden Satz eingebettet, sondern ihm in einer lockeren Weise angeschlossen. In vielen modernen Sprachen, z. B. TÜRKEITÜRKISCH, sind die meisten Imitationen dieser Art nicht mehr stilistisch akzeptabel. Stark fremdbeeinflußte Sprachen neigen jedoch zu getreueren Nachbildungen der Originale, z. B. das GAGAUSISCHE mit freien Subjunktoren wie *ani* 'wer, was, daß'.

4.11.3.1. Komplementsätze

Die Techniken der Komplementierung basieren auf Nomina actionis, paradigmatischen Verbalsubstantiven, deren syntaktische Funktionen im Matrixsatz durch Kasus- und Postpositionen markiert sind. Morphologisch entsprechen Komplementsätze Genitivkonstruktionen, z. B. TTÜ. *Orhan-'ın bil-diğ-i* (Orhan-GEN weis-PART-3POSS) ('Orhans Wissen') 'daß Orhan weiß/wußte'. Als Subjektskasus dient aber oft auch der Nominativ. Wo beide Kasus möglich sind, drückt der Genitiv oft Spezifizität aus, z. B. *para/para-nın kaybol-duğ-u* (Geld/Geld-GEN verschwind-PART-3POSS) 'daß Geld/das Geld verschwunden ist'. Zum analogen Gebrauch des Akkusativs vgl. 4.3.

Ein formaler Modusunterschied besteht oft zwischen faktiven und nonfaktiven Komplementsätzen. Erstere sind durch Suffixe wie *-GAn* und *-DIK* vertreten, z. B. USB. *Kel-gän-in-i bilämän* (komm-PART-3POSS-ACC weis-PRES-1SG) 'Ich weiß, daß er [usw.] gekommen ist'. Nonfaktive Sätze, die auf *-mA*, *-(I)š*, *-(U)w* usw. basieren, bilden u. a. Finalsätze wie TTÜ. *Ali gel-me-ler-in-i söylüyor* (Ali komm-INF-3PLPOSS-ACC sag-PRES) ('Ali sagt ihr Kommen') 'Ali sagt, daß sie kommen sollen' und durch modale Lexeme regierte Infinitivsätze wie USB. *Ket-iš-imiz keräk* (geh-INF-1PLPOSS nötig) ('unser Gehen nötig') 'Wir müssen gehen'. Infinitivsätze ohne Personalsuffixe implizieren meist Koreferenz mit dem Erstaktanten des Matrixsatzes, z. B. USB. *Men ič-iš-ni istäymän* (ich trink-INF-ACC mög-PRES-1SG) 'Ich möchte trinken'. Eine Infinitiv-Aversion ist nur in Balkan-Varietäten erkennbar.

4.11.3.2. Konverbsätze

Zur Bildung TÜRKISCHER Adverbialsätze dienen in der Regel Konverbmarker (Johanson 1995), während adverbiale Konjunktionen fehlen. Konditionalsätze werden zwar oft mit Kopien der PERSISCHEN Konjunktion *agar* 'wenn' eingeleitet, z. B. UIG. *ägär yaz-sam* (wenn schreib-COND-1SG) 'wenn ich schreiben sollte', aber das syntaktisch verankernde Element ist auch hier der Subjunktor *-sA*. Freie adverbiale Junktoren sind die versteinerten Konverbformen des Typs *dep*, *diye* (*de-* 'sagen'), die als Zitierpartikeln für direkte Rede und Gedankeninhalte dienen (3.9.) und oft mit optativischen und prospektivischen Finitformen Finalsätze und begründende Kausalsätze bilden, z. B. USB. *ket-sin de-b* (geh-OPT.3SG sag-CONV) ('sagend: möge gehen') 'damit er/sie geht'.

Subjekte von Konverbsätzen sind meist nominativisch. Einige Marker erfordern Koreferenz der Erstaktanten in Konverb- und Matrixsatz, z. B. JAK. *-A(:)n*, TTÜ. *-(y)Ip* (mit wenigen Ausnahmen). Die meisten Marker erfordern sie aber nicht, z. B. TTÜ. *Ali gel-ince Osman şaşırdı* (Ali komm-CONV Osman staun-PRET) 'Als Ali kam, staunte Osman'.

Die Türksprachen weisen auch Konverbsätze auf, die den Matrixsatz nicht semantisch modifizieren und also nicht „adverbial" im propositional restriktiven Sinne sind. Obwohl sie syntaktisch abhängig sind, haben sie den gleichen narrativen Wert wie der Matrixsatz. Zu den Subjunktoren, die nicht-modifizierend gebraucht werden können, gehören *-(I)p*, TTÜ. *-(y)Ip*, JAK. *-(A)n*, TSCHUW. *-sA*, TUW. *-GAš*. Zur Wiedergabe eignen sich oft deutsche koordinative Konstruktionen, z. B. TSCHUW. *Kil-se kurčě* (komm-CONV seh-PRET) 'Er/sie kam und sah (es)'. Non-modifizierende Konverbsätze können in den Skopus der Negation des Matrixsatzes einbezogen werden: TTÜ. *Gel-ip gör-me-din* (komm-CONV seh-NEG-PRET-2SG) 'Du kamst [nicht] und sahst es nicht'.

Diese Marker sind aspektuell terminal und daher propulsiv, d. h. können einen Handlungsablauf vorwärts führen, z. B. TTÜ. *Ali kay-ıp düş-tü* (Ali rutsch-CONV fall-PRET) 'Ali rutschte aus und fiel'. Deshalb sind sie zentrale textbildende Einheiten in periodischen Kettensätzen traditioneller Erzählstile. In derartigen Sätzen ist nur der abschließende finite Prädikatskern voll markiert, um eine endgültige aspektuelle, modale, temporale und illokutive Interpretation zu erlauben (Johanson 1992b).

Die alten weit verbreiteten konverbbasierten Textbaumuster schwinden heute immer mehr zugunsten europäischer Muster, die narrativ gleichgestellte Ereignisse nicht durch syntaktische Einbettung darstellen. Die langen OSMANISCHEN Kettensätze sind im TÜRKEITÜRKISCHEN stilistisch unannehmbar. Auch der Gebrauch von *-(I)p*-Sätzen mit anderen Erstaktanten als dem des Matrixsatzes nimmt ab. Der Gebrauch subordinativer Mittel richtet sich immer mehr nach europäischen Mustern. In der sowjetischen Turkologie galt der Beitrag des Russischen zur Eliminierung der angeblich semantisch vagen türkischen Konverbkonstruktionen als besonders günstig.

Infolge langer und intensiver Kontakte mit dem PERSISCHEN hat der Konverbgebrauch in einigen Varietäten, z. B. im USBEKISCH von Afghanistan und im CHALADSCHISCHEN radikal abgenommen. Das KASCHGAISCHE hat das -(I)p-Konverb und die dafür typischen Konstruktionen durch kopierte PERSISCHE Strukturen ersetzt.

4.11.3.3. Relativsätze

Relativsätze basieren auf partiziellen Subjunktoren. Wenn der Kopf mit dem Erstaktanten des Relativsatzes koreferentiell ist, wird kein Personalmarker verwendet, z. B. TAT. *kil-gän kěsě* (komm-PART Mann) 'ein/der Mann, der gekommen ist'. Dies gilt auch bei Koreferentialität des Kopfes mit einem Possessor des Erstaktanten, z. B. USB. *ånä-si käsäl bol-gän bålä* (Mutter-3POSS krank sei-PART Kind) 'ein/das Kind, dessen Mutter krank ist'.

Viele Sprachen gebrauchen das gleiche Muster bei Koreferentialität des Kopfes mit einem anderen Aktanten oder mit einer Einheit der Zeit, des Raumes usw. So mag ein isoliertes *kör-gän kiši* (seh-PART Person) sowohl 'eine/die Person, die gesehen hat' als auch 'eine/die Person, die man/jemand gesehen hat' bedeuten. Die präzise Relation wird durch pragmatische Mittel etabliert. Üblich sind somit unpersönliche Prädikationen, die auf keinen spezifischen Erstaktanten hinweisen, z. B. USB. *bår-gän yer* (geh-PART Platz) 'ein/der Platz, wo man/jemand hingegangen ist', KIRG. *jaz-γan qat* (schreib-PART Brief) 'ein/der Brief, den man/jemand geschrieben hat'.

Ein Erstaktant kann in solchen Fällen durch Nominativsubjekt ausgedrückt werden, z. B. AS. *men ač-an gapï* (ich öffn-PART Tür) 'eine/die Tür, die ich öffne(te)', KIRG. *aγam jazba-γan qat* (Vater-1SGPOSS schreib-NEG-PART Brief) 'ein/der Brief, den mein Vater nicht geschrieben hat'. Er kann auch durch ein possessives Personalsuffix ausgedrückt werden. Dieser Subjektvertreter kann am Kopf der Konstruktion stehen, z. B. USB. *bår-gän yer-im* (geh-PART Platz-1SGPOSS) 'ein/der Platz, wo ich hingegangen bin'. Ein entsprechendes Subjekt, das auf eine spezifische Entität referiert, steht normalerweise im Genitiv, z. B. TKM. *čaγa-nïŋ al-an kitab-ï* (Kind-GEN kauf-PART Buch-3POSS) 'das Buch, das das Kind gekauft hat'.

Der Subjektvertreter kann auch am Partizip stehen. Dies ist der Normalfall z. B. im TÜRKEITÜRKISCHEN, wo auch besondere Relativsubjunktoren, -DIK, -(y)AcAK usw., hierzu verwendet werden, z. B. *gel-diğ-im gün* (komm-PART-1SGPOSS Tag) 'der Tag, an dem ich ankam'. Formen mit Personalsuffix erfordern Subjekte im Genitiv, z. B. *Orhan-'ın gör-düğ-ü adam* (Orhan-GEN seh-PART-3POSS Mann) 'der Mann, den Orhan sieht/sah (etc.)'. Solche Konstruktionen finden sich auch bei Koreferenz des Kopfes mit einem Possessor, der im Relativsatz Nicht-Erstaktant ist, z. B. *baba-sı-nı tanı-dığ-ım çocuk* (Vater-3POSS-ACC kenn-PART-1SGPOSS Kind) 'das Kind, dessen Vater ich kenne (etc.)'.

Der Typ *gör-düğ-ün at* (seh-PART-2SGPOSS Pferd) 'das Pferd, das du siehst (etc.)' entspricht also dem KIRGISISCHEN Typ *sen kör-gön at* (du seh-PART Pferd). Auch TÜRKEITÜRKISCH kann aber den letztgenannten Typ wählen, wenn das Subjekt nicht-topikal und nicht-spezifisch ist und wenn der Kopf etwa einen Ort bezeichnet, z. B. *su ak-an yer* (Wasser fließ-PART Ort) 'ein Ort, an dem Wasser fließt'.

Die präzise Beziehung zwischen Relativsatz und Kopf geht also nicht immer aus der Konstruktion selbst hervor. Sie kann aber u. a. mittels possessivischer Postpositionen spezifiziert werden, z. B. TTÜ. *içine taşındığım ev* (Inneres-3POSS-DAT einzieh-PART-1SGPOSS Haus) 'das Haus, in das (in dessen Inneres) ich zog'.

Präpositive TÜRKISCHE Relativsätze sind nicht propulsiv, d. h. können den Handlungsablauf nicht über den vom Kopfsatz repräsentierten Zeitpunkt hinaus weiterführen, z. B. *Taşındığım bir ev aldım* (zieh-PART-1SGPOSS ein Haus kauf-PRET-1SG) '*Ich kaufte ein Haus, in das ich zog'.

Stark fremdbeeinflußte Sprachen wie KARAIMISCH, GAGAUISCH und iranotürkische Varietäten weisen auch kopierte postpositive Relativsätze und freie Relativjunktoren auf, z. B. GAG. *benim batüm ani polisdä čališer* (ich-GEN Bruder:1POSS REL.PRT Polizei-LOC arbeit-PRES) 'mein Bruder, der bei der Polizei arbeitet'. Dafür beschränken sich die präpositiven Strukturen hier auf einfache, wenig expandierbare Partizipialkonstruktionen.

5. Lexikalische Entwicklung

Das Lexikon der Türksprachen weist einen umfassenden, auf eine gemeinsame Ursprache zurückgehenden Grundwortschatz auf.

Andererseits hat eine gewisse lexikalische Differenzierung der verschiedenen Zweige stattgefunden. Typisch für Südwestsprachen sind z. B. Wörter wie *köpek* 'Hund', *bul-* 'finden', *ileri* 'vorwärts', *čoq* 'viel', während u. a. die Nordwestsprachen *it*, *tap-*, *murun*, *köp* usw. aufweisen. Der Wortschatz enthält etliche Beispiele für indirekte Sachverhaltsbezeichnung durch Tabuwörter, z. B. *qurt* 'Wurm' für 'Wolf'.

Zahlreiche Wörter wurden aus anderen Sprachen kopiert. Insgesamt dürfte der lexikalische Wandel durchgreifender gewesen sein als der Wandel auf anderen sprachlichen Ebenen. Im Lexikon ist auch eine Differenzierung nach Textsorten und Diskurstraditionen am sichtbarsten. In den Schriftkulturen wurden unterschiedliche Diskursanforderungen an die lexikalischen Systeme gestellt. Der Wortschatz der ALTUIGURISCHEN wurde ausgebaut, um den Anforderungen einer umfassenden Übersetzungsliteratur u. a. buddhistischen Inhalts zu genügen. Die meisten späteren Sprachen brauchten einen umfangreichen Wortschatz zum Ausdruck der Begriffe der islamischen Kultur. Moderne Sprachen entwickeln z. T. recht disparate Terminologien auf technischen, wissenschaftlichen und anderen Gebieten.

Zu Problemen des Wortschatzes s. u. a. Brands 1973, Doerfer 1988, Musaev 1984.

5.1. Wortschatzerweiterung mit einheimischen Mitteln

Ein Teil der Wortschatzerweiterung ist mit den einheimischen Mitteln der Komposition und Ableitung erfolgt. Die Wortbildungssuffixe haben durch ihren generalisierten Inhalt eine hohe Anwendbarkeit. So ist z. B. das Abstraktsuffix *-lIK* weitaus produktiver als seine DEUTSCHEN Äquivalente *-heit*, *-tum* usw. Die Nutzung des Potentials variiert erheblich. In älteren Sprachen und einigen heutigen sibirischen Sprachen können z. B. Adjektive ohne besondere Markierung auch als eigenschaftsbezeichnende Abstrakta dienen, z. B. JAK. *bāy* 'reich, Reichtum' (vgl. KRTSCH. *baylïq*). Die einzelnen Sprachen nutzen in sehr unterschiedlichem Maße die Mittel einer transparenten Wortbildung.

5.2. Kopierter Wortschatz

Alle Türksprachen haben Lehnwörter freizügig aufgenommen, die der Seßhaften besonders ARABISCH-PERSISCHE, die der Nomaden viele MONGOLISCHE. Auch Metaphorik und Idiomatik wurden weitgehend durch Sprachkontakte beeinflußt. Bereits die ältesten Texte weisen INDOIRANISCHE und CHINESISCHE Lehnwörter auf. Schriftsprachen wie TSCHAGATAISCH und OSMANISCH sind mit ARABISCH-PERSISCHEN Lexemen überladen. Besonders stark ist der iranische lexikalische Einfluß auf UIGURISCH, USBEKISCH und die Varietäten von Iran und Afghanistan. Die Einwirkung des MONGOLISCHEN ist vor allem nach dem Mongolensturm im 13. Jh. deutlich. Die südsibirischen Dialekte unterlagen auch später starken MONGOLISCHEN Einflüssen.

Viele Türksprachen, die sich unter russischer Dominanz, z. T. unter bilingualen Bedingungen, entwickelt haben, weisen große Mengen RUSSISCHER Lehnwörter und Lehnübersetzungen auf. In der sowjetischen Periode war der Einfluß besonders intensiv. Sprachen wie KARAIMISCH und GAGAUSISCH sind im Wortschatz stark slavisch geprägt. TSCHUWASCHISCH weist FINNOUGRISCHE, TATARISCHE, RUSSISCHE und sogar frühe ARABISCHE und PERSISCHE Lehnwörter auf.

Der Zufluß westlichen Wortgutes ist in der modernen Periode zunehmend wichtig geworden. Bereits im OSMANISCHEN begann ein Import u. a. GRIECHISCHER, ITALIENISCHER und FRANZÖSISCHER Lehnwörter. Die Sprachen der RUSSISCHEN Einflußsphäre erwarben ihren westlichen Wortschatz durch russische Vermittlung. Der lexikalische Aufbau der Türksprachen Chinas folgt dagegen CHINESISCHEN Mustern. Die Lexik der Sprachen Irans und Afghanistans ist nach wie vor PERSISCH geprägt.

5.3. Puristische Reformen

Die Dominanz nicht-türkischer Elemente in gewissen Varietäten hat im 20. Jh. puristische Maßnahmen angeregt. Als Reaktion gegen die ARABISCH-PERSISCH überladene OSMANISCHE Lexik wurde in der Türkei ein sog. *Öztürkçe* 'reines Türkisch') erstrebt und auch teilweise erzielt. Da der neue Wortschatz nicht nur aus echt TÜRKISCHEN Wörtern bestand, sondern z. T. künstlich geschaffen war, trug er wenig zur gegenseitigen Verständlichkeit mit anderen Türksprachen bei. Auch mehrere Sprachen der Sowjetunion wurden reformiert, allerdings nach andersartigen und meist disparaten Mustern. Die lexikalische Entwicklung vieler Türksprachen ist z. Z. in einer neuen kreativen Phase, allerdings mit schwer voraussagbaren Ergebnissen.

6. Spezielle Abkürzungen:

AS.	aserbaidschanisch
ATÜ.	alttürkisch
BASCHK.	baschkirisch
CHAK.	chakassisch
CHAL.	chaladschisch
JAK.	jakutisch
KAR.	karaimisch
KRTSCH.	karatschaisch
KAS.	kasachisch
KIRG.	kirgisisch
KUM.	kumükisch
NOG.	nogaisch
OSM.	osmanisch
SCHOR.	schorisch
TAT.	tatarisch
TSCHUW.	tschuwaschisch
TTÜ.	türkeitürkisch
TUW.	tuwisch
UIG.	uigurisch
USB.	usbekisch

Großbuchstaben und Klammern in der Notation von Suffixen bezeichnen sprachspezifische allomorphische Variationen (2.4.).

V Vokal

Bindestriche in Wortformen sollen nur die Identifizierung von Suffixen erleichtern. Für präzisere Angaben s. Johanson & Csató 1998.

7. Zitierte Literatur

Baskakov, Nikolaj A. (ed.) 1966. *Jazyki narodov SSSR, 2, Tjurkskie jazyki*. Moskva: Nauka.

Baskakov, Nikolaj A. 1975. *Istoriko-tipologičeskaja xarakteristika struktury tjurkskix jazykov*. Moskva: Nauka.

Berta, Árpád. 1996. *Deverbale Wortbildung im Mittelkiptschakisch-Türkischen*. (Turcologica, 24.) Wiesbaden: Harrassowitz.

Boeschoten, Hendrik & Verhoeven, Ludo (eds.) 1991. *Turkish linguistics today*. Leiden: Brill.

Brands, Horst Wilfrid. 1973. *Studien zum Wortbestand der Türksprachen. Lexikalische Differenzierung, Semasiologie, Sprachgeschichte*. Leiden: Brill.

Comrie, Bernard. 1981. *The languages of the Soviet Union*. Cambridge: Cambridge UP.

Comrie, Bernard. 1995. Rez. zu Johanson 1992a, *Rivista di Linguistica* 7: 391–394.

Csató, Éva Á. 1996. „Some typological properties of North-Western Karaim in areal perspektives". In: Boretzky, Norbert, Enninger, Werner & Stolz, Thomas (eds.). *Areale, Kontakte, Dialekte. Sprache und ihre Dynamik in mehrsprachigen Situationen*. (Bochum-Essener Beiträge zur Sprachwandelforschung, 24.) Bochum: Brockmeyer, 68–83.

Deny, Jean et alii (eds.) 1959. *Philologiae turcicae fundamenta*, 1. Aquis Mattiacis: Steiner.

Doerfer, Gerhard. 1971. *Khalaj materials*. (Indiana University Publications, Uralic and Altaic series, 115.) Bloomington, The Hague: Indiana UP.

Doerfer, Gerhard. 1988. *Grundwort und Sprachmischung. Eine Untersuchung anhand von Körperteilbezeichnungen*. (Münchener Ostasiatische Studien, 47.) Stuttgart: Steiner.

Doerfer, Gerhard. 1990. „Die Stellung des Osmanischen im Kreise des Oghusischen und seine Vorgeschichte". In: Hazai, György (ed.). *Handbuch der türkischen Sprachwissenschaft*, 1. Wiesbaden: Harrassowitz, 13–34.

Erdal, Marcel. 1991. *Old Turkic word formation. A functional approach to the lexicon 1–2*. (Turcologica, 7.) Wiesbaden: Harrassowitz.

Gabain, Annemarie von. 1974. *Alttürkische Grammatik*. 3. Aufl. Wiesbaden: Harrassowitz.

Hazai, György. 1978. *Kurze Einführung in das Studium der türkischen Sprache*. Budapest: Akadémiai Kiadó.

Johanson, Lars. 1971. *Aspekt im Türkischen. Vorstudien zu einer Beschreibung des türkeitürkischen Aspektsystems*. (Studia Turcica Upsaliensia, 1.) Uppsala: Almquist & Wiksell.

Johanson, Lars. 1979. *Alttürkisch als 'dissimilierende Sprache'*. (Akademie der Wissenschaften und der Literatur Mainz, Abhandlungen der Geistes- und sozialwissenschaftlichen Klasse, 1979: 2.) Wiesbaden.

Johanson, Lars. 1990. „Studien zur türkeitürkischen Grammatik". In: Hazai, György (ed.). *Handbuch der türkischen Sprachwissenschaft*, 1. Wiesbaden: Harrassowitz, 146–278.

Johanson, Lars. 1991. *Linguistische Beiträge zur Gesamtturkologie*. (Bibliotheca Orientalis Hungarica, 37.) Budapest: Akadémiai Kiadó.

Johanson, Lars. 1992a. *Strukturelle Faktoren in türkischen Sprachkontakten*. (Sitzungsberichte der Wissenschaftlichen Gesellschaft an der Johann Wolfgang Goethe-Universität Frankfurt am Main, 29: 5.) Stuttgart: Steiner.

Johanson, Lars. 1992b. „Periodische Kettensätze im Türkischen". *Wiener Zeitschrift für die Kunde des Morgenlandes* 82: 201–211.

Johanson, Lars. 1993. „Code-copying in immigrant Turkish". In: Extra, Guus & Verhoeven, Ludo (eds.). *Immigrant languages in Europe*. Clevedon: Multilingual Matters, 197–221.

Johanson, Lars. 1995. „Mehrdeutigkeit in der türkischen Verbalkomposition". In: Erdal, Marcel & Tezcan, Semih (eds.). *Beläk Bitig*. (Turcologica, 23.) Wiesbaden: Harrassowitz, 81–101.

Johanson, Lars. 1995. „On Turkic converb clauses". In: Haspelmath, Martin & König, Ekkehard (eds.). *Converbs in cross-linguistic perspective. Structure and meaning of adverbial verb forms – adverbial participles, gerunds*. (Empirical approaches to languages typology, 13.) Berlin, New York: Mouton de Gruyter, 313–347.

Johanson, Lars. 1996a. „Terminality operators and their hierarchical status". In: Devriendt, Betty, Goosens, Louis & van der Auwera, Johan (eds.). *Complex structures: A functionalist perspective.* (Functional Grammar Series, 17.) Berlin, New York: Mouton de Gruyter, 229–258.

Johanson, Lars. 1996b. „Kopierte Satzjunktoren im Türkischen". *Sprachtypologie und Universalienforschung* 49: 1–11.

Johanson, Lars. 1998. „Code-copying in Irano-Turkic". *Language Sciences* 20: 325–337.

Johanson, Lars. 1999a. „Viewpoint operators in European languages". In: Dahl, Östen (ed.). *Tense and aspect in the languages of Europe.* Berlin, New York: Mouton de Gruyter, 27–187.

Johanson, Lars. 1999b. „Frame-changing code-copying in immigrant varieties". In: Extra, Guus & Verhoeven, Ludo (eds.). *Bilingualism and migration.* (Studies on Language Acquisition, 14.) Berlin, New York: Mouton de Gruyter, 247–260.

Johanson, Lars. 1999c. „The dynamics of code-copying in language encounters". In: Brendemoen, Bernt & Lanza, Elizabeth & Ryen, Else (eds.). *Language encounters across time and space.* Oslo: Novus Press, 37–62.

Johanson, Lars & Csató, Éva Á. (eds.). 1998. *Turkic languages.* London: Routledge.

Johanson, Lars & Rehbein, Jochen (eds.). 1999. *Türkisch und Deutsch im Vergleich.* Wiesbaden: Harrassowitz.

Johanson, Lars & Utas, Bo (eds.). 1999. *Evidential. Turkic, Iranian and neighbouring languages.* Berlin, New York: Mouton de Gruyter.

Menges, Karl H. 1995. *The Turkic languages and peoples. An introduction to Turkic studies.* 2. Aufl. Wiesbaden: Harrassowitz.

Musaev, Kenesbaj. M. 1984. *Leksikologija tjurkskix jazykov.* Moskva.

Pritsak, Omeljan. 1963. „Das Alttürkische". In: Spuler, Bertold (ed.). *Handbuch der Orientalistik,* 1, 5: 1. Leiden & Köln: Brill, 27–52.

Róna-Tas, András. 1991. *Language and history. Contributions to comparative Altaistics.* (Studia Uralo-Altaica, 25.) Szeged: Universität Szeged.

Ščerbak, Aleksandr M. 1994. *Vvedenie v sravnitel'noe izučenie tjurkskix jazykov.* Sankt-Peterburg: Nauka.

Schönig, Claus. 1984. *Hilfsverben im Tatarischen. Untersuchungen zur Funktionsweise einiger Hilfsverbverbindungen.* Wiesbaden: Steiner.

Tekin, Talât. 1968. *A grammar of Orkhon Turkic.* (Indiana University Publications, Uralic and Altaic Series, 69.) Bloomington & The Hague: Indiana University Publications.

Tenišev, Ėdhem R. (ed.) 1984. *Srnavnitel'no-istoričeskaja grammatika tjurkskix jazykov. Fonetika.* Moskva: Nauka.

Tenišev, Ėdhem R. (ed.) 1988. *Srnavnitel'no-istoričeskaja grammatika tjurkskix jazykov. Morfologija.* Moskva: Nauka.

Lars Johanson, Universität Mainz
(Deutschland)

123. From Ancient Egyptian to Coptic

1. The language of Ancient Egypt
2. Phonology
3. Egyptian morphology
4. Egyptian syntax
5. Morphosyntax and typological patterns
6. Special abbreviations
7. References

1. The language of Ancient Egypt

1.1. General remarks

With its more than four millennia of productive written history (3000 BCE–1300 CE), the language of Ancient Egypt, from its earliest attestations in the Early Bronze Age down to Coptic in the Middle Ages, represents an ideal object of typological investigation (Loprieno 1995). In this article, rather than a contrastive presentation of synchronic states, the reader will find a selection of grammatical issues which lay down the main patterns of diachronic evolution from the earliest to the latest forms of this language.

The history of Ancient Egyptian is divided into two main phases, EARLIER EGYPTIAN and LATER EGYPTIAN, which are characterized by a major change from synthetic to analytic patterns (Junge 1985). Each of these two major phases can be further subdivided into three stages, which differ primarily in the sphere of graphemics (Kammerzell 1995).

1.2. Earlier Egyptian

Earlier Egyptian is the language of all written texts from 3000 to 1300 BCE and survives in formal religious texts until the third century CE. Its main stages are: (a) OLD EGYPTIAN (Edel 1955–64), the written language of the religious and funerary texts of the Old Kingdom and First Intermediate Period (2800–2000 BCE). (b) MIDDLE EGYPTIAN (Gardiner 1957), from the Middle Kingdom to the end of the 18th pharaonic dynasty (2000–1300 BCE). Middle Egyptian is the language of classical Egyptian literature. (c) TRADITIONAL EGYPTIAN, the language of religious texts from the 19th dynasty to the Greco-Roman period (1300 BCE–300 CE). During this time, Traditional Egyptian coexisted with Later Egyptian (see § 1.3.) in a situation of diglossia between a "higher" and a "popular" linguistic register (Vernus 1996: 560–564).

Earlier Egyptian is characterized by a preference for synthetic patterns, with morphological affixes indicating gender and number in the noun as well as deictic features in the verb. It displays the VSO order:

(1) EARLIER EG.
     sçm-f   n-k
     listen.PROSP-3M.SG to-2M.SG
     'May he listen to you.'

1.3. Later Egyptian

Later Egyptian is documented from the 19th pharaonic dynasty down to the Middle Ages (1300 BCE–1300 CE). Its main stages are: (a) LATE EGYPTIAN (Erman 1933; Junge 1996), the language of administration and entertainment literature from the 19th to the 26th dynasty (1300–700 BCE). Late Egyptian is not a homogeneous linguistic reality; the texts of this phase of the language show various degrees of interference with classical Middle Egyptian, with the tendency by older or formal texts to display a higher number of borrowings from the classical language, as opposed to administrative texts, where Middle Egyptian forms are much rarer (Winand 1992: 3–25). (b) DEMOTIC (Spiegelberg 1925; Johnson 1991), the language of administration and literature from the pharaonic Late Period to Late Antiquity (seventh century BCE–fifth century CE). While grammatically very close to Late Egyptian, it differs from it radically in its shorthand-like graphic system. (c) COPTIC (Till 1970; Lambdin 1983), the language of Christian Egypt (fourth–fourteenth century CE), written in a variety of Greek alphabet with the addition of a few Demotic signs to represent Egyptian phonemes absent from Greek. Coptic also differs from the earlier stages of the language because of the high percentage of lexical borrowings from Greek (Kasser 1991a). As a spoken, and gradually also as a written language, Coptic was superseded by Arabic from the ninth century onward, but it survives to the present time as the liturgical language of the Christian church of Egypt (Till 1970: 29–39) and in a few linguistic traces it left in the spoken Egyptian variety of Arabic (Vittmann 1991).

Besides displaying a number of phonological evolutions, Later Egyptian tends to develop analytic features: suffix markers of morphological oppositions are dropped and functionally replaced by prefixal classifiers; periphrastic SVO-patterns supersede the older VSO-formations (Hintze 1950):

(2) COPTIC
     mare-f-so:tǝm   (ʔ)ǝro-k
     OPT-3M.SG-listen to-2M.SG
     'May he listen to you.'

1.4. Dialects

Due to the centralized nature of the political and cultural models underlying the evolution of Ancient Egyptian society, there is hardly any evidence of dialect differences in pre-Coptic Egyptian (Osing 1975). There are indications, however, that the linguistic type represented by Earlier Egyptian may have had its origin in Northern Egypt, around the city of Memphis, which was the capital of the country during the Old Kingdom, whereas Later Egyptian represents a Southern variety of the language (Zeidler 1992: 208; Schenkel 1993: 148).

COPTIC is known through a variety of dialects which do not vary profoundly: they differ mainly in graphic conventions, to a limited extent in the lexicon, and only sporadically in morphology and syntax. In this article, the unmarked definition "Coptic" will refer to SAHIDIC, the Theban dialect of classical COPTIC literature; occasional reference will also be made to Alexandrian BOHAIRIC, which in the centuries following the Arabic invasion became the liturgical dialect of the COPTIC church (Kasser 1991b).

2. Phonology

2.1. Graphemes and phonemes

The exact phonological value of many Egyptian phonemes is obscured by difficulties in establishing reliable Afroasiatic correspondences (Schenkel 1990: 24–57). Vocalism and prosody can be partially reconstructed on the basis of Akkadian transcriptions of Egyptian words and phrases from the second millennium BCE, of GREEK transcriptions from the

Late Period (corresponding roughly to spoken Demotic), and of the Coptic evidence of the first millennium CE. The sketch of Egyptian phonology presented below prescinds from the problems of the graphic rendition of the phonemes, which are considerable in all stages of Egyptian, including Coptic (Kammerzell 1995: XLV–LII). The consonantal phonemes posited below for EARLIER EGYPTIAN, with the exception of /l/, may be rendered by one of the graphemes of the Egyptian writing system, the so-called "hieroglyphs," which by combining one-, two-, or three-consonant phonograms and semograms conveys the consonantal skeleton of a word, but allows no direct insight into vocalism or prosody; accordingly, vocalized Egyptian words are always scholarly reconstructions and, therefore, preceded by the asterisk. As for COPTIC, in spite of a certain number of graphic idiosyncrasies, all dialects share a relatively uniform phonological system, which is the one presented below. For example, the graphic conventions of SAHIDIC – as opposed to those of BOHAIRIC – do not distinguish between voiceless and ejective plosives (SAHIDIC ⟨tôre⟩, BOHAIRIC ⟨tʰôri⟩ = tʰo:rə 'willow' ~ SAHIDIC ⟨tôre⟩, BOHAIRIC ⟨tôri⟩ = ṭo:rə 'hand') or between velar and glottal fricatives (SAHIDIC ⟨hrai⟩, BOHAIRIC ⟨hrai⟩ = hrai̯ 'above' ~ SAHIDIC ⟨hrai⟩, BOHAIRIC ⟨xrai⟩ = xrai̯ 'below'). Yet, the presence of the corresponding oppositions in SAHIDIC can be established on the basis of comparative dialectology and of the different impact of these phonemes on their respective phonetic environment (Loprieno 1995: 40–50).

2.2. Consonants

In the Egyptian phonological system, the opposition between voiceless and voiced phonemes (Schenkel 1993: 138–146) appears limited to bilabial plosives (3a), whereas in the other series the articulatory opposition – when present – is between voiceless and ejective stop (3b–c). Voiceless plosives displayed the optional feature of aspiration in pretonic and high-sonority environments:

(3) (a) bilabial b ~ pʰ: BOHAIRIC COPTIC bo:k 'servant' ~ pʰo:k 'yours.M.SG'
(b) dental tʰ ~ ṭ: EARLIER EG. *tʰa:m 'to complete' ~ *ṭa:m 'to sharpen'
(c) palatal cʰ ~ ç: EARLIER EG. *cʰa:rat 'willow' ~ *ça:rat 'hand'

The dental series is typologically very complex: while it probably exhibited a tripartite opposition "voiceless-voiced-ejective" in the earliest periods, the voiced stop evolved to a pharyngeal fricative before the emergence of Middle Egyptian (Zeidler 1992: 206–210), and then to a glottal stop (and eventually zero) in Coptic (4a). During the second millennium BCE, the voiceless dental t shows the tendency to be dropped in final position (4b):

(4) (a) d > ʕ > ʔ/ø:
OLD EG. *da:ʃ > LATE EG. *ʕa:ʃ > COPTIC (ʔ)o:ʃ 'to call'
(b) t > ø / __#:
OLD EG. *sa:nat > LATE EG. *sa:nə(t) > COPTIC so:nə 'sister'

During the late second millennium BCE, the place of articulation of plosive consonants tends to be moved to the frontal region (Osing 1980: 946): uvulars and velars are palatalized (5a–c), palatals become dentals and dentals are dropped in final position (6a–b):

(5) uvular/velar > palatal(ized):
(a) LATE EG. *kʰaʔm > COPTIC kʲo:m 'garden'
(b) OLD EG. *qa:r > COPTIC kʲo:ʔ 'to cease'
(c) OLD EG. *qaṭ > COPTIC kʲot 'form'

(6) palatal > dental, dental > ø:
(a) OLD EG. *ça:rat > LATE EG. *ṭa:rə(t) > COPTIC ṭo:rə 'hand'
(b) OLD EG. *ra:mac > LATE EG. *ra:mə(t) > COPTIC ro:mə 'man'

During the first millennium BCE, the opposition between uvular and velars is neutralized: COPTIC exhibits a new tripartite opposition "palatalized-voiceless (with optional aspiration)-ejective" in the velar series (7a–c):

Table 123.1: Plosives in EARLIER EGYPTIAN

plosives	bilabial	dental	palatal	velar	uvular	glottal
voiced	b	(d)	–	–	–	–
voiceless	p(ʰ)	t(ʰ)	c(ʰ)	k(ʰ)	–	–
ejective	–	ṭ	ç	ḳ	q	ʔ

Table 123.2: Plosives in COPTIC

plosives	bilabial	dental	palatal	velar	glottal
palatalized	–	–	–	k^j	–
voiced	b	(d)	–	(g)	–
voiceless	p(ʰ)	t(ʰ)	c(ʰ)	k(ʰ)	–
ejective	–	ṭ	c̣	ḳ	ʔ

(7) $k^h \sim \underline{k} \sim q > k^j \sim k^h \sim \underline{k}$:
   (a) $k^h o{:}ʔ$ 'shrine' (from EG. *k^h) ~ $k^j o{:}ʔ$ 'to cease' (from EG. *$\underline{k}$)
   (b) $k^j o{:}b$ 'weak' (from EG. *$\underline{k}$) ~ $\underline{k}o{:}b$ 'to double' (from EG. *q)
   (c) $k^j ot$ "form" ~ $\underline{k}ot$ 'wheel' (both from EG. *q)

The opposition between voiceless and ejective plosives is neutralized as voiceless (unmarked) in posttonic position (8a) and voiced dentals and velars are only found in GREEK borrowings or as a result of assimilation of the corresponding voiceless in nasal environments (8b):

(8) (a) $so{:}təm < so{:}ṭəm$ 'to hear' ~ $so{:}təp < so{:}t(^h)əp$ 'to choose'
   (b) $to{:}unəg < to{:}unək$ 'stand up!'

In OLD EGYPTIAN, all fricative consonants are voiceless; in MIDDLE EGYPTIAN, as we just saw, a pharyngeal voiced /ʕ/ evolved from earlier /d/ via lateralization:

(9) (a) *$x > ʃ$:
   OLD EG. *$da{:}xam >$ LATE EG. *$ʕa{:}xəm >$ COPTIC $(ʔ)o{:}ʃəm$ 'to extinguish'
   (b) OLD EG. *$ç/ʃ > x$:
   OLD EG. *$θaçraw/θaʃraw >$ COPTIC sax 'scribe'
   (c) *$ç > x$:
   OLD EG. *$daça{:}mv(w)$ 'falcon' > LATE EG. *$ʕaça{:}m >$ COPTIC $(ʔ)axo{:}m$ 'eagle'

A similar neutralization affected in the first millennium BCE the opposition between pharyngeal /ħ/ and glottal /h/ (Osing 1976: 367–368):

(10) *$ħ, *h > h$:
   (a) OLD EG. *$ħu{:}rit >$ LATE EG. *$ħe{:}ʔə(t) >$ COPTIC $he{:}ʔ$ 'beginning'
   (b) OLD EG. *$haru{:}wv >$ LATE EG. *$haʔe{:}ʔ >$ COPTIC $he{:}ʔ$ 'season'

It should be noted that the voiced alveolar fricative z is only found in GREEK borrowings

Table 123.3: Fricatives in EARLIER EGYPTIAN

fricatives	labiodental	interdental	alveolar	alveopalatal	palatal	velar	pharyngeal	glottal
voiceless	f	θ	s	ʃ	ç	x	ħ	h
voiced	–	–	–	–	–	–	(ʕ)	–

The interdental θ merged very early with the alveolar s (θ > s). During the first millennium BCE, the tripartite opposition between fricatives in the palatal region (/ʃ/ ~ /ç/ ~ /x/) was reduced to a bipartite one (/ʃ/ ~ /x/), with a partial redistribution of the original articulation (Osing 1976: 401–402, 503):

or as a result of assimilation in nasal environments:

(11) COPTIC $(ʔ)anze{:}bə < (ʔ)anse{:}bə$ 'school'

Historical evolutions affecting nasals, liquids and glides during the second millennium

Table 123.4: Fricatives in COPTIC

fricatives	labiodental	alveolar	alveopalatal	velar	glottal
voiceless	f	s	ʃ	x	h
voiced	–	(z)	–	–	–

BCE (Loprieno 1995: 38) were the loss of the uvular vibrant /ʀ/ and its lenition to glottal stop /ʔ/ and eventually ø (12), and the loss of final vibrants and glides in the same environments in which a final voiceless dental *t* was dropped (13):

(12)   ʀ > ʔ > ø:
        OLD EG. *kʰaʀmaw > LATE EG. *kʰaʔm > COPTIC kʲoːm 'garden'

(13)   r, j, w > ø / __#:
    (a) OLD EG. *xaːpar > LATE EG. *xaːpə(r) > COPTIC ʃoːpə 'to become'
    (b) OLD EG. *nacʰuːra(w) > LATE EG. *nətʰeːrə 'gods' > COPTIC əntʰeːr 'idols'

Table 123.5: Sonorants in the Egyptian domain

sonorants	labial	dental	palatal	uvular
nasal	m	n		
vibrant		r		(ʀ)
lateral		l		
glide	w		j	

2.3. Vowels

The set of vowels posited for EARLIER EGYPTIAN (Osing 1976: 10–30) is the same as for most Afroasiatic languages in their earliest stage of development (Diakonoff 1965: 30–31):

Table 123.6: Vowels in EARLIER EGYPTIAN

vowels	short	long
high front	i	iː
low central	a	aː
high back	u	uː

This system underwent a certain number of historical changes, only some of which can be discussed here. First and foremost, because of the presence of a strong expiratory stress, Egyptian unstressed vowels were gradually phonologically reduced, until in COPTIC they are generally realized as schwa; only the short unstressed /a/ is maintained in pretonic position in specific phonetic environments (Schenkel 1990: 91–93):

(14) (a) OLD EG. *ramac-ni-kʰuːmat > COPTIC rəmənkʰeːmə 'Egyptian man'
    (b) OLD EG. *janak > COPTIC (ʔ)anok 'I'

Stressed vowels underwent a global sound shift: during the second millennium BCE, long /uː/ turned into /eː/, while short stressed /i/ and /u/ merged into /e/. In the main COPTIC dialects and unless followed by glottal stop, this /e/ evolved into /a/:

(15) (a) OLD EG. *rin > LATE EG. *ren > COPTIC (Sahidic and Bohairic) ran 'name'
    (b) OLD EG. *muʀdat > LATE EG. *meʔʕə(t) > COPTIC meʔ 'truth'
    (c) OLD EG. *kʰuːmat > LATE EG. *kʰeːmə(t) > COPTIC kʰeːmə 'Egypt'

Around 1000 BCE, long /aː/ became /oː/ resp. /uː/ after nasals — a shift that occurred simultaneously in NORTHWEST SEMITIC languages, where it is called the "Canaanite shift" — and short /a/ became /o/, a change limited to a part of the COPTIC linguistic domain, roughly the same to which (15a) applies:

(16) (a) OLD EG. *naːcar > COPTIC nuːtə 'God'
    (b) OLD EG. *san > COPTIC (SAHIDIC and BOHAIRIC) son 'brother'

Table 123.7: Vowels in COPTIC

vowels	unstressed	stressed short	long
high front			iː
	e		
	ə		eː
low central		a	
	a		oː
	o		
high back			uː

2.4. Stress and syllabic patterns

In EARLIER EGYPTIAN, the stress lay on the ultimate (oxytone) or penultimate (paroxytone) syllable of a word (Schenkel 1990: 63–86). Both closed (cvc) and open syllables (cv) can be found in pretonic, tonic, and posttonic position. The stressed vowel of a penultimate open syllable is always long (cvː); according to some scholars, extrasyllabic additions under oxytone stress could generate syllables of the type cvː(c) or cvc(c) (Loprieno 1995: 36–37):

Table 123.8: EARLIER EGYPTIAN syllabic structures

syllabic structures	pretonic	tonic	posttonic
open	cv	$'cv:$	$cv#
closed	cvc	$'cvc$	$cvc#
doubly-closed		$'cvcc#	
long		$'cv:c#	

These syllabic structures were modified under the influence of the strong expiratory stress which always characterized the Egyptian domain (Fecht 1960) and prompted significant typological changes in morphology and syntax (cf. § 3.5.). The gradual loss of short unstressed vowels led to the emergence of complex consonantal clusters in syllable onset in COPTIC (Loprieno 1995: 48–50):

Table 123.9: COPTIC syllabic structures

syllabic structures	pretonic	tonic	posttonic
open	cv #ccv$	$'cv:$ #'ccv:$	$cv#
closed	cvc #ccvc$	$'cvc$ #'ccvc$	$cvc#
doubly-closed		$'cvcc$ #'ccvcc$	
long		$'cv:c$ #'ccv:c#	

Examples for the evolution of oxytone (17) and paroxytone (18) patterns are:

(17) (a) cv'cvc > ccvc
   OLD EG. *waçaḥ > COPTIC wəṭaḥ 'fruit'
 (b) cvc'cvc > cvc'cvc
   OLD EG. *numḥiw 'poor' > COPTIC rəmheʔ 'free'

(18) (a) 'cvccvc > cvcc
   OLD EG. *xamtaw > BOHAIRIC ʃomt 'three'
 (b) cv'cvccvc > ccvcc
   OLD EG. *ḥijamwat > COPTIC hjomʔ 'women'
 (c) cv'cv:cvc > ccv:c
   OLD EG. *pisi:çaw > COPTIC psi:t 'nine'

3. Egyptian morphology

3.1. Root, stem, word

EARLIER EGYPTIAN is a language of the flectional (or fusional) type, in which morphemes are unsegmentable units combining many grammatical functions. Morphological forms exhibit a number of correspondences with the patterns of word formation in other AFROASIATIC LANGUAGES, and in spite of some problems — for example, the fact that, although it is the oldest documented AFROASIATIC language (at least seven centuries before AKKADIAN), Egyptian displays several typologically innovative features — Egyptian morphology is nonetheless conveniently described within the AFROASIATIC frame, which is capable of clarifying both the synchronic structures of the language and the remnants of earlier stages (Schenkel 1990: 94–121).

The basic structure of an Egyptian word is a lexical *root*, an abstract phonological entity consisting of a sequence of consonants or semiconsonants which vary in number from one to four, with an overwhelming majority of biconsonantal, triconsonantal, and so-called weak roots, which display a vocalic or semivocalic last radical or a gemination of the second radical. Superimposed on the root as a separate morphological tier is a vocalic or semivocalic pattern, which together with the root forms the so-called *stem*, the surface form acquired by the root; the stem determines the part of speech to which the word belongs. It is transformed into an actual *word* of the language by means of inflectional affixes (in Egyptian for the most part suffixes), which convey deictic notions and other grammatical functions such as gender, number, tense and aspect, and voice (Reintges 1994).

Vocalic skeletons generally determine the structure of nominal patterns and of basic conjugational forms, whereas semivocalic suffixes convey the expression of the plural, of adjectival forms of the verb (participles and relative forms), and of some conjugational patterns. A *j*- or *w*-prefix can be added to biconsonantal roots to form triradical nominal stems; conversely, a triconsonantal root may lose a semivocalic glide and be reduced to a biradical stem. Examples of consonantal additions to a root are *s*- for causative stems, *n*- for singulative nouns and reflexive verbs, and *m*- for nouns of instrument, place, or agent. While many of these morphological features are indeed shared by other AFROASIATIC languages, Egyptian stems

Table 123.10: Examples of derivation of EARLIER EGYPTIAN words

root	stem	affix	function	word
sn 'brother'	*san-	.ø	M.SG	*san 'brother'
		.at	F.SG	*saːnat 'sister'
	*sanu-	.aw	M.PL	*sanuːwaw 'brothers'
	*sansan-	.ø	INF	*sansan 'to befriend'
ncr 'god'	*nacar-	.ø	SG	*naːcar 'god'
	*nacur-	.aw	PL	*nacuːraw 'gods'
	*nucr-	.ij	M.ADJ	*nucrij 'divine'
		.it	F.ADJ	*nucrit 'divine'
sçm 'to hear'	*saçam-	.ø	INF	*saːçam 'to hear'
		.s	3F.SG	*saçaːmas 'hearing her'
	*saçma-	.ø	PROSP	*saçma-NP 'may NP hear'
		.f	3M.SG	*saçmáf 'may he hear'
	*saçim-	.na	PRET	*saçimna-N 'N heard'
		.c	2F.SG	*saçimnac 'you heard'
		.ø	ACT.PART	*saːçim 'hearer'
		.iw	PASS.PART	*sáçmiw 'heard' < **saçimiw
dḥd 'to stand'	*madḥid-	.wat	F.PL	*madḥídwat 'tomb(s)'
mn 'to be stable'	*man-	.ø	INF	*maːn 'to be stable'
	*simin-	.it	CAUS.INF	*simiːnit 'to establish'

resulting from the addition of a consonantal phoneme to a root tend to be lexicalized as new autonomous roots rather than treated as grammatical forms of the basic root: Egyptian, therefore, does not possess a full-fledged paradigm of verbal stems conveying semantic nuances of a verbal root similar to the SEMITIC *binyanim* (see also § 5.4.).

Common modifications of the root are: (1) the *reduplication* of the entire root or of a segment thereof. This pattern affects the semantic sphere, creating new lexemes: from *sn* 'brother,' *snsn* 'to befriend'; from *ḳmj* 'to find,' *nḳmḳm* 'to be gathered' (with the *n*-prefix of reflexivity); from *snb* 'to be healthy,' *snbb* 'to greet'; (2) the *gemination* of the last radical, which affects the grammatical sphere: *çt* 'to say' > *çṯṯt* 'what has been said,' *mrj* 'to love' > *mrr-j* 'that I love,' *sçm* 'to hear' > *sçmm-f* 'he will be heard' (Reintges 1994: 230–240). Examples of morphological structures are given in Table 123.10.

3.2. Nominal morphology

In EARLIER EGYPTIAN, nouns are built by adding to the stem a zero- or a non-zero suffix, depending on whether the stem ends in a consonant, in which case the suffix is zero, or a vowel, in which case a *w*-suffix is added. The feminine marker is a *t*-suffix added to the masculine noun; the plural displays a *w*- or *ww*-suffix; the dual has a *j*-marker added to the form of the plural in masculine, of the singular in feminine nouns:

Table 123.11: Nouns in EARLIER EGYPTIAN

nouns	masculine	feminine
singular	ø, w	t
dual	wj	tj
plural	ø, w, ww	t, jt, wt

Adjectives are morphologically and syntactically treated like nouns. In a very common derivational pattern, called *nisbation*, a morpheme masculine **ij*, feminine **it* is added to a stem, which may be different from the stem of the singular or plural noun, to form the corresponding adjective: **naːcar* 'god,' **nacuːra(w)* 'gods,' **nucrij*, **nucrit* 'divine.'

There are three sets of personal pronouns (Kammerzell 1991a). Stressed pronouns are used for the topicalized subject of noun clauses in the first and second person (19a), and for the focalized subject of verbal cleft sentences (19b):

(19) (a) MIDDLE EG.
    jnk   jtj-k
    1SG.TOP father-2M.SG
    'I am your father'
(b) *nts   s-ʕnx   rn-j*
    FOC3F.SG CAUS-live.PART name-1SG
    'She is the one who makes my name live.'

Unstressed pronouns are used for the object of VPs (20a), for the subject of adjective clauses (20b), and for the subject of adverb clauses (20c):

(20) (a) *hʀb-f   wj*
        send.PROSP-3M.SG 1SG.OBJ
        'He will send me'
(b) *nfr   cw   ḥnʕ-j*
    be.good.PART 2M.SG.SUBJ with-1SG
    'You are happy with me'
(c) *nn sj   m jb-j*
    not 3F.SG.SUBJ in heart-1SG
    'It was not in my heart.'

Suffix pronouns are used as subject of VPs, as possessive marker, and as object of prepositions:

(21) *cj-k   r-k   n-j*
      give.PROSP-2M.SG indeed to-1SG
      xt-j
      thing-1SG
      'You shall indeed (lit.: 'to-you') give me my possessions.'

Demonstratives are characterized by a deictic element preceded by the marker of gender and number and follow the noun they refer to (22a–b). In MIDDLE EGYPTIAN, the old plural forms are replaced by a partitive construction headed by an original neuter pronoun (22c):

(22) (a) *rmc pf* 'that man'
    (b) *ḥjmwt jptn* 'these women'
    (c) *nn nj srjww* 'these officials (lit. this-of-officials)'

The determinative pronoun *nj* is used primarily as a genitive marker; the relative pronoun *ntj* is morphologically derived from it. In EARLIER EGYPTIAN, these pronouns agree in gender and number with the head noun. Genitive constructions will be discussed in § 5.2., and relativization phenomena will be treated in § 5.3. Characteristic of EARLIER EGYPTIAN is the presence of a relative pronoun which semantically incorporates negation:

(23) *jwtj   pçr-f*
      who.not   vent.AOR-3M.SG
      çṭw   m   çt-f
      say.PART.IMPF.PASS in belly-3M.SG
      'He who does not vent what is said in his belly.'

Interrogative pronouns can be combined with prepositions or particles to form complex pronouns: *jn-m* (FOC-WH) 'who?,' *ḥr-m* (on-WH) 'why?'

Numerals precede the noun they refer to. The most common of them show etymological ties with other AFROASIATIC languages. The number "5" is derived from the word for "hand", "20" is the dual of "10," "50" through "90" represent the plural forms of the respective units "5" through "9". Ordinals are derived in Earlier Egyptian by adding a suffix (*-nw*) to the cardinal number (24a), in Later Egyptian through the prefixation of the participle *mḥ-* 'filling' (24b):

(a) EARLIER EG. *xmt-nw* 'third' (lit. '3-th')
(b) LATER EG. *mḥ-çwtj* 'twentieth' (lit. 'filling-20')

3.3. Verbal morphology

EARLIER EGYPTIAN finite VPs display a limited number of stems (three or four) indicating tense, aspect, and voice followed by the pronominal (25a) or nominal subject (25b):

(25) (a) OLD EG.
        **danxa-s*
        live.PROSP-3F.SG
        'She will live'
(b) **haʀbi-ḥijmat   θiʀ-vs*
    send.PFV-woman son-3F.SG
    'The woman sent her son.'

In addition to variations in the stem, a few verbal features are indicated by consonantal affixes inserted between the stem and the subject. The most important of these indicators are *n* for the preterite tense, *t* for non-paradimatic occurrences of the perfective aspect and for the prospective aspect of a few irregular verbs, *w* for prospective aspect and passive voice (in perfective stems) *tj* or *tw* for passive (in non-perfective stems).

A particular verbal stem of nominal (probably relative) origin displays the tonic vowel between the second and the third radical, and in weak verbal classes the reduplication of the second radical: *satap-* (choose.REL), *marar-* (love.REL). A similar verbal form indicates in SEMITIC languages the imperfective aspect; in Egyptian, its function is to mark the VP as pragmatic *theme* of the sentence in which it appears (Polotsky 1976: 4–25). In such sentences, the pragmatic *rheme* is usually an adverbial modifier or an adverb clause:

(26) MIDDLE EG.
      jrr   ḥm-k   r
      do.IMPF Majesty-2M.SG to
      mrt-f
      desire.REL.F-3M.SG
      'Your Majesty acts as he desires.'

The imperative has no suffix element in the singular, but sometimes, especially with weak verbs, a semivocalic suffix in the plural.

Egyptian also exhibits a verbal form, called Old Perfective, Stative or Pseudoparticiple, which indicates the wide semantic range of "perfectivity," from perfect aspect (with intransitive verbs) to passive voice (with transitive verbs). This form is built with a special set of suffixes that are etymologically linked to the forms of the Semitic suffix conjugation (Schenkel 1990: 104–108; Kammerzell 1991b: 165–199):

(27) *mk   wj   jj-kw*
      behold 1SG come-PERF-1SG
      'Look, I have come,' i. e. 'I am here.'

Non-finite forms of the Egyptian verb are (a) the participles, with nominal stems derived from the verbal root (e. g., **sa:ç̣im* 'hearer'), and (b) the infinitives, which display a suffix ø in the regular verbs (**sa:çam* 'to hear'), *t* in some classes of weak verbs (**mirjit* 'to love'), and *w* after verbs of negative predication, such as *tm* (**tam-ja:raw* 'not to do,' lit. to complete-to do.NEG.INF).

3.4. Prepositions and particles

The most frequent prepositions are *m* 'in, with'; *n* 'to, for'; *r* 'toward'; *mj* 'as, like'; *ḥr* 'on'; *ẓr* 'under'; *ḥnd* 'with'; *xft* 'according to'; *xnt* 'before.' Prepositional phrases follow the noun or the verb they modify. Particularly noteworthy is the presence of the preposition *xr* 'near', whose original semantic value 'beneath' was applied to any situation in which the two participants A and B belong to different hierarchical levels (28a–b):

(28) (a) OLD EG.
      ç̣t-f   xr msw-f
      say.PROSP-3M.SG by child.PL-3M.SG
      'He will say to his children'

(b) *jmRxy   xr ncr dR*
     honor.PART.PASS by god great
     'Honored by the Great God.'

The basic negative particle is *n*, which is used for contradictory negation (29a); if combined with the adverb *js* 'indeed,' this morpheme expresses contrariety (29b) (Loprieno 1991):

(29) (a) MIDDLE EG.
      n   rç-f   n-j   mw
      not give.PFV-3M.SG to-1SG water
      'He did not give me water'
      (b) *n-js   jtj-j   rçj*
      not-indeed father-1SG give.PART
      n-j
      to-1SG
      'It was not my father who gave (it) to me.'

A morphological variant of *n*, conventionally transcribed *nn*, is used in noun clauses to negate the existence (30a) and in verb clauses to negate the prospective aspect (30b):

(30) (a) *nn   mRʕtjw*
      not.exist trust.ADJ.PL
      'There are no trustworthy people'
      (b) *nn   mwt-k*
      not.exist die.PROSP-2M.SG
      'You shall not die.'

3.5. Developments in Later Egyptian

Under the pressure of a strong expiratory stress, which massively reduced the distinctive function of unstressed vowels, the flectional system underwent a profound crisis in LATER EGYPTIAN, requiring a reorganization of the carriers of morphological information. The general trend was to replace synthetic structures by analytic constructions: for example, nominalized participles (31) or abstract nouns (32) were replaced by lexicalized compounds with nominal classifiers (Till 1970: 71–75):

(31) EARLIER EG. > COPTIC
      PART > 'MAN-WHO'-V
      cʰRw   ref-cʰiwə
      steal.PART 'MAN-WHO'-steal.INF
      'Thief'

(32) ABSTRACT > 'THING-OF'-N
      rʔ   nj kʰmt
      mouth of Egypt
      mənt-rəm-ən-kʰe:mə
      'THING-OF'-man-of-Egypt
      'Egyptian language'

LATER EGYPTIAN develops two sets of articles. The indefinite article comes from the numeral *wdj* > *wʕj* 'one' (33); the definite article derives from a grammaticalized demonstrative pronoun (34):

(33) N[−SPEC] > INDEF.ART-N
 EARLIER EG. *snt* 'a.sister' > LATE EG. *wʕ(t)-sn(t)* > COPTIC *wə-soːnə* 'a-sister'

(34) N[+SPEC] > DEF.ART-N
 EARLIER EG. *rmc* 'the.man' > LATE EG. *pʔ-rm(t)* > COPTIC *p-roːmə* 'the man'

The definite article also attracts pronominal affixes indicating the possessor, which in EARLIER EGYPTIAN followed the head noun (35a). Similarly, deictics now precede the noun they modify (35b):

(35) (a) N-POSS > DEF.ART-POSS-N
 sn-f   *pe-f-son*
 brother-3M.SG the-3M.SG-brother
 'His brother'
 (b) N-DEM > DEM-N
 hjmt tn   *teị-shiːmə*
 woman this.F this.F-woman
 'This woman'

Thus, because of the described loss of regular flectional patterns, the only device by which COPTIC conveys the distinction between different patterns (masculine vs. feminine, nominal vs. verbal) is the presence of morphological markers preceding the noun (36a−c):

(36) (a) EARLIER EG. stem **ramac-* + M.SG ø = **raːmac* > COPTIC *p-roːmə* 'the man'
 (b) EARLIER EG. stem **san-* + F.SG *at* = **saːnat* > COPTIC *t-soːnə* 'the sister'
 (c) EARLIER EG. stem **xapar-* + INF ø = **xaːpar* > COPTIC *ø-ʃoːpə* 'to become'

The evolution towards a lexicalization of compound expressions also affected the verbal system (Winand 1992: 20). In many instances, an earlier verbal lexeme is replaced in LATER EGYPTIAN, particularly in COPTIC, by an auxiliary of generic meaning ('to do', 'to give', 'to take', etc.) followed by the verbal infinitive or by a noun object:

(37) VERBAL LEXEME > AUXILIARY + NOUN
 wcd   *(ʔ)ər-hap, ṭi-hap*
 judge.INF do.INF-law, give.INF-law
 'to judge'

Participles were superseded by analytic constructions with the relative pronouns (38a), while finite VS(O)-forms were replaced by a paradigm of SV(O)-constructions, called "sentence conjugations" or "clause conjugations" (Polotsky 1960), resulting from the grammaticalization of a form of the verb 'to do' followed by the infinitive (38b):

(38) (a) PARTICIPLE > RELATIVE CONSTRUCTION
 OLD EG. > LATE EG. > COPTIC
 *saːçim
 hear.PART.IMPFV
 p-ntj-(ḥr-)sṭm
 the.one-who-(on-)hear.INF
 p-et-soːtəm
 the.one-who-hear
 'the hearer'
 (b) VS(O) > AUX-SV(O)
 OLD EG. > LATE EG. > COPTIC
 scm-xr-f   *xr-jr-f-stm*
 hear-AOR-3M.SG AOR-do-3M.SG-hear.INF
 ʃa-f-soːtəm
 AOR-3M.SG-hear
 'He usually hears'

In this way, COPTIC ultimately maintains only two flectional patterns from most verbal roots: the infinitive for process predicates and the so-called "qualitative," derived from the 3M.SG (rarely 3F.SG) form of the Old Perfective, for statives (Polotsky 1990: 197−221):

(39) COPTIC
 f-ḳoːt   ~ *f-ḳeːt*
 3M.SG-build.INF 3M.SG-build.STAT
 'He builds'   'It is built'

Thus, with the productivity of root and stem variations massively reduced, LATER EGYPTIAN gradually moves toward the polysynthetic type which to a certain extent characterizes COPTIC:

(40) EARLIER EG.
 jw   *scm-n-j*   *xrw*
 'SITUATION' hear-PRET-1.SG voice
 > LATE EG.
 jr-j-sṭm   *wʕ-xrw*
 do.PRET-1SG-hearing a-voice
 > COPTIC
 (ʔ)a-ị-setm-wə-xrou̯
 PRET-1SG-hear-a-voice
 'I heard a voice'

4. Egyptian syntax

4.1. Noun clauses

In noun clauses, the predicate is a noun, either substantive or adjective (Loprieno 1995: 103−131). In categorical statements or qualifying adjectival sentences, the unmarked word order is PRED-SUBJ (41a); a demonstrative *pw* 'this' may be inserted as copula between the two phrases (41b):

(41) (a) MIDDLE EG.
 nfr mcn-j
 be.good.PART path-1SG
 'My path is good'
 (b) ṭmjt pw jmnt
 city.F COP West.F
 'The West is a city'

The order PRED-(COP-)SUBJ is modified to TOPIC-COMMENT in classifying sentences when the subject is a first or second person pronoun (42a), in identifying sentences when both the subject and the predicate are semantically determined or specified (42b), and in cleft sentences, in which the predicate is a participle and the subject is focalized (42c):

(42) (a) ntk jtj n nmḥw
 2M.SG father to orphan
 'You are a father to the orphan'
 (b) θçRW-f pw ḥrw
 scribe-3M.SG COP Horus
 'His scribe is Horus'
 (c) jn snt-j s-ʕnx
 FOC sister-1SG CAUS-live-PART
 rn-j
 name-1SG
 'My sister is the one who makes my name live.'

4.2. Adverb clauses

In adverb clauses, the predicate is an ADVP or a PP (Loprieno 1995: 144–172). The word order is always SUBJ-PRED. In EARLIER EGYPTIAN, main adverb clauses are often introduced by particles functioning as discourse markers (43a); in absence of a discourse marker, the clause is to be understood as syntactically dependent (43b):

(43) (a) jw nθw jr pt
 'SITUATION' king towards heaven.F
 'Now the king is (directed) towards heaven.'
 (b) xrt-k m pr-k
 rations.F-2M.SG in house.2M.SG
 '(Because) your rations are in your house'

4.3. Verb clauses

In verb clauses, the predicate is a VP (Loprieno 1995: 183–220); the word order is PRED-SUBJ:

(44) jj-n-j m nwt-j
 come-PRET-1SG from city.F-1SG
 'I came from my city.'

We saw in § 3.3. that the predicate of verb clauses may function as the theme of the utterance. In general, Egyptian verbal syntax displays a relatively high degree of topicalization and focalization phenomena (Loprieno 1988a: 41–52). The most common topicalization device is the extraposition of the topicalized argument through the particle *jr* 'concerning' (45a); used as a conjunction, the same particle introduces the protasis of a hypothetical clause (45b) (cf. Haiman 1985: 33–34):

(45) (a) jr sf wsjr pw
 concerning yesterday Osiris COP
 'As for "yesterday," it means "Osiris"'
 (b) jr jqr-k
 concerning be.important.PROSP-2M.SG
 ḳrḳ-k pr-k
 found.PROSP-2M.SG house-2M.SG
 'If you become wealthy, you should found a household.'

Unmarked VPs not introduced by discourse markers are less frequent than in related languages, mostly functioning as embedded or modal clauses:

(46) xʕy-k
 appear.PROSP-2M.SG
 'May you appear.'

4.4. Developments in Later Egyptian

Syntactic patterns prove rather stable throughout the history of Egyptian. COPTIC displays the same variety of sentence types as EARLIER EGYPTIAN:

(1) noun clauses (Polotsky 1987: 9–43) with an unmarked order PRED-SUBJ when the subject is a noun (47a), and with a marked order TOPIC-COMMENT in three environments: when the subject is a pronoun (47b), when both the subject and the predicate are semantically specific (47c), and in cleft sentences, in which the predicate is a participle and the subject is focalized (47d):

(47) (a) COPTIC
 wə-meʔ te te-f-mənt-məntreʔ
 a-truth COP POSS-3M.SG-thing-witness
 'His testimony is true'
 (b) (ʔ)anok wə-ʃoːs
 1SG-TOP a-shepherd
 'I am a shepherd'

(c) *t-arkhe: ən-t-sophia*
   the-beginning that.of-the-wisdom
   te t-mənt-mai̯-nu:tə
   COP the-thing-lover-god
   'The beginning of wisdom is piety'
(d) *p-nu:tə p-et-soun*
   the-god the.one-who-know.INF
   'God is the one who knows' (= 'Only God knows').

(2) Adverb clauses (Polotsky 1990: 203–224), in which the predicate is an AdvP or PP; the order is SUBJ-PRED:

(48) *ti-həm-pa-jo:t*
   1SG-in-POSS.1SG.father
   'I am in my father.'

(3) Verb clauses (Polotsky 1990: 175–202), in which the predicate is a VP built according to the SVO-patterns described in § 3.5.; in these patterns, the subject can be extraposed to the right of the predicate and anticipated by a cataphoric pronoun in the regular syntactic slot:

(49) *(ʔa-u̯-ri:mə*
   PRET-3PL-weep.INF
   ənkʲi-ne-sne:u̯
   namely-the-brother.PL
   'The monks wept.'

In COPTIC verbal sentences, the tendency to have VPs function as theme or rheme of the utterance reaches its full development: in the former case, the VP is preceded by a relative marker *e-* or *ənt-* and is described in Coptological literature as "second tense" (Polotsky 1987: 129–140); in the latter, the form is preceded by the circumstantial marker *e-* and is described as "circumstantial" (Polotsky 1990: 225–260):

(50) *ənt-a-n-cʰpo-f*
   REL-PRET-1PL-beget-3M.SG
   e-f-ʔo? ən-bəlle?
   'WHILE'-3M.SG-do.STAT as-blind
   'He was born to us blind.' (Lit. 'That we begot him was while he is as blind')

5. Morphosyntax and typological patterns

5.1. Case-marking and NP accessibility

Historical Egyptian displays no productive case-system, the only markers attached to NP-arguments being prepositions. Under the influence of a strong expiratory stress, old Afroasiatic case markers (nominative *-u, accusative *-a, genitive-possessive *-i) were probably lost already in prehistoric times: thus, a prehistoric **san-u* became *san 'brother,' the form we posit for EARLIER EGYPTIAN.

The case markers, however, left traces in the morphological behavior of the corresponding nouns (Zeidler 1992: 212–221). For example, the old case marker *-u, which was dropped in the stem of the singular of this word, reappears in the formation of the plural, attracting stress and vocalic length, developing a glide before the morpheme *-aw, and generating the form *sanu:waw. The ending *-u is still preserved in some singular patterns as well: when the original stem ended in a vowel, the ending was maintained as a glide, often graphically rendered ⟨w⟩ in the case of *-aw as opposed to ⟨ø⟩ in the case of *-iw or *-uw (Schenkel 1983: 186–187).

Remnants of the accusative (or absolutive) case in *-a are found in the vocalic ending of a preposition followed by a noun or a suffix pronoun (earlier Eg. *jaraf > Coptic *(ʔ)əro-f* 'to him'). As for the nominative *-u and the genitive *-i, a survival in historical times is offered by the vocalic pattern before pronominal suffixes, e. g. prehistoric Eg. nominative **har-u > Earlier Eg. *har > Coptic *ho?* 'face'; Earlier Eg. nominative *haru-f or genitive *hari-f > Coptic *hraf* 'his face'). The vocalization of an original derivational suffix can be reconstructed in the case of adjectives derived from nouns by means of the pattern known as *nisbation* (cf. § 3.2.): nominative **har-u > *har > *ho?* 'face,' with derivational *ij*-suffix Earlier Eg. *har-ij > Coptic *hraj* 'upper part' (lit. 'related to the face').

Egyptian displays many features of the nominative-accusative case-marking: throughout the history of the language, the roles of AGENT and SUBJECT are not distinguished in verbal sentences; in Old, Middle, and Late Egyptian, the grammatical relations SUBJ and OBJ are not expressed by any overt marker (51a); in Demotic and Coptic, OBJ is introduced by the marker *ən*, originally a preposition meaning 'in' (51b) (Polotsky 1990: 187–191):

(51) (a) MIDDLE EGYPTIAN
   jrr θj
   CO.IMPF (man)SUBJ
   mrrt-f m çrt-ncr
   (love.REL.F-3M.SG)OBJ in Necropolis'
   'A man does what he wishes in the Necropolis'

(b) COPTIC
(ʔ)a-f-roːhət   ən-nef-kʲic
PRET-3M.SG-strike OBJ-his.PL-hand
(ʔ)eçən-ne-u̯-ʔəreːu̯
on-POSS-3PL-companion
'He struck his hands together.'

This overt marker is obligatory except when the object is not an independent prosodic unit, as in (51b), but either follows the VP as part of the same prosodic unit, as in (40) above, or is conveyed by a suffix pronoun. This construction is optional in all VPs (52a), but it is not licensed in the present and imperfect tenses, which derive from an adverb clause and in which the use of the OBJ-marker is mandatory (52b) (Polotsky 1990: 216–221):

(52) (a) COPTIC
mere-p-cʰojs
love.IMP-the-lord
'Love the Lord!'
(b) *nere-jeːsuːs meʔ   əm-martha*
IMPF-Jesus   love.INF OBJ-Martha
'Jesus loved Martha' (Lit. 'Jesus was on loving Martha').

In the unmarked word order in verbal sentences (EARLIER EG. VSO > COPTIC SVO), the hierarchy of arguments is always SUBJ < OBJ < OBL (cf. Croft 1990: 101–111). This order is modified when the NP-argument is conveyed by a clitic pronoun, which tends to move to the position immediately following V, regardless of the semantic roles (V – PRON – N):

(53) (a) MIDDLE EG.
jnn-tw   n-f
bring.IMPF-PASS to-(3M.SG)OBL
jmt-prw   nb
(being.in-house)SUBJ each
'All testaments are brought to him'
(b) COPTIC
əmpe-f-ʔiːnə
PRET.NEG-(3M.SG)SUBJ-bring
nəmma-f   əm-p-nuːh
with-(3M.SG)OBL OBJ-the-rope
'He did not bring with him the rope.'

In spite of the predominance of the nominative-accusative case-marking, however, one can also find traces of the ergative-absolutive type (Comrie 1981: 104–110) which may have affected Egyptian in prehistoric times (cf. the discussion by Zeidler 1992: 210–212). In the passive voice, the role of AGENT or of CAUSE is introduced by the preposition *jn*:

(54) MIDDLE EG.
ꜥhꜥ-n   jn-kw   r jw
'stand.PRET' bring-1SG.PERF to island
pn jn wrw nj   wrç-wr
this by wave that.of green-great
'Then (< 'stand.PRET') I was brought to this island by a wave of the sea.'

This is the same morpheme used to build stressed (*jnk* 'I') and interrogative pronouns (*jn-m* 'who?', cf. § 3.2.) as well as to indicate the subject of the cleft sentence, which is the focalizing construction we already encountered in § 4.1., which is restricted to the AGENT of a VP:

(55) *jn   hm-f   rçj*
FOC majesty-3M.SG give.PART
jr-tw-f
do.PROSP-PASS-3M.SG
'It was His Majesty who let it be done.'

It is possible, therefore, that this morpheme was originally an ergative case-marker for AGENT, later reinterpreted as particle ('FOC') or as preposition ('by') within a nominative-accusative coding:

(56) MIDDLE EG.
kmt-f   jn   hm-f
find.INF-3M.SG AGENT majesty-3M.SG
Ergative coding: 'His Majesty found him' >
Nominative coding: 'Finding him by His Majesty.'

That Egyptian occupies an intermediate position between an earlier 'ergative-absolutive' and a more recent "nominative-accusative" coding (Dixon 1994: 193–203) is also shown by the fact that while subjects of finite VPs behave according to the former pattern, with an identical coding for both AGENT (*sçm-f* 'he hears') and SUBJ (*pr-f* 'he comes'), the adjective clause displays ergative features: pronominal subjects are expressed by unstressed pronouns and thus coded exactly like direct objects of VP (*nfr sj* 'she is good' vs. *sçm-f sj* 'he hears her'). In general, the suffix pronoun following a VP always represents its highest argument, i. e. SUBJ – the only exception being the suffix of a transitive infinitive, which, as shown in (56), encodes OBJ in the "nominative" strategy of historical Egyptian, but probably represents the vestige of a prehistoric "absolutive."

Particularly noteworthy in this respect is the presence of a rare antipassive construction (Dixon 1994: 146–152) in which the focalized grammatical subject (and logical object) of a passive VP is demoted to a peripheral function and marked by the preposition *m* 'in, as' (Loprieno 1995: 198–199; cf. especially Reintges 1997: 211–240):

(57) jr ʃm   θj   3   ḥr wRt
      if go.AOR man three on road.F
      ḳmm-tw   m   θj 2
      find.IMPF-PASS in man two
      'If three people leave on a road, only two survive.'

These EARLIER EGYPTIAN remnants of the ergative coding disappear in LATER EGYPTIAN: the cleft sentence is now built without any overt marker such as the particle *jn*, the pragmatically stressed function of subject being now marked by the absence of the copula. Compare the unmarked nominal sentence in (58a) and the cleft sentence in (58b):

(58) (a) COPTIC
          wə-meʔ pe
          a-truth COP
          p-et-i-ço:ʔ   əmmo-f
          the.one.M-which-1SG-say.INF   OBJ-3M.SG
          'I say the truth' (lit. 'What I say is the truth')
      (b) wə-meʔ t-et-i-ço:ʔ
          a-truth the.one.F-which-1SG-say.INF
          əmmo-s
          OBJ-3F.SG
          'It is the truth that I say.'

The expression of the passive also undergoes a radical typological change. In EARLIER EGYPTIAN (cf. Reintges 1997: 141–185), the PATIENT is encoded as SUBJ of a VP grammatically marked as passive, whereas the AGENT is introduced by the 'ergative' *jn* (59a). In LATER EGYPTIAN, on the contary, while the grammatical subject of the sentence is a generic 3PL, the role of PATIENT is – depending on the verb – encoded as direct object or as prepositional argument, whereas that of AGENT is introduced by a preposition meaning literally 'by the hand of' > 'by' (59b):

(59) (a) MIDDLE EG.
          çt-tw   rʔ   pn   jn   θj
          say.PROSP-PASS spell this FOC man
          'This spell should be recited by a man'
      (b) COPTIC
          əmpər-tre-u-çroʔ
          IMP.NEG-CAUS-3PL-become.strong
          (ʔ)əro-k hiṭəm-p-pet-hou̯
          to-2M.SG by-the.that.which-evil
          'Do not be overcome by evil'
          (Lit. 'do not cause that they become stronger than you by the hand of evil').

Adjective sentences of the EARLIER EGYPTIAN type, which survive down to LATE EGYPTIAN (60a), disappear in DEMOTIC and COPTIC, having turned into finite VPs resulting from their fusion with the aorist form of the verb *wnn* "to be" (60b):

(60) (a) EARLIER-LATE EG. > (b) Coptic
          nfr   sw nanu:-f
          be.good.PART   it be.good.AOR-3M.SG
          'it is good.'

5.2. Genitive and adjective constructions

Throughout Egyptian language history, genitival and adjectival modifiers follow the noun they refer to: N-GEN, N-ADJ. With pronominal possessors (61a), the genitive is conveyed in EARLIER EGYPTIAN by affixation of a suffix on the head noun. With nominal possessors, the genitival relation can be expressed in a twofold way: by direct juxtaposition of the modifier to the head noun (61b) or by insertion of a determinative pronoun agreeing in gender and number with the head noun (61c):

(61) (a) EARLIER EG.
          *san-uf
          brother-3M.SG
          'His brother'
      (b) pr-dnx
          house-life
          'Library' (lit. 'house of life')
      (c) θRt   nt   rmc pn
          daughter.F that.of.F   man this
          'This man's daughter.'

In LATER EGYPTIAN, as we observed in § 3.5., the indication of pronominal possessors is attached to the definite article. With nominal possessors, the indirect genitive construction becomes the only productive strategy; the determinative pronoun loses the agreement markers and acquires the function of an invariable linker (Croft 1990: 32):

(62) COPTIC
      t-ʃeʔrə   ən-pei-ro:mə
      the.F-daughter that.of-this-man
      'This man's daughter.'

We need to stress that only specific (i.e. definite or referentially unambiguous) head nouns can be modified by this type of genitive construction. Non-specific nouns, or nouns whose specificity is not determined by the genitival relation (for example, when preceded by a possessive morpheme), are modified by a prepositional phrase originally meaning 'in the hand of' (Erman 1933: 311–313):

(63)   COPTIC
       wə-faḭ-ʃiːnə
       a-carrier-message
       ənte-p-muːʔ
       'IN-THE-HAND-OF'-the-death
       'A messenger of death.'

The use of the construct genitive, on the other hand, tends to be gradually limited and to give rise to lexicalized compounds in which the distinct morphology of the two original components is no longer distinguishable (see also § 3.5.). In the oldest of these compounds, which had probably developed into lexicalized compounds already in EARLIER EGYPTIAN (Fecht 1960: 5–114), the prosodic stress affected the head noun (64a); in the more recent compounds, which were lexicalized in Later Egyptian, the stress fell on the modifier (64b):

(64)   (a) EARLIER EG. *ḥam-nacar 'servant of the god' > COPTIC hont 'pagan priest'
       (b) EARLIER EG. *harwu-miːsit 'day of birth' > COPTIC haṵmiːsə 'birthday.'

In COPTIC, these latter compounds belong to a structural paradigm also consisting of other types of lexicalizations, deriving for example from an indirect genitive (65a), a participle followed by its object (65b), or an adjective construction (65c):

(65)   (a) EARLIER EG. rmc (nj) kmt > COPTIC rəmənkʰeːmə 'Egyptian' (lit. 'man-of-Egypt')
       (b) EARLIER EG. cθj ḥRtj > COPTIC cʰasiheːt 'arrogant' (lit. 'lifter-of-heart')
       (c) LATE ERG. ʃrj ʕḥʔwtj > COPTIC ʃərhoṵt 'male child' (lit. 'son-male').

The typological similarities between genitive and adjective constructions are also displayed by two evolutions affecting the adjective in COPTIC. First of all, the adjective is introduced in this phase of the language by the same morpheme (ən-) which we already encountered as genitival linker, thus leading to a formal identity between genitive and adjective patterns (66a); however, unlike in genitive constructions, the morpheme ən- introducing the adjective is insensitive to the specificity of the head noun (66b), which means that the connection N-ADJ was stronger than N-GEN:

(66)   (a) COPTIC
            t-ʃeʔrə   ən-sabeː
            the.F-daughter that.who-wise.F
            'The wise daughter'
       (b) wə-ʃeʔrə   ən-sabeː
            a-daughter that.who-wise.F
            'A wise daughter.'

The second typological change affects the word order: the sequence N-ADJ appears sometimes reversed to ADJ-N, without any apparent rule governing the choice of this alternate sequence (67). This evolution is the effect of a universal tendency for the N-ADJ order to be less stable than other word orders, such as SUBJ-VERB, N-ADPOSITION, and N-GEN (Croft 1990: 210):

(67)   pi-ʔatmuːʔ   ən-roːmə
       the-immortal that.who-man
       'The immortal man.'

5.3. Relativization

The Egyptian domain displays the expected hierarchy of accessibility to relativization (Keenan & Comrie 1977):

SUBJECT < DIRECT OBJECT < INDIRECT OBJECT < OBLIQUE

Thus, the subject is never resumed by a pronoun in relative clauses, indirect objects and obliques always are, whereas direct objects are resumed by a pronoun when they are not local to the agreement carrier, i. e., the verbal form (Collier 1991). Compare (68a), where the object is resumed, with (68b), where it is not:

(68)   (a) MIDDLE EG.
            kRt-n-f   jrt-s
            devise.REL.F-PRET-3M.SG do.INF-3F.SG
            r-j   jr-n-j   st   r-f
            to-1SG do.PRET.1SG 3F.SG to-3M.SG
            'What he had planned to do to me, I did to him'
       (b) sqtw   jm-s   rx-n-k
            sailor.PL in-3F.SG kNOW-PRET-2M.SG
            'There are in it sailors whom you know.'

Example (68b) leads us to the discussion of the most important feature of Egyptian relative clauses, i. e., the different treatment of relative clauses modifying specific vs. non-specific antecedents, similar to the different treatment of specific vs. non-specific head nouns in genitive constructions (cf. § 5.2.). Definite antecedents (Loprieno 1995: 202–208) are resumed by an overt marker of relativization, such as the relative pronoun in adverb clauses (69a) or the agreement-marker in the relative VP: participle in presence of coreferentiality of antecedent and subject of the relative clause (69b), finite relative form in its absence (69c):

(69) (a) MIDDLE EG.
    mtr-n   wj   rmcw   kmt
    witness-PRET 1sg.OBJ man.PL Egypt
    ntjw   jm   ḥnʕ-f
    who.PL there with-3M.SG
    'Egyptians who where there with him bore witness for me'
(b) *cj-s   xt   nbt*
    give.PROSP-3F.SG thing.F every.F
    nfrt   wʕbt
    be.good.PART.F be.pure.PART.F
    prrt   ḥr   wcḥ-s
    exit.PART.F on altar-3F.SG
    'May she give every good and pure things which go up on her altar'
(c) *xRst   nbt*
    country.F every.F
    rwjt-n-j   r-s
    advance.REL.F-PRET-1SG against-3F.SG
    'Every country against which I advanced.'

Morphologically, finite relative forms of EARLIER EGYPTIAN probably originate from the insertion of a participial stem into the corresponding finite pattern, as displayed by their possibility to convey voice oppositions. Compare the active participle and the active relative form (derived from an active participle) in (70a) with the passive relative form (derived from a passive participle) in (70b):

(70) (a) OLD EG.
    mj   n-k   jrt-hrw
    take.IMP to-2M.SG eye.F-HORUS
    hpt   m-d   stʃ [...]
    escape.PART.PFV.F from Seth
    wppt-k   rʔ-k
    open.IMPF.REL.F-2M.SG mouth-2M.SG
    jm-s
    from-3F.SG
    'Take to yourself the Eye of Horus which escaped from Seth [...] and with which you open your mouth'
(b) MIDDLE EG.
    jtj-c   pw   msy-c
    father-2F.SG COP bear.PFV.REL-2F.SG
    n-f
    to-3M.SG
    'He is your father to whom you (fem.) were born.'

In LATER EGYPTIAN, as we observed in § 3.5., the use of the relative pronoun is generalized, both participles and relative VPs being superseded by analytic constructions with the relative pronoun (Polotsky 1987: 45−127):

(71) (a) COPTIC
    pa-ʔəsou
    POSS.1SG-sheep
    ənt-a-f-soːrəm
    which-PRET-3M.SG-go.astray
    'My sheep which had gone astray'
(b) *tei̯-rompə et-əs-na-muːʔ*
    this.F-year which-3F.SG-FUT-die
    ənheːt-əs
    in-3F.SG
    'This year in which she will die.'

Non-specific antecedents, on the other hand, are modified by relative clauses which lack overt agreement-markers (Loprieno 1995: 158−161): in EARLIER EGYPTIAN, as we saw in (68b), they are unmarked VPs embedded into the main clause, whereas in LATER EGYPTIAN they are introduced by a circumstantial marker:

(72) (a) *wə-hoːb e-f-hou̯*
    a-matter 'WHILE'-3M.SG-be.evil.STAT
    'An evil matter'
(b) *wə-hat e-ʔa-u̯-təbbo-f*
    a-silver 'WHILE'-PRET-3PL-purify-3M.SG
    'Pure silver' (lit. 'silver which has been made pure').

Egyptian and COPTIC syntax, therefore, shows clear parallels between genitive and relative constructions: while specific head nouns are modified by overt markers such as determinative pronouns or agreement-markers, non-specific antecedents can only be modified by prepositional phrases (for the genitive construction) or adverb clauses (for the relative clause).

5.4. Animacy hierarchy and grammaticalization

In this section, we will consider some examples of how the cross-linguistic person and animacy hierarchy (Croft 1990: 111−117):

1,2 PERS(PRON) < 3 PERS PRON < 3 PERSON ANIMATE < 3 PERSON INANIMATE

affected the evolution of the Egyptian grammatical patterns. A first interesting feature is the hierarchical treatment of the subject in classifying ('I am a man') or qualifying ('I am good') noun clauses, and in identifying (cleft) sentences, a construction in which the predicate is a participle and which, therefore, combines verbal and adjectival features ('I am the one who destroyed it'). In the first, and to a certain extent also in the second person, the opposition between unmarked and focalized subject is morphologically neutralized in these patterns, the stressed pronoun and the word order SUBJ-PRED being found with both functions:

(73) (a) MIDDLE EG.
ntk   jtj   n   nmḥw
2M.SG.TOP/FOC father to   orphan
'You are a father to the orphan'
(b) jnk   jrj
    1SG.TOP/FOC   make.PART.AOR
    xprw   m   Rx
    transformation in   spirit
    'I am someone who turned into a spirit.'

In the third person, on the other hand, the pragmatic opposition is conveyed by a different syntactic pattern: the unmarked third person subject is expressed by the unstressed pronouns and follows the word order PRED-SUBJ (74a), whereas the focalized subject is carried by the stressed pronoun or by a noun introduced by the focal marker jn (74b) (Loprieno 1988b: 77—98):

(74) (a) MIDDLE EG.
ḥʕj   sj   jm-f   r
rejoice.PART.AOR 3F.SG in-3M.SG to
ncr-sn
god-3PL
'She is happier with him more than with their god'
(b) nts   jct   cRw-f
    3F.SG.FOC   take.PART.AOR.F breath-3M.SG
    'She is the one who took his breath.'

The use of some finite verbal forms is restricted to the highest persons in the animacy hierarchy (cf. Croft 1990: 127—143): while all persons of the Stative can indicate a wide semantic range of "perfective" features, ranging from perfect aspect (in intransitive verbs) to passive voice (in transitive verbs), three of the more marked uses of this verbal form are hierarchically restricted: the "narrative" use to the first person (75a), the "exhortative" use to the second person (75b), and the "eulogical" use to the third person animate (75c):

(75) (a) OLD EG.
wṭ-kj   rn-j   r   bw
set.PFV-1SG   name-1SG to place
çrj   ncr
under.ADJ   god
'I set my name at the place where the god was'
(b) wçR-tj
    be.healthy.PFV-2SG
    'May you be healthy'
(c) nθw dnx-w   çt
    king live.PFV-3M.SG eternity.F
    'The King — may he live forever.'

This behavior is undoubtedly motivated by the tendency for the first and second person to be more "agentive" than the third and to select, therefore, the more foregrounding features within the semantic spectrum of the form, confining the third person to the expression of backgrounding features (Croft 1990: 160—164). Symmetrically, when the Stative ceases to be a productive verbal construction, it is the third, i. e. the least marked person, which survives in COPTIC as the "Qualitative," i.e. as the non-agentive counterpart to the Infinitive:

(76)
OLD EG. *danx-aw   >   COPTIC (ʔ)onx
        live.PFV-3M.SG   live.STAT
        'He is alive'   'to be alive'

The tendency of the higher persons on the animacy hierarchy to be more frequent than the third in agentive patterns is also evident in the COPTIC grammaticalization of the second person imperative and of the first person prospective of the verb 'to cause' (< 'to give') in two polysynthetic patterns ("sentence conjugations"), namely the "optative" (77a) and the "final" (77b) respectively:

(77) (a) COPTIC
ma-re-n-çoʔ-s
cause.IMP-do.PROSP-1PL-say-3F.SG
na-f
to-3M.SG
'Let us mention it to him'
(b) ʃiːnə
    seek.IMP
    ta-re-tən-kʲiːnə
    cause.PROSP.1SG-do.PROSP-2PL-find
    'Seek, and you shall find.'

The tendency for animate arguments to acquire the role of subject of the predication is also evident in the process of formation of a verb 'to have'. EARLIER EGYPTIAN does not express possession through a VP meaning 'to have', but rather by means of a PP with the preposition n 'to' and aspectual or modal features conveyed, when applicable, by a form of the verb wnn 'to be':

(78) (a) OLD EG.
jw   n-k   dnx
'SITUATION' to-2M.SG life
'You have life'
(b) MIDDLE EG.
jst   wn   ḥjmt-f
'MEANWHILE' be.AOR wife-3M.SG
'And he had a wife.'

A first typological change occurs in LATE EGYPTIAN with its preference for the prepositional pattern with *m-tj*, originally meaning 'in the hand of' > 'by'. This is the same preposition used for the genitive of a non-specific or deictically marked head noun (cf. § 5.2.):

(79) LATE EG.
wn   ḥmtj   jm   m-tj-k
be.AOR copper there by-2M.SG
'You have copper.'

In the more recent phases of LATER EGYPTIAN, the prepositional argument exhibits the tendency to be raised to the role of (animate) subject of the compound consisting of the V *wn-* and the PP 'by-N', reinterpreted as a VP 'N has'. Accordingly, what used to be the inanimate subject of an adverb clause is reanalyzed as overt object of a verb clause, the frequent use of a localizer ('there') being a remnant of the adverbial origin of the construction (Polotsky 1987: 72−78):

(80) COPTIC
wanṭa-f   əmmau   ən-wə-shiːmə
have-3M.SG there   OBJ-a-woman
'He has a wife.'

Finally, important evidence on the role of animacy in the formation of verbal paradigms is also provided by the study of causatives. In prehistoric Egyptian, as in other languages of the AFROASIATIC family, the addition of a prefix *s-* to a root was the most common device to form causative stems (Diakonoff 1965: 98):

(81) PROTO-EG. *dnx* 'to live' > *s-dnx* 'to make live'

We saw, however, that Egyptian stems resulting from the addition of a consonantal phoneme to a root were very soon lexicalized as new autonomous roots, ceasing to be treated as grammatical forms of the basic root (§ 3.5.). When these verbs survive down to COPTIC, the semantic connection with the original root has drifted considerably:

(82) OLD EG. *sdnx* 'to make live' > LATE EG. *sʕnx* > COPTIC *saʔnəʃ* 'to nourish'

In historical Egyptian, the productive device for the formation of causatives is to have the verb *rcj* 'to give, cause' control the prospective form of the main verb:

(83) OLD EG.   > MIDDLE EG.
sdnx-N   rct
make.live.INF-OBJ   cause.INF
ʕnx-N
live.PROSP-SUBJ
'To cause that N live'

We saw in § 3.5. that with the analytic reorganization of the verbal system in LATER EGYPTIAN, the only productive forms for most verbal roots remained the infinitive and the qualitative. In the case of causative constructions, the surviving form was a lexicalized compound consisting of the infinitive of the verb 'to cause' followed by what used to be the stem of the prospective form:

(84) LATE EG.   > COPTIC
*ṭi-ʕanxa-N   ṭanxoʔ
cause.INF-live.PROSP-N   make.live.INF
'To cause (N) to live'

The noun or pronoun following this new infinitive, therefore, historically the subject of the finite prospective form, is now functionally the object of the VP:

(85) COPTIC
(ʔ)a-f-taloʔ   ən-wə-thysia
PRET-3M.SG-offer   OBJ-a-sacrifice
'He offered a sacrifice' (< *'He caused a sacrifice to go up').

In some instances, an original 3PL subject, which the most unmarked person on the animacy hierarchy (Polotsky 1990: 181−184), is grammaticalized as part of the new infinitive compound and can of course itself be followed by a "new" suffix pronoun as object of the VP:

(86) COPTIC
əntof
3M.SG.FOC
p-ent-a-f-ṭənnou-t
the.one-who-PRET-3M.SG-'cause.bring.3PL'-1SG
'He is the one who sent me' (< *'who caused that they bring me').

These old causative infinitives, however, are in COPTIC themselves lexicalized remnants (Till 1970: 138−141). The productive causative construction is now a "clause conjugation" whose marker derives from the grammaticalization of the same infinitive of the verb 'to cause' followed by the conjugated prospective of the verb 'to make' and the infinitive of the basic verb (Polotsky 1987: 145−152):

(87) COPTIC
  (ʔ)a-i̯-tre-u̯-ʔiː?   (ʔ)əhuːn
  PRET-1SG-CAUS-3PL-come inside
  'I let them enter.'

5.5. Conclusion

Thus, besides a number of phonological evolutions (cf. §§ 2.1.−2.4.), the diachronic development of Egyptian displays a tendency to what has been named a "linguistic cycle" (Hodge 1970: 1−7), i. e. a first shift from the original synthetic structures of EARLIER EGYPTIAN to analytic solutions in LATER EGYPTIAN: suffixal markers of morphological oppositions are dropped and functionally replaced by prefixal indicators; the demonstrative "this" and the numeral "one" evolve into the definite and the indefinite article; older verbal formations with a VSO word order are superseded by SVO periphrastic patterns in which a conjugated form of the auxiliary verb 'to do' precedes the main verb (§§ 5.1.−5.3.). This first shift, however, is followed in COPTIC by a second major typological change in which originally analytic patterns are reanalyzed as polysynthetic structures (sentence and clause conjugations) marked by heavy prefixing and the concentration of many morphological markers into the same prosodic unit (§ 5.4.).

6. Special abbreviations

COP	copula
F	feminine
O(BJ)	object
OPT	optative
PART	participle
prosp	prospective
SPEC	specific
STAT	stative
S(UBJ)	subject

7. References

Collier, Mark. 1991. "The relative clause and the verb in Middle Egyptian". *Journal of Egyptian Archaeology* 77: 23−42.

Comrie, Bernard. 1981. *Language Universals and Linguistic Typology*. Chicago: Chicago University Press.

Croft, William. 1990. *Typology and Unviersals*. (Cambridge Textbooks in Linguistics.) Cambridge: Cambridge University Press.

Diakonoff, I. M. 1965. *Semito-Hamitic Languages. An essay in Classification*. (Languages of Asia and Africa.) Moscow: Akademia Nauk.

Dixon, R. M. W. 1994. *Ergativity*. (Cambridge Studies in Linguistics, 69.) Cambridge: Cambridge University Press.

Edel, Elmar. 1955−64. *Altägyptische Grammatik*. (Analecta Orientalia, 34−39.) Roma: Pontificium Institutum Biblicum.

Erman, Adolf. 1933. *Neuägyptische Grammatik*. Zweite Auflage. Leipzig: Wilhelm Engelmann.

Fecht, Gerhard. 1960. *Wortakzent und Silbenstruktur. Untersuchungen zur Geschichte der ägyptischen Sprache*. (Ägyptologische Forschungen, 21.) Glückstadt: J. J. Augustin.

Gardiner, Alan H. 1957. *Egyptian Grammar: Being an Introduction to the Study of Hieroglyphs*. Third edition. Oxford: Oxford University Press.

Haiman, John. 1985. *Natural Syntax*. (Cambridge Studies in Linguistics, 44.) Cambridge: Cambridge University Press.

Hintze, Fritz. 1950. "Konversion and analytische Tendenz in der ägyptischen Sprachentwicklung". *Zeitschrift für Phonetik und Allgemeine Sprachwissenschaft* 4: 41−56.

Hodge, Carleton T. 1970. "The linguistic cycle". *Language Sciences* 13: 1−7.

Johnson, Janet H. 1991. *Thus Wrote 'Onchsheshonqy. An Introductory Grammar of Demotic*. (Studies in Ancient Oriental Civilization, 45.) Second edition. Chicago: The Oriental Institute.

Junge, Friedrich. 1985. "Sprachstufen und Sprachgeschichte". In: *Zeitschrift der Deutschen Morgenländischen Gesellschaft. Supplement VI*. Stuttgart, 17−34.

Junge, Friedrich. 1996. *Einführung in die Grammatik des Neuägyptischen*. Wiesbaden: Otto Harrassowitz.

Kammerzell, Frank. 1991a. "Personalpronomina und Personalendungen im Altägyptischen". In: Mendel, Daniela & Claudi, Ulrike (eds.). *Ägypten im afro-orientalischen Kontext. Gedenkschrift Peter Behrens*. (Afrikanistische Arbeitspapiere. Special Issue.) Köln: Universität Köln, 177−203.

Kammerzell, Frank. 1991b. "Augment, Stamm und Endung. Zur morphologischen Entwicklung der Stativkonjugation". *Lingua Aegyptia* 1: 165−199.

Kammerzell, Frank. 1995. "Zur Umschreibung und Lautung". In: Hannig, Rainer. *Großes Handwörterbuch Ägyptisch-Deutsch (2800−950 v. Chr.)*. Mainz: Philipp von Zabern, XXIII−LIX.

Kasser, Rodolphe. 1991a. "Vocabulary, Copto-Greek". In: *The Coptic Encyclopedia*. Vol. 8. New York, 215−222.

Kasser, Rodolphe. 1991b. "Dialects; Dialects, Grouping and Major Groups of". In: *The Coptic Encyclopedia*. Vol. 8. New York, 87−88; 97−101.

Keenan, Edward & Comrie, Bernard. 1977. "Noun phrase accessibility and universal grammar". *Linguistic Inquiry* 8: 63–99.

Lambdin, Thomas O. 1983. *Introduction to Sahidic Coptic*. Macon: Mercer University Press.

Loprieno, Antonio. 1988a. "On the typological order of constituents in Egyptian". *Journal of Afroasiatic Languages* 1: 26–57.

Loprieno, Antonio. 1988b. "Der ägyptische Satz zwischen Semantik und Pragmatik: die Rolle von *jn*". In: *Studien zur Altägyptischen Kultur. Beiheft III.* Hamburg: Buske, Helmut, 77–98.

Loprieno, Antonio. 1991. "Topics in Egyptian Negations". In: Mendel, Daniela & Claudi, Ulrike (eds.), *Ägypten im afro-orientalischen Kontext. Gedenkschrift Peter Behrens.* (Afrikanistische Arbeitspapiere. Special Issue.) Köln: Universität Köln, 213–235.

Loprieno, Antonio. 1995. *Ancient Egyptian: a Linguistic Introduction.* Cambridge: Cambridge University Press.

Osing, Jürgen. 1975. "Dialekte". In: *Lexikon der Ägyptologie.* Band I. Wiesbaden: Otto Harrassowitz Verlag, 1074–75.

Osing, Jürgen. 1976. *Die Nominalbildung des Ägyptischen.* Mainz: Philipp von Zabern.

Osing, Jürgen. 1980. "Lautsystem". In: *Lexikon der Ägyptologie.* Band III. Wiesbaden: Otto Harrassowitz Verlag, 944–49.

Polotsky, Hans Jacob. 1960. "The Coptic Conjugation System". *Orientalia* 29: 392–422.

Polotsky, Hans Jacob. 1976. "Les transpositions du verbe en égyptien classique". *Israel Oriental Studies* 6: 1–50.

Polotsky, Hans Jacob. 1987–90. *Grundlagen des koptischen Satzbaus.* (American Studies in Papyrology, 27–29.) Atlanta: Scholars' Press.

Reintges, Chris. 1994. "Egyptian Root-and-Pattern Morphology". *Lingua Aegyptia* 4: 213–244.

Reintges, Chris. 1997. *Passive Voice in Older Egyptian. A Morpho-Syntactic Study.* (Holland Institute of Generative Linguistics. Dissertations, 28.) The Hague: Holland Institute of Generative Linguistics.

Schenkel, Wolfgang. 1983. "Zur Pluralbildung des Ägyptischen". In: Schenkel, Wolfgang. *Aus der Arbeit an einer Konkordanz zu den altägyptischen Sargtexten.* (Göttinger Orientforschungen, IV/12.) Wiesbaden: Otto Harrassowitz Verlag, 171–230.

Schenkel, Wolfgang. 1990. *Einführung in die altägyptische Sprachwissenschaft.* Darmstadt: Wissenschaftliche Buchgesellschaft.

Schenkel, Wolfgang. 1993. "Zu den Verschluß- und Reibelauten im Ägyptischen und (Hamito-)Semitischen. Ein Versuch zur Synthese der Lehrmeinungen". *Lingua Aegyptia* 3: 137–149.

Spiegelberg, Wilhelm. 1925. *Demotische Grammatik.* Heidelberg: Carl Winters Universitätsbuchhandlung.

Till, Walter C. 1970. *Koptische Grammatik.* (Lehrbücher für das Studium der orientalischen und afrikanischen Sprachen, 1.) Zweite Auflage. Leipzig: Verlag Enzyklopädie.

Vernus, Pascal. 1996. "Langue littéraire et diglossie". In: Loprieno, Antonio (ed.). *Ancient Egyptian Literature. History & Forms.* (Probleme der Ägyptologie, 10.) Leiden: E. J. Brill, 555–64.

Vittmann, Günther, 1991. "Zum koptischen Sprachgut im Ägyptisch-Arabischen". *Wiener Zeitschrift für die Kunde des Morgenlandes* 81: 197–227.

Winand, Jean. 1992. *Études de néo-égyptien, 1. La morphologie verbale.* (Aegyptiaca Leodiensia, 2.) Liège: CIPL.

Zeidler, Jürgen. 1992. "Altätyptisch und Hamitosemitisch. Bemerkungen zu den *Vergleichenden Studien* von Karel Petráček". *Lingua Aegyptia* 2: 189–222.

Antonio Loprieno, University of Basel, (Switzerland)

124. Vom Altäthiopischen zu den neuäthiopischen Sprachen

1. Hintergrund: Verbreitung und Klassifikation der äthiosemitischen Sprachen
2. Abstammung und sprachliche Kontinuität
3. Wortstellung
4. Adpositionen
5. Determination
6. Kasusmarkierung
7. Relativsatz/Relativkomplex
8. Koordination
9. Verbalsystem
10. Zusammengesetzte Verben
11. Phonologischer Typ
12. Typologischer Wandel und Sprachkontakt
13. Spezielle Abkürzungen
14. Zitierte Literatur

1. Hintergrund: Verbreitung und Klassifikation der äthiosemitischen Sprachen

Das Äthiosemitische ist eine Untergruppe der südsemitischen Sprachen, die im Gebiet der Staaten Äthiopien und Eritrea gesprochen wurde bzw. wird. Die äthiosemitischen Sprachen lassen sich in einen nordäthiopischen und einen südäthiopischen Zweig untergliedern (vgl. allgemein die Skizzen in Hetzron 1997: 242−260 und 424−549).

Nordäthiopisch:
Gəʿəz: Extinkte Schriftsprache, die seit dem 4. Jh. in Inschriften belegt ist, sowie in einer großen christlich geprägten Übersetzungsliteratur und einer umfangreichen nachklassischen Originalliteratur (hauptsächlich seit dem 13. Jh.). Das Aussterben des Gəʿəz als Umgangssprache steht sicherlich im Zusammenhang mit dem Niedergang des Reiches von Aksum. Genaueres lässt sich hier in Ermangelung einschlägiger Quellen nicht sagen. Spätestens seit dem 10. Jh. ist Gəʿəz auf den Gebrauch als Kirchen- und Schriftsprache reduziert. Gəʿəz ist damit immer nur Zweitsprache. Im ehemaligen Sprachgebiet des Gəʿəz spricht man jetzt TIGRINYA. Als Schriftsprache blieb Gəʿəz bis weit ins 19. Jh. vorherrschend, als Kirchensprache wird es bis in die Gegenwart gepflegt.
TIGRE: Nördlichste äthiosemitische Sprache, gesprochen in Eritrea; etwa 800.000 mehrheitlich muslimische Sprecher; nicht verschriftet.
TIGRINYA: Gesprochen in Eritrea und der Region Tigray (Äthiopien), hauptsächlich von der christlichen sesshaften Bevölkerung; vereinzelte Texte seit dem 19. Jh., in größerem Umfang seit 1942 als Schriftsprache verwendet; ca. 4 Mio. Sprecher; heute zusammen mit dem ARABISCHEN offizielle Sprache Eritreas.

Südäthiopisch:
AMHARISCH: Beheimatet im zentralen äthiopischen Hochland, seit dem Mittelalter Sprache der staatstragenden christlichen Bevölkerungsschicht Äthiopiens; Staatssprache seit der Mitte des 19. Jh. bis zum Ende des Mengistu-Regimes (1991); vereinzelte Texte seit dem 13. Jh. (vgl. Fellman 1979), in größerem Umfang als Schriftsprache erst seit dem 19. Jh. verwendet; 15 Mio. Sprecher (1988), darüber hinaus weite Verbreitung als lingua franca.
ARGOBBA: In der Nähe von Ankober gesprochen, früher auch noch in der Nähe von Harar (Leslau 1997a); dem AMHARISCHEN sehr nahe stehend.
GURAGE: Bündel von zwölf nicht verschrifteten Dialekten mit ca. 1,8 Mio. Sprechern in einem geschlossenen Gebiet südwestlich von Addis Abeba.
GAFAT: Früher in der Provinz Goǧǧam gesprochen, jetzt ausgestorben.
HARARI: Beheimatet in der Stadt Harar, ausschließlich von Muslimen gesprochen; ältere Texte in arabischer Schrift, etwa seit dem 18. Jh. (Wagner 1983); heute 8000 Sprecher in Harar, ein Mehrfaches davon in Diasporagemeinden.
Während die grundlegende Unterscheidung Nord- vs. Südäthiopisch unbezweifelt ist, wurde die Subklassifikation der südäthiopischen Sprachen kontrovers diskutiert (Leslau 1965, Leslau 1969, Leslau 1970, Hetzron 1972, Hetzron 1975, Goldenberg 1977, Fellman 1980). Einigkeit besteht darüber, dass das GURAGE-Bündel in sich keine genealogische Einheit darstellt. Hetzron (1972 und 1997: 6) unterscheidet die beiden Gruppen „Transverse South Ethiopic" (AMHARISCH, ARGOBBA, HARARI und die Ost-GURAGE-Dialekte) und „Outer South Ethiopic" (GAFAT, NORD-GURAGE, WEST-GURAGE).
Darüber hinaus teilen die äthiosemitischen Sprachen, insbesondere deren moderne Vertreter, eine ganze Reihe von Merkmalen mit KUSCHITISCHEN und OMOTISCHEN Sprachen des äthiopischen Konvergenzareals (Ferguson 1976; Raz 1989; vgl. § 13.).

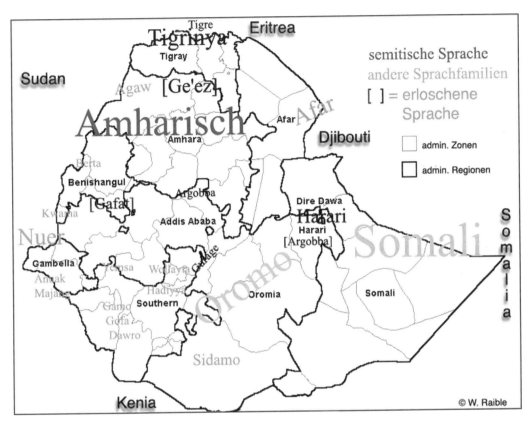

Karte 124.1 *Übersicht über die wichtigsten in Äthiopien gesprochenen Sprachen* (auf der Basis von Grimes, Barbara F. 2000. Languages of the World. Internet Version 14th edition).

2. Abstammung und sprachliche Kontinuität

Der vorliegende Beitrag soll zur Exemplifizierung diachronischer Aspekte von Sprachtypologie prominente typologische Entwicklungen vom Altäthiopischen zu den modernen äthiosemitischen Sprachen darstellen. Vor einer Untersuchung von Sprachwandel im typologischen Habitus der betroffenen Sprachen ist aber zunächst nach den tatsächlichen Abstammungsverhältnissen zu fragen, m. a. W. danach, ob die modernen äthiosemitischen Sprachen Tochtersprachen des altäthiopischen Gəʿəz sind. Zwar muss man mit Hetzron (1972: 19−21) davon ausgehen, dass keine der modernen äthiosemitischen Sprachen direkt vom Gəʿəz abstammt, sondern dass es sich quasi um jüngere Schwestersprachen handelt. Dennoch darf man annehmen, dass sie von Sprachen abstammen, die zumindest typologisch dem Gəʿəz sehr ähnlich waren. „Als Vertreter eines älteren Sprachstands für die semitischen Sprachen Äthiopiens muss, unbeschadet der noch immer keineswegs vollständigen Aufhellung seiner genauen Verwandtschaftsverhältnisse zu den heutigen notgedrungen das GEʿEZ beigezogen werden." (Correll 1983: 326; ähnlich schon Little 1974: 268 und Correll 1980: 47).

Um die Darstellung auf der Seite der modernen äthiosemitischen Sprachen nicht zu sehr ausdehnen zu müssen, werden im Folgenden hauptsächlich Beispiele aus dem TIGRINYA und dem AMHARISCHEN zitiert. Dies ist einerseits dadurch gerechtfertigt, dass sich die neuäthiopischen Sprachen einander typologisch ohnehin vielfach ähneln, andererseits dadurch, dass mit dem TIGRINYA als der Sprache, die zumindest geographisch als relativ direktester Nachfahre des Gəʿəz gelten muss, und dem AMHARISCHEN, als der Sprache, die als „diejenige semitische Sprache" gilt, „die am wenigsten vom altsemitischen Charakter besitzt" (Bergsträßer 1928: 112), und die daher als die innovativste anzusehen ist, die für unsere Zwecke wichtigsten Vertreter erfasst sind. Aus dem Zweck des vorliegenden Beitrages folgt auch, dass diejenigen typologischen Merkmale, die das Gəʿəz mit den modernen äthiosemitischen Sprachen teilt, im Folgenden nicht zur Sprache kommen werden, z. B. Wurzelstruktur, Introflexion, Präfixkonjugation, Gerundien/Konverben, Reflexiv-Passiv in Form abgeleiteter (T-)Stämme, Labiovelare, Vokalsystem usw.

3. Wortstellung

3.1. Grundwortstellung

Der wohl prominenteste Unterschied zwischen dem Gəʿəz und den modernen äthiosemitischen Sprachen besteht in der Grundwortstellung. Das Gəʿəz hatte eine liberale VSO-Grundwortstellung. Der geringere Grad an Verbindlichkeit zeigt sich daran, dass die Übersetzungsliteratur der aksumitischen Periode (4. Jh. bis etwa Ende 7. Jh.) im allgemeinen die Wortstellung der griechischen Übersetzungsvorlagen, soweit es die bedeutungstragenden Elemente betrifft, nachahmen kann. Doch hat dieser Umstand andererseits auch zur Folge, dass die Übersetzungstexte als Beleg für die Grundwortstellung praktisch unbrauchbar sind. Die Sprache der Inschriften zeigt, dass das Verb dem Subjekt und dem Objekt voransteht:

(1) Gəʿəz (RIÉ 187, 5)
 bahəya rakaba-na ʾabaʾalkəʿo
 dort traf-uns [Name]
 nəguśa ʾagwezāt
 König.CST [Name.PL]
 'Dort traf uns Abaʾalkəʿo, der König der Agwezāt.'

(2) Gəʿəz (RIÉ 188, 14)
 wa-qatalna saʿne wa-ṣawante
 und-wir.töteten [Name] und-[Name]
 'Und wir töteten (bzw. besiegten) [die Stämme] Saʿne und Ṣawante.'

Wenn es auch wegen des Stils der Inschriften nicht ganz leicht ist, einen unmarkierten Aussagehauptsatz mit explizitem, nicht pronominalisiertem Subjekt und Objekt zu finden, deuten zahlreiche Sätze wie die beiden voranstehenden doch auf die klassische westsemitische VSO-Wortstellung hin.

Im Gegensatz dazu haben die modernen äthiosemitischen Sprachen durchwegs SOV-Grundwortstellung, vgl. z. B. die folgenden Beispiele:

(3) TIGRINYA (Mk. 14, 63)
 šəʿu ʾəti liqä kahənat kədan-u
 dann ART alt.CST Priester.PL Kleid-sein
 ədidu
 reißen.CONV
 'Darauf zerriss der Hohepriester sein Kleid.'

(4) AMHARISCH (Gen. 1, 1)
 bä-mäǧämmäräya əgziʾabəḥer
 in-zuerst Gott
 sämay-ən-ənnā mədr-ən fäṭṭärä
 Himmel-DO-und Erde-DO schuf
 'Am Anfang schuf Gott Himmel und Erde.'

Der Versuch, das Amharische auf der Ebene der Tiefenstruktur als VSO-Sprache zu klassifizieren (Bach 1970), wurde von Hudson (1972) überzeugend zurückgewiesen.

3.2. Stellung des Attributs

Der Wandel VSO → SOV geht einher mit einem Wandel in der Stellung des Attributs. Gəʿəz hatte wohl eine deutliche Präferenz für die Stellung Substantiv − Attribut im unmarkierten Satz, die modernen äthiosemitischen Sprachen haben Attribut − Substantiv.

3.2.1. Stellung des Adjektivs

Im Gəʿəz folgt das attributive Adjektiv in der Regel dem Substantiv (vgl. 5), doch ist die Voranstellung zur Fokussierung ohne weiteres möglich (vgl. 6, wo der Übersetzer entgegen der griechischen Vorlage das Adjektiv voranstellt; weiter Gai 1981):

(5) Gəʿəz (Ex. 9, 18)
 wa-nāhu ʾana ʾazannəm
 und-sieh ich regnen.CAUS.IMPF.1SG
 geśama za-gize barada bəzuḫa
 morgen DEM-Zeit Hagel.ACC viel.ACC
 ṭəqqa
 sehr
 'Siehe, morgen um diese Zeit werde ich sehr schweren Hagel herabregnen lassen!'

(6) Gəʿəz (Gen. 21, 34)
 wa-nabara ʾAbrəhām wəsta
 und-blieb Abraham in
 mədra fələsṭəʾem bəzuḫa mawāʿəla
 Land.CST Philister viel.ACC Tage.ACC
 'Abraham blieb viele Tage im Lande der Philister.' (griech. Vorlage: hēméras pollás).

Auch in anderen Fällen ist die Voranstellung des attributiven Adjektivs nicht ungewöhnlich, etwa wenn es sich um religiöse Titel wie *bəḍuʿ* 'selig' handelt (Schneider 1959: 69).

Im TIGRE ist diese variable Wortstellung des attributiven Adjektivs erhalten (Raz 1983: 32). In den anderen modernen äthiosemitischen Sprachen steht das attributive Adjektiv stets voran:

(7) TIGRINYA (Leslau 1941: 172)
ʾab rəʾsu ṣaʿda šaš ṭəraḥ
auf Kopf.sein weiß Tuch nur
ʾasiru yəḵäyyəd
gebunden kommt
'Er kommt mit einem weißen Tuch (Turban) um den Kopf gebunden.'

(8) AMHARISCH (Leslau 1995: 208)
ṭəru tämari
gut Student
'ein guter Student'

3.2.2. Genitivattribut

Im Gəʿəz stehen Besitzer und Besitztum in der sogenannten Status-constructus-Verbindung. Das Nomen regens steht dabei im Status constructus (CST), der formal identisch mit dem Akkusativ ist (nach Konsonant *-a*; bei Nomina auf *-i* lautet er *-e*; bei anderen Vokalen nicht gekennzeichnet); das Nomen rectum steht virtuell im Genitiv, der sich morphologisch vom Nominativ nicht unterscheidet, also:

(9) Gəʿəz
beta nəguś
Haus.CST König
'Das Haus des Königs'

Die Wortstellung in der constructus-Verbindung ist fest. Die constructus-Verbindung kann auch mithilfe des suffigierten Personalpronomens und der Präposition *la-* umschrieben werden:

(10) Gəʿəz
bet-u la-nəguś
Haus-sein zu-König
'Das Haus des Königs'

Im TIGRINYA ist die alte Status-constructus-Verbindung des Gəʿəz nur noch als klar markierter Archaismus erhalten (Leslau 1941: 40; vgl. auch oben Beispiel 3):

(11) TIGRINYA
mängəstä səmayat
Reich.CST Himmel.PL
'Himmelreich'

Daneben existiert auch eine „moderne" Status-constructus-Verbindung mit der gleichen Wortstellung, jedoch ohne morphologische Kennzeichnung am Nomen rectum:

(12) Tigrinya (Gen. 3, 1)
kab kʷəllu ʾom gännät
von all Baum Garten
'von allen Bäumen des Gartens'

Während diese Konstruktion sich typologisch noch in Übereinstimmung mit dem Gəʿəz befindet, ist die alternative Konstruktion mit der Genitivpartikel *nay* eine Innovation:

(13) TIGRINYA (Leslau 1941: 181)
ətom nay-tu ʿaddi gʷaromsatat
ART.PL POSS-ART Dorf Jüngling.PL
'die jungen Männer des Dorfes'

Daneben soll auch die Möglichkeit bestehen, die Gruppe *nay* + Komplement dem Komplementierten nachzustellen (Leslau 1941: 41).

Anders ist der Befund im Amharischen: Das Komplement wird, mit dem Relativ-Element *yä-* eingeleitet, dem Komplementierten grundsätzlich vorangestellt:

(14) Amharisch (Leslau 1995: 193)
yä-təguh tämari däbtär
REL-aufmerksam Student Heft
'das Heft eines aufmerksamen Studenten'

Wo im AMHARISCHEN der alte Status constructus nach Art des Gəʿəz auftaucht, handelt es sich um Fremdwörter.

3.2.3. Attributiver Relativsatz

Ebenso wie die Stellung attributiver Adjektive und von Genitivattributen, hat sich auch die des Relativsatzes gewandelt. Im Gəʿəz steht der attributive Relativsatz meist nach dem Bezugsnomen:

(15) Gəʿəz (RIÉ 189, 1−5)
ʿezānā ... za-ʾay-yətmawwā
[Name] ... REL-NEG-wird.besiegt
la-ḍar
von-Feind
'Ezana ..., der vom Feind nicht besiegt wird'

Doch finden sich auch genügend Gegenbeispiele (Gai 1981: 260−261). Beispiel 16 zeigt, daß dies auch unabhängig von der Übersetzungsvorlage geschehen kann:

(16) Gəʿəz (Lev. 19, 9)
'i-tə'rayu   za-wadqa
NEG-sammeln.SBJV REL-fiel
'əkla
Getreide.ACC
'Lest das Getreide, das heruntergefallen ist, nicht auf!' (griech. Vorlage: kaì tà apopíptonta toû therismoû sou ou sylléxeis).

In den modernen äthiosemitischen Sprachen steht der Relativsatz voran (zum Relativsatz vgl. noch § 7.):

(17) TIGRINYA (Leslau 1941: 195)
zə-motä säb
REL-starb Mann
'der Mann, der gestorben war'

(18) AMHARISCH (Leslau 1995: 102)
yä-mäṭṭa-w säw-əyye wändəmm-e
REL-kam-ART Mann-ART Bruder-mein
näw
COP
'Der Mann der gekommen ist, ist mein Bruder.'

4. Adpositionen

Gəʿəz hat zahlreiche Präpositionen, die z. T. schon zum semitischen Erbe gehören, z. T. Innovationen sind. Es hat keine Postpositionen. Im Neuäthiopischen ist die Situation komplizierter. Während das konservative TIGRE ebenfalls nur Präpositionen aufweist, verfügt das TIGRINYA über eine Reihe von Postpositionen, wobei Präpositionen immer noch dominant sind. Im südäthiopischen AMHARISCH dagegen finden sich bei überwiegender Dominanz von Postpositionen dennoch einige ererbte Präpositionen (Leslau 1995: 597−659). Dabei werden durchaus auch Prä- und Postpositionen zu Zirkumpositionen zusammengestellt, wie im folgenden Beispiel mit der Präposition bä- („in") und der Postpositon gize („zur Zeit als"):

(19) AMHARISCH (Leslau 1995: 655)
bä-ṭorənnät-u gize əngliz agär
in-Krieg-ART Zeit englisch Land
näbbärku
ich.war
'Während des Krieges war ich in England.'

Im ARGOBBA scheint dieser Typ gängiger als bloße Postpositionen zu sein (Leslau 1997a: 95−97). Vgl. zur Problematik auch noch Greenberg (1980).

5. Determination

Gəʿəz ist eine artikellose Sprache, doch gibt es Möglichkeiten, mithilfe von suffigierten Possessivpronomina optional Determination auszudrücken (Correll 1991), vgl.:

(20) Gəʿəz (Gen. 37, 9)
ḥalamku kälə'a
träumen.PRF.1SG zweiter.ACC
ḥəlma wa-kama-zə ḥəlm-u
Traum.ACC und-so-DEM Traum-sein
'Ich träumte einen zweiten Traum, und so war der Traum: ...'

In dem Beispiel ist kein Element erkennbar, auf das sich das suffigierte (formal possessive) Pronomen der dritten Pers. mask. Sg. -u beziehen könnte. Läge ein anaphorisches Pronomen vor, müsste es in der 1. Person stehen, da der Sprecher ja von seinem eigenen Traum spricht. Es bezeichnet daher die Determination. Dieses Verfahren wird im Gəʿəz nur sporadisch genutzt.

Auch Demonstrativa können verwendet werden, um Determination auszudrücken, z. B.:

(21) Gəʿəz (Gen. 1, 8)
wa-samayo 'əgzi'abəḥer
und-nannte.ihn Gott
la-wə'ətu ṭafar samāya
für-DEM Dach Himmel.ACC
'Gott nannte das Dach 'Himmel'.'
(üb. tò stréōma)

Im Zusammenhang mit solchen Beispielen wurde der begründete Verdacht geäußert, dass der Gebrauch der Demonstrativa wie in Beispiel 21 durch den Artikel in den griechischen Übersetzungsvorlagen erst stimuliert sei (Hofmann 1969: 94−96; Kapeliuk 1994: 4).

Im Gegensatz zu diesen nur optionalen Verfahren zum Ausdruck der Determination, die auch nur vergleichsweise selten angewandt werden, haben die meisten modernen äthiosemitischen Sprachen Artikelsysteme (mit Ausnahme des HARARI, das eine optionale Determination nach Art des Gəʿəz beibehalten hat). In der Regel liegt die Opposition definiter Artikel vs. Ø vor, doch hat das AMHARISCHE auch einen indefiniten Artikel.

Aus dem im Gəʿəz angewandten Verfahren der optionalen Determination durch das Possessivpronomen hat z. B. das AMHARISCHE seinen Artikel entwickelt, vgl. bet „Haus" vs. betu „sein Haus" und „das Haus" (zur Verwendung des AMHARISCHEN Artikels, der insgesamt mit geringerer Frequenz verwendet wird als z. B. der ENGLISCHE oder der HEBRÄISCHE, vgl. Kapeliuk 1994: 10–60). Dasselbe Verfahren, nur mit einem anderen Pronomen, benutzt auch das CHAHA, ein GURAGE-Dialekt: *bet* „Haus" vs. *betäta* „sein Haus" und „das Haus".

Aus dem anderen im Gəʿəz angewandten optionalen Verfahren zur Determination, der Verwendung der Demonstrativa, hat das TIGRINYA seinen Artikel entwickelt: *bəʿray* „Rind" vs. *ʾətu bəʿray* „das Rind" (Leslau 1941: 38–39).

6. Kasusmarkierung

Das Gəʿəz bewahrt einen Teil des altsemitischen Kasussystems. Nominativ und Genitiv sind durch den Zusammenfall von kurzem **u* und **i* zu *ə*, das im Auslaut abfällt, äußerlich zusammengefallen, so dass sich folgendes Paradigma ergibt:

	Konsonant	auf -*i*
NOM/GEN	*bet*	*nolawi*
ACC	*beta*	*nolawe*

(*bet* = Haus; *nolawi* = Hirte)

Nomina auf -*ā*, -*e* und -*o* sind unflektierbar. Die Lebendigkeit der Kasusflexion zeigt sich auch daran, dass Relativ-, Demonstrativ- und Interrogativpronomina und mit suffigiertem Possessivpronomen versehene Substantive Akkusativformen aufweisen (z. B. *betu* 'sein Haus', Nom./Gen. vs. *beto* 'sein Haus' Akk.), sowie in Akkusativformen von einigen eher dem pronominalen Bereich zuzuordnenden Sonderbildungen wie *kʷəllu* 'all, ganz' (Nom.) vs. *kʷəllo* (Akk.). Die Kasusflexion erstreckt sich auch auf das Adjektiv, das somit kongruenzfähig ist:

(22) Gəʿəz (Apk. 5, 2)
wa-rəʾiku malʾaka ʿabiya
und-sah.1SG Engel.ACC groß.ACC
'Und ich sah einen großen Engel.'

Neben dieser morphologischen Kasusmarkierung treten im Gəʿəz, insbesondere bei determinierten Komplementen bzw. direkten Objekten, bereits häufig Periphrasen zur Umschreibung von Genitiv und Akkusativ auf. Diese setzen sich aus dem proleptischen suffigierten Personalpronomen und der resumptiven Präposition *la-* 'zu, hin' zusammen (vgl. oben § 3.2.2.):

(23) Gəʿəz (Ex. 1, 1)
zə-wəʾətu ʾasmāti-homu
DEM-er Name.PL-ihr(M.PL)
la-daqiqa ʾəsrāʾel
zu-Kinder.CST Israel
'Dies sind die Namen der Kinder Israels.'

(24) Gəʿəz (Ex. 1, 18)
wa-ṣawwəʿon nəguśa gəbṣ
und-rief.sie(F.PL) König.CST Ägypten
la-mawaləddāt
zu-Hebamme.PL
'Der König von Ägypten rief die Hebammen (zu sich).'

Kasusflexion ist im modernen Äthiosemitischen nicht vorhanden. Ihre Leistungen werden entweder von der Wortstellung oder von Klitika erfüllt. Zu adnominalen Konstruktionen („moderner" Status constructus und *nay* im TIGRINYA, *yä-* im Amharischen) wurde im Zusammenhang mit der Wortstellung des Genitivattributs bereits alles Notwendige gesagt (s. oben § 3.2.2.).

Das direkte Objekt ist in den modernen äthiosemitischen Sprachen häufig nur durch die Wortstellung gekennzeichnet:

(25) TIGRE (Raz 1983: 103)
gadəm ʾabbəkiki šāš bəzuḥ
nun Kiebitz Turban sehr
fatte-ʿala
liebte-DUR
'Nun, der Kiebitz [als er noch ein Mensch war] liebte den Turban sehr.'

(26) TIGRINYA (Leslau 1941: 42)
kahən ṣolot wäddiʾu
Priester Gebet beenden.CONV
'Der Priester hatte das Gebet beendet.'

(27) AMHARISCH (Leslau 1995: 182)
wəšša bäqlo näkkäsä
Hund Maultier biss
'Ein Hund biss ein Maultier.'

Eine periphrastische Markierung des direkten Objekts mit Hilfe von Präpositionen weisen auch das TIGRE und das TIGRINYA auf (Genaueres bei Raz 1983: 83):

(28) TIGRE (Raz 1983: 104)
ʾəgal kaləb waʿul ṭalmat ʾəttu
zu Hund absichtlich betrog.F ihn
'Sie (die Katze) betrog den Hund absichtlich.'

(29)   TIGRINYA (Leslau 1941: 160)
       nätu   q^wålʿa bə-šaš
       DO.ART Knabe mit-Musselin
       yəṭəmṭəməʾo
       einwickeln.F.PL.ihn
       'Sie wickeln den Knaben in ein Musselin-Tuch.'

Das AMHARISCHE hat einen suffigierten Marker *-n* zur Kennzeichnung des direkten Objekts. Dass ein klitisiertes Element und keine Kasusendung vorliegt, zeigt sich an der Tatsache, dass er gegebenenfalls hinter dem Artikel steht, und dass er, sofern ein Attribut vorhanden ist, nur einmal gesetzt wird und zwar nicht an den Kopf der Nominalphrase, sondern an das Attribut:

(30)   Amharisch (Leslau 1995: 184)
       wəšša-w   təlləq-u-n   bäqlo
       Hund-ART groß-ART-DO Maultier
       näkkäsä
       biss
       'Der Hund biss das große Maultier.'

Somit ist der alte Flexionskasus im Amharischen durch ein agglutinierendes Element ersetzt worden.

7. Relativsatz/Relativkomplex

Das Relativelement des Gəʿəz *za-* (fem. *ʾənta*, pl. comm. *ʾəlla*) leitet einen untergeordneten Satz ein (zur Wortstellung vgl. § 3.2.3.). Die Satzwertigkeit des Relativsatzes ist unabhängig davon, ob man *za-* etc. als Relativpronomen oder als Relativmarker betrachten will (so Hailu Fulass 1983).

(31)   Gəʿəz (Gen. 2, 16)
       ʾəm-k^wəllu ʾəḍ   za-hallo wəsta
       von-all   Baum REL-ist in
       gannat balāʿ
       Garten iss.IMPT
       'Iss von allen Bäumen, die im Garten sind.'

Weitere Beispiele mit Relativsatz s. o. § 3.4.3. Der relative Komplex des AMHARISCHEN unterscheidet sich in mehrfacher Hinsicht vom alten Relativsatz. Die Kongruenz mit einem vorhandenen Bezugsnomen ist endgültig aufgegeben. Die Form des Relativ-Elements richtet sich nach dem folgenden Verb: Vor dem Perfekt lautet es *yä-*, vor Imperfekt *yämm-*. *Yä-* leitet nicht den ganzen Relativsatz ein, sondern wird dem Verb präfigiert. Der Relativkomplex verhält sich in mancher Hinsicht wie ein Nomen. Dies zeigt sich nicht nur in der Stellung, die er mit dem Adjektiv teilt, sondern auch daran, dass er den bestimmten Artikel tragen kann:

(32)   AMHARISCH (Leslau 1995: 85)
       tələnt   yä-mäṭṭaš-wa   anči
       gestern REL-kommen.PERF.F-ART.F du
       näš
       COP
       'Der gestern gekommen ist, warst du.'

Demzufolge spricht man auch vom „relativen Verb" des AMHARISCHEN. Dessen Charakter zeigt sich auch an seinem Verhalten bei der Koordination mehrerer Verben. Sie werden nicht als koordinierte Prädikate ein und desselben Relativsatzes behandelt, sondern bekommen jedes für sich das Relativ-Element:

(33)   AMHARISCH (Leslau 1995: 89)
       əndä-ssu bəzu yämmibälla-nna
       wie-er   viel REL.isst-und
       yämiṭäṭṭa säw   yällämm
       REL.trinkt Mann ist.NEG
       'Es gibt keinen, der soviel isst und trinkt wie er.'

Zur Verwendung des relativen Verbs im Spaltsatz vgl. unten § 13.

8. Koordination

Das Gəʿəz verwendet zur Koordination von Satzteilen und Sätzen die ererbte, gemeinwestsemitische präfigierte Konjunktion *wa-*, vgl. z. B.:

(34)   Gəʿəz (Gen. 2, 1)
       wa-tafaṣṣama samāy wa-mədr
       und-vollenden.REFL.PRF.3M.SG Himmel und-Erde
       'Himmel und Erde waren vollendet.'

(35)   Gəʿəz (Gen. 3, 6)
       ... naśʾat fəre-hu   wa-balʿat
       ... nahm.F Frucht.ACC-sein und-aß.F
       wa-wahabat-o la-bəʾəsi-hā məslehā
       und-gab.F-ihn zu-Mann-ihr mit.ihr
       wa-balʿu   wa-tafatḥa
       und-aßen.PL und-öffnen.REFL.PRF
       ʾaʿyəntihomu wa-ʾaʾmaru
       Auge.PL.ihre und-erkannten.PL
       kama ...
       dass ...
       '... da nahm sie von seiner (des Baumes) Frucht und aß und gab sie ihrem Mann, der bei ihr war, und sie aßen. Da öffneten sich ihre Augen, und sie erkannten, dass ...'

Dabei ist die syndetische Anbindung durch *wa-* der unmarkierte Fall, Asyndese deutet dagegen auf die eine oder andere Art von Subordination hin. In den modernen äthiosemitischen Sprachen sind präfigierte Konjunktionen nur im TIGRE vorhanden, der nördlichsten der modernen äthiosemitischen Sprachen. Auch hier wird *wa-* sowohl zwischen Satzteilen als auch Sätzen verwendet:

(36) TIGRE (Raz 1983: 104)
      kaləb wa-dəmmu kəl'ot galgalāy
      Hund und-Katze zwei Freunde
      ma fatač 'alaw
      oder Kameraden waren
      'Der Hund und die Katze waren Freunde, oder Kameraden.'

(37) Tigre (Raz 1983: 89)
      wa-kəm ra'ayu ṭarqa 'əttu
      und-als sah.ihn kam zu.ihm
      ka-təsālamayu wa-mən 'aya
      dann-begrüßte.ihn und-von wo
      'ənta bello
      du sagte.zu.ihm
      'Und als er ihn sah, begrüßte ihn ihn, und fragte ihn: Von woher kommst du?'

In den anderen modernen äthiosemitischen Sprachen sind präfigierte koordinierende Konjunktionen weitgehend durch suffigierte ersetzt, vgl. z. B.:

(38) TIGRINYA (Leslau 1941: 169)
      'ətu mär'aw-ən 'əta mär'at-ən
      ART.M Bräutigam-und ART.F Braut-und
      'der Bräutigam und die Braut'

(39) AMHARISCH (Leslau 1995: 725)
      kä-gäbäya čäw-ənna bärbärre
      von-Markt Salz-und Pfeffer
      amäṭṭaʷh
      brachte.1SG
      'Ich brachte vom Markt Salz und Pfeffer.'

(40) AMHARISCH (Leslau 1995: 726)
      hid-ənna amṭa-w
      geh.IMPT-und bring.IMPT-es
      'Geh und bring es!'

Hauptsätze werden in aller Regel nicht durch Konjunktionen verbunden. Verbreitet ist auch die koordinierende Asyndese, z. B.:

(41) TIGRINYA (Leslau 1941: 146)
      'əṭan käbäro ṣänaṣəl
      Räucherwerk Trommel Sistren
      ḥizom yəmäṣu
      halten.CONV kommen.PL
      'Sie kommen mit Räucherwerk, Trommeln und Sistren.'

(42) AMHARISCH (Leslau 1995: 725)
      kä-gäbäya čäw bärbärre amäṭṭaʷh
      von-Markt Salz Pfeffer brachte.1SG
      'Ich brachte vom Markt Salz und Pfeffer.'

Es liegt also ein im Süden stärker als im Norden ausgeprägter Trend von obligatorischen präfigierten zu optionalen suffigierten Elementen der Koordination vor. Was die Koordination von Sätzen betrifft, ist zudem ein Trend von syndetischer zu asyndetischer Folge festzustellen. Dieser Koordinationstyp scheint mit der OV-Wortstellung im Zusammenhang zu stehen (Art. 64; 82).

9. Verbalsystem

Das klassische Gəʿəz der aksumitischen Zeit hat lediglich fünf morphologische Tempus- und Modus-Formen. Anhand der Beispielwurzel *qtl* lauten diese im Grundstamm:

Perfekt: *qatala* 'er tötete/wird getötet haben' (relative Vorzeitigkeit bzw. perfektiver Aspekt)
Imperfekt: *yəqattəl* 'er tötet/wird töten' (relative Gleich- und Nachzeitigkeit bzw. imperfektiver Aspekt)
Subjunktiv (Jussiv): *yəqtəl* 'er möge töten'
Imperativ: *qətəl* 'töte!'
Konverb (trad.: Gerund): *qatilo* 'getötet habend' (3SG. M)

Direkt verbunden werden diese Elemente nur mit den suffigierten Objektspronomina (nicht das Konverb!) und mit der präfigierten Negation *'i-* (nicht Imperativ und Konverb!). Der Ausbau dieses vergleichsweise schlichten Systems durch die Kombination mit kongruierenden Seinsverben ist im Gəʿəz nie über schwache Ansätze hinausgekommen (Weninger 1999; Weninger i. Dr.).

Im Gegensatz dazu hat die Verbalmorphologie in den modernen äthiosemitischen Sprachen einen erheblichen Ausbau erfahren und damit einen beträchtlichen Grad an Komplexität erreicht. So ist z. B. beim AMHARISCHEN allein beim Perfekt ein einfaches Perfekt *säbbärä* ('er brach'), ein negatives Perfekt *alsäbbärämm* ('er brach nicht') und die Fügungen mit den z. T. erstarrten Seinsverben *all(ä)*, *näbbär(ä)*, *nurʷall*, *yəhon* und *yəhonal* zu unterscheiden. Entsprechendes gilt für das Imperfekt, den Jussiv und das Gerund. Vergleichbares gilt auch für die anderen modernen äthiopischen Sprachen (vgl. z. B. Voigt 1977).

10. Zusammengesetzte Verben

Das Gəʕəz hat nur ein einziges mit 'sagen' zusammengesetzes Verb: ʼoho yəbe 'zustimmen', (wörtlich: 'ja sagen'; schon RIÉ 186, 6!). Dass diese Fügung tatsächlich lexikalisiert ist, zeigt der Kausativ ʼoho ʼabala 'überzeugen' (wörtlich: 'ja sagen lassen') (Leslau 1987: 12). Dieser Wortbildungstyp hat sich, sicherlich unter dem Einfluss KUSCHITISCHER Sprachen, im AMHARISCHEN stark ausgeweitet: $q^wa\ alä$ 'schnappen, klicken' (onomatopoetisch: 'q^wa sagen'), zəmm alä 'schweigen' (wörtlich: '"still!" sagen'); wədəqq alä 'hart / plötzlich fallen' (zu wäddäqä 'fallen'), läzzäbb alä 'etwas glatt sein' (zu ləzzəb 'glatt' etc.), $q^wəšəšš\ alä$ 'etwas schmutzig sein' (zu $q^wäšaša$ 'Schmutz, Abfall'), usw. (Rommel 1974; Leslau 1995: 580−596). Analoge Bildungen sind auch in den anderen modernen äthiosemitischen Sprachen belegt (Tigre, Raz 1983: 66; Tigrinya, Leslau 1941: 124; Argobba, Leslau 1997a: 89; Gurage, Leslau 1992: 275−276).

11. Phonologischer Typ

Das Konsonantensystem des Gəʕəz, soweit es sich auf der Basis der Orthographie, der traditionellen Aussprache, durch komparative Methodik und mit Hilfe vereinzelter Transkriptionen rekonstruieren lässt, verfügte u. a. über einen Satz von Laryngalen bzw. Pharyngalen (ʼ [ʔ], ʕ [ʕ], ḥ [ħ], h [h]) und wohl über zwei laterale Obstruenten (ḍ, ś), jedoch über keine Affrikaten oder palatalisierte Konsonanten (vgl. Voigt 1989, Gragg 1997 [lässt die Frage der Laterale offen], Weninger 1998). Damit steht dieses Konsonantensystem typologisch in weitgehender Übereinstimmung mit den anderen klassischen semitischen Sprachen (mit Ausnahme des AKKADISCHEN, das die Laryngale früh unter dem Substrateinfluss des SUMERISCHEN verloren hat). In unterschiedlich starkem Gegensatz dazu stehen die modernen äthiosemitischen Sprachen. Die lateralen Obstruenten sind in allen modernen äthiosemitischen Sprache mit den entsprechenden Sibilanten zusammengefallen. Was die Laryngale betrifft, so lässt sich auch hier ein Nord-Süd-Gefälle feststellen: In den nordäthiopischen Sprachen TIGRE und TIGRINYA sind sie vollständig erhalten (Raz 1983: 4−5; Leslau 1941: 6), im Südäthiopischen sind die Laryngale auf h reduziert (Leslau 1997b: 400 [AMHARISCH], Leslau 1992: 16−17 [GURAGE], Leslau 1997a: 1 [ARGOBBA]). Lediglich HARARI hat auch ḥ (Wagner 1997: 487). Alle modernen äthiosemitischen Sprachen haben eine gut ausgeprägte Reihe von Palatalen bzw. Präpalatalen entwickelt. Die Reihe č, ǧ, č̣, š, ž, ñ, y ist ebenso im nordäthiopischen TIGRINYA wie im südäthiopischen AMHARISCH oder im GURAGE vorhanden. Insgesamt ergibt sich so eine im Süden stärker als im Norden ausgeprägte Tendenz weg vom klassischen semitischen Typ eines Konsonantensystems mit Laryngalen und Lateralen zu einem System, das stark von Palatalen geprägt ist. (Vgl. allgemein auch Ullendorff 1955).

Dagegen ist die Glottalisierung der sogenannten emphatischen Konsonanten der äthiosemitischen Sprachen (ṣ, ṭ, č̣, ḳ) nicht, wie man früher z. T. annahm, eine Innovation unter dem Einfluss KUSCHITISCHER Sprachen (so z. B. Leslau 1945: 63). Denn seit fest steht, dass deren Kognaten im NEUSÜDARABISCHEN, wo KUSCHITISCHER Einfluss auszuschließen ist, ebenfalls glottalisiert sind (Johnstone 1975, vgl. Lonnet & Simeone-Senelle 1997: 348−349), hat sich in der Semitistik die Communis opinio durchgesetzt, dass die glottalisierte Realisation der Emphatica schon für das Ursemitische anzunehmen ist, und die pharyngalisierte Realisation im ARABISCHEN und im ARAMÄISCHEN sekundär ist. Dem entsprechend darf man Glottalisierung auch schon für das Gəʕəz annehmen, das damit in Übereinstimmung mit dem modernen Äthiosemitischen steht.

12. Typologischer Wandel und Sprachkontakt

Es hat sich immer wieder gezeigt, dass die Auswirkungen des drifts von einer VSO/NA-Sprache zu SOV/AN-Sprachen, der in Ansätzen schon im Gəʕəz sichtbar war, im Süden stärker ausgeprägt ist als im Norden. Dabei wird dennoch eine relative Einheitlichkeit des modernen Äthiosemitischen gegenüber dem Gəʕəz deutlich, das typologisch eher den anderen klassischen semitischen Sprachen ähnelt.

Schon Semitisten des 19. Jh. bemerkten, dass eine ganze Reihe dieser Entwicklungstendenzen, nebst einiger, die sich schon im Gəʕəz abzeichnen (z. B. das Gerund/Konverb), zu einer typologischen Ähnlichkeit der modernen äthiosemitischen Sprachen, insbesondere des AMHARISCHEN, mit den TÜRKSPRACHEN führen (→ Art. 122). So spricht

E. Rödiger (1842, zitiert bei Praetorius 1871: 2) vom „turanischen" Aussehen des AMHARISCHEN und Praetorius (1879: 3) schreibt, das AMHARISCHE wirke, „als habe ein Türke aus seiner Sprache unter Beibehaltung der türkischen Wortstellung ins Semitische übersetzt". Eine ganze Reihe von wichtigen typologischen Parallelen TÜRKISCHER und AMHARISCHER Syntax hat Polotsky (1960) zusammengetragen (vgl. weiter Kapeliuk 1990).

Der Kontakt der äthiosemitischen Sprachen mit verschiedenen Vertretern der KUSCHITISCHEN Sprachen, insbesondere mit den zentralkuschitischen Sprachen ist sehr alt. Er reicht in jedem Fall weit ins erste Jahrtausend v. Chr. zurück (Irvine 1978), wobei in dem äthiopischen Mosaik von Sprachgebieten und Sprachinseln nicht immer sicher auszumachen ist, welche Sprachen die Substrat- und welche die Superstratsprachen sind (Hudson 1978). Dass die äthiosemitischen Sprachen auf diese Weise unter dem Einfluss ihrer KUSCHITISCHEN Substrat- und Nachbarsprachen stehen, ist seit langer Zeit bekannt. So untersuchte z. B. schon im 19. Jh. F. Praetorius (1889; 1893) lexikalische Einflüsse KUSCHITISCHER Sprachen im Gəˁəz (vgl. zum Thema weiter Leslau 1945: 79—80; 1988). So auch in der Phonologie: Es ist naheliegend, die labialisierten Konsonanten der äthiosemitischen Sprachen kuschitischem Einfluss zuzuschreiben, da ein Merkmal „Labialisierung" in den asiatischen semitischen Sprachen unbekannt ist, und Labiovelare in den zentralkuschitischen AGAU-Sprachen vorhanden sind (Leslau 1945: 62). Etymologische Beziehungen der Art semitisch *kull 'all, ganz' → Gəˁəz kʷəll stehen dieser Annahme nicht im Wege. Des weiteren wurden z. B. Auswirkungen des KUSCHITISCHEN Substrats im Bereich des Pronominalsystems wahrscheinlich gemacht (Moreno 1949: 325), sowie einige Wortbildungssuffixe als KUSCHITISCH identifiziert (Leslau 1945: 66—68; vgl. zum Thema auch Leslau 1952; 1962).

Und so sind wohl auch eine ganze Reihe der typologisch relevanten Eigenschaften, die die modernen äthiosemitischen Sprachen vom Gəˁəz unterscheiden, KUSCHITISCHEM Einfluss zuzuschreiben (Nachweise für das Folgende, wo nicht anders angegeben bei Leslau 1945):

a) Der Wandel der alten VSO-Grundwortstellung zu SOV (vgl. oben § 3.1.): SOV ist die normale Wortstellung der kuschitischen Sprachen.

b) Voranstellung des Attributs vor das Bezugsnomen (vgl. § 3.2.): Die Stellung Attribut-Nomen, die in den meisten modernen äthiosemitischen Sprachen vorherrschend ist, ist in den KUSCHITISCHEN Sprachen die normale Stellung. Correll (1983) unternimmt den Versuch, die Voranstellung des Attributs im AMHARISCHEN unter Ausklammerung des KUSCHITISCHEN Einflusses aus „'echt semitischem' Sprachmaterial heraus zu erklären" (1983: 325), mit durchweg stichhaltigen Argumenten. Doch spricht die Herleitung aus SEMITISCHEN Syntagmen ja nicht dagegen, dass der Anstoß, der den Wandelprozess in Gang gebracht hat, aus der kuschitischsprachigen Umgebung kommt, sondern sie zeigt den Weg auf, den dieser Wandelprozess konkret genommen hat.

c) Der von Norden nach Süden zunehmende Trend zu Postpositionen (vgl. § 4.): Die KUSCHITISCHEN Sprachen haben überwiegend Postpositionen, und in der Regel nur wenige, oder keine Präpositionen.

d) Die stärkere Verbreitung der mit 'sagen' zusammengesetzten Verben (vgl. § 10.): Dieser Wortbildungstyp, der in den asiatischen SEMITISCHEN Sprachen unbekannt ist, und im Gəˁəz nur ein einziges Lexem bildet, ist in den KUSCHITISCHEN Sprachen weit verbreitet (vgl. auch Palmer 1974).

e) Palatalisierte und palatale Konsonanten (vgl. § 11.): Das in den modernen äthiosemitischen Sprachen weit verbreitete Merkmal Palatalisierung ist in zahlreichen KUSCHITISCHEN Sprachen vertreten. Zweifellos lassen sich zahlreiche Palatale auch durch regulären Lautwandel herleiten, z. B. Gəˁəz bet-əki (Haus-POSS.F) 'dein (fem.) Haus' → AMHARISCH bet-əš (Haus-POSS.F) 'dein (fem.) Haus'. Man könnte auch anführen, daß Palatalisierungen auch in asiatischen SEMITISCHEN Sprachen vorkommen (z. B. IRAK-ARABISCH č < k). Doch angesichts der weiten Verbreitung im modernen Äthiosemitischen und im KUSCHITISCHEN muss man wohl davon ausgehen, dass der Kontakt mit den KUSCHITISCHEN Sprachen bei solchen Lautwandelprozessen zumindest unterstützend mitgewirkt hat.

Die große Häufigkeit von Spaltsätzen (cleft sentences; Kopulasätze [Voigt 1977: 100]) mit Wiederaufnahme durch das relative Verb im modernen Äthiosemitischen, insbesondere im AMHARISCHEN (wie z. B. (43), vgl. auch den TIGRINYA-Satz 44), wurde ebenfalls KUSCHITISCHEM Einfluss zugeschrieben. Demgegenüber weisen Correll (1980) und Kapeliuk (1985) darauf hin, dass sich analoge

Strukturen nicht selten schon im Gəʿəz aufzeigen lassen (z. B. 45):

(43) AMHARISCH (Leslau 1995: 106)
tämaročču   əgər kʷas čwata
Studenten.ART Fuß   Ball Spiel
yämm-ihedu-t   nägä näw
REL-kommen.IMPF.3PL-ART morgen cop
'Morgen werden die Studenten zum Fußballspiel kommen.' (wörtlich: 'Morgen ist es, dass ...')

(44) TIGRINYA (Voigt 1977: 103)
tämäharti zə-säʾaluwo   ʾiyu
Schüler.PL REL-malen.3PL+3SG cop
'Die Schüler haben es gemalt.' (wörtlich: 'Die Schüler sind es, die ...')

(45) Gəʿəz (Lk. 3, 18)
wa-bāʿda-ni   bəzuḫa
und-anderes.ACC-auch viel.ACC
za-maharomu la-ḥəzb
REL-lehrte.sie zu-Volk
'Auch viel anderes lehrte er das Volk.'

Einschränkend ist bei der Frage nach dem KUSCHITISCHEN Einfluss natürlich anzuführen, dass alle KUSCHITISCHEN Sprachen erst in neuerer und neuester Zeit bezeugt sind. Der grundsätzliche methodologische Zweifel, ob das, was der Forschung in der Gegenwart als KUSCHITISCH entgegentritt, in allen Punkten schon so alt ist, dass es eindeutig die äthiosemitischen Sprachen beeinflusst haben kann, muss erlaubt sein. Manches könnte auch das Resultat einer gegenseitigen Beeinflussung durch den jahrhundertelangen engen Sprachkontakt im äthiopischen Konvergenzareal sein. Hier könnte das Beispiel des Lexikons instruktiv sein, wo Gragg (1991) eine ganze Reihe von Lexemen des Gəʿəz zusammengestellt hat, die zwar „äthiopisch" (im arealen Sinn!) sind, von denen sich allerdings nicht so einfach entscheiden lässt, ob sie (äthio-)SEMITISCH oder KUSCHITISCH sind. Eine umfassende Rekonstruktion des älteren KUSCHITISCHEN, unter Einbeziehung der südkuschitischen Sprachen (Kenia, Tansania), die außerhalb des Einflussbereichs der semitischen Sprachen liegen, könnte auch auf die Frage Licht werfen, inwieweit der typologische Wandel im Äthiosemitischen durch direkten Einfluss hervorgerufen wurde.

13. Spezielle Abkürzungen

COP   Copula
CST   (Status) constructus
RIÉ   Bernand, Drewes, Schneider (1991)
SBJV Subjunktiv

14. Zitierte Literatur

Bach, Emmon. 1970. „Is Amharic an SOV language?". *Journal of Ethiopian Studies* 8: 9−20.

Bergsträßer, Gotthelf. 1928. *Einführung in die semitischen Sprachen. Sprachproben und grammatische Skizzen.* München: Hueber.

Bernand, E. & Drewes, A. J. & Schneider, R. 1991 ff. *Recueil des inscriptions de l'Éthiopie des périodes pré-axoumite et axoumite.* I−II ff. Paris: Boccard.

Correll, Christoph. 1980. „Der 'abstrakte' Relativsatz im Amharischen: Ein Versuch, seine Entstehung zu klären". In: Diem, Werner & Wild, Stefan (eds.). *Studien aus Arabistik und Semitistik Anton Spitaler zum siebzigsten Geburtstag.* Wiesbaden: Harrassowitz, 42−59.

Correll, Christoph. 1983. „Einige sprachgeschichtliche Streiflichter auf den typologischen Wandel am Beispiel des Amharischen". In: Faust, Manfred (ed.). *Allgemeine Sprachwissenschaft, Sprachtypologie und Textlinguistik. Festschrift für Peter Hartmann.* (Tübinger Beiträge zur Linguistik, 215.) Tübingen: Narr, 325−34.

Correll, Christoph. 1991. „Gedanken zur nichtpossessiven Determination mit Hilfe von Possesivsuffixen im Altäthiopischen und Amharischen". In: Kaye, Alan S. (ed.). *Semitic Studies in Honor of Wolf Leslau on the occasion of his eighty-fifth birthday November 14th, 1991.* Wiesbaden: Harrassowitz, 252−66.

Fellman, Jack. 1979. „Lines on the history of Amharic". *Orbis* 28: 63−65.

Fellman, Jack. 1980 (1982). „Notes towards a classification of Modern Ethiopian Semitic". *Orbis* 29: 105−107.

Ferguson, Charles A. 1976. „The Ethiopian language area". In: Bender, M. Lionel (ed.). *Language in Ethiopia.* London: Oxford Univ. Press, 63−76.

Gai, Amikam. 1981. „The place of the attribute in Geʿez". *Journal of Semitic Studies* 26: 257−65.

Gragg, Gene. 1991. „'Also in Cushitic': How to account for the complexity of Geʿez-Cushitic lexical interactions?". In: Kaye, Alan S. (ed.). *Semitic Studies in Honor of Wolf Leslau on the occasion of his eighty-fifth birthday November 14th, 1991.* Wiesbaden: Harrassowitz, 570−76.

Gragg, Gene. 1997. „Geʿez Phonology". In: Kaye, Alan S. (ed.). *Phonologies of Asia and Africa (Including the Caucasus).* Winona Lake: Eisenbrauns, I 169−86.

Greenberg, Joseph H. 1980. „Circumfixes and typological change". In: Traugott, Elizabeth Closs & Labrum, Rebecca & Sheperd, Susan (ed.). *Papers from the 4th International Conference on Historical Linguistics.* (Amsterdam Studies in the Theory and History of Linguistic Science. Series IV: Current Trends in Linguistic Theory, 14.) Amsterdam: Benjamins, 233−41.

Hailu Fulass. 1983. „A note on Gəʿəz relative clauses". In: Segert, Stanislav & Bodrogligeti, András J. E. (eds.). *Ethiopian Studies dedicated to Wolf Leslau on the occasion of his seventy-fifth birthday*. Wiesbaden: Harrassowitz, 212–20.

Hetzron, Robert. 1972. *Ethiopian Semitic: Studies in classification*. (JSS Monographs, 2.) Manchester: Univ. Press.

Hetzron, Robert. (ed.). 1997. *The Semitic languages*. London: Routledge.

Hofmann, Josef. 1969. *Die äthiopische Johannes-Apokalypse kritisch untersucht*. (Corpus Scriptorum Christianorum Orientalium, 297. Subsidia, 33) Louvain: Secrétariat du Corpus SCO.

Hudson, Grover. 1972. „Why Amharic is not a VSO language". *Studies in African Linguistics* 3, 1: 127–65.

Hudson, Grover. 1978. „Geolinguistic evidence for Ethiopian Prehistory". *Abbay. Documents pour servir à l'histoire de la civilisation éthiopienne* 9: 71–85.

Irvine, A. K. 1978. „Linguistic evidence on ancient Ethiopia: The relationship of early Ethiopian Semitic to Old South Arabian". *Abbay. Documents pour servir à l'histoire de la civilisation éthiopienne* 9: 43–48.

Johnstone, T. M. 1975. „Contrasting articulations in the Modern South Arabian languages". In: Bynon, J. & Th. (eds.). *Hamito-Semitica*. La Hague: Mouton, 155–59.

Kapeliuk, Olga. 1985. „La phrase coupée en guèze". In: Robin, Christian (éd.). *Mélanges linguistiques offerts à Maxime Rodinson*. (Comptes rendus du Groupe Linguistique d'études chamito-sémitiques. Supplément, 12.) Paris: Geuthner, 191–204.

Kapeliuk, Olga. 1990. „Some striking similarities between Amharic and Turkish syntax". In: Bahner, Werner & Schildt, Joachim & Viewegler, Dieter (eds.). *Proceedings of the Fourteenth International Congress of Linguists*. Berlin: Akademie-Verlag, III 2376–79.

Kapeliuk, Olga. 1994. *Syntax of the Noun in Amharic*. (Äthiopistische Forschungen, 37.) Wiesbaden: Harrassowitz.

Leslau, Wolf. 1941. *Documents tigrigna (éthiopien septentrional). Grammaire et textes*. (Collection linguistique, 48.) Paris: Klincksieck.

Leslau, Wolf. 1945. „The influence of Cushitic on the Semitic languages of Ethiopia: A problem of substratum". *Word* 1: 59–82.

Leslau, Wolf. 1952. „The influence of Sidamo on the Ethiopic languages of Gurage". *Language* 28: 63–81. Nachdruck in Leslau 1992: 260–78.

Leslau, Wolf. 1962. „The influence of the Cushitic substratum on Semitic Ethiopic re-examined". In: *Proceedings of the 25th International Orientalists' Congress*. Moscow, I 387–390. Nachdruck in Leslau 1992: 603–6.

Leslau, Wolf. 1965. „Is there a Proto-Gurage?". *Proceedings of the International Conference on Semitic Studies*, Jerusalem: The Israel Academy of Sciences and Humanities, 152–171. Nachdruck in Leslau 1992: 226–45.

Leslau, Wolf. 1969. „Toward a classification of the Gurage dialects". *Journal of Semitic Studies* 14: 96–109. Nachdruck in Leslau 1992: 246–59.

Leslau, Wolf. 1970. „Classification of the Semitic languages of Ethiopia". *Proceedings of the third international conference of Ethiopian studies, Addis Ababa 1966*, Addis Ababa: Institute of Ethiopian Studies, II 5–22. Nachdruck in Leslau 1992: 559–76.

Leslau, Wolf. 1987. *Comparative Dictionary of Geʿez (Classical Ethiopic)*. Wiesbaden: Harrassowitz.

Leslau, Wolf. 1988. „Analysis of the Geʿez vocabulary: Geʿez and Cushitic". *Rassegna di studi etiopici* 32: 60–109.

Leslau, Wolf. 1992. *Gurage Studies: Collected articles*. Wiesbaden: Harrassowitz.

Leslau, Wolf. 1995. *Reference Grammar of Amharic*. Wiesbaden: Harrassowitz.

Leslau, Wolf. 1997a. *Ethiopic documents: Argobba. Grammar and Dictionary*. (Äthiopistische Forschungen, 47.) Wiesbaden: Harrassowitz.

Leslau, Wolf. 1997b. „Amharic Phonology". In: Kaye, Alan S. (ed.). *Phonologies of Asia and Africa (Including the Caucasus)*. Winona Lake: Eisenbrauns, I 399–430.

Little, Greta D. 1974. „Syntactic evidence of language contact: Cushitic influence in Amharic". In: Shuy, Roger W. & Bailey, Charles-James N. (eds.). *Towards tomorrow's linguistics*. Washington: Georgetown University Press, 267–75.

Lonnet, Antoine & Simeone-Senelle, Marie-Claude. 1997. „La phonologie des langues sudarabiques modernes". In: Kaye, Alan S. (ed.). *Phonologies of Asia and Africa (Including the Caucasus)*, Winona Lake: Eisenbrauns, I 337–72.

Moreno, M. M. 1949. „L'action du couchitique sur le système morphologique des langues sémitiques de l'Éthiopie". In: Lejeune, M. Michel (ed.). *Actes du sixième congrès international des linguistes*. Paris: Klincksieck, 325–32.

Palmer, F. R. 1974. „Some remarks on the grammar and phonology of the 'compound verbs' in Cushitic and Ethiopian Semitic". In: *IV Congresso Internazionale di Studi Etiopici*. Tomo II (Sezione linguistica). Roma: Accademia Nazionale dei Lincei, 71–77.

Polotsky, H. J. 1960. „Syntaxe amharique et syntaxe turque". In: *Atti del convegno internazionale di studi etiopici*. Roma: Accademia Nazionale dei Lincei.

Praetorius, Franz. 1871. *Grammatik der Tigriñasprache in Abessinien*. Halle: Buchhandlung des Waisenhauses.

Praetorius, Franz. 1879. *Die amharische Sprache*. Halle: Buchhandlung des Waisenhauses.

Praetorius, Franz. 1889. „Hamitische Bestandtheile im Aethiopischen". *Zeitschrift der Deutschen Morgenländischen Gesellschaft* 43: 317−26.

Praetorius, Franz. 1893. „Kuschitische Bestandtheile im Aethiopischen". *Zeitschrift der Deutschen Morgenländischen Gesellschaft* 47: 385−94.

Raz, Shlomo. 1983. *Tigre grammar and texts.* (Afroasiatic Dialects, 4.) Malibu: Undena.

Raz, Shlomo. 1989. „Areal features as a further criterion in elucidating the term 'Ethiopian Semitic'". *African Languages and Cultures* 2, 1: 93−108.

Rommel, Inge. 1974. „Studien zur Syntax des Amharischen: Substrat- und Adstratwirkung". In: Voigt, Wolfgang (ed.). *XVIII. Deutscher Orientalistentag. Vorträge.* (Zeitschrift der Deutschen Morgenländischen Gesellschaft. Supplement, 2.) Wiesbaden: Steiner, 606−9.

Schneider, Roger. 1959. *L'expression des compléments de verbe et de nom et la place de l'adjectif épithète en guèze.* Paris: Honoré Champion.

Ullendorff, Edward. 1955. *The Semitic languages of Ethiopia: A comparative phonology.* London: Taylor's.

Voigt, Rainer. 1977. *Das tigrinische Verbalsystem.* (Marburger Studien zur Afrika- und Asienkunde. Serie A: Afrika, 10.) Berlin: Reimer.

Voigt, Rainer. 1989. „The Development of the Old Ethiopic Consonantal System". In: Taddese Beyene (ed.). *Proceedings of the Eighth International Conference of Ethiopian Studies.* Addis Ababa: Institute of Ethiopian Studies, II 633−47.

Wagner, Ewald. 1983. *Harari-Texte in arabischer Schrift mit Übersetzung und Kommentar.* (Äthiopistische Forschungen, 13.) Wiesbaden: Steiner.

Wagner, Ewald. 1997. „Harari". In: Hetzron (ed.) 487−508.

Weninger, Stefan. 1998. „Zur Realisation des $ḍ$ (<*$ḍ$) im Altäthiopischen". *Die Welt des Orients* 29: 147 f.

Weninger, Stefan. (1999). „*kona qatala* zum Ausdruck der Vorvergangenheit im Gəʿəz?". In: Nebes, Norbert (ed.). *Tempus und Aspekt in den semitischen Sprachen.* (Jenaer Beiträge zum Vorderen Orient, 1.). Wiesbaden: Harrassowitz, 171−183.

Weninger, Stefan. (im Druck). *Das Verbalsystem des Altäthiopischen: Eine Untersuchung seiner Verwendung und Funktion unter Berücksichtigung des Interferenzproblems.* (Veröffentlichungen der Orientalischen Kommission.) Wiesbaden: Harrassowitz.

Stefan Weninger,
Universität Leipzig (Deutschland)

125. Die kaukasischen Sprachen

1. Die kaukasischen Sprachen
2. Zur Phonologie der KS
3. Der morphosyntaktische Typ der KS
4. Zur Aktantentypologie der KS
5. Aktanz in den grundsprachlichen Systemen
6. Spezielle Abkürzungen
7. Zitierte Literatur

1. Die kaukasischen Sprachen

1.1. Allgemeine Angaben

Unter „kaukasischen Sprachen" (KS) werden landläufig diejenigen Sprachen des kaukasischen Areals verstanden, die einer der drei Sprachfamilien *Südkaukasisch*, *Westkaukasisch* oder *Ostkaukasisch* zuzuordnen sind. Über die insgesamt 38 Sprachen hinaus werden (in kompakteren Gebieten) weiterhin Turksprachen (AZERI, QUMUQ, NOGAI, KARAČAI-BALQAR), iranische Sprachen (OSSETISCH, TATI, KURDISCH), ARMENISCH und RUSSICH gesprochen; hinzu tritt noch eine Reihe von Diaspora-Sprachen (GRIECHISCH, NEU-ARAMÄISCH usw.).

Die Angabe von 38 *kaukasischen* Sprachen ist als Minimum zu verstehen: Vor allem im Bereich der *ostkaukasischen* Sprachen ist die Grenzziehung zwischen Dialekt und Sprache in vielerlei Hinsicht problematisch (etwa in Bezug auf die CEZISCHEN Sprachen oder das DARGWA). Hinzu kommt, daß immer wieder Versuche unternommen werden, einzelne ausgestorbene, *asiande* Sprachen (etwa PROTO-HATTISCH, HURRITISCH-URARTÄISCH, GUTÄISCH) als „kaukasisch" zu klassifizieren. Da derartige Hypothesen (ebenso wie die baskisch-kaukasische Hypothese) bislang keinerlei überzeugenden Substantiierungen gefunden haben, sollen sie im Folgenden unberücksichtigt bleiben.

Die autochthonen *kaukasischen* Sprachen werden gewöhnlich in drei Gruppen eingeteilt: *Südkaukasisch* (jetzt vier Sprachen), *Westkaukasisch* (jetzt vier bis fünf Sprachen) und *Ostkaukasisch* (jetzt mindestens 29 Sprachen). Während *Südkaukasisch* und *Ostkaukasisch* mehr oder minder kompakte Sprachgebiete darstellen, ist das *westkaukasische* Areal durch eine relativ starke Partikularisierung einzelner Sprechgemeinschaften gekennzeichnet, die das Ergebnis einer massiven Intervention der zaristischen (zivilen und militärischen) Administration im vorigen Jahrhundert ist.

Die drei Sprachgruppen können jeweils *intern* als genetisch begründete Gruppen bezeichnet werden (vgl. 1.2.). Die Beziehungen *zwischen* den drei Sprachfamilien werden jedoch zum Teil kontrovers diskutiert: Während die südkaukasischen Sprachen aber höchstens über Konvergenzen in Beziehung zu den anderen Sprachen gesetzt werden können, existieren bezüglich der genetischen Beziehungen zwischen den beiden anderen Gruppen weitergehende Vermutungen, die auf ihre Subsumption unter *eine* gemeinsame Proto-Sprache (*Proto-Nordkaukasisch*) hinauslaufen (vgl. besonders Nikolayev/Starostin 1994). Da diese Hypothese aber — zurecht — bislang eher ablehnende Reaktionen gefunden hat, soll die Frage einer möglichen west-ostkaukasischen Sprachbeziehung zurückgestellt werden.

1.2. Die einzelnen Sprachgruppen

1.2.1. Südkaukasisch

Die südkaukasischen Sprachen (SKS) sind heute durch das GEORGISCHE, das LAZISCHE, das MINGRELISCHE und das SVANISCHE repräsentiert. Dabei wird gewöhnlich folgende Subklassifikation beschrieben (vgl. Schmidt 1962: 13):

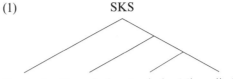

Demnach steht das SVANISCHE als relativ archaischer und marginaler Vertreter der SKS einer „zanisch-georgischen" Untergruppe gegenüber, die sich zunächst in einen GEORGISCHEN und einen „ZANISCHEN" oder LAZISCH-MINGRELISCHEN Zweig aufgespalten hatte, bevor letzterer sich als LAZISCH und MINGRELISCH vereinzelte. Lediglich das GEORGISCHE verfügt über eine nennenswerte schriftliche Tradition, die bis in das 4. Jahrhundert n. Chr. zurück reicht.

1.2.2. Westkaukasisch

Die westkaukasischen Sprachgruppe (WKS) wird durch ABXAZ, ABAZA, West- (ADYGHEI) und Ost-Čerkessisch (BESLENEY-KABARDA) konstituiert. Hinzu tritt das jetzt nahezu ausgestorbene UBYX. Alle Sprachen verfügen über mehr oder minder starke Sprechergruppen in der Diaspora (besonders in der Türkei, in Jordanien, Syrien und im Kosovo). Genetisch lassen sich die Verhältnisse in den WKS wie folgt darstellen (vgl. Smeets 1984: 41f., Colarusso 1992: 2):

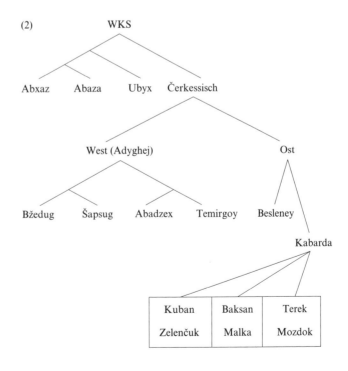

ABXAZ und ABAZA bilden die Südgruppe der WKS, zu der eventuell (in sehr entfernter Verwandtschaft) auch das UBYX zu stellen ist. Die (auch *Čerkessisch* genannte) Nordgruppe ist durch das komplexe Dialektkontinuum des Westčerkessischen (ADYGHEI) und das Ostčerkessische (BESLENEY-KABARDA) repräsentiert ((2) zeigt nur die Hauptdialekte an). Keine der genannten Sprachen verfügt über eine relevante, längere schriftliche Tradition (wohingegen die mündliche *Narten*tradition eine erhebliche Rolle spielt).

1.2.3. Ostkaukasisch

Unter der Etikette *Ostkaukasisch* (OKS) werden mindestens 29 Sprachen zusammengefaßt, die in ihrer hochgradigen Partikularisierung die arealen Gegebenheiten des Sprachgebiets (Nordosthänge des Großen Kaukasus bis zum Shah-Dagh-Gebirge) teilweise widerspiegeln. Diesbezüglich können *Flächensprachen* (etwa ČEČEN, AWAR, LAK, DARWGA, LEZGI) von *Dorfsprachen* unterschieden werden (etwa BAC (COVA-TUŠ), BOTLIX, BEŽITA, ARČI, XINALUG).

Die Subklassifikation der OKS, die auf ein bislang nur unzureichend erschlossenes, proto-ostkaukasisches Dialektkontinuum zurückzugehen scheinen, ist nur für einige Unterfamilien gesichert zu beschreiben. Die nachfolgende Übersicht gibt die Verhältnisse aus einer „konservativen" Sicht wieder (vgl. ausführlicher Schulze 1998: 134–186):

bung gibt eine Annäherung an die tatsächliche Lautung wieder.]

Als gesicherte Untergruppen ergeben sich 1) NAXISCH (mit BAC (COVA-TUŠ) als marginalem bzw. archaischerem Vertreter gegenüber dem innovativeren WAYNAX (ČEČEN und INGUŠ); 2) AWARO-ANDISCH (mit dem CEZISCHEN als vermutlich entferntem Verwandten); 3) die Samur-Gruppe der LEZGISCHEN Sprachen (alle „lezgischen" Sprachen außer ARČI, XINALUG und UDI). ARČI ist eine stark durch Konvergenzen zum awaro-andi-cezischen und lakischen Bereich gekennzeichnete LEZGISCHE (Nicht-Samur-)Sprache, während UDI näher zur Samur-Gruppe zu stellen ist. Der Status des XINALUG kann – wenn überhaupt – allenfalls als *lezgoid* bezeichnet werden. LAK und DARGWA bilden eine tentative Zentralgruppe der OKS, die allerdings bislang kaum weitergehend untermauert worden ist.

2. Zur Phonologie der KS

In phonologischer Hinsicht sind die WKS durch ein maximales Konsonantensystem gekennzeichnet (45–83 Phoneme), dem in der Regel ein (zum Teil erweitertes) diptotisches Vokalsystem (meist ə vs. /a/ [+ /e/ oder /a:/]) gegenüber steht. Die OKS verhalten sich demgegenüber etwas ausgeglichener, obschon auch sie in den meisten Fällen durch ein stark

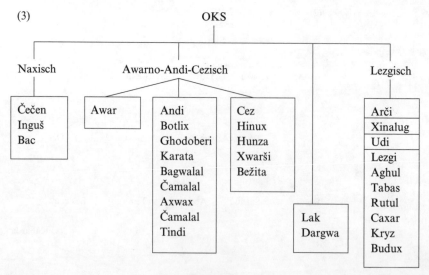

(3) OKS

[In der Bezeichnung der Einzelsprachen wird (wie im Falle der WKS) auf eine „Eindeutschung mittels *-(in)isch* verzichtet (dies gilt nicht für die bekannteren SKS); die Schrei-

differenziertes Konsonantensystem verfügen. Die Vokalsysteme basieren in der Regel auf den Kardinalvokalen /a/, /e/, /i/ und /u/, zu denen vor allem in den nördlicheren Sprachen noch /o/ tritt. Die SKS zeigen ein insgesamt harmonisierteres System, das über eine relativ geringe Zahl von Konsonanten und den Kardinalvokalen /a/, /e/, /i/, /o/ und /u/ operiert.

Typologisches Merkmal aller KS (mit Ausnahme des udischen Dialekts von NIDŽ) ist das Vorhandensein einer glottalisierten konsonantischen Reihe, die in den SKS und OKS auf Verschlußlaute und Affrikaten beschränkt ist, in den WKS aber auch auf den spirantischen Bereich ausgedehnt erscheinen kann. Dem gegenüber steht als basale Opposition das Paar [± stimmlos], das im Bereich der Labialen und Uvularen allerdings reduziert sein kann. Hinzu treten im konsonantischen Bereich in den WKS und OKS eine Reihe weiterer sekundärer (zum Teil kombinierter) Korrelationen, vornehmlich Labialisierung, Palatalisierung und Pharyngalisierung (in den WKS nur im Ubyx und vielleicht im ABXAZISCHEN Dialekt von Bzyp), sowie (in den OKS) zum Teil Gemination (oder Präruption) und Aspiration (besonders in manchen Samur-Sprachen). Als gemeinsames Merkmal der nördlichen WKS und der nördlichen OKS (mit Ausnahme des WAYNAXISCHEN) ist weiterhin das Vorhandensein einer (zum Teil defektiven) lateralen Reihe auszusehen (in den WKS fast ausnahmslos Frikative, in den OKS Affrikaten und Frikative).

In Bezug auf den Vokalismus ist Palatalisierung (Umlaut) in den SKS (z. B. einzelne Dialekte des SVANISCHEN) und den OKS (vor allem NAXISCH und LEZGISCH) zu beschreiben. Nasalierung und Längung sind selten und oftmals sekundärer Natur; Diphthongisierung tritt vornehmlich in den naxischen Sprachen auf.

3. Der morphosyntaktische Typ der KS

Analog zum phonologischen System verfügen nahezu alle KS über *ein* gemeinsames *formales* Merkmal, das gern als Bestandteil des kaukasischen Étalons beschrieben wird: Alle KS basieren (zumindest in diachroner Hinsicht) auf einem *ergativischen* Kodierungstyp (S=O;A). Allerdings ist dieses Merkmal in sehr unterschiedlicher Form morphosyntaktisch repräsentiert, weshalb davon Abstand genommen werden sollte, hierin in Bezug auf die Beziehung der drei Sprachgruppen untereinander mehr als eine zufällige Parallele sehen zu wollen. Dies gilt nicht für die einzelnen Gruppen selbst: Hier kann davon ausgegangen werden, daß auch die jeweiligen Proto-Sprachen über eine ergativische Basierung ihrer Morphosyntax verfügten. Abgesehen von diesem Merkmal (samt seiner Co-Paradigmatisierungen, etwa Personen- oder Empathie-Hierarchien) ergeben sich nur wenige und kaum prominente Strukturen, die von allen drei Sprachgruppen geteilt werden.

3.1. Die südkaukasischen Sprachen

Die SKS sind in typologischer Hinsicht unter anderem durch folgende morphosyntaktischen Merkmale gekennzeichnet:

Formale Architektur:
Präfix- und suffix-agglutinierend, starke Tendenzen zur Flexion;

Paradigmatische Architektur:
Nomen: Keine Nominalklassifikation oder Genera;
Numerus: Singular vs. Plural (vs. Kollektiva);
Kasus: Mäßig ausgeprägt; *casus rectus* vs. *casus obliquus* in älteren (pluralischen) Systemen;
Lokalisierung: Vornehmlich postpositional und über Präverbien;
NP: Gruppenflexion (am letzten Glied einer NP); partielle Kasuskonkordanz (besonders im Altgeorgischen);
Personalpronomen: Kein eigenständiges Flexionsparadigma für SAP; ABS/ERG/DAT-Identität bei SAP; Inklusiv/Exklusiv (1PL in AGR) im Svanischen; Schnittstelle in Agentivitätshierarchie: vornehmlich SAP vs. nSAP.
Deixis: Monozentrische oder (später) polyzentrische Systeme, Zwei- bis Dreiteilung der horizontalen Achse (*prox* (vs. *med*) vs. *dist*), keine Dreiteilung des Distals im vertikalen Schnitt;
Verb: Polypersonalität (bis zu zwei Aktanten); partielle Unterdifferenzierung einzelner Bereiche (bes. im aoristischen System, hier oft SAP vs. nSAP);
Spaltung des TAM-Paradigmas in drei Serien (Imperfektiv/Perfektiv/Stativ); Basierung von TAM-Formen auf eigenständiger Morphologie (Stammbildung) bzw. auf aspektueller Wirkung von Präverbien; ausgeprägte präverbiale Lokalisierungsstrategien; stark ausgeprägte SAP-zentrische Kodierungen (Medium bzw. *subjektive Version*);

Funktionale Architektur:
Aktanz: Aspektuell gespaltenes Paradigma: Akkusativische Architektur des Imperfektivs vs. partiell ergativische Architektur des Per-

fektivs (Aorist). Kasuelle Ergativität im Aorist mit AGR-Akkusativität (sowie mit Resten einer AGR-Ergativität) im GEORGISCHEN und SVANISCHEN; Ausdehnung (?) der kasuellen Ergativität auf alle nicht perfektivischen TAM im LAZISCHEN, auf aoristische Intransitiva im MINGRELISCHEN. Ansätze einer *split-S*-Typologie; Präferenz für Stellungsakkusativität (A(IO)(O)V); Inversion (IO-O-V) bei *verba sentiendi* und in stativischer Perfekt-Reihe;
NP: Dem-Num-ATTR-N (z. T. N-ATTR); kasuelle Possession (N-GEN N);
Perspektivierung: Passiv, Medium; Antipassiv als imperfektivische Reihe grammatikalisiert; Perspektivierungsmorpheme (*Version*);
Junktion: Ausgeprägte Subordination über Nebensätze; Relativsätze; akkusativischer A-*pivot*;
Topikalisierung: Links- und Rechtsverschiebungen; Topikpartikeln.

Demnach folgen die SKS einer ausbalancierten *head-dependent*-Typologie mit Tendenz zum *head marking*. Sie kodiert in morphologischer Hinsicht eine referenzdominierte Mittelstellung auf dem Akkusativ-Ergativ-Kontinuum (AEK), die durch ein mittelmäßig ausgeprägtes kasuelles System und durch komplexe Verfahren der Kongruenz signalisiert wird. In morphologischer Hinsicht ist der verbale Bereich stärker belastet, was eine größere Variabilität in Bezug auf die Relationierung von Aktanten anzeigt. Die Beispiele in (4)–(7) verdeutlichen einige dieser Aspekte:

(4) NEUGEORGISCH (*field notes*)
(a) *is   surat-s*
DIST:NOM Bild-DAT
da-u-χat'-av-d-a
PV-3:IO-malen-PRES-PAST-3:A
'Er/sie würde das Bild für ihn/sie gemalt haben.'
(b) *im   k'ac-ma   q'velaper-i*
DIST.OBL Mann-ERG alles-NOM
ga-i-g-o   rac
PV-SV-verstehen-3.:A:AOR REL
mo-i-sm-in-a
PV-SV-hören-CAUS-3:A:AOR
'Jener Mann verstand alles, was er sich anhörte.'
(c) *k'ac-s   ʒm-is(a)-tvis   c'eril-i*
Mann-DAT Bruder-GEN-für Brief.NOM
mi-u-c'er-ia
PV-3:IO-schreiben-3:S:PERF
'Der Mann hat dem Bruder einen Brief geschrieben.'

(d) ALTGEORGISCH (Mt 1,24)
gan-i-ǧviʒ-a   ioseb
PV-SV-erwachen-3:S:AOR Joseph.ABS
ʒil-isa   mi-s-gan   da
Schlaf-GEN ART-GEN-PP(ABL) und
q'-o   egre vitarca
machen-3:A:AOR so wie
u-brʒan-a   ma-s
3:IO-befehlen-3:A:AOR PROX-DAT
angeloz-man   upl-isa-man.
Engel-ERG   Herr-GEN-ERG
'Joseph erwachte aus dem Schlaf und machte [es] so, wie der Engel des Herren ihm befahl.'

(5) MINGRELISCH (Harris 1991b: 367 = Kluge 1916: 86[11])
ate uk'ulaši ʒima-k-ə
PROX letzter Bruder-ERG-EMPH
i-pirk-ə
SV-denken-3:S:AOR
'Der jüngste Bruder dachte nach.'

(6) LAZISCH (Holisky 1991: 450)
iy k'aoba   do iy p'at'oba
all Gutes.ABS und all Schlechtes.ABS
nena-k   i-kom-s
Zunge-ERG SV-machen.PRES-3:A
'Die ZUNGE macht alles Gute und Schlechte.'

(7) SVANISCH (Deeters 1930: 88)
ešxu ǧolya:ki:l
ein Lämmchen.ABS
x-e-q'ed-a-ì: eʒi
3:IO-RV-AUX-3:S:AOR-und DIST:ABS
čotʒie [ču-ad-x-o-ʒi-e]
hinunter-dorthin-3:IO-schlach-ten-3:A:AOR
'Sie hatte ein Lämmchen und das schlachtete sie.'

(4a) stellt eine einfache transitive Proposition mit „indirektem Objekt" dar. Das Verbum *dauχat'av-da* „würde gemalt haben" gehört zur präsentischen Serie, weshalb eine „akkusativische" Kodierung vorliegt. Hingegen ist *gaigo* „verstand" in (4b) eine aoristische Form, die eine kasuelle Ergativität erzwingt (*k'acma* (Mann-ERG)). In (4c) bedingt das perfektivische *miuc'eria* „ist/hat geschrieben" schließlich eine *inverse* Markierung (A>IO>AGR; O>S>AGR). (4d) gibt eine komplexe transitive Konstruktion im ALTGEORGISCHEN wieder: Markant ist hierbei einerseits der sogenannte *status absolutus*, der bei Eigennamen den Nominativ (-*i*) ersetzt; andererseits liegt in *ʒilisa misgan* und in *angelozman uplisaman* eine N-ATTR-Reihung vor, die in der zweiten NP zudem noch durch eine Kasusattrak-

125. Die kaukasischen Sprachen

tion (*upl-isa-man* (Herr-GEN-ERG)) gekennzeichnet ist.

(5) verdeutlicht das Übergreifen der ERG-Markierung im MINGRELISCHEN *(ǯima-k* (Bruder-ERG)) auf S-Aktanten im Aorist, während (6) die Generalisierung der ERG-Konstruktion in der präsentischen Reihe des LAZISCHEN belegt. Zudem wird die Position direkt vor dem Verb hier zur Fokussierung genutzt. In (7) schließlich liegt ein Beispiel für die ausgeprägte Tendenz des SVANISCHEN zum *pro-drop* vor.

3.2. Die westkaukasischen Sprachen

Die gern als *polysynthetisch* bezeichneten WKS operieren über eine komplexe Verbalmorphologie, der in der Regel ein schwach ausgebautes Paradigma der (pro)nominalen Flexion gegenüber steht.

Formale Architektur:
Präfix- und suffix-agglutinierend, polysynthetisch;

Paradigmatische Architektur:
Nomen: Keine Nominalklassifikation oder Genera;
Numerus: Singular vs. Plural (vs. Kollektiva);
Kasus: Kaum ausgeprägt; *casus rectus* vs. *casus obliquus* in den nördlichen WKS;
Lokalisierung: Postpositional oder über Prä-/Postverbien;
NP: Gruppenflexion (am letzten Glied einer NP);
Personalpronomen: Kein eigenständiges Flexionsparadigma (abgesehen von Numerus); ABS/ERG-Identität bei SAP; ansatzweise Inklusiv/Exklusiv (1PL und 2PL) im ABXAZ; Schnittstelle in Agentivitätshierarchie: vornehmlich SAP vs. nSAP.
Deixis: Monozentrische oder (später) polyzentrische Systeme, Zweiteilung bzw. Dreiteilung der horizontalen Achse (*prox/med/dist*), keine Dreiteilung des Distals im vertikalen Schnitt;
Verb: Polypersonalität (bis zu vier Aktanten); Sexus bzw. Klassendifferenzierung partiell in den südlichen WKS; Basierung von TAM-Formen auf eigenständiger Morphologie (z. T. mit Postpositionen verwandt); ausgeprägte prä- und postverbiale Lokalisierungsstrategien; stark ausgeprägte logozentrische Kodierungen;

Funktionale Architektur:
Aktanz: Verbale (AGR-)Ergativität mit ergativischer (zum Teil auch akkusativischer) Serialisierung der Personalzeichen (O-A-V bzw. (seltener) A-O-V); Pragmatische Effekte durch Stellungsvarianz in polypersonaler Kette; Präferenz für Stellungsakkusativität (A(IO)(O)V); Inversion (IO-O-V) bei *verba sentiendi*;
NP: Dem-Num[Ink]-N-ATTR; analytische (präfixale) Possession ((N) POSS-N);
Perspektivierung: Antipassiv und Passiv; Inkorporation; Perspektivierungspartikeln;
Junktion: In AGR reduzierte Subordination vornehmlich über Partizipien und Konverbien; Relativsätze (REL-*head*); akkusativischer A-pivot (mit *switch reference*-Markierung z. B. im KABARDA); Verbserialisierung;
Topikalisierung: Links- oder Rechtsverschiebung; Topikpartikeln.

Die nachfolgenden Beispiele sollen einzelne Aspekte der genannten Parameter verdeutlichen:

(8) KABARDA (Colarusso 1992: 135; 175)
(a) λ'ə-m   gʷaʒə-r
    Mann-OBL Weizen-REF:ABS
    Ø-y-ə-ʔʷəx̂ə-ž̌ə-aɣ-ś
    3:O-3:A-nPRES-entfernen-RES-PAST-AFF
    'Der Mann erntete den Weizen.'

(b) a-se-šx̂ʷa-m-k'ja
    DIST-Messer-groß-OBL-INSTR
    λ'ə-r   Ø-λ'a-ž̌ə-aɣ-ś
    Mann-REF:ABS 3:S-sterben-RES-PAST-AFF
    'Der Mann starb durch das/jenes Schwert'

(9) ADYGHEI (Smeets 1984: 69)
    sə-qə-b-de-kʷ'e-ž̌ə-śʷə-št-ep
    1:S-hierher-2:POSS-COM-gehen-FREQ-POT-FUT-NEG
    'Ich werde nicht mit dir zurückkehren können'

(10) ABXAZ (Gecadze 1979: 60)
     lara l-nap'ə   a-ćəmazaʕʷ
     3f   3f:POSS-Hand ART-krank
     l-xə
     3f:POSS-Kopf
     i-na-kʷ-l-k'ə-Ø-yt'
     3i:O-3i:POSS-SUPER-3f:A-legen-AOR-DYN:IND:ASS
     'Sie legte ihre kranke Hand auf ihren Kopf.'

(8a) gibt die transitive Standardkonstruktion im KABARDA wieder, wobei A in der NP über einen Obliquus (*-m*) angezeigt ist, während das overte O durch einen (Referenz etablierenden) Absolutiv (*-r*) kodiert wird. Beide Aktanten werden im Verb über AGR angezeigt. (8b) ist ein Beispiel für den intransitiven Bildungstyp (hier mit topikalisiertem Instrumental). (9) repräsentiert eine komplexe verbale Kette im ADYGHEI, die satzwertig ist.

(10) ist ein Beispiel für den kasuslosen Kodierungstyp des ABXAZ mit tri-aktantiellem Verb (O-IO(<LOC)-A).

3.3. Die ostkaukasischen Sprachen

Die Morphoyntax der OKS wird gewöhnlich unter Bezugnahme auf eine relativ einheitliche Typologie beschrieben, die mit dem Stichwort *nominalklassifizierende Ergativ-Sprachen* angezeigt wird. Tatsächlich erweist sich dieser Aspekt als zentrales Moment der Architektur vieler OKS, obschon kaum von einem „einheitlichen" Typus ausgegangen werden kann. Insgesamt sind die OKS durch die folgenden, basalen Aspekte gekennzeichnet:

Formale Architektur:
(Stark suffix-)agglutinierend, geringe Tendenzen zur Flexion;

Paradigmatische Architektur:
Nomen: Verdeckte (sekundär z. T. offene) Nominalklassifikation (zwei bis acht Klassen);
Numerus: Singular vs. (z. T. klassifizierender) Plural (vs. Kollektiva);
Kasus: Funktionale vs. lokale Kasus, partiell *casus rectus* vs. *casus obliquus*. Oftmals Basierung der Flexionsparadigmata auf z. T. klassifizierend wirkenden Stammerweiterungen (Absolutiv-, Obliquus-, Ergativ-, und Genitiv-Flexion);
Lokalisierung: Lokalkasus, postpositional (z. T. durch Präverbien gestützt);
NP: Partiell Klassenkonkordanz; Gruppenflexion (am Nomen), partiell attributive Obliquusmarkierungen (z. T. in determinierenden Funktion);
Personalpronomen: Partiell eigenständiges Flexionsparadigma; Inklusiv/Exklusiv in 50% der OKS; komplexe Schnitte innerhalb der Agentivitätshierarchie (z. B. SAP vs. nSAP; SAP(1) vs. nSAP(1), SAP. SG vs. SAP. PL usw.);
Deixis: Monozentrische oder (später) polyzentrische Systeme, Zweiteilung der horizontalen Achse (*prox* vs. *dist*), oftmals Dreiteilung des Distals im vertikalen Schnitt (dist →, dist ↑, dist ↓);
Verb: Monokongruenz über Klassenzeichen in etwa 75% der OKS, daneben polykongruente Systeme (Person/Klasse oder (im Tabasaran) Person/Person), monopersonale Systeme nur im Udi bzw. sonst in Ansätzen vorhanden;
Basierung von TAM-Formen auf Auxiliarstrukturen oder (Lokal-)Kasus; daneben eigenständige Tempusmorpheme; Aspektsysteme oft über Ablaut realisert; präverbiale Lokalisierungsstrategien;

Funktionale Architektur:
Aktanz: Kasusbasierte Ergativität mit ergativischer (zum Teil auch akkusativischer) Kongruenz; DOM in Agensbereich relevant (Agens<Instr<Lok), im Udi DOM auch im Patiensbereich (indet<det); partiell *split*-A-Strukturen (besonders bei SAP); Transitivitätsgrad oftmals über Auxiliare angezeigt, daneben *labile* Verben; Präferenz für Stellungsakkusativität (A(IO)(O)V); Inversion (IO-O-V) bei *verba sentiendi*;
NP: Dem-Num-Attr-N-Reihung; kasuelle Possession (N-GEN N);
Perspektivierung: Vornehmlich *bi-absolutive* Strukturen (A_j>ABS O_i>ABS AGR_i-V AUX-AGR_j), daneben partiell Antipassiv und (vornehmlich im Udi) Passiv;
Junktion: Subordination vornehmlich über Partizipien und Konverbien; Relativsätze nur im Udi; akkusativischer A- oder (seltener) ergativischer O-*pivot*.
Topikalisierung: Links- und Rechtsverschiebung oder Topikpartikeln (partiell über Klassen- oder Personalzeichen).

Die genannten Parameter erscheinen in den Einzelsprachen hochgradig partikularisiert, weshalb nur mit Schwierigkeiten von einem ostkaukasischen Étalon in der Morphosyntax ausgegangen werden kann (vgl. ausführlicher Schulze 2000). Folgende Beispielsätze können die diesbezügliche Variationsbreite andeuten:

(11)   HUNZA (Van den Berg 1995: 268[18])
bəl-a: bed boc'-lo-s
MED-ADV dann Schaf-OBL-GEN
reqen-no   m-iy(:)e-n-no
Herde(IV)-und IV-senden-GER:PRET-und
λ'odo   Ø-ãq'e-n   lo
oben   i-kommen-GER:PRET I.AUX:PRES
weˆxa.
Schafhirte(I).ABS
'Und so hat dann ein Hirte seine Schafherde ausgesandt und ist hinaufgekommen.'

(12)   KUBAČI (Magometov 1963: 327[2])
ˁab-a:g̃ʷe   duˆx-ub-žila
drei-vier   gehen-GER:PRÄT-bis=dann
wiy-b-e:q:ib-li-sa-w
PV(SUB.ABL)-III-bringen-GER:PRÄS-AUX:PRÄS-I
sa:l   bi:k'a-zi-b   ˁašak-ya
wieder   klein-ATTR-III Kessel(III).ABS-auch
b-e:n-kab-i-c:ul
III-PV(ILLATIV)-legen-GER:PAST-CV(PAST)
'Als drei vier [Tage] (ver)gangen waren, brachte [er] [ihn] zurück, nachdem er auch einen kleinen Kessel hineingelegt hatte.'

(13) UDI (Mt 4,22)
wa šo-t'-ǧ-on   t'e[s]sahat
und DIST-SE:OBL-PL-ERG sofort
k'ic'ke gämi-n-ax   waʕ ič-ǧ-o
klein   Boot-SE-DAT₂ und REFL-PL-GEN
bab-ax   bart-i
Vater-DAT₂ lassen-AOR
ta-q'un-c-i
PV-3pl:S-gehen:AOR-AOR
še-t'-a-qošt'an.
DIST-SE:OBL-GEN-hinter
'Und nachdem jene sofort ihr kleines Boot und ihren Vater verlassen hatten, gingen sie hinter ihm her.'

In Beispiel (11) ist der „kanonische" Kodierungstyp einer Reihe von OKS repräsentiert: O (*boc'olos reqen* „Schafherde") wird mittels des Klassenzeichens *-m-* (Klasse IV) am transitiven Verb wieder aufgenommen, während A im Verb nicht angezeigt ist. Kasuell wäre *wex̂a-l-lo* (Hirte-SE-ERG) statt absolutivischem *wex̂a* zu erwarten (vgl. *wex̂a-l-lo n-uq x̂o* (Hirte-SE-ERG V-essen.PRES Fleisch(V).ABS) „Der Hirte ißt Fleisch"), doch folgt das Hunza der in den OKS häufiger zu beobachtenden Tendenz, daß der A-pivot sich kasuell nach demjenigen Verb ausrichtet, dem er in einer verbalen Kette am nächsten steht (hier intransitives *ãq'en lo* „kommend"). Das Beispiel aus dem KUBAČI in (12) verdeutlicht ein bikongruentes Verfahren auf der Basis der Klassenmarkierung (*wiy-b-e:q:iblisa-w* „jemand [mask] hat etwas [-hum] zurückgebracht"). Die kasuelle Markierung folgt nicht dem zu erwartenden, biabsolutiven Schema (**id id wiybe:q:iblisaw*), sondern sie ist sekundär (nach der Univerbierung der Gruppe Verb.GER-AUX) nach dem ergativischen Schema ausgerichtet, vgl. *suq mallaras:it:in-ni-dil de:nil-c:il ʕašak b-iš-sabalčunni-sa-w* „Eines Tages lieh sich Mulla Nasreddin (ERG>AGR(-*w*)) von einem Nachbarn einen Kessel (ABS>AGR(*b*-))" (Magometov 1963: 327[1b]). Die verbale Gruppe ist von erheblicher Komplexität: präverbial markiert und der Verbstamm selbst über ein Ablautschema aspektuell markiert, das mit Gerundialsuffixen und Auxiliaren zur TAM-Bildung interagiert (in (12) erzeugt *wiybe:q:iblisaw* einen Inferential). Innerhalb der NP ist die durchgängige ATTR-Markierung (*bi:k'a-zi-b ʕašak* „kleiner Kessel") kennzeichnend für die zentralen OKS DARGWA (und eingeschränkt) LAK. (13) gibt einen Beleg für das monokongruente, personenbasierte System des UDI. Hier kongruiert das Personalzeichen grundsätzlich *akkusativisch*. Das System des UDI ist darüber hinaus durch die Einführung eines DOM-Typs gekennzeichnet, der auf der Spaltung von O nach [±det] oder [±ref] (ABS vs. DAT₂) beruht und die Charakterisierung von A als „Subjekt" ermöglicht (analog zur entsprechenden Kongruenz). Die ergativische Markierung von *šot'ǧon* „jene" in (13) ist nicht durch das finite Verb *taq'unci* (intr.) „sie gingen" bedingt, sondern durch das eingebettete, partizipiale *barti* „verlassen habend", was analog zur Regelung des HUNZA in (11) zu interpretieren ist: Der A-pivot richtet sich kasuell nach demjenigen Verb, dem er in einer verbalen Kette am nächsten steht.

4. Zur Aktantentypologie der KS

4.1. Vorbemerkungen

Die Ausgangslage der Empirie in den KS bedingt, daß Untersuchungen zur diachronen Typologie des Sprachgebiets nur in sehr geringem Umfang auf ältere Quellen zurückgreifen kann. Lediglich das GEORGISCHE verfügt über eine nennenswerte schriftliche Tradition (Spekulationen über die Möglichkeit, einige *agwanische* Inschriften aus Nordazerbaidschan bzw. Süddagestan (6.–9. Jh. n. Chr.) als eine frühe Form des UDI (oder einer anderen LEZGISCHEN Sprache) zu deuten, sollen hier unberücksichtigt bleiben). Die mündliche Tradierung nicht adaptierter Texte ist im Kaukasus nahezu unbekannt. Insofern müssen Hypothesen über die diachrone Dynamik der morphosyntaktischen Basisarchitektur der KS vornehmlich auf drei Verfahren beruhen: 1. Interne Rekonstruktion; 2. formale externe Rekonstruktion, 3. typologischer Vergleich und Bezugnahme auf universelle Tendenzen des Systemwandels. Dabei gilt, daß je einheitlicher ein System ist, d. h. je geringer die Zahl anzutreffender Variationen ist, desto weniger ist das Verfahren der internen Rekonstruktion anwendbar. Dies gilt innerhalb der KS vor allem für die WKS. Die externe Rekonstruktion ist um so erfolgversprechender, je geringer die Zahl der betroffenen Sprachen ist (auch wenn hierdurch bisweilen eine relativ geringe diachrone Tiefe erreicht wird). Dies gilt innerhalb der KS besonders für die SKS, aber auch für die Untergruppen der WKS und einzelne Untergruppen der OKS. Die Bezugnahme auf universelle Tendenzen des Systemwandels und typologische „Universalien" sollte als weitergehender Parameter immer dann herangezogen werden, wenn die Verfahren 1 und 2 zu schwachen Ergebnissen oder von solchen mit relativ geringer Plausibilität führen. In Bezug auf die Datenlage der KS sind die drei genannten Verfahren allerdings kaum zu trennen, weshalb ihr Ansatz im Folgenden auch nicht immer kenntlich gemacht wird. Zur Charakterisierung der Systemdynamik innerhalb der KS werden folgende paradigmatische bzw. kategorielle Größen (beispielhaft) ausgewählt: Aktantielle Funktionen und ihre Kodierung ((pro)nominale Kasus), Kongruenzverfahren, die Einbettung der Aktanz in TAM-Systeme sowie Perspektivierung. In einem ersten Schritt werden diese Systeme im einzelnen genauer vorgestellt, bevor in 5. Aspekte ihrer diachronen Typologie summarisch angesprochen werden.

4.2. Die Kodierung aktantieller Funktionen

4.2.1. Nomina

Wie bereits gesagt werden nahezu alle KS im nominalen Bereich vom einer kasuellen {S=O;A}-Typologie dominiert. Dabei ist der {S=O}-Bereich in der Regel unmarkiert (*Absolutiv*). Ausnahmen hiervon machen einerseits die SKS, die vermutlich schon grundsprachlich das Demonstrativum *ig-* als postponierten Artikel bei Absolutiva (> *-i*) verwendet hatten (Harris 1991a: 24). Relikte des Ø-markierten ABS finden sich in allen SKS (*casus indefinitus*). Die (sekundäre) Markierung des ABS mittels einer artikelähnlichen Struktur deutet darauf hin, daß im nominalen Bereich für die SKS grundsprachlich von einer {S=O}-dominierten kasuellen Ergativität auszugehen ist. Hinzu tritt im Georgischen eine erhebliche Tendenz zur (z. T. optionalen) Markierung des aoristischen {S=O}-Bereichs durch den Ergativ, wodurch eine Art von „Aktiv-Typologie" erreicht wird, die im Mingrelischen in einer grundsätzlichen Parallelkodierung von aoristischem A und S mittels des Ergativs vereinheitlicht worden ist. Andererseits haben die nördlichen WKS eine Markierung des *casus rectus* auf der Basis eines Morphems *-r* entwickelt, die eine eindeutige Referentialität der betreffenden NP anzeigt, vgl. (in (14a) ersetzt der Absolutiv zudem den erwarteten Ergativ):

(14) KABARDA (Colarusso 1992: 57;53)
 (a) *λə*   *Ø-y-a-ś'ə-f*
 Mann:ABS 3:O-3:A-PRES-machen-POT
 'Jeglicher Mann kann es machen'

(b) *λə-r*
 Mann-REF.ABS
 ma-a-k^w'ə-a
 3:S:INTR:PRES:DYN-PRES-bewegen-INTR
 'Der Mann kommt.'

(c) *λə-m*   *Ø-y-a-ś'ə-f*
 Mann-ERG 3:O-3:A-PRES-machen-POT
 'Der Mann kann es machen'

Tendenzen zur Markierung des {S=O}-Bereichs finden sich auch den OKS, wenn auch weniger systematisch: Hier ist vornehmlich der Bereich der nominalisierten Adjektive bzw. Pronomina angesprochen, vgl.:

(15) AGHUL (Dirr 1907: 79[27])
 alirq'^w-a-f
 sitzen-PART:PRES-NO:ABS
 arq'a-t:-i
 machen-PART:PRES-NO:OBL-ERG
 pu-na-y ...
 sagen.PRES-GER:PRET-PRET
 'Der, der Sitzgestelle zu machen pflegte, sagte ...' (lit. 'Sitzendes Machender sagte ...')

Der A-Bereich ist in den OKS in unmarkierten Fällen durch einen *casus ergativus* repräsentiert, der entweder eine eigenständige morphologische Größe darstellt oder synkretistisch mit anderen Funktionen zusammenfällt, vgl.:

(16) ERG
 ERG<INSTR
 ERG<INSTR<GEN
 ERG<{*casus obliqui*}

Als Beispiel für die ersten drei Typen sollen die folgenden Belege dienen:

(17) HUNZA (Van den Berg 1995: 43)
 (ERG)
 oλu-l   *b-uč'e*
 DIST:OBL-ERG IV-schneiden:PRES
 ēš   *č'it'o-d*
 Apfel(IV):ABS Messer-OBL-INSTR
 'Er/Sie schneidet den Apfel mit einem Messer.'

(18) UDI (*field notes*)
 (ERG<INSTR)
 še-t'-in   *e^sr ś-n-ux*   *mex-en*
 DIST-SE-ERG Apfel-SE-DAT₂ Messer-INSTR
 kac'-ne-xe
 (<erg) schneiden-3:A-AUX:PRES
 'Er/Sie schneidet den Apfel mit einem Messer.'

(19) LAK (Bouda 1949: 41)
      (ERG<INSTR<GEN)
      dina-**l**   mˤurši-s:a
      Dina-ERG   klein:ATTR
      ka-ru-nni-**l**
      Hand-PL-SE-INSTR (<ERG)
      ga-na-**l**
      DIST↓-SE[+MASC]-GEN(<ERG)
      huqa   k'unk'u   b-ull-ay
      Hemd(III).ABS berühren III-machen:
      b-iya
      DUR-PART:PRES III-AUX:AOR
      'Dina berührte sein Hemd mit ihren kleinen Händen.'

Die inhärente Gradierung des A-Bereichs kann über die offene Differenzierung von ERG vs. INSTR hinaus in vielen Fällen kasuell angezeigt werden (mit − wie zu erwarten − detransitivierender Wirkung). (20) ist ein Beispiel für die Verwendung lokaler Kasus zur Kodierung des Rollenaspekts <SOURCE>, (21) gradiert A über den Genitiv:

(20) ARČI (Alekseev 1979: 87)
      (a) quˤt'i-**li**   lo
          Donner-ERG Junge(III).ABS
          eˤwq'ni
          III.erschrecken.PRET
          'Der Donner erschreckte den Jungen.'
      (b) q'uˤt'i-li-λ:**iš**   lo
          Donner-SUB.ABL Junge(III).ABS
          eˤwq'ni
          III.erschrecken.PRET
          'Der Junge erschrak vor dem Donner.'

(21) ARČI (Alekseev 1979: 86)
      (a) to-w-**mu**   lur
          DIST-I-ERG:MASC Auge.PL.ABS
          c'anši   i
          blinzeln.PART IV.AUX.PRÄS
          'Er blinzelt mit den Augen'
      (b) to-w-mu-**n**   lur
          DIST-I-SE:OBL:MASC-GEN Auge.PL.ABS
          c'anši   i
          blinzeln.PART IV.AUX.PRÄS
          'Seine Augen blinzeln.'

Die Einbettung der ergativischen Funktion in den Funktionsbereich eines allgemeinen Obliquus ist für alle drei Gruppen der KS − wenn auch in unterschiedlichem Umfang − belegt: Im ALTGEORGISCHEN zum Beispiel erfolgt sie über die Opposition -*ni* (ABS) vs. -*t(a)* (OBL) als *eine* Form der Pluralmarkierung. Im Kabarda markiert das oblique Morphem -*m* Agens, Adressat, Benefaktiv, Lokativ (statischer Verben), Allativ (dynamischer

Verben), aber auch den Patiens in Antipassivkonstruktionen, vgl.:

(22) KABARDA (Colarusso 1992: 177)
      (a) pśaaśa-**m**   gʲaana-ha-**r**
          Mädchen-REF.ERG Hemd-PL-REF.ABS
          Ø-q'a-y-a-də-ha-r
          3:O-HOR-3:A-nähen-PL-PRES
          'Das Mädchen näht die Hemden.'
      (b) pśaaśa-**r**   gʲaana-ha-**m**
          Mädchen-REF.ABS Hemd-PL-REF.OBL
          Ø-q'ə-y-ha-a-də-a
          3:A-HOR-3:IO-PL-DAT-nähen-INTR
          'Das Mädchen versucht, die Hemden zu nähen.'

In den OKS spielt die Dichotomie ABS vs. OBL eine zentrale Rolle im Verfahren der nominalen und pronominalen Stammerweiterung. Hierbei wird der Obliquus durch ein zusätzliches Morphem gekennzeichnet, das entweder einem der funktionalen Kasus (gewöhnlich ERG oder GEN) entspricht, oder das die Basis für die Anfügung von Kasusmorphemen bildet. Das Verfahren der Stammerweiterung wird gern als Reflex eines ursprünglich diptotischen Kasussystems in den OKS gesehen (vgl. Topuria 1995, kritisch Schulze 1998: 210−213). Die erheblich ausgeprägte Polymorphie der Stammerweiterung in manchen OKS läßt vermuten, daß hierin *auch* alte semantische Klassifikationsverfahren repräsentiert sind, die zur Gradierung des A-Bereichs beigetragen haben.

Der IO-Bereich wird in den KS, die über Kasusmorpheme verfügen, gewöhnlich durch den Dativ (bzw. den Obliquus) angezeigt (in transitiven und intransitiven Propositionen). In den SKS (bis auf LAZISCH) übernimmt der Dativ auch die Funktion eines Akkusativs zur Kodierung des O-Bereichs mit Tempora der (präsentischen) „ersten Serie", vgl.:

(23) GEORGISCH (Aronson 1991: 273)
      p'ropesor-i   st'udent'-**s** c'ign-**s**
      Professor-NOM Student-DAT Buch-DAT
      ga-u-gzavn-i-s
      PV-3:IO-senden-SERIE.I-3:A
      'Der Professor wird dem Studenten ein Buch senden.'

4.2.2. Pronomina

Während die WKS als mehr oder weniger konsequente Pro-Drop-Sprachen bezeichnet werden können, spielen die Paradigmata der Personalpronomina in den übrigen KS meist eine wichtige Rolle in der Kodierung der aktantiellen Funktionen von Sprachaktteilnehmern (SAP) und Nicht-Sprechaktteilnehmern (nSAP). Dabei folgen alle SKS und etwa die Hälfte der OKS den Vorgaben der Personenhierarchie, d. h. die ABS/ERG-Dichotomie wird zugunsten einer *akkusativischen* (oder, im kasuellen Sinne), *neutralen*) Markierungstechnik zusammengefaßt, vgl.:

(24) GEORGISCH (Aronson 1991: 271)
čven šen g-xed-av-t
1PL.ABS 2SG.ABS 2:O-sehen-SERIE.I-PL
'Wir sehen dich.'

(25) AGHUL (CIRXE) (Magometov 1970: 215[9])
wun da-r-i-šin
2SG.ABS NEG-gehen-PRES-COND
čin was s:as:a s:e'
1.PL(e).ABS 2SG.DAT ein Maß.ABS
q'ur-an ye-s-i
Korn-SE-GEN geben-INF-AUX.PRÄS
'Wenn du nicht kommst, geben wir dir ein Maß Korn.'

Etwa 50% der OKS laufen der Silverstein-Hierarchie zuwider (vgl. Schulze (to appear)). Ihre Paradigmata der Personalpronomina sind in unterschiedlichem Umfang von einer ABS/ERG-Dichotomie betroffen, wobei folgende (nicht umfassende) Typologie erstellt werden kann:

(26) ABS = ERG   vs.   ABS ≠ ERG
      Alle   Ø
      SG   PL
      PL   SG
      1Sg   Rest
      2Sg   Rest
      1SG/PL   Rest
      1SG/PL(i)   Rest

Dabei ist zusätzlich zu unterscheiden, ob die morpohologischen Inventarien zur Kodierung des Ergativs primärer (pronominaler) oder sekundärer (nominaler) Herkunft sind (im BOTLIX wird der Ergativ der 1SG lexikalisch unterschieden: ABS *den(i)*, ERG *iš(:)kur*. Als Beispiel für eine ERG-Markierung von SAP mag dienen:

(27) AGHUL (KEREN) (Magometov 1970: 217[28])
zaš 'at:i-wu-čin
1SG.ERG herausreißen-AUX.PRES-COND
zus altuq-ra c'ay-wa
1SG.DAT Rest.ABS-TOP geben.PRES-Q
waš
2SG.ERG
'Gibst du mir den REST, wenn ich [es] herausreiße?'

Die Trennung von ABS und ERG kann im Andi und im Keleb-Dialekt des Awar weitergehend als Signal einer Frauen- (Andi) bzw. Männersprache (Keleb) genutzt werden (vgl. Cercvaʒe 1965: 198 ff., Mikailov 1959: 423). Ansonsten spielen Sexus-Differenzierungen in Bezug auf die Kodierung aktantieller Funktionen keine hervorragende Rolle. Eine lexikalische Sexus-Differenzierung ist nur in den südlichen WKS belegt (Abxaz: 2SG *wa(ra)* [+masc] vs. *ba(ra)* [+fem]), in den nominalklassifizierenden OKS erfolgt eine solche Differenzierung über das gesamte Paradigma hinweg mittels kongruierenden Klassenzeichen, vgl.:

(28) CAXUR (*field notes*)
zə Ø-ək'əyk'ar-as-or-na
1SG.ABS I-krank:RED-INF-AUX-1:S
'Ich [Mann] werde krank sein.'

(29) *ğu y-ək'əyk'ar-as-or-Ø*
2SG.ABS II-krank:RED-INF-AUX-n1:S
'Du [Frau] wirst krank sein.'

Der nSAP-Bereich wird gewöhnlich über zum Teil als *anaphoricum* spezialisierte Demonstrativpronomen realisiert. Dabei ist (mit Ausnahme der südlichen WKS) die ABS/ERG-Dichotomie in der Regel durchgeführt, vgl.

(30) LAK (Žirkov 1955: 69)
tay-nn-al tay-nn-an q:ata
3PL-SE-ERG 3PL-SE-DAT Haus(v).ABS
b-ay
v-bauen.PRES
'Sie bauen ihnen ein Haus.'

4.3. Aktanten und Kongruenz

Die Kodierung aktantieller Funktionen mit Hilfe von Kongruenzverfahren sollte in Bezug auf die Gegebenheiten der KS anhand des nachfolgenden Schemas beschrieben werden:

(31)

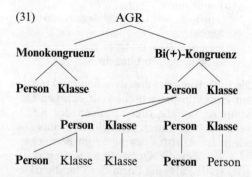

Demnach stellen die kategoriellen Größen *Person* und *Klasse* die zentralen Parameter der Kongruenz dar. In monokongruenten Systemen stehen sie sich diametral gegenüber, während in poly-, meist bikongruenten Systemen beide Größen gemischt erscheinen können. In diesem Fall liegt in den KS in der Regel (bis auf das ABXAZ) historisch gesehen eine Klassenbasierung vor, obwohl aktuell die Personenmarkierung (etwa im TABASARAN) dominanter sein kann. Die in den KS belegten Kongruenztypen sind in (31) durch Fettdruck kenntlich gemacht.

4.3.1. Monokongruente Systeme

Monokongruente Systeme, also solche, die ausschließlich *einen* (funktional fixierten) Aktanten am Verb kodieren, sind vornehmlich innerhalb der OKS dokumentiert. Darüber hinaus finden sich solche Verfahren auch in den SKS, hier in Abhängigkeit von dem zugrunde liegenden TAM-Split. Während die OKS-Systeme klassenkongruent sind, basiert die partielle Monokongruenz der SKS auf der Kategorie *Person*.

Prototypisch kann die Klassenkongruenz in den OKS dem {S=O}-Bereich zugeordnet werden. Sie basiert auf einer verdeckten, d. h. nicht am klassifizierten Nomen selbst erscheinenden Markierung (offene Markierungstechniken sind etwa bei Verwandtschaftstermini möglich), die zwischen zwei (TABASARAN) und acht Klassen (ČEČENISCHE Dialekte) etabliert. Auszugehen ist von einem Basissystem, das über vier Klassen operierte. Es ist zwischen phonetischer und semantischer Motiviertheit der Klassenallokation zu unterscheiden. Semantisch motiviert sind in jedem Fall die gewöhnlich „erste" und „zweite Klasse" genannten Kategorien (I = [MASC; HUM], II = [FEM; HUM], wobei der Schnittpunkt gegenüber den übrigen Klassen neben [HUM] u. a. auch [SPRECHFÄHIG], [INITIIERT] oder [ADULT] sein kann. Die zweite Klasse kann (besonders in den cezischen Sprachen) auch Inanimata beinhalten. Die beiden nichthumanen Klassen lassen nur bedingt eine semantische Motiviertheit erkennen, möglich scheint als prototypisches Schema: Klasse III [GROSS], [AUSGEDEHNT], [WICHTIG]; Klasse IV [KLEIN], [BEGRENZT], [MARGINAL] (vgl. Klimov 1977: 29, Schulze 1992, Schulze 1998: 220–233). Als Klassenmorpheme werden gewöhnlich folgende Elemente zum Ansatz gebracht:

(32) I   *w-
      II   *y- / *r-
      III *b-
      IV   *d-

KZ III und IV dienen in der Regel auch zur Kodierung pluralischer Konzepte, wobei eine Dichotomie [±human] etabliert wird: *b- > [HUMAN], *d- > [nHUMAN]. Neben diesem Verfahren verfügen viele OKS über sekundäre Klassifikationsstrategien, die vornehmlich über nominale Stammerweiterungen, Ergativmarkierungen oder attributive bzw. prädikative Markierungen von Adjektiven oder Partizipien definiert sind und sehr unterschiedliche, zum Teil kontrafaktische Kategorisierungen bewirken. Als Beispiel für einen komplexen Markierungstyp mag (33) dienen (die klassensensiblen Morpheme bzw. Klassenzeichen sind fett gedruckt):

(33) CAXUR (*field notes*)
kasib-na adam-e: čoǯ-us:-eb
arm-DEF:I Mann(I)-ERG:I Bruder-DAT-III
w-uk'ar-na   balkan
III-krank-DEF:III Pferd(III).ABS
aʲ̍a-b-t'-u
PV-III-nehmen-PRET
'Der arme Mann nahm das kranke Pferd von seinem BRUDER.'

Die standardmäßige Bindung der Klassenkongruenz an den {S=O}-Bereich verdeutlichen folgende Beispiele (die {S=O}-Kongruenz ist durch Fettdruck angezeigt):

(34) ČEČEN (Jakovlev 1940: 308[1]; 310[18])
(a) *šera-ču ara-xula cha **stag***
eben-OBL Feld-TRANS ein Mann(I).ABS
*xilla nowqa **w**-ödu-š*
AUX.INFER unterwegs I-gehen.PRES-GER
'Ein Mann war unterwegs auf einem weitem Feld.'

(b) ***y**-illi-na miska-ču stag-a*
IV-öffnen-INFER arm-OBL Mann-ERG
***baga**.*
Mund(IV).ABS
'Der arme Mann öffnete den Mund.'

Der durch diese Art der Klassenmarkierung grundsätzlich als *unpersönlich* zu beschreibende Typ vieler OKS bedingt, daß der Klassenkongruenz nur eine schwache Funktion der Kodierung referentieller Aspekte der ihnen zugeordneten (Pro)Nomina zukommt. Insofern sind Strukturen mit nicht expliziter NP (nominal oder pronominal) ambige, vgl.:

(35) HUNZA (Van den Berg 1995: 271[33]; 263[75])
(a) *bed-no šiyo **r**-uw-á*
dann-und was.ABS V-machen-INF
xazyayni-n iλ'e-n
Hauswirt(I)-FOC I.töten-GER.PRET
'Und was ist zu tun, nachdem (n)SAP den Hausherrn getötet hat?'

(b) *əgi dandi ãq'e-d*
dort entgegen I.kommen-COND
oλu-s dahab giho
DIST.OBL-GEN etwas dort=unten
rak'u n-eλ'-á
Herz(v).ABS V-gehen-AOR
'Wenn (n)SAP[masc] [zu ihm] geht, wird er ruhig sein'
(lit. 'Wenn SAP[masc] dorthin kommt, wird dessen Herz etwas hinunter gehen.')

Die Bindung der verbalen Klassenkongruenz an den durch ABS kodierten {S=O}-Bereich kann einzelsprachlich in unterschiedlichem Umfang variiert werden. Besonders markant ist die Ausdehnung der Kongruenz auf andere Aktanten, wodurch dann meist eine Fokussierung sei es des markierten Aktanten oder des {S=O}-Bereichs erreicht wird, vgl.:

(36) CAXUR (Schulze 1997: 63)
dak:^{j}-is-ər yed-is-ər
Vater(I)-DAT-I Mutter-DAT-I
ču-bi-ši-s-ər
Bruder-PL-SA-DAT-I
yiče-bi-ši-s-ər zə
Schwester-PL-SA-DAT-I ich(I).ABS
Ø-ək:an-o-r-na
I-lieben-NARR-I-1:SG
'VATER, MUTTER, BRÜDER und SCHWESTERN liebten mich.'

Durchgängig monopersonale Systeme sind in den KS insgesamt sehr schwach belegt. Die SKS operieren über eine Art *offener* Monopersonalität, d. h. Verben *können* durch die zusätzliche Einbindung eines weiteren Aktanten bikongruente Strukturen aufweisen, die allerdings nur in der perfektivischen Serie (IO-S-V) obligatorisch ist. In der Regel erfolgt die Kongruenzexpansion auf der Basis einer IO-Inkorporation, vgl.:

(37) GEORGISCH (Aronson 1982: 187)
(a) *gamq'idvel-man botl-i*
Kaufmann-ERG Flasche-NOM
araq'-i mi-q'id-a
Vodka-NOM PV-verkaufen.AOR-3:A
'Der Kaufmann verkaufte eine Flasche Vodka.'
(b) *gamq'idvel-man ivane-s-ac*
Kaufmann-ERG Ivane-DAT-auch
botli araq'i
Flasche-NOM Vodka-NOM
mi-h-q'id-a
PV-3:IO-verkaufen-3:A
'Der Kaufmann verkaufte auch Ivane eine Flasche Vodka.'

Der einzige Fall einer konsequent durchgeführten Monopersonalität ist durch das UDI repräsentiert. Im Gegensatz zum GEORGISCHEN sind die Markierungen von SAP und nSAP darüber hinaus isomorph, vgl. den folgenden Ausschnitt aus den Flexionsparadigmata („a, b, c" usw. stehen als Repräsentanten für spezifische Morpheme):

(38)	Georgisch		Udi
	Typ I	Typ II	
1SG	Präfix (a)	Suffix (a)	Affix (a)
2SG	Präfix (b)	Suffix (a)	Affix (b)
3SG	Suffix (c)	Suffix (b)	Affix (c)
1PL	Präfix (a)	Suffix (a)	Affix (d)
2PL	Präfix (b)	Suffix (a)	Affix (e)
3PL	Suffix (d)	Suffix (c)	Affix (f)

Wie im GEORGISCHEN sind die Personalzeichen akkusativisch auf den {S=A}-Bereich ausgerichtet, sofern keine *verba sentiendi* vorliegen, vgl.:

(39) UDI (Joh 19,23)
q'oši-n-en gena ewaxte
Krieger:COLL-SE-ERG aber als
čärčäräz-q'un-b-i isus-a
Qual-3PL:A-AUX:TRANS-AOR Jesus-DAT
a-q'un-q'-i šet'a
nehmen:3PL:A-AOR ANAPH-SE:OBL-GEN
partal-ax wa^ʕ
Kleid-DAT₂ Teil-3PL:A-AUX:TRANS-AOR
žok-q'un-b-i bip' ga-l-a
vier Teil-SE-DAT
'Die Krieger aber, nachdem sie Jesus gequält hatten, nahmen sein Kleid und teilten [es] in vier Teile.'

Im Gegensatz zu den SKS kennt das UDI auch monopersonale Verfahren, die nicht direkt dem Akkusativ-Ergativ-Kontinuum zuzuordnen sind. Hierzu zählen einerseits possessive Konstruktionen (vgl. 40), andererseits schwach kontrollierte *verba sentiendi*, die analog zu den übrigen KS in der Regel über eine spezifische Adressatenkodierung (Dativ oder Affektiv) operiert. Im UDI ist dabei ein unterschiedlicher, dialektal bestimmter Grad der Angleichung des Kongruenzverfahrens an das von (in)transitiven Strukturen zu beobachten (vgl. 41 (a = Vartašen, b = Nieder-Nidž, c = Ober-Nidž)):

(40) UDI (*field notes*)
me mex bak-i-bez
PROX Messer.ABS AUX-AOR-1SG:POSS
'Dieses Messer gehörte mir.'

(41) UDI (*field notes*)
  (a) ***me-t'-u*** / ***me-t'-in***   *t'e*
      PROX-SE-DAT / PROX-SE-ERG   DIST
      adamar-ax te-t'u-a-k'-sa
      Mann-DAT₂   NEG-3:SG:IO-sehen-PRES
      'Er/Sie sieht nicht jenen Mann.'
  (b) ***hun***   *mi-**n**-b-sa*
      2SG:ABS   frieren-2SG:S-AUX-PRES
      'Du frierst.'
  (c) ***hun***   *mi-**wa**-b-sa*
      2SG:ABS   frieren-2SG:IO-AUX-PRES
      'Du frierst.'

4.3.2. Polykongruente Systeme

Die polykongruenten Systeme der betreffenden KS sind in der Regel bikongruent, d. h. sie bilden zwei offen markierte oder verdeckte NPs am Verb ab. Die verbale Kodierung von mehr als zwei Aktanten ist besonders in den WKS anzutreffen, besonders mit Kausativa oder über die Inkoporation des IO-Bereichs oder postpositionaler Strukturen, vgl.:

(42) ABXAZ (Aristava et al. 1968: 129)
      i-w-z-d-aa-sə-r-ga-p'
      3SG:i:O-2SG:m-ADR-3PL:O(<A)-PV(ALL)-
      1SG:A-CAUS-bringen-FUT1
      'Ich werde sie es dir bringen lassen.'

(42) ist zugleich ein Beispiel für die polypersonale Architektur der WKS. Diese wird in den südlichen Sprachen zusätzlich von einem Klassifikationsverfahren dominiert, das im Bereich von SAP(2) und nSAP wirksam wird, vgl. (einige Allomorphe sind vernachlässigt):

(43) ABXAZ

	S=O	A	IO
1SG	sə	sə/zə	sə
2SG:m	wə	wə	wə
2SG:f	bə	bə	bə
3SG:m	də	yə	yə
3SG:f	də	lə	lə
3SG:i	yə	na	a
1PL	ħa	ħa	ħa
2PL	šʷə	šʷə	šʷə
3PL	yə	d/rə	d/rə

Die Tabelle verdeutlicht, daß entsprechend der Erwartungen der Silverstein-Hierarchie der SAP-Bereich in Hinblick auf aktantielle Rollen morphologisch kaum differenziert ist. Statt dessen operieren die WKS über eine relativ rigide Stellungsregelung, die – Ausnahmen seien hier vernachlässigt – vornehmlich über die ergativische Reihung S-IO bzw. O-IO-A definiert ist, vgl.:

(44) UBYX (Smeets 1984: 89)
  (a) ***sə-w-bğʲa-kʲa-n***
      1SG:S-2SG-PP(SUPER)-gehen-DYN
      'Ich besiege dich.' (lit. 'Ich gehe auf dich.')
  (b) ***a-w-bğʲa-sə-wtʷ'ə-n***
      3SG:i-O-2SG-PP(SUPER)-1SG:A-wegnehmen-DYN
      'Ich nehme es von dir weg.'

Das polypersonale Verfahren der WKS, das im Bereich der IO-Inkoporation eine tentative Analogie in den SKS findet, steht gegen die bikongruenten Systeme einer Reihe von OKS, die einerseits klassenbasiert, andererseits gemischt (Person–Klasse) erscheinen können. Während rein klassenbasierte Bikongruenz vornehmlich in subordinierten Strukturen zu finden sind, treten die gemischten Verfahren nahezu ausschließlich in Verben des Matrixsatzes auf. Klassenbasierte Bikongruenz kann als sekundärer Typ beschrieben werden, der durch die Behandlung eines klassenmarkierten Partizips als Attribut eines Nomens etabliert wird, wobei das Partizip zusätzlich über ein Klassenzeichen an das *determinatum* angebunden wird. Die gemischte Bikongruenz basiert auf der kanonischen Klassenkongruenz der OKS, die durch eine zusätzliche Personalisierung der verbalen Paradigmata gekennzeichnet ist. Der Grad der Personalisierung und ihre Motivation ist für die betreffenden OKS kaum nach einheitlichen Gesichtspunkten zu beschreiben. Sie ist oftmals co-paradigmatisiert, wobei als parallele Faktoren Kontrollgrad (BAC und SÜDTABASARAN), Fokussierung (UDI, TABASARAN, LAK, teilweise DARGWA), und TAM (u. a. ČEČENISCHE Dialekte, LAK, DARGWA, CAXUR, AXWAX, HUNZA, ZAKATAL'-AWAR) zu beschreiben sind. Zudem ist von Bedeutung, welche (n)SAP von einer Markierung betroffen sind. (45) listet die bislang bekannten Typen auf:

(45)

Markiert	Unmarkiert
SAP(1)	Rest
SA	PnSAP
SAP.SG	SAP.PL / nSAP
SAP(2)	Rest
SAP(2).SG	Rest
Rest	Inklusiv
SAP / n SAP	–

Während die SAP(2)-basierten Typen vor allem dem modalen (bzw. imperativischen) Paradigma entstammen, deuten diejenigen Paradigmata, die nur den SAP(1) markieren, auf eine entsprechende pragmatische Fokussierung dieser Person, vgl.:

(46)   NORD-AXWAX (Magomedbekova
       1967: 79 (a–b), 145[4–5] (c))
   (a) *de-de*   *w-ox̌-e-d-o*
       1SG-ERG I-nehmen-TV-AOR:1SG:A-I
       waša
       Junge(I).ABS
       'Ich nahm den Jungen.'
   (b) *me-de*   *y-ex̌-e-ri*
       2SG-ERG II-nehmen-TV-AOR
       yaše
       Mädchen(II).ABS
       'Du nahmst das Mädchen.'
   (c) *x̂ʷani-la*   *imix̌i-la*
       Pferd(III):ABS-und Esel(III):ABS-und
       qˤedo-qˤedo   *r-ikʷ'-a-ri*
       zurück-zurück III:PL-SEIN-TV-AOR
       'Das Pferd und der Esel blieben zurück.'

Derartige Strategien der pragmatischen Pointierung von SAP(1) beruhen in der Regel auf partizipialen Strukturen, die den unmarkierten Tempusstämmen der anderen (n)SAP gegenüber stehen (vgl. Schulze (im Erscheinen, Kap. II,4). In der AWARISCHEN Mundart von Katex ist dieses Verfahren auf den gesamten SAP-Bereich beim *präsens generale* ausgedehnt worden, vgl.:

(47)   KATEX-AWAR (*field notes*)
   (a) *dun*   / *mun*   *w-en-aw*
       1SG:ABS / 2SG:ABS I-gehen-SAP
       'Ich (Mann) gehe / du (Mann) gehst.'
   (b) *da-w*   *w-en-a*
       ANAPH:ABS-I I-gehen-nSAP
       'Er geht.'

Im LAK stellt die Trennung SAP vs. nSAP die erste Stufe in der Ausprägung eines komplexeren (TAM-abhängigen) Systems der Personalflexion dar, die die Sprechaktrollen grundsätzlich *en bloc* verarbeitet, vgl.:

(48)   Typ I   Typ II   Typ III
    SAP.SG   -w   -a   -ra
    SAP.PL   -w   -u   -ru
    nSAP   -Ø   -i   -r(i)

Das Beispiel in (46,a) zeigt, daß innerhalb eines Personalzeichens (hier SAP(1)) zusätzlich eine Klassendifferenzierung verbaut sein kann, vgl. auch:

(49)   CAXUR (Schulze 1997: 59)
   (a) *zə*   *dex̌*
       1SG:ABS Sohn(I).ABS
       gjetu-na
       I.schlagen.PAST-1SG:A(>I)
       'Ich schlug den Sohn.'
   (b) *zə*   *aslan*
       1SG:ABS Löwe(IV).ABS
       gjetu-yn
       IV.schlagen.PAST-1SG:A(>IV)
       'Ich schlug den Löwen.'

DARGWA, BAC und TABASARAN haben eine vollständige Differenzierung des SAP-Bereichs durchgeführt. Doch während Dargwa dieses Verfahren nur TAM-abhängig kennt, ist es in den beiden anderen Sprachen grundsätzlich durchgeführt. Kennzeichnend ist dabei, daß der nSAP-Bereich unmarkiert bleibt, und daß beide Sprachen die Personalflexion zur Kodierung von Kontrollgraden (partiell *fluid-S*) verwenden, vgl.:

(50)   SÜDTABASARAN (Magometov 1965: 199)
   (a) *uzu*   *uc:ura-zu*
       1SG:ABS krank.PRES-1SG:S_O
       'Ich bin krank.'
   (b) *uzu*   *hergra-za*
       1SG:ABS laufen.PRES-1:SG:S_A
       'Ich laufe.'

Die fokussierende Wirkung der PZ im TABASARAN wird vor allem dann deutlich, wenn sie einen Aktanten außerhalb des {S=O;A}-Bereichs kodieren, vgl. (51). Die beiden Belege zeigen weiterhin an, daß hierbei die Personenhierarchie wirksam wird:

(51)   SÜDTABASARAN ((a) Magometov 1965: 213, (b) *fieldnotes*)
   (a) *du-ğu*   *yas*   *čʷi*   *iži*
       ANAPH-ERG:M 1SG:POSS Bruder.ABS gut
       ip'urd-as
       machen.PRES-1:SG:POSS
       'Er behandelt MEINEN Bruder.'
   (b) *uzu*   *du-ğ-an*   *čʷi*   *iži*
       1SG:ABS ANAPH-SE-GEN Bruder.ABS gut
       ip'urd-as
       machen.PRES-1:SG:A
       'Ich behandle seinen Bruder.'

Die Polypersonalität des TABASARAN ist an das Vorhandensein eines agentivischen SAP(1) gebunden, vgl.:

(52)   NORDTABASARAN (Magometov 1965: 204)
   (a) *izu*   *iwu*
       1SG:ABS 2SG[HUM]:ABS
       d-iržu-nu-za-wu
       [HUM]-unterwerfen-AOR-1SG:A-2SG:O
       'Ich unterwarf dich.'
   (b) *iwu*   *izu*
       2SG:ABS 1:SG[HUM]:ABS
       d-iržu-nu-wa
       [HUM]-unter-werfen.AOR-2:SG:A
       'Du unterwarfst mich.'

In derartigen Fällen kann der nicht agentive Aktant auch durch einen peripheren Kasus markiert sein, vgl.:

(53) NORDTABASARAN (Magometov 1965: 211)
*iču   ič*ʷ*-uq*
1PL(e):ABS 2PL-POST.ESS
*q:iq:u-nu-ču-č*ʷ*uq*
hören-AOR-1PL(e):S-2PL.POST.ESS
'Wir hörten euch.'

Dieses Verfahren erlaubt es auch, eine NP des {S=A}-Bereichs, die durch ein persönliches Possessivpronomen determiniert ist, über das Possessivum am Verb abzubilden, vgl. (KL II = [-hum]):

(54) TABASARAN (Magometov 1965: 211)
yas   k'ask'ar
1:SG:POSS Messer(II).ABS
ga-w-q-un-as
PV(herunter)-II-fallen-AOR-1:SG:POSS
'MEIN Messer ist heruntergefallen.'

4.3.3. Funktionale Aspekte der Kongruenz
Die Dichotomie Personen- vs. Klassenkongruenz spiegelt sich in den basalen funktionalen Aspekten des jeweiligen Kongruenzverfahrens wider. Sofern keine zusätzlichen, pragmatischen Funktionen (etwa Fokussierung) relevant werden, kann grundsätzlich formuliert werden: Je persönlicher, d. h. SAP-ausgerichteter das Verfahren ist, desto stärker bindet es sich akkusativisch an den {S=A}-Bereich; umgekehrt gilt, daß Klassenmarkierungen vornehmlich ergativisch auf den {S=O}-Bereich abzielen. In Abhängigkeit davon, ob das jeweilige System der Aktantenmarkierung rollen- oder referenzdominiert ist, ergibt sich weitergehend die Zuordnung zum Bereich semantischer Rollen (Agens/Patiens usw.) bzw. syntaktischer Funktionen (Subjekt, Objekt usw.). In referenzdominierten Sprachen (etwa den SKS) etabliert die Personenkongruenz zunächst die Funktion „Subjekt" (oder *Vordergrund*), unabhängig davon, wie die betreffende NP kasuell markiert ist. Der sich besonders in den SKS andeutende Konflikt zwischen kasueller Ergativität und Akkusativität der Kongruenz wird noch verschärft, wenn verbal (in den SKS neben polypersonalen Aspekten vor allem numerusklassifizierende) Techniken der Abbildung des O-Bereichs transitiver Konstruktionen wirksam werden (Tuite 1998: 68−72), vgl.:

(55) ALTGEORGISCH (Gen 1,1)
dasabamad kmn-n-a
anfangs   schaffen.AOR-O:PL-3SG:A
γmert-man cay   da
Gott-ERG Himmel.NOM und
kweq'anay
Erde.NOM
'Am Anfang schuf Gott Himmel und Erde.'

Diejenigen OKS, die über eine Art persönlicher Kongruenz verfügen, verhalten sich bezüglich der Frage, welchen aktantiellen Bereich PZ signalisieren, relativ heterogen. Auch wenn eine deutliche Präferenz für den {S=A}-Bereich zu beobachten ist, operieren etwa TABASARAN und LAKO-DARGWA teilweise über hierarchische Bedingungen. Für transitive Sätze des Lak lassen sich diese Bedingungen für „nicht-assertive" Propositionen wie folgt zusammenfassen:

(56) (a) O = SAP ⇒ AGR(O)
     (b) O = nSAP ∧ A = SAP ⇒ AGR(A)
     (c) O = SAP ∧ A = nSAP ⇒ AGR(O)

Hieraus ergibt sich, daß die Kongruenz des LAK (sofern keine diathetischen Aspekte auftreten) eine deutliche Patiensprominenz aufweist. Diese wird lediglich durchbrochen, wenn die Hierarchie AG<PAT mit SAP< nSAP gekreuzt erscheint. Demgegenüber haben die darginischen Dialekte eine stärkere Agensprominenz ausgeprägt, was einher geht mit einer Ausdifferenzierung des SAP-Bereichs, vgl. den Überblick für KUBAČI:

(57)
	I	II	III
1SG	-d	-da	-de
2SG	-t(:e)	-de	-de
3SG	-Ø	AUX+KZ	-de
1PL	-da:	-da	-de
2PL	-t:a:	-da	-de
3PL	-Ø	AUX+KZ	-de

Zugrunde liegt hier eine allgemeine SAP-Markierung *-da*, die auf eine alte, zunächst an SAP(1) gebundene Fokuspartikel (*-ra*) zurückzuführen ist, und die vermutlich über das hochfrequente Auftreten von SAP(2) in Interrogativsätzen eine Sonderform für diesen Aktanten entwickelt hat (vgl. Schulze (im Erscheinen) Kap. IV). Die drei Typen der Personenkongruenz im KUBAČI sind TAM- und valenzabhängig, wobei Typ I (präsentisch/futurisch bzw. inferentiell) als der ausdifferenzierteste Typ beschrieben werden kann. Für die OKS kann allgemein beschrieben werden, daß je isomorpher das Paradigma der Personalzeichen mit dem der Personalpronomina bzw.

der (deiktischen) Anapher wird, desto stärker ist die {S=A}-Bezogenheit der PZ.

Die grundsätzliche Polypersonalität der Verben in den WKS deutet an, daß sich zumindest auf der formalen Ebene keine Präferenz der PZ für einen der beiden Bereiche {S=A}/{S=O} oder Subjekt/Objekt feststellen läßt. Innerhalb des SAP-Paradigmas finden sich nur sekundäre Differenzierungen in Hinblick auf diese Bereiche, weshalb als wichtigstes Kriterium das der Stellung der PZ zueinander gewertet werden kann. Dies gilt nicht für den Bereich der nSAP, die in der Regel auch morphologisch unterschieden sind, vgl. nochmals (43). Für den SAP-Bereich (und strukturell damit verbunden auch für den nSAP-Bereich) muß eine Präferenz für den {S=O}-Bereich in verbinitialer Stellung beschrieben werden. Der Bindungsgrad von S (und damit O) an den Verbstamm ist nicht so stark wie der von A, der in der Regel nur von Kausativmorphemen und einigen wenigen anderen Elementen vom Verbstamm getrennt werden kann. Die sich hieraus für die WKS ergebende Tendenz zu einer ergativischen Reihung der PZ korreliert mit der morphologischen Differenzierung im nSAP-Bereich (vgl. (43)). Diesem Befund steht die Tatsache gegenüber, daß die PZ in Bezug auf subjektspezifische Tests (Equi-NP, Preferred Subject Principle, Switch Reference usw.) einen deutlichen {S=A}-Bereich etablieren, weshalb von einer syntaktischen Akkusativität auszugehen ist. Diese bewirkt, daß die quasi-kasuelle Ergativität der PZ mit einer akkusativischen Ebene gekreuzt erscheint, die Reflex der „Spiegelarchitektur" des einfachen Satzes in den WKS ist (NP: {S=A}-O, Verb: {S=O}-A).

Im Gegensatz zur persönlichen Kongruenz ist die Klassenkongruenz der OKS in unmarkierten und nicht perspektivierten Sätzen eindeutig auf den {S=O}-Bereich ausgerichtet, also ergativisch. Inwieweit hierdurch auch eine Zuordnung von {S=O} zur Domäne „Subjekt" gegeben ist, hängt davon ab, ob eine referenzdominierte Morphosyntax vorliegt. In jedem Fall liegt in der Regel stets eine Korrelation von Absolutiv und Klassenkongruenz vor, wobei ein attributives Partizip zusätzlich in die Konkordanz einer NP eingebunden erscheinen kann, vgl.:

(58) AWAR (Charachidzé 1981: 69)
ğaka   *b-eč:'-u-le-y*
Kuh(III):ABS III-melken-TV-IND-II
č:užu...
Frau(II).ABS
'Die Frau, die die Kuh melkt ...'

Besonders in den zentralen OKS LAK und DARGWA besteht allerdings die Tendenz, eigentlich „bi-absolutive" Strukturen, die in der Auxiliargruppe kanonisch auf einen absolutivisch markierten A-Bereich referieren, ergativisch zu reanalysieren, mit der Folge, daß jetzt das entsprechende Klassenzeichen *auch* mit einem ergativisch angezeigten A-Bereich kongruieren kann, vgl.:

(59) KUBAČI (Magometov 1963: 328)
c:i⁽ˢ⁾q⁽ˤ⁾ča:-w-x̌-ub
erfreut-I-AUX-GER.PRET
kʷiy-sat:alčun-ni-sa-w
PV(aus den Händen)-nehmen.PERF-GER-AUX-I
kʷiyal ˤašak
beide Kessel:ABS
mallaras:it:in-ni-c:il
Mulla=Nasreddin-SE-ABL
de:n-il-dil.
Nachbar(I)-SE-ERG
'Erfreut nahm der Nachbar beide Kessel von Mulla Nasreddin.'

(60) LAK (Žirkov 1955: 189)
bu-t:a-l   *b-awx̌:u-nu*
Vater(I)-SE-ERG III-kaufen:III-AOR
ur   *ču.*
I:AUX.PRES Pferd(III):ABS
'Vater kaufte ein Pferd.'

Allerdings verletzt eine derartige Markierungstechnik weniger die grundsätzliche Orientierung von Klassenzeichen auf den {S=O}-Bereich; vielmehr basiert sie auf einer Hypertrophierung der ergativischen Markierung, die besonders im LAK auch den intransitiven Bereich berühren kann.

4.4. Aktanten und TAM

Lediglich in den SKS und (partiell) in den OKS ist das Verfahren der Aktantenmarkierung (kasuell oder mittels Kongruenz) paradigmatisch eingebettet in das jeweilige TAM-System. Für die SKS werden diesbezüglich drei *Serien* beschrieben: I = präsentisch-futurisch, II = aoristisch, III = perfektiv-inferentiell. Hinsichtlich der Kasusmarkierung von nominalen Aktanten ergibt sich folgendes basales Bild (hier nur Serien I und II):

(61)		A→O	S_O	S_A
GEO.	I	NOM>AKK	NOM	NOM
	II	ERG>NOM	NOM	ERG
MING.	I	NOM>AKK	NOM	NOM
	II	ERG>NOM	ERG	ERG
LAZ.	I	ERG>NOM	NOM	ERG
	II	ERG>NOM	NOM	ERG
SVAN.	I	NOM>AKK	NOM	NOM
	II	ERG>NOM	NOM	ERG

Die Auflistung verdeutlicht, daß in den SKS (bis auf das LAZISCHE) ein *split*-Verfahren vorliegt: Auf der kasuellen Ebene ist Serie I akkusativisch, Serie II aber ergativisch kodiert. Darüber hinaus zeigen sich in allen vier Sprachen Tendenzen der Spaltung des S-Bereichs in der Serie II (S_A vs. S_O). Zugrunde liegt vermutlich die Umdeutung einer alten antipassivischen Diathese in ein nicht-präteritales Tempussystem, vgl.:

(62) ERG: AG(ERG) → PAT(ABS)
     AP: AG(ABS) → PAT(OBL)

Der Absolutiv wurde bereits grundsprachlich durch eine deiktische Partikel *-i* (< *ig*) erweitert, während der Obliquus durch *-s* (genitivisch über *-s-i* zu *-š* oder *-s₁* verändert?) angezeigt war. Für den Ergativ wird gemeinhin grundsprachliches *-n/*-d angesetzt (Harris 1991a: 24). Residuen der Antipassiv-Morphologie findet sich in der Stammbildung der Präsensreihe, vgl. (die ehemalige ERG/AP-Morphologie ist fett angezeigt; (a) = ERG, (b) = AP):

(63) ALTGEORGISCH (Harris 1991a: 19)
  (a) *k'ac-**man*** *mšier-sa*
     Mann-ERG hungrig-DAT
     *mi-s-c-**Ø-a***
     PV-3SG:IO-geben-AOR-3SG:A
     *p'ur-**i***
     Brot:O-NOM(<ABS)
     'Der Mann gab dem Hungrigen Brot.'
  (b) *k'ac-**i*** *mšier-sa*
     Mann-NOM(<ABS) Hungrig-DAT
     *mi-s-c-**em-s***
     PV-3SG:IO-geben-PRES(<AP)-3SG:A(<S)
     *p'ur-**s***
     Brot:O(<IO)-DAT(<OBL)
     'Der Mann gibt dem Hungrigen Brot.'

In Bereich der ERG-Morphologie kann davon ausgegangen werden, daß entsprechend der Silverstein-Hierarchie 3>3-Strukturen grundsprachlich auch in der Kongruenz stärker patiens-orientiert waren, während die SAP eher akkusativisch kongruierten.

Die in den SKS stark ausgeprägte Interaktion von TAM-Systemen und Aktantentypologie finden in den übrigen KS nur sehr begrenzte Parallelen. Meist liegt – falls Perspektivierungsverfahren überhaupt angewendet werden – ein diathesenbasiertes System der Interaktion vor, also ein Verfahren, das den grundsprachlichen Zustand der SKS strukturell widerspiegelt. Eine den SKS in etwa analoge Technik ist durch den sogenannten Assertiv (ASS) im LAK belegt (Friedman 1994). Es handelt sich um einen bestätigenden oder bekräftigenden Modus, der vor allem in der Umgangssprache eine stark „subjektivische" (oder mediale) Diathese kodiert. Zugrunde liegt eine partizipiale Struktur, die durch die adjektivische Stammerweiterung *-s:a-* markiert ist. In nicht durativen Formen folgt der Assertiv mit der Inferenz ASS→RES einem grundsätzlich patiensorientieren, ergativischen Schema, während der Durativ (*-la-*) eine Pointierung des SAP-Bereichs erzwingt (ergativisch, wenn nSAP>SAP, akkusativisch, wenn SAP>(n)SAP), vgl.:

(64) LAK (*field notes*)
  (a) *ta-na-l*
     ANAPH-SE:M-ERG
     b-at:-ay-s:a-ru
     I/II:PL-schlagen-PART:PRES-ASS-2PL:O
     zu
     2:PL:ABS
     'Er schlägt sicherlich EUCH.'
  (b) *na Ø-at:-ay-s:a-r*
     1SG:ABS I-schlagen-PART:PRES-ASS-3SG:O
     ta:
     ANAPH:ABS
     'Ich schlage sicherlich IHN.'
  (c) *ta-na-l*
     ANAPH-SE:M-ERG
     b-atlati-s:a-ru
     I/II:PL-schlagen.DUR.PRES-ASS-2PL:O
     zu
     2PL:ABS
     'Er ist sicherlich dabei, EUCH zu schlagen.'
  (d) *na Ø-atlati-s:a-ra*
     I-schlagen.DUR.PRES-ASS-1SG:A
     ta:
     ANAPH(I):ABS
     'Ich bin sicherlich dabei, ihn zu schlagen.'

Modusspezifische Umstellungen der aktantiellen Markierung sind vor allem in den OKS dokumentiert. In der Regel sind der Potentialis oder die Modalität der Möglichkeit betroffen, wobei dann der {S=A}-Bereich (akkusativisch) durch einen Lokalkasus markiert wird, vgl.:

(65) XINALUG (Kibrik 1994: 400)
    gada-š riši
    Junge-POSS:LOC Mädchen(II):ABS
    χäšχ-in-k^{w}i-dä-mä
    stoßen-POSSIBLE-AUX-II-IND
    'Der Junge könnte das Mädchen stoßen.'

4.5. Diathesen

Diathesen als Ausdruck der Referenzdominiertheit finden sich vor allem in den SKS und WKS, während die OKS als eher rollendominierte Sprachen — wenn überhaupt — nur über eingeschränkte Verfahren der Perspektivierung mittels Diathese verfügen. Insgesamt können folgende Diathesetypen unterschieden werden:

(66) (a) Subjekt-Diathesen
    Passiv
    Antipassiv
    Bi-Absolutiv
    Labilität
  (b) Objekt-Diathesen

Da morphosyntaktische Verfahren der Objekt-Diathese nur marginal (in den WKS) belegt sind, sollen sie im Folgenden unberücksichtigt bleiben. Unter „Subjekt-Diathese" können in den KS alle Verfahren subsumiert werden, die das *foregrounding* eines Aktanten betreffen, womit das *backgrouding* eines in unmarkierter Stellung als „Subjekt" zu identifizierenden Aktanten verbunden sein kann. Umgekehrt kann sich das *foregrounding* als co-paradigmatischer Effekt der eigentlichen Funktion einer Diathese als *backgrounding* ergeben. Diesbezügliche Regelungen sind nur einzelsprachlich spezifizierbar. Der *cut-off point* in Bezug auf die Standardhierarchie AG<PAT<ADR<INSTR<LOC< TEMP liegt in den Passiv-Systemen in der Regel nach PAT, wohingegen Antipassiva auf AG beschränkt sind. Während in den SKS Antipassiva schon grundsprachlich als transitive (präsentische) Struktur umgedeutet worden sind, und sich heute nur passivische Variationen zeigen, operiert innerhalb der WKS beispielsweise das KABARDA über beide Typen der Subjekt-Diathese auch in synchroner Hinsicht. Dabei ist für Passiv und Antipassiv die Stellung der NPs in funktionaler Hinsicht relevant, vgl.:

(67) ERG: NP:A[OBL] − NP:O[ABS] − {O-A-VERB}
    PASS: NP:A[INSTR] − NP:O[ABS] − {S$_O$-VERB}
    NP: O[ABS] − NP:A[INSTR] − {S$_O$-VERB}
    AP: NP:O[OBL] − NP:A[ABS] − [S$_A$-IO$_O$-VERB]
    NP:A[ABS] − NP:O[OBL] − [S$_A$-IO$_O$-VERB]

Für Antipassiva ist die initiale Stellung des A-Bereichs besonders in der Subordination kennzeichnend, wobei ein „Beschäftigtsein mit etwas" markiert wird. O-initiale Strukturen hingegen zeigen vor allem ein „versuchen zu tun" an, vgl. (68) und (22b):

(68) KABARDA (Colarusso 1992: 177)
    g^{j}aana-ha-m pśaaśa-r
    Hemd-PL-OBL Mädchen-ABS
    Ø-q'ə-y-ha-a-də-a-wa
    3:SA-HOR-3:IO-PL-DAT-nähen-INTR-PRED
    '… daß das Mädchen mit dem Nähen von Hemden beschäftigt ist.'

Mit Passiva hat die Stellung des A-Bereichs direkt vor dem Verb eine fokussierende Wirkung, vgl.:

(69) KABARDA (Colarusso 1992: 176)
    wəna-r ƛ'ə-m-k^j'a
    Haus-ABS Mann-OBL-INSTR
    Ø-ś'ə-aλ   ma-x̌^{w}
    3:S$_O$-MACHEN-PAST 3$_O$:INSTR:DYN:PRES-AUX
    'Das Haus wurde von dem MANN (allein) gebaut.'

Die Passiv-Diathese der SKS steht in engem Zusammenhang mit der Bildung intransitiver Verben. Ausgangspunkt ist hierbei vor allem die Markierung eines Verbs durch die „mediale" (oder subjektive) Version (*-i-), wobei in vielen Fällen eine „unakkusativische" Lesart sinnvoll erscheint (Harris 1981, Kap. 13). Hinzu treten analytische Passiva, die im Gegensatz zu den synthetischen Passiva keine vollständige Ausblendung des A-Bereichs erzwingen.

(70) GEORGISCH (Aronson 1991: 276; 305)
  (a) *kartul-i   sit'q'va   advilad*
      georgisch-NOM Wort:NOM leicht
      i-c'er-eb-a
      SV-schreiben-PRES:STEM-3SG:S$_O$
      'Ein georgisches Wort ist leicht geschrieben.'
  (b) *es šroma   žapariʒ-is   mier*
      PROX Werk.NOM žaparidze-GEN PP(von)
      iq'o   da-c'er-iul-i
      sein:AOR:3:S PV-schreiben-PART:PRÄT-NOM
      'Dieses Werk wurde von Džaparidze verfaßt.'

Die stärker rollendominierten OKS kennen Verfahren der Subjekt-Diathese nur in eingeschränktem Umfang. Den typischsten Fall stellt der sogenannte Bi-Absolutiv dar, der auf einem *foregrounding* des A-Bereichs ohne entsprechender Maskierung des O-Bereichs (etwa Peripherisierung oder Tilgung) beruht. De facto liegt eine Doppelbesetzung des Vordergrunds, d. h. der Subjektfunktion vor, vgl.:

(71) XINALUG (Dešeriev 1959: 168)
(a) *muxtar-i   žanawar*
Muchtar-ERG Wolf:ABS
k'la-tʰ-mä
töten:nRES-AUX:LOC:PRES-IND
'Muchtar tötet einen/den Wolf.'
(b) *muxtar   čxi   žanawar*
Muchtar(I):ABS viel Wolf:ABS
k'la-tʰ-du-mä
töten:nRES-AUX:LOC:PRES-I-IND
'Muchtar ist einer, der viele Wölfe tötet.'

Semantisch ist der Bi-Absolutiv oftmals mit einer Dereferentialisierung bzw. Entindividuierung des O-Bereichs verbunden, womit eine Fokussierung des A-Bereichs einher geht. Dabei wird A analog zu Antipassiva oftmals in eine *typische* Relation zum O-Bereich gestellt, wodurch eine eher (intransitive) durative oder iterative Lesart, bisweilen auch eine Modalität im Sinne von „nicht vollendet" (etwa im GHODOBERI) etabliert wird. Hiermit ist wie zu erwarten die Basis für eine weitergehende Grammatikalisierung des Verfahrens in Hinblick auf TAM-Systeme (etwa im DARGWA) gegeben.

Wirkliche Antipassiva sind in den OKS relativ selten (Hewitt 1982). Belegt sind sie vor allem im Dargwa und in einigen andischen bzw. cezischen Sprachen. In funktionaler Hinsicht stellen sie eine Verstärkung der schon im Bi-Absolutiv angelegten Strategie zur Maskierung des O-Bereichs dar. Sie stellen eine Zwischenstufe auf der Detransitivierungsskala in den betreffenden OKS dar, die wie folgt dargestellt werden kann:

(72) Bi-Absolutiv < Antipassiv < Labile Verben

Diese Skala geht − mit Ausnahmen − einher mit einer Reduktion der morphologischen Dimension: Bi-Absolutive werden oftmals analytisch gebildet, während Antipassiva in der Regel durch ein spezifisches AP-Morphem am Verb gekennzeichnet sind. Labile Verben schließlich sind dadurch gekennzeichnet, daß sie keinerlei morphologische Mittel zur Unterscheidung von transitiven A>O-Verben und intransitiven $S_{A/O}$-Verben kennen, vgl.:

(73) GHODOBERI (Kibrik 1996: 136)
waša   ğuğ-e
Junge(I):ABS Taube(III):PL:ABS
r-ik:-at-a   wu-k'a
III-fangen-PRES-CV I-AUX.PAST
'Der Junge versuchte, Tauben zu fangen.'

(74) DARGWA (Abdullaev 1986: 228)
nu   žuz-li
ich(I):ABS Buch(III)-ERG
'-uč'ule-ra
I-lesen:PRES-1SG:S_A
'Ich bin dabei, ein Buch zu lesen.'

(75) AGHUL (RIČA) (Magometov 1970: 168)
(a) *zaš   k'ey-a   ħuč*
ich:ERG töten-PRES Wolf:ABS
'Ich töte den Wolf.'
(b) *zun   k'ey-a*
ich:ABS sterben-PRES
'Ich sterbe.'

(73) ist ein Beispiel für einen Bi-Absolutiv, (74) gibt einen Antipassiv wieder, während die beiden Belege in (75) ein labiles Verb verdeutlichen.

Im Gegensatz zu Bi-Absolutiven führen Antipassiva in den OKS kaum zur Inkorporation des O-Bereichs in das Verben. Häufiger ist die Ausblendung des O-Bereichs, womit stereotype Aktivitäten eines Aktanten angezeigt werden, vgl.

(76) GHODOBERI (Kibrik 1996: 137)
(a) *ʕali-di   q'iru*
Ali-ERG Weizen(III):ABS
b-el-at-a-da
III-dreschen-PRES-CV-COP
'Ali drischt den Weizen.'
(b) *ʕali   w-ol-a-da*
Ali(I):ABS I-dreschen-AP:CV-COP
'Ali ist am Dreschen.'

5. Aktanz in den grundsprachlichen Systemen

Auch wenn − wie bereits gesagt − nahezu alle KS von irgend einer Art Ergativität − sei es kasuell, über AGR oder syntaktisch/pragmatisch − dominiert sind, kann sicherlich nicht angenommen werden, daß die grundsprachlichen System auf ein einheitliches Verfahren der Aktantenmarkierung bzw. Aktantenmanipulation zurückgehen. Dies entspricht der Tatsache, daß die KS *insgesamt* keines gemeinsamen Ursprungs sind. Soweit wir wissen, unterschieden sich die Techniken der Strukturierung einfacher Sätze in den drei Gruppen der KS beträchtlich von einander. Dabei deutet sich eine Skala an, die den OKS eine eher kasuell bestimmte, patiens-orientierte Ergativität zuweist, während die SKS durch eine zwar ebenfalls kasuelle, aber eher agens-orientierte Ergativität gekennzeichnet sind. Die WKS schließlich sind vornehmlich von einer syntaktischen Stellungsergativität dominiert, die Aussagen über eine aktantielle Orientierung nur in geringem Umfang zuläßt.

Für SKS ist in grundsprachlicher Hinsicht zu vermuten, daß bereits hier die kasuelle Ergativität von nSAP mit einer AGR-gesteuerten, kasuellen Akkusativität der SAP entsprechend der Silverstein-Hierarchie in Konflikt geriet. Auch wenn bereits im KARTVELISCHEN auch der Bereich der nSAP zu einem akkusativischen AGR-Schema tendierten, kann davon ausgegangen werden, daß in einer früheren Stufe für nSAP eine Kongruenz dann gegeben war, wenn sie dem {S=O}-Bereich zugeordnet waren, vgl.:

(77) SAP → {S=A} → AGR({S=A})
      nSAP → {S=O} → AGR({O})

Dieses Schema wurde gekreuzt von der kasuellen Markierung, die SAP im {S=A}-Bereich unmarkiert ließ, während für den A-Bereich von nSAP (Nomen und Pronomen) eine spezifische ERG-Markierung gegeben war. Die tendenzielle Polypersonalität der SKS ist sicherlich schon grundsprachlich anzusetzen. Sie referierte auf den {O=IO}-Bereich, der zunächst vermutlich nur über eine Personen- oder Belebtheitshierarchie differenziert wurde. Dieses komplexe Schema war eingebunden in ein aspektuelles System, das über die Diathese ERG→perfektiv vs. AP→imperfektiv etabliert war, bevor in einem zweiten Schritt aus dieser Opposition eine TAM-Spaltung hervorging. Zusätzlich war das KARTVELISCHE von Techniken der *Version* dominiert, die einerseits distal lokalisierend (und − daraus grammatikalisiert − als Index des IO-Bereichs) wirken konnten, die aber andererseits über eine quasi proximale Semantik als spezifischer Index für den S_O-Bereich mediale (eigentlich „unakkusativische") Funktionen ausübten.

Die WKS unterscheiden sich grundsätzlich vom Typ der SKS. Auch wenn kasuelle Markierungen vor allem in den nördlichen Sprachen anzutreffen sind, kann davon ausgegangen werden, daß grundsprachlich eine isolierende Technik im Bereich der overten NPs vorlag, die über anaphorische, später am Verb klitisierte Pronomina wieder aufgenommen wurden. Die stärkere Bindung der Indizes für den {S=A}-Bereich am Verbstamm läßt vermuten, daß zunächst ein akkusativisches Verfahren der *cross-reference* dominant war. Dies gilt allerdings vornehmlich für den SAP-Bereich. Der nSAP-Bereich schien schon grundsprachlich ergativisch differenziert gewesen zu sein, wobei eventuell (sexus/genus-)klassifizierende Effekte eintraten, die auch für den SAP(2) gegeben waren. Somit folgte vermutlich auch das grundsprachliche System der WKS im wesentlichen den Erwartungen der Silverstein-Hierarchie.

Die OKS schließlich scheinen auf ein grundsprachliches System zurückführbar zu sein, das von einer erheblichen Patiens-Orientierung bestimmt war. Der {S=O}-Bereich wurde in einer frühen Phase durch anaphorische und nominalklassifizierende Pronomina am Verb wieder aufgenommen, das ursprünglich eine partizipiale Form darstellte und mit einem Auxiliar versehen eine Art *Fernattribut* zum {S=O}-Bereich darstellte. Diese *pragmatische* Pointierung des {S=O}-Bereichs wurde gekreuzt von einer *semantischen* Markierung des A-Bereichs: Die betreffenden Nomina und Pronomina wurden kasuell in Hinblick auf den Grad ihrer inhärenten Agentivität morphologisch markiert, wobei ein dem pragmatischen Verfahren der Klassenkongruenz entgegen laufendes Klassifikationsverfahren etabliert wurde (vornehmlich [MASK;HUMAN] < [REST] oder [HUMAN] < [nHUMAN] mit entsprechenden Metaphorisierungen).

Im Gegensatz zu den WKS und SKS waren von diesem Verfahren offensichtlich auch die SAP betroffen, d. h. Personalpronomina erhielten analog zu Nomina eine (allerdings spezifische) Agentivitätsmarkierung (Schulze 1999). Der morphologische Cluster, der zur Markierung des A-Bereichs diente, etablierte sich einerseits als nominale Stammerweiterung, andererseits als Ergativ-Morphem, wodurch die Basis für das Verfahren einer kasuellen Ergativität in den OKS gegeben war. Die semantische Basierung der morphologischen Ergativität in OKS verhinderte (bis auf den Bi-Absolutiv) die Ausprägung weitergehender diathetischer Verfahren, die vermutlich erst einzelsprachlich etabliert wurden.

Allen drei Gruppen der KS gemeinsam ist das Verfahren der *Inversion*, besser einer adressaten-orientierten Repräsentation spezifischer, meist unkontrollierten Sachverhalte (*verba sentiendi* usw.). Allerdings haben lediglich die SKS und die OKS dieses Verfahren auch kasuell etabliert (wohingegen die WKS hier − wie zu erwarten − stellungsbezogen operieren). Während die OKS eine semantische Basierung der Inversion beibehalten haben, ist sie in den SKS wohl schon grundsprachlich in eine stativische/perfektivische Struktur umgedeutet worden, die die Basis für die entsprechende TAM-Systematik der SKS bildete.

Setzt man abschließend einige zentrale Parameter der aktantiellen Typologie für die drei grundsprachlichen Systeme an, so ergibt sich folgendes tentatives Bild (P = „Proto-"):

(78)

	P-WK	P-SK	P-OK
Dominanz	{S=A}/O	[S=A]/O	O
Silverstein Kasuelle	ja	ja	nein
Ergativität	nein	ja	ja
AGR	SAP: S=A	SAP: S=A	O
	nSAP: S≠A	nSAP: O	
Diathese	?	AP	?
Version	ja	ja	nein
Inversion	ja	ja	ja

Hieraus ergibt sich, daß die südkaukasische Grundsprache einen intermediären Status zwischen grundsprachlichem Westkaukasisch und grundsprachlichem Ostkaukasisch einnimmt: In struktureller bzw. funktionaler Hinsicht teilt sie wesentliche Aspekte mit den Proto-Westkaukasischen, während es technisch eher dem Typus des Proto-Ostkaukasischen folgt. Bemerkenswert ist sicherlich, daß die strukturelle Nähe der süd- und westkaukasischen Grundsprachen im Zuge der Ausdifferenzierung der kaukasischen Einzelsprachen immer stärker verloren ging. Demgegenüber näherten sich die OKS dem südkaukasischen Typ auch strukturell, wobei als gemeinsamer Nenner eine starke Formalisierung der ergativischen Paradigmata zu beschreiben ist. Daß diese einzelsprachlich wieder semantisiert wurde (etwa über einen tendenziellen S-Split wie im GEORGISCHEN, BAC oder TABASARAN) zeugt davon, daß diese Formalisierung jedoch nicht zum Abschluß gekommen ist.

6. Spezielle Abkürzungen

A	Agentiv
ABS	Absolutiv
AFF	Affirmativ
AGR	Agreement
AP	Antipassive
ASS	Assertive
COP	Copula
CV	Converb
DAM	Differentiated Agentive Marking
DEF	Definite
dist↑	Distal
dist↓	Distal, above
dist→	Distal, horizontal
DOM	Differentiated Objective (or Object) Marking
DUR	Durative
DYN	Dynamic
EMPH	Emphatic
ESS	Essive
GER	Gerund
HOR	Horizon of interest
I, II, III	Noun classes
Inc	Incorporated
IND	Indicative
IO	Indirect Objective
med	Medial
n1	Non First Person
NARR	Narrative
NO	Nominalizer
nSAP	Non-Speech Act Participant
O	Objective
PART	Participle
POT	Potential
PP	Postposition
PRED	Predicative
prox	Proximal
PV	Preverb
Q	Question
RED	Reduplicated
REF	Referential
RES	Resultative
RV	Relative version
S	Subjective
SA	Stem augment
SAP	Speech Act Participant
SV	Subjective version
TAM	Tense, Aspect, Mode
TRANS	Translative
TV	Thematic vowel
V	Verb

7. Zitierte Literatur

Abdullaev, Zapir G. 1986. *Problemy èrgativnosti darginskogo jazyka.* Moskva: Nauka.

Alekseev, Michail E. 1979. „Funkcii èrgativnogo padeža v arčinskom jazyke". In: Mejlanova, Unejzat A. (otv. red.). *Imennoe sklonenije v dagestanskich jazykach.* Machačkala: DagFAN, 82–95.

Aristava, Š. K. et al. (red. koll.). 1968. *Grammatika abchazskogo jazyka. Fonetika i morfologija.* Suchumi: Alašara.

Aronson, Howard I. 1982. *Georgian. A Reading Grammar.* Columbus, Ohio: Slavica.

Aronson, Howard I. 1991. „Modern Georgian". In: Harris, Alice (ed.). *The Indigenous Languages of the Caucasus*, vol. 1: *The Kartvelian Languages.* Delmar, New York: Caravan, 219–312.

Bouda, Karl. 1949. *Lakkische Studien.* Heidelberg: Winter.

Cercvaʒe, Ilia. 1965. *Andiuri ena. Gramat'ik'uli ananlizi t'ekst'ebit.* Tbilisi: Mecniereba.

Charachidzé, Georges. 1981. *Grammaire de la langue avar.* Paris: Jean-Favard.

Colarusso, John. 1992. *A Grammar of the Kabardian Language.* Calgary, Alberta: University of Calgary Press.

Deeters, Gerhard. 1930. *Das Karthwelische Verbum.* Leipzig: Markert & Petters.

Dešeriev, Ju. D. 1959. *Grammatika chinalugskogo jazyka.* Moskva: Nauka.

Dirr, Adolf. 1907. „Agulskij jazyk. Grammatičeskij očerk, teksty, sbornik agulskich slov s russkim k nemu ukazatelem". *SMOMPK* 37,3. Tiflis: Tip. Imp. Velič. na Kavkaze.

Friedman, Victor. 1994. „The Lak Assertive". In: Aronson, Howard (ed.). *Non-Slavic Languages of the USSR. Papers From the Fourth Conference.* Columbus, Ohio: Slavica, 114–119.

Gecadze, Irina O. 1979. *Očerki po sintaksisu abchazskogo jazyke.* Leningrad: Nauka.

Harris, Alice. 1981. *Georgian syntax: A study in relational grammar.* Cambridge: Cambridge University Press.

Harris, Alice. 1991 a. „Overview on the History of the Kartvelian Languages". In: Harris, Alice (ed.). *The Indigenous Languages of the Caucasus*, vol. 1: *The Kartvelian Languages.* Delmar, New York: Caravan, 9–83.

Harris, Alice. 1991 b. „Mingrelian". In: Harris, Alice (ed.). *The Indigenous Languages of the Caucasus*, vol. 1: *The Kartvelian Languages.* Delmar, New York: Caravan, 313–394.

Hewitt, George. 1982. „'Anti-Passive' and 'Labile' Construction in North Caucasian". *General Linguistics* 22: 158–170.

Holisky, Dee Ann. 1991. „Laz". In: Harris, Alice (ed.). *The Indigenous Languages of the Caucasus*, vol. 1: *The Kartvelian Languages.* Delmar, New York: Caravan, 395–472.

Jakovlev, N. F. 1940. *Sintaksis čečenskogo literaturnogo jazyka.* Moskva, Leningrad: Izd. AN SSSR.

Kibrik, Andrej. 1996. „Transitivity in lexicon and grammar." In: Kibrik, Alexandr E. (ed.). *Godoberi.* München, Newcastle: LINCOM Europa, 108–147.

Kibrik, Alexandr E. 1994. „Khinalug". In: Smeets, Rieks (ed.). *The Indigenous Languages of the Caucasus,* vol 4: *The North East Caucasian Languages, part 2.* Demar, New York: Caravan, 367–406.

Klimov, Georgi A. 1977. *Tipologija jazykov aktivnogo stroja.* Moskva: Nauka.

Kluge, Theodor. 1916. *Beiträge zur mingrelischen Grammatik.* Berlin: Kohlhammer.

Magomedbekova, Zagidat M. 1967. *Achvachskij jazyk. Grammatičeskij analiz, teksty, slovar'.* Tbilisi: Mecniereba.

Magometov, Aleksandr A. 1963. *Kubačinskij jazyk. Issledovanie i teksty.* Tbilisi: Idz. AN Gr.SSR.

Magometov, Aleksandr A. 1965. *Tabasaranskij jazyk. Issledovanie i teksty.* Tbilisi. Mecniereba.

Magometov, Aleksandr A. 1970. *Agul'skij jazyk. Issledovanie i teksty.* Tbilisi: Mecniereba.

Mikailov, Š. I. 1959. *Očerki avarskoj dialektologii.* Moskva, Leningrad: Izd. AN SSSR.

Nikolayev, S. L. & Starostin, S. A. 1994. *A North Caucasian Etymological Dictionary.* Moscow: Asterisk.

Schmidt, Karl Horst. 1962. *Studien zur Rekonstruktion des Lautstandes der südkaukasischen Grundsprache.* Wiesbaden: Steiner.

Schulze, Wolfgang. 1992. „Zur Entwicklungsdynamik morphologischer Subsysteme: Die ostkaukasischen Klassenzeichen". In: Paris, Cathérine (éd.). *Caucasiologie et mythologie comparée.* Paris: Peeters, 335–362.

Schulze, Wolfgang. 1997. *Tsakhur.* München, Newcastle: LINCOM Europa.

Schulze, Wolfgang. 1998. *Person, Klasse, Kongruenz. Fragmente einer Kategorialtypologie des einfachen Satzes in den ostkaukasischen Sprachen. Band 1: Die Grundlagen.* München, Newcastle: LINCOM Europa.

Schulze, Wolfgang. 1999. „The diachrony of personal pronouns in East Caucasian". In: Van den Berg, Helma (ed.). *Studies in Caucasian Linguistics.* Leiden: CNWS, 95–111.

Schulze, Wolfgang. 2000. "Towards to a Typology of the Accusative Ergative Continuum: The Case of East Caucasian". In: *General Linguistics* 37.1–2: 77–155.

Schulze, Wolfgang (im Erscheinen). *Person, Klasse, Kongruenz. Fragmente einer Kategorialtypologie des einfachen Satzes in den ostkaukasischen Sprachen. Band 2: Die Person.* München, Newcastle: LINCOM Europa.

Smeets, Rieks. 1984. *Studies in West Circassian Phonology and Morphology.* Leiden: Hakuchi.

Topuria, Guram V. 1995. *Morfologija sklonenija v dagestanskich jazykach.* Tbilisi: Mecniereba.

Tuite, Kevin. 1998. *Kartvelian Morphosyntax.* München, Newcastle: LINCOM Europa.

Van den Berg, Helma 1995. *A Grammar of Hunzib.* München, Newcastle: LINCOM Europa.

Žirkov, L. I. 1955. *Lakskij jazyk. Fonetika i morfologija.* Moskva: Idz AN SSSR.

Wolfgang Schulze, Universität München (Deutschland)

Indexes / Register / Indexes

Index of names / Namenregister / Index de noms

A

Aarons, Debra 146
Aaronson, Doris 130
Aarsleff, Hans 223, 245, 246
Abad, May 1328
Abælard, s. Peter Abælard
Abaev, Vasilij I. 525
Abbi, Anvita 1532, 1537
Abdullaev, Zapir G. 1793
Abel, Fritz 1699
Abel-Rémusat, Jean-Pierre 603
Abelson, Robert P. 648
Abercrombie, David 1391, 1392
Abney, Steven P. 525
Aboh, Enoch Oladé 1079, 1081, 1090
Abraham, Werner 888, 1434, 1504
Abramson, Arthur 1383
Abusch, Dorit 563
Ackema, Peter 905, 1024
Ackerman, Farrell 891
Ackrill, John L. 726
Adam, Charles 86
Adam of Rotweil (= Adam von Rotweil) 216
Adams 285
Adams, Karen Lee 524
Adams, Valerie 702
Adamson, Lilian 1660
Adelung, Johann Christoph 230
Aebischer, Paul 1699
Åfarli, Tor 904
Agard, Frederick 1579
Agheyisi, Rebecca 1649
Agrell, Sigurd 16, 773
Agresti, Alan 430
Agricola, Erhard 642–644
Ahaghotu, A. 1278
Ahlgren, Inger 147, 149
Ahlsén, Elisabeth 126, 127
Aikhenvald, Alexandra Y. 894, 1132, 1137, 1164, 1165, 1275, 1298, 1674
Ailly, Pierre de 203
Aissen, Judith L. 890, 1044, 1064, 1067, 1312, 1442, 1449
Aitchison, Jean 709, 1648
Ajdukiewicz, Kazimierz 66

Akam, Michael 103
Akatsuka, Noriko 998–1000
Akmajian, Adrian 1061
Albert der Große 198
Albert, Martin L. 130, 132, 134, 135
Albert, Salich Y. 1360
Alberti, Gábor 1447
Alberti, Leon Battista 213, 214
Albertus, Laurentius 214
Albrecht, J. E. 159
Albrecht, Jörn 270, 271, 1151, 1152, 1157, 1163, 1564
Aldrete, Bernardo José 218
Alekseev, Michail E. 1783
Alemida, Michael J. 1137
Alexander de Villa Dei (= Alexandre de Villedien, Alexander von Villa Dei) 194, 211
Alexander the Great 236
Al-Fārābī (Al-Pharabius) 198
Alkuin 1687
Allan, Keith 825, 1275
Allan, Robin 696, 703
Allen, Margaret R. 701
Allen, William Sidney 733, 1317, 1319, 1682
Alleyne, Mervyn C. 1659
Allis, C. David 113
Almási, Judit 1248
Alpatov, Vladimir M. 309–312
Alpher, Barry 1210
Alsina, Alex 891
Altmann, Gabriel 26, 1477
Altmann, Hans 625
Alvares, Manuel 217
Ameka, Felix 728, 1081, 1093, 1199, 1498
Amikishiev, V. G. 116
Amith, Jonathan D. 1204
Ammann, Hermann 619
Ammon, Ulrich 1558, 1564, 1569, 1577, 1584
Anchieta, P. José de 254
Andersen, Elaine 1155, 1156
Andersen, Henning 401
Andersen, Paul Kent 894, 993
Andersen, Roger W. 1670, 1671
Anderson, Anne H. 456
Anderson, John 1327, 1329, 1330

Anderson, Lambert 1369
Anderson, Lloyd B. 495, 496, 505, 506
Anderson, R. C. 157
Anderson, Stephen R. 142, 527, 558, 580, 711, 712, 836, 913, 922, 930, 947, 1214–1220, 1223, 1338, 1368, 1624, 1633, 1636
André, Jacques 1151
Andrews, Avery 486–488, 920, 1415
Andriotis, Nicolaos P. 1510
Annius see Nanni, Giovanni
Anscombre, Jean-Claude 1602, 1604
Anselm of Canterbury (= Anselm von Canterbury) 195, 196
Antinucci, Francesco 20, 366, 1142, 1172
Antos, Gerd 441
Anward, Jan 6, 507, 726, 730, 733
Aoun, Joseph 1287
Apollonius Dyscolus (= Apollonios Dyscolos) 185–189, 279, 576
Apresjan, Jurij D. 1191
Apte, Mahadev L. 1535
Aquin, s. Thomas Aquinas
Arce-Arenales, Manuel 925
Archangeli, Diana 416, 681, 685
Arends, Jacques 1657, 1658
Arens, Hans 183, 184, 211, 218, 235, 1555
Arias Abellán, Carmen 1229, 1230
Ariel, Mira 1128, 1130, 1137
Aristar, Anthony R. 529, 968
Aristava, Šota Konstantinovic 1787
Aristoteles (Aristotle, Aristote) 9, 10, 14, 33, 87, 92, 105, 182–184, 192, 193, 195, 197–199, 202–209, 212, 237, 245, 246, 327, 479, 509–511, 563, 657, 726, 1144, 1310, 1311
Armstrong, David F. 142, 145

Arnaud, Jaqueline 1229
Arnauld, Antoine 244–246, 256
Aronoff, Mark 673, 682, 684, 1214–1216, 1221–1223
Aronson, Howard I. 1783–1786, 1792
Arrivé, Michel 643
Arutjunova, Nina D. 1135, 1137
Arvaniti, Amalia 1383, 1384
Asai, Kiyoshi 116
Ascham, Roger 240
Aschenberg, Heidi 436, 440, 473
Ascoli, Graziadio Isaia 1476, 1477
Asenova, Petja 1510, 1514, 1515
Ashby, William J. 1071, 1076
Asher, Nicholas 518, 1137
Asher, Ronald E. 526, 696, 700, 1107, 1460
Ashiwaju, Michael 771
Ashton, Ethel O. 956
Ashton, Roderick 135
Ashworth, Elisabeth J. 203
Askedal, John Ole 1624, 1629, 1634
Asper, Aemilius 188
Assmann, Aleida 1152
Assmann, Jan 49, 1152
Athanasiadou, Angeliki 998
Atherton, Catherine 184
Audax 188
Auer, Peter 49, 458, 459, 1320, 1343, 1391, 1392, 1395–1398
Augustinus, Aurelius (= St. Augustin) 188, 192, 193, 200, 245, 1648
Aurifaber, Johannes 203, 208
Auroux, Sylvain 211, 225–227, 231, 235, 245, 1555, 1576, 1586
Austerlitz, Robert 341
Austin, John Langshaw 55, 70, 72, 438, 445–448, 1038
Austin, Peter 894, 920, 922, 1434, 1435, 1437
Auxerre, s. Remigius von Auxerre
Avery, Oswald 105
Avicenna (Ibn Sīnā) 198
Awbery, G. M. 904
Awobuluyi, O. 1442
Ax, Wolfram 184
Axelrod, Melissa 925

B

Baarda, M. J. van 526
Babby, Leonard H. 889

Bach, Emmon 950, 1280, 1281, 1764
Bache, Carl 557, 561, 564, 565
Bacher, Wilhelm 216
Bachtin, Michail M. 2, 8, 50
Baciu, Ioan 1516
Back, Michael 1341, 1344
Backhouse, Anthony E. 1200
Bacon, Francis 86, 210, 213, 234, 243, 246, 247, 283
Bacon, Roger 200, 202, 218
Baddeley, Alan 1128, 1137
Badecker, William 124
Bagemihl, Bruce 1330, 1331
Bahan, Benjamin J. 149
Bahner, Werner 214
Bailey, Charles James N. 496, 1393, 1649
Bailey, Richard W. 241, 411
Bakeman, Roger 430
Baker, Carl L. 747, 749, 753, 1019, 1020
Baker, Gordon 70
Baker, L. 161
Baker, Mark C. 714, 718, 722, 723, 866, 919, 926, 974, 977, 1215, 1219, 1434–1439
Baker, Philip 1648
Bakhtin, Michail M. 2, 8, 50
Bakker, Dik 856, 865
Bakker, Egbert 918
Bakker, Peter 775, 776, 780, 1645, 1657–1660, 1675
Balagangadhara, S. N. 71
Baldauf, Ingeborg 167
Baldinger, Kurt 294, 1145, 1577, 1578, 1584, 1586
Balibar, Renée 1573
Bally, Charles 436, 972, 1152, 1157, 1161, 1168, 1170, 1172, 1693
Bamgbose, Ayo 696
Bandhu, Chudamani 900
Banniard, Michel 1573, 1687
Bar-Adon, Aaron 1683
Baratin, Marc 181, 184, 186
Barber, E. 906
Bardovi-Harlig, Kathleen 858
Bar-Hillel, Yehoshua 578
Barker, Muhammad Abd-al-Rahman 1438
Barnes, Betsy 1058
Barnes, J. 801
Barnes, Michael P. 1633
Baron, Naomi S. 886, 893
Barros, João de 214
Barsalou, Lawrence W. 1144
Barshi, Immanuel 971, 975–977
Bartels, Christine 1087
Bartlett, Barrie E. 225
Bartlett, Haley H. 1246
Bartoli, Matteo 1475, 1477, 1478

Bartsch, Renate 90, 530, 558, 787, 788, 857
Barwick, Karl 187
Barwise, John 478, 1279
Baskakov, Nikolaj A. 1721
Bastiaanse, Roelien 125
Bat-El, Outi 681, 686
Bates, Elizabeth 123, 125–128, 130
Batteux, Charles 230
Battison, Robbin M. 149
Battistella, Edwin L. 401–403, 407, 415
Battye, Adrian 288
Baudouin de Courtenay, Jan 87
Bauer, Gero 564
Bauer, Laurie 395, 702, 705, 1214, 1598, 1603
Bauer, Winifred 696
Bausani, Alessandro 85, 87, 89
Bavelier, Daphne 13
Bayer, Josef 124
Bayer, Klaus 439
Bayles, Kathryn 124
Bazin, Louis 1013
Bazzanella, Carla 641
Beaglehole, Ernest 1244
Beard, Robert 1217, 1223, 1225
Bearth, Thomas 1081, 1092, 1369
Beaufront, Louis de 87
Beauvais, s. Ralph of Beauvais
Beauzée, Nicolas 222, 223, 225–227, 229–231, 259–261, 623
Becanus, Johannes Goropius 239, 241
Bechert, Johannes 835, 839, 1484, 1492
Becker, Peter B. 112
Becker, Thomas 680, 1219, 1220
Beckman, Mary E. 1373, 1376, 1381, 1383, 1385–1388
Beckmann, Natanael 1501
Beffa, Marie-Lise 874
Behaghel, Otto 377, 623, 855, 858, 860
Behrens, Leila 500, 502, 503, 506, 1215, 1218
Belardi, Walter 181
Bell, Alan 419, 423, 425, 427, 431, 855, 1317, 1319, 1320, 1330–1332, 1461
Bellert, Irene 635–638, 646, 648
Belletti, Adriana 946, 1093
Bellugi, Ursula 99, 143–146, 149, 150
Bembo, Pietro 213, 214, 218
Benavente, Sonia 413
Bendor-Samuel, D. 957
Benedickt, Heinrich 86

Benešová, Eva 622
Bentolila, Simone 115, 116
Benveniste, Emile 338, 346, 1495, 1604
Benvoglienti, Bartolomeo 218
Bereiter, Carl 57, 155, 156
Berengar of Tours (= Berengar von Tours, de Tours) 194
Berg, Helma van den 1780, 1782, 1785
Berg, René van den 527
Berg, Thomas 1326
Bergel'son, Mira M. 318, 1117, 1122, 1125, 1133, 1134, 1137
Berger, Peter L. 43, 45, 445
Bergman, Brita 147−149
Bergmann, Jörg R. 49, 439, 468
Bergsträßer, Gotthelf 1764
Berlin, Brent 33, 415, 1149, 1151, 1178−1180, 1183, 1187, 1190, 1193−1195, 1228−1233, 1236, 1242, 1244, 1248, 1297
Berman, Ruth A. 607
Bernini, Giuliano 1484, 1492, 1498
Bernot, Denise 351, 352
Berquier, Anne 135
Berrendonner, Alain 643
Berruto, Gaetano 634
Berta, Árpád 1727
Bertinetto, Pier Marco 774, 781, 1391, 1393, 1469
Bertoni, Giulio 1477
Berwick, Robert C. 101, 114
Besch, Werner 1473
Besner, Derek 129
Béthune, s. Ebrard of Béthune
Betz, Werner 1606
Beyrer, Arthur 1699
Bezooijen, Renée van 1387
Bezuidenhout, Anne 513
Bhat, Darbne N. S. 501, 502, 1337, 1438
Biasci, Claudia 644
Biber, Douglas 2, 1135, 1137, 1564, 1569
Bibliander, Theodor 219
Bickel, Balthasar 374, 596, 597, 605, 1405
Bickerton, Derek 97, 100, 101, 410, 411, 779−781, 984, 1649, 1651, 1655, 1665
Bickmore, Lee S. 1328
Biermann, Anna 716
Bierwisch, Manfred 636, 1168, 1252, 1253, 1272
Biktimir, Tuvana 904
Biloa, Edmund 1080, 1093, 1094
Binder, Jeffrey 100
Binnick, Robert I. 557, 561−565

Birjulin, Leonid A. 312
Birner, Betty 1072, 1083
Bisang, Walter 524, 601, 603, 604, 611, 843−846, 850, 851, 1116, 1122, 1405, 1408
Bischoff, Bernhard 57
Bishop, Yvonne M. 429, 430
Bisle-Müller, Hansjörg 838
Bittner, Maria 1277
Black 1144
Black, Andrew 1362
Black, Max 1144
Blahoslav, Jan 215
Blake, Barry J. 367, 431, 483−490, 525, 705, 826, 1424, 1430
Blalock, Hubert M. Jr. 419, 422, 424
Blanche-Benveniste, Claire 1058
Blank, Andreas 1143, 1161, 1167, 1172, 1184, 1578, 1582, 1586, 1597, 1600, 1601, 1603, 1604, 1606
Blank, David L. 181
Blanke, Detlev 86−92
Blanken, Gerhard 124
Blevins, Juliette 1310, 1312, 1348, 1352
Bloch, Jules 1529−1531, 1683
Blommaert, Jan 414, 459
Bloom, Lois 1305
Bloom, Paul 101
Bloomfield, Leonard 250, 295, 338, 479, 697, 699−701, 834, 1133
Blumenberg, Hans 105
Blumenthal, Peter 1161, 1163, 1170, 1172
Blumer, Herbert 45, 46, 445
Blund, Robert 194
Boas, Franz 264, 695, 696, 704, 836, 837, 1126, 1228, 1427, 1439, 1540
Boccaccio, Giovanni 213
Bocheński, Innocentius 68
Bock, Hans Herrmann 1483
Bodnar, J. W. 117
Boeschoten, Hendrik 1721
Boethius, Dacus (= Bothius von Dacien) 203, 206, 208
Boethius, Anicius Manlius Severinus 192−195, 198, 208
Bogdanova, Ekaterina 750
Bogoras, Waldemar 696
Bohas, Georges 277, 683
Böhm, Roger 891
Boissin, Henri 1515, 1519
Bókay, Antal 636
Bolinger, Dwight L. 372, 378, 495, 502, 983, 984, 989, 1038, 1380, 1382, 1384, 1396
Bolkestein, Machtelt 982

Bolton, Ralph 1229, 1230
Bonaventura, St. (Giovanni di Fidanza) 198
Bondarko, Aleksandr V. 772, 774
Bonfante, Giuliano 1477
Boogaart, Ronny 562, 564
Booij, Geert 704, 1215, 1218, 1225, 1361
Boom, Holger van den 64
Bopp, Franz 1555
Boretzky, Norbert 1675
Borkin, Ann 984
Borowsky, Toni 1329, 1352
Borri, Cristoforo 254, 255
Borsche, Tilmann 267
Borst, Arno 86, 211, 220, 235, 238
Bortolini, Umberto 119
Bosch, Peter 638
Bossong, Georg 251, 252, 485, 873−876, 880, 1142, 1172, 1496, 1555, 1568, 1575, 1582, 1586
Bossuet, Jacques Bénigne 608, 609
Botas, Bécares 186
Botha, Rudolf P. 701
Bouda, Karl 1783
Bouhours, Dominique 242
Boulle, J. 352
Bourbaki group 9
Bourcey, Amable de 242
Boutroux, Émile 107
Bowerman, Melissa 571, 573
Bowers, John 1091
Boyes Braem, Penny 142
Boyle, Robert 223, 234
Boynton, Robert 1229, 1232
Brakel, Arthur 1396
Brakel, Jap van 1229
Brands, Horst Wilfried 1740
Brandt Corstius, Hugo 1278
Brandt, Margareta 55, 630, 645, 647, 1561
Brassai, Sámuel 627, 1442
Braun, Friederike 580
Brauner, Siegmund 771
Braunmüller, Kurt 836
Braunroth, Manfred 438
Brazil, David 641
Bréal, Michel 1604
Bredin, Hugh 1157
Breen, J. G. 1005
Breetvelt, I. 156
Brekle, Herbert Ernst 211, 215, 235, 239, 245, 246
Bremond, Claude 645
Brennan, Mary 147−149
Brennan, Susan 456, 457
Brennan, Virginia 1087
Brentari, Diane 145
Bresnan, Joan 1055−1057, 1069, 1070, 1424, 1435, 1437

Bricker, Victoria R. 1248
Brien, David 144
Brinker, Klaus 55, 441, 635, 644, 645, 930
Brinton, Laurel J. 562−565
Brito, s. Radulphus Brito
Britt, M. Anne 159
Britton, Bruce K. 157
Broca, Paul 13, 98, 100
Brocensis, s. Sanctius Brocensis, Franciscus
Brockhaus, Wiebke 1328
Brody, Michael 621, 1089, 1090, 1451, 1452
Brøndal, Viggo 271
Brooks, Bryan 817
Broschart, Jürgen 91, 326, 327, 337, 480, 485, 488, 501, 505, 506, 537, 548, 730
Broselow, Ellen 686, 1323, 1328, 1331
Brown, Cecil H. 1153−1156, 1178−1188, 1190, 1193, 1195, 1297
Brown, D. Richard 526
Brown, Gillian 435, 639, 642, 646, 648, 1581
Brown, Penelope 9, 17, 378, 448, 463, 570, 745, 1650
Brown, R. W. 745
Browning, Marguerite 747, 1091
Brozas, Sánchez de las 255, 256
Bruce, Gösta 1381, 1383
Bruder, Gail 1135
Brugmann, Karl 87, 562, 577, 581, 680
Bruneau-Ludwig, Florence 413
Brunel, Gilles 1179
Brunet, Roger 1483
Bruni, Francesco 1573
Brünner, Gisela 51, 446
Brunner, H. 166
Bruno, Giordano 86
Brunot, Ferdinand 629
Bruyn, Adrienne 1660
Buber, Martin 72
Buchanan, Lori 129
Buchholz, Kai 70, 73
Buchholz, Oda 834, 835, 997, 1516, 1527
Buck, Carl Darling 1180, 1304, 1305
Buck, Susanne 475
Budina Ladzina, T. 958
Buekens, Filip 445
Bühler, Karl 2−5, 7, 11, 44, 52, 56, 92, 154, 303, 408, 409, 435−437, 451, 458, 460, 577, 578, 580, 584, 587, 620, 1144, 1157, 1342, 1598
Bull, William E. 558, 559
Bullokar, William 215

Bulygina, Tat'jana 1137
Bunn, Gordon 1325
Bunn, Ruth 1325
Buntinx, Inge 99
Burgess, Don 962
Burgess, Eunice 1083
Buridan, s. Johannes Buridan
Büring, Daniel 620, 622, 625, 1444
Burkard, Franz-Peter 477
Burling, Robbins 100
Burne 269
Burridge, Kate 1707
Burrow, Thomas 700
Bursill-Hall, Geoffrey L. 245
Burzio, Luigi 314
Buscha, Joachim 1627
Bußmann, Hadumod 384, 398
Buszard-Welcher, Laura 1214
Butler, H. 1544, 1546
Bybee, Joan L. 7, 16, 318, 360, 373, 378, 421, 426, 432, 530, 537−539, 541−544, 547, 554, 557, 561−563, 586, 677, 688, 690, 709−713, 769−771, 773, 775−781, 784, 795−798, 815, 856, 900, 980, 983, 991, 1214−1220, 1223, 1297, 1405, 1462, 1463, 1466, 1579, 1581
Bynon, Theodora 25, 370, 380, 912
Byrne, Francis 1661
Byron, F. Robinson 430

C

Caesar, Julius Gaius 373
Calabrese, Andrea 1445
Calboli, Gualtiero 1692
Caldwell, Robert 1529, 1532
Calepinus, Ambrogius 215
Camargo, E. 353
Camden, William 241
Cameracanna, Emanuela 150
Campanella, Thomaso 247, 251, 255, 256, 260
Campbell, Lyle 36, 423, 432, 850, 986, 987, 1159, 1187, 1457, 1534, 1540−1548, 1551, 1577, 1624−1627, 1635, 1636, 1669−1674
Campbell, W. N. 1388
Cann, Rebecca 118
Cano Aguilar, Rafael 1566, 1573
Canterbury, Anselm of 195, 196
Cantrall, William R. 747
Capell, Arthur 503, 1280
Capella, Martianus 193, 194
Caplan, David 98
Caramazza, Alfonso 124

Caramuel y Lobkowitz, Juan 247
Caravolas, Jean-Antoine 211, 217
Carden, Guy 1662
Cardinaletti, Anna 625
Cardona, George 275
Carducci, Giosue 473
Carew, Richard 241
Carlson, Gregory 1443
Carlson, Lauri 774, 1088
Carlson, Robert 1134, 1401, 1407
Carlson, Thomas B. 56, 452
Carnap, Rudolf 54, 69, 80
Caron, Jean 1563, 1581
Carpenter, Patricia 157
Carstairs-McCarthy, Andrew (= Carstairs, Andrew) 390, 1214, 1222, 1223
Carstensen, Kai-Uwe 1252
Cartesius s. Descartes
Cartier, Alice 351, 352
Casacchia, Giorgio 278
Casad, Eugene H. 10
Casagrande, Joseph B. 1179
Casaubon, Meric 241
Cassiodorus 193
Cassirer, Ernst 1152
Casterline, Dorothy 144
Catford, John C. 435
Catts, Hugh W. 129
Causeret, Jean-François 353, 354
Cavalli, Giacomo 112
Cavalli-Sforza, Luigi Luca 117, 118, 1483, 1484
Cazden, Courtney B. 439
Celan, Paul 717
Cennamo, Michela 751
Čeremisina, Maja I. 319
Cerquiglini, Bernard 1570
Čertkova, Marina Ju. 319
Cervadze, Ilia 1784
Chadwick, J. 173
Chafe, Wallace L. 158, 159, 440, 483, 624, 777, 814, 833, 998, 1003, 1004, 1125−1130, 1135, 1298, 1306, 1566, 1568
Champeaux, s. William of Champeaux
Chang, Nien-Chuang 1383
Chang, Suk-Jin 1014
Chang, Zhang Yan 1229
Chao, Yuen Ren 1051, 1204, 1209, 1685
Chapman, George 240
Chapman, Shirley 696
Chappell, Hillary 377, 528, 965, 977, 1197
Charachidzé, Georges 1790
Chargaff, Erwin 105
Chari, P. 132, 135

Charles IV 215
Charles V 243
Charney, Rosalind 744
Charolles, Michel 593, 634, 637, 646, 649
Chary, Prithika 135
Chatterji, S. K. 1535
Chejne, Anwar G. 1682
Chelliah, Shobhana 1216
Chen, Matthew 1370, 1374, 1386
Cheng, Chao-Ming 130
Cheng, Lisa Lai-Shen 1019, 1020, 1024, 1025, 1095
Cherchi, Lucien 640
Chesterman, Andrew 838
Chevillard, Jean-Luc 276
Chiang, Wen-yu 1087
Chiara, Maria 1182
Chirinos Rivera, Andrés 414
Choe, Hyon-Sook 1442, 1444, 1448, 1449, 1452
Choe, Jae-Woong 1289
Choi, Gwon Jin 1210
Choi, Soonja 1259
Chomsky, Noam A. 14, 28, 36, 41, 66, 75, 76, 79–81, 95, 116, 127, 245, 258, 283, 284, 288, 289, 303, 370, 401, 403, 406, 479, 619, 622, 683, 684, 753, 790, 791, 866, 903, 908, 909, 942, 946, 947, 1088, 1089, 1094, 1168, 1310, 1314, 1337, 1338, 1352, 1385, 1409, 1603
Christmann, Hans Helmut 242, 243, 251, 267, 268, 271, 1476
Christophe, Anne 1363
Christophersen, Paul 833
Chrysippus 236
Chung, Sandra 560–565, 813, 913, 1005
Churchill, Don W. 99
Churchward, C. Maxwell 836
Chvany, Catherine V. 557, 676
Cicourel, Aaron V. 49, 439, 449, 455, 460
Cinque, Guglielmo 625, 1080, 1385
Citolini, Alessandro 1681
Claes, Franz 219
Clajus, Johannes 215
Clancy, Patricia 1124, 1127
Clark, Eve V. 528, 954, 1172
Clark, Herbert H. 50, 56, 57, 154, 444, 452, 456, 457, 1252
Clark, Ross 822, 836
Clarke, David D. 43
Classen, Constance 1304
Claudi, Ulrike 503, 528, 1549, 1609–1610, 1613, 1614
Clauss, Sidonie 87
Clayton-Smith, Jill 99

Clements, George Nick 684, 1094, 1132, 1312, 1317, 1318, 1326, 1329, 1348, 1387, 1452
Clenardus, Nicolas 217
Cloarec-Heiss, F. 351
Closs Traugott, Elizabeth s. Traugott, Elizabeth Closs
Cochran, William 419
Coe, Michael 174
Coelho, Francisco Adolfo 1649
Coenen, Herman 49
Coerts, Jane 148
Cohen, Antonie 1381
Colarusso, John 1775, 1779, 1782, 1783, 1792
Cole, Desmont T. 696, 699, 704
Cole, Peter 528, 638, 696, 700, 701, 802, 891, 917, 918, 921, 962, 1092, 1633, 1634
Colenso, William 1246, 1248
Colet, John 215
Collado-Vides, Julio 116
Collart, Jean 186
Collier, Mark 1756
Collins, Allan 45, 79
Collins, James 1314
Comenius, Johannes Amos 235, 244
Company Company, Concepción 1700
Compes, Isabel 718, 720
Comrie, Bernard 16, 25, 26, 32, 34, 54, 336, 341, 360, 364, 365, 389, 398, 406, 419, 478, 482–488, 525, 526, 528, 557–564, 592, 709, 716, 769, 771, 772, 774, 776–778, 792, 804, 851, 860, 875, 878, 880, 886, 887, 889–891, 893, 904, 928, 932, 957, 977, 989, 990, 998, 1000, 1014, 1018, 1025, 1026, 1100, 1216–1218, 1415, 1442, 1494, 1495, 1574, 1625, 1634, 1636, 1642–1644, 1721, 1722, 1754, 1756
Conches, s. William of Conches
Condillac, Étienne Bonnot de 90, 223, 226–231, 268, 608, 609
Confiant, Raphael 4
Conklin, Harold C. 744, 1229
Connell, Bruce 1387
Connolly, John H. 51
Consentius 188
Conte, Maria Elisabeth 634, 638, 639, 642, 649, 650, 1604, 1605
Cook, Eung-Do 526
Cooper, Robin 1279
Cooper, William E. 318
Cooreman, Ann 913
Corbett, Greville G. 34, 334, 525, 817, 819, 826, 857, 967, 1131, 1164, 1229, 1246, 1425

Corbin, Danielle 1216, 1219–1222
Corblin, Francis 639
Cordemoy, Géraud de 245
Corina, David 145
Cornish, Francis 638, 1128
Correas, Gonzalo 255, 256
Correll, Christoph 1763, 1766, 1771
Corver, Norbert 907
Coseriu, Eugenio 11, 17, 63, 64, 91, 181, 230, 250, 251, 266, 267, 270–272, 294, 338, 341, 436, 437, 441, 468, 469, 473, 558, 637, 642, 643, 647, 1143, 1145–1148, 1151, 1217, 1223, 1554, 1556, 1558–1562, 1564, 1565, 1572, 1574, 1575, 1581, 1583, 1596, 1598, 1602, 1623, 1682, 1692, 1697
Costa, Rachel 560
Coulmas, Florian 169, 1601, 1602
Coulter, Geoffrey R. 145
Coulthard, Malcolm 635, 642, 647
Couper-Kuhlen, Elisabeth 459, 641, 1391, 1392
Courtrai, s. Siger of Courtrai
Couturat, Louis 87, 89
Cowell, Mark W. 821
Crago, Martha B. 119, 120
Crago, Michael 99
Craig, Colette G. 900, 1275
Crain, Stephen 96
Cram, David 90, 91
Creider, Chet A. 623, 629, 1080
Creider, Jane T. 623, 629
Cresswell, Max 66
Crick, Francis 105
Crimmens, M. 478
Crisp, Peter 1229
Cristofaro, Sonia 1506
Croft, William 6, 7, 10, 15, 25, 280–282, 294, 360, 366, 370–378, 406, 407, 415, 485, 487, 502, 505, 506, 528, 669, 727, 732, 862, 863, 909, 910, 961, 1048, 1143, 1297, 1424, 1569, 1574, 1576–1579, 1581, 1636, 1754–1758
Croneberg, Carl G. 144
Crosson, Bruce 100
Crothers, Edward J. 649
Crowley, Terry 819
Cruse, D. Alan 1046, 1145, 1190, 1224
Cruttenden, Alan 1382–1384
Crystal, David 495, 496, 1142
Csató, Éva Á. 1721, 1722, 1741
Culicover, Peter W. 626, 1082, 1083
Curtiss, Susan 97

Curtius, Georg 385
Curto, S. 164
Cutler, Anne 554, 708–711, 856, 1214, 1220, 1217
Cyffer, Norbert 957

D

D'Andrade, Roy G. 1207
D'Achille, Paolo 474
Dacus, s. Johannes Dacus
Dahl, Östen 557–564, 619, 672, 677, 769–771, 774–781, 856, 863, 1005, 1116, 1122, 1204–1206, 1210–1212, 1424, 1466, 1469, 1495, 1496, 1501, 1506
Dahlenburg, Till 88, 89
Dahlmann, Hellfried 186
Dahlstrom, Amy 911
Dal Negro, Silvia 1674
Dalgarno, George 86–92
Dalrymple, Mary 909
Damasio, Antonio R. 13
Damasio, Hanna C. 13
Damourette, Jaques 2, 3
Dancygier, Barbara 608
Daneš, František 16, 350, 608, 619, 637, 641, 642, 644, 645, 648, 1171, 1442
Danon-Boileau, Laurent 576, 577
Dante Alighieri 7, 210, 213, 217, 219, 253, 254, 1681
Darbelnet, Jean 1152, 1161, 1170
Dardano, Maurizio 401, 408
Dardel, Robert de 1692, 1693
Darnell, Regna 1540
Darwin, C. J. 1392
Dascal, Marcelo 635, 643
Dasypodius, Petrus 215
Dauer, Rebecca M. 1393, 1396
Dauzat, Albert 268
Davidson, Donald 479, 480, 517, 519, 1446
Davies, John 696, 961, 1302, 1303
Davies, William 887
Davis, Stuart 1324, 1326, 1327
Davison, Alice 1113, 1114, 1122
Dawkins, Richard M. 1642, 1643
Dayley, Jon P. 696, 701, 956, 1426
De Angulo, Jaime 958
De Beaugrande, Robert Alain 155, 441, 593, 634–637, 643, 644, 648, 649
De Bleser, Ria 124–126
De Caen, Vincent 557
De Francis, John 163, 174

De Jongh, Dick 1136
De León, Lourdes 1543, 1548
De Reuse, Willem 1217
De Vreese, Luc P. 131
Dearden, Peter 103
DeCamp, David 1649
Déchaine, Rose-Marie 1663
Declerck, Renaat 558, 560
Décsy, Gyula 424, 1506
Dee, John 86
Dees, Anthonij 1479, 1480
Deeters, Gerhard 1778
DeGraff, Michel 1665
Dehaenne, Stanislas 13
Dekydtspotter, Laurent Pierre Aimé 1093
Delahunty, Gerald P. 1092
DeLancey, Scott 480, 485, 911, 1430
Delattre, Pierre 1393, 1396
DeLeón, Lourdes 570
Delin, Judy 627
Dell, F. 1330
Demers, Richard A. 730, 837
Deming, William Edward 423
Demirdache, Hamida K. 1094, 1095
Democritus 105
Den Os, Els 1391, 1392
Dench, Alan 1291
Denham, Kristin E. 1079
Denning, Keith 280
Dentler, Sigrid 1627
Deny, Jean 1721
Depraetere, Ilse 773
Derbolav, Josef 182
Derbyshire, Desmond C. 525, 527, 696, 729, 867, 967, 1081
Deroy, Louis 1606
Dervillez-Bastuij, Jaqueline 1252
Desbordes, Françoise 181
Descartes, René 86, 107, 234, 235, 244–248, 255
Desclés, Jean-Pierre 889
Deseriev, Ju. D. 1793
DeSilva, M. W. Sugahapala 1535
Despauterius, Johannes 212, 213
Desrosier, Jules 142
Dessaint, Micheline 351
Desző, László 267, 858
Detges, Ulrich 1580, 1581, 1586
Deuchar, Margaret 142, 146, 150, 795, 803
Deutsch, Georg 134
Devriendt, Betty 51
Dewey, John 445
Di Sciullo, Anna-Maria 705, 718
Diakonoff, Igor M. 1746, 1759

Dickinson, Connie 460, 461
Diderichsen, Paul 219
Diderot, Denis 230, 259
Diebold jr., A. Richard 1549
Diem, Werner 217
Diesing, Molly 1444, 1446
Diessel, Holger 832
Diewald, Gabriele 1579
Dijk, Teun A. van 157, 158, 160, 435, 438, 441, 634–636, 641, 643–648
Dijkhoff, Marta B. 980, 1409, 1658, 1666
Dik, Simon C. 51, 90, 294, 483, 488, 524, 611, 622, 643, 688, 985, 1079, 1085, 1087, 1092, 1093, 1107, 1171, 1230, 1305, 1404, 1415
Diller, Anthony 1193
Dilthey, Wilhelm 281
Dimmendaal, Gerrit Jan 696, 698
Dinnsen, Daniel 1337
Diogenes Laertios 237
Diomedes 188
Dionysius of Halicarnassus (= Dionys von Halikarnass) 182
Dionysius of Thracia (= Dionysios Thrax, Denys le Thracien) 182, 185, 211, 236, 741, 1310
Dirr, Adolf 1782
Dirven, René 998, 1147, 1148, 1252
Dittmann, Jürgen 124, 127
Dittmar, Norbert 439, 440
Dixon, Robert M. W. 489, 501, 525, 527, 703, 705, 728–731, 743, 825, 883, 886–893, 912, 913, 919, 961, 967, 979, 983, 984, 1170, 1195–1198, 1304, 1323, 1754
Dixon, Ronald 1540
Dodwell, Peter 1306
Doerfer, Gerhard 1721, 1740
Dokulil, Miklos 1223
Dolinina, Inga B. 312, 887
Domi, Mahir 1521, 1522
Dominicus Gundissalinus (= Domingo Gundisalvo 194, 198
Dominicy, Marc 223
Don, Jan 1218
Donabédian, Anaid 354
Donaldson, Tamsin 527, 802
Donat (Aelius Donatus) 187–189, 192, 193, 201, 206, 211, 214, 215
Donegan, Patricia J. 686, 1326, 1327, 1330, 1341, 1343, 1347, 1362, 1363, 1394
Dong, Shan 116

Index of names

Donnellan, Donald 513
Donnet, Daniel 186
Donovan, A. 1392
Dorfmüller-Karpusa, Käthi 640
Dorian, Nancy C. 1670–1674
Dositheus 187, 188
Dotter, Franz 141, 142, 150, 376
Dougherty, Janet W. D. 1180
Downing, Bruce T. 529
Downing, Pamela 1127, 1132, 1275
Dowty, David 296, 301, 484, 561–563, 866, 1171
Draper, Norman R. 429
Drayton, Michael 240
Drechsel, Emanuel J. 1648, 1652
Drescher, Martina 644
Dresher, B. Elan 1347, 1355, 1357, 1360
Dressler, Wolfgang U. 127, 372, 375, 405, 406, 408, 415, 441, 593, 629, 630, 635–644, 648, 649, 669, 671, 680, 682, 688, 712, 1162, 1215–1221, 1225, 1338–1342, 1605, 1670–1672, 1679
Droixhe, Daniel 1555, 1576
Drosaeus, Johannes 214
Drosée, Jean s. Drosaeus
Drossard, Werner 336, 487, 490, 537, 538
Drubig, Hans Bernhard 619, 621, 625, 1084, 1089, 1090, 1095
Dry, Helen 559, 562, 563
Dryer, Matthew S. 28, 37, 314, 316, 317, 363, 366, 423, 425, 431, 432, 529, 681, 696, 733, 827, 832, 843, 844, 855–858, 860–865, 869, 900, 901, 1198, 1280, 1292, 1462, 1464–1468, 1492, 1494, 1504, 1629, 1630
Du Bois, John W. 375
Du Fue, Veronica 817
Du Marsais, César Chesneau 223, 230, 231
Dube, K. C. 1113, 1122
Dubinsky, Stanley 930
Dubois, Jacques 214
Dubuisson, Colette 142, 148
Ducatez, Guy 1248
Ducatez, Jacky 1248
Duchan, Judith 1135
Ducrot, Oswald 562, 563, 644
Duffley, Patrick 984
Duhoux, Y. 173
Duličenko, Aleksandr 87
Dumézil, Georges 1108
Dunbar, Robin 100
Duns Scotus, s. Johannes Duns Scotus

DuPonceau, Peter S. 1126
Durand, Jacques 1329
Durante, Marcello 1573
Duranti, Alessandro 435, 438–440
Durbin, Marshall 1229
Durie, Mark 817, 886, 1193, 1414, 1419
Durkheim, Émile 20
Dürr, Michael 1545
Durrell, Martin 1252
Dutton, Thomas E. 743, 1646
Dyen, Isidor 1483
Dyskolos, s. Apollonios Dyscolus

E

Eades, Diana 705
Early, Robert 680
Ebbinghaus, Horst 142, 149
Ebert, Karen H. 610, 774, 837, 1531, 1533, 1537
Ebert, Robert P. 1707
Ebners, Ferdinand 72
Ebrard of Béthune (= Eberhard von Béthune, Evrart de Béthune) 194
Echegoyen, Artemisa 1543
Eckert, Gabriele 271
Eckert, Penelope 1
Eckman, Fred R. 1337
Eco, Umberto 86–88, 91, 92, 210, 211, 216, 239
Edel, Elmar 1742
Edmondson, Jerry A. 747, 750
Edmondson, Munro S. 1540
Edmondson, William H. 147
Edwards, Derek 1305
Efron, Bradley 430
Egli, Urs 184
Ehinger, Annette 124
Ehlich, Konrad 41, 46, 51, 56, 446, 577, 585, 1039, 1123, 1583
Ehrenfels, Christian von 8
Ehrich, Veronika 478, 583, 585
Ehrman, Madeline E. 696, 703
Eigler, Gunther 154, 155, 161
Eisenstein, Elizabeth 475
Ekman, Paul 1200
Elizabeth I 215, 240, 241
Elliott, Dale E. 1038, 1046
Elmedlaoui, Mohamed 1330
Elyot, Thomas 240
Embick, David 1007
Emeneau, Murray B. 1457, 1529–1531, 1533–1535, 1643, 1644
Emmorey, Karen 142, 145
Emonds, Joseph E. 288, 727, 844

Enç, Mürvet 560, 563, 796, 1443, 1445
Endress, Gerhard 1682
Endzelin, Janis 958
Engberg-Pedersen, Elisabeth 146–149
Engelhardt, Hiltraud 930
England, Nora C. 910, 962, 1546
Engler, Rudolf 371
Enkvist, Nils Erik 439, 636, 637, 641
Enrico, John 1442, 1449, 1452
Epée, Roger 1088, 1093
Epstein, Richard 1135
Erasmus of Rotterdam (Erasmus, Desiderius) 212, 213
Erbse, Hartmut 184
Erdal, Marcel 1727
Erdmann, Karl Otto 437
Erguvanli, Eser 1051, 1056, 1063, 1068–1071, 1073, 1076, 1442
Eriugena, s. John Scotus Eriugena
Erlandsen, Jens 1272
Erman, Adolf 1743, 1755
Eroms, Hans-Werner 624
Erteschik-Shir, Nomi 1084
Erting, Carol J. 149
Ertl, István 92
Ervin-Tripp, Susan 134, 449, 450, 459
Erwin, E. M. 879
Escalante Gutierrez, Carmen 414
Escalante Hernández, Roberto 1541
Eschbach, Achim 577
Estienne, Henri 218, 237
Estienne, Robert 212
Estival, Dominique 1634
Ettmayer, Karl von 1479
Evans, Nicholas 6, 503, 1194, 1199, 1204, 1211, 1277, 1282, 1289, 1291, 1308
Everaert, Martin 1214
Everett, Daniel 696, 1324
Ewart, A. K. 99

F

Faarlund, Jan Terje 1633, 1706, 1707, 1708, 1713
Fabricius-Hansen, Cathrine 586
Fagan 920
Faingold, Eduardo D. 407
Faithfull, R. Glynn 1681
Falk, Yehuda N. 891
Faltz, Leonard M. 757, 758, 920, 1289
Fanning, Buist M. 562, 563

Fanselow, Gisbert 41, 858, 1633
Farnetari, Edda 1392
Farwaneh, Samira 685
Fasold, Ralph W. A. 696
Fauconnier, Gilles 887
Fauriel 249
Fayol, Michel 642
Fecht, Gerhard 1747, 1756
Fehling, Detlev 1507
Feilke, Helmuth 49, 55, 455, 458
Feldman, H. 902, 1106
Felix, Sascha 41
Fellman, Jack 1762
Fenk-Oczlon, Gertraud 403
Fenn, Peter 564
Fenyvesi, Anna 1643
Ferdinand de Aragón 214, 215
Ferguson, Charles A. 1337, 1573, 1670, 1676, 1762
Ferro, Lisa 747
Fertig, David 373
Feuillet, Jack 1172, 1515
Fiedl, Günther 90
Fiedler, Wilfried 834, 835, 1516, 1527
Fiehler, Reinhard 41
Figge, Udo L. 648
Filimonova, Elena 281, 282
Fill, Alwin 1598
Fillenbaum, S. 132, 134
Filliozat, Jean 1682
Fillmore, Charles J. 76, 294, 301, 312, 478, 482−484, 488, 512, 569, 832, 942, 1039, 1046,1144, 1150
Finck, Franz Nikolaus 249, 266, 268−272, 503, 660, 962
Firbas, Jan 620, 623, 1084
Firth, John R. 438
Fischer, Olga 371−373, 375, 382
Fischer, Renate 141
Fischer, Susan 143
Fischer, Wolfdietrich 1248, 1403
Fisher, S. 352, 357
Fisher, Simon 120
Fisher, William 679
Fishman, Joshua A. 1684
Fisiak, Jacek 1583, 1624
Fitzpatrick-Cole, Jennifer 1349, 1357
Flaubert, Gustave 606, 640
Fleckenstein, Josef 1686, 1687
Fleischer, Wolfgang 705, 1598
Fleischman, Suzanne 250, 563, 640, 795, 815, 1570, 1578, 1579, 1586, 1700
Fletcher, Charles R. 160
Fletcher, Janet 1393
Flower, Linda 154−156

Fodor, Janet D. 366, 1596
Fodor, Jerry 76, 78, 80
Foley, James 1338
Foley, William A. 482, 484, 489, 504, 525, 528, 537, 538, 570, 571, 593, 605, 611−614, 696, 703, 704, 728, 729, 819, 835, 891, 899, 905, 907, 908, 981, 985, 966, 1115, 1122, 1124, 1130, 1133, 1195, 1196, 1201, 1305, 1419, 1434, 1438
Fónagy, Ivan 373
Fontana, Josep M. 1703
Foolen, Ad 755
Forgas, Joseph P. 1
Formigari, Lia 223, 228, 608, 1555
Forrest, Linda 905
Forrest-Pressley, Donna-Lynn 161
Forster, Peter 87, 89, 91
Forsyth, John 561, 562, 769
Fortescue, Michael 696, 698, 704, 900, 917, 918, 921, 1112, 1122
Fortunio, Giovanni Francesco 213
Foucault, Michel 1555
Fowler, Carol A. 1392
Fox, Barbara A. 528, 925, 1135
Fox, James A. 1648
Frachtenberg, Leo J. 695, 696
Fradin, Bernard 1058
Frajzyngier, Zygmunt 904, 983, 987
Franck, Dorothea 644, 646
François, Denise 1058
François, Frédéric 435
François, Jacques 483, 488
Frank, Barbara 469, 1570
Frank, Paul 526
Frank, Thomas 2, 87, 88, 91
Franke, Wilhelm 55
Fraser, N. M. 525
Frawley, William 478, 483
Frazier, Lyn 360, 858, 859
Fredborg, Karin M. 194−196
Frede, Michael 184
Frederiksen, Carl H. 155
Freed, Alice 562, 565
Freed, Barbara F. 1668
Freeland, J. S. 958
Freeze, Ray 943, 944, 949, 951, 952
Frege, Gottlob 209, 509−511, 519, 520, 806
Frei, Henri 385, 582, 878, 1582
Freidin, Robert 909, 1136
French, Patrice L. 1157
French, Peter 86
Fretheim, Thorstein 1054, 1064, 1071, 1076, 1129
Friederici, Angela D. 13, 124, 125

Friedman, Lynn A. 143
Friedman, Victor A. 778, 1791
Friedrich, Paul 563
Fries, Peter H. 487
Frishberg, Nancy 150
Fritsche, Johannes 644
Fritz, Gerd 1577, 1578, 1581, 1597
Frumkina, Rebecca 1246
Fu, Jialing 1685
Fuchs, Cathérine 642
Fudge, Erik C. 1327
Fujii Yamaguchi, Seiko 1008
Fujimura, Osamu 129
Fujisaki, Hiroya 1380
Fujitani, Nariakira 278
Fukui, Naoki 946

G

Gabain, Annemarie von 1720
Gabelentz, Georg von der 249−252, 266, 270, 481, 482, 487, 619, 842, 1442, 1575
Gadamer, Hans-Georg 1554
Gadet, Françoise 1569
Gahl, Susanne 1325
Gai, Amikam 1764, 1766
Gair, James W. 1097
Gal, Susan 1674
Galand, G. 351, 352
Galbraith, D. 154, 156
Galilei, Galileo 234, 255
Galloway, Brent D. 1240, 1248
Galton, Francis 425
Gambarara, Daniele 181
Gambhir, Vijay 1442
Gamillscheg, Ernst 835, 1699
Gamut, L. T. F. 68
Gardies, Jean-Louis 68
Gardiner, Alan H. 1743
Gårding, Eva 1381
Gardt, Andreas 211, 235
Garey, Howard B. 557, 565
Garfinkel, Harold 45, 439, 445
Garrod, Simon C. 158
Garvin, Paul 1495
Gauchat, Louis 1477
Gauger, Hans-Martin 91, 401, 1158, 1163, 1555, 1599, 1600
Gazdar, Gerald 857
Geach, Peter 515
Gébelin, Court de 230
Gebhard, Jerry G. 1651
Gecadze, Irina O. 1779
Geckeler, Horst 1145−1148, 1153, 1168, 1623
Geddes, W. R. 1228
Gee, James P. 145
Geeraerts, Dirk 81, 82, 1581
Gehlen, Arnold 1554, 1559
Gehring, Walter 115

Geis, Michael 1038
Geisler, Hans 1142, 1172, 1337, 1341, 1605
Gelderen, Elly van 756
Gelenius, Sigismundus 220
Geluykens, Ronald 1012, 1128
Genetti, Carol 850, 1002
Geniušienė, Emma 751, 920, 936, 937
Gensini, Stefano 214
Gensler, Orin D. 37, 1506
Gent, s. Henry of Ghent
Georgiev, Vladimir 1512, 1513, 1517, 1521
Georgopoulos, Carol 944, 946
Gerdts, Donna B. 714, 719
Gerhardi, Gerhard C. 243
Gerhardt, Carl Immanuel 87
Gerl, Hanna-Barbara 86
Germain, Claude 435
Gernsbacher, Morton Ann 159, 160, 649, 1130
Gerritsen, Marinel 1631, 1707
Gerth, Bernhard 330, 331
Gessinger, Joachim 222, 238
Gessner, Konrad 219
Gévaudan, Paul 1147, 1158, 1161
Ghini, Mirco 1351
Giacalone Ramat, Anna 382, 1581
Gibbon, Dafydd 641
Giegerich, Hans 1348
Giglioli, Pier Paolo 1
Gil, Alberto 643
Gil, David 730, 827, 858, 968, 1275−1280, 1287, 1289, 1290, 1347, 1363, 1420
Gilbert de la Porrée (= Gilbert von Poitiers, Gilbertus Porretanus) 194, 196, 197
Gilliéron, Jules 1473, 1474, 1477
Gilligan, Gary 285, 286, 708, 709, 1214, 1217, 1220, 1500
Gilman, A. 745
Ginneken, Jacques van 82
Giora, Rachel 642
Gipper, Helmut 141, 1152
Girard, Franck 117
Girard, Gabriel 230, 256−259, 261, 268
Givón, Talmy 4, 41, 51, 160, 301, 318, 370, 379−382, 403−406, 408, 410, 411, 460, 461, 477, 478, 480, 482, 484, 488, 501, 505, 528, 529, 611, 613, 623, 624, 638, 641, 649, 709, 727, 728, 790, 838, 855, 857, 860, 870, 884, 893, 903, 904, 907, 908, 911, 912, 921, 923, 954, 979, 983, 985, 998, 999, 1002, 1005, 1006, 1014,
1021, 1022, 1079, 1082, 1085, 1098−1100, 1125, 1127−1130, 1135−1137, 1171, 1276, 1400, 1566, 1582, 1609, 1612, 1649
Glavanov, Doris 158
Gleason, Henry A. 495
Gleitman, Lila R. 1305
Glinert, Lewis 696, 703, 704
Glück, Helmut 1142
Glymour, Clark 419, 427, 429−431
Göbels, Astrid 246, 247
Godart, Louis 173
Goddard, Cliff 224, 304, 742, 838, 1143, 1187, 1191−1194, 1196, 1199−1201
Goddard, Yves 1361
Goebl, Hans 1473, 1477, 1479−1483
Goedemans, Rob 1325
Goedsche, C. R. 557
Goethe, Johann Wolfgang von 1688
Goffman, Erving 9, 439, 451, 452, 462, 463
Goldap, Chistel 1545
Goldblum, Marie-Claire 130
Goldenberg 1762
Goldin-Meadow, Susan 97, 150
Goldsmith, John 684, 685, 1337, 1347, 1368, 1371
Golovko, Evgenij V. 894, 932, 938, 1675
Golston, Chris 682, 686, 687
Gómez, Paula 535, 548, 552
Gómez-Tortosa, Estrella 134
Gonda, Jan 700
Gonzáles Holguín, P. Diego 254
Goodale, Melvyn Alan 8, 1306
Goodenough, Ward C. 1207
Goodluck, Helen 1094
Goodwin, Charles 435, 438−440
Goodwin, R. 1305
Goody, Jack 1152
Goossens, Louis 1586
Gopnik, Myrna 99, 119, 120
Gordon, Barry 100
Gordon, D. 448
Gordon, Lynn 1306
Gotō, Toshifumi 888
Grabmann, Martin 203
Grabowski, Jürgen 578
Grabowski, Thomas J. 13
Graefen, Gabriele 51, 446
Graesser, Arthur C. 159, 161
Graetz, Patty 130
Grafton, Anthony 212, 213
Gragg, Gene 1770, 1772
Grasserie, Raoul de la 831
Grathoff, Richard 43, 44
Graumann, Carl-Friedrich 577, 1556

Graves, Nina 778
Gray, Russell 118
Green, David W. 134
Green, Ian 819
Green, Keith 578, 587, 1135
Green, Melanie 1090f.
Greenberg, Joseph H. 11, 15, 25, 27, 62−64, 90, 118, 250, 258, 259, 265, 280−282, 284, 306, 309, 314−317, 324, 325, 333, 338, 360, 363, 366, 368, 370, 376, 403, 419, 431, 527−530, 552, 629, 669, 708, 711, 741−744, 746, 821, 823, 831, 832, 835, 855−857, 860, 863−866, 869, 917, 1001, 1006, 1012, 1014, 1017, 1020, 1142, 1143, 1147, 1148, 1178, 1208, 1212, 1215, 1220, 1278, 1282, 1297, 1312, 1314, 1424, 1437, 1541, 1623, 1624, 1628, 1632, 1639, 1648, 1649, 1766
Greenfeld, Philip J. 1236
Greenfield, Pamela 96
Gregores, Emma 696, 863
Gregory of Rimini (= Gregor von Rimini) 203, 209
Greimas, Algirdas Julien 642, 643, 1145, 1150, 1272
Grennough, William T. 119
Grewendorf, Günther 285
Grice, Herbert Paul 71, 154, 445−449, 646, 809
Grice, Martin 1387
Grierson, George A. 958, 1529
Grimes, Barbara F. 142, 424, 638, 1541, 1763
Grimes, Joseph Evans 640, 647, 1129
Grimm, Jacob 1555
Grimshaw, Jane 1038, 1040, 1042
Grodzinsky, Yosef 125
Groenendijk, Jeroen 1136
Grønnum, Nina 1382, 1384
Groot, Casper de 774, 1120, 1122
Groß, Michael 1157
Große, Ernst Ulrich 55
Grosse, Rudolf 475
Grosu, Alexander 988
Gruber, J. S. 484
Gruntfort, J. 217
Grüßner, Karl-Heinz 1537
Gsell, René 352, 357
Guarini, Giovan Battista 212
Guarino Veronese 211
Guarisma, Gladys 351, 353
Guasti, Therese 1363
Guentchéva, Zlatka 345, 352, 357, 358, 889
Guéron, Jacqueline 1089
Guierre, Lionel 1384

Guilbert, Louis 1158
Guillaume, Gustave 334, 1612
Guillaume, Jean-Patrick 277, 683
Guchman, Mirra M. 1624, 1627, 1628
Gulgoz, S. 157
Gülich, Elisabeth 303, 441, 457, 636, 642, 644, 645
Gumbrecht, Hans Ulrich 468, 472
Gumperz, John J. 1, 439, 440, 457−460, 641, 1147, 1148, 1535, 1643
Gundel, Jeanette K. 620, 623, 1058, 1072, 1073, 1127−1129
Gundissalinus, s. Dominicus Gundissalinus
Günther, Hartmut 1565, 1598, 1600, 1603
Günther, Wilfried 604
Guo, Jiansheng 1057, 1064−1067, 1071
Gurd, Jennifer 124
Gussenhoven, Carlos 625, 1351, 1352, 1383
Gutenberg, Johannes 211
Gutiérrez Bravo, Rodrigo O. 720, 724
Guttman, Louis 496
Gutwinski, Waldemar 634, 644, 650
Gzell, Petr 215

H

Haag, Karl 1478
Haan, Ferdinand de 795
Haarmann, Harald 164, 167, 173, 176, 778, 1506
Haas, Cathy 151
Haas, Mary 1353, 1360
Haas, Walter 1577
Haas, Wim de 702
Habermas, Jürgen 44, 52, 71, 1557
Hacker, Peter 70
Haegeman, Liliane 36, 869
Haftka, Brigitta 626
Hagège, Claude 603, 605, 739, 753, 884, 920, 1132, 1574, 1609, 1612−1622
Haggblade, Elisabeth 230
Hagius, Hugh 184
Hahne, Anja 13
Haider, Hubert 284, 286−288, 858, 859, 864, 1708
Hailu Fulass 1768
Haiman, John 142, 366, 371−381, 387−389, 613, 614, 758, 835, 837, 843, 893, 957, 966, 989, 998, 1006, 1014, 1019, 1111−1114, 1118, 1120, 1122, 1134, 1406, 1431, 1752
Haiman, Larry M. 318
Hajičová, Eva 622, 641, 1087, 1442
Hale, Kenneth L. 18, 288, 528, 627, 680, 729, 829, 866, 1132, 1179, 1200, 1201, 1208, 1210, 1277, 1298, 1433−1435, 1713
Hale, Nick 1233
Halford, Brigitte K. 597
Halicarnasse, Denys d' 182
Hall, Christopher J. 708−711, 856
Hall, Robert A. 1478, 1658, 1692
Halle, Morris 401, 402, 684, 1310, 1314, 1320, 1337, 1338, 1347,1352, 1384, 1385, 1610
Halliday, Michael Alexander Kirkwood 1, 51, 409, 438, 477, 485, 487, 490, 619, 620, 630, 634, 635, 637, 638, 640−643, 1115, 1122, 1171, 1564, 1568
Hallig, Rolf 296
Halm, Carolus 1687
Halmøy, Jane-Odile 1112, 1120, 1122
Haloinus, Georgius 212
Hamasaki, Tomoyuki 129
Hamayon, Roberte 874
Hamblin, Charles L. 1012, 1038
Hammerich, Louis L. 503, 730
Hammond, Michael 1214
Hamp, Eric P. 1541
Hancock, Ian 1658
Händler, Harald 1479
Hankamer, Jorge 1312
Hanks, William F. 576
Hanson, Kristin 1068
Haraguchi, Shosuke 1376
Hard, Gerhard 1475
Hardin, Clyde 1297
Hare, Robert 241
Harkins, Jean 1199
Harlig, Jeffrey 858
Harlow, Ray 857, 858
Harré, Rom 741−744, 746
Harries-Delisle, Helga 1081, 1092
Harriot, Thomas 217
Harris, Alice 850, 901, 921, 986, 987, 1024, 1578, 1582, 1778, 1782, 1791, 1792
Harris, Catherine 80, 81
Harris, James 16, 231
Harris, John 1329
Harris, Martin 1586, 1625, 1634
Harris, Zellig 683−685
Harrison, Sheldon P. 528, 822, 1360
Harsdörffer, Georg Philipp 239, 240, 243
Hart, John 100
Hartmann, Dietrich 630, 837
Hartmann, Peter 272, 634
Harweg, Roland 577, 579, 593, 638, 639, 642, 650
Hasada, Rie 1005
Hasan, Ruqaiya 438, 487, 634−638, 640−643
Hasler, Juan A. 1540
Haspelmath, Martin 35, 601, 709, 712, 751, 752, 776, 843, 850, 888, 899−902, 906−908, 920−922, 926, 928, 965, 971−977, 986, 997, 1007, 1008, 1025, 1112−1215, 1122, 1193, 1215, 1217, 1277, 1289, 1291, 1298, 1403, 1405, 1424, 1472, 1484, 1492, 1493, 1496−1501, 1504, 1506, 1507, 1579
Haßler, Gerda 242, 245
Hasuike, Reiko 129
Hatakeyama, Katshuhiko 636
Hatcher, Anna Granville 702
Hatta, Takeshi 129
Haugen, Einar 778, 1329, 1606
Hausendorf, Heiko 454, 455, 459
Havers, Wilhelm 972, 973, 976
Haviland, John 570, 571, 1549
Hawkins, John A. 28, 30, 90, 314, 317, 360−365, 431, 529, 554, 623, 624, 629, 708−711, 833, 855, 856, 859−864, 988, 989, 1214, 1217, 1220, 1624, 1630, 1632, 1636
Hayes, Bruce 1320, 1324−1328, 1349, 1350, 1353−1355, 1360−1363, 1384
Hayes, John R. 154, 155
Hays, David G. 1229, 1230
Hayward, Richard (= Dick) 817, 819
Hazai, György 1721
Head, B. F. 1132
Healey, John F. 166
Heath, Jeffrey 660, 696, 1127, 1130, 1131, 1208, 1209, 1434
Heath, Shirley Brice 449
Hecht, Max 82
Hedberg, Nancy 1128
Hedin, Eva 776, 777
Heeschen, Volker 572
Hegel, Georg Wilhelm Friedrich 268
Heger, Klaus 14, 15, 293−305, 347, 406, 479−482, 485, 608, 634, 1143, 1150, 1571, 1574, 1586
Hegius, Alexander 203
Heid, Ulrich 1295

Heidegger, Martin 72, 203, 204
Heidolph, Klaus E. 638, 641
Heim, Irene 639, 1276
Heinämäki, Orvokki 776
Heine, Bernd 52, 382, 528, 573, 610, 677, 941, 954, 955, 961, 966, 967, 1023, 1095−1100, 1142, 1172, 1495, 1499, 1549, 1579, 1582, 1609−1615, 1636, 1649
Heinemann, Wolfgang 55, 635, 638, 644, 647−649
Heinrichs, Heinrich Matthias 837
Helbig, Gerhard 41, 482, 930, 1168, 1627
Held, Gerrit J. 1108
Helden, Jacques van 116
Helias, s. Petrus Helias
Helimski, Eugen 938
Henadeerage, Kumara 840
Hengeveld, Kees 523, 729, 730, 733, 787, 985, 1142, 1172, 1305, 1403
Henne, Helmut 453, 1566
Hennigfeld, Jochem 181, 184
Henry of Ghent (= Heinrich von Gent) 198
Herbermann, Clemens-Peter 575
Hercus, Luise A. 696, 704, 1210
Herder, Johann Gottfried 223, 225, 227, 228, 230
Hering, Gunnar 1683
Heritage, John 445, 454
Hermann, Eduard 1310
Herne, Alf A. Gunnar 1228
Herring, Susan C. 623, 624, 629, 1027, 1083
Herrmann, Theo 578
Herskovits, Annette 568, 572, 573, 1252
Hesiod 236, 237
Hess, Thomas 837, 839
Hess, Wolfgang 1382
Hesseling, Dirk Christian 1649
Heßmann, Jens 142, 149
Hetland, Jorunn 620, 625
Hetzron, Robert 1082−1085, 1092, 1642, 1762, 1763
Heuven, Vincent J. Van 1383, 1388
Hewes, Gordon W. 142
Hewitt, B. George 30, 696, 1061, 1402, 1406, 1426, 1427, 1793
Hewitt, Lynne 1135
Heycock, Caroline 1088
Hickmann, Maya 2
Higginbotham, James 512, 1275
Higgins, Robert F. 1088

Hilbert, Richard A. 45
Hilbert, Vi 837, 839
Hildebrandt, Nancy 129
Hill, Archibald H. 1151
Hill, Clifford 569, 570
Hill, Deborah 576, 584, 1199
Hill, Jane H. 729, 1668, 1671
Hill, Robert H. 425
Himmelmann, Nikolaus P. 487, 506, 577, 730, 832, 833, 835, 837
Hincha, Georg 876
Hinde, Hildegarde B. 1236
Hinds, John 638, 650, 1013, 1026, 1129, 1405
Hines, Terence M. 134
Hinnenkamp, Volker 1653
Hinrichs, Erhard 558
Hintikka, Jaakko 70
Hinton, Geoffrey E. 78
Hirose, Takehiko 129
Hirschberg, Julia 1043, 1045, 1383
Hispanus, s. Peter of Spain
Hittmair-Delazer, Magarete 127
Hjelmslev, Louis 252−255, 260, 294, 346, 1145, 1148, 1149, 1153
Hlebec, Boris 1252
Hoard, James E. 1330
Hobbes, Thomas 234, 248
Hoberman, Robert P. 686, 692, 1291
Hock, Hans Henrich 1159, 1533, 1535, 1536, 1582, 1632
Hockett, Charles F. 11, 12, 117, 151, 182, 338, 627, 682, 683, 729, 733, 1326, 1329, 1330, 1555
Hoddinott, William G. 1298
Hoeksema, Jacob 712
Hoekstra, Teun 942
Hoequist, Charles Jr. 1392
Höfler, Manfred 1606
Hofmann, Johann Baptist 1568
Hofmann, Josef 1766
Hogness, D. S. 111
Hoh, Pau-San 1087
Hohepa, Patrick W. 913
Höhle, Tilman N. 620, 625
Hole, Daniel 748
Holenstein, Elmar 8
Holes, Clive 698, 840
Holinshed, Raphael 241
Holisky, Dee Ann 1430, 1778
Hollenbach, Barbara E. 1369, 1371, 1549
Holm, Catherine 1394
Holzinger, Daniel 141−144, 146, 150
Homer 184, 236, 237, 244
Homer, Kristin 1050

Hooker, James T. 173
Hooper, Joan Bybee 982, 1312, 1319, 1337, 1340, 1341
Hoosain, Rumjahn 135
Hopper, Paul J. 4, 6, 18, 54, 356, 377, 380, 382, 489, 490, 500, 501, 505, 524, 557, 562, 604, 613, 630, 645, 727, 732, 881, 884, 894, 923, 954, 957, 986, 1171, 1416, 1577, 1579−1581, 1609, 1611
Horace (= Horaz) 109, 114
Horie, Kaoru 980, 984−988, 990
Hörmann, Hans 455
Horn, Laurence R. 887, 893
Horne, Kibbey M. 250
Horning, Adolf 1477
Hornstein, Norbert 288, 559, 560
Horváth, Julia 620, 621, 869, 1080, 1090, 1442, 1451, 1453
Hottenroth, Priska-Monika 581, 584
Householder, Fred W. 181, 185, 864
Hovdhaugen, Even 181, 186, 217, 332, 523, 529, 836
Howatt, Anthony P. R. 241
Howson, Colin 419
Hrabanus Maurus (= Rabanus Maurus) 193
Hrubý Jelení, Zigmund 220
Hu, Chieh Fang 129
Huang, Cheng-Teh James 287, 290, 1409
Huang, Yan 1124, 1128, 1409, 1410
Hubel, David H. 8
Huber, Walter 124, 125, 128, 130
Hudak, Thomas John 696, 1428
Huddleston, Rodney D. 1011
Hudso, Joyce 1195
Hudson, Grover 1764, 1771
Hudson, Richard A. 681, 690, 1015
Hüllen, Werner 213, 215, 216, 219, 239−243, 246, 247
Hulst, Harry van der 145, 684, 1351, 1493
Humboldt, Wilhelm von 2, 10, 92, 249, 251−253, 255, 262, 264−272, 280, 294, 306, 338, 391, 603, 660, 669, 715, 817, 1147, 1148, 1540, 1555, 1584, 1635
Hume, David 224
Hume, Elisabeth V. 1348
Humphrey, Nicholas 100
Hundius, Harald 524
Hunger, Herbert 1682

Hunn, Eugene 1179
Hünnemeyer, Friederike 1609–1610, 1613, 1614
Hurch, Bernd 1337
Hurford, James R. 527, 1278
Hus, Jan 215
Husserl, Edmund 8, 43, 52, 68, 402
Hutchisson, Don 819, 820, 1134
Hyman, Larry M. 1076, 1081, 1095, 1097–1100, 1320, 1328, 1358, 1368, 1370, 1373, 1374, 1631
Hymes, Dell H. 41, 446, 1152
Hyslop, Catriona 582

I

Iatridou, Sabine 1007
Ibn Sīnā s. Avicenna
Idsardi, William 1320, 1347
Ifrah, Georges 164
Igla, Birgit 1675
Ikola, Osmo 778
Ildefonse, Frédérique 181
Immler, Manfred 478
Ineichen, Gustav 91
Ingalls, Daniel H. 892
Ingram, David 1134
Ingria, Robert 1327
Inhelder, Bärbel 538
Inkelas, Sharon 686
Iordanskaja, Lidija N. 999, 1000
Ioup, Georgette 1289
Irvine, A. K. 1771
Irving, Judith T. 265
Isabella de Castilia 214, 215
Isačenko, Aleksandr V. 933
Isaev, Magomet I. 168, 176
Isenberg, Horst 469, 635–639, 642–644, 647
Isermann, Michael 248
Isidor de Sevilla 189, 193, 1687
Itkonen, Esa 275, 279
Itô, Junko 1352
Iturrioz Leza, José Luis 16, 535, 537–540, 543, 547–550, 552, 721
Ivić, Pavel 1512
Iwata, Gayla A. 97, 129

J

Jaberg, Karl 1476, 1478
Jackendoff, Ray S. 80–82, 296, 301, 482, 620, 622, 625, 627, 726, 857, 1047, 1088, 1149, 1252, 1287
Jacob, Daniel 1561, 1562, 1570, 1574, 1575, 1576, 1583, 1586
Jacob, François 108
Jacob, Judith M. 696
Jacobi, Klaus 196–198
Jacobowitz, E. Lynn 146
Jacobs, Haike 1355
Jacobs, Joachim 619, 621, 622, 625, 627, 748, 857, 858, 862, 863, 1090, 1444, 1450
Jacobs, Peter 911
Jacobsen, Wesley M. 932, 938
Jacobson, William H. 597, 598, 729, 1133, 1134
Jacomo, François Lo 92
Jacquesson, François 353
Jaeggli, Osvaldo 287, 866, 870
Jäger, Ludwig 1556
Jakobson, Roman 27, 92, 118, 333, 338, 371, 373, 376, 400–402, 405, 408, 409, 605, 606, 741, 769, 772, 777, 784, 1143, 1157, 1209, 1312, 1313, 1394, 1492, 1610, 1652
Jakovlev, Nicolaj F. 1785
James, Deborah 558, 561
James, William 445
Jamieson, Carole 1547, 1548
Janich, Peter 70
Janik, Dieter 469
Janis, Wynne D. 146
Janssen, Theo A. J. M. 558
Janzen, Terry 799
Jarvelle, Robert 1136
Jaspers, Karl 72
Jasperson, Robert 983
Jauß, Hans-Robert 470
Jaxontov, Sergej E. 31, 32, 307–312, 669, 777, 928, 934, 938
Jechle, Thomas 156
Jefferson, Gail 45, 439, 445
Jelinek, Eloise 730, 837, 866, 868, 1056, 1126, 1434, 1435
Jenkins, James 62–64
Jensen, H. 171
Jensen, M. Kloster 1311
Jernigan, Terry 99
Jespersen, Otto 87, 93, 385, 495, 505, 559, 623, 699, 1163, 1310, 1312, 1329, 1611, 1632
Ji, Sungchul 117
Jiménez Montaño, Miguel Angel 116
Jin, L. 118
Joachim, Guido H. G. 142
Joas, Hans 45, 47, 48, 51, 449
Jochelson, W. 957
Johannes Buridan 509, 515–517
Johannes Dacus (= Johannes de Dacia) 203, 206
Johannes Duns Scotus 199, 200, 203
Johanson, Lars 601, 778, 1114, 1119, 1122, 1721, 1722, 1724, 1726, 1730, 1731, 1737, 1738, 1741
John Scotus Eriugena (= Johannes Scotus Eriugena) 194
Johns, Alana 730, 733
Johnson 1144
Johnson, Janet H. 1743
Johnson, Marion R. 557, 558, 562, 564
Johnson, Mark 51, 52, 76, 523, 1144
Johnson, Nancy S. 645
Johnson, Robert 143, 144
Johnson-Laird, Philip N. 80, 83, 158, 159, 578, 1272
Johnston, Judith 336
Johnston, Trevor 146, 147
Johnstone, Thomas M. 1770
Joly, André 231, 1099
Jones, Ch. 1329
Jones, Richard Foster 240, 244
Jones-Molfese, Victoria J. 1229
Jonsson, Niklas 1203–1214
Joos, Martin 558
Jordan, Fiona M. 118
Jordanus of Saxony (= Jordanus von Sachsen) 192, 203, 204
Joseph, Brian 991, 1513, 1632
Josephs, Lewis S. 984
Joshi, Smita D. 275, 891
Jun, Sun-Ah 1386
Juncos-Rabadán, Onémiso 130
Junge, Friedrich 1742, 1743
Junger, Judith 689, 692
Junius, Adrianus 215, 219
Junqué, Carme 132, 134
Jurafsky, Dan 1225
Just, Marcel A. 157
Justeson, John S. 420, 421, 431

K

Kabatek, Johannes 1583, 1586
Kabore, Raphaël 353
Kacori, Thoma 955
Kager, René 1314, 1320, 1323, 1347, 1350, 1355, 1364
Kageyama, Taro 1215, 1221
Kahn, Daniel 1326, 1329, 1351
Kahrel, Peter 527, 1499
Kail, Michèle 607
Kakati, Banikanti 1535
Kalinina, Elena Ju. 319, 956
Kallmeyer, Werner 439, 639, 642
Kalmár, Ivan 1152
Kambartel, Friedrich 72
Kamlah, Wilhelm 67, 68

Kammerzell, Frank 1742, 1744, 1747, 1750
Kamp, Hans 557, 559, 562, 563, 640, 1136
Kanngießer, Siegfried 71
Kant, Immanuel 1, 10, 200, 223, 266, 268, 447
Kapeliuk, Olga 839, 1766, 1767, 1771
Kaplan, David B. 578
Karanth, Prathibha 135
Karjalainen, Merja 696, 701, 703, 1019, 1024
Karlsson, Fred 696
Karttunen, Lauri 500, 982, 1012
Kasevič, Vadim B. 309, 669
Kasher, Asa 448
Kassai, Georges 351
Kasser, Rodolphe 1743
Kaster, Robert A. 186
Kastovsky, Dieter 886, 887, 1596, 1598
Katsoyannou, Marianne 354
Katz, Jerrold J. 82, 1596
Kaufman, Terrence 411, 1187, 1537, 1540, 1541, 1457, 1458, 1643, 1673, 1675, 1693
Kawahata, Nobuya 129
Kawkins, Johna A. 964
Kay, Jannice 128
Kay, Paul 33, 415, 1041, 1039, 1046, 1149, 1178, 1179, 1183, 1187, 1190, 1193, 1228−1233, 1236, 1239, 1240, 1242, 1244, 1246, 1248, 1297, 1649
Kaye, Jonathan 1328, 1329
Kayne, Richard 858, 859, 951, 1091
Kazenin, Konstantin I. 319, 912, 919−922, 1096
Keenan, Edward L. 16, 34, 304, 360, 364, 365, 368, 487, 488, 527−529, 558, 580, 756, 857, 901−905, 910, 920, 1279, 1414, 1415, 1756
Keesing, Roger M. 571, 742, 743, 1204
Kegl, Judy 97, 146
Keightley, David N. 164, 168
Keil, Henricus 187, 189
Kelkar, Ashok Ramchandra 1324
Keller, Jörg 145
Keller, Rudi 46, 398, 1577, 1597
Kellogg, Ronald T. 156
Kellogg, Samuel H. 664
Kemenade, Ans van 1707
Kemmer, Suzanne 280, 415, 747, 749−752, 891, 893, 918−920, 924−926
Kemmerling, Andreas 447, 449, 807

Kemp, Alan J. 185
Kenesei, István 1090
Kenny, James A. 432
Kenstowicz, Michael 1358, 1361, 1371
Kepler, Johannes 234
Kertesz, Andrew 124, 125
Kesik, Marek 638
Kessler, Brett 1327
Key, Harold H. 696
Keyser, Samuel Jay 887, 1326, 1329, 1360
Kibrik, Aleksandr E. 6, 306, 317−319, 484, 488, 592, 750, 829, 910, 912, 922, 926, 934, 1001, 1005, 1006, 1125, 1133, 1296, 1414, 1416, 1420, 1791
Kibrik, Andrej A. 900, 904, 908, 1118, 1122, 1125, 1126, 1128−1130, 1133−1135, 1418, 1419, 1793
Kiefer, Ferenc 619, 704
Kiesler, Reinhard 1159
Kilani-Schoch, Marianne 669, 680, 688, 1216, 1219, 1220, 1605
Kilcher, Andreas 216
Kilwardby, s. Robert Kilwardby
Kim, Alan Hyun-Oak 623, 629, 869
Kim, Karl H. S. 134
Kim, Nam-Kil 987
Kimball, Geoffrey David 1193
Kimenyi, Alexandre 983
Kimminich, Eva 92
Kim-Renaud, Young-Key 1397
King, Tracy H. 1442
Kinkade, M. Dale 730, 1242
Kinnander, Bengt 778
Kintsch, Walter 82, 157, 158, 160, 441, 648
Kiparsky, Carol 982
Kiparsky, Paul 275, 276, 982, 1328, 1329, 1352
Kirby, Simon 361
Kircher, Athanasius 86
Kirchhoff, Paul 1539
Kirk-Greene, Anthony H. M. 6, 771, 901
Kirsner, Robert S. 904, 984
Kirtchuk, Pablo 351, 352
Kiss, Katalin E. 621, 625, 627−629, 868−870, 1079, 1080, 1088, 1091, 1092, 1434, 1442, 1444, 1446−1448, 1451
Klaiman, Mimi H. 906, 909, 910, 923, 925, 1643
Klee, Carol A. 412
Kleiber, Georges 373−375, 415, 437, 638, 639, 643, 1144, 1151
Klein, Wolfgang 130, 134, 562, 564, 576, 577, 583, 587, 630, 645, 1136, 1137

Klijnsmit, Anthony J. 216, 217
Klima, Edward 143, 146, 149, 150
Kliment von Ohrid 167
Klimov, Georgij A. 319, 486, 1785
Klingenheben, August 1316
Kloss, Heinz 4, 842, 1582
Kluge, Theodor 1778
Kneepkens, Corneille H. J. M. 194−196
Knjazev, Jurij P. 937
Knobloch, Clemens 268, 480, 481
Knoop, Ulrich 1556
Knott, Judith 894
Kober, Alice E. 1229, 1230
Kobusch, Theo 201, 204−206
Koch, Harold J. 1210
Koch, Ildikó 1172
Koch, Peter 2, 3, 16, 49, 53, 301, 304, 410, 440, 457, 458, 468−475, 482, 484, 611, 612, 1143−1145, 1153, 1155, 1158, 1164, 1167, 1169, 1170−1172, 1559−1569, 1570, 1578, 1582−1586, 1596, 1602− 1604, 1684
Koch, Walter A. 644
Koda, Keiko 129
Koerner, Konrad 217, 230, 264
Kofod, Frances M. 1298
Kohler, Klaus J. 1392
Kok, Ans de 1693
Kokutani, Shigehiro 974
Kölver, Ulrike 524
Komensky, Jan Amos s. Comenius
Komlósy, Andrés 1085
König, Ekkehard 595, 747− 749, 752−756, 758, 842, 849, 850, 971−973, 976, 1003, 1004, 1007, 1008, 1081, 1115, 1118−1120, 1122, 1143, 1613
Koopman, Hilda 288, 946, 1658
Koptjevskaja-Tamm, Maria 426, 481, 843, 961, 963−966, 980, 981, 1112, 1113, 1122, 1204−1206, 1210−1212, 1459, 1506
Kordi, Elena E. 312
Kordon, Claude 117
Koreman, Jacques 1323, 1350, 1351
Kori, Shiro 1392
Körner, Karl Herrmann 1574
Kornfilt, Jaklin 752
Kornilov, G. E. 893
Korolija, Natascha 455
Kortmann, Bernd 371, 598, 606−609, 611, 842, 844, 846, 849−851, 1116, 1118−1120, 1122, 1504, 1584

Koselleck, Reinhard 1555
Koster, Jan 753, 919
Kotschi, Thomas 55, 457, 644
Koul, Omkar N. 700
Kouloughli, Djamel E. 277, 278, 683
Kourmoulis, George 1510
Kouwenberg, Norbertus J. C. 886
Kouwenberg, Silvia 1409, 1661, 1663, 1672
Koval', Antonina I. 900, 903, 904, 921
Kövecses, Zoltán 1248
Kozinceva, Natalia A. 312, 930, 936
Kozinskij (Kozinsky), Isaak Š. 6, 17, 18, 20, 306, 307, 314–317, 891
Kraft, Charles H. 6, 771, 901
Krahe, Hans 1506
Kramer, Johannes 1682–1684, 1688
Krámsky, Jiři 325, 529, 831, 835, 836, 839
Kranzhoff, Jörn A. 389
Kratzer, Angelika 787, 804, 1084, 1444, 1446
Krefeld, Thomas 4, 1341, 1342, 1561, 1579, 1586
Kreig, Martha F. 1230
Krejnovič, Eruxim A. 931
Kress, Bruno 1021
Kress, Gunther 52
Kretzmann, Norman 193
Kriegel, Sibylle 4, 594, 1583
Krifka, Manfred 1444, 1450
Krings, Hans 441
Kripke, Saul 509, 519–521
Kroch, Anthony S. 1088
Kroeber, Alfred L. 716, 717, 1147, 1148, 1207, 1540
Kroeger, Paul 903
Krötsch, Monique 641
Kruisinga, Etsko 908
Krupa, Victor 1134
Kruskal, Joseph B. 1483
Kubozono, Haruo 1387
Kučera, Henry 776
Kuen, Heinrich 271
Kühlwein, Wolfgang 218
Kühner, Raphael 330, 331
Kuiper, Franciscus B. J. 1530, 1532, 1534
Kuipers, Aert H. 730, 1330, 1427
Kukenheim, Louis 216
Kulikov, Leonid R. 887, 888, 890–894
Kumari, T. C. 700
Kumaxow, Muxaddin A. 1126
Kummer, Werner 646

Kuno, Susumu 623, 641, 942, 983, 984, 988, 1018, 1087, 1116, 1119, 1122, 1442, 1444
Kuon, Peter 472
Kuroda, Sige-Yuki 628, 946, 1442, 1444, 1445
Kürschner, Wilfried 185
Kuryłowicz, Jerzy 688, 692, 731, 732, 1327
Kuschel, Rolf 1246
Kuznecova, Ariadna 932
Kvist, Ulrika 733
Kwee, John B. 1112, 1122
Kyrillos (Konstantinos) 167

L

Labov, William 54, 439, 446, 780, 1577, 1584
Laca, Brenda 1222, 1224
Ladd, D. Robert 1054, 1382–1385, 1387, 1388
Ladefoged, Peter 389, 1312
Ladusaw, William A. 1085
Laertius, s. Diogenes Laertios
Lafford, B. A. 408
Lafitau, Joseph-François 503
Lafitte, Pierre 677
Lafon, René 217
Lafrenz, Peter G. 1252
Lahiri, Aditi 1323, 1347, 1349–1351, 1355, 1357, 1360, 1363
Lai, Cecilia S. L. 120
Laidig, Carol J. 818, 825
Laidig, Wyn D. 818, 825
Laine, Matti 128
Laka, Itziar 1090
Lakoff, George 51, 52, 76, 81, 83, 212, 448, 495, 523, 1144, 1156, 1581, 1597
Lakoff, Robin 245, 560
Lallot, Jean 185, 186, 189
Lamb, Sydney M. 690
Lambdin, Thomas O. 1743
Lambert, Johann Heinrich 223, 227–231
Lambert, Pierre-Yves 353
Lambert, Richard D. 1668
Lambert, Wallace E. 132, 134
Lambrecht, Knud 619, 622, 625, 629, 1040–1044, 1047, 1051, 1053–1055, 1057–1061, 1064–1069, 1071–1075, 1084, 1444
Lamy, Bernard 229, 245
Lancelot, Claude 3, 243–246, 256
Landaburu, Jon 1105
Landau, Barbara 1252, 1305
Landesman, Charles 68
Lane, Archibald 245, 247
Lane, Harlan 141

Lang, Ewald 643, 644, 799, 1143, 1169, 1150–1154, 1271, 1272
Lang, Jürgen 1579, 1581, 1586
Lang, R. 910, 912
Langacker, Ronald W. 76, 80–83, 374, 506, 689, 690, 729, 900, 964, 1000, 1128, 1279, 1579–1582
Langdon, Margaret 1218, 1396
Langendoen, D. Terence 1386
Langleben, Maria 637
LaPolla, Randy 1405
Larrivee, Pierre 1291
Larson, Richard K. 902, 1093
Las Casas, Bartholomé de 217
Lasnik, Howard 403, 1090
Lass, Roger 389, 391
Laszlo, Pierre 117
Latzel, Signert 781
Laufer, Natalia I. 318
Laughren, Mary 1200, 1201, 1208
Launey, Michel 881, 1543, 1545, 1547, 1548, 1551
Laury, Rita 832
Lausberg, Heinrich 271, 1691, 1695
Lavandera, Beatriz R. 439
Law, Vivien 185, 236
Laycock, Donald C. 741, 742, 1651
Lazard, Gilbert 11, 300, 336, 340, 344–352, 354, 356, 358, 478, 481, 485–489, 491, 802, 876–884, 1171, 1413, 1495–1497, 1504
Laziczius, Julius 1311
Le Nestour, P. 354
Le Normand, M. T. 119
Le Page, Robert B. 1648
Leach, Edmund 729
Leal, Fernando 341
Léau, Léopold 89
Leben, William R. 1375
Lebrun, Yvan 131, 132
Lecarme, Jaqueline 1442
Lee, Hansol H. B. 525
Lee, Jennifer 1671
Lees, Robert B. 702
Lefèvre, Claire 27, 837, 1093, 1434, 1438, 1658
Lehfeldt, Werner 26, 1477
Lehiste, Ilse 1391
Lehmann, Christian 16, 26, 267, 270, 271, 294, 324, 334, 341, 363, 366, 382, 406, 478, 481–484, 489, 524, 525, 528, 529, 612–614, 677, 739, 751, 843, 966, 973, 982, 1112, 1113, 1122, 1142, 1169, 1401, 1472, 1494, 1495, 1506, 1507, 1548, 1579–1581, 1596, 1598, 1602, 1609, 1612, 1616

Lehmann, Thomas 276, 1117, 1122
Lehmann, Walter 1540
Lehmann, Winfred P. 316, 855, 858, 860, 1624, 1625, 1628, 1630
Lehmus, Ursula 973
Lehnhoff, Howard 120
Lehrer, Adrienne 1142, 1143, 1147–1150, 1168
Leibniz, Gottfried Wilhelm 20, 87, 247, 1472
Leinbach, John 96
Leiner, Alan 98, 100
Leiner, Henrietta 98
Leinonen, Marja 778
Leischner, Anton 131, 133
Leisi, Ernst 240, 729
Leiss, Elisabeth 1577, 1579, 1582
Lemoine, Kevin 1057
Lemos, Cláudia T. G. de 930
Lenker, Ursula 1570
Lenneberg, Eric H. 95
Lenz, Friedrich 576, 577
Leonard, Henry S. 426, 427
Leonard, Laurence B. 99, 119
Leong, Che Kann 129, 130
Lerch, Eugen 271, 272
Leskien, August 87
Leslau, Wolf 1642, 1762, 1765–1772
Lesniewski, Stanislaw 66
Leucippus (= Leukipp) 105
Leumann, Manu 1223
Levelt, Willem J. M. 570, 578
Levi, Judith N. 702
Levinsohn, Stephen H. 1125, 1128
Levinson, Stephen C. 9, 17, 52, 378, 439, 447, 448, 463, 523, 527, 570–573, 575, 745, 1147, 1148, 1242, 1244, 1272, 1548, 1549
Lévi-Strauss, Claude 118, 1146, 1147
Levy, Elena 1124
Levy, Paulette 974, 1547
Lévy-Bruhl, Lucien 1152
Lewin, Bruno 17
Lewis, David 66, 521, 578, 1280
Lewis, Geoffrey L. 807, 838
Lewis, H. 957
Lewis, L. 956
Lewis, Mark 246, 247
Lewis, Morris M. 1209
Lewitz, Saveros 1248
Lewy, Ernst 266–269, 271, 272, 1506
Li, Charles N. 487, 526, 603, 627, 628, 809, 910, 912, 958, 979, 1016, 1026, 1027, 1106, 1116, 1122, 1127, 1131, 1410, 1411, 1414, 1419, 1442, 1447, 1601, 1624, 1635, 1643
Li, Fengxiang 894, 895
Li, Jie 129
Liberman, Anatoly 406
Liberman, Mark 1320, 1326, 1347, 1381, 1383
Lichtenberk, František 528, 826, 966, 1108
Liddell, Scott K. 143, 144, 146–148
Lieb, Hans Heinrich 64, 1564
Lieber, Rochelle 701, 710
Lieberman, Philip 98, 1380–1382
Liebermann, Wolf-Lüder 236
Liebert, Wolf-Andreas 1597
Liebig, Peter 88, 89
Liedtke, Frank 46, 448
Liedtke, Stefan 1540
Lightfoot, David 288
Ligorred, Francesc 1541
Lillo-Martin, Diane 149, 366
Lily, William 213, 215
Linacre, Thomas 212, 213, 245
Lindau, Mona 1381
Lindblom, Björn 1392
Lindemann, Margrete 219
Lindgren, Kaj B. 1627
Lindstedt, Jouko 769, 773, 775, 777–779, 1469
Linell, Per 455
Link, Godehard 1276, 1289
Lipka, Leonhard 1598, 1600, 1602–1604
Lipps, Hans 72
Little, Greta D. 1642, 1763
Litvinov, Viktor P. 31, 935, 939
Livnat, Michal Allon 1099
Lizotte, R. J. 954
Ljutikova, Ekaterina A. 319
Lloyd, Antony C. 184
Lo Cascio, Vincenzo 558–560, 564, 639, 640
Löbel, Elisabeth 334
Löbner, Sebastian 789
Locke, John 222–224, 234, 235, 248, 592
Locker, Ernst 954
Lockwood, William B. 967
Lodwick, Francis 86, 88–91
Loewe, Martha 1362
Löfstedt, Bengt 1692
Löfstedt, Einar 1692
Loftin, Colin 425
Loftus, Elizabeth 79
Lombard, Alf 1515, 1519, 1527
Lombardi, Linda 685
London, H. 1387
Longacre, Robert E. 641, 642, 842, 843, 848, 851, 1008, 1369
Longus 600
Lonnet, Antoine 1770
López Austin, Alfredo 1549
López Madera, Gregorio 218, 238, 239
Loprieno, Antonio 1742, 1744–1747, 1750–1752, 1755–1758
Lorch, Marjorie Perlman 126
Lord, Carol 987
Lorenz, Kuno 68
Lorenzen, Paul 66–68, 72
Lötscher, Andreas 644, 645
Lott, Julius 87
Lounsbury, Floyd G. 1207
Lowe, I. 814
Loweke, Eunice 1371
Lowenstamm, Jean 1328
Lowie, Robert H. 1207
Lü, Ching Fu 1236
Lucas, Ceil 142
Luckmann, Thomas 43–45, 47–49, 445, 455, 456, 468, 1567
Lucy, John A. 524
Lüdtke, Helmut 1571, 1577, 1586, 1602, 1678, 1679, 1682, 1684–1687, 1689
Lüdtke, Jens 592, 1218, 1220–1224
Ludwig, Otto 1565, 1583, 1586
Ludwig, Ralph 4, 373–376, 381, 405, 406, 409–415, 594, 599, 604
Luhmann, Niklas 44, 45, 53, 56, 452, 453
Lukas, Johannes 696, 704, 1107
Lullus, s. Raimundus Lullus
Lumer, Christoph 42
Lundin, Barbro 1305
Lundquist, Lita 636–638, 647, 648
Luther, Martin 211, 215
Lutz, Angelika 1315, 1317, 1320
Lutzeier, Peter 1598
Luutonen, Jorma 713
Lux, Friedemann 438
Luzzatti, Claudio 130
Lyons, Christopher 965
Lyons, John 93, 435, 438, 483, 490, 495, 500, 506, 523, 524, 527, 528, 557–559, 561, 563, 568, 741, 796, 920, 923, 942, 984, 1123, 1142, 1179, 1404, 1596
Lytkin, Vasilij I. 892

M

Maas, Utz 48, 56, 57, 646
Macaulay, Donald 1020
Macavariani, Maja 928

MacKay, Carolyn J. 1329
Macken, Elizabeth 148, 151
MacKevitt, Paul 8
Mackridge, Peter 699, 779, 1515
MacLaury, Robert E. 1228–1233, 1236, 1239–1242, 1244, 1246–1249
MacWhinney, Brian 96, 125–128
Maddieson, Ian 389, 432, 1340, 1369
Maes, Anny 463, 464
Maffi, Luisa 1233, 1239, 1242, 1244, 1246, 1297
Magomedbekova, Zagidat M. 1788
Magometov, Aleksandr A. 1780, 1781, 1784, 1786–1790, 1793
Mahecha, Nancy R. 132
Maienborn, Claudia 478, 479
Mair, Christian 600
Mair, Walter N. 1586
Majtinskaja, Klara E. 1134
Makkai, Adam 1038, 1039
Malblanc, Alfred 1152, 1161, 1170
Malbran-Labat, Florence 352, 354
Malchukov, Andrej L. 525
Malin, Jean-Pierre 125
Malinowski, Bronislaw 437, 438
Malkiel, Yakov 1219–1221
Mallinson, Graham 431, 485, 864
Malotki, Ekkehart 568
Malsch, Derry L. 378
Mańczak, Witold 1478
Mandel, Mark 147, 151
Mandler, Jean M. 645
Manet, Édouard 402
Manfredi, Victor 1663
Mann, Wiiliam C, 1129
Manning, Christopher 904, 909
Manrique Castañeda, Leonardo 1550
Manuel-Dupont, Sonia 130
Manzelli, Gianguido 527, 528, 961
Manzoni, Alessandro 665
Marácz, László 1434
Marbais, s. Michael of Marbais
Marchand, Hans 1220, 1224, 1604, 1605
Marchese, Lynell 1100, 1623
Marcus, Barcan 519
Marcus, Gary 96
Marello, Carla 635, 640
Margalit, Avishai 635, 643
Maric, Chrystelle 117

Marlett, Stephen A. 1330
Marlowe, Christopher 240
Marotta, Giovanna 1392
Marsack, C. C. 1109
Marshall, John C. 124
Marslen-Wilson, William D. 710, 1124
Martin, M. 166
Martin, Samuel E. 1001, 1113, 1114, 1122
Martinet, André 9, 62–64, 69, 385–388, 392
Martinus Dacus (= Martin of Dacia) 203, 204, 206, 208
Marty, Anton 628, 1445
Marx 214
Masica, Colin P. 36, 826, 913, 1116, 1121, 1122, 1457, 1475, 1496, 1530–1537, 1682, 1683, 1689
Maslov, Jurij S. 773, 776
Maslova, Elena S. 894, 1284, 1289
Massam, Diane 837
Mathesius, Vilém 266, 269, 270, 272, 619, 1442
Matisoff, James A. 956, 968, 1372
Matsuda, Yuki 1091
Matthaios, Stephanos 185
Mattheier, Klaus J. 1556, 1577
Matthews, Peter 211, 235–237, 1214–1217, 1598
Matthews, Stephen 696, 752, 756, 989, 1195
Matthiessen, Christian M. I. M. 1129
Mattissen, Johanna 496
Maturana, Humberto R. 44
Maue Capira, Alejo 414
Maurer, Philippe 599, 1659
Maurus, s. Hrabanus Maurus
Maxwell, Daniel 858
Maxwell, Grover 90, 91
May, Jean 1371
Mayerthaler, Eva 1337, 1340
Mayerthaler, Willi 54, 90, 373, 400, 402–407, 538
McCarthy, John J. 679–681, 683–687, 690–692, 1328, 1358–1362, 1364, 1386
McCawley, James D. 559–561, 564, 887, 1046, 1048
McCawley, Noriko 1048
McClelland, James L. 78
McCloskey, James 1091, 1095, 1448
McCoard, Robert W. 559, 564
McCrea, Nelson G. 1230
McDaniel, Chad K. 1149, 1229
McElhanon, K. A. 1278
McGregor, William 377, 528, 744, 965, 1650

Mchombo, Sam A. 1055–1057, 1069, 1070, 1424
Mcilvenny, Paul 149
McKay, Graham R. 742, 743
McKoon, Gail 159
McLelland, James L. 96
McMahon, April M. S. 1577, 1579, 1584
McManus, I. C. 1229, 1230
McPhail, R. M. 1531
McQuown, Norman A. 1540, 1550
McWhinney, Brian 96
McWhorter, John H. 4, 1665, 1666
Mead, George Herbert 45, 46, 445
Meermann, Horst 570
Meeuwis, Michael 414
Meggle, Georg 448
Megiser, Hieronymus 219
Megyesi, Beata 1212
Mei, Tsu-Lin 69
Meier, Richard P. 143, 149
Meier-Oeser, Stephan 9
Meigret, Louis 214
Meij, Sjaak de 1434
Meillet, Antoine 346, 347, 842, 875, 1579, 1609
Meinunger, André 1088, 1091, 1092
Meise, Katrin 8, 50, 441
Meisel, Jürgen 1669
Mel'čuk, Igor' A. 312, 317, 672, 886, 889, 1190, 1191, 1214–1219, 1222, 1223, 1425
Melanchthon, Phillip 213, 215
Meløe, Jakob 73
Mendel, Daniela 503
Mendelsohn, Susan 134
Menges, Karl H. 1721, 1736
Menn, Lise 125, 127, 1671
Mennecier, Philippe 351–353, 882
Mennen, Ineke 1383, 1384
Menninger, Karl 1278
Menovščikov, Georgij A. 892, 1644, 1645
Menze, Clemens 266
Mereu, Lunella 1084, 1093, 1099, 1442, 1449, 1452
Merlan, Francesca 718, 721, 728, 1208, 1209
Merleau-Ponty, Maurice 52, 57, 58, 449, 454
Merlini-Barbaresi, Lavinia 1216
Merrifield, M. E. 1230
Merrifield, William R. 1233
Mersenne, Marin 86
Meščaninov, Ivan I. 319
Mester, Armin 1352
Mesulam, M.-Marsel 98, 124
Metcalf, George J. 219

Index of names

Metley, Donald S. 150
Meunier, Annie 1248
Mey, Jacob 503
Meyer, Martin 13
Meyer, Paul 1476, 1477
Meyer-Drawe, Käte 462
Meyer-Lübke, Wilhelm 271, 1686
Michael, Ian 211
Michael of Marbais (= Michel de Marbais, Michael von Marbais) 203
Michaelis, Laura A., 564, 1039, 1040, 1043, 1044, 1047, 1053, 1067, 1075
Michaelis, Susanne 16, 597, 604, 610, 1583
Michailovsky, Boyd 351
Miège, Guy 241–243
Miescher, Friedrich 105
Mihatsch, Wiltrud 1151
Mikailov, Š. I. 1784
Mikame, Hirofumi 408
Mikhejev, Alexej V. 1246
Milan, Carlo 930
Milewski, Tadeusz 249, 1424
Miller, Christopher 144, 148, 149
Miller, D. G. 175, 179
Miller, George A. 76, 83, 578, 1272
Miller, J. Gary 887
Miller, Jim E. 502
Miller, Peggy L. 462
Miller, Roy Andrew 1689
Miller, W. 1671
Miller, Wick R. 1549
Mills, Carl 1229
Milner, A. David 8
Milner, Jean-Claude 1042, 1046
Milsark, Gary 942–952, 1084, 1278
Minsky, Marvin L. 78, 648
Misch, Georg 72
Misteli, Franz 249, 266, 268, 1145
Mithun, Marianne 597, 623, 715, 716, 718–721, 723, 729, 817, 826, 843, 868, 1106, 1108, 1126, 1134, 1218, 1436, 1439, 1625
Mitzka, Walter 1473
Möbius, A. F. 18, 596
Möbius, Bernd 1382
Mock, Carol C. 1371
Moeschler, Jacques 50, 640, 646, 647
Mohanan, Karavannur Puthavettil 1297, 1323, 1337, 1434, 1532
Molendijk, Arie 558, 560, 563, 564
Molnár, Valéria 619, 620, 625, 1444

Monberg, Toren 1246
Mondry, Henrietta 1246
Mønnesland, Svein 776
Monod, Jacques 104, 108
Monreal-Wickert, Irene 251, 258, 1576
Montague, Richard 66, 69, 79, 578, 796, 857
Montanari, Elio 183
Montaut, Annie 353–355
Monteil, Vincent 1683
Montgomery, James 119
Montgomery, Martin 642, 647
Montler, Timothey 837
Montoya, Antonio Ruiz de 254
Moore, John 685, 686, 886, 891
Moosbrugger, André-F. 342
Moravcsik, Edith 325, 367, 402, 403, 507, 527, 529, 726, 733, 747, 756, 837, 838, 851, 874, 1220
More, Thomas 240
Morel, Mary-Annick 576, 577, 1038
Moreno Cabrera, Juan C. 901
Moreno, Martino Mario 1642, 1771
Morford, Jill P. 150
Morgan, Gerry 1229, 1246
Morgan, Lewis H. 1206
Moritz, Carl Philipp 228
Morland, J. Kenneth 1229
Moro, Andrea 942
Morphy, Frances 705
Morris, Charles 54, 55, 80, 445, 578
Mosel, Ulrike 332, 334, 480, 482, 496, 523, 529, 836, 1198
Moser, Margaret Gamble 1090
Moskovitch, W. A. 503
Moss, A. E. 1248
Motsch, Wolfgang 55, 646, 647
Mourelatos, Alexander P. D. 776
Mous, Maarten 1645, 1675
Moutaouakil, Ahmed 1051, 1056, 1059, 1063, 1065, 1067, 1069, 1073, 1076, 1081
Moxon, Richard E. 117
Moyne, John A. 747, 751
Moyse-Faurie, Claire 351–354, 357
Mudersbach, Klaus 297, 298, 300–303, 608
Mufwene, Salikoko 408, 410, 558, 980, 1209, 1409
Mugler, Alfred 478
Mühlhäusler, Peter 4, 741–744, 746, 1648–1652, 1657
Mulcaster, Richard 241
Mulder, Jean G. 836
Mulder, René 942
Muller, Enrique 1664

Müller, Friedrich 306
Müller, Gereon 286
Müller-Bardey, Thomas 336, 597, 598
Müller-Gotama, Franz 31, 1142, 1168
Müller-Hauser, Marie-Louise 629
Müller-Lancé, Johannes 602
Mullie, Josef L. M. 1106
Munro, Pamela 906, 1117, 1122, 1134
Muntzel, Martha C. 1541, 1669–1674
Murane, Elizabeth 956
Murdock, George P. 432, 1207, 1209
Murray, Robert 1312, 1317
Murugaiyan, Appasamy 877, 878
Musaev, Kenesbaj M. 1740
Musters, George C. 1236
Muysken, Pieter 410, 887, 889, 1214–1217, 1434, 1438, 1442, 1444, 1448, 1452, 1645, 1663, 1665, 1666
Myers-Scotton, Carol 414, 1657, 1675
Myhill, John 1634
Mylius (van der Mijk), Abraham 239

N

Nababan, P. W. J. 696, 704
Nadeau, Stephen 100
Næss, Arne 67
Nagano-Madsen, Yasuko 1392
Nagarajan, Srikantan 119
Nagata, Ken 129
Nanni, Giovanni 218, 238, 239
Nänny, Max 371–373, 375
Naroll, Raoul 419, 424–431
Nash, David 701
Naumann, Hans 1597
Nebrija, Antonio de 213, 214, 217, 218, 237, 238
Nedjalkov (= Nedyalkov), Igor' V. 698, 792, 798, 844, 894, 933, 934, 1001, 1407, 1504
Nedjalkov, Vladimir P. 31, 32, 312, 601, 777, 844, 886–892, 894, 922, 928, 935, 938, 939, 1001, 1112–1125, 1119, 1122, 1405
Nedožerský s. Nudožerinus
Neeleman, Ad 905, 1024
Nef, Frédéric 68
Neidle, Carol 146, 148
Nencioni, Giovanni 1566
Nerlich, Brigitte 43
Nerlove, Sarah 1208

Nespor, Marina 1337, 1363, 1385, 1386, 1393
Neumann-Holzschuh, Ingrid 1579, 1581, 1586
Neustupny, J. V. 1689
Neville, Helen J. 13
Newell, Allan 154
Newman, Jean 688
Newman, John 1198
Newman, Paul 817, 1090, 1244, 1371
Newmeyer, Frederick J. 101, 370, 372, 374–377, 379, 381, 1142
Newport, Elissa 147
Newton, Brian 1672
Newton, Isaac 234
Nichols, Johanna 29, 30, 314, 367, 423–426, 431, 432, 662, 777, 814, 855, 865, 888, 903, 904, 913, 961, 963–966, 968, 1108, 1109, 1117, 1122, 1126, 1306, 1424–1431, 1456, 1459, 1460, 1462–1468, 1497, 1503, 1543, 1547, 1634
Nicklas, N. T. Dale 1108
Nicol, Janet L. 125, 126, 130
Nicole, Pierre 244, 256
Niederehe, Hans-Josef 217, 219
Niemeier, Susanne 1148
Niemi, Jussi 127, 128
Niepokuj, Mary 1424
Nikiforidou, Kiki 964
Nikintina, Tamara N. 887
Nikolaev, Sergej 1422
Nikolaeva, Irina 1502
Nikolayev, Sergej L. 1775
Nilsson, Birgit 877, 878, 881
Njalibuli, D. 900, 903, 904, 921
Nocentini, Alberto 874, 1494
Noonan, Michael 481, 482, 786, 790, 904, 905, 979, 980, 982, 988, 1135, 1214, 1400
Noordegraf, Jan 230
Nordlinger, Rachel 6, 18
Noreen, Adolf 605, 608
Noske, Roland 1326
Nöth, Winfried 578
Nudožerinus, Laurentius Benedicti 216
Nuyts, Jan 53, 54
Nye, Irene 638
Nyman, Martti 780
Nyrop, Kristoffer 1604

O

O'Neill, Wayne 1360
Oates, Lynette F. 1302
Öberg, Anton Bernhard 930
Obler, Loraine 123, 125–128, 130–132, 134, 135
O'Brien, E. J. 159
Ochs-Keenan, Elinor 449
Ockham, s. William of Ockham
O'Connor 1039, 1046
Odden, David 1080, 1081, 1091, 1375
Odé, Cecilia 1383
O'Dowd, Elizabeth 980
Oelingerus, Albertus 214
Oesterreicher, Wulf 2, 3, 11, 49, 410, 440, 457, 458, 468, 471, 475, 751, 1143, 1171, 1554–1570, 1573–1579, 1582–1584, 1586, 1602, 1630, 1631, 1684, 1693
Ogden, Charles K. 295
Ogihara, Toshiyuki 560, 563
Ogloblin, Aleksandr K. 312
Ohala, John J. 1312, 1382
Ohori, Toshio 611
Ohrid, s. Kliment von Ohrid
Ojeman, George A. 98
Oliveira, Fernão de 214
Olsen, Mari Jean Broman 559, 561, 563, 564
Olsen, Susan 1219
Olson, Conrad X. 1232
Olson, Ronald D. 1331
Ong, Walter J. 1152, 1566
Onishi, Masayuki 1193, 1197, 1199
Ono, Yoshiko 480, 489
Optat, Beneš 215
Ordóñez, Francisco 1093
Orth, Ernst W. 1555, 1556
Ortiz de Urbina, Jon 1442
Orwell, George 92
Osaka, Noayuki 129
Osborne, Andrea Gail 1096
Osborne, C. R. 957
Osgood, Charles 62–64, 134
Osing, Jürgen 1743–1746
Osmán-Sági, Judit 125–128
Östman, Jan-Ola 635
Ostrofrancus s. Albertus Laurentius
Oswalt, Robert L. 1306
Otaina, Galina A. 890, 929, 938
Otsuka, Akira 129
Ottósson, Kjartan G. 868
Ouhalla, Jamal 870, 1079, 1081, 1090, 1442, 1450, 1452
Owens, Jonathan 277, 683

P

Padden, Carol A. 146
Padley, G. A. 211, 213, 214, 239, 245, 246
Padučeva, Elena V. 888, 893, 1135, 1136
Pafel, Jürgen 861
Pagliuca, William 537, 538, 586, 769–771, 775–777, 779–781, 980, 983, 991, 1297
Palaemon, Quintus Remmius 188
Palek, Bohumil 638, 639
Palij, Michael 130
Palm, Christiane 1601
Palmer, Frank R. 483–486, 488, 815, 983, 999, 1402, 1771
Palsgrave, John 216
Panaccio, Claude 200, 202
Pandharipande, Rajeshwari V. 700
Pandit, Rama 125
Pāṇini 275, 276, 279
Paol, John Natu 696
Paolillo, John C. 1083
Papen, Robert A. 1645, 1675
Papert, Seymor 78
Paradis, Michel 128–135
Paramei, Galina 1246
Paris, C. 351, 352
Paris, Gaston 1476, 1477
Paris, Marie-Claude 376
Park, Hea Suk 134
Parker, Elisabeth 1134
Paro, Renato 111, 112, 113
Parpola, Asko 172
Parret, Herman 57, 642
Parson, Talcott 45, 46, 47
Parsons, John H. 1228
Partee, Barbara Hall 558, 559, 640, 1137
Pascal, Blaise 245
Pasquier, Estienne 242
Passerieu Bordeneuve, Jean C. 878
Pastika, Wayan 840
Patañjali 275
Patschke, Cynthia 147
Patte, M.-F. 351, 354
Pätzold, Matthias 1382
Paul, Hermann 586, 618, 1052, 1556, 1599
Pawley, Andrew 504, 840, 1194, 1197, 1201, 1305, 1597–1599
Paxman, David B. 243
Payne, Doris L. 629, 868, 911, 912, 971, 975–977, 1083, 1085
Payne, John R. 804, 863
Payne, Judith 1325
Payne, Thomas E. 930, 1125, 1127, 1129, 1130
Peano, Giuseppe 87
Pearson, Paul David 157
Pedersen, H. 957
Pederson, Eric 584
Peirce, Charles Sanders 11, 371–374, 445, 578

Pelletier, Francis Jeffry 1275
Penfield, Wilder 130
Pennanen, Esko V. 892
Peralta, Jesus T. 1239
Percival, W. Keith 203, 211–213, 216, 696
Perdue, Clive 573
Perecman, Ellen 131
Perel'muter, Il'ja A. 928, 931
Peretto, Niccolò 211, 215
Pérez González, Benjamin 1541
Pérez Rueda, Ernesto 116
Perfetti, C. A. 159
Perfetti, Charles 129
Pericliev, Vladimir 1207
Perkins, Revere D. 316, 423, 425, 426, 430, 432, 586, 769–771, 775–777, 779–781, 980, 983, 991, 1297, 1462
Perlmutter, David M. 144, 145, 712, 905, 909, 1215
Perm, s. Stephan von Perm
Perrot, Jean 351–353, 876
Perry, John 151
Peškovskij, Aleksej M. 318
Pesot, Jürgen 1157
Peter Abælard 194, 195, 197, 205, 209, 477
Peter of Spain (= Pierre d'Espagne, Petrus Hispanus) 593
Petőfi, János S. 57, 441, 634–637, 642–644, 646
Petrarch (Petrarca), Francesco 213, 467, 474
Petronio, Karen 366
Petrus Helias 192, 194–196
Pettie, George 240, 241
Peuser, Günther 133
Peyraube, Alain 376
Pfaff, Carol W. 1641
Pfeiffer, Rudolf 184
Philippaki-Warburton, Irene 1513
Philomates, Václav 215
Piaget, Jean 538
Pica, Pierre 758
Picard, Jean 218
Picard, Mark 1326
Pichon, Édouard 2, 3
Pickering, Martin 365
Pierrehumbert, Janet B. 1043, 1045, 1368, 1373, 1376, 1381, 1383, 1385, 1387
Pike, Evelyn G. 611, 1326
Pike, Kenneth Lee 611, 1326, 1343, 1368, 1376, 1391, 1381
Pilhofer, Georg 597, 598, 1406
Pilot-Raichoor, Christiane 351–354, 876–878
Pimentel, D. Francisco 1540
Pinault, Georges-Jean 275, 1687
Pinborg, Jan 181, 203

Pinkal, Manfred 435
Pinker, Steven 96, 97, 101, 119, 120
Pinkster, Harm 1692, 1697, 1700
Pinnow, Hans-Jürgen 316
Piñon, Christopher 1090
Pinsonneault, Dominique 148
Pinxten, Rik 71
Pirejko, L. A. 933
Piron, Claude 91, 92
Pirrotta, Vincenzo 112
Pisani, Vittore 1493
Pitres, Albert 132
Pizzuto, Elena 146
Plank, Frans 230, 281, 282, 334, 373, 381, 382, 479, 485, 487, 496, 528, 677, 739, 747, 750, 818, 840, 961–963, 1142, 1168, 1215–1217, 1221, 1278, 1344, 1347, 1362, 1363, 1416, 1627, 1631, 1634, 1636
Plato 81, 182–184, 192, 231, 236
Plautus 596
Plungian, Vladimir A. 351, 675, 785, 799, 814, 874, 875, 894, 1112, 1122
Podlesskaya, Vera 319, 971, 973, 1002, 1005
Poeck, Klaus 125
Poghirc, Cicerone 1511, 1521
Pohlenz, Max 184
Poitiers, s. Gilbert de la Porrée
Poizner, Howard 13
Pokorny, Julius 1506
Polinsky, Maria 886, 891, 977, 1084, 1671, 1674
Pollack, Jordan B. 157
Pollard, Carl 857
Pollnac, Richard B. 1229
Pollock, Jean-Yves 870
Polotsky, Hans Jacob 1750–1754, 1759, 1760, 1771
Pomorska, Krystyna 401, 402
Pompino-Marschall, Bernd 1312, 1392
Pop, Sever 1471, 1473
Popovich, Harold 6, 1134
Poppe, Nicholas 955, 1402
Porphyrius 202
Porter, Stanley E. 562, 563
Porterie-Gutierrez, Liliane 874
Portner, Paul 796
Porzig, Walter 562, 1168
Poser, William J. 1376
Posner, Rebecca 1602, 1625
Posner, Roland 54, 371, 630
Post, Marike 1663
Postal, Paul 905
Postel, Guillaume 218, 238, 239
Pott, Friedrich A. 1546
Pottier, Bernard 272, 294, 295, 878, 1599, 1145

Poulin, Christine 149
Prado, Marcial 401
Praetorius, Franz 1771
Prandi, Michele 49, 56, 450, 460
Pratt, Alice E. 1229
Prechtl, Peter 477
Prem, Hanns J. 1539
Premper, Waldfried 336, 491
Press, Ian 957
Press, Margareth 966
Preston, Dennis 1670, 1674
Price, Thomas R. 1230
Prideaux, Gary Dean 17
Priestly, T. M. S. 824
Prieto, Pilar 1383
Prillwitz, Siegmund 142–144, 149
Primus, Beatrice 367, 485, 641, 750, 861, 866–870
Prince, Alan 96, 415, 679–681, 685–687, 691, 692, 1313, 1320, 1326, 1328, 1358–1364, 1386
Prince, Ellen 528, 625, 627, 1043, 1047, 1052, 1054, 1059, 1072, 1073, 1083, 1085, 1092
Prinzhorn, Martin 288, 1708
Priscianus (= Priscian, Priscien) 188, 192–194, 196, 201, 203, 205–207, 211–214, 247
Pritsak, Omeljan 1728
Přívratská, Jana 220, 244
Progovac, Ljiljana 1703
Propp, Vladimír 645
Pu, Ming-Ming 1124, 1128
Puglielli, Annarita 1084, 1093, 1099, 1442, 1449, 1452
Pulgram, Ernst 1394, 1692
Pullum, Geoffrey 120, 867, 1465, 1467
Pusch, Claus Dieter 594, 610
Puskás, Genoveva 1090
Pustet, Regina 501
Putenham, George 240, 241
Putnam, Hilary 76, 209
Pütz, Martin 1148, 1147
Putzu, Ignazio 1506
Pythagoras 226

Q

Quasthoff, Uta M. 454, 455, 459
Quesada, J. Diego 565
Quian, Gaoyin 129
Quillian, Roger 79
Quine, Willard van Orman 68, 209, 1276
Quintilian 237, 1687

Quirk, Randolph 367, 495, 496, 812, 1112, 1122, 1564, 1598, 1603, 1604
Quondam, Amedeo 475

R

Rabel, L. 957
Rabofski, Birgit 412
Racine, Jean 606
Račkov, Genadij E. 1119, 1122
Radden, Günter 16
Rader, Margaret 440
Radford, Andrew 864
Radtke, Edgar 468, 473
Radulphus Brito 203
Rahden, Wolfart von 222, 238
Raible, Wolfgang 4, 7, 9, 10, 20, 49, 68, 93, 104, 105, 113, 114, 295, 303, 337, 376, 410, 413, 441, 469, 482, 535, 592–596, 599–601, 604, 605, 608, 610, 612, 636, 639, 643–645, 842, 850, 1143, 1557, 1558, 1561, 1574, 1576, 1581, 1582, 1583, 1586, 1692, 1697
Raichle, Marcus E. 100
Raimundus Lullus (= Ramón Llull) 86
Rainer, Franz 1215, 1601
Rakhilina, Ekaterina 971, 973
Ralph of Beauvais (= Ralph von Beauvais) 194
Ramamurthi, B. 132, 135
Ramanujan, Attipat K. 1530
Ramat, Anna Giacalone 382, 1581
Ramat, Paolo 230, 1484, 1492, 1498, 1574, 1578
Ramsden, Herbert 1703
Ramsey, Frank Plumpton 69, 481
Ramstedt, Gustav J. 1112, 1122
Ramus, Petrus 212, 213, 216, 238
Randquist, Madeleine G. 635
Rangamani, G. N. 135
Ransdell, Joseph 371
Ransom, Evelyn N. 986, 987
Rapcsak, Steven 128, 129
Raposo, Eduardo 1057
Rapp, Karin 1392
Rappaport, Gilbert C. 1117, 1118, 1120, 1122
Rask, Rasmus 1555, 1635
Rastatter, Michael P. 130
Rastier, François 6, 643, 1563, 1581
Ratcliff, R. 159
Ratliff, Martha 1284, 1289
Ratner, Vadim A. 116, 117
Raudaskoski, Pirkko 149

Rauh, Gisa 575
Rausch, P. J. 528
Ray, Verne F. 1228
Raymond, William R. 1050
Rayner, Keith 858
Raz, Shlomo 1762, 1765, 1767–1770
Read, A. F. C. 1120, 1122
Reboul, Anne 513
Rebuschi, Georges 352, 882, 1088, 1090
Recanati, Francois 514
Recorde, Robert 240
Redeker, Gisela 463, 464
Reesnik, Ger P. 837
Reformatskij, Aleksandr A. 311
Reh, Mechthild 610, 677, 1095–1100, 1609, 1612, 1615
Rehbein, Jochen 41, 446, 447, 1721
Rehbock 1566
Reich, Ulrich 1344, 1562, 1570
Reichenbach, Hans 559, 560, 563, 576, 586, 640, 770, 772
Reichmann, Oskar 1584
Reid, Nicholas 819, 824
Reifferscheid 215
Reifler Bricker, Victoria 1540
Reilly, Judy S. 86, 142
Reinecke, John E. 1651
Reinhart, Tanya 620, 625, 635, 646, 753, 758, 861
Reinholtz, Charlotte 1434, 1436
Reinisch, Leonhard 1107
Reintges, Chris 1747, 1755
Remigius of Auxerre (= Remigius von Auxerre) 192
Renou, Louis 1682
Renzi, Lorenzo 401, 408
Rescher, Nicholas 786, 802
Restle, David 1320, 1327
Rettich, Wolfgang 1156
Reuchlin, Johannes 216, 217
Reuland, Eric 753, 758, 919, 941, 942
Reyle, Uwe 1136
Rhodes, Richard 1083
Ribhegge, W. 211
Ribot, Théodule 132
Ricca, Davide 1150
Rice, Carl C. 1686
Rice, Keren 1386
Richards, Barry 564
Richards, Eirlys 1195
Richards, Ivor A. 295
Richter, Heide 459, 576
Richter, Helmut 641
Richter, Michael 1688
Ricken, Ulrich 229, 257
Rickheit, Gert 42, 159, 637, 649
Riddle, Elizabeth 984
Riedl, Rupert 13

Rieger, Burghard B. 648
Riemsdijk, Henk van 907, 909
Rijk, Lambert Maria de 195, 198
Rijk, R. P. G. de 1442
Rijkhoff, Jan 281, 316, 425, 426, 526, 529, 530, 859, 861, 862, 865, 1142, 1170, 1473
Rijlaarsdam, Gert 154, 156
Rimini, s. Gregory of Rimini
Ringmacher, Manfred 268
Rischel, Jørgen 525, 1278
Rivers, William H. R. 1246
Rizzi, Luigi 284–287, 946, 1089, 1090, 1704
Rjabova, Irina S. 1001
Roach, Peter 1391
Roberg, Heinz 840
Robering, Klaus 1252
Robert Kilwardby 192, 203
Robert of Paris 194
Roberts, Craige 1080
Roberts, Ian 288
Roberts, John R. 1002, 1116, 1122
Roberts, Lamar 130
Roberts, Sarah 97
Robins, Robert Henry 181, 182, 185, 188, 210, 212, 215, 216, 235, 236, 438, 495, 503
Rochemont, Michael S. 620, 626, 1079, 1082, 1083
Rock, Irvin 1307
Rödiger, Emil 1771
Rodriguez, João Tçuzzu S. J. 254
Roelcke, Thorsten 1624
Roeltgen, David 128, 129
Roeper, Thomas 701, 887
Rogers, Andy 1295
Rohdenburg, Günther 367
Rohlfs, Gerhard 665, 877, 878, 1321
Rohrbacher, Bernhard Wolfgang 286
Rohrer, Christian 271, 557, 559, 560, 562, 563, 640, 702
Rohs, Peter 478
Roldán, Mercedes 972
Rolf, Eckard 55, 447
Romaine, Suzanne 780, 987, 1650, 1657
Rombandeeva, Evdokija I. 892
Römer, Raúl 1666
Römer, Ruth 267
Rommel, Inge 1770
Romney, Kimball 1207, 1208, 1209
Róna-Tas, András 1721
Rondal, Jean A. 99
Ronneberger-Sibold, Elke 386, 388, 1628
Roodbergen, Jouthe A. F. 275

Index of names

Rooij, Vincent de 1666
Roos, Heinrich 203
Rooth, Mats E. 622, 627, 1047, 1450
Rosaldo, Michelle Z. 71
Rosch, Eleanor 4, 80, 415, 1144, 1151, 1180, 1224, 1144
Rosen, Carol 887
Rosén, Haiim B. 184, 1682, 1689
Rosen, Sarah T. 718, 723
Rosenbek, John C. 124
Rosenblueth, David A. 116
Rosengren, Inger 55, 620, 625, 627, 647, 1561
Rosenqvist, Arvid 1478
Rosetti, Alexandru 1511
Rosiello, Luigi 257
Rosier, Irène 9, 196, 204
Ross, John Robert 318, 495–499, 501, 505, 626, 980, 989, 1106, 1107
Ross, Malcolm D. 696, 1642, 1643
Rossipal, Hans 630
Rotweil, s. Adam of Rotweil
Roulet, Eddy 55, 644, 647, 648
Rountree, Catherine 1666
Rowlands, E. C. 696, 974
Rubach, Jerzy 1348
Rubba, Jo 681, 690
Rudin, Catherine 290, 1442, 1449
Ruhlen, Merritt 118, 424, 431, 1337, 1483
Rumelhart, David E. 78, 96, 645
Rumsey, Alan 1208, 1209
Rupp, Heinz 478
Russell, Bertrand 209, 512, 513, 576, 578
Russell, James A. 1200
Russell, Kevin 1133, 1434, 1436
Růžička, Rudolph 1119, 1122
Ryder, Mary Ellen 702

S

Saah, Kofi Korankye 1080, 1093, 1094
Sabban, Annette 641
Sacerdos, Marius Plotius 187, 188
Sacks, Harvey 45, 439, 445, 454, 456, 647
Saddy, Douglas 124
Sadler, Lousia 6, 18
Sadock, Jerrold M. 807–810, 814, 869, 1014, 1015, 1017, 1022, 1023
Saeed, John Ibrahim 1084, 1093

Saeki, Tetsuo 278
Sáenz-Badillos, Angel 1682, 1683
Safir, Ken 286, 287, 866, 870, 942
Sag, Ivan A. 857, 904
Saha, P. K. 1015
Saib, Jilali 1319
Saint Jacques Fauquenoy, Marguerite 1661
Saksena, Anuradha 890, 891, 893
Salas, Adalberto 413
Salmon, Vivian 86, 87, 88, 217, 245–247
Saltarelli, Mario 696, 864
Samaniego Aldazábal, José Luis 409
Samek-Lodovici, Vieri 1093
Samet, Jerry 648
Sanctius Brocensis, Franciscus 212, 237, 245
Sanctius s. Brozas, Sánchez de las
Sandalo, Filomena 1641
Sandfeld, Kristian 1510, 1512, 1514, 1517–1522, 1527
Sandler, Wendy 144, 145
Sanford, Anthony J. 158
Šanidze, Ak'ak'i 312
Sankoff, Gillian 743, 1649, 1650, 1652
Santen, Jan van 1383
Sapir, Edward 26, 91, 249–251, 264, 265, 280, 294, 306, 341, 347, 479, 669, 696, 703, 708, 716–718, 1217, 1439, 1540, 1717
Sasanuma, Sumiko 129, 134
Sasse, Hans-Jürgen 4, 478, 480–482, 498, 500, 502, 503, 505, 506, 621, 624, 628, 629, 718, 729, 870, 1083–1085, 1092, 1093, 1096, 1099, 1172, 1447, 1633–1635, 1668, 1671–1673, 1675
Sastri, Subrahmanya 276
Saunders, Barbara A. C. 1229, 1244
Saussure, Ferdinand de 2, 3, 4, 20, 41, 81, 91, 92, 252, 294, 295, 346, 347, 371, 471, 818, 1153, 1156, 1157
Sauvageot, Aurélien 1164
Sauzet, Patrick 1055
Savage-Rumbaugh, Sue 96
Saville-Troike, Muriel 441
Saxena, Anju 987, 1533
Scaliger, Joseph Justus 220
Scaliger, Julius Caesar 212, 245, 247
Scalise, Sergio 1214, 1216, 1217, 1596, 1603

Scardamalia, Marlene 155, 156
Scatton, Ernest A. 836
Ščerbak, Aleksandr M. 1721
Schachter, Paul 374, 526, 728, 731, 903, 1088, 1091, 1094, 1097, 1099, 1414, 1416, 1420, 1442
Schadeberg, Thilo C. 1376
Schächter, Josef 67
Schaefer, Edward F. 4, 452, 456, 457
Schaefer, Ronald P. 1248
Schaffar, Wolfram 1092
Schaller, Helmut Wilhelm 36, 1510–1512, 1520, 1521
Schaller, Susan 13
Schank, Gerd 440, 473, 475, 1584
Schank, Roger 79, 648
Schapp, Wilhelm 72
Schaub, Willi 527, 530
Schebeck, Bernard 1210
Scheerer, Otto 503
Schegloff, Emanuel A. 45, 439, 445, 454, 457, 647
Schenk, Wolfgang 237, 238
Schenkel, Wolfgang 1743–1747, 1750, 1753
Schenkeveld, Dirk M. 182, 184
Schenning, Saskia 573
Schepman, Astrid 1383
Schepping, Marie-Theres 1143, 1145, 1149, 1152, 1161, 1169, 1170
Scherer, Hans Siegfried 440
Scherer, K. R. 1387
Scherners, Max 441
Schick, Brenda 147
Schiffmann, Harold F. 1535
Schiffmann, Harvey Richard 1296
Schiffrin, Deborah 557
Schifko, Peter 1158
Schiltz, Guillaume 1479, 1480, 1482
Schlaps, Christiane 242
Schlegel, August Wilhelm von 249–251, 253, 257, 258, 262, 264, 271, 272, 306, 660, 1555, 1623, 1626
Schlegel, Friedrich von 222, 249, 251, 253, 257, 258, 262, 264, 306, 660, 669
Schleicher, August 249, 306
Schlenck, Klaus Jürgen 124
Schleyer, Johann Martin 87, 89, 91
Schlieben-Lange, Brigitte 40, 41, 243, 437, 446, 468, 469, 1253, 1272, 1558, 1560, 1561, 1567, 1568
Schmalhofer, Franz 158
Schmalstieg, William R. 778

Schmid, Hans-Jörg 1144, 1151, 1170
Schmid, Stephan 411
Schmidt, Annette 1670, 1673
Schmidt, C. 214
Schmidt, Karl Horst 674, 1634, 1775
Schmidt, Siegfried J. 49, 455, 636
Schmidt, Wilhelm 855
Schmidt-Riese, Roland 1561, 1576, 1585
Schmitter, Peter 236
Schneider, Hans Julius 66, 67
Schneider, Jacob Hans Josef 193, 194, 196–200, 203–206, 208
Schneider, Roger 1765
Schnelle, Helmut 73, 389
Schnotz, Wolfgang 161
Schnur-Wellpott, Margit 472
Schoemann, Georg Friedrich 185
Schoenthal, Gisela 440
Scholem, Gershom 86
Scholz, Arno 410
Schönig, Claus 1729
Schottelius, Justus Georgius 239, 240, 243
Schpak-Dolt, Nikolaus 1604
Schrödinger, Erwin 105
Schubert, Klaus 930
Schuchardt, Hugo 87, 912, 1649
Schuh, Russel G. 1373, 1374
Schultze, Ernst 1651
Schultze-Berndt, Eva 504
Schulz, Peter 1114, 1122
Schulze, Wolfgang 478, 1776, 1783–1786, 1788, 1794
Schumann, John H. 1648, 1649
Schunert, Klaus 87
Schusky, Ernest 1206
Schütz, Alfred 43–45, 48, 439, 445, 455, 456, 458
Schütze, Fritz 439
Schwabe, Kerstin 396
Schwall, Ulrike 564
Schwartz, Arthur 529
Schwartz, Linda 1127
Schwarze, Christoph 730, 1147, 1170, 1598, 1605
Schwegler, Armin 250
Schwemmer, Oswald 66, 67, 72
Schwenter, Scott A. 771
Schwyzer, Eduard 598
Scott, Graham 598, 1406
Scott, Ruby 1543–1545
Searle, John Roger 55, 70, 71, 115, 116, 297, 438, 445, 446, 448, 481, 509, 510, 514, 521, 727, 806, 807, 811, 1038
Sears, Donald A. 372

Sebba, Mark 27, 1657
Segall, Marshall 1181
Seidenberg, Mark 129
Seiler, Hansjakob 11, 17, 35, 64, 294, 297, 304, 323–326, 328, 330, 332, 334–337, 339, 341, 478, 490, 491, 499, 528, 530, 538, 608, 611, 612, 733, 954, 961, 967, 968, 976, 1323, 1575, 1576
Seldeslachts, Herman 185
Selig, Maria 469, 593, 757, 837, 839, 1570, 1586, 1699
Seliger, Herbert W. 1668, 1670, 1671, 1673
Selkirk, Elisabeth O. 620, 621, 710, 1317, 1327, 1329, 1386, 1444
Sells, Peter 920
Selting, Margret 459
Senft, Gunter 568–571, 573, 604
Senn, Alfred 1625
Sennholz, Klaus 575
Septfond, D. 351, 353
Serbat, Guy 1224
Serzisko, Fritz 480, 547
Seuren, Pieter A. M. 408
Sgall, Petr 622, 641, 1442
Sgoff, Brigitte 249
Shaffer, Barbara 799
Shakespeare, William 240
Shao, Zhaohui 112
Shapiro, Michael 1535
Sharadzenidze, T. 252
Sharma, V. Venkatarama 275
Sharp, Harriet 1157
Sharwood Smith, Michael A. 1670, 1671, 1673
Shaw, Daniel R. 572
Shaw, Karen A. 572
Sherry, Richard 240
Sherzer, Joel 1540
Shetler, Joanne 680
Shibatani, Masayoshi 25, 370, 380, 695, 887, 889, 891–894, 901, 902, 904, 906–908, 912, 923, 972, 978
Shillcock, Richard 365
Shimada, Mutsuo 129
Shlonsky, Ur 1093, 1409, 1410
Shopen, Timothy 25, 1214
Shubin, Neil 111
Shuy, Roger W. 496
Sībawaihi 277
Sicard, Roch Ambroise 258
Sidney, Sir Philip 240, 243
Siegel, Muffy E. A. 701
Siemund, Peter 747–750, 752–756, 758, 1501
Sievers, Eduard 1310, 1312, 1329, 1330

Siewierska, Anna 528, 530, 676, 733, 855, 856, 862, 865, 866, 870, 901, 905, 910, 968, 1500
Siger of Courtrai (= Zeger van Kortrijk, Siger de Courtrai, Siger von Kortrijk) 203
Siklaki, István 645
Sil'nickij, Georgij G. 886–889, 891, 892, 894
Silva-Corvalán, Carmen 1053, 1055, 1061, 1641
Silverstein, Michael 17, 18, 316, 489, 729, 913, 922, 1430, 1648, 1657
Silvestris, Bernhard 194
Simango, Silvester Ron 930
Simeone-Senelle, Marie-Claude 1770
Simeonov, Boris 1512
Simmons, Geoffrey 1252
Simon Dacus (= Simon von Dacien) 203
Simon, Herbert 154
Simon, Julian Lincoln 426, 427, 430
Simone, Raffaele 225, 371, 404
Simons, Berthold 127
Simons, L. 1134
Simpson, J. M. Y. 1472
Simpson, Jane 1433, 1435, 1438
Singler, John Victor 780
Singleton, Jenny L. 150
Sirridge, Mary 203
Sitta, Georg 578
Skalička, Vladimir 249, 251, 272, 341, 660, 669, 678, 679, 716, 717, 1142, 1153, 1154, 1161, 1173, 1604, 1624
Skinner, Leo E. 1369
Skribnik, Elena K. 319
Slama-Cazacu, Tatjana 435
Slaughter, M. M. 246
Sloan, K. 1330
Slobin, Dan Isaac 2, 125–127, 336, 381, 607
Sluijter, Agaath 1388
Sluiter, Ineke 185, 236
Smailus, Ortwin 1542, 1545
Smeets, Ineke 797
Smeets, Rieks 1775, 1779, 1787
Smith Stark, Thomas C. 1187, 1188, 1204, 1457
Smith, Adam 230, 262
Smith, B. 478
Smith, Carlota 557, 560–562
Smith, Harry 429
Smith, John Charles 583
Smith, Norval 684, 792, 1657, 1660
Smith-Stark, T. Cedric 825–827, 830
Smolensky, Paul 78, 415, 686
Smyth, Mary M. 1306

Sneath, Peter 1483
Sneddon, J. N. 955
Snow, David L. 1244
Sobrero, Alberto A. 1153
Söderbergh, Ragnhild 702
Soemarmo 1095
Sohn, Sung-ock 999
Sokal, Robert R. 1483, 1484
Sokolovskaja, Natal'ja K. 1134
Solentia, Claretus de 215
Solncev, Vadim M. 310
Solnceva, Nina V. 309–312
Sommer, F. 524
Song, Jae Jung 33, 886, 888–891, 893, 895
Southworth, Franklin C. 1535, 1536
Sowinski, Bernhard 634
Sözer, Emel 636, 645
Spagnolo, F. L. M. 959
Spang-Hansen, Ebbe 1252, 1272
Speas, Arie 918
Speas, Margaret 946, 1438
Spencer, Andrew 1214, 1222, 1349
Spenser, Edmund 240, 243
Sperber, Dan 16, 82, 381, 448, 449, 452, 646, 1581
Spiegelberg, Wilhelm 1743
Spinicci, Paolo 8
Spinoza, Baruch (Benedict de) 217, 234, 248
Spitzer, Leo 269, 271
Sportiche, Dominique 946
Sprat, Thomas 243
Spriggs, Ruth 334
Spring, Cari 1361
Springer, Sally P. 134
Sproat, Richard 288
Squartini, Mario 781, 1469
Sreedhar, M. V. 1535
Sridhar, Shikaripur N. 673, 700
Srubar, Ilja 43–45, 50
Stäbler, Cynthia K. 4, 599
Stachowiak, Franz-Josef 334
Stahlschmidt, Andrea 597, 598
Staib, Bruno 1604
Stalph, Jürgen 128
Stammerjohann, Harro 211, 235
Stampe, David 686, 1326, 1327, 1330, 1337, 1339, 1341, 1343, 1347, 1362, 1363, 1394
Stankiewizc, E. 215, 216, 219
Stanner, William E. H. 1209
Stanzel, Franz K. 243
Staples, Ruth 1229
Stark, Elisabeth 641, 1058, 1568, 1586
Stark, Jaqueline Ann 127, 130
Starostin, Sergej A. 1422, 1775
Stassen, Leon 478, 507, 708, 726, 727, 733, 954, 956–959, 981, 993–996, 1105, 1107, 1109, 1111, 1112, 1117, 1122, 1499, 1502
Stati, Sorin 643
Stavi, Jonathan 1279
Stechow, Arnim von 484, 1450
Steedman, Mark 1386
Steele, Susan 865, 866, 957, 1547
Steever, Stanford B. 817, 1157
Stefanini, Jean 196
Stefenelli, Arnulf 1578
Steger, Hugo 468, 473, 1566
Stegmüller, Wolfgang 68, 1475
Stehl, Thomas 1586
Stein, Gabriele 216
Stein, Mark 1276
Stein, Peter 470
Steiner, Erich 438
Steinitz, Renate 638, 642
Steinthal, Heymann 81, 82, 181, 249, 266–268, 271, 272, 1145, 1310, 1311
Stekeler-Weithofer, Pirmin 70
Stempel, Wolf-Dieter 470, 610, 1052, 1053, 1561, 1568
Stephan von Perm 167
Stephens, Laurence D. 420, 421, 431
Steriade, Donca 1312
Stewart, Stephen O. 1233
Stewart, William A. 1662
Stiernhielm, Georg 239
Stirling, Lesley 1116, 1118, 1123, 1134
Stocker, Frank 89
Stojanović, Danijela 1094
Stokhof, Martin 1136
Stokoe, William C. 142–146
Stolz, Christel 1252, 1253, 1267, 1268, 1273, 1550
Stolz, Thomas 737–739, 1492, 1502, 1503, 1506, 1549–1551, 1579
Stone, Gerald 745, 818, 1290
Stopa, Roman 1151
Stowell, Tim 942, 1090
Strahl, Brian D. 113
Strasser, Gerhard F. 86, 87
Strawson, Peter Frederick 68, 515
Strehlow, Theodor Georg Henry 1108
Strohner, Hans 42, 50, 159, 461
Strömsdörfer, Christian 1629, 1636
Stroomer, Harry J. 524, 526
Stubbs, Michael 1563, 1570
Stucky, Susan U. 1081
Stump, Gregory T. 595, 710, 712, 1119, 1123
Sturlese, Rita 86
Sturmius, Johannes 214
Stute, Horst 1083
Stutterheim, Christiane von 630, 645
Suárez, Jorge A. 696, 863, 1540–1542, 1547–1550
Subbiondo, Joseph L. 87, 90
Sulkala, Helena 696, 701, 793, 1019, 1024
Sullivan, T. 903
Sumangala, Lelwala 1097
Sunik, Orest P. 319
Supalla, Samuel J. 149
Supalla, Ted 141, 147, 150
Sutton, Peter 1209
Sutton, Valerie 144
Suzuki, Takao 1201
Svantesson, Jan-Olof 1330, 1331
Svartvik, Jan 1569
Švedova, Natal'ja J. 999
Svolacchia, Marco 1084, 1093, 1099, 1442, 1449, 1452
Svorou, Soteria 432, 573, 1252
Swadesh, Morris 730, 1191, 1192, 1428
Swanton, John R. 696, 704, 1540
Sweetser, Eve E. 848, 1001, 1304, 1579, 1581, 1582, 1612
Swift, L. B. 1278
Swiggers, Pierre 181–185, 187, 189, 217, 371
Sylvius, Jacobus 214
Szabó, Árpád 11, 637
Szabó, Zoltán 637
Szabolcsi, Anna 625, 947, 1444, 1445, 1450

T

T'Hart, Johan 1381
Tabouret-Keller, Andrée 1648
Tagliavini, Carlo 1183
Taglicht, Josef 625
Tai, James H.-Y. 376
Takizala, Alexis 1088, 1098–1100
Tallal, Paula 119, 120
Tallerman, Maggie 1448
Talmy, Leonard 17, 76, 83, 415, 506, 568, 571, 572, 689, 730, 804, 891, 1142, 1169, 1170, 1198
Tamaoka, Katsuo 129
Tanaka, Yasufumi 129
Tannen, Deborah 440, 441, 463, 635
Tannery, Paul 86
Tao, Liang 1128
Tarski, Alfred 54, 69
Tatevoscov, Sergej G. 319

Tavoni, Mirko 211, 212, 214, 216, 218, 219
Taylan, Eser E. 878
Taylor, Carolyn P. 1129
Taylor, Charles 50−52
Taylor, Daniel J. 181, 186
Taylor, E. G. R. 1182
Taylor, John R. 415, 496, 961, 964, 1144, 1149, 1151, 1252
Tekin, Talât 1720
Telchid, Sylviane 414
Tendeng, Odile 6
Tenišev, Ėdhem R. 1721
ter Meulen, Alice 941, 942
Terasawa, Jun 893
Ternes, Elmar 1493
Terrace, Herbert 96
Tervoor, Bernhard T. M. 142
Tesak, Jürgen 124, 127
Tesnière, Lucien 116, 260, 294, 300, 312, 481, 1169, 1170, 1171, 1425
Testelec (Testelets), Jakov G. 314, 1133
Theckhoff, Claude 887
Thelin, Nils B. 559, 562−564
Theophrastus 237
Thieroff, Rolf 558, 560, 781, 1504
Thom, René 19, 339
Thomas Aquinas (= Thomas von Aquin) 198, 199, 206, 209
Thomas von Erfurt 203, 206−208, 247
Thomas, Cyrus 1540
Thomason, R. 796
Thomason, Sarah Grey 411, 1458, 1537, 1541, 1643, 1645, 1673, 1675, 1693
Thompson, Chad 905, 911, 1127, 1133
Thompson, Laurence C. 696, 700, 1276, 1643
Thompson, Sandra A. 6, 18, 356, 377, 380, 489, 490, 500−502, 505, 526, 528, 603, 604, 613, 614, 627, 628, 727, 732, 809, 842, 843, 848, 851, 881, 884, 894, 910, 923, 954, 957, 958, 979, 984, 988, 1008, 1016, 1026, 1027, 1106, 1116, 1120, 1123, 1127, 1129, 1131, 1171, 1218, 1414, 1416, 1419, 1442, 1447, 1601, 1635
Thomsen, M.-L. 171
Thomson, Alexander 874
Thomson, James 111
Thongkum, Theraphan 1236
Thorndyke, Perry W. 645
Thorne, Alan 118
Thorne, David A. 698
Thorsen, Nina 1381

Thráinsson, Höskuldur 1633, 1714
Thrax, s. Dionysios of Thracia
Thümmel, Wolf 482
Tibshirani, Robert J. 430
Tiersma, Peter M. 830
Tikkanen, Bertil 1112, 1114, 1115, 1118, 1120, 1123
Till, Walter C. 1743, 1750, 1759
Timberlake, Alan 560−565, 813, 904, 1005
Todorov, Tzvetan 469, 645
Togeby, Ole 1252
Toldova, Svetlana Ju. 1133
Tomlin, Russell S. 317, 368, 420, 426, 427, 432, 457, 623, 641, 645, 855, 861, 870, 1083, 1124, 1128, 1129, 1467, 1468
Tommola, Hannu 777
Tomson, A. I. 880
Tonelli, D. A. 1108
Toole, Janine 1135
Tophinke, Doris 46, 55
Topuria, Guram V. 1783
Totman, Richard 2
Tournier, Jean 1605
Trabant, Jürgen 51, 57, 267, 441, 1147, 1148, 1540
Tracy, Destutt de 81
Tranel, Daniel T. 13
Trask, Robert L. 777, 784, 998, 999
Traugott, Elizabeth Closs 5, 54, 382, 411, 592, 842, 850, 986, 998, 1007, 1014, 1159, 1577−1580, 1582, 1586, 1609, 1611, 1613, 1636
Travis, Lisa 858
Treiman, Rebecca 1327
Trier, Jost 642, 1145
Trivedi, G. M. 1533
Trommelen, Mieke 702
Trubetzkoy, Nikolaj S. (= Trubeckoj) 90, 325, 401, 402, 1393, 1394, 1457
Trubinskij, Valentin I. 777, 929
Truckenbrodt, Hubert 1386
Trudgill, Peter 1651, 1670, 1672
Tryon, Darrell 1652
Tschenkéli, Kita 1403
Tschida, Alexander 641
Tsimpli, Ianthi Maria 1442, 1444
Tsitsipis, Lukas 1673
Tsonis, Anastasios A. 114
Tsunoda, Tasaku 18, 490, 728
Tugendhat, Ernst 70, 478
Tuggy, David 886, 894
Tuite, Kevin 1789
Tuller, Laurice 1080, 1088, 1090, 1094, 1451, 1453
Tung, T'ung-ho 837

Turgot, Anne-Robert 230
Turley, Jeffrey S. 756
Turner, Graham H. 148
Turner, Lorenzo D. 1661
Turner, William 241
Tyler, Lorraine K. 98, 710, 1124
Tyndale, William 241
Tzeng, Ovid J. L. 125, 127, 129

U

Uchikawa, Keiji 1229
Ugorji, E. 1278
Uhmann, Susanne 620, 1343, 1391
Ullendorff, Edward 1770
Ullmann, Stephen 294, 437, 1142, 1143, 1145, 1148, 1149, 1152, 1156−1158, 1161, 1163, 1172, 1173, 1604
Ulrich, Miorița 1442
Ultan, Russell 528, 561, 961, 993, 997, 1012−1018, 1020, 1021, 1337, 1343, 1501
Underhill, Peter A. 118
Underwood, Walter L. 1229
Ungerer, Friedrich 1144, 1151, 1170
Urbach, Peter 419
Urban, Wilbur Marshall 437
Ureland, P. Sture 1506
Uspenskij, Boris A. 249, 256, 310
Utas, Bo 1731
Uyechi, Lionda 144, 145
Uytfanghe, Marc van 1688

V

Väänänen, Veikko 1692, 1693
Vago, Robert M. 1668, 1670, 1671, 1673
Vaid, Jyotsna 125
Vaissière, Jaqueline 1382
Valderrama Fernandez, Ricardo 414
Valdés, Juan de 218
Valdes-Perez, Raul E. 1207
Valentine, Charles W. 1229
Valin, Roch 334
Valla, Lorenzo 203, 212, 214, 218, 237
Vallduví, Enric 620, 622, 623, 626, 1051, 1054, 1055, 1060, 1066, 1068, 1089, 1384, 1442, 1444, 1446, 1449
Valli, Clayton 142
Vamling, Karina 1402

Index of names

van der Auwera, Johan 285, 785, 799, 814, 842, 998, 1003, 1004, 1008, 1115, 1122, 1458, 1471, 1484, 1492, 1493, 1504, 1505
van Hoek, Karen 1128
Van Ness, Silke 1670
Van Valin, Robert D. 482, 484, 489, 537, 538, 593, 605, 611–614, 891, 899, 905–908, 981, 985, 986, 1115, 1116, 1123, 1126, 1130–1133, 1405, 1419, 1424, 1431, 1434–1437
Vandeloise, Claude 81, 82, 1252, 1253
Vapnarsky, Valentina 354
Varchi, Benedetto 1681
Varela, Francisco F. 44
Varga, László 1386
Varga-Weisz, Patrick D. 112
Vargha-Khadem, Faraneh 99
Varma, Siddheshwar 1317, 1319, 1320
Varro, Gabrielle 2
Varron (Marcus Terentius Varro) 186, 187, 279
Vassilaki, S. 354
Vater, Heinz 634, 635, 644, 645
Vater, Johann Severin 230
Veenstra, Tonjes 1661, 1663, 1664
Velázquez-Castillo, Maura 974
Velde, Roger G. van de 637, 649
Velten, H. V. 880
Venditti, Jennifer 1386
Vendler, Zeno 481, 483, 517–519, 561, 565, 773, 774, 776, 1276
Vendryès, Joseph 1061
Vennemann, Theo 25, 27, 90, 325, 530, 686, 855, 857, 858, 860, 1312–1321, 1324, 1326–1329, 1337, 1345, 1396, 1506, 1624, 1628, 1629, 1635, 1636
Verburg, Pieter A. 255
Vergnaud, Jean-Roger 970, 1320, 1328, 1384, 1385
Verhagen, Arie 891, 893
Verhoeven, Ludo 1721
Verkuyl, Henk J. 557, 561, 779
Verma, Manindra K. 1297, 1532
Vermeer, Hans J. 1529
Vernus, Pascal 1743
Veronese, Guarino 214, 237
Verschueren, Jef 447, 451, 452, 459
Verspoor, Marjolijn H. 1147, 1148
Versteegh, Cornelius (= Kees) 217, 277, 1682

Verstegen, Richard 241
Vet, Co 558, 560, 563, 564, 640
Viberg, Åke 728, 1295–1297, 1302, 1304–1307
Victorinus, Marius 188
Viehweger, Dieter 55, 635, 637, 638, 644, 646–649
Vikner, Sten 288
Vilkuna, Maria 778, 1053, 1054, 1071, 1442
Villa Dei, s. Alexander de Villa Dei
Villalón, Cristóbal de 216
Vinay, Jean-Paul 1152, 1161, 1170
Vincent, Nigel B. 367
Vittmann, Günther 1743
Voegelin, Charles F. 423, 424, 432
Voegelin, Florence M. 424, 432
Vogel, Irene 1385, 1386, 1393
Vogel, Petra Maria 595
Vogel, Roos 559–561, 563, 564
Vogt, Hans 1403
Voigt, Rainer 1769–1772
Voigtlander, Katherine 1543
Volodin, Aleksandr P. 312
Vološinov, Valentin N. 1135
Volterra, Virginia 148, 149
Voorhoeve, Clemens L. 572, 1397
Voorhoeve, Jan 1376, 1649, 1658, 1666
Vorlat, Emma 215
Vossius, Gerard Johannes 247
Vossler, Karl 271
Vygotskij, Lev S. 10

W

Waal, Frans de 100
Wachowicz, Krystyna 893
Wackernagel, Jacob 333, 1703
Wagner, Ewald 1770
Wagner, Heinrich 1506
Wahl, Edgar von 87
Wälchli, Bernhard 1459
Wald, Lucia 505
Waldenfels, Bernhard 44–47, 50, 52, 54, 57, 58, 447, 450, 451, 456, 462
Wales, Katie 743, 745, 746
Wali, Kashi 700
Walker, Christopher B. F. 164
Wallace, Anthony F. C. 1207
Wallace, Stephen 557, 562
Wallace, W. D. 1442
Wallesch, Claus-W. 124, 125
Wallis, John 234
Wallmann, Joel 96
Walsh, Michael 498, 501
Walter, Heribert 499, 500

Waltereit, Richard 1167, 1172, 1581, 1582, 1586
Waltz, David L. 157
Wandruszka, Mario 271, 1170
Wang, William S.-Y. 1483
Wanner, Dieter 743, 1586, 1703, 1704
Ward, Gregory 1052, 1072, 1083
Warkentin, Viola 1543–1545
Warren, Beatrice 702, 1157
Wartburg, Walther von 271, 296
Washio, Ryuchi 894
Wąsik, Zdzisław 1019
Wasow, Thomas 909, 930, 1084
Waßner, Ulrich Hermann 479
Watkins, Laurel J. 696, 829
Watson, James 105
Watt, Ian 1152
Watt, W. C. 176
Watters, J. 1442, 1453
Watters, John R. 1079, 1081, 1091, 1095, 1097–1099
Watzlawick, Paul 53, 57, 453, 463
Wauchope, Robert 1540
Waugh, Linda R. 408, 557–560, 564, 1157
Webb, Rebecca 141
Webelhuth, Gert 1434
Weber, Max 43, 46
Wegener, Heide 971
Wegener, Philipp 440, 577
Wehle, Winfried 472
Weidemann, Hermann 184, 193
Weidenbusch, Waltraud 473
Weil, Henri 618, 855, 1442
Weingartner, Paul 649
Weinhold, Norbert 1478
Weinrich, Harald 51, 52, 114, 271, 272, 451, 629, 639, 771, 778
Weischenberg, Siegfried 49
Weisgerber, Leo 271
Weissenborn, Jürgen 576, 577, 607
Weizenbaum, Joseph 76
Wekker, Herman 408
Welke, Klaus M. 415
Wellmann, Hans 475
Wells, Margaret A. 696, 699
Welmers, William E. 695, 931, 1109, 1305, 1368
Weltens, Bert 1668
Weninger, Stefan 1769
Wenk, B. 1395
Wenker, Georg 1473
Wenzel, Harald 45, 446
Werlich, Egon 636
Werner, Otmar 92, 386, 388
Wernicke, Carl 13, 98, 100
Werth, Paul 641

West, Candace 463
Westermann, Diedrich 696
Wetzer, Harrie 501–503, 505, 731, 957
Weydt, Harald 1253, 1272
Weyhe, Eyvind 1633
Whaley, Lindsay J. 250
Wheatley, Julian K. 525, 527
Whinnom, Keith 1650
White, Isobel M. 1210
Whitley, Stanley M. 1172
Whitney, William Dwight 385, 387, 699–701, 703
Whorf, Benjamin Lee 69, 92, 265, 294, 347, 478, 568, 729, 730, 733, 1147, 1148, 1492, 1504
Widmann, Angelika 1183
Wiegand, Herbert Ernst 1479
Wierzbicka, Anna 10, 91, 294, 296, 301, 304, 415, 501, 605, 726, 887, 892, 893, 972, 984, 1000, 1033, 1143, 1149, 1187, 1191–1196, 1198, 1200, 1201, 1246, 1298, 1304
Wiesemann, Ursula 746, 1133, 1134
Wilbur, Ronnie B. 143, 145, 147
Wilcox, Sherman E. 142, 145
Wilhelm, Raymund 469, 471–474
Wilkins, David P. 576, 838, 1082, 1134, 1155, 1199, 1308
Wilkins, John 86–92, 246–248
Wilks, Yorick 79
Willerman, Raquel 149
Willett, Thomas 777, 1305
William of Champeaux (= Wilhelm von Champeaux, Guillaume de Champeaux) 196
William of Conches (= Guillaume de Conches, Wilhelm von Conches) 192, 194–196
William of Ockham (= Wilhelm von Ockham, Guillaume d'Ockham) 199–202, 208, 209, 593
Williams, Edwin 705, 710, 718, 856, 909, 949, 1443
Williams, John E. 1229
Willis, John Christopher 1476
Willmes, Klaus 125
Wills, Christopher 117
Wilmet, Marc 334
Wilson, Deirdre 16, 82, 381, 448, 449, 452, 646, 1581
Wilson, Robert 1535, 1643
Wilson, Thomas 240
Winand, Jean 1743, 1751
Windisch, Rudolf 1605
Winkler, Heinrich 503

Winkler, Susanne 620
Winograd, Terry 76, 83
Winston, Elizabeth A. 145, 149
Winter, Alexander 156
Wioland, François 1395
Wiredu, Kwasi 70
Wirth, Jessica 402, 403
Wisch, Fritz-Helmut 141
Wise, Mary Ruth 894
Witkowski, Stanley R. 1154, 1178–1181, 1184, 1187, 1188, 1190, 1193
Witte, P. 1105
Wittgenstein, Ludwig 65–67, 69, 70, 73, 415, 445, 448, 477, 657, 806
Wodeham, Adam de 203, 209
Wohlgemuth, Carl 1543–1545
Wolf, Charles M. de 887, 903
Wolf, J. J. 1387
Wolfson, Nessa 557
Woll, Bencie 141
Woodbury, Antony C. 733, 910, 1133
Woodbury, Hanni J. 722
Woods, Anthony 419, 421, 422, 427
Woodworth, Nancy L. 433
Woodworth, Robert S. 1228
Wörner, Markus H. 9
Worrall, Linda E. 126, 127
Wouters, Alfons 181, 182, 184, 185
Wright, Beverly 119
Wright, Roger 1687
Wu, Yongyi 1210
Wüest, Jakob 1693
Wuillemin, Dianne 135
Wulfeck, Beverly 123, 128
Wunderli, Peter 642
Wunderlich, Dieter 56, 438, 446, 480, 646, 977, 1598
Wundt, Wilhelm 482
Wurm, Stephen A. 742, 743, 1652
Wurzel, Wolfgang Ullrich 54, 90, 381, 393, 394, 398–401, 404, 405, 410, 688, 717, 1252, 1602
Wydell, Taeko N. 129

X

Xolodovič, Aleksandr A. 31, 312, 890
Xrakovskij, Viktor S. 31, 312–314, 892, 998, 1005, 1038
Xu, Yi 129

Y

Yang, Mu-Jang 130
Yasugi, Yoshiho 1540, 1541, 1543–1547, 1550
Yates, Frances A. 86
Yimam, Baye 681
Yip, Moira 685, 1369
Yip, Virginia 696, 752, 756, 1195
Yiu, Edwin 126, 127
Yoichiro, Yamanai 278
Yule, George Udny 435, 639, 642, 646, 648, 1581

Z

Zacharski, Ron 1128
Zaefferer, Dietmar 799, 805, 807
Zahwe, Claudia 143
Zamenhof, Ludvik Lejzer 87, 89, 91
Zatorre, Robert J. 135
Zavala, Roberto 720
Zec, Draga 1328
Zee, Eric 1372
Zeidler, Jürgen 1743, 1744, 1753, 1754
Zelealem Leyew 1670, 1674
Zemp, Hugo 1369
Zeno 236
Žepić, Stanko 702
Zerubavel, Eviatar 1184, 1185
Zeshan, Ulrike 149
Zhang, Sulan 129
Zhou, Hengxiang 638
Zhurinskij, Andrej N. 1252
Zide, Arlene R. K. 889
Ziegler, Wolfram 124
Zimmer, June 147
Zimmer, Karl 878, 1064
Zimmermann, Thomas 578
Zipf, George K. 19, 114, 385, 846
Žirkov, L. I. 1784, 1790
Žirmunskij, Viktor M. 319
Ziv, Yael 1068, 1071, 1072, 1076
Žolkovskij, Aleksandr K. 317
Zribi-Hertz, Anne 747, 752, 753
Zubin, David 1136, 1259
Zubizarreta, Maria Luisa 887, 970, 1384
Zumthor, Paul 1570
Zwaan, Rolf A. 160
Zwanenburg, Wiecher 1217, 1223, 1225
Zwart, Jan-Wouter 859
Zwicky, Arnold M. 710, 745, 807, 808, 810, 814, 857, 869, 1014, 1015, 1039, 1040, 1045, 1048, 1425

Index of languages / Sprachenregister / Index de langues

A

Abadzex 1775
Abaza 1775, 1776
Abkhaz (= Abxaz) 29–30, 527, 696, 699, 756, 847, 888, 918, 931, 935, 1034, 1061, 1281, 1291, 1300, 1301, 1330, 1426–1427, 1494, 1502, 1775–1776, 1779–1780, 1784–1785, 1787
–, Bzyp dialect of 1777
Abkhaz-Adyghean 1493
Acehnese 886, 974, 1193, 1419
Adamawa-Ubangi languages 530
Adnyamadhanha (= Adnjamathanha) 742, 1210
Adygh
 s. Čerkessisch, West
African languages 69–70, 118, 148, 280, 288, 308–309, 353, 610, 696, 698, 728, 752–753, 771, 817, 851, 955, 991, 1081, 1088, 1092–1097, 1100, 1106, 1109, 1116, 1619–1620
–, East 995
–, North 955
–, North-East 1107
–, Sub-Saharan 956, 994, 1109
–, West 762, 894, 987, 1093, 1109
Afrikaans 287, 390, 988, 1266, 1628, 1649, 1651, 1706, 1708
Afro-Asiatic languages 37, 265, 374, 678, 681, 906, 921, 962, 1463, 1493, 1502, 1747
Afscharisch 1720
Agau languages 1771
Aghem 625, 628, 1079, 1082, 1090–1091, 1097, 1100, 1372, 1374, 1442, 1453
Aghul 1776, 1782
–, Cirxe 1784
–, Keren 1784
–, Riča 1793
Agta 1239
Aguacatec 718
Aguarana 1151
Ainu 666, 730, 991, 1278, 1440
Aka 1621
Akan 70, 625, 767, 1080, 1087, 1092–1098, 1100, 1611, 1655

Akhvakh (=Axwax) 829, 1296, 1776, 1787–1788
Akkadian 165–166, 172, 174–175, 315, 316, 352, 933, 935, 1747, 1770
Alabama 685
Alamblak 1434
Albanian 36, 220, 758, 834–836, 847–849, 865, 874, 876, 880, 955, 963, 1150, 1340, 1492, 1494–1501, 1503, 1505, 1511–1527, 1674
Aleut 389, 391, 932, 938–939, 1036–1037
–, Mednyj 1645–1646, 1675
Algonquian languages 217, 720, 729, 911, 995, 1434
Aljutor 912
Altaic languages 842, 844, 889, 894, 956, 1109–1110, 1119, 1121, 1619, 1732
Altay 1720–1721, 1726
Amanab 741
Amazonian languages 1105
Amele 868, 1002, 1116
American Indian languages (= Amerindian languages) 69, 118, 264–265, 351, 353–354, 391, 527, 528, 570, 670, 681, 685, 724, 763, 837, 881, 892, 894, 955, 967, 974–976, 995, 1061, 1066, 1108, 1387, 1426, 1427, 1434
American languages, Central 92, 282, 332, 597, 851
–, North 92, 217, 265, 280, 332, 496, 506, 597, 696, 817, 843, 851, 963, 968, 994, 1116
–, South 217, 280, 391, 696, 699, 991
American Sign language (ASL) 11, 13, 142, 145, 147, 149, 799, 803
Amharic 166, 175–176, 364, 666, 681, 756, 767, 839, 874, 880, 973, 1018, 1149, 1674, 1762–1772
Andi 1776, 1784, 1793
Andoke 1105, 1106
Anejom 1500
Anglo-Romani 1675
Angolar 666
Antwerp dialect 239
Añun 351

Apache 1236
Arabana-Wankangurru 696–697, 704
Arabian, New South 1770
Arabic 35, 166–168, 176–177, 216, 219, 255, 256, 265, 315, 363–364, 666–667, 679, 680, 683–685, 698, 708, 736–737, 756, 778, 876, 886, 888, 892, 894, 931, 934, 937, 939, 944, 1034, 1051, 1059–1060, 1067–1068, 1073, 1079, 1080, 1154, 1157, 1160–1161, 1163–1164, 1166, 1305, 1392, 1408, 1410, 1442, 1449–1450, 1493, 1502, 1605, 1606, 1622, 1672, 1682, 1688–1689, 1720, 1725, 1727, 1740, 1743, 1762
Arabic dialects 838, 874–875, 883, 1611
Arabic, Algerian 881, 883
–, Cairene 1356, 1364
–, Classical 275, 277–279, 365, 561, 663, 681–682, 684, 685, 687, 1056, 1059, 1063, 1065, 1115
–, Cypriot Maronite 1672
–, Egyptian 503, 663, 1019–1020, 1095, 1611
–, Galilean 1277
–, Gulf 840
–, Iraqi 686, 874, 877, 879–880
–, Lebanese 755
–, Modern 959, 1683
–, Morocco 389
–, Palestinian 944–945
–, Syrian 821
–, Written 1403
Arahuacan 1541–1542
Aramaic 176, 218, 239, 503, 874–876, 1013, 1770
–, Aradhin Christian 1291
–, Modern (= Neo-Aramaic) 682, 686–687, 691–692, 1672, 1774
–, Modern, Fellihi dialect 681
Aranda (= Arrernte) 838, 1108, 1193, 1197–1198, 1327
–, Lower 1210
Arawakan(-Maipuran) languages 354, 894
Arbore 817, 818

Archi 728, 931–935, 939, 980, 1005–1006, 1416, 1418, 1502, 1776, 1783
Argobba 1762, 1766
Arikara 718, 721
Armenian 176, 354, 628, 672–673, 847–848, 874, 929–937, 973, 1035–1036, 1442, 1493–1501, 1503, 1620, 1671, 1774
–, Classical 874, 876
–, Eastern 672, 874–876
Aromunian 1673
Arrernte, Mparntwe 838
Arumanian 1511–1512, 1515
Arvanitika 1670–1675
Asheninca 1325
Asian languages 125, 308–309, 603, 628, 844, 852, 991, 1095, 1114, 1252
–, Central 238, 1109
–, South-East 36, 255, 260, 310–311, 316, 524, 604, 696, 699, 844, 846, 901, 933, 955, 968, 977, 987, 994, 1622
Asmat 1397
Assamese 1530, 1535–1537, 1643
Athabaskan languages 7, 17, 679, 767, 900, 904, 911, 1079
Athpare 1537
Atsugewi 1170
Australian languages 308, 524, 568, 570, 572, 670, 696, 701, 719, 721, 728–729, 741–744, 832, 851, 865, 882–883, 894, 906, 910, 957, 961, 967, 975, 991, 994–995, 1005, 1108–1109, 1115, 1116–1117, 1434, 1713
–, Central 838
–, Northern 496, 498, 504
–, Southern 390, 742
–, Western 705
Australia-New Guinea 504, 696, 701
Austrian Sign Language s. Österreichische Gebärdensprache
Austro-Asiatic 957, 1529–1539
Austronesian languages 91, 310, 332, 378, 527, 670, 680–681, 685, 730, 743, 817–819, 821, 834, 837, 886, 894, 902, 944, 955, 966, 1004, 1017, 1108–1110, 1612
–, Eastern 332, 956, 994–995, 1109
–, Western 836, 941, 1643
Avar 351, 666, 956, 1776, 1790
–, Katex 1788
–, Keleb dialect of 1784
–, Zakatal 1787

Avow-Andi 1776
Awa 315
Awtuw 1106
Awyi 741
Axininca 1361
Axwax (= Akhvakh) 829, 1296, 1776, 1787
–, North 1788
Aymara 874–876
Aynallu 1720
Ayuana 315
Azerbaijani (= Azeri) 177, 848, 1644, 1720–1721, 1723–1726, 1730–1731, 1737, 1739, 1774
–, dialects of 1725
–, Middle 1720
Aztec 167, 715
Aztec-Tanoan languages 921

B

Baagandji 6
Babine-Witsuwit'en 1079, 1081
Babungo 285, 527, 1110
Bac s. Bats
Badaga 351–354, 877–880
Bafia 351–353
Bagwalal 1776
Bak languages 6
Baka 1621
Baksan 1775
Balangao 680–681, 685
Balinese 836, 840, 1284, 1286
Balkan languages 6, 36–37, 880, 991, 1492, 1496, 1499, 1501, 1504–1505
Balkar 938, 1720, 1721
Balochi 1643, 1644
Balti 1120
Baltic languages 778, 865, 883, 958, 997, 1459, 1469, 1493
Balto-Finnic languages 851, 865, 1459, 1493, 1504
Balto-Slavic languages 1492, 1496, 1498–1499, 1501
Baluchi 1497
Bambara 1401, 1407, 1620
Bamileke 1370
Bamileke-Dschang 561
Banda-Linda 351, 352
Bantoid languages 1110
Bantu languages 90, 351, 527, 679, 717, 751, 826, 880, 900, 903, 908, 943, 963, 1001, 1055, 1080–1081, 1091, 1093–1094, 1170, 1453, 1462–1463, 1644, 1655, 1675
–, North-East 956
–, North-West 994
Bare'e 315
Bari 959

Bariba 1375
Bashkir 311, 1013, 1720–1721, 1723–1725, 1728, 1734
Basque 216–218, 220, 260–261, 352, 363, 365, 367, 621, 625, 664, 675, 677, 696, 698, 737–739, 762, 764, 767, 842, 848, 850–851, 856, 863, 864, 868, 869, 882–883, 888, 901, 903, 910, 995–996, 1001, 1090, 1109, 1112, 1442, 1493–1503, 1506
–, Biscayan 740, 764
–, Guipuzcoan 764
Bats (= Batsbi, Tsova-Tush, Bac) 315, 1430, 1776, 1787–1788, 1795
Bavenda 1148–1149
Bayso 817, 819, 821, 823
Beja 681, 1107
Belgian 239
Belhare 374
Bella Coola 893–894, 905, 1330–1331
Bellonese 1246
Bemba 767, 1402
Bengali 753, 826, 1013, 1015, 1288–1289, 1349–13450, 1357, 1388, 1502, 1530, 1533, 1536–1537, 1643
Benue-Congo languages 530
Berber 315, 351–352, 708, 836, 856, 883, 1330, 1376
Berbice Dutch Creole 1655–1666, 1672
Besleney 1775
Bezhta (= Bezhita) 881, 883, 1417, 1776
Bhojpuri 1536
Bichelamar 1621
Blackfoot 720, 1017
Boni 629, 1096, 1098–1100
Botlix (= Botlikh) 1776, 1784
Brahui 1529, 1643–1644
Brazilian 1344
Breton 628, 712, 849, 957, 994, 1100, 1154, 1340, 1448, 1494–1501, 1504, 1670–1672
British Sign language (BSL) 142, 803
Budux (= Budukh) 1776
Buginese 315
Buin 742
Bukusu 1372, 1375
Bulgarian 36–37, 290, 307, 351–352, 357, 563–564, 773, 775, 777–779, 828, 836, 838, 847, 880, 966, 1002, 1024–1025, 1210, 1260, 1263–1264, 1269, 1442, 1449, 1494–1501, 1511, 1514–1527, 1622, 1627, 1719
Burman languages 956

Index of languages

Burmese 309, 351–352, 363, 525, 527, 627, 676, 741, 856, 901, 1503, 1621
Burushaski 315, 856, 1109, 1113–1114, 1117, 1121, 1529
Byelorussian (= Belorussian) 1037, 1265, 1493
Bzhedug 1775

C

Caddo 718, 721, 1001, 1004, 1066, 1170, 1298
Caddoan languages 718, 1298, 1440
Cahuilla 332, 341, 967, 1323
Cakchiquel 1244
Cambodian 696, 699, 703, 1408
Camling 1405, 1406, 1532
Campa 1361
Cantabrian 220
Cantonese s. Chinese
Cape Verdian 1666
Carib languages 729, 967, 994
Cashibo 892
Castilian 214, 216, 218, 767
–, Medieval 1700
–, Old 219, 238–239
Catalan 216, 469, 626, 628, 757, 771, 848, 868, 877–878, 944–945, 1055, 1057, 1060–1061, 1066, 1068, 1384, 1442, 1444, 1446, 1449, 1452, 1602, 1689, 1694, 1697, 1703
–, dialects of 757, 837, 839
Caucasian languages 18, 351, 628, 754, 842, 881, 1107, 1109, 1252, 1426–1427, 1430, 1642, 1774, 1777, 1781–1783, 1785–1787, 1791–1794
–, Eastern 336, 874, 1774, 1776–1777, 1780–1783
  s. also Nakh-Daghestanian
–, North 844, 851, 912
–, Northeast 1117
–, North-West 1108–1109
–, South 845, 1774–1778, 1781–1795
  s. also Kartvelian
–, West 1774–1777, 1779, 1781–1784, 1787, 1790, 1792–1795
Caxar 1776
Caxinaua 353
Caxur 1784–1785, 1787–1788
Cayapa 391–392, 1242
Cayuga 496, 498–500, 506, 718, 837, 1436, 1671–1675
Cayuvava 696, 315
Celtic languages 37, 216, 241, 288, 678–679, 838, 842, 850, 865, 957, 959, 973, 1111, 1464, 1469, 1492–1493, 1498, 1504, 1506, 1679
Celtic, Old 219
Cemuth 1369
Čerkessisch, Ost- (= Besleney-Kabarda) 1775, 1776
–, West- (= Adygh) 389, 1775–1776, 1779
Chíol 1543–1546
Chacobo 391–392, 1239
Chadic languages 374, 817, 848, 895, 910, 1090, 1094, 1442, 1453, 1611
Chagatay 1720, 1728, 1734, 1740
Chaha 1767
Chakassisch 1720–1721, 1727, 1734, 1737
Chaladschisch 1719–1724, 1728, 1735–1737, 1739
Cham 310
Chamalal 1776
Chamorro 945, 1004
Changana 924
Chaque 1186
Chatino 1369
Chechen 844, 1117, 1427, 1776, 1785
–, dialects of 1785, 1787
Chemehuevi 966
Chepang 905
Chibcha 1541–1542
Chibchan languages 1109
Chichewa 908, 943, 1055–1057, 1060, 1068–1070, 1375, 1439, 1440, 1498
Chichimec 1547
Chin 1096–1098
Chinantec, Palantla 1377
–, Usila 1369
Chinese 27–28, 69, 90, 126–129, 133, 165–171, 217, 226, 255, 257, 259–260, 265, 278, 286, 290–291, 308–311, 351, 376, 395, 603–604, 611, 613, 660, 666, 715–716, 739, 797, 809, 876, 878, 931–938, 943, 968, 981, 991, 994, 1022, 1051, 1056, 1058, 1067, 1071, 1087, 1096, 1098, 1100, 1116, 1147, 1150, 1153–1154, 1156–1157, 1161–1162, 1165, 1167, 1170, 1191, 1195, 1200, 1209–1210, 1260, 1281, 1368, 1372, 1374, 1376, 1378, 1381–1383, 1405, 1408, 1410–1411, 1439, 1442, 1447, 1604, 1609–1611, 1618–1619, 1622, 1626, 1644, 1666, 1685, 1740
–, Ancient 1612
–, Cantonese (= Yue) 169, 696, 699, 752–753, 756, 767, 1285–1287
–, Classical 1601
–, Hokkien 1285–1287
–, Mandarin 127, 169, 287, 290, 351, 357, 526–527, 603, 628, 660, 739, 747–748, 750–751, 753–754, 767, 798, 843–845, 850–852, 874–875, 901, 931, 958, 974, 979, 986, 1013, 1016, 1019, 1021, 1025–1027, 1043, 1056–1057, 1064–1065, 1106, 1193, 1197, 1225, 1236, 1258–1265, 1267–1273, 1276, 1284–1286, 1292, 1368–1369, 1374–1376, 1397, 1601, 1612, 1622
–, Old (= Wenyan) 163–168, 310, 313
–, Pekingese 365
–, Wutun 1643
Chinook 265, 856, 1061, 1657
– Jargon 1188, 1648, 1651, 1657
Chipaya 1331
Chipewyan 17
Chippewa 1094
Chirah-mbwa 1153
Chitimacha 1013, 1428
Chizigula 1371, 1375, 1378
Choctaw 685, 908, 1108
Chon languages 1108
Chontal 708, 1013
–, Oaxaca 708
Chrau 1184
Chru 310
Chuj 718
Chukchi (= Chukchee) 353, 357, 696, 698, 716, 728, 881, 883, 894, 930–939, 974, 1035, 1117, 1240, 1440, 1499, 1644
Chukchi-Kamchatkan languages 1035, 1037
Chukchi-Koryak 1035
Chuvash 167, 847–848, 874–875, 893, 1719–1728, 1732, 1736, 1738, 1740
Cibemba 1373
Circassian (= Cerkessisch) 352, 354–355, 389, 1112, 1775–1776, 1779
Coatzospan 1370
Cocama 798
Cockney 1315
Colorado 1242
Columbia 1330
Colville 767
Comanche 719
Comox 1643
Coos 996, 1436
Coptic 1743–1747, 1750–1751, 1753–1760
–, Bohairic 1743–1744

–, Sahidic 1743–1744
Corachol 1541
Cornish 957, 1679
Cree 1240, 1244, 1246, 1436, 1675
–, Plains 911
Creek 1352, 1355
creole languages 4–5, 20, 85, 96–97, 119, 381, 410, 431, 557, 569, 594, 599, 604, 756, 764, 780, 1093, 1162, 1583, 1604, 1611, 1619, 1621, 1679–1680
–, English based 1618
–, French-based 4–5, 16, 412–415, 604, 1602, 1618
Cretan 172–174
Croatian 36, 220, 1045, 1316, 1494–1501
Crow 1207
Cua 708
Cuitlatec 1541
Cushitic languages 681, 817, 819, 1084, 1093, 1107, 1642, 1675, 1762, 1770–1772
Czech 35, 176, 215, 220, 244, 628, 716, 776, 997, 1025, 1150, 1154, 1182, 1265, 1494–1501
–, Bohemian 220

D

Dabida 1001
Daco-Rumanian 1511
Dafla 958
Daga 956
Daghestanian languages 728–729, 829, 910, 912, 956, 1001, 1109, 1416–1418, 1420
Dagomba 996
Dakisch 1679
Dakota 695, 696, 704
Dalabon 1210
Daly languages 819
Dan 1369
Danish 241, 288, 696–699, 703–704, 836, 848–849, 900, 922, 949, 1150, 1154, 1220, 1393, 1497, 1613, 1706
–, Old 1706
Daonda 741
Dargwa 315, 1418, 1774, 1776, 1781, 1787–1790, 1793
–, dialects of 1789
Demotic (= Old Egyptian) 166, 1743–1744
Dhimotiki 1683
Diyari 906, 920, 922
Djapu 705
Djaru 1297, 1298, 1304
Djola 924

Dogon 351, 675, 677, 876–877, 880, 894, 932, 935, 938, 1112
Dogrib 1378
Dolganisch 1720
Dolomitic 1694
Dravidian languages 172, 308, 351, 354, 363, 366, 670, 874, 876–878, 991, 1107, 1109, 1117, 1121, 1297, 1407, 1529–1539, 1621, 1642–1643
–, South- Central 817
–, North 1113
Drehu 351, 354
Duala 994, 1093
Duka 285
Dumi 912
Dutch 127, 130, 213, 219, 242–243, 286, 526–527, 571, 572, 626–627, 703, 745, 767, 844, 847–848, 892–893, 904–905, 942, 944, 949, 995–996, 1004, 1008, 1024, 1150, 1218, 1230, 1266, 1269, 1273, 1323, 1351, 1358, 1361, 1387, 1392–1393, 1460, 1493, 1494–1501, 1504–1505, 1627, 1631, 1649, 1657, 1706, 1708
–, Brabants 755
–, Middle 1707
Dyimini 1242
Dyirbal 913, 919, 967, 979, 1195, 1417, 1419, 1421, 1434, 1670, 1673

E

Efik 529, 767, 931, 1098, 1393
Egyptian
–, Earlier 1742, 1744, 1747–1760
–, Later 1742, 1743, 1749–1752, 1755, 1757
–, Middle 1743–1759
–, Old 1742–1749, 1758, 1759
Elema 743
Enga 910
Engenni 1375
English 4–5, 10, 13, 16–17, 28–31, 33–34, 37, 53, 88–89, 92, 96, 99, 109, 114, 119, 123–124, 126–127, 130, 133, 175, 213, 215, 217, 235, 237–247, 260, 265, 282, 284–287, 290, 310, 313–314, 324, 353, 362–365, 374, 376–380, 382, 391–393, 397, 400, 487, 495–499, 502–503, 520, 524–529, 557, 560–561, 563–564, 568, 571–572, 580, 583, 590, 592, 596, 599, 600, 603–605, 609, 613, 621, 624,
626, 643–644, 666–667, 675, 678–679, 695–696, 699–702, 704, 708, 712, 716, 726, 731, 733, 740–748, 750–758, 760–762, 764, 767, 772–777, 779, 781, 784, 793, 795, 797–798, 804, 809, 812, 816–817, 819, 824–827, 829, 833, 836–838, 842–845, 848–851, 856, 858, 861, 866, 868, 870, 877, 880, 886–887, 891–893, 899, 901–904, 908–909, 916, 920, 924, 931–937, 941–945, 949–952, 954–955, 961, 964–965, 970, 973–974, 981–985, 988–990, 993, 995, 997, 999, 1002, 1005, 1008, 1011–1012, 1015, 1017–1026, 1032, 1035–1037, 1041, 1044–1054, 1056–1059, 1062, 1064, 1067, 1070, 1079, 1081–1083, 1087–1092, 1094, 1098, 1105–1107, 1109, 1112–1115, 1117–1120, 1145–1151, 1153, 1157–1158, 1161, 1163, 1165, 1167–1168, 1170, 1172–1173, 1180, 1183–1185, 1195–1197, 1199–1200, 1205–1207, 1209, 1220–1221, 1229, 1236, 1248, 1252, 1257–1262, 1266, 1268–1269, 1271, 1275–1282, 1284–1291, 1294, 1298, 1300, 1306, 1312, 1315, 1319, 1329–1330, 1349, 1351–1352, 1355, 1358–1359, 1368, 1376, 1382, 1384–1385, 1387, 1392–1393, 1396, 1402, 1428, 1434, 1439, 1444, 1447, 1451–1452, 1459–1460, 1480, 1493, 1494–1501, 1503–1505, 1573, 1596–1606, 1610, 1612, 1619, 1622, 1625, 1627–1628, 1633, 1634, 1641–1643, 1657, 1672–1673, 1678–1679, 1686, 1706–1707, 1730, 1767
–, American 1167, 1351, 1622
–, British 367, 745, 761, 1351, 1605
–, Early Modern 592, 1023
–, Indian 1278
–, Middle 1180, 1315, 1600, 1602, 1634, 1641, 1678, 1707
–, Old 220, 391, 757, 887, 1180, 1230, 1315, 1350–1351, 1356–1357, 1360, 1602, 1604, 1613, 1634, 1707
–, Scottish 761, 768, 996
Eskimo languages 120, 351–354, 569, 716, 730, 733, 881, 883, 910, 918, 931, 939, 994, 1012, 1017, 1019, 1036, 1112,

Index of languages

1153, 1207, 1217, 1219, 1299–1300, 1395, 1503, 1644
–, Asiatic 935, 937, 1644
–, Greenlandic 351, 500, 503, 696, 698, 704, 906, 917, 921, 1017, 1019, 1021–1023, 1112
–, Inuit 771, 900, 909
–, Inuktitut 1440
–, Yupik 26–27, 716, 826
–, Yupik Alaskan 826
–, Yupik Naukan 892
–, Yupik Siberian 26–27, 716
Esperanto 51, 87–92, 1651
Estonian 168, 175, 778, 973, 1326, 1448, 1459, 1494–1501, 1504, 1613
Eteo-Cyprian 175
Ethiopic, New 1766
–, Old 1763
Etruscan 218, 238–239, 1679, 1681
Etsako 1369
Eurasian languages 37, 177, 598, 601, 696, 698–699, 865, 994
European languages 16–17, 34, 36, 69, 88–90, 125, 218, 220, 239–242, 244, 253, 255, 260–261, 308, 499, 501, 503, 505, 568, 572, 596–607, 609, 611, 621, 625, 628–629, 699, 745, 752–754, 758, 771–774, 776, 778, 838, 842–846, 849–852, 855, 865, 868, 901, 926, 963, 968, 971–977, 991, 995, 997, 1012, 1024–1025, 1057, 1095, 1107, 1109, 1492, 1684
–, Central 177, 238, 776, 842
–, Eastern 776
–, South 177
–, Standard Average (SAE) 6, 92, 304, 487, 842–843, 899, 903, 910, 997
–, West 215, 256, 569, 571, 842, 1106
Evenki 309, 698, 792, 798, 931–938, 1001, 1034, 1113, 1499
Ewe 363, 696, 931, 987, 1036–1037, 1193, 1197, 1199, 1498, 1610, 1614, 1616, 1619

F

Fa D'Ambu 1663
Fanti 844, 1013
Faroese 967, 1317, 1459, 1493, 1625, 1633–1634, 1706
Fasu 1371, 1376–1377
Fijian 838, 1395
–, Boumaa 527

Finnic languages 775, 778, 860
Finnish 6, 18, 119, 126–128, 177, 179, 216, 220, 265, 285, 309, 351, 353, 363, 396, 525, 596, 599, 601–603, 609–610, 628, 670–671, 673, 696, 698, 701–704, 763, 767, 771, 775, 777, 848, 851, 852, 856, 860, 877, 880, 883, 892, 904, 943, 945, 962, 973, 980, 1013–1014, 1017, 1019–1024, 1053–1054, 1071, 1112–1113, 1116, 1118, 1120, 1150, 1154–1155, 1161, 1233, 1260, 1269, 1442, 1448, 1459, 1494–1501, 1503–1504, 1613
–, American 1671, 1673
Finno-Ugric languages 336, 670, 672, 675–676, 751, 843, 880, 892, 900, 1017, 1170, 1252, 1492, 1494, 1496, 1498, 1502, 1722–1723, 1740
Flemish 219
Fongbe 1655, 1662
Fore 598, 1406
Franconian, Old Low 1706
Franco-Provençal 1695
French 2–7, 10, 12, 14, 16, 33, 88, 119, 133, 168, 175, 212–214, 216–219, 225, 229, 230, 235, 237–245, 257, 259–261, 271, 310, 313, 334, 350–353, 357, 391, 392, 413–415, 457, 467, 469, 473, 558–564, 569, 572, 583, 586, 591–592, 596–599, 604–609, 613, 625, 629, 639, 643, 666, 670, 674, 702, 705, 716, 736–738, 741, 742, 745, 751–753, 755, 761–764, 767, 779, 781, 797, 798, 836–837, 844–845, 847–851, 866, 870, 878, 883, 886, 890, 904, 924, 937, 941–945, 948–951, 967, 976, 984, 989, 995, 997, 1013, 1015, 1017, 1026, 1035–1036, 1039, 1044–1048, 1051–1055, 1057–1068, 1070–1074, 1076, 1092, 1112, 1118, 1120–1121, 1145–1147, 1151–1153, 1157, 1161–1163, 1165, 1168, 1170, 1172–1173, 1183, 1185, 1193–1194, 1196–1199, 1209, 1220–1221, 1224–1225, 1229, 1265–1266, 1269, 1271, 1273, 1278, 1329, 1394, 1396–1397, 1428, 1460, 1480, 1493, 1494–1501, 1504–1505, 1507, 1520, 1566, 1568, 1572, 1577, 1578, 1582, 1584, 1597–1606, 1610, 1613, 1618–1622, 1625–1626,

1641, 1645, 1658, 1675, 1680, 1685, 1687, 1689, 1697, 1704, 1740
French Sign Language
  s. Langue de signes française
–, Ancient 1172
–, dialects of 560, 1099, 1100, 1597
–, Early Modern 1597
–, Late 745
–, Lousiana 4, 599
–, Middle 1577, 1578, 1600
–, Old 591, 659, 1577, 1578, 1601–1604, 1694
–, Quebec 1291
Frisian 1706, 1707
–, North 34, 837
–, North, Fering dialect 34
–, Old 1706
–, West 1627, 1631, 1633
Friulian 1694
Fulani (= Fula) 365, 900, 903–904, 906, 921–922, 924, 1018, 1094
Futunian (= Futunan) 352, 353
Fu-Yü 1722–1724, 1735

G

Gã 1289, 1612
Gadsup 315
Gaelic 1501
–, East Sutherland 1670, 1671
–, Irish 679
–, Scottish (= Gaelic Scots) 768, 848, 851, 943, 965, 996, 1020, 1111, 1448, 1501
Gafat 1376, 1762
Gagausisch 1720, 1725, 1737–1740
Galela 526
Galician 1699, 1703
Gallic 218, 1679
Gallo-Romance 1473, 1493
Garifuna (= Black Carib) 1542
Garo 1537
Gascon 610, 877, 1604
Gaulish 218
Gaulish, Old 238, 239
Gavião 1083
Gbadi 288
Gbe languages 1079
Ge 996, 1083, 1150
Ge'ez 315, 1762–1772
Gelb-Uigurisch 1720, 1722, 1724, 1731, 1735
Georgian 285, 309, 312, 663, 666, 712, 756, 775, 826, 847, 849, 868, 869, 892, 901, 906, 921, 924, 928–931, 933–935, 938, 1021–1024, 1260, 1279, 1289, 1290, 1330, 1402–1403,

1493–1501, 1503, 1775, 1778, 1781–1786, 1792, 1795
–, New 1778
–, Old 1777–1778, 1783, 1789, 1791
German 17, 19, 30, 33, 88, 90, 119, 124–127, 130, 133, 168, 176, 197, 214–216, 219, 228, 231, 235, 237–240, 243–244, 257, 260, 269, 271, 282–285, 290, 299, 300–303, 314, 324, 328, 330–335, 339, 341, 385, 388–397, 404–405, 473, 477, 500, 535–536, 542–544, 547, 560, 575–577, 579–585, 592, 596, 597, 599, 603–607, 610, 624–627, 630, 639, 643, 659–663, 666–667, 677–679, 686, 700, 703, 705, 716–717, 739–741, 745, 747–757, 762, 775, 778, 781, 784–815, 817, 837, 838, 844–845, 847–848, 851, 857–860, 865–868, 886–887, 892, 901, 904, 924, 929–938, 944, 949, 963, 966–967, 970–977, 986, 989, 995, 997, 1000–1004, 1008, 1011, 1014–1015, 1019, 1022, 1023–1026, 1036, 1043, 1045, 1047–1048, 1051–1055, 1069, 1074–1075, 1121, 1145, 1147, 1150–1152, 1154–1155, 1157, 1161–1162, 1165, 1167–1168, 1170, 1172, 1197, 1199–1200, 1218, 1220–1221, 1229–1230, 1233, 1236, 1246, 1248, 1252, 1257, 1265–1269, 1271, 1273, 1278, 1305, 1312, 1315, 1323, 1329–1330, 1349, 1358–1359, 1387, 1392–1393, 1396, 1413, 1426, 1437–1438, 1444–1445, 1473, 1493–1501, 1503–1505, 1507, 1520, 1597–1606, 1626–1632, 1634, 1641–1642, 1648, 1679, 1706, 1708, 1740
–, American 1671
–, dialects of 132, 214–215, 219, 564, 837, 1626–1627
–, Low 1706
–, Middle High 395, 397, 797–798, 1600, 1602, 1603, 1630–1631, 1707
–, Modern 1163
–, Modern Standard 328–330, 679, 860, 1626, 1628
–, New High 239, 395, 397, 399, 404, 1630–1631
–, Old High 390, 395, 397, 399, 404, 986, 1350, 1597, 1600–1602, 1706–1707
–, Pennsylvania (= Pennsylvania Dutch) 1651, 1670

–, Standard 836
Germanic languages 126, 210, 217–220, 237, 239–241, 260, 285–288, 334, 341, 363, 394, 503, 558, 572, 595, 678, 679, 701, 717, 732, 750–751, 754, 865, 888, 933, 944, 949–951, 955, 993, 1003–1005, 1007, 1019, 1163, 1209, 1225, 1260, 1273, 1355, 1451, 1459, 1469, 1492, 1499, 1602, 1625–1628, 1633–1634, 1679, 1686, 1688, 1706–1718
–, Ancient 1706–1718
–, Middle 1706
–, Modern 1631, 1706
–, North 836, 838
–, West 756, 997, 1356, 1715
Germanic, Proto- 1714
Gilyak
  s. Nivkh
Goajiro 996
Godoberi 973, 1418, 1776, 1793
Golin 729, 1325
Gooniyandi 961
Gothic 219, 239, 847–848, 1273, 1506, 1706–1707
Grebo 1013
Greek 6, 11, 105, 166, 167, 173–175, 181, 185, 187, 195, 212, 214, 216–220, 228, 230, 234–237, 239, 241–246, 253, 256, 265, 333, 341, 357, 363–364, 593, 608, 628, 758, 762, 840, 849, 865, 880, 997, 1230, 1317, 1382, 1384–1385, 1442, 1444, 1449, 1452, 1492, 1494–1501, 1505, 1511–1527, 1642, 1671–1675, 1682–1683, 1688–1689, 1706–1707, 1722, 1740, 1743, 1774
–, Aeolian dialect of 218
–, Ancient 3, 6, 11, 36, 88, 92, 166, 173, 271, 324, 330–332, 336, 487, 557, 561–564, 667, 670, 680, 777, 928, 931, 932, 936, 1121, 1160, 1162, 1166, 1401, 1506, 1621, 1681, 1688
–, Apulian 1683
–, Asia Minor 164–173, 1672
–, Attic dialect of 236
–, Calabrian 354, 1683
–, Classical 210, 240, 275, 577, 593, 596, 598, 600, 757, 779, 838, 847, 848, 900–903, 906, 917, 918, 922–924, 959, 980, 996, 1621, 1683
–, Modern 6, 11, 36, 119, 354, 599, 667, 673, 699, 757, 767, 774, 779, 847, 848, 863, 868, 900–901, 906, 921, 943, 955, 959, 961, 1002, 1147, 1150, 1154, 1157, 1166, 1269, 1396

–, Mycenean 165, 173, 175, 1683
Greenlandic
  s. Eskimo
Guadeloupe Creole 412–415, 594
Guajajara 957
Guaraní 351, 663, 696, 856, 863, 874–876, 892, 974, 1013, 1146, 1151, 1188
Gude 528
Gujarati 869, 1020, 1536
Gullah 1661
Gumbaynggir 705
Gungbe 1079–1081, 1090
Gunwinggu 721
Gunwinyuguan 1211, 1440
Gunya 1005
Gur family 996, 1094
Gurage 1762
Gurnu 6
Gusiilay 6, 18
Gutäisch 1774
Gutnish, Old 1706
Guugu Yimidhirr 570–571, 924, 1298
Guyanais 1661
Guyanese Creole 984, 1602
Gypsy languages 1675

H

Hadic languages 1080
Haida 1442, 1449, 1452
Haisla 1440
Haitian Creole 837, 1036, 1093, 1161, 1621, 1655, 1658, 1660, 1662, 1665
Halkomelem 1242
Hanunoo 33
Harari 1762, 1766
Haruai 29
Hattic, Proto- 1774
Hausa 6, 365, 374, 526, 625, 680, 756, 767, 770, 771, 901, 931, 933, 1013, 1090, 1161, 1316, 1368, 1397
Hawaiian 391, 687, 1207, 1613
Hawaiian Creole English 1193, 1649, 1655
Haya 1369–1370, 1372, 1374
Hayu 351
Hebrew 119–120, 125–126, 130, 166–168, 212, 214–217, 219, 220, 228, 237–239, 245, 255–256, 260–261, 315, 351–352, 364–365, 663, 680, 683, 686, 695–699, 702–704, 749, 756, 758, 874, 876, 943, 959, 965, 1013–1015, 1019, 1035–1037, 1054, 1057, 1093,

Index of languages

1229, 1280, 1283, 1460, 1604, 1682−1683, 1689, 1767
−, Biblical 237−238, 278, 708, 856, 875, 901, 919, 1278, 1682
−, Israeli 1622
−, Modern 681−682, 826, 988, 1277, 1280, 1282, 1284, 1286, 1289, 1291−1292, 1495, 1683
Heiltsuk 1331
Hinalugh 1001
Hindi 126, 353, 355, 529, 664, 666, 856, 874−876, 893, 901, 930−933, 935−937, 941, 943, 945, 947, 951−952, 973, 1020, 1113−1114, 1162, 1324, 1438, 1495, 1497, 1501−1502, 1532, 1536, 1617
Hindi-Urdu 353−354, 629, 869, 875, 1113−1114, 1535
Hindustani, Calcutta 1535
Hinux 1776
Hiri Motu 1646, 1649
− trade language 742, 743
Hittite 1236
Hixkaryana 398, 525, 527, 696, 698, 729, 967
Hmong (= Miao) 527, 1408
−, White 1284, 1286, 1289
Hokkien 968, 1281
Hopi 568, 597−598, 607, 829, 1020, 1145−1146, 1151, 1613
Hua 835, 837, 1006, 1014, 1406
Huastec 1156
Huautla 718
Huave 1541
Huichol 18, 282, 533−555, 602, 718, 720−722, 724
Hungarian 28−29, 126−128, 176, 220, 308, 310, 351, 385, 389, 396, 500−503, 527−528, 585, 621, 625−628, 670−673, 704, 756, 767, 775, 840, 847−848, 852, 860, 868−869, 910, 922, 924, 951, 973, 995, 1017, 1020, 1025, 1036−1037, 1080−1082, 1085, 1089−1091, 1094, 1118, 1120, 1146, 1150, 1154, 1157, 1161, 1167, 1212, 1248, 1260, 1269, 1271, 1277, 1284, 1286, 1299, 1382, 1384−1385, 1434, 1442, 1443−1444, 1446−1447, 1451−1452, 1493, 1494−1504, 1619
−, American 1643
Hunza 1776, 1780−1782, 1785, 1787
Huron 718
Hurritisch-Urartäisch 1774

I

Iaai 966
Iai 6
Iaia 742
Iatmul 1406
Ibero-Romance languages 1493, 1498
Icelandic 126, 216, 286−287, 391, 742, 848, 851, 868, 900, 920, 944, 949, 1021−1022, 1315, 1317−1318, 1459, 1493, 1625, 1627, 1633−1634, 1706, 1708
−, Old 1625, 1633, 1706
Ido (= Esperanto dialect) 87, 89
Ifugao 1244, 1246
Igbo (= Ibo) 1109, 1153, 1278, 1369, 1376
−, Aboh 1374
Ijaw (= Ijo) 843, 1619
−, Kalabari 1655−1657
Ijil 315
Ika 526
Ikalanga 1372
Ilgar 1206, 1211
Ilokano 744, 996, 1328
Indian languages 148, 628, 718, 913
Indic languages 166, 222, 700, 750−751, 754, 973, 1493−1494, 1499, 1643
−, Old 777, 1314
Indo-Aryan languages 869, 874, 876, 900, 1112−1113, 1297, 1529−1539, 1683, 1689, 1740
Indo-European
− languages (= Indo-Germanic languages) 29, 36, 118, 126, 216, 219, 256, 264, 280, 311, 314, 316, 333, 353, 374, 393−395, 431, 449, 503, 568−571, 577, 586, 593, 640, 659−662, 666, 670−673, 676, 679, 744, 816, 842, 887−888, 901, 933, 944, 950, 955−958, 961, 973, 977, 993−994, 1002, 1017, 1019, 1109, 1117, 1121, 1164, 1170, 1252, 1492−1493, 1500, 1502, 1533, 1618−1619, 1636, 1706, 1714
−, Old 777
−, Proto- 316, 1209, 1492, 1506, 1572
Indo-Iranian languages 351, 842−843, 933
Indonesian (= Bahasa Indonesia) 31, 311, 352, 680, 839, 840, 888, 904, 924, 989, 990, 1014, 1019−1020, 1035−1037, 1054, 1059, 1095, 1112, 1613
−, Jakarta 1291
−, Riau 1277, 1281, 1290−1291, 1420, 1422
−, West 995

Induna 1246
Ingush 1776
Inuit/Inuktitut
  s. Eskimo
Iranian languages 390, 874, 913, 962, 968, 1005, 1163, 1493, 1499, 1494, 1502, 1642−1643, 1722−1724, 1737, 1740
−, North-East 874−875
Irish 220, 260, 353, 757, 847−849, 851, 856, 904−905, 973, 1091, 1095, 1155, 1236, 1434, 1448, 1494−1501
−, Old 166, 1111, 1503
Iroquoian languages 496, 498, 503−504, 718, 729, 843, 881, 938, 1207, 1211, 1434, 1671
Ishkâshimi 874
Italian 28, 99, 119−120, 125−127, 130, 133, 214, 216, 218, 230, 237−243, 257, 260, 284−287, 352, 377, 391, 401, 467, 469, 471, 473−475, 564, 596, 599, 605, 609−610, 625, 628, 638, 640−641, 663, 665−667, 674, 738, 747−748, 751−757, 761−763, 774, 781, 840, 847−849, 870, 890, 901, 941, 944, 965, 973, 976, 982, 1013, 1024−1025, 1041, 1043−1047, 1051, 1054−1057, 1063, 1093, 1146, 1150−1151, 1157, 1161−1166, 1170, 1200, 1218, 1266, 1269, 1318, 1327, 1382, 1392, 1394, 1396−1397, 1449, 1452, 1480, 1494−1501, 1504, 1566, 1572, 1599−1606, 1681, 1689, 1694, 1697−1698, 1702, 1740
−, dialects of 213, 217−218, 467, 474, 564, 764, 877, 1702
−, Old 219, 1603
−, Southern 1469
−, Standard (= Tuscan) 213−214, 218, 238, 467, 474, 761, 763, 767
−, Tuscan 1153
Italic languages 36, 994, 1492
Italo-Celtic 1492
− -Romance languages 1493, 1498
Ivrit (= Modern Hebrew) 1683
Iwaidja 1211
Ixil 718

J

Jacaltec 900, 1094, 1150, 1449
Jakutisch (= Yakut, Sakha) 894, 1036, 1720−1724,

1726−1728, 1730−1732,
1735−1736, 1738, 1740
Jamaican Creole 1655
Jaminjung 504
Japanese 6, 17, 28, 33, 119,
126−129, 166−167, 170, 175,
254, 275, 278−279, 309−312,
314, 353−354, 365−366, 496,
603, 624−625, 628−629,
660−661, 663, 666, 685, 695,
704, 741, 747−750, 753−758,
767, 777, 809, 856, 860−861,
869, 887, 902−904, 906,
929−933, 936−945, 950, 952,
974, 976, 983, 984, 987−991,
999, 1001−1002, 1005, 1008,
1013−1014, 1018−1019,
1025−1026, 1056−1060,
1064, 1069, 1079, 1083,
1091−1092, 1110, 1113−1115,
1116, 1119, 1121, 1145, 1147,
1154, 1163, 1164−1165, 1170,
1172, 1191, 1193−1194, 1195,
1197, 1199−1201, 1221, 1260,
1264, 1267, 1269, 1270, 1280,
1381, 1386, 1387, 1390, 1396,
1402, 1405, 1407, 1437−1438,
1440, 1442, 1444, 1448,
1501−1502, 1613, 1616,
1619−1620, 1622, 1689,
1721−1722
−, Tokyo 1373, 1376−1377,
1383
−, Okinawan 756
Javanese 365, 378, 996, 1219
−, Old 741
Jewish-Arabic 351
− -Georgian 168
− -Tajik (Bukhara) 168
− -Tat 168
Jiwarli 1434, 1437
Juang 1532

K

K'ekchi 943, 951
Kabardian 919, 921−922, 1775,
1779, 1782−1783, 1792
Kabiyé 1610
Kadai languages 310
Kadiwéu 1641−1642
Kalam 504, 1191, 1193−1194,
1197−1198, 1200−1201, 1303
Kalispel 708
Kalkatunga (= Kalkatungu)
367, 525, 826, 865, 894, 975
Kalmyk 848, 1499
Kamanokafe 1236
Kammu 1330
Kanakuru 1090, 1094, 1371,
1453
Kanjobal 718−719

Kannada 700, 856, 905, 1019,
1023, 1535, 1642−1643
Kanuri 696, 704, 922, 957
Karachanidisch 1720, 1729
Karachay 1720−1721, 1724,
1728, 1730, 1735, 1740
Karachay-Balkar 844, 847−
848, 1721, 1728, 1735, 1774
Karagassisch (= Tofa) 1720,
1723
Karaim 167, 1672, 1720, 1722−
1723, 1725, 1735, 1737, 1739,
1740
Karakalpakisch 1720−1721
Karata 1776
Karo Batak 886, 893
Kartvelian languages 845, 850,
1109, 1493−1494, 1794
Kaschgaiasch 1720, 1722, 1739
Kashaya 1306
Kashmiri 700, 893, 1530
Kate 315, 597
Kawi
s. Javanese, Old
Kayapo 996
Kayardild 6, 1193, 1194
Kaytej 1210
Kazakh 1035, 1720−1723,
1725, 1728−1731, 1737
Keley-i 685
Kemant 1670−1671, 1674−
1675
Kera 365
Kerek 1035−1037
Ket 931, 935, 937, 939, 1109,
1112, 1117
Kewa 1153, 1407
Khanty 1502
Kharia 1530
Khasi 957, 1015, 1020−1021,
1025, 1530, 1532, 1537
Khmer 171, 310−311, 603, 850,
852, 984, 990, 1395
−, Shokchang (dialect) of 310
Khoisan languages 389, 839,
895, 955, 1109, 1463
Khvarshi 1417−1418
Kihunde 1374
Kihung'an 1098, 1100
Kikongo 1655
Kiksht 561
Kikuyu 610, 625, 708, 1094,
1368, 1442, 1452
Kilivila 604
Kimatuumbi 1080, 1081, 1097
Kinande 1373, 1375
Kinyarwanda 34, 983, 1319
Kiowa 696, 697, 829
Kiptschakisch 1719, 1720
−, Armeno- 1720
Kiranti languages 1532
Kirgiz 1720−1721, 1724−1728,
1731, 1732, 1734−1736, 1739

Kirundi 767, 1375
Kituba 1210
Klamath 888, 1035, 1434, 1438
Koasati 685
Kobon 696, 961, 995, 1302−
1303
Kodava 1531−1532
Kom 1371, 1374
Komi 778, 1494−1501
Komi-Zyrian 167, 874, 892
Korean 166−167, 176, 308,
365, 525, 571, 624, 663, 676,
753, 809, 860, 869, 891, 894,
902, 933, 974, 976, 983, 987−
991, 999, 1013−1014, 1020,
1025, 1034, 1048, 1113, 1119,
1121, 1150, 1168, 1210,
1257−1262, 1264−1265,
1267, 1269−1270, 1376, 1386,
1407, 1442, 1444, 1448−1449,
1452, 1503, 1689, 1721−1722
Koryak 1349, 1440
Koyra Chiini 660
Koyukon 767
Kpelle 377, 695, 764, 767, 1305
Kriol 1652
Kru languages 288, 1378, 1621
Kryz 1776
Kubachi 1780−1781, 1789−
1790
Kuban 1775
Kui-Kuwi 1643
Kukuya 1371
Kuku-Yalanji 883
Kuliak 1614
Kumükisch (= Kumyk) 1720−
1721, 1728, 1730
Kurdish 973, 1774
Kurukh 1113, 1529, 1532, 1621,
1643
Kusaie 719
Kutenai 1280, 1281, 1292
Kwa languages 1013, 1079−
1080, 1109, 1619, 1655
Kwaio 742, 743
Kwakiutl 1643
Kwakw'ala 836, 1219, 1240,
1244, 1246
Kxoe 895

L

Labu 1500, 1160, 1368, 1369
Laccadive 869
Ladin 877
Laha 310−311
Lahu 363, 719, 956, 1056, 1058
Lak 912, 1418, 1776, 1781−
1784, 1787−1791
Lakota (= Lakhota) 366, 718,
837, 886, 892, 1289, 1434,
1436−1437

Index of languages

Lamang 895
Lango 980, 982
Langue de signes française (LSF) 11, 799
Lani 1233
Lao 1193, 1198–1200, 1291
Lapp
  s. Saami
Lardil 729, 1210, 1358
Larike 818–822, 824–825
Latin 177, 181, 185–188, 193, 195–197, 201, 210–220, 225, 228–230, 234, 236–239, 241, 243–247, 252–261, 265, 271, 307, 316, 367, 389, 392, 396, 404, 487, 557, 562, 564, 569, 577, 581, 596, 598, 600, 602, 605, 608, 610, 662, 665–666, 670–672, 713, 745, 747, 752, 757, 761, 763–765, 767, 772, 774, 776, 779, 798, 815, 832, 835, 839, 845, 847–849, 863, 865, 875, 892, 901, 906, 921–924, 959, 982, 994, 995, 1014, 1020, 1022, 1025, 1034, 1112, 1117, 1121, 1145–1147, 1151, 1163, 1183, 1220–1221, 1225, 1230, 1278, 1289, 1304, 1317, 1319, 1322, 1325, 1327, 1352, 1355, 1413, 1497, 1506–1507, 1559, 1577, 1578, 1597, 1601–1604, 1626, 1627, 1632, 1679–1684, 1687–1689, 1692–1704
–, Classical 210, 214, 216, 218, 238, 240, 247, 275, 593, 602, 610, 994, 1393, 1630, 1692
–, Early 1630
–, Late 593, 839, 1604, 1685, 1692, 1699
–, Medieval 210–211, 1682
–, Old 1506
–, Vulgar 218, 237, 271, 1602, 1603, 1625, 1692
Latino sine flexione 87
Latvian 168, 775, 778, 847–849, 903, 939, 958, 1021, 1459, 1494–1501
Laz 850, 856, 868, 1499, 1775, 1778, 1791
Lenca 1541, 1547
Lendu 1372
Lewo 680
Lezgian (= Lezgi) 666, 749, 751–753, 758, 844, 847–848, 851, 943, 973, 1019, 1023, 1298, 1494–1501, 1497, 1503, 1776
– (= Lezgic) languages 1776–1777, 1781
Lhota 1530
Lifou 392
Lillooet 1240, 1242

Limbu 351, 1530
Lingua Franca 1649
Lingua Geral Brasilica 1651
Lithuanian 168, 775–778, 847–849, 904, 909, 931, 932, 935–937, 964, 1014, 1021, 1115, 1121, 1150, 1154, 1459, 1494–1501, 1503, 1625
Livonian 778
Logoli 1149
Lolo (= Yi) 174–175
Longgu 570, 1193
Luganda 956, 1373–1375
Luiseño 956, 957
Luo 315–316, 1298
Lushootseed 837, 839
Luvale 708

M

Ma'a 1645–1646, 1675
Maasai (= Masai) 364, 856, 905, 1080, 1093, 1372, 1620
Macedonian 36, 778, 836, 847, 880, 1511–1514, 1520–1522
Machu-Tungusic 1113
Macro-Carib 1105
– -Siouan 1004
Maidu 703
Maisin 1643
Maithili 1497, 1531, 1536
Makua 1081
Malagasy 34, 365, 368, 398, 876–877, 902–904, 988, 1094
Malay 365, 1017, 1043, 1045, 1145–1146, 1191, 1193–1194, 1196–1200, 1292, 1501
Malay, Kuala Lumpur 1291
– /Indonesian 1290–1291
Malayalam 700, 869, 1100, 1277, 1289, 1323, 1434, 1437, 1530
Malayo-Polynesian languages 818, 904
Malka 1775
Maltese 736, 826, 847–848, 874, 876, 957, 965, 1210, 1277, 1493, 1494–1501, 1503
Malto 1529, 1643
Mam 557, 719, 962, 1546
Mame 718
Manam 826, 1108, 1361
Manchu 894
Mandarin
  s. Chinese
Mande languages 377, 503, 764
Mangap-Mbula 1193
Mangarayi 728, 865, 1499
Mangbetu 708
Manipuri 1530

Mansi (= Vogul) 351–352, 671–672, 675, 874, 892–893
Manx 848, 851
Mao Naga 1530, 1537
Maori 175, 696, 698, 856, 1198, 1246
Mapuche (= Mapudungu) 411–413, 797
Mara 696, 697
Marathi 700, 909, 1530–1531, 1534–1536, 1643
Margany 1005
Margi 798
Mari 167, 713, 1503
–, Eastern 675
Maricopa 1277, 1279, 1281, 1290, 1306
Maringi 767
Marrithiyel 819
Martuthunira 767
Mathimathi 1325, 1327
Maung 364
Mauritius Creole 594, 1604, 1621
Mayali 1277, 1282
Mayan languages 164, 166, 174, 354, 364, 570, 718–720, 724, 882, 888, 900–901, 910, 943, 951, 956, 962, 994, 1067, 1170, 1426, 1442, 1541, 1543, 1546
Mazatec 1547, 1548
Mbugu 1675
Mbui 1374
Mbula 1194, 1197
Mbum 1620
Media Lengua 1645–1646, 1675
Megleno-Rumanian 1511
Melanesian languages 351, 392, 571, 1108, 1110
Melanesian Pidgin English 1652
Mele-Fila 822–823
Mende 1368
Menomini 995
Meroitic 167
Meso-America 36
Messapisch 1679
Michif (= Mitchif) 1645–1646, 1675
Micmac 1244, 1246
Micronesian languages 719, 724, 966
Mikasuki 1185
Mikir 1530, 1537
Minangkabau 365, 1291
Mingrelian 845, 1775, 1778–1779
Minoan 173
Miogliola 1351
Miskito Coast Creole English 1665

Miskuti 1198
Misumalpan 1193, 1541, 1542
Mixe-Zoque 1541, 1547, 1550
Mixtec 167, 1549
–, Acatlán 1372
–, Yosondua 943
Mizo 1530
Mlabri, Minor 525, 1278
Mo 1244
Mobilian Jargon 1188, 1648
Mohawk 718, 721–724, 919, 926, 1376, 1436–1440
Mojave 988
Mokilese 528, 719, 822, 823, 1359
Moluccan language, Central 818
Mongolian 931, 934, 935, 937–939, 955, 1035–1036, 1264, 1269, 1270, 1402, 1407, 1497, 1721–1722, 1740
–, Classical 1402
Mongolic languages 1121
Mon-Khmer languages 901, 957, 1343–1344, 1535
Moore 353, 1621
Mopan 570
Mordvinian 874, 876, 880, 883, 1494
–, Erzia 167, 351, 675
More 1094
Morwap 741
Mota 743
Mozdok 1775
Munda languages 316, 1343–1344
–, Proto- 316
–, South 1121
Mundari 994, 1120, 1395, 1530, 1532
Mundo-lingue 87
Mupun 983
Murrinh-Patha 496, 498, 506, 1239
Muskogean languages 1108, 1434
Naga languages 1530
Nagala 742
Nagamese 1535
Nahali 1529
Nahuatl 666, 715, 718, 721, 729, 881, 886, 894, 903, 1188, 1436, 1439–1440, 1495, 1544–1545, 1670–1671
–, Central Guerrero 1211
–, Classical 715, 1541, 1543, 1545–1547, 1549
–, Proto- 1547
Nakanai 894
Nakh (= Naxisch) 1776–1777
– -Daghestanian languages 926, 1493–1494, 1498
Nama 704, 733, 839–840, 988, 1499

Nambikwara (=Nambiquara) 814, 1240
Nanai 938
Nandi 315
Nasioi 528
Navajo (= Navaho) 391, 629, 900–901, 908, 943, 1147, 1153, 1419
Ndje'bbana 742, 743
Ndjuka 764, 766–767
Negerhollands 1649, 1655, 1660–1662
Nenema 315
Nenets 848, 852, 1494–1501
Nepali 900, 911, 1530–1531, 1533, 1535
New Guinea languages 598, 605, 1108–1109
Newari 987, 1002, 1531–1533, 1621
Nez Perce 1170
Ngamambo 1370
Nganasan 1034, 1036
Ngandi 1436
Ngan'gikurunggurr 819
Ngan'gityemerri 819, 823–824
Ngan'giwumirri 819
Ngankikurungkurr 1298
Ngarinjin 1302–1304
Ngizim 848, 1290, 1453
Nicaragua Sign Language (NSL) 97
Niger-Congo languages 6, 675, 762, 764, 834, 843, 844, 924, 963, 1013, 956, 994, 996, 1109–1110, 1164, 1462–1463, 1609–1610
– -Kordofanian languages 377
Nigumak 315
Nilo-Saharan languages 922, 957, 959, 1107, 1463
Nilotic languages 1080, 1093, 1620
Nimboran 572
Nitinat (= Nitinaht) 730, 1619
Nivkh (= Gilyak) 32, 525, 890, 929, 931, 933–935, 937–939, 1034
Nocte 1530, 1533
Nogai 1720–1721, 1730–1731, 1774
Noni 1372
Nootka 69, 265, 730
Nordic 1706
–, Ancient 1706
–, East 1706
–, West 1706
Norse, Old 1626, 1630, 1706–1718
Norwegian 754, 757, 904–905, 929, 935, 937, 963, 967, 1054, 1057, 1064, 1071, 1076, 1494–1501, 1625–1626, 1629, 1633, 1706

–, Modern 963, 1625, 1630
–, Nynorsk 758, 1628
–, Old 1706
Novial 87
Nuba 1240
Numic languages 957
Nunggubuyu 865, 1434, 1440
Nupe 1099, 1372
Nyungar 1650

O

Ob-Ugric languages 351, 672
Ocaina 1240, 1242
Occidental 87
Occitan
s. Provençal
Oceanic languages 316, 528, 570, 680, 696, 817, 819, 881, 966, 991, 1620
Oghuz 1719–1720, 1724, 1728
Ogurisch 1719, 1724
Oirot 1721
Ojibwa 1083, 1170, 1198
Olmec 163, 167
Oluteco 720
Omotic languages 1762
Ona-Shelknám 1108
Oneida 718
Onge 1305
Ono 1407
Onondaga 718, 721–724, 952
O'odham, Tohono (= Papago) 680, 685, 900, 921
Oowekyala 1331
Oriental languages 242, 255
Oriya 1530, 1533, 1534, 1536
Oromo 524, 526, 1299
Oscan-Umbrian 1679
Osmanisch 1720–1721, 1726–1727, 1731, 1733, 1735, 1738, 1740
Ossetic 525, 836, 843–844, 874, 876, 1642–1643, 1774
Österreichische Gebärdensprache (ÖGS) 142, 146
Ostyak 351, 352
Otomanguean languages 943, 958, 1109, 1541, 1543, 1546–1547, 1550
–, Proto- 1550
Otomi 315, 1543

P

Paamese 819
Pacific languages 568, 570
Paiute, Southern 930–931
Palau (= Palauan) 880, 941–945, 951, 952, 1020, 1095, 1612

Index of languages

Palenquero 1655
Paleosiberian languages 319, 353
Pama-Nyungan languages 496, 924, 967, 1108, 1297
Pangwa 924
Panjabi 1536
Panyjima 767
Papiamento (= Papiamentu) 599, 1244, 1409, 1621, 1655–1666
Papua New Guinea languages 334, 504, 569, 742, 819, 865, 910, 912
Papuan languages 388, 504, 728, 729, 741–743, 835, 837, 955, 956, 994–995, 1002, 1014, 1106, 1113, 1116, 1305
–, South-East 956
Paraci 875
Parengi 315–316, 1532
Pashto 351–353, 877, 880
Paumarí 696, 705
Pawaian 1368
Pawnee 718, 721
Paya 1542
Persian 239, 663, 666, 751, 838, 851, 875–880, 882, 901, 950, 973, 1002, 1147, 1154, 1163, 1165, 1300, 1408, 1495, 1501–1503, 1620, 1641, 1720, 1722, 1725, 1735–1740
–, Modern 673, 955
Philippine languages 33, 71, 506, 680, 744, 902
Phoenician 165–166, 176
Phrygian 219
Pidgin English 1648
–, Samoan Plantation 741
Pidgin German 1652
Pidgin languages 4, 5, 20, 85, 97, 119, 381, 569, 741, 744
–, Atlantic 980
Pintupi 1354
Pinyin
  s. Chinese
Pipil 1547
Pirahã 696, 698–699, 1324, 1327
Piro 894
Pitcairnese 1646
Pitjantjatjara 1194
Pitta-Pitta 6, 894
Podoko 1080
Polabisch 1679
Polish 16, 126, 176, 313, 628, 666, 847, 848, 865, 880, 904, 1000–1001, 1013, 1024–1025, 1147, 1150, 1191, 1193, 1196, 1199, 1218, 1248, 1260, 1263, 1265–1269, 1273, 1299, 1340, 1494–1501, 1503
Polynesian languages 92, 332, 353, 357, 378, 506, 676, 719,
724, 836, 838–840, 883, 913, 943, 955, 994, 1109, 1170
–, Proto- 1246
Pomattertitsch 1674
Ponape 719
Ponca 836
Portuguese 4, 7, 176, 214, 219, 254, 564, 599, 667, 676, 755, 757, 768, 774, 848, 943, 950–951, 1057, 1150, 1166, 1172, 1185, 1266, 1315–1316, 1321, 1344, 1392, 1494–1501, 1573, 1599, 1601, 1641, 1658, 1664, 1689, 1694
–, Brazilian 755, 756
–, Portugal 667
Príncipe Creole 604
Proto-Sinaitic 166
Provençal 216, 771, 877, 1055–1056, 1070, 1493, 1498, 1602, 1694, 1702
Punjabi 1500
Pupeo 310

Q

Quechua 260, 351, 411–414, 610, 624–625, 628, 663, 666, 670, 675, 889–892, 904, 943, 994, 1156, 1434, 1438, 1440, 1442, 1444, 1448, 1452, 1645, 1675
–, Ancash 1112
–, Cochabamba 285
–, Cuzco 1217
–, Ecuadorian 1666
–, Imbabura 528, 696, 700–701, 802, 887, 906, 916, 918, 921, 962
–, Peruvian 1188
Quiché 1244, 1541
–, Chiquimula 1246
Quileute 762, 768, 1220, 1613
Qumuq 1774

R

Rapanui 817
Rendille 1099
Rhaeto-Romance (= Rheto-Romansh) 18, 756, 1602, 1697
–, Vallader 18
Romance dialects 880, 1683–1684, 1686
– languages 4, 7, 17, 36, 92, 126, 210, 218–219, 235–237, 239, 241, 243, 247, 253–257, 259–260, 271, 285, 341, 363, 376, 475, 503, 559–561, 572, 595, 600, 605–606, 609–610, 613, 640, 663–666, 674, 736,
743, 750–751, 754–757, 761, 764, 774–776, 779, 781, 865, 874–875, 878, 888, 890, 933, 944, 950–951, 955, 959, 983, 997, 1055, 1093, 1147, 1161, 1163, 1170, 1172–1173, 1200, 1218, 1220–1221, 1225, 1260, 1469, 1492, 1499, 1501, 1504–1505, 1507, 1573, 1579, 1582, 1586, 1601, 1605, 1627–1628, 1630–1632, 1683, 1686–1689, 1692–1704
– languages, Eastern 1694
–, Medieval 1692
–, Proto- 1692
Romani 848, 962, 965, 1503, 1675
  s. also Anglo-Romani
–, Hungarian 1469
Romany, Welsh 713
Rotokas 388, 389
Rotuman 1015, 1149
Ruang 315, 316
Rumanian (= Romanian) 36–37, 609, 628, 756, 836, 847–849, 856, 862–864, 868, 874–875, 880, 965, 967, 1017, 1145, 1147, 1161, 1163, 1166, 1172, 1229, 1289, 1442, 1449, 1452, 1494–1501, 1503, 1505, 1511–1527, 1602, 1694, 1697–1698, 1700, 1702
Russenorsk 1648–1649
Russian 17, 26, 30–31, 35, 88, 126, 168, 256, 306–308, 310, 313, 364, 402, 525, 557, 561–564, 580, 627, 628, 664, 666, 670, 672, 712, 747, 749, 751, 753, 757–761, 769, 773–775, 779, 781, 816, 817, 821–822, 828–829, 847–849, 851, 880, 883, 887–889, 900–903, 906, 909, 912, 916, 918–922, 924, 928, 931–937, 941–947, 950, 959, 967, 971, 973, 980, 999, 1000–1003, 1007, 1014, 1017, 1018, 1021, 1024, 1026, 1030–1034, 1036–1037, 1051, 1054, 1069, 1112, 1117–1119, 1147, 1150, 1154, 1156–1157, 1167–1168, 1191, 1194, 1196, 1200, 1222, 1229, 1246, 1260, 1263–1265, 1267–1269, 1271, 1273, 1278, 1284–1286, 1289, 1299–1300, 1312, 1329, 1340, 1376, 1384, 1392, 1397, 1413, 1426, 1493, 1494–1501, 1504, 1619, 1622, 1625, 1628, 1671, 1727, 1738, 1740, 1774
– dialects 936
– dialects, North 777, 904, 933
–, American 1671, 1674
Rutul 1776

S

Saami 260, 874
Sabaic 708
Sadani 1113
Sadari 1535
Sadri 1113
Sahaptian 1434, 1438
Saharan languages 1107
Sakao 708
Salarisch 1720, 1722, 1724, 1731
Salina 265
Salish (= Salishan) 1230, 1242, 1244, 1434
– languages 730, 837, 839, 900, 1643
Sam family 1096
Samaritan 315
Samish 1244, 1246
Samoan 332, 496, 523, 529, 719, 836, 839, 910, 1109, 1193, 1197, 1205, 1244, 1246
Samoyedic languages 874, 878, 1035, 1722
Samu 572
Samur languages 1776–1777
Sango 956, 1021, 1621
Sanskrit 3, 275, 276, 278, 666, 670, 697, 700, 703–704, 715, 824–825, 886–887, 892, 909, 924, 1114, 1118, 1121, 1314, 1316, 1318–1319, 1438, 1115, 1529, 1532–1533, 1534, 1682–1683, 1687, 1689
Santali 1531–1533, 1537
São Tomé Portuguese Creole 1655, 1657
Sapsug 1775
Saramaccan 739, 1649, 1656, 1658–1662, 1666
Sarcee 526
Sardinian 757, 839, 877, 1153, 1494–1501, 1694, 1697, 1700, 1702
–, Sassarese 768
Saxon 241, 1273
–, Middle 1706
–, Old 1706
Scandinavian languages 241, 282, 288, 754, 756, 758, 778, 851, 924, 973, 1376, 1458, 1469, 1494, 1505, 1625
–, Modern Mainland 1625–1626, 1628, 1634, 1708
Scythian 219, 239
Sechelt 1240, 1242, 1244, 1246
Selepet 1278
Selkup 931–932, 938
Semitic languages 69, 166, 255–256, 260, 264, 557, 663, 670, 679, 681, 684–688, 690–691, 751, 836, 842, 901, 962, 965, 1035, 1055, 1109, 1164, 1170, 1220, 1464, 1494, 1672, 1750
–, Ethiopic 1641, 1642, 1762
–, South 1762
Seneca 718, 1066
Sepik languages 819, 1106
Serbian 36, 1494–1501, 1511
Serbo-Croatian 36, 127, 847–848, 997, 1150, 1154, 1156, 1299, 1376, 1428, 1513, 1521
Seri 1236, 1330
Seselwa
  s. Seychelles Creole
Setswana 1043, 1047, 1298
Seychelles Creole (= Seselwa) 594, 597, 610, 1655–1657
Shaba Swahili 1666
Shanghainese 943
Sherpa 869
Shor 1720–1723, 1737
Shoshone 696
Shughni 875
Shuswap 708, 900, 1242
Siberian Yupik Eskimo
  s. Eskimo
sign languages 11, 13–14, 85, 97, 141–150, 258, 795
Simog 741
Singlish 1285–1286
Sinhala 837–838, 840, 901, 1083, 1097–1098, 1100
Sinhalese 1503
Sinitic languages 976, 1106
Sino-Japanese 1163
– -Tibetan languages 374, 627, 678, 956, 958, 968, 1106, 1109
Sioux languages 718
Siroi 696, 699
Slave 7, 1440
Slavic languages (= Slavonic languages) 34–36, 126, 210, 215, 219–220, 230, 243, 257, 562–564, 670, 750–751, 773–776, 778–779, 865, 888, 937, 967, 997, 1013, 1024, 1033, 1035, 1119, 1163, 1209, 1220, 1273, 1492, 1496, 1504–1505, 1625, 1628, 1679, 1688, 1722, 1724, 1727, 1737
–, South 824, 955
–, West 216, 818, 955, 1273
Slovak 628, 933, 1150, 1260, 1265–1269, 1273
Slovene (= Slovenian) 365, 824–825, 1035, 1150, 1393, 1469, 1494–1501
Slovinzisch 1679
Somali 625, 1084, 1093, 1099–1100, 1368, 1376–1377, 1442, 1449, 1452, 1620–1621
Songhai 894
Sora 315–316, 1395, 1530, 1532
Sorbian 1290, 1625
–, Upper 818, 821–822, 1035
Sotho 560
Spanish 7, 10, 16–18, 88, 119, 130, 230, 237–243, 257, 260, 302, 307, 352, 357, 364, 378, 401, 404, 413–414, 469, 536, 542–544, 547, 550, 581, 583, 592, 594, 596, 599–602, 604–605, 609, 663–666, 674, 676, 720, 742, 745, 751–752, 755, 757, 771, 774, 838, 845, 848–850, 874–876, 878, 880, 906, 917, 922, 937, 944, 950–951, 971, 979, 983, 988, 1024–1025, 1053–1054, 1061, 1150, 1153, 1157, 1161, 1163, 1165–1166, 1172, 1183–1185, 1193, 1195, 1218, 1220–1221, 1223, 1225, 1229, 1266, 1271, 1273, 1304, 1315, 1322, 1392, 1396, 1403, 1440, 1448, 1494–1501, 1545, 1566, 1573, 1578, 1599, 1601, 1602, 1605, 1606, 1627, 1645, 1658, 1662–1664, 1675, 1694–1698, 1702
  s. also Castilian
–, Chilean 412, 594
–, European 17
–, Latin American 17, 261, 410–414, 851
–, Medieval 1700, 1703
–, Mexican 1622
–, Old 1606
–, Peruvian 412–413
Squamish 708, 893, 911
Sranan 27, 1409, 1411, 1655–1658, 1660–1662
Sre 901
Standard Average European languages
  s. European languages
Sudan languages 90
Sudanese 1207
Suena 1369
Suk 315
Sumerian 163–165, 168, 171–172, 174, 1770
Supyire 1019, 1401, 1408
Surinam Creole 764
Surselvan 1700
Sursurunga 819–823
Svan 1775, 1777–1779
Swahili 166, 309, 392, 708, 762–763, 768, 832, 880, 893, 963, 1019, 1116, 1145–1146, 1151, 1154, 1156, 1164–1165, 1166, 1407, 1503, 1610, 1644
Swedish 126–127, 239, 260, 388, 397, 564, 731, 733, 754, 777–778, 836, 868, 944, 949, 965, 971, 997, 1022–1024,

Index of languages

1150, 1154, 1167, 1206, 1266, 1273, 1299, 1303, 1305, 1377, 1448, 1628–1629, 1706
– Sign Language (SSL) 142
–, Old 1706

T

Tabas 1776
Tabasaran 315, 1785, 1787–1789, 1795
–, North 1788–1789
–, South 1788
Tadzhik 1642
Tagalog 285, 503, 667, 680, 768, 827, 834–836, 840, 943, 945, 947, 949, 988, 1018, 1200, 1276, 1277, 1279, 1280, 1281, 1285, 1286, 1288–1290, 1292, 1416, 1420
Takelma 696, 703
Takia 1643
Talysh 848
Tamazight 994, 1319
Tamil 275–279, 351, 365, 526, 629, 696, 699–700, 703, 762, 768, 869, 877–878, 902, 910, 981, 1027, 1083, 1107, 1114, 1117, 1157, 1170, 1503, 1531–1534
–, Old 276, 277, 1114
Tanga 894
Tangele 1453
Tanoan languages 718, 723, 1440
Tarahumara, Western 962
Tarantschi 1720
Tarascan 1541
Tariana 894, 1298, 1674
Tasmanian 431
Tat 168
Tatar (= Tartar) 167, 220, 308, 1033, 1494–1501, 1720–1723, 1725–1728, 1731, 1735–1740
–, Crimean 1720, 1729
–, Kazan 1720
–, Mischär 1720
–, Volga 1285–1287
–, Westsiberian dialects of 1720
Tati 1774
Tayo 1652
Telugu 363, 869, 1094, 1392, 1533
Temiar 708
Temirgoy 1775
Teop 334
Tepecano 1244, 1246
Tequistlatec-Jicaque 1541
Tera 1094, 1244
Terek 1775

Tewa (= Southern Tiwa) 718, 723
Thai 171, 309, 310, 352, 357, 364, 524, 603, 696–699, 850, 852, 901, 991, 1014–1015, 1153, 1193, 1197, 1281, 1383, 1405, 1408, 1428, 1495, 1611
Tibetan 69, 265, 308–309, 311, 678, 1372
–, Anduo 1643
–, Classical 1112
Tibeto-Burman languages 309, 351, 719, 850, 911, 958, 996, 1002, 1096, 1121, 1160, 1529–1539, 1621
– -Karen languages 374
Ticuna 1369
Tigre 906, 921, 1762, 1765
Tigrinya 1762–1772
Tindi 1776
Tiwa, Northern 1185
–, Southern 1436
Tiwi 957, 1670, 1671
Tlapanec 1231, 1236
Toba-Batak 365, 696, 702, 704, 904, 996
Tocharian 674, 1121
Tofalar 1036
s. also Karagassisch
Tok Pisin 569, 572, 737–739, 741, 743, 987, 1648–1649, 1652, 1655
– Whiteman 1648
Tokelau (= Tokelauan) 357
Tolai 332, 1110
Tolomako 768
Tolowa (Athabaskan) 1314, 1316
Toltec 167
Tondano 955
Tonga 1246, 1368
Tongan 357, 719, 724, 836, 881, 910, 931, 943–944, 948–949
Tonkawa 315–316
Torzhok (dialect of Russian) 929
Toscian 1322, 1511
Totonac 1329, 1547
Totonac-Tepehua 1541
Trique 1369, 1549
–, Copala 1369, 1371
Trukese 943
Tsakhur 1420
Tsez 35, 973
Tsezic languages 1774, 1776, 1793
Tsimshian languages 315, 836
Tsoneca 1236
Tsou 837
Tsova-Tush
s. Bats
Tswana 696, 699, 704
Tubu 1107

Tuki 1080, 1093–1095
Tumpisa 696
Tungusic languages 309, 319, 894, 903–904, 1001, 1721–1722, 1732
Tunica 315, 1186
Tunumiisut 351–353
Tupi 1188
Tupi languages 957, 1083
Tupi-Guaraní languages 720, 863, 911–912
Tupinambá 720
Turkana 696, 698, 705
Turkic languages 308–311, 319, 598, 601, 670, 676, 750–751, 754, 778, 839, 851, 874, 890, 900, 956, 1034, 1036, 1121, 1493, 1502, 1636, 1642, 1719–1722, 1728–1730, 1733–1740, 1770, 1774
– languages, Iran 1723, 1736, 1739
–, Chorassan 1720
–, Choresm 1720
–, Chulym 1720
–, Saian 1720, 1722, 1724, 1731
–, Turkia 1720–1739
Turkish 365, 394–397, 404, 500, 503, 628–629, 663, 664, 666, 674, 738, 751–754, 758, 768, 778, 807, 837–838, 847–848, 856, 860, 868–869, 874, 876–878, 880–881, 886, 888–890, 892, 900, 904, 909, 922, 924, 943, 951, 956, 973, 1006, 1013, 1018, 1043–1048, 1051, 1056–1057, 1060, 1063–1064, 1068–1071, 1073, 1076, 1114, 1119, 1121, 1147, 1154, 1157, 1163–1166, 1260, 1267, 1277, 1289, 1290, 1305, 1397, 1407, 1442, 1494–1501, 1503, 1511, 1606, 1613, 1619, 1643, 1719–1722, 1726–1727, 1732, 1737, 1771
–, Modern 1114
–, Old 1719, 1726, 1728–1729
–, Old, Arghu dialect 1719
–, Old Anatolian 1720
–, Old-East 1720, 1723–1735
–, Yenisey 1720, 1722
Türkmenisch 1720, 1723, 1725–1727, 1731, 1736, 1739
Tuscarora 718, 723
Tuvan (= Tuvin) 890, 894, 1117–1120, 1726, 1729, 1731–1735, 1738
Tuyuca 801, 802
Twi 1369
Tzeltal 570–572, 745, 901, 1153, 1180
Tzeltal, Tenejapa 570

Tzotzil 315, 570, 975, 1044, 1064, 1180, 1198, 1219, 1543
Tzutujil 696, 698, 701, 956, 1426

U

Ubangian languages 351, 530, 956
Ubyx (= Ubykh) 666, 1108, 1499, 1775–1777, 1787
Udi 874, 1776–1777, 1780–1782, 1786–1787
Udmurt 671–672, 675, 778, 843, 848, 860, 906, 921–922, 1494–1501
Uigur 1719–1728, 1731–1738, 1740
–, New 1721
–, Old 1720, 1737, 1740
Ukrainian 1037, 1150, 1246, 1469, 1493
Ulch (= Ulcha) 903
Ulwa 1360
Umanakaina 315
Unami 1360, 1361
Unserdeutsch 1652
Uralic languages 118, 778, 839, 842, 852, 874, 876, 889, 995, 1109, 1119, 1121, 1493, 1619, 1722
Urdu 353, 1153, 1495, 1497, 1502, 1535, 1642–1643
Urhobo 365
Usarufa 315
Ute 903–905, 1014, 1021–1022, 1619
Uto-Aztecan languages 332, 533, 597, 680, 718–720, 894, 900, 957, 962, 967, 1109, 1211, 1428, 1434, 1541, 1543, 1546, 1668
Uzbek 931, 933, 936–939, 1642, 1720–1723, 1725, 1727–1740
–, Afghanistan 1739–1740
–, dialects of 1728
–, Kiptschak 1720

V

Vach 351
Vagla 1242
Vai 965
Vallader
  s. Rhaeto-Romance
Vanimo 1500
Vasconic 1506
Vata 288
Vedic 888, 900, 1115, 1314
Vietnamese 26–27, 166–167, 171, 254, 255, 310–311, 603, 696, 699–700, 850–851, 901, 943, 1006, 1013, 1025, 1045, 1260, 1263, 1269, 1273, 1278, 1284–1286, 1289, 1372, 1395, 1397, 1405, 1408, 1644
Vogul
  s. Mansi
Volapük 87, 89–90, 92

W

Waikurúan languages 1641
Wakashan languages 729, 730, 1619, 1643
–, North 836, 837
Wakhi 874
Walmajarri 1195
Wanggumara 390
Waorani 1185
Wappo 988
Wargamay 1323, 1356, 1364
Warlpiri (= Walbiri) 367, 529, 701, 866, 1170, 1200–1201, 1277, 1298, 1433–1439
Waropen 1108
Warrgamay 825, 961
Waskia 696
Waynax 1776, 1777
Welsh 37, 260, 288, 365, 628, 679, 698, 840, 848, 851, 856, 901, 904–905, 1014, 1448, 1494–1501
Wenyan
  s. Old Chinese
Weri 742
Western Desert 1013
Wichita 718, 721
Witotoan languages 1105
Wiyot 1330
Wolof 762, 768

X

X*u* 389
Xârâcùù 352, 354
Xavante 1083
Xerente 6
Xiamen 1370, 1372
Xinalug 1776, 1791, 1793
Xinca 1541, 1674
Xwarshi 1776

Y

Yag Dii 6
Yagua 1083
Yakut
  s. Jakutisch
Yana 265
Yankunytjatjara 838, 1191, 1193–1196, 1198–1199
Yao 1236
Yapese 719
Yaqui 900
Yatye 768
Yawelmani 681, 685
Yebamba 285
Yél 1242
Yélîdne 1244, 1246
Yellow Uigur
  s. Gelb-Uigurisch
Yeniseian languages 1117, 1121, 1722
Yi (= Lolo) 174–175
Yiddish 168, 287, 391, 848, 1014, 1460, 1706–1707
Yidiny 883, 894
Yimas 525, 696, 698, 703–704, 819, 821, 823, 865, 1196, 1201, 1434, 1438–1440
Yinhawangka 1291
Yolngu Matha 1199
Yoruba 625, 696, 703, 728, 974, 1014, 1019, 1093, 1147, 1157, 1160, 1162, 1300, 1331, 1374, 1376, 1383, 1387, 1392, 1395, 1397, 1439, 1442, 1495, 1611, 1616
Yucatec 524, 576, 679, 718–720, 724, 966, 973, 1252, 1260, 1264, 1267–1269, 1541, 1544, 1548, 1616
Yue
  s. Cantonese Chinese
Yukaghir 935, 938, 957, 1037, 1284–1286, 1298
Yuman 1211
Yupik
  s. Eskimo
Yurak 874, 878
Yurok 495

Z

Zande 529
Zanisch 1775
Zapotec 167, 708, 856, 958, 1019, 1371, 1544–1546, 1549
–, Ixtlan 958
–, Santa Ana del Valle 763, 766, 768
Zapotecan, Proto- 1550
Zarma 351
Zaza 1502
Zhilha 708
Zulu 708, 1094

Index of subjects / Sachregister / Index de matières

A

A-bar binding 1094
A-bar movement 1093
abductions 1597
ablativus absolutus 602
Ablaut 278
absolute participles 1117
absolute state 962
absolute tenses 557, 772
absolutive affix 975, 1548
− case 488, 881, 922, 1112, 1529, 1782
abstraction 335, 1610
acategoriality 501
accent//Akzent 205, 621, 1096, 1381, 1512
Accessibility Hierarchy 360, 364−365, 1756
accidence 245−246
accomplishment 516, 557, 773
accusative 277, 875
− language 356
accusativity//Akkusativität 301
accusativus cum infinitivo (ACI) 197, 600, 1697, 1704
− cum participio (ACP) 600
achievement 516, 773
acronymy 1605
actancy 348, 485−490
actant//Aktant 298, 300, 301, 348, 480
− model//Aktantenmodell 14, 294, 298−303, 479, 482
action nominal 496, 1121
− sentences 515
actional adverbs 937
− passives 931, 937
− verb 929
actionality 557, 772
activation threshold hypothesis 133
activator 108
active 318, 917
− language 319, 1419, 1782
− possessor 968
activity 516, 557
actor 484, 899
− defocusing 907
Adamic language 235, 244
addition 1119, 1120
adessive case 336
adjacency 367−368
adjectival agreement 1115

− article 1699
− genitives 965
adjectivalization 957
adjective//Adjektiv 146, 501, 522, 529, 863−864, 1659, 1764
adjunct 1082
admirative 1516
adnominal attribute 968
adnominal genitive 333
− modification 522−533, 968
− NP 956
− possession 954, 960−970, 973
− possessor 963, 970, 971, 976
− predicate complement construction 988
adposition 485, 1119, 1120, 1426, 1544, 1766
Adstrat 1511, 1519
Adverb 207, 527, 576, 930, 937, 995, 1580
adverbal complement 1117
− particles 1033
adverbial clause 598−599, 998, 1402, 1403, 1527
− comparative 994−995
− conjunction 598, 611, 842
− converb 1120
− function 994
− participle 1112
− phrase 1119
− subordination 598−599, 611−612, 1112, 1113
− suffixes 1121
adversative conjunction 1005
− Konditionalität 376, 606−608
− passive 906
affectedness 489, 910, 976
affix 312, 856, 1001, 1013, 1033
Afrikanistik 280
age-and-area hypothesis 1476, 1478
agent 313, 873, 899, 917−919, 925, 930, 933, 1029
− agreement 922
agentive 1416−1417
− complement/phrase 313, 938−939
agentivity scale 490
agent-oriented resultative 932−933
agglutination 26, 92, 250, 264, 267, 311, 386, 991, 1344,

1362, 1395, 1421, 1624, 1625, 1645
agglutinative/agglutinating language 126, 168, 171−172, 306−310, 395−397, 539, 875, 893, 1363, 1379, 1635, 1643, 1673, 1674, 1727
Aggregation 595−606, 609, 643
Aggregativität 413
Agrammatism//Agrammatismus 98, 124−125, 1671
Agraphie 128
agreement 146, 276, 335, 817, 901, 1115, 1400, 1402, 1406, 1427, 1697
− alternation 931
− phrase 287
Akrostichon 86
Aktantenfunktion 301
Aktionsart 16, 546, 549, 557, 561−565, 772, 1119
Aktivität 301
Aktiv-Typologie 1782
Akzentsilbengesetz 1321
akzentzählende Sprache 1322, 1391−1399
akzidentelle Bestimmungen 194, 195
Alexandrian grammarians 184, 505
Alexie 128
alienable/inalienable possession 952−955, 959, 961, 965−973, 1503
Alienation 377
alignment types 1429, 1465
allative 336, 994, 995
Alliteration 1394
Allophonie 1336
alphabetische Orientierung 1311
Alphabetschriften//alphabetic script 105, 166, 175−179
Alterität 11, 1554
alternation 1119
alternative concessive conditionals 1007−1008
− interrogatives 1011−1012, 1016
ambigènes 1516
ambiguous types of resultatives 929−930
Ambisyllabizität// ambisyllabicity 1322, 1328−1329, 1351, 1397

ambitransitive 887
amerikanischer Pragmatismus 445
Amerind hypothesis 1540
amorphous 308
analogical levelling 1671
analogous languages 230, 268
analytic causative 886
 – passive 901–902
 – possessive NPs 962, 963
 – vs. synthetic 271, 306–308, 961, 1626, 1671, 1696
analytical order 229–231
analytische Philosophie 446–447
 – Sprache 250, 265, 1394
anamnestischer Verweis 577
anaphora 160, 575, 592–593, 639, 1007
anaphoric persistence 1083
 – pronouns 924, 968, 1007
 – reference 334
 – reflexive 916
anaphorical ellipsis 593
anchoring of clitics 1703
anchors 964
AND-languages 1109, 1502
Angelman's Syndrome 99
Anglizismen 1573
anglo-amerikanische Sprachwissenschaft 400
animacy 489, 967
 – hierarchy 17, 18, 316, 946, 967, 976, 1757
animal language 96
animation 877, 1021
Anredeformen 409
antecedent 998
anterior converbs 1119
 – perfect 776
 – tenses 559
 – /terminal converb 1114
anteriority 845
anterior-modal converb 1113
Anthropologie 265, 266, 401, 419
anticausative 888, 902, 906, 921–926, 1497
anti-impersonal verb 352
antimédiatif 353
antipassive 352, 355, 489–490, 912–913, 883, 922, 1417, 1754, 1778, 1783, 1793
Antiquité classique 181–192
antithesis 1119
A-oriented 928
Aorist 557, 779, 936, 1515, 1730
apathischer Sprachverlust 1313
Aphaeresis 1604
aphasia//Aphasie 14, 97–100, 123–130, 398, 402, 1671
apocope 1604, 1627

apodosis 998–1000, 1002–1003, 1006–1008
appendix 1322, 1330
applicative 894, 974, 975, 977
apposition 525
apprehension 334–335, 339
approbative 1005
appurtenance 325–326, 333, 335
Äquativ 1728
Arab linguistic tradition 277
Arbeitsgedächtnis 156
arbiträr 176
arbitrariness/Arbitrarität 11, 142, 151, 224, 227–228, 371
archaeology 1540
Archilexem 643
Architektur 1564, 1565
areal linguistics 855, 1456–1457, 1460, 1510, 1529
 – patterns 316, 963, 977, 1400
 – typology 36–127, 1456–1491, 1540, 1722
areale Diffusion 1535
Arealnormen 1475, 1477
A-resultative 928, 931–933, 936, 937, 938
argument structure//Argumentstruktur 298, 480, 485–488, 536, 542, 621, 970, 973, 975, 977, 979, 1099
Argumentfunktionen 299
aristotelische Logik 192
artes liberales 193–194
article 226, 325, 331, 333, 522, 529, 831, 858, 965, 1421, 1494, 1698, 1701
 – copulatif 1518–1519
Artificial Intelligence 96, 441
Aspect//Aspekt 319, 378, 557–567, 587, 768, 883, 930, 932, 980–981, 1004–1006, 1034, 1096, 1099, 1115, 1118, 1513, 1548
aspectivizer/aspectualizer 562, 1531
aspectual verbs 1659
aspectuality 772
aspiration 1337, 1351, 1533
Assertion 297–298
Assertivität 534, 982
assertorische Präsupposition 303
assimilation 397, 1374, 1395, 1397
assistive 892
Association for Linguistic Typology (ALT) 282
association with focus 622
associative particle 963
 – -anaphoric use 833
asyndesis/asyndetic link 614, 982, 1114

asyndetic NP-coordination/asyndeton 1106
Atomismus 66, 105
attributive constructions 331, 341, 502, 513
audiology 119
Aufklärung 258, 1555
augment 779
Ausbau 4, 20, 1562
 – languages 842, 850
Aussagesatz 193
Außenperspektivierung 1571
authorship 964
autism 99
Autogenese 44
autonome Syntax 41
Autopoiesis 44
autosegmental phonology 1337, 1383
auxiliary 858, 901, 953, 1617
 – focus 1098
 – languages 86
axe paradigmatique/syntagmatique 1610, 1615

B

balancing/deranking construction 981
Balkan Sprachbund 1492, 1457–1458, 1510–1528, 1697, 1701
barbarism 237, 242
bare-infinitive complement 985
Basic plan 280
 – Word Order 90, 429, 855
basilektale Grammatik 381
Baumgraphen 294
beat retraction 1396
Bedeutung 66, 194–195, 295
 – vs. Referenz 194–195
Behaviorismus 47
benefactive 540, 925, 1439, 1617
Beobachter-Paradoxon 1570
Bequemlichkeit 385, 1343
Bewegungs-/Halt-Modell 144–145
Bewegungsverben 576
Beziehungsaspekte 444–467
Bi(+)Kongruenz 1784
 – Absolutiv 1792
bible 219, 238, 241
biclausal sentences 886
bilingualism 414, 1641
binäre Opposition 401
binding scale 985
bio-cultural sphere 961
biological foundations 95–103
biologische Metapher 1681
biology 316
bioprogram 118

bipersonal paradigm 315–316
bleaching 1581
blending 1605
body action verb 918, 919
– -part noun 932, 966, 1544, 1662
Bondedness hierarchy 611
bonding rules 1345
borrowing 503, 851, 1606, 1640, 1670, 1672
bound 775
– pronoun 1427
– resultative forms 931
boundary shift 1431
boundedness 773–774
bounder 773
branching direction 860
breath group 1381
Broca area 13, 19
Buchstabe 166, 193, 205, 1686
Buridan's law 509, 515
Burzio's generalization 314
Byblos-Schrift 166
Byzance 188

C

cabbalistic mysticism 216
calculus 510
CAPS/READER-Model 156
Cartesian ideas 107, 244, 258
case 276, 279, 1022, 1517, 1693
– assimilation and attraction 961
– concord 1434
– frames 482
– Grammar//Kasusgrammatik 294, 301, 512
– hierarchy 489, 867
– marking 337, 977, 979, 1406, 1413, 1427, 1626
– roles 483–485
casus indefinitus 1782
cataphora 638
cataphoric participants 1085
cataphoric persistence 1082
catastrophic evolution 101
catégories interlangagières 358
causal theory of reference 519
causality 595, 606–607, 1120
causative 32, 312, 337, 377, 540, 886–898, 986, 999, 1007, 1417, 1734, 1759
cause 32, 1119
center embedding 360, 363–364, 1113
Centre National de la Recherche Scientifique 344
centre-periphery pattern 1458, 1463
Cercle de Vienne 76
Charakterologie 266

Charlemagne Sprachbund 1484, 1493, 1505
Chereme 143
chinesische Schrift 86, 278
chi-squared tests 421
'chômeur' 974
Chorem 1475, 1483
chromatin 112, 117
circonstants 301
circum-Baltic area 1506
circumfix 901
circum-Pacific linguistic area 1550
circumstantial relations 842
clarté 271
class prefixes 963
classical languages 241
classification des verbes 351–352
clause chaining 597, 1115, 1121, 1407, 1418
– combining/linkage 590–614, 981–982, 1116, 1121
– expansion 1118
– final position 1014, 1015, 1020
– integration 595–606, 981, 1002, 1003
– types 1011
– -boundness 919, 920
– -initial position 1015, 1017, 1019–1020, 1023–1024
– -level syntax 977
cleft construction 593–594, 626, 1020, 1079, 1085, 1088, 1091–1092, 1095, 1451, 1752, 1754
cleft focus 1081–1082, 1092–1094
– -based WH-questions 1095
clipping 1604
clitic 979, 1013, 1525
– doubling 1518, 1525–1526
– raising/climbing 1703
cliticization 956
closed interrogatives 1011
cluster map 1504
coalescence 351, 590, 611–612
coda 1348
code switching 131, 414, 440, 1675, 1679
coercive 892
cognate 220
cognition, spatial 571
– -utterance verbs 985
cognitive complexity 405
– map 297, 607
– motivation 977
– parameters 954
– psychology 8–9, 222, 224, 415
cognitivisme 76, 80
collective noun 524

color terms 33, 328, 1550
combined (resultative) forms 931
comitative 956, 959, 1106, 1108, 1502, 1728
comma intonation 597
comment 409, 563
common functional denominator 324
communicative dynamism 590–591, 608, 620
– genres 1–2, 49
comparative construction 993–997, 1499, 1501, 1522, 1550
– psychology 96
comparison 845
– of equality 993, 997, 1499
– of inequality 993, 995
compensatory lengthening 1350–1351
competence 41
competing motivations 366–368, 387
competition model 126
complement article 835, 837
– clause/complementation 599–600, 832, 979–993, 1400, 1403, 1436, 1738
complementizer 610, 858, 869, 979, 985–987, 988
completive aspect 775
completive focus 1085–1087, 1526
Complex NP Constraint 989
compositionality 504
compression 982
conative function 408
concentric/egocentric languages 1424
conceptual semantics 296
conceptual unit 1106
concession/concessive 595, 606, 845, 852, 1008, 1119–1120
concessive conditionals 845, 1007
concomitance 1120
condition 606–607, 1119–1120
conditional clause 148, 288, 558, 606–607, 986, 998–1001, 1006–1008, 1011, 1096
– conjunction 1027
– construction 998–1010
– converbs 1006
– markers 1001–1004, 1006, 1014–1015
– resumptive 1002, 1003
conditionals 1006
configurationality 104, 117, 627, 865, 1433–1441, 1623, 1633
  s. also discourse configurationality
conformational interactions 104

conformations 117
conjoined comparative 994, 996, 1499
conjunct participles 1115
conjunction 147, 207, 611–612, 644, 1115, 1119–1120, 1403, 1502
conjunction reduction 1632
–, coordinating 610
–, subordinating 610
conjunctional adverb 844
– marker 956
– possessive 955, 957, 959
conjunctions, adverbial 611
conjunctive 600, 606, 1006, 1032, 1401
conjunctor 1105
connectedness effects 1088, 1091
connectionism 76–77, 96, 156
connective 1119
connotatio 436
Consecutio Temporum 560
consecutive/narrative tenses 1116
consecutivity 595
consequence 1119
Consistent Head Serialization (CHS) 855, 860
constant components 1032
constituent focus 1097
– interrogatives 1011–1013, 1017–1026
– order 316, 1012, 1629–1631
– questions 1080
– Recognition Domain 362, 366, 859
construct state 962, 1756
constructed numbers 829
constructeurs de langue 1609
construction biactancielle majeure 348, 873
– markers 961
Constructional Focus Principle 1082
constructions 481
constructivisme 84
contact-induced change 1639–1640, 1668, 1672
content space 156
contentive typology 319
contextual converb 1001, 1120
continuous aspect 930
continuum 20, 34, 265, 324, 329–330, 332, 335, 339, 346, 358, 481, 487, 495, 499, 503, 564, 596, 887, 899, 1401, 1565, 1567
contour 1013
– tone//Konturton 1368, 1394
contrary-to-fact 999
contrast 318, 1120
contrastive focus 1079, 1082, 1083, 1087, 1097

contrastive linguistics//kontrastive Linguistik 1573, 1624
contrastive topic 1444
contrastive WH-question 1087
control 483, 954, 1113
– verb 1698
convenience sample 424
converb//Konverb 308, 601, 602, 605, 929, 931, 1006, 1112, 1407–1408, 1418, 1495, 1504, 1529, 1531, 1536, 1619, 1729, 1732, 1738, 1769, 1779
– -prominent languages 1121
convergence 1666
converse 929
conversion 1604
coordinating adverb 996
– conjunction 610, 996, 998
coordinating particle 956, 1105
coordination 4, 595, 611, 958–959, 979, 981–982, 1003, 1105, 1107, 1116, 1421, 1522, 1642, 1737, 1768
– ellipsis 396
copredicative participles 1115
copula 65, 200, 511, 950, 951, 957, 959, 1082, 1091, 1099, 1100, 1548, 1659, 1672
– -supported clefts 1092
copulative converbs 1113, 1119
copy pronoun 365–366
core 923, 981
– argument 917, 925, 971, 1415
– coordination/cosubordination 612, 986
– function 926
– subordination 595–596, 981, 986
coreference 353, 916, 918, 919, 925, 926, 1116
corpus linguistics 1563, 1569
correlations 315, 926, 957–959, 1429, 1574
correptio Attica 1317
corruption 218
cosubordination 611, 612, 981
Co-Text 435
count nouns 825, 832
counterfactual 612, 1000, 1004–1006, 1008
coverbs 504
covert movement 1089
CP 1091
creativity 11, 114
creoles/creolization 5, 20, 96, 432, 780, 1573, 1645, 1655–1667
Crescendo-Decrescendo-Modell 1327
cross-categorial harmony 856
– -reference 917, 921, 1007
cue validity 126–127

– -cost-Faktor 126–127
cumulative expression 1415
current relevance 776
cursus-Sprache 1394
cybernétique 75, 77
cyclicity 1634

D

daß-Satz 197, 209
dative subject 1496, 1532
dativ//Dativ 875, 955, 971, 973, 974, 1498
de dicto/de re reading 197, 563
deaccenting 1384, 1386
decausative 888
declarative 892, 1011, 1013, 1018, 1020, 1026
declension class 1694
declination 186, 1387
decomposition 506
Deduktion 292, 479
deep cases 483
definite article 328, 334, 341, 527, 593, 964, 966, 977, 1518, 1625, 1755
– attribute 964
– description 512
definiteness//Definitheit 296, 351, 525, 529, 831, 877, 942, 967, 1085
degrammaticalization 1597
degree of control 957
deictic articles 837
De-Ikonisierung 150, 381
deixis/deictic 52, 142, 326, 334, 336, 412, 557, 569–570, 575–589, 983, 1414, 1698
delocutivity 1604
demarking 1092, 1093
demonstratives//Demonstrativa 324–325, 327, 331, 334, 341, 497, 522, 527, 529, 576, 577, 831, 840, 864, 983, 1519
demotion 904, 975
Demotivation 1600
dénomination 183
denotation 518
deobjective 922
deontic attitudes 999
– modality 553, 983
dependency grammar//Dependenzgrammatik 14, 88, 116, 300, 301, 862
– relations 367
dependent marking 314, 855, 961–963, 1108, 1424–1432, 1437
– dependent taxis 1119
dephrasing 1386
depictive value 1120
deponent 924, 1696

deranked construction 956, 958, 981, 995, 996, 1113, 1121
Derivation 1727
dérivation délocutive 1604
derivational approach 923
– morphology 395, 1748
– verbal form 919
derived case 995
– statives 928
– /non-derived reflexives 917–918
– -case comparatives 993
description, definite 512
–, indefinite 512
désémanticisation 1612
desententialization 602, 614, 982, 1401
Desiderativ 543, 987, 1729
designator 509
Deskriptive Grammatik 269
detached converbal clause 1118
determinants 328, 1601
determinate number 821
determination 325
Determinativ-/Logogrammsysteme 165
Determinatum 1601
determiner 329, 855
– genitives 965
– Phrase 525
detransitivization 900, 911, 918–920, 926
diachronische Soziolinguistik 1584
diachrony//Diachronie 7, 20, 218, 280, 282, 341–342, 606, 860, 865, 870, 875, 895, 913, 966, 986–988, 991, 1002, 1422, 1554–1556
diagrammatische Ikonizität 371, 373
diakritische Zeichen 171, 176
dialect continuum 1458
dialectique stoïcienne 184
dialectology//Dialektologie 1456, 1458, 1471–1491, 1536
dialects 218
Dialektik 268
Dialektometrie 1477, 1479, 1483–1484
Dialog 55, 72, 1567
Dialogizität 1568
Diaphasik 1565, 1568
Diaspora 1775
Diastratik 1565
diasynthetica 9, 208
Diasystem 1564
Diathese//diathesis (s. also voice) 15, 301, 306, 312, 313, 351–352, 355, 378, 489, 593–594, 608, 881, 1728, 1792
Diatopik 1565

Dichtekarten 1478
different subject 1002
differential object marking//marquage différentiel de l'objet 18, 351, 873–885
different-subject converb 1117
Diglossie 1573
dimensional adjective 1550
– view 326
Diphthong 1316, 1337, 1395
diptotisches Kasussystem 1783
direct causative 892
– object 989, 994, 995
– perception complement 986
– quote 987
– reference theory 514
– reflexive 918–919
– speech causation 1028
– /indirect objects 314
directional 981
directionnalité de la grammaticalisation 1622–1623
directive constructions 1026, 1030, 1728
– speech acts 1029
direkte/indirekte Rede 148
discontinuous constituents 1434, 1437
discourse configurationality//Diskurskonfigurationalität 627–628, 867, 1079, 1442–1455
discourse frame 955
– Iconicity Principle 623
– referent 500
– topic 955
– tradition 592, 1596
– Unit 454
– -familiar information 1083
discrete 1369
Disjunction/Disjunktion 644, 1011, 1012, 1016
Diskursanalyse 647–648
Diskursgattungen 468
diskursives Ensemble 1562–1563
Diskursivität 11, 1554
Diskursmarker 455
Diskursnormen 1559
Diskurspartikel 149
Diskurspragmatik 303, 1583
Diskurstradition 1, 2, 4, 467–477, 1559, 1561, 1582
Diskursuniversen 468
Dispersion 548
displaced focus 1085
– subject 1083
displacement 1079, 1081, 1091
Disrupted Language Transmission 1669
Dissimilation 1321, 1375
distal 977
Distinction Principle 318

distinguishability 924, 925
distributive 894
distributive quantifier 1446
ditransitive 32, 482, 868, 888
DNA 103, 110
Domain Integrity 861
domain minimization 362
– of reality 983
– of speech 983
double articulation 11, 107
– causative 893
– marking 145, 961–963, 1425, 1429
– negation 1701
– object construction 974, 1660
– subject construction 974, 1447
downdrifting 1369
downgrading 605, 609
Down Syndrome 99
downstep 1369, 1387
D-Teil 579, 582
dual 316, 818
– terminative 929
dummy subject 314, 944, 948, 1447
durative 929, 930
dyads 820
Dynamic Stereotype Principle 318
dynamicity 479, 939, 968
Dysarthrien 124
dyslexia 120
dysphasia 98

E

Early Immediate Constituents (EIC) 362, 859
– Modern Period 234–249
Ebenen der Textverarbeitung 158
échantillon 875
échelle d'individuation 352, 880
echo questions 1026
Echowörter 1533
École Pratique des Hautes Études 344
economy//Ökonomie 19, 113, 318, 366–367, 371, 375, 384–400, 846, 1314
egocentric system 570
egressive 562, 1621
Eigennamen 68
elaboration 982
Elision 1319
Ellipse//ellipsis 212, 637, 639–640, 963, 1012, 1604
embedded clause 982, 987, 1096

embedded interrogatives 496, 1012, 1026
embedded verb 923, 1097
emotional involvement 973
emotive verb 929
empathy hierarchy 489
empiricism 229
empty pronoun 594, 595, 1409
− word/full word 278
enchaînement 1397
encoding option 981
encyclopaedic knowledge//enzyklopädisches Wissen 132, 590, 593, 642, 649, 1598
encyclopédie 87, 231
endocentric constructions 325
Endreim 1327
enérgeia 2, 338
englischer Strukturalismus 435
énonciation 182−183
Entity Type Hierarchy 1404
Entlehnung 413, 1340, 1568
Entscheidungsfragen 148
enunciational epiphanies 225−231
enunciative 594
Epenthese 1337, 1349, 1396
Epiphänomene 226, 292
episodic verb 1084
epistemic modality 983, 998−999, 1004, 1007, 1731
epistolary tenses 557
equality 993
equative constructions 997, 1499
equipollent opposition 917
Ergänzungsfragen 148, 301
ergative/ergativity//Ergativ/Ergativität 18, 301, 314, 316, 318, 352, 356, 390, 488, 867, 875, 881, 887, 910, 912−913, 919, 933, 1402, 1414, 1416, 1422, 1425, 1465, 1533, 1624, 1632, 1635, 1754, 1777−1778, 1782, 1793
ergativité syntaxique 349
érgon 2, 338
eroded copula morphemes 1099
erosion 1578
Erstspracherwerb 372, 376, 381, 1313
Erzählen 449, 472
esoteric/exoteric languages 571
essence 327
essentialist metaphysics 223
Ethnomethodologie 42, 45, 445, 455, 460
etymology 230, 335
Eurasian linguistic area 1492
europäische Aufklärung 251
− Linguistik 280
europäischer Strukturalismus 294

Europäisierung 1737
European vernaculars 242
Europeanism 1493
EUROTYP 606, 629, 1471, 1484
Euroversals 851
Eurozentrismus 92, 1461
evaluation of languages 234−249
evaluative attitudes 999
− modalities 986, 999−1000, 1004
event 478, 515, 984
− frame 562
− vs. proposition 984−985
eventiveness 1082
event-related brain potential (ERP) 13
evidential 558, 777, 1516, 1731
evolution 113
exceed comparative 994−996, 1499
Exceptional Case Marking (ECM) 903, 1697
exclamative 1011, 1520, 1523
existential constructions 941−953, 955, 958−959, 1445
− order 945
− perfect 777
− quantifier 1025
exons 104
exoteric languages 571
expanding focus 1086
experiencer 968, 1414, 1417, 1443
− dative 1443
− diathesis 605
experiential 564, 938, 1410
− perfect 777
− predicates 1496
explanation 337−338, 360, 857, 866, 995, 996
expletive 286, 314, 866, 868, 949, 1082, 1091, 1448
explicitness of linking 614, 982
Explikatorverben 1531, 1536
Expressivität 413−414
exprimendum 325, 327, 340
extended demotion 890
− Pidgin 1648
− Right Capture 1351
extensionality 326−327
Exteriorität 11, 19, 1554
external possessor 970−978
extra-clausal coreferentiality 920
extraction 284−286, 1113
extra-inflectional affix 900
Extrametrikalität 1325−1326, 1355
extraposition 593−594, 988, 1113
extra-thematic arguments 973
ezafe-markers 962, 968

F

facework 17, 463
factitive hortative sentences 1031
− interpretation 1030
factivity 892, 982, 1738
Factuality Hierarchy 1404
facultative number 822
falling intonation 1013
Familiolekt 53
featuredness 400
Feldlehre 435
figura etymologica 641
Fillers First 366
final devoicing 1548
Finalfunktion 301
Finalgesetz 1319−1320
Fingeralphabet 141, 149
finite clause/verb 496, 613, 981, 989, 1002, 1017, 1659
finiteness 601, 603, 610, 613, 843, 979−981, 1400−1413
Finitheitsgrade 379, 613
first causative 893
− person inclusive 820
− -order entities 500
fixation of word order 1701−1704
fixed-case comparatives 993, 995
flectional/flective (fusional) language type 171, 250, 306−308, 310, 1344, 1362−1363, 1395, 1421, 1747
Flexion 256, 265, 267, 309
Flexionsformen 125
Flexionsklassen 390, 392, 404
Flexionsmorpheme 395
floated (or free) marking 1428
floating L tone 1370
flow dimension 1414, 1419−1420
focalization 1752
FocP (Focus phrase) 629, 1088, 1091−1093, 1095
focus background structure 1081
focus configurationality 869, 1633
− criterion 1090
− fronting 907, 1088, 1093
− marking 624−627, 1007, 1081, 1095, 1099, 1100, 1108
− morphology 1100
− movement 1089, 1451−1452
− of assertion 1079
− operator construction 1088, 1093
− particle 610, 1084, 1092, 1094, 1119
− prominence 1090, 1449−1453

− restrictions 1118
Fokus 374, 409, 413, 563, 618, 619, 621, 1017, 1079, 1094, 1368, 1420, 1433, 1449
Fokusbinder 621
fokus-sensitive Partikeln 627
Fokus-Verschiebung 160
fonctionnalisme 76, 84, 349
foot 1346, 1352−1359
foregrounding 1792
formal linguistics 1409−1411
formale Semantik 578
formant 309−310
fortition 1341
Fragesatzstrukturen 288−289
frames 155, 648, 1581
französische Klassik 271
free dative 971
− indexing 1094
− indirect discourse/speech 560, 606
− word order 275, 278, 865, 1438
− /bound morphemes 309, 1002
freies Thema 625
French Academy 242
− Enlightenment 608
frequency 403, 405, 408, 1013
frequentativity status 1004
Frühsilbengesetz 1322
Fugenlaut 1601
full word/empty word 278
function 313, 943
function words 124, 308−310, 1001, 1002, 1671
functional explanation 307, 324, 926, 932, 941, 966
− Grammar 487, 622, 985
− head 287, 290, 864
− magnetic resonance imaging (fMRI) 14
− proximity 1000, 1007
− Sentence Perspective//funktionale Satzperspektive 16, 28, 349, 619, 629, 630, 641
functionalism 269, 272, 281, 294, 317, 319, 370, 405, 1341, 1400
functional-typological approach 304, 371, 871
functor-argument structures 857
funktionale Grammatik 41, 51, 88, 1579
− Kategorie 287, 289
− Pragmatik 51, 446
− Kohärenz 271−272
− Oppositionen 270
Funktor 299
Fusion 307, 311, 386, 395, 1616
fusional inflection 1625
− language 26, 264, 395

future tense 770, 1695
futurum præteriti 1514
fuzziness 305

G

Galton's Problem 425
gap-filling 1087
gapping 996
Gattungen 1, 2, 4, 468, 1559
Gattungswandel 471
Gebärdensprache 141−154, 372
Gebrauchsfrequenz 386
Gelenkspartikel 1699
geminate consonant 1395, 1397, 1512
gender 30, 392, 865, 1034, 1430, 1516, 1693
− agreement 1115
− and number marking 1021
Genera verbi see Diathese
general grammar 222, 226−228
− meaning//Gesamtbedeutung 401, 769, 817
− noun 524
generalized alignment constraint 1386
generative grammar/linguistics 28, 35, 41, 51, 75, 95, 142, 144, 276, 283−284, 294, 325, 370, 401, 487, 512, 620, 622, 627, 858, 865, 870, 908, 1338, 1442
generative Phonologie 403, 1337, 1338
generative Semantik 296, 622, 1596
generelle Typologie 281
generic expression/NP 1000, 1443
Generizitätspostulat 470
Genesis 327
genetic alphabet 105
− classification 7, 855
− reconstruction 228
− relationship//genetische Verwandtschaft 7, 936−937, 1458, 1721
− /areal relatedness 7, 1424
genetics 11, 103
genitive 277, 389, 956, 961, 962, 964, 965, 970
genitive/dative syncretism 1519, 1524
genitivus subjectivus 389
genius 230−231, 235, 243
genius of language//génie de la langue 242, 259, 267−268
genome 103
Geographie//geography 1460, 1471, 1472
Geolinguistik 1460, 1471

Geotypen 1476, 1479
Germanistik 1471
germanophone Linguistik 400
gerund//Gerundium 376, 495, 595, 981, 983, 1112, 1114
Gesamtbedeutung//general meaning 401, 769, 817
Geschichtlichkeit 1554
Geschlechtsrolle 463
geschriebene/gesprochene Sprache 200, 436, 1566
Gesprächsanalyse 40
Gesprächsverhalten 463
Gestalt 1345
Gestaltpsychologie 18, 435
Gestaltwahrnehmung 1345
Gestik/Mimik 142
Glagolica 167
glottal stop//Glottalverschluß 1314, 1349
Glottalisierung 1642, 1770, 1777
glottochronology 118
goal 961, 967, 1023
governance 277
Government and Binding 512
− patterns 313
gradients 499
Gradpartikeln 621
gradual death 1669
gram 769
− family/gram type 769, 1466, 1469−1470
− types 780
grammaire générale 222
− raisonnée 231
− universelle 76
grammairiens-philosophes 226, 229
grammars of vernaculars 234
grammatica speculativa 9, 194, 198, 202−208
grammatica universalis 9, 203
grammatical relations 30, 314, 487−488, 890
− relations hierarchy 313, 890
− subject 487
− weight sensitivity 1083
grammaticality 226, 1089
grammaticalization 4, 9, 16, 282, 304, 314, 325, 349, 353, 358, 360, 372, 382, 504, 506, 540, 552, 573, 603−605, 609, 614, 775, 831, 891, 956−957, 959, 982, 986−987, 996, 1016, 1095−1096, 1100, 1108, 1120, 1430, 1468, 1577, 1579−1582, 1596, 1597, 1608−1623, 1668, 1674, 1700, 1757
− area 1549
− cline 781, 1468
− path 779, 850, 1100, 1730

- pattern 967−968
- source 967
- strategy 1004
- theory 406, 1424
grammaticography//
  grammaticographie 187, 189, 211, 216, 234
Grammatikalisierungsgrad 539
Grammatikalisierungsprozesse 52, 280, 303, 381, 1562, 1726
Grammatikalisierungsskala 548
grapheme-phoneme correspondence 1743
Graphophonie 1687−1688
Greek/Roman philosophy/linguistics 188, 237
Greenbergian universals 363, 1001, 1006
Grenzknoten 284, 285
griechische Antike 371
grounding 456, 590, 609
Grundwortstellung 90
Guttman scale 496

H

habitual aspect 776, 1621
- conditionals 1000, 1005
Handform/Handstellung 143
Handlungsformen 57
Handlungstheorie 40−62
Hand-Tier-Modell 144
hanging topic 625
Haplologie 1321
harmonic context 983
Hauptwort 496
HAVE-Drift 956, 957
- -perfect 977, 1495, 1513
- -Possessive 955, 957, 959
head 525, 855−865, 1311
- marking 29, 314, 961−963, 966, 968, 1108, 1424−1432, 1437, 1543
- proximity 861
headedness 1425
head-external/internal relative clause 1092
headward migration 1431
heavy constituent 988
Heavy NP Shift 626, 1082, 1083
Hermeneutik 72, 281
hesitation phenomena 1568
hesternal 560
Hiatgesetz 1318−1319
hidden Markov models 116
hierarchy 107, 324, 489
Hieroglyphen 86, 166, 172
Hintergrund 619
Hintergrundwissen 159
Hiragana 128, 166, 175, 1617
Hirnschaden 124

Hispanicization 1549
historical-comparative linguistics 252, 258, 855, 1422, 1458, 1576
- method 1424
historicity//Historizität 11, 470, 1554−1563, 1585−1586
historische Soziolinguistik 474
historisches Präsens 587
Historismus 1555
hodiernal 560, 771
Höflichkeit 16, 17, 378, 463
holistic descriptions 1623
holistic/partial typologies 26, 369, 1574
holistisch 251, 272, 281
holophrastic expressions 337
holy languages 237
home sign 97
homeobox genes 110
Homonymie 373, 375, 389
Homöorhese 1679
homophony 114, 169
honorific articles 836
honorifics 17
Hörer 451, 580
horizontal assimilation 1374
hortative constructions 1028−1034
hortatory discourse 820
human referent 18, 1021
Humangenetik 1483
Humanismus 212−213, 216, 234, 252
humanitude 875, 877
hybrid categories 495
hypercorrection 1674
hyperessive 336
hyperroles 484, 488, 1416
hypersupercompound tenses 560
hypotaxis 596−601, 843, 1115
hypothetical mood/conditional 998, 1000, 1005, 1008

I

iamb/iambic 858, 1352, 1396
iconicity//iconicité 11, 54, 111, 142, 150−151, 271, 318, 328−329, 337−339, 369−384, 388, 397, 404, 408−409, 487, 538, 578, 893, 957, 959, 966, 985, 1118, 1324, 1609
ico-semantic distinction 982
ideal language 228
Idealisierung 1564, 1576
idealistische Sprachwissenschaft 270
identification 325, 328
identificational focus 1079, 1449−1450

Identität 461−464
Ideogramm 164−165, 171
Ideographie 163, 167
ideographische Symbole 169
idiomatic expressions/idiomaticity 510, 523, 973, 976, 1599
if-clause 998
Ikone 371
ikonische Anordnung 148
- Bilderschrift 144
- Zeichen 164, 578
illocutionary conditional 1000
- force 514
Illokution 55, 438
illokutionäre Akte 70
- Rollen 448
Illokutionshierarchien 646
Illokutionstypen 296−297, 303
Imagepflege 463
imaginary plurals 1504
immediate constituents 362
- perception construction 985
imperative 312, 869, 1006, 1011, 1030−1034, 1731
imperfect tense 559
imperfective aspect 561, 604, 769, 774, 883
impersonal constructions 1117
- passive 904, 905, 1523
implicational hierarchies/patterns 304, 338, 361, 365, 370, 821, 903, 935, 987, 1437, 1649
implicational universals 19, 32, 371, 855, 918, 1440, 1575, 1649
implicativity 15, 19, 982
implicit-possessor construction 971
Implikationsrelation 403
Implikaturen 448, 646
inactive possessors 968
inactivization 908
inalienability hierarchy 977
inalienable possession 946, 952−954, 961, 965−966, 970, 973, 977, 1430
inceptive 312, 562
inclusive/exclusive „we" 1431, 1503, 1529, 1548, 1643
incomplétif 883
inconsistency 1636
inconsistent linearization 1630
incorporation 311, 317, 351, 498, 537, 544, 880−881, 904, 950, 956, 974, 1108, 1114, 1440, 1548
indeclinable words 279, 829
indefinite 954
- article 341, 977
- description 512
- noun phrase 1085

– object deletion 923
– pronoun 1011, 1534
indefiniteness 529
indeterminateness 1408
index of fusion/synthesis 26
indexation 485, 1425
indexikalische Zeichen 460, 578
Indexikalität
India 275
Indian Linguistic Area 1529
indicative 318, 600, 980, 1032
indicativity 18, 324, 327, 330, 339, 489
Indices 371
indirect causative 892
– directive speech acts 1030
– discourse/speech 560, 983, 986
– object 902, 1629, 1632
– passive 902
– reflexive 918, 925
– speech acts 1026
– statement 1027
indirective//Indirektiv 777, 1731
indistinction indexes 500
individual-level predicate 1446
individuation 489, 879, 1085
individuelle Typologie 281
Indogermanistik 381, 1477
Induktion 1479
inequality 993
inessive 336, 610
inférences conversationnelles 1613
inferential 778, 938, 1092
– construction
– statistics 420
inferentiality 558
Inferenz 159, 649, 1581
infinitive 308, 313, 481, 495, 595, 601, 980, 983, 1115, 1117, 1400, 1697
– loss 1526, 1658, 1697
– -converb 1117
infix 901
in-focus form 1097
– verb forms 1096
information flow 1118, 1414
– focus 1079, 1449–1450
– interrogatives 1011
– modalities 986
– structure// Informationsstruktur 371, 617–633, 1079, 1081, 1084, 1096, 1736
Informationsrelief 617
informatique linguistique 79
ingressive 300, 562, 1621
inherence 327
inherent possession 336
Initialgesetz 1319
Innere (Sprach-)Form 267, 269–271

Innovation 1583
Input-Output-Beziehungen 284
Inschriften 1720
in-situ language 1019, 1020, 1023
institutionalization 1598
instrument 301, 1120
instrumental passive 902
integral vs. partial typology 341
Integrale Sprachtypologie 270, 271
integration 595–606, 609
integrative intonation 597
Integrativität 413
intensifiers 1501
intensionality 326–327
intensity 938
intensive 894
interaktionistische Ansätze 445
interclausal semantic relations (hierarchy) 842, 986
interdental fricatives 1642
Interferenzen 131
Integration 643
Interjektion 199, 207, 1568
interlacing 982
Interlinguistik 87
interlude 1329
internal possessor construction 970–978
International Phonetic Association (IPA) 25
interne Diglossie 1684
interpersonelle Funktion 409
interpolation 1703
interpretator 592, 605, 609–610
Interpretierbarkeit 637
Interpunktion 642
interrogative cleft construction 1094
– construction 1010–1028, 1520
– intonation 1030
– particle 1011–1016, 1020, 1026
– pronoun 290, 963, 1011, 1022–1024, 1494
intertwining 1657, 1675–1676
intonation 596–597, 1003, 1008, 1011–1013, 1018, 1026, 1030, 1032, 1380–1390, 1445
intonational languages 1081
– phrase 1373, 1381
Intransitive predicates 482
intransitivization 928
intrinsische Orientierung 578
introflection 1624
introns 104
invariants 297
inverse construction/conjugation 910–911, 1700

inverse number 829
inversion 230, 1017, 1019, 1082–1083
inverting language 1017
IP 1091
Ironie 447
irrealis 558, 980, 982–983, 998, 1001, 1401
Islamic cultural sphere 275
island constraints 1080, 1089, 1093
– sensitivity 1093
Isochronie(hypothese) 1343, 1391, 1398, 1504
isogloss 1475, 1478, 1493, 1536
Isoglossenbündel 1481, 1533–1534
isolating type languages 26, 168, 250, 255–256, 264, 267, 306–307, 309–311, 386, 991, 1379, 1395, 1439, 1467, 1604, 1671
isomorphism 372–373, 846
isophorie/allophorie 353
isopleth 1458, 1505
Isotopie 643, 648
iterative 310, 312, 557, 894

J

Japanese linguistics 275
Jargon 1648
Jesuiten 254
junction 596, 599
juncture 611, 981
Junggrammatiker 1338
Junktion 299, 376, 414, 643
Junktor 65
jussive//Jussiv 986, 1515, 1769
juxtaposition 843, 961, 979, 1106, 1427–1428

K

Kabbala 86
Kakuminallaut 1572
Kana 128
Kanji 128, 166
karolingische Reform 1688
Kasusmarkierung 378, 1767
Kasussysteme 389
Katakana 128, 166
kategorematische Termini 201
Kategorialgrammatik 66–67
Kategorien, grammatische 293
kausale Relation 300, 376, 607, 608
Kausalfunktion 301
Kausalität 379
Keilschrift 172, 175
Kerbschrift 1724

kernel concept 334
kinship of languages 230
− terms 954, 966, 977, 1517
Kladogenese 1679
Klasseme 642
Klassifikation 257
Klassifikatoren 147
Klitika 290
Klitisierung 287
Koda 1311
Kodagesetz 1316
Kognition 156, 449, 648
Kognitive Grammatik 374
− Linguistik 42, 305, 1557
− Pragmatik 50, 461
Kognitiver Ausgangszustand 283
Kohärenz 155, 441, 634−637
Kohärenzbildung 159
Kohäsion 155, 634, 637
koiné 237
Kölner Universalienprojekt (s. also Unityp) 64
Kommentar 618
Kommunikantenrollen 444−467
Kommunikation 449, 1564
Kommunikationstheorie 40−62
Kommunikationswissenschaft 42
kommunikative Distanz 1565−1567
− Kompetenz 41
− Nähe 1565, 1567
− Regreßpflicht 297
kommunikativ-pragmatische Wende 41
Komparativ 403, 1533, 1728
Kompensationseffekt 1392
kompensatorische Dehnung 1327
Komposita 394, 1735
Komprimierungseffekt 1392
Kondensation 53
Kongruenz 287, 546, 1784, 1789
s. also agreement
Konjunktiv s. conjunctive
Konnektive 643, 644
Konnexität 636, 637
Konsonantenalphabet 165
Konsonantenharmonie 1311
Konsonantensysteme 389
konsonantische Stärke 1311
konstruktioneller Ikonismus 538
Konstruktionen 292
konstruktionistische Hypothese 159
Konstruktivismus 72, 1475
Kontext 435−444
Kontextinformation 575
Kontextualisierung 49, 457−461

Kontextwissen 579
Kontiguitätsrelationen 1581
Konversationsanalyse 45, 439, 445
Konversations-Implikaturen 447
Konversationsmaxime 71, 445
Konversion 550−551
konzeptionelles Kontinuum 1566, 1567
konzeptionelle Mündlichkeit/ Schriftlichkeit 1567
Konzil von Tours 1686
Kooperationsprinzip 447
Kopfattraktivitätsgesetz 1320
Kopfgesetz 1314
Kopfmaximierung 1317
Koproduktion 46
Koproduktivität 453−461
Körper 1311
Körperlichkeit 51
Kreativität 1554
Kreislaufmodell des Sprachwandels 1580
Kreolsprachen 410, 1583, 1679
Kulturgeographie 1478
Kulturpsychologie 265
Kultursemiotik 402
künstliche Intelligenz 161, 637
− Sprachen 85−95
Kyrillica 167

L

Labialharmonie 1726
Labialisierung 1777
labile verbs 887, 917
language acquisition 10, 19, 95, 317
− Bioprogram Hypothesis 96, 97, 780
− change 19, 219, 325, 338, 855
− contact 1424, 1507, 1550
− death 1669
− deprivation 96−97
− evaluation 236
− evolution 100
− isolates 432
− mixture 242
− obsolescence 4, 20, 599, 1668−1677
− shift 1458, 1668
langue 2, 20, 41, 252, 295
large linguistic areas 316
lateralisation 129, 134
Lautgesetze 1337
Lautharmonie 1725
Lautsprache 141
Lautveränderungen 381, 385
Law of Abbreviation 846
− Increasing Constituents 860

learnability 338
Lebenswelt(theorie) 40−62
Lebenszyklus 1678
Leerstelle 287, 436
left dislocation (s. also clefting) 625
− -branching 314, 858
Lehnprägung 1606
leichte Silben 1322
lektale Markierung 412, 414−415
lengthening process 1359
lengua general 1549
Leningrad school 306, 312
Lenisierung//lenition 1337, 1341
Leseaussprache 1687
levels of linking 596−606, 848
lexeme 298, 389−390
lexical aspect 561, 772
− decomposition 296
− ellipsis 1604
− focus phrase 1094
− fusion 985
− head 287, 864
− insertion 1596
− -Functional Grammar 1435
lexicalization 351, 382, 506, 604, 1595−1608
lexie 1599
lexifier language 1648
lexikalische Phonologie 1337
− Semantik 374
− Solidaritäten 643
Lexikostatistik 1483
LF movement 1089
liaison 183, 1397
light verbs 28, 1084
lineage 1461
Linear B 166
Linearität 106, 147, 164, 227, 1574
linguae francae 1682
linguistic area 36, 865, 1456, 1492−1509, 1530, 1533, 1539−1553
− evolution 361
− relativity hypothesis 571
− sign 236, 247
linguistica spaziale 1456
linguistique cognitive 75, 79−80
− informatique 79
linking article 834
linking clauses 590−617
linking pronouns 963
Linksversetzung 625
literacy 598, 611, 842
literarische Texte 160
Literaturwissenschaft 303, 1561
loan translation 1543
loanblends 1606
loanword//Lehnwort 1550, 1606, 1640, 1673, 1725, 1743

Index of subjects

localist hypothesis 523
locality conditions/restrictions 284–285, 1085, 1089, 1093
localization 326, 336, 537, 545, 548, 569–570, 1558
location 964, 1022–1023
– argument 942–943
– Schema 967
locational possessive construction 955–959
– /locative 955, 959, 994–995, 1007
locative adjuncts/adverbials 930, 968, 973
– comparatives 1499
– paradigm 941, 946–947, 950–952
– phrase 971
– preposition 974
– proform 944–945, 946, 949, 952–953
– subject 944, 948–949, 952
locuteurs-auditeurs 1612
logic 225
Logical Form (=LF) 14, 289, 515, 1089
– subject 69, 487
Logik 193, 196, 198, 437
logischer Empirismus 69
Logogramme 172, 174
Logographie 163, 168–169, 1689
logophoric pronoun 920, 1617
Logosmystik 223
lokale Verbesserung 399
long distance binding
– anaphora/binding 919–920, 1409
long-distance WH-movement 28
L-Teil 579, 582, 588
ludic potential 1673
Lullismus 86

M

Magnetic Resonance Imaging (MRI) 14, 100
maintenance of reference 591
Makroparadigma 390
manipulative verbs 985
manner adverb 1023, 1119, 1522
manuelle Parameter 143
marked word order 1100
markedness 19, 308, 313, 371, 398–419, 504, 769, 917, 1080, 1312
– hierarchies 360
– reversal 335
masking 119
mass noun 524

material relation 964
matrix clause 981, 987
– language 1657
Max Planck Institute 570, 573
maximal onset principle 1317
Maximen der Qualität/Quantität 447
maximising the onset 1348
Meaning-Text framework 317
measuring constructions 334
medial verb 1115–1116
médiaphorique 1621
mediopassive//médio-passif 352, 1513, 1523
Mediterranean area 1506
Mehrsprachigkeit 193
melody 1371
mensural classifiers 524
mental language 223–225, 230
– perception construction 985
mentalisme//Mentalismus 82, 265
merals 328
Merkmalhaftigkeit 400
Mesoamerican linguistic area 1492, 1539–1553
metalanguage//Metasprache 92, 132, 194, 225, 228, 256, 295–296, 304
metaphor//Metapher 106, 150, 194, 372, 1382, 1599, 1610
metaphorische Ikonizität 371
Metathese 1321, 1337
metatypy 1642
metonymy//métonymie 1599, 1603
metrical approach 1383
– coherence 1360, 1365
– structure 1314, 1346
– tenses 557, 560–561
metrische Phonologie 1337
microsatellites 117–118
Middle Ages 192–209, 1506–1507, 1628
– voice (s. also diathesis) 899, 906, 908, 920, 923–926
Mimik 145
Minderheitensprache 141
Minimal Attachment 869
– word 1357
Minimalistisches Programm 14, 288–289, 291
Minimize Domains 362
minnesong 1596
missionary linguistics 217
Mittelalter s. Middle Ages
Mittelfeldgrenze 285
mixed branching 858
– languages 1645
Möbius-strip 18, 339
modal meaning 983
– verbs 985, 1031

modality 302, 534, 541, 553, 647, 771, 986, 999, 1515, 1527
– in conditionals 1004–1006
Modalkategorien 302
Modallogik 438
Modalpartikel 378, 630
Modelling Analysis 958–959
modi intelligendi 9, 199
– significandi 9, 199, 200, 202
modification 325
Modifikation, verbale 533–556
Modisten 9, 10, 202–208, 252
molecular grammar 117
Monem 302, 386
Monoflexion 1628
Monokongruenz 1784
Monophthong 1316
Monophthongierung 1316
mono-pivotal subjectless languages 1420
monosemic 312
monosyndetic coordination 1107
monothetische Sprachen 170–171
– /polythetische Klassifikation 1477
mood 558, 983, 999, 1115, 1119
– in conditionals 1004–1006
mora//More 1325, 1393
Moraic representation 1349
– trochees//moraische Trochäen 1325, 1354
morpheme 147, 307, 389–390, 395, 1002
– -order changes 1643
morphemics 306
morphogenesis 110
morphographisches Schriftsystem 133
morphological causatives 886, 1530, 1536
– focus marking 1095, 1097, 1099
– processing 360
– typology 26, 264, 269, 306, 309, 991, 1623
morphologische Natürlichkeitstheorie 403
Morphologisierung 1725
morphophonemic fusion 1602
morphosyllabism 316
morpho-syntactic bondedness 961
Morse code 105
mother node 864
motion of body marks 932
motivation 372, 375
mouvance du texte 1570
movement transformation 859
– verb 1528
mRNA 104, 111

mtDNA 118
multilingualism 1460, 1645
multi-pivotal language 1415, 1419–1420
multiple topic construction 1448
multi-predicate construction 1418
Mundbild 143
Mundgestik 144
Mündlichkeit/Schriftlichkeit 406, 410, 440–441, 1340, 1565, 1570, 1573
Musterkennung 1475
muttersprachliche Kompetenz 292
Mystik 86
Mythologie 437

N

Nagari-Schrift 1682
Nähe-Distanz-Kontinuum 1567, 1571, 1573
nähesprachlich/ distanzsprachlich 1566
namegiving 335
Narratio-Formel 469
narrative converb 1113
– intonation 1030
– tenses 771
narrow focus 1079, 1088, 1093
Nasalisierung 1395
Nationalcharakter 265, 280
nationalism 244
natural order 230
– Semantic Metalanguage 852
natürliche generative Phonologie 1337, 1340
– Phonologie 1337, 1338
– Syntax 387
Natürlichkeitstheorie 90, 92, 408, 1313, 1338–1341, 1721
Nebenprädikation 550
Nebensilbe 1330
negated universal quantifier 1659
negation 883, 998, 1006, 1010, 1115, 1507, 1701
negative conditional 1000
– coordination 1504
– polarity item 1410–1411
– pronouns/quantifiers 1090, 1498
negator 856, 863
neogrammarian framework 1632
neolinguistic school/Neolinguistica 1456, 1477
Neologismen 92
nerbs 498
Neuplatonismus 68

neurolinguistics 14
neuronale Netzwerke 156
Neutralisation 407
new information 1083
Newsworthiness Principle 623
nexus 611, 981
Nezessitativ 1734
noematic structure 482
Noematik 293–294
Noemen 206, 295
nominal aspect 526
– clause 337, 1751–1752
– determination 328
– head 990
– number 816
– sentence 278
nominalismus 294
nominalization 326, 336, 481, 543, 550, 908, 980, 1096, 1400–1402, 1407
nominative 277
– experiencers 1495
– -accusative system 318
nominativus pendens 1449
Nominator 68
non-anchoring relation 964
– -animate 1021
– -argument position 1091
– -canonical word order 1007
– -combined (resultative) forms 931
– -configurational language 868
s. also configurationality
– -derived reflexive 917–918
– -detached converbal clause 1118
– -factive complement clause 982
– -finite verb/clause 276, 286, 366, 613, 958, 983, 1001, 1430
– -human referent 1021
– -identical subjects 959
– -restrictive relative clause 1100
– -specific subject 1446
– -stopped syllables 1368
– -testimonial 1516
– -Western approaches 275
Normativität 1576
notwendige Universalien 64
noun 496, 522, 816
– class 527
– incorporation 919, 1439
– phrase accessibility hierarchy 890
– phrase coordination 1105
– phrase/NP 522, 916
– /verb distinction 6, 18, 506
nouniness 495–508, 596, 602, 605, 979
Novosibirsk school of syntactic typology 319

NP accessibility 1753
– -articles 835
– -coordinators 1108
nuclear coordination/cosubordination 611, 612, 986
– operator 981
nucleus 981, 1348
Nukleusgesetz 1316
null anaphora 593, 1007
– pronoun 1439
Nullartikel 639
Null-Klitika 286
– -Subjekt 286, 287
– -Subjekt-Phänomen (pro-drop) 284, 285
– -Topik 286, 287
number agreement 1115
– Hierarchy 821, 824
– words 827
– //Numerus 265, 816
– -agreement properties 942
numeral 147, 522, 527, 529–530, 1520, 1735
– classifier 335, 524, 1548
Numeralklassifikatoren 1534, 1536
numeration 289, 337
numerische Klassifikation 1478, 1483
Numerologie 164

O

object 487, 1023
– agreement 880, 980
– conjugation 881
– marking 1753–1754
– of comparison 993
objective conjugation 500
– genitive 857
object-to-subject-raising 989
Objekt 544
Objektdeixis 580–582
Objektsprache/Metasprache 193–194, 198
objet 873, 875
objet coalescent 881
objet partitif 6, 880
obligatoriness 832, 1099, 1404
obligatory focus marking 1099
oblique (participant) 1415
– case 875
– stem 829, 1532
– subjects 1633
observable state 934–935
observational conditional 1001
obviate 911
obviative marking 1645
Ogham 166
Old European hydronymy 1506
– /new information 563, 1083, 1097

omnipredicativity 1551
one-form system 925
— -one-meaning-principle 866
— -strategy 924
onomasiologisch 11, 294–296, 300
onomatopoeia//Onomatopöie 150, 372, 380, 1604
onset 1348
ontogeny//Ontogenese 402, 554–556, 607
ontological categories 506
Ontologie 192
open conditional 998
— interrogatives 1011
— proposition 1010
operand 325, 857
operations 326
operator 325, 857, 981, 985, 1013, 1085, 1090, 1119
— focus 1079
— status of focussed constituents
oppositeness 337
optative 1006, 1032, 1515, 1758, 1731
Optimality Theory//Optimalitätstheorie 403, 415, 1313, 1364, 1386
optimierte Sprachsysteme 1313
order of affixes 314, 318
— of constituents 1011, 1016
ordinal numerals 526, 1503
ordinary language philosophy 445
ordre analytique 229
organisch-holistischer Ansatz 253
Organismus 267, 268, 270
organologische Theorie 267–268, 271
Organonmodell 44, 303, 408, 436
Orientierung im Raum 577
—, intrinsische 578
Origo 577, 580, 584
Orthographie 133
Orthosprache/Orthosyntax 66
Ortsdeixis 582–585
out-of-focus verb form 1096, 1099
overdetermination 840
overlay model of intonation 1382
overt focus movement 1089

P

Palatalisierung 1337
pan-Amerindianism 1551
panchronic 1510

Paradigmatische Ökonomie 387, 390
Paragrammatismus 128
Paragraph 642
parallel distributed processing 96
— focus 1086
parameter 499, 503, 1098, 1434
Parametrisierung 283, 284, 287
Paraphasie 124
paratactic complements 980
— construction/parataxis 612, 614, 982, 980, 1100
parole 2, 3, 41
parsing 859
Pars-Totum 299
part of speech//partie du discours 9, 181–182, 185–186, 211, 217, 225–228, 231, 314, 319, 495
partial interrogatives 1011
Participation 336–337, 339, 477–495, 534, 541
Participatum 480–481, 612
participial passive 1496
— /gerund construction 1644
participle//Partizip 207, 376, 308, 495, 499, 980, 1114, 1731
particle 307, 995, 1080
— comparative 995–996, 1499
particule de discours 875
partielle Typologien 1574
Partikularismus 252
partitive//partitif 875, 1519
part-whole relations 964, 977
passive/passif//Passiv 275, 313, 314, 352, 355, 489, 546, 624, 891, 894, 920–921, 923, 925, 928, 930, 932, 936, 938–939, 1417, 1447, 1523, 1631, 1635, 1663, 1695–1697, 1734, 1754–1755
passive converb 1120
— nominalization 908
— of state 930
— participle 928, 1495
— voice 899–916, 921
— /resultative 930–931
passivization 989
past tense 770, 1466
patient 313, 873, 917–919, 922, 925, 968
paucal 819
perfect 557, 769, 776, 930–933, 936–938, 1769
perfect and resultative 930
— language 243
perfective aspect 562, 552, 769, 774, 1006
— participle 931
performance 41, 360, 368
Performance-Grammar Correspondence Hypothesis 361

performative 448, 983
period intonation 1003
peripheral coordination/subordination/cosubordination 982, 986
periphery 923, 981
periphrasis 10, 1577, 1697, 1700
periphrastic causative 886
— perfect 1513, 1626
periphrastic resultative 931
permissive 892
— imperative 1034
— interpretation 1031
permutatio litterarum 218
person 1023
Personendeixis 296, 580
person-number agreement 1001
Perspektivierung 478, 540, 552, 578
Perspicuitas 271
Phänomenologie// phénoménologie 43, 52, 77, 81, 284
phänomenologisch-existentialistische Tradition 70
Pharyngalisierung 1777
pharyngealized consonants 1642
phasal adverbials 1504
philosophical grammar 213, 246
philosophie analytique 77, 80
— du langage 181–192
philosophische Pragmatik 438
Phonation 1342
Phonem 346, 386, 1344
— -Graphem-Konversion 129
phonemicization 1641
Phoneminventar 389, 399
Phonemsysteme 1313
Phonetic Form 289, 1090
Phonetik 143, 1338, 1391
phonetischer Symbolismus 150
Phonogramm 164
phonographische Schriften 166–167
phonological phrase 1385
— process 1356
— properties 1023
phonologie 142–143, 346, 401
phonologische Prozesse 1336–1347
phonologisches Wort 1326
phrasal article 834
phrasal compounding 1658
— rhythm 1363
phrase structure 947, 1434
physical contact 929
Physiologismus 1338, 1339
pidgin 5, 20, 1535, 1645, 1657
pidginization 1647–1654
pied piping 496–497

Piktographie 171, 163
piktographisch 168
pitch accent 1013, 1367, 1362, 1376, 1381, 1393
– range 1387
pivot 1415
pivotless languages 1420
Plansprache 50, 86–87
platonisierend 266
pluperfect 558
plural 818
Pluralität der Handlung 552
Plurizentrik 1573
poetische Sprache 85
Poisson distributions 421
polar interrogatives 1007, 1011–1017, 1020, 1026, 1501
– tone 1375
polarisation 876, 879
polarisation de l'objet 355
polarity 999, 1096, 1099
– in conditionals 1004–1006
– projection 1090
– status 1004
polite imperative 1006
politeness 9, 17, 1031
polyfunctionality 845
Polygonisierung 1478
Polygraphie 86
polypersonal agreement 921
polypredicative constructions 319
polysemy 114, 846, 917, 920–922, 931–932, 938, 1025, 1032
– of resultative markers 935–938
– of verbal reflexive markers 920
polysyndetic construction 1107
Polysynthesis Parameter 1440
polysynthetic language type 26, 171, 250, 265, 543, 506, 926, 974, 1012, 1427, 1433, 1624, 1645, 1751, 1760, 1779
polytonische Sprache 1394
polyvalence 174
Populationsgenetik 1483
P-oriented 928
Porphyrischer Baum 296
Port Royal Grammar 3, 222, 244–246, 225, 256
Portemanteau-Ausdruck 539
position in space 934–935
Positionsklassen 537
Positron Emission Tomography (PET) 14, 100
possessive affixes 500, 963
– article 839, 1699
– classifiers 963, 966
– clitics 966
– construction 29, 325, 335–336, 961, 928, 942–944, 947–951, 954, 957–958, 1543
– dative 971
– encoding types 954
– markers 1113
– NP 960
– prefixes 962
– pronoun 328, 331, 522, 528, 552, 840, 963, 1520
– relation 929, 955, 976
Possessivity 326
possessor 933, 943, 951–952, 954, 961, 964–968, 970, 973–974, 1426
possessor raising 970, 974–975
possibilitive 1005, 1006
possible worlds 517, 518
post-Creole continuum 1648
post-determination 328, 330
posterior tenses 559
posteriority 845
Postposition 1732
postspecification (right-branching) 1629
postspecifying language 860
postulats de signification 80
Postverbien 1729, 1733
potential 902, 922, 983
potentiality 983
poverty of the stimulus 95
Prädikatenlogik 65, 298, 578
Prädikation 68, 300–301
Prädikationshierarchie 296
Prädikativfunktion 301
Prädikativität 541
Prädikator 68, 298
Prädizierung 1558
praesens tabulare 587
Präferenzgesetze 1312
pragmatic explanation 977, 978
– mode 4
– motivation 977
Pragmatik 54, 68, 380–381, 444
pragmatische Inferenz 447
– Universalien 70–73
pragmatischer vs. syntaktischer Modus 1566
Prague School 269, 401, 619–620, 623, 1336, 1337, 1393, 1442
Präposition s. preposition 207
Präsumptive 1731
Präsupposition 619, 646
Präverbien 1777
preadaptation 101
predetermination 328
predeterminers 330
predicate adjectivals 502
– calculus 510, 511
– cleft 1660
– focus 1661
– locative 945–947, 950, 952
– logic 479
– -internal subject theory 946
predication 183, 326, 481–482, 509–522, 985
– base 480
– operator 1091
predicative adjective 957
predicative possession 954–956, 958–959, 1495
predicativity 324, 327, 330, 339, 501
predicator 479
preposition 207, 282, 309, 1618, 1661–1662
prescriptive grammar 237
prescriptor 1029, 1032
present tense 318, 770
presentational focus 1079, 1087
– interpretation 1093
presentative construction 1085
– movement 1082–1083, 1085
prespecification (left-branching) 1629
prespecifying language 860
P-resultative 928, 931–933, 935–939
Presupposedness Hierarchy 1404
presuppositional opacity 1118
preterite 558
– decay 1504
Preuve par Anachronie 1617
primates 100
Primitiva 296
primitive languages 505
Prim-Operationen 64
Principal (hyperrole) 1419–1421
Principe de Contradiction Inaperçue 1611
Principle of Least Effort 19
Principle of Maximation of Contrast 912
Principle of Natural Serialization 857
Principle of Scope 862
Principles and Parameters 28, 35, 284, 1400, 1409
Priority Principle 318
PRO („big pro") 1409
pro („little pro") 1409
probability samples 421, 424
processing principles 360
proclitic 963
Prodessiv 1728
pro-drop 28, 284–287, 866, 870, 1435, 1437–1438, 1500, 1783
productivity 504
proform 941, 948–949, 952
proform existential 944, 948
progressive 310, 563, 774, 883, 930, 938, 1359, 1621

– and resultative 931
– aphasia 98
prohibitive 1515
Projection Principle 1435
promotion of the possessor 975
pronom proleptique 1526
pronominal anaphora 594, 1002, 1113
– Argument Hypothesis 1435, 1437, 1440
– articles 838
– cataphora 594
– clitic 286, 287, 1694–1705
– copies 1093
Pronominalaffixe 544
pronominalization 326, 396, 1007
pronoms conjoints 1525
pronoun//Pronomen 146, 206, 277, 513, 576, 816, 1694, 1749
proper names 513, 518
property concepts 502
proposition 109, 155, 302, 478, 481, 509, 513–515, 1010
propositional act 509
– attitudes 514
– calculus 510
propositionaler Gehalt 297
propriety suffix 498
Prosodem 1394, 1396
prosodic features 1080, 1311
– prominence 1080–1081
– trough 1371
prosodische Konstituenten 1393
prospective 557
protasis/apodosis 998, 1000–1002, 1004–1007, 1015
Proto-Agent 867, 870
protolanguage 100
Proto-Patient 867, 868
– -Recipient 868
prototype (theory) 16, 33, 51, 272, 304, 371, 380, 406, 415, 495, 1557
pro-verb 302, 1727
proximate 911, 977
Prozessphonologie 1336
pseudo-clefts 1092
psych-action 986
psychoakustisch 1312
psycholinguistics 76, 141–142, 361, 368, 859
psychological subject 487
psychologisches Subjekt 618
pure focus particles 1081
puristische Reformen 1740
Puritans 241
purpose relation 845, 964, 1117, 1119

Q

quadral 819
qualification 326
quality 964
quantification 326, 942
quantified expression 1436
quantifier 324, 331, 522, 1095, 1119
– //Quantor 65, 861, 998, 1438, 1445
– -like operator 1088
quantitative valence 482
querelle des anciens et des modernes 229
question 1115
– word interrogatives 1011
– words 1662–1663
–: embedded 1026
–: rhetorical 1026, 1027
questione della lingua 219, 1681
quidditas 200
quotative 564, 606, 1026, 1120

R

raddoppiamento sintattico 1396
Radical Death 1669
raising 496, 903, 989
rank shifted clauses 1115
rationalism//Rationalismus 229, 249–263
Raumdeixis 582
real conditional 998
realis 558, 983
reanalysis 987, 1581, 1602, 1604, 1615, 1635
reason 1023, 1119
Rebusprinzip 169
recessive 917
recipient 961
– design 456–457
reciprocal 312, 894, 902, 919, 921, 923, 925–926
recognitional use 833
Redeteil 192, 194, 198, 201
Redeuniversum 437
redoublement de l'objet 880, 1525–1606
reduced clefts 1092, 1095
réduction phonique 1616
Reduktionsvokal 1331
reduplication 931, 1025, 1331, 1327, 1397, 1359, 1503, 1601, 1658, 1748
reference 68, 295, 481, 509–522, 638
– grammars 3
– point 768, 770, 964
– time 559

– tracking 593–594, 608, 1002, 1405
referent structure 1032
referential attributes 964
– distance 907
Referentialisierung 1558
referentiality 501
reflexive construction 352, 380, 902, 908, 920–923, 1662–1663, 1734
– pronoun/anaphor 544, 861, 909, 916–917, 919, 963, 1501, 1434, 1659
reflexives and antipassives 922
– and indefinite object deletion 922
reflexives and potentials 922
reflexivization 1418
regimen 196
regio 583
register tone 1368
regulating proteins 107, 111
reification 983
Reim 1311, 1394
Reimattraktivitätsgesetz 1320
reiterant speech 1392
Rektionsphonologie 1328
relatedness indicators 962
relation identifiers 962
relational classifiers 963, 966
– Grammar 487
– inheritance 974, 977
– noun 964, 1428, 1544
– theory of focus 1090
relationality 504
relations grammaticales 349
relative clause//Relativsatz 148, 261, 324–325, 331, 340, 366, 374, 522, 601, 968, 990, 1000, 1020, 1025, 1095–1097, 1099, 1408, 1494, 1527, 1529, 1739, 1765, 1768
relative particles 1507
– pronoun 331, 1011, 1025, 1494, 1507, 1751
– tense 557, 559–560, 772, 1119
– -clause construction 979
relativism 244–248
relativization 16, 325–326, 330, 360, 364, 1756
relevance//Relevanz 16, 538, 378, 537–538, 646
relexification 1649, 1657, 1666
Reliefgebung 617–633, 645
remoteness 771
remotivation 1600
Renaissance 87, 210–222, 234–249, 252, 1506, 1555
replacing focus 1086
replica language 1669
replication 114
réponse elliptique 353

reportative 564, 778, 920
repraesentandum 338
représentations symboliques 76
repressors 108
reset 1381
residual zone 1460
restricting focus 1086
- particles 1007
restrictive relative clause 367, 528, 1000
resultative/résultatif 31, 312, 564, 776, 928, 930, 1621
resultative Aktionsart 930
- and passive 937
- and perfect 935-937
- and progressive 938
- contructions 928-940
resumptive focus construction 1094
resumptive pronoun 1085, 1095, 1444, 1449, 1662
Resyllabierung 1329, 1337, 1348
retroflexe Konsonanten 1529-1530, 1536
Reziprokkonstruktion 379
Rhema 563, 1079
rhetoric 226, 229
rhetorical question 1026, 1027
- space 156
Rhetorik 1561
rhétorique 181, 187
rhetorische Frage 297
Rhotazismen 1337
rhyme 1348
rhythm 1391
rhythmic patterns 858
rhythmische Organisation 1336
rhythmischer Fuß 1392
Rhythmusgesetz 1322
Ribots Regel 132
rich agreement inflection 866
right-branching 314, 858
rightward displacement 1082
rigid designator 513, 518
- word order 865
rising intonation 1013
Rivalc 15, 344
RNA 104
Role and Reference Grammar 1405, 1436
role dimension 1414
- structure 1032
- -dominated languages 1416-1419
Rollendeixis 580
Romanistik 271, 1471, 1586
Romantik 231, 262, 266
root reduplication 931
Royal Society 243, 247
Russian linguistics 317

S

Sachverhalte 477
sacred languages 216, 239
salience 408
Salienzhierarchie 146, 581
sample
sampling 314, 316, 340, 419-435, 855, 1461, 1472
satellite-framed 17
satellites 572
Satz 302
Satzendform 598
Satzinnenform 598
Satzjunktion 298
Satzspaltung 626
Satzverkettungstechniken 376
Satzwörter 395
scalar concessive conditionals 1007
- phenomena 1401
scale of informativeness 1120
scalogram 496
Schale 1311
scheduled future 771
Schiefe 1482-1483
Schlagwortprinzip 172-173
Schnalze 1572
Scholastik 113, 223, 234, 246, 253
Schriftbild 1684
Schriftgeschichte 163-180
Schriftlichkeit/Mündlichkeit 48-49, 56, 410, 438, 456, 1565-1569
Schriftsprache 133, 167, 1535, 1720
Schriftsysteme 128
schwere Silben 1322
sciences cognitives 75-85
scope of verbal reflexive 919-920
scrambling 627, 1438
script 111, 648, 1581
scriptio continua 113
scripturality 596
Scythian tradition 219, 239
second causative 893
- language acquisition 1649, 1657, 1669
secondary A-resultative 933
sekundäre Kausativierungen 1530
selectional restrictions 862
selective focus 1086
selector genes 111
semantic change 607
- decomposition 482
- dependency 970, 971
- mapping 1580
- maps 297, 304, 505
- Motivation Principle 318
- parameters 954

- primes 223-225
- restrictiveness 1120
- role 30, 275, 276, 301, 318, 483, 485, 486, 858, 891, 1414
- space 847
- universals 224, 296
semanticity 11, 15
Semantik 65, 195, 437-438
sémantique cognitive 79-83
- générative 76
semantische Primitiva 91, 295
semantisches Netzwerk 637
Semantizität 1554
semasiologisch 295, 296
Semem 295
Semiosis 1574
semiotics//Semiotik 54, 223, 227-228, 294-295, 371, 445, 578, 1337, 1342, 1382
semi-speakers 1669
sensualistisch 226, 248, 257, 268
sentence accent 1099
sentence adverbials 1108, 1444
sentence-focus construction 1084
sentential arguments 312
Sentential Subject Constraint 497, 989
separatist expression/coding 1416, 1422
separative comparative 994
sequence of tense 560
sequentielle Ikonizität 376-377
seraspectial verbs 1116
serial verbs 27, 337, 845, 1108, 1408, 1661-1662
Serialisierungs-Ikonismus 397
serialization 504
set nouns 524
shift situations 1640
shortening process 1359
sign 224
signe linguistique 346
Signed English 141
Signemränge 14
Signemranghierarchie 294, 298, 302, 303
signifiant//Signifikant 346, 348, 372
signifié//Signifikat 295, 346, 348, 372
Silbe 150, 205
Silbenbeginn 1391
Silbengelenk 1329
Silbengewicht 1322
Silbengipfel 1391
Silbengrenze 1393
Silbenkontakt 1317
Silbenkontaktgesetz 1317
Silbenkonzepte 144
Silbenqualität 1325
Silbenrhythmus 1394

Silbenschnitt 1311
Silbenschrift 166, 170
Silbensprache 1393, 1396
Silbenstruktur 174−175, 1310−1336, 1396, 1724
silbenzählende Sprache 1322, 1391−1399
silent operator 1091
similative 1729
similative sentence 997
simplification 1668, 1670
simulfix 1621
Simultaneität 150, 151, 845, 955
simultaneous action 986
single-source/dual-source Pidgins 1651
singulative 1747
situation 477−495, 768
situational knowledge 591
Situationswissen 575
situative Ellipse 396
Sitz im Leben 1561
Smith-Stark (Animacy) Hierarchy 826
social dialects 1564
− intelligence 100
− relations 954
− semiotic 1
Societas Jesu 217
sociolinguistics 1456
sociology 316
solecism 237, 242
Sonorisierung 1724
Sonoritätsskala 1310−1312, 1329, 1348, 1353
Sonority Sequencing Generalization 1312
S-oriented 928
sort noun 524
sortal classifier 524, 527
sound symbolism 1382
source 967, 1023
− Schema 967
South Asian linguistic area 1492
SOV languages 278, 282, 288, 944, 1017, 1020, 1091, 1092
soziale Beziehungssysteme 40
− Rollen 461−464
− Wirklichkeit 43
Sozialphänomenologie 462
Soziolinguistik 40, 439−440
space 568−574
Spaltsätze (cleft sentences) 374, 1771
spatial cognition 571
speaker's positive evaluation 1005
special interrogatives 1011
specific articles 834
− attributes 964
− Language Impairment 99, 119

− NP 1443
specificity 832
specifier 287, 947
speech act 1, 2, 329, 509, 592
speech-act conditional 1000
speech act participant 976, 1415
− qualifiers 848
− theory 1029
− verbs 599, 923
spekulative Grammatik 199
spelling pronunciation 1602
Spell-out 289
split ergativity 18, 316, 1430, 1436, 1636
split marking 1429
split possession 965−967
spoken language 596, 599
Spontansprache 1683, 1685
Sprachatlanten 1471, 1474, 1477
Sprachbewußtsein 1556, 1571
Sprachbund 36, 1456−1458, 1492, 1529, 1540
Sprachcharakteristik 267−269, 271, 281
Sprachenmischung 134
Sprachentod 1558, 1573, 1679, 1723
Spracherwerb 288, 398
Sprachgebrauch 196
Sprachgeist 281
Sprachgenealogie 280
Sprachgeographie 1471
Sprachgeschichte 473−475, 1554
Sprachgesellschaften 240
Sprachklassifikation 268, 280
Sprachkontakt 141, 410, 412, 1770
sprachliche Zeichen 163, 294, 371, 387
sprachliches Handeln 444−467
Sprachlogik 196−202
Sprachmischung 131
Sprachpathologie 123−140
Sprachpsychologie 577
Sprachreflexion 1556
Sprachspiel 72, 73, 445
Sprachtechniken 1560
Sprachursprung 86
Sprachvariation 1554−1594
Sprachverarbeitung 124
Sprachverbesserung 1313
Sprachverschiedenheit 1556, 1560, 1750−1576
Sprachwandel 53, 92, 375, 381, 386, 391, 393, 395, 398, 399, 405, 1314, 1340, 1554−1595
Sprachwerk 2, 3
Sprachzeichen 193, 197, 199
spread zone 1460
Sprechakt 193, 297, 446, 647

Sprechaktspezifizierung 297
Sprechakttheorie 55, 56, 209, 298, 445, 448
Sprechakttypen 470
Sprechbund 1551
Sprecher 451, 580
Sprecher-Präsupposition 303
Sprecherwechsel 454
Sprechpraxie 124, 129
Sprechsituation 435−444
Sprechtätigkeit 1558, 1559
Sprechzeit 579, 587
squish 495
squishiness 330
S-resultative 928, 932−933, 938
St. Petersburg (formerly Leningrad) typological school 31, 306, 312
stadial typology 319
Stafettenkontinuität 1678
stage-level property 1084
Stammbaum model 1456
Standard Average European 92, 568, 899, 903, 910, 997, 1492−1509
− deviations 420
standards of comparison 862
starting point of movement 967
statal passive 930, 931, 937
− perfect 930
states of affairs 477
statistical and absolute universals 63, 314−315, 361, 855, 968, 1467
statistical methods 419−435
stative 928, 930, 933
− verb 929, 1031, 1428
− -active alignment 1430
stativization 908, 923
status absolutus 1778
− constructus 1765
stem 828
− alternations 830
− cells 111
Stichprobe 281, 1398, 1471
stock 1429
stød 1311
Stoics//stoïciens 184, 236
stranding 1662
structuralism//Strukturalismus 8, 41, 270, 272, 280, 303, 450, 478, 769
stress 1033, 1346, 1381, 1746
− timed 1391, 1343, 1362
− -focussed constituent 1080
strict agreement 1500
− universal 855
strong islands 1080
structural genius 265, 280
structuralisme fonctionnaliste européen 346
structures diathétiques 345
strukturelle Semantik 94, 247, 437

strukturell-funktionelle Linguistik 271
style indirect libre 598, 606
stylistically marked construction 1083
subcategorization frames 313
subclauses 1012
Subjazenz 284, 285, 288, 292, 1095, 1449
subject 304, 314, 353, 487, 543, 869–871, 933, 1414, 1663
– agreement 870
– and object agreement 315
– assignment 304
– position 989
– /predicate 1442
subjective assessment of the reality 998
– genitive 857
subjectless languages 1413–1423
– passives 899
subject-oriented languages 1413–1423
– -prominence 1447–1508
– -verb-agreement 980
Subjekt, psychologisches 618
subjektive Version 1777
Subjektivität 43
subjunctive (s. also conjunctive) 277, 600, 980, 983, 985, 1408, 1410, 1515, 1526, 1695
subordinate clause 842, 974, 1090
subordinating conjunction 29, 610, 955, 1618, 1644
subordination 4, 148, 595, 611, 644, 980, 981, 1003, 1113–1115, 1568, 1642, 1644, 1737
subordinator 843, 850, 1533
substance 245
substantialist approach 770
Substrat 1506, 1511, 1722, 1771
Subtraktion 405
Südasien 1529–1538
suffixing preference 856
sujet 353
superlative//Superlativ 403, 997, 832
superstrate 1511
suppletion 386, 828
suppositio-Lehre 437
Suppositionstheorie 202, 593
suppositive 1515
suppositum/appositum 196, 211, 213
surcomposé 560
SVO languages 1014, 1017, 1020
switch reference 612, 1002, 1116, 1118, 1406, 1547
Syllabar 165, 170
– Linear B 173

syllabic trochee 1354
Syllabierungsgesetz 1321
syllable quantity 1349–1350
– structure 1642, 1746
– timed 1343, 1391
– weight 1349–1350, 1378
– -timing 1362
Syllabogramme 172–175
Syllogismus 299
Symbole 371
Symbolfeld 460, 577
symbolische Verfahren 265
– Zeichen 578
symbolischer Interaktionismus 45, 445
sympathetic dative 971
synchrony-diachrony distinction 1457
syncopation 1348
syncretism 307, 311, 333, 1521, 1543, 1691, 1693, 1696
syndesis 614, 982
synharmonism 311
Synonymie 114, 373, 389
syntactic bondedness hierarchy 986
– categories 66, 332, 495
– causatives 886
– doubling 890
– Expression of Semantic Dependencies (SESD) 861
– functions 487–488
– islands 1085
– relations 265, 375, 976, 1414
syntagmatic article 963
syntagmatische Ökonomie 387
syntaktische Metapher 67
Synthese 1467, 1727
Synthesegrad 265
synthetic passive 900–901
– type languages 250, 265, 306, 307, 961
– /analytic 271, 1624, 1742, 1750
Systemangemessenheit//system-congruity 404, 409

T

Tabuwörter 85
tag 1012, 1019
Tail 622
target language 1640
tautology 518
Tautosyllabierung 1317
taxis 772
Teleologie 1392
teleonomic character of language 338
telic(ity) 483, 773
Telosfunktion 301
Temperamentenlehre 269

temporal clause 986, 1000, 1096
– deixis 1118
– interrogative words 1023
temporal sequence 957–959, 995, 996
temporality 557–567, 1120
temporary possession 954, 959
Tempus s. tense
Tempusikonizität 379
– tense//Tempus 557, 587, 639–640, 768, 980, 1004, 1034, 1096, 1099, 1115, 1118, 1400, 1514
tense forms 1081
– system 261, 932
– /aspect 1466, 1729, 1749, 1750
– -aspect-modality 979, 985, 999, 1006, 1008, 1657
tensedness 502
tenses, absolute 557
–, anterior 559
–, hypersupercompound 560
–, metrical 557, 560–561
–, relative 557, 559–560
Term 985
Termination 1013
Terminativ 535, 1728
terminative verbs 928, 938
terminologie linguistique 347
terrace-level 1369
tertium comparationis 10, 20, 292, 293, 296, 304, 324, 347, 478, 481, 596, 1572
text 302, 634
– types 2
Textdeixis 577, 579
Textgattung 49, 467
Textgliederung 469
Textkohärenz 634–656
Textkohäsion 634–656
Textlinguistik 40, 55, 302, 303, 436, 441, 468, 634
Textpragmatik 645–648
Textproduktionsforschung 154–162
Textrelief 380
Textsemantik 642–645
Textsorten 1559
Textsyntax 635, 638–642
textual genre 591, 592
Textualität 49
Textverstehensforschung 154–162
that-clause 496, 612
Theaterdialog 450
Thema/Rhema-Verteilung (s. also communicative dynamism) 303, 349
thematic continuity 1403
– element 968
– hierarchy 867

Index of subjects

- relations 484
- roles 313, 483, 512, 542, 866

thematicité 878
thématisation 352
thematische Progression 645
theme 409, 563, 618, 645
- argument 942, 943, 946, 947, 951
- First Principle 623

Theologie 194, 1561
thetic sentence 628, 1084, 1085, 1445, 1447
Thiessen-Methode 1478
Tiefenstruktur 66, 197, 258, 441
time 964, 1023, 1119
- depth 423
- stability 483, 504, 954
- -Dependency Hierarchy 1404

Tobler-Mussafia Law 1703
token identification 1022
- -Frequenz 394

Ton 316, 1096, 1397, 1665
tonal crowding 1383
tone cluster 1369
- difference 1097
- group 1370

tone language 1081, 1381, 1383, 1391
- level 1369
- rule 1373–1376
- sandhi 1370, 1376
- -bearing unit 1368

Toneme 170, 171
tonogenesis 1372, 1644
Tonstufenkorrelation 1394
Tonverlaufkorrelation 1394
topic 409, 480, 511, 563, 618, 959, 1006–1008, 1084, 1401, 1442
- and focus 1504
- continuity 1082
- marker/Topikmarkierung 624–627, 974
- movement 1444, 1448
- persistence 907
- Possessive 955–958
- prominence 1442–1449
- Schema 968

topicalization//Topikalisierung 155, 374, 552, 626, 907, 909, 923, 958, 1091, 1631, 1752
topic-comment 641
- -prominent language 287, 291, 910
Topic-Wechsel 160
topikkonfigurationelle Sprachen 628
Topikzeit 587
totality 774
tote Sprachen 1678–1690
Tough Movement 989

Tower of Babel//Turmbau zu Babel 86, 217, 220, 237, 238, 241, 244
Trabantenwörter 1578
Traditionalität 467–468
Traditionssprachen 1682
Trägheit 1343
transcendental particles 247
transcription 105, 106, 108
transformatif 886
transformation 908
Transformationsgrammatik 63, 212
Transformativität 1729
transitive predicates 482
Transitivierung 536
Transitivität//transitivity 18, 304, 337, 356, 378, 489–491, 542, 883, 917, 922, 956, 957
transitivity scale 491
translatability 338
Transliteration 169, 170
transnumeral 817
Transparenz 54, 397, 404, 409
transposition of clauses 1003
transpositional languages 230
transpositive languages 268
Transzendentalpragmatik 72
Trapezmodell 295
traumatic aphasia 98
trial 818
Trivium 193, 211
tRNA 115
trochee 858, 1352
truth value 955, 998
truth-conditions 1013
turning point (s. also continuum) 334
turn-taking 454
Typentheorie 68
Typik 43, 52, 158
typological change/typologischer Wandel 1623–1639, 1721
typologie actancielle 347–350
typologische Inkohärenz 270
typologisches Denken 249–263

U

übersetzen 73, 131
Umfelder 436
unaccusative 975, 976, 1084
uncertainty 1013
undergoer 484
unergative subject 975, 976
ungrammaticality 497
unidirectional grammaticalization 987
unidirectional historical development 319
Uniformität 54, 404, 1636
uninflectives 506
union linguistique (= Sprachbund) 1510
Unityp 15, 17, 35, 64, 323–343, 499, 541
Univerbation 1700
Universal Base Hypothesis 289, 291
- concessive conditionals 1007, 1008
- grammar//Universalgrammatik 14, 18, 51, 95, 143, 253, 260, 282, 283, 288, 370, 403, 505, 1082, 1668
- implications 63
- Language 247
- quantification 1446, 1450
- quantifier 1008, 1025

Universalien, absolute 10, 11, 281, 282
-, deduktive 282
-, empirische 64
-, essentielle 11, 91, 1554–1555
-, implikative 281, 282
-, statistische 10, 11, 282

Universalienbegriff 10, 11, 62–65, 297, 529
Universalienstreit 1475
universalism 244–248, 252
Universalpragmatik 40, 71
universals of comparative type choice 995
Universalsprache 85–95, 254
University of Paris 214
unreleased stop 1397
unrestricted universals 63
unsichtbare Hand 398
upstepping 1372
usualization 1596

V

valence change 480, 488–490, 894, 900, 923, 926, 930, 931
valence/valency 15, 300, 378, 480, 485–488, 535, 604, 873, 929, 930, 970, 975, 977
valency grammars (s. also Dependenzgrammatik) 862
valeur rhématique 875, 879
Validität 1472
vanitas mundi 235
variable word order 862–863
variation grammar 1649
variations d'actance 345
Variationslinguistik 1564
Varietätenlinguistik 2, 3, 1561, 1563, 1567
Varietätenraum 1564, 1582, 1584
vector verb 1531
verb 1099

- agreement 1631
- fronting 1017, 1501
- initial languages 1014
- patterners 844
- serialization 376, 602, 612

verbal adverb 1112, 1121
- noun 1407
- number 816, 817
- reflexive 916–927

verbale Modifikation 533–556
verbants 1621
verbe sériel 875
Verben der Bewegung 576
verb-final language 277, 1083
- -final syntax 1641
- -framed 17, 572

verbiness 495–508, 596, 602
verbs of affinity 932
- of cognition 923
- of grooming and body care 924
- of measure 1031
- of mental acquisition 932
- of motion 146
- of non-physical actions 934
- of non-translational motion 924
- of passive perception 1031
- of speech causation 1030
- of translational motion 923, 924

verbum substantivum 196, 198
verbzentrierte Sprachen 543
Verb-Zweit-Phänomen 284, 287
Vergangenheitstempora 1572
vernacular grammar 216
vernaculars 210–216, 238
Vernersches Gesetz 1337
Verschmelzung 1319
Verschriftung 163
Versdichtung 473
Version 1794
vertical assimilation 1374
Verum-Fokus 625
Verwandtschaftsbeziehungen 296
vices of speech 237
Vierfelderschema 3
vigesimal numeral system 1545, 1550
V-initial type 952
virtues of speech 237
visée communicative 351, 876
VO order 1116

voice (s. also diathesis) 306, 312–314, 489, 490, 889, 908, 932, 980, 1120
Vokalelision 1396
Vokalharmonie 541, 1311, 1397
Vokalsystem 389, 391, 1396, 1511, 1691, 1746
Völkerpsychologie 272
Volksbewußtsein 268
Volksetymologie 397
Volksgeist 267, 270
Volkspsyche 269
Volkssprache 1684, 1688
vouns 498
VP 1444
- -deletion 1448
- -ellipsis 1433
- -fronting 1433
VS order 1084
VSO-language 277, 278, 1017, 1020

W

Weak Crossover Effect 1089, 1093, 1095
- islands 1080
Wechselform 598
Weltanschauung 269
Weltbild 227
Welthilfssprachen 86–88
Weltwissen 437, 575, 581, 583, 642, 1581
WH-adverbials 1080
- -extraction 1080
- -fronting 1095
- -interrogatives 1011
- -movement 907, 1080, 1085, 1090
- -operator 1088, 1453
- -phrase 1086, 1096
- -pronoun 1451
- -question 28, 366, 1007, 1008, 1086, 1094, 1385
- -words 869
wide focus 1079, 1085, 1088, 1093, 1096, 1097
Williams syndrome 99, 101, 120
Wissenstransformation (knowledge transforming) 156
Wissenswiedergabe (knowledge telling) 155
WITH-drift 1110
- -languages 1109, 1502
- -possessive 956

Witterungsverben 287
word classes//Wortklassen 13, 195, 205, 246, 260, 277–279, 301, 302, 405, 436, 495, 1604
s. also part of speech
word knowledge 573
- order types 1003–1004, 1014, 1429
- order typology// Wortstellungstypologie 25, 27, 250, 284, 855–873, 1575
- order//Wortstellung 126, 268, 314, 316, 319, 328, 329, 360, 947, 968, 1007, 1033, 1083, 1119, 1362, 1463, 1530, 1546, 1660, 1661, 1764–1766
- prosody 1493
- stress 1346, 1384
- -form 308–310
- -formation 1603
Wortakzent 1322, 1394, 1395
Wortfeld 437, 642
Wortfindungsstörungen 131
Wortlänge 394
Wortrhythmus 1394
Wortsprache 1396
writing system 1744
Wurzelakzent 625

Y

yes-no question 1004, 1007, 1011, 1385

Z

Zeichen/Zeichentheorie 54, 67, 371, 445, 578
Zeigegeste 581
Zeigfeld 577
Zeitdeixis 585–588
Zeitkern 1584
zero anaphora 597
- derivation 1604, 1658
zero-marking 1106
Zitationsform (s. also quotative) 195
Zitierpartikel 1532, 1534
Zustandspassiv 930
Zwei-Ebenen-Semantik 622
Zweifelderlehre 577